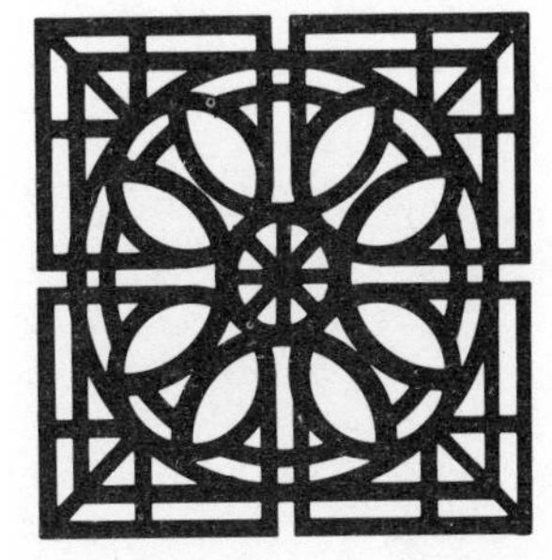

Evangelical Dictionary of Theology

Edited By;
Walter A. Elwell

Marshall·Pickering

Marshall Morgan & Scott Publications Ltd.
3 Beggarwood Lane, Basingstoke, Hants, RG23 7LP, UK

First published by Baker Book House in the United States.
First British edition by Marshall Pickering, 1985.

British Library Cataloguing in Publication Data

Evangelical dictionary of theology.
1. Theology—Dictionaries
230′.03′21 BR95

ISBN 0 551 01272 2

Printed and bound in Great Britain at The Bath Press, Avon

Preface

After several decades of trying to find answers for our deepest questions in everything from biochemistry to computer science, it has dawned upon us once more that these questions are theological and that only theological answers will do. This has created a newer, more friendly climate for the study of religion and a genuine need for serious, yet understandable reference works. Older works, good as they are, addressed the situation of earlier generations and simply do not provide what is needed today. Hence this volume, *Evangelical Dictionary of Theology*. It is a new work, designed to succeed *Baker's Dictionary of Theology*, which, since its publication in 1960, has nobly served almost two generations of seminarians and theological students.

The EDT, although considerably larger than its predecessor in the number of both entries and words, is still limited in scope because of its one-volume format. This limitation did have one good effect. It discouraged the inclusion of anything unnecessary. A beginning collection of over 8,000 entries was cut back several times until approximately 1,200 entries remained. Differences of opinion obviously will exist as to whether or not these 1,200 are the most significant. But the reader is humbly requested to consider how difficult it is to decide what should go or stay.

Several special features of the EDT need to be understood in order to use it most effectively. First, each article stresses the theological dimension of its subject. So, for example, items drawn from church history, Bible, or biography attempt to emphasize that entry's theological significance, rather than its significance *per se*. Second, contributors are sympathetic to the subjects on which they write. They are not, however, uncritically sympathetic, and in many instances they include critical evaluations. Third, the EDT is written in popular language. The editor, contributors, and publisher sincerely hope that the dictionary communicates well. Our goal was this: that the scholar find it correct; the layman, understandable. Fourth, cross references at the end of an article direct one to related material, enabling one to study thoroughly the whole subject. Fifth, the bibliographies are intended to be not exhaustive, but selective. For the most part they are limited to works in English, because that is the only language most of the dictionary's readers can use.

Needless to say, in a work written by approximately two hundred people, differences of opinion appear. No attempt was made to force uniformity upon it all. That differences of opinion exist in this dictionary is only testimony to the fact that such differences exist in the evangelical community at large. Nothing in EDT, though, casts doubt on any fundamental truth of the Christian faith, or on the absolute trustworthiness of the Bible.

Special acknowledgment is due to those who played a special role in the production of this work: Lauris Mays, who did all the secretarial work cheerfully and efficiently; my wife, Louan Elwell, whose patience and organizational skills kept the project on track; Allan Fisher of Baker Book House, whose guidance and understanding were exceptional; Jean Hager, whose final editorial work was invaluable; and finally Wheaton College, which granted a sabbatical in the fall of 1982.

Contributors

Adie, Douglas K. Ph.D., University of Chicago. George F. Bennett Professor of Economics, Wheaton College, Wheaton, Illinois.

Akers, John N. Ph.D., University of Edinburgh. Special Assistant, The Billy Graham Evangelistic Association, and Adjunct Professor of Bible, Montreat-Anderson College, Montreat, North Carolina.

Allis, Oswald T. Ph.D., University of Berlin. Sometime Professor of Old Testament, Westminster Theological Seminary, Philadelphia, Pennsylvania.

Allison, C. FitzSimons. D.Phil., Oxford University. Bishop, Diocese of South Carolina, Charleston, South Carolina.

Anderson, Marvin W. Ph.D., University of Aberdeen. Professor of Church History, Bethel Theological Seminary, St. Paul, Minnesota.

Archer, Gleason Leonard, Jr. Ph.D., Harvard University. Professor of Old Testament and Semitic Languages, Trinity Evangelical Divinity School, Deerfield, Illinois.

Atkinson, David J. Ph.D., University of London. Chaplain, Corpus Christi College, Oxford, England.

Babbage, Stuart Barton. Ph.D., University of London; Th.D., Australian College of Theology. Registrar, Australian College of Theology, Sydney, Australia.

Baird, John S. S.T.D., Temple University. Denise Professor of Homiletics and Ministry, University of Dubuque Theological Seminary, Dubuque, Iowa.

Baker, William H. Th.D., Dallas Theological Seminary. Associate Professor of Bible and Theology, Moody Bible Institute, Chicago, Illinois.

Barabas, Steven. Th.D., Princeton Theological Seminary. Sometime Professor Emeritus of Theology, Wheaton College, Wheaton, Illinois.

Beegle, Dewey M. Ph.D., Johns Hopkins University. Professor of Old Testament, Wesley Theological Seminary, Washington, D.C.

Benner, David G. Ph.D., York University. Professor of Graduate Psychological Studies, Wheaton College, Wheaton, Illinois.

Benton, W. Wilson, Jr. Ph.D., University of Edinburgh. Pastor, Covenant Presbyterian Church, Cleveland, Mississippi.

Bishop, Russell K. Ph.D., McGill University. Professor of History, Gordon College, Wenham, Massachusetts.

Blaising, Craig A. Th.D., Dallas Theological Seminary. Assistant Professor of Systematic Theology, Dallas Theological Seminary, Dallas, Texas.

Bloesch, Donald G. Ph.D., University of Chicago. Professor of Theology, University of Dubuque Theological Seminary, Dubuque, Iowa.

Boettner, Loraine. Th.M., Princeton Theological Seminary. Sometime theological writer.

Borchert, Gerald L. Ph.D., Princeton Theological Seminary. Professor of New Testament Interpretation, Southern Baptist Theological Seminary, Louisville, Kentucky.

Brandon, Owen Rupert. M.Litt., University of Durham. Formerly Tutor and Librarian, Lecturer in Theology and Psychology, London College of Divinity, London, England; Fellow and Librarian, St. Augustine's College, Canterbury, England.

Bromiley, Geoffrey W. Ph.D., Litt.D., University of Edinburgh. Senior Professor of Church History and Historical Theology, Fuller Theological Seminary, Pasadena, California.

Broomall, Wick. Th.M., Princeton Theological Seminary. Sometime Minister, Westminster Presbyterian Church, Augusta, Georgia.

Brown, Colin. Ph.D., University of Bristol. Professor of Systematic Theology, Fuller Theological Seminary, Pasadena, California.

Bruce, F. F. M.A., University of Aberdeen; M.A., Cambridge University; M.A., University of Manchester. Formerly Rylands Professor of Biblical Criticism and Exegesis, University of Manchester, Manchester, England.

Burge, Gary M. Ph.D., University of Aberdeen. Assistant Professor, Bible and Religion, King College, Bristol, Tennessee.

Burke, Gary T. Ph.D., University of Iowa. Associate Professor of Religion, Eastern New Mexico University, Portales, New Mexico.

Butman, Richard Eugene. Ph.D., Fuller Theological Seminary. Assistant Professor of Psychology, Wheaton College, Wheaton, Illinois.

Cameron, William John. M.A., University of Edinburgh. Professor Emeritus of New Testament Language, Literature, and Theology, Free Church of Scotland College, Edinburgh, Scotland.

Carson, Don A. Ph.D., Cambridge University. Professor of New Testament, Trinity Evangelical Divinity School, Deerfield, Illinois.

Caulley, Thomas Scott. Dr.Theol., University of Tübingen. Assistant Professor of Religion, Eastern New Mexico University, Portales, New Mexico.

Chappell, Paul G. Ph.D., Drew University. Associate Dean of Academic Affairs, School of Theology, Oral Roberts University, Tulsa, Oklahoma.

Clark, Gordon H. Ph.D., University of Pennsylvania. Formerly Professor of Philosophy, Covenant College, Lookout Mountain, Tennessee.

Cleveland, Howard Z. Th.D., Dallas Theological Seminary. Formerly Chairman of Language Department, Oak Hills Christian Training School, Bemidji, Minnesota.

Clouse, Robert G. Ph.D., University of Iowa. Professor of History, Indiana State University, Terre Haute, Indiana.

Coates, Richard John. M.A., University of Bristol. Sometime Vicar of Christ Church, Weston-Super-Mare, Somerset, England; Lecturer, Tyndale Hall, Bristol, England.

Collins, George Norman MacLeod. B.D., Knox College. Professor Emeritus of Church History, Free Church of Scotland College, Edinburgh, Scotland.

Colquhoun, Frank. M.A., Durham University. Canon Emeritus, Norwich Cathedral, Norwich, England.

Corduan, Winfried. Ph.D., Rice University. Associate Professor of Philosophy and Religion, Taylor University, Upland, Indiana.

Corlett, Lewis T. B.A., Peniel College. Formerly President of Nazarene Theological Seminary, Kansas City, Missouri.

Craigie, Peter C. Ph.D., McMaster University. Dean, Faculty of Humanities, University of Calgary, Calgary, Alberta.

Craston, Richard Colin. B.D., University of London. Vicar of St. Paul with Emmanuel and Rural Dean of Bolton, England.

Crum, Terrelle B. M.A., Harvard University. Sometime Dean of the College, Providence-Barrington Bible College, Providence, Rhode Island.

Cruz, Virgil. Ph.D., Free University. Professor of Biblical Studies, Western Theological Seminary, Holland, Michigan.

Culbertson, Robert G. Ph.D., University of Cincinnati. Professor of Criminal Justice Sciences, Illinois State University, Normal, Illinois.

Danker, Frederick W. Ph.D., University of Chicago. Professor, Christ Seminary, Seminex, Chicago, Illinois.

Davids, Peter H. Ph.D., University of Manchester. Visiting Professor of New Testament, Regent College, Vancouver, British Columbia.

Davis, Creath. M.Div., Southwestern Baptist Theological Seminary. Executive Director, Christian Concern Foundation, Dallas, Texas.

Davis, Donald Gordon. Ph.D., University of Edinburgh. Sometime Professor of Church History, Talbot Theological Seminary, La Mirada, California.

De Koster, Lester. Ph.D., University of Michigan. Editor Emeritus, *The Banner.*

Demarest, Bruce A. Ph.D., University of Manchester. Professor of Systematic Theology, Denver Conservative Baptist Theological Seminary, Denver, Colorado.

DeVries, Paul Henry. Ph.D., University of Virginia. Associate Professor of Philosophy, Wheaton College, Wheaton, Illinois.

Diehl, David W. Ph.D., Hartford Seminary Foundation. Professor of Religion, The King's College, Briarcliff Manor, New York.

Dieter, Melvin E. Ph.D., Temple University. Professor of Church History and Historical Theology, Asbury Theological Seminary, Wilmore, Kentucky.

Donnelly, John Patrick, S.J. Ph.D., University of Wisconsin-Madison. Associate Professor of History, Marquette University, Milwaukee, Wisconsin.

Douglas, J. D. Ph.D., Hartford Seminary Foundation. Editor and writer, St. Andrews, Fife, Scotland.

Drickamer, John M. Th.D., Concordia Seminary, St. Louis. Pastor, Immanuel Lutheran Church, Georgetown, Ontario.

Dunbar, David G. Ph.D., Drew University. Assistant Professor of Systematic Theology, Trinity Evangelical Divinity School, Deerfield, Illinois.

Dyrness, William A. D.Theol., Strasbourg University. President and Professor of Theology, New College Berkeley, Berkeley, California.

Earle, Ralph. Th.D., Gordon Divinity School. Distinguished Professor Emeritus of New Testament, Nazarene Theological Seminary, Kansas City, Missouri.

Edman, V. Raymond. Ph.D., Clark University. Sometime President, Wheaton College, Wheaton, Illinois.

Eller, David B. Ph.D., Miami University. Associate Professor of History, Bluffton College, Bluffton, Ohio.

Ellis, E. Earle. Ph.D., University of Edinburgh. Research Professor of New Testament Literature, New Brunswick Theological Seminary, New Brunswick, New Jersey.

Elwell, Walter A. Ph.D., University of Edinburgh. Professor of Bible and Theology, Wheaton College, Wheaton, Illinois.

Enroth, Ronald M. Ph.D., University of Kentucky. Professor of Sociology, Westmont College, Santa Barbara, California.

Erickson, Millard J. Ph.D., Northwestern University. Professor of Theology, Bethel Theological Seminary, St. Paul, Minnesota.

Estep, William R., Jr. Th.D., Southwestern Baptist Theological Seminary. Professor of Church History, Southwestern Baptist Theological Seminary, Fort Worth, Texas.

Farrer, Michael Robert Wedlake. M.A., Oxford University. Vicar, St. Paul's Church, Cambridge, England.

Feinberg, Charles L. Th.D., Dallas Theological Seminary; Ph.D., Johns Hopkins University. Dean Emeritus and Professor Emeritus of Semitics and Old Testament, Talbot Theological Seminary, La Mirada, California.

Feinberg, John S. Ph.D., University of Chicago. Associate Professor of Biblical and Systematic Theology, Trinity Evangelical Divinity School, Deerfield, Illinois.

Feinberg, Paul D. Th.D., Dallas Theological Seminary. Professor of Biblical and Systematic Theology, Trinity Evangelical Divinity School, Deerfield, Illinois.

Ferguson, Duncan S. Ph.D., University of Edinburgh. Chairman, Department of Religion and Philosophy, Whitworth College, Spokane, Washington.

Ferguson, Everett. Ph.D., Harvard University. Professor, Abilene Christian University, Abilene, Texas.

Field, David H. B.A., Cambridge University. Vice-Principal, Oak Hill College, London, England.

Finger, Thomas N. Ph.D., Claremont School of Theology. Associate Professor of Systematic Theology, Northern Baptist Theological Seminary, Lombard, Illinois.

Fisher, Fred Lewis. Th.D., Southwestern Baptist Theological Seminary. Director and Professor in Residence, Southern California Center, Golden Gate Baptist Theological Seminary, Mill Valley, California.

Fletcher, David B. Ph.D., University of Illinois. Assistant Professor of Philosophy, Wheaton College, Wheaton, Illinois.

Frame, John M. M.Phil., Yale University. Associate Professor of Apologetics and Systematic Theology, Westminster Theological Seminary in California, Escondido, California.

Franklin, Stephen T. Ph.D., University of Chicago. Professor of Systematic Theology, Wheaton College, Wheaton, Illinois.

Freundt, Albert H., Jr. M.Div., Columbia Theological Seminary. Professor of Church History and Polity, Reformed Theological Seminary, Jackson, Mississippi.

Fry, C. George. Ph.D., Ohio State University; D.Min., Winebrenner Theological Seminary. Associate Professor of Historical Theology, Concordia Theological Seminary, Fort Wayne, Indiana.

Gallatin, Harlie Kay. Ph.D., University of Illinois. Professor of History, Southwestern Baptist University, Bolivar, Missouri.

Gasque, W. Ward. Ph.D., University of Manchester. Vice-Principal, Regent College, Vancouver, British Columbia.

Gay, George Arthur. Ph.D., University of Manchester. Senior Associate Professor of New Testament, Fuller Theological Seminary, Pasadena, California.

Geisler, Norman L. Ph.D., Loyola University of Chicago. Professor of Systematic Theology, Dallas Theological Seminary, Dallas, Texas.

German, Terence J., S.J. Ph.D., Oxford University. Professor of Systematics, Marquette University, Milwaukee, Wisconsin.

Gerstner, John H. Ph.D., Harvard University. Professor at Large, Ligonier Valley Study Center, Ligonier, Pennsylvania.

Gill, David W. Ph.D., University of Southern California. Dean and Associate Professor of Christian Ethics, New College Berkeley, Berkeley, California.

Glasser, Arthur F. D.D., Covenant Theological Seminary. Dean Emeritus, School of World Mission, and Senior Professor of Theology and East Asian Studies, Fuller Theological Seminary, Pasadena, California.

Goddard, Burton L. Th.D., Harvard University. Dean Emeritus, Gordon-Conwell Theological Seminary, South Hamilton, Massachusetts.

Goldberg, Louis. Th.D., Grace Theological Seminary. Professor of Theology and Jewish Studies, Moody Bible Institute, Chicago, Illinois.

Gouvea, Fernando Q. M.A., University of São Paulo. Formerly Assistant Professor of Mathematics, University of São Paulo, São Paulo, Brazil.

Granberg, Lars I. Ph.D., University of Chicago. Peter C. and Emajean Cook Professor of Psychology, Hope College, Holland, Michigan.

Grider, J. Kenneth. Ph.D., Glasgow University. Professor of Theology, Nazarene Theological Seminary, Kansas City, Missouri.

Griffith, Howard. M.Div., Gordon-Conwell Theological Seminary. Associate Pastor, Stony Point Reformed Presbyterian Church, Richmond, Virginia.

Grudem, Wayne A. Ph.D., Cambridge University. Associate Professor of New Testament, Trinity Evangelical Divinity School, Deerfield, Illinois.

Gruenler, Royce G. Ph.D., University of Aberdeen. Professor of New Testament, Gordon-Conwell Theological Seminary, South Hamilton, Massachusetts.

Gundry, Stanley N. S.T.D., Lutheran School of Theology at Chicago. Executive Editor, Academic Books, Zondervan Publishing House, Grand Rapids, Michigan.

Guthrie, Donald. Ph.D., University of London. Formerly Vice-Principal, London Bible College, London, England.

Habermas, Gary R. Ph.D., Michigan State University. Associate Professor of Apologetics and Philosophy, Liberty Baptist College and Seminary, Lynchburg, Virginia.

Hall, Joseph H. Th.D., Concordia Seminary, St. Louis. Associate Professor of Church History and Librarian, Covenant Theological Seminary, St. Louis, Missouri.

Harm, Frederick R. Th.D., American Divinity School. Pastor, Good Shepherd Lutheran Church, Des Plaines, Illinois; Visiting Professor of Systematic Theology, Concordia Seminary, St. Louis, Missouri.

Harris, R. Laird. Ph.D., Dropsie College. Professor Emeritus of O!d Testament, Covenant Theological Seminary, St. Louis, Missouri.

Harrison, Everett F. Th.D., Dallas Theological Seminary; Ph.D., University of Pennsylvania. Professor Emeritus of New Testament, Fuller Theological Seminary, Pasadena, California.

Harrison, R. K. Ph.D., University of London. Professor of Old Testament, Wycliffe College, Toronto, Ontario.

Hasel, Gerhard F. Ph.D., Vanderbilt University. Dean and Professor of Old Testament, Andrews University, Berrien Springs, Michigan.

Hawthorne, Gerald F. Ph.D., University of Chicago. Professor of Greek, Wheaton College, Wheaton, Illinois.

Healey, Robert M. Ph.D., Yale University. Professor of Church History, University of Dubuque Theological Seminary, Dubuque, Iowa.

Hein, Rolland N. Ph.D., Purdue University. Professor of English, Wheaton College, Wheaton, Illinois.

Heinze, Rudolph W. Ph. D., University of Iowa. Lecturer in Church History, Oak Hill College, London, England.

Henry, Carl F. H. Th.D., Northern Baptist Theological Seminary; Ph.D., Boston University. Distinguished Visiting Professor of Religion, Hillsdale College, Hillsdale, Michigan.

Hesselgrave, David J. Ph.D., University of Minnesota. Professor of World Mission, Trinity Evangelical Divinity School, Deerfield, Illinois.

Hexham, Irving. Ph.D., University of Bristol. Assistant Professor of Religion, University of Manitoba, Winnipeg, Manitoba.

Higginson, Richard Edwin. B.D., University of London. Formerly Lecturer in Tyndale Hall, Bristol, England.

Hoehner, Harold W. Th.D., Dallas Theological Seminary; Ph.D., Cambridge University. Professor of New Testament Literature and Exegesis, Dallas Theological Seminary, Dallas, Texas.

Hoffecker, W. Andrew. Ph.D., Brown University. Professor of Religion, Grove City College, Grove City, Pennsylvania.

Hoover, A. J. Ph.D., University of Texas. Professor of History, Abilene Christian University, Abilene, Texas.

Hope, Norman Victor. Ph.D., University of Edinburgh. Archibald Alexander Professor of Church History Emeritus, Princeton Theological Seminary, Princeton, New Jersey.

Horn, Carl, III. J.D., University of South Carolina. Attorney, Civil Rights Division, United States Department of Justice, Washington, D.C.

Houston, James M. D.Phil., Oxford University. Chancellor and Professor of Spiritual Theology, Regent College, Vancouver, British Columbia.

Howe, E. Margaret. Ph.D., University of Manchester. Professor of Religion, Western Kentucky University, Bowling Green, Kentucky.

Hubbard, David A. Ph.D., St. Andrews University. President, Fuller Theological Seminary, Pasadena, California.

Hughes, Philip Edgcumbe. D.Litt., University of Cape Town; Th.D., Australian College of Theology. Professor Emeritus, Trinity Episcopal School for Ministry, Ambridge, Pennsylvania.

Hummel, Horace D. Ph.D., Johns Hopkins University. Professor of Old Testament Exegesis, Concordia Seminary, St. Louis, Missouri.

Imbach, Stuart R. Diploma in Bible, Prairie Bible Institute. Communications Department Director, Overseas Missionary Fellowship, Singapore.

Inch, Morris A. Ph.D., Boston University. Professor of Theology, Wheaton College, Wheaton, Illinois.

Ippel, Henry P. Ph.D., University of Michigan. Professor of History, Calvin College, Grand Rapids, Michigan.

Jewett, Paul K. Ph.D., Harvard University. Professor of Systematic Theology, Fuller Theological Seminary, Pasadena, California.

Johnson, Alan F. Th.D., Dallas Theological Seminary. Professor of Biblical Studies, Wheaton College, Wheaton, Illinois.

Johnson, James E. Ph.D., Syracuse University. Professor of History, Bethel College, St. Paul, Minnesota.

Johnson, John F. Th.D., Concordia Seminary, St. Louis; Ph.D., St. Louis University. Associate Professor of Systematic Theology, Concordia Seminary, St. Louis, Missouri.

Johnson, S. Lewis. Th.D., Dallas Theological Seminary. Professor of Biblical and Systematic Theology, Trinity Evangelical Divinity School, Deerfield, Illinois.

Johnston, O. Raymond. M.A., Oxford University. Director, Christian Action, Research and Education Trust, London, England.

Johnston, Robert K. Ph.D., Duke University. Dean, North Park Theological Seminary, Chicago, Illinois.

Justice, William G., Jr. D.Min., Luther Rice Seminary. Director of Pastoral Care, East Tennessee Baptist Hospital, Knoxville, Tennessee.

Kantzer, Kenneth S. Ph.D., Harvard University. President, Trinity College, Deerfield, Illinois; Dean Emeritus, Trinity Evangelical Divinity School, Deerfield, Illinois.

Kelly, Douglas F. Ph.D., University of Edinburgh. Visiting Professor of Systematic Theology, Reformed Theological Seminary, Jackson, Mississippi.

Kent, Homer A., Jr. Th.D., Grace Theological Seminary. President, Grace College and Theological Seminary, Winona Lake, Indiana.

Kerr, David W. Th.D., Harvard University. Sometime Professor of Old Testament, Gordon Divinity School, Beverly Farms, Massachusetts.

Kerr, William Nigel. Th.D., Northern Baptist Theological Seminary; Ph.D., University of Edinburgh. Professor of Church History and Missions, Gordon-Conwell Theological Seminary, South Hamilton, Massachusetts.

Kevan, Ernest F. Ph.D., University of London. Sometime Principal, London Bible College, London, England.

Kistemaker, Simon J. Th.D., Free University. Professor of New Testament, Reformed Theological Seminary, Jackson, Mississippi.

Klooster, Fred H. Th.D., Free University. Professor of Systematic Theology, Calvin Theological Seminary, Grand Rapids, Michigan.

Klotz, John W. Ph.D., University of Pittsburgh. Professor of Practical Theology and Director, School for Graduate Studies, Concordia Seminary, St. Louis, Missouri.

Knight, George W., III. Th.D., Free University. Professor of New Testament, Covenant Theological Seminary, St. Louis, Missouri.

Knox, David Broughton. D.Phil., Oxford University. Formerly Principal of Moore College, Sydney, Australia.

Kroeger, Catherine Clark. M.A., University of Minnesota.

Kroeger, Richard C. S.T.M., University of Iowa. Formerly Assistant Professor of Religion, Eastern New Mexico University, Portales, New Mexico.

Kromminga, Carl Gerhard. Th.D., Free University. Professor of Practical Theology, Calvin Theological Seminary, Grand Rapids, Michigan.

Kubricht, Paul. Ph.D., Ohio State University. Associate Professor of History, LeTourneau College, Longview, Texas.

Kuhn, Harold B. Ph.D., Harvard University. Professor Emeritus of Philosophy of Religion, Asbury Theological Seminary, Wilmore, Kentucky.

Kyle, Richard. Ph.D., University of New Mexico. Professor of History and Religion, Tabor College, Hillsboro, Kansas.

La Bar, Martin. Ph.D., University of Wisconsin-Madison. Professor of Science, Central Wesleyan College, Central, South Carolina.

Ladd, George Eldon. Ph.D., Harvard University. Sometime Professor Emeritus of New Testament Theology and Exegesis, Fuller Theological Seminary, Pasadena, California.

Lamorte, André. Th.D., Montpellier University. Sometime Professor of Theology at Aix-en-Provence, France.

LaSor, William Sanford. Th.D., University of California, Los Angeles; Ph.D., Dropsie University. Professor Emeritus of Old Testament, Fuller Theological Seminary, Pasadena, California.

Laurin, Robert B. Ph.D., St. Andrews University. Dean, American Baptist Seminary of the West, Berkeley, California.

Lewis, Gordon R. Ph.D., Syracuse University. Professor of Theology and Philosophy, Denver Conservative Baptist Theological Seminary, Denver, Colorado.

Liefeld, Walter L. Ph.D., Columbia University. Professor of New Testament, Trinity Evangelical Divinity School, Deerfield, Illinois.

Lightner, Robert P. Th.D., Dallas Theological Seminary. Associate Professor of Systematic Theology, Dallas Theological Seminary, Dallas, Texas.

Linder, Robert D. Ph.D., University of Iowa. Professor of History, Kansas State University, Manhattan, Kansas.

Lindsell, Harold. Ph.D., New York University. Editor Emeritus, *Christianity Today*.

Lowery, David K. Th.M., Dallas Theological Seminary. Assistant Professor of New Testament Literature and Exegesis, Dallas Theological Seminary, Dallas, Texas.

Lundin, Roger. Ph.D., University of Connecticut. Associate Professor of English, Wheaton College, Wheaton, Illinois.

Lyon, Robert W. Ph.D., St. Andrews University. Professor of New Testament Interpretation, Asbury Theological Seminary, Wilmore, Kentucky.

McClelland, Scott E. Ph.D., University of Edinburgh. Assistant Professor of Religion, The King's College, Briarcliff Manor, New York.

McComiskey, Thomas Edward. Ph.D., Brandeis University. Professor of Semitic Languages and Old Testament, Trinity Evangelical Divinity School, Deerfield, Illinois.

McDonald, H. D. Ph.D., D.D., University of London. Formerly Vice-Principal, London Bible College, London, England.

Macdonald, Michael H. Ph.D., University of Washington. Professor of German and Philosophy, Seattle Pacific University, Seattle, Washington.

McGavran, Donald A. Ph.D., Columbia University. Dean Emeritus and Senior Professor of Mission, Fuller Theological Seminary, Pasadena, California.

McIntire, C. T. Ph.D., University of Pennsylvania. Senior Member in History, Institute for Christian Studies, Toronto, Ontario.

McKim, Donald K. Ph.D., University of Pittsburgh. Assistant Professor of Theology, University of Dubuque Theological Seminary, Dubuque, Iowa.

McRay, John R. Ph.D., University of Chicago. Professor of New Testament and Archaeology, Wheaton College, Wheaton, Illinois.

Magnuson, Norris A. Ph.D., University of Minnesota. Professor of Church History, Bethel Theological Seminary, St. Paul, Minnesota.

Marchant, George John Charles. B.D., University of Durham. Archdeacon Emeritus, Durham Cathedral, Durham, England.

Mare, W. Harold. Ph.D., University of Pennsylvania. Professor of New Testament, Covenant Theological Seminary, St. Louis, Missouri.

Marshall, Caroline T. Ph.D., University of Virginia. Professor of History, James Madison University, Harrisonburg, Virginia.

Martin, Dennis D. Ph.D., University of Waterloo. Editor and Visiting Instructor, Institute of Mennonite Studies, Associated Mennonite Biblical Seminaries, Elkhart, Indiana.

Masselink, William. Th.D., Free University; Ph.D., Southern Baptist Theological Seminary. Sometime Teacher of Reformed Doctrine, Reformed Bible College, Grand Rapids, Michigan.

Mathew, C. V. Th.M., Serampore University. Lecturer in Religion and Society, Union Biblical Seminary, Pune, India.

Mennell, James E. Ph.D., University of Iowa. Associate Professor of History, Slippery Rock State College, Slippery Rock, Pennsylvania.

Mickey, Paul A. Ph.D., Princeton Theological Seminary. Associate Professor of Pastoral Theology, Duke University, Durham, North Carolina.

Miller, Douglas J. Ph.D., Claremont School of Theology. Professor of Christian Social Ethics, Eastern Baptist Theological Seminary, Philadelphia, Pennsylvania.

Moberg, David O. Ph.D., University of Minnesota. Professor of Sociology, Marquette University, Milwaukee, Wisconsin.

Morris, Leon. Ph.D., Cambridge University. Formerly Principal, Ridley College, Melbourne, Australia.

Motyer, J. A. B.D., Trinity College, Dublin. Minister of Christ Church, Westbourne, Dorset, England.

Motyer, Stephen. M.Litt., University of Bristol. Lecturer in New Testament, Oak Hill College, London, England.

Mounce, Robert H. Ph.D., University of Aberdeen. President, Whitworth College, Spokane, Washington.

Mounce, William D. Ph.D., University of Aberdeen. Assistant Professor of New Testament, Azusa Pacific University, Azusa, California.

Moyer, James C. Ph.D., Brandeis University. Professor of Religious Studies, Southwest Missouri State University, Springfield, Missouri.

Mueller, J. Theodore. Th.D., Xenia Theological Seminary; Ph.D., Webster University. Sometime Professor of Doctrinal and Exegetical Theology, Concordia Seminary, St. Louis, Missouri.

Nicole, Roger. Ph.D., Harvard University. Andrew Mutch Professor of Theology, Gordon-Conwell Theological Seminary, South Hamilton, Massachusetts.

Noll, Mark A. Ph.D., Vanderbilt University. Associate Professor of History and Church History, Wheaton College, Wheaton, Illinois.

Noll, Stephen F. Ph.D., University of Manchester. Assistant Professor of Biblical Studies, Trinity Episcopal School for Ministry, Ambridge, Pennsylvania.

Obitts, Stanley R. Ph.D., University of Edinburgh. Professor of Philosophy, Westmont College, Santa Barbara, California.

Oliver, O. Guy, Jr. B.D., Louisville Presbyterian Theological Seminary. Associate Professor of Christian Mission, Erskine Theological Seminary, Due West, South Carolina.

O'Malley, J. Steven. Ph.D., Drew University. Professor Church History, School of Theology, Oral Roberts University, Tulsa, Oklahoma.

Omanson, Roger L. Ph.D., Southern Baptist Theological Seminary. Assistant Professor of New Testament Interpretation, Southern Baptist Theological Seminary, Louisville, Kentucky.

Osborne, Grant R. Ph.D., University of Aberdeen. Associate Professor of New Testament, Trinity Evangelical Divinity School, Deerfield, Illinois.

Osterhaven, M. Eugene. Th.D., Princeton Theological Seminary. Albertus C. Van Raalte Professor of Systematic Theology, Western Theological Seminary, Holland, Michigan.

Packer, James I. D.Phil., Oxford University. Professor of Historical and Systematic Theology, Regent College, Vancouver, British Columbia.

Parker, Thomas Henry Louis. D.D., Cambridge University. Formerly Reader in Theology, University of Durham, Durham, England.

Payne, J. Barton. Ph.D., Princeton Theological Seminary. Sometime Professor of Old Testament, Covenant Theological Seminary, St. Louis, Missouri.

Perkin, Hazel W. M.A., McGill University. Principal, St. Clement's School, Toronto, Ontario.

Pfeiffer, Charles F. Ph.D., Dropsie College. Sometime Professor of Ancient Literatures, Central Michigan University, Mount Pleasant, Michigan.

Pierard, Richard V. Ph.D., University of Iowa. Professor of History, Indiana State University, Terre Haute, Indiana.

Piggin, F. Stuart. Ph.D., University of London. Senior Lecturer in Religious History, University of Wollongong, Wollongong, Australia.

Preus, Robert D. Ph.D., University of Edinburgh; D.Theol., Strasbourg University. President, Concordia Theological Seminary, Fort Wayne, Indiana.

Proctor, William Cecil Gibbon. B.D., Trinity College, Dublin. Formerly Lecturer in the Divinity School, Trinity College, Dublin, Ireland.

Pun, Pattle P. T. Ph.D., State University of New York at Buffalo. Associate Professor of Biology, Wheaton College, Wheaton, Illinois.

Ramm, Bernard. Ph.D., University of Southern California. Professor of Christian Theology, American Baptist Seminary of the West, Berkeley, California.

Rausch, David A. Ph.D., Kent State University. Professor of Church History and Judaic Studies, Ashland Theological Seminary, Ashland, Ohio.

Rayburn, Robert G. Th.D., Dallas Theological Seminary. Professor of Practical Theology, Covenant Theological Seminary, St. Louis, Missouri.

Rayburn, Robert S. Ph.D., University of Aberdeen. Pastor, Faith Presbyterian Church, Tacoma, Washington.

Rehwinkel, Alfred Martin. B.D., St. Stephen's Theological College. Formerly Professor of Theology, Concordia Seminary, St. Louis, Missouri.

Reid, William Stanford. Ph.D., University of Pennsylvania. Professor Emeritus of History, University of Guelph, Guelph, Ontario.

Rennie, Ian S. Ph.D., University of Toronto. Dean and Professor of Church History, Ontario Theological Seminary, Willowdale, Ontario.

Renwick, Alexander MacDonald. D.D., University of Edinburgh. Sometime Professor of Church History, Free Church of Scotland College, Edinburgh, Scotland.

Reymond, Robert L. Ph.D., Bob Jones University. Professor of Systematic Theology and Apologetics, Covenant Theological Seminary, St. Louis, Missouri.

Ringenberg, William C. Ph.D., Michigan State University. Professor of History, Taylor University, Upland, Indiana.

Ro, Bong Rin. Th.D., Concordia Seminary, St. Louis. Executive Secretary, Asia Theological Association, Taichung, Taiwan.

Roberts, Arthur O. Ph.D., Boston University. Professor of Religion and Philosophy, George Fox College, Newberg, Oregon.

Roberts, Robert C. Ph.D., Yale University. Associate Professor of Philosophy, Western Kentucky University, Bowling Green, Kentucky.

Robinson, Donald W. B. Th.D., Australian College of Theology. Archbishop of Sydney, Sydney, Australia.

Robinson, William Childs. Th.D., Harvard University. Sometime Professor of Church History and Polity, Columbia Theological Seminary, Columbia, South Carolina.

Ross, Alexander. M.A., University of Edinburgh. Sometime Professor Emeritus, New Testament Exegesis, Free Church of Scotland College, Edinburgh, Scotland.

Rule, Andrew Kerr. Ph.D., University of Edinburgh. Formerly Professor of Church History and Apologetics, Louisville Presbyterian Theological Seminary, Louisville, Kentucky.

Ryrie, Charles C. Th.D., Dallas Theological Seminary; Ph.D., University of Edinburgh. Professor of Systematic Theology, Dallas Theological Seminary, Dallas, Texas.

Saucy, Robert L. Th.D., Dallas Theological Seminary. Professor of Systematic Theology, Talbot Theological Seminary, La Mirada, California.

Schnucker, Robert V. Ph.D., University of Iowa. Professor of History and Religion, Northeast Missouri State University, Kirksville, Missouri.

Scholer, David M. Th.D., Harvard Divinity School. Dean of the Seminary and Professor of New Testament, Northern Baptist Theological Seminary, Lombard, Illinois.

Scott, J. Julius, Jr. Ph.D., University of Manchester. Professor of Bible and Theology, Wheaton College, Wheaton, Illinois.

Seerveld, Calvin G. Ph.D., Free University. Senior Member in Philosophical Aesthetics, Institute for Christian Studies, Toronto, Ontario.

Shelley, Bruce L. Ph.D., University of Iowa. Professor of Church History, Denver Conservative Baptist Theological Seminary, Denver, Colorado.

Shelton, R. Larry. Th.D., Fuller Theological Seminary. Director, School of Religion, Seattle Pacific University, Seattle, Washington.

Simpson, Dale. Ph.D., Georgia State University. Clinical Director, Family Life Counseling Services, Bryan, Texas.

Singer, Charles Gregg. Ph.D., University of Pennsylvania. Professor of Church History and Systematic Theology, Atlanta School of Biblical Studies, Atlanta, Georgia.

Skillen, James W. Ph.D., Duke University. Executive Director, Association for Public Justice, Washington, D.C.

Skoglund, Elizabeth R. M.A., Pasadena College. Marriage, Family, and Child Counselor and Writer, Burbank, California.

Smith, Stephen M. Ph.D., Claremont School of Theology. Assistant Professor of Systematic Theology, Trinity Episcopal School for Ministry, Ambridge, Pennsylvania.

Smith, Wilbur M. D.D., Dallas Theological Seminary. Sometime Professor of English Bible, Fuller Theological Seminary, Pasadena, California.

Spiceland, James D. Ph.D., Oxford University. Associate Professor of Philosophy, Western Kentucky University, Bowling Green, Kentucky.

Sprunger, Keith L. Ph.D., University of Illinois. Professor of History, Bethel College, North Newton, Kansas.

Stanton, Gerald Barry. Th.D., Dallas Theological Seminary. President, Ambassadors International, West Palm Beach, Florida.

Steeves, Paul D. Ph.D., University of Kansas. Professor of History, Stetson University, De Land, Florida.

Stein, Robert H. Ph.D., Princeton Theological Seminary. Professor of New Testament, Bethel Theological Seminary, St. Paul, Minnesota.

Synan, Vinson. Ph.D., University of Georgia. Executive Director, Department of Evangelism, Pentecostal Holiness Church, Oklahoma City, Oklahoma.

Taylor, Stephen. M.A., Wheaton College.

Tenney, Merrill C. Ph.D., Harvard University. Professor Emeritus of Bible and Theology, Wheaton College, Wheaton, Illinois.

Thomas, Robert L. Th.D., Dallas Theological Seminary. Professor of New Testament Language and Literature, Talbot Theological Seminary, La Mirada, California.

Thomson, J. G. S. S. Ph.D., University of Edinburgh. Professor of Hebrew and Old Testament, Columbia Theological Seminary, Columbia, South Carolina.

Tinder, Donald G. Ph.D., Yale University. Associate Professor of Church History, New College Berkeley, Berkeley, California.

Tongue, Denis Harold. M.A., Cambridge University. Formerly Lecturer in New Testament, Tyndale Hall, Bristol, England.

Toon, Peter. D.Phil., Oxford University. Director of Postordinational Training, Diocese of St. Edmundsbury and Ipswich, Boxford, England.

Troutman, Richard L. Ph.D., University of Kentucky. Professor of History, Western Kentucky University, Bowling Green, Kentucky.

Tuttle, Robert G., Jr. Ph.D., University of Bristol. Professor of Historical Theology, School of Theology, Oral Roberts University, Tulsa, Oklahoma.

Unger, Merrill F. Ph.D., Johns Hopkins University; Th.D., Dallas Theological Seminary. Sometime Chairman of Old Testament Department, Dallas Theological Seminary, Dallas, Texas.

Unmack, Robert V. Th.D., Central Baptist Theological Seminary. Sometime Professor of New Testament, Central Baptist Theological Seminary, Kansas City, Kansas.

VanderMolen, Ronald J. Ph.D., Michigan State University. Professor of History, California State College, Stanislaus, Turlock, California.

Van Engen, John. Ph.D., University of California, Los Angeles. Professor of History, University of Notre Dame, Notre Dame, Indiana.

Van Gemeren, Willem A. Ph.D., University of Wisconsin-Madison. Associate Professor of Hebrew and Old Testament Literature, Reformed Theological Seminary, Jackson, Mississippi.

Vos, Howard F. Th.D., Dallas Theological Seminary; Ph.D., Northwestern University. Professor of History and Archaeology, The King's College, Briarcliff Manor, New York.

Waetjen, Herman Charles. Th.D., University of Tübingen. Robert S. Dollar Professor of New Testament, San Francisco Theological Seminary, San Francisco, California.

Wallace, David H. Ph.D., University of Edinburgh. Formerly Associate Professor of Biblical Theology, California Baptist Theological Seminary, Covina, California.

Wallace, Ronald Stewart. Ph.D., University of Edinburgh. Professor Emeritus of Biblical Theology, Columbia Theological Seminary, Columbia, South Carolina.

Walls, Andrew Finlay. B.Litt., Cambridge University. Professor of Religious Studies, University of Aberdeen, Aberdeen, Scotland.

Walter, Victor L. Th.M., Princeton Theological Seminary. Pastor, Calvary Mennonite Church, Aurora, Oregon.

Walvoord, John F. Th.D., Dallas Theological Seminary; D.D., Wheaton College. President, Dallas Theological Seminary, Dallas, Texas.

Ward, Wayne E. Th.D., Southern Baptist Theological Seminary. Professor of Theology, Southern Baptist Theological Seminary, Louisville, Kentucky.

Weaver, J. Denny. Ph.D., Duke University. Professor of Religion, Bluffton College, Bluffton, Ohio.

Weber, Timothy P. Ph.D., University of Chicago. Associate Professor of Church History, Denver Conservative Baptist Theological Seminary, Denver, Colorado.

Webster, Douglas D. Ph.D., University of Toronto. Professor of Theology, Ontario Theological Seminary, Willowdale, Ontario.

Weinrich, William C. Th.D., University of Basel. Associate Professor of Early Church History and Patristic Studies, Concordia Theological Seminary, Fort Wayne, Indiana.

Wenger, J. C. Th.D., University of Zurich. Professor of Historical Theology, Goshen Biblical Seminary, Elkhart, Indiana.

Wheaton, David H. M.A., University of London. Principal, Oak Hill College, London, England.

White, R. E. O. B.D., University of London. Theological writer.

White, Ronald C., Jr. Ph.D., Princeton University. Associate Director of Continuing Education and Lecturer in Church History, Princeton Theological Seminary, Princeton, New Jersey.

Whitlock, Luder G., Jr. D.Min., Vanderbilt University. President, Reformed Theological Seminary, Jackson, Mississippi.

Williams, J. Rodman. Ph.D., Columbia University. Professor of Christian Theology, School of Biblical Studies, CBN University, Virginia Beach, Virginia.

Wilson, Marvin R. Ph.D., Brandeis University. Ockenga Professor of Biblical Studies, Gordon College, Wenham, Massachusetts.

Wolf, Herbert M. Ph.D., Brandeis University. Associate Professor of Old Testament, Wheaton College, Wheaton, Illinois.

Wood, James E., Jr. Ph.D., Southern Baptist Theological Seminary. Simon and Ethel Bunn Professor of Church-State Studies and Director, Institute of Church-State Studies, Baylor University, Waco, Texas.

Woolley, Paul. Th.M., Princeton Theological Seminary. Professor Emeritus of Church History, Westminster Theological Seminary, Philadelphia, Pennsylvania.

Woudstra, Marten H. Th.D., Westminster Theological Seminary. Professor of Old Testament Studies, Calvin Theological Seminary, Grand Rapids, Michigan.

Wright, David F. M.A., Cambridge University. Senior Lecturer in Ecclesiastical History, University of Edinburgh, Scotland.

Wright, John Stafford. M.A., Cambridge University. Formerly Principal, Tyndale Hall, Bristol, England.

Wyngaarden, Martin J. Ph.D., University of Pennsylvania. Sometime Professor of Old Testament Interpretation, Calvin Theological Seminary, Grand Rapids, Michigan.

Youngblood, Ronald. Ph.D., Dropsie College. Professor of Old Testament and Hebrew, Bethel Seminary West, San Diego, California.

Zerner, Ruth. Ph.D., University of California, Berkeley. Associate Professor of History, Lehman College, City University of New York, New York, New York.

Transliteration

Hebrew

Consonants		Vowels	
א	ʾ	ָ	*ā*
ב	*b*	ַ	*a*
ג	*g*	ֶ	*e*
ד	*d*	ֵ	*ē*
ה	*h*	ִ	*i*
ו	*w*	ָ	*o*[1]
ז	*z*	ֹ	*ō*
ח	*ḥ*	ֻ	*u, ū*[2]
ט	*ṭ*		
י	*y*		
כ, ך	*k*		
ל	*l*	הָ	*â*
מ, ם	*m*	ֶי	*ê*
נ, ן	*n*	ֵי	*ê*
ס	*s*	ִי	*î*
ע	ʿ	וֹ	*ô*
פ, ף	*p*	וּ	*û*
צ, ץ	*ṣ*		
ק	*q*		
ר	*r*	ֳ	*ŏ*
שׂ	*ś*	ֲ	*ă*
שׁ	*š*	ֱ	*ĕ*
ת	*t*	ְ	*ĕ*[3]

1. *qāmeṣ ḥāṭûp*
2. *u* = short, *ū* = long defective
3. vocal *šĕwâ*

Greek

α	*a*	ξ	*x*
β	*b*	ο	*o*
γ	*g, n*	π	*p*
δ	*d*	ρ	*r*
ε	*e*	σ, ς	*s*
ζ	*z*	τ	*t*
η	*ē*	υ	*y, u*
θ	*th*	φ	*ph*
ι	*i*	χ	*ch*
κ	*k*	ψ	*ps*
λ	*l*	ω	*ō*
μ	*m*	ʽ	*h*
ν	*n*		

Abbreviations

ANF	*The Ante-Nicene Fathers*, ed. A. Roberts and J. Donaldson
APTR	*The American Presbyterian and Theological Review*
AQ	*American Quarterly*
ASR	*American Sociological Review*
ATR	*Anglican Theological Review*
Aug	*Augustinianum*
AugS	*Augustinian Studies*
AUSS	*Andrews University Seminary Studies*
AV	Authorized Version of the Bible
BJRL	*Bulletin of the John Rylands University Library*
Blunt	*Dictionary of Doctrinal and Historical Theology*, ed. J. H. Blunt
BR	*Biblical Research*
BRM	*Biblical Research Monthly*
BS	*Bibliotheca Sacra*
BT	*The Bible Today*
BTB	*Biblical Theology Bulletin*
CathDi	*Catholic Digest*
CBQ	*The Catholic Biblical Quarterly*
CCen	*The Christian Century*
CCri	*Christianity and Crisis*
CGT	Cambridge Greek Testament for Schools and Colleges
CH	*Church History*
CHR	*The Catholic Historical Review*
Chu	*Churchman*
CJ	*The Classical Journal*
Con	*Concilium*
CongQ	*Congregational Quarterly*
CQ	*Covenant Quarterly*
CQR	*Church Quarterly Review*
CT	*Christianity Today*
CTJ	*Calvin Theological Journal*
CTM	*Concordia Theological Monthly*
CTQ	*Concordia Theological Quarterly*
CW	*The Catholic World*
DBSup	*Dictionnaire de la Bible*, supplement, ed. L. Pirot
DCB	*A Dictionary of Christian Biography, Literature, Sects and Doctrines*, ed. W. Smith and H. Wace
DCE	*Baker's Dictionary of Christian Ethics*, ed. C. F. H. Henry
DNB	*Dictionary of National Biography*
DOP	*Dumbarton Oaks Papers*
DTC	*Dictionnaire de théologie catholique*, ed. A. Vacant, E. Mangenot, and É. Amann
EB	*Encyclopaedia Biblica*, ed. T. K. Cheyne and J. S. Black
EJ	*Encyclopaedia Judaica*
EncyBrit	*Encyclopaedia Britannica*
ER	*An Encyclopedia of Religion*, ed. V. Ferm
ERV	English Revised Version of the Bible
Eter	*Eternity*
EvQ	*Evangelical Quarterly*
Exp	*The Expositor*
ExpT	*The Expository Times*
FH	*Fides et Historia*

Abbreviations

GM	*The Gospel Magazine*
Greg	*Gregorianum*
HBD	*Harper's Bible Dictionary*, M. S. Miller and J. L. Miller
HDAC	*Dictionary of the Apostolic Church*, ed. J. Hastings
HDB	*A Dictionary of the Bible*, ed. J. Hastings
HDCG	*A Dictionary of Christ and the Gospels*, ed. J. Hastings
HDSB	*Harvard Divinity [School] Bulletin*
Her	*Hermes*
HERE	*Encyclopaedia of Religion and Ethics*, ed. J. Hastings
HLR	*Human Life Review*
HMPEC	*Historical Magazine of the Protestant Episcopal Church*
HTR	*Harvard Theological Review*
HUCA	*Hebrew Union College Annual*
HZNT	*Handbuch zum Neuen Testament*
IB	*The Interpreter's Bible*
IBD	*The Illustrated Bible Dictionary*, ed. W. C. Piercy
ICC	The International Critical Commentary
IDB	*The Interpreter's Dictionary of the Bible*, ed. G. A. Buttrick
IDB Supplement	*The Interpreter's Dictionary of the Bible*, supplementary volume, ed. K. Crim
IEJ	*Israel Exploration Journal*
Int	*Interpretation*
IRM	*International Review of Mission*
ISBE	*The International Standard Bible Encyclopaedia*, ed. J. Orr
ISBE (rev.)	*The International Standard Bible Encyclopedia*, ed. G. W. Bromiley
ITQ	*Irish Theological Quarterly*
JAAR	*Journal of the American Academy of Religion*
JAOS	*Journal of the American Oriental Society*
JASA	*Journal of the American Scientific Affiliation*
JBL	*Journal of Biblical Literature*
JCMHS	*The Journal of the Calvinistic Methodist Historical Society*
JCR	*The Journal of Christian Reconstruction*
JCS	*Journal of Church and State*
Jeev	*Jeevadhara*
JEH	*The Journal of Ecclesiastical History*
JETS	*Journal of the Evangelical Theological Society*
JHBS	*Journal of the History of Behavioral Sciences*
JHI	*Journal of the History of Ideas*
JJS	*Journal of Jewish Studies*
JNES	*Journal of Near Eastern Studies*
JPH	*Journal of Presbyterian History*
JPSP	*Journal of Personality and Social Psychology*
JPT	*Journal of Psychology and Theology*
JQR	*The Jewish Quarterly Review*
JR	*The Journal of Religion*
JRH	*Journal of Religion and Health*
JSS	*Journal of Semitic Studies*
JTS	*The Journal of Theological Studies*
Kat	*Katallagete*
LCC	The Library of Christian Classics
Lesh	*Leshonenu*
LTK	*Lexikon für Theologie und Kirche*, ed. M. Buchberger, J. Höfer, and K. Rahner
LUA	*Lunds Universitets Arskrift*
LXX	Septuagint
MarS	*Marian Studies*
McCQ	*McCormick Quarterly*
MissRev	*Missiology: An International Review*
MP	*Modern Philology*
MQR	*The Mennonite Quarterly Review*
MSt	*Cyclopaedia of Biblical, Theological, and Ecclesiastical Literature*, ed. J. McClintock and J. Strong
NAB	New American Bible
NASB	New American Standard Bible
NatGeo	*National Geographic*
NBC	*The New Bible Commentary*, (1st edition) ed. F. Davidson, (3d edition) ed. D. Guthrie and J. A. Motyer
NBD	*The New Bible Dictionary*, ed. J. D. Douglas

NCE	*New Catholic Encyclopedia*
NEB	New English Bible
NEQ	*The New England Quarterly*
NIDCC	*The New International Dictionary of the Christian Church*, ed. J. D. Douglas
NIDNTT	*The New International Dictionary of New Testament Theology*, ed. C. Brown
NIV	New International Version of the Bible
NKJV	New King James Version of the Bible
NovT	*Novum Testamentum*
NPNF	*[A Select Library of] The Nicene and Post-Nicene Fathers*, ed. P. Schaff and H. Wace
NT	New Testament
NTS	*New Testament Studies*
NZSTR	*Neue Zeitschrift für systematische Theologie und Religionsphilosophie*
ODCC	*The Oxford Dictionary of the Christian Church*, ed. F. L. Cross
OT	Old Testament
OTS	*Oudtestamentische Studiën*
PAPS	*Proceedings of the American Philosophical Society*
PBA	*Proceedings of the British Academy*
PC	*The Presbyterian Communique*
PEQ	*Palestine Exploration Quarterly*
PI	*The Public Interest*
PP	*Pastoral Psychology*
PPR	*Philosophy and Phenomenological Research*
PRE	*Realencyklopädie für protestantische Theologie und Kirche*, ed. J. J. Herzog and A. Hauck
Presb	*Presbyterion*
PRR	*The Presbyterian and Reformed Review*
Pru	*Prudentia*
PTR	*The Princeton Theological Review*
Rat	*Ratio*
RB	*Revue biblique*
RCDA	*Religion in Communist Dominated Areas*
RE	*Review and Expositor*
RelEd	*Religious Education*
RelS	*Religious Studies*
Rev	*Revelation*
RevM	*The Review of Metaphysics*
RGG	*Die Religion in Geschichte und Gegenwart*
RQ	*Restoration Quarterly*
RQum	*Revue de Qumran*
RR	*Reformed Review*
RRR	*Review of Religious Research*
RSCHS	*Record of the Scottish Church History Society*
RSV	Revised Standard Version of the Bible
RTR	*The Reformed Theological Review*
RTWB	*A Theological Word Book of the Bible*, ed. A. Richardson
RUS	*Rice University Studies*
RV	Revised Version of the Bible
SBk	*Kommentar zum Neuen Testament aus Talmud und Midrasch*, ed. H. Strack and P. Billerbeck
Sci	*Science*
SciAm	*Scientific American*
SCJ	*The Sixteenth Century Journal*
SCPJ	*SCP Journal*
Sem	*Semeia*
SHERK	*The New Schaff-Herzog Encyclopedia of Religious Knowledge*, ed. S. M. Jackson
SJT	*Scottish Journal of Theology*
SwJT	*Southwestern Journal of Theology*
Tar	*Tarbiz*
TB	*Tyndale Bulletin*
TDNT	*Theological Dictionary of the New Testament*, ed. G. Kittel and G. Friedrich
TDOT	*Theological Dictionary of the Old Testament*, ed. G. J. Botterweck and H. Ringgren
Them	*Themelios*
Theol	*Theology*
TheolEd	*Theological Education*
Tht	*Thought*
TJ	*Trinity Journal*
TS	*Theological Studies*

TWOT	*Theological Wordbook of the Old Testament*, ed. R.L. Harris, G.L. Archer, Jr., and B.K. Waltke
TZ	*Theologische Zeitschrift*
VC	*Vigiliae Christianae*
VoxT	*Vox Theologica*
VT	*Vetus Testamentum*
WBE	*Wycliffe Bible Encyclopedia*, ed. C. F. Pfeiffer, H. F. Vos, and J. Rea
WitD	*The Wittenburg Door*
WlTJ	*Wesleyan Theological Journal*
WmTJ	*The Westminster Theological Journal*
ZAW	*Zeitschrift für die alttestamentliche Wissenschaft*
ZKT	*Zeitschrift für katholische Theologie*
ZNW	*Zeitschrift für die neutestamentliche Wissenschaft*
ZPEB	*The Zondervan Pictorial Encyclopedia of the Bible*, ed. M. C. Tenney
ZTK	*Zeitschrift für Theologie und Kirche*

Aa

Abaddon. This is the name given to a satanic angel in Rev. 9:11, who appears as king of a horde of hellish locust-monsters sent to plague rebellious mankind. The Greek translation of the name is *ho Apollyōn*, "the Destroying One." In the OT *'ăbaddôn* occurs several times as an epithet of Sheol or Hades and signifies literally "destruction" (from the root *'ābad* meaning "become lost, be destroyed"). It occurs, e.g., in Ps. 88:11: "Shall thy covenant-love be celebrated in the grave, thy faithfulness in [the place of] destruction [*'ăbaddôn*]?" (similarly Prov. 15:11; 27:20; Job 26:6; 28:22; 31:12.) G. L. ARCHER, JR.

See also SATAN; BAAL-ZEBUB.

Abba. The word occurs three times in the NT. Mark uses it in Jesus' Gethsemane prayer (14:36). Paul employs it twice for the cry of the Spirit in the heart of a Christian (Rom. 8:15; Gal. 4:6). In every case it is accompanied by the Greek equivalent, *ho patēr.*

Abba is from the Aramaic *abba.* Dalman (*Words of Jesus,* p. 192) thinks it signifies "my father." It is not in the LXX. Perhaps Jesus said only "Abba" (*HDCG,* I, p. 2), but Sanday and Headlam think both the Aramaic and Greek terms were used (ICC, *Romans,* p. 203). Paul's usage suggests it may have become a quasi-liturgical formula. R. EARLE

See also FATHER, GOD AS; GOD, NAMES OF.

Bibliography. O. Hofius, *NIDNTT,* I, 614–21; T. M. Taylor, "'Abba, Father' and Baptism," *SJT* 2:62–71; J. Jeremias, *The Central Message of the NT,* 9–30, *NT Theology,* 61–68, and *The Prayers of Jesus,* 11–65; G. Kittel, *TDNT,* I, 5–6.

Abelard, Peter (1079–1142). Philosopher, theologian, and teacher, Peter Abelard lived in constant personal turmoil and confrontation with authority. Born in Brittany, he studied with some of the most respected theologians of his day and eventually became the brightest intellectual star of the Cathedral School of Paris. But for his tragic love affair and marriage with the beautiful and talented Héloise, he undoubtedly would have been the dominant thinker of the century.

In philosophy during Abelard's time the ruling doctrine of universals was that of Boethius (d. *ca.* 524), who considered them to be realities. This traditional realism was then under attack by nominalists, who looked upon universals simply as words. Abelard worked out a moderate realism that avoided the dangers and salvaged the strong points of both nominalism and extreme realism. He accomplished this by demonstrating the logical consequences of some important distinctions, such as that between the word that stands for a thing, the thing itself, and the concept of the thing in the mind. Thus, universals are not mere sounds or words, as the nominalists held, nor are they things-in-themselves, as extreme realists thought. Rather, they are concepts in the mind that have an objective reality derived from a process of mental abstraction. Abelard's philosophy placed universals in a distinct category of reality, so that God was not a universal, nor were particulars the only reality.

In theology Abelard's view of the atonement is usually called the moral influence theory. He rejected the position set forth by Anselm in the previous generation that the satisfaction made by Jesus was necessary for the forgiveness of sins, arguing instead that God had forgiven sins as an unqualified act of grace before Christ came. In contrast to Anselm, he declared that God is love, and had voluntarily assumed the burden of suffering brought on by human sin. This act of God's grace—taken freely and without any demand for compensation for sin—awakens in people gratitude and love for God. In Jesus Christ, the God-man, individuals see what they should be; by contrast are brought to a realization of their sin; and, by God's love as seen in Jesus, are won to a response which releases new springs of love, resulting in right conduct. In this fashion, the forgiven sinner becomes a truly new creation.

Even more important was Abelard's *Sic et Non* (*Yes and No*), written around 1120, in which he participated in the main philosophical dispute of the time over the role of faith and reason in theology, suggested several seminal methodological innovations, and demonstrated the inadequacy of extracts from the church fathers then used for significant theological work. In *Sic et Non* he listed 158 theological propositions and cited the authorities affirming and denying each one, thus emphasizing that merely quoting authorities was methodologically insufficient. Instead, students had to apply their own intellectual skills to the question and to the opinions about it. In short, *Sic et Non* suggested that reason must play as large a role as revelation and tradition in determining truth. This method made Abelard the main representative of a new school of speculative theologians and prepared the way for the work of Thomas Aquinas in the thirteenth century. Thus Abelard was one of the pioneers of medieval scholasticism.

However, during the latter part of Abelard's life Bernard of Clairvaux accused him of misleading students and employing unorthodox theological methods. In 1141 several of Abelard's teachings were condemned by the Council of Sens. He appealed to the pope but died in 1142 near Cluny on his way to Rome. R. D. Linder

See also Atonement, Theories of the; Nominalism; Realism; Scholasticism.

Bibliography. Abelard, *Historia Calamitatum* (*The Story of My Misfortunes*), tr. J. T. Muckle; J. R. McCallum, *Abelard's Christian Theology;* É. Gilson, *Héloise and Abelard;* A. V. Murray, *Abelard and St. Bernard;* D. E. Luscombe, *The School of Peter Abelard;* L. Grane, *Peter Abelard;* R. Pernoud, *Héloise and Abelard;* B. Radice, ed., *The Letters of Abelard and Héloise;* K. M. Starnes, *Peter Abelard: His Place in History.*

Abide. The Greek word for abide is *menō.* The papyri as well as the NT usage is best seen by dividing it with reference to place, time, and condition. With reference to place, it means to tarry as a guest, to lodge, to sojourn, maintain unbroken fellowship. With reference to time, it means to continue to be, to endure, to survive. With reference to condition, it means to remain as one is.

In the LXX there are no less than sixteen Hebrew words used for the Greek *menō.* The principal ones are: (1) *yāšab,* meaning to live in, to dwell, to sit down; (2) *'āmad,* meaning to stand; (3) *qûm,* meaning to rise; and (4) *lîn,* meaning to lodge, tarry, dwell, spend the night. A few LXX examples will suffice: "let the maiden remain with us" (Gen. 24:55); "behold, the plague remains [stands or is checked] before him" (Lev. 13:5); "but the counsel of the Lord remains [stands or rises up] forever" (Prov. 19:21). Other OT usages are "to stand fast in battle" or "to abide by a conviction."

In the NT the verb is used both transitively and intransitively. The transitive usage means to await, be in store for, withstand or endure (cf. Jer. 10:10; Mal. 3:2; Acts 20:23; Heb. 13:14). The intransitive sense is to continue in a place or state in which one now is, to reside, to last, especially in the face of trial (cf. Luke 8:27; Acts 27:31; John 15:5; I Cor. 3:14). The word is used in composition with at least nine prepositions in the NT.

Menō is used around 118 times, especially by the apostle John, where there are 40 occurrences in the Gospel and 26 occurrences in the Epistles. John 15 provides an excellent example of how John uses the word. On the way to Gethsemane, Christ taught the disciples the imperative need of remaining in him by using the figure of the vine and branches. With the vine, the organic union with the trunk means life for the branches. This speaks of the essential union that must exist between Christ and believers. In 15:4 we have a divine imperative when Jesus said, "Abide in me." Of course, there is a distinction between the natural order and the spiritual. The natural branch does not exercise its own will to choose whether or not to abide in the vine. It either remains in the vine or dies. But in the spiritual sense there is a definite act of the will on the disciple's part. The sense of urgency can be seen in the Savior's imperative statement *meinate en emoi.* This immediately shows any disciple that there is responsibility on his part. Jesus' simple statement is true that in him there is fruitbearing but without him there is barrenness (15:5). This sense of dependency is found throughout the NT. Christ had taught earlier of a mutual responsibility which describes a true and genuine relationship (6:56; 15:4). The Master not only sustains life so as to produce fruitful branches, but he is also the very source and origin of life (1:3).

In the First Epistle of John the author speaks of this vital union with Christ by the words "in him remaining" (2:5). This expression is similar to Paul's thought *en Christō einai.* By the end of the first century, with the second coming so long delayed, this vital relationship of "abiding in Christ" needed to be interpreted in terms of long duration rather than tarrying for a short time. So today, this abiding is the pulse beat of the believer.

R. V. Unmack

See also Godliness; Sanctification.

Bibliography. A. Murray, *Abide in Christ* and *Absolute Surrender;* E. Best, *One Body in Christ;* F. Godet, *Gospel of John,* II; R. H. Lightfoot, *St. John's Gospel,* ICC; J. H. Bernard, *Gospel According to St. John,* II; A. E. Brooke, *Johannine Epistles.*

Abolitionism. Movement in America and Western Europe to abolish the slave trade and slavery. The term was often applied to those urging immediate (instead of gradual) emancipation of slaves.

By the end of the seventeenth century slavery was legally recognized in Britain's American colonies. Throughout the eighteenth century, however, there were increasing questions about its morality, coming from both religious leaders and secular thinkers influenced by the Enlightenment's emphasis on personal liberty. Some of the strongest opposition came from Quakers, who by the late eighteenth century had banned slaveholding by members. In Great Britain, William Wilberforce, who had been deeply influenced by evangelical Christianity, vigorously led the successful fight in Parliament to abolish the slave trade (1807). In 1808 the importation of slaves became illegal in the United States, and many hoped slavery would eventually die out. Such hopes were doomed, however, by the invention of the power loom and the cotton gin, which enormously increased the demand for slave-cultivated cotton.

As slavery became more firmly entrenched in the American South, its opponents sought a practical way to eliminate it. One proposal was to send freed slaves back to Africa, a scheme which led to the formation of the American Colonization Society (1817). It established the colony of Liberia on the west African coast for freed slaves, but was unable to gather widespread support. The implicit racism of colonization also offended some slavery opponents.

More significant was the emergence of groups favoring immediate abolition. Best known was the American Anti-Slavery Society, formed in Philadelphia (1833) primarily through the efforts of William Lloyd Garrison, fiery editor of *The Liberator,* and Lewis and Arthur Tappan, two wealthy brothers involved in many evangelical causes. At its height the society had 150,000 members. Many of its leaders had been influenced by the revivals of Charles Finney and saw their antislavery convictions as a logical outcome of their evangelical faith.

Militant abolitionism had a galvanizing effect on the South, which became increasingly withdrawn and intolerant of dissent. The strident tone of some abolitionists also offended many Northerners who favored gradual emancipation. Nevertheless, the lectures and writings of such abolitionists as Harriet Beecher Stowe (*Uncle Tom's Cabin*), Theodore Weld, and James Birney had enormous influence. Although many Northerners did not identify with the abolitionists, their efforts gradually persuaded many that slavery was an evil that only radical measures could eliminate. Abolitionist goals were finally achieved through the Civil War and the Thirteenth Amendment to the Constitution (1865). Abolitionism was the most important reform movement of the nineteenth century.

J. N. Akers

Bibliography. J. M. McPherson, *Struggle for Equality;* L. Ruchames, ed., *Abolitionists;* G. Sorin, *Abolitionism: A New Perspective;* J. L. Thomas, ed., *Slavery Attacked;* R. G. Walters, *American Reformers 1815–1860.*

Abomination of Desolation. In this precise form these words are found in the AV in Matt. 24:15 and Mark 13:14, but there is an interpretative expression in Luke 21:20. The phrase is undoubtedly taken from Dan. 11:31 and 12:11, where the AV reads "the abomination that maketh desolate"; it is possible also that Dan. 8:13 and 9:27 contribute to the conception. Most expositors have been of the opinion that the passages in Daniel allude to the idolatrous desecration of the temple by Antiochus Epiphanes. On Dec. 15, 168 B.C., a pagan altar was built on the site of the great altar of burnt sacrifices, and ten days later heathen sacrifice was offered on it. The Alexandrian Jews interpreted Daniel's prophecy in this way. I Macc. 1:54 reads: *ōkodomēsen bdelygma erēmōseōs epi to thysiastērion.*

The altar was erected to Zeus Olympios, the Hebrew rendering of which name was *ba'al šāmayim.* S. R. Driver points out that the title *ba'al šāmayim* is often found in Phoenician and Aramaic inscriptions. By a change of the first word and a pun on the second this Aramaic title for "Lord of Heaven" was contemptuously reduced to *šiqqūṣ šōmēm,* meaning "abomination of horror" or "abomination of desecration." Moffatt renders it "appalling horror," but this seems to represent only one side of its significance. The term *šiqqûṣ* stands for that which is foul, disgusting, and hateful; *šōmēm* signifies that which desecrates or destroys what is good. The phrase therefore stands for that which utterly desecrates a holy thing or place. It can thus refer to the idolatrous image set up by Antiochus Epiphanes or to any other abhorrent object, person, or event which defiles that which is holy.

The passages in the NT are, of course, not exhausted by the historical fulfillment of the intertestamental period, and they must be studied in their own right. The Greek phrase *bdelygma tēs erēmōseōs* may be rendered "a detestable thing that brings desolation." The emphasis appears to be more on the first word than on the last and draws attention to the objectionableness of the thing denoted. The word *bdelygma* refers to that which causes nausea and abhorrence: see the use of the word in Luke 16:15 and Rev. 17:4. It is a frequent LXX rendering of *šiqqûs* in the sense of an idol or false god, but it was not limited to that. Anything which outraged the religious feelings of the Jewish people might be so described.

The attempt to understand our Lord's allusion in the use of this expression seems partly involved in the view taken about the apocalyptic nature of the passage. If it is merely predictive and apocalyptic, then some idolatrous image may possibly be intended; but if our Lord's words are to be construed as prophetic in style, displaying that spiritual insight which belongs to true prophecy, then it may not be necessary to look for such an image but rather for something having a vital bearing on the behavior of the Jewish nation. Interpretative guidance is given in the record preserved by Luke, which reads: "When ye shall see Jerusalem compassed with armies, then know that the desolation thereof is nigh" (21:20). Writing for Gentiles, it would seem that Luke has replaced the obscure and mysterious word *bdelygma* by a term more intelligible to his readers. This is not, as some have said, to alter the Lord's meaning, but to explain it. On the principle of interpreting Scripture by Scripture, therefore, the "abomination of desolation" must mean the Roman troops. Matthew's reference to the abomination standing "in the holy place" does not require to be understood of the temple, but may equally indicate the holy "land." The historical fulfillment of the prophecy occurred first under Cestius (Gallus) in A.D. 66, then under Vespasian (A.D. 68), then under Titus (A.D. 70). It is possibly a superficial mistake to associate the abomination with the eagles of the Roman standards, for these had already been in the "land" long enough. It was the encirclement (*kykloumenēn*) of Jerusalem by besieging forces of the Roman army that constituted the sign. The participle is in the present tense and shows that the Christians were to flee when they saw the city "being compassed" with armies. The presence of the Roman army was thus a *bdelygma* of the worst kind and one that presaged coming ruin. The word *bdelygma* was not too strong an expression to describe this invasion, for it was detestable indeed that heathen feet should defile the holy land and that the ungodly should come into the heritage of the Lord. (The participle "standing" is masculine and possibly points away from the thought of an altar or image and might suggest "the abominable *one*.")

Alford rejects the view that the encirclement of Jerusalem with armies is identical with the *bdelygma* and argues that Matthew and Mark, writing for Jews, give the *inner* or domestic sign of the coming desolation, this being some desecration of the holy place by factious Jewish parties, and that Luke gives the *outward* state of things corresponding to this sign. Conceiving of the "abomination of desolation" as one thing and the encircling Roman armies as another, he nevertheless unites them in the event which occurred at the historical moment of which the Lord speaks. The question is an open one, of course, and Alford's view has much to commend it; but it seems preferable to take the simpler view, which explains the abomination in terms of the Roman army. It would appear that Jesus intends to foretell a desecration of the temple and city in a manner not unlike that brought about by Antiochus Epiphanes. The words of Daniel seemed to find a second fulfillment, and Rome has taken the place of Syria. E. F. KEVAN

See also ANTICHRIST.

Bibliography. D. Daube, *The NT and Rabbinic Judaism;* C. H. Dodd, *More NT Studies;* W. Foerster, *TDNT,* I, 598ff.; A. T. Robertson, *Word Pictures in the NT,* I; S. R. Driver in *HDB;* F. E. Hirsch, *ISBE,* I, 16–17; H. W. Fulford in *HDCG;* H. B. Swete, *St. Mark;* G. R. Beasley-Murray, *Jesus and the Future* and *NIDNTT,* I, 74–75.

Abortion. An abortion is an induced termination of pregnancy in a manner designed to kill the embryo or fetus. Although miscarriage is sometimes referred to as "involuntary abortion," this article will concern itself only with "voluntary abortion."

The general Christian view of abortion, in contrast to the views of pre-Christian paganism, is well summarized by Harold O. J. Brown: "The overwhelming consensus of the spiritual leaders of Protestantism, from the Reformation to the present, is clearly anti-abortion. There is very little doubt among biblically oriented Protestants that abortion is an attack on the image of God in the developing child and is a great evil" (*The Human Life Review,* Fall, 1976, p. 131).

Karl Barth's view appears to be normative: "The unborn child is from the very first a child. It is still developing and has no independent life. But it is a man and not a thing, nor a mere part of the mother's body. . . . He who destroys germinating life kills a man. . . . The fact that a definite

No must be the presupposition of all further discussion cannot be contested, least of all today" (*Church Dogmatics*, III/4, 415ff.).

It has been observed that the great European theologians of this century who have discussed abortion have strongly opposed it. See, e.g., Emil Brunner, *The Divine Imperative*, 367ff.; Dietrich Bonhoeffer, *Ethics*, 130–31 (where Bonhoeffer refers to abortion as "murder"); and Helmut Thielicke, *The Ethics of Sex*, 227–28.

Public debate of the abortion issue has escalated dramatically since the 1973 Supreme Court decision in *Roe v. Wade*. Although opinion polls have shown that the Court's decision is widely misunderstood as legalizing abortion only in the first three months of pregnancy, the Court actually held that abortion could be constitutionally performed during the full nine months. The Court held that in the first trimester (three months) of pregnancy the abortion decision must be left entirely to a woman and her physician. During the second trimester the state may only enact laws which regulate abortion in ways "reasonably related to maternal health" (such as requiring that only medical doctors perform abortions, or imposing public health requirements on locations offering abortion services). During the final trimester, the Court held, the state could prohibit abortions except where necessary to preserve the mother's "life or health." However, the Court went on to broadly define the word "health" to include psychological and emotional health, thus making it "unconstitutional" to prohibit abortions in such cases even up until the day of delivery. Practically speaking, this means that abortion cannot be prohibited throughout the full term of pregnancy if there is a doctor willing to perform the abortion and to attest that carrying the child to term would result in psychological or emotional harm to the mother.

Advocates of a liberal abortion policy make three key arguments in support of their position. The foremost argument is that the abortion decision is properly a part of the woman's "freedom of choice" (also referred to as the woman's "right of privacy" or her right of "control over her own body"). The antiabortion response, simply stated, is that one's freedom to act only extends to the point where it impinges upon another's right not to be acted upon. Abortion involves the rights of the mother and the rights of the unborn child. The antiabortion response rejects the view that the unborn child is a mere appendage of the mother's body, and holds that the unborn child is a valuable human being in his or her own right.

A second argument commonly made in support of a permissive abortion policy is that to hold otherwise would be to impose a particular view of morality, a particular value system, upon our law. The assumption, sometimes explicitly stated but more often implicitly accepted, is that such "legislation of morality" is inappropriate in a pluralistic society. The antiabortion response is that there is no position in which "values neutrality" is possible. It is not a question of *whether* but *whose* morality or values will be reflected in our law and public policy. The antiabortion response further contends that the closest our law could have come to values neutrality—at least as that concept is understood in a democratic society—would have been for the Supreme Court to have left abortion subject to state regulation, as it was prior to 1973. Indeed, the argument goes, in overturning the community judgments of all fifty states, it is the Supreme Court and those favoring its 1973 abortion decisions who are the offenders seeking to impose their unrepresentative views on a pluralistic populace.

A third key argument frequently made by abortion proponents is that it is necessary to protect the "quality of life" of the mother and those children who are allowed to be born. Thus a "quality of life" ethic, in contrast to the traditional Judeo-Christian "sanctity of life" ethic, is urged upon our policy makers. By concentrating on the so-called hard cases (pregnancy following rape, incest, or teen-age sex, or where the mother has a history of child abuse) this argument has a certain emotional appeal to many who are sensitive to human suffering. Thus, doctors, scientists, politicians, philosophers, and others appear to take the compassionate role as they argue that they be given the legal right to determine who should be born and which "products of conception" should be "terminated." The antiabortion response is to reject as morally and theologically repugnant the contention that fetuses' right to life depends upon their being "wanted," upon their genetic or physical endowment, or upon how much it will cost their parents or society to rear them. Malcolm Muggeridge and others have effectively shown that the argument for quality of life over sanctity of life, which they view as diabolical, applies with equal force to those who have been born or have become "defective," reminiscent of Hitler's Nazi death camps. There is a "slippery slope," the argument goes, from permissive abortion to active euthanasia, and our society's law and public values appear to be moving rapidly in that direction.

In addition to the primary issue of whether abortion should be allowed, and if so under what circumstances, a number of secondary issues have arisen in the courts and legislatures. Does the constitutional right to have an abortion require that the abortion be paid for with public funds? May a state require that parents be notified, or their consent obtained, before abortions are performed on their minor daughters? Can abortions be limited to licensed hospitals? What say, if any, should a husband have in his wife's decision whether or not to abort? Is it permissible to require that the abortionist fully describe the fetus and the abortion procedure prior to performing it, and, if so, may a subsequent waiting period be further required to ensure "informed consent"? Can those who engage in "sidewalk counseling" in the proximity of an abortion clinic, attempting to dissuade women from aborting their unborn children, be legally convicted of trespassing? These are just a few of the many questions that have been addressed by courts and legislatures since the Supreme Court's decision in *Roe v. Wade*.

Fundamentalists and evangelicals, while generally opposed to permissive abortion, have nevertheless been unable to agree as to the most appropriate response to the drastic changes which have taken place in the law. Until very recently the fundamentalist doctrine of separation from the world was understood to discourage involvement in social and political issues. Under this view "the world" is seen as so utterly corrupt and evil that little can be done to redeem its structures and institutions. Hope is placed instead in the return of Christ, the final judgment, and the creation of a new heaven and a new earth. However, the 1980 elections saw a massive surge of fundamentalist political involvement, and abortion was one of several issues on their much publicized agenda. One rather ironic effect of this renewed fundamentalist interest in social and political issues is that it has left their evangelical brethren at least appearing to be the more "separated" of these two conservative Protestant groups.

In spite of the fact that most evangelicals are personally opposed to abortion, a number have remained ambivalent about efforts to amend the Constitution or otherwise to pursue legislative remedies. Those who have not joined the ranks of "prolife" activists suggest several reasons for their inaction. Some evangelicals consider abortion a matter of private morality which they view as inappropriate for public legislation. Others are persuaded in varying degrees by the "quality of life" argument, particularly in the "hard cases." Still others cite the stridency or the political overtones of the right-to-life movement as being responsible for their inability to identify with its purposes. Finally, the proabortion pronouncements of a number of mainline Protestant denominations have contributed to the view of a number of evangelicals that abortion is too complex an issue for there to be one Christian position.

C. Horn, III

Bibliography. H. O. J. Brown, *Death Before Birth;* J. S. Garton, *Who Broke the Baby?* G. Grisez, *Abortion: The Myths, the Realities and the Arguments;* T. Hilgers, D. Horan, and D. Mall, eds., *New Perspectives on Human Abortion;* B. N. Nathanson and R. N. Ostling, *Aborting America;* J. T. Noonan, Jr., *A Private Choice: Abortion in America in the Seventies;* J. Powell, *Abortion: The Silent Holocaust;* C. E. Rice, *The Vanishing Right to Live;* J. C. Willke, *Handbook on Abortion.*

Abraham. Abraham stands in the unique position of being the father of a nation and the father of all believers. God told Abraham to leave his homeland and go to the land of Canaan. There God entered into a covenant with him (Gen. 12:1–3; 15:12–21). Abraham was the progenitor of the Hebrew nation and of several Arabic peoples. All Jews regard themselves as his descendants, a special people chosen by God (Isa. 51:1–2).

But beyond the physical posterity lies the spiritual dimension, for "all peoples on earth will be blessed through you" (Gen. 12:3; 18:18; 22:18; 26:4; 28:14). This is perhaps the first great missionary text in the Bible. Paul referred to it as the same gospel which he preached (Gal. 3:8). The blessing came through Christ, "the son of David, the son of Abraham" (Matt. 1:1). All who believe in Christ are the children of Abraham, even the Gentiles (Gal. 3:7–14). They too are "Abraham's seed, and heirs according to the promise" (Gal. 3:29). In fact, faith in Christ is more important than physical descent when it comes to determining who the children of Abraham really are (Matt. 3:9; John 8:33). God's promises to Abraham and the rest of the patriarchs find their unique fulfillment in Christ (Acts 3:25–26), though in a limited sense any godly king who sat on David's throne fulfilled the Abrahamic covenant (cf. Ps. 72:17). The covenant was unconditional and eternal, but kings and other individuals who disobeyed God would find themselves cut off from the covenant (Gen. 17:13–14; 18:18–19).

The NT mentions Abraham more than any other OT figure except Moses, and it stresses his significance as a man of faith. When called to leave Mesopotamia, Abraham "obeyed and went, even though he did not know where he was going" (Heb. 11:8). Even after reaching Canaan, Abraham still remained a stranger and did not live to see the fulfillment of the promises (Heb. 11:9–10). He did believe that God would give him a son and that his offspring would someday become as numerous as the stars. On the basis of this faith God "credited it to him as righteousness" (Gen. 15:4–6). Paul cites this passage as his first illustration of justification by faith in Rom. 4:1–3. In the same chapter Paul notes that Abraham dared to believe that Sarah would give birth to the promised child, even though she was past the age of childbearing and he was a hundred years old (Rom. 4:18–19). Abraham's unwavering faith in the promises of God remains a challenge to all people to "believe in him who raised Jesus our Lord from the dead" (Rom. 4:20–24).

The greatest test of Abraham's faith came when God instructed him to sacrifice Isaac on Mt. Moriah. In spite of the fact that God's previous promises were intertwined with the life of Isaac, Abraham obeyed and was ready to plunge the knife into his dear son. According to Heb. 11:17–19, Abraham reasoned that God would bring Isaac back to life, so deep was his confidence in God's promises. This experience of nearly sacrificing his only son placed Abraham in the position of God the Father, who sent his one and only Son to Mt. Calvary, not far from Mt. Moriah (II Chr. 3:1). The Greek word that describes Christ as the "only begotten" or "one and only son," *monogenēs,* is applied to Isaac in Heb. 11:17. A ram was substituted on the altar for Isaac (Gen. 22:13), but God "did not spare his own son"(Rom. 8:32). The pain and agony felt by Abraham at the prospect of sacrificing Isaac in some small way helps us understand the suffering of the Father when he offered up his Son for us all.

Abraham's fellowship with God is also illustrated through his prayer life. In Gen. 20:7 Abraham is called a prophet who will pray for the healing of a Philistine king and his family. Earlier, in Gen. 18:22–33, Abraham stood before the Lord and interceded in behalf of the city of Sodom. His boldness in prayer encourages the believer to lay petitions before the throne of grace. Because of his close walk with the Lord, Abraham is sometimes called the friend of God (II Chr. 20:7; Isa. 41:8; James 2:23). Both the Hebrew and the Greek words for "friend" include the idea of "the one who loves God." Abraham loved God more than anything else in the world (Gen. 22:2). His obedience to the Lord is emphasized also in Gen. 26:5. Before the law was written, Abraham kept God's requirements, commands, and laws.

Abraham was rightly called a prophet because he received divine revelation (Gen. 12:1–3). God spoke to him in a vision (Gen. 15:1) and appeared to him in a theophany (Gen. 18:1).

H. M. Wolf

Bibliography. J. Walvoord, "Premillennialism and the Abrahamic Covenant," *BS* 109:37–46, 293–303; G. von Rad, *OT Theology,* I, 170–75; J. B. Payne, *The Theology of the Older Testament;* J. Jeremias, *TDNT,* I, 8–9; R. Longenecker, "The 'Faith of Abraham,'" *JETS* 20:203–12; W. Kaiser, Jr., *Toward an OT Theology;* R. E. Clements, *TDOT,* I, 52–58.

Abraham's Bosom. In Luke 16:22–23 Lazarus is carried by the angels into Abraham's bosom. It is most natural and in keeping with NT thought elsewhere to think of the heavenly banquet to which Lazarus is now admitted. Reclining at table at Abraham's side (cf. John 13:23), Lazarus is thus enjoying the privileges of a guest of honor (cf. Matt. 8:11). Rabbinic Judaism used the expression also in a different sense, namely, that of rest from the toil and neediness of earthly life in intimate fellowship with the father of the race, who is still alive and blessed in death.

Hades and Abraham's bosom are distinct places, not two compartments of the same place. If Abraham's bosom was intended to refer to one of the divisions of Hades, then the other division would have been mentioned with equal precision. Hades is mentioned in connection with Dives only; the other place is "afar off." Hades is associated with being in torment; the latter appears to be the consequence of being in Hades. If Hades were a neutral concept here, then the contrast with the rich man's former sumptuous state would not have been expressed.

M. H. Woudstra

See also Intermediate State; Hades.

Bibliography. R. Meyer, *TDNT,* III, 824–26; *SBk,* II, 225ff.

Absolution. The word comes from the Latin *absolvo,* "set free." It is used in theology to denote the forgiveness of sins, being specifically used by Roman Catholics of the remission given through or by the church. It is a suitable word in that the truly free person is one against whom no accusation of sin can be made.

In the Bible. The Bible teaches God's willingness to forgive human sin and his provision whereby justice and mercy are reconciled in the transaction. This study is properly made under the subject of the atonement. Here we simply note the biblical teaching that all sin is sin against God ("Against thee, thee only, have I sinned," Ps. 51:4), and therefore sin can be forgiven only if it is forgiven by God. In the last analysis, then, absolution is the sole prerogative of God. This is basic in the whole conception of absolution.

But one's sin affects one's fellow men as well as offending God, and in particular the sins of a

Christian affect the whole church and his relationship with the church. We find this fact revealed in our Lord's teaching concerning forgiveness. He links the disciples' forgiveness of one another with God's forgiveness of them: "Forgive us our debts, as we also have forgiven our debtors." Several of his parables teach the same lesson (e.g., the unforgiving servant). And in our Lord's words (spoken first to Peter and afterward to all the disciples), "Whatever you bind on earth shall be bound in heaven, and whatever you loose on earth shall be loosed in heaven" (Matt. 16:19; 18:18), he clearly gives them their share in the matter of forgiveness of sins. Finally, the words spoken to the disciples in the upper room after the resurrection give unmistakable expression to the fact that the church has a part to play in conveying the sense of forgiveness to a penitent soul: "Jesus . . . said to them again, Peace be unto you: as the Father hath sent me, even so send I you. And when he had said this, he breathed on them, and saith unto them, Receive ye the Holy Spirit: whose soever sins ye forgive, they are forgiven unto them; whose soever sins ye retain, they are retained" (John 20:21–23).

Thus we conclude from biblical teaching that absolution comes from God alone; but, in that his church on earth is concerned with the sins of its members, it too has a ministry and commission in this matter, being given a special "inspiration" of the Holy Spirit for the purpose. How, then, has this been carried out by the church through history?

In the Church. There is ample evidence to show that in the early church the practice was for the penitent to make public confession of his sin before the congregation, whereupon he was received back by the congregation as a whole with prayer and the imposition of the hands of the bishop. As time went on, a natural alternative to such public confession was for the penitent to confess before a minister of the church (the bishop or a presbyter) in private. In both of these methods a prayer for absolution was used, asking God to forgive the sins so confessed and to restore the penitent "to the bosom of thy holy church" (from the Apostolic Constitutions).

In the eighth century and later, when the Eastern and Western churches were beginning to fall apart, we find a development taking place in the Latin church whereby the presbyter (priest), hearing confessions, assumed more and more the position of a judge, inquiring into every department of the penitent's life and finally giving absolution in a declaratory form as distinct from the earlier precatory form. Thomas Aquinas was the first formally to defend this type of absolution, which is now used in the church of Rome as follows: *Ego te absolvo a peccatis tuis in nomine Patris et Filii et Spiritus Sancti.*

The Reformers of the sixteenth century sought to restore the matter to its scriptural teaching and early church usage. The confessional with its declaratory form of absolution was abolished by all the Protestant churches. Differences of procedure sprang up in the different denominations, but the same basic idea may be found in all, namely, to stir the conscience to an inner acknowledgment of sin, so that on confession to God it may be absolved directly by God himself. This stirring of the conscience is mainly effected by preaching and prayer, and if there is any declaration of forgiveness it has the form of a proclamation of the gospel promises. In most cases opportunity is given for a public confession in divine worship, whether representatively by the minister or corporately by the whole congregation.

Protestant thought in general, however, does not overlook the need sometimes for the confession of a sin which is burdening the conscience of an individual. In Anglicanism provision is made for this by invitation to come to "a learned minister of God's Word"; and in other bodies, and often in evangelistic missions, opportunity is given for private consultation with a "counselor" or other Christian friend. In each case the Scriptures are the basis of instruction, and prayer is used to bring peace to the troubled mind and to kindle renewed faith in Christ.

To conclude, absolution is primarily identical with the divine remission. It is used especially of the declaration of forgiveness, i.e., the assuring of a penitent sinner that he is forgiven. It is received on the confession of sin to God, and its declaration is an integral part of the evangelical ministry of the church. W. C. G. Proctor

See also Atonement; Confession; Forgiveness; Penitence; Repentance.

Bibliography. M. H. Seymour, *The Confessional.*

Abstinence. A refraining from various external actions, such as drinking, eating, marriage, and participation in human society. In its wider meaning abstinence includes the whole negative side of biblical spirituality and morality, but its usual sense involves abstinence from food or drink.

The law given to Moses contained various dietary rules for the people of Israel (Lev. 11), but only required them to fast once during the year, on the day of atonement (Lev. 16:29). Zech. 8:19 refers to four annual fasts, which appear to have been introduced after the exile.

The practice of fasting appears to have been

widely followed by the Jews during the lifetime of Jesus, and he appears to have expected his followers to fast (Matt. 6:16–18), though possibly not until after his death (Mark 2:18–20).

Although Jesus' entry upon his public ministry was preceded by forty days of fasting during the temptation in the wilderness, he cannot be viewed as an ascetic in either his practice or his teaching. He did not withdraw from society—weddings, feasts, etc.—nor subject himself to austere practices. He was accused by the meticulous Pharisees of being "gluttonous and a winebibber" (Matt. 11:18–19). The joyful inner attitude of devotion to Christ precluded mourning and fasting by Jesus' followers (Matt. 9:14–15).

The early church fasted before important appointments were made (Acts 13:2–3; 14:23). At the Council of Jerusalem, when the question of the position of Gentile converts vis-à-vis the law was discussed, the only abstinence required of them was "from what has been sacrificed to idols and from blood and from what has been strangled and from unchastity" (Acts 15:29). The Didache (possibly early second century A.D.) speaks (8:1) of the importance of Christians fasting "not as the hypocrites" (i.e., the Jews) on Monday and Thursday, but on Wednesday and Friday (the latter called the Preparation, possibly a reminder that it was the day on which Jesus suffered; cf. John 19:14).

The medieval church encouraged fasting as a means of gaining merit in the sight of God, and the Roman church distinguished between abstinence, when meat is proscribed, and fasting, which allows only one meal in twenty-four hours. The English Reformers abolished this distinction by retaining certain "days of fasting, or abstinence," and the *Book of Common Prayer* prescribes for this purpose the forty days of Lent, the ember and rogation days, and the Fridays of the year. On these days some church people avoid meat at a main meal. The Homily of Fasting in the *Book of Homilies* explains how Reformed churchmen see the significance of this.

In modern times many Christians of all traditions have reintroduced this discipline in order to give themselves to prayer or other devotional exercises. Paul suggests in I Cor. 7:5 that on occasion a married couple might abstain from intercourse in order to give themselves to prayer, but this should only be a temporary arrangement by mutual consent. D. H. Wheaton

See also Alcohol, Drinking of; Fast, Fasting.

Bibliography. D. Smith, *Fasting.*

Abyss. *See* Bottomless Pit.

Accommodation. The theological term that designates that characteristic of biblical literature which allows a writer, for purposes of simplification, to adjust his language to the limitations of his readers without compromising the truth in the process. The concern here is to discriminate between the legitimate and the illegitimate application of this principle.

The following illustrations indicate the legitimate use of accommodation: (1) In the realm of theology proper God is often described as having physical properties (hands, eyes, etc.). This feature is called anthropomorphism. It serves a useful purpose. (2) In the realm of cosmology the facts of nature (the sun sets, etc.) are often pictured in the language of appearance rather than in the language of exact science. This allows the Bible to speak in ordinary language. (3) In the realm of ethics a stronger brother may, in matters indifferent, accommodate himself to the scruples of a weaker brother (I Cor. 8; Gal. 2:3–5). (4) In the realm of didactics parabolic language may be employed to accommodate the deeper mysteries to the minds of the unenlightened (Matt. 13:10–17).

The following illustrations indicate the illegitimate use of accommodation: (1) The claim that Christ accommodated himself to the prejudices and erroneous views of the Jews is a false use of accommodation. The scholars who make this claim practically nullify Christ's authority on critical questions. (2) The claim that the early church invested OT prophecies with a meaning they cannot bear is another false use of accommodation. The scholars who advance this claim practically empty the OT of real messianic prophecy. (3) The claim that the writers of Scripture adopted ideas from pagan religions and then, after some purging, accommodated these ideas to the religion of Israel or to the theology of the nascent NT church is another erroneous use of accommodation. God's revelation cannot be intermingled with human error. W. Broomall

See also Anthropomorphism.

Bibliography. *Blunt; MSt;* R. Hofman, *SHERK,* I, 22–24; J. R. Willis in *HDCG;* L. M. Sweet, *ISBE,* I, 28–33; G. T. Ladd, *The Doctrine of Holy Scripture,* I; W. Broomall, *Biblical Criticism.*

Accountability. *See* Responsibility.

Accountability, Age of. *See* Age of Accountability.

Acolyte. *See* Minor Orders.

Active Obedience of Christ. *See* Obedience of Christ.

Acts of Uniformity. *See* UNIFORMITY, ACTS OF.

Adam. The Hebrew word transliterated "Adam" is found about 560 times in the OT. In the overwhelming majority of cases it means "man" or "mankind." This is true of some of the references at the beginning of Genesis (in the creation and Eden stories), and many scholars hold that up to Gen. 4:25 all occurrences of "Adam" should be understood to refer to "man" or "the man." But there is no doubt that the writer on occasion used the word as the proper name of the first man, and it is with this use that we are concerned. It is found outside Genesis in I Chr. 1:1 and possibly in other passages such as Deut. 32:8 (where "the sons of men" may be understood as "the sons of Adam"), and in some important NT passages.

Adam in OT Teaching. We are told that God created man "in his own image" and that he created them "male and female" (Gen. 1:27), statements made about no other creature. Man was commanded to "be fruitful and multiply, and fill the earth and subdue it" (Gen. 1:28). He was not to be idle but was given the task of tending the Garden of Eden. He was forbidden to eat "of the tree of the knowledge of good and evil" (Gen. 2:15–17). The man was given the privilege of naming all the animals (Gen. 2:20), but no suitable help for him was found among them, so God made woman from a rib taken from the man's body (Gen. 2:21–23). The serpent beguiled the woman into breaking God's command not to eat of the tree of the knowledge of good and evil, and she then persuaded her husband to do likewise. They were punished by being expelled from the garden, and in addition the woman was to have pain in childbirth and be subject to her husband, while Adam would find the ground cursed so that it would bring forth thorns and thistles and he would have to toil hard all his days (Gen. 3). But curse is not all; there is the promise of a Deliverer who will crush the serpent (Gen. 3:15). We are told of the birth of two sons of Adam, Cain and Abel; of Cain's murder of Abel (Gen. 4:1–16); and of the birth of Seth (Gen. 4:25).

The meaning of these passages is disputed. Some OT scholars regard them as primitive myth, giving early man the answers to such questions as "Why do snakes lack legs?" or "Why do men die?" Others see them as mythological, but as expressing truths of permanent validity concerned with man's origin and constitution or, as others hold, with "a fall upward." This latter view sees man as originally no more than one of the animals. At this stage he could no more sin than any other animal could. It was accordingly a significant step forward when man became aware of something he was doing as wrong. But it is highly doubtful whether the writer had in mind any such ideas. Clearly he thought of Adam and Eve as the first parents of the human race, and he is telling us of God's purpose that those into whom he had breathed "the breath of life" should live in fellowship with him. But Adam and Eve fell from their original blissful state as a result of their first sin. And that sin has continuing consequences for the whole human race. In later times the magnitude of the fall has sometimes been emphasized by affirming that Adam was originally endowed with wonderful supernatural gifts, lost when he sinned (in Sir. 49:16 Adam is honored "above every living being in the creation"; cf. the medieval stress on Adam's supernatural graces). But this is speculation.

The creation narratives tell us at least that man is related to the rest of creation (he is made "of dust from the ground," Gen. 2:7; for the beast and the birds cf. vs. 19), and that he is related also to God (he is "in the image of God," Gen. 1:27; cf. 2:7). He has "dominion" over the lower creation (Gen. 1:26, 28), and this is symbolized by his naming of the other creatures. The fall passage speaks of the seriousness of his sin and of its permanent effects. This is not a topic to which there is frequent reference in the OT, but it underlies everything. It is a fundamental presupposition that man is a sinner, and this marks off the literature of the Hebrews from other literatures of antiquity. The solidarity of Adam with his descendants is in the background throughout the OT writings, as is the thought that there is a connection between sin and death. Whatever problems this poses for modern expositors, there can be no doubt about the fact that the OT takes a serious view of sin or that sin is seen as part of man's nature.

Adam in Intertestamental and NT Thought. During the intertestamental period there are some striking expressions of solidarity with Adam, such as Ezra's impassioned exclamation: "O Adam, what have you done? For though it was you who sinned, the fall was not yours alone, but ours also who are your descendants" (II Esd. 7:48 [118]; cf. 3:21; 4:30; Wis. 2:23–24; the blame is assigned to Eve in Sir. 25:24). Adam was seen not as a lone sinner, but as one who influenced all mankind.

In the NT Adam is mentioned in Luke's genealogy (Luke 3:38) and in a similar reference in Jude, where Enoch is "the seventh from Adam" (Jude 14). Little need be said about these passages. They simply mention the name of Adam to locate him in his genealogical place. There is perhaps an implied reference to Adam but without mention of his name (Matt. 19:4–6; Mark 10:6–8). Then there are three important passages with theological import (I Tim. 2:13–14; Rom. 5:12–21; I Cor. 15:22, 45).

In I Tim. 2:13–14 the subordinate place of woman is argued from two facts: (1) Adam was created first, and (2) Eve was deceived though Adam was not. This passage presumes that the Genesis stories tell us something of permanent significance about all men and women.

Romans 5 stresses the connection of mankind at large with Adam. It was through that one man that sin came into the world, and the consequence of his sin was death. This happened long before the law was given, so death cannot be put down to law-breaking. And even though people did not sin in the same way as Adam, they were caught in the consequences of sin: "death reigned from Adam to Moses" (Rom. 5:12–14). This brings Paul to the thought that Adam was a "type" of Christ, and he goes on to a sustained comparison of what Adam did with what Christ did. There are resemblances, mainly in that both acted representatively so that what each did has incalculable consequences for those he heads. But the differences are more significant. Adam's sin brought death and condemnation to all; it made people sinners. When law came in, that only increased the trespass. It showed up sin for what it was. The end result is disaster. By contrast Christ brought life and acquittal; such words as "free gift," "grace," and "justification" emphasize the significance of Christ's death. The end result is blessing. Paul concludes by contrasting the reign of sin in death with the reign of grace "through righteousness to eternal life through Jesus Christ our Lord."

In Paul's magnificent treatment of the resurrection we read: "As in Adam all die, so also in Christ shall all be made alive" (I Cor. 15:22). The thought is not unlike that in Rom. 5. Adam was the head of the race and brought death to everyone in it; Christ is the head of the new humanity and brought life to all within it. Some have argued that the two uses of "all" must refer to the same totality, the entire human race. There is no question but that this is the meaning in respect to Adam. The argument runs that similarly Christ raises all from the grave, though some are raised only for condemnation. However, "made alive" seems to mean more than "raised to face judgment." It is probably best to understand "made alive" to refer to life eternal, so that "all" will mean "all who are in Christ." All these will be made alive, just as all who are in Adam die.

A little later Paul writes, "'the first man Adam became a living being'; the last Adam became a life-giving spirit" (I Cor. 15:45). Adam became "a living being" when God breathed life into him (Gen. 2:7). Physical life was all the life Adam had and all he could bequeath to his posterity. But "the last Adam" gave life in the fullest sense, eternal life. Again there is the thought that Christ cancels out the evil Adam did. But the emphasis is not negative. It is on the life Christ gives.

The scriptural use of Adam, then, stresses the solidarity of the human race, a solidarity in sin. It reminds us that the human race had a beginning and that all its history from the very first is marked by sin. But "the last Adam" has altered all that. He has replaced sin with righteousness and death with life. L. Morris

See also Adam, The Last; Fall of Man; Sin; Man, Origin of.

Bibliography. C. K. Barrett, *From First Adam to Last;* K. Barth, *Christ and Adam;* B. S. Childs, *IDB,* I, 42–44; W. D. Davies, *Paul and Rabbinic Judaism;* J. Jeremias, *TDNT,* I, 141–43; A. Richardson, *An Introduction to the Theology of the NT;* H. Seebass, *NIDNTT,* I, 84–88; A. J. M. Weddeburn, *IBD,* I, 14–16.

Adam, The Last. In I Cor. 15:45 Paul refers to Jesus Christ as "the last Adam" (*ho eschatos Adam*) in contrast to "the first man Adam" (*ho prōtos anthrōpos Adam*). In this antithetic parallelism there is a continuity of humanity, but the second person who represents the new humanity so far excels the first that he is described as the one who became an active "life-giving spirit" (*pneuma zōopoioun*), where the original Adam (Gen. 2:7) became only "a natural living being" (*psychēn zōsan*). The contrast is heightened by Paul's pointed antithetic style, setting Adam as over against Christ in I Cor. 15:46–49:

	First Adam	Second Adam
46:	"natural" (*psychikon*)	"spiritual" (*pneumatikon*)
47:	"the first man" (*ho prōtos anthrōpos*) "from the earth, of dust" (*ek gēs, choikos*)	"the second man" (*ho deuteros anthrōpos*) "from heaven" (*ex ouranou*)
48:	"as was the man of dust, so are those who are of dust" (*hoios ho choikos, toioutoi kai hoi choikoi*)	"as is the man of heaven, so are those who are of heaven" (*hoios ho epouranios, toioutoi kai hoi epouranioi*)
49:	"as we have borne the image of the man of dust" (*kathōs ephoresamen tēn eikona tou choikou*)	"we shall also bear the image of the man of heaven" (*phoresomen kai tēn eikona tou epouraniou*)

The same contrast was also made earlier in I Cor. 15:21–22 and linked with death and resurrection:

	First Adam	Second Adam
21:	"since by a man came death" (*epeidē gar di' anthrōpou thanatos*)	"so also by a man has come the resurrection of the dead" (*kai di' anthrōpou anastasis nekrōn*)
22:	"For as in Adam all die" (*hōsper gar en tō Adam pantes apothnēskousin*)	"so also in Christ shall all be made alive" (*houtōs kai en tō Christō pantes zōopoiēthēsontai*)

The contrast is expressed again in Rom. 5: 14–19, where Paul describes the first Adam as follows: disobedience ➧ trespass ➧ judgment ➧ condemnation ➧ death ➧ many = all. But Jesus Christ as the second Adam is described in the following antithetic terms: obedience ➧ grace ➧ free gift ➧ justification ➧ acquittal ➧ righteousness ➧ life ➧ many/all. The powerful effect of Christ as the second Adam is summed up in one of Paul's favorite expressions, "how much more" (*pollō mallon*, 5:15, 17, and 8, 10), which makes explicit the Christological implications of the "how much more" in Jesus' own proclamation (Matt. 6:30; 7:11). These ideas may also be found in John 5:21–29; Rom. 1:3–5; 6:5–11; II Cor. 5:1–4, 17; Phil. 2:5–11. R. G. Gruenler

See also Adam; Incarnation.

Bibliography. C. K. Barrett, *From First Adam to Last;* O. Cullmann, *The Christology of the NT;* R. Scroggs, *The Last Adam;* W. D. Davies, *Paul and Rabbinic Judaism.*

Adiaphora, Adiaphorists. Adiaphora (Gk. "indifferent things"; German *Mitteldinge*, "middle matters") refers to matters not regarded as essential to faith which might therefore be allowed in the church. In particular the Lutheran confessions of the sixteenth century speak of adiaphora as "church rites which are neither commanded nor forbidden in the Word of God."

Historically the Adiaphorists were those Protestants who, with Philip Melanchthon, held certain Roman Catholic practices (e.g., confirmation by bishops, fasting rules, etc.) to be tolerable for the sake of church unity. This issue became the focal point for a bitter controversy prompted by the Augsburg Interim forced on the Lutherans in 1548 by Emperor Charles V and accepted by Melanchthon and others in the Leipzig Interim. The Gnesio-Lutherans, led by Nicholas von Amsdorf and Matthias Flacius, objected to the presuppositions and judgments concerning adiaphora that led the Saxon theologians (the "Philippists") to forge the Leipzig Interim. The "Gnesios" set down the basic principle that in a case where confession of faith is demanded, where ceremonies or adiaphora are commanded as necessary, where offense may be given, adiaphora do not remain adiaphora but become matters of moral precept. Those who supported the Interims argued that it was better to compromise appearances in terms of rites and customs than to risk the abolition of Lutheranism in Saxony. Although the controversy over the Interims became unnecessary after the Religious Peace of Augsburg in 1555, the dispute continued, and nearly two hundred tracts appeared discussing one stance or the other.

In 1577 the Formula of Concord brought an end to the question for Lutherans by setting forth three fundamental points concerning the nature of genuine adiaphora. First, genuine adiaphora is defined as ceremonies neither commanded nor forbidden in God's Word and not as such, or in and of themselves, divine worship or any part of it (Matt. 15:9). This evangelical principle is integral to the very cornerstone of Reformation theology; it cuts off at the source all false claims of human tradition and authority in the church. The second major point about genuine adiaphora is that the church does have the perfect right and authority to alter them so long as this is done without offense, in an orderly manner, so as to redound to the church's edification (Rom. 14; Acts 16, 21). The third assertion goes to the heart of the entire matter: at a time of confession, when the enemies of God's Word seek to suppress the pure proclamation of the gospel, one must confess fully, in word and deed, and not yield, even in adiaphora. Here it is not a question of accommodating oneself to the weak, but of resisting idolatry, false doctrine, and spiritual tyranny (Col. 2; Gal. 2, 5). In sum, the Formula of Concord's position included adiaphora within the domain of Christian liberty, which may be defined as consisting of the freedom of believers from the curse (Gal. 3:13) and coercion (Rom. 6:14) of the law and from human ordinances. This liberty is the direct result of justification (I Tim. 1:9; Rom. 10:4).

Outside the Lutheran tradition more rigid forms of Protestantism developed, such as the English Puritans, who tended to hold that everything not explicitly allowed in the Bible was forbidden. Others, such as the Anglican communion, were less stringent and regarded many traditional practices, though without scriptural warrant, as adiaphora. Adiaphoristic debates continued to develop periodically. In 1681 a controversy arose between Lutherans regarding participation in amusements. J. F. Johnson

See also Concord, Formula of; Melanchthon, Philip; Flacius, Matthias; Amsdorf, Nicholas von.

Bibliography. R. Preus and W. Rosin, eds., *A Contemporary Look at the Formula of Concord.*

Administration, Gift of. *See* Spiritual Gifts.

Adonai. *See* GOD, NAMES OF.

Adoption. A relatively infrequent term in the Scriptures, "adoption" is of theological importance, for it relates to how Israel and the Christian may be "sons" and "heirs" of God although they are not uniquely or by nature so, as in the case of Christ.

In the OT. The term "adoption" does not appear in the OT. There are no provisions for adoption in Israelite law, and the examples which do occur come from outside the Israelite culture (Eliezer, Gen. 15:1–4; Moses, Exod. 2:10; Genubath, I Kings 11:20; Esther, Esth. 2:7, 15). For the Israelites polygamy and levirate marriage were the more common solutions to infertility. Yet adoption was not unknown in their literature (cf. Prov. 17:2; 19:10; 29:21, which may all refer to adoption of slaves), and it may have been the means by which children fathered by a master on a slave mother inherited property (Gen. 16:1–4; 21:1–10; 30:1–13). Outside of Israel adoption was common enough to be regulated in the law codes of Babylon (e.g., Hammurabi's Code, sect. 185–86), Nuzi, and Ugarit. Not infrequently these refer to the adoption of a slave as an heir.

For Israel as a whole there was a consciousness of having been chosen by God as his "son" (Hos. 11:1; Isa. 1:2; Jer. 3:19). Since Israel had no myth of descent from the gods as the surrounding cultures did, adoption was the obvious category into which this act, as well as the deliverance from slavery in Egypt, would fit, as Paul indicates in Rom. 9:4. Likewise the kings succeeding David were God's "son" (II Sam. 7:14; I Chr. 28:6; Ps. 89:19). Ps. 2:7, e.g., uses "You are my son," which is probably the adoption formula used in the enthronement ceremony of each successive Davidic ruler. Together these ideas laid the basis for later NT usage of adoption imagery.

In the NT. In the NT the term "adoption" (*huiothesia*) is strictly a Pauline idea, occurring only in Rom. 8:15, 23; 9:4; Gal. 4:5; and Eph. 1:5. While John and Peter prefer the picture of regeneration to portray the Christian sonship, Paul has characteristically chosen a legal image (as in justification), perhaps due to his contact with the Roman world.

In Greek and Roman society adoption was, at least among the upper classes, a relatively common practice. Unlike the oriental cultures in which slaves were sometimes adopted, these people normally limited adoption to free citizens. But, at least in Roman law, the citizen so adopted became a virtual slave, for he came under the paternal authority of his adoptive father. Adoption conferred rights, but it came with a list of duties as well.

Paul combines several of these pictures in his thought. While Gal. 4 begins with a picture of the law enslaving the heirs until a given date (e.g., majority or the death of the father), there is a shift in vs. 4 to the adoption image in which one who was truly a slave (not a minor as in vss. 1–3) becomes a son and thus an heir through redemption. The former slave, empowered by the Spirit, now uses the address of a son, "Abba! Father!"

The reason for adoption is given in Eph. 1:5: God's love. It was not due to his nature or merit that the Christian was adopted (and thus receives the Spirit and the inheritance, Eph. 1:14–15), but to God's will acting through Christ. Adoption is a free grant to undeserving people solely from God's grace.

As in Galatians and Ephesians, adoption is connected to the Spirit in Romans as well. It is those who are "led by the Spirit" who are sons, who have received the "spirit of sonship," not that of slavery (Rom. 8:14–15). Again the Spirit produces the cry "Abba!" and indicates by his presence the reality of the coming inheritance.

Adoption, however, is not entirely a past event. The legal declaration may have been made, and the Spirit may have been given as a down payment, but the consummation of the adoption awaits the future, for the adoption of sons includes "the redemption of our bodies" (Rom. 8:23). Thus adoption is something hoped for as well as something already possessed.

Adoption, then, is deliverance from the past (similar to regeneration and justification), a status and way of life in the present (walking by the Spirit, sanctification), and a hope for the future (salvation, resurrection). It describes the process of becoming a son of God (cf. John 1:12; I John 3:1–2) and receiving an inheritance from God (cf. Col. 3:24). P. H. DAVIDS

See also INHERITANCE.

Bibliography. J. I. Cook, "The Concept of Adoption in the Theology of Paul," in *Saved by Hope*, ed. J. I. Cook; F. Lyall, "Roman Law in the Writings of Paul—Adoption," *JBL* 88:458–66; L. H. Marshall, *The Challenge of NT Ethics;* W. v. Martitz and E. Schweizer, *TDNT*, VIII, 397–99; W. H. Rossell, "New Testament Adoption—Graeco-Roman or Semitic?" *JBL* 71:233–34; D. J. Theron, "'Adoption' in the Pauline Corpus," *EvQ* 28:6–14; J. van Seters, "The Problem of Childlessness in Near Eastern Law and the Patriarchs of Israel," *JBL* 87:401–8.

Adoptionism. Put most simply, adoptionism is the theory that Jesus was in nature a man who became God by adoption.

The earliest extant work which expresses this position is the Shepherd of Hermas, thought to be written by the brother of the bishop of Rome about A.D. 150. It taught that the Redeemer was a virtuous man chosen by God, and with him the Spirit of God was united. He did the work to which God had called him; in fact, he did more than was commanded. Therefore he was by divine decree adopted as a son and exalted to great power and lordship. Adherents of this Christology who were declared heretics in the third century asserted it had at one time been the dominant view in Rome and that it had been handed down by the apostles.

This view was perpetuated in the second and third century church by the dynamistic monarchians, who taught that Christ was a mere man on whom the power of God came and who was then adopted or constituted the Son of God. A leader in that general movement was Theodotus, who came to Rome from Byzantium about 190. He taught that Jesus was a man who was born of a virgin through the operation of the Holy Spirit. After the piety of his life had been tested, the Holy Spirit descended on him at the baptism. By this means he became Christ and received the power for his special ministry. But he was still not fully God; that was achieved through resurrection. Theodotus was excommunicated by the Roman Church, and the effort of his followers to found a separate church early in the third century had little success.

Adoptionism was an attempt to explain the divine and human natures in Christ and their relation to each other. And as the great Christological debates raged during the fourth and fifth centuries, there were always a few who could be accused of taking this position. It did not flare again extensively, however, until the latter part of the eighth century, when it produced a commotion in the Spanish and Frankish churches.

Elipandus, bishop of Toledo from *ca.* 780, in his writings on the Trinity expressed the view that Christ was an adopted son; Felix, bishop of Urgel in the Pyrenees, taught a similar position soon thereafter. Numerous local churchmen opposed them; and their teachings were condemned by three synods under Charlemagne, who assumed the position of ruler of the church in his realm and who was concerned with its unity. Pope Adrian I also became involved, and the recantation of both men was obtained. They had a numerous following, however, and extensive efforts were required to bring these people back into the fold. The effects of the controversy lasted for decades in Toledo. Possibly remnants of the old Arian heresy contributed to the popularity of adoptionism at this time.

A sound refutation of adoptionism was never made, and leanings in that direction appeared in some scholastic writings during the late Middle Ages.

H. F. Vos

Bibliography. A. Harnack, *History of Dogma;* A. Hauck, *SHERK,* I, 48–50.

Adultery. In Scripture "adultery" denotes any voluntary cohabitation of a married person with any other than his or her lawful spouse. But at times the Bible designates this sin also by *porneia,* "fornication" (I Cor. 5:1), though this properly designates the offense of voluntary cohabitation between an unmarried person and one of the opposite sex. Where the two kinds of wrongdoing are to be distinguished, Scripture designates them by different terms: *pornoi,* "fornicators," and *moichoi,* "adulterers" (I Cor. 6:9).

Adultery is forbidden in the Scriptures especially in the interest of the sanctity of the home and family (Exod. 20:14; Deut. 5:18). More specifically the sin is described in Lev. 18:20: "Thou shalt not lie carnally with thy neighbor's wife to defile thyself with her." The wrong is regarded as so great that its penalty was death (Lev. 20:10; John 8:5). While the law of Moses did not specify how this penalty was to be executed, it is explained in the NT as stoning: "Moses commanded us to stone such" (John 8:5). In Deut. 22:22 the mode of punishing an adulteress is not prescribed, though in Ezek. 16:40; 23:43–47 stoning is mentioned as the proper punishment. So also in Deut. 22:23–24 an adulterous young woman betrothed to a man should be stoned together with her guilty partner. Various indications in Jewish tradition suggest that at times the punishment was inflicted by strangulation.

Since the death penalty could be inflicted only upon a person "taken in adultery, in the very act" (John 8:4), the woman suspected by her husband of having committed adultery had to undergo an ordeal to establish her innocence or be made manifest as a sinner by a divine judgment (Num. 5:11–31).

Though adultery was condemned in the divine law as a heinous crime (Job 31:9–11), it could not be rooted out, and both men and women were often found guilty of this grave offense (Job 24:15; 31:9; Prov. 2:16–19; 7:5–22). Even David became guilty of adultery and, as a result of this sin, of murder (II Sam. 11:2–5), of which, however, he earnestly repented (Ps. 51:1 ff.). Adultery filled the land especially through the influence of profane prophets and priests (Jer. 23:10–14; 29:23).

While the penal laws in the Scriptures consider only the actual transgression of the commandment of chastity, the moral law condemns also adulterous practices committed with the eye and the heart (Job 31:1, 7). Emphasis on this kind of transgression was urged especially by Christ in the Sermon on the Mount (Matt. 5:28), where he pronounced the person guilty of adultery who merely looked upon a woman to commit adultery with her, he having committed adultery with her already in his heart. Equally severe was our Lord's rebuke of the offensive hypocrites who condemned adultery while they themselves were guilty of unchastity (John 8:7). However, while he reproved the wicked accusers he did not condone the sin of the adulteress when he dismissed her with the command to go and sin no more (John 8:11). His words must be regarded rather as his solemn absolution of a sinner who was penitent.

When our Lord testified against the lax divorce practices of the Jews who followed the loose interpretation of Deut. 24:1–3 advocated by Hillel, he excepted adultery as the only cause justifying divorce (Matt. 5:32; 19:9), supporting in this the stricter school of Shammai, which likewise limited divorce to adultery. As a prevailing vice of perverted mankind, adultery will always be a continuing offense. For this reason the NT so earnestly warns against it (I Cor. 6:9; Heb. 13:4; James 4:4). In view of the corruption of the human heart it behooves also every Christian daily to pray with great seriousness David's penitential prayer (Ps. 51:2, 10–12).

Paul does not contradict Christ, who in Matt. 5:32; 19:9 permits the putting away of the wife because of fornication, when in his directions on marriage in I Cor. 7:10–13 he commands the faithful Christian spouse to be at peace in case the unbelieving husband or wife should break the marriage union by malicious desertion. In vss. 10 and 11 he forbids Christians to break the marriage union, and that as a word of the Lord, the reference being very clearly to Matt. 5:32; 19:9, with Christ's express statement "except it be for fornication" clearly understood. In vss. 12 and 13 Paul addresses to Christians joined in mixed marriages to unbelievers a new provision, which Christ had not considered when addressing Jews; namely, that if the unbelieving spouse desires to break the marriage bond by deserting the Christian, the latter is not bound, but is free to marry. J. T. Mueller

See also Fornication; Divorce; Marriage, Theology of.

Bibliography. H. Reisser *et al., NIDNTT,* I, 497ff., II, 582ff., III, 535ff.; H. Thielicke, *The Ethics of Sex;* E. Schillebeeckx, *Marriage in the History of the Church;* F. Hauck, *TDNT,* IV, 729ff.

Advent (*adventus,* coming, arrival). The season of the ecclesiastical year when the church prepares to celebrate the birth of Jesus Christ (Christmas) and engages in self-examination in expectation of his second coming in glory to judge the living and the dead. The collects and Scripture readings embrace these two themes. It begins in the West on the Sunday nearest to St. Andrew's Day (Nov. 30) and always includes four Sundays. However, in the East the period is longer, beginning earlier in November. During the Middle Ages and earlier the period was marked by discipline and fasting (based on "watch and pray"), but in modern times this emphasis has not been prominent. P. Toon

See also Christian Year.

Bibliography. A. A. Arthur, *The Evolution of the Christian Year.*

Adventism. The belief that Christ's personal second coming is imminent and will inaugurate his millennial kingdom and the end of the age. Chiliasm, apocalypticism, and millennialism are cognate theological terms. Adventism in this general sense has been espoused by many diverse groups throughout Christian history (e.g., Montanists, Anabaptists, Fifth Monarchy Men, Plymouth Brethren and other premillennialists, and Jehovah's Witnesses).

Adventism is most commonly used, however, to denote the movement which sprang up in the 1830s from the teachings of William Miller, a Baptist minister in New York. Miller confidently prophesied the imminent return of Christ and set 1843–44 as the time for the event. The Millerite movement spread rapidly among the churches of the Northeast. When the expected return did not occur as Miller originally had predicted, a reinterpretation of the Scripture set Oct. 22, 1844, as the correct date. The faithful met in their local gathering places on the appointed day worshiping and waiting. The "Great Disappointment" which followed the failure of the prophecy led many Millerites to forsake the movement and slip back into the churches from which they had never formally dissociated themselves. Miller himself acknowledged his error and dissociated himself from the movement and all further attempts to redeem it.

A series of new signs, visions, and prophecies, however, fed the lagging spirits of those who refused to give up their adventist hopes. As early as the day following the Great Disappointment, Hiram Edson, an adventist leader, had a vision which confirmed the prophetic significance of the Oct. 22, 1844, date, but indicated that it marked a heavenly rather than an earthly event. On that day Christ had moved into the holy of holies of the heavenly sanctuary to begin a new phase of his ministry of redemption. That ministry was ultimately defined in the adventist doctrine of investigative judgment; Christ entered the sanctuary to review the deeds of professing Christians to determine whose names should be included in the Book of Life. Other revelations subsequent to the Great Disappointment came to Ellen G. Harmon, a young disciple of Miller in Portland, Maine. She was quickly accepted as a prophetess and her teachings were accepted as authoritative. The revived movement also adopted sabbatarianism and the belief that the acceptance of the seventh-day sabbath was the mark of the true church. Seventh-day observance and Christ's ministry of investigative judgment, confirmed by the prophetic revelation of Mrs. Ellen (Harmon) White, completed the foundations of contemporary adventism. Most adventist groups also adhere to belief in soul sleep and annihilation of the wicked. Their strong emphasis on OT teaching also led to a strong traditional concern for diet and health.

Two major adventist bodies represent the movement today—the Advent Christian Church and the numerically predominant Seventh-day Adventists. They vary somewhat in their adherence to the adventist doctrines outlined above. The Seventh-day Adventists traditionally have been identified as a cult among Christian churches. Such classification results from the contention by Christian theologians that the authority which the church grants to Mrs. White's prophecies compromises the finality of scriptural revelation. They further charge that the doctrine of investigative judgment compromises the biblical doctrine of justification by faith alone and leads to an assurance of salvation based on perfect obedience rather than faith. In recent years, however, Seventh-day Adventist theologians have tended to regard Mrs. White's prophecies as subject to judgment by the canonical Scriptures and have put forth a more evangelical understanding of justification by faith. As a result some evangelical leaders, although by no means all, have begun to include the Seventh-day Adventists within the pale of orthodoxy. This division of opinion as to the theological stance of the movement is echoed within the group itself by the intense theological debate of these issues in recent years.

The Seventh-day Adventist Church has experienced rapid growth in the post–World War II period. This church, however, still tends to keep to itself among Christian denominations. It has consistently kept the education of its children under its own auspices. The Adventists have been especially well known for their health-care ministries. Their traditional dietary concerns, including their proscription of coffee and tea and their advocacy of vegetarianism, predated by many decades other contemporary movements in these areas.

The centrality of the events surrounding the return of Christ in the premillennialism which became so critical in the development of the fundamentalist movement and the contemporary emphasis upon the imminent second coming of Christ in evangelical churches in general show the continuing significance of general adventism in the Christian tradition. M. E. Dieter

See also Sabbatarianism; Soul Sleep; White, Ellen Gould; Millennium, Views of the; Annihilationism.

Bibliography. P. G. Damsteegt, *Foundations of the Seventh-day Adventist Message and Mission;* L. E. Froom, *The Prophetic Faith of Our Fathers*, 4 vols.; W. Martin, *The Kingdom of the Cults;* F. D. Nichol, *The Midnight Cry;* G. Paxton, *The Shaking of Adventism; Seventh Day Adventists Answer Questions on Doctrine;* A. A. Hoekema, *The Four Major Cults.*

Advent of Christ. *See* Birth of Jesus Christ; Second Coming of Christ.

Advocate. *See* Holy Spirit.

Aeon. *See* Age, Ages.

Aesthetics, Christian View of. A Christian view of aesthetic theory differs from a secular perspective on the discipline in showing how the field and its development relate to the lordship of Jesus Christ.

Development of a Theology of Beauty. For centuries before the historical incarnation of God in Jesus Christ reflection on beauty, epitomized by the dialogues of Plato, set up what became perhaps the major stumbling block to a fruitful theory of art, a down-to-earth sense of the aesthetic, and a hermeneutics that can trust imaginative knowledge.

Plato posited an absolute beauty outside the visible, temporal world as a pearl of great price men should desire to know. A good Greek mind would persist in pursuit of such transcending perfection until it came to contemplate the unspeakably well-proportioned, noetic form of Beauty itself. Then one's immortal soul would be saved from the curse of bodily, earthly transience (*Symposium* 209e–212a). The only prayer in Plato's works has Socrates intone the words, "O Pan, grant me to become beautiful inside" (*Phaedrus* 279b8–9).

The Hellenist Plotinus and even Augustine carried on the Platonic tradition with a chain-of-being ontology that allowed them to declare everything is beautiful insofar as it is. Worms are beautiful (*On True Religion* 41:77), and evil too with its punishment fits harmoniously into the balancing mosaic of God's goodness (*Confessions* 7:18–19). Although Thomas Aquinas thought in Aristotelian categories and maintained an analogical distance between creature and Creator, his doctrine of beauty retained the highly mathematical, Platonized dogma that proportion, perfection, and now brilliance constituted the attribute of God the Son (*Summa Theologica* I,39.8) which pleases us in its more mundane forms as "the beautiful."

The Reformer John Calvin understood the visible beauty of creation to be a mirroring of God's glory; art then became God's gift to humankind to help men and women recognize beauty, a kind of general revelation of God. The 1898 Princeton lectures of Abraham Kuyper followed through on Calvin and formulated somewhat idealistically what has become almost the mainline tradition among evangelical Protestant thinkers: art has the mystical task of reminding those who are homesick for heaven of the beauty that once was lost and of the perfect luster that is coming.

In the context of comparative religion Gerardus van der Leeuw developed an apologetic for the "beautiful" as an ancillary or penultimate step toward what is "holy." Thomist Jacques Maritain in his 1952 Mellon lectures presented a complex theology of artistic and transcendental beauty in which he confessed "that all great poetry awakens in us one way or another, the sense of our mysterious identity, and draws us toward the source of being."

Christian thinkers who adopt a theology of beauty are beset by the problems which attend natural theology and all theodicies: How radical and disfiguring is the reality of sin and the necessity of Christ's redemption? Can beautiful nature and art be evil? And, if human art is beautiful, is it not naturally good? Also, whether beauty is taken to be an elemental harmony in the world or a fitting and satisfying quality of human artifacts, the concepts of balanced order, form, and delight are at best analogues of aesthetic reality. Such properties of "beauty" do not define the peculiar character of artistry, nor do they explain art's special province of oblique meaning.

Struggle for a Foolproof Hermeneutics. Modern debate in aesthetic theory has largely converted beauty into a problem of taste and then argued about the kind and reliability of "aesthetic" judgments. There is concern with how to read and interpret art and literature with a critical mind that can be sure its exegesis is correct.

In the eighteenth century Alexander Gottlieb Baumgarten conceived the aesthetic realm to be one of fused image-knowledge, which lacks the precise distinctness of ideas that is requisite for higher, logical knowledge. Immanuel Kant identified taste as an autonomous, disinterested form of sensitivity which involved the satisfying use of one's cognitive faculties but which was not a source of knowledge; human sensitivity to beautiful and especially to sublime affairs was important to Kant, because such aesthetic activity is analogous and propaedeutic to morality.

Hegel, however, was influential in cutting concerns about taste and aesthetic judgment at large more narrowly down to examination of art, and art as a kind of secular theophany. Such romantic idealist philosophers of fine art as Herder and Schelling strongly supported the idea of artistic genius and intellectually intuitive creativity, which give art, music, and especially poetry a revelational character that transcends logical examination. Critique of literature soon became largely a matter of empathic discernment of the "spirit" of the text and its prophetic meaning for the present; past historical settings became largely immaterial for interpretation, next to the imaginative inspiration for humanity afforded by the piece.

Wilhelm Dilthey aimed to overcome the problem of historical relativity of artworks by making a rigorously descriptive, psychological analysis of the structure shaping poetic imagination. He believed he might be able to fashion a scientific method for interpretation that would distill the lasting, typical knowledge of literary art relevant for any time thereafter. Positivist I. A. Richards undid this hope in English-speaking lands by divorcing poetry as important emotive language from scientific prose that had semiotic referents. It remained for a new critique of poetic language (the "new critics"), harking back to Kant, to find a format that would keep distinct yet in synthesis the formal, textural devices of poetry which demand close, professional reading, and the paraphraseable message.

Marxist thinkers like Georg Lukács and Leon Trotsky made more clear than many confessing Christians how deeply permeated all art and literature is with the committed perspective of the artist forming the work. Marxist aesthetics is normally so partisan, however, and its literary hermeneutic so dictated by class-conscious, orthodox political dogmas, that the theory and the reading of texts became more a predictable diatribe than genuine analysis and exegesis. Quite differently, Hans-Georg Gadamer has reintroduced a Hegelian dialectic, humanized and authorized by Platonic dialogue on the beautiful, as the model for critical interpretation of art. Gadamer's hermeneutics mutes Heidegger's belief in the oracular nature of poetry to a conviction of the mediating power of language to bridge time and transmit the cultural heritage of literary art, if a reader's consciousness is free to be playfully charmed out of the darkness of prejudices into the light of "adequate knowledge" of the speaking text.

Christians working in literary theory and the aesthetics of art and literary criticism, as well as ordinary expositors of the Bible, have usually, unfortunately, followed secular trends at a distance. The neo-idealist concern for the "spiritual content," never mind the technical details, converted to Bultmann's demythologizing attempt to get at the *kerygma* core of Scripture, let the trappings go. The subsequent positivist creed, that only rational, logical knowledge (preferably scientifically verified) is trustworthy, has encouraged a teaching of literature that separates cleanly (1) neutral, technical description, from (2) orthodox evaluation of the world view. The idea that holy Scripture is not a true story so much as "propositional revelation" also owes a debt to the positivist commitment. Current schools of French structuralist aesthetics and the "deconstructivist" critics who treat texts with the arbitrary originality of dada artists, and whose focus is above all on the reader and the spectator, seem to have a curious echo in the praxis of those who do not mind eisegesis of the biblical Scriptures so long as the result is an orthodox point. There seems to be great ferment and much confusion at present, because imaginative (literary) knowledge still lacks a Christian philosophical home as *bona fide* knowledge.

Problematics of Systematic Aesthetic Theory. A theoretical aesthetics informed by knowledge that we inhabit a world created by the Lord God revealed in Jesus Christ will posit an ordinance for aesthetic reality, for the style of ordinary life, and for the professional construction of artworks. An aesthetic theory that has its analysis cast from a biblic‹ ly Christian orientation will also recognize that performers and critics as well as leaders in style and composers of artworks have breathed a holy or evil spirit into their respective artistic results, and each needs to be examined as to how the legitimate exercise of his tasks has served the public with insight or with curses.

One major attempt to think these matters through with Christian sensitivity takes the incarnation of Jesus Christ as the paradigm for artistic acts. Artists give the "flesh" of sensible matter to the content of spiritual ideas. Such a "theological aesthetics" tends to accept a theology of transcendental beauty, to think within a God-artist analogy, and to proffer an apologetics that treats all art as essentially sacramental.

A different current attempt to formulate a radically Christian philosophical aesthetic theory asks for a thoroughgoing reformation of received tradition and thinks out of a different categorical framework. The defining law of God for the aesthetic side of life and style to be obeyed is the ordinance of allusivity, where activity is to be ruled by playfulness and surprise—what would make God smile. Artists are called to catch things and events in creation with an imaginatively crafted miming characterized by the quality of nuancefulness. Artists are understood not as imitators of Christ taking on flesh but as diaconal workers skilled in forming symbols pregnant with meaning for whoever has eyes to see and ears to hear. Artworks are at core metaphors and parables that need to be treated as expressions of seriously committed, living human subjects under Christ's coming rule. If the artwork is vain, it needs to be charitably humbled; if weak, it should be aided by informed wisdom; if fruitful, it should be praised with thanks. Christian aesthetic theory will fashion an encyclopedia of the special arts and literature that avoids any ranking hierarchy. It will welcome art bound to special tasks such as commemorative portraiture, monuments, advertising, and liturgy, but will also promote theater, concerts, paintings in museums, and novels, which have their own special contribution to make as art in society. Christian aesthetics makes clear that our style, artworks, critique, and theory of the aesthetic and artistic in history will be judged for its redemptive fruit on the final Lord's day.

C. G. SEERVELD

See also ART, CHRISTIAN.

Bibliography. A. Kuyper, "Calvinism and Art," in *Lectures on Calvinism;* G. van der Leeuw, *Sacred and Profane Beauty;* J. Maritain, *Creative Intuition in Art and Poetry;* W. Tatarkiewicz, *A History of Six Ideas;* H. W. Frei, *The Eclipse of Biblical Narrative;* M. Murray, *Modern Critical Theory;* F. Lentricchia, *After the New Criticism;* S. K. Langer, *Feeling and Form;* C. G. Seerveld, *A Christian Critique of Art and Literature* and *Rainbows for the Fallen World; The New Orpheus,* ed. N. A. Scott, Jr.; N. Wolterstorff, *Art in Action;* R. Paulson, *Shakespeare, Milton, and the Bible.*

Affliction. *See* PAIN.

Affusion. *See* BAPTISM, MODES OF.

Agape. *See* LOVE FEAST; LOVE.

Age, Ages. ***OT Usage.*** The Hebrew word *ʿôlām* means a long indefinite period of time, whether past or future, whose limits are determined only by the context or the nature of the thing spoken of.

Undefined Past Time. Amos 9:11 foresees the restoration of the tabernacle of David as in "days of antiquity." Events in past history are referred to in Isa. 63:9; Mic. 7:14; Mal. 3:4. Jer. 5:15 speaks of "a nation of antiquity," Isa. 58:12 of "ruins of antiquity," and Jer. 18:15 of "roads of antiquity." The expression "from antiquity" can refer to events in the indefinite past (Jer. 2:20; Josh. 24:2; Jer. 28:8). It can also include the whole sweep of human history (Joel 2:2; Isa. 64:4).

The word is used of God's acts and relationships to Israel in the undefined past (Isa. 63:16; Ps. 25:6). It can also refer to the totality of God's dealings with humanity (Isa. 63:19); and it can also designate merely an indefinite time (Isa. 42:14). In Prov. 8:23 it reaches to a point in time before the creation of the earth. The hills are called "everlasting" (Gen. 49:26). This refers to their antiquity and not to the eternity of matter.

These references show that the temporal determination of the word must be derived from its context. Therefore when it refers to God's existence, as in Ps. 93:2, "Thou art from everlasting," no point of beginning can be conceived, and the word takes on the idea of an eternity in the past. See "God of antiquity" in Gen. 21:33; Isa. 40:28; Jer. 10:10. When the idiom is applied to the messianic ruler in Mic. 5:2, linguistically it can mean either his antiquity or his eternity. Context alone must decide.

Indefinite Future Time. The word *'ôlām* means an indefinite reach of future time—e.g., as long as a man will live (Deut. 15:17; I Kings 1:31; Ps. 61:7). The "eternity" of the earth (Pss. 104:5; 148:6) is only relative, for the earth is to be shaken in the final act of judgment and redemption (Hag. 2:6). An indeterminate future is seen in Isa. 32:14; I Sam. 13:13; Ezek. 25:15. Enduring without end are God's salvation (Isa. 51:6–8), his dwelling in Jerusalem (I Chr. 23:25), his covenants (Gen. 17:7; Isa. 55:3), the Mosaic institution (Exod. 27:21; 30:21; Lev. 3:17; 7:34; 10:9; Num. 10:8), the passover observance (Exod. 12:24), Solomon's temple (I Kings 9:3; II Kings 21:7), the Holy City (Ps. 125:1), and Messiah's rule (Ps. 45:6; Isa. 9:7). That some of these institutions have passed away illustrates again that the precise meaning of the phrase is to be derived from its context.

When the phrase is applied to the existence of God, the full idea of eternity emerges (Isa. 40:28; Deut. 32:40; Dan. 12:7).

The plural, "ages," is sometimes used to intensify the idea of an unending future: Isa. 45:17, "everlasting salvation" (salvation of ages); Dan. 9:24, "everlasting righteousness"; Isa. 26:4, "everlasting rock"; Ps. 145:13, "an everlasting kingdom" (a kingdom of all ages).

Past and Future. The indefinite past and future, "from antiquity and unto futurity," are brought together, referring to the existence of God (Pss. 90:2; 106:48); God's love (Ps. 103:17); praise to God (Neh. 9:5); the promise of the land of Israel (Jer. 7:7; 25:5).

NT Usage. *Aiōn as Indefinite Time.* The word *aiōn*, like *'ôlām*, is used to mean an indeterminate period of time. The age of the prophets is "from the age," i.e., from long ago (Luke 1:70; Acts 3:21). God's revelation to Israel was "from the age" (Acts 15:18). The phrase "from the age" in John 9:32 means from all past time. Jude 25 has a variant form, "before all the age," meaning before all time.

The expression "unto the age" occurs twenty-seven times. The precise meaning must be determined from the context. In Matt. 21:19; Mark 3:29; John 13:8; I Cor. 8:13 it means "never." In other contexts the idea of a future eternity is apparent (John 6:51, 58; 10:22; 11:26; 12:34; 14:16; II Cor. 9:9; Heb. 5:6; 6:20; 7:17, 21; I Pet. 1:25; I John 2:17; II John 2; Jude 13).

The plural, "ages," is used to strengthen the idea of endlessness. (1) In the past: "before the ages" (I Cor. 2:7); "from the ages" (Col. 1:26; Eph. 3:9). In Eph. 3:11 we have the "purpose of the ages," i.e., God's eternal purpose. (2) In the future: "unto the ages" (Matt. 6:13; Luke 1:33; Rom. 1:25; 9:5; 11:36; II Cor. 11:31; Heb. 13:8). Jude 25 reads "unto all the ages." The parallelism of ages and generations in Col. 1:26 suggests that the plural form conceives of time as consisting of a succession of many ages or generations, and this leads to the further thought that the ages are long but not unlimited periods of time.

The eternity of the future is further strengthened by doubling the form: (1) in the singular: "unto the age of the age" (Heb. 1:8); (2) in the plural: "unto the ages of the ages." This expression occurs twenty-one times, all in Paul or Revelation with the exception of Heb. 13:21; I Pet. 4:11; 5:11.

A number of variant expressions are Eph. 3:21, "unto all the generations of the age of the ages," and II Pet. 3:18, "unto the day of the age."

The lordship of God over all time is seen in the expression "king of the ages" (I Tim. 1:17; Rev. 15:3).

Aiōn as a Segment of Time. Theologically the most important usage of *aiōn* in the NT is that which designates two distinct periods of time: this age and the age to come. This structure provides the background for the eschatological character of the work of redemption. This idiom views redemptive history not as a series of unending ages but as two distinct and contrasting periods of time.

Several verses reflect this two-age structure without emphasizing it. Blasphemy against the Holy Spirit will never be forgiven in this age or in the age to come (Matt. 12:32). Christ is exalted above all authority both in this age and in the age to come (Eph. 1:21). Discipleship of Jesus, even though it brings its rewards, often involves the loss of possessions and family in this time, but it will mean eternal life in the age to come (Mark 10:29–30; Luke 18:28–30). This saying involves a slight variation in form: "time" (*kairos*) is substituted for "age" in the first member. This same idiom, "this time," is found in Rom. 3:26; 8:18; 11:5; II Cor. 8:13.

This age will come to its end with the parousia of Christ (Matt. 24:3). At the consummation of this age the Son of man will send his angels to separate the wicked from the righteous (Matt. 13:39–42). The age to come will be the age of immortality in contrast to this age. "Those who are accounted worthy to attain to that age" will be "sons of the resurrection" and will be like the angels in one aspect: they will no longer be subject to death (Luke 20:34–35).

The age to come is the age of eternal life (Mark 10:30), when the righteous will "shine forth as the sun in the kingdom of their Father" (Matt. 13:43). Mark 10:24, 30 equate the age to come with both eternal life and the kingdom of God; and in Matt. 25:34, 46 the righteous inherit the kingdom of God and enter into eternal life when the Son of man comes in his glory (Matt. 25:31) at the end of this age (Matt. 25:41).

The character of this age stands in sharp contrast to the coming age. It is evil (Gal. 1:4) because Satan is "the god of this age," holding men in darkness (II Cor. 4:4). This age stands in opposition to the kingdom of God; for, when the word of the kingdom is sown, "the care of the age" tends to choke it so that it does not become fruitful (Matt. 13:22). Love for this age caused Demas to forsake Paul (II Tim. 4:10). Paul describes those who live according to "the age of this world" in Eph. 2:1–2 as dead in sins, sons of disobedience following a satanic leading, pursuing the passions of the flesh; therefore they are under God's wrath. This phrase "the age of this world" closely associates the temporal and the spatial words. Indeed, the expression "this world" is a parallel expression (John 8:23; 9:39; 11:9; 12:25; 13:1; 16:11; 18:36; I John 4:17; I Cor. 3:19; 5:10; 7:31). The debater of this age and the wisdom of this world are both folly to God (I Cor. 1:20; 2:6), for God can be known only by revelation, not by wisdom (I Cor. 2:6). The rulers of this age who in ignorance crucified the Lord of glory are doomed to pass away (I Cor. 2:6, 8). Some interpreters find in this verse a reference to the demonic hosts of "the God of this age," but this is not proved.

In brief, this age is the period of Satan's activity, of human rebellion, of sin and death; the age to come, introduced by the parousia of Christ, will be the age of eternal life and righteousness, when Satan is destroyed and evil swept from the earth.

This dualistic structure is shared by the NT with contemporary Judaism (see IV Esd. 6:7–9; 7:20–31, etc.); but both are derived from elements implicit in the OT, which sees the world, the scene of human existence, in need of a miraculous transformation by the direct act of God before God's people can enjoy the fullness of the redemptive blessings (Isa. 65:17ff.).

However, at one important point the NT stands apart from its Jewish environment: in Christ the blessings of the age to come have entered into this evil age. Jesus, who will come in glory as the Son of man to inaugurate the age to come, has already appeared on earth in humility to bring to men in the midst of this evil age the life of the age to come. We already taste the powers of the coming age (Heb. 6:5). Through the death of Christ we are now delivered from this present evil age (Gal. 1:4). We are no longer to be conformed to this age but are to be transformed by an inner power (Rom. 12:2). It is possible that, in I Cor. 10:11, "upon whom the ends of the ages are come" may refer to this overlapping of the two ages and mean that, while Christians live bodily in this age of sin and death, they live spiritually in the age of righteousness and life. This phrase, however, like Heb. 9:26, "the consummation of the ages," may mean that in Christ, God's purpose in the ages of redemptive history has been fulfilled. In any case, the NT does teach an overlapping of the ages. Therefore, eternal life, which belongs to the age to come (Mark 10:30; Matt. 25:46; John 12:25; Rom. 2:7), is a present possession (John 3:36; 6:47). Justification, which really means acquittal from guilt in the final judgment (Matt. 12:36–37; Rom. 8:33–34), is already accomplished (Rom. 3:24; 5:1). Salvation which belongs to the future (Rom. 13:11; I Pet. 1:5, 9) is also present (II Cor. 6:2; Eph. 2:8). The kingdom of God which belongs to the age to come (Matt. 25:34; I Cor. 15:50) has invaded this age, bringing to men its blessings in advance (Matt. 12:28; Luke 17:20; Col. 1:13; Rom. 14:17). In brief, the redemptive realities are eschatological; they are the blessings which belong to the age to come, but in Christ they have been given to believers who still live in this age. Christians live in two ages; they enjoy the powers of the age to come while living in the end of this age.

Aiōn as a Spatial Concept. Sometimes *aiōn* refers not so much to a period of time as to that which fills the time period. The creation of the ages in Heb. 1:2 refers to all that fills the ages—the world. In Heb. 11:3 "the ages" is further described by the phrase "that which is seen"—the visible world which fills the ages of time.

Since *aiōn* can bear spatial connotations, it can be used interchangeably with *kosmos*, "world." See "the coming world" in Heb. 2:5 and "the coming age" in Heb. 6:5, "the wisdom of this world" (I Cor. 1:20; 3:19) and the "wisdom of this age" (I Cor. 2:6). Possibly the "care(s) of the age," in Mark 4:19 and Matt. 13:22, is synonymous with the care for the things of the world in I Cor. 7:33; and the assertion that God is the King of the ages (I Tim. 1:17) means not only that he is Lord of time but of all that fills time.

Aiōn as a Person. In hellenistic religion *aiōn* was used of semidivine beings standing between God and the world. Some scholars have found this meaning in the NT. Eph. 2:2 is said to be the *aiōn* who rules over this world; Col. 1:26 and Eph. 3:9; 2:7 are said to refer to heavenly spirits from whom God concealed his redemptive purpose and over whom Christ is to triumph. This interpretation is highly improbable.

The biblical concept of "the ages" stands in contrast to the Greek idea of the time-eternity relationship, in which eternity is qualitatively other than time. Biblically, eternity is unending time. The future life has its setting in a new redeemed earth (Rom. 8:21; II Pet. 3:13) with resurrection bodies in the age to come. It is not deliverance from the realm of time and space but from sin and corruption. Rev. 10:6 does not mean that time is to end.

G. E. Ladd

See also Time; Eternity; This Age, The Age to Come; Kingdom of Christ, God, Heaven; Second Coming of Christ.

Bibliography. E. D. Burton, *The Epistle to the Galatians*, ICC; O. Cullmann, *Christ and Time;* G. Vos, *The Pauline Eschatology;* G. E. Ladd, "Eschatology and the Unity of NT Theology," *ExpT* 68:268–73; H. Sasse, *TDNT,* I, 197ff.; J. Guhrt *et al., NIDNTT,* III, 826ff.; J. Ban, *Biblical Words for Time;* S. J. De Vries, *Yesterday, Today and Tomorrow.*

Age, This. *See* This Age, The Age to Come.

Age of Accountability. This theme stems from the dual biblical emphasis on the righteous judgment of God on all mankind and the personal responsibility of each individual to ready himself for this divine encounter. Hence theologians often stress the necessity of personal decision on the individual's part in which he either accepts Christ and is redeemed (an initial freedom from condemnation) or continually decides for Christ in ethical living (a perseverance of Christlike character). In either case, the chief question centers on the extent of God's grace in view of human shortcoming and the time at which one is fully responsible. Therefore at the outset accountability is tied to one's ability to be responsible. The *locus classicus* for this theme is Rom. 14:12: "Each of us shall give account of himself to God." Here, to halt divisions stemming from Christians judging one another, Paul reminds the church that an account will be demanded on all this human activity (cf. Rom. 1:20; 2:20; II Cor. 5:10).

The age of accountability is generally viewed as the chronological stage in a person's life when he is responsible for his conduct before God. This, however, is not a fixed age, but is relative depending on the growth of moral consciousness in the individual. Indicators for this development are often found in the ability to discern right and wrong: when the general premises of good and bad can be given specific application (Burroughs). More precisely, the individual should be able to reason from the universal ethical principle and reach a specific conclusion. Often social or parental conditioning may teach behavior that is only imitative, and therefore stress must always be laid on free moral choice. In biblical thought authentic freedom brings with it the knowledge of good and evil and, essentially, the knowledge of God and the possibility of rejecting him. In any event, the divine demand for accountability lies behind the repeated biblical call for decision.

G. M. Burge

Bibliography. J. Stalker, *ISBE* (rev.), I, 28–29; A. Burroughs, *NCE,* XII, 118; D. Fyffe, *Dictionary of Religion and Ethics,* X, 739–41.

Age of Man. *See* Man, Origin of.

Aging, Christian View of. The aging of the world's population is paralleled by even more rapid graying of the membership in most churches. Challenging opportunities for Christian ministries with and for the aging emerge from applying biblical values to current realities.

Demographic Data. United Nations studies reveal an accelerating increase in the world's aging population. In 1975, 343,151,000 or 8.5 percent of the population were past age 60; by the year 2000 the figure is expected to be 579,995,000 or 9.4 percent. The increases will be much greater in Africa, Latin America, and South Asia than in Europe and North America, where already significant increases will bring the proportion past 60 to about one fifth of the population.

In the United States people past 65 increased by 27.9 percent from 1970 to 1980, while those under 65 increased only 9.7 percent. In 1980, 25,544,000 people (11.3 percent or one in every nine) were past age 65, the statistical beginning of old age. The proportions ranged widely from a low of 2.3 percent in Alaska to a high of 17.3 percent in Florida, but there is a much wider spread in local communities; in some, more than one fourth are past age 65. Only 41 of every 1,000 people in the U.S. in 1900 were past age 65; the 1980 figure of 113 is expected to increase to 122 by the year 2000, with the fastest growth rate among those past 85. If fertility remains low, the figure will be even higher.

The proportion of church membership past 65 is generally higher for several reasons. Many churches do not include young children in their membership. Older people tend to retain their membership more tenaciously than young adults, and, on the basis of several criteria, they are the "most religious" segment of the population. Graying hair and wrinkled skin characterize a majority of the active members in many congregations.

In 1900 life expectancy at birth was 47.3 years in the U.S. By 1978 this had risen to 73.3, but for women it was 77.2, compared to 69.5 for men. (The figures are about eight months higher for whites and four years lower for other races.) Since life expectancy increases with each decade of survival, the white male who reached age 75 in 1978 could expect to live another 8.6 years, compared to 11.5 for the white female and, surprisingly, 9.9 for the male and 12.5 for the female of other races.

In 1980 there were 131 women for every 100 men in the 65–74 age group but 229 among those past 85. Over three fourths (78 percent) of the older men were married, but over half (51 percent) of the women were widows, a figure that rose to about 70 percent for women past age 75. There were 1,333,000 widowers past 65 in 1980, compared to 7,121,000 widows. Women also greatly exceed men among the elderly divorced and single population.

These differences have profound implications for churches. The increasingly unequal numbers of men and women are linked by a few Christians with the biblical prophecy that seven women will fight over each man, asking him to marry them (Isa. 4:1). Men generally die earlier, marry women younger than themselves, and find it much easier to remarry after widowhood or divorce.

Social Circumstances. Less than 1 in every 20 of the elderly live in nursing homes, hospitals, or other institutions, so churches that serve only them are ignoring the other 95 percent. One fifth (20.3 percent) of all U.S. households in 1980 were headed by a person past 65. Although they had a higher level of home ownership than younger heads, one third lived in housing that had problems (12.3 percent inadequate, 0.5 percent adequate but crowded, and 19.2 percent burdened by housing expenses exceeding 30 percent of their income). Among renters the corresponding figures were substantially higher (19.2, 0.5, and 48.3 percent).

Older economic units have only about half the income of their younger counterparts. Upon retirement, income typically is reduced by one half to two thirds, so many middle-class people are thrust into poverty or near poverty. As of 1980, 12.7 percent of the under-65 population but 15.7 percent of those over 65 lived in households that were below the official poverty level. The figures were much higher for blacks (38.1 percent) and people of Spanish origin (30.8 percent); in each category they were much higher for women than for men. The median (middle) income of families headed by older persons was $12,881 compared to $22,548 for those headed by persons under 65.

Much poverty among the elderly is invisible. They tend to retain middle-class attitudes and try to remain self-sufficient, keeping up the appearance of an earlier life style so well that their economic plight is overlooked by others. Inflation eats away the buying power of savings; except for Social Security benefits most income does not increase with rising costs. Poverty among young adults can be viewed as temporary; among the elderly it is permanent and hopeless.

Economic problems influence self-concepts. Retirement not only brings reduced income but also contributes to a loss of personal identity (who am I without a job title?), feelings of inferiority, and a spirit of self-pity among many people.

The necessity to live on a reduced income affects other activities. Retired people usually have extra discretionary time to spend as they wish, yet the costs of membership dues, luncheon meetings, transportation, and other expenses may prevent participation in social activities. To hold down the cost of living some save money on food at the expense of an imbalanced diet, which in turn increases the susceptibility to illness. Some discontinue telephone subscriptions or change to a reduced level of service which restricts the amount of communication with other people. They may also avoid making advisable medical appointments because of costs that exceed insurance coverage or fear that an unpleasant condition may be discovered.

Over two thirds (68 percent) of the noninstitutionalized older persons studied in 1979 reported their health to be good or excellent, compared with others their own age, and only 9 percent reported it poor. Yet close to half (45 percent) had some limitation on their usual activity because of a chronic condition (17 percent unable to perform it at all, 22 percent limited in its amount or kind, 6 percent limited outside of it). The most common chronic conditions were arthritis (44.3 percent), hypertension (38.5 percent), hearing impairment (28.2 percent), heart disease (27.4 percent), arteriosclerosis (12.0 percent), visual impairment (11.9 percent), and diabetes (8.0 percent). The older the age category, the higher is the proportion of disability. Three fourths of the deaths of older people are caused by heart disease, stroke, and cancer.

Ageism, discrimination against people simply because of their age, is evidenced by compulsory retirement programs, preferential offering of services to younger people, the high status accorded to youthfulness, and the removal of capable older persons from leadership positions. Much of it stems from the prejudice of gerontophobia, an inner, often unconscious, anxiety or fear of what might happen to the discriminator in his or her own later years. It also results from the observed fact that the later years of life tend to be a period of material, physical, and social losses.

Many problems of old age hence result as much from the reactions of people to the aging process as from aging itself. When people have attitudes of ageism and gerontophobia, a self-fulfilling prophecy occurs; some of the predicted results of aging become a reality largely because of their expectations.

Biblical Values. References to elderly persons and aging appear throughout the Bible. In Genesis a long life is viewed as normal and desirable; the aged are respected, but long life is not automatically equated with goodness, wisdom, or competence. The shortening of the lifespan to 120 years (Gen. 6:3) is charged to human evil, not to creation or human nature.

The Ten Commandments include respect for parents (Exod. 20:12; Deut. 5:16), and the Mosaic law commanded similar respect to all the elderly (Lev. 19:32). Some Christians interpret this and related passages (e.g., Eph. 6:1–3; I Tim. 5:3–16) to mean that the full responsibility for covering all needs of the aging resides in their own children. Many, however, have no children or none with the capacity to care for their needs. About 6 percent of the elderly have never married, and one tenth of those who did have not borne children. Even among those who have, the children may have died, become incapacitated, or be living under financial and physical disabilities of their own old age.

Everyone is aging and should recognize the brevity of life, spending the allotted years wisely as good stewards (Ps. 90). We should remember our Creator in the days of our youth before the "days of trouble" (Eccles. 12), but even the old can be born again (John 3:4). People who are properly related to God will still be fruitful in old age (Ps. 92:12–15). They will serve others to the very end of life on earth, reaping blessings for themselves and others as a result. Spiritual growth continues long after other losses and declines begin.

The royal law to love our neighbor as we love ourselves (James 2:8) summarizes the ethical teachings of Scripture pertinent to all ages, but this is not a one-way relationship. "It is more blessed to give than to receive" (Acts 20:35), so we must encourage the elderly to share in the joy that comes from giving to others by helping them discover opportunities for service. Biblical ethics imply that Christians should work *with* the aging, not merely provide services *for* or *to* them. Doing for others whatever we would want them to do for us (Matt. 7:12) similarly requires respect for their individual uniquenesses, autonomy, interdependencies, and abilities. No single approach to all elderly people is valid; providing alternatives enables each older person to choose what best fits personal desires and needs.

Ministries with and for the Aging. The range of potential and actual services to the aging by churches is extremely broad. Besides ministries that serve all ages, church-sponsored housing and nursing care facilities help to meet needs at various levels of care. An expanding range of home care services is also desirable. Most gerontologists recommend that people be helped to remain in their own homes as long as possible, both to promote their sense of well-being and to reduce the overall economic costs. Volunteer services and exchanges of labor can help to meet this need. A daily telephone reassurance call and regular assistance with housework, laundry, bathing, home maintenance, and transportation to necessary out-of-the-home services can extend the years during which many are capable of residing at home.

Senior citizen programs help to meet many physical, material, educational, social, psychic, and spiritual needs when they are wisely planned and directed. They also give older persons the opportunity to serve others. Day care services can provide for the daytime needs of dependent older persons while household members are at work or school. Churches can supplement public social service programs and in the process provide older persons the opportunity to help others, thus helping themselves.

Careful examination of the circumstances of the aging in one's community will often reveal basic problems in social institutions. Whether these pertain to inequities and injustices in Social Security rules and regulations; the limitations of Medicare; administration of service programs, nursing homes, or federal policies, they ought to be addressed by Christians who, like Jesus, care about the whole person. Jesus' concern was for people individually and collectively, thus for both personal needs and structural problems of society (Matt. 9:36).

An expanding set of published literature and numerous agencies provide educational services, advice, and other assistance to church-related programs with and for the aging. Most large denominations provide materials. Local social service agencies can be helpful. Several theological schools provide resources to help churches and pastors.

The elderly should be remembered in all church ministries, including evangelism. They are an important asset. Their presence is a living witness to God's faithfulness. Their prayers provide important support to the pastor and other leaders. The active service of the "young old" can significantly enlarge the scope of church ministries. As their spiritual needs are met, they in turn minister to the needs of others.

D. O. Moberg

Bibliography. H. B. Brotman, *Every Ninth American;* W. M. Clements, ed., *Ministry with the Aging;* D. F. Clingan, *Aging Persons in the Community of Faith;* T. C. Cook, Jr., and D. L. McGinty, eds., *Spiritual and Ethical Values and National Policy on Aging;* C. B. Freeman, *The Senior Adult Years;* R. M. Gray and D. O. Moberg, *The Church and the Older Person;* S. Hiltner, ed., *Toward a Theology of Aging;* C. and P. LeFevre, eds., *Aging and the Human Spirit;* J. M. Mason, *The Fourth Generation;* R. W. McClellan, *Claiming a Frontier: Ministry and Older People;* D. O. Moberg, *Spiritual Well-Being: Background and Issues;* T. R. Smith, *In Favor of Growing Older;* F. Stagg, *The Bible Speaks on Aging;* J. A. Thorson and T. C. Cook, Jr., eds., *Spiritual Well-Being of the Elderly;* C. W. Tilberg, ed., *The Fullness of Life;* J. H. Ziegler, ed., "Education for Ministry in Aging: Gerontology in Seminary Training," *TheolEd* 16, 3.

Agnosticism. A term generally used for the view that we do not know either in practice or in principle whether there is a God or not. Although etymologically the term is applicable to any kind of skepticism, T. H. Huxley coined the term to signify religious skepticism. Huxley first used the word in 1869 at a meeting of what later became the Metaphysical Society. There are conflicting accounts of how Huxley came to use the term. He said that he used the word as antithetical to the Gnostics of early church history. Agnosticism is to be contrasted with atheism and pantheism, as well as theism and Christianity. The theist asserts God's existence, the atheist denies it, while the agnostic professes ignorance about it, the existence of God being an insoluble problem for him. R. H. Hutton remembers the origin of the term as related to the reference which Paul made to the inscription on the altar to the unknown God (Acts 17:23).

Agnosticism is now used in a number of senses: (1) as the suspension of judgment on all ultimate issues, including God, free will, immortality; (2) to describe a secular attitude toward life, such as the belief that God is irrelevant to the life of modern man; (3) to express an emotionally charged anti-Christian and anticlerical attitude; (4) as a term roughly synonymous with atheism.

While Huxley has been credited with giving the term its present popularity, there were many historical antecedents. Socrates in Plato's *Republic* is praised by the oracle of Delphi as the wisest man in the world because he was aware of what he did know and what he did not know. By far the most important and immediate precursors of modern agnosticism were David Hume and Immanuel Kant. In Hume's *Enquiry Concerning Human Understanding* he examines the notion of a "cause." He argues that one cannot know the cause of anything *a priori*. The idea of a cause arises primarily from the constant conjunction of two objects or things. Moreover, Hume rejects the possibility of belief in miracles. Such a belief is based upon testimony. The testimony for a miracle is always counterbalanced by the universal testimony to the regularity of the natural law. In *Dialogues Concerning Natural Religion* Hume thoroughly criticizes the argument from design. Two of his most important points are that the order observable in the universe may be the result of a principle inherent in matter itself rather than external to it and imposed upon it, and that the argument can never establish the moral attributes of God because of the widespread presence of evil in the world.

Kant was concerned with the limits of human knowledge. He argues that we cannot have any knowledge of things that are not possible objects of experience. Since God is not a possible object of our experience, we have no knowledge of him based upon pure reason. There may be practical reasons for believing in God, but classical theistic proofs were in principle doomed to failure.

Thus, by the end of the nineteenth century there were a number of factors which contributed to the intellectual respectability of agnosticism. The limits of human knowledge had been widely set at the limits of sense experience. Further, it was generally accepted that natural theology had failed, leading to a critical attitude toward standards of evidence and argument in religious matters. Religious beliefs could not meet the rigorous standards applied to scientific beliefs. Moreover, the physical sciences seemed to be at odds with biblical history and cosmology. Finally, questions were being raised about the divine government of the world. John Stuart Mill, for instance, argued that the world was poorly made and arbitrarily managed. The goodness of God was questioned since he was the creator of hell.

In the present intellectual climate agnosticism has taken a somewhat different form in the English-speaking world. Many logical positivists and analytic philosophers have argued that the problem with theism is not one of evidence or argument, but of meaning and logical coherence. If religious discourse is understood as quasi-scientific statements about the nature of reality and a transcendent being, insoluble problems arise. "God exists" and "God loves me" should be understood as meaningless about reality. That is, there is nothing in sense experience that will count for or against their truth.

Many who reject theism and Christianity prefer to characterize themselves as agnostics rather than atheists. The perceived advantages are twofold. First, agnosticism avoids the social stigma associated with atheism. Socially, atheism is not as respectable as agnosticism. Second, agnosticism at least appears to avoid the burden of proof. To assert or deny anything requires a reason. The profession of ignorance, however, needs no reasons.

While there may be a certain intellectual respectability to embracing agnosticism, William James points out there is great practical danger. James notes that there are some questions that are live, momentous, and forced. One must believe or disbelieve, even if the evidence is ambiguous, or risk great loss. The question of God's existence is such a question for James. For Christians, however, the evidence for God's existence and the truth of Christianity is decisively decided in God's self-revelation in the Bible and the incarnation of Jesus Christ. P. D. Feinberg

See also God, Arguments for the Existence of; Pascal's Wager.

Bibliography. R. A. Armstrong, *Agnosticism and Theism in the Nineteenth Century;* J. Collins, *God in Modern Philosophy;* T. H. Huxley, "Agnosticism" and "Agnosticism and Christianity," in *Collected Essays,* V; J. Pieper, *Belief and Faith;* R. Flint, *Agnosticism.*

Agricola, Johann (*ca.* 1494–1566). Theologian, pastor, and teacher, Johann Agricola (family name Schneider or Schnitter) was born in Eisleben more than a decade after Martin Luther. Agricola went to Wittenberg in 1515 to study with Luther and remained there for ten years. He was with Luther when he posted his Ninety-five Theses in 1517 and when he burned the papal bull of excommunication in 1520, and he served as his secretary at the Leipzig debate in 1519.

Agricola was sent by Luther to help reform Frankfurt in 1525, but later that year he returned to Eisleben, where he became pastor and schoolmaster. In 1536 Luther invited him back to Wittenberg to teach theology. He signed the Smalcald Articles in 1537 and helped formulate the Augsburg Interim in 1548.

It was during his second Wittenberg period that Agricola became the eye of the storm over what was to become the first major theological dispute in the Lutheran movement—the so-called antinomian controversy. This bitter dispute can be partly attributed to Agricola's prickly personality which, at various times over the years, put him at odds with Philip Melanchthon, Johannes Bugenhagen, and Justus Jonas. Moreover, his general carelessness, presumptuousness, and stubbornness in dealing with theological issues compounded the problem. But the main cause of the conflict was a difference between Agricola and Luther over the proper relationship between the law and the gospel.

The antinomian controversy lasted intermittently from 1537 to 1540 when, just ahead of a trial for heresy, Agricola hastily left Wittenberg to become court preacher for the elector Joachim II of Brandenburg. Agricola argued that people were sufficiently motivated by hearing of Christ's sacrifice for their sins and that the preaching of the law was unnecessary and perhaps even harmful. Luther responded that although the severity of Christ's sacrifice indeed demonstrated the enormity of human sin, the law still needed to be preached forcefully, and people still had to be convicted of their sin by the law.

After Agricola and Luther had written several works defending their own views and attacking those of the other, and after at least three different recantations by Agricola, a permanent settlement of the dispute still could not be effected.

Even though, in retrospect, Agricola's position does not appear to have been as extreme as Luther believed, and even though Agricola finally returned to what most judged to be complete orthodoxy, Luther to his dying day never forgave him. As for his part, Agricola died convinced that Luther had merely misunderstood him.

R. D. LINDER

See also ANTINOMIANISM; LUTHER, MARTIN.

Aids, Gift of. *See* SPIRITUAL GIFTS.

À Kempis, Thomas. *See* THOMAS À KEMPIS.

Albertus Magnus (1193–1280). Dominican scholar, theologian, and churchman. A Swabian of noble birth, he became a monk (1223) and taught in convents in Germany from 1228 to 1240. He attended the University of Paris and taught there from 1245 to 1248. His most famous student was Thomas Aquinas. In 1248 he returned to Cologne to establish a new course of studies for his order. Later he served as head of the German province of the Dominicans and became Bishop of Regensburg (1260–62). After retiring from administrative duties he spent his time as a teacher, writer, and controversialist.

Albert was the dominant intellectual of his age. He lived at a time when the scientific works of Aristotle along with the comments on them by Islamic scholars were being translated and studied in the universities of Europe. He was the first to master this material, sharing his understanding in many of the twenty-one massive volumes that he wrote. These included a commentary on the *Sentences* of Peter Lombard and commentaries on the Major and Minor Prophets, Job, and the Gospels. The most significant of his works were his explanation of Aristotle's scientific writings and his attempt to harmonize theology and philosophy in the *Summa theologiae*. His scientific studies dealt with physics, psychology, geography, mineralogy, botany, zoology, and life processes in general. Differing from many medieval writers, he did not comment on each line of Aristotle but rather paraphrased the text and added digressions based on his own observations. Albert's other major interest, a synthesis between Aristotle's philosophy and Christianity, was not as successful as was the work of Aquinas, but he did begin the defense of the integrity of both the realm of revelation and the realm of reason. He believed that secular knowledge must be acquired so that one may relate it to faith and that Christians can never learn too much about philosophy or science. However, he clearly taught that knowledge in the ultimate sense cannot contradict divine revelation.

Albert lived during the "Golden Age of Scholasticism," and despite an enormously busy and varied life he mastered the knowledge available at his time to a greater extent than any of his contemporaries. In a sense he was a unique man, observing nature as well as reading books and constantly trying to fit the details into a coherent scheme. His scientific interest led to accusations that he was a miracle worker in touch with supernatural power. His impressive learning resulted in posterity rewarding him with the title of "the great," a term generally reserved for military conquerors.

R. G. CLOUSE

See also SCHOLASTICISM.

Bibliography. M. Albert, *Albert the Great;* É. Gilson, *A History of Christian Philosophy in the Middle Ages;* T. M. Schwertner, *St. Albert the Great;* J. A. Weisheipl, ed., *Albertus Magnus and the Sciences;* F. J. Kovach and R. W. Shahan, *Albert the Great.*

Albigenses. Adherents of a series of dualistic sects that flourished in Western Europe during the twelfth and thirteenth centuries. Although their theology was heretical, they shared many of the attitudes and teachings of more orthodox groups. An emphasis on bodily purity, the rejection of wealth, the devotion to the gospel, the condemnation of violence and power, and opposition to the Roman hierarchy were views held by the Waldenses and in part by the Beguines and the early Franciscans. These attitudes were encouraged by weaknesses in the medieval church and by a reaction against the growing urban culture of Europe with its money-making materialism and its disregard of human needs.

It is not known whether dualism came to Europe from the East as a complete system or whether Eastern ideas merged with extant heresies, but by the midtwelfth century various Gnostic and Manichaean beliefs appeared along the trade routes into northern Italy and southern France. Some groups of dualists were called Bogomils or Cathari, but the most common European name for them was Albigenses because the movement centered in Albi in Languedoc. Albigenses taught that there are two opposing forces in the world, one good and the other evil. It was debated as to whether the power of evil was independent of the Spirit of God or was one of his fallen angels. In either event it was the evil spirit who created the world. Consequently the physical world was evil because it had entrapped spirit in matter. Human beings were in a difficult position in this system due to the fact that the soul is spiritual and therefore good, but the body is evil. Therefore a person must try to liberate his soul from the evil flesh as effectively as possible. By living the proper life one could escape the flesh; otherwise the spirit would be doomed to reincarnation.

From this doctrine Albigenses derived a fanatical puritanism which condemned marriage, procreation, food, war, civil government, and the use of objects in worship. These extreme positions were often compromised in practice, but many Albigenses refused to take oaths or eat any product of coition. They divided themselves into the few, or perfect, who lived up to the strict code of their faith and the many, or believers, who tried to purify themselves. One became perfect by receiving the sacrament of *consolamentum.* If this was not done during a person's active life, it was administered when he was dying.

The Roman Church was horrified by the Albigenses, and through the Inquisition, the establishment of new mendicant orders, and the use of crusades the movement was crushed. In the process the brilliant Provençal civilization of southern France was destroyed. R. G. Clouse

See also Bogomils; Cathari; Manichaeism.

Bibliography. M. Lambert, *Medieval Heresy;* S. Runciman, *The Medieval Manichee, A Study of the Christian Dualist Heresy;* R. I. Moore, *The Origins of European Dissent;* W. L. Wakefield and A. P. Evans, *Heresies of the High Middle Ages;* D. Walther, "A Survey of Recent Research on the Albigensian Cathari," *CH* 34:146–77.

Albright, William Foxwell (1891–1971). Rightly called the dean of American biblical archaeologists, W. F. Albright was born in Coquimbo, Chile. In his early years he suffered from grinding poverty as the son of a Methodist missionary and minister, and although he had severe physical handicaps—extreme myopia and a crippled left hand—he also had a fierce determination to succeed. He earned an A.B. at Upper Iowa University in 1912 and the Ph.D. at Johns Hopkins in 1916. Though his wife converted to Catholicism, a fact which created many problems for him, he remained a lifelong Protestant.

Albright's influence has been felt in every facet of Near Eastern studies. It was exerted through his professorship in Semitic languages at Johns Hopkins University (1929–58), where he directed innumerable doctoral studies and during which time he interacted with countless others concerning their research and publications. His insistence on the highest possible standards of accuracy helped to transform the field of Near Eastern studies. His influence was extended through his editorship of the *Bulletin of the American Schools of Oriental Research* for thirty-eight years (1931–68), as vice-president and trustee of the ASOR for more than thirty years, and as director of the ASOR (1921–29) and its school in Jerusalem (now called the Albright Institute). His archaeological chronology, developed by 1935 from his excavations at Tell Beit Mirsim (which became the type-site for Palestine), gave new order to all subsequent archaeological studies in Palestine.

Albright's writings generally have made an enormous impact. There are over a thousand entries in his bibliography, including major and minor articles on almost every aspect of the ancient Near East. Among his major works are his pace-setting *From the Stone Age to Christianity, Archaeology and the Religion of Israel, The Archaeology of Palestine and the Bible, Yahweh and the Gods of Canaan, The Excavations at Tell Beit Mirsim,* and *The Archaeology of Palestine.*

Finally, Albright's impact on American theological and biblical thinking has been tremendous. He relentlessly attacked the prevailing views of OT scholarship spawned by the Wellhausen school from an archaeological point of view. He was especially opposed to literary and historical reconstructions that operated without the controls of external data or reasoning based on knowledge of the cultural context. An important presentation of his case occurred in his presidential address to the Society of Biblical Literature on December 27, 1939 (published in *History, Archaeology and Christian Humanism*). H. F. Vos

Bibliography. L. G. Running and D. N. Freedman, *William Foxwell Albright.*

Alcohol, Drinking of. A number of chemical compounds are classified under the rubric of alcohol, but only one can be utilized as a beverage ingredient—ethyl alcohol (ethanol). This is both an energy source (one gram yields seven calories when metabolized) and a drug that affects the central nervous system and depresses sensory functions. The desired effects of alcoholic drinks are, personally, a sense of euphoria; an easing of tension, stress, and worry; a general elevation of spirits; and, socially, the relaxation of barriers among people and promoting good fellowship within a group. But when alcohol is imbibed excessively, intoxication or "drunkenness" results. This involves impairment of speech and motor control, outbursts of aggressive behavior, and finally unconsciousness. Alcoholism goes beyond mere drunkenness and is a condition in which an individual's uncontrollable dependence upon alcohol interferes significantly with his or her physical and mental health, interpersonal relations, and social and economic functions. Specialists in the treatment of alcoholism agree that if the addiction pattern is not reversed, it leads to serious medical complications, even insanity or death, but they are divided as to whether its underlying causes are primarily physical in nature (a disease or genetic factors that render one incapable of drinking in moderation) or moral and psychological (sin or personality disorders).

Alcoholic Drinks. Since the dawn of history people have produced alcoholic beverages by utilizing a process of yeast enzyme fermentation which converts plant sugars into ethyl alcohol. Mead (fermented honey) was used in ancient India and Greece, beer (brewed from barley or other cereals) was produced in Egypt and the Greco-Roman world, and pulque (a beer from the maguey plant) was common in pre-Columbian America. However, by far the best-known alcoholic beverage in antiquity was wine. Viniculture was practiced throughout the Mediterranean world and the more temperate areas of Europe and Asia, and European emigrants have taken it to other parts of the world in modern times. The process involves crushing the grapes to obtain the juice, fermentation of the juice, and storing the wine properly so as to allow for its maturation while preventing spoilage. The earliest recorded instance of wine usage is found in the Bible (Noah's inebriation, Gen. 9:21), and both testaments contain an abundance of references to wine-making procedures.

Fermented beverages, whether made from grapes, cereals, or a wide range of other plants, have a fairly low ethanol content, at most 14 percent, but even before the Christian era the Chinese developed a means of distilling rice wine which significantly increased the alcohol proportion. Around A.D. 800 this was replicated by an Arab chemist and called *al-kuhul*, from which came the origin of the word "alcohol." The process was utilized by medieval European priests and physicians to produce brandies and liqueurs from a fruit base for medicinal purposes and as dessert wines. Brandies were gradually supplanted in importance by more potent distilled drinks such as whiskey, gin, and rum, which were made from a grain or sugar base and possessed an ethanol content ranging upward to 50 or 60 percent. At one time these were commonly referred to as "spirits," but the term is out of vogue today.

Public Concern About Alcohol. Drinking has been a matter of public concern for thousands of years. Through the centuries, beginning with the Code of Hammurabi (*ca.* 1800 B.C.), rules have limited the number of drinking establishments, regulated tavern operations, restricted the availability of drink to certain classes of people, and curbed the quantities and types of beverages that could be sold. Neither Judaism nor Christianity requires abstinence, unlike Buddhism and Islam, but Christians in particular have from time to time confronted the evils of excessive drinking. Some medieval religious orders required abstinence, and in the sixteenth century appeared the first temperance societies that combated drunkenness. The amount of alcoholism resulting from the wide distribution of distilled drinks and their ready availability to the lower classes in the later eighteenth and the nineteenth centuries led to the formation of numerous temperance organizations in North America, Britain, and Europe. While most of them called only for moderation or nonuse of distilled drinks, the movement for total abstinence by Christians quickly gathered steam. In the United States the temperance forces utilized the techniques of modern pressure politics to secure the enactment of national legislation prohibiting the manufacture and sale of alcoholic beverages, but this highly controversial measure was repealed in 1933 after fourteen years of bitter controversy. Since then the level of alcohol abuse has risen dramatically in most Western and Communist-bloc nations and has reached crisis proportions in some places, but fortunately considerable attention is now being placed on the scientific study of alcoholism and alcohol education.

Strong Drink in the Bible. The only alcoholic beverage identified by name in the Bible is wine (*yayin* and *tîrôš*, OT; *oinos*, LXX and NT). Another word, *šēkār*, is translated "strong drink" in the AV and "beer" in the NIV. No evidence whatsoever exists to support the notion that the wine mentioned in the Bible was unfermented grape juice. When juice is referred to, it is not called wine (Gen. 40:11). Nor can "new wine" (*tîrôš*, OT; *gleukos*, NT) mean unfermented juice, because the process of chemical change begins almost immediately after pressing. The new wine mentioned in Acts 2:13 must have been fermented, because nearly eight months had passed since the last grape harvest. The term correctly signifies the wine made from the first drippings, which had a higher sugar content before fermentation and therefore was stronger. In the Bible wine is wine, not grape juice.

It was used symbolically in the OT as a token of God's blessing and was acceptable to him when offered on the altar (Gen. 27:29; Exod. 29:40). Metaphorically, it represented something good he prepared for those who received it (Prov. 9:5; Isa. 55:1). Jesus performed his first miracle at Cana by changing water to wine, illustrated a point by referring to the current practice of putting new wine in new wineskins, was caricatured by his enemies as a tippler, and at the Last Supper instituted the Communion service, which included drinking a cup of wine in remembrance of his shed blood (John 2:1–11; Mark 2:22; Matt. 11:19; Luke 7:34; Matt. 26:27–29; Mark 14:23–25; Luke 22:20; I Cor. 11:25–26). Wine gladdened the heart, refreshed those caught in what seemed to be hopeless situations, and possessed medicinal value (Ps. 104:15; Prov. 31:6; I Tim. 5:23).

At the same time, its use was fraught with peril. It befuddled the mind, prevented rulers from acting wisely in their roles as lawmakers and judges, caused poverty, and led to outright humiliation, as the behavior of Noah and Lot while drunk illustrated (Isa. 28:7; Prov. 31:4–5; Gen. 9:21; 19:30–38). It was called a mocker that led one astray and destroyed his understanding (Prov. 20:1; Hos. 4:11). The whore of Babylon made the inhabitants of the earth drunk with the wine of her adulteries (Rev. 17:2).

Drunkenness and Temperance. The Scriptures are unequivocal in their condemnation of immoderate use of strong drink. Followers of Christ are commanded not to get drunk on wine but to be filled with the Holy Spirit, and they should not even associate with those who call themselves "brothers" but are drunkards (Eph. 5:18; I Cor. 5:10). Drunkenness is an act originating from one's fleshly or sinful nature, labeled a deed of darkness, and is a deterrent to inheriting the kingdom of God (Gal. 5:21; Rom. 13:12–13; I Cor. 6:10). People who are appointed to leadership positions in the church must not imbibe excessively (I Tim. 3:3, 8; Titus 1:7; 2:3). The biblical abhorrence of drunkenness can best be seen in the vivid description of the destructive impact alcoholism has on a person (Prov. 23:29–35).

The biblical norm is temperance, a term which means self-control and moderation in all of one's behavior, not total abstinence from beverage alcohol (Gal. 5:23; II Pet. 1:6; Titus 2:2). There are several examples of abstinence in the Bible, but these are special cases and not normative. Priests were not to drink before they entered the tabernacle to minister (Lev. 10:9). The Nazirite vow prohibited drinking, but this included all contact with grapes as well and it was to be for a specific period of time (Num. 6:3–5). The Rechabite clan had adopted abstinence as part of their program of rejecting a settled agricultural existence in order to follow a nomadic life like that of the people of Israel in the wilderness and thereby prophetically demonstrate faithful living with God (Jer. 35). Daniel and his friends rejected not only the wine offered by Nebuchadnezzar but also the fine food, and they prospered because of the total effect of a more austere but nutritious diet (Dan. 1:8–16). The abstinence of John the Baptist reflected his prenatal selection to become a prophet and the ascetic life style that accompanied this calling (Luke 1:15).

Paul teaches that strong Christians ought not to have problems with food and drink, but at the same time they should be considerate of the tender conscience of the "weak brother." If one's indulgence might cause this person to stumble spiritually, it would be better to abstain. Biblical temperance requires considered restraint in one's drinking practices and abstinence, if necessary, to shore up the faith of weaker brethren (Rom. 14; I Cor. 8). To be sure, Christian liberty permits one either to abstain or to partake in moderation, but the total abstainer is not justified in upholding his practice as the more biblical, virtuous, or spiritual of the two. Drunkenness, however, is inimical to a healthy Christian life and clearly must be proscribed by the church to its members. R. V. Pierard

Bibliography. R. S. Shore and J. M. Luce, *To Your Health: The Pleasures, Problems, and Politics of Alcohol;* J. A. Ewing and B. A. Rouse, *Drinking: Alcohol in American Society;* J. S. Blocker, Jr., *Alcohol, Reform, and Society;* J. F. Sutherland, *HERE,* V, 94–100; J. F. Ross, *IDB,* IV, 488, 844–52; D. M. Edwards, *ISBE,* II, 879–81; B. S. Easton, *ISBE,* V, 3086–88.

Alcuin (*ca.* 735–804). Outstanding Christian scholar and educator during the reign of Charlemagne. Born in England, Alcuin received his education at the noted Cathedral School in York; later he became its head. While on a trip to Rome in 781 he met Charlemagne; the following year he accepted the Frankish monarch's invitation to become head of a school attached to the imperial court. Charlemagne, as part of his policy of encouraging a renaissance of culture in his realm, was committed to elevating the educational standards of his kingdom, especially among the clergy. He gathered a number of scholars around him to assist in this program, of whom Alcuin was the most outstanding. Alcuin became a trusted adviser to Charlemagne, and under his direction many schools were founded. In 796 Alcuin became abbot of the Monastery of St. Martin of Tours, which under his leadership became an important center of medieval scholarship. He continued to act as adviser to Charlemagne in promoting learning until his death. He had little interest in the politics of Charlemagne's reign and generally confined his advice to nonpolitical matters.

Although Alcuin was said to be gentle in spirit, he played a significant role in several theological controversies. He vigorously defended the traditional Christology of the church against the adoptionism of the Spanish theologians Elipandus of Toledo and Felix of Urgel, and was the main influence at the Synod of Aachan at which Felix recanted his heretical views. A prolific writer, Alcuin wrote a number of biblical commentaries, theological treatises, hymns, poems, and several biographies of important ecclesiastical figures. Of special significance was his leadership of a group of scholars who revised the text of the Latin Vulgate Bible, making use of the most reliable manuscripts available. He also was responsible for the development of the Caroline minuscule script, the forerunner of Roman type faces. Some of his liturgical innovations have had a lasting impact on Roman Catholic worship.

Although Alcuin remained in Charlemagne's favor until his death, he opposed the latter's use of force in converting conquered peoples to Christianity and insisted that adult candidates for baptism should be thoroughly instructed in the Christian faith. J. N. AKERS

Alexander, Archibald (1772–1851). The first professor at Princeton Theological Seminary and progenitor of the "Princeton Theology," which held sway at the institution for over a century. Alexander came to the seminary in 1812 after service as an itinerant evangelist in his native Virginia, as president of Hampden-Sidney College (1796–1807), and as pastor of the Pine Street Presbyterian Church in Philadelphia (1807–12). His successors in Princeton's chair of theology—Charles Hodge, Archibald Alexander Hodge, and B. B. Warfield—expanded, clarified, and deepened the major themes of his thought but did not go measurably beyond them. The Bible—as interpreted by the Reformed theology of the Westminster standards, the orthodox Protestant theologians of seventeenth century Europe, and the principles of Scottish commonsense philosophy—was the indispensable standard for teaching and practice. Human reason was a powerful tool for demonstrating the validity of Scripture and exegeting its meaning. Religious experience under the direction of the Holy Spirit was crucial to spiritual life, but should never be allowed to drift into "enthusiasm." Alexander was not as substantial an exegete as Charles Hodge nor as skillful in polemics against New England and other forms of Arminianism; he was not as effective a popularizer as A. A. Hodge; and he was not as careful a reasoner as Warfield. Yet perhaps because of the scope of his earlier experience, he possessed more personal warmth and often displayed more insight into the human condition than his erudite successors. M. A. NOLL

See also PRINCETON THEOLOGY, OLD.

Bibliography. Alexander, *Evidences of the Authenticity, Inspiration, and Canonical Authority of the Holy Scriptures, Thoughts on Religious Experience,* and *Outlines of Moral Science;* J. W. Alexander, *The Life of Archibald Alexander;* J. A. MacKay, "Archibald Alexander (1772–1851): Founding Father," in *Sons of the Prophets,* ed. H. T. Kerr.

Alexander, Samuel (1859–1938). Jewish philosopher born in Sydney, Australia, and educated partly at Oxford. He made his philosophical contributions while professor at Manchester (1893–1924).

Alexander is best known for his Gifford Lectures, *Space-Time and Deity,* in which he sought to reconcile science (or philosophy of science) with the ideas of his day (including evolution and materialism). He started with Spinoza's static pantheistic concept of the god-world and never got beyond Spinoza's pantheism. But he gave it a certain dynamic quality as he linked it with "emergent evolution," a view of which he was one of the developers.

His "emergent evolution" was somewhat analogous to Bergson's idea of "creative evolution." He taught the emergence of the world order out of a more primitive space-time matrix. "Emergents" were new and not completely predictable outcomes of previously existing conditions. According to Alexander, ultimate reality was space-time and matter "emerged" from space-time. With the rise of certain physiochemical complexes life emerged. Out of certain configurations of living complexes arose consciousness. Out of a hierarchy of qualities arose "deity," which is the highest quality of God, whose "body" is the whole universe. Hence in his pantheism he distinguished between deity and God. As he saw the quality of "deity" continuing to evolve with the universe, he taught that personal religion consisted in advancing the world toward deity, which to him involved the triumph of good over evil in human affairs.

Alexander's chief works were *Moral Order and Progress* (1906); *Space-Time and Deity* (1920); *Spinoza and Time* (1921); *Beauty and Other Forms of Value* (1933). H. F. VOS

Alexander of Hales (*ca.* 1170–1245). Born at Hales Owen, in Shropshire, England, Alexander studied at the University of Paris, where he became a master of theology in 1221 and began to teach that same year. In 1236 he joined the

Franciscan Order of Friars, which had been founded in 1209, but he did not give up his teaching position until 1241. His importance in the history of theology is threefold. First, he began the association of the Franciscan Order with the universities and academic theology, hitherto neglected by the Order. Second, early in his teaching career he replaced the custom of lecturing on the Bible with lectures on the *Sentences* of Peter Lombard, which became the standard textbook on the subject and on which he wrote a commentary. Third, though rooted in the Augustinian tradition, he recognized something of the importance for theological study of the recently discovered Aristotelian philosophy, and he attempted to come to terms with it in his theological expositions. Though his work in this area was fragmentary, he paved the way for the assimilation of Aristotelianism into Christian theology by such men as Thomas Aquinas. The *Summa Theologica* traditionally associated with Alexander's name has been shown to be only partly of his authorship, since it incorporates material from others such as his pupil Bonaventure. N. V. Hope

Bibliography. M. C. Wass, *The Infinite God and the Summa Fratris Alexandri;* É. Gilson, *History of Christian Philosophy in the Middle Ages.*

Alexandrian Theology. It is probable that Christianity came to Alexandria in apostolic times, though the tradition that it was first brought by John Mark cannot be verified. The indications are that Christianity was well established in middle Egypt by A.D. 150 and that Alexandria was its port of entry and supporting base.

Clement of Alexandria became head of the Catechetical School about 190. A philosopher throughout his life, Clement saw Greek philosophy as a preparation for Christ, even as a witness to divine truth. Plato was a cherished guide. Sin is grounded in man's free will. Enlightenment by the Logos brings man to knowledge. Knowledge results in right decisions. These draw a man toward God until he is assimilated to God (*Stromata* iv. 23). The Christian lives by love, free from passion. His life is a constant prayer. Clement set forth its pattern in minute detail in the *Paedagogos.* He took an optimistic view of the future of all men, but knowledge would be rewarded in the world to come. An allegorical exegesis of Scripture supported these views.

Around 202 Clement was succeeded in the Catechetical School by the much abler Origen. A biblical student and exegete of great ability, Origen produced the *Hexapla* text of the OT. He wrote commentaries, scholia, or homilies on all the biblical books; but they were based on three senses of Scripture, the literal, moral, and allegorical. The Bible was inspired, useful, true in every letter, but the literal interpretation was not necessarily the correct one. Indebted, like Clement, to the Greeks, Origen was not as admiringly dependent upon them. His conception was of a great spiritual universe, presided over by a beneficent, wise, and personal being. Alexandrian Christology makes its beginnings with Origen. Through an eternal generation of the Son, the Logos, God communicates himself from all eternity. There is a moral, volitional unity between the Father and the Son, but an essential unity is questionable. The world of sense provides the theater of redemption for fallen creatures who range from angels through men to demons. By the incarnation the Logos is the mediator of redemption. He took to himself a human soul in a union that was a *henōsis.* It was, therefore, proper to say that the Son of God was born an infant, that he died (*De princ.* II. vi. 2–3). By teaching, by example, by offering himself a propitiatory victim to God, by paying the devil a ransom, Christ saves men. Men gradually free themselves from the earthy by meditation, by abstinence, by the vision of God. A purging fire may be needed in the process. Although this world is neither the first nor the last of a series, there will ultimately come the restoration of all things. Flesh, matter, will disappear, spirit only will remain, and God will be all in all. How long human freedom will retain the power of producing another catastrophe is not clear, but ultimately all will be confirmed in goodness by the power of God's love.

After Origen's departure from Alexandria his disciples diverged. One group tended to deny the eternal generation of the Logos. Dionysius, Bishop of Alexandria (247–65), sympathized with this party and declared the Logos to be a creation of the Father, but the future in Alexandria belonged to the opposite wing, which emphasized the divine attributes of the Logos. The Sabellian party was strong in Cyrenaica and Libya, and this influence affected Alexandria. When the presbyter Arius began, perhaps about 317, to proclaim that the Logos was a creation in time, differing from the Father in being, he attracted disciples, but Bishop Alexander opposed Arius. As Emperor Constantine found it impossible to restore harmony by exhortation and influence, he called for a general meeting of bishops. The resulting Council of Nicaea in 325 was attended by an Alexandrian delegation which included the deacon Athanasius. For the remaining years of his life Athanasius was to champion the Nicene conclusion that the Son was *homoousios* with the Father. The adoption of this term in spite of its checkered Gnostic and Sabellian background was a work of providential genius.

In 328 Athanasius succeeded Alexander as the Alexandrian bishop. In spite of some dictatorial tendencies he possessed a superb combination of the talents of a successful administrator with great depths of theological insight. From this time on, Alexandria emphasized vigorously the identity in being of the Father and the Son. Athanasius presented, in his *On the Incarnation of the Logos*, the indispensability of the union of true God with true man for the Christian doctrine of salvation through the life and death of Christ. Wholly God and wholly man the Savior must be. Through many false charges and five periods of exile Athanasius maintained his insistence upon one God, Father and Son of the same substance, the church the institute of salvation, not subject to the interference of the civil state. Athanasius also set forth the view that the Spirit is *homoousios* likewise with the Father and the Son, thus preparing the way for the formula *mia ousia, treis hypostaseis.*

That Christ need not be wholly divine and wholly human was a view which Apollinaris of Laodicea did not succeed in fastening upon Alexandria in spite of his efforts in that direction. His view that the *pneuma* of the Logos replaced the human spirit was rejected. His emphasis upon the unity of the personality of Christ, however, became increasingly an Alexandrian emphasis and was strongly stressed by Cyril, who became bishop in 412. The Logos took a full human nature upon himself, but the result was *henōsis physikē,* and Cyril loved the formula *mia physis,* one even though originally *ek duo.* The incarnation was to the end of salvation. God became man that we might become God. Cyril supported this by allegorical exposition of the Scripture of both testaments, especially the Pentateuch. The phenomenal allegory of the facts is designed to yield the noumenal meaning. His most famous writing is his series of twelve anathemas against Nestorius, attacking what appeared to him to be denials of the unity and full deity of Christ and of the crucifixion and resurrection of the Word. In 433 Cyril accepted, with the Antioch leaders, a profession of faith which declared that a unity of the two natures of Christ had come into existence (*henōsis gegone*) and used the term for which Cyril had so vigorously contended against Nestorius, *Theotokos,* as a description of the Virgin Mary.

Dioscurus continued the Cyrillian emphasis on unity in the person of Christ but pushed it to an extreme. At the Council of Chalcedon (451) the Alexandrian radicals suffered defeat with the adoption in the Chalcedonian Definition of the phrase *en dyo physesin.* The final Alexandrian tendencies produced schism after Chalcedon. The great bulk of Egyptian Christendom rejected Chalcedon and became monophysite. Monothelitism proved to be only a temporary enthusiasm in Alexandria. The arrival of Islamic rule ended it.

The Alexandrian school with its Platonic emphasis was the popular school of its time. In its more moderate form it set the Christological pattern for many centuries. The love of allegorical interpretation was characteristic. The intervention of the divine in the temporal was stressed, and the union of the natures of Christ with overriding emphasis on the divine component was dangerously accented.

P. Woolley

See also Clement of Alexandria; Origen; Logos; Monarchianism; Athanasius; Cyril of Alexandria; Monophysitism; Monothelitism.

Bibliography. E. R. Hardy, Jr., *Christian Egypt;* E. Molland, *The Conception of the Gospel in the Alexandrian Theology;* E. F. Osborn, *The Philosophy of Clement of Alexandria;* R. B. Tollinton, *Clement of Alexandria;* J. Daniélou, *Origen;* A. Robertson, *Select Writings and Letters of Athanasius, NPNF* 2nd series, IV; J. E. L. Oulton and H. Chadwick, eds., *Alexandrian Christianity;* E. R. Hardy, ed., *Christology of the Later Fathers,* LCC, III; R. V. Sellers, *Two Ancient Christologies;* C. Bigg, *The Christian Platonists of Alexandria;* R. B. Tollinton, *Alexandrian Teaching on the Universe.*

All. The Hebrew and Greek words of the OT and NT respectively which are represented by "all" in English translations are among the most frequently used words in Scripture. No conviction was held more firmly by the Hebrews than that the God of Israel created, sustains, and directs all things in heaven and on earth, visible and invisible. Even his special selection of Israel is not to be seen as an act of exclusivity but "that all the families of the earth shall be blessed" through Israel's hearing of the Word of God (Gen. 12:3).

The theme is expressed also in terms of redemption. The total healing of all the consequences of the fall is the fundamental vision of the prophets. In the restoration of all things the wolf will lie down with the lamb (Isa. 11:6–7), nations shall no longer learn war (Isa. 2:4), through the new law written on the heart all will know the Lord (Jer. 31:34).

The same themes are expressed Christocentrically in the NT. All creation has come into being through Christ as mediator in creation (John 1:3; I Cor. 8:6; Col. 1:16; Heb.1:2). Not only this, but the created order is sustained through him (Heb. 1:3; Col. 1:17). The NT speaks also of the redemptive work of Christ in inclusive terms.

The totality of creation is to experience reconciliation through his blood (Col. 1:20; cf. Rom. 8:21–22; Eph. 1:10). The call to repentance and faith goes out to all nations (Matt. 28:19–20; Luke 24:47; Acts 17:30). Finally, there is the vision of the day when every knee shall bow and every tongue confess the lordship of Jesus Christ. Such material is not to sustain a universalism but to declare the totality of the lordship of Christ and the inclusiveness of the call to faith. R. W. LYON

See also MANY.

Allegorical Sense of Scripture. *See* INTERPRETATION OF THE BIBLE.

Allegory. An oral or literary device which attempts to express immaterial truths in pictorial forms. Allegory usually occurs as an extended metaphor in narrative form; examples can be found in both the OT and NT (e.g., Ps. 80: Israel as a vine from Egypt; John 10:1–16: Jesus as the Good Shepherd). The device employs a point-for-point comparison between the intangibles under discussion and specified representations which are recognizable to the intended audience. For this reason knowledge of the text's cultural milieu is indispensable to a proper interpretation of the device. In Scripture the use of allegory is either specifically indicated (Gal. 4:21ff.) or is identified clearly through the context (Prov. 5:15ff.).

The literary use of allegory should be distinguished from the method of interpretation known as "allegorizing." This method is characterized by the search for a deeper meaning in the literal statements of a text that is not readily apparent in the text itself. The method often indicates more of the thought patterns of the interpreter than that of the original author.

Historically, allegorizing originated in Greece (sixth century B.C.), influenced Judaism through Philo at Alexandria (second century B.C.), and entered Christian use through such notables as Origen, Jerome, and Augustine. Their use of the method developed into an accepted fourfold interpretive approach to Scripture: (1) literal; (2) allegory; (3) moral (typology); (4) anagogy. This approach lasted throughout the Middle Ages only to be questioned by Aquinas, deemphasized by Nicholas of Lyra, and totally rejected by the Reformers. Emanuel Swedenborg's writings in the eighteenth century provide a more contemporary example of this method.

S. E. MCCLELLAND

Bibliography. D. C. Allen, *Mysteriously Meant: The Rediscovery of Pagan Symbolism and Allegorical Interpretation in the Renaissance;* R. Grant, *The Bible in the Church;* C. S. Lewis, *The Allegory of Love;* J. MacQueen, *Allegory: The Critical Idiom;* A. B. Mickelsen, *Interpreting the Bible;* H. A. Wolfson, *Philo;* J. Wood, *The Interpretation of the Bible.*

Alleine, Joseph (1634–1668). Puritan preacher and writer, Alleine is representative of the many who came up through the state church system in England and later defected from it. His experience also points up the fact that generally during early modern times in Western Christendom state churches were maintained, and dissenters from them were not dealt with kindly.

Alleine was born in Deviges, Wiltshire. His "being born again" occurred in 1645 when his eldest brother, Edward, a minister, died at the age of twenty-seven. He begged his father to be educated to succeed his brother in the ministry, and in 1649 entered Lincoln College, Oxford. Two years later he gained a scholarship at Corpus Christi College, Oxford, and graduated in 1653. At the university he came under the influence of John Owen and other outstanding Puritans. Resisting numerous opportunities to serve in state offices, he accepted the invitation to be assistant to George Newton, the outstanding minister of St. Mary Magdalene in Taunton, in 1654.

In 1662 both the senior and junior ministers at Taunton along with two thousand others were ejected from the established church under the Clarendon Code, which sought to remove from the ministry and government all who did not subscribe to the liturgy and doctrines of the Church of England. Alleine and John Wesley, grandfather of John and Charles, carried on an itinerant evangelistic ministry. For this he was fined and cast into prison (May 26, 1663) and treated with great indignity. After a year in jail he was released and more zealously propagated the gospel. When he was imprisoned again for sixty days in 1665, his confinement aggravated a developing disorder and he died November 16, 1668.

Alleine is said to rank with Richard Baxter as the most affectionately cherished of all Puritans. He is best known for his *Alarm to the Unconverted,* which sold 20,000 copies on its appearance in 1672; three years later it sold 50,000 when it was republished as *Sure Guide to Heaven.* Often reprinted, it influenced George Whitefield and Charles Spurgeon. Also a thoughtful scientific experimentalist and observer, Alleine wrote *Theologia Philosophica* (now lost) and other works. H. F. VOS

Alleluia, Alleluiah. *See* HALLELUJAH.

All Saints Day. From early times the church commemorated its great leaders and heroes, especially those who had suffered martyrdom, by observing the dates of their death. This gave rise to the sanctoral section of the liturgical calendar, and it was customary for those churches whose members had included great Christians or martyrs to gather for a Communion service at the martyr's tomb, which was sometimes used as a Communion table. At a later stage churches were built over these sites, and thus began the practice of dedicating churches in honor of specific saints.

Because there were other Christians whose faith and service (and even martyrdom) went unrecorded, and because some centers of the church gained more martyrs than could be commemorated in the days of the year, the practice of a general commemoration on All Saints Day developed. Originally celebrated on May 13, this festival was transferred in 835 to November 1, and medieval ideas of purgatory led to the following day being observed as All Souls Day, when the souls in purgatory were remembered.

At the Reformation the latter festival was dropped. Reformed churches use All Saints Day to thank God for the faithful departed.

D. H. Wheaton

See also Christian Year; Halloween.

Bibliography. M. Perham, *The Communion of Saints.*

Almighty. *See* God, Names of.

Alms, Almsgiving. Acts of personal charity have always played a major role among the people of God. They are not simply an obligation, but stem from the mercy God himself has already exhibited. Thus the term for alms, *eleēmosynē* (appearing thirteen times in the NT), comes from the word group for mercy (*eleos*). Alms are benevolent acts of mercy which compassionately meet the needs of the poor.

In the OT one is struck with the common standard of living in the Israelite towns, especially before the monarchy. Generosity to the poor was strongly commended (Deut. 15:7–11; Ps. 112:9). But to ensure a comprehensive system of welfare, the OT established various institutions to provide for the needy: the law stipulated that arable lands, vineyards, and orchards were to be left fallow every seventh year "for the poor" (Exod. 23:10–11); every third year a tithe of the land's produce was to go to the poor (Deut. 14); the poor could eat their fill as they passed through a neighbor's vineyard or field (Deut. 23:24–25); and finally at harvest the gleanings, the borders, and the corners of the fields were to be left for the poor (Lev. 19:9–10).

The prophetic disdain for the acquisition of riches should be seen as a result of the growing aristocracy in the later years of the monarchy and the widespread poverty resulting from foreign conquests (especially the Exile). Amos typically derides those who "trample the poor" (8:4–8) and Isaiah scorns the denial of justice to the poor especially among landowners and judges (5:8–10; 10:1–3). In Isa. 58 Judah's sins in neglecting its alms are carefully listed.

In the intertestamental period Judaism focused so much attention on almsgiving that charity took on a salvific and atoning value. "Righteousness" (Heb. *ṣedeq*) came to mean almsgiving, as the translation of the LXX attests (cf. the textual variant in Matt. 6:1: *dikaiosynē* vs. *eleēmosynē*) and especially as the Apocrypha affirmed: "Water extinguishes a blazing fire; so almsgiving atones for sin" (Sir. 3:30). Rabbinic teaching stressed three principles: (1) Generous almsgiving was incumbent on all, even the poor. A popular story told of two sheep who wanted to swim across a river. One sheep gave its wool and crossed without harm. The other kept its wool and drowned. Almsgiving was the virtue of the righteous. (2) But generosity was to have limits. The rabbis were well aware that imprudent giving could produce poverty for the giver. Thus the Mishnah stipulated a limit of 20 percent from anyone's earnings. (3) Acts of charity should protect the honor of the recipient. This checked the attitude of the giver and even provided for a "secret chamber" in the temple where the poor of good family could find aid without notice.

In Jesus' day an impressive system of welfare tended the poor. In addition to the OT legislation, synagogues filled "poor chests" each sabbath, a daily "poor bowl" circulated with food, and weekly a "poor basket" brought food and clothing to the needy. Jesus affirmed this activity completely (Matt. 6:1–4; John 13:29) and commended liberality in almsgiving (Matt. 5:42; Luke 6:38). The stories of Zacchaeus (Luke 19:1–10) and the rich young ruler (Matt. 19:16–22) no doubt illustrate Jesus' attitude to those who had severely abused the Jewish system. But at the same time Jesus cautioned against almsgiving for the sake of recognition (Matt. 6:2–3) and taught that alms of any sort could never be substituted for authentic spiritual piety (Luke 11:41; 12:33; Matt. 5:23–24).

It seems clear that the generous almsgiving of Judaism provided the impetus for the communal life style of the early Christian church. Possessions were sold and the proceeds distributed (Acts 2:42–47; 4:32–33). Ananias and Sapphira were no doubt examples of false participation (Acts 5:1ff.), and Acts 6 describes an administrative adjustment to the distribution of aid. Again, charity was one hallmark of righteousness, as seen in Tabitha (Acts 9:36) and Cornelius (10:2). Paul participated actively in almsgiving with his aid to Jerusalem in Acts 11 and the collection during his third missionary journey.

For Paul, an important theological connection existed between the mercy shown by God (Eph. 2:4–9; Titus 3:5) and the mercy surrounding almsgiving: the believer should pass on the mercy he has received (Rom. 12:1; II Cor. 4:1). In contrast, being without mercy (*aneleēmonas*) in Rom. 1:29–32 represents the full negation of God. James similarly exhorts the believer to be "full of mercy and good fruits" (3:17; cf. Heb. 13:16) because to reject this is to invite the merciless judgment of God on oneself (James 2:13).

As a rule the early church continued to grow in the postapostolic era as a body sharing its wealth, serving the poor, and remaining suspicious of riches. Didache 1:6 remarks, "To every man that asks of you, give, and ask not back; for the Father desires that gifts be given to all from his own bounties." In 15:4 almsgiving is listed with prayer as an equal Christian responsibility. II Clement 16:4 makes the remarkable assertion, "Almsgiving therefore is a good thing, even as repentance from sin. Fasting is better than prayer, but almsgiving than both . . . for almsgiving lifts off the burden of sin." As the church entered the mainstream of society, it wrestled with the questions of private property and the spiritual value of charity (see Clement of Alexandria, *The Rich Man's Salvation,* and Cyprian of Carthage, *On Good Works and Almsgiving*) and quickly affirmed both. However, wealth remained suspect, and those who were prosperous were obliged to take the lead in social reform. In all events, almsgiving retained the theological center found in Paul: The Christian must imitate God, who himself has taken the initiative in expressing unlimited charity and mercy. G. M. Burge

Bibliography. *SBk,* I, 429–31; R. Bultmann, *TDNT,* II, 477–87; R. deVaux, *Ancient Israel,* I, 72–74; G. H. Davies, *IDB,* I, 87–88; D. M. Lloyd-Jones, *Studies in the Sermon on the Mount,* II, 9–20; R. Schnackenburg, *The Moral Teaching of the NT;* J. Jeremias, *Jerusalem in the Time of Jesus;* M. Hengel, *Property and Riches in the Early Church;* H.-H. Esser, *NIDNTT,* II, 594–98.

Alpha and Omega. The rendering of the Greek expression *to Alpha kai to Ō,* which is found in three places in the NT (Rev. 1:8; 21:6; 22:13). It is also found in the Textus Receptus of Rev. 1:11, but modern scholarship largely regards it as not genuine in this place.

In this phrase there is probably a reference to the Jewish employment of the first and last letters of the Hebrew alphabet to indicate the totality of a thing. "The symbol *ṯ'* was regarded as including the intermediate letters, and stood for totality; and thus it fitly represented the Shekinah" (H. B. Swete, *The Apocalypse of St. John,* p. 10). It is a natural transition to the thought of eternity when the expression is related to time.

The expression is essentially the same as Isaiah's words, "I am the first, and I am the last; and beside me there is no God" (Isa. 44:6). Thus it is a claim that the one to whom it refers is the Eternal One.

The expression in Rev. 1:8, due to the explanatory phrases that modify the subject, refers to the eternity and omnipotence of the Lord God. In 21:6 it is further defined by the words "the beginning and the end," and in 22:13 by the words "the first and the last." The thought conveyed in the second and third occurrences is the same.

In patristic and later literature the expression referred to the Son. It seems clear, however, that the first two occurrences refer to the Father (1:8; 21:6), while the third properly refers to the Son. On its last occurrence (22:13) Swete remarks, "The phrase is applicable in many senses, but perhaps it is used here with special reference to our Lord's place in human history. As creation owed its beginning to the Word of God, so in His incarnate glory He will bring it to its consummation by the Great Award" (p. 307). S. L. Johnson

See also God, Names of; God, Doctrine of.

Altar. In OT Hebrew *mizbēah,* a place of slaughter or sacrifice. In NT Greek *bōmos* (only in Acts 17:23), an elevated place and frequently used in the LXX to translate *mizbēaḥ; thysiastērion,* a place of sacrifice.

In the OT. *Materials and Forms.* There were two basic types of altars in the OT. The first was an altar of no prescribed shape or material constructed of earth and stones. In some instances it is stated that the altar took this form, and in others the context suggests, that this was the form. This type of altar generally had a nonpriestly or lay use.

The second type had a prescribed form and was made of either wood and bronze or wood and gold. In particular, the two altars associated with the tabernacle and its priestly service (and that of its temple successors) followed definite patterns and were constructed by skilled craftsmen.

Uses and Functions. Altars could be put to legitimate or illegitimate uses. In the latter category were those of Israel's heathen neighbors (Exod. 20:25–26; 34:13–16; Deut. 7:5–11; Judg. 6:25–32). Israel's worship was to be entirely separate from theirs and faithful to the one true God who had revealed himself to them and the patriarchs. Unfortunately, Israel was all too prone to ignore these prohibitions and become involved with heathen gods, sacrifices, and altars (Num. 25:2–5; Judg. 6:25, 30; I Kings 12:32; 16:32; 22:43; II Kings 16:4, 10–16; Hos. 8:11; 11:2; Amos 3:14). Elijah complained that Israel had torn down God's altars and killed his prophets (I Kings 19:10), and later Jehu and Josiah each destroyed the altars of Baal (II Kings 10:18–28; II Chr. 34:1–7).

But altars just as clearly had a legitimate function. In fact, the Sinaitic regulations concerning altars were intended to preserve their legitimate functions distinct from the illegitimate ones. When we think of the lawful uses of altars we think first of the symbolism of ascending prayers, as with the altar of incense (Exod. 39:38; 40:5; cf. Rev. 8:3–5), or of substitutionary atonement, as with the offering of the ram in the place of Isaac on Mt. Moriah (Gen. 22:1–3). But altars and their sacrifices could have other significances. The first reference to an altar in Scripture is to the one built by Noah (Gen. 8:20); the context seems to suggest that Noah's sacrifices on the altar were an expression of thanksgiving for deliverance from the flood.

Abraham built altars at Shechem, Bethel-Ai, and Hebron (Gen. 12:7–8; 13:18); they were associated with his worship of God and claiming the land God had promised to him and his descendents (cf. Gen. 26:23–25). Moses built an altar as a memorial (Exod. 17:14–16); and when Israel affirmed the covenant with God, Moses built an altar at the foot of Mt. Sinai and sacrificed on it, apparently in affirmation of the covenant (Exod. 24:4–8).

Nonpriestly and Priestly Altars. That altars could be built and used by individuals other than the tabernacle priests is self-evident from the discussion above. There was no priesthood prior to Sinai, yet altars were built and used in the worship of God by the patriarchs. God told Moses to instruct the people of Israel concerning the proper construction and use of such "lay altars" (Exod. 20:24–26). That they continued to be built is clear from Josh. 8:30–35; Judg. 6:24; 21:4; I Sam. 7:17; 14:35; and II Sam. 24:25.

But at Mt. Sinai God also revealed to Moses the specifications for two altars associated with the tabernacle and the priestly ministry. The bronze altar or altar of burnt offerings was 7½ feet square, 4½ feet tall, made of acacia wood covered with bronze, and had horns on the four top corners. It was constructed in a manner so that it could be carried. When set up it stood between the entrance to the courtyard and the door of the tabernacle. The animal and cereal offerings were made here (Exod. 27:1–8; 31:2–5, 9; 38:1–7; 40:6, 29). Sacrifices offered here (Lev. 1–7) signified that atonement for sin was necessary before one could enter the presence of God.

The second altar was the gold altar or altar of incense. It was 18 inches square, 3 feet high, made of acacia wood covered with gold, and had four horns on the top corners. It too was constructed so it could be carried. It was probably situated just before the curtain separating the Holy Place from the Holy of Holies (Exod. 40:26; but cf. Heb. 9:4). On the gold altar the high priest offered incense morning and evening, and once a year the high priest applied atoning blood to its horns (Exod. 30:1–10; 40:5, 26–27). The smoke of incense arising and filling the tabernacle signified offered prayer (cf. Rev. 8:3).

It is not known what happened to either the bronze or gold altars of the tabernacle. But when Solomon built the temple, it was provided with counterparts of the two tabernacle altars. The new bronze altar was larger (30 feet square and 15 feet high, II Chr. 4:1), but little is known of the new gold altar except that it was made of cedar overlaid with gold (I Kings 6:20–22). The returned exiles presumably restored both altars in the second temple (Ezra 3:3; cf. I Macc. 1:21, 54; 4:44–49). Later, counterparts of the two altars were to be found in Herod's temple (Matt. 5:23–24; 23:18–20; Luke 1:11).

Ezekiel, the exilic prophet, had a vision of a rebuilt temple (Ezek. 40–44). An altar of burnt offering is described in some detail, its dimensions differing from earlier altars (43:13–17); but there is no mention of an altar of incense, unless that is the intended reference of 41:22. Some interpreters feel the vision was intended to focus the attention of the exiles on God's renewed dealings with Israel in a rebuilt Jerusalem and temple. Others see a fulfillment of Ezekiel's vision in a still future millennial temple and sacrificial ritual. Opponents of this view argue that a resumption of animal sacrifices is unthinkable in view of the fulfillment of the typological significance by Christ's work on the cross (cf. esp. the Epistle to the Hebrews). But proponents of the view argue that such sacrifices would have commemorative significance and in principle be no different from the present observance of the Lord's Supper. It is a difficult question and is intertwined with many other considerations involving ecclesiology and eschatology.

In the NT. Most NT references to altars refer to the altars in Herod's temple (see above). But there are also references to the altar of incense in the heavenly temple (Rev. 6:9; 8:3–5; 9:13; 14:18; 16:7). It is significant that in the heavenly temple there is apparently no altar of burnt offering, for atonement is complete. But the prayers of the saints like the sweet incense of the gold altar will always rise to God and be a pleasure to him.

Some theological traditions (in particular Eastern Orthodoxy, Roman Catholicism, High Church Anglicanism, and highly liturgical Protestant churches) consider the reference to "altar" in Heb. 13:10 to be a reference to the Communion table. This interpretation hardly fits the context of Hebrews in that in this case one material thing would be substituted for another; this would undermine the previous argument of the epistle. Heb. 13:10 is better understood as a reference to the cross as the altar on which Christ was offered. Since these same theological traditions regard the Communion table as an altar, it is natural that they consider the "table of the Lord" (I Cor. 10:21) to be synonymous with the Christian altar.

In Church History. Beginning with the early second century, the understanding of what happened in the Lord's Supper became ever more literalistic. At first the bread and wine were considered in some figurative sense to be an offering of the body and blood of Christ. This view gradually evolved over a period of centuries in a more literal direction, so that the offering of bread and wine eventually was considered to be quite literally the sacrificial offering of the body and blood of Christ by priests. It came to be called, even at a very early date, the "sacrifice of the altar" and finally culminated in the Roman Catholic doctrines of transubstantiation and the sacrifice of the Mass. Concommitant with these developments was the evolution of the Communion table from a simple house table on which the bread and wine were served to an altar on which Christ was in some sense offered. The more literally the elements were thought to be Christ, the more literally the table was considered to be an altar. Christian altars have always taken the tabular form, although there was a development from wood to metal and stone materials.

This perception of the Communion table as an altar came to prevail in both Eastern Orthodoxy and Roman Catholicism. However, even Protestant traditions that stress the "real presence" of Christ in the elements are likely to speak of the Communion table as an altar. As such it is the focal point of worship in the Communion service and in congregational prayers, praise, thanksgiving, and the offering of gifts. Traditions that understand the elements in more symbolic and/or spiritual terms (i.e., a spiritual presence) are more likely to speak simply of "the Lord's table."

Churches within the revivalist Protestant tradition have still another use of the term "altar." In those groups that stress the importance of public confession of Christ or public dedication of one's life to Christ, there is an "altar call" at the conclusion of most public services. At this time people are invited to come forward and sacrificially offer themselves to God (at the altar). In such cases the so-called altar is a rail, a bench, or simply the front row of seats. In fact, in some cases the altar may be only a manner of speaking, not identified with a particular object. In the revivalist tradition the altar is no longer the place where Christ is offered. It does not refer to the Communion table at all. It refers to the place where the individual offers himself to God. S. N. GUNDRY

See also OFFERINGS AND SACRIFICES IN BIBLE TIMES; LORD'S SUPPER; LORD'S SUPPER, VIEWS OF.

Bibliography. J. Bodensieck, ed., *Encyclopedia of the Lutheran Church; TDOT;* H. Wolf, *TWOT,* I, 233–35; E. H. Klotsche, *The History of Christian Doctrine;* B. Lohse, *A Short History of Christian Doctrine; NCE.*

Althaus, Paul (1888–1966). German Lutheran theologian. Born in Obershagen, near Hannover, he was the son of Paul Althaus, Sr., also a well-known theologian. Chief influences on his thought were his father, Carl Strange, and Adolf Schlatter. He taught at the universities of Göttingen (1914–20), Rostock (1920–25), and Erlangen (1925–66). In 1926 he succeeded Karl Holl as president of the *Luthergesellschaft,* where he remained as a major figure for the rest of his active life. He was cofounder of the *Zeitschrift für systematische Theologie.*

Althaus focused his attention on eschatology (*Die letzten Dinge,* 1922), Christian political theory (*Religiös Sozialismus,* 1921), Luther's doctrine of justification by faith (*Paulus und Luther über den Menschen,* 1938; *Die Theologie Martin Luthers,* 1962), the relationship between fact and faith in the church's proclamation of Jesus (*Die sogenannte Kerygma und der historische Jesus,* 1958), and, above all, Christian ethics (*Grundriss der Ethik,* 1931; *Die Ethik Martin Luthers,* 1965). He was critical of both Karl Barth (for his rejection of natural theology) and Rudolf Bultmann (for his denial of the essential link between faith and history in the kerygma). His image as a church leader was severely compromised by his involvement in the German National Party, which entered into a coalition with the National Socialist Party (Nazi) and helped to bring Hitler to power. Also, some of his writings between 1931 and 1938

seemed to be supportive of the policies of the Nazi government. Althaus was a careful student of the NT and was concerned to communicate the results of careful theological exegesis to the educated layperson, hence his involvement in the celebrated commentary series *Das Neue Testament Deutsch* and his popularity as a preacher (cf. his influence on H. Thielicke). In the words of Walter von Loewenich, he embodied the old axiom: "A theology is only as valuable as one is able to preach it." His five volumes of published sermons remain as a rich legacy to the church.
W. W. GASQUE

Bibliography. W. Kenneth and W. Joest, eds., *Dank an Paul Althaus;* H. Grass, *NZSTR* 8:213–41; W. Lohff, "Paul Althaus," in *Theologians of our Time,* ed. L. Reinisch; H. Grass, *Theologische Realenzyklopaedie,* II; W. von Loewenich, *Erlebte Theologie.*

Ambrose (*ca.* 340–397). One of the Doctors of the Church and a leading foe of Arianism. Ambrose was born in Trier into one of the Roman noble and senatorial families which had become Christian. His father, the Praetorian prefect of Gaul, died during Ambrose's youth, and the family returned to Rome, where Ambrose and his brother Satyrus received a classical education to prepare them for government service. It was in Rome that Marcellina, Ambrose's sister, received the consecration of a virgin at the hands of Pope Liberius and his mother entered the dedicated life of Christian widowhood. Such were his family influences that five of his extant works deal with Christian virginity and widowhood.

In 370 Ambrose was made governor of Aemilia-Liguria with headquarters at Milan, which at this time had replaced Rome as the West's imperial city. He became respected and popular because of his integrity, so when he attempted to calm the Arian and Catholic controversy at the election conclave for a new bishop of Milan in 374, he was acclaimed bishop by the crowd. Upon the approval of the emperor he received baptism, various orders, and the office of bishop all in one week. He was consecrated Bishop of Milan on December 7, 374. He chose to receive his office from the hands of a Catholic bishop and worked against the Arian party until his death. Backed by two able Roman popes, Damasus (366–84) and Siricius (384–99), Ambrose lived to see Arianism largely defeated in the Western church. To that end he called and presided over numerous synods, the most notable of which was the Synod of Aquilia (381), which deposed the Arian leaders Palladius and Secundianus.

Ambrose was part of the golden age of church fathers which included such strong prelates as Athanasius, Hilary, and Augustine. His own stormy but strong episcopacy weathered the opposition of the Arian imperial court (though he was banished briefly in 392), the invasion of the Gauls, and the beginning of the struggle between church and state. In 386 in withstanding the Arian dowager Empress Justina's effort to seize a basilica in Milan, Ambrose introduced the singing of hymns and chants into the Catholic crowds he kept in the contested building. In 390 he set a critical precedent by forcing the Catholic Emperor Theodosius to do public penance for his slaughter of seven thousand persons at the Thessalonican circus, insisting that the Emperor was within the church and not over it. He is perhaps best remembered for his influence on Augustine, who after his conversion was instructed and baptized by Ambrose.

Because of his classical education Ambrose was as fluent in Greek as he was in Latin. He read and used the thinkers of the Christian East, especially Origen and Basil of Caesarea. He introduced the thinking of Greek Christianity into the Latin Church and thus played a crucial role in the unity of the church even as the empire foundered. Thirty-five of his treatises are extant. They are written in a homiletical commentary style. *De officiis ministrorum,* a book on Christian ethics for clergy, is one of these and one of the earliest such works in the church. Ninety-one of his episcopal letters survive as well as a few of his hymns. "O Splendor of God's Glory," "Now Hail We Our Redeemer," "Savior of the Nations, Come," "O Trinity, Most Blessed Light" are still sung in contemporary churches.
V. L. WALTER

See also ARIANISM.

Bibliography. F. H. Dudden, *The Life and Times of St. Ambrose,* 2 vols.

Ambrosians. Name of a number of Roman Catholic ascetic movements, both of men and of women. One of the first was that of the Oblationaries of St. Ambrose, Milan, Italy, which originated in the ninth century. By the late twentieth century it was represented by only ten poor men and ten poor women. The fourth century Ambrose had nothing to do with their founding.

One of the chief bodies was that of the Brothers of St. Ambrose of the Grove, which had its origin under three men in the fourteenth century: Alexander Crivelli (or Grivelli), Antonio Pietrasancta, and Alber Bezozzi. This order took St. Ambrose as their patron. Gregory XI took note of them in 1375, addressing a bull to them. They were located in the diocese of Milan.

As early as 1408 there was an Ambrosian

order of nuns, founded by Dorothea Morosini, Eleanore Contarini, and Veronica Duodi. They were given canonical standing in 1471. A similar group of Ambrosian nuns was founded in 1474 by Catherine Morigia. Their habit resembled that of the Brothers of Saint Ambrose of the Grove—the group which originally met in a grove.

In 1441 Pope Eugene IV ordered the men's groups of Ambrosians to merge into one body. Until that time there had been similar groups here and there, but not united.

In 1578 another Italian, Charles Borromeo, founded the Oblates of St. Ambrose.

Less than a century later, in 1646, Pope Innocent X gave the Ambrosians a nonofficial status by administratively dissolving the order.

The Ambrosians did not serve as parish priests, but they preached and did good works in society.

There was also a small sixteenth century group of Anabaptists, a radical Protestant group, who were nicknamed Ambrosians. They emphasized an immediate contact with God, basing their doctrine on John 1:9—the light which illuminates every person coming into the world. They felt no need to look to priests or ministers for interpretation of the Bible. J. C. Wenger

See also Radical Reformation.

Amen. This Hebrew word originally was an adjective meaning "reliable, sure, true" or an adjectival verb, "it is reliable or true." The related verb *'āman* meant "to support, sustain"; in the niphal stem: "prove oneself steady, reliable, loyal"; in the hiphil stem: "to regard someone as reliable, trustworthy, or truthful," and hence, "to believe." *'Āmēn* by itself was used as a formula ("Surely!" "In very truth!") at the end of (a) a doxology, such as: "Blessed be Jehovah forever" (where the *Amen* signifies: "Yes indeed!" or, "May it be so in very truth!"); cf. Pss. 41:13; 72:19; 89:52; 106:48; also I Chr. 16:36 and Neh. 8:6, where the audience assents to and adopts their leader's praise of God; (b) a decree or expression of royal purpose, where the obedient listener indicates his hearty assent and cooperation (I Kings 1:36; Jer. 11:5). The one who prays or asseverates or joins in the prayer or asseveration of another, by the use of "Amen," puts himself into the statement with all earnestness of faith and intensity of desire. The usage is the same in the NT. Isa. 65:16 speaks of Jehovah as the God of Amen, meaning that he speaks the truth and carries out his word. The same is implied by the Lord Christ when he calls himself "The Amen" in Rev. 3:14.

It is significant that Jesus introduces matters of importance with a solemn *amēn, legō hymin* (Truly, I say unto you), thus affirming the truthfulness of what he is about to say. This is peculiar to Jesus in the NT and probably reflects his divine self-consciousness. He does not need to wait until after he has spoken to ratify what is said; *all* that he says has the mark of certain truth. G. L. Archer, Jr.

Bibliography. H. Bietenhard, *NIDNTT,* I, 97ff.; H. Schlier, *TDNT,* I, 335ff.; H. W. Hogg, "Amen," *JQR* 9:1ff.; G. Dalman, *The Words of Jesus.*

Americanism. The "Americanist" controversy of the late nineteenth century represents one of the rare occasions when an event in the United States has exerted a direct theological influence in Europe. It began with the suspicions of recent Catholic immigrants that American bishops were accommodating Catholic principle to American Protestant practice. It came to a head when Fr. Walter Elliot's biography of Isaac Hecker, founder of the American Paulist order, was translated into French in 1897. Hecker (1819–88) had grown up a Methodist before becoming a Catholic in 1844, after which time he labored both to aid Catholic immigrants and to convert other Protestants to Rome. As part of the latter effort he contended that the Catholic Church was completely compatible with the forms of American democracy. He also tended to stress the authority of the Holy Spirit in the individual believer at the expense of traditional Roman insistence upon the church's power.

The Archbishop of St. Paul, John Ireland (1838–1918), had provided a warm introduction to the American edition of Elliot's biography. Ireland was joined by American bishops John Keane and James Gibbons as leaders of the effort to make the Catholic Church more responsive to American culture. European conservatives were suspicious of that effort generally. Their concern turned to active opposition when a young French progressive, Abbé Felix Klein, praised Hecker, in an introduction to the European edition, as the priest of the future.

Pope Leo XIII appointed a committee of cardinals to study the affair. After they reported, he issued on January 22, 1899, a papal letter, *Testem benevolentiae,* to remedy the situation. The letter said that if American Catholics really taught certain doctrines—for example, that the Church should "show some indulgence to modern popular theories"—they should cease and desist. Leo spoke kindly of nonreligious institutions in America, but he insisted that Catholic doctrine not be compromised in its New World setting. The church must not shade its teachings to win converts, the church must remain the supreme spiritual authority, and the church's vows must not be indicted as an affront to religious liberty.

The "progressive" prelates in America quickly submitted while denying that they held the condemned doctrines. The Roman Catholic Church emerged unshaken from the controversy in an era when its major attention was devoted to silencing the more obviously menacing threat of "modernism." Yet issues raised about the accommodation of universal Catholic teaching to changing times and places would appear again in the wake of the Second Vatican Council sixty years later.

M. A. Noll

Bibliography. R. D. Cross, *The Emergence of Liberal Catholicism in America;* G. P. Fogarty, *The Vatican and the Americanist Crisis;* T. T. McAvoy, *The Americanist Heresy in Roman Catholicism, 1895–1900;* D. P. Killen, "Americanism Revisited: John Spalding and Testem Benevolentiae," *HTR* 66:413–54; T. E. Wangler, "The Birth of Americanism: Westward the Apocalyptic Candlestick,'" *HTR* 65:415–36.

Ames, William (1576–1633). Prominent Puritan preacher and theologian of England and the Netherlands. Educated at Christ's College, Cambridge (B.A. 1598, M.A. 1601), he stayed on to become a fellow and teacher of Christ's. As a student he was converted by the Puritan preaching of William Perkins, and throughout his life he associated himself with the more extreme Puritans. In 1610 Ames was expelled from Cambridge because of his Puritanism, and thereafter his career was destroyed in England.

Ames took refuge in the Netherlands, joining the large English-Scottish refugee community. During his immigrant years he served first as a military chaplain and then as professor of theology at the University of Franeker (1622–33), where he earned a doctor of theology degree. He was a strong Calvinist and opposed the Arminians, which reputation drew him to the Synod of Dort (1618–19) as an adviser to the Synod president. He died at Rotterdam.

He was often known as "the Learned Doctor Ames" because of his great intellectual stature among Puritans. As a Puritan intellectual he combined Calvinist doctrine, Ramist philosophy (from Peter Ramus), and Puritan practical divinity. His best known books are *The Marrow of Sacred Divinity* (1627, in Latin and English), and *Conscience,* or *Cases of Conscience* (1630, also in Latin and English). Both went through many seventeenth century editions, and the *Marrow* has been reprinted as recently as 1968. He wrote many books against Dutch Arminianism and against the episcopal system in England.

Ames stressed that theology must combine orthodox doctrine, which he defined as Calvinistic, and moral practice. Theology divides into a Ramist dichotomy: faith and observance. In church practices he experimented with new ideas. He believed in independent, voluntary congregations, but not separatism. He was one of the founders of the Congregationalist movement among Puritans. Just before his death he had accepted a call to become copastor with Hugh Peter of the English church of Rotterdam. This church was one of the earliest Congregationalist churches (1632).

Ames enjoyed a great reputation among Nonconformist English Puritans and among the Puritans of New England. Cotton Mather of Boston called him "that profound, that sublime, that subtil, that irrefragable,—yea that angelical doctor."

K. L. Sprunger

Bibliography. J. E. Eusden, ed., *The Marrow of Theology;* L. W. Gibbs, ed., *William Ames, Technometry;* D. Horton, *William Ames by Matthew Nethenus, Hugo Visscher, and Karl Reuter;* P. Miller, *The New England Mind: The Seventeenth Century;* K. L. Sprunger, *The Learned Doctor William Ames.*

Amillennialism. *See* Millennium, Views of the.

Amish. *See* Mennonites.

Amsdorf, Nicholas von (1483–1565). Considered one of the four or five greatest Lutheran Reformers—although he was not a strong creative personality in the usual sense of the word. He was born in Saxony, and studied theology and earned his master's degree at the University of Wittenberg in 1504. When Luther arrived at Wittenberg, the two became close friends. He accompanied Luther to the Leipzig debate in 1519, was at Worms with him in 1521, and assisted him with his translation of the OT.

The Elector John Frederick appointed Amsdorf first bishop to the Lutheran diocese of Naumburg-Zeitz. After Luther's death he was expelled from Naumburg (1547). He returned to Magdeburg, where much of his previous reforming activity had been carried on, and led the opposition to the compromising tendencies of Melanchthon and the Philippist party.

From 1552 until his death Amsdorf lived in Eisenach, without formal office but acknowledged as "Secret Bishop of the Lutheran Church." He was involved in several theological controversies eventually addressed in the Formula of Concord (1577), including the Majoristic controversy in which he rebutted the thesis of Georg Major, "Good works are necessary to salvation," with the proposition, "Good works are detrimental to salvation." No doubt he wanted to capture one of Luther's emphases, but failed to clarify his statement by adding that "good works" if *trusted in* are injurious to salvation. As a result Amsdorf's position was severely rebuked by other Lutheran theologians. J. F. Johnson

See also Majoristic Controversy; Adiaphora, Adiaphorists.

Bibliography. R. Kolb, *Nicholas von Amsdorf;* W. G. Tillmanns, *The World and Men Around Luther.*

Amyraldianism. The system of Reformed theology propounded by the French theologian Moise Amyraut and associates at the Saumur Academy in the seventeenth century. Its distinctives teachings vis-à-vis other systems (e.g., orthodox Calvinism, Arminianism, Lutheranism) focused on the doctrines of grace, predestination, and the intent of the atonement.

Fundamentally Amyraut took issue with contemporary Calvinists who shaped their system of theology around the decree of predestination. The entire body of divinity in much of seventeenth century Reformed theology was subsumed under the doctrines of sovereign election and reprobation. Amyraut insisted that the chief doctrine of Christian theology is not predestination but the faith which justifies. Commitment to justification by faith as the overarching theme denoted a theology as truly reformational. Moreover, Amyraut rightly argued that Calvin discussed predestination not under the doctrine of God but following the mediation of salvation blessings by the Holy Spirit. For Amyraut predestination is an inscrutable mystery, which offers an explanation of the fact that some accept Christ whereas others reject him.

Amyraut also developed a system of covenant theology alternative to the twofold covenant of works–covenant of grace schema propounded by much of Reformed orthodoxy. The Saumur school postulated a threefold covenant, viewed as three successive steps in God's saving program unfolded in history. First, the covenant of nature established between God and Adam involved obedience to the divine law disclosed in the natural order. Second, the covenant of law between God and Israel focused on adherence to the written law of Moses. And finally the covenant of grace established between God and all mankind requires faith in the finished work of Christ. In Amyraldianism the covenant of grace was further divided into two parts: a conditional covenant of universal grace and an unconditional covenant of particular grace. For actualization the former required fulfillment of the condition of faith. The latter, grounded in God's good pleasure, does not call for the condition of faith; rather it creates faith in the elect.

Amyraut's covenant theology—particularly his division of the covenant of grace into a universal conditional covenant and a particular unconditional covenant—provided the basis for the unique feature of Amyraldianism, namely, the doctrine of hypothetical universal predestination. According to Amyraut there exists a twofold will of God in predestination—a universal and conditional will, and a particular and unconditional will. Concerning the first, Amyraut taught that God wills the salvation of all people on the condition that they believe. This universal, conditional will of God is revealed dimly in nature but clearly in the gospel of Christ. Implicit in this first will is the claim that if a person does not believe, God has not, in fact, willed his or her salvation. Without the accomplishment of the condition (i.e., faith) the salvation procured by Christ is of no avail. Amyraut based his doctrine of hypothetical universal predestination on such biblical texts as Ezek. 18:23; John 3:16; and II Pet. 3:9.

Amyraut contended that although man possesses the natural faculties (i.e., intellect and will) by which to respond to God's universal offer of grace, he in fact suffers from moral inability due to the corrupting effects of sin upon the mind. Thus unless renewed by the Holy Spirit the sinner is unable to come to faith. Precisely at this point God's particular, unconditional will, which is hidden in the councils of the Godhead, comes to bear. Since no sinner is capable of coming to Christ on his own, God in grace wills to create faith and to save some while in justice he wills to reprobate others. Amyraut underscored the fact that God's particular, unconditional will to save is hidden and inscrutable. Finite man cannot know it. Hence the creature must not engage in vain speculation about God's secret purposes of election and reprobation. In practice the Christian preacher must not ask the question whether a given individual is elect or reprobate. Rather he must preach Christ as the Savior of the world and call for faith in his sufficient work. Only the universal, conditional will of God is the legitimate object of religious contemplation. Amyraldianism thus involves a purely ideal universalism together with a real particularism.

The issue of the intent or extent of Christ's atonement is implicit in the foregoing discussion. Amyraldianism postulated a universalist design in the atonement and a particular application of its benefits. The salvation wrought by Christ was destined for all persons equally. Christ legitimately died for all. Nevertheless only the elect actually come into the enjoyment of salvation blessings. Amyraldianism thus upheld the formula: "Jesus Christ died for all men sufficiently, but only for the elect efficiently."

Amyraut believed that his teachings on the twofold will of God and twofold intent of the atonement were derived from Calvin himself. He viewed his theology as a corrective to much of seventeenth century Calvinism, which denied the universal, conditional will of God in its preoccupation with the unconditional decree. And he disputed with Arminianism, which failed to see that a person's salvation was effectively grounded in the absolute purpose of God conceived on the basis of his own sovereign pleasure. And finally Amyraldianism provided a rapprochement with Lutheranism and its interest in justification by faith and the universality of Christ's atoning work. Some later Reformed theologians such as Charles Hodge, W. G. T. Shedd, and B. B. Warfield insisted that Amyraldianism was an inconsistent synthesis of Arminianism and Calvinism. Others, however, such as H. Heppe, R. Baxter, S. Hopkins, A. H. Strong, and L. S. Chafer maintained that it represents a return to the true spirit of Holy Scripture. B. A. DEMAREST

See also ATONEMENT, EXTENT OF THE; AMYRAUT, MOISE.

Bibliography. B. G. Armstrong, *Calvinism and the Amyraut Heresy;* R. B. Kuyper, *For Whom Did Christ Die?* B. B. Warfield, *The Plan of Salvation; Encyclopedia of Christianity,* I, 184–93.

Amyraut, Moise (1596–1664). French Protestant theologian, born in Bourgueil and died in Saumur. Amyraut earned a degree in law at the University of Poitiers (1616), but influenced by the Protestant minister at Saumur and by reading Calvin's *Institutes* he pursued instead a career in theology. He studied under John Cameron, the distinguished Scottish theologian, at the Academy at Saumur and was later ordained to the Protestant ministry. After briefly serving the Reformed church in St. Aignan, Amyraut was called in 1626 to minister at Saumur. The young clergyman quickly rose to prominence in the Reformed Church of France. In 1631 he was chosen to present to King Louis XIII a list of infractions against the Edict of Nantes (1598), which was intended to protect the rights of the Protestant minority.

In 1633 Amyraut was installed as professor of theology at Saumur. Under the leadership of Amyraut and his colleagues L. Cappel and J. de la Place the Saumur Academy became the leading theological school of French Protestantism. A prolific writer, Amyraut published some thirty books in addition to a number of sermons and essays. Chief among his works are *A Treatise Concerning Religions* (1631), *A Short Treatise on Predestination* (1634), and the six-volume *Christian Ethics* (1652–60).

A master of the literature of Calvin, Amyraut held to the main tenets of Calvinistic theology. Nevertheless he sought to revise what he judged to be the unacceptable teachings of seventeenth century scholastic Calvinism on grace and predestination and to forge a return to Calvin himself. In addition, he sought to create at the theological level a bridge with Lutherans who were offended by the pronouncements of the Synod of Dort (1618–19) regarding the intent of the atonement. In pursuit of these ends Amyraut propounded a view of hypothetical universal predestination, whereby God was said to will the salvation of all people on the condition that they believe. Thus ideally Christ's atonement was sufficient for all, but because of universal human depravity, in practice it was efficient only for the elect.

Staunch opposition arose to Amyraut's teaching on universal grace in Switzerland, the Netherlands, and in France itself. Amyraut was tried for heresy at three national synods in 1637, 1644, and 1659, but was acquitted in each case. The Formula Helvetic Consensus (1675) was prepared by the Swiss Reformed Church largely to counter the Saumurian theology of Amyraut and his colleagues. Notwithstanding such protests, Amyraut's interpretation of Calvin exercised considerable influence upon later Reformed theology. B. A. DEMAREST

See also AMYRALDIANISM.

Bibliography. E. F. K. Müller, *SHERK,* I, 160–61; *HERE,* I, 404–6.

Anabaptists. *See* RADICAL REFORMATION.

Anagogical Sense of Scripture. *See* INTERPRETATION OF THE BIBLE.

Analogia Fidei. *See* ANALOGY OF FAITH.

Analogy. Analogy means similarity. With respect to religious language it stands in contrast to two other views: the univocal and the equivocal. Univocal language expresses entirely the *same* meaning. An equivocal word has entirely *different* meaning (e.g., "bark" may mean coating of a tree or noise from a dog). Analogous language, by contrast, expresses a meaning that is *similar,* but neither identical nor totally different.

Historically the mystics stressed equivocal religious language. With their stress on the *via negativa* (way of negation), they claimed that one could not make positive affirmations about God which were actually true. Such views were held by Plotinus, Pseudo-Dionysius, and Meister Eckhart. John Duns Scotus argued for univocal God-talk, insisting that anything else leads to skepticism. Between these two extremes there are other theologians who insist on analogous religious language. Thomas Aquinas, for example, argued that since God is infinite, it follows that none of our finite concepts can apply to him univocally. He insisted also that since God created the world, then he cannot be totally different from it, for the creature must bear some similarity to the Creator.

Analogies are usually divided into two kinds: metaphysical and metaphorical. The former apply to God literally and the latter do not. For instance, in the sentence "God is good" the term good" applies to God literally. But in the sentence "God is a rock" the term "rock" applies to God only metaphorically. Likewise, when the Scriptures refer to God's arms, ears, and eyes, these are only metaphorical analogies usually called anthropomorphisms.

Some theologians distinguish between metaphorical and metaphysical analogies on the basis of what is called an intrinsic or extrinsic causal relation. An intrinsic causal relation is one where the cause produces an effect like itself, as when hot water is the cause of making an egg hot. In this kind of intrinsic causal relation both the cause and the effect have the property in question (e.g., heat in the above illustration). An extrinsic causal relation is one where the effect has a property which was caused by the cause but which the cause does not itself possess. For instance, hot water causes an egg to become hard, but the water is not itself hard. Thus in extrinsic causal relations the analogy is metaphorical. God can make a rock even though he is not literally a rock. In this sense "rock" is applied to God only metaphorically because there is only an extrinsic causal relation.

It is clear that if we are to avoid total skepticism in our knowledge of God, then at least some causal relations must be intrinsic. Thus since God created man in his image, one can look at man and know God by way of analogy. This is the point Paul made when he wrote, "Being then the offspring of God, we ought not to think that the Divine Nature is like gold or silver or stone" (Acts 17:29). Likewise, the psalmist argued for an analogy between man and God when he wrote, "He who planted the ear, does he not hear? He who formed the eye, does he not see?" (Ps. 94:9).

Objections to intrinsic analogy between creatures and God are often built on the fallacy of confusing an instrumental cause with an efficient cause. They say a pen is not like the letter it writes. However, a pencil is only an instrumental cause of the letter. The author is the efficient cause, and the letter does bear a resemblance (analogy) to the mind of the author. Some objections to analogy confuse accidental characteristics with essential characteristics. For instance, it is not essential that a musician give birth to a musician. But it is essential that humans give birth to humans. Therefore, when seeking to describe the way God really is, it is necessary for the theologian to use essential characteristics which flow from the efficient cause (God) to the effect (creation) and not to expect a resemblance to either the instrumental or accidental features involved in the analogy. After all, analogy means only similar, not identical. There are also ways in which God is unlike creatures. As the psalmist said, "There is none to compare with thee" (40:5). And Isaiah added, "To whom then will you liken God? Or what likeness will you compare with him?" (40:18). N. L. Geisler

Bibliography. N. L. Geisler, *Philosophy of Religion;* F. Ferré, *Encyclopedia of Philosophy,* I, 94–96; B. Mondin, *The Principle of Analogy in Protestant and Catholic Theology;* Aquinas, *Summa Theologica* I, 13, and *Summa contra Gentiles* I, 29–34.

Analogy of Faith. The expression is a biblical concept. Paul in Rom. 12:6 teaches that he who has the gift of prophecy should prophesy "in proportion to his faith." The apostle enjoins the believer to exercise his gift of prophecy to the extent that individual faith will allow. The "proportion" or "analogy of faith" (*analogia tēs pisteōs*) thus is similar to the "measure of faith" (*metron pisteōs*) mentioned by Paul in Rom. 12:3.

Later usages of the analogy of faith (*analogia fidei*) represent a development of the original Pauline meaning. Indeed, throughout history the term has assumed a wide range of meanings. As a general hermeneutical principle, analogy of faith connotes that an obscure text or passage may be illumined by other texts of Scripture whose meaning is clear. Since God is the author of Holy Scripture, what is taught in one Scripture cannot contradict what is taught in another Scripture on the same subject. In fact, the meaning of a given text often is established only after a careful consideration of other passages which speak to the issue. For example, Paul's negative attitude toward the law in Rom. 10:4 and Gal. 3:13 is clarified by consideration of his positive endorsement of the law, as in Rom. 7:12, 14, 16. When the full sweep of Pauline teaching is examined, it will be seen that the apostle repudiates law-keeping as a means of salvation, although as an expression of the moral will of God the law's precepts serve as a universal standard of conduct. The analogy of faith principle, operating under the modest assumption that Scripture interprets Scripture, may guard against a one-sided interpretation of the scriptural text.

As an extension of this principle Augustine insisted that the interpretation of Scripture should not violate the rule of faith summarized in the Apostles' Creed. If Scripture is alleged to mean something contrary to the universally accepted body of Christian truth, the validity of one's exegesis is suspect. In a similar vein, Luther argued that the primary interpreter of Scripture must be Scripture. When appealing to the analogy of faith in this latter sense Christian authorities sought to guard against the practice of interpreting Scripture on the basis of any sources outside of Scripture.

Roman Catholicism exceeds the modest use of the analogy of faith principle thus outlined by insisting that the Bible must be interpreted in accordance with the corpus of tradition. Origen, Irenaeus, Tertullian, and Jerome argued that difficult passages of Scripture are illumined by the rule of faith taught by the church. Indeed, the teachings commended may not have been in the mind of the biblical writer; but since approved by the church they are to be accepted as valid and binding. On this showing Scripture emerges as only one of the basic sources of belief. Reformation Protestantism with its principle of *sola Scriptura* rejected the claim that the meaning of Scripture is dependent upon normative interpretations imposed by the church.

As an exegetical principle the analogy of faith has been abused by the imposition of meanings that were not intended by the biblical writer. Some thus argue that even if a particular interpretation cannot be drawn from a given text, it may be imposed upon the passage provided the interpretation is found elsewhere in Scripture and provided it does not do violence to the literal meaning of the text. However, the attribution of such spiritual or allegorical significations to a text involves the danger that no end of meanings could be affixed to Scripture on the basis of the interpreter's subjective inclinations. But this would nullify the specific intention and normative meaning of the Spirit-guided prophetic or apostolic writer. Rather, the interpreter should strive via the practice of sound grammatical-historical exegesis to unfold the meaning which was in the mind of the inspired biblical writer. The exegete will also bear in mind that his interpretation must not contravene what is taught elsewhere in Scripture, and that in unfolding the meaning of a text other inspired Scriptures may help clarify the specific intention of the biblical writer.

B. A. Demarest

Bibliography. D. P. Fuller, "Biblical Theology and the Analogy of Faith," in *Unity and Diversity in NT Theology,* ed. R. A. Guelich; W. C. Kaiser, *Toward an OT Theology; NCE,* I, 468–69; M. Terry, *Biblical Hermeneutics.*

Anathema. *See* Curse.

Ancient of Days. *See* God, Names of.

Anderson, Robert (1841–1918). Influential Presbyterian layman who made an impact for the gospel through the legal profession, preaching, and writing.

Born in Dublin, he was educated at Trinity College there and entered the legal profession in Ireland in 1863. In 1868 he became adviser to the British Home Office in London in matters relating to political crime and showed considerable ability in dealing with plots of Irish and American-Irish conspirators. Leaving public service in 1877, he was called back by the government in 1880; and from 1888 to 1901 he headed the Criminal Investigation Department of Scotland Yard.

He began preaching soon after his conversion at nineteen and ministered to people in all walks of life in churches and missions. He spoke at numerous Mildmay Conferences and was associated with the Lawyers' Prayer Union, Prophecy Investigation Society, the Evangelical Alliance, the Bible League, and other organizations.

Sir Robert wrote extensively but centered his efforts on the fields of apologetics and Bible prophecy. He had a deep respect for the fundamental truths of the Bible and boldly attacked the higher criticism of his day. His approach to the interpretation of Scripture was dispensational, and he was a leading popularizer of that position. In that connection, he taught a distinction between the Pauline gospel for the church and the gospel of the kingdom as a message for the Jews.

Among his better-known works are *The Coming Prince, Daniel in the Critic's Den, The Bible and Modern Criticism, The Silence of God,* and *The Gospel and Its Ministry.*

H. F. Vos

Andover Controversy. The theological dispute from 1886 to 1892 involving the faculty of Andover Theological Seminary, significant as an example of transition from New England Calvinism to liberal theology. The seminary was founded in 1808 in Andover, Mass., in reaction to the Unitarian influence at Harvard. There was a determined effort by the founders to preserve orthodoxy at Andover by requiring the faculty to subscribe publicly to a Calvinistic creedal formula once every five years.

After the retirement of Professor E. A. Park in 1881 Andover became a champion of liberal theology. In 1884 the *Andover Review*, a theological journal, was published by the faculty for the purpose of rethinking and restating Christian theology in contemporary terms. It contained a series of editorials written by members of the faculty exploring central Christian doctrines under the title "Progressive Orthodoxy." The controversy centered on a question regarding the destiny of those who died without saving faith. Was the gospel absolutely necessary for salvation? The answer indicated that God will judge each person only after that person has had the opportunity to accept or reject the gospel. If God does not make himself known in Christ to that person in this life, then he will do so in a future state. This doctrine was referred to as future probation. Newman Smyth, brother of Egbert C. Smyth, president of the seminary, introduced this idea in America, and it became a major factor in the decision of the Board of Visitors not to appoint him to the chair of theology. The controversy over this and related matters raged for several years, and the American Board of Commissioners for Foreign Missions refused to send as missionaries any Andover graduates who consented to this view.

In 1886 E. C. Smyth and several of his colleagues were investigated. In June, 1887, the Board of Visitors dismissed Smyth. That decision was appealed to the Massachusetts Supreme Court, and in 1891, on technical grounds, the decision of the Board of Visitors was reversed. In 1892, after a new trial before the Board of Visitors, the matter was dropped.

The Andover Controversy went far beyond consideration of the doctrine of future probation. Ultimately it involved a careful rethinking of the nature of God, man, and the world in the light of the current evolutionary world view. Fueled by a sense of inadequacy to deal with social problems through traditional means, the Andover faculty attempted to point Christian theology to a new hope for human progress. Doctrine was modified by reason and experience. Incorporating the concepts of evolution and progress into Christian theology resulted in a radical reinterpretation of the doctrine of salvation. The Andover faculty shifted the emphasis from atonement to incarnation to salvation by the development of moral character.

L. G. Whitlock, Jr.

Bibliography. C. A. Briggs, *Whither?* E. C. Smyth, *The Andover Heresy;* J. LeConte, *Evolution, Its Nature, Its Evidences, and Its Relation to Religious Thought;* W. T. Tucker, *My Generation: An Autobiographical Interpretation;* D. D. Williams, *The Andover Liberals; A Study in American Theology;* G. F. Wright, "Some Analogies Between Calvinism and Darwinism," *BS* 37:49–74.

Andreae, James (1528–1590). Professor of theology at the University of Tübingen, leader of the Lutheran movement in Württemberg, and one of the major contributors to what became the Formula of Concord (1577).

Born in Waiblingen (the dukedom of Württemberg), Andreae enrolled in the preparatory school in Stuttgart. At the age of thirteen he matriculated at the University of Tübingen, and after four years of study in the liberal arts he advanced to the study of theology in 1545. However, Württemberg needed evangelical pastors, and consequently Andreae assumed the duties of deacon at the Hospital Church in Stuttgart just one year after he had begun to study theology. After the defeat of the evangelical forces at Mühlberg in April, 1547, the forces of Emperor Charles V moved to impose his interim religious settlement on evangelicals throughout the Holy Roman Empire. Andreae alone remained at his post when the Spanish occupation forces of the emperor began to implement the Augsburg Interim in Württemberg in November, 1548. He was transferred to Tübingen soon thereafter in order to avoid arrest. In Tübingen he served as a catechist for two congregations and undertook doctoral studies at the university.

During his university studies Andreae began his rise to prominence as an ecclesiastical adviser. In 1553 he assumed the duties of superintendent of the Lutheran churches in Göttingen. From this base Andreae was sent on a series of missions to help reconcile disputes which arose among Lutheran theologians in the wake of the Smalcaldic War. In 1557 Andreae published his first book, *A Short and Simple Statement Concerning the Lord's Supper,* in which he attempted to formulate a doctrine of the Lord's Supper consistent with Lutheran theology without offending the Calvinists.

Andreae's main contribution to Lutheran unity in the post-Reformation period was made through his *Six Christian Sermons* of 1573. These sermons treated the subjects over which the disputes had developed among the Lutherans, and they were suggested by Andreae as a basis for union between the Gnesio-Lutherans and the Philippists, the two main contending parties. In the winter of 1573–74 the sermons were recast into a more academic format entitled the Swabian Concord. This document, in turn, was revised by several Lutheran theologians in 1575–76, culminating in the Torgau Book and the Belgic book which together became the Formula of Concord. To be sure, the theological concerns and expressions of others altered and supplemented Andreae's views in the formula's final version. However, in and through the *Christian Sermons* Andreae not only helped create the text of the Formula of Concord but also fostered the climate in which such a formula could be written and accepted by the Lutherans. Without Andreae the princes had made little headway in forging Lutheran unity during the twenty years of trying to end the disputes of the theologians. Andreae was able to initiate the movement toward concord in part by emphasizing pastoral concern for clergy and laity who were being offended by controversy, and in part by taking his stance as a confessor of the central teachings of the Bible as he understood them from reading Luther. Both these factors placed him in the mainstream of Lutheranism by the time of his death. J. F. Johnson

See also Concord, Formula of.

Bibliography. T. Jungkuntz, *Formulators of the Formula of Concord;* R. Kolb, *Andreae and the Formula of Concord.*

Angel. *Angelos,* from which "angel" derives, is in itself a colorless word like its main Hebrew equivalent. It may denote either a human or a heavenly "messenger." Yet in the NT, except in Luke 7:24; 9:52; and perhaps Rev. 1:20, it is used only for heavenly beings. Rightly, therefore, the Vulgate introduced a distinction between *angelus* and *nuntius* which modern renderings and usage have maintained.

The term chosen by Scripture to denote angels gives us the clue to the function by which they are primarily to be known and understood. They are God's messengers or ambassadors. They belong to his heavenly court and service. Their mission in heaven is to praise him (Rev. 4:5). They devote themselves to doing his will (Ps. 103:20) and in this activity they behold his face (Matt. 18:10). Since heaven comes down to earth, they also have a mission on earth. They accompany God in his work of creation (Job 38:7), though they themselves are also creatures (Ps. 148:2, 5). They also assist in God's providential ordering of affairs (Dan. 12:1). Above all they are active in the divine work of reconciliation (from Gen. 19:1–2 onward). In fulfillment of their mission they declare God's word (e.g., Luke 1:26–27) and do his work (e.g., Matt. 28:2). There seems to be some ordering in their ranks; some are referred to as archangels, as over against those who are referred to as simply angels (I Thess. 4:16; Jude 9).

The function of angels may be seen clearly from their part in the saving mission of Jesus Christ. They are naturally present when this both begins with the nativity (Matt. 1; Luke 1–3) and ends with the resurrection (Matt. 28:2 and pars.) and ascension (Acts 1:10ff.). They also assist the church in its early ministry (e.g., Acts 5:19; 10:3). They will play an important part in the events of the end time (Rev. 7:1ff., etc.). Finally they will come with Christ when he returns in glory (Matt. 24:31) and separate the righteous and the wicked (Matt. 13:41, 49). They do not do the real work of reconciliation, which is Christ's prerogative. But they accompany and declare this work, praising the God of grace and glory and summoning men and women to participate in their worship (Luke 1:46). Interestingly, there seem to be only two angelic appearances between Christ's birth and resurrection: at the beginning of his way to the cross in the temptation (Mark 1:12) and then before the crucifixion itself in Gethsemane (Luke 22:43). This is perhaps because Jesus had to tread his way of atoning self-giving alone, and in his humiliation he is made a little lower than the angels (Heb. 2:9), though exalted far above them by nature (Heb. 1). Yet angels did not withdraw from the scene, for they rejoice at sinners repenting (Luke 15:10) and will hear the Son of man confess those who confess him (Luke 12:8–9).

The Bible offers only a few hints about the nature of angels. Belonging to the heavenly sphere, they cannot be properly conceived of in earthly terms. They are mostly described in relation to God, as *his* angels (e.g., Ps. 104:4). The two angelic names, Michael and Gabriel, emphasize this relationship with the *el* ending. It is as God's angels, perhaps, that they are called "elect" in I Tim. 5:21. Heb. 1:14 describes them as "ministering spirits" in a conflation of the two parts of Ps. 104:4. Elsewhere, in Job and Psalms, they figure as the "heavenly ones" (Ps. 29:1) or the "holy ones" (Job 5:1) who are set apart for God's service; both these terms occur in Ps. 89:6–7, though "sons of God" is here another rendering of "heavenly ones" in vs. 6 (cf. Ps.29:1). The "gods" of Ps. 82:1, in whose midst God holds judgment, are often thought to be angels too. Since Christians can also be called God's children, we need not infer from this usage, as did some of the apologists, that the angels are lesser deities.

Indeed, the Bible clearly warns us not to worship them (Col. 2:18; Rev. 19:10).

Among the heavenly beings mention is made of the seraphim (Isa. 6:2) and, more frequently, the cherubim. Cherubim guarded Eden after the expulsion of Adam and Eve (Gen. 3:24). They form God's chariot at his descent (Ps. 18:10). Figures of cherubim adorned the ark (Exod. 25:17ff.) and Solomon's temple (I Kings 6:23ff.), so that Yahweh is said to be enthroned above the cherubim (I Sam. 4:4; Ps. 80:1). Ezekiel offers an elaborate visionary description (Ezek. 1:10; 9:3; 10:15–22) in which their form is human (1:5) but symbolical traits stress their glory and spiritual excellence. Common paradise traditions may underlie Assyro-Babylonian parallels.

Of the angels named, Michael is called "the great prince" (Dan. 12:1) and the other angels seem to be led by him (Rev. 12:7), though God himself, of course, is the Lord of hosts and Prince of the host (Dan. 8:11). The man who appeared to Joshua in Josh. 5:13ff., usually taken to be an angel, says that he has come as commander of the army of the Lord. Gabriel, the other angel named in canonical Scripture, is the angel of the annunciation (Luke 1:26). Distinctions seem to be indicated in Rev. 4–5 with the references to the beasts and the elders, but the exact significance of these terms is disputed. The apocryphal writings provide three more angelic names, Raphael, Uriel, and Jeremiel. Tob. 12:15 calls Raphael one of the holy angels who present the prayers of the saints (cf. the seven who stand before God in Rev. 8:2 and the possible link between these seven and the "chief princes" of Dan. 10:13).

From the various statements about the nature of angels, and Paul's use of the terms "principalities," "powers," "thrones," "dominions," and "forces," early and medieval theology evolved a complex speculative account of the angelic world. Pseudo-Dionysius found separate entities in these, and he grouped them with the seraphim, cherubim, archangels, and angels in a threefold hierarchy of nine choirs. Aquinas, the Angelic Doctor, adopted a similar scheme in his full and acute discussion but was more interested in the nature of angels as individual, spatial, spiritual substances engaged primarily in the work of enlightenment and capable of rational demonstration (*Summa contra Gentiles* 91; *Summa Theologica* 50–64).

As Calvin saw, the error in so much angelology was to deal with angels apart from the biblical witness. Even regarding their function there was a tendency to rationalize or to focus interest on the idea of the guardian angel (cf. Matt. 18:10 and perhaps Acts 12:15). An inevitable reaction came in the age of the Enlightenment and liberal Protestantism when angels were either dismissed as fantastic, submitted to reinterpretation, or explained away as the relics of an original polytheism.

Some legitimate deductions may certainly be made from the biblical data. Though they come in human form, the angels are essentially noncorporeal. Present at creation, they are still creatures (Ps. 148:2, 5). They form an ordered unity, yet their plurality entails the existence of individuals within the totality, with a possible gradation in function. As compared with humans they have the advantage of being in God's immediate presence and serving as his direct messengers. They also guard the proprieties, if that is the meaning of I Cor. 11:10, and seem to play some role in or over the nations (Dan. 10). But when men and women respond to God's saving work in Christ they are raised above them, enjoy their ministry (Heb. 1:14), and will finally judge them (I Cor. 6:3), for even angels are not faultless in God's eyes (Job 4:18; 15:15).

Has there been a fall of angels? Jude 6 suggests this, and Irenaeus (*Against Heresies* iv. 37.1) and many fathers took this view. Certainly the Bible speaks of the dragon and his angels (Rev. 12:7) and also of powers of evil (Eph. 6:12), so that while we cannot be too dogmatic on the subject, we have to assume that there is a real kingdom of evil in grotesque caricature of the angelic kingdom. These angels and their leader were defeated at the cross (Col. 2:15) and will finally be condemned (Matt. 25:41).

A last question concerns the so-called angel of the Lord. In Judg. 13:2–3 this seems to be identical with God. Many have thought, then, that in the OT at least the reference is to the preincarnate Logos. Liberals have explained it as a softening of theophany to angelophany but without showing why this does not always apply. Another possible interpretation is that God speaks so fully through the angel that he himself is virtually speaking. Certainly the "angel of the Lord" of Luke 2:9 is not Christ, but this does not in itself rule out such an equation in the OT.

G. W. Bromiley

See also Angel of the Lord.

Bibliography. K. Barth, *Church Dogmatics* III/3, 51; H. Cremer *et al.*, *SHERK*, I, 174–78; *HDB*, I, 93; W. Grundmann *et al.*, *TDNT*, I, 74–87; J. M. Wilson, *ISBE* (rev.), I, 124–27.

Angel of the Lord. In the OT and NT the angel of the Lord (*mal'ak yhwh*) is represented as acting on behalf of the nation of Israel as well as of individuals. The lack of precise data in the OT with regard to the identification of this figure and his relationship to Yahweh has given rise to a number of conclusions. Eichrodt understands the presence of this figure in the literature of the OT as an attempt to express the concept of theophany in a less direct manner because of the early realization that it is impossible to see God. Von Rad suggests that the figure may have been inserted into some of the older traditions in place of an original Canaanite *numen*. However, this presupposes an already concrete idea of the concept and does not explain its origin or the nature of the concept in early Israelite religion.

Many understand the angel of the Lord as a true theophany. From the time of Justin on, the figure has been regarded as the preincarnate Logos. It is beyond question that the angel of the Lord must be identified in some way with God (Gen. 16:13; Judg. 6:14; 13:21–22), yet he is distinguished from God in that God refers to the angel (Exod. 23:23; 32:34), speaks to him (II Sam. 24:16; I Chr. 21:27), and the angel speaks to Yahweh (Zech. 1:12). The evidence for the view that the angel of the Lord is a preincarnate appearance of Christ is basically analogical and falls short of being conclusive. The NT does not clearly make that identification. It is best to see the angel as a self-manifestation of Yahweh in a form that would communicate his immanence and direct concern to those to whom he ministered.

T. E. McComiskey

See also Angel; Theophany.

Bibliography. H. Bietenhard *et al.*, *NIDNTT*, I, 101–5; W. Eichrodt, *Theology of the OT;* P. Heinisch, *Theology of the OT;* G. von Rad, *OT Theology.*

Anger. This emotion is rich in Hebrew terminology, being represented by seven words, but by only two in Greek. Because the nose was prominent in the hard breathing accompanying an increase in blood adrenalin, anger was commonly rendered by "nose," "nostril" (Heb. *'ap*) The intensity of anger was expressed by such words as "fury," "heat," "rage," "burn with anger" (Heb. *ḥēmâ, ḥārâ, 'ebrâ, zā'ap, qāṣap*) or "be irritated," "be grieved" (*pā 'am*). The NT employed *thymos* to describe emotionally intense wrath and *orgē* as the consequence of a moral judgment, but in the LXX the two terms were interchangeable.

The anger of God is a deliberate reaction to all that violates his holy nature. His covenant people were commanded to imitate God's holiness (Lev. 11:44), and when they failed to do so, they felt his anger, whether through natural circumstances (Num. 21:6) or other nations (Isa. 10:5). Even God's chosen servants experienced God's punishing wrath, as with Moses (Exod. 4:14), Miriam (Num. 12:9), Jonah (Jonah 1:4), and others. All violations of the covenant agreement exposed the Israelites to God's anger, which could only be averted by true repentance.

Jesus became angry with his disciples when they forbade children to be brought to him (Mark 10:14) and with the hardhearted members of the Capernaum synagogue (Mark 3:5). Similar expressions of anger were directed at the Sadducees (Mark 12:24–27), the scribes and Pharisees (Matt. 23:13–36), and Peter (Matt. 16:23), and on each occasion represented his rejection of unrighteousness. Human anger could be selfish (Gen. 4:5; Num. 24:10), righteous (Exod. 16:20; II Sam. 12:5), or a combination of both (Gen. 34:7; II Sam. 13:21). In the NT anger is usually condemned (Gal. 5:19–21; Col. 3:8).

R. K. Harrison

See also Emotion.

Bibliography. H. C. Hahn, *NIDNTT*, I, 105–13.

Anglican Communion. A worldwide fellowship of churches in communion with the Archbishop of Canterbury (England) and whose bishops are invited each decade (except during wartime) to the Lambeth Conference held in London since 1867. Anglicans hold that theirs is the church of NT times and the early church, reformed in the sixteenth century and waiting for the reunion of all Christians.

Bishops are the chief officers of Anglican churches, with archbishops or presiding bishops functioning as "first among equals" with national or provincial responsibilities and administrative authority. Only bishops may ordain clergy and consecrate other bishops. Some dioceses have assistant bishops called coadjutor or suffragan bishops. The latter does not automatically succeed the diocesan bishop, whereas the coadjutor does.

The basic unit in the church is the parish with its congregation and rector. A mission may be a congregation dependent upon a parish (or diocese). The diocese is that group of parishes and missions under a bishop whose representatives meet each year for a diocesan convention (or council). Each parish and mission is represented by laity as well as clergy, and laity are represented on all the significant governing committees. Bishops are elected at these conventions or councils in most Anglican churches, but some bishops are still appointed, as in the case of the Church of England and many mission dioceses.

The *Book of Common Prayer*, in one of its many derived forms, is used by all Anglican churches. It is regarded as the distinctive embodiment of Anglican doctrine following the principle of "the rule of prayer is the rule of belief" (*lex orandi, lex credendi*). The section of the Prayer Book called the Ordinal, by which clergy are ordained following their vows, is especially crucial for doctrinal standards. The Holy Scripture is declared to be the Word of God and to contain all that is necessary to salvation. The Nicene and Apostles' Creeds are accepted as confessing the faith of Scripture and classical Christianity.

The Thirty-nine Articles, dating from the Elizabethan settlement in the sixteenth century, are not required for explicit assent in most of the communion, but they are generally bound with the Prayer Book and regarded as an important historical statement and document. These articles explicitly reject the doctrine of transubstantiation and affirm the doctrines of justification by faith, the Trinity, and the person of Christ as "very God and very Man."

The worship in Anglican churches varies widely but is characterized by an attempt to follow the liturgical year; that is, to read the prescribed lessons designed to emphasize that portion of revelation from advent and the nativity (Christmas) through the manifestation of Christ to the Gentiles (Epiphany), Lent, Easter, and Pentecost. Worship is decisively biblical in that readings from both testaments are required at all normal services. The Prayer Book is saturated with Scripture in the phrases of the prayers, the versicles and responses, the canticles, and the Psalter (book of Psalms).

The Lord's Supper, or Holy Eucharist, is generally regarded as the central service, and gradually over the last century has come to be held with increasing frequency. The norm for public worship is to stand to sing, sit to listen, and kneel to pray. In recent revisions the Prayer Book has seen its most substantial changes from the sixteenth century work of Thomas Cranmer. The chief characteristics of the new books are flexibility, with options ranging from forms virtually identical to the traditional books to others which are exceedingly informal, replacing "thou" with "you" in addressing God, and giving modern synonyms for more obscure terms. In addition, the new revisions attempt to include more lay and congregational participation than was possible in the sixteenth century, when a literate congregation could not be assumed. The revisions have, however, met with considerable resistance on the part of many who feel the language to be inferior to Cranmer's and that some of the changes have unfortunate doctrinal implications.

The overall practical effect of this growing diversity among the Prayer Books will likely lead to more emphasis on Anglican identity being drawn from the pan-Anglican communion with the Archbishop of Canterbury than on the use of a common Prayer Book as has been the case in the past.

The basic intention of Anglican worship is expressed in the Prayer Book: "to render thanks for the great benefits that we have received at his hands, to set forth his most worthy praise, to hear his most holy word, and to ask those things which are requisite and necessary, as well as for the body as the soul." This is sought to be done with all the majesty, solemnity, and aesthetic quality possible, while at the same time making the mystery and awe as accessible and relevant as can be done to any and all conditions.

The wide diversity within Anglicanism is reflected by the astonishing growth and evangelical character of the church in East Africa, the highly sacramental and Anglo-Catholic tradition of the Province of South Africa, the liberal spirit and discomfort with classical expressions of orthodoxy on the part of the authors of *The Myth of God Incarnate*, and the conservative evangelicals who retain an unyielding loyalty to Scripture and the Thirty-nine Articles. C. F. ALLISON

See also THIRTY-NINE ARTICLES, THE; BOOK OF COMMON PRAYER; ANGLO-CATHOLICISM; HIGH CHURCH MOVEMENT; LOW CHURCH; LATITUDINARIANISM.

Bibliography. P. C. Hughes, *The Anglican Reformers;* S. Neill, *Anglicanism;* More and Cross, *Anglicanism;* W. Temple *et al., Doctrine in the Church of England.*

Anglo-Catholicism. The modern name for that tradition within Anglicanism that was previously termed "High Church." The name dates only from 1838 and occurred during the Tractarian or Oxford Movement. Edward Pusey, John Keble, and John Henry Newman were the leaders of this transition from the older high churchmanship with its emphasis on the established Erastian church-state relationship to an emphasis upon the distinctive claims of the church's authority in apostolic succession of bishops.

Earlier High Churchmen had tended to dismiss the claims of Free Church bodies on the ground that they were not a part of the Church of England, duly constituted by law. The Anglo-Catholics sensed a real threat to the church rather than a help in this relationship with an increasingly secular state. Instead they insisted that the church's authenticity lay in the essential nature of the episcopacy (Tract #1, 1833). Ordination by bishops was thus seen to be of the *esse* of the church without which a church is not a church.

At the same time less appreciation was given to the principles of the Anglican Reformation, and the movement became suspect in the eyes of many because of the large number of conversions to Rome out of Anglo-Catholicism, especially that of John Henry Newman.

Two major works indicate the best in scholarship and theological emphasis of this tradition: *Lux Mundi* (1889) and *Essays Catholic and Critical* (1926).

In modern times four strands of Anglo-Catholicism have been discerned: (1) The Cambridge Camden Society and its successors, who lay great and somewhat romantic emphasis upon English history and pre-Reformation English rites and vestments; (2) liberal Anglo-Catholicism, which is less authoritarian and more friendly to liberal theology; (3) evangelical Catholics, who attempt to blend the biblical and Reformation teachings on grace and gospel with the classical dogmas and distinctive polity; and (4) pro-Roman Anglo-Catholicism, whose main aim is the reunion of Anglicanism with Roman Catholicism, not merely in a general ecumenical way but by the sacrifice of the doctrine of the Anglican Reformation when it conflicts with the Council of Trent.

Anglo-Catholicism has emphasized the doctrine of the incarnation, sacramental theology, and ecclesiastical polity. It has appealed more to clergy than to laity. C. F. Allison

See also Anglican Communion; High Church Movement; Oxford Movement; Newman, John Henry; Pusey, Edward Bouverie; Keble, John.

Bibliography. W. L. Knox, *The Catholic Movement in the Church of England;* D. Stone, *The Faith of an English Catholic;* O. Chadwick, *The Victorian Church,* 2 vols.; C. Gore, ed., *Lux Mundi;* G. Selwyn, ed., *Essays Catholic and Critical;* O. Chadwick, ed., *The Oxford Movement;* M. Ramsey, *From Gore to Temple: An Era of Anglican Theology.*

Anguish. *See* Pain.

Annihilationism. The word is from the Latin *nihil,* "nothing," and expresses the position of those who hold that some, if not all, human souls will cease to exist after death. As observed by Warfield, this point of view may take three main forms: (1) that all human beings inevitably cease to exist altogether at death (materialist); (2) that, while human beings are naturally mortal, God imparts to the redeemed the gift of immortality and allows the rest of humanity to sink into nothingness (conditional immortality); (3) that man, being created immortal, fulfills his destiny in salvation, while the reprobates fall into nonexistence either through a direct act of God or through the corrosive effect of evil (annihilationism proper). The distinction between conditionalism and annihilationism, as indicated above, is frequently not observed, and these two terms are commonly used as practical synonyms. A fourth form of advocacy of the ultimate extinction of evil is the view that God will finally redeem all rational beings (universalism). Over against all the above positions, historic orthodoxy has always maintained both that human souls will eternally endure and that their destiny is irrevocably sealed at death.

The question whether or not man is naturally immortal pertains to the subject of immortality. The present article will be limited to stating and appraising briefly the main evidence advanced in support of the cessation of the wicked.

God alone, it is urged, has immortality (I Tim. 6:16; 1:17). This argument, if it proves anything, proves too much. In fact, God who alone has immortality in himself may and does communicate it to some of his creatures.

Immortality, it is urged, is represented as a special gift connected with redemption in Jesus Christ (Rom. 2:7; I Cor. 15:53–54; II Tim. 1:10). The same may be said of life, or eternal life (John 10:28; Rom. 6:22–23; Gal. 6:8; etc.). It is freely granted that in all such passages life and immortality are represented as the privileged possession of the redeemed, but it is claimed that in these connections these terms do not represent merely continued existence, but rather connote existence in joyful fulfillment of man's high destiny in true fellowship with God (John 17:3).

Cessation of existence, it is urged, is implied in various scriptural terms applied to the destiny of the wicked, such as death (Rom. 6:23; James 5:20; Rev. 20:14; etc.), destruction (Matt. 7:13; 10:28; I Thess. 1:9, etc.), perishing (John 3:16, etc.). But these expressions do not so much imply annihilation as complete deprivation of some element essential to normal existence. Physical death does not mean that body or soul vanishes, but rather that an abnormal separation takes place which severs their natural relationship until God's appointed time. Spiritual death, or the "second death" (Rev. 20:14; 21:8), does not mean that the soul or personality lapses into nonbeing, but rather that it is ultimately and finally deprived of that presence of God and fellowship with him which is the chief end of man and the essential condition of worthwhile existence. To be bereft of it is to perish, to be reduced to utter insignificance, to sink into abysmal futility. An automobile is said to be wrecked, ruined, destroyed, not only when its constituent parts have been melted or scattered away, but also when they have been so damaged and distorted that the car has become completely unserviceable.

It is inconsistent with God's love, it is urged, to allow any of his creatures to endure forever in torment. Furthermore, the continuance of evil would spell some area of permanent defeat for the divine sovereignty, a dark corner marring perpetually the glory of his universe. These considerations are not without weight, and a complete answer may not be possible in the present state of our knowledge. They are not adjudged by traditional orthodoxy as sufficient to overthrow the substantial weight of scriptural evidence to the effect that the wicked will be consigned to endless conscious sorrow. This is apparent from the expressions "fire unquenchable" (Isa. 66:24; Matt. 3:12; Luke 3:17), or "that never shall be quenched" (Mark 9:43, 45), the worm that "dieth not" (Isa. 66:24; Mark 9:44, 46, 48), "the wrath of God abideth on him" (John 3:36), as well as from the use of "everlasting" or "forever," applying to chains, contempt, destruction, fire or burning, punishment, torment (Isa. 33:14; Jer. 17:4; Dan. 12:2; Matt. 18:8; 25:41, 46; II Thess. 1:9; Jude 6–7; Rev. 14:11; 19:3; 20:10). It is worthy of note that, in the biblical record, those who spoke most about future punishment in its irrevocable finality are Jesus and the apostle John, the very ones who also represented most glowingly the supreme glory of God's love and the unshakable certainty of his ultimate triumph.

R. Nicole

See also Intermediate State; Conditional Immortality; Adventism.

Bibliography. B. B. Warfield, *SHERK,* I, 183–86; G. C. Joyce in *HERE.* In support of annihilationism: H. Constable, *The Duration and Nature of Future Punishment;* C. H. Hewitt, *A Classbook in Eschatology;* E. Lewis, *Life and Immortality;* F. L. Piper, *Conditionalism.* In opposition to annihilationism: H. Buis, *The Doctrine of Eternal Punishment;* R. Garrigou-Lagrange, *Life Everlasting;* W. G. T. Shedd, *Dogmatic Theology,* II, 591–640, 667–754.

Anoint, Anointing. In the ancient Near East anointing persons or objects with plain or perfumed oil was widespread for medicinal, preservative, and cosmetic purposes. Olive oil in particular was often applied after bathing (Ruth 3:3; Ezek. 16:9; Dan. 13:17; Ps. 104:15), on wounds (Isa. 1:6; Mark 6:13; Luke 10:34; James 5:14), on corpses (Mark 16:1; Luke 23:56; John 19:39), on released captives (II Chr. 28:15), and even on shields (II Sam. 1:21; Isa. 21:5). Specially prepared oils were also used to anoint the head (Ps. 23:5; Matt. 26:7; Luke 7:46) and feet (Luke 7:28, 46; John 12:3) of guests or venerated persons, and simply as perfumes (Deut. 28:40; Judg. 10:3; II Sam. 14:2; Dan. 10:3; Rev. 3:3). A sign of joy in these instances (Isa. 61:3; Matt. 6:7), it was something from which mourners were always to abstain.

In the OT. Anointing for such routine purposes, common to the entire ancient Near East, acquired distinctly religious significance in the OT. Anointing with oil set persons and objects apart as dedicated to divine service. According to legislation, elaborately prepared oils were used to dedicate the tabernacle, its furniture, and vessels (Exod. 30:22–33; 40:10–11), together with those from the high-priestly class of Levi who were to serve in it (Exod. 28:40–42; 29:1–46; 30:30–33). There are also scattered references to the anointing of prophets (I Chr. 19:16; Isa. 61:1). The greatest number of references by far is to the anointing of kings, which dates back to the beginnings of the monarchy (I Sam. 10:1; 16:13; I Chr. 1:39). As "anointed of the Lord" such kings were assured of succession and elevated to an inviolable status (I Sam. 24:7; 26:9, 11, 16).

The ancient Hebrews also looked forward to the coming of a king from the line of David who would be specially anointed of God to bring in his kingdom, and to this figure was given a name borrowed from the Hebrew word for anointing, the Messiah. OT prophetic descriptions of the Messiah vary widely in emphasis and content. Often depicted as a great and just king (Pss. 2; 7; 72; 110; Zech. 3), he invariably enjoys a unique relationship with God the Father and is fully endowed with extraordinary spiritual and charismatic gifts (Isa. 7:14; 9:1–6; 11:1–5; Mic. 5:1ff.). This figure was never lost sight of in the intertestamental period but did not play so prominent a role as in some of the later prophets.

In the NT. The entire NT testifies to the fact that Jesus of Nazareth was that Messiah. The equivalent Greek term for the "anointed one" (*Christos*) was applied to Jesus in every book except III John, and among the Greco-Roman communities where its original meaning was probably not understood it quickly lost the article and became a part of Jesus' name. The Gospel of Mark turns entirely upon the revelation that Jesus is the Messiah (Mark 8:29), whereas Matthew establishes it at the outset in his links to the line of David (Matt.1:16). The apostles preached this same message throughout the Acts (2:36; 4:27), and Paul spread it among the Gentiles. Jesus filled the office of Messiah with his own person, sometimes applying OT prophecies to himself, and so other titles or descriptions (Son of man, Son of God, Savior) rapidly overwhelmed the original Hebrew concept of the "anointed one," which simply was substantivized into a name, as in the first verse of Mark: the gospel of Jesus Christ, the Son of God. Ever since Bultmann a large modernist school has attempted in this century to deny that Jesus was himself conscious of being the "anointed one" or Messiah. But this rests upon an extremely arbitrary reading of the Gospels which conservative critics have learned in recent years how better to refute.

In Church History. Such numerous references to anointing in Scripture could not fail to have an impact upon Christians in the course of the church's history. Beginning in the eighth and ninth centuries kings and bishops were anointed with chrism (holy oil) upon their elevation into office. They were considered the vicars or placeholders of Christ, set apart, like the kings and high priests of the OT, for divine service. Anointing was extended to the thumbs and hands of Catholic bishops (with which they are to bless the people), and is still a part of the ritual today. Kings were anointed with catechumen's oil (a lesser oil to distinguish them from the sacerdotal office) into the nineteenth century. Beginning in the seventh and eighth centuries the hands of priests were anointed at their ordination in order to dedicate to the Lord that which was, in Catholic teaching, to confect and to hold the Body of Christ. Beyond these instances of ritual anointing there are two others which came to assume sacramental status in the Roman Catholic Church.

From at least the year 200 onward, the church practiced a postbaptismal anointing (see II Cor. 1:21; I John 2:20–27) and laying on of hands (see Acts 8:14–17; 19:1–6) in order to confer the gift of the Holy Spirit. In the early church and in large measure still in Eastern churches, this was not clearly distinguished from the baptism itself, and the rite took its name from the anointing or, more accurately, from the chrism it employed. In the course of the Middle Ages the Western or Catholic Church separated this rite from baptism and elevated it to the sacrament of confirmation, through which, its theologians taught, an increased or fortifying grace of the Spirit was conferred upon children or young adults.

The command to anoint the sick found in James 5:14 together with a suggestive reference in Mark 6:13 led to a practice which in the Catholic Church eventually came to be known as extreme unction and since Vatican II is once again called the anointing of the sick. From early Christian times until about 800 there are scattered references in both the Eastern and Western churches to the anointing of the sick with oil blessed by a priest or bishop, but such anointing was still repeatable and could be performed by laymen as well as clergy. Between 900 and 1300 Western practice linked it to penance done in mortal illness and the viaticum, the final reception of Communion, and thus it came to be regarded as the final forgiveness of sins, the healing of the soul which prepared it for heaven and the beatific vision. Medieval theologians often set it in parallel with cleansing infants of original sin at baptism (according to Catholic theology). Protestant Reformers uniformly rejected both the practice and its associated theology. In recent years, however, scattered Protestant groups have reconsidered the practice, which is now understood only with respect to prayer for physical healing. Just in the last decade the Catholic Church has also reconsidered the medieval practice and theology which had been reaffirmed at the Council of Trent. Pope Paul VI issued a constitution (*Sacram unctionem infirmorum,* 1972) which placed much greater emphasis upon prayer for healing, wholly ignored the old name of extreme unction, and deemphasized the notion of it as the final sacrament. J. Van Engen

See also Extreme Unction.

Bibliography. W. Grundmann *et al., TDNT,* IX, 493–580. On anointing of the sick, H. Vorgrimler in *Handbuch der Dogmengeschichte* 4.3, 215–34.

Anselm of Canterbury (1033–1109). One of the greatest of all medieval theologians, even though his influence was limited in his own day largely to a small circle of fellow monks. Born in northern Italy and educated at the best new schools of grammar and dialectic in northern France, he became a monk at age twenty-seven in an abbey (Le Bec in Normandy) renowned for its zealous religious life and its excellent abbot-teacher, Lanfranc. Anselm served in turn as prior (1063–78) and abbot (1078–93) at Bec before reluctantly agreeing to succeed Lanfranc as Archbishop of Canterbury (1093–1109). His twelve theological treatises, nineteen prayers, and three meditations, together with many of his letters (375 in all), rank as literary masterpieces. But all of them, even the most technical and logically demanding, presuppose a monastic setting in which he and his companions or students had given themselves over wholly to the contemplative life. Indeed his first written works were prayers and meditations (now available in an excellent English translation) which transformed the formal liturgical prayer of the early Middle Ages into a more intimate and intense expression of personal devotion to Christ, Mary, and the saints. His letters likewise became models for the sophisticated expression of warm personal and religious friendships. His theological works, on the other hand, were marked not so much by personal warmth as intuitive intellectual insight, clarity of exposition, and rigorous argument.

In the best tradition of Benedictine monasticism Anselm held that learning should serve the ends of the religious life. He always proceeded as one who already possessed faith and sought understanding, this tag ("faith seeking understanding") borrowed from an old Latin rendering of Isa. 7:9. But where other medieval monks made Scripture the end of their learning and the basis of their meditations; Anselm, fully trained in the rediscovered disciplines of grammar and dialectic, consciously set aside Scripture—much to Lanfranc's dismay—in order to speculate freely on the essential truths of the Christian faith. In his view the mind of man, created in the image of God, should seek to uncover the "necessary reasons" for things implicit in the Divine Being and implanted in all his works. With Augustine's arguments on the Trinity hovering ever in the background, he reflected therefore on the nature of the Highest Being, the attributes logically ascribable to him, his self-understanding and speech (the Word), and his relations to himself and others in love (the Spirit). This first work (1076/77) Anselm called initially an "example of meditating on the rationale of the faith," then shortened to *Monologion* [soliloquy] *on the Rationale of the Faith* (see Rom. 12:6). Next he sought in a style at once speculative and prayerful to capture the very essence and necessity of God's being in a single definition, the Being "than which no greater can be thought." The very heart of his *Proslogion* (colloquy), first entitled *Faith Seeking Understanding,* this the so-called ontological argument, in many ways less an argument than a way of perceiving and defining the nature of reality, has fascinated philosophers from the Middle Ages to the present, even though several great thinkers (Thomas Aquinas, Kant) have rejected it.

With the same combination of grammatical definition and logical exposition Anselm went on to treat matters pertaining to grammar, truth, and the devil's fall, the relationship of the virgin birth to original sin, the double procession of the Holy Spirit (at papal request), and the comportment of foreknowledge, predestination, and free will. Thus this philosophical theologian (in modern terms) ranged freely over issues later divided between general and special revelation or natural and revealed theology. This applies particularly to his consideration of *Why God Became Man,* the most influential of all his theological works. Setting aside all knowledge of Jesus Christ, Anselm attempted to produce necessary reasons for the coming of a God-man and his atoning sacrifice. The injury dealt to God's honor by man's fall into sin required man himself to render satisfaction to an upright God; yet only God himself could adequately make amends. Hence the God-man whose innocent sacrifice potentially made satisfaction for all men. Anselm may have aimed his argument partly at Jews, for their criticism of an incarnate God had become very vocal in his day. But its greatest impact was upon Christians. His "satisfaction" theory of the atonement effectively refuted early medieval notions of the devil's "rights" over fallen mankind and also displaced earlier Eastern emphases upon Christ as victor. Indeed this "satisfaction" theory shaped nearly all Catholic and Protestant thought on redemptive theology down to modern times.

J. Van Engen

Bibliography. *Anselmi Opera Omnia,* ed. F. S. Schmitt, 6 vols. (ET in 4 volumes by J. Hopkins); B. Ward, tr., *The Prayers and Meditations of St. Anselm; Eadmer, The Life of St. Anselm,* ed. R. W. Southern; *Memorials of St. Anselm,* ed. R. W. Southern and F. S. Schmitt; J. Hopkins, *A Companion to the Study of St. Anselm;* R. W. Southern, *St. Anselm and His Biographer;* G. R. Evans, *Anselm and Talking About God* and *Anselm and a New Generation.*

Anthropology. *See* Man, Doctrine of.

Anthropomorphism. The term (not found in the Bible—derived from Greek *anthrōpos,* man, and *morphē,* form) designates the view which conceives of God as having human form (Exod. 15:3; Num. 12:8) with feet (Gen. 3:8; Exod. 24:10), hands (Exod. 24:11; Josh. 4:24), mouth (Num. 12:8; Jer. 7:13), and heart (Hos. 11:8), but in a wider sense the term also includes human attributes and emotions (Gen. 2:2; 6:6; Exod. 20:5; Hos. 11:8).

This tendency toward anthropomorphism, common to all religions, found such full expression in Greek polytheism that the common man thought of the gods as mortal men. Xenophanes (*ca.* 570–480 B.C.) reacted strongly, accusing man of making the gods in his own image. Later developments in Greek thought considered men as mortal gods (an early form of humanism) or viewed God in the metaphysical sense of pure, absolute Being. The transcendentalism of the latter influenced the hellenistic Jews of Egypt so that the translators of the Greek OT, the LXX, made during the third and second centuries B.C., felt compelled to alter some of the anthropomorphisms. E.g., where the Hebrew reads "they saw the God of Israel" (Exod. 24:10) the LXX has "they saw the place where the God of Israel stood"; and for "I will speak with him mouth to mouth" (Num. 12:8) the LXX translates "I will speak to him mouth to mouth apparently."

However, the OT, if read with empathy and

understanding, reveals a spiritual development which is a corrective for either a crude, literalistic view of anthropomorphism or the equally false abhorrence of any anthropomorphic expressions. The "image of God" created in man (Gen. 1:27) was in the realm of personality, of spirit, not of human form. Because the Israelites "saw no form" (Deut. 4:12) at Sinai, they were prohibited images in any form: male or female, beast, bird, creeping thing, or fish (Deut. 4:15–19). The NT declaration of Jesus, "God is spirit, and those who worship him must worship in spirit and truth" (John 4:24), is anticipated by Job 9:32; Ps. 50:21; and Hos. 11:9.

The anthropomorphism of the Israelites was an attempt to express the nonrational aspects of religious experience (the *mysterium tremendum,* "aweful majesty," discussed by Rudolf Otto) in terms of the rational, and the early expressions of it were not as "crude" as so-called enlightened man would have one think. The human characteristics of Israel's God were always exalted, while the gods of their Near Eastern neighbors shared the vices of men. Whereas the representation of God in Israel never went beyond anthropomorphism, the gods of the other religions assumed forms of animals, trees, stars, or even a mixture of elements. Anthropomorphic concepts were "absolutely necessary if the God of Israel was to remain a God of the individual Israelite as well as of the people as a whole. . . . For the average worshipper . . . it is very essential that his god be a divinity who can sympathize with his human feelings and emotions, a being whom he can love and fear alternately, and to whom he can transfer the holiest emotions connected with memories of father and mother and friend" (W. F. Albright, *From the Stone Age to Christianity,* 2nd ed., p. 202).

It is precisely in the area of the personal that theism, as expressed in Christianity, must ever think in anthropomorphic terms. To regard God solely as Absolute Being or the Great Unknown is to refer to *him* or *it,* but to think of God as literally personal, one with whom we can fellowship, is to say *Thou.* Some object to this view, calling it anthropomorphic, but they are at a loss to explain how the creatures of an impersonal force became personal human beings conscious of their personality.

"To say that God is completely different from us is as absurd as to say that he is completely like us" (D. E. Trueblood, *Philosophy of Religion,* p. 270). Paradoxical as it may seem, there is a mediating position which finds the answer in the incarnation of Jesus the Christ, who said, "He who has seen me has seen the Father" (John 14:9). Finite man will ever cling to the anthropomorphism of the incarnation and the concept of God as Father (Matt. 7:11), but at the same time he will realize the impossibility of absolute, complete comprehension of God, for "my thoughts are not your thoughts, neither are your ways my ways, says the Lord" (Isa. 55:8). D. M. Beegle

Bibliography. W. Eichrodt, *Theology of the OT,* I; J. Hempel, "Die Grenzen des Anthropormorphismus Jahwes im Alten Testament: ein Vortrag," *ZAW* 57: 75ff.; G. D. Hicks, *The Philosophical Bases of Theism;* R. Otto, *The Idea of the Holy;* H. H. Rowley, *The Faith of Israel;* H. B. Swete, *An Introduction to the OT in Greek.*

Anthroposophy. A religious and philosophical system based on the theosophical ideas of Rudolf Steiner (1861–1925). Born in Hungary and raised a Roman Catholic, Steiner studied science at the University of Vienna, became an accomplished Goethe scholar, and acquired an intense interest in the occult. In 1902, while serving as editor of a literary magazine, he became general secretary of the German Theosophical Society but soon grew disillusioned with its overstress on Eastern religious thought. In 1913 Steiner broke with theosophy and founded the Anthroposophical Society, which joined certain Christian elements to its basically theosophical outlook. In 1922 Steiner and Friedrich Rittlemeyer, a former Protestant pastor, organized the movement into "Christian Fellowships" (*Christengemeinschaften*) where priests and priestesses performed mystical rites patterned after the Catholic Mass.

Like theosophy from which it came, anthroposophy includes elements from Hinduism, Neoplatonism, Gnosticism, and Sufism. It affirms the existence of spiritual as well as material worlds and teaches that salvation consists of escaping the confines of the material world by obtaining esoteric spiritual knowledge about the true nature of things. Unlike theosophy (wisdom of God), which holds that such knowledge comes from *avatars* (incarnations) and *arhats* (master teachers), anthroposophy (wisdom of man) teaches that people possess the truth within themselves. By cultivating one's occult powers through certain mental, physical, and spiritual exercises, anyone can become a *Hellseher,* a master of clear vision, and thereby gain extraordinary spiritual insight. According to Steiner's doctrine of the "seven lotus flowers," each person has seven bodies (physical, astral, etheric, the most intimate "I," etc.) which open out, like the lotus blossom, to new levels of truth. Once these spiritual organs are developed through meditation (yoga), one has access to "cosmic memory" through which he can understand all things.

Whereas theosophy views Christ as only one of many avatars, anthroposophy teaches that

Christ is the only avatar, an exalted solar being (*Sonnenwesen*) who entered human history as the full revelation of the spiritual world. Contact with Christ brings deeper penetration into his own knowledge of reality. Thus for anthroposophists celebration of the Eucharist has ultimate significance. Called the "Act of the Consecration of Man," the sacrament mystically joins the celebrant with the spirit and body of Christ, making him truly "man" and capable of realizing his own occultic powers.

Anthroposophy was condemned by the Roman Catholic Church in 1919. Followers today are most numerous in Germany, Britain, and the United States, and generally are drawn from "intellectuals" in search of more "effervescent" religious experience outside established religious channels. T. P. WEBER

Bibliography. G. A. Kaufmann, *Fruits of Anthroposophy;* R. Steiner, *The Story of My Life;* F. Rittlemeyer, *Reincarnation.*

Antichrist. Although the term "antichrist" occurs only in the Johannine letters, the conception of an archopponent of God and his Messiah is found in both testaments and in the intertestamental writings. Opposition is reflected in *anti,* which here probably means "against," not "instead of," although both ideas may be present: posing as Christ, Antichrist opposes Christ.

OT Background. Because Christ is not fully revealed, the OT offers no complete portrait of Antichrist but furnishes materials for the picture in descriptions of personal or national opposition to God.

Belial. Certain individuals, infamous for wickedness, are called "sons of [or men of] Belial" (*bĕlîya'al,* probably "without worth," "useless"). Idolatry (Deut. 13:13), sodomy and rape (Judg. 19:22; 20:13), drunkenness (I Sam. 1:16), disregard of God (I Sam. 2:12), sacrilege (I Sam. 2:17, 22), disrespect for authority (I Sam. 10:27; II Chr. 13:7), lack of hospitality (I Sam. 25:17, 25), perjury (I Kings 21:10, 13), and evil speech (Prov. 6:12; 16:27) are among the sins of these "empty men" (II Chr. 13:7), whom the good shun (Ps. 101:3).

Foreign Enemies. Opposition to God's kingdom is opposition to him. The nations' vain plot against the Lord's anointed king in Ps. 2 may be a foreshadowing of the antichrist idea. Similarly, the taunt songs against the rulers of Babylon (Isa. 14) and Tyre (Ezek. 28) vividly describe the calamitous fall of monarchs who usurp divine prerogatives. Gog's defeat (Ezek. 39:1–20; Rev. 20:7–10) seems to climax the fruitless struggle of nations to frustrate God's purposes by harassing his people.

The Little Horn. This rebellion is symbolized in Daniel's little horn. Chapter 7, the more eschatological, seems to depict the defeat of God's final enemy, while chapter 8 describes Antiochus IV Epiphanes (175–163 B.C.), the foreign ruler most hated by the Jews because of his personal wickedness and ruthless persecution of their religion.

The portrait of this "king of the north" (Dan. 11), the personification of evil, has helped significantly to shape the NT figure of Antichrist: (1) he abolished the continual burnt offering and erected the abomination of desolation in the temple (Dan. 11:31; Matt. 24:15; Mark 13:14; Rev. 13:14–15); (2) he exalted himself to the position of deity (Dan. 11:36–39; II Thess. 2:3–4); (3) his helpless death points to Christ's slaying of "the lawless one" (Dan. 11:45; II Thess. 2:8; Rev. 19:20). Whatever the antecedents of Daniel's beasts (W. Bousset, *Antichrist Legend,* holds that the battle of Antichrist and God stems from the Babylonian legend of Marduk's struggle with Tiamat), they are clearly nations opposing God and his people. The beast from the sea in Rev. 13:1 recalls Dan. 7:3, 7 and strengthens the link between Daniel's prophecy and the NT account of Antichrist.

Intertestamental Elaboration. Two emphases appear in the Apocrypha and Pseudepigrapha: (1) Rome replaces Syria as the national enemy, and Pompey supplants Antiochus IV as the epitome of opposition to God; (2) Belial (Beliar) is personified as a satanic spirit.

The "lawless one" (II Thess. 2:8) has been connected with Beliar, which rabbinic tradition interpreted as "without yoke" (*bĕlî'ōl*), i.e., refusing the law's yoke. This connection seems strengthened by the LXX translation of *belial* by *paranomos,* "lawbreaker" (Deut. 13:13, etc.). However, though Paul's description may partially reflect the Beliar tradition, he distinguishes Beliar from the lawless one: Beliar is a synonym of Satan (II Cor. 6:15), while Satan and the lawless one are differentiated (II Thess. 2:9).

NT Development. *The Gospels.* References to Christ's opponent are neither numerous nor specific. The disciples are warned that false Christs will attempt to deceive even the elect (Matt. 24:24; Mark 13:22). Similarly, Christ speaks of one who comes in his own name, whom the Jews receive (John 5:43). This may be a veiled reference to Antichrist or to any false Messiahs who present themselves to Judaism. Even the mention of the abomination of desolation (Matt. 24:15; Mark 13:14), recalling vividly Daniel's prophecy, is made with remarkable restraint. A single evil personality may be in view, but his portrait is not even sketched.

II Thessalonians. Paul gives a clearer picture of Christ's archenemy, whose outstanding characteristic is contempt of law. Two names—"man of lawlessness" (preferable to "man of sin") and "the lawless one" (II Thess. 2:3, 8–9)—stress this anarchistic attitude, recalling Dan. 7:25, where the little horn tries to change the times and law. Furthermore, Antichrist makes exclusive claim to deity (II Thess. 2:4) in terms reminiscent of Dan. 7:25; 11:36. Paul does not picture a pseudo-Messiah posing as God's messenger, but a pseudo-God viciously opposing all other religion. His model may have been the blasphemous emperor Gaius (A.D. 37–41).

He deceives many by wonders (II Thess. 2:9–10). Christ worked miracles by God's power, and the Jews attributed them to Satan (Matt. 12:24ff.); Antichrist will work miracles by satanic power, and many will worship him as God.

One of Antichrist's names—"son of perdition" (II Thess. 2:3; cf. John 17:12)—reveals his destiny: Christ will slay him by his breath and the brightness of his appearing (II Thess. 2:8; Rev. 19:15, 20; cf. Isa. 11:4).

Antichrist is the personal culmination of a principle of rebellion already working secretly—"the mystery of lawlessness" (II Thess. 2:7). When God's restraining hand which preserves law and order is withdrawn, this spirit of satanic lawlessness will become incarnate in "the lawless one."

The Johannine Letters. Though John recognized the expectation of a single antichrist, he turns his attention to the many antichrists who have come denying that Jesus is the Christ and thus denying the true nature of both Father and Son (I John 2:18, 22; 4:3). Contemporary docetists discredited Christ's humanity (II John 7), claiming that he *seemed* to have human form. To John they were the embodiment of the antichrist spirit. Their view taught that man was divine apart from God in Christ and left God and the world ununited.

John's account complements rather than contradicts Paul's. Following Daniel, Paul depicts a single archenemy, who claims the right to personal worship. John stresses the spiritual elements in these claims and the spiritual lie which made Antichrist seemingly strong.

Revelation. The Apocalyptist's beast (Rev. 13), dependent in spirit and detail on Daniel, combines the characteristics of all four OT beasts. Further, the NT beast has an authority belonging only to the little horn of Daniel's beast. John seemingly implies that the savage impiety of Antiochus will be embodied in a kingdom; for the beast, although he has some personal characteristics, is more than a person: his seven heads are seven kings (Rev. 17:10–12). The beast himself is an eighth king, springing from one of the seven. This complicated picture suggests that the beast symbolizes worldly power, the anti-God spirit of a nationalistic ambition (in Daniel's prophecy personified in Antiochus and in John's day in Rome) which will become incarnate in one great demagogue—Antichrist.

To Paul's account John adds at least one important element—the false prophet, a second beast who works under the authority of Antichrist, as Antichrist gains his authority from the dragon, Satan (Rev. 13:2, 11–12). After directing Antichrist's political and religious enterprises, the false prophet shares his fate at Christ's advent (Rev. 19:20).

Christian Interpretation. The fathers generally believed in a personal antichrist. His identity hinged on whether the "mystery of lawlessness" was interpreted politically or religiously. Politically, the most likely candidate was Nero, who, legend held, would reappear in resurrected form (*redivivus*) to continue his terrible reign. This interpretation, propounded by Chrysostom and others, has gained prominence in this century through preteristic interpreters of Revelation like R. H. Charles and C. A. Scott. Irenaeus and others who held that Antichrist would emerge from a religious context traced him to Dan on the basis of Gen. 49:17; Deut. 33:22; Jer. 8:16 (cf. the omission of Dan in Rev. 7:5ff.).

The Reformers equated Antichrist with the papacy, as had some medieval theologians—Gregory I, who taught that whoever assumed the title "universal priest" was Antichrist's forerunner; Joachim of Floris; and Wycliffe. Luther, Calvin, the translators of the AV, and the authors of the Westminster Confession concurred in this identification. Roman Catholic scholars retaliated, branding Rome's opponents Antichrist.

In the ideal or symbolic view Antichrist is an ageless personification of evil, not identifiable with one nation, institution, or individual. This idea gains support from the Johannine letters and has value in emphasizing the constancy of the warfare between Satan's manifold forces and Christ's.

Futurists (e.g., Zahn, Seiss, Scofield) hold that idealists fail to stress sufficiently the culmination of this hostility in a personal adversary. They believe that Antichrist will usher in a period of great tribulation at history's close, in connection with a mighty empire like a revived Rome, and will dominate politics, religion, and commerce until Christ's advent.

D. A. Hubbard

See also Abomination of Desolation; Mystery of Iniquity.

Bibliography. S. J. Andrews, *Christianity and Antichristianity;* G. G. Findlay, *Thessalonians,* CGT; G. Milligan, *Epistles to the Thessalonians;* H. H. Rowley, *Relevance of Apocalyptic;* G. Vos, *Pauline Eschatology;* W. Bousset, *The Antichrist Legend;* E. Kander, *NIDNTT,* I, 124ff.; G. C. Berkouwer, *The Return of Christ;* A. L. Moore, *The Parousia in the NT;* J. Jeremias, *Der Antichrist in Geschichte und Gegenwart;* A. A. Hoekema, *The Bible and the Future;* H. Ridderbos, *Paul.*

Anticlericalism. The term "anticlerical" probably first appeared in the early 1850s in Catholic France. It indicated opposition to Ultramontane revival with its reassertion of the sacral power of priests and of the primacy of the pope in the church. A staggering battle in Italy and Europe over the temporal power of the pope focused anticlerical attitudes in the 1850s and 1860s, especially in Italy, Belgium, Spain, and France. Thereafter, to this day, anticlericalism as attitude and as movement has been a considerable political factor in every Roman Catholic area, notably in Europe, Latin America, and Quebec. Anticlericalism has condemned priestly participation in national governments, municipalities, elections, education, and land and capital ownership.

Opposition to clerical authority, as well as fear and ridicule of priests, are age old within Catholic Christendom. In Catholic tradition, both before and after the creation of Protestant churches, clergy have claimed to be the sole authority in church government and doctrine as well as the only exercisers of sacramental power. They have put themselves forward as the leaders in faith and morals, and often as the guides of the laity in politics, economics, and intellectual and social life. In response there is a long tradition of popular satire in songs and tales against any clerical failings—irregular sexual behavior, religious hypocrisy, social pomp, intellectual stupidity, and arrogance. Moreover, excessive use of clerical power or usurpation of political and economic power has again and again evoked vigorous resistance. Anticlericalism has assumed that priests are constitutionally unable to keep their own standards, and are by nature inclined to dominate the whole of life.

The anticlerical factor in the Protestant movement of the 1500s contributed to the break with Rome and has continued to be a crucial element in anti-Catholicism to this day. In the 1700s the French *philosophes* were merciless against priests, and one Catholic state after another expelled the Jesuits. The French revolutionary governments tried to control priests by making them state employees. The revolutionaries in Catholic Europe in 1820, 1830, 1848, and 1870 explicitly regarded priestly power as an enemy. The Papal States, as a "government of priests," epitomized to anticlericals all that was evil. The liberal republics in Latin America were anticlerical. After 1870, in France, Spain, Italy, and Quebec, as well as in much of Latin America, politics polarized as the church and most clergy sided with the right against liberals, republicans, and socialists who built anticlericalism into their programs. Anticlericalism has usually contributed to secularization in Catholic cultures: since clergy have been the main agents of Christian presence in public life, opposition to priests in politics has entailed opposition to Christianity in modern society. Following Vatican II opposition to clerical domination within the church itself has contributed to a lay revival, but not yet to a termination of exclusively priestly authority in the church.

Anticlericalism has not been absent among Protestants. Many a Baptist pastor, Reformed dominie, or Lutheran minister has evoked anticlerical responses. Charismatics, Brethren, and Quakers have found they can do without clergy entirely. C. T. McIntire

Bibliography. O. Chadwick, "The Rise of Anticlericalism," in *The Secularization of the European Mind in the Nineteenth Century;* A. Mellor, *Histoire de l'anticlericalisme français;* R. Rémond, *l'Anticlericalisme en France, de 1815 à nos jours;* J. M. Diaz Mozaz, *Apuntes para una sociología del anticlericalismo.*

Antilegomena. A term meaning "disputed writings" used by the early church historian Eusebius to distinguish those NT era books which were neither universally accepted (Homologoumena) nor universally rejected as authoritative by the orthodox church.

Eusebius employed the term in its broadest sense for all disputed works. However, he also made a narrower distinction by using it to classify only those disputed books which were commonly accepted as canonical (James, II Peter, II and III John, Jude) as opposed to those which, though disputed, were commonly regarded as noncanonical (which he termed the *nothoi:* Acts of Paul, Shepherd of Hermas, Apocalypse of Peter, Epistle of Barnabas, Didache).

Eusebius's classifications were built upon two principles: canonicity and orthodoxy. The Homologoumena and the Antilegomena were understood to qualify as authoritative for the church on both counts. Those works found within the Antilegomena were regarded as disputed only because of a lack of testimony in the writings of early church fathers. S. E. McClelland

See also Bible, Canon of; Homologoumena.

Bibliography. Eusebius, *Ecclesiastical History* III.25 in *NPNF,* I.

Antinomianism. The word comes from the Greek *anti* (against) and *nomos* (law), and refers to the doctrine that it is not necessary for Christians to preach and/or obey the moral law of the OT. There have been several different justifications for this view down through the centuries. Some have taught that once persons are justified by faith in Christ, they no longer have any obligation toward the moral law because Jesus has freed them from it. A variant of this first position is that since Christ has raised believers above the positive precepts of the law, they need to be obedient only to the immediate guidance of the Holy Spirit, who will keep them from sin. A second view has been that since the law came from the Demiurge (as in Gnosticism) and not from the true, loving Father, it was a Christian's duty to disobey it. Third, others have said that since sin is inevitable anyway, there is no need to resist it. An extension of this view is the contention of some that since God, in his eternal decree, willed sin, it would be presumptuous to resist it. Finally, still others have opposed the preaching of the law on the grounds that it is unnecessary and, indeed, contrary to the gospel of Jesus Christ.

It was the first of these views that the apostle Paul had to address in various letters to Christian churches in the first century. For example, there were those in the Corinth church who taught that once people were justified by faith, they could engage in immorality since there was no longer any obligation to obey the moral law (I Cor. 5–6). Paul also had to correct others who obviously had drawn wrong conclusions from his teachings on justification and grace (e.g., Rom. 3:8, 31). Paul himself agonized over his own inability to meet the law's demands, but also exalted it as holy, spiritual, and good (Rom. 7). Elsewhere he taught that the law was the schoolmaster who brings sinners to a knowledge of their sin and therefore to Christ (Gal. 3:24). He concluded that the proper relationship was that of the stipulated works of the law flowing from the experience of saving grace rather than vice versa (Rom. 6–8).

Perhaps the most extreme form of antinomianism in early Christianity found expression in the Adamite sect in North Africa. The Adamites flourished in the second and third centuries, called their church "Paradise," condemned marriage because Adam had not observed it, and worshiped in the nude.

Many Gnostics in the first centuries of the Christian era held the second of these variations of antinomianism—that the Demiurge, not the true God, gave the moral law; therefore it should not be kept. Some forms of antinomian Gnosticism survived well into the Middle Ages. Moreover, various medieval heretical groups preached Corinthian-style freedom from the law, some going so far as to claim that even prostitution was not sinful for the spiritual person.

The two most famous antinomian controversies in Christian history occurred in the sixteenth and seventeenth centuries, and involved Martin Luther and Anne Hutchinson, respectively. In fact, it was Luther who actually coined the word "antinomianism" in his theological struggle with his former student, Johann Agricola. In the early days of the Reformation, Luther had taught that, after NT times, the moral law had only the negative value of preparing sinners for grace by making them aware of their sin. Agricola denied even this function of the law, believing that repentance should be induced only through the preaching of the gospel of salvation by grace through faith in Christ.

This first major theological controversy in Protestant history lasted intermittently from 1537 to 1540. During this time Luther began to stress the role of the law in Christian life and to preach that it was needed to discipline Christians. He also wrote an important theological treatise to refute antinomianism once and for all: *Against the Antinomians* (1539). The whole matter was finally settled for Lutheranism by the Formula of Concord in 1577, which recognized a threefold use of the law: (1) to reveal sin, (2) to establish general decency in society at large, and (3) to provide a rule of life for those who have been regenerated through faith in Christ.

There were several outbreaks of antinomianism in the Puritan movement in seventeenth century England. However, the major controversy over this teaching among Puritans came in New England in the 1630s in connection with an outspoken woman named Anne Marbury Hutchinson, who emigrated to Massachusetts Bay Colony in 1634. At the time, the New England Puritans were attempting to clarify the place of "preparation for conversion" in covenant (or federal) theology. They had come to the conclusion that salvation lay in fulfilling the conditions of God's covenant with humankind, including preparation for justification and a conscious effort toward sanctification. To some, including Hutchinson, this seemed like an overemphasis on the observance of the law, and she condemned it as a "covenant of works." Instead, she stressed the "covenant of grace," which she said was apart from the works of the law. She began to hold informal meetings in her home to expound her views and to denounce those of the preachers in Massachusetts.

In the context of the great stress of the times—it was only a few years before the civil war erupted in England and the colony lived in tense frontier circumstances—the New England clergy probably misunderstood her main concerns and overreacted to what they perceived to be a threat to the unity and internal security of the Puritan community. At a synod of Congregational churches in 1637 Hutchinson was condemned as an antinomian, enthusiast, and heretic, and banished from the colony. In 1638 she moved to Rhode Island.

In the twentieth century some have viewed existentialist ethics, situation ethics, and moral relativism as forms of antinomianism because these either reject or diminish the normative force of moral law. Certainly most orthodox Christians today agree that the law served the twin purposes of establishing the fact of human sin and of providing moral guidelines for Christian living. In general the various antinomian controversies in history have clarified the legitimate distinctions between law and gospel and between justification and sanctification.

The Christian community as a whole has rejected antinomianism over the years for several reasons. It has regarded the view as damaging to the unity of the Bible, which demands that one part of the divine revelation must not contradict another. Even more important, it has argued that antinomians misunderstood the nature of justification by faith, which, though granted apart from the works of the law, is not sanctification. In general, orthodoxy teaches that the moral principles of the law are still valid, not as objective strivings but as fruits of the Holy Spirit at work in the life of the believer. This disposes of the objection that since the law is too demanding to be kept, it can be completely thrust aside as irrelevant to the individual living under grace. R. D. LINDER

See also AGRICOLA, JOHANN; JUSTIFICATION; SANCTIFICATION.

Bibliography. E. Battis, *Saints and Sectaries: Anne Hutchinson and the Antinomian Controversy in the Massachusetts Bay Colony;* R. Bertram, "The Radical Dialectic Between Faith and Works in Luther's Lectures on Galatians (1535)," in C. S. Meyer, ed., *Luther for an Ecumenical Age;* D. D. Hall, ed., *The Antinomian Controversy, 1636–1638: A Documentary History;* F. F. Bruce, *New Testament History;* M. U. Edwards, Jr., *Luther and the False Brethren.*

Antiochene Theology. The book of Acts indicates that the term "Christian" was first used at Antioch and that there was a church there at the time of the early ministry of the apostle Paul (11:26). It was from Antioch that Paul began his three missionary journeys. It might be called the nearest approach which he had to a headquarters base. The decisions of the Apostolic Council at Jerusalem were published there (Acts 15:30–31).

The first monarchical bishop to secure notice was Ignatius of Antioch. He held the post in the early second century. In his seven epistles he shows himself to be a man eager to defend the full deity and full humanity of Christ. He particularly warns against docetism, and here appears an emphasis which is increasingly to characterize the school of Antioch. God came into flesh, was born of the Virgin Mary. Christ died to deliver men and women from ignorance and from the devil. He rose again from the dead for us. The believer is not only in Christ, he is also *christophoros.* The Supper is the flesh and blood of Christ, though there is no suggestion of a substantial change. Brotherly love is a cardinal emphasis in Ignatius.

Theophilus of Antioch, in the latter part of the second century, developed the Logos doctrine, referring to the logos *prophorikos* brought forth to create. The word *trias* is used to apply to the Godhead first by Theophilus.

Three quarters of a century later Paul of Samosata occupied the episcopal throne in Antioch. The emphasis on the human nature of Christ that was to characterize the later Antioch makes a clear appearance. With a monarchian stress, he found the Logos, a divine force, part of the mind of the Father, dwelling in Jesus from his birth, but apart from the Virgin. He manifested himself as *energeia.* Jesus was not to be worshiped though his enduement with the Logos was quantitatively unusual. His unity with God is one of purpose, of will, of love. While it is possible for Paul to speak of one *prosōpon* of God and the Logos, and to use the term *homoousios* of Christ and the Father, yet the Logos and the Son were not by any means identical. Paul was excommunicated and, after the Roman recapture of Antioch, well-nigh completely lost his influence. Paul's opponents did not approve the term *homoousios,* later to become a touchstone of orthodoxy.

Shortly after Paul's fall from power a schoolmaster, Lucian, came to prominence in Antioch. Lucian conceived of Christ on a higher plane than did Paul. Whether he considered him as equal with the Father in his deity is questionable. His work on the text of the Greek Bible was extensive, and he favored the historical and critical interpretation of the Scriptures.

In the decades following the Council of Nicaea, Antioch exhibited wide differences of opinion on the Arian question, but in this atmosphere John Chrysostom grew to maturity with his extraordinary ability as a preacher. Emphasizing the moral values of Christianity, he continued the stress on historical exegesis. One of Chrysostom's teachers, the presbyter Diodorus, became in due course Bishop of Tarsus and was recognized as a "normal" theologian by the Council of Constantinople in 381. But he did not find an adequate expression for the relationship between the divine and human natures of Christ. There seemed almost to be a dual personality in his conception. Another presbyter, Theodore, later Bishop of Mopsuestia, developed historical criticism much further. He failed to find the doctrine of the Trinity in the OT, and he minimized the messianic intimations in the Psalms. But he put heavy stress upon the importance of textual and historical study as a basis for exegesis. Theodore emphasized the difference between God and man. The Logos humbled himself and became man. The *prosōpon* of the man is complete and so is that of the Godhead. His disciple, the church historian Theodoret, carried on his work. Theodoret's exegesis is in the best historical tradition, his apologetic writing clear and well organized. He stressed the infinite difference between God and man. His Christological views were unquestionably influenced by his friend Nestorius, the most prominent representative of the Antiochene school. Impetuous, self-confident, full of energy, Nestorius was not a scholar. He emphasized the humanity of Jesus, but it is reasonably clear that what he intended to express was not a view that is heretical. The union of Godhead and manhood in Christ is voluntary, but it can be said that there is one *prosōpon* of Jesus Christ. Nestorius campaigned against the term *Theotokos* as applied to the Virgin Mary, yet he agreed that, if properly understood, the term was unobjectionable. It was the violence of his emphases, with their stress on the separateness of the human and the divine in Christ, which was dangerous.

Justinian's Edict of the Three Chapters in 543 was unfair to the School of Antioch in its condemnations of the writings of Theodore of Mopsuestia and of Theodoret. The Council of Constantinople of 553, called the Fifth Ecumenical, condemned writings of the Antioch school, but on the basis of falsified and mutilated quotations.

The separation from the imperial church of the bishops who led the Nestorian schism and the capture of Antioch in 637 by the rising power of Islam checked the further distinctive development of the School of Antioch. Its Aristotelian emphasis on rationality, on ethical quality, and on man's free agency was not popular. Yet it is to be valued for its stress on the genuine continuance in the Second Person of the properties of each nature and for its insistence upon the importance of grammaticohistorical exegesis.

P. Woolley

See also Logos; Monarchianism; Nestorius, Nestorianism.

Bibliography. C. C. Richardson, *The Christianity of Ignatius of Antioch;* G. Bardy, *Paul de Samosate* and *Recherches sur saint Lucien d'Antioche et son école;* F. Loofs, *Paulus von Samosata* and *Nestorius and His Place in the History of Christian Doctrine;* H. de Riedmatten, *Les Actes du procès de Paul de Samosate;* R. Devreesse, *Essai sur Theodore de Mopsueste;* J. F. Bethune-Baker, *Nestorius and His Teaching;* A. R. Vine, *An Approach to Christology;* R. V. Sellers, *Two Ancient Christologies.*

Antipaedobaptism. *See* Baptism, Believers'.

Anti-Semitism. The term was introduced in 1879 by Wilhelm Marr, a German political agitator. At that time it designated anti-Jewish campaigns in Europe. Soon, however, it came to be applied to the hostility and hatred directed toward Jews since before the Christian era.

Long and painful best describes the history of anti-Semitism. Among Jews, the tragic facts about anti-Semitism are well known, for it occupies a major portion of Jewish history. Today, after more than two millennia, this seemingly ubiquitous evil continues to exist. Hence, sensitivity to the wiles of the would-be anti-Semite is never far from the collective conscience of world Jewry. In Christian circles, however, the story of anti-Semitism—often sordid and self-indicting—remains generally untold. This is the case, it would seem, because the history of the church is about as long as the history of anti-Semitism—if not in the overt acts of Christians, certainly in their guilty silence.

In the ancient world the first major example of anti-Semitism occurred during the reign of Antiochus IV Epiphanes (175–163 B.C.). This Seleucid ruler's attempt to hellenize Jews of his day met with stiff opposition. Jews were monotheists and thus, for the most part, aloof from their Gentile neighbors. Gentiles viewed Sabbath rest as congenital idleness and adherence to dietary laws as gross superstition. Antiochus's attack on Jewish religion resulted in the desecration of the temple. A swine was sacrificed on the altar and its blood sprinkled upon Jewish scrolls. Jews were regarded by the Syrian rulers as nomadic wanderers, a homeless people worthy of destruction. Jews found the idolatry of the Greek world abhorrent and later, under the Romans, rejected emperor worship. Thus, Jews were viewed as the great dissenters of the Mediterranean world. To pagans they became *personae non gratae,* victims of discrimination and contempt.

The destruction of the temple in A.D. 70 marked a widespread dispersion of the Jews. In the second century the Roman emperor Hadrian 117–38) issued edicts forbidding the practice of Judaism. About this time the great Rabbi Akiba was tortured to death by the Romans by having his flesh stripped from his body with iron combs.

In 321 Constantine made Christianity the official religion of the Roman state. Jews were forbidden to make converts, serve in the military, and hold any high office. Several centuries later, under Justinian, Jews were barred from celebrating Passover until after Easter.

The roots of theological anti-Semitism derive from certain teachings which arose from the early Christian centuries. The Jewish revolt of A.D. 66–70 resulted in the death, exile, or slavery of thousands of Jews. Such hardship was thought by the rapidly expanding Gentile church to be chastisement, proof of divine rejection. Gradually the church saw itself as superseding Judaism, a "dead" and "legalistic" faith. Triumphantly, the church now stood over the synagogue as the new Israel of God, heir to the covenant promises. But Jews, as a people, still chafed under the Roman yoke. They failed to understand messianic redemption in terms of a suffering servant; they refused to believe that God had forever cast away his chosen.

The writings of several church fathers reflect a theological invective directed toward Jews. John Chrysostom, the "golden-mouthed," is a noted example. He taught that "the synagogue is a brothel and a theater, . . . a den for unclean animals. . . . Never has a Jew prayed to God. . . . They are all possessed by the devil."

In the Middle Ages, Jews were largely excluded from medieval Christian culture. They sought to avoid social, economic, and ecclesiastical pressures by living behind ghetto walls. They were, however, permitted to practice usury. This led Christians to accuse them of being a pariah people. Jews were required to wear a distinctive hat or patch sewn on their clothing. They were accused of having a peculiar smell, in contrast to the "odor of sanctity." Jews were also maligned as "Christ-killers," desecraters of the host, murderers of Christian infants, spreaders of the black plague, poisoners of wells and sucklers of sows. The First Crusade (1096) resulted in numerous mass suicides as Jews sought to avoid forced baptism. Toward the close of the Middle Ages many Jews became homeless wanderers. They were expelled from England in 1290, from France in 1306, and from cities in Spain, Germany, and Austria in the following years.

The Spanish Inquisition and expulsion of 1492 resulted in thousands of torturings, burnings at the stake, and forced conversions. In Germany, one generation later, Luther issued a series of vitriolic pamphlets attacking Jews. Of Jews he wrote, "Let us drive them out of the country for all time."

Toward the start of the modern ages a bloody revolt against the Cossacks occurred in Poland (1648–58). Caught in the middle, about half a million Jews were killed. In other European countries at the time Jews continued to be persecuted or, at best, viewed with suspicion or contempt.

In the latter part of the nineteenth century the largest Jewish population in the world (six million) was in czarist Russia. There Jews experienced a series of vicious pogroms which left thousands dead. Others, joining Jews from different European lands, fled to America. In this country they hoped to find a place earlier described by George Washington as offering "to bigotry no sanction, to persecution no assistance." Between 1880 and 1910 more than two million Jews immigrated to America through New York City. During this time the celebrated Dreyfus Affair in France (1894) drew the problem of anti-Semitism to world attention.

Rooted in the soil of Germany, the Holocaust of the twentieth century stands as an unparalleled event. Nazi propaganda stated that the human race must be "purified" by ridding it of Jews. The "final solution" to the Jewish "problem" was camps, gas chambers, and crematoria. Between 1933, when Hitler came to power, and the end of World War II some six million Jewish lives were destroyed. Today in Jerusalem the Yad Vashem (the name is taken from Isa. 56:5) stands as a memorial to Holocaust victims and as an institution for research and documentation.

At present anti-Semitism persists wherever Jews are found. Jews of Russia and France have been especially oppressed. In European countries and in the United States recent anti-Semitic incidents have included synagogue smearings and bombings, desecration of gravestones, vicious graffiti, Nazi pamphlets, and grotesque Jewish stereotypes in the press. At other times the so-called polite variety of anti-Semitism is found, namely discrimination and/or antipathy displayed toward Jews in the social, educational, and economic realms. The Anti-Defamation League and other Jewish agencies continue to make slow but steady progress in seeking to promote understanding among peoples of different races and religions.

M. R. Wilson

See also Zionism.

Bibliography. A. T. Davies, ed., *Anti-Semitism and the Foundations of Christianity; EJ,* III, 79–160; E. H. Flannery, *The Anguish of the Jews;* R. E. Gade, *A Historical Survey of Anti-Semitism;* C. Klein, *Anti-Judaism in Christian Theology;* R. Ruether, *Faith and Fratricide;* S. Sandmel, *Anti-Semitism in the NT.*

Antitrinitarianism. *See* Unitarianism.

Antitype. *See* TYPE, TYPOLOGY.

Anxiety. Anxiety is a universal experience. In contrast to fear, which is the apprehension of a real and present danger, anxiety anticipates nonexistent dangers in the future and helplessly dwells on how to reduce them. Even as many dangers and diseases are eliminated, our world grows increasingly worrisome, prompting many modern thinkers to call the last half of the twentieth century the "age of anxiety."

Modern psychology and medicine provide evidence that worry and anxiety have disastrous effects ranging from ulcers to chronic feelings of unhappiness. Psychological theories are constructed and therapeutic rituals formulated to stop the tide of anxiety. Psychological terror reigns in our world. We are our own torturers.

The profound passage of Matt. 6:25–32 records Jesus' view of anxiety, his reasoning, and his prescription. The Lord states clearly that worry is a complete waste of energy and should not be indulged because God provides for our needs. He then appeals to reason about the consequences of worry when he asks, "Can your worry add a single cubit to your life?" Care and fretting have never manipulated the future and will never do so. Jesus states that the ungodly fret over having their needs met, but that believers have security in the Father.

The position of the Lord regarding anxiety appears straightforward: (1) God the Father loves us and is in complete control; (2) God will meet our needs; (3) worry is useless and without effect. Jesus compares fretting over our basic needs to the ways of the ungodly and contrasts this with the spiritually mature life of faith.

The apostle Paul echoes this position in Phil. 4:6: "Be anxious for nothing but in everything by prayer and supplication with thanksgiving let your requests be made known to God." The reasoning for the Christian is that God is *the* person in complete control of life's events. But how does one translate reasoning down to the emotional and behavioral level?

The Scriptures give us the key: we are buttressed against worry through the power of the Holy Spirit. During a time when the natural response is to be anxious, the believer's relationship to the Holy Spirit is to sustain him or her. A practical example is in Luke 12:11–12, where Jesus told the disciples not to be afraid when the authorities brought them in because "the Holy Spirit will teach you that very hour what you ought to say." In II Tim. 1:7 we are told that "God has not given us a spirit of timidity but of power and love and discipline." Reducing worry is a process rooted in a relationship with the Spirit and not simply a matter of human willpower. The believer's confidence grows with the understanding that one's cares can be rolled onto God "because he cares for you" (I Pet. 5:7). For the Christian, overcoming worry is relationship, not a technique.

Jesus tells us in Matt. 6:33 what we should put in place of worry. Indeed, he gives us a contingency that tells us the *only* way to guarantee that one's needs will be met. If we "seek first his kingdom and his righteousness [then] all these things will be added to you [needs will be met]." It is only when we seek godliness in our lives that we are assured about our provision. Talking about meeting needs apart from a central relationship with the Creator is contradictory.

As Martha fussed over the preparations for dinner, Jesus said to her in Luke 10:41–42, "Martha, Martha, you are worried about so many things, but only a few things are necessary, really only one." Helping the Marthas of this world reduce worry involves a daily relationship with God combined with methods of deflecting attention away from irrational ideas and onto realistic beliefs. Overcoming anxiety is more than an injunction to stop. Learning to worry less is undergirded by a developing, daily walk with God. As the writer of Hebrews exclaims, "The Lord is my helper, I will not be afraid. What shall man do to me?" (13:6).

D. SIMPSON

Bibliography. G. R. Collins, *Overcoming Anxiety;* F. B. Minirth and P. D. Meier, *Happiness Is A Choice;* B. Narramore and B. Counts, *Freedom from Guilt;* C. Osborn, *Release from Fear and Anxiety;* P. Tournier, *Guilt and Grace.*

Apocalyptic. The word "apocalypse" (unveiling) is derived from Rev. 1:1, where it refers to the revelation to John by the ascended Jesus of the consummation of the age. The word has been applied by modern scholars to a group of Jewish books which contain similar literary and eschatological characteristics, not all of which are really apocalypses. An apocalypse is a book containing real or alleged revelations of heavenly secrets or of the events which will attend the end of the world and the inauguration of the kingdom of God.

Historical Background. Many apocalypses were produced by unknown Jewish authors between 200 B.C. and A.D. 100 in imitation of the book of Daniel. (Daniel is often described as the first of such apocalypses, but numerous traits linking Daniel closely to the prophetic writings lead to the conclusion that Daniel stands between the prophetic and apocalyptic types. There are also other reasons for dating Daniel earlier than Maccabean times.) The apocalypses arose out of a historical milieu involving a historical-theological problem consisting of three elements.

The Emergence of a "Righteous Remnant." In the prophetic period Israel continually lapsed into idolatry, forsaking the law of God. After the restoration there emerged circles of Jews who were loyal to the law. When Antiochus Epiphanes, in 168 B.C., attempted a forcible assimilation of the Jews to Greek culture and religion, these righteous, called Chasidim or Hasideans, refused to submit, choosing death rather than disobedience to the law. This spirit was preserved in their successors, the Pharisees. Another group, called the Qumran community, withdrew from the mainstream of Jewish life to seek a monastic retreat in the desert, giving themselves in complete devotion to the study and observance of the law.

The Problem of Evil. The prophets promised that a repentant, restored Israel would inherit the kingdom. Now Israel was restored to the land and was faithful to the law. According to the Jewish definition of righteousness, the conditions laid down by the prophets were satisfied; but the kingdom did not come. Instead came unprecedented suffering. Antiochus Epiphanes attempted to destroy the Jewish faith, inflicting tortures and martyrdoms upon the faithful. The religious liberty won by the Maccabean rebellion did not bring the kingdom of God. Instead of God's rule came the rule of the secular, worldly Hasmoneans and, after 63 B.C., Rome's native puppets and procurators. A righteous Israel which merited the kingdom met only suffering and political bondage.

The Cessation of Prophecy. Throughout these times of unparalleled evil God did not speak to explain this historical enigma. The voice of prophecy was stilled. No prophet appeared to announce "Thus saith the Lord" and to interpret to the afflicted people of God the riddle of the suffering of the righteous.

The apocalypses arose out of this milieu to provide an explanation of the sufferings of the righteous and the delay of the kingdom of God.

Literary Characteristics. Apocalyptic as a genre of literature succeeded the prophetic. At some points apocalyptic is a development of elements in prophecy; at other points it departs from the prophetic character. No sharp line can be drawn between the two types, and characterizations of apocalyptic differ considerably.

Revelations. The prophets often received their message by revelation, but their main concern was "the word of the Lord." Often the word of God came to the prophets as an overwhelming inner conviction apart from visions or dreams. In the apocalypses the word of the Lord has given way to revelations and visions. God does not speak by his Spirit to his servants. The seer must learn the solution to the problems of evil and the coming of the kingdom through dreams, visions, or heavenly journeys with angelic guides.

Imitative Literary Character. The prophets, out of experiences in which God disclosed his will, announced the divine will to the people. Scholars who reject any supernatural element admit real psychological experiences by the prophets. Possibly IV Ezra reflects real subjective experiences, but usually the revelations of the apocalyptists are only a literary form. The visions are literary fictions imitating the visions of the prophetic writings. Generally, therefore, prophecy was first spoken, while apocalypses were written.

Pseudonymity. The prophets spoke in the name of the Lord directly to the people. However, in the Maccabean period the voice of prophecy was stilled and the apocalyptists attributed their revelations to OT saints as a means of validating their message to their own generation. In this matter Daniel stands alone, for Daniel is unknown apart from his appearance in the apocalypse ascribed to him.

Symbolism. The prophets had often used symbols to convey the divine message. In the apocalypses symbolism becomes the main stock in trade, particularly as a technique for outlining the course of history without employing historical names. This technique appears first in Daniel and was imitated with bizarre proliferation in later apocalypses.

Rewritten History. The prophets took their stand in their own historical situation and proclaimed the word of God to their generation against the background of the future kingdom of God. The apocalyptists sometimes took their stand at a point in the distant past and rewrote history as though it were prophecy down to their own day, at which time the coming of the kingdom is expected. In some instances apocalypses can be dated by the latest events reflected in the alleged prophecy.

Religious Characteristics. The word "apocalyptic" is used also to describe the eschatology found in the apocalypses.

Dualism. Apocalyptic eschatology sees a contrast between the character of the present time of suffering and the future time of salvation that is so radical that it is finally described in terms of two ages: this age and the age to come. This age is characterized by evil; the age to come will see the kingdom of God. The transition from this age to the coming age can be accomplished only by a supernatural inbreaking of God. This dualism is not metaphysical or cosmic but historical and temporal. While this terminology of the two ages appears in the NT, it is found in the apocalyptic literature in fully developed form only in IV Ezra and the Apocalypse of Baruch.

Many critics attribute this development to the influence of Persian dualism, but it can also be explained as a historical development of ideas already implicit in the OT prophets. The prophetic expectation of the future kingdom includes a redeemed earth (Isa. 32:15–18; 11:6–9; 65:17; 66:22). This transformation will be accomplished only by a divine visitation, when God will shake the present order in judgment (Isa. 13:13; 34:4; 51:6; Hag. 2:7) and will cause a new order to emerge from the old.

Apocalyptic dualism is a development of this basic prophetic view of the world and redemption. The new order is usually described with Isaianic features of a new earth (Enoch 45:4–5; 51:1–5). Assumption of Moses 10:1 looks forward to a manifestation of God's kingdom "in all his creation." Sometimes more "transcendental" terms are employed (Enoch 62:16).

Some OT passages describe the new order in terms very similar to the present order, while others (Isa. 65–66) see a complete transformation involving new heavens and a new earth. Some apocalypses put together these two expectations and anticipate a temporal kingdom in this age followed by an eternal kingdom in the new order (IV Ezra 7:28–29). The age to come in Baruch is pictured as a new earth (32:6). The language of IV Ezra is difficult to interpret (7:36, 113).

Historical Perspective. The prophets took their stand within a specific historical situation and addressed their message to their environment. On the horizon was God's kingdom, and the future stands in a constant tension with the present. Isa. 13 describes the historical judgment of Babylon against the background of the eschatological visitation as though they were one and the same day. Historical judgments are seen as realized eschatology.

The apocalyptists have lost this tension between history and eschatology. They do not view the present against the background of the future, but their viewpoint encompasses the entire sweep of history for the purpose of interpreting history theologically. The apocalypses are theological treatises rather than truly historical documents.

Pessimism. It is not correct ultimately to call the apocalyptists pessimists, for they never lost their confidence that God would finally triumph and bring his kingdom. However, they were pessimistic as to the present age. The problem of the suffering of the righteous had led to the conclusion that God had withdrawn his aid from his people in the present age and that salvation could be expected only in the age to come (Enoch 89:56–75). IV Ezra sees the present age as hopelessly evil and the solution lying altogether in the future (4:26–32; 7:50; 8:1–3). The righteous can only patiently suffer while waiting a future salvation.

Determinism. This evil age has been predetermined and must run its course. The kingdom does not come even though the righteous deserve it, because fixed periods must intervene before the consummation. The kingdom must await its appointed time. God himself is pictured as waiting the passing of the times which he has decreed rather than bringing aid to the righteous (IV Ezra 4:36–37). This idea often led to the dividing of the course of time into determined periods of weeks or years.

Ethical Passivity. The apocalyptists lack moral or evangelical urgency. Their problem rests in the very fact that there *is* a righteous remnant which is overwhelmed by undeserved evil. The prophets continually warned Israel of the penalty of faithlessness; the apocalyptists comfort the faithful who need no correction. Therefore there is very little ethical exhortation in most of the apocalyptic writings. Such books as The Testaments of the Twelve Patriarchs and Enoch 92–105, which have considerable ethical exhortation, are least apocalyptic in character.

The NT Apocalypse. The Revelation of John shares numerous traits with Jewish apocalypses but at other important points stands apart from them. Although the similarities are usually stressed, the differences will be here emphasized.

First, the author designates his book as a prophecy (1:3; 22:7, 10, 18–19). The apocalyptic writings lost a prophetic self-consciousness; indeed they were written to fill the void caused by the absence of prophecy. Primitive Christianity witnessed a revival of the prophetic movement when God once more spoke directly through men. The Apocalypse, together with other NT books, is the product of the revival of the prophetic spirit. The visions given John were the means of conveying the word of God (1:2).

Second, John is not pseudonymous. The author merely signs his name: "John to the seven churches that are in Asia" (1:4). He appeals to no ancient saint for authority but writes out of the authority residing in him from the Spirit of God.

Third, John differs from the apocalyptic treatment of the future. The latter retraces history under the guise of prophecy. John takes his stand in his own environment, addresses his own contemporaries, and looks prophetically into the future to depict the eschatological consummation.

Fourth, John embodies the prophetic tension between history and eschatology. The beast is Rome and at the same time an eschatological antichrist which cannot be fully equated with historical Rome. While the churches of Asia were facing persecution, there is no known persecution in the first century A.D. which fits that portrayed in the Apocalypse. The shadow of historical Rome is so outlined against the darker shadow of the eschatological antichrist that it is difficult if not impossible to distinguish between the two. History is eschatologically interpreted; evil at the hands of Rome is realized eschatology.

Fifth, John shares the optimism of the gospel rather than the pessimism of apocalyptic thought. While John prophesies that the satanic evil of the age will descend in concentrated fury upon God's people in the end time, he does not see an age abandoned to evil. On the contrary, history has become the scene of the divine redemption. Only the slain Lamb is able to open the book and bring history to its eschatological denouement. The redemption which will be apocalyptically consummated is rooted in the event of Golgotha. Furthermore, it is probable that the first seal (6:2) represents the victorious mission of a conquering gospel in a world which is also the scene of war, famine, death, and martyrdom. God has not abandoned the age nor forsaken his people. The saints conquer the beast even in martyrdom and praise him who is the King of the ages (15:2–3).

Finally, the Apocalypse possesses prophetic moral urgency. It does indeed promise a future salvation but not one which can be taken for granted. The seven letters strike a note of warning and a demand for repentance (2:5, 16, 21–22; 3:3, 19). The outpourings of the divine wrath are not merely punitive but embody a merciful purpose whose intent is to bring all people to repentance before it is too late (9:20; 16:9, 11). The Revelation draws to its close with an evangelical invitation (22:17). Thus the book as a whole has a great moral purpose: judgment will fall upon a lax sleeping church, and the door is held open for the wicked to turn to God.

In summary, there is a prophetic and a nonprophetic apocalypse, and the Apocalypse of the NT stands in the first type. G. E. LADD

See also ESCHATOLOGY.

Bibliography. H. H. Rowley, *The Relevance of Apocalyptic* and *Jewish Apocalyptic and the Dead Sea Scrolls; EB,* I, 213–50; *HDB,* I, 741–49; D. S. Russell, *The Method and Message of Jewish Apocalyptic;* J. Bloch, *On the Apocalyptic in Judaism;* F. C. Burkitt, *Jewish and Christian Apocalypses;* F. C. Porter, *The Message of the Apocalyptical Writers;* S. B. Frost, *OT Apocalyptic;* R. H. Charles, *Testaments of the Twelve Patriarchs* and *The Book of Enoch;* J. R. Harris, *The Odes* and *Psalms of Solomon.*

Apocrypha, New Testament. A substantial collection of works that were published under the names of apostolic writers during the second and subsequent centuries. For the most part they were deliberate fabrications and never had any serious claim to canonicity. Hence, in this connection the word "apocrypha" is used in its meaning of untrue or spurious.

Evidently the NT Apocrypha arose primarily for two reasons. First, some sought to satisfy the curiosity engendered by the failure of the canonical Gospels to describe Christ's early life or numerous aspects of his personage. Others tried to supply details concerning the apostles omitted from the Acts. Second, those with heretical tendencies made an effort to gain an acceptance for their views by embedding them in works attributed to Christ and the apostles. Especially did the Gnostics seek to advance their cause in this way.

Writers of NT apocryphal works attempted to produce literary forms parallel to those of NT books. Hence their efforts may be classified as gospels, acts, epistles, and apocalypses.

The popularity of the NT Apocrypha is evidenced by the number of these works still in existence in whole or in part and the wide distribution of their use. To be sure, leaders in the church saw to it that the Apocrypha never received official sanction; but in more ignorant communities they were sometimes used without suspicion in the church service, and their contents continued to make a widespread impact on the popular piety. This fact is demonstrated by a study of the reliefs on sarcophagi of western Europe during the Middle Ages, as well as of the mosaics and stained glass windows of churches and cathedrals, the art of illuminated manuscripts, and themes of the mystery plays. All these drew some inspiration from the NT Apocrypha.

Therefore, if one is to understand many aspects of medieval life, it is necessary to study the Apocrypha. Moreover, one will gain important insights into the nature of Christianity during the postapostolic period. Heretical tendencies and popular beliefs and superstitions are writ large in these works. One can discern the slippage of the teachings of grace and a corresponding rise of legalism, a growing veneration of Mary, and an increase of sacramentalism. Furthermore, a study of these apocryphal works will demonstrate the superiority of the NT books in both content and form and will heighten respect for the canon and the validity of the canonical process.

As noted above, NT apocryphal works parallel in form the NT books. Something is known about over fifty apocryphal gospels. A few of these have been preserved in their entirety, others in fragments, and only the names are known of yet others. In these generally the author concealed his own name and ascribed his work to an apostle or disciple. Those available in their entirety are the Protevangelium of James (brother of the Lord), Gospel of Pseudo-Matthew, Gospel of the Nativity of Mary, History of Joseph the Carpenter, Gospel of Thomas, Gospel of the Infancy, Gospel of Nicodemus, Gospel of Philip, Gospel of the Egyptians.

Numerous Acts of the Apostles were also composed. Among the better known is the collection called the Leucian Acts because they were collected by Leucius. Five in number, these fragmentary works include the Acts of Paul, John, Andrew, Peter, and Thomas.

Apocryphal epistles are not so numerous because it was harder to fabricate them to have any appearance of authenticity. Among the better known are the Epistle of the Apostles, which dealt with heretical tendencies; the Epistle to the Laodiceans (cf. Col. 4:16), excerpts from Paul's letters (especially Philippians); Third Corinthians; and the Correspondence of Paul and Seneca.

Apocalypses were modeled somewhat on the book of Revelation. The most famous are the Apocalypse of Peter (second century) and the Apocalypse of Paul (fourth century). Among other things, both have visions of heaven and hell with scenes of blessedness and lurid descriptions of punishment.

One of the most significant finds of NT apocryphal works occurred in 1946 at Nag Hammadi, about thirty miles north of Luxor in Egypt. This included thirty-seven complete and five fragmentary works, generally with a Gnostic bias. All in Coptic, they were translated from Greek originals.

H. F. Vos

See also Apocrypha, Old Testament; Gnosticism; Bible, Canon of.

Bibliography. E. J. Goodspeed, *Strange New Gospels;* A. Helmbold, *The Nag Hammadi Gnostic Texts and the Bible;* M. R. James, *The Apocryphal NT;* R. M. Wilson, ed., *NT Apocrypha,* 2 vols.; J. M. Robinson, *The Nag Hammadi Library.*

Apocrypha, Old Testament. The word "apocrypha" is from the Greek *ta apokrypha,* "the hidden things," although there is no strict sense in which these books are hidden. Some thirteen books comprise the Apocrypha: I and II Esdras, Tobit, Judith, the Rest of Esther, the Wisdom of Solomon, Ecclesiasticus (which is also entitled the Wisdom of Jesus the Son of Sirach), Baruch, the Letter of Jeremiah, the Additions to Daniel, the Prayer of Manasses, and I and II Maccabees. Both the status of these books and the use of the term "apocrypha" have been in confusion since the early days of the church. In the restricted sense the word denotes the above-named books in contradistinction to the Pseudepigrapha, or false writings; but in the broader sense the word refers to any extracanonical scripture. Sometimes the term takes on a disparaging meaning, especially when used of the "apocryphal" gospels; this is to say they are spurious or heterodoxical. A further difficulty attending the restricted use of the term is that some of the Apocrypha are pseudonymous, whereas some of the Pseudepigrapha are not pseudonymous. R. H. Charles broke the accepted order by including III Maccabees in the Apocrypha and transferring II Esdras to the Pseudepigrapha. The ancient rabbinic practice was to regard all such writings as "outside books," and this designation was continued by Cyril of Jerusalem, who used Apocrypha in the same sense, i.e., scriptures outside the canon. In modern times C. C. Torrey has revived this signification so that all such books, including the Pseudepigrapha, are called Apocrypha. Therefore to use the term Pseudepigrapha is a concession to an unhappy usage.

How did the Apocrypha secure a place in some of our English Bibles? The Jews uniformly denied canonical status to these books, and so they were not found in the Hebrew Bible; but the manuscripts of the LXX include them as an addendum to the canonical OT. In the second century A.D. the first Latin Bibles were translated from the Greek Bible, and so included the Apocrypha. Jerome's Vulgate distinguished between the *libri ecclesiastici* and the *libri canonici* with the result that the Apocrypha were accorded a secondary status. However, at the Council of Carthage (397), which Augustine attended, it was decided to accept the Apocrypha as suitable for reading despite Jerome's resistance to their inclusion in the Vulgate. In 1548 the Council of Trent recognized the Apocrypha, excepting I and II Esdras and the Prayer of Manasses, as having unqualified canonical status. Moreover, anyone who disputed this ecclesiastical decision was anathematized. The Reformers repudiated the Apocrypha as unworthy and contradictory to the doctrines of the uncontroverted canon; however, Luther did admit that they were "profitable and good to read." The Coverdale and Geneva Bibles included the Apocrypha but set them apart from the canonical books of the OT. After much debate the British and Foreign Bible Society decided in 1827 to exclude the Apocrypha from its Bibles; soon afterward the American branch concurred, and this action generally set the pattern for English Bibles thereafter. Among Protestant communions only the Anglican Church makes much use of the Apocrypha today.

Many literary genres appear in the Apocrypha: popular narrative, religious history and philosophy, morality stories, poetic and didactic lyrics, wisdom literature, and apocalyptic. Most of these books were written in Palestine between 300 B.C. and A.D. 100, and the language of composition was either Hebrew or Aramaic, and occasionally Greek. They generally reflect the Jewish religious viewpoint of late OT times with certain additions which were emphasized. Almsgiving became an expression of good works meritorious to salvation (see Tob. 12:9). The Apocrypha, and to a greater extent the Pseudepigrapha, evince an amplified doctrine of the Messiah beyond what the OT reveals. Two types of messianic expectation predominate: the heavenly Son of man, taken from Daniel and embellished by Enoch, and the earthly Davidic king described in the Psalms of Solomon. The doctrine of resurrection of the body, so seldom mentioned in the OT, is ubiquitous in the Apocrypha and shows an advance over the OT idea of Sheol. The hope for immortality was greatly influenced by Greek thought. Throughout the Apocrypha is a highly developed angelology which is a natural consequence of the impact of dualism upon Jewish religious thought after the Exile. The NT cites none of the books of the Apocrypha, although there are frequent parallels of thought and language, as in the case of Eph. 6:13–17 and Wisd. Sol. 5:17–20, and Heb. 11 and Ecclus. 44. But to admit these parallels is not necessarily to admit dependence by NT authors upon the Apocrypha, and even if a clear case of dependence can be made, it does not follow that the NT author regarded these books as authoritative.

D. H. WALLACE

See also APOCRYPHA, NEW TESTAMENT; BIBLE, CANON OF.

Bibliography. R. H. Charles, *Apocrypha and Pseudepigrapha of the OT,* I; B. M. Metzger, *An Introduction to the Apocrypha;* W. O. E. Oesterley, *The Books of the Apocrypha;* R. H. Pfeiffer, *A History of NT Times with an Introduction to the Apocrypha;* E. J. Goodspeed, *The Story of the Apocrypha;* C. C. Torrey, *The Apocryphal Literature;* H. M. Hughes, *The Ethics of Jewish Apocryphal Literature;* H. Wace, ed., *Apocrypha,* 2 vols; J. H. Charlesworth, ed., *The OT Pseudepigrapha, Apocalyptic Literature and Testaments.*

Apokatastasis. The noun *apokatastasis* is found in the NT only in Acts 3:21: "Jesus . . . must remain in heaven until the time comes for God to restore everything, as he promised long ago through his holy prophets." The verb *apokathistēmi* occurs eight times in the sense of "to restore" or "establish." In the LXX it translates the Hebrew *šûb,* "to bring back," "restore," used of Israel's return from exile (Jer. 16:15; 24:6) and its eschatological restoration (Ezek. 16:55).

Stoic thought, from the perspective of a cyclical view of history, envisaged a restoration of the universe to its original status of perfection. Peter in Acts 3:21, from a different point of view, asserted that at Christ's parousia there would occur the restoration of all that was proclaimed by the OT prophets—e.g., conversion of the Jews, gathering of the elect, righteous reign of the Messiah on earth, and creation of a new heaven and a new earth. The end-time restoration Christ would effect is affirmed by the verb in Acts 1:6 and by wider teaching in Rom. 8:18–25; I Cor. 15:24–28; and II Pet. 3:13.

The claim that the apokatastasis includes the salvation of all mankind (some would add the devil and fallen angels) was advanced by Origen, Gregory of Nyssa, John Scotus Erigena, F. Schleiermacher, F. D. Maurice, and others. Jerome, Augustine, and most evangelicals, while insisting on an eschatological restoration by Christ, deny the corollary assertion of the ultimate salvation of all men.

B. A. DEMAREST

See also UNIVERSALISM.

Bibliography. H.-G. Link, *NIDNTT,* III, 146–48; C. A. Beckwith, *SHERK,* I, 210–12.

Apollinarianism. A heresy of the fourth century bearing the name of its originator, Apollinaris (or Apollinarius) the Younger. Apollinaris was born sometime between 300 and 315 and died shortly before 392. He apparently lived out his entire lifetime in Laodicea, which is southwest of Antioch. He was a man of such unusual ability and gracious saintliness that even his staunchest opponents paid tribute to his sterling character. As a young man he became a reader in the church of Laodicea under Bishop Theodotus and *ca.* 332 was briefly excommunicated for attending a pagan function. In 346 he was excommunicated a second time by the Arian Bishop George. However, the Nicene congregation of Laodicea selected him bishop sometime around 361.

Evidence would suggest that Apollinaris put more time into teaching and writing in nearby Antioch than in ecclesiastical administration. As a revered teacher he was the friend of Athanasius, consultant by correspondence to Basil the Great, and numbered among his pupils Jerome in 373 or 374.

Apollinarianism seemed to have emerged gradually as an independent strand of Christianity as its opponents succeeded in getting it condemned. A synod at Alexandria in 362 condemned the teaching but not the teacher. Basil the Great moved Pope Damasus I to censure it *ca.* 376, and in 377 Apollinaris and Apollinarianism both were condemned by a Roman synod. The general Council of Constantinople in 381 anathematized Apollinaris and his doctrine. Emperor Theodosius I then issued a series of decrees against Apollinarianism in 383, 384, and 388. But the elderly heretic apparently continued serenely writing and teaching in Antioch and Laodicea, pursuing his scholar's passion for truth with a saint's serene confidence in his own rightness.

Apollinarianism had become a definite schism by 373, for when the Emperor Valens deported certain Egyptian bishops to Diocaesarea, Apollinaris approached them with greetings and an invitation to enter into communion. They in turn rejected his overtures. By 375 Vitalis, a disciple of Apollinaris, had founded a congregation in Antioch. Vitalis was consecrated bishop by Apollinaris, who also engineered his friend Timothy's election to the bishopric of Berytus. Apollinarians held at least one synod in 378, and there is evidence that there may have been a second Apollinarian synod subsequently. After Apollinaris's death his followers split into two parties, the Vitalians and the Polemeans or Sinusiati. By 420 the Vitalians had been reunited with the Greek Church. Somewhat later the Sinusiati merged into the monophysite schism.

Apollinarianism was the harbinger of the great Christological battles which pitted Antioch against Alexandria, with Rome as referee, and finally issued in Christendom's permanent monophysite schism after the Council of Chalcedon in 451.

Diodore of Tarsus, leader of the Antiochene school from *ca.* 378 to his death *ca.* 392, typified the Christology of that literalist school of Bible interpretation. To defend the immutability and eternity of the Logos he spoke of Christ as Son of God and Son of Mary by nature and grace respectively. Their union was a moral one. If this was not Christological dualism, it was perilously close.

In contrast the Alexandrian school approached Christology in a word-flesh manner. The Word or Logos assumed human flesh at the incarnation, and Alexandrians were apt to deny or ignore Christ's possession of a human soul or mind.

It was undoubtedly as a representative of Alexandrian thinking countering the trend in Antioch that Apollinaris began to teach and write Christology and to move toward his own extreme.

The central deviation of Apollinarianism from the later Chalcedonian orthodoxy began in a Platonic trichotomy. Man was seen to be body, sensitive soul, and rational soul. Apollinaris felt that if one failed to diminish the human nature of Jesus in some way, a dualism had to result. Furthermore, if one taught that Christ was a complete man, then Jesus had a human rational soul in which free will resided; and wherever there was free will, there was sin. Therefore it followed that the Logos assumed only a body and its closely connected sensitive soul. The Logos or Word himself took the place of the rational soul (or spirit or *nous*) in the manhood of Jesus. Thus one can speak of "the one sole nature incarnate of the Word of God." This doctrine was developed by Apollinaris in his *Demonstration of the Divine Incarnation,* which was written in 376 in response to the initial papal condemnation.

Apollinaris was a prolific writer, but following his anathematization in 381 his works were assiduously sought out and burned. Thus Apollinarianism leaves little literature except as cited in the works of its critics. The general principle on which Apollinarianism was condemned was the Eastern perception that "that which is not assumed is not healed." If the Logos did not assume the rational soul of the man Jesus, then the death of Christ could not heal or redeem the rational souls of men. And as the church wrestled with this perception it rejected Apollinarianism and moved toward the Chalcedonian Definition, which rebuked and corrected both Antioch and Alexandria in their extremes: "This selfsame one is perfect both in deity and also in humanness; this selfsame one is also actually God and actually man, with a rational soul and a body."

V. L. Walter

See also Chalcedon, Council of.

Bibliography. C. E. Raven, *Apollinarianism;* G. L. Prestige, *Fathers and Heretics;* B. Altaner, *Patrology;* P. A. Norris, *Manhood and Christ;* J. N. D. Kelly, *Early Christian Doctrines.*

Apollyon. *See* Abaddon.

Apologetics. The English word comes from a Greek root meaning "to defend, to make reply, to give an answer, to legally defend oneself." In NT times an *apologia* was a formal courtroom defense of something (II Tim. 4:16). As a subdivision of Christian theology apologetics is a systematic, argumentative discourse in defense of the divine origin and the authority of the Christian faith. Peter commanded Christians to be ready to give a reason for the hope they have (I Pet. 3:15).

Broadly defined, apologetics has always been a part of evangelism.

Christianity is a world view that asserts some very precise things—e.g., that the cosmos is not eternal and self-explanatory, that a Creator exists, that he chose a people and revealed himself to them and worked miracles among them, and that he incarnated himself in a particular Jew at a precise time in history. All of these claims need to be substantiated. This involves apologetics. The only way to get apologetics out of the faith is to drop its truth claims.

Throughout Christian history apologetics has adopted various styles. One could divide them into two broad classes: the subjective and the objective.

The Subjective School. This includes such great thinkers as Luther, Pascal, Lessing, Kierkegaard, Brunner, and Barth. They usually express doubt that the unbeliever can be "argued into belief." They stress instead the unique personal experience of grace, the inward, subjective encounter with God. Such thinkers seldom stand in awe of human wisdom, but on the contrary usually reject traditional philosophy and classical logic, stressing the transrational and the paradoxical. They have little use for natural theology and theistic proofs, primarily because they feel that sin has blinded the eyes of man so that his reason cannot function properly. In Luther's famous metaphor, reason is a whore.

Thinkers of the subjective school have a keen appreciation of the problem of verification. Lessing spoke for most of them when he pointed out that "accidental truths of history can never become the proof of necessary truths of reason." The problem of going from contingent (i.e., possibly false) facts of history to deep, inward, religious certainty has been called "Lessing's ditch."

Kierkegaard complained that historical truth is incommensurable with an eternal, passionate decision. The passage from history to religious certainty is a "leap" from one dimension to another kind of reality. He said that all apologetics has the intent of merely making Christianity plausible. But such proofs are vain because "to defend anything is always to discredit it."

Yet, for all his anti-intellectualism, Kierkegaard still had a kind of apologetic for Christianity, a defense developed strangely out of the very absurdity of the Christian affirmation. The very fact that some people have believed that God appeared on earth in the humble figure of a man is so astounding that it provides an occasion for others to share the faith. No other movement has ever suggested we base the eternal happiness of human beings on their relationship to an event occurring in history. Kierkegaard therefore feels that such an idea "did not arise in the heart of any man."

Even Pascal, who discounted the metaphysical proofs for God and preferred the "reasons of the heart," eventually came around with an interesting defense of the Christian faith. In his *Pensées* he recommended the biblical religion because it had a profound view of man's nature. Most religions and philosophies either ratify man's foolish pride or condemn him to despair. Only Christianity establishes man's true greatness with the doctrine of the image of God, while at the same time accounting for his present evil tendencies with the doctrine of the fall.

And we are told that, in spite of his energetic *Nein!* there is an apologetic slumbering beneath the millions of words in Karl Barth's *Church Dogmatics.*

The Objective School. This places the problem of verification clearly in the realm of objective fact. It emphasizes external realities—theistic proofs, miracles, prophecies, the Bible, and the person of Jesus Christ. However, a crucial distinction exists between two schools within the objectivist camp.

The Natural Theology School. Of all the groups this takes the most cheerful view of human reason. It includes such thinkers as Thomas Aquinas, Joseph Butler, F. R. Tennant, and William Paley. Behind all these thinkers is an empirical tradition in philosophy that can be traced back to Aristotle. Such thinkers believe in original sin, but they seldom question the basic competency of reason in philosophy. Perhaps reason was weakened by the fall but certainly not severely crippled.

Aquinas sought for a common ground between philosophy and religion by insisting that God's existence could be demonstrated by reason but was also revealed in the Scriptures. He employed three versions of the cosmological argument and the teleological argument in his proofs for God.

In his *Analogy of Religion* (1736), Butler used the basic Thomistic approach but toned it down a bit with his emphasis on probability, "the very guide of life." He thus developed an epistemology very close to the pragmatic attitude of the scientist. Butler argued that geometrical clarity has little place in the moral and religious spheres. If a person is offended by an emphasis on probability, let him simply reflect on the fact that most of life is based on it. Man seldom deals with absolute, demonstrative truths.

Apologists of this school often have a naïve, simplistic approach to the evidence for Christianity. They feel that a simple, straightforward presentation of the facts (miracles, prophecies) will suffice to persuade the unbeliever.

The Revelation School. This includes such giants of the faith as Augustine, Calvin, Abraham Kuyper, and E. J. Carnell. These thinkers usually admit that objective evidence (miracles, proofs of God, prophecies) is important in the apologetic task, but they insist that unregenerate man cannot be converted by mere exposure to proofs because sin has seriously weakened human reason. It will take a special act of the Holy Spirit to allow the evidence to be effective.

One should not conclude from this that the revelation school considers the external evidence worthless. On the contrary, the work of the Spirit presupposes the external Bible and the historical Jesus Christ. If faith is largely a creation of the Holy Spirit, it still remains true that you could not have the faith apart from the facts. In sum, the Holy Spirit is the *sufficient* cause of belief while the facts are a *necessary* cause of belief.

The revelation school, therefore, borrows valuable insights from both the subjective school and the natural theology school. From one they acquire a distrust of unregenerated reason, from the other a proper appreciation of the role of concrete facts in the Christian faith. As Luther said, "Prior to faith and a knowledge of God, reason is darkness, but in believers it is an excellent instrument. Just as all gifts and instruments of nature are evil in godless men, so they are good in believers."

Oddly, both objectivist schools tend to use the same body of evidence when they do apologetics; they just differ on how and when the proofs persuade the unbeliever. Through the centuries Christian apologists of the objectivist school have used a variety of material: (1) Theistic proofs—the ontological, cosmological, teleological, and moral arguments. (2) OT prophecies—predictions about the Jewish Messiah that are fulfilled in Christ, such as Isa. 9:6; Mic. 5:1–3; and Zech. 9:9–10. (3) Biblical miracles—signs of the power of God which occur in great clusters in the Scripture, the two biggest centering around the Exodus and the coming of Christ. (4) The person of Christ—the unparalleled personality and character of Christ, illustrated by his demonstrations of love and concern for all kinds of people, especially the outcasts. (5) The teachings of Christ—the unparalleled doctrines, the beautiful sayings and parables of Jesus. (6) The resurrection of Christ—the greatest miracle of all Scripture, the capstone for the entire building of apologetics. (7) The history of Christianity—the benign influence of the Christian faith on the human race.

A. J. HOOVER

See also GOD, ARGUMENTS FOR THE EXISTENCE OF; THEODICY; EVIL, PROBLEM OF.

Bibliography. F. F. Bruce, *The Apostolic Defense of the Gospel;* A. Dulles, *A History of Apologetics;* J. H. Newman, *Apologia pro Vita Sua;* W. Paley, *A View of the Evidences of Christianity;* B. Pascal, *Pensées;* B. Ramm, *Varieties of Christian Apologetics;* J. K. S. Reid, *Christian Apologetics;* A. R. Vidler, *Twentieth Century Defenders of the Faith;* O. Zöckler, *Geschichte der Apologie des Christentums.*

Apostasy. A deliberate repudiation and abandonment of the faith that one has professed (Heb. 3:12). Apostasy differs in degree from heresy. The heretic denies some aspect of the Christian faith but retains the name Christian. The transfer of membership from one denomination to another of the same faith is not apostasy. It is also possible for a person to deny the faith, as Peter did, then reaffirm it at a later time.

Isa. 1:2–4 and Jer. 2:1–9 offer illustrations typical of the numerous defections during the history of Israel. Both leaders and people jettisoned their faith for various forms of idolatry and immorality. Several examples are mentioned in the LXX also: Ahaz in II Chr. 29:19 and Manasseh in II Chr. 33:19.

Perhaps the most notorious NT example is Judas Iscariot. Others include Demas (II Cor. 4:10) and Hymenaeus and Alexander (I Tim. 1:20). Paul the apostle was accused of teaching Jews to abandon their Mosaic religion (Acts 21:21). John encountered this problem (I John 2:18–19). The apostles warned about the rise of apostasy in the church, culminating in the appearance of the man of sin (I Tim. 4:1–3; II Thess. 2:3). The NT offers frequent warnings against the danger of apostasy. There are also references to the consequences of falling away from the faith (Heb. 6:5–8; 10:26).

Ten periods of persecution intensified the problem for the early church. A public confession of guilt and repentance was required before the offenders could be pardoned. Emperor Julian (361–63), who renounced the Christian faith and made such a vigorous effort to reestablish paganism in the Roman Empire, became known as "the Apostate."

L. G. WHITLOCK, JR.

Apostle, Apostleship. The biblical use of "apostle" is almost entirely confined to the NT, where it occurs seventy-nine times: ten in the Gospels, twenty-eight in Acts, thirty-eight in the epistles, and three in the Apocalypse. Our English word is a transliteration of the Greek *apostolos,* which is derived from *apostellein,* to send. Whereas several words for *send* are used in the NT, expressing such ideas as dispatch, release, or dismiss, *apostellein* emphasizes the elements of commission—authority of and responsibility to the sender. So an apostle is properly one sent on a definite mission, in which he acts with full authority on behalf of the sender and is accountable to him.

The noun occurs only once in the LXX. When the wife of Jeroboam came to Ahijah seeking information about the health of her son, the prophet answered, "I am sent unto thee with heavy tidings" (I Kings 14:6). Here *apostolos* renders the Hebrew *šālûah*, which became a somewhat technical term in Judaism. A *šālûaḥ* could be one who led the synagogue congregation in worship and thus represented it, or a representative of the Sanhedrin sent on official business. The priesthood was included under this term also, and a few outstanding personalities of OT story who acted strikingly on God's behalf. But in no case did the *šālûaḥ* operate beyond the confines of the Jewish community. So there is no anticipation in the *šālûaḥ* of the missionary emphasis associated with the NT *apostolos.*

Christ as Apostle. In Heb. 3:1 Jesus is called "the apostle . . . of our confession," in conscious contrast to Moses, to whom Judaism ascribed the term *šālûaḥ*. Jesus spoke more directly from God than Moses was able to do. Repeatedly he made the claim of being sent by the Father. When he declared that he was sending his chosen disciples into the world even as the Father had sent him, our Lord was bestowing on apostleship its highest dignity (John 17:18).

The Twelve as Apostles. These men are most often called disciples in the Gospels, for their primary function during Christ's ministry was to be with him and learn of him. But they are also called apostles because Jesus imparted to them his authority to preach and to cast out demons (Mark 3:14–15; 6:30). Just because this activity was limited while Jesus was with them, the term "apostle" is rarely used. After Pentecost this situation was changed.

The number twelve recalls the twelve tribes of Israel, but the basis of leadership is no longer tribal, but personal and spiritual. Evidently the college of apostles was regarded as fixed in number, for Jesus spoke of twelve thrones in the coming age (Matt. 19:28; cf. Rev. 21:14). Judas was replaced by Matthias (Acts 1), but after that no effort was made to select men to succeed those who were taken by death (Acts 12:2).

Apostles receive first mention in the lists of spiritual gifts (I Cor. 12:28; Eph. 4:11). Since these gifts are bestowed by the risen Christ through the Spirit, it is probable that at the beginning of the apostolic age these men who had been appointed by Jesus and trained by him were now regarded as possessing a second investiture to mark the new and permanent phase of their work for which the earlier phase had been a preparation. They became the foundation of the church in a sense secondary only to that of Christ himself (Eph. 2:20).

The duties of the apostles were preaching, teaching, and administration. Their preaching rested on their association with Christ and the instruction received from him, and it included their witness to his resurrection (Acts 1:22). Their converts passed immediately under their instruction (Acts 2:42), which presumably consisted largely of their recollection of the teaching of Jesus, augmented by revelations of the Spirit (Eph. 3:5). In the area of administration their functions were varied. Broadly speaking, they were responsible for the life and welfare of the Christian community. Undoubtedly they took the lead in worship as the death of Christ was memorialized in the Lord's Supper. They administered the common fund to which believers contributed for the help of needy brethren (Acts 4:37), until this task became burdensome and was shifted to men specially chosen for this responsibility (Acts 6:1–6). Discipline was in their hands (Acts 5:1–11). As the church grew and spread abroad, the apostles devoted more and more attention to the oversight of these scattered groups of believers (Acts 8:14; 9:32). At times the gift of the Holy Spirit was mediated through them (Acts 8:15–17). The supernatural powers which they had exercised when the Lord was among them, such as the exorcism of demons and the healing of the sick, continued to be tokens of their divine authority (Acts 5:12; II Cor. 12:12). They took the lead in the determination of vexing problems which faced the church, associating the elders with themselves as an expression of democratic procedure (Acts 15:6; cf. 6:3).

Paul as Apostle. The distinctive features of Paul's apostleship were direct appointment by Christ (Gal. 1:1) and the allocation of the Gentile world to him as his sphere of labor (Rom. 1:5; Gal. 1:16; 2:8). His apostleship was recognized by the Jerusalem authorities in accordance with his own claim to rank with the original apostles. However, he never asserted membership in the Twelve (I Cor. 15:11), but rather stood on an independent basis. He was able to bear witness to the resurrection because his call came from the risen Christ (I Cor. 9:1; Acts 26:16–18). Paul looked on his apostleship as a demonstration of divine grace and as a call to sacrificial labor rather than an occasion for glorying in the office (I Cor. 15:10).

Other Apostles. The most natural explanation of Gal. 1:19 is that Paul is declaring James, the Lord's brother, to be an apostle, agreeable to the recognition James received in the Jerusalem church. In line with this, in I Cor. 15:5–8, where James is mentioned, all the other individuals are apostles. Barnabas (along with Paul) is called an apostle (Acts 14:4, 14), but probably in a restricted sense only, as one sent forth by the Antioch church, to which he was obligated to report when his mission was completed (14:27). He was not regarded as an apostle at Jerusalem (Acts 9:27), though later on he was given the right hand of fellowship as well as Paul (Gal. 2:9). Andronicus and Junias are said to be of note among the apostles (Rom. 16:7). Silvanus and Timothy seem to be included as apostles in Paul's statement in I Thess. 2:6. The references in I Cor. 9:5 and 15:7 do not necessarily go beyond the Twelve.

It is reasonably clear that in addition to the Twelve, Paul and James had the leading recognition as apostles. Others also might be so indicated under special circumstances. But warrant is lacking for making "apostle" the equivalent of "missionary." In the practice of the modern church, prominent pioneer missionaries are often called apostles, but this is only an accommodation of language. In the apostolic age one who held this rank was more than a preacher (II Tim. 1:11). All disciples were supposed to be preachers, but not all were apostles (I Cor. 12:29). Curiously, at one point in the church's life all were busy preaching except the apostles (Acts 8:4). Paul would not have needed to defend his apostleship with such vehemence if he were only defending his right to proclaim the gospel. Alongside the distinctive and more technical use of the word is the occasional employment of it in the sense of messenger (Phil. 2:25; II Cor. 8:23).

E. F. HARRISON

See also APOSTOLIC SUCCESSION; CHURCH, AUTHORITY IN.

Bibliography. A. Fridrichsen, *The Apostle and His Message;* F. J. A. Hort, *The Christian Ecclesia;* K. Lake in *The Beginnings of Christianity,* V, 37–59; J. B. Lightfoot, *St. Paul's Epistle to the Galatians;* T. W. Manson, *The Church's Ministry;* C. K. Barrett, *The Signs of an Apostle;* W. Schmithals, *The Office of Apostle in the Early Church;* K. E. Kirk, ed., *The Apostolic Ministry;* E. Schweizer, *Church Order in the NT;* J. Roloff, *Apostalat—Verkündigung—Kirche;* G. Klein, *Die Zwölf Apostel, Ursprung und Gehalt einer Idee;* K. H. Rengstorf, *TDNT,* I, 398ff.; J. A. Kirk, "Apostleship Since Rengstorf," *NTS* 21:249ff.; D. Müller and C. Brown, *NIDNTT,* I, 126ff.

Apostles' Creed. For hundreds of years Christians believed that the twelve apostles were the authors of the widely known creed that bears their name. According to an ancient theory, the twelve composed the creed with each apostle adding a clause to form the whole. Today practically all scholars understand this theory of apostolic composition to be legendary. Nevertheless, many continue to think of the creed as apostolic in nature because its basic teachings are agreeable to the theological formulations of the apostolic age.

The full form in which the creed now appears stems from about A.D. 700. However, segments of it are found in Christian writings dating as early as the second century. The most important predecessor of the Apostles' Creed was the Old Roman Creed, which was probably developed during the second half of the second century. The additions to the Apostles' Creed are clearly seen when its present form is compared to the Old Roman version:

> I believe in God the Father Almighty. And in Jesus Christ his only Son our Lord, who was born of the Holy Spirit and the Virgin Mary; crucified under Pontius Pilate and buried; the third day he rose from the dead; he ascended into heaven, and sits at the right hand of the Father, from thence he shall come to judge the quick and the dead. And in the Holy Spirit; the holy Church; the forgiveness of sins; the resurrection of the flesh.

Still earlier fragments of creeds have been discovered which declare simply: "I believe in God the Father Almighty, and in Jesus Christ his only Son, our Lord. And in the Holy Spirit, the holy Church, the resurrection of the flesh."

The Apostles' Creed functioned in many ways in the life of the church. For one thing, it was associated with entrance into the fellowship as a confession of faith for those to be baptized. In addition, catechetical instruction was often based on the major tenets of the creed. In time, a third use developed when the creed became a "rule of faith" to give continuity to Christian teachings from place to place and to clearly separate the true faith from heretical deviations. Indeed, it may well have been that the main factor involved in adding clauses to the Old Roman Creed to develop the Apostles' Creed was its usefulness in these varied ways in the life of the church. By the sixth or seventh century the creed had come to be accepted as a part of the official liturgy of the Western church. Likewise, it was used by devout individuals along with the Lord's Prayer as a part of their morning and evening devotions. The churches of the Reformation gladly gave their allegiance to the creed and added it to their doctrinal collections and used it in their worship.

The Trinitarian nature of the Apostles' Creed is immediately evident. Belief in "God the Father Almighty, Maker of heaven and earth" is affirmed first. But the heart of the creed is the confession concerning "Jesus Christ, his only Son, our Lord," with special attention given to the events surrounding his conception, birth, suffering, crucifixion, resurrection, ascension, exaltation, and coming judgment. The third section declares belief in the Holy Spirit. To this Trinitarian confession are added clauses related to the holy catholic church, communion of saints, forgiveness of sins, resurrection of the body, and life everlasting.

The polemical nature of the Apostles' Creed is likewise evident. Emphasizing the unity of God's fatherhood and sovereignty disputed Marcion's rejection of the same. The affirmation of the reality of Christ's humanity and historicity denied the contention of Marcionite and docetic heretics that he was not a fully human person who could be born, suffer, and die. His conception by the Holy Spirit and birth of the Virgin Mary as well as his exaltation after resurrection affirmed Jesus' deity over against those who denied it. Other clauses may well have been added to deal with particular crises faced by the church. For example, the confession regarding forgiveness of sins may have related to the problem of post-baptismal sins in the third century. Likewise, affirming the holy catholic church may have dealt with the Donatist schism.

The Apostles' Creed continues to be used today much as it was in the past: as a baptismal confession; as a teaching outline; as a guard and guide against heresy; as a summarization of the faith; as an affirmation in worship. It has maintained in modern times its distinction as the most widely accepted and used creed among Christians.

O. G. Oliver, Jr.

See also Creed, Creeds.

Bibliography. J. N. D. Kelly, *Early Christian Creeds;* W. Barclay, *The Apostles' Creed for Everyman;* S. Barr, *From the Apostles' Faith to the Apostles' Creed;* P. Fuhrmann, *The Great Creeds of the Church;* W. Pannenberg, *The Apostles' Creed in the Light of Today's Questions;* J. Smart, *The Creed in Christian Teaching;* H. B. Swete, *The Apostles' Creed;* H. Thielicke, *I Believe: The Christian's Creed;* B. F. Westcott, *The Historic Faith.*

Apostleship, Gift of. *See* Spiritual Gifts.

Apostolic Succession. This theory of ministry in the church did not arise before A.D. 170–200. The Gnostics claimed to possess a secret tradition handed down to them from the apostles. As a counterclaim the Catholic church pointed to each bishop as a true successor to the apostle who had founded the see and therefore to the truth the apostles taught. The bishop, as an authoritative teacher, preserved the apostolic tradition. He was also a guardian of the apostolic Scriptures and the creed. In a generation when the last links with the apostles were fast dying out this emphasis on apostolic teaching and practice was natural. In the third century the emphasis changed from the open succession of teachers to the bishops as the personal successors of the apostles. This development owed much to the advocacy of Cyprian, Bishop of Carthage (248–58). Harnack regards this as a perversion rather than a development.

The terminology is not found in the NT. *Diadochē* ("succession") is absent from the NT and the LXX. There is little evidence for the idea in the NT (cf. II Tim. 2:2). All early succession lists were compiled late in the second century.

There is also a difference between the Roman- and Anglo-Catholic viewpoint. The former is a centralized autocracy with a papal succession traced back to Peter. The Tractarian teaches that all bishops alike, however insignificant the see, have equal power in a corporation. Thus an apostle transmitted to a bishop, through "the laying on of hands" and prayer, the authority which Christ had conferred on him. This theory of sacramental grace is a barrier to reunion in the Reformed churches, since the nonepiscopal bodies are regarded as defective in their ministry.

The weakness of the argument of *The Apostolic Ministry* (ed. K. E. Kirk) was its failure to explain the absence of the idea in the first two centuries of the Christian era. Ehrhardt does not supply the defect by postulating a priestly succession derived from the Judaizing church of Jerusalem as it laid stress on the new Israel and the continuity of its priesthood. The idea was in the air in the second century.

Bishop Drury affirms that the apostles left behind them three things: their writings; the churches which they founded, instructed, and regulated; and the various orders of ministers for the ordering of these churches. There could be no more apostles in the original sense of that word. The real successor to the apostolate is the NT itself, since it continues their ministry within the church of God. Their office was incommunicable. Three kinds of succession are possible: *ecclesiastical*—a church which has continued from the beginning; *doctrinal*—the same teaching has continued throughout; *episcopal*—a line of bishops can be traced unbroken from early times. This does not necessarily mean that the episcopal office is the same as the apostolic.

R. E. Higginson

See also Church, Authority in.

Bibliography. A. Erhardt, *The Apostolic Succession in the First Two Centuries of the Church;* C. H. Turner, "Apostolic Succession," in *Essays on the Early History of the Church,* ed. H. B. Swete; C. Gore, *The Ministry of the Christian Church;* H. Bettenson, *Documents of the Christian Church.*

Aquinas, Thomas. *See* Thomas Aquinas.

Archangel. *See* Angel.

Archbishop. *See* Bishop; Church Officers.

Archdeacon. *See* Deacon, Deaconess; Church Officers.

Archpriest. *See* Church Officers.

Arianism. The birth date for Arius, the North African priest who gave his name to one of Christianity's most troublesome schisms, is uncertain. He seems to have been born in Libya. He was in all probability a pupil of Lucien of Antioch. During the bishopric of Peter of Alexandria (300–311) Arius was made a deacon in that city and began the stormy pastoral career which is known to history. He was in rapid succession excommunicated for his association with the Melitians, restored by Achillas, Bishop of Alexandria (311–12), and given priestly orders and the church of Baucalis. Sometime between 318 and 323 Arius came into conflict with Bishop Alexander over the nature of Christ. In a confusing series of synods a truce was attempted between adherents of Alexander and followers of Arius; in March of 324 Alexander convened a provincial synod which acknowledged the truce but anathematized Arius. Arius responded with his publication of *Thalia* (which exists only as it is quoted in refutation by Athanasius) and by repudiating the truce. In February, 325, Arius was then condemned at a synod in Antioch. The Emperor Constantine was intervening by this time, and it was he who called the first ecumenical council, the Council of Nicaea. This council met on May 20, 325, and subsequently condemned Arius and his teaching. Present in the entourage of Alexander at this council was Athanasius. He took little part in the affairs of the Council of Nicaea, but when he became Bishop of Alexandria in 328, he was to become the unremitting foe of Arius and Arianism and the unflagging champion of the Nicene formula.

Following his condemnation Arius was banished to Illyricum. There he continued to write, teach, and appeal to an ever broadening circle of political and ecclesiastical adherents of Arianism. Around 332 or 333 Constantine opened direct contact with Arius, and in 335 the two met at Nicomedia. There Arius presented a confession which Constantine considered sufficiently orthodox to allow for the reconsideration of Arius's case. Therefore, following the dedication of the Church of the Resurrection in Jerusalem the Synod of Jerusalem declared for the readmittance of Arius to communion even as he lay dying in Constantinople. Since Arian views were being advanced by many active bishops and members of the court, and Arius himself had ceased to play a vital role in the controversy, his death in 335 or 336 did nothing to diminish the furor in the church. Instead of resolving the issues, the Council of Nicaea had launched an empire-wide Christological debate by its condemnation of Arius.

Arius was a thoroughgoing Greek rationalist. He inherited the almost universally held Logos Christology of the East. He labored in Alexandria, the center for Origenist teachings on the subordination of the Son to the Father. He blended this heritage into a rationalist Christology that lost the balance Origen had maintained in his subordinationist theology by his insistence on the eternal generation of the Son.

The guard against the error of Arius and the Arianism erected by the symbol and anathemas adopted by the Council of Nicaea serve as an outline of Arius's fundamental position.

Nicaea's "in one Lord Jesus Christ the Son of God, begotten of the Father, only-begotten, that is from the substance of the Father" was to offset Arius's central assertion that God was immutable, unique, unknowable, only one. Therefore Arians felt no substance of God could in any way be communicated or shared with any other being. The council's "true God from true God, begotten not made" set aside Arius's contention that, since God was immutable and unknowable, Christ had to be a created being, made out of nothing by God, first in the created order certainly, but of it. This limited the concept of the preexistence of Christ even while adapting the dominant Logos Christology to Arianism. The Logos, first born, created of God, was incarnate in the Christ but, asserted Arius, "there was when he was not."

Nicaea's "of one substance with the Father" made the Greek term *homoousios* the catchword of the orthodox. Arianism developed two parties, one of which felt Christ was of a substance like the Father (*homoiousios*). A more extreme wing insisted that as a created being Christ was unlike the Father in substance (*anomoios*). Arius himself would have belonged to the first or more moderate party.

The council's anathemas were extended to all

those who claimed "there was once when he was not"; "before his generation he was not"; "he was made out of nothing"; "the Son of God is of another subsistence or substance"; and "the Son of God [is] created or alterable or mutable." The last anathema attacked another Arian teaching. Arius and subsequent Arians had taught that Christ grew, changed, matured in his understanding of the divine plan according to the Scriptures, and therefore could not be part of the unchanging God. He was not God the Son; rather, He was simply given the title Son of God as an honor.

An observer in that day might well have thought Arianism was going to triumph in the church. Beginning with Constantius the court was often Arian. Five times Athanasius of Alexandria was driven into exile, interrupting his long episcopate. A series of synods repudiated the Nicene symbol in various ways—Antioch in 341, Arles in 353; and in 355 Liberius of Rome and Ossius of Cordoba were exiled and a year later Hilary of Poitier was sent to Phrygia. In 360 in Constantinople all earlier creeds were disavowed and the term substance (*ousia*) was outlawed. The Son was simply declared to be "like the Father who begot him."

The orthodox counterattack on Arianism pointed out that the Arian theology reduced Christ to a demigod and in effect reintroduced polytheism into Christianity, since Christ was worshiped among Arians as among the orthodox. But in the long run the most telling argument against Arianism was Athanasius's constant soteriological battle cry that only God, very God, truly God Incarnate could reconcile and redeem fallen man to holy God. It was the thorough work of the Cappadocian Fathers—Basil the Great, Gregory of Nyssa, Gregory of Nazianzus—which brought the final resolution that proved theologically acceptable to the church. They divided the concept of substance (*ousia*) from the concept of person (*hypostasis*) and thus allowed the orthodox defenders of the original Nicene formula and the later moderate or semi-Arian party to unite in an understanding of God as one substance and three persons. Christ therefore was of one substance with the Father (*homoousion*) but a distinct person. With this understanding the Council of Constantinople in 381 was able to reaffirm the Nicene Creed. The able Emperor Theodosius I threw himself on the side of orthodoxy and Arianism began to wane in the empire.

The long struggle with Arianism was not over yet, however, for Ulfilas, famous missionary to the Germanic tribes, had accepted the Homoean statement of Constantinople of 360. Ulfilas taught the similarity of the Son to the Father and the total subordination of the Holy Spirit. He taught the Visigoths north of the Danube, and they in turn carried this semi-Arianism back into Italy. The Vandals were taught by Visigoth priests and in 409 carried the same semi-Arianism across the Pyrenees into Spain. It was not until the end of the seventh century that orthodoxy was to finally absorb Arianism. Yet Arianism has been reborn in the modern era in the form of extreme Unitarianism, and the Jehovah's Witnesses regard Arius as a forerunner of C. T. Russell.

V. L. Walter

See also Nicaea, Council of; Athanasius.

Bibliography. J. Daniélou and H. Marrou, *The Christian Centuries*, I, chs. 18–19; J. H. Newman, *The Arians of the Fourth Century;* R. C. Gregg and D. E. Groh, *Early Arianism;* T. A. Kopecek, *A History of Neo-Arianism*, 2 vols.; H. M. Gwatkin, *Studies in Arianism;* E. Boularand, *l'Hérésie d'Arius et la foi de Nicée*, 2 vols.

Aristotle, Aristotelianism. The Greek philosopher Aristotle (384–322 B.C.) was the son of the court physician to the king of Macedon. At the age of seventeen he went to Plato's Academy in Athens, where he remained for twenty years (367–347) as a student and then a teacher. After the death of Plato he spent the next twelve years away from Athens, serving for three of these years as the tutor to the son of Philip II of Macedon, Alexander the Great. In 335 he returned to Athens to open a new school called the Lyceum, where he taught for the next twelve years. Upon the death of Alexander anti-Macedonian feelings threatened the school, forcing Aristotle to flee to Euboea, where soon afterward he died.

The majority of Aristotle's writings, which have survived substantially intact, consist of unpublished treatises that either served as his lecture notes or were used as texts by his students. He did do some writing in dialogue form, but only fragments quoted by later writers have survived. Among his major works are *Ethics; Physics; Metaphysics;* his works on logic called the *Organon;* a variety of treatises on natural science—e.g., *On the Heavens, On the Soul, On the Parts of Animals; Politics; Rhetoric;* and *Poetics.*

Traditionally Aristotle's writings have been regarded as expressing a finished philosophical system. However, in this century there have been attempts to find development within Aristotle's thought. Much of the early work on this issue was influenced by Werner Jaeger's division of his life into three periods. In the first period (to 347) he was taken to be a loyal Platonist, presenting material in dialogue form. He espoused Plato's view of the soul and the forms. The second period (347–335) was one of increasing unhappiness with Platonism. Aristotle became critical in particular of the doctrine of forms. In the final period he became a defender of empiricism, finally rejecting all the essential features of Platonic speculative metaphysics. More recent assessments of his philosophy, however, have reversed the direction of the development of his thought. Aristotle's earliest writings, it is held, reflect a hostility to Plato's philosophy. As he matured, there is the evolution of more sophisticated views, which, while not Plato's, are closer (in spirit) to Plato's.

Classification of the Writings. The subject matter of Aristotle's writings may be divided into four major groups: (1) The logical treatises, commonly called the *Organon.* Included in these writings are *Categories, De interpretatione, Prior Analytics, Posterior Analytics,* and *Topics.* (2) Writings on natural philosophy and science. The most significant of these works are *On Coming into Being and Passing Away, De caelo, Physics, De historia animalium, De partibus animalium, De generatione animalium,* and the *De anima* on human nature. (3) A collection of works known as the *Metaphysics.* (4) Works on ethics and politics. The most important of these are *Eudemian Ethics, Nicomachean Ethics, Politics, Rhetoric,* and the fragmentary *Politics.*

Logic. Aristotle does not speak of logic as a definite part of philosophy; rather, he sees it as a methodological tool involved in all science and philosophy. While the term "tool" (*organon*) is not Aristotle's, it is nevertheless true to his understanding. His logic may be divided into three parts: (1) basic modes of being that are apprehended by single concepts and definitions (*Categories*); (2) the union and separation of these modes of being as expressed by judgments (*De interpretatione*); and (3) the way the mind passes from reasoning about known truth to unknown (*Prior* and *Posterior Analytics*).

Aristotle lists the modes of being and kinds of concepts as ten in number: substance (man or horse); quantity (ten feet long); quality (green); relation (less than); place (Athens); date (400 B.C.); situation or position (sitting); state or having (sober); action (cutting); and passion (being cut). In some lists (e.g., *Posterior Analytics*) situation and state are omitted. Extramental entities exist as substances, qualities, relations, and so on. The basic concepts grasp these modes of being.

Truth and falsity relate to propositions and judgments, not isolated concepts. Propositions combine or separate two categorical concepts. If these concepts are, for example, combined in both the proposition and reality, then the proposition is true. If not, then it is false.

All science is universal and is known inductively from sense experience of individual substances and their properties. Certain subjects and predicates gained by induction are seen by the mind to be necessarily connected. These form the premises of science in the strict sense, making its foundations self-evident and without need of proof. Further, knowledge can be deduced by syllogistic reasoning. This process is described in *Prior Analytics* and requires the discovery of a middle term for its execution.

Natural Philosophy. Nature, for Aristotle, is characterized by change. Therefore, natural philosophy is fundamentally an analysis of the process of change. Change is always discontinuous. There is always an initial privation which is acquired in the final form. However, change is also continuous. Something does not come out of nothing. Thus, there must be a substratum, matter, which endures all change. Aristotle identifies four types of change. The most fundamental is the emergence of a new substance from some preceding substance or substances. Once in existence, any substance may be subject to the other three kinds of change: quality, quantity, and place.

All change may be explained in terms of four causes. There is the material cause, or matter from which the thing has evolved, as well as the formal cause, which gives it shape or structure. The efficient cause imposes the form on the matter, while the final cause is the end to which that substance emerges and which requires the efficient cause to act in a determinate way.

Change also has an important relationship to potentiality. It involves the actualization of the potential. Since there is movement from potentiality to actuality, there must be an external efficient cause that accounts for an object's origin and continued existence. Aristotle held that such an efficient cause was needed for the physical universe as a whole. Therefore, there must be a first, unmoved mover, who is not subject to change. Because there is regularity throughout nature, it may be concluded that this first cause is intelligent.

Aristotle thought that the earth was at the center of the physical universe. It was surrounded by a number of revolving spheres, which explained the movement of the planets. The outermost sphere has the stars and is moved by an aspiration of the unmoved cause.

There are different kinds of material substance. Most basic are the elements and their combinations that make up the realm of nonliving substances. These are moved only by external causes. Among the living substances there are many organisms. There are plants which have differentiated parts and act on one another. They are reproduced and grown of themselves. Animals also have vegetative functions of plants but possess sense organs which make interaction with the environment possible. Through these organs they meet needs and escape danger.

The highest earthly being is man. Aristotle gives a whole treatise, *De anima*, to the study of human nature. Man is a material substance and thus is part of nature. This means that, like other natural entities, man is composed of an underlying matter from which the human body has emerged and a soul which gives form or structure to the body. Both body and soul are essential to man.

The human soul is made of three united parts. There is the vegetative part, which allows the human to nourish himself, grow, and reproduce. The animal part makes him able to sense and desire objects, as well as move from place to place. The third part is distinctively human; it is the rational part. Through it man is able to perform the distinctively human functions.

Metaphysics. The most fundamental reality is being itself. All categories are restricted kinds of being. Metaphysics is the study of being *qua* being. Everything, whether it changes or is unchanging, whether it is quantitative or nonquantitative, falls within the subject matter of metaphysics. From this perspective the most basic structure of the world is understood. Unlike Plato, who held that the ultimate causes of all things were found in the forms which existed apart from the natural world, Aristotle held that formal structures are to be found in the individual things they determine.

The foundation of reality is not an abstract essence but an individual substance (e.g., this boat or this man). Individual substances are a combination of matter and form. The matter is like a substratum, while the form determines and actualizes the matter. Form makes an entity a certain kind. Other categories such as place, time, action, quantity, quality, and relation inhere in substance as accidents. As such, they cannot exist without substances.

God, or the first mover, is the first cause of all finite existence. He is total actuality and lacks all potentiality, otherwise there would be the need for something prior to himself to actualize him. The actualization of something potential involves change. Since God is only actuality, he must be changeless, eternal, and immaterial because matter is a form of potency. Being immaterial, he is a mind, not dependent on external objects for reflection but contemplating his own perfect being.

Practical Philosophy. Theoretical philosophy and science seek truth for its own sake. On the other hand, practical philosophy desires truth to guide human action. Action is of three kinds: transitive action, which is directed outside the agent to some external entity; immanent action, whereby a human being tries to perfect himself; and immanent actions of human beings who cooperate to perfect themselves in a human community.

The proper guide to action is individual ethics. Aristotle's earlier treatment of this topic is found in the *Eudemian Ethics,* and his more mature reflection is recorded in the *Nicomachean Ethics.*

Man has a complex nature, which like other substances tries to complete or perfect itself. However, unlike other substances, this nature does not include a set of fixed tendencies that automatically attain the aforementioned goal. Man does have reason, which makes possible the apprehension of the ultimate end and guides him to it. The various human appetites must be ruled by reason.

The goal toward which all men strive with more or less clarity is happiness or well-being. Happiness is the operation of all parts of human nature under reason for an entire life. Some material things will be needed as instruments of action. More important, this life will require that all tendencies respond to and act under the influence of reason. To bring these tendencies under reason requires the learning of basic moral virtues. These virtues are the rational habits to act in a certain way. At first the habit comes from without. Parents may punish and reward behavior, but moral virtue has not really been learned until the habit is internalized and the act done for its own sake.

Moral virtue is related to the golden mean. Every virtue is the mean between two extremes. For instance, courage is the mean between cowardice on the one hand and foolhardiness on the other. This mean is not a mathematical or quantative average but an intellectual mean. With our passions guided and controlled by reason and good fortune, a happy life may be lived. However, the intellectual virtues, since they are most distinctly human, are the crowning pleasures of a happy life. Contemplation and prayer are the most fundamental intellectual virtues because they underlie the rest. They demand less physical aid and may be enjoyed without the help of others.

Aristotle also thinks that man is a political animal in need of community to attain to his highest perfection. Community is needed because there the common good takes precedence over individual good, which is only a part of it.

The proper goal of politics is happiness and virtue for all citizens.

Aristotelianism. This may be divided into two branches. First, there is the Greek European branch, which grew out of Aristotle's disciple Theophrastus. He took over the Lyceum upon Aristotle's death, elaborating on a number of his teacher's doctrines. It was not long before Aristotelian logic was used and absorbed by such groups as the Stoics and Skeptics. In the first century B.C. the Aristotelian corpus was collected and edited by a group of scholars headed by Andronicus of Rhodes.

Plotinus (A.D. 204–70), the father of Neoplatonism, took what he needed from Aristotle and rejected the rest. He accepted the doctrine of the separate intellect but attacked the ten categories. Porphyry of Tyre (234–*ca.* 305), a follower of Plotinus, wrote an introduction (*Isagoge*) to five concepts: species, genus, differentia, property, and accident. The *Isagoge* became a part of the *Organon* and was the inspiration for the medieval doctrine of the five voices. The importance and popularity of this work was assured by Boethius, who wrote a commentary on it.

During the early Middle Ages, Aristotle's logical works received the greatest attention. Contrasts between substance and accident, matter and form, became important theological distinctions. In the thirteenth century the influence of Aristotle was increased enormously with the translation of his works into Latin from Arabic. Equally important was the availability of Arabic commentaries by major Islamic philosophers. For example, the work of Averroes (1126–98) was more honored in the West than in his homeland. His influence was most directly felt in the work of Albertus Magnus and Thomas Aquinas. Albertus Magnus first came in contact with Averroes' commentaries on Aristotle at the University of Paris. However, it was Albertus's pupil, Thomas Aquinas, who produced a synthesis of Christian thought and Aristotelianism. But Aristotelianism got a bad name through Averroes, who advocated the eternality of the universe, leading the church to condemn the work of Aristotle and Averroes in 1277.

With the canonization of Aquinas and the study of his works Aristotelianism regained favor. The influence of Aristotle can be seen in the scholastic theologians Duns Scotus and William of Ockham. During the Renaissance the emphasis on humanism and classical languages led to the scholarly revival of interest in Plato and Aristotle.

The sixteenth through the eighteenth centuries saw another reaction in the West against Aristotelianism. The response was at least partly the result of the astronomical views of such thinkers as Copernicus (1473–1543), whose views were in conflict with many of those of Aristotle. The Catholic Church, however, put its seal of approval on Aquinas's work with Pope Leo XIII's encyclical *Aeterni Patris* in 1879.

Aristotelianism developed a second branch, called the Arabic Middle branch, which contrasted sharply with the Greek European. In the West, Aristotelianism emerged through the grid of medieval scholasticism, while in the East the formulation of Aristotelian philosophy took a form that very likely would have been rejected by Aristotle. Islamic philosophers read Aristotle through Neoplatonic spectacles, leading to a rather cavalier treatment of his doctrines.

Aristotle's influence in the East reached its zenith in the writings of Avicenna (980–1037) and Averroes. Avicenna was Islam's great Neoplatonist. He wrote works dealing with metaphysics, logic, and the natural sciences. Averroes was a Spanish Muslim who wrote commentaries on Aristotle's works. P. D. FEINBERG

See also NEOPLATONISM; ALBERTUS MAGNUS; THOMAS AQUINAS; AVERROES; DUNS SCOTUS, JOHN; WILLIAM OF OCKHAM.

Bibliography. W. D. Ross, ed., *The Works of Aristotle Translated into English,* 12 vols.; F. Copleston, *Medieval Philosophy;* É. Gilson, *History of Christian Philosophy in the Middle Ages;* F. van Steenberghen, *Latin Aristotelianism* and *The Philosophical Movement in the 13th Century.*

Arius. *See* ARIANISM.

Ark of the Covenant. A rectangular boxlike structure of acacia wood, about 4′ by 2′ by 2′, with a lining and an external sheathing of pure beaten gold. It was covered by a lid of solid gold to which was affixed a carved golden cherub at each end. These celestial beings looked down upon the lid, and their wings covered the ark (Exod. 25:10–40). The gold lid to which the cherubim were fastened was called the "mercy seat" (Heb. *kappōret,* "cover"), and it was from between the cherubim that God communed with his people (Exod. 25:22). The ark was the only item of furniture in the most holy place of the tabernacle, and contained duplicate tablets of the law (Exod. 25:16; II Kings 11:12), a pot of manna (Exod. 16:33–34), and Aaron's rod (Num. 17:10). When the ark was moved, it was carried by priests using poles (Num. 4:5), and anyone who touched the ark was liable to die (cf. II Sam. 6:6–7). The ark survived until the Exile, when it was probably taken to Babylon (cf. II Kings 24:13). R. K. HARRISON

See also TABERNACLE, TEMPLE.

Armageddon. This locality (Gk. *harmagedōn*) is mentioned once in the Bible at Rev. 16:16, where the prophet describes the sixth bowl/vial. In this place the "kings of the whole world" will be assembled together under the inspiration of "demonic spirits" (16:14) in order to engage in battle. While the prophet's explanation that this name is Hebrew is meant to aid the interpreter, scholars have generally joined Jeremias in concluding that "the riddle of Har Magedon still awaits a solution."

The chief problem is that the name (h)armageddon does not appear in any extant Hebrew writing. The most popular solution is that we have here a reference to the mountain (*har*) of Megiddo (*magedōn*). This has merit in that Megiddo was a military stronghold (Josh. 12:21; 17:11; Judg. 1:27; II Kings 8:27) and many famous battles were fought in the area: Israel and Sisera (Judg. 5:19) as well as Josiah and the Pharaoh Neco (II Kings 23:29). On the other hand, R. H. Charles wonders if a corruption in the language (*'ar ḥemdâ*, city of desire; or *har migdô*, his fruitful mountain) should not point to Jerusalem, the mountain of Israel. Prophetic expectation seems to point to a climactic battle in the neighborhood of Zion (Joel 3:2; Zech. 14:2; I Enoch 56:7). Further, if the apocalyptic imagery of Rev. 16–20 derives from Ezek. 38–39, here again we have a picture of the final battle in the "mountains of Israel" (Ezek. 38:7ff.; 39:2). Still others (e.g., Beasley-Murray) suggest that no geographic locality is meant; rather, this name stands for an event. Here the culmination of history is found in the final clash between the forces of God and Satan/evil.

In contemporary theology "Armageddon" often adopts this symbolic meaning. In biblical thought the day of the Lord which climaxes history will come amid multinational war (Joel 3:9–15; Zech. 14:1–5; Zeph. 3:8; cf. Mark 13:7, 14ff., 24ff.). In Rev. 19:11–21 the armies of heaven engage the kings of the earth in the battle for the millennial kingdom. Therefore rebellion against God and his Messiah will hallmark the end of the age. The thought that devastating war will typify the end of the world enters even secular thinking. The First World War was termed "Armageddon" and the recent film by Francis Coppola, *Apocalypse Now*, contained apocalyptic imagery. Indeed, many conservatives speculate about the threat of nuclear war in modern politics and argue for the imminent fulfillment of the biblical Armageddon. Hal Lindsey's well-known book, *The Late Great Planet Earth*, suggests that Armageddon will come when armies of the West are arrayed against 200 million soldiers from China in a fierce land battle "with the vortex centered at the Valley of Megiddo."

G. M. Burge

Bibliography. R. D. Culver, *ZPEB*, I, 311; J. Jeremias, "Har Magedon (Apoc. 16, 16)," *ZNW* 31:73–77, and *TDNT*, I, 468; R. H. Charles, *The Revelation of St. John*, II, 50–51; J. F. Walvoord, *The Revelation of Jesus Christ*; R. Mounce, *The Book of Revelation*.

Arminianism. The theological stance of James Arminius and the movement which stemmed from him. It views Christian doctrine much as the pre-Augustinian fathers did and as did the later John Wesley. In several basic ways it differs from the Augustine–Luther–Calvin tradition.

This form of Protestantism arose in the United Netherlands shortly after the "alteration" from Roman Catholicism had occurred in that country. It stresses Scripture alone as the highest authority for doctrines. And it teaches that justification is by grace alone, there being no meritoriousness in our faith that occasions justification, since it is only through prevenient grace that fallen humanity can exercise that faith.

Arminianism is a distinct kind of Protestant theology for several reasons. One of its distinctions is its teaching on predestination. It teaches predestination, since the Scripture writers do, but it understands that this predecision on God's part is to save the ones who repent and believe. Thus its view is called conditional predestination, since the predetermination of the destiny of individuals is based on God's foreknowledge of the way in which they will either freely reject Christ or freely accept him.

Arminius defended his view most precisely in his commentary on Romans 9, *Examination of Perkins' Pamphlet*, and *Declaration of Sentiments*. He argued against supralapsarianism, popularized by John Calvin's son-in-law and Arminius's teacher at Geneva, Theodore Beza, and vigorously defended at the University of Leiden by Francis Gomarus, a colleague of Arminius. Their view was that before the fall, indeed before man's creation, God had already determined what the eternal destiny of each person was to be. Arminius also believed that the sublapsarian unconditional predestination view of Augustine and Martin Luther is unscriptural. This is the view that Adam's sin was freely chosen but that, after Adam's fall, the eternal destiny of each person was determined by the absolutely sovereign God. In his *Declaration of Sentiments* (1608) Arminius gave twenty arguments against supralapsarianism, which he said (not quite correctly) applied also to sublapsarianism. These included such arguments as that the view is void of good news; repugnant to God's wise, just, and good nature, and to man's free nature; "highly dishonorable to Jesus Christ"; "hurtful to the salvation of men"; and that it "inverts the order of the gospel of Jesus Christ" (which is that we are justified after we believe, not prior to our believing). He said the arguments all boil down to one, actually: that unconditional predestination makes God "the author of sin."

Connected with Arminius's view of conditional predestination are other significant teachings of "the quiet Dutchman." One is his emphasis on human freedom. Here he was not Pelagian, as some have thought. He believed profoundly in original sin, understanding that the will of natural fallen man is not only maimed and wounded, but that it is entirely unable, apart from prevenient grace, to do any good thing. Another teaching is that Christ's atonement is unlimited in its benefits. He understood that such texts as "he died for all" (II Cor. 5:15; cf. II Cor. 5:14; Titus 2:11; I John 2:2) mean what they say, while Puritans such as John Owen and other Calvinists have understood that the "all" means only all of those previously elected to be saved. A third view is that while God is not willing that any should perish, but that all should come to repentance (I Tim. 2:4; II Pet. 3:9; Matt. 18:14), saving grace is not irresistible, as in classical Calvinism. It can be rejected.

In Arminius's view believers may lose their salvation and be eternally lost. Quoting as support of this position such passages as I Pet. 1:10, "Therefore, brethren, be the more zealous to confirm your call and election, for if you do this you will never fall," Arminians still seek to nourish and encourage believers so that they might remain in a saved state. While Arminians feel that they have been rather successful in disinclining many Calvinists from such views as unconditional election, limited atonement, and irresistible grace, they realize that they have not widely succeeded in the area of eternal security. R. T. Shank's *Life in the Son* and H. O. Wiley's three-volume *Christian Theology* make a good scriptural case against eternal security from within the Arminian tradition, but the position has been unconvincing to Calvinists generally.

A spillover from Calvinism into Arminianism has occurred in recent decades. Thus many Arminians whose theology is not very precise say that Christ paid the penalty for our sins. Yet such a view is foreign to Arminianism, which teaches instead that Christ suffered for us. Arminians teach that what Christ did he did for every person; therefore what he did could not have been to pay the penalty, since no one would then ever go into eternal perdition. Arminianism teaches that Christ suffered for everyone so that the Father could forgive the ones who repent and believe; his death is such that all will see that forgiveness is costly and will strive to cease from anarchy in the world God governs. This view is called the governmental theory of the atonement. Its germinal teachings are in Arminius, but his student, the lawyer-theologian Hugo Grotius, delineated the view. Methodism's John Miley best explicated the theory in his *The Atonement in Christ* (1879). Arminians who know their theology have problems in such cooperative ministries with Calvinists as the Billy Graham campaigns because the workers are often taught to counsel people that Christ paid the penalty for their sins. But it is an important aspect of the Arminian tradition—from Arminius himself, through John Wesley, to the present—to be of tolerant spirit; so they often cooperate in these ministries without mentioning the matter to the leadership. Arminians feel that the reason Scripture always states that Christ suffered (e.g., Acts 17:3; 26:23; II Cor. 1:5; Phil. 3:10; Heb. 2:9–10; 13:12; I Pet. 1:11; 2:21; 3:18; 4:1, 13), and never that he was punished, is because the Christ who was crucified was guiltless because he was sinless. They also feel that God the Father would not be forgiving us at all if his justice was satisfied by the real thing that justice needs: punishment. They understand that there can be only punishment or forgiveness, not both—realizing, e.g., that a child is either punished or forgiven, not forgiven after the punishment has been meted out.

A spillover into Arminianism from Baptistic Calvinism is an opposition to infant baptism. Until recently the long Arminian tradition has customarily emphasized infant baptism—as did Arminius and Wesley (Luther and Calvin too, for that matter). It has been considered as the sacrament which helps prevenient grace to be implemented, restraining the child until such time as he becomes evangelically converted. Arminians believe that the several household baptisms mentioned in Acts 16–17 and I Cor. 1 imply that infants were baptized, and that this act is the NT counterpart of OT circumcision. But the untutored often feel that they should not baptize infants, because so many Baptist-type evangelicals do not.

Biblical inerrancy is another spillover. The Arminian tradition has been a part of the long Protestant tradition which Fuller Seminary's Jack Rogers discusses in his *Confessions of a Conservative Evangelical.* It is interested in the Bible's authority and infallibility, and expresses confidence that Scripture is inerrant on matters of faith and practice, while remaining open on possible mathematical, historical, or geographical errors. Its scholars in general do not believe that Harold Lindsell correctly interprets the long Christian tradition on Scripture in such works as *The Battle for the Bible,* when he says that until about 150 years ago Christians in general believed in the total inerrancy of Scripture.

Another spillover is in eschatological matters. Arminianism is not dispensationalist as such, has not committed itself to a given millennial view, and has little interest in specific prophecies (believing God would have us concentrate on what is clear in Scripture: Christ's redemption and a holy life). But many lay Arminians have succumbed to such popular prophetic books as those of Hal Lindsey, which teach unequivocally that present political events and trends fulfill specific biblical prophecies.

A considerable problem to Arminians is that they have often been misrepresented. Some scholars have said that Arminianism is Pelagian, is a form of theological liberalism, and is syncretistic. It is true that one wing of Arminianism picked up Arminius's stress on human freedom and tolerance toward differing theologies, becoming latitudinarian and liberal. Indeed the two denominations in Holland that issued from Arminius are largely such today. But Arminians who promote Arminius's actual teachings and those of the great Arminian John Wesley, whose view and movement have sometimes been called "Arminianism on fire," have disclaimed all those theologically left associations. Such Arminians largely comprise the eight million or so Christians who today constitute the Christian Holiness Association (the Salvation Army, the Church of the Nazarene, the Wesleyan Church, etc.). This kind of Arminianism strongly defends Christ's virgin birth, miracles, bodily resurrection, and substitutionary atonement (his suffering for the punishment believers would have received); the dynamic inspiration and infallibility of Scripture; justification by grace alone through faith alone; and the final destinies of heaven and hell. It is therefore evangelical, but an evangelicalism which is at certain important points different from evangelical Calvinism. J. K. GRIDER

See also ARMINIUS, JAMES; METHODISM; WESLEYAN TRADITION, THE.

Bibliography. *The Works of James Arminius,* 3 vols. (1853 ed.); J. K. Grider, *WBE,* I, 143–48; A. W. Harrison, *Arminianism* and *The Beginnings of Arminianism;* G. O. McCullough, ed., *Man's Faith and Freedom;* C. Pinnock, *Grace Unlimited.*

Arminius, James (1560–1609). Born at Oudewater, the Netherlands, Arminius was educated at the universities of Marburg (1575) and Leiden (1576–81), at the academy at Geneva (1582, 1584–86), and at Basel (1582–83). He was pastor of an Amsterdam congregation (1588–1603), and a professor at the University of Leiden from 1603 until his death.

He did not write a full systematic theology, as John Calvin had done, but he wrote considerably both during his fifteen year pastorate and while he was a professor at Leiden. His treatise on Romans 7 interpreted vss. 7–25 as depicting an awakened (vss. 12, 21), unregenerate (vss. 15, 18, 24) person. He wrote a treatise on Romans 9 in which he interpreted this passage, used by many Calvinists to teach unconditional predestination, to teach only conditional predestination. One of his most significant writings is his *Examination of Perkins' Pamphlet,* a "conditional predestination" answer to the view of Cambridge's William Perkins. His *Declaration of Sentiments* of 1608, which he presented to the governmental authorities at The Hague, gave his arguments against supralapsarianism (the view that each person's destiny was determined by God prior to Adam's fall). It also sought to secure favorable status in the United Netherlands for his own kind of conditional predestination teaching. In addition he wrote such treatises as an apology against thirty-one incorrect representations of his views that had circulated for some time; *Public Disputations;* and *Seventy-nine Private Disputations* (a posthumous publication of his theology class notes at Leiden).

Arminius was the ablest exponent of what various others had already been teaching: that God's predestination of the destiny of individuals is based on his foreknowledge of the way in which they will freely (in the context of prevenient grace) accept or reject Christ.

His teachings were promoted especially by John Wesley and the Methodists and, in our time, by the denominations which constitute the Christian Holiness Association. J. K. GRIDER

See also ARMINIANISM.

Bibliography. C. Brandt, *The Life of James Arminius;* C. Bangs, *Arminius.*

Armstrongism. This group founded by Herbert W. Armstrong has been made famous by his magazine, *The Plain Truth,* and radio broadcast, "The World Tomorrow." Its full name is the Worldwide Church of God, which has its headquarters at Ambassador College in Pasadena. Armstrongism is a blend of prophetic interpretation which applies a version of the teaching of British Israelitism to the American situation and a variety of other doctrines culled from

Adventists and Jehovah's Witnesses. Recently Armstrongism has been shaken by internal disputes between Herbert W. Armstrong and his son Garner Ted. These involve accusations of widespread immorality and corruption.

I. HEXHAM

See also ADVENTISM; BRITISH ISRAELITISM; JEHOVAH'S WITNESSES.

Bibliography. R. R. Chambers, *The Plain Truth about Armstrongism;* M. E. Jones, ed., *Ambassador Report;* L. F. Deboer, *The New Pharisaism;* J. Tuit, *The Truth Shall Make You Free.*

Art, Christian. Art that is Christian will be Christian art because the artwork meets the norm for art in the Lord's world and breathes a spirit of holiness which recognizes that our creaturely existence plagued by sin needs to be reconciled back to God in Jesus Christ.

Holy Spirited Art in History. During early Bible times the Lord raised up choreographers (Exod. 15:20), sculptors (Exod. 25:9–40), silversmiths (Exod. 31:1–11), songwriters (Psalms), composers (II Chr. 5:11–14), storytellers (Judg. 9:7–20, also Christ with his parables), poets (cf. Isa. 40), and artisans of many sorts (I Kings 7:13–22) who made a joyful noise to the Lord and praised God's name with the artistry of their hands, unafraid of violating the commanding Sinai word against making stupid images that might tempt people to idolatry. Despite the ancient oratory (Gen. 4:23–24) and architecture (Gen. 11:1–9) that was a testimony of godless vanity, artistry was from the beginning a gift with which God endowed human creatures (cf. Adam's poem about Eve in Gen. 2:23); God wanted artistry to be exercised as an obedient and edifying caretaking of the materials, sounds, shapes, sights, words, gestures, and the like which God had provided for men and women to tend.

Catechetical Art and Iconoclasm. By the time the church became a world power under Constantine, who converted to the Christian faith as emperor (313), arguments on whether images were incipient idolatry (Clement of Alexandria) or a proper, pictorial book of instruction for the illiterate (Gregory of Nyssa) had set the problematics for centuries of controversy on visual art.

Byzantine painting in Constantinople (after A.D. 330) synthesized earlier attempts at Christian art into a style of rich ornamentation but little figuration. The artisans employed to beautify the churches of Ravenna (sixth century), however, heirs perhaps of Syriac Christian insight, broke new ground in art. The monumentality of Greco-Roman temples and the illusionistic depiction of actual things, common in hellenistic mimesis, were replaced by a simple, jewellike splendor in mosaics that showed a sacramental quality. Whether human figures bearing gifts like magi or scenes of pastoral perfection representing the new earth were formed, the visible images of these Christian craftsmen seemed to make present and to certify a reality that was not yet visible. Even the originally Coptic, zoomorphic emblems of angel, lion, calf, and eagle for the evangelists bore a celebrative note that rather overpowered any didactic focus; the depictions and motifs in Ravenna are more richly liturgical than devotional.

The stand of Pope Gregory the Great (590–604) for catechetical use of images, a position later reaffirmed by the moderating Charlemagne (800–814), became embattled by the 726 edict of Emperor Leo III, which banned image worship; Leo's son, Constantine V (741–75), pursued a vigorous, outright iconoclastic policy that even suppressed images of the Virgin Mary. The Second Council of Nicaea (787), however, explicitly enunciated a doctrinal rehabilitation of images, using the precise distinction formulated by John of Damascus between veneration (*prosynesis*) for images and worship (*latria*) due God alone. Although antipathy toward picturing God persisted strongly in the church until 867, gradually popular practice not only received the requisite doctrinal justification for using images to teach the Bible stories but also, in line with the Neoplatonic position of Pseudo-Dionysius adopted by John of Damascus, affirmed that holy images were a means of grace. Icons, especially of Christ—who had come to earth in visible flesh—became beloved as mnemonic, mesmerizing aids, approved by the ecclesiastic hierarchy, for mediating communion between God and the ordinary worshiper.

Churched Art and Reformation. Monastic reform movements in the West from the tenth to twelfth century affected art with the ambivalence built in their combined tenets: *luxus pro Deo* (splendor for God, the Cluniac program of temporal power) opposite mystical renunciation (the Cistercian and later Franciscan Orders). Romanesque architecture insulated a determinate, impenetrable space from the lighted, outside world. But subsequent Gothic building of cathedrals, with flying buttresses and stained glass painting, embodied the principles of scholastic theology in which reason was meant to clarify faith with an exhaustive, concordant order that embraced everything under the sun and soared into a towering anonymity. The increasing presence of *Andachtsbilder,* cavernous pietà sculptures with relic overtones, and gargoyles hinted at an increasing individualistic and apprehensive fascination with the reality of death that stalked life.

A different spirit coursed through the *Canterbury Tales* of Geoffrey Chaucer, breathed in the graphic art of figures like Holbein, Dürer, Cranach, and Lucas van Leyden, and found shape in Huguenot psalmody of the Reformation. Now there was a colloquial bounce and an appreciation for creaturely phenomena and a joy of this earthly life lived before God's face, where faith was not seeking analogical understanding of the mysteries of God so much as itself providing a way to walk through the glories and miseries of historical turmoil. Unlike Dante's masterful, allegorical *Divina Commedia*, an *itinerarium mentis ad Deum* (the mind's road to God), Chaucer presents a kaleidoscope of society breathing pious grit and bawdy laughter that makes pilgrimage but does it with flesh and blood and peevishness. Following Luther's movement of institutional church reform, woodcuts and engravings began to flourish in northern Europe. Unlike sculpture and frescoes, art that was on paper lost the stigma of being an idol: you could hold the image in your hands and respond to its message anywhere, outside the precincts of the church. Luther's songs and the original psalm melodies of Louis Bourgeois and others in Geneva also drastically altered church music. Those who were not trained in Gregorian chant and its vocal decoration could now learn tunes with one note per syllable and with repeatable stanzas, so that song-praise came into the mouths of ordinary people, like folksongs.

Although the Council of Trent (1545–63) reasserted the priority of churched art in all its mannerist, baroque splendor as a proper catechetical tool, the possibility for art to be Christianly spirited but not under church hegemony—a striking tenet of the Reformation—became a culturally important legacy. In the seventeenth century, painting in the Netherlands by Rembrandt, Vermeer, and many others gave viewers eyes to find blessing in what is homely and to see glory in the creaturely commonplaces of sky and water. The great poet John Milton altered the reforming movement by combining an independentist streak in Protestantism (cf. his treatises on divorce and *Areopagitica*) with an enormously educated classical and Christian humanism, so that the art which embodied such a hybrid world-and-life vision took intellectual pains to "justify the ways of God to men" (in *Paradise Lost* and *Paradise Regained*). John Bunyan, however, became mouthpiece for a unadulterated biblical faith which was content to pass through life as a pilgrim while making progress not to an earthly Canterbury but toward the Heavenly City.

Confessional Art After Secular Enlightenment. Cultural leadership passed out of Christian hands in Western civilization as the deep-going secularizing trends of mathematical and empiricistic science, Encyclopedist philosophy, and warring mercantilism came to dominate European life in the 1700s. Disciples of Christopher Wren still built churches in England with a delicate, refined gravity; Isaac Watts and the Wesley brothers wrote hymns of simplified quatrains that comforted the many poor in society with gospel; but pietism, also flourishing in Germany, inhibited Christians both from losing themselves in a show of art and from giving direction in such matters of sensibility. In the new world of America, however, an amalgam of neoclassical rationality and the transcendentalist idealism of an Emerson could not stifle the resident Puritan consciousness of good struggling against the evil heart of darkness which surfaced in the rich, symbol-laden narratives of *The Scarlet Letter* (1850) and *Moby Dick* (1851), by Nathaniel Hawthorne and Herman Melville, respectively.

As industrialization complicated and upset traditional cultural patterns of privilege, and as a spirit of positivism, along with inventions such as photographic cameras (*ca.* 1830), faced art with the possibility of being leveled to mere fact, Christian artists like the Pre-Raphaelite Brotherhood in the midnineteenth century opted conservatively to fashion painting in an earlier illustrative style, with true-to-actual-daily-life detail and devout biblical or literary themes. Canvases like William Holman Hunt's *The Light of the World* came to serve as Victorian icons of sorts, mirrors to stimulate the viewer's subjective piety. The initiative of William Morris was more forward-looking, intent upon curing urban ugliness with good design and attention to craft; but the "arts-and-craft movement" still had a curious, old-fashioned, medieval feel to its program even while it trimmed architectural form and decorative arts to uncluttered lines. When Christian artisans are not busy setting the cultural pace of their day but look for norms and patterns of relevance in the past, they either tend, it seems, to introduce the faith thematically for confession inside their art or to suffer from touches of obsolescence.

Christian Art in a Pragmatistic Culture. Given the setback to cultural idealism in World War I and the profound jumble of avant-garde euphoria and huckster fashions since European dada and American jazz of the 1920s, the gradual supremacy of technocratic and commercialized interests over art has come to face professional artistry with a crisis: either art goes popular for a mass audience (television and tabloid), or art pulls back into an expensive, esoteric ghetto (the New York art gallery scene, for example). In such a pragmatistic and monopolistic context art that would be both viable and truly honoring of the Lord's rule in history will be relatively rare and of exceptional quality, or it will find a marginal home in Christian communities outside the hard-core, secular mainstream.

The engravings and paintings of Georges Rouault reinvest the Byzantine tradition with a somber, stained glass seriousness that is definitely biblical in its horror of modern dehumanizing atrocities, and is truly compassionate in composition, color, and gritty style that bespeaks Christian art, whether the topic be kings, prostitutes, or Jesus Christ's passion. The Nobel Prize winner for poetry in 1945, Gabriela Mistral of Chile, updates a Franciscan holiness and gives it a poignant, singing voice that casts halos of comfort around girlish hopes, forgotten prisoners, and even the nests of birds. Canadian painter William Kurelek weds a love for the Brueghel world of low life with a Roman Catholic slant on the poverty of success gained without the presence of the cross; his mark of pristine folk happiness is normally touched by an existential sense of nuclear war apocalypse, so the careful observer can never rest easy. Significant about such varied Christian art born out of Catholic sensitivities today is its unchurchly, worldwide, sorrow-sensitive aura.

A more hidden, "autonomous," or even tangential expression of biblical faith in art of the twentieth century deserves mention: the sculpture of German Ernst Barlach articulates with rough austerity a forceful cry in wood and metal for reconciliation with God and neighbor that so incurred the anger of the Nazi government it destroyed much of the work. The New York Jew Abraham Rattner not only conceived an enormous stained glass wall of apocalyptic emblems for a major Chicago synagogue but also grappled time and again in painting with the crucifixion of Christ, trying to exorcise both Golgotha and Auschwitz, as it were, from Jewish experience. Gabriel García Márquez of Colombia, 1982 Nobel prize winner for fiction, exposes small-town political corruption in South America with fantastic horizons that juxtapose real angels, supernatural forces, and the comic foibles of weak people.

The black spiritual song of American Civil War days takes on new evangelical fervor in the melodies and lyrics of Mahalia Jackson, whose simple Baptist roots act prophetically through the cascades of rhythmic beat and glorious sound. The paintings, prints, and constructions of Henk Krijger body forth reminiscences of both Bauhaus and German expressionism muted and melded into strong, restfully honed shapes and expertly chosen colors that reveal artistry integrated by the Reformation perspective that ordinary life is a vocation to be lived directly before God and to be redeemed while sharing sadness, humor, and hope.

New Ferment and Reforming Categories. Anglo-Catholics everywhere continue to renew the age-old vocabulary of liturgical artistic service. Native people like the Indians and Eskimos of North America and many tribal cultures in Africa who came to confess Jesus Christ as Lord through missionary efforts of the church are finding in the current generation their own non-Western idiom for art that shares biblical faith. Mennonites and various holiness communions are now looking for ways to practice Christian art, since the mass media no longer make a secluded escape from artistic praxis feasible. Christian liberal arts colleges in North America have come to form important pocket communities across the land for developing alternative, Christian formation of poetry, painting, music, and theater. Although the Nashville industry continues to break down Christian songwriters into formula sound that will sell well to the middle-class market, there are even large-scale events like the Greenbelt Festival in England which are probing pop and rock band music with an open-ended desire to find a truly new and powerful, integrated Christian art.

The old categories of "sacred" and "secular" art are misleading, as if art could be first of all "natural" or "neutral," and then sometimes "holy," if it is fitting for church or spells out a biblical message. It is indeed correct to understand that bona fide art may be appropriately harnessed or "encapsulated" into the specially limited service of church (for liturgy), state (in monuments), or business (as advertising). But art-as-such, like a novel or music concert, ballet or theater piece, is never uncommitted at the foundational level of human allegiance to Jesus Christ or to no-god. And art is not holy by virtue of its topic, any particular formula, or being blessed by church officials. When one realizes that Christian art is artistry infused with a genuinely holy spirit, in contrast to art subtly dictated by a Hindu, Buddhist, Muslim, or secular humanist spirit worshiping human hands, then the matter of Christian art will be rightly recognized as the fragile task and fruit of obedience in history performed by gifted artisans within Christ's body at large in the world. C. G. SEERVELD

See also AESTHETICS, CHRISTIAN VIEW OF.

Bibliography. E. Panofsky, *Gothic Architecture and Scholasticism* and "Art and Reformation," in *Symbols in Transformation;* E. Kitzinger, "The Cult of Images in the Age before Iconoclasm," *DOP* 8:83–150; É. Doumergue, *l'Art et le sentiment dans l'oeuvre de Calvin;* L. Wencelius, *Calvin et Rembrandt;* É. Mâle, *Religious Art from the Twelfth to the Eighteenth Century;* W. A. Visser 't Hooft, *Rembrandt and the Gospel;* D. Davie, *A Gathered Church: The Literature of the English Dissenting Interest, 1700–1930;* J. H. Hagstrum, *Sex and Sensibility, Ideal and Erotic Love from Milton to Mozart;* R. Paulson, *Shakespeare, Milton, and the Bible;* T. S. Eliot, *The Sacred Wood;* K. Harries, *The Meaning of Modern Art;* H. R. Rookmaaker, *Art and the Public Today* and *Modern Art and the Death of a Culture;* W. A. Dyrness, *Rouault: A Vision of Suffering and Salvation;* J. Barzun, *The Use and Abuse of Art;* R. Hughes, *The Shock of the New: Art and the Century of Change.*

Articles, The Thirty-nine. *See* THIRTY-NINE ARTICLES, THE.

Articles of Religion. A term commonly used for the standards of doctrine of the United Methodist Church. The Articles stem from the abridgment of the Thirty-nine Articles of the Church of England prepared by John Wesley for use in the American Methodist Episcopal Church organized in 1784; Wesley reduced the Thirty-nine Articles to twenty-four. The organizing conference added a twenty-fifth article (Article 23) outlining the church's relationships with the newly formed American government. This article replaced Article XXXVII of the *Book of Common Prayer*—a statement of the authority of the British monarch over the church—which Wesley had wisely omitted from his list.

The Articles of Religion as adopted by the 1784 Christmas Conference have remained intact throughout the history of the Methodist Episcopal Church and its successor bodies. The General Conference of 1808 helped to assure this continuity by removing the amendment of the Articles from the direct jurisdiction of succeeding General Conferences. It provided for amendment only upon a two thirds vote of any General Conference recommending change and a subsequent confirmation by a three fourths vote of all the Annual Conferences. The only change in the original doctrinal statement of the church has been the inclusion of the Confession of Faith of the United Brethren Church in the *Book of Discipline* at the formation of the present United Methodist Church in 1968. This addition introduced into the official doctrinal statement of the church, for the first time, an article on Christian perfection—a doctrine central to Wesleyan theology but never previously incorporated in the doctrines of the *Discipline.* M. E. DIETER

See also WESLEY, JOHN; WESLEYAN TRADITION, THE.

Bibliography. *The Book of Discipline of the United Methodist Church,* 1980; H. M. DuBose, *The Symbol of Methodism, Being an Inquiry into the History, Authority, Inclusions and Uses of the Twenty-Five Articles;* A. A. Jimeson, *Notes on the Twenty-Five Articles of Religion as Received and Taught by the Methodists in the United States.*

Asbury, Francis (1745–1816). The father of Methodism in the United States. Asbury was born near Birmingham, England. His parents, though poor, gave him a warmly religious upbringing and encouraged him to meet with Methodists for study and prayer after he experienced a religious awakening at the age of thirteen. He soon began to preach, a calling which he dignified with a lifetime of energetic labor. When John Wesley asked for volunteers to go to America as missionaries in 1771, Asbury responded eagerly.

Asbury arrived when the states were still colonies of Great Britain. Rapidly he assumed leadership among the four Methodist missionaries already in America. His colleagues favored a "settled" clergy located in populous areas, but Asbury was convinced that preachers should go where the gospel most needed to be heard—in taverns, jails, fields, and by the wayside. His authoritarian leadership, but even more the strength of his example, set the style for the itinerating, or traveling, Methodist minister in early America. Later he would exhort his associates to "go into every kitchen and shop; address all, aged and young, on the salvation of their souls." Asbury's desire to spread the gospel kept him on the move the rest of his life. During his ministry he traveled nearly 300,000 miles, mostly on horseback. He crossed the Appalachians more than sixty times to reach backwoods Americans. He probably saw more of the American countryside than any other person of his generation, and may have been the most well known person in North America.

In spite of Asbury's energetic efforts the Methodists did not grow rapidly at first. The War for Independence proved a major stumbling block. When violence erupted in 1775, all Methodist missionaries except Asbury returned to England. John Wesley's attacks on the move for independence did not make it any easier for American Methodists. Asbury himself attempted to remain neutral, but when he realized that independence was inevitable, he became a citizen of Delaware.

In the 1780s American Methodists set up an organization to bind established eastern centers with missionary outposts on the frontier. In 1784 Wesley appointed Asbury and Thomas Coke as "general superintendents" of the Methodists in the United States. In December of that year at the historic Christmas Conference in Baltimore, the Methodist Episcopal Church in America was officially organized, with Asbury as its guiding force. From that time the church grew rapidly, particularly west of the mountains where the roughness of life and the near-barbarism of the population discouraged representatives of more traditional denominations.

Asbury's message in city and wilderness alike was a traditional Protestant one, with the special Wesleyan emphases: God's free grace, mankind's liberty to accept or reject that grace, and the Christian's need to strive for the abolition of willful sin after conversion. Asbury's organization of "circuit riders" was perhaps an even greater cause of Methodist success than the doctrine of free grace. He early supported campmeetings and embraced revivals as means of evangelistic outreach. He also worked to solidify gains through the education of laity as well as through the circuit riders.

Throughout his life Asbury was a sterling example of devoted ministry. He preached a gospel, moreover, that reached beyond the inner life to the outer responsibilities of a Christian: he established academies and colleges, he willed his very modest estate to the Methodist "Book Concern," he argued against slavery, and he urged abstinence from hard liquor. Statistics never tell a whole story. But when Francis Asbury came to America in 1771, four Methodist ministers were caring for about 300 lay people. When he died in 1816, there were 2,000 ministers and over 200,000 Methodists devoted, as he phrased it, to "the dear Redeemer . . . of precious souls." M. A. NOLL

See also METHODISM.

Bibliography. *Journal and Letters of Francis Asbury,* 3 vols.; F. Baker, *From Wesley to Asbury: Studies in Early American Methodism;* L. C. Rudolph, *Francis Asbury.*

Ascension Day. Jesus ascended into heaven on the fortieth day after his resurrection (Acts 1:3, 9), and the subsequent period of waiting for the descent of the Holy Spirit appears to have lasted the ten days until Pentecost (Acts 2:1). During the third and early fourth centuries it seems that the festival of Pentecost commemorated both the ascension of the Lord Jesus and the descent of the Holy Spirit. This accords with the juxtaposition in thought in Eph. 4:8–11. Toward the end of the fourth century the two events were celebrated separately, and Ascension Day was kept on the fortieth day after Easter. Some modern scholars suggest that this was in fact Jesus' final ascension, and that he initially returned to heaven on the day of resurrection.

D. H. WHEATON

See also CHRISTIAN YEAR.

Bibliography. A. A. McArthur, *The Evolution of the Christian Year;* P. Toon, *Jesus Christ Is Lord.*

Ascension of Christ. That act of the God-man by which he brought to an end his postresurrection appearances to his disciples, was finally parted from them as to his physical presence, and passed into the other world, to remain there until his second advent (Acts 3:21). Luke describes this event in a word or two in Luke 24:51 and more fully in Acts 1:9. Even if the words "and he was carried up into heaven" are not part of the true text in Luke 24:51, we have good reason for saying, in the light of Luke's clear and unambiguous words in his second treatise, that the doubtful words in Luke 24:51 express what was in his mind. In accordance with the oral testimony of the apostles, he carries on his story of the life of Jesus as far as "the day that he was taken up" (Acts 1:22).

According to the Fourth Gospel our Lord referred on three occasions to his ascending into heaven (John 3:13; 6:62; 20:17). Paul speaks of Christ ascending far above all heavens in order to permeate the whole universe with his presence and power (Eph. 4:10). Such phrases as "received up in glory" (I Tim. 3:16), "gone into heaven" (I Pet. 3:22), and "passed through the heavens" (Heb. 4:14) refer to the same event. Paul exhorts the Colossian believers to "seek the things that are above, where Christ is, seated on the right hand of God" (Col. 3:1, ERV), and the numerous references in the NT to the session at the right hand of God presuppose the ascension.

In Eph. 1:20ff. Paul passes directly from the resurrection to the exaltation of Christ to the place of supreme power and authority in the universe. In passages like Rom. 8:34 and Col. 3:1 the session might seem to be thought of as the immediate result of the rising from the dead, thus leaving no room, as some have argued, for the ascension as a distinct event; but it is difficult to see that there is any force in any argument derived from Paul's silence in such passages when in Eph. 4:10 he states so emphatically his belief in the ascension. Our Lord's postresurrection appearances had, no doubt, shown that he belonged already to the upper world of light and glory; but with the ascension his fleeting visits to his disciples from that world came to an end, and the heavens received him from their sight. Yet, through the indwelling Holy Spirit they were to come nearer to him than ever before, and he was to be with them forever (John 14:16–18).

To object to the account of the ascension of Christ into heaven as implying a childish and outmoded view of the universe is, more or less, solemn trifling. While we may agree with Westcott when he says that "the change which Christ revealed by the ascension was not a change of place, but a change of state, not local but spiritual" (*The Revelation of the Risen Lord,* p. 180), on the other hand we are not unscientific when we think of the land where "the king in all His glory without a veil is seen" as the upper world of light and glory, high above us as good is above evil and blessedness above misery.

The Heidelberg Catechism suggests three great benefits that we receive from the ascension. (1) The exalted Lord in heaven is our Advocate in the presence of his Father (Rom. 8:34; I John 2:1; Heb. 7:25). As our High Priest he offered on the cross the one perfect and final sacrifice for sins forever (Heb. 10:12), and now, having sat down at the right hand of God, he has entered on his priestly ministry in heaven. As our King-Priest he communicates, through the Holy Spirit, to all believers the gifts and blessings which he died to win for them. "Christ's intercession in heaven," said the old Scottish preacher Traill, "is a kind and powerful remembrance of His people, and of all their concerns, managed with state and majesty; not as a suppliant at the footstool, but as a crowned prince on the throne, at the right hand of the Father." (2) We have our flesh in heaven, so that, as the subtle Scottish thinker "Rabbi" Duncan said: "The dust of the earth is on the throne of the majesty on high." In that, as the Heidelberg Catechism says, we have "a sure pledge that He, as our Head, will also take us, His members, up to Himself." (3) He sends us his Spirit, as the earnest of the promised inheritance.

That third benefit is of supreme importance. The Holy Spirit was not given, in the fullness of his gracious working in the souls of men, until Jesus was glorified (John 7:39). "Being by the right hand of God exalted, and having received of the Father the promise of the Holy Ghost, he hath poured forth this, which ye see and hear. For David ascended not into the heavens" (Acts 2:33–34, ERV). Thus was it demonstrated to the universe that, as Zahn has put it, "the risen Lord lives in heavenly communion with His and our Father, and that He takes an active part in the working of the power as well as of the grace of God in this world" (*The Apostles' Creed,* 162).

The ascended Lord is with us in the struggle here (Mark 16:19–20), and we know that he has gone to heaven "our entrance to secure, and our abode prepare" (John 14:2; Heb. 6:20).

A. Ross

Bibliography. *HDAC; HDB; HDCG;* W. Milligan, *The Ascension and Heavenly Priesthood of Our Lord;* A. M. Ramsey in *Studiorum Novi Testamenti Societas, Bulletin II;* H. B. Swete, *The Ascended Christ;* M. Loane, *Our Risen Lord.*

Ascetical Theology. Classically, ascetical theology has been defined as the branch of theology dealing with the ordinary means of Christian perfection—e.g., the disciplined renunciation of personal desires, the imitation of Christ, and the pursuit of charity. On this level it has been distinguished since the seventeenth century from moral theology (which deals with those duties essential for salvation and thus the avoidance of mortal and venial sins) and mystical theology (which deals with the extraordinary grace of God leading to infused contemplation and is thus a passive reception rather than an active pursuit). The borderline between moral and ascetical theology is hazy at best, while the distinction between it and mystical theology is often denied altogether. This fact becomes particularly clear when ascetical theology is divided in its usual manner into the purgative, illuminative, and unitive ways. The purgative way, which stresses the cleansing of the soul from all serious sin, clearly overlaps moral theology; the unitive way, which focuses on union with God, can easily include mystical theology. Only the illuminative way, the practice of positive Christian virtue, remains uncontested. Yet this threefold division of ascetical theology has been firmly established since Thomas Aquinas, although its roots can be traced to Augustine and earlier. Thus it is wisest to take ascetical theology in its broadest sense, meaning the study of Christian discipline and the spiritual life.

The postapostolic church, beginning, perhaps, with the Shepherd of Hermas, began producing works on how this discipline was to be pursued; that is, how the goal of perfect charity and fellowship with God was to be gained. Spiritual teaching was quickly connected first with martyrdom as its highest good and then, partially under the influence of Neoplatonism, with virginity as a type of living martyrdom. As the life (Matt. 7:13–27). One must also include the call for constant watchfulness (Matt. 24:42; 25:13, or "abiding" in John). Paul picked up this theme with his call for self-discipline (I Cor. 9:24–27), his exhortation to put off the "old man" (Eph. 4:22) or to put to death the flesh (Col. 3:5), and his demand that Christians walk by the Spirit (Rom. 8; Gal. 5). Similar examples could be discovered in James, John, or Peter. It is the unified witness of the NT that the Christian life is a discipline, a struggle, and that success in this struggle is enabled by the grace of God or his Spirit.

The postapostolic church, beginning, perhaps, with the Shepherd of Hermas, began producing works on how this discipline was to be pursued; that is, how the goal of perfect charity and fellowship with God was to be gained. Spiritual teaching was quickly connected first with martyrdom as its highest good and then, partially under the influence of Neoplatonism, with virginity as a type of living martyrdom. As the church became one with the Roman Empire, it was the monastic movement which took up and defended the rigor of the early period; this was to be the home of ascetical theology for much of the succeeding church history, producing the works of the desert fathers, Basil and the Eastern tradition of spiritual direction, and later the medieval monastic tradition, following in the steps of Augustine.

In the Reformation period ascetical theology split into several different streams, some of which were more influenced by the medieval stress on the meditation on and identification with the human life of Christ and others more by the spiritual internalization of the life of Christ in the *Devotio Moderna* as seen especially in Thomas à Kempis's *Imitation of Christ.* The most radical stream was the Anabaptist one, which aimed at a disciplined church with primitive purity: the whole church fulfilled the monastic ideal of imitating Christ. The Catholic stream focused more upon a group of elect "first class" Christians (Francis de Sales, Ignatius's *Spiritual Exercises*), preserving the tradition of deep meditation on the human sufferings of Christ. Lutheran pietism and especially Calvinist Puritanism mediated ascetical theology to their respective traditions with their stress on holy lives (Richard Baxter, and in some respects William Law's *Serious Call*). Finally, there is the whole holiness tradition, beginning with John Wesley. If these are classified as radical, catholic, state church, and holiness, one can find a place within these categories for the Quakers and others who, knowingly or unconsciously, repeat the calls of spiritual directors and writers on ascetical theology down the ages (e.g., Richard Foster, Watchman Nee, or George Verwer).

The common themes of ascetical theology in whatever its clothing are the following: (1) a stress on the call of God and thus on God's enabling grace to live the Christian life; ascetical theology is neither Pelagianism nor legalism in its basic forms; (2) a demand that one forsake sin, including practices that much of the church might find acceptable for ordinary church people; this demand is usually related to literal following of the NT ethic; (3) a call to mortify the flesh and its desires, to discipline oneself, which in its best forms is not connected to a Neoplatonic dualistic anthropology (this theme and the previous one form the purgative way); (4) an invitation to follow Christ and apply oneself to those virtues which he commanded; (5) a call to self-surrender to God's will as an act of radical faith, at times in the form of virtually a conversion experience or a second work of grace (the illuminative way); and (6) an expectation that through quiet prayer and meditation one will become closer to God and experience him spiritually as "the living word" (Anabaptist) or even as one's divine spouse (Catholic tradition, e.g., John of the Cross). This last is the unitive way. While all of this can become a very individualistic seeking of perfection, the best writers of the tradition are aware of the body of Christ and thus formed their own groups to jointly pursue the goal and/or expected that the pursuit of perfection would lead to a deeper service to the whole body of Christ (e.g., Fénelon).

In either its narrower classical sense or its broader sense including a large Protestant tradition ascetical theology is essentially that part of moral and pastoral theology which aims at the renewal of individuals and the church, deeper spiritual experience, and true holiness in primitive simplicity. As such it is a theological discipline indispensable to the proper functioning of the church. P. H. Davids

See also Spirituality; Purgative Way, The; Illuminative Way, The; Unitive Way, The; Mysticism; Unio Mystica; Devotio Moderna.

Bibliography. P. Brooks, *Christian Spirituality;* O. Chadwick, *Western Asceticism;* E. Cothenet, *Imitating Christ;* K. R. Davis, *Anabaptism and Asceticism;* A. Devine, *Manual of Ascetical Theology;* R. Foster, *Celebration of Discipline;* F. P. Harton, *The Elements of the Spiritual Life;* U. T. Holmes, *A History of Christian Spirituality;* K. E. Kirk, *The Vision of God;* J. Lindworsky, *Christian Asceticism and Modern Man;* R. Lovelace, *The Dynamics of Spiritual Life; Orthodox Spirituality;* L. C. Shepherd, *Spiritual Writers in Modern Times;* M. Thornton, *English Spirituality; Dictionnaire de spiritualité ascétique et mystique,* esp. I, 936–1010; H. von Campenhausen, *Tradition and Life in the Church;* R. Williams, *Christian Spirituality;* O. Wyon, *Desire for God.*

Aseity of God. *See* God, Attributes of.

Ash Wednesday. Traditionally the day for the beginning of Lent, Ash Wednesday gets its name from the custom observed in some churches of dabbing ashes on the head as a sign of penitence. This was originally a part of the discipline of public penitence and came to be used generally from the tenth century for all who attended this service: one explanatory formula read (from Gen. 3:19), "Remember, O man, that you are dust, and unto dust shall you return."

When Lent was regarded as the church's opportunity to enter into the Lord's discipline of forty days in the wilderness as preparation for ministry, it was recognized that the six weeks following the six Sundays of Lent allowed only for thirty-six days of fasting (Sunday always being a festival of the resurrection). So four preliminary days of fasting were added, and thus the season began (at Rome in the middle of the fifth century) on the Wednesday preceding the first Sunday in Lent.

By tradition preparations were made for the fasting season by using up scraps of fat, etc., on the previous day, which was known as Shrove Tuesday, and this gave rise to the custom of eating pancakes that day. D. H. Wheaton

See also Christian Year.

Bibliography. A. A. McArthur, *The Evolution of the Christian Year.*

Asian Theology. "Theological ideas are *created* on the European continent, *corrected* in England, *corrupted* in America, and *crammed* into Asia," said one theologian. Because of rising nationalism and reassertion of traditional values in Asia, shoving "the white man's Christianity" upon Asians is no longer advisable.

In order to understand Asian theology one must examine distinctions between Eastern and Western cultures. Since the end of World War II, Asian theologians have been seeking liberation from Western theologies in order to make the gospel more relevant to their own life situations.

Historically, the development of Asian theology is closely related to the development of indigenization in the early twentieth century and to the recent development of the concept of contextualization in missions. The International Missionary Council in Jerusalem in 1930 stressed that the Christian message must be expressed in national and cultural patterns with liturgy, church music, dance, drama, and building structures accentuating national features. This emphasis on using indigenous art forms and structures was carried over into the area of theology. For example, Kanzo Uchimura, founder of a noted Non-Church Movement in Japan, emphasized a Japanese theology: "If Christianity is literally just one, then what a monotonous religion it is." He stated that just as there are German, English, Dutch, and American theologies, Japan should have a Japanese theology. He wanted Christianity expressed from the viewpoint of the Japanese; he wanted a Japanese Christianity.

In the early 1970s the Theological Education Fund introduced a new term, "contextualization," during the Third Mandate Period (1972–77). The concept of indigenization was taken one step further by applying it in the area of mission, theological approach, and educational method and structure. Contextualization takes into account the processes of secularity, technology, and the struggles for human justice which characterize the history of nations in Asia. Asian theologians, therefore, have used the concepts of indigenization and contextualization to justify the development of Asian theologies.

Many theologians argue that God's revelation came to us in the Scriptures through a specific cultural form, such as in the NT when God used the Jewish and hellenistic cultures to record his revelation. Therefore the gospel must also be translated today into the particular forms of Asian cultures, and consequently numerous Asian theologies claim to represent Asian cultural forms: pain of God theology (Japan), water buffalo theology (Thailand), third-eye theology (for the Chinese), minjung theology (Korea), theology of change (Taiwan), and a score of other national theologies such as Indian theology, Burmese theology, and Sri Lanka theology. The proliferation of Asian theologies has escalated markedly since the 1960s and will continue to multiply in the future. This will undoubtedly produce enormous impact on as well as conflict and confusion in theological institutions and Christian churches in Asia.

The major proponents of Asian theology have been liberal theologians of mainline denominational seminaries. An increasing number of evangelical theologians have sharply reacted against the concept of Asian theology. Other evangelicals are insisting on the necessity of it.

Due to the existence of very divergent religious cultures in Asia, the content of Asian theology is also diversified. It can be classified in four main areas: (1) syncretistic theology, (2) accommodation theology, (3) situational theology, and (4) biblical theology which is relevant to Asian needs.

Syncretistic Theology. Some Christian theologians and other religious thinkers have tried to syncretize Christianity with a national religion (Hinduism, Buddhism, or Islam) in an attempt to contextualize theology into the national situation. The Programme Unit on Faith and Witness of the World Council of Churches (WCC) has sponsored a number of religious dialogues with the leaders of other living religions. Many of these dialogues have resulted in a mutual acceptance of each other's beliefs. The scope of Hinduism and Buddhism is large enough to accommodate all other religions including Christianity. Sri Ramakrishna, founder of the Ramakrishna Mission, meditated on Christ, recognized Christ's divinity as an avatar (incarnation) of the Supreme like Krishna and Buddha, and encouraged his disciples to worship Christ.

The idea of the cosmic Christ which was emphasized during the WCC Assembly in New Delhi in 1961 has become prominent among liberal theologians in India. Raymond Panikkar in his book *The Unknown Christ of Hinduism* stresses that Christ already indwells the heart of a Hindu and that the mission of the church is not to bring Christ *to* the Hindu but to bring Christ *out of* him.

Klaus Klostermaier, a Roman Catholic theologian from Germany, visited Vrindaban, one of the Hindu sacred places in India, to have dialogue with Hindu gurus. After his spiritual experiences with Hindu scholars he testified, "The more I learned of Hinduism, the more surprised I grew that our theology does not offer anything essentially new to the Hindu."

M. M. Thomas, a prominent church leader both in India and in the WCC, expanded the cosmic Christ into a form of secular humanism. He interpreted salvation as man finding his true humanness so that it is no longer suppressed by social injustice, war, and poverty. Thomas said, "I cannot see any difference between the accepted missionary goal of a Christian Church expressing Christ in terms of the contemporary Hindu thought and life patterns and a Christ-centered Hindu Church of Christ which transforms Hindu thought and life patterns within."

Accommodation Theology. Accommodation is another subtle attempt to contextualize theology in Asia. Just as a hotel or a family accommodates a guest, so theological accommodation considers prevailing customs and religious practices of another culture and accommodates good ideas from other religions. Christian attempts to accommodate other religious ideas are observable particularly in Buddhist countries.

The Thailand Bible Society selected the word *dharma* (law, duty, virtue, teaching, gospel) for the word Logos in John 1:1, because the *dharma* in Thai Buddhist culture is as meaningful as the Logos in the hellenistic world of NT times. In the same way Matteo Ricci, Roman Catholic Jesuit missionary to China in the sixteenth century, chose the words *Tien Chu* (Heavenly Lord) as the name for God because that was the popular Chinese Buddhist concept of God.

Kosume Koyama, a former Japanese missionary professor at Thailand Theological Seminary, in his *Waterbuffalo Theology* opposes syncretism for not doing justice to both parties. He advocates accommodation instead. Koyama believes that one cannot mix Aristotelian pepper with Buddhist salt in the North Thailand theological "kitchen." One must, therefore, emphasize good "neighborology" rather than mere Christology, because Koyama believes that every religion has positive as well as negative points and that Thai Christians must accept the positive elements of Buddhism in Thailand in order to change their life style.

Song Choan-Seng of Taiwan stresses a "third-dimensional theology" as seen from an Asian perspective in his book *Third-Eye Theology*. He says, for example, that just as the Holy Spirit works in a Westerner's consciousness to bring about Christian conversion, so he works in the Zen Buddhists of Japan to bring about *satori* (enlightenment of the mind). Since the same Spirit is working in both religions, the objective of Christian missions should not be evangelization, but rather the interaction of Christian spirituality with Asian spirituality.

Two noted theologians in Sri Lanka have had a similar interest in accommodating Buddhist terminologies and ideas to Christian theology. D. T. Niles, one of the key leaders in the East Asia Christian Conference (now Christian Conference of Asia), did not hesitate to use words such as *dharma* and *sangha* to describe Christian "doctrines" and the "body of Christ" in his *Buddhism and the Claims of Christ*. Lyn de Silva, a Methodist minister in Sri Lanka, believes that the teaching of earlier Buddhism on the three basic characteristics of existence—*anicca* (impermanence), *dukkha* (suffering), and *anatta* (no-self)—provides comprehensive analysis of the human predicament that can become a basis for Christian theology. *Anicca* affirms the status of constant change of all conditional things; *dukkha* affirms that attachment is the cause for human suffering; and *anatta* affirms no soul or any permanent entity in man. The concepts of *anicca* and *dukkha* can be easily accommodated into Christian theology, but *anatta* proves more difficult due to the biblical concept of immortality.

The accommodation of Asian religious terminologies and concepts such as *dharma*, *Tien Chu*, *anicca*, *dukkha*, and *anatta* into Christian theology can be accepted to a certain extent by many Christians as long as the biblical interpretation and meaning are added to such words and concepts. Yet the question of where to draw the line between syncretism and accommodation depends on whether the person is willing to accept the unique revelation of God in Jesus Christ and in the Scriptures in his accommodation. A person's answer to a question such as "Do Buddhists need to be converted to Jesus Christ for the forgiveness of their sins?" will reveal whether or not he believes that Jesus Christ is the only way to God.

Situational Theology. Another type of Asian theology derives directly from a particular situation. This situational theology may not be in agreement with the biblical and historical doctrines of the Christian church, and yet it speaks to concrete situations in Asia. Kazoh Kitamori's pain of God theology in Japan is an excellent illustration. He tried to demonstrate to the suffering people in Japan after their defeat in World War II that the God revealed in the Bible is the God of suffering and pain who could identify with the suffering Japanese.

The minjung theology (theology of the mass of the people) is another typical illustration. The main thrust of ecumenical theology today in Asia is toward the liberation of persons from social injustice, economic exploitation, political oppression, and racial discrimination. The minjung theology is a Korean version of liberation theology and teaches that Jesus Christ is the liberator of these oppressed people. The major papers from a conference on the minjung theology, October 22–24, 1979, were edited by Yong-Bock Kim, director of the Christian Institute for the Study of Justice and Development in Seoul, and published as *Minjung Theology: People as the Subjects of History.*

Need for Biblically Oriented Asian Theology. Theology in Asia has been taught by Western missionaries. The West has its own theological formulations derived out of its own cultural background—Calvinism, Arminianism, death of God, etc. Yet in Asia the circumstances facing Christians differ from the West. Asian Christians must make their theologies relevant to their living situations in Asia. Some of the main issues which Christians in Asia are facing today are communism, poverty, suffering, war, idolatry, demon possession, bribery, and cheating.

Most evangelical theologians see the value of Asian theology in allowing Asians to express their theological thoughts within their own contexts. Nevertheless, they are also very apprehensive of the danger of syncretism and of minimizing fundamental scriptural teachings during the process of contextualization.

At the Sixth Asia Theological Association Consultation in Seoul, Korea, 1982, some eighty evangelical theologians discussed Asian theology and jointly produced a twenty-page Asian evangelical theologians' declaration, *The Bible and Theology in Asia Today.* Although there is no particular Asian theology with an evangelical label which is widely accepted by evangelical theologians, this joint evangelical declaration has laid down a few guiding principles for theology in different religious contexts of Asia. (1) The authority of the Bible is reaffirmed as the only infallible, inerrant Word of God: "The Bible, not theologians, is to speak in our theology." (2) Jesus Christ, the only incarnate Son of God, is unique. (3) Mission-centered theology aiming to communicate the gospel to the lost is the best protection against syncretism. (4) Love should be the essential part of an Asian theology; only as Christians identify themselves with the needy do they contextualize the gospel.

Conclusion. The key issue in the whole argument around developing an Asian theology is whether in the process of contextualization the biblical and historical doctrines of the Christian church can be preserved without compromise. An analogy can be made with carrying the ark of the covenant in the OT. In OT times the ark was carried by ox cart. Today in several Asian countries the ark would be carried by rickshaw, horse, motorcycle, or car. Yet the meaning of the ark must not be changed. Many liberal theologians are trying to change the ark itself.

Asian Christians must listen to, evaluate, and be open-minded to different Asian theological views on contextualization and yet, without compromise, be faithful to the gospel and proclaim it in love, as the apostle Paul exhorts: "Be on the alert, stand firm in the faith, act like men, be strong. Let all that you do be done in love" (I Cor. 16:13–14).

B. R. Ro

See also PAIN OF GOD THEOLOGY.

Bibliography. G. H. Anderson, ed., *Asian Voices in Christian Theology;* D. J. Elwood, ed., *What Asian Christians Are Thinking;* D. J. Elwood and E. P. Nakpil, eds., *The Human and the Holy;* K. Kitamori, *Theology of the Pain of God;* K. Klostermaier, *Hindu and Christian in Vrindaban;* C. Michalson, *Japanese Contributions to Christian Theology.*

Assumption of Mary. *See* MARY, ASSUMPTION OF.

Assurance. Assurance of faith or assurance of salvation denotes the confidence of the believer in Christ that notwithstanding his mortal sinful condition he is irrevocably a child of God and an heir of heaven. If a president should pardon a convicted criminal, it is proper that he should bring this to the person's attention. Similarly, if God freely forgives our sins, we should expect that he will assure us of this fact. Thus just as he convicts the world of sin, righteousness, and judgment, the Holy Spirit, who cannot deceive, provides the believer with the certainty of his new standing in the family of God.

The doctrine of spiritual assurance is widely taught in the NT, particularly by Paul, John, and the writer of Hebrews. The apostle Paul plainly teaches that the Spirit of adoption produces in the Christian the assurance of sonship (Rom. 8:15–17; Gal. 4:6). By virtue of God's purposes and work in election, calling, justification, and glorification (Rom. 8:29–30), Paul is convinced that nothing earthly or heavenly can separate the believer from God's love (Rom. 8:38–39). The Christian possesses full certainty of God's ability to bring to completion the salvation that he has begun (II Tim. 1:12; Phil. 1:6). The Christian ought to possess "assured understanding" (Col. 2:2) and "full conviction" (I Thess. 1:5) of his spiritual heritage in Christ. John likewise writes that on the basis of scriptural testimony to Christ's saving work the believer can know with certainty that he possesses eternal life (John 5:24; I John 5:13). Moreover, the testimony of the Holy Spirit in the heart (I John 4:13; 5:10) and the presence of the fruits of the Spirit in the life (I John 3:18–19) provide assurance that a person is saved. The author of Hebrews concurs with these teachings when he writes of the "full assurance of hope" (Heb. 6:11) and the "full assurance of faith" (Heb. 10:22) the believer may enjoy by virtue of his new relation to Christ.

An examination of biblical teaching will disclose that assurance of salvation has both an objective and a subjective basis. First, on the objective authority of the Word of God the believer can know that God chose him from the foundation of the world, and that Christ made full atonement for his sins, rose from the dead for his justification, lives to make intercession, and will come again to receive him to glory. Assurance in the first place rests not on emotional experience but on the authoritative testimony to Christ's saving work. On the other hand, assurance also involves the deep personal conviction created by the Holy Spirit in the heart that sins have been forgiven, that I have been adopted into the family of God, and that I belong to him forever. The religious affections thus infallibly certify the saving benefits of the gospel.

Scripture makes it plain that one may be genuinely saved but lack full assurance of salvation (I John 5:13). Religious certainty may be weakened by sinful habits, neglect of God's Word, quenching of the Spirit, and even by physical or mental exhaustion. The normal experience of assurance achieved by faith and obedience results in security in an age of insecurity, selfless service to God and neighbor, and confidence in the face of death.

The doctrine of assurance was given full treatment by Luther, Calvin, and most post-Reformation divines. The Roman Catholic Church at the Council of Trent rejected the teaching that a Christian may be certain he is saved. Given the Roman doctrines of merit and purgatory, only a special revelation from God could provide the individual with assurance of final salvation. Arminians generally believe that the most one can enjoy is assurance at any given moment, since a believer may apostatize and forfeit his salvation. Methodism, under the lead of John Wesley, stresses as a central conviction the possession of assurance through the internal witness of the Holy Spirit and a life lived without voluntary sin.

B. A. Demarest

See also Backsliding; Perseverance.

Bibliography. L. Berkhof, *Systematic Theology,* 507–9; *Encyclopedia of the Lutheran Church,* III, 298–99; H. A. Ironside, *Full Assurance.*

Astrology. The ancient art or science that claims to discover and interpret the influence of stars and planets on persons or events. Some conclude that the planets actually exert an influence, while others believe that a study of their movements and positions will provide an indication or prediction of how a person or event will fare. Astrology is to be distinguished from astronomy in that the latter seeks information about the heavenly bodies and laws governing their movements, while the former deals with alleged meaning in the relationship of heavenly bodies to people and events on earth.

Astrological principles seem to have been developed first in Mesopotamia, among the Assyrians and Babylonians of the seventh-sixth centuries B.C. The interpretation of movements and positions of the heavenly bodies was one of the chief means at the disposal of priests for discovering the will and intentions of the gods. But horoscopes for individuals had not yet been developed; astrology was restricted to concerns of public welfare and the king as head of state. During the Persian period, in the late sixth century B.C., cultivation of astrology began in Egypt. After the death of Alexander the Great and the breakup of his empire, astrology found its way from the Seleucid Empire into the western Greek world. During the third century B.C. personal horoscopes became popular. In the first century B.C. astrological practices spread among the Romans. Augustus and Tiberius were first century A.D. emperors who subscribed to astrological practices.

Of great importance to the impact of astrology was Ptolemy (Claudius Ptolemaeus), the celebrated mathematician, astronomer, and geographer of second century Alexandria. Having established the view that the earth was spherical and that it was the center of the universe, he went on in his *Tetrabiblos* to provide the standard astrological text of the Middle Ages. In the credulous spirit of the Middle Ages both Jews and Christians were swept up in the practice of astrology. It was further developed by Muslim Arabs during the seventh to the thirteenth centuries. Enjoying considerable popularity even in political circles of the West during the fourteenth and fifteenth centuries, astrology lost its grip after the advent of the new astronomy of Copernicus and Newton during the sixteenth and seventeenth centuries and the subsequent arrival of the age of reason. The resurgence of astrology in recent years is due in part to the anxiety and uncertainty of the age and the decline of the influence of Christianity and biblical principles in Western civilization.

The OT is clear in condemning the worship of heavenly bodies (see, e.g., Deut. 4:19; 17:2–5; II Kings 17:16), a practice that Manasseh introduced in the southern kingdom (II Kings 21:5) and Josiah removed (II Kings 23:5). That was not the end of the matter, however; Jeremiah refers to Hebrew worship of the "queen of heaven" (Ishtar, the planet Venus; 7:18; 44:17–19) and more generally to worship of heavenly bodies (8:2; 19:13).

But such worship is not the same as the practice of astrology. Isaiah referred specifically to stargazers, to "those who divide the heavens," those who distinguished the signs of the zodiac (47:13). His condemnation of them was clear in his declaration that they could not even save themselves. Hebrews were to seek their God directly. The astrologers were also indirectly condemned in Daniel's day, when they could not meet the demands of Nebuchadnezzar. Daniel through divine enablement stepped into the gap (2:27; 4:7; 5:7, 11).

In the NT there may be two references to astrology. Some think that "height" and "depth" (Rom. 8:39) are to be considered as astrological terms, but more likely they are to be treated as astronomical terms and merely refer to celestial spaces above and below the horizon in which the stars move and from which they rise. The appearance of a star at the birth of Jesus has given rise to much astronomical and astrological discussion. Magi, perhaps Median priests, saw Jesus' star in the east (Matt. 2). Whether it was a nova, a comet, a conjunction of planets (e.g., Jupiter, Mars, and Saturn), or just some supernatural light in the sky, it signified to them the birth of a great ruler among the Jews. An isolated sign like this is no endorsement of astrology. God has the right to meet seeking hearts through a medium they would understand. If there was a sign in the heavens at Jesus' death (sun was darkened) and if there will be signs in the heavens at his second coming (cf. Luke 21:25), why should there not be a sign in the heavens at his first coming?

H. F. Vos

See also Occult, The.

Bibliography. F. Cumont: *Astrology and Religion Among the Greeks and Romans; Tetrabiblos,* ed. F. E. Robbins.

Athanasian Creed. One of the three ecumenical creeds widely used in Western Christendom as a profession of the orthodox faith. It is also referred to as the *Symbolum Quicunque* because the first words of the Latin text read, *Quicunque vult salvus esse*... ("Whoever wishes to be saved ...").

According to tradition Athanasius, bishop of Alexandria in the fourth century, was the author of the creed. The oldest known instance of the use of this name is in the first canon of the Synod of Autun, *ca.* 670, where it is called the "faith" of St. Athanasius. Although doubts concerning the Athanasian authorship had been expressed in the sixteenth century, Gerhard Voss, a Dutch humanist, demonstrated the impossibility of reconciling the facts known about the creed with the age of Athanasius. He published his findings in 1642. Subsequent scholarship, both Catholic and Protestant, has confirmed the verdict of Voss. Among other factors the Athanasian Creed is clearly a Latin symbol, whereas Athanasius himself wrote in Greek. Moreover, it omits all the theological terms dear to Athanasius such as *homoousion,* but it includes the *filioque* popular in the West.

There have been many suggestions as to the identity of the actual author. One of the more widely held theories is that the date of the creed was *ca.* 500, the place of composition a south Gaul location influenced by theologians of Lerins, and the special theological issues both Arianism and Nestorianism. These conclusions disqualify Ambrose of Milan even though several eminent scholars point to him as author. Caesarius of Arles perhaps comes closest to the above specifications. However, the question of authorship and origin remains open. The earliest copy of the text of the creed occurs in a sermon of Caesarius early in the sixth century. Other manuscripts containing the creed have been dated in the latter part of the seventh and eighth centuries. In these earliest mentions it appears that its functions were both liturgical and catechetical.

The creed was counted as one of the three classic creeds of Christianity by the time of the Reformation. Both Lutheran and Reformed confessional statements recognize the authoritative character of the *Quicunque* (with the exception of the Westminster Confession, which accords it no formal recognition). However, the contemporary liturgical use of the creed is largely confined to the Roman and Anglican communions.

Structurally the creed is composed of forty carefully modeled clauses or verses, each containing a distinct proposition. These clauses are divided into two clearly demarcated sections. The first centers on the doctrine of God as Trinity. The precise formulation of the doctrine is designed on the one hand to exclude unorthodox viewpoints, and on the other hand to express the insights explicit in the church under the influence of Augustine's teaching. Consequently this part of the creed expresses what the church felt to be the necessary understanding of God, the holy Trinity, calling it the *fides catholica.* The paradox of the unity and the Trinity of God is affirmed in the face of modalism, which attempted to solve the paradox by insisting on the unity while reducing the Trinity to mere successive appearances, and the Arians, who tried to resolve the difficulty by rejecting a unity of essence by dividing the divine substance.

The second section of the Athanasian Creed expresses the church's faith in the incarnation by affirming the doctrinal conclusions reached in controversies regarding the divinity and the humanity of Jesus. The creed does not hesitate again to affirm a doctrine which in human experience is paradoxical—that in the incarnation there was a union of two distinctly different natures, the divine and the human, each complete in itself, without either losing its identity. Yet the result of this union is a single person. The creed thus repudiates the teachings that Christ had but one nature (Sabellianism), or that the human nature was incomplete (Apollinarianism), or that the divine nature was inferior to that of the Father (Arianism), or that in the union of the two natures the identity of one was lost so that the result was simply one nature (Eutychianism).

It has been said that no other official statement of the early church sets forth, so incisively and with such clarity, the profound theology that is implicit in the basic scriptural affirmation that "God was in Christ reconciling the world to himself." The somewhat technical case of its phraseology notwithstanding, the concern of the Athanasian Creed is to assert a conception of the Triune God which is free from anthropomorphic polytheism and a conception of the incarnation which holds in tension the vital data concerning Christ's humanity and divinity. It is this doctrinal perspective which lends significance to the clauses at the beginning and end of the two parts of the creed ("whoever wishes to be saved must think thus" about the Trinity and the incarnation). They do not mean that a believer must understand all theological details to be saved or that he must memorize the language of the creed. What is intended is the fact that the Christian faith is distinctly Christocentric, trusting in Christ as Savior. The church knows no other way of salvation and therefore must reject all teachings which deny his true deity or his real incarnation.

The creed does not specify the authority, either the Bible or church, upon which it makes its affirmations. However, it is a scriptural creed because it uses the ideas and sometimes the words of Scripture. It is a church creed because it is a consensus within the Christian fellowship. The Athanasian Creed remains a superb compendium of Trinitarian and Christological theology and offers itself as a ready outline for catechetical purposes in keeping with its original intent.

J. F. Johnson

See also Creed, Creeds; Homoousion; Filioque; Athanasius.

Bibliography. J. N. D. Kelly, *The Athanasian Creed;* D. Waterland, *A Critical History of the Athanasian Creed;* C. A. Swainson, *The Nicene and Apostles' Creeds.*

Athanasius (*ca.* 296–373). Bishop of Alexandria from 328 to 373. An uncompromising foe of Arianism, Athanasius was particularly instrumental in bringing about its condemnation at the Council of Nicaea. He is regarded as the greatest theologian of his time.

Athanasius grew up within the order of the imperial church, an institution to which he held fast throughout his life. Of his early years little is known. It is said that he was the son of well-to-do parents, but in later years he made it clear that he was a poor man. As a youth he attracted the notice of Alexander, who presided over the see of Alexandria. At an early age Athanasius was taken into the household of the bishop and was provided the best training that the times could afford. His education was essentially Greek; he was a "classicist" and never seems to have acquired any knowledge of Hebrew. He demonstrated, of course, the influence both of his patron, Alexander, and of the earlier Alexandrian thinker, Origen. He numbered among his earlier acquaintances and tutors some who had suffered in the great persecutions, and he no doubt drew some of the intensity of his belief from the fervency engendered in those crucial years. Not long after he turned twenty, Athanasius plunged into writing and produced theological works of lasting importance. One was the *Contra Gentiles,* a defense of Christianity against paganism; another was the *De incarnatione,* an attempt to explain the doctrine of redemption.

During this period of writing Athanasius was acting as the secretary and confidant of his bishop, by whom he was personally made deacon. It was in this capacity that he attended the first general council held in Nicaea in 325. At the council the anti-Arian party led by Bishop Alexander won a resounding victory over Arian subordinationism. The council affirmed that the Son of God was "of one substance with the Father," which means that both share alike in the fundamental nature of deity. After the council concluded, Athanasius returned with his bishop to Alexandria and continued to work with him in establishing the faith that had been defined at Nicaea. In 328 Alexander died and Athanasius succeeded him in the see.

The tenure of Athanasius as Bishop of Alexandria was marked by five periods of exile. His vigorous defense of the Nicene formula caused him to be a target for the supporters of Arius, who rallied after the council. However, during his forty-six years as bishop there were enough years of relative peace in the empire and the church for Athanasius to accomplish much as a theologian. Admittedly he was a churchman and a pastor rather than a systematic or speculative theologian. However, this does not mean that his thought is not cogent, but that his work developed in response to the needs of each moment rather than on the basis of the requirements of a system. His works are pastoral, exegetical, polemical, and even biographical; there is no single treatise that attempts to present the totality of his theology. Nevertheless, for Athanasius the truth or falsity of a doctrine is to be judged on the basis of the degree in which it expresses two basic principles of the Christian faith: monotheism and the doctrine of salvation. These are the foci for his theological reflection.

In *Contra Gentiles,* Athanasius discusses the means by which God can be known. These are principally two: the soul and nature. God may be known through the human soul, for "although God Himself is above all, the road which leads to Him is not far, nor even outside ourselves, but is within us, and it is possible to find it by ourselves" (30.1). That is to say, by studying the soul we may infer something about the nature of God. The soul is invisible and immortal; therefore, the true God must be invisible and immortal. To be sure, sin prevents the soul from perfectly attaining the vision of God, but the soul was made according to the divine image and it was intended to be like a mirror in which that image, which is the Word of God, would shine. This is a Platonic theme that had become part of the Alexandrian tradition since Origen.

It is also possible to know God through his creation, which, "as though in written characters, declares in a loud voice, by its order and harmony, its own Lord and Creator" (*Contra Gentiles,* 34.4). But the order of the universe shows not only that there is a God but also that he is one. If there were more than one God, the unity of purpose that can be perceived throughout the cosmos would be impossible. Moreover, the order and reason within nature show that God has created it and rules it through his Word. For Athanasius, the Word of God who rules the world is the living Logos of God—that is, the Word who is God himself. This view of God indicates that Athanasius, even before becoming involved in the Arian conflict, had developed an understanding of the Word that was different, not only from the Arians, but also from that view held by many earlier theologians. Before Athanasius there was a tendency to establish the distinction between the Father and the Word on the basis of the contrast between the absolute God and a subordinate deity. This was, Athanasius insisted, incompatible with Christian monotheism.

The other pillar of Athanasius's theology was soteriology. The salvation of which humanity stands in need is continuous with creation, for it is in fact a re-creation of fallen humanity. In sin, man abandoned the image of God; an element of disintegration was introduced within creation through sin. It can be expelled only through a new work of creation. Consequently, the core of Athanasius's doctrine of redemption is that only God himself can save mankind. If the salvation that we need is really a new creation, only the Creator can bring it. This requires the Savior to be God, for only God can grant an existence similar to his.

The principles of monotheism and the doctrine of redemption influenced Athanasius in his formulation of arguments against the Arians. Whereas they usually appealed to logical analysis and subtle distinctions, Athanasius constantly referred to the two great pillars of his faith. In this sense, the importance of Athanasius lies not so much in his writings themselves as in the things he defended and preserved in a life full of tension and disturbance. In a critical moment in the church's history he maintained the essential character of Christianity in his struggles with Arians and emperors. But for him, Harnack has said (*History of Dogma,* II), the church would probably have fallen into the hands of the Arians.

J. F. Johnson

See also Nicaea, Council of; Arianism; Homoousion; Athanasian Creed.

Bibliography. H. von Campenhausen, *The Fathers of the Greek Church;* J. W. C. Wand, *Doctors and Councils;* F. L. Cross, *The Study of Athanasius.*

Atheism. The Greek word *atheos,* "without God," is found only once in the NT (Eph. 2:12). There it is used in the plural form to designate the condition of being without the true God. It refers to the deepest state of heathen misery (cf. Rom. 1:28). It is not found in either the LXX or the Apocrypha. Both the OT and NT begin with or assume the reality of God, not as some speculative premise, but as universally manifest in nature, man's reason and conscience, and divine revelation. The normal human state includes the knowledge of God; atheism is thus viewed as abnormal. Hebrew has no equivalent word for atheism. In the OT the form of atheism that one encounters is practical atheism—human conduct that is carried out without consideration of God (Pss. 10:4; 14:1; 53:1; cf. Isa. 31:1; Jer. 2:13, 17–18; 5:12; 18:13–15).

The Greeks used "atheism" in three senses: (1) impious or godless; (2) without supernatural help; (3) not believing in any god or the Greek conception of god. Because Christians denied the popular gods of the day, they were often accused of atheism by the pagans. Protestants at times have been called atheists because of their refusal to deify Mary and to worship saints. More and more in speculative circles the term came to mean a denial of God or the negation of the spiritual idea.

Just as the first century introduced a devotion to theism unique in its scope and depth, so the twentieth century has produced a somewhat parallel commitment to atheism. This century has seen the development of communism with its devotion to atheism, as well as the establishment in 1925 of the American Association for the Advancement of Atheism. The latter organization was formed to attack all religions through the distribution of atheistic literature. In 1929 its successor was formed, the League of Militant Atheists, with goals of the undermining of the religious foundations of Western society, the establishment of centers for atheistic lectures, the placement of atheistic professors, and the sponsorship of lectureships. By 1932 this organization claimed a membership of five and a half million.

Twentieth century atheism may be contrasted with older forms in two ways. (1) Today atheism is claimed to be the logical consequence of a rational system that accounts for all human experience without the need to appeal to God. Communism is such an organized and integrated system. At its heart is a materialistic view of history and the complete secularization of life. (2) Earlier atheists were thought to be vulgar and depraved. Today many serve on the faculties of the most prestigious universities, and more often than not the theist seems to be the obscurantist.

Thus, in modern usage four senses of "atheism" may be identified: (1) Classical atheism. This is not a general denial of God's existence but the rejection of the god of a particular nation. Christians were repeatedly called atheists in this sense because they refused to acknowledge heathen gods. It was also in this sense that Cicero called Socrates and Diagoras of Athens atheists. (2) Philosophical atheism. This position may be contrasted with theism, which affirms a personal, self-conscious deity (not a principle, first cause, or force). (3) Dogmatic atheism. This is the absolute denial of God's existence. This position is more rare than one might think, as people have more often declared themselves agnostics or secularists. There have, however, been those who claimed to hold this view (the eighteenth century French atheists). (4) Practical atheism. While God is not denied, life is lived as if there is no God. There is complete indifference to his claims, and often there is outspoken and defiant wickedness (Ps. 14:1). This form of atheism is widely prevalent, as can be seen from the Scriptures cited above.

Numerous arguments for atheism have been given. Some of the more important are: (1) The onus of proof is on the theist, since atheism is *prima facie* a more reasonable position. (2) Closely related is the belief that theistic proofs are inadequate. (3) Theism is harmful to society, as it leads to intolerance and persecution. (4) With the advances in modern science there is no need for God as an explanatory hypothesis. The supernatural is unneeded. (5) Belief in God is psychologically explainable. (6) The logical positivists argue that theism is neither true nor false because it is unverifiable (e.g., nothing counts for *or* against it) by public sense experience. (7) Classical theism is logically contradictory or incoherent. For instance, it has been claimed that the notion of necessary existence is incoherent and that the existence of an omnipotent, perfectly good God is inconsistent with the presence of evil in the world.

Finally, objections have been raised to atheism in its theoretical form: (1) It is against reason. The existence of something rather than nothing requires God. (2) It is contrary to human experience, where some knowledge of God, no matter how suppressed and distorted, has universally existed. (3) Atheism cannot account for design, order, and regularity in the universe. (4) It cannot explain the existence of man and mind.

P. D. Feinberg

Bibliography. E. Borne, *Atheism;* A. Flew, *God and Philosophy* and *The Presumption of Atheism;* J. Lacroix, *Meaning of Modern Atheism;* A. MacIntyre and P. Ricoeur, *Religious Significance of Atheism;* I. Lepp, *Atheism in Our Time;* C. Fabro, *God in Exile.*

Atheism, Christian. *See* Death of God Theology.

Atonement. The expression "to make atonement" is frequent in Exodus, Leviticus, and Numbers, but rare in the rest of the Bible. The basic idea, however, is widespread. The need for it arises from the fact that man is a sinner, a truth made plain throughout Scripture but infrequent outside the Bible.

In the OT sin is dealt with by the offering of sacrifice. Thus the burnt offering will be accepted "to make atonement" (Lev. 1:4), as also the sin offering and the guilt offering (Lev. 4:20; 7:7) and especially the sacrifices on the day of atonement (Lev. 16). Of course, sacrifice is ineffective if offered in the wrong spirit. To sin "with a high hand" (Num. 15:30), i.e., proudly and presumptuously, is to place oneself outside the sphere of God's forgiveness. The prophets have many denunciations of the offering of sacrifice as a merely external action. But to offer sacrifice as the expression of a repentant and trustful heart is to find atonement. Atonement is sometimes made by means other than the sacrifices, such as the payment of money (Exod. 30:12–16) or the offering of life (II Sam. 21:3–6). In such cases to make atonement means "'to avert punishment, especially the divine anger, by the payment of a *kōper,* a ransom,' which may be of money or which may be of life" (L. Morris, *The Apostolic Preaching of the Cross,* 166). Throughout the OT sin is serious; it will be punished unless atonement is sought in the way God has provided.

This truth is repeated and enlarged upon in the NT. There it is made clear that all men are sinners (Rom. 3:23) and that hell awaits them (Mark 9:43; Luke 12:5). But it is just as clear that God wills to bring salvation and that he has brought it in the life, death, resurrection, and ascension of his Son. The love of God is the mainspring (John 3:16; Rom. 5:8). We are not to think of a loving Son as wringing salvation from a just but stern Father. It is the will of the Father that men be saved, and salvation is accomplished, not with a wave of the hand, so to speak, but by what God has done in Christ: "God was in Christ reconciling the world to himself" (II Cor. 5:19), a reconciliation brought about by the death of Christ (Rom. 5:10). The NT emphasizes his death, and it is no accident that the cross has come to be accepted as the symbol of the Christian faith or that words like "crux" and "crucial" have come to have the significance that they possess. The cross is absolutely central to salvation as the NT sees it. This is distinctive of Christianity. Other religions have their martyrs, but the death of Jesus was not that of a martyr. It was that of a Savior. His death saves men from their sins. Christ took their place and died their death (Mark 10:45; II Cor. 5:21), the culmination of a ministry in which he consistently made himself one with sinners.

The NT does not put forward a theory of atonement, but there are several indications of the principle on which atonement is effected. Thus sacrifice must be offered—not the sacrifice of animals, which cannot avail for men (Heb. 10:4), but the perfect sacrifice of Christ (Heb. 9:26; 10:5–10). Christ paid sin's due penalty (Rom. 3:25–26; 6:23; Gal. 3:13). He redeemed us (Eph. 1:7), paying the price that sets us free (I Cor. 6:20; Gal. 5:1). He made a new covenant (Heb. 9:15). He won the victory (I Cor. 15:55–57). He effected the propitiation that turns away the wrath of God (Rom. 3:25), made the reconciliation that turns enemies into friends (Eph. 2:16). His love and his patient endurance of suffering set an example (I Pet. 2:21); we are to take up our cross (Luke 9:23). Salvation is many-sided. But however it is viewed, Christ has taken our place, doing for us what we could not do for ourselves. Our part is simply to respond in repentance, faith, and selfless living.

L. Morris

See also Atonement, Extent of the; Atonement, Theories of the; Blood, Sacrificial Aspects of.

Bibliography. R. S. Franks, *The Work of Christ;* L. W. Grensted, *A Short History of the Doctrine of the Atonement;* G. Smeaton, *The Doctrine of the Atonement According to Christ* and *The Doctrine of the Atonement According to the Apostles;* V. Taylor, *The Atonement in NT Teaching* and *Forgiveness and Reconciliation;* J. Owen, *The Death of Death in the Death of Christ;* J. Denney, *The Death of Christ;* A. A. Hodge, *The Atonement;* J. M. Campbell, *The Nature of the Atonement;* R. Wallace, *The Atoning Death of Christ;* J. K. Mozley, *The Doctrine of the Atonement;* C. R. Smith, *The Bible Doctrine of Salvation;* L. Morris, *The Apostolic Preaching of the Cross;* P. T. Forsyth, *The Cruciality of the Cross.*

Atonement, Day of. The day of atonement speaks of the Lord's gracious concern both to deal fully with his people's sins and to make them fully aware that they stand before him, accepted and covered in respect of all iniquity, transgression, and sin (Lev. 16:21).

The day of atonement (Lev. 16) centered on the high priestly ritual of the two goats (vss. 7–10, 15–17, 20–22). One goat is specified as a "sin offering" (vss. 9, 15). The priest would follow the rules of Lev. 4, except that now he sprinkles the blood within the veil (vs. 15). This was a concealed act (vs. 17), observed only by the priest. But the Lord would have his people know, by personal experience, what had thus taken place secretly. He therefore appointed a public ceremony (vss. 20ff.) which publicized what had been effected by the blood upon the mercy seat. The public ritual stresses, first, the truth of substitution. The laying on of hands (vs. 21; cf. 1:4; 3:2; 4:4) expresses the transference of sin from the guilty to the innocent, so that the latter actually becomes a "sin-bearer" (vs. 22; cf. Isa. 53:4, 6, 11–12). Secondly, atonement finally and irreversibly puts sin away: the sin-bearer goes, never to return, to the wilderness (vs. 10), a solitary (or "cut-off") land (vs. 22). In this connection the goat is said to be for "Azazel" (vss. 8, 10, 26), a word which, unused elsewhere, may mean a goat driven off (combining *'ēz*, "goat," with *'āzal*, "to go away"), or a precipice (symbolic of a remote, menacing place). Or it may be the name of a supposed desert demon, signifying not an offering to such a demon but the banishing of sin to the place of total separation from the Lord.

J. A. Motyer

See also Offerings and Sacrifices in Bible Times.

Bibliography. J. C. Rylaarsdam, *IDB*, I, 313–16; T. H. Gaster, *IDB*, I, 325–26; G. J. Wenham, *The Book of Leviticus;* R. K. Harrison, *Leviticus.*

Atonement, Extent of the. Although there are variations as to the basic ways in which this subject can be addressed, the choices boil down to two: either the death of Jesus was intended to secure salvation for a limited number or the death of Jesus was intended to provide salvation for everyone. The first view is sometimes called "limited atonement" because God limited the effect of Christ's death to a specific number of elect persons, or "particular redemption" because redemption was for a particular group of people. The second view is sometimes referred to as "unlimited atonement" or "general redemption" because God did not limit Christ's redemptive death to the elect, but allowed it to be for mankind in general.

Particular Redemption. The doctrine that Jesus died for the elect in particular, securing their redemption, but not for the world, arose as the implications of the doctrine of election and the satisfaction theory of the atonement were developed immediately following the Reformation. A controversy arose that resulted in the Synod of Dort (1618–19) pronouncing that Christ's death was "sufficient for all but efficient for the elect." This did not satisfy many theologians, even some Calvinists, so the controversy has continued to this day.

There are numerous arguments used to defend the doctrine of limited atonement, but the following represent some of the more frequently found.

First, in the Bible there is a qualification as to who will benefit by the death of Christ, thus limiting its effect. John 10:11, 15 says Christ died for "his sheep"; Acts 20:28 "his church"; Rom. 8:32–35 "the elect"; and Matt. 1:21 "his people." Second, God's designs are always efficacious and can never be frustrated by man. Had God intended all men to be saved by the death of Christ, then all would be saved. It is clear that not everyone is saved because the Bible clearly teaches that those who reject Christ are lost. Therefore it stands to reason that Christ could not have died for everyone, because not everyone is saved. To argue that Christ died for everyone is in effect to argue that God's saving will is not being done or that everyone will be saved, both of which propositions are clearly false. Third, if Christ died for everyone, God would be unfair in sending people to hell for their own sins. No law court allows payment to be exacted twice for the same crime, and God will not do that either. So God could not have allowed Christ to die for everyone unless he planned for everyone to be saved, which clearly he did not, because some are lost. Christ paid for the sins of the elect; the lost pay for their own sins. Fourth, to say that Christ died for everyone logically leads to universalism. It is true that not all of those who believe in general redemption believe in universalism; but there is no valid reason that they do not. If they were consistent they would, because they are arguing that Christ paid for everyone's sins, thus saving them. Fifth, Christ died not just to make salvation possible, but actually to save. To argue that Christ died only to provide the possibility of salvation is to leave open the question of whether *anyone* is saved. If God's designs are only of possibilities and not actualities, then no one is secure and everything is open to doubt. But the Bible clearly teaches that the death of Jesus actually secures salvation for his people, thus making it a certainty and limiting the atonement (Matt. 18:11; Rom. 5:10; II Cor. 5:21; Gal. 1:4; 3:13; Eph. 1:7). Sixth, because there are no conditions to be met in order to be saved (i.e., salvation is by grace and not by works, even an act of faith), both repentance and faith are secured for those for whom Christ died. If the design of the atonement were for everyone, then all would receive repentance and faith, but this is clearly false. Therefore, Christ's death could have been intended only for those who will repent and believe, namely, the elect. Seventh, the passages that speak of Christ's death for "the world" have been misunderstood. The word "world" really means the world of the elect, the world of believers, the church, or all nations. Finally, the passages that say Christ died for all men have also been misunderstood. The word "all" means "all classes" of men, not everyone.

General Redemption. The doctrine of general redemption argues that the death of Christ was designed to include all mankind, whether or not all believe. To those who savingly believe it is redemptively applied, and to those who do not believe it provides the benefits of common grace and the removal of any excuse for being lost. God loved them and Christ died for them; they are lost because they refused to accept the salvation that is sincerely offered to them in Christ. Those who defend general redemption begin by pointing out that it is the historic view of the church, being held by the vast majority of theologians, reformers, evangelists, and fathers from the beginning of the church until the present day, including virtually all the writers before the Reformation, with the possible exception of Augustine. Among the Reformers the doctrine is found in Luther, Melanchthon, Bullinger, Latimer, Cranmer, Coverdale, and even Calvin in some of his commentaries. For example Calvin says regarding Col. 1:14, "This redemption was procured through the blood of Christ, for by the sacrifice of his death, all the sins of the world have been expiated"; and on Mark 14:24, "*which is shed for many.* By the word 'many' he means not a part of the world only, but the whole human race." Even among the Calvinists there is a generalism, called hypothetical universalism, to be found with Moise Amyraut, Richard Baxter, John Bunyan, John Newton, and John Brown, among many others. Is it likely that the overwhelming majority of Christians could have so misread the leading of the Holy Spirit on such an important point?

The second point of the general redemption argument is that when the Bible says Christ died for all it means just that. The word ought to be taken in its normal sense unless some compelling reason exists to take it otherwise, and no such reason exists. Such passages as Isa. 53:6; I John 2:2; I Tim. 2:1–6; 4:10; and Heb. 2:4 make no sense if not taken in the normal way. Third, the Bible says Christ takes away the sin of the world and is the Savior of the world. A study of the word "world"—especially in John, where it is used seventy-eight times—shows that the world is God-hating, Christ-rejecting, and Satan-dominated. Yet that is the world for which Christ died. There is not one place in the entire NT where "world" means "church" or "the elect." Fourth, the several arguments that reduce to a charge of universalism are special pleading. Just because one believes that Christ died for all does not mean all are saved. One must believe in Christ to be saved, so the fact that Christ died for the world apparently does not secure the salvation of all. Those who assert this are simply wrong. Paul had no trouble saying that God could be the Savior of all, in one sense, and of those who believe, in another sense (I Tim. 4:10). Fifth, God is not unfair in condemning those who reject the offer of salvation. He is not exacting judgment twice. Because the nonbeliever refuses to accept the death of Christ as his own, the benefits of Christ's death are not applied to him. He is lost, not because Christ did not die for him, but because he refuses God's offer of forgiveness. Sixth, it is true that the benefits of Christ's death are referred to as belonging to the elect, his sheep, his people, but it would have to be shown that Christ died *only* for them. No one denies that Christ died for them. It is only denied that Christ died exclusively for them. Seventh, the Bible teaches that Christ died for "sinners" (I Tim. 1:15; Rom. 5:6–8). The word "sinner" nowhere means "church" or "the elect," but simply all of lost mankind. Finally, God sincerely offers the gospel to everyone to believe, not just the elect. How could this be true if Christ did not actually die for everyone? God would know very well that some people could never be saved because he did not allow Christ to pay for their sins. Even Berkhof, a staunch defender of limited atonement, admits, "It need not be denied that there is a real difficulty at this point" (*Systematic Theology,* p. 462).

Summary. Both points of view are trying to preserve something of theological importance. The defenders of limited atonement are stressing the certainty of God's salvation and the initiative he took in offering it to man. If salvation depended on our work, all would be lost. The defenders of general redemption are attempting to preserve the fairness of God and what to them is the clear teaching of Scripture. Salvation is no less certain because Christ died for all. It is the decision to reject it that brings about condemnation, and faith that puts one in a saving relationship with Christ who died that we might live. E. A. Litton attempts to mediate the two views in this fashion: "And thus the combatants may not be in reality so much at variance as they had supposed. The most extreme Calvinist may grant that there is room for all if they will come in; the most extreme Arminian must grant that redemption, in its full Scriptural meaning, is not the privilege of all men" (*Introduction to Dogmatic Theology*, p. 236). W. A. Elwell

See also Atonement; Atonement, Theories of the; Propitiation; Amyraldianism.

Bibliography. W. Rushton, *A Defense of Particular Redemption;* J. Owen, *The Death of Death in the Death of Christ;* A. A. Hodge, *The Atonement;* H. Martin, *The Atonement;* G. Smeaton, *The Doctrine of the Atonement According to the Apostles* and *The Doctrine of the Atonement According to Christ;* J. Davenant, *The Death of Christ;* N. F. Douty, *The Death of Christ;* A. H. Strong, *Systematic Theology;* J. Denney, *The Death of Christ;* J. M. Campbell, *The Nature of the Atonement;* L. Berkhof, *Systematic Theology.*

Atonement, Limited. *See* Atonement, Extent of the.

Atonement, Theories of the. Throughout the Bible the central question is, "How can sinful man ever be accepted by a holy God?" The Bible takes sin seriously, much more seriously than do the other literatures that have come down to us from antiquity. It sees sin as a barrier separating man from God (Isa. 59:2), a barrier that man was able to erect but is quite unable to demolish. But the truth on which the Bible insists is that God has dealt with the problem. He has made the way whereby sinners may find pardon, God's enemies may find peace. Salvation is never seen as a human achievement. In the OT sacrifice has a large place, but it avails not because of any merit it has of itself (cf. Heb. 10:4), but because God has given it as the way (Lev. 17:11). In the NT the cross plainly occupies the central place, and it is insisted upon in season and out of season that this is God's way of bringing salvation. There are many ways of bringing this out. The NT writers do not repeat a stereotyped story. Each writes from his own perspective. But each shows that it is the death of Christ and not any human achievement that brings salvation.

But none of them sets out a theory of atonement. There are many references to the effectiveness of Christ's atoning work, and we are not lacking in information about its many-sidedness. Thus Paul gives a good deal of emphasis to the atonement as a process of justification, and he uses such concepts as redemption, propitiation, and reconciliation. Sometimes we read of the cross as a victory or as an example. It is the sacrifice that makes a new covenant, or simply a sacrifice. There are many ways of viewing it. We are left in no doubt about its efficacy and its complexity. View the human spiritual problem as you will, and the cross meets the need. But the NT does not say how it does so.

Through the centuries there have been continuing efforts to work out how this was accomplished. Theories of the atonement are legion as men in different countries and in different ages have tried to bring together the varied strands of scriptural teaching and to work them into a theory that will help others to understand how God has worked to bring us salvation. The way has been open for this kind of venture, in part at least, because the church has never laid down an official, orthodox view. In the early centuries there were great controversies about the person of Christ and about the nature of the Trinity. Heresies appeared, were thoroughly discussed, and were disowned. In the end the church accepted the formula of Chalcedon as the standard expression of the orthodox faith. But there was no equivalent with the atonement. People simply held to the satisfying truth that Christ saved them by way of the cross and did not argue about how this salvation was effected. Thus there was no standard formula like the Chalcedonian statement, and this left men to pursue their quest for a satisfying theory in their own way. To this day no one theory of the atonement has ever won universal acceptance. This should not lead us to abandon the task. Every theory helps us understand a little more of what the cross means and, in any case, we are bidden to give a reason of the hope that is in us (I Pet. 3:15). Theories of the atonement attempt to do just that.

It would be impossible to deal with all the theories of the atonement that have been formulated, but we might well notice that most can be brought under one or the other of three heads: those which see the essence of the matter as the effect of the cross on the believer; those which see it as a victory of some sort; and those which emphasize the Godward aspect. Some prefer a twofold classification, seeing subjective theories as those which emphasize the effect on the believer, in distinction from objective theories which put the stress on what the atonement achieves quite outside the individual.

The Subjective View or Moral Influence Theory. Some form of the subjective or moral view is held widely today, especially among scholars of the liberal school. In all its variations this theory emphasizes the importance of the effect of Christ's cross on the sinner. The view is generally attributed to Abelard, who emphasized the love of God, and is sometimes called the moral influence theory, or exemplarism. When we look at the cross we see the greatness of the divine love. This delivers us from fear and kindles in us an answering love. We respond to love with love and no longer live in selfishness and sin.

Other ways of putting it include the view that the sight of the selfless Christ dying for sinners moves us to repentance and faith. If God will do all that for us, we say, then we ought not to continue in sin. So we repent and turn from it and are saved by becoming better people. The thrust in all this is on personal experience. The atonement, seen in this way, has no effect outside the believer. It is real in the person's experience and nowhere else. This view has been defended in recent times by Hastings Rashdall in *The Idea of Atonement* (1919).

It should be said in the first instance that there is truth in this theory. Taken by itself it is inadequate, but it is not untrue. It is important that we respond to the love of Christ seen on the cross, that we recognize the compelling force of his example. Probably the best-known and best-loved hymn on the passion in modern times is "When I Survey the Wondrous Cross," a hymn that sets forth nothing but the moral view. Every line of it emphasizes the effect on the observer of surveying the wondrous cross. It strikes home with force. What it says is both true and important. It is when it is claimed that this is all that the atonement means that we must reject it. Taken in this way it is open to serious criticism. If Christ was not actually doing something by his death, then we are confronted with a piece of showmanship, nothing more. Someone once said that if he were in a rushing river and someone jumped in to save him, and in the process lost his life, he could recognize the love and sacrifice involved. But if he was sitting safely on the land and someone jumped into the torrent to show his love, he could see no point in it and only lament the senseless act. Unless the death of Christ really does something, it is not in fact a demonstration of love.

The Atonement as Victory. In the early church there seems to have been little attention given to the way atonement works, but when the question was faced, as often as not the answer came in terms of the NT references to redemption. Because of their sin people rightly belong to Satan, the fathers reasoned. But God offered his son as a ransom, a bargain the evil one eagerly accepted. When, however, Satan got Christ down into hell he found that he could not hold him. On the third day Christ rose triumphant and left Satan without either his original prisoners or the ransom he had accepted in their stead. It did not need a profound intellect to see that God must have foreseen this, but the thought that God deceived the devil did not worry the fathers. They took that as evidence that God is wiser than Satan as well as stronger. They even worked out illustrations like a fishing trip: The flesh of Jesus was the bait, the deity the fishhook. Satan swallowed the hook along with the bait and was transfixed. This view has been variously called the devil ransom theory, the classical theory, or the fishhook theory of the atonement.

This kind of metaphor delighted some of the fathers, but after Anselm subjected it to criticism it faded from view. It was not until quite recent times that Gustaf Aulén with his *Christus Victor* showed that behind the grotesque metaphors there is an important truth. In the end Christ's atoning work means victory. The devil and all the hosts of evil are defeated. Sin is conquered. Though this has not always been worked into set theories, it has always been there in our Easter hymns. It forms an important element in Christian devotion and it points to a reality which Christians must not lose.

This view must be treated with some care else we will finish up by saying that God saves simply because he is strong—in other words, in the end might is right. This is an impossible conclusion for anyone who takes the Bible seriously. We are warned that this view, of itself, is not adequate. But combined with other views it must find a place in any finally satisfying theory. It is important that Christ has conquered.

Anselm's Satisfaction Theory. In the eleventh century Anselm, Archbishop of Canterbury, produced a little book called *Cur Deus Homo?* ("Why did God become Man?"). In it he subjected the patristic view of a ransom paid to Satan to severe criticism. He saw sin as dishonoring the majesty of God. Now a sovereign may well be ready in his private capacity to forgive an insult or an injury, but because he is a sovereign he cannot. The state has been dishonored in its head. Appropriate satisfaction must be offered. God is the sovereign Ruler of all, and it is not proper for God to remit any irregularity in his kingdom. Anselm argued that the insult sin has given to God is so great that only one who is God can provide satisfaction. But it was done by one who is man, so only man should do so. Thus he concluded that one who is both God and man is needed.

Anselm's treatment of the theme raised the discussion to a much higher plane than it had occupied in previous discussions. Most agree, however, that the demonstration is not conclusive. In the end Anselm makes God too much like a king whose dignity has been affronted. He overlooked the fact that a sovereign may be clement and forgiving without doing harm to his kingdom. A further defect in his view is that Anselm found no necessary connection between Christ's death and the salvation of sinners. Christ merited a great reward because he died when he had no need to (for he had no sin). But he could not receive a reward, for he had everything. To whom then could he more fittingly assign his reward then to those for whom he had died? This makes it more or less a matter of chance that sinners be saved. Not very many these days are prepared to go along with Anselm. But at least he took a very serious view of sin, and it is agreed that without this there will be no satisfactory view.

Penal Substitution. The Reformers agreed with Anselm that sin is a very serious matter, but they saw it as a breaking of God's law rather than as an insult to God's honor. The moral law, they held, is not to be taken lightly. "The wages of sin is death" (Rom. 6:23), and it is this that is the problem for sinful man. They took seriously the scriptural teachings about the wrath of God and those that referred to the curse under which sinners lay. It seemed clear to them that the essence of Christ's saving work consisted in his taking the sinner's place. In our stead Christ endured the death that is the wages of sin. He bore the curse that we sinners should have borne (Gal. 3:13). The Reformers did not hesitate to speak of Christ as having borne our punishment or as having appeased the wrath of God in our place.

Such views have been widely criticized. In particular it is pointed out that sin is not an external matter to be transferred easily from one person to another and that, while some forms of penalty are transferable (the payment of a fine), others are not (imprisonment, capital punishment). It is urged that this theory sets Christ in opposition to the Father so that it maximizes the love of Christ and minimizes that of the Father. Such criticisms may be valid against some of the ways in which the theory is stated, but they do not shake its essential basis. They overlook the fact that there is a double identification: Christ is one with sinners (the saved are "in" Christ, Rom. 8:1) and he is one with the Father (he and the Father are one, John 10:30; "God was in Christ, reconciling the world to himself," II Cor. 5:19). They also overlook the fact that there is much in the NT that supports the theory. It is special pleading to deny that Paul, for example, puts forward this view. It may need to be carefully stated, but this view still says something important about the way Christ won our salvation.

Sacrifice. There is much about sacrifice in the OT and not a little in the NT. Some insist that it is this that gives us the key to understanding the atonement. It is certainly true that the Bible regards Christ's saving act as a sacrifice, and this must enter into any satisfying theory. But unless it is supplemented, it is an explanation that does not explain. The moral view or penal substitution may be right or wrong, but at least they are intelligible. But how does sacrifice save? The answer is not obvious.

Governmental Theory. Hugo Grotius argued that Christ did not bear our punishment but suffered as a penal example whereby the law was honored while sinners were pardoned. His view is called "governmental" because Grotius envisions God as a ruler or a head of government who passed a law—in this instance, "The soul that sinneth, it shall die." Because God did not want sinners to die, he relaxed that rule and accepted the death of Christ instead. He could have simply forgiven mankind had he wanted to, but that would not have had any value for society. The death of Christ was a public example of the depth of sin and the lengths to which God would go to uphold the moral order of the universe. This view is expounded in great detail in *Defensio fidei catholicae de satisfactione Christi adversus F. Socinum* (1636).

Summary. All the above views, in their own way, recognize that the atonement is vast and deep. There is nothing quite like it, and it must be understood in its own light. The plight of sinful man is disastrous, for the NT sees the sinner as lost, as suffering hell, as perishing, as cast into outer darkness, and more. An atonement that rectifies all this must necessarily be complex. So we need all the vivid concepts: redemption, propitiation, justification, and all the rest. And we need all the theories. Each draws attention to an important aspect of our salvation and we dare not surrender any. But we are small-minded sinners and the atonement is great and vast. We should not expect that our theories will ever explain it fully. Even when we put them all together, we will no more than begin to comprehend a little of the vastness of God's saving deed.

L. Morris

Bibliography. D. M. Baillie, *God Was in Christ;* K. Barth, *The Doctrine of Reconciliation;* E. Brunner, *The Mediator;* H. Bushnell, *The Vicarious Sacrifice;* J. M. Campbell, *The Nature of the Atonement;* S. Cave, *The Doctrine of the Work of Christ;* R. W. Dale, *The Atonement;* F. W. Dillistone, *The Significance of the Cross;* J. Denney, *The Death of Christ* and *The Christian Doctrine of Reconciliation;* R. S. Franks, *The Work of Christ;* P. T. Forsyth, *The Cruciality of the Cross* and *The Work of Christ;* L. Hodgson, *The Doctrine of the Atonement;* T. H. Hughes, *The Atonement;* J. Knox, *The Death of Christ;* R. C. Moberley, *Atonement and Personality;* J. Moltmann, *The Crucified God;* L. Morris, *The Apostolic Preaching of the Cross* and *The Cross in the NT;* R. S. Paul, *The Atonement and the Sacraments;* V. Taylor, *Jesus and His Sacrifice* and *The Atonement in NT Teaching;* L. W. Grensted, *A Short History of the Doctrine of the Atonement;* R. Wallace, *The Atoning Death of Christ.*

Attributes, Communication of. *See* Communication of Attributes, Communicatio Idiomatum.

Attributes of God. *See* God, Attributes of.

Auburn Affirmation (1924). A document issued by liberal Presbyterian ministers in opposition to what they believed was a fundamentalist assault on the church's unity and liberty. Thanks to a conservative majority, the 1923 General Assembly of the Presbyterian Church in the U.S.A. affirmed the "doctrinal deliverance" of 1910 and 1916, which required all ministerial candidates to accept five "essential and necessary" doctrines: biblical inerrancy, the virgin birth, the death of Christ as a sacrifice to satisfy divine justice, the physical resurrection of Jesus, and his miracles.

Meeting in Auburn, New York, 150 clergy published *An Affirmation* in January, 1924, which attacked the action as intolerant and unconstitutional. Without rejecting the truth of the five essentials *per se*, the document distinguished between the *facts* of religion and the *theories* (i.e., the theological formulations) devised to explain them. While holding earnestly to the "great facts and doctrines" underlying the deliverance, the signers argued that the General Assembly had erred in forcing particular theories on the whole church. Other theories were equally plausible from the Scriptures and Presbyterian standards. Thus, the Affirmation stated, "All who hold to these facts and doctrines, whatever theories they may employ to explain them, are worthy of all confidence and fellowship." Furthermore, the document claimed that by singling out certain theological theories and requiring them for ordination, the General Assembly had amended the church's constitution without the necessary concurrence of two thirds of the presbyteries. In May, 1924, on the eve of the next General Assembly, the Affirmation was reissued, this time with 1,274 signatures.

The Auburn Affirmation demonstrated the radically different approach to doctrine and the basis for church unity among Presbyterian conservatives and liberals. Conservatives, for the most part, saw the church as a voluntary society made up of those who agreed on doctrinal issues. In his *Christianity and Liberalism*, Princeton professor J. Gresham Machen argued that historic Christianity and theological liberalism were two totally distinct religions that could never coexist in the same church. Liberals, on the other hand, believed that their differences with conservatives were not over essential matters and that doctrinal agreement was not the most important basis for church unity. In the long run, most northern Presbyterians (who were moderate to conservative theologically) sided with the spirit of the Auburn Affirmation, preferring a more inclusivist policy than the fundamentalists desired. T. P. Weber

See also Fundamentalism; Liberalism, Theological.

Bibliography. L. A. Loetscher, *The Broadening Church;* G. Marsden, *Fundamentalism and American Culture;* E. H. Rian, *The Presbyterian Conflict.*

Auburn Declaration (1837). A statement by New School Presbyterians to prove their loyalty to the Calvinist standards of the church. In the early nineteenth century Presbyterians in the United States divided into Old and New School parties over revivalism, interdenominational cooperation, and conformity to the Westminster Confession. In the mid-1830s the more conservative Old School tried unsuccessfully to oust a number of New School ministers for espousing the New Haven theology of Nathaniel Taylor, which allowed greater human participation in the salvation process than did traditional Calvinism. In 1837, however, the Old School mustered enough votes to "exscind" four New School synods (Western Reserve in Ohio and Utica, Genesee, and Geneva in New York) from the General Assembly, thereby cutting New School support by one half and essentially eliminating its voice in the church.

In August of the same year about two hundred New School ministers and lay people met in Auburn, New York, to protest this action and proclaim their faithfulness to Presbyterian standards. Their declaration answered the Old School's charges of widespread "Taylorism" in the New School. It affirmed that election was based on the secret counsel of God's will, not on his foreknowledge of future faith and obedience. It stated that all Adam's posterity suffered the consequences of his sin and that salvation depended solely on the regenerating power of the Holy Spirit, not human initiative or cooperation.

By any measurement, the Auburn Declaration was well within the boundaries of moderate, nineteenth century Calvinist orthodoxy. But it probably understated the degree of theological diversity in the New School at the time. As a result, the framers of the Declaration were unable to bring about reconciliation with the Old School until 1868, when conservatives were finally convinced that the statement was an accurate reflection of New School sentiments as a whole.

T. P. Weber

See also New Haven Theology; Taylor, Nathaniel William; Old School Theology; New School Theology.

Bibliography. S. J. Baird, *A History of the New School;* L. Cheeseman, *Differences Between the Old and New School Presbyterians;* G. Marsden, *The Evangelical Mind and the New School Presbyterian Experience;* S. E. Mead, *Nathaniel William Taylor, 1786–1858;* H. S. Smith, *Changing Conceptions of Original Sin.*

Augsburg Confession (1530). The basic Lutheran confession of faith or statement of what is believed in loyalty to Christ and his Word. It was presented at the Diet of Augsburg in 1530. Philip Melanchthon was its author, but its teachings are clearly those of Martin Luther.

Charles V called a diet, or convention, of the rulers of the Holy Roman Empire to meet in Augsburg in 1530. The emperor was staunchly Roman Catholic and wanted the empire to be loyal to Romanism. He directed those rulers supporting different teachings to present statements of what they believed. Charles wanted religious unity so that the empire could present a united front against foreign enemies, especially the Turks.

Lutheran theologians drafted various preliminary documents, including the Marburg, Schwabach, and Torgau Articles. Luther had a hand in their preparation, but he could not attend the diet. He had been outlawed by the Edict of Worms (1521), and the Elector of Saxony could not protect him at Augsburg. Since he had been declared a heretic, his presence would have shifted the focus away from doctrinal issues. His martyrdom would have served no purpose. Luther remained at the Coburg but was in constant correspondence with those in Augsburg.

Luther's co-worker, Philip Melanchthon, produced the final draft of the Augsburg Confession. At that time he was in doctrinal agreement with Luther, who approved of the confession wholeheartedly. Luther did note that it might have dealt with a few more errors and abuses, and that he would not have used such a mild tone. The doctrine of the confession is clearly that of the Reformer himself.

The Augsburg Confession was read publicly at the diet in German on the afternoon of June 25, 1530, by Chancellor Christian Beyer of Electoral Saxony. Both the German and the Latin copies were handed in as official. Melanchthon altered later editions, partly to render it ambiguous on points such as the real presence of Christ's body and blood in the Lord's Supper. He was inclined to compromise on doctrinal issues. That is why Gnesio-Lutherans have often referred to the Unaltered Augsburg Confession. The Augsburg Confession was included in the Book of Concord (1580) as the basic Lutheran confession.

The Augsburg Confession was signed by seven princes and representatives of two independent cities. They believed that the doctrine it taught was biblical and true. They were the ones to sign it because the diet was precisely a convention of the rulers of the empire. But the confession was not intended to present the teachings of some governmental authority. It stated what was being taught in the churches in those parts of Germany. The first article begins: "The churches among us teach with great consensus . . ." (Latin text).

In addition to a preface and a brief conclusion the Augsburg Confession has twenty-eight articles. The first twenty-one present the Lutheran teaching and reject contrary doctrines. The last seven reject abuses in Christian life. The confession is too brief fully to present the biblical proof or the testimony of previous theologians. In response to a Roman Catholic answer, the Confutation, Melanchthon published in 1531 the Apology of the Augsburg Confession, which deals with the controverted issues at greater length.

To discuss the teachings of the Augsburg Confession at length would constitute a theology textbook. We can at best give some idea of what it says. It teaches the Trinity; original sin as true sin that would condemn if not forgiven; the deity and humanity of Jesus; his sacrifice for all human sin; justification by grace through faith without our works; the gospel, baptism, and the Lord's Supper as actual tools of the Holy Spirit to create and sustain faith; good works as a result, not a cause, of salvation, motivated by the good news that salvation has been earned for us by Christ. Much more could be said, but this indicates that the Augsburg Confession simply teaches the position which Lutherans consider biblical.

The abuses corrected include various false ideas and practices in the Lord's Supper; clerical celibacy; the misuse of confession and absolution; the dietary laws of medieval Romanism; and the idea of a hierarchy in visible Christendom having divine authority in matters of conscience.

J. M. Drickamer

See also Confessions of Faith; Melanchthon, Philip; Luther, Martin.

Bibliography. F. Bente, *Historical Introduction to the Symbolical Books of the Evangelical Lutheran Church;* H. Fagerberg, *A New Look at the Lutheran Confessions 1529–1537;* C. P. Krauth, *The Conservative Reformation and Its Theology;* J. M. Reu, *The Augsburg Confession.* The text is available in English in *Concordia Triglotta,* ed. F. Bente, and *The Book of Concord,* ed. T. G. Tappert.

Augustine of Canterbury (d. 604?). The first Archbishop of Canterbury. His early years are uncertain, and his death can be placed no more exactly than 604–9, sometime after that of Gregory I, his papal patron. Augustine began as prior of Pope Gregory the Great's own Monastery of St. Andrew in Rome. This was the Gregory whose heart was stirred toward a rebirth of Roman Catholic missions by the auctioning of Anglo-Saxon slave boys in Rome's marketplace *ca.* 586. Sometime before 590 Gregory set off himself to go but was recalled only three days journey from Rome. In 590 Gregory used papal revenues to buy Anglo-Saxon slave boys to be trained as Christians and returned to England. Then in 596 he appointed Augustine to head a mission of thirty or forty monks to England.

Augustine did not wish the appointment and went only "under obedience." As he traveled through Gaul, he heard such tales of English savagery that he returned to Rome. Gregory sent him right back, however, so Augustine landed in Thanet early in 597. He was received kindly by King Aethelbert of Kent, whose queen, Bertha, was a Christian. She and her chaplain, the Frankish bishop Liudhard, maintained worship in St. Martin's Church. Aethelbert gave Augustine and his monks a living place and authority to preach in Canterbury. In rapid succession Augustine converted Aethelbert, baptized him and his subjects (ten thousand on Christmas Day, 597), began building Christ Church and the Monastery of Saints Peter and Paul (which now bears Augustine's name), and in 604 consecrated bishops for London (Mellitus) and Rochester (Justus).

The England Augustine reached was largely pagan because Anglo-Saxon invasions had isolated Christians in the northwest and Wales. Augustine labored in vain to unite these remnant British or Celtic clergy to Rome. Suspicion toward Augustine and differences over liturgy, baptism, and Easter doomed the effort. The conversion of pagans and reestablishment of Roman Catholicism succeeded only in Kent and Essex in Augustine's decade of ministry, but Gregory responded to these successes. In 597 he called Augustine to Arles to be consecrated bishop, and in 601 he sent the pallium and gave Augustine authority over all English bishops.

Two things in addition to establishing England as a see separate from Gaul flowed from Augustine's ministry in close contact with Pope Gregory. One was the development of English rites, for Gregory advised his new archbishop to establish worship adapting the usages of other churches to English needs. The second was of importance to the entire medieval church, for when Augustine inquired of his papal patron how to use church income, Gregory laid down the principle that was to characterize Roman practice: divide income into four equal parts—one for the bishop, one for the priest, one for relief of the poor, and one for upkeep of the church. V. L. WALTER

Bibliography. J. R. H. Moorman, *A History of the Church in England.*

Augustine of Hippo (354–430). Perhaps antiquity's greatest theologian, Augustine was born in Tagaste, North Africa (Algeria), to Patricius, a pagan, and Monica, a Christian. He studied grammar at Madaura and rhetoric in Carthage, and was intellectually stimulated by reading Cicero's *Hortensius.* After a carnal life during his school days he joined the Manichaean religion (373). He taught grammar and rhetoric in North Africa (373–82) and then in Rome (383), where he abandoned the Manichaeans and became a skeptic. He moved to Milan to teach (384), where he was later influenced by the reading of Neoplatonic philosophy and by Ambrose's sermons. He was converted through an exhortation, overheard in a garden, from Rom. 13:13–14, was baptized by Ambrose (387), and was reunited with his mother, who died shortly thereafter.

After years of retreat and study Augustine was ordained a priest in Hippo, North Africa (391), where he established a monastery and where he later became bishop (395). The rest of his life can best be seen by the controversies he engaged in and the writings he produced. Augustine died August 28, 430, as the Vandals laid siege to Rome.

Major Writings. Augustine's works fall roughly into three periods.

First Period (386–96). The first category in this period consists of philosophical dialogues: *Against the Academics* (386), *The Happy Life* (386), *On Order* (386), *On Immortality of the Soul* and *On Grammar* (387), *On the Magnitude of the Soul* (387–88), *On Music* (389–91), *On the Teacher* (389), and *On Free Will* (*FW,* 388–95). The second group is the anti-Manichaean works such as *On the Morals of the Catholic Church* (*MCC*) and *On the Morals of the Manicheans* (388), *On Two Souls* (*TS,* 391), and *Disputation Against Fortunatus the Manichean* (392). The last category is made up of theological and exegetical works such as *Against the Epistle of Manichaeus* (397), *Diverse Questions* (389–96), *On the Utility of Believing* (391), *On Faith and Symbol* (393), and some *Letters* (*L*) and *Sermons.*

Second Period (396–411). This group of writings contains his later anti-Manichaean writings such as *Against the Epistle of Manichaeus* (397), *Against Faustus the Manichean* (*AFM,* 398), and *On the Nature of the Good* (399). Next were some ecclesiastical writings, as *On Baptism* (400), *Against the Epistle of Petilian* (401), and *On the Unity of the Church* (405). Finally there were some theological and exegetical works such as the famous *Confessions* (*C*, 398–99), *On the Trinity* (*T*, 400–416), *On Genesis According to the Literal Sense* (400–415), *On Christian Doctrine* I–III (*CD*, 387). *Letters, Sermons*, and *Discourses on Psalms* were also written during this period.

Third Period (411–30). The works in the final period of Augustine's writings were largely anti-Pelagian. First against the Pelagians he wrote *On the Merits and Remission of Sins* (*MRS*, 411–12), *On the Spirit and the Letter* (*SL*, 412), *On Nature and Grace* (415), *On the Correction of the Donatists* (417), *On the Grace of Christ* and *On Original Sin* (418), *On Marriage and Concupiscence* (419–20), *On the Soul and Its Origin* (*SO*, 419), *The Enchiridion* (*E*, 421), and *Against Julian* (two books, 421 and 429–30). The second group of anti-Pelagian writings include *On Grace and Free Will* (*GFW*, 426), *On Rebuke and Grace* (426), *On Predestination of the Saints* (428–29), and *On the Gift of Perseverance* (428–29). The last writings in this period are theological and exegetical, including perhaps his greatest work, *The City of God* (*CG*, 413–26). *On Christian Doctrine* (*CD*, Book IV, 426) and the *Retractations* (426–27) fit here, as well as numerous *Letters, Sermons*, and *Discourses on Psalms*.

Translations of Augustine's works can be found in numerous sources, including *Ancient Christian Writers; Catholic University of America Patristic Studies; The Works of Aurelius Augustinus; The Fathers of the Church; Library of Christian Classics;* and *A Select Library of Nicene and Post-Nicene Fathers.*

Theology. Augustine is the father of orthodox theology.

God. Augustine argued for aseity (*CG* XI, 5), absolute immutability (*CG* XI, 10), simplicity (*CG* VIII, 6), and yet a triunity of persons (*L* 169, 2, 5) in this one essence. God is also omnipresent (*CG* VII, 30), omnipotent (*CG* V, 10), immaterial (spiritual) (*CG* VIII, 6), eternal (*T* XIV, 25, 21). God is not in time but is the creator of time (*C* XI, 4).

Creation. For Augustine creation is not eternal (*C* XI, 13, 15). It is *ex nihilo* (out of nothing) (*C* XII, 7, 7), and the "days" of Genesis may be long periods of time (*CG* XI, 6–8). Each soul is not created at birth but is generated through one's parents (*SO* 33). The Bible is divine (*E* 1, 4), infallible (*CG* XI, 6), inerrant (*L* 28, 3), and it alone has supreme authority (*CG* XI, 3) over all other writings (*AFM* XI, 5). There are no contradictions in the Bible (*CD* VII, 6, 8). Any error can be only in the copies, not in the original manuscripts (*L* 82, 3). The eleven books of the Apocrypha are also part of the canon (*CD* II, 8, 12) because they were part of the LXX, which Augustine believed to be inspired, and because they contain many wonderful stories of martyrs (*CG* XVIII, 42). Augustine recognized that the Jews did not accept these apocryphal books (*CG* XIV, 14). The canon was closed with the NT apostles (*CG* XXXIX, 38).

Sin. Augustine believed sin originated with free will, which is a created good (*TR* XIV, 11). Free will implies the ability to do evil (*CG* XII, 6). It is a voluntary (*TR* XIV, 27), noncompulsory (*TS* X, 12), self-determined act (*FW* III, 17, 49). Augustine appears to have later contradicted this view when he concluded that Donatists could be forced to believe against their will (*Correction of the Donatists* III, 13). With the fall man lost the ability to do good without God's grace (*E* 106), yet he retains the ability of free choice to accept God's grace (*L* 215, 4; *GFW* 7). True freedom, however, is not the ability to sin but the ability to do good (*CG* XIV, 11), which only the redeemed have (*E* 30).

Man. Augustine believed man was directly created by God without sin (*On the Nature of God*, 3), which the whole race derived from Adam (*CG* XII, 21). When Adam sinned, all men sinned in him seminally (*MRS* 14). Man is a duality of body and soul (*MCC* 4, 6), and the image of soul is in the soul (*CD* I, 22, 20). The fall did not erase this image (*SL* 48), although man's nature was corrupted by sin (*Against the Epistle of Manichaeus* XXXIII, 36). Human life begins in the womb at the time of animation (*E* 85). Miscarriages before this time simply "perish" (*E* 86). Man's soul is higher and better than his body (*CG* XII, 1), which is man's adversary (*C* X, 21, 43; *TR* 111, 103). There will be a physical resurrection of the bodies of all men, just and unjust (*E* 84, 92), to eternal bliss or agony respectively.

Christ. Augustine believed that Christ was fully human (*On Faith and the Creed* [*FC*] IV, 8), yet without sin (*E* 24). Christ assumed this human nature in the virgin's womb (*FC* IV, 8), yet he was also God from all eternity, of the same essence as the Father (*T* I, 6, 9). Christ, however, was only one person (*E* 35). Yet these two natures are so distinct (*L* CXXXVII, 3, 11) that the divine nature did not become human at the incarnation (*T* I, 7, 14).

Salvation. The source of salvation is God's eternal decree (*CG* XI, 21), which is unchangeable (*CG* XXII, 2). Predestination is in accord with God's foreknowledge of man's free choice (*CG* V, 9). Both those who are saved and those who are lost are so predestined (*SO* IV, 16). Salvation is wrought only through Christ's substitutionary death (*E* 33). It is received by faith

(*E* 31). Infants, however, are regenerated by baptism apart from their faith (*On Forgiveness of Sins, and Baptism* I, 44).

Ethics. For Augustine love is the supreme law (*CG* XV, 16). All the virtues are defined in terms of love (*MCC* XII, 53). Lying is always wrong, even to save a life (*L* 22, 23). In conflicting situations it is for God, not us, to determine which sins are greater (*E* 78, 79). God sometimes grants exceptions to a moral command so that killing is permissible in a just war (*CG* XIX, 7) and even in cases such as Samson's self-sacrificing suicide (*CG* I, 21). N. L. Geisler

Bibliography. A. H. Armstrong, *St. Augustine and Christian Platonism; AugS;* R. W. Battenhouse, ed., *A Companion to the Study of Saint Augustine;* G. Bonner, *St. Augustine of Hippo;* V. J. Bourke, *Augustine's Quest for Wisdom;* P. Brown, *Augustine of Hippo;* J. Burnaby, *Amor Dei: A Study of the Religion of St. Augustine;* M. P. Garvey, *Saint Augustine: Christian or Neo-Platonist;* É. Gilson, *The Christian Philosophy of Saint Augustine;* M. J. McKeough, *The Meaning of the Rationes Seminales in St. Augustine;* H. I. Marrou, *Saint Augustine and His Influence Through the Ages;* A. D. R. Polman, *The Word of God According to Saint Augustine;* E. R. TeSelle, *Augustine the Theologian;* Augustinian Institute, *St. Augustine Lectures* 1959; T. Miethe, *Augustinian Bibliography 1970–1980;* T. Van Bauel, *Repertoire bibliographique de Saint Augustine* 1950–1960; F. van der Meer, *Augustine the Bishop;* N. L. Geisler, *What Augustine Says;* E. Przywara, *An Augustine Synthesis.*

Aulén, Gustaf Emanuel Hildebrand (1879–1978). Swedish theologian and scholar. Aulén was appointed professor of theology at the University of Lund in 1913, remaining there until 1933. He then became bishop in Strängnäs (1933–52) and was deeply involved in the Swedish resistance to Nazism. In 1952 he returned to teaching at Lund and also continued his leading role in the ecumenical movement, playing an important part in the first assembly of the World Council of Churches in 1948.

Aulén's theological works span more than half a century. His *Faith of the Christian Church* was first published in 1923. The English translation of the fifth Swedish edition is still in print and a model of constructive, ecumenical Lutheran theology. At the age of ninety-four he wrote *Jesus in Contemporary Historical Research.* Here he has given his analysis of the work of biblical NT scholarship on the life and significance of Christ in the 1960s and early 70s. Translations of his *Church, Law and Society* and *Eucharist and Sacrifice* make his concerns available to an English-speaking audience.

Aulén is best remembered for his classic analysis of theories of the atonement in *Christus Victor,* written while still a professor at the University of Lund (1930). After discussing the biblical and historical aspects of three theories of the atonement—the subjective, Latin (penal), and the classic—Aulén attempts to breathe new life into the classic theory, where Christ's death is seen as the act of God in continuity with his victorious life and resurrection. The atonement is a divine victory overcoming the destructive powers of hell and death, making available and visible the reconciling love of God.

Aulén is also noted in the Swedish Lutheran Church as a composer of widely used church music. S. M. Smith

Authority in the Bible. *See* Bible, Authority in.

Authority in the Church. *See* Church, Authority in.

Authority of the Bible. *See* Bible, Authority of.

Auxiliary Bishop. *See* Bishop; Church Officers.

Avenger of Blood. Forbidding personal vengeance, OT law required exact equivalence between crime and punishment. The death penalty for murder was apportioned by due process of law, but an older practice of family vengeance had not died out and had to be regulated. The "avenger of blood," whose right to avenge his kinsman is assumed, is mentioned only in passages which counter the possibility of an unlimited vendetta by providing cities of refuge (Num. 35:9–28; Deut. 19:1–13; Josh. 20:1–9). In the case of premeditated murder, but then only after public trial, the avenger was allowed to exact a life for a life. "Avenger" translates *gō'ēl,* from *gā'al,* "to redeem," used of a next of kin taking upon himself a kinsman's need. J. A. Motyer

See also Civil Law and Justice in Bible Times.

Averroes (1126–1198). The Islamic philosopher and theologian Ibn Rushd, or Averroes, was born into a learned family of civil judges in Cordoba, Spain, and died at the caliph's court in Marrakesh, Morocco. He held several high civil posts in Islamic Spain and attended one of the caliphs as his personal physician. Though best known for his work in philosophy and theology, which comes at the very end of an Islamic attempt to synthesize all Greek philosophy, Averroes was also famous for his knowledge of law (especially his grasp of Islamic legal traditions), medicine (a textbook), and astronomy (attempts to prove the earth round). Against the philosophical view prevailing in the small circle of Islamic philosophers, essentially a Neoplatonic interpretation of Aristotle, Averroes attempted to recover the true Aristotle, that is, to establish the autonomy of philosophical investigation unimpeded by religious and theological considerations. To do so, he commented on nearly all the works of Aristotle, explaining the text word by word in three different versions of varying length and complexity. From those commentaries three problems emerged to confound Islamic and Christian theologians alike.

Truth is one, but there are three different ways to discover it, religious instruction (by way of the Koran or the Bible) being the lowest and philosophical thought the highest. If discrepancies between revealed and reasoned truths should emerge, religious language, meant for all the people, must be interpreted symbolically and yield to the philosophical. This is the foundation for the "double-truth theory" later associated with Averroes' name that suggested religion and philosophy might arrive at or teach truths which seem contrary. Averroes held, secondly, to the eternity of the world and regarded God chiefly as the essential "motor" thereof, the unmoved mover. Finally, he taught that the soul is the substantial form of the body, suggesting it was also mortal, while each individual intellect, though pure form, is passive (or potential), activated toward understanding by a single agent intellect (usually equated with God or his ideas) which is alone immortal.

Averroes' implied attacks upon divine revelation, creation, and the immortality of the soul put him out of favor with most Muslim thinkers, and many of his works have been lost in their original Arabic version. But they were translated almost immediately into Hebrew and Latin, and exercised an enormous influence from the thirteenth to the seventeenth centuries. From the 1230s onward, medieval philosophers and theologians learned their Aristotle through Averroes and regarded him simply as "the Commentator." Some, especially from the arts faculty (Boethius of Dacia, Siger of Brabant), seemed much too dangerously receptive to his views on the autonomy of philosophical investigation, while others (preeminently Thomas Aquinas) learned much from him but neutralized or refuted the most aberrant positions in behalf of Christian orthodoxy. Despite (or perhaps in reaction to) papal condemnations of Averroist positions in 1270 and 1277, John of Jandun and John Baconthorpe openly defended the autonomy of philosophical truths, and thus initiated a tradition of "Latin Averroism" which continued into the seventeenth century, linked most often to the University of Padua, Italy. J. VAN ENGEN

Bibliography. *Encyclopedia of Philosophy,* I, 220–23; *Theologische Realenzyklopädie,* V, 51–61; F. E. Peters, *Aristotle and the Arabs;* F. Van Steenberghen, *Thomas Aquinas and Radical Aristotelianism.*

Awakenings, The Great. *See* GREAT AWAKENINGS, THE.

Awe. A profound reverence and respect for God which is tempered with fear. This acute reverence is characterized by solemn wonder mingled with dread in view of the great and terrible presence of the Supreme Being. The Hebrew word *yir'â* and the Greek word *phobos* are used most commonly to refer to this holy fear or "fear of God." Awe is the most characteristic meaning of the term "fear" in the Bible and is based upon one's recognition and awareness of the holiness and supreme majesty of God. Foundational to this sense of holy fear is a person's perception of God's unmerited and gratuitous love toward him. This reverential awe of God stimulates within the believer the concomitant responses of fascination, adoration, trust, and worship, yet a sense of fear and anxiety. Awe is an essential element in the worship and service of God.

The Bible often speaks of this godly reverence (Gen. 20:11; Ps. 34:11; Acts 9:31; Rom. 3:18). It is a holy fear provided by God that serves as a stimulus to reverence God's authority, to be obedient to his commandments, to walk in his ways, and to abhor evil (I Sam. 12:14; Eccles. 12:13; Ps. 2:11; Prov. 8:13; Jer. 32:40). According to the NT this holy fear stimulates one to pursue a life of holiness (II Cor. 7:1; Phil. 2:12). Job and the psalmist identify it as the beginning of wisdom and knowledge (Job 28:28; Prov. 1:7; Ps. 111:10). The Bible further describes it as a feature of the people in whom God takes pleasure (Ps. 147:11) and is to be reflected in one's relations with others (Eph. 5:21). P. G. CHAPPELL

See also FEAR; NUMINOUS, THE.

Bibliography. S. Terrien, *IDB,* II, 256–60; R. Otto, *The Idea of the Holy;* R. Bultmann, *TDNT,* II, 751–54; R. H. Pfeiffer, "The Fear of God," *IEJ* 5:41–48.

Azusa Street Revival. An abandoned Methodist church at 312 Azusa Street in the industrial section of Los Angeles became in 1906 the originating center of modern Pentecostalism. William J. Seymour, a mild-mannered black Holiness preacher, founded the Apostolic Faith Gospel Mission on Azusa Street, where a new emphasis on the work of the Holy Spirit rapidly became a local sensation and eventually a worldwide phenomenon. Before coming to Los Angeles, Seymour had been influenced by the ministry of Charles Fox Parham, who had grown up in Methodist and Holiness circles. In his schools in Kansas and Texas, Parham taught that a baptism of "the Holy Ghost and fire" should be expected among those who had been converted and who had also gone forward to the perfect sanctification which John Wesley and American Holiness bodies had proclaimed. Parham had also pioneered the teaching that a special sign of the Holy Spirit baptism would be "speaking with other tongues." With many others in the Methodist and Holiness traditions at the end of the nineteenth century, he also placed a stronger emphasis generally on the gifts of the Spirit, including that of healing.

The revival which began on Azusa Street in 1906 rapidly attracted attention from such secular media as the *Los Angeles Times.* More importantly it soon became the center of attraction for thousands of visitors from around the world, who often went back to their homelands proclaiming the need for a special postconversion baptism of the Holy Spirit. These included Florence Crawford, founder of the Apostolic Faith movement in the northwestern United States; missionary T. B. Barratt, who is credited with the establishment of Pentecostalism in Scandinavia and northwestern Europe; William H. Durham of Chicago, early spokesman for Pentecostalism in the Midwest; and Eudorus N. Bell of Fort Worth, first chairman of the Assemblies of God.

Meetings at Azusa Street, which went on daily for three years, were marked by spontaneous prayer and preaching, a nearly unprecedented cooperation between blacks and whites, and the active participation of women. Observers at the time linked Azusa Street with the great Welsh Revival of 1904 and 1905 and the "Latter Rain" movement, which had pockets of influence throughout the United States. Azusa Street remains a potent symbol for the activity of the Holy Spirit to the now more than 50,000,000 Pentecostals worldwide. M. A. NOLL

See also PENTECOSTALISM.

Bibliography. V. Synan, *The Holiness-Pentecostal Movement in the United States;* W. E. Warner, ed., *Touched by the Fire: Eyewitness Accounts of the Early Twentieth Century Pentecostal Revival;* R. M. Anderson, *Vision of the Disinherited: The Making of American Pentecostalism.*

Bb

Baali. The word appears in Hos. 2:16, in a context that portrays Israel as adulterous and having forsaken her husband (God). The prophet asserts that in a future day when Israel is repentant and restored, she would again address God as Ishi (my husband) rather than Baali (a near synonym which was repugnant because it contained the name Baal—meaning "master"—a Canaanite deity). Baal was the most important god of the Canaanite pantheon. A god of fertility, he was worshiped extensively in western Asia from Babylonia to Egypt. In the OT his worship rivaled that of Yahweh and seems to have reached its height in Israel during the days of Ahab and Jezebel.

H. F. Vos

Baal-zebub. King Ahaziah, in an act of apostasy, sent to inquire of "Baal-zebub, the god of Ekron," one of the Philistine cities (II Kings 1:2–16). The two parts of "Baal-zebub" mean "lord of the fly." Baal (lord) was the Canaanite god of fertility and fire, one of the chief deities of the area. *Zĕbûb* means fly or poisonous insect (the same word is used of one of the plagues of Egypt, Exod. 8:20–32). The Philistines may have actually worshiped the fly, or the Jews may have changed *zĕbūl* ("dwelling," esp. in the temple or in heaven; hence "the lord of heaven," or "the Supreme Baal") to *zĕbûb,* the term for the hated insect.

In Mark 3:22 (= Matt. 12:24; cf. 9:34; Luke 11:15) the Pharisees denigrate Jesus and attempt to explain his power over demons as itself of demonic origin by saying, "He has Beelzebub, the prince of the demons." Here Beelzebub (and its archaic form Be-Elzebub) clearly means Satan. The precise meaning of Beelzebub is uncertain. Yet it certainly is related to the name of the pagan deity associated with the perennial enemy of Israel. Its use for Satan is best explained by the principle, "The god of one religion is the demon of another."

Jesus countered saying that he cast out demons, not by Beelzebub, but by God's power through which the "strong man" (Satan) was bound. This proved the presence of the kingdom of God.

J. J. Scott, Jr.

See also Satan.

Bibliography. F. C. Fensam, "A Possible Explanation of the Name Baal-Zebub of Ekron," *ZAW* 79: 361–64; W. Foerster, *TDNT,* I, 605–6; L. Gaston, "Beelzebub," *TZ* 18:247–55.

Babylon. Like Jerusalem, Babylon has a threefold significance in Scripture—historic, prophetic, and symbolic (or typical). Historically, it may refer to the great city on the Euphrates River, to the kingdom of Babylon, or to the plain referred to as Babylonia. The empire of Babylon was used by God in the final defeat of Judah and the destruction of Jerusalem. Nebuchadnezzar begins the times of the Gentiles (Jer. 27:1–11; Dan. 2:37–38). The final and complete destruction of Babylon is foretold in the prophets (Isa. 13:17–22; Jer. 25:12–14). The city fell to the Medes in 539 B.C., but the vast desolation spoken of by the prophets has not yet come to pass.

Three primary passages (Isa. 13; 14; 47; Jer. 50; 51; Rev. 16:17–19:5) predict Babylon's ultimate destiny. The universal sweep, particularly in Isaiah's prophecy, exceeding the scope of Babylon even in the days of its greatest glory, suggests that many aspects of this prediction have not yet been fulfilled. God did not change the whole earth when Babylon fell; in fact, the city was not destroyed at that time.

Our chief concern is with the significance of Babylon in the book of Revelation. The characteristics of the people of the land of Shinar—rebellion against God, self-sufficiency, lust for power and glory (Gen. 8:10; 11:1–9)—have marked the history of Babylon through the centuries and are basic in the Babylon passage of the Apocalypse.

The exact meaning of the term "Babylon" in Revelation has been disputed from the times of the church fathers. Called a harlot repeatedly (17:1, 5, 15, 16), she is said to be seated on many waters, which are defined as peoples (vs. 15). She is also portrayed as sitting upon a scarlet beast, who represents worldly powers arrayed against the Lamb of God. The beast ultimately turns upon the harlot to destroy her. In Rev. 18 Babylon is given prominence as a commercial power.

What is the meaning of Babylon in these passages? The older commentators tended to make it a prophecy of the evil world. Others have insisted on a specific geographical reference, such as Jerusalem. But the mention of rivers and ships and extensive commercial activity does not fit the holy city. Others have identified Babylon with the city of Rome, basing the identification largely on the mention of seven hills (Rev. 17:9). The fundamental objection to this interpretation is that the persecution of the Christians by the Roman Empire stopped at the advent of Constantine, whereas Rome was taken by the barbarians only a century later. Still another view refers the passage to literal Babylon on the Euphrates, which is now a heap of sand and ruins. Others believe that the reference is symbolical, that Babylon is not to be defined geographically but ecclesiastically. Some in this group interpret Babylon as the papacy, which through the centuries has persecuted multitudes of the saints of God. The Reformers shared this view. Others of this group understand the passage as a description not so much of the Roman Church at the end of this age as of apostate Christendom as a whole.

Whatever be the final conclusion on the identity of Babylon, the following factors are clear: (1) at the end of this age two powerful forces, a federation of nations and an ecclesiastical apostate body, will unitedly exercise jurisdiction over the world; (2) there will be a persecution of the saints of God; (3) a godless, economic, commercial worldwide activity will hold sway; (4) a dual judgment will bring this condition of abomination to an end; (5) the ecclesiastical power will be torn to pieces by the federation of nations; and (6) the whole ungodly system, staggering in the drunkenness of Babylonian pride, power, and wealth, will be destroyed by an act of God, which will bring rejoicing to the people of God (Rev. 18:20). If there is any chronological sequence in these last chapters of the book of Revelation, this judgment on Babylon will soon be followed by the battle of Armageddon. W. M. Smith

See also Eschatology; Second Coming of Christ.

Bibliography. I. T. Beckwith, *The Apocalypse of John;* G. B. Caird, *The Revelation of St. John the Divine;* K. G. Kuhn, *TDNT,* I, 514–17.

Backsliding. A temporary lapse into unbelief and sin following a spiritual conversion. The four relevant Hebrew words in the OT are variously translated (RSV) "backsliding" (Jer. 8:5), "apostasy" (Jer. 5:6), "turning away" (Hos. 11:7), and "faithlessness" (Hos. 14:4).

Backsliding in the OT primarily concerns Israel's forsaking of its covenant relation with Yahweh (see Jer. 2:19; 8:5; 14:7). The nation's turning from the Lord in disobedience is analogous to the breaking of a sacred marriage vow. (Jer. 3:6–22). Specific examples of backsliding in the OT include Saul (I Sam. 15:11–28), Solomon (I Kings 11:4–40), Rehoboam (II Chr. 12:1–2), and Asa (II Chr. 16:7–9). Although the word "backsliding" is not found in the NT, there are numerous examples of believers who draw away from fellowship with the Lord—e.g., the disciples (Matt. 26:56), Peter (Matt. 26:69–75), Demas (II Tim. 4:10), Corinthian Christians (II Cor. 12:20–21), and churches in Asia (Rev. 2:4, 14–15, 20).

The reason that some who are genuinely converted fall back into a life of sin is that the believer yet possesses the old nature that is "corrupt through deceitful lusts" (Eph. 4:22; cf. Rom. 7:13–24; I Cor. 3:1–3). Specific causes of spiritual backsliding include God-forgetfulness (Ezek. 23:35), unbelief (Heb. 3:12), bitterness (Heb. 12:15), preoccupation with the present world (II Tim. 4:10), love of money (I Tim. 6:10), and seductive philosophies (Col. 2:8). Backsliding displeases the Lord (Heb. 10:38), grieves the Holy Spirit (Eph. 4:30), incurs divine punishment (Lev. 26:18–25), including sorrow of heart (Lev. 26:16). Although backsliding brings untold hurt, most Christians believe that the backslidden believer is not eternally lost. The believer's union with Christ sealed by the Holy Spirit (Eph. 1:13–14), God's work of preservation (II Tim. 1:12), Christ's effectual intercession (Heb. 7:25), and the fact that the life Christ gives is eternal (John 3:16; 10:28) guarantee the final salvation of every blood-bought child of God.

According to Scripture, backsliding can be prevented by abiding in Christ (John 15:4–7), spiritual alertness (Eph. 6:18), constant prayer (I Thess. 5:17), and the maintenance of a good conscience (I Tim. 1:19). The promises of God to the backslider are exceedingly gracious: "Return to me, and I will return to you, says the Lord of hosts" (Mal. 3:7); "I will heal their faithlessness; I will love them fully" (Hos. 14:4).

B. A. Demarest

See also Assurance; Perseverance.

Bibliography. M. H. Smith, *Encyclopedia of Christianity,* I, 511.

Baillie, John (1886–1960). Scottish theologian. Born in a Free Church manse, he studied in Scotland and Germany, and held theological chairs at Auburn Theological Seminary (1920) and Union Theological Seminary (1930) in New York, and Emmanuel College, Toronto (1927), before becoming divinity professor (1934) and principal (1950) at New College, Edinburgh. One of the Church of Scotland's greatest scholars of this century, Baillie was said in theological outlook to have combined the old liberalism and Barthianism with a strong mystical tendency. He warmly supported the ecumenical movement, became a president of the World Council of Churches, and displayed his gift of statesmanship at the early assemblies, Amsterdam (1948) and Evanston (1954). He unsuccessfully commended a 1957 scheme of union between the national churches of Scotland and England. Among his many books were *Our Knowledge of God* (1939) and *Belief in Progress* (1950), but it is for two less technical little works that he is best remembered: *A Diary of Private Prayer* (1936) and *Invitation to Pilgrimage* (1942). Of the former it was said that in it "he set up a chain of prayer across the world."

J. D. Douglas

Balfour Declaration (1917). An official statement by British Foreign Secretary Arthur James Balfour on November 2, 1917, announcing the approval by the British government of a Jewish homeland in Palestine. The document was drafted in concert with Jewish leadership and issued to Lord Rothschild, who was representing the Zionists.

The Declaration reads: "His Majesty's Government view with favour the establishment in Palestine of a national home for the Jewish people, and will use their best endeavours to facilitate the achievement of this object, it being clearly understood that nothing shall be done which may prejudice the civil and religious rights of existing non-Jewish communities in Palestine, or the rights and political status enjoyed by Jews in any other country."

The Balfour Declaration was the first significant political victory achieved by the Zionist movement. Until this affirmative action by the British cabinet, since the Jewish dispersion no world power had ever granted official recognition to the claim of world Jewry to Eretz Yisrael. It has, accordingly, been compared to the edict of King Cyrus of Persia (Ezra 1:2–4).

Issued during World War I, the declaration was generally regarded as an effort to enlist Jewish support for the Allies. Though the Arab leadership at the time gave consent to the declaration, in the Arab–Israeli struggle in later years Arabs have often referred to the declaration as "the original sin."

M. R. Wilson

See also Zionism.

Bibliography. H. H. Ben-Sasson, ed., *A History of the Jewish People; EJ,* IV, 130–36; W. Laqueur, ed., *The Israel-Arab Reader;* C. Pfeiffer, *The Arab-Israeli Struggle;* A. Rubinstein, ed., *The Return to Zion.*

Bampton Lectures. Named for John Bampton (1689–1751), graduate of Oxford and canon of Salisbury, these originated in an endowment that provided for eight divinity lectures to be delivered annually in the Church of St. Mary the Virgin, Oxford. Bampton, who left his entire estate for the purpose, stipulated that the subject should be the exposition and defense of the Christian faith, with particular reference to the divine authority of the Scriptures, the authority of patristic writings, and the articles of the Apostles' and Nicene creeds. The lectures, the first series of which was given in 1780, were normally to take place between the day before Palm Sunday and the day before Whitsunday. Because of falling income they have been delivered only on alternate years since 1895. Chosen by Oxford college heads, the lecturer must be at least a Master of Arts of Oxford or Cambridge. No scholar may be invited a second time to undertake the project. Publication of the lectures is obligatory, and among the famous publications so sponsored have been those of T. B. Strong (1895), W. R. Inge (1899), N. P. Williams (1924), and R. H. Lightfoot (1934). In recent years some criticism has been expressed that the benefactor's concern for the upholding of orthodoxy has not always been shared by the appointed lecturer. J. D. Douglas

Banquet, Messianic. *See* Marriage Feast of the Lamb.

Baptism. Deriving from the Greek *baptisma,* "baptism" denotes the action of washing or plunging in water, which from the earliest days (Acts 2:41) has been used as the rite of Christian initiation. Its origins have been variously traced to the OT purifications, the lustrations of Jewish sects, and parallel pagan washings, but there can be no doubt that baptism as we know it begins with the baptism of John. Christ himself, by both precedent (Matt. 3:13) and precept (Matt. 28:19), gives us authority for its observance. On this basis it has been practiced by almost all Christians, though attempts have been made to replace it by a baptism of fire or the Spirit in terms of Matt. 3:11.

In essence the action is an extremely simple one, though pregnant with meaning. It consists in a going in or under the baptismal water in the name of Christ (Acts 19:5) or more commonly the Trinity (Matt. 28:19). Immersion was fairly certainly the original practice and continued in general use up to the Middle Ages. The Reformers agreed that this best brought out the meaning of baptism as a death and resurrection, but even the early Anabaptists did not think it essential so long as the subject goes under the water. The type of water and circumstances of administration are not important, though it seems necessary that there should be a preaching and confession of Christ as integral parts of the administration (cf. Acts 8:37). Other ceremonies may be used at discretion so long as they are not unscriptural and do not distract from the true action, like the complicated and rather superstitious ceremonial of the medieval and modern Roman Church.

Discussion has been raised concerning the proper ministers and subjects of the action. In the first instance there may be agreement with Augustine that Christ himself is the true minister ("he shall baptize you," Matt. 3:11). But Christ does not give the external baptism directly; he commits this to his disciples (John 4:2). This is taken to mean that baptism should be administered by those to whom there is entrusted by inward and outward calling the ministry of word and sacrament, though laymen have been allowed to baptize in the Roman Church, and some early Baptists conceived the strange notion of baptizing themselves. Normally baptism belongs to the public ministry of the church.

As concerns the subjects, the main difference is between those who practice the baptism of the children of confessing Christians and those who insist upon a personal confession as a prerequisite. This point is considered in the two separate articles devoted to the two positions and need not detain us in this exposition of positive baptismal teaching. It may be noted, however, that adult baptisms continue in all churches, that confession is everywhere considered important, and that Baptists often feel impelled to an act of dedication of children. Among adults it has been a common practice to refuse baptism to those unwilling to leave doubtful callings, though the attempt of one sect to impose a minimum age of thirty years did not meet with common approval. In the case of children, there has been misgiving concerning the infants of parents whose profession of Christian faith is very obviously nominal or insincere. The special case of the mentally impaired demands sympathetic treatment, but there is no warrant for prenatal or forced baptisms, and even less for baptism of inanimate objects such as was practiced in the Middle Ages.

A clue to the meaning of baptism is given by three OT types: the flood (I Pet. 3:19–20), the Red Sea (I Cor. 10:1–2), and circumcision (Col. 2:11–12). These all refer in different ways to the divine covenant, to its provisional fulfillment in a divine act of judgment and grace, and to the coming and definitive fulfillment in the baptism of the cross. The conjunction of water with death and redemption is particularly apt in the case of the first two; the covenantal aspect is more particularly emphasized in the third.

When we come to the action itself, there are many different but interrelated associations. The most obvious is that of washing (Titus 3:5), the cleansing water being linked with the blood of Christ on the one side and the purifying action of the Spirit on the other (see I John 5:6, 8), so that we are brought at once to the divine work of reconciliation. A second is that of initiation, adoption, or, more especially, regeneration (John 3:5), the emphasis again being placed on the operation of the Spirit in virtue of the work of Christ.

These various themes find common focus in the primary thought of baptism (in the destructive, yet also life-giving, power of water) as a drowning and an emergence to new life, i.e., a death and resurrection (Rom. 6:3–4). But here again the true witness of the action is to the work of God in the substitutionary death and resurrection of Christ. This identification with sinners in judgment and renewal is what Jesus accepts when he comes to the baptism of John and fulfills when he takes his place between two thieves on the cross (Luke 12:50). Here we have the real baptism of the NT, which makes possible the baptism of our identification with Christ and underlies and is attested by the outward sign. Like preaching and the Lord's Supper, "baptism" is an evangelical word telling us that Christ has died and risen again in our place, so that we are dead and alive again in him, with him, and through him (Rom. 6:4, 11).

Like all preaching, however, baptism carries with it the call to that which we should do in response or correspondence to what Christ has done for us. We, too, must make our movement of death and resurrection, not to add to what Christ has done, nor to complete it, nor to compete with it, but in grateful acceptance and application. We do this in three related ways constantly kept before us by our baptism: the initial response of repentance and faith (Gal. 2:20); the lifelong process of mortification and renewal

(Eph. 4:22–23); and the final dissolution and resurrection of the body (I Cor. 15). This rich signification of baptism, which is irrespective of the time or manner of baptism, is the primary theme that ought to occupy us in baptismal discussion and preaching. But it must be emphasized continually that this personal acceptance or entry is not independent of the once for all and substitutionary work of Christ, which is the true baptism.

It is forgetfulness of this point which leads to misunderstanding of the so-called grace of baptism. This may be by its virtual denial. Baptism has no grace apart from its psychological effects. It is primarily a sign of something that we do, and its value may be assessed only in explicable religious terms. The fact that spiritual gifts and even faith itself are true gifts of the Holy Spirit, with an element of the mysterious and incalculable, is thus denied.

On the other hand, it may be by distortion or exaggeration. Baptism means the almost automatic infusion of a mysterious substance which accomplishes a miraculous but not very obvious transformation. It is thus to be regarded with awe, and fulfilled as an action of absolute necessity to salvation except in very special cases. The true mystery of the Holy Spirit yields before ecclesiastical magic and theological sophistry.

But when baptismal grace is brought into proper relationship to the work of God, we are helped on the way to a fruitful understanding. First, and above all, we remember that behind the external action there lies the true baptism, which is that of the shed blood of Christ. Baptismal grace is the grace of this true reality of baptism, i.e., of the substitutionary work of Christ, or of Christ himself. Only in this sense can we legitimately speak of grace, but in this sense we can and must.

Second, we remember that behind the external action there lies the inward operation of the Spirit moving the recipient to faith in Christ's work and accomplishing regeneration to the life of faith. Baptismal grace is the grace of this internal work of the Spirit, which cannot be presumed (for the Spirit is sovereign) but which we dare to believe where there is a true calling on the name of the Lord.

Third, the action itself is divinely ordained as a means of grace, i.e., a means to present Christ and therefore to fulfill the attesting work of the Spirit. It does not do this by the mere performance of the prescribed rite; it does it in and through its meaning. Nor does it do it alone; its function is primarily to seal and confirm, and therefore it does it in conjunction with the spoken and written word. It need not do it at the time of administration; for, under the gracious sovereignty of the Spirit, its fruition may come at a much later date. It does not do it automatically; for, whereas Christ is always present and his grace remains, there are those who respond to neither word nor sacrament and therefore miss the true and inward meaning and power.

When we think in these terms, we can see that there is and ought to be a real, though not a magical, baptismal grace which is not affected greatly by the detailed time or mode of administration. The essentials are that we use it (1) to present Christ, (2) in prayer to the Holy Spirit, (3) in trustful dependence upon his sovereign work, and (4) in conjunction with the spoken word. Restored to this evangelical use, and freed especially from distorting and unhelpful controversy, baptism might quickly manifest again its power as a summons to live increasingly, or even to begin to live, the life which is ours in Christ crucified and risen for us. G. W. Bromiley

See also Baptism, Believers'; Baptism, Infant; Baptism, Modes of; Baptismal Regeneration; Baptism for the Dead.

Bibliography. G. W. Bromiley, *Baptism and the Anglican Reformers;* J. Calvin, *Institutes* 4; W. F. Flemington, *The NT Doctrine of Baptism;* Reports on Baptism in the Church of Scotland; G. R. Beasley-Murray, *Baptism in the NT;* A. Oepke, *TDNT,* I, 529–46.

Baptism, Believers'. Where the gospel is first preached or Christian profession has lapsed, baptism is always administered on confession of penitence and faith. In this sense believers' baptism, i.e., the baptism of those who make a profession of faith, has been an accepted and persistent phenomenon in the church. Yet there are powerful groups among Christians who think that we should go further than this. Believers' baptism as they see it is not merely legitimate; it is the only true baptism according to the NT, especially, though not necessarily, in the form of immersion.

This is seen first from the precept which underlies its institution. When Jesus commanded the apostles to baptize, he told them first to make disciples and said nothing whatever about infants (Matt. 28:19). In other words, preaching must always precede baptism, for it is by the word and not the sacrament that disciples are first made. Baptism can be given only when the recipient has responded to the word in penitence and faith, and it is to be followed at once by a course of more detailed instruction.

That the apostles understood it in this way is evident from the precedents which have come down to us in Acts. On the day of Pentecost, for example, Peter told the conscience-stricken people to repent and be baptized; he did not mention any special conditions for infants incapable of repentance (Acts 2:38). Again, when the Ethiopian eunuch desired baptism, he was told that there could be no hindrance so long as he believed, and it was on confession of faith that Philip baptized him (Acts 8:36ff.). Even when whole households were baptized, we are normally told that they first heard the gospel preached and either believed or received an endowment of the Spirit (cf. Acts 10:45; 16:32–33). In any case, no mention is made of any other type of baptism.

The meaning of baptism as developed by Paul in Rom. 6 supports this contention. It is in repentance and faith that we are identified with Jesus Christ in his death, burial, and resurrection. To infants who cannot hear the word and make the appropriate response, it thus seems to be meaningless and even misleading to speak of baptism into the death and resurrection of Christ. The confessing believer alone knows what this means and can work it out in his life. In baptism, confessing his penitence and faith, he has really turned his back on the old life and begun to live the new life in Christ. He alone can look back to a meaningful conversion or regeneration and thus receive the confirmation and accept the challenge that comes with baptism. To introduce any other form of baptism is to open the way to perversion or misconception.

To be sure, there is no direct prohibition of infant baptism in the NT. But in the absence of direction either way it is surely better to carry out the sacrament or ordinance as obviously commanded and practiced than to rely on exegetical or theological inference for a different administration. This is particularly the case in view of the weakness or irrelevance of many of the considerations advanced.

Christ's blessing of the children, for example, shows us that the gospel is for little ones and that we have a duty to bring them to Christ, but it says nothing whatever about administering baptism contrary to the acknowledged rule (Mark 10:13ff.). Again, the fact that certain characters may be filled with the Spirit from childhood (Luke 1:15) suggests that God may work in infants, but it gives us no warrant to suppose that he normally does so, or that he does so in any given case, or that baptism may be given before this work finds expression in individual repentance and faith. Again, the children of Christians enjoy privileges and perhaps even a status which cannot be ascribed to others. They are reckoned in some sense "holy" by God (I Cor. 7:14). But here too there is no express connection with baptism or the baptismal identification with Jesus Christ in death and resurrection.

Reference to the household baptisms of Acts is of no greater help. The probability may well be that some of these households included infants, yet this is by no means certain. Even if they did, it is unlikely that the infants were present when the word was preached, and there is no indication that any infants were actually baptized. At very best this could only be a hazardous inference, and the general drift of the narratives seems to be in a very different direction.

Nor does it serve to introduce the OT sign of circumcision. There is certainly a kinship between the signs. But there are also great differences. The fact that the one was given to infant boys on a fixed day is no argument for giving the other to all children some time in infancy. They belong, if not to different covenants, at least to different dispensations of the one covenant: the one to a preparatory stage, when a national people was singled out and its sons belonged naturally to the people of God; the other to the fulfillment, when the Israel of God is spiritual and children are added by spiritual rather than natural regeneration. In any case, God himself gave a clear command to circumcise the male descendants of Abraham; he has given no similar command to baptize the male and female descendants of Christians.

Theologically, the insistence upon believers' baptism in all cases seems better calculated to serve the true significance and benefit of baptism and to avoid the errors which so easily threaten it. Only when there is personal confession before baptism can it be seen that personal repentance and faith are necessary to salvation through Christ, and that these do not come magically but through hearing the word of God. With believers' baptism the ordinance achieves its significance as the mark of a step from darkness and death to light and life. The recipient is thus confirmed in the decision which he has taken, brought into the living company of the regenerate, which is the true church, and encouraged to walk in the new life which he has begun.

This means that in believers' baptism faith is given its proper weight and sense. The need for faith is recognized, of course, in infant baptism. It is contended that infants may believe by a special work of the Spirit, or that their present or future faith is confessed by the parents or sponsors, or that the parents or sponsors exercise vicarious faith, or even that faith is given in, with, or under the administration. Some of these notions are manifestly unscriptural. In others there is a measure of truth. But none of them meets the requirement of a personal confession of personal faith as invariably fulfilled in believers' baptism.

Again, believers' baptism also carries with it a genuine, as opposed to a spurious, baptismal grace. The expression of repentance and faith in baptism gives conscious assurance of forgiveness and regeneration and carries with it an unmistakable summons to mortification and renewal. Properly understood, this may also be the case with infant baptism, as in the Reformed churches. But a good deal of embarrassed explanation is necessary to make this clear, and there is always the risk of a false understanding, as in the medieval and Romanist view of baptismal regeneration. Baptism on profession of faith is the only effective safeguard against the dangerous notion that baptism itself can automatically transfer the graces which it represents.

To the exegetical and theological considerations there may also be added some less important but noteworthy historical arguments. First, there is no decisive evidence for a common Jewish practice of infant baptism in apostolic times. Second, the patristic statements linking infant baptism with the apostles are fragmentary and unconvincing in the earlier stages. Third, examples of believers' baptism are common in the first centuries, and a continuing, if suppressed, witness has always been borne to this requirement. Fourth, the development of infant baptism seems to be linked with the incursion of pagan notions and practices. Finally, there is evidence of greater evangelistic incisiveness and evangelical purity of doctrine where this form of baptism is recognized to be the baptism of the NT.

G. W. BROMILEY

See also BAPTISM; BAPTISM, INFANT; BAPTISMAL REGENERATION.

Bibliography. K. Barth, *The Teaching of the Church Regarding Baptism* and *Church Dogmatics* IV/4; A. Booth, *Paedobaptism Examined;* A. Carson, *Baptism in Its Modes and Subjects;* J. Gill, *Body of Divinity;* J. Warns, *Baptism;* K. Aland, *Did the Early Church Baptize Infants?* D. Moody, *The Word of Truth.*

Baptism, Infant. In a missionary situation the first subjects of baptism are always converts. But throughout Christian history, attested as early as Irenaeus and Origen with a reference back to the apostles, it has also been given to the children of professing believers. This has not been solely on grounds of tradition, or in consequence of a perversion, but for what have been regarded as scriptural reasons.

To be sure, there is no direct command to baptize infants. But there is also no prohibition. Again, if we have no clear-cut example of an infant baptism in the NT, there may well have been such in the household baptisms of Acts, and there is also no instance of the child of Christians being baptized on profession of faith. In other words, no decisive guidance is given by direct precept or precedent.

Yet there are two lines of biblical study which are thought to give convincing reasons for the practice. The first is a consideration of detailed passages or statements from the OT and NT. The second is a consideration of the whole underlying theology of baptism as it comes before us in the Bible.

To begin with the detailed passages, we naturally turn first to the types of baptism found in the OT. All these favor the view that God deals with families rather than individuals. When Noah is saved from the flood, his whole family is received with him into the ark (cf. I Pet. 3:20–21). When Abraham is given the covenant sign of circumcision, he is commanded to administer it to all the male members of his house (Gen. 17; cf. Col. 2:11–12 for the connection between baptism and circumcision). At the Red Sea it is all Israel (men, women, and children) which passes through the waters in the great act of redemption that foreshadows not only the sign of baptism but the work of God behind it (cf. I Cor. 10:1–2).

In the NT the ministry of our Lord is particularly rich in relevant statements. He himself becomes a child, and as such is conceived of the Holy Spirit. The Baptist, too, is filled with the Spirit from his mother's womb, so that he might have been a fit subject for baptism no less than circumcision very early in life. Later, Christ receives and blesses the little ones (Matt. 19:13–14) and is angry when his disciples rebuff them (Mark 10:14). He says that the things of God are revealed to babes rather than the wise and prudent (Luke 10:21). He takes up the statement of Ps. 8:2 about the praise of sucklings (Matt. 21:16). He warns against the danger of offending against little ones that believe in him (Matt. 18:6), and in the same context says that to be Christians we have not to become adults but to become as children.

In the first preaching in Acts it is noticeable that Peter confirms the covenant procedure of the OT with the words: "The promise is unto you, and to your children." In the light of the OT background and the similar procedure in proselyte baptisms, there is little reason to doubt that the household baptisms would include any children who might belong to the families concerned.

In the epistles children are particularly addressed in Ephesians, Colossians, and probably I John. We also have the important statement in I Cor. 7:14 in which Paul speaks of the children of marriages that have become "mixed" by conversion as "holy." This cannot refer to their civil status, but can only mean that they belong to the covenant people, and therefore will obviously have a right to the covenant sign.

It will be noted that in different ways all these statements bring before us the covenant membership of the children of professing believers. They thus introduce us directly to the biblical understanding of baptism that provides the second line of support for baptizing infants.

As the Bible sees it, baptism is not primarily a sign of repentance and faith on the part of the baptized. It is not a sign of anything that we do at all. It is a covenant sign (like circumcision, but without blood-shedding), and therefore a sign of the work of God on our behalf which precedes and makes possible our own responsive movement.

It is a sign of the gracious election of the Father who plans and establishes the covenant. It is therefore a sign of God's calling. Abraham no less than his descendants was first chosen and called by God (Gen. 12:1). Israel was separated to the Lord because he himself had said: "I will be your God, and ye shall be my people" (Jer. 7:23). Of all disciples it must be said: "Ye have not chosen me, but I have chosen you" (John 15:16). The elective will of God in Christ extends to those who are far off as well as nigh, and the sign of it may be extended not only to those who have responded, but to their children growing up in the sphere of the divine choice and calling.

But baptism is also a sign of the substitutionary work of the Son in which the covenant is fulfilled. As a witness of death and resurrection, it attests the death and resurrection of the One for the many without whose vicarious action no work even of repentance and faith can be of any avail. It preaches Christ himself as the One who is already dead and risen, so that all are dead and risen in him (II Cor. 5:14; Col. 3:1) even before the movements of repentance and faith which they are summoned to make in identification with him. This substitutionary work is not merely for those who have already believed. It may and must be preached to all, and the sign and seal given both to those who accept it and to the children who will be brought up with the knowledge of what God has already done for them once for all and all-sufficiently in Christ.

Finally, baptism is a sign of the regenerative work of the Holy Spirit by which individuals are brought into the covenant in the responsive movement of repentance and faith. But the Holy Spirit is sovereign (John 3:8). He works how and when and in whom he pleases. He laughs at human impossibilities (Luke 1:37). He is often present before his ministry is perceived, and his operation is not necessarily coextensive with our apprehension of it. He does not disdain the minds of the undeveloped as fit subjects for the beginning, or if he so disposes the completion, of his work. So long as there is prayer to the Spirit, and a readiness to preach the evangelical word when the opportunity comes, infants may be regarded as within the sphere of this life-giving work which it is the office of baptism to sign and seal.

Where infant baptism, or paedobaptism, as it is sometimes called, is practiced, it is right and necessary that those who grow to maturity should make their own confession of faith. But they do so with the clear witness that it is not this which saves them, but the work of God already done for them before they believed. The possibility arises, of course, that they will not make this confession, or do so formally. But this cannot be avoided by a different mode of administration. It is a problem of preaching and teaching. And even if they do not believe, or do so nominally, their prior baptism as a sign of the work of God is a constant witness to call or finally to condemn them.

On the mission field adult baptism will naturally continue. In days of apostasy it can and will be common even in evangelized lands. Indeed, as a witness to the fact that our response is really demanded it is good for the church that there should always be a Baptist section within it. But once the gospel has gained an entry into a family or community, there is good scriptural and theological ground that infant baptism should be the normal practice. G. W. Bromiley

See also Baptism; Baptism, Believers'.

Bibliography. G. W. Bromiley, *The Baptism of Infants;* J. Calvin, *Institutes* 4.16; O. Cullmann, *Baptism in the NT;* P. C. Marcel, *The Biblical Doctrine of Infant Baptism;* Reports on Baptism in the Church of Scotland; W. Wall, *The History of Infant Baptism;* J. Jeremias, *Infant Baptism in the First Four Centuries;* H. Thielicke, *The Evangelical Faith,* III.

Baptism, Lay. The NT affords neither precept nor precedent for the administration of baptism except by an ordained minister. From an early period, however, laymen did give baptism where ministers were not available. The custom was defended by Tertullian and later theologians on the ground that what is received may be passed on, that the sacrament is more important than order, and that the rule of love permits it. Some early authorities insisted on certain qualifications (e.g., monogamy or confirmation), and the medieval church drew up an order of precedence. Luther approved of the practice, seeing in it an exercise of the priesthood of the laity. But the Reformed school rejected and suppressed it on the ground that it is not scriptural, destroys good order, and is linked with the false idea of an absolute necessity of baptism. Baptism by midwives was particularly disliked. The practice was fully debated in the Church of England, and eventually discontinued after the Hampton Court Conference in 1604. G. W. Bromiley

Bibliography. J. Bingham, *Works*, VIII; G. W. Bromiley, *Baptism and the Anglican Reformers.*

Baptism, Modes of. There are, generally speaking, two opinions regarding the proper manner of administering baptism: that only immersion is lawful and that the mode is a matter of indifference. It would not be correct to identify the immersionist as the Baptist position, for some Baptists do not accept the necessity of immersion. The early Anabaptists as a rule baptized by pouring, and still today certain writers who strongly condemn infant baptism are indifferent as to mode (e.g., Karl Barth).

The immersionist position is founded on three arguments. (1) It is argued that the word *baptizein* means "to immerse" and therefore the command to baptize is itself a command to immerse. *Baptizein* in classical usage generally meant "to dip." Immersionists maintain that this meaning continues unaltered in NT usage and that this is confirmed by the use of the prepositions "in" and "into" with *baptizein* and by certain circumstantial references to baptism being administered in places where large supplies of water could be found (Luke 3:3; John 3:23). (2) Because baptism signifies union with Christ in his burial and resurrection (Rom. 6:4; Col. 2:12), immersionists contend that only sinking under and coming up out of the water adequately express the symbolism of the sacrament. (3) Immersionists lay claim to the testimony of the early church, for which immersion was the primary mode.

The second position is essentially a negative one. It denies the immersionist insistence that baptism is rightly administered only by immersion; instead, it contends that in the NT baptism, in its external form, is simply a washing, a cleansing, which can as well be effected by pouring (affusion) or sprinkling (aspersion) as by immersion.

While there is widespread agreement that *baptizein* in classical Greek means "to immerse," because *baptizein* has become a technical theological term in the NT it is maintained that the classical and secular usage cannot by itself be normative. The term *diathēkē*, for example, universally means "testament" in the Greek of the NT period, but it cannot be given that meaning in its NT usage. That in its biblical and theological use *baptizein* has come to mean simply "to wash" or "to purify with water" is indicated by certain occurrences of the term in the LXX and NT where *baptizein* cannot mean immerse (Sir. 34:25; Luke 11:38; Acts 1:5; 2:3–4, 17; I Cor. 10:1–2; Heb. 9:10–23). The last text in particular is a reminder that the purificatory water rites of the OT, the biblical antecedents of baptism, were never immersions. It is further maintained that it is at least implausible that certain baptisms recorded in the NT were immersions (Acts 2:41; 10:47–48; 16:33). Nor, it is contended, can appeal be made to the use of the prepositions "in" and "into" which are ambiguous and, if pressed, in Acts 8:38 would require the immersion of both subject and minister.

While baptism certainly signifies union with Christ in his death and resurrection, it is denied that this has relevance for the mode. In Rom. 6:6 union with Christ in his crucifixion and in Gal. 3:27 being clothed with Christ are included in the signification of baptism, but no mode illustrates these aspects of the symbolism of baptism. Further, water is a singularly unlikely symbol for the earth into which one is buried, as the immersionist contends. Actually, sprinkling is as well established in Ezek. 36:25 and Heb. 9:10, 13–14; 10:22.

It is conceded that immersion was the primary mode in the early church, but it is pointed out that other modes were permitted (cf. Didache 7; Cyprian, *Epistle to Magnus* 12), the earliest artistic representations depict baptism by pouring (affusion), and that some of the influences contributing to the popularity of immersion well may not have been healthy. In general, the nonimmersionist contends that rigor in matters of form is contrary to the spirit of NT worship, contrary to the universal indifference to the mode of celebrating the Lord's Supper, and subject to the scandal that, in principle, the immersionist depopulates the church of most of its membership and most of its finest sons and daughters.

R. S. Rayburn

See also Baptism.

Bibliography. A. Carson, *Baptism, Its Mode and Its Subjects;* T. J. Conant, *The Meaning and Use of Baptizein;* J. Warns, *Baptism;* J. Gill, *Body of Divinity;* A. H. Strong, *Systematic Theology;* A. Oepke, *TDNT,* I, 529–46; B. B. Warfield, "How Shall We Baptize?" in *Selected Shorter Writings of Benjamin B. Warfield,* II; W. G. T. Shedd, *Dogmatic Theology;* R. L. Dabney, *Lectures in Systematic Theology;* R. Watson, *Theological Institutes;* R. G. Rayburn, *What About Baptism?* J. Murray, *Christian Baptism.*

Baptismal Regeneration. Twice in the NT a connection is made between water, or washing in water, and regeneration. In John 3:3 we are told that a man must be born of water and of the Spirit to enter the kingdom of God. And in Titus 3:5 we read that we are saved "by the washing of regeneration and renewal of the Holy Spirit." In view of these passages, of the interrelationship of baptism with Christ's resurrection, and of the fact that it is the sacrament of initiation, it is inevitable that there should be some equation between baptism and regeneration. This equation is most strongly made in the phrase "baptismal regeneration."

The phrase as such is not wholly objectionable so long as the following points are kept clearly in view. The new life of the Christian is in Christ born, crucified, and risen for us. Incorporation into Christ is the work of the Holy Spirit. The true baptism behind the sacramental rite is this saving action of Christ and the Holy Ghost. The rite itself, in conjunction with the word, attests this work and is a means used by the Holy Spirit to its outworking in the believer. Baptism is not regeneration, however, nor is regeneration baptism, except in this deeper sense and context.

Unfortunately, medieval theology was tempted into a twofold isolation, that of the believer's regeneration from the substitutionary work of Christ, and that of the rite from baptism in its full and basic sense. In these circumstances the relationship between baptism and regeneration was necessarily misunderstood. "Regeneration" became the supernatural transformation of the believer and "baptism" a divinely appointed means of operation automatically efficacious so long as no bar (e.g., of insincerity) is opposed. The presuming of an absolute necessity of baptism, the emptying of regeneration of any true significance, and the whole problem of postbaptismal sin were evils which resulted from this perverted doctrine.

The Reformers clearly saw and rejected this perversion. But they did not make the mistake of breaking the relationship and treating baptism only as a symbolic rite with psychological effects. Rather, they tried to work back to the true and biblical understanding corrupted in the Romanist scheme. This certainly involves the danger of fresh misunderstanding, as emerges in the famous Gorham controversy in England. Hence the actual phrase "baptismal regeneration" is much better avoided. But in the long run the best antidote to perversion is the true and positive doctrine.

G. W. Bromiley

See also Baptism.

Bibliography. G. W. Bromiley, *Baptism and the Anglican Reformers;* J. B. Mozley, *The Baptismal Controversy;* J. C. S. Nias, *Gorham and the Bishop of Exeter;* A. Oepke, *TDNT,* I, 529–46; K. Barth, *Church Dogmatics* IV/4.

Baptism for the Dead. The problem of baptism for the dead arises out of the question asked by Paul in I Cor. 15:29: "Otherwise, what do people mean by being baptized on behalf of the dead? If the dead are not raised at all, why are people baptized on their behalf?" Various interpretations have been suggested for this verse. Some take it that the apostle refers to a practice of vicarious baptism as later reported among the Marcionites and Novatianists. On this view, he is not necessarily approving it, but using it for the sake of the argument. The Cataphryges seem to have derived from it a baptizing of corpses. Others construe it as a baptism of the dying or the administration of the sacrament "over dead men's graves." Most commentators try to avoid any connection with an actual practice, and there is again a wide range of suggestion. Baptism is to fill up the ranks left vacant by the dead, or under the inspiration of their witness, or with a view to death and resurrection in Christ, or more specifically in token that we are dead but may seek our new and true life in the resurrected Christ. Whatever the exact signification, the wider meaning is undoubtedly that baptism is a witness to the resurrection. Baptism loses its meaning if death is not followed by resurrection.

G. W. Bromiley

Bibliography. H. A. W. Meyer, *I Corinthians,* II; A. Plummer, *HDB,* I, 245; A. Robertson and A. Plummer, *I Corinthians,* ICC, 359; J. Weiss, *1 Kor.;* H. Preisker, "Die vikariatstaufe I Kor 15[29]—ein eschatologischer, nicht sacramentaler Brauch," *ZNW* 23:298ff.

Baptism of Jesus. The baptism of Jesus at the hands of John the Baptist is recounted in some detail in Matthew (3:13–17), told more briefly in Mark (1:9–11), only mentioned in Luke (3:21–22), and unrecorded though probably presumed in John (1:29–34). In all four accounts the anointing of Jesus with the Spirit and the declaration of his sonship are directly linked to the baptism.

Mark and Luke tell us only that Jesus was baptized in the Jordan by John, but Matthew adds that John the Baptist was hesitant and felt unworthy. Jesus, however, urges compliance with the call of God to "fulfill all righteousness." Mark suggests that Jesus was baptized during the ministry of John to all the people, while the structure of the text in Luke indicates that the baptism of Jesus by John was the culmination ("after all the people had been baptized, then Jesus also was baptized") of John's ministry. The Fourth Evangelist says only that John saw Jesus coming to him and then there follow certain Christological declarations by John.

The fundamental feature of all the narratives is that on the occasion of his baptism Jesus is anointed with the Spirit (Matt. 3:16; Mark 1:10; Luke 3:22; John 1:32). It is this anointing with the Spirit that inaugurates the ministry of Jesus which is characterized in the Synoptic Gospels by the power of the Spirit of the new age (Matt. 12:18, 28; Luke 4:18; 11:20; cf. Acts 10:38).

The anointing by the Spirit is the initial act of fulfillment (Luke 4:18, citing Isa. 61:1–2) which characterizes the whole story of Jesus and the subsequent story of the early church. This fulfillment motif is seen at two points. First, in all three of the Synoptic Gospels the temptation experience in the desert immediately follows the anointing of the Spirit; indeed Jesus is led by the Spirit (Mark: driven by the Spirit; Luke: led in the Spirit) into the desert. In a paradigmatic narrative the Spirit of the new age is confronted by the spirit who dominates the present. Jesus' conquest in the desert becomes the pattern for the rest of the Gospels as they report the power of Jesus to heal the sick and cast out demons. The presence of the Spirit of the new age raises the specter of the "unpardonable sin" against the Spirit, namely the sin of ascribing to the power of this age the healing work of the Holy Spirit (Matt. 12:31; Mark 3:28; Luke 12:10).

The link between Jesus' anointing with the Spirit and the fulfillment motif is to be noted also in the fact that Jesus inaugurates his ministry immediately after his baptism and the temptation. "Time is fulfilled: the kingdom of God is before you; repent and believe the good news" (Mark 1:15; cf. Matt. 4:17). Jesus declares the demise of the old and the initial thrust of the new. The promise of prophets is offered and people are invited to enter. From this point on, the burden of the word and work of Jesus is to invite, to initiate newness, to portray the freedom created by the Spirit, as well as to speak judgment upon the old system ruled by law, whose only fruit is oppression.

This significance of Jesus' anointing by the Spirit at his baptism is further noted in the words by which Jesus confirmed John the Baptist. No one is greater than John, yet anyone in the kingdom is greater. He is the final figure who concludes the old and introduces the new. He is the forerunner (Matt. 11:11–14). The anointing of Jesus at his baptism is the specific midpoint in redemptive history; it is the beginning of fulfillment.

It should be noted that the coming of the Spirit upon Jesus is not the promised baptism in the Spirit, for Jesus himself is the one who shall baptize. Further, the baptism in the Spirit is a baptism of judgment and grace. The experience of the Spirit at the baptism of Jesus is a bestowal that establishes the messianic character of his ministry. This is noted in the voice from heaven, "You are my Son, my beloved" (or "chosen"). Jesus' self-understanding of his sonship to the Father underlies his messianic office. The OT allusion may be either Isa. 42:1 or Ps. 2:7 or perhaps both. The significance here of the sonship is service to the Father rather than any particular reference to Jesus' divine nature. The expression is teleological rather than ontological.

Special significance is to be seen in the fact that Jesus submitted to the baptism of John, which was a baptism of repentance for the forgiveness of sins. John has called a sinful and self-righteous people to turn quickly before an impending judgment descends. "Already the ax is laid to the root of the tree." Matthew's narrative focuses on the issue, for in it the Baptist attempts to protest the inappropriateness of Jesus coming to be baptized. The baptism of Jesus marks his solidarity as the messianic servant with his people. He takes upon himself by this cultic act their condition and their predicament. He becomes their representative. Coming to them and speaking to them he takes his place with them. Incarnation is not only coming to earth but also assuming the burden of life in the flesh. He not only speaks to them but also speaks for them. The Father's Son becomes the intercessor to the Father. The significance of the baptism of Jesus is set forth in stark terms by Paul: "He who knew no sin became sin for us in order that in him we might become the righteousness of God" (II Cor. 5:21). The baptism is the formal act of "emptying himself" (Phil. 2:7), of "becoming poor" (II Cor. 8:9).

It is with reference to this act of solidarity that we see again the significance of the temptations in the desert, for there he experiences in an intense way the predicament of the human condition. He resists the fundamental temptation to use his power—a temptation thrown at him even in his last hour (Matt. 27:40, 42)—in order to bring redemption from below. In his baptism he prepares himself for death—the ultimate expression of nonpower—for the people with whom he identifies, and makes the identification complete.

R. W. Lyon

See also Jesus Christ.

Bibliography. C. K. Barrett, *The Holy Spirit and the Gospel Tradition;* G. W. H. Lampe, *The Seal of the Spirit;* J. D. G. Dunn, *Jesus and the Spirit;* W. F. Flemington, *The NT Doctrine of Baptism.*

Baptism of the Spirit. Among the greatest blessings conferred by the Christian gospel is the personal indwelling and enduement of the divine Spirit. First conceived as the invisible energy of God active in nature and in history, but occasionally coming upon artists, prophets, leaders, or kings with enabling power, the Spirit of God was promised as the personal and permanent equipment of Messiah for his work (Isa. 11:1–2; 61:1–3). Other prophets extended a similar promise to all God's people (Joel 2:28–29; cf. Ezek. 36:26–27).

In the NT. In due time the prophet John, seeking to prepare the Jews for the Messiah, emphasized one aspect of this remarkable prophecy. He warned of a radical inward and personal purification, accompanying an outward national purgation by judgment. The one alternative he offered to such an immersion (baptism) in "Spirit and fire" was to accept his baptism in water as a symbol of total repentance and reformation of life (Matt. 3:11–12; Luke 3:7–17).

In this way the promise of the Spirit first became associated with the language of baptism—a baptism with the Holy Spirit. But far more authoritative and compelling in establishing this connection of the coming of the Spirit with water baptism was the model experience of Jesus. In the moment of his baptism, all four Gospels insist, the Spirit descended like a dove and abode upon him (Matt. 3:16; Mark 1:10; Luke 3:22; John 1:32; cf. Acts 10:38). Thenceforth water baptism and the reception of the Spirit must ever be linked in Christian minds.

John's contrast of baptism with water and baptism with Holy Spirit, as alternatives, was given a deeper significance, however, when his words were repeated by Jesus (Acts 1:5), echoed by Peter (Acts 11:16), recalled again by the evangelist John (1:26, 33) and by Paul (Acts 19:4–6; cf. I Cor. 12:13). In these references the Christian's reception of the Holy Spirit is no longer the alternative to a water baptism of repentance, but at least its fitting analogue, more probably its supplement and fulfillment. Since for Judaism, for John, and for the apostolic church baptism by water was a rite of initiation into the people of God, the initial experience of the Spirit's indwelling and enduement came to be called a "baptism in" or "with" the Holy Spirit.

In Greek, the preposition is here ambiguous: *en* may be local, meaning "within" water or Spirit; or, following Hebrew idiom, it may be instrumental, meaning "by means of" water or Spirit. But, as in the parallel phrases, "baptism in or with fire" or "suffering" (see Mark 10:38–39), the difference between "in" and "with" is more theoretical then practical.

This Judaic and Johannine background explains the strange, and possibly misleading, expression "baptism in or with the Holy Spirit." For it carries with it the suggestion that God's Spirit is an element, an energy or instrument, rather than a person. The outpouring of the Spirit (Joel 2:28–29; Acts 2:17, 33) similarly reflects the OT thought of the Spirit as God's invisible power, manifest only in its results. When the fully Christian conception of the Spirit is reached, as a divine person, as Christ's "other self" (John 14:17; 16:7; II Cor. 3:17; "the Spirit of Jesus," Acts 16:7), then to speak of "pouring" or "baptism in" the Spirit would seem no longer completely appropriate.

This distinction between the Spirit as person and the Spirit as element or energy is of practical importance, lest a careless use of words lead us to suppose we can manipulate the Spirit's power rather than surrendering to the Spirit's will (see I Cor. 12:11). That danger noted, the phrase "baptism in the Spirit" is not more vague or nebulous than "baptism into Christ" (Gal. 3:27), "baptized into his death" and resurrection (Rom. 6:3, 5), "baptized into one body" (of Christ, I Cor. 12:13). In NT thought baptism signified an experience so deep, radical, transforming, and effectual that only such telescopic phrases could describe its immeasurable consequences.

In particular, the indwelling and enduement with the Holy Spirit, which became available through Christ to all who believe, came inevitably to be linked with, and described in the language of, that crucial public step by which individuals first became Christians and were accepted as members of the Spirit-filled, Spirit-led, Spirit-empowered church of Christ. Quite naturally the experience came to be described as being baptized in or with the Holy Spirit.

In Modern Experience. In modern discussion, however, a slightly different phrase, "the baptism of the Spirit," has replaced the scriptural phrases, especially in Pentecostal and charismatic circles. In its most common use this new expression has tended to place less emphasis upon the indwelling of the Spirit, with the illumination of mind (John 14:26; 16:8–15), the refinement of character (the fruit of the Spirit, Gal. 5:22–23; love, I Cor. 12:27–13:13), and the gifts of peace, power, and joy that the Spirit bestows. Instead, while not denying these, the phrase has become associated specifically with the initial and continuing enduement of individuals by the Spirit with miraculous powers, gifts, abilities, and emotional resources, manifest in spiritual healing, speaking in unknown tongues, prophesying, leadership, exuberant emotion, and other forms of equipment for Christian service.

Alongside this difference of emphasis as to

what qualities of life and service most clearly demonstrate the power of the Spirit, opinion is divided also on how and when the initial reception of the Spirit may be expected.

Some insist that the earliest experience of the Spirit coincides with conversion. They resist any suggestion that so vital an experience could depend in any degree upon a merely ritual event like water baptism. They underline the necessary ministry of the Spirit in bringing any soul to Christ. Without the Spirit no one can call Jesus Lord (I Cor. 12:3), or be born into the kingdom (John 3:5), or become Christ's at all (Rom. 8:9). Thus, to receive the Spirit is an essential part of salvation itself.

Some insist that in the NT pattern of initiation reception of the Spirit accompanies baptism in water. These argue that apostolic baptism was certainly no mere ritual but a deliberate, and often perilous, public and irrevocable commitment to the lordship of Christ. It was accompanied by the confession of Christ before men, which was essential to saving faith (Rom. 10:9; cf. Matt. 10:32–33), on the part of each repentant believer. Defending the close association of the experience of the Spirit with such a baptism in water, they point to the plain implication of the metaphor itself—"baptism" of the Spirit. They insist that Christ's own baptismal experience sets the norm for every Christian baptism. And they recall, beside the oft-repeated words of John linking water baptism with the promised baptism of the Spirit, Peter's clear instruction and promise at Pentecost: "Repent, and be baptized . . . and you shall receive the gift of the Holy Spirit" (Acts 2:38–39).

With perhaps a little more hesitation, defenders of the view that Spirit baptism ought to accompany water baptism draw attention to Paul's action at Ephesus, which sought to repair a baptism which had not conferred the Spirit by one that did (Acts 19:1–6). They also suggest that, on this view, expressions like "born of water and the Spirit" (John 3:5), "washed . . . sanctified . . . justified in the name of the Lord Jesus" (I Cor. 6:11), and "the washing of regeneration and renewal in the Holy Spirit" (Titus 3:5) are more easily understood.

Others again insist that the baptism of the Spirit is an experience subsequent to conversion and entirely independent of water baptism, possibly replacing it. It is a second blessing, an "infilling" of the Spirit, supplementing conversion as the young Christian advances to maturity. These would argue that the supposed NT pattern has certainly not been familiar in the historic church. They emphasize that Pentecost was for the first disciples later than, and consequent upon, introduction to Jesus. They recall that some already Christians are urged to "be filled with the Spirit" (Eph. 5:18). Above all, they point to the poverty of spiritual experience of many professing (and baptized) Christians as proof that something more than conversion and baptism are needed for a Spirit-filled life.

Differing exegesis and theological debate must not be allowed to obscure the primary truth: that the Spirit of the living Christ seeks to enrich, enable, empower, and use Christians in every generation. The spiritual significance of apostolic baptism and of that prevalent in the modern church is so different that for most Christians the "fullness of the Spirit" will be an experience long subsequent to baptism. But how we describe the experience is less important than that we open mind, heart, and will to the power and joy which the Spirit offers to confer. The contemporary church and the modern world sadly need Christians baptized with the Spirit.

R. E. O. White

See also Holy Spirit; Charismatic Movement; Pentecostalism; Spiritual Gifts.

Bibliography. W. H. Griffith Thomas, *Holy Spirit of God;* J. D. G. Dunn, *Baptism in the Holy Spirit;* T. A. Smail, *Reflected Glory;* H. Berkhof, *Doctrine of the Holy Spirit.*

Baptist Tradition, The. It is a popular misunderstanding about Baptists to think that their chief concern is with the administration of baptism. The convictions of Baptists are based primarily on the spiritual nature of the church, and the practice of believers' baptism arises only as a corollary of this and in the light of the NT teaching. The theological position taken up by Baptists may be presented as follows.

Membership of the Church. According to Baptist belief the church is composed of those who have been born again by the Holy Spirit and who have been brought to personal and saving faith in the Lord Jesus Christ. A living and direct acquaintance with Christ is, therefore, held to be basic to church membership. Negatively, this involves a rejection of the concept that equates a church with a nation. Membership in the church of Christ is not based on the accident or privilege of birth, either in a Christian country or in a Christian family. Baptists therefore repudiate the Anglican and Presbyterian view by deleting the phrase "together with their children" from the definition of the church. Positively, this view of church membership indicates that the church is entered voluntarily and that only believers may participate in its ordinances. All members are equal in status although they vary in gifts.

Nature of the Church. In distinction from churches of the institutional or territorial kind, the Baptist conviction is expressed in the concept of the "gathered church." The members of the church are joined together by God into a fellowship of life and service under the lordship of Christ. Its members are pledged to live together under his laws and to enter into the fellowship created and maintained by the Holy Spirit. The church conceived of in this way is perceived the most clearly in its local manifestation. Thus, although the church invisible consists of all the redeemed, in heaven and in earth, past, present, and future, it may be truly said that wherever believers are living together in the fellowship of the gospel and under the sovereignty of Christ there is the church.

Government of the Church. Christ is the only head of the church, and the early Baptist pioneers earnestly contended for what they called "the crown rights of the Redeemer." The local church is autonomous, and this principle of government is sometimes described as the "congregational order of the churches." Baptists believe in the competence of the local fellowship to govern its own affairs, and because of the theological importance of the local church in contradistinction to connectional systems (episcopal, presbyterian) of church government, Baptists do not speak of the denomination as "the Baptist Church," but as "the Baptist churches" in any given area. The congregational order of the churches—i.e., the government of the church through the mind of the local congregation—is not to be equated with the humanistic concept of democracy. Democracy is too low and too small a word. The Baptist belief is that the church is to be governed not by an order of priests, nor through higher or central courts, but through the voice of the Holy Spirit in the hearts of the members in each local assembly. Whereas in a strictly democratic order of church government there would be a government of the church *by* the church, the Baptist position makes recognition of Christ's rule in the church *through* the church. From the equality of status of every church member and the recognition of the diversity of gifts, two things follow. First of all, it is acknowledged that each member has a right and duty in the government of the local church, and secondly, that the church gladly accepts the guidance of its chosen leaders.

Baptist churches are usually regarded as independent in their government, but they do not glory in independence for its own sake. The independence of a Baptist church relates to state control, and the Baptists of the seventeenth century in England were in the foremost rank of those who fought for this freedom. Baptists have always recognized the great value of association between churches, and associations of Baptist churches have been characteristic of Baptist life down the centuries. All such association is voluntary, however, and the mistake must not be made of assuming that the Baptist Union or the Baptist World Alliance is coextensive with the Baptist community.

Ordinances of the Church. These are normally spoken of as two, namely, believers' baptism and the Lord's Supper, though it would be more proper to speak of three and to include the ordinance of preaching. Baptists have normally preferred to use the word "ordinance" rather than "sacrament" because of certain sacerdotal ideas that the word "sacrament" has gathered to itself. The word "ordinance" points to the ordaining authority of Christ which lies behind the practice. Baptists regard the Lord's Supper somewhat after the Zwinglian manner. The bread and the wine are the divinely given tokens of the Lord's saving grace, "but the value of the service lies far more in the symbolism of the whole than in the actual elements" (Dakin). Henry Cook writes: "Being symbolic of facts that constitute the heart of the Gospel, they [the ordinances] arouse in the believing soul such feelings of awe and love and prayer that God is able by His Spirit to communicate Himself in a vitalising and enriching experience of His grace and power." Baptists acknowledge that the ordinances are thus a means of grace, but not otherwise than is also the preaching of the gospel. The position has been epitomized by saying that the ordinances are a special means of grace but not a means of special grace. It is also part of the Baptist position on this subject that believers' baptism and the Lord's Supper are church ordinances, that is to say, they are congregational rather than individual acts. Priestly mediation is abhorrent to Baptists and derogatory to the glory of Christ, who is the only priest.

Ministry of the Church. The ministry is as broad as the fellowship of the church, yet for the purposes of leadership the term "ministry" has been reserved for those who have the responsibility of oversight and instruction. Baptists do not believe in a ministerial order in the sense of a priestly caste. The Baptist minister has no "more" grace than the one who is not a minister; he does not stand any nearer to God by virtue of his official position than does the humblest member of the church. There are diverse gifts, however, and it is recognized that the gift of ministry is by the grace of God, as Paul himself intimated in Eph. 3:8. Pastors and deacons are chosen and appointed by the local church, though their appointment is frequently made in the wider context of the fellowship of Baptist churches.

A Baptist minister becomes so by virtue of an inward call of God which, in turn, receives confirmation in the outward call of a church. Public acknowledgment of this call of God is given in a service of ordination, which ordination, it is held, does not confer any kind of superior or ministerial grace but merely recognizes and regularizes the ministry within the church itself. The importance of ordination lies in the fact that the church itself preaches through the minister; and, though ordination is not intended to imprison the activity of the Holy Spirit within the bounds of ecclesiastically ordained preachers, there is, nevertheless, considerable importance attached to the due authorization of those who are to speak in the name of the church.

Ecumenicity of the Church. It might seem that the idea of unity would be foreign to Baptists, given their strong views on independence and their doctrine of the autonomy of the church, but such is not the case. It all depends on what is meant by unity. For Baptists unity can mean one of three things: organic union, which is generally looked on unfavorably; cooperation with other denominations, which is encouraged within limits; and cooperation with other Baptists, which is almost unqualifiedly acceptable. Let us look briefly at each of these.

Baptist organizations are largely voluntary, cooperative ventures that have no legal binding force over their members. This is part of the Baptist ethos, allowing for freedom and concerted action to exist at the same time. Hence the denominations (and there are many) do not exist as units, but are simply collections of individual Baptist churches. It came as no surprise then that when the Consultation on Church Union was inaugurated in the 1960s, Baptists were cool to the idea of joining, especially since some form of episcopacy and recognition of apostolic succession (i.e., authoritative ecclesiastical structure) would be required of them. Only the American Baptists showed any interest, but when a general survey showed that fewer than 20 percent were interested in full participation, any plans of union were effectively scrapped. Organic union with other denominations, if it requires giving up Baptist distinctives, is simply out of the question.

Cooperation with other groups is a different matter. As early as the American colonial period Baptists cooperated with Quakers and Roman Catholics in the protection of religious freedom. In 1908 the Northern Baptist Convention was one of the founding members of the Federal Council of Churches; it has actively supported both the World Council of Churches and the National Council of Churches. Baptists are also active in the American Bible Society, various mission boards, and numerous civic and social organizations. It should be noted, however, that not all Baptists favor this form of cooperation; Baptists in the North are more inclined to cooperate than those in the South. In fact, this has been a source of tension among various Baptist groups. But most Baptists consider cooperation with non-Baptists appropriate.

Cooperation with other Baptists is strongly encouraged. Among the various Baptist groups exists a deep sense of comradeship that has historical, theological, and psychological roots. Although rather striking differences of style and expression exist among them, Baptists have managed to cooperate in supraregional groups (such as the American Baptist Convention and the Southern Baptist Convention) and in the international Baptist World Alliance, which claims over 33 million members in 138 countries. What unites them all is the express purpose of the alliance, to express "the essential oneness of the Baptist people in the Lord Jesus Christ, to impart inspiration to the brotherhood, and to promote the spirit of fellowship, service, and co-operation among its members." E. F. KEVAN

See also LANDMARKISM; BAPTISM, BELIEVERS'.

Bibliography. A. C. Underwood, *History of English Baptists;* H. W. Robinson, *Baptist Principles;* H. Cook, *What Baptists Stand For;* A. Dakin, *The Baptist View of the Church and Ministry;* O. K. and M. Armstrong, *The Baptists in America;* R. G. Torbet, *A History of the Baptists,* 2 vols.; S. L. Stealey, ed., *A Baptist Treasury;* W. S. Hudson, *Baptists in Transition;* T. Crosby, *The History of the English Baptists,* 4 vols.

Barclay, Robert (1648–1690). The outstanding theologian of early Quakerism. His theology was forged on the anvil of persecution out of materials gleaned from classical and biblical studies. At age twenty-eight he wrote his great work, *Apology for the True Christian Divinity,* which Voltaire claimed was the finest church Latin he had ever read. Barclay translated the *Apology* into English two years later, and many editions have followed since 1678. The *Apology* and Barclay's ability in public debate revealed a scholarly foundation in the Quaker movement that made its arguments impressive.

Barclay's most controversial thesis is his concept of "direct and unmediated revelation." In brief, Barclay (and other Quakers) held that the primary religious authority is direct experience of Jesus as the living and present Christ. The Scriptures as the "true and faithful record" of the historic revelation outwardly corroborate the primary inward experience. Barclay denied that this doctrine of the light of Christ led to anarchic antinomianism, although he was fully aware of the religious and political significance of this doctrine in undercutting preemptive claims by church and state to interpret Scripture and tradition. The doctrine also implied the universal and saving light of Christ as a golden mean between alternatives—arbitrary election or universalism.

Barclay was a tireless advocate of peace, religious liberty, and political rights. He used his influence with royalty on behalf of imprisoned or abused Friends. A. O. ROBERTS

See also FRIENDS, SOCIETY OF.

Bibliography. D. E. Trueblood, *Robert Barclay.*

Barclay, William (1907–1978). Scottish biblical scholar. Born in Wick and educated at the universities of Glasgow and Marburg, he was ordained in 1933 and served a Church of Scotland parish in industrial Clydeside. From 1947 he lectured in NT at Glasgow University, where he was promoted to professor in 1964. His *Daily Study Bible* (NT) won acclaim worldwide and was published in many languages. His gift of communicating with ordinary people, many of them with no religious connection, was further confirmed by a successful television series on the Christian faith. Barclay always urged his students to have some nonreligious interests and to keep abreast of current topics. Doctrinally, he was a universalist who rejected the substitutionary view of the atonement. Reticent about the authority of Scripture, he rejected also the virgin birth and regarded miracles as merely symbolic of what Jesus can still do in the world. At one point late in life he advocated a two-tier system of church membership—the first for those who were deeply attracted to Christ, the second for those prepared to make total commitment. Barclay retired in 1974, but continued work on the OT part of his *Daily Study Bible* until just before his death.

J. D. DOUGLAS

Bibliography. Barclay, *A Spiritual Autobiography;* R. D. Kernohan, ed., *William Barclay: The Plain Uncommon Man.*

Barmen, Declaration of (1934). An important declaration of the Confessing Church in Germany, agreed upon at the Synod of Barmen in 1934.

At the Braune Synod held in Saxony in 1933, the *Deutsche Christen* (German Christians) had attempted to provide Hitler's National Socialist movement with a theological justification, speaking of a new Christ striving for expression in the German people's community and claiming that a people's state was a central tenet of true religion. The opposition which this generated culminated in the Synod of Barmen.

The Barmen Confession, which contains six main paragraphs, attempts to resist the subordination of the Christian gospel and church to any political or social movement as its writers believed the *Deutsche Christen* had done. It stresses the absolute necessity for submission to, and dependence upon, Jesus Christ as the living Word of God. It also emphasizes the Scriptures, each paragraph developing a scriptural theme. The church, it proclaims, cannot recognize any source of final divine revelation other than Jesus Christ. He and he alone must be its Lord. The Barmen Declaration openly proclaimed its loyalty to what its signers believed to be the historic Protestant Christian faith, and it resisted the compromise of the *Deutsche Christen.*

It was in large part written by the theologian Karl Barth. J. D. SPICELAND

See also NEO-ORTHODOXY; BARTH, KARL.

Barnes, Albert (1798–1870). One of the most influential American Presbyterian clergymen during the middle third of the nineteenth century and a central figure in the Old School–New School controversy that led to the 1837 denominational division. Born in Rome, New York, he graduated from Hamilton and Princeton. While serving his first charge in Morristown, New Jersey, he attracted attention because of an 1829 revival sermon entitled "The Way of Salvation," which denied the doctrine of original sin and insisted that man was a free moral agent who could choose for or against Christian salvation. The Old School conservatives became increasingly alarmed when he accepted a call to the prestigious First Church of Philadelphia and also began a long-standing habit of expressing his biblical interpretations in the form of semischolarly, very widely read commentaries for laymen entitled *Notes: Explanatory and Practical.* Twice in the 1830s the Philadelphia Synod charged Barnes with doctrinal error, only to have the Presbyterian General Assembly acquit him. These difficulties influenced Barnes to join other New School ministers as an early leader of the independently controlled Union Theological Seminary in New York City.

While Barnes promoted and practiced the New School concept of revivalism that stemmed from the Second Great Awakening, he also led the New School Presbyterians in emphasizing that social concern should be the logical consequence of personal regeneration. Accordingly he vigorously participated in a variety of reform movements, including prohibition and abolition.

W. C. Ringenberg

See also New School Theology.

Bibliography. Barnes, *Sermons on Revivals, Scriptural Views of Slavery, The Church and Slavery,* and *Life at Three Score and Ten;* G. M. Marsden, *The Evangelical Mind and the New School Presbyterian Experience;* A. J. Stansbury, *Trial of the Rev. Albert Barnes.*

Barnhouse, Donald Grey (1895–1960). Probably the best known and most widely followed American Bible teacher during the early middle decades of this century. Born in Watsonville, California, he gained his training in a broad variety of institutions including Biola, Princeton Seminary, Eastern Seminary, and the University of Pennsylvania.

In 1927 Barnhouse accepted the pulpit of Tenth Presbyterian Church in downtown Philadelphia, and it was from this church, where he continued the rest of his life, that he built his national and international empire. As early as 1928 and continuing through most of his career he spoke over radio networks of up to 455 stations, using the Bible expository method of teaching. The popularity of these broadcasts and later telecasts led to many invitations to conduct Bible conferences, and the increasing demand of these conferences led him, after 1940, to be absent from his pulpit six months a year. Also serving as an outlet for his sermons, Bible studies, essays, and editorials were the two magazines which he founded and edited, *Revelation* (1931–49) and *Eternity,* which continues to the present.

Barnhouse's theology was an eclectic yet independent mix of dispensationalism, Calvinism, and fundamentalism. As a dispensationalist he developed elaborate eschatological schemes, yet he departed significantly from much dispensationalist teaching. His fearless and brusque attacks upon liberal Presbyterian clergymen led the Philadelphia Presbytery to censure him in 1932, yet he opposed the fundamentalist concept of separation, and in his later years gradually grew more mellow in his relations with the Presbyterian Church and the National Council of Churches.

W. C. Ringenberg

Bibliography. Barnhouse, *His Own Received Him Not, But—, God's Methods for Holy Living, Life by the Son, Teaching the Word of Truth, Guaranteed Deposits, Man's Ruin, God's Wrath, God's Remedy,* and *God's River;* also see Barnhouse's many articles and essays in *Rev* and *Eter* magazines; C. A. Russell, "Donald Grey Barnhouse: Fundamentalist Who Changed," *JPH* 59:33–57.

Barth, Karl (1886–1968). Perhaps the most influential German theologian of the twentieth century. The son of a Reformed minister and professor at Bern, Barth was ordained in 1908. His realization of the ethical bankruptcy of liberal Protestant theology while pastor at Safenwil during World War I brought him to question his own position. In 1919 he published the first edition of *Der Römerbrief.* The book brought him to a chair in Reformed theology at Göttingen and is recognized as the beginning of neo-orthodoxy, or dialectical theology, or theology of crisis. Although Barth is acknowledged as its founder, others were involved, including Friedrich Gogarten, Eduard Thurneysen, Heinrich Barth, and Emil Brunner. By 1930 Barth was teaching in Bonn, where he began to oppose the Nazi movement and allied himself with the Confessing Church. In 1934 the opposition produced the Barmen Declaration, a strong protest against fascism and the Nazis basically written by Barth. The next year he was expelled from Germany and went to Basel. After the war his *Against the Stream* revealed his doubts about capitalism and communism. He was a prodigious author, writing over five hundred books, articles, and papers, the most famous being the thirteen-volume *Church Dogmatics.*

There are at least three key ideas in his early thought critical for his later writings. The first is the absolute transcendent sovereign God in contrast to sin-dominated mankind. Second is a dialectical theological method which poses truth as a series of paradoxes. For example, the infinite became the finite; eternity entered time; God became human. Such paradoxes create tension, in which one finds both a crisis and truth. The crisis, the third idea, involves humans. The individual discovers in the tension of the dialectic a crisis of existence, judgment, separation, belief/unbelief, acceptance/rejection of the ultimate truth of God concerning mankind as revealed in the Word.

Barth's view of the absolute sovereignty of God coupled with his view of the fall meant the will, emotions, and reason were ruined and incapable of allowing one to discover God. Humans respond to God's self-disclosure but have no role in the self-disclosure. The *analogia entis* of Aquinas and others, important for natural theology, was rejected and replaced by the *analogia fidei.* This helps to explain Barth's *Nein* to Brunner's point of contact.

Another theme is the Christocentric Word as the only source of the knowledge of God. Christ is God's Word incarnate; the Word is in Scripture but the Scripture is not necessarily the Word; and the Word is that of proclamation. The Word is God's communication to humans; his self-disclosure in Jesus Christ; the one and only revelation; and humans are totally dependent upon it. The content of the Word is judgment and grace. The Word descends; it does not ascend from creation. As the Word, Jesus Christ is the *God*-man, and as the God-*man* takes humanity into partnership with God. This was part of the original covenant broken by the fall but restored in the Word made flesh. The Bible, seen as inspired, unique, to be taken with great seriousness, is not to be confused with the Word. It is a human document and becomes the Word only as the Holy Spirit testifies to it; thus use of higher and lower criticism is permissible and necessary.

Barth rejected the Christian faith as a series of propositional truths. The Christian faith is the result of the dynamic between being grasped by the truth of the gospel and being in a sinful world to which one must witness and proclaim the Word. It is from this existential approach that Barth came to reject infant baptism.

Barth's theology has not gained universal acceptance. Some, for example, object to his view of Scripture. Although Barth saw Scripture as having authority, he did not subscribe to verbal inspiration as the basis of scriptural authority. Biblical authority is also weakened for some by the possibility of fallibility. Further, if Scripture has authority only as it witnesses to the Word, then it has no authority in and of itself. Since many evangelicals feel it does have such authority, Barth's view of Scripture is seen to be seriously flawed.

The high Christology of Barth has come under attack. First, it is viewed as a procrustean bed for the OT, as seen in Wilhelm Vischer's commentary on Genesis. Second, the Christology seems to lead to universalism. As a correlate to the Christology, Barth's rejection of natural theology is often interpreted as a rejection of natural revelation, and the dispute with Brunner on the *imago Dei* highlights this problem.

Barth's view of sin is also challenged. He believed in a fallen world, yet the fall does not seem to have historical existence. One might argue that evangelicals believe in a profane fall, a fall at a point in time, while Barth believed in a sacred fall where time is irrelevant. For Barth the fall is a paradigm for all humans in all time and not an event at a point in time. This use of "history" raises questions concerning the incarnation and resurrection as sacred or profane, with many Christians accepting Christianity as profane; i.e., it is a historical faith involving specific points in time.

Other objections are made to his doctrines of predestination, grace, atonement, and so on. Yet whether or not Barth's theology ought to have conformed to that of evangelicals is a meaningless debate. He exposed the bankruptcy of nineteenth century Protestant thought and thus served as a corrective; his stress on Christology called Protestantism back to a central tenet of its faith; and the broad richness of his thought coupled with a fiery compassion for the truth of the gospel has set a standard for theologians yet to be matched in the latter half of the century.

R.V. SCHNUCKER

See also NEO-ORTHODOXY; BRUNNER, HEINRICH EMIL.

Bibliography. Barth, *The Epistle to the Romans, Dogmatics in Outline, Evangelical Theology*, and *Letters: 1961–1968;* J. Hamer, *Karl Barth;* H. Hartwell, *Theology of Karl Barth, an Introduction;* H. Küng, *Justification: The Doctrine of Karl Barth and a Catholic Reflection;* T. H. L. Parker, *Karl Barth;* T. F. Torrance, *Karl Barth: An Introduction to His Early Theology;* C. Van Til, *Christianity and Barthianism;* G. G. Bolich, *Karl Barth and Evangelicalism;* H. U. von Balthasar, *The Theology of Karl Barth;* C. Brown, *Karl Barth and the Christian Message;* J. Brown, *Subject and Object in Modern Theology*.

Basel, First Confession of (1534). This twelve-article statement of the Protestant faith was composed by Oswald Myconius in 1532 and approved and published by the city council of Basel, Switzerland, in 1534 as the official creed of the city. The nearby German city of Mühlhausen approved it in 1536; hence it is also known as the Confession of Mühlhausen.

The First Confession of Basel is to be distinguished from the First Helvetic Confession of 1536, also known as the Second Confession of Basel, which contained twenty-seven articles and was endorsed by seven Swiss cities. It is also to be distinguished from the Second Helvetic Confession of 1566, composed by Heinrich Bullinger, with thirty extensive chapters and widely endorsed throughout the Reformed world.

Johannes Oecolampadius came to Basel in 1522 and saw the Reformation officially embraced there in 1529. A month before his death in 1531 he addressed the Synod of Basel and included a brief personal confession of faith and paraphrase of the Apostles' Creed. It is generally believed that his successor, Oswald Myconius, used that draft in composing the First Confession of Basel.

The confession is a simple, warm expression of the Protestant faith expressed in contrast to both Roman Catholicism and Anabaptism. The twelve articles deal with God, man, providence, Christ, the church, the Lord's Supper, church discipline, the state, faith and works, the final judgment, God's commands, and infant baptism. Although it lacks a separate article on Scripture, the confession ends this way: "Finally, we desire to submit this our confession to the judgment of the divine Biblical Scriptures. And should we be informed from the same Holy Scriptures of a better one, we have thereby expressed our readiness to be willing at any time to obey God and His holy Word with great thanksgiving."

From 1534 until 1826 the confession was read annually from Basel pulpits during Easter week. It continued in force as Basel's official creed until 1872, when it was set aside under the influence of the liberalized thinking that began with the Enlightenment. F. H. KLOOSTER

See also CONFESSIONS OF FAITH.

Bibliography. P. Schaff, *Creeds of Christendom,* I, 385–88; A. C. Cochrane, *Reformed Confessions of the 16th Century;* F. Buri, *Basler Bekenntnis heute.*

Basil the Great (*ca.* 330–379). Bishop of Caesarea. He was born into a wealthy Christian family in Pontus. After receiving a good education both at home and in Athens, he returned to Caesarea in 356 as a teacher of rhetoric. A year later he was baptized and, following a visit to monastic communities in the eastern Mediterranean, retired to a hermitage on his family estate, where he began his career as a literary defender of the faith. In 364 he left his hermitage at the request of Eusebius, Bishop of Caesarea, who ordained him presbyter in that year and whom he succeeded in office in 370. He continued in that office until death, establishing an impressive record as an eloquent defender of Nicaean Christianity.

Basil is known for lasting contributions in three fields. (1) He introduced the idea of a communal monasticism based on love, holiness, and obedience, which replaced individual asceticism. The Rule of St. Basil remains today the basic structure of Eastern monasticism. (2) He established the principle of social concern for both monastic communities and for bishops. While defending the judicial independence of the local bishop from the Bishop of Rome (whose lead he accepted in doctrine), he established administrative control over the monasteries and other works of the church. Using this control and setting the example by giving away his own wealth, he organized and administered great works of charity—hospitals, schools, and hostels. (3) He defended orthodox doctrine, particularly the doctrine of the Trinity. In *De Spiritu Sancto* he defended the deity of the Holy Spirit against the Pneumatomachai. His *Adversus Eunomium* attacked the Arian heresy, which was at that time being pushed on the church by the Emperor Valens. In this defense of the faith he gave exact meanings to the terms for the Trinity, fixing the formula one substance (*ousia*) and three persons (*hypostaseis*) and thus preparing the way for the Council of Constantinople (381). In all of this work he, along with his friend Gregory of Nazianzus and his brother Gregory of Nyssa, mediated between East and West. His books, homilies (especially on the Psalms), commentary on Isa. 1–6, and letters have been of lasting value to the church, revealing the heart of not just a learned man, but also a loving Christian. P. H. DAVIDS

See also CAPPADOCIAN FATHERS.

Bibliography. H. Chadwick, *The Early Church;* W. C. Clark, *The Ascetic Works of St. Basil;* R. S. Deferrari, tr., *St. Basil: The Letters;* J. N. D. Kelly, *Early Christian Doctrines;* H. von Campenhausen, *The Fathers of the Greek Church;* J. W. C. Wand, *Doctrines and Councils.*

Baur, Ferdinand Christian (1792–1860). German Protestant theologian, founder of the Tübingen School of NT criticism. From 1826 until his death he was professor of theology at the University of Tübingen, where he put forward radical views concerning the origin of Christianity and the NT writings. Being convinced that the traditional Christian interpretation of Christian origins (viz., a revelation from God, the incarnation, the bodily resurrection of Christ, etc.) could not be right, he sought to provide a "strictly historical" (nonsupernatural) interpretation of early Christianity. He found in the contemporary philosophy of history espoused by Hegel a ready instrument for his reshaping of historical theology (P. C. Hodgson's attempt to deny Hegel's influence on Baur cannot be sustained; cf. works by Geiger and Harris).

Although no one in nineteenth century Germany exerted a greater influence on the development of the historical-critical method, Baur was more of a philosophical theologian than a biblical scholar or historian. Yet he published five books and a number of significant essays in the area of NT research. *Paul the Apostle of Jesus Christ* (2 vols., 1845) offers his most extensive exposition of his views. His basic thesis concerning the nature of early Christianity and its resulting documents was first put forward in 1831 in an essay on the so-called Christ-party of Paul's Corinthian correspondence. His thesis—which remained essentially unchanged throughout his life—was that, in spite of the impression of uniformity of doctrine and practice in the early church gained from a superficial reading of the NT, early Christianity was marked by a severe conflict between two groups who represent very different theologies: a Jewish (Petrine) party and a Gentile (Pauline) party. Thus it becomes necessary to approach each NT document in terms of its *Tendenz,* its special theological point of view within the context of the history of primitive Christianity. Baur thought that the NT could be divided into three groups: Palestinian/Jewish (e.g., Matthew, which he considered to be the first Gospel to have been written), hellenistic/Pauline (Romans, I and II Corinthians, and Galatians, the only genuine Pauline letters), and Catholic/conciliatory (Acts and most of the rest of the NT). Baur dated Acts in the midsecond century A.D.; it goes without saying that it is wholly untrustworthy as a source of the history of A.D. 30–60.

Although no one today would hold the detailed critical opinions of Baur, some of his assumptions come down to us in the writings of contemporary NT critics—viz., a cleavage between the Palestinian apostles and Paul, the unreliable nature of Luke-Acts, and the inadequacy of traditional orthodoxy. His most famous students were D. F. Strauss, A. Ritschl, and E. Zeller. The first two broke with their mentor in later years; Zeller became his son-in-law.

W. W. GASQUE

See also TÜBINGEN SCHOOL.

Bibliography. W. W. Gasque, *A History of the Criticism of the Acts of the Apostles;* W. Geiger, *Speculation und Kritik: Die Geschichtstheologie F. C. Baurs;* H. Harris, *The Tübingen School;* P. C. Hodgson, *The Formation of Historical Theology: A Study of F. C. Baur.*

Bavinck, Herman (1854–1921). Alongside Abraham Kuyper, a leading theologian of the neo-Calvinist revival initiated a century ago in the Dutch Reformed Church and still represented in North America by the Christian Reformed Church. Trained at the University of Leiden and the Theological Seminary at Kampen, Bavinck served a church at Franeker (1881–82) before becoming professor of systematic theology first at Kampen (1882–1902) and then at the Free University of Amsterdam (1902–20). His major work was *Gereformeerde Dogmatiek* (*Reformed Dogmatics*) in four volumes, first published between 1895 and 1901, of which only the second volume has been translated into English as *The Doctrine of God.*

In piety and life style Bavinck always remained close to his separatist origins, but in his scholarly work he showed a remarkable openness and sensitivity to nineteenth century developments. Thus he wrote many important essays on education, ethics (family, women, war, etc.), and even the new discipline of psychology. His first concern, however, was to apply the full scholarly resources of his own age to a renewal of the dogmatic tradition represented by seventeenth century Reformed scholastic theology. Bavinck considered theology to be the systematic study of the knowledge of God as Christ revealed that regarding himself and creation in his Word, a revelation made to the church as encapsulated in its creedal confessions and received in faith by the individual theologian. Bavinck's philosophical orientation, as revealed in his prolegomena, was more realist, in contrast to Kuyper's inclination to German idealism, and included a genuine appreciation for the contemporary neo-Thomist revival among Catholics. He sometimes spoke of certain "ideas" found in God and evident as well in creation, in man's image-likeness to God, and even in predestination. Yet he always insisted upon the primacy of Scripture. Toward the end of his life he encouraged younger colleagues to take up, from a conservative perspective, the difficult problems raised by newer biblical studies. Throughout his life he also insisted on the primacy of God's gift of grace in the justification of man, rejecting faith in particular or any other human act as preceding or invoking God's grace. Bavinck deeply influenced many Dutch and American Reformed theologians, though most of their works—e.g., Louis Berkhof's *Systematic Theology*—show much less of his broad grasp of the history of theology and his notable philosophical capacity.

J. VAN ENGEN

Bibliography. Bavinck, *The Doctrine of God, Our Reasonable Faith, The Philosophy of Revelation,* and *The Certainty of Faith.*

Baxter, Richard (1615–1691). Generally classified among the top rank of Puritan theologians, Baxter is known for his exemplary ministerial work as well as his approximately two hundred writings. Attaining his education largely through self-instruction, he was ordained in 1638 in the Church of England. His ministry at Kidderminster (1641–60) was marked by a dramatic transformation of the whole life of the community. He supported Parliament in its battle against the king, serving briefly as a military chaplain. He sided with the Nonconformist party and was eventually ejected from the Church of England along with two thousand other clergy in 1662. Throughout his ministry Baxter sought to increase cooperation and tolerance among the Episcopalians, Presbyterians, and Independents in church polity. Although forbidden to serve as pastor after 1662, he continued his ministry through writing and preaching.

Three of his writings have been reprinted frequently. *The Saint's Everlasting Rest* (1650) expounds "the blessed state of the Saints in their enjoyment of God in glory." It continues to be one of the classics of Christian devotional literature—although its one thousand pages are usually abridged. *The Reformed Pastor* (1656) describes the oversight pastors are to exercise over themselves first and then over their flock. It includes practical guidance for dealing with the pastor's perennial problems of instructing and guiding the church. *A Call to the Unconverted* (1657) shows Baxter's evangelistic concern. It consists of an earnest and reasoned appeal to the unconverted to turn to God and accept his mercy. Other important works of Baxter are his *Méthodus Theologiae Christianae* (1681), written in Latin, which sets forth his theology most systematically, and his autobiography, *Reliquiae Baxterianae* (1695). These and his other writings are filled with evangelical zeal for the lost, genuine piety, and a desire to bring reconciliation to the warring divisions of Christians in his day.

Baxter's theology was moderate. He attempted to avoid the acidity of polemical positions and to find truth in the theological center between the extremes. He always sought to isolate the element of truth in erroneous teachings. In theology no less than ecclesiology Baxter sought to be a peacemaker. Thus, his theology made him unpopular among many of his age. For example, Calvinists were offended by his acceptance of universal redemption, while Arminians were offended by his acceptance of personal election. Nevertheless, to his critics Baxter sought to vindicate his views by appeal to the Scriptures and to reason. O. G. Oliver, Jr.

Bibliography. W. Orme, ed., *Practical Works of Richard Baxter,* 23 vols.; W. M. Lamont, *Richard Baxter and the Millennium;* G. Nuttall, *Richard Baxter;* F. J. Powicke, *A Life of the Reverend Richard Baxter;* R. Schlatter, ed., *Richard Baxter and Puritan Politics;* J. Stalker, *Richard Baxter;* H. Martin, *Puritanism and Richard Baxter;* W. B. T. Douglas, "Politics and Theology in the Thought of Richard Baxter," *AUSS* 15:115–26, 16:305–12; R. S. Paul, "Ecclesiology in Richard Baxter's Autobiography," in *From Faith to Faith,* ed. D. Y. Hadidian.

Beatification. A legal process in the Roman Catholic Church whereby a departed "servant of God" is adjudged worthy of a public cult in a particular place. Such beatified persons, called "blessed," gain recognition only in particular churches, dioceses, or regions, and are distinguished iconographically by a simple circular diadem. In the ancient and medieval church such cults sprang up locally and often spontaneously. Since the seventeenth century the Roman See, specifically the Congregation of Rites, has claimed control of the process.

The ordinary process originates still with the local bishop, who appoints a postulator to handle the case in Rome. He must establish that all the person's writings are above suspicion, that his or her holiness was manifest in heroic virtue, and that at least two miracles have been done by his or her intercession. Once all this information has been gathered, verified, and printed, the pope may choose to "introduce the cause," which transfers jurisdiction to the Roman See where a similar investigation takes place. If on the recommendation of the Congregation of Rites a person is formally beatified at a public ceremony in the Vatican, the "blessed" then becomes an authorized model of Christian sanctity worthy of imitation in life and veneration in a public cult. This is the first and most significant step toward full canonization. Theologically, the person has been judged by the church to reign now in glory among the blessed and to intercede in behalf of the faithful who call on him or her. J. Van Engen

See also Canonization.

Bibliography. *NCE,* III, 55–61; *DTC,* II, 493–97; Benedict XIV, *Heroic Virtue.*

Beatific Vision. In Roman Catholic theology the beatific vision (*visio Dei*) refers to the direct, intuitive knowledge of the triune God which perfected souls will enjoy by means of their intellect; that is, the final fruition of the Christian life, in which they will see God as he is in himself. Many of the earliest church fathers—Ignatius, Theophilus, and especially Augustine—already interpreted in this way the numerous scriptural texts which speak of "seeing" and "knowing" God. Although Scripture teaches plainly that God dwells in inaccessible light and that man cannot "see" him in this life, several NT texts (Matt. 5:8; I Cor. 13:12; Heb. 12:14; I John 3:2, 6; Rev. 22:4) were understood to teach a qualitatively different knowledge and vision of God in eternity.

Medieval theologians, especially Thomas Aquinas and others heavily influenced by Aristotelian philosophy, defined the vision of God as a direct intuition or perception of his very being (*essentia*), as an eternal act of the intellect (though Augustinians such as Bonaventure and Duns Scotus continued to emphasize the role of love and the will), and as wholly supernatural in character, requiring special means (*medium*) known as the "light of glory" (*lumen gloriae*). They then disputed man's access to that vision in this life and Christ's retention of it throughout his earthly days; but they all insisted, contrary to Irenaeus and Pope John XXII, that man could enjoy that vision immediately upon death and not only after his resurrection. Protestant theologians rejected most of this as too narrow and too philosophical a conception of man's eternal blessedness, but without entirely abandoning the term and its associated theological problems. In recent years Roman Catholic and Protestant scholars alike have interpreted the biblical language of "seeing God face to face" much more broadly as living joyfully and everlastingly in the immediate presence of God. J. VAN ENGEN

Bibliography. K. E. Kirk, *The Vision of God;* G. C. Berkouwer, *The Return of Christ; DTC,* VII, 2351–94; *LTK,* I, 583–91; *NCE,* II, 186–93.

Beelzebub, Beelzebul. *See* BAAL-ZEBUB.

Begotten. *See* ONLY BEGOTTEN.

Being. Considered to be the most general property common to everything there is. In early Greek philosophy being was usually contrasted with becoming or change. Being was associated with perfection, and perfection could not change, since any change would be for the worse. Parmenides held that the world did not change and that the apparent change was only an illusion.

Aristotle held that being and unity could not be genera. Taking this hint, others have argued that "there is" and "there are" must be understood differently when applied to objects that belong to different categories. Moreover, Aristotle insisted that to say that something "is," is not to add anything to its description. From this discussion arose the medieval doctrine of the transcendentals. Aquinas identified "being," "one," "true," "thing," "something," and "good" as transcending the categories and as applicable to everything. These transcendentals are often included among the syncategorematic terms—terms which set forth the properties of being *qua* being, an idea originated by Aristotle, who thought it was the subject matter of metaphysics.

It is not unusual to distinguish different kinds of being. Existence is contrasted with subsistence and other notions. Alexius Meinong, for instance, held that material objects in time and space, as well as shadows and gravitational fields in time and space, *exist.* Universals, numbers, fictional or imaginary beings (e.g., unicorns) neither exist nor subsist, but possess *sosein,* which literally means "being so" or essence. Others insist that these latter items *subsist.* That is, they have being in some sense and are not simply reducible to mere words as the nominalists claim.

The discussion of fictional and nonexistent objects relates metaphysics to philosophical logic. Gotlieb Frege and Bertrand Russell sought a means for dealing with such objects in the language of first order predicate logic. They developed theories about logically proper names and definite descriptions. W. V. O. Quine examined the metaphysical commitment of formal logic and concluded that "to be is to be the value of a variable."

The discussion of being has had significance for the field of theology. The ontological argument raises the question as to whether existence is strictly speaking a predicate or property. Aristotle, quite apart from this argument, insisted that it was not. Descartes, on the other hand, argued that existence must be a perfection and used the argument for the existence of a most perfect being, God. It was the assumption that existence was a predicate that was severely criticized by David Hume and Immanuel Kant. To say that something exists is not to add to its description. Modern logicians have followed Aristotle, Hume, and Kant. To express existence or existential import one uses the existential quantifier.

As natural theology developed in the late Middle Ages, the nature of being became a central issue. God was pure actuality, and as such was immutable. He was a necessary being. That is, God is not in need of anything outside of his own being for his existence. On the other hand, all other beings are contingent beings. This means that they depend on something or someone outside themselves for their existence. This distinction becomes fundamental to the cosmological argument. This argument was developed in two directions. As a causal argument, it has been argued that a contingent being needs a first, necessary cause or an infinite regress results. As a contingency argument, it is maintained that a contingent being remains unexplained without reference to a necessary being who needs no explanation.

The objections to the cosmological argument are that an infinite regress is not intellectually unacceptable, that the idea of a necessary being is either inconsistent or incoherent, and that other contingent beings or causes do explain contingent beings.

In modern theology the concept of being has taken a quite different course. Paul Tillich insisted that God tends to become a being among beings. Eventually God is reduced to a way of speaking about human existence and ideals, making him unbelievable and dispensable. This is the essence of atheism for Tillich. God is "being itself" or "the ground of being." As such, Tillich's God is "the God beyond the God of theism." This view of God has been criticized as perilously close to pantheism and so obscure as to disappear in the depths of philosophical speculation.

In process theology there is an attempt to

synthesize the old antithesis between being and becoming. God is thought to be di- or bipolar. The static pole gives the subjective aim and potentiality to objects in reality. The dynamic pole is in constant becoming. Through it, God prehends the process, taking into himself value left by the perishing of objects. P. D. FEINBERG

Bibliography. É. Gilson, *Being and Some Philosophers* and *The Philosophy of St. Thomas Aquinas;* P. T. Geach, "Form and Existence," in *Aquinas,* ed. A. Kenny; J. Owens, *The Doctrine of Being in the Aristotelian Metaphysics.*

Belgic Confession (1561). Sometimes known as the Walloon Confession, this was composed in 1561 by Guido de Bres as an apology for the persecuted band of Reformed Christians in the Lowlands who formed the so-called churches under the cross. Translated from French into Dutch in 1562, it gained synodical approval at Antwerp in 1566, at Wesel in 1568, at Emden in 1571, and definitively at Dordrecht in 1618. Together with the Heidelberg Catechism and the Canons of Dort, it provided the confessional foundation for all Dutch Reformed churches, and remains binding still today for members of the Christian Reformed Church in North America. De Bres, a courageous pastor to French-speaking communities in the Lowlands who was martyred at Valenciennes in 1567, modeled his work on the so-called Gallic Confession adopted for all French Reformed churches at Paris in 1559. Like Calvin's *Institutes,* the text breaks down roughly into three parts: the triune God and the knowledge of him from Scripture (Arts. 1-9), Christ's work of creation and redemption (10-23), and the Spirit's work of sanctification in and through the Christian church (24-37)—this last part subdivided again in Calvin. De Bres quoted Scripture liberally and often used the pronoun "we" to personalize this confession of faith. To distinguish his community from the feared and "detested" Anabaptists (with whom Catholics had often confused them), de Bres asserted the full humanity of Jesus Christ (18), the public rather than sectarian nature of the true church (28-29), infant baptism (34), and the God-given character of civil government (36). As for the Catholics, who had brought the Inquisition down upon them, de Bres sought to find as many common beliefs as possible, especially the Trinity (1, 8, 9), the incarnation (10, 18, 19), and a catholic Christian church (27-29). But he also upheld distinctively Protestant emphases such as the unique authority of Scripture apart from the Apocrypha (3-7), the all-sufficiency of Christ's atoning sacrifice and intercession (21-23, 26), and the nature of good works (24) and of the two sacraments, Holy Baptism and the Holy Supper (34-35). Distinctively Reformed elements may be found in the articles on election (16), sanctification (24), the government of the church (30-32), and the Lord's Supper (35). There is no evidence that the Catholic authorities ever seriously read or were impressed by this little work, but Reformed Christians in the Lowlands quickly adopted it as their own confession of faith.
J. VAN ENGEN

See also CONFESSIONS OF FAITH.

Bibliography. J. N. Bakhuizen van den Brink, *De Nederlandse Belijdenisgeschriften;* A. C. Cochrane, *Reformed Confessions of the 16th Century.*

Belief, Believe. *See* FAITH.

Believer. *See* CHRISTIANS, NAMES OF.

Bellarmine, Robert (1542-1621). A Doctor of the Church, Bellarmine joined the Jesuit Order in Rome in 1560, taught theology at Louvain (1569-76) and Rome (1576-88), then perhaps the two leading intellectual centers of the Counter-Reformation, and concluded his life as a cardinal in the service of the Roman curia, deeply involved in numerous important political and ecclesiastical missions. Firmly grounded in Aristotelian philosophy and scholastic theology, Bellarmine helped to establish Thomas Aquinas's *Summa Theologica* as the basic textbook for Jesuit and eventually all Catholic theological education. But he was also a well-trained humanist who demonstrated that rhetorical and historical skills could also be applied to the service of the Roman Church—for instance, in his *De Scriptoribus ecclesiasticis,* a literary history of church authors since the early church. His theological lectures in Rome, published as *Disputations Concerning Controversies of the Christian Faith Against the Heretics of Our Time* (1586-93), proved the most forceful theological response to Protestantism to issue from the Counter-Reformation, and was widely used in teaching Catholic apologetics down to the early twentieth century. Theologically Bellarmine insisted upon the visible, hierarchical church culminating in the Roman papacy as the only true church, thus excluding Protestants and Orthodox alike; and he ascribed to the papacy an "indirect power" in temporal affairs. His theology of grace defended man's free will and "natural inclination to the beatific vision" in a form which went somewhat beyond Aquinas to approach the positions of Molina and other Jesuits. J. VAN ENGEN

See also COUNTER-REFORMATION.

Bibliography. *DTC,* II, 560-99; *Theologische Realenzyklopädie,* V, 525-31; J. Brodrick, *Robert Bellarmine, Saint and Scholar.*

Benediction. An act or pronouncement of blessing. The Aaronic benediction was given to Aaron and his sons as a part of their ministry in God's behalf toward the people, and is epitomized as a putting of God's name upon them (Num. 6:22–27). The NT parallel is the apostolic benediction (II Cor. 13:14), which reflects the progress of revelation by its emphasis on the Trinity. Other passages, notably Eph. 3:20–21; Heb. 13:20–21; and Jude 24–25, are often treated as benedictions by members of the clergy. The question is whether these are true benedictions or whether they are prayers. In the benediction the minister acts on behalf of God in pronouncing a blessing upon the congregation, whereas in a prayer he is the representative of the people, voicing a supplication to God on their behalf. It appears that in the strict application of the term there is only one benediction in the OT and one in the NT. The benediction is to be distinguished even more sharply from the salutation, which is a common feature of the opening portion of the NT epistles (e.g., Gal. 1:3). Such salutations are the counterpart of the greetings found in the everyday letters of the hellenistic period, but they inject a spiritual flavor into the greeting which lifts it above the commonplace. It hardly need be said that the practice of inventing benedictions which are not framed in the language of Scripture is of doubtful propriety.

In Roman Catholic theory the virtue of the benediction, which is regarded as quasi-automatic in its efficacy, increases with the rank of the one who pronounces it. "The higher the hierarchical position of him who bestows the blessing, the more powerful it is" (Achelis). It is common practice to "bless" objects also, giving them either a temporary or a permanent character of holiness. In modern times Romanism has introduced the Benediction of the Blessed Sacrament. The priest, having taken the host and placed it in the monstrance, then incenses the Blessed Sacrament. After appropriate singing and prayer, the priest makes the sign of the cross with the monstrance (still containing the host) over the people. This benediction is given in silence. E. F. Harrison

See also Bless, Blessed, Blessing.

Bibliography. E. C. Achelis, *SHERK*, II, 49–50; W. H. Dolbeer, *The Benediction.*

Berdyaev, Nikolai Aleksandrovich (1874–1948). Russian personalist philosopher-theologian. Born in Kiev, he was exiled by the czarist government as a Marxist in 1898. After the Bolshevik Revolution he was professor of philosophy at Moscow University until deported to Europe by the Soviets in 1922 because of the Christian premises of his socialism. Berdyaev lived as an unwilling exile until his death in France, where he propagated his thought as director of the Religious-Philosophical Academy and editor of the journal *The Way* and the YMCA Press. A freethinker in early years, Berdyaev embraced the Russian Orthodox Church on the eve of World War I, and though often openly critical of it he conscientiously remained a member and as such participated in conferences of the ecumenical movement. Nevertheless, by his own admission his thought was atypical within Orthodoxy, though he acknowledged his affinity to Origen and Gregory of Nyssa.

In over twenty books and dozens of articles Berdyaev presented no orderly system; disjointed ideas fill his works, and frequent aphorisms obscure more than clarify his conceptions. But this is in line with his confession that his vocation was "to proclaim not a doctrine but a view." He freely admitted that his theology was man-centered, because of his conviction that humanity had been deified by the incarnation.

Berdyaev's theology is rather conventionally Trinitarian, incarnational, and redemptive: the Second Person of the eternal Trinity became man to free humanity from evil and transform all creation into God's kingdom. His distinctiveness lies in his radical stress on freedom and creativity. He spoke of freedom as uncreated, independent of God, and eternal. It is the nothingness (*Ungrund*) out of which God produced his good creation; it also is the occasion for evil and thus pain and suffering. Creativity constitutes the likeness between God and man, created in the divine image and set free by the incarnation to achieve his destiny. Christ, the God-man, destroyed the radical disjunction between man and God and joined the two in the task of transforming "this evil and stricken world."

From this perspective derived Berdyaev's eschatological motif pointing to the achievement of perfect justice for human existence. But unlike Marxism, to which he otherwise remained sympathetic, Berdyaev declared the futility of this hope within history, since any society created by purely human effort would inevitably destroy freedom and creativity. The goal of history lies beyond history, in man's divine-human destiny, his obligation to God to express his creativity freely. Every creative act strikes a blow against the evil that enslaves man and it unites the actor with God. The proper relation of man to God, then, is not the objective act of worship but the subjective union of the two in the act of creation.

Berdyaev himself typified the spiritual turn

of many Russian intellectuals away from naturalism after 1900, generally called the Russian religious renaissance; appropriately, his writings now provide a principal impetus to the ongoing Soviet religious renaissance, a revival of interest in spirituality, especially Orthodoxy, within a segment of the young intelligentsia of the U.S.S.R.

P. D. STEEVES

See also ORTHODOX TRADITION, THE.

Bibliography. Berdyaev, *Dream and Reality: An Essay in Autobiography* and *Truth and Revelation;* O. F. Clarke, *Introduction to Berdyaev;* M. Vallon, *An Apostle of Freedom;* N. Zernov, *The Russian Religious Renaissance of the Twentieth Century.*

Berkeley, George (1685–1753). Irish-born philosopher who presented classic arguments in favor of idealist metaphysics. He produced most of his philosophical work early in life: *An Essay Towards a New Theory of Vision* in 1709 and *A Treatise Concerning the Principles of Human Knowledge* in 1710. Later he turned to other things—attempts to establish a college in Bermuda and service as an Anglican bishop in Cloyne, Ireland, beginning in 1734.

As an immaterialist Berkeley believed that material substance does not exist. Two kinds of things exist: spirits that perceive ideas and the ideas they perceive. Ideas do not represent something else; the idea of a body or a desk is not related to any material body or desk. According to Berkeley, this immaterialism protects us from skepticism: we have no reason to doubt whether our ideas correctly resemble material objects in the world because there are no material objects. All we know are the ideas present to our minds, and of these we are directly and indubitably aware. Berkeley found no distinction between appearance and reality; appearance is the only reality we have.

Berkeley's basic doctrine is that for something to exist, it must be perceived. If something is an odor it must be smelled; if it is a color it must be seen, etc. Moreover, sense information is the only basis for knowledge. We have no way of claiming that there is some material object that we sense because we cannot get beyond our senses to find out.

Do things cease to exist when no human is perceiving them? Berkeley said no, because God continues to perceive them. God also coordinates our ordinary perceptions to give them a lawlike regularity. This regularity simplifies the world for God, who does not have to maintain both a material world and our ability to perceive the world. He merely maintains our perceptions.

Berkeley's idealism need not be considered unorthodox. He believed that Jesus was fully God and fully man. Jesus was just as much in the flesh as you and I are, though flesh is seen as an "idea." Neither the incarnation nor the world at large is an illusion. On the contrary, God himself maintains all such true perceptions in an orderly fashion.

P. H. DEVRIES

Bibliography. J. Wild, *George Berkeley, a Study of His Life and Philosophy.*

Berkhof, Louis (1873–1957). Theologian of the Christian Reformed Church. He was born in Emmen, the Netherlands, and came to Grand Rapids, Michigan, in 1882. After earning diplomas at Calvin College (1897) and Calvin Theological Seminary (1900), he was ordained in the Christian Reformed Church. A two-year pastorate at Allendale, Michigan, was followed by two years of study at Princeton Theological Seminary (B.D., 1904). He then returned to Grand Rapids to serve the Oakdale Park Christian Reformed Church for two years.

In 1906 Berkhof began a thirty-eight-year teaching career at Calvin Theological Seminary, serving also as the first president of the seminary from 1931 until his retirement in 1944. The first twenty years were devoted to the biblical area, at first both OT and NT subjects but after 1914 NT studies only. In 1926 Berkhof became professor of dogmatics or systematic theology and continued in that field for the next eighteen years. He is best known as a systematic theologian.

English became the language of instruction at Calvin Seminary in 1924, and Berkhof's publications were aimed at the needs of his students. In 1932 his class lectures were published in two volumes as *Reformed Dogmatics.* A revised and expanded edition appeared in 1938, a single volume of 784 pages entitled *Systematic Theology.* This is the volume for which he is best known. In addition to this standard work covering the six main branches (loci) of systematic theology, Berkhof added an *Introductory Volume to Systematic Theology* (1932) on prolegomena issues, which was also subsequently revised and enlarged. He also added a volume on the *History of Christian Doctrines* (1937), which traced the development of Christian doctrine from the apostolic fathers to the liberalism of Schleiermacher and Ritschl.

In his work on systematic theology Berkhof followed in the line of John Calvin and embraced the development of Reformed theology by the Dutch theologians Abraham Kuyper and Herman Bavinck. The specific influence of the latter's four-volume *Gereformeerde Dogmatiek* is most evident. Berkhof was not an original or a speculative theologian; he followed well-tried paths. His major significance lay in setting forth the riches of the Reformed heritage in contrast to the major theologies of history. His writing was solid and well organized for classroom use as well as for private study. His *Systematic Theology* has been widely used in theological seminaries and Bible institutes throughout the United States and Canada, as well as in conservative circles throughout the world. A Spanish translation appeared in 1969.

In 1921 Berkhof delivered the Stone Lectures at Princeton Theological Seminary; they were published under the title *The Kingdom of God* (1951). He took an active part in the life of the church and published extensively in the denominational papers. The following monographs deserve special mention: *The Assurance of Faith* (1928), *Vicarious Atonement Through Christ* (1936), *Principles of Biblical Interpretation* (1950), *Aspects of Liberalism* (1951), *The Second Coming of Christ* (1953), and *Riches of Divine Grace* (1948), the latter a collection of ten sermons.

F. H. KLOOSTER

See also REFORMED TRADITION, THE; KUYPER, ABRAHAM; BAVINCK, HERMAN.

Bibliography. P. De Klerk, ed., *A Bibliography of the Writings of the Professors of Calvin Theological Seminary.*

Bernard of Clairvaux (1090–1153). The best known and most widely acclaimed man of his age, canonized in 1174 and made Doctor of the Church in 1830. Preeminently a monk, Bernard founded the monastery at Clairvaux but was active all his life along a broad spectrum of endeavor. He helped to heal the papal schism of 1130; was the "hammer of heretics" including Henry of Lausanne, Arnold of Brescia, and Peter Abelard; wrote voluminous mystical, theological, and devotional works; and carried on an extensive personal correspondence with emperors, popes, wayward monks, and theologians.

His theology was deeply appreciated by both Luther and Calvin, the latter quoting only Augustine more frequently. As a man of action, contemplation, mystical experience, doctrinal orthodoxy, and administrative skill, Bernard was the theological personification of the "medieval synthesis" for Dante. In *Paradise* he is the symbol of that contemplation through which man is given the vision of God; it is he who replaces Beatrice as guide in the final steps of salvation. Bernard's mysticism is largely devoid of any Gnostic and Manichaean quality of later fourteenth and fifteenth century mystics.

Bernard was the official preacher of the Second Crusade, and its outcome was bitterly disappointing to him. His devotion to the Virgin Mary gave great impetus to that movement, which previously had been relatively insignificant in the West. His theology is marked more by ardent piety and synthesis of the best of his age than by brilliance or originality. He was at times both impetuous and obstinate, but his selfless and passionate commitment to his vocation seems to give his work and life an uncommon authority.

Among hymns attributed to him are "Jesus, the Very Thought of Thee," "O Sacred Head Sore Wounded," and "Jesus Thou Joy of Loving Hearts."

C. F. ALLISON

See also MYSTICISM; SPIRITUALITY.

Bibliography. W. W. Williams, *Studies in St. Bernard of Clairvaux;* B. S. James, *St. Bernard of Clairvaux.*

Beza, Theodore (1519–1605). The undisputed leader in Geneva as John Calvin's successor. While his spiritual hegemony was unmarked by significant departures from Calvin's direction, Beza did differ in particular ecclesiastical emphases.

Born in Vézelay, Burgundy, into a well-to-do family, Beza early displayed academic ability and was sent to study under Melchior Wolmar, a crypto-Lutheran professor in Orléans. He became recognized as a major Latin poet after publication of a collection of humanistic poems, *Juvenalia.* His conversion followed a critical illness, after which he became identified with the Reformation movement.

Beza served as professor of Greek at the Academy of Lausanne from 1549 to 1558, when he was called to the post of both rector and professor at the newly formed Academy of Geneva. Being also an ecumenist he served tirelessly to bring about a united Protestantism.

Beza's chief contributions to the Swiss Reformation were securing Calvin's gains in Geneva and solidifying the Presbyterian system. He freely borrowed from both Calvin and Martin Bucer. In his pivotal doctrine of the church Beza, following Bucer, distinguished three marks of the true church: the word of God, the twofold sacraments, and discipline. He viewed the church as the company of the elect. However, election was not the central focus of Beza's ecclesiology. Rather, following Calvin, he treated election under the rubric of the person and work of Christ. Yet Beza created tension in this doctrine by treating it elsewhere in a scholastic manner along rather rigid supralapsarian lines.

Beza posited presbyterian church government as the only acceptable NT polity. He adopted Calvin's view that this order comprises pastors, doctors, elders, and deacons, but he applied this system in the various synodical and local levels more rigidly than did Calvin. Beza's doctrine of the church may be found in his three-volume collection *Tractationes Theologicae*, especially in his *Ad Tractationem de Ministrorum Evangelii... Responsio*, where he takes Anglican prelacy to task.

Other key scholarly works are his 1582 edition of the Greek NT and his three-volume *Histoire ecclésiastique des églises réformées... de France*. Concern for the welfare of the church prompted volumes of sermons, commentary, a French translation of many psalms for the Huguenot Psalter, a joint translation with Calvin of the French NT, and an influential confession of faith.

J. H. Hall

Bibliography. H. M. Baird, *Theodore Beza: The Counsellor of the French Reformation, 1519–1605;* J. S. Bray, *Theodore Beza's Doctrine of Predestination;* T. Maruyama, *The Reform of the True Church: The Ecclesiology of Theodore Beza;* J. Raitt, *The Eucharistic Theology of Theodore Beza.*

Bible. The English word "Bible" is derived from the Greek *biblion*, "roll" or "book." (While *biblion* is really a diminutive of *biblos*, it has lost this sense in the NT. See Rev. 10:2 where *biblaridion* is used for a "little scroll.") More exactly, a *biblion* was a roll of papyrus or byblus, a reed-like plant whose inner bark was dried and fashioned into a writing material widely used in the ancient world.

The word as we use it today, however, has a far more significant connotation than the Greek *biblion*. While *biblion* was somewhat neutral—it could be used to designate books of magic (Acts 19:19) or a bill of divorcement (Mark 10:4) as well as sacred books—the word "Bible" refers to the Book *par excellence*, the recognized record of divine revelation.

Although this meaning is ecclesiastical in origin, its roots go back into the OT. In Dan. 9:2 (LXX) *ta biblia* refers to the prophetic writings. In the Prologue to Sirach it refers generally to the OT Scriptures. This usage passed into the Christian church (II Clem. 14:2) and about the turn of the fifth century was extended to include the entire body of canonical writings as we now have them. The expression *ta biblia* passed into the vocabulary of the Western church and in the thirteenth century, by what Westcott calls a "happy solecism," the neuter plural came to be regarded as a feminine singular, and in this form the term passed into the languages of modern Europe. This significant change from plural to singular reflected the growing conception of the Bible as one utterance of God rather than a multitude of voices speaking for him.

The process by which the various books in the Bible were brought together and their value as sacred Scripture recognized is referred to as the history of the canon. Contrary to prevailing critical opinion, there existed, prior to the Exile, a large body of sacred literature. Moses wrote "all the words of the Lord" in the "book of the covenant" (Exod. 21–23; 24:4, 7). Joshua's farewell address was written "in the book of the law of God" (Josh. 24:26). Samuel spoke concerning the manner of the kingdom and "wrote it in a book" (I Sam. 10:25). "Thus saith the Lord" was the common preface to the utterances of the prophets.

This revelatory literature, although not reaching a fixed form until late in the second century B.C., was nevertheless regarded from the very first as the revealed will of God and therefore binding upon the people. The "oracles of God" were held in highest esteem, and this attitude toward the Scriptures was quite naturally carried over into the early church. Few will deny that Jesus regarded the OT as an inspired record of God's self-revelation in history. He repeatedly appealed to the Scriptures as authoritative (Matt. 19:4; 22:29). The early church maintained this same attitude toward the OT, but alongside of it they began to place the words of the Lord. While the OT canon had been formally closed, the coming of Christ had, in a sense, opened it again. God was once again speaking. Since the cross was the central redemptive act of God in history, the NT became a logical necessity. Thus the voice of the apostles, and later their writings, were accepted as the divine commentary on the Christ event.

Viewed as a historical process, the formation of the NT canon occupied some 350 years. In the first century the various books were written and began to be circulated through the churches. The rise of heresy in the second century—especially in the form of Gnosticism with its outstanding spokesman, Marcion—was a powerful impulse toward the formation of a definite canon. A sifting process began in which valid Scripture distinguished itself from Christian literature in general on the basis of such criteria as apostolic authorship, reception by the churches, and consistency of doctrine with what the church already possessed. The canon was ultimately certified at the Council of Carthage (397).

The claim of the Bible to divine origin is amply justified by its historical influence. Its manuscripts are numbered in the thousands. The NT had barely been put together before we find translations in Latin, Syriac, and Egyptian. Today there is not a language in the civilized world that does not have the word of God. No other book has been so carefully studied or had so much written on it. Its spiritual influence cannot be estimated. It is preeminently *the Book*—God's word in man's language.

R. H. Mounce

See also Bible, Authority of; Bible, Canon of; Bible, Inerrancy and Infallibility of; Bible, Inspiration of; Word, Word of God, Word of the Lord.

Bibliography. F. F. Bruce, *The Books and the Parchments;* B. F. Westcott, *The Bible in the Church;* P. R. Ackroyd *et al.*, eds., *The Cambridge History of the Bible,* 3 vols.; D. E. Nineham, ed., *The Church's Use of the Bible;* A. Harnack, *Bible Reading in the Early Church;* N. O. Hatch and M. A. Noll, *The Bible in America;* B. Smalley, *The Study of the Bible in the Middle Ages;* A. Richardson, *The Bible in the Age of Science;* J. Barr, *The Bible in the Modern World.*

Bible, Authority in. Authority is the concept of rightful power. It is used in the Bible with a good deal of elasticity. Although the English term itself is not used of God in the OT as it is in the NT (usually for *exousia*), the assumption permeating both testaments is that God alone is the ultimate authority and he alone the ultimate source of authority for others.

God's Authority. His sovereign, universal, and eternal rule over the entire universe gives evidence of his authority (e.g., Exod. 15:18; Job 26:12; Pss. 29:10; 47; 93:1–2; 95:3–5; 103:19; 146:10; 147:5; Isa. 40:12ff.; 50:2). He has fixed by his authority times or epochs (Acts 1:7) and "does according to his will in the host of heaven and among the inhabitants of the earth" (Dan. 4:34–35). This authority over man is compared to that of a potter over his clay (Rom. 9:20–23). So ultimate is God's authority that all authority among humans comes from God alone (Rom. 13:1). God's authority includes not only the authority of providence and history, but also the demand for submission and accountability from man, expressed, e.g., in the garden of Eden, the Ten Commandments, the gospel and its evangelical demands. Inherent in God's authority is the awesome power to cast the one who does not fear him into hell (Luke 12:5) and the glorious power to forgive sins and declare righteous those in Christ (Rom. 3:21–26). In the day of God's wrath and mercy, God's rightful authority as Creator (Rev. 4:11) and Redeemer in Christ (Rev. 5:12–13) will be acknowledged in an undisputed way.

Jesus Christ's Authority. As the God-man, the incarnate Son of God, Jesus Christ manifests his authority in a dual capacity. On the one hand, his authority is that of one who is the Son of God and is intrinsic to him and not derived. On the other hand, as the incarnate Son, who is the Son of man, he acts in submission and obedience to the Father. So he can say in one and the same breath concerning his plans to lay down his life: "No one has taken it away from me, but I lay it down on my own initiative. I have authority to lay it down, and I have authority to take it up again," and "this commandment I received from my Father" (John 10:18). But because his life as the promised Son of man is one of acting representatively for God on behalf of men as one who is also a man (cf. Dan. 7:13–14), Jesus speaks almost always of his authority in terms of acting for God the Father. In doing so he exercises all the prerogatives of God—e.g., forgives sins (Mark 2:5–8), heals (Mark 1:34), exorcises demons (Mark 1:27), controls the power of nature (Luke 8:24–25), raises the dead (Luke 7:11–17; John 11:38–44), teaches with authority (Matt. 7:28–29; cf. his "I say," Matt. 5:21–48), and demands that men submit to his authority both on earth (Luke 14:25–35) and at the judgment (Matt. 7:22–23). As the obedient Son he acknowledges and follows the word of his Father, the Scriptures, and appeals to them as the final authority (Matt. 4:1–10; 22:23–46; John 10:33–36).

By Christ's victory over sin and death in his death and resurrection, the usurped authority of the evil one and his angels is broken (Heb. 2:14–15; I John 3:8; Col. 2:15). Thus all authority in heaven and on earth is given to Jesus to exercise in his messianic role (Matt. 28:18–20) until he has completed his task of finally subduing all God's enemies and delivering up the kingdom to God the Father (I Cor. 15:24–28). In the interim Christ exercises leadership and authority in a providential way over all things for the good of his church (Eph. 1:20–23). With a redeeming authority and power that enables as well as commands, he authoritatively demands both evangelization of all the nations and obedience to all his commandments (Matt. 28:19–20; Acts 1:8; Rom. 6:1ff.; 8:1ff.; Phil. 2:12–13).

The Apostles' Authority. The authority of God is exercised in the OT not only by various direct means but also through those to whom he gave authority to act in his behalf—priests, prophets, judges, and kings. In the NT the authority of the Father and especially of Jesus Christ is expressed in a unique way through the apostles, who are by definition the direct and personal ambassadors of Jesus Christ (Matt. 10:1, 40; Mark 3:14; John 17:18; 20:21; Acts 1:1–8; II Cor. 5:20; Gal. 1:1; 2:8), speaking and acting with his authority (Gal. 1:11ff.; 2:7–9). They claim to speak for Christ and under the Spirit's direction in terms of both content and form of expression (I Cor. 2:10–13; I Thess. 2:13), to give the permanent norm for faith (Gal. 1:8; II Thess. 2:15) and conduct (I Cor. 11:2; II Thess. 3:4, 6, 14), as is indicated also by the self-conscious reference to "all the churches" (cf., e.g., I Cor. 7:17; 14:34), and even to designate their rulings on a question as "the commandment of the Lord" (I Cor. 14:37). They establish the order or government of the church so that a shared rule by a group of men, often but not always designated as bishops or elders, is universal in the NT period, as evidenced not only in the meeting at Jerusalem (Acts 15) but also in the various writings and geographical locations (Acts 14:23; I Tim. 3:1ff.; I Pet. 5:1ff.; cf. 1:1; Phil. 1:1; I Thess. 5:12–13; Heb. 13:7, 17; James 5:14). Alongside this leadership a diaconal ministry is established by the apostles (Acts 6:1–6; Phil. 1:1; I Tim. 3:8–13). Not only do they set the order of the church, they also prescribe discipline in Christ's name and with his authority (I Cor. 5:4; II Thess. 3:6). In so acting they have functioned as the foundation of the church (Eph. 2:20; 3:5; cf. I Cor. 12:28) who have no successors and whose foundational authority has been put permanently in place by their writings, which have conveyed, at Christ's command and in fulfillment of his promise, the truth he would have the church always teach and obey (cf. John 14:26; 16:13). So they are recognized as authoritative alongside "the rest of the Scripture," i.e., the OT (II Pet. 3:15–16).

Various Spheres of Authority. The Bible recognizes within its pages various spheres in which God has entrusted authority into the hands of leaders.

The Church. Christ has given authority to certain men to be leaders (often termed elders or bishops) in his church. Their task is to shepherd the church with love and humility as the servants of Christ and his people (I Tim. 3:5; I Pet. 5:1–4). A loving submission to their leadership is urged on Christians (I Thess. 5:12–13; Heb. 13:7, 17).

Marriage and the Family. Women as equals of men in both creation and redemption (cf. I Pet. 3:7; Gal. 3:28) are asked to submit to their own husbands as heads of the home because of the pattern established by God at creation (I Cor. 11:3, 8–9; I Tim. 2:12–15; Eph. 5:22; I Pet. 3:1–6). Both husbands and wives are asked to offset the effects of sin on this God-ordained authority relationship by their attitude and conduct, i.e., the husband exercising headship with love, honor, and without bitterness (Eph. 5:28; Col. 3:19; I Pet. 3:7) and the wives, with respect, as unto the Lord, and with a gentle spirit (Eph. 5:22, 33; I Pet. 3:4). Children are commanded to obey their parents (Eph. 6:1–3; Col. 3:20) and to care for them in times of need (I Tim. 5:4).

Civil Government. Christians are to recognize that God has granted authority in this realm to those who by his providence "exist" (Rom. 13:1; cf. John 19:11). Thus they are called dutifully to subject themselves to civil authorities (I Pet. 2:13–17) who are described as God's servants to prevent evildoers and to encourage good behavior (Rom. 13:1ff.). This authority requires not only subjection but also the rendering of various taxes, respect, and honor (Rom. 13:7).

Other Authorities in Human Life. The NT recognizes human institutions that will exist within human society, among which civil government is the prime example. Its word of instruction is that Christians, for the Lord's sake, should submit to every appropriate human institution (I Pet. 2:13). The word of qualification assumed but not stated in every one of these spheres is found explicitly in Acts 5:29 in reference to the civil and religious sphere; namely, "we must obey God rather than men" (cf. 4:19). When the human authority clearly contravenes one's allegiance to God's authority, one is authorized to appeal to God's authority and obey it in contradistinction to that of any human authority. For in that situation the authority structure has so opposed the one who gives it its validity that it forfeits its authority.

Satan's Authority. The exercise of power by the evil one and the demons is also regarded as a power or authority, but a usurped one which is only under God's ultimate authority (Luke 4:6; Acts 26:18; Col. 1:13; cf. Job 1). Such angelic beings, who are called powers or authorities, have been disarmed by Christ (Col. 2:15) and have no other final outcome than that of the devil's final doom (Rev. 20:10). G. W. Knight, III

Bibliography. W. Foerster, *TDNT,* II, 562–75; O. Betz and C. Blendingen, *NIDNTT,* II, 606–11; T. Rees, *ISBE,* I, 333–40; J. Denney, "Of Christ," *HDCG;* W. M. McPheeters, "In Religion," *HDCG;* J. Rea, *WBE,* I, 179–80; H. D. McDonald, *ZPEB,* I, 420–21; J. I. Packer, *IBD;* G. W. Bromiley, *ISBE* (rev.), I, 364–70; J. N. Geldenhuys, *Supreme Authority;* B. Ramm, *Patterns of Authority.*

Bible, Authority of. In its personal reference authority is the right and capacity of an individual to perform what he wills and who, by virtue of his position or office, can command obedience. It has also an application to words spoken or written whose accuracy has been established and whose information can consequently be trusted.

In the NT the Greek word *exousia* is sometimes translated "right" (NEB), or "power" (AV; e.g., Matt. 9:6; John 1:12; 17:2; 19:10), and sometimes "authority" (e.g., Matt. 7:29; 8:9; 21:23; John 5:27; Acts 9:14). What emerges from its various occurrences is that the possession of *exousia* is of a power held by right. In some contexts the emphasis falls on the authority which the possession of power rightfully gives; in other instances it falls on the reality of the power which conditions the right use of authority.

Authority may be bestowed or inherent. When Jesus was asked by what authority he taught and acted (Matt. 21:23–24) the implication was that his authority was external. His questioners supposed him to be exercising a representative or conferred authority only. On the other hand, in the declaration that Jesus taught with authority (Matt. 7:29) and "with authority and power" expelled unclean spirits (Luke 4:36) the locus of such authority was in his own being. It was, that is to say, an ontological authority. Thus, while the authority for his words and acts was not his own but came from the one who sent him (John 14:10; 17:8), yet these same words and acts had their *raison d'être* in his own person because grounded in his filial relationship with God his Father.

As in the case of Christ in whom both aspects of authority, the bestowed and the inherent, combined, so is it with the Bible. Because the Bible points beyond itself to God, it has a conferred authority. Yet the Bible has a real authority in itself as the authentic embodiment of God's self-disclosure. Liberal theologians refuse the Bible this ontological authority, granting it at most a borrowed authority. Some, like Karl Barth, allow this authority to be bestowed by God while insisting that the Bible itself is essentially a human product. Others—e.g., Rudolf Bultmann and Paul Tillich—regard the Bible as a fallible collection of religious writings on which the early church arbitrarily imposed an authority which evangelical piety has continued to uphold. But by refusing to the Bible an ontological authority, liberal theology uncovers its fundamental inconsistency, thereby pronouncing its own condemnation. For insofar as it wishes the acceptance of its own unbiblical speculations, it has to decry the authority of the Bible. Yet insofar as it is concerned to retain the label Christian, it appeals to the Bible as its authoritative source.

An approach to the subject of biblical authority must begin with God himself. For in him all authority is finally located. And he is his own authority, for there is nothing outside him on which his authority is founded. Thus, in making his promise to Abraham, he pledged his own name since he had no greater by whom to swear (Heb. 6:13). This authority of God is, then, the authority of what God is. But what God is, is made known in his self-disclosure, since only in his revelation can God be known. Revelation is therefore the key to God's authority, so that the two, revelation and authority, may be regarded as two sides of the same reality. In revelation God declares his authority.

The prophets of the OT found their certainty in God's revelation. In uttering their message they knew themselves to be declaring God's authoritative will. As God's ambassadors they proclaimed what God required of his people. For Christian faith Christ is known as God's final revelation. In him God's imperial authority is most graciously expressed. Thus is Christ the sum of all that is divinely authoritative for the life of man. But this progressive unveiling of God, which culminated in Christ, has been given perpetual form in the biblical writings. Scripture consequently participates in God's authority, so that Christ's relation thereto is decisive as vindicating its authority.

Jesus read "all the Scriptures" of the OT as a prophetic outline of what he came to accomplish; and he took its very language to be the natural, and at the same time the supernatural, expression of his Father's will. By his attitude to and use of the OT Christ truly validated its divinity. With the same conviction of its divine authority the NT writers accepted it and quoted it; and in its light they themselves, as the inspired interpreters of the saving significance of Christ's person and work, put their own writings on an equal footing with the OT Scriptures as divinely authoritative. In the words of his elect apostles the full measure of God's revelation in Christ was brought to completion so that Paul could declare, "In the sight of God speak we in Christ" (II Cor. 12:19). Thus do the apostles claim an absolute authority for their writings (e.g., II Cor. 10:11; I Thess. 2:13; 5:27; II Thess. 2:15; 3:14).

The authority of the Bible is established by its own claims. It is the word of God. Such declarations as, "Thus says the Lord," or its equivalent, occur so frequently in the OT that it can confidently be asserted that the whole account is dominated by the claim. The NT writers also refer to these Scriptures as having God for their source. In the NT itself both Christ and the gospel are spoken of as "the word of God" and so demonstrate the fact that the tie between the two is a vital and necessary one. Specifically is the gospel in its central content and many aspects, through the action of the Holy Spirit, brought into written form by Christ's appointees as God's authoritative word for the church and in the world. Both testaments therefore belong together under the one designation, "the word of God." As God's word the Bible consequently carries in itself God's authority.

It is the scripture of truth. In the OT the Hebrew word *'ĕmet,* rendered "truth" in the AV and frequently translated "faithfulness" in the RSV (e.g., Deut. 32:4; Ps. 108:4; Hos. 2:20), is constantly predicated of God. God as true is absolutely faithful (cf. Ps. 117:2), and this absolute faithfulness of God assures his complete trustworthiness. This truthfulness of God passes over as an attribute of what God is in himself to characterize all his works (cf. Ps. 57:3) and especially his word. Thus is his word both true and faithful (cf. Ps. 119:89). The whole OT, then, as "the word of God" is to be designated "the scripture of truth" (Dan. 10:21 AV). It partakes of God's own character, of the fundamental truthfulness of him who declares himself to be "not a man, that he should lie" (Num. 23:19; cf. I Sam. 15:29; Ps. 89:35). Ps. 31:5 declares that the Lord is the God of truth, while Ps. 119:160 affirms his word as the word of truth. In both places the same Hebrew term is employed. The same truth is thus predicated of God and his word.

In the NT the word *alētheia* has the same fundamental meaning of genuineness and truthfulness as opposed to what is false and unreliable. So God is both true (I John 5:20; John 3:33; 7:28; 8:26; 17:3; I Thess. 1:9) and truthful (Rom. 3:7; 15:8, etc.). And as God is, so too is his word. His word is truth (John 17:17). The gospel is presented with truthful words (II Cor. 6:7; cf. Col. 1:5; James 1:18), and the truth of the gospel (Gal. 2:5) is identical with the truth of God (Rom. 3:7).

The Bible is, then, the book of God's truth; and such truth is, as the Westminster Catechism says, "infallible truth." As it is wholly trustworthy regarding its truth, so must it be wholly reliable regarding its facts. And because it is both, it is our divine authority in all things that pertain to life and godliness. H. D. McDonald

See also Bible, Inspiration of; Bible, Inerrancy and Infallibility of.

Bibliography. R. Abba, *The Nature and Authority of the Bible;* H. Cunliffe-Jones, *The Authority of the Biblical Revelation;* R. E. Davies, *The Problem of Authority in the Continental Reformers;* C. H. Dodd, *The Authority of the Bible;* P. T. Forsyth, *The Principle of Authority;* N. Geldenhuys, *Supreme Authority;* F. J. A. Hort, *The Authority of the Bible;* G. H. Hospers, *The Reformed Principle of Authority;* R. C. Johnson, *Authority in Protestant Theology;* D. M. Lloyd-Jones, *Authority;* H. D. McDonald, *Theories of Revelation;* L. Oswald, *The Truth of the Bible;* B. Ramm, *Patterns of Authority;* A. Richardson and W. Schweitzer, eds., *Biblical Authority for Today;* J. Rogers, ed., *Biblical Authority;* J. W. C. Wand, *The Authority of the Scriptures;* B. B. Warfield, *The Inspiration and Authority of the Bible;* R. R. Williams, *Authority in the Apostolic Age.*

Bible, Canon of. The term "canon" in Christianity refers to a group of books acknowledged by the early church as the rule of faith and practice. Deriving from the Greek *kanōn,* which designated a carpenter's rule (possibly borrowed from a Hebrew term, *qāneh,* referring to a measuring reed six cubits long), the word has been used to identify those books considered to be spiritually superlative, by which all others were measured and found to be of secondary value in general church use.

Both Jews and Christians have canons of scripture. The Jewish canon consists of thirty-nine books; the Christian consists of sixty-six for Protestants and eighty for Catholics (whose canon includes the Apocrypha, regarded by most as of deuterocanonical status). Sacred books are found in all literate religions. The book is generally secondary to the faith, the book or books being a deposit of the faith. The use of a canon varies in world religions—for liturgy, renewal of faith, evangelism, or authority in faith and practice.

The process by which these books came to be generally regarded as exclusively authoritative is not known for either the Hebrew or Christian canon. That it transpired under the influence of the Spirit of God is commonly accepted among Christian people. Inspired literature formed only a part of the total religious literature of God's people at any time in their history, and only a portion of the inspired literature finally emerged as canonical in all parts of the ancient world. All inspired literature was authoritative, but it was not all equally beneficial to local groups and thus did not achieve universal or empire-wide acceptance. That is to say, local lists of books were not necessarily identical with the general list, the canon, which eventually consisted of the books common to all the local lists.

OT Canon. The faith of Israel existed independently of a book for hundreds of years between the time of Abraham and Moses. None of the patriarchs before Moses is recorded as having written sacred literature, although the art of writing was well developed at that time in the homeland of Abraham, as the recently discovered Ebla tablets have dramatically reaffirmed. The Sumerians and Babylonians already had highly developed law codes, and accounts of such events as the great flood appear in their literature. Moses, however, was the first known Hebrew to commit sacred history to writing (Exod. 24:4, 7).

Subsequent to the composition of the Pentateuch, it is recorded that Joshua wrote in the book of the law of God (Josh. 24:26). The law was always considered to be from God (Deut. 31:24; Josh. 1:8). The other two divisions of the Hebrew canon, the prophets and writings, were eventually selected out of a larger literature, some of which is mentioned in the OT itself ("book of the Wars of the Lord," Num. 21:14; "book of Jasher," Josh. 10:13; "book of the Acts of Solomon," I Kings 11:41; "book of Samuel the seer, book of Nathan the prophet, book of Gad the seer," I Chr. 29:29, etc.; fifteen or more such books are named in the OT).

The oldest surviving list of the canonical scriptures of the OT comes from about A.D. 170, the product of a Christian scholar named Melito of Sardis, who made a trip to Palestine to determine both the order and number of books in the Hebrew Bible. Neither his order nor his contents agree exactly with our modern English Bibles. There is no agreement in order or content in the existing manuscripts of Hebrew, Greek, or Latin Bibles. The modern English Protestant Bible follows the order of the Latin Vulgate and the content of the Hebrew Bible. It is important to remember that the OT was more than a thousand years in writing—the oldest parts being written by Moses and the latest after the Babylonian exile. During the entire period of biblical history, therefore, the Jews lived their faith without a closed canon of Scriptures, such a canon therefore not being essential to the practice of the Jewish religion during that time. Why then were the books finally collected into a canon? They were brought together evidently as an act of God's providence, historically prompted by the emergence of apocryphal and pseudepigraphical literature in the intertestamental period and the increasing need to know what the limits of divine revelation were. By the time of Jesus the OT, called Tanaach by modern Judaism, consisted of the law, prophets, and writings (the first book of which was the Psalms, Luke 24:44). Opinions about the full extent of the canon seem not to have been finalized until sometime after the first century A.D.

NT Canon. The earliest list of NT books containing only our twenty-seven appeared in A.D. 367 in a letter of Athanasius, Bishop of Alexandria. The order was Gospels, Acts, General Epistles, Pauline Epistles, Revelation. In the first century Peter spoke of Paul writing "in all his letters" (II Pet. 3:16), and by the early second century the letters of Ignatius were being collected. Evidence of exclusive collections being made in the second century is seen in the writings of Justin Martyr, who argues for only our four Gospels. Discussion about authorship and authority of various letters appears in writers of the second century, and one canonical list which has been dated from the second to the fourth century, the Muratorian Canon, differentiates between books that are suitable to be read in worship and those that should be read only in private devotion.

The fact that other books formed a larger deposit out of which the twenty-seven eventually emerged is seen in the reference to a prior letter to the Corinthians in I Cor. 5:9, a letter to the Laodiceans in Col. 4:16, and the inclusion of I and II Clement in the fifth century manuscript of the Greek NT, Codex Alexandrinus, as well as Barnabas and Hermas in the fourth century Codex Sinaiticus. Eusebius cited a letter from the second century Bishop of Corinth, Dionysius, stating that Clement's letter was read in the church there "from time to time for our admonition" (*Ecclesiastical History* IV.23.11).

The formation of the NT canon was not a conciliar decision. The earliest ecumenical council, Nicaea in 325, did not discuss the canon. The first undisputed decision of a council on the canon seems to be from Carthage in 397, which decreed that nothing should be read in the church under the name of the divine Scriptures except the canonical writings. Then the twenty-seven books of the NT are listed as the canonical writings. The council could list only those books that were generally regarded by the consensus of use as properly a canon. The formation of the NT canon must, therefore, be regarded as a process rather than an event, and a historical rather than a biblical matter. The coming of the Word of God in print is only slightly more capable of explication than the coming of the Word of God incarnate.

J. R. McRay

See also ANTILEGOMENA; HOMOLOGOUMENA.

Bibliography. B. F. Westcott, *A General Survey of the History of the Canon of the NT;* C. R. Gregory, *The Canon and Text of the NT;* A. Souter, *The Text and Canon of the NT;* E. J. Goodspeed, *The Formation of the NT;* R. M. Grant, *The Formation of the NT;* P. R. Ackroyd and C. F. Evans, eds., *The Cambridge History of the Bible,* I; H. von Campenhausen, *The Formation of the Christian Bible;* R. L. Harris, *Inspiration and Canonicity of the Bible;* W. R. Farmer, *Jesus and the Gospel;* W. Brueggemann, *The Creative Word;* J. A. Sanders, *Torah and Canon* and "Text and Canon: Concepts and Methods," *JBL* 98:5–29; A. C. Sundberg, Jr., "Canon Muratori: A Fourth Century List," *HTR* 66:1–41; S. Z. Leiman, *The Canon and Massorah of the Hebrew Bible;* H. E. Ryle, *The Canon of the OT.*

Bible, Inerrancy and Infallibility of. The question of authority is central for any theology. Since Protestant theology has located authority in the Bible, the nature of biblical authority has been a fundamental concern. The Reformation passed to its heirs the belief that ultimate authority rests not in reason or a pope, but in an inspired Scripture. Thus, within conservative Protestantism the question of inerrancy has been much debated.

The two words most often used to express

the nature of scriptural authority are "inerrant" and "infallible." Though these two terms are, on etymological grounds, approximately synonymous, they are used differently. In Roman Catholic theology "inerrant" is applied to the Bible, "infallible" to the church, particularly the teaching function of pope and *magisterium.* Since Protestants reject the infallibility of both the pope and the church, the word has been used increasingly of the Scriptures. More recently "infallible" has been championed by those who hold to what B. B. Warfield called limited inspiration but what today is better called limited inerrancy. They limit the Bible's inerrancy to matters of faith and practice, particularly soteriological issues. Stephen T. Davis reflects this tendency when he gives a stipulative definition for infallibility: the Bible makes no false or misleading statements about matters of faith and practice. In this article the two terms shall be used as virtually synonymous.

Definition of Inerrancy. Inerrancy is the view that when all the facts become known, they will demonstrate that the Bible in its original autographs and correctly interpreted is entirely true and never false in all it affirms, whether that relates to doctrine or ethics or to the social, physical, or life sciences.

A number of points in this definition deserve discussion. Inerrancy is not presently demonstrable. Human knowledge is limited in two ways. First, because of our finitude and sinfulness, human beings misinterpret the data that exist. For instance, wrong conclusions can be drawn from inscriptions or texts. Second, we do not possess all the data that bear on the Bible. Some of that data may be lost forever, or they may be awaiting discovery by archaeologists. By claiming that inerrancy will be shown to be true after all the facts are known, one recognizes this. The defender of inerrancy argues only that there will be no conflict in the end.

Further, inerrancy applies equally to all parts of the Bible as originally written. This means that no present manuscript or copy of Scripture, no matter how accurate, can be called inerrant.

This definition also relates inerrancy to hermeneutics. Hermeneutics is the science of biblical interpretation. It is necessary to interpret a text properly, to know its correct meaning, before asserting that what a text says is false. Moreover, a key hermeneutical principle taught by the Reformers is the analogy of faith, which demands that apparent contradictions be harmonized if possible. If a passage appears to permit two interpretations, one of which conflicts with another passage and one of which does not, the latter must be adopted.

Probably the most important aspect of this definition is its definition of inerrancy in terms of truth and falsity rather than in terms of error. It has been far more common to define inerrancy as "without error," but a number of reasons argue for relating inerrancy to truth and falsity. To use "error" is to negate a negative idea. Truth, moreover, is a property of sentences, not words. Certain problems are commonly associated with views related to "error." Finally, "error" has been defined by some in the contemporary debate in such a way that almost every book ever written will qualify as inerrant. Error, they say, is *willful deception;* since the Bible never willfully deceives its readers, it is inerrant. This would mean that almost all other books are also inerrant, since few authors intentionally deceive their readers.

Some have suggested that the Bible itself might help in setting the meaning of error. At first this appears to be a good suggestion, but there are reasons to reject it. First, "inerrancy" and "error" are theological rather than biblical terms. This means that the Bible applies neither word to itself. This does not mean that it is inappropriate to use these words of the Bible. Another theological term is "trinity." It is, however, more difficult to define such words. Second, a study of the Hebrew and Greek words for error may be classified into three groups: cases of error where intentionality cannot be involved (e.g., Job 6:24; 19:4), cases of error where intentionality may or may not be involved (e.g., II Sam. 6:7), and cases where intentionality must be involved (e.g., Judg. 16:10–12). Error, then, has nothing to do with intentionality.

Admittedly, precision of statement and measurement will not be up to modern standards, but as long as what is said is true, inerrancy is not in doubt.

Finally, the definition states that inerrancy covers all areas of knowledge. Inerrancy is not limited to matters of soteriological or ethical concern. It should be clear that biblical affirmations about faith and ethics are based upon God's action in history. No neat dichotomy can be made between the theological and factual.

Arguments for Inerrancy. The primary arguments for inerrancy are biblical, historical, and epistemological in nature.

The Biblical Argument. At the heart of the belief in an inerrant, infallible Bible is the testimony of Scripture itself. There is some disagreement as to whether Scripture teaches this doctrine explicitly or implicitly. The consensus today is that inerrancy is taught implicitly.

First, the Bible teaches its own inspiration, and this requires inerrancy. The Scriptures are the breath of God (II Tim. 3:16), which guarantees they are without error.

Second, in Deut. 13:1–5 and 18:20–22 Israel is given criteria for distinguishing God's message and messenger from false prophecies and prophets. One mark of a divine message is total and absolute truthfulness. A valid parallel can be made between the prophet and the Bible. The prophet's word was usually oral, although it might be recorded and included in a book; the writers of Scripture communicated God's word in written form. Both were instruments of divine communication, and in both cases the human element was an essential ingredient.

Third, the Bible teaches its own authority, and this requires inerrancy. The two most commonly cited passages are Matt. 5:17–20 and John 10: 34–35. Both record the words of Jesus. In the former Jesus said that heaven and earth will pass away before the smallest detail of the law fails to be fulfilled. The law's authority rests on the fact that every minute detail will be fulfilled. In John 10:34–35 Jesus says that Scripture *cannot* be broken and so is absolutely binding. While it is true that both passages emphasize the Bible's authority, this authority can only be justified by or grounded in inerrancy. Something that contains errors cannot be absolutely authoritative.

Fourth, Scripture uses Scripture in a way that supports its inerrancy. At times an entire argument rests on a single word (e.g., John 10:34–35 and "God" in Ps. 82:6), the tense of a verb (e.g., the present tense in Matt. 22:32), and the difference between a singular and a plural noun (e.g., "seed" in Gal. 3:16). If the Bible's inerrancy does not extend to every detail, these arguments lose their force. The use of any word may be a matter of whim and may even be an error. It might be objected that the NT does not always cite OT texts with precision—that as a matter of fact precision is the exception rather than the rule. This is a fair response, and an adequate answer requires more space than is available here. A careful study of the way in which the OT is used in the NT, however, demonstrates that the NT writers quoted the OT not cavalierly but quite carefully.

Finally, inerrancy follows from what the Bible says about God's character. Repeatedly, the Scriptures teach that God cannot lie (Num. 23:19; I Sam. 15:29; Titus 1:2; Heb. 6:18). If, then, the Bible is from God and his character is behind it, it must be inerrant and infallible.

The Historical Argument. A second argument for biblical inerrancy is that this has been the view of the church throughout its history. One must remember that if inerrancy was part of the corpus of orthodox doctrine, then in many discussions it was assumed rather than defended. Further, the term "inerrancy" may be a more modern way of expressing the belief in the English language. Nevertheless, in each period of the church's history one can cite clear examples of those who affirm inerrancy.

In the early church Augustine writes, "I have learned to yield this respect and honour only to the canonical books of Scripture: of these alone do I most firmly believe that the authors were completely free from error."

The two great Reformers, Luther and Calvin, bear testimony to biblical infallibility. Luther says, "But everyone, indeed, knows that at times they [the fathers] have erred as men will; therefore I am ready to trust them only when they prove their opinions from Scripture, which has never erred." While Calvin does not use the phrase "without error," there can be little question that he embraced inerrancy. Of the writers of the Gospels he comments, "The Spirit of God . . . appears purposely to have regulated their style in such a manner, that they all wrote one and the same history, with the most perfect agreement, but in different ways."

In modern times one could cite the works of Princeton theologians Archibald Alexander, Charles Hodge, A. A. Hodge, and B. B. Warfield as modern formulators and defenders of the full inerrancy and infallibility of Scripture.

The biblical and historical arguments are clearly more important than the two that follow. Should they be shown to be false, inerrancy would suffer a mortal blow.

The Epistemological Argument. Because epistemologies differ, this argument has been formulated in at least two very different ways. For some, knowledge claims must, to be justified, be indubitable or incorrigible. It is not enough that a belief is true and is believed on good grounds. It must be beyond doubt and question. For such an epistemology inerrancy is essential. Inerrancy guarantees the incorrigibility of every statement of Scripture. Therefore, the contents of Scripture can be objects of knowledge.

Epistemologies that do not require such a high standard of certitude result in this argument for inerrancy: If the Bible is not inerrant, then any claim it makes may be false. This means not that all claims *are* false, but that some might be. But so much of the Bible is beyond direct verification. Thus, only its inerrancy assures the knower that his or her claim is justified.

The Slippery Slope Argument. Finally, some see inerrancy as so fundamental that those who give it up will soon surrender other central Christian doctrines. A denial of inerrancy starts one down a slope that is slippery and ends in even greater error.

Objections to Inerrancy. The arguments for inerrancy have not gone unchallenged. In what follows, responses by those who object to each argument will be given and answers will be offered.

The Slippery Slope Argument. This argument is both the least important and most disliked by those who do not hold to inerrancy. What kind of relationship exists between the doctrine of inerrancy and other central Christian doctrines, they ask, that the denial of all inerrancy will of necessity lead to a denial of other doctrines? Is it a logical relationship? Is it a causal or psychological relationship? On close examination, none of these seems to be the case. Many people who do not affirm inerrancy are quite clearly orthodox on other matters of doctrine.

What has been said to this point is true. It should be noted, however, that numerous cases do support the slippery slope argument. For many individuals and institutions the surrender of their commitment to inerrancy has been a first step to greater error.

The Epistemological Argument. The epistemological argument has been characterized by some as an example of overbelief. A single error in the Bible should not lead one to conclude that it contains no truth. If one finds one's spouse wrong on some matter, one would be wrong to conclude that one's spouse can never be trusted on any matter.

This objection, however, overlooks two very important matters. First, while it is true that one error in Scripture would not justify the conclusion that everything in it is false, it would call everything in Scripture into question. We could not be sure that everything in it is true. Since the theological is based on the historical and since the historical is open to error, how can one be sure that the theological is true? There is no direct means for verification. Second, while the case of the errant spouse is true as far as it goes, it does not account for all the issues involved in inerrancy. One's spouse does not claim to be inerrant; the Bible does. One's spouse is not omniscient and omnipotent; the God of the Bible is. God knows everything, and he can communicate with man.

The Historical Argument. Those who reject inerrancy argue that this doctrine is an innovation, primarily of the Princeton theologians in the nineteenth century. Throughout the centuries the church believed in the Bible's authority but not its total inerrancy. The doctrine of inerrancy grew out of an apologetic need. Classical liberalism and its growing commitment to an increasingly radical biblical criticism made the orthodox view of Scripture vulnerable. Therefore, the Princeton theologians devised the doctrine of total inerrancy to stem the rising tide of liberalism. This represented a departure from the views of their predecessors in the orthodox tradition. Calvin, for example, speaks of God "accommodating" himself to man in the communication of his revelation. Calvin also says that the Bible's teaching does not need to be harmonized with science, and that anyone who wishes to prove to the unbeliever that the Bible is God's Word is foolish.

These objections to the historical argument do not do justice to the evidence. They fail to reckon with the host of clear affirmations of inerrancy by Christian theologians throughout the church's history, only a few of which were given above.

Moreover, the treatment of figures like Calvin is unfair. While Calvin talks about accommodation, he does not mean accommodation to human error. He means that God condescended to speak in language that finite human beings could understand. In one place he says that God spoke only baby talk. He never implies that what God said is in error. On matters of science and proof, the same sort of thing is true. Calvin nowhere says that the Scriptures *cannot* be harmonized with science or that they *cannot* be proven to be the Word of God. He felt rather that such an exercise is futile in itself because of man's sin. Hence, he relied on the testimony of the Holy Spirit to the unbeliever. The problem is in man, not in the Scriptures or the evidence for their origin. The theologians of the church may have been wrong in their belief, but they did believe in an inerrant Bible.

The Biblical Argument. A common objection to the biblical argument is that the Bible nowhere teaches its own inerrancy. The point seems to be a subtle one. Those who make this point mean that the Bible nowhere says "all Scripture is inerrant" in the way that it teaches "all Scripture is given by inspiration of God" (II Tim. 3:16). While it is true that no verse says explicitly that Scripture is inerrant, biblical inerrancy is implied by or follows from a number of things the Bible does teach explicitly.

Another objection is that inerrancy is unfalsifiable. Either the standard for error is so high that nothing can qualify (e.g., even contradictions have difficulty in qualifying), or the falsity or truth of scriptural statements cannot be demonstrated until all the facts are known. The doctrine of inerrancy is not, however, unfalsifiable in principle; it is unfalsifiable only at present. Not everything that bears on the truth and falsity of the Bible is yet available. How then is it possible to affirm so strongly the doctrine of inerrancy now? Should one be more cautious or even suspend judgment? The inerrantist wants to be true to what he or she thinks the Bible teaches. And as independent data have become available (e.g., from archaeology), they have shown the Bible to be trustworthy.

Another criticism is that inerrancy fails to recognize sufficiently the human element in the writing of Scripture. The Bible teaches that it is a product of human as well as divine authorship. This objection, though, underestimates the divine element. The Bible is a divine-human book. To deemphasize either side of its authorship is a mistake. Furthermore, this criticism misunderstands man, implying that humanity requires error. This is false. The spokesmen of God were human, but inspiration kept them from error.

The objection has been raised that if one uses the methods of biblical criticism, one must accept its conclusions. But why? One need accept only the methods that are valid and the conclusions that are true.

Finally, it has been objected that since the original autographs no longer exist and since the doctrine applies only to them, inerrancy is meaningless. The identification of inerrancy with the original autographs is a neat hedge against disproof. Whenever an "error" is pointed out, the inerrantist can say that it must not have existed in the original autographs.

Limiting inerrancy to the original autographs could be such a hedge, but it need not be. This qualification of inerrancy grows out of the recognition that errors crop up in the transmission of any text. There is, however, a great difference between a text that is initially inerrant and one that is not. The former, through textual criticism, can be restored to a state very near the inerrant original; the latter leaves far more doubt as to what was really said.

It might be argued that the doctrine of inerrant originals directs attention away from the authority of our present texts. Perhaps inerrantists sometimes fail to emphasize the authority of our present texts and versions as they should. Is the remedy, however, to undercut the base for their authority? To deny the authority of the original is to undermine the authority of the Bible the Christian has today. P. D. Feinberg

See also Bible, Authority of; Bible, Inspiration of.

Bibliography. For inerrancy: D. A. Carson and J. D. Woodbridge, eds., *Scripture and Truth;* N. L. Geisler, ed., *Inerrancy;* J. W. Montgomery, ed., *God's Inerrant Word: An International Symposium on the Trustworthiness of Scripture;* B. B. Warfield, *The Inspiration and Authority of the Bible;* J. D. Woodbridge, *Biblical Authority: A Critique of the Rogers/McKim Proposal.* Against inerrancy: D. M. Beegle, *Scripture, Tradition and Infallibility;* S. A. Davis, *The Debate About the Bible;* J. Rogers, ed., *Biblical Authority;* J. Rogers and D. McKim, *The Interpretation and Authority of the Bible.*

Bible, Inspiration of. The theological idea of inspiration, like its correlative revelation, presupposes a personal mind and will—in Hebrew terminology, the "living God"—acting to communicate with other spirits. The Christian belief in inspiration, not alone in revelation, rests both on explicit biblical assertions and on the pervading mood of the scriptural record.

Biblical Terminology. Today the English verb and noun "inspire" and "inspiration" bear many meanings. This diverse connotation is already present in the Latin *inspiro* and *inspiratio* of the Vulgate Bible. But the technical theological sense of inspiration, largely lost in the secular atmosphere of our time, is clearly asserted by the Scriptures with a special view to the sacred writers and their writings. Defined in this sense, inspiration is a supernatural influence of the Holy Spirit upon divinely chosen men in consequence of which their writings become trustworthy and authoritative.

In the AV the noun appears twice: Job 32:8, "But there is a spirit in man; and the inspiration of the Almighty giveth them understanding"; and II Tim. 3:16, "All scripture is given by inspiration of God, and is profitable for doctrine, for reproof, for correction, for instruction in righteousness." In the former instance both the ASV and the RSV substitute "breath" for "inspiration," an interchange which serves to remind us of the dramatic fact that the Scriptures refer the creation of the universe (Ps. 33:6), the creation of man for fellowship with God (Gen. 2:7), and the production of the sacred writings (II Tim. 3:16) to the spiration of God. In the latter instance, the ASV renders the text "Every scripture inspired of God is also profitable," a translation abandoned as doubtful by the RSV, "All scripture is inspired by God and profitable."

Biblical Teaching. Although the term "inspiration" occurs infrequently in modern versions and paraphrases, the conception itself remains firmly embedded in the scriptural teaching. The word *theopneustos* (II Tim. 3:16), literally God-"spirated" or breathed out, affirms that the living God is the author of Scripture and that Scripture is the product of his creative breath. The biblical sense, therefore, rises above the modern tendency to assign the term "inspiration" merely a dynamic or functional significance (largely through a critical dependence on

Schleiermacher's artificial disjunction that God communicates life, not truths about himself). Geoffrey W. Bromiley, translator of Karl Barth's *Church Dogmatics,* points out that whereas Barth emphasizes the "inspiring" of Scripture—that is, its present use by the Holy Spirit toward hearers and readers—the Bible itself begins further back with the very "inspiredness" of the sacred writings. The writings themselves, as an end product, are assertedly God-breathed. Precisely this conception of inspired *writings,* and not simply of inspired *men,* sets the biblical conception of inspiration pointedly over against pagan representations of inspiration in which heavy stress is placed on the subjective psychological mood and condition of those individuals overmastered by divine afflatus.

While the Pauline passage already noted lays proximate emphasis on the spiritual value of Scripture, it conditions this unique ministry upon a divine origin, in direct consequence of which the sacred record is profitable (cf. *ōpheleō,* "to advantage") for teaching, reproof, correction, and instruction in righteousness. The apostle Paul does not hesitate to speak of the sacred Hebrew writings as the veritable "oracles of God" (Rom. 3:2). James S. Stewart does not overstate the matter when he asserts that Paul as a Jew and later as a Christian held the high view that "every word" of the OT was "the authentic voice of God" (*A Man in Christ,* p. 39).

Emphasis on the divine origin of Scripture is found also in the Petrine writings. The "word of prophecy" is declared to be "more sure" than that even of the eyewitnesses of Christ's glory (II Pet. 1:17ff.). A supernatural quality all its own, therefore, inheres in Scripture. While involving the instrumentality of "holy men," Scripture is affirmed nonetheless to owe its origin not to human but to divine initiative in a series of statements whose proximate emphasis is the reliability of Scripture: (1) "No prophecy of scripture is of any private interpretation" (RSV, "is a matter of one's own interpretation"). Although the passage is somewhat obscure, it provides no support for the Roman Catholic view that the ordinary believer cannot confidently interpret the Bible but must depend on the teaching ministry of the church. While theologically acceptable, the *Scofield Reference Bible* comment that no individual verse is self-sufficient but the sense of Scripture as a whole is necessary is exegetically irrelevant. Everett F. Harrison notes that *ginetai* has the meaning of "emerging," compatibly with 1:21, and that *epilyseōs* may point to origination rather than to interpretation of Scripture. But the emphasis here may fall on divine illumination as the necessary corollary of divine inspiration so that, while the sense of Scripture is objectively given and determinable by exegesis, it must be discriminated nonetheless by the aid of the same Spirit by whom it was first communicated. In any event, the text precludes identifying the content of Scripture as an original product of the human writers.

(2) "Prophecy came not in old time by the will of man" (RSV, "no prophecy ever came by the impulse of man"). If the previous passage denies man's ultimate right to interpret Scripture, the present declaration emphatically denies the dependence of Scripture upon human initiative for its origin. (3) "Holy men of God spake . . . moved by the Holy Ghost." The RSV strengthens the divine quality of the sacred words: "men moved by the Holy Spirit spoke from God." Only through a determining and constraining influence of the Holy Spirit did the human agents actualize the divine initiative. The word translated "moved" is *pherō* (literally, "to bear along," "to carry"), and implies an activity more specific than mere guidance or direction.

Jesus' View of Scripture. If the passages already cited indicate something not only of the nature but of the extent of inspiration ("all scripture"; "the word of prophecy," elsewhere a summary term for the entirety of Scripture), a verse from the Johannine writings indicates something of the intensity of inspiration and at the same time enables us to contemplate Jesus' view of Scripture. In John 10:34–35, Jesus singles out an obscure passage in the Psalms ("ye are gods," Ps. 82:6) to reinforce the point that "the Scripture cannot be broken." The reference is doubly significant because it also discredits the modern bias against identifying Scripture as the word of God, on the ground that this assertedly dishonors the supreme revelation of God in the incarnate Christ. But in John 10:35 Jesus of Nazareth, while speaking of himself as indeed the one "the Father consecrated and sent into the world," nonetheless refers to those in a past dispensation "to whom the word of God came (and scripture cannot be broken)." The unavoidable implication is that the whole of Scripture is of irrefragable authority.

This is the viewpoint also of the Sermon on the Mount reported in Matthew's Gospel: "Think not that I have come to abolish the law and the prophets; I have come not to abolish them but to fulfil them. For truly, I say to you, till heaven and earth pass away, not an iota, not a dot, will pass from the law until all is accomplished. Whoever then relaxes one of the least of these commandments and teaches men so, shall be called least in the kingdom of heaven" (Matt. 5:17–19 RSV). Attempts to turn the repeated declarations, "You have heard that it was said . . . But I say to you" into a sustained criticism of the Mosaic law have not made their case convincingly against the probability that Jesus' protest is leveled rather against traditional reductions of the actual claim and inner intention of that law. Indeed, the necessary fulfillment of all that is written is a frequent theme on our Lord's lips (Matt. 26:31; 26:54; Mark 9:12–13; 14:19, 27; John 13:18; 17:12). Whoever searches the Gospel narratives faithfully in view of Jesus' attitude toward the sacred writings will be driven again and again to the conclusion of Reinhold Seeberg: "Jesus himself describes and employs the Old Testament as an infallible authority (e.g., Matt. 5:17; Luke 24:44)" (*Text-book of the History of Doctrines,* I, 82).

OT View. In both speech and writing the OT prophets are marked off by their unswerving assurance that they were spokesmen for the living God. They believed that the truths they uttered about the Most High and his works and will, and the commands and exhortations they voiced in his name, derived their origin from him and carried his authority. The constantly repeated formula "thus saith the Lord" is so characteristic of the prophets as to leave no doubt that they considered themselves chosen agents of the divine self-communication. Emil Brunner acknowledges that in "the words of God which the Prophets proclaim as those which they have received directly from God, and have been commissioned to repeat, as they have received them . . . perhaps we find the closest analogy to the meaning of the theory of verbal inspiration" (*Revelation and Reason,* p. 122). Whoever impugns the confidence of the prophets that they were instruments of the one true God in their disclosure of truths about his nature and dealings with man is driven, consistently if not necessarily, to the only possible alternative of their delusion.

From this same prophetic tradition it is impossible to detach Moses. Himself a prophet, rightly called "the founder of prophetic religion," he mediates the law and the priestly and sacrificial elements of revealed religion in the firm belief that he promulgates the veritable will of Jehovah. God will be the prophet's mouth (Exod. 4:14ff.); Moses is to be God, as it were, to the prophet (Exod. 7:1).

The Old and the New. The NT observations about Scripture apply primarily, of course, to the OT writings, which existed in the form of a unitary canon. But the apostles extended the traditional claim to divine inspiration. Jesus their Lord had not only validated the conception of a unique and authoritative corpus of sacred writings, but spoke of a further ministry of teaching by the Spirit (John 14:26; 16:13). The apostles assert confidently that they thus speak by the Spirit (I Pet. 1:12). They ascribe both the form and matter of their teaching to him (I Cor. 2:13). They not only assume a divine authority (I Thess. 4:2, 14; II Thess. 3:6, 12), but they make acceptance of their written commands a test of spiritual obedience (I Cor. 14:37). They even refer to each other's writings with the same regard as for the OT (cf. the identification in I Tim. 5:18 of a passage from Luke's Gospel, "The laborer is worthy of his hire" [Luke 10:7] as Scripture, and the juxtaposition of the Pauline epistles in II Pet. 3:16 with "the other scriptures").

Historical View. The traditional theory—that the Bible as a whole and in every part is the word of God written—held currency until the rise of modern critical theories a century ago. W. Sanday, affirming that the high view was the common Christian belief in the middle of the last century, comments that this view is "substantially not very different from that . . . held two centuries after the Birth of Christ," indeed, that "the same attributes" were predicated of the OT before the New (*Inspiration,* pp. 392–93). Bromiley notes certain rationalizing tendencies that have arisen on the rim of the high view: the Pharisees' rejection of Jesus of Nazareth as the promised Messiah despite their formal acknowledgment of the divine inspiration of Scripture; the attribution of inspiration to the vowel points and punctuation by seventeenth century Lutheran dogmaticians; and a depreciation (e.g., in the Middle Ages) of the role of illumination in the interpretation of Scripture ("The Church Doctrine of Inspiration" in *Revelation and the Bible,* ed. C. F. H. Henry, pp. 213ff.). The Protestant Reformers guarded their view of the Bible from the errors of rationalism and mysticism. To prevent Christianity's decline to mere metaphysics they stressed that the Holy Spirit alone gives life. And to prevent decline of the Christian religion to formless mysticism they emphasized the Scriptures as the only trustworthy source of the knowledge of God and his purposes. The historic evangelical view affirms that alongside the special divine revelation in saving acts, God's disclosure has taken the form also of truths and words. This revelation is communicated in a restricted canon of trustworthy writings, deeding fallen man an authentic exposition of God and his relations with man. Scripture itself is viewed as an integral part of God's redemptive activity, a special form of revelation, a unique mode of divine disclosure. In fact, it becomes a decisive factor in God's redemptive activity, interpreting and unifying the whole series of redemptive deeds, and exhibiting their divine meaning and significance.

Critical Theories. The postevolutionary criticism of the Bible carried on by Julius Wellhausen and other modern scholars narrowed the traditional confidence in infallibility by excluding matters of science and history. How much was at stake in a weakening of trust in the historical reliability of Scripture was not at first obvious to those who placed the emphasis on reliability of the Bible in matters of faith and practice. For no distinction between historical and doctrinal matters is set up by the NT view of inspiration. No doubt this is due to the fact that the OT history is viewed as the unfolding of God's saving revelation; the historical elements are a central aspect of the revelation. It was soon apparent that scholars who abandoned the trustworthiness of biblical history had furnished an entering wedge for the abandonment of doctrinal elements. Theoretically such an outcome might perhaps have been avoided by an act of will, but in practice it was not. William Newton Clark's *The Use of the Scriptures in Theology* (1905) yielded biblical theology and ethics to the critics as well as biblical science and history, but reserved the teaching of Jesus Christ as authentic. British scholars went further. Since Jesus' endorsement of creation, the patriarchs, Moses, and the giving of the law involved him in an acceptance of biblical science and history, some influential critics accepted only the theological and moral teaching of Jesus. Contemporaries swiftly erased even this remainder, asserting Jesus' theological fallibility. Actual belief in Satan and demons was insufferable to the critical mind, and must therefore invalidate his theological integrity, while the feigned belief in them (as a concession to the times) would invalidate his moral integrity. Yet Jesus had represented his whole ministry as a conquest of Satan and appealed to his exorcism of demons in proof of his supernatural mission. The critics could infer only his limited knowledge even of theological and moral truths. The so-called Chicago school of empirical theologians argued that respect for scientific method in theology disallows any defense whatever of Jesus' absoluteness and infallibility. Harry Emerson Fosdick's *The Modern Use of the Bible* (1924) championed only "abidingly valid" experiences in Jesus' life that could be normatively relived by us. Gerald Birney Smith went another step in *Current Christian Thinking* (1928); while we may gain inspiration from Jesus, our own experience determines doctrine and a valid outlook on life.

Simultaneously many critical writers sought to discredit the doctrine of an authoritative Scripture as a departure from the view of the biblical writers themselves, or of Jesus of Nazareth before them; or, if admittedly Jesus' view, they sought to dismiss it nonetheless as a theological accommodation, if not an indication of limited knowledge. The internal difficulties of such theories were stated with classic precision by Benjamin B. Warfield ("The Real Problem of Inspiration," in *The Inspiration and Authority of the Bible*). This attempt to conform the biblical view of inspiration to the looser modern critical notions may now be said to have failed. The contemporary revolt strikes more deeply. It attacks the historic view of revelation as well as of inspiration, affirming in deference to the dialectical philosophy that divine revelation does not assume the form of concepts and words—a premise that runs directly counter to the biblical witness.

Whatever must be said for the legitimate rights of criticism, it remains a fact that biblical criticism has met the test of objective scholarship with only qualified success. Higher criticism has shown itself far more efficient in creating a naïve faith in the existence of manuscripts for which there is no overt evidence (e.g., J, E, P, D, Q, first century nonsupernaturalistic "gospels" and second century supernaturalistic redactions) than in sustaining the Christian community's confidence in the only manuscripts the church has received as a sacred trust. Perhaps the most significant gain in our generation is the new disposition to approach Scripture in terms of primitive witness instead of remote reconstruction.

While it can shed no additional light on the mode of the Spirit's operation on the chosen writers, biblical criticism may provide a commentary on the nature and extent of that inspiration, and on the range of the trustworthiness of Scripture. The admittedly biblical view has been assailed in our generation especially by an appeal to such textual phenomena of Scripture as the Synoptic problem and apparent discrepancies in the reporting of events and numbers. Evangelical scholars have recognized the danger of imputing twentieth century scientific criteria to the biblical writers. They have noted also that the OT canon so unqualifiedly endorsed by Jesus contains many of the difficulties of the Synoptic problem in the features of the books of Kings and Chronicles. And they concede the proper role of an inductive study of the actual phenomena of Scripture in detailing the doctrine of inspiration derived from the teaching of the Bible.

C. F. H. Henry

See also Bible, Inerrancy and Infallibility of; Plenary Inspiration; Verbal Inspiration.

Bibliography. K. Barth, *The Doctrine of the Word of God;* C. Elliott, *A Treatise on the Inspiration of the Holy Scriptures;* T. Engelder, *Scripture Cannot Be Broken;* L. Gaussen, *Theopneustia: The Plenary Inspiration of the Holy Scriptures;* C. F. H. Henry, *God, Revelation, and Authority,* 4 vols., and (ed.), *Revelation and the Bible;* J. Orr, *Revelation and Inspiration;* N. B. Stonehouse and P. Woolley, eds., *The Infallible Word;* J. Urquhart, *The Inspiration and Accuracy of the Holy Scriptures;* J. F. Walvoord, ed., *Inspiration and Interpretation;* B. B. Warfield, *The Inspiration and Authority of the Bible;* J. C. Wenger, *God's Word Written;* J. I. Packer, *God Has Spoken;* H. D. McDonald, *What the Bible Teaches About the Bible;* P. Achtemeier, *The Inspiration of Scripture;* F. E. Greenspan, ed., *Scripture in Jewish and Christian Tradition.*

Bible, Interpretation of. *See* INTERPRETATION OF THE BIBLE.

Biblical Theology Movement. The standard definition for the "biblical theology movement" has been provided by OT scholar Brevard S. Childs. He perceptively describes the background, rise, flowering, and demise of the American aspect of the movement from the middle of the 1940s to the early part of the 1960s. In a more general sense the biblical theology movement was made up of biblical scholars in North America and Europe who shared liberal, critical assumptions and methods in an attempt to do theology in relation to biblical studies. This new way of doing theology was most fundamentally concerned to do justice to the theological dimension of the Bible, which previous generations of liberal scholars had almost completely neglected. Accordingly the movement reflected an interest of European neo-orthodox theologians of the 1920s and beyond. Neo-orthodoxy and the biblical theology movement shared the common concern to understand the Bible as a fully human book to be investigated with the fully immanent historical-critical method and yet to see the Bible as a vehicle or witness of the divine Word. This meant a meshing of the modern naturalistic-evolutionary world view as developed by natural science, modern philosophy, and critical history with the biblical view of a God who gives meaning and coherence to this world in his personal acts in history.

It has been shown by James Barr and James D. Smart that the biblical theology movement is not a uniquely American phenomenon (so Childs). In Great Britain and on the European continent the same tendencies inherent in the American aspect of the movement were present, although the setting in Europe was different. In any case, the biblical theology movement, international in scope, was broader than the scene in North America, and Barr claims it "can well be seen in the organized study programs of the international ecumenical movement." Even though there was no formal organization of the movement nationally or internationally, and although there existed varieties of emphases among its proponents, there were nevertheless overriding characteristics that were so typical of the movement that they gave a fairly well defined coherence.

Characteristics. Without attempting to be exhaustive, it will be useful to enumerate typical features that are common to the movement in America and Europe. Among those that characterize both its relative coherence and its distinctiveness are the following:

Reaction to Liberalism. The biblical theology movement was a reaction against the study of the Bible in previous liberal theology where the source criticism of the historical-critical method atomized the biblical text into separate sources, frequently consisting of small isolated entities or fragments of documents. These reconstructed sources were placed in new sociological, political, and cultural contexts in the ancient world and interpreted from this newly reconstructed context. A part of this scholarly reconstruction by means of the presuppositions and procedures of the historical-critical method, which reached its total victory over conservative approaches in Europe by the end of the 1900s and in America by the middle of the 1930s, consisted of a redating and reordering of the biblical materials along the lines of naturalistic-evolutionary developmentalism. Joined to this was the axiom that Israel borrowed extensively from the surrounding pagan cultures and religions and that Israelite and NT faith is best understood from the point of view of natural theology. All of this meant a lack of concern regarding the theological interests of the Bible for church, community, and individual. This sterile liberal theology, devoid of meaning for church and life, remained incompatible to significant segments of Christianity, particularly American Protestantism, which had only reluctantly given in to the historical-critical method in the long and devastating fundamentalist-modernist controversy. The biblical theology movement directed its efforts against the extremes of the historical-critical approach to the Bible, while itself remaining faithful to the historical-critical method, its presuppositions, and its procedures. The attempt of the movement was to move beyond the older liberal position within the liberal framework of the study of the Bible.

Alliance with Neo-orthodoxy. The biblical theology movement was fostered by the neo-orthodox reaction to theological liberalism that developed under the influence of Karl Barth and Emil Brunner in Europe and H. Richard Niebuhr and Reinhold Niebuhr in America. The neo-orthodox reaction against Protestant liberalism's reduction of the Christian faith to universal human and religious truths and moral values became a powerful impetus for the biblical theology movement. It must be noted, however, that neo-orthodoxy was not a return to older Protestant orthodoxy, which held that all Scripture was divinely inspired. By and large the biblical theology movement joined the neo-orthodox view of revelation and inspiration. Revelation is essentially God revealing himself in Christ, and Scripture may become a witness to this revelation. The Bible is not the word of God but may become the word of God in its witness to Christ. Particularly useful to the movement was Brunner's view on revelation in which he attacked classical Protestant and American fundamentalists on the one hand and classical liberals on the other. The biblical theology movement could join ranks with the neo-orthodox theology to wage a common battle against both liberalism in theology and fundamentalism among conservative segments in America.

Greek Versus Hebrew Thought. The biblical theology movement constantly opposed the influence of modern philosophy and its constructs as modes to understand biblical thought. It also tended strongly to reject an understanding of the Bible on the basis of Greek thought and its categories. In its rejection of the domineering effect of modern philosophy it shared once again a concern of neo-orthodoxy. The attempt was to understand the Bible outside certain modern or ancient philosophical norms and patterns of thought. It was argued that the Bible must be understood "in its own categories" (James Muilenburg) and the scholar must put himself "within the world of the Bible" (B. W. Anderson). The contrast between Greek and Hebrew thought (T. Boman and others) became rather important. Although the NT was written in Greek, the Hebrew mentality was common to both testaments. The idea of the Hebrew mentality led to significant studies of words in both testaments. The outlines of the Hebraic thought patterns were reflected in the words of the Hebrew language, and this Hebraic thought content was also communicated through the vehicle of language (Greek) of the NT.

The Bible Within Its Culture. Another characteristic of the biblical theology movement was an emphasis on the distinctiveness of the Bible in its environment. G. E. Wright's book *The OT Against Its Environment* (1950) is typical, reflecting in part the concern of the Albright school. The consensus emerged that when there is borrowing or even syncretism, or when there are plain similarities, the differences between the literature of Israel and that of the surrounding nations are far more remarkable than its points of contact. The movement claimed that the most significant things in Israel were not the things it held in common with its neighbors but the things where it differed from them. When the Bible was compared with other contemporary cultures and religions, its uniqueness became apparent. Further, this distinctiveness is not a matter of faith but a matter of scientific historical study. The uniqueness of the biblical faith was determined by historical study and subject to its norms.

Biblical Unity. A concomitant aspect of the distinctiveness of the Bible is its unity, particularly the unity of both testaments. "The attempt to deal with both testaments in a unified way came as a protest against the tendency of increased specialization which had characterized American and British scholarship in the preceding generation" (Childs, p. 36). The biblical theology movement rejected allegory, typology, and Christology as modes of unity between the testaments. The unity of the Bible was unity in diversity, such as "unity of Divine revelation given in the context of history and through the medium of human personality" (H. H. Rowley), unity of purpose, covenant relation, and divine revelation (Muilenburg), or simply a "higher unity" (R. C. Dentan) or a "kerygmatic unity" (J. S. Glenn). There were others who suggested a fundamental unity in history.

Revelation in History. One of the major tenets of the biblical theology movement was the concept of divine revelation in history. "It provided the key to unlock the Bible for a modern generation and at the same time to understand it theologically" (Childs, 39). The emphasis on revelation in history was used to attack both the conservative position, which holds that the Bible contains eternal truths and serves as a deposit of right doctrine, and the liberal position, which claims that the Bible contains a process of evolving religious discovery or simply progressive revelation. The emphasis on revelation stressed the divine self-disclosure and shifted the content away from propositional revelation and doctrine to the neo-orthodox concept of encounter without propositional content. The corresponding emphasis on history meant that the revelational encounter in history provided the bridge of the gap between past and present in that Israel's history became the church's history and subsequently our modern history. In the church's liturgy the believer and the community of faith participate in the same redemptive event by means of recital.

Decline and Evaluation. The biblical theology movement flourished for about a generation, from *ca.* 1945 to 1965. Childs sees its demise as a major force in American theology in the early 1960s. He is supported by Barr. Against this position it is held that "biblical theology is not a movement or a brand of theology but simply an enlargement of the dimensions of biblical science" (Smart, 11) which is continuing to function on an international scale. Childs appears to have overstated the case in claiming the death of the American biblical theology movement in 1963, but has been correct in his description of the characteristics of the movement as a coherent force within twentieth century liberal theology. By 1969 such a prominent member of the movement as G. E. Wright appears to have moved from his earlier position supporting a God who acts in history.

There is no easy way of evaluating and assessing the biblical theology movement because it is part of a trend in modern liberal theology and in part an overlapping with the neo-orthodox movement in our century. The following features may serve as major points of issue that are called for in an assessment of the movement:

The Problem of Hermeneutics. The issue of the adequacy of biblical interpretation within the framework of the historical-critical method remained unresolved. The theologians of the biblical theology movement remained with both feet planted in the historical-critical method. They affirmed the modern world view with its secular understanding of the spatiotemporal world process, i.e., the world of history and of nature. While the movement was critical of its forefathers in the liberal tradition of theology on a number of points as noted above, in a major sense the members of the biblical theology movement continued the liberal tradition. The secular-scientific (and liberal) understanding of the origin and development of the world along the evolutionary Darwinian model was accepted as axiomatic, and the liberal understanding of the movement of history along general historicist lines was not radically questioned. Onto the contemporary scientific understanding of both nature and history theologians of the biblical theology movement attempted to graft the biblical understanding of God as Creator and Lord who is dynamically active in the process of history (G. E. Wright). This meshing of a "secular" or "atheistic" (A. Schlatter) historical-critical method and a naturalistic-evolutionary world view with the God of the Bible who gives meaning and coherence to this world in his personal acts in history was "at best only an uneasy dualism" (Gilkey, 91). Childs notes incisively that "the historical-critical method is an inadequate method of studying the Bible as the Scriptures of the church," setting up "an iron curtain between the past and the present" (Childs, 141–42).

The Issue of "What It Meant" and "What It Means." The biblical theology movement attempted to put aside the dichotomy between the past and the present, the historical-critical and theological study of the Bible, or the descriptive and the normative approach to the Bible. The interest in the theological dimension of the Bible was of major concern. Nevertheless, the distinction of "what it meant" as that which is descriptive, objective, and scientific as compared to "what it means" as that which is theological and normative (see K. Stendahl) put a wedge between what the movement attempted to overcome. While Stendahl's distinction of "what it meant" and "what it means" remains highly debated (see Hasel, *OT Theology,* 35–75), it struck a blow at the heart of the movement.

The Problem of the Bible. Among the unresolved problems of the biblical theology movement is that of the Bible as a "fully human book and yet as the vehicle for the Divine Word" (Childs, 51). No consensus ever emerged whether the element of revelation claimed for the Bible lay *in* the text, *behind* the text, in text *and* event, or in some other mode. Likewise, the modes of unity within the testaments and between the testaments as expounded by such leaders as G. E. Wright, H. H. Rowley, O. Cullmann, R. C. Dentan, F. V. Filson, and others (see Hasel, *NT Theology,* 140–203) did not lead to a consensus.

The Concept of Revelation in History. The issue of history as the locus of divine revelation turned out to be ill-defined and drew heavy attack from several scholars (among them L. Gilkey, W. King, and J. Barr). Among the ambiguities of the concept of revelation in history are those related to the nature of the revelatory events, the sense of history, the relation between revelation and history as well as history and interpretation. Over against these ambiguities from the perspective of the modern historical-critical school of thought, conservative scholars have tended to base their case on the formal statements in Scripture about Scripture itself. In the last analysis history cannot be the authenticating factor of revelation, but the biblical revelation itself is self-authenticating. The concept of revelation in history as an alternative to propositional revelation on the one hand or general revelation on the other did not prove successful. The more recent attempt to replace revelation in history with the view that the OT is "story rather than history" (Barr) does not overcome the ambiguities of history but merely replaces them with those connected with story. Biblical revelation carries within itself its own validation by enabling the recipient of revelation to grasp the content of revelation and to be grasped by the truth of revelation. Due to the fact that biblical revelation is self-authenticating, there can be no external proofs that stand as judges over the revelation of the Bible.

In short, the biblical theology movement was a major attempt for a full generation in the twentieth century to correct liberal theology from within itself. It did not succeed because it ultimately remained a captive of the basic modes, thought patterns, presuppositions, and methods of liberal theology itself. It provided, therefore, an additional impetus to more recent attempts that show the basic method of liberalism, i.e., the historical-critical method, as bankrupt (W. Wink) or announce its end (G. Maier) and seek for new methods of the study of the Bible and its theology whether it be a theological-historical method (G. F. Hasel) or structuralism (D. Patte).

G. F. Hasel

Bibliography. D. L. Baker, *Two Testaments: One Bible;* J. Barr, *IDB* Supplement, 104–11; B. S. Childs, *Biblical Theology in Crisis;* L. Gilkey, *Naming the Whirlwind* and "Cosmology, Ontology, and the Travail of Biblical Language," *JR* 41:194–205; G. F. Hasel, *NT Theology: Basic Issues in the Current Debate* and *OT Theology: Basic Issues in the Current Debate;* G. Maier, *The End of the Historical-Critical Method;* J. D. Smart, *The Past, Present, and Future of Biblical Theology;* D. Patte, *What Is Structuralism?* K. Stendahl, *IDB,* I, 418–32; W. Wink, *The Bible in Human Transformation: Toward a New Paradigm for Bible Study.*

Biblicism, Bibliolatry. Two closely related terms most frequently used pejoratively of strong attachment to the Bible as the objectively authoritative word of God. The former refers primarily to an excessively literal method of interpretation. It emphasizes individual words, rejects any form of the historical-critical method, and frequently employs some form of free association or taking verses out of their context to prove a point (hence, proof texts). Some evangelicals may use biblicism to indicate their commitment to the absolute authority of the Bible in all matters of faith and practice.

"Bibliolatry" implies that the Bible is being turned into an idol. It is used to castigate those suspected of placing too high a value on the Bible, particularly when interpreted literally, by suggesting they have made it an object of worship.

J. J. Scott, Jr.

Binding and Loosing. These are technical terms for the exercise of disciplinary authority bestowed by Christ in conjunction with the keys of the kingdom, first to Peter in Matt. 16:19, then to all the disciples in 18:18. This does not mean that they are empowered to hand down decisions in matters of conduct; that is, in prohibiting or permitting specific duties or moral functions.

What is implied is the authority to exclude from, as well as to reinstate in, the community of believers. Although the equivalent Greek verbs *deō* and *lyō* do not bear this technical sense in themselves, they are translations from the Aramaic *'āsar* and *šĕrā',* which represent the Jewish formula for excommunication and reinstatement. It is to be noted, however, that binding and loosing in Judaism also mean "to prohibit" and "to permit" in matters of casuistry.

Related to the Matthean sense of binding and loosing is John 20:23. Exclusion from the community is always due to some offense and, therefore, presupposes the retaining of sins, while readmission includes the forgiveness of sins.

This understanding of binding and loosing is found among the church fathers—Tertullian, Cyprian, and Origen. In the Reformation, Luther likewise interpreted this power as (1) that of retaining and remitting sins, and (2) granted to all Christians to be exercised in preaching and private absolution. The Council of Trent recognized the former but declared that Matt. 18:18 applied only to bishops and priests.

H. C. Waetjen

See also Keys of the Kingdom.

Bibliography. O. Cullmann, *Peter: Disciple—Apostle—Martyr.*

Bioethics. An interdisciplinary branch of ethics in which doctors, philosophers, lawyers, and theologians collaborate to resolve difficult ethical and moral questions raised in the context of modern health care. In one sense bioethics is a very new field, one so new that the term does not appear in any but the most recent dictionaries. In another sense, however, the questions which are the subject of heated debate today are really timeless: What is the nature and value of human life? How are we to understand and respond to human suffering and imperfection? Where there are differences of opinion—e.g., on whether or not to extend routine medical care to handicapped newborns—who decides? Theologians and philosophers? Doctors? The family? The courts? In any event, modern technology and the general secularization of society have made bioethics one very strategic area for thoughtful Christian involvement.

The number of issues in bioethics that are

immediately recognizable as matters of current interest is surprising: abortion, euthanasia, genetic engineering, "test-tube babies," treatment of handicapped newborns, and population control. Other issues lurk just under the surface of popular media attention: the use of "surrogate mothers" who are artificially inseminated and give birth for another individual or couple, sperm banks (including one which carries only the sperm of "geniuses"), fetal experimentation, legal claims of "wrongful birth" (alleging failed contraception—the defense being, in part, that the mother could have aborted), amniocentesis, and cyrogenics (the practice of freezing bodies in the hope that a future "cure" of death will be discovered, enabling them to be brought back to life and health). This article will examine these and other issues and subissues.

James M. Gustafson has observed that Protestant and Catholic ethics have taken rather widely divergent paths. The primary difference, of course, is the *magisterium,* or teaching authority of the Roman Catholic Church, which is foreign to all but the most liturgical Protestants. Protestants stand on *sola Scriptura,* which seems to have been more helpful toward Protestant ethical pronouncements before the dominant social and cultural underpinnings of modern American society lost their vital connection to a Judeo-Christian world view. Gustafson argues persuasively that both Protestants and Catholics would benefit from rapprochement of the two traditions in the context of addressing common ethical concerns. Protestants would bring to such discussions an openness to current problems and issues which allows for fresh and creative ways to counsel and act. Catholics would contribute the riches of centuries of ordered thought on moral and ethical questions. Each would assist the other in identifying its own shortcomings and blindspots; Protestants would be encouraged to avoid the vagueness and relativism which often attend "open-mindedness" and Catholics would be encouraged to go beyond rigid and closed positions to where legitimate reconsideration is possible.

It is precisely this realization of the paramount need to avoid ethical relativism which has most animated evangelical consideration of these issues. Joseph Fletcher's *Situation Ethics: A New Morality* (1966) typified all that evangelicals most feared in liberal Protestant theology and philosophy. "Situation ethics" or "ethics of consequences," as it was sometimes called, was resoundingly condemned by evangelicals of all stripes, including Carl F. H. Henry and other evangelical academicians. Evangelicals and other conservative Christians who affirm the orthodox Christian faith have been correct to attack such obvious affronts to traditional teachings on moral principles and values. Yet the battle has been a long one and the warriors are weak; a new enthusiasm is needed to defend old ground and to respond to the numerous novel issues now under discussion. The challenge, however, remains much the same: to balance that which never changes, about which no compromise is possible, with a fresh and Spirit-filled willingness to identify with and help solve problems which oppress people in the trenches of life, where openness and creativity are the order of the day.

Abortion. In order to offer intelligent Christian counsel on bioethical issues it is first necessary to know the factual contexts in which the issues arise. Because abortion is the most widely discussed of the bioethical issues, it is appropriate to begin the inquiry there. It is fair to say, with a few relatively small qualifications, that the Christian position on abortion is to be against it. As Harold O. J. Brown has written, "The overwhelming consensus of the spiritual leaders of Protestantism, from the Reformation to the present, is clearly anti-abortion. There is very little doubt among biblically oriented Protestants that abortion is an attack on the image of God in the developing child and is a great evil." Yet, since the Supreme Court discovered a right of abortion in the Constitution in 1973, liberal Protestant voices have managed to leave an impression in the public mind that Christian teaching on abortion is vague and ambiguous. Some Protestants have gone so far as to argue that Christian "compassion" requires that abortion as one way to deal with an unwanted pregnancy must be baptized with Christian approval. Such arguments, while spurious, have had their regrettable effect on evangelicals, including those writing and teaching on abortion and other bioethical issues.

Christian opposition to abortion is based upon belief in the sanctity of human life. Modern secularist views are, to the contrary, viewing human life as only a slightly higher form of animal life—the result of an impersonal evolutionary process without any supernatural element or implications whatever. Thus, the first challenge for the Christian ethicist is to bridge what one writer has described as "a deep philosophical chasm between two radically distinct and diametrically opposed moral visions of humanity." Evangelicals and other conservative Christians must learn to respond with conviction and clarity to the arguments made for liberal abortion policy. Those arguments, and a brief answer to each, might be summarized as follows:

(1) *Argument:* A woman has a right to control

her own body, and this includes the right to choose abortion. *Response:* One's freedom to act extends only to the point that it impinges another's right not to be acted upon. There are two affected by the abortion decision—the unborn child is not a mere appendage of his or her mother. To kill one for the convenience of another is and always has been morally repugnant. (2) *Argument:* Those who oppose abortion are imposing their views or "legislating their morality" in a pluralistic society. *Response:* There is no "values neutrality," a condition this argument appears to assume. It is not a question of *whether* but *whose* morality, or values, will be reflected in the law and public institutions of our pluralistic society. Proposals in this regard, from whomever they might come, must compete in the marketplace of ideas. Moreover, it can be persuasively argued that the closest we could have come to the standard of "values neutrality" would have been for the Supreme Court to have left abortion subject to state regulation, as it was before the 1973 decision. Indeed, in overturning community judgments on abortion in all fifty states, it is the Supreme Court and those supporting their exercise of what Justice White properly termed "raw judicial power" who are imposing their unrepresentative views on a pluralistic populace. (3) *Argument:* What is really important is the quality of life of the mother and of the child to be allowed to be born. A child has a right to be wanted. *Response:* Of all the arguments for abortion this one is clearly the most specious. Consider what is being argued—that someone's precious right to life depends upon being able to meet certain genetic or physical standards or, even worse, that this person is wanted (with whether the child can be afforded often being a part of the latter consideration). Malcolm Muggeridge and other insightful social commentators have effectively shown how readily these same arguments are used to support the killing, by commission or omission, of those who have already been born. There is a "slippery slope," the Muggeridge argument goes, from permissive abortion to active euthanasia, and our society's laws and public values are dangerously tilting in that direction.

Euthanasia. After abortion, the bioethical issue which has gotten the most attention in modern times is euthanasia. Also referred to as "mercy killing," euthanasia enthusiasts and their opponents have inspired minor movements of their own. Parading under banners such as "the right to die" and "death with dignity," proponents of liberalized euthanasia laws have focused their efforts on amending state statutes to redefine "death" and to provide for "living wills." The idea in regard to the latter is to allow individuals to state their preference concerning medical treatment while they are alert and not in a state of medical emergency. The Karen Ann Quinlan case in New Jersey is the primary factual context in which such proposals are considered, which causes many problems for those who remain unpersuaded that this is a desirable way for society to move. As the axiom goes, hard cases make bad law (and bad ethics). The emotional exploitation of hard cases has resulted in our permissive national abortion policy, and opponents of liberalized euthanasia laws contend that we are in danger of the same result on euthanasia.

The traditional Christian view of euthanasia has distinguished between active and passive euthanasia. Active euthanasia, as the name suggests, involves an act to terminate the life of another such as administering a lethal dose of pain killer or sleeping pills. Christian ethicists have traditionally condemned active euthanasia. Passive euthanasia involves the withholding of certain forms of treatment and has generally been upheld as moral so long as the measures not taken were extraordinary and not ordinary ones. This latter distinction has been increasingly a difficult one, due in large measure to the constant improvements in medical technology which make today's extraordinary measures tomorrow's ordinary ones. This difficulty, plus the temptation toward relativism in defining these terms, has led Christian ethicist Paul Ramsey to recommend that they be replaced with what he calls a "medical indications policy." Simply stated, Ramsey would favor medical treatment except where it is medically indicated that death is certain and impending. This policy proceeds out of his conviction that one should always choose life where possible. To choose death, as in the case of suicide or murder, is to throw the gift back into the face of the Giver of life, to reveal a lack of confidence that God will be with us in all the exigencies of life, and to surrender to what the Bible calls "the last enemy." Ramsey quotes with approval a distinction made by Arthur Dyck between choosing death (which is disapproved) and choosing how to live while dying (which is approved). As Dyck puts it, "choosing how to live while dying" stands in diametrical opposition to actions that "have the immediate intention of ending life (one's own or another's)"—only the latter of which "repudiates the meaningfulness and worth of . . . life."

One very tragic application of the arguments for euthanasia or mercy killing has been to handicapped newborns. Baby Boy Doe, born in Bloomington, Indiana, in 1982, is an example.

This child not only had esophagal atresia—a condition which prevented him from taking nourishment orally. He also had Down's Syndrome. The esophagus problem could have been corrected by surgery, but the parents refused consent. They also refused to allow him to be fed intravenously while his fate was being determined by the courts. Three Indiana courts, including the state supreme court, declined to interfere with that decision. Baby Boy Doe was placed in an isolation room where he died without treatment or nourishment, a week after his birth.

Unfortunately, the Baby Doe situation is not an isolated one. George Will, who himself has a son with Down's Syndrome, wrote in response to this incident that "the freedom to kill inconvenient life is being extended, precisely as predicted, beyond fetal life to categories of inconvenient infants, such as Down's Syndrome babies." Although exact numbers are unavailable, every indication is that the practice of infanticide of handicapped newborns is widespread and growing. In a 1973 study published in the *New England Journal of Medicine* it was reported that 14 percent of the babies in the Yale–New Haven Hospital's intensive care unit died from "nontreatment." The current surgeon general, Dr. C. Everett Koop, has written persuasively on this subject, pointing out that "nontreatment" is often a euphemism which includes failure to feed—known in a less complex era as starvation and homicide. A more recent news article reported that at Children's Medical Center in Washington, D.C., for example, the decision not to extend medical treatment is made in about 17 percent of the cases. Whatever the precise statistics are, the philosophical acceptance of infanticide by the medical establishment is a grievous situation which cries for a Christian response.

Here the questions asked at the outset of this article are highly relevant. What is the nature and value of human life? How are we to understand and respond to human suffering and imperfection? Where there are differences of opinion, who decides? Ramsey has said what needs to be said in regard to the latter question: "If physicians are going to play God under the pretense of providing relief for the human condition, let us hope they play God as God plays God. Our God is no respecter of persons of good quality. Nor does he curtail his care for us because our parents are poor or have unhappy marriages, or because we are most in need of help." In stark contrast are the views of much of the present medical establishment and many of society's leading ethicists. Typical of their more "progressive" views is the opinion of one of the physicians at the Yale–New Haven Hospital that to be safe from a medical death warrant a baby must be "lovable." Similar is the argument of Millard S. Everett in his book *Ideals of Life* that "no child should be admitted into the society of the living" who has "any physical or mental defect that would prevent marriage or would make others tolerate his company only from a sense of mercy." To opinions such as these our current policymakers are altogether too open. It is essential that Christians with more traditional views become involved in this vital area of public life, affirming unequivocally the God-given dignity and right to life of each of God's creatures irrespective of "condition of dependency."

Other Issues. Many other bioethical issues might be raised and discussed, but space allows mention of only a few. Each of the following questions is the subject of public controversy.

Does a law prohibiting an individual or couple from paying another woman to have a child for them (after being artificially inseminated with the husband's or another's sperm) violate their "constitutional" right of privacy? Assuming there is no law in a particular state prohibiting a "surrogate mother" to put up her womb for rent, what happens to the baby when the contracting parent or parents decide they do not want the baby after all?

What limitations should be placed on "sperm banks"? This high-tech notion received official chill when it was reported that a couple had bought "genius sperm" and given birth to a healthy daughter. Enthusiasm quickly waned when the couple's prior efforts at child rearing were revealed. Convicted felons, the couple had lost custody of previous children for such things as beating them with a leather strap for homework errors, sending a son to school in his pajamas wearing a sign proclaiming him a bedwetter, and posting "Dummy" on one of their children's foreheads. The sperm bank was rather embarrassed at these disclosures, apparently manifestations of the parents' desire to have smart kids. Now they have a "half genius." Officials at the sperm bank promised to look into the criminal records of applicants for sperm purchase in the future.

What are the appropriate parameters of the regulation of what is commonly referred to as "genetic engineering"? At what point does responsible pursuit of academic/scientific discovery have to encounter legal and ethical limits? Who should decide what those limits should be?

How ethical is the current national policy in regard to population control of Third World countries? At what point do education and encouragement become manipulation and indoctrination?

In this highly controversial area whose values should be reflected in our law and public programs?

Where there is a legitimate shortage of medical equipment or technology, such as is the case in regard to kidney dialysis, who should be allowed the benefit of these scarce resources? When, if ever, should a "cost/benefit analysis" be permitted where human lives are at issue?

What is the extent of medical experimentation on fetuses that survive the disgusting and sickening abortion procedure? What is the best way to monitor and prevent such experimentation in the future?

What is the Christian response to the legal pioneers seeking to create a new "cause of action" for "wrongful life"? Briefly stated, the legal theory depends upon proving that the individual should never have been allowed to be born. Such a suit may be brought by disgruntled parents against a doctor after birth control measures fail or, more alarmingly, by a third party arguing that it would have been in the best interest of the child to have been aborted.

Is submitting to amniocentesis, a medical procedure whereby the possibility of handicaps are identified and where the only prescribed remedy in the event of a positive prognosis is abortion, ever moral? If so, under what circumstances?

How can Christians provide timeless ethical guidance on questions so futuristic (e.g., on cyrogenics, the patenting of crude life forms, or test-tube babies) without appearing hopelessly out of touch with modern realities? Asked another way, what is the wisdom of God which is "the same yesterday, today, and forever" and what is our human finitude in regard to the complex technology available for the delivery of modern health care?

The questions raised are not simple, but there are clear Christian principles which have stood the test of time that are too often ignored when they are publicly debated. The Christian begins by assuming that God the Creator loves his creation. This is what we mean when we contend for the "sanctity of life." It is fair to say that the conflicts in bioethics, at least on the most fundamental level, are a result of the modern rejection of this assumption. Although referred to here as a Christian assumption, it would be more accurate to speak of it as the Judeo-Christian ethic. In its place, sometimes consciously and sometimes unconsciously, a "quality of life ethic" is offered. It is an offer which should and must be rejected, not only by traditional Jews and Christians but by anyone wishing to preserve anything remotely resembling the accumulated moral consensus of Western civilization. The bioethical issues may not be all black and white, but neither, as so many of the modern experts imply, are they all gray. The quality of life ethic, which is little more than warmed-over situation ethics, must be unequivocally rejected by Christians seeking to make a faithful and responsible contribution to bioethics. For too long this field has been dominated by the misplaced compassion and specious arguments of ethical relativists, a situation those who affirm the sanctity of life must now give the highest priority.

C. Horn, III

See also Abortion; Euthanasia; Ethical Systems, Christian; Situation Ethics; Social Ethics.

Bibliography. K. Barth, *Church Dogmatics*, III/4, 397–470; *Bibliography of Bioethics;* H. O. J. Brown, *Death Before Birth; Encyclopedia of Bioethics;* J. M. Gustafson, *Protestant and Roman Catholic Ethics;* M. Scharlemann, *DCE*, 1–3; T. Hilgers, D. Horan, and D. Mall, eds., *New Perspectives on Human Abortion;* D. Horan and M. Delahoyde, eds., *Infanticide and the Handicapped Newborn;* D. Horan and D. Mall, eds., *Death, Dying, and Euthanasia; The Human Life Review;* J. Powell, *Abortion: The Silent Holocaust;* P. Ramsey, *Ethics at the Edge of Life;* C. E. Rice, *The Vanishing Right to Live.*

Birth, New. *See* Regeneration.

Birth of Jesus Christ. Jesus was born in Bethlehem, a small village in the northern part of Judea, about six miles south of Jerusalem. It was known also in the OT as Ephrath, a little place among the clans of Judah which was to produce a ruler in Israel (Mic. 5:2). The prophecy in Micah was well known to be messianic in the first century and was cited to Herod by the chief priests and scribes as pointing to the birthplace of the Messiah (Matt. 2:4–6). A cave beneath the Church of the Nativity in Bethlehem has been held to be the site of his birth for at least fifteen hundred years—perhaps even longer, since Justin Martyr stated in the second century that Joseph "took up his quarters in a certain cave near the village, and while they were there Mary brought forth the Christ" (*Dialogue* 78).

The exact time of his birth is not known. Luke's much disputed statement (2:2) that he was born at the time a census was conducted by Quirinius has received strong support very recently by E. Jerry Vardaman's discovery of micrographic lettering on coins and inscriptions of the time of Christ that state that Quirinius was proconsul of Syria and Cilicia from 11 B.C. until after the death of Herod the Great in 4 B.C. Perhaps a longstanding rejection of Luke's accuracy on this point will now be laid to rest. Confidence in the overall accuracy of Luke in reporting the facts of the birth of Christ was established decades ago by Sir William Ramsay and more recently by I. Howard Marshall and Raymond E. Brown. Papyri from Egypt have shown in three separate instances that a census was conducted every fourteen years in the Roman Empire during this time, and citizens were required to return to their place of birth for enrollment and taxation.

Theologically the advent of Christ marks the beginning of the last stages of God's fulfillment of his promise to Abraham that in his seed God would bless all the nations of the earth (Gen. 12:2; Gal. 3:16). It is in these last days that God has spoken to us in his Son (Heb. 1:2), and thus in the fullness of time God sent forth his Son (Gal. 4:4). He was not only born of woman but of one who had never had sexual union with a man (Matt. 1:18, 25; Luke 1:34). The conception of Jesus was by the Holy Spirit (Luke 1:35; Matt. 1:20) and he was born of a virgin. It should be remembered that the NT does not speak of a "virgin birth" but of a virgin conception. It was the conception that was miraculous, not the birth. Jesus was born like all other human beings are born. The importance of the miraculous conception of Jesus lay in the nature of the incarnation, a theological fact that transcends the understanding of mortal man. It is perhaps because of this that the virgin birth is never again mentioned in the NT outside its narration by Matthew and Luke. It was thus not considered as important a witness to the deity of Jesus in the first century as it has become in modern theology. This is probably due to the fact that by its very nature it could actually be witnessed by only one person, the Virgin Mary, and her testimony would have been considered as suspect to everyone as it was initially to Joseph. She of all people would have had reason to lie if it were not true, stoning by death being the required penalty for adultery.

On the other hand, the resurrection of Christ from the dead is appealed to frequently for confirmation of his deity by NT authors because it was witnessed by hundreds (I Cor. 15:3ff.). It strikes the modern exegete as incredible that neither Mark nor John felt the miraculous nature of the birth of Jesus sufficiently important to their work to include it. But it would be well to remember that Mark demonstrates the deity of Christ rather by his conquest of Satan through exorcising demons and resurrection from the dead, and John dwells on the preincarnate state of the Christ as the Word of God, manifest through his signs. It is the other evidence of his deity that confirms our faith in the miraculous conception of Jesus and not vice versa.

Alarm was unnecessarily felt over the Hebrew term *'almâ* as "young woman" rather than "virgin" in Isa. 7:14. The NT teaching on the virginity of Mary is confirmed independently of the OT prophecies. Furthermore, virtually all modern translations, including the RSV, render Matthew's (1:23) quotation of Isaiah as "virgin." Matthew, it should be remembered, quotes the Greek LXX and not the Hebrew Bible, and the Greek text contains the word "virgin." Why the LXX rendered the Hebrew word by the Greek *parthenos* (virgin) is another matter. Matthew has "virgin" in his quote because it was there in the LXX. In any event, the key word in the passage is probably not virgin but Emmanuel, a word appearing three times in key places in Isaiah (7:14; 8:8, 10). It was the birth of Jesus that brought to the world the meaning of Emmanuel, i.e., "God with us."

All of history was changed by his birth. Since Christ came into the world mankind has known the meaning of perfect love and has witnessed the life of a sinless human being. Those who witnessed that life were transformed, and they in turn altered the history of the world. His name was called Jesus because he would save his people from their sins (Matt. 1:21). J. R. McRay

See also Virgin Birth of Jesus.

Bibliography. R. E. Brown, *The Birth of the Messiah;* T. Boslooper, *The Virgin Birth;* J. Finegan, *The Archeology of the NT;* J. G. Machen, *The Virgin Birth of Christ;* I. H. Marshall, *Theologian and Historian;* J. R. McRay, "The Virgin Birth of Christ," *RQ* 3:61–71; J. Orr, *The Virgin Birth;* W. Ramsay, *Was Christ Born in Bethlehem?* J. T. Willis, "The Meaning of Isaiah 7:14 and Its Application in Matthew 1:23," *RQ* 21:1–18; E. Martin, *The Birth of Christ Recalculated.*

Bishop. One who is an overseer (pastor, shepherd) of the flock of God (the church). In the NT period it appears that the title "bishop" described the function of the presbyter (elder). In Acts 20:17–28 and Titus 1:5–7 these two terms may be interchangeable. The qualifications for the work of a bishop as well as its duties are supplied in I Tim. 3:2 and Titus 1:7. He is to be of wholesome character and a good teacher.

A clear distinction between the office of bishop and presbyter is seen in the letters of Ignatius, himself the sole bishop of Antioch. Written *ca.* 117 they testify to the emergence (at least in one geographical area) of what is often called the monarchical episcopate. Each church had a bishop, who was assisted by several presbyters and deacons. Thus there was a threefold order of ordained ministry. The bishop was seen as the chief celebrant in worship, the chief pastor of the flock, and the chief administrator of the people of God and their possessions. Further to the emergence of the episcopate as distinct from the presbyterate there came a theology of apostolic succession. By *ca.* 150 it was widely held that bishops were the direct successors of the apostles and the chief guardians of the teaching of the church. This particular theology was expanded in later centuries.

The emergence of the office of bishop as distinct from that of presbyter (priest) may be accounted for by identifying sociological pressures inside and outside the churches in the first century, pressures which necessitated leadership by one man (in contrast to leadership by a group of presbyters). Without denying these human realities it is also possible to see this development as part of the will of God and as initiated by the apostles as they came to the end of their ministries.

However we account for the origin of bishops as chief pastors, the historical fact is that they became universal in the church from early times until the sixteenth century. As the church expanded and adopted the geographical divisions of the Roman Empire, bishops became chief pastors of areas containing several or many churches. Those bishops in important cities or with large dioceses were called by such titles as pope, patriarch, metropolitan, and archbishop. To assist diocesan bishops there emerged suffragan, auxiliary, assistant, and coadjutor bishops.

During the Protestant Reformation some of the new churches abandoned the office of bishop, arguing that in the NT there is no distinction between a bishop and a presbyter. This approach has been dominant within Protestantism since that time. However, the Church of England and certain Scandinavian Lutheran churches retained the traditional office of bishop. Thus it is now found in the Roman, Orthodox, Eastern, Anglican, Old Catholic, and some Lutheran churches.

The title "bishop" is used in certain Protestant denominations where there is no claim that the bishops are in the apostolic succession. Here the word means either pastor or chief pastor.

The traditional office of the bishop is understood in the following ways: (1) He has been ordained by other bishops who are themselves in the apostolic succession. He thereby becomes a sign of the unity of the church in space and time. (2) He alone has the right to ordain deacons and presbyters (priests) and to share in the ordination of other bishops. (3) He is the chief pastor, celebrant, and administrator of the diocese and as such he may delegate these duties to others.

The Roman and Orthodox churches require bishops to be celibate. As signs of his office a bishop wears both a pectoral cross and an episcopal ring and he carries a pastoral staff. The method of choosing bishops varies from the democratic vote of the representatives of a diocese (as in parts of Anglicanism) to the decision of the pope (in Roman Catholicism). P. Toon

See also Church Officers; Elder.

Bibliography. R. E. Brown, *Priest and Bishop;* K. Rahner and J. Ratzinger, *The Episcopate and the Primacy;* WCC Faith and Order Paper 102, *Episkope and Episcopate;* B. Cooke, *Ministry of Word and Sacrament;* R. P. Johnson, *The Bishop in the Church;* W. Telfer, *The Office of a Bishop.*

Black Theology. The definition advanced by James Cone necessitates viewing black theology in conjunction with black history and black power. "Black history is recovering a past deliberately destroyed by slave masters, an attempt to revive old survival symbols and create new ones. Black power is an attempt to shape our present economic, social and political existence according to those actions that destroy the oppressor's hold on black flesh. Black theology places our *past* and *present* actions toward black liberation in a theological context, seeking to destroy alien gods and to create value-structures according to the God of black freedom" ("Black Theology and Black Liberation," 1085). While there are many currents in the modern discipline of black theology, most proponents affirm Cone's contention that its essential tasks are to form a new understanding of black dignity among black people and to oppose and eventually destroy white racism. Most spokespersons also analyze the situation of black persons in the light of God's revelation in Jesus Christ and seek to demonstrate the biblical character of resultant conclusions.

Thus, black theology is engaged theology, committed to the amelioration of the condition of black people and consciously locked in battle with white racism. The latter is regularly considered to be a religion and is termed variously "white religion," "whitianity," and "Christianity" (in contrast to true Christianity). G. S. Wilmore's historical research indicates that from the earliest period of blacks in America, deliberate distortions of Christianity were perpetrated so that Christianity would not change the existing relationship between master and slave but would rather lend sanction to the status quo. The white anthropologist J. Oliver Buswell, III, documents erroneous interpretations by which slavery and subsequently discrimination of all sorts were justified.

Rationale. Beginning with the generally accepted principle that the God of Israel and the church act in history to effect the salvation of men and women, black theologians contend that to view salvation as having an exclusively "spiritual" connotation is an irresponsible truncation of its meaning; rather, inherent in the concept are also economic, political, and social dimensions. Attention is directed to the Exodus event in which these dimensions are clearly evident. The conclusion is drawn that God's election of his people and his liberation of them from a variety of conditions of bondage are inextricably related. An additional conclusion is that God is not neutral; on the contrary, Cone quotes Karl Barth's deduction: "In the relations and events in the life of his people, God always takes his stand unconditionally and passionately on this side alone; against those who already enjoy right and privilege and on behalf of those who are denied it and deprived of it" (*Black Theology and Black Power,* 45; cf. Cone's reference at this juncture to Pss. 10:34; 72:12).

Regarding the NT material, a case is made for Jesus' intentional identification with the same categories of individuals based both upon the accusations of his enemies (Matt. 11:19) and upon his own teaching. Luke 4:18–19 functions as the primary text for black theology (and for most theologies of liberation), for here it is perceived that Jesus' work is essentially one of liberation.

Both testaments, therefore, are viewed as witnessing to the fact that recognition of God's liberating activity is integral to an understanding of his dealing with his people. Cone and others then conclude that, given this unmistakable commitment to the poor and the oppressed, it may be assumed that in the twentieth century Christ's radical identification would be with blackness, for just as identification with Israel clearly spoke to God's taking the side of the weak and the oppressed in the ancient world, so identification with blackness would be the most effective and easily discerned symbol of that choice in contemporary American society. It follows that obedience to God in the present requires of Christians a similar identification with the poor and oppressed, i.e., with blackness. Cone consequently defines heresy as "any activity or teaching that denies the Lordship of Christ or a word that refuses to acknowledge his liberating presence in the struggle for freedom. Heresy is the refusal to speak the truth in light of the One who is the Truth" (*God of the Oppressed,* 36).

Origin. Black theology's date of origin and its founder are vigorously debated. Among his contemporaries James Cone is *primus inter pares* due to the number of his publications and, more importantly, because they contain near normative formulations of the discipline. However, not everyone would grant him the status of originator. William Jones, for example, who observes that one's identification of a founder has unmistakable implications for one's definition of black theology, commends the adoption of 1964, the year of the publication of *Black Religion,* as an expedient date of origin and, by implication, Joseph Washington—its author—as founder. With the presence of the adjective "black" in his title Washington meets Jones's criterion of indicating "a self-conscious effort to express [his] position in determined opposition to its complement, an alleged white theology, . . . the precondition for undertaking a black theology [being] the prior conclusion that an unacknowledged white theology exists" ("Toward an Interim Assessment of Black Theology," 514).

In the opinion of the present writer James Cone should indeed be considered the originator of the contemporary expression of black theology. A series of factors combined to inspire him and to create a context of receptivity for his theological program. Significant were the collapse of colonialism and the rise of the Third World, the impact upon the black community of returning black soldiers at the conclusion of World War II manifesting increasing unwillingness to accept prejudicial treatment, and the influence of the Black Muslim movement with its emphasis upon black pride. Cone further maintains that this crucial reversal in attitude can also be explained in terms of existential philosophy, i.e., that blacks' reaction to the absurdity of the denial of equality in a nation claiming to be democratic was to reject that denial and to commence the struggle for black freedom. The culmination and summary of these aspects is black power, a necessary prerequisite for the emergence of black theology.

The concepts central to black theology, however, have long been articulated by a host of witnesses, among whom are Marcus Garvey, active and highly influential in the period 1916–27 as an advocate of black pride, black self-determination, black capitalism and economic development, a black church and a black Christ; Nat Turner, leader of a slave rebellion in 1828 and honored by Cone and others not for his bloody uprising but for his perception of God as liberator (not unlike the religious mystics who led peasant revolts in medieval Europe); additional unnamed black religious leaders who, inspired by insights that have never been completely absent in the black community throughout all its generations, kept alive the message of liberation which today is again being declared.

Black Theology in Dialogue. One external debate in which black theologians are involved is the issue: Is black theology *bona fide* theology? Whether prompted by benign or malicious intent, the questioner, most frequently a white Christian, and the black respondent have difficulty in establishing mutually acceptable evaluative criteria for this discipline which incorporates at many points an attack upon the former's theological position.

An equally lively exchange with potential for reciprocal benefit is under way between black theologians and representatives of the theology of hope. Internal dialogue is likewise extensive. In *Liberation and Reconciliation: A Black Theology,* J. Deotis Roberts, although uncompromisingly committed to liberation for black people, insists that to remain Christian, black theology also "must speak of reconciliation that brings black men together and of reconciliation that brings black and white men together" (152). To do otherwise is to move, perhaps unwittingly, from black Christian theology to "the religion of Black Power." Another critic, Major Jones, detects in Cone and others a tendency toward "theological justification for views akin to black racism." In the development of his own position Jones acknowledges indebtedness to the nonviolence of Martin Luther King, Jr.

Other spokespersons, focusing upon Cone's theological method, question particularly his dependence upon German abstract theology, and conclude that "linguistically and conceptually [his program indicates withdrawal] from the cultural and symbolic goal of its *raison d'être,* the black experience" (review of *God of the Oppressed* by Hycel B. Taylor in *Union Seminary Quarterly Review,* Summer, 1976).

William Jones of Yale criticizes not only Cone but Albert Cleague, Major Jones, Deotis Roberts, and Joseph Washington as well, faulting them individually and as a group on theodicy, in his opinion the central question for black and for Jew alike. He declares, e.g., that "given [Washington's] description of God's sovereignty over human history and his activity within it, God's malice for blacks seems the most probable explanation of black suffering" (*Is God a White Racist?* 79). Maintaining that attempts of the leading black theologians to reconcile the experience of oppression with the premise of God's benevolence are not convincing, Jones reconstructs black theology to provide a new foundation, termed by him humanocentric theism, as alternative to the benevolence-centered theism which underlies the work of others. Jones's position seeks to recognize the functional ultimacy of man by transferring to man "areas of control and some of the primary functions that previous theological traditions reserved for God alone" (187). It may be surmised that few black theologians will decide to trust Jones's fundamentally humanistic perspective.

In a major review of Cone's initial work (*Union Seminary Quarterly Review,* Summer, 1970) the Howard scholar Cain Felder recognizes Cone's significant contributions to black theology. At one point Felder notes his equivocal attitude toward violence as an option in the liberation struggle. This moderate position is dismissed by Felder in the light of the example of Jesus who, he maintains, was a first century zealot (denied by most NT scholars). Felder adds that violence should be espoused because of the "growing number of disillusioned blacks who believe that white America is beyond salvation and must, with her church, be destroyed now."

Appraisal. Black theology is regarded as one of the very few authentically indigenous North American theological movements. In the future it will undergo additional revision as the result of continuing internal dialogue and continuing research into such areas as its African roots. Confrontation with adversaries will also have an impact on it. Alteration will likewise come from dialogue with other liberation movements (feminist theology, Latin American theology of liberation, African theology), which after having received inspiration and strategy from black theology now in turn influence it from their respective positions.

The potential for good for the entire church is present if it joins in this dialogue. "If the major portion of the Bible is written by those who, in their own social situation, are the powerless and oppressed, if it is their perspective on the activity of God that is given us by Scripture, then surely a more accurate interpretation of the biblical word can be gained by those who currently stand in a parallel place in our own societies than by those who are powerful" (J. and C. González, *Liberation Preaching,* 16). All parties may discover that "the Lord has more light and truth to break forth out of his holy Word." It is conceivable that black theology will serve as an important catalyst in the effecting of this wider dialogue (note B. Reist's exploration of a mutual openness in *Theology in Red, White, and Black*).

The primary focus of black theology remains, however, a biblically mandated message of liberation. While acknowledging that blacks as well as whites are sinners, in the contemporary social setting it is particularly the white who must be called to a repentance that not only will mean a relinquishing of racial intolerance but will result in identification with blackness. And in Cone's words, "Being black in America has very little to do with skin color. To be black means that your heart, your soul, your mind, and your body are where the dispossessed are" (*Black Theology and Black Power,* 151). V. CRUZ

Bibliography. J. O. Buswell, III, *Slavery, Segregation and Scripture;* J. Cone, *Black Theology and Black Power, God of the Oppressed,* and "Black Theology and Black Liberation," *CCen,* Sept. 16, 1970; J. and C. González, *Liberation Preaching;* M. Jones, *Black Awareness: A Theology of Hope;* W. Jones, *Is God a White Racist?* and "Toward an Interim Assessment of Black Theology," *CCen,* May 3, 1972; B. Reist, *Theology in Red, White, and Black;* J. D. Roberts, *Liberation and Reconciliation;* J. Washington, *Black Religion;* G. S. Wilmore, *Black Religion and Black Radicalism;* G. S. Wilmore and J. Cone, eds., *Black Theology, A Documentary History 1966–1979;* C. Smalley and R. Behan, *What Color Is Your God?* T. Skinner, *How Black Is the Gospel?* W. H. Bentley, *The Relevance of a Black Evangelical Theology for American Theology;* A. Evans, *Biblical Theology and the Black Experience.*

Blasphemy. In general the word means simply slander or insult and includes any action (e.g., a gesture) as well as any word that devalues another person or being, living or dead. This general secular idea was made more specific in religious contexts, where blasphemy means to insult, mock, or doubt the power of a god.

In the OT it is always this religious use that is intended. Blasphemy is the direct or indirect detracting from the glory and honor of God and therefore the opposite of praising or blessing God. A Hebrew could blaspheme God directly by insulting "the Name" or indirectly by flaunting God's law (Num. 15:30), but in either case blasphemy, as idolatry (which was the ultimate blasphemy, Isa. 65:7; 66:3; Ezek. 20:27), was punishable by death by stoning (Lev. 24:10–23; I Kings 21:9–10). Generally, of course, it is pagans who have never experienced the God of Israel who blaspheme, although Israel's failures may incite them to it (II Sam. 12:14). The Assyrians blasphemed the Lord by equating him with the gods of other states; they received a sentence of doom (II Kings 19:4, 6, 22; Isa. 37:6, 23). The Babylonians mocked God in the exile of Israel (Isa. 52:5), when Edom and other enemies also mocked the forlorn state of the nation (Ezek. 35:12; Ps. 44:14; 74:10, 18; I Macc. 2:6).

In the NT blasphemy occurs in its wider Greek meaning as well as its specifically religious sense, for people are slandered, not just God (Rom. 3:8; I Cor. 10:30; Eph. 4:31; Titus 3:2). In fact, such slander and abusive language was a danger to Christians; it had been their preconversion habit and was the example of their culture. They were tempted to use it when falling back into old habits of speech. This is roundly condemned (Mark 7:22; cf. Eph. 4:31; Titus 3:2). Men, as James would argue (James 3:1–12), are made in God's image: to insult even the vilest person while claiming to bless God is inconsistent and evil. All people represent God to some degree.

It is also evil to mock angelic or demonic powers. The devil himself is not to be the object of insult. The NT looks on such mockery as gross presumption, a pride based on a false claim to knowledge and power (Jude 8–10; II Pet. 2:10–12).

The most common form of blasphemy in the NT, however, is blasphemy of God. In some cases God is directly insulted (Rev. 13:6; 16:9), while in others his word is mocked (Titus 2:5). In still others his revelation and its bearer are derided (Moses in Acts 6:11; Paul in I Cor. 4:12). But it is with respect to Jesus that the word is mainly used. When Jesus forgave sins (Mark 2:7) he was accused of blasphemy on the grounds that he, being a man, made himself God (John 10:33–36). The same charge was the basis of his condemnation at his trial (Mark 14:61–64), for the Sanhedrin judged his claim to be Christ a mockery of God. The real blasphemy to the NT writers was the mockery of Jesus (Matt. 27:39; Mark 15:29; Luke 23:39), which continues in the persecutors of the church who mock the baptismal vow "Jesus is Lord" (James 2:7) or try to force Christians to curse it (cf. Acts 26:11). Christians themselves expected to be maligned (I Cor. 4:13; I Tim. 1:13; Rev. 2:9; cf. Acts 13:45; 18:6), but they themselves could blaspheme not just by apostasy, but also by false doctrine (Rom. 3:8; II Pet. 2:2) or unloving actions which degrade the name of Christ (Rom. 2:24; Titus 2:5).

While blasphemy is forgivable (Mark 3:28–29; Matt. 12:32), it is serious. Without repentance one has no choice but to turn the guilty person over to Satan (probably expecting his death) so that he will be taught the necessary lesson (I Tim. 1:20). P. H. DAVIDS

Bibliography. H. W. Beyer, *TDNT,* I, 621–25; H. Wahrisch, C. Brown, and W. Mundle, *NIDNTT,* III, 340–47.

Blasphemy Against the Holy Spirit. A sin mentioned only in Mark 3:28–29; Luke 12:10; Matt. 12:31. The context in Mark makes it clear that this sin is not just any serious moral failure, or persistence in sin, or insulting or rejecting Jesus or God due to ignorance or rebellion: it is the willful and conscious rejection of God's activity and its attribution to the devil. The Pharisees saw a notable miracle and heard Jesus' own teaching, but they chose darkness (John 3:19) and called good evil (Isa. 5:20) by attributing the miracle to the devil. It is the enlightened, willful, high-handed nature of such a sin that makes it unforgivable (not forgiven at death, as the Jews thought, but punished through eternity). First John 5:16 speaks of a sin unto death and Heb. 6:4–6 speaks of those no agreement can bring to repentance: that is this type of sin. The person is not ignorant, but chooses to reject God, to call God the devil. There is nothing more that can be said to such a person, nor any miracle or evidence that would help him. By definition, then, no one who worries over committing this sin could have done it, for it rules out a troubled conscience. Instead it stands as a severe warning to those who know God's truth not to turn from it or to abandon their faith. P. H. Davids

See also Sin unto Death; Eternal Sin.

Bless, Blessed, Blessing. ***Bless.*** The verbs so translated in the OT and the NT respectively are *bārak* and *eulogeō*. Both have the meaning "to pronounce blessed," but the primary meaning of the former is to convey a gift by a potent utterance (Gen. 1:22–28). When one is said to bless God, the reference is to praise and thanksgiving, such blessing being always preceded by some realization of the divine blessing which prompts it (Ps. 145:1–2; Neh. 9:5; Luke 1:64, RV; 24:53). In blessing man, God bestows good, at the time or later. This takes various forms, the direction of the blessing being sometimes indicated by a synonym (Gen. 12:2; Num. 6:23; Ps. 28:9). It includes both temporal and spiritual well-being in the OT (Gen. 26:12–13; I Chr. 4:10), but is more particularly associated with spiritual benefit in the NT (Acts 3:26; Eph. 1:3; Gal. 3:8–9).

In some passages, where the sense of the word is either to express a wish or to make a prophetic utterance, men are said to bless their fellows (Gen. 24:60; 27:4; 48:15). In a number of instances, such as the blessing of bread, thanksgiving is implied (Mark 6:41; 8:7; Matt. 26:26; I Cor. 14:16).

Blessed. *Bārûk* usually applies to God in the OT (Gen. 9:26; 24:27; I Sam. 25:32). Sometimes it describes men as blessed of God (Gen. 24:13; 26:29; I Sam.15:13). *Eulogētos* is used only of God and Christ in the NT (Luke 1:68; II Cor. 1:2; Eph. 1:3). On the other hand, *'ašĕrê* and *makarios* always refer to men, or to a state. The former indicates earthly blessing (I Kings 10:8), a state in which blessing is possessed (Isa. 56:2) and is the result of God's gracious favor (Ps. 32:1–2; 65:4; 94:12; 112:1). With few exceptions the word stands for spiritual blessing in the NT. In addition to the eight beatitudes (Matt. 5:3–10), the frequent occurrence of single sayings in this form shows the prominence of the thought of blessedness in the teaching of Jesus (Matt. 11:6; 13:16; 16:17; Luke 11:28; 12:37; John 13:17, RV; 20:29).

Blessing. *Bĕrākâ* is opposed to the divine curse (Deut. 23:5; 28:2; 33:23). Sometimes it represents the good ensured by God's favor (Gen. 28:4; 45:25; Exod. 32:29). *Eulogia*, the parallel term in the NT, generally means saving blessing (Eph. 1:3; I Pet. 3:9). Two exceptions occur in Hebrews (Heb. 6:7; 12:17). Both words may also express the word of blessing pronounced by men or the good designated (Gen. 27:12, 35–36; II Chr. 5:1; James 3:10; Gen. 33:11; I Sam. 25:27; II Cor. 9:5).

W. J. Cameron and G. W. Knight, III

See also Benediction.

Bibliography. J. N. Oswalt, *TWOT*, I, 132–33; H. W. Beyer, *TDNT*, II, 754ff.; V. P. Hamilton, *TWOT*, I, 80–81; F. Hauck and G. Bertram, *TDNT*, IV, 362–70; H. G. Link and U. Becker, *NIDNTT*, I, 206ff.; A. C. Myers, *ISBE* (rev.), I, 523–24; J. Jeremias, *The Eucharist Words of Jesus;* D. Daube, *Studies in Biblical Law.*

Blood. The main question here is, Does the blood of Christ mean the death of Christ or the life of Christ released from the body? The second meaning would not normally occur to us, but some scholars hold that this is the view of the OT and that it is taken over into the NT.

The view is based on such passages as Lev. 17:11: "For the life of the flesh is in the blood; and I have given it for you upon the altar to make atonement for your souls; for it is the blood that makes atonement, by reason of the life." Sometimes it is said that "the blood is the life" (Deut. 12:23; cf. Gen. 9:4). It is claimed that such passages show that the Hebrews thought of life as somehow resident in the blood. When in the offering of sacrifice the blood of an animal was presented in the prescribed way, it is held that this means that the life of the animal, now released from the body, was presented to God. It was unfortunate for the animal that it died in the process, but that is seen as incidental. The important thing is the freeing of life from the bonds of the body and its presentation to God.

It is contended that when we read in the NT of the blood of Christ, we should understand that Christ's life was set free for a higher purpose, that of bringing salvation. It is not easy to see what this view means. To say that we are saved by the death of Christ is meaningful, but it is not at all obvious how the life of Christ released from the body saves us. If that was the way of it, why did that life come to be in a body in the first place?

Despite the confident claims of those who put it forward, the view that this gives of the OT concept of sacrifice is not easy to sustain. The OT employs the word *dām,* "blood," 362 times, of which 203 refer to death and violence, 103 to the blood of sacrifices, 7 connect life and blood, with which we should link 17 which refer to eating meat with blood (as Lev. 17:14). The remaining 32 examples do not bear on our problem. These numbers show that when a Hebrew heard the word "blood," the most likely association it would arouse would be "death."

No evidence is brought forward to prove that in sacrifice the important idea is the presentation of life. This is held to be obvious once the link between life and blood is pointed out. But that link means that there is a close connection between life and blood: when the blood is shed, the life is ended. However, the ceremonial manipulation of the blood in sacrifice seems to be the ritual presentation before God of the evidence that a death has taken place in obedience to his command. The words certainly do not unambiguously support the view that life is being released and presented to God.

In the OT in the overwhelming majority of cases blood means death. The passages that link it with life are exceptional. Again, the universal OT view is that sin is so serious that it is punished by death: "The soul that sins shall die" (Ezek. 18:20). The shedding of blood in the sacrifices is most naturally understood as connected with this penalty. Indeed, most of the accounts of the sacrifices include some mention of the death of the victim while they say nothing about its life (e.g., Lev. 1:5). Again, to speak of the life as continuing to exist after the slaying of the animal is to overlook the strong Hebrew connection of life with the body. Man's life after death means the resurrection of the body, not the immortality of the soul. If a man's life was not thought of apart from the body, it is not easy to see a reason for holding that an animal's life was set free when released from the body. Again, where atonement is brought about by means other than blood, it is never by life, though it may be by death, as when Phinehas slew Zimri and Cozbi (Num. 25:13) or when David delivered seven descendants of Saul to be hanged (II Sam. 21:3ff.). The OT evidence is that blood means death, in the sacrifices as elsewhere.

As in the OT, the largest group in the ninety-eight occurrences of the word in the NT is that for death by violence (twenty-five times). The blood of animal sacrifices (twelve times) will also point to death if our conclusions from the OT are valid.

Some of the references to the blood of Christ must signify his death. Thus Col. 1:20 refers to "the blood of his cross." Little blood was shed in crucifixion, so that must mean simply his death. Again, Paul speaks of being "justified by his blood" and "saved by him from the wrath of God," statements parallel to "reconciled to God by the death of his Son" and "saved by his life" (Rom. 5:9–10). There are references to death in the immediate context and this is surely the force of "blood" also. Other passages where "blood" plainly means the death of Christ include John 6:53–56 (note the separation of flesh and blood); Acts 5:28; Eph. 2:13; I John 5:6; Rev. 1:5; 19:13.

The references to Christ's blood as a sacrifice (Rom. 3:25, etc.) also point to death, as Heb. 9:14–15 shows. The context indicates that sacrifice is in mind, but it goes on to refer to death.

The witness of Scripture is clear. Only by a particular interpretation of a few passages can a case be made for thinking that blood means life. When evidence is surveyed as a whole, there is no reasonable doubt that blood points, not to life set free, but to life given up in death. References to blood are a vivid way of saying that we owe our salvation to the death of Christ. L. MORRIS

See also ATONEMENT; BLOOD, SACRIFICIAL ASPECTS OF; OFFERINGS AND SACRIFICES IN BIBLE TIMES.

Bibliography. J. Behm, *TDNT,* I, 172–77; S. C. Gayford, *Sacrifice and Priesthood;* B. Kedar-Kopfstein, *TDOT,* III, 234–50; L. Morris, *The Apostolic Preaching of the Cross,* ch. 3; A. M. Stibbs, *The Meaning of the Word "Blood" in Scripture;* F. J. Taylor, *RTWB,* 33–34; V. Taylor, *Jesus and His Sacrifice;* H. C. Trumbull, *The Blood Covenant.*

Blood, Avenger of. *See* AVENGER OF BLOOD.

Blood, Sacrificial Aspects of. Lev. 17:11 is the OT's central statement about the significance of blood in the sacrificial system, and what it asserts remains true throughout the regulations for individual sacrifices. (1) The blood of sacrifice is a divine provision: "I have given it to you." This counters any theory of sacrifice which sees in it a human gift designed to attract or excite divine favor. (2) The use of blood in sacrifice is a price-paying act: to make atonement. The meaning of blood must suit the function it fulfills. The verb (*kipper*) takes its meaning from the related noun (*kōper*), "redemption price" (cf. Exod. 21:30; 30:12; Job 33:24; etc.). It means to pay whatever price matches (and cancels) the offense. If the blood pays the price, then its significance is not, as many hold, life released from the flesh and made available to become somehow a gift to God, but life forfeited or laid down in payment for sin. "The life of the flesh is in the blood" in the ordinary sense that flesh and blood united make a living being or a living creature, while the separation of blood from flesh is the death of the creature. Thus, in biblical secular usage to shed blood is to kill (cf. Gen. 9:6). (3) The shedding of the blood of sacrifice is a substitutionary act: the last clause of Lev. 17:11 should be translated either the blood "makes atonement at the cost of the life" (i.e., the animal's life), or "makes atonement in the place of the life" (i.e., the sinner's life). For the use of the Hebrew preposition *bĕ* of price paying, see I Kings 2:23; Prov. 7:23; of exact equivalence or substitution, see Deut. 19:21; II Sam. 14:7. Heb. 9:11–18 confirms in the NT the symbolism of blood as death and applies Lev. 17:11 to the sacrifice of the Lord Jesus Christ.

J. A. Motyer

See also Blood; Atonement; Offerings and Sacrifices in Bible Times.

Bibliography. G. J. Wenham, *The Book of Leviticus;* L. Morris, *The Apostolic Preaching of the Cross;* J. A. Motyer, "Priestly Sacrifices in the OT," in *Eucharistic Sacrifice,* ed. J. I. Packer.

Boasting. Jer. 9:23–24 epitomizes the biblical perspective on boasting: "Let not a wise man boast of his wisdom, and let not the mighty man boast of his might, let not a rich man boast of his riches, but let him who boasts, boast of this, that he understands and knows me, that I am the Lord who exercises lovingkindness, justice, and righteousness on earth." This passage, as do the entire OT and NT, repudiates boasting oriented to man as misplaced praise and enjoins boasting in God, which is appropriately directed praise offered to one worthy of praise. The theological premise for the impropriety of man's boasting in himself and the propriety of his boasting in God is the creature/Creator distinction and the assumption that what man is and does is a gift from God (I Cor. 4:7) and what God is and does is intrinsic to him. For man to boast in himself is to claim the praise and glory that belongs to God; it is arrogance (cf. James 4:16). For man to boast in God is to give God the praise and glory that are rightfully his.

As is evident in Jer. 9:23–24, the same word can be used for the man-oriented boasting which is forbidden (e.g., I Kings 20:11; Pss. 10:3; 49:6; 52:1; 97:7; Prov. 20:14; 25:24; 27:1) and the God-oriented boasting which is encouraged (e.g., Pss. 34:2; 44:8). This is true of the most frequently used terms, the OT Hebrew root *hālal* and the NT Greek *kauch* terms (negatively I Cor. 3:21; James 4:16; positively II Cor. 1:12; II Thess. 1:4). Other terms—e.g., the NT Greek *alaz* terms—are used negatively (Rom. 1:30; II Tim. 3:2; James 4:16).

Paul is the one in the NT who has the most to say about boasting—fifty-seven out of sixty-three occurrences of the *kauch* family of words (five instances are in James and one in Hebrews). He repudiates all boasting in one's righteousness, wisdom, or status before God (Rom. 2:23; 3:27; 4:2; I Cor. 1:29; Eph. 2:8–9). For Paul the one appropriate form of boasting is, "Let him who boasts, boast in the Lord" (Jer. 9:24 cited in I Cor. 1:31). Boasting in God which is "through our Lord Jesus Christ" (Rom. 5:11) and "in the cross of our Lord Jesus Christ" (Gal. 6:14) encompasses all the aspects of God's work in one's life, and thus these also become occasions through which one may boast in praise and thanks to God. Thus Paul may boast of individual churches (II Cor. 1:14; 7:4, 14; 8:24; Phil. 2:16; I Thess. 2:19; II Thess. 1:4) and even of God's work in his own life (II Cor. 1:12) because to do so is to give praise to God for what God has done.

G. W. Knight, III

See also Glory; Pride.

Bibliography. H. C. Hahn, *NIDNTT,* I, 227–29.

Bodily Presence. *See* Lord's Supper, Views of.

Bodily Resurrection. *See* Resurrection of the Dead.

Bodily Resurrection of Christ. *See* Resurrection of Christ.

Body, Biblical View of the. In the OT there is no single term corresponding to the NT *sōma,* the physical body which is distinct from the soul and/or spirit. The Hebrew terms *bāśār* ("flesh") in Lev. 14:9; 15:2; *nĕbēlâ* ("corpse, carcass") in I Kings 13:22, 24; and *gĕwîyâ* in I Sam. 31:10, 12 are among those most frequently translated *sōma* in the LXX and "body" in some of the English translations.

In the NT the word "body" is used approximately 150 times. The English term "body" is translated from *kōlon* ("a limb") one time (Heb. 3:17); *chrōs* ("skin") one time (Acts 19:12); *sarx* ("flesh") two times (Col. 2:5; Heb. 9:10); *ptōma* ("corpse") six times (Matt. 14:12; Mark 6:29; 15:45; Rev. 11:8–9); and *sōma* ("body") approximately 140 times. It is this last usage that will be the concern of this article.

Physical Body. In addition to the human body the bodies of animals are referred to (Gen. 15:11; Judg. 14:8–9; Dan. 7:11; Heb. 13:11; James 3:3). Only one passage refers to the body of a plant (I Cor. 15:37–38). Also, there is one reference to terrestrial and celestial bodies (I Cor. 15:40). Although there is no specific reference to angels having bodies, they seem to have an appearance similar to men because they are at times confused with them (Gen. 18:2, 16; Ezek. 9:2; Dan. 10:5–6, 10, 18; 12:6–7; Rev. 20:1).

Earthly Body. Clearly, the predominate usage

in the Bible refers to the human body. It has become axiomatic to think of the body as more than the physical body; it is the person as a whole. This concept has been challenged by R. H. Gundry, who examines the usage of *sōma* in extrabiblical and biblical literature and concludes that it has reference to man's physical body.

Another term for the physical body is the "flesh" (*sarx*). *Sarx* can refer to the bodily substance of man (John 3:6; Gal.2:20; 4:13; Phil. 1:22, 24) or of Christ (Col. 1:22; Rom. 8:3). Although the *sōma,* like the *sarx,* is subject to lusts (Rom. 6:12) and is mortal (Rom. 6:12; 8:11; cf. II Cor. 4:11), it is different in several respects. (1) The body, which can be transformed, is the dwelling place of the Holy Spirit (Rom. 8:11; I Cor. 6:19), whereas in the flesh nothing good dwells (Rom. 7:18). (2) The body is for the Lord and is to glorify him (I Cor. 6:13, 20), whereas the flesh cannot please God (Rom. 8:8). (3) The body is to be an instrument of righteousness rather than sin (Rom. 6:12–13), whereas the flesh only serves as a beachhead for sin (Gal. 5:13) and is at enmity with God (Rom. 8:7; Gal. 5:16–17). (4) The body awaits redemption and resurrection (Rom. 8:23; I Cor. 15:35–49), whereas the flesh cannot be resurrected (I Cor. 15:50) but is destined for death. (5) Since the body will be resurrected, it will face the judgment seat of Christ to be judged for the deeds done in the body (II Cor. 5:10). The essential difference between the body and flesh is that the body can be transformed whereas the flesh cannot. The body can be used as an instrument for sin or righteousness, but the flesh cannot be an instrument for righteousness but only for sin. J. A. T. Robinson stated it succinctly: "While *sarx* stands for man, in the solidarity of the creation, in his distance from God, *sōma* stands for man, in the solidarity of creation, as made for God" (*The Body,* 31).

Bultmann with his existential theology postulates that the *sōma* is speaking of the whole person rather than the physical body. Robert Jewett says: "Bultmann has turned *sōma* into its virtual opposite: a symbol for that structure of individual existence which is essentially nonphysical" (*Paul's Anthropological Terms,* 211). Gundry has responded with a needed correction by showing that the Scriptures present man as "a duality—i.e., a proper unity of two parts—of spirit and body. The spirit is that part through the instrumentality of which man lives in the material and eventful world" (*Sōma in Biblical Theology,* 201). Therefore, man is more than just a body; he is physical and immaterial; he is body and soul and/or spirit. The scriptural dualism is not the same as Greek dualism, where the soul is the prisoner of the body, but rather the body is the instrument through which the immaterial expresses itself. The material and immaterial parts of a person are on a par with each other. Both need redemption and both live eternally. Man is not just body or just soul/spirit but the combination of them.

Resurrected Body. When a person dies, there is the separation of the immaterial from the material part. At the time of death the material or physical part continues to exist, although it is in the process of decay. For the Christian the body is described as being asleep, awaiting the coming of the Lord (I Cor. 15:6, 18; I Thess. 4:13–16). The immaterial part, at least for the believer, departs immediately to be with the Lord (II Cor. 5:6–8). Since a person is both immaterial and material, it is thought by many that between death and the resurrection there is an intermediate body. However, since this theory is based primarily on inferences in the story of the rich man and Lazarus (Luke 16:19–31), one cannot be too dogmatic regarding the nature of the intermediate state.

In I Cor. 15:35–49 Paul describes the resurrected body. It is contrasted with the preresurrected body, which is set forth as a "soulish body" or a material body which is governed by the soul. In the creation of Adam, God made him from the dust of the earth and breathed into him and he became a living soul (Gen. 2:7; I Cor. 15:45). The body of man was designed for earthly existence and is mortal. The resurrected body is described as a "spiritual body" (I Cor.15:44). This does not describe its composition but states rather that it is a material body governed by the spirit. It is immortal and designed for a heavenly existence (I Cor. 15:50–53). Certainly the resurrected body was matter that could be observed because Paul demonstrated Christ's resurrection by the many people who had seen Christ in his resurrection body (I Cor. 15:5–8). Also, in the Gospel and Acts narratives Christ was seen by his disciples (Matt. 16:20; 28:9–10; Mark 16:9, 12, 14–18; Luke 24:13–52; John 20:14–21:25; Acts 1:1–11). Although the resurrected body of Christ did have some similarities to the preresurrected body in that he breathed (John 20:22), ate (Luke 24:42–43), and was recognizable (John 20:27–29), it also was different because he was not always immediately recognizable (Luke 24:16–31; John 20:14; 21:4); he could walk through doors or walls (John 20:19, 26; Luke 24:36) and rapidly traverse great distances (Matt. 28:7–10). In conclusion, even though the pre- and postresurrected bodies are contrasted by Paul as perishable/imperishable, dishonor/glory, weakness/power, soul/spiritual (I Cor. 15:42–44), both are nevertheless physical or material.

Body of Christ. *Physical Body.* The NT specifically speaks of Christ's physical body in connection with his death (Matt. 27:58–59; Mark 15:43–45; Luke 23:52; 24:3, 23; John 19:38, 40; 20:12; Col. 1:22; Heb. 10:10). Furthermore, it was a body that could be seen, touched, and heard (I John 1:1–3; John 1:14; Acts 2:20). Jesus' body had characteristic members of a normal human body. Also, characteristically Jesus was hungry and ate, drank, and became weary. Nothing in the Gospels indicates that Jesus had a body other than a normal human body; neither his friends nor enemies made any remarks to that effect. While on earth he had the frailties of other humans in their bodies.

Communion. At the Last Supper, after he broke the bread, Jesus said, "This is my body" (Matt. 26:26; Mark 14:22; Luke 22:19; I Cor. 11:24). With the Passover meal being the setting of that Last Supper, the breaking of the bread symbolized the sacrifice of Jesus' body as a substitutionary death for all mankind. Paul warns the Corinthians that whoever eats the bread in an unworthy manner is guilty of profaning the body of the Lord (I Cor. 11:27) and whoever eats and drinks brings judgment upon himself if he does not discern the body (vs. 29). Hence the desecration of the Lord's Supper brings shame to Jesus' physical death as the sacrifice for sin and, in the case of many of the Corinthians, it brought judgment upon their physical bodies (vs. 30).

Body of Believers. The theological usage of *sōma* refers to the body of Christ or the church (Rom. 12:5; I Cor. 10:16–17; 12:12–27; Eph. 1:23; 2:16; 4:4, 12, 16; 5:23, 30; Col. 1:18, 24; 2:19; 3:15). Here one sees the metaphorical use of "body"; the believers are united by the Holy Spirit to Christ in one body. The usage of the individual members of the body and their relationship to each other vividly depicts both the relationship of believers with one another and with Christ and the diversity and unity within the body of Christ (I Cor. 12:12–30). A theological development of the body of Christ is seen. In Rom. 12:4–8 and I Cor. 12:12–30 Paul speaks of the body of Christ as believers with various spiritual gifts unified in their function in the local church setting. Although this same concept is expressed in Paul's later writings (cf. Eph. 4:4–12; 5:30; Col. 3:15), there is the additional feature of Christ being the head of the church (Eph. 1:22; 4:15; 5:23; Col. 1:18; 2:19) with greater emphasis on the universal aspect (Eph. 2:16–18; 3:6; 4:4–13). Therefore, "body" is used metaphorically in "the body of Christ," and it is compared with the human physical body to denote diversity and unity.

Conclusion. Outside the metaphorical use of "body" with reference to the body of Christ, the term "body" is consistently used as meaning the physical or material body. Even in the metaphorical usage of the body it is compared with the physical or material body. Man is more than just a physical or material body; he is a combination of both the material and immaterial.

H. W. Hoehner

See also Man, Doctrine of; Flesh.

Bibliography. C. B. Bass, *ISBE* (rev.), I, 528–31; J. C. Beker, *Paul the Apostle;* E. Best, *One Body in Christ;* R. Bultmann, *Theology of the NT,* I, 192–203; R. H. Gundry, *Sōma in Biblical Theology;* D. Guthrie, *NT Theology;* R. Jewett, *Paul's Anthropological Terms* and *IDB* Supplement, 117–18; G. E. Ladd, *A Theology of the NT;* S. V. McCasland, *IDB,* I, 451–52; H. Ridderbos, *Paul: An Outline of His Theology;* J. A. T. Robinson, *The Body;* E. Schweizer and G. Baumgärtel, *TDNT,* VII, 1024–94; S. Wibbling, *NIDNTT,* I, 232–38.

Body, Soul, and Spirit. *See* Man, Doctrine of; Trichotomy.

Body and Soul. *See* Man, Doctrine of; Dichotomy.

Body of Christ. *See* Church, The.

Boehme, Jakob (1575–1624). German Lutheran mystic and theosophist. A sickly child who received only an elementary education, he became a shoemaker in Görlitz and throughout his life was active as a merchant and family man, living during some of the difficult times of the Thirty Years' War. Such activities stand in sharp contrast to his mystical experiences, which began in 1600 with a vision induced by a reflection of the sun in a pewter dish. This vision and his subsequent mystical insights led him to write numerous books, including *Aurora* or *Day Dawning, On the Three Principals of Divine Being, Six Theosophical Points, Six Mystical Points,* and *The Way to Christ.*

Although he relied heavily on his own mystical approach, Boehme's work shows the influence of Schwenckfeld, Paracelsus, Valentine Weigal, Renaissance Neoplatonism, and Jewish mysticism. The obscure and unusual terminology he used makes the interpretation of his works difficult. His dependence upon myth and symbol rather than concepts leads to a manner of expression that is contemplative rather than discursive.

His thought centers on the problem of the unity of good and evil, of Yes and No. Much of his work involves an elaborate sevenfold system which explains the divine activity as reflected in nature. These seven qualities divide into two triads, a higher and a lower, between which there is creative energy called the flash. The lower group consists of individualization, diffusion, and the struggle between the two. The higher triad consists of love, expression, and the kingdom of God. People must choose between the lower world of sensation, or die to self and live on the higher plane. The true Christian life is an imitation of the sacrifice and triumph of Christ.

These teachings, when coupled with Boehme's opposition to scholastic Protestantism, led to his condemnation by a Lutheran pastor, and for a time he ceased his publications (1612–19). Despite such troubles his influence has been very great in Germany, where the pietist, romantic, and idealist movements each owed something to his teaching, and in England, where the Cambridge Platonists, John Milton, Isaac Newton, William Blake, William Law, and the Behmenists followed his ideas. R. G. CLOUSE

See also MYSTICISM.

Bibliography. Boehme, *The Way to Christ*, tr. P. Erb; F. Hartman, *Jacob Boehme: Life and Doctrines;* R. M. Jones, *Spiritual Reformers in the 16th and 17th Centuries;* J. J. Stoudt, *Sunrise to Eternity: A Study of Jacob Boehme's Life;* N. Thune, *The Behmenists and the Philadelphians.*

Boethius, Anicius Manlius Torquatus Severinus (*ca.* 480–524). Called by many "the last of the Romans and the first of the scholastics." A man of prodigious activity and brilliant intellect, Boethius bridged the gap between the ancient and medieval by his enormous literary output. His goal was to translate into Latin all of Aristotle and Plato; thus these works were made accessible to the Middle Ages. In addition to translations his writings are in four areas: theological (five survive); philosophical (*The Consolation of Philosophy*, which has been translated repeatedly into almost every European language); works on the four arts of the *quadrivium;* and logic (most of these survive).

Boethius saw the task of theology as that of making distinctions between reason and faith. Reason was to be marshaled to support faith. He set out to explain the Trinity in terms of Aristotelian categories. God is supersubstantially one with the three persons as internal relations. Since God is and wills the good, evil has no positive existence. Such an approach shows both that Boethius was indebted to Neoplatonism and Stoicism and that he was the logical forerunner of Thomas Aquinas.

Boethius was born in Rome into the Christian family of Anicii, one member of which, Olybrius, was briefly emperor in 472. After his father died in 487, he was raised by the able Senator Symmachus whose daughter, Rusticiana, he married. Boethius became a friend of the Ostrogothic ruler of Rome, Theodoric, who made him a consul of Rome in 510. He may have been head of the Senate, and *ca.* 520 he was made *magister officiorum*, head of all civil and other services of Rome. But in 522, shortly after he greeted his two children in the Senate as joint consuls, he was accused of treason by Theodoric, who had become suspicious of all Romans and Catholics. It is uncertain whether Boethius was conspiring against Theodoric, but among the charges against him were conspiracy in favor of Emperor Justin I of Constantinople, writing seditious letters, and the practice of magic. Theodoric banished him to prison in Pavia and beheaded him without trial in 524 or 525. It was while he was in prison that Boethius wrote his greatest work, *The Consolation of Philosophy.*

V. L. WALTER

Bibliography. H. R. Patch, *The Tradition of Boethius;* H. M. Barrett, *Boethius: Some Aspects of His Times and Work;* L. Cooper, *A Concordance of Boethius;* H. F. Stewart, *Boethius: An Essay.*

Bogomils. Christian heretics especially prevalent in the eleventh century in Bulgaria. The name means "friends of God." Little is known of the movement's origin and development; as with other medieval heretical groups most information comes from the writings of opponents.

The Bogomils were dualistic in theology and owed much to older Manichaean and docetic thought. They rejected the OT except for Psalms and the prophetic books. In their view the material world was created by Satanael, a powerful evil deity. He formed man from mud, but when he found he could not breathe life into his creatures, he reached an agreement with the supremely good God by which man would receive life and would belong equally to both Satanael and God. Satanael deceived man by giving him the Mosaic law, but God sent the Logos as an emanation from himself to bring salvation. The Logos appeared to be virgin born, die on a cross, and experience bodily resurrection; in reality, however, the incarnation was not physical but spiritual, since anything material was evil. Water baptism and the Lord's Supper were rejected for their materialism, as was the use of images (including the cross) in worship. They tended toward a Sabellian view of the Trinity.

The Bogomils were severely persecuted under Emperor Alexius in the twelfth century, although they continued to have influence for several centuries afterward. J. N. AKERS

Bibliography. D. Obolensky, *The Bogomiles.*

Bonaventure (1221–1274). Franciscan scholastic theologian; Doctor of the Church (Seraphicus) canonized in 1482. Born near Viterbo, in Tuscany, and baptized John Fidanza, in or around the year 1234 he began the study of theology under Alexander of Hales in Paris, where he taught from 1248 to 1255. In 1256 he was appointed to a chair of theology in Paris; but for local reasons the university did not confer its doctorate, with the right officially to occupy the chair, till a year later. By that time Bonaventure, who had entered the Franciscan Order in or about 1238, was chosen as general of the Order, and thereafter never resumed his teaching activity. In 1273 he was created Cardinal Archbishop of Albano; next year he attended the Council of Lyons, but died unexpectedly there.

Bonaventure's main written works were a commentary on the *Sentences* of Peter Lombard, the standard theological textbook of that day; *Itinerarium mentis ad Deum* (journey of the mind, or soul, toward God); and *Breviloquium*. One central theme of his theology is the journey, or rather the ascent, of the human soul toward God. In this pilgrimage there are three stages. First, since God has left his footprints in the visible world, which he called into being, reason can argue from effects to cause and deduce the existence and power of the Creator from his earthly creation. Since man is made in God's image, the second stage in this journey is to turn to the inner world of man's soul, with its powers of memory, intellect, and will. This will deepen and enhance the sense of God's being and unity. The doctrine of the Trinity, however, can be known only by supernatural revelation, which discloses that God the Father, who is infinitely good and ever active, gives rise to two processions, one of the Son and the other of the Holy Spirit. The third and final stage of the ascent to God goes beyond reason. It is the mystical contemplation of the ineffable joys of the divine presence, and is the pure gift of the Holy Spirit.

Although Bonaventure allowed Aristotle a limited place in his system, his viewpoint is fundamentally Augustinian in its basic religious orientation and philosophical principles.

N. V. Hope

Bibliography. Bonaventure, *The Mind's Road to God*, tr. G. Boas; É. Gilson, *The Philosophy of Saint Bonaventure*.

Bonhoeffer, Dietrich (1906–1945). Lutheran pastor and theologian whose life and legacy have exerted a worldwide influence upon theological thought, Christian imagination, piety, and practice in the post–World War II era. Born in Breslau, Germany, Bonhoeffer was executed at the age of thirty-nine in a Nazi concentration camp. At that time he had not attained the international recognition and fame that have been accorded him since the 1950s. It was after the posthumous publication and translation of his *Letters and Papers from Prison* (first released in 1951) that Bonhoeffer came to the attention of Christendom throughout the world. This volume of his collected correspondence, smuggled out of his prison cell in Berlin-Tegel, was never intended by Bonhoeffer for publication, and yet it has become the most popular of his many books. When he wrote the letters, he was imprisoned on charges connected with the smuggling of fourteen Jews to Switzerland and safety.

Bonhoeffer's earlier life hardly pointed him toward a prison cell. A brilliant student, one of eight children in the family of a leading psychiatrist at the University of Berlin, Bonhoeffer received his doctorate in theology from the University of Berlin at the age of twenty-one. After postgraduate work at Union Theological Seminary in New York City, he became Lutheran chaplain and lecturer at the University of Berlin, where he was ministering when Hitler came to power in 1933. Bonhoeffer joined the Confessing Church, consisting of one third of the Protestant clergy, led by Martin Niemoeller, and concerned laity, who in the Barmen Declaration of 1934 protested Nazi inroads and challenges to the integrity of the Christian church in Germany.

After two years as pastor of a German congregation in London (1933–35), Bonhoeffer became director of the Confessing Church seminary in Finkenwalde. Not only was this seminary closed by the Nazi regime in 1937, but Bonhoeffer was eventually forbidden to publish or to speak publicly. Although he considered the possibility of accepting the safety of an American teaching position in 1939, he finally decided that if he wanted to serve his fellow Germans as a Christian minister during the impending war, he would have to return to his homeland and to suffer with them. His brother-in-law, Hans von Dohnanyi, brought Bonhoeffer into the inner circles of the anti-Nazi resistance and employed him as a double agent in the German military intelligence office (*Abwehr*). Ostensibly using his international ecumenical connections for *Abwehr* purposes, Bonhoeffer actually transmitted to the British messages from the group of Germans planning to kill Hitler.

His two years as a Nazi prisoner (1943–45), although initially a time of intense spiritual testing, led Bonhoeffer to develop a routine of disciplined contemplation and creativity, resulting in writings focused on contemporary and future challenges facing the Christian church. Assessing

Christianity's role in "a world come of age," Bonhoeffer's Tegel theology (his prison letters) described a Christian as "a man for others" and the church as existing "for others." "Who is Christ for us today?" was his piercing query.

One of Bonhoeffer's most divergently understood concepts concerns a nonreligious interpretation of Christianity. "Religionless Christianity," a term sometimes taken out of context, was used by Bonhoeffer in a letter written to his friend Eberhard Bethge, with whom he shared a common theological heritage and understanding. The phrase is based on a critique of "religion" found in the works of Martin Luther and Karl Barth, both of whom distinguished between faith and religion. According to Luther, religion comes from the flesh, faith from the spirit. For Bonhoeffer the religious act was always something partial, while faith involved the whole of one's life; he understood the call of Jesus "not to a new religion, but to life." The Christian, said Bonhoeffer, participates in the suffering of God in the secular life. His emphasis on a "secular interpretation" of Christianity reflects his perception of Europe's historical movement toward a "completely religionless time." Although some of his fragmentary Tegel thoughts were later used by theologians who may not have shared his original presuppositions and world view ("death of God" theologians), Bonhoeffer's earlier works continually stir resonances in traditional centers of Christian piety, both evangelical Protestant and Roman Catholic. Most popular in these circles are *The Cost of Discipleship* (emphasizing obedience, "costly grace" versus "cheap grace") and *Life Together* (focusing on the discipline and balance of Christian community life).

Sparking responses in both conservative and liberal wings of Christianity, in secular and Marxist writings, Bonhoeffer has also been a source of inspiration and strength for all contemporary Christians who suffer under oppressive political regimes and for Christians in the Third World, especially in Latin America, where liberation theology has drawn on the model of his life and thought. Born to privilege, but with a special sensitivity to life's boundary experiences, Bonhoeffer spoke of the incomparable value of learning to see the world with "the view from below"—the perspective of the outcast, the powerless, and the oppressed. Thus he articulated and anticipated the central lesson which Christians, particularly in the privileged West, still need to learn today. R. Zerner

Bibliography. E. Bethge, *Costly Grace: An Illustrated Biography of Dietrich Bonhoeffer* and *Bonhoeffer: Exile and Martyr;* W.-D. Zimmermann and R. G. Smith, eds., *I Knew Dietrich Bonhoeffer;* A. Dumas, *Dietrich Bonhoeffer, Theologian of Reality;* J. Godsey and G. B. Kelly, eds., *Ethical Responsibility: Bonhoeffer's Legacy to the Churches;* J. Godsey, *The Theology of Dietrich Bonhoeffer;* C. J. Green, *Bonhoeffer: The Sociality of Christ and Humanity;* A. J. Klassen, ed., *A Bonhoeffer Legacy;* M. Marty, ed., *The Place of Bonhoeffer;* H. Ott, *Reality and Faith: The Theological Legacy of Dietrich Bonhoeffer;* L. Rasmussen, *Dietrich Bonhoeffer: Reality and Resistance;* R. G. Smith, ed., *World Come of Age.*

Book of Common Order. The title used historically by the Church of Scotland and associated Presbyterian churches for their liturgical handbooks. The latest edition bearing the name was published for the Church of Scotland in 1979 and contains forms of service in the traditional "Thou" style of addressing God as well as in more contemporary "You" form.

Contents of this book are the divine service (three full and one shortened orders for Holy Communion together with an outline order of service for public worship when the Lord's Supper is not celebrated), services for Christian initiation, the celebration of marriage, funerals, and the ordination and admission of elders. It also contains a lectionary, two sets of collects, and proper prefaces for the Christian year.

The first book to bear this title was published by authority of the General Assembly of the Church of Scotland in 1562 and contained texts for the ministration of the sacraments. Two years later a further edition included material for all purposes, including metrical psalms and versions of other portions of Scripture. The first edition had been largely based on what was known as John Knox's Genevan Service Book (1556), introduced by that Reformer for the English congregation in Geneva, which consisted largely of exiles from the reign of Mary. The attempt to replace the *Book of Common Order* by the so-called Laudian Liturgy of 1637 precipitated the Solemn League and Covenant, but in 1644 it was displaced by the *Directory of Public Worship.*

As the *Book of Common Order* had never been an absolute formulary like the *Book of Common Prayer* in England, but rather a standard and model of worship, the minister was given freedom for extempore prayer as well as flexibility of usage. This led to very "free" types of services in some churches during the eighteenth and nineteenth centuries, but this century has seen the resurrection of the *Book of Common Order.* The United Free Church of Scotland published a book of this title in 1928, and then the Church of Scotland itself, after reuniting with that church, produced the 1940 edition of the *Book of Common Order,* later revised in 1952. As well as the usual services, this handbook had interesting forms for the dedication of various church buildings and furniture as well as some useful devotional material in prayers for special occasions and graces. D. H. WHEATON

Bibliography. W. D. Maxwell, *An Outline of Christian Worship;* H. Davies, *Worship and Theology in England,* I, 274–93, IV, 370–72.

Book of Common Prayer. Historically there have been three books which have borne this title in the Church of England, though the title has also been applied to books in other provinces of the Anglican Communion that have been largely derived from these three.

In 1549 the English Parliament passed an Act of Uniformity requiring the clergy to use from the Feast of Pentecost in that year "the Booke of the Common Prayer and Administracion of the Sacramentes and other Rites and Ceremonies of the Church after the Use of the Church of England." This revised and reformed handbook of worship was largely the work of the Archbishop of Canterbury, Thomas Cranmer, and in his Preface, Cranmer explained that it was to provide common prayer in two senses of the word. From that time the worship of the Church of England, hitherto almost entirely in Latin, was to be in the common tongue ("suche language . . . as they mighte understande and have profite by hearying the same"), and a common usage in every diocese (previously there had been several different uses).

In conducting worship the clergy had previously needed the missal (for the Mass), breviary (for daily offices), manual (for the occasional offices), and pontifical (for episcopal services). The new book contained all of these except the ordinal (for daily services), which was published separately in 1550 and revised and bound up in the editions of 1552 and 1662. In addition it included a calendar and lectionary and the litany, together with Coverdale's translation of the Psalter.

The first prayer book met with little favor. Protestants felt that it did not go far enough in its reforms, and in 1551 Martin Bucer published a Censura, or critique, in which he set out in detail the areas where the book obscured clear biblical teaching. Further, those who leaned toward Roman Catholicism (notably Bishop Gardiner of Winchester) claimed that the book still taught the old doctrines of the Mass. In consequence Cranmer produced a second prayer book in 1552 in which the Protestant position was much more clearly adopted. These books are known as the First and Second Prayer Books of King Edward the Sixth.

When Mary Tudor ascended the English throne in 1553, this second prayer book was proscribed as she reestablished the teaching and practices of the Church of Rome and leading Protestants were martyred. In 1559 Elizabeth I restored the second book with minor alterations. During the next century with the accession of James I in 1603 and the restoration of Charles II in 1660 the ongoing struggle between extreme Puritans and Episcopalians smoldered continuously, and the Hampton Court (1604) and Savoy (1661) conferences were held in an attempt to resolve the matters at issue. In the end relatively few changes were made, and the 1662 Act of Uniformity introduced a third *Book of Common Prayer* which was basically that of 1552 in its theological emphasis.

In 1637 the High Church Archbishop of Canterbury, William Laud, had attempted to impose on the Scottish church a book which was much more akin to that of 1549 in its doctrinal outlook. Although he was unsuccessful, his book formed the basis of the *Book of Common Prayer* adopted by the Scottish Episcopal Church in 1764. By a strange quirk of history the Protestant Episcopal Church in America drew on this book in compiling its liturgy, and thus today the Anglican Communion embraces provinces of more Catholic or Protestant theological outlook depending on whether their liturgy is ultimately derived from the 1549 or 1552 archetype.

In 1872 the Act of Uniformity Amendment Act allowed certain modifications in the way the services of the prayer book were used in the Church of England, permitting certain omissions, mainly on weekdays; hence the act became known as the Shortened Services Act. However, no amendment of the text was made at this stage.

A revision of the *Book of Common Prayer* was proposed in the Church of England in 1927, and although it was approved by the church's Convocations and House of Laity of Church Assembly, the book was rejected by Parliament largely because it reintroduced controversial pre-Reformation ideas, particularly in the Communion service. Since then the Worship and Doctrine Measure of 1974 has given the Church of England greater freedom to control its liturgy, and in consequence the *Alternative Service Book* was published in 1980 to supplement with modern services, but not to supersede, the *Book of Common Prayer.* Authorization of the latter can still be withdrawn only by Parliament.

D. H. WHEATON

Bibliography. G. J. Cuming, *A History of Anglican Liturgy;* C. O. Buchanan, B. T. Lloyd, and H. Miller, eds., *Anglican Worship Today.*

Book of Concord. *See* CONCORD, BOOK OF.

Book of Life. In ancient cities the names of citizens were recorded in a register until their death; then their names were marked out of the book of the living. This same idea appears in the OT (Exod. 32:32–33; Ps. 69:28; Isa. 4:3). From the idea of being recorded in God's book of the living (or the righteous) comes the sense of belonging to God's eternal kingdom or possessing eternal life (Dan. 12:1; Luke 10:20; Phil. 4:3; Heb. 12:23; Rev. 13:8; 17:8; 20:15; 21:27). For Christ to say that he will never blot out the overcomer's name from the book of life (Rev. 3:5) is the strongest affirmation that death can never separate us from Christ and his life (cf. Rom. 8:38–39). A person enrolled in the book of life by faith remains in it by faithfulness and can be erased only by disloyalty. There is some evidence that a person's name could be removed from the city register before death if he were convicted of a crime. In the first century Christians who were loyal to Christ were under constant threat of being branded political and social rebels and then stripped of their citizenship. But Christ offers them an eternal, safe citizenship in his everlasting kingdom if only they remain loyal to him.

In Rev. 13:8 it has been debated whether the words "from the creation of the world" (also 17:8) belong grammatically with "have not been written" or with "that was slain." In other words, is it the Lamb who was slain from the creation of the world? In Greek either interpretation is grammatically acceptable. But the reference in Rev. 17:8 implies that the word order in the Greek (not the grammar) favors the latter view and suggests that John is deliberately providing a complementary thought to 17:8. In the former instance, the emphasis would rest on the decree in eternity to elect the Son as the redeeming agent for mankind's salvation (13:8; I Pet. 1:20); in the latter, stress lies on God's eternal foreknowledge of a company of people who would participate in the elect Son's redeeming work (17:8). In any event, the words "from the creation of the world" cannot be pressed to prove eternal individual election to salvation or damnation, since Rev. 3:5 implies that failure of appropriate human response may remove one's name from the book of life.

A. F. Johnson

Booth, Catherine (1829–1890). "Mother of the Salvation Army." Born Catherine Mumford in Derbyshire, a Wesleyan preacher's daughter, she was among those expelled from her church in 1848 for ideas regarded as overenthusiastic. William Booth ministered to this group. He and Catherine married in 1855, and thereafter she played a prominent part in founding the movement that became the Salvation Army in 1878. She was a pioneer in establishing and defending the right of women to preach and in combating the exploitation of women and children (she herself was the mother of eight). Within the Army she consolidated the principle that women have absolute equality with men in privilege, position, and dignity, and she played no small part in winning the sympathy of the upper classes for the new movement. She published a number of papers on practical religion, godliness, aggressive witnessing, popular Christianity, and the Army's position in relation to church and state. In 1888 she was stricken with cancer, and died in 1890 after great suffering. About this she would say, "God must have permitted it for a great and worthy purpose."

J. D. Douglas

See also Booth, William.

Bibliography. F. Tucker, *The Life of Catherine Booth,* 2 vols.; D. Lamb, "Catherine Booth," in *Great Christians,* ed. R. S. Forman; C. Bramwell-Booth, *Catherine Book;* C. T. Stead, *Mrs Booth.*

Booth, William (1829–1912). Founder of the Salvation Army. Born in Nottingham, he grew up amid poverty, became a pawnbroker's assistant, was converted at fifteen, and subsequently became a Methodist pastor. A missing dimension in his ministry, however, made him restless. For Booth, the Lord's requirements involved loosing the chains of injustice, freeing captive and oppressed, sharing food and home, clothing the naked, and carrying out family responsibilities. Victorian England, on the other hand, upheld God-appointed stations, especially for the poor. William Booth argued that to speak of godly poverty was no indication that God approved destitution. For him this was no theological issue: people did not stop dying in hopelessness and squalor while theologians discussed nice points of divinity.

Aided by the remarkable Catherine, whom he married in 1855, he began the Christian Mission as a rescue operation in London's East End. Renamed the Salvation Army thirteen years later (1878), it waged war on a dual front—against the pinch of poverty and the power of sin. Mainline churches shunned the new movement; magistrates and police offered little protection when mobs jeered, threw stones, broke windows, vandalized the Army's property. Booth pressed on, seeking castaways, exposing vice, providing homes and food, employment and medical care, reconciling families, and giving unwelcome publicity to frightful social conditions that no other agency would tackle.

On the basis that the devil was a proud spirit who could not bear to be mocked, Booth identified him as the chief enemy, challenged his monopoly of "all the best tunes," and used the big drum to deafen him. Booth fearlessly waged war against such contemporary evils as the sweat shops and girls sold into prostitution. In 1890 he published *In Darkest England—and the Way Out,* which set the tone for the Army's increasing emphasis on its social program for which, rather than for the message of "blood and fire," the movement is best known today.

His Army spread throughout the world, but Booth was always very much in control. A writer sent to interview him said he expected to meet a visionary and saint, and found instead the astutest businessman in the city of London. Booth was responsible for a whole network of social and regenerative agencies; Lord Wolseley once described him as the world's greatest organizer.

Criticism came because his Army observed no sacraments. Booth denied he was against them. Perhaps the wranglings these had caused in other churches did not encourage him to change his mind. By the time the century closed, Booth had won his fight: freeman of London, honorary doctor of Oxford, guest at the coronation of Edward VII and of the United States Senate, which he opened with prayer. In 1912 "the General laid down his sword"—and people of all ranks were among the thousands of funeral mourners. J. D. DOUGLAS

See also BOOTH, CATHERINE.

Bibliography. H. Begbie, *Life of William Booth,* 2 vols.; S. J. Ervine, *God's Soldier,* 2 vols.; R. Collier, *The General Next to God;* F. Coutts, *Bread for My Neighbour* and *No Discharge in This War;* E. H. McKinley, *Marching to Glory.*

Born Again. *See* REGENERATION.

Bossuet, Jacques Bénigne (1627–1704). Perhaps the leading French churchman of the seventeenth century. An important figure in the entourage of Louis XIV, he served as tutor to the king's son and as defender of the independent authority of the French church in opposition to papal claims. He was also a great orator, controversialist, and a formulator of philosophy of history.

Born in Dijon, Bossuet began his studies at the Jesuit school there and completed them at the College of Navarre in Paris. After seven years as canon and archdeacon in Metz (where he tangled with the Reformers), he went to Paris in 1659 and soon became preacher in the royal chapel. In 1681 he became bishop of Meaux, a position he held until his death.

While tutor to the dauphin, Bossuet wrote three important works. The first, a theological *Treatise,* was a discussion of the nature of God and the nature of man. The second, *Discourse on Universal History,* followed in the tradition of Augustine's *City of God* and took the position that the whole course of history was guided by providence. In this work he covered history chronologically from the creation to the reign of Charlemagne. The *Politique* reminded the dauphin that sovereigns have duties as well as rights and looked forward to a time when France would become a utopia with a Christian philosopher on the throne.

Just as Bossuet became bishop of Meaux, he found it necessary to preside over a conclave of French clergy which the king called to defend royal powers and the rights of the French church against the claims of the pope. In his later years he became embroiled in various controversies with rationalist, pantheistic, mystical, and Protestant groups. H. F. VOS

See also GALLICAN ARTICLES, THE FOUR.

Bibliography. Bossuet, *Complete Works,* 10 vols.; K. Löwith, *Meaning in History;* W. J. Simpson, *A Study of Bossuet.*

Boston, Thomas (1676–1732). Scottish evangelical minister and leader in the Marrow Controversy. Educated at Edinburgh, he became a noted authority on the Hebrew Bible. Finding a copy of *The Marrow of Modern Divinity* left in Scotland by a Commonwealth soldier, he was intrigued and had the work republished in 1718. This English Puritan work (attributed by some to Edward Fisher) was a compendium of the opinions of the leading Reformation divines on the doctrine of grace and the offer of the gospel. It immediately set off a storm of controversy, being condemned by the General Assembly of the Scottish church for its alleged antinomianism and defended by twelve divines including Boston. The "Marrow Men," as they were subsequently called, played a large role in the attempt within Scottish Presbyterianism to withstand the growing movement toward Arminianism, which also involved the corollary issue of limited versus universal atonement.

The conflict arose when the Auchterarder Presbytery would not ordain a man who refused to assent to the following proposition: "I believe that it is not sound and orthodox to teach that we must forsake sin in order to our coming to Christ, and instating us in Covenant with God." The Assembly overruled the Presbytery, and Boston argued against the Assembly.

Boston's influence was enhanced by his faithful and exemplary dedication to his parochial tasks and by his popular writings, which include *The Fourfold State of Human Nature, The Crook in the Lot,* and his autobiography. C. F. ALLISON

See also Marrow Controversy.

Bibliography. Boston, *Whole Works,* 12 vols., ed. S. McMillin; A. Thompson, *The Life of Thomas Boston.*

Bottomless Pit. The bottomless pit or abyss (from Heb. *tĕhôm,* "the deep") refers to the underworld as (1) a prison for Satan and certain demons (Luke 8:31; Rev. 20:1, 3; cf. II Pet. 2:4; Jude 6); (2) the realm of the dead which the living cannot enter (Rom. 10:7) and the place from which the beast or Antichrist arises (Rev. 11:7; 17:8). That God alternately imprisons and releases the demonic spirits signifies his ultimate power over the satanic evil realm. The concept provides an additional complementary image to hell of the place of terror filled with demons. Hell (Gehenna) is the eschatological fiery destination of all the wicked (man and demons), while the abyss is the present abode of demonic spirits.

A. F. Johnson

See also Hell; Hades; Deep, The.

Bibliography. H. Bietenhard, *NIDNTT,* II, 205; J. Jeremias, *TDNT,* I, 9.

Bousset, Wilhelm (1865–1920). German NT scholar and leader (with W. Wrede, H. Gunkel, J. Weiss, and W. Heitmüller) of the history of religions approach to biblical study. He taught at Göttingen (1896–1916) and Geissen (1916–20). With Heitmüller he edited the influential journal *Theologische Rundschau* (1897–1917) and, with Gunkel, the monograph series *Forschungen zur Religion und Geschichte des AT und NT* (1903–20). In his influential commentary on the Apocalypse (Meyer series, 1896), *Die Religion des Judentums im NTlichen Zeitalter* (1902), *Die Hauptprobleme des Gnosis* (1907), and *Kyrios Christos* (1913) he attempted to show that intertestamental Judaism was influenced by Iranian and hellenistic concepts and that primitive Christianity can only be understood against the background of late Judaism and hellenistic religious syncretism. A significant change took place in the early church as Gentile hero worshipers transferred their allegiance from other "lords" to Jesus the Lord (*Kyrios*). The disappointment of the early Palestinian church when the parousia of the Son of man failed to materialize hastened this decisive development in early Christianity. In contrast to earlier scholars Bousset dated this theological change at the middle of the first century rather than the end. Bousset's conclusions were a major influence on Rudolf Bultmann and his disciples.

W. W. Gasque

Bibliography. H. Gunkel, *Evangelische Freiheit* 42:141–62; L. Thomas, *DBSup,* I, 989–92; K. Kamlah, *RGG,* I, 1373–74.

Branch. The translation of over twenty Hebrew and Greek words, the more important of which are as follows. Hebrew: *zĕmôrâ,* especially "branch of grapevine"; *yôneqet,* "suckling, twig"; *nēṣer,* "sprout, shoot"; *ʿānāp,* "bough or branch" of tree or vine; *ṣemaḥ,* "bud, growth"; *qāneh,* "reed, cane"; Greek: *klados,* "branch" of tree; *klēma,* "branch," especially of grapevine. Most of these are self-explanatory in their contexts, referring to various kinds of branches and shoots of different trees, vines, or herbs.

The words calling for special mention are *nēṣer* and *ṣemaḥ* of messianic import. *Nēṣer* is used literally of branches in Isa. 14:19 and 60:21; figuratively, of a royal scion in Isa. 11:1 and Dan. 11:7. In Isa. 11:1 the parallel phrase seems to refer to a humble stump of the line of Jesse, from which root a sprout will grow. The awful invasions of the Assyrians in the days of Ahaz and Hezekiah had brought the Davidic house very low. It is impossible to divorce Isa. 11:1 from the messianic hope of a wonderful child of David's line who would bring miraculous deliverance. The child was called Immanuel in Isa. 7:14; 8:8; 10:8, given a fivefold divine name in 9:6, and promised the throne of David in 9:7. This could not be Hezekiah, as he was already a grown boy when Ahaz took the throne. The following passage of Isa. 11:2–16 also is clearly messianic and is so referred to in Rom. 15:12.

The similarity of *nēṣer* to Nazareth is doubtless alluded to in Matt. 2:23. There is no relation to the word Nazarite. It may be questioned whether Matthew urges a derivation of Nazareth from *nēṣer* or is only giving a play on words. The derivation of Nazareth is uncertain. The town is not mentioned in the OT. The derivation of the word Nazarene from Nazareth is defended philologically by W. F. Albright (*JBL* 65:397–401).

Ṣemaḥ is used seven times of a bud or growth. The messianic usages are in Isa. 4:2; Jer. 23:5; 33:15; and Zech. 3:8; 6:12. Apparently these messianic references become more clear as revelation progresses. The context of Isa. 4:2 is rather general, not even attaching the branch of the Lord to the Davidic dynasty. It foretells a time of blessing for Jerusalem. Jer. 23:5 is more specific. A righteous branch shall be raised to David. He shall reign and prosper (the same word translated "deal wisely" in the messianic passage of Isa. 52:13). His name is the Lord our Righteousness. His days shall be the time of final deliverance for Israel. Jer. 33:15 is very similar. Indeed, if an old vocalization be adopted which is witnessed to in Ugaritic and elsewhere, Jer. 33:15 may also be translated "and this is the name they shall call him, the Lord our Righteousness." Both passages thus foretell the messianic king.

In Zech. 3:8 and 6:12 this messianic title is significantly fastened upon Joshua, the son of Josedech the high priest. Not of David's line, Joshua is not himself to be the branch, but he and his fellows were "men wondered at" (Heb. "men of a sign"). Their crowns were to be given, then removed for future days. The prophecy speaks, not of Joshua, but of the future messianic king-priest in line with the messianic Ps. 110.

Remark should further be made of the passage in John 15 in which Christ calls his followers to an intimate vital union with himself, typified as the union of the branch with the vine. An overliteralness has found in John 15:2 a teaching against security. Rather, the point of the simile is to emphasize the necessity of abiding in him.

In Rom. 11 Israel is likened to an olive branch cast off during this age while the Gentile church is grafted in. There is added a promise that the natural branch, Israel, will be grafted in again in the day when the Redeemer will come out of Zion (Rom. 11:26).

R. L. Harris

See also Messiah.

Bibliography. J. G. Baldwin, "Semaḥ as a Technical Term in the Prophets," *VT* 14:93–97.

Breaking of Bread. *See* Lord's Supper.

Brethren of the Common Life.

Religious society in the Netherlands between the fourteenth and early seventeenth centuries. It reportedly developed out of regular meetings held in Deventer, where Gerhard Groote and some of his friends foregathered at the home of Florent Radewijns. Groote, an unordained preacher, was the first leader of the new community, which consisted of both clergy and laity. Members took no vows, joined no religious order, but sought to live in God's presence a life of total dedication and to prepare themselves for eternal life. In addition, however, this mystic strain was healthily complemented by active philanthropy toward the poor and by the setting up of hostels for students. Out of this there grew some of the best schools of the fifteenth century. Among those who benefited from training by the Brethren was Erasmus, the greatest humanist of his time. Thomas à Kempis, another student and subsequently community member, produced his *Imitation of Christ,* which reflects much of the movement's spirit and ideals.

The Brethren represented a reaction against the contemporary moral slackness and lack of religious zeal. Many of their communities (which had spread into Germany and on to Switzerland) derived their income from copying manuscripts, notably Bibles, missals, and prayer books. "You should order the work of your hands," copyists were instructed, "to the end that it may lead you to purity of heart, because you are weak and cannot be always at spiritual exercises, and for this reason was handiwork instituted." Florent assumed the leadership after Groote's death in 1384; he and some others further expanded Brethren interests by becoming Augustinian canons and founding the famous congregation of Windesheim. Known sometimes as the *Devotio Moderna,* the movement was overtaken by the Reformation, and did not long survive the opening of the seventeenth century.

J. D. Douglas

See also Devotio Moderna; Thomas à Kempis; Groote, Gerard.

Bibliography. A. Hyma, *The Brethren of the Common Life* and *The Christian Renaissance;* S. Kettlewell, *Thomas à Kempis and the Brethren of the Common Life,* 2 vols.

Bride of Christ. *See* Church, The.

British Israelitism.

The ideas of this group can be traced back to John Sadler's book, *The Rights of the Kingdom* (1649), but its modern form originated with John Wilson's *Our Israelitish Origin* (1814). The first society to propagate British Israelite views was the Anglo-Saxon Association founded in England in 1879. Today British Israelitism is in decline and only a few scattered groups remain; however, their influence in a somewhat distorted form is to be found in publications like Herbert W. Armstrong's *The Plain Truth.*

There is no authorized version of British Israelitism, but the following outline summarizes their main views. In the Bible God promised Abraham that as long as the sun and moon and stars endure Israel would survive as a nation. From promises found in the OT it is clear that Israel must exist somewhere today and must have had a continuous existence as a national entity right back to the time of Abraham. This required continuity means that the state of Israel, which came into existence in 1948, cannot be the nation of Israel. The present state of Israel is Jewish and therefore must not be confused with the historic nation of Israel. Marshaling a variety of arguments from the Bible and history, British Israelitism argues that the Anglo-Saxon people are the true Israel.

British Israelites claim that after the destruction of David's kingdom, Zedekiah's daughters (Jer. 41:10) escaped death in Egypt (Jer. 44:12–14) and took refuge (Isa. 37:31–32) in one of the "isles of the sea" (Jer. 31:10) to which they sailed in a ship with Jeremiah. These "isles" were Ireland, from where their descendants reached England and became the royal house. Thus the British royal family is directly linked to the house of David. The common people, however, reached England after wandering through the continent of Europe, where they were "sifted through many nations" (Amos 9:9). In the course of this sifting some true Israelites remained in western Europe, enabling British Israelitism to claim members in Germany, the Netherlands, and other parts of the Anglo-Saxon world.

With the Israelite origins of the British people established, OT prophecies are applied to the history of the British empire. America is included in the scheme by the application of Gen. 49:22, which is said to predict the emigration of the Pilgrim fathers, who left their relatives behind to establish a new nation. In addition to taking a highly literalist view of the Bible, British Israelites claim that the Great Pyramid of Egypt enshrines these truths in its measurements, which are sacred.

British Israelitism is not a sect or a cult but rather a fellowship which is to be found in many churches. At its height, around 1900, it claimed over two million members. Today its membership consists of several thousand rather elderly people. A careful examination of the texts used by British Israelites to support their arguments shows that they flout the rules of biblical exegesis. Even if their arguments were true, Paul's comment in Col. 3:11 would indicate that they are unimportant. British Israelitism fails to recognize that the promises of God in the OT were sometimes conditional (Deut. 28:58–68; I Sam. 2:30), while in other places prophetic language has a symbolic or poetic quality. The historical arguments of British Israelites are equally tenuous and no reputable historian supports them. Although the Bible does not explicitly state the fact, it is clear that the so-called lost tribes of Israel were largely absorbed into the tribe of Judah. I. HEXHAM

See also GLASTONBURY.

Bibliography. H. L. Goudge, *The British Israel Theory;* M. H. Gayer, *The Heritage of the Anglo-Saxon Race;* B. Wilson, ed., *Patterns of Sectarianism,* ch. 10; J. Tuit, *The Truth Shall Make You Free;* L. Deboer, *The New Phariseeism.*

Brother. *See* CHRISTIANS, NAMES OF.

Brown, William Adams (1865–1943). American Presbyterian theologian and social and ecumenical activist. Brown was born in New York City and educated at Yale, at Union Seminary in his hometown, and at Berlin under Harnack. He returned in 1892 to Union, serving on the faculty forty-four years. He was perhaps the most influential liberal theologian of his time and thoroughly representative of that viewpoint. Brown emphasized the life, personality, and certain teachings of the historical Jesus rather than the traditional orthodox doctrines about Christ. He held to the moral influence view of the atonement. He was confident that God works uniquely through Jesus to promote transformation in the lives of his followers, and through them to introduce gradually a better social order, the kingdom of God.

Believing that the proof of Christianity was in the practices it motivated, Brown was actively involved in ministry to slum dwellers and supported such causes as the emerging labor movement. Rather than trying to do everything, Brown felt the church should cooperate with home, school, workplace, and government in order to bring about a Christianized society (see *The Church in America,* 1922). In later writings, such as *God at Work* (1933), there were mild indications of the more realistic influence of neo-orthodoxy.

Brown saw denominational barriers as impediments to the practical task of the church. Accordingly he actively promoted the emerging ecumenical movement by involvement with several strands that would lead to the World Council of Churches. *The Church: Catholic and Protestant* (1935) and *Toward a United Church* (1946) dealt with this concern.

But Brown was primarily a theological professor, and significantly his autobiography is entitled *A Teacher and His Times* (1940). His influence spread widely beyond his own classes because of *Christian Theology in Outline* (1906), which was one of the two most widely used texts of liberal theology, the other being by William Clarke. D. G. TINDER

See also LIBERALISM, THEOLOGICAL.

Bibliography. S. M. Cavert and H. P. Van Dusen, eds., *The Church Through Half a Century: Essays in Honor of William Adams Brown.*

Brunner, Heinrich Emil (1889–1966). Swiss Reformed theologian, one of the "Three Bs" (Barth, Brunner, and Bultmann) who dominated twentieth century theological studies in the Christian world. A part of the circle which developed a new theological movement known variously as the theology of crisis, dialectical theology, neo-orthodoxy, and Barthian theology, Brunner represented the movement's middle ground. Karl

Barth and Brunner were the pioneers of what came to be known popularly as neo-orthodoxy, each developing his thought independently of the other.

Born at Winterthur, near Zurich, Brunner studied at the universities of Zurich and Berlin, earning his Th.D. from the latter in 1913. The period 1913–24 included a year of teaching in England, service in the Swiss militia during World War I, pastoral experience in Switzerland, marriage, and a year of study at Union Theological Seminary in New York (1919–20). From 1924 to 1955 he was professor of systematic and practical theology at the University of Zurich. During these years he made frequent lecture tours in Europe, Britain, and America, and in 1953–55 served as visiting professor at the newly established International Christian University in Tokyo. Returning from Japan in 1955, Brunner suffered a stroke which permanently impaired his speech and writing. However, in spite of a series of subsequent strokes he continued to work on a limited basis for several more years and managed to complete the third volume of his magisterial *Dogmatics* in 1960.

During forty-nine years of active writing Brunner published at least 396 books and scholarly journal articles, of which twenty-three books were translated into English. *The Mediator* (1927), which was the first attempt to treat the doctrine of Christ in terms of the new dialectical theology, established his reputation and led to his wide popularity as a visiting lecturer. In this work Brunner's thought was deeply influenced by Søren Kierkegaard's dialectic and Martin Buber's I-Thou concept.

A breach between Brunner and Barth over the issue of natural theology culminated in 1934 with the publication of Brunner's *Nature and Grace: A Discussion with Karl Barth* and Barth's categorical reply, *No!* In essence, Brunner, unlike Barth, accepted natural theology and the continuing presence of God's image in humans after the fall. As he diminished his contacts with Barth, however, he expanded them with other Christians in the context of the ecumenical movement, though his emphasis in this area was always on spiritual rather than institutional brotherhood established firmly on biblical rather than liberal theology.

Brunner's thought was characterized by a high Christology; an emphasis on personal encounter in Jesus Christ as the centerpiece of the Christian faith; an ethical system that attempted to maintain a balance between individualism and community; and a view of the church rightly patterned on the NT *ecclesia* as a fellowship of persons in Christ and wrongly constituted by men as an externally organized community. His doctrine of man stressed the paradoxical nature of man as both the image of God and a sinner, on one hand, and as both an individual and a member of a community, on the other. Brunner was highly influential in all these areas of his thought except, perhaps, that of the church.

However, his greatest enduring impact has been in the field of Christology and in his insistence that God can be known only through personal encounter. In Christology, Brunner was a part of the wrecking crew which attacked the body of then current theological liberalism with its humanistic and essentially unitarian picture of Jesus. In its place he attempted a fresh restatement of what he regarded as the indispensable Christian belief that the appearance of Jesus Christ was unique and unrepeatable—that Jesus was not just a great teacher or a humanitarian martyr but the one and only incarnation of the Word of God. In this Brunner stressed the incarnation and the resurrection as cornerstones of the Christian faith and accepted the definition of Chalcedon that Jesus Christ is at once true God and true man.

Related to his Christology was his belief that the truth about the Lord is discovered not through theorizing about his nature but through personal encounter with him, which was for Brunner a primary category of faith and theology. He tried to avoid a false objectivism (which he regarded as typical of unquestioning biblical literalists and dogmatic Roman Catholics) and a false subjectivism (which he regarded as characteristic of certain mystics, romantic liberals, and millenarian and Pentecostal enthusiasts). Thus, in *The Divine-Human Encounter* (1938) he took a middle ground between historic Calvinism and traditional Arminianism, arguing that the biblical witness shows God always to be God-approaching-man and man as always man-coming-from-God, and their meeting point as Jesus Christ. Moreover, he taught that although only God can take the initiative in arranging this meeting, God does not overwhelm his creature but treats each person as a free and responsible being whom he loves and whose choice is either to accept divine grace in faith or reject it in sin. The primary place in which this revelatory encounter takes place is Jesus Christ, for God reveals himself as Lord and Savior uniquely and decisively in Jesus. However, Brunner also believed that God's revelation of himself and his invitation to encounter continue in several areas of history and experience—namely, in the Scriptures, in the faith of the church, and in the personal testimony of the Holy Spirit in the hearts of individuals. Therefore, since God's revelation is neither timeless nor confined to a certain point in time, God keeps on encountering people.

Orthodox Christians are indebted to Brunner for his telling criticism of theological liberalism—especially of its sentimental and degrading portrayal of Jesus, its optimistic view of the essential goodness of humans, and its progressive idea of history as inevitably leading to the kingdom of God. Moreover, Brunner successfully rehabilitated and restated for the twentieth century many historic Christian doctrines: sin, the incarnation and resurrection of Christ, the centrality of Jesus in salvation, the need for a personal faith, and the church as a fellowship rather than an institution. Finally, and probably most importantly, he reestablished the Scriptures as the norm for faith and practice in Christian churches.

However, Brunner also has been sharply criticized by more orthodox theologians on several counts. For example, they find his rejection of certain doctrines such as the virgin birth and hell and his dismissal of the Adam and Eve account as symbolic to be subbiblical and even inconsistent with other of his doctrinal emphases. They point out that at times he seemed almost arbitrary in delineating what was biblical and what was not. For instance, though he appeared to assume that creation out of nothing and the image of God in man were biblically true, he rejected the virgin birth and hell as not widely supported in Scriptures. In so doing, it would seem that Brunner's judgment in these matters was obviously rational, despite his belief that he consistently stressed the supremacy of divine revelation over human knowledge, reason, and experience. Further, Brunner is sometimes accused of universalism on the basis of his teachings on the last judgment and ultimate redemption because of his ambiguity on these points. However, since one of his strongest emphases throughout his theology is that of personal responsibility and accountability, it seems unlikely that this was his real intent.

Others have denounced Brunner for system-building, for too much emphasis on structure, for being obsessed with form and content, and for his dialectical approach. However, the most telling criticisms have come from more conservative theologians who have disapproved of his doctrine of the Scriptures, especially in regard to the matter of inspiration. There is no doubt that Brunner accepted biblical authority as the norm for Christian theology. However, he regarded inspiration as only one aspect of the larger doctrine of revelation and felt that any attempt to indicate "the how" of it led to unwarranted speculative theory—such as that expressed in the doctrine of inerrancy. It seems fair to point out, however, that he could have said more about the meaning of inspiration for the production and preservation of Scripture, even if he did not believe in the plenary verbal view. Finally, like all neo-orthodox theologians Brunner, from the viewpoint of more traditionally orthodox Christian scholars, appeared arbitrary and capricious at times in his handling of the biblical text.

Brunner and Barth probably did more than any other twentieth century thinkers to prepare the way for the resurgence of historic biblical Christianity in the Western world in the last half of the twentieth century. In the final analysis, as time passes, historians and historical theologians appear more and more inclined to see Brunner as a scholar with an open and basically liberal mind who arrived at a basically conservative theological position. In any case, his thought, although clearly in what has been labeled the neo-orthodox camp, will continue to be valuable to more conservative theologians in their own attempts to interpret biblical truth to the modern mind.

R. D. Linder

See also Barth, Karl; Neo-orthodoxy.

Bibliography. Brunner, *Revelation and Reason, The Divine Imperative,* and *Dogmatics,* 3 vols.; P. K. Jewett, *Emil Brunner: An Introduction to the Man and His Thought;* C. W. Kegley, ed., *The Theology of Emil Brunner;* J. E. Humphrey, *Emil Brunner.*

Buber, Martin (1878–1965). Jewish religious thinker whose writings have influenced some Christian theologians. Raised in central Europe during the beginning years of Zionism, Buber became involved with that movement soon after his university education was completed. But from 1904 to 1909 he withdrew from public life to learn more about the Hasidism to which his grandparents had introduced him as a boy. Hasidism, a religious movement arising in the mid-eighteenth century among eastern European Jews, stressed loyalty to the covenant and piety. Around the rabbinic leaders of the movement communities formed which yet lived in and with the world. By the "hallowing of the everyday," by affirming every person in his or her wholeness, it was believed that one can transform oneself and the world for God. This concern to develop true humanity under God through communal relationships in everyday life came to spark all of Buber's thought and activity as an educator, writer, editor, and lecturer.

In 1938 he left Germany to become professor of sociology at the Hebrew University of Jerusalem. Here he enjoyed a distinguished career as a world-renowned proponent of what he took to be the true Hebrew humanism expressed in the

Hasidic teaching that "God is to be seen in everything, and reached by every pure deed."

Particularly through his widely read book *I and Thou,* Buber's ideas on true life as relation became known outside the Jewish world. He claims that in one's life with nature, with other persons, and with spiritual existences, a person can become an "I" only when the object with which one has to do is seen as a "Thou" rather than as an impersonal "it." In and through such relational events there is a meeting with the absolute Other, the eternal Thou, God. This is not so much a mystical union, or the transcendent becoming immanent, as it is an existential encounter taking place in faith.

Buber's concept of the "I-Thou" relationship has been adopted by several Christian theologians, notably Friedrich Gogarten, Karl Heim, Karl Barth, Dietrich Bonhoeffer, and Rudolf Bultmann. S. R. Obitts

Bibliography. Buber, *Between Man and Man, Two Types of Faith,* and *A Believing Humanism;* P. Schilpp and M. Friedman, eds., *The Philosophy of Martin Buber;* G. Schaeder, *The Hebrew Humanism of Martin Buber;* W. Herberg, ed., *The Writings of Martin Buber;* R. G. Smith, *Martin Buber;* M. Friedman, *Martin Buber's Life and Work;* M. Cohn and R. Buber, eds., *Martin Buber: A Bibliography of His Writings 1897–1978.*

Bucer, Martin (1491–1551). A leading figure in the European and English reformation movements. Bucer entered the Dominican Order in 1506, but his eventual emphasis on the work of the Holy Spirit in many ways made him a spiritual ancestor of John Wesley. Born at Schlettstadt in Alsace, he was introduced to Luther's theology in 1518 at Heidelberg. Convinced of the merits of the Reformation, in 1521 he received papal dispensation from his religious vows. His excommunication for preaching Lutheran theology (1523) was preceded by his marriage as a priest in 1522.

Captivated by Luther's disputation against medieval scholasticism (Heidelberg, 1518), Bucer, although a member of Tetzel's order, rose to Luther's defense. His *Summary,* a brief treatise, clearly established Bucer as a disciple of Luther and also as one possessed of an independent and free theological spirit. In *Summary* he heralds the Lutheran theme that men are justified by faith alone. Anyone who cannot so trust or teaches contrary to *sola fide* is the antichrist. A second, more independent theme—the power and guidance of the Holy Spirit in the reading of Scripture—is amplified. The word separated from the Spirit and from faith is divorced from Jesus Christ and salvation. This latter theme is exploited systematically by Bucer's most illustrious pupil, John Calvin.

Bucer gradually moved from a Lutheran doctrine of the Eucharist and under the influence of Zwingli and Carlstadt embraced a more symbolic interpretation of the sacraments. More radical than Luther, Bucer had no stomach for a doctrine of the ubiquity of the body of Christ; he found solace in Zwingli's notion that Christ's body is in heaven. Unable to embrace Zwingli's claim that the Lord's Supper is not in the strict sense a means of grace, Bucer moved to a middle position that rejected Luther's claim for the ubiquity of Christ's body but subscribed to the Lutheran notion that the sacrament is a means by which God graciously feeds his church; thus, the Lord's Supper is a means of grace. Affirming Zwingli's insistence that Christ's body is in heaven at the right hand of God, Bucer parted company with Zwingli's claim that the Lord's Supper is a memorial only, void of sacramental energy.

His mediating position thrust Bucer into several conciliatory efforts on the continent and in England. With Wolfgang Capito he coauthored the Tetrapolitan Confession (1530), an attempt drawn up at the Diet of Augsburg to effect reconciliation between the Reformed and evangelical wings. Again in the Concord of Wittenberg (1536) he collaborated with Melanchthon to assist Saxon Lutheran theologians in achieving unity over the doctrine of the bodily/spiritual presence of Christ in the sacrament. In England he developed a doctrine of the church as a living extension of the incarnation, committed to transforming the entire political and social order with its stress on discipline, visibility, and transformation of personal and corporate entities. These views were published posthumously as *De regno Christi* (1557).

Bucer's mediating position endeavored to adjudicate the hostilities between the Zwinglians and Lutherans on the continent. In England his views, especially his emphasis on the work of the Holy Spirit in the individual believer, put him at odds with Luther because Bucer could not take Luther's stance that justification automatically imputes sinful impulses, setting aside the law and the old man. Bucer therefore committed himself to a two-stage doctrine of justification. First is forgiveness of sin through Jesus Christ, without benefit of any human effort or contribution. In the second stage—and the controversial one—one is justified as one begins to perform works of love. This second stage (*justificatio legis*) opens the door for Wesley's doctrine of perfectionism and the Puritan call for visible evidences of the pure life.

In his latter years as Regius Professor of Divinity at Cambridge he played a significant role in the creation of the Ordinal of 1550 and in the reform of the *Book of Common Prayer* (1552). Bucer's doctrine of the church emerged as a significant contribution to the discussion of the church in the Reformation period. His dual emphasis on the church and the Holy Spirit probably influenced Calvin's doctrine of double predestination: only the elect have the Spirit; fruits of the Spirit are evidence that one is among the elect. P. A. MICKEY

See also TETRAPOLITAN CONFESSION; WITTENBERG, CONCORD OF.

Bibliography. W. Pauck, *Heritage of the Reformation.*

Buchman, Frank. *See* MORAL REARMAMENT.

Building. The metaphor of the church as a building is based on the words of Jesus himself. In Matt. 16:18 he declared, "Upon this rock I will build my church." The verb is *oikodomeō,* from *oikos,* house, normally used for erecting a building, but here used metaphorically. In all three Synoptic Gospels, Jesus is recorded as quoting Ps. 118:22: "The stone which the builders rejected, the same was made the head of the corner." Jesus is the keystone that holds the building together (cf. I Pet. 2:7).

Paul wrote to the Corinthians, "Ye are God's building" (I Cor. 3:9). Jesus Christ is the only foundation (I Cor. 3:11) of this "spiritual house" (I Pet. 2:5). The noun *oikodomē* is often translated "edifying" or "edification." R. EARLE

See also CHURCH, THE.

Bulgakov, Sergei Nikolaevich (1870–1944). Russian economist and theologian. Though a son of a Russian Orthodox priest, he abandoned the views of the church during his early life. Graduating from Moscow University (1894), he studied in Berlin, Paris, and London before returning to Russia to teach. He held professorships in political economics at the Polytechnic Institute of Kiev (1901–6), Moscow Institute of Commercial Science (1906–17), and Moscow University (1917–18). Meanwhile he had taken a doctorate in political economics at Moscow University (1912). In 1906 he was a member of the Second Duma (parliament), which sought to liberalize the Russian political system. Gradually returning to the faith of the Eastern Orthodox Church, he was ordained to the priesthood in 1918. Thereafter he served as professor at the University of Sympheropol in the Crimea. Expelled from Russia by the government in 1923, he went first to Prague to teach and then to Paris (1925), where he was professor and dean of the Orthodox Theological Institute.

Bulgakov's intellectual pilgrimage took him from Marxism to idealism to mysticism. He came to believe that the world was animated by a world soul and that God had created the world out of nothing. During his later years his goal was to interpret the main teachings of the Christian church in the light of the doctrine of Sophia or Holy Wisdom, a third being that mediated between God and the cosmos. Though his orthodoxy was challenged in some quarters, he was never subjected to official interrogation or censure.

Among his many publications are *The Unfading Light* (1917), *Jacob's Ladder* (1929), *The Orthodox Church* (1935), *The Comforter* (1936), and *The Wisdom of God, a Brief Summary of Sophiology* (1937). H. F. VOS

Bibliography. L. Zander, *God and the World: The World Conception of Father S. Bulgakov.*

Bullinger, Johann Heinrich (1504–1575). As successor to Zwingli in Zurich, Bullinger played a major role in the Protestant Reformation. He was the son of a parish priest. While studying theology at Cologne he was stimulated through his study of the early church fathers to a fresh investigation of the Scriptures. After he returned home to Zurich, he joined with Zwingli in the move to reform the church. Four years later, after Zwingli's death, Bullinger became the leader of the Zurich branch of the Swiss Reformation. Although the center of Reformed leadership soon passed from Zurich to Geneva and to John Calvin, Bullinger's influence continued for some forty years among those who adhered to Zwingli's version of the Protestant faith. He regularly preached and taught the Scriptures, delivered commentaries on the books of the Bible, set forth theological treatises on the disputed questions of the day, sought to establish and maintain fraternal relations with other Reformed Christians, and wrote a multivolume history of the Reformation.

The best summary of Bullinger's theology is his *Decades.* This work consisted of fifty long sermons dealing with the major tenets of Christian doctrine. They were published during 1549–51 and soon translated into English, Dutch, and French. In England the *Decades* served as the officially appointed theological guide for clergy who had not obtained a master's degree. Bullinger also wrote major studies on providence, justification, and the nature of the Scriptures. All told, his works number approximately 150.

Bullinger played an important role in uniting Protestants. He and Calvin sought to avert potential schisms in the Protestant movement through their proposal of the Zurich Agreement (1549). They agreed that believers receive Christ spiritually and are united to him through the Lord's Supper. Later Bullinger authored the Second Helvetic Confession, published in 1566, which became the bond of unity for Calvinistic churches scattered throughout Europe.

Like the other leaders of the Reformation, Bullinger emphasized the centrality of the Scriptures. The first sermons in his *Decades* deal with the giving of Scripture as God's all-sufficient revelation to all people for their salvation and sanctification. To comprehend fully the biblical message requires an awareness of the importance of the analogy of faith, reading texts in context, comparing Scripture with Scripture, and, most importantly, "a heart that loves God and seeks his glory." Ultimately the reader is dependent on the Holy Spirit to give understanding of the text.

Bullinger's ecclesiology agreed with that developed by the other Reformers. The invisible church is composed of all the elect, while the visible church consists of all professing Christians. Only God knows perfectly the members of each. The true church is characterized by proper preaching of the word of God and faithful administration of the two sacraments of baptism and the Lord's Supper. The true apostolic succession is found not in historical descent through bishops but in preaching and teaching those truths given by the apostles. While rejecting the papacy and its authoritative claims, Bullinger was willing to judge the Roman Catholic Church as well as Protestantism by the word proclaimed and the two sacraments administered correctly.

O. G. Oliver, Jr.

See also Helvetic Confessions; Zurich Agreement.

Bibliography. G. W. Bromiley, *Historical Theology* and (ed.) *Zwingli and Bullinger;* P. Schaff, *History of the Christian Church,* VIII, 204–14.

Bultmann, Rudolf (1884–1976). One of the twentieth century's most influential theologians. Professor in the University of Marburg, he was well known for his scholarly historical and interpretive writings on the NT. But his scholarship was never mere historical curiosity; he was at heart a churchman, seeking by his scholarship to make the Christian message live for his contemporaries.

In Bultmann's view the most pressing task facing theologians in the twentieth century was to discover a "conceptuality" in terms of which the NT could be made understandable to modern man, and then to work out the details of this interpretation. Bultmann believed that he had found such a conceptuality in the existentialist philosophy of Martin Heidegger, and spent virtually his entire career reading the NT as a Heideggerian document and using historical-critical methods to eliminate from the text elements resistive to existentialism.

According to Heidegger's philosophy as Bultmann read it, man in his truest nature is a being utterly different from anything that can be found in the world, and his distinctiveness is the fact that he is a maker of decisions. If decision making is man's essence, then the future rather than the past is his spiritual element, because only the future holds options, and only where there are options can there be decisions. According to Bultmann man does many things to avoid facing the fact that he is a decision maker. He often lives by dead traditions; he lets legalistic ethical systems make his decisions for him; he thinks of himself as having fixed character traits from which his actions issue rather than from decisions; he identifies himself by reference to his social roles and relations to other people, thus refusing total responsibility for his identity. In these and other ways man is "inauthentic"—that is, not him*self.* Bultmann thinks that when the NT speaks of man as a "sinner" and under the sway of "death," this inauthenticity is what it has in mind.

Salvation, then, is "radical openness to the future," which is the same as man's full acknowledgment that he is a decision maker. The secular existentialists tend to think man can become authentic by forthrightly confronting his own death and insecurity and meaninglessness, but Bultmann, being a Christian, maintains that man finds salvation only if he receives it as a gift. Thus he argues that man is in need of a savior, and even goes so far as to say that authenticity can be achieved only through Jesus Christ.

For Bultmann NT ideas such as the resurrection of the body, blood atonement for sins, everlasting life, an ethical ideal of human nature, and a salvation history only serve to mislead people about what salvation really is. These are primitive, "mythological" ideas which need to be reinterpreted in existentialist terms. In the 1940s he began to call this interpretive activity "demythologizing," and it is this word above all which is associated, in the popular mind, with the name of Bultmann.

R. C. Roberts

See also Demythologization; Existentialism; New Hermeneutic, The.

Bibliography. Bultmann, *Jesus and the Word, Jesus Christ and Mythology, Kerygma and Myth,* and *Theology of the NT,* 2 vols.; A. Malet, *The Thought of Rudolf Bultmann;* R. C. Roberts, *Rudolf Bultmann's Theology: A Critical Interpretation;* W. Schmithals, *An Introduction to the Theology of Rudolf Bultmann;* A. C. Thiselton, *The Two Horizons: NT Hermeneutics and Philosophical Description.*

Bunyan, John (1628–1688). One of the most influential authors of the seventeenth century. Although he had a bare minimum of education, a hyperconscientious religious sensitivity which at times seemed almost paralyzing led him into the depths of the gospel of grace that he discovered in the Bible.

Active as a lay preacher in the Parliamentary army and during the Commonwealth, he continued to preach during the Restoration and was imprisoned twelve years for doing so. Declining to be freed on the condition that he no longer preach, his famous reply was: "If I am freed today I will preach tomorrow."

During his imprisonment he wrote *Pilgrim's Progress*, the greatest book of its kind in English; *Grace Abounding to the Chief of Sinners*, a spiritual autobiography; and *Defense of Justification by Faith*, an uncompromising criticism of the rising tide of Pelagianism among Nonconformity and latitudinarianism among the Anglican establishment. He was attacked by Bishop Edward Fowler in a book, *Dirt Wiped Off*, but favorably mentioned by the illustrious Bishop of Lincoln, Thomas Barlow.

Macauley claims that *The Holy War*, written after his imprisonment, "would be the best allegory ever written if *Pilgrim's Progress* did not exist." Except for the Bible itself, no book was held in such respect among the lower and middle classes of England during the eighteenth century as *Pilgrim's Progress*. In Scotland and colonial America, Bunyan's popularity exceeded that in England. Jonathan Swift and Samuel Johnson acknowledged his greatness, but on the whole he was ignored in literary circles until the romantic movement in the nineteenth century.

He is duly appreciated for his literary genius by contemporary scholars who have indicated some influences upon him not previously noticed but which have not detracted from their profound appreciation of the "sublime tinker." This literary interest, unfortunately, has not been matched by a comparable appreciation of his doctrine. The unforgettable imagery and unusual blend of thought and passion were grounded in the classical Reformation teachings concerning man's fallen nature, grace, imputation, justification, and the atonement—all of which Bunyan seemed to have derived directly from Scripture with little mediation through theologians.

C. F. Allison

Bibliography. T. B. Macauley, *Critical and Historical Essays*, I; J. Brown, *John Bunyan: His Life, Times and Work;* R. M. Frye, *God, Man, and Satan;* O. E. Winslow, *John Bunyan;* R. Sharrock, *John Bunyan;* R. Greaves, *John Bunyan.*

Burnt Offering. *See* Offerings and Sacrifices in Bible Times.

Bushnell, Horace (1802–1876). Known as "the father of American theological liberalism," Bushnell was a complex figure who incorporated into his thought many of the traditional Puritan elements that later theological conservatives would also preserve. His theology combined the Puritan sense of covenant, influences from Europe and England, a great confidence in the future of America, and an organic view of God's work in history. He was a resident of Connecticut his entire life, but his thought—whether about great doctrines like the atonement or about national crises like the Civil War—was never provincial.

Bushnell was converted in part through the influence of Samuel Taylor Coleridge's writings. He attended Yale Divinity School and began a lengthy association with Hartford's North Church in 1833. The members of this church, to save their respected minister from charges of heresy made by other Congregationalists, eventually left their local consociation. Bushnell enjoyed an unusual ability to reconcile competing theological ideas. His work was a penetrating synthesis of many of the more advanced ideas of his age. He was, for his times, the Christian's answer to Ralph Waldo Emerson.

Bushnell's major works spell out the main currents of his thought. *Christian Nurture* (1847) focused new attention on the religious training of young people. It argued, in contrast to the dominant revivalism of the day, that long-range education was the surest way to inculcate the Christian faith. His most important theological work followed soon thereafter, a "Dissertation of Language" prefaced to *God in Christ* (1849). This essay contended that human language is inadequate to the realities of spiritual existence, which always demand symbolic representation. Bushnell himself may not have intended this work as an open invitation to recast orthodox understandings of Christianity, but many who followed in his train used it in that way. *Nature and the Supernatural* (1858) suggested that all things, natural and supernatural, shared a common spiritual character. His *Vicarious Sacrifice* (1866) arose out of a deep sense of tragedy at the unfolding of the Civil War combined with a lifetime's reflection on the nature of Christ's work. His conclusion was that the death of Christ was intended primarily as an example for the human race to follow in self-giving sacrifice.

Bushnell's influence hastened the acceptance in America of Friedrich Schleiermacher, Coleridge, and their romantic picture of the world.

Bushnell's theology enjoyed a large following among Americans who were suspicious of revival, optimistic about American democracy, uneasy about American vulgarity, and impressed with European innovations. To this kind of audience Bushnell offered a theological perspective which, while not itself completely divorced from traditional Protestantism, helped clear the way for a thorough liberalization of the faith. M. A. NOLL

See also LIBERALISM, THEOLOGICAL.

Bibliography. H. S. Smith, ed., *Horace Bushnell;* B. M. Cross, *Horace Bushnell: Minister to a Changing America.*

Butler, Joseph (1692–1752). A leading eighteenth century opponent of deism who is credited with considerable success in his defense of the theistic position.

Born in a Presbyterian home in Wantage, Berkshire, he was intended for the Presbyterian ministry, but chose not to throw in his lot with the dissenters and entered the ministry of the Church of England instead. After studies at Oxford he was ordained in 1718. He was preacher at Rolls Chapel, London (1719–26), rector of Haughton-le-Skerne (1721–25), rector of Stanhope (1725–40), chaplain to the lord chancellor (1733–36), clerk of the closet to Queen Caroline (1736–37), bishop of Bristol (1738–50), dean of St. Paul's (1740–50), clerk of the closet to George II (1746–50), and bishop of Durham, the richest see in England (1750–52). He declined the archbishopric of Canterbury in 1747. From the above list, it is clear that he was a pluralist—i.e., he held more than one church post at a time. In addition, he received various stipends from the church. He was not greedy, however, and was known for his generosity. He was a shy, sensitive man and never married. It is also clear that Butler enjoyed high positions in English church and state.

Butler lived during the "golden age of English deism," and he sought to cut the ground from under his deistic opponents. His great literary effort composed to that end was *The Analogy of Religion Natural and Revealed to the Constitution and Course of Nature* (1736). He took the position that the order in nature is paralleled by the order in revelation, intimating that God was author of both. He argued that the order and beauty of nature reveal a creating intelligence with some conscious design in view. So influential was this book that it did more to defeat deism than any other work and was for generations a text on apologetics in college and seminary.

Butler was also intensely practical, as his *Fifteen Sermons Preached at the Rolls Chapel* (1726) demonstrates. In this he sought to justify to practical men the practice of common virtues (benevolence, compassion, and the like). Practicality also dominated his *Six Sermons,* one of which was a defense of foreign missions and another an appeal for London hospitals. Most of the rest of his writings were destroyed after his death, according to his instructions. H. F. VOS

See also DEISM.

Bibliography. *DNB,* III, 519–24; I. Ramsey, *Joseph Butler.*

Cc

Caird, John (1820–1898). Scottish theologian. Born the son of a Greenock blacksmith, he served Church of Scotland parishes from 1845 to 1862, when he became professor of divinity and later principal (1873) of Glasgow University. A widely acclaimed sermon preached before Queen Victoria was hailed by his famous brother Edward as showing "the hollowness and worthlessness of any religion that wastes itself in feeling, in zeal for orthodoxy, or in the formalities of worship, and fails to consecrate the whole secular existence of man." His more Calvinistic colleagues condemned his brand of practical Christianity as creedless and heretical, and were appalled when he said he would not trouble to cross the street to convert a man from one denomination to another. Nonetheless he was a champion of the Kirk in those difficult post-disruption years and a trainer and encourager of theological students. An acknowledged authority on Spinoza, Caird reflected also strong neo-Hegelian tendencies in his *Introduction to the Philosophy of Religion* (1880) and in his Gifford Lectures published as *The Fundamental Ideas of Christianity* (1899). He condemned the unreality of making hard divisions between sacred and secular, but he was fiercely criticized for secularizing special revelation and for floating "a spurious semi-biblical theism in terms of philosophy of religion." J. D. Douglas

Bibliography. C. L. Warr, *Principal Caird.*

Cajetan, Thomas de Vio (1469–1534). Protestants remember Cajetan for his dramatic encounter with Martin Luther, but Roman Catholics give him his due as a philosopher, theologian, Bible scholar, and cardinal. He studied in the universities at Bologna and Padua; joined the Dominican Order in 1484; became a member of the Paduan theological faculty in 1493; served in Rome as procurator general for the Dominican Order, 1501–8; and was master general of the Dominican Order, 1508–18. He was given a cardinal's hat in 1517 and became Bishop of Gaeta in 1518. In his career he published about 115 works. Some of these were commentaries on Scripture translated and exegeted from Greek and Hebrew texts; they were intended to answer Protestant polemics based on exegesis from the original languages. But as an author and scholar Cajetan made his mark as a major Thomistic philosopher/theologian with his classic commentary on Thomas Aquinas's *Summa Theologica.*

In 1511 Cajetan became a leading defender of the power of the pope and the monarchical concept of the papacy against the claims of the Council of Pisa (a council not recognized by the Roman Catholic Church because it was not convened by a pope). It is not surprising, then, that Pope Leo X commissioned Cajetan, his legate at the time to the German Imperial Diet, to summon the upstart Martin Luther to Augsburg and to examine and pass judgment on the orthodoxy of Luther's views. Luther and Cajetan met on three successive days in mid-October, 1518. In the confrontation Cajetan argued that the pope was above church councils, the entire church, and Scripture. Luther replied that the pope was under the Word of God and asserted that some popes had twisted Scripture. The three days ended at an impasse with Cajetan ordering Luther to leave his presence and not to return unless he was ready to recant. That night Luther was secretly taken from Augsburg and safely returned to Wittenberg. In 1520 Cajetan helped draft the papal bull *Exsurge Domine* condemning Luther.

In spite of their sharp differences Luther recognized Cajetan as a person of learning and integrity. Indeed, though staunchly loyal to the Roman Church and Thomistic theology, Cajetan was an active advocate of reform of the abuses within the church. S. N. Gundry

See also Luther, Martin.

Bibliography. Thomas de Vio, *The Analogy of Names and the Concept of Being* and *Commentary on Being and Essence;* J. Wicks, ed., *Cajetan Responds: A Reader in Reformation Controversy.*

Call, Calling. The developed biblical idea of God's calling is of God summoning men by his word, and laying hold of them by his power, to play a part in and enjoy the benefits of his gracious redemptive purposes. This concept is derived from the ordinary secular meaning of the word (LXX and NT, *kaleō*)—i.e., summon, invite (see Matt. 2:7; 22:3–9)—by the addition of that quality of sovereign effectiveness which Scripture ascribes to the words of God as such. Divine utterance is creative, causing to exist the state of affairs which it declares to be intended (cf. Isa. 55:10–11; Gen. 1:3; Heb. 11:3). The thought in this case is of an act of summoning which effectively evokes from those addressed the response which it invites. The concept passes through various stages of growth before it reaches its final form in the NT epistles.

In the OT. Throughout the OT, Israel regards itself as a family which God had called first from heathendom, in the person of its ancestor (Isa. 51:2), and then from Egyptian bondage (Hos. 11:1), to be his own people (Isa. 43:1), serving him and enjoying his free favor forever. This conviction is most fully stated in Isa. 40–55. Here the central thought (developed in reference to the coming return from captivity) is that God's gracious once-for-all act of calling sinful Israel into an unbreakable covenant relation with himself guarantees to the nation the eventual everlasting enjoyment of all the kindnesses that omnipotent love can bestow (Isa. 48:12ff.; 54:6ff.; etc.). The calling of individuals receives mention only in connection with Israel's corporate destiny, either as the prototype of it (Abraham, Isa. 51:2), or as a summons to further it and bring the Gentiles to share it (Cyrus, Isa. 46:11; 48:15; the servant, 42:6; 49:1). The essence of the thought here is not verbal address (indeed, Cyrus, though called "by name"—i.e., announced as God's "shepherd" and "anointed"—does not know God's voice, Isa. 45:4; cf. 5:26ff.; 7:18ff.); "calling" signifies rather a disposition of events and destinies whereby God executes his purposes. The prophet's argument rests entirely on the assumption that God's callings express determinations which are unconditional, irreversible, and incapable of frustration (cf. Rom. 11:29). He views God's callings as sovereign acts, the temporal execution of eternal intentions.

In the NT. The thought of calling in the NT has to do with God's approach to the individual. In the Synoptics and Acts the term denotes God's verbal summons, spoken by Christ or in his name, to repentance, faith, salvation, and service (Mark 2:17 = Luke 5:32; Mark 1:20; Acts 2:39). The "called" (*klētoi*) in Matt. 22:14 are the recipients of this summons, as such; they form a larger company than the "chosen" (*eklektoi*), those who respond. In the epistles and Revelation, however, the concept is broadened, in accordance with the Isaiahic development noted above, to embrace God's sovereign action in securing a response to his summons. The verb "call" and the noun "calling" (*klēsis*) now refer to the effective evocation of faith through the gospel by the secret operation of the Holy Spirit, who unites men to Christ according to God's gracious purpose in election (Rom. 8:30; I Cor. 1:9; Gal. 1:15; II Thess. 2:13–14; II Tim. 1:9; Heb. 9:15; I Pet. 2:9; II Pet. 1:3, etc.). The "called" are those who have been the subjects of this work, i.e., elect believers (Rom. 1:6–7; 8:28; Jude 1; Rev. 17:14, etc.). This is the effectual or internal calling of classical Reformed theology, the first act in the *ordo salutis* whereby the benefits of redemption are conveyed to those for whom they were intended (see Rom. 9:23–26). This "upward," "heavenly" calling to freedom and felicity (Phil. 3:14 RSV; Heb. 3:1; Gal. 5:13; I Cor. 7:22 RSV; I Thess. 2:12; I Pet. 5:10) has ethical implications: it demands a worthy walk (Eph. 4:1) in holiness, patience, peace (I Thess. 4:7; I Pet. 1:15; 2:21; I Cor. 7:15; Col. 3:15), and sustained moral exertion (Phil. 3:14; I Tim. 6:12).

The terminology of calling has two subordinate applications in the NT: (1) to God's summons and designation of individuals to particular functions and offices in his redemptive plan (apostleship, Rom. 1:1; missionary preaching, Acts 13:2; 16:10; high priesthood, Heb. 5:4; cf. the calling of Cyrus mentioned above and of Bezaleel (Exod. 31:2); (2) to the external circumstances and state of life in which a man's effectual calling took place (I Cor. 1:26; 7:20). This is not quite the sense of "occupation" or "trade" which the Reformers supposed that it bore in the latter verse; but their revaluation of secular employment as a true "vocation" to God's service has too broad a biblical foundation to be invalidated by the detection of this slight inaccuracy. J. I. Packer

See also Elect, Election; Vocation.

Bibliography. R. Macpherson in *HDCG;* T. Nicol in *HDAC;* systematic theologies of C. Hodge (II, 639–732), L. Berkhof (IV. v–vi, 454–72); L. Coenen, *NIDNTT,* I, 271ff.; K. L. Schmidt, *TDNT,* III, 487ff.; H. H. Rowley, *The Biblical Doctrine of Election.*

Calovius, Abraham (1612–1686). German Lutheran theologian recognized as one of the leading representatives of seventeenth century Lutheran orthodoxy. Born in East Prussia, he entered the University of Königsberg at age fourteen, received an MA at twenty and an STD at twenty-five. After experience elsewhere as both a professor and pastor, Calovius joined the faculty of the University of Wittenberg as professor of theology in 1650. Later he became primarius and superintendent.

Calovius was rigidly orthodox, but at the same time he was known for his personal, practical piety. He was sympathetic with the concerns of Johann Arndt and Philipp Jakob Spener. His concern for orthodoxy extended to the most precise details of theological formulation, with every biblically based theological point regarded as a fundamental of the faith. This conviction put Calovius in direct opposition to fellow Lutheran George Calixtus, who held that the teaching of the early church as embodied in the Apostles' Creed was the criterion for fundamental truth. It was a complete doctrinal norm for all time and needed no further definition. Calixtus called upon all churches who accepted the Apostles' Creed to recognize and cooperate with one another. This, of course, included the Lutheran, Reformed, and Roman Catholic churches.

Calovius labeled Calixtus's view as "syncretism" and charged that on his view Arians, Socinians, Arminians, and Anabaptists could not be charged with heresy. By way of contrast, Calovius held that all revealed truth is fundamental for salvation. In 1664 Calovius proposed a new confession for Lutherans that is typical of his position. It rejected the following as heresies: that the Trinity is not revealed in the OT; that the angel of the Lord is not Christ; that OT believers did not know and believe the doctrine of Christ's person and office; that creationism is an explanation for the origin of souls; that the existence of God does not need to be proved by theology; that newly born children do not have real faith; and that Romanists and Calvinists can belong to the true church, can have hope of salvation, and are not condemned to eternal death.

It is difficult to escape the conclusion that Calovius's *de facto* definition of the fundamentals of the Christian faith was divine revelation as defined by Calovius. And it should come as no surprise that Calovius exercised his polemic skills not only against fellow Lutheran syncretists but also against Socinians, Calvinists, Arminians, Anabaptists, Roman Catholics, mystics, and the views of Hugo Grotius. *Systema locorum theologicorum,* regarded by some as the high point of Lutheran scholasticism, was his major work in systematic theology; *Biblia illustrata,* written to refute Grotius's commentaries, was his major exegetical work.

S. N. Gundry

See also Scholasticism, Protestant.

Bibliography. *Encyclopedia of the Lutheran Church,* I; O. W. Heick, *A History of Christian Thought,* II; W. Elert, *The Structure of Lutheranism,* I.

Calvin, John (1509–1564). Father of Reformed and Presbyterian doctrine and theology. Calvin was born in Noyon, Picardie. His father was a notary who served the bishop of Noyon, and as a result Calvin, while still a child, received a canonry in the cathedral which would pay for his education. Although he commenced training for the priesthood at the University of Paris, his father, because of a controversy with the bishop and clergy of the Noyon cathedral, now decided that his son should become a lawyer, and sent him to Orléans, where he studied under Pierre de l'Étoile. Later he studied at Bourges under the humanist lawyer Andrea Alciati. It was probably while in Bourges that he became a Protestant.

On his father's death Calvin returned to Paris, where he became involved with the Protestants there and as a result had to leave, eventually spending some time in Italy and in Basel, Switzerland. In the latter city he published the first edition of the *Institutes of the Christian Religion* (1536). After wandering around France, he decided to go to Strasbourg, a Protestant city, but while stopping overnight in Geneva he was approached by William Farel, who had introduced the Protestant movement there. After considerable argument Calvin was persuaded to stay and help. Calvin and Farel, however, soon ran into strong opposition and were forced out of the city, Calvin going to Strasbourg, where he stayed for three years (1538–41), ministering to a French Protestant refugee congregation. Called back to Geneva in 1541, he remained there for the rest of his life as the leader of the Reformed Church.

While Calvin was the pastor of the Église St. Pierre and spent much of his time preaching, his greatest influence came from his writings. Both his Latin and his French were clear and his reasoning lucid. He wrote commentaries on twenty-three of the OT books and on all of the NT except the Apocalypse. In addition he produced a large number of pamphlets—devotional, doctrinal, and polemical. But most important of all, his *Institutes* went through five editions, expanding from a small book of six chapters to a large work of seventy-nine chapters in 1559. Calvin also translated the original Latin versions into French. All these works were widely distributed and read throughout Europe.

Not only was Calvin's influence widespread in

his own day through his writings, but his impact on the Christian church has continued down to the present day. His works have been translated into many different languages, one of the most recent being the translation of the *Institutes* into Japanese. The result has been that his theological teachings as well as his political and social views have wielded a strong influence on both Christians and non-Christians since the Reformation.

W. S. Reid

See also Calvinism.

Bibliography. T. H. L. Parker, *John Calvin;* W. S. Reid, ed., *John Calvin: His Influence on the Western World;* G. E. Duffield, ed., *John Calvin;* J. Cadier, *The Man God Mastered;* T. B. Van Halsema, *This Was John Calvin;* G. Harkness, *John Calvin, the Man and His Ethics;* J. Moura and P. Louvet, *Calvin: A Modern Biography;* B. B. Warfield, *Calvin and Augustine;* R. Stauffer, *The Humanness of John Calvin;* F. Wendel, *Calvin.*

Calvinism. John Calvin, often regarded as "the systematizer of the Reformation," was a second-generation Protestant Reformer of the sixteenth century who brought together biblical doctrine systematically, in a way that no other Reformer before him had done. At the same time, he was not an ivory-tower scholar but a pastor who thought and wrote his theological works always with an eye to the edification of the Christian church. Although his views have not always been popular and have at times been grossly misrepresented, his system of theology has had a very wide influence down to the present time, as indicated by the fact that all Reformed and Presbyterian churches look back to him as the founder of their biblical-theological doctrinal position.

Scripture. The formal principle and source of Calvin's theological system is embodied in the Latin phrase *sola Scriptura* (Scripture only). In a strict sense Calvin was primarily a biblical theologian. Trained in the techniques of historico-grammatical exegesis through his humanistic and legal studies, he went to the Scriptures to see what they clearly said. He rejected the medieval fourfold interpretation which allowed allegorizing, spiritualizing, and moralizing, insisting that the literal meaning of the words was to be taken in their historical context. On this basis he sought to develop a theology that would set forth in a systematic form the teaching of Scripture. He was, however, no rationalist, for he constantly stressed the fact that while the Bible reveals God and his purposes to us, yet there is always the mystery of the divine Being and counsel which no human thought can penetrate. Deut. 29:29 was a verse to which he referred many times.

The stress which he laid upon the Scriptures was the result of his belief that they were the Word of God and therefore were the final authority for Christian belief and action. He did not believe in a doctrine of dictation, although he did on occasion refer to the writers as God's amanuenses, but held that the Holy Spirit in different and often mysterious ways revealed God's will and work and guided the writers in their recording of them. Thus, the Bible is authoritative in all matters with which it deals, but it does not deal with everything, such as astronomy. The individual comes to recognize the Bible as the Word of God not primarily because of logical, historical, or other arguments but by the enlightenment of the Holy Spirit's "internal testimony."

God. This raises the question of how Calvin regarded the God who had so revealed himself. In this he accepted the historic doctrine of the triunity of God, who is Father, Son, and Holy Spirit, the same in substance and equal in power and glory. Further, he laid great stress upon the fact that God is sovereign. This means that God is perfect in all respects, possessor of all power, righteousness, and holiness. He is eternal and completely self-sufficient. Therefore, he is not subject either to time or to any other beings, nor is he reducible to spaciotemporal categories for human understanding and analysis. To his creatures God must always be mysterious, except insofar as he reveals himself to them.

This sovereign God is the source of all that is. But he is not the source because everything which exists apart from him is an emanation of the divine Being; he is the source of all things because he is their creator. He has brought everything into existence, including the creation from nothing of both time and space. How he created everything neither Calvin nor his followers have attempted to explain, for that is in the realm of the mystery of God's action. Nor did God create because he was forced to do so by any necessity. He freely created according to his own plan and purpose, which resulted in a universe that was good.

To Calvin and his followers it is also important to realize that the triune God did not turn away from creation after it was formed, but continues to sustain and maintain its existence and operation. The physical laws which govern the material universe are the result of the continual work and action of the Holy Spirit. Such a doctrine had an important influence on the development of physical science in the late sixteenth and seventeenth centuries, being influential in the thinking of Pierre de la Ramée, Bernard Palissy, and Ambroise Paré in France; Francis Bacon, Robert Boyle, and Isaac Newton in England; and other early physical scientists.

As God sovereignly sustains all his creation, so in his providence he rules over and guides it to the accomplishment of his ultimate purposes that all things might be to the glory of God alone (*soli Deo gloria*). This rule included even the free actions of man, so that history might achieve the end which God has determined from all eternity. Here again is a mystery which the Calvinist is prepared to accept, since he is prepared to accept the ultimate mystery of God's being and action.

Man. Human beings were created in the image of God, with true knowledge, righteousness, and holiness. Man saw himself as God's creation, placed in creation as the steward of God's handiwork. Being in the image of God, he also had free will, which meant that he had the capacity freely to obey or disobey God's commands. In dealing with man God entered into a covenant relationship with him, promising his favor and blessing, in return for which man was to rule over and subdue nature, recognizing his office as the lord of creation under the sovereign authority of the triune God. This is known in Calvinistic theology as the covenant of works.

Despite this covenant relationship and God's manifest revelation of himself, man chose to think that he could declare his independence of the sovereign God. Tempted by Satan, man asserted himself as an independent being worshiping the creature rather than the Creator and thus fell under the judgment of God. The outcome was God's condemnation of man, resulting in man's rejection by God, his total corruption, and his bequeathing of this corruption to his descendants throughout history. Only by the general or common grace of God man's corruption did not, and does not, work itself out fully or completely in this life.

The sovereign God, however, did not allow his plans and purposes to be frustrated. Already in eternity as part of his secret counsel he had chosen a great number of his fallen creatures for himself, to be reconciled to him. Why he did so God never reveals, except to say that he chose to do this in his mercy, for he quite justly could have rejected the whole human race for its sins. In pursuance of this plan and purpose of redemption the Father sent the Son, the second person of the Trinity, into the world to pay the penalty for the sin of the elect and to fulfill completely the righteousness of God's law on their behalf. In the OT the prophets and patriarchs looked forward to the coming of Christ, trusting in his promised redemption, while in the NT church, which continues down to today, Christians look back to what Christ accomplished for them in history.

To those who are God's chosen ones the Holy Spirit is sent, not only to enlighten them to understand the gospel set forth in the Scriptures but to enable them to accept God's promise of forgiveness. By this "effectual calling" they come to faith in Christ as the one who has redeemed them, trusting in him alone as the one who has met all God's requirements on their behalf. Thus it is by faith alone (*sola fidei*) that they are saved, through the regenerating power of the Holy Spirit. Thereafter, as God's people they are to live lives which, while never perfectly holy, should manifest the fact that they are his people, seeking always to glorify him in thought, word, and deed.

The Church. The life which God's people now live they live as those who are God's covenant people. From all eternity the sovereign God purposed to make a covenant with his elect in and through their representative, the Son, who in history redeemed them by his spotless life and sacrifice on Calvary's cross. Therefore, as citizens of his kingdom they are now called to serve him in the world, which they do as the church. This obligation is laid upon both adult believers and their children, for the covenant is made with parents and children, as it was with Abraham and his descendants in the OT and with believers and their descendants in the NT. Baptism signifies this entry into the membership of the visible body of Christ's people for both children and adults, although in both cases the baptismal vows taken by the adults may be later repudiated. The Lord's Supper is the continuing sacrament of which Christ's people partake in remembrance of him and of his redemptive work for them. But again, it is only as the elements are received and partaken of in faith that the Holy Spirit blesses those who receive the bread and wine, by making them spiritual participants in the body and blood of the Lord.

In the matter of the organization of the church Calvinists have generally agreed on the view that the church is to be governed by elders, those who teach and those who rule or supervise, elected by the church. Some, however, believe that an episcopal form of church government is the proper, or at least the allowable, form of organization. But all agree that as far as possible the outward, visible unity of the church should be maintained, for all Christians are members of the one body of Christ. On the other hand, Calvinists have also allowed for the pluriformity of the church, recognizing that the church is not perfect, but have also insisted that there must be basic uniformity or congruence of doctrine.

Calvinism in History. Although Calvin was the systematizer of the Reformation theology, since his day those who have accepted his structure of theology have continued to develop many of his ideas. During his own lifetime he himself developed his thought in the successive editions of his *Institutes of the Christian Religion.* With the writing of various Calvinistic confessions such as the Heidelberg Catechism (1563), the Canons of the Synod of Dort (1618), and the Westminster Confession and Catechisms (1647–48) additions to and further developments in theological thought have appeared. Various theologians also during the succeeding years have elaborated various points which Calvin had raised but had not fully examined. The nineteenth century in particular saw a very considerable expansion of Calvinistic thought under the influence of Abraham Kuyper and Herman Bavinck in the Netherlands, Auguste Lecerf in France, and A. A. Hodge, Charles Hodge, and B. B. Warfield in the United States. The tradition established by these men has been carried on in the present century by John Murray, J. Gresham Machen, and Cornelius Van Til in the United States; Herman Dooyeweerd and D. H. Th. Vollenhoven in the Netherlands; and many others in various countries around the world.

Calvin's influence has by no means been limited to the theological sphere, however, for the implications of his beliefs even in his own day had a wide influence in other areas of thought. His view of the state and the right of the subjects and subordinate magistrates to remove an oppressive ruler helped to lay the foundation for the development of democracy. His views on art have also been important in giving a theological-philosophical foundation for the development of pictorial art in the Netherlands, England, Scotland, and France, to mention only a few countries. Much the same could be said of other fields of human endeavor such as science, economic activity, and social reform. Moreover his thought has spread beyond the confines of the Western world to exercise an influence in places such as Africa, where Calvinists have gone as missionaries. In all these ways Calvinism has wielded, and still does wield, an important influence in the world, seeking to set forth the biblical doctrine of God's sovereign grace. W. S. Reid

See also Calvin, John; Reformed Tradition, The.

Bibliography. Calvin, *The Institutes of the Christian Religion,* 2 vols., ed. J. T. McNeill; J. T. McNeill, *The History and Character of Calvinism;* J. H. Bratt, ed., *The Heritage of John Calvin;* D. E. Holwerda, ed., *Exploring the Heritage of John Calvin;* B. B. Warfield, *Calvin and Calvinism;* W. Niesel, *The Theology of Calvin;* J. T. Hoogstra, ed., *John Calvin, Contemporary Prophet;* A. Kuyper, *Lectures on Calvinism;* A. Lecerf, *Études Calvinistes;* H. Clavier, *Études sur Calvinisme;* W. H. Neuser, ed., *Calvinus Theologus;* G. E. Duffield, ed., *John Calvin.*

Calvinistic Methodism. A movement established in Wales by Griffith Jones (1684–1761), Howell Harris (1714–73), and Daniel Rowlands (1713–90), revivalists who had significant contacts with the English Methodists. First meeting as an association in 1743, the group ended its loosely knit organization under the influence of George Whitefield. It harbored no desire to break away from the Church of England at its inception, and not until 1795 did separation from the Establishment occur. However, the church did not ordain its own pastors until 1811. By 1823 a Confession of Faith patterned after the Westminster Confession was adopted.

The Calvinistic Methodist or Presbyterian Church of Wales had to wait to secure its autonomy in spiritual affairs until 1933. Active in educational, missionary, social, and political activities, the church's constituency of some 1,350 congregations is heavily Welsh speaking. Its Constitutional Deed (adopted 1823) organizes the church into presbyteries that are united with associations, which in turn comprise a General Assembly. Similar to the Wesleyan Methodist movement in its populist and social appeal, the church remains Calvinistic in its theology and polity. P. A. Mickey

See also Methodism; Calvinism; Reformed Tradition, The; Whitefield, George.

Bibliography. W. Williams, *Welsh Calvinistic Methodism; JCMHS.*

Cambridge Platform (1648). A document summarizing the thinking of Massachusetts's early Puritan leaders on questions of theology and church practice. The government of Massachusetts first called for a synod of churches in 1646. It was concerned that either the Presbyterian drift of England's Puritan Revolution or the radical proposals for church government which that revolution unleashed would undermine New England's traditional distinctives. The synod's first draft leaned in a Presbyterian direction by liberalizing guidelines for baptizing the colony's children. But conditions in England had changed by the time the synod finally issued its "platform" in 1648. With congregationalist sentiments on the rise there, Puritans in New England reaffirmed the congregational convictions of their earliest leaders.

The Platform accepted the Westminster Confession, which had recently appeared in England, on doctrinal matters. But it amended that confession's treatment of the church by incorporating the positions of New World leaders like John Cotton, John Davenport, and Thomas Hooker.

The Massachusetts Puritans agreed that the universal church consisted of all whom God had chosen to save. Local churches, however, were to be made up only of professed Christians and their children. The Platform condemned extreme separatism, but did proclaim the substantial independence of each local congregation. It authorized synods of ministers to play an advisory role, but no more, for the churches at large. It sanctioned the established practice whereby godly magistrates sometimes intervened in church affairs. And it named pastors, teachers, ruling elders, and deacons as the only legitimate church officers.

The Massachusetts Assembly endorsed the Platform, and the Platform was readily accepted also in the other Puritan colonies—Connecticut, Plymouth, and New Haven. It remains the best place to look for a general statement of what early New England congregationalists thought their churches should be. M. A. Noll

Bibliography. W. Walker, *The Creeds and Platforms of Congregationalism.*

Cambridge Platonists. An important philosophical and theological movement in seventeenth century England. The leaders were graduates of Cambridge University, and each was an Anglican clergyman. Some also became fellows of their college at Cambridge. The major leaders were Ralph Cudworth and Henry More. Others included Benjamin Whichcote, John Smith, Nathaniel Culverwel, and Peter Sterry. These men were called Platonists because of a general interest in the metaphysical perspectives of people from the Platonic tradition, from Plato to Plotinus. They were committed not so much to particular doctrines as to a general Platonistic perspective: a love of truth, a contempt for worldliness, and a concern for justice. They also believed that goodness is eternal and is not in any way based on personal choice—whether our choice or God's choice. Their primary emphasis was the moral life, which they saw to be the essence of Christianity.

The Cambridge Platonists trusted heavily in the human faculty of reason. As a result, they were critical of English empiricism. They rejected the empiricists' belief that the mind has no innate capacities for knowledge because that view seemed to suggest a materialistic picture of human nature, a view that would not give full weight to human rationality. Similarly, they attacked Calvinism because it seemed to them that Calvinists put faith above reason. They also felt that Calvinists were too dogmatic.

The Cambridge Platonists claimed that God is essentially rational. God ordains what is good because it is good; it is not good just because he ordains it. A good Christian shares in this divine rationality, and thus has a developed sense of discrimination for what is good. Enthusiastic sects failed their criterion for adequate religion, for the Cambridge Platonists believed that there is no real religion when the mind is not composed.

For the Cambridge Platonists reason is the very voice of God. The absolute values for life which reason dictates are self-evident to those who sincerely seek to live morally. Even the very existence of God can be proved on the basis of the idea of an infinitely perfect being which we find in our minds. This strong emphasis on reason brought them very close to the rationalism of Descartes. Nevertheless, they strongly disagreed with Descartes's sharp distinction between mind and body that made it possible for bodies to be thoroughly mechanical. For them the material world was not so alienated from the influence of God and reason. P. H. deVries

Bibliography. J. Tulloch, *Rational Theology and Christian Philosophy in England in the Seventeenth Century;* J. Redwood, *Reason, Ridicule and Religion;* F. J. Powicke, *The Cambridge Platonists.*

Campbell, Alexander (1788–1866). A founder of the Christian Church (Disciples of Christ). Son of Thomas Campbell, a Scotch-Irish Presbyterian minister of the Secession Church, Alexander Campbell was born in County Antrim, Ireland. After studying for a year at Glasgow University, in 1809 he migrated to America, where his father had gone in 1807. Joining the Christian Association of Washington (Pennsylvania), which his father had started, Campbell was ordained to its ministry in 1812, speedily sharing his father's leadership and spending the following years in itinerant preaching in Kentucky, Ohio, Indiana, West Virginia, and Tennessee, making converts to his group, whose members called themselves "Disciples of Christ." He expounded his ideas in two monthly magazines, *The Christian Baptist* (1823–30) and its successor, *The Millennial Harbinger* (1830–64). In 1840 he founded Bethany College in West Virginia, serving as its president for over twenty years.

Campbell claimed to derive his theology and churchmanship straight from the Bible, especially the NT, in which the basic pattern of Christian faith and practice was displayed. Church membership was based on personal confession of Jesus Christ as divine Savior and baptism by immersion, this sacrament being not only an act of obedience to Christ's command, but "a means of receiving a formal, distinct, and specific absolution, or release from guilt." The local congregation was the basic cell unit of Christianity, enjoying complete autonomy; but it was expected to cooperate with other Christian groups, both locally and beyond. Two classes of office-bearers were recognized: bishops or elders to give congregational leadership in matters spiritual and deacons to handle temporal concerns. The other Christian sacrament, the Lord's Supper, was observed weekly, according to NT practice.

Campbell hoped that his NT-based churchmanship would promote unity among Protestant evangelicals. But the only lasting merger he brought about was with Barton W. Stone's group, which called themselves "Christians." This union was begun in 1832 and completed during the next few years—though Stone's eastern followers did not join. The resulting group, called the Christian Church (Disciples of Christ), has become "the largest indigenous body having its inception in America." Campbell's followers were earlier called Campbellites. N. V. HOPE

Bibliography. A. Campbell, *The Christian System;* D. R. Lindley, *Apostles of Freedom;* R. Richardson, *Memoirs of Alexander Campbell,* 2 vols.

Campbell, John McLeod (1800–1872). Scottish theologian. After five years as minister of Row (modern Rhu), he was arraigned before Dumbarton presbytery and found guilty of preaching "the doctrine of universal atonement and pardon through the death of Christ, and also the doctrine that assurance is of the essence of faith and necessary to salvation." The Church of Scotland traditionally held that the atonement referred "only to a certain elected portion of the human family," and stressed God's justice more than they did God's love. Following the presbytery's condemnation, the next general assembly (1831) deposed Campbell from the ministry. His pastoral zeal and saintliness of character, acknowledged even by opponents, were reflected in his ministry in an independent congregation in Glasgow (1833–59).

Such was Campbell's restraint that *The Nature of the Atonement* was not published until 1856. In it he argued that Christ had effected the requisite repentance on behalf of humanity and had fulfilled the condition of forgiveness. This move away from a legal interpretation of the doctrine reportedly created "a brighter, clearer, theological atmosphere purged of Calvinistic gloom." The condemnation of Campbell was one of the dying shots of a system that was losing its firm hold over men's consciences, the relinquishing of which grip paved the way to a deeper spirituality. Hailed by James Denney and others as one of Scotland's greatest theologians, Campbell was partially rehabilitated by 1869, when Glasgow University made him an honorary D.D. His book on the atonement has gone through many editions, the latest of which, introduced by E. P. Dickie, was published in 1959. Campbell's *Reminiscences and Reflections,* edited by his son, was published in 1873. J. D. DOUGLAS

Campbellites. *See* CAMPBELL, ALEXANDER.

Camp Meetings. *See* REVIVALISM.

Canon. *See* CHURCH OFFICERS.

Canonization. A legal process in the Roman Catholic Church whereby a departed "servant of God," already beatified, is declared a saint. Such persons are entered into the "canon" or catalog of saints invoked at the celebration of Mass. Beyond the heroic virtue and miraculous power verified already at beatification, saints must perform at least two additional miracles.

In the early church elevation to sainthood was essentially a local affair and not distinguished from beatification. In an effort to curb superstitious abuses Pope Alexander III (1159–81) ruled that the Roman See would henceforth approve all canonizations. This led eventually to the complicated legal processes worked out by Pope Urban VIII in the seventeenth century and given authoritative exposition in Pope Benedict XIV's *Heroic Virtue* in the nineteenth.

There are several noteworthy differences between beatification (the first step) and canonization. Since Vatican Council I canonization is considered an infallible papal act, thus guaranteeing that these saints are indeed worthy of veneration and able to intercede for the faithful. The beatified receive only local recognition, while saints are venerated throughout the Catholic Church. The cult of the beatified is only permitted, while that of the saints is mandated. Saints alone become patrons of churches and are portrayed with the nimbus (gloriole). However, both beatification and canonization are judgments (the latter infallible) by the church that the person now reigns in glory, is worthy of veneration and imitation, and is able to intercede for the faithful. J. VAN ENGEN

See also BEATIFICATION.

Bibliography. *NCE,* III, 55–61; *DTC,* II, 493–97; E. W. Kemp, *Canonization and Authority in the Western Church.*

Canon Law. The word "canon" derives from the Greek *kanōn* meaning "measuring rod," "rule," "list." Hence canon law may be simply defined as the rules of the church for purposes of order, ministry, and discipline. At first these consisted of *ad hoc* pronouncements by leaders or councils in a local setting. Particularly important were those which came from the greater centers, and especially the canons adopted at Nicaea (A.D. 325). Indeed, it was not long before canons were put out under the name of the apostles or great figures of the first centuries, and a necessary process of collection and codification continued through the Dark Ages, with much standardization in the West under Charlemagne. Gratian was the man who brought this process to a virtual culmination in the Roman communion with his famous *Decretum* (A.D. 1140), which underlies the developed study of canon law in the Middle Ages and is the basis of the modern *Corpus iuris canonici.* The Protestant churches have naturally disowned this whole body of legislation and generally avoid the terms "canon" or "canon law," but insofar as any church must make rules for the ordering of its life and work, various forms of canon law are naturally found in all churches.

G. W. Bromiley

Canon of the Bible. *See* Bible, Canon of.

Capital Punishment. The penalty of death for the commission of a crime is an issue that tends to defy the application of reason. Almost everyone has an opinion on the death penalty; however, few have done the necessary study to understand the complexity of the issue. Supporters of capital punishment cite numerous scriptural passages which seem to lend support to their position. In the OT persons put to death included those who made sacrifices to false gods (Exod. 22:20), the blasphemer (Lev. 24:13), the witch (Exod. 22:18), those who labored on the sabbath (Num. 15:32), and those who committed similar offenses against the faith and cult of Israel.

On the other hand, those who oppose the death penalty note scriptural exceptions. Cain was not put to death for slaying his brother Abel. The death penalty was not appropriate for a homicide which had no previous enmity (Deut. 19:1–7). Those opposing capital punishment contend Jesus was opposed to the death penalty. In the case of the adulteress Jesus said, "That one of you who is faultless shall throw the first stone" (John 8:2–11). Teaching his disciples about punishment he said, "You have learned that they were told 'eye for eye, tooth for tooth.' But what I tell you is this, 'Do not set yourself against the man who wrongs you. If someone slaps you on the right cheek, turn and offer him your left'" (Matt. 5:38–39).

Basic issues in the study of capital punishment are deterrence, protection, and economy. The most frequently advanced argument supporting the death penalty is that the threat of death deters people from committing offenses. Unfortunately, claims of deterrence are personal opinions based on intuition and common sense that are not supported by scientific evidence. Supporters of capital punishment, for example, contend that this punishment deters people from killing law enforcement officers. Those who oppose capital punishment cite the research conducted by Sellin, which indicated that the risk of a police officer being killed was lower in states that did not have the death penalty. Numerous studies have been conducted on the deterrent effect of capital punishment, and there is no evidence to support this position. This is not surprising. Criminologists generally agree that certainty, not severity, leads to deterrence. The absence of certainty is obvious. The year-end prisoner count for those on death row in the United States in 1978 was 445. No death sentence was carried out in that year, and there was only one execution in 1977. Those opposing capital punishment contend that this form of punishment is not a deterrent; it is only a threat that is rarely carried out.

A second argument for capital punishment is protection. Supporters of the death penalty claim that it saves lives because murderers sentenced to life imprisonment will kill other prisoners and guards, and that if released by pardon or parole will likely kill again. These assumptions seem reasonable. Those who oppose capital punishment note that available evidence does not support this argument. The overwhelming majority of homicides that occur in prisons occur in death penalty states. Parolees from sentences for willful homicide are not the most likely to murder again. Persons paroled from sentences for armed robbery, aggravated assault, and rape are more homicidal than those incarcerated for willful homicide.

The third argument espoused by those supporting capital punishment is based on the utilitarian notion that it is cheaper to execute than to incarcerate. This argument also has a number of flaws noted by those who oppose capital punishment. Murder trials are very expensive, often lasting weeks. The cost of incarcerating a person on death row is great. A life-termer, if given the opportunity through prison industries, can support himself and contribute to the maintenance of dependents. In some cases he can make payments to persons deserving of restitution. Those who oppose capital punishment ask how far the argument of economy can be carried.

Should we execute all prisoners who are not self-supporting? The humanitarian feelings of the American public would not tolerate mass executions for economic reasons.

Those who oppose capital punishment contend that supporters of the death penalty fail to consider the complexities of our criminal justice system. They contend most Americans believe the criminal justice system favors the rich over the poor. To execute people in a process known for its inefficiency, ineptness, and occasional incompetence makes little sense. Because of a wide range of systemic problems in the areas of law enforcement, courts, and corrections, those opposing capital punishment see this punishment as extremely unjust.

The complexity of the philosophical and theological issues is reflected in the contentions made by those who support and those who oppose capital punishment. Supporters contend that through the penalty of death we demonstrate to society the importance we place on life. Those who oppose capital punishment contend that the death penalty devalues the worth of life. The fact is, we seldom execute. The absence of an even small number of executions indicates serious problems with capital punishment when it is to be applied. Those who oppose capital punishment contend that this enormous inconsistency is equivalent to legislative hypocrisy and that if the sanction is not going to be applied, it should be abolished. R. G. CULBERTSON

See also CIVIL LAW AND JUSTICE IN BIBLE TIMES; CRIMINAL LAW AND PUNISHMENT IN BIBLE TIMES.

Bibliography. K. E. Madigan and W. J. Sullivan, *Crime and Community in Biblical Perspective;* J. A. McCafferty, *Capital Punishment;* S. T. Reid, *Crime and Criminology;* T. Sellin, *The Penalty of Death.*

Capito, Wolfgang Fabricius (1478–1541). Known for his contributions to the Reformation, Capito was a Roman Catholic priest from the family Köpfel. Friend of Erasmus, Capito corresponded with Luther and Zwingli. Appointed to Strasbourg in 1523, the year of Bucer's arrival, he soon joined the ranks of the Reformers.

In the disputes between the Zwinglians and Lutherans he collaborated with Bucer to write the Tetrapolitan Confession (1530), which endeavored to effect a compromise between the Protestants and Evangelicals. Known for his tolerance of the radical, Anabaptist wing of the Reformation, Capito along with Bucer was instrumental in making Strasbourg relatively tolerant of religious dissent. Along with Bucer he prepared the Wittenberg Concord (1536), another effort at compromise and mediation between the Lutherans and Zwinglians. He served as professor of theology in Strasbourg, opening his home to many of the Reformers. P. A. MICKEY

See also TETRAPOLITAN CONFESSION; WITTENBERG, CONCORD OF.

Bibliography. D. Steinmetz, *Reformers in the Wings.*

Cappadocian Fathers. Three men of the fourth century, two of them brothers, are known as the Cappadocian Fathers. Basil the Great and Gregory of Nyssa were brothers; Gregory of Nazianzus was their friend from youth. Basil and Gregory of Nazianzus are now classed (along with John Chrysostom and Athanasius) as Doctors of the Greek Church.

Basil and Gregory of Nyssa were born into an aristocratic Christian family in Pontus. Basil was ordained *ca.* 365 and elected Bishop of Caesarea in Cappadocia in 370. He labored for effective administration, charity, and the unity of the Eastern churches, which were rent by the Antioch schism after 362 and rivalries between Antioch and Alexandria. He is remembered for his monastic rule and administration. His brother, Gregory of Nyssa, was appointed Bishop of Nyssa in 372. He was deposed by Emperor Valens and the Arians in 376 and restored in 378. The most philosophical of the trio, he was the most loyal to the thought of Origen. He was important at the Councils of Constantinople in 381 and 394 in supporting Trinitarian orthodoxy.

Gregory of Nazianzus, the theologian of the three, was born at Arianzus to Christian parents and became a friend of Basil's while studying in Athens. His father, Bishop of Nazianzus, baptized and ordained him. Basil made him Bishop of Sasima in a jurisdictional dispute, but Gregory never went there. When his father died in 374 he administered Nazianzus but refused the office. He labored for the Nicene party in Constantinople from 370 to 381 and was elected Bishop of Constantinople by that council in 381. In a step of personal sacrifice to avoid further controversy he resigned and returned to Nazianzus and then to his estate to write.

The Cappadocian fathers integrated Origen's best thought into orthodoxy, and by insisting on the formula "three persons but one essence" they preserved that Nicene Trinitarian orthodoxy from Arian and semi-Arian corruption. V. L. WALTER

See also BASIL THE GREAT; GREGORY OF NAZIANZUS; GREGORY OF NYSSA; ORIGEN.

Bibliography. H. von Campenhausen, *The Fathers of the Greek Church;* J. Quasten, *Patrology,* III.

Cardinal. A senior official of the Roman Catholic Church who is now always a bishop. Originally a cardinal was a clergyman attached to a parish church or cathedral. Thus the first Roman cardinals were the clergy of the diocese of Rome. From this body the present college of cardinals has evolved. Each member is nominated by the pope, and since 1962 has been raised to the office of bishop if he did not hold it already. In the sixteenth century there was a fixed rule of seventy cardinals, but now there are over one hundred. As a body they advise the pope, help in the government of the church from the Vatican, and when a vacancy arises they elect the new pope (who is usually one of their number). If a cardinal is over eighty years he cannot now participate in this election. Cardinals are required to reside in Rome unless they are diocesan bishops. They wear a special cassock and red skull cap and have the title of "Eminence." P. TOON

See also CHURCH OFFICERS.

Cardinal Virtues, Seven. The seven cardinal virtues as enunciated by the medieval church are faith, hope, love, justice, prudence, temperance, and fortitude. They are "cardinal" in that all other Christian virtues "hinge" (*cardo*) upon one or another of them.

These virtues are of two kinds. The first three are named "theological" and represent the Pauline triad in I Cor. 13:13 (cf. I Thess. 1:3; Gal. 5:5–6; Col. 1:4–5). The other four are "natural" (or "moral") virtues and find their origin in the philosophical thought of ancient Greece. This fourfold classification of virtue was held by Plato to correspond to the natural constitution of the soul. Prudence corresponded to the intellect, temperance to feeling, and fortitude to will. Justice was a social virtue and regulated the others.

It is understandable that pagan morality could not find a place within Christianity without first undergoing a radical transformation. This process begins in earnest with Augustine, who reinterpreted the virtues from a Christian perspective and redirected them toward a new object—devotion to God. The three theological virtues are placed alongside as representing the inner disposition in which the external virtues have their source. Thus while the moral ideas of the past are gradually baptized into Christianity, they become new creations in the process. Even though the schoolmen return to Aristotle as a source of moral speculation, the end product is always Aristotle read in the light of Augustine.

As the natural virtues can be referred to a psychological basis, so also can the theological. Faith relates to intellect, hope to desire, and love to the will. Thus virtue is that moral excellence in which the whole man (in both inner disposition and external act) is rightly oriented to his Creator. R. H. MOUNCE

See also VIRTUE, VIRTUES.

Bibliography. *HERE,* XI, 430–32; K. E. Kirk, *Some Principles of Moral Theology;* J. Stalker, *The Seven Cardinal Virtues.*

Care. *See* ANXIETY.

Carlstadt, Andreas Bodenstein von (1477–1541). German Protestant Reformer. He studied at Erfurt and Cologne before being assigned in 1505 to teach at the new University of Wittenberg, where as a member of the theological faculty he was known as a defender of the scholastic system of Thomas Aquinas. It was Carlstadt who conferred on Luther the doctor of theology degree in 1512. Like Luther, he underwent a spiritual transformation in which he repudiated his Thomist beliefs and became a supporter of the mobilizing Protestant movement. In 1518 he wrote against Johann Eck in support of Luther, stressing that the Bible itself was to be preferred over the authority of the whole church and its councils. When Eck demanded a public debate, Carlstadt gamely agreed and debated him at Leipzig in 1519. Carlstadt was condemned with Luther and others by a papal bull in 1520.

While Luther was in hiding at Wartburg, Carlstadt and Philip Melanchthon took the lead in guiding the Reformation. A natural leader, Carlstadt led the Wittenberg community in reform. On Christmas day, 1521, he celebrated Communion in the Castle Church without priestly dress and without sacrifice or elevation of the host. He even offered the cup to the laity. In January, 1522, he married and instructed that all ministers should marry. He also opposed church music, religious images, begging, and religious fraternities. While Luther could endorse many of these changes in the next few years, he believed Carlstadt's reforms to be dangerous to the Reformation movement at that juncture. This would lead to division between the two men. Luther returned to Wittenberg to "calm" the situation. Carlstadt went to Orlamünde in Thuringia, became a popular preacher there, and continued on his path of reform. He renounced his academic degrees, dressed as a peasant, and desired to be called "Brother Andrew" in deference to the priesthood of all believers.

By 1524 Luther was complaining about Carlstadt's books and reform in Orlamünde. He was sent by the Saxon authorities to Thuringia, debated Carlstadt, and a series of tracts were later exchanged. In September, 1524, the Saxon authorities banished Carlstadt, forcing him to leave behind his child and a pregnant wife. Allowed to return in 1525 on the condition that he would not lecture, he was again forced to leave and finally settled in Switzerland. Here his symbolic understanding of Communion was welcomed, and he held a professorship at Basel from 1534 to his death.

Most scholars have taken at face value Luther's polemic against Carlstadt, portraying him as petty, extreme, and divisive. Some recent scholarship has contended, however, that theological differences were not the crux of the separation in 1522 and that Carlstadt was a brilliant and decent man placed in an impossible political situation—a Reformer sensitive to the needs of the laity. D. A. Rausch

See also Reformation, Protestant; Luther, Martin.

Bibliography. H. Barge, *Andreas Bodenstein von Karlstadt;* J. S. Preus, *Carlstadt's "Ordinaciones" and Luther's Liberty;* G. Rupp, *Patterns of Reformation;* K. Müller, *Luther und Karlstadt.*

Carnell, Edward John (1919–1967). A leader among those post–World War II evangelical theologians in the United States who aimed to correct certain fundamentalist emphases and to restate classical orthodox theology in an intelligent and persuasive manner.

Like all persons Carnell's intellectual development was heavily influenced by his personal experiences. From his childhood in a Baptist parsonage in Antigo, Wisconsin, he came to see both the admirable qualities of fundamentalists and their negative attitudes and legalisms.

Carnell attended Wheaton College (Illinois), where he was influenced by Gordon Clark, a Christian rationalist interested in the defense of orthodoxy. Carnell gained his Th.B. and Th.M. degrees from Westminster Theological Seminary with an apologetics major under Cornelius Van Til. His first doctorate was in theology from Harvard University with a dissertation later published under the title *The Theology of Reinhold Niebuhr* (1950). He completed another doctorate in philosophy at Boston University under E. S. Brightman. His Boston dissertation was later published as *The Burden of Søren Kierkegaard* (1965).

Carnell commenced his teaching career in 1945 as professor of philosophy and religion at Gordon College and Divinity School. In 1948 he moved to Fuller Theological Seminary, where he remained until his death, serving as president for five years (1954–59) and, in his later years, as professor of ethics and philosophy of religion.

Carnell first came to theological prominence in 1948 with *An Introduction to Christian Apologetics,* a prize-winning volume which found its way into many classrooms as a textbook for apologetics. He followed with *A Philosophy of the Christian Religion* (1952). In the *Introduction,* Carnell tried to show that Christianity satisfies the demands of reason. In the *Philosophy* he argued that Christianity addresses the values of the heart.

Two later books, *Christian Commitment* (1957) and *The Kingdom of Love and the Pride of Life* (1960), preserved Carnell's respect for propositional revelation but moved into new realms of evangelical thought. They broadened Carnell's apologetic to include "knowledge by acquaintance" and a more existential defense of Christianity's answer to man's moral predicament. In 1960 Carnell wrote *The Case for Orthodoxy,* his sharpest critique of fundamentalism.

B. L. Shelley

Bibliography. J. A. Sims, *Edward John Carnell: Defender of the Faith.*

Caroline Divines. Those seventeenth century theologians named for the period under Charles I and Charles II. In practice, however, the term more widely refers to Anglicans writing generally in the seventeenth century. The term became current during the Tractarian movement in the nineteenth century.

Attention was drawn to the massive scholarship and extensive learning on the part of these men by the publication in the nineteenth century of the multivolume *Library of Anglo-Catholic Theology.* They were seen to exemplify an Anglicanism which had appropriated the value of the Reformation, avoided the excesses of Puritanism, and provided Christendom with a "middle way" between Geneva and Rome.

Among the leading figures were Lancelot Andrewes (1555–1626) and William Laud (1573–1645). The former is justly renowned for his scholarship, preaching, and devotional writings. Andrewes has been held up by T. S. Eliot as a model of the blend of thought and passion, form and substance that was a mark of the early seventeenth century. Laud was too soon orbited into affairs of state to be ranked with Andrewes in scholarship, but his role in enforcing uniformity against the Puritans has given his name to the high church reaction at the Restoration.

Much appreciation has been given in modern times to the so-called metaphysical poets: John Donne, George Herbert, Thomas Traherne, and

Henry Vaughan. The works of these Caroline figures are characterized by rich metaphor and a strong appreciation of Christian dogma blended in simple piety and worship. C. F. Allison

See also Laud, William.

Bibliography. H. R. McAdoo, *The Spirit of Anglicanism;* More and Cross, *Anglicanism;* C. F. Allison, *The Rise of Moralism: The Gospel from R. Hooker to R. Baxter;* T. Wood, *English Casuistical Divinity During the Seventeenth Century.*

Case, Shirley Jackson (1872–1947). Although he held several academic and administrative appointments, Case is probably best remembered as a former dean of The University of Chicago Divinity School. He was a prolific writer, with sixteen books, approximately ninety articles, and numerous reviews to his credit, to which must be added his extensive editorial activity.

Case's major contribution to the theological scene related to the study of Christian origins. He attacked both those skeptics who imagined that Christianity could have come about without reference to a historical figure and those "fundamentalists" who argued for the uniqueness of Christianity as a supernaturalistic faith. The former face the herculean task of disposing of the Pauline letters and the Gospels; the latter fail to appreciate how Christianity merely borrowed and adapted the devices of ancient paganism in order to demonstrate its superiority.

Case saw the continuing relevance of the Christian faith in the effort to realize the kingdom of God on earth, as the contemporary church triumphs over obstacles both similar and dissimilar to those encountered by the early church. He spoke with deep appreciation of "the striving social gospel," but emphasized the difficulty and persistence of those forces that stand in the way of Christian success. He concluded that the kingdom of God comes about through the "strenuous endeavor on the part of men who serve him from generation to generation throughout the evolving centuries." M. A. Inch

See also Chicago School of Theology.

Bibliography. Case, *The Evolution of Early Christianity, The Christian Philosophy of History,* and *The Origins of Christian Supernaturalism;* L. Jennings, "The Bibliographer and Bibliography of Shirley Jackson Case," *JR* 29; W. Hynes, *Shirley Jackson Case and the Chicago School.*

Casuistry. The art of applying moral laws, which tend to be general, to specific cases. Ever since Aristotle called attention to what he termed the need for equity, a method for deciding what is the right or wrong act in concrete situations has been an important part of the study of ethics. Indeed, it has been called the goal of ethics.

Christianity, as any other system which includes moral values, has engaged in casuistry. One of the earliest examples is the apostle Paul's rulings about the eating of meat sacrificed to idols and the remarriage of divorced persons. But as a systematically developed science it is more closely identified with Judaism and Roman Catholic Christianity. Jesus' attack upon the scribes and Pharisees for becoming so involved in their casuistry that they were missing the point of the law is well known. In the Roman Catholic Church casuistry has been carefully pursued because of the need for a clerical confessor and his penitent or a private penitent to have ready access to the church's position on the guilt of a past fault or obligation in a future situation. By the fifth century "penitential books" were appearing which included questions for the confessor to ask and exhaustive lists of sins and the corresponding penance.

In the sixteenth century casuistry became dominated by a doctrine called probabilism. It held that in cases where the rightness or wrongness of an act is in doubt, the appropriate response is whatever is probably required on the side of freedom from the regulation in question, even though submission to the regulation is more probably the truth of the matter. In the seventeenth century probabilism came to be considered too lax and was replaced by probabiliorism. This held that in cases of doubt, an act should be considered to fall under the law unless freedom is more probably called for. The eighteenth century saw the revival of a mediating form of probabilism called equiprobabilism, which has remained the preferred position up to the present. S. R. Obitts

Bibliography. G. W. Bromiley, *DCE,* 85–86; *NCE; ODCC,* 244.

Catechisms. A catechism is a popular manual of instruction (Gr. *katēcheō,* to instruct) in Christian beliefs, normally in question and answer form. The word is not used in this sense until the early sixteenth century.

Catechesis originated very early as the teaching given to converts before baptism and developed into the formalized catechumenate (cf. Hippolytus, *Apostolic Tradition*). It reached its heyday in the fourth and fifth centuries, incorporating quasiliturgical ceremonies like the oral transmission (*traditio*) by the catechist and rendition (*redditio*) by the catechumen of the Creed and Lord's Prayer. The system was designed to safeguard the integrity of the church and the secret discipline (*disciplina arcani*) of its inner life. From the weeks of concentrated preparation prior to the baptism at Easter (the origin of Lent) there survive series of catechetical addresses by Cyril of Jerusalem, Ambrose, Chrysostom, and Theodore of Mopsuestia. Augustine wrote *How to Catechize the Uninstructed* and Gregory of Nyssa a *summa* for catechists, his *Great Catechetical Oration.*

As infant baptism became the norm, the catechumenate declined. During the medieval era no regular ecclesiastical catechesis was provided for children, but various forms of popular teaching materials, based chiefly on the Apostles' Creed, Decalogue, and Lord's Prayer, were produced, from Alcuin's question and answer explanation of the Creed and Lord's Prayer to John Gerson's *ABC des simples gens.* In the late Middle Ages confessional manuals multiplied—e.g., *The Mirror of a Sinner* (*ca.* 1470), requiring of penitents responsive participation. In these the Decalogue was dominant, but other formulas were involved, such as the Hail Mary, lists of virtues and vices or capital sins, works of charity, and sacraments. Devotional dialogues, such as *The Mirror of a Christian Man* (*Faith*) of the 1480s, the first lay catechism in German, also used questions and answers. The Waldensians had a catechism in print by 1489, incorporating the traditional formulas but structured around faith, hope, and love (a pattern derived from Augustine's *Enchiridion*). The Bohemian Brethren's *Questions for Children* (1522), which was known to Luther, was almost certainly based on the Waldensians' book.

With the Reformation an explosion of catechism production took place, with many a Lutheran pastor compiling his own. Thousands never got beyond manuscript form, and no listing has ever approached completeness. Most of them were detached from any precise connection with baptism or Communion. By far the most influential was Luther's Small Catechism of 1529, published a month after his Great Catechism, which was based on a series of sermons of 1528. Both were intended as aids to pastors. The Small Catechism dealt with the Decalogue, Apostles' Creed, Lord's Prayer, and sacraments, the standard ingredients of subsequent Protestant catechisms. In gestation since his popular expositions of the Decalogue beginning in 1516 and anticipated especially by *A Short Form of the Ten Commandments . . . the Creed . . . and the Lord's Prayer* of 1520, it was also a response to the lamentable ignorance exposed by visitations in Saxony in 1528. Espousing the principle of habituation by verbal repetition, it represented a partial shift of conviction in Luther from the freedom of word and spirit to discipline and regulation. He had no doubt of its significance: "I have brought about such a change that nowadays a girl or boy of fifteen knows more about Christian doctrine than all the theologians of the great universities used to know." He was happy to remain forever "a child and a disciple of the catechism." Teaching children recalled the gospel summons to become like little children, and these catechisms inculcated the Lutheran gospel, reflecting in content its law-faith-prayer sequence. They also stressed social behavior, especially on the fourth and seventh commandments, expanding the narrowly religious focus of late medieval manuals.

Luther's productions had been preceded by some thirty Lutheran catechisms, notably by Johann Brenz, Melanchthon, Wolfgang Capito, Urbanus Rhegius, and Johann Agricola. The first to be entitled "Catechism" was by Andreas Althamer of Brandenburg-Ansbach in 1528. An extraordinary profusion followed Luther's example of 1529, until in the later sixteenth century his Small Catechism became the norm virtually everywhere in Lutheranism. Church ordinances normally legislated for the use of catechisms in church, especially compulsory Sunday afternoon classes for children, and in home and school. They were turned into primers, dialogues, hymns, and pictures for use with children. Other major target audiences were the rural populace and the urban hired laboring class.

Catechisms were anti-Roman from the outset. From around 1530 a catechism for the young was regarded as a salient mark of the reform movement's break with the past, and was regularly one of the first innovations of reformed states and cities. All this is observable in the Genevan Reformation. Calvin produced a French catechism in 1537 (Latin 1538), but far more significant was its simpler 1541 successor (Latinized in 1545). He claimed to be recovering ancient practice long corrupted. He reordered the four sections so that Decalogue followed Creed, indicating his understanding of the law as a guide for Christian life. Despite the tendency to verbosity which became typical of Reformed catechisms, his catechism served as prototype of numerous others, such as John à Lasco's 1554 Emden Catechism, used in East Friesland until superseded by the Heidelberg Catechism of 1563, which has had the widest appeal of all Reformation catechisms. Produced at the order of Elector Frederick III by Zacharias Ursinus and Casper Olevianus, professors at Heidelberg University, for use in the churches and schools of the Palatinate, it is predominantly Calvinist but has enough of Luther in it to constitute a mediating document, "a happy blend of Calvinist precision and comprehensiveness with Lutheran warmth and humanity" (W. A. Curtis). It has three parts: misery (brief), redemption (the Creed, including word and sacraments), and gratitude (including Decalogue and Lord's Prayer). It was approved unrevised by the Synod of Dort (1618), and has been widely used in numerous languages.

In Reformed Protestantism catechizing was often viewed as leading to an evangelically reformed confirmation (cf. Calvin, *Institutes* 4.19.4, 13). This issued in part from a response, especially by Bucer, to Anabaptist criticisms of infant baptism. The reformed Anglican Catechism appeared simply as part of the confirmation service in the first Prayer Book of 1549. It was probably largely Cranmer's work, drawn partly from popular manuals such as the Bishops' Book (1537) and the King's Book (1543), and William Marshall's *A Goodly Primer in English* (1534), which contained material from Luther's Small Catechism. It had a shortened version of the commandments and, exceptionally, nothing on the sacraments. The full Decalogue appeared in 1552, a section of the sacraments was added after the Hampton Court Conference of 1604, and further minor changes took place by 1662. It retained a commendable brevity and a much less confessional tone than most sixteenth century catechisms and was well suited for worldwide use in the spread of Anglicanism.

Continental productions such as Oecolampadius's and Bullinger's also circulated in England. Cranmer translated in 1548 Justus Jonas's catechism for Brandenburg-Nuremberg, in successive editions diluting its Lutheranism and revealing his transition to Swiss Reformed theology. *A Short Catechism... for All Schoolmasters to Teach* by John Ponet, Bishop of Winchester, was printed with versions of the Articles from 1553, and Alexander Nowell's two forms of 1570 and 1572 likewise met the need for a longer catechism than the Prayer Book provided. The Church of England approved a Revised Catechism in 1962.

Catechisms came thick and fast in Scotland. Archbishop Hamilton's Catechism (1552) was a reforming Catholic document, giving too little too late. Already circulating were the metrical catechism sections of largely Lutheran origin published in *The Gude and Godlie Ballatis*, probably largely the work of John Wedderburn and his brothers. The 1541 Genevan Catechism was replaced by the Catechism of the Scottish Reformer John Craig (1581). This first successful Scottish production was superseded partly by the Heidelberg Catechism and conclusively by the Westminster Shorter Catechism. Though lengthy, it is distinctive in presenting only one-line answers. Answers had tended to become either longer and longer or simply affirmatives responding to statements masquerading as questions. Craig's Short Catechism of 1592 was explicitly "A Form of Examination before Communion," indicating a distinctive role in a kirk which had no equivalent to confirmation.

The Shorter and Larger Catechisms of the Westminster Assembly (1647) largely displaced all others in Reformed/Presbyterian churches. They abandon the Creed but incorporate other traditional ingredients, while purveying the Calvinists' distinctive Calvinism in matters such as God's decrees and the Christian Sabbath. The Shorter Catechism is a work of great dignity, and has exercised unparalleled influence in Scotland.

The Catholic Counter-Reformation also stimulated the production of catechisms, although the Catechism of the Council of Trent (1566), while based on traditional formulas, is a polemical confession and manual for clerical use. Among popular catechisms the most serviceable proved to be *The Sum of Christian Doctrine* (1555) of the Jesuit Peter Canisius. The Roman Church has produced normally local catechisms, with none attaining general use. In the wake of Vatican Council II the General Catechetical Directory issued by Paul VI in 1971 laid down guidelines for local hierarchies to follow. The controversial Dutch volume of 1968, *A New Catechism*, is not a catechism in the normal sense.

Other traditions have had their own catechisms. Robert Browne's pioneer *Statement of Congregational Principles* (1582) consists of 185 questions and answers. Robert Barclay's Catechism of 1673 reflects the convictions of the first Quakers, while William Collins and Benjamin Keach were responsible for the Baptist Catechism of 1693, often known as Keach's Catechism. William Nast compiled two popular nineteenth century Methodist catechisms.

In the Orthodox world Peter Mogilas, the metropolitan of Kiev, produced around 1640 in the form of a catechism the Orthodox Confession of the Catholic and Apostolic Eastern Church, which from the Synod of Jerusalem (1672) became standard throughout the Greek and Russian churches. Directed against both Jesuit Romanism and Cyril Lucar's Calvinism, its three heads are faith (Nicene Creed), hope (Lord's Prayer and Beatitudes), and love (including the Decalogue). It was eventually superseded in the nineteenth century by the Christian Catechism of the Orthodox Catholic Eastern Greco-Russian

Church compiled in 1823 by Philaret, the scholarly and saintly metropolitan of Kiev. After revisions it was finally approved in 1839. It follows the pattern of Mogilas's work. Philaret produced a shorter catechism in 1840.

The formality of catechetical dialogue has scarcely survived the diversification of teaching methods in recent years. So far as their use persists, catechisms are more aids for teachers than precise patterns for learning. D. F. WRIGHT

See also CONFESSIONS OF FAITH; LUTHER'S SMALL CATECHISM; WESTMINSTER CATECHISMS.

Bibliography. J. Daniélou and R. du Charlat, *La Catéchèse aux premiers siècles;* E. W. Kohls, *Evangelische Katechismen der Reformationszeit vor Luthers kleinem Katechismus;* S. Ozment, *The Reformation in the Cities;* G. Strauss, *Luther's House of Learning;* T. F. Torrance, *The School of Faith;* H. Bonar, *Catechisms of the Scottish Reformation;* A. F. Mitchell, *Catechisms of the Second Reformation;* P. Schaff, *Creeds of Christendom,* 3 vols.; J. Geffcken, *Bilderkatechismus des fünfzehnten Jahrhunderts;* F. E. Brightman, *The English Rite,* I, 35–36, 120ff., 177ff., II, 776–91; J. M. Reu, *Dr. Martin Luther's Small Catechism: A History of Its Origin, Its Distribution and Its Use* and *Quellen zur Geschichte des kirchlichen Unterrichts in der evangelischen Kirche Deutschlands zwischen 1530 und 1600,* I.

Catechist. One who instructs others in the Christian faith. The word was originally used in the early church of the person who taught converts the faith and morals of the church in the period leading up to baptism. In traditional Western missionary work local pastors, leaders, and teachers have been called catechists, which was an order of ministry below that of the ordained clergyman. Since 1962 with the revival of the catechumenate in Roman Catholic missions the catechist is often the priest. P. TOON

Catechumen. In the early centuries of the church a convert to Christianity was expected to attend Sunday worship (but not take Holy Communion) and to receive instruction before being baptized (usually at Easter). Such a person was known as a catechumen, and he or she, having professed a desire to believe and live as a Christian, was instructed in the faith and morals of Christianity so that a true commitment could be made in baptism. This period of preparation lasted anywhere from one to three years and ended with rigorous examination and discipline during Lent. The latter included being exorcised, fasting, and an all-night vigil before Easter Sunday. It was possible to offer this kind of rigorous preparation when the church was small and when converts were comparatively few. Details of the catechumenate for the third century are given in Hippolytus's *Apostolic Tradition.*

After the rule of Constantine the Great, as the church became more acceptable and was more accepted, converts grew, and with a large number of catechumens the period of preparation was reduced, often being an intensive course during Lent. This involved instruction in the meaning of the Creed, exorcism, and learning appropriate teaching by heart (so that it could always be repeated). Examples of the type of instruction given may be seen in the catechetical lectures of Cyril of Jerusalem and of Augustine of Hippo. In this period infants were brought during Lent for exorcism and prayer before their baptism on Easter Day. This practice did not last long, for it became the practice to baptize infants within a week of birth. However, the Lenten ceremonies (chiefly exorcism) were compressed into the first part of the order of baptism for infants used in the medieval period.

The catechumenate is still a feature of the Roman Catholic Church, especially where it is working in the developing world or gaining large numbers of adult converts. The preparation is modeled on that of the early church. Other churches perhaps have a similar aim through classes for confirmation (where there are baptized children) or for baptism (where there are adult converts). P. TOON

Bibliography. J. D. C. Fisher, *Christian Initiation: Baptism in the Christian West;* T. Maertens, *Histoire et pastorale du rituel du catéchuménat et du baptême.*

Cathari. This term has been applied to several groups in church history. The basic idea in the word came from the Greek word for "pure" and referred to the groups' special emphasis on purity in life. The most famous group, and the one usually particularized by the term, emerged in Germany in the twelfth century. In other areas of Europe the name was applied to groups such as the Albigenses and the Bogomils. The Cathari were condemned as heretical by the church and persecuted by the Inquisition. By the fourteenth century their influence was destroyed.

The doctrinal teaching of the Cathari revolved around their attempts to solve the problem of evil. They held to a form of dualism whereby God as the author or principle of good was engaged in battle with an evil principle or spirit. Some Catharists believed this struggle to be an eternal one. From this dualism came a set of faulty teachings: creation was not good since it resulted from the activity of evil spirits; Christ, while the highest of created beings, was neither fully man nor fully God; redemption involved the rescue of the human spirit from the bondage of matter, which was itself viewed as evil; and sin resulted from contact with the world which had been created by the evil spirit. Sins especially despised by the Cathari were owning of earthly possessions, lying, war, killing of animals, and sexual intercourse even within marriage. The only path to cleansing from sinfulness was by renouncing the world and being admitted to the Cathari church, outside of which there was no hope of salvation. Within the Cathari church were two kinds of members: one known as "believers" and the other known as "perfected ones." To become a "perfected one" involved the laying on of hands, called *consolamentum*, and it could be received only from one who had already been perfected. The Cathari believed that this *consolamentum* removed the guilt of original sin and bestowed immortality, but it could be invalidated by the commission of a single transgression afterward. Therefore, many "believers" postponed their *consolamentum* as long as possible.

Catharism's claim to be the only true church placed it in a struggle to the death with the established Roman Catholic Church. Given its exclusivism and claims to superiority, Catharism was doomed to destruction. However, its call to purity of life and committed spirituality in a day of moral and religious laxity earned it a place among those who have sought renewal in the Christian movement and, perhaps, helped prepare the way at some points for the Protestant Reformation. O. G. OLIVER, JR.

See also ALBIGENSES; BOGOMILS.

Bibliography. M. D. Lambert, *Medieval Heresy* and "The Motives of the Cathars: Some Reflections," in *Religious Motivation*, ed. D. Baker; G. H. Shriver, "A Summary of 'Images of Catharism and the Historian's Task,'" *CH* 40:48–54; W. Wakefield, *Heresy, Crusade, and Inquisition.*

Catholic. A transliteration of the Greek *katholikos*, "throughout the whole," "general," this word has been used in a variety of senses during the history of the church. In the earlier patristic period it had the denotation of universal. This is its meaning in the first occurrence in a Christian setting—"Wherever Jesus Christ is, there is the catholic church" (Ignatius *Smyr.* 8:2). Here the contrast with the local congregation makes the meaning "universal" mandatory. Justin Martyr could speak of the "catholic" resurrection, which he explains as meaning the resurrection of all men (*Dialogues* lxxxi). When the term begins to appear in the Apostles' Creed—"the holy catholic church" (*ca.* 450)—as it had earlier appeared in the Nicene—"one holy catholic and apostolic church"—it retains the sense of universality and thus accents the unity of the church in spite of its wide diffusion. The catholic epistles of the NT were so designated by Origen, Eusebius, *et al.*, to indicate that they were intended for the whole church rather than a local congregation.

A second meaning emerges toward the end of the second century, when heresy had become a menace. Catholic becomes the equivalent of orthodox. The Muratorian Canon (*ca.* 170) refers to certain writings "which cannot be received in the catholic church, for gall cannot be mixed with honey." For the logical connection between this meaning and the former, see Lightfoot on Col. 1:6. Vincent of Lérins (*Commonitorium*, 434) in his famous maxim, "What all men have at all times and everywhere believed must be regarded as true," combines the ideas of universality and orthodoxy.

In Reformation times the word became a badge of those churches which adhered to the papacy in contrast to those groups which identified themselves with the Protestant cause. The designation Roman Catholic emerged in connection with the controversy between Rome and the Anglican Church, which insisted on its right to use the term catholic as linking it with the ancient apostolic church. Rome, on the other hand, put forth its claim as the true church because of organizational continuity. Churches could not be regarded as properly "Catholic" unless they submitted to the government of the Roman hierarchy.

Two modern uses should be noted. One is the designation of an individual as a Catholic, a member of the Roman Catholic Church. The word is sometimes employed also to indicate a breadth of spirit or outlook in contrast to that which is regarded as rigidly narrow. This vague use of the word, at times quite latitudinarian, is completely different from the ancient significance, where universality was coupled with precision of Christian belief.

Historians refer to the Old Catholic church as that phase of the development of Christianity which followed the apostolic and preceded the Roman Catholic. E. F. HARRISON

Bibliography. J. B. Lightfoot, *The Apostolic Fathers*, Part II, Vol. II, 310–12; J. Pearson, *An Exposition of the Creed;* H. E. W. Turner, *The Pattern of Christian Truth.*

Catholic Church, Roman. *See* ROMAN CATHOLICISM.

Catholicism, Liberal. A response by a minority of Catholic intellectuals to the French Revolution and nineteenth century European liberalism, liberal Catholicism may also be seen as a chapter in the history of reform Catholicism which has long contended with the majority, conservative, and authoritarian tradition within Roman Catholicism.

The characteristics of liberal Catholicism are best exemplified in its chief exponents. The pioneer of the movement was the passionate French priest and prophet H. F. R. de Lamennais (1782–1854), who developed a new apologetic for Catholicism. The Catholic religion, he maintained, is not evidenced chiefly by miracles and fulfilled prophecies but by its capacity to perpetuate those beliefs which mankind has found essential to an ordered social life: monotheism, the difference between good and evil, the immortality of the soul, and reward or punishment in a future life. Testifying to these beliefs is the *sensus communis* or general reason, the collective judgments derived from custom, tradition, and education. Hence society is the vehicle of revelation, a belief of great democratic potential. Lamennais's apologetics led to politics. His mission was to promote the social regeneration of Europe through the renaissance of Catholicism. The Catholic church should break with all royalist and absolutist regimes; the papacy should be the guardian of liberty and the champion of democracy; and the people, in whom was hidden the Word of God, should be sovereign.

In a daily newspaper, *L'Avenir*, with its motto "God and Liberty," Lamennais advanced his revolutionary program: freedom of conscience and religion (necessitating the abolition of concordats between the papacy and civil governments and the stopping both of state payment of clergy and of state intervention in the appointment of bishops); freedom (not a monopoly) for the church in education; liberty of the press; freedom of association; universal suffrage; and decentralization of government.

C. R. F. de Montalembert (1810–70), historian and publicist, entered the French Parliament in 1837, seeking to catholicize liberals and to liberalize Catholics. His greatest political victory was the passage in 1850 of the Falloux law, which allowed the development of a Catholic secondary education system independent of the state system.

The commitment by liberal Catholics to education was accompanied by an emphasis on preaching, then unusual in the Roman Catholic Church. The greatest liberal Catholic preacher was the Dominican J. B. H. Lacordaire (1802–61), who attracted vast crowds especially to his Lenten conferences at Notre Dame Cathedral, where his impassioned sermons combined the call for liberty in church and state with ultramontanism (centralization of papal authority in matters of church government and doctrine).

The majority of liberal Catholics remained orthodox, seeking to modernize the church through the political emancipation of the laity and the separation of church and state. A later generation of liberal Catholics, including Lord Acton (1834–1902) in England and J. J. I. von Döllinger (1799–1890) in Germany, advocated autonomy for the laity in doctrinal matters.

The currents of liberal Catholicism led at the beginning of the twentieth century to the much stormier waters of Catholic modernism, which tended to be antidogmatic and anthropocentric. The leading Catholic modernists—Alfred Loisy, George Tyrrell, Baron Friedrich von Hügel, Edouard Le Roy, Maurice Blondel, and Ernesto Buonaiuti—were concerned to reconcile traditional Catholic doctrine with the results of critical scriptural exegesis.

The papacy has consistently criticized and frequently condemned liberal Catholicism for its rationalism and naturalism. Lamennais's political liberalism was condemned by Gregory XVI in the encyclical *Mirari vos* of 1832. In 1834 in *Singulari nos* Gregory condemned Lamennais's doctrine that the evolution of truth was part of the progressive evolution of the people (a view later called immanentism). Montalembert concluded that it was not possible to be a Catholic and a liberal after Pius IX's encyclical *Quanta Cura* and the Syllabus of Errors (both 1864). Acton and Döllinger withdrew their active support of Rome after the promulgation in 1870 of the dogma of papal infallibility. Modernism was condemned in 1907 by Pius X in the decree *Lamentabili* and the encyclical *Pascendi gregis*.

F. S. Piggin

See also Roman Catholicism; Von Hügel, Friedrich; Tyrrell, George; Ultramontanism.

Bibliography. Lord Acton, *The History of Freedom and Other Essays;* J. L. Altholz, *The Liberal Catholic Movement in England;* E. E. Y. Hales, *Pio Nono: A Study in European Politics and Religion in the Nineteenth Century* and *Revolution and Papacy, 1769–1846;* D. Holmes, *The Triumph of the Holy See: A Short History of the Papacy in the Nineteenth Century;* T. M. Loome, *Liberal Catholicism, Reform Catholicism, Modernism: A Contribution to a New Orientation in Modernist Research;* J. N. Moody, ed., *Church and Society: Catholic Social and Political Thought and Movements, 1789–1950;* B. M. G. Reardon, *Liberalism and Tradition: Aspects of Catholic Thought in Nineteenth-Century France;* A. R. Vidler, *Prophecy and Papacy: A Study of Lamennais, the Church and the Revolution.*

Cause, Causation. Roughly, the relation between two events or states of affairs where the first is necessary or sufficient or both for the occurrence of the second. Reflection on this topic has been an important part of Western thought.

The pre-Socratics speculated about the elements from which all things were formed: earth, air, fire, and water. There is in this a loose similarity to Aristotle's concept of a material cause. However, the pre-Socratics were unable to account for the fact that the universe was ordered and intelligible. Plato's understanding of the causes of things bears similarities to Aristotle's formal cause. He treats the forms or ideas as if they are substances in their own right. Aristotle gave "cause" a much wider definition than it generally has today. He found Plato's doctrine of the forms unacceptable. He tried to explain the existence of all things in terms of themselves, without reference to a distinct metaphysical realm. He distinguished between four types of causes. All material objects have matter and form. Matter, or the material cause, is the "stuff" of which a thing is made. Matter is a relative term for Aristotle; it is relative to the structure that holds it together. For instance, the elements are the material cause of tissue, while tissues are the material cause of bodily organ. Bodily organs are the material cause of the living body.

The formal cause is the shape or structure that a thing takes. The blueprints are the formal cause of the airplane. For Aristotle the formal and material cause are usually inseparable; one requires the other.

Beyond the material and formal cause a thing must have an agent or force that imposes the form on the matter. This is the efficient cause. The builder of the airplane is the efficient cause. This cause most closely approximates the contemporary idea of a cause.

The fourth cause is the final cause. It is the end, goal, or purpose to which a thing aims and terminates. The final cause of an airplane might be said to be to transport things or people.

Medieval philosophers accepted Aristotle's idea of four causes; they also regarded an effect as flowing from the nature or essence of its cause. The medievals held three beliefs about causality to be indisputable: nothing comes from nothing; nothing can give what it does not itself possess; and a cause must have as much perfection or being as its effects.

Modern discussions of causality stem from David Hume's claim that the idea of causation cannot be gained in any simple way from reason or observation. Reason can give only logical relations, and cause and effect are not logical relations. Observation can tell what is really "out there," but these are only regularities of nonnecessary constant conjunction. That is, observation confirms that some things regularly follow on other things. Experience leads the observer to expect that certain perceptions will always be joined to others in a predictable way. Thus, the necessity that one feels is due to custom or habit.

Immanuel Kant accepted Hume's criticisms as decisive. He saw that such an analysis was damaging to a belief in scientific truths that were universal and necessary. His solution to the problem of the credibility of scientific laws and the questionable character of causality was to argue that causality is a necessary, universal, *a priori* category of the mind. For man to have knowledge objects must conform to this and other categories of the understanding.

While causation may involve regularity, philosophers have asked, Is that all? Regularities may be significant or accidental. More recently causation has been analyzed in terms of counterfactual conditionals: "If c_1 had not occurred, e_2 would not have occurred." However, it is not clear what makes such an analysis true.

Heisenberg's uncertainty principle has had a profound effect upon the notion of causality. He argued that it is in principle impossible to discover both the momentum and position of a fundamental particle. (It should be noted that it has been a matter of dispute whether particles have both momentum and position.) It is possible to state the behavior of such particles in terms of probabilities, so that one can predict with virtual certainty the behavior of masses of particles (i.e., objects). Such a position raises some questions about causality. Has physics given up or undermined causation? Is it sensible to think that individual subatomic movements are caused, although these causes in principle can never be discovered?

The whole matter of causality has been of interest to Christian theology. Two of the theistic proofs for God's existence depend heavily upon Aristotelian and medieval notions of causality. Both the causal and contingency forms of the cosmological argument depend on the idea that God alone can be the first cause. All other causes are secondary. These secondary causes never explain ultimately their effects. The teleological argument depends heavily, at least in some forms, on the idea that a cause cannot give to its effect what it does not itself have. Therefore, since the world exhibits intelligent design, its cause must be intelligent. Modern understanding of causality, as well as a widespread belief in evolutionary theory, has made these arguments less convincing to many today.

P. D. Feinberg

Bibliography. D. Hume, *A Treatise of Human Nature;* I. Kant, *Critique of Pure Reason;* D. Lerner, ed., *Cause and Effect;* B. Russell, *Our Knowledge of the External World.*

Celebration. Celebration is at the core of worship and service for the people of God. Although the word does not occur very frequently in Scripture, the concept is significant and is best understood in terms of its elements, qualities, subject, and occasions as seen in the festivals of Israel, the Lord's Supper, and the celebrative poetry of the Bible (such as I Sam. 2:1–10; Pss. 95; 100; Luke 1:46–55, 68–79).

Elements. In the biblical occasions and expressions of celebration praise, thanksgiving, singing, commemoration, reenactment, anticipation, and obedient service are the essential elements. Praise is directed to God as an exultation, even a boasting or glorying, in the majesty of his person and his acts in history. Thanksgiving celebrates the goodness and justness of God and expresses one's dependence on him. Singing is one of the vehicles for expression of celebration and is frequently mentioned in both the OT and the NT. Commemoration is often prominent in celebration; it celebrates the memory of God's works of creation and redemption. Reenactment is closely linked with commemoration. Reenactment is ritual that symbolically commemorates the redemptive acts of God, as in the Passover and the Eucharist. Celebration also incorporates the element of anticipation. In the very act of commemorating what God has redemptively done in the past, we anticipate the final redemption in the future consummation of all things. Finally, genuine celebration moves on to obedient service and ministry. Scripture does not allow for a dichotomy between hearing and doing or worship and service. Those who truly hear do, and those who truly worship serve. Such are the elements of celebration.

Qualities. These may be identified much more briefly, though they are no less important than the elements. These qualities are self-evident in the biblical examples of celebration: joy, the happy expression of the heart; sincerity, the absence of hypocrisy and pretense; spontaneity, the opposite of compulsion and conditioning; awe and reverence, the sense of the creature in the presence of the Creator; earnestness, the intensity that springs from within; beauty, the aesthetic dimension that should characterize the expressions of celebration; participation, the fact that to celebrate is actually to participate. All these qualities are found in the biblical examples of celebration.

Subject. This may be simply but profoundly put: God, for who he is and what he does as Creator and Redeemer.

Occasions. In Scripture these were both formal and informal. Formal occasions were those stated times set aside for celebration, as in the festivals of Israel and the Communion service in the church. But informal occasions, both individual and corporate, abound, as Hannah's song (I Sam. 2:1–10), the psalms of David (e.g., Ps. 103), the Magnificat of Mary (Luke 1:46–55), and the celebration of the early church (Acts 2:46–47).

Since there is considerable misunderstanding in the contemporary church about the nature of celebration and worship, it is also important that we clearly indicate what celebration is not. It is not mere formalism or ritual. It is not entertainment. It is not a mere addendum to the service to be rushed through. It is not a mere performance only to be observed by spectators, whether the performance be that of musicians, preachers, or priestly functionaries. It is not the repetition of meaningless clichés or pious platitudes. And celebration can never be grudging or compulsory.

S. N. Gundry

See also Worship; Worship in the Church.

Bibliography. R. Allen and G. Borror, *Worship: Rediscovering the Missing Jewel;* R. P. Martin, *Worship in the Early Church;* R. E. Webber, *Worship: Old and New;* J. F. White, *New Forms of Worship.*

Celibacy. The state of being unmarried for purposes of religious devotion and ethical purity. The practice has been a feature of many Christian groups and has also been observed by other religions for a variety of reasons. Since the fourth century celibacy has been a standard imposed on Roman Catholic clergy despite recurring agitation to have it laid aside. The Protestant Reformers denied the biblical validity of imposed celibacy; Luther, Zwingli, and Calvin all married.

The major influence giving rise to celibacy was the pagan dualism which replaced the healthy emphasis on marriage and family life the early church inherited from both the Old and New Testaments. This dualism was common to many religious movements and philosophies of the time. Its underlying theme was the rejection of all things physical as evil in contrast to the goodness of the spiritual. It soon became the accepted practice in the Western church for those fully devoted to God's service to separate themselves from physical realities such as sexual relations and their obvious setting in Christian marriage. Celibacy thus became the norm for monastics and priests. The Eastern church made an exception in not imposing celibacy upon clergy ordained after marriage.

Alongside its emphasis on the normalcy of marriage, including sexual relations and the family structure, the NT teaches the value of celibacy. John the Baptizer, Paul, and Jesus himself might be cited as examples of celibates. Further, in Matt. 19 and I Cor. 7 the Scriptures speak of the value of celibacy. Both Paul (I Cor. 7:7) and Jesus (Matt. 19:12) indicate such celibacy is a gift from God not given to all persons. Those receiving the gift are to forgo the married state for the sake of greater freedom and less worldly entanglements in serving God. This does not mean that to marry is sinful, as Paul indicates in I Cor. 7:9, 28, 36, 38. To forbid marriage is considered demonic in I Tim. 4:1–3. The normal expectation is that church leaders will be married and maintain an exemplary family life (I Tim. 3:1–3; Titus 1:6). While no Christian should be forced to practice celibacy, those receiving the gift of celibacy from God should be encouraged to do so as an expression of their service in the kingdom. O. G. OLIVER, JR.

Bibliography. W. Bassett and P. Huzing, eds., *Celibacy in the Church;* C. Frazee, "The Origins of Clerical Celibacy in the Western Church," *CH* 41:149–67; G. Frein, ed., *Celibacy: The Necessary Option;* H. Lea, *History of Sacerdotal Celibacy in the Christian Church,* 2 vols.; B. J. Leonard, "Celibacy as a Christian Life-Style in the History of the Church," *RE* 74:21–32; H. J. M. Nouwen, "Celibacy," *PP* 27:79–90; P. Schaff, *History of the Christian Church,* II, 397–414.

Cereal Offering. *See* OFFERINGS AND SACRIFICES IN BIBLE TIMES.

Ceremonial Law. *See* LAW, BIBLICAL CONCEPT OF.

Chafer, Lewis Sperry (1871–1952). Born into a minister's family and educated in music at Oberlin College and Conservatory of Music, Chafer began his ministry as a traveling gospel singer. Later he turned to an evangelistic ministry. However, his contact with C. I. Scofield from 1903 until Scofield's death in 1921 redirected Chafer's service to Bible teaching.

In 1922 he moved to Dallas, Texas, for the express purpose of establishing the Dallas Theological Seminary, which came into existence in 1924 and which he served as president and professor of systematic theology until his death.

The study and teaching of theology was thrust on Chafer by the death of W. H. Griffith Thomas, who was slated to teach theology at the new seminary but who died the summer before it opened. Chafer's theology may be characterized as biblical, Calvinistic, premillennial, and dispensational; but chiefly he was a strong exponent of the grace of God. This central concept was related to his Calvinism (though he taught unlimited redemption); to his understanding of the distinctiveness of the church, the body of Christ, in the program of God (thus his dispensationalism); to his emphasis on the faithfulness of God to fulfill his promises to Israel (thus his premillennialism); and to grace as the ruling principle of the Christian life, coupled with an emphasis on the ministry of the Holy Spirit.

Chafer was a skilled theologian, as may be seen in his excellent and often unique treatment of soteriology and pneumatology, and his theological writings gave academic status to his dispensational premillennial viewpoint. Undoubtedly his teaching and his written and popular ministry exerted a major influence for biblical understanding on the church in the twentieth century.

C. C. RYRIE

See also DISPENSATION, DISPENSATIONALISM.

Bibliography. Chafer, *Dispensationalism, Grace, The Kingdom in History and Prophecy, Major Bible Themes, Salvation,* and *Systematic Theology.*

Chalcedon, Council of (451). The Council of Chalcedon, the fourth ecumenical council of the church, was summoned by the Eastern Emperor Marcion. It was convoked specifically to establish ecclesiastical unity in the East, and its definitive formulation, the Chalcedonian Creed or Definition, became and remains the measure of orthodoxy for Christological statements concerning the two natures of Christ.

The work of Chalcedon can be understood only in the light of a series of Christological declarations beginning with the Council of Nicaea (325). The Nicene Creed declared that Christ is of the same divine substance with the Father, against Arius, who taught that Christ had a beginning and was only of similar substance. The Council of Constantinople (381) both ratified and refined the Nicene Creed, in opposition to continuing Arianism, and declared against Apollinarianism, which stated that Christ's human soul had been replaced by the divine Logos. Moreover, Constantinople declared that the Holy Spirit proceeds from the Father and the Son.

In the post-Constantinople period the heresies were Nestorianism and Eutychianism. The former posited a dual personality in Christ, whereas the latter, reacting to Nestorianism, declared that the incarnate Christ had only one nature. Nestorianism was defeated at the Council of Ephesus in 431, but Eutychianism was upheld by the so-called Robber Council held in Alexandria in 449. This set the stage for the Council of Chalcedon two years later.

Marcion ascended the imperial throne in 450 and immediately sought to bring about church unity, which was imperiled by dissension concerning the two natures of Christ. Pope Leo I wished a general council to be held in Italy, but settled for Chalcedon in Asia Minor as nearer the capital.

The Council of Chalcedon met in October, 451, with more than five hundred bishops and several papal legates in attendance. There existed a general consensus among the bishops simply to ratify the Nicene tradition interpreted by Constantinople along with the letters of Cyril of Alexandria to Nestorius and John of Antioch and Pope Leo's letter to Flavian (the so-called Tome, or *Epistola Dogmatica*). Had majority opinion prevailed there would have existed no need for further defining the faith. Nevertheless, the imperial commissioners deemed it necessary, in the interest of unity, to define the faith as it related to the person of Christ.

The council proceeded in three steps to its work of unification. First, it reaffirmed the Nicene tradition; second, it accepted as orthodox the letters of Cyril and Leo; and third, it provided a definition of the faith.

There existed two overarching concerns—maintenance of the unity of Christ's person and establishment of the two natures of Christ. Use was made of letters of both Cyril and Leo along with a letter of Flavian. The first draft of the definition, which is not extant, was deemed deficient in not clearly allowing for two natures. With much effort the council passed a definition which both negated the one-nature incarnational theory of Eutyches and affirmed the two-nature declaration as orthodox. Mary was declared to be the "God-bearer" (*Theotokos*) of God the Son, who at the incarnation became "truly man." Thus Christ was declared as to his deity "consubstantial with the Father," and as to his humanity "consubstantial with us in manhood."

The council then dealt with the unity of the two natures and concluded that the deity and humanity of Christ exist "without confusion, without change, without division, without separation." Thus the two natures coalesced in one person (*prosōpon*) and one substance (*hypostasis*).

Thus the Chalcedonian Creed safeguarded both the divine and human natures of Christ existing in one person in unchangeable union. Since salvation was uppermost in the minds of the framers of this definitive creed, they knew that only a Christ who was truly God and man could save men.

Although the Chalcedonian Creed became, and continues to be, the standard for Christological orthodoxy, it did not prevent continuing opposition from those seeking to coalesce the two natures into one, such as the monophysite and monothelite heresies in the succeeding two centuries. J. H. Hall

See also Councils, Church.

Bibliography. *NPNF*, series II, vol. XIV; P. T. R. Gray, *The Defense of Chalcedon in the East;* J. S. Macarthur, *Chalcedon;* R. V. Sellers, *The Council of Chalcedon.*

Channing, William Ellery (1780–1842). The most important spokesman for Unitarianism in the first half of the nineteenth century. He grew up in Rhode Island under the preaching of the strict Calvinist Samuel Hopkins, and he had a conversion experience as a Harvard undergraduate—experiences which, in spite of his later beliefs, he never regretted. In 1803 he became the minister of Boston's Federal Street Congregational Church, where he remained for the rest of his life. His presence along with a liberal Harvard College made Boston the Unitarian stronghold. It was not in Boston, however, but in Baltimore in 1819, at the ordination of Jared Sparks, that Channing preached a sermon which set out the basic outlines of his Unitarian beliefs. Here he denied the traditional understanding of the Trinity. He qualified severely the sense in which Christ should be considered divine. And he went further than the evolving convictions of New England's moderate Calvinists in softening concepts of depravity and the substitutionary atonement. In other works he affirmed the perfectibility of humanity, the fatherhood of God, and the moral perfection of Christ. As a nineteenth century "evangelical" Unitarian, Channing continued to affirm the reality of the resurrection and genuineness of other NT miracles. To him these constituted solid rational proof for the supernatural character of Christianity. He believed that the Bible recorded inspiration but felt, as he said in 1819, that it is "a book written for men, in the language of men, and that its meaning is to be sought in the same manner as that of other books." He would later in life criticize others, such as the transcendentalist Ralph Waldo Emerson, for taking further exceptions to traditional Christianity. Emerson, nonetheless, later in his own life looked back on Channing as the "bishop" of transcendentalism in the 1830s. Channing's moderate and temperate personality did much to spread his views. He also took strong stands against slavery and the use of liquor. M. A. Noll

See also Unitarianism.

Bibliography. *The Works of William Ellery Channing;* E. P. Peabody, *Reminiscences of Rev. William Ellery Channing;* C. Wright, *The Beginnings of Unitarianism in America.*

Charismata. *See* Spiritual Gifts.

Charismatic Movement. An expression used to refer to a movement within historic churches that began in the 1950s. In the earlier stages the movement was often termed "neo-Pentecostal"; in more recent years it has frequently been referred to as the "charismatic renewal" or the "charismatic renewal movement." Therefore, participants are usually described as "charismatics."

On the American scene it is possible to date significant charismatic beginnings to the year 1960 with the national publicity given to certain events connected with the ministry of Dennis Bennett, at that time Episcopal rector in Van Nuys, California. Since then there has been a continuing growth of the movement within many of the mainline churches: first, such Protestant churches as Episcopal, Lutheran, and Presbyterian (early 1960s); second, the Roman Catholic (beginning in 1967); and third, the Greek Orthodox (about 1971). The charismatic movement has affected almost every historic church and has spread to many churches and countries beyond the United States. This continuing growth has resulted in a multiplicity of national, regional, and local conferences, the production of a wide range of literature, and increasing attention to doctrinal and theological questions both within and outside the movement. The challenge to the churches may be seen in the fact that since 1960 well over one hundred official denominational documents—regional, national, continental, and international—on the charismatic movement have been produced.

The immediate background of the charismatic movement is "classical Pentecostalism" dating from the early twentieth century, with its emphasis on baptism with (or in) the Holy Spirit as an endowment of power subsequent to conversion, speaking in tongues as the initial evidence of this baptism, and the continuing validity of the spiritual gifts (charismata) of I Cor. 12:8–10. Because of such distinctive emphases these early "Pentecostals"—as they came to be called—found no place in the mainline churches (they either freely left or were forced out) and thus founded their own. As a result there gradually came into being such "classical" Pentecostal denominations as the Assemblies of God, the Pentecostal Holiness Church, the Church of God (Cleveland, Tennessee), the Church of God in Christ, and the International Church of the Foursquare Gospel. The charismatic movement, while related historically and doctrinally to classical Pentecostalism, has largely stayed within the historic church bodies or has spilled over into interdenominational church fellowships. In neither case has there been any significant movement toward the classical Pentecostal churches. Hence today the charismatic movement, despite its "classical" parentage, exists almost totally outside official Pentecostal denominations.

Special Emphases. Particular emphases are reflected variously in the charismatic movement.

Baptism with the Holy Spirit. There is common recognition of baptism with the Holy Spirit as a distinctive Christian experience. It is viewed as an event wherein the believer is "filled with" the presence and power of the Holy Spirit. Baptism with the Holy Spirit is understood to result from "the gift of the Holy Spirit," wherein the Spirit is freely "poured out," "falls upon," "comes on," "anoints," "endues" the believer with "power from on high." This event/experience is the moment of initiation into the Spirit-filled life. Spirit baptism is said to occur either at the time of conversion (through repentance and forgiveness) or subsequent thereto. Baptism with the Holy Spirit, accordingly, is not identified with conversion. It is viewed as a being filled with the Holy Spirit that brings about powerful witness to Jesus Christ. Through this Spirit baptism the exalted Christ carries forward his ministry in the church and world.

The gift of the Holy Spirit wherein Spirit baptism occurs is understood as an act of God's sovereign grace. Accordingly, the gift may be received only through faith in Jesus Christ, who is the mediator of the gift and the baptism. Participants in the charismatic movement emphasize the centrality of Christ (not the Holy Spirit) and the unique instrumentality of faith in him. It is the same Christ who through his life, death, and resurrection saves and forgives the lost who also through his exaltation to "the right hand of the Father" sends forth the Holy Spirit upon the redeemed. So it is by the same faith that both turning from sin and empowering for ministry are to be received from him. Charismatics generally hold that conversion and the gift of the Spirit, though both received by faith, may or may not happen at the same time. The book of Acts is viewed as exhibiting two patterns: a separation (however brief or long) between conversion and the gift of the Holy Spirit (the original 120, the Samaritans, Saul of Tarsus, and the Ephesian twelve), and a simultaneous reception of both (the centurion household in Caesarea). Hence, it is by way of faith—not necessarily at the initial moment—that the gift of the Spirit is received.

Participants in the charismatic movement also frequently point to the pattern of Jesus' own life, which includes both his conception by the Holy Spirit and the later descent of the Holy Spirit upon him. Jesus was therefore both born of the Spirit as Savior and anointed with the Spirit as he began his ministry. So it is said that correspondingly there is needed both a birth of the Spirit for salvation and an anointing of the Spirit for ministry in his name.

This leads to the emphasis of charismatics on such matters as prayer, commitment, and expectancy as the context for the gift of the Holy Spirit. So it was with Jesus' life leading up to the descent of the Spirit; also with the 120 disciples who waited in the upper room prior to Pentecost; likewise a number of others according to several additional accounts in the book of Acts. Prayer preceding the reception of the Holy Spirit particularly stands out in the accounts of the Samaritans, Saul of Tarsus, and the centurion household in Caesarea. Seeing a similar pattern in the life of Jesus, the original disciples, and the early church, many charismatics affirm that in a spirit of prayer, commitment, and expectancy they were visited by the Holy Spirit. Such an event, it is claimed, did not occur by dint of human effort, not through some work beyond faith; rather it happened to those who in faith were open to receive what God had promised to give.

Whereas the basic purpose of Spirit baptism is power for ministry and service, charismatics speak of a number of effects. Since it is the Holy Spirit who is given (not something he gives), many speak primarily of a strong sense of the reality of God, the Holy Spirit dynamically present, bearing witness to Jesus Christ and glorifying the Father. There is testimony to an enhanced sense of the Scriptures as the written Word of God, since the same Holy Spirit who inspired them fully is now said to be moving freely in the lives of the believers. Many charismatics also testify to an abounding joy, a deeper assurance of salvation, a new boldness for witness to Jesus Christ, and an enriched fellowship with other Christians. On this last point, one of the most noticeable features of the charismatic movement is the sense of *koinonia* that binds them together not only in a local fellowship but also across ancient denominational barriers. Accordingly, many claim that the charismatic movement is the true fulfillment of the Lord's prayer to the Father "that they may all be one" (John 17:21).

Speaking in Tongues. In the charismatic movement speaking in tongues—glossolalia—occupies a significant place. Speaking in tongues is generally understood to be communication with God in language that is other than one known to the speaker. A person does the speaking—that is, he freely uses his vocal apparatus—but it is claimed that the Holy Spirit gives the utterance. It is viewed as transcendent speech by the enabling of the Holy Spirit.

Speaking in tongues is considered by some charismatics to be the miraculous utterance of an unlearned foreign language (so in classical Pentecostalism). This is claimed, first, on the basis of the narrative in Acts 1, that since the Scripture says that the disciples "began to speak in other tongues" and "each one heard them speaking in his own language," the disciples must have been speaking the languages or tongues of the listeners. Second, there is the frequently given testimony that on many occasions people have heard their own language spoken by someone who was totally ignorant of what he was saying. However, many charismatics hold that the otherness of tongues is qualitative rather than quantitative, that "other tongues" are not natural (i.e., human languages) but spiritual. Accordingly, if someone says that he heard a person speaking in his own language, this is viewed as occurring because the Holy Spirit immediately interpreted what was said (hence it was not a hearing *of* but a hearing *in* one's own language). From this perspective there is no difference between the tongues referred to in Acts 2 and I Cor. 12–14. The former were not foreign languages and the latter ecstatic speech; both are utterances of the Holy Spirit that can be understood only when interpreted by the Holy Spirit. Charismatics who have embraced this understanding of "other tongues" believe that it best harmonizes the biblical witness, that it retains the spirituality of tongues, and that it accords with the empirical fact that there are no concrete data (for example, from the study of recordings of tongues) of an unknown language being spoken.

The essential charismatic claim about glossolalia is that this is the vehicle of communication par excellence between man and God. It is the language of transcendent prayer and praise. In tongues there is speech to God which goes beyond the mental into the spiritual. Charismatics frequently state that in tongues there is a fulfillment of the intense desire to offer total praise to God not only with the mind but also with the heart and spirit. Therein one goes beyond the most elevated of earthly expressions—even "hosannas" and "hallelujahs"—into spiritual utterance: the praise of God in language given by the Holy Spirit. In the regular life of prayer tongues are said to occupy a primary place. Such prayer is identified with praying in the spirit or with the spirit, which, since it is not mental, can be done at all times. This spiritual prayer does not intend to eliminate mental prayer, i.e., prayer with the understanding, but to afford the continuous undergirding and background for all conceptual prayer. The ideal is prayer with the spirit and with the mind (in that order). Where prayer passes into praise it may likewise be singing with the spirit and singing with the mind. For the charismatic movement at large singing in the spirit—singing in tongues—occupies an important place, particularly in situations of community worship. Therein both words and melody are free expressions believed to be given spontaneously by the Holy Spirit. This, often combined with more usual singing, is seen as the apex of worship: it is the worship of God in psalms and human and (climactically) spiritual songs.

Speaking in tongues is understood to be not irrational but suprarational utterance. It is not the forsaking of the rational for the nonsensical—hence gibberish—but the fulfillment and transcendence of the rational in the spiritual. Charismatics are not disturbed by linguists who claim that glossolalia has no observable language structure, for if such were the case, speaking in tongues would not be spiritual but rational speech. Further, speaking in tongues is not viewed as ecstatic utterance—in the sense of uncontrolled, highly emotional, perhaps frenzied activity. While containing a strong emotional (even a rational) element, glossolalia runs deeper than the emotions. Both reason (or mind) and emotions are aspects of the human psyche (*psychē*), whether on the conscious or subconscious level. Speaking in tongues is thus understood to be transpsychical; it belongs to the realm of the spirit (*pneuma*).

Most persons in the charismatic movement view speaking in tongues as directly connected with the event of Spirit baptism. The Scriptures in Acts which specifically record speaking in tongues (2:4; 10:46; 19:6) state that it occurred with persons who had just received the gift of the Holy Spirit. Glossolalia in Acts therefore is closely linked with Spirit baptism, as an immediately ensuing activity. Hence, most charismatics believe that there can be no speaking in tongues without prior Spirit baptism (this is the opposite of saying that there can be no Spirit baptism without speaking in tongues). The reason would seem to follow from the very nature of baptism in the Spirit: a fullness of the Spirit that overflows into transcendent prayer and praise. Granted this fullness—the outpouring of the Spirit—glossolalia may be expected. Further, according to Acts when speaking in tongues occurred, the Scriptures state or imply that everyone present did so. Thus charismatics generally conclude that speaking in tongues is not limited to some, but is the province of all. Also these very tongues may thereafter become an ongoing part of the life of prayer and worship. Such tongues are sometimes called "devotional tongues," and are viewed as an important part of the prayer life of the Spirit-baptized believers.

In addition to viewing glossolalia as a concomitant of Spirit baptism and belonging to the Spirit-filled life, most charismatics affirm that though one may speak in tongues as a consequence of Spirit baptism, he may not have "the gift of tongues" for ministry in the body of believers. This is based not on Acts but on I Cor. 12, where Paul depicts tongues as one of several manifestations of the Holy Spirit for the common good. In this situation tongues are to be spoken as the Spirit apportions, by the few not the many, and only when there is one present to interpret. Though all may be able to speak in tongues (Paul's expressed desire), not all are so directed by the Holy Spirit. The phenomenon of tongues is the same—whether in Acts or I Corinthians, whether in the life of prayer or in the body of believers; it is addressed not to men but to God. However, the practice of tongues is said to be quite different in that what belongs to the life of the Spirit-filled believer is not necessarily exercised by him in the Christian fellowship.

Finally, there are those in the charismatic movement who place little emphasis on speaking in tongues. They do not disregard glossolalia, or by any means rule it out, but, focusing almost entirely on I Cor. 12–14, view speaking in tongues as only one of several manifestations of the Holy Spirit. Hence if one does not speak in tongues, this does not signify any lack of Spirit baptism; it is only that the Holy Spirit has not apportioned to such a person that particular gift. Such a view, based more on the distribution of gifts in I Corinthians than the association of glossolalia with Spirit baptism in Acts, is obviously quite different from what has previously been described. Accordingly, to many other charismatics this failure to relate glossolalia primarily to the gift of the Spirit as its concomitant and as an ensuing expression in the life of prayer and praise is to overlook the basic purpose of tongues.

Spiritual Gifts. By definition the charismatic movement is concerned with *charismata*, the Greek term for "gifts of grace." Everywhere throughout the charismatic movement there is the claim that all the charismata, or charisms, mentioned in Scripture are, or should be, operational in the Christian community. Whereas in large sectors of Christendom many of the gifts have been viewed as belonging only to first century Christianity, the charismatic movement stresses their continuing importance. Many charismatics prefer the name "charismatic renewal" to "charismatic movement" to lay emphasis on a renewal of the gifts in our time.

It is generally recognized that the biblical charismata include a wide range of gifts as described in Rom. 12:6–8; I Pet. 4:10–11; and I Cor. 12–14. (The word "charisma" is also used in Rom. 1:11; 5:15–16; 6:23; I Cor. 1:7; 7:7; II Cor. 1:11; I Tim. 4:14; II Tim. 1:6; "charismata" in Rom. 11:29.) All these gifts, charismatics hold, should be functional in the body of Christ. The focal point of charismatics, however, is I Cor. 12–14, especially 12:4–11. They suggest a number of reasons for this: (1) These charismata alone are described as "the manifestation of the Spirit," hence have a unique importance as the direct expression and action of the Holy Spirit. The spiritual gifts, accordingly, make for a dynamic, vital community life. (2) The spiritual gifts are "power tools" for the upbuilding of the community. Each one functioning properly is essential to the full life of the body. (3) The exercise of the spiritual charismata by all makes for total ministry. It is not just the few (e.g., pastors, elders, deacons) who are to be channels for the Spirit's manifestation, but each person in the community. (4) A body of Christians in which spiritual gifts—along with other gifts and ministries—are operating is a community of spontaneity in worship, dynamism in ministry, and rich fellowship with one another. (5) It is through the exercise of these spiritual gifts that the church comes alive to "high voltage" Christianity: an extraordinary sense of the exalted Lord's presence in the Spirit moving powerfully among his people.

A profile on charismatic understanding of the spiritual gifts would include the following. All the gifts of the Spirit are viewed as extraordinary, supernatural, and permanent. The spiritual charismata as described in I Cor. 12:8–10 are not arranged in a hierarchy so that "word of wisdom" is the highest and "interpretation of tongues" the least. The greatest gift at a given time is that which edifies most. All the spiritual gifts, especially prophecy (the direct utterance of God to his people in their own language), are earnestly to be desired (I Cor. 14:1); thus an attitude of "seek not" about any gift is a violation of God's intention for his people. The gifts of the Spirit, because of their high potency and possible abuse, need to be carefully ordered. Abuse, however, does not call for disuse but proper use. The spiritual gifts will not cease until we see him "face to face"; then they will be no longer needed for the edification of the community. Love is the "way" of the gifts—without love they profit nothing—and love will endure forever.

A word should be added about the relation of baptism with the Holy Spirit to the gifts of the Spirit. Charismatics often state that baptism in the Spirit is initiation into the dynamic dimension; the gifts of the Spirit are dynamic manifestation. Hence baptism with the Spirit is for living in power and glory; the spiritual charismata are works of power and glory. Many charismatics affirm that whenever Spirit baptism occurs, the gifts, which are already resident in the Christian community, become all the more freely and fully exercised.

Finally, charismatics generally recognize that spiritual gifts cannot substitute for spiritual fruit. The fruits of the Spirit—love, joy, peace, etc. (Gal. 5:22)—represent the maturation of the believer in Christ. The most immature believer, if he is open to the Holy Spirit, may be Spirit-filled and exercising extraordinary gifts, and yet have experienced little of the Spirit's sanctifying grace. Such a person needs all the more to grow up into Christ.

Evaluations. Outside evaluations of the charismatic movement vary today from outright rejection to mixed acceptance. The more than one hundred official denominational documents earlier mentioned demonstrate on the whole an increasing openness, but with reservations, to many of its features. Critics of the theology of the charismatic movement have expressed disagreements variously. (1) Baptism with the Holy Spirit: some hold that it is improper, biblically and theologically, to refer to this as an experience possibly subsequent to conversion; others claim that whereas Spirit baptism may be a second experience, the primary purpose is not empowering but sanctification. (2) Speaking in tongues: some do not recognize glossolalia as having any longer a connection with Spirit baptism (the book of Acts being viewed as transitional) but consider it as only a lesser gift of the Holy Spirit available to some, or no longer available at all. (3) Spiritual gifts: some divide the spiritual gifts into "temporary" and "permanent," claiming that the former have been withdrawn whereas the latter continue; tongues and prophecy in particular are said to have ceased with the completion of the canon of Scripture. It is apparent from such criticisms that much more theological work needs to be done.

J. R. Williams

See also Pentecostalism; Spiritual Gifts; Baptism of the Spirit; Tongues, Speaking in.

Bibliography. Charismatic: D. J. Bennett, *The Holy Spirit and You;* L. Christenson, *Speaking in Tongues and Its Significance for the Church;* S. Clark, *Baptized in the Spirit and Spiritual Gifts;* H. M. Ervin, *These Are Not Drunken As Ye Suppose;* M. Harper, *Power for the Body of Christ;* K. McDonnell, ed., *The Holy Spirit and Power: The Catholic Charismatic Renewal;* J. Rea, *The Layman's Commentary on the Holy Spirit;* R. P. Spittler, ed., *Perspectives on the New Pentecostalism;*

L. J. Cardinal Suenens, *A New Pentecost?* J. R. Williams, *The Era of the Spirit, The Pentecostal Reality,* and *The Gift of the Holy Spirit Today.* Documentary: K. McDonnell, *Presence, Power, Praise: Documents on the Charismatic Renewal in the Churches, 1960–1980.* Noncharismatic: F. D. Bruner, *A Theology of the Holy Spirit: The Pentecostal Experience and the NT Witness;* J. D. G. Dunn, *Baptism in the Holy Spirit;* A. A. Hoekema, *Holy Spirit Baptism;* J. F. MacArthur, *The Charismatics: A Doctrinal Perspective;* J. R. W. Stott, *The Baptism and Fullness of the Holy Spirit.*

Chasten, Chastisement. *See* DISCIPLINE.

Chemnitz, Martin (1522–1586). A leading influence in consolidating Lutheran doctrine and practice in the generation after Luther's death. A popular adage runs: "*Si Martinus non fuisset, Martinus vix stetisset*" ("If Martin Chemnitz had not come along, Martin Luther would hardly have survived").

Chemnitz was born at Treuenbrietzen, near Wittenberg. Recognized as a child of superior intellectual gifts, he was sent to the Latin school in Wittenberg. He left school to lend a hand in the family clothmaking trade, but returned to school at Magdeburg (1539–42). In 1545 he went to the University at Wittenberg to study under Philip Melanchthon. When the Smalcald War disrupted Wittenberg temporarily, Chemnitz went to Königsberg, where he earned the degree of magister. It was here that he developed a deep interest in the study of theology. He was appointed librarian of the ducal library at Königsberg and in 1554 he was admitted to the philosophical faculty of Wittenberg. His large student audiences were a testimony to his effectiveness as a teacher. However, he soon moved to Brunswick, where he accepted a call as a preacher and coadjutor to the Lutheran superintendent of churches. He continued to serve Brunswick faithfully until his death.

Chemnitz is justly famous as churchman and preacher; nevertheless, his abiding significance rests on his work in connection with the controversies between the Roman Catholic Church and the churches which adhered to the Augsburg Confession and the strife which rent the latter churches after Luther's death. The first led to his *Examen* of the canons and decrees of the Council of Trent; the second to his large part in the production and acceptance of the Formula of Concord in 1577.

A short writing by Chemnitz against the Jesuit order brought him into conflict with Jacob Andrada, who sought to discredit Chemnitz's critique of the Jesuits by defending the theology of Trent. In response to Andrada, Chemnitz produced the *Examen*—a four-volume analysis of the decrees of Trent showing from Scripture and from both the most ancient and modern teachers of the church where the Tridentine formulations departed from the teachings of the Bible. In the first of these volumes Chemnitz worked out the so-called formal principle of the Reformation, that Scripture, and not tradition or a combination of Scripture and tradition, is the source and norm of doctrine in the Christian church. In the remaining three volumes he treated the sacraments and the abuses in the Roman Church which the Council of Trent had sought to defend. The *Examen* is widely acknowledged as not only a masterful polemic against the decrees of Trent but also a thorough exposition of the teaching of Reformation Lutheranism.

The serious dissensions which broke out among the Lutherans following Luther's death involved the understanding of several specific doctrines—original sin and conversion, the Lord's Supper, and ecclesiastical ceremonies. Chemnitz was one of several leaders who attempted to clarify the points at issue and allay the controversies. He wrote and rewrote the separate articles of the Formula of Concord and helped persuade pastors and princes to subscribe to the final document.

Chemnitz was a prolific writer. His works include *De Duabus Naturis,* a treatise on the two natures in Christ, and *Harmony of the Four Gospels,* which he did not manage to finish but which was carried to completion by Polycarp Leyser and Johann Gerhard and published posthumously. J. F. JOHNSON

See also CONCORD, FORMULA OF.

Bibliography. T. Jungkuntz, *Formulators of the Formula of Concord;* R. D. Preus, *The Theology of Post-Reformation Lutheranism,* 2 vols.

Cherub, Cherubim. *See* ANGEL.

Chesterton, Gilbert Keith (1874–1936). Christian writer and apologist. Born of Anglican parents in London, Chesterton from 1900 gained a reputation as a literary figure. His whimsical way with words was pressed into Christian service as his faith grew. In *Orthodoxy* (1908) he declared that anyone could fall into fads from Gnosticism to Christian Science. "But to have avoided them all," he continued, "has been one whirling adventure; and in my vision the heavenly chariot flies thundering through the ages, the dull heresies sprawling and prostrate, the wild truth reeling but erect." Against R. J. Campbell he argued that belief in sin as well as in goodness was more favorable to social reform than was the woolly optimism that refused to recognize evil. He held that the acid test of all religions lay in the question: what do they *deny?* He became a Roman Catholic in 1922; he would have done it earlier, but he was "much too frightened of that tremendous Reality on the altar."

Like his friend Ronald Knox, he was both entertainer and Christian apologist. He concluded that "in all that welter of inconsistent and incompatible heresies, the one and only really unpardonable heresy was orthodoxy." He complained that "the act of defending any of the cardinal virtues has today all the exhilaration of a vice." He saw clearly the crossroads at which Western civilization stood on deserting the path of religion and a God-centered universe. He blamed personal and national greed for World War I. Too many people were paying too much attention to the spice of life and too little attention to life itself. "Each day," he said, "is a special gift; something that might not have been." Chesterton early discovered the value of paradox as "truth standing on its head to gain attention." He could make others think by statements bizarre enough to pass their defenses and explode devastatingly within their minds. Most of his theological works came after he became a Roman Catholic, including *The Everlasting Man* (1925) and *Avowals and Denials* (1934). C. S. Lewis and Ronald Knox acknowledged their intellectual and spiritual debt to him. J. D. Douglas

Bibliography. A. L. Maycock, *The Man Who Was Orthodox;* D. Barker, *G. K. Chesterton;* M. Ward, *Gilbert Keith Chesterton.*

Chicago School of Theology. From the early 1900s scholars at the Divinity School of the University of Chicago worked toward a modernist theology. These scholars accepted the historical-critical approach to the Bible, to Christian origins, to church history, and to the development of Christian theology. Many of them—although on this issue some strongly dissented—also accepted a philosophical approach to the modern restatement of Christian theology. The philosophy was, depending on the individual scholar, either pragmatism or a process form of empiricism. This community of scholars and its modernist, historical-critical, and pragmatic or process-empirical point of view are known as the Chicago school of theology. In the mid-1960s the department of theology in the Divinity School appointed a number of faculty who, particularly on the issue of using process forms of philosophy to restate Christian doctrine, represented other points of view. The resultant pluralism marked the end of the Chicago school of theology.

The early years of the Chicago school produced men such as George Burman Foster who, at the turn of the century, agonized over the import of the "death of God" for Christianity. Shirley Jackson Case applied the historical-critical method to Scripture, while his colleague Shailer Mathews applied the same method to the development of Christian doctrine. For Case and Mathews the historical-critical method meant looking for social, psychological, economic, and other causes for the emergence of the Bible and Christian doctrine. Mathews also emphasized the immanence of God and the nature of Christianity as a social movement. Edward Scribner Ames focused on the psychology of religion and on pragmatism as the context for modern theology.

During its first two and a half decades the Divinity School self-consciously functioned as a center for the promotion of the modernist movement, both academically and in the Protestant churches. The faculty produced a wide variety of materials for popular audiences, preached endless sermons, and spoke at an amazing variety of local clubs. They vigorously fought the theological conservatives, convinced that the future was theirs. Shailer Mathews took World War I as the opportunity to suggest to the Chicago *Daily News* that the conservative premillennialists were probably being supported by the Germans, and he recommended a government investigation. Shirley Jackson Case, on the contrary, in his essay "The Premillennial Menace" suggested a link between premillennialism and the communists of the I.W.W.

In 1927 Henry Nelson Wieman joined the Chicago faculty, bringing an increased emphasis on philosophical theology. Wieman's first contribution to the Divinity School was to explicate the process philosophy of Alfred North Whitehead. This increased focus on philosophical theology seems to have had two sources. First, while the early historical-critical scholars could assume cosmic—that is, divine—support for modernist values, their studies had reached the level of sophistication where this cosmic support needed to be justified. Second, many people after World War I were not all convinced that humane, liberal, and progressive values could be found at the heart of modern culture. The claim that such values, derived from Christianity and cosmically supported, were immanent in modern democratic culture was the heart of modernism. Neoorthodox theology, however, was based precisely on the skepticism about modern culture. Neoorthodox theologians such as Barth in Europe and the brothers Niebuhr in America presented a profound challenge to the modernism of the

Chicago school—a challenge that evoked an increased philosophical sophistication in the Chicago men. In a significant sense the Chicago men considered the neo-orthodox as their foes until the breakup of the school.

While Wieman's own interests later shifted away from Whitehead, other scholars carried on the philosophical tradition of process empiricism. The strictest Whiteheadian was Bernard M. Loomer, who served as dean of the Divinity School from 1945 to 1953. As dean, Loomer encouraged the organization of the school's curriculum largely on a Whiteheadian basis. Daniel Day Williams and Bernard Eugene Meland sought to use process philosophy as a foundation for restating Christian doctrine, but both men were sensitive to philosophical resources in addition to Whitehead. Holding a joint appointment in the Divinity School and the philosophy department was Charles Hartshorne. As a young man at Harvard, Hartshorne had been a junior colleague of Whitehead's. While the paramount expositor of Whitehead, Hartshorne worked out his own version of process philosophy which, especially in its doctrine of God, depended less on a Whiteheadian type of empiricism and more on strictly logical considerations.

Although after 1927 process philosophy typically provided the foundation for constructive theology, it never completely dominated the Divinity School, even its department of theology. Historical theologians Wilhelm Pauck and Jaroslav Pelikan provided critiques of the use of philosophy, and of process philosophy in particular, as the foundation for Christian theology. By the mid-1960s, however, all the men mentioned previously had moved from Chicago or had retired, and their replacements represented a pluralism of theological methodologies. While the contemporary faculty accepts the historical-critical method, it no longer focuses primarily on modernist theology. And while Whiteheadian and process forms of theology continue to be vigorously pursued, they are now but one of many options. Perhaps the old Chicago school of theology lives, not so much in Chicago alone, but in the contemporary reemergence of process theology throughout the United States and Canada, many of the leaders of this revival having taken their doctorates at Chicago. S. T. FRANKLIN

See also PROCESS THEOLOGY; CASE, SHIRLEY JACKSON; MATHEWS, SHAILER; LIBERALISM, THEOLOGICAL.

Bibliography. C. H. Arnold, *Near the Edge of Battle;* B. E. Meland, ed., *The Future of Empirical Theology;* W. Hynes, *Shirley Jackson Case and the Chicago School.*

Chief Priest. *See* PRIESTS AND LEVITES.

Children of God. This highly controversial group grew out of a house meeting in Los Angeles organized by David Berg in 1967. Berg's group was one of the first to work with "the hippies and freaks" of that area and began as a legitimate protest against a dead orthodoxy. During 1970 Berg assumed the name Moses David, or "Mo." In 1971 his fledgling community experienced a period of rapid growth. During that year they sent their first missionaries to Europe and began their worldwide expansion. Organizationally the group developed into a number of colonies. Berg communicated with them by means of his "Mo letters." During this period the organization of the group became increasingly complex and a series of schisms appeared. At its peak in mid-1976, the Children of God had approximately 4,500 full-time members plus about 800 children of the members organized into over 600 colonies in 70 countries. Since then the movement has gone into rapid decline. However, because of the secretive nature of the group, it is difficult to obtain accurate information on its membership.

Originally the theology of the Children of God was a form of evangelical Christianity. In it one can find the influence of the Holiness Movement, Pentecostalism, Brethren ideas about the local church, and premillennialism. One of the first indications of their departure from orthodoxy was the development of a prophetic tradition in their communities. In 1970 Berg visited and became disillusioned with the State of Israel. This seems to have shattered his premillennial assumptions and an identity crisis occurred. Berg now portrayed himself as a prophet and quickly developed his distinctive views. Christian sexual ethics were rejected, and an amalgam of beliefs, including reincarnation, astral projection, and astrology, were incorporated. One of the most controversial developments appeared in his famous Mo letter of 1976, where he introduced the concept of "flirty fishes," by which he legitimated ritual prostitution as a form of evangelism. Today the group's theology is in constant flux and depends entirely on the "revelations" of Berg. I. HEXHAM

See also CULTS.

Bibliography. J. E. Richardson, ed., *Organized Miracles;* J. W. Drakeford, *Children of Doom;* R. M. Enroth, E. E. Ericson, Jr., and C. B. Peters, *The Jesus People.*

Chiliasm. *See* MILLENNIUM, VIEWS OF THE.

Choose, Chosen. *See* ELECT, ELECTION.

Christ, Jesus. *See* JESUS CHRIST.

Christ, Offices of. *See* OFFICES OF CHRIST.

Christening. This word would appear to have two derivations, and thus to be used with twofold significance. From the Greek *chriō* ("I anoint"), it was used to describe the anointing with oil (the chrism) by the bishop when baptism, anointing, and sometimes the laying on of hands were all administered as one rite in the ancient church. This symbol was seen as pointing to the imparting of the gift of the same Holy Spirit who came upon (or christened, made into Christ) Jesus at his baptism (Mark 1:10–11). Middle English used the word loosely as an equivalent to baptism (i.e., making a Christian). The word then came to be applied to the giving of the name in baptism, and from the sixteenth century it has been used as a synonym for naming. D. H. WHEATON

Bibliography. E. C. Whitaker, *The Baptismal Liturgy.*

Christian. *See* CHRISTIANS, NAMES OF.

Christian Calendar. *See* CHRISTIAN YEAR.

Christian Ethics. *See* ETHICAL SYSTEMS, CHRISTIAN.

Christianity and Culture. The relations between Christianity and culture have varied according to circumstances and particular perceptions of culture. Although modern social science has given us a more detailed understanding of culture, we are basically concerned with the way God's work of redemption—both in Scripture and in history—has confronted and changed the social order in its created context, and also with the ways believing communities have viewed and responded to their environment. The church confronts these issues whenever it seeks to live its faith and give a credible witness in the place to which God has called it.

The world "culture" originally referred to cultivating the ground, and it has never completely lost this rapport with natural productivity. While the word is often used more narrowly for the fine arts, culture is better understood as the total pattern of a people's behavior, and it is in this latter sense that the word will be used in this article. Culture includes all behavior that is learned and transmitted by the symbols (rites, artifacts, language, etc.) of a particular group and that focuses on certain ideas or assumptions that we call a world view.

Biblical and Theological Framework. *OT.* The Bible has no word for culture as such, but it is clear from the beginning that God created man and woman as creatures of culture. The early chapters of Genesis present the created order as an interrelated community in which relations with God, the earth, and human beings all played a part. There is an implied covenant between man and God that must be lived out in a social context by a people embedded in creation. Clearly the order was good (Gen. 1:31), and the human process of having dominion was good as well.

The fall following Adam and Eve's rebellion against God's instructions resulted in a disordered community and a culture that reflected human pride (Gen. 11:4). God's intervention, from the choosing of Abraham to the deliverance from Egypt, should be seen in terms of God's purpose to restore and renew the created order through a people reflecting his character.

It is a mistake to see the law as an expression of God's desire for his people to have a unique cultural system. Much of Israel's culture was common to other nations of the ancient Near East. True, contact with other cultures was forbidden upon entrance into Canaan (Josh. 6:18), but this was because they were subject to God's wrath due to their wickedness, not because they were foreign.

Indeed, anthropologists studying the OT recognize that Israel, due to its geography, had greater exposure to influences from neighboring peoples than almost any other ancient nation. Bible scholars have begun to appreciate how biblical practices—e.g., the ornamentation of the temple or even the covenant idea—have close parallels in neighboring cultures. So in the process of revelation God is not concerned to give his people a special culture, but to intervene and reveal his will so that institutions and practices that already existed could be reformed and become suitable vehicles of his glory. Of course this meant that much from neighboring cultures had to be forbidden, and even those institutions that Israel had in common with its neighbors—like the priesthood or kingship—were transformed under the impact of God's instructions (e.g., Deut. 17:14–20).

As Israel prospered during the monarchy, it forgot that its institutions were a means of furthering God's purposes and saw them as ends in themselves, so that God had to expel Israel from the land and send it to live in an alien culture. Even there God promised a sprout from the stump of Jesse would encompass the renewal of all creation (Isa. 11); in the meantime they must seek the welfare of the land in which they were dwelling (Jer. 29:5–7).

NT. God's desire to redeem and restore human

cultural patterns is implied in the ministry of Christ, who came with a clear consciousness of fulfilling the redemptive purpose of the OT. His earth-shattering re-creative work focused on the resurrection, ascension, and Pentecost, which were seen as fulfillment of the OT promises for covenant life and community.

The oft-repeated remark that the NT is indifferent to culture holds only for a very narrow view of culture. The Christian experience with Christ was seen to have great implications for culture (cf. Paul's advice to Philemon). And if the OT vision of earthly and human renewal is borne in mind, it can be seen that Christ's earthly work started a process of transformation that will be gloriously completed when he returns to judge the world, a consummation which by our response of faith and obedience we are already made to taste.

As in the OT, the environment of the NT church was highly cosmopolitan. Roman administration and Greek language and culture all favored the exchange of ideas. NT writers often used terms familiar to a broad spectrum of people: John makes use of words like *logos* or *sophia* to express the transforming reality of the Word made flesh; Paul shows respect for a great variety of cultural practices (I Cor. 10:23–33; Rom. 14; Col. 2:16; I Tim. 4:3–4) to underline the genuine liberation that comes from being in Christ. This is not to say that the gospel was compatible with any and every cultural pattern. There were fundamental encounters with Judaizers who insisted on a Jewish culture for all believers and with Greeks who believed wisdom expressed an immanent order discoverable by human reason. For these, the coming of Christ was the decisive element; new meaning was given to the witness of the Jewish law and to the Greek quest for human wisdom.

Historical Perspective. *The Early Church.* The church was born in the midst of major intellectual traditions. Some, such as Justin Martyr, felt that good culture was a reflection of the divine Logos and preliminary training for the gospel. Others agreed with Tertullian, who insisted that culture was the locus of sin and that salvation involved an ethical separation from surrounding influences. But it soon became clear that if the church was to communicate its faith in terms the world understood, it too, like the NT church, must make use of current expressions. The ideas of infinitude and eternity, which the Greeks were reluctant to apply to God, were used to describe the Christian God; the Near Eastern idea of a transcendent source of all things influenced later formulations of the doctrine of creation; and Plotinus's intelligible world was used to describe the New Jerusalem and to formulate a way to God from within. At other points, however—as in views of history and providence—Christianity broke sharply with these influences.

The conversion of Emperor Constantine (A.D. 312) decisively changed the position of Christianity in the world, if not the character of Christianity itself, and made it possible for a particular civilization to be identified with Christianity. The temptation was to view the faith in an institutional way rather than as the power of God to reform individuals and communities. Augustine contributed the first general interpretation of history and culture in his *City of God.* There he argued that history involved a continuous struggle between the city of man ruled by *cupiditas* (or covetousness) and the city of God ruled by love. With the fall of classical culture Augustine had come to feel a certain pessimism about human achievement and the need to rely on God's grace. The fall, he believed, created a split in human consciousness which could be healed only by submission to the church and an appropriation of its art and liturgy as a way of achieving oblique knowledge of God. Biblical imagery then replaced the classics as the basis for a "Christian culture" (cf. his *On Christian Doctrine*), thus laying the foundation for medieval art and worship.

Meanwhile in the East theologians stressed the earth as a potential vehicle of God's spirit and saw redemption in terms of divinization (Athanasius), a restoring of its "image" of God. This recaptured some OT echoes lost in the West and led to the rich mystical traditions of the Orthodox Churches.

Middle Ages. From Augustine there developed the view that everything on earth conformed to some heavenly pattern. Bonaventure pictured the world as a road leading to God where he could be read in every object. For Aquinas culture as a reflection of man's natural end must conform to natural law. Since "it is natural for man to be a social and political animal," life in society is prescribed by natural law. Grace, God's assistance, perfects rather than judges what is naturally good, since our end is implicit in our nature. This view understood the eternal significance of human achievement—our work "bears eternal fruit," as Dante put it in the *Divine Comedy*—even as it reduced its historical significance and sometimes elicited uncritical loyalty to particular embodiments of Christian civilization.

Reformation. The decisive critique of the medieval view of culture came with the Reformation. The Copernican revolution and the voyages of discovery focused on the possibilities of earthly life. The static medieval world view was broken, and the Reformers began to define Christian purposes not in terms of imaging some eternal pattern but in realizing a future ideal. John Calvin emphasized the sovereign interventions of God and the definitive victory of Christ which the resurrection highlights. The ascension implies the filling of all things with his glory, and so the Christian can be optimistic about this world order. The dynamic kingdom of Christ presses through the church to bring all mankind under the sway of the gospel.

Martin Luther, on the other hand, reacting against medieval pretensions of Christian culture, emphasized the sinful character of human work and the need for grace. Cultural forms then have no positive value and serve only to restrain evil. The spontaneous act of love which God produces in the believer can be performed as well in any calling and in any case will not be fully manifest until Christ returns. The church leavens society, but its influence is often visible only to faith.

The radical stream of the Reformation—sometimes called Anabaptism—picked up ascetic and perfectionist currents in the church and stressed personal conversion and a separated Christian community. Their view of the pervasive character of sin, their emphasis on the immanent return of Christ, and perhaps their minority status made them generally pessimistic about the possibilities of human culture.

Enlightenment. The Reformation conscience and the Renaissance emphasis on this world both contributed to a process of secularization in the West wherein the Christian consensus of the Middle Ages gradually gave way to the goals of the secular state. Christian ideals were often influential on society (as they are to this day), but belief in the Christian reality was given up. By the late eighteenth century, during what is known as the Enlightenment, the world was understood in immanent terms; God was distant and uninvolved; man had come of age. Lying behind this faith was the conviction that "the human situation is fundamentally characterized by conflict with nature" rather than conflict with God (H. R. Niebuhr). Moreover, there was every confidence that this conflict was being won, and the way was open to identify Christianity with Western European (and later North American) culture and to the cultural imperialism of the nineteenth and twentieth centuries.

Hegel's idea of the immanent development of spiritual reality in human cultures marked a final stage of the influence of Christianity on European culture. Soon Nietzsche announced that God was dead and all values must be reformulated. Karl Löwith calls the resulting nihilism "the only real belief of educated people" at the end of the nineteenth century.

Modern Period. World War I seemed to conform Nietzsche's cynicism and the absence of all Christian influences on culture and dashed the hopes of some who had believed it possible to bring in the millennium. Not surprisingly, most Christians were negative about the drift of Western culture and contented themselves with fighting on very narrow fronts. In an early attempt to make a critical judgment on modern post-Christian culture, T. S. Eliot in 1934 argued that modern literature was ruled by secularism and individualism. More recently evangelicals Francis Schaeffer and H. R. Rookmaaker traced the alienation of modern culture to the surrender of Christian values since the Renaissance. B. I. Bell and C. S. Lewis have described the manipulation and dehumanization that have resulted from modern consumer society and the resultant "starved sensibilities." More positively Paul Tillich has pointed out that modern cultural forms still express basic religious or absolute commitments and make possible an experience of depth.

The most far-reaching influence on Christian thinking about culture since World War II has come about by the growing impact of the social sciences. These studies have shown us that culture is more than an intellectual world view; it is also a complex of symbols—including objects, words, and events—by which a people orient themselves in the world. The meaning and thus the implications of the Christian commitment are seen to be pervasive throughout human culture, making possible a new, holistic understanding of the gospel. Cross-cultural communication of the faith has suggested the need to appropriate the resources of both sender and receptor cultures to achieve a fuller comprehension of Christian truth. In all communities there is the growing awareness that the Word of God, not some particular culture, will correct faults and redeem strengths, and every cultural perception of Christian truth and Scripture can be used to enhance our understanding of the gospel "until we all attain to the unity of the faith and of the knowledge of the Son of God" (Eph. 4:13).

Typology. The history of the encounter between Christianity and culture shows certain typical responses that reflect varying theological emphases and historical contingencies. At the risk of arbitrary division, we may suggest three typical views that have been influential on evangelical thinking.

Anabaptist. Throughout Christian history a

radical and rigorist stream has appeared emphasizing the fallen character of this world order and the necessity of creating alternative structures that more closely follow the model of the church's crucified Lord. Finding its clearest expression in the Radical Reformation, that view has continued to influence Christians through churches in this tradition and the many pietist groups that share its spirit. An extreme expression of this point of view is Watchman Nee, who believed that salvation involved the total severance of a person from this world's system. The Christian lives in the world as in an alien environment—like a diver in water—and so should develop an attitude of detachment. The earthly work of the Christian is always under death sentence; his only hope is God's final deliverance. A more moderate proponent of this view is Jacques Ellul, who argued that civilization looks to a new work of God wherein the New Jerusalem will displace this fallen city. Meanwhile we continue to work, realizing "we are participating in a work of death which is under a curse." A more positive and influential expression of this tendency comes from J. H. Yoder. For Yoder, Jesus came to effect a social revolution by the formation of a new voluntary community rather than by an encounter with the powers. Christ founded a new order with alternative patterns of leadership and life style that will eventually condemn and displace the old dying order. The way of the cross, Yoder believes, is an "alternative to both insurrection and quietism." This view has given clear expression to the apocalyptic and transcendent elements of Christianity, and many representatives have exerted a strong prophetic influence, though they have hesitated to engage in active public efforts to improve existing conditions.

Anglo-Catholic. Other Christians have insisted more on the distinction between the spheres of grace and nature. Continuing the medieval tradition, thinkers of this bent believe the area of human culture is indifferent to religious values. J. H. Newman gave a classic expression to this view a century ago when he claimed that culture has value on its own (natural) level but it cannot be the locus of virtue: "Intellectual cultivation is not the cause or proper antecedent of anything supernatural." In our century C. S. Lewis has taken a similar view. He believes the NT is unmistakably cold toward culture, which must be dispensed with the minute it conflicts with the service of God. The good of culture may be analogous to Christian good but it is not the same—he does not know, he confesses, how spiritual and cultural goods are to be reconciled. These thinkers correctly give priority to spiritual values, but they are not able to suggest critical perspectives shaped by Christian truth and so tend to support the cultural status quo.

Reformed. Since Justin Martyr there have been Christians convinced that culture can be taken captive to the lordship of Christ. Emphasizing the creative power of God and the victorious work of Christ, these thinkers tend to be more optimistic about human structures, feeling that however wicked and depraved certain institutions may appear, they do not lie outside of Christ's kingship. Calvin gave classic expression to this position, and he has been followed by the tradition of Reformed and Presbyterian Christianity. Early in our century Abraham Kuyper gave a concise expression to this view, which places the self-glorification of God in the center of Christian thinking about culture. All human labor collectively exhibits the image of God and by common grace is given to honor Christ, the mediator of creation. Culture then can be the means of controlling the influence of sin and, because of Christ's work which restores creation in its root, can begin to reflect the triumph of Christ's restored kingship which will be consummated at the second coming. Kuyper believes that genuine development in society will carry over into eternity (Rev. 21:24) even if the last days display an apostasy in spiritual things. This view has had a great influence on societies where it is present and exhibits an attractive emphasis on the lordship of Christ and the actuality of his kingdom; its weakness has been a tendency to triumphalism that underestimates the power and extent of evil.

Theological Conclusion. From the evidence surveyed, is it possible to suggest some guidelines for a Christian approach to culture? Some agree with H. R. Niebuhr that the relativities of our faith and station suggest we leave our options open. But certain biblical parameters may be proffered. Evangelicals have been properly concerned that cultural influences not challenge or dilute the authority of Christ and his Word. But clearly this problem cannot be solved by an avoidance of culture; it is impossible to commit oneself to Christ in isolation from our culture. A measure of solidarity with our environment is inevitable; we are products of it, and as Christians we are responsible to it as salt and light. Sin moreover is rebellion against God and his Word, and so the basic struggle in culture is not with nature but with the forces of evil. It follows that we cannot avoid the struggle for righteousness in the cultural sphere. As Milton put it: "It is one thing to be naïve and ignorant of moral options; it is quite another to be aware of options and choose to obey God." For visible purity, while it comes from God, cannot be realized except by trial, and trial comes by what is contrary.

The basic need for Christians through the ages has been a faith large enough to include the whole of the biblical material—that sees God as Creator and Sustainer; that honors Christ as both Logos and Lord; and that envisions in redemption both the reconciliation of the sinner and the renewal of the created order. This leads to a realistic optimism, for commitment to God frees us from subservience to lesser principles and helps us keep them in proper perspective. Scripture is the norm for all peoples and times, but the supracultural element must always be expressed in some particular cultural form, even if those forms are transformed as the Holy Spirit applies the reality of the kingdom. Meanwhile in our families and communities let us pray for the delight of the child who is astonished simply to be and for the wisdom of the sage to discern and contend for the truth. For the "little deeds of little men and women, all incomplete and imperfect . . . , are crucial and have their place in God's great schemes" (H. R. Rookmaaker).

W. A. Dyrness

Bibliography. E. Caillet, *The Christian Approach to Culture;* T. S. Eliot, *Notes Toward a Definition of Culture* and "Religion and Literature," in *Selected Essays;* J. Ellul, *The Meaning of the City;* C. Geertz, "Religion as a Cultural System," in *Reader in Comparative Religion,* ed. Lessa and Vogt; C. H. Kraft, *Christianity in Culture;* A. Kuyper, *Lectures on Calvinism;* C. S. Lewis, "Christianity in Culture," in *Christian Reflections;* W. Nee, *Love Not the World;* E. A. Nida, *Customs and Culture;* H. R. Niebuhr, *Christ and Culture;* F. Schaeffer, *How Should We Then Live?* J. Stott and R. Coote, eds., *Down to Earth: Studies in Christianity and Culture;* P. Tillich, *Theology of Culture;* J. H. Yoder, *The Politics of Jesus.*

Christian Liberty. *See* Liberty, Christian.

Christians, Names of. ***Christian.*** The name by which followers of Jesus Christ are now generally known among themselves and in the world achieved its preeminence only gradually. According to Acts 11:26 the name originated in Antioch. In the narrative of Acts it occurs once more (26:28) on the lips of Agrippa. I Pet. 4:16 is the only other occurrence in the NT, again with the suggestion of use by unbelievers. From Roman writers (Tacitus, *Annals* xv, 44; Suetonius, *Nero* xvi; Pliny, *Epistles* X.xcvi) comes the evidence that "Christian" was in common use among the citizenry of Rome by the reign of Nero and elsewhere in the empire by the end of the first century. Ignatius, also from Antioch, is the only one of the apostolic fathers to employ the term (*Mag.* 10; *Rom.* 3; *Phld.* 6), but by the end of the second century it was well established in the church. It was too fitting not to use ("You belong to Christ," Mark 9:41).

Though a controverted point, it seems likely that the name did not originate with the Christians themselves (contra Chrysostom, *Homily on John* xix, 3). Certain facts converge to suggest a pagan origin: it achieved general acceptance in the church slowly; it is not employed as a self-designation in the NT; its early use by pagans. So far as the evidence goes, the usages are uniformly set in the context of the persecution of Christians, and the Jews would hardly have dignified their enemies with a name derived from *christos,* the anointed one, whom they also were expecting.

Whether originally intended as a jibe, as the common title for believers in the Roman world, it soon became the name for which followers of Jesus Christ were persecuted (I Pet. 4:16; Pliny, *Epistles* X.xcvi). Perhaps largely as a result, in the second century "I am a Christian" became the triumphant confession of many martyrs (Martyrdom of Polycarp 10; Eusebius, *History* V.i, 19).

The name itself is formed after the usual Latin manner to signify the followers or adherents of a man named Christ (cf. "Herodians," Mark 3:6). This indicates that the originators of the name took Christ as a proper name and not as the designation of his office, the Anointed One. This fact invalidates the argument, though not the conclusion, of some older writers who saw in the name "Christian" the doctrine that believers are united to the Lord Jesus in his anointing and thus participate in his messianic offices and functions, becoming in him, in a subordinate way, prophets, priests, and kings (P. Mastricht, *Theoretico-Practica Theologia* V.iii.16, 40). The pagan origin of the name need not set aside, however, the suggestion of Eusebius, among others (*History* I.iv, 4), that Christian is the "new name" prophesied in Isa. 65:15.

Disciple. The characteristic name for those who gathered around Jesus during his ministry was "disciple." He was the teacher or master; they were his disciples (*mathētai*), a term involving too much personal attachment and commitment to be rendered adequately by "pupil." The name was carried over into Acts, where it frequently has the general sense of Christian (cf. Acts 14:21). The use of the term in Acts for those who had no acquaintance with Jesus during the days of his flesh serves as a reminder that the relationship of subsequent generations of Christians to the exalted Christ is not essentially different from that enjoyed by those who walked with him on the earth. It further indicates that the Lord's solemn sayings regarding the nature and cost of discipleship must be given their full weight in the construction of a doctrine of the Christian life (cf. Luke 6:40; 14:25–33).

However common the term may be in Acts, it disappears completely from the rest of the NT. Apparently disciple was no more adequate as a permanent title for Christians than teacher or rabbi was for Jesus, whose lordship was now fully revealed and understood. It had the further disadvantage that the term was common in Greek and Jewish circles (cf. in the Gospels disciples of John the Baptist, of the Pharisees, of Moses) and thus required some elaboration to be distinctively Christian (e.g., "disciples of the Lord," Acts 9:1).

The term was revived as a title for Christians in the second century, but primarily with reference to martyrdom. It thus became honorific (cf. Ignatius, *Eph.* 1).

Brother. This word occurs as frequently as "disciple" in Acts as a name for Christians. The parallel use of these titles, as in Acts 18:27, indicates that as technical terms they were virtually synonymous. Unlike "disciple," however, "brother" survived as a common self-designation in the rest of the NT and in early Christian literature. As a title it is expressive of the spiritual bond between fellow believers and of the obligation to love one another (Rom. 12:10; I Pet. 3:8). Christians did not always live up to this name (I Cor. 6:8).

The terminology of brotherhood has roots in the OT (Exod. 2:11; Ps. 22:22), in Jewish custom (cf. Acts 28:21), and in the teaching of Jesus (Matt. 23:8). In a few cases the term indicates the primary relationship between Christians and Christ himself (Matt. 28:10; John 20:17; Rom. 8:29; Heb. 2:11–12, 17).

Some NT occurrences of this name are illustrations of the profound reconciliation which the gospel effects between hitherto estranged men (Acts 9:17; Philem. 16). It is the supernatural character of Christian brotherhood which sets it apart from what was and is a common idea in other religions and in society generally.

So central to Christian experience was the brotherhood of believers and thus so common was this self-designation that it became well known in the pagan world and was often the object of ridicule (Tertullian, *Apology* xxxix). Nevertheless, even pagan commentators were forced to admit that the name did correspond to Christian conduct (e.g., Lucian, *De Morte Peregrini* xiii).

The term, as a general name for Christians, is found only sporadically after the third century, surviving primarily in clerical circles. It reappeared in the later Middle Ages (e.g., Brethren of the Common Life) and has been employed by some groups in the modern church.

Saint. Though rare in Acts, this is a common title in Paul and Revelation, appearing almost exclusively in the plural as a collective. It is an OT name for God's people (Ps. 34:9 *qĕdōšîm*, LXX *hagioi;* Ps. 85:8 *ḥăsîdîm*, LXX *hosioi*) and derives from the doctrines of God's intrinsic holiness and the holiness of his people by reason of their relationship to him (Deut. 7:6; Lev. 19:1; 20:26). In the NT also the fundamental idea of sainthood is separation to God or belonging to God. Thus the "holiness" of Christians is, in the first place, objective (I Cor. 7:14). They are saints or holy by virtue of their being people of God (Eph. 2:19–22), chosen and loved by God (Col. 3:12), called (Rom. 1:7), in Christ (I Cor. 1:30; Phil. 1:1), and the objects of the work of the Holy Spirit (II Thess. 2:13). The ethical dimension, subjective holiness or sainthood, is thus secondary, though no less important (Eph. 5:3; Heb. 12:14). The name thus bound believers to their holy God, to the great acts by which he separated them to himself, and to a life corresponding to his holiness.

The name survived as a general title for Christians only through the second century. Perhaps as a result of the juxtaposition of sainthood and martyrdom in Revelation (16:6; 17:6), it gradually became an honorific title for confessors, martyrs, and ascetics.

Believer. Given the centrality of faith in the NT it is predictable that a name for Christians should emerge from this direction. This is another title which is rooted in the OT (Gen. 15:6; Isa. 7:9; Hab. 2:4). In the verbal form (e.g., Acts 5:14 *pisteuontes*) the connection with the NT doctrine of faith as trust and confidence in God's mercy apprehended in Christ is clear (cf. John 20:31; Rom. 3:22). The absolute form (e.g., Acts 16:1; Eph. 1:1 *pistos*) is ambiguous. It can mean "believer" or "faithful, trustworthy." In any case, certain occurrences in the NT substantiate its technical use as a title for Christians (II Cor. 6:15; I Tim. 4:10, 12).

Follower of the Way. Six times in Acts, and all in connection with Paul, the Christian faith and community are designated "the Way" (*hē hodos*, 9:2; 19:9, 23; 22:4; 24:14, 22), making Christians "followers of the Way" or "those who belong to the Way." Acts 24:14 suggests that this was a Christian self-designation.

The background of this title is to be found in the OT use of "way" (*derek*) for the behavior of men (Ps. 1:6), the will of God (Gen. 18:19; Isa. 30:21), and the saving action of God (Ps. 67:2; Isa. 40:3) and in Christ's teaching about the two ways, one leading to life and the other to destruction (Matt. 7:13–14), and in his identification of himself as the way (John 14:6), the only avenue of salvation (cf. Heb. 9:8; 10:20). From the Dead Sea Scrolls we learn that the Qumran community also designated itself and its life "the Way."

Though "follower of the Way" did not survive as a title, the concept may be found in the exposition of the two ways in Didache 1–6 and Barnabas 18–21.

Friend. It is not certain whether "the friends" (*hoi philoi*) in Acts 27:3 and III John 15 are Christians in general or merely actual acquaintances. If the former, the title, like "brother," links the Christian with God and Christ (John 15:13–15; James 2:23) and with his fellows. It was apparently a popular title in Gnostic circles and was revived by certain medieval mystics (Friends of God) and later still by the Society of Friends (Quakers).

Nazarene. Coming from a Jew in Acts 24:5 this name is clearly a slur. In this the church found itself bearing its master's reproach (cf. John 1:46). According to Tertullian (*Against Marcion* iv, 8), it continued to serve Jews as a name for Christians. Later it was used by the Persians and Muslims. Similar to Nazarene is Galilean, which, though not used as a title for Christians in the NT (cf. Acts 2:7), was later used scornfully by enemies of the church such as the emperor Julian (Gregory of Nazianzus, *Oratation* 4). Both terms on hostile lips are suggestive of meanness of origin and culture.

Designations. In addition to these titles there is a large number of designations for Christians which never achieved the status of names by which Christians addressed one another or were addressed by unbelievers. Some of the more theologically important of these are "children of God" (Rom. 8:16; I John 3:1), "servant" (Acts 4:29; Rom. 1:1), "soldier" (II Tim. 2:3), "heir" (Rom. 8:17; Gal. 3:29), and "elect" (I Pet. 1:1).

Further, there is a set of such designations which directly identify Christians with OT Israel, among which may be mentioned "people of God" (Rom. 9:25), "sons of God" (Rom. 8:19; Gal. 3:26), "children of promise" (Gal. 4:28), "sons of Abraham" (Gal. 3:7), "seed of Abraham" (Gal. 3:29), "Israel" (Gal. 6:16; Heb. 8:8), and "circumcision" (Phil. 3:3).

Finally, there are descriptive phrases such as "those who call upon the name of our Lord Jesus Christ" (I Cor. 1:2) and "those who obey God's commandment and hold to the testimony of Jesus" (Rev. 12:17).

The names for Christians taken together furnish the materials for a theology of the Christian life. In particular, they bind Christians to their Lord and Master, to one another, to the OT and the history of salvation, and to their high and holy calling. It is a significant but unhappy observation that some of the richest of these titles fell out of use quite early and have never been restored to their original importance.

R. S. Rayburn

Bibliography. H. J. Cadbury, *The Beginnings of Christianity,* V, 375–92; A. Harnack, *The Mission and Expansion of Christianity in the First Three Centuries;* E. J. Bickerman, "The Name of Christians," *HTR* 42:109–24; H. B. Mattingly, "The Origin of the Name *Christiani,*" *JTS* new series 9:26–37.

Christian Science. *See* Church of Christ, Scientist.

Christian Socialism. *See* Socialism, Christian.

Christian Year. The Christian year includes the various seasons of the year designated by the church. It does not begin on January 1 but on the first Sunday of Advent, which usually falls about a month before Christmas. The central feast within the seasons of the year is Easter rather than Christmas. Time is made holy within this yearly experience, and it helps lead human beings toward heaven. The various feast days of the seasons help mankind to remember aspects of the life of Jesus Christ and various saints who have sought to follow in the footsteps of Christ.

Vatican Council II discusses the year in its Constitution on the Sacred Liturgy. The seasons and feasts all have a liturgical aspect since each of them has the worship of God as its ultimate purpose. Vatican Council II is very careful to show how the feasts of the saints and of the Blessed Virgin Mary are related to the mysteries of Christ. The paschal mystery is shown forth in the life of Mary and the lives of the saints. Pius XII in his writing *Mediator Dei* asks Christians to concentrate ever more seriously upon the paschal mysteries in order to more clearly realize how they are redeemed by Christ. He insists that the year of the church is not a boring record of a previous time period, but rather a vibrant reliving of the paschal mysteries.

There are actually two levels in the year. One deals with the feasts of Jesus Christ while the other deals with the feasts of Mary and the saints. The feasts of the saints grew out of the celebrations of various particular communities. As these communities corresponded among themselves, they began to copy feasts and to devise a kind of temporal sequence concerning them. Pius V decided to schematize the year more clearly in the sixteenth century. By the twentieth century there were over 250 feasts. It was feared that the feasts of the saints were overshadowing the celebration of the mysteries of Jesus Christ, so Pius X made it very clear in his writings that all feasts had to be centered ultimately upon Jesus Christ. In 1960 some of the feasts of the saints were actually dropped from the year for various reasons. Vatican Council II attempted to simplify things to an even greater extent. The feasts which are still celebrated always involve remembering a particular historical happening. In reference to saints, their deaths rather than their births are celebrated. It is believed that their death has become their birth or entrance into heaven.

Many feast days are movable in the sense that they can happen on various dates within the year, but some feasts are fixed to a particular day in the year. Easter is the most notable movable feast, whereas Christmas is the most notable fixed feast day. Some fixed feast days cannot be celebrated if they occur on a Sunday because Sunday always celebrates God as Father, Son, and Holy Spirit. The feasts always must draw one to reflect upon God as Father, Son, and Holy Spirit in one way or another.

The most important parts of the Christian year celebrate the historical aspects of the redeeming power of Jesus Christ in union with events in his own life. Every Sunday celebrates the paschal event of Jesus Christ. The apostles began the custom of celebrating Sunday, but many of the Jewish Christians retained sabbath worship together with Sunday for several decades.

For some reason Fridays and Wednesdays became more important days in between Sundays. They were declared to be fasting days. Friday was usually held to be more important than Wednesday. Sometimes the fasting on these two days was related to a series of prayers which helped prepare the early Christians for Sunday celebrations. The least important weekday was Saturday.

The Easter Season. The prime feast of the Christian year is Easter. The Sunday called Septuagesima begins the preparation of the faithful for Easter. The Easter celebration in a sense does not end until the celebration of Pentecost. Easter celebrates not only the resurrection of our Lord Jesus Christ but also his passion and death within the context of his resurrection. His death and resurrection must always be held together in the minds of the faithful.

Holy Week is the most important preparation for Easter. Holy Week begins with Palm Sunday. It introduces us to the life of Jesus as he advances toward his passion and death. Monday, Tuesday, and Wednesday of Holy Week are not too important, but Holy Thursday celebrates in vivid form the Last Supper of our Lord Jesus Christ and his apostles. Part of the vividness involves the washing of feet in remembrance of Christ, who washed the feet of his apostles to demonstrate his humility and his desire to serve mankind. Good Friday celebrates the passion and death of Christ. No Mass is celebrated on Good Friday. Holy Communion consecrated on Holy Thursday is retained for Good Friday, when it is distributed to the faithful. The veneration of the cross is the most moving experience for many of the faithful on Good Friday because it dramatically reminds them of the death of their Lord Jesus Christ. Holy Saturday consists in quiet and reflective preparation for Easter itself.

Easter is celebrated as an octave lasting eight days. Each day deals with various aspects of the resurrected Christ. The faithful experience how the life of the resurrected Christ affects them in the order of redemption by seeing how he affected the early Christians after his resurrection and before his ascension into heaven. The entire Easter season is to be a period of joy culminating in the happiness surrounding the placing of Jesus at the right hand of God, his Father, in heaven. The season closes with Pentecost, which celebrates the coming of the Holy Spirit to the early Christians so that they might rejoice in their strength and find the inspiration to go out and convert the world to Jesus Christ.

The Christmas Season. The Christmas period is second in importance to Easter, although some of the faithful appear to place more stress upon Christmas—although the stress may not be for a spiritual reason. The Christmas season not only celebrates the birth of Christ; it also celebrates his childhood with Mary and Joseph. As part of the Christian year the Christmas season developed later than the Easter season, although the feast of Christmas itself comes from Roman times. The feast of Christmas was developed by the church to combat a pagan feast which was celebrated yearly on December 25. The Advent period deals with the coming of Christ and the preparation the faithful should make to receive him in their hearts. His incarnation celebrates not only his birth but also his messianic age, which is the beginning of the end of the world as it marches toward eternity. Advent combines some recognition of sin on the part of the faithful with the joy that Jesus, their Savior, is coming.

The feast of the Epiphany ends the Christmas season, but the Sundays after the Epiphany have themes which are related to it. (The Sundays after Pentecost appear to be quite separate from the Easter season.) The only real order in those Sundays revolves around the fact that each of them is celebrating the paschal mysteries of our Lord Jesus Christ.

Feasts of the Saints. The Christian year as

described above revolves around Jesus Christ. Within this Christian year on a less important level are the feasts of the saints. Many of these involve a celebration of the early martyrs. When Constantine declared Christianity to be the religion of the Roman Empire, the martyrs began to be revered for the suffering and death they experienced previous to the time of Constantine. The deaths of the martyrs were related to the death of Christ. Relics of the martyrs also became important aspects of various feasts. Charlemagne continued the celebration of the martyrs after the Roman Empire fell apart.

Martyrs still today are considered to be the most important representatives of the saints in their feast days. There are about 120 feasts of martyrs. Some of the feasts are suspect, in part in reference to the exploits of certain martyrs. The positivist approach to the historicity of some martyrs and their exploits cannot, however, take too much away from the symbolic lessons which various feasts of martyrs seek to teach to the faithful. A martyr must have shed his blood for Christ, which reminds the faithful symbolically of the shedding of Christ's blood for our redemption.

Confessors are not martyrs in the strict sense of having shed their blood for Christ, but it is required of a confessor that he or she should have suffered in one way or another for Christ. Ascetics and bishops on occasion were considered to be types of confessors of the faith. Ascetics led a life of partial suffering in an effort to be like the martyrs of the age of persecution.

The notion that virginity was a very holy way of living caused the faithful to revere various women. Some virgins or "holy women" who were widows were also truly martyrs. Agatha and Perpetua are revered not only for being martyrs, but also for their courage when tortured for refusing to submit sexually to their tormentors.

The church has a series of feasts celebrating various aspects of the life of the Virgin Mary. Devotion to the Blessed Virgin developed in the early church. One of the first feasts somewhat related to Mary was the Feast of the Purification, which has Jesus as its central aspect. Although the assumption of the Blessed Virgin Mary did not become a dogma of the church until much later, the Feast of the Assumption was being celebrated as early as the eighth century. Some people overdid their devotion to Mary, so that Vatican Council II has trimmed back Marian devotions.

The Christian year must always ultimately seek to immerse the faithful in the experiences of the life, death, and resurrection of our Lord Jesus Christ in union with the other paschal mysteries. Ultimately the Blessed Virgin Mary and the saints are revered as a means of leading the faithful closer to Jesus Christ and also as an encouragement to the faithful that they too can become saints if they seek to be like Christ.

T. J. German

See also Maundy Thursday; Good Friday; Holy Saturday; Holy Week; Palm Sunday; Easter; Ascension Day; Pentecost; All Saints Day; Halloween; Advent; Christmas; Lent.

Bibliography. P. Parsch, *The Church's Year of Grace;* A. Löhr, *The Year of Our Lord;* I. H. Dalmais, *Introduction to the Liturgy;* H. Jenny, *The Paschal Mystery in the Christian Year;* O. Rousseau, *The Progress of the Liturgy.*

Christmas. The day observed by Christians in commemoration of the birth of Jesus Christ. The Scriptures do not reveal the exact date of Christ's birth, and the earliest Christians had no fixed time for observing it. However, by the late fourth century Christmas was generally celebrated in the churches, although on differing dates in different locales. Various methods were used in an attempt to compute the day of Christ's birth; among dates suggested by early churchmen were January 2, April 18, April 19, May 20, and December 25. December 25 eventually became the officially recognized date for Christmas because it coincided with the pagan festivals celebrating Saturnalia and the winter solstice. The church thereby offered the people a Christian alternative to the pagan festivities and eventually reinterpreted many of their symbols and actions in ways acceptable to Christian faith and practice. For example, Jesus Christ was presented as the Sun of Righteousness (Mal. 4:2) replacing the sun god, Sol Invictus. As Christianity spread throughout Europe, it assimilated into its observances many customs of the pagan winter festivals such as holly, mistletoe, the Christmas tree, and log fires. At the same time new Christmas customs such as the nativity crib and the singing of carols were introduced by Christians.

In every period of Christian history the observance of Christmas has been opposed by a minority of Christian leaders. Usually one or more of three factors have been involved in this opposition: (1) a rejection of ecclesiastical authority in its attempt to establish official feast days, of which Christmas is one; (2) an objection to the drinking, partying, and immorality associated in every age with Christmas festivities; (3) the long-standing and continuing associations of Christmas with pagan religious ideas and practices. Some Protestants, especially those in the Calvinistic tradition—including Calvin himself, Knox, the English and American Puritans, and many Presbyterians—refused to celebrate Christmas. However, the Lutherans, the continental Reformers, and most other Protestants defended the observance of Christmas and sought to emphasize its deeper truth expressed in the doctrine of the incarnation. By the midtwentieth century Christmas had come to be observed almost universally in some form or another by Christians throughout the world. With the expansion of Christianity into the cultures of Africa, Asia, and Latin America, many new customs and ideas were incorporated into the Christian celebration of Christmas.

O. G. Oliver, Jr.

See also Christian Year.

Bibliography. L. W. Cowie and J. S. Gummer, *The Christian Calendar;* O. Cullmann, "The Origin of Christmas," in *The Early Church;* P. Schaff, *History of the Christian Church,* III, 394–400.

Christ Mysticism. In an influential monograph entitled *Die neutestamentliche Formel "in Christo Jesus"* (1892), Adolf Deissmann found the idea of union with Christ, as expressed in the familiar phrase "in Christ," at the heart of Paul's theology. His views were later popularized in *Paul: A Study in Social and Religious History* (1911). He coined the terms "Christ-intimacy" (*Christus-Innigkeit*) and "Christ-mysticism" (*Christus-Mystik*) to describe what Paul meant by the phrase. Paul is not a mystic in the sense of the medieval mystics who lost themselves in the reality of the divine essence; rather, he is one for whom fellowship with Christ is the most important thing. He "lives 'in' Christ, 'in' the living and present spiritual Christ, who is about him on all sides, who fills him, who speaks to him, and speaks in and through him. Christ is for Paul not a person of the past . . . but a reality and power of the present, . . . whose life-giving powers are daily expressing themselves in him, and to whom, since that day at Damascus, he has felt a personal-cult dependence" (*Paul,* pp. 135–36).

Many have concurred with Deissmann that the formula "in Christ" is central to Paul's thought. Albert Schweitzer understood Paul's "Christ mysticism" in terms of an eschatological mysticism: "I am in Christ; in Him I know myself as a being who is raised above this sensuous, sinful, and transient world and already belong to the transcendent; in Him I am assured of resurrection; in Him I am a Child of God" (*The Mysticism of Paul the Apostle,* p. 125). The Scottish theologian James S. Stewart has written a most attractive exposition of Paul's theology in these terms (*A Man in Christ,* 1935). Recent writers have recognized that it is an oversimplification to interpret all of the 164 occurrences of "in Christ" or "in the Lord" in Paul's letters in personal-mystical terms. While it obviously includes the idea of personal fellowship with Christ, the phrase seems to have a decidedly communal emphasis. To be "in Christ" is to be a Christian, viz., to be in the body of Christ, the church.

W. W. Gasque

Bibliography. E. Best, *One Body in Christ;* A. Wikenhauser, *Pauline Mysticism.*

Christology. ***NT Christology.*** In the NT the writers indicate who Jesus is by describing the significance of the work he came to do and the office he came to fulfill. Amidst the varied descriptions of his work and office, always mainly in terms of the OT, there is a unified blending of one aspect with another, and a development that means an enrichment, without any cancellation of earlier tradition.

Jesus in the Gospels. His humanity is taken for granted in the Synoptic Gospels, as if it could not possibly occur to anyone to question it. We see him lying in the cradle, growing, learning, subject to hunger, anxiety, doubt, disappointment, and surprise (Luke 2:40; Mark 2:15; 14:33; 15:34; Luke 7:9), and finally to death and burial. But elsewhere his true humanity is specifically witnessed to, as if it might be called in question (Gal. 4:4; John 1:14), or its significance neglected (Heb. 2:9, 17; 4:15; 5:7–8; 12:2).

Besides this emphasis on his true humanity, there is nevertheless always an emphasis on the fact that even in his humanity he is sinless and also utterly different from other men and that his significance must not be sought by ranking him alongside the greatest or wisest or holiest of all other men. The virgin birth and the resurrection are signs that here we have something unique in the realm of humanity. Who or what he is can be discovered only by contrasting him with others, and it shines out most clearly when all others are against him. The event of his coming to suffer and triumph as man in our midst is absolutely decisive for every individual he encounters and for the destiny of the whole world (John 3:16–18; 10:27–28; 12:31; 16:11; I John 3:8). In his coming the kingdom of God has come (Mark 1:15). His miracles are signs that this is so (Luke 11:20). Woe, therefore, to those who misinterpret them (Mark 3:22–29). He acts and speaks with heavenly regal authority. He can challenge men to lay down their lives for his own sake (Matt. 10:39). The kingdom is indeed his own kingdom (Matt. 16:28; Luke 22:30). He is the One who, in uttering what is simply his own mind, at the same time utters the eternal and decisive word of God (Matt. 5:22, 28; 24:35). His word effects what it proclaims (Matt. 8:3; Mark 11:21) as God's word does. He has the authority and power even to forgive sins (Mark 2:1–12).

Christ. His true significance can be understood only when his relationship to the people in whose midst he was born is understood. In the events that are set in motion in his earthly career God's purpose and covenant with Israel is fulfilled. He is the One who comes to do what neither the people of the OT nor their anointed representatives—the prophets, priests, and kings—could do. But they had been promised that One who would rise up in their own midst would yet make good what all of them had utterly failed to make good. In this sense Jesus of Nazareth is the One anointed with the Spirit and power (Acts 10:38) to be the true Messiah or Christ (John 1:41; Rom. 9:5) of his people. He is the true prophet (Mark 9:7; Luke 13:33; John 1:21; 6:14), priest (John 17; Hebrews), and king (Matt. 2:2; 21:5; 27:11), as, e.g., his baptism (Matt. 3:13ff.) and his use of Isa. 61 (Luke 4:16–22) indicate. In receiving this anointing and fulfilling this messianic purpose, he receives from his contemporaries the titles Christ (Mark 8:29) and Son of David (Matt. 9:27; 12:23; 15:22; cf. Luke 1:32; Rom. 1:3; Rev. 5:5).

But he gives himself and receives also many other titles which help to illuminate the office he fulfilled and which are even more decisive in indicating who he is. A comparison of the current messianic ideas of Judaism with both the teaching of Jesus himself and the witness of the NT shows that Jesus selected certain features of messianic tradition which he emphasized and allowed to crystallize round his own person. Certain messianic titles are used by him and of him in preference to others, and are themselves reinterpreted in the use he makes of them and in the relationship he gives them to himself and to one another. This is partly the reason for his "messianic reserve" (Matt. 8:4; 16:20; John 10:24; etc.).

Son of Man. Jesus used the title "Son of man" of himself more than any other. There are passages in the OT where the phrase means simply "man" (e.g., Ps. 8:5), and at times Jesus' use of it corresponds to this meaning (cf. Matt. 8:20). But the majority of contexts indicate that in using this title Jesus is thinking of Dan. 7:13, where the "Son of man" is a heavenly figure, both an individual and at the same time the ideal representative of the people of God. In the Jewish apocalyptic tradition this Son of man is regarded as a preexistent one who will come at the end of the ages as judge and as a light to the Gentiles (cf. Mark 14:62). Jesus sometimes uses this title when he emphasizes his authority and power (Mark 2:10; 2:28; Luke 12:19). At other times he uses it when he is emphasizing his humility and incognito (Mark 10:45; 14:21; Luke 19:10; 9:58). In the Gospel of John the title is used in contexts which emphasize his preexistence, his descent into the world in a humiliation which both conceals and manifests his glory (John 3:13–14; 6:62–63; 8:6ff.), his role of uniting heaven and earth (John 1:51), his coming to judge men and hold the messianic banquet (John 5:27; 6:27).

Though "Son of man" is used only by Jesus of himself, what it signified is otherwise expressed, especially in Rom. 5 and I Cor. 15, where Christ is described as the "man from heaven" or the "second Adam." Paul here takes up hints in the Synoptic Gospels that in the coming of Christ there is a new creation (Matt. 19:38) in which his part is to be related to and contrasted with that of Adam in the first creation (cf., e.g., Mark 1:13; Luke 3:38). Both Adam and Christ have the representative relationship to the whole of mankind that is involved in the conception "Son of man." But Christ is regarded as One whose identification with all mankind is far more deep and complete than that of Adam. In his redeeming action salvation is provided for all mankind. By faith in him all men can participate in a salvation already accomplished in him. He is also the image and glory of God (II Cor. 4:4, 6; Col. 1:15) which man was made to reflect (I Cor. 11:7) and which Christians are meant to put on in participating in the new creation (Col. 3:10).

Servant. Jesus' self-identification with men is brought out in passages that recall the suffering servant of Isaiah (Matt. 12:18; Mark 10:45; Luke 24:26). It is in his baptismal experience that he enters this role (cf. Matt. 3:17 and Isa. 42:1) of suffering as the One in whom all his people are represented and who is offered for the sins of the world (John 1:29; Isa. 53). Jesus is explicitly called the "servant" in the early preaching of the church (Acts 3:13, 26; 4:27, 30), and the thought of him as such was also in Paul's mind (cf. Rom. 4:25; 5:19; II Cor. 5:21).

In the humiliation of his self-identification with our humanity (Heb. 2:17; 4:15; 5:7; 2:9; 12:2) he fulfills the part not only of victim, but also of high priest, offering himself once for all (Heb. 7:27; 9:12; 10:10) in a self-offering that brings about forever a new relationship between God and man. His "baptism," the fulfillment of which he accomplishes in his earthly career culminating in his cross (cf. Luke 12:50), is his self-sanctification to his eternal priesthood, and in and through this self-sanctification his people are sanctified forever (John 17:19; Heb. 10:14).

Son of God. The title "Son of God" is not used by Jesus himself to the same extent as "Son of man" (though cf., e.g., Mark 12:6), but it is the name given to him (cf. Luke 1:35) by the heavenly voice at his baptism and transfiguration (Mark 1:11; 9:7), by Peter in his moment of illumination (Matt. 16:16), by the demons (Mark 5:7) and the centurion (Mark 15:39).

This title "Son of God" is messianic. In the OT, Israel is the "son" (Exod. 4:22; Hos. 11:1). The king (Ps. 2:7; II Sam. 7:14) and possibly the priests (Mal. 1:6) are also given this title. Jesus, therefore, in using and acknowledging this title is assuming the name of One in whom the true destiny of Israel is to be fulfilled.

But the title also reflects the unique filial consciousness of Jesus in the midst of such a messianic task (cf. Matt. 11:27; Mark 13:32; 14:36; Ps. 2:7). This has the profoundest Christological implications. He is not simply a son but *the* Son (John 20:17). This consciousness, which is revealed at high points in the Synoptic Gospels, is regarded in John as forming the continuous conscious background of Jesus' life. The Son and the Father are one (John 5:19, 30; 16:32) in will (4:34; 6:38; 7:28; 8:42; 13:3) and activity (14:10) and in giving eternal life (10:30). The Son is in the Father and the Father in the Son (10:38; 14:10). The Son, like the Father, has life and quickening power in himself (5:26). The Father loves the Son (3:35; 10:17; 17:23–24) and commits all things into his hands (5:35), giving him authority to judge (5:22). The title also implies a unity of being and nature with the Father, uniqueness of origin and preexistence (John 3:16; Heb. 1:2).

Lord. Though Paul also uses the title "Son of God," he most frequently refers to Jesus as "Lord." This term did not originate with Paul. Jesus is addressed and referred to in the Gospels as Lord (Matt. 7:21; Mark 11:3; Luke 6:46). Here the title can refer primarily to his teaching authority (Luke 11:1; 12:41), but it can also have a deeper significance (Matt. 8:25; Luke 5:8). Though it is most frequently given to him after his exaltation, he himself quoted Ps. 110:1 and prepared for this use (Mark 12:35; 14:62).

His lordship extends over the course of history and all the powers of evil (Col. 2:15; I Cor. 2:6–8; 8:5; 15:24) and must be the ruling concern in the life of the church (Eph. 6:7; I Cor. 7:10, 25). As Lord he will come to judge (II Thess. 1:7).

Though his work in his humiliation is also the exercise of lordship, it was after the resurrection and ascension that the title of Lord was most spontaneously conferred on Jesus (Acts 2:32ff.; Phil. 2:1–11) by the early church. They prayed to him as they would pray to God (Acts 7:59–60; I Cor. 1:2; cf. Rev. 9:14, 21; 22:16). His name as Lord is linked in the closest association with that of God himself (I Cor. 1:3; II Cor. 1:2; cf. Rev. 17:14; 19:16; and Deut. 10:17). To him are referred the promises and attributes of the "Lord" God (*Kyrios*, LXX) in the OT (cf. Acts 2:21 and 38; Rom. 10:3 and Joel 2:32; I Thess. 5:2 and Amos 5:18; Phil. 2:10–11 and Isa. 45:23). To him are freely applied the language and formulas which are used of God himself, so that it is difficult to decide in a passage like Rom. 9:5 whether it is the Father or the Son to whom reference is made. In John 1:1, 18; 20:28; II Thess. 1:12; I Tim. 3:16; Titus 2:13; and II Pet. 1:1, Jesus is confessed as "God."

Word. The statement, "The Word became flesh" (John 1:14), relates Jesus both to the Wisdom of God in the OT (which has a personal character, Prov. 8) and to the law of God (Deut. 30:11–14; Isa. 2:3) as these are revealed and declared in the going forth of the Word by which God creates, reveals himself, and fulfills his will in history (Ps. 33:6; Isa. 55:10–11; 11:4; Rev. 1:16). There is here a close relationship between word and event. In the NT it becomes clearer that the Word is not merely a message proclaimed but is Christ himself (cf. Eph. 3:17 and Col. 3:16; I Pet. 1:3 and 23; John 8:31 and 15:17). What Paul expresses in Col. 1, John expresses in his prologue. In both passages (and in Heb. 1:1–14) the place of Christ as the One who in the beginning was the agent of God's creative activity is asserted. In bearing witness to these aspects of Jesus Christ it is inevitable that the NT should witness to his preexistence. He was "in the beginning" (John 1:1–3; Heb. 1:2–10). His very coming (Luke 12:49; Mark 1:24; 2:17) involves him in deep self-abasement (II Cor. 8:9; Phil. 2:5–7) in fulfillment of a purpose ordained for him from the foundation of the world (Rev. 13:8). In the Gospel of John he gives this testimony in his own words (John 8:58; 17:5, 24).

Yet while his coming from the Father involves no diminution of his Godhead, there is nevertheless a subordination of the incarnate Son to the Father in the relationship of love and equality which subsists between the Father and the Son (John 14:28). For it is the Father who sends and the Son who is sent (John 10:36), the Father who gives and the Son who receives (John 5:26), the Father who ordains and the Son who fulfills (John 10:18). Christ belongs to God who is the Head (I Cor. 3:23; 11:13) and in the end will subject all things to him (I Cor. 15:28).

Patristic Christology. In the period immediately following the NT, the apostolic fathers (A.D. 90–140) can speak highly of Christ. We have a sermon beginning: "Brethren, we ought so to think of Jesus Christ, as of God, as the Judge of the quick and the dead" (II Clement). Ignatius with his emphasis on both the true deity and humanity of Christ can refer to the "blood of God." Even if their witness falls short of this, there is a real attempt to combat both Ebionitism, which looked on Christ as a man born naturally, on whom the Holy Spirit came at his baptism, and also docetism, which asserted that the humanity and sufferings of Christ were apparent rather than real.

The apologists of the next generation (e.g., Justin, *ca.* 100–165, and Theophilus of Antioch) sought to commend the gospel to the educated and to defend it in face of attacks by pagans and Jews. Their conception of the place of Christ was determined, however, rather by current philosophical ideas of the *logos* than by the historic revelation given in the gospel, and for them Christianity tends to become a new law or philosophy and Christ another God inferior to the highest God.

Melito of Sardis at this time, however, spoke clearly of Christ as both God and man, and Irenaeus, in meeting the challenge of Gnosticism, returned also to a more biblical standpoint, viewing the person of Christ always in close connection with his work of redemption and revelation, in fulfillment of which "he became what we are, in order that he might make us to become even what he is himself." He thus became the new Head of our race and recovered what had been lost in Adam, saving us through a process of "recapitulation." In thus identifying himself with us he is both true God and true man. Tertullian also made his contribution to Christology in combating Gnosticism and the various forms of what came to be known as monarchianism (dynamism, modalism, Sabellianism), which has reacted in different ways against the apparent worship of Christ as a second God beside the Father. He was the first to teach that the Father and Son are of "one substance," and spoke of three persons in the Godhead.

Origen had a decisive influence in the development of Christology in the East. He taught the eternal generation of the Son from the Father and used the term *homoousios.* Yet at the same time his complicated doctrine included a view of Christ as an intermediate being, spanning the distance between the utterly transcendent being of God and this created world. Both sides in the later Arian controversy, which began *ca.* 318, show influences which may be traced to Origen.

Arius denied the possibility of any divine emanation, or contact with the world, or of any distinction within the Godhead. Therefore the Word is made out of nothing before time. Though called God, he is not very God. Arius denied to Christ a human soul. The Council of Nicaea (325) condemned Arius by insisting that the Son was not simply the "first born of all creation" but was indeed "of one essence with the Father." In his long struggle against Arianism, Athanasius sought to uphold the unity of essence of the Father and Son by basing his argument not on a philosophical doctrine of the nature of the Logos, but on the nature of the redemption accomplished by the Word in the flesh. Only God himself, taking on human flesh and dying and rising in our flesh, can effect a redemption that consists in being saved from sin and corruption and death, and in being raised to share the nature of God himself.

After Nicaea the question was raised: If Jesus Christ be truly God, how can he be at the same time truly man? Apollinaris tried to safeguard the unity of the person of the God-man by denying that he had complete manhood. He assumed that man was composed of three parts: body, irrational or animal soul, and rational soul or intellect (*nous*). In Jesus the human *nous* was displaced by the divine *Logos.* But this denied the true reality of Christ's humanity and indeed of the incarnation itself and therefore of the salvation. The most cogent objection to it was expressed by Gregory of Nazianzus: "The unassumed is the unhealed." Christ must be true man as well as true God. Apollinaris was condemned at Constantinople in 381.

How, then, can God and man be united in one person? The controversy became focused on Nestorius, Bishop of Constantinople, who refused to approve the use of the phrase "mother of God" (*Theotokos*) as applied to Mary, who, he asserted, bore not the Godhead but "a man who was the organ of the Godhead." In spite of the fact that Nestorius clearly asserted that the God-man was one person, he seemed to think of the two natures as existing side by side and so sharply distinguished that the suffering of the humanity could not be attributed to the Godhead. This separation was condemned, and Nestorius's deposition at the Council of Ephesus (431) was brought about largely by the influence of Cyril in reasserting a unity of the two natures in Christ's person so complete that the impassible Word can be said to have suffered death. Cyril sought to avoid Apollinarianism by asserting that the humanity of Christ was complete and entire but had no independent subsistence (*anhypostasis*).

A controversy arose over one of Cyril's followers, Eutyches, who asserted that in the incarnate Christ the two natures coalesced in one. This implied a docetic view of Christ's human nature and called in question his consubstantiality with us. Eutychianism and Nestorianism were finally condemned at the Council of Chalcedon (451), which taught one Christ in two natures united in one person or hypostasis, yet remaining "without confusion, without conversion, without division, without separation."

Further controversies were yet to arise before the mind of the church could be made up as to how the human nature could indeed retain its complete humanity and yet be without independent subsistence. It was Leontius of Byzantium who advanced the formula that enabled the majority to agree on an interpretation of the Chalcedonian formula. The human nature of Christ, he taught, was not an independent hypostasis (anhypostatic), but it was enhypostatic, i.e., it had its subsistence in and through the Logos.

A further controversy arose as to whether two natures meant that Christ had two wills or centers of volition. A formula was first devised to suit the monothelites, who asserted that the God-man, though in two natures, worked by one divine-human energy. But finally, in spite of the preference of Honorius, Bishop of Rome, for a formula asserting "one will" in Christ, the Western church in 649 decreed that there were "two natural wills" in Christ, and this was made the decision of the whole church at the sixth ecumenical council at Constantinople in 680, the views of Pope Honorius I being condemned as heresy.

Further Development. The theologians of the Middle Ages accepted the authority of patristic Christology and allowed their thought and experience to be enriched by Augustine's stress on the real humanity of Christ in his atoning work, on his important as our example in humility, and on mystical experience. But this emphasis on the humanity of Christ tended to be made only when he was presented in his passion as the One who mediates between man and a distant and terrible God. In their more abstract discussion of the person of Christ there was a tendency to present One who has little share in our real humanity. The humanity of Jesus, however, became the focus of mystical devotion in Bernard of Clairvaux, who stressed the union of the soul with the Bridegroom.

At the Reformation, Luther's Christology was based on Christ as true God and true man in inseparable unity. He spoke of the "wondrous exchange" by which, through the union of Christ with human nature, his righteousness becomes ours, and our sins become his. He refused to tolerate any thinking that might lead to speculation about the God-man divorced either from the historical person of Jesus himself or from the work he came to do and the office he came to fulfill in redeeming us. But Luther taught that the doctrine of the "communication of attributes" (*communicatio idiomatum*) meant that there was a mutual transference of qualities or attributes between the divine and human natures in Christ, and developed this to mean a mutual interpenetration of divine and human qualities or properties, verging on the very commingling of natures which Chalcedonian Christology had avoided. In Lutheran orthodoxy this led to a later controversy as to how far the manhood of the Son of God shared in and exercised such attributes of divine majesty, how far it was capable of doing so, and how far Jesus used or renounced these attributes during his human life.

Calvin also approved of the orthodox Christological statements of the church councils. He taught that when the Word became incarnate he did not suspend nor alter his normal function of upholding the universe. He found the extreme statements of Lutheran Christology guilty of a tendency toward the heresy of Eutyches, and insisted that the two natures in Christ are distinct though never separate. Yet in the unity of person in Christ, one nature is so closely involved in the activities and events which concern the other that the human nature can be spoken of as if it partook of divine attributes. Salvation is accomplished not only by the divine nature working through the human but is indeed the accomplishment of the human Jesus, who worked out a perfect obedience and sanctification for all men in his own person (the humanity being not only the instrument but the "material cause" of salvation). This salvation is worked out in fulfillment of the threefold office of prophet, priest, and king.

There is here a divergence between the Lutheran and Reformed teaching. The Lutherans laid the stress upon a union of two natures in a communion in which the human nature is assumed into the divine nature. The Reformed theologians refused to think of an assumption of the human nature into the divine, but rather of an assumption of the human nature into the divine person of the Son, in whom there was a direct union between the two natures. Thus, while keeping to the patristic conception of the *communicatio idiomatum,* they developed the concept of the *communicatio operationum* (i.e., that the properties of the two natures coincide in the one person) in order to speak of an active communion between the natures without teaching a doctrine of mutual interpenetration. The importance of the *communicatio operationum* (which also came to be taken up by Lutherans) is that it corrects the rather static way of speaking of the hypostatic union in patristic theology, by seeing the person and the work of Christ in inseparable unity, and so asserts a dynamic communion between the divine and human natures of Christ in terms of his atoning and reconciling work. It stresses the union of two natures for his mediatorial operation in such a way that this work proceeds from the one person of the God-man by the distinctive effectiveness of both natures. In this light the hypostatic union is seen as the ontological side of the dynamic action of reconciliation, and so incarnation and atonement are essentially complementary.

Since the early nineteenth century the tendency has been to try to depart from the Chalcedonian doctrine of the two natures on the ground that this could not be related to the human Jesus portrayed in the Gospels, and that it made use of terms which were alien both to Holy Scripture and to current modes of expression. Schleiermacher built up a Christology on the basis of finding in Christ a unique and archetypal consciousness of utter filial dependence on the Father. In Lutheran Christology there was a further important development, the attributes of the humanity of Jesus being regarded as limiting those of his deity, according to the "kenotic" theory of Thomasius. On this view, the Word, in the incarnation, deprived himself of his "external" attributes of omnipotence, omnipresence, and omniscience, yet still retained the "essential" moral attributes. Though always remaining God, he ceased to exist in the form of God. Even his self-consciousness as God was absorbed in the single awakening and growing consciousness of the God-man. Ritschl, too, stressed the importance of the ethical attributes of the person of Christ and of refusing to speculate beyond the revelation of God found in the historic Jesus, who must have for us the value of God and whose perfect moral nature is both human and divine. Early in the twentieth century modern conceptions of personality and scientific and philosophical doctrines of evolution enabled theologians to produce further variations in the development of nineteenth century Christology.

The middle years of the twentieth century saw a return to the use of the Chalcedonian doctrine of the two natures, particularly as interpreted in the Reformed tradition, and a realization that this apparently paradoxical formula is meant to point toward the mystery of the unique relationship of grace set up here between the divine and human in the person and work of the God-man. This mystery must not be thought of apart from atonement, for it is perfected and worked out in history through the whole work of Christ crucified and risen and ascended. To share in this mystery of the new unity of God and man in Christ in some measure is also given to the church through the Spirit. This means that our Christology is decisive in determining our doctrine of the church and of the work of sacraments as used in the church. Our Christology must indeed indicate the direction in which we seek to solve all theological problems where we are dealing with the relation of a human event or reality to the grace of God in Christ. In this Christological pattern the whole of our theological system should find its coherence and unity.

Nor must this mystery be thought of in abstraction from the person of Jesus shown to us in the Gospels in the historical context of the life of Israel. The human life and teaching of the historical Jesus have to be given full place in his saving work as essential and not incidental or merely instrumental in his atoning reconciliation. Here we must give due weight to modern biblical study in helping us to realize both what kind of a man Jesus was and yet also to see this Jesus of history as the Christ of faith, the Lord, the Son of God. Through the study of his office and work we come to understand how his humanity is not only truly individual but is also truly representative.

Modern theological discussion continues to be a witness to the centrality of Jesus Christ himself in matters of faith and is dominated by the two closely related questions: "Who is Jesus Christ?" and "What has he done for the world?" The context in which these questions are raised has, however, changed. In the nineteenth century many of the radical restatements of Christological belief were often felt to imply a rejection of orthodox faith, and were argued for as such. It is often claimed today, however, that restatements of this type, if they arise from a sincere response to Jesus, deserve to be regarded as valid modern interpretations of the same truth to which the older statements bore witness in their day. Those who formulated the earlier creeds, it is held, were expressing in their statements simply their own contemporary experience of being redeemed by Jesus. Their statements need not be interpreted literally in order to be confessed truly, even if their language continues to be occasionally used.

It is held, moreover, that modern man with his secular and scientific outlook cannot possibly be asked seriously to think of the universe as providing the background necessary to give credibility to talk of a preexistent Son of God descending into our midst from heaven and finally ascending. The early church, when it affirmed such things of Jesus, was simply using the pictures given by current religious myths of the time in order to give expression to the new liberty and self-understanding given to them as they found themselves addressed by God as Jesus, especially in the proclamation of his cross. Some church theologians believe that what the early witnesses meant by their statements can today be adequately reexpressed without recourse even to talk of an incarnation. Discontent continues to be expressed, exactly as it was in last century, with words like "essence," "substance," and "nature." It is claimed that these are now mere dictionary terms of no current use in making meaningful statements.

In the midst of such desire to express the meaning of Christ in new ways, Jesus is often spoken of simply as an agent through whose mediation and example we are enabled to find authentic self-expression and new being, and enter into a meaningful experience of reality and the world. Doubt is raised about our need for his continuing work and ministry. Even when we are directed to his person, it is as if to One who is symbolic of something else, and who points entirely beyond himself. We seem at times to be confronted by an Arianism content to affirm that the Son is simply "of like substance" with the Father, at times with a docetism for which the reality of the human nature is of little importance.

Much recent NT study has, however, been undertaken in the belief that the Gospels do provide us with sufficient historical detail about Jesus to give us a reliable picture of the kind of man he actually was. The importance of regaining such a genuine understanding of his humanity as a basis for our Christology has been stressed. Wolfhart Pannenberg has criticized Karl Barth and others who have followed him for beginning their Christological thought from the standpoint of God himself: i.e., by first assuming the Trinity and the incarnation, and then arguing downward, viewing the humanity of Jesus against this transcendent background. Pannenberg himself believes that such initial presupposition of the divinity of Jesus will involve us inevitably in a Christology marked by disjunction and paradox, and will pose insoluble problems in relation to the unity of his person. Moreover, it will obscure our understanding of his true humanity.

Pannenberg seeks to form a "Christology from below," moving upward from Jesus' life and death toward his transformation in his resurrection and exaltation through the grace of God. Pannenberg believes that there are legendary elements in the Gospel history (e.g., the virgin birth). He stresses the need to interpret Jesus and his death from the standpoint of our own experience of history as well as from the standpoint of the OT. Karl Rahner, on the Roman Catholic side, also pursues a Christology beginning with the humanity of Jesus and based on anthropology.

We have to question whether the NT accounts of Jesus allow us to make such a one-sided approach and to follow such a method. Consistently Jesus is presented in the Gospels as one who is both truly man and truly God. The first witnesses did not try to present him to us in a manhood existing apart from the mystery of his unique union with God. It does not seem possible, therefore, that we ourselves should have access to the reality to which they are pointing unless we try to grasp him in the strange interpenetration of these two aspects that seems to mark their accounts of him. That the "Word became flesh" seems to imply that we cannot have the flesh apart from the Word nor the Word apart from the flesh.

What the Gospel writers intended to give us in their witness must therefore determine both our own approach and the method we adopt in our investigation. Hans Frei has more recently produced a study in Christology in which he attempts to face the problems of our approach to the Gospel narratives. He insists that Jesus Christ is known to the Christian believer in a manner that includes personal knowledge but also at the same time surpasses it mysteriously. Moreover, "we can no longer think of God except as we think of Jesus at the same time nor of Jesus except in reference to God." Frei also insists that while we can think of other people rightly without them being present, we cannot properly think of Jesus as not being present. We cannot indeed know his identity without being in his presence.

R. S. Wallace

See also Jesus Christ; Logos; Messiah; Word, Word of God, Word of the Lord.

Bibliography. H. R. Mackintosh, *The Person of Christ;* D. M. Baillie, *God Was in Christ;* O. Cullmann, *The Christology of the NT;* E. Brunner, *The Mediator;* L. B. Smedes, *The Incarnation, Trends in Modern Anglican Thought;* H. Relton, *A Study in Christology;* K. Barth, *Church Dogmatics,* IV/1 and IV/2; *RGG,* I, 1745–89; H. Vogel, *Gott in Christo* and *Christologie;* M. Fonyas, *The Person of Jesus Christ in the Decisions of the Ecumenical Councils;* W. Pannenberg, *Jesus—God and Man;* H. W. Frei, *The Identity of Jesus Christ;* E. Schillebeeckx, *Christ, Jesus,* and *Jesus and Christ;* R. A. Norris, *The Christological Controversy;* J. A. Dorner, *History of the Development of the Doctrine of the Person of Christ,* 4 vols.

Chrysostom, John (*ca.* 347–407). One of the Doctors of the Greek Church. Born at Antioch, Syria, and raised by his widowed Christian mother, he excelled in rhetorical and legal studies under the famous teacher Libanius. Unsatisfied as a lawyer, John abandoned his career to devote himself to Christian asceticism. He was baptized by Bishop Meletius and instructed in Christianity by Diodorus, teacher of the Antiochene School and later Bishop of Tarsus. For some years John lived as a monk at home while caring for his mother and assisting Meletius in worship services as a reader. About 373, after his mother's death, he left Antioch to take up a more rigorous monasticism in the mountains. The severity of the discipline ruined his health and forced him to adopt a less strenuous life style in the city. He was ordained deacon in 381. The new bishop, Flavius, made him elder in 386 and assigned him the task of preaching. In this role his rhetorical skills amplified by his scholarship and piety earned him a reputation as a biblical expositor second to none. Later generations have affirmed his greatness on the basis of his published sermons, treatises, and letters. Sixth century churchmen began regularly referring to him as "Chrysostomos" (golden mouthed).

In 398 John became Patriarch of Constantinople. He labored to reform the laxness of the clergy and the corrupt life of the city. Soon powerful enemies including Eudoxia, the emperor's wife, and several bishops conspired against him. With the help of the jealous Patriarch Theophilus of Alexandria they tried more than once to depose John. In 404, after defying an imperial order, Chrysostom was exiled to the eastern frontier. Three years later he was ordered to march to a more remote location and died on the way from exposure and exhaustion.

John's theology was expressed primarily in his sermons and was neither systematic, precise, nor original. His sermons drew spiritual and moral applications from a literal and grammatical exegesis of the Scriptures, most effectively from the Pauline Epistles, Matthew, and John. He played no active part in any major controversy, but he was the most popular and unquestionably orthodox of the Antiochene Fathers.

H. K. Gallatin

See also Antiochene Theology.

Bibliography. D. Attwater, *St. John Chrysostom, Pastor and Preacher;* P. C. Bauer, *John Chrysostom and His Time,* 2 vols.; D. Burger, *Complete Bibliography of Scholarship on the Life and Works of St. John Chrysostom;* S. C. Neill, *Chrysostom and His Message;* J. Pelikan, *The Preaching of Chrysostom;* P. Schaff, "The Life and Work of St. John Chrysostom," *NPNF,* IX, 3–23; R. V. Sellers, *Two Ancient Christologies;* W. R. W. Stephens, *Saint Chrysostom: His Life and Times;* B. Vanderberghe, *John the Golden Mouth.*

Church, Authority in. This subject is made difficult not only by the rich diversity of the NT witness, but also by the diverse trajectories of ecclesiastical traditions from postapostolic times on.

The Locus of Authority. Arguably, the strongest authoritative human voices in the earliest churches were the apostles (in the narrow sense of that flexible term, i.e., the Twelve [Matthias replacing Judas] plus Paul). Their authority extended beyond the local congregation, even beyond congregations they had been instrumental in founding (for how else could Peter's influence be felt in Corinth and Paul's in Colossae?), but it was not without limit. A Peter could prove inconsistent in practice (Gal. 2:11–14), and a Paul could be mistaken in judgment (Acts 15:37–40; cf. II Tim. 4:11). The objective truth of the gospel, Paul insists, enjoys an antecedent authority; if even an apostle tampers with that, he is to be reckoned anathema (Gal. 1:8–9). So an authoritative gospel must be passed on. That Paul in an early epistle can speak of the old covenant as being read (II Cor. 3:14) not only presupposes that Christians enjoy a new covenant but anticipates a reading of the new covenant (and therefore a NT canon) with scriptural authority analogous to that of the OT (II Pet. 3:15–16). In such cases, however, whether the penman be an apostle or not, the authority rests in the resulting inspired Scriptures, not the human being who inscripturates them (II Tim. 3:16).

Analogous things could be affirmed of OT prophets. Indeed, it can be argued rather compellingly that the true NT analogue of the OT prophet is not the NT prophet but the NT apostle (in the narrow sense). The apostles enjoy a self-conscious authority as God-chosen custodians of the gospel; and if they prefer to exercise their authority with meekness in an effort to win spiritually minded consensus (e.g., I Cor. 5:1–10; II Cor. 10:6; I Pet. 5:1–4), they are also prepared, if need be, to impose their authority without seeking consensus, and even against the consensus (e.g., Acts 5:1–11; I Cor. 4:18–21; II Cor. 10:11; 13:2–3; III John 10). Their authority is especially prominent in their role as interpreters both of the OT Scriptures and of the teachings of Jesus, as well as of his ministry, death, resurrection, and ascension. The church devoted itself to the apostles' teaching (Acts 2:42).

NT prophets likewise enjoyed wide authority. Some of them may have been itinerant, not restricting their ministrations to one congregation. "Prophecy" in the NT ranges from Spirit-empowered preaching to direct propositional messages from God; but the degree or kind of inspiration and the corresponding authority status of the prophet are limited. It is virtually impossible to conceive of I Cor. 14:29 being applied to OT prophets (once their credentials were accepted) or to NT apostles.

Those who seem consistently to enjoy the greatest authority at the level of the local congregation are the elders, almost certainly the same as those also labeled bishops (or overseers) and pastors (Acts 20:17–28; cf. Eph. 4:11; I Tim. 3:1–7; Titus 1:5, 7; I Pet. 5:1–2). The first term stems from the synagogue and from village organization; the second reflects genuine oversight and authority; and the third betrays an agrarian background ("pastor" derives from a Latin root meaning "shepherd"). In a typical list of qualifications for this office/function (e.g., I Tim. 3:1–7) we discover that almost every entry is mandated elsewhere of *all* believers. What is distinctive about the elder reduces to two things: (1) He must not be a novice. Clearly this is a relative term, largely dictated by how recently the church in question came into being, since Paul appoints elders mere months after their conversion in some instances (e.g., Acts 14:23). (2) He must be able to teach, which presupposes a growing grasp of the gospel and of the Scriptures and an ability to communicate them well. The other qualifications mentioned (e.g., an overseer must not be a woman, must be given to hospitality, etc.) suggest that he must excel in the graces and deportment expected of all believers. He who would lead the church must himself be a good reflection of it, not a mere professional.

In general, the sphere of responsibility and authority for these bishops-elders-pastors is the local church; there is little compelling evidence for the view that a bishop, for instance, unlike elders, exerted authority over several congregations. A plurality of elders, if not mandated, appears to have been common, and perhaps the norm. On the other hand, only "church" (*ekklēsia* in the sing.) is used for the congregation of all believers in one city, never "churches"; one reads of churches in Galatia, but of the church in Antioch or Jerusalem or Ephesus. Thus it is possible, though not certain, that a single elder may have exercised authority in relation to one house group—a house group that in some cases constituted part of the citywide church—so that the individual elder would nevertheless be one of many in that citywide "church" taken as a whole.

The apparent anomalies to this limitation on the sphere of elders can be credibly explained. The writer of II John and III John labels himself an "elder," even though he is seeking to influence the affairs of other churches; but most likely this particular elder is writing with apostolic prerogatives. The same is true of Peter when he refers to himself as an elder (I Pet. 5:1). The position of James in Acts 15 is peculiar, but the evidence is being stretched when interpreters conclude that James chaired the proceedings. The case is laid before the apostles and elders (15:4); "the apostles and elders, with the whole church" (15:22), make the final decisions; and the apostles and elders write the letter (15:23). Peter speaks as an apostle, James as an elder; it is not obvious that either "chaired" the meeting. But even if James did so, the crucial decisions were taken by the apostles, elders, and the church in concert.

Deacons may trace the origin of their office/function to the appointment of the seven (Acts 6), but this is uncertain. When lists of qualifications are presented elsewhere (e.g., I Tim. 3:8–13), stress is laid (as in the case of elders) on features which signify spiritual maturity; but in this instance teaching is not required. Deacons were responsible to serve the church in a variety of subsidiary roles, but enjoyed no church-recognized teaching authority akin to that of elders.

Patterns of Authority. The more difficult question is how these two offices/functions—viz., elders/pastors/overseers and deacons—relate their authority to the authority of the local church or to some broader grouping of churches. Historically one of three avenues has been followed, with many variations.

Congregationalism tends to place the ultimate choices in the hands of the entire congregation. In part this stance is a reaction against the interposition of a priestly class between God and man; the priesthood of all believers (I Pet. 2:9) is central. Churches decide alongside the apostles and elders (Acts 15:22); churches are responsible to protect themselves against false teachers (Galatians; II Cor. 10–13; II John); churches become the final court of appeal (Matt. 18:17); and even when the apostle Paul wants some discipline to be exercised, he appeals to the entire local church in solemn assembly (I Cor. 5:4).

Episcopacy labels its chief ministers bishops and lesser ones presbyters (or priests) and deacons. Some within this camp see the function of the bishops as heir to the apostles; others point to the intermediate roles of Timothy and Titus as portrayed in the Pastoral Epistles—men who had power themselves to appoint elders (Titus 1:5), as had the apostles in the churches they founded (Acts 14:23). Certainly the threefold ministry was defended as early as Ignatius (*ca.* A.D. 110), without, apparently, a traumatic debate reflecting change.

Presbyterianism points out that presbyters in the NT occupy the most important place after the apostles; and in any location the plurality of presbyters (or elders) seems to argue for a committee or college of presbyters who exercised general oversight over the congregation in the area (I Thess. 5:12–13; Heb. 13:17).

As most frequently practiced, all three of these prevailing patterns raise questions. Presbyterianism has raised an inference from Scripture to the status of principle. Episcopacy makes disjunctions between bishop and elder that cannot be defended from the NT, and therefore appeals to Timothy and Titus as paradigms are futile, not least because their functions are best explained on other lines (and in any case they are not called "bishops" over against some lesser clergy status). Congregationalism tends to read principles of democratic majority vote into NT churches. Ironically, some forms of congregationalism elevate the pastor, once he has been voted in, to near papal authority, in practice if not in theory.

The problem may lie in the fact that we have too often envisaged church authority flowing in straight lines, whether up or down, instead of recognizing the somewhat more fluid reality of the NT. The normal responsibility for and authority of leadership in the NT rests with the bishops-elders-pastors; but if they are interested in pursuing biblical patterns of leadership, they will be concerned to demonstrate observable growth not only in their grasp of truth but also in their lived discipline (I Tim. 4:14–16). They will comprehend that spiritual leadership, far from lording it over others (Matt. 20:25–28), is a balanced combination of oversight (I Tim. 4:11–13; 6:17–19; Titus 3:9–11) and example (I Tim. 4:12; 6:6–11, 17–18; I Pet. 5:1–4) which, far from being antithetical, are mutually reinforcing. By the same token such leaders prefer not to dictate terms but to lead the church into spiritually minded consensus. Whereas Christians are encouraged to support and submit to spiritual leadership (e.g., Heb. 13:17), such encouragement must not be considered a blank check if churches are responsible for and have the authority to discipline false teachers and to recognize an antecedent commitment not to a pastor but to the truth of the gospel. Modern models are not so much wrong as frequently lopsided, favoring a prejudicial selection of the NT data. Similarly, the Ignatian defense of a threefold ministry was not so much a rebellious aberration as an attempt to ground the rising monarchial episcopate in Scripture in order to use it to ward off traveling preachers who were frequently found spreading Gnostic heresy.

Spheres of Authority. The spheres in which ecclesiastical authority (however such authority is to be manifested) operates are primarily three. First, the early Christian churches exercised discipline, which ranged all the way from private and thoughtful admonition (e.g., Gal. 6:1) to excommunication (a severe social pressure when the entire church was cooperating) and even the handing over of a person to Satan (e.g., I Cor. 5:5; cf. Matt. 16:19; 18:18). Calvin was not wrong to identify church discipline as the third distinguishing mark of the NT church. Second, they enjoyed responsibility for and authority over a substantial range of questions affecting internal order—e.g., arrangement for collection of monies for relief of the poor (II Cor. 8–9) or the administration of the Lord's Supper (I Cor. 11:20–26). Third, churches had some responsibility and authority in the selection of deacons and elders and delegates (e.g., Acts 6:3–6; 15:22; I Cor. 16:3).

In no case were decisions established by mere majority approval; nor were these spheres of authority the exclusive prerogatives of the entire congregation. Apostles appointed elders, and Timothy had hands laid on him both by the apostle Paul and by the presbytery (II Tim. 1:6; I Tim. 4:14). This need not mean such appointment was made without close consultation with the church; but if the authority granted Titus is significant (Titus 1:5), it appears that oversight, especially in the case of fledgling churches, was exercised first by the apostles and then by their appointees.

In sum, there is dynamic tension among the constituent parts of the church as far as the authority of each is concerned. Two boundaries, to say the least, are fixed: (1) the church is not at liberty to ignore or countermand or contravene the authority of the gospel itself, now at last inscripturated, without sooner or later calling into question its own status as church. (2) The church of the NT does not expect its authority to be administered directly to the surrounding world, but to be felt through the transformed and redemptive lives of its members. D. A. CARSON

See also CHURCH DISCIPLINE; CHURCH GOVERNMENT.

Bibliography. W. Bauer, *Orthodoxy and Heresy in Earliest Christianity;* G. Bertram, *TDNT,* V, 596–625; J. Calvin, *Institutes* 4.3ff.; R. W. Dale, *Manual of Congregational Principles;* E. J. Forrester and G. W. Bromiley, *ISBE* (rev.), I, 696–98; J. Gray, "The Nature and Function of Adult Christian Education in the Church," *SJT* 19: 457–63; W. Grudem, *The Gift of Prophecy in 1 Corinthians;* E. Hatch, *The Organization of the Early Christian Churches;* C. Hodge, *Discussions in Church Polity;* F. J. A. Hort, *The Christian Ecclesia;* K. E. Kirk, ed., *The Apostolic Ministry;* T. A. Lacey, *Authority in the Church;* J. B. Lightfoot, "The Christian Ministry," *Commentary on Philippians;* T. W. Manson, *The Church's*

Ministry; B. H. Streeter, *The Primitive Church;* H. B. Swete, ed., *Essays on the Early History of the Church and Ministry;* H. von Campenhausen, *Ecclesiastical Authority and Spiritual Power in the Church of the First Three Centuries;* R. R. Williams, *Authority in the Apostolic Age.*

Church, The. The English word "church" derives from the late Greek word *kyriakon,* the Lord's house, a church building. In the NT the word translates the Greek word *ekklēsia.* In secular Greek *ekklēsia* designated a public assembly, and this meaning is still retained in the NT (Acts 19:32, 39, 41).

In the Hebrew OT the word *qāhāl* designates the assembly of God's people (e.g., Deut. 10:4; 23:2–3; 31:30; Ps. 22:23), and the LXX, the Greek translation of the OT, translated this word with both *ekklēsia* and *synagōgē.* Even in the NT *ekklēsia* may signify the assembly of the Israelites (Acts 7:38; Heb. 2:12); but apart from these exceptions, the word *ekklēsia* in the NT designates the Christian church, both the local church (e.g., Matt. 18:17; Acts 15:41; Rom. 16:16; I Cor. 4:17; 7:17; 14:33; Col. 4:15) and the universal church (e.g., Matt. 16:18; Acts 20:28; I Cor. 12:28; 15:9; Eph. 1:22).

Origin. According to Matthew, the only Gospel to use the word "church," the origin of the church goes back to Jesus himself (Matt. 16:18). Historical problems, though, arise in regard to this passage. For only in Matt. 16:18 and 18:17 does Jesus use the word "church," and there are no good reasons that Mark would omit the words of Matt. 16:17–19 if they were spoken by Jesus. Further, if Jesus expected God to establish his kingdom soon (cf. Mark 9:1; 13:30), then he would not have foreseen the need to establish a church with regulations for binding and loosing, i.e., to decide which actions are permissible and not permissible according to the teachings of Jesus. Matt. 16:18–19 may well be the Syrian church's declaration of independence from the synagogue and may derive from that early community which identified itself with Peter.

The question thus arises: Did Jesus intend to establish the church? The answer to this question must be based not on statements of church dogma but on careful interpretation of the NT writings. Here one's conclusions will be affected by the degree to which one assigns various statements of Jesus to Jesus himself or to the postresurrection church and by one's interpretation of terms such as "Son of man" and parables such as the fish net, the leaven, and seeds of growth (Matt. 13:47–50; 13:33; Mark 4:1–20). Critical study of the Gospels reveals that Jesus probably did not give teachings for the purpose of establishing and ordering the church. Rather his whole life and teaching provide the foundations upon which the church was created and called into being through its faith in the risen Lord.

Nature. Throughout most of history the nature of the church has been defined by divided Christians trying to establish the validity of their own existence. The Donatists of North Africa in the early centuries focused on the purity of the church and claimed to be the only church that measured up to the biblical standard. In the Middle Ages various sects defined the church in such ways as to claim that they, and not the Roman Catholic Church, were the true church. The Arnoldists emphasized poverty and identification with the masses; the Waldenses stressed literal obedience to Jesus' teachings and emphasized evangelical preaching. Roman Catholics claimed that the only true church was that over which the pope was supreme as successor of the apostle Peter. The Reformers Martin Luther and John Calvin, following John Wycliffe, distinguished between the visible and invisible church, claiming that the invisible church consists of the elect only. Thus an individual, including the pope, might be a part of the visible church but not a part of the invisible and true church.

If one is to be true to the NT testimony, it must be acknowledged that there is a multiplicity of images and concepts that contribute to an understanding of the nature of the church. In the appendix of *Images of the Church in the New Testament,* Paul Minear lists ninety-six images which he classifies as (1) minor images, (2) the people of God, (3) the new creation, (4) the fellowship in faith, and (5) the body of Christ. Listing only a few of these will demonstrate the great diversity of images: the salt of the earth, a letter from Christ, branches of the vine, the elect lady, the bride of Christ, exiles, ambassadors, a chosen race, the holy temple, priesthood, the new creation, fighters against Satan, the sanctified slaves, friends, sons of God, household of God, members of Christ, spiritual body.

Though such a plethora of images exists, it is nonetheless possible and useful to find the major concepts that hold these many images together. From the Council of Constantinople in 381 and reaffirmed at Ephesus (431) and Chalcedon (451) the church has affirmed itself to be "one, holy, catholic, and apostolic."

The Church Is One. According to the *World Christian Encyclopedia* (1982), there were an estimated 1,900 church denominations at the beginning of the twentieth century. Today there are an estimated 22,000. Do not such numbers effectively refute the theological assertion that the church is one? The answer must be no.

First of all, the NT witness is clear regarding the unity of the church. In I Cor. 1:10–30 Paul warns against divisions in the church and urges the people to be united in Christ. In this same letter (ch. 12), he states that while there are many gifts, there is one body (cf. Rom. 12:3–8). The Gospel of John speaks of the one shepherd and the one flock (10:16), and Jesus prays that his followers may be one even as Father and Son are one (17:20–26). In Gal. 3:27–28 Paul declares that in Christ all are one, with no distinction of race, social status, or sex. Acts 2:42 and 4:32 are likewise eloquent testimony to the oneness of the church. Perhaps the most stirring passage on this point is Eph. 4:1–6: "There is one body and one Spirit, just as you were called to the one hope that belongs to your call, one Lord, one faith, one baptism, one God and Father of us all, who is above all and through all and in all" (vss. 4–6).

Unity, however, does not demand uniformity. Indeed, from the beginning the church has manifested itself in many local churches (in Jerusalem, Antioch, Corinth, Ephesus, etc.); and the one NT church had neither uniformity of worship nor structures, or even a uniform theology. Certainly the ecumenical movement which arose in this century out of the missionary movement of the nineteenth century has challenged the church today to recognize that "God wills unity" (Faith and Order Conference, Lausanne, 1927). The challenge for Christians today is to live in unity without insisting that our worship, structure, and theology be more uniform than that of the NT church. Unity is possible when we stop thinking of our church or denomination as the vine and all others as the branches. Rather, Jesus is the vine and all of us are branches.

The Church Is Holy. According to I Corinthians, Christians there were guilty of incest (5:1), suing one another in pagan courts (6:6), defrauding each other (6:8), having sexual relations with prostitutes (6:16). In Rome the weak Christians were judging the strong Christians, and the latter despised the former (Rom. 14:10). Such is the partial testimony of the NT concerning the reality of sin in the church, but then one scarcely needs to leave the twentieth century church to verify this reality. Does not the presence of sin refute the theological assertion that the church is holy? Again, the answer is no.

Various solutions have been proposed in the history of the church to reconcile the fact that the holy church is a sinful church. Donatists as well as Gnostics, Novationists, Montanists, Cathari, and other sects solved the problem by claiming that they alone were holy while all others were not really members of the church. But I John 1:8 reminds one that the church which has no sin to confess simply does not exist. Others have claimed that the members are sinful but the church is holy. But the church does not exist in the abstract; it is sinful people who constitute the church. Gnostics claimed that the body was sinful while the soul was holy. But biblical anthropology declares that it is the whole, undivided human being who is sinful.

The solution lies in the awareness of what "holy" means in the Bible. To be holy is to be separated from what is profane and to be dedicated to the service of God. It does not mean that the Christian is free of sin. The apostle Paul said of himself: "Not that I have already obtained this or am already perfect" (Phil. 3:12*a*), and in the greetings to the Corinthian Christians he calls them "sanctified" and "saints." Christians are holy in that they are separated for God's service and set apart by God (II Thess. 2:13; Col. 3:12, etc.).

The Church Is Catholic. The word "catholic" derives from the Latin *catholicus*, which in turn derives from the Greek *katholikos*, meaning "universal." Although the word is not used in the NT to describe the church, the concept which it expresses is biblical. Ignatius of Antioch wrote in the early second century, "Wherever the bishop is, there his people should be, just as where Jesus Christ is, there is the Catholic Church" (*Smyr.* 8:2). Only from the third century on was "catholic" used in a polemical sense to refer to those who were "orthodox" Christians as opposed to schismatics and heretics. To speak of the catholicity of the church is thus to refer to the entire church, which is universal and which has a common identity of origin, lordship, and purpose.

While the local church is an entire church, it is not *the* entire church. As catholic, the church includes believers of past generations and believers of all cultures and societies. It is unfortunate that the church in the Western world has for far too long formulated theology and mission strategy in isolation from the churches of Africa, Asia, and Latin America, the churches of the two-thirds world. The *World Christian Encyclopedia* shows that whites now represent 47.4 percent of the Christian population of the world, the first time in 1,200 years that whites are not the majority. Two hundred eight million Christians speak Spanish, 196 million speak English, 128 million speak Portuguese, followed by German, French, Italian, Russian, Polish, Ukrainian, and Dutch.

The Church Is Apostolic. Eph. 2:20 states that the church is "built upon the foundation of the apostles and prophets, Christ Jesus himself being the cornerstone." Apostles are those who were eyewitnesses of the ministry of Jesus, and prophets are Christian prophets who were spokesmen for the risen Jesus. Previous centuries of Christians assumed that the NT manuscripts were written by the apostles or else by someone who was closely associated with them. Many critical scholars today question apostolic authorship for all four Gospels, Acts, James, I and II Peter, Jude, and Revelation, and further question or reject Pauline authorship of Ephesians, Colossians, I and II Timothy, Titus, and Hebrews. Yet the truth is that regardless of who wrote these Gospels and letters, the church canonized these writings and accepted them as normative for faith and practice. The message of these documents is thus the norm by which the life of the church is to be measured; and the church can be one, holy, and catholic only if it is an apostolic church.

To claim that the church is apostolic is not to assert a direct line of succession through specific individuals. It is to recognize that the message and the mission of the apostles as mediated through Scripture must be that of the whole church.

The adjectives "one, holy, catholic, apostolic" are terms specific enough to describe the essential nature of the church and yet allow for differences within denominations and churches in the ways in which each fulfills the mission and ministry of the church in the world. As previously mentioned, the NT uses nearly a hundred images that relate to the church. One major image, the body of Christ, is especially rich in what it communicates about the nature of the church.

The Body of Christ. Of the NT writers only Paul uses this term. It is significant that he speaks of the church as the body of Christ but never as a body of Christians. Scholars debate how literally Paul intended this phrase to be understood. One may safely say that though the image may perhaps be taken too literally, it cannot be taken too seriously.

Christians are one body in Christ with many members (Rom. 12:4–5; I Cor. 12:27). Indeed, the church is the body of Christ (Eph. 1:22–23; 4:12), who is the head of the body (Eph. 5:23; Col. 1:18); and the body is dependent on its head for its life and growth (Col. 2:19). The church is never directly called the bride of Christ, but is so understood by Paul's analogy in which the husband-wife relationship is said to be like the Christ-church relationship (Eph. 5:22–33). Husband and wife are to be one flesh, and this is the same regarding Christ and the church (Eph. 5:31–32).

Through this image several important theological concepts are expressed concerning the church. Christians form a unity both with Christ and with one another, and Christ is acknowledged as both the authority who stands over the church and the one who gives life and growth. Also, this image is a strong assertion regarding the need for and proper appreciation of the diverse gifts that God gives to the church.

Purpose. God has called the church out of the world for a purpose. He intended for his creation to have fellowship with him. When that fellowship was broken, God called the people of Israel to be "a light to the nations" (Isa. 42:5–8); but when Israel failed, God called a remnant (Isa. 10:20–22). In the fullness of time God himself entered fully into human history in the birth of Jesus Christ, whom Simeon at the temple called "a light for revelation to the Gentiles, and for glory to thy people Israel" (Luke 2:32). Jesus then called twelve disciples as symbolic of the new Israel of the end time which he was creating (Matt. 19:28). These twelve formed the nucleus of God's new people, the church, which like Israel of old has been called into being to be the means by which all of humanity is restored to fellowship with its creator (Acts 1:8; Matt. 28:18–20).

The church has a dual purpose; it is to be a holy priesthood (I Pet. 2:5) and is to "declare the wonderful deeds of him who called you out of darkness into his marvelous light" (I Pet. 2:9). It is the whole church in relationship to the world which is to exercise the tasks of priesthood. As a priesthood the church is entrusted with the responsibility of bringing God's word to mankind and of interceding with God on behalf of mankind.

In addition to the priestly function the church also has a missionary function of declaring God's wonderful deeds. The missionary task of the church is not optional, for by its very nature the church is mission. Furthermore, mission is in and to the world, not in and to itself.

R. L. Omanson

Bibliography. K. Barth, *Church Dogmatics* IV/1–3; G. C. Berkouwer, *The Church;* E. Brunner, *The Christian Doctrine of the Church, Faith, and the Consummation;* R. N. Flew, *Jesus and His Church;* H. Küng, *The Church;* J. H. Leith, ed., *Creeds of the Church;* P. Minear, *Images of the Church in the NT;* K. L. Schmidt, *TDNT,* III, 501ff.; H. Schwarz, *The Christian Church;* E. Schweizer, *The Church As the Body of Christ;* D. D. Bannerman, *The Scripture Doctrine of the Church;* E. G. Jay, *The Church;* D. Watson, *I Believe in the Church;* F. J. A. Hort, *The Christian Ecclesia;* A. Cole, *The Body of Christ.*

Church and State. The phrase refers to an ancient differentiation between two kinds of institutions that have structured and defined the lives of human beings. In this arrangement one of these authority structures—the state—has been primarily concerned with temporal life as an end in itself, while the other—the church—has been concerned with temporal life as a means to spiritual ends. Moreover, "church and state" designates a certain kind of tension implicit in any society that contains these two institutions, even in those in which there is no attempt to separate them.

The issue of the most desirable relationship between church and state is older than the Christian faith, and has been a persistent theme in its history. Jesus clearly taught the principle of separating the two realms. His dictum to "render therefore to Caesar the things that are Caesar's, and to God the things that are God's" (Matt. 22:21) marked the beginning of a new epoch in the history of relations between religion and the state. For the first time, a formal distinction was made between the obligations owed to both.

Unfortunately, Jesus did not indicate where the exact line of demarcation lay; consequently, since at least the fourth century Christian theologians and other scholars have argued over where it should be drawn. The resulting discussions stretching over the centuries since that time constitute an almost impenetrable historical-theological swamp. The debate continues in the Christian world today and is especially intense in highly pluralistic societies like the United States.

Historical Background. Christian thinkers made no attempt to formulate a theory of church-state relations until Christianity became a state religion in the fourth century. Before that time, even though they had no legal right to exist, believers generally followed Paul's admonition to "be subject to the governing authorities" (Rom. 13:1) except when that subjection conflicted with explicitly understood commands of God or the preaching of the gospel (Acts 5:29). Moreover, the duty of obedience to civil rulers was always qualified by the condition that these authorities were doing their work of restraining evil and seeking peace and safety (cf. Rom. 13:1–7 and Rev. 13).

Widespread persecution of the early Christians was frequent, beginning at least as early as the reign of Nero in the midfirst century. The final effort to eradicate Christians from the Roman world took place under Diocletian in 303. It failed, and with the Edict of Milan in 313 Christianity became an officially recognized religion in the Roman Empire. Moreover, by the end of the century the Roman rulers had decreed that Christianity was the sole official religion of the empire.

This new arrangement created a need for closer definition of the relationships between church and state, but such theory developed only gradually. For one thing, it was during this period that the church became an institution in the modern sense. For another, the Emperor Constantine I, in keeping with previous custom, regarded himself as the religious leader of the realm (*pontifex maximus*) and assumed the right to intervene in church affairs. Later rulers gave up this title but continued to consider themselves responsible for directing church activities.

The removal of the capital from Rome to Constantinople (Byzantium) in 330, among other factors, led to a different conception of church-state relations in the East than that in the West. In the Eastern Roman Empire (later the Byzantine Empire) and consequently in Eastern Orthodoxy the prevailing theory and practice came to be caesaropapism—that is, supreme authority over the church exercised by the secular ruler, even in doctrinal matters. In the West, the church had more freedom from direct control by the civil authorities.

Partly because of the ineffective political leadership in the Western Empire and partly because of the inherent authority accorded the church in Rome, the Roman bishops had to take responsibility for judicial affairs, military defense, and other secular matters. It was in this context that Bishop Gelasius I initially stated the doctrine of the two swords in 494: "There are two powers by which this world is chiefly ruled; the sacred authority of the popes and the royal power. Of these the priestly power is much more important because it has to render account for the kings of men themselves at the divine tribunal. . . . You know that it behooves you, in matters concerning the reception and reverent administration of the sacraments, to be obedient to the ecclesiastical authority rather than to control it."

During the Middle Ages (*ca.* 500–1500) the theory of the two spheres, the spiritual and the temporal, was generally accepted, but the question of supremacy remained undefined. To be sure, the state was universally considered a Christian institution in this period, obligated to nourish, protect, and further the faith. Church law held that the state was obligated to punish heretics, and this obligation was accepted by the state. But there was also endless debate among theologians and canon lawyers over the real meaning of Gelasius's two swords theory. The text of his statement was analyzed and the etymological significance studied in order to deduce the implications of spiritual supremacy for temporal affairs. Eventually the concept of a single society with two aspects, each with its own responsibilities, was worked out. However, it was a painful and slow process.

During the early Middle Ages the church

struggled to free itself from intrusion by secular rulers. For example, after the sixth century, emancipated from direct control from Byzantium, the popes increased in prestige and power, in both the spiritual and temporal realms. But an important event in church-state relations took place in 800 when Pope Leo III crowned Charlemagne as emperor. Charlemagne had tried to revive the empire in the West and held views close to caesaropapism. He would have liked to limit the role of the pope to purely spiritual affairs, but he had no competent heirs to continue his policies. For their part, later popes used the precedent of Charlemagne's coronation to show that emperors received their crowns from the papacy. On the other hand, later emperors claimed the right to approve those elected to papal office. Thus, by the eleventh century the elements of a major confrontation between pope and emperor, church and state, were present.

When Pope Gregory VII, an advocate of reform, challenged the right of Emperor Henry IV to appoint the Archbishop of Milan, the investiture controversy ensued. In 1075 Gregory issued a decree forbidding lay investiture and asserted that popes had the power to depose emperors. After considerable maneuvering by both parties—including Gregory's dramatic but temporary triumph at Canossa in 1077—a compromise was worked out by the Concordat of Worms in 1122. Bishops in the empire were to be chosen according to canon law but invested with their insignia by an ecclesiastical officer. The practice was copied elsewhere and tensions eased somewhat.

However, the issues of the right of the popes to depose kings and the role of the secular rulers in selecting appointees to high church offices were worked out only gradually over the decades, the papacy eventually becoming dominant. This trend culminated in the reign of Pope Innocent III (1198–1216), the most powerful pontiff in Christian history. Under Innocent, and for about a century thereafter, it was clear that royal power was subordinate to pontifical authority. The thirteenth century was the zenith of papal power in terms of church-state relations. However, the aspirations of kings to consolidate their national strength and the discrediting of the papacy during the period of the Babylonian Captivity of the Church (1309–77) and the Great Papal Schism (1378–1417) which followed led to the curtailment of papal influence and prestige. These factors and the growth of the Renaissance papacy in the fifteenth century further weakened the papal office and helped set the stage for the coming of the Protestant Reformation.

The Reformation and Its Aftermath. The Protestant Reformers challenged the authority of the church in general and the papacy in particular, in both the spiritual and political realms. This further diminished the ability of the church to control and/or intervene in political affairs. Moreover, in place of the late medieval theory of ultimate pontifical authority in church-state matters, the Reformers posited a variety of different approaches. Martin Luther sharply distinguished the temporal from the spiritual but considered many ecclesiastical functions, such as administration, as nonessentials. Therefore, most of the Lutheran states developed an Erastian territorial system in which the princes supervised church affairs. John Calvin tried to make a clear distinction between the spheres of church and state, believing that it was the duty of the latter to maintain peace, protect the church, and follow biblical guidelines in civil affairs. In general, Geneva and the Reformed churches of Europe attempted to follow his views and avoid civil domination. The Church of England adopted an Erastian position by substituting the king for the pope as the head of the church and by designating king and Parliament to regulate ecclesiastical government, worship, and discipline.

However, the Anabaptists and other Radical Reformers insisted that the correct biblical emphasis was to separate completely the spheres of church and state. Their position seemed so anarchical at the time that they were severely persecuted by all other parties, Protestant and Catholic alike. In turn, the Anabaptists passed on their views on church and state to related movements in seventeenth century England—Baptists, Quakers, and Independents.

More than any other religious group in the seventeenth and eighteenth centuries, those of Baptist views—John Smyth, Thomas Helwys, Leonard Busher, John Murton, John Bunyan, John Clarke, Roger Williams, Isaac Backus, and John Leland, among others—championed the concept that the logical corollary to the doctrine of religious liberty was the principle of the separation of church and state. On the basis of such Scriptures as Matt. 22, Rom. 13, and James 4:12 they argued that this was the only way to safeguard religious freedom and the priesthood of the believer. By this they meant that the state had no right to interfere with the religious beliefs and practices of individuals or congregations, and that the church for its part had no claim upon the state for financial support. To receive public money was to invite government control and the loss of religious identity.

Also in the eighteenth century Enlightenment

natural rights theorists such as John Locke and Hugo Grotius popularized the view that civil government was rooted in a social contract rather than in God's appointment. Armed with this concept the emerging national states tended to make the church subservient to the common good of society and came to expect institutional religion to steer clear of political issues. However, the development of this concept in Europe and the remainder of the world was uneven, and attempts at state control of the church recurred. Only in the newly created United States of America did the government clearly agree to a new system that sought to guarantee religious freedom through separation of church and state.

The American Experiment. Conditions in the American colonies prior to 1776 were not favorable to the establishment of a single church. To be sure, during most of the period many of the individual colonies had an established church—Congregationalism in New England and the Church of England in most other places. However, there was no state church in Rhode Island, Pennsylvania, New Jersey, or Delaware, while in many other places large numbers of Baptists and Quakers opposed those that existed. Numerous dissenters and the need to attract settlers regardless of religious persuasion made it difficult to enforce establishment. By the time of the revolution, when the new states wrote their constitutions, most of them disestablished their churches. Gradually all would abandon the concept. Vestiges of an establishment lingered in Massachusetts until 1833.

The U.S. Constitution forbade religious tests for public office and its First Amendment provided that "Congress shall make no law respecting an establishment of religion, or prohibiting the free exercise thereof." A new experiment in church-state relations had been inaugurated with the strong backing of Baptists, Mennonites, Quakers, and most Methodists and Presbyterians—all of whom were Bible-believing Christians who wanted to protect the freedom of the churches and individual consciences from the state—and the support of the founding fathers—most of whom were rationalist deists who wanted to protect the state from clerical domination. Moreover, there was the practical matter of the prevailing denominational pluralism in the new nation that made it impossible to agree upon which church to establish.

Although the original intentions of the founding fathers and their supporters are now debated, it appears that Thomas Jefferson and his party and the vast majority of evangelical Protestants, the dominant religious group of the early national period, assumed that there was a "wall of separation" between the two institutions which should be maintained at all costs, for the good of the republic and the health of true religion. They considered that government best which governed least, regarded religion as primarily a private affair between an individual and God, and saw no reason for conflict between politics and religion. Although they wanted a strict separation of the institutions of church and state, they did not try to segregate religion from national life. General references to the majority religion were acceptable in what was then a largely homogeneous nation. This common view dominated church-state relations in America throughout the nineteenth century.

However, there was also a minority view, expressed by John Adams and others, that the main concern of the First Amendment was to keep the federal government from interfering with religious matters so that each state could handle such questions. Some eventually extended this to a claim that the goal was to make the United States a Christian nation, but neutral in respect to particular denominations.

As America became more religiously and culturally heterogeneous in the twentieth century, the dominant nineteenth century view of a rather rigorous separation of church and state was increasingly challenged. Many now argue that there was actually no unanimity among those who voted for the First Amendment and that it is impossible to determine their original intent. This has resulted in a sharp division in interpretation, with some arguing for a veritable "Berlin Wall" of separation that would clearly secularize society by excluding anything religious from national life and others arguing for a more porous wall that would allow for the flow of a virile civil religion into the stream of national affairs.

Historically speaking, this new period of church-state relations began in the 1920s when the old Protestant establishment committed cultural suicide in the internecine fundamentalist-modernist controversy. Theologically speaking, it dates from the wave of theological liberalism that engulfed Protestantism in the first quarter of the twentieth century, thus diminishing the ability of American society to resist the encroachments of secular humanism and to assimilate the great waves of new immigrants which came to America in this period. Legally and politically speaking, it stems from 1940, when a landmark decision by the Supreme Court (*Cantwell et al. vs. State of Conn.*) resulted in a dramatic shift in church-state cases from state to federal jurisdiction. Since that time the court has dealt with a number of critical religious issues related in some way to the First Amendment: laws governing business on Sundays, taxation of church property, religion and prayers in the public schools, public support for parochial education, church lobbying, conscientious objection, abortion, pornography and censorship, and resistance to war taxes. Currently in the offering are other questions concerning church and state, such as the status of military chaplains and legislation to limit the activities of so-called cults.

In the period since 1940 several principles have been established by the Supreme Court in dealing with church-state matters. For example, it invoked the "child benefit theory" in 1947 (*Everson vs. Bd. of Ed., N.J.*). In 1971 (*Earle vs. DiCenso* and *Lemon vs. Kurtzman*) it established the principle of "evidence of excessive entanglement" of church and state. Nevertheless, it has been difficult for the Supreme Court to decide what is and is not equivalent to "an establishment of religion" in twentieth century America and to determine where the freedom of an individual or group conflicts with the freedom of others or with obligations to the larger good of the community. Moreover, the competing forces of diverse religious and ethnic groups along with a lack of a clear national consensus on moral values have made it difficult to reach decisions on church and state acceptable to a clear majority of Americans.

Theologians, historians, and other scholars have not contributed a great deal to the discussion of church-state issues since World War II. The monumental work of Anson Phelps Stokes and Leo Pfeffer is an exception and provides the beginning point for any analysis of current church-state relations in America. James E. Wood, Jr., and the *Journal of Church and State* have also provided vigorous leadership in this area, and such organizations as Americans United for Separation of Church and State remain in the forefront of such discussion and analysis. But even AUSCS, long an advocate of the "wall of separation," appears to be less "united" on the issues than it once was. Finally, there is considerable evidence that the increasing number of adherents of authoritarian religious cults and denominations and the presence of the new religious right in America will have a profound role in altering the meaning of "separation of church and state" in the years to come—probably in the direction of more government involvement in religion.

Conclusions. Islam, Hinduism, and most of the other major religions of the world have not produced a doctrine of separation of church and state comparable to that championed by evangelical Protestants and Enlightenment rationalists and eventually implemented in the United States. For example, in many Muslim countries there is no separation of church and state in the Western sense. In others there is formal separation of the institutions but a close link between them in terms of favored treatment and anticonversion laws.

On the other hand, the validity of the principle of church-state separation has been increasingly recognized all over the world in the twentieth century. Nearly every European country has disestablished former state churches, and in some nations, such as France, a radical separation has been effected. Even in most Marxist states, such as the Soviet Union and China, church and state are constitutionally separated, not in order to ensure religious freedom but in order to make certain that religious groups stay out of government affairs and to keep them under supervision.

In one sense the concept of separation of church and state has come almost universally to have normative value. Most secular governments prefer to have some kind of line of demarcation between the sacred and the profane, at least in terms of institutional expression. On the other hand, the principle has not yet been definitively articulated, not even in its American homeland. Moreover, there are emerging movements—such as Islamic republicanism in Iran—which renounce any attempt to separate the institutions. In America growing numbers of people appear to have abandoned the more traditional emphasis on a "wall of separation" in favor of some kind of bland civil religion that will allow for more open-ended cooperation between the two institutions. It remains to be seen if people today can distinguish between the impossibility of separating religion from politics, on the one hand, and the desirability of keeping church and state on their respective sides of the religious-political wall, on the other. R. D. LINDER

See also CHURCH, THE; CIVIL RELIGION; GOVERNMENT.

Bibliography. *JCS* (1959–); *RCDA* (1973–); O. Cullmann, *The State in the NT;* R. H. Bainton, *The Travail of Religious Liberty;* J. C. Bennett, *Christians and the State;* F. H. Littell, *From State Church to Pluralism;* R. F. Drinan, *Religion, the Courts, and Public Policy;* A. G. Huegli, ed., *Church and State Under God;* K. F. Morrison, *The Two Kingdoms;* A. P. Stokes and L. Pfeffer, *Church and State in the United States;* B. Tierney, *The Crisis of Church and State, 1050–1300;* J. F. Wilson, ed., *Church and State in American History;* P. R. Coleman-Norton, *Roman State and Christian Church,* 3 vols.; E. A. Smith, ed., *Church-State Relations in Ecumenical Perspective;* L. Pfeffer, *Church,*

State and Freedom and *God, Caesar and the Constitution;* J. E. Wood, Jr., *The Problem of Nationalism in Church-State Relationships;* W. R. Estep, Jr., *The Anabaptist Story;* A. J. Menendez, *Church-State Relations: An Annotated Bibliography;* F. J. Sorauf, *The Wall of Separation;* M. J. Malbin, *Religion and Politics;* E. Helmreich, ed., *Church and State in Europe;* W. C. Fletcher, *Soviet Believers;* H. B. Clark II, ed., *Freedom of Religion in America;* J. L. Garrett, Jr., *Our Heritage of Religious Freedom.*

Church Councils. *See* COUNCILS, CHURCH.

Church Discipline. As an ecclesiastical function discipline is mandated by the Great Commission's "Go and make disciples" (Matt. 28: 19–20). A disciple is one who voluntarily places himself under the discipline of a master—meaning for the Christian believer learning to "do all that I have commanded you" and meaning for the church the schooling of would-be disciples in doing the Lord's revealed will. The universal form of discipline, then (though not always so perceived), is the preaching of the Word of God—confessed in Protestantism as one of the keys to the kingdom of Heaven (Matt. 16:19; 18:18).

Because the believer is formed as disciple by what comes out in behavior as obedient response to what goes in as Word (Matt. 15:11), and because a saving faith is evidenced by the fruit of good works (James 2:17), the church's disciplining includes active supervision of each member's conduct. The Head of the body requires such "guardianship" at the hands of church leaders (Acts 20:28) by whatever title designated; and the believer is required to pay heed to their admonition (Heb. 13:17). In this stricter sense disciplinary supervision of members' faith and life is confessed in the church as a second key to the kingdom.

Procedures for the administration of ecclesiastical discipline—from loving admonition (Gal. 6:1) to excommunication (I Cor. 5:13)—are commonly prescribed by denominational polities. They will usually move, as required, from private, personal counsel by representatives of the congregation's ruling body, through meeting with that body, through announcement to the congregation (usually at first anonymously) with request for urgent supplication, to public naming of the disciplinee, culminating in eventual excommunication—assuming that there has been stubborn refusal to acknowledge sin and pursue amendment (Matt. 18:15–17 sets the pattern). Throughout these steps the recalcitrant member is usually placed under "silent censure," i.e., advised not to partake of the Lord's Supper (I Cor. 11:27–32)—a separation confirmed, if unrepented, by excommunication.

The disciplinary process seeks the restoration of the wandering member to the body. Heaven rejoices with local congregation when the erring one repents (Luke 15:7). This is *love.*

The ultimate disciplinary act of excommunication aims at both (1) etching out the awesome issue involved, leading still to restoration of the severed membership; and (2) maintaining the integrity of the church—for the body not only risks spreading rebellion when instances of it are ignored (I Cor. 5:7), but is blemished before the world by sins winked at (Jude 5–13). Moreover, God himself is blasphemed by the Christian's unrepented misbehavior (Rom. 2:23–24). Discipline due but ignored is not love but *sentimentality,* love's counterfeit.

Creating disciples through discipline has characterized the church from Adam and Abraham. It is the burden of "the law and the prophets" (Matt. 5:17–20) and the thrust of the NT.

For Protestantism the church universal takes on visibility in the local congregation. It is there that the keys are exercised and discipline is thus administered. In a time when the universal church is dispersed into churches, the administration of discipline seems to be complicated by the probability that the disciplinee will flee to—and be welcomed by—another congregation. This likelihood, combined with the rage for "church growth," tends to give discipline a flabby and indecisive character. But the local congregational leadership does well to remember that the Lord requires of their hands an accounting of the blood of each member (Ezek. 3:20–21; Acts 20:26–27). What the disciplined member does becomes his responsibility; what the leaders fail to do is ineradicably theirs. L. DE KOSTER

Bibliography. L. DeKoster and G. Berghoef, *Elders' Handbook;* Augsburg Confession (28); Belgic Confession (32); Westminster Confession (30).

Church Government. Basically there are three types of church government—the episcopal, the presbyterian, and the congregational—each of which takes on features from the others. Episcopalianism, for example, finds a large place for presbyters in its synods and elsewhere, and its congregations have many functions of their own. Presbyterian congregations also play a large part, while the appearance of moderators attests a movement toward episcopal supervision. The very existence of such groupings as Congregational and Baptist Unions with their presidents shows that churches with a basically congregational polity are yet alive to the value of other elements in the Christian tradition. Yet the general categories do apply.

Episcopacy. In this system the chief ministers of the church are bishops. Other ministers are presbyters (or priests) and deacons. All these are mentioned in the NT, although there bishops and presbyters seem to be identical. Those who see an episcopal system in the NT point to the function of the apostles, which some think was passed on to bishops whom the apostles ordained. They see as important the position of James of Jerusalem, which is not unlike that of the later bishop. The functions of Timothy and Titus as revealed in the Pastoral Epistles show these men to have been something of a transition between the apostles and the bishops of later times. The apostles are said to have practiced ordination by the laying on of hands (Acts 6:6; I Tim. 4:14), and they appointed elders in the churches they founded (Acts 14:23), presumably with the laying on of hands. On this view the apostles were the supreme ministers in the early church, and they took care that suitable men were ordained to the ministry. To some of them they entrusted the power to ordain and so provided for the continuance of the ministry in succeeding generations.

It is further alleged that the organization of the church subsequent to NT days supports this view. In the time of Ignatius the threefold ministry was clearly in existence in Asia Minor. By the end of the second century it is attested for Gaul and Africa by the writings of Irenaeus and Tertullian. Nowhere is there evidence of a violent struggle such as would be natural if a divinely ordained congregationalism or presbyterianism were overthrown. The same threefold ministry is seen as universal throughout the early church as soon as there is sufficient evidence to show us the nature of the ministry. The conclusion is drawn that episcopacy is the primitive and rightful form of church government.

But there are objections. There is no evidence that bishops differed from presbyters in NT days. It is going too far to say that all the ministry of these times was of apostolic origin. There were churches not of apostolic foundation, like that in Colossae, which do not seem to have lacked a ministry. Again, some of the early church orders, including the Didache, are congregational in outlook. The case is far from proven.

Nevertheless, episcopacy is undoubtedly early and practically universal. In time divisions appeared, notably the great schism in 1054 when the Orthodox Church in the East separated from the Roman Catholic Church in the West. Both continue to be episcopal and hold to the doctrine of apostolic succession. But there are differences. The Orthodox Church is a federation of self-governing churches, each with its own patriarch. The Roman Catholic church is more centralized, and its bishops are appointed by the pope. There are doctrinal differences, such as different views of the *filioque* clause in the Nicene Creed.

At the Reformation there were further separations. The Church of England rejected Roman supremacy but retained the historic episcopate. Some of the Lutheran churches opted for an episcopal system but did not remain in the historic succession. In more recent times other churches have decided to have bishops—e.g., some Methodist churches—and these too have rejected the historic succession. There have been other divisions, such as the separation of the Old Catholics when the dogma of papal infallibility was proclaimed. More Christians accept episcopacy than any other form of church government, but episcopal churches are for the most part not in communion with one another.

Presbyterianism. This system emphasizes the importance of elders, or presbyters. Its adherents do not usually hold that this polity is the only one in the NT. At the Reformation the Presbyterian leaders thought that they were restoring the original form of church government, but this would not be vigorously defended by many Presbyterians today. It is recognized that there has been much development, but it is held that this took place under the guidance of the Holy Spirit and that in any case the essentials of the presbyterian system are scriptural. It is beyond question that in the NT presbyters occupy an important place. They are identical with the bishops and form the principal local ministry. In each place there appears to have been a group of presbyters who formed a kind of college or committee which was in charge of local church affairs. That is the natural conclusion to which exhortations like Heb. 13:17 and I Thess. 5:12–13 point. From the account of the Council of Jerusalem in Acts 15 we see that the presbyters occupied an important place at the very highest levels of the early church. In the subapostolic age the bishop developed at the expense of the presbyters. This was due to such circumstances as the need for a strong leader in times of persecution and in the controversies against heretics and perhaps also to the prestige attaching to the minister who regularly conducted the service of Holy Communion.

There is much that is convincing in this case. But we must also bear in mind the considerations urged by upholders of the other ways of viewing church government. What is beyond doubt is that from the Reformation onward the presbyterian form of church government has been of very great importance. John Calvin organized the four churches in Geneva on the basis of his understanding of the NT ministry as fourfold: the pastor, the doctor (or teacher), the deacon, and the presbyter (or elder). It was the pastor who had the care of the congregation. This was not the full presbyterian system, but it laid the foundation for it, and presbyterianism developed in Switzerland, Germany, France, the Netherlands, and elsewhere. On the continent the name "Reformed" is used for these churches.

Another important development in Geneva took place in a congregation of exiles from Queen Mary's England. They met under their elected pastors, John Knox and Christopher Goodman, and developed along presbyterian lines. After the accession of Elizabeth, Knox returned to Scotland, and his work led in time to the full emergence of the Presbyterian Church in that country, from where it spread to northern Ireland. England for a number of reasons did not accept presbyterianism as wholeheartedly as did Scotland, but a presbyterian church emerged there also. From this church Welsh presbyterianism took its origin. From Europe, more particularly from Britain, the church spread to America, where it became one of the most significant groups of Christians. In the great missionary movement of modern times missionaries carried the presbyterian form of the church far and wide, and national presbyterian churches were formed in many parts of the world.

Presbyterian churches are independent of one another, but they have in common that they accept such standards as the Belgic Confession, the Heidelberg Catechism, or the Westminster Confession and that they practice a presbyterial form of church government. The local congregation elects its "session," which governs its affairs. It is led by the minister, the "teaching elder," who is chosen and called by the congregation. He is, however, ordained by the presbytery, which consists of the teaching and ruling elders from a group of congregations over which it exercises jurisdiction. Above it is a General Assembly. In all courts parity between teaching and ruling elders is important. There has been a tendency for smaller bodies of presbyterians to appear among those who are dissatisfied with the laxity (as they see it) in the way some of the larger churches hold to classic presbyterianism.

Congregationalism. As the name implies, this puts the emphasis on the place of the congregation. Perhaps it would not be unfair to say that the chief scriptural buttresses of this position are the facts that Christ is the head of his church (Col. 1:18, etc.) and that there is a priesthood of all believers (I Pet. 2:9). It is fundamental to NT teaching that Christ has not left his church. He is the living Lord among his people. Where but two or three are gathered in his name, he is in the midst. Nor is it any less fundamental that the way into the very holiest of all presences is open to the humblest believer (Heb. 10:19–20). Other religions of the first century required the interposition of a priestly caste if anyone wished to approach God, but the Christians would have none of this. Christ's priestly work has done away with the necessity for any earthly priest as the mediator of access to God. Added to this is the emphasis on the local congregation in the NT. There, it is maintained, we see autonomous congregations, not subject to episcopal or presbyterial control. The apostles, it is true, exercise a certain authority, but it is the authority of founders of churches and of the Lord's own apostles. After their death there was no divinely instituted apostolate to take their place. Instead the local congregations were still self-governing, as we see from local church orders like the Didache. Appeal is also made to the democratic principle. The NT makes it clear that Christians are all one in Christ and there is no room for any absolute human authority.

Congregationalism as a system appeared after the Reformation. Some among the Reformed decisively rejected the idea of a state church and saw believers as forming a "gathered church," those who have heard the call of Christ and have responded. An Englishman, Robert Browne, published in Holland a famous treatise, "Reformation Without Tarrying for Any" (1582), in which he affirmed the principle of the gathered church, its independence of bishops and magistrates, and its right to ordain its ministers. Denied the freedom to put all this into practice in England, many crossed into Holland. It was from the church at Leiden that the Pilgrim fathers sailed for America in 1620 and established congregationalism in the new world, where it became very important.

Congregationalism is much wider than the church that bears the name. Baptists, for example, usually have congregational polity. They see the local congregation as independent and not subject to any outside authority. So is it with several other denominations. In addition there are Christians who from time to time set up their own congregations with no links with anyone. Congregationalists generally oppose creedal tests. This leads to an admirable toleration. But it also opens up the way to a distortion of NT Christianity, and some congregationalists have passed over into unitarianism. Nevertheless congregationalism remains a widely held form of Christianity, and it undeniably points to important NT values.

Conclusion. A consideration of all the evidence leaves us with the conclusion that it is impossible to read back any of our modern systems into the apostolic age. If we are determined to shut our eyes to all that conflicts with our own system we may find it there, but scarcely otherwise. It is better to recognize that in the NT church there were elements that were capable of being developed into the episcopal, presbyterian, and congregational systems and which in point of fact have so developed. But while there is no reason that any modern Christian should not hold fast to his particular church polity and rejoice in the values it secures to him, that does not give him license to unchurch others whose reading of the evidence is different. L. MORRIS

See also CHURCH, AUTHORITY IN; CHURCH OFFICERS.

Bibliography. R. W. Dale, *Manual of Congregational Principles;* E. Hatch, *The Organization of the Early Christian Churches;* K. E. Kirk, ed., *The Apostolic Ministry;* J. B. Lightfoot, "The Christian Ministry," *Commentary on Philippians;* T. W. Manson, *The Church's Ministry;* J. Moffatt, *The Presbyterian Church;* J. N. Ogilvie, *The Presbyterian Churches of Christendom;* B. H. Streeter, *The Primitive Church;* H. B. Swete, ed., *Essays on the Early History of the Church and Ministry;* W. Telfer, *The Office of a Bishop.*

Church Growth Movement. The church of Jesus Christ has grown enormously. From 120 on the day of Pentecost to more than a billion souls in 1982, and from a small band of believers to great companies of Christians, the church has grown tremendously. It has also grown unevenly. In places it remains static for generations. In places it declines. Many denominations in the United States in the last few years have declined. The missionary movement, cresting in the early decades of the twentieth century, produced a tremendous surge of church growth in some regions of the world, but large areas remain non-Christian. The modern Church Growth Movement must be seen against that background.

The modern Church Growth Movement was caused by theological convictions. The Bible teaches that all children of God, of whatever race or religion, language or culture, are lost until they believe on and follow Jesus Christ. God wants his lost children found. Jesus commanded his followers to preach the gospel to all and to disciple *panta ta ethnē*—all the peoples, classes, tribes, and other segments of society. All must be discipled (enrolled) in his body, the church. After declaring that he has become all things to all men that he might save some, the apostle Paul says, "Be imitators of me as I am of Christ." Denying oneself and making every effort to save men and women is essential Christian behavior. This conviction underlies the modern Church Growth Movement.

True, the growth of the church will produce more members. They will give more, build more beautiful sanctuaries, and pay their ministers more. But none of these are good reasons for church growth. The good reasons are Christ's commands and example to seek and save the lost. While Christians are properly concerned with the physical man, the Bible is clear that salvation is an infinitely greater good than a full belly or a warm bed. The Church Growth Movement is driven by a conviction that heaven, even if to get there entails being eaten by lions in the Colosseum, is preferable to hell after living a comfortable life.

Furthermore, the Bible is clear that if we want brotherhood, equality, and justice in the world, there is no surer way of getting it than to lead multitudes to become spirit-filled followers of Jesus Christ. The kingdom of God is not an ethical paradise in which men of every philosophy and shade of opinion gather. The kingdom of God first and foremost is that nation in which all citizens believe in Jesus Christ the King. As a result, the kingdom exhibits far more kindness, mercy, justice, and brotherhood than any association of unconverted men and women. Multitudes must become followers of Christ. The Church Growth Movement has been built on biblical bedrock.

Origin. The Church Growth Movement was conceived when Donald McGavran, missionary to India, noticed that though thousands of missionaries were doing a tremendous amount of good work—feeding the hungry, teaching the ignorant, healing the sick, caring for victims of leprosy, rearing orphans, and sheltering refugees—most missionaries were seeing little church growth in their areas. Many were seeing none at all. They might be all things to all men, but they were not winning some.

As McGavran studied the districts where many were being saved and churches were multiplying, and districts where a single nongrowing congregation continued for decades, a vast curiosity arose within him. Why do churches grow and multiply? Why do they stagnate and decline? He made this his life study. He studied it in the towns and districts where his mission worked, and in those where other missions labored. He journeyed to Kenya, Rwanda, the Belgian Congo, Nigeria, the Gold Coast, and to Jamaica, Thailand, Mexico, Puerto Rico, Japan, Orissa, and the Philippines to study church growth there. Out of this wide experience, firm convictions were formed as to why churches grow and do not grow.

After twenty-six years studying and working at church growth, in January of 1961 McGavran established the Institute of Church Growth at Northwest Christian College in Eugene, Oregon. The modern Church Growth Movement was born in 1961. At Winona Lake, Indiana, in September of that year, he spoke to the executives of the Evangelical Foreign Missions Association, and an annual Church Growth Seminar at Winona Lake was established. During the next ten years more than one thousand career missionaries attended this and went away resolving to carry on missions in order to bring the multitudes to believe in Christ and become practicing members of his church.

In the spring of 1965 Fuller Theological Seminary determined to start a Graduate School of World Mission and called McGavran to be the founding dean of the school. He was commissioned to recruit faculty. In four years he called Alan Tippett, Ralph Winter, Charles Kraft, J. Edwin Orr, Arthur Glasser, and C. Peter Wagner. They added valuable dimensions to the study of effective evangelism, which is church growth. In 1970 appeared *Understanding Church Growth,* the definitive book on church growth.

Church Growth in America. In 1971 C. Peter Wagner conceived the idea that church growth was desperately needed in the United States also. He recruited twenty pastors and eminent laymen of the area for a regular seminary class on church growth. He asked McGavran to teach half the sessions. Out of that creative move came the conviction that church growth was not only greatly needed but was eagerly grasped by pastors in America.

Out of that group also came two other developments. First, Win Arn established the Institute of American Church Growth and was soon holding church growth seminars all across America. Second, there arose in the Fuller Evangelistic Association a determination to push American church growth as a most needed aspect of effective evangelism in North America.

The School of World Mission required all degree candidates to produce theses and dissertations (original researches in church growth in the nations where these missionaries worked). The best of these were published and spoke to specific situations in Japan, Korea, Taiwan, the Philippines, Indonesia, India, Pakistan, Africa, Latin America, Brazil, and other regions of the globe. Each book reached a different group of readers. Each therefore touched with the magic wand of church growth a new set of pastors, missionaries, national leaders, mission executives, and professors of mission.

Methods. The world is a vast mosaic made up of tens of thousands of different pieces. The church grows differently in every piece. The gospel must be proclaimed in many different languages and cultural settings. The abilities of the proclaimers vary enormously. Some are illiterate tribesmen. Some are college graduates from affluent lands. Some are welcomed, some rejected. Some missionaries stay for a year, some for a lifetime. Some pastors spend all their time in their study or calling on the saints. Others spend half their time seeking the lost. Differences are multitudinous. Each piece requires a different method.

Consequently, it is not possible in any brief article to set forth all the methods of church growth. What can be done is to indicate a few ways of acting which God has blessed to the increase of his church. Of the hundreds, only seven will be mentioned.

(1) It is essential to measure and see exactly what is happening. How many lost are being found? In what section of society is the church stagnant and in what growing? To what unreached people is God calling his church to rescue the perishing?

(2) Mankind is a vast mosaic and it is crucial to view it in this way. The particular piece being evangelized needs to be understood well. Is it Jewish or Gentile? Of this class or that? Proud and resistant, or open and receptive?

(3) The message must be contextualized—spoken in the language and thought process of that unit of mankind.

(4) The congregation formed grows best if it is of one people. The church is a place to feel at home. For example, a few Hispanics may join English-speaking congregations, but many more will obey Christ's call if they can join Hispanic churches.

(5) An important strategy is winning close relatives and friends. Andrew went and found his brother—Simon. The gospel flows fastest along lines of relationship.

(6) It is helpful to set goals. Denominations which set out to double in twenty years are much more likely to do it than those which set no goals.

(7) It is vital to enlist at least some of the laity in purposeful evangelism. God has given to many gifts of evangelism. They should be encouraged to use these.

Continuous Expansion. The Church Growth Movement has far outgrown its humble beginnings on the West Coast of America. New congregations and denominations catch the vision.

The Holy Spirit says to this Christian and to that: "Wake your sleeping comrades. Look on the fields. They are white to harvest. Go. Bring in the sheaves." Canada, England, Scandinavia, Kenya, Guatemala, the Philippines, North Ireland, and many more suddenly hear the call and surge out to find and fold the lost, multiply new companies of the redeemed, new cells of the body.

The coming decades, if the Lord tarry, will be the most fruitful the church has ever seen. Three billion souls await the gospel. Our Lord commands, "Go! Disciple all the peoples." Obeying that command is church growth.

D. A. McGAVRAN

See also MISSIOLOGY.

Bibliography. M. Watkins, *Literacy, Bible Reading, and Church Growth;* J. W. Pickett *et al., Church Growth and Group Conversion; Church Growth Bulletin;* A. R. Tygsett, *Church Growth and the Word of God;* D. A. McGavran, *Understanding Church Growth, How Churches Grow,* and (ed.), *Church Growth and Christian Mission;* J. Morikawa, *Biblical Dimensions of Church Growth;* E. Gibbs, *I Believe in Church Growth;* M. Harper, *Let My People Grow;* D. A. McGavran and W. Arn, *Ten Steps to Church Growth;* C. P. Wagner, *Church Growth and the Whole Gospel* and *Your Church Can Grow;* A. F. Glasser and D. A. McGavran, *Contemporary Theologies of Mission.*

Church of Christ, Scientist. An organization founded by Mary Baker Eddy in an effort to reinstate primitive Christianity and its lost element of healing. In 1876 Eddy formed the Christian Scientists Association and three years later chartered the Church of Christ, Scientist. The church was reorganized into its present form in 1892. The First Church of Christ, Scientist, of Boston is known as the mother church, and other Christian Science churches are considered branches, although each is independently governed. The tenets and bylaws of the church were incorporated by Eddy into the church manual of 1895. The church's fundamental theological teachings are presented in Eddy's *Science and Health with Key to the Scriptures.*

Theologically, the Church of Christ, Scientist, does not concur with the basic tenets of historic orthodox Christianity. Although it uses the theological vocabulary of traditional Christianity, it assigns metaphysical meanings to the terms. The sources of authority for the church are the Bible and Eddy's writings. Members accept Eddy's writings as divine revelation and interpret the Bible allegorically through her works. The most significant authority for the church is *Science and Health,* which was published in 1875 and regularly revised until Eddy's death in 1910. Eddy referred to this volume as containing the perfect word of God, and thus was divine and infallible teaching.

Christian Science's view of God is monistic. God is divine principle, not a supreme being. God is mind, and mind is all. Nothing possesses reality or exists which is not mind. The characteristics and attributes of God become God. The Trinity is constituted by the threefold nature of divine principle (God): life, truth, and love. God, Christ, and Holy Spirit are not persons. The Christology of Christian Science denies a physical incarnation of Christ and insists Mary conceived Christ only as a spiritual idea. Since God is mind and spirit, and nothing exists which is not spirit, there can be no matter or flesh; these are only illusions. Thus Christ did not possess a body and did not die on a cross. The need of an atonement is nullified since sin, evil, sickness, and death are delusions, not reality. God is good, and nothing can exist which is not good. Christian Science teaches man is created in God's image as spirit, mind, and good; thus man is incapable of sin, sickness, and death. Man is placed on a plane of equality with God in his origin, character, and eternity. The metaphysical presuppositions of the church insist that heaven and hell are present states of man's thoughts, not real future dwelling places.

Christian Science church services are simple and uniform worldwide. They focus upon the uniform lesson-sermons which are read aloud from the Bible and *Science and Health* by readers elected from the congregation. There is no clergy or priesthood. The sacraments are not special rites. Baptism means the spiritual purification of daily life and the Eucharist is silent spiritual communion with God. No visible elements are used. Salvation to the Christian Scientist is the gaining of the understanding that man's life is wholly derived from God the Spirit, and is not mortal and material.

P. G. CHAPPELL

See also EDDY, MARY BAKER.

Bibliography. C. S. Braden, *Christian Science Today;* E. M. Ramsay, *Christian Science and Its Discoverer;* L. P. Powell, *Christian Science, the Faith and Its Founder;* R. Peel, *Christian Science: Its Encounter with American Culture;* E. S. Bates and J. V. Dittemore, *Mrs. Eddy, the Truth and the Tradition.*

Church Officers. ***Archbishop.*** One who presides over a "province" in the Church of England or the Roman Church. A province is a geographical area in which a number of dioceses are grouped together for administrative purposes: the bishop of the chief see or archdiocese is termed the archbishop or metropolitan. The term, derived from the Roman Empire, dates from *ca.* A.D. 350. (Derivations: Gr. *archi,* "chief," and *episkopos,* "overseer, bishop.")

Archdeacon. A cleric who exercises delegated administrative authority under a bishop. The duties are of a general disciplinary character; they also include a particular responsibility for the temporal property of the church. Originally, an archdeacon was the chief of the deacons who assisted the bishop (hence the name *oculus et manus episcopi*). The office has occasionally carried the right of succession.

Archpriest. The term describes a priest who occupies a position of preeminence, e.g., the senior priest of a city. An archpriest in the early church often performed liturgical and administrative duties during the absence of the bishop. At a later date the archdeacon was responsible for administrative functions and the archpriest for sacerdotal. In the Roman Church and Eastern Orthodoxy the title is essentially an honorific one.

Auxiliary Bishop. In the early church the bishop was the leader of the local Christian community. With the growth of churches and the formation of geographical groups of churches into dioceses it became necessary for the responsibilities of spiritual oversight and episcopal ministry to be shared. Various titles have been used to describe the bishops created for this role, such as assistant, auxiliary, coadjutor, and suffragan, and each of these has its own significance. The term "auxiliary" is most commonly used in the Roman Catholic Church on both sides of the Atlantic and, unlike "coadjutor," carries with it no implications of succession.

Bishop. In NT times the leader of a congregation was called a bishop or elder. Very soon the two became separate offices and the bishop became the chief pastor ruling over several churches in one geographical area. During the Reformation some of the newly formed Protestant churches abandoned the title of bishop and reverted to the title of elder. Bishops of large or important areas are called variously pope, patriarch, metropolitan, and archbishop.

Canon. A member of the chapter of a cathedral. Appointment is by either nomination or election. "Residentiary canons" form part of the salaried staff of a cathedral and have general responsibility for the maintenance of services, the care of the fabric, etc. "Nonresidentiary" canons (or honorary canons) are unsalaried but enjoy certain privileges, including a cathedral stall. The title derives from the fact that in the Middle Ages chapters were usually composed of clergy living under a rule (canon) of life.

Cardinal. In the Roman Catholic Church the cardinals rank immediately after the pope and, when assembled in consistory, act as his immediate counselors. When a vacancy occurs they meet in secret session to elect a pope. There are three ranks: cardinal-priests, cardinal-deacons, and cardinal-bishops.

Coadjutor Bishop. A bishop who assists the diocesan bishop to administer and serve the diocese. In the Roman Catholic Church since Vatican Council II the coadjutor bishop always has the right of succession whereas an auxiliary bishop does not. This custom is not necessarily the case in Anglicanism. The coadjutor is a true bishop in every sense (rightly ordained with the power to ordain), but he needs the permission of the diocesan bishop to act in the diocese.

Curate. Originally a clergyman who had the "cure" of souls; today a clergyman (either deacon or priest) who assists a parochial clergyman. Curate is the term popularly used to describe an assistant or unbeneficed clergyman.

Deacon, Deaconess. An office in the early church that emphasized service, modeled on a similar office in the Jewish synagogue. Deacons and deaconesses were to free the apostles for other works of ministry (Acts 6:1–6). Their qualifications are mentioned in I Tim. 3:8–13, and women were admitted to this order (Rom. 16:1; I Tim. 3:11).

Dean. The head of a cathedral church ranking immediately after the bishop. He presides over the chapter and is responsible for the ordering and government of the cathedral. The title is also used in a nonecclesiastical sense, e.g., the dean of a college or the dean of a faculty.

Elder. A leader of the NT church, synonymous with bishop in the early period; his function was to rule the church for the spiritual good of the people. A congregation could have more than one elder. The qualifications for elder are found in Titus 1:5–9.

Metropolitan. The title of a bishop exercising provincial, and not merely diocesan, powers. The title first appears in the fourth canon of the Council of Nicaea (325). Metropolitans are commonly called archbishops or primates.

Moderator. In the Presbyterian Church the moderator is the presbyter or elder who presides over a presbytery, synod, or General Assembly. He has only a casting vote. He is *primus inter pares* and holds office for a limited period (generally one year).

Patriarch. A title (dating from the sixth century) for the bishops of the five chief sees: Rome, Alexandria, Antioch, Constantinople, and Jerusalem.

Prebendary. The occupant of a cathedral benefice. The title dates from the Middle Ages, when "prebends" were usually endowed from the revenue of various cathedral estates. The title has generally been superseded by that of "canon."

Presbyter. Another name for elder.

Rector. Historically, a rector, as distinguished from a vicar, is a parish incumbent whose tithes are not impropriate. With the commutation of tithes this distinction no longer exists. The title is used in Scotland for the head of a school and in Europe for the secular head of a university. It is also the title for the head of a Jesuit house.

Rural Dean. The title for the clergyman who is appointed by a bishop as head of a group of parishes. The rural dean acts as a link between the bishop and the clergy, but his functions have been increasingly overshadowed and superseded by those of the archdeacon.

Suffragan Bishop. The term may be applied to bishops in two main senses. First, all diocesan bishops are suffragans when they join with the archbishop or metropolitan in synod and cast their "suffrage." Second, and more generally, assistants to diocesan bishops are described as suffragans.

Superintendent. In the Church of Scotland superintendents were first appointed under the *First Book of Discipline* (1560) to oversee various territorial districts. While enjoying a certain measure of superiority, they are subject to the control and censure of the other ministers associated with them. In the Lutheran Church there are also superintendents, but in the Scandinavian churches the title "bishop" is retained. The term is also found in some Methodist churches.

Vicar. In medieval times, when a church was appropriated to a monastery, the revenue was paid to the monastery, and a monk was employed to perform the duties of the parish. Later, a secular priest, called a vicar (Lat. *vicarius,* "a substitute"), was employed. Today, the vicar is simply the incumbent of a parish with the same status and duties as a rector. S. B. BABBAGE

See also CARDINAL; PATRIARCH; MINISTER; CLERGY; MINOR ORDERS; MAJOR ORDERS; ORDERS, HOLY; ORDAIN, ORDINATION; BISHOP; DEACON, DEACONESS; ELDER; PAPACY; CHURCH GOVERNMENT.

Church of Jesus Christ of Latter-day Saints. *See* MORMONISM.

Circumcision. An operation performed on the male organ of propagation for the removal of the foreskin. Although practiced also among other nations, within Israel circumcision has a distinct meaning. As a sign of the covenant with Abraham (Gen. 17:11) it partakes of the characteristics of this covenant. It appears capable of a progressive deepening of import and teaches ethical and spiritual truth. The external rite, whose observance is strictly enjoined (Gen. 17:12ff.; Exod. 4:24ff.; Josh. 5:2ff.), ought to be the sign of an internal change, effected by God (Deut. 10:16; 30:6). The uncircumcised as well as the unclean are barred from the "holy city" (Isa. 52:1; cf. Ezek. 44:7, 9). Humility and acceptance of God's punishment are to take the place of the uncircumcised heart before God will restore his covenant (Lev. 26:41).

The NT echoes this teaching and brings it to its completion. Circumcision being a sign of the righteousness of faith (Rom. 4:10–11) and having lost its relevance for justification through Christ's coming (Gal. 5:6), no NT believer can be compelled to submit to it (Acts 15:3–21; cf. Gal. 2:3). In the light of this NT fulfillment circumcision now applies equally to Jewish and Gentile Christians alike (Phil. 3:3) since in the "circumcision of Christ" all those who are baptized have put off the body of the flesh (Col. 2:11–12).

M. H. WOUDSTRA

See also ISRAEL, THE NEW.

Bibliography. G. Vos, *Biblical Theology;* F. Sierksma, "Quelques remarques sur la circoncision en Israël," *OTS* 9:136–69; H. C. Hahn, *NIDNTT,* I, 307ff.; R. Meyer, *TDNT,* VI, 72ff.; J. B. Payne, *The Theology of the Older Testament.*

Civil Disobedience. An intentional act that is prohibited by the civil authority or a refusal to perform an act that is required by the civil authority. Civil disobedience may be carried out by an individual or a group, and it may be directed at a very specific issue or more generally at the governing authorities. Illegal meetings, speeches, publications and demonstrations, sit-ins at racially segregated establishments during the civil rights movement, refusal to register for the military draft, and refusal to surrender personal or financial records to the state—these are all examples of civil disobedience. While violence technically may be a form of civil disobedience, discussions of the topic usually are restricted to the range of actions from passive noncooperation to nonviolent resistance.

For Christian theology and ethics the problem of civil disobedience is raised by two facts. First, Christians are called to an unqualified obedience to their Lord and God (Deut. 13:4; Jer. 7:23; John 14:15). Second, Christians are called to submit to the governing authorities and to recognize that, even where the civil authority is not Christian, God uses (or can use) it as his servant for good (cf. Rom. 13:1–7; I Pet. 2:13–17). Civil disobedience becomes an issue when these two claims come into conflict, i.e., when God commands us to do something which the civil authority prohibits or the civil authority commands us to do something which God prohibits.

That the conflict is real and that civil disobedience may be a Christian option is acknowledged by much of the church throughout history and, most importantly, by the Bible itself. Daniel's illegal prayer (Dan. 6), Peter's illegal preaching (Acts 5:27–32), and Paul's refusal to leave his prison cell as ordered (Acts 16:35–40) are but three examples of biblical civil disobedience. Prominent examples in the history of the church would include illegal preaching and assembly, illegal printing and dissemination of

Scripture, refusal to take oaths, refusal of military service, refusal to baptize children, refusal to worship the emperor, and violation of racially segregationist laws.

While the basic principle is clear—"We must obey God rather than men" (Acts 5:29)—careful discernment is necessary to distinguish a biblically warranted occasion for civil disobedience from a mere rationalization of illegal protest growing out of other motives and interests. Rigorous and prayerful searching of the Word of God must be accompanied by careful analysis of the sociopolitical situation. While individual conscience is finally responsible before God, great emphasis must be placed on the church as a community of moral discernment and support. The burden of proof falls on individuals who deviate from the consensus of a praying, biblically informed community.

The clearest indication for civil disobedience has always been an overt conflict between civil authority and the central tasks of discipleship: prayer and worship together in the presence of God, proclamation of the gospel in all its dimensions, and the various tasks of healing (Mark 3:14–15; Luke 9:1–2). The Ten Commandments, the message of the prophets on God's justice, the Sermon on the Mount, and the apostolic teaching on the social implications of the gospel are other essential sources for a clear perception of the command of God which supersedes all other commands.

If it becomes apparent that there is a real conflict between the demands of biblical justice and love and the demands of the state, and if all available legal avenues of reform are exhausted, then civil disobedience may be warranted. And while Christians are ruled by the call to faithfulness much more than the call to measurable effectiveness, civil disobedience probably should be avoided if its practice is likely to produce, directly or indirectly, an increase in repression or injustice for others.

Finally, the choice of tactics must receive careful attention. What are the means appropriate to the end that is sought? The range of options runs from passive noncooperation to more active obstruction, demonstration, and nonviolent resistance. Beyond this range some would argue that sabotage, destruction of property, and even violent revolt may on occasion be warranted. The critical factor from the standpoint of Christian theology and ethics is to recognize the indissoluble link between means and end. The means affect the character of the end and thus should exhibit as much as possible the character of the desired end (peace, justice, truthfulness, etc.). Godly ends are achieved by godly means.

Those who are led to engage in civil disobedience must remain humble and rigorously self-critical. Many Christians would also argue that while disobedience is possible, insubordination is not. This means that during and after the disobedience the practitioners should remain subordinate to the penalties and consequences meted out by the civil authority (jail, punishment, exile, etc.) and/or flee rather than attempt to evade these consequences by direct, violent overthrow of the superordinate powers.

D. W. Gill

See also Social Ethics.

Bibliography. J. Childress, *Civil Disobedience and Political Obligation;* S. C. Mott, *Biblical Ethics and Social Change,* ch. 8; D. B. Stevick, *Civil Disobedience and the Christian.*

Civil Law and Justice in Bible Times. The discussion of any aspect of law in the OT must come, sooner or later, to Lev. 19, a microcosm of the whole legal principle of Scripture. From the point of view of this present article, the testimony of Lev. 19 is that, while civil law in the OT is expressed in enactments appropriate to its purposes, it is not to be distinguished in principle from any of the other commandments of God, domestic, moral, ceremonial, or personal. Lev. 19 seems to be almost designedly without pattern or structure; it sweeps together into one place rules and directives of every kind. A principle of kindness (vs. 14) lies between one of commercial honesty (vs. 13) and integrity in justice (vs. 15); sexual purity (vs. 20), sound husbandry (vs. 23), the avoidance of pagan religious practice (vss. 26–28), family honor (vs. 29), sabbath keeping (vs. 30), respect for the aged (vs. 32) and for the immigrant (vs. 33) all seem to be on the same level—and essentially they are, for all alike arise from one common consideration, "I am the Lord."

What is thus true in Lev. 19 is capable of wide illustration in the OT. To Amos, social violence (3:10) and personal self-indulgence (3:15) are alike "transgressions" for which the Lord will "visit" (3:14) and are alike offenses against his holiness (4:2). The law of the Lord is one law, and the legal procedure and principles of jurisprudence are, within their own sphere, manifestations of the holy nature of the Lord who gave them. It is important for us to realize this lest we should think that what was enacted for a time and a society so seemingly different from our own has no testimony to bear to us or no word of direction for the present day.

Forms and Procedures. The development of legal procedures in the OT partakes of the distinctive nature of biblical progression of truth whereby nothing is lost en route but old truth is caught up and perpetuated by the newer truth which followed on.

The Patriarchal Period. There is no record of

law throughout the period of Abraham, Isaac, and Jacob, though incidents like the transaction over the cave of Machpelah (Gen. 23) and the status of the servant Eliezer as Abram's adopted son (Gen. 15:3) reflect norms and forms known from outside the Bible. We may suppose that Noahic covenantal law with its prescription of the death penalty would have remained in force, but the only misdemeanor occurring in the narratives is sexual: the perverted sexual life of Sodom (Gen. 19), the lie told by Isaac about Rebekah (26:7), the "folly" of 34:7, and the "sin against God" of 39:9. Gen. 38, dealing with the same area of misconduct, reveals that justice was dispensed by a family court convened by the head of the family to whom the offense had to be reported and who pronounced sentence. The same incident shows that such justice was not arbitrary but according to the facts received in evidence.

The Mosaic Settlement. Circumstances compelled Moses to decentralize the administration of justice (Exod. 18:13–26), and he did so in a far-reaching fashion, right down to what must have been a minor rank of officials (rulers of tens, vs. 25). Possibly it was at this point that the older system of family justice was interleaved with the newer procedures, leaving the head of the family to continue as the first tier of judicial administration.

Moses made provision for lower and higher courts (Exod. 18:26), and it is plain that this practice continued even though details of procedure are not stated. Thus, in Deut. 22:28–29 it seems to be the father of the family who enforces the prescribed penalty, whereas in vss. 13–21 he brings the case to the elders. Above the court of the elders was that of the priests (Deut. 17:8–13). During his lifetime Moses was the supreme court, and it may be that the special place given to the high priest in cases of murder and manslaughter (Num. 35:25, etc.) indicates that Moses envisaged the high priest would become the supreme court for the post-Mosaic period—or, possibly, the high priest in conjunction with some sort of national tribunal as expressed by the word "congregation" in Num. 35:24.

Under the Monarchy. The period covered by Judg. 1–I Sam. 12 was plainly one in which the simplicity of the earlier provisions for the maintenance and execution of justice were proving insufficient for the growing complexity of life within the twelve-tribe confederacy. The scintillating charismatic figures of the judges achieved no more than limited stability and security for the people. The recurring refrain that "the land had rest for . . . years" (e.g., Judg. 5:31; 8:28) is more a confession of failure than anything else. Within the testimony of the book of Judges it is part of the evidence that another form of government, productive of enduring benefits, was required (cf. 17:6; 18:1; 19:1; 21:25). Even in the case of Samuel this was so. His achievements were great, including a national revival of religion (I Sam. 7:2ff.), but his area of administrative control was comparatively circumscribed (7:15–17) and the attempt to introduce his sons as deputies was a disaster (8:1–4). There is nothing, therefore, to counter the revelation given in Judges that the land was in religious (17:1–13), social (18:1–31), moral, and political (19:1–21:25) disarray—a situation which, as Judges saw it, only monarchy could remedy.

The eldership continued through the period of the judges (Judg. 8:16; 11:5; 21:16) and of Samuel (I Sam. 4:3; 8:4), into the monarchies of Saul (I Sam. 16:4; 30:26), David (II Sam. 17:4; 19:11), Solomon (I Kings 8:1), and the divided kingdoms (I Kings 21:8; II Kings 23:1). On to this the kings superimposed a palace-based bureaucracy (II Sam. 8:15–18; I Kings 4:1–6) and, at least in the case of Solomon, a new administrative division of the land (I Kings 4:7–19). Some, possibly overmuch, of the administration of justice remained directly in the king's own hand (cf. I Kings 3:28). Absalom was able to make a good deal of headway for his rebellion because of the inefficiency of the royal courts (II Sam. 15:1–6). And even as late as King Zedekiah (Jer. 38:7) it appears that the causes of the tribes came before the royal court.

Principles of Jurisprudence. *The Lex Talionis.* The basic principle of OT jurisprudence was absolute equity, enunciated in the striking and memorable form "an eye for an eye and a tooth for a tooth." This is often unthinkingly criticized as if it were a license for savagery, but reflection establishes that its intention was to secure as exact an equation as is humanly possible between crime and punishment.

The law is stated three times. The first statement (Exod. 21:23) simply requires that equity must govern all court practice; indeed, words could not make the great principle of equivalence clearer. The second statement (Lev. 24:19–20) adds that the rule of equity applies to all alike, alien as well as nativeborn. The third (Deut. 19:19–21) goes further by claiming that this absolutely equal apportionment of justice promotes a wholesome society and acts as an effective deterrent. Far from being a charter for excess, the *lex talionis* guards the rights of the guilty (who must not be punished beyond their deserts) as much as it maintains the dignity of the law. Far from being a piece of ancient barbarism, it should still apply—and God help the state, ancient or modern, where it does not.

The Death Penalty and Theories of Punishment. The OT, then, insists that the punishment must match the crime, no more, no less. In this way earthly courts seek to reproduce the absolute justice of the God of Israel. For, ideally considered, coming before the courts was coming before God (Exod. 22:8; Deut. 19:17), and the legal process was meant to be one aspect of the obedience-blessing/disobedience-cursing syndrome which the OT teaches to be the Lord's providential order in the whole course of history. In his law the Lord has testified to his own nature, and the upholding of the dignity of the law is a duty in honor of God.

The clearest example the OT affords of the working of the *lex talionis* was that "life shall go for life." The case for the death penalty is not argued: there is a special seriousness in the crime of murder in that a particular despite is done to the image of God in man (Gen. 9:6) and the principle of equity must be invoked. Can anything else vindicate the law in the face of this violation, when life is arrogantly and highhandedly taken by murder?

The OT does not seem to say anything about punishment as reformative of the criminal, though Lev. 26:23 reveals that the Lord is moved by a reformatory impulse in punishing his people, and Deut. 4:36 (using the same verb) teaches that the giving of the law had itself a reformatory aim. But reformation is not developed in the OT as a theory of punishment. On the other hand, the purging of society and the deterrence of other potential offenders are both taken into account (e.g., Lev. 20:14; Deut. 13:5, 11; 17:7; 19:19–20). But these ends are not achieved by punishments either of obvious leniency or of notable severity but by the steady application of the *lex talionis:* the apportionment to each crime of its due reward. To purge society and to deter others are by-products of the retribution theory of punishment which the OT affirms.

We have no evidence other than in the case of the death penalty about the application in detail of the principle of equivalence. The OT recognized a practice of commuting punishments and of substituting monetary fines. Ordinarily the principle of the *lex talionis* would have been safeguarded by the payment of carefully assessed damages to the offended party (e.g., Exod. 21:19, 22, 33–34; 22:1–15). Likewise the OT took note of degrees of murder (e.g., Exod. 21:13) and provided cities of refuge for cases of manslaughter (Num. 35:9–15; Deut. 19:1–13). Yet, even so, the city of refuge was not a soft option: the closeness of the city-arrest (Num. 35:26–28) and the continuing threat that the "avenger" would exact his penalty indicate the sense of moral outrage with which the OT viewed even unintentional taking of life.

The Value of the Person. The cry of the defenseless has often gone unheard in every society at every period of history, but it is doubtful if there was ever a legal system which, in its intention, was so committed to protecting people from injustice and repression. The prophets were outraged when the upright figure of Justice was made to lie prone and when sectional, influential interests used the forms of legality to secure personal ends (cf. I Kings 21:17ff.; Isa. 5:8–10; Amos 8:4ff.). The messianic forecast of the perfect king stressed his concern for the needy (e.g., Ps. 72:2–4, 12–14; Isa. 11:4). This was doubtless in contrast to many a Davidic ruler, yet it ever held up to such the ideal inherent in his office. As ever in the Bible, this concern for the needy had a theological basis: according to Deut. 10:17–19 the God of Israel, who knows no favoritism and is not open to bribes, reaches out specially to the helpless and in this is to be imitated by his people.

In this same spirit the OT forbids favoritism and insists on even-handed justice (e.g., Exod. 23:3; Lev. 19:15). To foster this Moses extended the legal system down to the family unit (rulers of tens) so as to make justice available to all. He insisted on integrity on the judicial bench (Deut. 16:18–20); he established rules of evidence (Num. 35:30; Deut. 17:6; 19:15); he regulated punishment so as to preserve the personal dignity of the guilty; he insisted that the law should take its course in a humane way (Exod. 22:25–27); and, more than any other legislator, he concerned himself with the protection of women—the slave girl (Exod. 21:7–11), the female prisoner of war (Deut. 21:10–14), the "hated" wife (Deut. 21:15–17), and even the extraordinary rules for the case of husbandly suspicion (Num. 5:11–31) where, surely, the ceremony was devised to favor the suspected wife. Just as the OT shows that when law is flouted love evaporates, so also it insists that without law love is not liberated to flourish and, furthermore, that law itself must be infilled with love if it is to reflect the character of the God in whose name it was administered. J. A. MOTYER

See also CRIMINAL LAW AND PUNISHMENT IN BIBLE TIMES; LAW, BIBLICAL CONCEPT OF; CAPITAL PUNISHMENT.

Bibliography. J. A. Motyer, *Law and Life* and *The Image of God: Law and Liberty in Biblical Ethics;* O. O'Donovan, *Measure for Measure: Justice in Punishment and the Sentence of Death;* B. N. Kaye and G. J. Wenham, eds., *Law, Morality and the Bible;* A. Phillips, *Ancient Israel's Criminal Law.*

Civil Religion. Also called civic, public, or political religion, civil religion refers to the widespread acceptance by a people of a body of religio-political traits connected with their nation's history and destiny. It serves to relate their society to the realm of ultimate meaning, enables the self-interpretation of the society, and functions as the integrating symbolism of the nation. It is the "operative religion" of a society (Will Herberg), the system of rituals, symbols, values, norms, and allegiances that function in the ongoing life of the community and provide it with an overarching sense of unity that transcends all internal conflicts and differences. A civil religion is distinctive in that it has reference to power within the state yet transcends that power by focusing on ultimate conditions. Theoretically it gives both the justification for power and a basis for criticizing those who exercise power. "Civil" faith must in some sense be independent of the church as such or it will merely be an ecclesiastical legitimization of the state, and it must be genuinely a "religion" or it will be just secular nationalism (Phillip Hammond). It requires a "civil theology" because this provides the society with meaning and a destiny, interprets the historical experience, and affords a sense of dynamism, uniqueness, and identity (Maureen Henry). Reduced to its bare essentials, civil religion means that the state utilizes a consensus of religious sentiments, concepts, and symbols—either directly or indirectly, consciously or unconsciously—for its own political purposes. Commentators view it as a "general" religious faith and contrast it with the "particular" faith of sectarian or denominational groups which can claim the allegiance of only a segment of the population.

Although the traits commonly associated with civil religion appear as far back as classical antiquity when each Greek *polis* had its own gods, dogmas, and worship, Plato developed the outlines of a civil theology in *The Republic*, and the Roman emperor functioned both as the chief priest in the state cult and as an object of worship, the term was actually coined by Jean Jacques Rousseau in the *Social Contract* (1762). He identified the civil faith as something that could deal with religious diversity and at the same time cement people's allegiance to civil society, thereby achieving and ensuring social peace after the long era of disruptive, religiously inspired wars. It was, however, not until the 1950s and 1960s that civil religion became a major topic of theological discussion. The catalyst that propelled it into the center of scholarly attention was a paper presented by sociologist Robert N. Bellah in 1965 which boldly asserted: "Few have realized that there actually exists alongside of and rather clearly differentiated from the churches an elaborate and well-institutionalized civil religion in America." What followed was a heated debate in academic circles as to the nature of the public faith and whether in fact it even was a valid concept.

The key problem was that of definition, and this continues to be a matter of contention and intense confusion among scholars of civil religion. Russell E. Richey and Donald G. Jones attempted to resolve the difficulty by sketching out five broad, essentially interrelated meanings advanced by various writers, especially ones who treat the American phenomenon. They are (1) folk religion—the common religion that emerges out of the ethos and history of the society and competes with particularistic religion; (2) transcendent universal religion of the nation—a common faith that stands in judgment over the folkways of the people and the nation and as a corrective against idolatrous tendencies in particular forms of Christianity and Judaism; (3) religious nationalism—the nation takes on a sovereign, self-transcendent character and becomes the object of adoration and glorification; (4) the democratic faith—the humane values of equality, freedom, and justice that exist without necessary dependence on a transcendent deity or a spiritualized nation represent civil religion at its best; (5) Protestant civic piety—the fusion of Protestantism and nationalism in the American ethos which is reflected by moralism, individualism, activism, pragmatism, and missionizing the world.

An alternative offered by Martin E. Marty proposes that there are two kinds of civil religion, one that sees an objective, transcendent deity as the reference point for the social process (the nation under God) and the other which stresses national self-transcendence. Within these are two approaches—the "priestly," which is celebrative, affirmative, and culture-building, and the "prophetic," which is dialectical but tends toward the judgmental. In the first category he includes Dwight Eisenhower as priest and Jonathan Edwards, Abraham Lincoln, and Reinhold Niebuhr as prophets. In the national self-transcendent grouping he places Robert Welch, Richard Nixon, and J. Paul Williams as priests and Sidney Mead and Robert Bellah as prophets. Arguing in a totally different direction, John Murray Cuddihy maintained that the American faith is nothing more than "religious civility," a complex code of rites which instructs people in the ways of being religiously inoffensive, tolerant, and sensitive to the beliefs of others. John F. Wilson suggested that the ambiguities of the civil religion debate stem from the "uncritically mixed modes of analysis and the confusion of models by different interpreters," and he delineated four major "constructions," each based on a distinctive set of premises and intellectual traditions. The models are: (1) societal—emphasizes every collectivity or social entity as sacred; (2) cultural—oriented toward analysis of the way in which a particular set of values functions in terms of interaction among the members of a given social order, that is, the symbolic unity and coherence of a society; (3) political—looks at the role of religious behavior and beliefs within a political society; (4) theological—places the content of public religion in an overarching framework of meaning that provides norms for the political order, general culture, and society as a whole.

Although it is obvious that civil religion is an

extremely vague and controversial concept, writers have detected its manifestations in a wide range of countries and societies, especially England, South Africa, Japan, and the United States. Most attention has been paid to the American scene, where a civil religion appeared which allowed the nation to be understood in a transcendent manner while at the same time religious pluralism flourished at the grass-roots level. Since there was a need for common symbols of national purpose which no single church could supply and since people, whether or not they were church members, felt at liberty to use religious symbols, the so-called secular institutions and their personnel occupied a preeminent role in the civil religion. The ideology that underlay this alliance between politics and religion was: (1) there is a God; (2) his will can be known through democratic procedures; (3) America has been God's primary agent in history; and (4) the nation has been the chief source of identity for Americans. They were viewed as God's chosen people who made the exodus to the promised land across the sea and became a city on a hill, a light to the nations, proclaiming the message of democracy as the salvific doctrine that would lead mankind to freedom, prosperity, and happiness. Evidences of the civil faith include the biblical imagery and references to Almighty God and providence that have pervaded the speeches and public documents of American leaders from the very earliest times, the prominent display of the nation's flag in church sanctuaries, the inclusion of "under God" in the Pledge of Allegiance, and above all the national motto: "In God We Trust."

Supporters of civil religion insist that the ideas of transcendence and covenant hold the nation accountable, constitute cement in an otherwise heterogeneous society, challenge the country to fulfill its most noble ideals, and serve as instruments in the hands of wise political leaders (such as Lincoln and Martin Luther King, Jr.) to inspire people to higher levels of achievement. Critics condemn it for idolizing the nation, tempting patriotic enthusiasts to distort and even falsify national history in order to make it fit civil religion preconceptions, demeaning the dignity of God by reducing him to the level of a tribal deity, providing a tool for public leaders to drum up support for questionable policies and ventures, and ignoring the needs of suppressed minorities within the national community. Many regard a biblical, evangelical faith and civil religion as incompatible, but there is no consensus in the conservative Protestant community on the question.

R. V. Pierard

Bibliography. R. V. Pierard and R. D. Linder, *Twilight of the Saints: Biblical Christianity and Civil Religion in America;* R. N. Bellah, *Beyond Belief* and *The Broken Covenant: American Civil Religion in Time of Trial;* R. N. Bellah and P. E. Hammond, *Varieties of Civil Religion;* C. Cherry, *God's New Israel;* R. T. Handy, *A Christian America;* D. G. Jones and R. E. Richey, eds., *American Civil Religion;* M. E. Marty, *A Nation of Behavers;* S. E. Mead, *The Nation with the Soul of a Church;* J. Moltmann *et al., Religion and Political Society;* T. D. Moodie, *The Rise of Afrikanerdom: Power, Apartheid, and the Afrikaner Civil Religion;* M. Henry, *The Intoxication of Power: An Analysis of Civil Religion in Relation to Ideology;* J. M. Cuddihy, *No Offense: Civil Religion and Protestant Taste;* J. F. Wilson, *Public Religion in American Culture;* R. J. Neuhaus, *Time Toward Home: The American Experiment as Revelation;* E. A. Smith, *The Religion of the Republic;* E. L. Tuveson, *Redeemer Nation: The Idea of America's Millennial Role.*

Civil Righteousness. To say that all men are totally depraved is to say only that the corruption of sinful nature permeates the whole man, including all the faculties of his being—intellect, emotion, will, personality, etc. This is not to say that all men are as evil as they can be, or that they give unrestrained expression to all forms of wickedness, or that they are completely void, in their natural state, of certain amiable qualities, or that they have no virtues in a limited sense, or that they cannot render a certain obedience to some legal standard or code of conduct. Those positive qualities and moral virtues which may be exhibited and the acts of civil obedience which may be performed constitute what theologians call civil righteousness (*justitia civilis*).

The fact that men, even in an unregenerate condition, can render some good is a result of God's common grace extended to human beings indiscriminately as image-bearers of the divine nature. This grace restrains the general destructive process of sin within the human race; enables men, although estranged from their Creator, to develop skills and abilities, to harness the forces of nature, and so make a positive contribution to the cultural, scientific, and social welfare of the world; and promotes within the conscience the praise of good and the condemnation of evil. It is, therefore, this grace which serves as the foundation from which all demonstrations of civil righteousness flow.

While it is true that the earthly existence of mankind is enhanced by the presence of civil righteousness, it must be stated categorically that such righteousness has no redemptive value. It cannot save men from eternal judgment nor earn for them eternal life. The manifestation of civil righteousness may evoke the approbation of men, but it will commend no one to a righteous God in whose eyes all human righteousness, including civil righteousness, is as filthy rags (Isa. 64:6).

W. W. Benton, Jr.

See also Grace.

Civil Rights. A civil right is an entitlement that citizens possess over against the state or other citizens as contained in a constitution and a statutory law. Civil rights may refer to more general rights such as the classic ones to freedom of speech, press, religion, and assembly. These are commonly called civil liberties. More often people use the phrase "civil rights" to designate more specific rights that have emerged as a response to the moral claims of powerless social groups, especially those that have been historically subjected to unfair treatment by the majority (or more powerful minorities). In Anglo-Saxon legal tradition criminal suspects, for example, are given procedural safeguards such as the right to a writ of habeas corpus and to a trial by jury.

To claim a right against another is clearly different from seeking a favor secured by their gracious consent. What rights may a citizen legitimately expect to claim? Some argue that these should be limited to the more procedural questions such as due process under the law. Others assert that they must include the requirements for equal material resources, or at least equal access to those conditions by which one's social well-being is guaranteed. This latter view is reflected in the United Nations' International Covenant on Economic, Social, and Cultural Rights (1966), which declares that citizens of all nations have a right to an adequate and continually improving standard of living. This includes rights to food, to a decent job, to adequate medical care, and even to "periodic holidays with pay." The debate about what constitutes one's civil rights underlies much of the civil strife in the modern world.

In Western Political Thought. Civil rights laws here rest upon fundamental moral principles that have been nurtured in the natural law tradition. The idea of natural law stretches back to the early Greek, Roman, and Christian writers who affirmed that certain "laws" were eternal and that every human being was capable of recognizing them. One significant corollary of natural law thinking was the insistence upon human equality. This provided a ready-made criterion which early social critics used to help undermine established institutions that treated groups of people unfairly. Roman jurisprudence, which fashioned Western legal practice, was greatly influenced by this development.

The success of natural law was facilitated by Christian writers who, influenced by Greek and Roman ideas, found the concept compatible with Paul's statement that the Gentiles "show that what the law requires is written in their hearts" (Rom. 2:15). Through the influence of Thomas Aquinas the natural law tradition provided the foundation for most civil and canon laws in the Middle Ages. By the eighteenth century natural law theory reached its political height. John Locke, for instance, believed that all humans are the workmanship of the one all-powerful and wise Maker and, consequently, the state of nature has a law of which nothing is more evident than that all people are equal. All rights and duties humans owe each other in the sociopolitical realm are derived from this claim. Both the United States and French Declarations of Independence affirm as "self-evident" truths or "simple and incontestable principles" that "all men are created equal" or are "born and remain free and equal in rights." Undergirding these truths was the declared assumption that all people possess an "equal station to which the laws of nature and nature's God entitle them."

The emphasis upon human rights in the West not only springs from natural law theory; it is also rooted in the soil which nurtured the Judeo-Christian faith. The earliest known law codes and documents recognized minimal civil rights for people belonging to vulnerable groups. Early Egyptians instituted a right for the poor to be ferried across a river if they could not pay and established positive legal duties to widows and orphans. Likewise, Babylonian, Assyrian, and Hittite law secured certain minimal rights for widows, children, concubines, slaves, debtors, and hirelings.

In the Bible. The Hebrew laws surpassed other contemporary codes in affirming the equal treatment of all citizens regardless of social standing. Some OT laws even surpass many contemporary progressive statutes in affirming civil rights. Since the laws which protected citizens were established by God, they were quite secure. Not even the king could neglect them with impunity; see Ahab and Jezebel's punishment for their evil action in killing Naboth to gain his vineyard (I Kings 21). These statutes not only established procedural guarantees before the law, but they also granted the powerless certain economic claims against the wealthy. Thus, the hungry had the right to glean food from another's crop (Lev. 19:9–10; Deut. 23:24; 24:19–22; Matt. 12:1). Debtors could expect their loans canceled after seven years (Deut. 15:7–11). The sojourners, widows, and orphans were given special rights to the food brought to the temple as a tithe (Deut. 14:28–29).

The Israelites' deep sense of social justice was a flowering of their belief in Yahweh's creative activity. The human creature as male and female was formed in the very image of God (Gen. 1:27) and could even be described as but a "little less" than God (Ps. 8:5). Since human beings are so highly praised, to oppress, afflict, and harshly treat them as did the Egyptians was an inherent violation of their dignity and roused both the compassion and wrath of God (Deut. 26:5–9). However, God chose the Hebrews not because they possessed merit, social status, or desirability, but rather because they were persons whose rights as humans created in God's image were being violated. God's purpose in delivering the people became the rationale for Israel's own system of civil rights for powerless groups (Lev. 19:34; Deut. 24:22).

Unfortunately, the rights of the poor were often neglected or even despised. The prophets, however, became an eloquent moral force in reaffirming the civil rights tradition. Their visions of the Holy God radicalized their understanding of sin and sensitized them to the extent of economic exploitation occurring in the land (Isa. 5:16; 6:3–5; Jer. 22:13ff.; Ezek. 18:5–18; Mic. 3:1–4; Hos. 6:4–9). The prophets were so insistent upon the restoration of civil rights that, on occasion, they linked spiritual activity with seeking justice (Amos 5:4–15; Isa. 58:3–9; Jer. 9:23–24; Mic. 6:8). The prophetic material is not alone in defending civil rights. The popular proverbs and religious hymns also highlight that concern (Prov. 14:31; 29:7; Ps. 15; 113:7–9).

The NT reflects the same strong civil rights position as embodied in the OT. The teachings of Jesus are well within the prophetic focus and are highly critical of unjust treatment for disenfranchised groups. On more than one occasion he reminded his adversaries that a human being is of great value (Matt. 12:12; Luke 14:5). In his "inaugural discourse" Jesus insisted that factors such as social status or national identity were irrelevant in God's care for people (see Luke 4:16–32, where God even heals an enemy Syrian.) Moreover, he saw himself as the champion of the underclasses, the messianic liberator of the oppressed (Luke 4:18). Jesus' teachings and activities continually reinforced the moral standing of the penniless (Mark 12:41–44), the diseased (Matt. 14:13–14), the aged (Matt. 15:4–6), women (John 4:7ff.), children (Mark 10:13–14), and other socially weak groups such as prisoners (Matt. 25:36) and the blind (Matt. 11:4–6).

The writings of Paul and the communal practices of the early church (Acts 2:44–45; 4:34–35) mediated the same moral and theological grounding for civil rights as was found in the OT and the teachings of Jesus. Paul's theological affirmations of human equality were unequivocal (Gal. 3:28; I Cor. 7:3–4; II Cor. 8:13–15), although on occasion he accommodated his beliefs to historical realities (see I Tim. 2:11, where Paul suggests that women who are uneducated should not lead in the church). Paul's doctrine of justification by faith, which implied that all humans come before God as sinners and not as meriting favor, may have been Christianity's greatest contribution to the development of civil rights in the West. After the Reformation the belief in justification by faith resulted in freedom of conscience and belief, a seedbed for other rights within the state.

In the United States. Civil rights in America have been historically linked to the struggle of blacks to gain full equality. The Civil Rights Act of 1866 granted citizenship to blacks and was the first major rights legislation in the United States. The Constitution was also amended to outlaw slavery and give blacks the right to vote, although these laws were often defied outright or watered down by court interpretations. Under the influence of black protests, which initially emerged from the black church under the general leadership of Martin Luther King, Jr., some important civil rights gains were made during the 1950s and 60s. These strides culminated in the Civil Rights Acts of 1964 and 1968, which outlawed discrimination in housing, employment, education, voting, and public accommodations.

The relative success of the civil rights movement has inspired other groups to press for their rights as citizens. These include women, Native Americans, Hispanics, prisoners, mental patients, homosexuals, tenants, the handicapped, the aged and children, aliens and refugees, the poor, the unborn, consumers, and employees. Many church groups and organizations of nearly all theological persuasions are actively engaged in supporting these various groups in procuring their civil rights.

D. J. Miller

Bibliography. E. Corwin, *The "Higher Law" Background of American Constitutional Law;* A. P. d'Entreves, *Natural Law: An Historical Survey;* G. Forell and W. Lazareth, eds., *Human Rights: Rhetoric or Reality;* C. Fisher, *Minorities, Civil Rights and Protest;* M. L. King, Jr., *Why We Can't Wait;* W. Laqueur and B. Rubin, eds., *The Human Rights Reader;* D. Lyons, *Rights;* A. Miller, ed., *Christian Declaration of Human Rights;* J. Miranda, *Marx and the Bible;* A. Muller and N. Greinacher, eds., *The Church and the Rights of Man;* P. Ramsey, *Basic Christian Ethics;* J. Rawls, *A Theory of Justice;* J. A. Sigler, *American Rights Policies;* H. Shue, *Basic Rights: Subsistence, Affluence, and U. S. Foreign Policy.*

Cleanness, Uncleanness. Like other ancient Near Eastern civilizations ancient Israel had a concept that we call ceremonial or ritual cleanness (*ṭāhôr*) and uncleanness (*ṭāmē'*). Therefore, the OT contains many laws describing what made one become unclean and the purification ritual necessary to return to the desirable status of being clean. These laws for cleanness concentrated on prohibited food (Lev. 11), bodily emissions (Lev. 15), various kinds of skin disease (Lev. 13), death (Num. 19:11–19), and places (Lev. 18: 24–30). Purification rituals varied but included a waiting period (Lev. 12:2–5), a cleansing agent such as water (Lev. 15:5), blood (Lev. 14:25), or fire (Num. 31:23), and a sacrifice or offering (Lev. 5:6).

Various explanations have been offered for these laws of cleanness and uncleanness. A summary of the more important ones follows.

The distinctions were *hygienic*. Unclean animals were unfit to eat because they were carriers of disease, while the clean animals were relatively safe to eat. Washing and purification have always been consistent with sound medical practice.

The distinctions were *cultic*. Unclean animals were closely associated with the negative religious practices of Israel's neighbors and therefore were to be shunned completely by ancient Israel.

The distinctions were *symbolic*. This is an anthropological approach developed by Mary Douglas (*Purity and Danger*). She suggests that systems of distinguishing cleanness and uncleanness were really ways of ordering the universe. Laws of cleanness symbolized wholeness and normality, while the laws of uncleanness symbolized chaos and disorder. Priests had to be free from physical deformity (Lev. 21:17–21); improper unions (Lev. 20:20) and mixtures (Lev. 19:19) were prohibited. Clean animals conformed to a standard (pure) type, while unclean animals departed from this standard in one way or another (Lev. 11).

Each of these explanations has some value, but the symbolic interpretation is more comprehensive and has been gaining additional supporters.

Israel's approach to cleanness was also connected to Yahweh and his holiness. Priests were to distinguish between both the holy and profane and the clean and unclean (Lev. 10:10). While cleanness and holiness were not identical, cleanness was one important aspect of holiness, and priests were extensively involved in many purification rituals. So we may conclude that the laws of cleanness were indirect aids to remind the ancient Israelite of the purity and holiness of his God (Lev. 11:44–45).

In the NT the ceremonial aspects of cleanness (*katharos*) and uncleanness (*akathartēs*) gave way to an emphasis on moral purity and impurity. Jesus stressed that it was not what went into a man that defiled him, but what came out of him (Matt. 15:1–20; Mark 7:1–23). Mark (7:19) added that Jesus declared all foods to be clean. However, this issue was not easily resolved in the early church. Unclean foods distinguished and divided Jews, including Christian Jews, from Gentiles (Acts 10 and 15). However, when Gentiles were incorporated into the church, the food laws lost their symbolic significance and were eventually dropped. Acts 15:9 indicates that both Jewish and Gentile believers were clean because of God's work of cleansing, not because of observing dietary laws. The book of Hebrews went on to show that the work of Christ made not only purification rituals but other OT ceremonial practices unnecessary. Rom. 14:14 sums up the NT position: "Nothing is unclean in itself; but it is unclean for anyone who thinks it unclean."

J. C. Moyer

Bibliography. G. J. Wenham, *Leviticus* and "The Theology of Unclean Food," *EvQ* 53:6–15; J. Hartley, *ISBE* (rev.), I, 718–23.

Clement of Alexandria (*ca.* 150–*ca.* 215). Titus Flavius Clemens, Greek theologian and writer, was the first significant representative of the Alexandrian theological tradition. Born of pagan parents in Athens, Clement went to Alexandria, where he succeeded his teacher Pantaenus as head of the Catechetical School. In 202 persecution forced him to leave Alexandria, apparently never to return.

Of Clement's writings four are preserved complete: *Protreptikos* (an exhortation addressed to the Greeks urging their conversion); *Paedagogos* (a portrayal of Christ as tutor instructing the faithful in their conduct); *Stromata* (miscellaneous thoughts primarily concerning the relation of faith to philosophy); "Who Is the Rich Man That Is Saved?" (an exposition of Mark 10:17–31, arguing that wealth, if rightfully used, is not un-Christian). Of other writings only fragments remain, especially of the *Hypotyposes*, a commentary on the Scriptures.

Clement is important for his positive approach to philosophy which laid the foundations for Christian humanism and for the idea of philosophy as "handmaid" to theology. The idea of the Logos dominates his thinking. The divine Logos, creator of all things, guides all good men and causes all right thought. Greek philosophy was, therefore, a partial revelation and prepared the Greeks for Christ just as the law prepared the Hebrews. Christ is the Logos incarnate through whom man attains to perfection and true *gnōsis*. Against the Gnostics who disparaged faith, Clement considers faith the necessary first principle and foundation for knowledge, which itself is the perfection of faith. Man becomes a "true Gnostic" by love and contemplation. Through self-control and love man rids himself of passions, reaching finally the state of impassibility wherein he attains to the likeness of God. With this idea Clement profoundly influenced Greek Christian spirituality.

W. C. Weinrich

See also Alexandrian Theology.

Bibliography. E. F. Osborn, *The Philosophy of Clement of Alexandria;* S. R. C. Lilla, *Clement of Alexandria: A Study in Christian Platonism and Gnosticism;* R. B. Tollington, *Clement of Alexandria: A Study in Christian Liberalism,* 2 vols.; E. Molland, *The Conception of the Gospel in the Alexandrian Theology;* J.

Quasten, *Patrology*, II: *The Ante-Nicene Literature after Irenaeus;* W. H. Wagner, "The Paideia Motif in the Theology of Clement of Alexandria" (Diss., Drew University, 1968); W. E. G. Floyd, *Clement of Alexandria's Treatment of the Problem of Evil;* D. J. M. Bradley, "The Transfiguration of the Stoic Ethic in Clement of Alexandria," *Aug* 14:41–66; J. Ferguson, "The Achievement of Clement of Alexandria," *RelS* 12:59–80.

Clergy. The word derives from the Greek *klēros*, "a lot," which points to a method of selection like that in Acts 1:26 (in Acts 1:17 "part" [AV] translates *klēros*). As early as Jerome it was pointed out that the term is ambiguous. It may denote those chosen to be God's, the Lord's "lot" (as in Deut. 32:9). Or it may signify those whose lot or portion is the Lord (cf. Ps. 16:5). In the NT the word is not used of a restricted group among the believers, and in I Pet. 5:3 the plural is used of God's people as a whole ("God's heritage," AV). But by the time of Tertullian it was used of the ordained office-bearers in the church, viz., bishops, priests, and deacons. Later the word came to include the minor orders, and sometimes, it seems, members of religious orders or even educated people generally. But this use did not last, and the term now denotes regular members of the ordained ministry of the church (without respect to denomination) as distinct from lay people generally.

L. Morris

Clergy, Secular. *See* Secular Clergy.

Coadjutor Bishop. *See* Church Officers; Bishop.

Cocceius, Johannes (1603–1669). Linguist and biblical theologian, Johann Koch (latinized to Cocceius) was born in Bremen. In his inaugural at Bremen in 1630, where he was appointed professor of Oriental languages, Cocceius defended the science of biblical philology and indicated his aversion to scholastic theology and philosophy. Six years later he accepted a similar position at the University of Franeker, where he continued to develop his own system of grammatico-historical exegesis. After fourteen years there he was appointed professor of theology at Leiden, where he remained until his death.

Cocceius's views are set forth in his *Doctrine of the Covenant and Testaments of God* (1648) and in his *Commentary on the Epistle to the Romans* (1655). Holding that Scripture should always be interpreted in context without foreign presuppositions, he opposed the prevailing Cartesian philosophical influences of his day and also the prevailing orthodoxy of the Reformed Church. In this latter he held, contrary to Voetius of Utrecht, who interpreted Scripture according to the conclusions of the Synod of Dort, that truth should be derived from Scripture itself, in the same manner as the Reformers had sought to understand it. Biblical subjects should be understood in biblical terms. Using a strict exegetical method, he developed a biblical theology in which he distinguished three different periods in the history of God's dealings with his people. In his relationship to mankind God established a covenant of works with Adam. This was supplanted by a covenant of grace made with Moses in which there were three periods—before, during, and after Moses' time. The new covenant is given in Jesus Christ. Using allegorical exegesis Cocceius found prophetic types of Christ throughout the OT and was accused of fanciful exegesis by his opponents. With a proper understanding of the "hidden sense of Scripture," Cocceius held, one could discover the seven periods of the history of the church.

Cocceius's distinction between the forgiveness of sins in the OT, which was imperfect and incomplete and which prevented God's people from having the assurance and blessing that Christians possess, and the forgiveness enjoyed after the event of the cross aroused opposition by those who felt that he was engaged in a dangerous historicizing of Scripture. Moreover, his belief that the sabbath was instituted in the desert, not in paradise, and that it is not binding on Christians got him into difficulty. Although famous as a covenantal theologian, his covenantal theology was not new; it is found in Olevianus, Bullinger, and others. The theological conflict begun in his lifetime was continued by his disciples and their opponents for a half century after his death.

M. E. Osterhaven

See also Covenant Theology; Federal Theology.

Bibliography. C. S. McCoy, "Johannes Cocceius: Federal Theologian," *SJT* 16:352–70; G. Schrenk, *Gottesreich und Bund in älteren Protestantismus.*

Cohabitation. The situation of those who live together in a sexual relationship but are not married. While cohabitation represents only a very small percentage of American households, it nearly tripled (from 500,000 to 1.5 million residences) in the decade 1972–82. If this same rate of increase continues, by the year 2012 nearly one half of all families in the United States would include unmarried people living together. Already in 1982 25 percent of students on college campuses reported that they had lived with someone of the opposite sex. Cohabitation covers a wide variety of relationships from temporary casual arrangements of convenience to more committed lifelong substitutes for marriage.

Some people believe that the rising incidence of cohabitation is due primarily to a general breakdown in personal morality. Others see an assortment of broader social forces contributing to its upswing. The changing sexual values and patterns, the emphasis upon individual human growth, the liberalization of living arrangements on college campuses, the phenomenon of extended adolescence and later marriage, more effective contraception, and the high cost of housing are all factors which encourage cohabitation. Moreover, tax and social security laws often tend to discourage some couples from marrying.

Most Christians stand firmly against cohabitation and are more than slightly alarmed by its increasing frequency and almost routine social acceptance. The moral problem of unwed people living together is grounded in the historical Christian belief that sexual activity outside marriage is an offense against God's law and a disservice to one's partner. Nevertheless, many people who cohabit claim to hold positive views toward marriage. They justify their action by asserting that love is the key ingredient of their relationship and a marriage license contributes scarcely anything to that love. While Christians have usually insisted that sexual activity must be nurtured by love, they have also maintained that its most sublime meaning is achieved when it is linked to marriage. This view has emerged from the belief in God's extraordinary activity in creation and consequent unique alliance with humans. When the world was commanded into being, God determined that human relationships would be guided by structured obligations so that the world might not revert to an enslaving social chaos (Gen. 2:15–25).

Throughout the Scriptures, God's relation to humans is described in covenantal terms with recognizable concrete stipulations. Human life is placed upon a moral footing and is fulfilled by the faithful exercise of stated responsibilities. Relationships between humans are likewise depicted as covenantal, with mutual responsibilities arising from contractual commitments. These human covenants acquire their power and durability because they spring from God's covenant-making activity (I Sam. 20:8–23). One corollary of this suggests that God created the state and its legal authority to provide the means whereby these human covenants might be fulfilled (Rom. 13:1–7). Marriage is one of the more significant legal covenants which God has provided. Thus, the claim is only partially true that human ties are made in heaven apart from the concrete legal arrangements. Rather they are also made on earth, as affirmed by a theology which describes God as creator of both heaven and earth.

The God-ordained provision of a marriage contract does not diminish the element of love in a couple's relationship, as is often implied by cohabitors. On the contrary, the Bible portrays the concept of love itself in covenantal terms. Thus, one of the Hebrew words for love (*ḥesed*) is often translated "loyal love" or "steadfast love," and is occasionally found in the idiom "covenant and steadfast love" (Neh. 1:5; 9:32; Deut. 7:9). Rather than stifling a couple's relationship, this type of covenantal love actually liberates it. At its highest point marriage provides mutual emancipation within the boundaries of certain expectations, responsibilities, and loyalties; i.e., marriage permits the most mature expression of love to develop. Cohabitation, on the other hand, permits mutual exploitation within the context of potential flight.

God's original command in creation was that male and female "cleave" to one another in covenantal partnership, or marriage (Gen. 2:24). This bond bestowed meaning upon their sexual activity as expressed by the phrase "one flesh" (Gen. 2:24). It highlights the complete interchange of the two selves, as in the bride's delightful declaration in the Song of Solomon, "My beloved is mine and I am his" (2:16). Sexual experience, as a pleasurable expression of a couple's bond, is the recurring sign of their mutual self-giving, and this includes the physical, moral/spiritual, and legal dimensions. In the NT Paul infuses meaning to sexual experience within marriage by deriving it from the "hidden truth" of Christ's total love for his bride, the church, and the church's resulting loyal love to him (Eph. 5:32).

A link exists between these biblical traditions and subsequent cultural expressions of love, sex, and marriage. Thus, in the West it is nearly impossible to escape the layers of moral and legal implications that underlie these activities. At its deepest level sexual pleasure is a presentation of the self to the other in a way that culturally symbolizes mutual commitment and bonding. Marriage affirms this by specifying and guarding certain expectations and responsibilities. This does not happen, however, in cohabitation. Thus far, all research has shown that, on the whole, cohabiting couples evidence less commitment than those who marry. Cohabitation is a form of social interaction which may communicate that a couple might be important to each other, but they are not so important that they wish to leap into a relationship of ultimacy and permanence. In cohabitation sexual expression is a structurally false symbol of a totally committed relationship.

Many Christians believe that the church should respond to cohabitation by neither condoning nor condemning the people who practice it. Rather it should oppose those questionable social forces which tend to encourage and even subsidize it. In this view parents, relatives, friends, and the church are urged to continue a gospel ministry of care to those who live together outside of marriage, helping the couple to deal with their own individual circumstances, while addressing the broader social trends which tend to perpetuate this life style. D. J. MILLER

See also MARRIAGE, THEOLOGY OF.

Bibliography. E. Achtemeier, *The Committed Marriage;* P. Bertocci, *Sex, Love, and the Person;* E. Macklin, "Review of Research on Non-marital Cohabitation in the United States," in *Exploring Intimate Life Styles,* ed. B. Murstein; W. H. Masters and V. Johnson, *The Pleasure Bond: A New Look at Sexuality and Commitment;* P. Ramsey, *Deeds and Rules in Christian Ethics;* L. Smedes, *Sex for Christians;* H. Thielicke, *The Ethics of Sex;* E. Wheat and G. Wheat, *Intended for Pleasure.*

Coke, Thomas (1747–1814). Probably the most important figure in the spread of worldwide Methodism in the generation following the death of John Wesley. Born in Brecon, Wales, he graduated from Jesus College, Oxford, in 1768, and was ordained an Anglican priest in 1772. While serving as a curate at South Petherton in Somerset, he gradually adopted Methodistic enthusiasm, open air meetings, and cottage services. These led to his dismissal, after which he formally joined the Methodists in 1777 and moved to London to become Wesley's assistant during the latter's declining years.

Following an appeal from American Methodists for ordained clergy to administer the sacraments, Wesley sent an organizational team headed by Coke as superintendent to the United States in 1784. Coke found Francis Asbury, the only English Methodist missionary to remain in America during the Revolution, well in control of American Methodism, and he largely accepted Asbury's natural authority. During the next two decades Coke made eight return visits.

Coke's contribution to Methodism was less that of innovator than that of zealous promoter and organizer. As a widely traveled preacher he skillfully and effectively presented Wesley's ideas, appealing to the hearts rather than the heads of his listeners. While he did not claim significance as a writer, he did produce a Bible commentary, a journal of his first five trips to America, and a history of the West Indies. His greatest contribution was that of promoter of Methodist missions from England and America to Ireland, Africa, the West Indies, and elsewhere during the formative period of Methodist missionary expansion. W. C. RINGENBERG

See also METHODISM.

Bibliography. Coke, *Journals, Plan of the Society for the Establishment of Missions Among the Heathen, Commentary on the Bible,* and *History of the West Indies;* J. A. Vickers, *Thomas Coke: Apostle of Methodism;* W. A. Candler, *Life of Thomas Coke.*

Collegialism. The teaching that church and state are *collegia,* voluntary associations or societies created by the will of the members to unite together. Each society is independent of the other in its aims and purposes. Thus the civil authority (king or magistrate) cannot interfere in the life of the church. Such teaching has its origin in the natural rights theories of Hugo Grotius and S. Pufendorf, but the actual word itself was probably coined by J. H. Boehmer of Halle (d. 1745). Collegialism normally presupposes one major church in each territory and is to be distinguished from both territorialism and Erastianism. P. TOON

See also TERRITORIALISM; ERASTIANISM.

Comforter. *See* HOLY SPIRIT.

Command, Commandment. *See* LAW, BIBLICAL CONCEPT OF.

Commandment, The New. Although the law of Moses contained an abundance of commandments from God for Israel, it was everywhere understood that the supreme commandment was to love God, with the result that the *Shema* (Deut. 6:4–9) was recited daily and posted on the doorpost of every home. A second command like it in importance was to love one's neighbor as oneself (Matt. 22:39), as required in Lev. 19:18. Jesus considered this second command to be of such importance that he referred to them both as one commandment when he said, "There is no other greater commandment than these" (Mark 12:31). But the same law demanded that one love not only his neighbor but also the stranger who lived with him (Lev. 19:34), and that he love them both as he loved himself (Lev. 19:18, 34). So when Jesus said he was giving his disciples a new commandment to love one another, he was undoubtedly referring to this requirement of the law but with an even deeper meaning, which was to love as he had loved them (John 13:34). Years later John thus wrote that the commandment was both old and new (I John 2:7–8; II John 5). Love, as understood in the Western world, is an emotion which cannot be commanded, but in the Semitic world of the Bible it was rather a matter of volition and included the keeping of God's commandments (John 14:15; I John 2:3–4). In the final analysis, love is the mark of discipleship (John 13:35). J. R. McRay

Bibliography. G. Quell and E. Stauffer, *TDNT*, I, 21–55; C. Brown, *NIDNTT*, II, 538–51; J. Moffatt, *Love in the NT.*

Commission, The Great. *See* Great Commission, The.

Common Grace. *See* Grace.

Common Order, Book of. *See* Book of Common Order.

Common Prayer, Book of. *See* Book of Common Prayer.

Communication of Attributes, Communicatio Idiomatum. The communication of attributes means that whatever can be attributed to (said about) either the divine or the human nature in Christ is to be attributed to the entire person. Whatever is true of either nature is true of the person. This is only a detailed discussion of the fact that Jesus Christ is one person, not two. It does not add to the statement that the God-man is one person.

Orthodox theologians have always taught that Jesus Christ is both true God and true man, yet only one person. This truth was rejected by Nestorianism but affirmed by the Councils of Ephesus (431) and Chalcedon (451). To deny that Christ is one person is to deny the incarnation (John 1:14).

In several respects Lutheran and Reformed theologians have disagreed about the communication of attributes since the Reformation. Because this doctrine is more characteristic of Lutheran than Reformed theology, it will be presented here in the categories common among Lutherans. Some Reformed disagreements will be noted.

Genus Idiomaticum (*Category of Attributes*). The properties of each nature are ascribed to the person, using any of his names or titles. For example, the Lord of glory was crucified (I Cor. 2:8). This is no word game. It is a reality according to the Bible.

Genus Maiestaticum (*Category of Majesty*). The divine attributes are communicated (given) to Christ's human nature. Christ received according to his human nature the omnipotence, omniscience, and omnipresence which he as true God always possessed (Matt. 11:27; 28:18–20; Col. 1:19; John 3:34–35). The divine nature does not receive human limitations because God cannot change. Reformed theologians claim that Christ's human nature received only finite gifts, not divine attributes.

Genus Apotelesmaticum (*Category of Works*). What Christ did for our salvation he did as the God-man. All his works for us are his works as God and man (I John 3:8; Heb. 2:14–15; Gal. 4:4). Reformed theologians have tended to designate Christ's acts as the acts of one nature or the other. J. M. Drickamer

Bibliography. M. Chemnitz, *The Two Natures in Christ;* F. Pieper, *Christian Dogmatics*, II; L. Berkhof, *Systematic Theology.*

Communion, Holy. *See* Lord's Supper.

Communion of Saints, The. For many centuries believers have affirmed in the Apostles' Creed their faith in "the communion of saints." The phrase is probably the latest addition to the creed, not being attested before the fifth century. It is absent from all the Eastern creeds.

This affirmation of belief has been interpreted in various ways. The traditional, and probably the best, interpretation refers the phrase to the union of all believers, living or dead, in Christ, stressing their common life in Christ and their sharing of all the blessings of God. Some medieval interpreters, including Thomas Aquinas, read the phrase as "the communion in holy things" (a reading which the Latin text allows), referring it to the sacraments, especially the Eucharist. Others, such as Karl Barth, have chosen a mixture of these views. As a rule the Reformers and the Reformed confessions follow the traditional interpretation, sometimes limiting the idea to living believers.

It has been common for Catholic and Anglo-Catholic interpreters to use this article of the creed as a justification of the practice of prayers for the dead. Since such prayers do not seem to have biblical sanction, this inference is unacceptable.

To the traditional view, that the phrase refers to the existing unity of all believers in Christ and their common sharing of his grace, must be added a more modern emphasis on the need for this unity to be actualized in the church. Believing in the communion of saints is more than affirming an existing unity, since it calls the church to fellowship, to mutuality, and to the sharing of "all good gifts" received from God.

F. Q. Gouvea

See also Apostles' Creed; Fellowship; Prayers for the Dead.

Bibliography. K. Barth, *Dogmatics in Outline;* J. Pearson, *Exposition of the Creed;* J. Köstlin, *SHERK,* III, 181–182.

Communitarianism, Community of Goods. In the early Christian church Christian life centered on worship. In the wake of Pentecost a desire to worship God appears to have led to a spontaneous sharing of goods in the church of Jerusalem (Acts 2:42–47; 4:32–37). In the Acts of the Apostles this sharing of goods was interpreted as a manifestation of the work of the Holy Spirit (Acts 5:3). Throughout the NT writings the welfare of other Christians is of constant concern. Hospitality and aid are continually advocated (I Cor. 16).

The idealism and communitarianism of the early church has served as an example throughout church history which various individuals and movements have sought to emulate. At different times the appeal of "having all things in common" has led to different syntheses of Christian thought with the prevailing philosophical ethos. Thus Jewish apocalyptic thought has often provided a motive for Christians to share their worldly goods as they awaited the end of the world. Similarly, certain forms of Greek philosophy have led Christians to scorn material pleasures and to organize movements that were stoic in their simplicity. Hermits, ascetics, and monastic orders have all sought to renounce private property and live in accordance with the demands of poverty. Within the Roman Catholic Church the monastic life has always been the ideal to which the layman was expected to aspire. The great example of such spiritual poverty in the Middle Ages was the Franciscans. But they and groups inspired by them, such as the lay Brethren of the Common Life, never developed consistent economic theories. Rather, they were united in a devotion to apostolic poverty as an ideal.

Both Wycliffe and Hus, forerunners of Luther, espoused theories of society which today we would call socialist. However, due to the persecution of their followers no society was developed based upon their theories.

During the Reformation some religious groups developed socialist views. These include the Anabaptist Hutterites, who followed Jacob Hutter, a reformer who was burned at the stake in 1536, and the Calvinist Levelers of Cromwell's England.

In American religious history communal groups have played an important role. These include the Shakers, who followed the teachings of Mother Ann Lee (1736–84), and the perfectionist Oneida Community of John Humphrey Noyes (1811–86). Although heretical in terms of traditional Christian theology, both these groups had considerable social impact upon American society. The Shakers are credited with inventing the washing machine, while the Oneida Community developed silver plating and became an important industrial enterprise.

During the nineteenth century the theology of F. D. Maurice played an important role in legitimating and promoting Christian socialism. In the twentieth century William Temple is an outstanding example of the British Christian socialist tradition. Ecclesiastically the work of Maurice helped inspire such High Church Anglican groups as the Community of the Resurrection, which was founded with the encouragement of Charles Gore in 1892.

Christian socialism has also had a considerable impact in North America, where it appears to have been inspired by both the liberal theology of Horace Bushnell and the evangelical revivalism of Charles Finney. In the United States, Christian socialism became associated with liberal theology and the social gospel movement in the early part of the twentieth century and has been largely rejected by evangelical Christians. Only in the mid-1970s, after several decades of staunch conservatism, did young evangelicals once more begin to examine the socialist heritage of certain forms of evangelical thought. In Canada the Christian socialist heritage has been relatively more successful, and its influence can be seen in the formation of both the Co-operative Commonwealth Federation (CCF), the forerunner of the present New Democratic Party (NDP), and the Social Credit movement of William Aberhart.

Today most North American Christians reject socialism in favor of some form of free enterprise capitalism. However, significant numbers of younger evangelicals in Europe, North America, and the Third World are reexamining and advocating some form of Christian socialism and communalism.

I. Hexham

See also Socialism, Christian; Utopianism; Monasticism.

Bibliography. D. Clark, *Basic Communities: Towards an Alternative Society;* R. Sider, *Rich Christians in an Age of Hunger;* R. Quebedeaux, *The Worldly Evangelicals.*

Comparative Religion. Although it is possible to trace the origin of comparative religion to the sixth century Greek thinker Xenophanes, who noted that different peoples tend to depict God in their own image, it was not until the nineteenth century that the study of comparative religion began in earnest. Under the influence of evolutionary theory a number of scholars found what they believed to be evolutionary links between various religious traditions. Chief among these were F. Max Müller, E. B. Tylor, and J. G. Fraser. The discipline gained rapid academic recognition, and chairs were established in various institutions, particularly the new universities of North America. In Britain the subject tended to serve the needs of the empire and was closely linked to the study of Asian languages. In Germany it took the form of the history of religions, which was seen as an adjunct to Christian theology. In the United States, under the influence of institutions like the University of Chicago, it became an important element in the expression of the American liberal consensus. As an undergraduate subject comparative religion became highly popular in the late 1960s and early 1970s, with the result that new religious studies departments were opened in many universities in Britain and North America.

In its crudest form comparative religion makes the assumption that all religions are essentially one. Thus the ten commandments of Judaism, the teachings of Jesus, the four noble truths of Buddhism, and various Hindu moral codes are compared to show that they all contain a common denominator such as the command to love one's neighbor. In a similar way it is often argued that despite apparent differences, all men worship a supreme being. However, serious study of various religions has revealed more disagreements than agreements. Thus, while it may be true that English housewives and African women in Uganda carry umbrellas, this information tells us very little about the actual life style of the women involved. Using an umbrella to protect oneself from the rain is not the same as using it to avoid the glare of the sun. Similarly, prayer to God in Christianity and meditation in Buddhism may look similar, but the object of each exercise is very different. Such a religion as Theravada Buddhism, in fact, presents a strong argument against crude forms of comparative religion because of its rejection of the importance of belief in God and denial of the existence of an individual self. As a result of considerations like these, the study of religion as a universal phenomenon with a variety of different expressions has become increasingly complex. Some scholars still retain a desire to find an underlying unity, while many others have abandoned this quest in favor of the study of a particular religious tradition which they recognize to be unique. I. HEXHAM

Bibliography. E. J. Sharp, *Comparative Religion;* M. Eliade and J. M. Kitagawa, eds., *The History of Religions;* N. Smart, *Reasons and Faiths.*

Conciliarism. A reform movement in the Western church of the fifteenth century arising from the Great Schism (1378–1417), during which first two and then three popes contended for the loyalty of Christendom. Such a scandalous situation effectively weakened the papacy as an institution, and led thinkers such as Jean Gerson, Pierre d'Ailly, and Francesco Zarabella to affirm, following William of Ockham and others, that, though God had indeed given the church final authority in matters of faith and morals, this authority was vested, not in the pope, but in the church as a whole, and that it should thus be exercised by a general council. These ideas led to the conciliarist movement, which reached the peak of its influence in the Council of Constance (1414–18). This council not only ended the schism by deposing all three popes, but also affirmed the authority of general councils over the pope. These decrees, which would have completely changed the authority structure of the church, were accepted at that critical moment. But they began to be disregarded as soon as another pope was elected, and were finally overturned by Pius II in his bull *Execrabilis* in 1460. This marked the end of conciliarism as a movement, though its ideas remained influential for some time.

From a Protestant point of view conciliarism, though a step in the right direction in its rejection of papal authority, was not sufficiently radical; it failed to see that, while the church does have authority (Matt. 16:19; 18:18), this is a relative authority, since it is controlled and limited by the inspired Word of God. F. Q. GOUVEA

See also CHURCH, AUTHORITY IN; PAPACY.

Bibliography. G. H. W. Parker, *The Morning Star;* G. Holmes, *Europe: Hierarchy and Revolt 1320–1450;* W. Walker, *A History of the Christian Church;* H. Bettenson, *The Documents of the Christian Church,* Pt. II, Sect. V; W. Ullman, *A Short History of the Papacy in the Middle Ages.*

Concomitance. This is a technical term used in the eucharistic theology of Roman Catholicism to describe the presence of both the body and blood of Christ in each of the species of bread and wine, and thus to afford a theological justification for the denial of the cup to the laity. More widely, it denotes the presence of the whole Christ, i.e., his human soul and Godhead, together with the body and blood in virtue of the hypostatic union. It is sometimes linked with grace to describe the divine operation which accompanies the human as distinct from the prevenient grace which precedes. G. W. Bromiley

See also Lord's Supper, Views of; Real Presence; Transubstantiation.

Concord, Book of (1580). Sometimes called *The Confessions of the Evangelical Lutheran Church* (German) or *Concordia* (Latin), this contains all the generally accepted symbols of the Lutheran Church. The *Book of Concord* comprises the following creeds and confessions: (1) the Apostles' Creed (*ca.* 186); (2) the Niceno-Constantinopolitan Creed (381); (3) the Athanasian Creed (*ca.* 350–600); (4) Luther's Large and Small Catechisms (1529); (5) the Augsburg Confession, written by Melanchthon and submitted by the elector of Saxony and other Lutheran princes at Augsburg in 1530; (6) the Apology of the Augsburg Confession (1531), written by Melanchthon against the Roman confutation which had rejected the Augsburg Confession; (7) the Smalcald Articles (1537), written by Luther and summarizing the Protestant understanding of the major articles of faith for a church council that was never called; (8) the Treatise on the Power and Primacy of the Pope (1537), written by Melanchthon to augment the Smalcald Articles; and (9) the Formula of Concord (1577), written to settle a number of disputes arising among Lutherans after Luther's death.

The *Book of Concord* was subscribed by over eight thousand pastors and by numerous territories and imperial cities of Germany. It was accepted in Sweden and Hungary, but only the confessions before 1531 were accepted officially in Denmark-Norway (although the later confessions were never rejected). Since 1580 most Lutheran pastors throughout the world have subscribed, at least formally, the *Book of Concord* at their ordination. None of the *Book of Concord* is confined to any national church, but all the confessions are considered ecumenical, i.e., orthodox and biblical and to be accepted by any Christian. All attempts since 1580 to add confessions to the *Book of Concord* have failed, although it has never been considered a sort of "closed canon." R. D. Preus

See also Concord, Formula of.

Bibliography. F. Bente, *Historical Introductions to the Book of Concord;* H. Fagerberg, *A New Look at the Lutheran Confessions (1529–1537);* R. Preus, *Getting into the Theology of Concord;* D. Scaer, *Getting into the Story of Concord;* E. Schlink, *The Theology of the Lutheran Confessions.*

Concord, Formula of (1577). The last symbol, or confession, representing the doctrinal position of the Evangelical Lutheran Church. It was completed in 1577 and was published in the *Book of Concord* in 1578. It culminated some thirty years of arduous theological study and labor expended by hundreds of faithful Lutheran theologians as they sought to settle a number of doctrinal controversies which beset Lutheranism after Luther's death. Upon his death Lutheranism quickly fell into two parties. The Philippists (sometimes called Synergists or Crypto-Calvinists) followed the more mediating spirit of Philip Melanchthon as he veered toward a synergistic doctrine of conversion and a weakening of total depravity and as he formulated a doctrine of the Lord's Supper which, although Lutheran, was couched in terminology acceptable to the Reformed. Opposing the Philippists were the Gnesio (authentic) Lutherans who pointed out the deviations of Melanchthon and his followers, particularly condemning Melanchthon for accepting the Leipzig Interim, a compromise and evangelical politico-theological statement of faith and practice imposed by Emperor Charles V on the Lutherans in the German Empire after their defeat in the Smalcald War (1547).

When the two parties could not settle their controversies, a third large group of younger theologians arose to heal the division. Chief among these were James Andreae, who spearheaded the effort toward concord, Martin Chemnitz, David Chytraeus, and Nikolaus Selnecker. These men, who had been students of Melanchthon and respected him highly, were also firmly committed to Luther's theology on the points at issue. They represented the best scholarship and most respected leadership among the Lutherans of the day. After almost thirty years of doctrinal discussion throughout Germany and many abortive attempts to construct doctrinal statements that would unite Lutherans again in the theology of Luther and the earlier Lutheran confessions, the Formula of Concord was written in 1577. The document, together with an Epitome written by Andreae, was submitted to the Lutheran pastors, churches, and princes and subscribed by thirty-five imperial cities, the electors of Saxony, Brandenberg, and the Palatinate, and about eight thousand pastors.

The Formula of Concord deals with the following articles of faith: (1) original sin (affirming total depravity); (2) bondage of the will (affirming monergism in conversion and salvation by grace alone); (3) justification (stressing the forensic nature of justification); (4) good works; (5) the distinction between law and gospel; (6) the third use of the law (i.e., the necessity of preaching law in the Christian community); (7) the Lord's Supper (confessing the Lutheran doctrine of the sacramental union and the real presence); (8) the person of Christ (emphasizing the communication of attributes of the two natures); (9) the descent into hell (Christ's actual descent and victory over the forces of evil); (10) adiaphora; (11) predestination (to salvation by grace for Christ's sake, but not to hell); (12) various heresies (Anabaptism, Schwenckfeldianism, Neo-Arianism, etc.). R. D. Preus

See also Concord, Book of.

Bibliography. F. H. R. Frank, *Die Theologie der Concordienformel;* E. F. Klug, *Getting into the Formula of Concord;* R. D. Preus and W. H. Rosin, eds., *A Contemporary Look at the Formula of Concord;* E. Schlink, *The Theology of the Lutheran Confessions.*

Concursus. Concurrence (*concursus divinus*) is the term used to denote the relationship between the divine activity and that of finite creatures within God's providential control of the world. Scripture frequently speaks about the absolute sovereignty of God; it also emphasizes the reality of human decision and responsibility. The cooperation between the divine and human wills was treated by Augustine in his anti-Pelagian writings, but the doctrine of concurrence was not worked out until later. In the schoolmen, particularly Aquinas (*Contra Gentiles* III.66–67; *Summa Theologica* i.q.105), the doctrine is elaborated with heavy reliance on philosophical terminology. Later debate was over the question whether God acts mediately or immediately, i.e., through the gifts which he has bestowed on creatures, such as intelligence and will, or more directly in influencing their actions. Whereas Lutheran theologians have shown sympathy with the treatment of the subject, Reformed theology in general has rejected the doctrine of concurrence as introducing into theological discussion philosophical notions about causation that are foreign to the Bible, and considers the doctrine of providence under the topics of preservation and government. M. E. Osterhaven

Bibliography. G. C. Berkouwer, *The Providence of God.*

Condemnation. *See* Judgment.

Conditional Immortality. The doctrine that immortality was not a natural endowment of man at creation, but is a gift from God to the redeemed who believe in Christ. Those who do not receive Christ ultimately lose all consciousness or existence. It is related to annihilationism, which teaches that all men were created immortal but that those who do not repent and believe in Christ will by a positive act of God be deprived of immortality and reduced to nonexistence at death.

Some of the early church fathers made statements which could be taken to support conditional immortality. Thus Irenaeus argued that free but mortal man must be obedient to God in order to become immortal. Disobedience brings death, but obedience results in immortality (*Against Heresies* 4.38.3; 5.23.1). This teaching enjoyed some degree of popularity in the nineteenth century through the writings of E. White, J. B. Heard, and the prebendaries Constable and Row in England, Richard Rothe in Germany, A. Sabatier in France, E. Petavel and Ch. Secretan in Switzerland, and in the United States through C. F. Hudson, W. R. Huntington, C. C. Baker, L. W. Bacon, and Horace Bushnell.

Beyond the historical support like that cited above, conditionalists appeal to the Scriptures for additional evidence. (1) Only God is said to be immortal (I Tim. 6:16); (2) eternal life is described as a gift from God imparted only to the believing person (John 10:27–28; 17:3; Rom. 2:7; 6:22–23; Gal. 6:8); and (3) the wicked are said to "perish" or to be "destroyed," which is taken to mean that the nonredeemed will be reduced to nonexistence.

Yet in each of the above cases a satisfactory alternative explanation is available. (1) While God alone has inherent immortality, he chooses to impart immortality to certain of his creatures. (2) All men have a derivative immortality. We should not blur the distinction between immortality of existence with God's gift of eternal life to the believer in Christ. Immortality is continued existence, while eternal life speaks of a special kind of continued existence in the fellowship and blessing of the triune God. (3) The destruction of the wicked cannot arbitrarily be assumed to mean their nonexistence. Rather, it speaks of their loss of well-being and deprivation.

Furthermore, the doctrine of the resurrection of the wicked to condemnation argues against conditional immortality (John 5:28–29; cf. Rev. 20:6, "the first resurrection" implying a second resurrection which is the "second death"). It is this doctrine of resurrection which strikes a blow at both the Greek concept of the immortality of the soul and the conditional immortality viewpoint. Thus the biblical view of man concerns total man (body and soul). Immortality is a gift to all men in virtue of their creation and it is the total man which is immortal, hence the biblical emphasis on the resurrection of the body for both the wicked and the redeemed.

A. F. Johnson

See also Annihilationism.

Bibliography. L. Berkhof, *Systematic Theology;* B. B. Warfield, *SHERK,* I, 183–86.

Confession. The Hebrew *yādâ* and Greek *homologeō* (plus derivatives and related concepts) convey the idea of confession, acknowledgment, and praise of God's character and glorious works, often with expression of man's confession of faith in God and in his Son, Jesus Christ; also man's confession to God of his sins and wicked works.

In the OT one acknowledges and praises God's name: "We give you thanks and praise your glorious name" (I Chr. 29:13; cf. Ps. 145:1). Also the very person of God is praised: thanks is given to God who is good (Ps. 106:1), whose name (and therefore person) is holy (Pss. 97:12; 99:3), great, and awesome (Ps. 99:3). Exalted above all, God is praised as God of gods and Lord of lords (Ps. 136:2–3) and the God of heaven (Ps. 136:26). He is praised for his works of creation (Pss. 89:5; 136:4–9) and providential acts to his people (Ps. 136:10–24) and creatures (Ps. 136:25). A believer's true commitment to God is implied in such praise.

In the NT emphasis is placed on the personal acknowledgment of Christ: "Whoever acknowledges me before men" (Matt. 10:32) and particular acknowledgment of him as Savior and Lord (Rom. 10:9; cf. Phil. 2:11). This confession of Christ includes acknowledging him in his deity as the Son of God (Matt. 16:16; I John 4:15) and in his humanity as incarnate in the flesh (I John 4:2; II John 7).

The Bible also teaches that one is to confess his sins to this sovereign God. In the OT levitical sacrifices this is portrayed when the worshiper confesses his sins over the head of the sacrificial animal (cf. Lev. 1:4; 16:21), a picture or type of Christ, the Lamb of God (John 1:29), bearing the sins of his people (Isa. 53:6; I Cor. 5:7). The OT also emphasizes the great confessions of Israel's sins (Ezra 10:1; Neh. 1:6; 9:2–3; Dan. 9:4, 20). Personal confession is seen in David's acknowledgment (Ps. 32:5).

Confession of sin is also emphasized in the NT (Matt. 3:6; Mark 1:5), and with it is connected the promise of forgiveness of sins (I John 1:9; cf. Matt. 6:12), a forgiveness which is based solely on the death of Christ (Eph. 1:7). That confession of sin, an acknowledgment that forgiveness is possible only through Christ the risen Lord, God uses as an instrument in bringing the sinner to salvation (Rom. 10:9–10). This is to be a sacrifice of praise to God (Heb. 13:15). Although confession of sin is to be made to God alone (Luke 18:13), on occasion believers are encouraged to share their confession with one another (James 5:16).

W. H. Mare

Bibliography. W. A. Quanbeck, *IDB*, I, 667–68; R. H. Alexander, *TWOT*, I, 364–66; O. Michel, *TDNT*, V, 199–219; V. C. Grounds, *ZPEB*, I, 937–39.

Confession of 1967, The. The United Presbyterian Church in the United States of America adopted the Confession of 1967 as part of its *Book of Confessions* in 1967. Included with this confession are the Nicene Creed, the Apostles' Creed, the Scots Confession, the Heidelberg Catechism, the Second Helvetic Confession, the Westminster Confession and Shorter Catechism, and the Declaration of Barmen.

The central theme of the confession is reconciliation. Its three parts are God's Work of Reconciliation, the Ministry of Reconciliation, and the Fulfillment of Reconciliation. Closely intertwined throughout are a view of covenant and a continuing focus on Jesus Christ as the one in whom reconciliation takes place.

Assuming the doctrines of the Trinity and the person of Christ, the confession describes Jesus of Nazareth as a Palestinian Jew in whom "true humanity was realized once and for all." As the risen Christ he is also the Savior for all joined to him by faith as well as the judge of all people. New life and hope are marks of those who respond to Christ in faith, repentance, and obedience. The Scriptures as the "word of God written" and the "witness without parallel" to Jesus Christ are where the church finds its faith and obedience nourished and regulated.

The church as the reconciling community is to serve God by speaking and acting appropriately in the world and by carrying the gospel to all people. Four problems are mentioned as particularly urgent for the church to act upon at the present time: discrimination, international conflicts, poverty, and sexual anarchy. The gifts of the church are cited, and the confession ends with an affirmation of the final triumph of God.

D. K. McKim

See also Confessions of Faith.

Bibliography. "A Symposium—A Confessional Church," *McCQ* 19, No. 2; E. A. Dowey, Jr., *A Commentary on the Confession of 1967 and an Introduction to "The Book of Confessions"*; J. B. Rogers, "Biblical Authority and Confessional Change," *JPH* 59:131–59; *The Book of Confessions.*

Confessions of Faith. Variations on the term "confession" are found in the NT (e.g., I Tim. 3:16; 6:13). In the early church the word was used to describe the testimony of martyrs as they were about to meet their deaths. Its most common usage, however, designates the formal statements of Christian faith written by Protestants since the earliest days of the Reformation. As such, "confessions" are closely related to several other kinds of brief, authoritative summations of belief. The term "creed" most frequently refers to statements from the early church which Christians in all times and places have recognized—the Apostles' Creed, the Nicene Creed, the Definition of Chalcedon, and (less frequently) the Athanasian Creed. While Orthodox Churches hold to the authority of seven ancient ecumenical creeds, and while the Roman Catholic Church continues to use the term for later doctrinal formulations (as "the Creed of the Council of Trent," 1564), it is not uncommon to speak of just the Apostles' or just the Nicene affirmations as *the* creed. "Catechisms" are structured statements of faith written in the form of questions and answers which often fulfill the same functions as confessions. Finally, the technical term "symbol" is a general designation for any formal statement—whether creed, confession, or catechism—which sets apart the community which professes it from those who do not.

The Reformation and Confessions. Conditions in the sixteenth century were ripe for the composition of confessions. The publications of Luther, Calvin, Zwingli, and other Reformation leaders had brought momentous theological questions to the fore. When entire communities, or just the leaders, turned to their teachings, an immediate demand arose for uncomplicated yet authoritative statements of the new faith. The leading Reformers were also deeply involved in the day-to-day life of the churches where they sensed the uneasiness of the people—whether at the abuses of Rome or at their own innovations. And they early on saw the necessity for brief theological summaries that all could understand.

In addition, the very nature of the Reformation and the very character of the sixteenth century greatly stimulated the urge to write confessions. The Reformers posed Scripture as the ultimate authority for all of life, even if this undercut received Catholic tradition. They spoke of the priesthood of believers and the internal testimony of the Holy Spirit, in spite of the fact that these teachings called the pronouncements of Rome's infallible *magisterium* into question. The Reformers also challenged Catholic influence in the state. They proposed a new reading of history to support their own push for reform. And they had a passion for restoring the NT purity of Christian belief and practice. Yet every assault on an established belief and every challenge to a traditional practice called for a rationale, a concise statement of the reasons for change.

It was not, however, merely in the religious sphere that change prepared the way for newer confessions of faith. Europe in general was passing through a period of rapid evolution. Virtually every support for traditional Roman Catholic belief was then under fire. If the Reformers challenged Catholic interference in the state and Catholic involvement in the economy, so too did monarchs of the new nation-states question the church's traditional political role, and the burgeoning class of merchants challenged its accustomed authority in the world of trade. If Luther and Calvin called upon Rome to rethink its interpretation of Scripture, so too did leaders of the Renaissance challenge other intellectual traditions in art, political theory, literature, and history. If the Reformation raised troubling questions in theology, so too had several generations of academicians raised troubling issues in philosophy. In short, the world of the sixteenth century needed new statements of Christian belief not just to reorient Christian life, but to reposition Christianity itself within the forces of early modern Europe.

The great outpouring of confessions in the first century and a half of Protestantism performed a multitude of functions. Authoritative statements of Christian belief enshrined the new ideas of the theologians, but in forms that could also provide regular instruction for the common faithful. They lifted a standard around which a local community could rally and which could make plain the differences with opponents. They made possible a regathering of belief and practice in the interests of unity, even as they established a norm to discipline the erring. And for Catholics, the writing of confessionlike statements made it possible to discriminate between acceptable modifications in its ancient faith and unacceptable deviations from its traditional norms.

The Confessions of Protestants. Very early in the Reformation, Protestants began to set down their vision of the faith. In little more than the first decade of reform in Switzerland, Ulrich Zwingli himself superintended the publication of four confessional documents—the Sixty-seven Articles of Zurich in 1523 (to bring his own canton to break with Rome), the Ten Theses of Berne in 1528 (to solidify reform in that city), the Confession of Faith to Charles V in 1530 (to inform the emperor of Protestant convictions), and the Exposition of the Faith to King Francis I in 1531 (to move the French sovereign to a more even-handed attitude toward Protestants). In Germany, meanwhile, Luther had published his Small Catechism in 1529 after a disappointing tour of Saxony revealed gross ignorance of elemental biblical material, not even to speak of the main Reformation principles. And in 1530 the Protestant princes of Germany confessed their faith before the emperor at Augsburg in a document written by Philip Melanchthon which has stood as the touchstone of Lutheran theology ever since. The same pattern appeared in other Protestant regions. Soon after the magistrates or the common people accepted Reformation teaching, a single individual or a small group would be commissioned to write a definitive statement of faith. The process was the same for Basel, Geneva, and Zurich, for the French Protestants, for Lutheran communities in Germany and Scandinavia, for Scotland, Holland, Bohemia, Poland, and England. And at the close of the Council of Trent (1545–63), which defined orthodox Catholicism in lengthy canons and decrees, Rome also recapitulated its faith in a brief, authoritative statement. (Since that time the Catholic Church has published many catechisms to communicate the Tridentine faith, including the Baltimore Catechism which has long been used in the United States.)

The very nature of Protestantism as a politically diverse movement prevented the formulation of a single inclusive confession. Yet in the Reformation's "second generation" considerable consolidation did occur. Lutherans wrote many confessions throughout the sixteenth century, but in 1580 they authorized the *Book of Concord* to designate the specific symbols which were to ground their teaching—the Apostles', Nicene, and Athanasian Creeds, the Smalcald Articles (1537), the Formula of Concord (1577), and especially Luther's Small and Large Catechisms (1529) and the Augsburg Confession (1530). Scandinavian Lutherans tended to consolidate even more thoroughly by neglecting the *Book of Concord* and rallying instead around just the Augsburg Confession.

In Reformed areas the same process was at work. The different Protestant cities of Switzerland wrote many catechisms and statements of belief, including several that attempted to mediate Protestant differences concerning the Lord's Supper. Eventually, however, several of them settled on the Second Helvetic Confession (1566), originally composed for his own use by Heinrich Bullinger, Zwingli's successor in Zurich. Although the Heidelberg Catechism (1563) was written to pacify Protestant strife in just that one city, it became a rallying symbol for Reformed groups in Germany, Holland, and elsewhere. Similar consolidation occurred in the British Isles, where the Thirty-nine Articles (1563) emerged with the sanction of Elizabeth I as the official statement of the English church. Those in England and Scotland who leaned more consistently to Calvinism were not entirely unhappy with the articles, but they still proposed modifications or alternative symbols of their own, a process which culminated in the 1640s with the Westminster Confession and Catechisms. Although Protestants continued to write confessions, certain of the earlier documents achieved a dominant position which they have retained to the present.

To be sure, the writing of confessions has never stopped, especially in the United States. The profusion of new denominations in America, or the branching off of old bodies into new configurations, has created a situation in which composition proceeds with great regularity. American Congregationalists, Baptists, Methodists, and Presbyterians among many others have rewritten Old World creeds to fit the New World situation (e.g., the Congregationalist Saybrook Platform of 1708 or the American Presbyterian revisions of the Westminster Confession in 1788). Others have composed altogether new documents (e.g., the New Hampshire Confession of Faith for Baptists in 1833). Americans have also issued confessionlike statements as the charters for new denominations (e.g., Thomas Campbell's "Declaration and Address" of 1809 which helped found the Disciples of Christ). They have written confessions in response to shifting theological perceptions (e.g., the Presbyterian Confession of 1967). And even the Lutherans, among the most conservative of Protestants, have at times proposed modifications in the Augsburg Confession, although these have been regularly turned back.

The writing of confessions is not by any means an exclusively American enterprise. Two of the most significant Protestant confessions of the twentieth century arose beyond the shores of the United States: the Barmen Declaration in 1934, in which German "confessing Christians" announced their determination to live by the Word of God come what may, and the Lausanne Covenant of 1974, which expressed the faith of evangelicals from around the world on theological and social matters. The ecumenical movement has also led to a series of important confessional statements in this century (e.g., "The Call to Unity" of the Lausanne Faith and Order Conference, 1927). And even the Catholics have experienced a kind of confessional activity with the decrees on papal infallibility from the first Vatican Council in 1870 and from Pope Pius XII on the assumption of the Virgin Mary in 1950.

The Place of Confessions in the Churches. Given the diversity of Protestants, it is not surprising that the heirs of the Reformation also put confessions to use in diverse ways. Some of the differences can be explained by the circumstances of their composition. Others arise from differing Protestant attitudes toward confessions themselves. Confessions, in the first place, reflect the developmental stage of the group for which they were written. Luther's Small Catechism of 1529, a manual for private and family instruction, has more spontaneity of expression and more concern for simplified essentials than the Augsburg Confession of 1530, composed for presentation to the emperor and to theologians, or the Formula of Concord of 1577, written to quiet a lengthy series of theological controversies among the Lutherans. Confessions also differ depending on the theological circumstances which called them into existence. The Christian Reformed Church holds both the Heidelberg Catechism and the Canons of Dort (1619) among its official confessional statements. They are, however, quite different documents, since the Heidelberg Catechism was written for pastoral and irenic purposes, while the Canons of Dort were a response to one set of narrow theological issues. It also makes considerable difference whether the confession came into being with the support of an entire community or as the outcry of a besieged minority. England's Parliament commissioned the Westminster Confession and gave its authors time and much support to write it. Quite predictably, it turned out to be a comprehensive and balanced statement. The Anabaptist Schleitheim Articles (1527), on the other hand, were written under duress by Michael Sattler, who was put to death for his convictions only three months after penning the document. Not surprisingly, it turns out to neglect general areas of Christian agreement in order to emphasize the distinctive doctrines and practices of the Swiss Brethren. Although they are sometimes forgotten, the historical conditions surrounding the composition of a confession sometimes explain a great deal about the thrust of the document.

Other distinctive features in the employment of confessions are related more to attitudes concerning authority or the church. Baptists who seek to ground faith exclusively on the Bible alone will regard the New Hampshire Confession as merely advisory; Anglicans and Episcopalians will differ among themselves over whether the Thirty-nine Articles are a current denominational standard or an antiquarian statement of merely historical interest; some smaller Presbyterian bodies will insist that their ministers and elders follow the Westminster Confession and Catechisms to the letter. In the past the denominations of greater centralization (episcopal or presbyterian) tended to place more weight on confessions than those of greater decentralization (congregational). But now some of the historically confessional bodies sit much looser to statements of faith than do independent churches and organizations.

Confessions also reflect different theological perspectives. Even in the great era of confession writing following the Reformation, it was possible to distinguish broadly between two sorts of statements—those which emphasized the drama of redemption and those which placed greater emphasis on the truth of the faith. The first gave heightened attention to the person of God and his loving mercy toward sinners, or at least moved these topics to the top of the agenda. They included the Augsburg Confession, Luther's Small Catechism, Zwingli's Sixty-seven Articles and Ten Theses of Berne, the Heidelberg Catechism, the Scots Confession (1560), and the Thirty-nine Articles. The second began with the truths of revelation in Scripture before going on to a discussion of God's activity. Among these were the First Helvetic Confession (1536), the Second Helvetic Confession, the French Confession of Calvin (1559), the Belgic Confession (1561), the Irish Articles of James Ussher (1615), and the Westminster Confession. Many of the two types of confessions were fully compatible with each other (e.g., the Reformation movement in Holland adopted both the Heidelberg Catechism and the Belgic Confession). But in structuring themselves along different lines, these documents testified to the way in which theological vision shapes confessional emphasis. In subsequent centuries a much wider range of theological convictions have found expression in a much less harmonious group of Protestant confessions.

The Propriety of Confessions. Confessions have served Protestants as bridges between scriptural revelation and particular cultures. They arise in response to a need for understanding Christian teaching concerning a particular problem or in a particular place. As such, many confessions have had their hour in the sun and passed quietly away. Others, because of affective power or balanced judiciousness, have endured. Some of these have become extremely important to their communions, so much so that in practice it is nearly unthinkable to challenge the confession openly while remaining a member in good standing. Yet even in these cases Protestants insist, as the great student of the creeds Philip Schaff once put it, that "the authority of symbols, as of all human compositions, is relative and limited. It is not coordinate with, but always subordinate to, the Bible, as the only infallible rule of the Christian faith and practice." Many Protestant confessions acknowledge this fact directly by including a statement that even the best of human documents are liable to error.

The realization that confessions err, combined with Protestant allegiance to Scripture, has led especially some independent groups to disparage confessions entirely. A rallying cry for this point of view, which gained popularity in America during the early nineteenth century, has been the slogan, "No creed but the Bible." In point of fact, however, all Protestant bodies have operated under the authority of either formal, written confessions or informal, unwritten standards that function like confessions. In the latter case a series of inarticulate guidelines, often regulating belief and practice to the minutest detail, shapes the thought and actions of the members of the communion.

Protestants who value written confessions make two arguments to those who play down their importance. The first is practical. They contend that a written confessional document encourages clarity of belief and openness in theological discussion. Unwritten standards, it is argued, are overly susceptible to the manipulation of power brokers or the vagaries of selective application. The second defense is scriptural. Those who affirm the value of confessions point to the many places in the NT where formalized summaries of belief are taken for granted as aids to faith and practice (e.g., "what we preach," I Cor. 1:21; "the truth," II Thess. 2:13; "the gospel," I Cor. 15:1–8; "the word," Gal. 6:6; "the doctrine of Christ," II John 9–10; "the sure word," Titus 1:9; "the standard of teaching," Rom. 6:17; "the traditions," I Cor. 11:2; "traditions," II Thess. 3:6; and even that which we "confess," I Tim. 3:16). Defenders of Protestant confessionalism regard these biblical precedents as ample warrant for the continued employment of confessions.

To be sure, Protestants do not ascribe to their confessions the status which the Roman Catholic Church gives to its doctrinal promulgations. Protestant confessionalists acknowledge the work of the Holy Spirit in the unfolding of doctrine throughout history and in the writing of confessions, but they regard that work always as an illumination or an extension of the absolute standards of Scripture. The churches have no independent capacity to compose confessions but are everywhere dependent upon the authoritative norm of Scripture. And they may certainly make mistakes. While Roman Catholics, on the other hand, also treat Scripture as a norm, they believe that the Holy Spirit inspires the teaching *magisterium* of the church in such a way as to make its definite pronouncements coordinate in authority with the Bible. The self-correcting statements of the Protestant confessions—that even the best of confessions must not encroach upon the ultimate authority of Scripture—differentiate the authority of Protestant confessions from Catholic dogmas.

Although Protestants do not regard confessions as absolute authorities in matters of faith and practice, many of them have found confessions to be valuable introductions to Christian belief, helpful summaries of Scripture, and dependable guides to the Christian life.

M. A. Noll

See also Augsburg Confession; Westminster Confession of Faith; Thirty-nine Articles, The; New Hampshire Confession; Luther's Small Catechism; Concord, Book of; Helvetic Confessions; Scots Confession; Heidelberg Catechism; Irish Articles; Smalcald Articles, The; Confession of 1967, The.

Bibliography. P. Schaff, *The Creeds of Christendom,* 3 vols.; J. H. Leith, *Creeds of the Churches;* C. Plantinga, Jr., *A Place to Stand: A Reformed Study of Creeds and Confessions;* T. G. Tappert, ed., *The Book of Concord;* A. C. Cochrane, ed., *Reformed Confessions of the Sixteenth Century.*

Confirmation. One of the seven sacraments of both the Roman Catholic and Eastern Orthodox church. The Roman Church teaches that it was instituted by Christ, through his disciples, for the church. Its early history is somewhat uncertain, and only gradually did it receive recognition as a sacrament. It was given a sacramental status by Peter Lombard in the twelfth century and by Thomas Aquinas in the thirteenth century, and finally by the Council of Trent in the sixteenth century. One of the two sacraments administered by a bishop in the Roman Catholic Church, its purpose is to make those who have been baptized in the faith strong soldiers of Jesus Christ. It is administered to children before they receive their first Communion, generally at about the age of twelve. Concerning it Aquinas wrote: "Confirmation is to baptism what growth is to generation." It is administered according to this form: "I sign thee with the sign of the Cross and confirm thee with the chrism of salvation." Since it confers an indelible character upon the recipient, it is administered but once. According to Roman Catholic theology, sanctifying grace is increased in the soul, and a special sacramental grace consisting of the seven gifts of the Holy Spirit is conferred upon the recipient. This has recently been reaffirmed by Pope Paul VI in the Apostolic Constitution on the Sacrament of Confirmation (1971), where he says, "Through the sacrament of confirmation, those who have been born anew in baptism receive the inexpressible Gift, the Holy Spirit himself, by which they are endowed . . . with special strength."

In the Lutheran Church confirmation is a rite

rather than a sacrament and the recipient offers it as a confirmation in his own heart of those baptismal vows which his parents assumed on his behalf. It is administered but once at about thirteen or fourteen years of age and admits the recipient to the Communion. In the Episcopal Church it is a sacramental rite completing baptism. C. G. SINGER

See also SACRAMENT; BAPTISM.

Bibliography. H. J. D. Denzinger, *Sources of Catholic Dogma;* G. W. Bromiley, *Sacramental Teaching and Practice in the Reformation Churches;* G. C. Richards, *Baptism and Confirmation;* G. Dix, *The Theology of Confirmation in Relation to Baptism;* G. W. H. Lampe, *The Seal of the Spirit;* L. S. Thornton, *Confirmation.*

Congregationalism. *See* CHURCH GOVERNMENT.

Conscience. The word is derived from the Latin *conscientia,* which is a compound of the preposition *con* and *scio,* meaning "to know together," "joint knowledge with others," "the knowledge we share with another." It stems from the same root as *consciousness,* which means "awareness of." Conscience is an awareness restricted to the moral sphere. It is a moral awareness. The Greek equivalent in the NT is *syneidēsis,* a compound of *syn,* "together," and *eidenai,* "to know," that is, to know together with, to have common knowledge together with someone. The German *Gewissen* has the same meaning. The prefix *ge* expresses a collective idea, the "together with," and *wissen* is "to know."

In the Bible. The word "conscience" does not appear in the OT. However, the idea is well known and is expressed by the term "heart." It appears at the very dawn of human history as a sense of guilt with Adam and Eve after the fall. We read of David that his heart smote him (II Sam. 24:10). Jobs says: "My heart shall not reproach me" (Job 27:6). And Pss. 32:1–5 and 51:1–9 are the cries of anguish of an aroused conscience.

The Babylonians, like the Hebrews, identified conscience with the heart. The Egyptians had no specific word for conscience but recognized its authority, as is evident from the Book of the Dead. The early Greeks and Romans personified conscience and depicted it as fiendish female demons called Erinyes and Furies respectively.

The word *syneidēsis* or "conscience" appears thirty times in the NT—nineteen times in the writings of Paul, five times in Hebrews, three times in the letters of Peter, twice in Acts, and once in the Gospel of John, although the correctness of the latter reading (8:9) has been questioned.

Description. Conscience is that faculty by which one distinguishes between the morally right and wrong, which urges one to do that which he recognizes to be right and restrains him from doing that which he recognizes to be wrong, which passes judgment on his acts and executes that judgment within his soul. Webster defines conscience as the sense or consciousness of right and wrong. Kant speaks of it as a consciousness of a court within man's being or the categorical imperative. Others have defined conscience as the ethical sense organ in man.

Conscience is innate. According to Rom. 2:14–15 conscience is innate and universal. It is not the product of environment, training, habit, or education, though it is influenced by all of these factors.

As to function, conscience is threefold. (1) Obligatory. It urges man to do that which he regards as right and restrains him from doing that which he regards as wrong. (2) Judicial. Conscience passes judgment upon man's decisions and acts. (3) Executive. Conscience executes its judgment in the heart of man. It condemns his action when in conflict with his conviction by causing an inward disquietude, distress, shame, or remorse. It commends when man has acted in conformity with his convictions.

Erring conscience. This is a misnomer. Conscience does not err, but the standard on the basis of which conscience acts might be in error.

The morbid, perverted, or narrow conscience. By this is meant a conscience out of proper balance, narrow, fanatic, bigoted.

Pathological and neurotic conscience. This has its origin in a psychic disorder or in a neurosis related to phobias, obsessions, fixed ideas, and compulsions.

Doubting conscience. One who acts in uncertainty. Rom. 14:23 declares such action to be sinful.

Dulled, calloused, or dead conscience. This is a condition wherein conscience ceases to function because of repeated disregard of its warning voice. Paul speaks of it as a seared conscience (I Tim. 4:2).

Good conscience. When man acts in conformity with his convictions, he is said to have a good conscience. "Faith cannot exist and abide with and alongside of a wicked intention to sin and to act against conscience" (Formula of Concord, Epitome IV).

Social conscience. The merging of the individual moral consciousness into a group moral consciousness results in the social conscience.

Freedom of conscience. The freedom to believe, practice, and propagate any religion whatsoever or none at all is referred to as freedom of conscience.

Conscience is a gift of God. It is a guardian of

morality, justice, and decency in the world. It is an irrefutable testimony to the existence of God.

A. M. Rehwinkel

Bibliography. A. M. Rehwinkel, *The Voice of Conscience;* C. A. Pierce, *Conscience in the NT;* H. C. Hahn and C. Brown, *NIDNTT,* I, 348ff.; R. Jewett, *Paul's Anthropological Terms;* C. Maurer, *TDNT,* VII, 898ff.; N. H. G. Robinson, *Christ and Conscience;* H. Thielicke, *Theological Ethics,* I, 298ff.; K. Stendahl, "The Apostle Paul and the Introspective Conscience of the West," *HTR* 56:199ff.

Conscientious Objection. *See* Pacifism.

Consensus Tigurinus. *See* Zurich Agreement.

Conservation. That continual activity of God whereby he maintains in existence the things which he has created, together with the forms, properties, and powers with which he has endowed them. While conservation presupposes creation, it is distinguished from it. In creation God acted to bring the universe into existence; in conservation God acts to sustain what he has already created. Creation is the production of something out of nothing; conservation is the maintenance of that something which already exists. Futhermore, in creation God is the sole cause of the universe, but in conservation there is a cooperation and concurrence of the first with second causes. In Scripture the two concepts, although inseparably related, are never confused: "all things were created by him . . . and by him all things consist" (Col. 1:16–17).

According to Scripture, the exercise of that omnipotent energy by which God sustains existence extends over all created things, animate and inanimate. Some texts assert in general terms that God sustains all things by the word of his power (Neh. 9:6; Col. 1:17; Heb. 1:3). Others refer to the regular operations of nature which are declared to be preserved in their efficiency by divine power (Pss. 104; 148). Still others indicate that both irrational animals and rational creatures owe their continual existence to God's sustaining power (Pss. 36:6; 66:8–9; Acts 17:28; I Tim. 6:13*a*). Such passages teach that the created order does not sustain itself; that, in fact, it would revert to nothingness if unsupported by God's power; that no creature continues in existence by an inherent principle of life, but by the will of the Creator; and that conservation includes not only essence and substance, but also the nature, attributes, and powers of all created things.

W. W. Benton, Jr.

See also God, Doctrine of; God, Attributes of.

Constantinople, Council of (381). The gathering in Constantinople of 150 Eastern bishops at the request of the Emperor Theodosius I was later regarded by the Council of Chalcedon (451) as the second great ecumenical council of the church. Most importantly it marked the end of over fifty years of Arian political and theological dominance in the East and the restoration and pneumatological extension of Nicene orthodoxy.

The path of history from Nicaea to Constantinople is twisted with various political and theological figures and several theological and synodal skirmishes between Arianism and orthodoxy. The varied array of heresies that emerged during this period is given in the council's first canon, where they are also anathematized. A brief examination of these will set the theological context.

Semi-Arians. This name was applied to those who tried to steer a middle course between Nicene orthodoxy and Arianism. Too sensitive to Sabellian implications and the biblical absence of the term *homoousion* to fully embrace Nicaea and recoiling from blatant Arian characterizations of the Son as a creature, they took refuge in the term *homoiousion.* By this they taught that the Son was like (*homoios*) the Father but not necessarily the same in essence. This ambiguous position was held by many who were very close to orthodoxy—e.g., Cyril of Jerusalem—as well as those who were more of an Arian disposition—e.g., Basil of Ancyra. Due to the efforts of Athanasius and Hilary of Poitiers many of this party were reconciled to orthodoxy, especially as more radical Arian positions developed.

Pneumatomachians. In the post-Nicene period attention was turned to the Holy Spirit and his relation to the discussions on the Father and the Son. About 360, Athanasius wrote to correct an Egyptian heresy advocated by the Tropici in which the Spirit was taught to have been created out of nothing. Athanasius maintained instead the deity of the Spirit and his *homoousia* with the Father and the Son. After this the pneumatomachians (literally "Spirit-fighters") appeared within the *homoiousion* party. Led by Eustathius of Sebaste (after 373), they tried to assert a nondivine, noncreaturely, intermediate status for the Spirit, even after affirming the *homoousia* of the Son. They were opposed by the Cappadocians, who taught the full deity and *homoousia* of the Spirit both implicitly (as in Basil, *On the Holy Spirit*) and explicitly (as in Gregory of Nazianzus, *Oration 31*). It is this Cappadocian (and Athanasian) theology which prevailed at the Council of Constantinople.

Eunomians or Anomoians. Founded by Aetius of Antioch and led by Eunomius of Cyzicus at the time of the council, these held the radical Arian position which refused any compromise with orthodoxy. They taught a Neoplatonic hierarchy of three beings which were in essence utterly unlike (*anomoios*) each other, though possessing relative divinity (thus confirming the charge of polytheism).

Eudoxians. These held a classical Arian position particularly advocated at the time of the council by the followers of Eudoxius, former bishop of Antioch (358) and Constantinople (360). He was known for the jest: "The Father is impious (since he worships no one), but the Son is pious (since he worships the Father)."

Sabellians, Marcellians, and Photinians. Since the Arians vigorously insisted that the *homoousion* logically reduced to Sabellianism, it was necessary for the council to repudiate this heresy. One who actually came close to espousing it was Marcellus of Ancyra, who resisted the Cappadocian Trinitarian development in which three *hypostases* were distinguished while maintaining one *ousia*. Marcellus preferred to speak of the expansion of an indivisible Monad (God) which resulted in the externalization of the (until then) immanently existing Logos (the Son) at the time of incarnation, with an expected future contraction of the Logos back into the Monad. Although he was exonerated of the Sabellian label at Rome (341) and Sardica (343), Constantinople condemned his deviant views. Photinus of Sirmium, a pupil of Marcellus, developed his teacher's views into an adoptionist Christology and was condemned for the heresy of Paul of Samosata at various councils.

Apollinarians. Constantinople brought a final condemnation on this Christological heresy which originated within the Nicene camp. A former friend of Athanasius, Apollinarius of Laodicea zealously advocated the deity of the Logos and upheld the *homoousion*. However, in his concern to avoid the dualistic personality of an adoptionistic Christology, he capitulated to the Arian error in which the Logos completely replaced the human soul and mind in the incarnate Christ. For this deficient humanity he was opposed reluctantly by Athanasius and vigorously by the Cappadocians.

The theology of the Council of Constantinople is set forth first by the condemnation of these heresies. More positively, it was expressed in a published statement of doctrine, a *tomos*, and the creed of the council. Unfortunately, the *tomos* is no longer extant except for what is reflected of it in the letter of the synod of 382. The creed is to be found not in the records of Constantinople, but in those of the Council of Chalcedon (451), where a creed attributed to Constantinople (C) was read along with the Nicene Creed (N). C happens to be the creed that is read in churches today under the title the Nicene Creed, but it is more appropriately known as the Niceno-Constantinopolitan Creed. Without recounting the scholarly debates on C, it seems most likely that it was a local form of N, adopted by Constantinople and amended to reflect the council's pneumatology. Thus the Council of Constantinople did not see itself as producing a new creed but rather reaffirming and upholding the faith of Nicaea. At Chalcedon, however, concern for the pure form of N led them to distinguish between N and C.

The pneumatological emendation of the Nicene faith followed the example of Basil by limiting itself to biblical words and phrases. The Spirit is confessed to be the "Lord" and "Life-giver," the one "who with the Father and the Son is together worshiped and together glorified." The *homoousia* of the Spirit is not explicitly affirmed here, probably because of a last-minute attempt to reconcile the pneumatomachians. However, the *homoousion* apparently was affirmed in the *tomos*, since the letter of the synod of 382 summarizes the council's doctrine as faith in the uncreated, consubstantial, and coeternal trinity.

Besides the reaffirmation of Nicene orthodoxy, this developed pneumatology, which made possible a full Trinitarian doctrine for the East, was the most important contribution of the Council of Constantinople. C. A. BLAISING

See also ARIANISM; NICAEA, COUNCIL OF; MONARCHIANISM; APOLLINARIANISM; HOMOOUSION.

Bibliography. "Canons of the One Hundred and Fifty Fathers," *The Seven Ecumenical Councils, NPNF;* *H. M. Gwatkin, Studies of Arianism;* J. N. D. Kelly, *Early Christian Creeds* and *Early Christian Doctrines;* C. E. Raven, *Apollinarianism;* R. Seeberg, *The Textbook of the History of Doctrines;* J. Taylor, "The First Council of Constantinople (381)," *Pru* 13:47-54, 91-97; W. P. DuBose, *The Ecumenical Councils.*

Constructive Theology. In the 1970s a group of American theologians of nonevangelical persuasion designed a long-range work group on constructive theology. The study group of approximately twenty-five theologians adopted as its agenda the task of clarifying how the church can meet and shape the actual world with a Christian message freed from bondage to arcane models of vertical transcendence. Their theme is that the traditional package of classical orthodox faith is discredited and must be reshaped to meet the needs of the modern world.

The character and objectives of the work group were first described by Julian Hartt in *Occasional Papers* of the Institute for Ecumenical and Cultural Research, March, 1979. The work group undertook its initial study under the auspices of the institute, and Hartt's article nicely summarizes the goals of the new theology. The members of the work group included, from Vanderbilt Divinity School, Edward Farley, John Forstman, Peter Hodgson, Eugene TeSelle, Sallie McFague, and Robert C. Williams. From other schools, Carl Braaten (Lutheran School of Theology, Chicago), David Burrell (Notre Dame), John Cobb (Claremont School of Theology), Stephen Crites (Wesleyan University), Langdon Gilkey and David Tracy (University of Chicago Divinity School), Gordon Kaufman and George Rupp (Harvard Divinity School), George Kehm (Pittsburgh Theological Seminary), David Kelsey (Yale Divinity School), Robert H. King (Millsaps College), Walter Lowe (Candler School of Theology), Schubert Ogden and John Deschner (Perkins School of Theology), George Stroup (Princeton Theological Seminary), and Robert R. Williams (Hiram College).

The first item on the agenda addresses the authority of Scripture. Hartt asserts that the faith of our fathers may be living still, but we are not under a divine mandate to accept our theological fathers' views and uses of Scripture. Indeed, he says, hardly anything better illustrates the power of historical relativism in our time than the need to produce constructive—constructive rather than past-regarding—views on the authority and function of Scripture in theological work. American theologians are not as tied to biblical theology as their European counterparts, and accordingly are not likely to claim direct scriptural warrant for every serious theological proposal about God, man, nature, and history. The group concludes that the authority of Scripture is a question that cannot be resolved by appealing directly to Scripture itself; the decision to make Scripture the ultimate norm of Christian life and thought cannot be shown to have been a decision made in Scripture, but is an inescapable theological decision that can be neither resolved nor vindicated by exegetical maneuvers.

The decision of the work group not to take a strong stand on the authority of Scripture reflects their tacit assumption regarding the question of authority in the Christian life: in a pluralistic society such as ours the matter is left as vague as possible. The assumption is that a devotedly pluralistic culture will not stand for a theology based on the absolutely normative authority of Scripture.

The large question the work group is wrestling with is the problem of theological method. The pattern that has emerged is Hegelian. Basic Christian doctrines have been assigned to various members who will follow a common format. First, a brief account of the historical development of the doctrine will be presented (thesis); then will follow an analysis of the factors in the modern world that have eroded the traditional meanings of the doctrine (antithesis); and finally the constructive work of the group will proceed to reformulate the traditional doctrine in terms acceptable to the mood of modernity (synthesis).

In this dialectical enterprise contemporary criticisms of traditional Christian doctrines determine the final reformulations. That this is clearly the case, and that the authority of Enlightenment modernity has replaced the authority of Scripture, comes out in a major presupposition of the work group. Much of the traditional package of the Christian faith has been discredited. Christian supernaturalism may be just an attachment of dubious classical philosophical systems to Christian faith. In any event, the work group feels that modern secularist attacks have overpowered the central element of "vertical transcendence," or the supernatural, in traditional theology. Accordingly, one of the principal questions the constructive theologians of the work group face, along with the minister in the pulpit, is whether the Christian message can be freed from bondage to arcane models of vertical transcendence; so bound, the church's message fails to reckon with the shape and movement of the actual world. The factor which works most powerfully to discredit the traditional package is the enormity of evil in our time.

The first published volume of the work group's research appeared in 1982 under the title *Christian Theology: An Introduction to Its Traditions and Tasks*, edited by Peter Hodgson and Robert King. The book is a collaborative venture that addresses the traditional doctrines of Christian faith: Scripture and tradition, God, revelation, creation and providence, human being, sin and evil, Christ and salvation, church, Holy Spirit and the Christian life, kingdom of God and the life everlasting, and world religions. The evangelical reader will gauge the effectiveness of this renewed attempt at an older venture of theological liberalism by the pluralistic and nonsupernatural assumptions expressed in the articles. The authors seem convinced that in this new age progressive theologians are aware, as their foremothers and forefathers were not, that theology is a constructive enterprise and that Christianity is but one religion among many.

Since this volume (with subsequent results of the collaborative process) is designed to be used as a textbook in colleges, universities, and seminaries, it warrants the careful scrutiny and reply of orthodox scholars. Primary concerns include the epistemological assumption of the work group that modern pluralism is normative over Scripture, that classical Christianity is arcane, discredited, and addresses the problem of evil less well in our time than constructive theology, and whether the adjective "constructive" properly describes an enterprise that promotes the deconstruction and demolition of biblical faith as a central task in the reconstruction of theology for our time. R. G. GRUENLER

Consubstantiation. *See* LORD'S SUPPER, VIEWS OF.

Consummation of the Age. *See* ESCHATOLOGY.

Contextualization of Theology. The genesis of the neologism "contextualization" must be understood in order to understand its meaning and method. An October, 1970, circular letter from Nikos A. Nissiotis (then director of the Ecumenical Institute of the World Council of Churches) regarding the imminent 1971 consultation on "Dogmatic or Contextual Theology" in Switzerland emphasized the need for a new point of departure in theologizing. His concern, subsequently reinforced by the consultation, was to give preference to a "contextual or experiential" theology that grows out of the contemporary historical scene and thought, in contrast to systematic or dogmatic theologies the aegis of which are discoverable in the biblical tradition and confessional statements based on the biblical text.

Along with other discussions, the 1971 consultation reflected the "Third Mandate" effort of the WCC's Theological Education Fund and its directors Shoki Coe and Aharon Sapsezian to discern the issues and challenges to theological education posed by secularism, technology, and a variety of social and religious struggles, especially in the Third World. In 1972 the TEF report *Ministry in Context* introduced "contextualization" as a term and approach designed to supersede the indigenization approach that had been dominant in mission theory for a century. The new emphasis was viewed as including the positive elements of the older term but going beyond this in order to take the new challenge into account in theologizing as well as ministering.

The rootage of contextualized theology is to be found in the Christian-Marxist dialogue; the impetus given to the secularization of the theology by Vatican II and the social encyclicals dealing with the *aggiornamento* of the church in the world; the economic and sociopolitical analyses of Latin America put forth at the Medellín meeting of CELAM (1968); and the Uppsala General Assembly of the WCC (1968), where the agenda of the world was taken as the agenda of the church and the idea of the unity of the church as a sign of the unity of mankind was introduced. Precursors of the kind of contextualization advocated in the conciliar movement include the theology of hope, the theology of liberation, and black theology. In accordance with these trends and concerns TEF leaders attempted to "press beyond" the more static indigenization (self-supporting, self-governing, self-propagating) concept in mission to one that is more dynamic, open to change, and future-oriented. Accordingly, contextuality has been defined by Shoki Coe as critically assessing contexts in the light of the *missio Dei,* and contextualization has been advocated as a new way of theologizing which takes into account the dialectic between contextuality and contextualization. The aegis of theologizing has been located in praxis within the world rather than in the exegesis of Scripture. And mission has become a matter of discerning what God is doing in the contemporary world and participating in that task rather than participating in a missionary task delineated in the NT. The mixed results of such theologizing are discoverable in the recent works of such scholars as John Mbiti, E. W. Fashole-Luke, Néstor Paz, Choan-Seng Song, and Kosuke Koyama (see *Mission Trends No. 3*). As an examination of the resultant theologies will show, the gains resulting from an increased awareness of the "cultural bent" of Western theologies and the need for taking non-Western cultural contexts much more seriously have been often undercut by a theological method which prizes analysis of cultural and sociopolitical contexts more than the grammaticohistorical interpretation of the Bible and consideration of the historic creeds of the church.

More conservative scholars have not been slow to respond. Along with potential gains of contextualized theology they see new digressions from the biblical mandate. The International Congress on World Evangelization in Lausanne (1972) gave some attention to contextualization. Brought together by the Lausanne Continuation Committee, a group of mostly conservative theologians and missiologists meeting at Willowbank, Bermuda (1974), studied the issues growing out of the developing contextualization theory and practice (see *Down to Earth*). Other responses by conservatives and evangelicals to contextualized theology in general and liberation theology in particular have been coming from a wide spectrum of conservative evangelicals. These responses are divergent. Some feel that the term is already so ambiguous and misleading that it should be abandoned altogether. A majority, however, take the approach of redefining the word and redirecting the method. This latter group differs in such matters as the importance to be attached to cultures; the relation between evangelism and humanitarian and sociopolitical action in mission; and the relationships between faith and theologizing, meaning and symbol, form and function, and meaning and relevance. A broad consensus among conservatives has emerged, however. It is understood, for example, that theologies developed in the Third World will give special attention to such issues as demonism, sorcery, and ancestor veneration and less emphasis to matters of classification and ontological/functional questions. At the same time, it is recognized that theological reflection without epistemological control and revelatory givens can lay no valid claim to being Christian. Western and Third World theologians who base their teachings on Scripture may indeed develop different theologies. But they will develop theologies that are complementary, not contradictory. Moreover, these Western and Third World theologians will be in a position to encourage one another to a richer understanding of the person, purpose, and provision of God and to challenge one another to faithfulness to his Word.

While adaptation to cultural contexts and existential situations is incumbent upon both theologians and participants in mission, adherence to the Scriptures must be viewed as basic to all authentic theologizing and missionizing.

D. J. Hesselgrave

Bibliography. G. H. Anderson and T. F. Stransky, eds., *Mission Trends No. 3: Third World Theologies;* B. C. E. Fleming, *Contextualization of Theology: An Evangelical Assessment;* B. J. Nicholls, *Contextualization: A Theology of Gospel and Culture;* J. R. W. Stott and R. T. Coote, eds., *Down to Earth: Studies in Christianity and Culture.*

Contingency Argument for God. *See* God, Arguments for the Existence of.

Contingent Being. *See* Being.

Continuous Creation. *See* Creation, Continuous.

Contribution, Gift of. *See* Spiritual Gifts.

Contrition. Sorrow for sin because it is displeasing to God. When we analyze the meaning of repentance, we realize that a person may repent of sin for two reasons: (1) the fear of punishment; (2) because he has offended a just and holy God. The term "attrition" is used in Roman Catholic theology (from the Middle Ages) to denote the first, and "contrition" the second. Obviously the first reason for repentance is not because sin is an evil thing, but because of possible unpleasant consequences to oneself. Such an attitude does not constitute penitence in the true sense (cf. II Cor. 7:9–10). The second is the proper attitude, and indicates real love of God and desire to please him. Even Roman Catholic theologians, though teaching the necessity of confession to a priest to receive absolution, allow that a true "act of contrition," without the presence of the priest, receives absolution from God. Evangelical theology and practice seeks to equate repentance with contrition, and always to stir up contrition in the heart of sinners.

W. C. G. Proctor

See also Penitence; Repentance.

Conventicle. The main usage of this term has been in relation to groups meeting together for religious worship outside and in opposition to the established order in the church. Thus some of the early Puritans in post-Reformation England formed conventicles when they associated for free worship, particularly after the passing of the 1604 canons. Whenever five or more persons gathered in a house in addition to the family and took part in some form of worship, this constituted an illegal conventicle as defined in the later legislation. The acts against conventicles were repealed in 1689 with the toleration and licensing of dissenting bodies.

G. W. Bromiley

Conversion. An integral concept in the Bible, though it does not always appear under this name in English translations. In the OT it is directly related to the Hebrew *šûb*, the twelfth most frequently used verb, which signifies to turn back, go back, come back, or return. It is also ssociated with the Hebrew *niḥam*, which means to be sorry or to regret. In the NT the two principal words indicating "to turn" are *epistrephō* and *metanoeō*. The latter and its cognates indicate a renewal of mind and heart, heartfelt repentance. A key passage in the Synoptic Gospels is Matt. 18:3: "Except ye be converted, and become as little children, ye shall not enter into the kingdom of heaven" (AV). In the NEB the first part reads, "Unless you turn round. . . ."

In the developing Catholic tradition conversion was more and more associated with the sacraments of baptism, penance, and confirmation. It was said that in baptism one receives the remission of sins, but for sins committed after baptism one must have recourse to the sacrament of penance, which entails confession of sins, absolution by the priest, and acts of penitence, which mitigate the severity of the temporal consequences of sin.

As mysticism penetrated Catholic spirituality,

conversion came to be associated with the first stage of the mystical way, purgation—which, it was hoped, would lead to illumination and finally to contemplative union. The beginning of the illuminative way was often marked by what was called a second conversion.

Monastic spirituality, heavily influenced by mysticism, saw a twofold blessing of the Spirit: in baptism and in monastic dedication. The latter was frequently referred to as both a second baptism and a second conversion. It was regarded as a new empowering of the Spirit for vocation. Conversion in this context means retiring from the world, commitment to the religious life.

In Reformation theology conversion was understood as the human response to regeneration, the infusion of new life into the soul. Conversion was held to be dependent on grace; it was seen as an act empowered and directed by divine grace. Calvinism was inclined to portray this grace as irresistible, with the result that conversion became a virtually spontaneous turning of the one who was elected to receive grace. Luther believed that conversion could be aborted and that one could fall away from one's conversion. Both Calvin and Luther envisaged the whole Christian life as a life of conversion.

Among the later evangelicals conversion came to be associated with a crisis experience that inaugurates the new life in Christ. In some circles it was regarded as an event involving total transformation. In the Holiness Movement conversion was seen as the initiation of Christian life and entire sanctification as the fulfillment of Christian life.

Karl Barth in the twentieth century has portrayed conversion (*Umkehr*) as the pivotal event in history, the liberation and renewal of the world in Jesus Christ. The awakenings to the reality of this event can be described as conversion (*Bekehrung*) in a secondary sense.

In an evangelical theology that seeks to be true to Scripture and the Reformation, conversion has two sides, divine and human. It represents the incursion of divine grace into human life, the resurrection from spiritual death to eternal life. It is commonly said that we are active in conversion just as we are passive in regeneration, but this must not be understood synergistically. We are active only on the basis of grace, only through the power of grace. We do not procure salvation, but we decide for salvation once our inward eyes are opened to its reality. Conversion is the sign but not the condition of our justification, whose sole source is the free, unconditional grace of God.

Conversion is both an event and a process. It signifies the action of the Holy Spirit upon us by which we are moved to respond to Jesus Christ in faith. It also includes the continuing work of the Holy Spirit within us purifying us of discord and contumacy, remolding us in the image of Christ. This work of purification is accomplished as we repent and cling to Christ anew.

Again, conversion is both personal and social. While it basically connotes a change in our relationship with God, it indicates at the same time an alteration in our attitudes toward our fellow human beings. Conversion is a spiritual event with far-reaching social implications. It entails accepting Christ not only as Savior from sin but also as Lord of all of life.

Finally, conversion must be seen as the beginning of our ascent to Christian perfection. What is needed is not a second conversion by which such perfection is secured but the continuing and maintaining of a conversion that is never completed in this life. Evangelical theology in the tradition of the Reformation contends that we can make progress toward perfection, but we can never attain it as a realized goal. Even the converted need to repent, even the sanctified need to turn again to Christ and be cleansed anew (cf. Ps. 51:10–12; Luke 17:3–4; 22:32; Rom. 13:14; Eph. 4:22–24; Rev. 2:4–5, 16; 3:19).

We cannot be converted through our own power, but we can repent and turn to Christ through the power of his Spirit. We cannot maintain our walk with Christ on the basis of our own resources, but we can maintain this walk with the aid of his Spirit. Conversion entails the promise of sanctification just as it reveals the gift of justification. D. G. BLOESCH

See also JUSTIFICATION; SANCTIFICATION; REGENERATION; SALVATION; GRACE; FAITH.

Bibliography. D. G. Bloesch, *The Christian Life and Salvation, The Crisis of Piety,* and *Essentials of Evangelical Theology,* II; J. Baillie, *Baptism and Conversion;* A. B. Crabtree, *The Restored Relationship;* K. Rahner, *The Christian Commitment;* B. Citron, *New Birth;* J. H. Gerstner, *Steps to Salvation;* A. Koeberle, *The Quest for Holiness;* W. G. T. Shedd, *Dogmatic Theology,* II, 529–37; H. Schmid, *The Doctrinal Theology of the Evangelical Lutheran Church;* E. Routley, *The Gift of Conversion;* K. Barth, *Church Dogmatics,* IV/4; J. Calvin, *Institutes of the Christian Religion* 2.2.3.14; P. S. Watson, *The Concept of Grace;* P. T. Forsyth, *The Work of Christ.*

Convocation. The AV and RSV use "holy convocation" for OT *miqrā'* (NEB "sacred assembly"). Sabbaths and special days like the day of atonement, on which no work was to be done, were "holy convocations" (Lev. 23). By extension Christian gatherings for worship and edification may be called convocations. Historically the Church of England used the term for the meetings, first of bishops, then also of other clergy, which from the days of Theodore (668–690) made and revised canons and later voted taxes. The Reformation and its aftermath tightened royal control, ended the right of taxing, and finally brought suspension in 1717. Revived and reorganized in the nineteenth century, convocation was incorporated into the Church Assembly by the Enabling Act of 1919. G. W. BROMILEY

Bibliography. E. W. Kemp, *Counsel and Consent;* D. B. Weske, *Convocation of the Clergy.*

Cooperation, Ecclesiastical. *See* ECUMENISM.

Cornerstone, Christ as. In the NT the people of God are viewed as a spiritual temple in which Jesus Christ is the cornerstone, Heb. *'eben pinnâ,* Gr. *akrogōniaios* (Isa. 28:16; Eph. 2:20; I Pet. 2:6). The theological significance of the term arises from this usage. The word appears to be practically the equivalent of the phrase "head of the corner," Heb. *rō'š pinnâ,* Gr. *kephalē gōnia* (Ps. 118:22; Matt. 21:42 and parallels; Acts 4:11; I Pet. 2:7). For example, in Ps. 118:22 the latter phrase is rendered *akrogōniaios* by Symmachus and, in turn, Isa. 28:16 is translated by the Peshitta as "head of the wall." There is a difference of opinion, however, regarding its precise connotation. Generally, it has been considered the first laid cornerstone above the foundation level of the building and, hence, the stone by which the other stones were measured or beveled and to which the design of the building conformed. Keil and Delitzsch (on Ps. 118:22 and Zech. 4:7) view *rō'š pinnâ* as designating the final topstone of the temple. Similarly, J. Jeremias argues that *akrogōniaios* is the capstone (*Abschlussstein*) which completes the building and which is placed at the summit or (probably) over the entrance. This use of the term occurs in some extracanonical Jewish literature and in IV Kings 25:17 (Symmachus), where the crown or capital of a column is so rendered. In either case the "cornerstone" signifies a keystone in which "the whole structure is welded together" (Eph. 2:21, Moffatt).

The "temple typology," of which the cornerstone is a part, expresses a basic theological concept in the NT. The true temple of God, "not made with hands," is superior to the material temple (Mark 14:58; Acts 7:48; 17:24; cf. Matt. 12:6). It is a spiritual house of which Christ is the builder (Mark 14:58; cf. Matt. 16:18), the cornerstone, and the high priest (Heb. 9:11). In fact, Christ's body is the very essence of the temple (John 2:21), and Christians, who are the "body" of Christ, are the "living stones" (I Pet. 2:5) of the temple. It is no little thing, therefore, that the Jewish "builders" should reject the stone which God has destined to be "head of the corner." The result is the rejection of the builders themselves. It is within this context that the Lord quotes Ps. 118:22 in which Israel, the stone, is rejected by the Gentile builders. The NT, typically, views Jesus Christ as "Israel" and unbelieving Jews as "Gentiles" and so applies the passage.

The "cornerstone" is a part of what Austin Farrer has called the great images of the NT. The concept is no less real for being in the language of imagery; rather, we may believe that in just this fashion it is best conveyed. E. E. ELLIS

Bibliography. E. G. Selwyn, *The First Epistle of St. Peter;* E. E. Ellis, *Paul's Use of the OT;* J. Jeremias, *TDNT,* I, 791ff.

Correction. *See* DISCIPLINE.

Cosmological Argument for God. *See* GOD, ARGUMENTS FOR THE EXISTENCE OF.

Councils, Church. A council is a conference called by the leaders of the church to give guidance to the church. The first council took place in Jerusalem (*ca.* A.D. 50) for the purpose of opposing Judaizing efforts and is recorded in Acts 15. The results of this first Council of Jerusalem were normative for the entire early Christian church. However, the Jerusalem Council must be distinguished from succeeding councils in that it had apostolic leadership.

A council may be either ecumenical and thus representative of the entire church, or it may be local, having regional or local representation. For example, twelve regional councils met to discuss the Arian heresy between the ecumenical councils of Nicaea in 325 and Constantinople in 381.

Whereas previously the term "ecumenical" meant a representation based on the widest geographical coverage, during our present millennium the meaning shifted to denote the pope's inherent authority to declare a council ecumenical. Thus the pope, understood as exercising Christ's rule on earth, has authority to declare or to reject a council as ecumenical. Although this papal prerogative was operative earlier, it finds explicit affirmation in the Vatican II decree "Light of the Nations," which states: "A council is never ecumenical unless it is confirmed or at least accepted as such by the successor of Peter." The situation became problematic with general councils that had been called by emperors, as was Nicaea in 325. These were declared ecumenical by the popes *ex post facto.*

It was precisely to this absolute authority of the pope to convene councils that Martin Luther directed one of his significant 1520 pamphlets, *Address to the Christian Nobility*. Luther viewed such papal prerogatives as one of the "three walls" that had to be broken down.

Historically, councils have been called by emperors, popes, and bishops. The first seven councils were convoked in the East by emperors and were thus typical of Eastern caesaropapism (state over church). In the Western church the pope typically convened councils, except for a time during the Great Schism (1378–1417) when the plurality of bishops both convened councils and deposed popes (conciliarism). Indeed, the Council of Constance in 1415 proclaimed the superiority of general councils over the pope. But their supremacy was short-lived. By 1500 the pontiff had overcome the conciliar movement and was again convening councils.

While both Roman Catholics and the Eastern Orthodox churches regard the first councils as ecumenical, Protestant churches also regard as valid many of the declarations of these councils. This is because these councils largely concerned themselves with controversies over the deity, person, and natures of Christ. After the split between the Roman Catholic (Western) and Orthodox (Eastern) churches each branch began its own authoritative councils.

The most significant of the early councils were Nicaea (325) and Chalcedon (451). The former settled the issue of the nature of Christ as God, whereas the latter dealt with the issues of the twofold natures of Christ and their unity. In the case of Nicaea a presbyter of Alexandria, Arius, maintained that Christ was not the eternal Son of God. Athanasius, Bishop of Alexandria, vigorously opposed that idea, declaring Christ to be of the same substance (*homoousios*) with God. Athanasius and orthodoxy prevailed. In general, this was the first binding theological declaration for the entire postapostolic church.

The Council of Chalcedon was called in 451 by the emperor Marcion for the purpose of settling disputes and clarifying the issue of the unity of the two natures of Christ. The resultant Chalcedonian Creed, or Definition, afforded the entire Christian Church a standard of Christological orthodoxy in declaring that Christ's two natures exist "without confusion, without change, without division, without separation."

Subsequent councils found it necessary to consolidate the gains of Chalcedon and to oppose further Christological errors. These councils terminated with the Third Council of Constantinople in 680–81.

In the West the Second Synod of Orange (529) was very significant in both combating semi-Pelagianism and setting forth the gracious character of salvation apart from works. Although it was not officially ecumenical, its declarations prevailed *de jure* but not *de facto* in the Roman Catholic Church down to the Reformation era.

After the separation of the Eastern and Western churches in 1054 it became characteristic of the pope to convene councils in the Roman Catholic Church. Beginning in 1123 a series of so-called Lateran Councils was held at Rome in the Church of St. John Lateran. The most important of these was the Fourth Lateran Council (1215) convened by the great Pope Innocent III. This council declared transubstantiation to be the accepted interpretation of Christ's presence in the Lord's Supper.

The next most significant council was the Council of Trent, 1545–63. This council should be viewed as both a counter to the Protestant Reformation and an establishing of key tenets of Roman Catholicism. Both Scripture and tradition were declared authoritative for the church. Salvation by grace alone through faith was jettisoned in favor of sacramental and works righteousness. Modern Roman Catholicism, in general, continues to be Tridentine Catholicism.

The two Vatican Councils each represent both the old and the new. Vatican I (1869–70) made official what had long been practiced—papal infallibility. Vatican II (1962–65) was attended by both traditional and radical Roman Catholics. Its pronouncements regarding the universal character of the church approach sheer universalism. Its more open stance toward the Bible is hailed by most Protestants as very salutary. Thus the term used at Vatican II, *aggiornamento* (modernization), has to some extent been realized in post–Vatican II Roman Catholicism.

J. H. HALL

See also ECUMENICAL COUNCILS; NICAEA, COUNCIL OF; CONSTANTINOPLE, COUNCIL OF; CHALCEDON, COUNCIL OF; EPHESUS, COUNCIL OF; TRENT, COUNCIL OF; VATICAN COUNCIL I; VATICAN COUNCIL II.

Bibliography. G. J. Cuming and D. Baker, eds., *Councils and Assemblies;* P. Hughes, *The Church in Crisis: A History of the General Councils 325–1870; The Seven Ecumenical Councils of the Undivided Church: Their Canons and Dogmatic Degrees, NPNF.*

Counter-Reformation. The label for the Roman Catholic revival of the sixteenth century. It emphasizes that the reaction to the Protestant challenge was the dominant theme of contemporary Catholicism. The movement is also labeled the Catholic Reformation and the Catholic renaissance, since elements of Catholic reform and revival predated the Protestant Reformation and were, like Protestantism, a response to the widespread aspiration for religious regeneration pervading late fifteenth century Europe. It is now better understood that the two reformations—Protestant and Catholic—though believing themselves to be in opposition, had many similarities and drew on a common past: the revival of preaching exemplified in the great pre-Reformation preachers like Jan Hus, Bernardino of Siena, and Savonarola; the Christ-centered, practical mysticism of the *Devotio Moderna;* the movement for ecclesiastical reform headed by Cardinal Ximénez de Cisneros in Spain but also well represented by reforming bishops in France and Germany.

The Counter-Reformation is sometimes described as a Spanish movement. Over three thousand mystical works are known to have been written in sixteenth century Spain, suggesting that mysticism was a popular movement. But the dominant Spanish mystics were three aristocrats: Teresa of Ávila (1515–82), John of the Cross (1542–91), and Ignatius of Loyola (1491–1556). Two of the three great instruments of the Counter-Reformation stemmed from Spain, namely the Society of Jesus and the Inquisition. The third was the Council of Trent, which was finally convened in 1545 after constant pressure from the Emperor Charles V, grandson of Spain's great reforming monarchs, Ferdinand and Isabella.

The Society of Jesus (Jesuits), incorporated in 1540, was the most remarkable of the new orders of reformed priests (clerks regular) who lived among the faithful rather than withdrawing into monasteries. Other orders included the Theatines (1524), Somaschi (1532), and Barnabites (1534). The founder of the Jesuits, Ignatius of Loyola, sought to prepare his followers for a life of triumphal service and heroic self-sacrifice through his *Spiritual Exercises,* a series of practical meditations. The Jesuits ministered to the poor, educated boys, and evangelized the heathen. Francis Xavier (1506–52) a Spanish Jesuit, traveled to Goa, South India, Ceylon, Malaya, and Japan on his amazing missionary journeys. When Ignatius died, the society had around 1,000 members administering 100 foundations. A century later there were over 15,000 Jesuits and 550 foundations, testifying to the sustained vitality of the Counter-Reformation.

The Roman Inquisition was established in 1542 by Pope Paul III to suppress Lutheranism in Italy. Cardinal Caraffa, its Inquisitor General, later Pope Paul IV (1555–59), directed that heretics in high places should be dealt with most severely, "for on their punishment, the salvation of the classes beneath them depends." The Roman Inquisition reached its peak during the pontificate of the saintly zealot Pius V (1566–72), systematically extirpating Italian Protestants and securing Italy as a base for a counteroffensive on the Protestant north.

The corrupt hierarchy of the Roman Catholic Church was dramatically reformed in the wake of the Council of Trent. Dioceses mushroomed in areas where there was felt to be a particular Protestant threat. Bishops carried out frequent visitations of their dioceses and established seminaries for the training of clergy. The number of church buildings and clergy increased markedly. The most vigorous of the reforming popes, Sixtus V (1585–90), established fifteen "congregations" or commissions to prepare papal pronouncements and strategy. Some Protestant gains were reversed under the direction of such theologians as Robert Bellarmine (1542–1621) and Peter Canisius (1521–97). The Counter-Reformation in general, and the Council of Trent in particular, strengthened the position of the pope and the forces of clericalism and authoritarianism. The genuinely spiritual foundations of these developments should not be denied.

F. S. Piggin

See also Trent, Council of; Reformation, Protestant; Society of Jesus, The.

Bibliography. H. Daniel-Rops, *The Catholic Reformation;* J. Delumeau, *Catholicism Between Luther and Voltaire;* A. G. Dickens, *The Counter-Reformation;* P. Dudon, *St. Ignatius of Loyola;* H. O. Evennett, *The Spirit of the Counter-Reformation;* B. J. Kidd, *The Counter-Reformation, 1550–1600; The Spiritual Exercises of St. Ignatius,* tr. A. Mottola; M. R. O'Connell, *The Counter-Reformation 1559–1610.*

Covenant. A compact or agreement between two parties binding them mutually to undertakings on each other's behalf. Theologically (used of relations between God and man) it denotes a gracious undertaking entered into by God for the benefit and blessing of man, and specifically of those men who by faith receive the promises and commit themselves to the obligations which this undertaking involves.

In the OT. Uniformly the word used to express the covenant concept is the Hebrew *bĕrît.* The original meaning of this word was probably "fetter" or "obligation," coming from a root *bārâ,* "to bind." This root does not occur as a verb in Hebrew, but it does occur in Akkadian as *bāru,* "to bind," and appears as a noun in the Akkadian *birîtu,* which means "bond" or "fetter." Thus a *bĕrît* would originally signify a relationship between two parties wherein each bound himself to perform a certain service or duty for the other. But some scholars prefer to derive this noun from the verb *bārâ* "to eat," which occurs in II Sam. 13:6; 12:17; etc., and thus interpret it as "a meal" or "food," with reference to the sacrificial meal which the contracting parties often ate together when ratifying their agreement before the deity who was invoked as protector and guarantor of the covenant. Still others trace it from a *bārâ* meaning "to perceive" or "to determine"; hence *bĕrît* would involve the basic idea of "vision." But neither of these explanations commends itself as being so fitting or appropriate to the basic character of a covenant as the idea of "bond" preferred by the majority of scholars.

A general characteristic of the OT *bĕrît* is its unalterable and permanently binding character. The parties to a covenant obligated themselves to carry out their respective commitments under the penalty of divine retribution should they later attempt to avoid them. Usually, although not necessarily, the promise of each was supported by some sort of legal consideration or *quid pro quo*. But where the one party to the agreement was greatly superior to the other in power or authority, the situation was a bit different: the ruler or man of authority would in the enactment of the *bĕrît* simply announce his governmental decree or constitution which he thought best to impose upon those under him, and they for their part expressed their acceptance and readiness to conform to what he had ordained. Doubtless it was true even in this type of covenant that the ruler implicitly committed himself to rule for the best interests of his people and to contrive for their protection against their foes.

But in the case of the promulgation of a covenant by God with his chosen people, this one-sided aspect of the transaction was even more apparent, since the contracting parties stood upon entirely different levels. In this case the covenant constituted a divine announcement of God's holy will to extend the benefits of his unmerited grace to men who were willing by faith to receive them, and who by entering into a personal commitment to God bound themselves to him by ties of absolute obligation. The characteristic statement of this relationship occurs in the formula "I will be their God and they shall be my people" (cf. Jer. 11:4; 24:7; 30:22; 32:38; Ezek. 11:20; 14:11; 36:28; 37:23; Zech. 8:8; etc.). This signifies that God unreservedly gives himself to his people and that they in turn give themselves to him and belong to him. Thus they are his "peculiar treasure" (*sĕgullâ*—Exod. 19:5; Deut. 7:6; 14:2; 26:18; Ps. 135:4; Mal. 3:17). His motive in adopting them as his own covenant children is stated to be "lovingkindness" or "covenant-love" (*ḥesed*), a term with which *bĕrît* is often associated (cf. Deut. 7:9; I Kings 8:23; Dan. 9:4). (Compare also I Sam. 20:8, where Jonathan is said to exercise *ḥesed* when he enters into his covenant relationship with David.) This presents a remarkable contrast to the motivation attributed by the heathen Semites to their gods, who were uniformly depicted as entering into covenant relations with their devotees for the purpose of extracting service and nourishment from their altars, more or less like the feudal lords of human society who extract their support from the labor of their vassals.

One very important element in God's covenant relations with Israel lay in the dual aspect of conditionality and unconditionality. Were his solemn promises, which partook of the nature of a binding oath (cf. Deut. 7:8), to be understood as capable of nonfulfillment, in case of the failure of man to live up to his obligations toward God? Or was there a sense in which God's covenant undertakings were absolutely sure of fulfillment, regardless of the unfaithfulness of man? The answer to this much-debated question seems to be: (1) that the promises made by Jehovah in the covenant of grace represent decrees which he will surely bring to pass, when conditions are ripe for their fulfillment; (2) that the personal benefit—and especially the spiritual and eternal benefit—of the divine promise will accrue only to those individuals of the covenant people of God who manifest a true and living faith (demonstrated by a godly life). Thus the first aspect is brought out by the initial form of the covenant with Abram in Gen. 12:1–3; there is no shadow of doubt but what God will truly make of Abram a great nation, and make his name great, and shall bless all the nations of earth through him and his posterity (cf. Gal. 3:8). This is set forth as God's plan from the very beginning; nothing shall frustrate it. On the other hand, the individual children of Abraham are to receive personal benefit only as they manifest the faith and obedience of Abraham; thus Exod. 19:5 ("Now therefore if ye will obey my voice indeed, and keep my covenant, then ye shall be a peculiar treasure unto me. . . . And ye shall be unto me a kingdom of priests and a holy nation"). In other words, God will see to it that his plan of redemption will be carried out in history, but he will also see to it that none partake of the eternal benefits of the covenant in violation of the demands of holiness. No child of the covenant who presents to him a faithless and insincere heart shall be included in its blessings.

This triumphantly enduring quality of the covenant of grace is especially set forth by the prophets in the form of the "new covenant." In the classic passage on this theme (Jer. 31:31–37) the earliest phase of the covenant (that was effected at Sinai) is shown to have been temporary and provisional because of the flagrant violation of it by the Israelite nation as a whole, and because of their failure to know or acknowledge

God as their personal Lord and Savior. But there is a time coming, says Jehovah, when he will put his holy law into their very hearts, so that their cordial inclination and desire will be to live according to his holy standard. Moreover he shall beget within them a sense of sonship toward himself, so that they shall have a personal knowledge and love of him that will not require artificial human teaching. Furthermore the carrying out of this redeeming purpose is stated to be as sure as the continued existence of sun, moon, and stars, or even of the foundations of heaven itself.

In the NT. The term for covenant employed in the NT is *diathēkē*, the word used constantly in the LXX for *bĕrît*. Since the ordinary Greek word for "contract" or "compact" (*synthēkē*) implied equality on the part of the contracting parties, the Greek-speaking Jews preferred *diathēkē* (coming from *diatithemai*, "to make a disposition of one's own property") in the sense of a unilateral enactment. In secular Greek this word usually meant "will" or "testament," but even classical authors like Aristophanes (*Birds* 439) occasionally used it of a covenant wherein one of the two parties had an overwhelming superiority over the other and could dictate his own terms. Hence the biblical *diathēkē* signified (in a way much more specific than did *bĕrît*) an arrangement made by one party with plenary power, which the other party may accept or reject but cannot alter. Johannes Behm (*TDNT*, II, 137) defines it as "the decree (*Verfuegung*) of God, the powerful disclosure of the sovereign will of God in history whereby he constitutes the relationship, the authoritative divine ordinance (institution), which introduces a corresponding order of affairs." There is just one passage in which the more usual secular significance of "will" or "testament" appears along with the covenantal idea: Heb. 9:15–17. A legal analogy is drawn from the fact that a testator must die before his will can take effect; so also in the enactment of the Mosaic covenant there was slain a sacrificial animal, representing the atonement of Christ, and it was the blood of that victim which was sprinkled upon the people and the covenantal document itself. But even here the predominant notion in *diathēkē* is "covenant" rather than "testament." G. L. Archer, Jr.

See also Covenant, The New.

Bibliography. G. R. Berry, *ISBE*, II, 727–29; A. B. Davidson, *The Theology of the OT;* G. E. Mendenhall, *Law and Covenant in Israel and the Ancient Near East;* G. Oehler, *Theology of the OT;* W. Oesterley and T. H. Robinson, *Hebrew Religion;* G. Vos, *Biblical Theology;* J. Behm and G. Quell, *TDNT*, II, 106ff.; G. Gurt, *NIDNTT*, I, 365ff.; W. Eichrodt, *Theology of the OT*, 2 vols.; D. J. McCarthy, *OT Covenant;* K. Baltzer, *The Covenant Formulary;* D. R. Hillers, *Covenant: History of a Biblical Idea;* M. G. Kline, *Treaty of the Great King.*

Covenant, The New. Jeremiah first speaks of a new covenant in his prophecy of a great work of salvation which God would perform sometime in the future (Jer. 31:31–34). In substance, Jeremiah's new covenant prophecy has strong affinities with other prophetic texts that depict the triumph and consummation of the kingdom of God in the world (cf. Jer. 32:36–41; 33:14–26; Isa. 11:6–9; 54:11–15; 59:20–21; Ezek. 16:59–63). The term is found six times in the NT (I Cor. 11:25; II Cor. 3:6; Heb. 8:8; 9:15; 12:24; and the disputed reading in Luke 22:20) though the idea of a new covenant is present elsewhere (cf. Rom. 11:27; Gal. 4:21–31). In II Cor. 3:4–18 the new covenant is contrasted with the old covenant in the context of Paul's contrasting his ministry with that of Moses. By the time of Tertullian, Old Covenant (*Vetus Testamentum*) and New Covenant (*Novum Testamentum*) appear as designations of the pre-Christian and Christian Scriptures respectively.

In Christian theology generally the new covenant has been identified with the Christian dispensation, the religiohistorical economy introduced by Christ and the apostles. Accordingly, it is the fulfillment of the promises of the old covenant and is better by degrees than that former covenant by virtue of its clearer view of Christ and redemption, its richer experience of the Holy Spirit, and by the greater liberty which it grants to believers.

Particularly in Reformed theology, as a result of its careful reflection on the scriptural doctrine of the covenants, the new covenant came to be given a double aspect. To account for the fact that there has ever been but one covenant of God with his people, of which Christ is the mediator, and the fact that in Jeremiah and the NT the term "new covenant" is a synonym for the gospel of Christ and the divine application of redemption, the new covenant was identified both strictly with that form of the covenant of grace manifested after the incarnation and broadly with the covenant of grace in general (cf. F. Turretin, *Institutio Theologiae Elencticae*, XII. VIII. v).

A better solution is to forsake altogether the religiohistorical identifications of the two covenants. Jeremiah's prophecy of a new covenant is a prophecy of the ultimate consummation of the kingdom of God, and in Paul and Hebrews the contrast between the old covenant and the new covenant has to do not with relative distinctions between the two dispensations of God's covenant of grace succeeding one another in time but with the radical antithesis of two subjective situations: the formalism, legalism, unbelief, and death of ancient Israel on the one hand and the genuine experience of salvation by all believers on the other. R. S. RAYBURN

See also COVENANT.

Bibliography. Irenaeus, *Against Heresies* 4; Augustine, *The Spirit and the Letter;* Calvin, *Institutes of the Christian Religion* 2.9–11; H. Witsius, *The Economy of the Covenants Between God and Man;* J. Murray, *The Covenant of Grace;* W. Kaiser, "The Old Promise and the New Covenant," *JETS* 15:11–23; W. B. Wallis, "The Pauline Conception of the Old Covenant," *Presb* 4: 71–83; R. S. Rayburn, *The Contrast Between the Old and New Covenants in the NT* (Ph.D. diss., University of Aberdeen); O. P. Robertson, *The Christ of the Covenants.*

Covenant of Grace. *See* COVENANT THEOLOGY.

Covenant of Redemption. *See* COVENANT THEOLOGY.

Covenant of Works. *See* COVENANT THEOLOGY.

Covenant Theology. The doctrine of the covenant was one of the theological contributions that came to the church through the Reformation of the sixteenth century. Undeveloped earlier, it made its appearance in the writings of Zwingli and Bullinger, who were driven to the subject by Anabaptists in and around Zurich. From them it passed to Calvin and other Reformers, was further developed by their successors, and played a dominant role in much Reformed theology of the seventeenth century when it came to be known as covenant, or federal, theology. Covenant theology sees the relation of God to mankind as a compact which God established as a reflection of the relationship existing between the three persons of the Holy Trinity. This emphasis on God's covenantal dealings with the human race tended to lessen what appeared to some to be harshness in the earlier Reformed theology which emanated from Geneva, with its emphasis on the divine sovereignty and predestination. From Switzerland covenant theology passed over into Germany, and from there into the Netherlands and the British Isles. Among its early and most influential advocates were, besides Zwingli and Bullinger, Olevianus (*Concerning the Nature of the Covenant of Grace Between God and the Elect,* 1585), Cocceius (*Doctrine of the Covenant and Testaments of God,* 1648), and Witsius (*The Oeconomy of the Covenants,* 1685). It was taken up into the Westminster Confession and came to have an important place in the theology of Scotland and New England.

The Covenant of Works. Having created man in his own image as a free creature with knowledge, righteousness, and holiness, God entered into covenant with Adam that he might bestow upon him further blessing. Called variously the Edenic covenant, the covenant of nature, the covenant of life, or preferably the covenant of works, this pact consisted of (1) a promise of eternal life upon the condition of perfect obedience throughout a probationary period; (2) the threat of death upon disobedience; and (3) the sacrament of the tree of life, or, in addition, the sacraments of paradise and the tree of the knowledge of good and evil. Although the term "covenant" is not mentioned in the first chapters of Genesis, it is held that all the elements of a covenant are present even though the promise of eternal life is there by implication only. Before the fall Adam was perfect but could still have sinned; had he retained his perfection throughout the probationary period, he would have been confirmed in righteousness and been unable to sin. Inasmuch as he was acting not only for himself but representatively for mankind, Adam was a public person. His fall therefore affected the entire human race that was to come after him; all are now conceived and born in sin. Without a special intervention of God there would be no hope; all would be lost forever.

The good news, however, is that God has intervened in behalf of mankind with another covenant. Unlike the earlier covenant of works, whose mandate was "Do this and you shall live" (cf. Rom. 10:5; Gal. 3:12), the covenant of grace is bestowed on men in their sinful condition with the promise that, in spite of their inability to keep any of the commandments of God, out of sheer grace he forgives their sin and accepts them as his children through the merits of his Son, the Lord Jesus Christ, on the condition of faith.

The Covenant of Redemption. According to covenant theology, the covenant of grace, established in history, is founded on still another covenant, the covenant of redemption, which is defined as the eternal pact between God the Father and God the Son concerning the salvation of mankind. Scripture teaches that within the Godhead there are three persons, the same in essence, glory, and power, objective to each other. The Father loves the Son, commissions him, gives him a people, the right to judge, and authority over all mankind (John 3:16; 5:20, 22, 36; 10:17–18; 17:2, 4, 6, 9, 24; Ps. 2:7–8; Heb. 1:8–13); the Son loves the Father, delights to do his will, and has shared his glory forever (Heb. 10:7; John 5:19; 17:5). The Father, the Son, and the Holy

Spirit commune with each other; this is one of the meanings of the Christian doctrine of the Trinity. On this foundation covenant theology affirms that God the Father and God the Son covenanted together for the redemption of the human race, the Father appointing the Son to be the mediator, the Second Adam, whose life would be given for the salvation of the world, and the Son accepting the commission, promising that he would do the work which the Father had given him to do and fulfill all righteousness by obeying the law of God. Thus before the foundation of the world, within the eternal being of God, it had been determined that creation would not be destroyed by sin, but that rebellion and iniquity would be overcome by God's grace, that Christ would become the new head of humanity, the Savior of the world, and that God would be glorified.

The Covenant of Grace. This covenant has been made by God with mankind. In it he offers life and salvation through Christ to all who believe. Inasmuch as none can believe without the special grace of God, it is more exact to say that the covenant of grace is made by God with believers, or the elect. Jesus said that all those whom the Father had given him would come to him and that those who come would surely be accepted (John 6:37). Herein is seen the close relation between the covenant of grace and the covenant of redemption, with the former resting on the latter. From eternity the Father has given a people to the Son; to them was given the promised Holy Spirit so that they might live in fellowship with God. Christ is the mediator of the covenant of grace inasmuch as he has borne the guilt of sinners and restored them to a saving relationship to God (Heb. 8:6; 9:15; 12:24). He is mediator, not only in the sense of arbitrator, although that is the sense in which the word is used in I Tim. 2:5, but in the sense of having fulfilled all the conditions necessary for procuring eternal salvation for his people. Thus Heb. 7:22 calls Jesus the "surety" or "guarantee" of the new covenant, which is better than that which came through Moses. Within the context of this last passage repeated mention is made of God's promise to Christ and his people. He will be their God and they will be his people. He will bestow on them the grace they need to confess his name and live with him forever; in humble dependence on him for their every need, they will live in trustful obedience from day to day. This latter, called faith in Scripture, is the sole condition of the covenant, and even it is a gift of God (Eph. 2:8–9).

Although the covenant of grace includes various dispensations of history, it is essentially one. From the promise in the garden (Gen. 3:15), through the covenant made with Noah (Gen. 6–9), to the day that the covenant was established with Abraham, there is abundant evidence of God's grace. With Abraham a new beginning is made which the later, Sinaitic covenant implements and strengthens. At Sinai the covenant assumes a national form and stress is laid on the law of God. This is not intended to alter the gracious character of the covenant, however (Gal. 3:17–18), but it is to serve to train Israel until the time would come when God himself would appear in its midst. In Jesus the new form of the covenant that had been promised by the prophets is manifest, and that which was of a temporary nature in the old form of the covenant disappears (Jer. 31:31–34; Heb. 8). While there is unity and continuity in the covenant of grace throughout history, the coming of Christ and the subsequent gift of the Holy Spirit have brought rich gifts unknown in an earlier age. These are a foretaste of future blessedness when this present world passes away and the Holy City, the New Jerusalem, comes down out of heaven from God (Rev. 21:2). M. E. Osterhaven

See also Covenant; Federal Theology.

Bibliography. L. Berkhof, *Systematic Theology;* C. Hodge, *Systematic Theology,* II; H. Heppe, *Reformed Dogmatics;* H. Bavinck, *Our Reasonable Faith;* G. Schrenk, *Gottesreich und Bund in älteren Protestantismus;* H. H. Wolf, *Die Einheit des Bundes.*

Covetousness. The word means primarily "inordinate desire." It has come to mean a desire for anything which is inordinate in degree, or a desire for that which rightfully belongs to another, especially in the realm of material things. In a general sense it means all inordinate desire for worldly possessions such as honors, gold, etc. In a more restricted sense, it is a desire for the increasing of one's substance by appropriating that of others.

The shades of meaning vary according to the particular word used and the context. The following are some of the uses; *beṣa',* dishonest gain (Exod. 18:21); *pleonexia,* the desire to have more than one possesses (Luke 12:15); an intense love or lust for gain (Rom. 1:29); greed (II Pet. 2:14 RSV); *philarguria,* an inordinate love of money (I Tim. 6:10).

Covetousness is a grave sin. It is labeled idolatry (Col. 3:5), for intensity of desire and worship are closely related. Its heinousness doubtless is accounted for by its being, in a very real sense, the root of many forms of sin. This is the reason Jesus warned against it so sternly (Luke 12:15).

L. T. Corlett

Creation, Continuous. The theory that the universe is a result of a new creation from moment to moment. God is regarded as both the originator of all being and the only cause of all natural effects in each successive moment. Thus sustenance or preservation is really continued creation.

This view was held by the New England theologians Edwards, Hopkins, and Emmons, and more recently by Rothe in Germany. Opponents stress that regular activity is not the mere repetition of an initial decision but an act of the will quite different in kind. Moreover, if God's will is the only force in the universe, the divine will must in that case be the author of human sin. Finally, continuous creation tends to pantheism; mind and matter alike become phenomena of one force and, in the end, the distinct existence and personality of God is lost.

The continuous creation theory of scientific cosmology is in contrast with theories which postulate a beginning to the universe (e.g., the "big bang" theory). In 1929 Edwin Hubble discovered the expansion of the universe. Many cosmologists now infer a time of origin in a highly localized sense. The continuous creation "steady state" cosmologists retain an expanding universe but posit a continuous creation of hydrogen in the intergalactic medium to keep the density of the universe constant. The identification and detection of the microwave background radiation in 1965 dealt a severe blow to the steady state and continuous creation theory, since this radiation is identified as being the remnant of the radiation from the "big bang." Some cosmologists also argue that continuous creation and its implications of an infinite age for the universe conflicts with the second law of thermodynamics, in which entropy (disorganization) increases with time. Further creation would be required to remove the accumulated entropy.

M. H. Macdonald

Bibliography. C. S. Lewis, *Mere Christianity;* A. H. Strong, *Systematic Theology;* G. O. Abell, *Exploration of the Universe;* H. L. Shipman, *Black Holes, Quasars, and the Universe;* J. M. Pasachoff, *Contemporary Astronomy.*

Creation, Doctrine of. Both the opening verse of the Bible and the opening sentence of the Apostles' Creed confess God as Creator. In Scripture the theme of God as Creator of the "heavens and the earth" (Gen. 1:1) is prominent in both the OT (Isa. 40:28; 42:5; 45:18) and NT (Mark 13:19; Rev. 10:6). God is the Creator of humans (Gen. 1:27; 5:2; Isa. 45:12; Mal. 2:10; Mark 10:6), of Israel (Isa. 43:15), indeed of "all things" (Eph. 3:9; Col. 1:16; Rev. 4:11). Creation occurs by God's word (Gen. 1:3, etc.) so that when he speaks, all comes into being (Pss. 33:9; 148:5). His word of command which calls into being things that had no prior existence is the Word who was with God and is God (John 1:1ff.). "All things were made through him, and without him was not anything made that was made" is the statement of John 1:3 with reference to the Word of God, Jesus Christ the Son who became flesh (John 1:14). Of Christ it is said that "in him all things were created" (Col. 1:16; cf. I Cor. 8:6), thus making Jesus Christ the agent of creation. The work of God's Spirit is also involved (Gen. 1:2; Job 33:4; Ps. 104:30). Creation is the work of the triune God and is an article of faith, as Heb. 11:3 clearly shows.

Theologically, the doctrine of creation as an act of the triune God is of great importance. The history of the church's early creeds and confessions indicates this plainly. Struggles with Gnosticism, Arianism, and Manichaeism revolved in part around God as Creator and the relation of the Creator to the Redeemer, Jesus Christ. The church's three creedal statements from the early period reflect its attempt to join creation and redemption in the one living God. The Apostles' Creed added the phrase "maker of heaven and earth" to the old Roman Creed and recognized the Creator as the Father of Jesus Christ. The Nicene Trinitarian statement (A.D. 325) spoke of the "maker of all things visible and invisible" who is "of the same substance" (*homoousios*) as the Son. The Council of Chalcedon (A.D. 451), after affirming earlier creeds that identified God as "Ruler of all, the maker of heaven and earth and of all things seen and unseen," confessed Jesus Christ as "very God and very man," thus again uniting Creator and Redeemer. The Creator God is not detached from the God who works for our salvation in Jesus Christ through his Holy Spirit.

Significance of Creation. Since God as Creator is the explanation for the existence of the world and for human existence, it is the activity of creation that establishes our deepest and most essential relation to God: as Creator and thus Lord. The doctrine of God as Creator, then, is perhaps the most basic conception of God that we know.

The church has held firmly to this doctrine over against other views of the relationship of God to the world. Pantheism teaches that "all is God." God is the world and all that is in it. Philosophically this is monism. Many dualistic systems have posited two equal and primary principles in the universe. In some of these "creation" occurs when two complementary principles unite in some way to produce a new "form" out of the already existing, independent "matter" or principles. Dualism is found in Eastern creation myths where a God of order subjugates a monster or principle of chaos. Perhaps the best-known form of a dualistic view is from the Platonic picture of creation in the *Timaeus,* where the Demiurge shapes the world out of chaos while viewing eternal "ideas" above him. Forms of dualism were the most prominent views of creation in the hellenistic world of early Christianity. Gnosticism and Manichaeism were both dualistic systems.

Against these and variations of these—such as emanationism, which explains the origins of reality by supposing a perfect and transcendent principle from which all else is derived by the process of "emanation"; and eternal generation (Aristotle), which posits the universe as having always existed; and deism, which gives a place to God as Creator but then totally removes him from any involvement in the world—the Christian doctrine of creation proclaims God as the Creator *ex nihilo.* This means God brought the world into existence "out of nothing" through a purposeful act of his free will. In this the Christian doctrine confesses God as the almighty and sovereign Lord of all existence. Dualistic systems, by positing another power besides God, limit this sovereignty and are thus to be rejected. By stressing God as Creator "out of nothing" instead of "out of matter" or what already existed, Christian theology rejects the moral dualism that often stems from metaphysical dualism (as in Manichaeism); namely, that matter must be evil since it is in principle opposed to God who is the source of good. The creative act of God sets God apart from all that is created, and thus monism is rejected as well. The Fourth Lateran Council (1215) made the term *ex nihilo* an official part of church teaching.

Theology of Creation. From the affirmation of God as Creator *ex nihilo* a number of theological points follow. Langdon Gilkey has cited three major dimensions of what this means theologically.

God Is the Source of All That There Is. God is the sovereign Lord over all things. No other principle or power can be coequal or coeternal with God. Since all that is comes from God's will as its source, nothing in existence is in itself evil. The biblical picture is of a good Creator whose creative word is powerful and wise (Jer. 10:12; Prov. 3:19) and who created all things good (Gen. 1:31). Creation *ex nihilo* by a good God points to the essential goodness of all things that can be directed and transformed by God's power. God as sole Creator means no thing or no one else may be worshiped. All forms of idolatry are prohibited. God's creative act *ex nihilo* was a unique act, unlike any natural or human act with which we are familiar. The relation between Creator and creature must thus be spoken of in a way that differs from how we speak of the relation of one finite event to another. Therefore the theological doctrine of creation cannot be examined in the fashion of contemporary science, which by definition deals only with the relations of finite events within limits and boundaries. The Christian doctrine of creation concerns ultimate origins, not the proximate origins with which science is concerned.

Creatures Are Dependent Yet Real and Good. The Christian doctrine over against monistic pantheism affirms that creaturely existence is real because God created it and is thus "good" if it is in relationship to God. Human creatures have been given freedom and intelligence which may be used either to affirm or deny the fundamental relationship of existence, dependence on God. From this arises understandings of sin and grace in which creatures rebel and reject their Creator or are "re-created" by him through Jesus Christ (II Cor. 5:17) into a relationship of love and fulfillment. The basic Christian view of the goodness of life helps make science possible by stressing the orderliness and relational aspects of life and value possible by nurturing the desire to control nature for positive human purposes.

God Creates in Freedom and with Purpose. Against theories of how the world was created by emanation, as rays of light from the sun, or generation through a process of mating and birth, or by craft, as a carpenter would form a box out of wood, the Christian doctrine of creation *ex nihilo* abandons any explanation of "how" creation took place. Creation was a free act of the free God. The act was an expression of the character of God which is variously described in the Scriptures but which finds its primary focus in love (I John 4:16), specifically in God's love for the world as shown in Jesus Christ (John 3:16). In creation and in God's continuing sustaining and providing for creation, God is working out his ultimate purposes for humanity and the world. This means human life can be meaningful, intelligible, and purposeful even in the face of evil or "anything else in all creation" because life can be grounded in "the love of God in Christ Jesus our Lord" (Rom. 8:39). This points finally to God's purpose of creating "new heavens and a new earth" (Isa. 65:17; cf. 66:22; II Pet. 3:13; Rev. 21:1).

Contemporary Thought on Creation. Contemporary conversations between theologians and philosophers and between theologians and scientists have often addressed matters of creation in relation to such diverse issues as time, evolution, origins of the cosmos, the nature of human knowledge, and language about God. The doctrine of creation must be in dialogue with such figures as Newton, Einstein, Planck, Polanyi, Sagan, and a host of others.

T. F. Torrance has studied particularly the relation of theology and science and specifically the topic of creation and science. He cites three "masterful ideas" developed in the early church from the doctrines of the incarnation and creation *ex nihilo* which have had a powerful and determinative influence on both natural science and theology through the centuries.

The Rational Unity of the Universe. God the Creator is the ultimate source of all order and rationality. God is the unity who unifies the "universe," and this means too that wherever one goes in the universe, it is open to rational inquiry.

The Contingent Rationality or Intelligibility of the Universe. There is a natural and intrinsic order in the universe which can be probed and discovered through science. This is created by God as a counterpart to the rational order of his creation.

The Contingent Freedom of the Universe. God as the transcendent Lord of all space and time is not indebted to the universe or bound to it. God does not need the universe to be God. But the universe is indebted to God and completely dependent on him for its origin and continuity. This means the universe is not enslaved to alien principalities or powers. Creation by God *ex nihilo* shattered cyclical views of time and history, which have built-in futilities because they are ruled by a power of inevitable fate. The Christian doctrine offered instead a linear view of time and history moving toward their consummation in the purposes of their Creator. The freedom to explore the universe is given to creatures, and that contingent freedom embraces inexhaustible possibilities of discovery that can lead to the praise and glory of the Creator God.

D. K. McKim

See also God, Doctrine of.

Bibliography. K. Barth, *Church Dogmatics,* III; E. Brunner, *The Christian Doctrine of Creation and Redemption;* L. Gilkey, *Maker of Heaven and Earth;* Z. Hayes, *What Are They Saying About Creation?* S. Jaki, *Cosmos and Creator, Science and Creation,* and *The Road of Science and the Ways to God;* E. Klaaren, *Religious Origins of Modern Science;* T. F. Torrance, *The Ground and Grammar of Theology.*

Creation, New; Creature, New. *See* New Creation, New Creature.

Creationism. *See* Soul.

Creed, Creeds. "Creed" derives from the Latin *credo,* "I believe." The form is active, denoting not just a body of beliefs but confession of faith. This faith is trust: not "I believe *that*" (though this is included) but "I believe *in.*" It is also individual; creeds may take the plural form of "we believe," but the term itself comes from the first person singular of the Latin: "*I* believe."

Biblical Basis. Creeds in the developed sense plainly do not occur in Scripture. Yet this does not put them in antithesis to Scripture, for creeds have always been meant to express essential biblical truths. Furthermore, Scripture itself offers some rudimentary creedal forms that provide models for later statements. The *Shema* of the OT (Deut. 6:4–9) falls in this category, and many scholars regard Deut. 26:5–9 as a little credo. In the NT many references to "traditions" (II Thess. 2:15), the "word of the Lord" (Gal. 6:6), and the "preaching" (Rom. 16:25) suggest that a common message already formed a focus for faith, while confession of Jesus as Christ (John 1:41), Son of God (Acts 8:37), Lord (Rom. 10:9), and God (John 20:28; Rom. 9:5; Titus 2:13) constitutes an obvious starting point for the development of creeds in public confession. Indeed, if Acts 8:37 is authentic, it offers at the very first a simple creedal confession in baptism. This is, of course, exclusively Christological (cf. baptism in Christ's name in Acts 8:16; 10:48), leading to the theory that creeds consisted originally only of the second article. Nevertheless, the NT also contains many passages, culminating in Matt. 28:19, which include either the Father or the Father and the Holy Spirit in a more comprehensive Trinitarian formulation of a doctrinal, confessional, or liturgical type.

Creedal Functions. *Baptismal.* When more fixed creedal forms began to emerge out of the biblical materials, they probably did so first in the context of baptism. A creed offered the candidates the opportunity to make the confession of the lips demanded in Rom. 10:9–10. At first the form of words would vary, but familiar patterns soon began to develop. Fragmentary creeds from the second century—e.g., the DerBalyzeh Papyrus—support the thesis that creeds quickly became Trinitarian, or were so from the outset. This is implied also in Didache VII.1 and substantiated by the *Apostolic Tradition* of Hippolytus. The common view is that the mode of confession was responsive rather than declaratory.

Instructional. With a view to the baptismal confession, creeds soon came to serve as a syllabus for catechetical instruction in Christian doctrine. The level of teaching might vary from simple exposition to the advanced theological presentation of the *Catecheses* of Cyril of Jerusalem in the fourth century. All candidates, however, were to acquire and display some understanding of the profession they would make. A sincere commitment was demanded as well as intellectual apprehension.

Doctrinal. The rise of heresies helped to expand the first rudimentary statements into the more developed formulas of later centuries. A phrase like "maker of heaven and earth" was probably inserted to counteract the Gnostic separation of the true God from the creator, while the reference to the virgin birth and the stress on Christ's death safeguarded the reality of Jesus' human life and ministry. The Arian heresy produced another crop of additions (notably "of one substance with the Father") designed predominantly to express Christ's essential deity. These modifications gave the creeds a new function as a key to the proper understanding of Scripture (Tertullian) and as tests of orthodoxy for the clergy.

Liturgical. Being used in baptism, creeds had from the very first a liturgical function. It was seen, however, that confession of faith is a constituent of all true worship. This led to the incorporation of the Nicene Creed into the regular eucharistic sequence, first in the East, then in Spain, and finally in Rome. Placing the creed after the reading of Scripture made it possible for believers to respond to the gospel with an individual or congregational affirmation of faith.

The Three Creeds. *Apostles'.* In Christian history three creeds from the early church have achieved particular prominence. The first was supposedly written by the apostles under special inspiration and thus came to be called the Apostles' Symbol or Creed (Synod of Milan, 390). Lorenzo Valla finally refuted the story of its origin, which the East never accepted, and scholars now recognize that while the old Roman Creed (expounded by Rufinus, 404) no doubt underlies it, it derives from various sources. In its present form it is known only from the eighth century and seems to have come from Gaul or Spain. Nevertheless it came into regular use in the West, and the Reformers gave it their sanction in catechisms, confessions, and liturgies.

Nicene. Despite its name, the Nicene Creed must be distinguished from the creed of Nicaea (325). Yet it embodies in altered form, and without the anathemas, the Christological teaching which Nicaea adopted in answer to Arianism. It probably rests on creeds from Jerusalem and Antioch. Whether it was subscribed at Constantinople I in 381 has been much debated, but Chalcedon recognized it (451) and Constantinople II (553) accepted it as a revision of Nicaea. The West on its own added the *filioque* clause ("and from the Son") to the statement on the Holy Spirit, but the East never conceded its orthodoxy or the validity of its mode of insertion. In both East and West this creed became the primary eucharistic confession.

Athanasian. The creed popularly attributed to Athanasius is commonly thought to be a fourth or fifth century canticle of unknown authorship. As a more direct statement on the Trinity it became a test of the orthodoxy and competence of the clergy in the West at least from the seventh century. It differs from the other two main creeds in structure, in its more complex doctrinal character, and in its inclusion of opening and closing monitions. The Reformers valued it highly, the Anglicans even making some liturgical use of it, but the East did not recognize it, and in general its catechetical and liturgical usefulness has been limited.

Conclusion. The dangers of creed-making are obvious. Creeds can become formal, complex, and abstract. They can be almost illimitably expanded. They can be superimposed on Scripture. Properly handled, however, they facilitate public confession, form a succinct basis of teaching, safeguard pure doctrine, and constitute an appropriate focus for the church's fellowship in faith.

G. W. Bromiley

See also Apostles' Creed; Athanasian Creed; Filioque; Nicaea, Council of; Confessions of Faith.

Bibliography. F. J. Badcock, *History of the Creeds;* W. A. Curtis, *History of the Creeds and Confessions of Faith;* O. Cullmann, *The Earliest Christian Confessions;* J. N. D. Kelly, *Early Christian Creeds* and *Athanasian Creed;* A. C. McGiffert, *Apostles' Creed;* P. Schaff, *The Creeds of Christendom,* 3 vols.; H. B. Swete, *Apostles' Creed.*

Criminal Law and Punishment in Bible Times. Our knowledge of ancient Near Eastern law derives mainly from law codes surviving intact or as fragments, as with the codes of Ur-Nammu (*ca.* 2050 B.C.), Bilalama (*ca.* 1925 B.C.), Lipit-Ishtar (*ca.* 1860 B.C.), and Hammurabi (*ca.* 1760 B.C.), the Hittite laws (*ca.* 1450 B.C.), the Assyrian code (*ca.* 1350 B.C.), and the Hebrew covenant code (Exod. 21–23; *ca.* 1250 B.C.).

The codes formalized existing law or else instituted reforms, often after a period of conquest or change of monarchy, and set out in detail the protection afforded the individual and the life style expected by both king and deity. Because divine intervention was frequently considered instrumental in the inspiration of law and its communication to man, crime was regarded as a rejection of deity, and thus there was little differentiation between religious, criminal, and civil law.

A group or tribe would covenant with a deity to follow certain religious practices and other more general daily behavior for community well-being, and this relationship helped to unify the diverse interests and activities of group members. By agreeing to a covenant the community trusted its future prospects to a deity, but the infractions punished by that deity, usually in the form of natural disasters or defeat in battle, resulted in punishment for the entire community. Some penalties for transgression, however, could be administered by the group.

Punishment was frequently limited to compensation of equal value ("an eye for an eye"), although severe penalties, including death, were prescribed for stealing animals, as in Hammurabi's code (section 8). In general, the less developed the culture (as with the Assyrian laws), the more savage was the punishment, which often involved death. Probably the most civilized of ancient law was the Hittite code, although biblical law had a stronger ethical content.

Religious Offenses. Concern to maintain monotheism was paramount among the Hebrews, and this resulted in crimes of idolatry—the worship of gods other than Jehovah (Exod. 20:4–5; Deut. 5:8–9), blasphemy (Lev. 24:11–16), and sabbath-breaking (Exod. 16:23; 20:9–10; Num. 15:32–36) becoming capital offenses. By contrast the Hittites, who were protecting an agricultural economy, enforced laws relating to the land, and frequently imposed fines for infractions while occasionally making death or facial mutilation the penalty. The Hebrews regarded infant sacrifice (Lev. 20:2), false prophecy (Jer. 26:8–9), or any form of premeditated crime as an offense against God, and this kind of religious violation was usually punished by death.

Personal Injury. Premeditated murder was punished by death (Exod. 21:12), but a man who had killed accidentally could be shielded and obtain sanctuary (Num. 35:10–28; cf. Exod. 21: 12–15, 18–23). Kidnapping also merited the death penalty (Exod. 21:16). Some laws related to accidental injury and prescribed recompense. In the code of Hammurabi the fine levied included payment for the physician who treated the injury (section 206). Among the Hebrews an offender whose assault caused a permanent injury or possibly the loss of an eye or limb suffered an identical injury as punishment. A slave who suffered permanent injury from his master received his freedom as compensation (Exod. 21:26–27).

Laws Concerning Property. Damage to property or crops caused willfully or through negligence was punished by fines or restitution (Exod. 22:6; code of Hammurabi 53–56). Injuries caused to or by animals, particularly oxen, figure prominently in the code of Hammurabi (sections 250–52) as well as in the covenant code (Exod. 21:28–22:4). Hammurabi's code legislated that an accident was forgivable whereas negligence was not, and compensation was paid according to the rank of the injured party.

In ancient times a woman was considered the property and/or the responsibility of a man. Before marriage she was the property of her father and after marriage of her husband. If widowed, she was often the responsibility of the nearest male relative (Ruth 3:13). The recognized victim in sexual offenses was thus the property owner, to whom compensation was paid; but because of the value society placed on a high moral standard and sexual purity in Israel for the continuation of a strong race, adultery, rape, or seduction was punished severely. If rape occurred out-of-doors, the seducer was put to death, the theory being that if the girl had cried out, she could not have been heard (Deut. 22: 25–27). If it occurred indoors, both were executed, the girl then being considered a willing partner in the crime. A child was the property of his parents and as such was expected to honor and obey them. Cursing a parent was punishable by death (Exod. 21:17), as was assault on a parent (Exod. 21:15). By Mosaic times a child could not be executed by the parent without an accusation first being brought before the council. If the son was found guilty by the elders of drunkenness, laziness, or persistent disobedience, the adult males would stone him to death (Deut. 21:18–21).

A convicted robber had to return what he had stolen, and in cases of robbery with violence an additional 20 percent in punitive damages was added as a deterrent (Lev. 6:2–7). In Babylonia a householder catching a burglar breaking into his house could have him executed and walled up in the breach he had made, according to the code of Hammurabi (section 21). Larceny, frequently of an animal, resulted in a three- to fivefold restitution (Exod. 22:1–4); but if unable to pay, the offender worked as a slave for an appropriate length of time.

Crimes Reflecting Life Style. In ancient society a man's word was his bond, and false accusations merited the resultant punishment for the crime of which the defendant was accused. In the code of Hammurabi the one falsely accusing a man of murder was to be put to death (section 1). Perjury was considered a crime against God as well as against a neighbor. The individual was expected to take personal and financial responsibility for property entrusted to him and to make restitution at the rate of 100 percent for loss or 200 percent for dishonesty or connivance (Exod. 22:9–11). Members of the community requiring special protection included widows, orphans, the poor, or foreigners. The punishment of their oppressors came directly from the Lord, who was likely to place their own families in similar jeopardy (Exod. 22:21–24, 26–27; 23:9; Deut. 23:20; 24:17). Sexual acts considered crimes were incest, intercourse during menstruation (Lev. 15:24; 18:19; 20:18), and bestiality (Lev. 18:23; 20:15–16). Other general laws included the removal of boundary markers (Deut. 19:14) and use of false weights (Deut. 25:15; Lev. 19:35; Mic. 6:11; Prov. 11:1; 20:23). Bribery was forbidden, but no penalty was specified (Exod. 23:8).

Punishments. Capital punishment took the form of stoning or beheading, the latter particularly for crimes against the king (II Sam. 16:9; II Kings 6:31–32). Execution by the sword was often used for religious crimes (Exod. 32:27; Deut. 13:15). Burning is mentioned for sexual offenses (Lev. 20:14; 21:9), although branding may sometimes have been inferred. The holy ground of Mount Sinai was sacred, and those defiling it were shot to death with arrows. As a deterrent corpses were exhibited by hanging, but hanging was not a form of execution (Gen. 40:19; Josh. 8:29; 10:26; II Sam. 4:12). The body was suspended over a wooden gallows. Execution by impalement on a wooden spike was frequent among the Assyrians. Crucifixion was used in 167–166 B.C. as punishment for those who refused to abandon their Jewish faith (Josephus *Antiquities* xii.5.4), and this form of execution remained popular in the Roman period. Death by stoning was used for religious offenses, for adultery, and for a disobedient child (Lev. 24:15–16; Num. 15: 32–36; Deut. 13:1–10; 17:2–7; 21:18–21; 22:22–24). In Roman times the victim was sometimes placed on a scaffold to be stoned.

Physical punishment included beating with rods (Exod. 21:20; Prov. 13:24; 26:3; Isa. 9:4; II Cor. 11:25) and scourging or flogging, which was done with a leather whip of several strands, sometimes with small pieces of bone or metal inserted in the ends. Forty lashes was the normal number (Deut. 25:1–3), later reduced by one (II Cor. 11:24). Scourging was also used as a form of persuasive interrogation (Acts 22:24). It was customary in Roman times for a prisoner to be scourged after being condemned to death, not before, as Jesus was (Luke 23:16, 22; John 19:1). Gouging out a prisoner's eyes was a normal practice in the Near East (Num. 16:14; Judg. 16:21; I Sam. 11:2; Prov. 30:17). Mutilation as punishment, or as self-inflicted in cultic practices, was also common except among the Hebrews, who regarded the body as sacred because it was made in God's image. They felt justified, however, in mutilating their enemies by cutting off their thumbs and large toes so that they could no longer fight. Mutilation of the face and hands was prescribed in the code of Hammurabi and the Assyrian enactments. The prophets Hanani (II Chr. 16:10) and Jeremiah (Jer. 20:2–3) were placed in the stocks, and in Roman times this could be used as a form of torture as well as an indignity.

Many punishments, even capital punishments, were to be carried out by the nearest living relative of the victim. Thus some form of vengeance seems involved, as well as possible clemency on occasions.

H. W. PERKIN

Bibliography. D. Amram, "Retaliation and Compensation," *JQR* new series 2:191–211; J. M. P. Smith, *The Origin and History of Hebrew Law;* G. R. Driver and J. C. Miles, *The Assyrian Laws* and *The Babylonian Laws,* 2 vols.; H. B. Clark, *Biblical Law;* D. Daube, *Studies in Biblical Law;* J. Pritchard, ed., *Ancient Near Eastern Texts;* G. E. Mendenhall, *Law and Covenant in Israel and the Ancient Near East;* M. Greenberg, "The Biblical Conception of Asylum," *JBL* 78:125–32; M. G. Kline, *Treaty of the Great King;* D. J. McCarthy, *Treaty and Covenant;* S. M. Paul, *Studies in the Book of the Covenant;* B. S. Jackson, *Theft in Early Jewish Law;* B. N. Kaye and G. J. Wenham, *Law, Morality and the Bible.*

Crisis Theology. *See* NEO-ORTHODOXY.

Cross, Crucifixion. The Greek word for "cross," *stauros,* literally refers to an upright, pointed stake or pale. The word *xylon* is usually "wood" or "tree." In the NT and in some other literature of the time both frequently refer to a particularly cruel and degrading form of capital punishment known as crucifixion. In both canonical and later Christian literature "cross" and "crucifixion" take on a particularly important significance because of their connection with the death of Jesus and his expectations of his disciples. Any understanding of crucifixion in the ancient world must include the facts related to the act itself, its effect upon the victim, and the sociocultural implications attached to it.

Method of Crucifixion. Crucifixion involved elevating the condemned upon a pole, some form of frame or scaffolding, or a natural tree, thus exposing him to public view and derision. In many cases the individual was put to death through some other means and all or a part of the body (usually the head) then elevated. In other circumstances it became the actual means of execution. Because of both the effect of crucifixion upon the body and the lengthy period which usually elapsed before death, it represented the most painful, cruel, and barbaric form of execution. Its roots are lost in history. In one form or another it is known to have been practiced by many groups (such as the Indians, Scythians, Celts, Germani, Britanni, and Taurians) but is most closely associated with the Persians, Carthaginians, Phoenicians, Greeks, and especially the Romans. Some evidence suggests that it may have been associated with religious human sacrifice as well as a means of punishment.

Earlier forms probably involved impaling the condemned on a single pole or suspending him by wedging the head between a "Y" at one end of the implement. By NT times there seem to have been several different forms of "crosses" commonly used by the Romans. In addition to the single pole (*crux simplex*), most involved the use of at least two separate pieces of wood to construct a frame. However, crucifixion gave executioners opportunity to use their most cruel and sadistic creativity; victims were occasionally hung in grotesque positions by a variety of means. The two cross forms most likely used for the execution of Jesus are the St. Anthony's cross (*crux commissa*), shaped like a "T," or the Latin cross (*crux immissa*), on which the vertical piece rises above both the horizontal cross-bar (*patibulum*) and the head of the victim; the statement in Matt. 27:37 (cf. Luke 23:38) that the inscription was placed "over his head" and most ancient tradition favor the latter.

Detailed descriptions of crucifixion are few; writers seem to have avoided the subject. Recent archaeological discoveries, including skeletal remains of a crucifixion in first century Palestine (at Giv'at ha-Mivtar in Jerusalem), have added considerably to knowledge of the act. It seems that the Gospel accounts of the death of Jesus describe a standard Roman procedure for crucifixion. After the pronouncement of sentence, the condemned was required to carry the horizontal piece to the place of execution, always outside the city. The leader of the four-man execution squad led the procession bearing a sign detailing the reason for the execution. There the victim was flogged (this seems to have preceded condemnation in the case of Jesus—possibly to elicit sympathy). The victim's outstretched arms were affixed to the cross-bar by either nails or ropes. This was then raised and secured to the perpendicular pole (which in some areas may have been left in place permanently, both for convenience and as a warning). A small board or peg may have been provided as sort of a seat to bear some of the weight of the condemned (this actually may have prolonged suffering by prohibiting suffocation). The feet were then secured in a manner forcing the knees into a bent position. Contrary to popular contemporary opinion, crosses were not high; the feet were probably only a few inches above the ground. The sign describing the accusation was secured to the cross.

Death usually came slowly; it was not unusual for persons to survive for days on the cross. Exposure, disease, hunger, shock, and exhaustion were the usual immediate causes of death. Occasionally death was "mercifully" hastened by breaking the legs of the condemned. In Jesus' case death came much more swiftly than usual. A spear was thrust into his side to assure he was really dead before the body was removed (John 19:31–37). Bodies of the crucified were often left unburied and eaten by carnivorous birds and beasts, thus adding to the disgrace.

The social stigma and disgrace associated with crucifixion in the ancient world can hardly be overstated. It was usually reserved for slaves, criminals of the worst sort from the lowest levels of society, military deserters, and especially traitors. In only rare cases were Roman citizens, no matter what their crime, crucified. Among the Jews it carried an additional stigma. Deut. 21:23, "A hanged man is accursed by God," was understood to mean that the very method of death brought a divine curse upon the crucified. Thus, the idea of a crucified Messiah posed a special problem for such Jews as Paul (cf. Gal. 3:13; I Cor. 1:27–29).

Significance of the Cross. NT writers assume the historicity of the crucifixion of Jesus and focus their attention upon its significance. In it they understand that he, "who was in the form of God, did not consider equality with God a thing to be grasped at," was willing to "humble himself," take "on the form of a servant," and endure "even the death on the cross" (Phil. 2:6–8). This demonstrates the ultimate of humiliation and degradation. Yet, they affirm, the crucifixion of Jesus, the Messiah (Christ), was the will and act of God with eternal and cosmic significance. At the simplest level, the crucifixion of Jesus was the means by which God provided salvation, the forgiveness of sins (cf. I Cor. 15:3). Christ crucified becomes the summary of the Christian message (I Cor. 2:2). The cross of Jesus, the beloved Son of God, is the supreme demonstration of the love God has for sinful man (cf. John 3:16; 15:16). In Jesus' death God deals concretely with the sin and guilt which offends his holiness and separates man from his Creator. Because of the cross God becomes both the righteous and just Judge and, at the same time, the one who makes forgiveness available and justifies believers (cf. Rom. 3:26). The condemning legal demands set against man have been "canceled," nailed to the cross (Col. 2:14). The word of the cross is God's word of reconciliation (II Cor. 5:19).

The cross is also the symbol of discipleship. To first century Palestinians, who often witnessed the condemned carrying the crossbar to the site of their final torture, Jesus' word, "If any man will come after me, let him take up his cross and follow me" (Mark 8:34; cf. Matt. 10:38; Luke 14:27), must have come with a jolting, graphic impact. Jesus insists that the humiliation and suffering that culminated in his crucifixion were to characterize the experience of his followers. "It is," he says, "for the disciple to be like his teacher" (Matt. 10:24). Crucifixion becomes a part of the identification between Christ and the believer who is "crucified with Christ" (Gal. 2:20). The negative side of the characteristics of the new life of the Christian consists in having "crucified" sinful natures and desires (Gal. 5:24).

When understood in its historical, social context, Paul's statement that the proclamation of Christ crucified is a "stumbling block" or "scandal" (*skandalon*) to the Jews and "foolishness" (*mōria*) to the Gentiles is both logical and clear. Yet for Christians it remains an act and demonstration "of the power and wisdom of God" (I Cor. 1:23–24). J. J. Scott, Jr.

Bibliography. B. Siede *et al., NIDNTT,* I, 389–405; J. F. Strange, *IDB* Supplement, 199–200; M. Hengel, *Crucifixion.*

Crown. A headdress worn to symbolize honor, joy, victory, or official standing. In the OT there are four types of crowns. (1) The high priest's crown was a gold plate inscribed with "Holy to the Lord" and fastened to his turban by blue lace; it symbolized his consecration to represent the people to the Lord (Exod. 29:6; 39:30; Lev. 6:9; 21:12). (2) Hebrew kings normally wore a light crown, a narrow band of silk studded with jewels (II Sam. 1:10). The crown symbolized their divine appointment (II Kings 11:12; Pss. 21:3; 89:39; 132:18; Ezek. 21:25–26). (3) Pagan kings and idols wore massive crowns of gold and jewels, which were at times taken by Israelites and worn as a sign of empire (II Sam. 12:30; I Chr. 20:2; Zech. 9:16; Esth. 1:11). Zechariah made such a crown for Joshua, the high priest, symbolizing the unity of priestly and royal office (Zech. 6:11, 14). (4) A crown or wreath of flowers was used at banquets as a symbol of joy and celebration (Isa. 28:1; Song of S. 3:11; Wisd. Sol. 2:8). The word "crown" was also used symbolically to indicate royalty (Nah. 3:17; Prov. 27:24), glory (Job 19:9; Ps. 8:5; Isa. 28:5; Ezek. 16:12), joy (Ezek. 23:42), or pride (Job 31:36; Isa. 28:1, 3).

In the NT two words for crown are used. One, *stephanos,* is strictly speaking a chaplet or circlet, usually a laurel wreath worn at banquets or given as a civic or military honor. Paul contrasts this withering crown to the Christian's imperishable one (I Cor. 9:25; II Tim. 2:5), seeing his converts as his own garland (Phil. 4:1; I Thess. 2:19).

The Christian is urged to train as an athlete to gain his crown (I Cor. 9:25), which God will award in the last day (II Tim. 4:8), and to beware of losing it (Rev. 3:11). As a victor's wreath a crown is the glory of Christ (Heb. 2:7, 9), the eternal life won by Christians who persevere (James 1:12; I Pet. 5:4; Rev. 2:10), and the victory of Christ (Rev. 6:2; 14:14) and others (Rev. 9:7; 12:1). Normally *stephanos* does not indicate royalty, for *diadēma* (diadem) is the royal crown; but Christ's crown of thorns, while apparently in part an ironic parody of the victor's wreath (Mark 15:17), was in combination with robe and scepter a royal symbol (Mark 15:26), showing a flexibility in the use of the term. The bleeding Christ was mocked as a comic king as well as a helpless victor.

Diadem (*diadēma*) is rare in the NT. It is a symbol of royalty in each use: the dragon, the beast from the sea, and Christ (Rev. 12:3; 13:1; 19:12). P. H. Davids

Bibliography. C. J. Hemer, *NIDNTT,* I, 405–6; H. St. J. Hart, "The Crown of Thorns in John 19:2–5," *JTS* new series 3:66–75; W. M. Ramsay, *The Letters to the Seven Churches;* K. A. Kitchen, *IBD,* I, 345.

Crucifixion. *See* Cross, Crucifixion.

Crypto-Calvinism. In the sixteenth century questions arose about how much the influence of Calvin should be allowed to penetrate into Lutheranism. Philip Melanchthon and some of his followers (Philippists) were accused of being too accommodating to Calvin's doctrines and of thus practicing Crypto-Calvinism, or "secret" Calvinism, whereby Calvin's views were covertly being held by members of the Lutheran church. In particular, controversies raged over the Lord's Supper, with debates taking place in Heidelberg, Bremen, and Saxony.

In 1552 Joachim Westphal, an ardent Lutheran, published a book which pointed out divergences between Luther and Calvin, including their differences on the Lord's Supper. Strict Lutherans held views of the ubiquity (omnipresence) of Christ's glorified body, its physical presence in the supper, and the partaking of Christ's body by unbelievers. Melanchthon, however, inclined toward Calvin's view on these issues that Christ was genuinely present at the supper but in a spiritual way, but he did not wish to commit himself publicly. His spirit of conciliation toward the Reformed had earlier led him to change his Augsburg Confession by omitting from its article on the supper the phrase "truly present" and the condemnation of opposite views (1542). But after Melanchthon's death, his views were declared to have been the same as Luther's.

The Elector Augustus of Wittenberg declared the Philippists to be enemies of the state, expelling or imprisoning all of their leaders. In 1574 a commemorative medal was struck celebrating true Lutheranism's victory. The Formula of Concord (1577) formalized theologically the rejection of the view of Calvin and his followers that the "true, essential, and living body and blood of Christ" become truly present in the Holy Supper only "spiritually by faith." D. K. McKim

See also Concord, Formula of; Melanchthon, Philip.

Bibliography. J. L. González, *A History of Christian Thought,* III; K. R. Hagenbach, *A Text-Book of the History of Doctrines,* II; *Mst,* II, 597; R. Seeberg, *Text-book of the History of Doctrines;* D. C. Steinmetz, *Reformers in the Wings.*

Cults. Defining a cult is far more difficult than is often appreciated. Many evangelical Christians support the activities of Jews for Jesus and see them as a legitimate missionary group. But members of the Jewish community regard them as an evil and deceptive cult, a fact that well illustrates the problems surrounding the word. In its modern form the word "cult" was originally used by Ernst Troeltsch in his classic work, *The Social Teaching of the Christian Churches* (1912), where he classifies religious groups in terms of church, sect, and cult. For Troeltsch the cult represents a mystical or spiritual form of religion that appeals to intellectuals and the educated classes. At the heart of the cult is a spirituality which seeks to enliven a dead orthodoxy. Thus for Troeltsch the early Luther, many Puritans, and pietism can be seen as examples of cultic religion. Although Troeltsch's ideas about the distinction between church and sect generated a vigorous debate, little attention has been paid to his views on the cult. However, several liberal writers influenced by Troeltsch have seen evangelical Christianity in terms of a cult.

More important for the modern usage of the word "cult" has been the development of evangelical polemics against groups which they have seen as heretical. The classic work on this subject, which probably gave the word its modern usage, is Jan van Baalen's *The Chaos of Cults* (1938). In this work van Baalen expounds the beliefs of various religious groups such as theosophy, Christian Science, Mormonism, and Jehovah's Witnesses and subjects them to a rigorous theological critique from an evangelical perspective. In the last twenty years a large number of evangelical books dealing with cults have appeared. Over the course of time these have increasingly concentrated on the allegedly fraudulent claims of the cults, the immoralities of their leaders, and the ways in which their followers are deceived. As a result, in many cases a transition has occurred from a theological argument refuting the claims of various religious groups to a reliance upon psychological arguments which suggest that members of these groups are in some way brainwashed. This development poses a great danger for evangelical Christianity as can be seen from William Sargent's *The Battle for the Mind* (1957). In this book Sargent takes evangelical conversion as a classic example of brainwashing. More recently this argument has been developed by Jim Siegelman and Flo Conway in their popular book *Snapping* (1979), where the experience of born-again Christians is compared to the process by which people join groups like the Moonies. Such books as these and stories in the media about brainwashing have led to considerable pressure on governments in various American states, Canada, Britain, and Germany for anticonversion laws. These laws are supposedly aimed at groups like the Moonies. But because of their lack of definition (cf. the Lasher Amendment, State of New York in Assembly, 11122-A, March 25, 1980) they are in practice aimed at any form of change of life style brought about by a religious conversion.

Today the real problem of cults is the propaganda value of the word "cult" in a secular society. Although there are reliable statistics to show that the total membership of groups like the Children of God, the Unification Church (Moonies), and Hare Krishna is less than 35,000 in the United States and even fewer in other Western countries, these groups are presented as a major threat to society. As a result secularists are able to urge the acceptance of laws which replace religious freedom by a grudgingly granted religious toleration. Rather than persisting with the use of a word which has now become a propaganda weapon, the academic practice of calling such groups "new religious movements" should be followed. An alternative to this neutral terminology available for Christians who oppose such groups on theological grounds would be to revive the usage of "heretic" or simply call such groups "spiritual counterfeits." Such a procedure would move the debate away from psychological theories that can be used by secularists against Christianity to the arena of theological discussion and religious argument. I. Hexham

See also Sect, Sectarianism; Heresy.

Bibliography. M. Hill, *Sociology of Religion;* W. R. Martin, *The Kingdom of the Cults;* H. W. Richardson, ed., *New Religions and Mental Health;* C. Y. Glock and R. N. Bellah, eds., *The New Religious Consciousness;* I. I. Zaretzky and M. P. Leone, eds., *Religious Movements in Contemporary America;* T. Robbins and D. Anthony, eds., *In Gods We Trust;* R. S. Ellwood, *Religious and Spiritual Groups in Modern America;* J. Needleman and G. Baker, eds., *Understanding the New Religions.*

Culture and Christianity. *See* Christianity and Culture.

Curate. *See* Church Officers.

Curse. The Scriptures employ the term "curse" (OT noun forms, *qĕlālâ* and *ḥĕrem;* verb, *'ārar;* NT noun forms, *katara* and *anathema;* verb, *kataraomai*) in certain well-defined significations. In general usage a curse is an imprecation or an expressed wish for evil. If it be directed against God, it is blasphemy (Job 1:5, 11; 2:5, 9). It may be a desire uttered to God against another person or thing. A curse was considered to have an innate power to carry itself into effect (Zech. 5:1-3, where the curse inevitably found its victim). Curses among the heathen were supposed to be possessed of the power of self-realization (Num. 22-24 with Balaam). In Scripture a curse was invariably related to sin (Gen. 3) and disobedience (Prov. 26:2). In certain cases the concept of oath suffices to convey the meaning (Judg. 17:2; Isa. 65:15).

In its specific usage the curse was an act of dedicating or devoting to God. Things or persons thus devoted could not be used for private purposes (Lev. 27:28). In time of war a city was devoted to the Lord. This included the slaying of men and animals (Deut. 20:12-14; Josh. 6:26); the redeeming of children and virgins (Deut. 21:11-12); the burning of combustibles (Deut. 7:25); the placing of metals in the temple (Josh. 6:24); and the imposition of the ban on those who violated these provisions (Josh. 6:18). How literally the ban was carried out may be seen from the tragic history of Achan and his family, and the experience of Hiel the Bethelite (Josh. 7:1ff. and I Kings 16:34). The Canaanites as a nation were set apart for this kind of destruction (Josh. 2:10; 6:17).

In its higher significance the curse indicates a thing devoted to an exclusively sacred use. It amounts then to a vow. Compare the consecration of John the Baptist (Luke 1:15; 7:33), and the misuse of the vow among the people of Israel by an evasion instituted by their religious leaders (Mark 7:11ff.). It denotes, as seen, the ban of extermination and occurs frequently in the OT, but there is no clear instance of this in the NT. The ban of annihilation was replaced at times by the discipline of excommunication (John 9:22; 12:42; 16:2; Matt. 18:17). Ezra 10:8 is understood to approximate the later rabbinic practice of excommunication (Matt. 18:17; Luke 6:22). Admittedly, the Lukan reference may have a wider application.

One regular use of the word is in contrast to blessing. When the term is so employed, there are no sacred associations, and the word runs the gamut from divine to satanic. Before the people of Israel entered Canaan they were given the choice of obedience and God's blessing or disobedience and the curse. The curse was placed symbolically on Mount Ebal, while the blessings were attached to Mount Gerizim (Deut. 27:13-26). The rarity of the curse in the NT is in keeping with the spirit of the new age (Matt. 21:19ff.; Mark 11:12ff.).

The curse has a definite Christological reference. Paul states that Christ became a curse for us (Gal. 3:13) by bearing the penalty of the law (Deut. 21:23). The curse of the law (Deut. 27:26) fell upon him by the manner of his death as well as the fact of it. It was a criminal's death and so under the curse. C. L. Feinberg

Bibliography. D. Anst, *NIDNTT,* I, 413ff.; J. B. Payne, *Theology of the Older Testament;* J. B. Lightfoot, *Galatians;* J. Behm, *TDNT,* I, 353ff.

Cyprian (200-258). Caecilius Cyprianus was born in North Africa to a wealthy and highly cultured pagan family. After having distinguished himself as a master of rhetoric he was converted to Christianity and renounced his wealth and pagan culture. He was quickly raised through the presbytery to become Bishop of Carthage about 248. He had an influential pastoral ministry and produced various writings before his martyrdom in 258.

Cyprian was not primarily a theologian as was Tertullian, to whom he looked with respect. However, in his handling of certain pastoral and schismatic problems he expressed certain views which decisively shaped the church's ecclesiology until Augustine and also down through the Middle Ages. The most serious of these problems was the Novatian schism, a split beginning in Rome among orthodox parties over the treatment of lapsed Christians during the Decian persecution (Cyprian's own views advocating degrees of penance became the accepted practice and contributed to the Roman Catholic doctrine of penance). In order to condemn the schism Cyprian contended that the unity of the church was episcopal, not theological. The oneness of the church was to be found in the union of the college of bishops. Disassociation from the bishops was *ipso facto* separation from the true church. He taught that the episcopal unity was expressed in Christ's mandate to Peter (Matt. 16:18). The bishops as the successors of the apostles manifest this unity.

There are two versions of Cyprian's argument in *On the Unity of the Church,* both apparently genuinely Cyprian. The papal version is that he argues for the primacy of Peter, the other that he contends for coequality among all apostles and therefore all bishops. Cyprian goes on in this treatise to make the classic statements: "He is not a Christian who is not in Christ's church"; "He cannot have God for his father who has not the church for his mother"; and "There is no salvation outside the church."

Cyprian strongly contended for the correlation of Spirit baptism and regeneration with water baptism, resisting those (including Stephen of Rome) who were inclined to separate them. He also is important in the development of the doctrine of the Mass, as he taught that the supper was a sacrifice of Christ's body and blood which the priest, functioning in Christ's stead, offers up to God the Father on behalf of the people.

C. A. Blaising

See also Donatism; Novatian Schism.

Bibliography. J. N. D. Kelly, *Early Christian Doctrines;* J. Quasten, *Patrology,* II; M. Sage, *Cyprian.*

Cyril of Alexandria (d. 444). Patriarch of Alexandria 412–44. During Cyril's patriarchate his ministry was racked by controversy with Nestorius regarding the person of Christ.

Personal, theological, and political factors all doubtless played a part in the controversy, which reached a climax with the Council of Ephesus in 431. Deep-seated theological differences between Antioch and Alexandria came to sharp expression in 428 when Cyril accused Nestorius, Patriarch of Constantinople, of heresy because he insisted that Mary could be called *Christotokos* but not *Theotokos.* Cyril was determined to recognize the unity of Christ which, in his opinion, Nestorius had compromised by his excessive distinction between the divine and human natures.

The Roman Synod of 430 appointed Cyril as representative to ask Nestorius to recant. Ensuing correspondence between the two became increasingly intense, including reciprocal anathemas. The controversy stirred up such troubles that a general council was called by imperial order to settle the matter. When the council met at Ephesus in 431, Cyril presided over an action, prior to the arrival of Syrian delegates sympathetic to Nestorius, condemning and deposing Nestorius. In following days as other delegates arrived the action was reversed. Ultimately, however, Nestorius was exiled.

In order to resolve difficulties between the two positions represented, a Formula of Union was agreed upon. Cyril abided by it until his death. He affirmed a "hypostatic union" in which the humanity and divinity of Christ were seen as two distinct, inseparable natures. Some confusion occurred because he used *physis* to refer to the divine *Logos* but not to the humanity of Christ. He spoke of "one nature of God the Word incarnate," which was an Apollinarian phrase. Such emphasis and formulations opened the way for the monophysite position to predominate in Alexandrian theology after his death.

The relationship of the two natures of Christ has continued to be a point of contention in spite of the declaration of the ecumenical councils. Since the eighteenth century objections have found expression in the higher critical tradition, which emphasizes the humanity of Christ, reducing him to a historical man.

L. G. Whitlock, Jr.

See also Nestorius, Nestorianism; Ephesus, Council of; Adoptionism; Hypostatic Union; Alexandrian Theology; Antiochene Theology.

Bibliography. J. L. González, *A History of Christian Thought,* I; A. Grillmeier, *Christ in Christian Tradition;* C. E. Raven, *Apollinarism: An Essay on the Christology of the Early Church;* R. V. Sellers, *The Council of Chalcedon* and *Two Ancient Christologies.*

Dd

Dabney, Robert Lewis (1820–1898). One of the outstanding Presbyterian theologians of the nineteenth century and the most important and influential theologian in the Presbyterian Church, U.S., from 1865 to 1895. A native of Virginia, he was ordained to the ministry in 1847. In 1853 he was appointed as professor at his alma mater, the Union Theological Seminary in Richmond. Except for a brief period of military service, he remained at Union until 1883. He concluded his career as professor of mental and moral philosophy and political economy at the newly established University of Texas, during which time he cofounded the Austin School of Theology, later renamed the Austin Presbyterian Theological Seminary.

He was recognized as an unusually effective preacher and teacher. He was also a prolific writer. The most important of his works was his *Lectures in Systematic Theology*, which became the standard theological textbook in Southern Presbyterian seminaries and remained so at Union in Richmond until 1930. Some of the more important articles have been preserved in a two-volume collection entitled *Discussions: Evangelical and Theological.* As had J. H. Thornwell, Dabney championed the Calvinism of Old School Presbyterianism and was so effective that this theology and general point of view prevailed as that of the denomination during the whole Reconstruction period and at Union Seminary well into the twentieth century.

As a result of his service as chief of staff to General T. J. "Stonewall" Jackson, he wrote a biography of the noted commander. He was a vigorous, articulate defender of the South, as revealed in his volume *A Defense of Virginia.*

L. G. Whitlock, Jr.

See also Old School Theology; Thornwell, James Henley.

Bibliography. R. L. Dabney, *Social Rhetoric;* T. C. Johnson, *The Life and Letters of Robert Lewis Dabney;* E. T. Thompson, *Presbyterians in the South.*

Damnation. *See* Judgment; Hell.

Darby, John Nelson (1800–1882). The most influential British leader of the separatist Plymouth Brethren movement (also known as Darbyites) and systematizer of dispensationalism. His ideas pervaded late nineteenth century millenarianism in England and America and became a prominent element in American fundamentalism. Although born in London, Darby was educated at Trinity College and began his practice of law in Ireland at the age of twenty-two. Following his conversion and call to the ministry he was a zealous deacon and priest in the Established Church and led a spiritual awakening among his parishioners and their Roman Catholic neighbors. However, he became deeply disillusioned when he perceived a sharp contrast between the moral and spiritual laxness of the contemporary church and the spiritual vitality of NT believers narrated in Acts. Declaring the church to be in ruins, Darby left Anglicanism in 1828 and joined the Brethren movement, nondenominational groups who met in private homes for Bible study and spiritual edification.

Under Darby's forceful leadership Brethren groups grew rapidly. Darby distinguished the signs of a true church as spiritual unity and fellowship, and obedience to Scripture under a ministry guided by the Holy Spirit. Such criteria were juxtaposed against the visible, ordained ministry and worldly, manmade systems of church government in the Established Church and other dissenting denominations.

After 1840 sharp divisions between Darby and other Brethren teachers erupted over increasingly narrow theological and ecclesiastical questions. As a result Darby became the leader of the Exclusive group after a bitter controversy with B. W. Newton. In a series of lectures delivered at Lausanne, Darby synthesized his idea of the apostasy of the contemporary church with his interest in biblical prophecy and developed an elaborate philosophy of history. He divided history into separate eras or dispensations, each of which contained a different order by which God worked out his redemptive plan. The age of the church, like all preceding periods, has ended in failure due to man's sinfulness. Darby broke not only from previous millenarian teaching but from all of church history by asserting that Christ's second coming would occur in two stages. The first, an invisible "secret rapture" of true believers, could happen at any moment, ending the great "parenthesis" or church age which began when the Jews rejected Christ. Then literal fulfillment would resume OT prophecy concerning Israel, which had been suspended, and fulfillment of prophecy in Revelation would begin the great tribulation. Christ's return would be completed when he established a literal thousand-year kingdom of God on earth, manifest in a restored Israel.

Darby popularized dispensationalism and attempted to proselytize converts to Brethrenism by travels to Europe, New Zealand, and seven trips to Canada and the United States between 1862 and 1877. His views gained gradual acceptance, as his basic theological assumptions of verbal inspiration of Scripture, human depravity, and the sovereignty of God's grace were compatible with traditional Calvinism. His eschatological views were propagated through a series of prophecy conferences such as the Niagara Bible Conference, an evangelical fellowship which met annually from 1883 to 1897 to uphold biblical truth. Although many Baptists and Old School Presbyterians accepted Darby's eschatology and his view that the church was often corrupt, few actually left their denominations. And many leaders criticized Brethrenism for weakening the church by its proselytizing.

Darby's eschatological views figured prominently in American fundamentalism in the 1920s as conservative Christians such as dispensationalists and Princeton Calvinists joined forces to counter liberalism's rejection of biblical teaching.

W. A. Hoffecker

See also Dispensation, Dispensationalism; Fundamentalism; Millennium, Views of the; Rapture of the Church; Tribulation; Niagara Conferences.

Bibliography. C. B. Bass, *Backgrounds to Dispensationalism;* F. R. Coad, *A History of the Brethren Movement;* J. N. Darby, *Collected Writings,* ed. W. Kelly, 34 vols.; H. A. Ironside, *A Historical Sketch of the Brethren Movement;* C. N. Kraus, *Dispensationalism in America;* E. R. Sandeen, *The Roots of Fundamentalism: British and American Millenarianism 1800–1930;* G. Marsden, *Fundamentalism and American Culture.*

Darkness. Beyond the literal meaning of the Hebrew *ḥōšek, 'ōpel,* and the Greek *skotia, skotos, zophos,* there is a wealth of metaphor. Concerning man, darkness means ignorance (Job 37:19), calamity (Ps. 107:10), death (Ps. 88:12), wickedness (Prov. 2:13; John 3:19), damnation (Matt. 22:13). These metaphors are grounded in the truth that God is light (I John 1:5) and in creation and redemption (II Cor. 4:6) he has conquered darkness, the forces which oppose his rule (Luke 22:53; Eph. 6:12). Darkness is associated with divine interventions, firstly, as in Deut. 4:11, because God is hidden except he reveal himself; secondly, because the light of revelation (Isa. 60:2) becomes darkness and condemnation to those who refuse it (Amos 5:18; Zeph. 1:15).

J. A. Motyer

See also Light.

Dark Night of the Soul. The phrase is taken from the title of a book by John of the Cross. It refers, however, to a universal experience of spiritual and mystical writers. The contemplative life is often at first a life of great spiritual experiences. Conversion is exciting as the works of evil are stripped away and the person experiences the power of God in a new way, both in physical provision and in spiritual experience (from visions to the simple perception of God's love and fellowship). Growth in spiritual knowledge and insight is perceptible.

Then comes a period when all of this is removed. God had seemed very close; now he seems distant or even absent. One had been experiencing great spiritual fervor; now one experiences nothing. In fact, prayer, Scripture, church, and devotion may seem boring or dull. The person keeps on, but only because he is disciplined and knows he should. Previously one rejoiced in freedom from sin as obvious worldliness was left behind; now he is deeply conscious of his sinful state. Sins such as lust, anger, and evil thoughts which were believed conquered rise up like so many demons from hell. Sins of which one was totally unconscious are suddenly discovered. The person feels utterly sinful, unworthy, and unfit for God's presence. On a deeper level there may for some be a fascination with death, a longing to be closer to God, and a feeling that only death will free one from the clinging sinfulness.

This period was described in the older literature as aridity, or dryness in the soul. *The Cloud of Unknowing* describes it as a dark cloud between the person and God. John of the Cross calls it the dark night of the soul. The goal of the experience is the purification of the person. The intense feeling of sinfulness and struggle with internal sins not only produce a deeper holiness but also a deeper humility as the person experiences how he can never be worthy. The lack of experience of God's nearness means the person must operate on faith, trusting that God is near, although not experienced. The lack of spiritual "highs" and other gifts means the person discovers whether he loves God or only the pleasant feelings spiritual life produces and the gifts God gives. As faith, love, and humility develop to a mature state, the person reaches a point of self-abandonment in which anything God may do with him is acceptable to him. This is the goal of aridity. When it is reached after however many weeks or even years in "the valley," the person often experiences even higher "mountaintops" of union with God than before. But he realizes it is all a gift, all of grace. P. H. Davids

See also John of the Cross; Mysticism.

Bibliography. E. Underhill, *Mysticism;* John of the Cross, *Dark Night of the Soul, Ascent of Mount Carmel,* and *The Cloud of Unknowing;* A. Bloom, *Beginning to Pray.*

Day. ***Natural Meanings.*** The greatest number of uses of day (*yôm; hēmera*) refer to natural time units; but in the progress of revelation its theological use increases to such an extent that in the Synoptic Gospels almost one third of all uses of *hēmera* is eschatological.

Hours of Daylight. Any given day between dawn and dusk (Gen. 1:5, 16, 18). The Lord Jesus spoke of a day of twelve hours, assuredly of light since man does not stumble (John 11:9). Day is used to indicate the dawn (Josh. 6:15; II Pet. 1:19), midday (I Sam. 11:11; Acts 26:13), late afternoon or evening hour (Judg. 19:9; Luke 9:12). A large number of references speak of day as opposed to night (Isa. 27:3; Mark 5:5; Luke 18:7; I Tim. 5:5).

Legal or Civil Day. A period of twenty-four hours' duration. The sabbath is from dusk to dusk (Lev. 23:32). There are six days and a sabbath in a week (Luke 13:14). The Lord's resurrection is after three days (Mark 8:31; Luke 24:46). The period between the resurrection and the ascension is forty legal days (Acts 1:3). The legal day is contrasted with the hour and month and year in Rev. 9:15.

A Longer Period. Although day is used in the singular to designate long periods of time, as the "day" of Christ (John 8:56), or the day of salvation (Isa. 49:8; II Cor. 6:2), it is more generally used in this respect in the plural in such expressions as "the days of Adam" (Gen. 5:4), "the days of Abraham" (Gen. 26:18), "the days of Noah" (Matt. 24:37), "the days of the Son of man" (Luke 17:26). Christ's presence is "always" (lit. "all the days") with those who go out to preach his word (Matt. 28:20).

Theological Meanings. *General.* The antithesis of day and night in the literal sphere is seen in the description of believers as children of the day and unbelievers as children of the night (I Thess. 5:5–8). The Lord Jesus indicates that the day is the time of opportunity for service that will end with the coming night (John 9:4). Paul, however, teaches that the period up to the time of eschatological salvation is the night, and this will issue in the glorious day of Christ (Rom. 13:11–13).

Eschatological. In the records of man's earliest history the word "day" came to be associated with special days set aside as belonging to Jehovah (Gen. 2:3; Exod. 20:8–11; 12:14, 16; Lev. 16:29–31). In the total OT concept they were designed for judgment of sin in nations or individuals (Isa. 2:12; 13:9, 11; Ezek. 7:6–8; Zeph. 1:14–18; Obad. 15), but they also had the purpose of salvation, vindication, or restoration of God's chosen ones (Gen. 7:10–13, 23; Mic. 2:12; Isa. 4:3–6). The local days of Jehovah visited on Israel and Judah (Ezek. 7:4–8) or upon pagan nations (Isa. 13:9) were just a foretaste of one climactic *dies irae* to come upon the whole world (Joel 2:31; Mal. 4:5; Isa. 2:12; Jer. 25:15). Immediately following this supernatural intervention on the plane of history God would set up his eternal kingdom (Dan. 2:28, 44) in which he alone would be sovereign and exalted (Isa. 2:11).

In the NT the day of Jehovah, or final day of reckoning, is designated by various phrases (I Thess. 5:4; John 6:39; Matt. 10:15; I Pet. 2:12), principally in combination with the name of Jesus Christ (Phil. 1:6, 10; I Cor. 1:8; 5:5; Acts 2:20; II Pet. 3:10), but they contain the same basic concepts as in the OT, i.e., God's judgment, salvation, sovereignty, and exaltation.

The phrase "the last days" (Acts 2:17; Heb. 1:2; II Tim. 3:1; II Pet. 3:3–4) seems to include, in its greatest extension, the whole period from the cross to the second advent. More specifically, day in its plural form is used to designate that final terrible period immediately before the parousia, including the great tribulation (Matt. 24:19–22;

Luke 17:26–30; cf. Rev. 4–11). In the singular form it designates the parousia itself (Matt. 24:30–31, 36; II Thess. 2:1–2) and also the postparousia period up to the creation of the new heavens and earth (II Pet. 3:8–13).

The theological connotations of day do not rob it of its literalness when referring to the parousia. Rather, God's choice of the term "day" only serves to emphasize its literal reality. When the Lord himself makes his second appearance on earth, then will begin what Peter calls "the day of eternity" (II Pet. 3:18, Gr.). G. A. GAY

See also DAY OF CHRIST, GOD, THE LORD; ESCHATOLOGY; LAST DAY, DAYS.

Bibliography. O. Cullmann, *Christ and Time;* W. G. Kümmel, *Promise and Fulfilment;* H. W. Robinson, *Inspiration and Revelation in the OT;* H. H. Rowley, *The Faith of Israel;* S. J. De Vries, *Yesterday, Today, and Tomorrow;* G. von Rad and G. Delling, *TDNT,* II, 943ff.

Day of Atonement. *See* ATONEMENT, DAY OF.

Day of Christ, God, the Lord. In Semitic thought it was customary to designate events of importance with the term "day." These could be decisive events in Israel's history (the day of Jerusalem's destruction, Ps. 137:7) or random events which took on symbolic value (the day of trouble, Ps. 77:2). Among Israel's prophets the term often took on an eschatological tenor describing a future climactic day of judgment (the day of the Lord of hosts, Isa. 2:12). This day of the Lord was anticipated by Israel as a future day of Yahweh's visitation. It would inaugurate some hopeful era for God's people. But as the earliest reference in Amos (5:18–20) makes clear, this visitation would not reaffirm Israel's hopes. As G. Ladd writes, "Amos shattered this shallow nonreligious hope with an announcement that the future holds disaster rather than security." Jerusalem would be destroyed (Amos 2:5) and foreign powers would raze Israel (3:9–11). Other prophets confirmed this same picture (Isa. 2:12; Zech. 14:1). Joel writes that "the day of the Lord is near—it will come like destruction from the Almighty" (1:15, NIV). Zephaniah in particular gives this theme increased attention when he describes the coming catastrophe (1:7, 14) and employs images descriptive of an impending battle (1:10–12, 16–17; 2:5–15).

Alongside this desperate outlook, however, another prophetic word is evident. The prophets not only view historical events as ushering in the day of the Lord's visitation, but they look to an ultimate eschatological event. Even for Amos this will be a day of universal judgment (8:8–9; 9:5) when at last salvation and genuine hope will come to Israel: "In that day I will raise up the booth of David that is fallen . . . and rebuild it as in the days of old. . . . I will restore the fortunes of my people Israel" (Amos 9:11–15; cf. Zeph. 3:9–20). Therefore this "day" is both near and far, both historical and eschatological for Israel. It may be a divine visitation within history as well as a final visitation that climaxes history.

The NT maintains this futurist expectation consistently but adds that the second coming of Jesus Christ (or the parousia) will hallmark the day of the Lord. It will be a day of Christ's revealing (I Cor. 1:8; 5:5; cf. II Thess. 2:2) and thus may be termed "the day of the Lord Jesus" (II Cor. 1:14) or simply "the day of Christ" (Phil. 1:10; 2:16). It will be a day of surprise (I Thess. 5:2; II Pet. 3:10) ushering in a climactic battle (Rev. 16:14) and universal judgment (II Pet. 3:12). This surprising climactic denouement to history parallels the eschatological Son of man sayings in the Gospels ("For as lightning flashes and lights up the sky, . . . so will the Son of man be in his day," Luke 17:24).

The most important development in NT eschatology is the early Christian view that in some fashion the eschatological era had been inaugurated with the coming of Christ and the Spirit. Thus in Acts 2, Peter can cite Joel 2 and interpret the experiences of Pentecost in light of eschatological fulfillment. This therefore somewhat parallels the OT notion of a special divine visitation within history. But still, while the promise may be partially realized, NT writers are clear that its fulfillment is future. Thus the church experiences a religious tension. While it has already acquired some benefits of the day of the Lord, it still awaits a thoroughgoing future bestowal at the second coming of Christ. G. M. BURGE

See also ESCHATOLOGY; REALIZED ESCHATOLOGY; SECOND COMING OF CHRIST; LAST DAY, DAYS.

Bibliography. E. Jacob, "The Consummation," in *Theology of the OT;* G. von Rad, "The Origin of the Concept of the Day of Yahweh," *JSS* 4:97–108, and "The Day of Yahweh," in *The Message of the Prophets;* G. von Rad and G. Delling, *TDNT,* II, 943–53; M. Rist, *IDB,* I, 783; E. Jenni, *IDB,* I, 784–85; G. Ladd, *The Presence of the Future.*

Days, Last. *See* LAST DAY, DAYS.

Deacon, Deaconess. While the office of elder was adopted from the Jewish synagogue, the early church instituted something new with an order of deacons. The word group surrounding *diakoneō,* "to serve" (*diakonia,* service; *diakonos,* server), initially referred to a waiter at a meal (John 2:5, 9). This meaning expanded to include care for the home and finally any personal help or care. But still for Judaism religious service as a "deacon," or server, was uncommon. In Judaism service was exercised through alms, not serving. Hence in the Greek OT *diakonos* refers only to professional court servants. Waiting at table was considered below the dignity of the Jewish freeman (cf. Luke 7:44–45; so Hess). In this sense *diakonos* often appears in the NT referring to servants and their masters (Matt. 22:13). Similarly, Christians are to be known as servants (*diakonoi*) of Christ (John 12:26), who not only himself served as a *diakonos* (Rom. 13:4; 15:8; Gal. 2:17) but directed each of us to serve in a similar fashion (Mark 9:35; 10:43; cf. II Cor. 3:6; 11:15, 23; Col. 1:7). Again, this language of pious service employing the term *diakoneō* was uncommon in the first century. The church on the other hand viewed its work on the model of Christ, who engaged in humble service. Even fellowship around a table (the Lord's Table) would inspire the use of such language as a descriptive title for Christian service (cf. John 13:1–30).

The beginnings of a formal *diaconate,* or formal office of deacons, may be traced to Acts 6. A problem in distribution of aid led to the appointment of seven leaders who would free the apostles from "waiting on tables" (*diakoneō,* 6:2). The body elected the seven, who were ordained for service by the apostles (6:6). Luke's intimate knowledge of Paul's church organization and his extended interest in this passage no doubt suggest that he is here introducing what was for Paul an important office.

From Jerusalem the diaconate spread to the Gentile churches. Phil. 1:1 lists the deacons alongside the bishops in Paul's greeting and suggests two adjacent offices. But was this office universal? A mere functional description may appear in Rom. 12:6–8; I Cor. 12:28–31; and I Thess. 5:12. But in the list of offices in Eph. 4 deacons are absent (as are elders), and when Paul instructs Titus to appoint elders in every city of Crete (Titus 1:5) he fails to mention an order of deacons. Still, in I Tim. 3:8–13 there is a substantial paragraph devoted to the role of the deacon. This should be expected inasmuch as Paul here directly turns his thoughts to church organization. Deacons are to demonstrate an exemplary moral life style and a firm faith. They are to be practical servants (and not necessarily teachers, cf. 5:17). In fact, the description found in I Tim. 3:8–13 so closely parallels the description of bishops (3:1–7; cf. Phil. 1:1) that scholars have often wondered if the offices were once one. But this seems doubtful.

A brief glance at the patristic era shows that the office was soon formalized (I Clem. 42:4; Hermas, *Visions* 3, 5:1; *Similitudes* 9, 26:2; and Ignatius, *Eph.* 2:1; *Mag.* 6:1; 13:1; *Trall.* 2:3; 3:1; 7:2; *Pol.* 6:1). Lightfoot notes how Irenaeus labeled the seven in Acts 6 as "deacons." Eusebius even records how the Roman Church limited its diaconate to seven, preserving the memory of Stephen. By the third century Rome had forty-six elders but only seven deacons—and this tradition persisted through the fifth century. In the early fourth century the Greek Council of Neocaesarea ruled that any given city could boast only seven deacons (again viewing Acts 6 as the model).

It is certain that women served actively as deacons. This is clear not only in Rom. 16:1, where the deaconess Phoebe of Cenchreae is commended by Paul, but in I Tim. 3:11. Here the best exegesis would view the reference to women as meaning another order of deacons (*gynaikas hōsautōs*), namely women deacons (see J. N. D. Kelly, *The Pastoral Epistles,* pp. 83–84). A parallel development is found in I Tim. 5:3–16, where a women's order of widows was recognized for its ready service. Nevertheless, the patristic church enjoyed the service of an independent order of women deacons, as witnessed to in the Syriac Didascalia. From the fourth century on, their common title was "deaconess" (Gk. *diakonissa;* Lat. *diaconissa*).

Archdeacon is an order of ministry of relatively recent development which began to be recognized in the medieval period. The archdeacon is a cleric with specific administrative tasks usually assigned by a bishop. It is a common order in the Anglical tradition.

G. M. Burge

See also Church, Authority in; Church Officers; Major Orders.

Bibliography. R. Banks, *Paul's Idea of Community;* E. Best, "Bishops and Deacons: Phil. 1:1," *Studia Evangelica,* IV, 371–76; H. W. Beyer, *TDNT,* II, 81–93; J. G. Davies, "Deacons, Deaconesses and the Minor Orders in the Patristic Period," *JEH* 14: 1–15; K. Hess, *NIDNTT,* III, 544–49; J. B. Lightfoot, "The Christian Ministry," in *Philippians;* E. Schweizer, *Church Order in the NT.*

Dead, Abode of the. The concept is one which develops in Scripture. In the OT one descends at death to Sheol, which may simply mean the grave (Num. 16:30, 33), but usually means the underworld to which one "goes down" beneath the earth (Gen. 42:38; Prov. 15:24). The important theological concept is that Sheol is not just a place of darkness and forgetfulness (Job 10:21–22; Pss. 88:12; 94:17), but a place where Yahweh does not remember people (Ps. 88:5, 11; Isa. 38:18), a place of permanent decay (Job 14:21–22), whose inhabitants are permanently unclean and cut off from the cult and service of Yahweh. His praises are never sung there, and he is not remembered (Pss. 6:5; 30:9; 115:17). Because of the uncleanness and separation from the cult, worship of the dead was avoided in Israel and necromancy prohibited (I Sam. 28:7–25; Deut. 18:11).

On the positive side, existence in Sheol was among one's ancestors (Gen. 25:8; Ezek. 32:17–30) and it was not outside the reach of God's power (Ps. 139; Jonah 2:2; Amos 9:2). But still it could hardly be called life, for life existed for the Hebrew only in the presence of God (Ps. 16:10). It was only in exceptional cases and toward the end of the OT period that the writers began to express hope concerning the realm of the dead or to believe in an eventual resurrection (Job 14:13–22; 19:25–27; Pss. 49; 73:23–28; Dan. 12:1–2).

It was during the intertestamental period that a clear idea of the abode of the dead emerged. The OT word "Sheol" was translated by the Greek word "Hades." For some writers this was just a continuation of the old idea of a place of separation from God, but for others Hades was a place where the righteous were rewarded and the wicked tormented (I Enoch 22; 51:1; 102:5; II Macc. 6:23). Another name for the place where the wicked were tormented was Gehenna (from the OT site of child sacrifices, II Kings 16:3; I Enoch 90:20–27), while the Persian term Paradise was applied to the place where the righteous were rewarded.

While the NT basically adopts the intertestamental picture, it has relatively little to say about the abode of the dead—about thirty-five verses. What it does say is contained in a multitude of terms which are used with more than one meaning.

Hades is a place within the earth to which all dead go down (Matt. 11:23; 12:40; Luke 10:15), a place with gates which, however, cannot hold the Christian (Matt. 16:18), for Christ holds the key (Rev. 1:18). Believers will be raised from the dead to be with their Lord.

In another use of the term, Hades is the place of torment for the wicked dead (Luke 16:23); it is also called Gehenna, a place of fire and worms (Matt. 5:22; 18:9; Mark 9:45; James 3:6); outer darkness (Matt. 8:12; 22:13; 25:30); Tartarus (II Pet. 2:4); and the abyss, the prison of the devil and his angels (Rev. 9:1–11; 11:7; 17:8; 20:3; Matt. 25:41). In the end Gehenna or the lake of fire becomes the all inclusive term, for it swallows Hades and Death (since by then they hold none of the righteous who have been resurrected, Rev. 19:20; 20:10, 14–15; 21:8).

When spoken of separately, the righteous dead are said to enter a blessed state at death termed Abraham's Bosom (Luke 16:22) or Paradise (Luke 23:43; Paul and John place it in heaven, II Cor. 12:2–4; Rev. 2:7). Paul, after his own near brush with death (II Cor. 1:8–11), describes this as being with Christ and thus better than life (Phil. 1:23; II Cor. 5:8). Death has no power to separate Christians from God (Rom. 8:38–39); in fact, it unites them.

The devil in no way controls the place of the dead. Jesus has the key (Rev. 1:18), and it is distributed only to his messengers (Rev. 9:1; 20:1). Jesus himself upon his death descended to the place of the dead (Eph. 4:9; the rabbis used "the lowest earth" to refer to Sheol/Gehenna/Hades), and he preached there to imprisoned spirits, probably meaning the fallen angels of Noah's time (I Pet. 3:18–20; cf. Gen. 6:1–4). His preaching was surely an annunciation of victory. Thus for the Christian death, while sad, has lost its fearful aspect. Their leader has entered the stronghold of Hades and has reappeared victorious in resurrection. Whether thought of in terms of Paradise and Abraham's Bosom or in terms of the heavenly Jerusalem (Heb. 12:22), being under the heavenly altar (Rev. 6:9), or standing before God's throne (Rev. 7:9; 14:3), the abode of the righteous dead is one of union with Christ. P. H. Davids

See also Hades; Hell; Sheol; Abraham's Bosom; Heaven; Paradise; Death; Intermediate State.

Bibliography. H. Bietenhard, *NIDNTT,* II, 205–10; J. S. Bonnell, *Heaven and Hell;* J. Jeremias, *TDNT,* I, 9–10, 146–49, 657–58; L. Morris, *The Biblical Doctrine of Judgment.*

Dead, Prayers for the. *See* Prayers for the Dead.

Dead Sea Scrolls. The designation popularly given to manuscripts discovered since 1947 in the area west of the Dead Sea.

Qumran. The most important manuscripts are those found in eleven caves overlooking the Wadi Qumran—apparently the remnants of the library of a religious community which had its headquarters at Khirbet Qumran between *ca.* 145 B.C. and A.D. 68 (with a break of thirty years *ca.* 34–4 B.C.). This community, organized by a leader usually referred to by a phrase meaning "the Teacher of Righteousness," regarded itself as the godly remnant of Israel. It withdrew to the wilderness of Judea to prepare for the cataclysmic events which would bring the current "epoch of wickedness" to an end and introduce the kingdom of God. By diligent study and practice of the law of God its members hoped to win his acceptance and expiate the errors of their misguided fellow Israelites; they also expected to be the executors of his judgment on the ungodly at the end of the age.

They refused to recognize the priesthood that controlled the Jerusalem temple during the "epoch of wickedness" (the Hasmonean priesthood), partly because it did not belong to the family of Zadok and partly because of its moral unfitness for the sacred office. In their own ranks they preserved the framework of worthy priests and Levites, ready to resume a pure sacrificial worship in the temple of the new Jerusalem.

The men of Qumran believed in the absolute sovereignty of God. He knew the end from the beginning and disposed all things in accordance with his eternal purpose, despite attempts by man to frustrate it.

They were also strict predestinarians: men and angels alike have been allotted by God to the realm of light or the realm of darkness, each realm governed by its appropriate "prince." The idea of someone being redeemed from the realm of darkness to share the inheritance of the "sons of light" was scarcely contemplated; the impression is given, however, that it might be all too easy for sons of light to defect to the realm of darkness: only unremitting vigilance and divine grace could keep them true.

The schema of the realms of light and darkness may owe something to Zoroastrian influence, but there is no ultimate dualism in Qumran theology because the one God is supreme over both realms; the prince of light and the prince of darkness are alike created by him.

God has given his law to Israel. It is therefore for Israel to obey his law, but Israel as a whole has failed to do so. The faithful remnant, as a miniature Israel, set itself to render the obedience that Israel as a whole had failed to render, according to a radically strict interpretation of the law—considerably stricter than that of the Pharisees, whom the men of Qumran disparaged as "seekers after smooth things" or "givers of smooth interpretations" (cf. Isa. 30:10). The sabbath law and the marriage law were interpreted with special severity. But the members of the sect did not complain; they entered its ranks as "volunteers for holiness," setting themselves willingly to attain a standard of righteousness higher than that of the scribes and Pharisees (cf. Matt. 5:20).

But, while they knew they could not win God's approval without unremitting devotion to his law, they were far from supposing that such devotion could establish a claim on God. When they had done all, they were not thereby justified: their justification in God's sight depended entirely on his grace. His righteousness was understood by them, as later by Paul, in a twofold sense—not only of his personal character but also of his gracious act in justifying those who would not venture to regard their own righteousness as an adequate basis for being accepted by him.

The end of the current epoch of wickedness and the inauguration of the new age of righteousness would be marked by the rise of three figures foretold by the OT prophets. One of these was the prophet like Moses foretold in Deut. 18:15–19; another would be the warrior prince of the house of David; the third would be a great priest of Aaronic descent. The designation "messiah" is given to the second and the third (they are "the anointed ones of Israel and Aaron"); but when the Messiah as such is mentioned, the Davidic prince is intended. He, however, takes his orders from the great priest, who is to be the effective head of state in the new age, just as the prince in Ezekiel's new commonwealth is subordinate to the priesthood.

The Qumran library, of which over four hundred documents have been identified (most in very fragmentary condition), included biblical and nonbiblical texts. About a hundred out of the four hundred are biblical texts. All the OT books except Esther are represented, some of them several times over. These biblical manuscripts date from the closing centuries B.C. and the first century A.D. They attest at least three distinct textual traditions of Hebrew Scripture—not only the text (preserved in Babylonia) which underlies the later Massoretic recension, but also the text (of Egyptian provenance) underlying the Septuagint and a text (native to Palestine) akin to the Samaritan Pentateuch. The discovery of these manuscripts has reduced the gap separating the autographs from the oldest extant copies by about a thousand years and is of great importance for the textual history of the OT. In addition to copies of the type of Hebrew text used by the Septuagint translators, pieces of their actual Greek translation have also been identified.

The nonbiblical manuscripts, along with the archaeological evidence furnished by the excavation of Khirbet Qumran, give a picture of the beliefs and practices of this community, which almost certainly was an Essene group. The members practiced ceremonial ablutions; they held fellowship meals; they followed the solar calendar of the book of Jubilees; they cherished apocalyptic hopes; they interpreted prophetic Scripture in terms of persons and events of their own days and of the days immediately to follow.

Some of the most interesting documents are commentaries (*pěšārîm*) on biblical texts, from which may be learned the ideas of biblical interpretation favored by the community. The prophets, it was believed, knew by revelation what God was going to do at the end time, but they were not told when the end time would come. This further revelation was reserved for the Teacher of Righteousness, who imparted it to his followers. They accordingly congratulated themselves as men whom God had specially favored by initiating them into his wonderful mysteries. Their system of interpretation presents striking points of resemblance and contrast with the interpretation of the OT found in the NT.

Their expectations, however, were not fulfilled. The community was dispersed, and its headquarters destroyed, during the Roman suppression of the Judean revolt between A.D. 66 and 70.

The Qumran community has been compared to the primitive church in its eschatological outlook and its remnant mentality, as well as in its biblical interpretation. But the decisive difference between the two lies in the person and work of Jesus. The Teacher of Righteousness was exactly what his title suggests: he was no messiah or savior. Jesus was to the early Christians all that the Teacher was to the men of Qumran, but he was more. As Messiah, he was prophet and priest and king in one; and he fulfilled his messianic mission in terms of the portrayal of the suffering servant which the Qumran community may have endeavored to fulfill corporately. If (as appears possible) refugees from Qumran after the destruction of their headquarters made common cause in Transjordan with the refugee church of Jerusalem, they would have learned at last how Jesus fulfilled the hopes which had not been realized in the way they had formerly been led to expect.

Murabba'at. In caves in the Wadi Murabba'at about eleven miles south of Qumran, manuscripts were discovered around 1952. The most significant belonged to the period when Murabba'at was occupied by a garrison of Simeon Ben Kosebah (commonly called Bar Kochba), leader of the second Jewish revolt against Rome (A.D. 132–35). From some of the documents, including two letters from the leader himself, it was discovered for the first time that his proper patronymic was Ben Kosebah. The manuscripts included many fragments of biblical texts of the period, all of them showing a "proto-Massoretic" recension. From caves in neighboring wadis further manuscripts came to light, including a fragmentary copy of the minor prophets in Greek.

Khirbet Mird. Another collection of manuscripts was unearthed at Khirbet Mird, north of the Wadi en-Nar (Kidron Valley), midway between Qumran and Murabba'at. This collection dates between the fifth and eighth centuries A.D., is of Christian origin, and contains several biblical texts in Greek (including fragments of uncial codices of Wisdom, Mark, John, and Acts) and in Palestinian Syriac (including fragments of Joshua, Luke, John, Acts, and Colossians).

Masada. During the excavations of the rock fortress of Masada between 1963 and 1965 several manuscripts were found. These had been left there since the place was stormed by the Romans early in A.D. 74. They included portions of Psalms, Leviticus, Ecclesiasticus (the Wisdom of Ben Sira), and Jubilees, as well as a liturgical text already known from the Qumran finds—all in Hebrew.

F. F. BRUCE

See also ESSENES.

Bibliography. F. F. Bruce, *Biblical Exegesis in the Qumran Texts;* J. H. Charlesworth, ed., *John and Qumran;* F. M. Cross, Jr., *The Ancient Library of Qumran and Modern Biblical Studies;* R. de Vaux, *Archaeology and the Dead Sea Scrolls;* T. H. Gaster, *The Dead Sea Scriptures;* J. T. Milik, *Ten Years of Discovery in the Wilderness of Judaea;* J. Murphy-O'Connor, ed., *Paul and Qumran;* G. Vermes, *The Dead Sea Scrolls in English* and *The Dead Sea Scrolls: Qumran in Perspective.*

Dean. *See* CHURCH OFFICERS.

Death. Death has preoccupied Christian thought for centuries, either in its physical aspects as the cessation of bodily life and how one ought to prepare for it or in its spiritual aspects as separation from God and how it may be overcome. These perspectives developed out of a variety of strands in the biblical literature.

OT and Intertestamental Periods. In the OT death is usually seen as a natural part of human existence: Adam was not seen as created immortal. The goal was to live a long, full life and to die in peace. An early death was a great evil (II Kings 20:1–11) and indicated God's judgment for sin (Gen. 2–3; Deut. 30:15; Jer. 21:8; Ezek. 18:21–32). As death cut one off from the people of God, worship, and God himself (only rarely and in later literature does God comfort one in the face of death or is present to the dead, Pss. 73:23–28; 139:8), it was not a good thing. Thus suicide was rare (I Sam. 31; II Sam. 17:23) and the death penalty ("he shall be cut off from his people") severe.

In the intertestamental period the idea that death itself is an evil, first seen in Eccles. 3:19–29, grows under Greek influence and further reflection. Not just premature death, but all death is the result of sin (II Apoc. Bar. 54:19; II Esd. 3:7). There is also the growth of the idea that the whole person does not die, but only his body. The soul lives on either to await resurrection (I Enoch 102) or to enjoy its natural immortality free from the body (Wis. 3:4; 4:1; IV Macc. 16:13; 17:12), which was an essentially Greek idea. There is thus an increasing acceptance of suicide being in some cases better than an ignoble life (e.g., Josephus, *War* 7.325ff.). On the other hand, those who believed in resurrection also spoke of an eternal death which corresponded to resurrection life (II Esd. 7:31–44).

The NT. In the NT, which focuses on a crucified and resurrected Lord, death is a theological problem. Immortality belongs to God alone (I Tim. 6:16), so humans naturally live in fear of death (Matt. 4:16; Heb. 2:15). But if God is the source of all life (Rom. 4:17), death must be the result of being cut off from God, a process which Adam began (Rom. 5:15, 17–18; I Cor. 15:22) and in which every human being now participates (Rom. 3:23; 5:12), bringing upon himself the inevitable result of such separation from God (Rom. 6:23; Heb. 9:27). Death, then, is a power dominating the present life of the individual, not just something that happens at the end of life. It is in separation from God, a spiritual death, that the person lives all his life. Death or estrangement from God is the common factor in all natural human life (life according to the flesh, Rom. 8:6; I John 3:14), for sin with its resulting death lives within the person despite God's law (Rom. 7:9; I Cor. 15:56; James 1:15). The archrebel Satan is the lord of death (Heb. 2:14); indeed death itself may be seen as a demonic power (I Cor. 15:26–27; Rev. 6:8; 20:13–14).

The good news in the NT is that Christ who did not need to die (since he was sinless) entered into death (Phil. 2:7; I Cor. 5:7; I Pet. 3:18), dying "for us" (Mark 10:45; Rom. 5:6; I Thess. 5:10; Heb. 2:9), and conquered the devil and death, ascending with power over them (Heb. 2:14–15; Rev. 1:17–18, the keys of death). Christ, then, breaks the power of death over his followers, those who are joined to him or "baptized into Christ" (Rom. 6:3–4) and thus die with him to the world and to sin (Rom. 7:6; Gal. 6:14; Col. 2:20). The Christian passes through the experience of death in Christ but is now separated, not from God, but from the world and sin, which are dead in the sense of separation, for the life in him is the life of Christ (II Cor. 4:10; 5:14–15; Col. 3:3). In other words, the effect of Jesus' ministry was to give life or to raise the dead, not in the end of the age only, but immediately. Those who commit themselves to Christ pass now from death to life (John 5:24) and never see real death (John 8:51–52), although the world as a whole is already dead (Rev. 3:2) and headed toward eternal separation from God, a second death (Rev. 20:14).

Christians are still mortal, so they die physically, but they die "in Christ" (I Thess. 4:16) or "fall asleep" (Acts 7:60; John 11:11–14; I Cor. 7:39; 15:6, 18, 20, 51; I Thess. 4:13–15). Physical death is an enemy potentially conquered by Christ, but still undefeated in individual physical experience (Rom. 8:9–11; I Cor. 15:26). Yet its teeth are pulled, for it cannot separate the Christian from Christ, but rather puts him even closer to Christ (Rom. 8:38–39; II Cor. 5:1–10; Phil. 1:20–21), who as the resurrected one will call all believers back to transformed physical life as well as the spiritual life they already enjoy (I Cor. 15:20; Col. 1:12).

The Church. The early church lived in the consciousness of both the tragedy and mortality of human physical existence and the victory of Christ over death in which Christians shared. Death for them was the door to eternity, a great step forward on the road from estrangement in sin to life in God. Thus the death of martyrs could be celebrated and the death of the faithful, while sorrowful, could be spoken of with confidence and joy. While at times this was combined with a body-denying Greek dualism that virtually rejected the possibility of possessing God's life before physical death, this early view was largely shared down through the ages, including the Reformation. Death was not denied nor sorrow suppressed, but death was seen as hopeful, an event in Christ, an event for which one could prepare. This idea produced a literature on holy dying and elaborate descriptions of the deathbeds of holy persons. For the Christian death was an enemy whose sting had been pulled; thus he could face death with confidence and hope, since he already lived in Christ.

P. H. Davids

See also Dead, Abode of the; Hades; Hell; Sheol; Abraham's Bosom; Paradise; Intermediate State; Death, The Second.

Bibliography. F. F. Bruce, "Paul on Immortality," *SJT* 24:457–72; R. Bultmann, *TDNT,* III, 7–21; O. Cullmann, *Immortality of the Soul or Resurrection of the Dead?* J. D. G. Dunn, "Paul's Understanding of the Death of Jesus," in *Reconciliation and Hope,* ed. R. Banks; R. Martin-Achard, *From Death to Life;* J. D. McCaughty, "The Death of Death," in *Reconciliation and Hope;* J. Owen, *The Death of Death in the Death of Christ;* J. Pelikan, *The Shape of Death;* W. Schmithals, *NIDNTT,* I, 429–47; O. Kaiser and E. Lohse, *Death and Life;* J. McManners, *Death and the Enlightenment.*

Death, The Second. Christian use of the phrase "second death" is based upon its occurrence in Revelation, in which it is found four times (2:11; 20:6, 14; 21:8), the only biblical instances of this expression. It is defined as the "lake of fire" into which are placed at the very end of God's judgment all those not found in God's book of life and, finally, Death and Hades themselves. Those who are God's faithful people are promised that the second death has no claim on them. The expression presupposes that the first death is physical death at the end of one's life.

The identification of second death with the lake of fire may reflect the tradition within apocalyptic language identifying final judgment with fire (e.g., Ezek. 38:22; II Esd. 7:36–38; Matt. 25:41; Rev. 14:10). Presumably the "second death" terminology was a common phrase in at least some circles of ancient Judaism. Although not found in any Jewish text clearly prior to Revelation, it does occur in some Targums (TgDeut. 33.6; TgIsa. 22.14; 65.6, 15; TgJer. 51.39, 57) and in Pirque de Rabbi Eliezer 34 (18a).

In Christian theology second death refers to the final condition of those outside of God's salvation. There is debate as to whether the term indicates eternal punishment, probably the majority view of the church's theology, or annihilation, a view held by Adventists and others.

D. M. SCHOLER

See also FINAL STATE; LAKE OF FIRE; LAST JUDGMENT, THE; HELL.

Bibliography. M. McNamara, *The NT and the Palestinian Targum to the Pentateuch.*

Death of Christ. *See* CROSS, CRUCIFIXION; ATONEMENT; ATONEMENT, THEORIES OF THE.

Death of God Theology. Also known as radical theology, this movement flourished in the mid-1960s. As a theological movement it never attracted a large following, did not find a unified expression, and passed off the scene as quickly and dramatically as it had arisen. There is even disagreement as to who its major representatives were. Some identify two, and others three or four. Although small, the movement attracted attention because it was a spectacular symptom of the bankruptcy of modern theology and because it was a journalistic phenomenon. The very statement "God is dead" was tailor-made for journalistic exploitation. The representatives of the movement effectively used periodical articles, paperback books, and the electronic media.

History. This movement gave expression to an idea that had been incipient in Western philosophy and theology for some time—the suggestion that the reality of a transcendent God at best could not be known and at worst did not exist at all. Philosopher Kant and theologian Ritschl denied that one could have a theoretical knowledge of the being of God. Hume and the empiricists for all practical purposes restricted knowledge and reality to the material world as perceived by the five senses. Since God was not empirically verifiable, the biblical world view was said to be mythological and unacceptable to the modern mind. Such atheistic existentialist philosophers as Nietzsche despaired even of the search for God; it was he who coined the phrase "God is dead" almost a century before the death of God theologians.

Midtwentieth century theologians not associated with the movement also contributed to the climate of opinion out of which death of God theology emerged. Rudolf Bultmann regarded all elements of the supernaturalistic, theistic world view as mythological and proposed that Scripture be demythologized so that it could speak its message to the modern person. Paul Tillich, an avowed antisupernaturalist, said that the only nonsymbolic statement that could be made about God was that he was being itself. He is beyond essence and existence; therefore, to argue that God exists is to deny him. It is more appropriate to say God does not exist. At best Tillich was a pantheist, but his thought borders on atheism. Dietrich Bonhoeffer (whether rightly understood or not) also contributed to the climate of opinion with some fragmentary but tantalizing statements preserved in *Letters and Papers from Prison.* He wrote of the world and man "coming of age," of "religionless Christianity," of the "world without God," and of getting rid of the "God of the gaps" and getting along just as well as before. It is not always certain what Bonhoeffer meant, but if nothing else, he provided a vocabulary that later radical theologians could exploit.

It is clear, then, that as startling as the idea of the death of God was when proclaimed in the mid-1960s, it did not represent as radical a departure from recent philosophical and theological ideas and vocabulary as might superficially appear.

Nature. Just what was death of God theology? The answers are as varied as those who proclaimed God's demise. Since Nietzsche, theologians had occasionally used "God is dead" to express the fact that for an increasing number of people in the modern age God seems to be unreal. But the idea of God's death began to have special prominence in 1957 when Gabriel Vahanian published a book entitled *God Is Dead.* Vahanian did not offer a systematic expression of death of God theology. Instead, he analyzed those historical elements that contributed to the masses of people accepting atheism not so much as a theory but as a way of life. Vahanian himself did not believe that God was dead. But he urged that there be a form of Christianity that would recognize the contemporary loss of God and exert its influence through what was left. Other proponents of the death of God had the same assessment of God's status in contemporary culture, but were to draw different conclusions.

Thomas J. J. Altizer believed that God had actually died. But Altizer often spoke in exaggerated and dialectic language, occasionally with heavy overtones of Oriental mysticism. Sometimes it is difficult to know exactly what Altizer meant when he spoke in dialectical opposites such as "God is dead, thank God!" But apparently the real meaning of Altizer's belief that God had died is to be found in his belief in God's immanence. To say that God has died is to say that he has ceased to exist as a transcendent, supernatural being. Rather, he has become fully immanent in the world. The result is an essential identity between the human and the divine. God died in Christ in this sense, and the process has continued time and again since then. Altizer claims the church tried to give God life again and put him back in heaven by its doctrines of resurrection and ascension. But now the traditional doctrines about God and Christ must be repudiated because man has discovered after nineteen centuries that God does not exist. Christians must even now will the death of God by which the transcendent becomes immanent.

For William Hamilton the death of God describes the event many have experienced over the last two hundred years. They no longer accept the reality of God or the meaningfulness of language about him. Nontheistic explanations have been substituted for theistic ones. This trend is irreversible, and everyone must come to terms with the historical-cultural death of God. God's death must be affirmed and the secular world embraced as normative intellectually and good ethically. Indeed, Hamilton was optimistic about the world, because he was optimistic about what humanity could do and was doing to solve its problems.

Paul van Buren is usually associated with death of God theology, although he himself disavowed this connection. But his disavowal seems hollow in the light of his book *The Secular Meaning of the Gospel* and his article "Christian Education *Post Mortem Dei*." In the former he accepts empiricism and the position of Bultmann that the world view of the Bible is mythological and untenable to modern people. In the latter he proposes an approach to Christian education that does not assume the existence of God but does assume "the death of God" and that "God is gone."

Van Buren was concerned with the linguistic aspects of God's existence and death. He accepted the premise of empirical analytic philosophy that real knowledge and meaning can be conveyed only by language that is empirically verifiable. This is the fundamental principle of modern secularists and is the only viable option in this age. If only empirically verifiable language is meaningful, *ipso facto* all language that refers to or assumes the reality of God is meaningless, since one cannot verify God's existence by any of the five senses. Theism, belief in God, is not only intellectually untenable, it is meaningless. In *The Secular Meaning of the Gospel* van Buren seeks to reinterpret the Christian faith without reference to God. One searches the book in vain for even one clue that van Buren is anything but a secularist trying to translate Christian ethical values into that language game. There is a decided shift in van Buren's later book *Discerning the Way*, however.

In retrospect, it becomes clear that there was no single death of God theology, only death of God theologies. Their real significance was that modern theologies, by giving up the essential elements of Christian belief in God, had logically led to what were really antitheologies. When the death of God theologies passed off the scene, the commitment to secularism remained and manifested itself in other forms of secular theology in the late 1960s and the 1970s.

S. N. Gundry

See also Secularism, Secular Humanism; Existentialism; Bonhoeffer, Dietrich; Bultmann, Rudolf; Tillich, Paul.

Bibliography. T. J. J. Altizer, *The Gospel of Christian Atheism;* T. J. J. Altizer and W. Hamilton, *Radical Theology and the Death of God;* S. N. Gundry and A. F. Johnson, eds., *Tensions in Contemporary Theology;* K. Hamilton, *God Is Dead: The Anatomy of a Slogan;* P. M. van Buren, "Christian Education *Post Mortem Dei*," *RelEd* 60:4–10; G. Vahanian, *No Other God.*

Death Penalty. *See* Capital Punishment.

Decalogue, The. *See* Ten Commandments, The.

Decrees of God. God's "decree" is a theological term for the comprehensive plan for the world and its history which God sovereignly established in eternity. Paul refers to "the plan of him who works out everything in conformity with his will" (Eph. 1:11). The Westminster Shorter Catechism provides this classic definition: "The decrees of God are his eternal purpose, according to the counsel of his will, whereby, for his own glory, he hath foreordained whatsoever comes to pass" (Q.7).

There are analogies between God's decree and the decrees of human rulers, but important differences exist. Theologians distinguish God's will of decree from the will of precept; a closer parallel exists between God's will of precept and human decrees. The will of precept refers to the commands and laws that God sets for his creatures, commands which call for obedience but which are often transgressed. The will of decree, on the other hand, refers to the eternal, all-comprehensive, unchangeable, and efficacious plan of God which is carried out in history.

Some scriptural examples of human decrees are Darius's order to worship the image (Dan. 6:7–12), Cyrus's command to rebuild the temple (Ezra 5:13), and Caesar's decree for a census (Luke 2:1; cf. Acts 17:7). "Decree" (*dogma* in the Greek NT) is also used for the decisions of the Jerusalem Council (Acts 16:4) as well as for various Jewish legal regulations, ordinances, or rules (Eph. 2:15; Col. 2:14–15). Similar terms are used for God's decree against Nebuchadnezzar (Dan. 4:24), for his decree concerning rain and the sea (Job 28:26; Prov. 8:29), and for his laws governing human life (e.g., Ps. 119:5, 8, 12). There are also instances where God's decree refers to his regulations issued in history (Exod. 15:25; Rom. 1:32). Sometimes it is difficult to distinguish a decree that is the historical revelation of part of God's eternal plan from a regulation or order of God's in history that does not specifically refer to the eternal decree (see Ps. 2:7).

The theological discussion of God's decree is generally restricted to the eternal plan established before the creation of the world. In contrast to every human ruler, God has always existed. He existed before he created the world, and his decree or eternal plan was established before the creation; the elect were chosen "before the creation of the world" (Eph. 1:4; cf. Heb. 4:3; I Pet. 1:20; II Tim. 1:9; I Cor. 2:7; Eph. 3:11).

The relation of eternity and time, of divine sovereignty and human responsibility, makes human understanding of God's eternal decree very difficult. Several important distinctions are helpful. The decree is not eternal in exactly the same sense that God is eternal. The decree results from the free, sovereign will of God; it must be distinguished therefore from the necessary acts of God within the divine Trinity. The decree of God must also be distinguished from its execution in history. The decree to create is not the actual creation of the world "in the beginning" (Gen. 1:1). The decree to send Jesus Christ is not carried out until Jesus was born of Mary in the days of Caesar Augustus (Luke 2:1–7). Another important distinction arises when human agents are used in carrying out God's decree. Some decreed events occur by God's direct agency, as creation, regeneration, and the first and second comings of Jesus Christ. Other decreed events are carried out in history through human agency; sometimes this occurs through obedient human agents who live according to God's law, the will of precept, but sometimes the decree is fulfilled through sinful, disobedient human action, as in the crucifixion of Jesus Christ. The complex issues involved in the relation of divine sovereignty and human responsibility or irresponsibility in carrying out the eternal decree become clearer when one examines scriptural references to the crucifixion of Jesus Christ.

The eternal, divine decree clearly lies behind the cross of Christ. Before his death Jesus indicated that "the Son of man will go as it has been decreed" (Luke 22:22), and Peter told his Pentecost audience that Jesus of Nazareth "was handed over to you by God's set purpose [*boulē*] and foreknowledge [*prognōsei*]" (Acts 2:23). A little later a group of believers confess in their prayer that the crucifiers "did what your power and will decided beforehand should happen" (Acts 4:27–28; "the determinate counsel and foreknowledge of God," ASV). Yet the crucifixion was the most heinous crime of human history; the crucifiers transgressed God's commandments, his will of precept. Each of the three passages just mentioned also refers to the sin of those taking part in the crucifixion: Judas, Herod, Pilate, the Gentiles, and Israel. The crucifixion was part of God's eternal decree, and sinful human action was involved; but the guilt of such action is not minimized even when it functions as means to effectuate God's decree. Reflection on this crucial event of redemptive history is helpful since so many of the complex issues involved in understanding the relations of God's decree and human history are involved.

Scriptural references to God's decree are generally set forth in concrete relation to historical situations for the purpose of promoting comfort, security, assurance, and trust. In the words of the psalmist, "The Lord foils the plans of the nations" and "thwarts the purposes of the peoples"; but "the plans of the Lord stand firm forever, the purposes of his heart through all generations" (Ps. 33:10–11). Again, "Many are the plans in a man's heart, but it is the Lord's purpose that prevails" (Prov. 19:21).

The eternal decree of God also provides the explanation of predictive prophecy. The decree of God is largely secret and unrevealed; the crucifiers had no awareness of God's decree. Prophecy, however, reveals key features of God's eternal plan. The first such prophecy was the promise of a deliverer from the seed of the woman (Gen. 3:15), which runs like a golden thread through the entire Scripture. Isaiah frequently refers to God's decree and contrasts Yahweh with the idols; he makes "known the end from the beginning, from ancient times, what is still to come," and his "purpose will stand" (Isa. 14:24–27). Part of God's decree, not yet carried out in history but revealed by prophecy, provides the basis for the Christian's hope for the second coming of Jesus Christ in glory, for the consummation of God's kingdom, and for life everlasting in the new heaven and the new earth.

The doctrine of God's eternal decree receives consideration primarily in Augustinian, Reformed theology along with the doctrines of God's sovereignty and predestination. Pelagian and liberal theology deny this doctrine as inconsistent with human freedom and meaningful history. Semi-Pelagian and Arminian theologies restrict God's decree to foreknowledge of future events and compromise it by way of human initiative and cooperation.

The traditional objections to the doctrine of an eternal decree are that it is inconsistent with human responsibility, makes history meaningless, and makes God the author of sin. The distinctions referred to above and the illustration of Christ's crucifixion provide an answer to such objections. Failure to distinguish the will of decree and the will of precept, failure to distinguish the decree and the complex ways of its execution, may lead to fatalistic or deterministic concepts of God's decree. Then humans are considered robots and history is viewed as a programmed computer or a prerecorded sight-sound project. The meaningfulness of history is promoted, at least in part, by the secret, unrevealed nature of God's decree and his demand that our lives be governed by his revealed commands. Even though Adam's fall and Christ's crucifixion were included in God's decree, Scripture clearly indicates that the decree did not force the outcome. Humans acted freely but irresponsibly; they did precisely what God commanded them *not* to do. F. H. KLOOSTER

See also PREDESTINATION; ELECT, ELECTION; SOVEREIGNTY OF GOD; REPROBATION; SUPRALAPSARIANISM.

Bibliography. L. Berkhof, *Systematic Theology;* A. A. Hodge, *Outlines of Theology.*

Deep, The. The term (*ṣûlâ, mĕṣûlâ, tĕhôm*) most frequently refers to the sea in the OT. The suggestion that *tĕhôm* connotes a mythological water chaos is linguistically difficult. The root *thm* occurs in Ugaritic meaning only "sea."

In the NT the word *abyssos* is translated "the deep" in Luke 8:31 and Rom. 10:7. In the former passage it connotes the place of incarceration of demonic spirits (cf. Rev. 9:1–6), and in the latter passage it refers to the realm of the dead. The words *bathos* and *bythos* also refer to the sea.

T. E. MCCOMISKEY

See also BOTTOMLESS PIT.

Defilement. *See* CLEANNESS, UNCLEANNESS.

Deism. This word is customarily used to describe an unorthodox religious view expressed among a group of English writers beginning with Lord Herbert of Cherbury in the first half of the seventeenth century. It also denotes a certain movement of rationalistic thought that was manifested chiefly in England from the midseventeenth to the mideighteenth century. Deism (Lat. *deus,* god) is etymologically a cognate of theism (Gr. *theos,* god), both words denoting belief in the existence of a god or gods and therefore the antithesis of atheism. The term deism, as distinguished from theism, polytheism, and pantheism, does not designate a well-defined doctrine. In general, it refers to what can be called natural religion or the acceptance of a certain body of religious knowledge acquired solely by the use of reason as opposed to knowledge gained either through revelation or the teaching of a church.

Deism is sometimes used loosely to define a particular viewpoint with regard to the relationship between God and the world. It would reduce God's function in creation to that of first cause only. According to the classical comparison of God with a clockmaker, which is found as early as Nicolaus of Oresmes (d. 1382), God wound up the clock of the world once and for all at the beginning, so that it now proceeds as world history without the need for his further involvement.

The basic doctrines of deism are: (1) the belief in a supreme being; (2) the obligation to worship; (3) the obligation of ethical conduct; (4) the need for repentance from sins; and (5) divine rewards and punishments in this life and the next. These five points were stated by Lord Herbert, often called the father of deism. Deism contradicts orthodox Christianity by denying any direct intervention in the natural order by God. Although deists profess belief in personal providence, they deny the Trinity, the incarnation, the divine authority of the Bible, the atonement, miracles, any particular elect people such as Israel, and any supernatural redemptive act in history.

In England at the beginning of the seventeenth century this general religious attitude turned more militant, particularly in the works of John Toland, Lord Shaftesbury, Matthew Tindal, Thomas Woolston, and Anthony Collins. The ideal of these deists was a sober natural religion without many of the basic tenets of Christianity.

Deists were agreed in denouncing any kind of religious intolerance because, in their opinion, all religions are alternately the same. The deists were particularly opposed to any manifestation of religious fanaticism and enthusiasm. Here Shaftesbury's *Letter Concerning Enthusiasm* (1708) was probably the most important document in furthering their ideas. Shaftesbury denounced all forms of religious extravagance as perversion of true religion. All descriptions of God which depicted his vengeance, vindictiveness, jealousy, and destructive cruelty were considered blasphemous. The deist conceived God to be a gentle, loving, and benevolent being, who intended that mankind behave in a kind and tolerant fashion.

English deism was transmitted to Germany primarily through translations of Shaftesbury's works. Important German deists were Leibniz, Reimarus, and Lessing. Kant, the most important figure in eighteenth century German philosophy, stressed the moral element in natural religion. Moral principles are not the result of a revelation, but originate from the very structure of man's reason. Voltaire is generally considered to be the greatest of the French deists. Even though he consistently used the word "theist" in reference to himself, Voltaire was a deist in the tradition of the British deists, never attacking the existence of God but always the corruptions of the church. By the end of the eighteenth century deism had become a dominant religious attitude among intellectual and upper-class Americans. Among great Americans who considered themselves deists were Benjamin Franklin, George Washington, and Thomas Jefferson.

The late eighteenth and nineteenth century interpretation of deism restricts the meaning to belief in a God or first cause, who created the world and instituted immutable, universal laws that preclude any alteration as well as any form of divine immanence.

The legacy of deism continues into the twentieth century as a stress on mechanism. The tendency today is to seek explanation of almost everything by analogy with a machine. The so-called higher criticism of today may also be traced to the deism of earlier days. Thus, although deism is not widely held in our day, its significance historically has been great, and it still exerts influence on religious thought in our time.

M. H. MACDONALD

See also ENLIGHTENMENT, THE; LEIBNIZ, GOTTFRIED WILHELM; LESSING, GOTTHOLD EPHRAIM; KANT, IMMANUEL.

Bibliography. E. Cassirer, *The Philosophy of the Enlightenment;* J. Collins, *God in Modern Philosophy;* S. Hampshire, ed., *The Age of Reason: The 17th Century Philosophers;* J. Leland, *A View of the Principal Deistical Writers . . .*, 3 vols.; D. MacKay, *The Clockwork Image;* J. Orr, *English Deism: Its Roots and Its Fruits;* N. Torrey, *Voltaire and the English Deists;* C. Webb, *Studies in the History of Natural Theology;* A. R. Winnett, "Were the Deists 'Deists,'" *CQR* 161:70ff.; J. Yolton, *John Locke and the Way of Ideas.*

Deity of Christ. *See* CHRISTOLOGY.

Deliverance, Deliverer. The OT concept of deliverance embraces the themes of safety (*yĕšûʿâ, tĕšûʿâ*) and escape (*pĕlêṭâ*). Isaiah lamented that Israel had accomplished no deliverance in the earth (Isa. 26:18), but by contrast the psalmists attributed the nation's security to God's action (Pss. 18:50; 44:4), as did the writers of the historical books (Judg. 15:18; II Kings 5:1; 13:17; I Chr. 11:14). The prophets also expected that the future deliverance of the nation from various perils would result from God's protective power (Joel 2:32; Obad. 17). In the NT deliverance involved the idea of being released or liberated from some evil situation such as torture (Heb. 11:35) or bondage (Luke 4:18).

The personage of a deliverer in the OT drew naturally upon the root words describing deliverance, with the addition of the verb *nāṣal,* appearing in a causative participial form to describe a deliverer as one "snatching away" a people from destruction (Judg. 18:28). In the NT the deliverer was one who "loosed" (*lyō*) the Israelites from bondage in Egypt (Acts 7:35), or who would "deliver" (*rhyomai*) the nation from ungodliness (Rom. 11:26, quoting Isa. 59:20).

Undoubtedly the most characteristic act of deliverance in Israel's history occurred under Moses, when God rescued his people from bondage to the Egyptians and set them free in the Sinai wilderness (Exod. 12:31–14:31). This awesome humbling of mighty Egypt and the subsequent establishing of the Sinai covenant demonstrated the character of the liberty with which God makes his people free. The deliverance from Egypt was commemorated in the annual passover celebrations and by generations of historians and poets. The functions of such writers were combined in teaching compositions such as the "psalms of history" (e.g., Pss. 105–107), a tradition that was followed in Stephen's speech to the Jewish council (Acts 7).

The liberation of Israel from Egypt under Moses established the true nature of all such subsequent activity. It thus becomes clear in Israel's history that God does not free an individual or a group from some type of bondage merely to provide relief from an embarrassing or potentially disastrous situation. Instead, he liberates people, not to enable them to pursue their former way of life, but that they might be free to serve him and him alone. This concept was fundamental to the Sinai covenant, and has been an abiding principle of spirituality ever since.

God delivers his people from a wide variety of troubles and afflictions (cf. Pss. 33:19; 34:6; 107:6, 13, 19), and promises to liberate even creation from its bondage to decay (Rom. 8:21), thereby reversing the law of entropy. In Matt. 6:13 the heavenly Father delivers the believer "from evil," which probably means more accurately "from the evil one." This concept of deliverance from sin and the works of the devil is emphasized by Paul more fully in passages such as Acts 16:31; Eph. 2:8; and I Thess. 1:10.

The deliverer (Heb. *môšîa'; měpallēṭ; maṣṣîl;* Gk. *rhyomenos; lytrōtēs*) most prominent in the OT is God, who enters into a covenant relationship with his people, and by this and the promise of a Messiah brings about the ultimate redemption of the world in Christ's atoning death on Calvary. The deliverer thus makes for the sinner a way of escape (Ps. 40:17; cf. I Cor. 10:13) and also intervenes to save his people from their perils (Judg. 2:16; 3:9; Isa. 43:1–2; etc.). Those who serve as human agents of deliverance for Israel receive their authority and power from God (Isa. 49:3–6).

The term "deliverer" is used only twice in the NT, in reference to Moses (Acts 7:35) and to the deliverer from Zion (Rom. 11:26). Nevertheless, the work of the divine Deliverer is paramount in the NT, and is expressed in synonyms which describe various aspects of the redemptive and saving work of God in Christ. Nowhere in the NT is Jesus described as a "deliverer."

R. K. Harrison

Bibliography. *RTWB*, 62–63; R. L. Harris, *ZPEB*, II, 90.

Deluge, The. *See* Flood, The.

Demiurge. A term (from Gr. *dēmiourgos*) which means "craftsman" or "creator" and is used once in the NT (Heb. 11:10) to refer to God's creative activity. Plato and Epictetus employ the term to refer to the craftsmanship of the phenomenal or visible world by the Divine. The Gnostics, however, used the term in a derogatory sense to refer to the lower deity who was responsible for the creation of the world after the "fall" or straying of Sophia in the upper realm of deity. For the Gnostics the world is a negative place formed by a negative creator from which escape is necessary.

G. L. Borchert

See also Gnosticism.

Demon, Demon Possession. Biblical evidence abounds for the existence of evil supernatural beings who are subservient to Satan. Their origin, however, is a matter on which Scripture does not elaborate.

Basically there are two major theories for the origin of such beings. One theory holds that a multitude of angels fell into sin prompted by Lucifer's original rebellion against God (Matt. 25:41; II Pet. 2:4; Rev. 12:7–9). Another theory speculates that demons are the unnatural offspring of angels and antediluvian women (Gen. 6:2; Jude 6). These beings (*něpilîm*, giants), the theory states, issued forth evil spirits from their bodies once they were destroyed either in battle or in the flood. The Jewish Apocalyptic work I Enoch is a major source for this view (10:11–14; cf. "the watchers," 16:1; 86:1–4). This concept was accepted by the Christian apologist Justin Martyr and is even found to have influenced the views of Thomas Aquinas.

Origen developed the concept of a precosmic rebellion, understanding all intelligent creatures (man and angels) as being created with a free will. The diversity of these creatures' relationship to God is directly related to Lucifer's fall (*De princips* 2.9.6). Thus, demons are those angelic beings who were fully carried away with Satan's apostasy. This became the prevailing Christian view, adopted by, among others, Augustine (*De genesi ad literem* 3.10) and Peter Lombard (*Sentences* 2.6).

Rabbinic speculation concerning demonic origins varied greatly. Demons were viewed as unfortunate spirits that were left bodiless when God rested on the sabbath or as the builders of the Tower of Babel who were punished and transformed into demons.

Terminology. The Greek terms *daimōn* and *daimonion* originally held no inherently evil connotation. Although their etymology is uncertain (possibly signifying a disruption or "rending apart"), the terms appear to have been used to specify a god or a minor deity against the background of popular animistic beliefs. Homer appeared to differentiate *daimōn* from *theos* in that the former term constituted the divine power at work among men, while the latter isolated the concept of divine personality. Prior to the NT, however, *daimōn* was used for those personal intermediary beings who were believed to exercise supervision over the cosmos (Plato *Symposium* 202e). These beings, at least in popular belief, were considered to be spirits of the departed, who were endowed with supernatural power (Lucian *De morte peregrini* 27).

While the connection of demons with specifically evil practices slowly developed in Greek thought, this appears to have been consistently implied in the Hebrew use of such terms as *šēdîm* and *sĕʿîrîm*. Though the OT offers little speculation on the subject, the practices of idolatry, magic, and witchcraft were related to demonic forces (Deut. 32:17; Ps. 96:5). Since such practices clashed with Israel's monotheism, they were specifically prohibited for the people of God (Deut. 18:10–14; I Sam. 15:23). Demonic activity in the OT, then, is to be found as an opposing force to God and his own personal intermediary beings, the *malʾākîm* (angels).

Thus, when these Hebrew terms were translated into the LXX, the concept of demon was narrowed to that of an evil spirit. However, because of the positive nature of the Greek religious usage of *daimōn*, the LXX and the NT prefer the term *daimonion* to express the restricted concept.

In the NT, along with *daimonion*, the presence of demons is described with the terms "unclean" (*akatharton*, Mark 1:24–27; 5:2–3; 7:26; 9:25; Acts 5:16; 8:7; Rev. 16:13) and "evil" (*ponēra*, Acts 19:12–16) spirits. The majority of references to the work of these spirits occur with regard to their possession of individuals. There is no speculation offered concerning their origin, however; their existence and active operation is established.

Similar to the OT connection between idolatry and demons, the apostle Paul states that, while the so-called gods worshiped by idolators have no existence, demonic forces exist as those who instigate and propagate such worship and those to whom worship is directed and to whom the worshipers are subject (I Cor. 10:20–21; 12:2; cf. Rev. 9:20). It is the understanding of both Paul and the author of Revelation that the activity of demons will be on the increase in the latter days and that many men will be seduced to follow after them (I Tim. 4:1; Rev. 16:13–14). Perhaps the most comprehensive treatment of Paul's understanding of this theme occurs in Eph. 6:10–18. The Christian must be prepared to combat "rulers, . . . authorities, . . . powers, this dark world and the spiritual forces of evil in the heavenly realms."

Thus the NT seems to be consistent in its presentation of a conflict between two realms, the kingdom of Satan, the prince of this world, and the kingdom of God, which through the incarnation of Jesus Christ has broken into Satan's realm. There appears to be no recognition of a positive role for the *daimonion* as is found in the early hellenists. The NT rests solely within the Hebrew understanding that these beings are of a completely evil nature and are destined to share in the destruction which God has prepared for Satan (Matt. 25:41).

Possession. The majority of references to demonic activity in the NT occur in the Synoptic Gospels and deal with confrontations between Jesus and the demon-possessed. The specialized expression for demon possession (*daimonizomai*) is not found in Scripture. Some scholars trace the origin of the term to Josephus (*Antiquities* 8.47). The common Synoptic construction is *daimonion echein* ("to have a demon").

The major characteristics of the Synoptics' recording of Jesus' encounters with demons include: (1) There is a statement concerning the physical or mental affliction attributable to the possession—nakedness, mental anguish, and masochism (Matt. 8:28–33; cf. Mark 5:1–10; Luke 8:26–39); inability to speak (Matt. 9:32; 12:22); blindness (Matt. 12:22); lunacy (Matt. 4:24; 17:15; cf. Mark 9:17).

(2) Often the demon is said to have recognized and feared Jesus as the Holy One of God (Matt. 8:28; cf. Mark 5:7; Luke 8:28; Mark 1:24; cf. Luke 4:34).

(3) Jesus' power over the demons is demonstrated, usually by their exorcism through the power of his word (Matt. 4:24; 8:16; 8:28; cf. Mark 7:30) or by Jesus' permission for them to depart (Matt. 8:32; cf. Mark 5:13; Luke 8:32). This power was also to be found in Jesus' disciples (Luke 10:17; Acts 5:16; 8:7; 16:18; 19:12) and is promised to all believers (Mark 16:17).

Throughout the NT other noticeable characteristics of those who were demon possessed include superior or supernatural knowledge (James 2:19), the ability to foretell the future (Acts 16:16), and superior or uncontrollable strength (Matt. 8:28; 17:15; Acts 19:16).

The ability of Jesus and his followers to exercise authority over demons is established as an eschatological sign of the kingdom's inbreaking presence (Matt. 12:22; Luke 10:17) and is a cause for some of the popularity of Jesus' mission (Luke 4:36). The activity of exorcism, however, is usually associated with Jesus' healing ministry and that of the apostles. However, a distinction between demon possession and insanity (or other diseases) is implied.

Possession and Church History. In the postapostolic church a number of commentators developed a view of demon possession beyond what the teaching of Scripture would imply. Justin Martyr believed the pagan gods to be representations of demons who had fallen from a state of angelic guardianship over men (*Second Apology* 5). Aquinas developed Augustine's belief in demons' ability to attack men to a point where demons continued the practice, cited in I Enoch, of sinning with men and women sexually (*Summa Theologica* 1.51.3, 6; *De potentia* 6.8, 57). Apparently influenced by certain apocryphal writings, Origen believed that a good and an evil angel watched over each individual, both of whom attempt to influence one's thought patterns. He also believed that "vice demons" existed—so called since one such demon would be in control of a particular vice (*De princips* 3.2.2–4).

A distinction was made between demon possession and demonic influence, with the one being possessed called an "energumen." Some understood the demonic influence to include the inducement of evil thoughts directly into the minds of men (Augustine, Athanasius, Origen, Peter Lombard, Bede, Thomas Aquinas). This form of temptation was considered to be the demon's normal mode of operation, while possession was recognized as only an extraordinarily strong extension of a demon's control over man.

Methods of Deliverance. Justin Martyr records that the exorcism of demon-possessed individuals continued to be an active ministry of the postapostolic church. The rite of exorcism took on a variety of forms such as prayer, fasting, laying on of hands, burning of roots, or the sprinkling of holy water. However, one crucial element to a successful exorcism was the invocation of the name of Jesus Christ (*Second Apology* 6). Tertullian also witnesses to the power of Christ's name when invoked against a demon. When properly adjured, the demon would tell the truth about himself, and was made to obey the word of the exorcist (*Apology* 23).

Several other ecclesiastical rites incorporated an exorcistic (demon-expelling) or apotropaic (demon-repelling) dimension. Prior to baptism a candidate might endure certain rituals designed to cleanse him from demonic infestation associated either with original sin or idolatry and the eating of food offered to idols (*Clementine Recognitions* 21.71). The candidate might also be required to make public renunciation of Satan, his angels, and his ways, while the baptismal water itself would be exorcised and consecrated. The sign of the cross was also used as an apotropaic device.

In the Middle Ages the amount of superstition that developed around the various beliefs about demonic activity and the rites of exorcism soon led to large-scale persecutions of so-called witches and others who were deemed to be "in league" with the devil. The Protestant Reformation reacted against these abuses. The Lutheran Church first restricted and then abolished exorcism by the end of the sixteenth century. The Calvinists renounced the practice as applicable only for the first century. By 1614 Pope Paul V severely restricted the practice in the *Roman Ritual* (12, 13) and the rite was further defined by Pope Pius XI in this century.

Modern Views. The belief or disbelief in the existence of demons and, in some cases, in Satan himself has developed into one of the distinguishing marks between the modern liberal and fundamental/evangelical traditions in Christendom. On the liberal side of the issue, much of what was termed as demonic possession in Scripture is now recognized to include many psychological maladies that were unknown to the first century mind. Jesus' actions with regard to the supposed demonic activity, it is argued, actually amounted only to his accommodation to the contemporary beliefs of the Palestinian peasant and in no way reflected his own opinion as to the cause of individual afflictions.

However, with the increase of interest in, and practice of, occultism in more recent times the conservative acceptance of the existence of both Satan and demons appears to be confirmed.

Spiritism has developed into a widely recognized "religious" practice whereby individuals seek contact with spiritual forces in an effort to gain aid or information for their own personal use. Such psychic phenomena as levitation, apports, telekinesis, automatic writing, and materializations are associated with spiritism. These activities appear to increase in intensity in proportion to an individual's openness to the spiritual influence. There seems to be a parallel between the characteristics of those who practice spiritism and those cited in Scripture as being "possessed."

Deliverance from demonic subjection involves the confession of an individual's faith in Christ as Savior, the confession and repentance of the occult involvement, and reception of the liberation that can be found in Christ. It is notable that this emphasis on the deliverance from possession through the operative power of Jesus Christ is completely consistent with the NT and does not at all reflect the abuses or superstitions associated with the Middle Ages. S. E. McClelland

See also Occult, The; Satan; Satanism and Witchcraft.

Bibliography. M. F. Unger, *Demons in the World Today;* H. A. Kelly, *The Devil, Demonology, and Witchcraft;* D. G. Barnhouse, *The Invisible War;* S. V. McCausland, *By the Finger of God;* T. K. Oesterreich, *Possession, Demonological and Other;* H. Schlier, *Principalities and Powers in the NT;* K. E. Koch, *Christian Counselling and Occultism.*

Demythologization. A technical term which is usually associated with the interpretive principles of Rudolf Bultmann and which dates from a pastors' conference on April 21, 1941, in Frankfurt, Germany, when Bultmann delivered his famous lecture published in English as "New Testament and Mythology" (See *Kerygma and Myth,* pp. 1–44). Bultmann's thesis is that contemporary humanity, which depends upon a scientific world view, cannot accept the mythological world view of the Bible. Myth for him is the use of language symbols or images of this world and this life to conceptualize the divine or the otherworldly. Thus, ideas such as God's transcendence or heaven and hell are described in spatial terms that pertain to an ancient three-story *Weltanschauung* (concept of the universe or reality). For Bultmann ethical implications of up and down are unacceptable to the modern scientific mind.

While Bultmann was the great exponent of demythologization, he was indebted to a development of thought that reaches back through the history of religions school to David F. Strauss. But the process of demythologizing was begun much earlier among ancient thinkers such as the Gnostics like Ptolemaeus and Valentinus, who constructed elaborate mythologies for the purpose of expressing their philosophies of life and death.

Bultmann's concern was not the elimination of myth, as the English word "demythologize" might suggest. Rather, influenced by his colleague Martin Heidegger at the University of Marburg, Bultmann sought a reinterpretation of the mythological language of the Bible. The cosmological categories of the Bible, for Bultmann, must be reinterpreted in anthropological (man-oriented) or, better, existential (personal) categories. Thus, the fall of Adam is basically a statement of human sinfulness and finitude. The purpose of demythologization, accordingly, is the reinterpretation of the biblical images so as to provide self-understanding for the scientific mind of the twentieth century.

Bultmann's goal of reinterpreting the biblical myths was to highlight the nature of faith. In this emphasis upon faith he stood firmly in the traditions of Paul and Luther. Most of his critics, however, consistently charge that in his zeal for self-understanding and faith Bultmann abandons the kerygma or core content of the Christian message. The cross becomes to him a continuing challenge for humanity to undergo crucifixion with Christ. As such the once-for-allness and sacrificial nature of Jesus' death are regarded as untenable. The resurrection as a fact of history is to Bultmann "utterly inconceivable." Easter faith thus becomes faith in the preached word. Moreover, Bultmann finds the concepts of the preexistence of Jesus and the virgin birth to be irreconcilable attempts to express the myth of "Jesus Christ." Jesus, for Bultmann, is a man, whereas Christ is virtually the God of encounter.

Important to Bultmann's demythologizing thesis is his understanding of history. Unlike English, the German language provided Bultmann with two words for "history." The first, *Historie,* is used to refer to the facts of history. The second, *Geschichte,* is the term implying the meaning or significance of an event in history. By using these two words it is possible to differentiate between the meaning of an event and an actual fact. Thus, Easter may be a faith event (*Geschichte*) without the resurrection being a fact of history (*Historie*). A *geschichtliche* event is not unimportant. In fact, for Bultmann it is very important, because it is the basis of existential meaning. Statements which sound like *Historie* in the Bible, however, may have no reference to facticity. Some, indeed, Bultmann holds to be mere "legends," such as the empty tomb and the virgin birth, which have arisen in the Christian community to support the "myths" of the resurrection and the incarnation. Both myths are part of the church's larger mythological formula known as "Jesus Christ."

What, then, can be said of Bultmann and his demythologizing method by way of conclusion? First, his left-wing critics like Schubert Ogden and Karl Jaspers challenged him to carry his logic to its implied end and demythologize Christ. Bultmann would not go that far. His goal was to free Christ from myth. Second, Bultmann's students like Günther Bornkamm found their teacher's radical separation between Jesus and Christ to be an unnecessary bifurcation in expressing the Christian faith. Thus, they returned to the combined term. Third, the church in general should have learned from Bultmann's wrestling with faith that the abandonment of the kerygma must not be the price which is paid for a relevant message to the contemporary world.

G. L. Borchert

See also Bultmann, Rudolf; Myth; New Hermeneutic, The.

Bibliography. M. Ashcraft, *Rudolf Bultmann;* G. L. Borchert, "Is Bultmann's Theology a New Gnosticism?" *EvQ* 36:222–28; R. Bultmann, *Jesus Christ and Mythology;* H. W. Bartsch, ed., *Kerygma and Myth;* E. M. Good, "The Meaning of Demythologization," in *The Theology of Rudolf Bultmann,* ed. C. W. Kegley; K. Jaspers and R. Bultmann, *Myth and Christianity;* J. MacQuarrie, *The Scope of Demythologizing;* S. Ogden, *Christ Without Myth.*

Denney, James (1856–1917). Scottish theologian. Born in Paisley, near Glasgow, he studied classics and philosophy at Glasgow University, from which he graduated with the rare distinction of a double first (highest honors in both), and divinity at the Free Church College in Glasgow (under A. B. Bruce, J. S. Candlish, and T. M. Lindsay). In 1896 he was appointed minister of the East Free Church in Broughty Ferry, a suburb of Dundee, where he achieved a reputation for his thoughtful biblical exposition, including his contributions to *The Expositor's Bible* on I Thessalonians (1892) and II Corinthians (1894). In 1897 he became professor of systematic and pastoral theology at Glasgow Divinity College, moving to New Testament three years later, which position he occupied until his death. He served as principal from 1915 to 1917.

Denney concentrated his attention on the writings of Paul and the doctrine of the atonement, which he considered to be the touchstone of all genuine Christian theology. Chief among his writings are a commentary on Romans (*The Expositor's Greek Testament,* 1900), *The Death of Christ* (1902), *The Atonement and the Modern Mind* (1903), *Jesus and the Gospel* (1908), and *The Christian Doctrine of Reconciliation* (1917). His chief contribution lies in his exposition of the significance of the work of Christ and his defense of the doctrine of the substitutionary atonement. Christ's death on the cross is a revelation not merely of the love of God for us but also of his righteousness. Because of man's sin Christ's death is the necessary ground for our forgiveness: "if Christ had done less than die for us, . . . there would have been no atonement" (*Death of Christ,* 200). Something objective actually happened at the cross to change our status before God and to make it possible for us to enter into a new relationship with the Father.

Denney, with his colleague James Orr, was steadfast in his rejection of the subjective theology of the Ritschlians of his day, as he was of the "new" or liberal theology in general. In fact, he was hostile to speculative theology as such (see his *Studies in Theology,* 1894). On the other hand, he was not an obscurantist and accepted the basic approach of modern biblical criticism (minus its attendant skepticism). In Denney's ideal church the evangelists are the theologians and the theologians, evangelists. He had no use for a theology which could not be preached and did not lead men and women to commit themselves unreservedly to the God who has revealed himself in the cross of Calvary. W. W. Gasque

Bibliography. J. R. Taylor, *God Loves Like That;* I. H. Marshall, in *Creative Minds in Contemporary Theology,* ed. P. E. Hughes.

Denominationalism. Denominations are associations of congregations—though sometimes it might be said that congregations are localized subdivisions of denominations—that have a common heritage. Moreover, a true denomination does not claim to be the only legitimate expression of the church. A denominational heritage normally includes doctrinal or experiential or organizational emphases and also frequently includes common ethnicity, language, social class, and geographical origin. However, many or all of these once common features have usually evolved into considerable contemporary diversity, especially in older and larger denominations. This often results in as wide a range of differences within a denomination, despite organizational unity, as exists between denominations.

The term "denomination" in general refers to anything distinguished by a name. In religious contexts the designation has traditionally applied both to broad movements within Protestantism, such as Baptists and Methodists, and also to the numerous independent branches of such movements that have developed over the years primarily because of geographical expansion and theological controversy.

Even though denominations within Protestantism have come to be the largest expression of organized Christianity beyond the level of the congregation, there has never been much theological reflection on denominationalism. A look at theology textbooks or church creeds confirms this. Probably the simplest explanation for this omission is that the Bible in no way envisages the organization of the church into denominations. It instead assumes the opposite, that all Christians—except those being disciplined—will be in full fellowship with all others. Any tendencies to the contrary were roundly denounced (I Cor. 1:10–13). Paul could write a letter to the Christians meeting in various places in Rome or Galatia with every assurance that all would receive its message. Today, for any city or country, he would have to place the letter as an advertisement in the secular media and hope.

Denominationalism is a comparatively recent phenomenon. The theological distinction between the church visible and invisible, made by Wycliffe and Hus and elaborated by the Protestant Reformers, underlies the practice and defense of denominationalism that emerged among seventeenth century English Puritans, who agreed on most things but not on the crucial issue of how the church should be organized. The eighteenth century revivals associated with Wesley and Whitefield greatly encouraged the practice, especially in America, where it became dominant.

Although a true denomination never claims to be the only legitimate institutional expression of the church universal, it frequently thinks itself to be the best expression, the most faithful to the Scriptures and to the present activity of the Holy Spirit. Had it not thought so, at least when beginning, why else would it have gone through the trauma of separating from (or not joining with) an older denomination? A true denomination does not, however, make exclusive claims upon its members. It frees them to cooperate with Christians from other denominations in various specialized ministries.

In theory denominationalism is sharply contrasted with two much older approaches, catholicism and sectarianism. That catholic or sectarian groups are often called denominations reflects either an excessively loose use of the designation or historical development within the group.

Catholic or national churches at the period of their greatest growth are almost always supported, that is "established," by the civil government, whether imperial or tribal or—most commonly in recent centuries—national. Such churches usually have been able to survive even after that official support is withdrawn when the government became Muslim, Marxist, or secular. Catholic (from a Greek word for "the whole") churches see themselves as properly embracing from infancy all Christians within their territories, in contrast with the voluntary nature of individual affiliation with a denomination. When catholic churches, of which the Armenians have the oldest, are dispersed, then the basis for association becomes ethnic rather than territorial. Over the centuries catholic churches have usually recognized each other as having jurisdiction over the Christians of their respective territories or peoples. (The largest of them, the coalition mostly of southwest Europeans and their derivative national churches known as Roman Catholicism, has been recognizing others only in this century since its claims were universal.) This mutual recognition is facilitated by the catholic view—except in northwest Europe where the national churches became Protestant in theology—that the churches in each place are properly governed only by bishops in a supposedly traceable succession from the apostles. In recent decades, and especially in countries outside their homelands, most such churches have become in practice increasingly like denominations. That is, they have been willing to concede some legitimacy to and encourage their members to cooperate with other than catholic or national ecclesiastical bodies.

In theory denominationalism is also sharply distinguishable from sectarianism. Each Christian sect sees itself as the only legitimate institutional expression of the followers of Christ. Unlike catholic churches the sects have never embraced more than a small percentage of any population (with the possible exception of some short-lived medieval sects). Sects are frequently distinguished not only by their exclusive organizational claims but also by their disagreement with the fourth century understanding of the doctrine of the Trinity that is traditionally adhered to by all catholic churches and Protestant denominations. (Such professedly Christian movements as Spiritualism and New Thought may be said to be divided into denominations even as Protestantism is, but it is too confusing to blend these differing kinds of denominations given their widely divergent theologies.) Some sects, especially when they are Trinitarian, have been evolving into denominations. Conversely, some denominational branches so focus their energies on their distinctive beliefs and practices that they might as well be sects.

Besides attracting to its ranks the once clearly distinct catholic churches and some sects, denominationalism has brought forth several other institutional responses. These are related in various ways to the obvious discrepancy between denominational distinctiveness (or rivalry) and the biblical portrayal of a unity of all Christians as close as that of the Father and the Son, a unity perceived not just by faith but observable by the world (John 17:20–23).

One response has been to oppose denominations and urge all true Christians to leave them and meet simply as churches of Christ, Christian churches, churches of God, disciples, brethren, Bible churches, evangelical churches, and similar inclusive names. Despite obvious appeal in times of denominational confusion, strife, and declension, the reality is that no such movement has anywhere attracted most Christians to itself. Instead this has been just another way of increasing the number of denominations—and sects—usually with the group's reluctance to admit it.

Another response has been for local congregations to remain organizationally independent but to engage in cooperative endeavors with other Christian organizations near and far that have a variety of denominational links. In fact many congregations that have historical and legal ties to a denomination are functioning as if they did not. (Conversely, an independent congregation that isolates itself is in effect just a small sect.)

The practicality of congregational independency has been enhanced in this century by the growing numbers and kinds of nondenominational specialized ministries such as home and foreign missions; colleges and seminaries; camp and conference grounds; publishers of magazines, books, and Sunday school curricula; evangelistic teams; youth organizations; radio and television broadcasters; occupational fellowships; and many others. Such ministries stress the doctrines and practices held in common by all or at least many denominational families, perform many functions that once were handled mostly by denominational agencies, and enable both denominational and independent congregations to experience broader fellowship. Perhaps a biblical precedent could be the evangelistic team of "Paul and his company" (Acts 13:13). Such organizations have at least as much validity as do the denominations whose leaders frequently disparage them, but only as helpful supplements to and extensions of a vibrant congregational life rather than as a replacement for it.

Yet another response to denominationalism has been the attempt to promote more visible unity in this century through ecumenicity. The ecumenical movement has seen many denominational mergers, sometimes across family lines, as well as denominational cooperation at the higher official levels through councils of churches. Generally speaking, the nondenominational specialized ministries are unambiguously evangelical in theology, while the promoters of conciliar ecumenism are not.

Denominational identity is not nearly so accurate a predicter of theological stance, worship style, organizational preference, or social class as it once was. There is no indication that denominations will soon disappear, but neither does it appear that anyone is eager to justify them theologically. The trend seems to be toward a new kind of denominationalism, one that is no longer based primarily on associations of congregations with a common heritage. Such associations will no doubt continue, but increasing emphasis seems likely to be placed directly on the local congregation of whatever, if any, denomination, and on the network of specialized ministries supported by and extending the outreach of congregations and their members.

D. G. Tinder

See also Ecumenism.

Bibliography. R. E. Richey, ed., *Denominationalism;* R. P. Scherer, ed., *American Denominational Organization;* H. R. Niebuhr, *The Social Sources of Denominationalism.*

Depravity, Total. A proper definition of total depravity should not focus primarily on the questions of sinfulness vs. goodness or ability vs. inability, but on fallen man's relation to a holy God. Because of the effects of the fall, that original relationship of fellowship with God was broken and man's entire nature was polluted. As a result no one can do anything, even good things, that can gain soteriological merit in God's sight. Therefore, we may concisely define total depravity as the unmeritoriousness of man before God because of the corruption of original sin.

The concept of total depravity does not mean (1) that depraved people cannot or do not perform actions that are good in either man's or God's sight. But no such action can gain favor with God for salvation. Neither does it mean (2) that fallen man has no conscience which judges between good and evil for him. But that conscience has been affected by the fall so that it cannot be a safe and reliable guide. Neither does it mean (3) that people indulge in every form of sin or in any sin to the greatest extent possible.

Positively *total* depravity means that the corruption has extended to all aspects of man's nature, to his entire being; and total *depravity* means that because of that corruption there is nothing man can do to merit saving favor with God.

The Bible teaches this concept of total depravity in many places. The Lord recognized good people (Matt. 22:10), yet he labeled his own disciples as evil men (Matt. 7:11). The mind is affected (Rom. 1:28; Eph. 4:18), the conscience is unclean (Heb. 9:14), the heart is deceitful (Jer. 17:9), and by nature mankind is subject to wrath (Eph. 2:3). God sent the flood as a judgment on mankind's depravity (Gen. 6:5). Depravity, according to the Lord, is in the inner being and is the root of evil actions (Mark 7:20–23). With a string of OT quotations Paul also shows it is deep-seated, universal, and total (Rom. 3:9–18).

Calvinists trace depravity to an inherent corruption of man's nature which was inherited from Adam. Augustine stressed the idea that all were seminally present in Adam when he sinned and therefore all sinned in him. The semi-Pelagian reaction to Calvinism is found today in Arminian theology, which denies *total* depravity, the guilt of original sin, and the loss of freedom of the will, and which affirms involvement in the sin of Adam only to the extent of giving mankind a tendency toward sin but not a sinful nature.

The implications of depravity are especially crucial in relation to salvation. Man has no ability to save himself. He can do good and make choices, but he cannot regenerate himself (John 1:13). Unless the Holy Spirit enlightens an individual he will remain in darkness (I Cor. 2:14). Some theologians have labeled this "moral inability," an unclear term, since it implies that depraved people are devoid of morality. C. C. RYRIE

See also SIN.

Bibliography. L. Berkhof, *Reformed Dogmatics* and *Systematic Theology;* J. Miley, *Systematic Theology,* I, 441–553; W. G. T. Shedd, *Dogmatic Theology,* II, 257; H. C. Thiessen, *Lectures in Systematic Theology.*

Descartes, René (1596–1650). Modern philosophy is generally said to have begun with René Descartes. "Modern" is here applied to much of the thought of the seventeenth century to imply a break between medieval and postmedieval philosophy. Clearly there was with Descartes in France and Frances Bacon in England, and even more with the others who followed them, a shift of interest from theological themes to a study of nature and of man without explicit reference to God.

Descartes was occupied with problems which, in his opinion, would be solved by reason alone. He considered himself to be a philosopher and a mathematician, not a theologian. His fundamental aim was to attain philosophical truth by the use of reason. He wished to develop a system of true propositions, in which nothing would be presupposed that was not self-evident and indubitable. Thus there would be an organic connection between all the parts of the system and the whole edifice would rest on a solid foundation. His ideal of knowledge was an ordered system of propositions dependent on one another. This ideal was suggested in large part by mathematics.

Descartes's way of doing philosophy began with a methodological skepticism. By this method he systematically doubted each proposition that could possibly be doubted as a preliminary to the establishment of certain knowledge. Having subjected to doubt all that can be doubted, he arrived at the "simple" and indubitable proposition, *Cogito, ergo sum* (I think, therefore I am). However much I doubt, I must exist. Otherwise I could not doubt. Thus my existence is proven in the act of doubting. The *cogito, ergo sum* is therefore the indubitable truth on which Descartes proposed to found his philosophy.

Next Descartes attempted to prove the existence of God. This illustrates an essential feature of his thought and is very significant to later developments in the history of philosophy. So far Descartes had established only that he existed as a thinking being; now he proceeded entirely from the contents of his own consciousness to prove the existence of something else. Descartes proceeded in this "transcendental" way, proving first the existence of God and then working deductively from God's existence to other contingent beings and the "external" world. His method of working from the data of consciousness has remained important to subsequent thinkers, becoming the basis for many later subjectivist and idealist developments.

Descartes is among the most original philosophers and mathematicians of modern times and is generally acknowledged to be the most important French philosopher. M. H. MACDONALD

Bibliography. *Oeuvres de Descartes,* 12 vols., ed. C. Adam and P. Tannery; *Descartes: Philosophical Writings,* tr. G. E. M. Anscombe and P. T. Geach; *Descartes' Philosophical Writings,* ed. N. K. Smith; L. J. Beck, *The Method of Descartes;* N. K. Smith, *Studies in Cartesian Philosophy.*

Descent into Hell (Hades). In the NT Hades indicates the abode of the dead and is roughly equivalent to Sheol in the OT. It was believed that upon death both good and bad go to Hades, though in later biblical thought the good are seen to be in a higher compartment of Hades called Paradise (cf. Luke 16:19–31). In the intertestamental and NT periods there was disagreement among the rabbis as to whether Paradise was to be included in Hades or was indeed a separate realm altogether. Paul maintained that we are closer to God in Paradise than in our earthly, bodily existence (II Cor. 5:6–8). The Wisdom of Solomon and Maccabees spoke of the righteous as being in the very presence of God. Tertullian reflected the viewpoint of many church fathers in his contention that Paradise is not yet heaven but is higher than hell, affording an interval of rest to the souls of the righteous (*Against Marcion* iv.34). Hades as the intermediate state of the dead is to be distinguished from Gehenna, the future abode of the damned, the eschatological hell, as well as from Tartarus, the realm of darkness inhabited by the devil and his angels, though these distinctions were not always made in the early church.

Christ's descent into Hades after his crucifixion and death has a solid foundation in both Scripture and the early church. In the NT it is attested in Acts 2:31; Eph. 4:9–10; and I Pet. 3:19–20. The passages in Ephesians and I Peter seem to indicate the extension of the saving work of reconciliation and redemption to the souls in the nether world of Hades.

In the Gospels reference is made to the saints in the tombs (the nether world) who were raised with Jesus (Matt. 27:51–53; John 5:25–29). Jesus also spoke of forgiveness in this world and in the world to come (Matt. 12:31–32). He confidently expected that the gates of Hades could not prevail or hold out against his church (Matt. 16:18). In the book of Revelation it is said that Christ possesses the keys to the underworld and can open its gates (Rev. 1:18). Similarly, an angel is given the key to the bottomless pit in order to open it (Rev. 9:12; 20:1).

In the OT the ransoming or redemption of the dead from Hades is hinted at if not testified to in Ps. 49:15; Hos. 13:14; Jonah 2:2, 6; and Isa. 26:19. In an apocryphon cited from Jeremiah by both Justin and Irenaeus and still found in certain synagogue copies, the idea of a descent to the underworld is quite clear: "The Lord, the Holy One of Israel remembered his dead ones who slept in the dust of the earth, and descended to them to preach his salvation and save them." This apocryphon is similar to a Latin text of Ecclus. 24:32: "I [Wisdom] will penetrate all the lower parts of the earth, and will visit all that sleep, and will enlighten all that hope in the Lord."

The descent into Hades was not universally accepted as part of the Apostles' Creed until the eighth century, though it is mentioned in local forms of that creed in patristic times. The descent formula is included in the Athanasian Creed, composed about the middle of the fifth century and accepted by both East and West.

Christ's descent into Hades was almost universally affirmed by the church fathers, including Polycarp, Justin Martyr, Origen, Hermas, Irenaeus, Cyprian, Tertullian, Hippolytus, Clement of Alexandria, Athanasius, Ambrose, and Augustine. The earliest patristic references to the descent occur in the epistles of Ignatius about the beginning of the second century.

There was disagreement among the church fathers on who benefited from Christ's descent. Many restricted Christ's redemptive activity in the realm of the dead to the OT patriarchs and prophets (Ignatius of Antioch, Irenaeus, Tertullian). Others held that those who had died before the great flood were likewise redeemed (the Alexandrian theologians and Origen). Some thought that Jesus Christ redeemed all the dead with the exception of the very wicked (Melito, Gregory of Nazianzus, Marcion, Ephraem). Cyril of Alexandria spoke of Christ "spoiling all Hades," "emptying the insatiable recesses of Death," and "leaving the devil desolate and alone."

In the theological development in medieval thought the idea of an intermediate state of Hades was supplanted by heaven, hell, purgatory, the limbo of the patriarchs, and the limbo of unbaptized children. Thomas Aquinas contended that Christ descended to the underworld not to convert unbelievers but to put them to shame for their unbelief and wickedness. The just and holy souls of the patriarchs were indeed delivered by his descent but not the souls in the limbo of children.

At one stage in his life Luther taught with Melanchthon that Christ's preaching in Hades, as referred to in I Peter, might have effected the salvation of the nobler heathen. In a sermon at Torgau in April, 1533, Luther spoke of the descent of the whole Christ into hell, where he demolished hell and bound the devil. Luther and Lutheran orthodoxy saw the descent as the first stage in Christ's exaltation. Flacius, Calovius, and many other Lutheran theologians regarded the descent as a damnatory manifestation of judgment against the rejected.

In Reformed theology the descent into Hades has generally been interpreted as a figurative expression of the unutterable sufferings of Christ in his humanity. Reformed theology, following Calvin, saw the descent as part of the humiliation of Christ, not as the first stage of his exalted state as in Lutheranism.

In liberal Protestantism the idea of an intermediate state of Hades and Paradise has generally been discarded as a relic of an outmoded mythology. Some have interpreted the descent as simply denoting an ignominious place of death for the Prince of Life. Others see it as a symbolic portrayal of the fact of death.

It is well to note that the Gnostics, with the exception of Marcion, did not envision a descent of the Savior into the underworld, the abode of the dead. Instead, they preferred to speak of a premundane descent of the divine "aeon" or eternal power out of the *plērōma* to rescue the fallen *sophia* (wisdom) from the lower spheres. Those who are liberated are imperfect righteous souls in one of the lesser heavens.

While mythologies and other religions contain visits of a divinity, hero, or saint to the nether world of spirits, there is no parallel with the NT doctrine of the offer of redemption to the dead through preaching. A case can be made that a descent doctrine existed already in NT Christianity (anticipated even in the OT) without the aid of pagan myths.

To believe in the literal descent of Christ into Hades for the purpose of offering redemption does not imply universalism. Most of those who have held to this belief admit the possibility of rejecting the offer of salvation given by Christ. Again, this is not to be confounded with the doctrine of a second chance. What the descent doctrine affirms is the universality of a first chance, an opportunity for salvation for those who have never heard the gospel in its fullness.

D. G. Bloesch

See also Paradise; Purgatory; Hell; Hades; Limbo; Spirits in Prison; Dead, Abode of the.

Bibliography. J. A. MacCulloch, *The Harrowing of Hell;* T. A. Kantonen, *The Christian Hope;* T. F. Glasson, *Greek Influence in Jewish Eschatology;* R. H. Charles, *Eschatology: Doctrine of a Future Life in Israel;* G. J. Dyer, *Limbo: Unsettled Question;* C. W. Pilcher, *The Hereafter in Jewish and Christian Thought;* G. C. Studer, *After Death, What?* E. H. Plumptre, *The Spirits in Prison and Other Studies on the Life after Death.*

Descent of Man. *See* Man, Origin of.

Desire. A term used to describe the self in its longing to possess and enjoy some valued object or to fulfill some need or prized goal. God has created the human brain with specialized neural systems and pleasure/pain centers that govern desires, including the common drives such as hunger, thirst, rest, and sex. Desiring is so essential to human experience that some have described the self as being simply the aggregate of its desires. To lack basic desires, as illustrated by anorexia nervosa (a lack of the desire to eat) or inhibited sexual desire (ISD), is currently considered a mental illness that may be ruinous to the human personality.

The most common word for desire in the NT is *epithymia,* derived from *thyō,* meaning "to well up" or "boil." When the term is used in a morally negative sense, it is often translated as "lust" or "covetousness." In later Greek philosophy, *epithymia* signified the failure of human striving as it was either inferior to reason, directed toward evil objects, associated with pleasure, or it violated the golden mean of moderation. Some church fathers, most notably Augustine, were greatly influenced by this view. Augustine lashed out against the "disease of desire" as the "eager concupiscence which is always seeking pleasure," and even identified it with original sin.

In the NT the Greek view of associating desire with evil is tempered by Hebrew anthropology. The Hebrew term *nepeš* represents the total human self, but it spotlights the self in its unique longings for certain biological, psychic, social, and spiritual goods (Prov. 27:7; Song of S. 1:7; Isa. 26:8–9). Moreover, these desires themselves are good when they emanate from righteous people (Prov. 10:24; 11:23). Those who delight in the Lord and are concerned, for instance, to satisfy the desires of the hungry, will themselves be granted their hearts' desires (Ps. 21:2; 37:4; Isa. 58:11). However, in the story of the fall, these same desires, when quickened by the serpent's lure, selfishly attracted Adam and Eve to the forbidden tree's delightful food and its anticipated divine wisdom (Gen. 3:6). Humans are continually enticed to reject God, forget others, and selfishly indulge their desires (Deut. 31:20; Exod. 20:17; Ps. 112:10).

The NT writers continue the Hebrew tradition that human desires are normal dimensions of the created self (Matt. 13:17; Luke 16:21; Phil. 1:22–23). Jesus not only spoke favorably of human longings, but he felt them himself (Luke 17:22; 22:15). However, both Jesus and Paul affirmed that desires are the primary medium of sin in the fallen world as the forces of Satan battle the will of God (Mark 4:19; John 8:44; Eph. 2:3; Titus 2:12). Paul develops this idea in the context of both Christology and eschatology. The Christian lives simultaneously in this age, which is characterized by the evil powers that prey upon the weakness of the flesh, and in the juxtaposed age to come, represented by the reign of Christ (Rom. 8:12–27). The cosmic powers of this age, however, have invaded the self through its desires, whether they be sensual, moral, or religious desires, and have shaped them toward passionate but malicious self-seeking (Rom. 1:24ff.; Eph. 2:2–3; I Thess. 4:4–6). Thus, Paul rejected the notion that the desires nourish evil primarily because of their inferiority to reason, or their association with pleasure, or their evil objects, or their excessiveness. Rather, as a part of God's creation they are good, but they become evil when directed away from others to pure self-interest. These desires "of the flesh" are referred to as "deceitful" (Eph. 4:22), "evil" (Col. 3:5), "hurtful" (I Tim. 6:9), "worldly" (Titus 2:12), "youthful" (II Tim. 2:22), and "sinful" (Rom. 13:14).

In redemption Christ's spirit confronts the demonic powers in the arena of the desiring self (Rom. 7:7–8; Eph. 4:22–24; see also James 1:14–15; II Pet. 2:18; I John 2:15). The desires of the spirit (love, joy, peace, etc.) battle those of the flesh (fornication, idolatry, envy, party intrigues, etc.) and the battle itself points to Christ's victory won by his death and resurrection (Gal. 5:16–25). Thus, through the grace of God in Christ, the Christian is freed from surrendering to the fallen selfish desires. God takes possession of the person by seizing the desiring self and reshaping those desires into love for the neighbor (Gal. 5:13–15). Thus, every impulse to love, whether strong or weak, is a preamble to the unveiling of Christ's supreme rule in the world. D. J. Miller

See also Flesh.

Bibliography. F. Büchsel, *TDNT,* III, 167–72; R. Gundry, "The Moral Frustration of Paul Before His Conversion: Sexual Lust in Romans 7:7–25," in *Pauline Studies,* ed. D. Hagner and M. Harris; E. Käsemann, *Perspectives on Paul.*

Despair. That sense of utter hopelessness that characterizes those whose spirits have been so crushed by tragic events or by their own guilt that they do not see any meaning to their lives. In the Scriptures despair is described in such rich but bitter terms and images as "languish," "wailing," "anguish," "terror," "desolation," "gloom," "dwelling in darkness," "cowering in ashes," "torn to pieces," "wormwood and gall," "teeth grinding on gravel," "depths of the pit," "soul in tumult," "gnashing of teeth," "heavy chains" (see Lam., esp. 3:5–20). The "woe" cry, one of the more intense expressions of despair in the Bible, was often uttered by the prophets to intensify the hopelessness of those who despise God's justice (Amos 5:18). The future woes will bring such an avalanche of despair that the earth's inhabitants will scream for the mountains to bury them (Rev. 6:15–17; 8:13).

While hopelessness usually characterizes those who are alienated from God and experience God's wrath, there are moments when the person of faith reaches the boundaries of despair. In the presence of the holy and glorious God, Isaiah envisions his own uncleanness and is driven to declare, "Woe is me" (Isa. 6:5). Events can strike with such devastating force that both Job and Jeremiah curse the day of their birth and wish they had died in delivery (Job 3:3ff.; Jer. 20:14–18). As the saying went, Rachel in Ramah laments and weeps bitterly for her children and refuses to be comforted (Jer. 31:15). Koheleth despairs of the seeming vanity and injustice of human striving (Eccles. 2:20). The forsaken psalmist cries out day and night for the absent God (Ps. 22). Even Jesus experiences this same divine abandonment in bearing the total weight of human sin on the cross (Matt. 27:46). In each of these cases, however, the biblical writers counter with firm glimpses of hope and salvation. Paul describes his own life as reaching the border of despair in his helplessness before the law and the desertion, persecution, and perplexity that the life of faith brings. Yet he proclaims confidence in the power of Christ to deliver from sin, and he affirms that the Christian's precarious walk of faith does not ultimately lead to despair and destruction but rather brings life and joy (Rom. 7:7–25; II Cor. 4:8–12; see also Rom. 8:35–39).

That the Christian often lives near the edges of despair was noted by Augustine and theologically developed by Martin Luther. Luther maintained that despair (*Anfechtung*) is a redeeming force in the salvation of the sinner. However, it also plays a significant role in the life of the believer, since the believer is simultaneously saint and sinner (*simul justus et peccator*). Because of sin as well as God's determined mode of revelation, the Christian paradoxically confronts God as "hidden" in the passion of Christ; i.e., in his suffering, forsakenness, and death on the cross and in his descent into hell. Thus, the believer shudders before the crucified Christ as he or she experiences with Christ the painful withdrawal of God in the face of human sin. Luther asserted, "All honest and pious Christians are like Jonah; they are thrown into the sea, yes, into the depths of hell. . . . All saints must also descend with their Lord into the inferno." Nevertheless, at the cross the Christian also recognizes the overwhelming love of God expressed in Christ's sacrificial death. Thus, in the very midst of that despair caused by God's turning away from the Son who bears the world's sins, God's love is most fully comprehended and experienced.

Since Luther, one of the most profound and influential theological discussions of despair is encountered in Søren Kierkegaard's *The Sickness unto Death.* In this classical work he analyzes in great detail the various forms or stages of despair, and argues that underlying all despair is not the felt deprivation because of earthly misfortune, but rather a desperation at the loss of the true self and thus a loss of the eternal God who constitutes the self. Nevertheless, despair is the "passageway to faith" and, as it becomes more intense, it brings one nearer to salvation.

Kierkegaard's analysis of despair has greatly influenced contemporary writers. The present crisis of faith in God and the fear of mass human destruction have enticed some dispirited persons to embrace cynicism and nihilism. These sentiments have sparked modern theologies of despair culminating in the gloomy claim that God is dead. A few contemporary theologians have directly addressed the existential despair of this age. For example, Paul Tillich, following the lead of Luther and Kierkegaard, writes that a life of faith can be forged from the fires of despair. Simply put, the positive has meaning in recognition and acceptance of the negative. In the "courage of faith" present in despair, the Christian experiences unshakable confidence in the eternal God.

It is not unusual for Christians to be driven to the edges of darkness because of unforeseen tragic events or heinous sins they or others have committed. However, the children of God never lose hope by dwelling on the question "Why?" Rather, they ask, "What is God going to do through me now?" Thus, they humbly accept God's sovereignty and God's justifying acts with fortitude and with the expectation that they are instruments of God's redemptive change in a fragmented and misery-congested world.

D. J. Miller

Bibliography. C. S. Evans, *Despair: A Moment or a Way of Life;* P. Tillich, *The Courage to Be.*

Destruction. The idea of temporal calamity dominates the wide range of OT words on this topic, but of the twenty-two instances of *apōleia, olethros,* and *kathairesis* in the NT only five concern temporal distress; the rest refer to eternal loss. Where the truth of eternal life shines fully, it illumines the truth of eternal destruction.

The exceptions to the general OT notion are found in the word *'ăbaddôn.* This word occurs in parallelism with *šĕ'ôl, māweṯ* (death), *qeber* (grave), and *hōšek* (darkness). The suggestion of reference here to the state after death is borne out by examination of instances (though, as with Sheol, the teaching is nebulous and scanty). Thus, while Job 26:6 refers to Sheol and Abaddon in proof of God's power, Prov. 15:11 does so in proof of his moral discernment. This notion that moral distinctions are made hereafter is enforced by Job 31:12, where Abaddon is the ultimate destiny of the adulterer. Finally, in Ps. 88 the psalmist, in temporal distress, depicts himself as one who, already in Sheol (identified in vs. 11 with Abaddon), is under pressure of God's wrath (vs. 7) and cut off from God's fellowship (vss. 10–12).

The bridge between this unformulated OT doctrine and the full NT teaching is Rev. 9:11, where Abaddon is the name of the "angel of the abyss," also called Apollyon (cf. "son of *apōleia,*" John 17:12; II Thess. 2:3). Destruction meets those who have chosen the broad road (Matt. 7:13), oppose the cross (Phil. 3:19; II Pet. 2:1), are ungodly (II Pet. 3:7), pervert Scripture (II Pet. 3:16), and are unready for Christ's return (I Thess. 5:3). Destruction is the opposite of life (Matt. 7:13) and salvation (Phil. 1:28; Heb. 10:39); is swift, personally merited (II Pet. 2:13), inescapable (I Thess. 5:3), and by fire (II Thess. 1:8, 9; II Pet. 3:7); it results in eternal separation from God (II Thess. 1:9). The justice of this condemnation is guaranteed by the unimpeachable will of God (Rom. 9:22). J. A. Motyer

See also Abaddon; Death, The Second; Eternal Punishment; Hades; Hell; Sheol.

Determinism. *See* Freedom, Free Will, and Determinism.

Devil. *See* Satan.

Devil Ransom Theory. *See* Atonement, Theories of the.

Devotio Moderna. A devotional movement of the fifteenth and sixteenth centuries chiefly associated with the Brethren of the Common Life; their founder, Gerard Groote; and their best-known writer, Thomas à Kempis. The Brethren were a mixed lay and clerical group that founded houses especially in Germany and Holland, the best known of which was Windesheim (founded 1387). The movement was not monastic in the full sense, although it had much in common with the Franciscan Tertiaries and sought the reform of the whole church, including monasteries.

The *Devotio Moderna* was strongly Augustinian in tone, but without his stress on predestination. The chief marks of the movement included: (1) a focus on devotion to Christ, including meditation on his passion; (2) an emphasis on obeying Christ's commands and therefore on holiness, simplicity, and community; (3) a strong involvement in individual piety and spiritual life; (4) a call to repentance and reform; and (5) elements of nominalism, Christian humanism, and Franciscan asceticism. The adherents' biblical emphasis, encouragement of lay ministry, stress on a personal relationship to Christ, and rejection of indulgences and other medieval abuses made them appear precursors of the Reformers. But their individualism and call for a disciplined piety, as well as their independence and their refusal to rely on more than the Bible alone, means that they were more similar to the Anabaptists, who may indeed have been influenced by the movement, than to Luther, Zwingli, or Calvin, who accepted a mixed church as a necessity of their acceptance of state sponsorship. At the same time the *Devotio Moderna,* although controversial, was fully within the Catholic Church; its weak doctrine of the church universal and of the Spirit (due to the focus on Christ) meant it felt no need for a radical break, although its sacramental teaching moved in a Reformed direction.

The lasting value of this movement has been the literature it produced and its influence over Anabaptists and other Reformers, directly and indirectly. P. H. Davids

See also Brethren of the Common Life; Groote, Gerard; Thomas à Kempis.

Bibliography. K. R. Davis, *Anabaptism and Asceticism;* A. Hyma, *The Christian Renaissance;* à Kempis, *The Imitation of Christ.*

Diadem. *See* Crown.

Dialectical Theology. *See* Neo-orthodoxy.

Dichotomy. This term, which signifies a division into two parts (Greek *dicha,* in two; *temnein,* cut), is applied in theology to that view of human nature which holds that man has two fundamental parts to his being: body and soul. Usually the two are sharply contrasted, considered to have different origins and independent existence. Thus, the actual relationship between body and soul becomes the crucial question.

Plato taught that the body was perishable matter but the soul existed in the heavenly world of pure form or idea before its incarnation in the human body. The soul was therefore uncreated and immortal—a part of deity. The body is the prison house of the soul; the soul is locked in the body like an oyster in its shell. At death the soul leaves the body to return to the heavenly world or to be reincarnated in some other body.

Aristotle's adaptation of Plato by dividing the soul into its animal and rational aspects was further developed in Roman Catholic doctrine through Thomas Aquinas, who taught that the soul was created in heaven and placed in the forming body, probably at the time of "quickening" in the mother's womb. The new philosophy after Descartes affirmed the independent origin of body and soul, supposing that the apparent unity of them in the human personality is due to the coincidental correlation that occurs momentarily, as when the pendulums of separate clocks happen to swing together. Contemporary theology usually rejects this view, holding to the body-soul unity of man as set forth in Hebrew thought: "and man became a living soul" (Gen. 2:7).

W. E. Ward

See also Trichotomy; Man, Doctrine of.

Bibliography. R. Bultmann, *NT Theology,* I; G. P. Klubertanz, *The Philosophy of Human Nature;* R. Niebuhr, *The Nature and Destiny of Man;* H. W. Robinson, *The Christian Doctrine of Man;* E. C. Rust, *Nature and Man in Biblical Thought;* G. C. Berkouwer, *Man: The Image of God.*

Diocese. A territorial unit of the church administered by a bishop. The word was adopted from the territorial divisions of the Roman Empire (Gr. *diokēsis,* administrative unit) but only gradually achieved common usage in the church. Today it is the basic unit of the Roman, Anglican, Old Catholic, and some Lutheran Churches. The bishop is assisted in his shepherding of the diocese by assistant or suffragan bishops and by presbyter/priests. Usually the diocese is subdivided into parishes, which may be grouped into deaneries and archdeaneries. In the Orthodox and Eastern Churches diocese can refer to a much larger area—that supervised by a patriarch.

P. Toon

See also Church Officers; Bishop.

Dionysius the Pseudo-Areopagite. One of the influential streams by which the Christian Platonism of the early church was transmitted to the Middle Ages was through the writings of the "pseudo-Dionysius." This writer had been mistakenly identified as Dionysius the Areopagite who was converted by Paul (Acts 17:34). Instead, he lived *ca.* 500, probably in Syria. His writings paved the way for later Christian mysticism and became standard theological authorities in the Eastern church. Their Latin translation by John Scotus Erigena made them widely known in the West. Theologians such as Hugh of St. Victor, Bonaventure, Meister Eckhart, Albertus Magnus, and Thomas Aquinas knew the writings and used them.

Major themes of the pseudo-Dionysian writings include the hierarchical pattern of the universe, the soul's intimate union with God, and humanity's eventual deification. These are found in the treatises *Celestial Hierarchy, Ecclesiastical Hierarchy, Divine Names,* and *Mystical Theology.* Ten letters to monks, priests, and deacons also survive.

For pseudo-Dionysius, a series of hierarchically arranged beings relate God to the world. Each being springs directly from God, with Jesus serving as both the principle of creation and the consummation of all hierarchies. On earth the celestial hierarchy is mirrored in the ecclesiastical hierarchy of bishops, priests, deacons, etc.

Pseudo-Dionysius approached the knowledge of God both positively and negatively, though he expressed a preference for the *via negativa.* In *Divine Names* he argued that God is superior to all reason, speech, being, and name. To speak of God, then, one must do so only in a special sense. God is "hyper-[super-] Being," "hyper-Goodness," "hyper-Life," etc. Ultimately the name God deserves above all others with regard to creation is "the Good." With regard to God himself, the best name is "Being." God is "He Who Is" (Exod. 3:14).

On the other hand, in *Mystical Theology* pseudo-Dionysius has the mind begin by denying to God those characteristics farthest from him such as "drunkenness" or "fury." The mind then progresses to deny God all human characteristics until one comes to God as "the Darkness of Unknowing." God is absolutely unknowable. One is united to God through ecstatic, mystical experience which is a complete ignorance of God and also a knowledge beyond reason. God is thus beyond both affirmation and negation.

D. K. McKim

See also Mysticism; Neoplatonism.

Bibliography. F. Copleston, *A History of Philosophy,* II, Pt. 1; *Encyclopedia of Philosophy,* VI; É. Gilson,

History of Christian Philosophy in the Middle Ages; J. L. González, *A History of Christian Thought,* II; *ODCC,* 402–3; J. Pelikan, *The Emergence of the Catholic Tradition, The Growth of Medieval Theology,* and *The Spirit of Eastern Christendom;* M. de Wulf, *History of Medieval Philosophy,* I.

Discerning of Spirits. *See* SPIRITUAL GIFTS.

Disciple. *See* CHRISTIANS, NAMES OF.

Discipleship Movement. A term applied to the teachings and persons coming from the Fort Lauderdale, Florida, Shepherd's Church. Sometimes referred to as the Shepherding Movement, it represents a specialized group within the charismatic movement that arose in the early 1960s. It also has older roots in the Pentecostal movement that began in the United States in 1900. The principal teachers in the movement have been the leaders of the Fort Lauderdale congregation, including Bob Mumford, Charles Simpson, Derek Prince, Don Basham, Ern Baxter, and John Poole. The official name of their organization is Christian Growth Ministries, and its major publication is *New Wine* magazine.

The concept of discipling is related to the goal of encouraging and measuring growth in Christian discipleship through the behavioral change that would result from a consistent application of biblical principles to personal and corporate Christian living. According to Mumford, the shepherd is to nurture discipleship through a three-part program, including baptism by water, discipleship by a man "commissioned by God," and acknowledging the abiding presence of Christ with the shepherd (or disciple maker) and his disciples. Mumford advocates avoiding spiritual independence that would lead to religious anarchy in favor of embracing the yoke of Christ as a symbol of discipleship.

In a typical Discipleship community, household fellowships gather in closed weekly meetings. Often the leading shepherds in a community have been directly trained by one of the abovenamed leaders. The members are often obliged to submit to covenantal norms, such as tithing, obedience to the authority of the community (which also may have authority in the area of male-female relationships), and the requirement of job-holding for all but married women.

The leaders of the Discipleship Movement have extensively expressed their views on their roles. They are frequently concerned with the integrity of the shepherds, especially their motivation to serve God uncompromisingly, and with the need to develop disciplined Christian leadership for shepherding communities that can withstand moral oppression and economic havoc from the contemporary society. Not seeking to found a new denomination, they emphasize the realization of the kingdom of God that transcends existing ecclesiastical structures. They often picture their role in military terms, as captains of the Lord's army. They expect opposition from the contemporary society and often pray for divine strength to endure in the midst of an alien world.

A chief biblical text for the movement is the reference to pastor-teachers in Eph. 4:11, which designates for them a man "called and equipped to give oversight and care to God's people." Discipling is seen as a comprehensive word that denotes a God-given authority. Each shepherd understands that he is to give account of his stewardship to the chief shepherd. Just as Jesus regarded few of the professional religious leaders of his day as true shepherds, so the leaders of the Discipleship Movement often find unacceptable the ministry of those who are exercising ecclesiastical authority over people in their day. This criticism recalls that of Christian sectarian leaders in past history, such as Montanus, the Spiritual Franciscans, the Anabaptists, and the radical pietists.

The criteria for effective discipling also include the avoidance of selfish preoccupation with power and personal status, in line with the admonition in I Pet. 5:1–6. In addition, there is the responsibility for shepherds to equip the saints for ministry. This involves instructing and admonishing each member in public and in private.

Discipleship communities include those designed for celibate persons and for families. Covenantal norms frequently include poverty, or the renunciation of self-centered aims and self-provision, and yieldedness, or obedient reliance upon God through submission to the headship of the community leaders through whom Christ is to rule. In addition, communal sharing of lives and possessions is often emphasized, in accordance with Acts 4:32. Such communities view themselves as living on the frontiers of Christian commitment, although evangelism may be limited to shepherds, who are regarded as being spiritually mature. Common activities in discipling communities include corporate worship, prayer meetings, and the Eucharist; administration of these group activities is under the authority of an apostolate, a term that often refers to the total group of shepherds in a given community.

In 1975 response to the Discipleship Movement precipitated a controversy within the charismatic movement as a whole as several charismatic leaders, including Pat Robertson of the Christian Broadcasting Network, expressed public disagreement with the Fort Lauderdale group. In December of that year a representative group of pastors, teachers, and leaders met in Ann Arbor, Michigan, for a theological and pastoral evaluation of the controversy. This group agreed that much of it had resulted from poor communication and misunderstanding, and that the real differences that existed were within the bounds of the variety permitted in the body of Christ. Subsequent charismatic leaders' conferences have been held, such as the Oklahoma City meeting in 1976, that have sought to achieve reconciliation among the parties to the dispute.

Some critics do not believe that the Discipleship Movement is operating according to biblical principles, pointing out that Scripture teaches *all* Christians should submit to one another (Eph. 5:19–21). Some oppose the amount of control exercised by shepherds over such matters as the choice of a mate and the decision to have children. The movement is not always regarded by these critics as a cult, since it accepts the essential beliefs of Christianity, including the Trinity, Christ's incarnation and resurrection, salvation by grace through faith, and authority of Scripture. However, it is objected that the hypersensitivity and secrecy often to be found in the movement—even to the point of disallowing discussion of its doctrines and practices with others outside the group—tend to raise questions in people's minds. Others have questioned the tendency of the movement to separate itself from the concerns of the historical church. These objections notwithstanding, the significance of the impact of the Discipleship Movement upon the charismatic movement remains. J. S. O'Malley

See also Charismatic Movement.

Bibliography. C. Farah, *From the Pinnacle of the Temple;* R. J. Foster, *A Celebration of Discipline;* M. Harper, *A New Way of Living;* D. Hartman and D. Sutherland, *Guidebook to Discipleship;* W. A. Henricksen, *Disciples Are Made—Not Born;* R. A. Lovelace, *Dynamics of Spiritual Life;* J. S. O'Malley, *The Mystique of Godliness: Bishop John Seygert and the United Methodist Heritage;* J. C. Ortiz, *The Disciple;* R. G. Tuttle, *The Partakers;* D. Watson, *Called and Committed: World-Changing Discipleship.*

Discipline. Discipline implies instruction and correction, the training that improves, molds, strengthens, and perfects character. It is the moral education obtained by the enforcement of obedience through supervision and control. Usually the concept is translated chastening, chastisement, and instruction (Heb. *yāsar, mûsār;* Gr. *paideuō, paideia*). The discipline of the believer on the part of the heavenly Father is frequently illustrated by the correction made by the human father. "As a man chasteneth (*yāsar*) his son, so the Lord thy God chasteneth thee" (Deut. 8:5; Pss. 6:1; 38:1). He is taught not to despise the chastening, *mûsār,* of the Almighty (Job 5:17; Prov. 3:11). The value of discipline by a human father is stressed in Prov. 19:18.

The OT teaching is amplified in the NT, especially in Heb. 12:3–12, by considering carefully the suffering endured by the Savior. The Christian is reminded to value the discipline of the Almighty (*paideia*). The discipline is a sure evidence of sonship and of God's love.

Lack of chastening is an evidence of hatred rather than of love (Prov. 13:24). Furthermore, the end result of discipline which for the moment is grievous is the ultimate good of that one who is thereby instructed (Heb. 12:10–11).

Discipline may be severe but not disastrous, "as chastened, and not killed" (II Cor. 6:9; Ps. 118:18); and such chastisement delivers from condemnation with the world (I Cor. 11:33). Discipline is often by pain, sorrow, and loss (Job 33:19, *yākah*) whereby the Christian shares Paul's assurance of God's comfort (II Cor. 1:3–11; 12:7–10). There is a self-chastening (Dan. 10:10, Hithpael of *'ānâ*). The consequent fumbling and suffering are designed to deliver from temporal consideration (I Pet. 4:1–2; II Cor. 5:15; I John 2:15–17).

The purpose of discipline is the correction, the improvement, the obedience, the faith, and the faithfulness of God's child. The outcome is a happiness, a blessedness (Job 5:17; Ps. 94:12; and assurance of Rev. 3:19: "as many as I love, I rebuke and chasten"). V. R. Edman

See also Church Discipline.

Bibliography. H. Baltensweiler, *NIDNTT,* I, 494ff.; G. Bertram, *TDNT,* V, 596ff.

Discipline, Church. *See* Church Discipline.

Discrimination. The practice of treating people unfairly because they are members of a group marked by certain physical, religious, or social characteristics. Discrimination is not simply limited to isolated personal actions, but may also be embodied in structural arrangements such as laws, codes, ordinances, policies, community organizations, and broader social institutions.

Discrimination is fertilized by prejudice, the patterned attitude of hostility (blatant or hidden) toward other people. Its effects are usually devastating on the physical and spiritual well-being of its victims. Like a vicious circle the aftereffects of this victimization manage to reinforce further prejudice and stereotyping, which then contribute to even greater discrimination. In certain circumstances this cycle of discrimination could ultimately lead, as history itself has too often confirmed, to the most heinous of human crimes—genocide, the systematic extermination of whole groups of people. The Holocaust is the most recent brutal example of the logic of prejudice and discrimination. Because of such vicious outcomes, discrimination is seen as morally abhorrent by all people of good will.

For Christians discrimination is morally objectionable not only because of its evil consequences, but also because it violates the fundamental biblical motif of love, which assumes the equal worth of all human beings. It is not within the nature of God to show partiality against particular groups of people (Deut. 10:17; II Chr. 19:7; Acts 10:34; Rom. 2:11; Gal. 2:6). Because humans are created in the image of God's very nature, they are not only worthy of equal treatment themselves, but are summoned to treat others accordingly. The Israelites were sternly exhorted not to pervert justice, and this was clarified to mean "thou shalt not show partiality" (Deut. 16:19). All the people, including the poor and the small, even strangers and enemies, were to be treated lovingly (Lev. 19:1–5; Deut. 1:17; 24:17–18). This included provisions for special compensation to the poor because of their disadvantageous circumstances, often pejoratively referred to as "reverse discrimination" (Lev. 19:10; 25:35; Deut. 15:7–11; 24:19–22). The prophets, who reflected the mind of God, so vigorously condemned discrimination that they even predicted the demise of great cities and whole nations because they practiced partiality against the poor, orphans, widows, and other vulnerable groups (Isa. 1:21–23; 3:8–15).

Jesus continued the prophetic tradition when he claimed in his famous sermon that God's benefits are showered upon friend and foe alike (Matt. 5:45). Jesus is described even by his enemies as teaching the true way of God, which they interpreted as not showing partiality (Luke 20:21). This was not just idle flattery because he did, in fact, refuse to comply with discriminatory practices based upon common prejudices. He spoke with a Samaritan woman in public (John 4:7–9), ate with publicans and sinners (Matt. 9:10–13), defended a woman taken in adultery (John 8:1–11), and touched lepers (Matt. 8:3). According to Luke, Jesus' claim that God cares for a hungry "unclean" widow and even a leprous enemy general was so offensive to the "in-group" at Nazareth that they became a murderous mob (Luke 4:25–30).

The principle of impartiality gave impetus to the early church's worldwide evangelistic thrust as represented by Peter's realization that God shows no partiality against various ethnic groups (Acts 10:34; 11:12; 15:9). Nondiscrimination became such a fundamental element of the early church's ethic that in the book of James it is one of the major tests of true faith in Jesus Christ (James 2:9). Exhibiting the "royal law" of love is interpreted in the context of whether or not one makes a "dishonorable" distinction by preferring richly adorned people over shabbily dressed ones (vss. 2–9).

Today, even though great efforts have been made to eliminate discrimination through education and civil rights laws, it continues to be a most persistent and subtle reality in nearly every society. Tragically, nagging prejudice and discrimination have been perpetuated in Christian-oriented societies out of self-interest or perceived fear. This is often then coupled with a misreading of selective biblical texts. Fortunately, some of the strongest movements against sexual, racial, religious, and cultural discrimination, as illustrated by the contemporary black civil rights struggle, have been rooted in the Judeo-Christian ethic. This ethic will help to stimulate the Christian church to maximize its efforts to uproot prejudice and abolish discrimination through transformation of the heart, conversion of the mind, and social and legal reform. D. J. Miller

Bibliography. G. Allport, *The Nature of Prejudice;* G. S. Becker, *The Economics of Discrimination;* J. Feagin and C. Feagin, *Discrimination American Style: Institutional Racism and Sexism;* A. H. Goldman, *Justice and Reverse Discrimination;* F. Holmes, *Prejudice and Discrimination;* M. L. King, Jr., *Why We Can't Wait;* W. Laqueur and B. Rubin, *The Human Rights Reader;* V. Mollenkott, *Women, Men, and the Bible;* V. Mollenkott and L. Scanzoni, *Is the Homosexual My Neighbor? Another Christian View;* R. A. Ruether, *Liberation Theology;* G. E. Simpson and J. M. Yinger, *Racial and Cultural Minorities: An Analysis of Prejudice and Discrimination;* T. Skinner, *Black and Free.*

Dispensation, Dispensationalism. The Greek words, used about twenty times in the NT, mean "to manage, regulate, administer, and plan the affairs of a household." This concept of human stewardship is illustrated in Luke 16:1–2, where the ideas of responsibility, accountability, and the possibility of change are detailed. In other occurrences (Eph. 1:10; 3:2, 9; Col. 1:25) the idea of divine stewardship is prominent—i.e., an administration or plan being accomplished by God in this world.

Theological Usage. Building on the idea of God's administration of or plan for the world, dispensationalism describes the unfolding of that program in various dispensations, or stewardship arrangements, throughout the history of the world. The world is seen as a household administered by God in connection with several stages of revelation that mark off the different economies in the outworking of his total program. These economies are the dispensations in dispensationalism. Thus from God's viewpoint a dispensation is an economy; from man's it is a responsibility to the particular revelation given at the time. In relation to progressive revelation, a dispensation is a stage within it. Thus a dispensation may be defined as "a distinguishable economy in the outworking of God's program."

Number of Dispensations. At least three dispensations (as commonly understood in dispensationalism) are mentioned by Paul: one preceding the present time (Col. 1:25–26), the present arrangement (Eph. 3:2), and a future administration (Eph. 1:10). These three require a fourth—one before the law, and a prelaw dispensation would seem to need to be divided into pre- and postfall economies. Thus five administrations seem clearly distinguishable (at least within a premillennial understanding of Scripture). The usual sevenfold scheme includes a new economy after the Noahic flood and another with the call of Abraham.

Relation to Progressive Revelation. God did not reveal all truth at one time but through various periods and stages of revelation. This principle of progressive revelation is evident in the Scriptures themselves. Paul told his audience on Mars Hill that in a former time God overlooked their ignorance, but now commands all men everywhere to repent (Acts 17:30). The majestic opening of the book of Hebrews outlines the various means of progressive revelation (Heb. 1:1–2). One of the most striking verses that show different ways of God's dealing with mankind is John 1:17.

The concept of progressive revelation does not negate the unity of the Bible but recognizes the diversity of God's unfolding revelation as essential to the unity of his completed revelation.

Essential Characteristics. Dispensational theology grows out of a consistent use of the hermeneutical principle of normal, plain, or literal interpretation. This principle does not exclude the use of figures of speech, but insists that behind every figure is a literal meaning.

Applying this hermeneutical principle leads dispensationalism to distinguish God's program for Israel from his program for the church. Thus the church did not begin in the OT but on the day of Pentecost, and the church is not presently fulfilling promises made to Israel in the OT that have not yet been fulfilled.

Salvation. Doubtless the most frequent
heard objection to dispensationalism is that
allegedly teaches several ways of salvation. Th
arises from wrongly considering each dispens
tion as a way of salvation (therefore, there a
five, six, or seven ways) instead of inclusi
administrative arrangements which include
among many other things, sufficient revelatio
so that a person could be right with God. It als
comes from a misunderstanding of the use c
"law" and "grace" as labels for two of the di
pensations, as if to imply that these are two wa
of salvation. However, dispensationalists ha
taught and do teach that salvation is alwa
through God's grace. The *basis* of salvation i
every dispensation is the death of Christ; the *r*
quirement for salvation in every age is faith; th
object of faith is the true God; but the *content* c
faith changes in the various dispensations. T
affirm a sameness in the content of faith woul
of necessity deny progressiveness in revelatio
Nondispensationalists may sometimes be guilt
of reading the NT back into the OT in order t
be able to achieve a uniformity in the content c
faith.

Origins. Often dispensationalism is charge
with being recent in origin, and therefore untru
Of course, recency does not mean falsity an
more than antiquity guarantees truth. Unsystem
atic dispensationallike statements can be foun
from the writings of the church fathers on, bu
as a system dispensationalism did not begin t
develop until the early part of the eighteent
century in the writings of Pierre Poiret, Joh
Edwards, and Isaac Watts. Though these me
set forth dispensational schemes, it was the min
istry and writings of John Nelson Darby in th
nineteenth century that systematized the con
cept. His work was the foundation for later dis
pensationalists such as James H. Brookes, Jame
M. Gray, C. I. Scofield, and L. S. Chafer.

Other Dispensational Schemes. Some cov
enant theologians (those who view God operatin
under a single covenant of grace from the fa
on) use the concept of different dispensation
but as part of the covenant of grace. The OT an
NT dispensations are readily recognized, thoug
some add dispensations related to the call o
Abraham and the giving of the Mosaic law (e.g.
Charles Hodge). However, the unifying feature i
the covenant of grace and salvation under it, s
that any changes from one dispensation t
another are in the nature of anticipation in th
OT and accomplishment in the NT, rather tha
distinctive and actual changes in administratio

Though there are several branches of ultra
dispensationalism, they are characterized b
teaching the existence of two churches withi

the book of Acts. One was the Jewish church which began at Pentecost and ended when the second, the body of Christ church, began with the ministry of the apostle Paul at either Acts 9, 13, or 28). Ultradispensationalists often do not practice water baptism but usually observe the Lord's Supper. C. C. RYRIE

See also ULTRADISPENSATIONALISM; DARBY, JOHN NELSON.

Bibliography. C. B. Bass, *Backgrounds to Dispensationalism;* D. P. Fuller, *Gospel and Law;* C. N. Kraus, *Dispensationalism in America;* C. C. Ryrie, *Dispensationalism Today;* E. Sauer, *From Eternity to Eternity;* C. I. Scofield, ed., *The New Scofield Reference Bible.*

Divine Presence. *See* PRESENCE, DIVINE.

Divinity of Christ. *See* CHRISTOLOGY.

Divorce. Although there are few references to divorce in the early centuries of the Christian era, the evidence points toward a rejection of divorce with right of remarriage by the early fathers. By the sixth century the Eastern church had developed a tradition of allowing divorce with right of remarriage for a variety of causes, and the Eastern Orthodox tradition today has introduced the concept of the "moral death" of a marriage. The Western church, however, held firmly to the view that marriage was indissoluble. Augustine, to whom we owe the development of the view of marriage as a sacrament, believed that marriage was indissoluble, but in the sense of a moral obligation of permanence: marriage *should not* be dissolved. The medieval schoolmen in the West, however, developed a sacramental view of marriage as indissoluble in an absolute sense: valid marriage *could not* be dissolved. This view prevailed in the Roman Church, and is held by Christians of Catholic traditions. In the Middle Ages, alongside the rejection of divorce, a complex set of procedures for dispensation and annulment grew up by which burdensome marriages were dissolved, thus evading or overcoming the law of indissolubility.

The continental Reformers sought to return to a more biblical understanding of the nature of marriage. They rejected the elevation of marriage to the status of sacrament, and they disagreed with the absolute indissolubility of marriage. They objected to the annulment procedures that were bringing the divine ideal of permanence into disrepute. They believed that some parts of the NT allowed divorce with right of remarriage in certain circumstances.

The Reformers in England inherited ideas both from the Western Catholic tradition and from the continental Reformers. Had Cranmer's proposals for a revised canon law ever reached the statute book, they would have included provision of divorce for adultery, malicious desertion, prolonged absence without news, attempts against the partner's life, and cruelty. Severe punishment for adultery was prescribed but the innocent partner was allowed to remarry. Since Reformation times the Church of England has exhibited the tension of two opposing views. There has been a strong indissolubilist tradition, forbidding divorce on any grounds and so requiring the strictest discipline of any church. There has also been a significant nonindissolubilist influence. In the seventeenth century there were a number of divorces procured by special Act of Parliament, with subsequent remarriage in church. This tension still exists and underlies the recent Anglican reports "Marriage, Divorce and the Church" (1971) and "Marriage and the Church's Task" (1978), both of which (the second by a majority) recommended that the Church of England should relax its present strict convocation rule that no person with a former partner still living may be married in church, although divorced persons with special permission are welcome to Holy Communion.

Both sides believe that they are upholding a long-standing Christian tradition. Furthermore, both would claim biblical backing for their case. Indissolubilists insist that Jesus affirms the indissolubility of marriage in his teaching, forbidding divorce, thus abrogating the OT law. The nonindissolubilists believe that the NT does concede permission for divorce, in line with the Mosaic ruling, as a concession to the sinfulness of the human heart.

OT Background. On the assumption that the people of preexilic ancient Israel shared the attitudes and customs of their contemporary neighbors, it would appear (from *ca.* eighteenth century B.C. Mesopotamia: the laws of Hammurabi and the laws of Eshunna) that marriage was commonly arranged by parents; that financial considerations showed that marriage was intended to be lifelong; that husbands expected fidelity from their wives and could exact the death penalty for adultery. Divorce, although possible, was rare except to the very rich, because the cost was prohibitively high. In postexilic times (in comparison with fifth century Egypt) the customs were similar to earlier practices, although the cost of divorce had fallen; the death penalty was not exacted; and women as well as men could sue for divorce.

The Pentateuchal laws governing sexual relationships appear to be framed to preserve the view that in marriage a man and a woman are united together in what is intended to be a permanent, lifelong, exclusive union. It is from this context that we must examine the central OT paragraph concerning divorce, Deut. 24:1–4, which forms the background to some of the material in the Gospels.

The older translations make it appear that a man is *required* to divorce his wife if "some indecency" is found in her, but this is not so. The RSV agrees with modern commentators that this legislation is granting a permission, not giving a command. Indeed, the main point of the paragraph is concerned with remarriage: a woman who has been divorced by her husband because of some "indecency" (probably some serious sexual misconduct short of adultery), and who subsequently marries another who then later also divorces her, is not permitted to return to her first husband. The paragraph recognizes that divorces happen, though it does not command or encourage them. It also regulates divorce (the husband has to give the wife a bill of divorcement) to provide some protection to the wife. The curious prohibition about subsequent remarriage to the first husband may indicate a curb on male cruelty if there was some custom of "lending out" wives for a time.

It is important to note that the law is concerned with divorce and not only with separation. The word "divorce" in the phrase "bill of divorcement" is related to the word for hewing down trees, even cutting off heads. It indicates the severing of what was once a living union. Divorce, then, is a kind of amputation. It cannot happen without damage to the partners concerned. This OT legislation, therefore, affords recognition of the fact that marriages are sometimes broken, although divorce is not approved; it acknowledges the need of civil legislation for the sake of society (bill of divorcement); it serves to protect the divorced woman and to legislate against cruelty. In its own negative way, therefore, it is seeking to preserve the divine ideal for marriage as far as possible within a sinful world.

Looking briefly at postexilic practice in Israel, one finds possible hints that the practice of divorce had become easier: thus Malachi needs to reaffirm God's intention for marriage by reminding his readers that God hates divorce (2:16).

NT Teaching. Divorce is discussed in the NT in a context where both the OT law was held dear (although it was variously interpreted by different schools of Pharisees) and Greco-Roman customs were exercising some influence (thus Mark 10:12 coincides with the Roman permission for women to initiate divorce as well as men, but Matt. 19:9, written for a Jewish readership, does not say this).

In Jesus' day there was a dispute current between the Pharisaic schools about the interpretation of Deut. 24:1–4 and about what constituted permissible grounds for divorce. (This lies behind the way Matthew frames the question in 19:3: "Is it lawful to divorce one's wife *for any cause?*" cf. Mark 10:2.) The Shammaite Pharisees interpreted the Deuteronomic legislation in a strict way: divorce was permitted only for serious sexual sin. The more liberal Hillelite Pharisees (with whom Jesus might have been expected to side) understood "if she finds no favor in his eyes" (Deut. 24:1) to be permission to divorce for the most trivial of reasons (even if she spoils a dish for him). It may well be that even the Shammaites did not always practice what they preached (cf. Matt. 23:4), so that divorce on fairly trivial grounds may not have been uncommon in the time of Jesus—although rare by modern standards.

It seems very unlikely that in the time of Christ the Jewish courts were allowed to carry out the death penalty for adultery; as far back as Hosea's day the exaction of the death penalty for adultery does not seem to have been operative. In the NT it is assumed that divorce is the only penalty for adultery. Indeed, Israelite courts could *compel* a Jewish husband to divorce his wife on certain grounds. It is certain, therefore, that Jesus' hearers would have assumed that the law of divorce was relevant to the crime of adultery, and highly probable they would have assumed that divorce after adultery was mandatory. If Jesus was introducing anything radically new, we would expect this to be made clear.

The Synoptic material has given rise to considerable dispute among commentators. In the first place, Jesus responds to the Pharisees' question about the grounds for divorce by referring back to God's intention in creation (Matt. 19:4; Mark 10:6). In contrast to much of the church's concentration throughout its history on what we may call the externals of marriage—legalities, disciplines, ceremonies—the primary biblical emphasis is on marriage as a covenant relationship. Marriage language is used to describe God's covenant relationship with his people; God's relationship with his people, Christ's with his church, is given as the pattern for marriage relationships. A covenant is a personal relationship within a publicly known structure, based on promises given and accepted. It is to this personal relationship that Gen. 2:24 (to which Jesus refers in Matt. 19:5) points when it summarizes marriage thus: "leaving father and mother" (public declaration; the social dimension to marriage); "cleaving" (the word of committed covenant love-faithfulness); "becoming one flesh" (a complete unitary partnership of persons in relation, symbolized by and deepened through sexual union). Jesus sets this verse in the theological context of Gen. 1:27: the creation of man in the image of God, male and female. In other words, marriage answers to God's creation pattern for personal sexual relationship. A marriage is intended to be a relationship, healing and growing and maturing through time, a "harvest of the Spirit," which is patterned on and in turn displays something of God's covenant relationship. It thus requires predictability, continuity, reliability—that is, permanence. God's creation ideal, Jesus affirms, is for a lifelong, exclusive union which should not be broken.

Secondly, Jesus brings divorce and remarriage under the heading of adultery (Matt. 19:9; cf. 5:27–32). The Pharisees had trivialized divorce by reducing their concerns to the level of grounds for divorce and to the need for a certificate. Jesus says that in the light of God's creation intention every unfaithfulness, every breaking of the commitment of "one flesh," every "putting away" (*apolyō*) of one's partner is sin. The commandment "You shall not commit adultery" means "You shall not break the one flesh." Divorce, therefore, is covenant unfaithfulness; it breaks this command.

Some Christians believe that Jesus is speaking here not of divorce as such but of separation. The emphasis would then be on remarriage as adultery in the physical sense. Jesus is tightening up the Mosaic concession; he is being even more strict than the Shammaites. Divorce is not permitted. Remarriage is adultery. This is the reason for the shocked reaction of the disciples to this teaching (Matt. 19:10). Other Christians believe that Jesus really *is* talking about divorce and not just separation. It does not appear likely that he is using *apolyō* in the sense of separation without right of remarriage. Such separation was unknown in Jesus' day. If he was using the word in a new and restricted sense, particularly in a discussion of Deut. 24 in which remarriage (albeit restricted) was assumed—prompted by disagreements between Shammai and Hillel (both of whom also assumed remarriage)—would Jesus have been so understood without further explanation? It seems a natural assumption that divorce in the Synoptic material includes right of remarriage and that the sin of adulterous covenant-breaking is the sin of "putting away" one's partner.

To see divorce as covenant-breaking is thus to see it as a serious and sinful act. It is arguable that in circumstances in which sin traps us such that none of the ways open to us is good, divorce may in some circumstances be seen as a "lesser evil" choice. However, taking the divine covenant as our guide, divorce is never obligatory; even the sin of sexual unfaithfulness (Hosea's wife) can be an occasion for forgiveness and reconciliation.

The argument thus far is that two principles need to be held together: on one hand, the divine ideal for the permanence of the marriage relationship as a covenant partnership of personal ("one flesh") communion, growing by the grace of the Spirit to be increasingly in fact what it is initially in intention; on the other hand, a recognition that when breakdowns occur, all attempts at reconciliation having failed, in some circumstances caused by what Jesus called "hardness of heart" (Matt. 19:8) divorce as a concession may be a permitted last resort.

These two principles are expressed in different ways in the OT and in the Synoptic Gospels. They are also to be found in Paul. In Rom. 7:1ff. and I Cor. 7:10 the apostle gives the divine rule: marriage is permanent. But there is a small parenthetical concession acknowledging the reality of separation in I Cor. 7:11, and there seems to be a permission for divorce in the case of a Christian deserted by an unbelieving partner in I Cor. 7:15 ("the brother or sister is not bound").

Grounds for Divorce. There is further disagreement among Christians concerning the grounds on which divorce, if countenanced at all, may be permitted. At this point we must consider the exceptive clause in Matt. 19:9 and 5:32 (except on the ground of *porneia*). There is considerable disagreement about the meaning of this phrase, although it seems most likely that *porneia* refers to serious sexual sin, including adultery. But what function is this clause serving in Matthew, and why do Mark, Luke, and Paul not refer to it? There was an earlier view among biblical specialists that the clause was not authentic, but this has largely been abandoned: it is present in the best texts. The best explanation seems to be that Matthew, with his particular concern with law and order for his Jewish readership, recognized the civil requirement on a Jewish husband to divorce his wife if she was unfaithful to him. Mark and Luke give us the rule without the exception (which may have been assumed). Matthew is careful to include the exception. The exceptive clause points to the sort of concession to which Deut. 24:1–4 also referred. It recognizes that, despite being a sinful departure from God's intention for marriage, divorce may sometimes be permitted in a sinful world.

Is Jesus giving prescriptive legislation here? In other words, is divorce permitted only for *porneia?* The Deuteronomic law was framed largely to prevent *cruelty;* Matthew points us to *unlawful sexual misbehavior;* Paul seems to allow divorce as a consequence of *desertion* in some circumstances. These may well serve as paradigms in clarifying the extreme seriousness with which the question of divorce should be approached. They suggest the sort of circumstances which might allow the moral permissibility of divorce as a last resort. Recognition of the persistent "hardness of heart" in an as yet sin-affected society requires recognition of the human impossibility of healing some broken relationships. Divorce in some extreme circumstances with repentance, can be allowed as a lesser evil. Such a course inevitably presses the question, "Is it lawful to divorce one's wife for any cause?" The danger is that we may lose sight of Jesus' answer.

Pastoral Implications. If it is right to suggest that the Bible allows divorce as a lesser evil in some circumstances, though it always stands under divine judgment, what are the pastoral implications of this view?

In the first place we must work toward helping one another grow characters capable of committed love-faithfulness if there are to be growing numbers of marriages which display something of the nature of God's covenant. Secondly, the Christian community must become known as a context in which help is available to move marriages toward being environments of healing and nurture and growth in personal and mutual fulfillment. The church must be a haven of support for those whose relationships are in difficulties and an agency of reconciliation and of the ministry of forgiveness whenever possible.

When marriages are broken, however, the tasks of the church are primarily twofold. The first is acceptance. For too long the primary stance of the church toward divorced people has been one of rejection. This is not to say that church discipline is unimportant, nor is it to say that the church does not have a prophetic role in making clear God's opposition to divorce. But the Christian community is called also to display the character of God which is seen in the acceptance of sinners as persons, whatever their failure, and helping them toward a renewed experience of God's restoring grace. The second task is that of support and guidance in aiding divorced persons in their future. This will mean emotional and material care, and possibly considerable help over time with the complexities of readjustment and feelings of guilt and bereavement. It may for some involve searching out the rights and wrongs in the thorny question of remarriage.

D. J. Atkinson

See also Separation, Marital; Marriage, Theology of; Remarriage.

Bibliography. L. Boettner, *Divorce;* D. R. Catchpole, "The Synoptic Divorce Material as a Traditio-Historical Problem," *BJRL* 57; H. Crouzel, "Remarriage after Divorce in the Primitive Church," *ITQ* 38:21; J. Dominian, *Marital Breakdown* and *Marriage Faith and Love;* F. Dulley, *How Christian Is Divorce and Remarriage?* R. J. Erlich, "The Indissolubility of Marriage as a Theological Problem," *SJT* 23:291; M. Geldard, "Jesus' Teaching on Divorce," *Chu* 92:134; C. Jones, ed., *For Better, For Worse;* K. E. Kirk, *Marriage and Divorce;* J. Murray, *Divorce;* O. M. T. O'Donovan, *Marriage and Permanence;* J. H. Olthuis, *I Pledge You My Troth;* H. Oppenheimer, *The Marriage Bond;* J. P. Sampley, *And the Two Shall Become One Flesh;* E. Schillebeeckx, *Marriage: Human Reality and Saving Mystery;* D. W. Shaner, *A Christian View of Divorce;* J. R. W. Stott, "The Biblical Teaching on Divorce," *Chu* 85:165; H. Thielicke, *The Ethics of Sex;* B. Thornes and J. Collard, *Who Divorces?* W. R. Winnett, *Divorce and Remarriage and Anglicanism* and *Divorce and the Church;* D. Atkinson, *To Have and to Hold* and *Tasks for the Church in the Marriage Debate;* A. K. Mitchell, *Someone to Turn to: Experiences of Help before Divorce.*

Docetism. A term used to refer to a theological perspective among some in the early church who regarded the sufferings and the human aspects of Christ as imaginary or apparent instead of being part of a real incarnation. The basic thesis of such docetics was that if Christ suffered he was not divine, and if he was God he could not suffer. The combination of the two natures, Son of David and Son of God, affirmed by Paul in Rom. 1:3–4 was apparently already under attack in the Johannine community (see I John 4:2; II John 7). Docetic thinking became an integral part of the perspectives of Gnostics, who viewed Jesus as the alien messenger from outside the present evil world and one who was untouched by the evil creator. This alien Jesus came to awaken Gnostics to their destiny outside the realm of creation. While the framers of the Apostles' and Nicene Creeds were opposed to docetic teaching and clearly assumed the two natures of Jesus, the drafters of the Definition of Chalcedon (A.D. 451) made explicit the Christian teaching concerning Jesus Christ as "truly God and truly man."

G. L. Borchert

See also Chalcedon, Council of; Gnosticism.

Bibliography. J. N. D. Kelly, *Early Christian Doctrines.*

Dodd, Charles Harold (1884–1973). British Congregational minister and NT scholar. A graduate of Oxford, he served as lecturer in NT at Mansfield College, Oxford (1915–30), Rylands

Professor of Biblical Criticism and Exegesis at the University of Manchester (1930–36), and Norris-Hulse Professor of Divinity at Cambridge (1936–49). Following his retirement from formal academic life he served as general director of the translation committee for the New English Bible.

Dodd towered over British NT scholarship during his academic career and even in retirement. His work on the parables (1935) set the tone in the English-speaking world as Julicher's had done in Germany. His interpretation of the teaching of Jesus in terms of "realized eschatology" and his identification of a common outline of the early church's kerygma (in *The Apostolic Preaching and Its Developments,* 1936) focused the attention of NT theologians for several decades. In *According to the Scriptures* (1952) he stressed the unity of the NT writers in their handling of the OT and linked this to Jesus' teaching. In his commentary on Romans (1932) and elsewhere he argued that the biblical concept of the wrath of God should be understood as an impersonal process of retribution in human history rather than as the divine reaction to the sin of humankind. Along similar lines he rejected the idea of propitiation as essentially unbiblical. His *The Interpretation of the Fourth Gospel* (1953) and *Historical Tradition in the Fourth Gospel* (1963) represent the apex of his scholarly achievement and are perhaps the most important studies of the Gospel of John ever written. W. W. Gasque

See also Realized Eschatology.

Bibliography. F. W. Dillistone, *C. H. Dodd: Interpreter of the NT;* W. D. Davies and D. Daube, eds., *The Background of the NT and Its Eschatology.*

Doddridge, Philip (1702–1751). English Nonconformist minister, educator, author, and hymn writer. Born in London of pious Dissenter parents, Doddridge received a typical eighteenth century education at home, in grammar school, and at a private academy. He declined an opportunity to attend Oxford or Cambridge as preparation for service in the Church of England; instead he became an unordained Nonconformist minister in Kibworth, Leicestershire, in 1723. After transferring to Market Harborough, Northamptonshire, he joined with Isaac Watts and several other preachers in establishing an academy, which was modeled after the one he had attended in Kibworth and to which he was appointed head tutor. In 1729 he was ordained minister to a large Independent (Congregational) congregation in Northampton, where he also moved his academy. Here he remained until his death.

Doddridge's academy, predominantly a training school for the ministry, became one of the most prominent Dissenter academies in the eighteenth century, providing generations of preachers for Nonconformist churches. He encouraged the greatest freedom of inquiry among his students, insisting only that Scripture was the genuine standard of truth but exposing them to a wide spectrum of theological points. This liberal tradition did not stem the tide toward antitrinitarianism, and Doddridge himself did not please his fellow strictly orthodox Independents with his "sentiments on the head of the Trinity." He sought eagerly for Christian unity among his fellow Nonconformists. His friendship with John Wesley and the Countess of Huntingdon was considered unusual for his day, and his "middle way" between Calvinism and Arminianism identified him with the "Baxterian" tradition in theology.

His best-known theological work, *The Rise and Progress of Religion in the Soul,* reminiscent of Richard Baxter's works of an earlier generation, ranks with William Law's *Serious Call* as a remarkable display of evangelical commitment, spiritual perceptivity, and freedom from contention. He also wrote a six-volume paraphrase and commentary on the NT entitled *The Family Expositor,* which was extremely popular and reprinted numerous times. One of his best-known hymns, "Oh Happy Day, That Fixed My Choice," carries sentiments that can properly be ascribed to its author. H. P. Ippel

Bibliography. G. F. Nuttall, *Philip Doddridge; Correspondence and Diary of Doddridge,* 5 vols.; *Works,* 8 vols., contains his *Life* by J. Orton.

Dogma. In the NT the Greek *dogma* refers to a decree, ordinance, decision, or command (Luke 2:1; Acts 16:4; 17:7; Eph. 2:15; Col. 2:14; Heb. 11:23). In late Greek philosophy legal usage was subsumed under *dogma* as the doctrinal propositions that expressed the official viewpoint of a particular teacher or philosophical school.

Early Christian theology eventually came to use the term in the same way. Basil the Great in the middle of the fourth century distinguished between the Christian kerygma and Christian dogmas in the sense of propositions of faith. The church's first sanctioning of "dogmatic" statements was in 325 at the Council of Nicaea, where the consubstantiality of the Son with the Father was stated as a confession of faith.

In the Middle Ages the Roman Catholic Church developed the view of the *depositum fidei* ("deposit of faith"), in which the church was seen as having been entrusted with a certain treasury of truths whose ramifications could be rightfully developed by the church. Eventually, through the Council of Trent (1545–63) and the First Vatican Council (1870), the church's dogmatic pronouncements came to be considered as infallible. Thus, dogma was seen in Roman Catholicism even prior to the Reformation as a truth whose objective content is revealed by God and defined by the church. This is done through a church council, by a pope, or from the dogma's general propagation in church teachings.

Since the Reformation, Protestantism has rejected the association of dogma with infallible ecclesiastical pronouncements. In Reformation thought all dogmas must be tested against the revelation of God in Holy Scripture. As Karl Barth observed, "The Word of God is above dogma as the heavens are above the earth" (*Church Dogmatics,* I/1, 306). Also, for the Reformers faith is personal trust and relationship with God through Jesus Christ, not primarily assent to what the church says must be believed. Dogma has come to mean an expression of doctrinal truth that has achieved ecclesiastical status yet without claims to infallibility.

The 1845 work by John Henry Newman, *An Essay on the Development of Christian Doctrine,* was a seminal piece in raising questions about the traditions, developments, and continuities of Christian ideas. German scholars such as Ferdinand Christian Baur and Adolf Harnack subjected the historical developments of Christian dogmas and doctrines to critical scrutiny. From different perspectives so also did three Scottish theologians: William Cunningham, Robert Rainy, and James Orr.

Karl Barth reinterpreted the old Roman Catholic usage in modern Protestantism by defining dogma as "the agreement of Church proclamation with the revelation attested in Holy Scripture" (*Church Dogmatics,* I/1, 304). Dogmas are the forms in which dogma appears. Dogma becomes ultimately an "eschatological concept" since no human formulations will ever completely agree with the Word of God prior to the final kingdom of God, according to Barth. Dogmatic inquiry can be freed, however, to work with individual dogmas and to appreciate them as attempts to express the truth of revelation.

D. K. McKim

See also Dogmatics; Systematic Theology.

Bibliography. H. Berkhof, *Christian Faith;* B. Lohse, *A Short History of Christian Doctrine;* J. Orr, *The Progress of Dogma;* J. Pelikan, *Historical Theology;* W. E. Reiser, *What Are They Saying about Dogma?* R. Seeberg, *Text-book of the History of Doctrines,* P. Toon, *The Development of Doctrine in the Church;* O. Weber, *Foundations of Dogmatics,* I.

Dogmatics. That branch of theology which attempts to express the beliefs and doctrines (dogmas) of the Christian faith—to set forth "the whole counsel of God" (Acts 20:27) in an organized or systematic way. Since no dogmatic theologian deals only with the "dogmas" of the church, this discipline is now more commonly called "systematic theology" or simply "theology."

The terms "dogmatics" and "systematic theology" are used in both a broad and a narrow sense. In the broad sense the terms designate one of the four branches of theology, thus distinguishing systematic theology from biblical, historical, and practical theology. In the narrow sense the terms are used within that one branch of theology to distinguish the discipline from the history of doctrine, symbolics (the study of creeds and confessions), apologetics, and ethics. This article concentrates on the narrow sense of dogmatics (systematics).

Dogmatics or systematic theology generally deals with the doctrines of revelation (prolegomena), God (theology proper), man (anthropology), the person and work of Jesus Christ (Christology), the Holy Spirit and the application of salvation (soteriology), the church and the means of grace (ecclesiology), and the intermediate state and the second coming of Christ (eschatology). Even when using different terms and organizational arrangements, all systematic or dogmatic theologians deal with these subjects.

Dogmatic or systematic theologians are generally concerned with the biblical sources and support of the doctrines of faith, with the history of the development of such doctrines, with contrasting dogmas from other faith communities, and with the views of other theologians dealing with those doctrines. Because this discipline is concerned with the whole as well as with specific doctrines, systematic theology always reflects a particular faith community—Roman Catholic, Eastern Orthodox, Lutheran, Reformed, liberal, neo-orthodox, existentialist, etc.

The term "dogmatics" arose after the middle of the seventeenth century and was probably first used in 1659 as the title of a book by L. Reinhardt. Before that, when writing theology which appealed to Scripture, theologians used such terms as "sacred page" or "sacred doctrine." The most famous of the systematic theologians in the patristic period were Origen, Augustine, and John of Damascus, the latter representing the Greek Orthodox tradition. In the Middle Ages scholastic theology was represented by Peter Lombard and especially Thomas Aquinas. Philip Melanchthon reflected Protestant Lutheranism in the *Loci Communes,* while John Calvin expressed Reformed theology in his *Institutes of the Christian Religion.* In the following two centuries dogmatic works in the Protestant tradition multiplied.

The father of theological liberalism, Friedrich Schleiermacher, called his systematic work *The Christian Faith* (1821) to indicate his emphasis on the subjective faith of the believer rather than on church dogma or God's revelation. Neoorthodox theologians, partly in reaction to liberalism, again turned to the term "dogmatics." Emil Brunner published a three-volume *Dogmatics* and Karl Barth a thirteen-volume *Church Dogmatics.* However, Paul Tillich, an existentialist, produced a three-volume *Systematic Theology.*

A new theology of history in the Protestant tradition is evident in the systematic monographs of Wolfhart Pannenberg and Jürgen Moltmann. Karl Rahner and Hans Küng have written from new Roman Catholic perspectives. Donald G. Bloesch in the United States, Hendrikus Berkhof in the Netherlands, and Otto Weber and Helmut Thielicke in Germany have recently published dogmatic/systematic volumes.

Reformed theologians have been especially productive in this area during the nineteenth and twentieth centuries, some calling their works "dogmatics" and others "systematic theology." The Dutch theologians Abraham Kuyper, Herman Bavinck, and G. C. Berkouwer deserve mention, as do the Americans Charles Hodge, Louis Berkhof, John Murray, Herman Hoeksema, James Oliver Buswell, Jr., and Cornelius Van Til.

Francis Pieper has written from the perspective of confessional Lutheranism and Augustus Hopkins Strong from the Baptist tradition. Lewis Sperry Chafer wrote a dogmatics from the dispensationalist standpoint. F. H. KLOOSTER

See also DOGMA; SYSTEMATIC THEOLOGY.

Bibliography. J. J. Davis, ed., *The Necessity of Systematic Theology;* A. Lecerf, *An Introduction to Reformed Dogmatics;* L. Berkhof, *The History of Christian Doctrines;* G. P. Fisher, *History of Christian Doctrine;* G. Ebeling, *The Study of Theology;* P. Schaff, *Theological Propaedeutic: A General Introduction to the Study of Theology.*

Döllinger, Johann Joseph Ignaz von (1799–1890). German church historian and theologian. Ordained a Roman Catholic priest in 1822, he taught church history at Aschaffenburg (1823–26) and at the University of Munich (1826–72). Linguist and versatile scholar with a remarkable memory, Döllinger became part of a group in Munich that steadily upheld Catholic principles in society. Gradually his views, seen notably in *Reformation* (1845–48) and *Luther* (1851), took on a growing nationalism. He advocated a Catholic Church in Germany headed by a German metropolitan and encouraged the growth of a Catholic press. His protests against increasing papal absolutism and the revival of scholastic theology brought him into confrontation with the Jesuits, who tended to label opinions other than their own as heretical. His fears were confirmed when the immaculate conception (1854) was pronounced and the Syllabus of Errors (1864) published. He was drawn into the Vatican I controversy about papal prerogatives, wrote vigorously against them, but ruined his case by overstatement. He was excommunicated (1871) soon after publication of his *The Pope and the Council* (1869–70), was removed from his chair, but continued attendance at Mass.

Hailed as one of the organizers of the Old Catholic Church, he lost enthusiasm for it when it departed from some Roman practices (priestly celibacy, confession). Roman Catholic scholars have played down Döllinger's originality by linking his ideas with Gallicanism and Febronianism, but even they concede the weighty contribution he made in urging a historical approach to theology. J. D. DOUGLAS

See also FEBRONIANISM; GALLICANISM.

Donatism. A schismatic movement arising in the fourth century. In its first stage it was a North African expression of a doctrine of the church. In its second stage it was a popular rebellion that pitted the Berber and landless against the landed Latin Catholic elite. Donatus, schismatic Bishop of Carthage (313–47), sometimes spoken of as Donatus the Great, directed the schismatic church with vigor and a shrewd use of ethnic and social factors until the Roman emperor exiled him to Gaul or Spain in 347; he died there *ca.* 350. Parmenian, also an able leader, succeeded him.

Donatism grew out of the teachings of Tertullian and Cyprian. Following these two, Donatists taught that a priest's part in sacraments was substantial (he had to be holy and in proper standing with the church for the sacrament to be valid) rather than simply instrumental. The latter was the view of Rome and of Augustine, Bishop of Hippo and chief anti-Donatist spokesman. To Donatus the church was a visible society of the elect separate from the world, whereas Augustine developed the Catholic concept of an invisible church within the visible. Donatists also had a fierce reverence for every word of Scripture; therefore to pour a libation to the emperor or to surrender a Bible to Roman persecutors to burn was to be a heretic or a *traditore.* Any who had done so were forever outside the visible church unless they were rebaptized (being saved all over again). Augustine and the Catholics accepted *traditores* as they did any other backsliders; they were welcomed back into communion upon proper penance prescribed by their bishop. Donatists saw themselves as the only true church and Augustine and his Catholics as a mixed multitude.

The actual schism followed Diocletian's persecution (303–5), which was particularly widespread in North Africa. There priests and bishops were often permitted to escape death by surrendering Scriptures and regalia to authorities. In 311 Caecilian was elected and consecrated as Bishop of Carthage. Religiously the consecration was considered invalid because Caecilian himself may have handed over Scriptures for burning and because one of his three confirming bishops, Felix of Aptonga, was a *traditore*. Politically the consecration of Caecilian was suspect because the primate of Numidia, Secundus of Tigisi, was not involved, and for the previous forty years Numidia had claimed the right of ordaining the Bishop of Carthage. Secundus arrived in Carthage with seventy Numidian bishops, declared Caecilian's election invalid, and elected Majorinus as rival Bishop of Carthage. Majorinus died within two years, and Donatus was consecrated in his place in 313.

Constantine, after trying councils and conciliation, turned to severe oppression in 317; but when that failed he granted Donatists liberty of worship in 321. In 371 Donatists joined the anti-Roman revolt of Firmus. In 388 the fanatical Donatist Bishop Optatus of Thamugadi and organized bands of Donatist terrorists, called Circumcellions, led a revolt under Geldon that lasted to the deaths of Optatus and Geldon in 398. Donatism survived until the seventh century Muslim conquest of North Africa obliterated Catholics and Donatists alike. V. L. WALTER

See also AUGUSTINE OF HIPPO; CYPRIAN; TERTULLIAN.

Bibliography. W. H. C. Frend, *The Donatist Church;* W. J. Sparrow-Simpson, *St. Augustine and African Church Divisions;* R. A. Markus, "Donatism: The Last Phase," in *Studies in Church History,* I.

Doorkeeper. *See* MINOR ORDERS.

Dooyeweerd, Herman (1894–1977). Dutch Reformed philosopher. A graduate of the Free University of Amsterdam, Dooyeweerd worked as a civil servant until 1922, when he was appointed assistant director of the Kuyper Institute in The Hague, where he was responsible for editing the antirevolutionary *Staatkunde,* a monthly journal of the institute which dealt with a broad range of political and economic issues. In 1926 he was appointed to the chair of legal philosophy at the Free University, a position which he occupied until his retirement in 1965. Dooyeweerd is best known for his four-volume work, *A New Critique of Theoretical Thought* (1953–58).

Dooyeweerd drew his inspiration from the Dutch Calvinist tradition as developed during the nineteenth century by Groen van Prinsterer and Abraham Kuyper. In 1935 Dooyeweerd and his brother-in-law, D. H. Th. Vollenhoven, played a major role in the establishment of the Association for Calvinistic Philosophy and began the publication of the academic journal *Philosophia Reformata.* As Dooyeweerd's thought matured, he chose to replace the name Calvinistic Philosophy with the simpler title, Christian Philosophy. Although in many ways his attempt to establish a Christian philosophy has been neglected by the philosophical establishment and many Christian groups, Dooyeweerd nevertheless generated a small but dedicated following. His most widely known pupils were probably Hans Rookmaaker and Cornelius Van Til, while Francis Schaeffer served as the popularizer of his ideas.

Dooyeweerd was an innovative thinker who boldly faced the intellectual challenges of his day. His writing demands concentration and a familiarity with the intellectual history of the Western world, which he boldly challenges from a Christian perspective. The best-known part of his work is his transcendental critique of Western thought, which seeks to subject the Western philosophical tradition to a thorough examination. "Why is it," Dooyeweerd asks, "if philosophy is based upon reason, the various schools of philosophy can never agree with each other?" In answer to this question he argues that religious commitments rather than unbiased reason underlie the thought of all men. Having established this point and shown, to his own satisfaction at least, the weaknesses of various philosophical schools, Dooyeweerd goes on to develop a Christian philosophy that will be able to maintain a unified view of the world. To do this he constructs a complex system of hierarchically ordered interrelated realms of spheres which he claims are foundational to all reality and which exist in an increasingly complex structural framework.

Dooyeweerd's writings are to be compared to those of Kant, with whose philosophy he is in continuous debate. He rejected the analytic/synthetic distinction some thirty years before the Harvard philosopher W. V. O. Quine did, and was discussing the importance of what Thomas Kuhn was to call paradigms long before Kuhn did so. Another contemporary issue dealt with by Dooyeweerd is the sociology of knowledge.

Here again his contribution has been largely neglected.

Although many criticisms can be made of Dooyeweerd's work, he appears to be the only thinker nurtured by a conservative Christian community who has attempted to challenge the intellectual ideas of his day while remaining loyal to his religious roots. The value of his work lies not in the solutions he proposes but rather in the foundation he has laid and the example he provides of the Christian thinker who is unafraid of creatively interacting with modern thought.

I. HEXHAM

See also KUYPER, ABRAHAM.

Bibliography. L. Kalsbeek, *Contours of a Christian Philosophy;* A. L. Conradie, *The Neo-Calvinistic Concept of Philosophy;* V. Brummer, *Transcendental Criticism and Christian Philosophy;* R. Nash, *Dooyeweerd and the Amsterdam Philosophy;* J. M. Spier, *An Introduction to Christian Philosophy.*

Dorner, Isaac August (1809–1884). German Lutheran theologian. Born at Neuhausen, Würtemberg, Germany, the son of a Lutheran pastor, Dorner studied philosophy and theology at the University of Tübingen from 1827 to 1832. From 1832 to 1834 he acted as parish assistant to his father, and in the latter year became a teaching fellow at Tübingen, receiving promotion to an associate professorship four years later. In 1839 he accepted a full professorship at Kiel, moving in 1843 to Königsberg, in 1847 to Bonn, and in 1853 to Göttingen. In 1862 he was appointed to a chair at Berlin, where he taught till his retirement in 1883.

Dorner's importance for theology is threefold. (1) He was a cofounder of the journal *Jahrbucher für deutscher Theologie* in 1856 and was active in this publication until it was discontinued in 1878. (2) He wrote learned treatises on various aspects of theological history, particularly *History of the Development of the Doctrine of the Person of Christ* (5 vols., 1846–50), and *The History of Protestant Theology* (2 vols., 1867). (3) He expounded his constructive theology in *A System of Christian Doctrine* (4 vols., 1879–81).

In his theological system Dorner emphasized the central importance for Christianity of the person and work of Jesus Christ, the divine-human Savior. He interpreted the personal development of Jesus Christ during the days of his flesh in a distinctive way. Starting from the premise that God and man are not unlike but akin, he described the incarnation as the Logos, the divine principle of revelation and self-bestowal, himself entering into Jesus in his human nature, without partaking of nature's sinfulness, however, for he held Jesus to be sinless, thus creating a new humanity, destined to be the head of a redeemed human race, "the progenitor of spiritual humanity." Thus Dorner conceived of Jesus Christ's incarnation not as something completed at once but as continually increasing throughout his earthly life, inasmuch as God the Logos ever grasped and appropriated such new aspects of growth as were generated by Jesus' truly human development.

N. V. HOPE

Bibliography. C. Welch, *God and Incarnation in Mid-Nineteenth Century German Theology; APTR,* 1863, pp. 42–64, 251–80, 406–14.

Dort, Synod of (1618–1619). An international church assembly called by the States General of the Netherlands to settle certain ecclesiastical and doctrinal matters that had been troubling the Reformed Church of the Netherlands. It consisted of thirty-five pastors and a number of elders from the Dutch churches, five theological professors from the Netherlands, eighteen deputies from the States General, and twenty-seven foreign delegates.

The problems that faced the synod were complex. First, it had to deal with the ancient problem of Erastianism, the control of the church by the state. The Dutch church was by confession Calvinistic. It was Calvin's conviction that the church should be independent of the state while cooperating with it. By 1554 he had won that battle in Geneva, but until the time of Dort, and later, the Dutch church had in it a strong element, including such leaders as Oldenbarneveldt, Grotius, and Coolhaas, which favored state control over the church. Thus even the Prince of Orange in 1575 gave an order that consistories were to be appointed by local magistrates, a view which had wide support.

A second problem with which Dort had to wrestle was an anticonfessional humanism that was more hellenistic than biblical in spirit. Erasmus and Coornheert were its heroes. Although these men lived well before the meeting of the synod, their rejection of the doctrine of human depravity and adulation of free will was accepted by the Arminian party, named after James Arminius, a professor of theology at the University of Leiden. A major issue before the synod was the status of the creeds. The Arminian party, while having to admit that the church had a confession, disliked confessional confinement and sought to have the creeds revised.

The third problem with which Dort had to wrestle was one of fundamental Christian doctrine. Predestination was the doctrine most attacked, especially that part of it known as reprobation. The Arminian party was helped in its attack by extreme positions of some of its opponents. Furthermore, in their *Remonstrance* of 1610 and afterward the Arminian party, whose proponents then came to be called "Remonstrants," was unwilling to say that man is totally unable to save himself; it held rather that, while human nature has been impaired by sin, the will is still free and able to respond to the grace of God. It claimed that God determined to save all who believe, and it refused to accept the teaching that election is unto faith. It held that Christ died for all even though only believers benefit from his death; that grace is not irresistible; and that faith may be lost. Besides publicly challenging the doctrines of predestination, sin, grace, and the perseverance of the saints, the Remonstrants indicated that they were unsure of other doctrine as well; original sin, justification by faith, the atonement, and even the deity of Christ were called into question. That they doubted Christ's deity is not a well-known historical fact, but it contributed to the seriousness and bitterness of the controversy. It was not until after the death of Arminius in 1609 that the drift toward Socinianism, a version of Unitarianism, became noticeable. The appointment of Conrad Vorstius to the chair of theology at Leiden vacated by Arminius aroused suspicions; in 1622 he made his espousal of Socinianism public.

As a result of all this a strong party spirit developed throughout the country which threatened to split the church and provinces of the Netherlands. Arminian leaders got civil authorities to decree that no contested doctrines might be preached, and in some instances succeeded in getting pulpits closed against ministers. Reformed classes retaliated, and where the contra-Remonstrants, or orthodox, could not get a majority they sometimes worshiped in houses or barns, only to be punished by civil authorities. The situation deteriorated until it appeared in 1617 that there might be civil war. On November 11 of that year the States General decreed that a synod should be called to settle the questions troubling the country and bring it to peace. There had been numerous earlier calls for a national synod by classes, by the Remonstrants when they thought they might have a majority if the States General would select delegates, and by provincial synods and civil authorities.

When the Synod of Dort met in 1618, the Remonstrants expected that they would be recognized as equals and that the synod would be a conference to discuss disputed questions. Instead, the synod summoned the Remonstrants to appear before it as defendants, and in due time their doctrines were condemned. The Canons of Dort set forth: (1) Unconditional election and faith are a gift of God. (2) While the death of Christ is abundantly sufficient to expiate the sins of the whole world, its saving efficacy is limited to the elect. (3, 4) All are so corrupted by sin that they cannot effect their salvation; in sovereign grace God calls and regenerates them to newness of life. (5) Those thus saved he preserves until the end; hence there is assurance of salvation even while believers are troubled by many infirmities.

Dort thus preserved the Augustinian, biblical doctrines of sin and grace against the claim that fallen mankind has free will, that the human condition in sin is not as desperate as the orthodox party said it is, and that election is only God's response to man's decision to believe. It was such a prestigious gathering that it served as an example for the Westminster Assembly, which was held in Britain a generation later, and it set the course which the Dutch church was to follow for centuries. M. E. Osterhaven

See also Arminianism; Remonstrants; Calvinism.

Bibliography. M. G. Hansen, *The Reformed Church in the Netherlands;* P. Schaff, *The Creeds of Christendom,* I, III; J. Hale, *Golden Remains;* P. Y. DeJong, *Crisis in the Reformed Churches;* L. Boettner, *The Reformed Doctrine of Predestination;* H. E. Dosker, "Barneveldt, Martyr or Traitor," *PRR* 9:289–323, 438–71, 637–58; W. Cunningham, *Historical Theology,* II, 371–86; A. A. Hoekema, "A New English Translation of the Canons of Dort," *CTJ* 3:133–61.

Double Predestination. *See* Elect, Election.

Doubt, Religious. Just as belief may be propositional or personal, so one may doubt with respect to propositions or persons and objects. In regard to propositions, doubt is called a propositional attitude, i.e., a particular intellectual stance one takes toward a proposition. Such propositions may be about religious or nonreligious entities, but the doubt in all cases is such as to express an attitude of uncertainty about the truthfulness or falsity of the proposition. It should be noted that the proposition in question may in fact be true and even verified, but doubt or uncertainty relates to whether or not the proposition has been perceived to be true—i.e., it is a subjective attitude that need not have anything to do with the objective certainty (degree to which the proposition has been verified or even its truthfulness) of the proposition.

Doubt of a person may be reducible to propositional doubt. For example, to doubt God may mean nothing more than doubting the truth of the proposition "God exists." On the other hand, doubt of a person often involves much more than questioning the truth of a proposition about the person's existence. In particular, it often involves the matter of distrust. Thus, if one doubts God, he may not indicate any disbelief in God's existence but only that he does not find God to be reliable and thus feels he cannot trust and depend on him. An example of the importance of this matter of trust is seen in Jesus' words, "Let not your heart be troubled. Ye believe in God, believe also in me" (John 14:1). Jesus is clearly saying more than that the disciples should believe God and he exist. As they were in his presence, there would be no question that he existed, and for such monotheists as the disciples there would be no question of the existence of God. Instead, Christ's point was obviously that they should trust in him and commit themselves to him. These matters of mistrust and unwillingness to commit oneself most clearly distinguish doubting a person from doubting a proposition.

In regard to propositional doubt, there are various forms, and most can be illustrated in Scripture. First, there is philosophical doubt, and philosophers distinguish two forms of it. On the one hand, there is definitive doubt which can be called skeptical doubt, while on the other, there is provisional doubt (exemplified in the method of Descartes) which calls items into question for the sake of reaching a more dependable conclusion, i.e., doubt in order to learn. The skeptic doubts not only because he has no answer, but because he thinks there is no answer and could be none. Examples of skeptical doubt are rare in Scripture, but the Bible is replete with cases of provisional doubt. For example, the doubt of Thomas seems to fit this category, and it is important to note that there is not one word of rebuke to Thomas from the Lord or one word of repentance by Thomas. Evidently such doubt is not sinful.

A second broad kind of doubt is equivalent to denial. The individual does not pose a question in order to learn, nor need he be a skeptic. Instead, his doubts are meant as veiled assertions of denial. Such doubt simply says no in the presence of evidence (the skeptic's point is that there is no evidence). A prime example of such doubt is Satan's reaction to Eve in the garden. In Gen. 3:1 Satan asks, "Hath God said ye shall not eat of every tree of the garden?" He is obviously not asking for information, for his question is a veiled assertion of denial which in vss. 4–5 becomes unveiled. Likewise, the Pharisees' continuous request for another sign from Jesus despite all the previous miracles performed provides another example. In the face of the evidence, they refused to believe and requested another sign. Jesus recognized their request as a refusal to believe the evidence, and he responded by rebuking them and refusing to give another sign (Matt. 12:38–42).

Finally, there is a kind of doubt which may be labeled "ignorant doubt." It is doubt which seeks evidence in the face of evidence, but not because there is a rejection of evidence. Instead, the individual has enough evidence to believe, but he still doubts, because he thinks there is some further explanation that will resolve all doubt completely. In such a case he does not know what a final explanation would be, for if he did, he might realize that he already has it. Thus, such doubt is without rational ground. It is ignorant in that the person doubting is looking for something further but cannot explain what this would be. Though examples of such doubt are present in everyday life, they are not plentiful in Scripture. Perhaps the response of Agrippa to Paul in the face of the evidence (Acts 26) is an example of such doubt, but even that is unclear. His doubt could be an example of skepticism or even denial.

From this discussion of the various kinds of doubt it should also be evident that there are several elements involved in doubting. The most obvious element is the rational or intellectual. On the other hand, one may still doubt in the face of evidence, even evidence which he fully understands. In such a case it seems proper to argue that there are either emotional and/or volitional problems as well. That is, one may know the truth but not be comfortable with the way such a truth makes him feel, so he still withholds belief. Or it may be that one understands the implications in terms of change of life style if he were to commit himself to what he knows to be true, and so he chooses to withhold such commitment (volitional problem) and as a result begins to question the truth of the item in question. For example, in view of James 2:19 it is safe to say that the doubt and disbelief of Satan and demons is not primarily an intellectual but rather a volitional and emotional problem. In such a case the individual may have propositional belief in the intellectual sense but simply refuses to add to it belief in the person (trust and commitment). On the other hand, Scripture also indicates and theologians have argued that there are several elements to saving faith—viz., an intellectual element (one must know the facts of the gospel to be saved), an emotional element (assent—agreement that what one knows in general is appropriate for oneself), and a volitional element (the element of commitment of life to what one knows to be the case).

J. S. Feinberg

See also Faith; God, Arguments for the Existence of.

Bibliography. R. Descartes, *Meditations on First Philosophy;* N. Malcolm, *Knowledge and Certainty;* H. H. Price, "Belief 'in' and Belief 'That,'" in *The Philosophy of Religion,* ed. B. Mitchell; L. Wittgenstein, *On Certainty.*

Doxology. The term, which is derived from the Greek *doxa* (glory), denotes an ascription of praise to the three persons of the Blessed Trinity. In its commonest form, known as the *Gloria Patri* or "Lesser Doxology," it is rendered: "Glory be to the Father, and to the Son, and to the Holy Ghost: As it was in the beginning, is now, and ever shall be, world without end. Amen." Its use at the end of the Psalms, as directed, e.g., in the *Book of Common Prayer,* dates from the fourth century. It is thus a symbol of the duty of Christianizing the Psalms and serves at the same time "to connect the Unity of the Godhead as known to the Jews with the Trinity as known to Christians" (*Tutorial Prayer Book,* p. 101).

The so-called Greater Doxology is the *Gloria in Excelsis,* "Glory be to God on high." On account of its opening words, taken directly from Luke 2:14, it is sometimes known as the Angelic Hymn. This doxology is of Greek origin (fourth century) and was used at first as a morning canticle. Later it became incorporated into the Latin Mass, where it occupied a place at the beginning of the service. In the English Communion Service of 1552 the Reformers transferred the hymn to the end of the office, no doubt in accordance with the usage at the first Eucharist: "When they had sung an hymn, they went out" (Matt. 26:30). In this position it forms a fitting conclusion to the Christian sacrifice of praise and thanksgiving.

It is now generally agreed that the doxology at the end of the Lord's Prayer is not part of the original text of Matt. 6:9–13. It may be regarded as an ancient liturgical addition to the prayer, which was adopted by the Greek church but not by the Latin. F. COLQUHOUN

See also WORSHIP IN THE CHURCH.

Drechsel, Thomas. *See* ZWICKAU PROPHETS.

Drink Offering. *See* OFFERINGS AND SACRIFICES IN BIBLE TIMES.

Drunkenness. *See* ALCOHOL, DRINKING OF.

Dualism. A theory in interpretation which explains a given situation or domain in terms of two opposing factors or principles. In general, dualisms are twofold classifications which admit of no intermediate degrees. There are three major types: metaphysical, epistemological or epistemic, and ethical or ethicoreligious.

Metaphysical dualism asserts that the facts of the universe are best explained in terms of mutually irreducible elements. These are often considered to be mind and matter, or as by Descartes, thought and extension. Mind is usually conceived as conscious experience, matter as occupying space and being in motion. They are thus two qualitatively different orders of reality.

Epistemological dualism is an analysis of the knowing situation which holds that the idea or object of judgment is radically other than the real object. The "object" of knowledge is held to be known only through the mediation of "ideas." This type of thinking raises the important question of the manner in which knowledge can bridge the gap between the idea of an object and the object itself.

Ethical or ethicoreligious dualism asserts that there are two mutually hostile forces or beings in the world, the one being the source of all good, the other the source of all evil. The most clear-cut type of ethicoreligious dualism is that of the ancient Iranian religion, usually associated with the name of Zoroaster, in which Ahura Mazda and Ahriman represent the projection into cosmology, respectively, of the forces of good and evil. The universe becomes the battleground for these opposing beings, identified respectively with light and darkness. More moderate forms of dualism pervade most religions, expressed, for example, by the distinction between sacred and profane, or by the analysis of reality in terms of yang and yin in Chinese thought.

Christian theology generally accepts a modified moral dualism, recognizing God as supremely good and Satan as a deteriorated creature bent everywhere upon the intrusion of evil. This, however, is not dualism in the sense of its usual definition, since Christian theology does not consider Satan to be ultimate or original, and sees him ultimately excluded from the universe.

H. B. KUHN

See also MANICHAEISM; ZOROASTRIANISM.

Bibliography. D. Runes, *Dictionary of Philosophy,* 84–85.

Dulia. Both a disposition to honor those persons whose lives deserve it and the honoring act itself. The word originally could mean the honor due from a slave to his or her master. Because of this meaning dulia has been deemphasized since Vatican Council II; the council insisted upon the communality and basic equality of the people of God. T. J. GERMAN

See also HYPERDULIA; LATRIA.

Bibliography. H. Delehaye, *Sanctus: Essai sur le culte des saints dans l'antiquité.*

Duns Scotus, John (1266–1308). Franciscan scholastic theologian, born in Scotland and educated at Oxford and the University of Paris. Details of his life are vague, but it is known that he taught at Oxford, Paris, and Cologne. His teaching is preserved in a commentary on the *Sentences* of Peter Lombard, glosses on Aristotelian texts, and disputations about various subjects. Although he is venerated as a saint within his order, other groups within Roman Catholicism have not accepted his status.

Scotus is a difficult thinker to interpret for several reasons. These include the fact that he never wrote a full presentation of his system, that his works are preserved in very poor condition—often being available only from students' notes—and that he coined new terms and concepts to explain his ideas. Consequently his work has been interpreted in numerous ways. Some have claimed that he represented the most complex development of scholastic reason, while others believe that he separated philosophy from theology and reason from faith to such an extent that he taught a system called the double truth, similar to Siger of Brabant. This outlook held that there are some conclusions that one accepts in philosophy but cannot accept in faith, and when such contradictions occur one must accept the conclusions of faith.

Scotus's ideas were formed in an atmosphere of opposition to the earlier philosophical position of Thomas Aquinas. Scotus felt that faith was a matter of the will rather than a process based on logical proofs. Even though he relied on some arguments for the existence of God, he taught that the most basic Christian truths such as the resurrection and immortality must be accepted by faith. Emphasizing the love of God, he used this characteristic to explain creation, grace, the incarnation, and heaven. His ideas have influenced later Franciscan thought, and his views about the immaculate conception have contributed to Catholic belief in a more general manner.

Given the title *Doctor Subtilis* by his admirers, Scotus has been ridiculed by others, including the humanists and the Protestant Reformers. These groups, unsympathetic to scholastic theology, have used his name as an epithet, calling someone whose ideas are obscure a "duns" or dunce. Despite this, individuals as diverse as C. S. Peirce and Gerard Manley Hopkins have regarded his insights as profound. R. G. CLOUSE

See also SCHOLASTICISM.

Bibliography. F. Copleston, *A History of Philosophy,* II, Pt. 2; A. Maurer, *Medieval Philosophy;* J. K. Ryan and B. Bonansea, eds., *Studies in Philosophy and the History of Philosophy,* III; J. Weinberg, *A Short History of Medieval Philosophy.*

Duty. What is morally necessary or required; what one is morally obliged to do as distinct from what one is merely pleased or inclined to do. Duties are reasons for action. As reasons for action duties do not function like causes. One could have a duty to act in a certain way without either acting in that way or even being inclined to so act.

Generally when people speak of duties, they think in terms of deontological ethics. According to deontological ethics one ought to give primary focus to rules and principles in making moral decisions. From the deontological viewpoint the consequences of one's actions are relatively unimportant. For example, the Stoics believed that people had duties to virtue and reasonable action quite apart from any calculation or expectation of human happiness.

The most outstanding representative of the deontological approach was Immanuel Kant. According to Kant, we should not seek to acquire happiness but to be worthy of it through developing a good will, a will that acts only on the basis of duty. One's duties are defined by the basic moral law, which he called the "categorical imperative." This basic principle is categorical because it applies to every person at every time and is unresponsive to particular prudential goals. According to one version of the categorical imperative, I should always act in such a way that I could will that the rule of my action should become a universal law. The point is not that I should legislate my rules for others, but that I should not treat myself as a special case. Whatever rules I adopt for myself, I have to be able to legislate for others. The categorical imperative is like the Golden Rule except for two qualifications. First, Kant explicitly included duties to ourselves in the categorical imperative. Second, Kant explicitly denied any moral concern for the results of our actions, whereas a person following the Golden Rule may consider results to be morally relevant.

An alternative to the deontological approach is teleological ethics—focusing primarily on the results or consequences of our actions. Moral principles become for teleologists important practical rules of thumb for acquiring valued results. The critical thing is to discover what results are the most valuable. Some seek personal happiness; others seek the greatest total happiness for a group of people; still others seek the advancement of the kingdom of God, reconciliation, the glorification of God, or the growth of love relationships. Teleologists argue that fulfilling one of these goals is our highest duty and that our commitment to any rule should depend on the effectiveness of the rule to help us achieve our highest goal. Critics argue that teleologists merely seek to justify their means by the ends they desire.

A third approach to ethics might be called the ontological approach, arguing that we have certain duties to obey rules and other duties to achieve goals because of the kinds of beings we are. Moral duties can be seen as derived from laws of nature—laws that we can discover within our own selves or in our relationships to God or the world.

However one sees his duties, whether in terms of principles or goals or nature, conflicting duties are possible. Ethics must include methods for resolving these conflicts. Also, there are duties that apply to all humanity as well as duties that apply to particular roles such as father or husband. Not everyone's duties need to be exactly the same.

It is not obvious that all our duties are contained within an ethical system. Kierkegaard argued that our duty to God involved a "teleological suspension of the ethical." Regardless of the system of ethics that I have, I must be responsive to God's voice to do what may even seem to be unethical. Others have argued that God's way is best discerned through a system of deontological, teleological, or ontological ethics. That is, God's will is most effectively understood within a set of principles, the selection of the best goals, or the working of our best self-understanding.

To talk about duties or laws seems to imply that we have a duty or law *to* someone. Ethics seems to be pointless without responsibility to another being. Certainly we have duties to ourselves and duties to other humans, but the seriousness of ethical responsibility (e.g., our inability to merely negotiate ethical duty into nonexistence) may suggest an ongoing duty to Someone greater than ourselves. Kant argued that in order to understand the role of ethical duty, it is necessary to believe in the existence of a Supreme Judge who observes our actions in every circumstance. In addition, Kant believed that ethics necessarily include a belief in immortality so that beyond this life we are able to receive the rewards for our actions.

While our understanding of our duties may vary from person to person and from culture to culture, many have sought for and found duties that are broadly shared among people of many cultures. Discovering such a common core of duties, C. S. Lewis took this as evidence for a common Lawgiver to whom all humans are responsible. Moreover, Lewis argued that our professed moral beliefs make sense only if we believe that all our moral actions make a difference even if no other human is watching. The actual use of our concept of duty seems to require the existence of Someone to whom we have these duties.

Ludwig Wittgenstein and some of his followers have argued that the essence of a religious commitment is a commitment to a set of moral duties. While moral duties certainly seem central, it is doubtful that this interpretation of religious commitment can account for either the importance of historic events for the Christian religion or the personal relationship with God.

P. H. DEVRIES

See also ETHICS; ETHICS, BIBLICAL; ETHICAL SYSTEMS, CHRISTIAN; SITUATION ETHICS.

Bibliography. Aristotle, *Nicomachean Ethics;* W. Frankena, *Ethics;* I. Kant, *Critique of Practical Reason* and *Foundations of the Metaphysics of Morals;* S. Kierkegaard, *Fear and Trembling;* J. S. Mill, *Utilitarianism;* Plato, *The Republic.*

Dwight, Timothy (1752–1817). Congregational minister, author, and educator, born in Northampton, Massachusetts, and educated at Yale. After graduation Dwight taught school and then became a clergyman and a chaplain in the Continental Army. Later he accepted the pastorate of the Congregational church at Greenfield Hill, Connecticut, serving from 1783 to 1795. During these years he rose to prominence because of his role in founding educational institutions, his activities as an author, and the leadership that he gave to the Congregational cause in Connecticut. In 1795 he was chosen president of Yale, a post that he held for the remainder of his life. Not only was he a successful administrator, broadening the curriculum to include scientific and medical training, but he also taught rhetoric, logic, metaphysics, ethics, and theology. He became the champion of the conservative Calvinists in New England. This led him to encourage a religious revival and to foster an antidemocratic federalism. Despite opponents who called him "Pope Dwight," his supporters who looked on him as a second St. Paul seemed to win the victory with the advent of the Second Great Awakening.

Dwight's literary works include *The Conquest of Canaan* (1785) and *Greenfield Hill* (1794). He also left a multivolume record of *Travels in New*

England and New York and a series of sermons that had been repeated over a regular four-year cycle at Yale and were published under the title *Theology Explained and Defended* (5 vols. 1818–19). Much of what he said and wrote during his years as president of Yale was meant to stem the tide of infidelity that he identified with the Enlightenment. Despite such efforts he was himself affected by the eighteenth century rationalist movement and has been credited with furthering the Scottish philosophy in America.

R. G. Clouse

See also Great Awakenings, The; New England Theology; Scottish Realism.

Bibliography. C. E. Cunningham, *Timothy Dwight, 1752–1817;* J. Haroutunian, *Piety Versus Moralism: The Passing of the New England Theology;* K. Silverman, *Timothy Dwight.*

Ee

Earth, Age of. The earth's age is of theological importance for two reasons. First, the Bible speaks about the past; second, evolutionary views of origins require an age amounting to billions of years.

Genesis has been used to estimate the age of the earth. Archbishop James Ussher suggested that the earth was created in 4004 B.C. Others, such as John Lightfoot, have gone so far as to fix the date and hour of the first day of creation. Such estimates require assumptions: the data are complete and accurate; the days of Gen. 1 were brief and consecutive; and the events described in Gen. 1 began soon after the formation of the earth.

Bible genealogies cannot legitimately be used to construct chronologies. Comparison shows names omitted (e.g., compare Matt. 1:8 and I Chr. 3:10–12).

There is controversy over the days of Gen. 1, and opinions range from holding that they were consecutive twenty-four-hour periods to supposing that they were long periods of time, not necessarily consecutive. Reasons for doubting the twenty-four-hour day theory include: the seventh day is still in progress (see John 5:10–19; Heb. 4:1–11); the sixth day is still in progress (John 5:17); and the sixth day, described in detail in Gen. 2, contained more events than could have occurred in a twenty-four-hour period. Proponents of the last view claim that the Hebrew word usually translated as "now" in Gen. 2:23 actually indicates "at last" or "at length."

If the days of Gen. 1 actually were long periods of time, it still appears impossible to reconcile the sequence of the events listed there with current evolutionary theory. Birds, appearing on the fifth day, could not have been descendants of reptiles appearing on the sixth day, and if the sea creatures of day five included any mammals, they could not have had land mammals from the sixth day as ancestors.

The *Scofield Reference Bible* popularized the concept that there is a gap of time between Gen. 1:1 and 1:2, citing Jer. 4:23–26; Isa. 24:1; 45:18. However, this gap theory is not accepted by most Bible scholars because they hold it to be inconsistent with the original language and doubt that Satan had the power to destroy God's original creation.

The earth's age, then, cannot be deduced unequivocally from biblical evidence. Most scientists, including some who hold to the verbal inspiration of the Bible, believe that the dates proposed by various kinds of geological evidence are approximately correct and that the earth is five billion years old or older. Others, questioning the conclusions of radioactive dating and historical geology, are convinced that the earth is only a few thousand years old. It seems, as Heb. 11:3 says, that we can fully comprehend God's creative acts only by faith.

M. La Bar

See also Gap Theory.

Bibliography. J. Block, "Origins and the Bible," *JASA* 29:64–67; J. O. Buswell, III, "Warfield and Creationist Anthropology," *JASA* 18:117–20; U. Cassuto, *A Commentary on the Book of Genesis;* D. J. Krause, "Apparent Age and Its Reception in the 19th Century," *JASA* 32:146–50; H. M. Morris, *The Genesis Record;* R. C. Newman and H. J. Eckelmann, Jr., eds., *Genesis One and the Origin of the Earth;* P. H. Seeley, "The Antiquity of Warfield's Paper on the Antiquity of Man," *JASA* 18:28–30; J. C. Whitcomb, Jr., *The Early Earth,* J. C. Whitcomb, Jr., and H. M. Morris, *The Genesis Flood;* D. A. Young, *Creation and the Flood* and *Christianity and the Age of the Earth.*

Earth, New. *See* New Heavens and New Earth.

Easter. The annual day and season commemorating the resurrection of Christ. As the oldest and most important movable feast, its date determines the arrangement of the Christian liturgical year.

In Germanic languages the words used (English *easter;* German *ostern*) are thought to derive either from the name of an obscure Germanic goddess of spring, Eastre (a view popularized by the English monk Bede), or, more likely, from an Old German root for dawn or east (the time and place of the rising sun). At an early date and for obscure reasons these Germanic words came to translate the Greek *pascha* (from the Hebrew *pesaḥ*), the biblical word for the paschal (passover) feast used by most of the Romance languages (French *pâques;* Italian *pasqua*).

The early development of the celebration of Easter and the attendant calendar disputes were largely a result of Christianity's attempt to emancipate itself from Judaism. Sunday had already replaced the Jewish sabbath early in the second century, and despite efforts in Asia Minor to maintain the Jewish passover date of 14 Nisan for Easter (hence the name Quartodecimans), the Council of Nicaea adopted the annual Sunday following the full moon after the vernal equinox (March 21). Unfortunately, different methods of Easter reckoning devised to reconcile the Jewish lunar and Roman solar calendars led to several disputes, such as the one in seventh century Britain between Celtic and Roman Christianity. Even the notable calendar reform sponsored by Pope Gregory XIII in 1582 was primarily an attempt to keep Easter in the spring by correcting the drift (eleven days at the point) of the less accurate Julian calendar. Since Eastern Orthodoxy still follows the old calendar, it can be as much as five weeks at variance with the other churches in celebrating Easter. In recent years concern for Christian unity has led to proposals for a universal fixed date such as the second Sunday in April. This in turn would make possible the creation of a uniform world liturgy.

Originally Easter was a unitary night celebration (like passover), recalling both the death and resurrection of Christ. The ceremony included the lighting of the paschal candle, prayer, readings from Scripture, and the joyful celebration of Eucharist. This also became the ideal occasion for baptisms (with resurrection life symbolized by white robes) and led in turn to the lengthening of the brief preparatory period into the forty days of Lent (paralleling Christ's forty-day fast before his passion). Accordingly, after the fourth century the unitary feast was broken up into several parts and the resurrection came to be celebrated separately on Easter Sunday morning, with Eastertide extending another forty or fifty days. Over the centuries many popular customs have been added reflecting pagan spring folklore (Easter egg and rabbit) as well as Jewish and Christian sources. R. K. Bishop

See also Paschal Controversies; Christian Year.

Bibliography. L. Cowie and J. Gummer, *The Christian Year;* G. Dix, *The Shape of the Liturgy;* D. Jones, G. Wainwright, and E. Yarnold, *The Study of the Liturgy;* F. Weiser, *The Easter Book;* E. Zerubavel, "Easter and Passover: On Calendars and Group Identity," *ASR,* Apr., 1982.

Ebionites. Ascetics who chose poverty as a way of life and who may have drawn their name from this term for poor men (*'ebyônîm*). Four Scripture verses seem central to the Ebionites. Matt. 5:3 mentions the poor in spirit; Luke 4:18 and 7:22 speak of the poor. Deut. 18:15 was as central to their theology as the other references were to their chosen life style. They accepted Jesus of Nazareth as the "prophet like me from among you." This meant that the Ebionites were to be classed among the various early Christian sects. On the whole they rejected the Pauline epistles, clinging instead to aspects of the Jewish law; therefore they are to be numbered among the Jewish Christian sects.

Origen knew of two groups of Ebionites, those who accepted the virgin birth and those who saw Jesus as a prophet fathered by Joseph; he states they observed Easter with the Jews. Eusebius adds that the Ebionites who did accept the virgin birth still rejected the preexistence of Christ, and he associated the Gospel of Hebrews with them. Epiphanius was the first of the church fathers to say that they originated after the destruction of the temple in A.D. 70 among the Christians who fled to Pella. Epiphanius credits their founding to Ebion, who, he says, moved to Kochaba near Karnaim and came out of a Jewish Christian group called Nazaranes. Jerome adds that they practiced circumcision and lived by the law but looked forward to the return of Christ and the millennium. Ebionites therefore seem to be a continuing reflection in the early church of the Judaizers seen in Acts and the epistles as opponents of Paul. They came into relative prominence after A.D. 70 and waned after the fourth century.

In addition to accepting Jesus as the prophetic successor to Moses (whether virgin born or born of Joseph) and practicing asceticism, particularly poverty, Ebionites tended to deny the preexistence of the Logos; venerate Jerusalem; see Christianity as obedience to a moral code that was higher than or fulfilled the law; see Jesus as made the Anointed One at his baptism; teach that Jesus was so selected because he kept the law perfectly; stress the Epistle of James and reject Pauline soteriology. Some may have tended toward a Gnostic dualism. Many were vegetarians and practiced various ritual ablutions culminating in baptism. Modern scholars feel Ebionites are probably responsible for portions of the Clementine Homilies and Recognitions and the Gospel of the Ebionites; but Klijn and Reinink have made a good case for disassociating them from the Gospel of the Hebrews. V. L. WALTER

See also JUDAIZERS.

Bibliography. A. F. J. Klijn and G. J. Reinink, *Patristic Evidence for Jewish-Christian Sects;* H.-J. Schoeps, *Jewish Christianity.*

Eck, Johann (1486–1543). Born Johann Maier at Eck (or Egg) in Swabia, Eck is little remembered except as an opponent of Luther. After studying at Heidelberg, Tübingen, and Freiburg, in 1510 he achieved a doctorate in theology and joined the faculty at Ingolstadt, later becoming prochancellor. He made a reputation as a humanist and attracted attention with his defense of a modest rate of interest (1514). At first friendly with Luther, he replied to the Ninety-five Theses with the tract *Obelisks* (1518), to which Luther responded with *Asterisk.* Speaking for the papacy at the Leipzig disputation (1519), Eck displayed a fine memory, sound learning, and a tactical mastery of debate which confused Carlstadt and forced Luther to admit some solidarity with Hus and to set infallible Scripture above fallible popes, councils, and fathers. Eck followed up his campaign by helping to secure Luther's condemnation in the bull *Exsurge Domine* (1520) and defending papal authority in the treatise *On the Primacy of Peter* (1521). He then composed a frequently republished work (1525), *A Manual of Commonplaces against Luther and the Other Enemies of the Church* (Melanchthon and Zwingli). At the Diet of Augsburg (1530) he presented 404 propositions against Luther and wrote a *Confutation* of the Confession. To counteract Luther's Bible he attempted his own version (1537), but with little success. His presence at Worms (1521), Hagenau (1540), and Regensburg (1541) did nothing to promote the desired restoration of unity. While perhaps surpassing Luther in pure scholarship, Eck hardly compares with him in theological perception. Justly, then, he is remembered largely for his negative function.

G. W. BROMILEY

See also LUTHER, MARTIN; LEIPZIG DISPUTATION.

Bibliography. T. Wiedermann, *Dr. Johann Eck.*

Eckhart, Meister. *See* MEISTER ECKHART.

Ecumenical Councils. Councils that originated from the link between the Christian church and Roman state during the fourth century. Originally summoned by emperors to promote unity, the early councils were intended to represent the whole church. Through the centuries the Roman Catholic canon law came to stipulate that an ecumenical council must be convened by the pope and be duly representative of the dioceses of the Roman Church (although decision making was subordinated to papal confirmation). Because of this switch in policy and representation, Christians have disagreed on which councils were "ecumenical." While the Roman Catholic Church accepts twenty-one, the Coptic, Syrian, and Armenian churches accept only the first three in the Roman Catholic list. Most Protestant groups and the Eastern Orthodox Church accept the first seven. To the Roman Catholic Church the ecumenical or universal council binds the whole church, while a particular council binds only one part of the church.

The first eight councils that were called by emperors and had a representation of both Eastern and Western bishops were the councils of Nicaea I (325); Constantinople I (381); Ephesus (431); Chalcedon (451); Constantinople II (553); Constantinople III (680–81); Nicaea II (787); and Constantinople IV (869–70).

With the First Lateran Council (1123) the papacy initiated and assumed control, continuing this policy with Lateran II (1139); Lateran III (1179); Lateran IV (1215); Lyon I (1245); Lyon II (1274); and Vienne (1311–12). During the conciliar movement, when the papacy had reached a low ebb, the Council of Constance (1414–18) and the Council of Basel (called 1431, transferred to Ferrara in 1438 and Florence in 1439) were convened. During the sixteenth century the Fifth Lateran Council (1512–17) and the Council of Trent (1545–63) were called to meet challenges to the Roman Church. In the modern period the papacy has convened two councils nearly a century apart—Vatican I (1869–70) and Vatican II (1962–65). D. A. RAUSCH

See also COUNCILS, CHURCH.

Ecumenism. The organized attempt to bring about the cooperation and unity of all believers in Christ. The word "ecumenical" comes from the Greek *oikoumenē,* "the entire inhabited earth" (Acts 17:6; Matt. 24:14; Heb. 2:5).

Early Ecumenism. The theological basis for Christian unity is rooted in the NT. Jesus prayed that his followers "may be one, Father, just as you are in me and I am in you. May they also be in us so that the world may believe that you have sent me" (John 17:21). Likewise, Paul urged the Ephesians to "keep the unity of the spirit through the bond of peace" because "there is one body and one Spirit, . . . one Lord, one faith, one baptism" (Eph. 4:3–5). Throughout his ministry, the apostle worked to maintain the unity of the church in the face of theological deviation (Galatians and Colossians) and internal division (I and II Corinthians).

In the postapostolic church the early fathers tried to maintain this unity, despite the distances that separated congregations and the different cultures in which they were located. In his discussion of the *regula fidei*, Irenaeus claimed that the church, "although scattered throughout the whole world, yet, as if occupying but one house, carefully preserves [the faith]. . . . For, although the languages of the world are dissimilar, yet the import of the tradition is one and the same." Early Christians considered themselves united by their allegiance to the apostolic gospel as expressed in the apostolic canon and preserved by the apostolic clergy. When heresies and doctrinal disagreements threatened to destroy this catholic (universal) unity, church leaders met in ecumenical councils to settle disputes. This early ideal was clearly articulated in the Nicene Creed (325): we believe in the "one, holy, catholic, and apostolic Church."

Despite such attempts to maintain ecclesiastical unity there arose numerous divisions over matters of faith and practice. The early ecumenical councils often failed to prevent schism and heresy. For a variety of reasons, Eastern and Western churches excommunicated each other in 1054, driving a wedge down the center of Christendom. The Western church was split by the Protestant Reformation of the sixteenth century, which in turn opened the door to a rapid and extensive proliferation of denominations and sects.

Many Christians have not been satisfied with this state of affairs and have worked to at least restore some measure of cooperation between the various churches, if not bring about a more visible unity. For example, in the early nineteenth century American Christians from a variety of Protestant denominations cooperated in the establishment of numerous evangelistic, missionary, benevolent, tract, and Bible societies. In 1846 individuals from over fifty British and American denominations formed the Evangelical Alliance to promote religious liberty and various cooperative evangelistic and educational activities. In 1908 thirty-one American Protestant denominations formed the Federal Council of Churches, which was absorbed by the larger National Council of Churches of Christ in 1950.

The Modern Ecumenical Movement. This began in Edinburgh in 1910 at the International Missionary Conference. Under the leadership of American Methodist John R. Mott, the thousand delegates who attended caught the vision for Christian unity. As a result, three organizations were established to continue the work and realize the promise of the Edinburgh Conference. The International Missionary Council (Lake Mohonk, New York, 1921) attempted to bring about cooperation between Protestant mission agencies; the Conference on Life and Work (Stockholm, 1925) sought to unify efforts to solve social, economic, and political problems; and the Conference on Faith and Order (Lausanne, 1927) addressed the theological basis of church unity. By 1937 the conferences on Life and Work and Faith and Order agreed that a new, more inclusive organization was needed and proposed the establishment of a World Council of Churches (WCC). The coming of World War II prevented speedy implementation of the proposal, but finally in 1948, 351 delegates representing 147 denominations from 44 countries gathered in Amsterdam and formed the World Council, under the leadership of W. A. Visser 't Hooft. Later General Assemblies of the WCC were held at Evanston, Illinois (1954), New Delhi, India (1961), Uppsala, Sweden (1968), Nairobi, Kenya (1975), and Vancouver, British Columbia (1983). At the New Delhi assembly the Russian Orthodox Church joined the Council, the International Missionary Council was brought under WCC control, and the confessional "Basis" was adopted: "The World Council of Churches is a fellowship of Churches which confess the Lord Jesus Christ as God and Savior according to the Scriptures and therefore seek to fulfil together their common calling to the glory of one God, Father, Son, and Holy Spirit."

Conspicuously absent from most of these ecumenical endeavors has been the Roman Catholic Church. For decades disagreements over the primacy of the Roman pontiff, the meaning and practice of the Eucharist, and the like have kept Roman Catholics and Protestant ecumenists far apart. In the Second Vatican Council, Pope John XXIII opened the door to greater ecumenical dialogue. In the council's Decree on Ecumenism (1964), Rome maintained its traditional insistence that "only through the Catholic Church of Christ, the universal aid to salvation, can the means of salvation be reached in all their fulness." But for the first time it was willing to recognize that there were authentic Christians ("separated brethren") outside the Roman fold. The Eastern churches, for example, are not far from Rome in their doctrine, church order, and liturgy. The Anglican Communion has also retained much of Catholic tradition, while other churches, though more seriously defective, nevertheless have preserved some important elements of Catholic truth. The decree declared the hope that on the basis of the Christian rite of initiation, all "brothers by baptism" may work to achieve the fully integrated unity that the Roman Church already possesses.

As a reflection of this new spirit, in December, 1965, the Roman pope and the patriarch of Constantinople mutually lifted the excommunication that had divided the Roman Catholic and Eastern Orthodox churches since 1054. Furthermore, a number of ecumenical contacts have occurred under the auspices of the Vatican's Secretariat for the Promotion of Christian Unity.

Evangelicals and Ecumenism. The conservative evangelicals are the last group to remain outside the ecumenical movement. Almost from the beginning of modern ecumenism, evangelicals have questioned the attempt to unify the churches on the "federation" model. They cite, for example, the rather nebulous doctrinal basis of the WCC and its seemingly weak commitment to evangelism. Furthermore, in more recent times most evangelicals object to what they consider to be the WCC's political support of Third World leftist movements.

This reticence to become actively involved in the ecumenical movement does not necessarily mean that evangelicals are against all collective action. Since the evangelical awakenings of the eighteenth century evangelicals have cooperated in evangelism and foreign missions. In the 1940s American evangelicals founded two cooperative organizations, the National Association of Evangelicals (NAE) and the American Council of Christian Churches (ACCC). Both groups were historically orthodox in doctrine, though they differed in their approach to "separation." The NAE accepted into membership any group or individual that was broadly evangelical, while the ACCC demanded adherence to a much narrower doctrinal statement and rejected anyone who had any dealings with the WCC or the National Council of Churches. Both organizations clearly were more interested in fostering evangelism and mutual support than in bringing about union on the federation model.

On the international scene evangelicals have worked to encourage united efforts on a number of fronts. In 1951 the World Evangelical Fellowship (WEF) was organized. Membership in the WEF is open to national evangelical fellowships that subscribe to an orthodox statement of faith. The WEF assists in theological education around the world, undertakes humanitarian relief, and promotes Bible and evangelistic ministries.

On the whole, however, evangelicals seem to be most interested in promoting evangelism. Growing out of the ministry of Billy Graham, the World Congress on Evangelism was held in Berlin in 1966, drawing delegates from over a hundred countries. In 1974 over 2,700 participated in the International Congress on World Evangelization in Lausanne, Switzerland. The Lausanne congress marked a new maturity in evangelical unity efforts. It recognized that "the church's visible unity in truth is God's purpose." The unity of the church is a gift of God through the Spirit, made possible through Christ's redemptive work on the cross. This unity, the congress declared, is based on truth (adherence to the historic gospel) and is required by the divine mandate to declare a gospel of reconciliation to all people. How can the church declare a gospel of peace to the world, while remaining fragmented and unreconciled itself? As a result of the congress, a forty-eight-member Continuation Committee for World Evangelization was established "to encourage and assist where necessary in the formation of regional and national committees to advance world evangelization in every area."

In summary, then, by the 1980s two models of "ecumenism" were evident among Christians. The federation model of the World Council of Churches tended to downplay the necessity of doctrinal agreement and evangelism while stressing concerted social and political action in Christ's name. The cooperative model of conservative evangelicals sought to restore evangelism to primary place in the church's mission in the hope that more visible kinds of unity would follow. T. P. WEBER

See also UNITY; MOTT, JOHN RALEIGH.

Bibliography. R. Rouse and S. C. Neill, eds., *A History of the Ecumenical Movement, 1517–1948;* H. Fey, ed., *A History of the Ecumenical Movement, 1948–1968;* R. M. Brown, *The Ecumenical Revolution;* N. Goodall, *The Ecumenical Movement* and *Ecumenical Progress: A Decade of Change in the Ecumenical Movement, 1961–1971;* J. D. Douglas, ed., *Let the Earth Hear His Voice;* B. Leeming, *The Vatican Council and Christian Unity;* J. D. Murch, *Cooperation Without Compromise: A History of the National Association of Evangelicals.*

Eddy, Mary Baker (1821–1910). Founder of the Church of Christ, Scientist, and author of its famous textbook, *Science and Health with Key to the Scriptures.* Born Mary Morse Baker, she was reared in a devout Congregationalist home, but later rejected her parents' strict Calvinism.

Although her formal education was limited due to chronic ill health, she studied such subjects as natural science, moral philosophy, logic, Greek, and Hebrew under the tutelage of her brother, a Dartmouth graduate. In 1843 she married George W. Glover, who died before the birth of their first child. Her second marriage, to David Patterson (1853), ended in divorce. In 1877 at age fifty-six she married one of her first Christian Science students, Asa Gilbert Eddy.

Suffering poor health throughout most of her life, Mary was preoccupied with questions of health. In search of healing she submitted herself to the metaphysical teachings of Phineas P. Quimby and was healed. Suffering a serious fall in 1866, she was healed by reading the Bible and practicing metaphysical principles. She regarded that incident as the discovery of Christian Science. Her metaphysical system gradually evolved and was published as *Science and Health with Key to the Scriptures* in 1875. Although her followers consider this work as divinely inspired, her critics contend that it is deeply indebted to the works of Francis Lieber and Quimby. The following year she founded the Christian Scientist Association, which three years later became the Church of Christ, Scientist.

Eddy's theological position has little in common with historic orthodox Christianity. It is entirely built upon a metaphysical base. She uses the theological vocabulary of traditional Christianity but substitutes metaphysical meanings for the terms. For her, God is "All-in-All"; he is mind; he is the divine principle of all existence, not a person. As the only cause of existence, God is reality and nothing apart from him can be real. Since God is Spirit and is All, matter cannot exist. Since all reality is divine and God is good, all reality is good. There cannot exist evil, sin, sickness, or death. Imperfections of every sort are illusory and unreal—delusions of the carnal mind.

The Trinity is defined by Eddy as the principles of life, truth, and love. The historic view of three persons in one Godhead is labeled heathen. Christ is not considered a person but rather the true idea of God, and his death or resurrection could not have occurred since evil and sin have no existence.

Eddy's major writings include *The People's Idea of God* (1886), her autobiography *Retrospection and Introspection* (1891), *Unity of Good* (1891), *Manual of the Mother Church* (1895), and *Miscellaneous Writings* (1896). P. G. Chappell

See also Church of Christ, Scientist.

Bibliography. S. Wilbur, *Life of Mary Baker Eddy;* R. Peel, *Mary Baker Eddy: The Years of Discovery;* E. M. Ramsey, *Christian Science and Its Discoverer;* C. Smith, *Historical Sketches from the Life of Mary Baker Eddy;* W. Martin, *The Christian Science Myth;* M. F. Bednarowski, "Outside the Mainstream: Women's Religion and Women Religious Leaders," *JAAR* 48:207–31.

Edification. This term occurs four times in the NT (AV: Rom. 15:2; I Cor. 14:3; II Cor. 10:8; 13:10). In every case it translates the noun *oikodomē,* which literally means "building." This same Greek noun is translated "edifying" seven times (I Cor. 14:5, 12, 26; II Cor. 12:19; Eph. 4:12, 16, 29) and "wherewith one may edify" once (Rom. 14:19). The corresponding abstract noun *oikodomia* is rendered "edifying" in I Tim. 1:4. Furthermore, the verb *oikodomeō,* which literally means "build a house," is translated "edify" seven times (Acts 9:31; I Cor. 8:1; 10:23; 14:4 [twice], 17; I Thess. 5:11).

A glance at the above Scripture references will show that the thought of edification was dominant with the apostle Paul. All the references but one are from his epistles. Repeatedly the great apostle expresses his concern for the spiritual strengthening of the believers and their congregations. It is also clear that it was the church at Corinth which particularly needed to be strengthened in love and unity.

As already noted, the primary idea of the Greek words for "edify" and "edification" is "build" or "building up." This is brought out well in the NIV: "Each of us should please his neighbor for his good, to build him up" (Rom. 15:2); "the authority the Lord gave us for building you up rather than pulling you down" (II Cor. 10:8; cf. 13:10). This communicates the spiritual meaning of "edification" more clearly to the modern reader. Paul was concerned for the building up, in faith and love, of individual believers and congregations, and also the entire church of Jesus Christ. R. Earle

Edwards, Jonathan (1703–1758). Massachusetts Congregational minister who produced one of the most thorough and compelling bodies of theological writing in the history of America. Edwards, the son of a Congregational minister, entered the ministry in 1726 after a bachelor's degree at Yale, further independent study, and brief service as a Yale tutor and in the Presbyterian church of New York City. His first charge was Northampton, Massachusetts, where he served until dismissed in 1750 after a controversy with his congregation over standards for church admission. He then labored in frontier Stockbridge, Massachusetts, as minister to congregations of Indians and whites. His death from inoculation for smallpox came on March 22,

1758, only a few weeks after he began his work as president of the College of New Jersey.

Edwards's claim to be regarded as America's greatest evangelical theologian, and perhaps the greatest of any variety, rests on both the depth and breadth of his writing and his importance for both practical and theoretical religion. He was the theologian of the First Great Awakening, and every bit as important in explicating that movement as George Whitefield had been in promoting it. He was also the eighteenth century's most powerful exponent of experimental Calvinism. In between his active labors as a pastor and his more popular preaching and writing, he found time to compose works of rarified theological construction which challenge scholars to this day. The ongoing publication of a definitive edition of Edwards's works by Yale University Press makes clear how large his contributions were, not only in several divisions of theology defined more narrowly, but also in metaphysics, ethics, and psychology.

Theology. Edwards is most often studied for his Augustinian description of human sinfulness and divine all-sufficiency. In such early sermons as "God Glorified in Man's Dependence" (1731), "A Divine and Supernatural Light" (1733), and "Sinners in the Hands of an Angry God" (1741), he anticipated in a popular way the themes that would inform his later theological treatises. The root of human sinfulness was antagonism toward God; God was justified in condemning sinners who scorned the work of Christ on their behalf; conversion meant a radical change of the heart; true Christianity involved not just an understanding of God and the facts of Scripture but a new "sense" of divine beauty, holiness, and truth.

Edwards eventually summarized many of these insights in 1754 when he published *A Careful and Strict Inquiry into the Modern Prevailing Notions of that Freedom of Will, Which is Supposed to be Essential to Moral Agency, Virtue and Vice, Reward and Punishment, Praise and Blame.* In this commanding treatise Edwards argued that the "will" was not an independent faculty but an expression of more basic human motivation. To "will" something was to act in accordance with the strongest motives prevailing within a person. Edwards was here arguing in traditional Augustinian and Calvinistic fashion that human action is always consistent with human character. But he bent his dialectic skill especially to show that modern versions of "free will" served merely to obviate human responsibility and reduce analysis of human choice to a nonsensical infinite regression.

Uppermost in Edwards's mind were the implications for conversion which this view of human nature entailed. It meant that a sinner *by nature* would never choose to glorify God unless God himself changed that person's character or—as Edwards phrased it—implanted a new "sense of the heart" to love and serve God. Regeneration, God's act, was the basis for repentance and conversion, the human actions.

In a posthumously published volume, *Original Sin* (1758), Edwards defended the view of human nature which underlay the argument in *Freedom of Will.* This volume contended that all humanity was present in Adam at the fall and that all people, as a consequence, shared the bent toward sinning which Adam had brought upon himself. Edwards felt that he could show in this way how individuals were responsible for their own sinfulness and yet also were bound to the dictates of a fallen nature until converted by God's sovereign grace. Edwards's willingness to postulate a nearly Platonic connection between Adam and the rest of humanity also provided a glimpse of the recondite philosophical reasoning with which he had been filling his private notebooks for years.

As a result of his Calvinistic convictions as well as his experiences in the Great Awakening, Edwards also propounded important ideas on the church and on eschatology. To Edwards the church was the bride of Christ, which, as such, should be made up only of the professedly regenerate. While in the last analysis God must be the judge of the heart, the church on earth had the responsibility to preserve its character, and especially its administration of the Lord's Supper, as purely as possible. It was this conviction which drove Edwards to repudiate the belief of his grandfather, Solomon Stoddard, that the Lord's Supper should be thrown open to all nonscandalous people in a community, even those without a profession of faith. And it was this conviction which ultimately cost Edwards his pulpit in Northampton.

Encouraged by the early successes of the Great Awakening, Edwards countenanced the idea that the millennial dawn was about to break in New England. A series of sermons, published eventually in 1744 as *A History of the Work of Redemption,* expressed his fondest hopes for the beginning of the realized kingdom as a result of the Holy Spirit's work in the awakening. Later, as revival fires cooled, Edwards universalized his hopes for the eschaton and planned to write a full account of God's activity in world history. Death prevented his completion of that project, but he did complete a related work, *A Dissertation Concerning the End for Which God Created the World* (published 1765), which set out a more general vision of God's glory as the end to which all history moved.

Psychology. Edwards's examination of religious psychology arose directly out of his experiences in the Northampton revivals and, later, in the colonial Great Awakening as a whole. A letter to Boston's Benjamin Colman in 1736, later published as *Narrative of Surprising Conversions,* was the first of a series of works examining the nature and expression of awakened religious experience. This work analyzed events occurring during a local revival in Northampton, but soon Edwards published *Some Thoughts Concerning the Present Revival of Religion in New England* (1743) to take account of the wider movement. In particular, he responded to charges by anti-revivalists that the revival was all emotion, froth, and disorder. Edwards conceded that the emotionalism of the awakening could undercut authentic Christianity, but he also defended the revival by pointing to the more intense worship and to the permanently changed lives it left in its wake.

Three years later Edwards published his most mature examination of this subject, *A Treatise on the Religious Affections,* a book which has—with justice—been likened in its acuity to William James's *Varieties of Religious Experience.* This volume argued that true religion resides in the heart, or the seat of affections, emotions, and inclinations. But it also detailed with painstaking scrutiny the kinds of religious emotions that are largely irrelevant to any determination of true spirituality. The book closed with a description of twelve "marks" which indicate the presence of true religion. The first of these was a religious affection arising "from those influences and operations on the heart, which are spiritual, supernatural and divine." The last was the manifestation of true religion—genuinely gracious affections—in Christian practice. Edwards's careful analysis of genuine faith emphasized, in sum, that it was not the quantity of emotions which indicated the presence of true spirituality, but the origin of such emotions with God and their manifestation in works in accord with the law of God.

Metaphysics. Edwards's metaphysical speculations also deserve consideration as part of his religious convictions, since they were so intensely theological. They have been largely ignored in the subsequent history of American evangelical theology, but they still represent a compelling effort to view reality in strictly theistic terms. Edwards recorded most of his metaphysical work in notebooks which have begun to be published only in recent years. But these more substantial reflections are consonant with modes of thought present in *Freedom of Will* and other works published during his life.

In broadest terms Edwards's metaphysical reflections demonstrate the truthfulness of James Ward Smith's contention that Edwards alone of eighteenth and nineteenth century American theologians understood the "deeper spirit" as well as the "superficial corpus" of the new science associated with Newton and Locke. Edwards read these two giants with intense interest and considerable pleasure. He also accepted important aspects of their thought, such as Newton's description of the relationship among physical entities (i.e., universal gravitational attraction) and Locke's notions of memory and, with some qualifications, sensation. Yet Edwards was not tied uncritically to these two, and he profited as well from his wide reading in other seventeenth century philosophers, including the Cambridge Platonist Henry More.

Edwards's most important metaphysical commitment was to idealism. Physical reality and physical laws are not self-explanatory, according to Edwards, but are the result of God's constant and voluntary choices. With this conviction Edwards was still able to accept most of Newtonian science. As he put it: "To find out the reasons of things in natural philosophy is only to find out the proportion of God's acting. And the case is the same . . . whether we suppose the world [is] only mental in our sense, or no." Yet Edwards repudiated the dualism between mind and matter which Newton assumed and which was the heart of Locke's epistemology. Rather, as Edwards phrased it in his notes on "The Mind": "That which truly is the substance of all bodies is the infinitely exact and precise and perfectly stable idea in God's mind, together with his stable will that the same shall gradually be communicated to us, and to other minds, according to certain fixed and exact established methods and laws."

For Edwards this idealism was an outgrowth of his surpassingly high view of God. All reality, not just all religious occurrences, depended upon the harmony, goodness, consistency, and orderliness of God.

Ethics. Most of the major themes of Edwards's theology came together in the ethical interests which dominated the last period of his life. In particular he was concerned to argue against "the new moral philosophy" of the eighteenth century Enlightenment. This was a tendency, traceable to the Third Earl of Shaftesbury (1671–1713), the Scottish moralist Francis Hutcheson (1694–1746), and to many other ethicists of the seventeenth and eighteenth centuries, who argued that human beings possessed some natural faculty or sense which, when cultivated properly, could point the way to a truly virtuous life. In response to this broad intellectual tendency, which was the ethical counterpart to the generally ameliorative views of human nature prominent in his century, Edwards reacted strongly by contending that true virtue could not be understood apart from God and his revelation. It was Edwards's argument, especially in the posthumously published *Nature of True Virtue* (1765), that genuine morality arises only from God's regenerating mercy.

In his ethical deliberations Edwards returned constantly to the contribution of grace to ethical behavior. His dilemma was to show how his well-developed theology of the renewed heart (an Augustinian motif shared by Puritans such as William Ames) differed from the natural sentimentalism of Shaftesbury and Hutcheson. Edwards's goal was to give seventeenth century conceptions of Puritan piety, which tied true virtue to God's work in the heart, a respectable philosophical defense for his own century.

Edwards's approach involved three steps. He first acknowledged a limited value in the work of the new moralists. People by nature, because of God's common grace, did possess the capacity to act ethically in a carefully qualified sense. Natural conscience did have a prudential value in regulating conduct, sentiments of symmetry and beauty did provide insights into the nature of human morality, piety and familial affection did help stabilize society, and a natural "moral sense" did reveal some truths about the ethical world.

Secondly, however, Edwards insisted that the socially useful benefits of natural virtue fell far short of true virtue. For him the unshakable foundation remained the regenerating grace by which God quickened the sinner. In his own words: "Nothing is of the nature of true virtue, in which God is not the first and the last." In sum, Edwards was asserting in ethics what he had previously asserted concerning the inner life in *Religious Affections* and concerning conversion in *Freedom of Will*. No truly good thing, speaking strictly, exists which is not always and everywhere dependent upon God.

Thirdly, Edwards also tried to show that the picture of virtue presented by the new moral philosophers was merely a confusing description of prudence, self-seeking, and self-love. In these efforts Edwards was striving to preserve the particularity of grace. By so doing, he hoped to reassert the unique goodness of God as the sole legitimate source of true virtue.

Edwards's thought has been a theological landmark for many subsequent American Christians, but only a very few have seriously tried to maneuver by his coordinates. This lack of successors to continue his theological emphases may be due to the changing conditions of an increasingly democratic America; it may be due to weaknesses in his thought; or it may be due to the incapacity of those who called themselves "Edwardseans." In any event, the theology of Jonathan Edwards remains of great interest both for historians of the eighteenth century and for some modern theologians, especially those who sense a need for a renewed presentation of philosophically sophisticated Calvinistic and Augustinian theology in the modern world. M. A. Noll

See also New England Theology; Great Awakenings, The.

Bibliography. Edwards, *The Nature of True Virtue*, ed. W. K. Frankena, and *Representative Selections*, ed. C. H. Faust and T. H. Johnson. *The Works of Jonathan Edwards: Freedom of the Will*, ed. P. Ramsey; *Religious Affections*, ed. J. E. Smith; *Original Sin*, ed. C. A. Holbrook; *The Great Awakening*, ed. C. C. Goen; *Apocalyptic Writings*, ed. S. J. Stein; *Scientific and Philosophical Writings*, ed. W. E. Anderson. C. Cherry, *The Theology of Jonathan Edwards: A Reappraisal;* E. H. Davidson, *Jonathan Edwards: The Narrative of a Puritan Mind;* N. Fiering, *Jonathan Edwards's Moral Thought and Its British Context;* P. Miller, *Jonathan Edwards;* H. P. Simonson, *Jonathan Edwards: Theologian of the Heart;* J. W. Smith, "Religion and Science in American Philosophy," in *The Shaping of American Religion*, ed. Smith and A. L. Jamison; O. E. Winslow, *Jonathan Edwards, 1703–1758.*

Effectual Calling. *See* Call, Calling.

Efficacious Grace. *See* Grace.

Egotism. *See* Self-Esteem, Self-Love.

El. *See* God, Names of.

Elder. ***In the OT.*** The "elders of the people" or the "elders of Israel" are frequently associated with Moses in his dealings with the people (Exod. 3:16; 4:29; 17:5; 18:12; 19:17; 24:1, 11; Num. 11:16). They later administer local government (Judg. 8:14; Josh. 20:4; Ruth 4:2) and have a hand in national affairs (I Sam. 4:3) even after the institution of the monarchy (I Sam. 8:4; 30:26; II Sam. 3:17; 5:3; I Kings 21:8). They achieve fresh prominence during the Exile (Jer. 29:1; Ezek. 7:1; 14:1; 20:1) and after the return are associated both with the governor in his functions (Ezra 5:9ff.; 6:7) and with local administration (Ezra 10:14). They have by themselves certain juridical functions (Deut. 22:15; 25:7ff.) and are associated with the judges, who are probably appointed from their number, in the administration and execution of justice (Deut. 16:18; 21:2ff.; Ezra 7:25; 10:14). They are also associated with Moses and Aaron in conveying the word of God to the people (Exod. 3:14; 4:29; 19:7) and in representing the people before God (Exod. 17:5; 24:1; Num. 11:16) on great occasions. They see to the passover arrangements (Exod. 12:21).

Other nations had elders (cf. Gen. 50:7; Num. 22:7), the right to the title being due to age, or to the esteem in which an individual was held, or to the holding of a definite office in the community (cf. Saxon *alderman*, Roman *senator*, Greek *gerousia*). The elder in Israel no doubt at first derived his authority and status as well as his name by reason of his age and experience.

In the Maccabean period the title "elders of Israel" is used of the members of the Jewish Sanhedrin, which was regarded as having been set up by Moses in his appointment of the seventy elders in Num. 11:16ff. At the local level a community of 120 (cf. Acts 1:15) or more could appoint seven elders (Mishna, *Sanhedrin* 1:6). These were called the "seven of a city," and it is possible that the seven appointed in Acts 6 were regarded as such elders (cf. D. Daube, *The NT and Rabbinic Judaism*, 237). In the Gospels the elders are associated with the scribes and chief priests as those at whose hands Jesus (Matt. 16:21; 27:1) and the apostles (Acts 6:12) suffered.

In the NT. Elders or "presbyters" (*presbyteroi*) appear early in the life of the church, taking their place along with the apostles, prophets, and teachers. At Jerusalem they are associated with James in the government of the local church after the manner of the synagogue (Acts 11:30; 21:18), but in association with the apostles they also share in the wider, or more sanhedral, government of the whole church (Acts 15:2, 6, 23; 16:4). An apostle can be a presbyter (I Pet. 5:1).

Presbyters do not appear at Antioch during Paul's stay there (Acts 13:1), nor are they mentioned in Paul's earlier epistles. Possibly government was then a matter of minor importance. But Paul and Barnabas on their first missionary journey had presbyters appointed in all the churches they founded (Acts 14:23).

The presbyters whom Paul addressed at Ephesus (Acts 20:17ff.) and those addressed in I Peter and Titus have a decisive place in church life. Besides their function of humble pastoral oversight, on them largely depend the stability and purity of the flock in the approaching temptation and crisis. They are in a position of authority and privilege that can be abused. They share in the ministry of Christ toward the flock (I Pet. 5:1–4; Acts 20:28; cf. Eph. 4:11).

It is often asserted that in the Gentile churches the name *episkopos* is used as a substitute for *presbyteros* with identical meaning. The words seem to be interchangeable in Acts 20:17, 28; and Titus 1:5–9. But though all *episkopoi* are undoubtedly *presbyteroi*, it is not clear whether the reverse is always true. The word *presbyteros* denotes rather the status of eldership while *episkopos* denotes the function of at least some elders. But there may have been elders who were not *episkopoi*.

In I Tim. 5:17 teaching as well as oversight is regarded as a desirable function of the presbyter. It is likely that when the apostles and teachers and prophets ceased to be able to minister to the whole church in their travels, the function of teaching and preaching would fall on the local presbyters, and thus the office and the qualifications of those holding it would develop. This, again, may have led to distinction within the presbyterate. The presidency of the body of presbyters, in both the ordering of the congregation and the celebration of the Lord's Supper, would tend to become a permanent office held by one man.

The "elder" in II and III John refers merely to someone highly esteemed within the church. The twenty-four elders who appear so frequently in the visions of the book of Revelation are examples of how all authority should humbly adore God and the Lamb (Rev. 4:10; 5:8–10; 19:4). It is to be noted that even these presbyters seem to minister in heaven to the church on earth (Rev. 5:5, 8; 7:13).

In Church History. At the time of the Reformation, Calvin found that the office of elder was one of the four "orders or offices" which Christ had instituted for the ordinary government of the church, the others being pastors, doctors (teachers), and deacons. The elders, as representatives of the people, along with pastors or bishops were responsible for discipline. In Scotland the elder was later ordained for life, without the laying on of hands, and was given the duty of examining communicants and visiting the sick. He was encouraged to teach. The theory arose, through I Tim. 5:17, that ministers and elders were both presbyters of the same order, the former being the teaching elder, the latter the ruling elder. But, as a whole, the Presbyterian Church has held that there is a distinction between ordination to the ministry and that to the eldership, ordination being determined by the end to which it is directed. The elder has been regarded as a representative of the people (though not appointed by or responsible to the people) in the ordering of church affairs, and has fulfilled many of the functions appropriate to the diaconate in the NT. The pattern of the elder's work within the church corresponds closely to that of the OT "elder of the people."

R. S. WALLACE

See also CHURCH GOVERNMENT.

Bibliography. T. M. Lindsay, *The Church and Ministry in the Early Centuries;* B. H. Streeter, *The Primitive Church;* G. D. Henderson, *The Scottish Ruling Elder;* J. M. Ross, *What Is an Elder?* A. A. Hodge, *What Is Presbyterianism?* G. Bornkamm, *TDNT,* VI, 651ff.

Elect, Election. Scripture employs a rich vocabulary to express several aspects of God's sovereign election, choice, and predestination. Five types of election call for distinction. (1) There is only one reference to "the elect angels" (I Tim. 5:21; cf. I Cor. 6:3; II Pet. 2:4; Jude 6). (2) Election to service or office is evident in God's sovereign choice of David as Israel's king (I Sam. 16:7–12) and in Jesus' choosing of the disciples and apostles (Luke 6:13; John 6:70; 15:16; Acts 9:15; 15:7). (3) The election of Abraham's descendants to form the theocratic nation of Israel is a common biblical theme (Deut. 4:37; 7:6–7; 10:15; I Kings 3:8; Isa. 44:1–2; 45:4; 65:9, 15, 22; Amos 3:2; Acts 13:17; Rom. 9:1–5). The election of Israel originated in God's sovereign choice, expressed his covenantal love, and served the goal of redemptive history culminating in Jesus Christ. (4) The election of the Messiah is a fourth type of election. Isaiah referred to the servant of the Lord as "my chosen one" (42:1; cf. Matt. 12:18). Of the Synoptics only Luke refers to Jesus as the Chosen One (9:35; 23:35). Peter echoes another Isaiah reference (28:16) in I Pet. 1:20 and 2:4, 6. These references indicate the unique mediatorial office of Christ and the Father's pleasure in him. It is an election basic to the final type, (5) election to salvation, with which the rest of this article is concerned.

The most common NT reference to election is God's eternal election of certain persons to salvation in Jesus Christ. The subject is dealt with comprehensively in Eph. 1:3–11 and Rom. 8:28–11:36. John Calvin, who became a major defender of the Reformed doctrine, saw the whole doctrine of election summarized in Eph. 1. All the Reformed confessions include divine election, but the Canons of Dort, reflecting the controversy with the Arminians, provide the greatest detail. Election is part of God's eternal decree and it has a soteriological role: "That some in time are given faith by God and that others are not given faith proceeds from His eternal decree" (I.6). Election is then defined as "the unchangeable purpose of God whereby, before the foundation of the world, out of the whole human race, which had fallen by its own fault out of its original integrity into sin and ruin, He has, according to the most free good pleasure of His will, out of mere grace, chosen in Christ to salvation a certain number of specific men, neither better nor more worthy than others, but with them involved in a common misery" (I.7).

Double predestination is the typical Reformed doctrine. The Canons of Dort distinguish election and reprobation because the Scripture "declares that not all men are elect but that certain ones have not been elected, or have been passed by in the eternal election of God. These God out of His most free, most just, blameless, and unchangeable good pleasure has decreed to leave in the common misery into which they have by their own fault plunged themselves, and not to give them saving faith and the grace of conversion" and "finally to condemn and punish them eternally" for all their sins (I.15). Predestination thus includes election and reprobation, and reprobation involves both a sovereign passing by (preterition) and a just condemnation.

Principles of Election. Six main features of election deserve attention.

(1) Election is a sovereign, eternal decree of God. The elect have been "predestined according to the plan of him who works out everything in conformity with the purpose of his will" (Eph. 1:11). God chose us in Christ "before the creation of the world" (Eph. 1:4). God's sovereign decree is not arbitrary; "in love he predestined us . . . in accordance with his pleasure and will" (Eph. 1:5; cf. Rom. 8:29). This perspective is reflected in the definition of election quoted above from Dort (I.7).

(2) The presupposition of God's eternal decree of election is that the human race is fallen; election involves God's gracious rescue plan. It is not based on human works or God's foreknowledge of works (Rom. 9:11). The elect are chosen "to be holy and blameless in his sight"; they are "adopted as his sons through Jesus Christ" (Eph. 1:4–5). Hence election leads to "redemption through his blood, the forgiveness of sins" (Eph. 1:7). The same perspective is evident in Romans, for those whom "God foreknew he also predestined to be conformed to the likeness of his Son" (8:29). The presupposition is that they are fallen, and hence God's predestination includes calling, justification, and glorification. This presupposition, that the fallen race is the object of predestination, reflects the infralapsarian perspective which is also that of the Canons of Dort (cf. I.1,8,15).

(3) Election is "election in Christ"; election involves rescue from sin and guilt and receiving the gracious gifts of salvation. Election in Christ is evident in the words already quoted from Eph.

1:4–5, 11, and Rom. 8:29. Christ is not merely a subsequent means to effectuate a decree of election; election is in Christ and through Christ. This is clearly expressed in the Canons of Dort: "He has . . . chosen in Christ to salvation. . . . From eternity He has also appointed Christ to be the Mediator and Head of all the elect and the foundation of their salvation. Therefore He decreed to give to Christ those who were to be saved, and effectually to call and draw them into His fellowship through His word and Spirit" (I.7). Thus God's election is in Christ, and Christ is both the foundation of election and the foundation of salvation. Calvin also referred to Christ as the mirror of our election.

(4) Election involves both the elect's salvation and the means to that end. This is already evident in the repeated references to election in Christ, but it is made even more specific. God chose the elect "to be holy and blameless in his sight, . . . to be adopted as his sons" (Eph. 1:4–5); the elect are those whom God "foreknew . . . predestined . . . called . . . justified . . . glorified" (Rom. 8:29–30). God chose the elect "to be saved through the sanctifying work of the Spirit and through belief in the truth" (II Thess. 2:13). Hence the preaching of the gospel is indispensable in effecting God's election (Rom. 10:14–17; cf. Acts 18:9–11). The salvation of the elect has its decretive origin before time, is realized through means in history, and culminates in eternal glorification. This is echoed in the Canons of Dort: "He decreed to give them true faith in Him, to justify them, to sanctify them, and, after having powerfully kept them in the fellowship of His Son, finally to glorify them, for the demonstration of His mercy and the praise of the riches of His glorious grace" (I.7). This feature of election negates the objection that if one is elect, one will be saved regardless of whether or not one believes. It also excludes the objection that election leads to a libertine spirit; unbelief and careless living are inconsistent with the scriptural doctrine of election.

(5) Election (as well as reprobation) is individual, personal, specific, particular. Ephesians refers repeatedly to "us" and "we" in connection with election (1:4–5, 12). In Romans, Paul refers to "those" whom God foreknew, predestined, called, justified, and glorified (8:29–30). Rom. 9 indicates that personal election unto salvation was operative within the election of Israel. Paul states that "not all who are descended from Israel are Israel" (9:6, 8) and he shows that "God's purpose in election" distinguished between Isaac and Ishmael, between Jacob and Esau (9:7, 11–13). This is also the implication of the expressions in John 6:37–40; 10:14–16, 26–29; 17:2, 6, 9, 24. Hence the Canons of Dort refer to election as the selection of "a certain number of specific men" (I.7) and also state that "not all men are elect but that certain ones have not been elected" but passed by in God's decree (I.15). The Westminster Confession expresses this even more emphatically when it refers to the predestined as "particularly and unchangeably designed, and their number so certain and definite that it cannot be either increased or diminished" (III.4). The Arminians held to an indefinite, conditional election, the election of those who believe. The Reformed view took the above Scripture references seriously as well as the comforting assurance that nothing "shall separate us from the love of Christ" and that "in all these things we are more than conquerors through him who loved us" (Rom. 8:35–39). Particular, personal election leads to the believer's comfort and does not promote carelessness or false confidence.

(6) Finally, the ultimate goal of election is the glory and praise of God. Election to salvation involves personal privilege, blessing, security, and comfort for the elect. But Scripture makes clear that it is "to the praise of his glorious grace" that everything leads (Eph. 1:6). The elect have been chosen and predestined "in order that we . . . might be for the praise of his glory" (Eph. 1:12). God's goal is "to bring all things in heaven and on earth together under one head, even Christ" (Eph. 1:10; cf. I Pet. 1:1; 2:9; Matt. 13:27–30; 24:31). When Paul finished his long discussion of election in Romans, he concluded with doxology (Rom. 11:33–36). That praise is also echoed in the Reformed confessions; the final glorification of the elect is "for the demonstration of His mercy and praise of the riches of His glorious grace" (Canons of Dort I.7). The Westminster Confession concludes its discussion of God's eternal decree and predestination with similar words: "So shall this doctrine afford matter of praise, reverence, and admiration of God; and of humility, diligence, and abundant consolation to those that sincerely obey the Gospel" (III.8).

F. H. Klooster

See also Decrees of God; Predestination; Reprobation; Supralapsarianism; Sovereignty of God.

Bibliography. G. C. Berkouwer, *Divine Election;* L. Boettner, *The Reformed Doctrine of Predestination;* J. Calvin, *Institutes* 3.21–24; P. Y. De Jong, ed., *Crisis in the Reformed Churches: Essays in Commemoration of the Great Synod of Dort, 1618–1619;* F. H. Klooster, *Calvin's Doctrine of Predestination;* B. B. Warfield, "Predestination," in *Biblical Doctrines,* "Predestination in the Reformed Confessions," in *Studies in Theology,* and "Election," in *Selected Shorter Writings of B. B. Warfield,* I, 285–98.

El-Eloe-Israel. *See* God, Names of.

El Elyon. *See* God, Names of.

Elements, Elemental Spirits. The root meaning of this NT expression (*ta stoicheia*) is "belonging to a series." It was used to describe, among other things, the order of letters in the alphabet, and hence the elementary principles (the ABCs) of any science or system. This usage is reflected in Heb. 5:12, where immature Christians are criticized for failing to grow out of their doctrinal infancy. *Stoicheia* was also widely used in NT times for the four primary elements of the physical world (earth, water, air, and fire). So II Pet. 3:10, 12, foretells the destruction of the elements on the eschatological day of the Lord.

The meaning Paul attaches to *stoicheia* is not so clear (Gal. 4:3, 9; Col. 2:8, 20). By "the elements of the world" he may simply mean world order; that is, the elementary truths of natural religion, expressed in basic ethical precepts, which structure the lives of ordinary people (cf. NIV "basic principles"). Many commentators, however, believe that Paul had supernatural powers in mind (cf. RSV "elemental spirits"). He certainly appears to personify the *stoicheia* (Gal. 4:2–3) and to link them with angel worship (Col. 2:18). Jewish and early Christian sources attest a widespread belief in spiritual agencies behind the natural elements (Jub. 2:2; II Esd. 6:3; Aristides, *Apology* 3–6, 7.4). If the heresy under attack in Colossians is a syncretistic combination of Eastern religion and Jewish law, Paul's sights may also have been set on the worship of astral deities (*stoicheia* came in time to mean "stars"; cf. I Enoch 80:6).

The main argument against this interpretation is that all the known instances of *stoicheia* with a spiritual reference occur after the first century A.D. Paul also links bondage to the *stoicheia* with Jewish legalism. Whatever the Judaizers' failings, it is hard to believe that he meant to accuse them of star worship. Identifying the elemental spirits with the angels who mediated the giving of the law (Gal. 3:19) only aggravates the problem by suggesting an un-Pauline disparagement of the law itself (*contra* Rom. 9:4–5).

Whether Paul meant to spiritualize the "elements" or not, the theological thrust of his argument is clear. The *stoicheia* stand for all religious and ethical practices, whether Jewish law-keeping or pagan worship of "no-gods" (Gal. 4:3–5, 8–9), which belong to life outside Christ. Compared to him, they are all "weak and miserable" (Gal. 4:9). He has triumphed over them, and intends his followers to be free from their bondage (Col. 2:20).

D. H. Field

Bibliography. G. Delling, *TDNT*, VII, 670–87; H.-H. Esser, *NIDNTT*, II, 451ff.; E. Lohse, *Colossians and Philemon;* D. Guthrie, *NT Theology;* G. E. Ladd, *Theology of the NT.*

Elijah. Of four persons so named in the OT, the life of only one is known in detail: Elijah the Tishbite, one of the prophets, who came from the region of Gilead in Transjordan. The name means "Yahweh is God." Elijah's prophetic ministry was conducted in the northern state of Israel, *ca.* 875–850 B.C., during the Omride Dynasty, principally during the reign of King Ahab and his foreign wife, Jezebel.

In the OT, the principal sources of Elijah's life are to be found in I Kings 17–19; 21:17–29; and II Kings 1–2. A series of incidents in his life and ministry are known, but it is not possible to reconstruct a complete biography. Elijah is described only in the historical narratives of the OT; unlike many other prophets, no book has been named after him. Key incidents in his life include raising the widow's son, the contest on Mount Carmel with the prophets of Baal, the encounter with God at Mount Horeb, and his departure from this world in a chariot of fire. He was succeeded by his distinguished disciple Elisha.

In Israel's religion Elijah stood firmly in the tradition of the Mosaic faith and championed a return to the old ways, against the encroachments of the foreign religion introduced in Israel by Jezebel. He emphasized a number of important perspectives in Israel's faith. (1) He stressed the dangers of syncretism; the true faith would be lost if it became fused with the religion of Baal-Melqart. (2) He emphasized the intimate relationship between faith and ethics. The incident of Naboth's vineyard (I Kings 21) illustrates the championing of the just cause of an individual against a monarch's authority. (3) He perceived the international nature of God's power; even an evil foreign king could be used to achieve God's purposes.

In later Judaism, Elijah came to be seen as a forerunner of the messianic age; this view was based in part on his translation and on the prophecy of Malachi (4:5–6). In addition, he is referred to frequently in the Talmud and in the later mystical writings of Judaism as one who visited the rabbis and mystics, instructing them in the meaning of the Torah. In the contemporary Jewish ritual of circumcision Elijah is believed to be present; an empty chair is set out for him, his presence symbolizing faithfulness to the covenant.

Continuity with the Jewish tradition can be

observed in NT references to Elijah. Many persons hesitated to accept the message of Jesus, claiming that the kingdom could not come until Elijah had returned; Jesus indicated that Elijah had already appeared in the person of John the Baptist (Mark 9:11–13). Indeed, many people thought that Jesus himself was Elijah (Mark 8:27). At the transfiguration Jesus talked with Moses and Elijah, who represented the law and the prophets.

Elijah is also a significant figure in Islam, being referred to several times in the Koran. His attempt to turn people away from the worship of Baal, back to the true faith, is used in Muhammad's preaching to exemplify true prophecy.

P. C. Craigie

Bibliography. J. Gray, *I and II Kings;* H. H. Rowley, "Elijah on Mount Carmel," *BJRL* 43:190–210; G. E. Saint-Laurent, "Light from Ras Shamra on Elijah's Ordeal on Mount Carmel," in *Scripture in Context,* ed. C. D. Evans, W. W. Hallo, and J. B. White.

Elohim. *See* God, Names of.

El Shaddai. *See* God, Names of.

Elyah. *See* God, Names of.

Emanation. The English word used to describe the Greek *aporroia,* "a flowing down from," which became a technical term for Greek philosophers such as Empedocles, who employs the idea of emanation to connect external realities with mind perceptions. In Philo the Logos doctrine becomes the first stage of bridging the gap between the transcendent God and the world of sense perception or between the realm of unity and world of plurality. Plotinus seeks to interpret the move from transcendence to the world of sense by an analogy to light and its weakened intensity as it moves farther from its source.

In the Gnostic systems the concept of emanation becomes the basis for explaining the problem of evil through the development of a defect in the godhead itself. The emanation process in a Valentinian structure begins with a transcendent pair of deities—"ultimate depth" and "silence"—and ends with a defective "Sophia" or "wisdom" who is subject to a "fall" or defection from her intended state.

In the Middle Ages the Neoplatonic ideas of Plotinus and others were mixed with Christian perspectives and gave birth to the mysticism of thinkers like John Scotus Erigena. The universal is real and a causal process gives birth to the particular. Thus, the created order is really God unfolded into particularities. This unfolding process is basically the emanation process of Plotinus, and the angels of Christian mysticism are conceived according to Neoplatonic order.

G. L. Borchert

See also Neoplatonism; Gnosticism; Mysticism.

Ember Days. In Roman Catholicism and Anglicanism Wednesday, Friday, and Saturday of the four Ember weeks. They occur in the weeks after the Feast of St. Lucy (Dec. 13), Ash Wednesday, Pentecost, and Holy Cross Day (Sept. 14). Originally in the fifth century there were three Ember weeks corresponding to the agricultural festivals of sowing time, corn harvest, and vintage time. A fourth was added by the seventh century. The twelve days were seen as times for prayer, fasting, and almsgiving. In modern times they have been retained but with modifications in their intentions. They can be associated either with special prayer for those to be ordained in the church or with special prayer for the needs of the world.

P. Toon

Emerson, Ralph Waldo (1803–1882). American transcendentalist, essayist, poet. A child of the Puritans, Emerson fathered a cultural tradition his spiritual ancestors might well have deplored. He helped to sever the final ties of that tradition to the historic Christian faith, and he is considered the central figure in the birth and growth of a distinct American literature. Because of his immediate impact upon Thoreau, Hawthorne, Whitman, Melville, and Dickinson, and his continuing influence upon figures as diverse as William James, Robert Frost, and Henry Ford, it is all but impossible to imagine the development of American literary and cultural life without Emerson.

Like his father, who had been the pastor of one of Boston's most influential churches, Emerson also trained for the ministry. But even though the Unitarianism of Emerson's day required little specific theological commitment, Emerson found even its limited requirements stifling. He resigned his own pastorate in 1832 in a dispute over the Lord's Supper. True radical Protestant that he was, Emerson questioned both the morality and efficacy of any historical event or ritualistic practice that claimed in any way to mediate the soul's direct experience of God.

To the training in liberal Christianity and commonsense realism he had received at home and at Harvard, Emerson added, through wide reading in early adulthood, the influences of the controversial sectarian Emmanuel Swedenborg, the Neoplatonist philosopher Plotinus, the English poet and critic Samuel Taylor Coleridge, and through Coleridge the German philosopher Immanuel Kant. Countless scattered references to these and other sources made their way into Emerson's journals and eventually into the lectures and essays through which he established his fame in the late 1830s and 1840s. Having abandoned pulpit and sermon, he found in lectern and lecture a forum perfectly suited to his needs.

In that forum he preached a message of romantic idealism that was distinctly his own and distinctly American. In *Nature* (1836), *Essays, First Series* (1841), *Essays, Second Series* (1844), and *Representative Men* (1850), Emerson exhorted his audiences to lead lives of self-reliant rectitude and purpose. He took many underlying themes in the American experience—a disdain for the past, a distrust of authority, an unbridled faith in the future—and made them the manifest content of his artistic and religious faith. "Imitation is suicide," Emerson proclaimed in "Self-Reliance," and he repeatedly preached the need for American writers to free themselves from bondage to the formal and thematic traditions of English literature and the need for American spirituality to break with historic Christianity. Instead of a faith bound to what he thought to be the dead letter of Scripture and tradition, Emerson called, in "The Divinity School Address," for "a faith like Christ's in the infinitude of man." In his loftier moments Emerson foresaw nothing less than the total regeneration of historical life, a secularized millennium ushered in through the exercise of American principles. R. LUNDIN

See also TRANSCENDENTALISM.

Bibliography. *The Complete Works of Ralph Waldo Emerson*, 12 vols.; *The Journals and Miscellaneous Notebooks of Ralph Waldo Emerson*, I-XIV; F. O. Matthiessen, *American Renaissance: Art and Expression in the Age of Emerson and Whitman;* J. Porte, *The Representative Man: Ralph Waldo Emerson in His Time;* G. W. Allen, *Waldo Emerson: A Biography.*

Emmanuel. *See* IMMANUEL.

Emotion. Emotions have been viewed by Christians in a variety of ways. Some see them as one of God's finest gifts to mankind, reflecting something of the divine nature and bestowing richness on personal functioning. Others have viewed them as a serious complication to life; sometimes they are even seen to be a result of the fall. This ambivalence has been heightened in recent years by the attention given to emotions by modern psychology, with some psychologists even telling us to trust our emotions as a guide for behavior. Sensitivity groups encourage free emotional expression. Many Christians have recoiled from this culture of emotionality.

An understanding of the intended role of emotions in personality must begin with the creation account in Scripture. God created man in his image and pronounced that the created product was good. Emotionality was part of the original creation and not a consequence of the fall. This is clear from the record of Eve experiencing delight in considering the fruit of the tree of the knowledge of good and evil (Gen. 3:6).

But if man was created with emotions and described as being in God's image, then God must have emotions. Indeed, the biblical record makes it abundantly clear that this is the case. God is described as experiencing sorrow (Gen. 6:5–6), anger (Deut. 13:17), pleasure (Ps. 149:4), and a number of other emotions. An examination of the life of Jesus makes this point even more forcefully. Jesus is reported to have experienced anger on numerous occasions (John 2:14–22; Mark 3:1–5; Matt. 23). He also experienced fear (Matt. 26:38–39), grief (John 11:35), sadness (Luke 19:41–42), joy (John 15:11), compassion (Mark 1:41), and love (John 14:31). So characteristic were emotions of our Lord that we call him the Man of Sorrows.

In the Bible a great deal of emphasis is given to emotional states in the description of individuals. In fact, Scripture not only speaks about emotions, it also speaks to and through our emotions. The Bible itself is emotional literature, filled with emotional expression and designed not just to communicate with our rationality but also to stir us emotionally, thus affirming our emotionality.

Yet discovering God's affirmation of emotions does not answer our question about their intended role in personality. God makes us emotional creatures because he is emotional in nature and wished to create us like himself. But how are we to respond to our emotions? Can they be trusted as a guide for behavior?

An answer to these difficult questions must begin with the realization that our emotionality bears the marks of the fall. Expressions of emotion can be sinful; for example, Paul warns us that such can be the case with our anger (Eph. 4:26, 31). However, Christ's example teaches us that it is possible for the expression of anger to be an act of righteousness (Mark 3:5). It would seem that any emotional expression has the potential of being either God-honoring or God-displeasing.

The response of some Christians to this realization has been to suppress emotional expression. They feel that while they may not be able to control the experience of the emotion, they certainly can control its expression. Rather than have their life complicated by deciding between appropriate and inappropriate expressions, they simplify matters by attempting to minimize emotional expression. However, such emotional suppression is not only the cause of many psychological problems, it should probably also be seen as a sinful response to emotion in that it violates God's intentions. Emotions were given in order to energize behavior and were intended by God to be a catalyst for action. Because of the fall they are imperfect guides to behavior, so we cannot simply "do as we feel." But we must pay attention to our feelings. Only when they are acknowledged can the appropriate response be made.

Christianity alone of the world's religions gives man's emotional life a balanced place. In contrast to the Stoics, who viewed emotion as irrational, and the Epicureans, who acquiesced to the inevitability of emotions, Jesus realistically faced emotion in man's life and provided us with guidelines for emotional expression. Life gains an intensity and richness when emotions are used as valid means of relating to the world, other people, and to God. Therefore Christians should thank God for their emotions and allow them to enrich their lives in the ways God intended.

D. G. Benner

Bibliography. B. B. Warfield, "The Emotional Life of Our Lord," in *The Person and Work of Christ;* J. E. Pedersen, "Some Thoughts on a Biblical View of Anger," *JPT* 2:210–15; J. E. Eccles, *The Human Psyche;* E. Lutzer, *Managing Your Emotions.*

Empiricism, Empirical Theology. The philosophical theory that all ideas are derived from experience, asserting that both internal and external experience are the sole foundation of true knowledge and of science. While Enlightenment figures such as John Locke and Francis Bacon have been associated with the empiricist approach, David Hume is the clearest representative of empiricism. In his *An Enquiry Concerning Human Understanding,* Hume maintained that all of one's knowledge of the world is the product of experience. While man can know the relation between ideas with certainty, their actual reality cannot be established beyond probability. Thus, the true nature and scope of ordinary and scientific knowledge can be revealed only by a "science of man," founded on experience and observation. In Hume's view observation and experience teach that all thoughts are derived from past experience. In contrast to the blind person, for example, men can think about colors because they have seen them. It is from man's impressions that all of his ideas are ultimately derived. Impressions are man's forceful and lively perceptions, whereas ideas are nothing but faint copies of impressions. A remembered pain, according to Hume, is obviously less vivid a perception than a felt pain.

Hume's empiricism established a criterion for meaning and significance which has been adopted by many since his time. Complex ideas are only combinations of simple ideas. Thus, the idea of a "golden mountain" is only the joining together of two previously experienced simple ideas, "gold" and "mountain." Since the simple ideas are copies of impressions, one can test the meaningfulness of both scientific and philosophical statements by asking, "From what impression is that supposed idea derived?" If it is impossible to assign any, one should be suspicious of that statement. Any truth discoverable by thought alone never tells one about the world, but only about internal relations between one's ideas. Such a truth is a statement true only by definition, the denial of which is self-contradictory; e.g., "All spinsters are unmarried." Therefore, in the empirical approach, all reasoning about relations of ideas—e.g., logic, arithmetic, geometry, algebra—is analytic and based on the principle of noncontradiction; all reasoning about matters of fact—e.g., physics, chemistry, one's everyday knowledge—is based upon merely probable past observations and experiences.

While "all ideas are derived from experience" is the crux of empiricism, the word "empirical" has been overused and misapplied to such an extent that in the last two centuries ideological incompatibles such as Francis Bacon, Thomas Hobbes, Immanuel Kant, William James, Henri Bergson, Rudolf Carnap, and Edmund Husserl have been designated at one time or another as empiricists. Most of this confusion results from differences in definition and interpretation of "ideas," "derived from," and "experience." Since Hume comes closest to a thoroughgoing empiricism, the problems with the empiricist approach are seen perhaps most clearly in his criteria. When his criteria are applied consistently, they narrow the scope of genuine knowledge almost to a vanishing point. For example, when Hume applied his criteria to the scientific method (induction), he concluded that because empirical generalization is founded on the principle of cause and effect, and because cause and effect cannot itself be clearly confirmed by experience, the scientific method has no certain foundations. In fact, such empirical principles led Hume to declare that one could not know whether physical things (such as a body, house, or tree) actually existed. All one could ascertain was that there have been and are particular impressions and ideas of physical things.

The root problem with any form of empiricism is that of the relation of discourse concerning experience to the factual or empirical data. It involves the relation between experiences and the "meanings" by which experiences can be conceptualized, articulated, and communicated. Since there may be a variety of interpretations of what constitutes an experience, any appeal to experience as the sole arbiter of meaning and significance is problematical. Such an appeal is completely dependent on which interpretation of the experience one applies. This problem was particularly apparent when twentieth century logical positivists attempted to construct a unified approach to all areas of knowledge and science. This attempt failed because logical positivists were unable to keep theoretical interpretations from entering into their "observation" language.

Empiricism has been applied to theology in various ways. Hume believed in studying religion scientifically because there was nothing unique about religious experience. Friedrich Schleiermacher did believe that religious experience was unique, and he believed that theology could only provide symbols for describing the great diversity of man's religious experiences. Therefore, every man must have a private description of his feelings, an individual theology. Some would suggest that Schleiermacher is the source of all the "religious experience" theories current today. Liberal theologians of the latter nineteenth and early twentieth centuries applied the scientific method to religion, attempting to reconstruct the Christian faith in accordance with the "modern" findings of science. Thus, a proper Christian understanding of the world and its progress required the empirical method. This desire to harmonize the Christian faith with the empirical method of science is not merely a modern liberal phenomenon but also can be found in the eighteenth century natural theologies of conservative writers such as William Paley and Bishop Butler. Some modern conservatives, such as John Warwick Montgomery, have continued this trend.

D. A. Rausch

See also Hume, David.

Bibliography. A. Pasch, *Experience and the Analytic;* H. Morich, ed., *Challenges to Empiricism;* J. W. Montgomery, *The Shape of the Past.*

Encratites. A group who practiced an ascetic mode of life, including permanent abstinence from eating meat, drinking wine, and marriage. They appeared first in the second century. The early church viewed such permanent abstinence as wrong because it denigrated God's creation. While it cannot be decisively proved that the Encratites were Gnostics, they were considered heretical by some early writers—e.g., Irenaeus, Hippolytus, and Eusebius of Caesarea. Their stress on permanent abstinence was certainly a Gnostic trait. Some of the best-known followers of this extremely ascetic mode of life were Tatian, Marcion, and Saturninus. These men added theological heresy to the practical heresy of extreme asceticism.

J. H. Hall

Bibliography. Eusebius, *Ecclesiastical History,* IV. 29; R. M. Grant, "The Heresy of Tatian," *JTS* new series 5:62–68; *DCB,* II, 118–20.

End of the World. *See* Eschatology.

Endurance. The word does not occur in the AV translation of the NT. "Enduring" is found once (II Cor. 1:6) as the translation of the noun *hypomonē.* Unfortunately, in the AV this Greek noun is translated "patience" twenty-nine out of the thirty-two times it occurs in the NT—altogether too weak a rendering for *hypomonē.* It comes from the verb *hypomenō,* which literally means "remain under." The AV translators did a much better job with the verb, rendering it "endure" eleven out of its seventeen NT occurrences.

The verb plays a significant role. Jesus said that "he who stands firm to the end will be saved" (Matt. 10:22; 24:13; Mark 13:13, NIV). This is a solemn warning about the essential importance of endurance. It is not enough to be born again. One must stand firm in the faith to the end of one's life on earth.

The noun *hypomonē* is perhaps even more significant. The AV does well in translating it "patient continuance" in Rom. 2:7. The NIV has "persistence," which is the basic idea of the term. Not so fortunate is the AV translation of this noun in Heb. 12:1: "Let us run with patience the race that is set before us." No one ever won a race by simply being patient. The Christian race is a long distance marathon—a term very familiar to the people of Paul's day. It can be won only by running with "perseverance" (NIV).

Another significant passage is II Thess. 1:4, where Paul speaks of "your perseverance and faith in all the persecutions and trials you are enduring" (NIV). The last verb is *anechō,* which means "hold up (under)." All Christians have "persecutions" of some kind (Acts 14:22) as well as "trials" of many kinds. What is needed is endurance to hold up under these hardships.

R. Earle

Energumen. *See* Demon, Demon Possession.

Enlightenment, The. The Age of Enlightenment (German *Die Aufklärung*) covers roughly the eighteenth century. It is sometimes identified with the Age of Reason, but the latter term covers both the seventeenth and eighteenth centuries. Although the Enlightenment had some of its roots in seventeenth century rationalism, the ideas which characterize the Enlightenment went far beyond the rationalism of Descartes, Spinoza, and the thinkers of their time.

In 1784 Immanuel Kant wrote an article in answer to the question "What is enlightenment?" He replied that enlightenment was man's coming of age. It was man's emergence from the immaturity which caused him to rely on such external authorities as the Bible, the church, and the state to tell him what to think and do. No generation should be bound by the creeds and customs of bygone ages. To be so bound is an offense against human nature, whose destiny lies in progress. Kant admitted that the eighteenth century was not yet an enlightened age, but it was the age of enlightenment. The barriers to progress were coming down; the field was now open. The motto of enlightenment was *Sapere aude*—"Have courage to use your own understanding."

Kant wrote his article at a point almost midway between the American and French Revolutions. It was not accidental that such leading figures and thinkers in the American Revolution as Jefferson, Franklin, and Paine enjoyed close ties with their French enlightened counterparts. Both the Declaration of Independence of the United States of America (1776) and the Statement of Human and Civil Rights ratified by the French National Assembly (1789) bear the stamp of enlightened thinking. Both appealed to truths which were deemed to be self-evident. Although some reference to God or a Supreme Being was retained, such concepts as life, liberty, and the pursuit of happiness (American) and freedom, property, security, and the right to protect oneself from violence (French) were regarded as naturally valid.

Linked with these ideas was an enlightened philosophy of government that implicitly rejected the idea that kings and governments had been appointed by God with inalienable rights to govern. Governments were now said to derive their authority from the consent of the governed. Essential sovereignty resides in the nation as a whole and not simply in those who govern. Laws may be changed to meet the needs and desires of the subjects. Likewise governments may be changed when they become injurious to the governed. Underlying all this was the idea of the social contract, which had been put forward by Thomas Hobbes in the seventeenth century and restated by John Locke and Jean-Jacques Rousseau. The latter saw society based on an implicit social pact that combined freedom with just government in the interests of the majority. All society involves compromise by which individual members accept certain constraints in order to achieve the maximum liberty for all.

The classic documents of the American and French Revolutions with their allusions to God represent a middle stage between the traditional Christian view of the state and modern secular democracy. Calvin had seen the state as a divinely appointed instrument for the protection of law and order, the maintenance of morals, and the promotion of true religion, all based on the Word of God. The enlightened view of the state did not dismiss God altogether. In general enlightened thinkers adopted a deistic view of God, acknowledging his existence as Creator but leaving the conduct of life to man and his reason. The enlightened view of the state acknowledged the deity but proposed essentially humanistic goals for society, insisting that both the ends and the means should be determined by reason acting in accordance with nature.

The theme of nature figured large in enlightened thought. Nature embodied both the beautiful and the good. It was also eminently accessible to the right use of reason. The high esteem in which nature was held was linked in part to the fact that it was simply there as self-evident reality and in part to the prestige of modern science, exemplified in Isaac Newton's mechanistic view of a world governed by rational laws. In France the enlightened view of an orderly, rational world found expression in the *Encyclopedia* (1751–65) edited by Diderot and d'Alembert. It described itself as "an analytical dictionary of the sciences, arts and trades." It proved to be a platform for skeptical attacks on religion and for progressive political views.

Not all enlightened thinkers went so far as the atheism of Baron d'Holbach, but many shared the convictions expressed in his *System of Nature* (1770) that man is unhappy because he is ignorant of nature. D'Holbach saw religion as a barrier to a true understanding of nature. Somewhat earlier Jean-Jacques Rousseau had eulogized the myth of the noble savage. Repudiating the Christian doctrine of the fall, Rousseau held that man is noble by nature. He is born free, but everywhere he finds himself in chains. His enslavement is due to the corruption of society, for which religion must bear a large share of the blame. As a remedy Rousseau proposed a theory of education based on nature. Ideally, children would be educated away from the harmful influences of society and the church. The child would be allowed to follow its own inclinations. It would not be coerced into learning or adopting patterns of behavior. It would find things out for itself, happily turning to the teacher whose role would be to facilitate the child's free inquiry. In this way Rousseau and the Enlightenment laid the foundations for much modern educational theorizing.

In France, Rousseau and Voltaire led the attack on the church and institutional Christianity. At the same time they both professed belief in a Supreme Being. Rousseau's religion denounced all creeds beyond the assertion that natural religion was based on feeling and that all beliefs should be brought "to the bar of reason and conscience." God was not a fit subject for argument and debate. He is known already in the depths of our being. Voltaire, on the other hand, professed a theism based on the order and rationality of the world. Just as a watch proves a watchmaker, so a universe proves a God. On this basis Voltaire urged tolerance of all religions except that of the institutionalized church, against which he directed his celebrated slogan, "Blot out the infamous one."

Voltaire's thoughts on religion were heavily indebted to the English deists, whose ideas he got to know during his exile in London. The deists claimed that true religion was the religion of reason and nature, and that Christianity should be made to conform to this view. They were highly critical of the traditional appeal, made by Christian apologists, to fulfilled prophecy and miracles as proof of divine attestation of Christianity. They argued that the OT passages that were alleged to be fulfilled did not really predict the events concerned and that the NT miracles did not really happen.

The ideas of the deists also influenced Hermann Samuel Reimarus, the Hamburg schoolteacher who is widely credited with having initiated the quest of the historical Jesus. Reimarus wrote a private *Defence of the Rational Worshippers of God,* which portrayed Jesus as a simple Galilean preacher whose moral teaching got mixed up with politics and eschatology and who died a disillusioned man, having vainly tried to establish the kingdom of God on earth. Christianity is based on the fraudulent claims of the resurrection and the second coming of Christ, which the disciples invented after Jesus' death. Extracts from Reimarus's manuscript were posthumously published by Gotthold Ephraim Lessing, the dramatist and essayist, who pretended to have discovered them in the library of the Duke of Brunswick. Lessing suggested that they might have been the work of a long-deceased heretic. He himself did not defend Reimarus's ideas. Instead, he questioned whether the truth of any religion could be settled by appeals to history. Like other enlightened thinkers, Lessing viewed the major religions as different expressions of the one true religion whose role is to provide a moral education for the human race, teaching all men to live as brothers.

To many men of similar persuasions in the eighteenth century Freemasonry offered an attractive ideal, combining altruistic beliefs with esoteric ritual, seeming to offer the enlightened thinker a superior view of life and reality. On both sides of the Atlantic, Freemasonry enjoyed renewed popularity among the enlightened.

The Age of Enlightenment was characterized by the desire for a superior, more rational view of everything. It was a desire which contained within itself the seeds of its own destruction. In the hands of the Scottish philosopher David Hume, enlightened criticism was turned back on itself. Hume used skeptical, empirical philosophy to question the powers of the human mind. Not only was Hume critical of religion; he was skeptical of man's knowledge of the world outside himself and of the power of the human mind to know anything for certain. Kant's philosophy of the mind was in part an answer to Hume, but many felt that Kant had given back Hume's problem as if it were the answer. Kant's philosophy was the last great attempt by an enlightened thinker to work out a truly enlightened philosophy of reality. Kant reduced religion to ethics and ethics to humanistic, rational principles. However, his teaching left unanswered the question why man should base his behavior on the principles that Kant proposed. It failed to do justice to religious experience, and it superimposed a rationalistic interpretation on the Bible.

By the beginning of the nineteenth century the Enlightenment had already given way to idealism in philosophy, and to classicism and romanticism in the arts. Hume and Kant had shaken confidence in man's rational capacities, and the Enlightenment's lofty confidence in man's innate goodness and rationality seemed increasingly misplaced as the French Revolution took its course and the Napoleonic Wars plunged Europe into turmoil. Nevertheless, the Enlightenment left its mark on the modern mind. Many of the ideas which are taken for granted in Western society have their origin in the Age of Enlightenment.

C. Brown

See also Deism.

Bibliography. K. Barth, *Protestant Theology in the Nineteenth Century;* C. L. Becker, *The Heavenly City* *of the Eighteenth-Century Philosophers;* L. I. Bredvold, *Brave New World of the Enlightenment;* J. B. Bury, *The Idea of Progress;* E. Cassirer, *The Philosophy of the Enlightenment;* F. Copleston, *A History of Philosophy,* V, VI; H. N. Fairchild, *The Noble Savage;* P. Gay, *The Enlightenment;* E. Halévy, *Growth of Philosophic Radicalism;* P. Hazard, *The European Mind, 1680–1715* and *European Thought in the Eighteenth Century;* J. F. Lively, *The Enlightenment;* R. O. Rockwood, ed., *Carl Becker's Heavenly City Revisited;* F. J. Teggart, ed., *The Idea of Progress,* 1925.

Envy. In the OT *qānā'* and its derivatives are translated "envy" and, in some cases, "jealousy" or "zeal." The root meaning of the Hebrew verb is "to become intensely red," i.e., the blush resulting from emotion.

OT representative occurrences are Gen. 30:1—where Rachel becomes envious ("jealous" in NASB, NEB, TEV) of her sister Leah, who gives children to their husband Jacob while she remains barren—and Gen. 37:11, where Joseph's brothers are jealous (RSV, NASB, NEB, TEV) of him after hearing the interpretation of his dream.

In several OT passages there is anthropomorphic reference to God's jealousy (Exod. 20:5, in the context of the commandment against worship of other Gods; Deut. 4:24, the admonition against worship of images). Calvin observes regarding the second commandment: "This is as if [God] were saying that it was he alone to whom we ought to hold fast. . . . We are not to transfer to another what belongs to him" (*Institutes* 2; 8.16.18).

The OT expressions "evil eye" and "to eye" also indicate envy and jealousy. In I Sam. 18:9 the verb designates Saul's envy of David following the latter's publicly acclaimed victories. A further implication is that the envy results from Saul's being overtaken by an evil spirit after the Spirit of God had departed from him (I Sam. 16:14–16). Consistent with OT rejection of dualism, the evil spirit is characterized as being from God.

The term "evil eye" also occurs in the NT (Mark 7:22 where, in a catalog of sinful acts, it clearly means envy). Envy and jealousy in the NT are chiefly translations of *phthoneō* and *phthonos.* The verb is used in Gal. 5:26, "envying one another," which is contrasted with being led by the Spirit. As D. H. Field observes, envy is featured in several of the lists of vices found in the Pauline Epistles. In Rom. 1:29 it is "an identification of those given up by God to a base mind"; Gal. 5:21, a work of the flesh; Titus 3:3, a characteristic of life prior to conversion that is to be put off by those who have experienced salvation; and in I Tim. 6:4, "it is symptomatic of pseudo-Christian teaching which trades on controversy and wordy dispute."

Envy, not loyalty to Rome, no doubt motivated the Jews to deliver Jesus to trial and to call for his crucifixion (see esp. Mark 15:10), a fact discerned by Pilate (Matt. 27:18).

The meaning of *phthonos* in James 4:5 is widely debated. The reference may be either to the envious nature of the human spirit given to mankind by God (so TEV, NEB), or to the characteristic of God who "yearns jealously [cf. Exod. 20:5] over the spirit which he has made to dwell in us" (RSV). S. Laws gives a full review of the discussion.

While jealousy may in rare instances have a good connotation, envy is universally bad. The most telling biblical example is its ruinous and deadly effect upon Saul, whose envy of David "did more to break his health than his advancing years" (R. McCracken). Envy merits well its place among the cardinal sins. V. Cruz

Bibliography. D. H. Field, *NIDNTT,* I, 557–58; S. Laws, *The Epistle of James;* R. J. McCracken, *What Is Sin? What Is Virtue?*

Ephesus, Council of (431). There were two Councils of Ephesus. The first, held in 431, is reckoned by all as the third ecumenical council (following Nicaea in 325 and Constantinople in 381). The second is termed the Robber Synod of Ephesus. It occurred in 449 and by manipulation and force attempted to exonerate Eutyches and compromise orthodoxy. Pope Leo I immediately denounced it, giving it the label by which it has been known.

At issue in Ephesus in 431 were the Christological concept *Theotokos* (mother of God) as applied to the Virgin Mary, the personality of Nestorius, Patriarch of Constantinople, and the rivalry between Alexandria and Constantinople. Cyril of Alexandria supported the concept of Mary as the mother of God, i.e., that Jesus Christ was God the Word and man fully joined. Nestorius apparently believed that in Jesus Christ the Logos and a human person were joined in a harmony of action but not in a single personhood; he objected to the term *Theotokos.* The final actions of this council included the condemnation of Nestorius, the excommunications of John of Antioch, Theodoret of Cyr, and their adherents, and the banning of any creed other than the Nicene.

In character the Council of Ephesus in 431 was almost as turbulent as the Robber Synod. It was convoked by Emperor Theodosius II; convened June 7, 431, by Cyril of Alexandria before the Eastern bishops arrived; on June 22 Nestorius was condemned; June 26 the Eastern bishops arrived with John of Antioch and held their own council condemning Cyril; Emperor Theodosius II then issued a rescript annulling the premature decisions of Cyril and his council. The papal legates arrived, and in their presence Cyril's half of the council met again on July 10–11 and again condemned Nestorius. In August, Theodosius issued a rescript ordering the bishops home and deposing Nestorius, Cyril, and Memnon and ordering their arrest. Cyril escaped and returned to Alexandria in triumph, while Nestorius was confined to a monastery. It was not until 433 that Cyril and John of Antioch hammered out a compromise accepting Mary as *Theotokos* "because the Word of God has become flesh and is made man," asserting that Christ's natures were distinguishable but united in one person, and condemning Nestorius. Pope Sixtus III then ratified Cyril's Ephesus Council, and the Council of Chalcedon in 451 confirmed this certification of Ephesus as the third ecumenical council. V. L. WALTER

See also CYRIL OF ALEXANDRIA; NESTORIUS, NESTORIANISM.

Bibliography. W. P. Dubose, *The Ecumenical Councils.*

Epicureanism. Epicurus (341–270 B.C.) established a school in ancient Athens which became famous for its teachings on ethics in the hellenistic world. Reality was understood to be composed of indivisible, qualitatively similar atoms of matter eternally "falling" in empty space. To account for human agency in a mechanistically material universe Epicurus posited an unexplainable swerve in the travel of some atoms that caused them to strike other atoms unpredictably. This, in turn, caused a chain reaction which resulted in the physical world we know inhabited by human agents.

As the present life is all a person will have, and as there are no supernatural beings to fear or obey, the good life is the one bringing the most pleasure or happiness now. However, the wise person will learn to distinguish between natural desires and unnatural ones. Not only are unnatural desires impossible to satisfy, but they also cause negative repercussions in the person who tries to satisfy them. Of the natural desires the one to choose for supreme happiness is the desire for physical and mental repose. Since the greatest disturbers of mental repose are the fear of death and the fear of a supernatural meddling in human affairs, elimination of these beliefs through the espousal of mechanistic materialism is advantageous.

The kinds of acts which Epicurus held to be the most pleasure-producing are those characterized by justice, honesty, and simplicity. But he failed to notice that unless everyone would derive the most pleasure from such actions always, these virtuous acts would hinder or compete with attainment of the highest good, which is pleasure. He was so much a part of his culture that he assumed what it regarded as virtuous, such as honesty, would bring the most pleasure. He does not seem to have considered the possibility that a dishonest act might bring more pleasure to someone, thereby being a more virtuous act. Apparently Epicurus was confused as to whether honesty is a means to an end—i.e., pleasure—or an end in itself. This confusion lies behind the fact that "Epicureanism" has come to be a term used for profligacy and luxury. Pleasure of the individual—egocentric hedonism—as the highest good can just as easily lead to debauchery and extreme selfishness as it can to the simple, honest life style of Epicurus.

The apostle Paul preached to a group of Epicureans in Athens, emphasizing the incarnation and resurrection of Jesus (Acts 17:16–32). They were evidently not very impressed with what he had to say. S. R. OBITTS

Bibliography. C. Bailey, *Epicurus: The Extant Remains* and *The Greek Atomists and Epicurus;* A. H. Armstrong, *An Introduction to Ancient Philosophy.*

Epiphany. This word is a transliteration of the Greek *epiphaneia,* which means a disclosure or unveiling. In the history of the Christian church it has been used to refer to various occasions on which the incarnate Lord Jesus Christ was revealed to various groups of men at his birth, the coming of the magi, his baptism, and the wedding at Cana (first miracle), as well as when he will be revealed at his second coming. Consequently the word has come to be used liturgically to refer to the festival at which this revelation of Christ is celebrated. By the fourth century the Eastern church remembered all these facts on January 6. Clement of Alexandria had earlier referred to a Gnostic sect who kept a feast on this day in honor of Jesus' baptism. The Western church (certainly in Rome) appears to have observed December 25 as the birthday of Jesus from at least 336, and so January 6 was then kept as a day for commemorating his subsequent manifestation to the Gentiles at the visit of the magi.

The origins of the festival are far from clear, and the issue has been further confused by variations in calendar between Eastern and Western churches, some following the Julian and others the Gregorian. D. H. WHEATON

See also CHRISTIAN YEAR.

Bibliography. P. G. Cobb in Jones, Wainwright, and Yarnold, eds., *The Study of Liturgy;* J. Gunstone, *Christmas and Epiphany;* A. A. McArthur, *The Evolution of the Christian Year.*

Episcopacy. *See* CHURCH GOVERNMENT.

Episcopius, Simon (1583–1643). Remonstrant leader. A native of Amsterdam and student at the University of Leiden under Arminius, Episcopius was banished by the Synod of Dort for his able defense of the Arminian position. He published *Confessio* (1622) while in exile. Returning to Holland in 1634, he published a systematic exposition of Arminianism in four volumes, *Institutiones Theologicae* (1650–51).

Challenging four of the basic tenets of orthodox Calvinism, the Remonstrant movement achieved its fullest statement in Episcopius, who was less interested in speculative theology than in the practical, daily, disciplined pilgrimage of the believer. Consequently, he was accused of Pelagianism, and some unhappy Calvinists leveled an unfounded charge, based on his emphasis on practical Christianity and the freedom of the human spirit, that Episcopius was influenced by Socianism.

P. A. MICKEY

See also REMONSTRANTS; DORT, SYNOD OF; ARMINIANISM.

Bibliography. V. Ferm, *A Protestant Dictionary; Encyclopedic Dictionary of Religion,* I, 1221; Bihlmeyer-Tüchle, *RGG,* III, 202; W. F. Dankbaar, *RGG,* II, 531–32.

Epistemology. The branch of philosophy that is concerned with the theory of knowledge. It is an inquiry into the nature and source of knowledge, the bounds of knowledge, and the justification of claims to knowledge.

Nature and Source of Knowledge. The question of the nature and source of knowledge has been dominated by the rationalist/empiricist debate. Rationalists (e.g., Plato and Descartes) have held that the ideas of reason innate to the mind are the sole source of knowledge. The mind through its activity can originate the content of knowledge. While the rationalist often speaks of experience, it is to denigrate it. It is the source of error. At best it can lead one to opinion. Empiricists (e.g., Locke and Hume) have argued that sense experience is the primary source of human knowledge. The content of the mind is built upon what it passively receives from the senses or through reflection. The mind begins as a *tabula rasa,* or blank tablet.

Both rationalism and empiricism have been criticized as inadequate. Rationalism has been objected to on the grounds that, while it offers certainty for its claims, such certainty applies only to mathematical and logical propositions. Such knowledge remains only in the realm of concepts, symbols, and deductive inferences, and none of these tells us anything about the real world. Empiricism, on the other hand, is in no better position. It seems as if the simplest statements about material objects deal with far more than momentary sense impressions. Knowledge is "built up" by interpreting these impressions by means of a complex and rich set of concepts and principles (e.g., cause and effect). These concepts and principles are different from sense impressions; e.g., they lack the immediacy of the impressions.

It has been argued that Kant marks a significant point in the debate between rationalism and empiricism. He is responsible for synthesizing the two views. In a sense this is true. Like the rationalists Kant argued that there was an *a priori* element to knowledge. He held that the forms of intuition (space and time) and the categories of the understanding (e.g., causality) were the *a priori* conditions of knowledge. Any objects that did not conform to these structures could not ever be possible objects of knowledge. But concepts alone were empty. Knowledge required sensation. However, there is a sense in which Kant stands over against both rationalism and empiricism. Both systems are reductivistic. Kant is not.

The Meaning and Justification of Knowledge Claims. In contemporary Anglo-American philosophy, under the influence of philosophers like G. E. Moore and Ludwig Wittgenstein, the concerns of the epistemologist have shifted. The two questions that have dominated discussion are the meaning of knowledge claims and their justification. A commonly held view is that when a subject claims to know a proposition, he or she is making this kind of claim: (1) the subject believes the proposition; (2) the proposition is true; and (3) the subject has good reasons for believing the proposition.

Another alternative analysis of the meaning of knowledge claims was provided by J. L. Austin. Austin distinguished between constative and performative utterances. This was roughly similar to Gilbert Ryle's distinction between knowing *that* and knowing *how.* On this analysis, to say that one knows is to be able to tell or to go on (e.g., continue on in a multiplication table). Austin later came to include his earlier views in his speech act theory. On this account, every speech act had these elements: a locution (roughly the statement in a language), an illocution (what the speaker intends by uttering the statement), and a perlocution (the effect the utterance has on the hearer). Thus, a performative element is retained in both the illocutionary force of a statement and its perlocution.

On the matter of justification two distinguishable positions characterize modern epistemology. First, foundationalism is the view that there are epistemologically basic propositions or beliefs. Generally it is argued that these are not justified in terms of anything more basic. In turn these epistemologically basic beliefs justify other higher-level beliefs or propositions. The idea of basic and higher-level beliefs gives the schema the name "foundationalism."

Second, coherentism or contextualism is the position that there are no epistemologically basic beliefs. Rather, the justification of any knowledge claim is more like a web of belief. Propositions support or justify one another at various points.

The Bounds of Knowledge. For an epistemologist like Plato knowledge was confined to a suprasensible world of forms or ideas. Most philosophers, however, have rejected Plato's view. Kant insisted that knowledge was limited to the world of experience. Anything that was not a possible object of experience was not a possible object of knowledge. Still others have held that our knowledge is not restricted to the world of experience. Knowledge includes not only what is observed but also what is beyond observation in any straightforward way (e.g., God).

Religious Epistemology. Religious epistemology is the inquiry into the nature of knowledge about God and the justification of claims to religious knowledge.

In the contemporary Anglo-American scene the two questions that have dominated epistemological discussions in general have influenced inquiry into religious epistemology. Philosophers like A. J. Ayer and Antony G. N. Flew charged that religious language was meaningless because it was impossible to either verify or falsify in sense experience. Religious statements were compatible with any and all states of affairs.

Responses to this charge took three forms. First, there were those like John Hick, who argued that religious language was in fact verifiable but not in this life. He advocated what has become known as eschatological verification. Verification of religious statement is not presently possible because of the ambiguity of our experience. However, there is a future unambiguous state, promised as a part of Christian theology, where the verification of religious language would be possible. Second, there were those who challenged the applicability of verifiability as a criterion of meaningfulness. It was claimed that at worst the principle itself could not be verified, and was thus meaningless. At best, it was an arbitrary rule of language that could either be accepted or rejected. Moreover, it became clear that every formulation of a verification principle was either too exclusive or too inclusive. Third, other philosophers argued that religious language was not descriptive in character but served some other function. For example, R. B. Braithwaite held that religious language was conative language. It did not describe, but rather committed one to a way of life.

Following the lead of this last group of philosophers, analysis of the meaning of religious utterances moved from verification to function. The meaning of religious statements was seen in their use. For instance, religious language was a part of a language game, which in turn was embedded in a form of life. Religious language could not be analyzed in the abstract but had to be understood in its context.

As the question of meaning has diminished in importance, the problem of the justification of claims to religious knowledge received greater attention. Recently Alvin Plantinga has contended that belief in God, at least for some, is epistemologically basic. That is, it needs no justification in terms of something more basic.

Other philosophers of religion have sought to justify belief in God in terms of the concept of God (e.g., the ontological argument) or some set of sense impressions (e.g., the cosmological or teleological argument). Following Hume and Kant, they have objected that the concept of God does not guarantee the instantiation of this concept in reality. Nevertheless, Descartes argued that God was the only being for whom essence (concept) and existence (reality) are the same. Those who object to an appeal to sense impressions in defense of religious belief point out that no conceivable set of impressions can justify an infinite, eternal, omniscient being. Moreover, if it is argued that there is an analogy between an object and its maker, and the world and its creator, then it must be admitted that the creator is evil as well as intelligent, because both evil and design are found in the creation.

Revelation is often appealed to as the ultimate ground of knowledge about God. Yet this does not eliminate questions of justification. Are there grounds for accepting a revelation as from God? On what grounds is its authority justified? If there are historical data, then are these data well based?

P. D. Feinberg

Bibliography. R. M. Chisholm, *Theory of Knowledge;* D. W. Hamlyn, *Theory of Knowledge;* B. Mitchell, *The Justification of Religious Belief;* A. D. Woozley, *Theory of Knowledge: An Introduction.*

Equiprobabilism. *See* CASUISTRY.

Erasmus, Desiderius (1466?–1536). The leading Christian humanist of the Reformation era, who wished to reform the church through scholarly effort. Educated at Deventer by the Brethren of the Common Life (1475–84), he spent six years as a monk and then attended the Collège de Montaigu in Paris (1494). In 1499 he visited England, where he met John Colet and Thomas More. This experience influenced him to employ literary talent, intellectual brilliance, and clever wit in the service of Christ. He became fascinated with the prospect of studying Scripture in addition to the classical heritage that so impressed him.

With a new outlook Erasmus returned to Paris and Louvain, where he began the most productive period of his life. He published the *Adages* (1500), an annotated collection of classical proverbs; the *Enchiridion* (1503), a handbook of practical theology; editions of Cicero and Jerome; and a critical edition of the *Annotations of the NT* by Lorenzo Valla. A constant traveler, he went back to England in 1505, where he began his translation of the NT, and in 1506 he journeyed to Italy, where he had direct contact with humanistic culture.

In 1509 Erasmus was back in England once again and had finished *The Praise of Folly.* He continued traveling, translating the NT, and preparing critical editions of Jerome, Seneca, Plutarch, and Cato. In 1516 he published his Greek edition of the NT together with his own Latin translation, perhaps his most important work. Another publication from the same period, the *Education of a Christian Prince,* advocated toleration, peace, education, and social justice. By this time he had settled in Basel, where except for some short excursions he was to live and work for many years.

Erasmus was a prolific writer, and each main category of his work reveals something of his personality. First, he produced many scholarly books including historical material, lexicons, translations, and critical editions of earlier books. His purpose was to combat ignorance. He believed that truth was attainable through clarity of expression. A second element of his approach is revealed in satirical works such as *The Praise of Folly.* Here Erasmus ridicules humanists and scholars who take themselves too seriously, but he saves his most biting satire for bigoted churchmen, pompous lawyers, and warmongering rulers. A final category of his work, the more overtly Christian writings, demonstrates that neither scholarship nor humor was to be an end in itself. These elements were pursued to reach the goal of the restoration of primitive Christianity. Erasmus felt called to cleanse and purify the church through the application of humanistic scholarship to Christian tradition. For him truth and piety were not the result of ritual and sacraments but of historical research. Erasmus reached the height of his fame at the beginning of the Protestant Reformation. At first he encouraged Luther, but after the Leipzig debate (1519) he began to criticize him. Finally, he publicly broke with Luther in his *Diatribe on Free Will* (1524). In a sense, history passed Erasmus by, leaving him to defend his position against Reformers and Counter-Reformers.

R. G. CLOUSE

See also HUMANISM, CHRISTIAN.

Bibliography. R. H. Bainton, *Erasmus of Christendom;* R. L. DeMolen, ed., *Erasmus of Rotterdam: A Quincentennial Symposium;* J. B. Payne, *Erasmus: His Theology of the Sacraments;* M. M. Phillips, *Erasmus and the Northern Renaissance;* J. K. Sowards, *Desiderius Erasmus;* J. D. Tracy, *Erasmus: The Growth of a Mind* and *The Politics of Erasmus.*

Erastianism. Erastianism takes its name from Thomas Erastus (1524–83), who was born at Baden, studied theology at Basel, and later medicine, becoming professor of medicine at Heidelberg. He was a friend of Beza and Bullinger and was a Zwinglian.

A controversy arose in Heidelberg over the powers of the presbytery. Erastus emphasized strongly the right of the state to intervene in ecclesiastical matters. He held that the church has no scriptural authority to excommunicate any of its members. As God has entrusted to the civil magistrate (i.e., the state) the sum total of the visible government, the church in a Christian country has no power of repression distinct from the state. To have two visible authorities in a country would be absurd. The church can merely warn or censure offenders. Punitive action belongs to the civil magistrate alone. The church has no right to withhold the sacraments from offenders.

In practice, the term "Erastianism" is somewhat elastic. Figgis calls it "the theory that religion is the creature of the state." Generally it signifies that the state is supreme in ecclesiastical causes, but Erastus dealt only with the disciplinary powers of the church. When the Roman emperors became Christian, the relations of civil and ecclesiastical rulers became a real problem. It became universally accepted until modern times that the state could punish heretics or put them to death.

The name Erastian emerged in England in the Westminster Assembly (1643) when outstanding men like Selden and Whitelocke advocated the supremacy of the state over the church. The assembly rejected this view and decided that church and state have their separate but coordinate spheres, each supreme in its own province but bound to cooperate with one another for the glory of God. A. M. RENWICK

See also CHURCH AND STATE.

Bibliography. W. Cunningham, *Historical Theology;* J. N. Figgis, "Erastus and Erastianism," *JTS* 2:66ff.

Erigena, John Scotus (810–877). Irish philosopher who played a significant role in interpreting Greek thought to the West. He was involved in two major theological controversies. One was with the monk Gottschalk over predestination; the other focused on the Eucharist and was begun by Paschasius Radbertus.

As a philosopher Erigena helped direct and develop the emergent scholasticism through his translations and expositions of the Neoplatonic writer Dionysius the Pseudo-Areopagite and also the Aristotelian logic of Boethius. For Erigena, philosophy and theology were identical. His goal was to give an exhaustive, rational explanation of Christian doctrine from Scripture and the early church theologians. He accepted Scripture's authority but argued that proper biblical interpretation was that which best coincided with reason. Thus he could write that "reason and authority come alike from the one source of divine wisdom, and cannot contradict each other." His work helped signal the beginning of a philosophical shift from Platonic thought to that of Aristotelian reasoning as a dominant force in Europe. While Scripture was the main source of the knowledge of God for Erigena, it was the function of reason, as illuminated by God, to study and expound the biblical data supplied by authority.

Erigena's views on nature and creation were portrayed in his greatest work, *De divisione naturae.* In the thirteenth century this work was condemned. It divided nature into four categories, urging a sharp distinction between God and creation and describing the emanation of the created order from God. While denying that creatures are part of God, Erigena also claimed that God is the only true reality. Elements of pantheism are strong in his thought.

D. K. MCKIM

See also SCHOLASTICISM; NEOPLATONISM; ARISTOTLE, ARISTOTELIANISM.

Bibliography. F. Copleston, *A History of Philosophy,* II/1, chs. 12–13; *Encyclopedia of Philosophy;* É. Gilson, *History of Christian Philosophy in the Middle Ages;* J. González, *A History of Christian Thought,* II; *ODCC,* 460–61.

Error in the Bible. *See* BIBLE, INERRANCY AND INFALLIBILITY OF.

Eschatology. Traditionally defined as the doctrine of the "last things" (Gr. *eschata*), in relation either to human individuals (comprising death, resurrection, judgment, and the afterlife) or to the world. In this latter respect eschatology is sometimes restricted to the absolute end of the world, to the exclusion of much that commonly falls within the scope of the term. This restriction is unwarranted by biblical usage: the Hebrew *bĕ'aḥărît hayyāmîm* (LXX *en tais eschatais hēmerais,* "in the last days") may denote the end of the present order or even, more generally, "hereafter."

The biblical concept of time is not cyclical (in which case eschatology could refer only to the completion of a cycle) or purely linear (in which case eschatology could refer only to the terminal point of the line); it envisions rather a recurring pattern in which divine judgment and redemption interact until this pattern attains its definitive manifestation. Eschatology may therefore denote the consummation of God's purpose whether it coincides with the end of the world (or of history) or not, whether the consummation is totally final or marks a stage in the unfolding pattern of his purpose.

Individual Eschatology in the OT. A shadowy existence after death is contemplated in much of the OT. Jesus indeed showed that immortality was implicit in men and women's relation to God: the God of the fathers "is not God of the dead, but of the living; for all live to him" (Luke 20:38). But this implication was not generally appreciated in OT times. Perhaps in reaction against Canaanite cults of the dead, the OT lays little emphasis on the afterlife. Sheol is an underworld where the dead dwell together as shades; their former status and character are of little account there. The praises of Yahweh, which engaged so much of a pious Israelite's activity on earth, remained unsung in Sheol, which was popularly thought to be outside Yahweh's jurisdiction (Ps. 88:10–12; Isa. 38:18). Occasionally a more hopeful note is struck. According to Pss. 73 and 139 one who walks with God in life cannot be deprived of his presence in death: "If I make my bed in Sheol, thou art there!" (Ps. 139:8). While Job and his friends generally discount the possibility of life after death (Job 14:10–12) and do not suppose that the comforts of a future existence can compensate for the sufferings of the present, Job asserts, in a moment of triumphant faith, that if not in this life then after death he will see God rise up to vindicate him (Job 19:25–27).

The hope of national resurrection finds earlier expression than that of individual resurrection. In Ezekiel's vision of the valley of dry bones, where the divine breath breathes new life into corpses, a national resurrection is in view: "These bones are the whole house of Israel" (Ezek. 37:11). National resurrection may also be promised in Isa. 26:19: "Thy dead shall live, their bodies shall rise." Individual resurrection first becomes explicit in Dan. 12:2.

The persecution of martyrs under Antiochus Epiphanes gave a powerful impetus to the resurrection hope. Henceforth belief in the future resurrection of at least the righteous dead became part of orthodox Judaism, except among the Sadducees, who claimed to champion the old-time religion against Pharisaic innovations. With this new emphasis goes a sharper distinction between the posthumous fortunes of the righteous and the wicked, in Paradise and Gehenna respectively.

World Eschatology in the OT. The day of Yahweh in early Israel was the day when Yahweh would publicly vindicate himself and his people. It was possibly associated with an autumnal festival at which Yahweh's kingship was celebrated. If the "enthronement psalms" (Pss. 93; 95–100) provide evidence for this festival, his kingship was commemorated in his work of creation, his seasonal gifts of fertility and harvest, his dealings of mercy and judgment with Israel and other nations. His sovereignty in these spheres would be fully manifested at his coming to "judge the world in righteousness" (Pss. 96:13; 98:9).

In the earliest significant mention of this "day of the Lord" (Amos 5:18–20) the Israelites are rebuked for desiring it so eagerly because it will bring not light and joy (as they hope) but darkness and mourning. Since Yahweh is utterly righteous, his intervention to vindicate his cause must involve his judgment on unrighteousness wherever it appears, especially among his own people, who had exceptional opportunities of knowing his will.

Psalmists and prophets recognized that, while Yahweh's kingship was exercised in many ways, the reality which they saw fell short of what they knew to be the ideal. Even in Israel Yahweh's sovereignty was inadequately acknowledged. But one day the tension between ideal and reality would be resolved; on the day of Yahweh his kingship would be universally acknowledged, and the earth would be filled with "the knowledge of the Lord" (Isa. 11:9; Hab. 2:14). His effective recognition as "king over all the earth" is portrayed in terms of a theophany in Zech. 14:3–9.

The decline of the Davidic monarchy emphasized the contrast between what was and what ought to be. That monarchy represented the divine kingship on earth, but its capacity to do so worthily was impaired by political disruption, social injustice, and foreign oppression. As the fortunes of David's house sank ever lower, however, there emerged with increasing clarity the figure of a coming Davidic king in whom the promises made to David would be fulfilled and the vanished glories of earlier times would be restored and surpassed (Isa. 9:6–7; 11:1–10; 32:1–8; Mic. 5:2–4; Amos 9:11–12; Jer. 23:5–6; 33:14–22).

This hope of a Davidic Messiah, Yahweh's permanent vicegerent, dominates much subsequent Jewish eschatology. In some portrayals of the new age, however, the Davidic ruler is overshadowed by the priesthood, as in Ezekiel's new commonwealth (Ezek. 46:1–10) and later in the Dead Sea Scrolls, where the Davidic Messiah is subordinate to the chief priest, who will be head of state in the coming age.

Another form of eschatological hope appears in Daniel. No king reigns in Jerusalem, but the Most High still rules the kingdom of men and successive world emperors attain power by his will and hold it so long as he permits. The epoch of pagan dominion is limited; on its ruins the God of heaven will set up an indestructible kingdom. In Dan. 7:13 this eternal and universal dominion is given at the end time to "one like a son of man," who is associated, if not identified, with "the saints of the Most High" (Dan. 7:18, 22, 27).

NT Eschatology. OT eschatology is forward looking, its dominant notes being hope and promise. These notes are present in the NT, but here the dominant note is fulfillment—fulfillment in Jesus, who by his passion and resurrection has begotten his people anew to a living hope (I Pet. 1:3), because he has "abolished death and brought life and immortality to light through the gospel" (II Tim. 1:10).

Jesus' Galilean preaching, summarized in Mark 1:15 ("The time is fulfilled, and the kingdom of God is at hand; repent, and believe in the gospel"), declares the fulfillment of Daniel's vision: "The time came when the saints received the kingdom" (Dan. 7:22). In one sense the kingdom was already present in Jesus' ministry: "If it is by the finger of God that I cast out demons, then the kingdom of God has come upon you" (Luke 11:20; cf. Matt. 12:28). But in another sense it was yet future. Jesus taught his disciples to pray, "Thy kingdom come" (Luke 11:2). In this sense it would come "with power" (Mark 9:1)—an event variously associated with the resurrection of the Son of man or with his advent "with great power and glory" (Mark 13:26).

The expression "the Son of man" figures prominently in Jesus' teaching about the kingdom of God, especially after Peter's confession at

Caesarea Philippi (Mark 8:29). It echoes Daniel's "one like a son of man" (Dan. 7:13). In Jesus' teaching he himself is the Son of man. But while he speaks occasionally, in Daniel's terms, of the Son of man as "coming with the clouds of heaven" (Mark 14:62), he more often speaks of the Son of man as destined to suffer, in language reminiscent of the servant of Yahweh in Isa. 52:13–53:12. This portrayal of the Son of man in terms of the servant is quite distinctive, in that Jesus undertook to fulfill personally what was written of both. As Daniel's "one like a son of man" receives dominion from the Ancient of Days, so Jesus receives it from his Father. As Daniel's "saints of the Most High" receive dominion, so Jesus shares his dominion with his followers, the "little flock" (Luke 12:32; 22:29–30). But its fullness must await the suffering of the Son of man (Luke 17:25).

Sometimes Jesus uses "life" or "eternal life" (the life of the age to come) as a synonym for "the kingdom of God"; to enter the kingdom is to enter into life. This links the kingdom with the new age, when the righteous are brought back from death to enjoy resurrection life.

In the apostolic teaching this eternal life may be enjoyed here and now, although its full flowering awaits a future consummation. The death and resurrection of Christ have introduced a new phase of the kingdom, in which those who believe in him share his risen life already, even while they live on earth in mortal body. There is an indeterminate interval between Christ's resurrection and parousia, and during this interval the age to come overlaps the present age. Christians live spiritually in "that age" while they live temporally in "this age"; through the indwelling Spirit of God they enjoy the resurrection life of "that age" in anticipation.

This outlook has been called "realized eschatology." But the realized eschatology of the NT does not exclude an eschatological consummation to come.

Realized Eschatology. If the *eschaton,* the "last thing" which is the proper object of eschatological hope, came in the ministry, passion, and triumph of Jesus, then it cannot be the absolute end of time, for time has gone on since then. In the NT the "last thing" is more properly the "last one," the *eschatos* (cf. Rev. 1:7; 2:8; 22:13). Jesus is himself his people's hope, the Amen to all God's promises.

According to Albert Schweitzer's "consistent eschatology," Jesus, believing himself to be Israel's Messiah, found that the consummation did not come when he expected it (cf. Matt. 10:23) and embraced death in order that his parousia as the Son of man might be forcibly brought to pass. Since the wheel of history would not respond to his hand and turn round to complete its last revolution, he threw himself on it and was broken by it, only to dominate history more decisively by his failure than he could have done by attaining his misconceived ambition. His message, Schweitzer held, was thoroughly eschatological in the sense exemplified by the crudest contemporary apocalypticism. His ethical teaching was designed for the interim between the beginning of his ministry and his manifestation in glory. Later, when his death was seen to have destroyed the eschatological conditions instead of bringing them in, the proclamation of the kingdom was replaced by the teaching of the church.

Schweitzer's interpretation of Jesus' message was largely a reaction against the liberal nineteenth century interpretation, but it was equally one-sided and distorted in its selection from the gospel data.

Later Rudolf Otto and C. H. Dodd propounded a form of realized eschatology. Dodd interpreted Jesus' parables in terms of the challenge to decision which confronted his hearers in his announcement that the kingdom of God had arrived. Dodd viewed the kingdom as coming in Jesus' life, death, and resurrection; to proclaim these events in their proper perspective was to proclaim the good news of the kingdom of God. Jesus' future coming did not, at first, come into the picture. His redeeming work constituted the decisive or eschatological manifestation of the power of God operating for the world's salvation; the later concentration on a further "last thing" in the future betokened a relapse into Jewish apocalypticism, which relegated to a merely "preliminary" role those elements of the gospel which were distinctive of Jesus' message. (As time went on, Dodd made more room for a future consummation: what came to earth with Christ's incarnation was finally decisive for the meaning and purpose of human existence, so that, at the ultimate winding up of history, humankind will encounter God in Christ.)

Joachim Jeremias, who acknowledges indebtedness to Dodd, found that Jesus' parables express an eschatology "in process of realization"; they proclaim that the hour of fulfillment has struck and compel hearers to make up their minds about Jesus' person and mission.

Dodd's pupil, J. A. T. Robinson, interprets Christ's parousia not as a literal event of the future but as a symbolical or mythological presentation of what happens whenever Christ comes in love and power, displaying the signs of his presence and the marks of his cross. Judgment day is a dramatic picture of every day. Robinson denies that Jesus used language implying his return to earth from heaven. His sayings which have been so understood express the twin themes of vindication and visitation—notably his reply to the high priest's question at his trial (Mark 14:62), where the added phrase "from now on" (Luke 22:69) or "hereafter" (Matt. 26:64) is taken to be an authentic part of the reply. The Son of man, condemned by earthly judges, will be vindicated in the divine law court; his consequent visitation of his people in judgment and redemption will take place "from now on" as surely as his vindication.

Instead of realized eschatology, Robinson (following Georges Florovsky) speaks of an "inaugurated eschatology"—an eschatology inaugurated by Jesus' death and resurrection, which released and initiated a new phase of the kingdom in which "hereafter" God's redeeming purpose would achieve its fulfillment. To Jesus' ministry before his passion Robinson applies the term "proleptic eschatology" because in that ministry the signs of the age to come were visible in anticipation.

Conclusion. Jesus' use of OT language was creative and cannot be confined to the meaning which that language had in its original context. He probably did point forward to his personal coming to earth—not only to manifest his glory but to share that glory with his people, raised from the dead by his quickening shout. When the consummation to which his people look forward is described as their "hope of glory," it is their participation in Jesus' resurrection glory that is in view; that hope is kept bright within them by his indwelling presence (Col. 1:27) and sealed by the Spirit (Eph. 1:13–14, 18–21).

There is a tension between the "already" and the "not yet" of the Christian hope, but each is essential to the other. In the language of the seer of Patmos, the Lamb that was slain has by his death won the decisive victory (Rev. 5:5), but its final outworking, in reward and judgment, lies in the future (Rev. 22:12). The fact that we now "see Jesus crowned with glory and honor" is guarantee enough that God "has put all things under his feet" (Heb. 2:8–9). His people already share his risen life, and those who reject him are "condemned already" (John 3:18). For the Fourth Evangelist, the judgment of the world coincided with the passion of the incarnate Word (John 12:31); yet a future resurrection to judgment is contemplated as well as a resurrection to life (John 5:29).

Some much canvassed questions, such as the chronological relation of the parousia to the great distress of Mark 13:19, to the manifestation of the man of lawlessness of II Thess. 2:3–8, or to the millennial reign of Rev. 20, are marginal to the main course of NT eschatological teaching, belonging rather to the detailed exegesis of the passages concerned. The eschatological outlook of the NT is well summed up in the words: "Christ Jesus our hope" (I Tim. 1:1). F. F. Bruce

See also Apocalyptic; Second Coming of Christ; Tribulation; Millennium, Views of the; Rapture of the Church; Age, Ages; This Age, The Age to Come; Kingdom of Christ, God, Heaven; Day of Christ, God, the Lord; Last Day, Days; Judgment; Judgment Seat; Judgment of the Nations, The; Israel and Prophecy.

Bibliography. G. R. Beasley-Murray, *Jesus and the Future* and *The Coming of God;* R. H. Charles, *A Critical History of the Doctrine of a Future Life;* O. Cullmann, *Christ and Time;* C. H. Dodd, *The Parables of the Kingdom, The Apostolic Preaching and Its Developments,* and *The Coming of Christ;* J. E. Fison, *The Christian Hope;* T. F. Glasson, *The Second Advent;* J. Jeremias, *The Parables of Jesus;* W. G. Kümmel, *Promise and Fulfilment;* G. E. Ladd, *The Presence of the Future;* R. Otto, *The Kingdom of God and the Son of Man;* H. Ridderbos, *The Coming of the Kingdom;* J. A. T. Robinson, *In the End, God...* and *Jesus and His Coming;* A. Schweitzer, *The Quest of the Historical Jesus;* E. F. Sutcliffe, *The OT and the Future Life;* G. Vos, *The Pauline Eschatology.*

Essence. The noun "essence" comes from the Latin verb *esse,* meaning "to be." We observe that every existing thing in the world of our experience perpetually changes and yet maintains its identity. External manifestations change, yet their inner core or form remains the same. The essence of a thing may be said to be that which remains stable in change. On this basis essence means what necessarily belongs to a thing and most determines its character. Thus, without its essence, a thing would not be what it is.

That in some sense or other there are essences, universals, abstract objects—i.e., objects of thought rather than of sense perception—no philosopher or theologian would wish to dispute; the difficulties begin when we try to be more precise. In saying of two or more objects that each is a table, or square, or white, or made of brass, we are saying that there is something common to the objects which may be shared by many others and in virtue of which the objects may be classified into kinds.

An analysis of essence involves problems related to definition that constantly recur in theological and philosophical discussion—although there is a widespread tendency to assume that they have been solved. One important view of definition, the essentialist view, stresses that an accurate definition must deal with the essence of the object, and since an essence is thought of as perfect and unchanging, a definition is a precise and certain truth. This view was first proposed by Socrates and Plato. Plato (*Republic* VI) distinguished two kinds of objects of knowledge (sensible things and forms) and two modes of knowledge (sense perception and intellectual vision). What Plato, Aristotle, and later Kant have in common is their interest in idea or essence (Kant, *noumenon*), knowledge of which is acquired (if at all) through the intellect and not sense perception. When one works toward an understanding of essence, one is soon likely to be involved in matters of God, freedom, and immortality. M. H. MACDONALD

See also EXISTENCE.

Bibliography. Aristotle, *Metaphysics;* Thomas Aquinas, *Being and Existence;* H. H. Price, *Thinking and Experience;* R. Robinson, *Definition;* N. Wolterstorff, *On Universals: An Essay in Ontology.*

Essenes. An important Jewish group which flourished in Palestine from the late second century B.C. to the late first century A.D.

Sources. Our understanding of the Essenes is determined to a large degree by how we delimit our sources. Certainly the sources which explicitly mention the Essenes are pertinent. The most valuable among these are Philo's *Apology for the Jews* (now lost but preserved in part by Eusebius, *Praeparatio evangelica* 8.2) and *Every Good Man Is Free,* both written in the first half of the first century A.D.; Flavius Josephus's *The Jewish War* and *The Antiquities of the Jews,* dating from about A.D. 75 and 94 respectively; and the elder Pliny's *Natural History,* completed in about A.D. 77. Also of some independent value is Hippolytus's *Philosophumena,* written in the third century A.D.

Though they explicitly mention the Essenes, these sources present several problems. None of them gives a firsthand, inside view of the Essenes. Furthermore, these sources generally cater to Greek or hellenized readers and thus, on some points, misrepresent Essene practices, doctrines, and motives. Finally, it is doubtful that any of these sources has anything to say, by way of description, about the Essenes as they existed before the reign of Herod the Great (37-4 B.C.).

In the last thirty years scholars have sought to mitigate these difficulties by using information derived from the Dead Sea Scrolls. This approach has problems of its own, however. The relationship between the Essenes and the Qumran sectaries is uncertain. The name "Essene" never appears in the Qumran literature, and viable cases have been made for identifying the Qumran sectaries with Pharisees, Zealots, Sadducees, and other Jewish and Christian groups. Nevertheless, on the basis of archaeological and literary evidence most scholars now believe that the Qumran sectaries were Essenes—though not necessarily *the* Essenes. The inhabitants of Qumran may have been the leaders, or perhaps only a small branch, of a broad Essene movement. In either case it is impossible to know just how and to what extent the Qumran documents reflect standard Essene practices and beliefs. For this reason, it would seem prudent to make at least a provisional distinction between what Philo and Josephus claim to know about the Essenes and the potentially relevant evidence of Qumran. Of the Qumran documents the Manual of Discipline, the Damascus Document, the War Scroll, the recently published Temple Scroll, and the various *pesher*-type commentaries on the Minor Prophets are proving to be the most useful in the discussion of Essene life, doctrine, and history.

Name. "Essenes" is an English transliteration of the Greek *Essēnoi.* The derivation and meaning of the Greek word have been a mystery since the first century A.D. Philo, our earliest source (*ca.* A.D. 40), speculated that "Essenes" was derived from the Greek *hosios,* meaning "holy." Modern scholars have preferred to go back to Semitic originals. The two most probable etymologies offered to date are from the Aramaic *'āsên, 'āsayyâ,* "healers," and from the East Aramaic *ḥasên, ḥasayyâ,* "the pious." The first etymology would suggest a link between the Essenes and the Therapeutae (Gr. "healers"), a similar Jewish group flourishing contemporaneously in Egypt. The second etymology would imply a historical relationship between the Essenes and the Hasidim (Hebrew: "pious ones"), the faithful Jews who distinguished themselves during the Maccabean revolt (*ca.* 167 B.C.). Extant evidence will not allow a firm decision between the two etymologies, though it would seem that the latter currently enjoys more credence. In any case, there is no reason to assume that "Essenes," or its Semitic equivalent, was a self-designation. It may have been a label applied to the group by outsiders. As such, it would point to the manner in which the Essenes were perceived by their contemporaries.

Life and Doctrine. Philo, Josephus, Pliny, and Hippolytus generally agree quite closely on the main characteristics of the group. Asceticism was a central trait. Many Essenes were devoted to the celibate ideal, though Josephus mentions a group who married. They eschewed luxury items, such as oil, and avoided all unnecessary social and economic contacts with non-Essenes. Their highly regimented life centered on prayer, rigorous work, frequent lustrations, and the study of Scriptures.

Essene life was also communal. Not only was property held in common, but it seems that many, if not all, of their meals were taken together as well. An Essene traveler could always be certain of finding free lodging wherever fellow Essenes lived. Essene communities were highly structured with four different classes of membership divided according to seniority. It would seem that priests occupied the top rung of the Essene social ladder; Josephus explicitly mentions that the ones who administered the communal finances were priests. The internal social structure of Essene communities was maintained by careful and exacting discipline. An entrance procedure requiring a three-year novitiate and solemn vows ensured a committed membership.

There is some disagreement between Philo and Josephus on the Essene attitude toward the temple and sacrifices. Philo claims that the Essenes abstained from animal sacrifices altogether, while Josephus reports that, because of their views on purity, the Essenes were excluded from the temple courts and for this reason sacrificed among themselves.

Finally, Josephus says that the Essenes were thoroughgoing predestinarians, and that along with a belief in the immortality of the soul they held to a doctrine of preexistence.

This picture of Essene life and doctrine is, on the whole, corroborated by the information derived from Qumran and its documents. As one might expect, however, the agreement is not perfect; there are some outright contradictions. For example, the Manual of Discipline mandates a two-year, not a three-year, novitiate. According to Philo, the Essenes eschewed oaths, but the Damascus Document prescribes several oaths for the Qumran sectaries. These and other incongruities highlight the uncertainties of using the Dead Sea Scrolls to illuminate Essenism. Even if one assumes that Philo and Josephus were mistaken on some points (and this is quite probable), one must still reckon with the possibility that the Dead Sea Scrolls do not reflect universal Essene characteristics.

Yet, with this possibility in mind, one can still appreciate the tremendous value of the Qumran scrolls for Essene studies. The scrolls give clear evidence that at least some of the Essenes followed a solar, 364-day calendar as opposed to official Judaism, which used a lunar one. Moreover, the scrolls intimate that the Qumran Essenes (if no others) were implacable foes of the Hasmonean high priests. In fact, it seems that many Essene leaders were Zadokites—members of the high priestly family displaced by the Hasmoneans. This information has in turn shed light on the vexing problem of the Essenes and temple sacrifices. It seems that the Qumranians abstained from temple sacrifices because of a rift with the ruling priests in Jerusalem, not because they repudiated the sacrificial system, as Philo implies. Finally, the scrolls expose an Essenism which was thoroughly eschatological in outlook. The writers of the scrolls believed themselves the true remnant of Israel living in the last days. They eagerly awaited the appearance of both a political messiah and an eschatological high priest.

In general it can be said that the Dead Sea Scrolls have preserved a place for Essenism within the mainstream of Judaism. Josephus's and Philo's accounts show it was difficult to fit the Essenes into what was known about late second temple Judaism. The Essenes were often regarded as syncretistic monastics, imbued with a hellenistic asceticism. Recent studies on the Qumran scrolls, however, have revealed an ascetic and communal life style not based on some Greek philosophical ideal but on an overwhelming concern for ritual purity. Regardless of the identity of the Qumran sectaries, it is now possible to understand the Essenes as one of the numerous purity-conscious groups which flourished in Judaism before A.D. 70.

History and Influence. Our explicit sources contain very little information of a historical nature. The Qumran documents are full of historical allusions, but they are notoriously ambiguous. Moreover, the history of the Qumran community may not accurately reflect the history of Essenism as a whole. By using a combination of sources, however, scholars have developed the following tentative outline of Essene history. The Essenes seem to have arisen after the Maccabean revolt (*ca.* 167–160 B.C.). Sometime between 152 and 110 B.C. at least some of the Essenes—perhaps only the leaders—retreated to Qumran, on the shores of the Dead Sea. There they stayed until the Parthian invasion of 40 B.C. or the earthquake of 31 B.C. forced them to leave. At that time they settled in the regions around Jerusalem. Soon after Herod the Great's death (4 B.C.) at least some of the Essenes returned to Qumran. Some seventy years later Essenes were involved in the revolt against the Romans. The survival and persistence of the Essenes as a separate group after A.D. 70 is still debated. Many scholars have found traces of Essenism within such later sects as the Ebionites, the Mandaeans, and the Karaites.

Also still undecided is the importance and influence of Essenism within pre–A.D. 70 Judaism and early Christianity. It has often been dismissed as a peripheral Jewish sect or hailed as the very seedbed of the Christian faith. Both of these positions are too extreme. It is more likely that the Essenes were one expression of a widespread pietistic reaction to the pragmatic and tepid spirit of official Judaism. From the ranks of such a reaction the early church would have drawn heavily. S. TAYLOR

See also DEAD SEA SCROLLS; PHARISEES; SADDUCEES.

Bibliography. G. Vermes, *The Dead Sea Scrolls in English;* A. Dupont-Sommer, *The Jewish Sect of Qumran and the Essenes;* M. Burrows, *The Dead Sea Scrolls;* F. F. Bruce, *Second Thoughts on the Dead Sea Scrolls;* W. S. LaSor, *The Dead Sea Scrolls and the NT;* R. deVaux, *Archaeology and the Dead Sea Scrolls;* J. H. Charlesworth, "The Origin and Subsequent History of the Authors of the Dead Sea Scrolls: Four Transitional Phases among the Qumran Essenes," *RQum* 10:213–33; C. D. Ginsburg, *The Essenes.*

Eternal Generation. Deriving from Origen, this is the phrase used to denote the inter-Trinitarian relationship between the Father and the Son as is taught by the Bible. "Generation" makes it plain that there is a divine sonship prior to the incarnation (cf. John 1:18; I John 4:9), that there is thus a distinction of persons within the one Godhead (John 5:26), and that between these persons there is a superiority and subordination of order (cf. John 5:19; 8:28). "Eternal" reinforces the fact that the generation is not merely economic (i.e., for the purpose of human salvation as in the incarnation, cf. Luke 1:35), but essential, and that as such it cannot be construed in the categories of natural or human generation. Thus it does not imply a time when the Son was not, as Arianism argued. Nor is there to be expected a final absorption of the Son. Nor does the fact that the Son is a distinct person mean that he is separate in essence. Nor does his subordination imply inferiority. In virtue and not in spite of the eternal generation, the Father and the Son are one (John 10:30).

Objections have been lodged against the phrase on the ground that it is rhetorical, meaningless, and ultimately self-contradictory. Yet it corresponds to what God has shown us of himself in his own eternal being, and, if it carries an element of mystery (as is only to be expected), it has rightly been described by O. A. Curtis (*The Christian Faith,* p. 228) as "not only conceivable" but "also one of the most fruitful conceptions in all Christian thinking." It finds creedal expression in the phrases "begotten of his Father before all worlds" (Nicene) and "begotten before the worlds" (Athanasian). G. W. BROMILEY

See also ONLY BEGOTTEN.

Bibliography. H. Bettenson, *Documents of the Christian Church;* J. N. D. Kelly, *Early Christian Doctrines;* C. W. Lowry, "Origen as Trinitarian," *JTS* 37: 225–40; G. L. Prestige, *God in Patristic Thought;* J. Stevenson, *A New Eusebius.*

Eternality of God. *See* GOD, ATTRIBUTES OF.

Eternal Life. Though anticipated in the OT, the concept of eternal life seems to be largely a NT revelation. The common translation, "eternal life" or "everlasting life," is the translation of *zōē* (life) and *aiōnion* (eternal), an expression found throughout the NT, but especially in the Gospel of John and I John. *Zōē* is found 134 times, translated "life" in every instance in the AV except one (Luke 16:25). The verb form *zaō* is found 143 times and is similar in meaning. *Aiōnion* appears 78 times, usually translated "eternal" (42 times in AV), but also "everlasting" (25) and once "for ever."

Both the terms "eternal" and "life" are difficult to define except descriptively. *Zōē* is used in many shades of meaning in Scripture, sometimes little different from *bios,* which occurs only eleven times in the NT and refers to earthly life only. *Zōē* is found in the following meanings: (1) life principle, or that which makes one alive physically (John 10:11, 15, 17; 13:37); (2) life time, or duration of man's life—similar to *bios* (Heb. 7:3; James 4:14); (3) the sum of all activities comprising life (I Cor. 6:3–4; I Tim. 2:2; 4:8); (4) happiness or state of enjoying life (I Thess. 3:8, verb form; cf. John 10:10); (5) as a mode of existence given by God, whether physical or spiritual (Acts 17:25); (6) spiritual or eternal life, a state of regeneration or renewal in holiness and fellowship with God (John 3:15–16, 36; 5:24; 6:47); (7) the life which is in Christ and God—divine life itself (John 1:4; I John 1:1–2; 5:11).

Though *zōē* is sometimes used without adjective to denote eternal life (I John 5:12), in many instances *aiōnion* is used to distinguish eternal life from ordinary physical life. The adjective *aiōnion* corresponds to the noun *aiōn,* which refers to life in general, or the age in which a life is lived. The idea of eternity seems to be derived from the fact that eternity is a future age which eclipses in importance all other ages, and thus is the age preeminent. Hence, eternal life or age life is that which anticipates and assures fellowship with God in eternity as well as having promise of entering into that eternal fellowship in time.

The Scriptures describe but do not formally define eternal life. The nearest approach to a definition is given in John 17:3, where Christ stated: "This is life eternal, that they might know thee the only true God, and Jesus Christ, whom thou has sent." Eternal life is described in its experimental aspect of knowing God and having fellowship with God through his Son, Jesus Christ.

Eternal life is contrasted in Scripture with ordinary physical life. One having physical life without eternal life is described as "dead in trespasses and sins" (Eph. 2:1). The lack of eternal life is equated with the state of being unsaved, condemned, or lost, in contrast to those who have eternal life who are declared to be saved, and promised that they shall never perish (John 3:15–16, 18, 36; 5:24; 10:9).

Even in the case of the elect, eternal life is not possessed until faith in Christ is exercised (Eph. 2:1, 5). Eternal life is not to be confused with efficacious grace, or that bestowal of grace which is antecedent to faith. Nor is it to be confused with the indwelling of the Holy Spirit or of Jesus Christ, though this accompanies and manifests eternal life. Eternal life is to be identified with regeneration and is received in the new birth. It is resultant rather than causative of salvation, but is related to conversion or the manifestation of the new life in Christ.

Eternal life is given by the work of the Holy Spirit at the moment of faith in Christ. As in the case of the incarnation of Christ, however, the Trinity is related to the impartation of life. According to James 1:17–18, the Father is said to beget his spiritual children. The life which is bestowed upon the believer is identified with the life which is in Christ (John 5:21; II Cor. 5:17; I John 5:12). In other passages the Holy Spirit is declared to be the one who regenerates (John 3:3–7; Titus 3:5).

The impartation of eternal life is embodied in three principal figures in the Scripture. (1) Regeneration is described first as a new birth, being "born . . . of God" (John 1:13), or "born again" (John 3:3). The bestowal of eternal life therefore relates the believer to God in a father and son relationship. (2) The new life in Christ is described as a spiritual resurrection. Not only is the believer "raised together with Christ" (Col. 3:1) but is "alive from the dead" (Rom. 6:13). Christ anticipated this in his prophecy: "The hour cometh, and now is, when the dead shall hear the voice of the Son of God; and they that hear shall live" (John 5:25). (3) The bestowal of new life is compared to the act of creation. As Adam became a living soul by the breath of God, so the believer becomes a new creation (II Cor. 5:17). The possessor of eternal life is declared to be "created in Christ Jesus unto good works (Eph. 2:10). The concept of a new creation not only carries with it the possession of eternal life, but involves a new nature which corresponds to the life: "old things are passed away; behold, they are become new" (II Cor. 5:17 ASV).

J. F. WALVOORD

See also LIFE; SALVATION; REGENERATION; NEW CREATION, NEW CREATURE; MAN, OLD AND NEW.

Bibliography. "Life" and "Eternal Life" in *HDB, Unger's Bible Dictionary;* J. J. Reeve, *ISBE*, III, 1888–90; L. Berkhof, *Systematic Theology;* L. S. Chafer, *Systematic Theology*, IV, 24–26, 389, 400–401; VII, 142, 227; A. H. Strong, *Systematic Theology;* J. F. Walvoord, *The Holy Spirit.*

Eternal Punishment. It is plain from the Bible that sin will be punished (Dan. 12:2; Matt. 10:15; John 5:28–29; Rom. 5:12–21), and the duration of this punishment is sometimes expressed in the NT by the use of *aiōn* or one of its derivatives (e.g., Matt. 18:8; 25:41, 46; II Thess. 1:9). *Aiōn* means "an age," and it was used of the never ending "age to come," which gave to the corresponding adjective *aiōnion* the meaning "eternal," "everlasting." These words are used of "the King of ages" (I Tim. 1:17), of "the eternal God" (Rom. 16:26), and when glory is ascribed to God "for ever" (Rom. 11:36) and God is blessed "for ever" (II Cor. 11:31). The concept of endless duration could not be more strongly conveyed; the use of these expressions for the eternity of God shows conclusively that they do not mean limited duration. It is important that the same adjective is used of eternal punishment as of eternal life (Matt. 25:46 has both). The punishment is just as eternal as the life. The one is no more limited than the other.

A similar idea is conveyed by the use of other terminology. Thus Jesus said, "It is better for you to enter life maimed than with two hands to go to hell, to the unquenchable fire" (Mark 9:43; cf. Luke 3:17). He referred to "hell, where their worm does not die, and the fire is not quenched" (Mark 9:47–48). He spoke of fearing God because he, "after he has killed, has power to cast into hell" (Luke 12:5). He said that there is a sin that "will not be forgiven, either in this age or in the age to come" (Matt. 12:32). Similarly John writes, "He who does not obey the Son shall not see life, but the wrath of God rests upon him" (John 3:36). The awful finality of Christ's warnings implies permanence. He spoke of the door being shut (Matt. 25:10), of being "thrown into the outer darkness" (Matt. 8:12; "thrust out," Luke 13:28), of an impassable gulf (Luke 16:26). It is not always realized that Jesus spoke of hell more often than did anyone else in the NT. And nowhere is there a hint of any possible reversal of the last judgment.

More could be cited. And against the strong body of NT teaching that there is a continuing punishment of sin we cannot put one saying which speaks plainly of an end to the punishment of the finally impenitent. Those who look for a different teaching in the NT must point to possible inferences and alternative interpretations. But if Jesus wished to teach something other than eternal retribution, it is curious that he has not left one saying which plainly says so. In the NT there is no indication that the punishment of sin ever ceases.

In the light of the cross we can be sure that the mercy of God reaches as far as mercy can reach. God does all that can be done for man's salvation. Beyond that, and the teaching of the permanence of the doom of the wicked, we cannot go. It may be that the dread reality is other than men have usually pictured it, as C. S. Lewis suggests. It must be borne in mind that Scripture uses symbolic terms of necessity to refer to realities beyond the grave. The imagery Christians have tended to stress is that of "the hell of fire" (Matt. 5:22). But there are references also to "the unquenchable fire" (Mark 9:43), "the outer darkness" (Matt. 8:12), the "worm" that "does not die" (Mark 9:48), weeping and gnashing of teeth (Luke 13:28), "the resurrection of judgment" (John 5:29), "being sentenced to hell" (more literally, "the judgment of hell," Matt. 23:33), receiving "a severe beating" (Luke 12:47; or being "beaten with many stripes," AV), being "lost" (Matt. 10:6), "perishing" (I Cor. 1:18), death (Rom. 6:23), losing the life (Luke 9:24). With such a variety of terms, it is unwise to press one as though that gave the complete picture. We should beware of oversimplifying; it is impossible to envisage what the reality is which can be described so variously. But we should beware also of yielding to the sentimental demand that we water down such expressions. That there is a grim reality Scripture leaves us in no doubt.

But from early days some Christians have rejected this teaching. Origen taught that all will finally be saved. Such views did not attract a wide following until modern times. A group of nineteenth century poets popularized this line (cf. Tennyson and "the larger hope"), and in this century universalism is widely accepted.

The basic reason is that it is not easy to reconcile the idea of hell with the love of God. It is argued that the love of God would be defeated if only one sinner were left to suffer in eternity. Such an approach must be treated with respect, but it is not found in Scripture. Some passages are adduced, such as those that express God's goodwill toward all (I Tim. 2:4; II Pet. 3:9); the universal scope of the cross (II Cor. 5:19; Col. 1:20; Titus 2:11; Heb. 2:9; I John 2:2); and the wide outreach of Christ's atoning work (John 12:32; Rom. 5:18; Eph. 1:10). But to interpret such passages as meaning that in the end all will be saved is to go beyond what the writers are saying and to ignore the fact that in the contexts there are usually references to God's condemnation of the wicked, or to the final separation between good and evil, or the like.

Another idea is that man is no more than potentially immortal. If he puts his trust in Christ and enters into salvation, he attains immortal life. If he fails to do so, he simply dies and that is the end of him. This might accord with passages that speak of "death" as the lot of the wicked, but not with those referring to Gehenna or the like. If we are to be true to the whole teaching of Scripture, we must come to the conclusion that the ultimate fate of the wicked is eternal punishment, though we must add that we have no way of knowing in exactly what that punishment consists.

L. MORRIS

See also HELL; ANNIHILATIONISM; UNIVERSALISM; APOKATASTASIS.

Bibliography. C. S. Lewis, *The Great Divorce;* J. Orr, *ISBE,* IV, 2501–4; A. Richardson, "Hell" in *RTWB;* S. D. F. Salmond, *The Christian Doctrine of Immortality;* H. Buis, *The Doctrine of Eternal Punishment;* F. C. Kuehner, "Heaven or Hell?" in *Fundamentals of the Faith,* ed. C. F. H. Henry; J. A. Motyer, "The Final State: Heaven and Hell," in *Basic Christian Doctrines,* ed. C. F. H. Henry.

Eternal Security of the Believer. *See* PERSEVERANCE.

Eternal Sin. The expression does not occur in the AV translation of the NT. But in Mark 3:29 instead of *kriseōs* ("judgment") the very oldest Greek manuscripts have *hamartēmatos* ("sin"). So the best translation is not "in danger of eternal damnation" (AV) but "guilty of an eternal sin" (NASB, NIV)—which is actually far worse morally. It is the sin of blasphemy against the Holy Spirit, for which there is no forgiveness (Matt. 12:31; Mark 3:29; Luke 12:10).

R. EARLE

See also BLASPHEMY AGAINST THE HOLY SPIRIT.

Eternal State. *See* FINAL STATE.

Eternity. The word suggests transcendence of the temporal and is employed in various senses: durability ("the eternal hills"); time without end ("passing to his eternal reward"); time without beginning (speculative conceptions of the universe as "an eternal process"); infinite time (the ascription of temporality to the nature of God). Beyond this the term traditionally has been used by theology and philosophy to designate God's infinity in relation to time—i.e., to designate the divine perfection whereby God transcends temporal limitations of duration and succession and possesses his existence in one indivisible present.

In Greek philosophy the eternity of divine being simultaneously implied the shadow-reality and insignificance of the temporal, a speculative view contradictive of biblical theism with its emphasis on redemptive revelation in time and place. Parmenides already had shaped the Greek prejudice: only the unchanging and permanent is real, all else is illusory. By another route Plato and Aristotle reached the same conclusion: genuine significance pertains only to eternal realities, never to the temporal.

Biblical theology and philosophy, however, affirmed the unique eternity of God without ruling out the created and conditional reality of the time-space order and its momentous significance. The doctrines of creation, preservation, providence, incarnation, and atonement all involved a strategic role for the world of time and history.

Prompted by Hegel, modern philosophy lodged time (and the universe) in the very nature of the Absolute. The immanental speculations conceived the whole of reality as temporal, as the Absolute in process of logical evolution. Thus the idea of an insignificant temporal order was subverted, but so also was the conception of the self-sufficient God. Hegel indeed distinguished the Absolute's indivisible timeless inner unity from the Absolute's temporal differentiation as nature and spirit. But this ambiguity led post-Hegelian thinkers in two directions. F. H. Bradley declared temporal distinctions unreal in the Absolute's experience, while most post-Hegelian scholars rejected divine timelessness. Josiah Royce proposed a mediating position. While affirming the temporality of all experience, he asserted that the Absolute knows all events in a single time span, a unitary act of consciousness, in contrast with the long successions of time spans involved in our finite knowledge. But Royce's formula transcended the duality of eternity and time only verbally, since on his theory time would not exist for the Absolute in the same sense as for its parts, nor would events as known by finite selves carry absolute significance. Edgar S. Brightman vigorously asserted the divine temporality of his finite God. As naturalism more and more displaced idealism as the influential modern philosophy, its exponents affirmed the ultimacy of time.

In reaction to the modern temporalizing of deity, neo-orthodox theology stresses the "infinite qualitative difference" between eternity and time. It emphasizes not only the ontological transcendence of God as Creator and his moral transcendence of man as sinner, but sketches his epistemological transcendence in such a way that, in the exposition of the *imago Dei*, it curtails the role of cognition and the significance of the forms of logic in the human reception of divine revelation. It minimizes the historical aspect of redemptive revelation, moreover, by assigning God's disclosure a superhistorical locus in man's encounter with deity. Later writings of Barth and Brunner somewhat moderate their more extreme early statements; nonetheless, although now emphasizing the created reality of time and the crucial importance of the incarnation and atonement, they evade the direct identification of history at any point with divine revelation.

To repair this gulf between the temporal order and the Deity some recent theologians in turn discard the definition of eternity as pure timelessness or nontemporality. While thus avoiding Hegel's identification of the temporal order with God's direct self-manifestation, they lodge time in the very nature of God instead of viewing it as in created dependency. Oscar Cullmann drops the whole idea of timelessness with reference to the eternal. He maintains that eternity is simply infinitely extended time: the former, boundless time; the latter, bound by creation at the one end and by eschatological events at the other.

Here the philosophical and theological repudiation of nontemporal eternity meet, though the philosophical motives are avowedly speculative, while Cullmann's are professedly biblical and exegetical. From the NT use of *aiōn* for a period of time, both defined and undefined in duration, alongside its use of this term for eternity, Cullmann argues that eternity is not timeless but rather is unending time. Since the same term is applied both to this age and to the next, the temporal and eternal worlds are presumably not qualitatively distinguishable in respect to time. The eschatological drama, moreover, requires the idea of time progression. Hence the qualitative disjunction of eternity and time is dismissed as Greek rather than biblical in outlook. Instead of binding time to the creation alone, Cullmann affirms that time falls into three eras: precreation; from creation to "the end of the world"; and posteschatological. The first is unbegun, the last unending.

No objection can be taken to Cullmann's aim, which is to preserve the absolute significance of redemptive history and to prevent a dissolution of the Christ-event as the decisive center of history from which both time and eternity are to be understood. His detection of docetic and hellenic influences in the theology of Kierkegaard, Barth,

Brunner, and Bultmann, moreover, gains its point from their excessive formulations of divine transcendence. But the repudiation of the unique eternity or nontemporality of God is not required to preserve the reality and significance of historical revelation and redemption; indeed, the temporalizing of the Eternal poses theological problems all its own.

Admittedly many biblical representations suggest nothing beyond an exaltation of God above all temporal limitations of the universe (John 17:24; Eph. 1:4; II Tim. 1:9). Recourse to Exod. 3:14, "I am who I am," where the French render the name of Jehovah as the Eternal, is unavailing, for the comfort of the oppressed Israelites in Egypt must surely have sprung from an assurance that God intervenes redemptively in fallen history, and not especially from his nontemporality.

But the nontemporality of God nonetheless can be firmly supported. The constant use of *aiōn* for the spatial world (cosmos) suggests the concomitance of time and space; hence not simply the temporality but also the spatiality of God—an assumption objectionable to biblical theists—would seem to be implied by a one-sided reliance on *aiōn*. From this circumstance the conviction gains support that time and space belong to the created order as distinct from the divine essence and that eternity is an incommunicable divine attribute. Moreover, the biblical contrast of divine and temporal duration frequently looks beyond a quantitative or proportional to a qualitative contrast. Temporal categories are viewed as inapplicable to Jehovah (cf. Ps. 90:2) and the word *'ôlām* gains theological significance. This qualitative connotation is more fully carried by the later use of *'ôlām* in plural form for God's eternity, a turn of phrase required by the absence of alternatives in Hebrew vocabulary to express a qualitative differentiation.

"The plural cannot mean the literal addition of a number of indefinite, unbounded temporal durations; it can only be read as a poetic emphasis by which a quantitative plural is a symbol for a qualitative difference" (*RTWB*, 266). The NT translation of *'ôlām* by *aiōn* and *aiōnios* is instructive, moreover. The primary thrust of the familiar terms "eternal life" and "eternal death" is qualitative, and not simply quantitative. The former phrase depicts a quality of life fit for eternity, in which the believer already participates through regeneration (John 5:24), although it does not, of course, imply nontemporality; the latter, eternal death, is spiritual death which, in the case of the impenitent unbeliever, is transmuted at physical death into an irrevocable condition. Finally, the attribute of eternity cannot be disjoined from God's other attributes. The biblical emphasis on divine omniscience supports the view of his supertemporal eternity. If God's knowledge is an inference from a succession of ideas in the divine mind, he cannot be omniscient. Divine omniscience implies that God knows all things in a single whole, independent of a temporal succession of ideas. C. F. H. Henry

See also God, Attributes of; God, Doctrine of; Time; Age, Ages; This Age, The Age to Come.

Bibliography. O. Cullmann, *Christ and Time;* C. F. H. Henry, *Notes on the Doctrine of God;* J. Marsh, "Time," in *RTWB.*

Ethical Systems, Christian. For generations Christians have found directions for daily life in the records of Jesus and the occasional counsels of the apostles; the church has never attempted to systematize its ethical teaching as it did its theology. The earliest attempts to commend Christian morality to the ancient world presented it as either the fulfillment of the Judaic system of ethics or the culmination of pagan moral philosophy. The first of all Christian ethical "systems"—that of Ambrose—followed the Roman pattern.

The Early Church and Middle Ages. Ambrose's concern was to equip the church for ministry to a Christian state. His *Duties of the Clergy* is explicitly a Christian adaptation of Cicero's *De officiis.* Accordingly, Ambrose constantly appealed to the Stoic law of nature (leading to later Christian moralists' preoccupation with natural law) and to the philosophical mean—moderation in all things. He defined the Christian virtues on the Stoic model, holding that Scripture illustrates Greek insights with supreme clarity.

Theological controversy prompted the great church councils, but from them issued authoritative decisions governing church discipline which, with counsels and adjudications of outstanding leaders, attained the status of canon law (codified by Gratian in the twelfth century). This was accompanied by a penitential system allotting penalties to breaches of church rules governing private and public life; Christian ethics was here reduced to ecclesiastical discipline, perpetuating the legalism and casuistry characteristic of Judaism.

Meanwhile the more contemplative, ascetic, "Greek" trend in Christian thought, desiring to escape the active world rather than to control it with Ambrose, retreated into monasteries for intense cultivation of the inner life, seeking the vision of God by internal and external imitation of Christ. Soon there arose the need for "Rules" of discipline (e.g., Benedict's) in which monastic vows of poverty, chastity, and humility were spelled out in detailed guidance for corporate living, useful work, and Christlike ministry.

Similar summaries of Christian morality were produced in more individualist and mystical Christian circles in innumerable books of spiritual counsel (à Kempis's *Imitation of Christ* is one of many), in which emotional and contemplative devotion is concentrated upon inward imitation, especially in renunciation, purgation, humility, and prayer.

Earlier Augustine, immersed in controversies, wrestled to elucidate the place of ethics within a theology of salvation which assumed the helplessness of man's will, corrupted by original sin, and the consequent necessity of divine grace to the accomplishment of any good in man. At the same time, faced with social and moral disintegration of the empire, Augustine expounded the Christian social ideal as the coming City of God.

Augustine's far-ranging thought embraced a privative theory of evil as the absence of good; man's responsibility (as free of external restraint) for not choosing the good; available irresistible grace, an internal dynamic which alone can create a good disposition of will; and the principle that one cannot do evil, even in persecuting heretics, if love be the motive. Augustine's basic position was eudaemonist: morality is pursuit of the good, which will bring happiness; all seek happiness, differing only in *where*. Christians find it in the spiritual satisfaction of loving God as chief good—the only *summum bonum* which can satisfy such a creature as man.

From this Augustine derived all personal Christian virtues, the social love of neighbor on every level, and a whole series of practical counsels on marriage, property, the state, the just war, not with academic precision of analysis but with the informal system imposed by a single profound mind.

The first thoroughgoing attempt at systematization was that of Aquinas, sitting at the feet at once of Augustine and Aristotle, and producing the most massive of all intellectual expressions of Christian thought. In ethics he set out from the purposive nature of every act of will to discover man's supreme goal in the vision of God, which only revelation can make known, only right reason can apprehend (the moral law being natural to a rational creature), and only faith, created by the infusion of divine grace, can hope to attain. Within this framework Aquinas explains the seven cardinal Christian virtues; the complex meaning of law; the place of right emotions, dispositions, and habits in the formation of character; and the outworking of such faith in man ("a social and political animal").

The Reformation. While Luther's thought is anything but systematic, his fertile thought (*On Liberty, Good Works, Authority and Obedience, Galatians, The Decalogue*) exercised such influence that his ethic must be mentioned. Starting from a dynamic view of man as ever active, he defined the central issue as man's freedom to act, which as creature, sinner, "curved in upon himself," fallen man does not possess; he is enslaved under moral law, but not saved by it. Only faith in the saving initiative of God can create man anew, justifying him before God. Such faith is then ever active in love and good works, becoming "a sort of Christ" to its neighbors; it lives within the secular world, not withdrawn from it, exercising a new freedom bestowed by Christ—though that may lead to imitation of Christ's crucifixion.

The social consequences of salvation are expounded on the basis of the Decalogue in generally conservative terms, preserving the established orders of society as divinely instituted and defending existing structures, marriage, commercial order, political authority, the traditional just war. Luther's doctrine of "two kingdoms" differentiated sacred and secular spheres while insisting that the secular, too, is God's.

The nearest Protestant equivalent to Aquinas's architectural structure is Calvin's monumental *Institutes*. Starting from the absolute sovereignty of God, Calvin summarizes Christian ethics as the discipline of the individual life and the creation of a sanctified society, both to God's glory. God's sovereignty confronts the individual as law, first in nature and then in revelation through the Decalogue, interpreted in the light of later insights. To keep this law means perfection for the believer.

But Adam's disobedience corrupted man's nature into moral helplessness; repentance (including mortification and reform), which God in grace bestows and faith receives, so regenerates human nature as to produce righteousness, the image of God, and holiness. The resulting moral life is disciplined, energetic, free, charitable, imitating Christ. Discipline is the central principle and includes self-denial, a "calling," chastity within marriage and outside it.

God's sovereignty confronts man corporately with the ideal of a sanctified society. The commercial world would be brought under God's rule as the sense of vocation developed faithfulness in work, justice and compassion in the ownership of property, investment for fair interest (a wholly novel principle in Christian ethics). The political world would be brought under God's sovereignty as civil institutions regulated and restrained manners according to God's natural law, exercizing divine authority in promoting true religion, defending the weak, and punishing the wicked, all with Christian support. But only under God: rulers are neither above criticism nor to be obeyed when misgovernment becomes intolerable. War is simply the extension of the magistrate's "power of the sword" against international crime, rightly claiming Christian loyalty. Thus church and state cooperate to make this world again God's kingdom.

Modern Ethical Systems. Various attempts to replace the external ecclesiastical authority repudiated at the Reformation by an internal autonomous authority of conscience (Butler), moral reason (Kant), or the inner light of the Spirit (Barclay) failed to achieve a system of ethics, and systematizing fell out of fashion.

The nineteenth century saw the emergence of a unifying movement to set Christian ethics on a new basis, to express the common thinking (or feeling) behind very many attempts at Christian social amelioration and prevention of evils. Numerous propagandists contributed, usually starting from strongly evangelical compassion, but the new thrust's intellectual formulation owed most to F. D. Maurice, who emphasized Jesus' teaching on the kingdom of God as the heart of the gospel: "The kingdom of God is the great existing reality that is to renew the earth."

Walter Rauschenbusch likewise stated that "Christ's concept of the kingdom came to me as a new revelation," and his social gospel (emphasizing both words equally) sought the establishment of Christ's rule in all human relationships. Sin and salvation, the Christian goal, he saw as essentially social; the task of Christian ethics was "the Christianizing of the social order." Against the more idealistic aspects of the movement Reinhold Niebuhr insisted upon Christianity's limitations in the political field, with a realism which Dietrich Bonhoeffer, confronting Nazism, sought to adapt into an existentialist, secular, "religionless" Christianity. This would accept the secular world as already, and in fact, redeemed and in process of being conformed to "the form of Christ." This world is not separate from God; a world "come of age" must not look for divine interventions. Christians must work to conform this world to Christ by living for others, under certain divine mandates of labor, marriage, government, and church. In Bonhoeffer's posthumous and fragmentary *Ethics* is material which might have become a new system of Christian ethics on radical social lines.

Instead, on one side Christian ethical thought has turned to existentialism expressed as "situation ethics," which almost implies the denial of all system and consistency. On another side it has turned to "the theology of the Word"—again more a movement than a system, but marked by a consistent pattern thoroughly pursued. Reasserting the transcendence of God and the givenness of revelation against overemphasis upon religious experience, Karl Barth rejected natural morality in favor of the objective authority of the word God speaks to men in Christ. Ethics is the doctrine of God's command implied within all Christian theology: within creation (God commanding in nature), within reconciliation (God commanding in salvation), and within final redemption (God commanding for glory); and the command is always concrete ("situational"), never in abstract principles. Obligation, then, is really privilege, and obedience is man's acknowledgment that God is right in all he does and asks. This is man's freedom, too, and the expression of his love.

Emil Brunner carried Barth's main emphasis further: the good is not what is natural to man, but what God wills. But Brunner gave greater place to man's responsibility—his ability to respond—to the given, saving act of God in Christ, which becomes the very center of life: (1) by revealing what the good is, namely love, whose prescriptions cannot be known beforehand, but whose endeavor exceeds justice as needs exceed right; (2) by achieving the good, as faith lets God, by the Spirit, have his way with us. Love constitutes community—of life (in marriage and parenthood), of labor (working to use and serve creation), of the state (God's order for a sinful world), of culture (enriching common life), and of the church (molding the institutions of society).

To this emphasis on the Word of God Rudolf Bultmann added the existential overtone, that the Word comes to the soul in the very act of the proclamation of Christ, received in faith. The death and resurrection of Christ attain meaning only in my dying and rising with him. To receive the proclamation is to participate in it, in obedience and love. Ethics is the unfolding of faith itself, in "authentic existence."

Here again a common mind appears to be shaping a system. After several generations of diverse analysis, any ethical synthesis is attractive if it promises clarity and authority. But when it emerges, certain unfailing constants that have marked all truly Christian systems will no doubt characterize the new formulation. It will uphold a given, objective moral standard; it will demonstrate the relation of ethics to human nature as God made it; it will offer to sinful men not merely moral counsel but incentive, dynamic, and hope; it will be as relevant to society as to the individual, as flexible to changing situations as it is loyal to the given unchanging ideal that unites obligation with love—the imitation of Christ.

R. E. O. White

See also ETHICS; ETHICS, BIBLICAL; SITUATION ETHICS; SOCIAL ETHICS; GOOD, THE GOOD, GOODNESS.

Bibliography. W. Beach and H. R. Niebuhr, eds., *Christian Ethics;* T. Aquinas, *Summa contra Gentiles* III and *Summa Theologica* II; E. G. Rupp, *The Righteousness of God;* K. Barth, *Church Dogmatics,* II/2, III/4; E. Brunner, *The Divine Imperative;* R. E. O. White, *Christian Ethics;* B. Häring, *Free and Faithful in Christ;* C. F. H. Henry, *Christian Personal Ethics.*

Ethics. The inquiry into man's moral nature so as to discover what are his responsibilities and the means by which he may fulfill them. Ethics shares with certain other human enterprises the quest for truth, but is distinct in its concern for what man ought to do in the light of the truth uncovered. It is not simply descriptive, but prescriptive in character.

The field of ethical inquiry can be divided into philosophical, theological, and Christian ethics. Philosophic ethics approaches man's responsibility from what can be known by natural reason and in respect to temporal existence. Theological ethics deals with what may be gained from the alleged insight of any given religious community as to this life or that to come. Christian ethics is the Christian instance of theological ethics. It allows that "God, after he spoke long ago to the fathers in the prophets," has "in these last days spoken to us in his Son" (Heb. 1:1–2). It weighs man's moral obligations in the light of this distinctive revelation.

It is also common to distinguish between personal and social ethics, although this is somewhat misleading because man is a social being and any conduct has social significance. However, social ethics deals with the moral considerations that relate to our corporate identity, as we form associations and establish societal policies. While the distinction may seem rather contrived, it reminds us that ethics involves not simply how one relates to others, but how groups associate so as to act responsibly.

Ethical inquiry is a reflective activity and, as such, human and fallible. Whatever the belief of the individual or group concerning a revelation of God, it is never thought to be exhaustive or all-encompassing. The features of life change with the times, so that man must weigh now and again what are the implications of truth perceived in the past for the present. And there are also the cross-cultural barriers that must be overcome in pressing to understand man's obligation in some particular setting.

It has been customary to speak of conscience as man's ethical faculty, but this way of expressing the matter has increasingly fallen into disuse since the demise of faculty psychology. It remains that man makes decisions not simply with reference to strictly pragmatic concerns, but to what he perceives as right and proper. He reasons and acts in reference to some ethical norm.

There is within theological ethics as a rule and Christian ethics in particular a concern for "the higher order." One's religious commitment takes precedence over the obligation to human authority, legitimate as the latter might otherwise be. One must obey God rather than man (cf. Acts 4:18–19). In any case, we see our responsibility within the scope of whatever integrating factor or ideal that is operative. M. A. INCH

See also ETHICAL SYSTEMS, CHRISTIAN; ETHICS, BIBLICAL; SITUATION ETHICS; SOCIAL ETHICS.

Bibliography. K. Baier, *The Moral Point of View;* E. Brunner, *The Divine Imperative;* W. Elert, *The Christian Ethos;* N. Geisler, *Ethics: Alternatives and Issues;* J. Hospers, *Human Conduct;* C. H. Whiteley, "On Defining 'Moral,'" in *The Definition of Morality,* ed. G. Wallace and A. D. M. Walker; G. Winter, ed., *Social Ethics.*

Ethics, Biblical. Ethics finds place in a theological dictionary precisely because neither in Judaic nor in Christian thought can ethics be separated, except for the purpose of concentration, from its theological context. All biblical theology has moral implications which comprise the biblical ethic.

In the OT. In recognizing the OT as Christian Scripture the church adopted some embarrassing moral precedents: burning of witches, the poisoned trial cup, family punishment, polygamy, concubinage, and much violence and war. But it also fell heir to a great deal of moral instruction, warning, example, high inspiration, and moral faith that immeasurably increased Christianity's ethical resources.

Chief among gains was undoubtedly the theocratic foundation of ethics as the will of God, holy, faithful, and good, and based upon what God had already done as creator and redeemer of his people. Thus the Decalogue opens with "I am the Lord your God who brought you out of the land of Egypt, out of the house of bondage"; while the unique covenant which bound Israel to its God, not in a natural bond (as though God were the remotest ancestor) but in a moral relationship, originating in God's choice, promise, and deliverance and answered by Israel's grateful obedience and trust, lent an unparalleled quality of humility and confidence to Jewish ethical thought. Properly understood, obedience did not aim at divine favor but was inspired by it.

The Decalogue itself (perpetuating even older ideals) is a remarkable ethical document, its received form embracing a dual code of religious (Exod. 20:3–12) and social (vss. 13–17) duties, though bringing both areas (worship, prohibition of idols, the oath, the sacred day, and filial piety on the one hand, and the sanctity of life, marriage, property, truth, and desire on the other) under direct divine authority. Inevitably this form of commandment gave its tone to Judaic morality, although the final commandment against coveting enters a realm where legalism is helpless.

The development of this ethical basis in the "book of the covenant" (Exod. 20:22–23:19; see 24:7) reflects a simple nomadic and agricultural background, bringing a sense of justice and measured responsibility into primitive conditions; capital offenses are numerous, slavery accepted, but equity and piety begin to affect social life.

Deuteronomy emphasizes a humanitarian spirit, a liberality, sympathy, and inward holiness ("Thou shalt love the Lord thy God," 6:5) entirely in accord with the teaching of the prophets. Amos made ethics essential to Israel's relation to God, and his morality was pure, self-disciplined, passionately defensive of the poor and oppressed, passionately opposed to cruelty, deceit, luxury, and selfishness. Isaiah and Micah demanded a religion consonant with the character of the Holy One of Israel. Jeremiah, Ezekiel, and Isaiah 40–66 apply the bitter lessons of the Babylonian exile in relentlessly ethical ways, though always within the context of God's unswerving purpose for his people. Israel's God is emphatically the author and guardian of the moral law, requiring above all that men do justly, love mercy, and walk humbly with their God (Mic. 6:8).

Later Jewish moral teaching included (in Proverbs, Ecclesiastes, Job, Sirach) valuable ethical "wisdom" whose aim was to simplify duty into practical reverence for God, the merest common sense in those who know themselves creatures of the Eternal: "the fear of the Lord is the beginning of wisdom" (Ps. 111:10). Wisdom's ideal is eloquently expressed in Job 31.

The Babylonian exile and the foreign domination that followed so threatened Jewish self-identity that immense emphasis was laid upon the written and oral law, which enshrined everything distinctively Jewish. Piety, nationalism, and pride combined to produce an exaggerated legalism, burdensome to most and a source of moral blindness, hypocritical casuistry, and self-righteousness to many. Hence arose "religious" opposition to Jesus, for whom legalism held no divine authority, and Christianity's emphasis upon freedom.

In the NT. A long ethical tradition was summarized, therefore, when John the Baptist appeared demanding purity, righteousness, honesty, and social concern (Luke 3:10–14). But especially illuminating is the discrimination of Jesus as he took up from Judaism its ethical monotheism, its social conscience, and the relation of religion to morality, while rejecting the tendency to self-righteousness, the hard, external legalism, the nationalism, the cultivation of merit, and the failure to differentiate ritual from morality. On the other hand, Jesus pressed the demand for righteousness still further than the law, into the mind and motive behind behavior (Matt. 5:17–48), back to the original purposes of God (Mark 2:27; Matt. 19:3–9), or to the sufficient and overriding commandment of love to God and neighbor (Matt. 22:35–40). In this summary of all duty, religious and social, as *love* lies Jesus' most characteristic contribution to ethical thought, as his example of love's meaning and his death in love for men comprise his most powerful contribution to ethical achievement.

Religion and ethics meet again in Christ's gospel of the kingdom of God, his version of the messianic hope and of the prophets' vision of God as Lord of history; Christ's description of life in the kingdom, its opportunities and obligations, applies his radical and realistic idea of righteousness and love to family life, stewardship of wealth, responsibility toward the state, social evils, the fact of sin's sickness and cruelty. In all realms obedience to the will of God constitutes the kingdom and ensures its blessings; though it may involve loss of the self-life, that will gain eternal profit.

But the King is also Father, and the citizens of the kingdom are his sons, sharing a status and life which reflect the character of God, in a fellowship and forgiveness, a freedom and trust, that make obedience glad. Beneath all else is the personal attachment of men to Jesus himself as Savior and Lord; in that love (John 14:15; 21:15–17) the desire to be like Christ becomes a moral incentive of immense emotional power. Such love delights to keep Christ's commandments.

There is good reason to believe that the apostolic church offered considerable moral training to converts, covering abstinence from old sins and pagan ways, steadfastness under persecution, the fostering of fellowship, and submission to leaders. This probably included lists of duties as husband, wife, parent, child, servant, slave, neighbor (see Colossians and I Peter). The earliest development of Christian ethical teaching is perhaps best illustrated in I Peter, where the emphasis falls upon holiness and submission—to civil powers (2:13–17), to slave-masters (2:18–25), to husbands (3:1–7), and within the fellowship (3:8–9; 4:8–11; 5:5–6). This unexpected theme not only spells out the meaning of life under divine rule; it follows from the biblical view of the essence of sin as self-will.

Illustration of the earliest Christian moral life is best seen in Luke's impressive gallery (in Acts) of essentially good, happy, socially useful, courageous, and transformed people, closely corresponding to his picture of Jesus in his Gospel. James, too, probably presents an early picture of the church's moral stance, in a series of meditations on great words of Jesus in the manner of Jewish wisdom literature.

Paul's ethical concern was to counter the legalism which had failed in his own life and which threatened to confine the church to a Jewish sect, by insisting on the sufficiency of faith to save Jew and Gentile alike and on the freedom of the Christian to follow the leading of the Spirit (so Galatians). While handing on to converts the common tradition of ethical teaching (Rom. 6:17; II Thess. 2:15; 3:6), Paul especially explicated the ethical significance of faith and the nature of life in the Spirit.

Faced with the challenge that if justification is by faith alone the believer may continue in sin with impunity, Paul replies that the faith which saves involves such a personal identification with Christ in death to sin, self, and the world, and in resurrection to a new life of freedom, surrender, and triumph, that to continue in sin while exercising such faith is inconsistent, unnecessary, and impossible (Rom. 6; Gal. 2:20). For Paul, the faith that saves sanctifies. If any believer finds this not so, it is because he is failing to be what in Christ he has become—dead to sin, alive to God.

Paul's other ethical theme contends that what the law can never do, through the weakness of human nature, "the rule of the Spirit of life in Christ Jesus" does accomplish, so that the law is fulfilled in us (Rom. 8:1–4). Already Jeremiah and Ezekiel had linked the invisible power of God in creation and history (Spirit) with the new heart and will needed in Israel. Luke, by showing Jesus as the bearer and bestower of the Spirit, and John, by describing the Spirit as Jesus' other self, reveal how in early Christian thought the whole idea of the divine Spirit had become stamped with the image of Jesus (Acts 16:7). Paul spells out the effect of this identification as producing the Christlike character—the fruit of the Spirit—in every willing believer (Gal. 5:22–23; Rom. 5:5; 8:9–14). This transformation of men by the inner dynamic of the Christ Spirit is one of the central ethical motifs of Christianity.

The other is the theme common to all NT ethical teaching, the imitation of Christ. The Synoptic Gospels present this as simply following Jesus. John expounds the ideal of *Christus Exemplar* as loving (13:34; 15:12), obeying (9:4; 15:10), standing firm (15:20), and humbly serving (13:14–15) as Jesus did for us. First John links it with the Christian hope (3:2). Peter connects imitation especially with the cross (I Pet. 2:21–25; 3:17–18; 4:1, 13). Paul makes it the goal of worship (II Cor. 3:18), of ministry (Eph. 4:11–13), of exhortation (I Cor. 11:1), and of God's providence (Rom. 8:28–29), defining its inmost meaning as having "the mind of Christ" (I Cor. 2:16; Phil. 2:5), "the Spirit of God" (I Cor. 7:40).

Summary. In contrast with philosophical systems, the enduring marks of biblical ethics are its foundation in relationship with God; its objective, imposed obligation to obedience; its appeal to the deepest in man; its down-to-earth social relevance; and its capacity for continual adaptation and development.

The final biblical formulation of the ideal as Christlikeness is related directly to love and gratitude kindled by the experience of redemption; it is rooted in objective history (as the obvious ethical implicate of the incarnation); it appeals strongly to man's finest moral intuitions; it calls to Christlike ministry among the needy of the world and to the fulfillment of God's kingdom on earth; and through the Christian centuries its many forms and interpretations have proved its flexible adaptability to changing conditions. The early biblical command, "Be ye holy, for I am holy," finds clear echo in the latest biblical promise, "We shall be like him." R. E. O. White

See also Ethical Systems, Christian; Ten Commandments, The; Kingdom of Christ, God, Heaven; Imitation of Christ.

Bibliography. W. O. E. Oesterley and T. H. Robinson, *Hebrew Religion;* J. H. Houlden, *Ethics of the NT;* W. Lillie, *Studies in NT Ethics;* L. H. Marshall, *Challenge of NT Ethics.*

Ethics, Sexual. *See* Sexual Ethics.

Ethics, Situation. *See* Situation Ethics.

Ethics, Social. *See* Social Ethics.

Eucharist. *See* Lord's Supper.

Euthanasia. The word is derived from two Greek words meaning "good" and "death." It refers to any attempt to prevent the process of death from being prolonged and/or painful in situations of inevitable and painful death. Often heavy medical expenditures are a factor. The heightening of the issue of euthanasia is in part a by-product of medical success. Persons who formerly would have died at a relatively early age are now kept alive to the point of contracting diseases of older age or experiencing the general physical deterioration which so often accompanies advanced years. With a rapidly increasing population of older persons in our society, euthanasia will become a larger issue.

Euthanasia may be classified on the basis of several criteria. It may be passive or active. Passive euthanasia involves simply allowing the person to die through withholding or discontinuing treatment that would prolong life. Active euthanasia involves some positive step to terminate life, such as administration of a toxic substance or injection of an air bubble into the bloodstream. Euthanasia may also be classified as voluntary or involuntary. Voluntary euthanasia is the case where the subject has indicated his desire for life to end. In involuntary euthanasia the decision is made for the subject by some third party, usually the closest relative. Thus there are four possible classes of euthanasia: voluntary passive, involuntary passive, voluntary active, and involuntary active.

Passive euthanasia is in fact quite widely practiced today. Typically the situation is one in which there is no medical prognosis of recovery or even of improvement. The patient is ordinarily in great discomfort or even acute pain. Frequently great sympathetic distress is felt by the patient's loved ones as well, and in addition, crushing economic burdens may be imposed upon the family by prolonged costly medical care.

Some opponents of euthanasia advance what has been called the sanctity of life argument. On these terms life itself is a good, a gift from God. It should therefore be preserved by all means. However, while Scripture does accord a high value to life, it is questionable whether it is an absolute value, in disregard of other considerations. On the other side is the natural death argument. God is the giver and taker of life. There is a time for death and when this time comes, the person is to die. We should not interfere with this occurrence. The difficulty with this argument is that it would preclude *any* medical assistance, even first aid, since that could be interpreted as (and might actually be) interference with the inevitability of death. This has caused some to distinguish between more customary medical treatment and the more unusual (sometimes termed "heroic measures"), maintaining that we are obligated to take all normal steps to conserve life but need not take heroic measures. The difficulty with this approach is the relativity of the terms. What is extraordinary treatment now may be routine ten years from now.

Sooner or later, death is God's will (Heb. 9:27). Mercy may call for permitting it, especially where the patient has declared that to be his wish. The use of a "living will" enables the next of kin to know the patient's wish when he may no longer be capable of expressing it. Nonetheless, such a step is a sobering one, particularly where the patient is not a Christian, since it cuts off the last opportunity of accepting Christ. Christians will want to make certain that such persons have heard the gospel.

Active euthanasia presents somewhat different issues. Although it is currently illegal in most countries, appeals are being made for its legalization. Some simply reject this either as murder or as assisted suicide. It should be noted, however, that biblically not all cases of homicide were treated as murder. There was condemnable killing (murder), excusable killing (accidental death), and even mandatory killing (warfare and capital punishment). Murder was intentional, premeditated, malicious taking of the life of someone not deserving of capital punishment and contrary to the wishes of the person. While involuntary active euthanasia contains too many of these features to be acceptable, voluntary active euthanasia is neither contrary to the wishes of the subject nor done for the purpose of inflicting harm.

Nor is the effort to treat this as suicide convincing. The Bible does not speak clearly regarding suicide, the cases (Abimelech, Judg. 9:50–57; Saul, I Sam. 31, cf. II Sam. 1:1–16; and Judas Iscariot, Matt. 27:5) being simply reported rather than given any moral evaluation. The first two are most like euthanasia, but appear to have been motivated by desire to avoid disgrace rather than pain. And not all cases of self-willed death are regarded as suicide. There is self-sacrifice, commended by Jesus (John 15:13) and even practiced by him. Suicide involves willing a death which would presumably not otherwise occur for some time and which may terminate an otherwise useful life. Euthanasia merely hastens the end of a life that is possibly already largely useless and alters the circumstances of the death.

Some, recognizing the lack of clear-cut biblical statements about euthanasia, have attempted to resolve the difficulty by appealing to biblical principles. Those who oppose euthanasia usually cite the sanctity of life and the sovereignty of God. Those favoring it appeal to the principles of mercy and love. While relevant, none of these considerations appear compelling, however.

Great caution should be observed in dealing with this difficult issue. Both revealed and nonreligious principles suggest that active euthanasia is less than God's best: the value of life; the finality of death; the possibility of diagnostic errors; the possible danger of abuse; and the biblical perspective that suffering is not an unqualified evil but may have a purifying or strengthening effect. It is desirable, therefore, that the present laws prohibiting euthanasia be retained while further thorough study is done. Other options, including the possibility of passive euthanasia, the use and development of painkillers, the sustaining power of God, and the encouragement of believers, should be explored and utilized.

M. J. ERICKSON

Bibliography. P. R. Baelz, "Voluntary Euthanasia," *Theol* 75:238–51; A. B. Downing, ed., *Euthanasia and the Right to Death;* D. C. Maguire, *Death by Choice;* K. Vaux, ed., *Who Shall Live: Medicine, Technology, Ethics.*

Eutychianism. *See* MONOPHYSITISM.

Evangelicalism. The movement in modern Christianity, transcending denominational and confessional boundaries, that emphasizes conformity to the basic tenets of the faith and a missionary outreach of compassion and urgency. A person who identifies with it is an "evangelical," one who believes and proclaims the gospel of Jesus Christ. The word is derived from the Greek noun *euangelion,* translated as glad tidings, good or joyful news, or gospel (a derivative of the Middle English *godspell,* a discourse or story about God), and verb *euangelizomai,* to announce good tidings of or to proclaim as good news. These appear nearly one hundred times in the NT and have passed into modern languages through the Latin equivalent *evangelium.*

Biblically the gospel is defined in I Cor. 15:1–4 as the message that Christ died for our sins, was buried, and rose again on the third day in fulfillment of the prophetic Scriptures and thereby provided the way of redemption for sinful humanity. Three times the NT calls one who preaches the gospel an *euangelistēs* (evangelist).

Theological Meaning. Evangelicalism has both a theological and historical meaning. Theologically it begins with a stress on the sovereignty of God, the transcendent, personal, infinite Being who created and rules over heaven and earth. He is a holy God who cannot countenance sin, yet he is one of love and compassion for the sinner. He actively identifies with the sufferings of his people, is accessible to them through prayer, and has by his sovereign free will devised a plan whereby his creatures may be redeemed. Although the plan is predetermined, he allows them to cooperate in the attainment of his objectives and brings their wills into conformity with his will.

Evangelicals regard Scripture as the divinely inspired record of God's revelation, the infallible, authoritative guide for faith and practice. Inspiration is not mechanical dictation; rather, the Holy Spirit has guided the various biblical authors in their selection of words and meanings as they wrote about matters in their respective places and times. Thus the words and imagery are culturally conditioned, but God has nonetheless conveyed his eternal, unconditional Word through them. The Scriptures are inerrant in all that they affirm and serve as the adequate, normative, and wholly reliable expression of God's will and purpose. But the heavenly teaching of the Bible is not self-evident, and the guidance and illumination of the Holy Spirit is required to bring out the divine meaning embedded in the text and to apply it to our lives.

Denying the Enlightenment doctrine of man's innate goodness, evangelicals believe in the total depravity of man. All the goodness that exists in human nature is tainted by sin, and no dimension of life is free from its effects. Man was originally created perfect; but through the fall sin entered the race, making man corrupt at the very core of his being, and this spiritual infection has been passed on from generation to generation. Sin is not an inherent weakness or ignorance but positive rebellion against God's law. It is moral and spiritual blindness and bondage to powers beyond one's control. The root of sin is unbelief, and its manifestations are pride, lust for power, sensuousness, selfishness, fear, and disdain for spiritual things. The propensity to sin is within man from birth, its power cannot be broken by human effort, and the ultimate result is complete and permanent separation from the presence of God.

God himself provided the way out of the human dilemma by allowing his only Son, Jesus Christ, to assume the penalty and experience death on man's behalf. Christ made atonement for sin on Calvary's cross by shedding his blood, thereby redeeming man from the power of spiritual death by dying in his place. Christ's substitutionary or vicarious atonement was a ransom for mankind's sins, a defeat of the powers of darkness, and a satisfaction for sin because it met the demand of God's justice. Then when Christ arose from the grave, he triumphed over death and hell, thus demonstrating the supremacy of divine power in a sin-cursed world and laying the foundation for the eventual redemption of all creation from sin's corrupting influence. To affirm the atonement, Christians are called upon to bear witness by following their Lord in a life of demanding discipleship and bearing the burdens, sufferings, and needs of others.

Evangelicals believe that salvation is an act of

unmerited divine grace received through faith in Christ, not through any kind of penance or good works. One's sins are pardoned, and one is regenerated (reborn), justified before God, and adopted into the family of God. The guilt of sin is removed immediately, while the inward process of renewing and cleansing (sanctification) takes place as one leads the Christian life. By grace believers are saved, kept, and empowered to live a life of service.

Heralding the Word of God is an important feature of evangelicalism. The vehicle of God's Spirit is the biblical proclamation of the gospel which brings people to faith. The written word is the basis for the preached word, and holy living is part of the process of witness, since life and word are inseparable elements of the evangelical message. Holiness involves not withdrawal from the world and detaching oneself from evil but rather boldly confronting evil and overcoming its effects both personally and socially. In this fashion the church brings the lost to a knowledge of Christ, teaches the way of discipleship, and engages in meeting human needs. Social service thus becomes both the evidence of one's faith and a preparation for the proclamation of the gospel. The preevangelism of works of mercy may be just as important as preaching itself in bringing people into the kingdom of God.

Finally, evangelicals look for the visible, personal return of Jesus Christ to set up his kingdom of righteousness, a new heaven and earth, one that will never end. This is the blessed hope for which all Christians long. It will consummate the judgment upon the world and the salvation of the faithful.

It should be stressed that these are special emphases of evangelicals and that they share many beliefs with other orthodox Christians. Among them are the Trinity; Christ's incarnation, virgin birth, and bodily resurrection; the reality of miracles and the supernatural realm; the church as the body of Christ; the sacraments as effectual signs or means of grace; immortality of the soul; and the final resurrection. But evangelicalism is more than orthodox assent to dogma or a reactionary return to past ways. It is the affirmation of the central beliefs of historic Christianity.

Historical Meaning. Although evangelicalism is customarily seen as a contemporary phenomenon, the evangelical spirit has manifested itself throughout church history. The commitment, discipline, and missionary zeal that distinguish evangelicalism were features of the apostolic church, the fathers, early monasticism, the medieval reform movements (Cluniac, Cistercian, Franciscan, and Dominican), preachers like Bernard of Clairvaux and Peter Waldo, the Brethren of the Common Life, and the Reformation precursors Wycliffe, Hus, and Savonarola. At the Reformation the name "evangelical" was given to the Lutherans who sought to redirect Christianity to the gospel and renew the church on the basis of God's authoritative Word. With the onset of Lutheran orthodoxy and the domination of many churches by civil rulers, unfortunately much of the spiritual vitality evaporated. Soon the word came to be applied collectively to both Lutheran and Reformed communions in Germany. Congregations belonging to the Prussian Union Church (founded 1817) utilized it as well, and in contemporary Germany evangelical (*evangelisch*) is synonymous with Protestant.

A recovery of the spiritual vigor of the Reformation resulted from three movements in the late seventeenth and the eighteenth centuries—German pietism, Methodism, and the Great Awakening. Actually these were rooted in Puritanism with its strong emphasis on biblical authority, divine sovereignty, human responsibility, and personal piety and discipline. The pietism of Spener, Francke, and Zinzendorf stressed Bible study, preaching, personal conversion and sanctification, missionary outreach, and social action. It directly influenced developments in Britain and America and laid the foundations for the later revival in Germany.

To be sure, the Enlightenment had a chilling effect on spiritual movements, but this was countered by the Methodist revival of John and Charles Wesley and George Whitefield in Britain and the Great Awakening in America prior to the Revolution. The new fervor spread within the Anglican Church at the end of the century where the "Evangelical" party of John Newton, William Wilberforce and his Clapham sect, and numerous others fought social ills at home and abroad and founded Bible and missionary societies. Similar developments occurred in the Scottish church under Thomas Chalmers and the Haldane brothers, while the Baptists, Congregationalists, and Methodists all created foreign mission agencies. In Germany, where the old pietism had waned, a new wave of evangelical enthusiasm spread across the land, the *Erweckung,* which cross-fertilized with British movements, while a parallel development occurred in France and Holland, the *Reveil.*

The nineteenth century was clearly the evangelical age. The Anglican party, represented by such distinguished personalities as Lord Shaftesbury and William E. Gladstone, occupied a central position in public life, while Nonconformist groups like the Baptists with their silver-tongued orator Charles H. Spurgeon and the Christian (Plymouth) Brethren reached many with the gospel. Other instances of British evangelical vitality included the YMCA founded by George Williams, the Salvation Army of Catherine and William Booth, the social ministries of George Mueller and Thomas Barnardo, the China Inland Mission of J. Hudson Taylor, and the Keswick movement. In Germany were the *Gemeinschaft* (fellowship) movement, the charitable endeavors of J. H. Wichern, and the spiritual preaching of the Blumhardts, while in Holland the Calvinist theologian and political leader Abraham Kuyper had a major impact.

In America revivalism was the hallmark of evangelical religion. The urban efforts of Charles Finney and D. L. Moody as well as rural and frontier movements among the Baptists, Methodists, Disciples of Christ, and Presbyterians and the growth of holiness perfectionism all helped to transform the nation's religious landscape. Evangelicalism reached to the grass roots of white America, while the black community, in both slavery and freedom, was sustained and held together by its churches, which expressed a deep, personal evangelical faith. Evangelicalism shaped the nation's values and civil religion and provided the vision of America as God's chosen people. Political leaders publicly expressed evangelical convictions and suppressed non-Protestant and "foreign" elements who did not share in the national consensus. Not only unbelief but also social evil would be purged, and revivalism provided the reforming vision to create a righteous republic. The antislavery and temperance campaigns, innumerable urban social service agencies, and even the nascent women's movements were facets of this.

The Protestant nations of the North Atlantic region shared in the great foreign missionary advance that carried the gospel to every corner of the earth, and before long the evangelical revivals that had repeatedly swept the Western world began to occur in Africa, Asia, and Latin America as well. The Evangelical Alliance was formed in London in 1846 to unite Christians (but not churches or denominations as such) in promoting religious liberty, missions, and other common interests. National alliances were formed in Germany, the United States, and many other countries. In 1951 the international organization was replaced by the new World Evangelical Fellowship.

The Twentieth Century. In the early twentieth century, however, evangelicalism went into a temporary eclipse. A decorous worldliness characterized by a stress on material prosperity, loyalty to the nation-state, and a rugged individualism inspired by social Darwinism virtually severed the taproot of social concern. Orthodox Christians seemed unable to cope with the flood of new ideas—German higher criticism, Darwinian evolution, Freudian psychology, Marxist socialism, Nietzschean nihilism, and the naturalism of the new science—all of which undermined confidence in the infallibility of the Bible and the existence of the supernatural. The bloodbath of World War I shattered the optimistic, postmillennial vision of ushering in the kingdom of God as soon as the hold of social evil was broken at home and the Great Commission of carrying the gospel to all parts of the globe was fulfilled. Emerging from the struggle against theological liberalism and the social gospel in Britain and North America was a narrow fundamentalism that internalized the Christian message and withdrew from involvement in the world. In addition, communism in the Soviet Union, nazism in Germany, and secularism throughout the world contributed to declining church attendance and interest in Christianity in general.

After World War II things turned around dramatically. Foreign missionary endeavors, Bible institutes and colleges, works among university students, and radio and literature ministries blossomed, while the evangelistic campaigns of the youthful Billy Graham had a global impact. A party of "conservative evangelicals" emerged in Britain and *Evangelikaler* in Germany, and their strength was reflected in such developments as the National Evangelical Anglican Congress and the German-based Conference of Confessing Fellowships. In the United States the foundation of the National Association of Evangelicals (1942), Fuller Theological Seminary (1947), and *Christianity Today* (1956) were significant expressions of the "new evangelicalism," a term coined by Harold J. Ockenga in 1947.

The new or "neo" evangelicalism took issue with the older fundamentalism. Ockenga argued that it had a wrong attitude (a suspicion of all who did not hold every doctrine and practice that fundamentalists did), a wrong strategy (a separatism that aimed at a totally pure church on the local and denominational levels), and wrong results (it had not turned the tide of liberalism anywhere nor had it penetrated with its theology into the social problems of the day). Edward J. Carnell maintained further that fundamentalism was orthodoxy gone cultic because its convictions were not linked with the historic creeds of the church and it was more of a mentality than a movement. Carl F. H. Henry insisted that fundamentalists did not present Christianity as an overarching world view but concentrated instead on only part of the message. They were too otherworldly, anti-intellectual, and unwilling to bring their faith to bear upon culture and social life.

Although the new evangelicalism was open to ecumenical contacts, rejected excessive legalism and moralism, and revealed serious interest in the social dimension of the gospel, many of its spokespersons remained tied to the political and economic status quo. Groups of more "radical" Christians within mainstream evangelicalism—e.g., the Chicago Declaration of 1973, the Sojourners Community, and the British Shaftesbury Project—began calling attention to needs in this area. As more attention was given to defining an evangelical, it became clear that the numbers were far greater than had been believed. But the variations among the groups—Mennonites, Holiness, Charismatics, Christian Brethren, Southern Baptists, black churches, separatist-fundamentalists, "nondenominational" bodies, and evangelical blocs within the traditional denominations—were enormous and probably unbridgeable.

Nevertheless, evangelical ecumenism has proceeded apace. The Billy Graham organization has been a major catalyst, especially in calling the World Congress on Evangelism (Berlin, 1966) and the International Congress on World Evangelization (Lausanne, 1974). The subsequent consultations sponsored by the Lausanne committee together with the activities of the World Evangelical Fellowship and the regional organizations formed by evangelicals in Africa, Asia, Latin America, and Europe have done much to foster closer relations and cooperative efforts in evangelism, relief work, and theological development. With the indigenization of mission society operations, the multinational character of relief and evangelistic organizations, and the sending of missionaries by people in Third World countries themselves, evangelicalism has now come of age and is truly a global phenomenon.

R. V. Pierard

Bibliography. B. L. Ramm, *The Evangelical Heritage;* D. F. Wells and J. D. Woodbridge, *The Evangelicals;* D. G. Bloesch, *Essentials of Evangelical Theology,* 2 vols., and *The Evangelical Renaissance;* K. S. Kantzer, ed., *Evangelical Roots;* K. S. Kantzer and S. N. Gundry, eds., *Perspectives on Evangelical Theology;* M. Erickson, *New Evangelical Theology;* B. L. Shelley, *Evangelicalism in America;* J. D. Woodbridge, M. A. Noll, N. O. Hatch, *The Gospel in America;* W. G. McLoughlin, ed., *The American Evangelicals;* D. W. Dayton, *Discovering an Evangelical Heritage;* T. L. Smith, *Revivalism and Social Reform;* D. O. Moberg, *The Great Reversal: Evangelism and Social Concern;* G. M. Marsden, *Fundamentalism and American Culture;* D. E. Harrell, Jr., *Varieties of Southern Evangelicalism;* J. B. A. Kessler, *A Study of the Evangelical Alliance in Great Britain;* R. O. Ferm, *Cooperative Evangelism;* J. R. W. Stott, *Fundamentalism and Evangelism;* R. H. Nash, *The New Evangelicalism;* C. F. H. Henry, *Evangelicals in Search of Identity, The Uneasy Conscience of Modern Fundamentalism, A Plea for Evangelical Demonstration,* and *Evangelicals at the Brink of Crisis;* R. V. Pierard, *The Unequal Yoke: Evangelical Christianity and Political Conservatism;* R. Quebedeaux, *The Young Evangelicals;* R. Webber and D. Bloesch, eds., *The Orthodox Evangelicals;* R. E. Webber, *Common Roots: A Call to Evangelical Maturity;* R. G. Clouse, R. D. Linder, and R. V. Pierard, eds., *The Cross and the Flag;* S. E. Wirt, *The Social Conscience of the Evangelical;* R. J. Sider, ed., *The Chicago Declaration;* C. E. Armerding, ed., *Evangelicals and Liberation;* M. A. Inch, *The Evangelical Challenge;* R. K. Johnston, *Evangelicals at an Impasse: Biblical Authority in Practice;* J. Johnston, *Will Evangelicalism Survive Its Own Popularity?* J. Barr, *Fundamentalism;* R. P. Lightner, *Neoevangelicalism Today;* J. C. King, *The Evangelicals;* J. I. Packer, ed., *Anglican Evangelicals Face the Future;* J. D. Douglas, ed., *Let the Earth Hear His Voice: International Congress on World Evangelization;* C. R. Padilla, ed., *The New Face of Evangelicalism;* D. E. Hoke, ed., *Evangelicals Face the Future.*

Evangelism. The proclamation of the good news of salvation in Jesus Christ with a view to bringing about the reconciliation of the sinner to God the Father through the regenerating power of the Holy Spirit. The word derives from the Greek noun *euangelion,* goods news, and verb *euangelizomai,* to announce or proclaim or bring good news.

Evangelism is based on the initiative of God himself. Because God acted, believers have a message to share with others. "For God so loved the world that he gave his one and only Son" (John 3:16). "But God demonstrates his own love for us in this: While we were still sinners, Christ died for us" (Rom. 5:8). Like a father who longs for the return of his lost son, a woman who searches diligently for a lost coin, and a shepherd who leaves the rest of his flock to find a lost sheep (Luke 15), God loves sinners and actively seeks their salvation. God is always gracious, "not wanting anyone to perish, but everyone to come to repentance" (II Pet. 3:9).

God, in turn, expects his people to share in his quest to save the lost. In order to believe the gospel people must first hear it and understand it (Rom. 10:14–15). Thus God has appointed ambassadors, agents of his kingdom, to be his ministers of reconciliation in the world (II Cor. 5:11–21).

A comprehensive definition of evangelism came out of the International Congress on World Evangelization (1974). According to the Lausanne Covenant, "To evangelize is to spread the good news that Jesus Christ died for our sins and was raised from the dead according to the Scriptures, and that as the reigning Lord he now offers the forgiveness of sins and the liberating gift of the Spirit to all who repent and believe. Our Christian presence in the world is indispensable to evangelism, and so is that kind of dialogue whose purpose is to listen sensitively in order to understand. But evangelism itself is the proclamation of the historical, biblical Christ as Saviour and Lord, with a view to persuading people to come to him personally and so be reconciled to God. In issuing the gospel invitation we have no liberty to conceal the cost of discipleship. Jesus still calls all who would follow him to deny themselves, take up their cross, and identify themselves with his new community. The results of evangelism include obedience to Christ, incorporation into his church and responsible service in the world."

The Message. In light of this statement evangelism may be broken down into its component parts. First, there is the message. To be biblical, evangelism must have content and convey information about the true nature of spiritual things. It should address the nature of sin and the plight of the sinner (Rom. 3). It should stress the love of God and his willingness to be reconciled to the lost (John 3; II Cor. 5). It must include a clear statement about the centrality of Jesus Christ in God's plan of redemption: that God was in Christ reconciling the world to himself and that Christ died for our sins and was raised from the dead, according to the Scriptures (I Cor. 15; II Cor. 5; Rom. 10). The evangelistic word must also contain the promise of forgiveness of sins and the regenerating gift of the Holy Spirit to everyone who repents of his sin and puts his faith and trust (i.e., believes) in Jesus Christ (Acts 2; John 3). In short, the evangelistic message is based on the Word of God; it seeks to tell the story that God has already acted out.

The Method. Second, there is the method. Good news can be told in a variety of ways. Scripture does not designate a single method of transmitting the gospel. In the NT believers shared their faith through formal preaching and teaching, in their personal contacts and chance encounters. Consequently Christians have felt free to devise different ways of doing evangelism: personal, mass (i.e., revival campaigns), saturation (i.e., blanketing of a given area), friendship, etc. They have learned how to use various media in spreading the gospel, including the latest in printed and telecommunications fields. All of these means are allowable if they present the message clearly, honestly, and compassionately. Overaggressiveness, manipulation, intimidation, and a well-intentioned misrepresentation of the gospel message actually subvert effective evangelism, though they may appear to bring "results." Whereas there is a legitimate place for aggressiveness and even confrontation in evangelism, integrity and love should be the foundation on which all methods are built. Furthermore, sharers of the good news should know their hearers well enough to speak to their needs, in ways that they can understand (I Cor. 9:19–23). When it comes to evangelistic method, Paul's words still speak with authority and insight: "And pray for us too, that God may open a door for our message . . . so that I may proclaim it clearly, as I should. Be wise in the way you act toward outsiders; make the most of every opportunity. Let your conversation be always full of grace, seasoned with salt, so that you may know how to answer everyone" (Col. 4:3–6).

The Goals. Finally, there are the goals of evangelism. Basically evangelism seeks to bring people into a new relationship with God through Jesus Christ. Through the power of the Holy Spirit it endeavors to awaken repentance, commitment, and faith. Its goal is nothing less than the conversion of the sinner to a radically new way of life. How, then, do we know when evangelism has taken place? When the message has been given? When the message has been adequately understood? When the hearer has been brought to the point of deciding for or against the message he has received? Theologically, of course, the results of evangelism are in the hands of the Spirit, not the evangelist. But practically, the bearer of the message determines to a large extent the scope of the hearer's response because he has stated the terms of the invitation. This means that though evangelism by definition concentrates on the need to respond to God in initial repentance and faith, its message must also contain something about the obligations of Christian discipleship.

In their enthusiasm for sharing the benefits of the gospel evangelists dare not neglect the obligations that come with receiving it. In many evangelical circles, for example, people make a distinction between accepting Christ as Savior and accepting him as Lord. This often leaves converts with the impression that they can obtain the forgiveness of sins without committing themselves to obedience to Christ and service in his church. Such notions are not found in the NT and may be part of the reason that so many modern converts have so little staying power. They have been offered and have accepted "cheap grace" rather than the free but costly grace of the gospel. "Counting the cost" is an essential part of responding to the gospel message, not something that can be put off until a later time.

Conversion to Jesus Christ entails more than the forgiveness of sins. It includes obedience to the commands of God and participation in the body of Christ, the church. As Jesus said, "Therefore go and make disciples of all nations, baptizing them in the name of the Father and of the Son and of the Holy Spirit, and teaching them to obey everything I have commanded you" (Matt. 28:19–20).

One way to maintain the connection between conversion and discipleship is to keep proclamation and demonstration together in evangelism. In the ministry of Jesus and in the life of the apostolic church, preaching and acting, saying and doing were always joined (e.g., Luke 4:18–19; Acts 10:36–38; Rom. 15:18–19). Proclaiming salvation without demonstrating its transforming power in the fruit of the Spirit and goods works is as inadequate as showing the effects of new life in Christ without explaining their source. Announcing the good news of salvation without showing the love of Christ in personal and social concern is not evangelism in the style of the NT. In this holistic approach to evangelism we do not fail to distinguish between regeneration and sanctification, but do contend that the two should be held closely together. T. P. WEBER

See also GOSPEL; CONVERSION; REGENERATION.

Bibliography. D. Watson, *I Believe in Evangelism;* J. I. Packer, *Evangelism and the Sovereignty of God;* J. D. Douglas, ed., *Let the Earth Hear His Voice;* J. Engel and W. Norton, *What's Gone Wrong with the Harvest?* A. Johnston, *The Battle for World Evangelism.*

Evangelism, Gift of. *See* SPIRITUAL GIFTS.

Eve. Adam gave his wife the name Eve because she would become the mother of all the living (Gen. 3:20). The Hebrew word for Eve, *ḥawwâ,* is very similar to the word "living," *ḥay* (fem. *ḥayyâ*), and the LXX actually translated her name as Life (*Zōē*). *Ḥawwâ* is virtually identical to the Ugaritic word for life, *ḥwt.* Eve was created because it was "not good for the man to be alone," so God made "a helper suitable for him" (Gen. 2:18, 20). The word translated "suitable" is a compound preposition meaning "corresponding to" or "opposite" him. It expresses the complementary nature of a person equal to him and able to respond to him and even challenge him. The uniqueness of the husband-wife relationship is seen in that this compound preposition occurs nowhere else in the OT. The closest parallel is a preposition that describes antiphonal choirs standing opposite one another and responding to one another (Neh. 12:24).

Unfortunately, the joyful mutuality that marked this perfect relationship came to an end when Eve succumbed to the serpent's clever urging and ate the forbidden fruit (Gen. 3:1–6). Rather than obeying the simple command of God, she looked at the attractiveness of the fruit and its reward of "wisdom" and then shared the fruit with her husband. Sin now marred their relationship and the lives of their children. In II Cor. 11:3 Paul warns the believers not to be deceived like Eve by the serpent's cunning but rather to stay true to the gospel of Christ. In I Tim. 2:11–14 Paul denies to women the right "to teach or have authority over a man," because Adam was created before Eve and because Eve was the one who was deceived. Although Eve's sinful act had led to death, it would be her offspring who would crush the serpent's head (Gen. 3:15). Christ's death and resurrection defeated the Evil One and opened the way for Adam and Eve's descendants to have eternal life. At the birth of her first child Eve acknowledged that the Lord was the author of life (Gen. 4:1). H. M. WOLF

See also ADAM; WOMAN, BIBLICAL CONCEPT OF.

Bibliography. W. Foerster, *TDNT,* V, 580–81; W. Kaiser, Jr., *Toward an OT Theology;* A. Kapelrud, *TDOT,* IV, 257–60.

Evening Prayer, Evensong. In the Anglican Church evening prayer and evensong mean the same thing, referring to the evening service which is said or sung daily throughout the year. In origin this service is a conflation of the medieval services of vespers and compline. It is composed chiefly of Scripture—OT and NT lessons, biblical canticles (e.g., the Magnificat), biblical versicles, and responses with the Lord's Prayer. To these are added the Kyrie Eleison, creed, and prayers. In Roman Catholicism evening prayer is sometimes used to describe the evening office of vespers found in the new breviary (1971). P. TOON

See also OFFICE, DAILY (DIVINE).

Everlasting Life. *See* ETERNAL LIFE.

Everlasting Punishment. *See* ETERNAL PUNISHMENT.

Evidences of Christianity. *See* APOLOGETICS.

Evil. The bad (moral evil) or the harmful (natural evil). Natural evil, although distinct from moral evil, is not separate from it.

According to the Bible, natural evil is the consequence of moral evil. At first, while still sinless, man is placed in an idyllic garden, where he lives in a happy relationship with his Creator, his wife, and his animals. There is the possibility of eternal life. The "day" that he disobeys God, i.e., commits moral evil, he is covered with shame, confusion, and anxiety, is condemned by God and ejected from the garden. The man must bring forth the fruit of the earth, the woman the fruit of the womb, in agony (Gen. 3).

In the OT. This view prevails throughout the OT (Deut. 27:14; Ps. 1; Prov. 14:31; Mal. 4:1–6). Although Job was convinced for a time that natural suffering had come upon him without his deserving, at the end he humbles himself under the divine rebuke (Job 42:1–6). The prophets predict the Messiah's advent, whose righteous role shall return the natural order to the Edenic state (Isa. 11:1–9; Hos. 2:18). The experience of Job presents in biographical form what Ps. 91 states didactically: that catastrophe "shall not come nigh thy soul," that is, though natural evil exists in this sinful world, it shall not be able to harm the soul of the godly person.

In the NT. This same theme is caught up in the teaching of Christ, whose doctrine may be summarily stated in five points. First, sin and punishment are interrelated. His revelation of hell is most pertinent here (Matt. 10:28; 23:33; Luke 16:23). The Galileans on whom the tower fell (Luke 13:4f.), although no more sinful than others, were assumed to have been sinful and therefore serve to warn the rest of sinful mankind. Second, the cancellation of sin removes punishment. This is especially clear in the healing of the paralytic (Mark 2:3–4). Third, faith is necessary to receive this forgiveness and deliverance (Matt. 9:22; Mark 6:56; Luke 8:48; 17:19). Fourth, the purpose of some suffering is benign. This is revealed especially in the case of the man born blind (John 9:1ff.), particular affliction coming upon him that its healing might be an occasion for the revelation of the glory of God in Christ. Fifth, the resurrection of the bodies of the righteous and the wicked is in order that each group should be placed in the natural state appropriate to its moral state (John 5:29).

The rest of the NT, especially Paul, maintains the same doctrine. "The wrath of God" is revealed against all unrighteousness (Rom. 1:18). "The wages of sin is death" (Rom. 6:23). The death here mentioned represents not only the ultimate natural evil of temporal life, but also of eternal existence, for it is set in contrast to the eternal life which is through Christ. John closes the NT (Rev. 22:14–15) with an apocalyptic vision of the world to come in which there will be a place filled with nothing but moral evil and natural evil or suffering (hell) and a place filled with nothing but moral good and natural good or blessedness (heaven). Thus the Bible represents God as permitting moral evil and its consequent, natural evil (cf. esp. Rom. 8:22–23), and restoring some persons to a state of moral goodness and natural blessedness. According to Paul, all this is with a view to revealing his power in vessels of wrath, no less than his grace in vessels of mercy (Rom. 9:22–23).

In Christian Thought. The extrabiblical development shows considerable variety. Augustine echoes the theodicy of Paul (*City of God,* esp. XI), as do Aquinas and Calvin. While the Pauline-Augustinian tradition sees this twofold purpose of evil, a tradition from Origen to Karl Barth sees only a benign purpose. The evil of men is interpreted as functional to the good, and the wrath of God is an aspect of his love. This optimistic universalism, shared approximately by the philosopher Leibniz, is in stark opposition to the pessimism of Schopenhauer and von Hartmann, who find evil to be ultimate. The other philosophy of evil is embodied in the dualism of Zoroastrianism wherein, however, the good principle conquers in the end time.

Those who deny the realism of the Bible, the optimism of universalism, or the pessimism of Schopenhauer are faced with irreducible "surd" evil. One group sacrifices God's goodness to his power; the other, his power to his goodness. The one affirms that God is certainly powerful, and since he does not prevent evil he must not be altogether good. The other says, God is certainly good, and since he does not prevent evil he must not be altogether powerful. He wants to eliminate evil and he is partly successful in overcoming it, but not completely. Plato found a recalcitrant matter outside of God which prevented the full expression of the highest Idea or the Good. E. S. Brightman internalized the recalcitrant element which he called the "given," and saw a "finite God" struggling with himself. But whether it be a dualist like Plato, a mystic like Boehme, a pragmatist like William James, or limited theists such as Brightman and Berdyaev, they all solve the problem of evil by yielding belief in some of the attributes of God. J. H. GERSTNER

See also EVIL, PROBLEM OF; THEODICY; SIN.

Bibliography. Augustine, *City of God* and *Enchiridion;* J. S. Candlish, *The Biblical Doctrine of Sin;* J. Edwards, *The Great Christian Doctrine of Original Sin;* G. W. Leibniz, *Théodicée;* C. S. Lewis, *The Problem of Pain;* J. Mueller, *The Christian Doctrine of Sin;* R. A. Tsanoff, *Nature of Evil.*

Evil, Problem of. The issue of God and evil is a most important matter for a proselyte considering the claims of a given religion. He wants to know if the religion commits him to belief in a

God who does evil or who fails to do good. On the other hand, the problem of evil is a question about the logical consistency of several propositions central to various theological systems. The phrase "the problem of evil" is actually a label for a series of such problems involving God and evil.

Historically the problem of evil has been raised in many forms. One of its initial statements in its more abstract form was by Epicurus, but the problem has reappeared in many forms all the way down to the present. In biblical literature, though the problem is explicitly covered in greatest detail in the book of Job, the particular question of why the righteous suffer is also treated in various portions of Scripture such as I Pet., James 1, and Rom. 5. The problem of evil, then, is a problem of both theological and philosophical interest as well as a matter of religious import, and it arises not only in Western religion and philosophy but also in various other world religions.

The problem of evil has been put to various uses in philosophical and nonphilosophical discussions. Four are particularly worthy of note. First, some have raised the problem merely to show that a particular theological system is internally self-contradictory and thereby to be rejected. It is claimed that such a system has no way to justify the existence of evil, as the system perceives of evil, in light of the claim that an all-loving, all-powerful God exists. A second and more frequent use of the problem is to argue not only that one theistic position is problematic in this way, but that all theistic positions are so deficient. In other words, many atheists have argued that theism and religion in general are not worthy of adherence because of an alleged inability of all theistic positions to solve their problem of evil. A third and corollary use is to argue from the existence of evil to the nonexistence of God. In such a case the critic is not primarily concerned about the overall consistency or inconsistency of any theological position. He simply uses the problem of evil to reject belief in any god whatsoever. Finally, there are those who use the problem of evil to argue specifically against the Judeo-Christian concept of God. They are not willing to become atheists altogether, but their claim is either that the Judeo-Christian God does not exist or that an acceptable account of God must differ from perceptions of him found in Judaism and Christianity.

Other intellectual problems arise in connection with the problem of evil. Since this problem arises within a theological system, it will take the particular shape of the system in which it arises. Of course, each system has its own peculiar understanding of human freedom, ethics, and metaphysics. Consequently, in the process of handling the problem of evil, one is confronted with such questions as how his system synthesizes its understanding of human freedom with its understanding of God's sovereignty.

Nature of the Problem. Generally theists and atheists alike have perceived the problem of evil to be a problem about the internal consistency of the following three propositions: "God is all-loving," "God is all-powerful," and "Evil exists in a world created by such a God." It is generally assumed that all theologians within the Judeo-Christian tradition have the same understanding of God and evil, and thus that one and only one problem of evil confronts such theists. Atheists are convinced that there is no way for a classical theist to solve the problem of evil. The problem as it is perceived can be portrayed in the following propositions, which form an argument for the inconsistency of theistic positions: (1) God is omnipotent; (2) God is wholly benevolent, i.e., totally disposed to will and do those things which promote the happiness of others; (3) evil consequences resulting from actions and events befall mankind; (4) the omnipotent and wholly benevolent being of 1 and 2 eliminates every evil insofar as it can; (5) there are no nonlogical limits to what an omnipotent being can do; (6) therefore, God eliminates every evil which is logically possible for him to remove. Propositions 1, 2, 4, 5, and 6 entail the negation of 3, and thus the set of six is said to be self-contradictory.

Though there is much truth in this general perception of the problem of evil, there are some important mistakes which must be noted. Without a proper understanding of the nature of the problem any hope of resolving it is lost. The first mistake is thinking there is only one problem of evil confronting all theistic positions. As a matter of fact, there is no such thing as *the* problem of evil, for there are many problems of evil. This is true in two different but very important senses. There is no one problem because there are various kinds of problems of evil, and all are different. First, there is a religious problem. This is a problem about some concrete instance of evil that someone is actually experiencing. In view of the experienced affliction the individual's personal relation with God is strained. Someone caught in the throes of this problem asks such questions as "Why is God allowing this to happen to me?" and "Can I continue to worship a God who does not remove the evil which is now besetting me?" Second, there is the philosophical/theological problem of evil. Normally this can be divided into two more specific problems, the problem of moral evil (evil produced by activities of moral agents) and the problem of natural evil (evil which occurs in the process of the functioning of the natural order). The philosophical/theological problem, as opposed to the religious, is an abstract problem. It is not about a specific evil, nor is it about someone's relationship to God. Instead, it is a general question about why there should be any evil in a world created by an all-loving, all-powerful God. Even if there were no God and no evil, such a question could be posed as follows: How would the existence of an all-powerful, all-loving God, if such a God should exist, square with the existence of evil in the world, if there should be such evil?

There are also problems about the degrees of evil, the intensity and the gratuitousness of evil. That is, one can ask why God needs so much evil in the world to do whatever he is doing with evil. Could he not accomplish his ends with a lesser degree of evil? One could likewise ask why the evil which is present is as intense as it is. For example, whatever God wants to accomplish through someone's cancer, can he not do so without the pain being so intense or lasting so long? Finally, there is some evil which seems to serve no useful purpose whatsoever. Even if one can explain away the other evil in the world, how can one justify the ways of God to man in virtue of the apparent gratuitousness of so much evil? Answers to one kind of problem are not necessarily relevant to—or appropriate as—answers to another problem. For example, if someone experiencing the religious problem because of cancer asks why this should be happening, and if the response is that evil comes from the abuse of free will, the answer will not suffice. Free will is relevant to a problem of moral evil but inappropriate as an answer to someone suffering from cancer.

Even the philosophical/theological problem of evil is not just one problem. As noted, a problem of evil is always a problem that confronts some theological position. However, it should be obvious that not all theological positions even within Judaism or Christianity are identical. Thus, there will be as many philosophical/theological problems of evil as there are theological positions according to which (1) God is omnipotent, in some sense of "omnipotent"; (2) God is said to be benevolent in the sense of willing the removal of evil, in some sense of "evil"; and (3) evil, in the sense mentioned, is said to be present in the world. The point is that not all theological positions have identical perceptions of God and evil. Consequently, contrary to perceptions of atheists and even some theists, the same problem of evil cannot confront all theological systems. Each system has its own problem and requires its own answer.

The Problem of Internal Consistency. A second major point relevant to a proper understanding of the nature of a problem of evil is that a problem of evil in whatever form or system it arises is always a problem about the *internal* consistency of a theological position. Thus, the crucial question is not whether a theological position contradicts another theistic system or even whether it contradicts the atheist's views, but whether it contradicts *itself.* This point has important implications for both theists and critics of theism. For the theist, the implication is that he must so structure his theology as to contain views of God, evil, and human freedom which, when put together, do not result in a contradictory system. In particular, he must be careful to avoid a system in which God is said to be both good and able to remove evil, despite the system's admission of the existence of evil. Such a system will most assuredly succumb to its problem of evil. The implication for the critic of theism is that he must specify a problem which actually arises within the views held by some theist. It is always possible to create a problem for the theist if the atheist is allowed to attribute some of his own views to the theist and then tell the theist there is a problem. Obviously there will be a problem, but not a problem of internal inconsistency.

Unfortunately, many atheistic attacks on theistic systems for their alleged inadequacy in handling evil amount to nothing more than a rejection of the theist's account of God, evil, or freedom. It is legitimate for an atheist to claim that the theistic account of these items is inadequate. It is illegitimate, however, for the atheist to claim that a theist cannot solve his problem of evil *on such a basis.* If the theist, on his own views, can resolve the problem of evil generated by his system, then his system is internally consistent, regardless of whether the atheist or other theists like the intellectual commitments of the system. Once one takes this matter of internal consistency seriously, he finds there are many theistic systems which can solve their own problem of evil, for they can be shown to be self-consistent. One might reject the system as a whole because of some inadequacy in its fundamental intellectual commitments, but such a rejection cannot be on grounds of any alleged internal inconsistency or any inability of the system to resolve its problem of evil.

Perception of God. A final point in clarifying the nature of the problem of evil is that while it is always an attack on a theological perception of God, it is not necessarily an attack on God himself. But if the theological position does reflect the true and living God, then the problem of evil which arises for that system is in fact an attack on God himself. Thus, one needs verification independent of the discussions on the problem of evil that a particular system's God is the true and living God. Consequently, any use of a problem of evil to argue ultimately to the nonexistence of God would be misguided, unless it could be shown that the perception of God being attacked is the correct perception.

In response to the problem of evil there have been many attempts to present answers. Such answers are known as theodicies or defenses, attempts to establish that God is just in spite of the evil present in the world. Generally speaking, the key premise in the argument about evil is that a good God removes every evil insofar as he can. The basic strategy of theodicists has been to suggest that while the premise is true, there is some key reason that God, though all-powerful and all-loving, still cannot remove the evil present in the world. Such a reason would justify the evil present in the world and resolve the theological position's problem of evil. J. S. FEINBERG

See also THEODICY; PAIN; EVIL.

Bibliography. M. B. Ahern, *The Problem of Evil;* J. S. Feinberg, *Theologies and Evil;* J. Hick, *Evil and the God of Love;* J. L. Mackie, "Evil and Omnipotence," in *Philosophy of Religion,* ed. B. Mitchell; E. Madden and P. Hare, *Evil and the Concept of God;* H. J. McCloskey, "God and Evil," in *God and Evil,* ed. N. Pike.

Evil One. *See* SATAN.

Evil Spirits. *See* DEMON, DEMON POSSESSION.

Evolution. Since the publication of *The Origin of Species* by Charles Darwin in 1859, a storm of controversy has raged among theologians and scientists. Some proponents of Darwin's theory have elevated it as a new paradigm to be used to reinterpret the human experience. Other people have identified the theory of evolution as the work of the devil without any scientific merit. Most people stand somewhere in between these two opinions. This article will attempt to examine these various views and relate them to the interpretation of the Genesis account. A critique of each of these views is also presented.

Liberal Views. Auguste Comte, a contemporary of Darwin, devised an evolutionary explanation of religion with three stages of development: (1) *fetishism:* separate will animating material subjects; (2) *polytheism:* many gods acting through inanimate things; (3) *monotheism:* a single, abstract will controlling everything in the universe. The liberals have extrapolated this view of religion in the form of progressive revelation to exegete the Bible. They believe that the revelation of God has progressed from the crude OT God, a fearful, merciless tyrant who treated individuals as merely temporary members of social groups without personal significance. The concept of God evolved during the shattering exilic experience of the Israelites through the anticipation of a personal God in the Psalms and finally culminated in Jesus Christ of the NT, the personal Savior and Lord of every Christian.

The rise of higher criticism also gave impetus to the liberal interpretation of the Bible. While challenging the Mosaic authorship of the Pentateuch, liberals also cast doubts on the originality and authenticity of the biblical records of creation and the flood because of their alleged similarities to the Babylonian versions in *Enuma elish.* The Bible has since been treated by liberal scholars as a great literary work full of human errors and outdated teachings despite its essential message of vital personal realization.

Catholic theologian and anthropologist Pierre Teilhard de Chardin (1881–1955) incorporated the entire evolutionary concept into the biblical framework. The Christian message is reinterpreted according to evolution. Original sin is treated not as an act of disobedience of the first human couple, but rather the negative forces of counterevolution—evil. This evil is a mechanism of the creation of an incompletely organized universe. God has been creating since the dawn of time through a continuous transformation from within the universe and individuals. The blood of Christ is a symbol of revitalization that is essential in the ascent of the creation and the progress of the world as represented by the cross of Christ. Accordingly, Christ is no longer the Savior of the world from the damnation of sins, but rather the culmination of evolution which gives direction and meaning to the world. Christianity, then, is primarily a faith in the progressive unification of the world in God. The mission of the church is the alleviation of human suffering rather than spiritual redemption of the world, the former being in direct harmony with the inevitable progress fostered by evolution.

Evangelical Positions. Evangelical Christians accept the Bible as the inspired Word of God, the only unerring guide of faith and conduct. However, there are at least four widely held theories in the contemporary dialogue among evangelicals relating the interpretation of Genesis to the findings of modern science. They are (1) the pre-Adamites theories, (2) fiat creationism,

(3) theistic evolutionism, and (4) progressive creationism.

Pre-Adamites Theories. These take two forms. The gap theory states that after the creation of the heavens and the earth and before the situation described in Gen. 1:2, a long period of time elapsed in which a great cataclysm desolated the earth. Jer. 4:23–26; Isa. 24:1; and 45:18 are cited as evidence of this cataclysmic judgment of God. This theory attributes early human fossils to pre-Adamites in the first creation in Gen. 1:1, who were destroyed before the rest of the creation events in Gen. 1. The two Adams theory states that the first Adam of Gen. 1 was the old stone age Adam, which has since been extinct, and the second Adam of Gen. 2 was the new stone age Adam, who is the ancester of mankind today. This theory suggests the rest of the Bible is concerned with the fall and salvation of the new stone age Adam and his descendants.

Fiat Creationism. This includes all of the literal views which insist on a twenty-four-hour creation day in Gen. 1. It demands a young earth approximately ten thousand years of age and a universal deluge that accounts for most if not all of the sedimentary deposits and fossils of today. It rejects all the scientific data pertaining to the concept of an ancient earth. It adopts essentially the chronology worked out by Archbishop James Ussher (1581–1656) and John Lightfoot based on the assumption that biblical genealogies were intended to be used for the construction of chronology. Fiat creationists also reject any form of evolutionary development of life by attributing the differences in related organisms today to variations of the original stocks created by God. They believe that evolution is the culmination of the atheistic offensive to undermine the trustworthiness of the Scriptures by destroying the creation account. Thus any evolutionary compromise in the interpretation of Gen. 1 is detrimental to the Christian faith.

Theistic Evolutionism. This view allegorizes the Genesis account to be a poetic representation of the spiritual truths of man's dependence on God his Creator and the symbolic acts of man's disobedience in the fall from God's grace. Theistic evolutionists accept the trustworthiness of the Scriptures. They also accept the processes of organic evolution as the ways God used to create humans. They believe that the Bible only tells us that God created the world but does not tell us how. Science provided a mechanistic explanation of life in terms of evolution. The two levels of explanation should complement instead of antagonize each other. Despite the necessity to dispense with the historicity of the human fall, theistic evolutionists feel the fundamental Christian doctrines of original sin and the human need for redemption are unshaken by the incorporation of organic evolution into the Christian interpretation of life and origins.

Progressive Creationism. This view stresses the complementarity between science and Scripture in the explanation of God's truth. Progressive creationists are willing to reinterpret the Scriptures if this is necessitated by the findings of modern science. Therefore in light of the overwhelming evidence supporting the antiquity of the earth, they accept the traditional day-age theory of the creation account in Genesis. This view revolves around the usage of "day" as depiction of a period of time rather than a twenty-four-hour solar day. They find this interpretation exegetically sound and demanded by the antiquity of the earth.

Progressive creationists are also cautious in their evaluation of the scientific theory of evolution. They accept only the microevolutionary theory, which states that mutations selected by natural forces give rise to the diversification of varieties in a biological species, as scientifically demonstrable. They are skeptical about macroevolution (from ape to man) and organic evolution (from molecule to man) because these theories are increasingly being divorced from the well-documented mechanism of natural selection. Therefore, to the progressive creationists the present-day varieties of organisms are the result of the diversification process through microevolution from the prototypes originally created by God. There are also at least three versions of the day-age theory: (1) day–geological age, which assigns different geological eras to the creation days in Gen. 1; (2) modified intermittent day, in which each creative era is preceded by a twenty-four-hour solar day; (3) overlapping day-age, with each creative era delimited by the phrase, "There was evening and there was morning," and overlapping with each other.

A Critique. *Liberal Evolutionism.* Humanistic influence in theology, with its overextended attitude of analytical criticism that attempts to remove all unreasonable and supernatural factors from the Bible, has downgraded the Bible to be merely a great book of religion instead of the Word of God. The only message of the Bible with all its outgrown traditions is the human experience, exemplified by the Hebrew's aspiration for personal deliverance and culminating in the person of Jesus Christ. However, the desire to reduce the essence of the Bible to a vague and undefined quest for inward salvation as self-fulfillment has been a failure. Too often it has become a rather diffuse sentimentalism that operates without any regard for the truth or historicity of the biblical account.

Liberal evolutionism has placed man in an ethically relative box with no moral standard by which he can evaluate the conflicting moral values he observes in himself and others.

Pre-Adamites Theories. According to J. Oliver Buswell, Jr., the gap theory is untenable because of two serious weaknesses: (1) it has no exegetical evidence in the Bible; (2) it was invented by Christian geologists to attempt to harmonize the apparent conflicts of the creation of light and vegetation before the appearance of the sun and the antiquity of human fossils. The reference to Jer. 4:23–26; Isa. 24:1; and 45:18 as supporting a cataclysmic divine judgment on God's creation before the events of Gen. 1:2 is farfetched. The contexts of these passages clearly indicate that they are references to future events. The word "was" in Gen. 1:2, which was taken to mean "became" in the gap theory, is more exegetically justified to be translated as "was" since the context does not indicate otherwise. The word "replenish" in Gen. 1:28 should mean simply "to fill" instead of "fill over again," as stipulated in the gap theory to depict a once occupied earth that was devastated. The two Adams theory is not exegetically sound, and it seems to impinge on the fundamental concept of the unity of the human race held by all anthropologists and orthodox theologians.

Fiat Creationism. The major hurdle facing the fiat creationists is the antiquity of the earth. Since the dominant atheistic view of evolution requires a vast amount of time, fiat creationists maintain that the acceptance of the ancient-earth concept is a compromise with atheistic evolution detrimental to the Christian faith. Therefore, they reject the principle of uniformitarianism ("the present is the key to the past") and all of the dating methods that point to the antiquity of the earth in favor of a universal cataclysm. However, due to the lack of visible evidence of the universal deluge and the intriguing patterns of the distribution of animals in different continents, the theory of a universal flood is still far-fetched. They have also ignored the vast amount of data supporting the observable micro-evolutionary processes in nature and the laboratory. The refusal to be open-minded to scientific inquiry because of the espousal of a particular interpretation of the Bible has impressed others as the continuation of the medieval obscurant mentality of the church in the Copernican revolution.

Theistic Evolutionism. If man is a product of the chance events of natural selection, theistic evolutionists have the problem of convincing the secular world of the biblical basis of humans as created in the image of God and of the first sin. The figurative interpretation of the Genesis account of creation seems to weaken these two fundamental doctrines of the Christian faith. By denying the historicity of the first Adam, this position also invites skepticism about the meaning of the cross of Christ, the second Adam (Rom. 5:12–21), as a historical event and thus endangers the whole structure of the Christian message.

The materials in Gen. 1:1–2:4 are formal and are arranged in balanced structure with recurring formal phrases. This has led some theistic evolutionists to treat the formal structures as "poetic." However, this interpretation is untenable for two reasons. First, the creation account in Gen. 1:1–2:4 bears no resemblance to any known form of poetic arrangement. Second, the account has nothing of the emotional tone of poetry. The abundance of Hebrew poetry in biblical and extrabiblical Semitic literature provides no comparison with the Genesis account and thus does not lend itself to the support of the poetical interpretation of this passage. The commandment to honor the sabbath day is rooted in the sequential events of the creation week (Exod. 20:8–11). A figurative interpretation would provide no factual basis for this commandment, and thus it would be untenable.

The eleven tablets each ending with "These are the names (generations, descendants) of ..." found in the first thirty-six chapters of Genesis seem to depict a historical account of primeval and patriarchal life (Gen. 1:1–2:4; 2:5–5:1; 5:2–6:9*a;* 6:9*b*–10:1; 10:2–11:10*a;* 11:10*b*–27*a;* 11:27*b*–25:12; 25:13–19*a;* 25:19*b*–36:1; 36:2–9; 36:10–37:2). The NT also regards certain events of Gen. 1 as actually having taken place (e.g., see Mark 10:6; I Cor. 11:8–9).

The creation of Eve (Gen. 2:21–22) also constitutes an enigma for the theistic evolutionists who accept the naturalistic explanation of humanity as being genetically derived from a nonhuman ancestor. Furthermore, in Gen. 2:7 it is stated that "the Lord God formed man from the dust of the ground and breathed into his nostrils the breath of life, and man became a living being" (NIV). Although the process of formation is not specified, it seems to convey the thought of special creation from inorganic material rather than derived creation through some previously living form.

The Hebrew words for "living being" in Gen. 2:7 are the same as the words translated "living creatures" or "living and moving thing" in Gen. 1:20–21, 24. The word *nepeš* ("soul") is used in both instances. The difference between humans and beasts is that humans were created in God's image whereas the beasts were not. Therefore, Gen. 2:7 seems to imply that humans became living beings just as other beasts. The interpretation that humans are derived from a preexisting living being is entirely inappropriate in light of this consideration.

Theistic evolutionists also give too much credence to the as yet poorly formulated theory of organic evolution. In their efforts to reconcile the naturalistic and theistic approaches to the origin of life they have inadvertently put themselves into the inconsistent position of denying the miracles of creation while maintaining the supernatural nature of the Christian message. This is caused in part by Bube's dictum that reality can be analyzed at many levels, each one more or less complete in itself. This runs into the difficulty (from a Christian holistic perspective) of compartmentalizing reality into separate spiritual and physical realms. A dualism of this sort seems almost to be implicit in the theistic evolutionist position of the human being, with a body that is a product of naturalistic evolution and a spiritual capacity that is given by God in a supernatural act.

Progressive Creationism. Progressive creationists maintain that aside from the scientific data supporting the antiquity of the earth, there is adequate exegetical data to demonstrate that the days of Gen. 1 can be considered long indefinite periods of time, and that the genealogies of the Bible were not intended and cannot be used for the construction of an accurate chronology.

That the creative day is taken to denote a period longer than a twenty-four-hour solar day is supported by the following arguments: (1) The sun's visible function of defining days and years did not begin until the fourth creative day when the sun was revealed. Therefore the first four days were definitely not twenty-four-hour solar days. (2) The citation of the fourth commandment to argue against the day-age interpretation is not necessarily valid, since it is based on analogy but not identity. The establishment of a sabbath year (Exod. 23:10–11; Lev. 25:3–7) seems to corroborate the interpretation that the substance of keeping the sabbath is rest instead of the strict interpretation of "day." People must rest for one day after six days of work and lands must rest for one year after six years of cultivation since God also worked in six creative periods and rested in the seventh. (3) The citation of "and there was evening and there was morning" found at the end of every creative narrative to support the twenty-four-hour solar day interpretation is not conclusive. Since "day" can be taken to also mean a period of time of undesignated length (Gen. 2:4; Ps. 90:1–4) and periods of light as contrasted with darkness (Gen. 1:5), the components of "day" can similarly be interpreted figuratively (Ps. 90:5–6). Moreover, the evening and the morning make a night, not a day, if one wants to press the literal interpretation of these two items. (4) Events that transpired in the sixth day of creation as recorded in Gen. 2 seem to take up a considerable amount of time. The most important time consideration seems to be the Hebrew word *happa'am,* translated in Gen. 2:23 as "at last" (RSV) or "now" (NIV, NASB), in Adam's exclamation. The word seems to imply that Adam had waited a long time for a mate, and finally his desire was satisfied. This interpretation is supported by the usage of the word in the OT in contexts of elapsed time (Gen. 29:34–35; 30:20; 46:30; Exod. 9:27; Judg. 15:3; 16:18).

As to the biblical genealogies, noted OT scholar W. H. Green, a contributor to the famous *Fundamentals* papers, analyzed these and concluded that they were not intended and cannot be legitimately used to construct a chronology. His conclusion has been corroborated by other biblical scholars. His major observations were that abridgment and omission of unimportant names form the pattern in the genealogies of the Bible; the genealogies include significant names; and "father," "son," and "begot" were used in a broad sense.

The traditional day-age interpretation of creation assigns days to various geological periods. However, it is difficult to align the creative days to the actual fossil records. In addition, the creation of land plants that bear seeds and trees that bear fruits with seeds before the creation of land animals poses a problem, since many land plants with fruits and seeds depend on insects for pollination and fertilization. Both the modified intermittent day and overlapping day-age models overcome this problem by assuming the overlapping or contemporaneousness of the creation of the fruit-bearing land plants with some of the land animals. The current popular star formation model of the origin of the earth and the solar system can be nicely harmonized with the Genesis account. This theory (the "big bang" theory of the galaxies) depicts the universe as expanding from a superdense state that exploded thirteen billion years ago and subsequently cooled down to form the interstellar products, including the earth and the planets. The events in the first three creative eras seem to be consistent with the scientific model of a dark nebula containing water vapor which eventually cleared up as oxygen was given off by plants that underwent photosynthesis.

All three of these models allow for processes

of change to take place after the creation of each prototype of living creatures. In the interpretation of God's rest in the seventh day, the overlapping day-age model assumes creation was ended at the conclusion of the sixth day (Gen. 1:31) and God is resting on the seventh. This agrees with the traditional view. However, the modified intermittent day model suggests that we are still living in the creative period initiated by the sixth creative solar day, which intervenes between the sixth and seventh days. God is still creating through the changes and developments of the inorganic as well as the organic world. The seventh day, on which God absolutely rests (Heb. 4:1–11), will commence only at the inception of the new heavens and new earth (Rev. 21:1–8). This latter position seems to strain the interpretation of Gen. 2:1, which states, "Thus the heavens and the earth were completed in all their vast array" (NIV).

The hurdles faced by the progressive creationists are less insurmountable than those confronting the other models because there is a conscientious attitude in relating science to Scripture. Two of the more perplexing problems are: (1) How does the antiquity of humans fit in with the seemingly advanced civilization of Gen. 4? Despite the lack of artifacts associated with the early human fossils, physical anthropology suggests that humans have been on earth for perhaps millions of years. The large gap that exists between the first human and the advent of human civilization, which is dated to 9000 B.C., is a major problem. Attempts to ameliorate the difficulties include the alleged meager description of Cain's and Abel's civilization and the postulate, based on Gen. 4:12, of lost civilization because of the prevalence of sin. It is possible that human culture was rediscovered at the advent of the Neolithic Age some eleven thousand years ago. (2) What is the extent of the Noachian deluge? Since there is a lack of visible evidence for a universal flood, most progressive creationists subscribe to some form of local flood theories which suggest that the flood was confined to the Mesopotamian areas. The major argument of the local flood theory is that there is a sort of metonymy commonly employed by the ancient Near Eastern culture to speak of a considerable part as a whole (see Gen. 41:57; Deut. 2:25; I Kings 18:10; Ps. 22:17; Matt. 3:5; John 4:39; Acts 2:5). Therefore, the universality of the flood may simply mean the universality of experience of those who reported it. It is difficult to conceive how Moses would perceive the universal flood if he did not know the entire scope of the earth at his time.

Conclusion. In summary, liberal evolutionism casts doubts on the validity of human moral judgment. Among the evangelical views, fiat creationism seems to adhere to certain theological traditions that suppress the objectivity of science. Theistic evolutionists apparently concede important theological grounds to the atheists and the liberals by allegorizing the Genesis account of creation and the fall. The position of the progressive creationists seems to be able to maintain scriptural as well as scientific integrity.

P. P. T. PUN

See also CREATION, DOCTRINE OF; MAN, ORIGIN OF; EARTH, AGE OF.

Bibliography. R. J. Berry, *Adam and Ape: A Christian Approach to the Theory of Evolution;* R. Bube, *The Human Quest;* J. O. Buswell, Jr., *Systematic Theology of the Christian Religion;* H. M. Morris, *Biblical Cosmology and Modern Science;* R. C. Newman and H. J. Eckelmann, Jr., *Genesis One and the Origin of the Universe;* E. K. V. Pearce, *Who Was Adam?* P. P. T. Pun, *Evolution: Nature and Scripture in Conflict?* B. Ramm, *The Christian View of Science and Scripture;* J. C. Whitcomb and H. M. Morris, *The Genesis Flood;* E. J. Young, *Studies in Genesis One.*

Exaltation of Jesus Christ. *See* STATES OF JESUS CHRIST.

Ex Cathedra. The phrase means "from the throne" and is used to describe certain statements or pronouncements made by the pope in his capacities as head of the church on earth and vicar of Christ on earth. Such utterances are accepted by Roman Catholics as infallible. However, there are no infallible criteria by which it is possible to determine when a statement is actually *ex cathedra.* Not all papal statements are regarded as of this particular kind. P. TOON

See also INFALLIBILITY.

Excommunication. The most extreme disciplinary measure of the church, excommunication is the exclusion of a contumacious sinner from the communion of the faithful. In most periods of the church's history excommunication has been understood primarily as a medicinal measure, to recall to repentance and obedience. A secondary purpose is to safeguard the community's purity. When excommunication is rightly understood, punishment has never been the object.

Excommunication is said to have originated with the teaching of Jesus on binding and loosing (Matt. 16:19; 18:18; John 20:23). The sinner is bound in his sinful alienation from God's people and loosed following repentance. Excommunication came to be seen, then, as a responsibility of the true church derived from its Lord. The procedure for disciplining sinners and the three steps to be taken prior to excommunication were also delivered to the church by Jesus. The straying one is first to be corrected privately (Matt. 18:15), the object being his reclamation, not the purity of the community of believers. If he will not listen, he is to be corrected before witnesses (Matt. 18:16) whose task is to protect the offender (cf. Deut. 19:15), since the admonisher may be in error, or they might find the right reproof when he does not. Thirdly, the unrepentant offender is to be brought before the society of believers (Matt. 18:17), who are to sever all ties with him if he remains obdurate.

Two related disciplinary practices are revealed in the writings of Paul. First, private sins are to be corrected privately; open sins are to be corrected publicly (I Tim. 5:20; for an example see Gal. 2:14). Second, Paul excommunicated a particularly scandalous sinner as soon as he was informed of the offense, a sentence he requested the dilatory community of believers to confirm at a special meeting (I Cor. 5:3–5). Paul's severity, however, is in the interests of the sinner's cure, not his destruction (cf. II Thess. 3:14–15).

The practice of the church up to the sixth century emphasized the close connection between excommunication and repentance. A grave offender who wished to make his peace with God presented himself to the bishop, who, by a liturgical excommunication, assigned him to the category of "penitent" and prescribed for him a period of public penitential works. When these were completed, the bishop lifted the excommunication, and with other clergy received the penitent back into communion by the laying on of hands, an action which Cyprian called the "peace." The society of believers was also required to consent.

From the seventh century a form of excommunication developed apart from the sacrament of penance. The strict requirement that all excommunicated persons should be avoided was relaxed so that, by the fifteenth century, a clear distinction was made between excommunicates (the *vitandi*) who were to be shunned because of their flagrant offenses, and those less serious offenders (the *tolerati*) who were to be excluded only from the sacraments.

The Reformation recalled the church to a more biblical position on ecclesiastical discipline, which was of major concern to the second generation of Reformers, especially Martin Bucer and John Calvin. Calvin maintained that discipline according to the word of the Lord is the "best help" to sound doctrine, order, and unity, and that banishing blatant sinners and the contumacious is to exercise a spiritual jurisdiction invested by the Lord in the assembly of believers. To Calvin excommunication has a threefold purpose: first, "that God may not be insulted by the name of Christians being given to those who lead shameful and flagitious lives"; second, "that the good may not . . . be corrupted by constant communication with the wicked"; and third, "that the sinner may be ashamed, and begin to repent of his turpitude." Mindful of the examples of Paul and the early church fathers, Calvin insisted that the whole assembly of believers should witness any excommunication.

The Council of Trent also addressed the problem of abuses in the practice of excommunication within the Roman Catholic Church. Bishops were asked not to allow themselves to be made tools of the state, excommunicating according to the wish of temporal rulers. They were also enjoined to be moderate in the use of excommunication, for the widespread use of the penalty for slight offenses provoked contempt. The primary medicinal function of excommunication was reconfirmed.

Modern Catholic teaching on excommunication, incorporated in canon law (*Codex Iuris Canonici*, 1917, canons 2257–67), denies to the excommunicate the sacraments, Christian burial, ecclesiastical office, and revenue from ecclesiastical sources. He is not thereby deprived of divine grace, for that is forfeited only by mortal sin. Neither does he cease to be a Christian, since excommunication cannot remove the indelible character imprinted on the soul by baptism. He loses the rights of membership in the church but is not released from the obligations, acquired at baptism, of his affiliation with it. A nonjuridical form of excommunication imposed on non-Catholics is a barrier to the acceptance by the Roman Catholic Church of intercommunion (full sharing in the Lord's Supper by separated Christians).

Formal excommunication is now rarely exercised in Protestant churches, although it is still countenanced by the revised canons (1969) of the Church of England. F. S. PIGGIN

See also CHURCH DISCIPLINE.

Bibliography. J. Calvin, *Institutes of the Christian Religion* 4.12.1–13; F. E. Hyland, *Excommunication: Its Nature, Historical Development and Effects;* R. P. McBrien, *Catholicism; NCE,* V, 704–7; E. Schweizer, *The Good News According to Matthew.*

Exemplarism. *See* ATONEMENT, THEORIES OF THE.

Exhortation. One of the fundamental elements of the Word of God throughout the history of the people of God. From the election of Abraham to the founding of the church, instruction in righteousness, the call to obedience, and exhortation have been part of God's address to his people. Torah (usually translated "law," but better understood as "instruction" and exhortation) is basically a call to the people to structure their community and order their worship in a way that will reflect their own distinctiveness and his lordship.

Immediately after release from bondage in Egypt the Israelites were faced with questions of how to preserve their identity, how to organize community life and worship so as not to be contaminated by heathen worship, and how to secure their existence in a hostile environment. Early hortatory material seeks to meet those needs. Under the new covenant the church faced the same issues, and the paraenetic material of the NT is a response to those needs.

Exhortation underscores the social and community character of life in Christ. Faith is a social experience, breaking down barriers of alienation (Eph. 2:14–15; Gal. 3:28) and creating a unity through the common gift of the Spirit (Eph. 4:3). But while unity is a reality, it is also a "not yet" (Eph. 4:13). The NT church was a new phenomenon and struggled to work out its community life. The struggle was particularly intense in the Gentile world, where the members of the believing community had limited contact with the ethical monotheism of Judaism.

The NT writers, following the OT prophets, set forth the close relationship between the gift of salvation and the call to obedience. Logically the latter flows from the former, so that we have in several of the letters a natural division (e.g., Rom. 1–11, 12–15; Eph. 1–3, 4–6). The Reformation reinforced this logical formula by way of *sola fidei* and *sola gratia.* But experientially the two cannot be separated, as though we are saved by faith and then follow that faith up with obedience. While faith and obedience are not identical, such texts as Matt. 7:21; 25:31ff.; James 1:21–22; I John 3:17 show that there is overlapping. The people of God are called to both faith and faithfulness.

The content of the NT exhortation reflects the newness of the kingdom of God. This is a kingdom of inverse values whose citizens are called to embrace paradox. They are to seek no public recognition (Matt. 6); they are to exalt concrete servanthood (John 13); they are to set themselves over against "the world" (Rom. 12:1–2). The center of exhortation in the church is the command to love, which gives fullness to the whole law. Without love every gift and virtue is meaningless (I Cor. 13:1–3). Biblical perfection consists in indiscriminate love (Matt. 5:43–48). The care of the poor is the quintessence of love (James 1:27; I John 3:17–18; Luke 4:18) and Christian duty.

Alongside this social paraenetic are those that seek to preserve the identity and character of the church from the world with its principalities and powers which always seek to subvert and undermine (cf. Rom. 12:1–2; John 17:14–16; Eph. 6:12–20).

R. W. Lyon

Exhortation, Gift of. *See* Spiritual Gifts.

Existence. In its most general meaning the word refers to the fact or state of existing. If taken to mean total reality, existence must include the supernatural and the reality of freedom, by virtue of which guilt, sin, and redemption can be accepted. It is interesting to compare the Greek and Judeo-Christian understanding of existence. The main interest of the Greeks (of the Platonic tradition) was in ultimate and permanent nature. History, as that which comes into being and passes away, was ultimately not worth knowing. Plato himself thought of his ideal state as isolated from its neighbors and even from its own past. It was so detached from time that once it was founded it would always remain the same. In contrast, the enlightenment of Israel came from God's revelation and inspiration to them about their own history. They learned that they were a people with one God, a God very close to his people, who demanded from them faith and obedience. Israel's revelation is made complete by Christianity, based on belief in the God of Israel who became man in Jesus of Nazareth, through whom salvation is offered to all men. Man is continuously affected by this offer of grace, which means that man, as he in reality exists, is in the theological sense always more than mere nature.

The term "existentialism" covers various forms of philosophical thinking which all have one thing in common: existence is not the actualization of an essence, as the scholastics understood *existentia,* but the active realization of man's existence, which in every case is an individual act.

M. H. Macdonald

See also Existentialism; Essence.

Bibliography. M. Heidegger, *Being and Time;* K. Jaspers, *Philosophie,* II: *Clarification of Existence;* N. Wolterstorff, *On Universals: An Essay in Ontology.*

Existence of God, Arguments for. *See* God, Arguments for the Existence of.

Existentialism. The term embraces a variety of philosophies and attitudes to life which flourished in Germany from the time of the First World War and in France during and immediately after the Second World War. In the postwar period its influence was felt in Britain, North America, and in Western culture generally. Although existentialism is associated with major philosophers such as Karl Jaspers and Martin Heidegger, many of its leading advocates have been writers, including Albert Camus and Jean-Paul Sartre, whose interests embraced literature as well as philosophy. To them the novel or the play was a better vehicle for describing and analyzing existence than was the scholarly paper. For existentialism has been concerned above all with the problems of human life in the modern, secular world.

Existentialism has been described as the attempt to philosophize from the standpoint of the actor rather than (as in many past schemes of philosophy) from that of the detached spectator. But the resultant philosophy varies enormously, depending on whether the philosopher concerned believes in God or whether he or she is an atheist.

Nineteenth Century Origins. The origins of existentialism are frequently traced back to the nineteenth century Danish philosopher Søren Kierkegaard, the German philosopher and poet Friedrich Nietzsche, and the Russian novelist Fëdor Dostoevski. Whether any of these three could be called an existentialist in the modern sense of the term is doubtful. But in their different ways each anticipated ideas that became pronounced in existentialism. All three questioned the accepted values and philosophies of their day, and all three were concerned with the need of the individual to discover truth which was valid for him in the struggles of his personal existence.

Kierkegaard's earlier writings contained a series of attacks on the confusions and irrelevance of Hegel's idealism as a guide to life and to the truth about God. His later writings attacked the confusions and irrelevance of institutionalized Christianity. Whereas later existentialist thinkers taught that, since God does not exist, man must make up his own values, Kierkegaard taught exactly the opposite. Underlying all his writings is the conviction that God exists, that he has become incarnate in Jesus Christ, and that this is the most important of all facts for human existence. But whereas previous thinkers had given formal acknowledgment to the transcendence of God, Kierkegaard explored its radical significance. Since God is wholly other, he can never be identified with anything finite. Even in revelation God's divinity remains hidden from our sight and the capacity of our reason to grasp it. When people saw Jesus Christ on earth, they saw a man. His divinity remained hidden. The infinite cannot be changed into the finite, and the eternal cannot be reduced to the temporal. In the incarnation God was incognito. That his true identity can be seen only by the eyes of faith testifies to the paradox of the divine and human together.

For Kierkegaard the existence of God and the divinity of Christ could never be proved by reason, because reason is capable of dealing only with the finite. Only from the standpoint of faith can one get a true view of God and the world. But this in turn requires the commitment of one's whole being to a life of discipleship, for the truth of existence is grasped only in the total commitment of faith. Kierkegaard has been strongly criticized for his alleged irrationalism. But in some respects he stands close to evangelical presuppositionalism with its faith commitment to the God of the Bible as the ground of our knowledge.

Friedrich Nietzsche, on the other hand, was openly hostile to Christianity and religion in general. He declared that God is dead and that mankind must learn to live without him. This meant a revaluation of all values. Christian ethics and the Christian way of life must be rejected along with Christian theology. Nietzsche despised the Christian virtues. For him the ideal man, the superman, is completely self-possessed. He has no fear of others, of himself, or of death. He is characterized by a will to power. Nietzsche believed that his philosophy was compatible with a scientific view of the world, but he believed that his values transcended science, for there was no meaning in life other than that which man gives it. In a sense man is his own creator. If he is ever to rise above the flux of meaningless existence, he must choose a way of life that has meaning and dignity for him, even though it might bring suffering to himself and to others. Although Nietzsche ridiculed theology and the metaphysical systems of others, he indulged in a theological system of his own, which revived the Greek notion of the eternal recurrence of all things.

Whereas Nietzsche claimed scientific justification for his views, including his doctrine of eternal recurrence, much of Dostoevski's work was devoted to attacking the pretensions of scientific humanism and urging the necessity of faith and of God as the basis of human freedom. Man seeks freedom but is bound by the institutions of society. Dostoevski rejected the idea that man is bound by scientific laws and is thus totally determined by physical factors, whether he realizes it or not. He also rejected the idea that everything is governed by reason. Reason does not exist apart from the minds of the reasoners. Truth is not something absolute and timeless; it depends upon our wills. Freedom is both the supreme good and the supreme evil. If God did not exist, everything would be allowed. God appears to pose a threat to human freedom, but true, saving freedom is to be found in conditionless religious faith and commitment.

Twentieth Century Existentialists. The themes sounded by Kierkegaard, Nietzsche, and Dostoevski have been taken up by twentieth century existentialists, though no two existentialist thinkers share identical views. In some respects existentialism is characterized by a protest against theological and metaphysical systems into which human life is made to fit. But both Heidegger and Sartre have erected metaphysical systems of their own on the basis of their analysis of existence. In common with others, Heidegger rejected the idea of a personal Creator who exists over and above the universe and upon whom the universe depends for its existence. Instead, he drew a distinction between Being and beings who participate in Being. His analysis of being-in-the-world, nothingness, time, dread, facticity, and destiny resulted in an elaborate ontology, reminiscent of pantheism and idealism but replete with his own idiosyncratic vocabulary.

Sartre's atheistic existentialism also developed a complex ontology, full of Sartre's own private, technical jargon. The world as a whole is absurd and meaningless. Man finds himself dumped into it, unable to turn to anyone for guidance but himself. Since God does not exist, man cannot turn to the Bible or the church for help. Nor can man resort to Christian ethics, now that it has lost its foundation. Nevertheless, man has choices to make which determine his existence. In a sense man creates himself, for the choices that he makes shape what will become of him. The slogan "Essence precedes existence" reverses the traditional view, which sees man as having a relatively fixed nature. Inevitably man finds himself in a state of anxiety, for life is like a relentless conveyer belt, carrying one to the grave. Life is meaningless apart from the meaning that one chooses to give it. Man craves for freedom, but is subject to remorseless social, political, and economic pressures. The free act of one individual means the curtailment of someone else's freedom. What is left is suicide as the ultimate act of freedom.

A distinction frequently drawn by existentialists is that between authentic and inauthentic existence. But there seems to be no consensus of agreement as to how to define these ideas, and it is questionable whether such a distinction is legitimate for an atheistic existentialist, since the idea of authentic existence implies that one form of existence is not merely preferable but right. However, it is difficult to see how anyone could say that one act is intrinsically better than another in a world in which man alone determines values. Even the claim that authentic existence is characterized by the decision to choose rather than allow choices to be made for one is questionable, as the latter possibility could well be authentic for the person concerned, though not necessarily for someone else.

Existentialism and Theology. Existentialism has affected contemporary theology, notably in the teaching of Rudolf Bultmann, Paul Tillich and Karl Barth. But none of these was a pure existentialist. Bultmann made use of Heidegger's terminology, especially his distinction between authentic and inauthentic existence, to describe the distinction between the life of faith and life in the flesh in the context of his demythologizing program. But the framework of Bultmann's thought was a neo-Kantian view of God that affirmed God's transcendence but questioned man's capacity to know God directly. Tillich also made use of existential categories, but did so in the context of an ontology that revived the philosophy of being, advocated by the early nineteenth century German idealists. Barth's view of revelation was indebted to Kierkegaard, but his teaching, like Kierkegaard's, was a restatement of a theistic view of God and the world which was not characteristic of later existentialism.

C. Brown

See also Kierkegaard, Søren; Heidegger, Martin; Neo-orthodoxy.

Bibliography. W. Barrett, *Irrational Man;* H. J. Blackham, *Six Existentialist Thinkers;* R. Bultmann, *Essays: Philosophical and Theological;* F. Copleston, *Contemporary Philosophy: Studies of Logical Positivism and Existentialism* and *A History of Philosophy,* IX; M. Green, *Introduction to Existentialism;* M. Heidegger, *Being and Time* and *An Introduction to Metaphysics;* W. Kaufmann, ed., *Existentialism from Dostoevsky to Sartre;* C. W. Kegley, ed., *The Theology of Rudolf Bultmann;* J. Macquarrie, *An Existentialist Theology* and *The Frontiers of Philosophy and Theology, 1900–1960;* J.-P. Sartre, *Existentialism and Humanism* and *Being and Nothingness;* A. Thatcher, *The Ontology of Paul Tillich.*

Ex Nihilo, Creatio. *See* Creation, Doctrine of.

Ex Opere Operato. The historic Roman Catholic view of the way sacraments are effective is that they operate *ex opere operato* ("from the work done"). This position became official at the

Council of Trent (1545–63). Canon VIII of the seventh session opposed the view that "grace is not conferred through the act performed, but that faith alone in the divine promise suffices for the obtaining of grace." The condition for the recipient is only that one does not place an obstacle (*obex,* sinful act or disposition) against the sacrament's administration. Grace is given by God when the sacrament is conferred rightly by the church. This *ex opere operato* working makes the sacraments unique conductors of divine grace.

The Reformers rejected this view. Calvin said it contradicted the nature of the sacraments. Protestants have stressed the need for faith to be present in the recipient for a sacrament to have validity. Sacraments are the instruments used by God to confirm the word of his promise to those who believe.

D. K. McKim

See also Sacrament; Grace; Opus Operatum.

Bibliography. G. C. Berkouwer, *The Sacraments; ODCC;* R. Seeberg, *Text-book of the History of Doctrines;* P. Schaff, *Creeds of Christendom,* II; P. Tillich, *A Complete History of Christian Thought.*

Exorcism. *See* Demon, Demon Possession.

Exorcist. *See* Minor Orders.

Expediency. The character of an act in which any predetermined goal is sought by whatever means will enable one to achieve the goal most directly and advantageously without regard to the moral implications of these means.

The relationship between expediency and moral values may be set forth in different ways. According to utilitarians the two areas coalesce; what is really expedient constitutes the right.

According to the Stoics and Kant the two areas overlap. The good must always be followed for the sake of duty alone; but where no moral standard for conduct is applicable, expediency becomes the only sensible path to follow.

A third type of relationship between expediency and moral principles sets them apart as mutually exclusive guides to conduct and as usually in conflict. The expedient, therefore, must never be followed because it is expedient, but every act must be morally determined.

Christians generally have followed the second view and argued for an area of adiaphora where expediency has a place, but some have tended to hold to the third view. All Christians have insisted that, however inexpedient the right course of action may sometimes appear to be, in the overruling providence of God the believer may know that the morally good always works out ultimately to his best advantage (Rom. 8:28).

K. S. Kantzer

See also Adiaphora, Adiaphorists; Ethical Systems, Christian; Casuistry; Situation Ethics.

Experience, Theology of. Experience can be understood as a source of knowledge deriving from a direct perception or apprehension of reality. Experiential knowledge can be gained either externally or internally, the given presenting itself immediately either to the natural sense or to the inner world of the spirit. Experiencing something is to be distinguished from reflecting about it or hearing a report on it. The experience has greater force ("you should have been there") and provides a sense of certitude ("but I saw it") that reflection and reportage do not. The personal nature of experience, however, is an important qualifier, for experience can never be fully transmitted or re-presented. Moreover, apart from authentic reflection experience, however vivid, remains arbitrary, unclear, and open to false claims. Experience and reflection must therefore be understood as complementary and interactive, although no easy formula spells out adequately their interrelation.

Encounters with the transcendent can be labeled religious experience. Defined thus, religious experience is essential to all religions, including Christianity. Within the history of Christianity, however, there have been certain movements that have distinguished themselves by stressing the primacy and authority of experience over other sources of knowledge, i.e., the church (tradition) and the word (Scripture). In the modern period pietism, revivalism, the Holiness Movement, and Pentecostalism have all given preeminence to the experience of the believer. Such movements have not viewed themselves as being in opposition to the witness of Scripture or the true teaching of the church. They have challenged a recurring conceptualist orthodoxy and/or rigid scholasticism. Without the complementary life of the Spirit the letter remains dead (II Cor. 3:6).

At the beginning of the nineteenth century liberal theology arose, understanding experience as the basis for Christian reflection. Friedrich Schleiermacher offered the classic formulation. Rather than emphasize God's action with regard to humankind, he sought to clarify Christianity in terms of humankind's experience of God. Remembering the pietism of his youth and reacting to contemporary rationalistic and ethical reductions of religion, seen in Hume and Kant, Schleiermacher wrote his *On Religion:*

Speeches to Its Cultured Despisers (1799), arguing for the centrality of feeling in religion. Religion is not action (morality), nor is it metaphysics (theoretical knowledge). Rather, as he later characterized it, religion is based in the "feeling of absolute dependence."

Schleiermacher (and those following his lead) has often been criticized for both his subjectivism and his pantheism—charges that are mistaken unless carefully qualified. A more trenchant critique has to do with his one-sided stress on religious feeling. There is throughout his discussion, despite occasional disclaimers, a false compartmentalization of human activity into feeling, doing, and thinking. The result is a downplaying and/or rejection of orthodox Christian thought, for ideas about God remain secondary for him and are ultimately unimportant.

A theology based in experience need not deny orthodox Christian reflection, however. Such a theology is chiefly distinguishable not by its sometimes liberal orientation, but by its Trinitarian emphasis on the Holy Spirit (on one's experience of God in creation and redemption). Within present-day evangelicalism both those stressing a charismatic understanding of the Christian faith (e.g., Dennis Bennett, Michael Harper) and those focusing on a relational approach (e.g., Keith Miller, Bruce Larson) can be said to be experiential theologians. Neither movement desires to ignore or reject the authority of the Word. Rather, both want to stress the fundamental and initiatory role of the Spirit, whether in creation (relational theology's interest in our being fully human) or in re-creation (charismatic theology's interest in a Spirit-filled, separated life).

Experiential theology has important strengths. It has arisen historically within Christianity in reaction to a sterile intellectualism and/or a rote traditionalism. Moreover, its emphasis on the role of the Spirit continues to help the church attain a balanced Trinitarian perspective. But there are also dangers: (1) Christian experience must never be viewed individualistically but nurtured and evaluated within the Christian community past and present. (2) Experience and reflection must not become isolated from each other. Word and Spirit must remain complementary expressions of the Trinity. (3) The Spirit who is experienced cannot be reduced to only the Spirit in creation, or Christianity risks degeneration into psychology (cf. Feuerbach's critique). Neither can Christian theology be concerned only with the Spirit of redemption, for then Christianity risks isolationism and mysticism.

A biblically based theology of experience will stress the Spirit's ongoing role in creation and redemption (cf. Acts 14:15–18; Rom. 8; Gal. 4:6–7). It will also recognize that a focus upon the Spirit will open naturally and authentically into an emphasis on Christ the Word (I John 4:2; I Cor. 12:3). Finally, an experiential theology will always be a corporate church theology (I Cor. 12; Rom. 12).

R. K. Johnston

See also Schleiermacher, Friedrich Daniel Ernst; Pietism; Revivalism; Pentecostalism; Holiness Movement, American.

Bibliography. K. Lehmann, "Experience," *Sacramentum Mundi*, 307–9; R. Otto, *The Idea of the Holy;* W. James, *The Varieties of Religious Experience;* J. Edwards, *Religious Affections;* R. Johnston, "Of Tidy Doctrine and Truncated Experience," *CT*, Feb. 18, 1977; B. Larson, *The Relational Revolution.*

Expiation. *See See* Propitiation.

External Calling. *See* Call, Calling.

Extreme Unction. An anointing with oil of the sick used as a sacrament in the Roman Catholic Church. "Extreme" may refer to the fact that the unction is the last of the three sacramental unctions, the former at baptism and confirmation, or to the fact that it is administered when the patient is *in extremis*. The Council of Trent states that it was instituted by Christ. No reference is given, but it is said to be implied in Mark. Its sacramental status and effects are based on an interpretation of James 5:14–15. Oil, consecrated by the bishop, is the matter; unction with prayer by the priests the sign; the grace given on condition of repentance and faith is forgiveness of sins, renewed health, and strength of soul and also of body if God sees fit. Our Lord used varied means in healing the sick, but there is no actual record of his use of oil unless we infer it from apostolic practice in Mark 6:13. Was the use of oil medicinal or symbolical? The Roman Church makes the oil symbolical of the Holy Spirit. Prayer for the blessing of oil for the sick is found in the *Apostolic Tradition* of Hippolytus (*ca.* A.D. 225) and in the *Euchologion* of Serapion (*ca.* A.D. 365). From the fifth century references to anointing are more frequent. The rite was included among the seven sacraments in the thirteenth century, and its doctrine defined at Trent.

R. J. Coates

See also Sacrament; Anoint, Anointing.

Bibliography. F. W. Puller, *The Anointing of the Sick in Scripture and Tradition.*

Ff

Fairbairn, Andrew Martin (1838–1912). British theologian. Born into a strict Presbyterian family in Fife, he had little early schooling, but after taking classes at Edinburgh University and the Evangelical Union Academy, he was ordained and served Congregational churches in Bathgate and Aberdeen (1860–77). During visits to Germany he sat under Dorner, Tholuck, and Hengstenberg, and thereafter his theology was broader than that of his Scottish contemporaries. He was subsequently principal of Airedale Theological College, Bradford (1877–86), and the first principal when Mansfield College, Oxford, was founded in 1886. The summer school he began there (modeled on the American pattern he had seen at Chautauqua and Yale) was criticized as a mere vehicle for the support of higher criticism, but Fairbairn was unrepentant, holding that through it "we know the New Testament as it was never known before." Always he insisted that criticism involved construction. Neither Nicaea nor Chalcedon interpreted God adequately in terms of the consciousness of Christ, he said, and now was the time to put this right, since the available material was fuller and richer than ever before.

Much of his viewpoint is reflected in his best-known book, *The Place of Christ in Modern Theology* (1893), which quickly went through twelve editions. The *Spectator* hailed it as valuable and comprehensive, but a German review more perceptively noted the volume's neglect of eschatological considerations in estimating the consciousness of Christ. Fairbairn clashed with J. H. Newman, declaring that the latter's *Grammar of Assent* was "pervaded by the intensest philosophical scepticism." Fairbairn's mediating type of theology is less durable because of his preoccupation with controversies of his time. Fairbairn also took a leading part in organizing theological teaching in the Welsh universities, and was one of the earliest fellows of the British Academy.

J. D. Douglas

Bibliography. W. B. Selbie, *Life of Andrew Martin Fairbairn.*

Faith. Noun corresponding to the verb "believe," for which the Hebrew is *he'ĕmîn,* the hiphil form of *'āman,* and the Greek (LXX and NT) *pisteuō.* The latter is a key word in the NT, being the term regularly used to denote the many-sided religious relationship into which the gospel calls men and women—that of trust in God through Christ. The complexity of this idea is reflected in the variety of constructions used with the verb (a *hoti* clause, or accusative and infinitive, expressing truth believed; *en* and *epi* with the dative, denoting restful reliance on that to which, or him to whom, credit is given; *eis* and, occasionally, *epi* with the accusative—the most common, characteristic, and original NT usage, scarcely present in the LXX and not at all in classical Greek—conveying the thought of a movement of trust going out to, and laying hold of, the object of its confidence). The Hebrew noun corresponding to *'āman* (*'ĕmûnâ,* rendered *pistis* in the LXX), regularly denotes faithfulness in the sense of trustworthiness, and *pistis* occasionally bears this sense in the NT (Rom. 3:3, of God; Matt. 23:23; Gal. 5:22; Titus 2:10, of man). The word *'ĕmûnâ* normally refers to the faithfulness of God, and only in Hab. 2:4 is it used to signify man's religious response to God. There, however, the contrast in the context between the temper of the righteous and the proud self-sufficiency of the Chaldeans seems to demand for it a broader sense than "faithfulness" alone—the sense, namely, of self-renouncing, trustful reliance upon God, the attitude of heart of which faithfulness in life is the natural expression. This is certainly the sense in which the apostolic writers quote the text (Rom. 1:17; Gal. 3:11; Heb.

10:38), and the sense which *pistis*, like *pisteuō*, regularly carries in the NT, where both words are used virtually as technical terms (John preferring the verb, Paul the noun) to express the complex thought of unqualified acceptance of, and exclusive dependence on, the mediation of the Son as alone securing the mercy of the Father. Both normally bear this whole weight of meaning, whether their grammatical object is God, Christ, the gospel, a truth, a promise, or is not expressed at all. Both signify commitment as following from conviction, even in contexts where faith is defined in terms of the latter only (e.g., compare Heb. 11:1 with the rest of the chapter). The nature of faith, according to the NT, is to live by the truth it receives; faith, resting on God's promise, gives thanks for God's grace by working for God's glory.

Some occasional contractions of this broad idea should be noticed:

(1) James, alone of NT writers, uses both noun and verb to denote bare intellectual assent to truth (James 2:14–26). But here he is explicitly mimicking the usage of those whom he seeks to correct—Jewish converts, who may well have inherited their notion of faith from contemporary Jewish sources—and there is no reason to suppose that this usage was normal or natural to him (his reference to faith in 5:15, e.g., clearly carries a fuller meaning). In any case the point he makes—namely, that a merely intellectual "faith," such as the demons have, is inadequate—is wholly in line with the rest of the NT. For example, when James says, "Faith without works is dead" (2:26), he is saying the same as Paul, who says in essence, "Faith without works is not faith at all, but its opposite" (cf. Gal. 5:6; I Tim. 5:8).

(2) Occasionally, by a natural transition, "the faith" denotes the body of truths believed (e.g., Jude 3; Rom. 1:5[?]; Gal. 1:23; I Tim. 4:1, 6). This became standard usage in the second century.

(3) From Christ himself derives a narrower use of "faith" for an exercise of trust which works miracles (Matt. 17:20–21; I Cor. 12:9; 13:2), or prompts the workings of miracles (Matt. 9:28–29; 15:28; Acts 14:9). Saving faith is not always accompanied by "miracle-faith," however (I Cor. 12:9); nor vice versa (cf. Matt. 7:22–23).

General Conception. Three points must be noted for the circumscribing of the biblical idea of faith:

Faith in God Involves Right Belief about God. The word "faith" in ordinary speech covers both credence of propositions ("beliefs") and confidence in persons or things. In the latter case some belief about the object trusted is the logical and psychological presupposition of the act of trust itself, for trust in a thing reflects a positive expectation about its behavior, and rational expectation is impossible if the thing's capacities for behavior are wholly unknown. Throughout the Bible trust in God is made to rest on belief of what he has revealed concerning his character and purposes. In the NT, where faith in God is defined as trust in Christ, the acknowledgment of Jesus as the expected Messiah and the incarnate Son of God is regarded as basic to it. The writers allow that faith in some form can exist where as yet information about Jesus is incomplete (Acts 19:1ff.), but not where his divine identity and Christhood are consciously denied (I John 2:22–23; II John 7–9); all that is possible then is idolatry (I John 5:21), the worship of a manmade unreality. The frequency with which the epistles depict faith as knowing, believing, and obeying "the truth" (Titus 1:1; II Thess. 2:13; I Pet. 1:22, etc.) show that their authors regarded orthodoxy as faith's fundamental ingredient (cf. Gal. 1:8–9).

Faith Rests on Divine Testimony. Beliefs, as such, are convictions held on grounds, not of self-evidence, but of testimony. Whether particular beliefs should be treated as known certainties or doubtful opinions will depend on the worth of the testimony on which they are based. The Bible views faith's convictions as certainties and equates them with knowledge (I John 3:2; 5:18–20, etc.), not because they spring from supposedly self-authenticating mystical experience, but because they rest on the testimony of a God who "cannot lie" (Titus 1:2) and is therefore utterly trustworthy. The testimony of Christ to heavenly things (John 3:11, 31–32), and of the prophets and apostles to Christ (Acts 10:39–43), is the testimony of God himself (I John 5:9ff.); this God-inspired witness is God's own witness (cf. I Cor. 2:10–13; I Thess. 2:13), in such a sense that to receive it is to certify that God is true (John 3:33), and to reject it is to make God a liar (I John 5:10). Christian faith rests on the recognition of apostolic and biblical testimony as God's own testimony to his Son.

Faith Is a Supernatural Divine Gift. Sin and Satan have so blinded fallen men (Eph. 4:18; II Cor. 4:4) that they cannot discern dominical and apostolic witness to be God's word, nor "see" and comprehend the realities of which it speaks (John 3:3; I Cor. 2:14), nor "come" in self-renouncing trust to Christ (John 6:44, 65), till the Holy Spirit has enlightened them (cf. II Cor. 4:6). Only the recipients of this divine "teaching," "drawing," and "anointing" come to Christ and abide in him (John 6:44–45; I John 2:20, 27). God is thus the author of all saving faith (Eph. 2:8; Phil. 1:29).

Biblical Presentation. Throughout Scripture, God's people live by faith; but the idea of faith develops as God's revelation of grace and truth, on which faith rests, enlarges. The OT variously defines faith as resting, trusting, and hoping in the Lord, cleaving to him, waiting for him, making him our shield and tower, taking refuge in him, etc. Psalmists and prophets, speaking in individual and national terms respectively, present faith as unwavering trust in God to save his servants from their foes and fulfill his declared purpose of blessing them. Isaiah, particularly, denounces reliance on human aid as inconsistent with such trust (Isa. 30:1–18, etc.). The NT regards the self-despairing hope, world-renouncing obedience, and heroic tenacity by which OT believers manifested their faith as a pattern which Christians must reproduce (Rom. 4:11–25; Heb. 10:39–12:2). Continuity is avowed here, but also novelty; for faith, receiving God's new utterance in the words and deeds of Christ (Heb. 1:1–2), has become a knowledge of present salvation. Faith, so regarded, says Paul, first "came" with Christ (Gal. 3:23–25). The Gospels show Christ demanding trust in himself as bearing the messianic salvation. John is fullest on this, emphasizing (1) that faith ("believing on," "coming to," and "receiving" Christ) involves acknowledging Jesus, not merely as a God-sent teacher and miracle worker (this is insufficient, John 2:23–24), but as God incarnate (John 20:28), whose atoning death is the sole means of salvation (John 3:14–15; 6:51–58); (2) that faith in Christ secures present enjoyment of "eternal life" in fellowship with God (John 5:24; 17:3). The epistles echo this, and present faith in various further relationships. Paul shows that faith in Christ is the only way to a right relationship with God, which human works cannot gain (see Romans and Galatians); Hebrews and I Peter present faith as the dynamic of hope and endurance under persecution.

History of Discussion. The church grasped from the first that assent to apostolic testimony is the fundamental element in Christian faith; hence the concern of both sides in the Gnostic controversy to show that their tenets were genuinely apostolic. During the patristic period, however, the idea of faith was so narrowed that this assent came to be regarded as the whole of it. Four factors together caused this: (1) the insistence of the anti-Gnostic fathers, particularly Tertullian, that the faithful are those who believe "the faith" as stated in the "rule of faith" (*regula fidei*), i.e., the Creed; (2) the intellectualism of Clement and Origen, to whom *pistis* (assent on authority) was just an inferior substitute for, and stepping stone to, *gnōsis* (demonstrative knowledge) of spiritual things; (3) the assimilation of biblical morality to Stoic moralism, an ethic not of grateful dependence but of resolute self-reliance; (4) the clothing of the biblical doctrine of communion with God in Neoplatonic dress, which made it appear as a mystical ascent to the supersensible achieved by aspiring love, having no link with the ordinary exercise of faith at all. Also, since the doctrine of justification was not understood, the soteriological significance of faith was misconceived, and faith (understood as orthodoxy) was regarded simply as the passport to baptism (remitting all past sins) and to a lifelong probation in the church (giving the baptized opportunity to make themselves worthy of glory by their good works).

The scholastics refined this view. They reproduced the equation of faith with credence, distinguishing between *fides informis* ("unformed" faith, bare orthodoxy) and *fides caritate formata* (credence "formed" into a working principle by the supernatural additon to it of the distinct grace of love). Both sorts of faith, they held, are meritorious works, though the quality of merit attaching to the first is merely *congruent* (rendering divine reward fit, though not obligatory), and only the second gains *condign* merit (making divine reward due as a matter of justice). Roman Catholicism still formally identifies faith with credence, and has added a further refinement by distinguishing between "explicit" faith (belief which knows its object) and "implicit" faith (uncomprehending assent to whatever it may be that the church holds). Only the latter (which is evidently no more than a vote of confidence in the teaching church and may be held with complete ignorance of Christianity) is thought to be required of laymen for salvation. But a mere docile disposition of this sort is poles apart from the biblical concept of saving faith.

The Reformers restored biblical perspectives by insisting that faith is more than orthodoxy—not *fides* merely, but *fiducia*, personal trust and confidence in God's mercy through Christ; that it is not a meritorious work, one facet of human righteousness, but rather an appropriating instrument, an empty hand outstretched to receive the free gift of God's righteousness in Christ; that faith is God-given, and is itself the animating principle from which love and good works spontaneously spring; and that communion with God means, not an exotic rapture of mystical ecstasy, but just faith's everyday commerce with the Savior. Confessional Protestantism has always maintained these positions. In Arminianism there resides a tendency to depict faith as the human work upon which the pardon of sin is suspended—as, in fact, man's contribution to his own salvation. This would be in effect a Protestant revival of the doctrine of human merit.

Liberalism radically psychologized faith, reducing it to a sense of contented harmony with the Infinite through Christ (Schleiermacher), or a fixed resolve to follow Christ's teaching (Ritschl), or both together. Liberal influence is reflected in the now widespread supposition that "faith," understood as an optimistic confidence in the friendliness of the universe, divorced from any specific creedal tenets, is a distinctively religious state of mind. Neo-orthodox and existentialist theologians, reacting against this psychologism, stress the supernatural origin and character of faith. They describe it as an active commitment of mind and will, man's repeated "yes" to the repeated summons to decision issued by God's word in Christ; but the elusiveness of their account of the content of that word makes it hard sometimes to see what the believer is thought to say "yes" to.

Clearly, each theologian's view of the nature and saving significance of faith will depend on the views he holds of the Scriptures, and of God, man, and of their mutual relations. J. I. Packer

Bibliography. E. D. Burton, *Galatians;* B. B. Warfield in *HDB* and *Biblical and Theological Studies;* G. H. Box in *HDCG;* J. G. Machen, *What is Faith?* B. Citron, *New Birth;* systematic theologies of C. Hodge (III, 41–113) and L. Berkhof (IV, viii: 493–509); D. M. Baillie, *Faith in God;* G. C. Berkouwer, *Faith and Justification;* J. Hick, *Faith and Knowledge;* O. Becker and O. Michel, *NIDNTT,* II, 587ff.; A. Weiser, *TDNT,* VI, 174ff.; D. M. Emmet, *Philosophy and Faith.*

Faith, Gift of. *See* Spiritual Gifts.

Faithfulness. Faithfulness characterizes God's loyalty to his covenant people and becomes a divine requirement pressing upon man the need for a similar loyalty in his relationship with God. The Hebrew term *'āman* (in various forms) conveys this notion with the meaning "firmness," "fixity," or "stability." The LXX introduced the idea of "trustworthiness," sometimes translating *'āman* with *alētheia,* although the usual term (employed sixty-seven times in the NT) was *pistos,* from the frequent term *pistis* (faith).

Perhaps the most important OT theme in this regard is the connection between God's faithfulness and his covenant love (*ḥesed*). Deut. 7:9 says, "Know therefore that the Lord your God is God, the faithful God who keeps covenant and steadfast love with those who love him and keep his commandments" (cf. Gen. 24:27; Exod. 34:6). The stress on this found in the psalms is especially noteworthy; "All the paths of the Lord are steadfast love and faithfulness" (Ps. 25:10; cf. 40:10–11; 85:10; 88:11; 115:1; esp. 136), and this faithfulness of God becomes the basis of appeals for divine aid (Pss. 40:11; 54:5; 57:3; 69:13; 86:15–16; 143:11–12; esp. 89). In this connection it is God's faithfulness to his covenant people that enables the prophets to assure Israel of God's continuing trustworthiness in spite of impending disaster. Hosea eloquently uses a marriage metaphor to this end: "And I will betroth you to me forever; I will betroth you to me in righteousness and in justice; in steadfast love and in mercy. I will betroth you to me in faithfulness" (Hos. 2:19; cf. Isa. 49:7; Jer. 32:41; Mic. 7:20).

Faithfulness is also to be found among God's people. In the OT, however, while God's loyalty to his people is a gracious act, human loyalty to God is a "dutiful response" (Verhey). This faithfulness is not required to sustain God's favor or covenant love; it is simply the only appropriate response open to man. Hence in numerous psalms faithfulness is paralleled to obedience to divine law (Pss. 119:30; 111:7–8). Also, the connection between faithfulness and *ḥesed* (steadfast love) appears here as well, but only as a feature of man's relation to the covenant community (Prov. 3:3; 14:22; 16:6). It is incumbent on God's people, therefore, to exhibit a reciprocal faithfulness that reflects the trustworthiness already shown by God.

The NT affirms this completely. The faithfulness of God confirms the Christian in his calling (I Cor. 1:9), especially in that God remains loyal to all his promises (Heb. 11:11; cf. 10:23). God faithfully preserves his people until Christ's second coming (I Thess. 5:23) and offers strength in temptation (I Cor. 10:13), before evil (II Thess. 3:3), and in the turmoil of suffering (I Pet. 4:19). The tenacity of God's faithfulness takes on dimensions of his OT covenant love which cannot be moved by man's erratic commitment: "if we are faithless, he remains faithful—for he cannot deny himself" (II Tim. 2:13). Since Jesus reflects this disposition of God, the Apocalypse gives *pistos* a titular significance for him: Jesus is the Faithful One (Rev. 3:14; 19:11, *pistos kai alēthinos*).

Faithfulness also hallmarks the life of the Christian. Various leaders are given the approving description of being "faithful": Tychicus (Eph. 6:21; Col. 4:7), Epaphras (Col. 1:7; 4:12), Onesimus (Col. 4:9), and Timothy (I Cor. 4:17). Hebrews is consistent in its Christology and presents Christ as the model of faithfulness (2:17; 3:2, 5–6; cf. 11) which in turn should give encouragement to the believer. For Paul, faithfulness is especially incumbent on the witness and minister. Paul himself had been deemed thus (I Tim. 1:12), and from this he can explain his pastoral calling. Likewise, Timothy is exhorted to appoint teachers in whom faithfulness is a prominent characteristic. Ultimately faithfulness to God and his people is a virtue generated by the Spirit (Gal. 5:22) which should be at the center of normative Christian experience.

In Biblical theology, therefore, faithfulness lies at the heart of the covenant relationship. God pledges consistent fidelity to his promises, and this is why he expresses himself through covenants. God pledges a lasting relationship, and we are invited—indeed called—to commit our lives with a commensurate faithfulness. G. M. Burge

See also God, Doctrine of; Lovingkindness.

Bibliography. A. D. Verhey, *ISBE* (rev.), II, 273–75; R. Bultmann, *Theology of the NT,* I, 314–24; J. Calvin, *Institutes of the Christian Religion* 3.2; O. Michel, *NIDNTT,* I, 593–606; A. Weiser and R. Bultmann, *TDNT,* VI, 174–228.

Faith Healing. *See* Heal, Healing.

Fall of Man. The fall denotes Adam and Eve's disobedience and commission of sin which brought tragic spiritual, physical, and social deprivation to the entire human race. The record of the fall is set forth in stark simplicity in Gen. 3. That the account is firmly historical (so Tertullian, Athanasius, Augustine, Calvin) is proven by Paul's juxtaposition of the "one man" Adam with Moses and with Christ (Rom. 5:12, 15–19; cf. I Cor. 15:20–22) and by the apostle's face-value acceptance of the reality of the tempter and the ensuing temptation (II Cor. 11:3; I Tim. 2:14). In addition, Luke traces the genealogy of Jesus, the universal man, from Joseph through David to Adam.

The Biblical Account. By way of background to the fall, Gen. 1 and 2 depict man as a sinless being created in the image of God for fellowship with his Creator. Adam and Eve were endowed with intellect, with emotion, and with a will which, although inclined toward God, was free either to obey or to disobey. Scripture indicates that God placed the first man in the garden under a probationary arrangement whereby his obedience and loyalty to God would be tested. To be authentically man Adam must be given opportunity to choose between the competing loyalties of God or self. The record implies that the reward of obedience would be confirmation in holiness as a spiritual son of God and the reward of disobedience spiritual and physical death. In the state of probation Adam acted not only for himself but representatively for the entire race.

Adam's probation centered around two trees—the tree of life and the tree of the knowledge of good and evil (Gen. 2:9). God's command to Adam was clear. He could freely eat of every tree except the tree of the knowledge of good and evil. Should he eat of the latter he would die (Gen. 2:16–17). Since no reason is given why Adam ought not eat the fruit of the tree of knowledge, we may assume that it stood as a sheer test of obedience. Through their choices made in respect of the trees Adam and Eve were confronted with the will of God to which they must respond with a Yes or a No.

The two principal trees possessed no intrinsic magical potency, but only symbolic meaning. The tree of life symbolized an eternal life of fellowship with God (cf. Rev. 2:7; 22:2, 14). Had our first parents eaten obediently of the tree of life instead of the tree of knowledge, they would have secured eternal life as the reward of their faith. The tree of knowledge, it seems clear, was a tree which, if the fruit thereof were eaten, would impart experimental ethical knowledge. Strong suggests that by partaking of the fruit man would know good by the loss of it and evil by bitter experience. Somewhat differently, Machen avers that formerly Adam knew good, but by eating disobediently he would come to know evil, whereas the good would become but a memory. However one understands the symbolism of the tree of knowledge, God's prohibition against eating was a test of man's loyalty and obedience. Would Adam submit to the will of God, or would he assert his own will independently of the Creator?

The record indicates that our first parents, who possessed everything needful for the realization of their destiny, were enticed by the serpent (Gen. 3:1). Was the serpent merely a figurative description for Satan (Buswell), or did the serpent become the instrumentality of the devil's dark workings (Hodge, Berkhof)? The latter interpretation seems preferable, since in judgment God permanently cursed the reptile (Gen. 3:14). Nevertheless, it is clear from NT teaching that the real tempter was Satan (I John 3:8; Rev. 12:9). The devil in the guise of a serpent sought to beguile Eve by tempting her first to distrust God's goodness (Gen. 3:1–3) and then to disbelieve God's Word (Gen. 3:4–5). The devil, as John would put it, was a liar from the beginning (John 8:44). Enticed by the serpent Eve saw that the tree was "good for good," "a delight to the eyes," and "to be desired to make one wise" (Gen. 3:6). The attraction of the tree of knowledge could be likened to the material ("lust of the flesh"), aesthetic ("lust of the eyes"), and intellectual ("pride of life") aspects of the world's allurement (I John 2:16). Lured by Satan, Eve was struck with ambition, pride, and the quest for self-realization apart from God.

The fall of our first parents is set forth simply and briefly. Eve "took of its fruit and ate; and she also gave some to her husband, and he ate" (Gen. 3:6). Various Jewish and Christian authorities have interpreted the tree of knowledge as the rise of sexual awareness and Eve's eating of the forbidden fruit as sexual intercourse. But since Eve and Adam each ate independently, and since God had earlier commanded them to be fruitful and multiply (Gen. 1:28; cf. 2:24), this viewpoint must be rejected. More accurate is the assertion that when faced with the choice of submitting to the will of God or unlawfully asserting her own will, Eve chose the latter course, which in turn manifested itself in the act of eating the forbidden fruit. First Eve and then Adam violated the divine command, thus disclosing their decision to cut themselves loose from God and to forge their future alone. By means of this free act of the will sin entered the human family through Adam and Eve, the progenitors of the race.

The Results. The remainder of Gen. 3 unfolds the disastrous results of the fall. First there are the effects of sin upon Adam and Eve and, by imputation, upon the race as a whole. Immediately following their willful transgression Adam and Eve experienced personal guilt, evidenced by attempts to make garments to cover their nakedness. Next, efforts to hide themselves from the presence of the Lord suggest that Adam and Eve suffered a breach in relationship with God, or spiritual death. The pair's evasive answers to God's interrogation and casting of blame upon the other further illustrate the depravity which had overcome the human heart. Finally, the fall resulted in physical death, or the dissolution of man's body-soul unity (vss. 22–24). Adam and Eve were driven out of the garden and prevented from eating of the tree of life, by means of which they would have lived forever. The cherubim and flaming sword guarding the tree of life symbolize the barrier that now exists between sinful man and a holy God.

Mankind after the fall suffers extensive spiritual deprivation. Although the image of God in man survives (Gen. 9:6), reason has lost its soundness (II Cor. 4:4), the will is no longer free to choose God and the good (John 8:34), and man is both spiritually blind (I Cor. 2:14) and spiritually dead (Eph. 2:1, 5). Once able not to sin (*posse non peccare*), the sinner now is incapable of not sinning (*non posse non peccare*, Jer. 13:23; II Pet. 2:14). Man's grim life of sin following the fall is outlined by Paul in Rom. 1:21–32 and 3:9–18. In response to sinners' deliberate love for and practice of sin, God "gave them up" to the painful consequences of their spiritual rebellion (Rom. 1:24, 26, 28).

The results of the fall to Satan and the serpent follow (Gen. 3:14–15). Because the reptile served as the instrument of Satan's deception, God cursed the serpent above all the wild animals. The repulsion which people sense when confronted with a snake would seem to be a consequence of God's curse upon it. The prophecy is then given that Satan is doomed to be crushed. A perpetual enmity would exist between the devil and the line of spiritual humanity which culminated in Christ. Satan would inflict hurt upon the people of God, but the seed of the woman would deliver a fatal wound upon the archenemy of the saints. Satan was struck a mighty blow at Christ's cross and resurrection (Col. 2:15), but his final doom awaits the Lord's second coming (Rom. 16:20; Rev. 20:2).

The fall would have far-reaching implications for the female sex (Gen. 2:16). With the onset of sin and death as the law of human existence, women must bear additional children with the consequent increase of physical pain. In God's plan the woman would also experience a psychosexual desire for her husband. And in a sinful world God ordained that within the framework of the ontic equality of male and female there should be a functional subordination of the wife to the husband (cf. I Cor. 11:3; Eph. 5:22–24; I Pet. 3:1, 5, 6).

The fall also had a direct impact upon the existence of the man (Gen. 3:17–19). The ground, which now offers resistance to man's efforts, exacts toil and sweat in order to make it produce. But in a fallen world labor would serve as a brake to sin. Moreover, in fulfillment of Gen. 2:17 man is condemned to death. Raised from the dust to live, sinful man is now consigned to return to the same dust in death.

The fall's effects impinge even upon the inanimate creation as God curses the ground upon which man treads. Paul teaches that since the rebellion of man the entire material universe languishes in a state of disfunction (Rom. 8: 20–22). The effects of Adam's sin thus are truly cosmic in scope.

Finally, the fall of Adam and humanity in him (Rom. 5:12, 15–19; I Cor. 15:21–22) has an impact on the God who created man and woman (Gen. 3:21). God's act of making clothing of skins for Adam and Eve typifies the fact that God then began the long process of covering sin, first by the sacrifice of animals and then through the sacrifice of his own Son (cf. II Cor. 5:4).

The Fall and Theology. The historical reality and import of the fall have been denied in some circles. Judaism generally holds that Adam's transgression affected only Adam and resulted in physical, not spiritual, death. The Pelagians likewise taught that Adam's sin had no impact on his offspring. Man is born into the world morally capable of obeying God and actualizing the good. Modern liberalism, postulating the evolutionary ascent of man, uniformly denies the historicity of Adam's fall and the hereditary transmission of sin. Neo-orthodox theologians such as Barth and Brunner argue that the Genesis account of the fall is not history but saga or legend. According to Barth, Adam is a general title for Everyman. We dare not ask how, when, and where the fall took place. A function of primal history (*Urgeschichte*), the fall conveys the fundamental truth that man is subject to the law of sin and death. Traditional Roman Catholicism postulates that Adam was created morally neutral, but was subsequently endowed by God with the superadded gift of righteousness (*donum superadditum*). Hence the fall did no more than return Adam to his condition as originally created. B. A. DEMAREST

See also ADAM; SIN; DEPRAVITY, TOTAL.

Bibliography. C. Hodge, *Systematic Theology*, II, 123–29; C. S. Lewis, *The Problem of Pain*, ch. 5; J. G. Machen, *The Christian View of Man*, ch. 14; A. H. Strong, *Systematic Theology;* N. P. Williams, *The Ideas of the Fall and of Original Sin.*

False Christs. This expression, formed on the analogy of "false apostles" (II Cor. 11:13) and "false brothers" (II Cor. 11:26), is derived from the Greek *pseudochristoi*, and is used in Matt. 24:24 and Mark 13:22 to denominate those who falsely claim to be Israel's deliverer. Gamaliel alludes to a revolt (A.D. 6) led by a Judas of Galilee and to a certain Theudas who perished with four hundred followers (Acts 5:36–37). The military tribune (Acts 21:38) mentions a certain Egyptian who led four thousand daggermen (*sikarioi*) to the Mount of Olives and bade them wait until, at his command, the walls fell flat. When the attack failed the Egyptian conveniently hid himself. The tribune erroneously thought that the Jewish leaders had identified Paul as the Egyptian and were exacting vengeance for his self-imposed exile. During the revolt against Rome John of Giscala, leader of the Zealots, and Simon bar Gioras (i.e., son of the proselyte) opposed one another with ruinous consequences terminating in the debacle of A.D. 70. The last of the false Christs in the early Christian era was Simon bar Cochba (A.D. 132–35), to whom Rabbi Akiba referred in Num. 24:17.

In its broader application, as the phrase "in my name" (Matt. 24:5) suggests, the term "false Christs" suggests a problem prompted by consideration of the apparent contradiction between Jesus' claims to lordship and the disappointing evidence of his sovereignty inside history. The temptation is to have the chasm bridged by more patent demonstrations of Jesus' sovereignty rather than to live in constant faith that Jesus Christ's purposes ripen fully not within but outside history. F. W. DANKER

See also ANTICHRIST; SECOND COMING OF CHRIST.

Bibliography. G. R. Beasley-Murray, *A Commentary on Mark Thirteen*, pp. 83–85; *HDCG*, I, 600ff.

Farrar, Frederic William (1831–1903). Anglican writer and theologian. Born in Bombay, son of a missionary clergyman, he was educated at London and Cambridge universities, and was greatly influenced by the thinking of S. T. Coleridge and F. D. Maurice. He was ordained in 1854, and was for more than twenty years a schoolmaster, in which field his pioneering methods led to his election (rare for a churchman) as a fellow of the Royal Society. He later became canon (1876) and archdeacon (1883) of Westminster.

In 1877 Farrar aroused controversy over a series of five sermons he preached in Westminster Abbey on the soul and the future life, in the course of which he challenged the doctrine of eternal punishment. The sermons were published as *Eternal Hope* (1878) and ran to eighteen editions before his death. E. B. Pusey, the Tractarian leader, was among many who replied, and Farrar to some extent modified his position in *Mercy and Judgment* (1881). While he could never quite discard his evangelical upbringing, it was Farrar who suggested that Darwin be buried in Westminster Abbey, and he himself preached the funeral sermon on the scientist's life and character. Farrar wrote a number of other books, notably a *Life of Christ* (1876), which proved immensely popular in America, and a *Life of Saint Paul* (1879), which also had a great impact on Victorian England. Some of Farrar's more liberal views had a brief vogue among United Presbyterians in Scotland. J. D. DOUGLAS

Bibliography. R. Farrar, *The Life of Frederic William Farrar.*

Farrer, Austin (1904–1968). Administrator, pastor and preacher, NT scholar, philosopher, theologian, poet, and author. He did his undergraduate studies at Oxford University and was made a Doctor of Divinity by the university. He was the chaplain of Trinity College, Oxford (1925–60), and warden of Keble College, Oxford (1960–68). He delivered the Bampton Lectures in 1948 and the Gifford Lectures in 1957. His published works include sermons, devotional books, theology, philosophy of religion, and Bible commentaries.

These books reveal a man bringing together faith and reason and a philosopher-theologian-scholar who was concerned for matters of the heart as well as the mind. His sermons in particular show his concern for both theology and spirituality. For twenty-five years he and C. S. Lewis were Oxford dons together; they shared an affection and appreciation for one another. What Farrer said of Lewis could also be said of Farrer: He could think about all that he strongly felt, and he could feel the realities about which he thought. At the core of his theological understanding was the conviction that belief in God must be lived as well as thought; but without being thought it cannot be lived. Theology and practice cannot be separated.

Farrer, the son of a Baptist minister, converted to Anglicanism as a young man. For Farrer, to be Anglican was to be catholic. He avoided ecclesiastical party loyalties, but described his understanding of Christianity as Reformed. His intention was to be orthodox in his theology and to center the faith on Christ.

Of Farrer's many books, *The Glass of Vision* is the most important for seeing the wide range of his thought. S. N. Gundry

Bibliography. A Farrer, *Finite and Infinite: A Philosophical Essay* and *A Rebirth of Images: The Making of St. John's Apocalypse;* C. C. Hefling, Jr., *Jacob's Ladder: Theology and Spirituality in the Thought of Austin Farrer.*

Fast, Fasting. The act of total or partial abstinence from food for a limited period of time, usually undertaken for moral or religious reasons. Religious dicta concerning fasting range from Zoroastrianism, which forbade it, to Jainism, which teaches that the believer's goal is a life of passionless detachment culminating ideally in death by voluntary starvation.

Nearly all religions promote or sanction fasting in some form or another. In primal religions it is often a means to control or appease the gods, a way to produce virility, or preparation for a ceremonial observance—such as initiation or mourning. The fast was used by the ancient Greeks when consulting oracles, by the American Indians to acquire their private totem, and by African shamans to make contact with spirits. Many Eastern religions use it to gain clarity of vision and mystical insight. Judaism, several branches of Christianity, and Islam all have fixed fast days, and usually associate fasting with the discipline of the flesh or with repentance for sin. Islam undertakes the annual fast of Ramadan, an entire month when Muslims are obliged to abstain from all food and water from sunrise to sunset.

In Judaism the day of atonement is the only public fast day prescribed by the law (Lev. 16:29–31; 23:26–32; Num. 29:7–11). However, the OT also refers to many special public and private fasts, usually coupled with prayer, to signify mourning (I Sam. 31:13; II Sam. 1:12), to show repentance and remorse (II Sam. 12:15–23; I Kings 21:27–29; Neh. 9:1–2; Joel 2:12–13), or to demonstrate serious concern before God (II Chr. 20:1–4; Pss. 35:13; 69:10; 109:24; Dan. 9:3). However, fasting that was not accompanied by genuine repentance and righteous deeds was denounced as an empty legal observance by the prophets (Isa. 58; Jer. 14:11–12).

Jesus himself apparently fasted during his so-called wilderness experience as a part of the preparation for his formal ministry (Matt. 4:1–2; Luke 4:1–2). However, the Gospels report that he spoke only twice about fasting—once to warn his disciples that it was to be a private act of simple devotion to God and once to indicate that it would be appropriate for his followers to fast after he left them (Matt. 6:16–18; 9:14–15; cf. Mark 2:18–20; Luke 5:33–35). It is clear that he did not stress fasting, nor did he lay down any rules concerning its observance as had John the Baptist and the Pharisees for their disciples.

The early Christian community did not emphasize fasting but observed it in connection with certain occasions of solemn commitment (Acts 13:2–3; 14:23). Moreover, Jewish Christians apparently followed the Jewish custom of fasting and prayer on Mondays and Thursdays until around the end of the first century when Wednesdays and Fridays were observed, probably in reaction against the Judaizers. However, such fasts were usually concluded by midafternoon and were not universally enforced. Also, from the second century on, two intensive fast days were observed in preparation for Easter.

In the fourth century, when Christianity finally became the only recognized faith of the Roman Empire, the consequent institutionalization of the church led to a much greater stress on form, ritual, and liturgy. Fasting thus became increasingly linked with a legalistic theology and the concept of meritorious works. For example, the early church's two-day fast before Easter came, in the fourth century, to be a Lenten observance of forty fast days, which by the tenth century was obligatory upon the entire Western church. In addition, fasting was a common element of discipline in the early monastic communities from the second century onward. When the monastic way replaced martyrdom as the highest act of devotion of the Christian life in the fourth century, monastic practices such as fasting were also elevated in the eyes of the faithful.

The church of Rome added a number of fast days to the calendar of the Christian year during the Middle Ages. It adopted the days of the chief agricultural operations in Italy as obligatory fasts called ember days: the Wednesday, Friday, and Saturday following the first Sunday in Lent; Pentecost; and September 14. A fourth season of fasting from December 13 to Christmas was added later. Also during the Middle Ages the Eastern Orthodox Church added obligatory fast days beginning November 15 during Advent, from Trinity Sunday until June 29, and the two weeks prior to August 15.

The Protestant Reformers of the sixteenth century, with the exception of the Anglicans, rejected obligatory fast days along with much of the other prescribed ritual and formal religious acts of the Roman Church. The Anabaptists, more than any other reform group of the period, relegated fasting once more to the private sphere, leaving it up to the individual believer to determine its appropriateness for enhancing self-discipline and prayer.

The Roman Catholic Church maintained its church calendar of fast days until the twentieth century, when it was modified by several acts related to Vatican Council II. Moreover, the modern Catholic approach has been to link fasting to the call to love one's neighbor and to see it as a symbol of the Christian's identification with the poor and hungry of the world. In some Christian circles—Catholic and non-Catholic, evangelical and nonevangelical—there is the growing custom of meeting for a simple repast and giving the cost of the normal meal to relieve world hunger as a kind of modern-day version of fasting. Twentieth century Pentecostal charismatics have written extensively about the benefits of the fast, nearly always linking it with prayer, as a means to deepen spiritual life and/or to obtain God's favor. Some charismatic leaders even claim that the course of history can be shaped by prayer and fasting.

As with any religious practice, there are dangers in fasting, especially when emphasized at the expense of other biblical teachings or misused for selfish ends. The Bible notes such abuses as fasting as a means of getting things from God, as a substitute for genuine repentance, as a mere convention and therefore an end in itself, and as an occasion for outward religiosity (Isa. 58; Zech. 7:5; Matt. 6:16). Moreover, there is psychological evidence that fasting lends itself to self-induced visions which sometimes prove harmful. On the other hand, there is biblical evidence that fasting and prayer practiced together can be a useful part of individual and congregational life, though the practice should never be allowed to degenerate into an empty formal observance or a device for attempting to manipulate God.

R. D. Linder

Bibliography. H. Franke, *Lent and Easter;* A. Wallis, *God's Chosen Fast;* J. L. Beall, *The Adventure of Fasting;* D. Prince, *Shaping History Through Prayer and Fasting;* E. N. Rogers, *Fasting: The Phenomenon of Self-Denial;* A. Cott *et al., Fasting: A Way of Life;* A. M. Fulton, ed., *The Fasting Primer;* D. Dewelt, *What the Bible Says about Prayer and Fasting.*

Fate, Fatalism. Fate, personified by the Greeks under the name of Moira, signified in the ancient world the unseen power that rules over human destiny. In classical thought fate was believed to be superior to the gods, since even they were unable to defy its all-encompassing power. Fate is not chance, which may be defined as the absence of laws, but instead a cosmic determinism that has no ultimate meaning or purpose. In classical thought as well as in Oriental religion fate is a dark, sinister power related to the tragic vision of life. It connotes not the absence of freedom but the subjection of freedom. It is the transcendent necessity in which freedom is entangled (Tillich). Fate is blind, inscrutable, and inescapable.

Christianity substituted for the hellenistic concept of fate the doctrine of divine providence. Whereas fate is the portentous, impersonal power that thwarts and overrules human freedom, providence liberates man to fulfill the destiny for which he was created. Fate means the abrogation of freedom; providence means the realization of authentic freedom through submission to divine guidance. Providence is the direction and support of a loving God, which makes life ultimately bearable; fate is the rule of contingency that casts a pall over all human striving. Whereas fate makes the future precarious and uncertain, providence fills the future with hope. Fate is impersonal and irrational; providence is supremely personal and suprarational.

Fatalism was present among the ancient Stoics, and it pervades much of the thought of Hinduism, Buddhism, and Islam. Modern philosophers who have entertained ideas akin to fate are Oswald Spengler, Herbert Spencer, John Stuart Mill, and Arthur Schopenhauer.

D. G. Bloesch

See also Freedom, Free Will, and Determinism; Providence of God.

Bibliography. W. C. Greene, *Moira: Fate, Good and Evil in Greek Thought;* R. Guardini, *Freedom, Grace, and Destiny;* P. Tillich, "Philosophy and Fate," in *The Protestant Era,* and *The Courage to Be;* H. Ringgren, ed., *Fatalistic Beliefs in Religion, Folklore, and Literature;* J. Den Boeft, *Calcidius on Fate.*

Father, God as. There is nothing in the Bible to support the heathen notion of a literal divine fatherhood of clans or nations. Several passages of Scripture imply that God is the Father of angels and men as their Creator (Job 1:6; 2:1; 38:7; Ps. 86:6; Luke 3:38). But it is chiefly in connection with Israel, the Davidic king, and Messiah that references to the fatherhood of God occur in the OT. By the historical event of deliverance from Egypt, God created the nation of Israel and subsequently cared for them, establishing a special relationship with them. Allusions to his fatherly regard for them look back to this crisis as the time of the nation's origin. Their emancipation marked them off from other people as his adopted children. His care for them is frequently compared to that of a father (Hos. 11:1; Deut. 14:1; II Sam. 7:14; Pss. 2:7; 89:26; Deut. 1:31; 8:5; Isa. 1:2). On the other hand, a response of filial love expressed in obedience was required from them (Jer. 3:9; Mal. 1:6), and since it was so often refused, a more restricted conception of the fatherhood of God resulted. According to this deeper view, he is the Father of the God-fearing among the nation rather than of the nation as a whole (Ps. 103:13; Mal. 3:17).

This later mode of thought finds expression also in the literature of the intertestamental period (Jub. 1:24; Ps. Sol. 13:8; 17:30; Ecclus. 23:1, 4) and is endorsed by the teaching of Jesus. He gave largely increased prominence to the doctrine of the fatherhood of God. The number of instances of the word "Father" as applied to God in the Gospels is more than double the number found in the remaining books of the NT. In the Gospel of John alone 107 occur. Two points in connection with Jesus' use of this title are of special interest. (1) He never joins his disciples with himself in allusions to his relationship with the Father in such a way as to suggest that their relationship to God is of the same kind. He was aware of standing in an intimate and unparalleled relation. He claimed to be the preexistent eternal Son, equal with the Father, who became incarnate for the fulfillment of his purpose of salvation, being appointed by him sole Mediator between God and men (Matt. 11:27; John 8:58; 10:30, 38; 14:9; 16:28; 3:25; 5:22). (2) When he speaks of God as the Father of others he almost always refers to his disciples. While accepting the teaching of the OT that all persons are children of God by creation and receive his providential kindness (Matt. 5:45), he also taught that sin has brought about a change in men, necessitating rebirth and reconciliation to God (John 3:3; 8:42; 14:6). In accordance with this, the apostles teach that one becomes a child of God by faith in Christ and thus receives the Spirit of adoption (John 1:12; Gal. 3:16; 4:5; Rom. 8:15). Sonship leads to likeness and inheritance (Matt. 5:16; Rom. 8:29; I John 3:2; Rom. 8:17). The Father is revealed as sovereign, holy, righteous, and merciful. Prayer may confidently be offered to him in Jesus' name (Matt. 6:32; John 17:11, 25; 14:14).

W. J. CAMERON

See also GOD, NAMES OF; GOD, ATTRIBUTES OF; GOD, DOCTRINE OF; ABBA.

Bibliography. T. A. Smail, *The Forgotten Father;* A. P. F. Sell, *God Our Father;* S. Lidgett, *The Fatherhood of God;* J. Jeremias, *NT Theology: The Proclamation of Jesus,* 36–37, 61–68.

Fathers, Church. Ecclesiastically, the fathers are those who have preceded us in the faith, and are thus able to instruct us in it. In this sense, ministers and particularly bishops are often referred to as fathers. More particularly, however, the term has come to be applied to the first Christian writers of acknowledged eminence. Already in the fourth century it was used in this way of the teachers of the preceding epoch, and later all the outstanding theologians of at least the first six centuries have come to be regarded as fathers. This is the normal usage of the term today, although sometimes the patristic era is extended and Protestants may also speak of the Reformation fathers (e.g., Luther, Zwingli, and Calvin).

The question arises how a given author may be classified as a father. The mere survival of his work is not enough, for many heretical writings have come down to us, together with others of doubtful value. Four main characteristics have been suggested as necessary qualifications: first, substantial orthodoxy; second, holiness of life; third, widespread approval; and fourth, antiquity. It is allowed that fathers may be in error on individual points, as necessitated by the many disagreements, but they can still be counted and read as fathers so long as they satisfy these general requirements (cf. esp. the cases of Origen and Tertullian).

Various answers may be given to the question of patristic authority. From the Roman Catholic standpoint, the fathers are infallible where they display unanimous consent, although even in this regard Aquinas clearly ranks them below Scripture. Otherwise they may err, but are always to be read with respect. Protestants naturally insist that the fathers too are subject to the supreme norm of Scripture, so that their statements or interpretations may call for rejection, correction, or amplification. On the other hand, they deserve serious consideration as those who have preceded us in faith and made a serious attempt to express biblical and apostolic truth. Their support is thus valuable, their opinions demand careful study, they are to be set aside only for good reason, and their work constitutes no less a challenge to us than ours to them.

To list the fathers is hardly possible in so brief a compass, nor is it easy to classify them except perhaps in terms of the broad distinction between Greek and Latin. Mention may be made of the immediate postapostolic fathers who have given us our earliest Christian literature outside the NT (e.g., Clement of Rome, Ignatius of Antioch, and Polycarp). The Alexandrian school (Clement and Origin) at the end of the second and early in the third century deserves notice, as do such writers as Irenaeus, Tertullian, Hippolytus, and Cyprian. The fourth century, which was already referring to the fathers, provides us with some of the greatest of all in men like Athanasius, Hilary, Basil, Gregory of Nyssa, Gregory of Nazianzus, Ambrose, Augustine, Chrysostom, and Jerome. Among others who may be mentioned are the Cyrils, Theodoret, the two popes Leo I and Gregory I, and at the very end of the patristic period John of Damascus and Isidore of Seville. But these are only a selection from the great company of writers who over a wide and complex front gave to the church its earliest magnificent attempt in theology. G. W. BROMILEY

See also AUGUSTINE OF HIPPO; AMBROSE; CLEMENT OF ALEXANDRIA; CHRYSOSTOM, JOHN; CYPRIAN; CYRIL OF ALEXANDRIA; CAPPADOCIAN FATHERS; HIPPOLYTUS; GREGORY I, THE GREAT; ORIGEN; TERTULLIAN.

Bibliography. LCCI–VIII; *ANF* and *NPNF;* G. W. Bromiley, *Historical Theology*, Pt. I; G. W. H. Lampe in *A History of Christian Doctrine*, ed. H. Cunliffe-Jones; J. N. D. Kelley, *Early Christian Doctrines;* B. Altaner, *Patrology.*

Fear. No fewer than fifteen Hebrew nouns and ten verbs are translated by "fear" in the OT (AV), thus giving it a strikingly large place in the Hebrew Scriptures.

A common expression is "the fear of the Lord," which occurs fourteen times in the book of Proverbs. It is declared to be "the beginning of knowledge" (1:7), "the beginning of wisdom" (9:10), "a fountain of life" (14:27), and "the instruction of wisdom" (15:33). We are told that "the fear of the Lord is to hate evil" (8:13), that it prolongs life (10:27), that it gives "strong confidence" (14:26), that it keeps people away from sin (16:6), that it leads to life (19:23), and that the reward of humility and the fear of the Lord are "riches, honor and life" (22:4).

It should be obvious that "the fear of the Lord" does not mean being afraid of God. Rather, it is a reverential trust in God that makes us want to please and obey him. And yet there is a wholesome feeling of being sure that we do not disobey or displease him.

Another interesting expression is "the Fear of Isaac" (Gen. 31:42; cf. vs. 53). It appears to be an appellation for God, meaning the one for whom Isaac had fear (that is, reverential trust).

Somewhat different is the fear of God spoken of in Gen. 20:11. When Abraham came to Gerar, he thought, "Surely there is no fear of God in this place." This would probably mean being afraid of God.

An interesting combination is that found in Exod. 20:20: "And Moses said to the people, 'Do not be afraid; for God has come in order to test you, and in order that the fear of him may remain with you, so that you may not sin.'" The people were not to be afraid of God, but they were to have a proper sense of reverence that would include a fear of displeasing him.

In the NT there is one main noun for "fear," *phobos*, and one main verb, *phobeō*. The element of fright or terror seems to be inherent in these terms, but as is the case in the OT, the idea of reverential trust predominates.

A favorite phrase in the NT that occurs also in a number of places in the OT is "Fear not," or, "Do not be afraid" (NASB, NIV). This occurs especially with the sudden appearance of angels (Matt. 28:5; Luke 1:13, 30; 2:10). Here it seems to indicate the feeling of terror or fright that the angel's presence brought.

Jesus used it in the sense of being afraid of the future. He comforted his disciples with the words: "Don't be afraid: you are worth more than many sparrows" (Luke 12:7). In verse 32 of the same chapter he says: "Do not be afraid, little flock, for your Father has been pleased to give you the kingdom." Fear as a preventative has value. But fright or terror has no place in the Christian's life, at least in his relationship to God.

R. EARLE

See also AWE.

Feasts and Festivals, Christian. *See* CHRISTIAN YEAR; FIXED FEASTS; MOVABLE FEASTS.

Feasts and Festivals, Old Testament. The general word for festival is *môʿēd* (pl. *môʿădîm*). The word signifies a place or a time that has been set apart for a particular purpose. In cultic usage it may form a compound ("tent of meeting," *'ōhel/mô'ēd*) or have a designation of a time appointed for a religious festival. Festivals are characterized by several qualities: great joy (Hos. 2:11), except for the day of atonement; special offerings and sacrifices (Lev. 23:37–38; Num. 28, 29); special prayers (Isa. 1:14–15); special ceremonies for each of the festivals, such as eating of unleavened bread or bringing of first fruits. The Pentateuchal festivals are sabbath; the new moon; passover; first fruits; the new year; the day of atonement; and tabernacles. The postexilic festivals are Purim and Hanukkah. All feasts are festivals, but not all festivals are feasts.

The word "feast" comes from the root *ḥgg* (to celebrate) and is related to the root *ḥûg* (to circle). The roots *ḥgg* and *ḥûg* are so closely related that it is difficult to ascertain to which the word "feast" is related. Though all festivals except for the day of atonement were times of celebration and rejoicing, only three festivals are designated as feasts. Each is a pilgrimage feast: (1) passover, unleavened bread (Heb. *pesaḥ*); (2) first fruits, harvest, weeks (Heb. *šābū'ôt*); (3) tabernacles, booths, ingathering, succoth (Heb. *sukkôt*).

Prescriptive Texts. The shortest regulation on the festivals is given in Exod. 23:14–17, where they are listed as the feasts of unleavened bread, harvest, and ingathering. The requirement at each feast is that all males appear before the Lord. The times and offerings are not given. A more extensive regulation of the feasts is given in Exod. 34:18–23. The feast of unleavened bread is to be celebrated for seven days in the month Abib. The feast of weeks is at the conclusion of the wheat harvest, and the feast of ingathering at the turning of the year. Again, each feast is an occasion where all males must come before the Lord, but the location is not specified. From all appearances the feasts are agricultural feasts. Only in Deuteronomy is the place of assembly more specifically referred to as "the place which he will choose" (16:16). In Deut. 16:1–17 the three feasts are called passover, connected with the feast of unleavened bread (vss. 1–8, 16); the feast of weeks, celebrated seven weeks after the harvest of the first ears of grain (vss. 9–12); and the feast of booths, which is also a harvest festival (vss. 13–15). The emphasis is very much on rejoicing (vss. 11, 14) because of the abundance of Yahweh's blessings (vss. 10, 15, 17). Hence, the pilgrimage feasts are opportune times for bringing a gift "in accordance with the blessing of Yahweh" to the place which he will choose (vss. 16–17). In Leviticus the regulations are more clearly set forth pertaining to calendar, rituals, and offerings. The pilgrimage feasts are integrated into an extensive list of festivals that includes the sabbath, the day of acclamation (trumpets), and the day of atonement. The regulations also speak of days of rest or "holy convocations," when absolutely no work was to be done. For the development of the interpretation of the prescriptive texts and the practices in Judaism, see the Mishnaic tractate *Mô'ēd*.

The Jewish Festival Calendar. *Festival of the New Moon* (*Rō'š Ḥōdeš*). Held on the first of each month the festival of the new moon was a minor festival. It was a day of gladness (Num. 10:10). Fasting was prohibited. There were prescribed sacrifices (Num. 28:11–15; cf. Ezek. 46: 6–8). Work was permitted in Jewish practice (Babylonian Talmud, tractate *Ḥagigah*, 18a), but since it became customary to rest (Amos 8:5) or at least to refrain from heavy labor, it became an opportune time for special gatherings (II Kings 4:23; I Sam. 20:5–6; Neh. 10:33). In order to celebrate the new moon uniformly in the diaspora, two witnesses had to appear before the high court in Jerusalem to testify that they had seen the crescent of the moon. Thus, the Jews throughout the diaspora were informed by beacons lighted on mountains or by runners.

Feast of Passover and Unleavened Bread (Pesaḥ, Maṣṣôt). This was held on the fourteenth through the twenty-first of Abib (Nisan). The Torah differentiates between the passover as the first day of the celebration and the feast of unleavened bread as the seven days which follow. The passover ritual includes the slaughter of an unblemished one-year-old male sheep or goat (Exod. 12:5) which had been set aside on the tenth day (Exod. 12:3). The meat could be eaten only by circumcised males (Exod. 12:48) and by those who belonged to the family. All the meat had to be eaten that evening and whatever was left over had to be burned (12:10). The next seven days, the people ate unleavened bread (12:15–20; cf. Lev. 23:6). The first and the seventh days were "holy convocations," as no work could be performed (Lev. 23:7–8). Special sacrifices were offered (Lev. 23:8; Num. 28:19–24), and the first fruits of the harvest were presented to the priests (Lev. 23:10–14).

The passover liturgy has undergone extensive development. The NT gives a glimpse of Jesus' practice with his disciples. Jesus had celebrated the feast from his youth (Luke 2:42) and went to Jerusalem as a pilgrim (John 2:13; 11:55). The ceremony of the last supper included a meal, a blessing over the bread and over the wine, and the singing of a hymn (Matt. 26:21–30), probably one of the Hallel psalms (115–118). The Mishnaic tractate *Passover* gives in great detail the celebration of the passover. Today's celebration can best be studied by looking at a passover Haggadah of which traditional and contemporary versions exist.

Feast of First Fruits (*Šābū'ōt*). Celebrated fifty days after the sabbath of the passover (Lev. 23:15–16, 21), this was one of the three pilgrimage feasts. A difference of interpretation arose with respect of the word "sabbath" in Lev. 23:15: "from the day after the sabbath, . . . you shall number seven weeks." The Sadducees took the word "sabbath" to refer to the seventh day and hence decided that the feast of first fruits always had to fall on Sunday. The interpretation of the Pharisees favored the general meaning of Sabbath in the sense of a holy convocation. Since the first day of the feast of unleavened bread is a holy convocation, the feast of first fruits fell fifty days later and hence could be celebrated on any day of the week. Special offerings were presented in the temple (Lev. 23:17–20), where the pilgrims were met with the Levitical singers (Mishnah, tractate *Bikkurim* 3:2–4). The custom of celebrating the giving of the law is an early medieval interpretation of Exod. 19:1, according to which the law was given on Mount Sinai the third month after the Israelites left Egypt. In the Bible the feast is mentioned as having been observed in the times of Solomon (II Chr. 8:13), Hezekiah (II Chr. 31:3), and after the Exile (Ezra 3:4; Zech. 14:16, 18–19).

The Festival of Acclamation. Celebrated on the first day (new moon) of the seventh month (Tishri), it is the festival on which the ram's horn (shofar) was blown (Lev. 23:23–25; Num. 29:1–6). The psalmist sang about it in these words:

> Sound the ram's horn at the New Moon,
> and when the moon is full, on the day
> of our Feast;
> this is a decree for Israel,
> an ordinance of the God of Jacob.
> (Ps. 81:3–4)

Ezra read the law to the people on the first day of the seventh month (Neh. 8:1–8). Nehemiah spoke of that day as a day of feasting (8:10). The festival was the beginning of a series of high holy days and was not equated with New Year (Rosh ha-Shanah) until postexilic times. The rabbis differed in their interpretation of its significance. Some identified it with the beginning of the world and others as the day on which mankind will be judged. Jewish liturgies reflect both traditions.

The shofar is the instrument blown on the festival. It became an important part of the ceremony, as is evident from the traditions (cf. tractate *Rosh Hashanah* in the Mishnah and Babylonian Talmud). Rabbi Josiah suggested that at the sound of the shofar the Creator rises from his throne of judgment and moves over to his throne of mercy (*Lev. Rabbah* 29:4).

The Day of Atonement. This fell on the tenth of the seventh month (Tishri; Lev. 23:27–32; Num. 29:7–11). It was a holy convocation on which the Israelites humbled themselves before the Lord. Special sacrifices were presented as an atonement for the sins of the priests and the people (Lev. 16); "because on this day atonement will be made for you, to cleanse you. Then, before the Lord, you will be clean from all your sins" (Lev. 16:30). Special offerings were also presented (Num. 29:8–11). In the year of jubilee the blowing of the shofar solemnized the freeing of slaves (Lev. 25:9–10).

The Feast of Tabernacles (*Sukkôt*). This was held for seven days from the fifteenth through the twenty-first of the seventh month (Exod. 23:16–17; 34:22; Lev. 23:33–44). It was the third pilgrimage feast. The first day and the day after the feast were solemn assemblies. All Israelite families were required to live in booths made of branches of trees, including the poplar and palm (Lev. 23:40, 42). Because it was a harvest feast, special offerings were presented in the temple (Lev. 23:37–38). It was a feast marked by great joy (Deut. 16:13–15).

Hanukkah. The feast of lights or dedication is celebrated for eight days beginning on the twenty-fifth of Kislev. The word Hanukkah comes from a Hebrew root meaning "to dedicate." The festival celebrates the dedication of the second temple on the twenty-fifth of the month Kislev (165/164 B.C.). Judas Maccabeus had subdued the Seleucid forces, marched into Jerusalem, and cleansed the temple (I Macc. 4:36–57), which had been desecrated by Antiochus IV Epiphanes' sacrifice of a pig. The Jews celebrated it for eight days with great joy. Judas decreed it to be a perpetual observance (vs. 59). The tradition developed of burning one additional light each day until eight lights had been lit on the eighth day. The day of dedication had become the day of lights. In Jesus' time the temple was all lit up with lamps. The lights and their reflection on the marble and gold of the temple made Jerusalem a magnificent sight to behold from the Mount of Olives in the evening. During one of the festivals Jesus was in Jerusalem and taught in the temple precincts (John 10:22–23).

Purim (Lots). This was celebrated on the fourteenth and fifteenth of Adar. The origin of the festival is given in the book of Esther. Haman's plot to have the Jews of the Persian Empire executed was foiled by Esther the queen. King Ahasuerus (Xerxes, 485–465 B.C.) permitted the Jews to defend themselves on the day of the thirteenth of Adar. Haman had determined by "lots" to rid the kingdom of the Jews (Esth. 3:7). On the thirteenth and fourteenth of Adar the Jews were victorious in repelling their enemy, and thus they were saved. It was decreed to celebrate Purim as the festival of lots (probably from Akkadian *puru*, "stone"); it is characterized by eating and drinking and giving gifts (Esth. 9:20–22, 24, 26). There may be an allusion to Purim in John 5:1.

The Theology of the Feasts and Festivals. Each feast expresses a theological statement. The passover is the feast of Yahweh's redemption of Israel from Egypt. He showed himself powerful and victorious over the enemies of his people (Exod. 12:17; 13:7–9, 14–16). The redemption from Egypt was viewed as an act of love (Exod. 19:4) and of covenantal loyalty (Pss. 105:6, 37, 42, 43; 111:9). The feast of weeks celebrates the gift of the land of Canaan, where the Israelites received the blessings of God in the form of rain and a plentiful harvest. By permitting the poor to glean the fields and to harvest the "corners" of the field, all of God's people had reason to rejoice before the Lord (Deut. 16:11–12). The celebration of the new moon was a reminder of God's goodness in giving another month of covenant life. The seventh new moon festival (today's New Year) not only marked the midpoint of the religious calendar; it also was the beginning of the special days (atonement and tabernacles). At later times it was associated with God's work of creation, his judgment of the world, and his mercy on Israel. The day of atonement was the only day on which Israel did not rejoice, but humbled itself by fasting. Five days later it celebrated the feast of tabernacles. The feast of tabernacles is also a harvest festival, but its historical emphasis lies in the remembrance of the forty years in the wilderness, when Israel lived in tents. Hanukkah marked God's continued redemption of the people. They were forced to assimilate, and Judaism was in danger of abandoning its heritage had it not been for men, zealous for the law of God and the temple, who through victories in war were granted to free the temple and to consecrate it. Purim similarly speaks of God's providence and his continued care for his people, even when they are in the dispersion.

The Jews in the second temple period, when Jesus was on earth, had developed elaborate rituals and theological justifications of these ancient festivals. The festivals bound together Jews in Judea and Galilee and Jews and proselytes living in the diaspora. All celebrated the festivals. During the pilgrimage feasts they made efforts to be in Jerusalem. The diverse origins of the people are shown by Luke as he reports on the crowds present in Jerusalem during the Pentecost feast (Acts 2:5–11). Our Lord participated in the pilgrimages, and along the way he continued his ministry (Matt. 19:1–20:34). The apostle Paul expressed a desire to be in Jerusalem for the feast of Pentecost (Acts 20:16).

The customs had developed extensively over the years after the Exile until they were codified by Rabbi Judah the Prince in the Mishnah (*ca.* A.D. 200). They continued to show their dynamics in a development which formed a cohesive element for Jews all over the globe. The NT witnesses to one such development. In the OT there is no ritual of a pouring out of water associated with the feast of tabernacles. But it was practiced in the first century A.D. It is this custom of pouring out water on the last day of the feast of tabernacles as a symbolic prayer for rain that forms the background for Jesus' invitation to come to him and be satisfied with the living water of the Spirit (John 7:37–39).

Since Jesus' coming the relevance of the Jewish religious calendar has been reduced to a shadow of things to come. Jesus is portrayed as the passover lamb (I Cor. 5:7–8). Christians celebrate the Lord's Supper instead of the passover. With the destruction of the temple, pilgrimages and special temple offerings have come to an end. The death of Christ, particularly, is portrayed in the NT as the final sacrifice by which man can be reconciled to God (Heb. 7:27; cf. ch. 8). The apostle Paul clearly taught that the observance of sabbaths, new moons, and festivals is not a criterion by which godliness is to be judged (Col. 2:16–17; cf. Rom. 14:5–6). Some have even concluded that all sabbath observances have come to an end. Others posit that the word "sabbaths" must be interpreted in a pharisaic sense as "solemn assemblies," i.e., the days of rest associated with the festivals. The practice of sabbath observance lacks uniformity in the Christian community. The celebration of Easter has completely supplanted the observance of passover. Recently a renewed interest in some Christian circles has been expressed in the celebration of the passover. The unity experienced by God's people in the OT during the celebration of the feasts and festivals (Ps. 133:1) has not found expression in the Christian community, where unity has been more confessionally oriented.

W. A. Van Gemeren

Bibliography. G. F. Moore, *Judaism*, II, 40–45; E. Auerbach, "Die Feste im alten Israel," *VT* 8:1–18; E. Rackman, *Sabbath and Festivals in the Modern Age;* R. deVaux, *Ancient Israel*, II, 468–517; H. Schauss, *Guide to Jewish Holy Days* and *The Jewish Festivals;* A. P. Bloch, *The Biblical and Historical Background of the Jewish Holy Days;* entries on the individual festivals in *EJ.*

Febronianism. The name given by Roman Catholics to an eighteenth century German theological movement begun by John Nicholas von

Hontheim, Bishop of Treves. Under the pen name of Justinus Febronius, Hontheim wrote tracts disputing the doctrine of papal infallibility. In 1768 he published a tract arguing that Christ gave Peter the keys of the kingdom to empower not Peter and his papal descendants but the church as a whole. Accordingly, Hontheim believed that all Christians could claim equal authority in deciding matters of faith and doctrine. A consequence of this position would be that any body of Christians, such as the bishops as a whole, wielded more power than the pope. This approach shifted infallibility to the church away from the pope, whose function became to preserve the church canon, not to alter it.

Hontheim's system would have drastically weakened papal authority. Therefore many Roman Catholics considered it an extreme and entirely unacceptable form of Gallicanism. While Gallicanism must certainly have influenced Hontheim, its goals differed widely from those of Febronianism. Hontheim's purposes were apolitical; by reducing papal authority he wanted to reconcile the Protestant and Catholic views, not to increase the power of secular government.

The papacy opposed any form of Hontheim's ideas. Pope Clement XIII condemned the Febronian position, and Hontheim responded with an abridgment of his pamphlet in 1777. This compromise failed to satisfy the papacy, however. In 1778 Pope Pius VI forced Hontheim to make an outright retraction. Nevertheless, he published a restatement of his original beliefs in 1781.

P. A. Mickey

See also Gallicanism.

Bibliography. *The Protestant Dictionary; The New Catholic Dictionary.*

Federal Theology. The name of Johannes Cocceius (1603–69) stands in the closest association with federal theology because of the prominence into which he brought it in the theological schools. But federal theology finds clear exposition in I Cor. 15 and Rom. 5. "As in Adam all die," writes Paul, "even so in Christ shall all be made alive" (I Cor. 15:22). Adam, as the first man, was the natural head of the race, and represented all mankind as the human party to the covenant of works into which God entered with him. As the natural head, he stood in a federal (*foedus,* Latin "covenant") relationship to all posterity. His obedience, had it been maintained, would have transmitted an entail of blessedness to them; his disobedience involved them with him in the curse which God pronounced upon the transgressors of his law.

This argument is developed in Rom. 5:15–21. The entire human race is summarized in the two Adams. The first Adam was the federal head of the race under the covenant of works; the second Adam, the Lord Jesus Christ, is the federal head of all believers under the covenant of grace. Thus as the sin of Adam was legally and effectively *our* sin, so the obedience of Christ is legally and effectively the righteousness of all believers. The federal relationship in which Adam stood to the race was the ground of the imputation of his guilt to them and the judicial cause of their condemnation. And the law which condemned them could not justify them unless an adequate reparation should be made for the wrong done, a reparation which they were incapable of making because of the corruption which they inherited from Adam as their natural and federal head. To provide their salvation, the needed reparation had to be made by another who was not of federal connection with Adam and therefore was free from the imputation of his guilt. Federal theology represents these requirements as being met in Christ, the second Adam, in whom a new race begins. God had entered into covenant with him, promising him the salvation of all believers as the reward of his obedience. But the obedience required of him as the federal head of his people was more than the mere equivalent of that required of Adam. His representative obedience must include a penal death. And thus his resurrection victory is also the victory of the new humanity which has its source in him.

The various theological schools differ with regard to the implications of the imputation of Adam's guilt to his posterity. Pelagius (late fourth and early fifth centuries) denied that there was any necessary connection between the sin of Adam and that of his descendants. Cocceius himself did not found his federal theology on the doctrine of predestination, after the manner of Calvin. The earlier Arminians held that man has inherited his natural corruption through Adam, but that he is not implicated in the guilt of Adam's first transgression. The later Arminians, however, particularly those of the Wesleyan following, admitted that man's inborn corruption also involves guilt. Yet notwithstanding these and other modifications, there is a broad agreement between the Roman, Lutheran, and Reformed theologies that man's loss of original righteousness is the consequence of Adam's first sin as the covenant head of the race. "Nothing remains," writes Augustine, "but to conclude that in the first man all are understood to have sinned, whereby sin is brought in with birth and not removed save by the new birth." Any other view tends to break the analogy that is so clearly set forth in Rom. 5:19: "For as by one man's disobedience many were made sinners, so by the obedience of one shall many be made righteous." A real imputation of the righteousness of Christ as federal head of his people requires a real imputation of the guilt of Adam to his posterity. For, as Calvin argues against the Pelagian view, if the imputation of Adam's sin means no more than that Adam became our example in sin, then the strict application of Paul's analogy of the two Adams would mean no more than that Christ became the example of his people in righteousness, and not the cause of their righteousness. Their vital union with Christ is the cause of their righteousness and also the guarantee of their growth in personal sanctification.

G. N. M. Collins

See also Cocceius, Johannes; Covenant Theology.

Bibliography. J. Cocceius, *Summa Doctrinae de Foedere et Testamentis Die;* J. Calvin, *Commentary on Romans;* C. Hodge, *Commentary on I Corinthians;* A. A. Hodge, *Outlines of Theology;* L. Berkhof, *Manual of Reformed Doctrine;* J. W. Beardslee, *Reformed Dogmatics;* H. Heppe, *Reformed Dogmatics;* J. W. Baker, *Heinrich Bullinger and the Covenant.*

Feeling, Theology of. *See* Experience, Theology of.

Felix Culpa. *See* Fortunate Fall, The.

Fellowship. The basic meaning conveyed by the Greek term *koinōnia* is that of participation. Both fellowship and communion, as translations of this term, are to be understood in this light. There is normally no sense of abstraction in the use of the word, in either noun or verb form, but rather that of actual participation in that to which the term refers. It is striking that the noun does not appear in the Gospels. Perhaps the sense conveyed by the early church's use of the term is that which was only appropriate in the close-knit fellowship of its Spirit-filled membership. The verb form appears only twice in the Gospels, where it has no connotation of anything uniquely Christian (Matt. 23:30; Luke 5:10).

The sense of sharing and self-sacrifice that is inherent in the word is clearly evident in those references to financial support in the early church as *koinōnia* (Rom. 12:13; 15:26; Gal. 6:6; Phil. 4:15 verb; II Cor. 8:4; 9:13; Heb. 13:16 noun). It is clear in these passages that Paul viewed the contribution for the needy Jewish Christians in Jerusalem, taken up from the poverty-stricken Gentile Christians in the hellenistic world, as the ultimate expression of fellowship among Christian people. It was more than simple sharing of material possessions by those taught with their teachers. For Paul it was a theological expression of the validity of his work among Gentiles, a sure sign that they had been completely accepted into God's work among the Jews. Friendship is a supreme expression of fellowship. The early church maintained this fellowship daily (Acts 2:42), as is evidenced in its communalism described in Acts 4 and 5.

But just as one may participate in wholesome activities with a fellow human being, he may also have fellowship with another's sins (I Tim. 5:22), another's wickedness (II John 11), and even with demons (I Cor. 10:16). When this happens, it is a sure sign that Christ is not dwelling in the heart of the believer; light and darkness do not have fellowship with one another, just as Christ has no fellowship with Belial (II Cor. 6:14). The true believer has fellowship in (i.e., participates in the implications of) the sufferings of Christ (Phil. 3:10; I Pet. 4:13), the sufferings of the apostles (II Cor. 1:7), and the sufferings of his fellow man (Heb. 10:33).

The unity in the fellowship of the early church was not based upon uniformity of thought and practice, except where limits of immorality or rejection of the confession of Christ were involved. The capacity to fellowship with one with whom there were disagreements extended beyond the corporate church into the home itself. A believing wife was exhorted by Paul to remain married to an unbelieving husband as long as he was content to dwell with her, and likewise husband with wife (I Cor. 7:12–16).

There is a sense in which the Lord's Supper constitutes a fellowship or participation in the blood and body of Christ (I Cor. 10:16). This is perhaps one of the meanings of the fellowship of the Spirit (II Cor. 13:14; Phil. 2:1) and one of the ways we become partakers (*koinōnia*) of the divine nature (II Pet. 1:4) and of the glory that is to be revealed (I Pet. 5:1). The communion between man and God in the eating of the Supper was probably based less on sacramental presuppositions than on the cultural/theological implications inherent in the experience of Jew and Gentile, male and female, slave and free (Gal. 3:28) sitting down together to eat and drink with him in his kingdom (Mark 14:25; Luke 22:30).

J. R. McRay

Bibliography. F. Hauck, *TDNT,* III, 804ff.; J. Eichler and J. Schattenmann, *NIDNTT,* I, 635ff.; G. W. H. Lampe, *IDB,* I, 664ff.

Festivals. *See* Feasts and Festivals, Old Testament; Christian Year.

Fideism. A theological term coined at the turn of the century by Protestant modernists in Paris

(Menegoz, Sabatier) to describe their own thought, but since used pejoratively to attack various strands of Christian "irrationalism." Fideists, following Kant (who argued that reason cannot prove religious truth), are said to base their understanding of the Christian faith upon religious experience alone, understanding reason to be incapable of establishing either faith's certitude or credibility. Among others, Luther, Kierkegaard, Van Til, Schleiermacher, and Barth have been accused of fideism. The term, however, is used too imprecisely to be of much value. Certainly none of these theologians would deny the use of reason altogether. If helpful at all, the term functions to describe an excessive emphasis upon the subjective dimensions of Christianity. R. K. JOHNSTON

See also EXPERIENCE, THEOLOGY OF.

Filioque. The term means "and from the Son" and refers to the phrase in the Western version of the Nicene Creed which says that the Holy Spirit proceeds from the Father and the Son. Originally this was not in the confessions agreed to at Nicaea (325) and Constantinople (381). It seems to have been first inserted at the local Council of Toledo (589) and in spite of opposition gradually established itself in the West, being officially endorsed in 1017. Photius of Constantinople denounced it in the ninth century, and it formed the main doctrinal issue in the rupture between East and West in 1054. An attempted compromise at Florence in 1439 came to nothing. Among the fathers Hilary, Jerome, Ambrose, Augustine, Epiphanius, and Cyril of Alexandria may be cited in its favor; Theodore of Mopsuestia and Theodoret against it; with the Cappadocians occupying the middle ground of "from the Father through the Son."

On the Eastern side two points may be made. First, the relevant verse in John (15:26) speaks only of a proceeding from the Father. Second, the addition never had ecumenical approval. Two points may also be made for the *filioque.* First, it safeguards the vital Nicene truth that the Son is consubstantial with the Father. Second, the Son as well as the Father sends the Spirit in John 15:26, and by analogy with this relationship to us we are justified in inferring that the Spirit proceeds from both Father and Son in the intratrinitarian relationship. Not to say this is to divorce the Spirit from the Son in contradiction of the passages that speak of him as the Spirit of Christ (cf. Rom. 8:9; Gal. 4:6). G. W. BROMILEY

Bibliography. K. Barth, *Church Dogmatics* I/1 §12,2; J. N. D. Kelly, *Early Christian Doctrines;* H. Thielicke, *The Evangelical Faith,* II, 181ff.; H. B. Swete, *History of the Doctrine of the Procession of the Holy Spirit.*

Final State. The theological term used for the two eternal destinies of heaven and hell. Jesus himself spoke often of both these eternal states, sometimes together: "And these will go away into eternal damnation, but the righteous into eternal life" (Matt. 25:46 NASB).

The OT is not so explicit in its teaching concerning eternal punishment as the final state of the wicked as is the NT. In at least one OT passage it is clearly taught: "And many of those who sleep in the dust of the ground will awake, these to everlasting life, but the others to disgrace *and* everlasting contempt" (Dan. 12:2).

Although it is not easy to conceive of a final state of punishment, this eternal state is clearly the teaching of Scripture, especially of the NT. The NT does not teach either universalism or the annihilation of the impenitent. It teaches instead that after a "great white throne judgment," everyone will be ushered into one of two final states: eternal heaven or eternal hell: "And I saw a great white throne and Him who sat upon it.... And I saw the dead, the great and the small, standing before the throne ... and the dead were judged.... And if anyone's name was not found written in the book of life, he was thrown into the lake of fire" (Rev. 20:11–15; see also Luke 16:26; Matt. 25:41, 46). And Paul said, "And these will pay the penalty of eternal destruction, away from the presence of the Lord and from the glory of His power" (II Thess. 1:9). J. K. GRIDER

See also HEAVEN; HELL; JUDGMENT; JUDGMENT SEAT.

Finney, Charles Grandison (1792–1875). Between 1824 and 1832 Finney established the modern forms and methods of revivalism in America; he then spent the last forty years of his life constructing a theology of revival and Christian life.

Raised and educated in upstate New York, he settled down as a lawyer in Adams, New York, in 1820. The next year an intense experience of religious conversion induced him to prepare for the ministry of the church. He then studied under the local Presbyterian pastor in Adams and received ordination in the Oneida Presbytery (1824). For the next eight years he led revival meetings in upper New York state and in major cities from Wilmington to Boston, including New York City. Next (1832–36) came the pastorate of Chatham Street Chapel (Presbyterian) in New York City, where he initiated his pattern of lawyerlike theological lectures. He became professor at what was soon called Oberlin College in Ohio (1836) and, as he developed his belief in "Christian perfection," became a Congregational minister. He remained at Oberlin until his death, serving as the second president (1851–66). He conducted a few revivals in the 1840s and 1850s, including one tour in Great Britain in 1859/60.

His *Lectures on Revival* (1835) sought to preach a "right view of both classes of truths," namely, God's sovereignty and free human agency. He detailed the means he believed God had established for humans to promote revival among both "backslidden Christians" and "unconverted sinners." Christians needed to have "a burning love for souls," to "grow in grace," and to ask sinners to "give their hearts to God." He expected revival to sweep America, bringing progress and social reforms—democracy, abolition of slavery, temperance, education, eschewing of luxury and fashionable display. In his *Letters on Revival* (1845) he confessed he had been too optimistic. He nonetheless wished to use Oberlin to prepare "a new race of revival ministers" and, as he explained in *Lectures to Professing Christians* (1837) and later writings, to awaken people to the attainable duty of practicing Christian perfection as commanded by Matt. 5:48. C. T. McIntire

See also Oberlin Theology; Revivalism.

Bibliography. C. G. Finney, *Lectures on Revivals of Religion;* W. G. McLoughlin, *Modern Revivalism: Finney to Billy Graham;* W. R. Cross, *The Burned Over District: Enthusiastic Religion in Western New York, 1800–1850;* T. Smith, "The Doctrine of Sanctifying Christ: Charles G. Finney's Synthesis of Wesleyan and Covenant Theology," *WITJ* 13:92–113.

Fire, Lake of. *See* Lake of Fire.

Firstborn. Primogeniture, the exclusive right of inheritance belonging to the firstborn, is traceable back to patriarchal times. Ishmael, though the eldest son of Abraham, was not accounted a firstborn because his mother was a slave (Gen. 21:10). Esau bartered his birthright and thereby opened himself to the charge of profanity, for he had spurned his right of inheritance (Gen. 25:33).

The idea of firstborn in the NT is indicated by *prōtotokos,* which occurs eight times, most of them referring to Christ, sometimes historically, sometimes figuratively. That the term is a messianic title is suggested by the Greek of Ps. 89:27. The NT alludes to Christ as the firstborn in three aspects. (1) In Col. 1:15 he is said to be the "firstborn of all creation," and Heb. 1:6 also describes him by this word. The Arians used these passages as evidence that our Lord was a created being, but the proper understanding is implied by the context in Colossians, viz., that it refers to the preincarnate Christ. Moreover, the term declares Christ to be the Lord of creation, for as the firstborn he is the heir of the created order. (2) Col. 1:18 and Rev. 1:5 use firstborn in a sense similar to the first fruits of I Cor. 15:20. Christ is the firstborn from the dead because he was the first to be raised. (3) Rom. 8:29 teaches that Christ is the "firstborn among many brethren," which affirms that believers have joined the family of which Christ is the eldest Son. Heb. 12:23 projects the idea so that all who believe are given the status of firstborn sons and therefore heirs of God. D. H. Wallace

Bibliography. W. Michaelis, *TDNT,* VI, 871ff.; K. H. Bartels, *NIDNTT,* II, 667ff.

First Day of the Week. *See* Lord's Day.

First Resurrection. *See* Resurrection of the Dead.

Fixed Feast. A fixed feast differs from a movable feast within the various types of feasts celebrated in the Christian year. Easter is a movable feast because its historical development states that it may appear on various dates during the year. Christmas is a fixed feast because its historical development states that it must fall every year on December 25. T. J. German

See also Movable Feasts; Christian Year.

Bibliography. N. M. Denis-Boulet, *The Christian Calendar.*

Flacius, Matthias (1520–1575). Lutheran theologian born in the Adriatic peninsula of Istria, whose Croatian name of Vlacic was Latinized as Flacius Illyricus was added to indicate his homeland, resulting in his being commonly called Matthias Flacius Illyricus. He studied with humanistic scholars in Venice (1536–39), and later through the influence of his uncle he attended the universities of Basel, Tübingen, and Wittenberg. While studying at Wittenberg he was converted to evangelical doctrine and subsequently became a professor at the institution (1544) lecturing on Hebrew, Aristotle, and the Scriptures. His opposition to the Augsburg Interim led him to leave Wittenberg and settle at the University of Jena. Here he helped to establish a center of conservative Lutheran doctrine.

Brilliant and controversial, Flacius became involved in many of the struggles that plagued later sixteenth century Lutheranism. These included the adiaphoristic, the majoristic, and the synergistic controversies. Flacius and his supporters founded the Gnesio-Lutheran ("true Lutheran") faction, which attacked Melanchthon and his followers for being too conciliatory toward Roman Catholicism and proceeded to develop a Lutheran teaching not only in distinction from Catholicism but also in opposition to the doctrine of the more moderate Lutherans (the Philippists). In the most basic of these struggles, the adiaphoristic controversy, Flacius condemned his opponents for making concessions to Catholicism in the matter of church ceremonies. The "true Lutheran" view, he believed, held that nothing is an adiaphoron (a matter of indifference) if it touches on any aspect of Christian truth. By 1561 his constant polemics led to his dismissal from Jena. Subsequently he lived in Regensburg, Antwerp, Strasbourg, and Frankfurt.

In addition to his personal role in developing the Lutheran position, Flacius is well known for his books. These include the *Clavis,* or key to the Scriptures, which sets forth his hermeneutical principles, and a history of the church, the *Magdeburg Centuries.* The latter work, written by Flacius and six other Lutheran scholars, is a monumental attempt to present in thirteen volumes the story of the Christian church to the year 1308. The work is highly polemical, viewing history as a struggle between God and Satan in which the pope and the Roman Church represent Satan's power on earth. The biased tone of these volumes led to an impassioned response from Cesare Baronius entitled the *Annales ecclesiastici* (1588–1607). R. G. Clouse

See also Adiaphora, Adiaphorists; Majoristic Controversy; Synergism; Monergism; Melanchthon, Philipp.

Bibliography. H. W. Reimann, "Matthias Flacius Illyricus," *CTM* 35:69–93.

Flesh. Certain obvious meanings, literal and figurative, are expressed throughout the Bible by the word "flesh." The words *šĕʾēr* and *bāśār* in the OT, and *sarx* in the NT, describe the vehicle and circumstances of man's physical life in this world. Thus, in Phil. 1:22–24 Paul contrasts abiding "in the flesh" with departing to be "with Christ." Regularly, "flesh" is used along with "bones," "blood," or "body" (e.g., Prov. 5:11; I Cor. 15:50) to isolate for inspection the physical aspect of man's nature. From its use for the outer covering of the body (Gen. 2:21), there arose a figurative sense of "outward appearance," "worldly standards" (I Cor. 1:26; Eph. 2:11). More important is the recognition of the contrast between two modes of being signified by the words "flesh" and "spirit" (Isa. 31:3; Jer. 17:5; John 1:13). By comparison with God, mankind is seen as sharing in a common flesh, and the expression "all flesh" customarily acknowledges the solidarity of the race (Gen. 6:12; Matt. 24:22; I Pet. 1:24). It is no distance from this to the use of "flesh" to mean "next of kin" (Lev. 18:12) or, more remotely, "human ancestry" (Rom. 4:1).

In the OT. Here the first thing which becomes clear from the use of the word "flesh" is the outright opposition to anything that savors of Gnosticism. While there is general recognition that man is psychical as well as physical—Ps. 63:1 shows man, in both aspects, longing for God—there is total absence of any suggestion that these are separable as far as a doctrine of human nature is concerned, or that "flesh" is lower in the scale of personality than "spirit." In fact, man's psychical capacities are more often than not instanced by reference to physical organs. Thus, Ps. 73:26 speaks of the end of earthly life and hope as the failing of "flesh" and "heart," and the corresponding use of "reins" or "bowels" is too well known to need exemplification. The unity of human personality in its psychophysical nature could not be seen more clearly than by recalling that, according to the Bible, the act of sexual intercourse is spoken of as "knowing" (Gen. 4:1), and the result of that act is that "they shall be one flesh" (Gen. 2:24; Matt. 19:5; I Cor. 6:16). "To know" is not here used euphemistically but literally. Marriage, in God's plan, is intended to bring two people into the deepest and most intimate knowledge of each other. This ultimate interpenetration of personalities is called becoming "one flesh."

While there is nothing in the OT corresponding to the NT view of the "flesh" as the central and dynamic principle of fallen humanity, yet the OT, with its emphasis on man's "flesh-personality," offers the background against which the NT can paint its picture of human nature held in thrall by a dynamism which has captured the citadel of its essential unity. This, in turn, illuminates the constantly fleshly terms in which the holy life is expressed. In Gen. 17:13 God says that his covenant is "in your flesh," and the prophets (e.g., Jer. 4:4) use the same symbol of circumcision to express a consecrated return to God. There can be no salvation which is not a salvation of "flesh," and when Ezekiel looks forward to God's act of regeneration, he declares that God will "take away the stony heart out of your flesh, and will give you an heart of flesh" (36:26). Herein he implies what Paul states: that the flesh has become perverted, and that God plans for humanity that which we have learned to call the "resurrection of the body."

In the NT. The NT doctrine of the flesh is chiefly but not exclusively Pauline. The "flesh" is a dynamic principle of sinfulness (Gal. 5:17; Jude 23). The unregenerate are "sinful flesh" (Rom. 8:3); they are "after the flesh" (Rom. 8:5). In them the flesh, with its "passions and lusts" (Gal. 5:24), works "death" (Rom. 7:5). The flesh, producing "works" (Gal. 5:19) in those who live "after the flesh" (Rom. 8:12), is characterized by "lust" (I John 2:16; Gal. 5:16; I Pet. 4:2; II Pet. 2:10), which enslaves the bodily members and also dominates the mind (Eph. 2:3), so that there is a complete mental affiliation called "the mind of the flesh" (Rom. 8:5, 7). Under these circumstances life is given to fleshly satisfactions (Col. 2:23) and is described as "sowing unto the flesh," whence is reaped a harvest of fleshly corruption (Gal. 6:8). Such people are dominated by "sinful passions" (Rom. 7:5), unable to obey God's law (Rom. 8:3) or to please God (Rom. 8:8). Even their religious practice is astray from God's will because of fleshly thinking (Col. 2:18). They are "children of wrath" (Eph. 2:3).

Very different are those who have experienced God's regeneration. They remain "in" the flesh, but they are no longer "after" the flesh (II Cor. 10:3; Gal. 2:20). They need to be watchful. For the fact of the flesh means dullness of spiritual perception (Rom. 6:19), and though the Christian need pay none of the claims of the flesh (Rom. 8:12), yet he must remember that in his flesh there is nothing good (Rom. 7:18), and that if he should repose his trust there again (Phil. 3:3; Gal. 3:3) he would lapse into bondage (Rom. 7:25). He has become the recipient of a new principle of life sufficient to oust the old principle of death (Rom. 8:4, 9, 13; Gal. 5:16–17), "the life of Christ" in his "death-bound body" (II Cor. 4:10–11).

We have thus traced the notion of the flesh from its pure conception in the Creator's plan to the depths of its self-wrought corruption and to the re-creation in Christ. It remains to show how the work of Christ is expressed in the same terminology. Here also Christ redeemed us from the curse by becoming the curse himself: "The Word became flesh" (John 1:14). The sinlessness of Jesus is preserved by the careful statement that God sent his Son "in the likeness of sinful flesh" (Rom. 8:3; cf. Heb. 4:15), and the blessed truth is declared that the Son became one with us at the point of our need (Heb. 2:14) in order to deal with sin at the point of its strength (see Rom. 8:3, ERV). "Flesh" is constantly used to teach the genuine manhood of the Savior (Rom. 1:4; 9:5; I Tim. 3:16; Heb. 5:7). Yet it is not his flesh as displayed in its perfection, but his flesh as "given" (John 6:51–56) which avails for the life of the world. It was by his being made "an offering for sin" that he condemned sin in his flesh (Rom. 8:3, ERV). The flesh is the sphere and instrument of his redeeming work (Col. 1:22; I Pet. 3:18; 4:1). This was the sublime purpose of the incarnation (Heb. 10:5–20). He took flesh in order that in and by his flesh he might loose us from the bondage of "the flesh" and fulfill the prophecy by making us "epistles of Christ . . . written not with ink, but with the Spirit of the living God; not in tables of stone, but in tables that are hearts of flesh" (II Cor. 3:3; Ezek. 36:26). J. A. MOTYER

See also MAN, DOCTRINE OF; SIN.

Bibliography. O. Cullmann, *Immortality of the Soul or Resurrection of the Dead?* W. D. Davies, *Paul and Rabbinic Judaism;* W. P. Dickson, *St. Paul's Use of the Terms Flesh and Spirit;* A. C. Thiselton, *NIDNTT,* I, 671ff.; R. Jewett, *Paul's Anthropological Terms;* E. Schweizer *et al., TDNT,* VII, 98ff.; W. Barclay, *Flesh and Spirit;* W. G. Kümmel, *Man in the NT;* J. A. T. Robinson, *The Body;* W. D. Stacey, *The Pauline View of Man.*

Flood, The. The biblical flood is an outstanding example of the sudden deluges which, according to archaeological excavations, plagued ancient Mesopotamia. A deluge is a sudden, heavy, extensive, and devastating deposit of water. Such a flood is usually a combination of heavy rain and overflowing rivers, but sometimes tidal waves resulting from earthquakes are the main factor. In Mesopotamia violent thunderstorms at the northern ends of the Tigris and Euphrates caused enormous amounts of water to build up in the rivers and flood the lower plains. A high water table in the area slowed the dispersal of the deluge, which was often in evidence many hours after the original storm had passed.

Many ancient cultures have preserved traditions of a devastating flood that exterminated life over a wide area, but whether these describe separate incidents or are diverse accounts of one original deluge is hard to determine. Excavations in Mesopotamia have uncovered levels of water-laid clay at different sites, including an eight-foot-thick layer at Ur. Unfortunately none of these agrees in date with the others, making it difficult to identify a specific deposit with the Genesis flood.

Noah's deluge is a genuine historical event of catastrophic proportions, which involved tidal waves as well as heavy rain (Gen. 7:11) and perhaps underground springs. From southern Mesopotamia the flood stretched northward to the mountains of Urartu (Ararat), the peaks of which were covered. All living things died, and the storm only began to diminish after 150 days, the earth finally drying out 371 days from the beginning of the storms.

The extent of the flood has aroused much debate. The word translated "earth" can also mean a country, and "heaven" can describe the amount of sky visible within one's own horizon (I Kings 18:45). While some arguments may suggest a limited flood, the fact that the mountains were submerged implies a more extended one (Gen. 7:19–20). Genesis thus supports arguments for both a local and a universal deluge, with traditional biblical teaching favoring the latter and regarding the flood as a punishment for unrepented wickedness (Gen. 6:5).

Ancient wooden fragments recovered from Mount Ararat have been supposed to comprise remains of Noah's ark, but the exact age of the material is debatable, and more definite evidence will be necessary before positive identification can be made. Adherents to a "young earth" theory date the flood about 2500 B.C., but others assign greater antiquity to it. R. K. HARRISON

Bibliography. H. M. Morris and J. C. Whitcomb, Jr., *The Genesis Flood;* F. A. Filby, *The Flood Reconsidered;* H. F. Vos, *ISBE* (rev.), II, 316–21.

Followers of the Way. *See* CHRISTIANS, NAMES OF.

Foot Washing. A religious act in some segments of the Christian church based upon the performance and command of Jesus at the Last Supper. However, the wearing of open sandals, the dry climate, and dusty roads made foot washing upon entering a home a familiar practice in Eastern hospitality. The custom was at least as early as Abraham (Gen. 18:4; 19:2), and continued in the nation of Israel (Judg. 19:21). Usually it was performed by the person himself, but at times by a servant. For the host to perform it was an unusual favor (I Sam. 25:41). Failure to provide such amenities was a discourtesy (Luke 7:44).

The practice was given special prominence by Jesus when he washed his disciples' feet (John 13:1–20). His statement that the disciples "ought to wash one another's feet" (John 13:14) gave added importance to the act.

While recognizing that Jesus' performance utilized the common custom, most interpreters understand that the explanation to Peter, "What I do thou knowest not now" (John 13:7), reflected more than a forgotten courtesy. Jesus' washing of feet is usually explained as teaching the need for humility in the light of the disciples' obvious lack of self-abasement in the upper room (Luke 22:24–30). Yet the point of the matter lay elsewhere, for Jesus said that if he did not do so, Peter, not Jesus, would be the one deficient (John 13:8).

Spiritual cleansing was the primary emphasis in the act. Lack of cleansing was stated regarding Judas (John 13:10–11). All except Judas had been "bathed" (*leloumenos*—complete bath), but they still needed their feet washed (*nipsasthai*—partial washing). The complete bath represented salvation as symbolized by baptism. The washing of the feet symbolized the need that believers have for repeated cleansing from defilement through contact with a sinful world.

Many Christians have understood Jesus to have intended this act to be perpetuated on the basis of John 13:14–15. The practice of the pedilavium may be seen in the early church from I Tim. 5:10 and from patristic notices in Tertullian (*De Corona* 8) and Athanasius (*Canon 66*). The Synod of Toledo (694) prescribed it. It has been observed by Roman and Greek churches and in such Protestant groups as Brethren, Mennonites, Waldensians, Winebrennarians, and some Baptists. H. A. KENT, JR.

Bibliography. P. Tschackert, *SHERK*, IV, 339–40; *MSt*, III, 615–16; M. H. Shepherd, Jr., *IDB*, II, 308; R. D. Culver, *ZPEB*, II, 588; H. A. Hoyt, *This Do in Remembrance of Me;* J. R. Shultz, *The Soul of the Symbols.*

Foreknowledge. Scripture uses the term "foreknow" for God's prescience or foresight concerning future events. Foreknowledge is thus an aspect of God's omniscience. All things, past, present, and future, external and internal, material, intellectual, and spiritual, are open to God. The Lord knows all things (I Sam. 2:3) or everything (I John 3:20). All creatures are open to his eyes (Heb. 4:13). Israel is not hid from him (Hos. 5:3). He knows every secret sin (Ps. 90:8). His knowledge is too wonderful for us, encompassing words and thoughts and our total being (Ps. 139). He knows all the ways of all his creatures; not a sparrow falls to the ground without him (Matt. 10:29). He notes our tossings (Ps. 56:8). He knows the way of the righteous (Ps. 1:6) and is not ignorant, uncaring, or impotent when the wicked afflict his people (Ps. 94:5ff.). His knowledge is complete, allowing for no confusion, obscurity, deficiency, or error. It is like the full light of day: God is light and in him is no darkness (I John 1:5).

Omniscience naturally includes prescience. God does not just know what is happening or has already happened. He knows what is still to happen. This comes out most plainly in Isa. 40ff. God boldly announces the fall of Babylon and the liberation of his people. He challenges all comers to show comparable knowledge: "Tell us what is to come hereafter" (41:23); "New things I now declare; before they spring forth I tell you of them" (42:9). Nor is God's foreknowledge displayed only here; it underlies the element of foretelling in all prophecy. Micaiah tells Ahab his end (I Kings 22:13–24). Elisha announces the relief of Samaria (II Kings 7). Jeremiah and Ezekiel declare the ineluctability of the fall of Jerusalem. Daniel offers visions of complex future events (11:2ff.). Details about the coming Messiah include his Davidic descent (Isa. 11:1), his birth at Bethlehem (Mic. 5:2), his death with the wicked and burial among the rich (Isa. 53:9). It is true that full knowledge of past and present, too, belongs to God alone, but perfect knowledge of the future is a particular mark of deity which arrogant humanity, having no claim to such knowledge, consistently denies or disparages—e.g., in its handling of the predictive element in Scripture.

Foreknowledge stands in obvious relation to the divine eternity. God is the "high and lofty One who inhabits eternity" (Isa. 57:15). "A thousand years in his sight are but as yesterday when it is past" (Ps. 90:4, cf. II Pet. 3:8). Past, present, and future are all present to God. He sees the end from the beginning and the beginning at the end. Being part of creation, time does not limit or condition God. As Lord of time he does not live or act in abstraction from it. He eternally "comprehends" it, being before, with, and after it. Having total knowledge of all that has been and is, he also has total knowledge of all that will be.

God's foreknowledge stands related to his will and power. What he knows, he does not know merely as information. He is no mere spectator. What he foreknows he ordains. He wills it. In his challenge to the gods in Isa. 40ff. he can "declare the end from the beginning, . . . things not yet done," because "my counsel shall stand, and I will accomplish all my purpose" (46:10). Nor does he know merely because he wills. He knows because, willing, he has the power to do his will. "I have spoken, and I will bring it to pass" (46:11); "I work and who can hinder it?" (43:13).

By reason of the totality of will and power in God's prescience, the "pre" in the word has more than temporal meaning. With his prior knowledge of things God is the presupposition of their being. As Augustine says, we know things because they are, but things are because God knows them. All that exists does so first and eternally in God's knowledge. We must not press this to the point of saying that his foreknowledge is the cause of all things. God knows what is possible as well as actual, but did not cause it. He also knows the devil and sin, but plainly is not their cause. Furthermore, he knows the contingent decisions of human wills but causes them only insofar as they have their origin in him. Prescience is the presupposition of all things as the prescience of the God of will and power.

In regard to the decisions of human wills, a collision seems to arise between divine foreknowledge and human freedom. God plainly foreknows and foreordains everything. Nothing outside him restricts or conditions his own freedom. He is always free to be himself and to will and act as such. This rules out pantheism, dualism, and every form of Pelagianism. Nevertheless, Scripture no less plainly teaches human responsibility in moral decision (cf. Acts 4:27–28; Eph. 1:11; Rom. 8:29–30 for divine sovereignty; Deut. 30:19; I Kings 18:21 for human responsibility). Divine foreknowledge must not be confused with determinism or fatalism, difficult though the reconciling of prescience and human choice might be.

The task of putting the two biblical truths together has led on the one hand to some valid and important distinctions. Thus God's necessary knowledge of himself is distinguished from his free knowledge of creatures. His speculative or contemplative knowledge is distinguished from his practical or active knowledge. His knowledge of possibility is distinguished from his knowledge of actuality. His approving knowledge of good is distinguished from his disapproving knowledge of evil (cf. the "I never knew you" of Matt. 7:23). All things are not known to God in the same way.

Some more dubious differentiations have arisen on the other hand. Thus Molina postulated a "middle" knowledge between God's necessary and free knowledge—i.e., a knowledge of what is only conditionally future, of what might have happened, or might happen, given certain contingencies, decisions, or circumstances (cf. I Sam. 23:11–12; Matt. 11:21–22). Arminius, with a special focus on predestination, separated God's foreknowledge from his foreordination. God foreordains the salvation of all those who, freed by his Spirit, trust in Christ, and he foreknows who will make this decision and stick to it. On this view neither foreordination nor foreknowledge affects the individual decision but at the cost of breaking the chain of Rom. 8:29–30, robbing foreordination of its point, and separating the knowledge of God from his will and power.

Perhaps a more fruitful approach is from the recognition that, whether in providence or predestination, divine prescience means that God is in fact the presupposition of all things, including our wills, choices, and decisions. Nothing we do can inform or surprise him or impose conditions on him. He knows us omnipotently as our Creator and Lord. Yet he does not destroy us with this knowledge, but with it originates and guarantees our authentic freedom. Only as sinners opposing God's will do we experience his foreknowledge as burden and bondage. True freedom, however, does not imply the possibility of defying God but of serving him. We are foreknown and foreordained in the real self-determination which sees no problem in its being self-determination in and under the divine prescience.

G. W. Bromiley

See also Elect, Election; Scientia Media.

Bibliography. K. Barth, *Church Dogmatics* II/1, 552ff., 558ff.; R. Bultmann, *TDNT*, I, 689ff., 515–16.

Foreordination. *See* Predestination.

Forgiveness. Seven words in Scripture denote the idea of forgiveness: three in Hebrew and four in Greek. In the Hebrew OT they are *kipper*, "to cover"; *nāśā'*, "to bear"—take away [guilt]; *sālaḥ*, "to pardon." *Nāśā'* is used of both divine forgiveness and human forgiveness. The other two are used only of divine forgiveness.

In the Greek NT the words for forgiveness are *apolyein*, *charizesthai*, *aphesis*, and *paresis*. *Apolyein* is found numerous times as "to put away," e.g., a wife (Matt. 5:31), but only once to signify forgiveness (Luke 6:37). *Paresis* is found only once (Rom. 3:25) and suggests "putting aside" or "disregarding." In order for the righteous God to do this, for "sins previously committed," Christ Jesus had to be "displayed publicly as a propitiation" (Rom. 3:25 NASB). *Charizesthai* is used only by Luke (Luke 7:21; Acts 3:14; etc.) and Paul, and only by the latter in the sense of "to forgive sins" (II Cor. 2:7; Eph. 4:32; Col. 2:13; 3:13; etc.). It especially expresses the graciousness of God's forgiveness. Thus its use in connection with Christ's bestowing sight (Luke 7:21) and in Paul's thought that God freely gives us "all things" (Rom. 8:32).

The most common NT word for forgiveness is *aphesis*. This noun is found fifteen times and is generally translated "forgiveness" (e.g., Matt. 26:28 RSV, NASB, NIV). It conveys the idea of "sending away" or "letting go." The verb with the same meaning is found about forty times.

No book of religion except the Bible teaches that God completely forgives sin, but there it is frequently taught, for example, "I will heal their waywardness, I will love them freely" (Hos. 14:4 NIV); "God for Christ's sake hath forgiven you [*echarisato*, graciously forgiven]" (Eph. 4:32 AV); "Their sins and iniquities will I remember no more" (Heb. 10:17). The initiative of this forgiveness is with God, especially in Paul's use of *charizesthai* (II Cor. 12:13; Col. 2:13). It is a ready forgiveness, as is shown in the prodigal son or "gracious father" parable (Luke 15:11–32).

There is only one sin for which the Father does not promise forgiveness: blasphemy against the Holy Spirit (Mark 3:29; Matt. 12:32). The contexts seem to suggest that this sin is attributing to unclean spirits the work of the Holy Spirit, but many interpreters (including Augustine) have understood it to include a deliberate persistence in such evil. This sin is also considered by some to be the unforgiving spirit (see Matt. 18:34–35). It might be the same as the "sin unto death" of I John 5:16.

There are to be no limitations whatever to the forgiveness of one's fellows. In Luke 17:4 it is to be "seven times in a day," and until "seventy times seven" in Matt. 18:22, both of which probably signify limitlessness. It is to be an attitude of mind even before the offending party requests forgiveness, as is implied by Jesus' "unless you forgive your brother from your heart" (Matt. 18:35 NIV).

For us to receive forgiveness, repentance is necessary (Luke 17:3–4). For the holy God to extend forgiveness the shedding of blood (Heb. 9:22) until no life is left (Lev. 17:11) is prerequisite—ultimately, the once-for-all (Heb. 9:26) spilling of Christ's blood and his rising again (Rom. 4:25).

J. K. Grider

Bibliography. P. Lehmann, *Forgiveness;* H. R. Mackintosh, *The Christian Experience of Forgiveness;* E. B. Redlich, *The Forgiveness of Sins;* V. Taylor, *Forgiveness and Reconciliation.*

Form. The concept of form played an important role in Greek philosophy. In Plato it was the unchanging element in an object, considered apart from the changing manifestations of the object in sense experience.

Aristotle later took the view that, while there must be things other than sensible objects and these are universals, it does not follow that universals are forms and ideas in Plato's sense. The key to Aristotle's rejection of the Platonic forms lies in his doctrine of substance, where he distinguishes between primary substance, i.e., particular men, horses, and so on, and secondary substances, i.e., the species and genera to which the individuals belong.

Medieval thinkers distinguished several kinds of forms, the more important being (1) "substantial forms," which are the principles determining the primary matter of a particular nature; (2) "accidental forms," which determine substances to some accidental mode of being, e.g., whiteness or greatness; (3) "separated forms," which exist apart from matter, thus the angels and human souls after death.

In modern philosophy the conception of form is applied to the order of thought, insofar as it rests on the subjective structure of the human mind. Kant distinguishes between the two forms of perception, viz., space and time, and the forms of thought arranged in twelve "categories" of unity, plurality, totality, etc., which are valid *a priori.*

Form is also thought of today as synonymous with structure and contrasted with the formless and the structureless. Recently some have called for a new and unstructured kind of Christianity separate from the ecclesiastical tradition that came from the past. However, critics stress that the God of the Bible is also the God of Abraham, Moses, the apostles, and the whole postapostolic church; this is the overall form/structure which binds us all to Christ and his church universal.

M. H. MACDONALD

See also EXISTENCE; ESSENCE.

Bibliography. Plato, *Phaedo;* Aristotle, *Physics, Metaphysics, On the Ideas;* I. Kant, *Critique of Pure Reason;* J. R. W. Stott, *Basic Christianity* and *Balanced Christianity;* N. Wolterstorff, *On Universals: An Essay in Ontology.*

Formula of Concord. *See* CONCORD, FORMULA OF.

Fornication. In its more restricted sense fornication denotes voluntary sexual communion between an unmarried person and one of the opposite sex. In this sense the fornicators (*pornoi*) are distinguished from the adulterers (*moichoi*), as in I Cor. 6:9. In a wider sense *porneia* signifies unlawful cohabitation of either sex with a married person. In this meaning it is used interchangeably with *moicheia,* as in Matt. 5:32, where Christ says that anyone who divorces his wife except for *porneia* causes her to become the object of adultery (*moicheuthēnai*) since he who marries her commits adultery (*moichatai*). The same use of *porneia* in the sense of adultery (*moichatai*) is found in Matt. 19:9. In its widest sense *porneia* denotes immorality in general, or every kind of sexual transgression. In I Cor. 5:1 *porneia* is rightly translated in the RSV by "immorality," which term it properly uses also in I Cor. 5:11, where the word stands without any further modification (cf. 6:18). The plural "fornications" (*dia tas porneias*) is best taken in the sense of "temptations to immorality" (I Cor. 7:2; cf. RSV). While other sins must be overcome by spiritual crucifixion of the flesh (Gal. 5:24), the sin of immorality (*porneia*) is one from which the Christian must flee in order to keep pure (I Cor. 6:18). Since God's close relation to his people is regarded as a marriage bond (Eph. 5:23–27), all forms of apostasy are designated in Scripture as adultery, and this indeed very fittingly, as the pagan cults were usually connected with immorality (Hos. 6:10; Jer. 3:2, 9; Rev. 2:21; 19:2). The use of the verb *porneuein* and of the noun *pornos* (and *pornē*) is similar to that of the abstract *porneia.* It proves the greatness of divine grace in Christ Jesus that our Lord permitted Rahab (Heb. 11:31; Matt. 1:5) and other fornicators to be numbered in his genealogy.

J. T. MUELLER

See also ADULTERY.

Bibliography. H. Reisser, *NIDNTT,* I, 497ff.

Forsyth, Peter Taylor (1848–1921). Evangelical theologian hailed as a modern prophet by both his admirers and critics. Born in Aberdeen, Scotland, Forsyth entered Aberdeen University in 1864, graduating with first class honors in classics. He spent a semester at the University of Göttingen in 1870 studying under Albrecht Ritschl. Having been called to the Congregational church in Shipley, Yorkshire, he was ordained in 1876. In 1904 he became chairman of the Congregational Union of England and Wales. He spent his last twenty years as principal of Hackney College, a Congregational theological seminary. In 1907 he gave the Lyman Beecher lectures at Yale University.

Forsyth sought to relate the gospel to the modern mind without surrendering its unique claims. In contrast to much traditionalist orthodoxy he accepted the findings of historical criticism, but unlike liberal theology he believed that criticism must be subjected to the scrutiny of a higher norm—the gospel. Against the more conservative evangelicals he contended that there was a need for a fresh restatement of the biblical faith, but he had marked reservations concerning apologetics, which seeks to build on a criterion held in common with unbelief. He based his theology on Holy Scripture but appealed always to the pivotal center of Scripture—the gospel of redeeming grace.

In Forsyth's view the heart of evangelical faith lies in the message of the cross. Soteriology was even more important for him than Christology, the atonement more crucial than the incarnation. He rejected the crude theories of the atonement fashionable in orthodox circles of his time in which Jesus was portrayed as being punished by an angry God. The truth of the atonement is that Cod himself in the person of his Son entered into our sufferings, identifying himself with our pain and anguish. Christ's confession of the holiness of the Father is the ground of forgiveness and the new life in Christ. Forsyth saw the cross of Christ as the creative moral crisis of history, the point where divinity and humanity, time and eternity, judgment and grace met for a new creation.

This Christocentric stance led Forsyth to combat humanitarianism, in which human virtue was praised over divine grace, as well as an evolutionary naturalism in which man's ascent to divinity overshadowed God's descent to sinful humanity in Jesus Christ. Forsyth was especially critical of the liberal theology that portrayed God exclusively as love. In his view love, grace, and judgment are all to be seen as aspects of God's holiness.

Forsyth also pioneered in the area of spirituality. He declared that the best documents are human sacraments. It is holy souls who furnish the most potent argument for the gospel, apart from the gospel itself. Whereas Augustine had rediscovered the lost truth of salvation by grace and Luther justification by faith, the emphasis in our time should be justification by holiness (i.e., by the holy God) and for holiness (life in communion with God).

Yet Forsyth was highly critical of the often vague spirituality associated with a theology of experience. The gospel is not a projection of man's innate spirituality but a transforming reality that profoundly alters man's spiritual and ethical life. Our focus should not be on cultivating piety in order to raise ourselves to divinity; instead, we should acquaint ourselves with God's saving work of redemption in Jesus Christ. Our spirituality should stress ethical obedience rather than detachment from the world for the purpose of inward purification.

Forsyth saw prayer not as meditation or contemplation on the ground of being but as supplication and intercession before a holy God. He made a prominent place for importunity in the life of prayer, even speaking of wrestling with God in prayer. He believed that God is glorified not only when we submit to his will but also when we resist his will in order to discover more fully his ultimate design for our lives.

Though warning against the idolatry of the preacher and calling for a rediscovery of the sacraments in both evangelical and liberal Protestantism, he nonetheless subordinated the sacraments to the proclaimed Word. He regarded the sacraments as the visible Word and saw them as channels and not merely symbols of grace. Yet he attacked the doctrine of baptismal regeneration and the traditional understanding of the Lord's Supper as a sacrifice. It is not the absence of the sacraments that damns but their contempt.

Forsyth is highly relevant for our time, when theological authority is being eroded and when the battle for social justice tends to overshadow the hope for the righteousness of the kingdom of God. Forsyth is widely regarded as a forerunner of the neo-orthodoxy of Karl Barth and Emil Brunner.

D. G. Bloesch

Bibliography. R. M. Brown, *P. T. Forsyth: Prophet for Today;* S. J. Mikolaski, ed., *The Creative Theology of P. T. Forsyth;* D. G. Miller, B. Barr, and R. S. Paul, *P. T. Forsyth: The Man, The Preacher's Theologian, Prophet for the Twentieth Century;* J. H. Rogers, *The Theology of P. T. Forsyth;* A. M. Hunter, *P. T. Forsyth: Per Crucem ad Lucem;* G. C. Griffith, *The Theology of P. T. Forsyth;* W. L. Bradley, *P. T. Forsyth: The Man and His Work.*

Fortitude. *See* Cardinal Virtues, Seven.

Fortunate Fall, The. The concept of "fortunate fall" or *felix culpa* (happy crime) is an ancient one, rooted in early Christian liturgy, medieval and Reformed theology, and ultimately in the biblical text. It expresses the believer's confidence in God's beneficial control of evil. On the evening before the victorious celebration of Easter churches using the Roman Missal sang these words from the *Exsultet: O felix culpa, quae talem ac tantum meruit habere redemptorem!* ("O happy crime, which merited such and so great a Redeemer!") The author of these words is unknown, but they may go back as early as the fifth century. The same concept was expressed much later in the fifteenth century English carol, "Adam Lay Ybounden":

> Ne had the apple taken been,
> The apple taken been,
> Ne had never our lady
> A-been heavene queen.
>
> Blessed be the time
> That apple taken was.
> Therefore we moun singen
> Deo Gracias!

Augustine stated: "God judged it better to bring good out of evil than to suffer no evil to exist" (*Enchiridion* 8.27). The church's major theologians continued this insight down to the Reformation, which placed a renewed emphasis upon it. According to Musculus, "Through Christ we are more happily restored after the fall than we had been when created" (H. Heppe, *Reformed Dogmatics,* p. 304). The Reformed held that "God resolved . . . to use Adam's fall as a means to a new and higher revelation of His nature" (ibid., p. 371).

Similarly in Scripture, Joseph says: "Ye thought evil against me; but God meant it unto good" (Gen. 50:20). Paul affirms: "But where sin abounded, grace did much more abound" (Rom. 5:20), and "All things work together for good to them that love God" (Rom. 8:28). D. F. Kelly

See also Theodicy; Evil, Problem of; Fall of Man; Providence of God.

Fosdick, Harry Emerson (1878–1969). American Protestant minister and one of the most influential clergymen of the first half of the twentieth century, Fosdick was among the major popularizers of modern theological liberalism. Born in Buffalo, New York, the son and grandson of Baptist schoolteachers, he renounced his childhood evangelical faith in 1896 while an undergraduate at Colgate University after reading Andrew Dickson White's powerful attack on biblical Christianity entitled *A History of the Warfare of Science with Theology in Christendom.* This set Fosdick on the road which led him from what he called "scriptural obscurantism" to the theological liberalism that he eventually embraced.

Fosdick's professors at Colgate University and Union Theological Seminary (New York), where he earned his A.B. and B.D. degrees respectively in 1900 and 1904, convinced him that he need not give up his goal of the Christian ministry along with his evangelical theology. Instead, learned theologians like William Newton Clarke led Fosdick to embrace the new liberalism with its stress on the evolution of divine revelation and human goodness.

Finding the Baptists unfriendly toward his new theology, Fosdick was ordained by the Presbyterians in 1903. However, he took a Baptist pastorate in 1904 in Montclair, New Jersey. While there he was appointed professor of practical theology at Union Seminary, a post which he held from 1908 to 1946. From 1918 to 1924 he served as regular "guest minister" of the First Presbyterian Church in New York. In this position he became the lightning rod in the early years of the fundamentalist-modernist controversy when in 1922 he preached and later published an attack on the fundamentalists entitled "Shall the Fundamentalists Win?" In response, conservative Presbyterians and Baptists dubbed him "the Moses of modernism" and "the Jesse James of the theological world"—and in 1924 Fosdick left his guest pastorate under fire. However, his friend J. D. Rockefeller, Jr., offered Fosdick the pulpit of his own family's congregation, the Park Avenue Baptist Church in New York. Fosdick finally accepted only after Rockefeller agreed to build him a spacious new edifice and to change the membership requirements to make the church, in effect, interdenominational. Thus in 1926 Fosdick was installed as the pastor of what soon became the famed Riverside Church, which he served until his retirement in 1946. During that period he was the nation's most influential Protestant preacher.

Fosdick spent his last years writing and lecturing. In his autobiography, published in 1956, he expressed confidence that liberalism was the final and supreme expression of Christianity and that it would survive the criticisms of the neo-orthodox theologians. However, during the last decade of his life he became more conservative in his general outlook, stressed that he had always been a moderate "evangelical liberal," and searched the Bible once more for those spiritual verities which he was certain that it contained.

A dynamic preacher and a polished writer, Fosdick used his thirty books, his weekly radio ministry, and his popular pulpit to discredit traditional nineteenth century Protestantism with its emphasis on evangelism, its uncritical use of the Bible, and its lack of interest in scientific educational theory. In place of these he attempted to incorporate into Christian thinking biblical criticism, insights from the psychology of religion, the teachings of evolution, and the values expressed in modern political and social movements, while accenting the ethical rather than the doctrinal aspects of the Christian faith. Fosdick also stressed the personal peace and power of religion—as in his enormously popular *On Being a Real Person* (1943)—but always took care to keep his counsels within the parameters of Christian theology albeit in its liberal form. Moreover, he greatly influenced American preaching through his "problem-centered" homiletical style.

Like most theological liberals, Fosdick contributed little to a realistic understanding of institutional power, social structures, or human depravity. It appears that few of his works will withstand the critique of the neo-orthodox and conservative theologians or the test of time. Only his autobiography remains to provide an insightful link to that now bygone era when a dynamic liberalism was king of Western theology.

R. D. Linder

See also Liberalism, Theological; Fundamentalism.

Bibliography. H. E. Fosdick, *The Modern Use of the Bible* and *The Living of These Days: An Autobiography;* W. K. Cauthen, *The Impact of American Religious Liberalism;* W. R. Hutchison, *The Modernist Impulse in American Protestantism;* J. R. Scruggs, *Baptist*

Preachers with Social Consciousness: A Comparative Study of Martin Luther King, Jr. and Harry Emerson Fosdick.

Fourfold Sense of Scripture. *See* INTERPRETATION OF THE BIBLE.

Four Spiritual Laws, The. An evangelistic aid written by Bill Bright, president of Campus Crusade for Christ. Originally prepared for the staff of his worldwide evangelistic organization, the laws have since been given wide circulation, with well over twenty-five million printed copies being distributed by 1980. The laws attempt to distill the essence of the gospel and to present it simply, yet convincingly, to the non-Christian.

Bright believes there are spiritual laws which govern one's relationship with God, just as there are similar physical laws controlling the universe. In his pamphlet he supports these laws with scriptural texts, diagrams, brief explanations, a suggested prayer of personal commitment, and preliminary counsel for the person having newly received Christ as Savior and Lord.

The four laws Bright formulates are: (1) God loves you and offers a wonderful plan for your life (John 3:16; 10:10). (2) Man is sinful and separated from God. Therefore, he cannot know and experience God's love and plan for his life (Rom. 3:23; 6:23). (3) Jesus Christ is God's only provision for man's sin. Through him you can know and experience God's love and plan for your life (Rom. 5:8; I Cor. 15:3–6; John 14:6). (4) We must individually receive Jesus Christ as Savior and Lord; then we can know and experience God's love and plan for our lives (John 1:12; 3:1–8; Eph. 2:8–9; Rev. 3:20).

Bright's schematic has proved a useful aid for Christians who desire to communicate the gospel to others but lack the necessary skills. The simple outline has been used by the Holy Spirit to bring large numbers into personal faith. Moreover, it has been a corrective within the church in two regards. By giving priority through its first law to God's grace toward humankind, the fourfold presentation has countered evangelism based on fear of divine judgment. By calling people to personal decision, the laws have also challenged a church willing to rest content at times with only an intellectual knowledge of Christianity.

Despite their proven utility, the laws also have their limitations. Their impersonality and structure fail to speak convincingly to many. Moreover, in an age when advertising has made increasing numbers suspicious of promotions (particularly when sold aggressively), this prepackaged presentation has sometimes proved offensive. Lastly, Bright's fourfold summary of the gospel lacks sufficient biblical focus on the costly, ethical demands of the Christian faith. The message of John is quoted but not that of I John; Paul is referred to but not James.

R. K. JOHNSTON

Bibliography. B. Bright, *Have You Heard of the Four Spiritual Laws?* R. Quebedeaux, *I Found It! The Story of Bill Bright and Campus Crusade;* "Door Interview: Bill Bright," *WitD* (Feb.-Mar., 1977).

Fox, George (1624–1691). Founder of the Society of Friends, otherwise known as Quakers. Son of a Leicestershire weaver, he had evidently little formal education or regular occupation, but at the age of eighteen he left home in search of enlightenment. After many painful experiences that made him regard his fellow men less trustingly, he tells of having found One who spoke to his condition. In 1646 he announced his reliance on the "Inner Light of the Living Christ." He rejected outward sacraments, paid clergy, even church attendance, and taught that truth is to be found primarily not in Scripture or creed but in God's voice speaking to the soul. So emerged the "Friends of Truth." Fox taught the priesthood of all believers and advocated a simple life style for his colleagues, who later included William Penn. The Friends traveled widely in England. Their anticlerical views, disrespect of authority, and refusal to take oaths often led to arrest and imprisonment. At Derby in 1650 Fox was charged with blasphemy; then it was that the term "Quakers" was born in a magisterial jibe after Fox had urged the bench to "tremble at the word of the Lord." Persecution was stepped up after the monarchy was restored in 1660, and altogether Fox served eight jail sentences with a total of six years. His travels extended also to the Netherlands, the West Indies, and America (notably Maryland and Rhode Island). Whenever he could, he established local congregations. Fox was also a true pacifist, and his use of group silence was a brake on impetuous conduct. Later he moved his base from northwest England to London, where he spent his final years crusading against social evils, fighting for religious toleration and the promotion of education. His famous *Journal* gives valuable insights into the turbulent conditions in England during the latter half of the seventeenth century.

J. D. DOUGLAS

See also FRIENDS, SOCIETY OF.

Bibliography. R. M. Jones, *George Fox, Seeker and Friend;* H. E. Wildes, *The Voice of the Lord;* Fox's *Journal,* ed. J. L. Nickalls.

Franciscan Order. One of four thirteenth century orders of mendicant (begging) friars (Franciscan, Dominican, Carmelite, Augustinian) established to meet the urgent challenge of spiritual decline, urban growth, and the rapid spread of heresy (especially in southern France and northern Italy). It was founded by Francis of Assisi and formally approved by Innocent III in 1210. Unlike earlier monasticism, the friars lived active lives within the world as preachers and ministers to the needy.

Francis' deep suspicion of formal organization and learning and his extreme view of poverty (even physical contact with money was to be avoided) became the center of bitter conflicts within the Order. Early on, tension arose between the Zealots, who advocated strict observance of the founder's rule, and those factions (the Laxists, the Community) who favored various accommodations to reality. Under papal auspices the Order was fully organized by 1240 as one international body with only clerics eligible for office (another departure from the spirit of Francis, who favored laity), and provision was made for property to be held in trusteeship to get around the prohibition against ownership. During the years 1257–74 tensions abated under the conciliatory minister general Bonaventure, who established a moderate balance between structure and vitality. As an outstanding scholar, he also represented the increasing influx of Franciscans into the world of learning within the urban-based universities.

Following the death of Bonaventure a bitter debate ensued over the nature of apostolic poverty. The extreme view of the Spirituals (formerly the Zealots) was rejected by Pope John XXII, who in 1322 officially approved corporate ownership of property, arguing that Christ and the apostles as leaders of the church had owned property. Spirituals who fled became known as Fraticelli. Even outstanding figures such as the minister general Michael of Cesena and William of Ockham went into exile and denounced the pope.

Difficult conditions of plague, warfare, and papal schism during the century and a half before the Reformation led to a general decline within the Order, but another movement for restoration of the strict rule emerged—the Observants. They were opposed by the more moderate Conventuals, who preferred urban residence to remote hermitages. Failure to unite these factions led Pope Leo X in 1517 to officially separate the Order into two independent branches—the Friars Minor of the Regular Observants (strict) and the Friars Minor Conventuals (moderate). Given their reforming instincts, the Observants soon divided into several factions—Discalced (shoeless), Recollects, Reformed, and Capuchins (pointed cowl). The latter played a significant role in the Counter-Reformation and by 1619 had gained complete autonomy. Again, internal division and the external challenge of the Enlightenment and revolutionary Europe weakened the Order until mounting pressure led Pope Leo XIII in 1897 to unite all Observant branches (except the Capuchins, who retained their independence).

Alongside the Order of Friars Minor, with the three independent branches of Observants, Conventuals, and Capuchins, there emerged two other Franciscan Orders—the Second Order of nuns (Poor Clares), founded by Francis and his follower Clare in 1212, and the Third Order (Tertiaries) of mainly lay persons.

The Franciscans, along with their rivals the Dominicans, represented a new spiritual force within the thirteenth century church. As advocates of the simpler apostolic life of poverty and preaching, they struck a responsive chord among the growing number of townspeople who had become alienated from the monastic and hierarchical establishment. Nonetheless, instead of becoming rebellious heretics, the friars were obedient servants of the established church. Like the town, the university became a major focus of their activity as they sought to prepare intellectually for their worldwide mission—confronting infidel, heretic, and indifferent alike with the truth of Christianity. Virtually every outstanding scholar of that age was a friar—including Bonaventure, John Duns Scotus, and William of Ockham among the Franciscans. Contrary to the spirit of Francis, however, the Order became aggressively associated with the repressive Inquisition and the anti-Jewish activities of the Western church during its effort to consolidate Christian society.

R. K. BISHOP

See also FRANCIS OF ASSISI; MONASTICISM; SCHOLASTICISM; MYSTICISM.

Bibliography. R. Brooke, *The Coming of the Friars;* J. Cohen, *The Friars and the Jews;* L. Little, *Religious Poverty and the Profit Economy in Medieval Europe;* J. Moorman, *A History of the Franciscan Order from Its Origin to the Year 1517.*

Francis of Assisi (1182–1226). The universally admired founder of the Order of Friars Minor (Franciscans). Born Francesco Bernardone, son of a wealthy cloth merchant from Assisi, he was a popular, high-spirited youth, much inspired by chivalric ideals of the troubador and the knight. In his early twenties he experienced a gradual but profound religious conversion, expressed in a number of dramatic gestures such as the exchanging of clothes with a beggar and kissing the diseased hand of a leper. After he had sold family merchandise in order to rebuild a local church, his enraged father, disgusted by the son's unworldly instincts, brought him to judgment before the bishop's court. Here Francis freely renounced his inheritance and, in a memorable act, stripped off his clothes as well to signify total abandonment to God.

Francis spent the next several years living as a hermit in the vicinity of Assisi, ministering to the needy, repairing churches, and attracting a small band of followers to his simple rule. Pope Innocent III's approval of the fledgling order in 1210 was a major triumph; rather than being rejected as yet another threatening, heretical movement, the "little brothers" were embraced as a powerful current of reform within the established church.

Following a preaching mission in the Islamic East (including a remarkable audience with the sultan in Egypt), Francis returned home in 1219 to face a crisis. The movement now numbered some five thousand adherents, and pressure was mounting to establish a more formal organization. Distressed by this drift away from earlier spontaneity and simplicity, Francis increasingly withdrew to live out his mission by personal example. Intense meditation on the suffering of Christ led to the famous experience of the stigmata—signs in his own flesh of the wounds of his Master. And although he was more a preacher than a writer, in 1223 he completed a second rule (adapted as the official Rule of the Order) and about 1224 his most famous piece, "Canticle of the Sun," a paean of praise for God and his creation. Ill and nearly blind, he was finally brought back to Assisi from his remote hermitage and died on October 3, 1226. He was canonized by his friend Gregory IX in 1228, and his body was soon moved to the newly constructed basilica bearing his name.

The key to Francis's life was his uncompromising attempt to imitate Christ of the Gospels through absolute poverty, humility, and simplicity. He loved nature as God's good handiwork and had a deep respect for women (such as his beloved mother and Clare, his follower). At the same time, his willing obedience to the papacy and the priesthood allowed them to embrace this otherwise radical reformer and saint.

R. K. Bishop

See also Franciscan Order; Mysticism; Monasticism.

Bibliography. M. Bishop, *St. Francis of Assisi;* L. Cunningham, *St. Francis of Assisi;* O. Englebert, *Saint Francis of Assisi;* A. Fortini, *Francis of Assisi;* J. H. Smith, *Francis of Assisi.*

Francke, August Hermann (1663–1727). One of the foremost leaders of pietism. Francke studied at Erfurt, Kiel, and Leipzig, and taught at Leipzig (1685–87 and 1689–90). His teaching was well received by some but also aroused opposition. Through the influence of P. J. Spener he became professor at the recently founded University of Halle in 1692 and taught there until his death. Halle became a center of pietism. Francke's students carried his influence to various parts of Germany and to Scandinavia and Eastern Europe. Francke also pastored a nearby congregation. In 1695 he founded an orphanage, the first of several educational and charitable institutions funded entirely by contributions. He was active in supporting foreign mission work in India. His writings include exegetical, practical, and polemical works, a copious correspondence, and a few hymns.

Francke had been raised a Lutheran, but he followed the pietistic line of thinking and so departed from orthodox Lutheranism. The essence of pietism was its stress on religious experience for the assurance of salvation. Francke had had a sudden conversion experience. As did many of the pietists, he generalized his own experience as though it should be the same for all Christians. Accordingly he placed a great deal of importance on the feeling of sorrow and terror at sin and the feeling of being forgiven by God. Such experience would necessarily be decisive for the life of the individual and would become apparent in many good works. He saw the conversion experience as especially necessary for leadership among Christians.

Orthodox Lutherans opposed this stress on experience or feeling as the assurance of salvation. For Lutherans the assurance of salvation was in the means of grace (the gospel, absolution, baptism, the Lord's Supper). From the Lutheran perspective, Francke was replacing the gospel with the law by finding the assurance of salvation in man instead of in the Word of God. Stressing experience instead of the Word, Francke also deemphasized the importance of purity of doctrine and so tended to disregard the doctrinal differences between the Lutherans and the Reformed. Pietism in general crossed confessional lines.

J. M. Drickamer

See also Pietism; Spener, Philipp Jakob; Experience, Theology of.

Bibliography. C. Bergendoff, *The Church of the Lutheran Reformation; The Concordia Cyclopedia;* F. E. Stoeffler, *The Rise of Evangelical Pietism.*

Freedom, Free Will, and Determinism. There are three basic positions concerning man's choices: determinism, indeterminism, and self-determinism. Determinism is the belief that all of man's actions are the result of antecedent factors or causes. Naturalistic determinists, such as Thomas Hobbes and B. F. Skinner, argue that man's behavior can be fully explained in terms of natural causes. Theistic determinists, such as Martin Luther and Jonathan Edwards, trace man's actions back to God's controlling hand. The opposite position to determinism is indeterminism. On this view there are no causes for man's actions, antecedent or otherwise. The final position is self-determinism, or free will. This is the belief that man determines his own behavior freely, and that no causal antecedents can sufficiently account for his actions.

Determinism. The belief that man's actions are the result of antecedent causes has been formulated naturalistically and theistically. The naturalistic view sees human beings as part of the machinery of the universe. In such a world every event is caused by preceding events, which in turn were caused by still earlier events, *ad infinitum.* Since man is part of this causal chain, his actions are also determined by antecedent causes. Some of these causes are the environment and man's genetic make-up. These are so determinative of what man does that no one could rightly say that a given human action could have been performed otherwise than it in fact was performed. Thus, according to determinism, Bob's sitting on the brown chair rather than the blue sofa is not a free choice but is fully determined by previous factors.

A contemporary example of naturalistic determinism is B. F. Skinner, the author of *Beyond Freedom and Dignity* and *About Behaviorism.* Skinner believes that all human behavior is completely controlled by genetic and environmental factors. These factors do not rule out the fact that human beings make choices; however, they do rule out the possibility that human choices are free. For Skinner, all human choices are determined by antecedent physical causes. Hence, man is viewed as an instrumental cause of his behavior. He is like a knife in the hands of a butcher or a hammer in the grip of a carpenter; he does not originate action but is the instrument through which some other agent performs the action.

A philosophical argument often given for determinism can be stated as follows. All human behavior is either completely uncaused, self-caused, or caused by something external. Now human behavior cannot be uncaused, for nothing can happen without a cause—nothing cannot cause something. Human behavior cannot be self-caused either, for each act would have to exist prior to itself to cause itself, which is impossible. Thus the only alternative is that all human behavior must be completely caused by something external. Naturalistic determinists maintain that such things as heredity and environment are the external causes, whereas theistic determinists believe that God is the external cause of all human behavior.

There are several problems with this argument. First, the argument misinterprets self-determinism as teaching that human acts cause themselves. Self-determinists, for example, do not believe that the plays in a football game cause themselves. Rather they maintain that the players execute the plays in a football game. Indeed it is the players that choose to play the game. Thus the cause of a football game being played is to be found within the players of the game. Self-determinists would not deny that outside factors, such as heredity, environment, or God, had any influence. However, they would maintain that any one of the people involved in the game could have decided not to play if they had chosen to do so.

Second, the argument for determinisim is self-defeating. A determinist must contend that both he and the nondeterminist are determined to believe what they believe. Yet the determinist attempts to convince the nondeterminist that determinism is true and thus ought to be believed. However, on the basis of pure determinism "ought" has no meaning. For "ought" means "could have and should have done otherwise." But this is impossible according to determinism. A way around this objection is for the determinist to argue that he was determined to say that one ought to accept his view. However, his opponent can respond by saying that he was determined to accept a contrary view. Thus determinism cannot eliminate an opposing position. This allows the possibility for a free will position.

Third, and finally, if naturalistic determinism were true, it would be self-defeating, false, or be no view at all. For in order to determine whether determinism was true there would need to be a rational basis for thought, otherwise no one could know what was true or false. But naturalistic determinists believe that all thought is the product of nonrational causes, such as the environment, thus making all thought nonrational. On this basis no one could ever know if determinism were true or not. And if one argued that determinism was true, then the position would be self-defeating, for a truth claim is being made to the effect that no truth claims can be made. Now if determinism is false, then it can be rationally rejected and other positions considered. But if it is neither true nor false, then it is no view at all, since no claim to truth is being made. In either case, naturalistic determinism could not reasonably be held to be true.

Another form of determinism is theistic determinism. This is the view that all events, including man's behavior, are caused (determined) by God. One of the more famous advocates of this view was the Puritan theologian Jonathan Edwards. He maintained that the concept of free will or self-determinism contradicted the sovereignty of God. If God is truly in control of all things, then no one could act contrary to his will, which is what self-determinism must hold. Hence, for God to be sovereign he must cause every event, be it human or otherwise.

Edwards also argued that self-determinism is self-contradictory. For if man's will were in equilibrium or indifferent to any given event or decision, then his will would never act. Just as a scale cannot tip itself unless an outside force upsets the balance, so man's will could never act unless God moved it. Thus to speak of human acts as self-caused would be like speaking of nothing causing something. But since every event must have a cause, self-determinism, which denies this, must be self-contradictory.

During Edwards's own day some thinkers objected to his view on the grounds that it ran contrary to the biblical evidence which supported human freedom (e.g., Prov. 1:29–31; Heb. 11:24–26). Edwards responded in his *Freedom of the Will* that human freedom is not the power to do what one decides but rather what one desires. The cause of man's desires is God, and man always acts in accordance with them. Thus freedom is not uncaused, which is nonsensical, but caused by God.

Like naturalistic determinism, theistic determinism may be objected to on several grounds. First, to view freedom as that which one desires is inadequate. People do not always do what they desire; no one desires to carry out the garbage or clean a dirty oven. Further, people often desire to do what they do not decide to do, such as taking revenge on someone for wronging them.

Second, according to self-determinism, Edwards's position evidences a misunderstanding of free will. The acts of free human beings are not uncaused but self-caused. To say they are self-caused is not to say that they arise out of nothing or exist prior to themselves. Such would be an uncaused or self-caused *being*, which is nonsensical. However, self-determinism maintains that man's exercise of his freedom is self-caused *becoming*, which is not contradictory. In other words, persons exist and can freely cause their own actions (not their own being).

Third, Edwards's argument suffers from a faulty view of man. Human beings are not like a machine (scale) which cannot be moved until some outside force tips it in one direction or another. Rather, man is a person created in the image of God as a personal living soul (Gen. 1:26–27; 2:7), and he retains this image even after the fall (Gen. 9:6; I Cor. 11:7). This image includes the ability to make choices and act upon them. Hence, since man is personal, it is at best inadequate to illustrate his behavior by impersonal, mechanical models, such as a scale.

And fourth, Edwards is mistaken when he argues that human freedom is contrary to God's sovereignty. God sovereignly gave man his freedom by creating him a free creature, and God sovereignly continues to allow man to exercise his freedom by sustaining him moment by moment in existence (Col. 1:17). Thus the sovereignty of God is not thwarted by human freedom but glorified through human freedom. For God gave man free will, he sustains man so he can act freely, and he brings about all his purposes without violating man's free will. As the Westminster Confession puts it, "Although in relation to the foreknowledge and decree of God, the first cause, all things come to pass immutably and infallibly, yet by the same providence he ordereth them to fall out, according to the nature of second causes, either necessarily, freely, or contingently" (V, ii).

Indeterminism. This view contends that human behavior is totally uncaused. There are no antecedent or simultaneous causes of man's actions. Hence, all of man's acts are uncaused; hence, any given human act could have been otherwise. Some indeterminists extend their view beyond human affairs to the entire universe. In support of the indeterminacy of all events Heisenberg's principle of uncertainty is often invoked. This principle states that it is impossible to predict where a subatomic particle is and how fast it is moving at any given moment. Thus, it is argued, since subatomic events are inherently unpredictable, how much more so are complex human acts. From this they conclude that human and nonhuman events are uncaused. Two noted exponents of indeterminism are William James and Charles Peirce.

There are at least three problems with this view. First, Heisenberg's principle does not deal with causality but with predictability. Heisenberg maintained that the movement of subatomic particles was unpredictable and unmeasurable; he did not maintain that their movement was uncaused. Thus this principle cannot be used to support indeterminism. Second, indeterminism unreasonably denies the principle of causality, namely, that every event has a cause. Simply because one does not know what the cause is, is not proof that an event is not caused. Such lack of knowledge only reflects our ignorance. Third, indeterminism strips man of any responsible behavior. If human behavior is uncaused, then no one could be praised or blamed for anything he did. All human acts would be nonrational and nonmoral, thus no act could ever be a reasonable or responsible one.

Indeterminism is unacceptable for a Christian. For if indeterminism is true, then either the existence of God or any causal connection between God and the universe would have to be denied. But clearly a Christian could not hold this, for the Christian position is that God created the world and he providentially sustains it and intervenes in its affairs (Matt. 6:25–32; Col. 1:15–16).

Self-determinism. On this view a person's acts are caused by himself. Self-determinists accept the fact that such factors as heredity and environment often influence one's behavior. However, they deny that such factors are the determining causes of one's behavior. Inanimate objects do not change without an outside cause, but personal subjects are able to direct their own actions. As previously noted, self-determinists reject the notions that events are uncaused or that they cause themselves. Rather, they believe that human actions can be caused by human beings. Two prominent advocates of this view are Thomas Aquinas and C. S. Lewis.

Many object to self-determinism on the grounds that if everything needs a cause, then so do the acts of the will. Thus it is often asked, What caused the will to act? The self-determinist can respond to this question by pointing out that it is not the will of a person that makes a decision but the person acting by means of his will. And since the person is the first cause of his acts, it is meaningless to ask what the cause of the first cause is. Just as no outside force caused God to create the world, so no outside force causes people to choose certain actions. For man is created in God's image, which includes the possession of free will.

Another objection often raised against self-determinism is that biblical predestination and foreknowledge seem to be incompatible with human freedom. However, the Bible does clearly teach that even fallen man has freedom of choice (e.g., Matt. 23:37; John 7:17; Rom. 7:18; I Cor. 9:17; I Pet. 5:2; Philem. 14). Further, the Bible teaches that God predestines in accordance with his foreknowledge (I Pet. 1:2). Predestination is not based on God's foreknowledge (which would make God dependent upon man's choices) nor is it independent of God's foreknowledge (since all of God's acts are unified and coordinate). Rather, God knowingly determines and determinately knows those who will accept his grace as well as those who will reject him.

A further argument for free will is that God's commandments carry a divine "ought" for man, implying that man can and should respond positively to his commands. The responsibility to obey God's commands entails the ability to respond to them, by God's enabling grace. Furthermore, if man is not free, but all his acts are determined by God, then God is directly responsible for evil, a conclusion that is clearly contradicted by Scripture (Hab. 1:13; James 1:13–17).

Therefore, it seems that some form of self-determinism is the most compatible with the biblical view of God's sovereignty and man's responsibility. N. L. GEISLER

Bibliography. Augustine, *The Free Choice of the Will* and *On Grace and Free Will;* B. Holbach, *The System of Nature,* chs. 11, 12; W. James, "The Dilemma of Determinism," in *Pragmatism;* M. Luther, *The Bondage of the Will;* R. Taylor, *Metaphysics,* ch. 4; A. Farrer, *The Freedom of the Will.*

Freewill Offering. *See* OFFERINGS AND SACRIFICES IN BIBLE TIMES.

Friend. *See* CHRISTIANS, NAMES OF.

Friends, Society of. Known also as Quakers, the Society of Friends can best be understood through the lives of the early leaders. The founder was George Fox, whose youth saw the rule of Charles I and his marriage to a French princess who was a Roman Catholic, the Petition of Right, Archbishop Laud's harsh rules for Nonconformists, the Puritan emigration to America, and the meetings of the Long Parliament. His public career coincided with the defeat and execution of Charles I, the Puritan Commonwealth under Cromwell, the Stuart Restoration and the rule of James II, the Bill of Rights, and the "Glorious Revolution" of 1688. Some of his contemporaries were Locke, Hobbes, Milton, Dryden, Bunyan, Cromwell, Newton, Harvey, Baxter, and Ussher.

In 1647 Fox experienced a profound change in his religious life. In 1652 he said that he had a vision at a place called Pendle Hill; from that point on, he based his faith on the idea that God could speak directly to any person.

Some of the first converts of Fox were called "Friends" or "Friends in Truth." The term "Quaker" was described by Fox as follows. "The priest scoffed at us and called us Quakers. But the Lord's power was so over them, and the word of life was declared in such authority and dread to them, that the priest began trembling himself; and one of the people said, 'Look how the priest trembles and shakes, he is turned a Quaker also.'" According to Fox, the first person to use the term was Justice Bennet of Derby. Among the early converts were English Puritans, Baptists, Seekers, and other Nonconformists. The work spread to Ireland, Scotland, and Wales.

Quakerism took on certain characteristics such as simplicity in the manner of living, encouraging women to be ministers, spiritual democracy in meetings, absolute adherence to truth, universal peace and brotherhood regardless of sex, class, nation, or race. Quakers refused to remove their hats to those in authority and used the singular "thee" and "thou" in their speech, while the common people were supposed to address their betters as "you." In turn, they influenced the thought and social ethics of the English-speaking world far out of proportion to their numbers. Fox was imprisoned eight times during his life, but he pioneered care for the poor, aged, and insane, advocated prison reform, opposed capital punishment, war, and slavery, and stood for the just treatment of American Indians.

George Fox died in 1691, and the movement went into a quiet period. The center shifted to America. The first Friends to visit America were Mary Fisher and Anne Austin, who arrived in Massachusetts in 1656. They were sent away by the magistrates, but others arrived after them. In 1659 William Robinson and Marmaduke Stephenson were hanged on Boston Common, as was Mary Dyer the following year.

Probably the best known historical figure in the Society of Friends was William Penn. Born in 1644, he became a Quaker in 1667 and was an embarrassment to his father, Admiral Penn. King Charles II gave young William a grant of land in America to repay a debt to his father, and thus was launched Pennsylvania, a "holy experiment." By 1700 there were Friends meeting in all of the colonies.

Penn's tolerant policies attracted immigrants from many places. Difficulties arose from the fact that the Quakers wanted only to be at peace, while the British expected them to support the colonial wars against the French and Indians. A similar situation arose when the colonists revolted against the British in 1776.

A division occurred in the Society of Friends about 1827, with one group supporting the views of Elias Hicks, who believed that one should follow the inner light. The other group was influenced by the evangelical movement and put great emphasis on belief in the divinity of Christ, the authority of the Scriptures, and the atonement.

Friends were also active in the antislavery movement. John Woolman, Anthony Benezet, Lucretia Mott, and John Greenleaf Whittier were involved in such activities as the underground railroad and the Colonization Society. Benjamin Lundy's ideas were presented in *The Genius of Universal Emancipation.*

The tradition of caring for others carried on through the American Civil War, and the American Friends Service Committee was formed in 1917. The purpose of the organization was to provide young conscientious objectors with alternative service opportunities during wartime. A red and black star was chosen to symbolize the group.

The Society of Friends are optimistic about the purposes of God and the destiny of mankind. Their ultimate and final authority for religious life and faith resides within each individual. Many, but not all, seek for this truth through the guidance of the inner light. They believe that they are bound to refuse obedience to a government when its requirements are contrary to what they believe to be the law of God, but they are willing to accept the penalties for civil disobedience. They practice religious democracy in their monthly meetings. After discussion of an issue, for example, the clerk states what appears to be the mind of the group; but if a single Friend feels that he cannot unite with the group, no decision is made. Their stand for religious toleration is symbolized by the inscription on the statue of Mary Dyer across from Boston Common: "Witness for Religious Freedom. Hanged on Boston Common, 1660."

The Society of Friends has no written creed. Their philosophical differences can be seen in the fact that Richard Nixon was born into the group, while Staughton Lynd joined because of their teachings. They do have an interest in education, with the founding of Haverford, Earlham, Swarthmore, and other colleges. The teaching by example has caused some to ask why Quakers do not preach what they practice. Their ideal is to pursue truth at all costs, and it is hard to imagine a higher calling here on earth.

J. E. Johnson

See also Fox, George.

Bibliography. H. Barbour, *The Quakers in Puritan England;* W. C. Braithwaite, *The Beginnings of Quakerism* and *The Second Period of Quakerism;* R. M. Jones, *The Later Periods of Quakerism;* E. Russell, *The History of Quakerism;* D. E. Trueblood, *The People Called Quakers;* M. H. Bacon, *The Quiet Rebels;* A. N. Brayshaw, *The Quakers: Their Story and Message;* H. H. Brinton, *Friends for Three Hundred Years;* W. R. Williams, *The Rich Heritage of Quakerism.*

Fullness. The Greek word *plērōma* denotes that which fills, fulfills, or completes. In classical and hellenistic Greek it may mean the entire contents, or sum total. It is used, e.g., of the full strength of a military corps, or of a ship's complement. Philo applies it to the collection of animals in Noah's ark; he also describes a soul as having a full cargo (*plērōma*) of virtues.

Nontheological Occurrences in the NT. Of the seventeen instances of *plērōma* in the NT, eleven have no technical sense; they may be classified as follows. The word is used (1) of the patch put in to "fill up" the rent in an old garment (Matt. 9:16–Mark 2:21); (2) of the leftover fragments which "filled" several baskets after the miraculous feedings (Mark 6:43; 8:20); (3) of the earth's contents, in a quotation from Ps. 24:1 (LXX 23:1), representing Hebrew *mĕlô'* (I Cor. 10:26); (4) of the final sum total of believing Jews and Gentiles respectively (Rom. 11:12, 25); (5) of love as the "fulfillment" of the law (Rom. 13:10); (6) of the "fullness" of Christ's blessing which Paul hopes to bring to Rome (Rom. 15:29); (7) of the completion of an appointed period of time (Gal. 4:4).

Theological Occurrences in the NT. The remaining six instances have the following connotations:

(1) The "fullness" of Christ (John 1:16), i.e., the inexhaustible resources of his grace ("grace upon grace") on which his people may freely draw.

(2) The "fullness" of Christ (Eph. 4:13), i.e., the spiritual maturity to which believers attain as members of his body.

(3) The "fullness" of God (Eph. 3:19), i.e., the full realization in believers of that eternal purpose toward which God is working.

(4) The "fullness" which by God's decree resides in Christ (Col. 1:19), i.e., the "fullness" of deity which is embodied in him (Col. 2:9). In Colossians Paul refutes an incipient Gnosticism which evidently used *plērōma* as a technical term, denoting the plenitude of the divine nature as distributed among several emanations, intermediaries between God and the world. Paul insists that Christ, the one Mediator between God and men, embodies the fullness of the Godhead, and in addition imparts his fullness to his people. Without him they remain incomplete fragments; incorporated in him they share a common life in which he and they complement each other as the head does the body and the body the head.

(5) This last thought probably underlies the use of *plērōma* in Eph. 1:23, where the church, the body of Christ, is called "the *fullness* of him who fills all in all"—or (as others translate) "the *complement* of him who is being perpetually filled" (with the fullness of deity). Whether the verb is middle ("fills") or passive ("is being filled"), "fullness" is probably in apposition with "body." Another view treats the clause "which is his body" as parenthetical and takes "fullness" in apposition with "him" (vs. 22), making Christ the Father's *plērōma* or "complement." So, according to Charles John Vaughan, *plērōma* in Eph. 1:23 "seems very likely to refer to *Christ*—'gave him, Christ, I say, as the fulness of him who is filled with (*or* in respect of) all things'—or middle, 'who fills the universe with all things.' 'The fulness of him,' i.e., the fulness of God, is what Christ is here said to be. This view seems supported by Col. 1:18." For the same view cf. A. E. N. Hitchcock, *ExpT* 22:91; C. F. D. Moule, *ExpT* 60:53. It involves unnecessary awkwardness in construing the text.

Gnostic Usage. In Valentinianism *plērōma* denotes the totality of the divine attributes. These attributes are expressed mythologically as thirty "aeons" emanating from God, but distinct from him and from the material world. They correspond to the Platonic "ideas"; sometimes each aeon is called a *plērōma* by contrast with the defectiveness of its earthly copies. Again, an individual's spirit counterpart is called his *plērōma;* in this sense Heracleon on John 4:16 says that the Samaritan woman was told to fetch her *plērōma.* Each of the aeons imparted its peculiar excellence to Jesus, so that he appeared on earth as "the perfect beauty and star of the *plērōma*" (Irenaeus, *Against Heresies* i.14.2). In the Valentinian Gospel of Truth the word comes forth from the *plērōma,* which is its place of repose.

F. F. Bruce

Bibliography. J. B. Lightfoot, *Colossians and Philemon;* J. A. Robinson, *Ephesians;* C. A. A. Scott, *Christianity According to St. Paul;* F. C. Burkitt, *Church and Gnosis;* E. Percy, *Probleme der Kolosser- und Epheserbriefe;* P. Benoit, "Corps, tète et plērōme dans les Épìtres de la Captivité," *RB* 63:5ff.; C. F. D. Moule, *Colossians and Philemon;* E. K. Simpson and F. F. Bruce, *Ephesians and Colossians;* G. Delling, *TDNT,* VI, 283ff.; T. Brandt *et al., NIDNTT,* I, 728ff.

Fullness of Time. The expression appears twice in the NT: Gal. 4:4 and Eph. 1:10. These two verses encompass the totality of God's redemptive plan in history, or *Heilsgeschichte* (history of salvation, holy history).

Gal. 4:4 refers to the period before Christ's birth. Israel had waited centuries for a Messiah. The Exile had come, the return had happened, Persia had fallen, Greece had fallen, the Seleucid oppression had come and gone, and finally Rome had arisen. Where was the redemption? Why did Israel still groan? These questions could be asked whether one looked for Israel's spiritual purification or political restoration. Paul uses this expression (which literally indicates the time set for a child's majority) to indicate that only when history had "matured" to the proper point was God ready to act. Traditionally this maturity has been seen as a combination of the widespread Greek language and culture with the Roman political pacification and transportation system making the spread of the gospel easier. One could add the socially oppressive situation in Palestine and the existence of legally protected Jewish synagogues around the Mediterranean. Paul, however, is thinking of something deeper. Just as in Gen. 15:16 God was not ready to act, so God patiently waited until the inward and outward aspects of history were "just right" before he sent his Son. There was no accident, but God worked through and controlled history (cf. Mark 1:15; Matt. 13:11, 16–17).

In Eph. 1:10, however, Paul is looking in the other direction. He realizes that redemption was accomplished at the cross, but it is marked out in history. The "mystery" (Rom. 16:25–26; Eph. 1:9; 3:4–5; Col. 1:26), which is this plan to unite all things in Christ, is being worked out in the church as the gospel spreads, people are joined to Christ, and the gospel transforms the social situation of the world. But Paul was deeply aware that the "already" of the foretaste he saw happening even in his ministry was combined with the "not yet" of rejection and endless frustration around him (cf. Rom. 8:18–25). The result was not despair, but a realization that God also had a time when this age will come to full ripeness or maturity, and his plan or purpose is the revelation of Jesus Christ as head over all things, a position he potentially holds since the ascension but will actualize only in his parousia (second coming). P. H. Davids

Bibliography. O. Cullmann, *Christ and Time;* G. E. Ladd, *A Theology of the NT;* C. L. Mitton, *Ephesians;* E. Sauer, *From Eternity to Eternity.*

Fundamentalism. A movement that arose in the United States during and immediately after the First World War in order to reaffirm orthodox Protestant Christianity and to defend it militantly against the challenges of liberal theology, German higher criticism, Darwinism, and other isms regarded as harmful to American Christianity. Since then, the focus of the movement, the meaning of the term, and the ranks of those who willingly use the term to identify themselves have changed several times. Fundamentalism has so far gone through four phases of expression while maintaining an essential continuity of spirit, belief, and method.

Through the 1920s. The earliest phase involved articulating what was fundamental to Christianity and initiating an urgent battle to expel the enemies of orthodox Protestantism from the ranks of the churches.

The series of twelve volumes called *The Fundamentals* (1910–15) provided a wide listing of the enemies—Romanism, socialism, modern philosophy, atheism, Eddyism, Mormonism, spiritualism, and the like, but above all liberal theology, which rested on a naturalistic interpretation of the doctrines of the faith, and German higher criticism and Darwinism, which appeared to undermine the Bible's authority. The writers of the articles were a broad group from English-speaking North America and the United Kingdom and from many denominations. The doctrines they defined and defended covered the whole range of traditional Christian teachings. They presented their criticisms fairly, with careful argument, and in appreciation of much that their opponents said.

Almost immediately, however, the list of enemies became narrower and the fundamentals less comprehensive. Defenders of the fundamentals of the faith began to organize outside the churches and within the denominations. The General Assembly of the northern Presbyterian Church in 1910 affirmed five essential doctrines regarded as under attack in the church: the inerrancy of Scripture, the virgin birth of Christ, the substitutionary atonement of Christ, Christ's bodily resurrection, and the historicity of the miracles. These were reaffirmed in 1916 and 1923, by which time they had come to be regarded as the fundamental doctrines of Christianity itself. On a parallel track, and in the tradition of Bible prophecy conferences since 1878, premillenarian Baptists and independents founded the World's Christian Fundamentals Association in 1919, with William B. Riley as the prime mover. The premillennialists tended to replace the miracles with the resurrection and the second coming of Christ, or even premillenarian doctrine as the fifth fundamental. Another version put the deity of Christ in place of the virgin birth.

The term "fundamentalist" was perhaps first used in 1920 by Curtis Lee Laws in the Baptist *Watchman-Examiner,* but it seemed to pop up everywhere in the early 1920s as an obvious way to identify someone who believed and actively defended the fundamentals of the faith. The Baptist John Roach Straton called his newspaper *The Fundamentalist* in the 1920s. The Presbyterian scholar J. Gresham Machen disliked the word, and only hesitatingly accepted it to describe himself, because, he said, it sounded like a new religion and not the same historic Christianity that the church had always believed.

Through the 1920s the fundamentalists waged the battle in the large northern church denominations as nothing less than a struggle for true Christianity against a new non-Christian religion that had crept into the churches themselves. In his book *Christianity and Liberalism* (1923), Machen called the new naturalistic religion "liberalism," but later followed the more popular fashion of calling it "modernism."

Even though people like Harry Emerson Fosdick professed to be Christian, fundamentalists felt they could not be regarded as such because they denied the traditional formulations of the doctrines of Christianity and created modern, naturalistic statements of the doctrines. The issue was as much a struggle over a view of the identity of Christianity as it was over a method of doing theology and a view of history. Fundamentalists believed that the ways the doctrines were formulated in an earlier era were true and that modern attempts to reformulate them were bound to be false. In other words, the fundamentals were unchanging.

Church struggles occurred in the Methodist Episcopal Church, the Protestant Episcopal Church, and even in the southern Presbyterian Church, but the grand battles were fought in the northern Presbyterian and northern Baptist denominations. Machen was the undisputed leader among Presbyterians, joined by Clarence E. Macartney. Baptists created the National Federation of the Fundamentalists of the Northern Baptists (1921), the Fundamentalist Fellowship (1921), and the Baptist Bible Union (1923) to lead the fight. The battles focused upon the seminaries, the mission boards, and the ordination of clergy. In many ways, however, the real strongholds of the fundamentalists were the Southern Baptists and the countless new independent churches spread across the south and midwest, as well as the east and west.

In politics fundamentalists opposed the teaching of Darwinian evolution in public schools, leading up to the famous Scopes trial (1925) in Dayton, Tennessee. William Jennings Bryan, a Presbyterian layman and three times candidate for the American presidency, was acknowledged leader of the antievolution battle.

Late 1920s to the Early 1940s. By 1926 or so, those who were militant for the fundamentals had failed to expel the modernists from any denomination. Moreover, they also lost the battle against evolutionism. Orthodox Protestants, who still numerically dominated all the denominations, now began to struggle among themselves. During the Depression of the 1930s the term "fundamentalist" gradually shifted meaning as it came to apply to only one party among those who believed the traditional fundamentals of the faith. Meanwhile, neo-orthodoxy associated with Karl Barth's critique of liberalism found adherents in America.

In several cases in the north fundamentalists created new denominations in order to carry on the true faith in purity apart from the larger bodies they regarded as apostate. They formed the General Association of Regular Baptist Churches (1932), the Presbyterian Church of America (1936), renamed the Orthodox Presbyterian Church, the Bible Presbyterian Church (1938), the Conservative Baptist Association of America (1947), the Independent Fundamental Churches of America (1930), and many others. In the south fundamentalists dominated the huge Southern Baptist Convention, the southern Presbyterian Church, and the expanding independent Bible church and Baptist church movements, including the American Baptist Association. Across the United States fundamentalists founded new revival ministries, mission agencies, seminaries, Bible schools, Bible conferences, and newspapers.

During this period the distinctive theological point that the fundamentalists made was that they represented true Christianity based on a literal interpretation of the Bible, and that *de facto* this truth ought to be expressed organizationally separate from any association with liberals and modernists. They came to connect a separatist practice with the maintenance of the fundamentals of the faith. They also identified themselves with what they believed was pure in personal morality and American culture. Thus, the term "fundamentalist" came to refer largely to orthodox Protestants outside the large northern denominations, whether in the newly established denominations, in the southern churches, or in the many independent churches across the land.

Early 1940s to the 1970s. Beginning in the early 1940s the fundamentalists, thus becoming redefined, divided gradually into two camps. There were those who voluntarily continued to use the term to refer to themselves and to equate it with true Bible-believing Christianity. There were others who came to regard the term as undesirable, having connotations of divisive, intolerant, anti-intellectual, unconcerned with social problems, even foolish. This second group wished to regain fellowship with the orthodox Protestants who still constituted the vast majority of the clergy and people in the large northern denominations—Presbyterian, Baptist, Methodist, Episcopalian. They began during the 1940s to call themselves "evangelicals" and to equate that term with true Christianity. Beginning in 1948 a few called themselves neoevangelical.

Organizationally this split among largely northern fundamentalists was expressed on one hand by the American Council of Christian Churches (1941), which was ecclesiastically separatist in principle, and on the other by the National Association of Evangelicals (1942), which sought to embrace orthodox Protestants as individuals in all denominations. The term "fundamentalist" was carried into the 1950s by the ACCC as well as by a vast number of southern churches and independent churches not included in either body. It was proudly used by such schools as Bob Jones University, Moody Bible Institute, and Dallas Theological Seminary, and by hundreds of evangelists and radio preachers. The International Council of Christian Churches (1948) sought to give the term worldwide currency in opposition to the World Council of Churches.

The term "fundamentalist" took on special meaning in contrast with evangelical or neoevangelical, rather than merely in contrast with liberalism, modernism, or neo-orthodoxy. Fundamentalists and evangelicals in the 1950s and 1960s shared much; both adhered to the traditional doctrines of Scripture and Christ; both promoted evangelism, revivals, missions, and a personal morality against smoking, drinking, theater, movies, and card-playing; both identified American values with Christian values; both believed in creating organizational networks that separated themselves from the rest of society. However, fundamentalists believed they differed from evangelicals and neoevangelicals by being more faithful to Bible-believing Christianity, more militant against church apostasy, communism, and personal evils, less ready to cater to social and intellectual respectability. They tended to oppose evangelist Billy Graham, not to read *Christianity Today,* and not to support Wheaton College or Fuller Theological Seminary. Instead they favored their own evangelists, radio preachers, newspapers, and schools. Fundamentalists tended to differ greatly among themselves and found it difficult to achieve widespread fundamentalist cooperation.

Meanwhile people in North America and Great Britain who were neither fundamentalist nor evangelical tended to regard both as fundamentalist, noting their underlying similarities.

Late 1970s and the 1980s. By the late 1970s and in particular by the 1980 campaign of Ronald Reagan for the American presidency, fundamentalists entered a new phase. They became nationally prominent as offering an answer for what many regarded as a supreme social, economic, moral, and religious crisis in America. They identified a new and more pervasive enemy, secular humanism, which they believed was responsible for eroding churches, schools, universities, the government, and above all families. They fought all enemies which they considered to be offspring of secular humanism—evolutionism, political and theological liberalism, loose personal morality, sexual perversion, socialism, communism, and any lessening of the absolute, inerrant authority of the Bible. They called Americans to return to the fundamentals of the faith and the fundamental moral values of America.

Leading this phase was a new generation of television and print fundamentalists, notably Jerry Falwell, Tim La Haye, Hal Lindsey, and Pat Robertson. Their base was Baptist and southern, but they reached into all denominations. They benefited from three decades of post–World War II fundamentalist and evangelical expansion through evangelism, publishing, church extension, and radio ministry. They tended to blur the distinction between fundamentalist and evangelical. Statistically, they could claim that perhaps one fourth of the American population was fundamentalist-evangelical. However, not all fundamentalists accepted these new leaders, considering them to be neofundamentalists.

The fundamentalists of the early 1980s were in many ways very different people from their predecessors, and they faced many different issues. But they continued important traits common to fundamentalists from the 1920s through the early 1980s. They were certain that they possessed true knowledge of the fundamentals of the faith and that they therefore represented true Christianity based on the authority of a literally interpreted Bible. They believed it was their duty to carry on the great battle of history, the battle of God against Satan, of light against darkness, and to fight against all enemies who undermined Christianity and America. Faced with this titanic struggle they were inclined to consider other Christians who were not fundamentalists as either unfaithful to Christ or not genuinely Christian. They called for a return to an inerrant and infallible Bible, to the traditional statement of the doctrines, and to a traditional morality which they believed once prevailed in America. To do all this, they created a vast number of separate organizations and ministries to propagate the fundamentalist faith and practice.

C. T. McIntire

See also Evangelicalism; Fundamentals, The.

Bibliography. G. W. Dollar, *A History of Fundamentalism in America;* R. Lightner, *Neo-Evangelicalism;*

L. Gasper, *The Fundamentalist Movement, 1930–1956;* J. Falwell, E. Dobson, and E. Hindson, eds., *The Fundamentalist Phenomenon;* G. M. Marsden, *Fundamentalism and American Culture;* C. A. Russell, *Voices of American Fundamentalism;* N. F. Furniss, *The Fundamentalist Controversy, 1918–1931;* E. R. Sandeen, *The Roots of Fundamentalism;* J. I. Packer, *"Fundamentalism" and the Word of God;* James Barr, *Fundamentalism.*

Fundamentals, The. A series of twelve volumes of articles published in Chicago between 1910 and 1915 as a witness to the central doctrines and experiences of Protestant Christianity, and as a defense against numerous modern movements, cults, and criticisms of orthodoxy.

The Fundamentals, subtitled "A Testimony to the Truth," is associated with the founding of fundamentalism as a restatement of orthodox Christianity against the liberal theology and modernism of the time. Three million individual copies of the volume were distributed free to English-speaking Protestant ministers, missionaries, and workers around the world. They were financed anonymously by "two Christian laymen," Lyman and Milton Stewart, wealthy California oil capitalists who donated the income from interest on some of their securities investments.

The Fundamentals originated out of and was editorially controlled by persons in the Bible school, revival, and independent church movements associated with the Bible Institute of Los Angeles and Moody Bible Institute. But the authors were a broad selection of Presbyterians, Anglicans, Baptists, Independents, and others, from England, Scotland, Canada, as well as the United States. As a group they represented the last of Victorian orthodoxy; all but nine of the thirty-seven most prominent were deceased by 1925, and of those, only six stood with the fundamentalists in the church battles of that decade.

The eighty-three articles covered these main themes: (1) a statement and apologetic defense of main Christian doctrines (e.g., God, revelation, the incarnation, the atonement, the resurrection, the Holy Spirit, inspiration); (2) a defense of the Bible against German higher criticism; (3) a criticism of movements considered non-Christian (e.g., Romanism, Eddyism, Mormonism, rationalism, Darwinism, socialism); (4) an emphasis on evangelism and missions; (5) a sample of personal testimonies by people telling how Christ worked in their lives.

The Fundamentals, especially in the first seven or eight volumes, was an attempt to be broad and well-rounded, doctrinal as well as experiential, educational and intelligently apologetic, and tolerant and considerate of those they criticized. Their aim was to help equip Protestant workers in their ministries to understand the new situation in Christianity when alternatives to and departures from orthodoxy were both numerous and successful.

A look at how two or three themes were treated will illustrate *The Fundamentals.* Many articles are devoted to a defense of Scripture against German higher criticism. Dyson Hague, lecturer at Wycliffe College, Toronto, had read the Germans carefully and appreciated their attempts to understand the authorship, literary forms, and sources of the biblical texts. In an appeal even to the critics themselves he pointed out that their scholarship depended upon the *a priori* of naturalism and that there were valid alternative treatments of the higher critical questions. Professor James Orr from Glasgow carefully distinguished between Darwinism and evolutionary theory. Darwinism, he said, unwarrantly opposed a scientific theory to the biblical accounts; by contrast some form of evolutionary theory may describe how God created the living creatures, including humans. C. T. McIntire

See also Fundamentalism.

Bibliography. *The Fundamentals for Today* (reprinted 1958, 1964); G. M. Marsden, *Fundamentalism and American Culture;* E. R. Sandeen, *The Roots of Fundamentalism.*

Future Life. The witness of Scripture can be cited to support what might be termed a universal hope—that man will survive his own death.

The OT concept of Sheol, though presented as a shadowy, inert experience (Job 10:21–22; Ps. 143:3), is nevertheless also described in terms relating to consciousness and recognition (Isa. 14:12). The translations to heaven of Enoch (Gen. 5:24; cf. Heb. 11:5) and Elijah (II Kings 2:11) give further credence to those passages suggestive of a resurrection hope (Pss. 16:8–11; 17:15; Isa. 26:19; Dan. 12:2; etc.).

Jesus' life and teachings exhibit this hope as a reality. The transfiguration (Mark 9:2–13), assurance to the dying thief (Luke 23:43), and the resurrection confirm that God is "of the living" (Matt. 22:32). Man is promised an eternal future life if he "has the Son" (I John 5:12), who currently prepares a place for us in his Father's house (John 14:2–4).

Paul and Hebrews represent such life as a higher, happier state of completion (II Cor. 5:8; Phil. 1:23; I Thess. 4:13; etc.; Heb. 11:13–16; 12:23).

Recent scientific studies of near-death phenomena lend support to the view that man's consciousness continues to exist and to undergo some common postmortem experiences.

S. E. McClelland

See also Eternal Life; Heaven; Hell.

Bibliography. P. Badham, *Christian Beliefs About Life After Death;* J. Hick, *Death and Eternal Life;* R. A. Moody, *Life After Life.*

Gg

Gaebelein, Arno Clemens (1861–1945). A central figure in the development of the fundamentalist movement in the later nineteenth and early twentieth centuries. Gaebelein was born in Thuringia (now part of East Germany) and emigrated to the United States in 1879 at the age of eighteen. While working in a wool mill in Lawrence, Massachusetts, this same year he received his call to the ministry and diligently studied the Bible and ancient languages. In 1881 he was asked to become the assistant at Louis Wallon's German Methodist Episcopal Church on Second Street in New York City. He boarded with Wallon's father, who gave him his first taste of premillennial eschatology. Following successful pastorates in Baltimore, Harlem, and Hoboken, Gaebelein returned to New York and began the Hope of Israel Movement, a mission dedicated to the Jewish people and their needs. *Our Hope* magazine (1894–1957) originated as an arm of this missionary enterprise to teach Christians about the Jewish people, to foster prophetic study, and to combat anti-Semitism. As Gaebelein's national—and later worldwide—ministry as a Bible teacher and conference speaker grew, *Our Hope* expanded into an influential Bible study magazine. It attracted readers from a broad spectrum of denominations and vocations.

Gaebelein was most famous in the realm of prophecy. C. I. Scofield, who asked him to contribute in this area to the *Scofield Reference Bible,* stated in a letter to Gaebelein: "I sit at your feet when it comes to prophecy." Gaebelein was adept at more than prophecy, however, writing nearly fifty books and scores of pamphlets on a variety of biblical topics. Known as an irenic spirit and calming influence in a movement that progressively gained a reputation for divisiveness and invective, Gaebelein never lost his love for the Jewish people. Under his editorship *Our Hope* firmly denounced Adolf Hitler and provided readers with up-to-date details of the plight of the Jews during the Holocaust, in contrast to the many other periodicals of that time that doubted the truth of the reports coming out of Germany. Gaebelein died on Christmas day in 1945, believing that the Jewish state he had supported for over fifty years would soon be established in Palestine.

D. A. Rausch

Bibliography. A. C. Gaebelein, *Half A Century: The Autobiography of a Servant;* D. A. Rausch, *Zionism Within Early American Fundamentalism,* chs. 6, 8; and "Our Hope: An American Fundamentalist Journal and the Holocaust," *FH* 12:89–103.

Gallican Articles, The Four (1682). Drawn up at a specially convened assembly of the French bishops at Paris in March, 1682, these articles sought to delineate as clearly as possible the respective powers of popes, kings, and bishops in the French Catholic Church. The immediate occasion for this gathering was a dispute that had broken out between the French king Louis XIV and Pope Innocent XI, concerning the right of nomination to vacant bishoprics and the disposition of their revenues. The 1682 assembly adopted four proposals drafted by Bossuet, Bishop of Meaux, on the basis of an earlier pronouncement of the theological faculty at the Sorbonne. These articles declared: (1) that popes have no control over matters temporal, that kings are not subject to any ecclesiastical authority in civil affairs, that kings could not legitimately be deposed by the church, and that their subjects could not be released from their political allegiance by any papal decree; (2) that the papacy is subject to the authority of general councils of the church, as decreed by the Council of Constance (1414–18); (3) that papal authority must be exercised with due respect for local and national church usages and customs; (4) that, though the pope has "the principal part in questions of faith," pending the consent of a general council, his judgments are not irreformable.

The articles—a classic expression of Gallicanism, i.e., French national Catholicism—were ordered by Louis XIV to be taught in all French universities; but since they were not acceptable to the papacy, a number of French bishoprics remained vacant for years. In 1693 Pope Alexander VIII allowed the French king to retain the revenues from vacant bishoprics, in return for abandonment of the Gallican Articles; but they continued to be taught in France throughout the eighteenth century. N. V. Hope

See also Gallicanism.

Bibliography. W. H. Jervis, *The Gallican Church;* S. Z. Ehler and J. B. Morrall, *Church and State Through the Centuries;* A. Galton, *Church and State in France, 1300–1907.*

Gallicanism. A French movement with the intent of diminishing papal authority and increasing the power of the state over the church. It was viewed as heretical by the Roman Catholic Church. Its earliest exponents were the fourteenth century Franciscans William of Ockham, John of Jandun, and Marsilius of Padua. Marsilius's writings helped to cause the schism in the church which resulted in two rival popes (1275–1342). Conciliarism, an early form of Gallicanism, was the attempt to patch up the breach between the opposing factions in the Catholic Church. In the conciliar spirit a church council's authority would prevail over the edicts of any pope. The Council of Constance (1414–18) adopted conciliarism as a stance, hoping that it would permit the election of a pope acceptable to both Catholic factions. John Gerson (1363–1429) and Peter d'Ailly (1350–1420) were influential figures in the development of Gallicanism during the early fifteenth century.

Thus far Gallicanism had remained an ecclesiastical affair, but in 1594 Pierre Pithou brought it into the secular political arena. Pithou, a Parisian lawyer, wrote *The Liberties of the Gallican Church* that year. The Gallican Liberties, as Pithou's proposals came to be called, infringed on the traditional rights of the papacy in favor of increased governmental power over the church. The liberties explicitly claimed royal authority to assemble councils and make church law. They crippled communication between the pope and his bishops in France: the bishops were made subject to the French sovereign, they were prevented from traveling to Rome, papal legates were denied visits to the French bishops, and any communication with the pope without express royal consent was prohibited. Furthermore, publication of papal decrees in France was made subject to royal approval, and any papal decision could lawfully be appealed to a future council.

In 1663 the Sorbonne endorsed Gallicanism. Bossuet drew up the Gallican Articles, published by the Assembly of the Clergy in 1682. These attempted to clarify the theological justification of the Gallican Liberties by appealing to the conciliar theory and reasoning that Christ gave Peter and the popes spiritual authority but not temporal. In support of the conciliar theory Bossuet attributed direct authority from Christ to the ecclesiastical councils. He declared that papal decisions could be reversed until they were ratified by the whole church, and he advocated faithfulness to the traditions of the Church of France (significantly, not the Church of Rome). The Gallican Articles became an obligatory part of the curriculum in every French school of theology, and the movement flourished during the seventeenth century. The French Revolution struck a fatal blow to Gallicanism near the end of the next century by forcing the French clergy to turn to Rome for help when they, along with the government, came under attack. Eventually the movement died out. P. A. Mickey

See also Febronianism; Gallican Articles, The Four; Bossuet, Jacques Bénigne.

Bibliography. A. Barry, "Bossuet and the Gallican Declaration of 1682," *CHR* 9:143–53; C. B. du Chesnay, *NCE;* F. P. Drouet, "Gallicanism," *The New Catholic Dictionary;* J. A. Hardon, *Modern Catholic Dictionary,* 225; W. H. Jervis, *The Gallican Church and the Revolution.*

Gallic Confession (1559). French Protestant statement of religious belief. Protestantism began to take hold during the second and third quarters of the sixteenth century, mainly under the sponsorship of Calvin's Geneva. In 1555 a congregation was organized in Paris, holding regular services and having a formal organization; and during the years immediately following, similar groups sprang up elsewhere in France. In May, 1559, representatives of these congregations met in Paris under the moderatorship of François de Morel, the local pastor, for their first national synod, at which a system of church discipline was approved. This assembly received from Geneva a draft confession of faith in thirty-five articles and expanded it into forty. These articles began with the Triune God, revealed in his written Word, the Bible. Then they affirmed adherence to the three ecumenical creeds—Apostles', Nicene, and Athanasian—"because they are in accordance with the Word of God."

Then they proceeded to expound basic Protestant beliefs: man's corruption through sin, Jesus Christ's essential deity and vicarious atonement, justification by grace through faith, the gift of the regenerating Holy Spirit, the divine origin of the church and its two sacraments of baptism and the Lord's Supper, and the place of the political state as ordained by God "for the order and peace of society." They asserted the doctrine of predestination in a moderate form.

This revamped confession was adopted by the synod, and in 1560 a copy was presented to King Francis II with a plea for tolerance for its adherents. At the seventh national synod, held at La Rochelle in 1571, this Gallic Confession was revised and reaffirmed. It remained the official confessional statement of French Protestantism for over four centuries. N. V. Hope

See also Confessions of Faith.

Bibliography. A. C. Cochrane, *Reformed Confessions of the Sixteenth Century;* P. Schaff, *The Creeds of Christendom,* I, 490–98.

Gap Theory. The gap or reconstruction theory is a scheme to reconcile the long geologic ages in the earth's history with the Genesis creation account. It basically advocates that the first two verses of Genesis 1 describe a condition that lasted an indeterminate length of time and preceded the six days of creation in Gen. 1:3ff. There was creation (1:1), followed by a catastrophe (1:2), in turn followed by a re-creation (1:3ff.). All the needed geologic ages in earth's pre-Adamic history may be found either between 1:1 and 1:2 or during 1:2.

Early expressions of the view can be traced to Episcopius (d. 1643), a theologian who taught at the University of Leiden in the Netherlands, and to the scientist J. G. Rosenmuller (d. 1815). In nineteenth century England it was espoused by the theologian Thomas Chalmers, geologist William Buckland, biblical scholar John Pye Smith, and church historian J. H. Kurtz. In the United States the view was widely disseminated by G. H. Pember, Harry Rimmer, and the first edition of the *Scofield Reference Bible* (1909).

For many today the day-age theory has replaced the gap theory as the best explanation of the geologic ages and Genesis 1. Others have adopted flood-catastrophism. Criticism of the gap theory has arisen from various circles, and summaries may be found in the works of Allis, Ramm, and Young cited below. In essence the criticism involves (1) the improbability that only one verse (Gen. 1:1) deals with the original creation while so many sentences are devoted to a secondary or re-creation process; (2) the lack of solid exegetical evidence to support the rendering of the Hebrew verb "was" in Gen. 1:2 as "became"; (3) the sense of "without form" and "void" meaning nothing more than "empty," "uninhabited"; (4) elaborate theories of angelology and demonology derived from Isa. 14 and Ezek. 28 and inserted in Gen. 1:2 being unjustified; and (5) such a theory turning the entire field of geology over to the geologists since the Bible yields no reference to earth's earliest formation.

A. F. Johnson

See also Evolution; Creation, Doctrine of.

Bibliography. O. T. Allis, *God Spake by Moses;* B. Ramm, *The Christian View of Science and Scripture;* D. A. Young, *Christianity and the Age of the Earth.*

Gehenna. The Greek transliteration of the Aramaic *gēhinnām,* which itself goes back to the Hebrew *gê hinnōm:* "Valley of Hinnom" (also "valley of the son (sons) of Hinnom"; cf. II Chr. 28:3; II Kings 23:10, etc.). Original reference was to a valley to the south and west of Jerusalem. Near where this valley joined the Kidron Valley, on the south and east, was Topheth, early site of Baal worship and the abominable practice of sacrifice of children to Molech (cf. II Kings 16:3 and 21:6 for involvement respectively of Ahaz and Manasseh; and II Kings 23:10 for condemnation by Josiah, the reformer king). In Jer. 7:32 and 19:6 is the prophecy that this place of shame will become the place of punishment by God.

Because of such associations, by the first century B.C. gehenna came to be used metaphorically for the hell of fire, the place of everlasting punishment for the wicked. This understanding is discernible in Jewish apocalyptic literature (e.g. II Esd. 7:36). Talmudic literature abounds in references to gehenna with fascinating opinions—e.g., that the depth of gehenna is immeasurable or that the sinner is relegated to a depth commensurate with his wickedness. References to a fiery hell are found in both Philo and Josephus and also in the Qumran literature.

Of the twelve occurrences of gehenna in the NT eleven are in the Synoptic Gospels and one in James. All the Synoptic references are to words of Jesus and have the same meaning as above. In addition to the word itself, scholars agree that there are several occurrences of the concept, e.g., Matt. 25:41 and Rev. 20:4. Gehenna shares some common ground with Hades/Sheol; however, the latter is more consistently the interim abode of both good and bad souls after death prior to judgment, while gehenna is the final and everlasting place of punishment for the wicked following the last judgment.

The numerous references to gehenna tell

forcefully against a doctrine of universalism. Attempts to soften or ignore this material concerning the lot of those who refuse to repent of sin constitute distortion of the biblical witness.

V. Cruz

See also Eternal Punishment; Hell; Hades; Sheol.

Bibliography. H. Bietenhard, *NIDNTT*, II, 205–10; L. Blau, *Jewish Encyclopedia*, V, 582–83; H. Buis, *The Doctrine of Eternal Punishment;* L. Morris, *The Biblical Doctrine of Judgment.*

General Confession, The. This term has a specific and a general meaning. In the Anglican *Book of Common Prayer* there is a prayer at the beginning of matins and evensong to be said by all present. In this there is confession of sins, request for forgiveness, and prayer for grace to live better. Traditionally this is called the General Confession. In Roman Catholicism a general confession is a private prayer in which the penitent makes a confession of the whole of (or part of) the sins of his life, even though he believes that he has already been forgiven for some or all of them. Such a practice is particularly associated with having committed a mortal sin or before entering into a new state of life (e.g., entering a religious order).

P. Toon

General Revelation. *See* Revelation, General.

Generation, Eternal. *See* Eternal Generation.

Genevan Catechism (1537). This catechism by John Calvin was published in French in 1537 as *Instruction and Confession of Faith according to the Use of the Church of Geneva;* it was also published in Latin the following year. Along with a confession of faith and articles on church government which appeared in 1537, the catechism was part of Calvin's original program for the perfecting of the reformation and organization of the church during his first period in Geneva.

The catechism was in fifty-eight sections, and its treatment included the following topics: the knowledge of God, the difference between false and true religion, man, free will, sin and death, salvation, the law of God (including the Ten Commandments), the aim of the law, faith, election and predestination, justification and sanctification, sanctification and obedience to the law, repentance and regeneration, faith and good works, the Apostles' Creed, hope, prayer (including the Lord's Prayer), sacraments, baptism, the Lord's Supper, church pastors and their power, human traditions, excommunication, and the magistrate. The confession of faith that was appended was actually shorter than the catechism and was an extract from the catechism. Both documents restated doctrines that appeared earlier in Calvin's *Institutes* (1536) and were intended as summaries of the faith to which the Genevan community was expected to pledge itself. The catechism was really a manual of theology and was thus too lengthy and profound for the instruction of children. When Calvin returned from exile in 1541, this catechism was replaced by a new catechism in question and answer form. The significance of the 1537 catechism is that it was the first systematic exposition of Calvinist thought in the French language.

A. H. Freundt, Jr.

See also Calvinism; Catechisms.

Bibliography. Calvin, *Catechism, 1538*, tr. F. L. Battles, and *Opera Quae Supersunt Omnia*, ed. J. W. Baum, E. Cunitz, and E. Reuss.

Gerhard, Johann (1582–1637). Considered the third most important theologian in the history of Lutheranism, next to Martin Luther and Martin Chemnitz. His pastor, Johann Arndt, encouraged him to study theology, and he studied at Wittenberg, Jena, and Marburg. As a young man he was already a successful administrator, serving as superintendent of Heldburg and then of Coburg. His academic inclinations and his poor health led away from this strenuous administrative work to a more sedate theological professorship at Jena in 1616. He taught there until his death, in spite of many requests to teach elsewhere. He received numerous requests for advice.

Gerhard wrote in many theological fields, including exegesis, dogmatics, history, polemics, and sermonic and devotional material. His sermons were well received by hearers and readers. His devotional writings show that Lutheran orthodoxy was not at all dead but was conducive to vibrant Christian faith. The best known and most influential of his works was his multivolume dogmatics, *Loci Theologici.*

Gerhard was no innovator as far as the content of Christian doctrine was concerned. He faithfully followed the doctrinal stance of the Lutheran confessions, believing it to be thoroughly biblical. In *Loci Theologici* he drew heavily on exegesis and historical theology in the presentation of doctrine and also showed the practical use of each doctrine. He organized theology according to the synthetic method, as indicated by the word *Loci* ("topics"). Each doctrine was taken up in turn, and all the Bible said on each topic was considered. There was no attempt to turn theology into a philosophical system. Each doctrine was brought into relation to other doctrines, especially to the main doctrine, the gospel of the forgiveness of sins because of Jesus' death on the cross.

In Gerhard's day Aristotelian terminology came back into fashion in academic circles and he introduced such terminology into Lutheran theology, especially analysis in terms of causes. Gerhard was careful not to let this influence the content of his theology, however. Later seventeenth century Lutheran theologians followed Gerhard in continuing to use these terms.

J. M. DRICKAMER

See also LUTHERAN TRADITION, THE.

Bibliography. *The Concordia Cyclopedia;* R. D. Preus, *The Theology of Post-Reformation Lutheranism;* H. Schmid, *The Doctrinal Theology of the Evangelical Lutheran Church.*

Ghost, Holy. *See* HOLY SPIRIT.

Gifford Lectures. Named for Adam, Lord Gifford (1820–87), a leading Scottish judge, these lectures have been delivered in the four ancient Scottish universities since 1888. Their prescribed aim: "for promoting, advancing, teaching, and diffusing the study of natural theology, in the widest sense of that term, in other words, the knowledge of God" and the study of "the foundation of ethics." Many prestigious publications have resulted from the series, among the participants in which have been W. R. Inge, Friedrich von Hügel, William Temple, Karl Barth, and Reinhold Niebuhr.

J. D. DOUGLAS

Gifts, Spiritual. *See* SPIRITUAL GIFTS.

Gill, John (1697–1771). Baptist minister, theologian, and biblical scholar. Born in Kettering, Northamptonshire, England, he attended the local grammar school where he learned Latin and Greek. With a tremendous thirst for knowledge, he later taught himself other subjects, including Hebrew, theology, and philosophy. In 1716 he made a profession of faith in the local Particular (Calvinistic) Baptist Church and soon began preaching. In 1719 he became pastor of the church at Horsleydown, Southwark, in London, a congregation which he served until his death. In addition, from 1729 to 1756 he lectured on Wednesday evenings in Great Eastcheap. He was also one of the Lime Street lecturers (1730–31). A diligent student, he read widely, particularly in Puritan and Reformed authors and in rabbinic literature. He was recognized in 1745 for his scholarship in biblical literature, Oriental languages, and Jewish antiquities by an honorary D.D. degree from Marischal College, Aberdeen University.

Gill was a very prolific and controversial writer and, although his style was somewhat prolix and ponderous, his writings were appreciated in the Particular Baptist circles among which he became a prominent authority. He defended staunch Baptist principles and what he believed to be orthodox Calvinism against contemporary heterodoxical views on the Trinity, the person of Christ, and the five points of Calvinism. He actually espoused an extreme form of Calvinism, teaching the doctrines of the eternal justification and adoption of the elect and of an eternal covenant of grace. Believing that an elect person is passive in conversion as well as regeneration, he denied that grace should be freely offered to unconverted sinners; it was not his practice to address them or to urge acceptance of the gospel.

Gill's principal writings include *The Doctrine of Justification by the Righteousness of Christ Stated and Defended* (1730), *The Doctrine of the Trinity Stated and Vindicated* (1731), *The Doctrine of God's Everlasting Love to His Elect and Their Eternal Union to Christ* (1732), *The Cause of God and Truth* (1734–38), *The Necessity of Good Works unto Salvation Considered* (1739), *Exposition of the New Testament* (3 vols., 1746–48), *Exposition of the Old Testament* (6 vols., 1748–63), *The Doctrine of Predestination Stated and Set in Scripture-Light* (1752), *The Doctrine of the Saints' Final Perseverance Asserted and Vindicated* (1752), *Dissertation Concerning the Antiquity of the Hebrew Language, Letters, Vowel-Points and Accents* (1767), *A Body of Doctrinal Divinity* (2 vols., 1767), and *A Body of Practical Divinity* (1770). Some of these are still valued and occasionally appear in reprints, such as his biblical expositions and divinity volumes. He was little interested in the evangelical awakening of the eighteenth century, and the influence of Gill and his fellow Hyper-Calvinists explains why this revival was slow in having an effect upon the Particular Baptists.

A. H. FREUNDT, JR.

See also CALVINISM; REFORMED TRADITION, THE.

Bibliography. J. W. Brush, "John Gill's Doctrine of the Church," in W. S. Hudson, ed., *Baptist Concepts of the Church;* J. Rippon, *A Brief Memoir of the Life and Writings of the Late Rev. John Gill, D.D.;* P. Toon, *The Emergence of Hyper-Calvinism in English Nonconformity, 1689–1765.*

Gladden, Washington (1836–1918). A popularizer of liberal theology and one of the most well-known advocates of the social gospel at the turn of the twentieth century in the United States. An ordained Congregationalist minister, Gladden served lengthy pastorates in Springfield, Massachusetts, and Columbus, Ohio. He also lectured widely and authored more than thirty-five books. Theologically Gladden was in the vanguard of liberalism. He emphasized God's loving care as a Father for his children. He regarded the atonement as "the reconciliation of suffering with love" that brought us Christ's victory over evil and his love for God. And under the influence of Horace Bushnell, he regarded all of nature romantically as the arena of God's imminent activity. Such works as *Who Wrote the Bible?* (1891) adapted evolutionary views of Christian origins and human potential to the higher criticism of Scriptures.

Gladden was a tireless champion of social reform. His interests focused on the economic sphere, where he argued against industrial exploitation of workers and for the rights of unions. He felt that education could improve the lot of laborers in order to equip them for fuller participation in the economy. He once urged his denomination to refuse a gift from the Standard Oil Company as tainted money. Much more than most of his contemporaries, Gladden preserved the social activism that had characterized nineteenth century American Christianity in general. But he did not preserve its basically orthodox theology. It was the kingdom of God, understood in social terms, with a renewed America bringing it to fruition, that occupied his concern. Gladden was also the author of hymns, including the well-known "O Master, Let Me Walk with Thee."

M. A. Noll

See also Social Gospel, The; Liberalism, Theological.

Bibliography. J. H. Dorn, *Washington Gladden: Prophet of the Social Gospel;* C. H. Hopkins, *The Rise of the Social Gospel in American Protestantism: 1865–1915;* R. T. Handy, ed., *The Social Gospel in America: 1870–1920.*

Glastonbury. During the Middle Ages the town of Glastonbury in Somerset, England, was a major center of pilgrimage. In the twelfth century, following a fire at the abbey, the monks of Glastonbury claimed to have found the remains of the legendary King Arthur. In addition to promoting legends about Arthur, the monks of Glastonbury said that the abbey was founded by Joseph of Arimathea. At the Reformation, Glastonbury Abbey was destroyed. During the eighteenth and nineteenth centuries its ruins attracted sporadic visitors, including the poet and visionary William Blake. In the twentieth century both the Roman Catholic and Anglican Churches have organized regular pilgrimages to Glastonbury. After 1906 the abbey ruins were restored as a historical monument by the Church of England, which employed the architect Fredrick Bligh Bond to supervise the work. Bond began experimenting with automatic writing and claimed to receive instructions from the spirits of long-dead monks. His occult activities embarrassed the Bishop of Wells, who removed him from his post.

During the 1920s and 30s an artistic festival was organized in Glastonbury. This festival aimed at reviving English folk arts and had a particular interest in Arthurian legends. Among others the Christian writer C. S. Lewis was influenced by this movement, and his book *That Hideous Strength* is set in Glastonbury. Two important writers in Glastonbury during this period were the ritual magician Dion Fortune, who published *Avalon of the Heart* in 1939, and Mrs. K. E. Maltwood, whose *Guide to Glastonbury's Temple of the Stars* (1938) describes a massive prehistoric earthwork she claimed to have discovered in the hills surrounding Glastonbury. This monument she named the Somerset Zodiac. In the 1940s Major W. Tudor Pole started a religious retreat known as the Chalice Well House and claimed to have received spiritual communications about Glastonbury. In *A Man Seen Afar* (1965) he describes a vision of Christ returning to Glastonbury. A variety of other books have been written containing spiritual messages about Glastonbury. In 1965 the British Israelites opened their national conference center there.

During the late 60s the British counterculture made Glastonbury a center for pilgrimage and popularized both the traditional legends and the more recent occult writings. Since then, the Findhorn community has established itself in Glastonbury and is using the prestige which the town holds in British occultist circles to promote its own views. In addition to groups already mentioned, others calling themselves the Druids, the Essenes, and a variety of similar off-beat organizations make regular visits to Glastonbury.

I. Hexham

See also British Israelitism.

Bibliography. O. L. Reiser, *This Holiest Erthe.*

Glorification. This refers especially to the time when, at the parousia, those who died in Christ and the living believers will be given the resurrection of the body—a final and full "redemption of our body" (Rom. 8:23), preparatory for and suited to the final state of the Christian believer. As a theological term it is a synonym of immortality—when immortality is thought of as the glorification which believers will receive, and not, as erroneously thought of, as simply the continued existence of both the believers and the finally impenitent.

Glorification, therefore, is only for believers, and it consists of the redemption of the body. At that time "this perishable" will "put on the imperishable," and "this mortal," the body, will "put on immortality" (I Cor. 15:53). Then death, the Christian's last enemy (I Cor. 15:26), will be swallowed up in victory (I Cor. 15:54).

The finally impenitent will be resurrected, but this is a second resurrection, to damnation—the "second death" (Rev. 2:11). Scripture does not refer to this second resurrection as either immortality or glorification.

Our special glory seems to consist, in part, in the hope we hold to: that we will be glorified. Paul also seems to teach that after the believers are glorified, the whole created world will undergo a fundamental renewal: "For the anxious longing of the creation waits eagerly for the revealing of the sons of God. For the creation was subjected to futility, . . . in hope that the creation itself will be set free from its corruption into the freedom of the glory of [or glorification of] the children of God" (Rom. 8:19–21 NASB).

J. K. Grider

See also Heaven.

Glory. The principal word in the Hebrew for this concept of *kābôd,* and in the Greek *doxa,* which is derived from *dokeō,* "to think" or "to seem." These two meanings account for the two main lines of significance in classical Greek, where *doxa* means opinion (what one thinks for himself) and reputation (what others think about him), which may shade into fame or honor or praise.

In the OT. Since *kābôd* derives from *kābēd,* "to be heavy," it lends itself to the idea that the one possessing glory is laden with riches (Gen. 31:1), power (Isa. 8:7), position (Gen. 45:13), etc. To the translators of the LXX it seemed that *doxa* was the most suitable word for rendering *kābôd,* since it carried the notion of reputation or honor which was present in the use of *kābôd.* But *kābôd* also denoted the manifestation of light by which God revealed himself, whether in the lightning flash or in the blinding splendor which often accompanied theophanies. Of the same nature was the disclosure of the divine presence in the cloud which led Israel through the wilderness and became localized in the tabernacle. So *doxa,* as a translation of *kābôd,* gained a nuance of meaning which it did not possess before. At times *kābôd* had a deeper penetration, denoting the person or self. When Moses made the request of God, "Show me thy glory" (Exod. 33:18), he was not speaking of the light-cloud, which he had already seen, but he was seeking a special manifestation of God which would leave nothing to be desired (cf. John 14:8). Moses had a craving to come to grips with God as he was in himself. In reply, God emphasized his goodness (Exod. 33:19). The word might be rendered in this instance "moral beauty." Apart from this the eternity of God as a subject of human contemplation might be depressing. This incident involving Moses is the seed plot for the idea that God's glory is not confined to some outward sign which appeals to the senses, but is that which expresses his inherent majesty, which may or may not have some visible token. Isaiah's vision of him (6:1ff.) included both the perception of sensible features and the nature of God, particularly his holiness (cf. John 12:41). The intrinsic worth of God, his ineffable majesty, constitutes the basis of warnings not to glory in riches, wisdom, or might (Jer. 9:23) but in the God who has given all these and is greater than his gifts. In the prophets the word "glory" is often used to set forth the excellence of the messianic kingdom in contrast to the limitations of the present order (Isa. 60:1–3).

In the NT. In general *doxa* follows rather closely the pattern established in the LXX. It is used of honor in the sense of recognition or acclaim (Luke 14:10), and of the vocalized reverence of the creature for the Creator and Judge (Rev. 14:7). With reference to God, it denotes his majesty (Rom. 1:23) and his perfection, especially in relation to righteousness (Rom. 3:23). He is called the Father of glory (Eph. 1:17). The manifestation of his presence in terms of light is an occasional phenomenon, as in the OT (Luke 2:9), but in the main this feature is transferred to the Son. The transfiguration is the sole instance during the earthly ministry, but later manifestations include the revelation to Saul at the time of his conversion (Acts 9:3ff.) and to John on the Isle of Patmos (Rev. 1:12ff.). The fact that Paul is able to speak of God's glory in terms of riches (Eph. 1:18; 3:16) and might (Col. 1:11) suggests the influence of the OT upon his thinking. The display of God's power in raising his Son from the dead is labeled glory (Rom. 6:4).

Christ is the effulgence of the divine glory (Heb. 1:3). By means of him the perfection of the nature of God is made known to men. When James speaks of him as the Lord of glory (2:1), his thought seems to move along the lines of the revelation of God in the tabernacle. There the divine presence was a gracious condescension but also an ever-present reminder of God's readiness to mark the sins of his people and to visit them with judgment. So the readers of James's epistle are admonished to beware of partiality. The Lord is in the midst of his people as of yore.

The glory of Christ as the image of God, the Son of the Father, was veiled from sinful eyes during the days of his flesh but was apparent to the men of faith who gathered around him (John 1:14).

Even as the preincarnate Son had dwelt with the Father in a state of glory (with no sin to mar the perfection of the divine mode of life and intercourse), according to his own consciousness (John 17:5), so his return to the Father can properly be called an entrance into glory (Luke 24:26). But more seems to be involved here than a sharing with the Father of what he had enjoyed in ages past. God now gives him glory (I Pet. 1:21), in some sense as a reward for the faithful, full completion of the Father's will in relation to the work of salvation (Phil. 2:9–11; Acts 3:13). So it is that both the taking up of Christ from the earth (I Tim. 3:16) and his return (Col. 3:4; Titus 2:13) and the representations of his presence and activity as the future judge and king (Matt. 25:31) are also associated with a majesty and radiance which are largely lacking in the portrayals of Jesus in the days of his humiliation.

While the contrast is valid, therefore, between the sufferings of Christ and the glory (literally, the glories) to follow (I Pet. 1:11), John's Gospel reveals a further development, namely, that the sufferings themselves can be viewed as a glorification. Jesus was aware of this and expressed himself accordingly. "The hour is come that the Son of man should be glorified" (John 12:23). This word "hour" in the Fourth Gospel points regularly to the death of Christ. Jesus was not seeking to invest the cross with an aura of splendor which it did not have, in order to conjure up a psychological antidote to its pain and shame. Rather, glory properly belongs to the finishing of the work which the Father had given him to do, since that work represented the perfect will of God.

Eschatological glory is the hope of the Christian (Rom. 5:2). In this future state he will have a new body patterned after Christ's glorified body (Phil. 3:21), an instrument superior to that with which he is presently endowed (I Cor. 15:43). Christ within the believer is the hope of glory (Col. 1:27). He is also the chief ornament of heaven (Rev. 21:23).

The word "glory" is found in the plural to denote dignitaries (Jude 8). It is not easy to determine whether the reference is to angels or men of honor and repute in the Christian community.

A somewhat specialized use of the word is that which it has in the doxologies, which are ascriptions of praise to God for his worth and works (e.g., Rom. 11:36).

On several occasions glory is used as a verb (*kauchaomai*) where the meaning is to boast, as in Gal. 6:14.

E. F. Harrison

See also Boasting; Honor.

Bibliography. I. Abrahams, *The Glory of God;* A. von Gall, *Die Herrlichkeit Gottes;* G. B. Gray and J. Massie in *HDB;* E. C. E. Owen, "Doxa and Cognate Word," *JTS* 33:132–50, 265–79; A. M. Ramsey, *The Glory of God and the Transfiguration of Christ;* G. von Rad and G. Kittel, *TDNT,* II, 232ff.; S. Aalen, *NIDNTT,* II, 44ff.

Glossolalia. *See* Tongues, Speaking in.

Gnesio-Lutherans. *See* Adiaphora, Adiaphorists; Flacius, Matthias.

Gnosticism. Prior to the first half of the twentieth century such early heresiologists (defenders of Christianity against heresy) as Irenaeus, Tertullian, Hippolytus, and Epiphanius were our principal sources of information concerning the Gnostics. These heresiologists were scathing in their denunciations of the Gnostics, who were perceived as leading Christians astray by the manipulation of words and the twisting of scriptural meanings. Of particular interest to Gnostic interpreters were the stories of Genesis, the Gospel of John, and the epistles of Paul. They used the biblical texts for their own purposes. Indeed, Gnostics such as Heracleon and Ptolemaeus were the first commentators on the Fourth Gospel. But Irenaeus likens such interpretations to someone who takes apart a beautiful picture of a king and reassembles it into a picture of a fox (*Adversus Haereses* 1.8.1).

The heresiologists regarded Gnosticism as the product of the combination of Greek philosophy and Christianity. For instance, after detailing the Gnostic heretics, Tertullian announces: "What indeed has Athens to do with Jerusalem? What concord is there between the Academy and the Church? What between heretics and Christians? . . . Away with all attempts to produce a mottled Christianity of Stoic, Platonic, and dialectic composition" (*On Prescription Against Heretics* 7). The heresiologists' view concerning Gnosticism was generally regarded as acceptable even at the end of the nineteenth century, when Adolf Harnack defined Gnosticism as the "acute secularizing of Christianity."

The history of religions school, of which Hans Jonas is a contemporary exponent, has challenged this definition. According to Jonas, Gnosticism is a general religious phenomenon of the hellenistic world and is the product of the fusion of Greek culture and Oriental religion. The "Greek conceptualization" of Eastern religious traditions—i.e., Jewish monotheism, Babylonian astrology, and Iranian dualism—is viewed as the basis for Gnosticism. While R. M. Wilson and R. M. Grant reject such a broad definition and affirm instead a primary basis in hellenistic Judaism or Jewish apocalyptic, the advantage of Jonas's view is that it recognizes the broad spectrum within Gnosticism. The weakness is that the definition encompasses almost everything within the concept of hellenistic religions.

The breadth of Gnostic orientations, however, has been confirmed by the discovery of a Gnostic library at Nag Hammadi in Egypt. In the thirteen ancient codices are included fifty-two tractates of which six represent duplicates. The tractates are of various types and orientations. A large number clearly present a Christian Gnostic perspective, the most familiar being the three so-called Valentinian gospels: the Gospel of Thomas (composed of a series of brief sayings of Jesus), the Gospel of Philip (a collection of sayings, metaphors, and esoteric arguments), and the Gospel of Truth (a discourse on deity and unity reminiscent of the language of the Fourth Gospel but definitely bent in the direction of Gnostic mythology and possibly related to the Gospel of Truth by Valentinus noted in Irenaeus). Also among the Christian Gnostic tractates are the Apocryphon of James, the Acts of Peter and the Twelve Apostles, the Treatise on the Resurrection, the long collection known as the Tripartite Tractate, and three editions of the Apocryphon of John (the fascinating story of creation which involves a reinterpretation of the Genesis accounts).

But not all the tractates reveal a pseudo-Christian orientation. The Paraphrase of Shem seems to reflect a Jewish Gnostic perspective. The Discourse on the Eighth and the Ninth is patently a Hermetic treatise. The longest tractate in the library (132 pages) bears the designation Zostrianos and purports to be from Zoroaster. One of the interesting features of this library is the presence of two editions of Eugnostos the Blessed, which seems to be a non-Christian philosophic document which has apparently been "Christianized" in a redacted tractate called the Sophia of Jesus Christ. Finally, the presence of a segment from Plato's *Republic* among these documents gives further witness to the syncretistic nature of Gnostic thinking. As a result of Gnostic borrowing, readers will sense a certain fluidity in the Gnostic designations.

Types of Gnosticism. Despite a fluidity within Gnosticism, however, Jonas identifies two basic patterns or structures of Gnostic thought. Both are mythological structures which seek to explain the problem of evil in terms of its relationship to the process of creation.

Iranian. This branch of Gnosticism developed in Mesopotamia and reflects a horizontal dualism associated with Zoroastrian worship and is epitomized in its later Gnostic form of Manichaeism. In this pattern light and darkness, the two primal principles or deities, are locked in a decisive struggle. This struggle has been positionalized by the fact that, since light transcends itself and shines beyond its own realm, light particles were subjected to capture by its jealous enemy, darkness. In order to launch a counterattack and recapture its lost particles, therefore, light gives birth to (or "emanates") a series of subordinate deities that are emanated for the purpose of doing battle. In defense, darkness likewise sets in motion a comparable birthing of subdeities and arranges for the entombment of the light particles in a created world. This cosmic realm becomes the sphere of combat for the protagonists. The object of the struggle is the winning of the human beings who bear the light particles and the effecting of their release from the prison of this world so that they may reenter the sphere of heavenly light.

Syrian. This type arose in the area of Syria, Palestine, and Egypt and reflects a much more complex vertical dualism. In this system the ultimate principle is good, and the task of the Gnostic thinkers is to explain how evil emerged from the singular principle of good. The method employed is the identification of some deficiency or error in the good.

The Valentinian solution to the problem of evil is that the good god (the ultimate depth) with his consort (silence) initiates the birthing process of (or "emanates") a series of paired deities. The last of the subordinate deities (usually designated as Sophia, wisdom) is unhappy with her consort and desires, instead, a relationship with the ultimate depth. This desire is unacceptable in the godhead and is extracted from Sophia and excluded from the heavenly realm (*plērōma*). While Sophia is thus rescued from her lust, the godhead has lost a portion of its divine nature. The goal, therefore, is the recovery of the fallen light.

But the excluded desire (or lower Sophia) is unaware of its fallen nature, and depending on the various accounts, either it or its offspring, the Creator, begins a "demiurgical" or birthing process which partially mirrors the "emanating" process in the *plērōma* and ultimately results in the creation of the world. The upper godhead (*plērōma*) by its divine messenger (often called Christ or the Holy Spirit) tricks the Creator-

Demiurge into breathing into man the breath of life, and thus the light particles are passed to a light-man. The defense strategy of the lower godhead (realm of the Demiurge) is that the light-man is entombed in a body of death which, under the direction of the Demiurge, has been formed by its pseudosubdeities, also known as "the fates" or identified with the realm of the planets.

The Garden of Eden story is then transformed so that the biblical tree of the knowledge of good and evil becomes a vehicle of knowledge (*gnōsis*) established by the heavenly or pleromatic realm. But the tree of life becomes a vehicle of bondage and dependence established by the demiurgical realm. The divine messenger from the *plērōma* encourages man to eat from the tree of knowledge; and in so eating, man discovers that the jealous Creator-Demiurge (often linked with misspelled forms of Yahweh such as Yaldabaoth or Yao) is not in fact the ultimate God but really an enemy of God. Man, as a result of divine help, thus comes to know more than the Creator. In anger the Creator casts man into an earthly body of forgetfulness, and the pleromatic realm is forced to initiate a process of spiritual awakening through the divine messenger.

The divine messenger is frequently identified with the figure of the Christian's Jesus Christ, but such identification has some very significant alterations. Since the divine realm is basically opposed to the creation of the lower realm, bodies at best are part of the created process and therefore need only to be regarded as vehicles which the divine may use for its own purposes. The divine messenger Christ, for the purpose of modeling the divine perspective, "adopted" the body of Jesus at a point such as the baptism and departed at a point such as just prior to the crucifixion. It is the risen "Jesus" or Christ, devoid of bodily restrictions, that based on the modeling has power to awaken man from his sleep of forgetfulness. This assumption of the body of Jesus by the divine messenger is generally termed as "adoptionism" and is related to docetism, wherein Christ merely appears to be a man.

Gnostics are those set within a world where they are the spiritual persons (*pneumatikoi*) who possess the light particles and need only to be awakened in order to inherit their destinies. In the world there are also said to be psychic persons (*psychikoi*), who are a grade lower and need to work for whatever salvation they may be able to attain. The Gnostics often identified such psychics with Christians and understandably irritated the Christian heresiologists such as Irenaeus. The third division of this view of humanity is composed of material persons (*hylikoi* or *sarkikoi*), who have no chance to inherit any form of salvation but are destined for destruction. Accordingly, it should be obvious that such a view of anthropology is very deterministic in orientation.

The Valentinian goal is reentry into the *plērōma*, which is often symbolized by terms such as "union" or "unity." In documents such as the Gospel of Philip, however, the use of the term "bridal chamber" may suggest a sacrament of union. Such expressions highlight the fact that in many Gnostic documents sexually suggestive terminology is employed. For some Gnostics sexual interests may be attached to a spiritual alternative within an ascetic life style which seems to issue in warnings not to fragment further the light particles in one's self through conjugation or sexual intercourse. For others, however, such as the followers of Marcus, spiritual awareness was apparently transferred through copulative activity outside of marriage.

At death the Gnostics, who had experienced awakening, shed the rags of mortality as they ascended through the realms of the fates (or planets). Thus, passing through the purgatory of the planets, they came at last to the limit (*horos*) or border (sometimes called the "cross") where, devoid of all that constitutes evil, they are welcomed into the eternal realm. The concept of purgatory in the Roman Catholic tradition is not unrelated to the purging pattern in Gnostic thought.

The above description is a pattern for understanding the Syrian type of Gnostic structure. While this structure should provide a helpful model for readers in interpreting Gnostic documents, it is imperative to recognize the syncretistic nature of Gnosticism and the wide variety of forms which are evident. The Sethians, for example, used Seth as their human figurehead, whereas the Ophites concentrated on the role of the serpent in giving knowledge. The vast possibilities for variation in structure make Gnostic studies both an intriguing and exercising enterprise.

The Gnostics obviously used sources such as Platonic dualism and Eastern religious thought, including ideas derived from Christianity. Their use of sources, however, often resulted in an attack upon those sources. For example, the Gnostics employ the concept of wisdom (the goal of Greek philosophy) in such a way that it is made the cause of all evil in the world. Such an ingenious attack on the concept of wisdom is far more hostile than Paul's statements in I Cor. 1:22–2:16.

In addition to the Valentinian system and its

many related forms Hermetic literature provides a somewhat similar vertical-structured dualism. This arose in Egypt, and most of the writings seem to be generally unrelated to Christianity or Judaism, although the principal tractate of the Corpus Hermeticum known as Poimandres may not be totally unlike the thought world of the Fourth Gospel. Hermetic literature thus raises the problem of Gnostic origins.

The Problem of Dating. Because of the methodological problems concerning Gnostic origins, it is imperative to mention briefly Mandaeanism. In the 1930s many scholars were referring to Mandaeanism as being pre-Christian, in spite of the fact that the documents used in the interpretive process were obtained from the small contemporary sect in Persia. There is of course no doubt that the traditions of this baptismal sect (which refers to John the Baptist) come from a much earlier time. But how long before the rise of Islam—which considered Mandaeans a valid religious group possessing both sacred writings and a prophet prior to Mohammed—is totally unknown. The matter of dating is, therefore, extremely problematic in the entire study of Gnosticism. Some documents like the Hermetic materials seem to evidence very few influences from Christianity, whereas a few documents, such as the Sophia of Jesus, may be Christianized redactions of earlier non-Christian documents. But the question that still remains to be answered is: When did Gnosticism arise? Clearly by the middle of the second century A.D. Gnosticism had reached its flowering. But contrary to Schmithals (*Gnosticism in Corinth*) the opponents of Paul in Corinth were hardly Gnostics. Were the opponents described in Colossians or Ephesians Gnostics? Were the opponents in the Johannine letters Gnostics? It is hard to read the NT and gain any secure feeling at the present that canonical writers were attacking the Gnostic devotees or mythologizers. G. L. BORCHERT

See also MANDAEANS; HERMETIC LITERATURE.

Bibliography. D. M. Scholer, *Nag Hammadi Bibliography 1948–1969,* plus annual supplementary bibliographies beginning in 1971 by the same author in *NovT;* J. Robinson, ed., *The Nag Hammadi Library in English;* R. M. Grant, ed., *Gnosticism: A Source Book of Heretical Writings from the Early Christian Period;* W. Foerster, *Gnosis: A Selection of Gnostic Texts,* 2 vols.; B. Aland, *Gnosis: Festschrift für Hans Jonas;* G. L. Borchert, "Insights into the Gnostic Threat to Christianity as Gained Through the Gospel of Philip," in *New Dimensions in New Testament Study,* ed. R. N. Longenecker and M. C. Tenney; R. M. Grant, *Gnosticism and Early Christianity;* H. Jonas, *The Gnostic Religion;* E. Pagels, *The Gnostic Gospels;* G. Quispel, *Gnosis als Weltreligion;* W. Schmithals, *Gnosticism in Corinth* and *Paul and the Gnostics;* R. M. Wilson, *The Gnostic Problem* and *Gnosis and the New Testament;* E. Yamauchi, *Pre-Christian Gnosticism.*

God, Arguments for the Existence of. The arguments for the existence of God constitute one of the finest attempts of the human mind to break out of the world and go beyond the sensible or phenomenal realm of experience.

Certainly the question of God's existence is the most important question of human philosophy. It affects the whole tenor of human life, whether man is regarded as the supreme being in the universe or whether it is believed that man has a superior being that he must love and obey, or perhaps defy.

There are three ways one can argue for the existence of God. First, the *a priori* approach argues from a conception of God as a being so perfect that his nonexistence is inconceivable. Second, the *a posteriori* approach gives evidence from the world, from the observable, empirical universe, insisting that God is necessary to explain certain features of the cosmos. Third, the existential approach asserts direct experience of God by way of personal revelation. This approach is not really an argument in the usual sense, because one does not usually argue for something that can be directly experienced.

The* A Priori *Approach. This approach is the heart of the famous ontological argument, devised by Anselm of Canterbury though adumbrated earlier in the system of Augustine. This argument begins with a special definition of God as infinite, perfect, and necessary.

Anselm said that God cannot be conceived in any way other than "a being than which nothing greater can be conceived." Even the fool knows what he means by "God" when he asserts, "There is no God" (Ps. 14:1). But if the most perfect being existed only in thought and not in reality, then it would not really be the most perfect being, for the one that existed in reality would be more perfect. Therefore, concludes Anselm, "no one who understands what God is, can conceive that God does not exist." In short, it would be self-contradictory to say, "I can think of a perfect being that doesn't exist," because existence would have to be a part of perfection. One would be saying, "I can conceive of something greater than that which nothing greater can be conceived"—which is absurd.

The ontological argument has had a long and stormy history. It has appealed to some of the finest minds in Western history, usually mathematicians like Descartes, Spinoza, and Leibniz. However, it fails to persuade most people, who seem to harbor the same suspicion as Kant that "the unconditioned necessity of a judgment does not form the absolute necessity of a thing." That is, perfection may not be a true predicate and thus a proposition can be logically necessary without being true in fact.

The* A Posteriori *Approach. Popular mentality seems to appreciate the *a posteriori* approach better. The ontological argument can be made without ever appealing to sensation, but the cosmological and teleological arguments require a careful look at the world. The former focuses on the cause, while the latter stresses the design of the universe.

The Cosmological Argument. This has more than one form. The earliest occurs in Plato (*Laws,* Book X) and Aristotle (*Metaphysics,* Book VIII) and stresses the need to explain the cause of motion. Assuming that rest is natural and motion is unnatural, these thinkers arrived at God as the necessary Prime Mover of all things. Thomas Aquinas used motion as his first proof in the *Summa Theologica* (Q.2, Art.3). Everything that moves has to be moved by another thing. But this chain of movers cannot go on to infinity—a key assumption—because there would then be no first mover and thus no other mover. We must arrive, therefore, at a first mover, Aquinas concludes, "and this everyone understands to be God."

This argument from motion is not nearly as cogent for our scientific generation because we take motion to be natural and rest to be unnatural, as the principle of inertia states. Many philosophers insist that the notion of an infinite series of movers is not at all impossible or contradictory.

The most interesting—and persuasive—form of the cosmological argument is Aquinas's "third way," the argument from contingency. Its strength derives from the way it employs both permanence and change. Epicurus stated the metaphysical problem centuries ago: "Something obviously exists now, and something never sprang from nothing." Being, therefore, must have been without beginning. An Eternal Something must be admitted by all—theist, atheist, and agnostic.

But the physical universe could not be this Eternal Something because it is obviously contingent, mutable, subject to decay. How could a decomposing entity explain itself to all eternity? If every present contingent thing/event depends on a previous contingent thing/event and so on *ad infinitum,* then this does not provide an adequate explanation of anything.

Hence, for there to be anything at all contingent in the universe, there must be at least one thing that is not contingent—something that is necessary throughout all change and self-established. In this case "necessary" does not apply to a proposition but to a thing, and it means infinite, eternal, everlasting, self-caused, self-existent.

It is not enough to say that infinite time will solve the problem of contingent being. No matter how much time you have, dependent being is still dependent on something. Everything contingent within the span of infinity will, at some particular moment, not exist. But if there was a moment when nothing existed, then nothing would exist now.

The choice is simple: one chooses either a self-existent God or a self-existent universe—and the universe is not behaving as if it is self-existent. In fact, according to the second law of thermodynamics, the universe is running down like a clock or, better, cooling off like a giant stove. Energy is constantly being diffused or dissipated, that is, progressively distributed throughout the universe. If this process goes on for a few billion more years—and scientists have never observed a restoration of dissipated energy—then the result will be a state of thermal equilibrium, a "heat death," a random degradation of energy throughout the entire cosmos and hence the stagnation of all physical activity.

Naturalists from Lucretius to Sagan have felt that we need not postulate God as long as nature can be considered a self-explanatory entity for all eternity. But it is difficult to hold this doctrine if the second law is true and entropy is irreversible. If the cosmos is running down or cooling off, then it could not have been running and cooling forever. It must have had a beginning.

A popular retort to the cosmological argument is to ask, "If God made the universe, then who made God?" If one insists that the world had a cause, must one not also insist that God had a cause? No, because if God is a necessary being—this is established if one accepts the proof—then it is unnecessary to inquire into his origins. It would be like asking, "Who made the unmakable being?" or "Who caused the uncausable being?"

More serious is the objection that the proof is based on an uncritical acceptance of the "principle of sufficient reason," the notion that every event/effect has a cause. If this principle is denied, even if it is denied in metaphysics, the cosmological argument is defanged. Hume argued that causation is a psychological, not a metaphysical, principle, one whose origins lay in the human propensity to assume necessary connections between events when all we really see is contiguity and succession. Kant seconded Hume by arguing that causation is a category built into our minds as one of the many ways in which we order our experience. Sartre felt that the universe was "gratuitous." Bertrand Russell claimed that the question of origins was tangled in meaningless verbiage and that we must be content to declare that the universe is "just there and that's all."

One does not prove the principle of causality easily. It is one of those foundational assumptions that is made in building a world view. It can be pointed out, however, that if we jettison the idea of sufficient reason, we will destroy not only metaphysics but science as well. When one attacks causality, one attacks much of knowledge *per se*, for without this principle the rational connection in most of our learning falls to pieces. Surely it is not irrational to inquire into the cause of the entire universe.

The Teleological or Design Argument. This is one of the oldest and most popular and intelligible of the theistic proofs. It suggests that there is a definite analogy between the order and regularity of the cosmos and a product of human ingenuity. Voltaire put it in rather simplistic terms: "If a watch proves the existence of a watchmaker but the universe does not prove the existence of a great Architect, then I consent to be called a fool."

No one can deny the universe *seems* to be designed; instances of purposive ordering are all around us. Almost anywhere can be found features of being that show the universe to be basically friendly to life, mind, personality, and values. Life itself is a cosmic function—that is, a very complex arrangement of things both terrestrial and extraterrestrial must obtain before life can subsist. The earth must be just the right size, its rotation must be just right, its distance from the sun must be within certain limits, its tilt must be correct to cause the seasons, its land-water ratio must be a delicate balance. Our biological structure is very fragile. A little too much heat or cold and we die. We need light, but not too much ultraviolet. We need heat, but not too much infrared. We live just beneath an airscreen shielding us from millions of missiles every day. We live just ten miles above a rock screen that shields us from the terrible heat under our feet. Who created all these screens and shields that make our earthly existence possible?

Once again we are faced with a choice. Either the universe was designed or it developed all these features by chance. The cosmos is either a plan or an accident!

Most people have an innate repugnance to the notion of chance because it contradicts the way we ordinarily explain things. Chance is not an explanation but an abandonment of explanation. When a scientist explains an immediate event, he operates on the assumption that this is a regular universe where everything occurs as a result of the orderly procession of cause and effect. Yet when the naturalist comes to metaphysics, to the origin of the entire cosmos, he abandons the principle of sufficient reason and assumes that the cause of everything is an unthinkable causelessness, chance, or fate.

Suppose you were standing facing a target and you saw an arrow fired from behind you hit the bull's eye. Then you saw nine more arrows fired in rapid succession all hitting the same bull's eye. The aim is so accurate that each arrow splits the previous arrow as it hits. Now an arrow shot into the air is subject to many contrary and discordant processes—gravity, air pressure, and wind. When ten arrows reach the bull's eye, does this not rule out the possibility of mere chance? Would you not say that this was the result of an expert archer? Is this parable not analogous to our universe?

It is objected that the design argument, even if valid, does not prove a creator but only an architect, and even then only an architect intelligent enough to produce the known universe, not necessarily an omniscient being. This objection is correct. We must not try to prove more than the evidence will allow. We will not get the 100 percent Yahweh of the Bible from any evidence of natural theology. However, this universe of ours is so vast and wonderful we can safely conclude that its designer would be worthy of our worship and devotion.

Many object that the theory of evolution takes most of the wind out of the design argument. Evolution shows that the marvelous design in living organisms came about by slow adaptation to the environment, not by intelligent creation. This is a false claim. Even if admitted, evolution only introduces a longer time-frame into the question of design. Proving that watches came from a completely automated factory with no human intervention would not make us give up interest in a designer, for if we thought a watch was wonderful, what must we think of a factory that produces watches? Would it not suggest a designer just as forcefully? Religious people have been overly frightened by the theory of evolution.

Even the great critics of natural theology, Hume and Kant, betrayed an admiration for the teleological argument. Hume granted it a certain limited validity. Kant went even further: "This proof will always deserve to be treated with respect. It is the oldest, the clearest and most in conformity with human reason. . . . We have nothing to say against the reasonableness and utility of this line of argument, but wish, on the contrary, to commend and encourage it."

The Moral Argument. This is the most recent of the theistic proofs. The first major philosopher to use it was Kant, who felt that the traditional proofs were defective. Kant held that the existence of God and the immortality of the soul were matters of faith, not ordinary speculative reason, which, he claimed, is limited to sensation.

Kant reasoned that the moral law commands us to seek the *summum bonum* (highest good), with perfect happiness as a logical result. But a problem arises when we contemplate the unpleasant fact that "there is not the slightest ground in the moral law for a necessary connexion between morality and proportionate happiness in a being that belongs to the world as a part of it." The only postulate, therefore, that will make sense of man's moral experience is "the existence of a cause of all nature, distinct from nature itself," i.e., a God who will properly reward moral endeavor in another world. In a godless universe man's deepest experience would be a cruel enigma.

In his *Rumor of Angels*, Peter Berger gives an interesting negative version of the moral argument, which he calls "the argument from damnation." Our apodictic moral condemnation of such immoral men as Adolf Eichmann seems to transcend tastes and mores; it seems to demand a condemnation of supernatural dimensions. Some deeds are not only evil but monstrously evil; they appear immune to any kind of moral relativizing. In making such high-voltage moral judgments, as when we condemn slavery and genocide, we point to a transcendent realm of moral absolutes. Otherwise, all our moralizing is pointless and groundless. A "preaching relativist" is one of the most comical of self-contradictions.

Most modern thinkers who use the moral argument continue Kant's thesis that God is a necessary postulate to explain moral experience. Kant thought the moral law could be established by reason, but he called in God to guarantee the reward for virtue. Modern thinkers do not use God so much for the reward as for providing a ground for the moral law in the first place.

The moral argument starts with the simple fact of ethical experience. The pressure to do one's duty can be felt as strongly as the pressure of an empirical object. Who or what is causing this pressure? It is not enough to say that we are conditioned by society to feel those pressures. Some of the greatest moralists in history have acquired their fame precisely because they criticized the moral failings of their group—tribe, class, race, or nation. If social subjectivism is the explanation of moral motivation, then we have no right to criticize slavery or genocide or anything!

Evolutionists attack the moral argument by insisting that all morality is merely a long development from animal instincts. Men gradually work out their ethical systems by living together in social communities. But this objection is a two-edged sword: if it kills morality, it also kills reason and the scientific method. The evolutionist believes that the human intellect developed from the physical brain of the primates, yet he assumes that the intellect is trustworthy. If the mind is entitled to trust, though evolved from the lower forms, why not the moral nature also?

Many people will go part way and accept moral objectivism, but they want to stop with a transcendent realm of impersonal moral absolutes. They deny that one must believe in a Person, Mind, or Lawgiver. This seems reductive. It is difficult to imagine an "impersonal mind." How could a *thing* make us feel duty bound to be kind, helpful, truthful, and loving? We should press on, all the way to a Person, God, the Lawgiver. Only then is the moral experience adequately explained.

The Question of Validity. How valid are all these theistic proofs? This question raises issues in a number of fields: logic, metaphysics, physics, and theory of knowledge. Some thinkers like Aquinas feel that the proofs reach the level of demonstration. Others like Hume say that we should just suspend judgment and remain skeptics. Still others like Pascal and Kant reject the traditional proofs but offer instead practical grounds or reasons for accepting God's existence. Pascal's famous wager is an appeal to pragmatism; it makes sense, in view of the eternal consequences, to bet on the existence of God.

Paul seems to demand a high view of the theistic proofs when he says that the unbelievers are "without excuse." "What can be known about God is plain to them, because God has shown it to them. Ever since the creation of the world his invisible nature, namely his eternal power and deity, has been clearly perceived in the things that have been made" (Rom. 1:19–20).

Paul was not necessarily affirming that the arguments are deductive, analytical, or demonstrative. If someone rejected a proposition of high probability, we could still say that he was "without excuse." The arguments, in their cumulative effect, make a very strong case for the existence of God, but they are not logically inexorable or rationally inevitable. If we define proof as probable occurrence based on empirically produced experiences and subject to the test of reasonable judgment, then we can say the arguments prove the existence of God.

If God truly exists, then we are dealing with a

factual proposition, and what we really want when we ask for proof of a factual proposition is not a demonstration of its logical impossibility but a degree of evidence that will exclude reasonable doubt. Something can be so probable that it excludes reasonable doubt without being deductive or analytical or demonstrative or logically inevitable. We feel that the theistic proofs—excluding the ontological argument—fall into this category.

Natural theology, however, can never establish the existence of the biblical God. These proofs may make one a deist, but only revelation will make one a Christian. Reason operating without revelation always turns up with a deity different from Yahweh, the Father of Our Lord Jesus Christ. One can confirm this easily by comparing Yahweh with the deities of Aristotle, Spinoza, Voltaire, and Thomas Paine. A. J. HOOVER

See also REVELATION, GENERAL.

Bibliography. J. Baillie, *Our Knowledge of God;* D. Burrill, *The Cosmological Argument;* G. H. Clark, *A Christian View of Men and Things;* R. E. D. Clark, *The Universe: Plan or Accident?* H. H. Farmer, *Towards Belief in God;* R. Hazelton, *On Proving God;* J. Hick, *The Existence of God;* D. Hicks, *The Philosophical Basis of Theism;* A. J. Hoover, *The Case for Christian Theism;* S. Jaki, *The Road of Science and the Ways to God;* C. E. M. Joad, *God and Evil;* J. Maritain, *Approaches to God;* E. L. Mascall, *The Openness of Being;* G. Mavrodes, *The Rationality of Belief in God;* A. Plantinga, ed., *The Ontological Argument;* R. C. Sproul, *If There Is a God, Why Are There Atheists?* A. E. Taylor, *Does God Exist?*

God, Attributes of. God is an invisible, personal, and living Spirit, distinguished from all other spirits by several kinds of attributes: metaphysically God is self-existent, eternal, and unchanging; intellectually God is omniscient, faithful, and wise; ethically God is just, merciful, and loving; emotionally God detests evil, is long-suffering, and is compassionate; existentially God is free, authentic, and omnipotent; relationally God is transcendent in being, immanent universally in providential activity, and immanent with his people in redemptive activity.

The essence of anything, simply put, equals its being (substance) plus its attributes. Since Kant's skepticism of knowing anything in itself or in its essence, many philosophers and theologians have limited their general ways of speaking to the phenomena of Jewish or Christian religious experience. Abandoning categories of essence, substance, and attribute, they have thought exclusively in terms of Person-to-person encounters, mighty acts of God, divine functions, or divine processes in history. God is indeed active in all these and other ways, but is not silent. Inscripturated revelation discloses some truth about God's essence in itself. Conceptual truth reveals not only what God does, but who God is.

Biblical revelation teaches the reality not only of physical entities, but also of spiritual beings: angels, demons, Satan, and the triune God. The Bible also reveals information concerning attributes or characteristics of both material and spiritual realities. In speaking of the attributes of an entity, we refer to essential qualities that belong to or inhere in it. The being or substance is what stands under and unites the varied and multiple attributes in one unified entity. The attributes are essential to distinguish the divine Spirit from all other spirits. The divine Spirit is necessary to unite all the attributes in one being. The attributes of God, then, are essential characteristics of the divine being. Without these qualities God would not be what he is—God.

Some have imagined that by defining the essence of God human thinkers confine God to their concepts. That reasoning, however, confuses words conveying concepts with their referents. Does a definition of water limit the power of Niagara Falls? The word "God" has been used in so many diverse ways that it is incumbent upon a writer or speaker to indicate which of those uses is in mind.

God Is an Invisible, Personal, Living, and Active Spirit. Jesus explained to the Samaritan woman why she should worship God in spirit and in truth. God is spirit (John 4:24). The noun *pneuma* occurs first in the sentence for emphasis. Although some theologies consider "spirit" an attribute, grammatically in Jesus' statement it is a substantive. In the pre-Kantian, first century world of the biblical authors, spirits were not dismissed with an *a priori,* skeptical assumption.

As spirit, God is *invisible.* No one has ever seen God or ever will (I Tim. 6:16). A spirit does not have flesh and bones (Luke 24:39).

As spirit, furthermore, God is *personal.* Although some thinkers use "spirit" to designate impersonal principles or an impersonal absolute, in the biblical context the divine Spirit has personal capacities of intelligence, emotion, and volition. It is important to deny of the personal in God any vestiges of the physical and moral evil associated with fallen human persons.

In transcending the physical aspects of human personhood God thus transcends the physical aspects of both maleness and femaleness. However, since both male and female are created in God's image, we may think of both as like God in their distinctively nonphysical, personal male and female qualities. In this context the Bible's use of masculine personal pronouns for God conveys primarily the connotation of God's vital personal qualities and secondarily any distinctive functional responsibilities males may have.

Christ's unique emphasis upon God as Father in the Lord's Prayer and elsewhere becomes meaningless if God is not indeed personal. Similarly, the great doctrines of mercy, grace, forgiveness, imputation, and justification can only be meaningful if God is genuinely personal. God must be able to hear the sinner's cry for salvation, be moved by it, decide and act to recover the lost. In fact, God is superpersonal, tripersonal. The classical doctrine of the Trinity coherently synthesizes the Bible's teaching about God. To place the name of God upon a baptismal candidate is to place upon the candidate the name of the Father and the Son and the Holy Spirit (Matt. 28:19).

The unity of the one divine essence and being emphasized in the NT concept of a personal spirit implies simplicity or indivisibility. Neither the Trinitarian personal distinctions nor the multiple attributes divide the essential unity of the divine being. And that essential, ontological oneness is not torn apart by the incarnation or even the death of Jesus. Relationally or functionally (but not essentially) Jesus on the cross was separated from the Father who imputed to him the guilt and punishment of our sin.

In view of the indivisibility of the divine Spirit, how than are the attributes related to the divine being? The divine attributes are not mere names for human use with no referent in the divine Spirit (nominalism). Nor are the attributes separate from each other within the divine being so that they could conflict with each other (realism). The attributes all equally qualify the entirety of the divine being and each other (a modified realism). Preserving the divine simplicity or indivisibility, God's love is always holy love, and God's holiness is always loving holiness. Hence it is futile to argue for the superiority of one divine attribute over another. Every attribute is essential; one cannot be more essential than another in a simple, nonextended being.

God as spirit, furthermore, is *living and active.* In contrast to the passive ultimates of Greek philosophies the God of the Bible actively creates, sustains, covenants with his people, preserves Israel and the Messiah's line of descent, calls prophet after prophet, sends his Son into the world, provides the atoning sacrifice to satisfy his own righteousness, raises Christ from the dead, builds the church, and judges all justly. Far from a passive entity like a warm house, the God of the Bible is an active architect, builder, freedom fighter, advocate of the poor and oppressed, just judge, empathetic counselor, suffering servant, and triumphant deliverer.

As an invisible, personal, living spirit, God is no mere passive object of human investigation. Such writers as Pascal, Kierkegaard, Barth, and Brunner have helpfully reminded Christians that knowing God is not like studying soils. However, these writers go too far in claiming that God is merely a revealing subject in ineffable personal encounters and that no objective, propositional truth can be known of God. Members of a creative artist's family may know him not only with passionate, personal subjectivity, but also objectively through examination of his works, careful reading of his writings, and assessment of his résumé. Similarly God may be known not only in passionate subjective commitment, but also by thought about his creative works (general revelation), his inspired Scripture (part of special revelation), and theological résumés of his nature and activity. Knowledge of God involves both objective, conceptual validity and subjective, personal fellowship.

We have considered the meaning of asserting that God is spirit: the divine being is one, invisible, personal, and thus capable of thinking, feeling, and willing, a living and active being. There are, however, many spirits. The subsequent discussion of the divine attributes is necessary to distinguish the divine Spirit from other spirit-beings.

While considering the meaning of each attribute it is well to be aware of the relation of the attributes to the being of God. In the Scriptures the divine attributes are not above God, beside God, or beneath God; they are predicated of God. God is holy; God is love. These characteristics do not simply describe what God does, they define what God is. To claim that recipients of revelation can know the attributes of God but not the being of God leaves the attributes ununified and belonging to nothing. The Scriptures do not endorse worship of an unknown God but make God known. The attributes are inseparable from the being of God, and the divine spirit does not relate or act apart from the essential divine characteristics. In knowing the attributes, then, we know God as he has revealed himself to be in himself.

This is not to say that through revelation we can know God fully as God knows himself. But it is to deny that all our knowledge of God is equivocal, something totally other than we understand by scripturally revealed concepts of holy love. Much of our knowledge of God's attributes is analogical or figurative, where Scripture uses figures of speech. Even then, however, the point illustrated can be stated in nonfigurative language. So all our understanding of God is not exclusively analogical. The revealed, nonfigurative knowledge has at least one point of meaning the same for God's thought and revelationally informed human thought. Some knowledge of God, then, is called univocal, because when we assert that God is holy love, we assert what the Bible (which originated, not with the will of man, but God) asserts. We may be far from fully comprehending divine holiness and divine love, but insofar as our assertions about God coherently convey relevant conceptually revealed meanings, they are true of God and conform in part to God's understanding.

The divine attributes have been differently classified to help in relating and remembering them. Each classification has its strengths and weaknesses. We may distinguish those attributes that are absolute and immanent (Strong), incommunicable or communicable (Berkhof), metaphysical or moral (Gill), absolute, relative, and moral (Wiley), or personal and constitutional (Chafer). Advantages and disadvantages of these groupings can be seen in those respective theologies. It is perhaps clearer and more meaningful to distinguish God's characteristics metaphysically, intellectually, ethically, emotionally, existentially, and relationally.

Metaphysically, God Is Self-existent, Eternal, and Unchanging. Other spirits are invisible, personal, one, living, and active. How does the divine spirit differ? Significant differences appear in several respects, but we first focus upon the metaphysically distinctive characteristics of God.

First, God is *self-existent.* All other spirits are created and so have a beginning. They owe their existence to another. God does not depend upon the world or anyone in it for his existence. The world depends on God for its existence. Contrary to those theologians who say we cannot know anything about God in himself, Jesus revealed that God has life in himself (John 5:26). The ground of God's being is not in others, for there is nothing more ultimate than himself. God is uncaused, the one who always is (Exod. 3:14). To ask who caused God is to ask a self-contradictory question in terms of Jesus' view of God. Another term conveying the concept of God's self-existence is "aseity." It comes from the Latin *a,* meaning from, and *se,* meaning oneself. God is underived, necessary, nondependent existence. Understanding that God is noncontingent helps to understand how God is unlimited by anything, or infinite, free, self-determined, and not determined by anything other than himself contrary to his own sovereign purposes.

God is *eternal* and omnipresent (ubiquitous). God's life is from within himself, not anything that had a beginning in the space-time world. God has no beginning, period of growth, old age, or end. The Lord is enthroned as King forever (Ps. 29:10). This God is our God forever and forever (Ps. 48:14). Although God is not limited by space or time, or the succession of events in time, he created the world with space and time. God sustains the changing realm of succeeding events and is conscious of every movement in history. The observable, changing world is not unimportant or unreal (*maya* in Hinduism) to the omnipresent Lord of all. No tribe, nation, city, family, or personal life is valueless, however brief or apparently insignificant. God's eternal nature is not totally other than time or totally removed from everything in time and space. The space-time world is not foreign or unknown to God. History is the product of God's eternally wise planning, creative purpose, providential preservation, and common grace. God fills space and time with his presence, sustains it, and gives it purpose and value. The omnipresent and ubiquitous One is Lord of time and history, not vice versa. God does not negate time but fulfills it. In it his purposes are accomplished.

In Christianity, then, eternity is not an abstract timelessness, but the eternal is a characteristic of the living God who is present at all times and in all places, creating and sustaining the space-time world and accomplishing his redemptive purposes in the fullness of time.

God is *unchanging* in nature, desire, and purpose. To say that God is immutable is not to contradict the previous truth that God is living and active. It is to say that all the uses of divine power and vitality are consistent with his attributes such as wisdom, justice, and love. God's acts are never merely arbitrary, although some may be for reasons wholly within himself rather than conditioned upon human response. Underlying each judgment of the wicked and each pardon of the repentant is his changeless purpose concerning sin and conversion. Unlike the Stoic's concept of divine immutability, God is not indifferent to human activity and need. Rather, we can always count upon God's concern for human righteousness. God changelessly answers prayer in accord with his desires and purposes of holy love. Hence, although speaking in terms of human experience God is sometimes said in Scripture to repent, it is in fact the unrepentant who have changed and become repentant or the faithful who have become unfaithful.

God is the same, though everything else in creation becomes old like a garment (Ps. 102:25–27). Jesus shared that same unchanging nature (Heb. 1:10–12) and vividly exhibited it consistently throughout his active ministry in a variety of situations.

The immutability of God's character means that God never loses his own integrity or lets others down. With God is no variableness or shadow of turning (James 1:17). God's unshakable nature and word provide the strongest ground of faith and bring strong consolation (Heb. 6: 17–18). God is not a man that he should lie (Num. 23:19) or repent (I Sam. 15:29). The counsel of the Lord stands forever (Ps. 33:11). Though heaven and earth pass away, God's words will not fail (Matt. 5:18; 24:35).

Intellectually, God Is Omniscient, Faithful, and Wise. God differs from other spirits not only in being but also in knowledge. God's intellectual capabilities are unlimited, and God uses them fully and perfectly.

God is *omniscient.* God knows all things (I John 3:20). Jesus has this attribute of deity also, for Peter says, "Lord, you know all things; you know that I love you" (John 21:17). God knows all inward thoughts and outward acts of humanity (Ps. 139). Nothing in all creation is hidden from God's sight. Everything is uncovered and laid bare before the one to whom we must give account (Heb. 4:13). Isaiah distinguished the Lord of all from idols by the Lord's ability to predict the future (Isa. 44:7–8, 25–28). Clearly the Lord's knowledge of the future was communicable in human concepts and words. In the context Isaiah made predictions concerning Jerusalem, Judah, Cyrus, and the temple. These concepts were inspired in the original language and are translatable in the languages of the world.

How can God know the end from the beginning? In a way greater than illustrated in a person's knowledge of a memorized psalm, Augustine suggested. Before quoting Psalm 23 we have it all in mind. Then we quote the first half of it and we know the part that is past and the part that remains to be quoted. God knows the whole of history at once, simultaneously because not limited by time and succession, but God also knows what part of history is past today and what is future, for time is not unreal or unimportant to God (*Confessions* XI, 31).

The belief that God knows everything—past, present, and future—is of little significance, however, if God's knowledge is removed from human knowledge by an infinite, qualitative distinction. The frequent claim that God's knowledge is totally other than ours implies that God's truth may be contradictory of our truth. That is, what may be true for us is false for God or what is false for us may be true for God. Defenders of this position argue that because God is omniscient, God does not think discursively line upon line, or use distinct concepts connected by the verb "to be" in logical propositions. This view of divine transcendence provided an effective corrective in the hands of Barth and Bultmann against the continuity modernism alleged between the highest human thought and God's thought. And that influence finds additional support from the Eastern mystics who deny any validity to conceptual thinking in reference to the eternal. Relativists from many fields also deny that any human assertions, including the Bible's, are capable of expressing the truth concerning God.

From a biblical perspective, however, the human mind has been created in the divine image to think God's thoughts after him, or to receive through both general and special revelation truth from God. Although the fall has affected the human mind, this has not been eradicated. The new birth involves the Holy Spirit's renewal of the person in knowledge after the image of the Creator (Col. 3:10). Contextually, the knowledge possible to the regenerate includes the present position and nature of the exalted Christ (Col. 1:15–20) and knowledge of God's will (Col. 1:9). With this knowledge Christians can avoid being deceived by mere fine-sounding arguments (Col. 2:4). They are to strengthen the faith they were taught in concepts and words (Col. 2:7). And the content of the word of Christ can inform their teaching and worship (Col. 3:16).

In these and many other ways the Scriptures presuppose an informative revelation from God, verbally inspired and Spirit illumined, to minds created and renewed in the divine image for the reception of this divine truth. Insofar as we have grasped the contextual meaning given by the original writers of Scripture, our scripturally based assertions that God is spirit, God is holy, or God is love are true. They are true for God as he is in himself. They are true for the faith and life of Christians and churches.

The propositional truth that the Bible conveys in indicative sentences that affirm, deny, contend, maintain, assume, and infer is fully true for God and for mankind. Of course God's omniscience is not limited to the distinctions between subjects and predicates, logical sequence, exegetical research, or discursive reasoning. But God knows the difference between a subject and a predicate, relates to logical sequence as much as to temporal sequence, encourages exegetical research and revelationally based discursive reasoning. Although God's mind is unlimited and knows everything, it is not totally different in every respect from human minds made in his image. As omniscient then, God's judgments are formed in the awareness of all the relevant data. God knows everything that bears upon the truth concerning any person or event. Our judgments are true insofar as they conform to God's by being coherent or faithful to all the relevant evidence.

God is *faithful* and true. Because God is faithful and true (Rev. 19:11), his judgments (Rev. 19:2) and his words in human language are faithful and true (Rev. 21:5; 22:6). There is no lack of fidelity in God's person, thought, or promise. God is not hypocritical and inconsistent.

We may hold unswervingly to our hope because he who promised is faithful (Heb. 10:23). He is faithful to forgive our sins (I John 1:9), sanctify believers until the return of Christ (I Thess. 5:23–24), strengthen and protect from the evil one (II Thess. 3:3), and not let us be tempted beyond what we can bear (I Cor. 10:13). Even if we are faithless, he remains faithful, for he cannot disown himself (II Tim. 2:13).

Not one word of all the good promises God gave through Moses failed (I Kings 8:56). Isaiah praises the name of God, for in perfect faithfulness God did marvelous things planned long ago (Isa. 25:1). Passages like these convey a basic divine integrity in both life and thought. No contrast can be drawn between what God is in himself and what God is in relation to those who trust him. God does not contradict his promises in his works or in other teaching by dialectic, paradox, or mere complementarity. God knows everything, and nothing can come up that was not already taken into account before God revealed his purposes.

Because God is faithful and consistent, we ought to be faithful and consistent. Jesus said, "Simply let your Yes be Yes and your No, No" (Matt. 5:37). Paul exhibited this logical authenticity in his teaching about God. As surely as God is faithful, he said, our message to you is not Yes and No (II Cor. 1:18). Those who imagine that talk about God in human language must affirm and deny the same thing at the same time and in the same respect (in dialectic or paradox) have a different view of the relation between the divine mind and the godly person's mind than did Paul. Because God is faithful, we must be faithful in our message about him. Since God cannot deny himself, we ought not to deny ourselves in speaking to God.

Knowing the connection between personal and conceptual faithfulness in God we know that the idea that faithful persons ought not to contradict themselves did not originate with Aristotle. He may have formulated the law of noncontradiction in a way that has been quoted ever since, but the ultimate source of the challenge to human fidelity in person and word is rooted in God himself. The universal demand for intellectual honesty reflects in the human heart the ultimate integrity of the Creator's heart.

God is not only omniscient and consistent in person and word, but also perfectly *wise*. In addition to knowing all the relevant data on any subject, God selects ends with discernment and acts in harmony with his purposes of holy love. We may not always be able to see that events in our lives work together for a wise purpose, but we know that God chooses from among all the possible alternatives the best ends and means for achieving them. God not only chooses the right ends but also for the right reasons, the good of his creatures and thus his glory.

Although we may not fully understand divine wisdom, we have good reason to trust it. After writing on the great gift of the righteousness that comes from God, Paul exclaims, "To the only wise God be glory forever through Jesus Christ! Amen." (Rom. 16:27). He had earlier alluded to the incomprehensible depth of the riches of the wisdom and knowledge of God (Rom. 11:33).

The interrelation of the attributes is already evident as the divine omniscience is aware not only of what is but also of what ought to be (morally); divine faithfulness and consistency involve moral integrity and no hypocrisy; and wisdom makes decisions for action toward certain ends and means in terms of the highest values. It is not so strange then when we read that the fear of the Lord is the beginning of knowledge (Prov. 1:7).

Ethically, God Is Holy, Righteous, and Loving. God is distinct from and transcendent to all his creatures, not only metaphysically and epistemologically, but also morally. God is morally spotless in character and action, upright, pure, and untainted with evil desires, motives, thought, words, or acts. God is *holy,* and as such is the source and standard of what is right. God is free from all evil, loves all truth and goodness. He values purity and detests impurity and inauthenticity. God cannot approve of any evil, has no pleasure in evil (Ps. 5:4), and cannot tolerate evil (Hab. 1:13). God abhors evil and cannot encourage sin in any way (James 1:13–14). Christians do not stand in awe of the holy as an abstraction, but of the Holy One (Isa. 40:25). The Holy One is not merely an object of emotional fascination, but of intellectual hearing and volitional obedience.

Holiness is not solely the product of God's will, but a changeless characteristic of his eternal nature. The question Plato asked therefore needs to be reworded to apply to the Christian God: "Is the good good because God wills it? Or does

God will it because it is good?" The question relates not to God's will or to some principle of goodness above God, but to God's essence. The good, the just, the pure, the holy is holy, not by reason of an arbitrary act of the divine will, nor of a principle independent of God, but because it is an outflow of his nature. God always wills in accord with his nature consistently. He wills the good because he is good. And because God is holy, he consistently hates sin and is repulsed by all evil without respect of persons. The Holy Spirit is called holy not only because as a member of the divine Trinity he shares the holiness of the divine nature, but because the Spirit's distinctive function is to produce holy love in God's redeemed people. We are to seek to be morally spotless in character and action, upright, and righteous like the God we worship.

God is just or *righteous*. God's justice or righteousness is revealed in his moral law expressing his moral nature and in his judgment, granting to all, in matters of merit, exactly what they deserve. His judgment is not arbitrary or capricious, but principled and without respect of persons. OT writers frequently protest the injustice experienced by the poor, widows, orphans, strangers, and the godly. God, in contrast, has pity on the poor and needy (Ps. 72:12–14). He answers, delivers, revives, acquits, and grants them the justice that is their due. In righteousness God delivers the needy from injustice and persecution. Eventually God will create a new heaven and a new earth in which righteousness will dwell (Isa. 65:17).

God's wrath is revealed as sinners suppress his truth and hold it down in unrighteousness (Rom. 1:18–32), both Jews and Gentiles (Rom. 2:1–3:20). In the gospel a righteousness from God is revealed, a righteousness that is by faith from first to last (Rom. 1:17; 3:21). Believers are justified freely by God's grace that came by Jesus Christ, who provided the sacrifice of atonement (Rom. 3:24). Hence like Abraham, those who are fully persuaded that God can do what he has promised (Rom. 4:21) find their faith credited to them for righteousness (Rom. 4:3, 24). God in his justice graciously provides for the just status of believers in Christ. Righteousness in God is not unrelated to mercy, grace, and love.

In mercy God withholds or modifies deserved judgment, and in grace God freely gives undeserved benefits to whom he chooses. All of these moral characteristics flow from God's great love. In contrast to his transcendent self-existence is his gracious self-giving, agape love. He who lives forever as holy, high, and lofty also lives with him who is contrite and lowly in spirit (Isa. 57:15).

It is not that God is lacking something in himself (Acts 17:25), but that God desires to give of himself for the well-being of those loved, in spite of the fact that they are unlovely and undeserving. God not only loves but is in himself *love* (I John 4:8). His love is like that of a husband toward his wife, a father toward his son, and a mother toward her unweaned baby. In love God chose Israel (Deut. 7:7) and predestined believing members of the church to be adopted as sons through Jesus Christ (Eph. 1:4–5). God so loved the world that he gave his one and only Son, that whoever believes in him shall not perish but have eternal life (John 3:16).

Love cares for the aged, the oppressed, the poor, the orphans, and others in need. The loving God of the Bible is not unmoved by people with real needs (or impassible). The God of Abraham, Isaac, Jacob, Job, Jeremiah, Jesus, Judas, Peter, and Paul suffered, indeed was long-suffering. In empathy God enters through imagination into the feelings of his creatures. Beyond that, God incarnate entered through participation into our temptations and sufferings. As H. W. Robinson has said, "The only way in which moral evil can enter into the consciousness of the morally good is as suffering." In all Israel's afflictions God was afflicted (Isa. 63:9). What meaning can there be, Robinson asks, in a love that is not costly to the lover? The God of the Bible is far from apathetic in regard to the vast suffering of people in the world. In love God sent his Son to die that ultimately suffering might be done away and righteousness restored throughout the earth as the waters cover the seas.

Since love involves commitment for the well-being of others, a responsible commitment, a faithful commitment, it is not classed as primarily emotional. Love is a settled purpose of will involving the whole person in seeking the well-being of others.

Emotionally, God Detests Evil, Is Long-suffering, Compassionate. A. H. Strong says God is devoid of passion and caprice. Indeed God is devoid of caprice, injustice, or emotions out of control. We have earlier sought to negate any passions unworthy of God. Strong rightly adds, there is in God no selfish anger. However, God is personal and ethical, and both senses call for healthy emotions or passions. One who delights in justice, righteousness, and holiness for the well-being of his creatures can only be repulsed by the injustice, unrighteousness, and corruption that destroys their bodies, minds, and spirits. Hence the Bible frequently speaks of God's righteous indignation at evil. Righteous indignation is anger aroused, not by being overcome by emotions selfishly but by injustice and all the works of fallen "flesh." God *detests evil.*

Jesus and the Scriptures in general speak more often of God's wrath at injustices such as persistent mistreatment of the poor and needy than of love and heaven. Although the Lord is slow to anger, he will in no way leave the guilty unpunished, but will pour out his fury upon them (Nah. 1:3). None can withstand his indignation, which is poured out like fire and shatters rocks before him (Nah. 1:6). Apart from understanding God's wrath against evil, it is impossible to understand the extent of divine love in the incarnation, the extent of Christ's suffering on the cross, the propitiatory nature of his sacrifice, the prophetic Scriptures speaking of the great day of God's wrath, the great tribulation, or the book of Revelation.

God is patient and *long-suffering.* Properly jealous for the well-being of the objects of his love, God is angry at injustice done to them but suffers without losing heart. Long-suffering with evildoers God, without condoning their sin, graciously provides them with undeserved temporal and spiritual benefits. God promised the land to Abraham, but the iniquity of the Amorites was not yet full (Gen. 15:16). After over four hundred years of long-suffering restraint God in the fullness of time allowed the armies of Israel to bring just judgment upon the Amorites' wickedness. Later Israel worshiped the golden calf and deserved divine judgment like other idolators. But God revealed himself at the second giving of the law as "the Lord, the Lord, a God merciful and gracious, slow to anger, and abounding in steadfast love and faithfulness" (Exod. 34:6). The Psalmist could write, "But Thou, O Lord, art a God merciful and gracious, slow to anger and abounding in steadfast love and faithfulness" (Ps. 86:15). However, the day of God's grace has an end. Eventually, without respect of persons, God's just judgment fell upon Israel for its pervasive evils. God's long-suffering is a remarkable virtue, but it does not exclude or contradict God's justice.

Although theologians in the Thomistic tradition have taught the impassibility of God, the Scriptures do not hesitate to call God *compassionate.* Because of his great love we are not consumed, for his compassions never fail (Lam. 3:22). Even after Israel's captivity God will again have compassion on her (Mic. 7:19). The God of the Bible is not an apathetic God, but one who deeply cares when the sparrow falls. Jesus beautifully displayed this divine-human compassion for the hungry (Matt. 15:32), the blind (Matt. 20:34), the sorrowing (Luke 7:13). And Jesus taught the importance of compassion in the account of the good Samaritan (Luke 10:33) and that of the father's concern for his lost son (Luke 15:20).

The incarnate Christ felt what humans feel in all respects but did not yield to the temptations involved. As God in literal human experience, Jesus wept with those who wept and rejoiced with those who rejoiced. He remembered the joyful glory he had with the Father before the foundation of the world (John 17:5, 13). The divine-human author of our salvation, however, was made perfect or complete through suffering in this life (Heb. 2:10). Because he himself suffered, he can help those who suffer and are tempted (Heb. 2:18). The God revealed in Jesus Christ is no apathetic, uninvolved, impersonal first cause. The Father who Jesus disclosed is deeply moved by everything that hurts his children.

Existentially, God Is Free, Authentic, and Omnipotent. The modern concerns for freedom, authenticity, fulfillment should not be limited to mankind. Biblical writers seem even more concerned that God be understood to be free, authentic, and fulfilled.

God is *free.* From all eternity God is not conditioned by anything other than himself contrary to his purposes. Good things, as we have seen, are purposed with divine pleasure and enduement. Evil things are permitted with divine displeasure. But God is self-determined, either way. Self-determination is that concept of freedom which emphasizes that personal thought, feeling, and volition are not determined by external factors but by one's self.

God is not free to approve sin, to be unloving, to be unwise, to ignore the hard facts of reality, to be unfaithful to what is or ought to be, to be uncompassionate or unmerciful. God cannot deny himself. God is free to be himself, his personal, eternal, living, intellectual, ethical, emotional, volitional self.

God is *authentic,* authentically himself. The God who in Christ so unalterably opposed hypocrisy is himself no hypocrite. We have emphasized his intellectual integrity or faithfulness above. Here we emphasize his integrity ethically, emotionally, and existentially. God is self-conscious, knows who he is and what his purposes are (I Cor. 2:11). He has a keen sense of identity, meaning, and purpose.

God knows that he is the ultimate being, that there are in reality none to compare with him. In calling upon people to turn from idols, therefore, God in no way is asking something of us not in accord with reality. In steadfastly opposing idolatry he seeks to protect people from ultimate concerns destined to disillusion and disappoint. God desires our worship for our sakes, that we not succumb eventually to despair as one after another of our finite gods lets us down.

In the next place, God is *omnipotent* (Mark 14:36; Luke 1:37). God is able to do whatever he wills in the way in which he wills it. God does not choose to do anything contrary to his nature of wisdom and holy love. God cannot deny himself, and God does not choose to do everything by his own immediate agency without intermediate angelic and human agents. Although God determines some things to come to pass unconditionally (Isa. 14:24–27), most events in history are planned conditionally, through the obedience of people or their permitted disobedience to divine precepts (II Chr. 7:14; Luke 7:30; Rom. 1:24). In any case, God's eternal purposes for history are not frustrated, but fulfilled in the way he chose to accomplish them (Eph. 1:11).

God has not only the strength to effect all his purposes in the way in which he purposes them, but also the authority in the entire realm of his kingdom to do what he will. God is not a subject of another's dominion, but is King or Lord of all. By virtue of all his other attributes—his wisdom, justice, and love, for example—God is fit for the ruling of all that he created and sustains. God is a wise, holy, and gracious sovereign. As just, the power of God itself cannot punish sinners more than they deserve. To whom much is given, of him much shall be required; to whom little is given, of him little shall be required. But in the bestowing of undeserved benefits and gifts God is free to dispense them as he pleases (Ps. 135:6). Having permitted sin, God is great enough to limit its furious passions and to overrule it for greater good, as at Calvary (Acts 4:24–28). God can defeat the nations and demonic hosts that rage against him. No one can exist independent of divine sovereignty. The attempt to go one's own way independent of God is sinful insolence on the part of creatures who in him live and move and have their being. Only a fool could say that there is no God, when God sustains the breath the atheist uses to deny divine dominion over him.

Relationally, God Is Transcendent in Being, Immanent Universally in Providential Activity, and Immanent with His People in Redemptive Activity. As *transcendent,* God is uniquely other than everything in creation. God's distinctness from the being of the world has been implied in previous discussions of God's attributes metaphysically, intellectually, ethically, emotionally, and existentially. God is "hidden" relationally because so great in all these other ways. God's being is eternal, the world's temporal. God's knowledge is total, human knowledge incomplete. God's character is holy, humanity's character fallen and sinful. God's desires are consistently against evil yet long-suffering and compassionate; human desires fluctuate inconsistently and often intermingle evil with the good. God's energy is untiring and inexhaustible; the world's energy is subject to depletion through entropy. Hence God is over and above persons in the world in all these respects.

The incomparable divine transcendence involves a radical dualism between God and the world that ought not be blurred by a resurgent monism and pantheism. Although made like God and in the divine image, mankind is not (like Christ) begotten of God or an emanation from God of the same divine nature. The ultimate goal of salvation is not reabsorption into the being of God but unbroken fellowship with God. The unity Christians seek is not a metaphysical unity with God but a relational unity, a oneness of mind, desire, and will. To seek to be as God in a biblical perspective is not deeper spirituality but rebellious idolatry or blasphemy. Christians may respect nature as a divine creation but not worship nature as divine. Christians may respect the founders of the world's religions but cannot bow to any guru as the divine manifest in human form. Only Jesus Christ is from above; all others are from below (John 8:23). Because God is separate from the world, Christians cannot bow to any earthly power as God, whether that power be economic, political, religious, scientific, educational, or cultural. The inestimable benefit of bowing to a transcendent Lord of all is that it frees one from every finite, fallen tyranny.

A biblical theist not only believes that the one, living God is separate from the world, as against pantheism and panentheism, but also that God is continuously active throughout the world providentially, in contrast to deism. God is not so exalted that he cannot know, love, or relate to natural law in the world of everyday experience. A study of divine providence as taught in Scripture shows that God sustains, guides, and governs all that he created. The nature psalms reflect upon God's activity in relation to every aspect of the earth, the atmosphere, vegetation, and animal (e.g., Ps. 104). God also preserves and governs human history, judging corrupt societies and blessing the just and the unjust with temporal benefits like the sunshine, rain, food and drink. Through God's universal providential activity the cosmos holds together and his wise purposes of common grace are achieved.

But God is *immanent* in the lives of his people who repent of their sin and live by faith to accomplish the goals of his redemptive grace. "For this is what the high and lofty One says—he who lives forever, whose name is holy; I live in a high and holy place, but also with him who is contrite and lowly in spirit, to revive the spirit of the lowly and to revive the heart of the contrite" (Isa. 57:15). Just as persons may be present to one another in varying degrees, God may be present to the unjust in one sense and to the just in a richer way. A person may simply be present as another rider on a bus, or much more significantly as a godly mother who has prayed daily for you all of your life. God is graciously present in forgiving love with the converted, who by faith have been propitiated, reconciled, and redeemed by Christ's precious blood. They become his people, he becomes their God. God dwells in them as his holy place or temple. The relational oneness of thoughts, desires, and purposes grows through the years. That unity is shared by other members of Christ's body who are gifted to build each other up to become progressively more like the God they worship, not metaphysically, but intellectually, ethically, emotionally, and existentially.

Summary. In summary, God is a living, personal Spirit worthy of whole-soul adoration and trust (because of his many perfect attributes), separate from the world, and yet continuously active in the world.

Unlimited by space, God nevertheless created and sustains the cosmos, scientific laws, geographical and political boundaries.

Beyond time, God nevertheless actively relates to time, to each human life, home, city, nation, and to human history in general.

Transcendent to discursive knowledge and conceptual truth, God nevertheless intelligently relates to propositional thought and verbal communication, objective validity, logical consistency, factual reliability, coherence and clarity, as well as subjective authenticity and existential integrity.

Unlimited by a body, God is nevertheless providentially related to physical power in nature and society, industrially, agriculturally, socially, and politically. God knows and judges human stewardship in the use of all the earth's energy resources.

God transcends every attempt to achieve justice in the world, but righteously relates to every good endeavor of his creatures personally, economically, socially, academically, religiously, and politically.

Although free from unworthy and uncontrolled emotions, God is caringly related to the poor, the unfortunate, the lonely, the sorrowing, the sick, the victims of prejudice, injustice, anxiety, and despair.

Beyond all the apparent meaninglessness and purposelessness of human existence, God personally gives significance to the most insignificant life.

G. R. Lewis

See also God, Doctrine of; Revelation, General; Revelation, Special; Trinity; Impassibility of God.

Bibliography. H. Bavinck, *The Doctrine of God;* D. Bloesch, *Essentials of Evangelical Theology;* J. M. Boice, *The Sovereign God;* E. Brunner, *The Christian Doctrine of God;* J. O. Buswell, Jr., *A Systematic Theology of the Christian Religion;* L. S. Chafer, *Systematic Theology;* S. Charnock, *The Existence and Attributes of God;* C. F. H. Henry, *God, Revelation and Authority,* 4 vols.; J. Lawson, *Comprehensive Handbook of Christian Doctrine;* G. R. Lewis, "Categories in Collision?" in *Perspectives on Evangelical Theology,* ed. K. Kantzer and S. Gundry; G. R. Lewis, *Decide for Yourself: A Theological Workbook* and *Testing Christianity's Truth Claims;* J. I. Packer, *Knowing God;* W. W. Stevens, *Doctrines of the Christian Religion;* A. H. Strong, *Systematic Theology;* H. Thielicke, *The Evangelical Faith,* 2 vols.; O. C. Thomas, *Introduction to Theology;* A. W. Tozer, *Knowledge of the Holy;* H. O. Wiley, *Christian Theology,* I.

God, Doctrine of. The most fundamental teaching of the Bible and Christian theology is that God exists and is ultimately in control of the universe. This is the foundation on which all Christian theologizing is built.

The Biblical Concept of God. *Existence.* Questions concerning the reality of God are not discussed in the Scriptures; his existence is everywhere assumed. The opening passage which reveals God as Creator and Sovereign of heaven and earth sets the pattern for the remainder of the Bible in which God is viewed as foundational for a view of life and the world. The biblical question is therefore not does God exist, but who is God?

The Scriptures do recognize the existence of a professed atheism. But such atheism is considered primarily a moral rather than an intellectual problem. The fool who denies God (Ps. 14:1) does so not from philosophical reasons (which are, in any case, incapable of disproving the absolute except by affirming such), but from the practical supposition that he can live without considering God (Ps. 10:4). The Scriptures also recognize the possibility of a willful and therefore culpable "suppressing" of the knowledge of God (Rom. 1:18).

Knowledge of God. According to the Scriptures, God is known only through his self-revelation. Apart from his initiative in disclosing himself God could not be known by man. Human attempts to reason to God by various means, including the so-called proofs of God, while they can provide evidence for the need of a god, do not yet attain to the knowledge of the true God (cf. I Cor. 1:21*a*). Limited to the realm of creation, whether external nature or human subjective experience, man is incapable of reasoning to a valid knowledge of the transcendent Creator. God alone knows himself and discloses himself to whom he wills by his spirit (I Cor. 2:10–11). As the subject of his revelation God at the same time makes himself the object of human knowledge so that man can know him truly.

God has also revealed something of himself in his creation and preservation of the universe (Rom. 1:20), and to the extent that human reason yields a concept of a god it is undoubtedly related to this general or natural revelation. But the entrance of sin and its alienating effect blinds man from truly seeing God through this means (Rom. 1:18; Eph. 4:18). Moreover, the Bible indicates that even prior to the fall man's knowledge of God was derived not solely from the creation surrounding him, but from a direct personal communication with God.

While God communicates himself to man through a variety of means, including actions and words, human knowledge is fundamentally a conceptual matter and therefore the Word is the primary means of God's revelation. Even his actions are not left as mute works but are accompanied by the interpretive Word to give their true meaning. The revelation of God climaxed in the person of Jesus Christ, who was not simply the bearer of the revelatory Word of God as were all who spoke God's Word prior to his coming, but the personal divine Word. In him "all the fullness of deity" dwelt in bodily form (Col. 2:9). Thus in his work as Creator and Redeemer and through his words, God makes himself known to man.

The revelation of God does not totally exhaust his being and activity. He remains the incomprehensible one that man cannot totally fathom, both in his essence and ways (Job 36:26; Isa. 40:13, 28; cf. Deut. 29:29). Finitude cannot comprehend infinity, nor can human thought patterns, which are associated with the created environment, completely grasp the transcendent realm of God.

On the basis of this limitation of human reason modern rationalism has at times argued for the unknowability of God. Man's knowledge is said to be limited to the world of human experience, thus excluding the knowledge of a transcendent God. Such an equation of the incomprehensibility of God with unknowability is valid only on the premise that man's knowledge of God is derived through human reason. But the incomprehensible God of the Scriptures is the God who reaches out to man with the revelation of himself. The knowledge thus derived, although limited according to his good pleasure, is nevertheless a true knowledge of his being and work.

In giving us a knowledge of himself God gives his Word a finite form compatible with human creatureliness. Despite this necessary accommodation to the limitations of human understanding, the revealed knowledge of God is nevertheless an authentic knowledge of God. Theories which use the difference between God and man to deny the possibility of a genuine communication of true knowledge do not do justice to at least two biblical facts: (1) the truth that God created man in his own image, which certainly includes a likeness sufficient for communication; (2) the omnipotence of God, which implies that he can make a creature to whom he can truthfully reveal himself if he so wills. To be sure, there remains a hiddenness in relation to the total comprehension of God. But God himself does not remain hidden, for he has given true though partial knowledge of himself through self-revelation understandable to man.

The nature of our knowledge of God has been the subject of much discussion in Christian theology. Some have emphasized the negative character of our knowledge—e.g., God is infinite, nontemporal, incorporeal. Others, notably Aquinas, have advocated an analogical knowledge that is similar to God's knowledge and yet dissimilar because of his infinite greatness. Suffice it to say that even the negative (such as infinite) conveys a positive concept of greatness, and, while the position of analogy may be used to acknowledge a distinction in depth and breadth of understanding, there is finally a sense in which man's knowledge of divine things is the same as God's. For if man does not know God's meaning, he does not know the true meaning. Interestingly, the Scriptures view the problem of a true knowledge of God as moral rather than noetic.

Definition of God. From the biblical viewpoint it is generally agreed that it is impossible to give a strict definition of the idea of God. Defining, which means limiting, involves the inclusion of the object within a certain class or known universal and the indication of its distinguishing features from other objects in that same class. Since the biblical God is unique and incomparable (Isa. 40:25), there is no universal abstract category of the divine. Studies in comparative religions reveal that "god" is, in fact, conceived in the most different ways. Attempts to provide a general definition that encompasses all concepts of the divine, such as Anselm's "that than which nothing greater is conceivable," or "the supreme Being," do not convey much of the specific characteristics of the God of Scripture. Instead of a general definition of God, therefore, the Bible presents descriptions of God as he has revealed himself. These are conveyed through express statements as well as through the many names by which God identifies himself. Fundamental to the nature of God, according to the biblical description, are the truths that he is personal, spiritual, and holy.

God Is Personal. Over against any abstract neutral metaphysical concept, the God of Scripture is first and foremost a personal being. He reveals himself by names, especially the great personal name Yahweh (cf. Exod. 3:13–15; 6:3; Isa. 42:8). He knows and wills self-consciously in accord with our concept of personality (I Cor. 2:10–11; Eph. 1:11). The centrality of God's personality is seen in the fact that while he is the Creator and Preserver of all nature, he is encountered in Scripture not primarily as the God of nature, as in pagan religions, but rather as the God of history, controlling and directing the affairs of man. The central place of the covenant by which he links himself in a personal relationship to men is further indication of the scriptural emphasis on the personal nature of God. Nowhere is the personhood of God more evident than in his biblical description as Father. Jesus constantly spoke of God as "my Father," "your Father," and "the heavenly Father." Beyond the unique Trinitarian relationship of the divine Son with the Father, which certainly involves personal traits, the fatherhood of God speaks of him as the source and sustainer of his creatures who personally cares for them (Matt. 5:45; 6: 26–32) and the one to whom man can turn in believing trust.

The personhood of God has been called into question on the basis of our use of the word "person" with respect to human beings. Human personhood involves limitation that allows relationship with another person or the world. To be a person means to be an individual among individuals. All of this cautions us against an erroneous anthropomorphizing of God. Biblically it is more proper to see the personhood of God as having priority over that of man and therefore to understand human personhood theomorphously, i.e., a finite replica of the infinite divine person. Despite the final incomprehensibility of God's suprahuman personhood, the Scriptures portray him as a real person who gives himself in reciprocal relationship to us as a genuine Thou.

The biblical concept of the personhood of God refutes all abstract philosophical ideas of God as merely First Cause or Prime Mover as well as all naturalistic and pantheistic concepts. Modern equations of God with immanent personal relations (e.g., love) are also rejected.

God Is Spiritual. The Scriptures preclude the reduction of the personhood of God to a human level by the description of God as spirit (John 4:24). As the word "spirit" has the basic idea of power and activity, the spiritual nature of God refers to the infinite superiority of his nature over all created life. The weakness of the forces of this world, including men and beasts which are but flesh, are contrasted to God who is spirit (cf. Isa. 31:3; 40:6–7).

As spirit, God is the living God. He is the possessor of an infinite life in himself (Ps. 36:9; John 5:26). Matter is activated by spirit, but God is pure spirit. He is fully life. As such he is the source of all other life (Job 33:4; Ps. 104:30). The spiritual nature also prohibits any limitations of God derived from a materialistic conception. For this reason images of God are prohibited (Exod. 20:4; Deut. 4:12, 15–18). He cannot be restricted to any particular place or in any sense be brought under man's control as a physical object. He is the invisible transcendent living power from whom all derive existence (Acts 17:28).

God Is Holy. One of the most fundamental features of God's being is expressed by the word "holy." He is the incomparable God, "the Holy One" (Isa. 40:25, cf. Hab. 3:3). The word "holy," which in both Hebrew and Greek has the root meaning of separateness, is used predominantly in Scripture for a separateness from sin. But this is only a secondary meaning derived from the primary application to God's separateness from all creation, i.e., his transcendence. "He is exalted above all the peoples." Therefore, "holy is he" (Ps. 99:2–3). He is "the high and exalted One . . . whose name is Holy," and he lives "on a high and holy place" (Isa. 57:15). In his holiness God is the transcendent Deity.

The transcendence of God expresses the truth that God in himself is infinitely exalted above all creation. The concept of revelation presupposes a transcendent God who must unveil himself to be known. Transcendence is further seen in God's position as Creator and Sovereign Lord of the universe. As the former he distinguishes himself from all creation (Rom. 1:25), and in his sovereignty he evidences his transcendent supremacy.

The transcendence of God is frequently expressed biblically in terms of time and space. He exists before all creation (Ps. 90:2), and neither the earth nor the highest heavens can contain him (I Kings 8:27). A certain anthropomorphic sense must be recognized in such expressions lest God's transcendence be conceived in terms of our time and space, as though he lives in a time and space like ours only beyond that of creation. On the other hand, it is biblically incorrect to conceive of God in his transcendence as existing in a realm of timeless nowhereness outside of creation. In a manner that exceeds our finite understanding God exists in his own infinite realm as transcendent Lord over all creaturely time and space.

God's transcendent holiness is biblically balanced with the teaching of his immanence, which signifies that he is wholly present in his being and power in every part and moment of the created universe. He is "over all and through all and in all" (Eph. 4:6). Not only does everything exist in him (Acts 17:28), but there is no place where his presence is absent (Ps. 139:1–10). His immanence is seen especially in relation to man. The Holy One who lives in a high and holy place also dwells with the "contrite and lowly of spirit" (Isa. 57:15). This dual dimension of God is seen clearly in the description "the Holy One of Israel" as well as in the name Yahweh, which describes both his transcendent power and his personal presence with and for his people.

The biblical teaching of both God's transcendence and immanence counters the human tendency throughout history to emphasize one or the other. A one-sided transcendence is seen in the Greek philosophers' concept of the ultimate ground of being as well as the later deists of the seventeenth and eighteenth centuries. The various forms of pantheism throughout history give evidence of the opposite emphasis on immanence. The attractiveness of these exaggerations to sinful man is in the fact that in both man no longer stands before God in any practical sense as a responsible creature.

The Trinity. Crucial to the biblical doctrine of God is his Trinitarian nature. Although the term "trinity" is not a biblical word as such, Christian theology has used it to designate the threefold manifestation of the one God as Father, Son, and Holy Spirit. The formulated doctrine of the Trinity asserts the truth that God is one in being or essence who exists eternally in three distinct coequal "persons." While the term "person" in relation to the Trinity does not signify the limited individuality of human persons, it does affirm the I-thou of personal relationship, particularly of love, within the triune Godhead.

The doctrine of the Trinity flows from the self-revelation of God in biblical salvation history. As the one God successively reveals himself in his saving action in the Son and the Holy Spirit, each is recognized as God himself in personal manifestation. It is thus in the fullness of NT revelation that the doctrine of the Trinity is seen most clearly. God is one (Gal. 3:20; James 2:19), but the Son (John 1:1; 14:9; Col. 2:9) and the Spirit (Acts 5:3–4; I Cor. 3:16) are also fully God. Yet they are distinct from the Father and each other. The Father sends the Son and the Spirit, while the Son also sends the Spirit (Gal. 4:4; John 15:26). This unified equality and yet distinctness is seen in the triadic references to the three persons. Christian baptism is in the name of the Father, Son, and Holy Spirit (Matt. 28:19). Likewise, all three are joined in the Pauline benediction in a different order suggesting the total equality of persons (II Cor. 13:14; cf. Eph. 4:4–6; I Pet. 1:2).

Although the Trinity finds its clearest evidence in the NT, suggestions of a fullness of plurality are already found in the OT revelation of God. The plural form of the name of God (Elohim) as well as the use of plural pronouns (Gen. 1:26; 11:7) and verbs (Gen. 11:7; 35:7) point in this direction. So also do the identity of the angel of the Lord as God (Exod. 3:2–6; Judg. 13:21–22) and the hypostatization of the Word (Ps. 33:6; 107:20) and Spirit (Gen. 1:2; Isa. 63:10). The Word is not simply communication about God nor is the Spirit divine power. They are rather the acting God himself.

As the product of the self-revelation of God, the Trinitarian formulation is not intended to exhaust his incomprehensible nature. Objections to the doctrine come from a rationalism that insists on dissolving this mystery into human understanding, i.e., by thinking of the oneness and threeness in mathematical terms and human personality. Attempts have been made to draw analogies of the Trinity from nature and the constitution of man. The most notable of these is Augustine's trinity of lover, the object of love, and the love which binds the two together. While this argues strongly for a plurality within God if he is eternally a God of love apart from creation, it along with all other suggestions from the creaturely realm proves finally inadequate to explain the divine being.

The doctrine of the Trinity developed out of the church's desire to safeguard the biblical truths of the God who is the transcendent Lord over all history and yet who gives himself in person to act within history. The natural human tendencies toward either a nonhistorical divine transcendence or the absorption of the divine into the historical process are checked by the orthodox concept of the Trinity. The first is the ultimate error of the primary distortions of the Trinity. Subordinationism, which made Christ less than God, and adoptionism, which understood Christ only as a human endowed with God's Spirit for a time, both denied that God truly entered history to confront man in person. Modalism or Sabellianism makes the persons of Christ and the Holy Spirit to be only historical roles or modifications of the one God. This error likewise tends to separate man from God; he is encountered not directly as he is in person, but as a role player who remains hidden behind a mask.

The Trinitarian doctrine is thus central to the

salvation kerygma of Scripture, according to which the transcendent God acts personally in history to redeem and share himself with his creatures. Origen rightly drew the conclusion that the believer "will not attain salvation if the Trinity is not complete."

The Doctrine in History. The history of Christian thought reveals persistent problems concerning the nature of God and his relation to the world. These involve the related issues of transcendence/immanence, personal/nonpersonal perspectives, and the knowability of God. The earliest Christian theologians, who attempted to interpret the Christian faith in terms of Greek philosophical categories, tended toward an emphasis on the abstract transcendence of God. He was the timeless, changeless Absolute who was the final and adequate cause of the universe. Little could be predicted of him, and his attributes were defined primarily in the negative. He was the uncaused (possessing aseity), absolutely simple, infinite, immutable, omnipotent Being, unlimited by time (eternal) and space (omnipresent).

Although Augustine's view was more balanced with a view of the personal immanent, condescending God in the revelation of Christ, this philosophical understanding of God dominated until the Reformation, reaching its climax in Thomas Aquinas and the medieval scholastics. Aquinas held that philosophical human reason could attain to the knowledge of the existence of God. His stress, however, was on the transcendence of God and how little he could be known.

With an emphasis on biblical rather than philosophical categories, the Reformers brought more recognition of the immanence of God within human history but maintained a strong emphasis on his transcendence, as evidenced in the definition of the Westminster Confession of Faith.

Reaction to the traditional Protestant and Catholic understanding of God with its stress on the transcendence of God came with the rise of liberal theology in the eighteenth and nineteenth centuries. The combination of new philosophies (e.g., Kant, Hegel) making the mind of man supreme for true knowledge, scientific advances that seemed to substantiate human abilities, and a new historical perspective that tended to relativize all tradition, including the Scriptures, led to a new understanding of ultimate reality. Because, as Kant argued, human reason could no longer establish the existence of a transcendent God, God became increasingly identified with the ideals of human experience. Talk of religious dependency (Schleiermacher) or ethical values (Kant, Ritschl) became talk of God. There was an almost exclusive emphasis on the immanence of God, with a tendency to see an essential kinship between the human and divine spirit.

World events including two world wars and the rise of totalitarian regimes brought the collapse of old liberalism with its immanentistic understanding of God and the reassertion of divine transcendence. Led by Karl Barth, theology sought to return not to the earlier philosophical concepts of God but to the categories of the Judeo-Christian Scriptures. Based upon a radical separation between eternity and time, the transcendence of God was exaggerated to the point that a direct revelation of God in human history was denied. According to this neoorthodox theology God did not speak directly in Scripture. As a result of this denial of a direct cognitive communication, with the consequent skepticism of any knowledge of God in himself, the accent on transcendence was gradually lost. The religious experience of man, usually interpreted according to existential philosophy, became increasingly viewed as the key to theological knowledge. God was understood primarily as the meaning he holds for the "existential experiences" of man.

This movement can be traced from Barth, whose theology maintained a strong divine transcendence, to Bultmann, who, while not denying God's transcendence, nevertheless focused almost entirely on God in the human existential experience, and finally to Tillich, who denied entirely the traditional God "out there" in favor of an immanent God as the "ground" of all being. Thus the transcendence of God has been lost in much of contemporary thought which seeks to do theology in the existential philosophical framework. Divine transcendence is simply equated with the hidden self-transcendence of human existence.

Other contemporary theologians seek to reconstruct theology in terms of the modern scientific evolutionary understanding of the universe. Such process theology, based on the philosophy of A. N. Whitehead, sees the fundamental nature of all reality as process or becoming rather than being or unchanging substance. Although there is an abstract eternal dimension of God which provides the potential for the process, he also is understood to encompass all changing entities in his own life and therefore to be in the process of change himself. As the universe is dynamic and changing, actualizing its potentialities, so also is God.

The wide variety of contemporary formulations of God that tend to define God in ways in which he is no longer the personal Creator and sovereign Lord of human history are the direct result of denying a knowledge of God through his cognitive self-revelation in the Scriptures and the sinful human propensity to autonomy.

R. L. Saucy

See also God, Arguments for the Existence of; God, Attributes of; God, Names of; Trinity; Revelation, General; Revelation, Special.

Bibliography. K. Barth, *Church Dogmatics,* II/1 and 2; H. Bavinck, *The Doctrine of God;* E. Brunner, *The Christian Doctrine of God;* J. S. Candlish, *The Christian Doctrine of God;* W. Eichrodt, *Theology of the OT,* I; C. F. H. Henry, *God, Revelation and Authority,* II; C. Hodge, *Systematic Theology,* I; Kleinknecht, Quell, Stauffer, Kuhn, *TDNT,* III, 65–123; G. L. Prestige, *God in Patristic Thought;* H. Thielicke, *The Evangelical Faith,* II; O. Weber, *Foundations of Dogmatics,* I.

God, Names of. ***The Divine Names as Vehicles of Revelation.*** Efforts to find the origins and significance of the Hebrew divine names in other ancient Near Eastern cultures have yielded generally disappointing results. One of the major reasons for this is that the ancient Hebrew theology invested these names with a uniqueness that renders investigation outside the narratives of the OT incapable of exploring fully their historical and religious significance.

Basic to ancient Hebrew religion is the concept of divine revelation. While God is conceived of as revealing his attributes and will in a number of ways in the OT, one of the most theologically significant modes of the divine self-disclosure is the revelation inherent in the names of God.

This aspect of divine revelation is established in the words of Exod. 6:3, "I appeared to Abraham, to Isaac and to Jacob, as God Almighty, but by my name the Lord [Yahweh] I did not make myself known to them." According to classical literary criticism, the verse teaches that the name Yahweh was unknown to the patriarchs. Thus, an ideological conflict exists between the Priestly author and the earlier Yahwist, who frequently put the name Yahweh on the lips of the patriarchs.

However, the words "by my name Yahweh I did not make myself known to them" have a somewhat hollow ring if the name Yahweh is understood only as an appellative. The reason for this is that Moses asks in Exod. 3:13, "What is his name?" (*mah-šĕmô*). M. Buber has demonstrated that the syntax of this question does not connote an inquiry as to the name of God but an inquiry into the character revealed by the name. He says, "Where the word 'what' is associated with the word 'name' the question asked is what finds expression in or lies concealed behind that name" (*The Revelation and the Covenant,* p. 48). J. Motyer also concludes, "In every case where *mâ* is used with a personal association it suggests enquiry into sort or quality or character, whereas *mî* expects an answer instancing individuals, or, as in the case of rhetorical questions, calling attention to some external feature" (*The Revelation of the Divine Name,* 19).

Exod. 14:4 also supports the view that the name Yahweh embodies aspects of God's character. It says, "and the Egyptians will know that I am Yahweh." It is hardly likely that the intent of this assertion is that they would learn only the name of the Hebrew God.

In the light of these observations, the use of the concepts of the name of God in the early narratives of the book of Exodus is far broader than simply the name by which the Hebrew God was known. It has a strong element of divine self-disclosure within it.

The corpus of divine names compounded with *'ēl* and a descriptive adjunct also support this concept. The very fact that the adjunctive element is descriptive is an indication of its value as a source of theological content.

Typical of this type of name is *'ēl rŏ'î* ("God who sees"; Gen. 16:13) and *'ēl 'ôlām* ("God eternal"; Gen. 21:33). These *'ēl* names sometimes emerge from a specific historical situation that illuminates their significance.

The Meaning of the Divine Names. *Yahweh, Jehovah* (Lord). Efforts to determine the meaning of the tetragrammaton (*YHWH*) through historical investigation have been rendered difficult by the paucity of informative data relative to the various forms of the name *ya* in historical sources outside the OT. For this reason the investigation has generally followed philological lines. G. R. Driver suggested that the form *ya* was originally an ejaculatory cry, "shouted in moments of excitement or ecstasy," that was "prologued to ya(h)wá(h), ya(h)wá(h)y, or the like." He suggested further that the name Yahweh arose from the consonance of an extended form of *ya* with the "imperfect tense of a defective verb." Thus, he saw the origin of the name in a popular etymology and asserted that its original form was forgotten (*ZAW* 46:24).

Mowinckel proposed the theory that the tetragrammaton should be understood as consisting of the ejaculatory element and the third person pronoun *hû',* meaning "O He!"

Another approach to the problem is to understand the tetragrammaton as a form of paronomasia. This view takes account of the broad representation of the name *ya* in extrabiblical cultures of the second millennium B.C. The name Yahweh is thus understood as a quadriliteral form, and the relationship of the name to *hāyâ* ("to be") in Exod. 3:14–15 is not intended to be one of etymology but paronomasia.

The most common view is that the name is a form of a triliteral verb, *hwy.* It is generally regarded as a 3 p. Qal stem imperfect or a 3 p. imperfect verb in a causative stem. Another suggestion is that it is a causative participle with a *y* preformative that should be translated "Sustainer, Maintainer, Establisher."

With regard to the view that the tetragrammaton is an elongated form of an ejaculatory cry, it may be pointed out that Semitic proper names tend to shorten; they are not normally prolonged.

The theory that the name is paronomastic is attractive, but when appeal is made to the occurrences of forms of *ya* or *yw* in ancient cultures, several problems arise. It is difficult to explain how the original form could have lengthened into the familiar quadriliteral structure. Mowinckel's suggestion is attractive, but speculative. It is also difficult to understand how the name Yahweh could have such strong connotations of uniqueness in the OT if it is a form of a divine name that found representation in various cultures in the second millennium B.C.

The derivation of the tetragrammaton from a verbal root is also beset with certain difficulties. The root *hwy* on which the tetragrammaton would be based in this view is unattested in West Semitic languages before the time of Moses, and the form of the name is not consonant with the rules that govern the formation of *lāmed hē'* verbs as we know them.

It is evident that the problem is a difficult one. It is best to conclude that the use of etymology to determine the theological content of the name Yahweh is tenuous. If one is to understand the theological significance of the divine name, it can be only by determining the theological content with which the name was invested in Hebrew religion.

Jah, Yah. This shorter form of Yahweh occurs twice in Exodus (15:2 and 17:15). The former passage is echoed in Isa. 12:2 and Ps. 118:14. It also occurs numerous times in the formula *halĕlûyâ* ("praise *yah*"). Its use in early and late poetic passages and its formulaic function in the Hallel psalms suggest that this form of Yahweh is a poetic stylistic device.

The compounding of *yah* with Yahweh in Isa. 12:2 (*yah yhwh*) indicates a separate function for the form *yah,* but at the same time an identification of the form with Yahweh.

Yahweh Ṣĕbā'ôt ("Lord of Hosts"). The translation "He creates the heavenly hosts" has been suggested for this appellative. It is based on the assumption that Yahweh functions as a verbal form in a causative stem. This conclusion is rendered difficult by the fact that the formula occurs in the expanded form *yhwh 'ĕlōhê ṣĕbā'ôt* ("Yahweh God of hosts"), which attributes the function of a proper name to Yahweh. The word *ṣĕba'ôt* means "armies" or "hosts." It is best to understand Yahweh as a proper name in association with the word "armies."

Elohim. The root of Elohim is El (*'ēl*). The form *'ĕlōhîm* is a plural form commonly understood as a plural of majesty. While the word occurs in Canaanite (*'l*) and Akkadian (*ilu[m]*), its etymology is uncertain. In the OT the word is always construed in the singular when it denotes the true God. In the Pentateuch the name *'ĕlōhîm* connotes a general concept of God; that is, it portrays God as the transcendent being, the creator of the universe. It does not connote the more personal and palpable concepts inherent in the name Yahweh. It can also be used to apply to false gods as well as to judges and kings.

El. El has the same general range of meaning as Elohim. It is apparently the root on which the plural form has been constructed. It differs in usage from Elohim only in its use in theophoric names and to serve to contrast the human and the divine. Sometimes it is combined with *yah* to become *Elyah.*

El Elyon ("God Most High"). The word *'elyôn,* an adjective meaning "high," is derived from the root *'lh* ("to go up" or "ascend"). It is used to describe the height of objects (II Kings 15:35; 18:17; Ezek. 41:7) as well as the prominence of persons (Ps. 89:27) and the prominence of Israel as a nation (Deut. 26:19; 28:1). When used of God it connotes the concept of "highest."

The name El Elyon occurs only in Gen. 14:18–22 and Ps. 78:35, although God is known by the shorter title Elyon in a significant number of passages.

There is a superlative connotation in the word *'elyôn.* In each case in which the adjective occurs it denotes that which is highest or uppermost. In Deut. 26:19 and 28:1 the superlative idea is apparent in the fact that Israel is to be exalted above the nations. The use of the word in I Kings 9:8 and II Chr. 7:21 may not seem to reflect a superlative idea, but there is, as C. F. Keil suggests, an allusion to Deut. 26:19 and 28:1, where the superlative idea exists. The superlative is also evident in the use of the word in Ps. 97:9, where it connotes Yahweh's supremacy over the other gods.

El Shaddai. The etymology of *šadday* is obscure. It has been connected with the Akkadian *šadū* ("mountain") by some. Others have suggested a connection with the word "breast," and still others have seen a connection with the verb *šādad* ("to devastate"). The theological significance of the name, if it can be understood fully, must be derived from a study of the various contexts in which the name occurs.

The name Shaddai frequently appears apart from El as a divine title.

El-Eloe-Yisrael. This appellation occurs only in Gen. 33:20 as the name of the altar that marked the place of Jacob's encounter with God. It denotes the unique significance of El as the God of Jacob.

Adonai. The root *'dn* occurs in Ugaritic with the meanings "lord and father." If the word originally connoted "father," it is not difficult to understand how the connotation "lord" developed from that. The basic meaning of the word in the OT is "lord."

Critical to the understanding of the meaning of the word is the suffix *ay.* It is commonly suggested that the ending is the first person possessive suffix on a plural form of *'ādôn* ("my lord"). This is plausible for the form *'ădōnay,* but the heightened form *'ădōnāy,* which also appears in the Massoretic text, is more difficult to explain, unless it represents an effort on the part of the Massoretes "to mark the word as sacred by a small external sign."

Attention has been drawn to the Ugaritic ending *-ai,* which is used in that language "as a reinforcement of a basic word." However, it is doubtful that this explanation should be applied in all cases. The plural construction of the name is evident when the word occurs in the construct as it does in the appellation "Lord of lords" (*'ădōnê hā'ădōnîm*) in Deut. 10:17. And the translation "my Lord" seems to be required in such vocative addresses as "my Lord Yahweh, what will you give me?" (Gen. 15:2; see also Exod. 4:10).

It appears, then, that it is best to understand the word as a plural of majesty with a first person suffixual ending that was altered by the Massoretes to mark the sacred character of the name.

Other Divine Names. The name Baali occurs only once, in Hos. 2:16 (AV; "My Baal," RSV) in a play on words. The word means "my husband," as does *'îšî,* the word with which it is paired.

Ancient of Days is an appellation applied to God in Dan. 7. It occurs with other depictions of great age (vs. 9) to create the impression of noble venerability.

Abba is an alternate Aramaic term for "father." It is the word that Jesus used to address God in Mark 14:36. Paul pairs the word with the Greek word for "father" in Rom. 8:15 and Gal. 4:6.

The *'ālep* that terminates the form *'abbā'* functions as both a demonstrative and a vocative particle in Aramaic. In the time of Jesus the word connoted both the emphatic concept, "the father," and the more intimate "my father, our father."

While the word was the common form of address for children, there is much evidence that in the time of Jesus the practice was not limited only to children. The childish character of the word ("daddy") thus receded, and *'abbā'* acquired the warm, familiar ring which we may feel in such an expression as "dear father."

The Theological Significance of the Divine Names. *Yahweh.* The parallel structure in Exod. 3:14–15 supports the association of the name Yahweh with the concept of being or existence. It says, "I AM has sent me to you" (vs. 14; "The LORD . . . has sent me to you" (vs. 15). The name "I AM" is based on the clause "I AM WHO I AM" found in 3:14 which, on the basis of the etymology implied here, suggests that Yahweh is the 3. p. form of the verb *'ehyeh* (I am).

The clause *'ehyeh 'ăšer 'ehyeh* has been translated in several ways, "I am that I am" (AV), "I am who I am" (RSV, NIV), and "I will be what I will be" (RSV margin). Recently the translation "I am (the) One who is" has been suggested. The latter translation has much in its favor grammatically and fits the context well.

The main concern of the context is to demonstrate that a continuity exists in the divine activity from the time of the patriarchs to the events recorded in Exod. 3. The Lord is referred to as the God of the fathers (vss. 13, 15, 16). The God who made the gracious promises regarding Abraham's offspring is the God who is and who continues to be. The affirmation of vs. 17 is but a reaffirmation of the promise made to Abraham. The name Yahweh may thus affirm the continuing activity of God on behalf of his people in fealty to his promise.

Jesus' application of the words "I am" to himself in John 8:58 not only denoted his preexistence but associated him with Yahweh. Jesus was the fulfillment of the promise given to Abraham, the fulfillment of which Abraham anticipated (John 8:56).

In the Pentateuch, Yahweh denotes that aspect of God's character that is personal rather than transcendent. It occurs in contexts in which the covenantal and redemptive aspects of God predominate. Cassuto says, "The name YHWH is employed when God is presented to us in His personal character and in direct relationship to people or nature; and *'Ĕlōhîm,* when the Deity is alluded to as a Transcendental Being who exists completely outside and above the physical universe" (*The Documentary Hypothesis,* p. 31). This precise distinction does not always obtain outside the Pentateuch, but Yahweh never loses its distinct function as the designation of the God of Israel.

The name Yahweh Sabaoth appears for the first time in Israel's history in connection with the cult center at Shiloh (I Sam. 1:3). It is there that the tent of meeting was set up when the land of Canaan had been subdued by the Israelites (Josh. 18:1). The name apparently had its origin in the period of the conquest or the postconquest period. It does not occur in the Pentateuch.

It is possible that the name was attributed to Yahweh as a result of the dramatic appearance to Joshua of an angelic being called the "commander of the host of Yahweh" at the commencement of the conquest (Josh. 5:13–15). The name would thus depict the vast power at Yahweh's disposal in the angelic hosts.

The association of this name with the ark of the covenant in I Sam. 4:4 is significant in that Yahweh is enthroned above the angelic figures known as the cherubim (II Sam. 6:2). Because the name was associated with the ark of the covenant, David addressed the people in that name when the ark was recovered from the Philistines (II Sam. 6:18). The name is often associated with the military activities of Israel (I Sam. 15:2–3; II Sam. 5:10).

The almighty power of Yahweh displayed in this name is manifested in the sphere of history (Pss. 46:6–7; 59:5). His power may be displayed in the life of the individual (Ps. 69:6) as well as the nation (Ps. 80:7). Sometimes he is simply referred to as "the Almighty."

The military connotation of the name was not lost, even in the eighth century, for Isaiah appeals to that name to depict the hosts of heaven that accompany Yahweh in his intervention in history (Isa. 13:4).

Elohim. This is the more general name for God. In the Pentateuch, when used as a proper name, it most commonly denotes the more transcendental aspects of God's character. When God is presented in relation to his creation and to the peoples of the earth in the Pentateuch, the name Elohim is the name most often used. It is for this reason that Elohim occurs consistently in the creation account of Gen. 1:1–2:42 and in the genealogies of Genesis. Where the context takes on a moral tone, as in Gen. 2:4*b*ff., the name Yahweh is used.

Throughout Genesis and the early chapters of Exodus *'ĕlōhîm* is used most often as a proper name. After Exod. 3 the name begins to occur with increasing frequency as an appellative, that is, "the God of," or "your God." This function is by far the most frequent mode of reference to God in the book of Deuteronomy. When used in this fashion the name denotes God as the supreme deity of a person or people. Thus, in the frequent expression, "Yahweh your God," Yahweh functions as a proper name, while "God" functions as the denominative of deity.

The appellative *'ĕlōhîm* connotes all that God is. As God he is sovereign, and that sovereignty extends beyond Israel into the arena of the nations (Deut. 2:30, 33; 3:22; Isa. 52:10). As God to his people he is loving and merciful (Deut. 1:31; 2:7; 23:5; Isa. 41:10, 13, 17; 49:5; Jer. 3:23). He establishes standards of obedience (Deut. 4:2; Jer. 11:3) and sovereignly punishes disobedience (Deut. 23:21). As God, there is no one like him (Isa. 44:7; 45:5–21).

The same connotations obtain in the use of the shorter form *'ēl.* He is the God who sees (*'ēl rŏ'î;* Gen. 16:13) and he is *'ēl* the God of Israel (Gen. 33:20).

As El Elyon, God is described in his exaltation over all things. There are two definitive passages for this name. In Ps. 83:18 Yahweh is described as "Most High over the earth," and Isa. 14:14 states, "I will ascend above the heights of the clouds, I will make myself like the Most High."

However, in the majority of cases the attributes of this name are indistinguishable from other usages of El or Elohim. He fixed the boundaries of the nations (Deut. 32:8). He effects changes in the creation (Ps. 18:13). El Shaddai occurs most frequently in the Book of Job, where it functions as a general name for the deity. As El Shaddai, God disciplines (Job 5:17); he is to be feared (Job 6:14); he is just (Job 8:3); he hears prayer (Job 8:5); and he creates (Job 33:4).

This name occurs six times in the patriarchal narratives. In most of those instances it is associated with the promise given by God to the patriarchs. Yet the name is often paired with Yahweh in the poetic material, and thus shares the personal warmth of that name. He is known for his steadfast love (Ps. 21:7) and his protection (Ps. 91:9–10).

The root of Adonai means "lord" and, in its secular usage, always refers to a superior in the OT. The word retains the sense of "lord" when applied to God. The present pointing of the word in the Massoretic text is late; early manuscripts were written without vowel pointing.

In Ps. 110:1 the word is pointed in the singular, as it usually is when it applies to humans rather than God. Yet Jesus used this verse to argue for his deity. The pointing is Massoretic, and no distinction would be made in the consonantal texts. Since the word denotes a superior, the word must refer to one who is superior to David and who bears the messianic roles of king and priest (vs. 4).

The name Abba connotes the fatherhood of God. This is affirmed by the accompanying translation *ho patēr* ("father") which occurs in each usage of the name in the NT (Mark 14:36; Rom. 8:15; Gal. 4:6).

The use of this name as Jesus' mode of address to God in Mark 14:36 is a unique expression of Jesus' relationship to the Father. Jeremias says, "He spoke to God like a child to its father, simply, inwardly, confidently. Jesus' use of *abba* in addressing God reveals the heart of his relationship with God" (*The Prayers of Jesus*, p. 62).

The same relationship is sustained by the believer with God. It is only because of the believer's relationship with God, established by the Holy Spirit, that he can address God with this name that depicts a relationship of warmth and filial love.

In a sense the relationship designated by this name is the fulfillment of the ancient promise given to Abraham's offspring that the Lord will be their God, and they his people (Exod. 6:7; Lev. 26:12; Jer. 24:7; 30:22). T. E. McComiskey

See also God, Doctrine of; God, Attributes of; Names in Bible Times, Significance of; Abba; Alpha and Omega; Holy One of Israel.

Bibliography. W. F. Albright, *From Stone Age to Christianity;* W. Eichrodt, *Theology of the OT,* I, 178ff.; L. Koehler, *OT Theology;* J. Schneider *et al., NIDNTT,* II, 66ff.; G. Oehler, *Theology of the OT;* M. Reisel, *The Mysterious Name of Y.H.W.H.;* H. H. Rowley, *The Faith of Israel;* H. Schultz, *OT Theology,* II, 116ff.; T. Vriezen, *An Outline of OT Theology;* H. Kleinknecht *et al., TDNT,* III, 65ff.

Godliness. The manner of life which is centered on God, with special reference to devotion, piety, and reverence toward him. It can be defined as the conjunction of an attitude of devotion to God and of the consequent right conduct.

The idea of godliness is in many ways typically hellenistic, with its emphasis on reverence and devotion to God. Its closest OT equivalent is the "fear of God," which has as its central meaning a life of active obedience to the law (cf. Lev. 19:14; 25:17; II Kings 17:34; Job 1:1; Ps. 128:1; Jer. 32:40).

The Greek word corresponding to godliness or piety is *eusebeia.* Its original meaning was the appropriate attitude to that which inspires reverence and awe, from social structures to God himself. It derives from a word meaning "to step back," or "to keep a distance." In its application to religious devotion it is connected to awe, reverence, and trepidation before God and, as such, is characteristic of Greek religiosity (Acts 17:23). This is very far from the idea of obedience to God's law and probably explains the almost total absence of the word and its cognates from the LXX.

This word group is largely absent from the NT, probably for the same reason. The words are principally confined to the book of Acts (3:12; 10:2, 7; 17:23), where they seem to refer to piety in general, without a specifically Christian content; the Pastoral Epistles; and II Peter, where they are given specifically Christian content. The fact that these words occur almost exclusively in these letters suggests that it may have taken some time for these hellenistic ideas to be integrated to Christian thought.

In the Pastoral Epistles *eusebeia* denotes a particular manner of life and comes close to the OT idea of "the fear of God." However, it does not focus upon the law, but on the individual believer's faith in Christ (I Tim. 3:16). The secret of the godly life is the revelation of God in Jesus Christ; godliness is basically following him in this life (Titus 2:12). It is thus presented as a Christian goal, to be earnestly sought after (I Tim. 2:2; 4:7–8), even if it leads to persecution (II Tim. 3:12). Godliness and sound doctrine are closely related. True doctrine is described as being "according to godliness" (I Tim. 6:3; Titus 1:1), while an appearance of godliness without true Christian content is characteristic of evil men (II Tim. 3:5). It is important to note that godliness is directly connected to proper respect for the family (I Tim. 5:4).

The usage of II Peter is similar to this. Godliness is one of a list of Christian virtues (1:6–7); it is related to the power of God (1:3). The use of the word in the plural in 3:11 suggests a reference to specific acts of piety.

Godliness is thus the honoring of God as Creator and Redeemer that is born of faith in Jesus Christ and expresses itself in daily living. It is the manifestation of faith in life and includes respect for the orders of creation, such as the family. As such, it is a criterion for soundness of doctrine, and should characterize all Christians.

F. Q. Gouvea

See also Ethics, Biblical.

Bibliography. W. Foerster, *TDNT,* VII, 168–96; W. Günther, *NIDNTT,* II, 90–95; A. Bowling, *TWOT,* I, 399–401.

Gogarten, Friedrich (1887–1967). German theologian. Gogarten was educated in the theological tradition of German idealism, writing his earliest book on the religious thought of Fichte. However, his was an uneasy liberalism, and he soon took issue with the idea that Jesus Christ represented the "source in us" in favor of One who stands over against us. He concluded that liberalism had taught us to look at all things as man's doing, but man's works have no permanence to them.

They not only begin, they also end: "We have all entered so deeply into the human as to have lost God."

When Gogarten lectured before the assembly of Friends of the Christian World, he left no doubt but that he had undertaken a new theological course. William Shafer recalls that "with Gogarten there stepped into the banqueting hall of the Wartburg Martin Luther . . . ready to fling his ink bottle at the head of the Devil."

Gogarten associated himself with a young Swiss pastor, Karl Barth, who was similarly disengaging himself from the earlier theological idealism and charting a course which would be variously described as "crisis theology," "dialectical theology," and "neo-orthodoxy." Gogarten's polemic advocated rethinking the Christian faith along historical rather than metaphysical lines. History implied for him the process of interaction in which being and meaning are re-created.

The nature of Christian responsibility consisted for Gogarten in receptivity (being-from-the-other), activity (being-for-the-other), and openness to "the absolute mystery which presses upon man's consciousness of responsibility for the world." Barth criticized Gogarten for courting the notion of history as a second source of revelation, and Gogarten countered with the charge that Barth held an abstract dialectic, lacking historical tangency. Gogarten vigorously defended Bultmann in the demythologizing controversy, but his criticisms of Bultmann were eventually picked up by such so-called post-Bultmannians as Gerhard Ebeling and Ernst Fuchs.

M. A. INCH

See also NEO-ORTHODOXY; DEMYTHOLOGIZATION.

Bibliography. F. Gogarten, *Demythologizing and History* and *The Reality of Faith;* T. Runyon, Jr., "Friedrich Gogarten," in M. Marty and D. Peerman, eds., *A Handbook of Christian Theologians;* L. Shiner, *The Secularization of History: An Introduction to the Theology of Friedrich Gogarten.*

Golden Rule. Jesus states what has come to be described as the Golden Rule: "However you want people to treat you, so treat them, for this is the Law and the Prophets" (Matt. 7:12; cf. Luke 6:31). The negative form was widely expressed in Judaism. The famed first century rabbi Hillel was reported to have taught, "Whatsoever you would that men should not do to you, do not that to them."

Similar references are found elsewhere in the literature of antiquity. Tzu Kung inquired of Confucius: "Is there any one word that can serve as a principle for the conduct of life?" To which the sage replied: "Perhaps the word 'reciprocity': Do not do to others what you would not want others to do to you" (Analects 15:23).

One ought not draw too simple a comparison between these references to reciprocity and the Golden Rule. Each has its own particular setting and significance. Reciprocity can degenerate to unbridled self-interest, where one hopes to secure good treatment by his behavior toward others. Jesus' teaching stands in stark contrast to such travesty when read in conjunction with the account of the good Samaritan (Luke 10:25-37).

M. A. INCH

Bibliography. P. Bertocci and R. Millard, *Personality and the Good;* L. H. DeWolf, *Responsible Freedom;* N. Geisler, *Ethics: Alternatives and Issues;* T. B. Maston, *Biblical Ethics;* J. Noss, *Man's Religions;* B. Ramm, *The Right, the Good and the Happy.*

Gomarus, Francis (1563–1641). Dutch Calvinist theologian. Born at Bruges, Gomarus studied at Strasbourg, Neustadt, Oxford, and Cambridge before taking his doctorate at Heidelberg in 1594. In 1586 he became pastor of the Dutch community at Frankfurt, and in 1594 was appointed professor of theology at Leiden. Here he emerged as a staunch upholder of Calvinistic orthodoxy; and after James Arminius joined him on the Leiden faculty in 1603, controversy developed between them. The main point in dispute between Gomarus and Arminius was this: Arminius maintained that in the work of salvation, man in some sense cooperates with God, whereas Gomarus held that in this work God and God alone is active. When the pro-Arminian Conrad Vorstius was appointed to succeed Arminius in 1610, Gomarus resigned his chair in protest. In 1611 he became minister of the Reformed congregation at Middleburg; from 1614 to 1618 he taught at the French Protestant seminary at Saumur; and from 1618 until his death he occupied a professorial chair at Groningen.

In 1610 the Arminian group published *The Remonstrance,* a manifesto expounding their theological viewpoint. Thereupon the Gomarists replied with a *Counter-Remonstrance.* This controversy dragged on till 1618, when the Synod of Dort was called to settle the dispute. This synod pronounced against the Arminians, asserting in its decrees the so-called five points of Calvinism: unconditional election, limited atonement, total depravity, irresistible grace, and the final perseverance of the saints. But Gomarus, who played a prominent role at Dort, was unable to persuade the synod to endorse his supralapsarianism—i.e., the idea that God's decree of election preceded the fall of man and contemplated man's fallen estate as part of the divine plan of predestination.

N. V. HOPE

See also ARMINIUS, JAMES; DORT, SYNOD OF; SUPRALAPSARIANISM.

Bibliography. A. W. Harrison, *The Beginnings of Arminianism;* P. Schaff, *The Creeds of Christendom,* I, 508–23, III, 550–97.

Good, the Good, Goodness. The word "good" is the most comprehensive term used when praising excellence of something. To speak about a good book or good food is to use "good" in typically *nonmoral* ways. However, good conveys a *moral* sense when someone says "he is a good man" or "she did a good deed/work." The man is being lauded for his excellent moral character and the woman for her effort in fulfilling a human need. As in these examples, the morally good refers to various aspects of personhood which include deeds, character traits, motives, intentions, desires, and needs. When an action is commended because of "transpersonal" factors, such as its conformity to principles, the term "right" is most often employed. The relationship between the right and the good has been the most persistent problem in ethics. The solution lies in the hotly contested search for the criteria or standards of goodness and has centered around the most compelling of all human questions, "What is the good?"

An answer to this question rests upon one's philosophical assumptions and/or religious beliefs. This has fostered a host of often clashing distinctions such as objective vs. subjective good, temporal vs. eternal good, greater vs. lesser good, real vs. apparent good, material vs. spiritual good, common vs. individual good, immutable vs. mutable good, good as an end vs. good as a means. Classical thinkers such as Socrates, Plato, and Aristotle tried to clarify and unify these various facets of the good. Their ideas greatly influenced Augustine and Thomas Aquinas who, with compelling rigor, related these discussions about the good to the Christian faith.

Both Augustine and Aquinas attempted to link the material and spiritual good by proposing the idea of "grades of goodness" with God being the highest good (*summum bonum*) and the source of all lesser goods. Moral evil (*concupiscence*) is present when one desires a lesser (nonmoral) good as an end in itself. But when the desire for a lesser good is a means to love God (*caritas*), then the "mutable adheres to the immutable" and it becomes a blessing (moral good). With their theocentric focus these theologians took an important step in unifying the concept of the good. Nevertheless, because of their dependence upon Greek ideas they were unable to affirm the goodness of some things such as physical pleasures, especially sexual passion. Thus, the integration they sought tended to evaporate. Also their notion that human effort was involved in achieving the highest good was later to be dramatically challenged by Luther and the other Reformers.

God Is All Good. While the classical theologians failed to fully integrate the concept of the good, they did underscore its proper source and reference. For the Christian the meaning and unity of the good rests completely and absolutely in God as revealed by the word. Declarations that God is good, acts with goodness, and is the source of all good superabound throughout Scripture and are usually tied to human gratitude and praise (e.g., II Chr. 5:13; 7:3; Pss. 25:8; 100:5; 106:1; Jer. 33:11; Nah. 1:7; Mark 10:18). The identity of the good with God is profoundly expressed by Amos in his unconventional use of the oft-repeated priestly teaching or call to worship, "Seek the Lord and live." He quotes this phrase three times, but on the third he substitutes the word "good" for "the Lord" and admonishes the people to "seek good and not evil that you may live" (Amos 5:4, 6, 14). To seek God is to seek the good.

God's absolute goodness was no more powerfully affirmed than when Jesus was confronted by the man who flippantly addressed him as good and assumed he would redefine its meaning. Rather, Jesus insisted that God is perfect goodness and that God alone decides and, in fact, has already determined (in Scripture and in Jesus himself) what is the good (cf. Mark 10:17–22; Matt. 19:16–22). The tragic fall of the first human pair when they ate from the tree of the knowledge of good and evil lay precisely in their rebellious attempt to be above God and assume God's sole prerogative to determine what is good and what is evil (Gen. 3:4–7).

God's Good Gifts. The Christian's unique understanding of the good is shaped by the Bible's unparalleled presentation of the triune God who acts by creating the world and by establishing an everlasting covenant of fellowship with that world. Already in the opening verses of Genesis the meaning of the good (*ṭôb, agathos, kalos*) is clarified. The phrase "and God saw that it was good (or pleasing)" is a postlude to each day's creative activity (Gen. 1:4, 10, 12, 18, 21, 25, 31; cf. I Tim. 4:4). Each declaration of goodness accents God's orderly design and fashioning of the universe, resulting in the interdependence of its structures and in the grouping of all life after its kind. The meaning of the good as the harmonious ordering and agreement among the parts is highlighted in Adam and Eve who, as physical and psychological beings, are created in total accord with their environment (note the linguistic relationship between *'ādām* and *'ădāmâ* meaning "earth"). Thus, the natural elements of the earth are "pleasant to the sight and good for food" (Gen. 2:9).

Because of this ordered agreement between the created self and the created world, the good is closely associated in Scripture with the desirable or the "pleasing." For instance, good figs are ripe ones, i.e., figs which are pleasing to eat (Jer. 24:2); honey is good because it is sweet on the tongue (Prov. 24:13); some women are good to look at, meaning they are pleasing to men (Gen. 6:2). The natural goods of life, however, are not simply limited to those things that agree with the physical senses. Wisdom, for example, is good because it finds accord with the soul.

Because the things pleasing to the body are often necessities for human life or even social status, they become economically valuable. Consequently, "goods" can refer to one's possessions, property, or wealth (Luke 6:30). These goods often constitute a part of God's promises. The Promised Land is a good land, i.e., a land flowing with milk and honey (Exod. 3:8). While the Lord bestows goods (blessings) upon those that wait upon him (Lam. 3:25), God's goodness is also granted to all people (Ps. 145:9). It is possible to overindulge in God's good gifts with the result that too much honey causes one to vomit (Prov. 25:16), or to grow fat and serve other gods (Deut. 31:20). Furthermore, one may deprive others of the natural goods to which they are entitled. In these contexts *the good* conveys a religiomoral meaning and pinpoints the moral excellence of who a person is and what a person does.

Being and Doing Good. The idea of the good as friendly agreement between the parts emerges from the theological conviction that God relates to humans in a covenantal way, i.e., in an ordered or commanded relationship between various parties (Gen. 6:18; I Sam. 20:8). The good person is the one who lives in fellowship with the Lord and acts in accord with God's dictates for assuring human community (Mic. 6:8). The one who does good is of God (III John 11), and thus the faithful are exhorted to choose good (Isa. 7:15); hold fast to the good (Rom. 12:9); diligently seek good (Prov. 11:27); love good (Amos 5:15); learn to do good (Isa. 1:17); and imitate good (III John 11). The good, however, is only possible by divine aid, since no one does good, but only evil continually (Rom. 3:12). As Jesus insisted, persons must be made good before they are able to produce good fruit (Matt. 12:33–35). According to Paul, Christians have been created in Christ Jesus for good works (Eph. 2:10). Then they become "lovers of good" (*philagathos,* Titus 1:8) and are able to distinguish good from evil (Heb. 5:14); to prove what is good (Rom. 12:2); to overcome evil with good (Rom. 12:21); to do good to those that hate them (Luke 6:35); and to be rich in good deeds (I Tim. 6:18; Matt. 5:16; II Cor. 9:8; II Tim. 2:21; 3:17; Titus 2:14). Goodness is a fruit of the Spirit (Gal. 5:22) and is closely tied to love (Matt. 19:16–19; Heb. 10:24). For this reason Christians are never to seek their own good, but the good of others, especially that of the community or the "common good" (cf. I Cor. 10:24 with 12:7).

Throughout Scripture the good is embodied in procedures of justice, deeds of kindness, and acts of liberation, all of which serve the poor and lowly in society (Isa. 1:17; Mic. 6:8). In these contexts the good becomes the right and is essentially linked to the practical goods of life. Goodness as justice guarantees that legal structures will be impartial in the distribution of natural goods that fulfill human existence (Amos 5:15; Mic. 3:1–4; II Cor. 8:12–14). Kindness is the personal distribution of these goods when the justice within structures fails (Mark 14:6–8; Isa. 59:14–15). Freedom as a good permits others to make choices necessary for their overall well-being (Jer. 34:8ff.; Luke 4:18). To those who do good to others, God will bestow good upon them and they shall have life (Jer. 32:39–42; John 5:29).

For the Christian, then, the right and the good are not finally at odds. The good as the right points to the necessary criteria for distributing natural goods. Nevertheless, these goods make the right worth pursuing. Since all good comes from God, goodness is, as Karl Barth correctly states, "the sum of everything, right, friendly and wholesome" (*Church Dogmatics,* II/2, 708).

D. J. Miller

Bibliography. Thomas Aquinas, *Summa Theologica;* Aristotle, *Nicomachean Ethics;* Augustine, *The City of God;* W. Eichrodt, *Theology of the OT,* II; R. M. Hare, *The Language of Morals;* A. Gewirth, *Reason and Morality;* C. F. H. Henry, *Christian Personal Ethics;* P. Lehmann, *Ethics in a Christian Context;* G. E. Moore, *Principia Ethica;* E. Beyreuther, *NIDNTT,* II, 98ff.; W. Grundmann *et al., TDNT,* I, 10ff.; II, 536ff.

Good Friday. The Friday before Easter Day. Its origins as a special holy day go back to the development of Holy Week in Jerusalem in the late fourth century. In the East it came to be called "Great" and in the West "Good" Friday. It is observed in the Western nations in many ways. For example, in Roman Catholicism the liturgy of the day, used between 3:00 P.M. and 8:00 P.M., has three parts—readings and prayers, adoration of the cross, and Holy Communion with bread consecrated a day beforehand. There is no celebration of the Eucharist on this day. In Anglicanism there is variety, including the use of the Roman liturgy, a three hour service (noon to 3:00 P.M.), or a simple service of morning or evening prayer. In some Protestant denominations there is a celebration of the Lord's Supper.

P. TOON

See also HOLY WEEK; CHRISTIAN YEAR.

Good News. *See* GOSPEL.

Good Works. *See* WORKS.

Gore, Charles (1853–1932). For a time, as Bishop of Oxford, the most influential leader in the Anglican Church. He worked toward bringing a reconciling and more liberal outlook to the Oxford Movement, which sought to restore the High Church ideals of seventeenth century Anglicanism.

Gore is characterized as a "liberal catholic." To him this was Anglicanism at its best. He noted three marks of catholicism as apostolic succession, high sacramentalism, and a common rule of faith. Gore's liberalism is seen in his concern to give reason wide reign whether in philosophy or science, historical criticism, or the spiritual experience of humankind.

National notoriety came when Gore edited and contributed to *Lux Mundi* (1889). The Oxford Anglican contributors to this volume wished to bring the catholic faith into line with modern scholarship and moral problems. Gore's essay "The Holy Spirit and Inspiration" rooted authority for the church in the Holy Spirit's guidance. The Spirit acts in the church to help Scripture, reason, and tradition interpret each other. The impact of this for Gore was that the church could be completely open to the new findings of biblical criticism. These views led to Gore's break with the older generation of conservative High Church leaders.

Gore's views were expanded in his Bampton Lectures, *The Incarnation of the Son of God* (1891), and his *Dissertations on Subjects Connected with the Incarnation* (1895). In these the *kenosis* or self-emptying of Christ became the key to the incarnation, the central doctrine of Christianity for Gore. This meant that during his "incarnate and mortal life" Jesus, out of his "self-restraining love," voluntarily limited himself so that his divine functions and powers, such as omniscience, were not exercised. Gore believed this was scriptural and permitted the Son of God, without ceasing to be God, to enter fully into human experience. Presupposed in all Gore's thought was the basic unity of nature and grace in which Jesus Christ is both creator and redeemer. In Jesus the Godhead's creative intention reached its highest fruition.

Gore's literary output was large after he resigned his bishopric in 1919. His *Reconstruction of Belief* (1926) was a single-volume publication of three earlier works. His strong social views were summarized in *Christ and Society* (1928).

D. K. MCKIM

See also OXFORD MOVEMENT; LIBERALISM, THEOLOGICAL.

Bibliography. J. Carpenter, *Gore: A Study in Liberal Catholic Thought;* P. E. Hughes, ed., *Creative Minds in Contemporary Theology;* G. Crosse, *Charles Gore: A Biographical Sketch;* J. C. Davies, "Charles Gore," *Theol* 25:259ff.; T. A. Langford, *In Search of Foundations: English Theology 1900–1920;* G. L. Prestige, *The Life of Charles Gore;* A. M. Ramsey, *From Gore to Temple; ODCC.*

Gospel. The English word "gospel" (from the Anglo-Saxon *god-spell,* i.e., God-story) is the usual NT translation of the Greek *euangelion.* According to Tyndale, the renowned English Reformer and Bible translator, it signified "good, mery, glad and ioyfull tydinge, that maketh a mannes hert glad, and maketh hym synge, daunce, and leepe for ioye" (*Prologue to NT*). While his definition is more experiential than explicative, it has touched that inner quality which brings the word to life. The gospel is the joyous proclamation of God's redemptive activity in Christ Jesus on behalf of man enslaved by sin.

Origin. *Euangelion* (neut. sing.) is rarely found in the sense of "good tidings" outside of early Christian literature. As used by Homer it referred not to the message but to the reward given to the messenger (e.g., *Odyssey* xiv. 152). In Attic Greek it always occurred in the plural and generally referred to sacrifices or thank offerings made in behalf of good tidings. Even in the LXX *euangelion* is found for sure but once (II Kings 4:10: Eng. versions, II Sam.) and there it has the classical meaning of a reward given for good tidings. (In II Kings 18:22, 25, *euangelion* should undoubtedly be taken as fem. sing. in harmony with vss. 20 and 27 where this form is certain.) *Euangelion* in the sense of the good news itself belongs to a later period. Outside of Christian literature the neuter singular first appears with this meaning in a papyrus letter from an Egyptian official of the third century A.D. In the plural it is found in a calendar inscription from Priene about 9 B.C. It is not until the writings of the apostolic fathers (e.g., Didache 8:2; II Clement 8:5) that we sense a transition to the later Christian usage of *euangelion* as referring to a book which sets forth the life and teaching of Jesus (Justin, *Apology* i. 66).

Against this background the frequency with which *euangelion* occurs in the NT (more than seventy-five times) with the specific connotation of "good news" is highly informative. It suggests that *euangelion* is quite distinctively a NT word. Its true significance is therefore found, not by probing its linguistic background, but by observing its specific Christian usage.

This is not to deny, of course, that the basic concept has its rightful origin in the religious aspirations of the nation Israel. Some seven centuries before Christ the prophet Isaiah had delivered a series of prophetic utterances. With vivid imagery he portrayed the coming deliverance of Israel from captivity in Babylon. A Redeemer shall come to Zion preaching good tidings unto the meek and liberty to the captives (Isa. 60:1–2). "How beautiful upon the mountains are the feet of him who brings good tidings" (Isa. 52:7). Jerusalem itself is pictured as a herald whose message is good tidings (Isa. 40:9).

Jesus saw in these prophecies a description of his own mission (Luke 4:18–21; 7:22). They expressed that same sense of liberation and exultation which was the true characteristic of his messianic proclamation. What was at first simply a literary allusion came easily to represent the actual message which was being proclaimed. *Euangelion* was the natural result of the LXX's *euangelizein.* Thus Mark could write that Jesus came into Galilee "heralding the *euangelion* of God" (Mark 1:14).

Euangelion *in the Gospels.* Upon examining the four Gospels we find that the word *euangelion* is used only by Matthew and Mark. The concept, however, is not foreign to Luke. He uses the verb form twenty-six times in Luke-Acts, and the noun twice in the latter book. In the Fourth Gospel there is no trace of either verb or noun.

In all but one instance Matthew further describes *euangelion* as the gospel "of the kingdom." This gospel is not to be distinguished from what Mark calls the "gospel of God" (many manuscripts read "the gospel of the kingdom of God") and summarizes in the words, "the time is fulfilled, and the kingdom of God is at hand" (Mark 1:14–15). On the other occasion Matthew writes "*this* gospel" (Matt. 26:13)—the context indicating that Jesus is alluding to his coming death. The phrase "preaching the gospel of the kingdom" is twice used in summary statements of the ministry of Jesus (Matt. 4:23; 9:35). This gospel is to be preached throughout the entire world prior to the consummation of the age (Matt. 24:14; cf. Mark 13:10).

The way in which Mark uses *euangelion* is suggested by his opening words, "The beginning of the gospel of Jesus Christ, the Son of God." Here *euangelion* is a semitechnical term meaning "the glad news which tells about Jesus Christ." Where Luke writes "for the sake of the kingdom of God" (Luke 18:29), the Markan parallel is "for my sake and for the gospel" (Mark 10:29). This gospel is of such tremendous import that for its sake a man must be willing to enter upon a life of complete self-denial (Mark 8:35). In the long ending of Mark, Christ commands his disciples to "preach the gospel to the whole creation" (Mark 16:15).

The Gospel According to Paul. Over against the six occasions (discounting parallels) on which *euangelion* is used by the Gospel writers, it is found a total of sixty times in the writings of Paul. *Euangelion* is a favorite Pauline term. It is evenly distributed throughout his epistles, missing only in his note to Titus.

Paul's ministry was distinctively that of the propagation of the gospel. Unto this gospel he was set apart (Rom. 1:1) and made a minister according to the grace of God (Eph. 3:7). His special sphere of action was the Gentile world (Rom. 16:16; Gal. 2:7). Since Paul accepted the gospel as a sacred trust (Gal. 2:7), it was necessary that in the discharge of this obligation he speak so as to please God rather than man (I Tim. 2:4). The divine commission had created a sense of urgency that made him cry out, "Woe to me if I do not preach the gospel" (I Cor. 9:16). For the sake of the gospel Paul was willing to become all things to all men (I Cor. 9:22–23). No sacrifice was too great. Eternal issues were at stake. Those whose minds were blinded and did not obey the gospel were perishing and would ultimately reap the vengeance of divine wrath (II Cor. 4:3; II Thess. 1:9). On the other hand, to those who believed, the gospel had effectively become the power of God unto salvation (Rom. 1:16).

Because Paul on occasion speaks of his message as "my gospel" (Rom. 2:16; II Tim. 2:8), and because in his letter to the Galatians he goes to some pains to stress that he did not receive it from man (Gal. 1:11ff.), it is sometimes maintained that Paul's gospel should be distinguished from that of apostolic Christianity in general.

This does not follow. I Cor. 15:3–5 sets forth with crystal clarity the message of primitive Christianity. Paul, using terms equivalent to the technical rabbinic words for the reception and transmission of tradition, refers to this message as something which he had received and passed on (vs. 3). In vs. 11 he can say, "Whether then it was I or they, so we preach and so you believed." In Galatians, Paul tells how he laid before the apostles at Jerusalem the gospel which he had preached. Far from finding fault with the message, they extended to him the right hand of fellowship (Gal. 2:9). What Paul meant by his earlier remarks is that the charges against his gospel as a mere human message were completely fraudulent. The revelation of the full theological impact of the Christ-event was God-given and stemmed from his encounter on the Damascus road. Thus he speaks of "my gospel" meaning his own personal apprehension of the gospel. On other occasions he can speak freely of "our gospel" (II Cor. 4:3; I Thess. 1:5).

For Paul, the *euangelion* is preeminently the "gospel of God" (Rom. 1:1; 15:16; II Cor. 11:7; I Thess. 2:2, 8–9). It proclaims the redemptive activity of God. This activity is bound up with the person and work of God's Son, Christ Jesus. Thus it is also the "gospel of Christ" (I Cor. 9:12; II Cor. 2:12; 9:13; 10:14; Gal. 1:7; I Thess. 3:2; vss. 16 and 19 of Rom. 15 indicate that these are interchangeable terms). This gospel is variously expressed as "the gospel of our Lord Jesus" (II Thess. 1:8), "the gospel of the glory of the blessed God" (I Tim. 1:11), "the gospel of his Son" (Rom. 1:9), and "the gospel of the glory of Christ" (II Cor. 4:4). It is a gospel of salvation (Eph. 1:13) and peace (Eph. 6:15). It proclaims the hope of eternal life (Col. 1:23). It is "the word of truth" (Col. 1:5; Eph. 1:13). Through this gospel, life and immortality are brought to light (II Tim. 1:10).

The Apostolic Preaching. If we wish to investigate more closely the specific content of the primitive gospel, we will do well to adopt the basic approach of C. H. Dodd (*The Apostolic Preaching and Its Developments*). While Dodd refers to the message as *kērygma,* he is ready to admit that this term is a virtual equivalent of *euangelion.* (*Kērygma* stresses the manner of delivery; *euangelion,* the essential nature of the content.)

There are two sources for the determination of the primitive proclamation. Of primary importance are the fragments of pre-Pauline tradition that lie embedded in the writings of the apostle. These segments can be uncovered by the judicious application of certain literary and formal criteria. While at least one purports to be the actual terms in which the gospel was preached (I Cor. 15:3–5), others take the form of early Christian hymns (e.g., Phil. 2:6–11), summaries of the message (e.g., Rom. 10:9), or creedal formulas (I Cor. 12:3; I Tim. 3:16).

A second source is the early Petrine speeches in Acts. These speeches (on the basis of their Aramaic background, freedom from Paulinism, and the general trustworthiness of Luke as a historian) can be shown to give reliably the gist of what Peter actually said and not what a second generation Christian thought he might have said.

These two sources combine to set forth one common apostolic gospel. In briefest outline, this message contained: (1) a historical proclamation of the death, resurrection, and exaltation of Jesus, set forth as the fulfillment of prophecy and involving man's responsiblity; (2) a theological evaluation of the person of Jesus as both Lord and Christ; (3) a summons to repent and receive the forgiveness of sins.

It will be noticed that the essential core of this message is not the dawn of the messianic age (as Dodd implies)—although this is most certainly involved—but that sequence of redemptive events which sweeps the hearer along with compelling logic toward the climactic confession that Jesus is Lord.

The gospel is not the product of a bewildered church pondering the theological significance of Good Friday. It is rather the result of a natural development which had its origins in the teachings of Jesus himself. The Passion sayings of Jesus—far from being "prophecies after the event" (cf. R. Bultmann, *Theology of the NT,* I, 29)—are undeniable evidence that Jesus laid the foundation for a theology of the cross. In his teaching regarding his own person Jesus furnished what R. H. Fuller has aptly termed "the raw materials of Christology" (*The Mission and Achievement of Jesus*). The resurrection was the catalyst which precipitated in the minds of the disciples the total significance of God's redemptive activity. It released the gospel!

This gospel is power (Rom. 1:16). As an instrument of the Holy Spirit it convicts (I Thess. 1:5) and converts (Col. 1:6). It cannot be fettered (II Tim. 2:9). Although it is good news, it is strenuously opposed by a rebellious world (I Thess. 2:2). Opposition to the message takes the form of opposition to the messenger (II Tim. 1:11–12; Philem. 13). Yet those who proclaim it must do so boldly (Eph. 6:19) and with transparent simplicity (II Cor. 4:2)—not with eloquence lest the cross of Christ be robbed of its power (I Cor. 1:17). To those who refuse the gospel it is both foolishness and a stumbling block (I Cor. 1:18ff.), but to those who respond in faith it proves itself to be "the power of God unto salvation" (Rom. 1:16).

R. H. Mounce

Bibliography. R. H. Strachan, "The Gospel in the NT," *IB,* VII; W. Barclay, *NT Wordbook;* A. E. J. Rawlinson, *EncyBrit* X, 536ff.; M. Burrows, "The Origin of the Term 'Gospel,'" *JBL* 44:21–33; W. Milligan, *Thess.,* Note E; A. Harnack, *Constitution and Law,* Appendix III; L. Clarke, "What Is the Gospel?" in *Divine Humanity;* V. Becker, *NIDNTT,* II, 107ff.; G. Friedrich, *TDNT,* II, 705ff.; R. H. Mounce, *The Essential Nature of NT Preaching.*

Gospel, Social Implications of. The gospel is the proclamation and demonstration of God's redemptive activity in Jesus Christ to a world enslaved by sin. Redemption is personal as men and women respond to the claims of Jesus Christ as Lord and Savior. Redemption is also social, but the nature, priority, and extent of the social implications of the gospel have not been as readily agreed upon.

Early Period. The social implications of the gospel have been evident in every era of the church's life. The early church, for example, expressed a social witness by faithfulness to the radical demands of Christian community (Acts 2:42–46). Limited in their social expression by virtue of being members of a persecuted sect, many Christians challenged cultural values in their refusal to bear arms.

The church continuously manifested its social conscience with a concern for the poor. Basil the Great, for example, created a whole complex of charitable institutions in the fourth century. The monastic movement generated much philanthropic activity. The institutional charities of the Roman Catholic Church take their impetus from this medieval social heritage.

The Reformation heralded a renewal of biblical faith, including the Scripture's social emphasis. Though Martin Luther denied that good works had any place in the drama of salvation, he nevertheless commended good works as the proper response to the gracious gift of redemption. John Calvin, a second-generation Reformer, gave greater attention to the implications of the gospel for society. Whereas for Luther the civil rule was a restraining force because of sin, for Calvin government should be a positive force for the common welfare. In Calvin's Geneva this meant a commitment to education and to welfare for refugees, and outside Geneva sanctioning, under certain circumstances, the right of resistance for peoples suffering under unjust rulers.

Modern evangelicalism traces its roots to the Reformation, but is more directly the result of a variety of post-Reformation movements. Puritanism grew up in England in the sixteenth century, but its spirit flowered in America in the seventeenth century. "The Puritan dilemma" in America was the tension between individual freedom and social order. The strong emphasis on the covenant, though, meant an impetus toward self-sacrifice for the common good. Puritanism is sometimes remembered for its individualism, but it deserves to be known as much for its contribution to the social realm, bequeathing elements that would help form the American political tradition.

German pietism infused new life into seventeenth century Lutheranism. Though often characterized as individualistic, legalistic, and otherworldly, the pietists nevertheless complained heartily against a lifeless orthodoxy that did not translate into love and compassion. Thus Philipp Jakob Spener challenged wealthy Christians to give their goods to the poor in order to eliminate begging. Spener's pupil, August Hermann Francke, transformed the University of Halle into a training center for pastors and missionaries, and in the town itself an orphanage and hospital were founded and the poor were both catechized and fed.

Fueled in part by the example of pietism, and especially the influence of the Moravians, an evangelical revival swept across Great Britain in the eighteenth century. John and Charles Wesley, along with George Whitefield, preached in fields and streets in an attempt to recapture the alienated poor for the church. Their emphasis on sanctification and the holy life energized their followers into opposing slavery, exhibiting concern for prisoners, and initiating reforms related to the industrial revolution.

In America the First Great Awakening, which began as a season of individual conversions, resulted in an intercolonial movement that reshaped the social order. Under the leadership of Jonathan Edwards and Whitefield the hierarchical nature of both church and society was challenged. Indeed, it is widely recognized that this movement, with its democratizing influence, helped prepare the way for the American Revolution.

Modern Period. The modern discussion about the social implications of the gospel has been shaped by a variety of movements and factors. Revivalism has been a crucial force in determining the nature of the discussion because of the prominence of revival leaders in molding modern evangelicalism. In the nineteenth century Charles G. Finney maintained that religion came first, reform second, but he sent his converts from the "anxious bench" into a variety of reform movements, including abolitionism. Energized by a postmillennial theology, Finney often said that "the great business of the church is to reform the world." Dwight L. Moody, on the other hand, saw little hope for society. As a premillennialist he pictured the world as a wrecked ship: "God had commissioned Christians to use their lifeboats to rescue every man they could."

This shift in the relationship between revivalism and reform, present in Moody and more pronounced in Billy Sunday, has been characterized by evangelical scholars as "the great reversal." Beginning at the end of the nineteenth century and continuing past the midpoint of the twentieth century, the social implications of the gospel were neglected, sometimes abandoned, and most often declared to be of secondary importance by those who called themselves conservatives or fundamentalists. Groups that had hitherto supported social reform retreated into a posture where the primary concern after conversion was the purity of individuals rather than justice in society.

At the same time, however, a movement was on the rise which challenged this uncoupling of evangelism and reform—the social gospel. Born in post–Civil War America, growing to maturity in the era of progressivism, the impact of the social gospel continued long after its formal demise following World War I. The social gospel has been defined by one of its adherents as "the application of the teaching of Jesus and the total message of the Christian salvation to society, the economic life, and social institutions . . . as well as to individuals." Interacting with the changing realities of an increasingly industrialized and urbanized nation, the social gospel viewed itself as a crusade for justice and righteousness in all areas of the common life.

Walter Rauschenbusch was its foremost theologian, and his own pilgrimage is typical. Reared in the piety of a German Baptist minister's family, Rauschenbusch began his first charge in the Hell's Kitchen neighborhood of New York City. Encountering conditions that stifled the lives of his people, he wrote that Hell's Kitchen "was not a safe place for saved souls." This experience forced Rauschenbusch to return to the Bible in search of resources for a more viable ministry. He discovered there both in the prophets and in the teaching of Jesus the dynamic concept of the kingdom of God. Later, as a professor of church history, he wrote that "the doctrine of the kingdom of God was left undeveloped by individualistic theology," so that "the original teaching of our Lord has become an incongruous element in so-called evangelical theology."

The discoveries of Rauschenbusch, Washington Gladden, and other social gospel leaders, however, helped exacerbate a deep division that was developing within American Protestantism. Because the social gospel was closely identified with theological liberalism, a popular logic developed whereby conservatives tended to reject social action as part of their rejection of liberalism. As a matter of record, not all social gospelers were liberals and not all liberals were social gospelers. Indeed, Rauschenbusch characterized himself as an "evangelical liberal." He and others like him were evangelical in their adherence to personal faith and piety, but liberal in their openness to critical biblical studies and their insistence on a social ministry based on the social conception of sin which demanded social action beyond individual acts of benevolence.

Recent Discussion. In the contemporary period there are numerous attempts to return to a balance of individual and social emphasis in the Christian faith. Carl F. H. Henry, in *The Uneasy Conscience of Modern Fundamentalism* (1947), decried the lack of social compassion among conservatives. Further, the civil rights crisis and the Vietnam war pricked the consciences of younger evangelicals who wondered whether their spiritual parents had not accommodated their faith to an American "civil religion." The last two decades have seen a rebirth of social concern. Evangelicals have been rediscovering their roots in Finney and earlier evangelical leadership. The Chicago Declaration of 1973 acknowledged that "we have not proclaimed or demonstrated [God's] justice to an unjust American society." Today organizations such as Evangelicals for Social Action and journals such as *Sojourners* and *The Other Side* advocate the involvement of evangelicals in all aspects of society.

A new perspective is the liberation theologies emanating from Latin America, Asia, and Africa. The demand is for theological reflection that begins, not in the classroom, but in the midst of the poverty and injustice that defines the human situation for many of the peoples of the world today. The call is for a theology of "praxis" (practice). Many evangelicals recoil from liberation theologies because of the use of Marxist analysis. But others believe that the affirmation that God is on the side of the poor is a starting place for yet more faithful understandings of the meaning of discipleship. Although the Third World liberation theologians state that their programs cannot be directly translated to North America, at the same time there has been fruitful interchange with black, feminist, and other theologians working out the meaning of justice.

In summary, historical study helps focus present options. As for priority the question remains: Are the social implications equal, secondary, or prior to the individual implications of the gospel? Continuing discussion about the nature and extent of social ministry revolves around such options as (1) individual and/or social action; (2) charity and/or justice. However one chooses, the challenge is to translate love and justice into meaningful strategies so that proclamation becomes demonstration. R. C. White, Jr.

See also Social Gospel, The; Social Ethics; Liberation Theology; Civil Rights; Evangelicalism.

Bibliography. D. W. Dayton, *Discovering an Evangelical Heritage;* G. Gutiérrez, *A Theology of Liberation;* D. O. Moberg, *The Great Reversal: Evangelism versus Social Concern;* W. Rauschenbusch, *A Theology for the Social Gospel;* W. Scott, *Bring Forth Justice;*

R. J. Sider, *Rich Christians in an Age of Hunger;* T. L. Smith, *Revivalism and Social Reform;* J. Sobrino, *Christology at the Crossroads;* J. Wallis, *Agenda for Biblical People;* R. C. White, Jr., and C. H. Hopkins, *The Social Gospel, Religion and Reform in Changing America;* J. H. Yoder, *The Politics of Jesus.*

Government. ***The Biblical Witness.*** From a biblical point of view government is one of the means God has established to rule his creation through human stewardship. In this general context government is similar to all other forms of human stewardship, including the responsibilities of parents, employers, teachers, artists, and so forth; each has a responsibility for administering part of God's creation under the authority of God (see, e.g., I Pet. 2:13–3:17; 5:1–7).

The call from God to any human steward is a call to obedience in particular realms of responsibility according to the normative law of God. The responsibility of governmental authorities is distinguishable from that of parents, teachers, or pastors, and therefore the governor must learn to know and fulfill the peculiar responsibilities of government. In doing so, the public official is obliged as a steward and servant to respond in obedience to God's universal dominion over the earth.

This general framework of human stewardship under God's dominion is evident, for example, in God's choosing of Moses and David for government responsibility (Exod. 3:11–12; 18:13–26; Deut. 17:14–20; I Sam. 16:12–13; II Sam. 7:1–29), in his challenges to Israel's governors through the prophets (I Sam. 13:11–14; Isa. 10:1–4; Jer. 22:1–30; Dan. 2:20–23; 4:34–37; Zech. 7:8–14), and in NT teaching about governmental authority at many points (John 18:33–37; 19:7–11; Rom. 13:1–7; Col. 1:15–16; Rev. 11:15–19).

The particular character and purpose of government is illuminated in biblical texts from early in the OT through to the end of the NT, though none of those texts is a treatise on government comparable to Greek, Latin, or modern European political essays. We learn about God's purpose for government in diverse biblical contexts where at one time God gives directions for Israel's entrance into the Promised Land, or at another time challenges the misuse of power by Israel's kings, or at another time instructs Christians about their proper obligations to government in a given situation. From these texts we do not obtain a political philosophy, but we do learn much about the normative meaning of justice and injustice, the peculiar tasks of earthly governors, and the proper relationship between governors and the governed. With respect to government the Bible is truly a light on our path (Ps. 119:105).

One of the things we learn from the Scriptures about the nature of government is that it has broad tasks of distribution and retribution for the sake of the entire community or society over which it governs (see, e.g., Exod. 21; Lev. 25; Deut. 24:1–22). Today we would call this a "public" responsibility. Society today is a diversity of families, businesses, schools, associations, churches, and so forth. Governments are called to look after the general public health and welfare of the whole society, but that does not give them the authority to disrupt or destroy the proper responsibilities that God has given to parents, pastors, teachers, employers, and other stewards. Rules and regulations for sanitation, transportation, contracts, and the punishment of crimes, for example, are all public laws that belong to the proper domain of government.

This domain of public responsibility, then, must be fulfilled as a trust from God, a stewardship of justice for the sake of the whole society. When justice is not done by the government to everyone who is subject to its authority, then the abuse of power manifests itself in that realm of responsibility. The proper use of public authority or the abuse of that authority shows up especially clearly when it comes to the use of force. From the beginning of the biblical witness God reveals that the use of force against another human being is wrong (Gen. 9:5–6; Exod. 20:13; 21:12–27). It deserves punishment by a God-appointed governor so that proper retribution can be made and so that justice can be affirmed as the basis of all interrelationships in society. One of the central responsibilities of government, then, is to restrain the use of force and to punish those who use violence against their neighbors.

When government itself uses force in illegal ways or in ways that do not restrain violence but only encourage it, then it displays irresponsibility and lack of obedience to God's norm of justice. Most of the political ideologies of the modern world contain elements that allow or even encourage governments to use force for purposes that are not just from a biblical point of view. Christians, therefore, should work not only to encourage governments to restrain and punish the violence perpetrated by individuals in society but also to encourage governments themselves to act justly and not be instigators of unjust violence through oppression, war, and self-aggrandizement.

Finally, we should remind ourselves regularly that biblical revelation shows government to be one of the means of God's self-revelation. God has revealed himself not only as father, shepherd, husband, counselor, gardener, brother, and friend, but also as king, judge, governor, and

Lord. Government, then, is not simply a human good that we have at our disposal for keeping some measure of peace and order on earth. Government is more than a this-worldly affair which may be discounted as less than important in God's overall plan for the creation. Government is as important in God's self-revelation as family life, farming, worship, and every other aspect of creational life that was made in and through and for Jesus Christ to reveal the glory of God (see Ps. 93; 94:1–3; 95:3; Isa. 9:6–7; Col. 1:16; Heb. 1:8–14; Rev. 1:5, 8; 19:11–21).

Christian Responses in History. The biblical witness about government and its place in God's plan for his human creatures has been much in dispute among biblical believers themselves. Whether it was Israel under the authority of Moses or under one of Israel's kings; whether during the fragmented period of the judges or in the period of exile; whether during Jewish or Christian persecution at the hands of the Romans—all these circumstances led to considerable difference of opinion about the responsibility of God's people with respect to the proper role of government.

After three hundred years of uncertain existence and persecution following the first coming of Christ, Christians were rather quickly given a protected place in the ancient Roman world when the emperors themselves became Christians. First Constantine and then one successor after another began to "Christianize" Rome. Was this God's providential blessing of protection for Christians, or was it the beginning of the fall from grace as Christians began to depend on the Roman imperial order for their life and security in this world? Could biblical teaching about the lordship of Christ be accommodated to the earthly sovereignty of an emperor? Does the church exist by the grace of imperial (or any other) authority, or does earthly government exist by the grace of Christ?

Before the end of the first millennium after Christ, Christians had established two divergent "empires" in the East and West. The Eastern one followed more closely the older Roman tradition of imperial sovereignty shepherding the church, while the West eventually developed a pattern of ecclesiastical sovereignty over feudal estates. All the while a minority within both traditions opposed this earthly entanglement and pride of the church, and sought a life of piety undefiled by earthly power, wealth, and property.

By the time of the Reformation in the sixteenth century protesters within the Western church had gained sufficient power to challenge the very existence of a Roman ecclesiastical dominance over politics and culture. Most of the Anabaptists drew strength from the long tradition of protest within the church and appealed for a total separation of church from state. Whatever government is within God's plan, it certainly exists "outside the perfection of Christ," they argued.

The Calvinists and Lutherans, on the other hand, adapted much more readily to the newly emerging centralized state structures in which they sought a relative freedom for the church within a political order that would protect the homogeneous orthodoxy of society (orthodoxy being defined by a Lutheran or Calvinist creed). The Roman Catholic church did not accept Calvinist, Lutheran, or Anabaptist reinterpretations of either ecclesiastical or political orders. In the East very little changed.

In the West most of the newly emerging states gradually took shape in ways that led to a *de facto* separation of political power from ecclesiastical establishment, though not many Catholics and Protestants actually accepted the Anabaptist interpretation of this reality. Thus, what we have today are largely "secular" states and a host of divergent opinions among Christians about how they should be related to those political authorities. The modern states are not simply disconnected from churches; in most cases they are based on ideologies that claim no relation to or dependence upon a biblical view of reality. Modern liberal, socialist, and communist ideologies all claim to be rooted in nothing more than the sovereignty and independence of human will and reason.

Many Christians, therefore, spend their time trying to weigh or even justify the relative merits of one of these ideologies from a biblical viewpoint. Others accept the incompatibility of biblical Christianity with modern political establishments and seek a purer Christian life and witness apart from political engagement. Still others try to recover one of the earlier Catholic or Protestant traditions of life and thought as a basis for reforming or engaging in political life. And finally there is a large number of Christians who simply ignore or remain apathetic about government and politics, treating that realm as inconsequential for their Christian witness. In the realm of politics and government today there appears to be very little agreement among Christians about the nature and task of government from a biblical viewpoint. Not only do the Eastern Orthodox, Roman Catholic, and various Protestant traditions continue to unfold with degrees of allegiance to past political viewpoints, but today, especially in the Third World, new interpretations of political life are emerging, many of them influenced by biblical as well as modern ideological influences.

Key Issues and Questions for Our Day. Considering the diversity of "Christian" approaches to political life in the light of the biblical witness, a few issues seem to stand out as most important for our consideration today.

First, Christians should not expect to find in biblical revelation some kind of ideal or unchanging model of government (or the state) by which to evaluate their responsibility in contemporary reality. Nowhere in the Bible does God put forward an ideal of monarchy or republicanism or some other political system as the unchanging truth for our aspiration. The search for a divine ideal comes from the Greek tradition of philosophy, not from biblical revelation. What we do find in the Bible is instance after instance of instruction and example regarding God's normative demand of justice. God's command to do justice required different responses when Israel was wandering in the wilderness, or when it had entered Canaan, or when it was sent into exile. A modern state is quite different from an ancient empire, and the contemporary problems of urban culture, nuclear weapons, environmental destruction, and greatly expanded human populations will require responses different from those offered in the sixteenth or eleventh or fifth centuries after Christ. Rather than debate about competing ideals, Christians should turn to a critical assessment of their political traditions and ideologies in the light of a deeper understanding of biblical revelation about justice.

Second, the character of the modern state is a phenomenon that requires a thorough understanding of political and economic history, and thus the kind of education that we give our children is crucial. It is not possible to read passages from the OT or NT about "government" and then simply impose them on the contemporary situation without careful interpretation. The Roman world in which Christianity arose, for example, had a very limited notion of "citizenship." Most people in that world were simply "subjects"—subject to a supposedly divine authority vested in the emperor. There were no political parties, no free newspapers, no separation of church and state. Most modern governments are tied to specific state constitutions and traditions of party or military government. The very idea of the state is relatively new, being unknown in the medieval period or even in ancient Greece, where the *polis* was more like a miniature religious kingdom than like a modern state. Without a grasp of the state's character and the modern ideologies that shape it, we cannot begin to consider a biblical view of it.

And finally, we must consider in a fresh way the meaning of the contemporary "global village." The world is rapidly becoming a closely interconnected network of communications systems, trade relations, military dangers, and environmental limits. The modern state system is itself showing its limits. Biblical revelation about the lordship of Christ over the whole earth, about the earth being God's footstool, about the challenge to Christ's sovereignty by Antichrist with a global design—all these dimensions of biblical revelation have direct bearing on the political life and governments of our day. The demand for justice is increasingly the demand for *global justice,* and Christians should be leading the way to an understanding of what the proper human stewardship of government means in response to Christ the King. J. W. Skillen

Bibliography. R. H. Bainton, *Christian Attitudes Toward War and Peace;* O. Cullmann, *The State in the NT;* A. F. Holmes, ed., *War and Christian Ethics;* R. E. M. Irving, *The Christian Democratic Parties in Western Europe;* R. Mouw, *Politics and the Biblical Drama;* H. E. Runner, *Scriptural Religion and Political Task;* T. G. Sanders, *Protestant Concepts of Church and State;* J. W. Skillen, *Christians Organizing for Political Service,* (ed.) *Confessing Christ and Doing Politics,* and *International Politics and the Demand for Global Justice;* W. Ullmann, *Medieval Political Thought;* J. H. Yoder, *The Politics of Jesus.*

Government, Church. *See* Church Government.

Government, Gift of. *See* Spiritual Gifts.

Governmental Theory of the Atonement. *See* Atonement, Theories of the.

Grace. Like many other familiar terms the word "grace" has a variety of connotations and nuances, which need not be listed here. For the purposes of this article its meaning is that of undeserved blessing freely bestowed on man by God—a concept which is at the heart not only of Christian theology but also of all genuinely Christian experience. In discussing the subject of grace an important distinction must be maintained between common (general, universal) grace and special (saving, regenerating) grace, if the relationship between divine grace and the human situation is to be rightly understood.

Common Grace. Common grace is so called because it is common to all mankind. Its benefits are experienced by the whole human race without discrimination between one person and another. The order of creation reflects the mind and the care of the Creator who sustains what he has made. The eternal Son, through whom all things were made, "upholds the universe by his word of power" (Heb. 1:2–3; John 1:1–4). God's gracious provision for his creatures is seen in the sequence of the seasons, of seedtime and harvest. Thus Jesus reminded his hearers that God "makes his sun rise on the evil and on the good, and sends rain on the just and on the unjust" (Matt. 5:45). The Creator's sustaining care for his creation is what is meant when we speak of divine providence.

Another aspect of common grace is evident in the divine government or control of human society. It is true that human society is in a state of sinful fallenness. Were it not for the restraining hand of God, indeed, our world would long since have degenerated into a self-destructive chaos of iniquity, in which social order and community life would have been an impossibility. That a measure of domestic, political, and international harmony is enjoyed by the generality of mankind is due to the overruling goodness of God. Paul actually teaches that civil government with its authorities is ordained by God and that to resist these authorities is to resist the ordinance of God. He even calls secular rulers and magistrates ministers of God, since their proper concern is the maintenance of order and decency in society. Insofar as they bear the sword for the punishment of wrongdoers in the interests of justice and peace, theirs is a God-given authority. And, significantly, the state of which the apostle was proud to be a citizen was the pagan and at times persecuting state of imperial Rome, at the hands of whose rulers he would be put to death. (See Rom. 13:1ff.)

It is due, further, to common grace that man retains within himself a consciousness of the difference between right and wrong, truth and falsehood, justice and injustice, and the awareness that he is answerable or accountable not merely to his fellowmen but also and ultimately to God, his Maker. Man, in short, has a conscience and is endowed with the dignity of existing as a responsible being. He is duty-bound lovingly to obey God and to serve his fellows. The conscience is the focus within each person, as a being formed in the image of God, not only of self-respect and of respect for others but of respect for God.

To common grace, then, we must thankfully attribute God's continuing care for his creation, as he provides for the needs of his creatures, restrains human society from becoming altogether intolerable and ungovernable, and makes it possible for mankind, though fallen, to live together in a generally orderly and cooperative manner, to show mutual forbearance, and to cultivate together the scientific, cultural, and economic pursuits of civilization.

Special Grace. Special grace is the grace by which God redeems, sanctifies, and glorifies his people. Unlike common grace, which is universally given, special grace is bestowed only on those whom God elects to eternal life through faith in his Son, our Savior Jesus Christ. It is to this special grace that the whole of the Christian's salvation is owed: "All this is from God, who through Christ reconciled us to himself," Paul writes of the believer's re-creation in Christ (II Cor. 5:18). God's regenerating grace is dynamic. It not only saves but also transforms and revitalizes those whose lives were previously broken and meaningless. This is graphically illustrated by the experience of Saul the persecutor who was dramatically changed into Paul the apostle, so that he was able to testify: "By the grace of God I am what I am, and his grace toward me was not in vain. On the contrary, I worked harder than any of them [the other apostles], though it was not I, but the grace of God which is with me" (I Cor. 15:10). All is thus ascribed to the grace of God, not merely the Christian's conversion but also the whole course of his ministry and pilgrimage. For the sake of convenience, the theme of special grace will now be developed under a number of customary theological heads or aspects, as prevenient, efficacious, irresistible, and sufficient.

Prevenient grace is grace which comes first. It precedes all human decision and endeavor. Grace always means that it is God who takes the initiative and implies the priority of God's action on behalf of needy sinners. That is the whole point of grace: it does not start with us, it starts with God; it is not earned or merited by us, it is freely and lovingly *given* to us who have no resources or deservings of our own. "In this is love," John declares, "not that we loved God but that he loved us and sent his Son to be the expiation for our sins"; consequently, "we love, because he first loved us" (I John 4:10, 19). God, in fact, showed his prior love for us by graciously providing this redemption precisely when we had no love for him: "God shows his love for us," says Paul, "in that while we were yet sinners Christ died for us," so that "while we were enemies we were reconciled to God by the death of his Son" (Rom. 5:8, 10; cf. II Cor. 8:9). God took action, moreover, when we were helpless (Rom. 5:6), without any ability to help ourselves or to make any contribution toward our salvation. The sinner's state is one of spiritual death, that is to say, of total inability, and his only hope is the miracle of new birth from above (John 3:3). That is why the apostle reminds the Ephesian believers that salvation came to them when they were "dead" in sins, from which there follows only one conclusion, namely, that it is by grace that they were saved. Both now and for all eternity the Christian will be indebted to "the immeasurable riches" of God's grace displayed in his kindness toward us in Christ Jesus; for, Paul insists, "by grace you have been saved through faith, and this is not your own doing, it is the gift of God—not because of works, lest any man should boast" (Eph. 2:5–9). But for the prevenience, or priority, of divine grace, all would be lost.

Efficacious grace is grace which effects the purpose for which it is given. It is efficacious simply because it is *God's* grace. What is involved here is the doctrine of God: what God purposes and performs cannot fail or come to nothing; otherwise he is not God. The indefectibility of redeeming grace is seen not only in the turning of sinners from darkness to light but also in the bringing of them to the consummation of eternal glory. "All that the Father gives to me will come to me," Jesus declared; "and him who comes to me I will not cast out; . . . and this is the will of him who sent me, that I should lose nothing of all that he has given me, but raise it up at the last day" (John 6:37, 39; cf. 17:2, 6, 9, 12, 24). There is no power in all the universe that can undo or frustrate the work of God's special grace: "My sheep hear my voice, and I know them, and they follow me," says the Good Shepherd; "and I give them eternal life, and they shall never perish, and no one shall snatch them out of my hand" (John 10:27–28). All, as we have seen, from beginning to end, is owed to the grace of Almighty God (II Cor. 5:18, 21). The whole of our redemption is already achieved and sealed in Christ: "For those whom [God] foreknew he also predestined to be conformed to the image of his Son; . . . and those whom he predestined he also called; and those whom he called he also justified; and those whom he justified he also glorified" (Rom. 8: 29–30). That the grace of God in Christ Jesus is efficacious, that it achieves now and for evermore the redemption it was designed to achieve, should be a source of the utmost confidence, strength, and security to the Christian. The fact that "God's firm foundation stands, bearing this seal: 'The Lord knows those who are his'" (II Tim. 2:19) should fill him with unshakable assurance. Since the grace of redemption is the grace *of God,* he may be absolutely certain "that he who began a good work in you will bring it to completion at the day of Jesus Christ" (Phil. 1:6). God's special grace is never in vain (I Cor. 15:10).

Irresistible grace is grace which cannot be rejected. The conception of the irresistibility of special grace is closely bound up with what has been said above concerning the efficacious nature of that grace. As the work of God always achieves the effect toward which it is directed, so also it cannot be resisted or thrust aside. No doubt it is true that most persons blindly struggle against the redemptive grace of God at first, just as Saul of Tarsus fought against the goads of his conscience (Acts 26:14); subsequently, however, he understood that God had not only called him through his grace but had set him apart before he was born (Gal. 1:15), indeed that those who are Christ's were chosen in him before the foundation of the world (Eph. 1:4). As creation was irresistibly effected through the all-powerful word and will of God, so also the new creation in Christ is irresistibly effected through that same all-powerful word and will. The Creator God is one and the same with the Redeemer God. This in effect is what Paul is affirming when he writes: "It is the God who said, 'Let light shine out of darkness' [that is, at creation; Gen. 1:3–5], who has shone in our hearts to give the light of the knowledge of the glory of God in the face of Jesus Christ [that is, in the new creation]" (II Cor. 4:6). The regenerating work of God in the believing heart, precisely again because it is *God's work,* can no more be resisted than it can come to nothing.

Sufficient grace is grace that is adequate for the saving of the believer here and now and hereafter to all eternity. As with the other aspects of special grace, its sufficiency flows from the infinite power and goodness of God. Those who draw near to him through Christ he saves "fully and completely" (Heb. 7:25, Phillips). The cross is the only place of forgiveness and reconciliation, and it is fully so; for the blood of Jesus shed there for us cleanses from all sin and from all unrighteousness (I John 1:7, 9), and he is the propitiation not for our sins only but also "for the sins of the whole world" (I John 2:2). Moreover, as we face the trials and afflictions of this present life the Lord's grace continues to be unfailingly sufficient for us (II Cor. 12:9). He has promised, "I will never fail you nor forsake you." "Hence," as the author of the Letter to the Hebrews points out, "we can confidently say, 'The Lord is my helper, I will not be afraid; what can man do to me?'" (Heb. 13:5–6; Ps. 118:6).

The fact that many who hear the call of the gospel fail to respond to it with repentance and faith, and continue in their unbelief, does not imply that there is any insufficiency in Christ's atoning sacrifice of himself on the cross. The fault rests entirely with them, and they are condemned because of their own unbelief (John

3:18). It is inappropriate to speak of divine grace in terms of quantity, as though it were sufficient only for those whom God justifies, or as though for its sufficiency to exceed these limits would mean a wastage of grace and to that extent an invalidation of Christ's self-offering. God's grace is boundless. How could it be anything else, seeing it is the grace of our Lord Jesus Christ, God himself incarnate? That is why it is all-sufficient. No matter how much we draw from it, the river of divine grace is always full of water (Ps. 65:9). Quantitative notions of God's saving grace make the universal offer of the gospel unreal for those who reject it and leave them rejecting something that is not even there for them to reject. And this in turn leaves no ground for their condemnation as unbelievers (John 3:18 again). More biblical is the distinction that has been propounded between the sufficiency and the efficiency (or efficaciousness) of special grace (though it would be foolish to imagine that this dissolves the mystery of God's gracious dealings with his creatures), according to which this grace is sufficient for all but efficient (or efficacious) only for those whom God justifies by faith.

It is important always to remember that the operation of God's grace is a deep mystery that is far beyond our limited human comprehension. God does not treat men as though they were puppets with no mind or will of their own. Our human dignity as responsible persons under God is never violated or despised. How could it be, since this dignity is itself given by God? By Christ's command the gospel of divine grace is freely proclaimed throughout the whole world (Acts 1:8; Matt. 28:19). Those who turn away from it do so of their own choice and stand self-condemned as lovers of darkness rather than light (John 3:19, 36). Those who thankfully receive it do so in full personal responsibility (John 1:12; 3:16), but then they give all the praise to God because their whole redemption is, in some wonderful way, due entirely to the grace of God and not at all to themselves. Confronted with this marvelous but mysterious reality, we can do no more than exclaim, with Paul: "O the depth of the riches and wisdom and knowledge of God! How unsearchable are his judgments and how inscrutable his ways! . . . For from him and through him and to him are all things. To him be glory for ever. Amen" (Rom. 11:33, 36).

P. E. Hughes

See also Grace, Means of.

Bibliography. C. R. Smith, *The Biblical Doctrine of Grace;* J. Moffatt, *Grace in the NT;* N. P. Williams, *The Grace of God;* H. H. Esser, *NIDNTT,* II, 115ff.; H. Conzelmann and W. Zimmerli, *TDNT,* IX, 372ff.; E. Jauncey, *The Doctrine of Grace;* T. F. Torrance, *The Doctrine of Grace in the Apostolic Fathers.*

Grace, Means of. The means of grace, or media through which grace may be received, are various. The primary means of grace is that of Holy Scripture, from which our whole knowledge of the Christian faith is derived and the chief purpose of which is to communicate to us the saving grace of the gospel of Jesus Christ (II Tim. 3:15; John 20:31). Preaching, which is the proclamation of the dynamic truth of the gospel, is, as the teaching and practice of Christ himself and his apostles show, a means of grace of the utmost importance (Luke 24:47; Acts 1:8; Rom. 1:16; 10:11–15; I Cor. 1:17–18, 23). Similarly, personal witness and evangelism are means for bringing the grace of the gospel to others.

If the above are essentially means of saving grace, there are also means of continuing or strengthening grace. The exposition of Holy Scripture for the instruction and edification of Christian believers is one such means, as also is the private study of the Bible. Another is prayer, in which the Christian communes with God, experiences his presence, and opens himself to his purpose and his power. Another is fellowship with other Christians in worship and witness. And yet another is participation in the sacrament of the breaking of bread which Christ instituted and commanded his followers to observe (Acts 2:42).

It is of particular importance that the means of grace should be rightly received, and to be rightly received they must be received with faith and gratitude; otherwise, instead of being means of grace they become means of condemnation. Thus the purpose of Christ's coming was not to judge but to save the world. The person, however, who in unbelief rejects Christ and his teaching is not saved but judged by Christ (John 12:47–48). The gospel must not only be heard; it must also be believed (John 5:24; I John 5:13; Rom. 10:9–14).

Similarly, the sacrament of the breaking of bread (known also as the Lord's Supper, Holy Communion, or the Eucharist) was instituted by Christ as a means of grace, and it is indeed such to all who thankfully receive it with faith in the Savior who died for sinners on the cross. Such persons truly eat Christ's flesh and drink his blood (John 6:35, 52–58). But those who receive in an unworthy manner are "guilty of profaning the body and blood of the Lord," and to them the sacrament becomes a means of condemnation, so that, in receiving it, they eat and drink judgment upon themselves (I Cor. 11:27–29). Accordingly, it is erroneous to imagine that this sacrament—or for that matter, baptism, or the hearing of the gospel, or attendance at church—is automatically a means of grace to any who partake of it, without regard to their disposition of faith or unbelief, as though the mere reception sufficed to guarantee the imparting of grace. That is why Paul speaks of the ministers of the gospel as being, in their witness and in their suffering, those who spread the fragrance of the knowledge of Christ—fragrance, however, which to those who are perishing through unbelief is "fragrance from death to death," while to those who are being saved through faith it is "fragrance from life to life" (II Cor. 2:14–16). P. E. Hughes

See also Grace; Lord's Supper; Baptism.

Great Awakenings, The. The theological significance of America's first two Great Awakenings lies in the effect which intense revivalism had upon the shape of Christian thinking. The First Great Awakening (*ca.* 1735–43) is associated with the labors of the Dutch Reformed clergyman Theodore Frelinghuysen, the Presbyterian Gilbert Tennent, the Congregationalist Jonathan Edwards, and especially the itinerant Anglican George Whitefield—all Calvinists whose theological commitments provided a definite shape for their work. The Second Great Awakening (*ca.* 1795–1830) was more diffuse, with origins in the frontier west under the leadership of Methodist, Baptist, and Presbyterian itinerants, and in the settled East with the Congregational ministers of New England and the special efforts of Yale President Timothy Dwight. The culminating theological figures of the Second Great Awakening were Yale divinity professor Nathaniel William Taylor, the driving organizational genius Lyman Beecher, and the dominant evangelist Charles Grandison Finney—all men who were far less Calvinistic than leaders of the earlier Awakening and more closely attuned to the democratic assumptions of the new United States.

The soteriology of the First Awakening was exemplified in the practice of George Whitefield and the thought of Jonathan Edwards. Whitefield regularly preached that salvation belonged completely to God, and that humans did not possess the natural capacity to turn to Christ apart from God's saving call. A Connecticut farmer, Nathan Cole, described what such preaching was like when he went to hear Whitefield on October 23, 1740: "My hearing him preach gave me a heart wound; by God's blessing, my old Foundation was broken up, and I saw that my righteousness would not save me; then I was convinced of the doctrine of Election: and went right to quarrelling with God about it; because that all I could do would not save me; and he had decreed from eternity who should be saved and who not."

Edwards provided a more systematic exposition of Augustinian and Calvinistic views in his many theological works. His *Freedom of Will* (1754) argued that the "will" was an expression of the whole person which always followed the heart's strongest motive. *Original Sin* (1758) showed how the heart's ultimate motives were selfish and turned from God because of humanity's participation in Adam's fall, until God's sovereign grace brought about a change in the heart. His *Religious Affections* (1746) suggested that true spirituality was an overflow of the redeemed heart and not a product of emotional or willful exertion. Edwards's rejuvenation of a basically Calvinistic soteriology was the longest-lived theological result of the First Awakening.

The First Awakening also influenced theologies of the church and of society. Under Edwards's leadership many New England Congregationalists and middle colony Presbyterians moved toward an ideal of a "pure church," the conviction that only professed believers should participate in the Lord's Supper or take their places as full members of a local congregation. This conviction, which grew out of the revival's heightened sense for the purity and holiness of God, overturned the Halfway Covenant and the yet more liberal ecclesiology of Edwards's grandfather, Solomon Stoddard, who had invited virtually all in a community to the Lord's Supper. The First Awakening had other ecclesiological effects, for it stimulated the efforts of Separate Congregationalists and Baptists to organize churches that were entirely distinct from New England governments. Edwards and the New Light party that shared his ideas did not feel that such a step was necessary, but Baptists and Separate Congregationalists believed that Edwards's own preaching on the church led inevitably in that direction.

The First Awakening also brought to an end the Puritan conception of society as a beneficial union of ecclesiastical and public life. The leaders of the Awakening called for purity in the churches, even if it meant destroying Puritanism's historically close association between church and state. On the other hand, opponents of the Great Awakening valued that connection so highly that they were willing to dilute the church's spiritual requirements to preserve the bond. The result was a series of competing theologies of public life, no one of which enjoyed the general acceptance of the older Puritan synthesis.

In the years between 1740 and 1800 the theology of the First Awakening underwent considerable change. In the first place, the heirs of

Jonathan Edwards modified his thought to bring it closer to the Enlightenment principles of fairness, justice, and equity that became so important in America. More important, however, was the effect of the American Revolution. The warfare and public disruption of the times were difficult for the churches. But the revolution's assumptions about human values posed even more difficulties for traditional Calvinism. The patriotic spirit encouraged more confidence in human capacities, less willingness to concede an absolute sovereignty to any being, including God, and a greater optimism about the human ability to overcome the evils of personal and public life.

The Second Great Awakening stimulated religious life on an unprecedented scale at the turn of the nineteenth century and beyond. It breathed new life into exhausted denominations and provided the impetus for the creation of many newer bodies. It also had important theological consequences for ideas of salvation, church, and society.

Particularly in the work of Nathaniel Taylor the soteriology of the Second Awakening moved away from that of Whitefield and Edwards. Taylor's conviction that individuals always possessed a "power to the contrary" when facing moral choices led him to a full belief in human free will. While Edwards and Whitefield had stressed the inability of sinful people to save themselves in order to preserve God's sovereignty in salvation, Taylor and the leading revivalists on the frontier tended to stress more the ability which God had bestowed on all people to come to Christ. This more Arminian approach to salvation received reinforcement from the increasing influence of Methodists in American life, even though many of the early American Methodists did not express quite the confidence in native human capacities that Taylor or Finney did. Taylor's soteriology was partially grounded in his faculty psychology, the conviction that the will was an independent arbiter which chose among options presented to it by the mind and the emotions. A reading of Scripture that was shaped by the Scottish philosophy of common sense and its presuppositions concerning human behavior also influenced Taylor's view of salvation.

The Second Awakening also had a great impact on ecclesiology. Under the libertarian influence of the Revolutionary age individual Christians insisted that the Bible and the Bible only, free from traditional interpretations, was the standard for organizing churches. So it was that following the Bible only, Disciples, Free Will Baptists, Calvinistic Methodists, Universalists, "Christians," and other new groups employed private interpretation of Scripture to break from historical denominations and start their own. The more democratic spirit of the early United States also lay behind the great success of voluntarism. Voluntary societies, separate from the denominations and organized for a specific goal, were a product of the Second Awakening's energetic efforts to Christianize and reform America. The theology of the church which underlay this voluntarism took seriously the universal spiritual unity of the church, but did not have as much room for the place of systematic theology or cohesive Christian thinking in the church.

Finally, the Second Awakening contributed to a theology of society which emphasized the potential of America and the promise of a millennial hope. As a result of the many conversions, the widespread revivals, and the great success of voluntary societies, many American Christians felt that God had poured special blessings on the United States. This vision nerved Christians to great feats of Christian service, due in no small part to the conviction that such a special outpouring of God's Spirit was a herald for the end of the age.

America's two early Awakenings were more important as theological events than were later revivals in the United States. The First Awakening stimulated a brief revival of Calvinism which, especially in the works of Jonathan Edwards, has been a fruitful source of study ever since. The Second Awakening was even more important, for it encouraged a revivalistic, aggressive, democratic theology that shaped all American Protestantism through the 1870s, provided one of the major sources of fundamentalism, and contributed an enduring legacy to modern evangelicalism. M. A. Noll

See also Revivalism; Edwards, Jonathan; Taylor, Nathaniel William; Finney, Charles Grandison; Dwight, Timothy; Whitefield, George; New England Theology; Stoddard, Solomon; Halfway Covenant.

Bibliography. E. S. Gaustad, *The Great Awakening in New England;* C. Cherry, *The Theology of Jonathan Edwards;* F. H. Foster, *A Genetic History of the New England Theology;* J. Haroutunian, *Piety Versus Moralism: The Passing of the New England Theology;* H. S. Smith, *Changing Conceptions of Original Sin: A Study of American Theology Since 1750;* N. O. Hatch, *The Sacred Cause of Liberty: Republican Religion and the Millennium in Revolutionary New England;* D. G. Mathews, "The Second Great Awakening as an Organizing Process, 1780–1830," *AQ* 21:23–43; J. B. Boles, *The Great Revival, 1787–1805;* S. E. Mead, *Nathaniel William Taylor, 1786–1858.*

Great Commission, The. This biblical injunction embodies the command of the Lord to carry and proclaim his gospel to all nations. Both the OT (Isa. 45:22; cf. Gen. 12:3) and NT (Matt. 9: 37–38; 28:19; Acts 1:8) teach this. The message to be carried includes the historical events of the incarnate Christ's life, particularly his crucifixion (I Cor. 15:3; Col. 2:14–15), his resurrection and ascension (Luke 24:46–48; Rom. 4:25; I Cor. 15: 3–4; Eph. 1:20–23), and his second coming (Acts 3:19–21).

The love that Christ poured out for his people in his death and resurrection (II Cor. 5:14–21) is the motive for proclaiming the gospel. He who is the Author of life (Acts 3:15) and the Lord of glory (I Cor. 2:8) and the one who has all authority in heaven and on earth commands his people to go and make disciples of all nations (Matt. 28:18–19).

Christ is the great example of carrying out the commission. He went around doing good (Acts 10:38), proclaiming his message of redemption (Mark 10:45), and seeking and saving the lost (Luke 19:10). Just as he taught and preached the good news of the kingdom (Matt. 4:23), so his disciples should teach and proclaim Jesus and his resurrection (Acts 4:2).

This gospel is to be carried to all peoples, starting from Jerusalem and Judea and nearby Samaria and extending to the ends of the earth (Luke 24:47–48; Acts 1:8). The message is for all kinds of people, first for the Jew (Acts 2:5–11) and then for the Gentile (Acts 13:46; Rom. 1:16). The message of the commission, seen applied from the time of the fall of Adam (Gen. 3:17) through the period before the cross (Rom. 3:25; Gal. 3:8–9), is to be proclaimed throughout this present age to the second coming of Christ (Matt. 24:14).

The Holy Spirit's indwelling and power are essential for the commission to be effective (Luke 24:49; Acts 1:8), for it is the Holy Spirit who convicts of sin (John 16:8), who is the author of regeneration (Titus 3:5), and who enables men to confess Jesus as Lord (I Cor. 12:3).

The method in carrying out the great commission involves preaching (II Tim. 4:2) and teaching the word (Matt. 28:20); accompanying these there should be good works extended to all men (Acts 9:36; Gal. 6:9–10; Eph. 2:10), all done for the glory of God (I Cor. 10:31). W. H. Mare

Bibliography. I. W. Batdorf, *IDB*, I, 663; D. M. Howard, *The Great Commission Today;* K. H. Rengstorf, *TDNT*, IV, 461; J. H. Kane, *ZPEB*, I, 927–28.

Great Tribulation, The. *See* Tribulation.

Grebel, Conrad (*ca.* 1498–1526). Organizer of the first Free Church congregation. He was born in Zurich, at that time a solidly Roman Catholic city. It is believed that young Grebel studied at the Latin School called the Carolina from his eighth to his sixteenth year. He then attended the University of Basel in 1514–15; the University of Vienna in 1515–18 (with a royal scholarship which his wealthy father extracted from the Austrian emperor); and finally the University of Paris in 1518–20 (this time with a royal scholarship from the king of France). He later secured a papal grant to attend the University of Pisa but this plan fell through. He was a brilliant humanist scholar, knew Greek, wrote Latin well, but lived a secular and rather wild life. In 1521 he came to know and love ardently a girl named Barbara, and in spite of the vigorous opposition of his parents, he married her on February 6, 1522, while his father was out of the city.

Grebel had long been an admirer of Zwingli and was in the inner circle of humanist scholars who gathered around the Zurich Reformer. Some months after his marriage Grebel was converted to the gospel of God's free grace, coupled with earnest discipleship, as taught by Zwingli. At first Grebel was an earnest and enthusiastic disciple of Zwingli, but by the fall of 1523 he had grown critical of Zwingli for his allowing the Zurich Council of the "200" to determine the tempo of the Reformation. And by the fall of 1524 Grebel had developed the major features of his own theological position. He and his followers (now called Mennonites) held to *sola Scriptura* with warmth; the Free Church concept; believer's baptism; a life of earnest obedience to the NT (called Christian discipleship); the rejection of the civil oath on the word of Christ; the rejection of all force and violence, including participation in the military; the concept of a suffering church coupled with the "believer's cross"; a simple and plain meetinghouse; religious toleration (no persecution of religious nonconformists); and the saved status of infants and children without any baptismal ceremony.

Grebel founded the first modern free church and inaugurated believer's baptism on January 21, 1525, after he and his followers faced fines and imprisonment for disrupting the religious unity of Zurich's new evangelical religious movement under Zwingli. He spent some time in prison, evangelized earnestly in northern Switzerland, and died of the plague the summer of 1526, a year and a half after founding his biblicist church. J. C. Wenger

See also Mennonites; Zwingli, Ulrich.

Bibliography. H. S. Bender, *Conrad Grebel;* J. L. Ruth, *Conrad Grebel of Zurich;* J. C. Wenger, *Conrad Grebel's Programmatic Letters.*

Gregory I, the Great (540–604). Pope whose papacy is generally considered the beginning of the medieval period. Gregory was born to a wealthy and pious Roman family. About the age of thirty he was appointed urban prefect of Rome; shortly afterward he resigned to devote himself to religious works. With his inherited wealth he established seven monasteries, including one on his family estate in Rome, which he entered as a monk. In 577 he became one of the seven deacons responsible for administering the Roman Church. Two years later he became papal nuncio to Constantinople, the most important diplomatic assignment in the church. Upon returning to Rome a few years later he resumed monastic life, but in 590 was elected to the papacy.

Gregory is especially significant for his role in increasing the power and authority of the papacy. He firmly believed the Roman pope was Peter's sole successor and therefore supreme head of the universal church, a view not accepted in some areas. In numerous ecclesiastical disputes he asserted the papacy's supremacy over the whole church. His efforts were not always successful, but by his death the authority of the papal office had been greatly enhanced. Equally significant was Gregory's assertion of political authority for the papacy. Italy was in turmoil due to the expansion of the Lombards. The emperor in Constantinople paid little heed to Italy's pleas for assistance, and Gregory, fearing that Rome would be overrun if he did not take action, became deeply involved in counteracting the Lombard threat. His actions foreshadowed the political involvements of later medieval popes.

A different side of Gregory's character is seen in his pastoral and evangelistic concerns. He strongly believed that the church must never lose sight of the spiritual needs of individuals. He vastly increased the benevolent work of the church, supported in large part by his careful administration of vast estates owned by the church. His practical book on pastoral care, *Pastoral Rule,* had enormous influence for centuries. He also exhibited a deep concern for the evangelization of unbelievers. In 596 he commissioned Augustine of Canterbury to bring the Christian faith to England. He also encouraged missionary efforts among Jews, although he rejected forced conversions.

Theologically Gregory owed much to his study of the church fathers, especially Augustine. He held a high view of Scripture as the Word of God, emphasizing its importance not only for doctrinal truth but for individual spiritual nourishment. At the same time his teachings included many elements that would become standard in later Roman Catholic theology, including the sacrificial nature of the Mass and the dogma of purgatory. J. N. AKERS

See also PAPACY.

Bibliography. P. Batiffol, *St. Gregory the Great;* C. Butler, *Western Mysticism;* E. Clausier, *St. Grégoire le Grand;* F. H. Dudden, *Gregory the Great,* 2 vols.; F. W. Kellett, *Pope Gregory the Great and His Relation with Gaul;* N. Sharkey, *St. Gregory the Great's Concept of Papal Power;* A. Snow, *St. Gregory the Great.*

Gregory of Nazianzus (*ca.* 329–*ca.* 389). One of the Cappadocian fathers, Gregory was born of aristocratic Christian parents near Nazianzus, where his father, also named Gregory, was bishop. In Athens he studied rhetoric with Basil, the future bishop of Caesarea, and Julian, the future emperor. Soon after his return to Nazianzus (*ca.* 358) Gregory, at Basil's invitation, assumed the monastic life in Pontus. Here he collaborated with Basil in the preparation of the *Philocalia* (selections from the writings of Origen) and the *Moralia* (monastic rules). Ordained priest against his will (*ca.* 362), Gregory assisted his father in Nazianzus until the latter's death in 374. Soon thereafter Gregory sought the monastic life at Seleucia in Isauria (375). Basil, in a jurisdictional dispute, had earlier (372) prevailed upon Gregory to accept the bishopric at Sasima, an insignificant village in Cappadocia. Gregory, however, never assumed his duties there.

In 379 Gregory took charge of the small Nicene community in Constantinople. His eloquent sermons in the Church of the Resurrection, which gave him the name "the theologian," were instrumental in defeating Arianism and establishing the Nicene confession in Christ's full deity as orthodox. During the Council of Constantinople (381) Gregory was elected bishop of Constantinople, but he resigned the see when his election was disputed. He retired to Nazianzus and then to his estate at Arianzus, where he died.

Gregory's *Orations* constitute his most significant writings. Of these, the five "Theological Orations" (*Orat.* 27–31), preached at Constantinople in 380, are the best known. In them Gregory defends the divinity of the Son and of the Holy Spirit. *Oration* 2 is a treatise on the priesthood which influenced John Chrysostom's *On the Priesthood* and Gregory I's *Pastoral Rule.* Of his many letters two (101 and 102) are important treatises against Apollinaris. The Councils of Ephesus (431) and Chalcedon (451) adopted Epistle 101 as a statement of orthodoxy. Some four hundred poems are also extant.

Theologically Gregory's significance lies in his clarification of the Trinitarian and Christological doctrines. While maintaining against the Arians the essential unity of the three divine persons, and therefore their equality, Gregory provided the terminology necessary to express the real distinctions between Father, Son, and Spirit, thereby safeguarding the Trinity from Sabellian tendencies. The distinctive property of each person refers to the origin of each: the Father is unbegotten (*agennēsia*), the Son is begotten (*gennēsia*), the Spirit proceeds (*ekporeusis*). Against the Apollinarian denial of Christ's human soul Gregory insisted upon the complete manhood of Christ, for salvation is incomplete if the Son's incarnation is incomplete. Salvation is essentially deification, the complete participation of human nature in the divine; therefore, in Christ there must be two complete natures inseparably united in one person. W. C. WEINRICH

See also CAPPADOCIAN FATHERS.

Bibliography. H. von Campenhausen, *The Fathers of the Greek Church;* T. R. Martland, "A Study of Cappadocian and Augustinian Trinitarian Methodology," *ATR* 47:252–63; J. F. Mitchell, "Consolatory Letters in Basil and Gregory Nazianzen," *Her* 96:299–318; H. Musurillo, "The Poetry of Gregory of Nazianzus," *Tht* 45:45–55; B. Otis, "The Throne and the Mountain: An Essay on St. Gregory Nazianzus," *CJ* 56:146–65; R. R. Ruether, *Gregory of Nazianzus.*

Gregory of Nyssa (*ca.* 335–*ca.* 394). One of the Cappadocian fathers, Gregory was born into a famous Christian family (father, Basil the elder; sister, St. Macrina; brothers, Basil of Caesarea and Peter of Sebaste). Although educated for the church's service, he determined for a career in rhetoric and it may be that he married. If so, upon his wife's death Gregory retired to Basil's monastery in Pontus, where he dedicated himself to asceticism and theological study. In 372 Basil, wishing to strengthen the orthodox position in Cappadocia, consecrated Gregory bishop of Nyssa. Arian opposition, aided by the Emperor Valens, led to Gregory's removal from Nyssa (376), but he triumphantly returned upon Valen's death (378). At the Council of Constantinople (381) Gregory vigorously defended the Nicene cause, and Emperor Theodosius I named him a standard of orthodoxy and touchstone of ecclesiastical fellowship in Pontus. Of Gregory's later life little is known, although on several occasions he was in Constantinople, to preach funeral orations for the Princess Pulcheria (385) and the Empress Flacilla (386) and to attend a council there (394).

Theological controversy determined much of Gregory's writing. His *Against Eunomius* represents a detailed refutation of Arianism's subordination of the Word. In *To Ablabius* Gregory defends the Trinitarian doctrine against tritheistic misinterpretations. Against Apollinaris he argues for a full incarnation in the treatise *Antirrheticus.* Gregory's *Catechetical Oration* presents a systematic treatment of Christian doctrine for the instruction of catechumens. His exegetical works show the influence of Origen's allegorical method and include *The Life of Moses* and homilies on the Song of Songs, Ecclesiastes, the Lord's Prayer, and the Beatitudes. Gregory's *On Virginity* and *Life of St. Macrina* are classics of Christian asceticism. Sermons, orations, and letters also remain.

Gregory ensured the triumph of Nicene orthodoxy by his detailed working out of Basil's distinction between *ousia,* the Godhead in which Father, Son, and Spirit share, and *hypostasis,* the individuality of each. The distinction between divine persons is maintained by their immanent mutual relations, while the true unity is seen by the oneness of attributes and external operation. A clear distinction between the two natures in Christ characterizes Gregory's Christology. He held the idea of the communication of attributes and the status of Mary as *Theotokos.* Gregory's debt to Origen is visible in his universalist belief in the salvation of all things (*apokatastasis*), although he rejected Origen's view of the soul's preexistence. Gregory's anthropology was an important contribution to Christian mysticism. Created in God's image, man's soul is like unto God's nature, enabling man intuitively to know God and through purification to become like God. W. C. WEINRICH

See also CAPPADOCIAN FATHERS.

Bibliography. J. F. Callaghan, "Greek Philosophy and the Cappadocian Cosmology," *DOP* 12:31–57; H. von Campenhausen, *The Fathers of the Greek Church;* H. F. Cherniss, *The Platonism of Gregory of Nyssa;* A. S. Dunstone, *The Atonement in Gregory of Nyssa;* Sr. T. A. Goggin, *The Times of Saint Gregory of Nyssa as Reflected in the Letters and the Contra Eunomium;* R. E. Heine, *Perfection in the Virtuous Life: A Study in the Relationship between Edification and Polemical Theology in Gregory of Nyssa's De vita Moysis;* J. E. Hennessy, "The Background, Sources and Meaning of Divine Infinity in St. Gregory of Nyssa" (Diss., Fordham University); G. B. Ladner, "The Philosophical Anthropology of St. Gregory of Nyssa," *DOP* 12:59–94; J. Quasten, *Patrology,* III, 254–96; J. H. Srawley, "St. Gregory of Nyssa on the Sinlessness of Christ," *JTS* 7: 434–41.

Gregory Palamas (1296–1359). Greek Orthodox mystic and theologian. Born and educated in Constantinople, in 1318 he entered the monastic life at Mt. Athos in Greece, where he became known for his asceticism and his emphasis on mystical exercises. After periods at several other monasteries he returned to Mt. Athos in 1331 and began the first of his numerous writings. In 1347 he was appointed archbishop of Thessalonica, a position he held until his death.

Palamas is best known for his pivotal role in the hesychast controversy, which had lasting effects on Eastern Christianity. The hesychast ("quiet") movement stressed certain spiritual exercises which, they contended, brought one into communion with the divine light that had shone on the Mount of Transfiguration. While the concept of mystical communion with the divine light had appeared in Eastern Christianity before, the hesychasts raised it to greater significance. Their practices included inducing a trancelike state by holding the breath and gazing intently at the navel. The movement was centered at Mt. Athos, and Palamas was its most noted advocate.

The hesychasts were attacked by Barlaam, a former Roman Catholic monk who had joined the Greek Church. He and his supporters mocked the practices of the hesychasts, and contended that the theology of mystical communion with God was faulty because God could not be known directly. Palamas answered that communion with the divine light was not equivalent to communion with the essence of God; the divine light was an activity of God that was inseparable from God and proceeded from him, but was not his essence.

The controversy was examined by a series of synods which eventually affirmed the views of Palamas. The Greek Church thus rejected the scholasticism of the Roman Church and established the emphasis on the mystical vision of the divine light that has been a part of Greek Orthodox theology since then. J. N. Akers

See also Mysticism; Hesychasm.

Groningen Theology. A theological movement that takes its name from the theological faculty of the University of Groningen in the city of that name in the Netherlands. About 1830 four young men were appointed professors of theology at Groningen. Led by Petrus Hofstede de Groot, they were strongly influenced by (1) a stream of mysticism that had run through the Dutch church for centuries, (2) the Platonism taught by the brilliant philosopher and teacher at Utrecht, Philip Willem van Heusde, and (3) Dutch nationalism. Convinced that much of the earlier theology and life of the church was out of touch with the needs of the day, these men believed that a "new construction was necessary," that they should devote themselves to the task, and that they should be guided in their efforts by the NT. They met together each Friday to read the NT and in 1835 began a theological society in which they were joined by others. In 1837 the society began the publication of a periodical, *Waarheid in Liefde* (*Truth in Love*), was holding monthly meetings, and found its influence spreading rapidly. In 1855 Hofstede de Groot published *De Groninger Godgeleerden in hunne eigenaardigheid* (*The Groningen Theologians in Their Distinctiveness*), in which the twenty-five years of service which he and his colleagues had given the University of Groningen was celebrated. By then the *Groninger Theologie* had come to be known as a distinct school of thought in the life of the nation.

Its central doctrine was that God has revealed himself in all of creation and supremely in Jesus Christ so that mankind may be conformed to his image. While God had been active among all men and women, his work is seen especially in Israel and in the life of Jesus. With little regard for the orthodox Christology of the church, with its insistence that Jesus is both God and man, the Groningen theology emphasized God's revelation in Jesus as an example to be followed. It claimed that Jesus had one spiritual nature that is shared by both God and mankind. It denied the doctrines of the Trinity and the atonement but accepted the miracles of Jesus as signs of his special mission. In his person, words, and works are seen the nature of God, the holy Father of mankind. In Christ, God shows us ourselves, our depravity, and our destiny as his saved people. Faith in Christ saves from guilt and the dominion of sin, God's forgiving love is experienced, and the faithful are filled with his Spirit. Christ founded the church, preserves and perfects it; it will triumph in the end. "It will be the nursery of light and warmth for every science and all art; it will conquer hearts for Christ in house and school and society."

The Groningen theology sought to infuse new life into the theology of the church at a time when the older orthodoxy seemed moribund and rationalism was undermining the faith of many. While helping to preserve an interest in religion in sectors of Dutch society, its foundation was that of humanism—e.g., it preferred Erasmus to Luther; it had an antipathy to church confessions; and it failed in an adequate theological interpretation of the Christian faith. It disclaimed indebtedness to Schleiermacher for its religious orientation, but it was remarkably similar to his thinking in many respects.

M. E. Osterhaven

Bibliography. J. H. Mackay, *Religious Thought in Holland During the Nineteenth Century;* S. D. van Veen, *SHERK,* V, 80–81, 314–15; K. H. Roessingh, *Het Modernisme in Nederland; Christelijke Encyclopedie,* III.

Groote, Gerard (1340–1384). Dutch mystic who was the moving spirit behind the Brethren of the Common Life and the *Devotio Moderna.* Born into a wealthy family, he studied in Germany and France, proved himself a versatile scholar with wide-ranging interests, and for a time taught at Cologne. After his conversion in 1374 he returned to his native Deventer. Finding self-discipline a problem, he entered a Carthusian monastery. In 1379 he was made deacon and, though never ordained priest, became a missionary preacher in the Utrecht diocese and beyond, with much acceptance by the common people. He denounced abuses in the church, while upholding its traditional teaching and seeking reform from within. The establishment predictably reacted adversely to his criticism, and withdrew his license to preach. He retired to Deventer, founded the Brethren of the Common Life, but died of the plague before many of his ideas had been implemented.

In his sermons and writings Groote stressed poverty, the communal (but not cloistered) life, commitment to Christ, and the necessity of being the church in the world. The Brethren were also concerned actively in the furtherance of education. Much of Groote's thinking is reflected in the work of his most famous follower, Thomas à Kempis, author of *The Imitation of Christ,* a book earlier attributed to Groote himself.

J. D. Douglas

See also Brethren of the Common Life; Devotio Moderna; Thomas à Kempis.

Bibliography. E. F. Jacob, "Gerard Groote and the Beginnings of the 'New Devotion' in the Low Countries," *JEH* 3:40–57; T. P. Van Zijl, *Gerhard Groote: Ascetic and Reformer;* A. Hyma, *The Brethren of the Common Life.*

Grotius, Hugo (1583–1645). Dutch jurist, statesman, theologian, and historian who was born at Delft and educated at the University of Leiden. After practicing law for a time and holding public office, in 1613 he was appointed pensionary of the city of Rotterdam, a post that carried with it a seat in the States General of Holland and later in the States General of the United Netherlands. This position brought him into Dutch politics at a time of intense struggle between the Calvinists and the Arminians. As a leader of the Arminians when the Calvinist side won, he was sentenced to life imprisonment (1618). In 1621 he escaped from prison in a book chest and made his way to France. He returned to Holland briefly in 1631, but most of the remainder of his life was spent in Paris, where he served fora time (1634–45) as Swedish ambassador.

Grotius is remembered as the "father of international law" on the basis of his *De Jure Belli et Pacis* (*Concerning the Law of War and Peace*), which appeared in 1625. This work contains an impressive knowledge of legal authorities, the classics, the Scriptures, and the church fathers, as well as the seventeenth century scientific outlook, used to prove that there is a common law between nations that is valid in times of peace and war. Consequently the rule of right reason and of law can be applied to the actions of sovereign states. The faith of Grotius in the orderliness of the world is basic to his work in both jurisprudence and theology. There is, he believed, a law of nature which even God cannot alter.

Grotius was an ardent student of religion who wrote on theology, scriptural interpretations, and church government. One of his most popular books, *On the Truth of the Christian Religion* (1627), was intended as a missionary manual for those who had contact with pagans and Muslims. It presented the evidences for the Christian faith based on natural revelation. Another work, *De Satisfactione Christi* (1617), espoused the governmental theory of the atonement. This view regarded God as the ruler of the world who could in a sense relax the law that death followed sin and allow Christ to suffer as a penal example so that sin could be forgiven and yet the fundamental law of the universe be upheld. Grotius also published commentaries on the NT, treating it on a level with other literature and applying rules of textual criticism to it. In works such as *Via ad Pacem Ecclesiasticum* (1642) he expressed a desire for the unity of the church and was willing to make such extensive concessions to restore union with Rome that he was accused of converting to Roman Catholicism. The reason for his irenic approach was his desire as a Christian and a statesman to bring peace and unity to a world torn by religious wars.

R. G. Clouse

Bibliography. E. Dumbauld, *The Life and Legal Writings of Hugo Grotius;* W. S. M. Knight, *The Life and Works of Hugo Grotius.*

Guardian Angel. *See* Angel.

Guilt. The state of a moral agent after the intentional or unintentional violation of a law, principle, or value established by an authority under which the moral agent is subject. The law may have been established by the head of a social order as a part of a greater legal system. It may have been established by God in his effort to lead and protect the highest well-being of mankind. Or the law may have been established by one's own authority and integrated into his or her own personal code of ethics.

In the Bible. When limited to its theological distinction, guilt is that state of a moral agent after the intentional or unintentional violation of a law (cf. Lev. 4:2, 13, 22, 27; 5:2, 3, 15) or principle established by God.

The Bible shows a progressive development in the concept of guilt. Early in the book of the law personal responsibility was not necessary for one to have been considered guilty. The priest's sins made "the people also become guilty" (Lev. 4:3). Even the common citizen's sin could bring guilt upon the whole land (Deut. 24:4). Individual personality and individual responsibility were undeveloped, with the individual merged into the body of the clan. A man's family, even if totally unaware of his sin, bore his guilt, and they and even his animals were subject to equal punishment with him (Josh. 7).

By the time of the prophets, however, we see a notable advance in the concept of sin and its consequent guilt in that they have become more clearly ethical and personal. The emphasis is less on ritual correctness and more on motive, inner spirit, and personal attitude (Isa. 1; 57:15; 58:1–12; Mic. 6:8). The idea of personal responsibility had arrived. The people could no longer hold an adage claiming that when their fathers ate sour grapes, their children's teeth were set on edge. When their teeth were on edge, they were reaping the results of personally having eaten sour grapes. They had to pay the natural consequences of their actions, and they would pay additionally by being punished (Ezek. 18:29–32; II Kings 14:6).

Jesus recognized even broader and deeper implications in guilt. He was concerned not only with the act and the inner attitude (Matt. 5:21–22), but he saw degrees of guilt dependent on knowledge and motive (Luke 11:29–32; 12:47–48). He made it clearer that the law had been made for man's benefit (Mark 2:27) and that which made him guilty not only brought suffering to the offender and possibly another human being, but it brought pain to the heart of God. Jesus, God incarnate, was already paying a price for the guilty people's sins even as he grieved over the city of Jerusalem (Matt. 23:37–39).

Their guilt and others' guilt was not only in the violation of rules, but in the violation of persons, whether the injury was to others or to themselves. The weight or seriousness of guiltiness is in its cost in terms of human injury. Jesus paid the ultimate price upon the cross. Since God loves humankind, any injury to man is an affront to God.

Management of Guilt. The word "guilt" carries with it the concept of deserved punishment or payment due, or even payment by punishment. This was established in the first judgments upon man's behavior and attitude that declared him guilty (Gen. 4:11–15) and was early incorporated into the written law (Lev. 4). The concept of payment for wrongdoing by punishment runs throughout the OT and into the NT. The concept of payment was significant in the atoning death of Christ upon the cross for the individual and collective sins of mankind, and the concept of payment is significant today among some religious sects in the form of flagellation as payment for their own sins. Current theological and psychological literature shows abundant evidence of the inner need of man to punish even himself, atoning for the violations of his own accepted ethical code. But inner psychodynamic forces make it possible for another to pay in his behalf. Though it is not widely discussed in secular literature, modern clinical studies help us understand the psychological mechanism that makes it possible for a person to accept a vicarious atoning payment for his sin.

Clouding the modern understanding of guilt is the common but erroneous use of the words "guilt" and "guilt feeling" as though they were interchangeable. Guilt is an after-the-fact reality or state that may or may not be accompanied by guilt feeling. Indeed, some remnants of humanity have enacted the most heinous crimes with no testable trace of any feelings of guilt.

Guilt feeling is a painful conglomerate of emotions that usually includes anxiety in anticipation of punishment; shame, with its sense of humiliation, dirtiness, and the need to hide; and grief, or depression, for the diminished sense of worth, dignity, and self-esteem. Though a source of intense emotional pain, the feelings of guilt do have value. They serve as an internal alarm system that alerts us to a keener awareness that we have violated our own value system. They goad us, correcting us toward more constructive behavior or attitude.

But since it is such an intense source of pain, man commonly draws from about three dozen methods of escaping, evading, or killing the pain of the guilty conscience, most of which bring further injury to human personality. The most constructive, healthy response of mankind to the pain of guilt is repentance and acceptance of the grace of forgiveness offered by God through the person of Jesus Christ.

W. G. Justice

Bibliography. *ER;* C. Houselander, *Guilt;* W. G. Justice, *Guilt and Forgiveness* and *Guilt: The Source and the Solution;* H. F. Rall, *ISBE,* II, 1309–10; E. V. Stein, *Beyond Guilt* and *Guilt: Theory and Therapy;* H. Hanse, *TDNT,* II, 828; C. Maurer, *TDNT,* VIII, 557–58.

Guilt Offering. *See* Offerings and Sacrifices in Bible Times.

Guyon, Madame (1648–1717). French mystic and quietist. Born Jeanne Marie Bouvier de la Mothe, at Montargis, France, she was educated in a convent and desired to enter a religious order. But in 1664 she was compelled by her mother to marry Jacques Guyon, an invalid twenty-two years her senior. This unhappy marriage ended with Guyon's death in 1676. After being widowed, Madame Guyon entered more deeply into a life of religious devotion. Influenced by the writings of the Spanish quietist Miguel de Molinos (1640–96), she took as her spiritual director a Barnabite friar, François La Combe, with whom she toured parts of France, Switzerland, and Italy for five years (1681–86) propagating her beliefs. The pair being suspected of heresy, La Combe was arrested in 1687 and imprisoned for life; Madame Guyon was arrested in 1688, but after eight months she was released from prison through the intervention of Madame de Maintenon, King Louis XIV's wife. In 1695 Madame Guyon was again arrested for alleged heresy and spent six years in prison at Vincennes and later in the Bastille. She was eventually released in 1703 and spent the final fourteen years of her life at Blois, at the estate of her son-in-law.

Madame Guyon was an exponent of mystic quietism. She maintained that a true Christian must pray and strive for spiritual perfection, a state of inner blessedness that consists of a wholly disinterested love of God, submits implicitly to his will, and is indifferent to all outward things, even to the church and its sacraments. Her major writings were *A Short and Easy Method of Prayer, Autobiography,* and *The Song of Songs.* N. V. Hope

See also Quietism.

Bibliography. T. C. Upham: *Life, Religious Opinions and Experiences of Madame de la Mothe Guyon.*

Hh

Hades. In the LXX, Hades (Gr. *hadēs*) is virtually synonymous with the Hebrew Sheol, the place-name of the abode of the dead. Thus the word has in itself no doctrine of reward or punishment: see, e.g., Acts 2:27; Rev. 20:13. It appears, however, in Matt. 16:18 as the locus of opposition to the church, and this leads on to Matt. 11:23 (Luke 10:15) and Luke 16:23 where Hades is the place of punishment of the wicked dead. This NT development is to be noted. The OT only begins to suggest a diversity of eternal destiny. However, when the Lord Jesus Christ brings life and immortality to light (II Tim. 1:10), he reveals both eternal gain and eternal loss. Even Hades, otherwise equivalent to Sheol, cannot resist this further significance. This simultaneous maturing of truth is ignored by every attempt to divest the NT of its grim, but dominical, doctrine of eternal punishment. J. A. Motyer

See also Hell; Sheol; Dead, Abode of the.

Bibliography. J. A. Motyer, "The Final State," *Basic Christian Doctrines,* ed. C. F. H. Henry, and *After Death;* L. Morris, *The Biblical Doctrine of Judgment.*

Halfway Covenant (1662). A major attempt by the American Puritans to preserve a Christian commonwealth in the New World. The "Puritan way" in Massachusetts had begun with close cooperation between church and society. Voting was open to all church members, but to no others. To become a church member an individual had to testify publicly that God had worked "savingly" in the heart. In Massachusetts's early years the system worked well. A steady stream of people came forward to testify to the "new birth," and as church members these converted people set the tone for the whole society.

Soon, however, difficulties arose. Children of the earliest settlers were not experiencing God's grace and hence not becoming church members. The Puritan leaders faced a serious problem. In the Puritans' Reformed theology the converted had the privilege of offering their infant children for baptism as a seal of God's covenanting grace. Now many of those who had been baptized as infants, but who were not making public profession of their own faith, were expressing the desire to have their children baptized. The Puritan leaders wanted to preserve the church for the professed believers, but they also wanted to keep as many people as possible under the influence of the church. Their solution was to create a "halfway" covenant relating just to church membership. Individuals from the second New England generation could bring their third generation children for baptism and halfway membership. But no one in the second or third generation could participate in the Lord's Supper or exercise other privileges of church membership unless they testified that God had done a gracious work in their heart.

Puritans thought they had preserved both the integrity of the church and a broad Christian influence in society. As it happened, the church in Massachusetts did prolong its impact through the halfway system. It also may have diluted its spiritual character. At least that is what Jonathan Edwards, America's greatest evangelical theologian, thought in the next century. His active opposition to the practice helped bring about its death in the second half of the eighteenth century. M. A. Noll

Bibliography. W. Walker, *The Creeds and Platforms of Congregationalism;* R. G. Pope, *The Half-Way Covenant;* E. S. Morgan, *Visible Saints.*

Hallelujah. The Hebrew term *halĕlû-yâ,* "praise the Lord," from a root meaning "to boast," "to praise," was translated into Greek as *allēlouia* and modified in English versions to *alleluia(h).* It is a liturgical expression which urged worshipers to indulge in one of the highest forms of devotion that can be offered to God. The term is restricted to songs of praise in Scripture, occurring twenty-four times in the Psalter and four times in Revelation. In its usage it extolled God's power in creation, in the liberation of the Israelites from Egyptian bondage, and in the blessings that he showers upon believers. In corporate worship this invocation or shout was uttered predominantly at the feasts of Passover, Pentecost, and Tabernacles, although it obviously had a constant place in private devotions as well.

In the synagogue period the "Egyptian Hallel" (Pss. 113–18) was recited as part of the domestic Passover ceremony, the first two psalms preceding the meal and the remainder sung at the conclusion (cf. Matt. 26:30). Psalms 135–36 were sung on the sabbath, while the "Great Hallel" (Pss. 120–36, or 135–36, or 145–50) was sung at the morning services. The NT closes with a heavenly choir thundering "Hallelujah," a word that has become a permanent part of Christian worship. R. K. Harrison

Hallow, Hallowed. To hallow is to make holy or honor as holy, to set apart for religious use, or to consecrate. That which is hallowed has been consecrated or is revered as sacred. The Bible speaks of setting apart many things or persons for sacred purposes, e.g., the priests (Exod. 29:1); the tabernacle and its equipment (Exod. 40:9); the children of Israel (Lev. 22:32); the sabbath (Jer. 17:22); the jubilee year (Lev. 25:10); the first-born (Num. 3:13); the temple (I Kings 8:64); and God himself (Lev. 22:32; Matt. 6:9; Luke 11:2).

H. F. Vos

Halloween (All Hallows Eve). The name given to October 31, the eve of the Christian festival of All Saints Day (November 1). How there came to be a feast of all the saints on November 1 is not known, but its observance seems to date back to the eighth century. The pagan festival of Halloween originated with the pre-Christian Druids of Gaul and Britain. The Druids believed that on this night ghosts and witches were most likely to wander about. The lighting of bonfires and feasting on Halloween also date back to Druid activities. Pagan peoples of western Europe also believed that their god (called the Devil by Christian observers) became incarnate in human or animal form (in Britain the bull, the dog, and the cat). Gradually, Druid practices were merged with the Roman fall festival in honor of the goddess Pomona and the Christian feast day. H. F. Vos

See also All Saints Day.

Hands, Laying on of. *See* Laying on of Hands.

Happiness. The contemporary definition of happiness may imply any degree of well-being, from mere contentment or the absence of sorrow to the most intense experience of joy or fulfillment. A fuller description of the content of happiness is found in the Scriptures and is verified in human experience.

Theological Issues. From a biblical point of view happiness is always the by-product of a greater value. Any person who makes his own happiness to be the top priority of his life will experience only frustration. Jesus clearly indicated that anyone who selfishly grasps his own life actually forfeits any chance of experiencing real life (Matt. 16:25).

What are the greater values which carry with them both contentment and joy?

(1) Happiness, according to the Psalmist and others, comes to those people who allow the living God to be God in their life (Ps. 144:15; Prov. 16:20). Man, being finite, must find an infinite reference point for his own existence or else his life will ultimately be absurd. Man was created in God's own image and made for fellowship with him. True happiness becomes a real possibility only when a man is properly related to his creator.

(2) Happiness never comes to those who have no moral base (Prov. 29:18; Ps. 128:1). To live without a moral base is to live on a subhuman level. God has not left mankind scrambling in the dark for moral absolutes. He gave the Ten Commandments as the basis for mental, moral, and spiritual health.

(3) Happiness comes only to those who learn how to relate well to others (Ps. 133:1; Matt. 19:18–19; I Cor. 13). It may be said that a person is as rich or as poor as the quality of his personal relationships. The Judeo-Christian faith has always been relational, God relating to us by grace through faith and enabling us to relate to one another in love. Without caring relationships we remain alone and discontent.

(4) Happiness comes to those who have mercy on the poor (Prov. 14:21). Generosity breeds contentment. To have the kind of compassion which compels one to respond to the needs of those who are dispossessed and who cannot give anything in return is to taste the quality of life that God himself possesses.

(5) Happiness comes to those who see their work as a gift from God (Gen. 2:15; Prov. 12:27; I Thess. 4:11; II Thess. 3:6–13). From the beginning it was intended that mankind would participate in a productive manner in the life process. God gave Adam, the first man, a place and a task. His

place needed his work. Man's labor actually was an expression of his affinity to God. With the fall of man came the distortion and drudgery of work (by the sweat of your brow you will eat your food, Gen. 3:19); yet God, in his redemptive activity, purposes to redeem man's work as well as man himself. It can rightly be said: happy is the person who thoroughly enjoys his work.

(6) Happiness comes to those who possess true wisdom (Prov. 3:13). Wisdom is the spiritual/intellectual ability to integrate truth as a whole. Wisdom begins with God who has clearly revealed himself in history (Prov. 9:10). The person who possesses wisdom will reflect a wholesome balance in his life (Phil. 4:5–9). That balance will include a profound acceptance of one's self, of others, and of life (Phil. 4:12). The wise person does not give himself to peripheral issues nor is he caught pursuing tangents (Matt. 23:23). His is a life of faith, wonder, gratitude, and hope, which produces an enthusiasm for living and opens the door for happiness.

Psychological Issues. The healthier a person is spiritually *and* psychologically the greater his potential for happiness. A person so preoccupied with his own safety, his own anxiety, his own depression that he cannot lay aside his defensiveness sufficiently either to form deep friendships or to respond to life spontaneously will experience little or no happiness.

(1) Healthy people do not distort reality to fit their wishes. True happiness must be reality-based—it is not an illusion.

(2) Happiness does not exclude pain or grief, but only depression and the sense of worthlessness.

(3) The person who is in the process of actualizing his own unique potential will have the greatest opportunity for experiencing happiness.

(4) The possibility for happiness is greatly increased when there is the freedom to learn through experience, the openness to change, and the flexibility to adapt to changing circumstances. Rigidity blocks the life process.

(5) The psychological necessity which is most important to every human being is love. From birth to the grave, being loved does more to fill the psyche with a sense of well-being than all else. Happiness is always connected to love.

C. Davis

See also Hedonism.

Bibliography. G. Bertram and F. Hauck, *TDNT*, IV, 364–70; S. H. Blank, *IDB*, II, 523; L. H. Durand, *The Psychology of Happiness;* V. J. McGill, *The Idea of Happiness;* F. B. Minirth and P. D. Meier, *Happiness Is a Choice.*

Hardening, Hardness of Heart. The action of hardening one's heart or the state of hardness of heart is the action or state of persistent and sometimes hostile rejection of the Word of God. This involves not simply a refusal to hear the Word but a refusal to respond in submission and obedience. The rejection may also extend to those who convey the Word, whether prophets, apostles, or the Logos himself, Jesus Christ. The objects of hardening may be individuals (e.g., Pharaoh in Exod. 4:21; 7:13, 22; 8:15, 19; 10:1) or whole communities of peoples or nations (most importantly Israel in Isa. 6:10–11; 29:9–14; Rom. 11:7–25; II Cor. 3:14; but also Gentiles in Josh. 11:20; Eph. 4:18). There is no one technical word or phrase for hardening in Scripture; rather a variety of words and phrases are used to describe the same phenomenon.

Most theological discussions are concerned with identifying the agent of the hardening, and opinion is divided between God as the sole agent (strict Calvinism) and man as solely responsible (Arminianism). Variations would be that God provides the opportunity for hardening or that he hardens on the basis of his foreknowledge of man's sin. Usually the attempt is made to tie hardening to reprobation or preterition, and thus the phenomenon is seen as directly concerning an individual's eternal destiny.

In Scripture both God and man are listed as agents of hardening. In the case of Pharaoh, he is said to harden his own heart (Exod. 8:15). But God is also said to harden Pharaoh's heart (Exod. 4:21; 10:1), and Paul's comment on the incident is that God hardens whom he will and has mercy on whom he will (Rom. 9:18). Scripture warns against hardening, implying responsibility on the part of the hearers (Ps. 95:8; Heb. 3:8, 15; 4:7). Noteworthy is the different rendering of Isa. 6:9–10 in the Massoretic Text and the LXX and the consequent usage of the passage in the NT. The former makes God the agent working through the instrument of the prophet, preventing repentance in Israel (see John 12:40). The LXX sees the people themselves as the agents refusing repentance (see Matt. 13:15 and Acts 28:27).

Hardening, therefore, is a complex phenomenon involving both divine and human agency. But instead of being the manifestation of predetermined reprobation, hardening is primarily presented in Scripture as a means of God's accomplishment of his purposes for history. Such can be seen in the case of Pharaoh through which God accomplished Israel's deliverance (cf. Josh. 11:20). It is also the case in the present hardening of Israel (Rom. 11:7–25) through which God is bringing salvation to the Gentiles. In such activity God's sovereignty must be clearly seen.

In each case, hardening results in a manifestation of mercy and grace.

Hardening is lifted only by God (II Cor. 3:15–16; 4:3–6). Scripture expects the present hardening of Israel to be followed by new covenant ministries of the Spirit in which the hard heart of the nation is replaced by a new heart of faith and obedience (Jer. 31:33–37; Ezek. 36:26–37:28; Rom. 11:25–32). C. BLAISING

Bibliography. G. Molin, *Encyclopedia of Biblical Theology,* II, 1136ff.; A. Kuyper, *The Work of the Holy Spirit;* L. J. Kuyper, "The Hardness of Heart According to Biblical Perspective," *SJT* 27:459–74; U. Becker, *NIDNTT,* II, 153ff.

Harnack, Adolf (1851–1930). German theologian and church historian. The son of a noted Luther scholar, Harnack was educated at Dorpat and Leipzig and occupied positions at Leipzig, Giessen, and Marburg before going to Berlin in 1891. He was a prolific and influential scholar, and controversy swirled around him because of his unorthodox views, but the government backed him against critics in the church. In 1905 he assumed the prestigious directorship of the Prussian State Library and in 1911 helped found and presided over the Kaiser Wilhelm Society for Fostering Scholarship. After the war he alienated many supporters by accepting the Weimar Republic and also suffered the defection of his leading pupil, Karl Barth.

Harnack's principal contributions were in NT studies and patristics. Major works available in English include *History of Dogma* (7 vols., 1894–99), *The Mission and Expansion of Christianity in the First Three Centuries* (2 vols., 1904–5), *The Constitution and Law of the Church in the First Two Centuries* (1910), *Luke the Physician* (1907), *The Sayings of Jesus* (1908), *The Acts of the Apostles* (1909), and *The Date of the Acts and of the Synoptic Gospels* (1911). His historical scholarship broke new ground and in some respects actually undermined the views of contemporary liberal biblical critics.

After an intellectual journey from orthodoxy through the historical-critical approach of the Tübingen School to Ritschlian liberalism, Harnack came to see religion in practical terms as reconciling culture and Christian faith, and properly ordering life. The unity of gospel and culture had been lost in the Enlightenment, but the power and revelation of God brought by Jesus—that gospel which is the eternal life in the midst of time—provides men with freedom and responsibility in all things and serves as the foundation of moral culture.

His most distinctive idea was that dogma in the early church was the natural outgrowth of the search for standards for membership, and this obscured the essential nature and practical thrust of Jesus' teachings. To penetrate back to these one must recognize that Jesus and the disciples were as timebound in their thoughts and actions as we are today, and must separate the "kernel" of the gospel, that which is permanently valid, from the "husk" of the changing forms of life and thought in which it was given. In the theological best seller *What Is Christianity?* (1901) he argues that the kernel of Jesus' message is the kingdom of God, where the victory over evil provides the inner link with God and gives ultimate meaning to life. Here is demonstrated the fatherhood of God and the infinite worth of the human soul, and Christians follow Jesus' example of the "higher righteousness" governed by the law of love, which exists independent of religious worship and technical observance.

Although love is the new life already begun, it is a highly individualistic approach to life and service that does not require one's active involvement in effecting political, social, and economic change. Such a theology left Christians at the mercy of the establishment and enabled Harnack to join with other intellectuals in giving unqualified support to the German war effort in 1914. R. V. PIERARD

See also LIBERALISM, THEOLOGICAL.

Bibliography. G. W. Glick, *The Reality of Christianity: A Study of Adolf von Harnack as Historian and Theologian;* W. Pauck, *Harnack and Troeltsch: Two Historical Theologians;* G. Bromiley, *Historical Theology: An Introduction;* W. Schneemelcher, *RGG,* III, 77–79; C. Brown, *NIDCC,* 452; P. D. Feinberg, *DCE,* 282.

Hartshorne, Charles. *See* PROCESS THEOLOGY.

Hate. The Hebrew is *śānē'* and the Greek *miseō.* Both words have as their basic meaning strong opposition to love. The direct opposite of hating is loving.

In the OT and the LXX the word is used when two are enemies of each other (e.g., Gen. 26:27; II Sam. 5:8; I Kings 22:8).

God is said to hate. All sin is hated by him because he is absolutely holy and altogether apart from it in his person. Special note should be made of the fact that God hates false worship (e.g., Deut. 12:31; 16:22; Jer. 44:4). Idolatry is an abomination to God (Amos 5:21; Hos. 9:15; Isa. 61:8). The hatred of God speaks of his total opposition and aversion to sin.

Those who claim God as theirs are said to hate evil also (Ps. 97:10). This hatred of evil by the righteous is because of their relation to and love for God (Exod. 18:21; Isa. 33:15; Ps. 119:104).

Such hatred of what God himself hates is the result of implicit faith in him, loving what he loves, and despising what he despises. Throughout Scripture the unrighteous love evil and hate the good, and the righteous love good and hate the evil.

God's rejection, in his sovereign wisdom, of Esau as the one through whom the Chosen Seed should come is described as "hate" (Mal. 1:2–3; cf. Rom. 9:13). This "hate" means not a passionate aversion to Esau but a refusal to choose him in the sense in which Jacob was chosen. It certainly stresses the free choice of God and the mystery of divine election.

Christ often reminded his own disciples of the hatred which would come to the people of God. It was present when he was on earth and would continue in the future (John 15:18–23).

The contrast between love and hate seems to reach a climax in the writings of John. Therein, the one who does evil hates the light and refuses to come to it for fear his evil deeds will be revealed (John 3:20). Since the world hates God the Son, it also hates God the Father (John 15:23). Because the people of God love the Father and the Son, the world hates them as well (John 15:18; 17:14). One who hates the believer lives in the very sphere of darkness and not light (I John 2:9, 11; 3:15; 4:20).

The Lord Jesus exhorted his disciples to love all men, even those who hated them (Luke 6:27). They were never to repay hatred with hatred. People of God are to have a strong dislike, a hatred for evil, but a deep, abiding love for God and righteousness. Hatred, as a malicious attitude, must never characterize the believer. This is not compatible with the Christlike spirit. It is one of the works of the flesh (Gal. 5:20). A true indication of how much one loves God is how much he hates evil. R. P. Lightner

Bibliography. W. Foerster, *TDNT,* II, 811–15; O. Michael, *TDNT,* IV, 683–94; G. Van Groningen, *TWOT,* II, 874; *WBE,* I, 758.

Head, Headship. As the determinative and most prominent part of the body, the head (Heb. *rō'š;* Gk. *kephalē*) frequently represents the whole man (Gen. 49:26; II Sam. 15:30; Isa. 43:4, LXX; Acts 18:6). Figuratively, "head" is used to designate the summit of a mountain (Gen. 8:5), a leader (Judg. 10:18), the source of a road (Ezek. 21:19, 21), and, generally, any position of superiority (Deut. 28:13; Isa. 7:8). The theologically significant uses of the term are confined almost exclusively to Paul.

In I Cor. 11:3 Paul designates God as "the head of Christ." The Arians appealed to this text to establish their doctrine of the ontological subordination of the Son to the Father. Taking *kephalē* to mean source or origin, others have found support here for the view, developed by the Cappadocian fathers and maintained in the Orthodox Church, that the Father is the cause or source of the Godhead, the Son and the Spirit deriving their personal subsistences from him. The Western fathers and most Protestant theologians argue that as "Christ" is the designation not of the second person of the Trinity, the eternal Son of God, but of the incarnate Son, the God-man, Paul means no more than that the incarnate Son of God is subject to the Father in his mediatorial office.

Paul ascribes to Christ a double headship. First, he is the head of all things (Eph. 1:10, 22) and head over every power and authority (Col. 2:10). Christ's headship over creation is by virtue of his being its creator, its sustainer, its ruler, its restorer, and himself its end and purpose (Eph. 1:10, 23; Col. 1:15–19). With these assertions Paul emphatically excludes the existence of anyone or anything outside of the authority of Christ and thus establishes the necessity of the church being subject to Christ alone (Col. 2:8–10, 16–20).

Second, Christ's headship over all things is exercised with a view toward the church over which he is the head in a special sense (Eph. 1:22–23). The special character of Christ's headship over the church is indicated by the designation of the church as the body of Christ. The relationship between these two metaphors of head and body poses a problem. The metaphor of the head sometimes occurs without any thought of a body which is attached to the head (I Cor. 11:3). The metaphor of the body is sometimes used without a view to Christ's headship, indeed with the head represented only as part of the body (I Cor. 12:14–27). Even in certain texts where head and body occur together, the church is represented as the whole body, that is, not as the trunk of the body without the head (Eph. 4:16). Apparently Paul is working with two separate metaphors, Christ the head and the church the body, and has at several points in Ephesians and Colossians brought them together.

Paul employs the concept of Christ's headship over the church to indicate that Christ is the source of the church's life, indeed that its life is in actuality a participation in his own (Eph. 1:23; 5:23; Col. 2:19); that the union between Christ and the church is deep and profoundly spiritual (Eph. 5:28–32); that Christ loves his church and is concerned for its welfare (Eph. 5:29–30); that he is the provider of all things needful for its growth and vitality (Eph. 4:7–16); that he is the Lord of the church and believers his subjects

(Eph. 5:23–24); and that believers united to Christ form a unity themselves (Eph. 4:15–16). The headship of Christ is a particularly rich Pauline theme and incorporates aspects of each of Christ's offices: prophet, priest, and king.

Christ's relationship to the church is depicted further in the ascription to him in the NT of the phrase from Ps. 118:22, "the head of the corner" (Gr. *kephalē gōnias* or *akrogōniaios;* Matt. 21:42; Acts 4:11; Eph. 2:20; I Pet. 2:6–7). Whether the phrase refers to the keystone above the door or, as is more probable, to the cornerstone of the foundation, it suggests the fundamental dependence of the church upon Christ.

In Protestant theology in general and Reformed theology in particular the doctrine of Christ's headship over the church occupied an important place in the polemics of church polity. This headship is appealed to as the chief bulwark of the spiritual freedom of the church from either the authority of the pope or that of the magistrate.

The idea of headship is also employed by Paul to describe the relationship between man and woman, husband and wife. In I Cor. 11:3 *kephalē* is normally understood to designate a position of superiority or rule. Others have suggested that it ought to be translated "source" or "origin." In this case, Paul would be pointing to the fact that, while man originates immediately from the creative act of Christ, woman is brought forth out of the man (cf. Gen. 2:18–25). In any case, for Paul the headship of the male does involve a superiority of rank and authority (I Cor. 11:7–9; Eph. 5:22–24).

R. S. Rayburn

Bibliography. H. Schlier, *TDNT,* III, 673–81; K. Munzer and C. Brown, *NIDNTT,* II, 156–63; Ambrose, *On the Christian Faith,* IV, iii; J. Bannerman, *The Church of Christ,* 187–210; J. Ainslie, *The Doctrine of Ministerial Order in the Reformed Churches of the 16th and 17th Centuries;* K. Barth, *Church Dogmatics* III/2, 309–16; III/4, 168–76; S. Bedale, "The Meaning of *kephalē* in the Pauline Epistles," *JTS* new series 5:211–15; H. Ridderbos, *Paul: An Outline of His Theology.*

Heal, Healing. The restoration of health (Ps. 41:3), the making whole or well whether physically, mentally, or spiritually. The Bible indicates that God's highest will for man is for him to "be in health, even as thy soul prospereth" (III John 2). Healing is a prominent topic in the Bible. Sickness is cured by the supernatural intervention of God with or without the use of earthly means. God himself proclaimed, "I am the Lord thy healer" (Jehovah-Rophi, Exod. 15:26), and Scripture clearly teaches that God heals all of man's diseases (Ps. 103:3). In the OT the word used most commonly to denote healing is *rapha',* in the LXX *iaomai* frequently stands for *rapha',* and in the NT healing is normally expressed by the words *therapeuō* and *iaomai.*

The Bible presents two basic views concerning healing and sickness. (1) In the OT Yahweh alone was the source for healing, just as he was considered the source for sickness. Summarizing the basic OT attitude concerning sickness and healing, Deut. 32:39 portrays God as the direct dispenser of sickness and disease as punishment for man's sin (e.g., Num. 12:9–15; II Chr. 21:18–19; 26:16–21), while healing is a reward for obedience, a manifestation of God's forgiveness, mercy, and love (e.g., Gen. 20:17; Ps. 41:5). This applied not only to individuals but also to entire nations (e.g., Exod. 23:22–25; Lev. 26:14–21; Num. 16:47; Deut. 7:15).

(2) The second view of healing and sickness is not as prominent in the OT, although it is demonstrated in the book of Job, in certain healing stories, and in the Psalms. It is the motif upon which Jesus based his teachings. This view accepts sickness as the consequence of the universal corrupt nature of man caused by original sin (Gen. 2:17; 3:19; Rom. 5:12–21). Thus as a result of the fall of man through Adam, mankind became naturally susceptible to disease. In the NT sickness and Satan continue to be closely related (Luke 13:16; Matt. 12:22–28); however, Jesus' teachings, like the book of Job, demonstrate that sickness is not always divine punishment for man's individual sins (although this remains possible, John 5:14), nor is it normative for God to use sickness as punishment. Before Jesus healed a blind man his disciples asked, "Master, who did sin, this man or his parents, that he was born blind? Jesus answered, neither hath this man sinned, nor his parents: but that the works of God should be made manifest in him" (John 9:1–3; cf. 11:4). Yet God does work through sickness to discipline and chasten his children (Heb. 12:6; Prov. 3:7–8, 11–12) and even to assist in developing faith, humility, and character, as in the case of Job and Paul (Job 40:4; 42:6; II Cor. 4:17). Nevertheless, sickness is basically an evil that contradicts and hinders God's will and desire for man.

In the healing ministry of Christ faith was a dominant factor. Normally faith on the part of the sufferer or by someone on his behalf was a prerequisite for healing and was assumed to be present, not initiated, by the healing itself (e.g., Matt. 9:2, 22, 29; 8:13; 15:28). Illustrating this, Mark 6:5–6 and Matt. 13:58 expressly record that Christ could not heal in Nazareth due to the people's lack of faith, and in Matt. 17:20 a healing was delayed because of a lack of faith. James 5:16

emphasizes that it is the prayer of faith that brings healing.

The most controversial theological aspect of divine healing is its relationship to the atonement. One view maintains that the privilege of physical healing is governed by the will and sovereignty of God—i.e., God heals whomever he wills. Most supporters of divine healing, however, believe that physical healing, like salvation, is an inheritance of every believer through the atoning death of Christ. Using Matt. 8:16–17 to interpret Isa. 53:4, this view concludes that Christ bore man's bodily as well as his spiritual suffering on the cross. Thus one receives his physical healing by faith just as he receives his salvation.

Because of faith's integral part in divine healing, some supporters of the doctrine believe the use of medical means and the supernatural are mutually exclusive. Since the root cause of sickness is sin and the only cure of sin is spiritual, they believe the only cure for sickness is spiritual. Any medical attempt at helping would imply a lack of faith in God's healing power. John Alexander Dowie's 1895 sermon entitled "Doctors, Drugs and Devils; or the Foes of Christ the Healer" illustrates this view that medical means are Satan's instruments to defeat the believer's exercise of true faith. The Bible, however, does not support this radical position. In both the OT and NT the medical means of the day were utilized (e.g., II Kings 20:2–11; Luke 10:34; I Tim. 5:23) unless they were connected with paganistic practices (e.g., Asa sought a physician who was the equivalent of a pagan magician, II Chr. 16:12). The Jews of the dispersion believed "the Lord created medicines out of the earth, and a prudent man will have no disgust at them" (Sir. 38:1–15). Matt. 9:12 shows that Christ himself considered it normal for people to consult physicians.

The healing ministry of Jesus was continued through his commissioning and sending out of the twelve (Mark 6:7–13; Matt. 10:1–5; Luke 9:1–6) and the seventy (Luke 10:9). The book of Acts and the epistles provide clear evidence of the continuance of divine healing throughout the apostolic church, and James 5:14–16 placed the healing of the sick through the prayer of faith as a permanent provision and promise of the "righteous man." There is also abundant evidence through the early Church Fathers (e.g., Irenaeus, Origen, Justin Martyr, Tertullian, Augustine) to verify the continued widespread practice of divine healing after the time of the apostles. Pope Innocent I described anointing and prayer for the sick as a right which every sick believer should expect. By the ninth century a significant decline in the practice of divine healing had begun. During the pre-Reformation period the practice of healing continued but only in isolated instances, as with Bernard of Clairvaux or the Waldensians. Luther and the English reformers renewed the practice in their ministries, and in the post-Reformation period such groups as the Brethren, Mennonites, Quakers, Moravians, and Wesleyans practiced the doctrine. In the nineteenth century a healing revival exploded in Europe under the leadership of Dorthea Trudel, Otto Stockmayer, Johannes Blumhardt, and William Boardman. In America during the nineteenth century the Holiness Movement began a distinctive divine healing ministry with such leaders as Charles Cullis, Carrie Judd Montgomery, A. B. Simpson, A. J. Gordon, R. A. Torrey, and John Alexander Dowie. Divine healing also became a major doctrine of the modern Pentecostal and charismatic movements.

From Genesis to Revelation, from the early church to the twentieth century, the record demonstrates that physical healing by divine intervention has been the experience of many of God's people.

P. G. Chappell

See also Spiritual Gifts.

Bibliography. K. M. Bailey, *Divine Healing, the Children's Bread;* W. E. Boardman, *The Great Physician (Jehovah Rophi);* F. F. Bosworth, *Christ the Healer;* H. Bushnell, *Nature and the Supernatural;* R. K. Carter, *The Atonement for Sin and Sickness* and *"Faith Healing" Reviewed After Twenty Years;* P. G. Chappell, "The Divine Healing Movement in America" (Ph.D. diss., Drew University); E. Frost, *Christian Healing;* A. J. Gordon, *The Ministry of Healing;* R. K. Harrison, *ISBE* (rev.), II, 640–47; M. T. Kelsey, *Healing and Christianity in Ancient Thought and Modern Times;* R. L. Marsh, *"Faith Healing": A Defense;* A. Murray, *Divine Healing;* F. W. Pullen, *The Anointing of the Sick;* O. Stockmayer, *Sickness and the Gospel;* R. A. Torrey, *Divine Healing;* B. B. Warfield, *Counterfeit Miracles.*

Healing, Gift of. *See* Spiritual Gifts.

Heart. ***Biblical Psychology.*** Hebrew and Christian views on the nature of man were developed in a religious setting: there is no systematized or scientific psychology in the Bible. Nevertheless, certain fundamental conceptions are worthy of note: (1) In the OT there is no very marked emphasis on individuality but, rather, on what is frequently now termed *corporate personality.* Yet (2) A. R. Johnson has shown that a fundamental characteristic of OT anthropology is *the awareness of totality.* Man is not a body plus a soul, but a living unit of vital power, a psychophysical organism. (3) The Hebrews thought of man as influenced from without—by evil spirits, the devil, or the Spirit of God—whereas in modern psychology the emphasis has tended to be placed on dynamic factors operating from within (though at the present time, fresh interest is being evoked in the study of environmental forces as factors influencing human behavior). (4) The study of particular words in the OT and NT affords a comprehensive view of the underlying Hebrew and Christian conceptions of man.

In the OT. In the English versions several Hebrew expressions are translated "heart," the main words being *lēb* and *lēbāb.* In a general sense, heart means the midst, the innermost or hidden part of anything. Thus, the midst (or heart) of the sea (Ps. 46:2); of heaven (Deut. 4:11); of the oak (II Sam. 14:18).

In the physiological sense, heart is the central bodily organ, the seat of physical life. Thus, Jacob's heart "fainted" (Gen. 45:26); Eli's heart "trembled" (I Sam. 4:13).

But, like other anthropological terms in the OT, heart is also used very frequently in a psychological sense, as the center or focus of man's inner personal life. The heart is the source, or spring, of motives; the seat of the passions; the center of the thought processes; the spring of conscience. Heart, in fact, is associated with what is now meant by the cognitive, affective, and volitional elements of personal life.

The book of Proverbs is illuminating here: The heart is the seat of wisdom (2:10; etc.); of trust (or confidence) (3:5); diligence (4:23); perverseness (6:14); wicked imaginations (6:18); lust (6:25); subtlety (7:10); understanding (8:5); deceit (12:20); folly (12:23); heaviness (12:25); bitterness (14:10); sorrow (14:13); backsliding (14:14); cheerfulness (15:13); knowledge (15:14); joy (15:30); pride (16:5); haughtiness (18:12); prudence (18:15); fretfulness (19:3); envy (23:17).

In the NT. The NT word is *kardia.* It, too, has a wide psychological and spiritual connotation. Our Lord emphasized the importance of right states of heart. It is the pure in heart who see God (Matt. 5:8); sin is first committed in the heart (Matt. 5:28); out of the heart proceed evil thoughts and acts (Matt. 15:19); forgiveness must come from the heart (Matt. 18:35); men must love God with all their heart (Matt. 22:37); the word of God is sown, and must come to fruition, in the heart (Luke 8:11–15).

Paul's use of *kardia* is on similar lines. According to H. W. Robinson, *The Christian Doctrine of Man,* in fifteen cases heart denotes personality, or the inner life, in general (e.g., I Cor. 14:25); in thirteen cases, it is the seat of emotional states of consciousness (e.g., Rom. 9:2); in eleven cases, it is the seat of intellectual activities (e.g., Rom. 1:21); in thirteen cases, it is the seat of the volition (e.g., Rom. 2:5). Paul uses other expressions, such as mind, soul, and spirit, to augment the conception of man; but, on the whole, it may be said that the NT word *kardia* reproduces and expands the ideas included in the OT words *lēb* and *lēbab.*

The Gospel of the New Heart. Since the heart is regarded as the center or focus of man's personal life, the spring of all his desires, motives, and moral choices—indeed, of all his behavioral trends—it is not surprising to note that in both Testaments the divine appeal is addressed to the "heart" of man.

The subject is too broad to allow of full treatment here; but the leading ideas may be outlined thus. The evil imagination, according to the rabbis, is located in the heart (Gen. 6:5); the heart is engraven with sin; it is deceitful and desperately sick (Jer. 17:1–10); but it can be cleansed (Ps. 51:10) and renewed (Ezek. 36:26), and can be made to bear the impress of the divine law (Jer. 31:33). God searches the heart (Rom. 8:27); he shines in our hearts with the light of the knowledge of his glory in the face of Jesus Christ (II Cor. 4:6); it is the pure in heart who attain to the beatific vision (Matt. 5:8). The important point is that, whether in Old or New Testaments, or in rabbinic teaching, it is in the heart, in the innermost recesses of his being, that man is illumined, cleansed, renewed, by attention to the word of God. It is an inward renewal, a new birth, a regeneration.

Conclusion. In view of modern trends in psychology, it is instructive to note this emphasis on the heart in early Hebrew and Christian literature. True, these early writers tended to think of man as influenced from without; but they saw clearly that it is in the heart of man that moral and spiritual battles must be fought and won. Hence the Psalmist's prayer (Ps. 19:14): "Who can discern his errors? Absolve me from faults unknown. . . . May the words of my mouth and the meditation of my heart be acceptable in thy sight, O Lord, my strength and my redeemer."

O. R. Brandon

See also Man, Doctrine of.

Bibliography. R. Bultmann, *Theology of the NT,* I, 220–27; A. R. Johnson, *The Vitality of the Individual in the Thought of Ancient Israel;* W. D. Stacey, *The Pauline View of Man;* L. S. Thornton, *The Common Life in the Body of Christ;* T. Sorg, *NIDNTT,* II, 180ff.; R. Jewett, *Paul's Anthropological Terms;* F. Baumgärtel *et al.; TDNT,* III, 605ff.; K. Rahner, *Theological Investigations,* III, 321ff.

Heaven. The most frequently used Hebrew word for heaven in the OT is *šāmayim,* signifying "heaved up things" or "the heights." In the Greek

NT it is *ouranos,* which denotes "sky," or "air." These words refer to the atmosphere just above the earth (Gen. 1:20, etc.); to the firmament in which the sun and moon and stars are located (Gen. 1:17, etc.); to God's abode (Ps. 2:4, etc.); to the abode of the angels (Matt. 22:30). The OT has no word for universe, and to express the idea there is the frequent "heaven and earth." We read of "the heaven and the heaven of heavens" (Deut. 10:14), and of a man's being "caught up into the third heaven" (II Cor. 12:2), but such references are probably to be thought of metaphorically.

Although some, like Plato, imagine heaven to be a disembodied state where naked minds contemplate the eternal, unchanging ideas, in the Bible this is not so. According to Paul, the whole person survives. Even the body is raised again, so that, if it is no longer flesh and blood (I Cor. 15:50), it nevertheless has a continuity with the present body, a sameness in form if not in material element (see Matt. 5:29, 30; 10:28; Rom. 8:11, 23; I Cor. 15:53). So there is nothing in the Bible (nor in the main creeds of the church) about disembodied spirits in the next world existing *in vacuo.* Yet there is no eating nor drinking (Rom. 14:17), nor appetite of sex (Matt. 22:30; Mark 12:25; Luke 20:35). Feasting there is evidently to be understood symbolically, according to Matt. 26:29 where Jesus speaks of that day when he will drink the fruit of the vine "new" with the disciples in his Father's kingdom. In heaven the redeemed will be in the immediate presence of God; will forever feed on the splendor of God's majesty, beholding the Father's face. In the present life men "see through a glass, darkly; but then face to face" (I Cor. 13:12). And the sons of God will see Christ "as he is" (I John 3:2). The childlike in faith, even as the angels do now, will "always behold the face" of the Father (Matt. 18:10). They will not so much glory in the presence of Supreme Reason, as the Greeks anticipated, but in the wonder of the All-Holy One (Isa. 6:3; Rev. 4:8). And this God is a Father, in whose house (John 14:2) the redeemed will dwell, where "they shall be his people," and where "God himself shall be with them" (Rev. 21:3).

There will be activities in heaven to engage man's highest faculties. For one thing, there will be governmental ministries. The "spirits of just men made perfect" (Heb. 12:23) will be in the "city of the living God, the heavenly Jerusalem" (Heb. 12:22), and men are to assist in governing the whole. Thus in the parable of the nobleman the good servant, who has been "faithful in a very little" on earth, is in heaven to be given "authority over ten cities" (Luke 19:17). In Matthew the servant who had been given five talents and who had "gained beside them five talents more" is told: "Well done, thou good and faithful servant: . . . I will make thee ruler over many things: enter thou into the joy of thy lord" (25:20–21). Perhaps new songs are to be written and sung (Rev. 5:9). The "redeemed from the earth," too, are to *learn* a "new song" (Rev. 14:3). And the kings of the earth are to "bring their glory and honour into it" (Rev. 21:24). So while there is to be on the part of the redeemed a continuous worship in heaven, it seems to be in the sense that all activities engaged in will be for the sole glory of God and will therefore partake of the nature of worship. J. K. GRIDER

See also FINAL STATE.

Bibliography. R. Lewis, *A New Vision of Another Heaven;* D. L. Moody, *Heaven;* K. Schilder, *Heaven: What Is It?* B. Siede *et al., NIDNTT,* II, 184ff.; J. S. Bonnell, *Heaven and Hell;* H. B. Swete, *The Ascended Christ;* W. M. Smith, *The Biblical Doctrine of Heaven;* G. von Rad *et al., TDNT,* V, 497ff.

Heavenlies, The. This phrase (*en tois epouraniois*) occurs five times in Ephesians (1:3, 20; 2:6; 3:10; 6:12) and nowhere else in the NT. It is translated "in the heavenly places" (AV, RSV, NASB) and "in the heavenly realms" (NIV). The "heavenlies" is the spiritual sphere where God, Christ, the spiritual powers, and believers exist together. Believers, while they live in the physical world, at the same time are seated with the risen Christ in the heavenlies, where they are enjoying their spiritual blessings and are engaged in the real battle for their souls with the demonic powers.

The Greek adjective used means "heavenly" and is used here substantivally (cf. John 3:12; Heb. 8:5; 9:23). Some translate "with/among the heavenly beings/things," but the phrase most likely denotes a spatial concept—"places." John 1:20 and 2:6 speak of being "seated" in the heavenlies, which implies a location, and 3:10 and 6:12 make sense only if "heavenlies" describes a place. The phrase appears to be a formula and its meaning is therefore probably consistent. Although "heavenlies" is a spatial concept, it is a spiritual and not a physical place. The plural "places" may be due to Semitic influence (e.g., the use of "heavens," in the plural), or it may have been used to emphasize the vastness of the spiritual arena.

God raised Christ to sit at this right hand in the heavenlies (Eph. 1:20; cf. Ps. 110:1; Heb. 8:1; 9:24; I Pet. 3:22). God also raised believers with Christ so that, while they are living on earth, at the same time they are also seated with Christ in the heavenlies (Eph. 2:6), enjoying their spiritual blessings given by God (Eph. 1:3; the blessings are enumerated in 1:4–14). This is not a Platonic dualism, for both the physical and spiritual realms are real and there is no necessary correlation between the two realms. It is also not a bodily dualism with part of man on earth and part in the heavenlies. It is an "in Christ" dualism. Eph. 1:3 and 2:6 say that we are "in the heavenlies" because we are "in Christ." We are therefore "in the heavenlies" in the same sense that we are "in Christ." This is also not to say that Paul's eschatology is fully realized. It is partially realized, but there is still a future element (cf. Eph. 1:14, 21; 2:7; 4:30; 5:5, 27; 6:8).

The heavenlies are also the arena of the real battle for believers' lives because it is here that the spiritual powers exist (Eph. 3:10). The believers' real battle is not fought against the things of this world but rather against the spiritual forces who are in the heavenlies (Eph. 2:6; cf. Job 1:6; Rev. 12:7).

Our real battle is not fought on earth: the real battle is a spiritual battle against spiritual foes. But we have won the victory because Christ is now in control of all (Eph. 1:21f.; cf. Acts 4:12; I Cor. 15:24; Eph. 1:10; 6:9; Phil. 2:10; Col. 1:16–20; I Pet. 3:22). We have our spiritual blessings and are now seated with Christ in the heavenlies.

W. D. Mounce

See also Principalities and Powers.

Bibliography. A. T. Lincoln, "A Re-examination of 'The Heavenlies' in Ephesians," *NTS* 19:468–83; H. Odeburg, *The View of the Universe in the Epistle to the Ephesians, LUA* (1934); R. M. Pope, "Studies in Pauline Vocabulary: 'Of the Heavenly Places,'" *ExpT* 23:365–68; H. Traub, *TDNT,* V, 538–43.

Heavens, New. *See* New Heavens and New Earth.

Heave Offering. *See* Offerings and Sacrifices in Bible Times.

Hedonism. From the Greek *hēdonē,* pleasure. Hedonism comprises all those ethical theories which identify the moral goal as happiness, pleasure. The ancient Cyrenaics assumed that accurate foresight of the pleasurable or painful results of actions constituted wisdom; later they emphasized present pleasure as the result always to be sought. Epicureans modified this, cultivating a total life of pleasure against merely momentary pleasures: "pleasure through prudence" ensuring sublety, variety, permanence, to satisfy a rational being. Neither "pure" nor "modified" hedonism provided truly moral guidance.

"Psychological hedonism" held that pleasure/pain governs all choices (Bentham); desiring anything and finding it pleasurable are inseparable (Mill). Certainly, any object must attract (move with anticipated pleasure) before it can be chosen: yet desire for some *object* must precede pleasure in its attainment; pleasure itself, nor even pleasant things, are not always chosen, since that would yield no moral guidance.

"Egotistic hedonism" (Hobbes) held that, general happiness being an abstraction, each should seek only his own; or, that each seeking his own would promote general happiness. But that even refined selfishness always promotes the general good contradicts all experience.

"Altruistic hedonism" (the very influential Utilitarianism) held that each should seek the greatest happiness of the greatest number (Mill), intellectual identification with others (Sidgwick), or emotional sympathy (Hume), making others' happiness necessary to one's own. But if *pleasure* be the goal, why should others' pleasure deny one's own? To appeal to justice and unselfishness introduces nonhedonist considerations. And can pleasure be so totaled, and shared out?

In general, hedonism is criticized for identifying happiness with pleasure; for arguing that because what one chooses must attract, therefore pleasure itself is the only goal, the object as well as the accompaniment of choice; for ignoring that a person can pursue many things (artistic excellence, freedom, faith) while indifferent to pleasures they might bring; for ignoring the truly moral question: with what ought I to be pleased, to what extent, at what cost? Also, for reducing morality to feeling, omitting its rational, ethical, social aspects; for providing no criteria to distinguish pleasures, higher from lower, worthy from unworthy, animal from spiritual, or to reconcile contradictory pleasures, or one person's with another's. Further, pleasure being intensely individualistic, society has no common center of feeling for pleasure or pain. Hedonism finds no place for sacrifice, disinterestedness, or duty. Obligation being dissolved into desire, morality descends to expediency, the pursuit of the comfortable. Attempts to evaluate pleasure goals led on to (nonhedonist) "value theory."

Nevertheless moral life does involve feeling. Promises of "reward" run all through Scripture, and Christianity, inheriting the idea that a loving God created man sentient, has never dispensed with hedonist considerations. It holds that right conduct will yield ultimate satisfaction, that love will ever promote happiness for others. Sixteen times Jesus pronounces certain attitudes and qualities "happy," and he describes life under divine rule in the language of feasting, wine, pearls, treasure, joy. Paul, too, expects Christians to be happy (Phil. 4:4ff.; note I Cor. 7:40).

Augustine expounded Christian "eudaemonism" (Gr. *eudaimonia,* happiness): morality being the pursuit of the good, what will obtain happiness, then what matters is where men seek it. There is no happiness in the satisfaction of every random desire, in things impermanent or in things of less value than the soul, but only in man's chief good—God. To love and enjoy God is happiness indeed. Ambrose and Aquinas include "felicity" in man's final end. Butler thought man's nature leads him to seek the greatest happiness possible; due concern and reasonable effort towards happiness is virtuous. "It deserves consideration whether men are at liberty . . . to make themselves miserable without reason than to make other people so." So Kant, convinced that man was made to require happiness within his ultimate End, posited God and immortality to reconcile the demands of duty with the inescapable need for happiness.

Most modern Christians are hedonist enough to expect happiness to follow dedication, though they translate pleasure into "blessing" and assume that God's love *means* divine concern to shelter, comfort, and reward the good. A mature Christian hedonism, while energetic for the happiness of others, would never make its own happiness a goal, but only a reward, if God so wills, for life devoted to disinterested service of Christ; while in "happiness" it would include total spiritual welfare, with felt divine acceptance.

R. E. O. White

See also Happiness.

Bibliography. Augustine, *Moral Behavior* iii.vi.xv; *Sermons* 3, 15, on Psalm 32; D. D. Raphael, *British Moralists 1650–1800;* W. R. Matthews, ed., *Butler's Sermons and Dissertation upon Virtue;* J. C. B. Gosling, *Case For Hedonism Reviewed;* P. B. Edwards, *Pleasures and Pains: A Theory of Qualitative Hedonism.*

Hegel, Georg Wilhelm Friedrich (1770–1831). German philosopher. He was born the son of a civil servant at Stuttgart, and nothing about his early life or schooling would indicate the great influence he would have. Upon his graduation from the University of Tübingen in 1793, his certificate commended his good character and fair knowledge of theology and philology, as well as his inadequate grasp of philosophy. After being a resident tutor for aristocratic families, Hegel accepted a teaching position at the University of Jena in 1801. Here he came under the influence of Schelling, with whom he worked in editing the *Critical Journal of Philosophy.* At Jena he also wrote his first major work, *The Phenomenology of Spirit.* Unfortunately, a military battle in 1807 forced the university to close, so Hegel briefly worked as an editor of a daily paper. In 1808 he became headmaster of a school in Nuremberg, where his philosophical work continued to blossom on his own time. In 1816 he began teaching philosophy at the University of Heidelberg. Finally, in 1818, he became a professor of philosophy at the University of Berlin, where he became famous and influential.

Hegel was the most influential of the German idealists. In his view, only mind is real; everything else is the expression of mind. Philosophy became a kind of theology for Hegel, because he saw all reality as an expression of the Absolute, who is God. All that exists is the expression of divine mind, so that the real is rational and the rational is real.

In terms of method, Hegel sought to accentuate what he considered to be contradictions in people's thinking in order to expose the weaknesses of their views. He thought that error is caused by either incompleteness of thought or abstraction. By his exposing "contradictions," people could see the incompleteness of their thoughts and be driven to an understanding of the particular and the real. Hegel thought of history itself as a forum in which the contradictions and inadequacies of finite thought and action are exposed, allowing the infinite mind of the Absolute to reach higher levels of cultural and spiritual expression.

According to Hegel, the state is man's highest social achievement. While he emphasized family love, he viewed the state as a higher and more universal expression of family love. The state provides the actuality of the ethical ideal; the mind of the nation is the divine, "the actual God," knowing and willing itself. The fact that the state imposes its will by force did not bother Hegel, who considered war beneficial. War prevents stagnation in history and preserves the health of nations. Two different nations could both be right and could both be divine expressions; war decides which "right" has to give way to the other.

Hegel divided religion into four different stages—four ways of gaining knowledge of the Absolute. First is natural religion, or animism, in which man worshiped trees, streams, and animals. The second stage represents God in human form, with temples built and statues honored. This stage also involves the development of self-consciousness in humans. Historic Christianity provides the third stage. Through the Incarnation God is present in the world—God and man together. Hegel valued the ethical teachings of Jesus, especially in the Sermon on the Mount. Jesus did not distinguish enemies and friends; he broke down inequalities. With Jesus, morals were a spontaneous expression of life—a participation in divine life. The fourth stage is the highest; it is Hegel's reformulation of Christian beliefs into concepts of speculative philosophy.

Hegel saw God manifested in the world in many ways. History itself is a study of divine providence. Through divine action, "contradictions" between antithetical movements or cultures are repeatedly resolved into a higher synthesis. God expressed himself fully in the Incarnation, for here his presence was not restricted beyond the world. Nevertheless, in the Incarnation God was too bound to a particular setting. A more general philosophical religion is necessary. God is love, so that while negation and opposition are historically necessary between theses and antitheses, reconciliation and synthesis are always essential. The dialectical movements of history are expressions of God's providence throughout time.

Interpretations of Hegel vary widely. Many consider his philosophized Christianity heretical, thinly veiled pantheism. For others, Hegel's system is a sincere attempt to articulate Christian truth in philosophical language. His influence has been far-reaching, extending to Marx's historical dialectic on one hand and Kierkegaard's concern for self-awareness and passion on the other. P. H. deVries

Bibliography. G. W. F. Hegel, *Lectures on the Philosophy of Religion, Phenomenology of Spirit, Philosophy of Right,* and *Science of Logic;* F. Copleston, *A History of Philosophy,* VII, chs. 9–11; J. N. Findlay, *Hegel: A Reexamination;* J. M. E. McTaggart, *Studies in Hegelian Cosmology;* G. R. G. Mure, *An Introduction to Hegel;* W. T. Stace, *The Philosophy of Hegel.*

Heidegger, Martin (1889–1976). A central figure in contemporary existentialist thought as well as a prime mover for new directions in hermeneutics. He was born in Baden, Germany. Early in his philosophical career he was a disciple of Husserl, being trained in Husserl's phenomenological method. When Heidegger wrote his most influential book, *Being and Time,* in 1927, he dedicated it to Husserl. Nevertheless, he later developed his own phenomenological method. Husserl had emphasized systematic, scientific, unchanging knowledge. He sought ideas and truth above the flux of historical change. In contrast, Heidegger concentrated on disclosing being within its historical expressions. His goal was to lay open what is hidden within the temporality of our existence. In 1933 Heidegger renounced Husserl. That same year he became the first National Socialist rector of the University of Freiburg. In this position he publicly gave enthusiastic support of the Third Reich. Extreme nationalism, as well as a belief in the superiority of the German language and culture, characterized his life.

In *Being and Time,* Heidegger characterizes everyday existence as inauthentic. We find ourselves thrown into our world, our mental universe. Each of us has his own world; for each of us our self and our world are inseparable. As a result, genuine being remains undiscovered. We give our attention to the pressing experience of everyday cares and events. Each human becomes merely a member of the crowd, hidden in the rat race of crises and moods. According to Heidegger, there is one and only one mood which leads humans to genuine self-knowledge and away from self-betrayal: that mood is dread. Instead of focusing on particular objects in our world, we should develop a sense of nothingness by facing the structure of our finite being-in-the-world. We develop the sense of nothingness by facing death: wholeness is found in "being-to-death." Death comes to us as individuals; by facing death we do not lose ourselves in the crowd. Also, our life develops a unity as we focus on its ending.

Heidegger sees human beings as primarily historical. We are necessarily related to the historical facts in which we find ourselves. To be authentic, I must resolve to make my historical situation vitally my own, and not just be inflicted by historical circumstances. I owe this resolution to myself, but I can never fully realize it, and am thus condemned to live with a sense of guilt. My destiny is to be authentically present, to freely play the role into which I have been cast (though not of my own choice). Why should I do this? I *am* this performance and nothing else. To live in the prospect of my own death is to realize that there is no substance, no deeper self. Humans are what they culturally interpret themselves to be. Humans are essentially self-interpreting beings; there is no bottom substance, for we are interpretation all the way down. Therefore, hermeneutics, the discipline of interpretation, is the central human task. Unfortunately, we seek to escape its challenge by clinging to facts and everyday activities.

While Heidegger was not a theologian, he expressed a deep religious concern in his writings. First, there is a constant focusing on our finitude and death. An awareness of death leads to authentic existence, though apart from any godly relationship. Second, Heidegger provided a constant religious critique of the contemporary world: we are too concerned with factual details and not concerned enough with true being. Because our age focuses on research and planning, we see our tasks in terms of limited, neat, manageable functions. He provides a biting religious critique of our neglect of genuine understanding and knowledge. Third, he nevertheless attacked Christianity for contributing to our self-betrayal. He believed that Christianity did not redeem but destroyed genuine culture. Along with other movements Christianity has made truth a matter of propositions rather than of existence. Fourth, Heidegger gives central importance to language: "Language is the house of Being." For him, the best of language is not found in logical or theological propositions but in the disclosures of poets. He sought to reorient theological and philosophical talk away from the modern scientific ideal.

Heidegger's influence on contemporary philosophy and theology is phenomenal. He deeply influenced strains of neo-orthodox thought, especially in the work of Bultmann and Tillich. His concept of hermeneutics has also generated new movements in that field. Under Heidegger's influence some have dropped grammatical-historical hermeneutics in favor of a more poetical, openended disclosure of being. P. H. deVries

See also Existentialism; Neo-orthodoxy; Bultmann, Rudolf; Tillich, Paul.

Bibliography. J. Wild, *The Challenge of Existentialism;* J. Collins, *The Existentialists: A Critical Study;* J. Macquarrie, *An Existentialist Theology;* H. Kuhn, *Encounter with Nothingness;* H. J. Blackham, *Six Existentialist Thinkers;* R. Marcic, *Martin Heidegger und die Existenz-philosophie;* M. Greve, *Martin Heidegger;* T. Langan, *The Meaning of Heidegger.*

Heidelberg Catechism (1563). Catechisms usually have three functions: instruction for all ages, preparatory training for confirmation, and the statement of a confessional position. The Heidelberg Catechism fulfills these three functions.

The Palatinate, south and west of Mainz, became Lutheran in 1546 under Elector Frederick II, but soon Calvinist ideas spread into the area and a series of acrimonious theological disputes broke out over the issue of the "real presence" in Holy Communion. When Frederick III the Pious (1515–76) inherited the area, he was aware of the disputes and studied both sides of the "real presence" argument. He came to the conclusion that Article XI of the Augsburg Confession was popish and opted for a Calvinist position. To foster his position, even though he was opposed by other Lutheran princes who pressured him to support the Peace of Augsburg, which did not recognize the Reformed position, Frederick staffed the theological faculty of the Collegium Sapientiae in Heidelberg, his capital, with those of Reformed persuasion, and he began to reform the worship of the churches in the Palatinate. In an effort to reconcile the theological parties, to bring about reform, and to defend himself against the Lutheran princes, Frederick asked the theological faculty to draw up a new catechism which could be used in the schools as a manual of instruction, a guide for preaching, and a confession of faith. Although many of the theological faculty were involved, as was Frederick himself, the two commonly acknowledged architects of the catechism were Caspar Olevianus and Zacharias Ursinus. The German text, with a preface by Frederick III, was adopted by a synod in Heidelberg on January 19, 1653. It was translated into Latin at the time of its publication.

The catechism is important for at least three reasons. (1) It came to be translated into numerous languages and was adopted by many groups, making it the most popular of Reformed statements. (2) Although born in the midst of theological controversy, it is irenic in spirit, moderate in tone, devotional and practical in attitude. It espouses Reformed theology as dictated by Frederick III, but Lutheran ideas were not slighted. The avoidance of polemics in the catechism, except for question 80, the use of clear language, and a sense of fervency helped to allay somewhat the theological controversies of that time and to guarantee an acceptance among the Reformed outside the Palatinate. (3) The organization of the catechism is most unusual. The 129 questions and answers are divided into three parts patterned after the book of Romans. Questions 1–11 deal with mankind's sin and misery; questions 12–85 are concerned with the redemption in Christ and faith; the last questions stress man's gratitude, expressed in action and obedience, for God's love. The questions are further structured so that the whole catechism can be covered in fifty-two Sundays. In addition, the catechism provides an exposition of the Reformed view of the Apostles' Creed and the Ten Commandments. The use of the first person singular encourages the catechism to be a personal confession of faith.

The Reformed theological perspective is found (1) in the doctrine of the sacraments, particularly the Eucharist, where believers are partakers in the true body and blood of Christ through the working of the Holy Spirit; (2) in the centrality of Scripture as authority; (3) in good works as the Christian response to divine grace; and (4) in the church as the true source of Christian discipline. The issue of predestination is found in question 54, where election is affirmed but reprobation and limited atonement are not. An example of Lutheran concepts is found in the section on man's sinful condition. R. V. Schnucker

See also Catechisms; Ursinus, Zacharias.

Bibliography. K. Barth, *Heidelberg Catechism;* H. Hoeksema, *The Heidelberg Catechism;* H. Ott, *Theology and Preaching;* C. Van Til, *Heidelberg Catechism;* Z. Ursinus, *Commentary on the Heidelberg Catechism.*

Heilsgeschichte. A German term meaning the "history of salvation." It sees the Bible as essentially such a history. While the Bible says much about other matters, these are merely incidental to its single purpose of unfolding the story of redemption. It traces in history and doctrine the development of the divine purpose in the salvation of men. Considered as a somewhat different approach from the "proof-text" method, which uses the Bible as the raw material for the shaping of a systematic theology, *Heilsgeschichte* stresses a more organic approach.

Johann Albrecht Bengel (1687–1752) is regarded as the father of this approach, but J. J. Beck of Tübingen (1804–78) and J. C. K. von Hofmann (1810–77) stand out as developers of the idea. However, it is interesting that Bengel's contemporary in New England, Jonathan Edwards, also conceived of presenting a "rational divinity" along these very lines, and his posthumously published *History of Redemption* may be considered as the first work of the American *Heilsgeschichte* school. His interest was apparently spontaneous since there is no evidence that Edwards knew of the work of Bengel. If we remember further that John Wesley was influenced by the work of Bengel, we can see the significant fact that German, English, and American pietism showed a simultaneous concern for our subject. It is not to be supposed, however, that this outflowering of *Heilgeschichte* was from a dry ground, for anticipations of the viewpoint are earlier seen in Irenaeus, Joachim of Flora, Luther, Cocceius, and many others. Furthermore, parallel developments appeared in the new science of the history of doctrine (over against the Roman contention that ecclesiastical dogma was incapable of improvement, being infallible). In the realm of apologetics, to take but one more example, the teleological argument came to be concerned more with the purposive structure of the whole universe than with the marvelous precision of its parts.

While the eighteenth century advocates of *Heilsgeschichte* used this approach as an ally of, rather than as substitute for, systematic theology and had no intention of circumventing the authority of the individual texts by the more general and organic view of Scripture as a whole, some later adherents, especially in this century, have so employed *Heilsgeschichte.* The Roman Catholic Church charges Protestantism with teaching that the Bible is authoritative only with respect to "faith and morals" and, by implication, abandoning verbal inspiration. While not every Protestant is guilty as charged, there can be no denying that many Protestants defend the Bible in the area of *Heilsgeschichte* alone, not concerned with its accuracy in history, astronomy, geology, and the like. This is not an essential of the *Heilsgeschichte* approach but merely a perversion of its original form that has become common today.

Many modern scholars are working in this field. Oscar Cullmann says: "I always come again to the same conclusion, namely, that the real centre of early Christian faith and thought is *redemptive history* (*Heilsgeschichte*)." W. G. Kümmel, C. H. Dodd, W. Vischer, G. von Rad, W. Zimmerli, and others are absorbed with the same subject in terms of promise and fulfillment. On the other hand, Rudolf Bultmann is an implacable foe of *Heilsgeschichte.* J. H. Gerstner

Bibliography. J. A. Bengel, *Gnomon Novi Testamenti;* B. S. Childs, "Prophecy and Fulfillment: A Study of Contemporary Hermeneutics," *Int* 12:259–71; Jonathan Edwards, *A History of the Work of Redemption;* G. Vos, *Biblical Theology;* G. Weth, *Die Heilsgeschichte;* O. Cullmann, *Christ and Time* and *Salvation in History;* E. C. Rust, *Salvation History.*

Heim, Karl (1874–1958). German Lutheran theologian. His professional career spanned more than fifty years. After teaching at Halle and Münster, he was appointed, at the age of forty-six, to the faculty of theology at Tübingen, where he spent the rest of his life, producing several important works.

Heim was a sensitive and perceptive observer of the modern world as well as a committed churchman. This sensitivity and commitment produced a tension which he was able to harness in a creative manner. He was persuaded that the church could not retreat from the challenge which the twentieth century's scientifically oriented world view presented to it. On the contrary, the church, if it was to retain its credibility, must enter into dialogue with the world outside and must direct its energies to answering the world's questions.

In his own work he attempted to uncover the intellectual bedrock of this scientifically oriented world view. This attempt left him convinced that science and its attendant world view were not equipped to answer the deepest existential questions of man, that the reality of a personal God belongs to a dimension which is different from everything accessible to scientific investigation. He therefore felt that modern man had two choices open to him: skepticism or a *decision* of faith. The world's conceptual scheme could lead only to an empty skepticism, faith in Jesus Christ to intellectual and spiritual wholeness.

During the traumatic years of the 1930s and

early 40s, his sympathies were with the confessional church. Several of his works have been translated into English, including *God Transcendent* (1935) and *Christian Faith and Natural Science* (1953).
J. D. SPICELAND

Heir. *See* INHERITANCE.

Hell. Generally speaking the word "hell" is used in Scripture to refer to a place of future punishment for the wicked dead. However, there are other meanings also. There are times when the word is used to refer to the grave, or to the place of the dead. Also, "hell" is used to speak of the place of disembodied spirits without any implication of either their bliss or torment.

One Hebrew word and two Greek words are each translated "hell" in the English translations of the Bible. These constitute the main teaching on the subject of hell and damnation. The Greek *tartaroō* appears once and is translated "hell" in the AV (II Pet. 2:4). In the Greek mind, this place was below Hades, where divine punishment was endured comparable to that in Hades.

The Hebrew *šĕ'ôl* is variously translated as "the grave," "hell," and "the pit." The word appears only once outside the OT, in Jewish Elephantine papyri, where it means grave. Derivation or etymology of the word is uncertain. In the OT it is used to refer to the grave several times (Job 17:13; Ps. 16:10; Isa. 38:10). It is also used for the place where the dead, both good and bad, abide (e.g., Gen. 37:35; Job 14:13; Num. 16:33; Ps. 55:15; Prov. 9:18). Darkness, gloom, forgetfulness, and distance from God are also implied in the word (Ps. 6:5; Isa. 38:18).

Jacob, at death, went down into Sheol (Gen. 37:35), but so did the wicked Korah and Dathan (Num. 16:30). Such teaching has led to the view that Sheol had two compartments—an upper and lower level. It is thought that Christ delivered the righteous in the upper level at the time of his resurrection (I Pet. 3:19; Eph. 4:9–10). Those who reject the two-compartment view of Sheol generally hold that Sheol had a double meaning. The word originally meant simply "the grave." Later it was more specialized and used to refer to hell. Hell does seem to be more in view in the later passages, but a few of the earlier ones seem to have this idea also.

The Greek word *hadēs* parallels the Hebrew Sheol. In the LXX, which is the Greek translation of the OT, "Hades" usually appears as the rendering of "Sheol."

Hades is used in the NT to refer to the underworld, the region of the departed. It defines the intermediate state between death and the future resurrection. Of the eleven times the word is used in the NT, it is rendered as "hell" by the AV with one exception (I Cor. 15:55, where "grave" appears).

On the one hand, Hades seems to be the gathering place of all souls (see Acts 2:27, 31, where it is the Greek translation of "Sheol" in Ps. 16:10). In Luke 16:23–26 all the dead are located in the underworld, but the word "Hades" itself is used only of the place where the wicked are punished.

Wherever the righteous dead went before Christ's resurrection—Hades or heaven—we know from Paul's testimony that to be absent from the body is to be present with Christ (II Cor. 5:8). Those who die in the Lord in this age go immediately into the presence of the Lord. Those who die without Christ go to Hades, where there is torment (Luke 16:19–31). They will later be brought from Hades to appear before the great white throne of judgment, after which they will all be cast into the lake of fire and experience eternal damnation (Rev. 20:11–15).

Gehenna, from the Greek *geenna*, is the eternal abode of the wicked. Whereas Hades is the intermediate state, Gehenna is eternal hell. Wherever it is used in the NT, it always means the place of eternal damnation.

The valley of Hinnom south of Jerusalem was the place where human sacrifices were offered to the pagan god Moloch in the days of Ahaz and Manasseh (II Kings 16:3; 21:6). The dead bodies were thrown and burnt there. The prophets warned of judgment to come because of such sins (Jer. 7:32; 19:6; cf. Isa. 31:9; 66:24), and because of these threats, the valley came to be a symbol for eternal judgment.

The scriptural teaching of hell goes beyond these three words, however. Frequently, especially in the Gospels, hell is seen as "unquenchable fire" (Matt. 3:12; cf. 5:22; 18:9), "damnation" (Matt. 23:33), "furnace of fire" (Matt. 13:42, 50), "blackness and darkness" (Jude 13), a "lake which burneth with fire and brimstone" (Rev. 21:8), a place "prepared for the devil and his angels" (Matt. 25:41).
R. P. LIGHTNER

See also ETERNAL PUNISHMENT; HADES; GEHENNA.

Bibliography. R. L. Harris, *TWOT*, II, 892–93; J. Jeremias, *TDNT*, I, 146–49; 657–58; R. A. Killen, *WBE*, I, 778–79; R. G. Rayburn, *WBE*, I, 418; M. F. Unger, *Unger's Bible Dictionary*, pp. 235, 467; H. Bietenhard, *NIDNTT*, II, 205–10.

Helps, Gift of. *See* SPIRITUAL GIFTS.

Helvetic Confessions. The First Helvetic Confession (*Confessio Helvetica prior*) is the same as the Second Confession of Basel. The First Confession of Basel was written in 1534 and had acceptance only in Basel and Mühlhausen. This fact of limited acceptance was characteristic of the Swiss in the 1520s–30s; they had no common confession.

Pope Paul III's call for a general council, the desire for some accommodation with the Lutherans, and the need for a common Swiss confession in preparation for the council prompted the magistrates of the Swiss cities to send delegates to Basel in 1536 to draw up a new confession. Bullinger, Oswald Myconius, Simon Grynäeus, and Leo Jud were asked to prepare the confession. Their efforts to effect an accommodation with the Lutherans did not succeed. The first draft appeared to be too Lutheran to some, and to others the doctrine of the "real presence" in the Lord's Supper was too Zwinglian. In the end, the twenty-seven articles of the first Reformed creed of "national" authority was not accepted by the Lutherans, although Luther viewed it with favor, and it was rejected by Strasbourg under Capito's leadership, and by Constance.

The issue of the "real presence" in the Lord's Supper was basically resolved for the Swiss in 1549 when Calvin and Farel visited Bullinger and they worked out the Zurich Consensus. From this point on the Zwinglian movement and the Calvinists were effectively one.

The Second Helvetic Confession began as Bullinger's personal confession written in Latin in 1562. Peter Martyr Vermigli read it shortly before his death and agreed with it—a good sign for its ultimate acceptance in the Reformed faith. In 1564 the plague broke out in Zurich, Bullinger's wife and three daughters died from it, and Bullinger contracted the disease but recovered. While the plague raged, he revised his 1562 confession and set it with his will to be delivered to the city magistrate in the event of his death.

Frederick III the Pious had come under attack for his Reformed position as seen in his church reforms in the Palatinate and in the publishing of the Heidelberg Catechism. He was accused by his Lutheran allies of being a heretic. So in 1565, in order to defend himself, he asked Bullinger to supply him with a clear exposition of the Reformed faith. Bullinger sent him a copy of his 1564 confession. Frederick was so pleased, he asked for and got permission from Bullinger to translate the confession into German. This was done prior to Frederick's appearance at the Imperial Diet in Augsburg in 1566.

At the same time the Swiss again felt the need for a new common confession, and a conference was called to meet in Zurich. Bullinger's confession was considered and a few changes were made in it, to which Bullinger consented. It was published in German and Latin on March 12, 1566, and had the approval of Berne, Biel, Geneva, The Grisons, Mühlhausen, Schaffhausen, and St. Gall. This Second Helvetic Confession (*Confessio Helvetica posterior*) was soon translated into a number of languages ranging from French to Arabic and was adopted by the Scots in 1566, the Hungarians in 1567, the French in 1571, and the Poles in 1578. The same month in which the confession was adopted at Zurich, Frederick III appeared before the Diet and so defended his position that he was not tried for heresy.

Due to its origin as Bullinger's personal confession, which followed the order of the twenty-seven articles of the First Helvetic Confession, the Second Helvetic Confession is really a theological treatise with thirty chapters and over twenty thousand words. This lengthy scholarly statement shows the consistency of the Reformed position with that of the Greek and Latin church fathers. Although the confession accepts the ecumenical creeds, it does not accept the primacy of Rome. Scripture is given primacy, and this is shown by the fact that the first two chapters emphasize that belief. Scripture is God's Word, which has precedence over the church fathers, councils, and church tradition. Chapters III–V deal with God, his unity, his trinity, the problem of idols, images, and with God's proper worship. The doctrine of providence and creation are the topics of chapters VI–VII, while chapters VIII–XI cover the fall, free will, predestination—where election to reprobation is not mentioned—and Christ as the true God-man and only Savior of the world. The next five chapters generally cover the way of salvation and the new life in Christ. Chapter XII discusses the law of God; XIII the gospel of Christ; XIV the repentance and conversion of mankind; XV justification of faith; XVI faith and good works where good works are done out of gratitude for God's grace and not for merit. Chapters XVII–XXI present the Reformed position on the church, the role of the ministry, and the two sacraments, baptism and the Lord's Supper. The last nine chapters cover church ordinances; XXII is on religious and ecclesiastical meetings; XXIII deals with prayers and singing; XXIV with holy days and fasting; XXV catechizing and visiting the sick; XXVI burial; XXVII rites and ceremonies; XXVIII possessions of the church; XXIX marriage and celibacy; and XXX the magistry, where the taking up of arms is affirmed but only in self-defense and as a last resort.

The Heidelberg Catechism and the Second Helvetic Confession are the two most widely adopted and authoritative of the Reformed statements of faith. R. V. SCHNUCKER

See also BULLINGER, JOHANN HEINRICH; CONFESSIONS OF FAITH.

Heresy. The Greek word *hairesis* means: (1) a choice, e.g., Lev. 22:18, 21 (LXX), where "gifts according to their choice" means free-will offering; (2) a chosen opinion, the only NT example being in II Pet. 2:1, where "destructive opinions" are caused by false teaching; (3) a sect or party (holding certain opinions), used in the NT (a) of the Sadducees and Pharisees (Acts 5:17; 15:5), (b) of the Christians (Acts 24:14; 28:22; in 24:14 Paul substitutes "way" for "heresy," possibly because he himself had given the word the bad meaning), and (c) a sect or faction within the Christian body (being synonymous with "schism" in I Cor. 11:19; Gal. 5:20), and resulting not so much from false teaching as from the lack of love and from self-assertiveness, which lead to divisions within the Christian community. It is the meaning given to *hairesis* in II Peter which came to predominate in Christian usage. Heresy is a deliberate denial of revealed truth coupled with the acceptance of error. The creeds were considered to contain the standard of truth and correct belief, and themselves formally contradicted various false teachings, e.g., Arianism, Apollinarianism, Nestorianism, and Eutychianism. The union of church and state after Nicaea led in time to legal penalties against heretics. Paul's and Luke's usage (#3 above) survives in, e.g., Eusebius's *History* X. v. 21–22, where Christianity is "our most sacred heresy," and Augustine *Epistle* 185, a valuable commentary on the early Christian idea of heresy.

The Roman Catholic Church distinguishes heresy from schism (disunity through lack of love) and apostasy (abandonment of Christianity). Heresy may be either "formal" (adherence to false doctrine by a baptized Roman Catholic) or "material" (false doctrine held in ignorance by a non-Roman). M. R. W. FARRER

See also SCHISM; EXCOMMUNICATION; CHURCH DISCIPLINE.

Bibliography. Augustine, *On the Gift of Perseverance* and *Epistle* 185; Cyprian, *On the Unity of the Church;* G. L. Prestige, *Fathers and Heretics;* J. V. Bartlet in *HDB;* H. E. W. Turner, *The Pattern of Christian Truth.*

Hermeneutic, The New. *See* NEW HERMENEUTIC, THE.

Hermeneutics. *See* INTERPRETATION OF THE BIBLE.

Hermetic Literature. This title designates a body of writings associated with Hermes Trismegistos, whom a popular account quoted by Lactantius equates with the fifth Mercury, called Thoth by the Egyptians. Although a man, he was very ancient, and his vast learning earned him the title Trismegistos (Thrice-great). He wrote many books on the knowledge of divine things, speaking of one God as Father, as Christians do (*Divine Institutes* i. 6). The Greek Hermes was thus assimilated into the Egyptian god Thoth. Hermes was associated with astrology in Alexandrine cults (Clement of Alexandria *Stromateis* vi. 4), and Festugière has shown the place of Hermes Trismegistos in Egyptian magical literature.

Of religious works, a corpus of eighteen Greek tractates, including the notable Poimandres, has been preserved; another, Asclepius, survives in Latin, while M. Puech announces a Coptic version found with Christian Gnostic works at Chenoboskion, where two more Hermetic opuscula have been found (*Coptic Studies in Honor of W. E. Crum,* pp. 91ff.); and Stobaeus and others quote fragments of other works.

Most of these writings belong, by common consent, roughly to the second and third centuries A.D. They are mystical, deeply influenced by Platonic and Stoic thought, but not always self-consistent. The use of the LXX seems indubitable, and the cosmogony of Poimandres presupposes Gen. 1–2. The Logos figures largely, and there are striking parallels of language with John's Gospel: direct borrowing either way is improbable, though Christianity perhaps influenced some Hermetica.

There is no evidence of a Hermetic "church." The literature represents one aspect of the movement of Gnostic personal religion as the Christian mission began. It is therefore essentially syncretistic. Whatever John and Hermes had in common, they could never share the cross of the personal Logos. A. F. WALLS

See also LOGOS; GNOSTICISM.

Bibliography. R. Reitzenstein, *Poimandres;* A. D. Nock and A. J. Festugière, *Corpus Hermeticum,* 4 vols. (texts and French translation); A. J. Festugière, *La révelation d'Hermès Trismégiste,* I; C. H. Dodd, *The Bible and the Greeks* and *The Fourth Gospel.*

Hesychasm. In the *koinē, hēsychazō* meant "to be quiet, be at rest, remain silent." Originally it designated certain Christian monastics who, though in communities, lived quietly in private cells. By the eleventh century, hesychasm referred to a contemplative movement in Eastern Orthodoxy known as "the way of stillness and repose." As it developed, this hesychastic mysticism found its focus in spiritual exercises designed to produce a beatific vision that could actually be seen with the physical eye. This vision consisted of an infusion of the "eternal, uncreated, divine light"—supposedly the same theophanic light that enveloped Jesus on the Mount of Transfiguration. The hesychasts believed the light to be communicable, gradually transforming the seeker, until at length he partook of the divine nature himself.

Some church historians believe that hesychasm had its origins in the so-called mystical interpretation of the Pauline "in Christ" formulation. This view sees Christ and the Holy Spirit as one, having a body compounded of divine light and glory which also dwells in and around the believer as air does around the physical man. Thus a mystical union with Christ is established when one is regenerated by the Holy Spirit. Apparently this hermeneutic emerged from the Alexandrian school of Christian thought and informed the theory and practice of monastic groups in Sinai and Asia Minor. A Studite mystic, Simeon the New Theologian (940–1022), adopted these early hesychastic traditions, many still in oral form, and gave them such significant theological and practical impetus that he has been called the father of hesychasm. The doctrine of the divine light became a cardinal doctrine of Eastern Orthodox faith, but not without a struggle. By the fourteenth century, the monastic community on Mt. Athos had become the mecca of hesychasm.

Adherents came to be known by noninitiates as "navel-souls" or "navel-gazers," although they protested that their spiritual exercises were but aids to the mystic encounter. Assuming a contemplative posture similar to modern yogic practice, with head pitched forward, chin on chest and gaze directed toward the region of the navel, the hesychast sought the light. The posture, he averred, enabled him to examine the state of his inner "heart." With breath carefully controlled, he repeated the "Jesus Prayer": "Lord Jesus Christ, Son of God, have mercy on me a sinner."

A Calabrian monastic theologian, Barlaam, about 1337, accused the hesychasts of heresy, charging that their view of the divine, uncreated light required a source in the very essence of God. The hesychasts replied that the light had its origin in the divine energy or operation, and not in the absolute essence of the transcendent God. This explanation appeared to Barlaam to indicate a belief in two gods: one transcendent and superior, the other immanent and inferior. He argued that man's knowledge of God was indirect at best, and that a mystical reception of the light could be only symbolic. Hesychasm was championed by the Mt. Athos leader, Gregory Palamas (1296–1359), who defended the distinction between the transcendent God, in essence unknowable and ineffable, and the immanent activity of divine energies or operations communicated to the seeking mystic by means of grace. The "divine and uncreated light," he maintained, was an operation of the divine energy and not a direct communication of God's essence. In defense of a real communication between God and man, he declared that man "will experience the divine once the passions of the soul in accord with the body have been changed and sanctified though not deadened." After considerable conflict, the views of Palamas were finally accepted by the Councils of Constantinople in 1341, 1347, and 1351.

Hesychasm teaches that the unregenerate human condition resembles the sleep of death, where no remembrance of God is possible. This state is called "prelest." In prelest, the fallen human being mistakes the "mirage" world in which he lives for the real world, and thus can never have a holistic relationship with himself or God. The "sleeping" self needs to be awakened through the process of contemplation and spiritual exercises. The Jesus Prayer is still widely used in Eastern Orthodoxy, although the physical exercises are generally discouraged. Hesychasm influenced the Bulgarian and Russian Orthodox Churches profoundly and experienced a revival in Russia in the nineteenth century.

R. C. Kroeger

See also Mysticism; Gregory Palamas; Beatific Vision; Unio Mystica.

Bibliography. J. Gregerson, *The Transfigured Cosmos: Four Essays in Eastern Orthodox Christianity;* J. Meyendorff, *St. Gregory Palamas and Orthodox Spirituality.*

Hibbert Lectures. A series established from 1878 and named for Robert Hibbert (1770–1849), a Jamaica merchant and slave owner, who was a graduate of Cambridge University. The lectures were part of the Hibbert trust, which he founded in 1847 for "the spread of Christianity in its most simple and intelligible form" and of "the unfettered exercise of the right of private judgment in matters of religion." The intention being to benefit the Unitarian ministry, the aims of his trust were anti-Trinitarian, and its participants must be "heterodox." In 1902, the trust also founded the *Hibbert Journal* as a "Review of Religion, Theology, and Philosophy," which amply fulfilled the resolve of the editors to treat philosophical and religious subjects from a liberal point of view.

J. D. Douglas

Hierarchy. A system of church government by a priesthood that has the following characteristics: (1) the priesthood is distinct from the laity and has the exclusive right to administer sacraments and govern the church; (2) the priesthood claims an unbroken line of descent from Christ and the apostles and stands as their representatives in the church; (3) the priesthood has a worldwide ordering of ranks or levels of authority (such as pope, bishops, priests).

Such a hierarchical system of church government is most fully developed within the Roman Catholic Church, where the hierarchy is divided into two parts: The hierarchy of *order* has authority to perform spiritual functions such as administering the sacraments and absolving sins; it consists of bishops (including the pope in his role as a bishop), priests, deacons, and several lesser offices (subdeacons, acolytes, etc.) instituted by the church. The hierarchy of *jurisdiction* (or pastoral government), on the other hand, has authority over church discipline and establishes rules of conduct and belief. This aspect of the hierarchy consists of the pope, bishops, cardinals, legates, and other lesser officers. Bishops thus belong to both aspects of the hierarchy.

The Church of England (the Protestant Episcopal Church in the U.S.) is partially hierarchical, since it claims direct succession from the apostles and has bishops, priests, and deacons. The Methodist churches have only a vestige of hierarchical structure with bishops, elders (or presbyters), and deacons, but no claim to apostolic succession and a much less sharp distinction between clergy and laity.

Most other Protestant churches do not have a hierarchical government but emphasize the NT teaching that all believers are priests before God (I Pet. 2:9; I Tim. 2:5; Heb. 7:23–28; 10:19–20). Furthermore, they would claim that there is no present-day equivalent to the unique office of apostle (John 14:26; Acts 1:2, 26; I Cor. 9:1; 15:7–9; II Cor. 12:12; Gal. 1:1; I Thess. 2:6; Rev. 21:14; the title is not applied to Timothy or any of Paul's assistants); that the place of the apostles is now taken not by people but by the NT books which the apostles wrote or authorized (John 14:26; Eph. 2:20; Heb. 1:1–2; I Cor. 14:37; II Cor. 13:2–3, 10; II Thess. 3:14; Jude 3); and that the term "bishop" (or "overseer") in the NT is simply a synonym for "elder" (Titus 1:5–7; Acts 20:17, 28; I Tim. 3:1–2 with 5:17–19; I Pet. 5:2).

W. A. Grudem

See also Church Government; Church Officers; Bishop; Papacy.

Bibliography. K. Mörsdorf, "Hierarchy," *Sacramentum Mundi,* III, 27–29; J. H. Crehan, "Hierarchy in the Early Church," *A Catholic Dictionary of Theology,* II, 15–19; *MSt,* IV, 233–35.

High Church Movement. A phenomenon found in some of the major Protestant churches but particularly used of a school of thought in the Church of England (Anglicanism). The "high" normally refers to a high view of the continuity of the church through history, and thus of its visibility; therefore, a particular denomination may claim to be a part of the continuing one, holy, catholic, and apostolic church. With this emphasis on visibility and continuity there usually exists a view of the two Gospel sacraments, baptism and the Lord's Supper, which sees them as important and even indispensable means of grace. Further, regular reception, after due preparation, of the Lord's Supper is encouraged. Other "signs" of being "high" include an emphasis on duly ordained and educated clergy, respect for Catholic tradition (especially the ecumenical creeds), and a search for good liturgy. Within Lutheranism (from the seventeenth century) and within Methodism (from the nineteenth century) such an ethos or movement has often been found, although it has not necessarily been called "high church."

In Anglicanism, where the term has been much used, it is important clearly to distinguish between the High Church movement and the Tractarian (or Anglo-Catholic) movement. The former is much older than the latter. It originated in the seventeenth century and represented then the opposite end of the spectrum to Puritanism (which wanted to make the Church of England more like the church in Geneva or Scotland, i.e., Calvinist). High Churchmen emphasized that the Church of England was a full member of the historical, continuing, and visible church of God, that its bishops could trace their "descent" back to the earliest times, that its liturgy contained original Catholic principles, that its sacraments were efficacious, and that its doctrine accorded with basic Catholic doctrine, being in harmony with that of the early centuries of the church. High Churchmen of distinction included such names as Lancelot Andrewes (1555–1626), Bishop of Winchester; George Herbert (1593–1633) the poet; Jeremy Taylor (1613–67), writer on spirituality; William Laud (1573–1645), Archbishop of Canterbury; and Henry Hammond (1605–60), a biblical commentator.

The term "low church" was used from the eighteenth century to describe the mentality of those who were latitudinarian or broad-minded in their attitude to doctrine, tradition, and liturgy. Only later was it used as a synonym for evangelical; at first low churchmen called "evangelicals" by such names as "enthusiasts."

When the Tractarian movement was born in

1833, the largest grouping in the Church of England was "high church" and there was a strong but small evangelical party. Tractarians came from both high church and evangelical ranks but it was soon recognized that Tractarianism was not just an enthusiastic "high church" movement. It was something more than this, for while the High Church movement had always opposed Roman Catholicism, both in doctrine and ritual, Tractarianism (led by John Henry Newman) spoke favorably of it and in some ways imitated it. Thus there was some tension between the enthusiastic Tractarians and some of the representatives of the old high church movement (e.g., as represented by Christopher Wordsworth [1807–85], bishop of Lincoln). However, by the end of the nineteenth century the High Church movement had been absorbed by the Tractarian or Anglo-Catholic movement, and thus Tractarianism, High Church, and Anglo-Catholic functioned as rough equivalents, as they do to this day in Anglicanism.

In recent decades there has been a move by evangelical Anglicans to recapture some of the ideals of the old High Church movement, and in this search they have been joined by evangelicals from other denominations. C. S. Lewis has often been the author to guide people in the search for that approach to worship, doctrine, and tradition represented by the High Church movement at its best (in the seventeenth century). Thus some people are happy to be called high church evangelicals. P. TOON

See also ANGLO-CATHOLICISM; OXFORD MOVEMENT; LAUD, WILLIAM; LOW CHURCH.

Bibliography. P. E. More and F. L. Cross, eds., *Anglicanism;* R. Webber and D. Bloesch, eds., *The Orthodox Evangelicals;* S. Neill, *Anglicanism.*

Higher Criticism. This term describes the study of Scripture from the standpoint of literature, as opposed to "lower criticism," which deals with the text of Scripture and its transmission. Higher criticism thus has three main concerns: (a) detecting the presence of underlying literary sources in a work; (b) identifying the literary types (*Gattungen*) that make up the composition; and (c) conjecturing on matters of authorship and date.

The term "higher criticism" might seem to carry either a mystic or a sinister meaning, but it is in fact a process that all scholars follow to varying degrees. In order to obtain a proper understanding of the nature of biblical writings it is important to investigate the character of the sources. Sometimes this brings history to bear upon the work, as in the book of Ezra, where a section of the edict of Cyrus liberating captive peoples in Babylonia in 538 B.C. is quoted (Ezra 1:2–4). In the same book, a state document in Aramaic which gave instructions about the rebuilding of the Jerusalem temple (Ezra 6:3–5) was recovered after a search of the archives, and found to have been written at Cyrus's command also. This memorandum supported Jewish claims that the temple was being rebuilt by royal authority.

The recognition of various types of literature is also important because they can be compared with secular counterparts. Thus OT legal enactments often have much in common with those of other Near Eastern nations, while the NT letters can be better understood by comparison with what is known about the form, style, and language of first century A.D. secular letters. The fact that a work is ascribed *to* an author need not mean that it was written *by* that person. Thus the Assumption of Moses, while seeming to come from an ancient, reputable author, proves on examination to be early first century A.D. in date, and therefore its contents and purpose must be judged accordingly.

Several other approaches have developed to assist the scholar in the use of higher criticism. One is form criticism, which encourages the recognition of literary units according to their form. This is helpful in studying the parables, miracles, and sayings of Christ, for example, or in the recognition that the Fourth Gospel is written in the form of an ancient Babylonian tablet, complete with title, text, and colophon. A close form critical examination of Genesis indicates that chapters 1–36 comprise eleven distinct sections marked off by the phrase "these are the generations of," and this material also appears in traditional Babylonian tablet form.

Another procedure is tradition criticism, which examines the way in which specific traditions were interpreted by the various biblical writers. By studying a well-established tradition such as the Exodus, it is possible to see the different emphases placed upon it by historians, psalmists, and apostles. An interesting though rather speculative study is redaction criticism, which arose from form criticism and investigates the editorial motivation involved in the production of a work with particular reference to the viewpoint expressed. Thus the chronicler was concerned almost exclusively with the Davidic succession and its continuity in postexilic Judea and, as a result, developed a theology of history that was unique in antiquity. Again, John's Gospel deals selectively with the data of Christ's life and presents them theologically to the readers so that they might be saved. This standpoint makes the Fourth Gospel distinctive as an evangelistic document.

While the processes of structuralism are interpreted in a variety of ways, its basic concept appears to be that form and content are so firmly united that the latter cannot be understood properly unless the significance of the former is grasped clearly. This reinforces the values of form criticism, and prevents the truth of God from being considered as a purely abstract concept.

As with other disciplines, higher criticism needs to be handled carefully because of the ease with which results can be obtained by pure speculation in the absence of external data. Since the Reformation, biblical study has been littered with unsubstantiated suppositions, hypotheses, and theories, not infrequently based upon some concept of organic evolution.

This can be seen clearly in the work of nineteenth century liberal scholars, whose studies were generally so lacking in external controls, such as archaeological evidence, that unwarranted liberties were taken with both biblical interpretation and historical processes. Because these approaches went far beyond the available relevant evidence in the conclusions adopted, they also cast doubt upon the reliability of the method involved.

Responsible critical scholarship will resist such tendencies, partly because the purely speculative can be so easily demolished by opposing factual evidence, but more particularly because the integrity of the Scriptures is thereby seriously undermined. R. K. HARRISON

See also TÜBINGEN SCHOOL; ENLIGHTENMENT, THE; INTERPRETATION OF THE BIBLE.

Bibliography. E. J. Young, *Introduction to the OT;* R. K. Harrison, *Introduction to the OT;* D. Guthrie, *NT Introduction;* G. L. Archer, *ZPEB,* I, 584–90; R. K. Harrison *et al., Biblical Criticism: Historical, Literary and Textual.*

High Priest. *See* PRIESTS AND LEVITES.

Hinnom, Valley of. *See* GEHENNA.

Hippolytus (*ca.* 170–*ca.* 236). A Greek-speaking presbyter in the church at Rome, Hippolytus led a schism against Bishop Callistus. He and a later bishop of Rome, Pontianus, were exiled to Sardinia during the persecution of the emperor Maximin (235). Callistus and Hippolytus were apparently reconciled before dying in Sardinia, and were both reckoned martyrs.

Hippolytus wrote several important documents. The *Refutation of all Heresies* (sometimes cited *Philosophumena*) deals principally with Gnostic sects and traces their errors to philosophy. The *Apostolic Tradition* is the fullest source on the organizational and liturgical customs of the ante-Nicene Church—covering baptism, eucharist, ordination, and love feast. The *Commentary on Daniel* is the earliest commentary from the Orthodox Church; it sets forth a chiliastic eschatology. The *Against Noetus* opposes an early form of modalism. A statue of Hippolytus, presumably prepared during his lifetime, bears an inscription listing his writings and giving a table for calculating the date of Easter.

Hippolytus's views were sharpened by his controversy with Callistus. Besides their personal differences (Callistus a former slave with little formal education and Hippolytus a cultured free man) and rivalry for the episcopate, the two men disagreed doctrinally on two important points. Hippolytus championed the Logos Christology and distinguished the Father and Christ to such an extent that Callistus called him a "ditheist"; Callistus and his predecessor Zephyrinus emphasized the divine unity to such an extent that Hippolytus saw no difference between their views and the modalism of Sabellius. Hippolytus took a rigorist view on church discipline, denying reconciliation to the church to those guilty of major sins, and leaving their forgiveness to God; Callistus took a laxer view, and was ready to grant the church's forgiveness, especially in cases of sexual sins. E. FERGUSON

Bibliography. C. Wordsworth, *Hippolytus and the Church of Rome;* J. J. I. von Döllinger, *Hippolytus and Callistus;* A. d'Alès, *La théologie de Saint Hippolyte;* R. H. Connolly, *The So-Called Egyptian Church Order and Derived Documents;* B. S. Easton, *The Apostolic Tradition of Hippolytus;* J. M. Hanssens, *La liturgie d'Hippolyte;* Gregory Dix, *The Treatise on the Apostolic Tradition of St. Hippolytus of Rome.*

History of Religion School. *See* COMPARATIVE RELIGION.

Hocking, William Ernest (1873–1966). American Protestant scholar of philosophy and religion. Hocking taught at Andover Newton Theological School, Yale, and Harvard. It was his conviction that philosophy, if it is to be a worthwhile pursuit, must not be limited to academic circles. It must help to clarify and resolve issues in the wider world, including the world of religion, his area of special interest. He was a prolific writer, producing eighteen books, including *The Meaning of God in Human Experience* (1912), *Human Nature and Its Remaking* (1918), *Re-thinking Missions* (1932), and *Living Religions and a World Faith* (1940), and some two hundred journal articles. In *Re-thinking Missions* he argued that missionaries should not limit themselves to evangelism—they should also be actively engaged in providing social work and medical services. This view, which was somewhat more controversial then than it is now, involved him in the liberal-conservative debates of the time.

His philosophical system is called objective idealism. In it he stresses the "other mind" of God. His work was both influenced by, and in turn influenced, the existentialist movements of European thought. He taught that the "I" and the "Thou" are inseparable, which was a fundamental revision of the views of Descartes. He also believed that man experiences God not only in the universal, but also in the particular, in sensation.

He was a widely traveled individual who was a perceptive and critical observer of other cultures. He lectured in England, Scotland, The Netherlands, Germany, Syria, China, and other countries. J. D. Spiceland

Bibliography. W. E. Hocking, *The Meaning of Immortality in Human Experience, The Meaning of God in Human Experience, Science and the Idea of God,* and *What Man Can Make of Man;* L. S. Rouner, ed., *Philosophy, Religion, and the Coming World Civilization.*

Hodge, Archibald Alexander (1823–1886). Eldest son and successor of theologian Charles Hodge. He continued the Calvinist tradition begun at Princeton Theological Seminary by Archibald Alexander, after whom he was affectionately named. Nurtured in a genuinely pious home, which he vividly described in *The Life of Charles Hodge* (1880), A. A. Hodge graduated from Princeton in 1841 and Princeton Seminary in 1846. He was then ordained by the Presbyterian Church as a missionary to Allahabad, India. Although he and his wife were forced by illness to return with their two daughters after less than three years' service, his experience contributed to his lifelong involvement in advocating missions.

Following his return, Hodge served several pastorates in Maryland, Virginia, and Pennsylvania. He wrote *Outlines of Theology* (1860) from his preaching on doctrinal themes at Sunday evening services. Although catechetical in form, the lectures were well received due to Hodge's power as a speaker. He defended natural theology, contrasted systems of thought such as Augustinianism and Pelagianism, and analyzed broad theological themes. Because of its clarity and precision, *Outlines* was translated into several languages and widely used as a theological text. In 1864 Hodge was called as professor of didactic theology at Western Seminary in Pittsburgh. While there, he published monographs titled *Atonement* (1867) and *Exposition of the Confession of Faith* (1869), and also pastored North Presbyterian Church.

In 1877, Princeton Seminary called Hodge to assist his father, whose health was failing. In his inaugural address Hodge affirmed his commitment to systematic theology and biblical preaching, which together are to nourish vital piety. After his father died in 1878, the younger Hodge succeeded him as professor of didactic and polemical theology, a position he held until his death eight years later.

Even though Hodge was not as prominent as his father in Presbyterian ecclesiastical affairs, he worked with Charles A. Briggs of Union Seminary on publishing eight articles on higher criticism in the *Presbyterian Review.* In 1881 Hodge and Benjamin B. Warfield upheld Princeton's opposition to post-Enlightenment biblical criticism in their article "Inspiration." Affirming plenary verbal inspiration of the original autographs, Hodge and Warfield defined the doctrine of inerrancy, which dominated Presbyterianism in the 1890s.

In *Popular Lectures on Theological Themes,* published posthumously in 1887, Hodge attempted to integrate his defense of Calvinism with cultural analysis. As nineteenth century thinkers mounted campaigns for religious neutrality in public life, Hodge argued that only a Reformed theological base could provide a sufficient cultural foundation for traditional American values and institutions such as family, law, education, and economics. Without Christian theism, which he believed was best expressed in Reformed theology, American life and its institutions would be drastically altered into a relativistic secular culture. W. A. Hoffecker

See also Hodge, Charles; Warfield, Benjamin Breckinridge; Princeton Theology, Old.

Bibliography. C. A. Salmond, *Princetonia: Charles and A. A. Hodge.*

Hodge, Charles (1797–1878). The most influential American Presbyterian theologian of the nineteenth century. He was educated at Princeton College, Princeton Seminary, and during a two-year tour of German theological institutions from 1826 to 1828. He taught biblical literature at Princeton Seminary from 1822 to 1840, when he became Archibald Alexander's successor as professor of exegetical and didactic theology, a position which he held until his death. Hodge used his position as editor of the *Biblical Repertory and Princeton Review* (founded 1825) to expound his own version of orthodox Calvinism and to attack theologies which deviated from it, such as the New Haven theology of N. W. Taylor, the revivalism of Charles Finney, and the Mercersburg theology of John W. Nevin. Hodge wrote widely on church politics (including the

Presbyterian schism of 1837 and reunion of 1868), popular piety (including his 1841 exposition for the American Sunday School Union, *The Way of Life*), books of the Bible (including commentaries on Romans, Ephesians, I and II Corinthians), and on contemporary affairs (including discussion of the Civil War and an attack on Darwinism). But he is most remembered for his *Systematic Theology*, a three-volume, 2,000-page work published in 1872–73. He was hard-working, earnest, prolific, and the most complex of the conservative theologians who shaped education at Princeton Seminary from 1812 to 1929.

Hodge's theology grew out of his commitment to an authoritative Bible, his respect for Reformed confessions and for the European Reformed theologians of the seventeenth century, and his belief in the necessity of living piety. He regularly employed the thought forms of inductivist science and the categories of Scottish commonsense philosophy. Yet except for the introductory remarks of his *Systematic Theology*, these philosophical assumptions were not as influential as they were for other Princeton theologians. Hodge's Calvinism exalted God as the source of salvation and of all good. It was the basis for his belief that the Catholic Church and the Oxford Movement overestimated the saving power of the church, that Charles Finney and Horace Bushnell, in their different ways, underestimated the affect of sin upon native human capacities, and that the New England theologians overindulged modern assumptions about sin and grace at the expense of biblical convictions. Although Hodge was known best in his own day as a polemicist and as a popular exponent of Calvinistic spirituality, he has received more attention in recent years for his efforts to defend the authority of the Bible in opposition to the early findings of higher criticism. M. A. Noll

See also Hodge, Archibald Alexander; Warfield, Benjamin Breckinridge; Princeton Theology, Old.

Bibliography. C. Hodge, *The Way of Life* and *Systematic Theology;* A. A. Hodge, *The Life of Charles Hodge;* W. A. Hoffecker, *Piety and the Princeton Theologians;* M. A. Noll, *The Princeton Theology 1812–1921.*

Hofmann, Johann Christian Konrad von (1810–1877). German Lutheran theologian, leader of the Erlangen School. Born in Nuremburg and educated in Erlangen (1827–29) and Berlin (1829–32), he began his theological career as a lecturer at Erlangen (1838–42). He was called to Rostock as professor in 1842 and from there back to Erlangen in 1845, where he was the dominant figure until his death. He espoused what has come to be known as the *heilsgeschichtlich* (salvation history) approach to biblical theology, stressing the history of the people of God, the inspiration of Scripture, and Jesus Christ as the goal of and key to the meaning of history. In his view, the purpose of biblical theology is to expound the history of salvation as contained in the books of the OT and NT.

Hofmann was active in the promotion of missionary work and general evangelical piety. His two great works were his *Weissagung und Erfüllung im Alten und Neuen Testament* (1841–44) and *Der Schriftbeweis* (1852–56). He began a commentary on the NT (*Die heiligen Schriften des Neuen Testaments,* 1862–78), which he never completed. The only one of his writings that has been translated into English is his *Biblische Hermeneutik* (1880), published in 1959 as *Interpreting the Bible.* Although he identified himself with Lutheran confessionalism as well as with the major concerns of evangelical life and theology, his conviction that the Bible did not teach the doctrine of Christ's substitutionary atonement caused him to be opposed by many orthodox Christians of his day. W. W. Gasque

Bibliography. *PRE,* VIII, 234–41; *RGG,* III, 420–22; K. G. Steck, *Die Idee der Heilsgeschichte: Hofmann–Schlatter–Cullmann.*

Holiness. The religious term par excellence. A close connection is to be found everywhere between religion and the holy. At the heart of religion is the numinous, the vastly mysterious (the *mysterium tremendum*—Otto), the supernaturally threatening. All are contained in the idea of "the holy." Holiness, in a great variety of expressions, is the inmost core of religious faith and practice.

In the OT. In the OT holiness is spoken of primarily in relation to God, e.g., "the Lord is holy!" (Ps. 99:9). Holiness refers to his essential nature; it is not so much an attribute of God as it is the very foundation of his being. "Holy, holy, holy is the Lord of hosts" (Isa. 6:3). Thrice holy, intensely holy is the Lord. Holiness, accordingly, is the background for all else declared about God.

The first use of the word "holy" in the OT (Exod. 3:5) points to the divine sacredness. "Do not come near"—God speaks to Moses from the burning bush—"remove your sandals from your feet, for the place on which you are standing is holy ground." The holy is God's inviolable sacredness. It is only after this encounter with the holy God that Moses is given the name of God as the Lord (Yahweh), the one who will graciously deliver Israel from Egypt. The Redeemer is first of all the holy God. At Mount Sinai, after this deliverance and preparatory to the giving of the law, the sacredness of God is again vividly shown forth: the Lord "descended upon it in fire . . . and the whole mountain quaked violently" (Exod. 19:18). The Israelites are not allowed to come up the mountain "lest he break forth upon them" (Exod. 19:24). Thus memorably is all Israel, like Moses earlier, confronted with the elemental divine holiness.

Holiness bespeaks also the majesty and awesomeness of God. He is majestic in holiness (Exod. 15:11), and the very being of God is such as to provoke awe and fear. Jacob at Bethel, in a dream beholding the exalted Lord, awakens to cry, "How awesome is this place! This is none other than the house of God, and this is the gate of heaven" (Gen. 28:17). The primary response to God's majestic holiness is wonder, awe, even dread. So does the psalmist proclaim: "Worship the Lord in holy array; tremble before him, all the earth" (Ps. 96:9). His majestic presence calls for the response of worship and reverence. It also makes for awe and trembling.

Holiness then denotes the separateness, or otherness, of God from all his creation. The Hebrew word for holy, *qādôš*, in its fundamental meaning contains the note of that which is separate or apart. God is totally other than the world and man: "I am God and no man, the Holy One in your midst" (Hos. 11:9). This separateness, or otherness, is first of all that of his very "Godness," his essential deity. God is not in any way (as in many religions) to be identified with anything else in all of creation. Secondly, it signifies God's total apartness from all that is common and profane, from everything unclean or evil.

Hence, holiness in relation to God refers climactically to his moral perfection. His holiness is manifest in total righteousness and purity. The holy God will show himself holy in righteousness (Isa. 5:16). His eyes are too pure to approve evil (Hab. 1:13). This moral, or ethical, dimension of God's holiness becomes increasingly significant in the witness of the OT.

Everything associated with God is also holy. The second use of the word "holy" in the OT is found in the expression "a holy assembly" (Exod. 12:16), an assembly called by God to celebrate his "pass over" (Exod. 12:13) of Israel. The sabbath instituted by the Lord is "a holy sabbath" (Exod. 16:23); the heaven above is God's "holy heaven" (Ps. 20:6); God sits on his "holy throne" (Ps. 47:8); Zion is God's "holy mountain" (Ps. 2:6). God's name is especially holy, and never to be taken in vain (Exod. 20:7; Deut. 5:11).

Accordingly, God's covenant people, chosen by him, are a holy people: "You are a people holy to the Lord your God; the Lord your God has chosen you . . . out of all the peoples who are on the face of the earth" (Deut. 7:6). Israel is a separated people—separated unto the Lord—and therefore is holy not first of all because of any virtue but simply because of its set-apartness. But Israel is also called to holiness, thus to be a consecrated people: "I am the Lord your God. Consecrate yourselves therefore, and be holy; for I am holy" (Lev. 11:44). Hence, the word holiness in relation to the people of God contains both the negative sense of separation and the positive of consecration. All in all, the mark of holiness is the highest expression of the covenant relationship between a holy God and his people.

Whatever is connected with the religious cultus (worship, sacrifice, etc.) is also holy. There are, e.g., holy days (in addition to the holy sabbath), holy priests, holy anointing oil, holy first fruits, holy utensils. Ceremonial cleansing and purity are required of everything—priests, vehicles of worship, the congregation itself—that participates in the cultic activity. Furthermore, the call to holiness (as in Lev. 11:44) may be put totally in terms of not eating unclean foods. Thus, in the OT there is marked stress on ritual holiness.

There is, however, also an increasingly strong emphasis on holiness in the moral, or ethical, sphere. A central feature of the day of atonement is that of inward cleansing: "You shall be clean from all your sins before the Lord" (Lev. 16:30). Also there are many expressions elsewhere in the OT relating to the need for inner holiness. For example, in reply to the question, "Who may stand in his holy place?" the answer is given: "He who has clean hands and a pure heart" (Ps. 24:3–4). In the OT, even as the holiness of God is more and more understood to have moral content, so it is with holiness in relation to the people of God.

In the NT. The NT bears further witness to many of the aforementioned matters regarding holiness. In regard to God himself, for all that is said about his grace and love, there is no less emphasis on his holiness. The God of love is Holy Father (John 14:11), Jesus Christ is the Holy One of God (Mark 1:24; John 6:69), and the spirit of God is the Holy Spirit. Indeed, the OT declaration "Our God is holy," stands forth all the more markedly with the triune God fully disclosed in the NT. Likewise, such previously noted aspects of divine holiness as sacredness, majesty, awesomeness, separateness, and moral perfection are all to be found in the NT record. Also, God's people are called to holiness: "You shall be holy, for I am holy" (I Pet. 1:16).

It is the ethical dimension of holiness that the NT highlights. Holiness moves beyond any idea of a nation outwardly holy by virtue of divine election, and demonstrating such holiness through ritual and ceremony, to a people who are made inwardly holy. Basic to this is the witness of Jesus himself, the Holy One of God, who also as the Son of man lived out a life of complete holiness, righteousness, and purity. He "committed no sin; nor was any deceit found in his mouth" (I Pet. 2:22). As a result of his work of redemption, believers in him are declared righteous, but also enter into true righteousness and holiness: "We have been made holy through the sacrifice of the body of Jesus Christ" (Heb. 10:10).

Holiness (*hagiōsynē*) in the NT, accordingly, belongs to all believers. A common term for all believers is holy ones (*hagioi*), usually translated as "saints." "Saints," therefore, does not refer to persons preeminent in holiness, but to believers generally: all true believers are holy through Christ. This is the central meaning of such a statement as "in Christ Jesus" is "our righteousness, holiness, and redemption" (I Cor. 1:30). Holiness, in the NT, is an internal reality for all who belong to Christ.

In addition, holiness in the sense of transformation of the total person is now envisioned. So, e.g., does Paul write: "May the God of peace himself sanctify you [i.e., make you holy] entirely ... spirit and soul and body" (I Thess. 5:23). Since God is totally holy, his concern is that his people likewise become completely holy. Hence, holiness is not only an internal reality for the believer but also that which is to be perfected: "Let us cleanse ourselves from all defilement of flesh and spirit, perfecting holiness in the fear of God" (II Cor. 7:1).

Believers, as the saints of God, are "a chosen race, a royal priesthood, a holy nation" (I Pet. 2:9). The holy nation is no longer Israel but the church, nor is holiness any longer that to which a people are set apart and consecrated, but that which has now become an inward reality and in which they are being gradually transformed. The final goal: "that he [Christ] might present to himself the church in all her glory, having no spot or wrinkle or any such thing, but that it should be holy and blameless" (Eph. 5:27).

In Church History. In the history of the church, holiness has been viewed from many perspectives. In the Roman Catholic and Eastern Orthodox traditions several may be noted: (1) Ascetic. The pursuit of holiness by fleeing the world (forsaking secular occupation, marriage, worldly goods), hence limited to the few; holiness to be achieved by prayer vigils, fasting, self-mortification; the saints, or the religious, being those who thereby have gained a higher level of holiness. (2) Mystical. Holiness to be attained not so much by fleeing the world as by rising above it, a ladder of holiness with various stages such as purgation, illumination, contemplation until there is spiritual absorption in God. The barrier to holiness is not so much human sin as human finitude, one's bondage to the creaturely and temporal. (3) Sacramental. Holiness imparted through the supernatural grace of the sacraments; hence sacramental (unlike ascetic and mystical) holiness is available to all. Moreover, this objective infusion of holiness, though of a lesser degree than that attainable by ascetic or mystic, is given objectively without all the struggle involved.

Classical Protestantism (sixteenth century) was largely a movement away from ascetic, mystical, and sacramental views of holiness into a more biblical perspective. Soon, however, a number of diverging emphases were to emerge: (1) Disciplinary. A stress on ecclesiastical discipline and obedience to God's commandments as the way of holy living; the cultivation of a serious, often austere, life viewed as the mark of a God-fearing and truly holy man (e.g., Scottish Presbyterians, English Puritans). (2) Experimental. A reaction in various ways against rigid orthodoxy, formalism, and the externals of faith—institution, ritual, creed (in some cases, even the Scriptures)—to get into the spiritual; the holy viewed as the inner life to be cultivated and practiced (variously, Anabaptists, Quakers, Lutheran pietists). (3) Perfectionist. Total holiness, "entire sanctification," possible not through works but by faith; in addition to the holiness given in initial faith and growth in holiness there is the call of God to complete holiness through the eradication of sin and the gift of perfect love (Wesley, later holiness movements).

From the preceding brief review of certain perspectives (Catholic, Orthodox, Protestant) on holiness, the need for a truly biblical and reformed understanding is apparent. Such renewed understanding could be one of the most significant theological undertakings of our time.

J. R. Williams

See also Spirituality.

Bibliography. *HERE*, VI, 743-50; O. R. Jones, *The Concept of Holiness;* A. Koeberle, *The Quest for Holiness;* A. Murray, *Holy in Christ;* S. Neill, *Christian Holiness;* R. Otto, *The Idea of the Holy;* J. C. Ryle, *Holiness;* S. Taylor, *Holy Living.*

Holiness Movement, American. Originating in the United States in the 1840s and 50s, this was an endeavor to preserve and propagate John Wesley's teaching on entire sanctification and Christian perfection. Wesley held that the road from sin to salvation is one from willful rebellion against divine and human law to perfect love for God and man. Following Wesley, Holiness preachers emphasized that the process of salvation involves two crises. In the first, conversion or justification, one is freed from the sins he has committed. In the second, entire sanctification or full salvation, one is liberated from the flaw in his moral nature that causes him to sin. Man is capable of this perfection even though he dwells in a corruptible body marked by a thousand defects arising from ignorance, infirmities, and other creaturely limitations. It is a process of loving the Lord God with all one's heart, soul, and mind, and it results in the ability to live without conscious or deliberate sin. However, to achieve and then remain in this blessed state requires intense, sustained effort, and one's life must be marked by constant self-renunciation, careful observançe of the divine ordinances, a humble, steadfast reliance on God's forgiving grace in the atonement, the intention to look for God's glory in all things, and an increasing exercise of the love which itself fulfills the whole law and is the end of the commandments.

In the midnineteenth century several factors converged that contributed to the renewal of the Holiness emphasis, among them the camp meeting revivals that were a common feature in rural America, the Christian perfectionism of Charles Finney and Asa Mahan (the Oberlin theology), the "Tuesday Meeting" of Phoebe Palmer in New York, the urban revival of 1857–58, and protests within the Methodist churches about the decline of discipline which resulted in the Wesleyan Methodist secession in 1843 and Free Methodist withdrawal in 1860. These two became the first denominations formally committed to Holiness. After the Civil War a full-fledged Holiness revival broke out within the ranks of Methodism, and in 1867 the National Camp Meeting Association for the Promotion of Holiness was formed. From 1893 it was known as the National Holiness Association (NHA) and in 1971 was renamed the Christian Holiness Association. Until the 1890s Methodists dominated the movement and channeled its enthusiasm into their churches.

The increasing number of Holiness evangelists, many of whom were unsanctioned by their superiors, a flourishing independent press, and the growth of nondenominational associations gradually weakened the position of mainline Methodism in the movement. By the 1880s the first independent Holiness denominations had begun to appear, and tensions between Methodism and the Holiness associations escalated. The gap between the two widened as Methodist practice drifted steadily toward a sedate, middle-class American Protestantism, while the Holiness groups insisted they were practicing primitive Wesleyanism and were the true successors of Wesley in America. The small schismatic bodies gradually coalesced into formal denominations, the largest of which were the Church of God, Anderson, Indiana (1880), Church of the Nazarene (1908), and Pilgrim Holiness Church (1897—merged with the Wesleyan Methodists in 1968 to form the Wesleyan Church). The polity of these bodies was a modified Methodism in that there was generally somewhat more congregational autonomy, and the "second blessing" of entire sanctification was an integral part of their theology. Most operated with a strict perfectionist code of personal morality and demanded from their adherents plain dress and abstinence from "worldly" pleasures and amusements. Also, nearly all of them allowed women to be ordained to the ministry and occupy leadership positions.

The Holiness movement quickly spread beyond the bounds of Methodism. A Mennonite group, the United Missionary Church (formerly Mennonite Brethren in Christ and since a merger in 1969 called the Missionary Church), adopted the doctrine of entire sanctification and Holiness standards of personal conduct. The Brethren in Christ (founded 1863) was of mixed Pennsylvania German pietist and Mennonite origins, but it also took on Wesleyan perfectionism. Four Quaker yearly meetings that had been influenced by Holiness doctrines came together in 1947 to form the Evangelical Friends Alliance. The Salvation Army also has had a firm commitment to Holiness. The Christian and Missionary Alliance with its emphasis on Christ as Savior, sanctifier, healer, and coming King has an affinity with the Wesleyan movement, and its two most prominent thinkers, A. B. Simpson and A. W. Tozer, are widely read in Holiness circles, but it never accepted the doctrine of the eradication of sin.

The growth of the independent churches was related to the decline of the Holiness emphasis within Methodism, and after World War II denominationalism turned the originally evangelistic NHA into a council of Holiness churches. But numerical growth and material prosperity led inexorably to compromise with contemporary culture, and the relaxation of personal discipline was reflected in the wearing of fashionable dress and jewelry and secular entertainments such as participation in athletics and television viewing. As a result, several conservative splinter groups seceded from the Holiness denominations and joined together in an interchurch organization in 1947 known as the Interdenominational Holiness Convention. This now sees itself as the defender of pristine Wesleyanism.

Pentecostalism is an offshoot of the Holiness

movement. It teaches that speaking in tongues is the evidence one has received the second blessing. At a Bible school in Topeka, Kansas, founded by a Holiness evangelist the "gift of the Spirit" came to a student in 1901, and the practice of glossolalia quickly spread. The Pentecostal revival made its greatest inroads in areas where Holiness movements were already prospering, and it attracted far more non-Methodists than had the earlier forms of perfectionism. Besides the emphasis on the baptism of the Holy Spirit, Pentecostalism recognized divine healing and demanded highly puritanical standards of personal conduct. Like the Holiness groups the Pentecostals were theological conservatives, and they comprised an important addition to the Arminian wing of Protestant conservatism in the period when the fundamentalist movement was gathering steam.

Some Holiness denominations, most notably the Church of the Nazarene, flatly reject the use of tongues, while others, the largest being the Church of God, Cleveland, Tennessee, and the Pentecostal Holiness Church, teach both glossolalia and entire sanctification. Denominationalism soon took hold in Pentecostalism, and before long it had more adherents than its parent in such bodies as the Assemblies of God, the black Church of God in Christ, and the International Church of the Foursquare Gospel.

More difficult to characterize is the Keswick movement which originated in Britain in 1875 at a "Convention for the Promotion of Practical Holiness" in the Lake District town of that name. Speakers at the annual Keswick conferences emphasized the "deeper life" instead of holiness, believing that the tendency to sin is not extinguished but is counteracted by victorious living through the Holy Spirit. The predominance of Reformed Anglicans along with like-minded Free Church evangelicals in the movement prevented the Wesley-Arminian view of sanctification from establishing a foothold.

In Germany the Holiness concept was institutionalized in the *Gemeinschaftsbewegung* (Fellowship Movement) which came into existence under the influence of Keswick and Methodist evangelists from Britain and the United States. Several societies were founded, the most important being the German Evangelization Association (1884), Gnadau Association (1888), and Blankenburg Alliance Conference (1905), which cultivated a deeper holiness among members of the territorial churches.

The Holiness movement contributed to a deepening of the spiritual life in a materialistic age, and it was a welcome contrast to the sterile intellectualism and dead orthodoxy that characterized so many churches at the time. However, it has been criticized for suggesting that a "second blessing" can provide some Christians with a higher kind of sanctification than that which flows from one's justifying faith. P. T. Forsyth said it is "a fatal mistake to think of holiness as a possession which we have distinct from our faith and conferred upon it. That is a Catholic idea, still saturating Protestant pietism." Other objections include the tendency to identify holiness with quietistic self-abasement and even loss of personality, an otherworldly asceticism that calls for the rejection of all secular culture as sinful, confining the grace of God to stereotyped forms of religious experience, an overemphasis on feeling, and claiming with overweening confidence the special action of the Holy Spirit in one's life and direct inspiration in the details of thought and action. R. V. PIERARD

See also WESLEYAN TRADITION, THE; METHODISM; PENTECOSTALISM; PERFECTION, PERFECTIONISM; OBERLIN THEOLOGY; KESWICK CONVENTION.

Bibliography. C. E. Jones, *A Guide to the Study of the Holiness Movement;* D. W. Dayton, *The American Holiness Movement: A Bibliographic Introduction;* M. E. Dieter, *The Holiness Revival of the Nineteenth Century;* C. E. Jones, *Perfectionist Persuasion: The Holiness Movement and American Methodism;* J. L. Peters, *Christian Perfection and American Methodism;* T. L. Smith, *Called Unto Holiness;* P. Scharpff, *History of Evangelism;* A. Clarke, *Commentary on the Holy Bible;* H. O. Wiley, *An Introduction to Christian Theology;* R. H. Coats, *HERE,* VI, 743–50; D. W. Dayton, *NIDCC,* 474–75; V. Synan, *The Holiness-Pentecostal Movement.*

Holiness of God. *See* GOD, ATTRIBUTES OF; GOD, DOCTRINE OF.

Holiness of the Christian. *See* GODLINESS.

Holl, Karl (1866–1926). German historian and theologian who made an important contribution to the study of Martin Luther. He rose to the prestigious rank of professor of history at Berlin University in 1906 where he became a leading expert on Luther. Had he never written a word about Luther's theology, Holl would still be an important Luther scholar, for he understood the need to clarify the Luther canon until it could be counted as reliable. This he did until he was able to discard several Luther works as not genuine, while several hitherto unknown works were proved to have been written by Luther.

Holl's knowledge of Luther's writings led him to analyze Luther's theology. He stressed that the foundation of Luther's faith was a "religion of conscience." By this Holl meant that Luther responded to something which arose from deep inner feelings with which he felt impelled to deal. Those experiences, said Holl, are central to Luther's theology, for Luther felt that he was standing alone in his sins before God. From this confrontation with God, said Holl, came Luther's theology.

This focus on Luther's personal experience with God as the foundation of his theology was a contribution because Holl clarified the basic reasons for Luther's rebellion against the church: an honest man who could do nothing but what his conscience bade him do, and an honest theologian who could think only what his conscience bade him think in spite of the church's teachings. But Holl's explanation of the means by which Luther reached his theological conclusions as a result of his personal experiences is controversial. He tends to stress that Luther's personal experiences and logic, rather than a rediscovery of biblical teachings, led Luther to this theology. J. E. MENNELL

Bibliography. K. Holl, *The Cultural Significance of the Reformation* and *What Did Luther Understand by Religion?*

Holocaust, The. Auschwitz, the Polish site of one of the largest Nazi concentration camps, has become a symbol of the mass murders and horrors of the Holocaust. Just as one of the many Nazi death camps represents in popular imagination the entire system of mass deportation, deprivation, degradation, and destruction of humans carried out by German conquerors throughout Europe during World War II, so "Holocaust," the term usually used to describe Nazi persecution, imprisoning, and pitiless eradication of six million Jews between 1933 and 1945, has become a paradigm for the extremes of human suffering and of evil, in institutionalized and personal manifestations, during the twentieth century. In the first half of this century, labeled "the Era of Violence" by *The New Cambridge Modern History,* two pinnacles of destruction dominate: the Holocaust and the atom bomb.

Scholars have probed the inadequate, indifferent responses of bystanders, both in Germany and abroad, to the Nazi persecution of the Jews. The Allied governments have been criticized for not focusing bombing raids on Auschwitz and its railroad lines during the war against Germany. Even Jewish organizations in America have been faulted for failing to do enough to save Jews in Europe. The greater burden of responsibility, however, falls upon Christian churches, especially in Germany, because of their apathy or sins of omission before and during the Holocaust; in addition, certain Christian teachings, historical attitudes, and actions nurtured a Christian anti-Judaism that contributed to the popular attitudes susceptible to strident anti-Semitic movements before 1933. Sinister shadows in the German Lutheran legacy were shaped by the virulent anti-Semitic remarks of Martin Luther in 1543 and by the anti-Semitism passionately proclaimed by Adolf Stoecker, who by 1874 became court preacher in Berlin. Moreover, the traditional Christian doctrine of the cursed Jews, linked to the guilt of deicide, was sometimes interpreted by the public as an encouragement of anti-Semitic policies and acts. In the post-Holocaust rethinking of Roman Catholic theology, the Second Vatican Council recognized the pernicious effects of this teaching in its 1965 statement that what happened in Christ's passion cannot be blamed on all the Jews then living, without distinction, nor upon the Jews of today. Protestants have also reappraised their teachings on Jews. In 1980 the Rhineland Synod of the German Evangelical [Protestant] Church overwhelmingly adopted a path-breaking document: "Resolution on the Renewal of the Relationship between Christians and Jews." Describing the Holocaust as a turning point and initial motivation, the declaration acknowledges "the co-responsibility and guilt of Christianity in Germany with respect to the Holocaust." It goes on to assert that the continuing existence of the Jewish people and the creation of the state of Israel are signs of God's faithfulness to his people. Affirming that both Jews and Christians are witnesses of God to the world and to each other, the resolution maintains that the church cannot exercise its witness to the Jewish people as it does to the nations of the world. Thus, the document also touches on the sensitive issue of Christian mission to the Jews, an activity which some Jews in the post-Holocaust era link to an attempt at spiritual genocide. They ask: Do Christians really want a world free of Jews (*Judenrein* in Nazi terminology)? At least one evangelist, Billy Graham, refrains from singling out Jews as Jews for evangelistic purposes.

Although Christian anti-Judaism contributed to ripening German antagonism toward Jews, the primary burden of guilt for the Holocaust falls upon Adolf Hitler, who made racial anti-Semitism the cornerstone of his policies, as well as the leaders of the Nazi party and their functionaries, who made the machinery of destruction function so effectively. Concentration camp doctors, trained as healers, became killers, as they supervised inhuman medical experiments and selected people for extermination. Technicians introduced a new killing device, Zyklon B gas, administered in chambers camouflaged as shower rooms. Even in the 1930s Jews, viewed as vermin by the Nazis, were given the worst treatment in concentration camps. During the 1940s the annihilation of Jews and other prisoners became the primary goal of six eastern European killing centers, inaugurating the industrialization of mass murder: Auschwitz, Belzec, Chelmno, Maidanek, Sobibor, and Treblinka. They were supplemented by a vast network of concentration camps, specializing in slave labor under the most deplorable physical and psychological conditions. Of an estimated eleven million civilians who died or were killed in these camps, six million were Jews. Thus, by 1945 the Nazis had eliminated two thirds of the European Jews (a figure representing almost one third of world Jewry).

Accelerated political and racial anti-Semitism in the late nineteenth and early twentieth centuries, as well as the economic and social chaos following World War I in Germany, created conditions conducive to Nazi extremist propaganda. After Hitler was appointed German chancellor on January 30, 1933, the Nazi regime's policies toward Jews evolved and intensified through four stages:

1933–1935. Sporadic economic and professional harassment included an economic boycott of Jewish businesses (Apr. 1, 1933), the elimination of Jews from civil service posts (Apr. 7, 1933) and from leading professions.

1935–1938. Legal disabilities culminated in the September, 1935, Nuremberg laws, depriving Jews of German citizenship and prohibiting intermarriage. "Aryanization" of Jewish property and wealth also began.

1938–1941. Deportations and pogroms started with "Crystal Night" (Nov. 9, 1938). Jewish businesses were expropriated and Jews sent to concentration camps.

1941–1945. The planned program of physical destruction of Jews began with the June, 1941, German invasion of Russia, when Jews were systematically killed by mobile killing units and gas vans in Russia. After the Jan. 20, 1942, Wannsee conference in Berlin, extermination camps (with gas chambers and crematoria) became centers of the killing operations.

"The final solution" of the Jewish problem was the Nazi phrase used at the Wannsee conference, held to coordinate with top government officials suitable treatment for the Jews. Both "Holocaust" (derived from the Greek word for a sacrifice wholly consumed by fire) and the Hebrew word *šôʼâ* (variously used in the Bible for disaster, destruction, darkness, or emptiness) are current designations for the mass annihilation of Jews in Europe. These two words surfaced in Israel as descriptions of the Nazi program against Jews; *šôʼâ* was first applied in 1940, and Holocaust was initially used between 1957 and 1959.

Worldwide revulsion against the Holocaust has had effects on the contemporary human rights movement, leading to the UN Genocide Convention, the Universal Declaration of Human Rights, and many national and international human rights groups. The resisters to Nazism and those courageous individuals like Raoul Wallenberg, who acted to save Jews, also provide historical models for current human rights activists. Many Christians as individuals helped Jews escape, but institutionalized Christianity failed both by silence and by lack of open, fearless, and concerted action to aid the oppressed. The German Protestant Confessing Church focused its public efforts on the plight of baptized Jews, not on the persecution of Jews as Jews.

Holocaust studies have been multidisciplinary, expanding perspectives in psychology, sociology, political science, literature, history, and theology. In addition to the inevitable ethical questions, new questions of theodicy have been raised, the Jewish roots of Christianity are being probed, and uniqueness versus the universality of the event has been debated. The special wisdom and grace of the survivors have surfaced in stories that instruct us all. R. Zerner

See also Anti-Semitism.

Bibliography. L. S. Dawidowicz, *The War Against the Jews, 1933–1945;* H. L. Feingold, *The Politics of Rescue: The Roosevelt Administration and the Holocaust, 1938–1945;* R. Hilberg, *The Destruction of the European Jews;* B. L. Sherwin and S. G. Ament, *Encountering the Holocaust: An Interdisciplinary Survey;* J. Sloan, ed., *Notes from the Warsaw Ghetto: The Journal of Emmanuel Ringelblum;* J. Blatter and S. Milton, *Art of the Holocaust;* T. Des Pres, *The Survivor: An Anatomy of Life in the Death Camps;* P. Friedman, *Their Brothers' Keepers;* L. L. Langer, *The Holocaust and the Literary Imagination;* I. Leitner, *Fragments of Isabella: A Memoir of Auschwitz;* E. Wiesel, *Night;* E. Berkovits, *Faith After the Holocaust;* E. Fleischner, *Auschwitz: Beginning of a New Era?* B. Klappert and H. Starck, eds., *Umkehr und Erneuerung;* C. Klein, *Anti-Judaism in Christian Theology;* F. Littell and H. G. Locke, eds., *The German Church Struggle and the Holocaust;* R. L. Rubenstein, *After Auschwitz* and *The Cunning of History: The Holocaust and the American Future;* R. Ruether, *Faith and Fratricide;* M. Bergman and M. Jucovy, eds., *Generations of the Holocaust;* H. Krystal, ed., *Massive Psychic Trauma.*

Holy Communion. *See* Lord's Supper.

Holy Ghost. *See* Holy Spirit.

Holy of Holies. *See* TABERNACLE, TEMPLE.

Holy One of Israel. This title for God occurs twenty-six times in the book of Isaiah and only six times in the rest of the OT. From the very first chapter (1:4), Isaiah contrasts the perfection and purity of God with the corruptness and sinfulness of Israel. A God so powerful and so holy deserved to be held in awe (8:13; 29:23), but instead the people of Israel spurned him and mocked him (5:19). It is against the background of Israel's blatant sin that Isaiah presents his vision of the Holy God in chapter 6. So overwhelming was his glimpse of the holiness of God in the heavenly temple that Isaiah acknowledged his sin and responded in obedience to the Lord.

Throughout the rest of the book Isaiah refers to "the Holy One of Israel" as the God set apart from all other Gods and worthy of all honor. Even the powerful king of Assyria is doomed to failure because he dared to defy this "Holy One of Israel" (37:23). Jeremiah announces the defeat of mighty Babylon for the same reason (Jer. 50:29). The Holy One is the judge of all the world.

Six times Isaiah links the "Holy One of Israel" with the word "redeemer" (41:14; 43:14; 47:4; 48:17; 49:7; 54:5). Just as God delivered his people from the slavery of Egypt, so will he bring them back from the Babylonian exile. God will build a highway for the redeemed, called "the way of holiness" (35:8–10). An incomparable and faithful God will once again come to the rescue of his chosen people (49:7).

It is likely that Isaiah patterns the name "the Holy One of Israel" after the title "the Mighty One of Jacob." This name for God first occurs in the patriarchal blessing of Gen. 49:24, and appears three out of six times in Isaiah (1:24; 49:26; 60:16). The first time it is given as "the Mighty One of *Israel*," rather than "*Jacob*," probably echoing "the Holy One of *Israel*" in 1:4. The God whom Jacob worshiped needed to be revealed in new power to the rebellious nation of Isaiah's day. H. M. WOLF

See also GOD, NAMES OF.

Bibliography. O. Procksch, *TDNT,* I, 93–94; T. McComiskey, *TWOT,* II, 786–88.

Holy Saturday. Part of Holy Week, which culminates with Easter Sunday, the celebration of the rising of our Lord Jesus Christ, from the tomb, after he died on the cross. It deals in a specific sense with the remembrance of the period of time during which Jesus lay in the tomb and borders on his rising. In a sense it celebrates the entire paschal mystery in a reflective mood. T. J. GERMAN

See also CHRISTIAN YEAR; EASTER; HOLY WEEK.

Bibliography. L. Bouyer, *The Paschal Mystery: Meditations on the Last Three Days of Holy Week.*

Holy Spirit. In the NT, the third person of the Trinity; in the OT, God's power.

The OT. In the OT the spirit of the Lord (*rûaḥ yhwh;* LXX, *to pneuma kyriou*) is generally an expression for God's power, the extension of himself whereby he carries out many of his mighty deeds (e.g., I Kings 8:12; Judg. 14:6ff; I Sam. 11:6). As such, "spirit" sometimes finds expression in ways similar to other modes of God's activity, such as "the hand of God" (Ps. 19:1; 102:25); "the word of God" (Ps. 33:6; 147:15, 18); and the "wisdom of God" (Exod. 28:3; I Kings 3:28; Job 32:8). The origins of the word "spirit" in both Hebrew (*rûaḥ*) and Greek (*pneuma*) are similar, stemming from associations with "breath" and "wind," which were connected by ancient cultures to unseen spiritual force, hence "spirit" (cf. John 3:8—note the association with air in English; e.g., "pneumatic," "respiration," etc.). The AV uses the term "Holy Ghost" for "Holy Spirit" based on an obsolete usage of the word "ghost" (from Middle English and Anglo-Saxon, originally meaning "breath," "spirit"—cf. the German *Geist*). Thus it is understandable that God's creative word (Gen. 1:3ff.) is closely akin to God's creative breath (Gen. 2:7). Both ideas are identified elsewhere with God's spirit. As an agent in creation, God's spirit is the life principle of both men and animals (Job 33:4; Gen. 6:17; 7:15).

The primary function of the spirit of God in the OT is as the spirit of prophecy. God's spirit is the motivating force in the inspiration of the prophets—that power which moved sometimes to ecstasy but always to the revelation of God's message, expressed by the prophets with "thus saith the Lord." Prophets are sometimes referred to as "men of God" (I Sam. 2:27; I Kings 12:22; etc.); in Hos. 9:7 they are "men of the Spirit." The general implication in the OT is that the prophets were inspired by the spirit of God (Num. 11:17; I Sam. 16:15; Mic. 3:8; Ezek. 2:2; etc.).

The phrase "Holy Spirit" appears in two contexts in the OT, but is qualified both times as God's holy Spirit (Ps. 51:11; Isa. 63:10–11, 14), such that it is clear that God himself is the referent, not *the* Holy Spirit which is encountered in the NT. The OT does not contain an idea of a semi-independent divine entity, the Holy Spirit. Rather, we find special expressions of God's activity with and through men. God's spirit is holy in the same way his word and his name are holy; they are all forms of his revelation and, as such, are set in antithesis to all things human or material. The OT, especially the prophets, anticipates a time when God, who is holy (or "other than/separate from" men; cf. Hos. 11:9) will pour out his spirit on men (Joel 2:28ff.; Isa. 11:1ff.; Ezek. 36:14ff.), who will themselves become holy. The Messiah/Servant of God will be the one upon whom the spirit rests (Isa. 11:1ff.; 42:1ff.; 63:1ff.), and will inaugurate the time of salvation (Ezek. 36:14ff.; cf. Jer. 31:31ff.).

Intertestamental Judaism. Within intertestamental Judaism several significant developments shaped the idea of "Holy Spirit" as it was understood in NT times. After the OT prophets had proclaimed the coming of the Spirit in the messianic age of salvation, Judaism had developed the idea that the spirit of prophecy had ceased within Israel with the last of the biblical prophets (Syriac Bar. 85:3; I Macc. 4:46; 14:41; etc.; cf. Ps. 74:9). Consequently, there arose from time to time a hope of the dawning of the new age, especially within the apocalyptic movement, which generally pointed to a supposed messiah and/or prophetic reawakening of some kind (cf. Acts 5:34ff.). The Qumran community is illustrative of this, since it understood itself to be involved in the fulfillment of Israel's messianic hope as the "preparers of the way of the Lord" (Isa. 40:3; cf. 1QS 8. 14–16). The Qumran literature also shows increased identification of the spirit of prophecy with "God's Holy Spirit" (1QS 8. 16; Zadokite Documents II. 12). The phrase, "the Holy Spirit," occasionally occurs in Judaism (IV Ezra 14:22; Ascension of Isa. 5:14; etc.), but, as in the rabbis, it generally meant "God's spirit of prophecy." Thus, the messianic expectation of Judaism, which included the eschatological outpouring of God's spirit (e.g., I Enoch 49:3, citing Isa. 11:2; cf. Sybilline Oracle III, 582, based on Joel 2:28ff.), was bound up with the conviction that the Spirit had ceased in Israel with the last of the prophets; the Holy Spirit was understood as God's spirit of prophecy, which would be given again in the new age to a purified Israel in conjunction with the advent of a messiah.

The concept of the Holy Spirit was broadened through the Wisdom Literature, especially in the personification of wisdom as that idea came into contact with the idea of Spirit. As early as Prov. 8:22ff. and Job 28:25ff. wisdom is presented as a more or less independent aspect of God's power (here as agent in creation), and wisdom is credited with functions and characteristics that are attributed to the Holy Spirit in the NT. Wisdom proceeded from the mouth of God and covered the earth as a mist at creation (Sir. 24:3); she is the breath of the power of God (Wisd. Solomon 7:25); and by means of his wisdom God formed man (Wisd. Sol. 9:2). The Lord poured out wisdom upon all his works, and she dwells with all flesh (Sir. 1:9–10). Moreover, wisdom is full of spirit, and indeed is identified with the Spirit (Wisd. Sol. 7:22; 9:1; cf. 1:5). Thus the Jews of NT times were familiar with the background of these ideas as they are variously expressed in the NT, ideas which use these background concepts but move beyond them to some unexpected conclusions. Indeed, Jesus taught that his messiahship and the corresponding outpouring of the Spirit were firmly rooted in OT understanding (Luke 4:18ff., citing Isa. 61:1–2), and, similar to intertestamental Judaism, understood the messianic Spirit of the Lord to be the Holy Spirit (Matt. 12:32), that spirit which had foretold through the prophets that the coming Messiah would inaugurate the age of salvation with the pouring out of the Spirit on all flesh. Jesus developed the idea of the Holy Spirit as a personality (e.g., John 15:26; 16:7ff.), specifically as God working in the church.

The NT. The NT teaching of the Holy Spirit is rooted in the idea of both the spirit of God as the manifestation of God's power and the spirit of prophecy. Jesus, and the church after him, brought these ideas together in predicating them of the Holy Spirit, God's eschatological gift to man. When Mary is "overshadowed" by the power of the Most High—a phrase standing in parallel construction to "the Holy Spirit" (Luke 1:35; cf. 9:35)—we find echoes of the OT idea of God's spirit in the divine cloud which "overshadowed" the tabernacle so that the tent was filled with the glory of the Lord (Exod. 40:35; Isa. 63:11ff. identifies God's presence in this instance as "God's Holy Spirit"). Luke records Jesus' power to cast out demons "by the finger of God," an OT phrase for God's power (Luke 11:20; Exod. 8:19; Ps. 8:3). This power is identified as the "Spirit of God" (Matt. 12:28), i.e., the Holy Spirit (Matt. 12:32). At Jesus' baptism the spirit came upon him (Mark 1:10; "the Spirit of God," Matt. 3:16; "the Holy Spirit," Luke 3:21), and he received God's confirmation of his divine sonship and messianic mission (Matt. 3:13ff., par.). Jesus went up from the Jordan full of the Holy Spirit (Luke 4:1), and after the temptation began his ministry "in the power of the Spirit" (Luke 4:14). Taking up the message of John the Baptist, Jesus proclaimed the coming of the kingdom of God (Matt. 4:17; cf. 3:1)—a coming marked by the presence of the Holy Spirit (Matt. 12:28ff., par.) as the sign of the messianic age of salvation (Luke 4:18ff.; Acts 10:38; etc.).

From the beginning of Jesus' ministry he identified himself with both the victorious messiah-king and the suffering servant figures of OT prophecy (Isa. 42:1ff.; cf. Mark 10:45), ideas which Judaism had kept separate. Jesus further defined the role of God's Messiah as proclaiming God's favor, God's salvation, in the new age—a message stressed far beyond that of "judgment of the nations," which the Jews had come to expect. At the synagogue in Nazareth (Luke 4:16ff.) when Jesus identified himself with the Messiah promised in Isa. 61:1–2*a* he stopped short of reading the "words of judgment" of Isa. 61:2*b* (even though Isa. 61:2*c*, "comfort to those who mourn," is part of Jesus' teaching at Matt. 5:4). This emphasis is made again when John the Baptist asks whether Jesus is indeed the one who was to come (Luke 7:18–23). Indeed, even though John the Baptist proclaimed Jesus to be the one who would "baptize in the Holy Spirit and in fire" as aspects of the new age (salvation *and* judgment, respectively—Luke 3:15ff.; note the clear judgment connections of "baptism with fire" in 3:17), Jesus' own focus was on the positive, salvific aspect of the new age as represented in the baptism with the Holy Spirit (Acts 1:5; 11:16).

Jesus understood the Holy Spirit as a personality. This comes out especially in John's Gospel, where the Spirit is called the "Paraclete," i.e., the Comforter (Counselor, Advocate). Jesus himself was the first Counselor (Paraclete, John 14:16), and he will send the disciples another Counselor after he is gone, i.e., the Spirit of truth, the Holy Spirit (14:26; 15:26; 16:5). The Holy Spirit will dwell in the believers (John 7:38; cf. 14:17), and will guide the disciples into all truth (16:13), teaching them "all things" and bringing them "to remembrance of all that [Jesus] said" to them (14:26). The Holy Spirit will testify about Jesus, as the disciples must also testify (John 15:26–27).

In Acts 2:14ff. Peter interpreted the Pentecost phenomena as the fulfillment of Joel's prophecy of the outpouring of the spirit upon all flesh in the messianic age (Joel 2:28ff.). The outpouring of the spirit upon all flesh was accomplished for the benefit of Jew and Gentile alike (Acts 10:45; 11:15ff.), and individual converts had access to this gift of the age of salvation through repentance and baptism into the name of Jesus Christ (Acts 2:38). This, according to Peter, put the converts in contact with the promise of Joel's prophecy, the gift of the Holy Spirit; "for to you is the promise . . . , for all whom the Lord our God will call" (Acts 2:39; Joel 2:32). The apostles and others carried out their ministries "full of the Holy Spirit" (4:31; 6:5; 7:54; etc.), and the Holy Spirit—identified in Acts 16:7 as the Spirit of Jesus—directed the mission of the fledgling church (Acts 9:31; 13:2; 15:28; 16:6–7). The salvific aspects of the new age practiced by Jesus—notably healing and exorcism—were carried out by the early church through the power of the Holy Spirit. Visions and prophecies occurred within the young church (Acts 9:10; 10:3; 10:10ff.; 11:27–28; 13:1; 15:32) in keeping with the Acts 2 citation of Joel 2:28ff. The experience of the early church confirmed that the messianic age had indeed come.

Paul taught that the Holy Spirit, poured out in the new age, is the creator of new life in the believer and that unifying force by which God in Christ is "building together" the Christians into the body of Christ (Rom. 5:5; II Cor. 5:17; Eph. 2:22; cf. I Cor. 6:19). Romans 8 shows that Paul identified the spirit, the spirit of God, and the spirit of Christ with the Holy Spirit (cf. the spirit of Christ as the spirit of prophecy in I Pet. 1:10ff.), and that these terms are generally interchangeable. If anyone does not have the spirit of Christ, he does not belong to Christ (Rom. 8:9); but those who are led by the spirit of God are sons of God (Rom. 8:14). We all have our access to the Father through one spirit (Eph. 2:18), and there is one body and one spirit (Eph. 4:4). We were all baptized by one spirit into one body, and we were all given the one spirit to drink (I Cor. 12:13). The believer receives the spirit of adoption or "sonship" (Rom. 8:15)—indeed, the spirit of God's own Son (Gal. 4:6)—by whom we cry, "Abba, Father," that intimate address of filial relationship to God pioneered by Jesus, the unique Son of God (Mark 14:36).

The believers are being built together into a dwelling place of God in the spirit (Eph. 4:22). To each one was apportioned grace according to the measure of the gift of Christ (Eph. 4:7; cf. Rom. 12:3), and Christ has given different ones to be prophets, apostles, evangelists, pastors, and teachers (Eph. 4:11) for the edification of the body. Similarly, the Spirit gives different kinds of spiritual gifts for different kinds of service (I Cor. 12:4–5; 7), all for the common good. The way of love is to be followed in all things; indeed, the fruit of the spirit is love, joy, peace, etc. (Gal. 5:22ff.). All of this is because God has initiated the new covenant (Jer. 31:31ff.; Ezek. 36:14ff.; 26) in the hearts of men by means of his eschatological spirit (II Cor. 3:6ff.). In this new age the spirit is the earnest of our inheritance (II Cor. 1:22; 5:5; Eph. 1:14), a "firstfruits," the seal of God (II Cor. 1:22; Eph. 1:13; 4:30). These phrases point out the "already vs. the not yet" tension of the new age: the new age has dawned, and the eschatological spirit has been poured out, yet all of creation awaits the final consummation. Even though the spirit bears witness with our spirit that we are sons of God (Rom. 8:16) and we truly have the firstfruits of the spirit (Rom. 8:23), we await the adoption as sons (8:23) at the final consummation. Until that time Christians have the Comforter, the Spirit who intercedes on behalf of the saints according to the will of the Father (Rom. 8:27).

Patristic and Medieval Theology. In the patristic period we encounter little that moves beyond the biblical ideas of the Holy Spirit. The apostolic fathers reflect the NT idea that the spirit is operative in the church, inspiring prophecy and otherwise working within individuals (Barnabas 12:2; Ignatius, *Phil.* 7:1). Itinerant Christian prophets are dealt with as a present reality in the Didache, but as time passes, such charismata are treated as theoretical. The view that the spirit of OT prophecy is one and the same Holy Spirit that inspired the apostles is periodically encountered (Justin, *Dialogues* 1–7; 51; 82; 87; etc.; Irenaeus, *Against Heresies* II, 6.4; III, 21.3–4), and the apostles emerge as the "Spirit-bearers" (*pneumatophoroi*)—a designation given to the OT prophets (Hos. 9:7, LXX). The Holy Spirit is credited with empowering the church—even with inspiring certain noncanonical writings—as late as the fourth century.

Even though the "trinitarian" formula of Matt. 28:19 is found in the apostolic fathers, the word "trinity" is first applied to the Godhead by Theophilus of Antioch (*To Autolycus* 2:15). Tertullian clearly taught the divinity of the Holy Spirit, an idea that was later to occupy the church in discussion for a thousand years. Tertullian wrestled with the problem of the tension between the authority of the Spirit in the church versus apostolic tradition and Scripture as received revelation. He espoused montanism for a time, a system which placed primary importance on the current inspiration of the Spirit in the body. The church, however, rejected montanism in favor of the objective authority of apostolic tradition as reflected in Scripture, and montanism eventually died out. The church's stand against the montanist heresy was largely responsible for the demise of Christian prophecy and other charismata. The Muratorian Canon (lines 75ff.) states that the number of prophets is settled, and even the *Apostolic Tradition* of Hippolytus, which elevates charismatic leadership above ecclesiastical structure, restricts the term "prophet" entirely to the canonical prophets. In the late fourth century John Chrysostom could speak of the spiritual gifts as belonging to an age in the past.

In the period immediately prior to Nicaea the church was preoccupied with the famous "Christological controversies" and paid scant attention to a doctrine of the Holy Spirit. The Nicene Creed confesses faith in the Holy Spirit, but without any development of the idea of the Spirit's divinity or essential relationship to the Father and the Son. This question became a major issue within the church in the late fourth century and following, and the Council of Constantinople added to the words of the Nicene Creed, describing the Holy Spirit as "the Lord and Giver of Life, proceeding from the Father, to be worshiped and glorified together with the Father and the Son." A controversy developed around the source of the Spirit, specifically concerning whether he ought not also be confessed as "proceeding from the Son." Following Augustine's teaching, the phrase *filioque* ("and the Son") was added by the Western church to the above creed at the Council of Toledo in 589. The Eastern church rejected the *filioque* doctrine, and the creed constituted confessional grounds for the split between East and West which had already taken place in practice.

Although other aspects of the Spirit were occasionally discussed, the procession of the Spirit continued to occupy theologians in the West. Anselm of Canterbury brought the debate into the era of scholasticism and, although reason as proof of doctrine was unevenly received, *filioque* remained the standard of the church. Peter Lombard argued from Scripture for *filioque,* and the fourth Lateran Council again espoused Trinitarianism and *filioque.* Although Aquinas rejected reason as a means to know the distinctions of the Divine Persons, he affirmed that the spirit proceeds from the special relationship that exists between the Father and the Son. Such discussions as this continued into the fifteenth century, when the Council of Florence again attempted to unite the Western and Eastern churches. The *filioque* idea was reaffirmed and, although a cosmetic change of wording was made in an attempt to satisfy the Eastern church, the Greek Orthodox Church rejected the substance of the creed. The position of the Roman Catholic Church has remained essentially unchanged, and the rift between East and West over this issue remains to the present.

The Reformation. Although other aspects of the Spirit's work were of importance in medieval theology—including sanctification and illumination—it was not until the Reformation that the work of the Spirit in the church was truly rediscovered. This was due at least in part to the rejection of Rome's dogma of church tradition as the guarantor of correct Scripture interpretation and formation of true doctrine. This reaction led to a Reformation stress on the idea of *sola Scriptura* and the work of the Spirit in salvation independent of the Catholic Church's "unbroken succession back to Christ." While Luther rejected "enthusiasm" (the subjective claim of direct guidance by the Spirit independent of Scripture or church structure, he stressed Spirit over structure, and understood the Spirit to be at work through the Word (the gospel), primarily in preaching, and in the sacraments, and therefore in salvation. The Spirit works in salvation by influencing the soul to reliance, by faith, on Christ. Faith is itself a mystical gift of God whereby the believers *mit Gott ein Kuche werden* (become kneaded into one cake with God). Without the grace and work of the Spirit man is incapable of making himself acceptable to God or of having saving faith (cf. *The Bondage of the Will*, 1525). This is accomplished by the Holy Spirit through the Word of God. Salvation is thus a gift bestowed by the grace of God, and Luther implies that the Word (the Gospel) as preached is primarily the efficacious Word of God *after* the Spirit works upon the heart of the hearer. For Luther, the Word is the main sacrament, for faith and the Holy Spirit are conveyed through the preaching and the teaching of the gospel (Rom. 10:17); baptism and the Lord's Supper are signs of the "sacrament of the Word," in that they proclaim the Word of God. Luther favored the preached Word over the written Word, but did not hold the two to be mutually exclusive. To be Christian the preaching of the church had to be faithful to the Scripture; but to be faithful to Scripture, the church had to preach.

The Word—primarily the incarnate Logos—is God's channel for the Spirit. Man brings the Word of the Scripture to the ear, but God infuses his Spirit into the heart; the word of Scripture thus becomes the Word of God (*Lectures on Psalms; Epistle to the Romans*). No one can rightly understand the Word of Scripture without the working of the Spirit; where the Word is, the Spirit inevitably follows. The Spirit does not operate independent of the Word. Luther resisted the enthusiasts' sharp distinction between inward and outward Word. On the other hand, he rejected the Roman Catholic idea that the Spirit is identified with church office and that the sacraments are effective in and of themselves (*ex opere operato*). Thus the Spirit makes Christ present in the sacraments and in Scripture; only when the Spirit makes Christ present in the word is it God's own living Word. Otherwise the Scripture is letter, a law—it merely describes, it is only history. But as preaching, the Word is gospel (as opposed to law); the Spirit makes it so. The Spirit is not bound to the Word; he exists in God's eternal glory, away from the Word and our world. But as revealing Spirit he does not come without the Word.

Melanchthon followed Luther with few exceptions. Although allowing more room for man's response to the gospel than did Luther, he still stressed the primary work of the Spirit in salvation. Melanchthon showed more flexibility than Luther in the issue of the real presence in the Lord's Supper (cf. the Wittenberg Concord), but was in basic agreement with Luther as seen in the Augsburg Confession and its *Apology*. Zwingli departed from Luther and Melanchthon over the work of the Spirit in the sacraments, denying the necessity of baptism and asserting the largely commemorative significance of the Lord's Supper. The radical Reformers, too, were at odds with Luther and Melanchthon, and taught the priority of immediate revelation over Scripture. Lutherans and Catholics alike were condemned by the *Schwarmer* (fanatics) for their dependence upon the letter of Scripture instead of making the Bible subject to tests of religious experience.

Calvin taught that the Spirit works in regeneration to illumine the mind to receive the benefits of Christ and seals them in the heart. By the Spirit the heart of a man is opened to the penetrating power of the Word and sacraments. Calvin went beyond Luther in asserting that not only is the preached Word the agent of the Spirit, but the Bible is *in its essence* the Word of God (Genevan Catechism). The Spirit works in the reading of Scripture as well as in the preaching of the Word, and the Word—preached or read—is efficacious through the work of the Holy Spirit. The divine origin of Scripture is certified by the witness of the Spirit; the Scripture is the Word of God given by the Spirit's guidance through limited human speech. Thus the exegete must inquire after God's intention in giving Scripture for us (e.g., in the modern application of the OT; *Institutes* 2.8.8). The highest proof of Scripture derives from the fact that God in person speaks in it, i.e., in the secret testimony of the Spirit (*Inst.* 1.7.4). We feel the testimony of the Spirit engraved like a seal on our hearts with the result that it seals the cleansing and sacrifice of Christ. The Holy Spirit is the bond by which Christ unites us to himself (*Inst.* 3.1.1). Although Calvin rejected rational proofs as a basis for authenticating Scripture, interconfessional battles later caused the rigidifying of Reformed thought, and a tradition of scholastic proofs was developed to overcome the subjectivism of Calvin's authentication theory (cf. the Canons of Dort).

A seventeenth century reaction to strict Calvinism arose in Holland among the followers of James Arminius. Arminius rejected strict predestination, allowing for man's freedom to reject God's offer of grace. The Arminian position was denounced by the Synod of Dort, but had great influence in England. John Wesley grew up in early eighteenth century England within this climate of Arminianism, and through him Methodism was given its distinctive Arminian character. For Wesley, God acts in cooperation with, but not in violation of, free human response in the matter of saving faith. God does not merely dispense upon man justifying grace, nor does man simply acquire such grace by believing. There is rather a unified process of God's giving and man's receiving. The Holy Spirit convicts of sin and also bears witness of justification. Thereafter the Holy Spirit continues to work in man in sanctification, such that the believer feels in his heart the mighty workings of the Spirit of God. God continually "breathes" upon man's soul, and the soul "breathes unto God"—a fellowship of spiritual respiration by which the life of God in the soul is sustained. Sanctification—the renewal of man in the image of God, in righteousness and true holiness—is effected by the Spirit through faith. It includes being saved from sin and being perfected in love. Works are necessary to a continuance of faith, and "entire sanctification," perfection, is the goal of every believer.

The Modern Period. While seventeenth century radical Puritanism produced the Quakers with their emphasis on subjective experience of the Holy Spirit (the Inner Light of George Fox)—such that Scripture is only a secondary source of knowledge for faith and practice (Robert Barclay, *Apology*)—eighteenth century Methodism expressed a more balanced approach to the work of the Spirit. The focus of later Methodism on the work of the Spirit after conversion as an experience of divine grace has found development in the modern Holiness Movement, represented by churches in the Christian Holiness Association.

Another development that can be traced to Methodism's stress on sanctification is the twentieth century reawakening of Pentecostalism. Stemming from earlier emphases upon "second experience," Pentecostalism has placed great importance upon the "baptism of the Holy Spirit," which is seen as the completion of a two-stage process of salvation. Since the inception of this modern movement at the turn of the century, speaking in tongues has been proclaimed as the main sign of Spirit baptism, although other "gifts of the Spirit"—notably healing—are also emphasized. From its fundamentalist/biblicist beginning the Pentecostal movement has grown into what is loosely called the charismatic movement, which now touches all of Protestantism and has made inroads into Roman Catholicism. This movement generally proclaims a distinct experience of "Spirit baptism" and, as a rule, focuses on speaking in tongues as the manifestation of that experience.

One of the most significant twentieth century developments in understanding the Holy Spirit was made in the teaching of Karl Barth. Barth was a Reformed theologian who was largely responsible for the introduction of neoorthodoxy, the so-called dialectical or crisis theology. Barth and others broke with classical liberalism in the first decades of the twentieth century, denying liberalism's theology of pious religious self-consciousness, its man-centeredness (Schleiermacher; Ritschl; Feuerbach). Barth emphasized the "infinite qualitative distinction" between man and God, and prophetically proclaimed God's *nein* to all of man's attempts at self-righteousness. Barth's *Letter to the Romans* sounded this note of man's "crisis"—the acknowledgment that what man knows of God, God has himself revealed. Barth developed his idea of God's self-revelation in terms of the doctrine of the Word of God (*Church Dogmatics* I/1 and I/2). First and most importantly, Jesus is the incarnate Logos, the Word of God. The Word of God is subsequently found in the preaching of the gospel, and "among the words of Scripture" (cf. Luther's doctrine of Spirit and Word). The Word of God is God himself in Holy Scripture. Scripture is holy and the Word of God, because by the Holy Spirit it became and will become to the church a witness to divine revelation. This witness is not identical to the revelation; it is not itself revelation, but the witness to it. Faith in Jesus as the Christ, specifically in Jesus' resurrection, is effected through the work of the Holy Spirit. The subjective "in Spirit" is the counterpart to the objective "in Christ." God's grace is manifested both in the objective revelation of God in Christ and man's subjective appropriation of this revelation through the Spirit. According to Scripture, God's revelation occurs in our enlightenment by the Holy Spirit to a knowledge of God's Word. The outpouring of the Spirit is God's revelation. In this reality we are free to be God's children and to know, love, and praise him in his revelation. The Spirit as subjective reality of God's revelation makes possible and real the existence of Christianity in the world. For, Barth observes, "where the Spirit of the Lord is, there is freedom" (II Cor. 3:17); God in his freedom discloses himself to man and so makes man free for him (*Evangelical Theology*, pp. 53ff.).

Concluding Observations. This sketch shows some of the diversity in the development of Christian thinking about the Holy Spirit. It is ironic that God's eschatological gift to man has so often been a point of contention and division among Christians. Since the road ahead appears no less difficult than the way we have come, we would do well to be humbly mindful of God's sovereignty and of our weakness.

Because God in Christ has initiated the messianic age with its outpouring of the Spirit, man's relationship to God has been forever changed. No longer can the law be used as a means of exclusion and oppression of the disenfranchised: Jesus has preached the messianic gospel of release to the captive, sight to the blind, and good news to the poor; the new law of life has been written on the hearts of men. Thus we must abhor any new legalism which uses the Scripture to exclude and oppress—this is to turn the good news of Christ into "the letter that kills." We must, rather, recognize the "God-breathed" character of Scripture, and the "Spirit that makes alive." Only so will the Scripture be profitable. Conversely, the Spirit cannot be claimed as the mark of an elite, as that which distinguishes and divides. The gospel of Jesus Christ includes the message that the Holy Spirit has been poured out on all flesh. All abuses of Scripture and the Spirit must hear God's message: "The promise is to those who are near, and to those who are afar off, as many as the Lord our God will call."

T. S. Caulley

See also God, Doctrine of; Spiritual Gifts; Tongues, Speaking in; Baptism of the Spirit; Charismatic Movement.

Bibliography. C. K. Barrett, *The Holy Spirit and the Gospel Tradition;* F. D. Bruner, *A Theology of the Holy Spirit;* J. D. G. Dunn, *Baptism in the Holy Spirit* and *Jesus and the Spirit;* M. Green, *I Believe in the Holy Spirit;* H. Gunkel, *The Influence of the Holy Spirit;* G. S. Hendry, *The Holy Spirit in Christian Theology;* G. T. Montague, *The Holy Spirit: Growth of a Biblical Tradition;* C. F. D. Moule, *The Holy Spirit;* P. D. Opsahl, ed., *The Holy Spirit in the Life of the Church;* M. Ramsey, *Holy Spirit;* E. Schweizer, *The Holy Spirit;* H. B. Swete, *The Holy Spirit in the Ancient Church* and *The Holy Spirit in the New Testament;* H. Watkins-Jones, *The Holy Spirit from Arminius to Wesley.*

Holy Week. The week preceding Easter, observing in a special manner the passion and death of Jesus Christ. It may also be called the Greater Week in remembrance of the great work performed by God during that week. It may be called the Paschal Week in reference to the coming resurrection. Athanasius of Alexandria used the phrase "Holy Week" in the fourth century. It is sometimes referred to as the week of remission because confession is one of the experiences asked of some Christians in preparation for the celebration of Easter. Eastern Christians sometimes call it the week of salvation.

In the early development of Holy Week only Good Friday and Holy Saturday were designated as holy days. Some areas referred to a triduum of three days, including Easter Sunday morning within Holy Week. Holy Thursday officially became a holy day in the fourth century. Wednesday was added to commemorate the plot of Judas to give Jesus over to his enemies. The other days of the week were added by the middle of the fourth century. In general, most of the Holy Week observances originated in Jerusalem and were adopted by Europe. Before the Council of Nicaea the great feast which was celebrated was the Christian Passover on the night of Holy Saturday.

After the medieval period Holy Week lost quite a bit of its appeal. Pius XII attempted to give it central importance to the church in the 1950s. It is now considered by many to be the heart of the Catholic Church's yearly celebration of the events of the life, death, and resurrection of Jesus Christ. The central mystery of redemption is relived during Holy Week.

Holy Thursday, or Maundy Thursday, as part of Holy Week is properly called Thursday of the Lord's Supper. It commemorates the changing of bread and wine into the body and blood of Jesus Christ. Mass on Holy Thursday is celebrated in the evening.

Good Friday is the anniversary of the crucifixion of our Lord; it is a day of sorrow. Its full title is "Friday of the passion and death of the Lord." The liturgical section includes (1) the reading service, (2) the veneration of the cross, (3) the Communion service. The service of the stations of the cross is optional.

Holy Saturday is usually a quiet day of prayer and reflection in preparation for the celebration of the resurrection of our Lord Jesus Christ on Easter Sunday.

T. J. German

See also Ash Wednesday; Maundy Thursday; Good Friday; Holy Saturday; Easter.

Bibliography. W. J. O'Shea, *The Meaning of Holy Week;* C. Howell, *Preparing for Easter;* J. Gaillard, *Holy Week and Easter;* L. Bouyer, *The Paschal Mystery: Meditations on the Last Three Days of Holy Week;* M. Tierney, *Holy Week: A Commentary.*

Homologoumena. Those writings of the NT universally recognized in the church as canonical, as opposed to those which are disputed. This classification was first made by Origen, who included in the homologoumena the four Gospels, thirteen epistles of Paul, I Peter, I John, Acts, and Revelation (Eusebius, *History* 6.25.3ff.). Eusebius of Caesarea follows Origen in this listing, but he includes Hebrews (among the epistles of Paul). Revelation is included "if it should seem correct to do so" (Eusebius, *History* 3.25.1ff.).

W. C. Weinrich

See also ANTILEGOMENA; BIBLE, CANON OF.

Bibliography. B. F. Westcott, *A General Survey of the Canon and Text of the NT;* C. R. Gregory, *Canon and Text of the NT.*

Homoousion. The word became an important theological term when it was employed by the Council of Nicaea in 325 to describe the relationship between the Son of God and the Father. Later it was used to describe the relationship of the Holy Spirit to the Father and the Son and thus was instrumental in the developing doctrine of the Trinity. *Homoousios* literally means same (*homo*) in substance (*ousia*) or, as it is sometimes translated, consubstantial.

However, in order to determine precisely what is meant when it is asserted that the son is *homoousios* with the Father, one needs to know the sense of sameness and of substance that is being appealed to. It is clear that the fathers at Nicaea did not think of *homoousios* from the standpoint of Aristotle's category of primary *ousia*, in which *ousia* is considered simply as an individual thing. In that sense, to say that the Father and the Son are *homoousios* would be to say that these are simply different terms representing the same single reality, expressing no difference, being numerically identical. There is evidence that the use of *homoousios* was condemned at the synod of Antioch in 268, because Paul of Samosata employed it precisely with this monarchian sense.

Neither did the fathers make complete use of Aristotle's secondary category in which *ousia* is taken as a genus to which various species belong. The Arians seemed to understand the orthodox view in this sense, for they objected that a doctrine of *homoousios* would have the illogical result of proposing a division of the indivisible divine substance. The fathers did use many analogies of relationships in this second category (such as man and mankind), but they also used analogies that express a much closer relationship than members of a genus (such as the relationship of rays to the sun or a river to a spring). At any rate, they were careful to point out the limitations of such analogies when applied to the Godhead.

In the teaching of Nicene and Post-Nicene orthodoxy the essential relationship between the Father and the Son (and this was applied by extension to the Holy Spirit also in the Post-Nicene period) was seen as one in which the Son derives his *ousia* from the Father, so that they are not numerically the same, and so that the Father is properly the source of the Son's being. Nevertheless, it was asserted that in this (eternal) derivation, the Son is and remains *homoousios* with the Father, so that what the Father is and has is exactly what the Son is and has. Thus there exists (in the classic statement of Archibald Robertson) a "full and unbroken continuation of the Being of the Father in the Son." While this use of *homoousios* still leaves many questions unanswered, the use of the term was regarded as a necessary one in that it seemed to express better than any other term an essential part of the biblical description of the Father-Son relationship in such a way as to decisively refute the Arian doctrine that the Son was a created being, wholly other from the Father, having his own beginning.

C. A. BLAISING

See also NICAEA, COUNCIL OF; HYPOSTATIC UNION.

Bibliography. Athanasius, *Defense of the Nicene Council;* J. N. D. Kelly, *Early Christian Doctrines;* G. C. Stead, *Divine Substance.*

Homosexuality. Sexual desire directed toward members of one's own sex. Female homosexuality is frequently called lesbianism, from Lesbos, where the Greek poetess Sappho (reputedly homosexual) lived *ca.* 600 B.C. Traditionally homosexuality was the sin for which Sodom was destroyed by divine judgment, hence the popular term "sodomy." This interpretation depends upon uncertain translation, while Ezek. 16:49ff. and Sir. 16:8ff. give other reasons for the judgment. The assumption of homosexuality in Sodom dates from the Greek occupation of Palestine, when "the Greek sin" seriously endangered Jewish youth and strong scriptural warning was necessary.

Homosexuality had been condemned in both Leviticus (18:22; 20:13), where it is abhorrent to God, defiling, punishable by death, and in Deuteronomy (23:18), where it is forbidden to bring the hire of harlot or homosexual ("dog") into the house of God in payment of religious vows, both being abhorrent to God. It is usually assumed that the male cult prostitutes common in heathen shrines but forbidden in Israel (Deut. 23:17), though sometimes prevalent (I Kings 14:24; 15:12; 22:46; II Kings 23:7), were homosexual.

Some hold that tolerance (and institutionalizing) of homosexual prostitution contributed much to the decay of Greek youth and army. Roman law punished it severely as early as the third century B.C., later protecting minors and forbidding the use of premises on pain of death—even by burning. Rome's concern was probably more military than moral.

Such laws show the practice ancient and widespread. Today, it has been claimed, 4–5 percent of white adult males are homosexual, 10–20 percent bisexual, the remainder heterosexual; but innumerable gradations must be recognized:

a "six point scale" of degrees of homo-, bi-, and heterosexuality oversimplifies the situation.

Early Christian reaction is expressed by Paul: homosexuals "will not inherit the kingdom of God" (I Cor. 6:9–10); because of idolatry God gave the heathen up "to dishonorable passions. Their women exchanged natural relations for unnatural, and the men likewise gave up natural relations with women and were consumed with passion for one another, men committing shameless acts with men and receiving in their own persons the due penalty for their error" (Rom. 1:26–27). Here the association with idolatry, the unnaturalness of the practice, and the divine judgment which abandons individuals to it (an echo of Sodom?) are all significant. The Sodom story recurs in Jude 7 ("unnatural lust") and II Pet. 2:6–7 ("lust of defiling passion"), perpetuating the tradition that homosexuals were under divine ban.

The Didache extends the commandments to forbid corrupting of boys; Athenagoras classes pederasty with adultery. Perhaps influenced by the Roman attitude, Christian canon law laid down penalties ranging from nine years' penance to permanent excommunication. On the whole, the church treated homosexuality as a sin needing spiritual cure rather than a crime for magistrates to punish—unless linked with heresy, when the punishment was death. Earthquakes threatening Byzantium ("Sodom") were blamed upon homosexuals.

In Britain from the sixteenth century the law prescribed (though rarely exacted) death. The jurist William Blackstone (eighteenth century) wrote: "Homosexuality, the crime against nature, one which the voice of nature and reason and the express law of God determine to be capital. Of which we have a signal instance long before the Jewish dispensation, in the destruction of the cities by fire from heaven, so that this is a universal not merely a provincial precept." In the nineteenth century imprisonment was substituted.

In recent decades the prevalence of blackmail and suicide, the difficulties of detection and punishment ("sending homosexuals to prison resembles sending alcoholics to a brewery"), led to reconsideration. Private acts by consenting adults of responsible age without duress are commonly no longer crimes. Some interpret this change as tacit public approval or indifference. Tolerance of homosexuals has greatly increased, within and outside the churches (and within the Christian ministry), largely through (misnamed) "gay" protestation, publicity, clubs, and by uninhibited discussion of the condition's causes.

Causes of Homosexuality. The attempt to understand causes is very recent, and important to a Christian judgment.

(1) Since the individual's earliest sexual curiosity and experience is usually with his own body, then with others of the same sex, a puberty phase of homosexual interest is normal. Some adult homosexual interest may therefore merely be arrested development, due to extreme shyness, introversion, disfigurement, fear of rejection, only-child inability to socialize, or some physical deficiency. This arrested-development explanation makes many heterosexual men treat homosexuals with contempt, as "just kids."

(2) Similarly, after normal heterosexual outturning to the other sex has taken place, an unhappy love affair, an illness, pathological fear of women/men, or the like may lead to regression, a return to the furtive but safer relief of early puberty.

(3) Environmental causes include artificial all-male society in one-sex school, army, or prison; a wrong relationship between, or with, parents, or with any oversexed adult; male resentment, or protest, against aggressive, predatory, overdominatng women, or by women against similar men; unfortunate conflict in childhood and/or puberty, with relatives, guardians, teachers who repressed, scorned, terrified, or disgusted the growing mind.

(4) Constitutional causes include genetic or hormone factors that condition the individual from birth to respond sexually to his or her own sex; there seems no doubt that in some cases the homosexual disposition can be inborn, prenatal in origin, wholly involuntary.

(5) Vicious causes include unbridled sensuality, flagrant exhibitionism, and the mischievous desire to shock; exploitation by the depraved of the young, the timid, the mentally unstable, for carnal indulgence; duress, bribery, or blackmail.

Even so slight an analysis of causes has important consequences. A homosexual tendency arising from psychological, accidental, or environmental influences is said sometimes to yield, as do some other deep-seated disorders, to psychological treatment by enticing the underlying, subconscious cause into full consciousness and self-understanding. Constitutionally homosexual disposition, on the other hand, is probably incurable.

Further, an involuntary predisposition, traceable to psychological distortion, infantile terrors, accidental situations, or congenital factors, whether or not complicated by later unhappy experiences, is obviously not a fitting target for moral condemnation or contempt, but for sympathy.

In Karl Barth's phrase, much homosexual inclination is "a moral malady"; it is no more to be blamed than left-handedness or colorblindness. To borrow convenient terms of distinction, it is the recognition of constitutional homosexuality, in men and women, that has moderated Christian judgments in recent years, even when homosexual practice (homosexualism) remains condemned.

A Christian View. This discrimination between condition and conduct is essential to a fair Christian reaction. Homosexual acts continue to arouse disgust. Though ignorance, and fear for the vulnerable, mingle with it, moral repulsion is sometimes a healthy reaction—as that toward wanton cruelty. Aquinas first articulated the age-old intuition reflected in Leviticus, in Deuteronomy (where homosexuality is linked with bestiality as perversion), and in Paul that homosexual activity is essentially unnatural, a perversion of the natural order linking sex with procreation, and so defiance of divine natural law. Society still disapproves, but discovery of homosexual situations involving those we have loved, trusted, and admired does affect our judgment of their character, trustworthiness, and quality. Secrecy and deceit are therefore still necessary. Known homosexual behavior alienates from "normal" society, making normal relationships more difficult to establish, thus leading to frustration and despair. Though the Sodom argument be abandoned, Scripture reprobates such practices, while Christian love must condemn the use, for sensual purposes only, of another's body, mind, and emotions if, as seems inevitable in unnatural relations, that degrades and undervalues the partner. Finally, in the constant conflict between flesh and spirit in Christian life, deliberate cultivation of homosexual sensuality can have no defensible place. For all these reasons, homosexual activity is wrong.

But the homosexual condition, until indulged, is innocent, and should be cleared of the guilt feeling that may drive into deeper introversion. Like all congenital deviations from the normal, established homosexuality has to be accepted and lived with. The resulting problem is acute, but no more so than for heterosexuals, the widower/widow, the impotent, the single who long to marry and cannot or (through inherited insanity) should not. For all such, prostitution or promiscuity may offer constant temptation, but one to be resisted by the help of God. For neither heterosexual nor homosexual is the situation culpable; but actions to which the situation may incline them remain sinful, as unnatural, degrading, contrary to Christian concern for total welfare of others, inimical to religious devotion and spiritual progress, and no solution to their problem.

But to say this is to acknowledge that the existence and acuteness of the problem challenge Christian compassion and ministry, and call for ever improving sex education in a Christian context. A mature society will recognize prevalent homosexual activity not as "liberation" but as a symptom of moral malaise; an alert church will not ostracize but befriend those whose constitution and circumstances make Christian living harder for them than for most. R. E. O. White

Bibliography. F. Lake, "The Homosexual Man," *First Aid in Counselling;* H. Kimball-Jones, *Toward a Christian Understanding of the Homosexual;* R. Lovelace, *Homosexuality and the Church;* R. Moss, *Christians and Homosexuality;* N. W. Pittenger, *Time for Consent.*

Honesty. Originally indicating whatever in conduct deserved to be honored (hence Acts 6:3; Rom. 12:17), honesty in later usage means truthfulness, openness, avoidance of deceit, either in practical affairs or in personal character. Thus, stealing and burglary are strictly forbidden (Exod. 20:15; 22:2); commercial fraud by false weights and measures, "balances of deceit," is frequently condemned by law (Lev. 19:35–36; Deut. 25:13–16) and by the prophets (Amos 8:4–5; Mic. 6:11; cf. Hos. 12:7; Ezek. 45:10ff., Ps. 24:3ff.). In the NT, thieves and liars are excluded from the kingdom and city of God (I Cor. 6:9–10; Rev. 21:8, 27; cf. I Pet. 4:15). The fraudulent stratagem of Ananias and Sapphira to obtain Christian charity as dependents while retaining private resources is punished with death. Paul takes special care to have representatives of contributing churches travel with him when delivering the collection for the poor at Jerusalem, so "providing things honest" and "avoiding blame" (Acts 20:4–5; Rom. 12:17; II Cor. 8:18–21).

In the more personal sense of integrity of character, Jesus demands complete honesty in his prohibition of oaths, urging in effect that your "yes" means "yes" and your "no" means "no" (Matt. 5:33–37), and also in his reiterated condemnation of hypocrisy. So "the Lord abhors . . . deceitful men" (Ps. 5:6); deceitfulness is specially condemned throughout Psalms and the Wisdom literature. For Paul it is a clear symptom of pagan decadence (Rom. 1:29; cf. 3:13). The Johannine writings relate knowing the truth with speaking truth, doing truth, and truth indwelling the soul; only such complete "walking in truth" is acceptable before God who is light, Christ who is the truth (e.g., John 8:12; I John 1:6, 8; 2:4; II John 1–2; III John 3).

The deepest motive for Christian honesty lies

in adoration of God as utterly true, faithful, "covenant-keeping," and requiring truth in the inward being (Ps. 51:6). Additional motives are the law of love (Rom. 13:9–10; I Cor. 6:8; Eph. 4:15) and Christian unity, which dishonesty destroys (Eph. 4:25–28; cf. Col. 3:9). Good faith, moreover, is listed among the fruits of the Spirit (Gal. 5:22).

In later Christian ethics honesty is usually treated as an element in social justice, until greatly overshadowed in modern thinking by avaricious materialism, the exigencies of war propaganda, situational sophistries, and political expediency. Of all Christian groups perhaps the Society of Friends has cultivated the tenderest conscience for the simple precision of speech and consistency of action with profession which Christian honesty requires. R. E. O. White

See also Ethics, Biblical.

Honor. The respect and esteem enjoyed by someone or something. In Scripture man is usually the subject, although honor is frequently applied to God. Man's honor is often associated with his rank in the community (Ps. 45:9) and his authority (Esth. 10:2). Honor is given to God because of who he is (Lev. 10:3; I Chr. 29:12) and what he has done (Dan. 4:37).

The meanings of the Hebrew root *kbd* and Greek *timē*—words translated "honor"—are much wider in scope than the English implies. *Kābēd* literally means "to be heavy, weighty" but is used almost exclusively in figurative ways, the most common being to be honorable. For a man to be "weighty" in society is understood figuratively as his being important, respected, and honored. *Timē* also includes the idea of value. Some of the other translations of the two words are splendor, majesty, beauty, respect, and glory, the latter being the most common.

Honor is often paired with other concepts. We read of honor and glory (Ps. 8:5), majesty (I Chr. 16:27), riches (Ps. 96:6), dignity (Esth. 6:3), peace (Rom. 2:10), praise and fame (Deut. 26:19), favor (Ps. 84:11), immortality (Rom. 2:7), life (Prov. 21:21), gifts and rewards (Dan. 2:6), humility (Prov. 15:33), possessions and wealth (II Chr. 1:11), light, gladness, and joy (Esth. 8:16), power, wisdom, might, and blessing (Rev. 5:12), and thanksgiving (Rev. 7:12).

Man is told to honor his parents (Deut. 5:16; Matt. 19:19), widows (I Tim. 5:3), the emperor (I Pet. 2:17), elders (I Tim. 5:17), the elderly (Lev. 19:32), masters (I Tim. 6:1), the good slave (Prov. 27:18), wives (I Pet. 3:7; I Thess. 4:4), one another (Rom. 12:10), all men (I Pet. 2:17), and men like Epaphroditus (Phil. 2:29). Contrary to secular custom, honor is to be given even to those of lower rank (I Cor. 12:23–24).

Likewise, we are to give honor to God (Rev. 4:11). Scripture makes this clear in many of its doxologies (I Tim. 1:17; 6:16; Rev. 5:12; 7:12; cf. 4:9, 11).

By virtue of their place in creation, human beings have been given honor (Ps. 8:5). God will also give honor to man if he will "embrace" wisdom (Prov. 4:8), honor God (I Sam. 2:30), and serve Christ (John 12:26). Honor will also be one of the believer's eschatological gifts (Rom. 2:7, 10).

Dishonor can be a sign of sin (Rom. 1:24), although not necessarily (cf. Job; II Cor. 6:8; I Pet. 3:13–14).

Honor is one of the distinctives which is to characterize the relationships between men and God. Man is to honor his fellow man (Rom. 12:10), Christ (John 5:23; Phil. 1:20), and God (Prov. 14:31). Christ honors God (John 8:49), and God honors man (John 12:26) and Christ (Heb. 2:9).

W. D. Mounce

See also Glory.

Bibliography. W. B. Wallis, *WBE*, I, 808; J. N. Oswalt, *TWOT*, I, 426–28; W. Harrelson, *IDB*, II, 639–40; J. Pedersen, *Israel, Its Life and Culture*, IV, 649ff.; S. Aalen, *NIDNTT*, II, 48–52; J. Schneider, *TDNT*, VIII, 169–80.

Hooker, Richard (1554–1600). A major Anglican theologian. Hooker was born near Exeter and educated at Oxford, after which he became a leading preacher in London. He was a noted opponent of the Puritans, who maintained that the established Church of England had failed to carry through a fully scriptural reformation. Hooker answered the Puritan critics of Anglicanism in his epoch-making *Laws of Ecclesiastical Polity* in eight books (only five were published in his lifetime). Whitgift, Archbishop of Canterbury, had encouraged this project, and Queen Elizabeth I praised its completion. In order to defend the Anglican establishment Hooker circumvented both the Puritan appeal to Scripture and the Catholic appeal to church tradition by going behind both to the primary source of authority: natural law, which is implanted in people's minds by God and comes to full expression in the state. The voice of the people is the voice of God, but is articulated through the civil magistrate. While Hooker held that Scripture contained what is necessary for salvation, still the law of nature was primary. As times change, specific laws (including Scripture) can be changed, though always in accordance with fundamental natural law. Thus the church cannot be held subject to the letter of Scripture or of tradition; it is free to adjust itself to its own historical context. In practice, Hooker's position tended to uphold

Erastianism (state control over the church) and royal absolutism, though his idea that government must ultimately rest on popular consent would later influence Locke and Burke in a libertarian direction. Hooker's Christology was, from the Calvinist perspective, somewhat subordinationist. He had little to say on the atonement. However, his *Laws* would remain the classical defense of the Anglican establishment, a monument of noble English prose, and an exemplar of massive scholarship. D. F. Kelly

See also Anglican Communion; Natural Law.

Bibliography. *The Works of Richard Hooker,* 3 vols.; J. S. Marshall, *Hooker and the Anglican Tradition;* P. Munz, *The Place of Hooker in the History of Thought;* C. J. Sisson, *The Judicious Marriage of Mr. Hooker and the Birth of "The Laws of Ecclesiastical Polity."*

Hope. *Elpis* (Hebrew *bāṭaḥ*) had in Greek and Roman times a neutral meaning as expectation of good or evil. Some, like Thucydides, treat it cynically; others, like Menander, extol it; Sanskrit poets class it among evils. Paul characterizes the Gentile world as *elpida mē echontes* (Eph. 2:12). For OT writers (except Ecclesiastes?) God is "the Hope of Israel" (Jer. 14:8). They trust in him (Jer. 17:7), wait passively upon him (Ps. 42:5), or actively anticipate his blessing (Ps. 62:5). Some Israelites cherished materialistic hopes for a messianic kingdom; but the Anglican Article VII denies that the old fathers looked only for transitory promises, since such as Daniel anticipated the resurrection (Dan. 12:2).

Christ himself is described as the Christian hope (I Tim. 1:1), and by his resurrection the specifically Christian virtue of hope is bestowed on the regenerate, who abound in hope through the Spirit (Rom. 15:13). (1) This hope relates to salvation and is an essential grace, like faith and love (I Cor. 13:13); but where faith refers to past and present, hope includes the future (Rom. 8:24–25). (2) Its object is the ultimate blessedness of God's kingdom (Acts 2:26; Titus 1:2). (3) It produces the moral fruits of joyful confidence in God (Rom. 8:28), unashamed patience in tribulation (Rom. 5:3), and perseverance in prayer. (4) It anticipates an actual righteousness (Gal. 5:5) and is thus good (II Thess. 2:16), blessed (Titus 2:13), and glorious (Col. 1:27). (5) It stabilizes the soul like an anchor by linking it to God's steadfastness (Heb. 3:6; 6:18–19). (6) It was generated in the OT fathers by God's promise first given to Abraham (Rom. 4:18), then embraced by Israel (Acts 26:6–7), and proclaimed by Paul as the hope of the gospel.

The one in whom hope is placed is sometimes called *elpis,* e.g., Jesus in I Tim. 1:1; the Thessalonians in I Thess. 2:19; or God in Jer. 17:7. Similarly the thing hoped for is *elpis* (I John 3:3; Col. 1:5), i.e., hope stored up in the heavens, expectation focused on the parousia and voiced in the cry *Maranatha.*

Elpis is a collective hope in the body of Christ. The Thessalonians are exhorted to hope for reunion with their deceased brethren (I Thess. 4:13–18), and ministers hope for their converts (II Cor. 1:7), desiring to present them perfect (Col. 1:28). Christ as the chief Shepherd expresses this hope that his own will together behold his glory (John 17:24), and this consummation is guaranteed by the earnest of the Spirit within Christian hearts and the church (Rom. 8:16–17).

D. H. Tongue

See also Hope, Theology of.

Bibliography. E. Hoffmann, *NIDNTT,* II, 238ff.; E. Brunner, *Eternal Hope;* E. H. Cousins, ed., *Hope and the Future of Man;* K. Hahnhart, "Paul's Hope in the Face of Death," *JBL* 88:445ff.; P. S. Minear, *Christian Hope and the Second Coming;* R. Bultmann and K. N. Rengstorf, *TDNT,* II, 517ff.; E. Hoffmann, *NIDNTT,* II, 238ff.

Hope, Theology of. In the late 1960s a new approach to theology emerged. Its early leaders were Germans who attempted to do theology and understand the mission of the church from a shift in interpretative perspective. This new approach is a resurrection-centered theology, in the awareness that Christ's resurrection is the beginning and promise of that which is yet to come. The Christian is to be seen as a "hoper," who is impatient with evil and death in this present age. The church is seen as a disquieting entity, confronting society with all its human securities, empires, and contrived absolutes. The church awaits a coming city and, therefore, exposes all the cities made with hands. This form of theology exists in dialogue with other visions of the future, especially Marxism, and it stands against the individualism of liberal pietist and existential theologies. In some ways it is orthodox, and yet politically it can be quite radical. Third World churches have been deeply influenced by the theology of hope.

Undoubtedly a central figure of this new theology is Jürgen Moltmann. The most influential work by Moltmann is his *Theology of Hope,* published in English in 1967. This book is merely part of a wealth of material now being produced by Moltmann. It is a work of sustained spiritual force and systematic power, written when Western culture was in great ferment. *Theology of Hope* speaks of an understanding of God as being ahead of us and the one who will make all things new. He is known now in his promises. It speaks to a world vividly aware of the "not yet" dimensions of human and social existence, and of the fact that hope at its human level is of the stuff of meaningful existence. Within this sort of situation, sustained by a renewed confidence in the eschatological or apocalyptic vision of Scripture, and reacting to the individualistic exaggerations of theological existentialism (e.g., Bultmann), Moltmann has sought to rethink theology.

Eschatology is not to be seen as the last chapter in a theology textbook but the perspective from which all else is to be understood and given its proper meaning. For Moltmann eschatology is the key or central concept from which everything else in Christian thought is set.

Moltmann sees the entire story of Israel as a unique historic pilgrimage as Israel is confronted by the God of promise. Israel's entire identity is in light of the promises of God. In Jesus Christ the future kingdom is present—but as future kingdom. His resurrection is the firstfruits of *the* resurrection and can have meaning only within that universal horizon of meaning. Christian life and salvation are firstfruits, living in the promise of the future of God in Christ.

The church is to be seen as the people of hope, experiencing hope in the God who is present in his promises. The coming kingdom gives the church a much broader vision of reality than a "merely" private vision of personal salvation. The church is to contest all the barriers that have been constructed by man for security; it challenges all structures that absolutize themselves, and all barriers erected between peoples in the name of the reality that is to come in Jesus Christ. The coming kingdom creates confronting and transforming vision for the mission of the people of God.

Although Moltmann is perhaps most conspicuous, he is not the only theologian of hope. Lutheran theologian Wolfhart Pannenberg is another who has become quite well known in the United States since the late 60s. His editorship of a programmatic work, *Revelation as History* (1968), and his *Jesus—God and Man* (1968) have already given him a significant place on the theological map. In *Revelation as History,* Pannenberg has produced a key essay containing "Dogmatic Theses on the Doctrine of Revelation." In this work we find an understanding of all reality in terms of the eschaton, the Christ event as the beginning, proleptically, of that future, and of the concept of God as the God of the future. Apocalyptic is the key theological category, for only at the end will God be seen as God, and only in the light of *this* end is the resurrection of Jesus Christ seen in its proper universal context. Pannenberg's massive work on Christology is a further attempt to rethink this crucial doctrine "from the end." Jesus Christ is defended as very God and very man, and the resurrection is defended as an event in history and given meaning by placing it within an apocalyptic conceptual horizon. Here, indeed, is a new and promising attempt to defend and affirm the church's witness to Christ as God and man.

From a much more political emphasis comes the work of Catholic theologian Johannes B. Metz. In his *Theology of the World* (1968) we have a serious attempt to rethink the mission of the church in light of the future orientation of biblical faith. Lutheran theologian Carl Braaten is perhaps the leading American advocate of this sort of theology and its meaning for theology and church. His programmatic work is *The Future of God* (1969).

It is, of course, true that since the publication of Albert Schweitzer's *The Quest of the Historical Jesus* at the turn of the century, the church has been vividly aware of eschatology. But what was to be done with it? Was it merely a first century conceptual "husk" (Harnack)? Was it the vivid mythological language of existential ultimacy (Bultmann)? Was it merely a mistake replaced by the church (Loisy)? *No,* say the theologians of hope. They have studied the biblical witness long and hard. They have listened seriously to the philosophical climate of their time, especially sharpening their historical awareness through the left wing of the Hegelian tradition (Feuerbach, Marx, and Bloch). They contend that the time has come to rethink theology in light of the *telos.*

Theological reflection can take several styles. One approach is to take one doctrine as central and *think from it* to the rest of one's theological agenda. The central doctrine becomes the hub and other doctrines are the spokes of a conceptual wagon wheel. Luther did this with great power with the doctrine of justification; Barth, likewise, with the incarnation of the Son. Theologians of hope have made eschaton their conceptual center. Their first move is to use this center to affirm the meaning and significance of Jesus Christ. The eschaton is not an embarrassment; rather, it gives Christianity both personal and universal significance in a world that thinks, plans, and dreams in terms of future fears, hopes, and schemes. Further, this form of doing theology provides a way of seeing the mission of the church in terms of the larger issues of man in community and the question of revolution. The promise of this effort remains to be fully seen. Surely from their own perspective no theological model can be absolute.

On the critical side, questions certainly arise. It seems that with all the focus on the end, a simple question arises about the beginning. How does the creation and fall fit in? Would it be as easy to conceptualize a sort of dualism with God finally "winning" in the end? Surely this is not contemplated—but what is? Further, Moltmann seems to have much difficulty incorporating any thought of a future judgment as condemnation. But if the Christ-event is the "presence of the future" and if it is the clue to the destiny of all, then is the church in its witness and mission anything more than the harbinger of the truth of all men? Is there no real discussion to be made? Is there no condemnation in the future? Resurrection in the Bible is unto either life *or condemnation.* Finally, is this theology no more than a sign of the times? Because our materialism and narcissism have blinded us to God as a living presence, have we now conjured a theology to somehow account for this by putting him into the future? Has virtue (hope) become the child of tragic necessity? Criticisms such as these, however necessary, need not keep us from exploring the possibilities of thinking "from the *telos.*"

S. M. Smith

Bibliography. F. Herzog, ed., *The Future of Hope;* M. E. Marty and D. G. Peerman, eds., *New Theology No. 5;* W. Capps, *Time Invades the Cathedral;* J. McQuarrie, *Thinking about God,* ch. 20; D. P. Scaer, "Theology of Hope," in *Tensions in Contemporary Theology;* J. M. Robinson and J. B. Cobb, Jr., eds., *Theology As History.*

Hosanna. The Greek form of the Hebrew salutation meaning, "Save now, we beseech thee" (see Ps. 118:25). The six occurrences of the word in the NT are all in connection with the triumphal entry of Jesus into Jerusalem. The cry was taken up not only by the multitude that followed our Lord but also by the children in the temple (Matt. 21:9, 15). These Gospel references indicate that the expression, while originally a prayer addressed to God, also assumed the form of a shout of homage or greeting, equivalent to "Hail" or "Glory to."

The word "hosanna" early passed into liturgical use in Christian worship as an interjection of joy and praise. It is thus found in the Didache (10:6)—"Hosanna to the God of David!" It occurs in the Latin Mass in a form which links it with the Gospel story: "Hosanna in the highest! Blessed is he that cometh in the name of the Lord!" On account of their association with the Roman dogma of transubstantiation, these words were omitted by the English Reformers from the Prayer Book of 1552.

F. Colquhoun

Host, Hosts of Heaven. The word "host" (Heb. *ṣābā'* or *ḥayil;* Gk. *stratia*) is associated in the OT with God's heavenly throne, with the created order, and with divine and human warfare. The heavenly host are the angels of God's council, also called "holy ones" or "sons of God" (I Kings 22:19; cf. Ps. 89:6, 8; Job 1:6; 2:1; 38:7). Although at times the biblical writers consider the heavenly bodies almost naturalistically as markers of time (Gen. 1:16; Isa. 40:26; cf. Neh. 9:6), elsewhere they describe them as exercising a delegated authority over the nations of the earth (Deut. 4:19; 32:8). While the heavenly host is as a whole subservient to God's will and offers him praise (Ps. 103:21), there are also elements of discord within its midst (I Kings 22:21; Job 1:6–12; 15:15), leading to God's final judgment (Ps. 82; Isa. 24:21).

The heavenly host also refers to God's army. The Lord of hosts (Heb. *yhwh ṣĕbā'ôt*) is a title associated with the ark of the covenant and the holy wars of early Israel (I Sam. 4:4; cf. Num. 10:36). In God's saving appearance (or theophany) in support of Israel's army, he is accompanied by heavenly warriors (Deut. 33:2; Judg. 5:20). The angelic leader of the heavenly host is called a "prince" (Heb. *śar*), a title later associated with the archangels (Josh. 5:14; Dan. 8:25; 10:13; 12:1).

The divine, cosmic, and military associations of the heavenly host reach far back into the biblical tradition and into the background of the ancient Near East, and they continue to flourish in the apocalyptic literature of the intertestamental period and to a lesser extent in the NT (e.g., in I Enoch 1; 14:22; 18:13; Luke 2:13; Rev. 12).

S. F. Noll

See also Angel; Principalities and Powers.

Bibliography. P. D. Miller, *The Divine Warrior in Early Israel;* L. I. J. Stadelmann, *The Hebrew Conception of the World;* W. Eichrodt, *Theology of the OT,* II, ch. 18.

Hosts, Lord of. *See* God, Names of.

Household Salvation. Both the OT and NT demonstrate a family solidarity that is alien to Western individualistic thought. The Abrahamic, Mosaic, and Davidic covenants involved the household in the covenant blessings. The OT formula "he and his house" referred to parents and their children of all ages. Thus, wagons were sent by Pharaoh to bring to Egypt those members of the households of Joseph's brothers who could not walk (i.e., old people and children, Gen. 45:18–19). When Saul destroyed Ahimelech's household (I Sam. 22:16–19), not even infants were spared. Household includes infants, as is seen in Gen. 17, where every male "in Abraham's house" was circumcised (including a baby eight days old). Deut. 6 shows the importance of teaching children the revealed way of blessing, while Exod. 12 includes children in the Passover meal.

The NT also involves the household in salvation. Acts 11:14 says: "Thou and all thy house shall be saved." In Acts 2:38–39 Peter states: "The promise is unto you and your children." Household baptisms show that the whole family was involved in salvation (Acts 16:15, 33; 18:8; I Cor. 1:16). In I Cor. 7:12–16 Paul counsels believers to remain married to unbelievers: "For the unbelieving husband is sanctified by the wife, and the unbelieving wife is sanctified by the husband: else were your children unclean; but now are they holy." Hence in some sense one believing parent sanctifies an entire household. Whether household salvation implies infant baptism is a disputed question. Nevertheless, scholars who disagree on baptism still unite in attributing high significance to the household in the economy of salvation. D. F. KELLY

Bibliography. J. Jeremias, *Infant Baptism in the First Four Centuries;* D. Kingdon, *Children of Abraham: A Reformed Baptist View of Baptism, the Covenant, and Children.*

House of God. *See* TABERNACLE, TEMPLE.

Hubmaier, Balthasar (*ca.* 1480–1528). South German Reformer and writer. Born in Friedberg near Augsburg, Hubmaier was sometimes known as Dr. Friedberger. He studied with the famous Johann Eck, Luther's later opponent, at the University of Freiburg, and earned his B.A. degree, but later followed Eck to the University of Ingolstadt, where he received both the licentiate and the doctorate in theology. He was a priest in the Regensburg Cathedral, in Waldshut in Breisgau (twice in each), and in Schaffhausen. He engaged in both friendly discussions and bitter debates with Zwingli in Zurich, and ended up imprisoned there (1525–26). He escaped with his life only by recanting. Like Luther, he at first sympathized with the demands of the German peasants but later opposed their armed revolt.

Hubmaier wrote voluminously. In 1524 he issued his eighteen theses, as well as his famous booklet against the burning of heretics. In 1525 he accepted baptism from Wilhelm Reublin, a colleague of the Zurich founder of Anabaptism, Conrad Grebel. By this time he had broken with Catholicism, as revealed in his marriage with Elisabeth Hügeline. He wrote several books on baptism which were powerful defenses of the baptism of believers. His catechism for the instruction of catechumens appeared in 1526. The next year he issued treatises on church discipline, baptism, the Lord's Supper, and free will. By 1527 he had broken with the Swiss, South German, and Austrian Anabaptists on the subject of nonresistance as set forth in his booklet on the sword; on that subject he stood closer to Luther.

Arrested in 1527, both Hubmaier and his wife were imprisoned in Vienna. He endured torture on the rack, which sufficiently broke his spirit so that he offered to "stand still" as to the practice of believer's baptism. But he steadfastly refused to recant. Strangely enough, he was granted a formal disputation with his old friend John Faber, a staunch Catholic theologian. For a time he was imprisoned in Kreuzenstein in northern Austria, but was soon taken back to prison in Vienna, from which he was led forth to the stake on March 10, 1528. His wife was drowned several days later. Some people compared his death with that of Jan Hus in 1415. J. C. WENGER

Bibliography. T. Bergsten, *Balthasar Hubmaier;* H. C. Vedder, *Balthasar Hubmaier; Mennonite Encyclopedia,* II, 834.

Hügel, Friedrich von. *See* VON HÜGEL, FRIEDRICH.

Humanism. *See* SECULARISM, SECULAR HUMANISM.

Humanism, Christian. The view that individuals and their culture have value in the Christian life. Justin Martyr appears to have been the first to offer a formulation of Christianity that included an acceptance of classical achievements as he stated in the *Apology* (1.46) that Christ the Word had put culture under his control. Such an approach, he believed, would restrain believers from leading vulgar lives while at the same time keeping them from attaching more importance to human culture than to the truths of the faith.

During the Middle Ages little attention was paid to humanism, but with the beginning of the Renaissance there was a revival of that perspective. Renaissance humanism was both an outlook and a method. It has been described as "man's discovery of himself and the world." The worth of earthly existence for its own sake was accepted, and the otherworldliness of medieval Christianity was disparaged. Humanists believed that the pursuit of secular life was not only proper but even meritorious. Closely allied to the new view of worldly life was a devotion to nature and its beauty as part of a broadened religious outlook. Yet Renaissance humanism must be viewed from another vantage point. Those involved in the movement were devoted to the *studia humanitatis,* or the liberal arts, including history, literary criticism, grammar, poetry, philology, and rhetoric. These subjects were taught from classical texts of the Greco-Roman period and were intended to help students understand and deal with other people. In addition, the humanists valued ancient artifacts and manuscripts and tried to revive classical life styles.

Many Christians, including Savonarola and Zwingli, reacted against the more secular approach of humanism; but others such as John Colet, Thomas More, and Erasmus felt that great benefits would come from the revival of classicism and the development of historical criticism. It has been pointed out that even John Calvin reveals the influence of humanism. The new Renaissance philological tools were helpful in studying the Bible, and the ancient view of man held the promise for better government and greater social justice. A wedding of the ethical and social concern of the Renaissance with the introspective force of Christianity held the possibility for church renewal in the minds of many sixteenth century scholars. Christian humanist teaching was kept alive by many Anglicans, by the moderates in the Church of Scotland, by certain German pietists, and through the philosophy of Kant. It continues in the twentieth century among such writers as Jacques Maritain and Hans Küng.

Those who believe that the Christian revelation has a humanistic emphasis point to the fact that man was made in the image of God, that Jesus Christ became man through the incarnation, and that the worth of the individual is a consistent theme in the teaching of Jesus. Indeed, when asked to give a summary of the life that pleases God, Christ advised his listeners to "love the Lord your God with all your heart, and with all your soul, and with all your mind" and to "love your neighbor as yourself" (Matt. 22:37, 39).

Christian humanists acknowledge the contributions of other forms of humanism, such as the classical variety that discovered the value of human liberty, and the Marxists, who realize that man has been estranged from the good life because he is dispossessed of property and subordinated to material and economic forces. However, they caution that these other forms can degenerate into excessive individualism or savage collectivism because they operate without God. The Christian humanist values culture but confesses that man is fully developed only as he comes into a right relationship with Christ. When this happens, a person can begin to experience growth in all areas of life as the new creation of revelation (II Cor. 5:17; Gal. 6:15). R. G. Clouse

See also Maritain, Jacques; Erasmus, Desiderius.

Bibliography. L. Bouyer, *Christian Humanism;* Q. Breen, *John Calvin: A Study in French Humanism;* H. Küng, *On Being a Christian;* J. Maritain, *True Humanism;* J. I. Packer, *Knowing Man;* G. Toffanin, *History of Humanism;* C. Trinkaus, *In Our Image and Likeness;* W. Bouwsma, *The Interpretation of Renaissance Humanism.*

Humanity of Christ. *See* Christology.

Hume, David (1711–1776). Scottish philosopher and historian. Born and educated in Edinburgh, Hume maintained a love affair with philosophy that would absorb his life and make him one of the key British philosophers of the Enlightenment. During a three-year visit in France (1734–37) he wrote *Treatise of Human Nature,* which was published in three volumes in 1739–40 after his return to London. Although he expected it to be quite popular, to Hume's chagrin its abstract nature and difficult language failed to interest the public. Immersing himself in more study, mainly in economic and political theory, he published in 1741 the first volume of his *Essays, Moral and Political* which, in contrast, was exceptionally well received. Nevertheless, he was unable to obtain a university professorship and, after a decade of application, received only the post of librarian at the Advocates' Library. Hume attained his greatest success as a man of letters during this period of excellent research facilities, publishing *Natural History of Religion* in 1757 and completing *Dialogues Concerning Natural Religion* which, upon the advice of friends, he withheld from publication until after his death.

Both deism and orthodox Christianity were attacked in Hume's literary works. Hume maintained that all of one's knowledge is the product of experience. While man can know the relation between ideas with certainty, their actual reality cannot be established beyond an appearance of probability. Thus, concepts of cause and effect do not come from logic, but rather from man's habit of association and man's custom. In *Dialogues* Hume declared that the argument of natural theology for the infinite cannot be inferred from the finite and that the existence of God cannot be proved by arguments from cause and effect. Hume did not say that God does not exist, but he did argue that the existence of God may not be established from reason or sense experience. In this fashion, he anticipated Kant by attacking ontological, cosmological, and teleological proofs of the existence of God.

In his "Essay on Miracles," which was a section of his *Philosophical Essays Concerning Human*

Understanding (1748), Hume argues that since all of one's knowledge comes from experience, and since this experience conveys the regularity of nature, the report of a miracle is much more likely to be a false report than an interruption in the uniform course of nature. Thus, a report of resurrection from the dead is in all probability a deceptive report. In *Natural History of Religion,* Hume suggests that all religious sentiments grow out of two human emotions, hope and fear—especially fear. He believed in studying religion scientifically, because there was nothing unique about religious experience. Therefore, it should be approached in the same secular fashion as any other form of human behavior. Hume contended that from polytheism man turned to monotheism through the observation of nature. Experiences of good and evil that conveyed to man benevolent and malevolent gods were transformed to belief in one powerful and arbitrary God through observation of strange occurrences and impressive natural phenomena. Hume found no connection between deity and morality, and he believed moral life was dominated by the passions of mankind.

Hume's philosophical works attained much more fame in France than in Britain, and he spent time with some of the most important French thinkers of the eighteenth century. He was a man of many talents. Between 1754 and 1762 he published *History of England,* which became a standard historical work and made him rich. He published numerous essays on a wide range of topics from demography to economics. An amiable and moderate individual in his relationships with others, Hume seemed to delight in the controversial nature of his literary works. D. A. RAUSCH

See also ENLIGHTENMENT, THE; EMPIRICISM, EMPIRICAL THEOLOGY.

Bibliography. V. C. Chappell, ed., *Hume: A Collection of Critical Essays;* J. C. A. Gaskin, *Hume's Philosophy of Religion;* T. H. Green and T. H. Grose, eds., *The Philosophical Works of David Hume;* R. Hall, *Fifty Years of Hume Scholarship;* E. Mossner, *The Life of David Hume;* B. Stroud, *Hume.*

Humiliation of Jesus Christ. *See* STATES OF JESUS CHRIST.

Humility. Usually looked down upon in the world, being too often confused with "ever-so-humbleness," with willful self-disparagement, or with conventional descriptions of (other) sinners as "guilty, vile, and helpless worms." In Christian tradition humility ranked high. With Barnabas it was part of "inward fasting"; with Chrysostom, "foundation of our philosophy"; Augustine said, "If you ask me what is the first precept of the Christian religion I will answer, first, second and third, Humility."

À Kempis and Bernard held humility necessary to imitation of Christ. Luther condemned "instead of being humble, seeking to excel in humility." "Unless a man is always humble, distrustful of himself, always fears his own understanding . . . passions . . . will, he will be unable to stand for long without offence. Truth will pass him by." Humility is "aptness for grace," the essence of faith.

For Calvin, humility alone exalts God as sovereign; it is part of self-denial, with the abandonment of self-confidence that constitutes faith, and of self-will. (Calvin insisted on being buried in an unmarked grave.) Puritans cultivated humility as an antidote to self-righteousness, by constant self-examination. Jonathan Edwards thought humility an essential test of religious emotionalism.

Such appreciation of humility springs from prophetic conviction that man, made of dust, totally dependent, and sinful, had nothing to be proud of except God's being mindful of him and visiting him (Ps. 8:4–5) with favor and redemption. God dwells with the humble (Isa. 57:15) and requires that man walk humbly with him (Mic. 6:8). Later legalism contradicted this with its doctrine of merit; Paul's reiterated repudiation of boasting illustrates where the Christian shoe pinched the Pharisee's foot.

So Jesus required, for receiving the kingdom or greatness within it, that one humble oneself as a child in "pure receptivity," the unself-conscious, unassuming readiness to accept favor, without considering desert, without injured pride, trusting the kindness of the giver. The example was set by Jesus' washing the disciples' feet as the Servant who humbled himself—"emptied himself" (Phil. 2:7–8). So, whoever would be first must be servant of all (Mark 10:43).

Thus, from humility toward God followed humility toward others ("in humility count others better than yourselves," Phil. 2:3, the classic passage) and also toward oneself ("not to think of himself more highly than he ought to think," Rom. 12:3). For the Christian knows he possesses nothing he has not received, is nothing but for the grace of God, and, apart from Christ, can do nothing. He remembers that God opposes the proud, giving grace to the humble; never presumes to repay God's goodness, but counts himself an unworthy servant; and recognizes that the highest goodness is always unconscious (Matt. 25:37). He never forgets he has been loved, saved, and made a son of God. R. E. O. WHITE

Hus, Jan (*ca.* 1372–1415). Early Czech reformer. Hus (also Huss) was born in the village of Husinec in southern Bohemia. He studied at the university in Prague, and in 1398 joined the arts faculty as a lecturer. He also took priestly vows. During these years he underwent a conversion, although the details are unclear. His choice of a priestly vocation had been largely motivated by a desire for prestige, financial security, and the camaraderie of academic society. As a result of his conversion, Hus adopted a simpler life style and manifested more interest in his spiritual growth.

Hus was appointed rector and preacher in Prague's Bethlehem chapel, the center of the Czech reform movement, in 1402. During these years many of John Wycliffe's ideas influenced Hus, especially those dealing with the spirituality of the church. However, Hus was not solely a product of Wycliffe's theology, because earlier Czech theologians, such as Matthew of Janov, shaped Hus's theological development as well.

By 1407 Hus was clearly identified with the reformists. His evangelical wing threatened not only the theological balance in Bohemia but also the ethnic status quo by challenging the power that Germans held in the Roman Catholic Church in Bohemia.

In 1409 Pope Alexander V empowered the Archbishop of Prague to root out heresy in his diocese. When the archbishop asked Hus to stop preaching, Hus refused, and was excommunicated in 1410. When Hus continued to attack the papal politics of the Great Schism and the sale of indulgences, rioting erupted in Prague against the church hierarchy. With no support from the king, and the pope threatening to place Prague under interdict, Hus left the city in 1412 to live in southern Bohemia.

In 1414, with a promise of safe conduct, Hus traveled to the Council of Constance, where he was imprisoned and placed on trial for heresy. He refused to admit that the charges against him were true unless proven so by Scripture. Nevertheless, he was judged guilty and burned at the stake on July 6, 1415.

Hus's sermons attacked clerical abuses, especially the immorality and high living of the clergy. His theology was a mixture of evangelical and traditional Roman Catholic doctrines. Hus preached against the veneration of the pope by stressing a strong Christocentric faith that emphasized an individual's responsibility before God. He believed only Christ could forgive sins and expected a coming day of judgment. However, he still accepted the Roman Catholic doctrine of purgatory. Hus believed that both the wine and the bread should be administered in the Lord's Supper, and held a view of the elements similar to the doctrine of consubstantiation. He emphasized preaching the Word of God to bring about moral and spiritual change in listeners' lives. To help them read the Scriptures, he also revised a Czech translation of the Bible.

As a theologian, Hus helped restore a biblical vision of the church, one that focused on Christ's teachings and example of purity. Moreover, his stress on preaching and the universal priesthood of believers became hallmarks of the later Protestant Reformation. He also encouraged congregational hymn singing, writing many songs himself. For Czechs, Hus was not only a spiritual leader but also a focal point of national inspiration in the centuries following his death.

P. Kubricht

Bibliography. J. Hus, *The Church*, tr. D. S. Schaff; M. Spinka, *John Hus and the Czech Reform; John Hus, a Biography;* and *John Hus' Concept of the Church;* M. Spinka, ed., *John Hus at the Council of Constance* and *The Letters of John Hus;* J. K. Zeman, *The Hussite Movement and the Reformation in Bohemia, Moravia and Slovakia (1350–1650): A Bibliographical Study Guide.*

Hutchinson, Anne (1591–1643). One of the most creative of New England's early religious thinkers, whose theology yet brought her into serious conflict with Puritan authorities. She came to Massachusetts in 1634 to remain under the preaching of her English pastor, John Cotton, who had migrated to Boston the year before. Hutchinson was especially taken by Cotton's emphasis on God's free grace. Once in New England, Mrs. Hutchinson began a midweek meeting to discuss Cotton's sermon of the previous Sunday and to encourage lay piety. All went well until word began to spread that Anne Hutchinson's views were tending toward antinomianism, the theological error that Christians do not need the law. In her meetings she suggested that a believer possesses the Holy Spirit and thus is not bound by the law. Further, mere obedience to external laws (for example, of Massachusetts) does not mean that one is truly a Christian.

Anne Hutchinson relied on the preaching of John Cotton and on her own wide knowledge of the Bible to support these views. They were in fact a legitimate, if unsettling, extension of Puritan concepts of salvation. The difficulty came in the potential damage of these opinions to the Puritan way in New England. If every believer were entirely under grace, how could the godly act together to build the society which Puritans longed for so dearly? The Massachusetts leaders soon demanded an explanation. Through many days of interrogation, Hutchinson held her own against the colony's most powerful ministers and magistrates by careful biblical argument and penetrating logic. Just when it seemed as if she had finally silenced her opponents, however, she made a fatal mistake. She claimed that the Holy Spirit communicated directly to her, apart from Scripture, and this the leaders could not tolerate. As a result, she and her followers were banished from the colony in 1638. She moved first to Rhode Island, then to Long Island, and finally to inland New York. Here she and most of her family were killed by Indians. One of her descendants, Thomas Hutchinson, eventually became the last colonial governor of Massachusetts, the very colony which had long before banished his ancestor, colonial America's ablest, if also most controversial, woman theologian. M. A. Noll

Bibliography. E. Battis, *Saints and Sectaries: Anne Hutchinson and the Antinomian Controversy in the Massachusetts Bay Colony;* D. D. Hall, ed., *The Antinomian Controversy, 1636–1638: A Documentary History.*

Hyperdulia. In Roman Catholic theology, hyperdulia is defined as that form of veneration offered to the Blessed Virgin Mary in her capacity of being the Mother of God. Hyperdulia as a veneration may be seen as a form of adoration if one remembers that adoration ultimately is offered to the Trinity. The cult of dulia therefore differs from the cult of latria, which is adoration directly to God. In *Lumen Gentium* the Second Vatican Council restated that "veneration" of Mary is part of the "devotion" to Mary which proceeds from true faith. T. J. German

See also Latria; Dulia.

Bibliography. B. Häring, *The Law of Christ;* L. Bouyer, *Rite and Man: Natural Sacredness and Christian Liturgy.*

Hypocrisy. The NT concept of hypocrisy has probably been influenced by two sources: (1) the Hebrew *ḥānēp,* "polluted," "impious"; (2) the Attic Greek *hypokrisis,* "an actor's response," hence stage-playing or acting. Pedersen lists the root *ḥnp* among words which denote "antagonism to what is sacred" (*Israel,* III–IV, 271). In Job, where the majority of OT occurrences are found, the word parallels "all who forget God" (Job 8:13), "wicked" (Job 20:5; 27:8), etc. The LXX renders *ḥānēp* with a variety of words meaning lawlessness and impiety: *anomos* (Isa. 9:17), *asebēs* (Job 8:13; 20:5, etc.), *paranomos* (Job 17:8), etc. Occasionally *hypokritēs* is used (Job 34:30; 36:13). The RSV "godless" and "godlessness" convey accurately the OT idea that hypocrisy is not so much duplicity or insincerity as impiety and disregard of God's law.

In Christ's stern denunciations of the scribes and Pharisees in the Synoptics (the only NT occurrences of *hypokritēs*), the OT meaning "godless" is strongly felt—e.g., Matt. 22:18; 23:13–29, and 24:51, where the parallel (Luke 12:46) has "unfaithful." Furthermore, while Mark 12:15 reads "hypocrisy," Matt. 22:18 and Luke 20:23 have "wickedness" and "craftiness." As A. G. Hebert has noted, Jesus' point is not that the scribes were deliberately acting a part, but that, while outwardly religious, inwardly they were profane and godless (*RTWB,* p. 109). In Gal. 2:13 it is probably not so much acting a part as unprincipled action that Paul condemns.

Elsewhere, the Greek idea of acting appears to be in the forefront. Hypocrite in Matt. 6:2, 5, 16 seems to mean play-actor as does the sole occurrence of the verb *hypokrinesthai* in Luke 20:20. The adjective *anypokritos,* "genuine," "sincere," "without hypocrisy" (Rom. 12:9; I Tim. 1:5; James 3:17, etc.), also seems to reflect the influence of the Greek drama.

It is not impossible that both NT concepts "godlessness" and "play-acting" may be explained from Hebrew or Aramaic without recourse to Greek thought, for *ḥānēp* in the postbiblical period comes to mean hypocrite, flatterer, or insincere person. D. A. Hubbard

Hypostasis. The word is a transliteration of the Greek *hypostasis,* "substance," "nature," "essence" (from *hyphistasthai,* "stand under," "subsist," which is from *hypo,* "under," and *histanai,* "cause to stand"), and denotes a real personal subsistence or person. In philosophy it signifies the underlying or essential part of anything, as distinguished from attributes which may vary. It developed theologically as the term to describe any one of the three real and distinct subsistences in the one undivided substance or essence of God, and especially the one unified personality of Christ the Son in his two natures, human and divine. The classic Chalcedonian definition of God, one essence in three hypostases (*mia ousia, treis hypostaseis*), was unfortunately translated into Latin as "one substance [Gr. *hypostasis*] in three persons" (*una substantia, tres personae*). This not only confused threefold substance with the one *ousia* (Lat. *essentia,* "essence"), but the Latin word *persona* ("face" or "mask") sounded like Sabellian modalistic monarchianism to the Greeks. The Council of Alexandria (362) tried unsuccessfully to resolve the conflict by defining *hypostasis* as synonymous with the very different word *persona.* Although much confusion still reigns, orthodoxy has generally held to the one substance of God, known in the three persons of Father, Son, and Holy Spirit.

W. E. WARD

See also GOD, DOCTRINE OF; TRINITY; CHALCEDON, COUNCIL OF.

Bibliography. H. P. Van Dusen, *Spirit, Son, and Father;* L. Hodgson, *The Doctrine of the Trinity;* C. C. Richardson, *The Doctrine of the Trinity;* C. Welch, *In This Name: The Doctrine of the Trinity in Contemporary Theology.*

Hypostatic Union. The doctrine of the hypostatic union, first set forth officially in the definition of faith produced by the Council of Chalcedon (451), concerns the union of the two natures (*dyo physes*) of deity and humanity in the one *hypostasis* or person of Jesus Christ. It can be stated as follows: In the incarnation of the Son of God, a human nature was inseparably united forever with the divine nature in the one person of Jesus Christ, yet with the two natures remaining distinct, whole, and unchanged, without mixture or confusion so that the one person, Jesus Christ, is truly God and truly man.

Several important Christological issues are highlighted by this doctrine: (1) the unipersonality of the Savior. Nestorianism, which divided the natures as persons, is ruled out. There is only one who is at the same time God and man. Obviously this doctrine excludes any separation between the Christ of faith and the Jesus of history. (2) The continuity of the Savior's personality. Jesus Christ is the same person who was the preexistent Logos, the Son of God (John 1:1, 14; 8:58). Thus, every form of adoptionism is ruled out, since the hypostatic union excludes the independent personal subsistence of the human nature. (3) The complexity of the Savior's personality. While there is continuity of identity, there is this difference. It is no longer the divine nature alone which is expressed in his person. The human nature, not an impersonal appendage, has its personal subsistence in the Logos. The incarnate Christ is *theanthrōpos,* the God-man. (4) The distinction of the natures. Eutychianism, which confused the natures into a *tertium quid,* is excluded along with every form of monophysitism. (5) The perfection of the natures. Every Christology which diminishes either the deity or the humanity of Jesus Christ, from docetism to Socinianism, from Arianism to Apollinarianism, would be considered inadequate from the standpoint of this doctrine. Jesus Christ is truly, perfectly, and wholly God, and he is truly, perfectly, and wholly man.

Admittedly, this doctrine leaves many metaphysical questions unanswered. However, it should be noted that this doctrine was not produced as the fruit of philosophic speculation on the possible singulary cosubsistence of the finite and the infinite. Rather it was offered as a precise description of the incarnation recorded in Scripture, drawn from the greatest extent of biblical data and making use of whatever language that might help in that descriptive task (such as the introduction of a technical distinction between *physis* and *hypostasis*). The considered biblical data include all the major passages on the incarnation (such as Phil. 2:6–11; John 1:1–14; Rom. 1:2–5; 9:5; I Tim. 3:16; Heb. 2:14; I John 1:1–3), as well as the Gospel narratives and epistolary references where the attributes of both natures are manifested in one person, the *communicatio idiomatum.*

C. A. BLAISING

See also CHALCEDON, COUNCIL OF; COMMUNICATION OF ATTRIBUTES, COMMUNICATIO IDIOMATUM; MONOPHYSITISM.

Bibliography. K. Barth, *Church Dogmatics* I/2; L. Berkhof, *Systematic Theology;* G. C. Berkouwer, *The Person of Christ;* A. Grillmeier, *Christ in Christian Tradition,* I; C. Hodge, *Systematic Theology,* II; J. N. D. Kelly, *Early Christian Doctrines;* R. Norris, Jr., ed., *The Christological Controversy;* R. V. Sellers, *The Council of Chalcedon.*

Ii

"I Am" Sayings. A diversity of "I am . . ." formulae in the OT by which Yahweh repeatedly discloses himself. He reveals himself as the God of the patriarchs (Gen. 15:7; 17:1; 28:13; etc.), or as "the Lord your God, who brought you out of Egypt" (e.g., Exod. 20:2 at the beginning of the Decalogue), or more simply in the words "I am Yahweh" (e.g., Ezek. 33:29; 36:36). The disclosure of Exod. 3:14, often rendered "I am who I am" or "I am the existing one," may well be an instance of paronomasia; but more importantly, like the repeated "I am he" or "I myself am he" utterances (Deut. 32:39; Isa. 41:4; 43:10, 13, 25; 45:18; 46:4; 48:12; 51:12; 52:6), Yahweh presents himself in antithesis to the finite gods of the prevalent polytheism. In most instances the context precludes a rendering "I am this or that," but presupposes something like "I am the Absolute One." Especially in Isa. 40ff., the surrounding verses show that the meaning of God as the Absolute works out in an array of attributes: he is sovereign, uncreated, unimaginable, personal, master of history, holy, and the universal monarch whose purposes cannot ultimately be thwarted. Moreover, the formula here is *self*-revelatory: Yahweh is not addressed in this way, but uses these expressions of himself, thereby demonstrating that he graciously chooses to reveal himself to men.

In the NT, many "I am" sayings are supplied with a subjective completion (e.g., "I am the light of the world," John 8:12) and therefore do not qualify as "I am" utterances in the absolute sense. More difficult are the few instances outside John's Gospel where the text offers a simple *egō eimi* (lit. "I am") but where the context makes clear that the meaning is "It is I" or "I am he"—with the antecedent of the "I" or "he" apparent in the surrounding verses. These are probably at best ambiguous self-disclosures of deity, hints for those familiar with the OT; for many of Jesus' prepassion self-revelations adopt such a stance of planned ambiguity. For instance, when Jesus walks to his frightened disciples across the surface of the water, he calms their fears by saying, *egō eimi*. The context demands the conclusion that Jesus is identifying himself ("It is I"), showing that what they perceive is not a ghostly apparition (Mark 6:50). Yet not every "I" could be found walking on water: it would be premature to discount all reference to OT theophany. Again, Jesus warns his disciples against those who will lead many astray by claiming "I am" (Mark 13:6; Luke 21:8); but the context demands this be interpreted as "I am the Christ"—as Matt. 24:5 makes explicit. Jesus uses identical language at his trial (Mark 14:61–62) and similar language after his resurrection (Luke 24:39), in each case bearing some ambiguity.

The Fourth Gospel raises new questions. Although many of Jesus' "I am" utterances recorded by John are supplied with explicit predicates ("I am the true vine," "I am the good shepherd," "I am the bread of life," "I am the resurrection and the life"), two are undeniably absolute in both form and content (8:58; 13:19) and constitute an explicit self-identification with Yahweh who had already revealed himself to men in similar terms (see esp. Isa. 43:10–11). Jesus' opponents recognize this claim to unity with Yahweh (John 8:58–59); in 13:19–20, Jesus himself proceeds to make it explicit. These two occurrences of the absolute "I am" suggest that in several other passages in John, where "I am" is *formally* absolute but a predicate might well be supplied from the context (e.g., 4:26; 6:20; 8:24, 28; 18:5, 6, 8), an intentional double meaning may be involved.

D. A. Carson

See also Sayings of Jesus.

Bibliography. B. J. Beitzel, "Exodus 3:14 and the Divine Name," *TJ* 1:5–20; R. E. Brown, *The Gospel*

According to John I, 532–83; D. A. Carson, *Christ the Lord;* D. Daube, *The NT and Rabbinic Judaism;* P. B. Horner, *The "I Am" of the Fourth Gospel;* H.-G. Link, *NIDNTT,* II, 278–83; W. Manson, *Jesus and the Christian;* E. Stauffer, *TDNT,* II, 343–62.

Ibn Rushd. *See* AVERROES.

Identification with Christ. The theological doctrine of identification with Christ which derives from various Scriptures that regard Christians as being "in Christ." In a general way Christ is identified with mankind as the second Adam, and identified with Israel as the predicted Son of David. In these cases the identity is a physical fact. In contrast to these relationships the theological concept of identification with Christ relates a Christian to the person and work of Christ by divine reckoning, by the human experience of faith, and by the spiritual union of the believer with Christ effected by the baptism of the Holy Spirit.

Identification with Christ is accomplished by the baptism of the Holy Spirit, an act of divine grace and power sometimes expressed as being baptized into (*eis*) the body of Christ, the church (I Cor. 12:13), sometimes described as being baptized into Christ (Gal. 3:27). This new relationship of being "in Christ" was first announced by the Lord to his disciples in the upper room in the statement, "Ye in me [*en emoi*], and I in you" (John 14:20). The new relationship of the believer in Christ is defined as a new position, "in Christ," resulting from a work of God. That it is more than merely a position created by divine reckoning is revealed by the companion revelation, "I in you." The resultant doctrine is embraced in the word *union,* which is commonly taken as a synonym for identification.

Various figures are employed in Scripture to illustrate this union and identification. The vine and the branches is employed by Christ himself in John 15:1–6. Here the union is manifested by communion, spiritual life, and fruit as a result of the union of branch and vine. The branch is in the vine and the life of the vine is in the branch. Another figure is that of the head and the body (cf. Eph. 1:22–23; 4:12–16; 5:23–32). Here also there is organic union of the body and the head, depicting the living union of Christ and the church. Intrinsic in the figure is the thought that the identification of the body with the head does not imply equality but carries with it the obligation of recognizing the head as the one who directs the body.

Close to the figure of the head and the body is that of the marriage relation of Christ and the church presented in the same section as the figure of the head and the body in Ephesians 5:23–32. Here the relationship is compared to the identification of a wife with her husband stated in the declaration that they are "one flesh."

Various expressions are used to signify this identification. Most frequent is the terminology "in Christ" (*en Christō*), but others also are used such as "in" or "into Christ" (*eis Christon*), and "in the Lord" (*en kyriō*). Though some distinction may be observed between the use of the prepositions *en* and *eis* ("in" and "into"), the resultant doctrine is much the same.

Important theological truths are related to the doctrine of identification in Scripture. The believer is identified with Christ in his death (Rom. 6:1–11); his burial (Rom. 6:4); his resurrection (Col. 3:1); his ascension (Eph. 2:6); his reign (II Tim. 2:12); and his glory (Rom. 8:17). Identification with Christ has its limitations, however. Christ is identified with the human race in his incarnation, but only true believers are identified with Christ. The identification of a believer with Christ results in certain aspects of the person and work of Christ being attributed to the believer, but this does not extend to possession of the attributes of the Second Person, nor are the personal distinctions between Christ and the believer erased. Taken as a whole, however, identification with Christ is a most important doctrine and is essential to the entire program of grace.

J. F. WALVOORD

See also ABIDE; MURRAY, ANDREW; MYSTICISM; UNIO MYSTICA; UNITIVE WAY, THE.

Bibliography. L. Berkhof, *Systematic Theology;* E. Best, *One Body in Christ;* L. S. Chafer, *Systematic Theology,* IV, 54–143; A. Deissmann, *St. Paul;* A. Schweitzer, *The Mysticism of Paul the Apostle;* A. H. Strong, *Systematic Theology;* H. C. Thiessen, *Lectures in Systematic Theology;* J. F. Walvoord, *The Holy Spirit.*

Idolatry. The worship of an idol or of a deity represented by an idol, usually as an image. Idolatry, as a form of religious practice, was common in both OT and NT times. Literary and archaeological evidence for the practice has survived from Mesopotamia, Syria-Palestine, Egypt, and from the Roman Empire.

One of the most distinctive features of Hebrew religion during the OT period was the absence of idolatry. Its practice was prohibited among the Hebrews, and the archaeological evidence indicates that the prohibition was observed for the most part.

There were two prevalent forms of idolatry in OT times, both banned by the Decalogue: (1) The first commandment prohibited the Israelites from worshiping any other god than the Lord

(Exod. 20:3), thereby eliminating the false forms of idolatrous religion practiced in neighboring nations. (2) The second commandment forbade the worship of the God of Israel in the form of an image or idol (Exod. 20:4–6).

Of the two prohibitions, the latter was crucial to the integrity of Israel's theology. To worship God in the form of an idol would be to reduce God the Creator to the substance of creation (that which was represented in the idol), thereby undermining fundamentally the conception of the transcendent creator God. The idol gave to devotees a sense of the physical proximity of a deity and perhaps also the conviction that the deity's power could be harnessed by human beings. The God of Israel was immanent, but that immanence could not be expressed in physical or tangible form; it remained the essence of faith and of experience.

Despite the prohibition of idolatry in Hebrew law, it clearly remained a fundamental form of temptation throughout Israel's history, whether in worshiping false gods through their idols or in reducing the worship of the one true God to idolatrous form. Hence, the denunciation of idolatry in its various forms is a recurrent theme in both the law and the prophets (Deut. 7:25–26; 29:16–17; Isa. 40:18–23).

In NT times idolatry was practiced in various forms throughout the Roman empire and was steadfastly resisted by the early Christian church. It was understood as a sign of human folly (Rom. 1:22–23), representing a perversion of true religion. More frequently, however, the NT writers used the concept of idolatry in a metaphorical sense, particularly with respect to covetousness (Eph. 5:5, Col. 3:5); covetousness is an "idol" by virtue of becoming the immediate focus of a person's desires and "worship," displacing the worship of God.

In the later history of Christianity, idolatry in the strict sense has continued to be opposed in the terms of the ancient biblical prohibitions. But the continuing danger has more commonly returned in the metaphorical sense delineated in the NT; it is the "worship" (i.e., the total dedication of a person) of that which is seen and tangible, the goals of covetousness, rather than the unseen spiritual being that is God. P. C. Craigie

Bibliography. O. Barfield, *Saving the Appearances: A Study of Idolatry;* P. C. Craigie, *The Book of Deuteronomy;* R. de Vaux, *Ancient Israel.*

Ignatius of Loyola (1491–1556). The founder of the Society of Jesus (Jesuits). Ignatius was born of Basque noble parents in Guipúzcoa. Although early destined for a church career, he served as a courtier until 1521, when battle wounds forced convalescence during which his reading of the lives of Christ and the saints resulted in a religious conversion. He is frequently stereotyped as the soldier-saint, but his military career lasted only a few months, and the stereotype detracts from any real understanding of Loyola.

After his conversion he spent eleven months in prayer and fasting at Manresa in Catalonia. His religious experiences there became the basis and core of his *Spiritual Exercises,* published in 1548 after much revision. The *Spiritual Exercises,* a classic of Christian spirituality which has been published in five thousand editions in some thirty languages, is a manual designed to share Loyola's mystical experiences at a lower level with ordinary but sincere Christians and to help them reorder their lives to a single-minded service of God.

Loyola completed a pilgrimage to Jerusalem in 1523 and, returning to Europe, determined that he could serve his fellowman more effectively if he had an education. He therefore enrolled in a grammar school at Barcelona for two years before entering the University of Alcalá, where he attracted a few disciples. Opposition from the Inquisition forced him to transfer to the University of Salamanca. There he was imprisoned by the Inquisition; although acquitted, he was forbidden to speak on religious topics until he had completed theological studies. Thereupon, Loyola transferred to the University of Paris where he studied from 1528 to 1535 and gathered around him companions, such as Francis Xavier and Diego Lainez, who were to be the founding fathers of the Society of Jesus. In 1534 Loyola and six companions vowed perpetual poverty and chastity and promised to work for souls in Palestine if that were possible. After a short visit to Spain he was reunited with his companions at Venice, but war between Venice and the Turks prevented their departure for Palestine. Instead, they preached in the north Italian cities and then placed themselves at the disposal of Pope Paul III. Loyola was ordained a priest in 1537. Gradually the companions realized that only the structure of a religious order would preserve and perpetuate their union and apostolic work. Paul III authorized the Society of Jesus in 1540. Loyola was elected the first superior general and was commissioned to draw up constitutions.

Loyola lived in Rome from 1537 until his death in 1556, writing the Jesuit *Constitutions* and supervising the rapid expansion of the new order. His correspondence (all but a handful of 6795 items relate to the Roman years) mirrors the first decades of Jesuit history. Meanwhile, his mystical experiences, which had abated during his years of study, returned with increased force. In his last years, Loyola was at once a mystic and a religious bureaucrat. He husbanded some time for an active apostolate to those he considered most needy: he set up a halfway house for ex-prostitutes; a hospice for young girls; and charitable agencies for abandoned boys, Jewish converts, and impoverished noblemen. His autobiography, dictated to a subordinate, covers his life up to 1537. J. P. DONNELLY

See also SOCIETY OF JESUS, THE.

Bibliography. J. Brodrick, *St. Ignatius: The Pilgrim Years, 1491–1538;* P. Dudon, *St. Ignatius of Loyola;* M. Foss, *The Founding of the Jesuits 1540;* H. Rahner, *Ignatius the Theologian;* F. Wulf, *Ignatius Loyola: His Personality and Spiritual Heritage, 1556–1956.*

Ignorance. A lack of knowledge, either in general or with respect to a particular fact or subject.

Biblical Description. The OT describes ignorance as a failure (1) to know clearly (Deut. 19:4; Ps. 73:22; Isa. 56:10) or (2) to act acceptably (Lev. 4:2, 22, 27; 5:15, 18; Num. 15:24–29). Divine provision for those who had committed sins of ignorance was found in the sin offering (Lev. 4:2–12) and the cities of refuge (Deut. 19:4–10; Josh. 20:2–6). Guilt for such acts was recognized, but the extent of culpability diminished.

The NT expresses ignorance (*agnoeō* and *agnoia*) as (1) failure to understand or perceive (Mark 9:32; Luke 9:45); (2) to be uninformed, not to know, as in the phrase "I would not have you to be ignorant, brethren" (Rom. 1:13; 11:25; I Cor. 10:1; 12:1; II Cor. 1:8; I Thess. 4:13); (3) ignorance that leads astray (I Tim. 1:13; Heb. 5:2); and (4) not knowing as a consequence of the willful closing of one's mind to the appeal of truth (Acts 13:27; Rom. 10:3). Once again sin is acknowledged, but culpability is tempered by the dimension of ignorance involved.

Ethical Implications. Ethicists have long sought an equitable mode for determining the extent of culpability for acts performed in ignorance. A useful formula is expressed by distinguishing between avoidable and unavoidable ignorance (some use the terms "vincible" and "invincible").

In events involving unavoidable ignorance we exonerate the agent from responsibility, as in the case of a man's failure to appear for an appointment because he was ignorant of the fact that he would be engaged in an accident on the way. Obviously such ignorance is unavoidable. On the other hand, a judge does not excuse a defendant who claims he did not know that a gun was loaded for the agent could have taken the time to inform himself on this point, and since the gun is a lethal weapon, he should have informed himself before pressing the trigger. However, it is important to recognize that not all avoidable ignorance is deemed inexcusable. If a professor of physics were not able to explain $E = MC^2$ we would find this inexcusable; on the other hand, if he pleaded ignorance as to the evolution of the English preposition we might well excuse him even though he could have added such material to his fund of knowledge. It becomes clear, therefore, that determining the extent of man's culpability in certain contexts is dependent upon numerous factors.

The Christian rejoices in the fact that the final judgment of mankind resides with a mind more penetrating, a will more discerning, and a heart more loving than his own.

Theological Synthesis. Man, the sinner (Rom. 3:23), is constitutionally ignorant. Having lost the pristine knowledge of God in the fall, he is aware of the existence of deity but totally incapable of knowing how to effect peace with him (Rom. 1:19–20; Eph. 2:12; 4:18). Man's ignorance is most clearly expressed in this inability to recognize the Son of God when he appeared; this failure issued in Christ's rejection and death (Acts 3:17; I Cor. 2:7–8). Only divine intervention has prevented man from perishing in his ignorance (Hos. 13:9 AV). As the gospel is proclaimed (I Cor. 15:1–3) faith is created (Rom. 10:17) and a knowledge provided that eventuates in man's salvation (John 17:3; II Tim. 3:15). In eternity, the ignorance of redeemed man will be superseded by consummate knowledge (the beatific vision, I Cor. 13:12). F. R. HARM

See also ETHICS, BIBLICAL; RESPONSIBILITY.

Bibliography. E. Schütz and E. D. Schmitz, *NIDNTT,* II, 390–409; J. Hardon, *The Catholic Catechism;* A. C. Schultz, *DCE,* 311–12; J. Hospers, *Human Conduct;* J. Macquarrie, ed., *Dictionary of Christian Ethics.*

Illumination. (1) A general enlightening that Christ brings to all men especially through the gospel (John 1:9; II Tim. 1:10); (2) the enlightening experience of salvation (Heb. 6:4; 10:32); (3) the understanding of Christian truth (Eph. 1:18; 3:9); and (4) the searching character of future judgment (I Cor. 4:5). Biblically, the verb *phōtizō* is used in such references.

Theologically, the word has been applied to various concepts. (1) In the early church, baptism was frequently described as illumination (e.g., Justin, *First Apology* 61). (2) Applied to biblical inspiration, the illumination theory holds that the perception and understanding of the biblical writers were elevated or intensified to a degree greater than that of other men. (3) Illumination and revelation are confused in the neo-orthodox view of the Bible's becoming the Word of God, for that makes man's discovery of truth the locus of revelation.

Specifically, the doctrine of illumination relates to that ministry of the Holy Spirit that helps the believer understand the truth of Scripture. In relation to the Bible, the doctrine of revelation relates to the unveiling of truth in the material of the Scriptures; inspiration concerns the method by which the Holy Spirit superintended the writing of Scripture; and illumination refers to the ministry of the Spirit by which the meaning of Scripture is made clear to the believer.

The unregenerate man cannot experience this illuminating ministry, for he is blinded to the truth of God (I Cor. 2:14). The Lord promised his followers that when the Spirit came on the day of Pentecost he would lead them into the truth (John 16:13–16), and this includes understanding the deep things of God (I Cor. 2:9–10). However, such understanding is not without conditions. The believer must himself be maturing and in fellowship with the Lord to experience this full perception of truth, for carnality in his life will hinder the ministry of the Spirit (I Cor. 3:1–3). He also would expect to benefit from the Spirit ministering through others who have the gift of teaching (Rom. 12:6–7), and such ministry can be experienced orally or through the printed page or various other media. But ultimately it is the Spirit who is the direct connection between the mind of God as revealed in the Scriptures and the mind of the believer seeking to understand the Scriptures. C. C. Ryrie

Bibliography. L. S. Chafer, *Systematic Theology,* I, 105–13; B. Ramm, *The Witness of the Spirit;* C. C. Ryrie, *The Holy Spirit.*

Illuminative Way, The (Latin: Via illuminativa). The second of the three stages of the mystic way, being intermediary between the purgative way, in which the person learns to reject sin, and the unitive way, in which the person enters the pure love of God, the mystic union. This second stage, also called the Way of the Proficients, finds the person being disengaged from his attachment to the things of this world, even those that are good or are associated with religious meanings. Instead the soul is enlightened concerning the pure world of the spirit and is thus prepared to appreciate God more deeply. While found in its basics as early as Basil the Great, the classic expression of this way is found in the writings of John of the Cross, particularly the first part of the *Dark Night of the Soul.*

P. H. Davids

See also Beatific Vision; John of the Cross; Mysticism; Purgative Way, The; Unitive Way, The.

Illyricus. *See* Flacius, Matthias.

Image of God. The doctrine that man is created in the divine image. The Bible answers the question of the nature of man by pointing to the *imago Dei.* That man by creation uniquely bears the image of God is a fundamental biblical doctrine—as is also that this image is sullied by sin and that it is restored by divine salvation. Man's nature and destiny are interwoven with this foundational fact, and speculative philosophies inevitably strike at it when they degrade man to animality or otherwise distort his personality.

Biblical Data. The biblical data pertaining to the *imago Dei* in man are found in both New and Old Testaments. Their setting throughout is revealed religion, and not speculative philosophy. Dependence of the Pauline view on the hellenic mystery religions has been asserted by the comparative religions school. Reitzenstein has affirmed (*Die hellenistischen Mysterienreligionen,* pp. 7ff.) that Paul's teaching on the image is indebted to the private mystery cults in Egypt, Phrygia, and Persia, particularly those of Isis, Attis and Cybele, and Mithra, with their goal of salvation secured through personal union with the god or goddess. But H. A. A. Kennedy has argued convincingly in *St. Paul and the Mystery Religions* that the basic NT ideas are forged against the background of Hebrew theology, rather than of the hellenistic cults, and that even in respect to the image the resemblance between the Pauline concepts and the mysteries is superficial. David Cairns also emphasizes that "the New Testament writers make almost no use"—he might properly have deleted the word "almost"—of notions so frequently found in the mystery cults such as the divinization of the believer and human absorption into the Deity.

Hebrew-Christian theology frames the doctrine of the *imago* in the setting of divine creation and redemption. "The gist of the doctrine of Creation is surely this," Cairns would remind us, in respect to the image, "that man's being, though linked with the divine, is itself essentially not divine, but created, and thus dependent on God, and of a different order from His own being though akin to it" (p. 63). Bible doctrine does not, therefore, simply affirm in a religious manner what speculative philosophies express more generally in their emphasis on the inherent dignity and worth of man, or on the infinite value and sacredness of human personality. For Scripture conditions man's dignity and value upon the doctrine of creation, and not upon an intrinsic divinity, and assuredly it does not obscure the fact of man's fall and of his desperate need of redemption. Those who, like Kingsley Martin, profess to find in Stoicism a superior and sounder basis for human dignity than that afforded by biblical theology seem little to realize that in such a transition to pantheism the Hebrew-Christian dimensions of the *imago* are actually abandoned.

The biblical discussion turns on the Hebrew words *ṣelem* and *dĕmût*, and the corresponding Greek terms *eikōn* and *homoiōsis*. Scripture employs these terms to affirm that man was fashioned in the image of God, and that Jesus Christ the divine Son is the essential image of the invisible God. The passages expressly affirming the divine image in man are Gen. 1:26, 27; 5:1, 3; and 9:6; I Cor. 11:7; Col. 3:10; and James 3:9. The doctrine is implied also in other passages in which the precise phrase "image of God" does not appear, particularly in Ps. 8, which J. Laidlaw called "a poetic *replica* of the creation-narrative of Genesis 1 as far as it refers to man" (*HDB*, II, 452a), and in the Pauline reference on Mars Hill to man and his Maker. The terms "image and likeness" in Gen. 1:26 and 5:3 do not distinguish different aspects of the *imago*, but state intensively the fact that man uniquely reflects God. Instead of suggesting distinctions within the image, the juxtaposition vigorously declares that by creation man bears an image actually corresponding to the divine original. In Gen. 1:27 the word "image" alone expresses the complete idea of this correspondence, whereas in Gen. 5:1 the term "likeness" serves the same purpose.

Although man images God by creation—a fact which the divine prohibition of graven images (which obscure the spirituality of God) serves pointedly to reinforce—man's fall precludes all attempts to read off God's nature from man's. To project God in man's image is therefore a heinous form of idolatry confounding the Creator with the creaturely (Rom. 1:23). This confusion reaches its nadir in worship of the beast and his image or statue (Rev. 14:9ff.).

Recent Theological Studies. Granted that the terms "image" and "likeness" denote an exact resemblance, in what respect does man reflect God? What of the vitiating effects of his fall into sin? Is the NT conception of the *imago* in conflict with the OT conception? Is it in conflict with itself? These questions are among those most energetically debated by contemporary theology.

The importance of a proper understanding of the *imago Dei* can hardly be overstated. The answer given to the *imago*-inquiry soon becomes determinative for the entire gamut of doctrinal affirmation. The ramifications are not only theological, but affect every phase of the problem of revelation and reason, including natural and international law, and the cultural enterprise as a whole. Any improper view has consequences the more drastic as its implications are applied to regenerate and to unregenerate man, from primal origin to final destiny.

The new theology supports a "Christological" or "eschatological" interpretation of the divine image in man. This orientation is formally commendable, since the God-man assuredly exhibits the divine intention for man, and the glory of redeemed humanity will consist in full conformity to Christ's image. In the past a type of Christian rationalism has sometimes unfortunately emerged, seeking on the basis of anthropology alone, independently of Christology, to delineate man's true nature and destiny. Such expositions, which arbitrarily identify the *imago* in fallen man with that of Christ, blur easily into speculations of a personalistic and idealistic nature.

But there is also need for caution over the new theology, since it often incorporates an evasive turn into its Christological appeal. It diverts attention from the important question of man's primal origin—that is, from the creation and fall of the first Adam—because of a reluctance to challenge the modern evolutionary philosophy from the standpoint of the Genesis creation account.

By the *imago* the Protestant Reformers had understood especially man's state of original purity, in accord with Gen. 1 and 2, wherein Adam is depicted as fashioned for rational, moral, and spiritual fellowship with his Maker. The existentializing philosophy of our times, however, finding this representation too abruptly contradictory of current scientific views, confers upon the first Adam only a mythical status, regarding him—in respect to deviation from perfection—as simply a type of every man. The *imago* is then no longer conceived as a state, but as a relation—since an original state of Adamic purity is set aside. Hence neo-orthodox theology not only rejects, in common with Protestantism generally, the Roman Catholic exposition of the image in Thomistic terms (of *analogia entis*, a "being" which Creator and creature share in different degrees), but also sets aside the traditional Protestant confidence in the Genesis creation narratives as a scientifically relevant account of origins.

Just because the Christological or eschatological view looks to the end rather than to the beginning, it does not by itself do full justice to the biblical representation. It subordinates the exhibition of the divine image as God's gift in creation, and is vulnerable also to universalistic expositions of redemption. For while the image of the Godhead (Gen. 1:26) on the basis of creation has an anticipatory reference to the God-man, it is not as such the image of Jesus Christ the Redeemer. Although the redemption-image truly presupposes the creation-image, and the creation-image prepares the way for the redemption-image, Karl Barth's emphasis that all divine revelation is redemptive ignores significant considerations. If the original image is in fact a reflex of *grace,* if man *is* God's image only by promise (whereas Jesus Christ is *actually* God's image), can universalism really be avoided? We may note: (1) The creation-image was once-for-all wholly given at the creation of the first Adam; the redemption-image is gradually fashioned. (2) The creation-image is conferred in some respect upon the whole human race; the redemption-image only upon the redeemed. (3) The creation-image distinguishes man from the animals; the redemption-image distinguishes the regenerate family of faith from unregenerate mankind. (4) The creation-image was probationary; the redemption-image is not.

Statements of the *imago Dei* in current theology, while equating the image with those features by which man transcends the animals, often give to the biblical passages a bizarre tone of novelty. Barth has proposed at least two interpretations of the image, and Emil Brunner, three, and their most recent recensions are not devoid of difficulties. The conclusion to be drawn from such adjustment and readjustment is that theologians today seek to comprehend the image within a framework that is unsatisfactorily narrow. While pantheizing liberalism formerly set aside sin and the need for redemption, and mistakenly regarded the natural man as destined for Christ simply on the basis of creation, neo-orthodox writers exaggerate the transcendence of God to the dilution of the *imago* in man as both created and fallen. The recent dialectical reconstructions of the *imago* almost invariably profess to honor the Protestant Reformers, who are credited with first having controlled the *imago* idea in terms of the "true *dialectical* or christological principle." But Calvin's stress on continuity and discontinuity of man's *imago* with his Maker is said to have lacked a proper working balance which the dialectical approach now provides. The new speculation conceives their unity "eschatologically"; that is, neither original righteousness nor the fall are conceded a place in a past empirical time-series, but are held to be known only in faith-response. So it is that the Christological and eschatological expositions of the *imago* today are surfeited with dialectical and existential elements.

Recent denials that the *imago* survives in fallen man reflect an extreme point of view. Barth has championed this position at an earlier stage, contending that humanity and personality have no significance for the image. T. F. Torrance has professed to find it in Calvin. Brunner has readily acknowledged that the image formally survives the fall, but has vacillated over the question of its material content. Nonetheless, the divergences of neo-orthodox theologians are not as significant as their agreements, especially their exclusion of the forms of logic and of a conceptual knowledge of God from the *imago.* The result is their depreciation of the rational element in revelation, both general and special. This modern revision of the noetic aspect of the *imago* is tapered to the limitation of human reason in conformity with the dialectical philosophy; the admission of such conceptual knowledge of God would undermine the possibility of and necessity for the dialectic.

Evangelical expositors of the biblical revelation find the created image of God to exist formally in man's personality (moral responsibility and intelligence) and materially in his knowledge of God and of his will for man. Hence the image is not reducible simply to a relation in which man stands to God, but rather is the precondition of such a relationship. The fall of man is not destructive of the formal image (man's personality) although it involves the distortion (though not demolition) of the material content of the image. The biblical view is that man is made to know God as well as to obey him. Even in his revolt man stands condemned by the knowledge he has, and he is proffered God's redemptive revelation in scriptural (i.e., in propositional) form. The objections that the admission of such a rational content to the *imago* implies pantheism, or a capacity for self-salvation by reflection through its supposed assertion of an undamaged spot in human nature, loses force when the support for such objections is seen to rest on exaggerations of divine transcendence from which the dialectical view itself arises, rather than on biblical considerations.

Although the Old and New Testaments seem to conflict—since the former reiterates the survival of the image in man after the fall, while the latter stresses the redemptive restoration of the image—there is no real clash. The OT conception is presupposed also in the New, which is a legitimate development. For the NT also speaks of the divine image in the natural man (I Cor. 11:7; James 3:9). But its central message is redeemed man's renewal in the image of Christ.

Wider Implications. The Bible depicts man primarily from the perspective of his relation to God because his nature and destiny can be grasped only from this standpoint. Its interpretation of man is therefore primarily religious. The creation narratives are not written expressly to answer the questions posed by twentieth century science, although attempts to discredit them as unscientific sooner or later are embarrassed by inevitable reversals of scientific opinion. Recent evangelical discussions of the harmony of Scripture and science on such matters as the origin, unity, and antiquity of the human race may be found in *Contemporary Evangelical Thought* (C. F. H. Henry, ed., "Science and Religion") and *Theology and Evolution* (R. Mixter, ed.). The Bible does not discriminate man from the animals in terms of morphological considerations, but rather in terms of the *imago Dei.* Man is made for personal and endless fellowship with God, involving rational understanding (Gen. 1:28ff.), moral obedience (2:16–17), and religious communion (3:3). He is given dominion over the animals and charged to subdue the earth, that is, to consecrate it to the spiritual service of God and man.

Nor does Scripture detail a science of psychology in the modern sense, although it presents a consistent view of man's nature. Its emphasis falls on man as a unitary personality of soul and body. Their disjunction is due to sin (2:17); man's reconstitution as a corporeal being in the resurrection is part of his destiny. While the soul survives in the intermediate state between death and resurrection, this is not the ultimate ideal (II Cor. 5:1–4), in sharp contrast to Greek philosophy. The dispute over dichotomy or trichotomy too often loses sight of the unitary nature of human personality. It is not possible to assert separate distinctions within man's nature simply on the basis of the different scriptural terms for soul, spirit, mind, and so forth. Heb. 4:12, often cited in behalf of trichotomy ("the dividing asunder of soul and spirit, and of the joints and marrow"), does not establish soul and spirit as different entities, but as different functions of the one psychic life of man, as is evident from the parallel phrase "the joints and marrow" in relation to the body.

To the OT picture of man, the NT adds the graphic exposition of his divine sonship through the adoption of grace (John 1:12) and his new role, subsequent to his rescue from an unregenerate race, in the family of redemption. As a member of the church, the body of Christ, whose head has already passed through death and resurrection, the redeemed man already has an existence in the eternal order (Eph. 1:3), so that the sudden end of this world order would disclose the exalted Redeemer as the true center of his life and activity. At the same time, the crowned Christ mediates to the members of the body powers and virtues that belong to the age to come as an earnest of their future inheritance (II Cor. 1:22; Gal. 5:22; Eph. 1:14). Man's destiny is therefore not simply an endless existence, but is moral—either a life redeemed and fit for enternity, or a life under perpetual divine judgment.

C. F. H. Henry

See also Man, Doctrine of.

Bibliography. K. Barth, *Church Dogmatics,* III/2; G. C. Berkouwer, *Man: The Image of God;* E. Brunner, *Man in Revolt;* D. Cairns, *The Image of God in Man;* G. H. Clark, *A Christian View of Men and Things;* J. G. Machen, *The Christian View of Man;* J. M. Miller, "The 'Image' and 'Likeness' of God," *JBL* 91:289ff.; W. Mundle *et al., NIDNTT,* II, 284ff.; R. Niebuhr, *The Nature and Destiny of Man;* J. Orr, *God's Image in Man;* H. W. Robinson, *The Christian Doctrine of Man;* M. Smith, *The Image of God;* T. F. Torrance, *Calvin's Doctrine of Man.*

Images, Veneration of. Honor directed to God, saints, or angels through visual representations such as paintings, statues, and other symbols.

Christian history has been marked by recurring tension between those who revere images (iconodules) and those who reject them (iconoclasts). The iconoclasts' position derives from the biblical prohibition against making images. The iconodules rejoin that even under the old dispensation Moses approved image-making in the form of the cherubim above the ark. Moreover, in the new dispensation God himself assumed human form; the incarnation thus conveyed divine sanction for images. Iconoclasts consider image veneration idolatry; iconodules insist that veneration involves no ascription of any divinity to the image.

In the ancient church, public veneration of images developed slowly because of the aversion to idolatry. In the spirit of the Decalogue, such fathers as Tertullian, Eusebius, and Augustine condemned artistic representations of sacred persons. The Gentile church, however, gradually incorporated symbols into worship as paintings from the catacombs attest. Early images seldom portrayed human form but employed suggestive figures, e.g., a lamb or cross for Christ, a dove for the Holy Spirit or apostles. After Constantine, as Christians enjoyed more opportunity to decorate churches, reverence toward images increased. In the sixth century, Gregory I cautiously approved paintings as media to instruct the illiterate, but he explicitly forbade worship of images.

An important stage in the history of Christian

images was reached when the Quinisext Council decreed that Christ must be represented in his human form and not as a lamb. To counter the monophysite and monothelite heresies, which taught that Christ's humanity had been abridged by his divinity, the council found representation of the human form necessary to declare the reality of the incarnation. As John of Damascus, the chief systematizer of this Christological rationale, explained inasmuch as the invisible God had become visible, it is proper to represent artistically "what is visible in God," namely Christ's flesh. In this respect, the icon is a pictorial creedal statement.

But while the conciliar approval of images determined Orthodox Christology, it spawned the bitter "iconoclastic controversy," leading to the explicit requirement of images by Nicaea II. Clarifying the image's role in piety, the council stated that in viewing the representation, the faithful are moved to love and worship the prototype with veneration (*proskynesis*), though not with the adoration (*latria*) proper only to divinity.

The Catholic West was reserved in its acceptance of the Nicaean commendation, preferring to honor saints in their relics. Trent defined Catholic doctrine in response to the revival of iconoclasm in the Protestant Reformation, affirming that it is proper to venerate images of Christ, the Virgin, and other saints, not because of any virtue in the images but because honor given to them passes to the persons depicted.

P. D. Steeves

Bibliography. J. Gibbons, *The Faith of Our Fathers; St. John Damascene on Holy Images;* J. Meyendorff, *Byzantine Theology;* L. Ouspensky, *Theology of the Icon;* J. Pelikan, *The Christian Tradition,* III: The Spirit of Eastern Christendom.

Imago Dei. *See* Image of God.

Imitation of Christ. The basic biblical concept that man is God's child and reflects his attributes. Accordingly Christians are to imitate not evil, but good (III John 11), Paul's conduct (I Cor. 4:16; Phil. 3:17; II Thess. 3:7, 9), the apostles, even as they imitate Christ (I Cor. 11:1; I Thess. 1:6), the heroes of faith (Heb. 6:12; 13:7), and God the Father (Eph. 5:1). In I Thess. 2:14 Paul commends the Thessalonian church for imitating the churches of Judea in steadfastness under persecution.

From these passages, and more particularly from those indicating that man is made in God's image, we derive the popular notion of imitating Christ. The sad facts of sin teach us all that God's image in man is either partially or totally destroyed. But the Bible declares that restoration of the image is possible through Christ. Hence the desire to imitate Christ as the only exact and full image of God (Col. 1:15; 2:9). Likeness to Christ is achieved not by legalistically trying to mold one's action after the divine pattern but by the inward processes of salvation which change heart attitudes, producing good works and Christlike virtues (Rom. 12:2; Eph. 2:8–10; Phil. 2:12–13). The image becomes more like Christ through our attending to him (II Cor. 3:18), but is not finally completed until we see him on the day of resurrection (I John 3:2; Rom. 8:29–30).

From the beginning many desired to imitate the Master, requesting, for example, a model prayer (Luke 11:1–4) which we still repeat today. This ambition prompted the zealous declaration of James and John that they could drink Jesus' cup and undergo his baptism (Mark 10:38–39). It moved Paul, as he sought to let the indwelling Spirit of Christ speak and act through him (Gal. 2:20; Phil. 1:21); so he exhorted others to imitate him even as he imitated Christ.

In Acts 7:60 we find Stephen imitating the dying words of Jesus (Luke 23:34). In Paul's letters the theme of exhibiting Christ's humility, sufferings, and death constantly recurs (e.g., Rom. 8:17, 18, 36; Phil. 1:29–30; 2:5; 3:10–21) and Peter says explicitly (I Pet. 2:21–23) that we are to follow in Christ's steps in suffering and death.

In the postapostolic literature there is a conscious effort to point out how the martyrs imitated Christ in their humility, in being betrayed, in their Spirit-prompted utterances, and triumphant dying (e.g., Ignatius; To the Ephesians 10:3; To the Romans 6:3; Martyrdom of Polycarp 1:1–2; 17:3; 19:1; Diognetus 10:4–5). This literature fortified thousands who nobly imitated their Lord during the terrible Roman persecutions. When Constantine legalized Christianity "second quality" Christians flooded the churches and the imitation of Christ was confined more and more to the monasteries. Mystical experiences corresponding to those of both Christ and the saints multiplied, culminating in the stigmata of Francis of Assisi, a literal physical reproduction of the wounds of Christ. Such mystical experiences continue to our day.

During the fifteenth century and afterward the quiet mysticism of Thomas à Kempis's book, *The Imitation of Christ,* influenced all branches of the church. In our time James Stalker's *Imago Christi* (1889) is perhaps the best, although *In His Steps* by Charles Sheldon (1899) has sold more copies. It is debatable whether John Bunyan's devotional classic, *Pilgrim's Progress,* should be classified here, but devotion takes many forms;

consciously or unconsciously all of them reproduce an image of Christ in the devotee, more or less complete, more or less enlightened.

Modern psychology throws much new light on the perennial desire to imitate Christ by stressing man's need to identify the self with strong personalities (mother figure, father, saint, etc.) in order to build the personality, and by stressing the importance of the subconscious as a reservoir from which our actions rise.

T. B. Crum

See also Brethren of the Common Life; Pietism; Francis of Assisi; Identification with Christ; Mysticism; Thomas à Kempis; Unio Mystica.

Immaculate Conception. The idea that the Mother of God did not have original sin at her conception nor did she acquire elements of original sin in the development of her life, whereas all other human beings have original sin from their conception due to the fall of Adam. The immaculate conception is an article of faith for Roman Catholics. The Mother of God, the Virgin Mary, did not have original sin because of the direct intervention of God. Mary was immaculate as a divine privilege. The Roman Catholic Church considers the doctrine of the immaculate conception of the Virgin Mary to be part of apostolic teaching related to both the Bible and tradition.

The doctrine is referred to, at least implicitly, in the Bible in Gen. 3:15, which indicates a woman who will battle Satan. The woman ultimately wins the battle. Pope Pius IX said that this section of the Bible foretells the immaculate conception. He described his view in "Ineffabilis Deus."

In the early church Mary was often referred to as "all holy." Luke 1:28 which relates Gabriel's greeting to Mary "Hail, full of grace" is said to be a reference to her immaculate conception. In the eighth century the church in England began to celebrate a feast of Mary's conception. Thomas Aquinas and Bernard of Clairvaux opposed the introduction of the feast into France. Duns Scotus favored the feast and explained that Mary was more indebted to the redemptive power of Jesus Christ than any other human being because Christ prevented her from contracting original sin because of the foreseen merits of Christ. By 1685 most Catholics accepted the notion of the immaculate conception. Clement XIII strongly favored the doctrine in the eighteenth century. In the nineteenth century devotion to the feast grew swiftly. Pope Pius IX, after consulting with all bishops of the church, stated the dogma holding that "the most blessed Virgin Mary was preserved from all stain of original sin in the first instant of her conception." This took place in 1854. The immaculate conception is a special feast for the Catholics of the United States.

T. J. German

See also Mariology; Mary, Assumption of; Mary, the Blessed Virgin; Mother of God.

Bibliography. J. B. Carol, *Fundamentals of Mariology;* E. O'Connor, ed., *The Dogma of the Immaculate Conception;* M. Jugie, *l'Immaculée Conception dans l'Écriture Sainte et dans la tradition orientale.*

Immanence of God. *See* God, Attributes of.

Immanuel. Literally "with us [is] God." Occurring three times in the Bible (Isa. 7:14; 8:8; Matt. 1:23), the Hebrew word *'immānû'ēl* (Gr. *Emmanouēl*) is employed as a proper name in all three verses, and as such is the name of the promised offspring of the *'almâ* ("unmarried woman") of Isa. 7:14 and the *parthenos* ("virgin") of Matt. 1:23, who owns (Isa. 8:8) and protects (vs. 10) the land and people of Israel.

As a proper name it is also descriptive of both this child's divine nature and his messianic work of grace. Taken by itself, this name, of course, does not prove that this virgin's son would also be the Son of God, the Second Person of the Holy Trinity. But when one learns from New Testament revelation that Mary's offspring was in fact God incarnate (John 1:1, 18; 20:28; Rom. 9:5; Titus 2:13; Heb. 1:8; II Pet. 1:1; I John 5:20; cf. Luke 1:35; Col. 2:9; I Tim. 3:16), then it becomes apparent that his name was intended to indicate more than the idea that God was merely active through Jesus to govern and protect his people; it actually becomes descriptive of the incarnate Christ's divine nature.

How this name implies his gracious work is apparent from the preposition "with" in his name. When one reflects on the two parties on either side of the preposition: on the one hand, God, infinitely holy, in whom there is no darkness at all (I John 1:5), who is of purer eyes than to behold evil with any degree of approbation (Hab. 1:13); and on the other hand, men, of whom none is righteous (Rom. 3:10) and who are all children deserving God's wrath (Eph. 2:3); one could hardly blame God had he sent his Son as "God against us" or "God opposed to us." When, however, he reveals his Son as "God *with* us," the messianic task, full of grace and the promise of salvation, is suggested.

That his ministry fulfills the Messianic task promised by the name Immanuel Jesus himself affirms when he declares, "Surely I will be with you always" (Matt. 28:20). And the hope that it holds forth is finally and fully satisfied in the new heaven and new earth when "God himself will be with [men] and be their God" (Rev. 21:3).

R. L. Reymond

Immersion. *See* Baptism, Modes of.

Imminence. The doctrine that Christ can return at any moment and that no predicted event must intervene before that return. This view is held primarily by those who believe the church will be raptured before the seven-year tribulation (also known as the seventieth week of Daniel). It is the view typically held by dispensational premillennialism.

Traditionally, most pretribulation rapturists have considered the imminence of Christ's return to be one of the strongest evidences that the rapture will occur before, rather than after, the tribulation. The argument runs like this: The NT presents Christ's return as a comforting hope (John 14; I Thess. 4:17–18; Titus 2:13; James 5:7–8). Believers wait for Christ (I Thess. 1:10) and are exhorted to watch and be sober (5:6); consequently, it is a purifying hope (I John 3:1–3; cf. Rom. 13:11–12; I Pet. 4:7). If the hope is a blessed and comforting hope, no events of predicted trial and tribulation are expected to occur before Christ returns for the church. Otherwise, believers would dread the approach of Christ's return because of the preceding events to be endured. If Christ's return is the basis for exhortation to godly living, that return must be expected at any moment; events thought to be some distance away because of predicted intervening events do not serve well to promote purity and readiness. Finally, believers are exhorted to live in watchfulness and expectation of Christ's return, not of intervening events. According to pretribulationists, all these considerations imply that the event believers await is imminent, and a rapture that comes after a seven-year tribulation cannot be imminent. Therefore the rapture must be pretribulational.

Posttribulation rapturists reply by insisting that the passages in question only imply the believer's attitude of expectancy, but do not imply imminence. They also argue that the NT clearly implies certain necessary intervening events in the early church before Christ's return, such as time to carry out the Great Commission (Matt. 28:18–20; Acts 1:8) or the assurance to Peter he would reach old age (John 21:18–19; II Pet. 1:14). Thus, for the NT church the exhortations to watch could not have implied imminence. Why, then, should they now?

The doctrine of imminence has been most characteristic of pretribulation rapturists. However, some who hold to a midseventieth week rapture accept at least a limited imminence by maintaining that the beginning of the seventieth week cannot be known. Also, those who either understand the tribulation or seventieth week to be already fulfilled or who spiritualize it can hold to the imminence of Christ's return. A few posttribulational premillennialists accept the imminence of Christ's return on this basis. Amillennialists are hesitant dogmatically to espouse a strict imminence doctrine, but they do not subscribe to a seven-year period necessarily occurring before Christ's return. Though amillennialists are uncomfortable describing Christ's coming as strictly imminent, they do think it may be described as impending and as something the believer should always be ready and watchful for.

S. N. Gundry

See also Eschatology; Rapture of the Church; Second Coming of Christ; Tribulation.

Bibliography. R. H. Gundry, *The Church and the Tribulation;* G. E. Ladd, *The Blessed Hope;* J. F. Walvoord, *The Blessed Hope and the Tribulation* and *The Rapture Question.*

Immortality. The quality or state of being immortal. The concept of immortality is expressed directly in the Bible only in the NT. The words used are *athanasia, aphtharsia,* and its cognate adjective *aphthartos. Athanasia* is the exact equivalent of the English immortality, and it is used in I Cor. 15:53–54 where it describes the resurrection body as one which is not subject to death: and in I Tim. 6:16, where God is said to be the one who alone has immortality. He alone in his essence is deathless. *Aphtharsia* has the basic meaning of indestructibility and, by derivation, of incorruption, by which it is rendered in the familiar resurrection paean in I Cor. 15:42ff. in the AV. The translation *immortality* is used, however, in Rom. 2:7, where the reference is to the life of glory and honor to which the believer aspires: in II Tim. 1:10, where it is said that Christ "abolished death and brought life and *immortality* to light." The adjective *aphthartos* is used to describe God as not being subject to diminution or decay (Rom. 1:23; I Tim. 1:17); or of things which are not perishable, such as the crown awarded to the successful Christian (I Cor. 9:25), the inheritance which is reserved for the Christian (I Pet. 1:4), the seed of which the Christian is born (I Pet. 1:23).

It may be said, therefore, that immortality in the biblical sense is a condition in which the individual is not subject to death or to any influence which might lead to death. God is uniquely immortal in that he is without beginning or end of life and is not in any way affected by change or diminution. Man, on the other hand, is immortal only by derivation and when his mortal body has been replaced by one which is immortal. This article is concerned with human immortality.

The biblical idea of immortality thus differs from all others in certain important respects. One of these is that in nonbiblical teaching man is inherently immortal. Another is that it is the spiritual aspect of human nature only which is thought to be immortal. The human soul or spirit survives death. A corollary of these two is that the human body is usually thought of as a kind of prison house of the spirit, or, at best, as a very transitory part of the human personality. In biblical thought man is not inherently immortal; it is the whole man, body and soul, that is immortal even though the body must undergo a transformation in order to achieve immortality.

In the OT as well as in the NT, man is a complete being only as his body and spirit are in union. He is then a living soul, or person (Gen. 2:7). While some have understood the Genesis narrative as teaching that man was created immortal and that sin brought mortality, it would seem better to interpret the account as teaching that man would have gained immortality through a period of testing in which he would be obedient to the divine commands. If death was the penalty for sin, life was to be the reward for obedience.

Throughout the OT the dead are described as going down to Sheol, a place of obscurity, forgetfulness, and relative inactivity (Job 10:20–22, 14:13ff.; Ps. 88:10–12; *et al.*). Sheol, however, was not outside the Lord's purview (Ps. 139:8; Amos 9:2), and it was indicated through some OT writers that there would be a deliverance from it (Job 19:25–27; Ps. 16:10; 49:14ff.). This deliverance would take the form of a resurrection, though this climax of OT hope finds expression only in Dan. 12:2.

In the NT it is implied that OT believers did not have a full knowledge of the meaning of immortality, since our Lord Jesus Christ brought life and immortality (*aphtharsia*) to light through the gospel (II Tim. 1:10). Christians have been begotten in Christ to an immortal (*aphtharton*) inheritance (I Pet. 1:3–4). The inheritance is described as one of glory, honor, incorruption (*aphtharsia*), and eternal life. To be without the life in Christ is not to have immortality, in the biblical sense of the term.

Immortality, for the Christian, involves the resurrection and may be fully attained only after it. While it is said that believers who have died are present with the Lord when they are absent from the body (II Cor. 5:8), they are nevertheless to be changed at Christ's appearing. Both those who have died and those who are alive upon earth will receive a body like the resurrection body of Jesus Christ (Phil. 3:21). Those who are the children of God will be like Christ (I John 3:2), perfected in righteousness (Phil. 1:6), from all sin, sorrow, pain, or death (Rev. 22:3ff.), and they will serve God continually. D. W. Kerr

See also Annihilationism; Conditional Immortality; Heaven; Intermediate State; Resurrection of the Dead; Sheol.

Bibliography. S. D. F. Salmond, *Christian Doctrine of Immortality;* J. Orr, *Christian View of God and the World,* Lects. iv, v, and app.; O. Cullmann, "Immortality of the Soul and the Resurrection of the Dead," *HDSB,* 7–36.

Immortality, Conditional. *See* Conditional Immortality.

Immutability of God. *See* God, Attributes of.

Impanation (Lat. *impanare,* "to embody in bread"). An explanation of Christ's presence in the Lord's Supper which maintains that he is embodied in the bread. Christ is locally and physically present in the host. Guitmund of Aversa (d. before 1195) taught this doctrine, comparing Christ's incarnation at Christmas with his impanation in the Eucharist. John of Paris (d. 1306) said "the Body of Christ is 'impanated,'" i.e., "has become bread." The Roman Catholic Church rejected this view, affirming instead transubstantiation, the doctrine that at the consecration the bread is changed into the body of Christ in a "wonderful and singular conversion," so that the accidents of bread (outward appearance) remain but the substance (inward reality) is body. Impanationists disagreed, insisting on both the continuing existence of bread and the presence of Christ's body. A communicant receives not just the body of Christ, as in transubstantiation, but also bread. This position is often attributed to Lutherans, who are said to teach consubstantiation, the view that in the Lord's supper one receives body and bread mixed together. Individual Lutherans may hold such opinions. The Lutheran confessions, however, do not try to explain the mode of union between Christ's body and the bread in the Supper. It is regarded as a "mystery." Lutherans officially rejected impanation, condemning it in the Formula of Concord of 1577, confessing that they "do not believe that the body and blood of Christ are locally enclosed in the bread" (SD.14), but testifying that while they receive "natural bread" they also obtain his body "in a supernatural, incomprehensible manner" (SD.64).

C. G. Fry

See also Lord's Supper, Views of.

Impassibility of God. The doctrine that God is not capable of being acted upon or affected emotionally by anything in creation.

Passibility, Thomists argued, involves potentiality and potentiality involves change. Unrealized potential and change in the Deity seemed to contradict their understanding of God's immutability, transcendence, self-existence, self-determination, and perfection. Suffering, furthermore, seemed incompatible with perfect divine blessedness. Thus the Thirty-nine Articles of the Church of England affirm that God is without body, parts, or passions.

However, that view seemed to others to convey the idea that God was devoid of an affectional nature essential to personality and *agape* love. As early as the Bishops Conference of 1786 the word "passions" was omitted. Hence, the Methodist statement stops with saying God is without body or parts.

The two hypotheses, that God is passible and that God is impassible, need to be put to the test of relevant scriptural evidence, along with their assumptions concerning the meaning of other divine attributes.

The OT portrays God as folding Israel in his arms like a shepherd (Isa. 40:11), redeeming and restoring his scattered children (43:5–7), loving with a love greater than a mother's tenderness (49:15), and comforting as a mother comforts her child (66:13). Jesus constantly referred to God as Father to convey the fact that God personally cares about his children by creation and regeneration.

All of these anthropomorphic expressions are figurative, but the figures of speech illustrate a nonfigurative point. The God of Abraham, Isaac, and Jacob is not without feeling, not without the capability of loving and feeling the hurt of love spurned. The relationship of love to suffering stands out in God's suffering servant (Isa. 53). With some things God is pleased, with others God is displeased. God pours out his righteous indignation upon the ungodly who persecuted his people (63:1–6), but God suffered as his people suffered. "In all their distress he too was distressed, and the angel of his presence saved them. In his love and mercy he redeemed them; he lifted them up and carried them all the days of old" (vs. 9). When his people turn against him, the Holy Spirit can be grieved (vs. 10; Eph. 4:30).

The heavenly Father was so moved by human sin that he sent his Son into the world to suffer as humans suffer, to sacrifice himself, and to lay the foundation for the church. The Father suffered with Jesus and with the poor, the orphans, the widows, and the strangers empathically. But the Father did not die on the cross. The Father suffers, but contrary to Kitamori and Moltmann does not die, even symbolically. But before Jesus can establish his future kingdom, he must suffer many things and be rejected by this generation (Luke 17:25). Missing the impact of the Father's imputed wrath and Jesus' agony as forsaken by the Father, we miss the pathos of the gospel.

Dietrich Bonhoeffer in his *Letters and Papers from Prison* asks, did not Jesus himself use distress as his point of contact with men? We are challenged to participate in the sufferings of God at the hands of a godless world. By ranging themselves with God in his suffering, Bonhoeffer claimed, Christians distinguish themselves from the heathen. H. Wheeler Robinson saw that suffering rises from love. Because God loves mankind he permits, or suffers, sin, but takes no pleasure in it. The only way moral evil can enter the consciousness of the morally good is as suffering. What meaning can there be in a love, Robinson asks, that is not costly?

We do not worship, as Dorothee Sölle alleged, an apathetic God. Just as God perfectly uses his intellectual and volitional powers, he perfectly uses his emotional powers. Negatively, God has no physical pains, and no emotions, inconsistent with all his other attributes. God is not overcome by emotions, has no emotions out of control, out of balance, or inappropriate. God does not suffer emotional disorders. Affirmatively, the God of the Bible has appropriate, healthy, self-controlled emotional experience. As exhibited in Jesus, the Father may be viewed as weeping with those who weep and rejoicing with those who rejoice.

A biblically active, rather than a philosophically passive, view of God's other attributes avoids the alleged antinomy Leonard Hodgson thinks irresolvable. God's immutability does not reduce the living, active, personal Lord of all to an impersonal, static principle. It affirms that God in all his thoughts, words, and acts dynamically moves in ways consistent with his own essence and purposes. Let passibility involve change. Change that does not deny any of God's essential attributes is in harmony with a biblical view of God. God is not only transcendent, but also immanent, relating to both the just and the unjust. Though God alone has life in himself, God has granted life to many others in order to participate in personal relationships with them. God's perfect joy is surely not an unrealistic one, but is inseparable from his knowledge of all the evils and values of creation. Suffering accepted as inevitable, Kitamori has observed, is depressing, but suffering born of love produces power and life. G. R. LEWIS

See also GOD, ATTRIBUTES OF.

Bibliography. J. O. Buswell, Jr., *A Systematic Theology of the Christian Religion;* J. Gill, *Body of Divinity;* V. A. Harvey, *A Handbook of Theological Terms;* L. Hodgson, *For Faith and Freedom;* K. Kitamori, *Theology of the Pain of God;* J. Y. Lee, *God Suffers for Us;* G. R. Lewis, *ZPEB,* V, 530–33; J. Moltmann, *The Crucified God;* J. K. Mozley, *The Impassibility of God;* H. W. Robinson, *Suffering, Human and Divine;* D. Sölle, *Suffering;* A. H. Strong, *Systematic Theology;* H. O. Wiley, *Christian Theology.*

Impeccability of Christ. *See* SINLESSNESS OF CHRIST.

Imprecatory Psalms. The psalms containing passages seeking the hurt of someone else (e.g., 5:10; 10:15; 55:15; 109:9ff.) and which compel the question whether they can have any place in Christian Scripture. Two background remarks are in place. First, imprecations are found in the NT also, not least the maledictions of the Lord himself (e.g., Matt. 23:13ff.) and the apostolic anathema (Gal. 1:8ff.; cf. Rev. 6:10; 18:20). Second, the notably imprecatory Ps. 69 is used by the Lord Jesus (John 15:25) and of the Lord Jesus (John 2:17; Rom. 15:3), and its divine inspiration is affirmed (Acts 1:16, 20; see also Rom. 11:9ff.).

It is impossible, therefore, to dismiss the imprecatory psalms as OT morality, especially when we recall that the OT itself forbids vengeance and grudge-bearing (Lev. 19:17–18), teaches that the Lord hates violence (Ps. 5:6), and insists that vengeance must be left to him (Ps. 7:4; Prov. 20:22; etc.). Furthermore, the imprecatory psalms themselves cannot be treated as if they were somehow out of step with the rest of the OT or were perhaps exemplary of a lower morality than the OT came to hold; for alongside the imprecations, these very psalms display a spirituality we would covet (Ps. 139 is a case in point).

In a positive appraisal of the imprecatory psalms it must be noted first that all the imprecations are prayers. They are not a declaration of intent on the part of the psalmist, but a commitment of the problem to the Lord and a leaving of vengeance to him; they show an obedient faith godward and an unretaliatory intent manward. Second, the imprecations express a holy, moral indignation. These psalmists longed for the vindication of God's name (9:19ff.; 83:16–17; etc.), and were lifted up to experience a perfect hatred (139:21–22). Third, the imprecations were expressed with realism: a realistic acceptance of what God had revealed of his certain judgment (cf. 109:13 with Exod. 20:5) and a realistic awareness of the outworking of just retribution in the experiences of this life (cf. Ps. 137:9, tr. "O how right he will be"). J. A. MOTYER

Bibliography. J. A. Motyer, *The New Bible Commentary Revised;* F. D. Kidner, *The Psalms,* I, 25–32; C. S. Lewis, *Reflections on the Psalms.*

Imputation. A broad concept finding its theological center in the atonement. The Latin *imputare* literally means "to reckon," "to charge to one's account," and is an adequate rendering of the Greek term *logizomai.* This forensic notion of imputation has its partial roots in the commercial and legal language of the Greco-Roman world; one who has something imputed to him is accountable under the law. It is in this sense that Paul asks Philemon to have Onesimus's debts transferred to Paul (Philem. 18: "If he has wronged you ... charge that to my account"). Imputation also has its distinctively Hebraic roots (cf. *ḥāšab,* "to count for, to reckon"), being used, for example, in reference to the sacrificial system (cf. Lev. 7:18: "neither shall it be credited to him"; Lev. 17:4). It is also important to note that the OT uses the term to include even those judgments that have no direct, objective basis (e.g., Gen. 31:15: "Are we not regarded by him as foreigners?" II Chr. 9:20).

In the NT, Christians are said to receive the "alien righteousness" of God as a "free gift in the grace of that one man Jesus Christ" (Rom. 5:15). Just as God reckoned Abraham as righteous on the basis of Abraham's belief alone (Gen. 15:6; Rom. 4:3), so others are similarly blessed as the Lord does not impute their iniquity to them (Ps. 32:1–2; Rom. 4:7–8). This divine judicial act is based, not on human merit, but on God's love (Rom. 5:6ff.).

In arguing for a forensic, communal grace rooted solely in the Lord Jesus Christ, through whom we receive our reconciliation, Paul contrasts the work of Christ with the sin of Adam, by which sin, guilt, and death came into the world (Rom. 5:12–14). Just as it is in Christ that we are redeemed, so it is in Adam that we are judged sinners (Rom. 5:15–21; cf. I Cor. 15:21–22). The exact meaning of this comparison has caused heated debate through much of church history. Can it be said that humankind is judged according to an "alien guilt"? Is not such a notion irrational, harsh, arbitrary, and even fatalistic, not in keeping with the larger biblical witness that people act freely and are responsible for their own sins (cf. Ezek. 18:1–20)?

Pelagius in the fifth century substituted for the notion of *imputation* the less severe concept of *imitation.* He argued that as free and responsible agents who are born with the capacity not to sin, all people nevertheless sin concretely following Adam's example. Pelagius was opposed by Augustine, and his view concerning human possibility has since been repeatedly rejected by the orthodox church (although it has proven a recurring notion, e.g., in Protestant liberalism).

How then is the imputation of Adam's sin to humankind to be understood? Some have argued that God's justice demands that imputation be considered not as forensic, but as real, all humankind having in fact sinned with Adam. Guilt thus is a proper guilt and in no sense alien. Such "realists" have difficulty in explaining how we might be actually present with Adam, however.

An alternate solution, one argued by the Westminster Confession, for example, is to understand Adam as our representative. God, in creating the human community, covenanted with all humanity through its head, Adam. The decision of the public figure Adam to sin is thus our decision as well, and his guilt, ours too. Such an explanation is often labeled federalism, after a federalist notion of government.

Although the exact nature of divine imputation remains a mystery, a biblically based understanding of the concept would want to maintain the following: (1) as formulated by Paul, the notion of imputation is included as part of a doxology to God for his grace in Christ. Imputation has to do ultimately with salvation, with our "alien righteousness," with being reckoned *as if* we were righteous. (2) Not only is Christ the theme of Paul's discussion, he is the starting-point as well. Only in the context of God's yes to us on the cross (and in the law) do we understand the full horror of his no to humankind (Rom. 5:13). In Adam, God judged the entire human race guilty, but only in Jesus is this fact fully understood (cf. Jesus' cry, "My God, my God, why hast thou forsaken me," Mark 15:34; cf. Isa. 53:4–6; II Cor. 5:21).

(3) The doctrine of the imputation of sin has never had as its purpose the denial of personal freedom and guilt. Rather, it has been intended to emphasize universal complicity on the part of humanity. The notion of imputation provides sin neither an excuse nor an explication, only a judgment. We stand in need of God's grace (cf. Rom. 6:23).

(4) The stress on the corporate and original nature of human sin, on the human solidarity of guilt, is but one pole of a full biblical understanding. Sin's social dimension needs the continual, yet paradoxical, balancing of sin's individual and personal dimensions (I John 1:9–10). As fallen men and women, we live out a life of sin (i.e., of independence from God) and actualize our sins. Given God's judgment on humankind, his alienation from us, we can only worship creature and not Creator. And yet, it is we who choose no longer to submit and to follow instead our independent passions.

(5) The analogy between Adam and Christ is not simple or total. While the imputation of righteousness is *arbitrary,* a free and undeserved act of grace whose reality remains forensic, the imputation of guilt is *appropriate,* its consequence affirming the judgment. Paul himself emphasizes the danger of taking the analogy too far, distinguishing the "free gift" from the "trespass" (Rom. 5:15). (6) The divine imputation of sin and guilt, being a forensic act of God, needs have no objective basis in the life of the person (cf. II Cor. 5:21: "For our sake he made him [Christ] to be sin who knew no sin, so that in him [Christ] we might become the righteousness of God"). Nevertheless, the consistent biblical witness, validated by all who have followed after Adam, is that it does (cf. Rom. 3:23: "all have sinned and fall short of the glory of God"). God is not capricious, but righteous and loving (Ezek. 18:25–32). Humankind has not merely been declared guilty; it has acted out its guilt. R. K. Johnston

See also Adam; Fall of Man; Sin.

Bibliography. G. C. Berkouwer, *Sin;* A. A. Hodge, *The Atonement;* H. W. Heidland, *TDNT,* IV, 284–92; J. Murray, *The Imputation of Adam's Sin.*

Incarnation (Lat. *in* and *carō,* stem *carn,* meaning "flesh"). In the context of Christian theology, the act whereby the eternal Son of God, the Second Person of the Holy Trinity, without ceasing to be what he is, God the Son, took into union with himself what he before that act did not possess, a human nature, "and so [He] was and continues to be God and man in two distinct natures and one person, forever" (Westminster Shorter Catechism, Q. 21). Scripture support for this doctrine is replete, e.g., John 1:14; Rom. 1:3; 8:3; Gal. 4:4; Phil. 2:7–8; I Tim. 3:16; I John 4:2; II John 7 (cf. also Eph. 2:15; Col. 1:21–22; I Pet. 3:18; 4:1).

The Nature of the Incarnation. Like many other theological terms, this term can be misleading. It might suggest that the eternal Logos by the act of incarnation was *confined* to the human body of Jesus of Nazareth. The implication of such a construction of the result of the incarnation is that God the Son, kenotically "emptying" himself, divested himself of his attribute of being always and everywhere immediately present in his universe. But to hold such a view is tantamount to contending that he who enfleshed himself as Jesus of Nazareth, while doubtless more than man, is not quite God. Divine attributes are not, however, characteristics separate and distinct from God's essence that he can set aside when he desires. To the contrary, it is precisely the sum total of God's attributes that constitutes the essence of his deity and expresses his divine glory. Jesus, during the days of his flesh, claimed omnipresence for himself in Matt. 18:20 and 28:20. Recognizing this, the Council of Chalcedon (A.D. 451), whose creedal labors produced the Christological definition that fixed the boundaries for all future discussion, declared that Jesus Christ possessed "two natures without confusion, *without change,* without division, without separation, the distinctiveness of the natures being by no means removed because of the union, but *the properties of each nature* being preserved" (emphasis added; cf. also Calvin, *Inst.* 2.13.4; Heidelberg Catechism, Q. 48). The doctrine, thus clarified, means that in the incarnation the divine Logos, while in the body of Jesus and personally united to it, is also beyond the bounds of the human nature he assumed.

It is very important, in light of what has just been said, to underscore that in the incarnation the divine Logos did not take into union with himself a human person; otherwise, he would have been *two* persons, *two* egos, with *two* centers of *self*-consciousness. The Scriptures will not tolerate such a view. Never does Jesus Christ, when referring to himself, say "we" or "us" or "our"; he always uses "I" or "me" or "my." What the divine Logos, who was already and eternally a person, did do, through the operation of the Holy Spirit, was to take into union with himself a human *nature* with the result that Jesus Christ was *one* person with a divine nature (i.e., a complex of divine attributes) and a human nature (i.e., a complex of human attributes). This is not to say that the human nature of Christ is impersonal; "the human nature of Christ was not for a moment impersonal. The Logos assumed that nature into personal subsistence with Himself. The human nature has its personal existence in the person of the Logos. It is in-personal rather than impersonal" (L. Berkhof). John Murray writes: "The Son of God did not become personal by incarnation. He became incarnate but there was no suspension of his divine self-identity."

The Effecting Means of the Incarnation. The means, according to Scripture, whereby the incarnation came about is the virginal conception (a more accurate description than virgin birth) of the Son of God by the Holy Spirit in the womb of Mary (Isa. 7:14; Matt. 1:16, 18, 20, 23, 25; Luke 1:27, 34–35; 2:5; 3:23; Gal. 4:4). Due to the interpenetration of the persons within the Godhead (cf. John 14:20; 17:21–23; Heb. 9:14), the Holy Spirit, by means of the virginal conception, insured the divine personality of the God-man without creating at the same time a new human personality. As Berkhof says: "If Christ had been generated by man, He would have been a human person, included in the covenant of works, and as such would have shared the common guilt of mankind. But now that His subject, His ego, His person, is not out of Adam, He is not in the covenant of works and is free from the guilt of sin. And being free from the guilt of sin, His human nature could also be kept free, both before and after His birth, from the pollution of sin."

Scriptural Representations of the Incarnate Person. Because Jesus Christ is the God-man (one person who took human nature into union with his divine nature in the one divine person), the Scriptures can predicate of his person whatever can be predicated of either nature. In fact, the person of Christ may be *designated* in terms of one nature while what is *predicated* of him so designated is true by virtue of his union with the other nature (cf. Westminster Confession, VIII, vii). In other words:

1. The person, and not a nature, is the subject of the statement when what is predicated of Christ is true by virtue of all that belongs to his person as essentially divine and assumptively human; e.g., redeemer, prophet, priest, and king.

2. The person, and not a nature, is the subject of the statement when what is predicated of him, designated in terms of what he is as human, is true by virtue of his divine nature; e.g., in Rom. 9:5 Christ is designated according to his human nature ("Christ according to the flesh"), while what is predicated of him is true because of his divine nature ("God over all, blessed forever"). The Scriptures do not confuse or intermingle the natures. It is the person of Christ who is always the subject of the scriptural assertions about him.

3. The person, and not a nature, is the subject of the statement, when what is predicated of him, designated in terms of what he is as divine, is true by virtue of his human nature; e.g., in I Cor. 2:8 Christ is designated according to his divine nature ("the Lord of glory"), while what is predicated of him is true because of his human nature (man "crucified" him). Again, there is no confusion here of the divine and human natures

of Christ. It is not the divine nature as such which is crucified; it is the divine person, because he is also human, who is crucified.

R. L. Reymond

See also Christology.

Bibliography. L. Berkhof, *Systematic Theology;* C. Hodge, *Systematic Theology,* II; J. Murray, *Collected Writings,* II; B. B. Warfield, *The Person and Work of Christ.*

Indian Theology. The attempt to reformulate biblical theology in Indian categories of thought, in a manner relevant to the Indian context. Until recently Western theology has dominated the Indian theological scene, and Christianity has come under criticism from Hindu thinkers in this regard. The pioneers of Indian theology were not Christians but enlightened Hindus who came under the strong influence of Western thought and Christianity. These enlightened nationalists wanted to reform Hinduism and Indian society, thereby counterbalancing Christian missionary activities. For Indian Christian leaders, Indian theology is an attempt to meet the criticism that Christianity is a foreign and dangerous denationalizing force. It represents a search for and an expression of self-identity in India and in the field of Christian theology. It is an attempt to conceptualize the urge for being Christian and Indian simultaneously. It faces the challenges of renascent Hinduism in its relegation of Christianity to a subordinate status. Moreover it stands for the concern of Indian theologians to communicate the gospel in thought patterns familiar to the Indian mind. It is to present "the water of life in an Indian cup."

Trends in Indian Theology. No uniform pattern or common trends can be traced in Indian theology. Corresponding to the diversified historical context and socioreligious needs, there are varied theological expressions of response to the gospel.

(1) There are attempts to harmonize Christianity, rather than Christ, with Hinduism. Raam Mohan Roy (1772–1833), the father of modern India, and his successor Keshab Chandra Sen (1838–1884) interpreted Jesus in Indian traditions. Jesus is portrayed as an Asiatic. His ethical precepts, independent of his person, provide the way to happiness and peace. His "Divine Humanity" is explained within the framework of Hindu mystic traditions. Jesus Christ and the "best elements" of Christianity are conveniently accommodated under the wide umbrella of Hinduism. Because of the universalistic and absorptive features of Hinduism, no tension is experienced in this.

(2) There is concern for dialogue. Christian theology in India finds itself in the midst of spirited and influential non-Christian religious systems, especially Hinduism, which claims the allegiance of eighty-four percent of Indians. Hindu religiocultural factors have, therefore, played a decisive role in the emergence of several significant issues of Indian theology, for instance, the uniqueness and finality of Christ and the nature and scope of Christian mission. A viable base has been found in the NT synthesis of Hebrew and Greek culture for synthesizing Christian and Hindu culture in India. Hinduism and its scriptures are treated as counterparts to Judaism and the OT in relation to the gospel. God speaks equally through other religions also. P. D. Devanandan and Raymond Panikkar's theologies emerge in this context of religiocultural pluralism. They advocate letting Christ reform Hinduism from within and so unveil the Christ who is already present there, though hidden and unacknowledged.

(3) There is frequently a polemic emphasis. God's special revelation is essential for knowing the truth, and Jesus is this divine special revelation. Without him intuition and inspiration fall short of "the rock of Christ" in knowing the truth.

(4) There is an apologetic emphasis. Renascent Hinduism stripped Christ and Christianity of everything that they claim and possess. Christ is made one among those who experienced the *advaitic* (monistic) experience. Christianity is treated as one of the earlier stages in the evolution of religion. The church has been accused of denationalism. The crucial issues reflected in Brahmabandab Upadhyaya's theology are to be judged in this context. He reformulated the doctrine of Trinity in which he portrayed Christ as "nothing but the highest." He was a Hindu-Catholic, i.e., at heart a Christian, yet culturally a Hindu.

(5) There is concern for evangelism. Jesus Christ is not a monopoly of the West. He is equally for India too. There he is to be presented, not in Western robes and image, but in terms and thought-forms intelligible to the Indian mind. Sadhu Sunder Singh's Christocentric theology is a conscious attempt toward this.

(6) One finds emphasis on relevancy. Indian theologians want to erase the ghetto mentality of the minority Christians. Their task is to help Christians see themselves as an integral part of the larger community in India and participate in the common life and experience. The struggles for socioeconomic development and humanization are seen as "Christ at work today." M. M.

Thomas and others contend that Christian theology has to be relevant in this context, and therefore the context and social dimension of the gospel are primary.

Summary and Evaluation. These attempts to explain, interpret, and formulate the essentials of Christianity in Indian thought-patterns have enabled Indian thinkers to contribute something to Christian theology. While contributing to the field of apologetics, these attempts to wed faith with reason, revealed theology with natural theology, have had only partial success. It has, to an extent, made the gospel relevant in the context of Indian nationalism, religiocultural pluralism, and socioeconomic development. It marks the beginning of Indian biblical scholarship and creative theological formulations. Yet none has managed to be faithful to Christian theology in its entirety, nor to the context and content simultaneously. Quite often "context" has become more decisive than the "text," and this is critical. The final authority seems to rest upon context and not the Bible. More than the special revelation in Scripture, various social sciences influence and determine the content and scope of Indian theology. Instead of being theocentric, God in relation to man, it becomes more anthropocentric, man in relation to man or structures. However, no one philosophy or sociology can provide an adequate framework for Christian theology that is faithful to revealed content of Scripture. The quest for relevance in theology, whether European, American, African, or Indian, should not be at the expense of commitment to the finality of the written and living Word.

C. V. Mathew

Bibliography. K. Baago, *Pioneer in Indigenous Christianity;* R. H. S. Boyd, *An Introduction to Indian Christian Theology;* H. Burkle and W. M. W. Roth, eds., *Indian Voices in Today's Theological Debate;* M. M. Thomas, *The Acknowledged Christ of the Indian Renaissance.*

Indulgences. The means by which the Roman Church claims to give remission before God of the temporal punishment due to sins, whose guilt has already been forgiven. The theology of this idea developed slowly in the Western church and from the sixteenth century in Roman Catholicism; it has often been the case that practice went ahead of the theory. Further, the granting of indulgences has sometimes been the occasion of abuse and controversy, e.g., the famous controversy between Martin Luther and J. J. Tetzel in 1517 in Germany at the beginning of the Protestant Reformation.

Basic to the theology of indulgences is the distinction between eternal and temporal punishment due to sin. Roman Catholics believe that in absolution, given by the priest following repentance, the repentant sinner receives the remission of sins and removal of eternal punishment by God, for the sake of Jesus Christ. The matter of temporal punishment of sins remains, however, and this can only be removed by penitential acts and effort. It is here that indulgences are believed to function, in that the church (via the pope or a bishop) grants indulgences to cover all or part of the temporal punishment of sins. In the case of an indulgence granted to a soul in purgatory the effect is to guarantee for that soul the intercession of the saints.

By what power does the church grant such indulgences? There is believed to exist a treasury of merits (those of Christ, the saints, and martyrs) available to the church in and through the communion of saints. The pope may make use of this merit and apply it via indulgences to Christian people in order to remit their temporal punishment. Since the Second Vatican Council the Roman Church has made efforts to revise and improve this whole system.

P. Toon

Bibliography. J. Neuner and J. Dupuis, eds., *The Christian Faith in the Doctrinal Documents of the Catholic Church;* P. Schaff, *Creeds of Christendom,* II, 205–9, 220, 433, 549.

Inerrancy and Infallibility of the Bible. *See* Bible, Inerrancy and Infallibility of.

Infallibility. The state of being incapable of error. The word "infallible" occurs in the AV in Acts 1:3 with reference to the resurrection of Christ. There is no corresponding word in the Greek, however, and it is omitted in later versions.

That the revelation of God in Jesus Christ is infallible, in the general sense that it presents mankind with the infallible way of salvation, would be accepted by all Christians, but the seat of infallibility is a matter of controversy. Three main lines of thought may be discerned corresponding to the three main divisions of Christendom. The Eastern Orthodox Church believes that general councils of the Church are guided by the Holy Spirit so as not to err; the Roman Catholic Church believes that the pope is personally preserved from error by God; and Protestant thought relies on the sufficiency of Holy Scripture as the guide to God's self-revelation. We can relate these three theories in the following way. Christians of all traditions accord to Holy Scripture a unique place in the determination of the gospel, and there exists an extensive body of common belief derived from it. This common belief is further described and defined by the councils held in the early centuries, four of which at any rate command universal approval. The Orthodox Church continues to rely on councils, the Latin Church has finally come to define the seat of infallibility as the papacy, while Protestants look to the Scriptures as the ultimate source of authority. Particular attention must be given to the doctrine of papal infallibility, and the Protestant doctrine of the sufficiency and supremacy of Scripture.

The doctrine of the infallibility of the pope was defined by the Roman Catholic Church in the year 1870. It declares that the pope is enabled by God to express infallibly what the church should believe concerning questions of faith and morals when he speaks in his official capacity as "Christ's vicar on earth," or *ex cathedra.*

Behind this dogma lie three assumptions which are disputed by other Christians: (1) that Christ established an office of "vicar" for his church on earth; (2) that this office is held by the bishop of Rome; and (3) that Christ's vicar is infallible in his declarations of faith and morals. The grounds upon which the Church of Rome bases these assumptions may be summarized as follows: (1) Our Lord's saying to Peter recorded in Matt. 16:18, "Thou art Peter, and on this rock I will build my church," implies that Christ made Peter the head of the church, or his "vicar on earth." (2) Peter was bishop at Rome, and thereby constituted this see the supreme bishopric over the church, transmitting to his successors the prerogative of being Christ's vicar. (3) The vicar of Christ must be infallible by the very nature of the case. All three arguments are necessary to the doctrine of papal infallibility, and all three display a fallibility which makes it impossible for the Orthodox and Protestant churches to accept them.

Recently, Roman Catholic attitudes toward papal infallibility have shifted somewhat in response to ecumenical dialogue, historical investigation, and most recently Hans Küng's book. Küng's challenge, provoked by the papal ruling on contraception, set off a large and still unresolved debate inside Catholicism. Küng argued that the papal teaching office (*magisterium*) had in fact made many contradictory and erroneous rulings over the centuries, and that Catholics should therefore speak only of an "indefectibility of the Church," a position strikingly similar to that of some Protestants, as many Catholics pointed out. The debate has forced all Catholics to define more clearly just what papal infallibility entails, thus cutting back many exaggerated notions of it; and many progressive Catholics have sought to include bishops, theologians, and even the whole church in their notion of an infallibly preserved tradition of the true faith. In the meantime historians have shown that indefectibility of the church was the received view in the West down to about 1200, slowly replaced then by infallibility of the church and finally by infallibility of the papacy, a position first proposed around 1300 but hotly debated in the schools and never officially sanctioned until 1870.

When we turn to Protestant or evangelical thought on this matter, we find that, in so far as it is used at all, infallibility is ascribed to the OT and NT Scriptures as the prophetic and apostolic record. It is so in the fourfold sense (1) that the word of God infallibly achieves its end, (2) that it gives us reliable testimony to the saving revelation and redemption of God in Christ, (3) that it provides us with an authoritative norm of faith and conduct, and (4) that there speaks through it the infallible Spirit of God by whom it is given.

In recent years concentration upon historical and scientific questions, and suspicion of the dogmatic infallibility claimed by the papacy, has led to severe criticism of the whole concept even as applied to the Bible; and it must be conceded that the term itself is not a biblical one and does not play any great part in actual Reformation theology. Yet in the senses indicated it is well adapted to bring out the authority and authenticity of Scripture. The church accepts and preserves the infallible Word as the true standard of its apostolicity; for the Word itself, i.e., Holy Scripture, owes its infallibility, not to any intrinsic or independent quality, but to the divine subject and author to whom the term infallibility may properly be applied.

Ironically, attacks upon biblical infallibility, which for over a century came mainly from liberal Protestants, have come in the last decade from conservatives, who argue that only "inerrancy" (another word not found in Scripture) adequately protects the utter truthfulness and reliability of the Bible. Mainstream evangelicals, therefore, especially those who accept some of the methods and findings of modern scriptural study, are forced to defend the traditional concept of biblical infallibility over against liberals as a necessary basis for receiving divine revelation, and over against conservatives as an adequate basis. W. C. G. PROCTOR AND J. VAN ENGEN

See also EX CATHEDRA; PAPACY; PETER, PRIMACY OF; ROMAN CATHOLICISM.

Bibliography. H. Küng, *Infallible?* G. Salmon, *The Infallibility of the Church;* B. B. Warfield, *The Inspiration and Authority of the Bible.*

Infant Baptism. *See* BAPTISM, INFANT.

Infant Salvation. The possibility of the salvation of infants, recognized from the earliest times of the NT church. Irenaeus, for instance, includes "infants and children" among those whom Christ came to save. The changing doctrine of the church, whereby the kingdom of God was identified with the external church, and the widespread acceptance of the belief that outside the visible church there could be no salvation, gave rise to the doctrine that baptism, the sacrament of admission to the external church, was necessary to salvation. No unbaptized infant therefore could be saved, although, in the view of medieval churchmen, the sufferings of lost infants are less intense than those of lost adults. Furthermore, Thomas Aquinas and others admitted the possibility that stillborn infants of Christian parents might, in the grace of God, be sanctified and saved in a way unknown to us.

The Council of Trent, which defined the position of the papal church as against the Protestant position, committed the Church of Rome to the view that infants dying unbaptized were damned, although it did not express a definite view as of the kind and degree of their punishment. Moreover, the belief was expressed that the desire and intention of godly parents to have their children baptized might be accepted in lieu of actual baptism in the case of stillborn babes. Eusebius Amort (1758) taught that God might be moved by prayer to grant salvation to such infants extrasacramentally. The inconclusiveness of the Tridentine declarations leaves the way open for widely differing conceptions as to what is to be understood by the exclusion of unbaptized children from heaven.

The Augsburg Confession commits Lutheranism to the view that baptism is necessary to salvation, although, in modification of this position, Lutheran theologians have taught that "the necessity of baptism is not intended to be equalized with that of the Holy Ghost." Luther believed that God would accept the intention to baptize the infant in lieu of actual baptism where circumstances made the latter impossible. Later Lutherans adopt the more cautious attitude that it would be wrong to assume that all unbaptized infants, including children of those who are outside the church, are lost. While not committing themselves to a belief in the salvation of all children dying in infancy, they tend to regard it as an uncontradicted hope.

The Reformed doctrine of the church carried with it a distinctive doctrine of infant salvation. The church of Christ being, not an external organization, but the true people of God everywhere, it follows that membership in this community is acquired, not by the external act of baptism, but by the internal action of the Holy Spirit in regenerating the soul. Zwingli took the position that all children of believers dying in infancy are saved, for they were born within the covenant, the promise being to believers and to their children (Acts 2:39). He even inclined to the view that all children dying in infancy are elect and saved. John Owen, a good spokesman of Puritan Calvinism, expresses the belief that infants may have an interest in the covenant even through more remote forebears than parents. And, since the grace of God is free and not tied to any condition, he has no doubt that many infants are saved whose parents are not believers. Whatever differing shades of opinion may be found in Reformed teaching with regard to infant salvation, the Reformed Confessions agree in teaching the possibility of infants being saved "by Christ through the Spirit, who worketh when, and where, and how he pleaseth" (Westminster Confession). They do not give confessional authority to the Zwinglian supposition that death in infancy may be taken as a sign of election, and thus of salvation, but with reverent caution assert only that for which they can claim the clear authority of Holy Scripture, namely, that all elect children shall be saved by God's mysterious working in their hearts although they are incapable of the response of faith. They have no claim, in themselves, to salvation, but are, as in the case of saved adults, the subjects of the sovereign election of grace, and the purchase of the redeeming blood of Christ. G. N. M. Collins

See also Baptism, Infant.

Bibliography. A. A. Hodge, *Class Book on the Confession of Faith;* Charles Hodge, *Systematic Theology,* I, 26–27; B. B. Warfield, *Studies in Theology.*

Infralapsarianism (Lat. for "after the fall," sometimes designated "sublapsarianism"). A part of the doctrine of predestination, specifically that which relates to the decrees of election and reprobation. The issues involved are God's eternal decrees and man's will—how can the one be affirmed without denying the other. If one argues for God's predetermination of mankind's fate, this tends to deny mankind's free will and threatens to make God responsible for sin. On the other hand, if one argues for the freedom of mankind's will, thus making man responsible for sin, this can threaten the sovereignty and power of God since his decrees then are contingent upon mankind's decisions. The argument/dilemma is not new. Pelagius and Augustine argued over the issue with the Synod of Orange, 529, which sided with Augustine. In the Middle Ages, Duns Scotus and William of Ockham questioned Augustine's position. Luther and Erasmus argued the issue in *Freedom of the Will* and *Bondage of the Will.*

Melanchthon got involved and was accused by Flacius of synergism, and by the end of the sixteenth century the position of Arminius stirred the controversy among the Reformed, who attempted to resolve the issue at the Synod of Dort.

What is the order of the eternal decrees of God? Infralapsarians argue for this order:

(1) God decreed the creation of mankind—a good, blessed creation, not marred or flawed.

(2) God decreed mankind would be allowed to fall through its own self-determination.

(3) God decreed to save some of the fallen.

(4) God decreed to leave the rest to their just fate of condemnation.

(5) God provides the Redeemer for the saved.

(6) God sends the Holy Spirit to effect redemption among the saved.

The key to the order of the decrees is that God decreed election to salvation after the fall—not before; hence the name of the view "infralapsarianism." The supralapsarian view would offer an order in which the decree for election and reprobation occurs before the creation. Those on both sides of the issue cite weighty arguments for their positions, quote Scripture as a foundation, and comb through Augustine, Calvin, and others for support. Generally most Reformed assemblies have refused to make either infra- or supralapsarianism normative, although the tendency has been to favor the former without condemning those who hold to the latter. R. V. SCHNUCKER

See also ARMINIUS, JAMES; CALVINISM; DORT, SYNOD OF; PREDESTINATION; SUPRALAPSARIANISM.

Inheritance. Property or other possessions received by an heir. The OT terms for heir, inheritance, do not necessarily bear the special sense of hereditary succession and possession, although they are found in laws concerning succession to the headship of the family, with consequent control of the family property (Gen. 15:3–5; Num. 27:1–11; 36:1–12; Deut. 21:15–17). The main roots are *nāḥal* (the substantival form, *naḥălâ*, occurs nearly two hundred times), and *yāraš*. Both signify possession in a general sense, though the former means receiving as one's share by lot. *Ḥēleq*, "portion," has the same idea.

A development of thought and spiritualizing of the concept of inheritance is apparent in the OT. From the first, the inheritance promised by Jehovah to Abraham and his descendants was the land of Canaan (Gen. 12:7; 15:18–21; 26:3; 28:13; Exod. 6:8). Israel's possession of the land rested solely on the gift of Jehovah, and, though only entered into with hard fighting, was not theirs by self-effort (Josh. 21:43–45; Ps. 44:3). Furthermore, the inheritance had to be divided by lot among the tribes, the allotting having divine sanction (Num. 26:52–56; 33:54; 34:13; Josh. 14:1–12; 18:4–10). The land was to be possessed "for ever" (Gen. 13:15), yet continued enjoyment and possession was conditional upon faithfulness to God (Deut. 4:26ff.; 11:8–9). Although given to Israel, the land also remained the inheritance of Jehovah, his special portion out of all the earth (Exod. 15:17; Lev. 25:23; I Sam. 26:19; II Sam. 21:3; Ps. 79:1; Jer. 2:7).

Alongside and developing from this concept of the land as Jehovah's inheritance is the thought that Israel, whom he has chosen and put in the land, was also his inheritance (Deut. 4:20; 7:6; 32:9). Likewise, Israel, and particularly the faithful of the nation, came to regard Jehovah himself, and not merely the land, as their inheritance (Pss. 16:5; 73:26; Lam. 3:24). Indeed, the Levites never had any inheritance but Jehovah (Num. 18:20–26). However, the earlier thought of the possession of the land was not lost, for in the messianic kingdom such possession is envisaged (Ps. 37:9; Isa. 60:21).

In the NT "heir," "inheritance," represent *klēronomos, klēronomia*, and derivatives (also used in LXX for *nāḥal* and *yāraš*). So basic an idea in the Old Covenant as inheritance must have its counterpart in the New Covenant. The Epistle to the Hebrews, particularly, shows that as Israel received her inheritance, so in the New Covenant a better inheritance is to be possessed by the New Israel. Furthermore, as is to be expected, the inheritance is "in Christ." In Mark 12:1–11 Christ claims to be the heir of God. This is confirmed in Heb. 1:2 and implied in Rom. 8:17. Here, more clearly than *nāḥal* or *yāraš*, *klēronomos* conveys the thought of hereditary possession. Rom. 8:17 shows that those "in Christ" are joint heirs with Christ of the inheritance. Whereas the inheritance is his by right, in that he is the only begotten Son, it is possessed by the believer by grace, as he is adopted as a son in Jesus Christ.

The inheritance is the kingdom of God with all its blessings (Matt. 25:34; I Cor. 6:9; Gal. 5:21). While enjoyment of it begins in this life, insofar as the kingdom is already present, the full possession must be future (Rom. 8:17–23; I Cor. 15:50; Heb. 11:13; I Pet. 1:3–4). R. C. CRASTON

Bibliography. W. D. Davies, *The Gospel and the Land;* W. Foerster and J. Herrmann, *TDNT,* III, 758ff.; J. D. Hester, *St. Paul's Concept of Inheritance;* W. Mundle, *NIDNTT,* II, 295ff.; J. Schneider, *TDNT,* IV, 294ff.

Inheritance of Adam's Sin. *See* SIN; IMPUTATION.

Iniquity. *See* SIN.

Inner Man (Gr.: *ho esō anthrōpos*). A term used by Paul in Rom. 7:22; II Cor. 4:16; and Eph. 3:16 to express graphically the human focus of God's work of regeneration. We should probably not understand him to be referring specifically to certain distinct areas lying near the center of the human personality. The term is deliberately vague and is used to express two paradoxical ideas:

(1) The work of God is at present secret, to be revealed at the eschaton. In II Cor. 4–5 Paul is afflicted, persecuted, yet possesses the treasure of the gospel (4:7–10), his eyes fixed on the unseen reality of future transformation (4:18–5:5). In Rom. 7 he describes a torturing moral conflict arising from the godward orientation of the "inner man," against which other instincts within him strive. This conflict too will only be resolved at the end (Rom. 8:11, 23).

(2) The work of God must embrace the whole of man's nature, penetrating every corner of his person. Eph. 3:16 literally runs, "that he may grant you . . . to be strengthened through his Spirit *into* the inner man": "into" expresses this penetration. Thus "inner man" means "the whole/essential man viewed from the perspective of God's secret work of transformation."

S. MOTYER

See also MAN, DOCTRINE OF; OUTWARD MAN.

Bibliography. J. Behm, *TDNT*, II, 698–99; R. Jewett, *Paul's Anthropological Terms;* W. D. Stacey, *The Pauline View of Man.*

Inspiration, Plenary. *See* PLENARY INSPIRATION.

Inspiration, Verbal. *See* VERBAL INSPIRATION.

Inspiration of the Bible. *See* BIBLE, INSPIRATION OF.

Intercession. *See* PRAYER.

Intercession of Christ. *See* OFFICES OF CHRIST.

Intermediate State. The period between death as an individual phenomenon and the final judgment and consummation. If Christian thought held to no final state of affairs for all creation, then perhaps one's final situation could be conceived as being settled at death, as in Greek philosophy. However, Christian creeds have always affirmed the resurrection of the body, the judgment of the living and the dead, and life everlasting. To affirm that each individual's destiny is caught up in the triumph of God in Christ has created the distinct possibility of reflection upon the individual's situation between death and that future event.

In the NT. The NT offers no sustained reflection on the intermediate state, and this is probably because the parousia was perceived as so real and imminent that it would have seemed irrelevant to reflect upon the state of the dead. In I Thess. 4:13–18 we find exactly this sort of thinking. Paul is here assuring the believers that those who are "asleep" in Christ have not lost out on the "day of the Lord." Indeed, "the dead in Christ will rise first." We need only note that the reflection here is not upon the present situation of "sleeping" Christians, but upon their future place in the parousia.

A further reason for the absence of reflection on the intermediate state could well be the profound awareness of human wholeness. Salvation is never the extrication of the soul from the body for participation in ethereal bliss. We can see this awareness reflected in II Cor. 5:1–10. Here Paul refers to the intermediate state paradoxically as being "unclothed" (vs. 4) and as being "at home with the Lord" (vs. 8). His true longing and expectation is that at the parousia he will put on his "heavenly dwelling" by being "swallowed up by life" (vss. 2–4). To die is "gain" because it is a departure to "be with Christ" (Phil. 1:21–23), yet Paul is only too clear that his hope is set upon the triumph of Christ when the last enemy, death, is destroyed (I Cor. 15:20–27). Salvation is ultimately resurrection (Rom. 8:18–23).

It should be noted that some have been so keenly aware of the importance of the parousia, the emphasis on human wholeness in Scripture, and the paucity of reflection on the intermediate state that other positions have been taken. Luther seemed sympathetic with the notion that the intermediate state was a kind of sleep, or soul sleep. The parousia was a real awakening. Others have so emphasized our body/soul unity that death is seen to be total; the parousia would then be the re-creation of our body/soul.

Perhaps the classic text contesting such views of *soul sleep* and the like is the parable of the rich man and Lazarus (Luke 16:19–31). Here we are given a unique (in the Bible) and vivid picture of the intermediate state in which destinies are fixed, bliss and torment are apportioned, and a "great chasm has been fixed" between the blessed and damned. Recent scholarship has made it altogether clear that the imagery depicting these contrasting fates was part of the popular lore of the time. Further, once this is understood, the real, final focus of the parable comes to light, namely the fate of the five remaining brothers and their self-pandering unbelief. With their life style they have shut themselves out of the possibility of hearing the Word of God. Perhaps the most such imagery is intended to teach is the real and eternal consequences resulting from our beliefs and consequent life styles. If we are rightly cautioned against pushing the imagery beyond Jesus' intention, we must also resist the claim that it has no meaning. If that were true, what would Jesus have meant when he said, "Today you will be with me in Paradise" (Luke 23:43)?

Purgatory. There has been a tragic side to the history of reflection on the intermediate state, in the emergence of the doctrine of purgatory. Purgatory in Roman Catholic thought developed during the Middle Ages and hardened into dogma in reaction to the Protestant rejection of it. The Council of Trent (1545–63) declared that those who reject the doctrine of purgatory are "anathema," accursed. Purgatory is the doctrine that the intermediate state is not only the place of fixed blessing and torment, but primarily the place of passage by punishment toward blessing as postbaptismal sins are atoned for. Since some sins are more grievous than others, the time of punishment varies. The church here "below" can also aid those being punished through prayers and masses. Even outright absolution has been granted through the exercise of the power of the keys of Peter—the pope. Recent Roman Catholic thought has seen purgatory in more positive terms as a preparing, cleansing, or maturing transition from life on earth to the joys of heaven.

This doctrine can be seen as a distortion of biblical truth for several reasons: (1) Clear scriptural warrant is absent. The only possibly supportive text is in the Apocrypha (II Macc. 12: 43–45). (2) The doctrine reflects an unacceptable ecclesiastical hubris that would claim to have clout in heaven concerning the extent of punishment of those already dead. This deprives God of his freedom and majesty as judge. (3) The doctrine reflects the loss of the triumphant awareness of the eschatological reality of justification through the cross of Christ. "There is therefore *now* no condemnation for those who are in Christ Jesus" (Rom. 8:1 RSV).

The doctrine of purgatory reflects pastoral problems relating to an earlier age in which church and society were coterminous and all baptism was of infants. How are postbaptismal sins to be dealt with and how is divine justice to be related to this form of sin of those who are dead? The theory of purgatory said, "You will not be lost, yet God will be just." At the present time, with much awareness of life as a process or evolution, purgatory has also allowed for speculation about the continued development of the soul. As such, it continues to be attractive for some in a greatly modified form.

Spirits in Prison. A further area of reflection has concerned itself with the language of I Pet. 3:18–22 and 4:6 about the preaching by the Crucified to the "spirits in prison." This imagery has been rather naturally related to the question of the state of all those who never heard the gospel, infants, and the impaired. Does (or did) Christ preach to these so that they too have the opportunity of belief? Is this what is behind the phrase "descended into hell"? It certainly has been interpreted this way from Origen to Luther (Calvin saw this phrase as a theological reflection on the meaning of Christ's death).

The reference to spirits in prison brings us to the biblical teaching that is the backdrop for the doctrine of the intermediate state, the OT doctrine of Sheol, translated Hades in the NT. Strictly speaking the early OT concept of Sheol is not part of the intermediate state. Here Sheol is either the grave or the realm of the dead where there is the absence of all we know as life, yet existence continues. Sheol is pictured as a gloomy prison where there is no hope (Job 17:13–16), an insatiable monster (Prov. 30:15–16). However, for some in the OT this is not all. Hope reaches beyond Sheol to rejoice in a future in the presence of God (Pss. 49:15; 73:24–26). As the full apocalyptic vision of a final judgment emerges in Dan. 12:2–3, Sheol has become the intermediate state. In the era between the testaments, distinctions within Sheol emerged, and Sheol became separate from paradise, yet connected. We see this in the parable discussed. Finally, the vision of the book of Revelation sees Sheol (Hades) as being destroyed in the lake of fire at the end (Rev. 20:14). This vision of the final judgment answers the cry of the souls of the martyred witnesses to Christ, "How long before thou wilt judge?" (Rev. 6:10). This last judgment will not be rendered till death and Hades gave up the dead in them (Rev. 20:13).

The intermediate state remains an area of inevitable concern for Christians both for practical pastoral reasons and as part of the meaning of salvation. However, it should remain clear that the hope of the Christian focuses on the parousia of Christ and the new creation. Speculation on the intermediate state should never diminish the certainty that flows from the cross or the hope in the new creation. S. M. SMITH

See also PURGATORY; SOUL SLEEP; SPIRITS IN PRISON.

Bibliography. H. Berkhof, *Well-Founded Hope;* J. Calvin, *Psychopannychia;* R. H. Charles, *Eschatology;*

K. Hahnhart, *The Intermediate State in the NT;* A. A. Hoekema, *The Bible and the Future;* D. Moody, *The Hope of Glory;* H. Schwarz, *On the Way to the Future.*

Internal Calling. *See* CALL, CALLING.

Internal Testimony of the Holy Spirit. The theological designation of the Holy Spirit's activity in bringing about the believing acknowledgment of Scripture's inherent authority. It thus identifies one of the many facets of the illuminating work of the Spirit by which the eyes of a sinner's heart are enlightened (Eph. 1:17–18) to receive and respond to God's word. In the succinct description of the Westminster Confession, "Our full persuasion and assurance of the infallible truth and divine authority [of Scripture], is from the inward work of the Holy Spirit bearing witness by and with the Word in our hearts" (I. v).

The doctrine of the internal testimony goes back in some form to Augustine and other patristic theologians. It became part of the general Protestant perspective, and was given its clearest expression by John Calvin in the *Institutes* (1.7–9). Since Calvin, it is generally known by the Latin term *testimonium Spiritus sancti internum,* and the doctrine has become part of such Reformed confessions as the French (IV), Belgic (V), Second Helvetic (I), and Westminster (I,v). In those confessions the internal testimony is more closely tied to the believer's acknowledgment of the canon and the infallibility of Scripture than it was in Calvin's *Institutes* and in the draft he personally submitted to the synod which adopted the French Confession in 1559. The doctrine is also implied in the Formula of Concord (2.2), is included in the works of Arminius (I.40), and found a place in several early Baptist confessions.

Although the words are not found directly in Scripture, the doctrine of the internal testimony of the Holy Spirit rests on the pervasive witness of Scripture to the depravity of the sinner's heart and mind and to the necessity of the Holy Spirit's work in bringing such sinners to faithful obedience to Christ and the Word. The whole of I Cor. 2 is relevant. Paul emphasizes that "the man without the Spirit does not accept the things that come from the Spirit of God, for they are foolishness to him, and he cannot understand them, because they are spiritually discerned" (2:14). The Spirit, however, enables such sinners to "understand what God has freely given us" (2:12) and gives believers "the mind of Christ" (2:16). Some related passages are John 16:13–15; I Thess. 1:5; and I John 2:20, 27.

Calvin and the Reformed confessions distinguish the internal testimony of the Holy Spirit from three alternative sources posited by the Roman Catholics, the Anabaptists, and the apologetic appeal to reason, respectively. Roman Catholicism, at least in practice, based a believer's certainty concerning the authority of Scripture on the testimony of the church (cf. *Inst.* 1.7.1–3). On the other hand, Anabaptists claimed new revelation by the Spirit to create this certainty (cf. *Inst.* 1.9). Others attempted to establish credibility in Scripture by apologetic arguments developed largely from extrabiblical materials and which appealed to human reason for conviction. Both Calvin and the Reformed confessions also reject that approach (*Inst.* 1.8; Belgic, V; Westminster, I, v). Calvin acknowledged that such "secondary aids to our feebleness" may be useful if "they follow that chief and highest testimony" of the Holy Spirit (1.8.13). However, the attempt "to prove to unbelievers that Scripture is the Word of God" is to act foolishly "for only by faith can this be known" and that is the result of the Spirit's testimony (1.8.13).

This doctrine of the internal testimony should not be confused with the Barthian view that regards Scripture as a fallible witness to revelation and acknowledges authoritative revelation only in an ever-recurring, present act of God. It should also be distinguished from existentialist views of revelation as well as from mystical and pietistic claims to new revelation. On the other hand, the classic doctrine may not be used to exclude the role of solid exegesis of the biblical text and of sound hermeneutical principles for biblical interpretation.

The internal testimony of the Holy Spirit is related to, but distinguished from, both the text of Scripture and the subjective conviction of the believer. The internal testimony relates to the external testimony of Scripture itself; it does not bring new revelation to supplement Scripture. Scripture clearly testifies to its own inspiration and authority. It is self-authenticating (*autopiston*), inherently authoritative. The Spirit's internal testimony does not make Scripture authoritative; rather, it contributes to the believer's conviction that Scripture is truly what it claims to be. Thus the same Spirit who inspired the authoritative Word awakens that conviction and acknowledgment in a sinner's heart through this internal testimony "by and with the Word."

The Spirit's internal testimony is a divine activity and should not be confused with the believer's experience of it. The Spirit's activity in the sinful heart is the cause; the believer's deep-rooted experience is the subjective result. The experience brings firm conviction, but the experience itself may not be appealed to as evidence of the truth of one's convictions; it may legitimately be referred to only as an explanation of how that conviction arose within one's heart. The Spirit testifies "by and with the Word"; hence the biblical text must be appealed to as evidence for the truth of personal conviction. Word and Spirit are correlative in bringing the subjective conviction; they may not be separated in accounting for that conviction.

The experience resulting from the Spirit's internal testimony is a firm conviction, however, not mere subjective feeling. Calvin described it as "a conviction that requires no reasons," as "a knowledge with which the best reason agrees," and as knowledge in "which the mind truly reposes more securely and constantly than in any reasons" (1.7.5). Nor is it an experience restricted to only a few; it is a conviction that every "believer experiences within himself," although Calvin adds, "my words fall far beneath a just explanation of the matter" (1.7.5). F. H. Klooster

Bibliography. A. Kuyper, *The Work of the Holy Spirit;* J. Murray, "The Attestation of Scripture," in *The Infallible Word;* B. Ramm, *The Witness of the Spirit;* P. Schaff, *The Creeds of Christendom,* III; B. B. Warfield, *Calvin and Calvinism.*

Interpretation of the Bible. An explanation of what is not immediately plain in the Bible. Because of the multifaceted character of the Bible, its interpretation takes a variety of forms. The biblical documents are ancient, written in Hebrew, Aramaic, and Greek at various times between 1200 B.C. (if not earlier) and A.D. 100, reflecting several different historical and cultural settings. A basic requirement for the understanding of these documents is their grammaticohistorical interpretation or exegesis—bringing out of the text the meaning the writers intended to convey and which their readers were expected to gather from it. This grammaticohistorical exegesis is commonly practiced in the classroom, and is distinguished from exposition, which is more appropriate to the pulpit. Exposition aims to apply the text and its meaning to men and women today, enabling them to answer the question: what message has this for us, or for me, in the present situation? To be valid, exposition must be firmly based on exegesis: the meaning of the text for hearers today must be related to its meaning for the hearers to whom it was first addressed. The study of the principles of interpretation—both the grammaticohistorical interpretation and the practical application of that interpretation in the pulpit—is called hermeneutics.

Grammaticohistorical Exegesis. Each biblical document, and each part of a biblical document, must be studied in its context—both its immediate literary context and the wider situation in which it appeared. This calls for an understanding of:

The Biblical Languages, their structure and idioms.

The Types of Literature Represented. Unless the literary character of a document is obvious from the first, one must ask whether it is prose or poetry, history or allegory, literal or symbolic. Some genres found in the Bible have peculiar features not readily paralleled elsewhere and call for special rules of interpretation, e.g., prophecy and apocalyptic.

The Historical Background. A sense of history, such as the biblical writers themselves had, is necessary for the understanding of their writings. The historical background is the whole span of Near Eastern civilization from the early fourth millennium B.C. to the period of the widest expansion of the Roman Empire (under Trajan, A.D. 98–117). The changes within this time span were so sweeping that a biblical document can be misinterpreted if it is related to the wrong chronological setting. An appreciation of this fact will save us from judging precepts and actions of the Late Bronze Age by the ethical principles of the Sermon on the Mount. Again, the book of Jeremiah may yield some devotional profit even when one ignores the revolutionary movements that took place during the prophet's ministry, but the book could not be expounded adequately without some appraisal of those movements and their relation to Jeremiah's message.

The Geographical Conditions. The influence of climate and terrain on the outlook and behavior patterns of a population is of the greatest importance. The religious conflicts of OT times cannot be understood apart from some acquaintance with Palestinian geography. The prevalent Baal worship resulted from the fact that Palestine depended for its fertility on regular rainfall (cf. Deut. 11:10–17; Hos. 2:8; Jer. 14:22). To the Canaanites, Baal was the rain god who fertilized the earth, and his worship was a magical ritual designed to make the rain fall and the crops grow. It was difficult for the Israelites, after their settlement in Canaan, to grasp the lesson that the God of their fathers, who had provided for them in the wilderness, was equally able to provide for them in this new environment—that it was he, and not Baal, who sent the rain and gave them good harvests. So much of the biblical language, literal and metaphorical, has direct reference to geographical conditions that a knowledge of these conditions is indispensable for understanding the language.

The Life Setting. What kind of people were those whom we meet in the Bible? The effort to get under their skin and see through their eyes is not easy, but it is necessary if we are to gain a sympathetic understanding of their unquestioned assumptions, their actions and words, their loves and hates, their motives and aspirations. Here trustworthy descriptions of everyday life in biblical times can be very helpful.

Theological Exegesis. For those who accept the Bible as a sacred text, the church's book, the record of God's unique self-revelation, its interpretation cannot be conducted on the grammaticohistorical level alone. That level is fundamental, but there is a theological level. The books of the Bible do not simply constitute an anthology or a library; they make up a canon—a canon in two stages: the canon of the Hebrew scriptures (common to Jews and Christians) and the canon of the Greek New Testament (recognized by the church). Thus, in addition to the forms of context of which grammaticohistorical exegesis takes account, the whole canon provides a theological context within which each document may be viewed and its contribution to the record of divine revelation and of human response to that revelation may be assessed. Whereas grammaticohistorical exegesis may bring out the variety of viewpoint and emphasis represented in the Bible, theological exegesis presupposes that there is an overall unity in the light of which the diversity can be appreciated in its proper perspective.

Jewish Exegesis. In traditional Jewish exegesis of the Hebrew scriptures, the Prophets and the Writings were treated largely as commentaries on the Torah. Alongside the surface meaning of the text, the *pěšaṭ*, was the more extended application, the *děraš*, which might appear farfetched at times, but not more so than the allegorization practiced in Alexandrian Judaism and in many areas of the Christian church. Leading rabbis set forth certain rules to be followed in scriptural interpretation: Hillel (*ca.* 10 B.C.) propounded seven, Ishmael (*ca.* A.D. 100) thirteen, and Eliezer ben Yose (*ca* A.D. 150) thirty-two. These remained normative into medieval times.

Early Christian Exegesis. The NT writers treat the OT oracles as a unity, teaching the way of salvation through faith in Jesus Christ and providing believers with all that is needed for the service of God (II Tim. 3:15–17). The basis of this unity is that those who "moved by the Holy Spirit spoke from God" (II Pet. 1:21) all bore witness to Christ. In the earliest Christian interpretation the OT is related to the NT as promise is to fulfillment. The promise is found in the histories that led up to Christ as well as in the prophecies that foretold his coming; the fulfillment is found in him. The writer to the Hebrews contrasts the "many and various ways" in which "God spoke of old to our fathers by the prophets" with his perfect and final revelation in Christ (Heb. 1:1–2). Paul traces God's dealings with the world through successive stages associated with Adam, Abraham, Moses, and Christ. This conception of the biblical revelation as historical and progressive is fundamental; it goes back to the creative insight of Christ himself. It traces a consistent pattern of divine action throughout the centuries, marked by repeated manifestations of judgment and renewal, until it found its definitive exemplification in the gospel.

The Postapostolic Age. Biblical interpretation in the postapostolic age is influenced by a Greek theory of inspiration that had as its corollary allegorical exegesis. If a poet like Homer was inspired, then what he said about the gods could be acceptable to thoughtful pagans only if it were taken to be a veiled allegorical presentation of truths otherwise attained by philosophical reasoning. This attitude influenced the OT interpretation of the Jewish philosopher Philo of Alexandria, and subsequently the biblical interpretation of the Alexandrian Christians, Clement and Origen. To them, much in the Bible that was intellectually incredible or morally objectionable if understood literally could be made intelligible and congenial if it was allegorized. By allegorization, it was believed, the intention of the Spirit who spoke through the prophets and apostles could be penetrated. But this approach was largely arbitrary, because the approved interpretation depended so largely on the interpreter's personal preference, and in practice it violated the original intention of the Scriptures and almost obliterated the historical relatedness of the revelation they recorded. Over against the school of Alexandria stood the school of Antioch which, while it did not completely reject allegorization, paid much more serious attention to the historical sense of the text. In the West, the anonymous Pauline commentator usually referred to as Ambrosiaster and, above all, Jerome attached supreme importance to the grammatical sense, while Ambrose and Augustine were more influenced by the allegorizing methods of Alexandria. But Augustine's theological insight, especially his recognition of divine love as the essential element in revelation, supplied him with a sound hermeneutical principle and kept his allegorization within scriptural limits.

The Middle Ages. The patristic distinction between the literal and "higher" senses of Scripture was elaborated in the Middle Ages. The schoolmen dwelt on the fourfold sense of Scripture: (1) the literal sense, which related the things done and said in the biblical record according to its surface meaning; (2) the moral sense, which brought out lessons for life and conduct; (3) the allegorical sense, which deduced doctrine from the text; (4) the anagogical sense, which derived heavenly meanings from earthly data. For example, a reference to water could denote on different levels (1) literal water, (2) moral purity, (3) the practice and doctrine of baptism, (4) eternal life in the heavenly Jerusalem (as in Rev. 22:1). Some of these could be further subdivided: thus varieties of the allegorical sense were the mystical sense and what is nowadays called the typological sense. A good example of the mystical sense is provided by Bernard of Clairvaux in his homilies on the Song of Songs. There was a parallel development (called *sōd*) in Jewish interpretation: this extracted the highest meaning, which led by knowledge through love to ecstasy and the beatific vision. The typological sense, when properly controlled, was based on a comparison of recurring instances of a particular pattern throughout Scripture. The typological sense of the material details of the wilderness tabernacle and the levitical sacrifices was found in the spiritual worship of the Christian order.

Alongside the cultivation of the derivative senses, many centers in Western Europe cultivated literal interpretation; this often went hand in hand with the study of Hebrew, knowledge of which was easily obtainable from rabbis. One such center was the Abbey of Saint Victor, Paris, where a vigorous school of literal interpretation, in the tradition of Jerome, flourished in the twelfth century. Nicolas of Lyra, the greatest Christian Hebraist of his age, produced commentaries on the whole Bible. These were both literal and figurative, but he stressed the primacy of the literal sense, which alone could yield proof. Luther, who was not a little influenced by him, called him "a fine soul, a good Hebraist and a true Christian."

New Beginnings. In the late fifteenth and sixteenth centuries a series of new developments halted the threatened divorce between grammaticohistorical and theological exegesis. Luther, in principle at least, refused to distinguish between these two forms of exegesis: "What is theology," he asked, "but grammar applied to the text?" But, a generation before Luther, others were expressing similar thoughts. The English scholar John Colet caused a sensation when he returned to Oxford from the Continent in 1496 and, in a course of lectures on the Pauline Epistles, expounded them in the light of their historical setting, according to the plain meaning of the text. His methods of exegesis influenced Erasmus.

To the insights of the Renaissance, Martin Luther added those of the Reformation, making the teaching of justification by faith in Christ alone the central principle of biblical interpretation as of so much else. He rejected allegory as rubbish, although he did have recourse to it from time to time. John Calvin was a systematic exegete of the grammaticohistorical school; his first exercise in this field was a commentary on a treatise of the Roman philosopher Seneca. His voluminous biblical commentaries are still consulted with profit.

The Counter-Reformation also made its contribution to the revival of sound exegesis. At a time when the Apocalypse was too often used as an arsenal for weapons to be used in the Reformation cleavage by one side against the other, F. Ribera and L. Alcasar went back to the earlier Christian fathers to find a more satisfactory method of interpreting that book. On the Reformed side, the first exegete to abandon the identification of antichrist with the papacy was the Dutch jurist Hugo Grotius, whose *Annotationes in Novum Testamentum* (1641–46) were so objective that he was criticized for rationalism.

Primary and Plenary Senses. Since the Bible is the church's book, a further context within which any part of it may be read is supplied by the whole of Christian history. What the Bible has come to mean in the experience of Christian readers, generation by generation, has added something to its meaning for Christian readers today. This increment of meaning makes up what is called the plenary sense (*sensus plenior*). The primary sense is what the author intended to convey, established by the grammaticohistorical method; but the plenary sense, provided it does not violate the primary sense, enriches the appreciation of the Bible both in the life of the church as a whole and in the personal experience of Christian men and women. The story of Jacob's wrestling with the angel at the ford of Jabbok (Gen. 32:22–32), for example, presents some interesting exegetical problems when studied in its original setting, but these do not impair the lessons readers of many ages have learned from it. Hosea in his day found significance in the story (Hos. 12:3, 4), and to later generations it has served as an illustration of the lesson learned by Paul from a different experience: "When I am weak, then I am strong" (II Cor. 12:10). To many Christians in the English-speaking world Charles Wesley's hymn "Wrestling Jacob" has provided a rich commentary on the incident, disclosing the plenary sense in a Christian idiom.

> And when my all of strength shall fail,
> I shall with the God-Man prevail.

This plenary sense, however, is acceptable because it is consistent with the primary sense, according to which it was not wrestling and scheming Jacob, but weeping, disabled, clinging Jacob that prevailed with God and secured his blessing.

Contemporary Trends. Since World War II the existential interpretation of Scripture (especially the NT) has been widely cultivated, largely under the influence of Rudolf Bultmann. Bultmann's own thinking was influenced by Wilhelm Dilthey, who insisted that the interpreter should project himself into the author's experience so as to relive it, and by Martin Heidegger, who conceived of the truly "authentic" man as experiencing freedom because he has faced reality. This conception of Heidegger provided the "pre-understanding" of Bultmann's theology and, not altogether surprisingly, Bultmann found this "pre-understanding" confirmed in the NT text. To his mind, Heidegger was saying, quite independently, what the NT writers had already said. Bultmann's disciple Ernst Fuchs regards the hermeneutical task as the creation of a "language event" in which the authentic language of the Bible encounters readers today, challenging them to decision, awakening faith, and achieving salvation.

Still more recent is the structuralist approach, which abandons all concern to keep the plenary sense in line with the primary sense. It may ignore all questions about the historical background of a text, its original life setting, and the course of its transmission; it may even be quite uninterested in the author's intention, since its concern is with the final form of the text as an independent linguistic phenomenon.

More fruitful approaches are the "salvation-history" hermeneutic represented preeminently by Oscar Cullmann and the "canonical exegesis" propounded by Brevard S. Childs—the former viewing the text in the light of the ongoing record of God's saving activity that finds its climax in Christ; the latter viewing it in the setting of the entire biblical canon. F. F. Bruce

See also Allegory; Bultmann, Rudolf; Demythologization; Dodd, Charles Harold; Heilsgeschichte; Higher Criticism; Type, Typology.

Bibliography. G. W. Anderson, ed., *Tradition and Interpretation;* J. Barr, *Old and New in Interpretation;* E. C. Blackman, *Biblical Interpretation;* C. E. Braaten, *History and Hermeneutics;* R. Bultmann, *Faith and Understanding,* I; B. S. Childs, *Exodus: A Commentary;* O. Cullmann, *Salvation in History;* C. H. Dodd, *According to the Scriptures;* F. W. Farrar, *History of Interpretation;* H.-G. Gadamer, *Truth and Method;* L. Goppelt, *Typos: The Typological Interpretation of the OT in the New;* R. M. Grant, *A Short History of the Interpretation of the Bible;* B. Lindars, *NT Apologetic;* I. H. Marshall, ed., *NT Interpretation;* D. E. Nineham, ed., *The Church's Use of the Bible Past and Present;* J. M. Robinson and J. B. Cobb, *The New Hermeneutic,* II; B. Smalley, *The Study of the Bible in the Middle Ages;* P. Stuhlmacher, *Historical Criticism and Theological Interpretation of Scripture;* A. C. Thiselton, *The Two Horizons;* G. Vermes, *Scripture and Tradition in Judaism;* J. Weingreen, *From Bible to Mishna;* J. D. Wood, *The Interpretation of the Bible.*

Interpretation of Tongues, Gift of. *See* Spiritual Gifts.

Invisible Church. *See* Church, The.

Invocation of the Saints. Requests to persons in heaven for their intercession before God in support of the petitioner's prayers.

The practice of invocation of saints derives from the doctrine of the communion of saints, the fellowship of all members of the Body of Christ, including the terrestrial church militant and the heavenly church triumphant. If Christian fellowship impels believers on earth to bear one another's burdens in prayer, it seems reasonable to conclude that the compassion of those who have died disposes them even more to pray for those who still struggle with evil and suffering, especially as the former no longer face their own cares.

Scriptural support for the practice is indirect. That believers should pray for others is explicit (Rom. 15:30; James 5:16); that the dead feel concern for the living appears from the rich man in Hades (Luke 16:27–28). Catholic and Orthodox teaching infers that the saints in heaven know the needs of the faithful and delight to aid their brethren for the sake of God's kingdom. In respectful gratitude, those on earth invoke the saints' efficacious intercession. Such intercession does not detract from, but rather honors, Christ the mediator, through whose merits all prayers are offered. While believers surely may pray directly to God, the praise of his glory is amplified by the joining of the prayers of the blessed in heaven to those from earth.

Having begun in the third century, the practice of invocation intensified during the Middle Ages in connection with the exaggerated veneration of patron saints and relics. The Council of Trent moderated the practice by declaring it "good and useful" to invoke the saints while not mandating invocation nor anathematizing those who denied its efficacy.

Reformation theology identified the notion that human souls hear prayer as blasphemy. Lutheran doctrine acknowledged that saints do pray generally for the church militant, but they do not receive its prayers. Calvin denied that departed saints "abandon their own repose to be drawn into earthly cares."

Modern Roman Catholic theology affirms the propriety of invocation while distinguishing between divine adoration (*latria*) and respect for saints (*dulia*). Recently, some non-Catholics have begun to reckon with the unity of living believers with the dead in Christ, whereby God is beseeched to receive by "comprecation" the praise of the blessed in heaven in unison with the church on earth. P. D. STEEVES

See also COMMUNION OF SAINTS, THE; VENERATION OF THE SAINTS.

Bibliography. P. Brown, *The Cult of the Saints;* J. Calvin, *The Institutes of the Christian Religion,* 3.20.20–27; J. Gibbons, *The Faith of Our Fathers;* T. G. Tappert, ed., The Augsburg Confession, Art. 21, in *The Book of Concord;* J. Pelikan, *The Christian Tradition,* III: The Growth of Medieval Theology.

Irenaeus (*ca.* 130–*ca.* 200). A Greek father of the early church. In his youth Irenaeus listened to Polycarp, bishop of Smyrna, disciple of John. In his maturity he was bishop of Lyons in Gaul. Irenaeus ("peaceful") sought to mediate between the churches of Asia Minor and Rome in the Montanist and the Quartodeciman disputes.

Two of his treatises survive. The *Demonstration* (or Proof) *of the Apostolic Preaching* may have been written for an apologetic or a catechetical purpose. It presents Christ and Christianity as the fulfillment of Old Testament prophecy. Salvation history is structured according to the various covenants of God with man.

Against Heresies ("Refutation and Overthrow of the Gnosis Falsely So Called") is a polemical work opposing Gnosticism. Against the Gnostics' mythological interpretation of Scripture, association of matter with evil, and spiritualizing eschatology, Irenaeus proposed an interpretation of Scripture according to a summary of the apostolic preaching (the "rule of truth"), the biblical doctrines of creation, redemption, and resurrection, and a chiliastic eschatology.

Irenaeus's most original contribution to theology was his doctrine of recapitulation (*recapitulatio*). The fully divine Christ became fully man in order to sum up all humanity in himself. What was lost through the disobedience of the first Adam was restored through the obedience of the second Adam. Christ went through all the stages of human life, resisted all temptation, died, and arose a victor over death and the devil. The analogy with Adam was extended to include Mary as a new Eve. The benefits of Christ's victory are available through participation in him.

Irenaeus contributed to the developing ecclesiastical organization the doctrine of apostolic succession. The Gnostics claimed a secret tradition from the apostles. Irenaeus argued that if the apostles had had any secrets to impart they would have delivered them to those men they appointed as bishops of the churches. The succession passed from one occupant of the teaching chair to the next in each church, not from ordainer to ordained. The public nature of the teaching given by the bishops and the uniformity of this teaching among all the churches guaranteed that it was the genuine apostolic tradition. The church of Rome, as founded by Paul and Peter and as mirroring all the churches, held an important place in this argument.

Irenaeus is the earliest author whose works survive to argue from Scripture as a whole: NT as well as OT and a range of NT writings approximating the present canon. E. FERGUSON

Bibliography. V. Ammundsen, "The Rule of Truth in Irenaeus," *JTS* 13:574–580; F. R. M. Hitchcock, *Irenaeus of Lugdunum;* J. Lawson, *The Biblical Theology of Saint Irenaeus;* E. Molland, "Irenaeus of Lugdunum and the Apostolic Succession," *JEH* 1:12–28; G. Wingren, *Man and the Incarnation;* E. P. Meijering, "God, Cosmos, History," *VC* 28:248–76; D. R. Schultz, "The Origin of Sin in Irenaeus and Jewish Pseudepigraphical Literature," *VC* 32:161–90.

Irish Articles (1615). One hundred and four articles of belief adopted at the first convocation of the Irish Episcopal Church. The articles are arranged under nineteen heads. They were written largely by James Ussher, then in charge of Trinity College Theological Faculty in Dublin, later Archbishop of Armagh. These articles affirm the absolute sovereignty of God, predestination, election and reprobation, and justification by faith, along with the importance of repentance and good works. They teach the Puritan view of the sabbath, identify the pope as antichrist, and recognize the king as head of both church and state. They mention neither the necessity of episcopal ordination nor the three orders of the ministry. These articles are considerably more Calvinist than the earlier (1563) Thirty-nine Articles of the Church of England. In 1635 the Irish Articles were officially replaced by the Thirty-nine Articles, although Archbishop Ussher continued to require subscription to both. The Westminster Confession of Faith (of the British Parliament's Assembly of Divines in the 1640s) draws more from the Irish Articles than from any other source. Thus the Anglican Irish Articles—mediated through the Westminster Confession—have had their greatest influence on the Presbyterian Churches of the English-speaking world. D. F. KELLY

See also THIRTY-NINE ARTICLES, THE; USSHER, JAMES; WESTMINSTER CONFESSION OF FAITH.

Bibliography. A. F. Mitchell, *Westminster Confession of Faith; A Contribution to the Study of Its History, and to the Defense of Its Teaching;* P. Schaff, ed., *The Creeds of Christendom,* I, 662–65; III, 526–44.

Ironside, Henry Allen (1876–1951). Popular Bible teacher, evangelist, pastor, and author. Born in Toronto, Canada, "Harry" Ironside moved with his family to California in 1886. There at the age of fourteen he was converted and began to preach. After a brief period as a Salvation Army officer, Ironside resigned because he no longer accepted the holiness view of "entire sanctification." He joined the Plymouth Brethren and started what would become a highly successful itinerant ministry of preaching and teaching. Though essentially self-taught, he was always in high demand as an expositor at Bible conferences and institutes. From 1925 to 1943, he served as a visiting professor at Dallas Theological Seminary. From 1930 to 1948 he was pastor of Moody Memorial Church in Chicago, a position that earned him considerable criticism from the Plymouth Brethren, who reject the idea of "one-man ministries" and of receiving a stipulated salary for preaching the gospel. During a preaching tour of New Zealand, Ironside suffered a fatal heart attack and was buried in Auckland in January, 1951.

In addition to his itinerant and pastoral ministries, Ironside is best known for his prolific literary output. He produced close to a hundred major books and pamphlets, mainly on expository and prophetic themes. Ironside was a major figure in the popularizing of dispensationalism among American evangelicals and for the most part followed the views of the *Scofield Reference Bible.* T. P. WEBER

See also DISPENSATION, DISPENSATIONALISM.

Bibliography. E. S. English, *Ordained of the Lord;* H. A. Ironside, *The Mysteries of God, The Lamp of Prophecy, A Historical Sketch of the Brethren Movement, The Great Parenthesis,* and *The Prophet Isaiah.*

Irrationalism. The philosophical belief which asserts that reality is contacted nonrationally. The real is either suprarational or transrational and requires, therefore, a nonrational approach to be contacted. The approach may be by intuition (Bergson), by the will (Schopenhauer), by emotion (romanticism), or by mysticism (Plotinus).

Irrationalism in theology is the belief that God is contacted nonrationally. Religious intuitionalism, mysticism, and existentialism are forms of theological irrationalism. Liberalism, rooted in romantic or pantheistic philosophy, has a strong overtone of irrationalism, as does much contemporary theology which has been influenced by Kierkegaard's doctrines of the dialectic and the paradoxical, and by existentialism's separation of existence and essence (also from Kierkegaard). B. RAMM

Irresistible Grace. *See* GRACE.

Irving, Edward (1792–1834). An evangelical Church of Scotland minister who sought to get back behind the anticharismatic stance of the Protestant Reformation and reintroduce the charismatic dimension to Protestantism. A man of creativity and singular powers of expression he became critical of his fellow evangelicals early in his ministry. Believing himself called as a prophet by God with a message—however yet unclear—to the British Protestantism of his day he jumped at the invitation to become minister of a small congregation in London in 1822. Here his pulpit gifts were soon recognized, and by 1827 the great Regent Square Church was erected to hold the crowds.

Fearful of liberalism and disillusioned with the entrepreneurial optimism of evangelicalism his romanticism led him, in company with so many Confessional Protestants, to seek the answers to the needs of the present in a golden age of the past. This age was the Reformation, but while most British Confessionalists sought the answer in Reformation doctrine, he as usual beat his own path. He discerned much of the power of the Reformation to lie in its sacramental theology, and thus he particularly stressed the presence and power of the Holy Spirit in baptism—a charismatic sacramentalism.

His expectations were heightened when he came in touch with some of the first Evangelical Anglican premillennialists. In the imminent return of Jesus Christ, he saw the removal of liberalism and evangelicalism; but even more he saw a brief period prior to the Second Advent when there would be a latter-rain outpouring of the Holy Spirit. With his exuberance and expectation he became the first major popularizer of nineteenth century premillennialism, leading such recognized fathers of the movement as J. N. Darby and other early Plymouth Brethren into this new understanding. He was now advocating a charismatic eschatology.

The next stage in Irving's development was his conviction that the "extraordinary" gifts of the Holy Spirit would be given once again just prior to the Second Coming. This he preached and for this he waited. During this period he also developed a charismatic Christology in which he taught that in the incarnation Jesus Christ received human nature after the fall, but that the activity of the Spirit kept him from sin. Such views created much opposition in the Church of Scotland, opposition that intensified when he announced that his new views opened up a universal triumph of Christ which could no longer bear with traditional Calvinism.

Then in the spring of 1830 word came that speaking in tongues had occurred in the west of Scotland, and within a year, manifestations were present in Regent Square Church. Debarred from his pulpit by the presbytery, and under threat of deposition by the Scottish General Assembly, Irving and his supporters, almost all former Evangelical Anglicans, found their way into what became known as the Catholic Apostolic Church. Those gifted with apostleship consigned Irving to a significantly lesser rank, which he accepted, only to die within a matter of months. I. S. RENNIE

Bibliography. M. Oliphant, *The Life of Edward Irving*, 2 vols.; G. Carlyle, *The Collected Writings of Edward Irving*, 5 vols.; A. L. Drummond, *Edward Irving and His Circle;* R. A. Davenport, *Albury Apostles;* E. Sandeen, *The Roots of Fundamentalism;* G. Strachan, *The Pentecostal Theology of Edward Irving;* W. Oliver, *Prophets and Millennialists.*

Ishi. According to Hos. 2:16–17, this is the new title by which Israel will address Yahweh her covenant lord (Heb. *ʾîšî*, "my husband"); no longer will she use the name Baal (Heb. *baʿălî*, "my master") in any context. Thus Hosea calls for a complete break from the syncretistic worship practiced in eighth century Israel (2:19), and he promises a new "marriage" covenant between Yahweh and his people (2:16, 20–22). S. F. NOLL

Israel, The New. A description of the church, arising from the conviction that the position of Israel as the elect people of God has been transferred to the church, so that the former can no longer claim it. The description is not actually used in the NT, but of course the NT may take this view of the relationship without using the expression. It has been used from the time of Tertullian, and it is plainly vital to theology to know whether the NT supports its use. So we ask, Could the church have been called the New Israel in the NT?

The NT presents a picture of both continuity and discontinuity between itself and the Old.

Discontinuity. There are some horrifying expressions of judgment upon Israel for her failure to accept the Christ (e.g., Matt. 23:37–38; Mark 13:2; Luke 19:41–44; John 8:24; Rom. 9: 27–29; 11:8–10; I Thess. 2:16), as well as some strong expressions of the inadequacy and provisional nature of the OT law (Rom. 3:20, 8:3; Gal. 3:23–25; Phil. 3:6–7; Heb. 8:13) and a polemic against Israelite institutions (e.g., the teaching office—Matt. 23:2ff.; the sacrificial system—Heb. 10:3–4, 11; the temple—John 2:13–22; Acts 7: 48–53; the synagogue worship—II Cor. 3:14–15).

Continuity. The NT also affirms the divine origin of the Old, and its compatibility with the gospel (Matt. 5:17–18; 22:41–46; John 5:37–39; 10:35; Rom. 3:2, 31; 7:12, 14; 13:8–10; 15:4), and consequently we find OT images, institutions, and prophecies applied to Christ and the church. Paul asserts the certainty of Israel's ultimate salvation (Rom. 11:25–26), and the early church (following Jesus' example) initially felt completely at home in, or took over for itself, the institutions of Israel (temple—Luke 2:49; John 5:1; Acts 3:1; teaching office and prophecy—Mark 1:21; Acts 13:15–16; synagogue—Luke 4:16; Acts 13:5).

Reconciliation. How are these two attitudes to be reconciled? Some have maintained that the NT writers simply could not clarify the relationship to Israel and the law, because they were too personally involved. But deep personal involvement is usually a vital spur to clarity of mind. Paul, for one, had to think very carefully about this issue, because in his Gentile mission it was raised on two opposing fronts: on the one hand, the "Judaizers" argued that the coming of Christ meant no alteration whatsoever in the preexisting state of affairs: Israel is still the elect people of God, so Gentile converts must join Israel (by circumcision) as well as the church (by baptism). Against them certain Gentile Christians argued that Israel had finally forfeited her special status, and that God had established in Christ a new Gentile order of salvation, in which the law had no place.

Paul steered a careful course between these extremes. Some scholars maintain that his response differs from that of other NT authors, but taking the NT as a whole the following picture emerges:

(1) *Christ, not any particular group of people, is the center of God's purposes.* "All the promises of God find their Yes in him," says Paul (II Cor. 1:20). In Galatians, Paul pictures Christ as the "seed of Abraham" when Abraham was given the promise "to you and to your seed" (Gen. 17:7–8), on which Israel's election was based (Gal. 3:16). In a sense, then, Christ is himself the people of God, embodying all that God intended for the elect.

Matthew makes the same point vividly when he shows Jesus reenacting the great events of Israel's election. He goes down to Egypt to avoid destruction (Matt. 2:13; Gen. 45:7; 50:20), and is brought up again as God's Son (Matt. 2:15; Exod. 4:22). He passes through the water like Israel (Matt. 3:13–17; I Cor. 10:1–2; Exod. 14:22), and is tempted in the wilderness (Matt. 4:1–11; Deut. 8:3). Finally he sits on a mountain and his disciples gather round him to hear his Torah, just as Moses climbed Sinai to receive the Torah from God (Matt. 5:1–12; Exod. 19:20–20:17).

(2) *It follows that the people of God and the OT must be understood Christocentrically.* Only in Christ, says Paul, are the promises made to Abraham fulfilled. Consequently, "If you are Christ's, then you are Abraham's offspring, heirs according to promise" (Gal. 3:29). Since all, whether Jew or Gentile, may embrace Christ by faith, it follows that Abraham is not merely the father of historical Israel but "the father of all who believe," whatever their national origin (Rom. 4:11; cf. Matt. 8:5–13). Conversely, the right to claim Abraham as father, and enjoy membership in Israel, is forfeited by Jews who refuse to believe (Rom. 9:6–7; John 8:39–44; cf. Rom. 2:28–29). So the name Israel is rightly applied only to those Jews who form the saved remnant in Christ (cf. Gal. 6:16: the phrase "Israel of God" here could refer to the whole church, Jews and Gentiles, but probably Paul is praying especially for Jewish Christians); and Gentile Christians may picture their position as that of "graft" onto the age-old "tree" of God's people (Rom. 11:17–24).

Christ thus provides the key to the right understanding of the OT. Its institutions (e.g., high priest—Heb. 4:14; Davidic king—Luke 1:32–33) and prophecies (e.g., prophet like Moses—Acts 3:22–23; John 5:46; servant of the Lord—Mark 10:45; Acts 3:13; New Covenant—Heb. 8:6–13) are applied to Jesus, and the law itself finds its meaning only in pointing to him (Rom. 3:21; 10:4; Gal. 3:24).

(3) *Judgment on Israel does not cancel her election.* Interpreting the OT through Christ does not mean any sudden changes of direction. Just as Zechariah proclaimed the fulfillment of the covenant in Christ (Luke 1:67–79), so Paul insists that God's word still stands (Rom. 9:6), that he has not rejected his people (Rom. 11:1), and that Israel will be saved (vss. 25–26), for "the gifts and the call of God are irrevocable" (vs. 29). But she will be saved through a judgment that will remove the dross and purify her once and for all (Rom. 9:27–29; Isa. 1:24–26).

(4) *OT ways of understanding God's people may be applied to the church.* The saving events of the OT, especially the Exodus, are used to illuminate salvation in Christ (e.g., John 6; I Cor. 10:1–11); the true meaning of OT religion is found in the gospel (e.g., Rom. 3:24–25; Heb.; I Pet. 1:18–19); and many times images for Israel are applied to believers (e.g., Luke 12:32; John 15:1; I Pet. 2:9).

Conclusion. We must conclude that the New Israel does not reflect the fullness of NT thinking. The renewed Israel would imply less of a dividing line between the testaments and would help us to take seriously today Paul's radical statement that the gospel concerns "the Jew first and also the Greek" (Rom. 1:16). S. Motyer

See also Church, The.

Bibliography. D. L. Baker, *Two Testaments: One Bible;* F. F. Bruce, *The NT Development of OT Themes;* W. D. Davies, *Paul and Rabbinic Judaism;* H. L. Ellison, *The Mystery of Israel;* D. J. Harrington, *God's People in Christ: NT Perspectives on the Church and Judaism;* W. Hendriksen, *Israel in Prophecy;* H. Räisänen, *Paul and the Law;* P. Richardson, *Israel in the Apostolic Church.*

Israel and Prophecy. The declaration of the Word of God to the people of God (Israel). In any discussion of Israel in the context of prophecy there is difficulty over the precise definition of terms. First, the word "prophecy" must be clearly understood, for if it is misused, it may distort any attempt to understand Israel's place in prophecy. The subject matter of prophecy, given the fundamental definition above, may vary. God's Word may relate to the past, present, or future, though in the first instance it will always have some relevance to its immediate present in the time of the prophet. When the divine Word is concerned with the distant future, it is merely one part of biblical prophecy, namely prophetic eschatology. As the OT prophets were Israelites, and as their message concerned the chosen people, it follows that almost all prophecy, including prophetic eschatology, has as its primary focus Israel (including the united kingdom, and after 922 B.C. the separate states of Judah and Israel). This statement of fundamental principles is crucial, for in popular English usage the word "prophecy" has become more or less synonymous with prediction and futurology. This popular and modern approach to prophecy is typified by a quotation in a modern popular paperback, "Prophecy is merely history written in advance." This approach to the subject is a fundamental misunderstanding of the OT notion of prophecy.

A second difficulty pertains to the use of the word "Israel." In modern discussions of the Bible's prophetic eschatology, frequent reference is made to Israel. But it is not always easy to determine in the sources whether the reference is to Israel in the OT sense (the nation of the chosen people) or in some future nationalistic sense (a restored Israel), or whether the reference is to the church, which may perhaps be referred to as the New Israel. Whereas the first difficulty arises simply from mistaken understanding, the second difficulty is related to the interpretation of such difficult texts as Gal. 6:16 (see Richardson).

The Basic Prophetic Message Concerning Israel. The prophets in general addressed the Word of God to Israel throughout the nation's history in OT times and during and after the Exile, continuing into the period when the chosen people no longer survived as a distinct and independent nation. Prior to the beginning of the Exile (587/6 B.C.), the prophets' message was that Israel's failure in the covenant relationship had been so fundamental that if there were no repentance, judgment would come; the covenant would be brought to an end. The message was designed to evoke repentance and thus avert judgment; the eventual failure of the nation to rediscover the essence of its covenant relationship with God culminated in the end of the independent state of Israel.

During and after the Exile, the prophets continued to address God's word to the Israel that survived, not as a nation, but as a people. In part, their message was addressed to those in exile and to those returning to the promised land. The prophets continued to speak of coming judgment, but with respect to the future they spoke also of a restoration of Israel that lay beyond the judgment. In the interpretation of particular prophetic passages, it is difficult to know sometimes whether the restoration of which they speak is fulfilled in the return of Israel to the promised land after the Exile and the consequent reestablishment of the temple worship, or whether they refer to a more distant future. While the distinction is often difficult to draw in a particular text, it is clear that in the prophetic writings as a whole a distinctive prophetic eschatology develops; the prophets gave expression to their anticipation of a new and restored Israel in a transformed world, in which violence and evil would be eventually eliminated. Yet, as one might expect when the divine message is declared through different persons, the substance of the various prophetic eschatologies differs in details; it is not that the respective messages contradict each other, but rather that the truth toward which they point eludes the descriptive capacity of human language. In profound symbolism, limited nevertheless by the inadequacy of human speech, the prophets anticipated a transformed world in which God's kingdom and rule would be eventually established.

From Prophecy to Apocalyptic. At the end of the OT period and continuing into intertestamental times, a transformation took place from prophecy to apocalyptic; that is, the proclamation of the divine Word in prophecy (especially that part having eschatological significance) gave way to apocalyptic writings in which the "secrets" of the future were affirmed in the account of visions, or in narratives written in the form of visionary accounts. The Book of Daniel, not technically a prophetic book, forms a bridge between OT prophecy and intertestamental and NT apocalyptic writings (notably the Revelation to John). Though the themes of prophetic eschatology continue to be present in the apocalyptic writings, their concern is less immediate than that of the prophets, who addressed God's Word urgently to their own generation. In the attempt to interpret the apocalyptic literature, one faces similar difficulties to those encountered in the interpretation of prophetic eschatology; it is not always easy to differentiate between that which clearly refers to events now lying in the past and that which still pertains to a future reality.

Problems of Interpretation. The place of Israel in prophetic eschatology and apocalyptic literature is the subject of considerable difficulty of interpretation. (1) While the Bible clearly affirms a faith about the future, namely, the return of Christ, a transformed world, and a new Israel, it also warns of the dangers of trying to determine the precise time of such events. It is one thing to be perpetually ready, but readiness must be accompanied by an awareness that we do not and cannot know the future precisely (Mark 13:22; Acts 1:6–7). (2) All language about the future must necessarily be mysterious and symbolic, insofar as it conveys truth beyond our present knowledge of historical reality. As such, the general truth of the language must be grasped, but one must not reduce prophetic statements to completely literal meaning, as if they constituted an airline schedule of departures and arrivals from heavenly places. (3) During the course of Christian history, each age has had interpreters who have identified the prophetic and apocalyptic "predictions" with the persons and events of their own age. Time has shown them to be fundamentally wrong over and over again; thus, while retaining readiness and an openness to God's intervention in human history, a healthy skepticism may be adopted to some of the popular "prophets" of our own age, whose interpretations of the biblical texts are no less suspect than those of their predecessors. (4) Attempts to relate the role of Israel in future history to the *millennium* referred to in Rev. 20:1–10 are equally fragile and should be presented with a good deal of caution, given the genuine difficulties in interpreting the biblical texts with respect to their modern and future implications. (5) The reestablishment of the modern state of Israel in 1948 has given rise, in both Judaism and Christianity, to renewed speculation about the restoration of Israel and the fulfillment of the eschatological anticipations of the prophets. It must certainly be recognized that this is an extraordinary event, and that the Zionist movement, during the last one hundred years, has been motivated in part by the prophetic expectations of the restoration of the nation and the return of the people of the diaspora. But even such an extraordinary event cannot be interpreted automatically as a fulfillment of the ancient prophetic hope. Within the state of Israel, there are parties of ultraorthodox Jews (e.g., the Neturei Karta) who are opposed to the government of Israel precisely because, in their view, the state was not established by the intervention of a messianic figure and as an act of God. Indeed, the Neturei Karta proclaimed the first government of Israel to be "a regime of blasphemers."

In summary, the biblical perspective emerging from the writings of the prophets is that human history has a direction and movement within the providence of God in which Israel has a continuing place. From the NT perspective, faith in the second coming of Christ, coupled with the prophetic eschatology concerning Israel, is something to be grasped by faith. To retain the vital faith in the culmination of human history as we know it, and yet to refrain from tying the prophetic message concerning Israel to our own intricate schemes and timetables, are the challenges perpetually facing us in attempting to understand Israel's place in prophecy.

P. C. Craigie

See also Eschatology; Millennium, Views of the; Second Coming of Christ.

Bibliography. C. E. Armerding and W. W. Gasque, eds., *Dreams, Visions, and Oracles;* G. E. Ladd, *ISBE* (rev.), I, 151–71; G. P. Richardson, *Israel in the Apostolic Church.*

Issy, Articles of (1695). Thirty-four articles composed by a commission of the Catholic Church in 1695 at Issy, near Paris. The commission, made up of J. B. Bossuet, L. de Noailles, and M. Tronson, was formed to condemn erroneous teachings in the writings of Madame Guyon, who was under the influence of Bishop Fénelon. At issue were the theories of quietism (not unlike the nineteenth century Protestant holiness and deeper life movement), which called for an abandonment of human effort and complete passivity of will in order to reach a state of spirituality pleasing to God. The need for petitionary prayer was set aside for a passive, contemplative state of soul. The active life of faith and repentance was inferior, if not a positive hindrance, to the quiet losing of the soul in God. It is doubtful that Madame Guyon or Bishop Fénelon actually held to the extreme doctrines of quietism such as indifference to the truth of the Trinity and the incarnation, or to the impossibility of sin in the yielded soul. Though Madame Guyon, F. Fénelon, and J. B. Bossuet all signed the Articles of Issy, Bossuet and Fénelon continued to wage literary battle until the church condemned Fénelon with twenty-three propositions in 1699.

D. F. Kelly

See also Guyon, Madame; Quietism.

Bibliography. J. de Guibert, *Documenta Ecclesiastica Christianae Perfectionis Studium Spectantia;* H. Heppe, *Geschichte der Quietistischen Mystik in der Katholischen Kirche;* R. A. Knox, *Enthusiasm;* B. B. Warfield, *Perfectionism.*

Jj

Jah. *See* God, Names of.

Jahweh. *See* God, Names of.

Jansen, Cornelius Otto (1585–1638). Flemish Catholic theologian. Jansen was born at Accoi, near Leerdam in southern Holland, and educated first at Louvain and then at Paris, where he received his doctorate in 1617. Shortly thereafter he was appointed director of the Saint Pulcherie Seminary in Louvain and professor of exegesis at the university. In 1630 he was named Regius Professor of Sacred Scripture, and in 1635 was University Rector. Next year he was consecrated Bishop of Ypres, where he died of the plague in 1638.

After Jansen's death some of the commentaries which he had written for his academic lectures on biblical books were published. More significant, however, was his major treatise on Augustine. Jansen had been interested in Augustine's religious thought since student days. In the early 1620s, coming to believe that Augustine's theology of efficacious predestinating grace was being threatened by the humanitarian tendencies of the Jesuit theologians of the Counter-Reformation, he embarked on an intensive study of Augustine's works, particularly his anti-Pelagian writings. The massive treatise which resulted from this work, entitled *Augustinus,* was published posthumously in 1640. Its three parts presented Augustine's theology of grace in a systematic and continuous synthesis. Part I described the Pelagian and semi-Pelagian heresies which Augustine sought to refute; Part II expounded Augustine's interpretation of man's original state of innocence and his subsequent fall; and Part III set forth his doctrine of salvation through God's redeeming grace in Jesus Christ.

The publication of this work touched off a heated controversy in Roman Catholic circles in European countries, particularly in France. Jansen's theology encountered strong opposition both from the ecclesiastical establishment and from the civil power. In 1653 five propositions, allegedly derived from Jansen, were condemned by Pope Innocent X in his bull *Cum Occasione.* These propositions, related to predestination, maintained that without God's enabling grace man cannot fulfill the divine commands and that the operation of God's grace, bestowed on his elect, is irresistible. Despite such official opposition, however, Jansenism, because it sought to defend traditional orthodoxy, to deepen personal piety, and to foster ascetic rigor in moral conduct, enlisted the support of certain notabilities. One of them was Blaise Pascal, whose *Povincial Letters* is one of the classic documents of this controversy. Other supporters included the theologian and philosopher Antoine Arnauld and his sister Jacqueline, abbess of the convent of Port Royal, which became an important center of Jansenist influence. But in 1709 Port Royal was closed down and its occupants dispersed; and in 1713 Pope Clement XI, in his bull *Unigenitus,* officially condemned certain propositions attributed to Pasquier Quesnel, a leading Jansenist theologian. Though the movement in France was thus seriously damaged, in 1723 the Jansenists of the Netherlands nominated a schismatic archbishop of Utrecht as their ecclesiastical leader, and this group has maintained its existence down to the present day, becoming in the later nineteenth century part of the Old Catholic Church.

N. V. Hope

See also Pascal, Blaise.

Bibliography. N. Abercrombie, *The Origins of Jansenism;* R. A. Knox, *Enthusiasm;* E. Romanes, *The Story of Port Royal;* A. Sedgwick, *Jansenism in Seventeenth Century France.*

Jansenism. *See* JANSEN, CORNELIUS OTTO.

Jaspers, Karl (1883–1969). German existentialist philosopher. Trained in medicine, he first practiced in psychiatry and then moved via psychology to philosophy, finally accepting a professorship in this at Heidelberg in 1921. He was ousted from his post during the Nazi era but returned to it after the war. His first major book, *General Psychopathology* (1913), dealt with the merits and limits of various psychological procedures, distinguishing between the internally comprehendible and the merely causally recognizable events in the life of the mind.

In subsequent works—*Psychologie der Weltanschauungen* (1919), *Philosophie* (3 vols., 1932), *Man in the Modern Age* (1932), *Reason and Existence* (1935), *Existenzphilosophie* (1938), and numerous others—he developed the central ideas of his existentialism. The nature of the self is discovered through the "illumination of existence," which discloses man as an entity seeking understanding and being. Existence is the authentic self and infinitely open to new possibilities. It cannot be conceptually determined by philosophy but is illuminated by reflection and communicated. It is the eternal in man and total freedom; but since life is a flux in which man seeks to find mooring, existence is necessarily limited by "boundary situations" such as death, suffering, guilt, and struggle. Man has freedom of choice, and when he chooses, he acts. But in so doing he takes chances, because the original choice determines his subsequent existence. Since there is no escape from man's limits, he is condemned to endless striving, but in the paradox between finite existence and the struggle for infinity is found transcendence, the ultimate symbol of his salvation.

In these and his major theological volumes—*Nietzsche and Christianity* (1946), *The Perennial Scope of Theology* (1948), and *Myth and Christianity* (1954)—Jaspers sees religious answers emerging from metaphysical descriptions of being. He rejects theism, pantheism, revealed religion, and atheism as mere "ciphers" or symbols which should not be taken literally, and argues that one should look to phenomenological descriptions of the fringes of inward and outer experiences for the understandings usually articulated by theology and metaphysics. He uses "the encompassing" to designate the ultimate but indefinite limits of being as we think, conceive, or conceptualize, while reserving "transcendence" for man's personal, devoted, and committed effort to reach the encompassing. In effect he calls for a "philosophical faith" in man's freedom and the transcendence which provides him with help and on which the world is grounded, and rejects the alleged "absolutism" of traditional Christianity for the openness and tolerance of this faith.

In his later years Jaspers turned more to social activism—*The Idea of the University* (1946), *The Question of German Guilt* (1946), *The Future of Mankind* (1957)—and published extensively in the history of philosophy as well. R. V. PIERARD

See also EXISTENTIALISM.

Bibliography. P. A. Schilpp, ed., *The Philosophy of Karl Jaspers;* E. T. Long, *Jaspers and Bultmann;* O. F. Bollnow, *RGG,* III, 549–50; P. Koestenbaum, *Encyclopedia of Philosophy,* IV, 254–58.

Jealousy. An intense emotion which may be seen in a positive light as zeal or in a negative light as envy. It is a single-minded devotion which, when turned inward to one's self, produces hatred and envy of others or, when turned beyond one's self, produces intense zeal leading to total selflessness.

The Hebrew word *qānā'* means "to become dark red" (Num. 5:14; Prov. 6:34). There is heightened color resulting from the deep personal emotions being felt. The Greek word *zēloō*, meaning "to boil," may be translated "zeal" or "jealousy" depending on the context. This term is used for both God and man (Deut. 32:21; Acts 7:9; Rom. 10:19; 11:11; I Cor. 10:22; 13:4).

God reveals himself as "a jealous God" (Exod. 20:5; 34:14). He alone is the true living God and has the exclusive right to the worship and service of his people. He is jealous for the well-being of his people (Zech. 1:14). He is a "consuming fire" against all evil both within and without Israel, but full of zeal on behalf of the salvation of his people (Deut. 4:24). God's jealousy is provoked by idolatry (Deut. 32:16) and by disobedience (Isa. 59:17–18) because such course destroys those who pursue it. The matter of absolutes—right and wrong—are always involved when God is concerned.

Man can also possess a jealousy or zeal for God and for the things of God. Elijah declared, "I have been very zealous for the Lord God Almighty" (I Kings 19:10). Paul speaks of his godly jealousy with regard to the Corinthian Christians: "I am jealous for you with a godly jealousy" (II Cor. 11:2). Paul also indicates that the godly sorrow of these same Christians created in them an intense zeal for doing right (II Cor. 7:11). A strong passion for God and for his purpose is the kind of motivation which causes his people to remain faithful to him.

Jealousy has a double meaning as it relates to man. In contrast to godly zeal there is envy.

Cain's murder of Abel in Gen. 4 is the first biblical illustration of the destructive and negative force of jealousy. Paul makes it clear that envy is the antithesis of love (I Cor. 13:4; II Cor. 12:20). He also identifies jealousy as being among the "works of the flesh" (Gal. 5:20). Jealousy in this sense is resentfulness toward others for what they have in possessions, advantages, relationships, or whatever. It destroys one's spirituality (Job 5:2; Prov. 14:30).

From a psychological perspective jealousy in its negative sense distracts a person from his own genius and productivity, and ultimately destroys him. Jealousy distorts one's entire perspective of the world, producing an enormous amount of tension and conflict. The jealous person is always an angry person who is filled with self-pity. For the jealous person both his past and his future seem empty, and the desire to cut other people down to his own size becomes intense. The jealous person responds defensively and is easily irritated. He develops a hypersensitivity toward everyone and interprets both the deeds and conversations of others in the most negative light possible. Jealousy sets a person at cross-purposes to everyone, robbing him of any feeling of belonging to the world. It has been found that jealousy is basic to all character disorders.

Nothing can liberate the envious person until he sees that he is the source of his own painful situation. C. Davis

Bibliography. E. M. Good, *IDB*, II, 806–7; *IBD*, II, 736–37; A. Stumpff, *TDNT*, II, 877–88; J. Pulsford, *The Jealousy of God;* M. and W. Beecher, *The Mark of Cain: An Anatomy of Jealousy.*

Jehovah. *See* God, Names of.

Jehovah's Witnesses. This name was adopted in 1931 by the movement founded by Charles Taze Russell in the 1870s. Russell was born in 1852 in Pittsburgh, Pennsylvania. His family were Congregationalists but Russell reacted strongly against his religious upbringing. At the age of eighteen he started a Bible class in Pittsburgh, and this group grew into the organization which we now know as the Jehovah's Witnesses. In 1876 Russell became the group's pastor, and in 1879 he started a magazine, *Zion's Watchtower,* the forerunner of today's *Watchtower.* Russell's organization became the Zion's Watch Tower Tract Society in 1884. In 1908 Russell moved the headquarters of his organization to Brooklyn, New York. The organization has been based in Brooklyn ever since.

In 1886 Russell published the first of a series of seven books entitled *Studies in the Scriptures.* Volume 6 appeared in 1904 and the seventh volume in 1917, a year after Russell's death. The publication of Volume 7 of *Studies in the Scriptures* led to a schism in the organization. The majority of members followed J. F. Rutherford, while a smaller group formed itself into the Dawn Bible Student's Association. This group is still in existence and publishes the *Dawn* magazine, which has a circulation of about 30,000 copies. The larger group following Rutherford became today's Jehovah's Witnesses. Their magazine, *The Watchtower,* has a circulation of over 64 million worldwide.

Following Russell's death in 1916 Judge Joseph Franklin Rutherford became the leader of the organization. An able organizer, he developed the group into its present organization. Rutherford wrote over a hundred books and fundamentally shaped the group's theology. He increased its hostility toward organized religion and developed a variety of highly successful missionary methods. Rutherford, who was born in 1869, died in 1942, leaving behind an organization which has continued to grow at a remarkable rate.

In 1981 the Jehovah's Witnesses were shaken by a series of schisms which led to a large number leaving the organization. The leader of the opposition to the Brooklyn headquarters group was Professor James Penton, a Canadian, whose family had been among Russell's earliest converts. Penton and those who sided with him sought to reemphasize the doctrine of justification by faith and return the group to its original interest in Bible study. The intention of Penton and other Witnesses who shared his ideas appears to have been to reform the group from within. The Brooklyn leadership strongly rejected their arguments and expelled anyone who supported their views. Although this division was a serious one, it appears that the majority of Witnesses remained within the official organization, which retained control over all of the group's assets.

As a religious organization the Jehovah's Witnesses are typical of many nineteenth century groups. Although their theology bears some resemblance to that of the Arians in early church history, they are essentially a modern group strongly influenced by rationalism. Like many other new religions in the nineteenth century the Witnesses represent a strong reaction to the scientific world view. The rationalism of the group can be seen in their rejection of Trinitarian doctrines and traditional teachings about the person and work of Jesus Christ. Their rationalistic attitude toward the Bible comes out in their literal interpretation of prophecy and failure to appreciate the symbolic character of biblical language. Their rejection of blood transfusions reflects this rejection of modern science as well as the extreme literalism of their exegesis.

In attempting to justify their interpretation of Christianity and rejection of orthodoxy the Witnesses produced their own translation of the Bible—*The New World Translation of the Christian Greek Scriptures* and *The New World Translation of the Hebrew Scriptures*—in 1950. Although this work claims to be a translation, the Witnesses have yet to name the translators or prove their credentials as competent scholars. What one finds in fact is a rendering of the Bible in terms of the theology of the organization.

Probably the best introduction to the theology of the Jehovah's Witnesses is their book *Let God Be True.* In addition to their rejection of the Christian doctrine of the Trinity they teach a number of distinct doctrines. In their view the atonement is a ransom paid to the God Jehovah by Jesus Christ which removes the effects of Adam's sin, laying the foundation for a new righteousness and enabling men to save themselves by their good works. They teach that Jesus was resurrected a divine spirit after offering this ransom to God. At death humans either sleep until the resurrection or, if they are evil, suffer annihilation. In their view Jesus Christ returned to earth spiritually in 1914 and is now proceeding to overthrow Satan's worldly organization and to establish a theocratic millennial kingdom. This kingdom will arrive in the near future with the battle of Armageddon. After Armageddon true believers will be resurrected to a life on earth while a select group of 144,000 will rule in heaven with Christ. In addition to holding these doctrines Jehovah's Witnesses reject a professional ministry and, until recently, the idea of church buildings. They are pacifists and call upon their members to have nothing to do with worldly politics.

Today there are over three million Witnesses worldwide. They have an extensive missionary network throughout the world and operate in most countries. In some places, particularly in Africa, the Witnesses have suffered severe persecution. In others, especially North America, they are rapidly coming to resemble a reasonably sized religious denomination. I. HEXHAM

See also CULTS.

Bibliography. W. R. Martin and N. Klawn, *Jehovah of the Watch Tower;* T. Dencher, *The Watch Tower versus the Bible;* J. Penton, *The End Delayed;* A. Hoekema, *The Four Major Cults.*

Jerome (*ca.* 347–419). Biblical scholar and translator who aimed to introduce the best of Greek learning to Western Christianity. He sensed the inferiority of the West, and he labored to add scholarship to the public glory of the church.

Jerome, whose Latin name was Eusebius Hieronomous, was born in the little town of Strido near the border of Italy and Dalmatia (today's Yugoslavia). His parents were well-to-do Catholics who sent their son to Rome for his higher education. There he heard the great grammarian Donatus, laid the foundation of his library of classical Latin authors, and adopted Cicero as his model of Latin style.

At the end of his studies, when about twenty years of age, he set off for Gaul. In Treves, the imperial capital, he experienced a type of conversion, renouncing a secular career for meditation and spiritual work. This change of career led him back to his home and to neighboring Aquilia, where he met Rufinus and other clergymen and devout women interested in asceticism. Thus began his career of cultivating ascetic and scholarly interests.

In 373 Jerome decided to travel to the East. He settled for a time in the Syrian desert southeast of Antioch. There he mastered Hebrew and perfected his Greek. After ordination at Antioch he went to Constantinople and studied with Gregory of Nazianzus. In 382 he returned to Rome, where he became the friend and secretary of Pope Damasus. We have Damasus to thank for the first impulse toward Jerome's Latin translation of the Bible, the Vulgate.

When Damasus died, late in 384, Jerome for the second time decided to go to the East. After some wandering, first to Antioch then Alexandria, he settled in Bethlehem, where he remained for the rest of his life. He found companions in a monastery and served as a spiritual adviser to some wealthy women who had followed him from Rome.

Jerome's greatest accomplishment was the Vulgate. The chaos of the older Latin translation was notorious. Working from the Hebrew OT and the Greek NT, Jerome, after twenty-three years of labor, gave Latin Christianity its Bible anew. Although the text became corrupted during the Middle Ages, its supremacy was reaffirmed by the Council of Trent in 1546, and it remains to this day the classical Latin Bible.

A second and related part of Jerome's heritage lies in his expositions of Scripture. Like all biblical interpreters of the early church, Jerome affirmed a threefold (historical, symbolic, and spiritual) meaning of Scripture and repudiated an exclusively historical interpretation as "Jewish." The mere letter kills. What he demanded was only that the historical interpretation should not be considered inferior to the allegorical (or spiritual).

Jerome was no creative theologian, no great teacher of the church. He engaged in one bitter controversy after another with vindictive passion. Yet for all his personal weaknesses, Jerome's reputation as a biblical scholar endures.

B. L. SHELLEY

Bibliography. H. von Campenhausen, *Men Who Shaped the Western Church;* J. N. D. Kelly, *Jerome;* C. C. Mierow, *Saint Jerome: The Sage of Bethlehem;* F. X. Murphy, ed. *A Monument to Saint Jerome;* J. G. Nolan, *Jerome and Jovinian;* J. Steinmann, *Saint Jerome and His Times.*

Jerusalem. The origins of the city are lost in antiquity; but evidence of civilization on the site stretches back to 3000 B.C., and the city is referred to by name in Egyptian texts as early as the beginning of the second millennium B.C. According to Ezek. 16:3, the site was once populated by Amorites and Hittites; and, if it is to be identified with Salem (Gen. 14:18; Ps. 76:2), it was ruled in Abraham's day by the petty king Melchizedek, who was also "priest of God Most High." Some hold that the "region of Moriah" (Gen. 22:2), where Abraham was tested with the sacrifice of Isaac, was what became the temple site, but this connection has not been proved.

Jerusalem in History. At the time of the conquest Jerusalem (otherwise known as Zion, the name originally given to the southeast hill where the earliest fortress was located) was populated by the Jebusites, a Semitic tribe ruled over by Adoni-zedek. Joshua soundly defeated an alliance of rulers headed by Adoni-zedek (Josh. 10) but never took Jerusalem, which became a neutral city between Judah and Benjamin. It was still administered by Jebusites, even though the men of Judah overran and burned at least parts of the city (Judg. 1:8, 21). This situation changed when King David decided to move his capital from Hebron. He decisively conquered the Jebusites (II Sam. 5:6–10) and established Jerusalem (or Zion) as his strategic center and political capital. Calling it the City of David (II Sam. 5:9), he fortified and beautified it until his death, and his successor, Solomon, pursued the same course even more lavishly.

The division of the kingdom immediately after Solomon's death marked the beginning of several stages of decline. Now the capital of the southern kingdom only, Jerusalem was plundered by Egyptians under Shishak as early as the fifth year of Rehoboam (I Kings 14:25–26). Fresh looting took place in Jehoram's reign, this time by a concert of Philistines and Arabs; and part of the walls were destroyed in skirmishes between Amaziah of the southern kingdom and Jehoash of the north. Repairs enabled the city under Ahaz to withstand the onslaught of Syria and Israel, and again the city providentially escaped when the northern kingdom was destroyed by the Assyrians. But eventually the city was captured (597 B.C.) and then destroyed (586 B.C.) by the Babylonians, and most of the inhabitants killed or transported.

Persian rule brought about the return of a few thousand Jews to the land and city, and the erection of a smaller temple than the majestic center built by Solomon; but the walls were not rebuilt until the middle of the fifth century under the leadership of Nehemiah. Jerusalem's vassal status continued under the Greeks when Alexander the Great overthrew the Persian Empire; but after his untimely death (323 B.C.) Jerusalem became the center of a brutal conflict between the Seleucid dynasty in the north and the Ptolemies of Egypt in the south. The struggle bred the Jewish revolt led by the Maccabees, who succeeded in rededicating the temple in 165 B.C. Infighting and corruption contributed to the decisive defeat of the city by the Romans in 63 B.C. and its pacification in 54 B.C.

Herod the Great came to power in 37 B.C. as a vassal king responsible to Rome, and embarked on the enlargement and beautification of the temple and other buildings, projects not completed until decades after his death. The Jewish revolt that began in A.D. 66 inevitably led to the destruction of the city by the Romans in A.D. 70. A further revolt under Bar Cochba in A.D. 132 led to the city's destruction once again (135). This time the Romans rebuilt the city on a smaller scale and as a pagan center, banning all Jews from living there—a ban that was not lifted until the reign of Constantine. From the early fourth century on, Jerusalem became a "Christian" city and the site of many churches and monasteries. Successive occupiers—Persians, Arabs, Turks, Crusaders, British, Israelis—have left their religious and cultural stamp on the city, which since 1967 has been unified under Israeli military might.

The Centrality of Jerusalem. From the time that Jerusalem became both the political and the cultic capital of the children of Israel, it progressively served as a bifocal symbol: on the one hand it reflected the people and all their sinfulness and waywardness; on the other it represented the place where God made himself known and the anticipation of all the eschatological blessing that God had in store for his people. In Scripture, Zion is the city of God (Ps. 46:4; 48:1–2) and therefore the joy of the whole earth (Ps. 48:2). The Lord himself has chosen Zion (Ps. 132:13–14), which consequently serves as his abode. But if Jerusalem thus becomes virtually equivalent to "temple," it can in other images represent all of God's covenant people; indeed, to be "born in Zion" is to know God and experience his salvation (Ps. 87:5). These strands come together at least in part because the temple is located on the holy hill called Zion (Ps. 15:1; Isa. 31:4; Joel 2:1); equally, the holy hill is set in parallel with Jerusalem (Isa. 45:13; Dan. 9:16–17). Hence Jerusalem is the holy city (Neh. 11:1; Isa. 48:2; 52:1), so much so that going up to Zion is virtually equivalent to approaching Yahweh (Jer. 31:6) and salvation out of Zion is of course from the Lord (Ps. 14:7; cf. Pss. 128:5; 134:3).

Jerusalem's Sin. Precisely because of these associations, the sin of its people is the more grievous. The prophets (esp. Isaiah, Jeremiah, Ezekiel, and Micah) speak of Jerusalem as a prostitute, fallen away from God, guilty of idolatry and of flagrant disregard of God's commandments. The city must stand under the judgment of God (e.g. Isa. 1:21; 29:1–4; 32:9ff.; Jer. 6:22ff.). Jerusalem's social and religious transgressions are so gross and persistent that Ezekiel labels it "the city of bloodshed" (Ezek. 22:2–3; 24:6). In its sin Jerusalem is counted as part of the pagan world (Ezek. 16:1–3) and will certainly be destroyed (Ezek. 15:6). The citizens of Jerusalem are worse than Samaria and Sodom (Lam. 4:6; Ezek. 16:44–58; cf. Amos 2:4–5; Mal. 2:11). The city taken by David will now be taken in judgment (Isa. 29:1–7).

Analogous to this bifocal casting of Jerusalem's symbolic significance stands the prophetic intertwining of threatened destruction and promised eschatological blessing. Because Jerusalem is so sinful, it must be judged and destroyed (Isa. 1:21; 32:13–14; Ezek. 22:19); the guilty must be brought to account (Zeph. 1:12). At one level this judgment is executed in the horrors of the Exile (II Kings 24:13, 20; Jer. 42:18; 44:13; Lam. 1–5); but according to Jesus this is not the only judgment Jerusalem must face (Matt. 23:37–39).

Jerusalem's Glory. Yet all is not gloom. Nations used by God to punish Jerusalem must themselves be called to account (Ps. 137:1, 4–9; Isa. 10:12). Promises for the restoration of Jerusalem following the Exile become linked with promises of eschatological blessing (Isa. 40:1–5; 54:11–17; 60; cf. Hag. 2:19; Zech. 1:12–17). Yahweh can no more forget Jerusalem than a woman can forget her child (Isa. 49:13–18). Ezekiel anticipates the return of Yahweh to Zion (43:1–9). In Zion, Yahweh will inaugurate his eschatological rule (Pss. 146:10; 149:2; Isa. 24:23; 52:7; Obad. 21; Mic. 4:7; Zeph. 3:15; Zech. 14:9), whether personally or through Messiah (Zech. 9:9–10), his servant (Isa. 40–66).

Although there are frequent demands that Jerusalem (and by metonymy all Israel) repent as a presage of the eschatological glory, yet ultimately Jerusalem's glory rests on God's saving intervention (Isa. 62; 66:10–15). He it is who washes away the filth of Zion's sin (Isa. 4:4). Jerusalem will become the eschatological capital (Isa. 16:1; 45:14), will be awarded a new name expressive of Yahweh's delight and rights (Isa. 62:4, 12; Jer. 3:17; 33:16; Ezek. 48:35; Zech. 8:3), will be built with unfathomable opulence (Isa. 54:11–17), and will be secure from all enemies (Isa. 52:1; Joel 2:32; 3:17). The redeemed who return to Zion constitute the holy remnant (II Kings 19:31; Isa. 4:3; 35:10; 51:11)—a theme which suggests that the early return to Jerusalem after the Exile constitutes an anticipation of an eschatological return (Isa. 27:13; 62:11; Zech. 6:8, 15). The temple is central to the city (Ezek. 40–48; cf. Isa. 44:28; Zech. 1:16).

The eschatological glory to be experienced by Zion is accompanied by a transformation of nature and by long and abundant life, heroic strength, economic prosperity, joy, and thankful praise (Isa. 11; 12:4–6; 61:3; 62:8–9; 65:20; Jer. 33:11; Zech. 2:4, 5). Although there is repeated assurance that the nations that have savaged Jerusalem will themselves be ravaged, in another emphasis the nations of the earth, after an unsuccessful campaign against Jerusalem (Isa. 29:7–8; Mic. 4:11), join in a great pilgrimage to Zion, where they are taught by Yahweh to live according to his will (Isa. 2:2–4; Jer. 33:9; Mic. 4:1–3; Zech. 2:11). In all this Jerusalem retains a central place.

Jerusalem in NT Teachings. In the NT "Zion" occurs only seven times: Rom. 9:33 and I Pet. 2:6 (citing Isa. 28:16), Rom. 11:26 (citing Isa. 59:20), Matt. 21:5 and John 12:15 (cf. Zech. 9:9; Isa. 40:9; 62:11—all with reference to the inhabitants addressed as the daughter of Zion), and in two independent uses, Heb. 12:22 and Rev. 14:1 (both "Mount Zion"). But "Jerusalem" occurs 139 times. Even many of the occurrences in the Gospels and Acts that at first glance seem to bear nothing more than topographical significance tend to fall into identifiable patterns. Jerusalem is still "the holy city" (Matt. 4:5; 27:53), the home of the temple and its priestly service, as well as the center of rabbinic authority. Jesus must die in the Jerusalem area (Matt. 16:21; Mark 10:33–34; Luke 9:31), in direct conflict with these central Jewish institutions. His death and resurrection stand in fulfillment of all they represented; but the irony and tragedy of the sacrifice is that the people connected with these institutions recognized little of this salvation-historical fulfillment. The temple had become a den of thieves (Mark

11:17), and Jerusalem itself lived up to its reputation as killer of the prophets (Matt. 23:37–39; cf. Luke 13:33). Jerusalem must be destroyed by foreign invaders (Matt. 23:38; Luke 19:43–44; 21:20, 24). In Acts, Jerusalem is the hub from which the gospel radiates outward (Acts 1:8), the site both of Pentecost and of the apostolic council; but if it is the moral and salvation-historical center of Christianity, it is also the ideological home of Judaizers who wish to make the entire Mosaic code a precondition for Gentile conversion to Jesus Messiah—a position Paul condemns (Gal. 1:8–9). Paul himself, however, is quick to recognize how beholden all other believers are to the Christian remnant of Jerusalem (Gal. 2:10; II Cor. 8–9) which in a salvation-historical sense is truly the mother church.

A still deeper connection links OT treatment of Jerusalem to the "heavenly Jerusalem" (Heb. 12:22), to which Christian believers have already come, and to "Jerusalem above" (Gal. 4:26), which in an extended typology embraces new covenant believers and relegates geographical Jerusalem and its children to slavery: Jesus *fulfills* and to that extent *replaces* the OT types and shadows that anticipated him. Jesus enters Jerusalem as messianic king (Mark 11:1–11 par.) and is concerned to see Jerusalem's temple pure (Mark 11:15–17 par.) precisely because the city and temple anticipate his own impending death and resurrection—events that shift the focal meeting place between God and man to Jesus himself (Mark 14:57–58; John 2:19–22). This constitutes part of a broader pattern, worked out in some detail in the Epistle to the Hebrews, in which the gospel and its entailments simultaneously fulfill OT institutions and expectations and render them obsolete (e.g., Heb. 8:13). The ultimate goal is the new Jerusalem.

Jerusalem and the Church. Difficulties in rightly relating OT and NT materials on Jerusalem have contributed to the church's changing perceptions regarding itself, the Jews, and Jerusalem. Especially in the wake of the destruction of A.D. 132–35 Christians saw themselves as the exclusive heirs of the covenant people of old: Christians constituted the true Jerusalem. Geographical Jerusalem became a focal point for Christian piety and tradition, an ideal location for monasteries and basilicas, especially after Helena, mother of Constantine, devoted so much attention to Christian sites around the city. The Constantinian settlement (early fourth century) continued to see Christianity as the legitimate heir of Judaism, but its mingling of ecclesiastical and spiritual authority led both to persecution of Jews and to substantial disillusionment when Rome, perceived as the successor of Jerusalem, was ransacked by barbarians. The latter event prompted Augustine to write his famous *City of God*, which shifted the focus of the true city from either Jerusalem or Rome to the spiritual dimension; but this stance was easily overlooked during the height of medieval Catholicism, when Rome's authority frequently extended itself to all temporal spheres. The Reformation, and especially the Puritan awakening in England, while preserving a certain harshness toward Jews, became progressively interested in Jewish evangelism—not in order to restore the Jews to Jerusalem, but to reincorporate them into the people of God and thus (in the case of the Puritan hope) to usher in the expected millennial age.

Modern theological treatments frequently focus on the replacement theme (W. D. Davies, *Gospel and Land*) or use the city as a cipher for a colorful intermingling of sociology and Barthianism (J. Ellul, *The Meaning of the City*). Conservatives tend to dispute how much of the OT promises regarding Jerusalem's restoration are taken up in NT typological fulfillment. Positions range from a thoroughgoing affirmation of typology (various forms of amillennialism) to equally thoroughgoing disjunction (various forms of dispensationalism). The typological cannot be ignored, nor can the NT's substantial silence on the future of Jerusalem and the land; but some passages, notably Luke 21:21–24, seem to anticipate the restoration of Jerusalem's fortunes.

D. A. CARSON

See also JERUSALEM, THE NEW.

Bibliography. F. F. Bruce, "Paul and Jerusalem," *TB* 19:3–23; M. Burrows, *IDB*, II, 843–66; G. Fohrer and E. Lohse, *TDNT*, VII, 292–338; J. Jeremias, *Jerusalem in the Time of Jesus;* K. M. Kenyon, *Digging up Jerusalem;* B. Mazar, *The Mountain of the Lord;* J. Munck, *Paul and the Salvation of Mankind;* G. F. Oehler, *Theology of the OT*, 509–21; D. F. Payne, *IBD*, II, 752–60; J. B. Payne, *ZPEB*, III, 459–95; G. N. H. Peters, *The Theocratic Kingdom*, III, 32–63; N. W. Porteous, "Jerusalem-Zion: the Growth of a Symbol," in *Living the Mystery;* G. A. Smith, *Jerusalem*, 2 vols.; Y. Yadin, ed., *Jerusalem Revealed.*

Jerusalem, The New. Already in Paul and in the Epistle to the Hebrews, Jerusalem becomes an antitypical symbol for the church, the new covenant community, the "Mount Zion" which is the locus of the firstborn (Gal. 4:26; Heb. 12:22). In the Apocalypse this theme extends to a further expression, "the new Jerusalem" (3:12; 21:2).

In the first occurrence (3:12) one of the rewards promised to the believers in Philadelphia (3:7–13) is "the name of my God and the name of the city of my God, the new Jerusalem, which is coming down out of heaven from my God." All seven of the letters of Rev. 2–3 utilize elements which speak loudly to the cultural and historical backgrounds of the immediate recipients. Philadelphia had suffered a series of disastrous earthquakes that had bred major insecurity; and the church, small and faithful but not strong, suffered from similar feelings of insecurity. The risen Christ therefore reassures his people by promising an eminently suitable reward: they will be made pillars in the temple of God (in an earthquake zone!), the temple they will never leave, and they will be characterized by the name of the new Jerusalem, the city of God. Whatever theological value rests in this rubric, it also symbolizes in this context the ultimate hope and reward of the church, the dwelling place of God, sovereignly interposed by God and characterized by massive stability and unending endurance.

The new Jerusalem receives extended treatment in Rev. 21–22. The ultimate state of the church, and her reward, is presented under diverse metaphors: the church is simultaneously "prepared as a bride beautifully dressed for her husband"—indeed, she is "the bride, the wife of the Lamb" (21:2, 9), and "the holy city, the new Jerusalem, coming down out of heaven from God" (21:2). The holy city is perfectly symmetrical (21:16) and is constructed with materials of fabulous wealth (21:18–21, using language from Isa. 54:11). It shines with the glory of God (21:11) and has foundations named after the apostles and gates named after the twelve tribes of Israel (21:12, 14). The water of life flows from the throne of God down the middle of the main street (22:1), and on each side of the stream the tree of life bears a different crop of fruit each month. The throne of God and of the Lamb is in the city (22:3); night and tears have both been banished (21:4; 22:5). Best of all, God's servants will see his face, and that will provide all the light they need (22:4–5). The "nations" are not other than the church, since they have free access to this city that does not admit anything impure (21:24–27; 22:2); rather, the city becomes the focal point of the existence of all the redeemed in the new heaven and new earth.

The rich symbolism reaches beyond our finest imaginings, not only to the beatific vision but to a renewed, joyous, industrious, orderly, holy, loving, eternal, and abundant existence. Perhaps the most moving element in the description is what is missing: there is no temple in the new Jerusalem, "because the Lord God Almighty and the Lamb are its temple" (21:22). Vastly outstripping the expectations of Judaism, this stated omission signals the ultimate reconciliation. D. A. Carson

See also Jerusalem; Church, The.

Jesuits. *See* Society of Jesus, The.

Jesus Christ. The expression is a combination of a name, "Jesus" (of Nazareth), and the title "Messiah" (Hebrew) or "Christ" (Greek), which means "anointed." In Acts 5:42, where we read of "preaching Jesus the Christ," this combination of the name and the title is still apparent. As time progressed, however, the title became so closely associated with the name that the combination soon was transformed from the confession—Jesus (who is) the Christ—to a confessional name—Jesus Christ. The appropriateness of this title for Jesus was such that even Jewish Christian writers quickly referred to Jesus Christ rather than Jesus the Christ (Cf. Matt. 1:1; Rom. 1:7; Heb. 13:8; James 1:1; I Pet. 1:1).

Sources of Information. The sources for our knowledge of Jesus Christ can be divided into two main groups: non-Christian and Christian.

Non-Christian Sources. These sources can be divided again into two groups: pagan and Jewish. Both are limited in their value. There are essentially only three pagan sources of importance: Pliny (*Epistles* x.96); Tacitus (*Annals* xv.44); and Suetonius (*Lives* xxv.4). All these date from the second decade of the second century. The main Jewish sources are Josephus (*Antiquities* xviii.3.3 and xx.9.1) and the Talmud. The non-Christian sources provide meager information about Jesus, but they do establish the fact that he truly lived, that he gathered disciples, performed healings, and that he was condemned to death by Pontius Pilate.

Christian Sources. The nonbiblical Christian sources consist for the most part of the apocryphal gospels (A.D. 150–350) and the "agrapha" ("unwritten sayings" of Jesus, i.e., supposedly authentic sayings of Jesus not found in the canonical Gospels). Their value is quite dubious in that what is not utterly fantastic (cf. Infancy Gospel of Thomas) or heretical (cf. Gospel of Truth) is at best only possible and not provable (cf. Gospel of Thomas 31, 47).

The biblical materials can be divided into the Gospels and Acts through Revelation. The information we can learn from Acts through Revelation is essentially as follows: Jesus was born a Jew (Gal. 4:4) and was a descendant of David (Rom. 1:3); he was gentle (II Cor. 10:1), righteous (I Pet. 3:18), sinless (II Cor. 5:21), humble (Phil. 2:6), and was tempted (Heb. 2:18; 4:15); he instituted the Lord's Supper (I Cor. 11:23–26), was transfigured (II Pet. 1:17–18), was betrayed (I Cor. 11:23), was crucified (I Cor. 1:23), rose from the dead (I Cor. 15:3ff), and ascended to heaven (Eph. 4:8). Certain specific sayings of Jesus are known (cf. I Cor. 7:10; 9:14; Acts 20:35), and possible allusions to his sayings are also found (e.g., Rom. 12:14, 17; 13:7, 8–10; 14:10).

The major sources for our knowledge of Jesus are the canonical Gospels. These Gospels are divided generally into two groups: the Synoptic Gospels (the "look-alike" Gospels of Matthew, Mark, and Luke) and John. The former are generally understood to "look alike" due to their having a literary relationship. The most common explanation of this literary relationship is that Mark wrote first and that Matthew and Luke used Mark and another source, now lost, which contained mostly teachings of Jesus (called "Q") and that they used other materials as well ("M" = the materials found only in Matthew; "L" = the materials found only in Luke).

Jesus of Nazareth. In Matthew and Luke we find accounts of the birth of Jesus. Both accounts point out that Jesus was born of a virgin by the name of Mary in the city of Bethlehem (Matt. 1:18–2:12; Luke 1:26–2:7; attempts to find allusions to the virgin birth in Gal. 4:4 and John 8:41 are quite forced). Attempts to explain these accounts as parallels to Greek myths stumble on the lack of any really substantial parallels in Greek literature and above all by the Jewish nature of these accounts.

The ministry of Jesus began with his baptism by John (Mark 1:1–15; Acts 1:21–22; 10:37) and his temptation by Satan. His ministry involved the selection of twelve disciples (Mark 3:13–19), which symbolized the regathering of the twelve tribes of Israel; the preaching of the need of repentance (Mark 1:15) and the arrival of the kingdom of God in his ministry (Luke 11:20); the offer of salvation to the outcasts of society (Mark 2:15–17; Luke 15; 19:10); the healing of the sick and demon-possessed (which are referred to in the Jewish Talmud); and his glorious return to consummate the kingdom.

The turning point in Jesus' ministry came at Caesarea Philippi when, after being confessed as the Christ by Peter, he acknowledged the correctness of this confession and proceeded to tell the disciples of his forthcoming death (Mark 8:27–31; Matt. 16:13–21). Advancing toward Jerusalem, Jesus cleansed the temple and in so doing judged the religion of Israel (note Mark's placement of the account between 11:12–14 and 11:20–21 as well as the contents of the following two chapters). On the night in which he was betrayed he instituted the ordinance of the Lord's Supper, which refers to the new covenant sealed by his sacrificial blood and the victorious regathering in the kingdom of God (Mark 14:25; Matt. 26:29; Luke 22:18; I Cor. 11:26). Thereupon he was arrested in the Garden of Gethsemane, tried before the Sanhedrin, Herod Antipas, and finally Pontius Pilate, who condemned him to death on political charges for claiming to be the Messiah (Mark 15:26; John 19:19). On the eve of the sabbath Jesus was crucified for the sins of the world (Mark 10:45) outside the city of Jerusalem (John 19:20) at a place called Golgotha (Mark 15:22) between two thieves who may have been revolutionaries (Matt. 27:38).

He gave up his life before the sabbath came, so that there was no need to hasten his death by crurifragium, i.e., the breaking of his legs (John 19:31–34). He was buried in the tomb of Joseph of Arimathea (Mark 15:43; John 19:38) on the eve of the sabbath. On the first day of the week, which was the third day (Friday to 6 P.M. = day 1; Friday 6 P.M. to Saturday 6 P.M. = day 2; Saturday 6 P.M. to Sunday A.M. = day 3), he rose from the dead, the empty tomb was discovered, and he appeared to his followers (Mark 16; Matt. 28; Luke 24; John 20–21). He abode forty days with the disciples and then ascended into heaven (Acts 1:1–11).

So ended the three-year ministry (John 2:13; 5:1; 6:4; 13:1) of Jesus of Nazareth.

The Christ of Faith. The unique self-understanding of Jesus can be ascertained by two means: the implicit Christology revealed by his actions and words, and the explicit Christology revealed by the titles he chose to describe himself.

Implicit Christology. Jesus during his ministry clearly acted as one who possessed a unique authority. He assumed for himself the prerogative of cleansing the temple (Mark 11:27–33), of bringing the outcasts into the kingdom of God (Luke 15), and of having divine authority to forgive sins (Mark 2:5–7; Luke 7:48–49).

Jesus also spoke as one who possessed authority greater than the OT (Matt. 5:31–32, 38–39), than Abraham (John 8:53), Jacob (John 4:12), and the temple (Matt. 12:6). He claimed to be Lord of the Sabbath (Mark 2:28). He even claimed that the destiny of all people depended on how they responded to him (Matt. 10:32–33; 11:6; Mark 8:34–38).

Explicit Christology. Along with the implicit Christology of his behavior Jesus also made certain Christological claims by means of the various titles he used for himself. He referred to himself as the Messiah or Christ (Mark 8:27–30; 14:61–62), and his formal sentence of death on political grounds (note the superscription on the cross) only makes sense on the basis of Jesus' having acknowledged that he was the Messiah. He referred to himself also as the Son of God (Mark 12:1–9; Matt. 11:25–27), and a passage such as Mark 13:32 in which he clearly distinguished between himself and others must be authentic, for no one in the church would have created a saying such as this in which the Son of God claims to be ignorant as to the time of the end.

Jesus' favorite self-designation, due to its concealing as well as revealing nature, was the title Son of man. Jesus in using this title clearly had in mind the Son of man of Dan. 7:13, as is evident from Mark 8:38; 13:26; 14:62; Matt. 10:23; 19:28; 25:31. Therefore, rather than being a title which stresses humility, it is clear that this title reveals the divine authority Jesus possesses as the Son of man to judge the world and his sense of having come from the Father (cf. here also Mark 2:17; 10:45; Matt. 5:17; 10:34). Many attempts have been made to deny the authenticity of some or all of the Son of man sayings, but such attempts founder on the fact that this title is found in all the Gospel strata (Mark, Q, M, L, and John) and satisfies perfectly the "criterion of dissimilarity," which states that if a saying or title like this could not have arisen out of Judaism or out of the early church, it must be authentic. The denial of the authenticity of this title is therefore based not so much on exegetical issues as upon rationalistic presuppositions which *a priori* deny that Jesus of Nazareth could have spoken of himself in this way.

The Christology of the NT. Within the NT numerous claims are made concerning Jesus Christ. Through his resurrection Jesus has been exalted and given lordship over all creation (Col. 1:16–17; Phil. 2:9–11; I Cor. 15:27). The use of the title "Lord" for Jesus quickly resulted in the association of the person and work of Jesus with the Lord of the OT—i.e., Yahweh. (Cf. Rom. 10:9–13 with Joel 2:32; II Thess. 1:7–10, I Cor. 5:5 with Isa. 2:10–19; II Thess. 1:12 with Isa. 66:5; I Cor. 16:22 and Rev. 22:20; Phil. 2:11.) His preexistence is referred to (II Cor. 8:9; Phil. 2:6; Col. 1:15–16); he is referred to as creator (Col. 1:16); he is said to possess the "form" of God (Phil. 2:6) and be the "image" of God (Col. 1:15; cf. also II Cor. 4:4). He is even referred to explicitly in a number of places as "God" (Rom. 9:5; II Thess. 1:12; Titus 2:13; Heb. 1:5–8; I John 5:20; John 1:1; 20:28; although the exegesis of some of these passages is debated, it is clear that some of them clearly refer to Jesus as "God").

The Quest for the Historical Jesus. The beginning of the quest for the historical Jesus can be dated to 1774–78 when the poet Lessing published posthumously the lecture notes of Hermann Samuel Reimarus. These notes challenged the traditional portrait of Jesus found in the NT and the church. For Reimarus, Jesus never made any messianic claim, never instituted any sacraments, never predicted his death nor rose from the dead. The story of Jesus was in fact a deliberate imposture of the disciples. In so portraying Jesus, Reimarus raised the question, "What was Jesus of Nazareth really like?" And so the quest to find the "real" Jesus arose. During the earliest part of the nineteenth century the dominating method of research in the quest was rationalism, and attempts were made to explain "rationally" the life of Christ (cf. K. H. Venturini's *A Non-Supernatural History of the Great Prophet of Nazareth*). A major turning point came when D. F. Strauss's *The Life of Christ* was published in 1835, for Strauss in pointing out the futility of the rationalistic approach argued that the miraculous in the Gospels was to be understood as nonhistorical "myths." This new approach was in turn succeeded by the liberal interpretation of the life of Jesus, which minimized and neglected the miraculous dimension of the Gospels and viewed it as "husk" which had to be eliminated in order to concentrate on the teachings of Jesus. Not surprisingly, this approach found in the teachings of Jesus such liberal doctrines as the fatherhood of God, the brotherhood of man, and the infinite value of the human soul.

The "death" of the quest came about for several reasons. For one, it became apparent, through the work of Albert Schweitzer, that the liberal Jesus never existed but was simply a creation of liberal wishfulness. Another factor that helped end the quest was the realization that the Gospels were not simple objective biographies which could easily be mined for historical information. This was the result of the work of William Wrede and the form critics. Still another reason for the death of the quest was the realization that the object of faith for the church throughout the centuries had never been the historical Jesus of theological liberalism but the Christ of faith, i.e., the supernatural Christ proclaimed in the Scriptures. Martin Kähler was especially influential in this regard.

During the period between the two World Wars, the quest lay dormant for the most part due to disinterest and doubt as to its possibility. In 1953 a new quest arose at the instigation of Ernst Käsemann. Käsemann feared that the discontinuity in both theory and practice between the Jesus of history and the Christ of faith was very much like the early docetic heresy, which denied the humanity of the Son of God. As a result he argued that it was necessary to establish a continuity between the historical Jesus and the Christ of faith. Furthermore he pointed out that the present historical skepticism about the historical Jesus was unwarranted because some historical data were available and undeniable. The results of this new quest have been somewhat disappointing, and the enthusiasm that greeted it can be said, for the most part, to have disappeared. New tools have been honed during this period, however, which can assist in this historical task.

The major problem that faces any attempt to arrive at the "historical Jesus" involves the definition of the term "historical." In critical circles the term is generally understood as "the product of the historical-critical method." This method for many assumes a closed continuum of time and space in which divine intervention, i.e., the miraculous, cannot intrude. Such a definition will, of course, always have a problem seeking to find continuity between the supernatural Christ and the Jesus of history, who by such a definition cannot be supernatural. If "historical" means nonsupernatural, there can never be a real continuity between the Jesus of historical research and the Christ of faith. It is becoming clear, therefore, that this definition of "historical" must be challenged, and even in Germany spokesmen are arising who speak of the need for the historical-critical method to assume an openness to transcendence, i.e., openness to the possibility of the miraculous. Only in this way can there ever be hope of establishing a continuity between the Jesus of historical research and the Christ of faith. R. H. Stein

See also Christology; Messiah; Logos; Resurrection of Christ; Virgin Birth of Jesus; Sayings of Jesus; Parables of Jesus; Sermon on the Mount; Baptism of Jesus; Second Coming of Christ; Preexistence of Christ; Sinlessness of Christ.

Bibliography. F. F. Bruce, *Jesus and Christian Origins Outside the NT;* D. Guthrie, *A Shorter Life of Christ;* E. F. Harrison, *A Short Life of Christ;* J. G. Machen, *The Virgin Birth of Christ;* G. E. Ladd, *I Believe in the Resurrection of Jesus;* T. W. Manson, *The Teaching of Jesus;* J. Jeremias, *The Parables of Jesus* and *The Problem of the Historical Jesus;* R. H. Stein, *The Method and Message of Jesus' Teachings* and *An Introduction to the Parables of Jesus;* I. H. Marshall, *The Origins of NT Christology* and *I Believe in the Historical Jesus;* R. N. Longenecker, *The Christology of Early Jewish Christianity;* A. Schweitzer, *The Quest of the Historical Jesus;* M. Kähler, *The So-Called Historical Jesus and the Historic, Biblical Christ;* H. Anderson, *Jesus and Christian Origins;* R. H. Stein, "The 'Criteria' for Authenticity," in *Gospel Perspectives,* I; D. E. Aune, *Jesus and the Synoptic Gospels.*

John, Theology of. For a man who has been so prominent in Christian thinking throughout the centuries John is a strangely shadowy figure. In the Gospels and Acts he is almost invariably accompanied by someone else and the other person is the spokesman (there is an exception when John tells Jesus that he forbade a man to cast out demons; Luke 9:49). He is often linked with Peter and with his brother James, and these three were specially close to Jesus (Matt. 17:1; Mark 14:33; Luke 8:51). He and James were called "sons of thunder" (*Boanērges;* Mark 3:17), which perhaps points to the kind of character revealed in their desire to call down fire from heaven on people who refused to receive Jesus (Luke 9:54).

We learn more from the writings linked with his name. The Fourth Gospel as it stands is anonymous, but there is good reason for thinking that John wrote it and that he was the beloved disciple who leaned on Jesus' breast at the Last Supper (John 13:23) and to whom the dying Jesus commended his mother (John 19:26–27). The impression we get is that John had entered into the mind of Jesus more than any of the other disciples had.

God as Father. From his Gospel we learn a good deal about the Father and, indeed, it is to John more than anyone else that Christians owe their habit of referring to God simply as "the Father." John uses the word "father" 137 times (which is more than twice as often as anyone else; Matthew has it 64 times, Paul 63). No less than 122 refer to God as Father, a beautiful emphasis which has influenced all subsequent Christian thinking. John also tells us that this God is love (I John 4:8, 16), and love is an important topic in both his Gospel and his epistles. We know love in the Christian sense because we see it in the cross (John 3:16; I John 4:10); it is sacrificial giving, not for worthwhile people, but for sinners.

The Father is constantly active (John 5:17); he upholds his creation and brings blessing on those he has made. He is a great God whose will is done, particularly in election and salvation. "No one can come to me," said Jesus, "unless the Father who sent me draws him" (John 6:44); and again, "You did not choose me, but I chose you" (John 15:16; cf. 8:47; 18:37).

The book of Revelation was written by John (Rev. 1:1–3), though which John is not specified. But there is good reason for seeing it as coming from John the apostle and as stressing an important aspect of Johannine thought, namely that of divine sovereignty. It is easy to get lost in a strange world of seals, trumpets, bowls, and animals with unusual numbers of heads and horns. But this is not the important thing. Throughout this book God is a mighty God. He does what he wills and, though wickedness is strong, in the end he will triumph over every evil thing. There is a great deal about the wrath of God in Revelation (and something about it in the Gospel), which brings out the truth that God is implacably opposed to evil and will in the end overthrow it entirely.

Christology. Throughout the Johannine writings there is a good deal of attention given to

Christology. The Gospel begins with a section on Christ as the Word, a passage in which it is clear that God has taken action in Christ for revelation and for salvation. Christ is "the Savior of the world" (John 4:42), and this is brought out when he is referred to as Christ (= Messiah), Son of God, Son of man, and in other ways. They all depend in one way or another on the thought that God is active in Christ in bringing about the salvation he has planned. John has an interesting use of terms like "glory" and "glorify," for he sees the cross as the glorification of Jesus (John 12:23; 13:31). Suffering and lowly service are not simply the path to glory; they *are* glory in its deepest sense. This striking form of speech brings out the truth that God is not concerned with the kind of thing that people see as glorious. The whole life of Jesus was lived in lowliness but John can say, "We have beheld his glory" (John 1:14).

Miracles. John's treatment of the miracles is distinctive. He never calls them "mighty works" as do the synoptists, but "signs" or "works." They point us to significant truth, for God is at work in them. "Work" may be used of Jesus' nonmiraculous deeds as well as those that are miraculous, which suggests that his life is all of a piece. He is one person; he does not do some things as God and others as man. But all he does is the outworking of his mission, a thought which means much to John. There are two Greek words for "to send," and John's gospel has both more frequently than any other book in the NT. Mostly he uses the words to bring out the truth that the Father sent the Son, though there are some important passages linking the mission of his followers with that of Jesus (John 17:18; 20:21). Being sent means that Jesus became man in the fullest sense, as is brought out by his dependence on the Father (cf. John 5:19, 30) and by statements about his human limitations (e.g. John 4:6; 11:33, 35; 19:28). John's Jesus is fully divine, indeed, but he is also fully human.

The Holy Spirit. John tells us more about the Holy Spirit than do the other evangelists. He is active from the beginning of Jesus' ministry (John 1:32–33), but the full work of the Spirit among man awaited the consummation of Jesus' own ministry (John 7:39). The Spirit is active in the Christian life from the beginning (John 3:5, 8) and there are important truths about the Spirit in Jesus' farewell discourse. There we learn among other things that he is "the Spirit of truth" (John 14:16–17), that he will never leave Jesus' people (John 14:16), and that he has a work among unbelievers, namely that of convicting them of sin, righteousness, and judgment (John 16:8).

The Spirit is active in leading Christians in the way of truth (John 16:13), and John has a good deal to tell us about the Christian life. He speaks of "eternal life," which seems to mean life proper to the age to come, life of the highest quality (cf. John 10:10). Entrance into life is by believing, and John uses this verb 98 times (though never the noun "faith"). Believers are to be characterized by love (John 13:34–35). They owe all they have to the love of God, and it is proper that they respond to that love with an answering love, a love for God that spills over into a love for other people. This receives strong emphasis in I John. John emphasizes the importance of light (for believers are people who "walk in the light"; I John 1:7) and of truth. Jesus is the truth (John 14:6) and the Spirit is the Spirit of truth (John 14:17). To know the truth is to be free (John 8:31–32).

John's is a profound and deep theology, though expressed in the simplest of terms. It sets forth truths which no Christian can neglect.

L. Morris

Bibliography. J. E. Davey, *The Jesus of St. John;* W. F. Howard, *Christianity According to St. John;* R. Kysar, *The Fourth Evangelist and His Gospel;* C. F. Nolloth, *The Fourth Evangelist;* N. J. Painter, *John: Witness and Theologian;* S. S. Smalley, *John: Evangelist and Interpreter;* D. G. Vanderlip, *Christianity According to John.*

John of the Cross (1542–1591). One of the leading teachers of Christian contemplation or the mystical way, as well as a founder of the Discalced Carmelite order. Born Juan de Yepes y Alvárez in Old Castile, Spain, to a poor family of noble stock, he entered the Carmelite order in 1563 and, after a study of theology at Salamanca, was ordained in 1567. At that time the discipline of the Carmelite Order was relatively lax, and many of its leaders favored the mitigated observance. John, distressed by their laxity, came under the influence of Teresa of Ávila and, following her advice, attempted to introduce reform into the order. While in and out of office and prison because of his combination of great ability and reforming zeal (which his superiors mistrusted and feared), he produced some of the greatest mystical theological literature in the history of the church. The order itself eventually split into Calced and Discalced branches, as the stricter group withdrew in 1578 under the leadership of Teresa and John. His death was the result of privations suffered in these struggles.

While John of the Cross is best known for his *Dark Night of the Soul,* that work is but the second part of *Ascent of Mount Carmel.* This latter work deals with the purgative way, while the former instructs in the illuminative and unitive ways. Through the progressive stages of purgation (the night of the senses) and spiritual growth (the night of the spirit) the soul is prepared for union with God, described in terms of marriage (*The Living Flame of Love*). While John was a strict monastic and a philosopher in the Thomistic tradition, and while he fed on Scripture, especially the hard sayings of Jesus and Paul, his poetic gentleness is evident in *The Spiritual Canticle* (begun while in prison), and his wisdom as a spiritual guide and counselor shines through his work, which is important to pastors in many traditions but is invaluable to people interested in more mystical spiritual experience of the nonimaged type. P. H. DAVIDS

See also MYSTICISM; PURGATIVE WAY, THE; ILLUMINATIVE WAY, THE; UNITIVE WAY, THE.

Bibliography. A. Cugno, *St. John of the Cross;* L. Christiani, *St. John of the Cross;* B. Frost, *St. John of the Cross;* E. A. Peers, *Spirit of Flame* and *Handbook of the Life and Times of Saint Teresa and Saint John of the Cross.*

John the Baptist. The son of Zechariah, the priest, and Elizabeth (also of priestly descent and a relative of Mary the mother of Jesus). Born in the hill country of Judah, his birth having been foretold by an angel (Luke 1:11ff.), he spent his early years in the wilderness of Judea (Luke 1:80). His public ministry began in the fifteenth year of the emperor Tiberius (*ca.* A.D. 27) when he suddenly appeared out of the wilderness.

The Gospels look upon John as the fulfillment of the *Elijah redivivus* expectation, for both the announcing angel (Luke 1:17) and Jesus (Mark 9:11–13) expressly taught this. Furthermore, John's garb of a "garment of camel's hair, and a leather girdle around his waist" (Matt. 3:4) was similar to the dress of Elijah (II Kings 1:8). Although John himself denied this identification (John 1:21–25), admitting only to being Isaiah's "voice in the wilderness" (John 1:23), it may be that he was disclaiming the popular hope for the literal resurrection of Elijah, accepting only the fulfillment of his spirit and power. Indeed this was the explicit promise of the angel.

John's message had a twofold emphasis: (1) the imminent appearance of the messianic kingdom, and (2) the urgent need for repentance to prepare for this event (Matt. 3:2). In true prophetic fashion his concept of the nature of the kingdom was not that of the popular mind, and thus was a proper preparation for Christ. The multitudes expected the "day of the Lord" to be happiness for all Israel, basing their hope on racial considerations. John proclaimed that the kingdom was to be a rule of righteousness, inherited only by those who exhibited righteousness by the way they lived. Thus his message of repentance was directed particularly to the Jew, for God was going to purge Israel as well as the world (Matt. 3:7–12). When Jesus appeared on the scene John's role as a forerunner was completed in his personal testimony to the fact of Jesus' messiahship (John 1:29).

The baptism of John complemented his preparatory task. In its basic sense it was a symbolic act for the cleansing away of sin, and was thus accompanied by repentance. So Matt. 3:6 says, "and they were baptized by him in the river Jordan while confessing fully (*exomologoumenoi*) their sins." But in its fullest sense it was an eschatological act preparing one for admission into the messianic kingdom. Thus when the Pharisees and Sadducees came for baptism, John said, "Who warned you to flee from the wrath to come?" (Matt. 3:7). Josephus's account of John's baptism (*Antiquities* xviii.5.2) is at variance with this, suggesting that its purpose was to provide a bodily purification to correspond with an already accomplished inward change. The historical background to John's baptism is probably Jewish proselyte baptism, with John emphasizing by this that both Jew and Gentile were ceremonially unclean as far as the true people of God were concerned. The baptism of Jesus by John (Matt. 3:13–15) is to be explained not as a sign that Jesus needed repentance, but rather that by this act he was identifying himself with mankind in the proper approach to God's kingdom.

It has long been felt that John was at one time connected with the Essenes, because of his ascetic habits and his location near the chief settlement of the sect. This has been given greater possibility by the recognized affinities between John and the Dead Sea Scroll (Qumran) sect, an Essenish group which dwelt on the northwest shore of the Dead Sea. This connection is certainly possible, for both John and the Qumran sect resided in the wilderness of Judea, both were of a priestly character, both laid emphasis on baptism as a sign of inward cleansing, both were ascetic, both thought in terms of imminent judgment, and both invoked Isa. 40:3 as the authority for their mission in life. But although John may have been influenced by the sect in the early stages of his life, his ministry was far greater. John's role was essentially prophetic; the sect's was esoteric. John issued a public call to repentance; the sect withdrew to the desert. John proclaimed an exhibition of repentance in the affairs of ordinary life; the sect required submission to the rigors of its ascetic life. John introduced the Messiah; the sect still waited for his manifestation.

John's denunciation of Herod Antipas for his marriage was the cause of his death by beheading (Matt. 14:1–12). Josephus tells us that this took place at the fortress of Machaerus near the Dead Sea. The Mandaeans were influenced by John, for he plays a large part in their writings. This connection may have come through John's disciples, who existed for at least twenty-five years after John's death (Acts 18:25; 19:3). R. B. LAURIN

Bibliography. C. H. Kraeling, *John the Baptist;* J. Thomas, *Le mouvement baptiste en Palestine et Syrie;* A. Plummer, *Gospel According to St. Matthew,* 30–31; M. Burrows, *More Light on the Dead Sea Scrolls;* W. Wink, *John the Baptist in the Gospel Tradition;* F. F. Bruce, *NT History;* E. Barnwell, "The Baptist in Early Christian Tradition," *NTS* 18:95ff.; C. H. H. Scobie, *John the Baptist.*

Joy. A delight in life that runs deeper than pain or pleasure. From a biblical perspective it is not limited by nor tied solely to external circumstances. Joy is a gift of God, and like all of his other inner gifts it can be experienced even in the midst of extremely difficult circumstances.

In both the OT and the NT joy is presented as a consistent mark of both the individual believer and the believing community. It is a quality of life and not simply a fleeting emotion. It is grounded in God himself and flows from him (Ps. 16:11; Rom. 15:13). Joy is not an isolated or occasional consequence of faith but rather an integral part of one's whole relation to God. The fullness of joy comes when there is a deep sense of the presence of God in one's life. From that awareness flows the strong desire to share what one is experiencing with others. It is too good to keep for one's self alone.

In the OT the most common Hebrew words for joy are *śimḥâ* (gladness, mirth); *gûl* or *gîl* (to spring about, be joyful); *māśôś* (joy, rejoicing), and *śāmēaḥ* (to shine, be glad). Both the experience and expression of joy were associated with God's mighty saving acts (Pss. 5:11; 9:2; 16:9; 32:11; 63:11; Isa. 35:10), with God's law (Ps. 119:14), and with God's Word (Jer. 15:16). This joy was celebrated at festivals with singing, shouting, clapping of hands, and dancing.

The NT words most commonly used are *chara* (joy) and *chairō* (to rejoice). Here joy is also connected with God's salvation (I Pet. 1:6). What God has made available to all men in his redemptive grace is cause for great rejoicing. Jesus made it clear that joy is inseparably connected to love and to obedience (John 15:9–14). Paul identifies joy as a vital part of the fruit of the Spirit (Gal. 5:22).

There can also be joy in suffering or in weakness when suffering is seen as having a redemptive purpose and weakness as bringing one to total dependency upon God (Matt. 5:12; II Cor. 12:9).

From a psychological perspective one cannot experience joy while being preoccupied with one's own security, pleasure, or self-interest. Freedom from inhibitions comes when one is caught up in something great enough to give meaning and purpose to all of life and to every relationship. God alone is the only adequate center for human existence, and he alone can enable us to experience life with joyous spontaneity and to relate to others with love. C. DAVIS

Bibliography. D. Harvey, *IDB,* II, 1000–1001; H. Conzelmann, *TDNT,* IX, 359–72; *IBD,* II, 820–21; J. Moffatt, *Grace in the NT.*

Judaism. The religion and culture of the Jewish people. Jewish civilization includes historical, social, and political dimensions in addition to the religious. The word "Judaism" derives from the Greek *Ioudaismos,* a term first used in the intertestamental period by Greek-speaking Jews to distinguish their religion from hellenism (see II Macc. 2:21; 8:1; 14:38). In the NT the word appears twice (Gal. 1:13–14) in reference to Paul's prior consuming devotion to Jewish faith and life.

Development. Hebrew religion began to give rise to Judaism after the destruction of the temple and the exile of Judah in 586 B.C. The term "Jew," in its biblical use, is almost exclusively postexilic. The Jewish religion of the biblical period evolved through such historical stages as the intertestamental, rabbinic, and medieval to the modern period of the nineteenth century with Orthodox, Conservative, and Reform Judaism.

Along the way Jewish religion took on new teachings and practices. But with the lengthy development of Judaism and its many changes it is incorrect to posit, as some have done, that Jewish history produced two separate religions: an OT religion of Israel and the postexilic religion of Judaism. Despite the shifting phases of its history, the essence of the religious teaching of Judaism has remained remarkably constant, firmly rooted in the Hebrew Scriptures (OT). Judaism is a religion of ethical monotheism. For centuries many Jews have sought to distill its essential features from one biblical verse that calls Israel "to act justly, to love mercy and to walk humbly with your God" (Mic. 6:8).

The Babylonian exile brought certain modifications in Jewish religious life. Deprived of land, temple, and cultic priestly ministrations, Judaism began to adopt a nonsacrificial religion. Jews began to gather in homes for the reading of Scripture, for prayer and instruction. Here may be traced the earliest roots of the synagogue. Now "lip sacrifice" (prayer and penitence) rather than "blood sacrifice" (sheep and goats) became central to the life of piety.

There was one thing Israel carried to Babylon and clung to dearly. It was the law, the Torah, for by it Israel was assured of its divine calling and mission. In the fifth century the "father of Judaism," Ezra the scribe, enacted religious reforms by appealing to the Torah. The priesthood was purified and mixed marriages dealt with as the principles of the law became applied to every detail of life. Gradually many Jews came to believe that here lay the only real proof of who was a true Jew: vigorous, unflinching obedience to the teachings of Torah.

Scribes became the priestly interpreters of the Torah, setting forth their own authoritative teachings. By the second century B.C. the Pharisees taught that the oral law carried the same authority as the law of Moses. Later Jesus denied that the traditions of men were equal in authority to the written law (Mark 7:1–23); in addition, Paul denied that man could be justified before God by perfect obedience to that law (Gal. 3).

The destruction of the temple in A.D. 70 and the scattering of thousands of Jews from the land brought a sudden demise to the priesthood. Johanan ben Zakkai, a Pharisee, was soon permitted by the Romans to open an academy at Jabneh. He took it upon himself to install rabbis as the keepers and legislators of Torah. By word of mouth the rabbis passed their teachings from generation to generation until the oral law (Mishnah) was written down about A.D. 200, Rabbi Judah ha-Nasi its chief editor. By A.D. 500 the Talmud was completed with the issuing of the Gemara, a rabbinical commentary on the Mishnah. The Talmud contains more than 6,000 folio pages and references to more than 2,000 scholar-teachers. It became the basic document of rabbinic Judaism, and still holds a major place in shaping Jewish thought.

Basic Doctrines and Beliefs. According to the teaching of Judaism there is no set of beliefs upon the acceptance of which the Jew may find salvation. Even Maimonides' thirteen articles of faith—as close as Judaism ever came to a catechism—is not binding on the conscience of Jews. Judaism has historically put more stress upon the deed (*miṣwâ*) than the creed (*'ănî ma'ămîn*, "I believe"). Nevertheless, from Talmudic times, as a way of life Judaism has been distinguished by giving special emphasis to certain beliefs and ethical values.

In the Mishnah (Abot 1:2) one sees the broad philosophy that governed the minds of the early rabbis: "By three things is the world sustained: by the law, by the [temple] service, and by deeds of lovingkindness." This basic teaching is further underscored by the threefold function of the synagogue as a "house of study" (for learning of Torah), "house of prayer" (for worship of God), and "house of assembly" (for the care of community needs).

Contemporary Judaism often speaks of four foundational pillars of the Jewish faith, each interacting as a major force as part of the covenant: (1) The Torah, always a living law as the written Torah is understood in light of the oral Torah; (2) God, a unity (one), spiritual (not a body), and eternal; (3) The people (Israelites/Jews), called into being by God as members of one family, a corporate personality, a community of faith; and (4) The land (known today as Eretz Yisrael), a bond going back to Abraham, the "father of the Hebrew people" (Gen. 17:7–8).

In its modern expression Judaism is also shaped by the following traditional beliefs:

(1) Man is pivotal in the universe. He sees himself as partner with God in the unending process of creation. In rabbinic thought, "God needs man as much as man needs God."

(2) Man is a responsible moral agent, fully accountable for his acts. He is free to shape his own destiny.

(3) Human progress is possible as man realizes the great potential within him. The nature of man is basically good, or neutral, free from the encumbrance of original sin. Thus man may be optimistic and hopeful about his future.

(4) "This-worldliness" is a distinguishing mark of Judaism. The Hebrew Scriptures focus more on earth and man than upon heaven and God. Hence, lengthy speculation about the afterlife and otherworldly realities has never occupied a major position in Jewish thought.

(5) All of life must be regarded as sacred. Man is to seek to imitate God in sanctifying his every action. Time must be imbued with the seeds of eternity.

(6) Man is to pursue peace, justice, and righteousness. Salvation is dependent upon the betterment of society through good deeds. Historically, Jews have seen the Messiah as God's anointed human representative (not a God-man) who would usher in a golden age of societal and spiritual redemption. Today, however, Reform Judaism teaches that the Messianic Age will appear

when humankind collectively, by its acts, reaches a level of true enlightenment, peace, and justice.

M. R. Wilson

See also Pharisees; Sadducees; Essenes; Zionism.

Bibliography. L. Baeck, *The Essence of Judaism;* H. Danby, *The Mishnah;* H. Donin, *To Be a Jew; EJ,* X, 383–97; A. Hertzberg, ed., *Judaism;* G. F. Moore, *Judaism,* 2 vols.; M. Steinberg, *Basic Judaism;* L. Trepp, *Judaism: Development and Life.*

Judaizers. Those Gentiles who followed certain religious practices and customs of Judaism. The Greek verb *Ioudaizō* "to judaize" (RSV "live like Jews"; NIV "follow Jewish customs") occurs in the NT only in Gal. 2:14. In this passage Paul relates how he opposed Peter at Antioch because Peter refused to eat with the Gentiles in the church there. By practicing social separation Peter was in effect saying to these Gentile Christians, "Unless you conform to Jewish dietary laws and a Jewish life style we cannot maintain fellowship with you." By his withdrawal Peter was compelling these Gentiles to "judaize."

Christ, however, had already instituted a change in regard to OT regulations on clean and unclean foods (Mark 7:1–23; cf. Lev. 11; Deut. 14). As "apostle to the Gentiles" (Rom. 11:13), Paul was against imposing a strict Jewish dietary code on non-Jews. Such might imply that the belief of Gentile Christians was defective in comparison with that of Jewish Christians; something else (i.e., conformity to Jewish custom) must be added to faith in Christ (cf. Acts 15:1, 5). Paul thus was opposed to judaizing. It had the potential to distort salvation by grace alone, divide the body, and be an argument for developing two separate assemblies: one for Jews and one for Gentiles.

The only OT reference to judaizing is found in Esth. 8:17, where the Hebrew *yĕhûdî* ("Jew") is used to form the Hithpael verb *mityahădîm,* "to become a Jew" or "profess oneself a Jew." The verb refers to those Gentiles in Persia who adopted the Jewish way of life out of fear for Esther's decree, which permitted the Jews to avenge themselves on their enemies (Esth. 8:13). The LXX uses *Ioudaizō* here and adds that they became circumcised. This normally would imply conversion. In this circumstance, however, they may only have pretended to be Jews in order to save their own lives by identification with the Jewish cause.

M. R. Wilson

Bibliography. F. F. Bruce, *The Epistle to the Galatians; EJ,* X, 398–402; F. V. Filson, *IDB,* II, 1005–6; E. F. Harrison, *ISBE* (rev.), II, 1150; C. Moore, *Esther,* 81–82; W. Gutbrod, *TDNT,* III, 383.

Judgment. Because we are born in sin and therefore cannot live up to God's righteous standards, condemnation (damnation, the older synonym, has other connotations today) hangs over our heads like the sword of Damocles (II Pet. 2:3; Rom. 1:18; Eph. 5:5–6; Col. 3:5–6). God himself is the one who condemns (Job 10:2; Jer. 42:18; John 12:48). His condemnation is based on his justice, and such condemnation is deserved (I Kings 8:32; Rom. 3:8; Gal. 1:8–9). Condemnation comes to the wicked and unrepentant (Matt. 12:41–42; Luke 11:31–32; John 5:29; Rom. 5:16, 18; II Thess. 2:12; Rev. 19:2) and results in eternal punishment (Matt. 23:33), but no OT believer who trusted in God (Ps. 34:22) or NT believer who trusts in Christ (John 3:18; 5:24) will be condemned. Jesus came to save rather than to condemn (John 3:17), and he frees us from final condemnation (Rom. 8:1–2).

Conscience may cause us to condemn ourselves (I John 3:19–21), but no one can justly condemn the righteous if God is on his side (Isa. 50:9; Titus 2:7–8). In fact, the Lord prevents or reverses unfair condemnation by our enemies (Pss. 37:33; 79:11; 102:19–20; 109:31). Self-righteous people should avoid condemning others (Job 32:3; Luke 6:37; Rom. 8:34; 14:3) because quickness to condemn may recoil on their own heads (Job 15:6; Ps. 34:21; Luke 6:37; Rom. 2:1; Titus 3:10–11). Needless to say, it is the height of arrogance and folly for sinful people to condemn a just and omnipotent God (Job 34:17, 29; 40:8).

Divine judgment is God's method of displaying his mercy as well as his wrath toward individuals and nations (Exod. 6:6, 7:4; Eccles. 3:17; 12:14; Dan. 7:22; Joel 3:2; II Cor. 5:10). As God is the one who condemns, so also he is the true and only Judge (Gen. 18:25; Ps. 82:1; Eccles. 11:9), an office and function shared by the Father (Gen. 31:53; John 8:50; Rom. 3:6) and the Son (Acts 10:42; 17:31; Rom. 2:16). Retributive or negative judgment is a direct result of sin (I Sam. 3:13; Ezek. 7:3, 8, 27; Rom. 2:12; Jude 14–15) and is therefore both just (Ezek. 33:20; II Tim. 4:8; I Pet. 2:23) and deserved (Pss. 94:2; 143:2; Ezek. 18:30). Rewarding or positive judgment relates to the believer's stewardship of his talents and gifts and is therefore characterized by divine compassion (Matt. 25:14–23; I Cor. 3:12–15; I Pet. 1:17). Although we experience judgment initially in this life, all of us are judged ultimately after death (Isa. 66:16; Jer. 25:31; Joel 3:12; John 12:48; Acts 17:31; Rom. 2:16; Rev. 20:12–13) at the judgment seat of God (Rom. 14:10) or Christ (II Cor. 5:10). Self-judgment, another manifestation of the same activity, is brought about by rebellion and willfulness (Rom. 13:2; I Cor. 11:29; I Tim. 5:12).

It is not only human beings who are judged, however. God also judges other gods, real or imagined (Exod. 12:12; Num. 33:4; Jer. 10:14–15), and angels as well (II Pet. 2:4; Jude 6). The devil himself is not exempt from such judgment (I Tim. 3:6). And although in the final analysis God is the only judge, he has chosen to allow us to participate with Christ in judging the world (Matt. 19:28; Luke 22:30; I Cor. 6:2; Rev. 20:4), including the angels (I Cor. 6:3).

The story of Noah's flood contains several principles concerning divine judgment that are worth careful consideration. (1) God's judgments are never arbitrary. Man's sin is God's sorrow (Gen. 6:5–6). The Lord is not capricious when he judges. He makes a considered and deliberate decision before unleashing his punishment. (2) God can be counted on always to judge sin (Gen. 6:7). No sin escapes his notice; his judgment on sin is inevitable (Rom. 2:3; Heb. 9:27; 10:26–27). (3) God always announces judgment beforehand (Gen. 6:13). He informs us that our evil deeds are condemned by him and will be judged by him. (4) God always gives sinners an opportunity to repent before judging them (see Acts 17:30–31; Rom. 2:4; II Pet. 3:9). There was a period of 120 years of grace for the people of Noah's day (Gen. 6:3). (5) God always follows through on his decision to judge (cf. Gen. 7:4 with vss. 12 and 23), once he has announced it and once people have had an opportunity to repent. His judgments are irreversible. (6) God's judgments always lead to death (see Jer. 51:18; Hos. 6:5). Gen. 7:17–24, the only paragraph in the flood narrative that does not contain the name of God, reeks with the smell of death. When judgment results in death, God is no longer there.

But the flood story teaches us also that (7) God's judgments always include elements of both justice and grace. Though the story of the flood begins with judgment, it ends with redemption; though it begins with a curse (Gen. 6:7), it ends with a covenant (9:11). If judgment always issues in death, grace and redemption always issue in life. Judgment is never God's last or best word to those who believe in him, because "mercy triumphs over judgment" (James 2:13).

R. Youngblood

See also Judgment Seat.

Bibliography. L. Morris, *The Biblical Doctrine of Judgment;* R. Youngblood, *How It All Began;* F. Büchsel, *TDNT,* III, 921–54; W. Schneider *et al., NIDNTT,* II, 361–71.

Judgment, The Last. *See* Last Judgment, The.

Judgment of the Nations, The. Amillennialism and premillennialism, the two prevailing approaches to eschatology among evangelical Protestants, have quite different views of the eschatological judgments. These differences are a reflection of the inherent differences of the systems and each one's schema of the unfolding of future events.

Amillennialists believe that the Bible teaches one general resurrection of all the dead at the end of the present age when Christ returns. This is taken to imply that there is also only one final judgment, since the judgment is said to follow the resurrection (Rev. 20:11–15). The so-called judgment of the nations (Joel 3:1–3), then, is subsumed under this one final judgment. Consequently, all people who ever lived, saved and unsaved, appear before Christ in this final judgment scene.

Premillennialists generally distinguish four judgments: the judgment of believers, the judgment of Israel, the judgment of the nations, and the "great white throne" judgment. These judgments are distinct from one another in subjects, time, and place. Premillennialists disagree among themselves on some aspects of these judgments (especially on those matters that are related to the time of the rapture), but there is general agreement on the judgment of the nations. They understand it to be a judgment of the living Gentile nations by Jesus Christ following his return in glory to the earth (cf. Joel 3:1–3; Isa. 2:4; Matt. 25:31–46). In the usual premillennial scheme this occurs after the seven-year tribulation but before the millennium. The main indictment in the judgment of the nations will be their treatment of Israel (Joel 3:2), but Isa. 2:4 could imply that other wrongs will also be brought to judgment. It must be emphasized that premillennialists understand this as a final judgment of the *living* nations when Christ returns to earth. The unrighteous living (the goats) go to eternal punishment; the righteous (sheep) who have treated Israel well and who submit to the messianic King enter the earthly millennial kingdom (cf. Isa. 60:12).

S. N. Gundry

See also Millennium, Views of the; Second Coming of Christ; Judgment Seat; Last Judgment, The.

Bibliography. L. Berkhof, *Systematic Theology;* C. L. Feinberg, *Premillennialism or Amillennialism?* A. A. Hoekema, *The Bible and the Future;* A. J. McClain, *The Greatness of the Kingdom.*

Judgments, Ordinances, and Statutes. The Hebrew term *mišpāṭ,* translated "judgments" (AV, NKJV) or "ordinances" (RSV), claims a long legal history. It apparently originated in a Semitic root meaning "to decide, arbitrate," describing the judgment pronounced in a civil court. This usage also occurs in Ugaritic, where Dan'el adjudicates with respect to widows and orphans (2 Aqht V:7–8). Ordinances or judgments are thus decisions rendered by judicial authorities, or precedents that have been established as guides for future civil verdicts. The nature of the *mišpāṭ* is well illustrated by the case law of Exod. 21:1–22:17, and the plural *mišpāṭîm* was probably a general title for the so-called Book of the Covenant (Exod. 20:22–23:33). This law, which was civil rather than moral or ceremonial, applied equally to the Israelites and resident aliens (Num. 15:15–16). Other derived meanings of *mišpāṭ* include "justice," "legal right," "legal case," and "what is appropriate." Case law (casuistic), introduced by the formula "if . . . then," is not wholly secular in character, for it was grounded in covenant love (Deut. 4:37) and in a demand for implicit obedience (Deut. 5:32), that the Israelites might submit to God's law of love wholeheartedly (Deut. 6:5) and enjoy his promises under the covenant (Deut. 6:2–3).

Ḥōq and *ḥuqqâ*, often rendered "statutes," are derived from a root meaning "to engrave, to cut," and in consequence refer to rules of behavior fixed in writing. *Ḥōq* has the wide meaning of anything prescribed by authority and recorded for the guidance of society, whether the enactment is sacred or secular in nature. *Ḥuqqâ* seems to carry the sense of a custom, law, or statute in a more restricted manner than *ḥōq*. The most common LXX Greek equivalent of these Hebrew terms is *dikaiōma*, translating *ḥōq* normally but in Ezekiel appearing as the rendering of *mišpāṭ*. In the NT the term described the righteousness that resulted from the act of justification which accounted an individual righteous before God. Hence it was used of an ordinance (Luke 1:6), the pronouncement of acquittal (Rom. 5:18), and as a description of a righteous act (Rev. 19:8). Another Greek word, *dogma*, also appears in the NT to describe a public decree or ordinance, whether promulgated by the Roman rulers of Palestine (Luke 2:1; Acts 17:7) or the apostles themselves (Acts 16:4). It was also used in connection with the ordinances of Jewish law (Eph. 2:15; Col. 2:14).

Because God is a God of order, not confusion, the ordinances and statutes of the law were necessary for Israel's instruction in attaining the divinely prescribed goal of becoming a kingdom of priests and a holy nation (Exod. 19:6). The social prescriptions reflected the distinctive moral and spiritual standards of the Lord of Sinai, with a specific emphasis upon divine holiness. For the Israelites, to exemplify holiness meant that they had to obey God's commandments implicitly, and by worshiping him alone to separate themselves from all forms of pagan religion. The type of worship practiced by the Canaanites, among whom the chosen people were to dwell, has been regarded as one of the most depraved and morally corrupt that the world has ever known. The Israelites had been chosen to bring the light of divine revelation into this moral darkness, and by their total dedication in worship and community living to the one true God to be his witnesses to the Near Eastern world.

The ordinances and statutes, because they are civil law, naturally reflect to some extent certain enactments of neighboring peoples where similar social circumstances were involved. In other respects, however, there were significant differences, if only because the laws of pagan nations were enacted in the names of deities that were fundamentally false. God revealed himself at Sinai as Redeemer in bringing Israel out of bondage in Egypt and as supreme King in binding a newly fledged nation to him in covenant relationship. Because Israel was intended to be a spiritual fellowship, the distinction between religious and civil law should not be applied too stringently. The statutes of Israelite law, even where they appear to be entirely secular in nature, manifest the loving concern of God for the welfare of his people. By contrast with modern legal codes, the collections of ordinances and statutes in the Torah commonly appear as though drawn up on an *ad hoc* basis and assembled without reference to any overall plan of organization. There is no doubt, however, about the consistency of their spiritual ethos. Crimes against society merited specific and appropriate punishments. Premeditated murder required the death of the murderer, whereas manslaughter did not. In instances where the punishment consisted of restitution, upper limits were set (Exod. 21:24–25) in the interests of equity, and it was commanded that slaves were to be treated in a humane manner, a provision unique in ancient Near Eastern legislation. Moral offenses against society were always considered serious, and the statutes emphasized the need for social justice and the love of persons for each other. The ordinances and statutes of Israel were designed to glorify God's love and mercy in Israelite community life, and to guide the nation in its covenant relationship with God so that the chosen people would reflect such spiritual qualities in their dealings with neighboring nations.

R. K. Harrison

See also Civil Law and Justice in Bible Times; Criminal Law and Punishment in Bible Times; Ten Commandments, The; Law, Biblical Concept of.

Bibliography. J. A. Wharton, *IDB*, III, 607–8; K. L. Barker, *ZPEB*, IV, 543–44; J. B. Payne, *Theology of the Older Testament.*

Judgment Seat. From the Greek *bēma;* literally a "step," referring to the platform upon which the civil magistrate sat during judicial proceedings. Also translated as "court" or "tribunal" (Acts 18:12, 16). This platform could be found in both public (John 19:13) or private (Acts 25:23) locations.

Figuratively the term found use as a picture of the final confrontation between man and Jesus Christ where an accounting would be held for the individual's earthly deeds. Such a judgment appears to be universal in scope, including (1) all the nations of the world (Matt. 25:32); (2) angels (Jude 6; II Pet. 2:4; cf. I Cor. 6:3, where Christians appear to participate in this judgment); (3) the unsaved dead at the "great white throne" (Rev. 20:5, 7); (4) individual Christians (II Cor. 5:10). While the predominant nature of these judgments indicates they are held to announce condemnation to the wicked (Matt. 25:31, 46; John 3:18; II Thess. 1:7–10; Rev. 20:14–15), the judgment of Christians appears to be one which is designed to evaluate the stewardship of their earthly life only (Rom. 14:10; I Cor. 3:12–15).

Chrysostom used the figure to warn schismatic Judaizers (Homily on Rom. 14:10) as well as to bring hope and correction to Christians (Homily on II Cor. 5:10). S. E. McClelland

See also Judgment; Last Judgment, The; Judgment of the Nations, The.

Bibliography. J. Bailey, *And the Life Everlasting;* O. Cullmann, *Christ and Time;* L. Morris, *Wages of Sin* and *The Biblical Doctrine of Judgment;* L. Boettner, *Immortality.*

Justice. Justice is a communicable attribute of God, manifesting his holiness. The biblical words thus translated, *ṣĕdāqâ, ṣedeq,* and *dikaiosynē,* are also rendered as "righteousness." Used of man, justice refers to right rule, right conduct, or to each getting his due, whether good or bad. God's *relative* justice has to do with his rectitude in and of himself; by his *absolute* justice is meant the rectitude by which he upholds himself against violations of his holiness. By *rectoral* justice he institutes righteous laws and establishes just rewards and penalties, as over against *distributive* justice, whereby he metes out just rewards (*remunerative* justice, expressive of his love) and punishments (*retributive* justice, expressive of his wrath).

God's moral excellence made necessary either the punishment of sinners or expiation whereby their condemnation would be removed. The sinner was without power to offer satisfaction for his sin, but righteousness was provided as Christ, the representative of man, met all the righteous demands of the law and paid the price of sin in the believer's place so that he, trusting only in Christ's righteousness, might be justified by God. The gospel, therefore, is the good news that through the Savior the requirements of divine justice have been met. B. L. Goddard

See also Righteousness; God, Attributes of; Cardinal Virtues, Seven.

Bibliography. L. Berkhof, *Reformed Dogmatics,* I, 51–52; S. Charnock, *Existence and Attributes of God,* I, 554–56; II, 181–86; C. Hodge, *Systematic Theology,* I, 416–27; W. Shedd, *Dogmatic Theology,* I, 365–85; R. Girdlestone, *Synonyms of OT;* G. Quell and G. Schrenk, *TDNT,* II, 192ff.; E. Brunner, *Justice and the Social Order;* N. Snaith, *Distinctive Ideas of the OT;* G. Rupp, *The Righteousness of God;* H. Seebass, *NIDNTT,* III, 352ff.

Justification. The basic fact of biblical religion is that God pardons and accepts believing sinners (see Pss. 32:1–5; 130; Luke 7:47ff.; 18:9–14; Acts 10:43; I John 1:7–2:2). Paul's doctrine of justification by faith is an analytical exposition of this fact in its full theological connections. As stated by Paul (most fully in Romans and Galatians, though see also II Cor. 5:14ff.; Eph. 2:1ff.; Phil. 3:4ff.), the doctrine of justification determines the whole character of Christianity as a religion of grace and faith. It defines the saving significance of Christ's life and death by relating both to God's law (Rom. 3:24ff.; 5:16ff.). It displays God's justice in condemning and punishing sin, his mercy in pardoning and accepting sinners, and his wisdom in exercising both attributes harmoniously together through Christ (Rom. 3:23ff.). It makes clear what faith is—belief in Christ's atoning death and justifying resurrection (Rom. 4:23ff.; 10:8ff.), and trust in him alone for righteousness (Phil. 3:8–9). It makes clear what Christian morality is—law-keeping out of gratitude to the Savior whose gift of righteousness made law-keeping needless for acceptance (Rom. 7:1–6; 12:1–2). It explains all hints, prophecies, and instances of salvation in the OT (Rom. 1:17; 3:21; 4:1ff.). It overthrows Jewish exclusivism (Gal. 2:15ff.) and provides the basis on which Christianity becomes a religion for the world (Rom. 1:16; 3:29–30). It is the heart of the gospel. Luther justly termed it *articulus stantis vel cadentis ecclesiae;* a church that lapses from it can scarcely be called Christian.

The Meaning of Justification. The biblical meaning of "justify" (Hebrew, *ṣādēq;* Greek, LXX and NT, *dikaioō*) is to pronounce, accept, and treat as just, i.e., as, on the one hand, not penally liable, and, on the other, entitled to all the privileges due to those who have kept the law. It is thus a forensic term, denoting a judicial act of administering the law—in this case, by declaring a verdict of acquittal, and so excluding all possibility of condemnation. Justification thus settles the legal status of the person justified. (See Deut. 25:1; Prov. 17:15; Rom. 8:33–34. In Isa. 43:9, 26, "be justified" means "get the verdict.") The justifying action of the Creator, who is the royal Judge of this world, has both a sentential and an executive, or declarative, aspect: God justifies, first, by reaching his verdict and then by sovereign action makes his verdict known and secures to the person justified the rights which are now his due. What is envisaged in Isa. 45:25 and 50:8, for instance, is specifically a series of events which will publicly vindicate those whom God holds to be in the right.

The word is also used in a transferred sense for ascriptions of righteousness in nonforensic contexts. Thus, men are said to justify God when they confess him just (Luke 7:29; Rom. 3:4 = Ps. 51:4), and themselves when they claim to be just (Job 32:2; Luke 10:29; 16:15). The passive can be used generally of being vindicated by events against suspicion, criticism, and mistrust (Matt. 11:19; Luke 7:35; I Tim. 3:16).

In James 2:21, 24–25 its reference is to the proof of a man's acceptance with God that is given when his actions show that he has the kind of living, working faith to which God imputes righteousness. James's statement that Christians, like Abraham, are justified by works (vs. 24) is thus not contrary to Paul's insistence that Christians, like Abraham, are justified by faith (Rom. 3:28; 4:1–5), but is complementary to it. James himself quotes Gen. 15:6 for exactly the same purpose as Paul does—to show that it was faith which secured Abraham's acceptance as righteous (vs. 23; cf. Rom. 4:3ff.; Gal. 3:6ff.). The justification which concerns James is not the believer's original acceptance by God, but the subsequent vindication of his profession of faith by his life. It is in terminology, not thought, that James differs from Paul.

There is no lexical ground for the view of Chrysostom, Augustine, and the medieval and Roman theologians that "justify" means, or connotes as part of its meaning, "*make* righteous" (by subjective spiritual renewal). The Tridentine definition of justification as "not only the remission of sins, but also the sanctification and renewal of the inward man" (Sess. VI, ch. vii) is erroneous.

Paul's Doctrine of Justification. The background of Paul's doctrine was the Jewish conviction, universal in his time, that a day of judgment was coming, in which God would condemn and punish all who had broken his laws. That day would terminate the present world order and usher in a golden age for those whom God judged worthy. This conviction, derived from prophetic expectations of "the day of the Lord" (Amos 5:19ff.; Isa. 2:10–22; 13:6–11; Jer. 46:10; Obad. 15; Zeph. 1:14–2:3, etc.) and developed during the intertestamental period under the influence of apocalyptic, had been emphatically confirmed by Christ (Matt. 11:22ff.; 12:36–37; etc.). Paul affirmed that Christ himself was the appointed representative through whom God would "judge the world in righteousness" in "the day of wrath and revelation of the righteous judgment of God" (Acts 17:31; Rom. 2:16). This, indeed, had been Christ's own claim (John 5:27ff.).

Paul sets out his doctrine of the judgment day in Rom. 2:5–16. The principle of judgment will be exact retribution ("to every man according to his works," vs. 6). The standard will be God's law. The evidence will be "the secrets of men" (vs. 16); the Judge is a searcher of hearts. Being himself just, he cannot be expected to justify any but the righteous, those who have kept his law (Rom. 2:12–13; cf. Exod. 23:7; I Kings 8:32). But the class of righteous men has no members. None is righteous; all have sinned (Rom. 3:9ff.). The prospect, therefore, is one of universal condemnation, for Jew as well as Gentile; for the Jew who breaks the law is no more acceptable to God than anyone else (Rom. 2:17–27). All men, it seems, are under God's wrath (Rom. 1:18) and doomed.

Against this black background, comprehensively expounded in Rom. 1:18–3:20, Paul proclaims the present justification of sinners by grace through faith in Jesus Christ, apart from all works and despite all demerit (Rom. 3:21ff.). This justification, though individually located at the point of time at which a man believes (Rom. 4:2; 5:1), is an eschatological once-for-all divine act, the final judgment brought into the present. The justifying sentence, once passed, is irrevocable. "The wrath" will not touch the justified (Rom. 5:9). Those accepted now are secure forever. Inquisition before Christ's judgment seat (Rom. 14:10–12; II Cor. 5:10) may deprive them of certain rewards (I Cor. 3:15), but never of their justified status. Christ will not call in question God's justifying verdict, only declare, endorse, and implement it.

Justification has two sides. On the one hand, it means the pardon, remission, and nonimputation of all sins, reconciliation to God, and the end of his enmity and wrath (Acts 13:39; Rom. 4:6–7; II Cor. 5:19; Rom. 5:9ff.). On the other hand, it means the bestowal of a righteous man's status and a title to all the blessings promised to the just: a thought which Paul amplifies by linking justification with the adoption of believers as God's sons and heirs (Rom. 8:14ff.; Gal. 4:4ff.). Part of their inheritance they receive at once: through the gift of the Holy Spirit, whereby God "seals" them as his when they believe (Eph. 1:13), they taste that quality of fellowship with God which belongs to the age to come and is called "eternal life." Here is another eschatological reality brought into the present: having in a real sense passed through the last judgment, the justified enter heaven on earth. Here and now, therefore, justification brings "life" (Rom. 5:18), though this is merely a foretaste of the fullness of life and glory which constitutes the "hope of righteousness" (Gal. 5:5) promised to the just (Rom. 2:7, 10), to which God's justified children may look forward (Rom. 8:18ff.). Both aspects of justification appear in Rom. 5:1–2, where Paul says that justification brings, on the one hand, peace with God (because sin is pardoned) and, on the other, hope of the glory of God (because the believer is accepted as righteous). Justification thus means permanent reinstatement to favor and privilege, as well as complete forgiveness of all sins.

The Ground of Justification. Paul's deliberately paradoxical reference to God as "justifying the ungodly" (Rom. 4:5)—the same Greek phrase as is used by the LXX in Exod. 23:7; Isa. 5:23, of the corrupt judgment that God will not tolerate—reflects his awareness that this is a startling doctrine. Indeed, it seems flatly at variance with the OT presentation of God's essential righteousness, as revealed in his actions as Legislator and Judge—a presentation which Paul himself assumes in Rom. 1:18–3:20. The OT insists that God is "righteous in all his ways" (Ps. 145:17), "a God . . . without iniquity" (Deut. 32:4; cf. Zeph. 3:5). The law of right and wrong, in conformity to which righteousness consists, has its being and fulfillment in him. His revealed law, "holy, just and good" as it is (Rom. 7:12; cf. Deut. 4:8; Ps. 19:7–9), mirrors his character, for he "loves" the righteousness prescribed (Ps. 11:7; 33:5) and "hates" the unrighteousness forbidden (Ps. 5:4–6; Isa. 61:8; Zech. 8:17). As Judge, he declares his righteousness by "visiting" in retributive judgment idolatry, irreligion, immorality, and inhuman conduct throughout the world (Jer. 9:24; Ps. 9:5ff., 15ff.; Amos 1:3–3:2, etc.). "God is a righteous judge, yea, a God that hath indignation every day" (Ps. 7:11, ERV). No evildoer goes unnoticed (Ps. 94:7–9); all receive their precise desert (Prov. 24:12). God hates sin, and is impelled by the demands of his own nature to pour out "wrath" and "fury" on those who complacently espouse it (cf. the language of Isa. 1:24; Jer. 6:11; 30:23–24; Ezek. 5:13ff.; Deut. 28:63). It is a glorious revelation of his righteousness (cf. Isa. 5:16; 10:22) when he does so; it would be a reflection on his righteousness if he failed to do so. It seems unthinkable that a God who thus reveals just and inflexible wrath against all human ungodliness (Rom. 1:18) should justify the ungodly. Paul, however, takes the bull by the horns and affirms, not merely that God does it, but that he does it in a manner designed "to shew his righteousness, because of the passing over of the sins done aforetime, in the forbearance of God; for the shewing, *I say,* of his righteousness at this present season: that he might himself be just, and the justifier of him that hath faith in Jesus" (Rom. 3:25–26, ERV). The statement is emphatic, for the point is crucial. Paul is saying that the gospel which proclaims God's apparent violation of his justice is really a revelation of his justice. So far from raising a problem of theodicy, it actually solves one; for it makes explicit, as the OT never did, the just ground on which God pardoned and accepted believers before the time of Christ, as well as since.

Some question this exegesis of Rom. 3:25–26 and construe "righteousness" here as meaning "saving action," on the ground that in Isa. 40–55 "righteousness" and "salvation" are repeatedly used as equivalents (Isa. 45:8, 19–25; 46:13; 51:3–6, etc.). This eliminates the theodicy; all that Paul is saying, on this view, is that God now shows that he saves sinners. The words "just, and" in vs. 26, so far from making the crucial point that God justifies sinners *justly,* would then add nothing to his meaning and could be deleted without loss. However, quite apart from the specific exegetical embarrassments which it creates (for which see V. Taylor, *ExpT* 50:295ff.), this hypothesis seems groundless, for (1) OT references to God's righteousness normally denote his retributive justice (the usage adduced from Isaiah is not typical), and (2) these verses are the continuation of a discussion that has been concerned throughout (from 1:18 onward) with God's display of righteousness *in judging and punishing sin.* These considerations decisively fix the forensic reference here. "The main question with which St. Paul is concerned is how God can be recognized as himself righteous and at the same time as one who declares righteous believers in Christ" (Taylor, p. 299). Paul has not (as is suggested) left the forensic sphere behind. The sinner's relation to God as just Lawgiver and Judge is still his subject. What he is saying in this paragraph (Rom. 3:21–26) is that the gospel reveals a way in which sinners can be justified without affront to the divine justice which, as shown (1:18–3:20), condemns all sin.

Paul's thesis is that God justifies sinners on a just ground, namely, that the claims of God's law upon them have been fully satisifed. The law has not been altered, or suspended, or flouted for their justification, but fulfilled—by Jesus Christ, acting in their name. By perfectly serving God, Christ perfectly kept the law (cf. Matt. 3:15). His obedience culminated in death (Phil. 2:8); he bore the penalty of the law in men's place (Gal. 3:13), to make propitiation for their sins (Rom. 3:25). On the ground of Christ's obedience, God does not impute sin, but imputes righteousness, to sinners who believe (Rom. 4:2–8; 5:19). "The righteousness of God" (i.e., righteousness *from* God: see Phil. 3:9) is bestowed on them as a free gift (Rom. 1:17; 3:21–22; 5:17, cf. 9:30; 10:3–10): that is to say, they receive the right to be treated and the promise that they shall be treated, no longer as sinners, but as righteous, by the divine Judge. Thus they become "the righteousness of God" in and through him who "knew no sin" personally, but was representatively "made sin" (treated as a sinner and punished) in their stead (II Cor. 5:21). This is the thought expressed in classical Protestant theology by the phrase "the imputation of Christ's righteousness," namely, that believers are righteous (Rom. 5:19) and have righteousness (Phil. 3:9) before God for no other reason than that Christ their Head was righteous before God, and they are one with him, sharers of his status and acceptance. God justifies them by passing on them, for Christ's sake, the verdict which Christ's obedience merited. God declares them to be righteous, because he reckons them to be righteous; and he reckons righteousness to them, not because he accounts them to have kept his law personally (which would be a false judgment), but because he accounts them to be united to the one who kept it representatively (and that is a true judgment). For Paul union with Christ is not fancy but fact—the basic fact, indeed, in Christianity; and the doctrine of imputed righteousness is simply Paul's exposition of the forensic aspect of it (see Rom. 5:12ff.). Covenantal solidarity between Christ and his people is thus the objective basis on which sinners are reckoned righteous and justly justified through the righteousness of their Savior. Such is Paul's theodicy regarding the ground of justification.

Faith and Justification. Paul says that believers are justified *dia pisteōs* (Rom. 3:25), *pistei* (Rom. 3:28), and *ek pisteōs* (Rom. 3:30). The dative and the preposition *dia* represent faith as the instrumental means whereby Christ and his righteousness are appropriated; the preposition *ek* shows that faith occasions, and logically precedes, our personal justification. That believers are justified *dia pistin*, on account of faith, Paul never says, and would deny. Were faith the ground of justification, faith would be in effect a meritorious work, and the gospel message would, after all, be merely another version of justification by works—a doctrine which Paul opposes in all forms as irreconcilable with grace and spiritually ruinous (cf. Rom. 4:4; 11:6; Gal. 4:21–5:12). Paul regards faith, not as itself our justifying righteousness, but rather as the outstretched empty hand which receives righteousness by receiving Christ. In Hab. 2:4 (cited Rom. 1:17; Gal. 3:11) Paul finds, implicit in the promise that the godly man ("the just") would enjoy God's continued favor ("live") through his trustful loyalty to God (which is Habakkuk's point in the context), the more fundamental assertion that only through faith does any man ever come to be viewed by God as just, and hence as entitled to life, at all. The apostle also uses Gen. 15:6 ("Abraham believed God, and it was reckoned unto him for righteousness," ERV) to prove the same point (see Gal. 3:6; Rom. 4:3ff.). It is clear that when Paul paraphrases this verse as teaching that Abraham's faith was reckoned for righteousness (Rom. 4:5, 9, 22), all he intends us to understand is that faith—decisive, wholehearted reliance on God's gracious promise (vss. 18ff.)—was the occasion and means of righteousness being imputed to him. There is no suggestion here that faith is the ground of justification. Paul is not discussing the ground of justification in this context at all, only the method of securing it. Paul's conviction is that no child of Adam ever becomes righteous before God save on account of the righteousness of the last Adam, the second representative man (Rom. 5:12–19); and this righteousness is imputed to men when they believe.

Theologians on the rationalistic and moralistic wing of Protestantism—Socinians, Arminians, and some modern liberals—have taken Paul to teach that God regards man's faith as righteousness (either because it fulfills a supposed new law or because, as the seed of all Christian virtue, it contains the germ and potency of an eventual fulfillment of God's original law, or else because it is simply God's sovereign pleasure to treat faith as righteousness, though it is not righteousness; and that God pardons and accepts sinners on the ground of their faith). In consequence, these theologians deny the imputation of Christ's righteousness to believers in the sense explained, and reject the whole covenantal conception of Christ's mediatorial work. The most they can say is that Christ's righteousness was the indirect cause of the acceptance of man's faith as righteousness, in that it created a situation in which this acceptance became possible. (Thinkers in the Socinian tradition, believing that such a situation always existed and that Christ's work had no Godward reference, will not say even this.) Theologically, the fundamental defect of all such views is that they do not make the satisfaction of the law the basis of acceptance. They regard justification, not as a judicial act of executing the law, but as the sovereign act of a God who stands above the law and is free to dispense with it, or change it, at his discretion. The suggestion is that God is not bound by his own law: its preceptive and penal enactments do not express immutable and necessary demands of his own nature, but he may out of benevolence relax and amend them without ceasing to be what he is. This, however, seems a wholly unscriptural conception.

The Doctrine in History. Interest in justification varies according to the weight given to the scriptural insistence that man's relation to God is determined by law and sinners necessarily stand under his wrath and condemnation. The late medieval theologians took this more seriously than any since apostolic times; they, however, sought acceptance through penances and meritorious good works. The Reformers proclaimed justification by grace alone through faith alone on the ground of Christ's righteousness alone, and embodied Paul's doctrine in full confessional statements. The sixteenth and seventeenth centuries were the doctrine's classical period. Liberalism spread the notion that God's attitude to all men is one of paternal affection, not conditioned by the demands of penal law; hence interest in the sinner's justification by the divine Judge was replaced by the thought of the prodigal's forgiveness and rehabilitation by his divine Father. The validity of forensic categories for expressing man's saving relationship to God has been widely denied. Many neo-orthodox thinkers seem surer that there is a sense of guilt in man than that there is a penal law in God, and tend to echo this denial, claiming that legal categories obscure the personal quality of this relationship. Consequently, Paul's doctrine of justification has received little stress outside evangelical circles, though a new emphasis is apparent in recent lexical work, the newer Lutheran writers, and the *Dogmatics* of Karl Barth. J. I. PACKER

See also FAITH; SANCTIFICATION.

Bibliography. Sanday and Headlam, *Romans;* E. D. Burton, *Galatians;* L. Morris, *The Apostolic Preaching of the Cross;* V. Taylor, *Forgiveness and Reconciliation;* Calvin, *Institutes* 3.11–18; J. Owen, *Justification by Faith;* J. Buchanan, *The Doctrine of Justification;* W. Cunningham, *Historical Theology,* II, 1-120; A. Ritschl, *Critical History of . . . Justification;* C. Hodge, *Systematic Theology,* III, 114–212; L. Berkhof, *Systematic Theology,* 510–26; G. Quell *et al., TDNT,* II, 174ff.; J. A. Ziesler, *The Meaning of Righteousness in Paul;* H. Seebass and C. Brown, *NIDNTT,* III, 352ff.; H. Küng, *Justification;* G. B. Stevens, *The Christian Doctrine of Salvation;* J. W. Drane, *Paul—Libertine or Legalist?* E. Käsemann, "The Righteousness of God in Paul," in *NT Questions of Today;* G. C. Berkouwer, *Faith and Justification.*

Justitia Civilis. *See* CIVIL RIGHTEOUSNESS.

Kk

Kabbalah (Heb. *qābal,* "to receive, tradition"). An esoteric mystic lore of Judaism, passed as secret doctrine to only the chosen few. Its origin is lost in antiquity, but one sees traces of ancient Jewish apocalyptic, talmudic, and midrashic literature and non-Jewish sources of Gnosticism and Neoplatonism in Kabbalah. Its first systematic development occurred among the Babylonian Jewish Gaonim scholars (A.D. 600–1000). As the Babylonian center waned, other areas became prominent—Italy, Spain, southern France, and Germany—and the development continued in the 1100s and 1200s. The most prominent book of Kabbalah is the *Zohar,* which appeared in 1300 under Moses de Leon. Once this material was recorded, everyone was able to study it. Further development occurred in the sixteenth century in Safed, Israel, under Isaac Luria, who initiated a distinctive emphasis of redemption and messianism. Rabbis at times denounced this form of study as so much speculation that would only lead Jewish people away from mainline Judaism's three great emphases: repentance, prayer, and good deeds to man and God.

Christians in the Middle Ages also became interested in Kabbalah—e.g., Lully, Pico della Mirandela, and John Reuchlin. As with Jewish people, there was also a reaction among some Christians against sterile belief, and it was thought that Kabbalah was a valid corrective. Christians also studied this material to find verification of their mystical beliefs.

Kabbalah pictures God as being above all existence; through a series of ten emanations the world was created. The system is somewhat pantheistic since everything that exists has its place in God. Through good deeds a pious Jew supposedly affects the various emanations, ultimately affecting God on behalf of mankind.

Kabbalah includes reincarnation. The pure soul, once the body dies, will be present among the emanations who control the world. An impure soul must be reborn in another body, and the process continues until it has been made pure. Evil is only the negation of good, and in the Jewish setting evil is overcome through the three great emphases, along with strict adherence to the law.

What is most distinctive is the hermeneutical principle of finding hidden meanings in the texts of Scriptures. Human language in Scripture is examined not only allegorically and analogically, but also through the interpretation of words and letters according to their numerical equivalents, and by interchanging numerical equivalents new letters and words could be created, thereby allowing for new interpretations.

Kabbalah influenced Jewish messianic movements, principally Hasidism, which developed a joyful religious expression that avoided sterile legalism.

L. GOLDBERG

Bibliography. J. Abelson, *Jewish Mysticism;* D. C. Ginsburg, "The Kabbalah," in *The Essenes; EJ,* II, 489–654; A. E. Waite, *Holy Kabbalah;* M. Waxman, "The Kabbalah," in *A History of Jewish Literature,* II, 337–421.

Kähler, Martin (1835–1912). German Protestant theologian. He was born near Königsberg in East Prussia, the son of a Lutheran pastor, and studied theology at the universities of Heidelberg, Tübingen, and Halle. Except for three years at Bonn (1864–67), his entire academic career as professor of systematic theology was spent at the University of Halle. His theological development was shaped by Rothe, Tholuck, Müller, Beck, and von Hofmann.

His principal theological work, a volume on dogmatics entitled *Die Wissenschaft der christlichen Lehre* (1883), had the doctrine of justification as its primary theme. His lectures on

Protestant theology, the *Geschichte der protestantischen Dogmatik im 19 Jahrhundert,* were published posthumously (1962). He is best known for a collection of essays entitled *Der sogenannte historische Jesus und der geschichtliche, biblische Christus* (1892), in which he resisted the current scholarly trend of separating the historical Jesus from the apostolic proclamation. He claimed that these attempts to isolate the historical Jesus were as filled with speculation as were the dogmatic Christological theories against which the historians of Jesus were reacting. The real Jesus is not the historically reconstructed Jesus of Nazareth but the Christ of faith.

Kähler, however, was not unconcerned about the historical issues. He claimed that the Christ of the kerygma attested to in the NT was the Jesus of history. In Kähler's thought there is no separation of the kerygmatic Christ from the historical figure of Jesus, nor was Jesus the mere starting point of the early Christian kerygma. Rather, Jesus was the basis and content of the kerygma, and hence the object of faith. Kähler's views anticipated those of J. Weiss, A. Schweitzer, and R. Bultmann, and have been important in recent theological discussion. D. S. FERGUSON

See also NEO-ORTHODOXY; BULTMANN, RUDOLF; DEMYTHOLOGIZATION.

Bibliography. C. E. Braaten, *New Directions in Theology Today,* II, 59–63, and "Martin Kähler on the Historic Biblical Christ," in *The Historical Jesus and the Kerygmatic Christ;* M. Kähler, *The So-Called Historical Jesus and the Historic, Biblical Christ,* tr. C. E. Braaten.

Kant, Immanuel (1724–1804). One of the most acute philosophers of all time. In his thought the Age of Enlightenment reached its peak. No other thinker has so profoundly influenced the course of nineteenth and twentieth century philosophy and theology.

Kant was born in Königsberg, East Prussia, where from 1755 until his death he taught philosophy at the university. In 1784 he wrote an article asking the question, "What is enlightenment?" He replied that enlightenment is man's emergence from immaturity. It is man learning to think for himself without relying on the authority of the church, the Bible, or the state to tell him what to do. Kant's philosophy was an attempt to reappraise human knowledge, ethics, aesthetics, and religion in the light of this ideal. As a necessary first step he undertook an examination of the scope and limitations of the human mind in relation to these subjects. This was the common theme of his three great critiques: *Critique of Pure Reason* (1781), *Critique of Practical Reason* (1788), and *Critique of Judgment* (1790). These dealt respectively with human knowledge, ethics, and aesthetics. He also dealt with ethics in his *Groundwork of the Metaphysic of Morals* (1785). He set out his enlightened view of religion in *Religion Within the Limits of Reason Alone* (1793).

Kant's approach to knowledge combined elements from both rationalism and empiricism. Kant agreed with the empiricists in saying that all our knowledge of the world outside us comes to us via our senses. But he held with the rationalists that the mind itself contributes to our knowledge of reality. Its role is to process the data provided by the senses. It does so by applying to sense data such notions as time and space, number, and cause and effect. The mind uses these ideas to interpret physical reality as related by the sense of sight, touch, smell, and sound. Without them we could not grasp anything at all. On the other hand, we know things only as they are conditioned by the mind with all its limitations. We do not know reality as it is in itself.

This led Kant to reject all metaphysical knowledge. Since our knowledge of even material things is conditioned by the mind, all claims to knowledge of reality over and above the physical must be likewise conditioned. Claims to metaphysical and theological knowledge involve hopeless contradictions that the human mind is not equipped to resolve.

Kant rejected the traditional arguments for the existence of God. He argued that the cosmological argument (arguing from causation to a first cause) and the teleological argument (arguing from evidence of design in the world to a great designer) rested upon the illegitimate ontological argument. The latter appealed to reason alone to infer the existence of God from the notion of God as the most perfect being, on the grounds that the latter would not be the most perfect being if he did not exist. Kant believed that the ontological argument rested on a tautology which merely defined God as a necessarily existing, perfect being without supplying any reasons for thinking that such a being actually did exist. It could no more prove the existence of God by asserting his existence than a merchant could increase his wealth merely by writing zeros in his ledger. Kant maintained that the cosmological and teleological arguments tacitly appealed to the ontological argument in order to convert the ideas of a first cause and great designer into an actually existing first cause and great designer.

Kant rejected the idea of ethics based on the will of God, although his own view begs the question of the source of our sense of moral obligation. He applied the categorical imperative as the test of the moral value of an action: "Act only on that maxim whereby thou canst at the same time will that it should become a universal law." The notions of God, freedom, and immortality were for Kant regulative principles. They were indemonstrable, but gave coherence to ethical thought and behavior.

Kant saw Christianity as a way of teaching ethics for the philosophically unsophisticated. Jesus was for him an enlightened moral teacher whose life exemplified his teaching.

In their different ways idealism, existentialism, and logical positivism were responses to the positions advocated by Kant. Liberal theology either followed Kant in stressing the ethical aspect of religion or Schleiermacher in his attempt to get around Kant by basing theology on religious feeling. C. Brown

See also Enlightenment, The.

Bibliography. K. Barth, *Protestant Theology in the Nineteenth Century;* E. Cassirer, *Kant's Life and Thought;* F. Copleston, *A History of Philosophy; VI, Wolff to Kant;* S. Körner, *Kant.*

Keble, John (1792–1866). A founder of the Tractarian (Oxford) Movement. Keble College, Oxford, is named in his memory. From 1823 until his death he was a parish priest. From 1831 to 1841 he combined that duty with the professorship of poetry at Oxford, where as a young man he had been a fellow of Oriel college. His first major publication was the cycle of poems he called *The Christian Year* (1827), which was often reprinted. He was regarded by J. H. Newman as the real founder of the Tractarian Movement because of the sermon he preached before the University of Oxford on July 14, 1833. In this he referred to the national apostasy displayed in the suppression of ten Irish bishoprics (Ireland was then part of Britain). He called for a higher view of the church as the church not of Parliament but of Christ. With Newman he wrote many of the ninety *Tracts for the Times* (1833–41). He edited the classic apology of Anglicanism, Richard Hooker's *Ecclesiastical Polity,* along with other works, and two years later, in 1838, he became one of the editors of the *Library of the Fathers.* To this he contributed a translation of the works of Irenaeus. After the defection of Newman to Rome in 1845, Keble shared with E. B. Pusey the leadership of the movement. He was known as its quiet saint, a strong moral and spiritual leader. His high view of the Eucharist is seen in his *Eucharistical Adoration* (1857). His hymns are often sung in Anglican churches. P. Toon

See also Anglo-Catholicism; Oxford Movement; Pusey, Edward Bouverie.

Bibliography. G. Battiscombe, *John Keble: A Study in Limitations.*

Kenosis, Kenotic Theology. "Kenosis" is a Greek term taken from Phil. 2:7, where Christ is spoken of as having "emptied himself" (RSV) and taken human form. There has been much discussion about this entire crucial passage (2:6–11), and several interpretations exist today. Kenotic theology is a theology that focuses on the person of Christ in terms of some form of self-limitation by the preexistent Son in his becoming man. Kenotic theology at the theoretical level is a way of conceiving of the incarnation that is relatively new in the history of reflection on the person of Christ. Some see this form of thought about Christ as the most recent advance in Christology; others see it as a blind alley.

History. Kenotic theology can be said to have begun as a serious form of reflection on Christology in the works of Gottfried Thomasius (1802–75), a German Lutheran theologian. In general kenotic theology was formulated in the light of three crucial concerns. The primary concern was to find a way of understanding the person of Christ that allowed his full humanity to be adequately expressed. Biblical studies had given the church an intensified awareness that Christianity began in the earliest encounters with the man Jesus. Critical scholarship was "recapturing" him in the light of his environment. It was becoming more sensitive to the limitations of that "prescientific" era and was seeing more clearly the Synoptic portrait of the human personality of the man Jesus. All this conspired to force upon theologians the need to affirm in new ways that Christ was truly man. He grew, he hungered, he learned, he appropriated his culture, and he exhibited its limitations. All this must be said about Christ himself, not merely about some abstract appendage called humanity "assumed" by God the Son.

A second, equally important concern was to affirm that God truly was in Christ. The creeds are correct: very God, very man. The problem is how this can be said without turning Christ into an aberration. If to be human is to learn, grow, etc., and to be God is to be omniscient, then how can we speak of one person? Must he not have had "two heads"?

The third concern stems in part from the first. The age was learning to think in terms of the categories of psychology. Consciousness was a central category. If at our "center" is our consciousness, and if Jesus was both omniscient

God and limited man, then he had two centers and was thus fundamentally not one of us. Christology was becoming inconceivable for some.

The converging of these concerns led to kenotic theologies in a variety of forms. All shared a need to affirm Jesus' real, limited humanity and limited consciousness along with the affirmation that he is very God and very man. The varying forms of the theory of divine self-limitation were the way this was attempted.

All forms of classical orthodoxy either explicitly reject or reject in principle kenotic theology. This is because God must be affirmed to be changeless; any concept of the incarnation that would imply change would mean that God would cease to be God.

Types. These concerns by no means force a uniformity of formulations; in fact, there are many different possibilities under the general category "kenotic theology." There is a variety of possibilities for a Christology in terms of the idea of a preincarnate self-limitation by God the Son. There are two broad categories for understanding kenotic theories. One concerns the relation of the kenotic theory to traditional orthodox formulas. A kenotic theory can have the function of being supportive modification of a traditional formula or it can be presented as an alternative. This is a key difference between the otherwise quite similar presentations given by Anglican Charles Gore in his Bampton Lectures, *The Incarnation of the Son of God* (1891), and Congregationalist P. T. Forsyth in his *Person and Place of Jesus Christ* (1909). Both writers clearly affirm a real commitment to an understanding of Christ as God and man, yet Gore's kenotic proposal functions to reinforce his consistent and articulate defense of Chalcedonian orthodoxy. Forsyth sees his theory as a biblical alternative to a static, Greek, outmoded formula found in the Chalcedonian Definition. Both Gore and Forsyth are altogether clear on their vision of Jesus' humanity, his growth, and limitations as part of the meaning of his identity.

A second distinction within kenotic theories concerns the place of the concept within the larger understanding of God's being and relation to the world. The work of A. E. Garvie in *Studies in the Inner Life of Jesus* (1907) shows the influence of a conservative form of Hegelian speculation on the nature of the Trinity. Here there is seen to be a movement or dialectic within God between fullness (Father) and self-limitation/expression (Son) that finds its historic expression in the incarnation kenotically understood. Thus kenotic theology is not intended to be an *ad hoc* device for making sense of the Christ event; rather the Christ event is the historic expression of the eternal dialectic within the Triune God. Others also see the relation of God as Creator to creation as a form of self-limitation, thus providing genuine human freedom and the broad context for the more specific instance of divine self-limitation in Jesus Christ. The contrast to these more speculative forms of kenotic theology would naturally be those forms which focus more specifically on the incarnation as the exclusive act of divine self-limitation for our salvation.

At least two broad areas of distinction can be made in understanding the potential range of kenotic theories. First is the crucial distinction on the relation of a proposed kenotic theology to the history of Christology. Is the theory to be seen as an alternative to existing dogma (Forsyth, Mackintosh) or a reinforcing modification (Garvie, Weston)? Secondly, is a kenotic theology to be seen in its uniqueness as the act of divine self-limitation (Forsyth), or is it to be seen as either the culminating historical instance of the Trinitarian dialectic (Garvie) and/or the kenotic relation of God to creation in general?

Criticism. Kenotic theology as formulated in Germany (1860–80) or in England (1890–1910) was clearly not without challenge. Indeed, many believe that the criticisms evoked have proven fatal.

A persistent criticism has been that kenotic theology is not biblical. If one were to hold some sort of developmental theory about the emergence of NT Christology—as do R. Bultmann, J. Knox, R. H. Fuller, e.g.—then the most that could be said would be that kenotic theology could at best reflect one of the emerging models. If one holds to the Christological unity of the NT, as do kenotic theorists in general, then the question is more pointed. What advocates of kenotic theology would uniformly contend is that as an interpretative scheme their understanding allows one to see Jesus Christ as a real, growing, limited man without creating a sense that God is not somehow deeply involved in exactly *this* man. It is not a question of the interpretation of Phil. 2, but a question of how one sees God and man in Jesus Christ. Did Christ know or not know the time of the end (Mark 13:32)? Orthodoxy said he *must* know, he is the presence of the omniscient God; however, for some reason he has chosen not to reveal this knowledge. Kenotic theorists insist that the text says what it says. He limited himself to his human and real development; he was genuinely dependent on his Father; he did not know. The problem of who is biblical cuts more than one way.

A second criticism clearly must focus on the

fundamental credibility of the concept of a divine self-limitation. We must be clear here. Theology has always countenanced a divine concealment for pedagogical purposes in Christ. He concealed his divine radiance and became tangible so as to meet us in our darkened, fallen world on our terms (Augustine). Kenotic theology goes a crucial step beyond this; in the incarnation, however conceived, there was a preincarnate act of limitation, whether it be a "laying aside" (Gore) or a "concentration" (Forsyth). It is something like whether or not a missionary were to take his two-way radio (and thus his link to his support system) with him into the jungle. How can Jesus Christ be God if we would simultaneously affirm that during the incarnate life he was not omniscient?

Following the lead of Thomasius, some argued that there are two kinds of attributes—internal (love, joy) and external (omnipotence, omnipresence, etc.). The eternal Son "set aside" the external attributes and revealed the internal. In him we see the love of Father-Son; in him we see God's "heart" made visible. A. M. Fairbairn carefully works this out in his pioneering work, *The Place of Christ in Modern Theology* (1895).

Others of a more speculative bent (e.g., Garvie) contend that self-limitation is *in* God in his "innertrinitarian" life. Thus what is revealed in Christ is not one act of self-limitation, but God the Son in his eternal self-limiting obedient relation to the Father. The incarnation is thus seen to be the revelation of the eternal relation of Father to Son and the saving love that would include others.

The third response focuses on the importance of goal or intention for God. If God can be said to have as his fundamental goal to bring lost children back to himself, then his omnipotence/omniscience is precisely that which achieves the goal. The greatest act of omnipotence can then be seen as the Son's becoming "poor" that we may become rich in him. Omnipotence is reconsidered more in terms of the goal in view than as an abstract category. Forsyth worked with this idea at length; he called it the "moralizing of God," that is, the reshaping of our view of God from what he called static categories to dynamic ones reflecting God's saving purposes seen in Christ. Thus there were several ways those holding a kenotic theology would attempt to make the concept of self-limitation credible. Further, the challenge was reversed. How, it was asked, can one make sense of Jesus Christ as an omniscient being simultaneously living as a growing, learning, limited man without creating a "two-headed" being? Is the union of natures conceivable without a divine self-limitation? Is not some form of docetism the only alternative? Did Jesus only look human?

The third criticism has focused on the supposed strength of kenotic theology, the consciousness of Jesus. Perhaps, it would be conceded, the person of the Incarnate is more of a unity, but have we not created a new duality between the preincarnate Son and the historical Jesus? Was there not an inconceivable loss (of knowledge) at Bethlehem? Further, if the Son simultaneously remained the transcendent Logos, is there not a radical, fatal discontinuity between the consciousness of the transcendent Logos and the earthly Jesus? It can be argued that at this point kenotic theology is most strained. However, the strain is fundamentally a relocation of the same strain orthodoxy faces when it attempts to affirm very God–very man in terms of the consciousness of the earthly Jesus. The problem cuts both ways. For kenotic theology the tension is in the cleavage between the preexistent and incarnate Son. For orthodoxy the tension is as great as it attempts to comprehend in some measure how Jesus can be both the presence of the omniscient God and a limited, growing man.

Summary. Kenotic theology is in reality a variant but new form of orthodox, biblical faith. It has appeared in a variety of forms over the last century. It has been vigorously debated, and interest in it remains. From one angle it can be seen as an attempt to give conceptual substance to the great hymn of Charles Wesley that speaks in awe that the Son would "empty himself of all but love" and die for a fallen humanity. From another angle kenotic theology represents an attempt to give central place to Jesus' limited yet sinless humanity while affirming that the ultimate significance of that humanity was and is that here on earth God the eternal Son has come, truly come, to redeem. S. M. Smith

See also Christology.

Bibliography. C. Welch, *God and Incarnation in Mid-Nineteenth Century German Theology;* C. Gore, *Dissertations on Subjects Connected with the Incarnation;* W. I. Walker, *The Spirit and the Incarnation;* F. Weston, *The One Christ;* A. B. Bruce, *The Humiliation of Christ;* H. E. W. Turner, *Jesus the Christ;* W. Pannenberg, *Jesus—God and Man.*

Kerygma. A Greek word meaning "proclamation." It may refer to the content of the gospel, to the message of the sermon, or to the preaching itself. The verb form, *kēryssō,* meaning "to preach" or "to proclaim," is used in reference to Jesus' message concerning the coming of the kingdom of God (Mark 1:14–15). In current NT scholarship the term is used to describe the content of the early Christian message. It contains within its scope the life and work of Jesus, with particular emphasis on his conflicts, suffering, death, and resurrection from the dead. In addition, the kerygma connected the events of Jesus' life and death with the history of Israel, seeing them as the climax of God's redemptive activity.

Kerygma is often distinguished from *didachē*, the former being the message of God's act in Christ calling people to the decision of faith and membership in the community of faith, the church, the latter being the instruction in belief and morals which the new converts received within the church.

It is now a commonly accepted practice to understand the kerygmatic proclamation as foundational for the beginnings of the Christian church. To be sure, there are differences among scholars regarding the details, but there is wide unanimity that the life, death, and resurrection of Jesus constitute the eschatological act of God which has ushered in the new age.

The NT as a whole may be said to be kerygmatic in character, but certain passages appear to contain quite specific kerygmatic formulations. In I Cor. 15:1–11 the apostle makes reference to the tradition which he has "received": (1) that Christ died for our sins in accordance with the Scriptures; (2) that he was buried; (3) that he was raised on the third day according to the Scriptures; and (4) that he appeared to Cephas, then to the twelve. Other NT passages which appear to contain kerygmatic formulations include Rom. 1:1–4; Acts 2:22–24; and I Tim. 3:16. These passages should be viewed as but examples of the way the kerygmatic proclamation came to be stated in specific form.

The theological debate around the term "kerygma" has focused on the relationship of the proclaimed message to the historical Jesus. To understand the Gospels as a kerygmatic witness to the risen Christ rather than biographical reports has been nearly universally accepted by theologians and NT scholars. But the question remains: Where does the historical Jesus fit into the theological scheme? Surely the kerygma without the Jesus of history is a shaky foundation for faith, and a Jesus without the kerygma allows for no faith at all.

Rudolf Bultmann has raised the question of the relationship between the kerygma and the Jesus of history with characteristic force. Faith, he argues, must never be allowed to rest on the results of historical scholarship but only on the kerygma. But, one might ask, is it not only one short step from this position to a removal of the earthly life of Jesus from the content of the kerygma? Bultmann refused to take this step, insisting, as a minimum, that the kerygma is linked to the bare fact of Jesus' historicity and his death on the cross. Many of his critics have pointed out the apparent inconsistency in his view; namely, on the one hand, his insistence that faith must not be tied to history but solely rooted in the kerygma and, on the other, his unwillingness to separate the Jesus of history from the kerygma. It would seem that even Bultmann cannot escape the charge he has often leveled at other theologians: that they make faith dependent upon historical inquiry.

It is certainly true that in the minds of the authors of the NT there is no separation of the kerygmatic proclamation from the Jesus of Nazareth who lived, preached, died, and rose again from the dead. He, indeed, was the one who was alive in the word of preaching. D. S. FERGUSON

See also GOSPEL; PREACH, PREACHING; BULTMANN, RUDOLF.

Bibliography. C. E. Braaten and R. A. Harrisville, eds., *Kerygma and History;* R. Bultmann, *Kerygma and Myth;* C. H. Dodd, *The Apostolic Preaching and Its Developments.*

Keswick Convention. An annual summer gathering of evangelical Christians, held since 1875 at Keswick in the Lake District of northern England. It had its origin in the Moody-Sankey evangelistic campaign in Britain in 1873–74 and in the writings of the American religious leaders Asa Mahan, W. E. Boardman, and especially Mr. and Mrs. Robert P. Smith. The first Keswick Convention was preceded by a number of similar smaller conferences held by Smith throughout England and by larger ones held at Broadlands and at Oxford in 1874 and at Brighton in 1875. T. D. Harford Battersby, vicar of the Anglican church in Keswick, held the first Keswick Convention on his own church grounds, and the meetings, lasting one week, have been held there every year since. This convention has become the mother of similar conventions not only in England but in many other countries throughout the world.

From the beginning the convention has had as its aim the deepening of the spiritual life. It differs from the average Bible conference in that it aims not merely to impart Bible knowledge and spiritual uplift, but to be a spiritual clinic where defeated and ineffective Christians may be restored to spiritual health. It stands for no particular brand of denominational theology. Its motto is "All One in Christ Jesus."

Since the convention has a definite aim and purpose to accomplish in its meetings, the teaching given during the week normally follows a progressive order. On the first day the addresses focus on sin and its disabling spiritual effects in the life of the believer. On the second day the addresses deal with the provision God has made through the cross to deal with the problem of sin, not only its guilt but also its power. Much is made of Rom. 6–8, where Paul states that the believer is identified with Christ in his death to sin and is therefore set free from slavery to sin. Keswick does not teach the possibility of the eradication of the sin nature or the attainability of sinlessness in this life. The third day is devoted to teaching on consecration, which is man's response to God's call for complete abandonment to the rule of Christ, involving both a crisis and a process. The fourth day is occupied with teaching on the Spirit-filled life. All Christians, it is taught, receive the Holy Spirit at regeneration, but all are not controlled by him. The fullness of the Spirit is made experiential by abandonment to Christ and abiding in that state of abandonment. On Friday the theme of the convention is Christian service, which is the natural result of a Spirit-filled life. Keswick has always stressed the importance of missions and has deeply influenced the missionary movement.

The majority of Keswick speakers have naturally come from England, but many have come from other parts of the world. Among the better known are Donald G. Barnhouse, F. B. Meyer, H. C. G. Moule, Andrew Murray, John R. W. Stott, Hudson Taylor, and R. A. Torrey. The addresses given at the convention are published annually in a volume usually called either *The Keswick Convention* or *The Keswick Week.* S. Barabas

Bibliography. S. Barabas, *So Great Salvation: The History and Message of the Keswick Convention;* C. F. Harford, *The Keswick Convention;* E. H. Hopkins, *The Law of Liberty in the Spiritual Life;* J. Pollock, *The Keswick Story.*

Keys of the Kingdom. A spiritual authority to preach the gospel and exercise church discipline on earth. The phrase occurs only once in Scripture. In Matt. 16:19 Jesus says to Peter, "I will give you the keys of the kingdom of heaven; and whatever you shall bind on earth shall have been bound in heaven and whatever you shall loose on earth shall have been loosed in heaven" (NASB).

Elsewhere in the NT a key always implies authority to open a door and give entrance to a place or realm (Luke 11:52; Rev. 1:18; 3:7; 9:1; 20:1; cf. Isa. 22:22). The keys of the kingdom of heaven therefore represent at least the authority to preach the gospel of Christ (cf. Matt 16:16) and thus to open the door of the kingdom of heaven and allow people to enter.

Peter first used this authority by preaching the gospel at Pentecost (Acts 2:14–42). But the other apostles also were given this authority in a primary sense (they wrote the gospel in permanent form in the NT). And all believers have this "key" in a secondary sense, for they can all share the gospel with others.

However, two factors suggest that the authority of the keys in Matt. 16:19 is broader than just preaching the gospel. First, the plural "keys" suggests authority over more than one door. Thus, more than just entrance to the kingdom is implied; some authority within the kingdom is also suggested.

Second, Jesus completes the promise about the keys with a statement about "binding" and "loosing." Although the rabbinic literature often uses the words "bind" and "loose" for forbidding and permitting various kinds of conduct, a much closer parallel in language, grammar, and authorship is Matt. 18:18, where "binding" and "loosing" mean placing under church discipline and releasing from church discipline (see Matt. 18:15–17). This sense is also suitable in the context of Matt. 16:19; after promising to build his church, Jesus also promises to give not only the authority to open the door of entrance into the kingdom, but also some administrative authority to regulate the conduct of people once they are inside.

The initial conversation with Peter in Matt. 16:16–19 does not indicate whether the disciplining authority of the keys would later be given to others. But in Matt. 18:18 this authority is broadened to the church generally whenever it meets and corporately exercises church discipline (as in Matt. 18:17).

The term "whatever" in both passages is neuter and refers not to persons but to specific actions that are subject to discipline. Yet the authority of the keys with respect to church discipline is not completely unlimited. It will only be effective against true sin (cf. Matt. 18:15), sin as defined by God's Word. The keys of the kingdom do not represent authority to legislate ethical standards in an absolute sense, for the authority to define right and wrong belongs to God alone (Rom. 1:32; 2:16; 3:4–8; 9:20; Ps. 119:89, 142, 160; Matt. 5:18). Nor can the authority of the keys involve authority to forgive sins, which in Scripture can be done only by God himself (Isa. 43:25; 55:7; Mark 2:7, 10; Ps. 103:3; I John 1:9). In John 20:23 the "forgiveness" of sins by the disciples is best understood as freeing from church discipline and restoring personal relationships in a sense similar to the "loosing" of Matt. 16:19 and 18:18.

Both Matt. 16:19 and Matt. 18:18 use an unusual Greek verb construction (periphrastic future perfect). It is best translated by the NASB, "whatever you shall bind on earth *shall have been bound* in heaven, and whatever you shall loose on earth *shall have been loosed* in heaven." Several other examples of this construction show that it indicates not just a future action ("shall be bound"), for which a common Greek tense was available (future passive), but rather an action that would be *completed* before some future point, with effects that would continue to be felt (see Luke 12:52; Gen. 43:9; 44:32; Exod. 12:6; Sir. 7:25; Hermas, *Similitudes* 5.4.2; *Letter of Aristeas,* 40). Thus, Jesus is teaching that church discipline will have heavenly sanction. But it is not as if the church must wait for God to endorse its actions; rather, whenever it enacts discipline it can be confident that God has already begun the process spiritually. Whenever it releases from discipline, forgives the sinner, and restores personal relationships, it can be confident that God has already begun the restoration spiritually (cf. John 20:23). Earthly church discipline involves the awesome certainty that corresponding heavenly discipline has already begun. W. A. Grudem

See also Kingdom of Christ, God, Heaven; Peter, Primacy of; Church Discipline.

Bibliography. D. Müller and C. Brown, *NIDNTT,* II, 729–34; J. Jeremias, *TDNT,* III, 744–53; J. Calvin, *Commentaries* on Matt. 16:19; W. O. Carver, *ISBE,* III, 1794–97.

Kierkegaard, Søren (1813–1855). Danish lay theologian and unintentional founder of existentialism. Born in Copenhagen, he inherited a melancholy disposition from his father, a wealthy and devout wool dealer. Kierkegaard spent ten years preparing for the Lutheran ministry at the University of Copenhagen (M.A. 1840) but was never ordained. Although his life was filled with personal tragedy and loneliness, he was familiar with the major literary, artistic, and intellectual movements of his day.

Kierkegaard's writings were significantly shaped by personal relationships. Perhaps the most important of these was his broken engagement to Regine Olsen. Although Kierkegaard loved her deeply, he ended the relationship convinced that the intimacy of marriage would destroy them both. His love for Regine became a symbol of Abraham's faith at being willing to sacrifice Isaac, a theme Kierkegaard returned to again and again.

The engagement ended, Kierkegaard sought refuge in Berlin. He returned shortly to Copenhagen with his first major work, *Either-Or* (1843). It is a brilliant, dialectical, and poetic discussion in which he sought to justify his actions but which also set forth a basic tenet of existentialism. Kierkegaard argued that each individual must choose—consciously and responsibly—among the alternatives that life brings.

Many Kierkegaard scholars divide his works into two groupings, although the division is arbitrary. The first writings—1843–46—are characterized by aesthetic and philosophical themes. Titles from this period include *Fear and Trembling* (1843), *Philosophical Fragments* (1844), *The Concept of Dread* (1844), and *Concluding Unscientific Postscript to the Philosophical Fragments* (1846).

Following a vicious attack on him in 1846 by a widely read literary paper, Kierkegaard became even more withdrawn and considered giving up writing. A second conversion experience in 1848, however, convinced him of the need to clarify for his contemporaries the true nature of Christianity. Titles characteristic of this later period include *Works of Love* (1847), *Christian Discourses* (1848), and *Training in Christianity* (1850).

Philosophically, Kierkegaard's target was the "system" (idealism) of G. W. F. Hegel. He attacked Hegel's attempt to systematize all of reality because Hegel left out the most important element of human experience, namely existence. Indeed, Kierkegaard felt that no philosophical system could explain the human condition. The experience of reality, such as the loss of a loved one, was what mattered, not the idea (concept) of it. Whereas Hegel emphasized universals, Kierkegaard argued for decision and commitment. Hegel sought an objective theory of knowledge. Kierkegaard believed in the subjectivity of truth.

This emphasis on the subjective led to Kierkegaard's paradoxical understanding of faith. Genuine faith calls for a "leap of faith," a passionate commitment to God in the face of uncertainty and objective reasoning. For Kierkegaard, the free choice of faith alone brings authentic human existence.

The last few years of his life were filled with writings harshly critical of the established Lutheran Church. Following the death in 1854 of his father's friend Bishop Jacob Pier Myster, Kierkegaard could not refrain from attacking the cold formality and indifference of the state church. He was especially hard on clerics, symbolized by Myster, who had become all too comfortable in secular society, and rather than striving to be followers of Christ were spiritually bankrupt civil servants. After two years of this crusade Kierkegaard's health was broken, and he died shortly thereafter.

During his lifetime Kierkegaard was little

known or read outside of Denmark. In the twentieth century, as his works have been translated, Kierkegaard has come to be widely appreciated for his affirmation of faith and critique of the human condition. D. B. ELLER

See also EXISTENTIALISM.

Bibliography. R. Bretall, ed., *A Kierkegaard Anthology;* W. H. Auden, *The Living Thoughts of Kierkegaard;* E. Carnell, *The Burden of Kierkegaard;* J. Collins, *Mind of Kierkegaard;* H. Diem, *Kierkegaard's Dialectic of Existence* and *Kierkegaard: An Introduction;* L. Dupré, *Kierkegaard as Theologian;* V. Eller, *Kierkegaard and Radical Discipleship;* W. Lowrie, *A Short Life of Kierkegaard;* L. Shestov, *Kierkegaard and the Existential Philosophy;* P. Sponheim, *Kierkegaard on Christ and Christian Coherence.*

King. The word designates a male sovereign; he would normally be the ruler of an independent state, though sometimes in the ancient world the title was retained by rulers of states that had colonial or provincial status, subject to some imperial ruler.

In the ancient Near Eastern states monarchy was a standard form of government; states were ruled by persons who held the title "king" (in Mesopotamia, Syria, Palestine) or "pharaoh" (Egypt), an essentially synonymous term. The title and position implied certain religious associations. In Egypt the pharaoh-king was believed to be in some sense divine, whereas in Mesopotamia and the Syro-Palestinian states the king was normally viewed as a god's representative on earth. A king's authority was in theory total, being derived from a high god (usually a god-king in the Asian world), but, in theory at least, the king was to exercise authority wisely. He was responsible not only for the maintenance and the defense of the state (and hence war), but also for matters of justice pertaining to the citizens of the state. Kingship in Near Eastern states was commonly hereditary, though the vicissitudes of war and politics were such that dynasties frequently changed.

In Israel the office of king emerged for the first time during the eleventh century B.C. when Saul became the first full monarch. Prior to that time the people had been led by prophetic-type figures (Moses, Samuel) and judges, for there had been resistance to introducing the office of king in Hebrew society. The resistance was probably in part a consequence of the awareness of how kingship had been abused in other states and the fear of similar abuse in Israel. But in addition, the true king of Israel was believed to be God, a theological awareness which had dawned in the exodus from Egypt (Exod. 15:18). Hence, in Hebrew law kingship was anticipated and permitted under certain controls (Deut. 17:14–20), but it was not perceived as the ideal form of human government.

From the time of Saul kingship in Israel extended throughout the history of Israel's independent statehood. There was first a united monarchy (Saul, David, Solomon); following the division of the kingdom into two separate states, kingship continued to be the norm of government in both the northern state of Israel and the southern state of Judah. Hereditary kingship was the norm, though in the northern state political turmoil resulted in a succession of different dynasties. In the southern state of Judah the dynasty established by King David continued to rule until the end of the state came through the defeat by the Babylonian Empire (586 B.C.).

Following the downfall of Judah the prophets and others reflected deeply on the nature of Israel's defeat and the termination of the succession of Davidic kings. The future hopes of many people were pinned on the possibility of establishing a new kingdom, to be ruled by a Davidic king. For many prophets, however, this hope took on a particular theological perspective. It was not a kingdom-state that was required, nor another human king; there developed rather the view of a future kingdom of God, in which a messianic king would hold sway. And in such a context the norms of kingship would be reversed; the power symbolized by a king's sword would be exchanged for power of peace (Zech. 9:9).

It is this radically revised concept of kingship that appears in the NT (Matt. 21:1–10). In Mark's Gospel the first summary statement of Jesus' preaching indicates that it was concerned with the kingdom of God (Mark 1:14–15), and the theme recurs throughout the Gospels. This kingdom has no geographical territory, no earthly government, and no mortal king; it transcends the boundaries normally ascribed to a nation-state, and includes all those who have responded to the message of the kingdom. The work of Christ, in death and resurrection, establishes the kingdom, in both a worldly and heavenly sense (I Cor. 15:24–28), though its consummation remains still in the future.

Throughout the history of Western Christianity kingship has been a common form of government in many of the states in which Christianity has flourished. From time to time attempts have been made to establish "the divine rights of kings," resorting essentially to the OT model, though failing to perceive the transformation of that model in the NT. In contemporary monarchies the king (queen) holds only limited and temporal power, though he (she) may assume such responsibilities as the "defender of the faith."

P. C. CRAIGIE

See also KINGDOM OF CHRIST, GOD, HEAVEN.

Bibliography. M. Buber, *Kingship of God;* J. Gray, *The Biblical Doctrine of the Reign of God;* A. R. Johnson, *Sacral Kingship in Ancient Israel.*

King, Christ as. *See* OFFICES OF CHRIST.

King, Martin Luther, Jr. (1929–1968). Christian advocate of nonviolent social change, and America's most visible civil rights leader from 1955 until his assassination in April of 1968. The son of a prominent black Baptist pastor in Atlanta, King studied at Morehouse College, Crozer Theological Seminary, and Boston University, where he received the Ph.D. At Boston he pursued studies in philosophy (personalism and Hegelianism) and theology (varieties of existentialism, liberalism, and more traditional orthodoxy) that would one day contribute to his civil rights activity. In 1955, while pastor of the Drexler Avenue Baptist Church in Montgomery, Alabama, he led a successful bus boycott which ended racial segregation in the city's public transportation. In 1957 he helped organize the Southern Christian Leadership Conference (SCLC), whose leaders, like King, were mostly black Baptist pastors.

King's personal prestige was at its height in the early to mid-1960s. His keynote sermon, "I Have a Dream," at the great march on Washington in August, 1963, was one of the most memorable such performances in American history. He also directed the well-publicized Selma to Montgomery march in the spring of 1965. The first of these events mobilized support for the Civil Rights Act of 1964, the second for the federal Voter Registration Act of 1965. King was awarded the Nobel Prize for Peace in 1964.

Toward the end of his life King had struck off on several new courses that put his influence in jeopardy. He traveled north (to Chicago in 1966, as an example) to campaign for civil rights, and this cost him the support of those who saw the issue in strictly southern terms. He also criticized the Vietnam war, which earned him distrust from the administration of President Lyndon Johnson. And he was caught in an ideological crossfire caused by rioting in American cities during the mid- to late 1960s. Critics claimed that King should answer for the violence because of his forceful promotion of civil rights. Some blacks felt that King betrayed their cause by continuing to repudiate the use of violence to attain racial justice.

During the 1950s and 1960s King's prominence gave many Americans their first glimpse of the richness of black preaching. His speeches and writings drew heavily on the vocabulary of black Christian history. Yet his thought reflected a number of influences. It drew upon an evangelical realism concerning the nature of evil and a scriptural defense of nonviolence ("love your enemies"). In classic black fashion, however, he made little distinction between spiritual and social problems involved in the civil rights struggle. Other elements also entered his thinking—the pacifism of Gandhi, the civil disobedience of Thoreau, the existentialist theology of Paul Tillich, the personalistic idealism which he had studied at Boston University, and the American public faith in democratic equality. The conviction which bound these various influences together was his belief that a history of suffering made the oppressed especially capable of proclaiming, and working toward, the ultimate triumph of God's righteousness. M. A. NOLL

See also CIVIL RIGHTS; BLACK THEOLOGY.

Bibliography. C. E. Lincoln, ed., *Martin Luther King, Jr.: A Profile;* F. Schulke, ed., *Martin Luther King, Jr.: A Documentary, Montgomery to Memphis;* H. Walton, Jr., *The Political Philosophy of Martin Luther King, Jr.*

Kingdom of Christ, God, Heaven. ***Terminology.*** "The kingdom of God" occurs four times in Matthew (12:28; 19:24; 21:31; 21:43), fourteen times in Mark, thirty-two times in Luke, twice in John (3:3, 5), six times in Acts, eight times in Paul, once in Revelation (12:10). "The kingdom of the heavens" occurs thirty-three times in Matthew, once in a variant reading in John 3:5, once in the apocryphal work the Gospel of the Hebrews 11. "Kingdom" occurs nine times (e.g., Matt. 25:34; Luke 12:32; 22:29; I Cor. 15:24; Rev. 1:9); also "thy kingdom" (Matt. 6:10; Luke 11:10); "his kingdom" (Matt. 6:33; Luke 12:31; I Thess. 2:12); "the kingdom of their [my] Father" (Matt. 13:43; 26:29); "the gospel of the kingdom" (Matt. 4:23; 9:35; 24:14); "the word of the kingdom" (Matt. 13:19); "the sons of the kingdom" (Matt. 8:12; 13:38); "the kingdom of our father David" (Mark 11:10). Twice "kingdom" is used of the redeemed (Rev. 1:6; 5:9).

"The kingdom of God" and "the kingdom of the heavens" are linguistic variations of the same idea. Jewish idiom often substituted a suitable term for deity (Luke 15:21; Matt. 21:25; Mark 14:61; I Macc. 3:50; Pirke Aboth 1:3). Matthew preserved the Semitic idiom while the other Gospels render it into idiomatic Greek. See Matt. 19:23–24 for their identity of meaning.

The kingdom of God is also the kingdom of Christ. Jesus speaks of the kingdom of the Son of man (Matt. 13:41; 16:28), "my kingdom" (Luke 22:30; John 18:36). See "his kingdom" (Luke 1:33; II Tim. 4:1); "thy kingdom" (Matt. 20:31; Luke

23:42; Heb. 1:8); "the kingdom of his beloved Son" (Col. 1:13); "his heavenly kingdom" (II Tim. 4:18); "the eternal kingdom of our Lord and Savior Jesus Christ" (II Pet. 1:11). God has given the kingdom to Christ (Luke 22:29), and when the Son has accomplished his rule, he will restore the kingdom to the Father (I Cor. 15:24). Therefore it is "the kingdom of Christ and of God" (Eph. 5:5). The kingdom of the world is to become "the kingdom of our Lord and of his Christ" (Rev. 11:15). There is no tension between "the power and the kingdom of our God and the authority of his Christ" (Rev. 12:10).

The Secular Use. *Basileia* is first the authority to rule as a king and secondly the realm over which the reign is exercised.

The Abstract Meaning. In Luke 19:12, 15 a nobleman went into a far country to receive a "kingdom," i.e., authority to rule. Rev. 17:12 speaks of ten kings who have not yet received a "kingdom"; they are to "receive authority as kings" for one hour. These kings give over their "kingdom," their authority, to the Beast (Rev. 17:17). The harlot is the great city which has "kingdom," dominion over the kings of the earth (Rev. 17:18).

The Concrete Meaning. The kingdom is also a realm over which a reign is exercised. The idea of a realm is found in Matt. 4:8 = Luke 4:5; Matt. 24:7; Mark 6:23; Rev. 16:10.

The Kingdom Is God's Reign. The "kingdom of God" means primarily the rule of God, the divine kingly authority.

OT Usage. The Hebrew word *malĕkût,* like *basileia,* carries primarily the abstract rather than the concrete meaning. A king's reign is frequently dated by the phrase "in the . . . year of this *malĕkût,*" i.e., of his reign (I Chr. 26:31; Dan. 1:1). The establishment of Solomon's *malĕkût* (I Kings 2:12) meant the securing of his reign. The reception of Saul's *malĕkût* by David (I Chr. 12:23) is the authority to reign as king. The abstract idea is evident when the word is placed in parallelism with such abstract concepts as power, might, glory, dominion (Dan. 2:37; 4:34; 7:14).

When *malĕkût* is used of God, it almost always refers to his authority or his rule as the heavenly King. See Pss. 22:28; 103:19; 145:11, 13; Obad. 21; Dan. 6:26.

In the NT. The kingdom of God is the divine authority and rule given by the Father to the Son (Luke 22:29). Christ will exercise this rule until he has subdued all that is hostile to God. When he has put all enemies under his feet, he will return the kingdom—his messianic authority—to the Father (I Cor. 15:24–28). The kingdom (not kingdoms) now exercised by men in opposition to God is to become the kingdom of our Lord and of his Christ (Rev. 11:15) and "he shall reign for ever and ever." In Rev. 12:10 the kingdom of God is parallel to the salvation and power of God and the authority of his Christ.

This abstract meaning is apparent in the Gospels. In Luke 1:33 the everlasting kingdom of Christ is synonymous with his rule. When Jesus said that his kingdom was not of this world (John 18:36), he did not refer to his realm; he meant that his rule was not derived from earthly authority but from God and that his kingship would not manifest itself like a human kingdom but in accordance with the divine purpose. The kingdom which men must receive with childlike simplicity (Mark 10:15; Matt. 19:14; Luke 18:17), which men must seek (Matt. 6:33; Luke 12:31), which Christ will give to the disciples (Luke 22:29), is the divine rule.

The Kingdom Is Soteriological. The object of the divine rule is the redemption of men and their deliverance from the powers of evil. I Cor. 15:23–28 is definitive. Christ's reign means the destruction of all hostile powers, the last of which is death. The kingdom of God is the reign of God in Christ destroying all that is hostile to the divine rule.

The NT sees a hostile kingdom standing over against God's kingdom. The "kingdom of the world" is opposed to God's kingdom (Rev. 11:15) and must be conquered. The kingdoms of the world are under satanic control (Matt. 4:8; Luke 4:5). Matt. 12:26 and Luke 11:18 speak of the kingdom of Satan, whose power over men is shown in demon possession. This world or age opposes the working of God's kingdom; the cares of the age will choke the word of the kingdom (Matt. 13:22). This opposition between the two kingdoms, of God and of Satan, is summarized in II Cor. 4:4. Satan is called the god of this age and is seen to exercise his rule by holding men in darkness. This statement must be understood in light of the fact that God remains the King of the ages (I Tim. 1:17; Rev. 15:3).

The kingdom of God is the redemptive rule of God in Christ defeating Satan and the powers of evil and delivering men from the sway of evil. It brings to men "righteousness and peace and joy in the Holy Spirit" (Rom. 14:17). Entrance into the kingdom of Christ means deliverance from the power of darkness (Col. 1:13) and is accomplished by the new birth (John 3:3, 5).

The Kingdom Is Dynamic. The kingdom is not an abstract principle; the kingdom *comes.* It is God's rule actively invading the kingdom of Satan. The coming of the kingdom, as John the Baptist preached it, would mean a mighty divine act: a baptism of judgment and fire (Matt.

3:11–12). God was about to manifest his sovereign rule in the Coming One in salvation and judgment.

The Kingdom Comes at the End of the Age. John looked for a single, though complex, event of salvation-judgment. Jesus separated the present and future visitations of the kingdom. There is a future eschatological coming of the kingdom at the end of the age. Jesus taught the prayer, "Thy kingdom come" (Matt. 6:10). When the Son of man comes in his glory, he will sit on the throne of judgment. The wicked will suffer the condemnation of fire; the righteous will "inherit the kingdom" (Matt. 25:31–46). The same separation at the end of the age is pictured in Matt. 13:36–43. This eschatological coming of the kingdom will mean the *palingenesia* (Matt. 19:28), the rebirth or transformation of the material order.

The Kingdom Has Come into History. Jesus taught that the kingdom, which will come in glory at the end of the age, has come into history in his own person and mission. The redemptive rule of God has now invaded the realm of Satan to deliver men from the power of evil. In the exorcism of demons Jesus asserted the presence and power of the kingdom (Matt. 12:28). While the destruction of Satan awaits the coming of the Son of man in glory (Matt. 25:41; Rev. 20:10), Jesus has already defeated Satan. The strong man (Satan) is bound by the stronger man (Christ) and men may now experience a new release from evil (Matt. 12:29). The mission of the disciples in the name and power of Christ casting out demons meant the overthrow of Satan's power (Luke 10:18). Thus Jesus could say that the kingdom of God was present in the midst of men (Luke 17:21). In the messianic works of Christ fulfilling Isa. 35:5–6, the kingdom manifested its power (Matt. 11:12. *Biazetai* is best interpreted as a middle form).

The Kingdom Is Supernatural. As the dynamic activity of God's rule the kingdom is supernatural. It is God's deed. Only the supernatural act of God can destroy Satan, defeat death (I Cor. 15:26), raise the dead in incorruptible bodies to inherit the blessings of the kingdom (I Cor. 15:50ff.), and transform the world order (Matt. 19:28). The same supernatural rule of God has invaded the kingdom of Satan to deliver men from bondage to satanic darkness. The parable of the seed growing by itself sets forth this truth (Mark 4:26–29). The ground brings forth fruit *of itself.* Men may sow the seed by preaching the kingdom (Matt. 10:7; Luke 10:9; Acts 8:12; 28:23, 31); they can persuade men concerning the kingdom (Acts 19:8), but they cannot build it. It is God's deed. Men can receive the kingdom (Mark 10:15; Luke 18:17), but they are never said to establish it. Men can reject the kingdom and refuse to receive it or enter it (Matt. 23:13), but they cannot destroy it. They can look for it (Luke 23:51), pray for its coming (Matt. 6:10), and seek it (Matt. 6:33), but they cannot bring it. The kingdom is altogether God's deed although it works in and through men. Men may do things for the sake of the kingdom (Matt. 19:12; Luke 18:29), work for it (Col. 4:11), suffer for it (II Thess. 1:5), but they are not said to act upon the kingdom itself. They can inherit it (Matt. 25:34; I Cor. 6:9–10, 15:50), but they cannot bestow it upon others.

The Mystery of the Kingdom. The presence of the kingdom in history is a mystery (Mark 4:11). A mystery is a divine purpose hidden for long ages but finally revealed (Rom. 16:25–26). The OT revelation looks forward to a single manifestation of God's kingdom when the glory of God would fill the earth. Dan. 2 sees four human kingdoms, then the kingdom of God.

The mystery of the kingdom is this: Before this eschatological consummation, before the destruction of Satan, before the age to come, the kingdom of God has entered this age and invaded the kingdom of Satan in spiritual power to bring to men in advance the blessings of forgiveness (Mark 2:5), life (John 3:3), and righteousness (Matt. 5:20; Rom. 14:16) which belong to the age to come. The righteousness of the kingdom is an inner, absolute righteousness (Matt. 5:22, 48) which can be realized only as God gives it to men.

The parables of Matt. 13 embody this new revelation. A parable is a story drawn from daily experience illustrating a single, fundamental truth; the details are not to be pressed as in allegory. The kingdom has come among men but not with power which compels every knee to bow before its glory; it is rather like seed cast on the ground which may be fruitful or unfruitful depending on its reception (Matt. 13:3–8). The kingdom has come, but the present order is not disrupted; the sons of the kingdom and the sons of the evil one grow together in the world until the harvest (Matt. 13:24–30, 36–43). The kingdom of God has indeed come to men, not as a new glorious order, but like the proverbial mustard seed. However, its insignificance must not be despised. This same kingdom will one day be a great tree (Matt. 13:31–32). Instead of a world-transforming power, the kingdom is present in an almost imperceptible form like a bit of leaven hidden in a bowl of dough. However, this same kingdom will yet fill the earth as the leavened dough fills the bowl (Matt. 13:33). In neither of these two parables is the idea of slow growth or gradual permeation important, for our Lord nowhere else used either idea. In Scripture natural growth can illustrate the supernatural (I Cor. 15:36–37).

The coming of the kingdom of God in humility instead of glory was an utterly new and amazing revelation. Yet, said Jesus, men should not be deceived. Although the present manifestation of the kingdom is in humility—indeed, its Bearer was put to death as a condemned criminal—it *is* nevertheless the kingdom of God, and, like buried treasure or a priceless pearl, its acquisition merits any cost or sacrifice (Matt. 13:44–46). The fact that the present activity of the kingdom in the world will initiate a movement that will include evil men as well as good should not lead to misunderstanding of its true nature. It *is* the kingdom of God; it will one day divide the good from the evil in eschatological salvation and judgment (Matt. 13:47–50).

The Kingdom as the Realms of Redemptive Blessing. A reign must have a realm in which its authority is exercised. Thus the redemptive rule of God creates realms in which the blessings of the divine reign are enjoyed. There is both a future and a present realm of the kingdom.

The Future Realm. God calls men to enter his own kingdom and glory (I Thess. 2:12). In this age the sons of the kingdom will experience suffering (II Thess. 1:5) and tribulations (Acts 14:22), but God will rescue them from every evil and save them for his heavenly kingdom (II Tim. 4:18). Men should be careful to assure entrance into the kingdom of Jesus Christ (II Pet. 1:11). Paul frequently speaks of the kingdom as a future inheritance (I Cor. 6:9–10; 15:50; Gal. 5:21; Eph. 5:5).

In the Gospels the eschatological salvation is described as entrance into the kingdom of God (Mark 9:47; 10:24), into the age to come (Mark 10:30), and into eternal life (Mark 9:45; 10:17, 30; Matt. 25:46). These three idioms are interchangeable. The consummation of the kingdom requires the coming of the Son of man in glory. Satan will be destroyed (Matt. 25:41), the dead in Christ raised in incorruptible bodies (I Cor. 15:42–50) which are no longer capable of death (Luke 20:35–36) to inherit the kingdom of God (I Cor. 15:50; Matt. 25:34). Before his death Jesus promised his disciples renewed fellowship in the new order (Matt. 26:29) when they would share both his fellowship and his authority to rule (Luke 22:29–30).

The stages of this consummation is a debated question. The Gospels picture only a single redemptive event at the return of Christ with resurrection (Luke 20:34–36) and judgment (Matt. 25:31–46). Revelation pictures a more detailed consummation. At the return of Christ (Rev. 19), Satan is bound and shut up in a bottomless pit, the first resurrection occurs, and the resurrected saints share Christ's rule for a thousand years (Rev. 20:1–5). In this millennial reign of Christ and his saints is found the fulfillment of such sayings as Rev. 5:10; I Cor. 6:2; Matt. 19:28; Luke 22:30. Only at the end of the millennium is Satan cast into the lake of fire (Rev. 20:10) and death finally destroyed (Rev. 20:14).

One interpretation understands this language realistically and looks for two future stages in the accomplishment of God's purpose, one at the beginning and one at the end of the millennium. This view is called premillennialism because it expects a millennial reign of Christ after his second coming. It explains the Gospel expectation in terms of progressive revelation. Dan. 2 does not foresee the church age; the Gospels do not foresee the millennial age; only Revelation gives the full outline of the consummation.

Others insist that there is only one stage of consummation and that the coming of Christ will inaugurate the age to come. The binding of Satan is the same as that in Matt. 12:29; the "first" resurrection is not bodily but spiritual (John 5:25; Rom. 6:5); and the reign of Christ and his saints is a present spiritual reality (Rev. 3:21; Heb. 1:3; Eph. 2:5–6). This interpretation is called amillennial because it does not expect a millennial reign after Christ's return. The thousand years is a symbolic number for the entire period of Christ's present reign through the church.

It is often overlooked that in both of these interpretations the final goal is the same—the consummation of God's kingdom in the age to come. The debate is about the steps by which God will accomplish his redemptive purpose and not about the character of God's redemptive purpose.

A Present Realm. Because the dynamic power of God's reign has invaded this evil age it has created a present spiritual realm in which the blessings of God's reign are experienced. The redeemed have already been delivered from the power of darkness and brought into the kingdom of Christ (Col. 1:13). Jesus said that since the days of John the Baptist the kingdom of God has been preached and men enter it with violent determination (Luke 16:16). The one who is least in the new order of the kingdom is called greater than the greatest of the preceding order (Matt. 11:11) because he enjoys kingdom blessings which John never knew. Other sayings about entering a present realm of blessing are found in Matt. 21:31; 23:13.

The present and future aspects of the kingdom are inseparably tied together in Mark 10:15.

The kingdom has come among men and its blessings have been extended in the person of Jesus. Those who now receive this offer of the kingdom with complete childlike trust will enter into the future eschatological kingdom of life.

The Kingdom and the Church. The kingdom is not the church. The apostles went about preaching the kingdom of God (Acts 8:12; 19:8; 28:23); it is impossible to substitute "church" for "kingdom" in such passages. However, there is an inseparable relationship. The church is the fellowship of men who have accepted his offer of the kingdom, submitted to its rule, and entered into its blessings. The kingdom was offered to Israel (Matt. 10:5–6), who because of their previous covenantal relationship to God were "sons of the kingdom" (Matt. 8:12)—its natural heirs. However, the offer of the kingdom in Christ was made on an individual basis in terms of personal acceptance (Mark 3:31–35; Matt. 10:35–37) rather than in terms of the family or nation. Because Israel rejected the kingdom, it was taken away and given to a different people (Matt. 21:43), the church.

Thus we may say that the kingdom of God creates the church. The redemptive rule of God brings into being a new people who receive the blessings of the divine reign. Furthermore it was the activity of the divine rule which brought judgment upon Israel. Individually the kingdom means either salvation or judgment (Matt. 3:11); historically the activity of the kingdom of God effected the creation of the church and the destruction of Israel (Matt. 23:37–38). This is probably the meaning of Mark 9:1. Within the lifetime of the disciples the kingdom of God would be seen manifesting its power in bringing a historical judgment upon Jerusalem and in creating the new people, the church. Paul announced the rejection of Israel and the salvation of the Gentiles (I Thess. 2:16; Acts 28:26–28). However, the rejection of Israel is not permanent. After God has visited the Gentiles, he will regraft Israel into the people of God, and "so all Israel will be saved" (Rom. 11:24–26), receive the kingdom of God, and enter into its blessings (see Matt. 23:39; Acts 3:19–20).

The kingdom also works through the church. The disciples preached the kingdom of God and performed signs of the kingdom (Matt. 10:7–8; Luke 10:9, 17). The powers of the kingdom were operative in and through them. Jesus said that he would give to the church the keys of the kingdom of heaven with power to bind and loose (Matt. 16:18–19). The meaning of the keys is illustrated in Luke 11:52. The scribes had taken away the key of knowledge, i.e., the correct interpretation of the OT. The key of understanding the divine purpose had been entrusted to Israel; but the scribes had so misinterpreted the oracles of God delivered to them (Rom. 3:2) that when Messiah came with a new revelation of God's kingdom, they neither entered themselves nor allowed others to enter. These keys, along with the kingdom blessings, are to be given to the new people who, as they preach the good news of the kingdom, will be the means of binding or loosing men from their sins. In fact, the disciples had already used these keys and exercised this authority, bringing men the gift of peace or pronouncing the divine judgment (Matt. 10:13–15). The kingdom is God's deed. It has come into the world in Christ; it works in the world through the church. When the church has proclaimed the gospel of the kingdom in all the world as witness to all nations, Christ will return (Matt. 24:14) and bring the kingdom in glory.

G. E. LADD

See also CHURCH, THE.

Bibliography. G. Dalman, *The Words of Jesus;* G. Vos, *The Teaching of Jesus Concerning the Kingdom of God and the Church;* W. G. Kümmel, *Promise and Fulfillment;* R. H. Fuller, *The Mission and Achievement of Jesus;* A. M. Hunter, *Introducing New Testament Theology;* K. L. Schmidt *et al., TDNT,* I, 564ff.; B. Klappert, *NIDNTT,* II, 373ff.; A. Robertson, *Regnum Dei;* R. Otto, *The Kingdom of God and the Son of Man;* H. Ridderbos, *The Coming of the Kingdom;* G. Lundström, *The Kingdom of God in the Teaching of Jesus;* G. E. Ladd, *Crucial Questions About the Kingdom of God* and *Jesus and the Kingdom;* R. Hiers, *The Kingdom of God in the Synoptic Tradition.*

Kingsley, Charles (1819–1875). Anglican writer and social reformer. Graduate of Cambridge, he was ordained and from 1844 held a living in Hampshire. He was also chaplain to Queen Victoria (1859); professor of modern history at Cambridge (1860–69), a post for which he was dubiously competent but which made few demands on his time; and canon of Westminster (1873). Influenced by Thomas Carlyle and F. D. Maurice, he was a founding member of the Christian Socialist movement in England, which views are reflected in many of his popular novels, notably *Alton Locke* (1850), which highlighted appalling industrial conditions. He called on the church to take vigorous social action and resented the description "muscular Christianity" that came to be applied to his teachings. Kingsley supported Darwin's theories and sought to reconcile Christianity and science, not least in his best-selling children's book, *The Water Babies* (1863). This led to a notorious dispute with J. H. Newman, the target of one of Kingsley's less felicitous utterances: "Truth, for its own sake, had never been a virtue with the Roman clergy." Out of the controversy came Newman's *Apologia pro Vita Sua* (1864), in which Newman outlined his religious development. Kingsley disliked asceticism of all kinds, and greatly disliked the Oxford Movement with its High Church sympathies. He was of the Broad Church party, but became more theologically conservative in later life. He worked selflessly on behalf of the working classes at a time when such crusades were unpopular among his contemporaries. "The age of chivalry is never past," he declared, "so long as there is a wrong left unredressed on earth." J. D. DOUGLAS

See also SOCIALISM, CHRISTIAN.

Bibliography. U. P. Hennessy, *Canon Charles Kingsley.*

Kneel, Kneeling. The various Hebrew and Greek words and phrases which express the idea of kneeling usually pertain to acts of worship, pronouncements of blessing, prayer, and homage to superiors. Kneeling is also the posture of giving birth (I Sam. 4:19) and even dying (Acts 7:60).

In the NT the Greek *gonypetein,* "to kneel," and *gony,* "knee," in the phrase "bow the knee" are the most common words used, but the close equivalent, *proskynein,* "to worship," can mean kneel in worship as well as complete prostration. For example, the soldiers knelt before Christ in mock homage (Mark 15:19), the apostle Paul bowed his knees before the Father in prayer (Eph. 3:14), and Cornelius worshiped Peter by falling at Peter's feet, apparently upon his knees (Acts 10:25). References to bowing the knees are rare among the Greeks and Romans in extrabiblical literature, but the word *proskynein* is used frequently to denote such posture.

The Hebrew *kāra',* "to bow down," is often connected with *berek,* "knee," in the OT, as in Isa. 45:23, "every knee shall bow." The Hebrew derivative, *bārak,* means "to bless" and implies that the one blessed kneels (I Sam. 23:21), except when God is blessed by men (I Chr. 16:36).

In both the OT and NT there are frequent references to kneeling in adoration and petition. Typical is the psalmist's exhortation, "Come, let us bow down in worship, let us kneel before the Lord our Maker, for he is our God" (Ps. 95:6-7). Solomon is pictured kneeling, as is Daniel: "Three times a day he got down on his knees and prayed" (Dan. 6:10). The Lord Jesus also "knelt down and prayed" (Luke 22:41), as did the apostles and followers: "On the beach we knelt to pray" (Acts 21:5). Stephen (Acts 7:60), Peter (Acts 9:40), and Paul (Acts 20:36) are pictured as kneeling. In the Gospels petitioners kneel before Jesus, as did the man who sought his son's healing (Matt. 17:14), the rich ruler (Mark 10:17), and the man with leprosy (Mark 1:40).

By Irenaeus's time the church worshiped while standing, prostrated, bowing, and kneeling. In standing the worshipers united with Christ and his resurrection. Other positions symbolized repentance, submission, and petition. Sitting during worship was unknown, though it was common in teaching sessions. The Apostolic Constitutions command prayer while standing thrice on the Lord's day honoring the risen Christ. In Chrysostom's time the deacon admonished, "Let us stand with reverence and decency." The Eucharist was first received by communicants while standing, and not until later was kneeling introduced. The Reformers received Holy Communion while sitting, since to kneel meant adoration to the host. The Anglican prayer book specified frequent kneeling during the service, to which the Puritans objected. Theodoret recounts that ordination candidates were "forced" to kneel, thus demonstrating their sense of unworthiness and the awesome nature of the office being accepted.

The Scripture and history show that the position of the body in worship is significant, though the perceptions of the meaning of those positions may vary. What is important is that one express true worship in terms of the current conception of that which expresses adoration, humility, and yieldedness.

In Scripture kneeling is a significant eschatological concept, summing up the goal of history—that Jesus will be acknowledged as Lord when "every knee bows" in worship to him (Phil. 2:10).

W. H. BAKER AND W. N. KERR

Bibliography. B. S. Easton, *ISBE,* III, 1815; S. Mowinckel, *The Psalms in Israel's Worship,* II, 44-52; A. Murtonen, "The Use and Meaning of the Words *lebarek* and *berakah* in the OT," *VT* 9:158-77; J. N. Oswalt, *TWOT,* I, 132-33; J. Scharbert, *TDOT,* II, 279-308; H. Schlier, *TDNT,* I, 738-40; H. Schonweiss, *NIDNTT,* II, 859-60; W. S. Towner, "'Blessed be Yahweh' and 'Blessed Art Thou, Yahweh'—The Modulation of a Biblical Formula," *CBQ* 30:386-99.

Knowledge. The problems of knowledge that are raised by the biblical revelation are chiefly two: first, what is the nature of God's knowledge, and, second, what is man's knowledge, particularly man's knowledge of God?

Perhaps the fullest summary of the biblical material on God's knowledge is found in Stephen Charnock's *Discourses upon the Existence and Attributes of God.*

The main point in considering God's knowledge is his omniscience: "His understanding is infinite" (Ps. 147:5). The items of God's knowledge are made in Scripture in great profusion: events past, "God remembered Rachel" (Gen. 30:22), and "a book of remembrance was written before him" (Mal. 3:16); events present, "Doth he not see all my ways and count all my steps" (Job 30:4); events future, "In that day there shall be a fountain opened" (Zech. 13:1), and "He shall reign over the house of Jacob forever" (Luke 1:33); and, as well, hypothetical events contrary to fact, "The Lord said, they will deliver thee up" to Saul if David stayed in Keilah (I Sam. 23:12).

Not so explicit but more important, God knows himself. When the apostle says, "The Spirit searches the deep things of God" (I Cor. 2:11), the word "search," as is also the case in Rev. 2:23, "I am he which searcheth the reins and heart" (cf. I Chr. 28:9; Rom. 8:27), does not imply that God had been ignorant previous to this search. In these cases "search" means to know exactly and completely. Furthermore, that God knows himself may be deduced from his omnipotence, his blessedness, and perfection, all of which are expressed in sundry passages and divers manners.

The idea of omnipotence, perfection, and blessedness requires God to know all things always. His knowledge is eternal. Such an immediate and uninterrupted knowledge has frequently been designated as *intuitive.* God sees all things at a glance, as it were. He does not learn. He was never ignorant, and he can never come to know more.

This intuitive knowledge is distinguished from both the reasoning and the empirical learning of man. A high school student learns the axioms of geometry and painfully deduces the hitherto unknown theorem that triangles contain 180 degrees. God does not reason in this fashion. This is not to say that God is ignorant of the logical relation between axioms and theorems. God's mind, i.e., God himself, is perfectly logical. But he does not reason in the sense of taking time to pass from one idea to another. That is to say, there is no succession of ideas in God's mind. He does not first know one item and then come to know another of which he was previously ignorant. All ideas are always in his mind.

But though there is no succession of ideas in God's mind, it does not follow that there is no idea of succession. The logical succession of conclusion upon premise is a part of omniscience. Similarly the idea of succession in time is known to God. God knows that one event follows another in time. Christ came after David, and David after Moses. But God's ideas do not follow one another in time, for Christ was slain before the foundation of the world. Therefore God did not learn that Christ was crucified or that David came after Moses by waiting for history to show it to him. God does not depend upon experience. His knowledge is entirely *a priori.* Otherwise prophecy would be impossible.

Charnock says, "As nothing that he wills is the cause of his will, so nothing that he knows is the cause of his knowledge; he did not make things to know them, but he knows them to make them. . . . If his knowledge did depend upon the things, then the existence of things did precede God's knowledge of them: to say that they are the cause of God's knowledge is to say that God was not the cause of their being."

Because of God's intuitive omniscience, as well as by reason of his omnipotence and omnipresence, God is incomprehensible. This idea, however, turns the subject from God's knowledge of himself to man's knowledge of God. Of course God comprehends himself. In this respect God is not merely comprehensible but is actually known, understood, and comprehended. But God is incomprehensible to man.

Unfortunately, the term "incomprehensible" carries undesirable connotations. The word sometimes means irrational, unintelligible, or unknowable. Now, obviously if man could know or understand nothing about God, Christianity would be impossible. It is absolutely essential to maintain that the human mind is capable of grasping truth. Incomprehensible therefore must be taken to mean that man cannot know everything about God. It is necessary to assert that man can know some truths about God without knowing everything that God knows.

In reaction against the optimistic modernism of the nineteenth century, contemporary neo-orthodoxy has insisted on the transcendence of God. But it has distorted the biblical concept of transcendence to the degree of making God completely unknowable. Some of its phraseology may be repeated as examples. God has been called the Wholly Other. Brunner writes, "God can, when he wants to, speak his word even through false doctrine." Another author denies that a proposition can have the same meaning for man as it does for God. Several theologians collaborated to say that "we dare not maintain that his [God's] knowledge and our knowledge coincide at any single point."

Now, it seems obvious that if a man knows any truth at all, he must know a truth that God knows, for God knows all truths. A sentence must mean to a man who knows its meaning precisely what it means to God; for if the man does not know God's meaning, he does not know the meaning of the sentence. Hence, if man is to know anything, it cannot be denied that there are points of coincidence between human and divine knowledge. Similarly God cannot be Wholly Other, for this would deny that man was created in the image of God.

Neo-orthodox theologians try to substitute a personal encounter with God for conceptual knowledge of him. Thought, they say, cannot grasp God, or indeed any persons. Persons are *met,* not thought. But in human relations wordless encounters do not produce friendship. There must be knowledge of character, and this comes mainly through intelligible conversation. Similarly, if God does not give us information about himself, information that is rationally understood, a personal encounter would leave our minds a religious blank.

The intricacies of theology and philosophy are very difficult. Epistemology is terrifyingly technical. Whether we learn by logic alone as Descartes and Spinoza taught; or whether we learn by experience alone as Berkeley and Hume taught; or whether we need Kant's *a priori* categories; or whether we can receive truth only by revelation—all these are subjects of interesting scholarly discussion. But however it may be, the Bible does not countenance skepticism. It is not anti-intellectual; it does not treat doctrine as unimportant, false, or "incomprehensible." Rather it places considerable emphasis on truth and understanding.

"Grace and truth came through Jesus Christ. ... And ye shall know the truth.... I tell you the truth.... Sanctify them through thy truth; thy word is truth" (John 1:17; 8:32; 16:7; 17:17; cf. 5:53; 8:45; 16:13). In the face of these utterances it is difficult to understand how anyone can seriously say that we can be sanctified through false doctrine.

Or, again, "We *know* that the Son of God is come and hath given us an *understanding,* that we might *know* him that is *true*" (I John 5:20. Cf. I Kings 17:24; Pss. 25:5; 43:3; 86:11; 119:43, 142, 147; Rom. 1:18; 3:7; II Cor. 6:7; 7:14; 11:10; Gal. 2:5, 14; Eph. 1:13, etc.).

These verses indicate that we can grasp God's meaning, that the truth can be known, and that God can be known. Christianity is the religion of a Book; it is a message of good news; it is a revelation or communication of truth from God to man. Only if the propositions of the Bible are rationally comprehensible, only if man's intellect can understand what God says, only if God's mind and man's mind have some content in common, only so can Christianity be true and only so can Christ mean something to us.

G. H. Clark

See also Epistemology; Truth; Revelation, General; Revelation, Special.

Bibliography. J. Maritain, *The Degrees of Knowledge;* J. O. Buswell, *A Christian View of Being and Knowing;* G. H. Clark, *A Christian View of Men and Things;* J. Orr, *A Christian View of God and the World;* H. Bavinck, *The Philosophy of Revelation;* N. Gillman, *Gabriel Marcel on Religious Knowledge;* B. J. F. Lonergan, *Insight: A Study of Human Understanding.*

Knowledge, Gift of. *See* Spiritual Gifts.

Knox, John (1514?–1572). Scottish Reformer, who pursued a vigorous and prolonged career of preaching and writing on behalf of Protestantism. After a short term of preaching at St. Andrews Castle and nineteen months of captivity as a galley slave of the French, Knox became pastor of an English congregation (1549–54). He then fled to the continent where, in Geneva from 1555 to 1559, he came under the effective influence of Swiss Reformed leaders, particularly John Calvin. Knox returned to Scotland in 1559, preaching at St. Giles Church in Edinburgh and working tirelessly for the establishment of a Reformed Church. At times he was in direct conflict with Mary, Queen of Scots. After Mary's abdication in 1567 Knox preached at the coronation of her son, James VI.

Knox saw his calling as primarily a preacher, not an academic theologian. His favorite characterization of his work was "to blaw his maisteris trumpet." Nevertheless, his literary output was prodigious, filling six volumes.

Knox's theology was Protestant. The principle which dictated the content of his thinking is that of *sola Scriptura,* that the Bible is the only authoritative basis upon which doctrine can be founded. Having been influenced by Luther's writing and by George Wishart, Knox early affirmed *sola fide,* justification by faith only. His theology was profoundly Calvinistic at its core. At the behest of Calvin in 1559, Knox wrote his only academic theological work, the *Treatise on Predestination,* of some 170,000 words. In it he follows closely the formulations of Calvin and Theodore Beza, teaching God's sovereign election of some to salvation, his choice of others to damnation, and affirming that man's salvation is by grace alone. In 1560 Knox coauthored the Scots Confession, a document which served as the confessional basis of the Scottish Church until the drafting of its heir, the Westminster Confession of Faith (1647). The Scots Confession is notable for the centrality of the work of Christ in each of its various topics, as well as for a richness of spirituality and warmth of expression.

In the same year Knox helped draft the First Book of Discipline, in which the authors formulated a plan for the ecclesiastical and social life of the nation. In a time when the people were moving from one kind of church to a completely different kind, Knox found it necessary to provide them with biblical criteria by which to judge a truly Christian church. The marks of a true church according to the *Book of Discipline* were the proper preaching of God's Word, the proper administration of baptism and the Lord's Supper, and the proper exercise of discipline.

The *Book of Discipline* also provided directions for worship. Knox's commitment to *sola Scriptura* is found clearly in his theology of worship. Exposition of Scripture and preaching are the center of true worship, according to the Reformer. Under the influence of Ulrich Zwingli and John Hooper, Knox taught that no practice is legitimate in public worship unless it is specifically commanded in Scripture (the so-called regulative principle). While in England in 1551 Knox brought this principle to bear on the *Book of Common Prayer,* by convincing Thomas Cranmer to state explicitly that kneeling during the reception of the Lord's Supper did not imply adoration of the bread and wine (the so-called black rubric). Knox's view of the Lord's Supper was similar to that of Calvin and Bucer: the presence of Christ is spiritual and received only by faith. Under the *First Book of Discipline* government of the church was not strictly presbyterian, but the presbyterian idea was present in seed form.

The Scottish Reformer's most distinctive contribution to Reformation theology was his concept of the relation of church and state. He tended to view the church and the state as comprising the same community. Not recognizing the NT view of the church as the fulfillment of the Israelite theocracy, Knox looked to the OT theocracy for a model of good civil government. In the Reformation period the religion of the prince was the religion of the people. Knox therefore constantly had to battle the Roman Catholic queens who persecuted the Protestants. Knox found a precedent in ancient Israel for the right of God's people to disobey civil authority when it contradicted the higher law of Scripture (*An Admonition or Warning,* 1554). He eventually taught that Christians are obliged to overthrow an idolatrous (i.e., Roman Catholic) monarch as the Israelites overthrew idolatrous kings. This idea he propounded in *The First Blast of the Trumpet Against the Monstrous Regiment of Women* (1558). Knox's affirmation of the state establishment of religion was incompatible with his affirmation of the right of the individual to be guided by Scripture alone. Nevertheless, his teaching gave impetus to the growth of religious freedom.

Although Knox opposed any extensive involvement of the church in affairs of government, he had a clear social vision. He stated the obligation of every Christian to care for the poor, and he devised a system by which each church would provide for its own needy and administer catechetical schools for all children, rich and poor. However, Knox was not a social revolutionary, nor would he have favored democracy as such.

John Knox can be seen as a forebear of Puritanism in his view of worship and the "regulative principle." His doctrine of the right of dissent from tyrannical government provided the lines for a doctrine of church and state that was developed by later Presbyterians and French Huguenots. The sense of man's utter dependence upon the grace of God which informed Knox's thought and life has been the heart of the life of the Reformed family of churches throughout its history.

H. Griffith

See also Scots Confession.

Bibliography. P. H. Brown, *John Knox,* 2 vols.; R. L. Greaves, *Theology and Revolution in the Scottish Reformation;* J. Knox, *History of the Reformation in Scotland,* ed. W. C. Dickinson, 2 vols., and *Works,* ed. D. Laing, 6 vols.; J. S. McEwen, *The Faith of John Knox;* W. S. Reid, *Trumpeter of God: A Biography of John Knox;* H. Watt, *John Knox in Controversy.*

Koinonia. *See* Fellowship.

Küng, Hans (1928–). Contemporary Roman Catholic theologian. Born in Switzerland, Küng received a varied education at the German College in Rome, the Gregorian University, and the Sorbonne, with additional study in Berlin, London, Amsterdam, and Madrid. Ordained in 1955, he first served as a parish priest; upon achieving prominence with his theological writing, he was appointed professor of theology on the Roman Catholic faculty at Tübingen in 1960. A progressive thinker with a gift of popularization, he helped to promote many of the reforms at the Second Vatican Council, being prepared to go much further, as his *Council, Reform and Reunion* (1961) testifies. In *Justification* (1964) he even advanced the startling thesis that the Calvinist and Catholic views of justification are substantially the same, the Council of Trent's teaching being an extreme which is defensible only as a necessary answer to the opposite extreme of Luther. This did not, he thought, compromise Trent's irreformability, since its presentation remained true in context even if it needed to be supplemented to achieve the total picture. Küng's concern for reunion led him to apply the same technique of supplementation to another debatable issue in *Apostolic Succession* (1968), a symposium in which he argued for a succession not only of apostles but also of prophets and teachers and all charismatic functions. Reservations about the papacy as a true pastorate, along with the publication of *Humanae Vitae* (on birth control), launched him into a fuller investigation of authority in *Infallible?* (1972), in which he claimed that historical relativity rules out infallibility and that the papal claim is more a political tool than a true doctrinal reality. The threat thus posed to a basic Roman Catholic principle could not pass unnoticed. An inquiry began which led to Küng's admonishment in 1975 and finally, when he refused to recant, to his deposition, not from the Tübingen faculty, but from his official status as a Roman Catholic teacher. If, however, Küng seemed to have been moving to a reformation position on justification and the Petrine office, he was going beyond it to liberal Protestantism with his denial of infallibility to holy Scripture as well, which on his view offers us only the normative language of faith. The implications of this denial came out plainly in his apologetic work *On Being a Christian* (1971), in which, while stressing Christ's centrality, he called many NT stories uncertain, contradictory, and legendary, rejected Chalcedonian Christology, weakened God's transcendence in favor of humanization, and seemed to present Christ more as an example to follow than a divine Savior in whom to trust. The work *Does God Exist?* (1980), though containing much of interest and value, continued on the same course of apologetics by concession. Not surprisingly, then, a more conservative Vatican refused in 1982 to accede to Küng's request for an audience until he withdrew the extreme opinions which according to *The Küng Dialogue* (1980) constituted the grounds for his loss of authorization as an official teacher of doctrine. G. W. Bromiley

Bibliography. L. Swidler, ed., *Küng in Conflict* and *Consensus in Theology;* C. M. LaCugna, *The Theological Methodology of Hans Küng;* P. Hebblethwaite, *The New Inquisition?* R. Nowell, *Hans Küng and His Theology.*

Kuyper, Abraham (1837–1920). Dutch theologian and statesman. Born in Maassluis, Kuyper was the son of a Reformed Church minister. At the University of Leiden he was a brilliant student who embraced liberalism and the latest theological views. During his first pastorate, in Beesd, he experienced an evangelical conversion. Influenced by the piety of his parishioners, he began anew his study of theology, drawing inspiration from the Dutch Calvinist tradition.

Following the death of Groen van Prinsterer in 1876 Kuyper became the leader of the small but growing Calvinist movement in both church and state. He wrote many books and hundreds of articles on theology, philosophy, politics, art, and social issues in which he sought to express a Christian world and life view.

Kuyper founded two newspapers, the daily political paper *De Standaard* and the weekly religious paper *De Heraut.* In 1874 he entered parliament as a representative of the newly formed Anti-Revolutionary Party. This was the first modern political party in the Netherlands. In 1878 he published *Ons Program,* the party's political manifesto, and in 1880 he founded the Free University of Amsterdam. Active in church politics, Kuyper led a secession movement from the state church in 1886 to form the independent Gereformeerde Kerk (Reformed Church).

In 1900 Kuyper's Anti-Revolutionary Party was elected to office and he became prime minister. He broke the crippling railway strike of 1902 but after a bitter election campaign in 1905 lost power. From 1908 he sat as a delegate in the Second Chamber of the Dutch Parliament and continued to exercise a political influence as editor of *De Standaard* until shortly before his death.

Kuyper is best remembered for his development of the theological doctrine of common grace and his views about the importance of the kingdom of God in Christian thinking, which were influenced by the work of F. D. Maurice. His social and political theory of sphere sovereignty is an attempt to give an intellectual justification to pluralism and create structural means of limiting the power of the state. Kuyper was keenly aware of the dangers of totalitarianism. He was a strong lover of liberty who recognized that business interests as well as government can oppress the weak; therefore he saw the function of the state as that of preserving God's justice in society. I. Hexham

See also Maurice, John Frederick Denison; Van Prinsterer, Guillaume Groen.

Bibliography. A. Kuyper, *Lectures on Calvinism, Principles of Sacred Theology, The Work of the Holy Spirit,* and *Christianity and the Class Struggle;* P. Kasteel, *Abraham Kuyper;* F. Vandenberg, *Abraham Kuyper.*

Ll

Labor. *See* WORK.

Lactantius (*ca.* 240–*ca.* 320). When the Emperor Diocletian established his capital at Nicomedia, he invited Lucius Caelius Firmianus Lactantius, probably from North Africa, to teach rhetoric there. Lactantius was converted to Christianity and lost his position. Later the Emperor Constantine chose him as tutor for his son Crispus, an act which brought him to Gaul about 313.

Lactantius used history, philosophy, and especially his own literary training to defend Christianity. *On the Manner in Which the Persecutors Died* describes the horrible deaths of enemies of the church. *On the Anger of God* deals with God's punishment of crime. *On the Workmanship of God* presents the marvels of the human body as a proof of the wisdom and goodness of God. His principal work is *The Divine Institutes,* of which he also prepared an epitome. Its first three books are a refutation of paganism, giving a systematic presentation of the themes of early Christian apologetics. Books 4 through 7 set forth a philosophy of religion emphasizing the true worship of the one God, justice, moral conduct, and the immortality of the soul. This work shows what aspects of Christian teaching appealed to the ruling circles around Constantine, to whom the work is addressed.

Christianity, according to Lactantius, combines true religion and true wisdom, the two things for which the nature of man is desirous. He gives abundant citation of pagan testimonies (especially from Latin literature) in support of Christian teaching. Lactantius followed Plato on the nature of the soul and body but combined this view with chiliasm. Although presenting a strong case for a Christian version of natural religion, he was weak on distinctively Christian doctrines, his views on the Trinity in particular being deficient. Lactantius has been called the "Christian Cicero," both for the excellence of his style and for the quantity of quotation and of ideas taken from Cicero. E. FERGUSON

Bibliography. R. Pichon, *Lactance;* P. Labriolle, *History and Literature of Christianity;* J. Stevenson, "The Life and Literary Activity of Lactantius," *Studia Patristica,* I, 661–77; R. M. Ogilvie, *The Library of Lactantius;* J. Fontaine and P. Perrin, eds., *Lactance et son temps.*

Laity. From *laos* ("people"), the laity ought strictly to denote whole people of God. Historically, however, it has come to be used of those who are not specifically ordained to the ministry (clergy). The distinction is particularly marked in the Roman Catholic and Eastern Orthodox Churches, with a strong emphasis on the fact that the duty of the laity is to be taught, to obey, and to make financial contribution. The discontent of the laity has found expression in the various church-state conflicts and in a deep-seated spirit of anticlericalism in many countries. Protestant churches find the term a convenient one when it is desired to distinguish between ministers and nonministers, but it seems to have no material validity in view of the fact that all Christians are priests and all constitute the real people of God. Hence it is perhaps better avoided in its traditional sense. G. W. BROMILEY

See also CLERGY.

Lake of Fire. The phrase occurs six times in Revelation and nowhere else in the NT or in Jewish literature. It is the place of eternal punishment for the wicked. The beast and false prophet are thrown alive into it before the millennial reign (19:20). After the final battle they are joined by Satan (20:10), and after the final judgment Death and Hades are also cast in (20:14; cf. Isa. 25:8; I Cor. 15:26) as well as those whose names are not in the book of life (20:15) and evil men (21:8; the author here is probably speaking of apostate believers).

Although "lake of fire" does not occur elsewhere, "fire" was commonly associated with punishment and destruction, often in connection with the final judgment. It is especially common in Revelation.

Three of the six occurrences of "lake of fire" speak of fire and sulphur (19:20; 20:10; 21:8; the AV translates "sulphur" as "brimstone"). This combination is common in the OT and NT (e.g., Gen. 19:24; Ps. 11:6; Ezek. 38:22; Luke 17:29; Rev. 9:17–18; 14:10). The imagery of a lake, fire, and sulphur within the context of punishment and destruction may have originated from the story in Gen. 19:24.

Rev. 20:14 and 21:8 equate the lake of fire with the second death (cf. Rev. 2:11; 20:6), a rabbinic term for the death of the wicked in the next world. After physical death (i.e., the first death) the soul resides temporarily in Hades and goes through the final judgment. The wicked are then condemned to the lake of fire (i.e., the second death) in eternal, conscious punishment (cf. Rev. 20:10; 14:11). There is no concept of annihilation in Revelation. John's lake of fire is also equivalent to the Synoptics' gehenna.

The conflict between Satan and man which began in the garden will most assuredly end with God's total victory. Satan and his followers have traded the new creation for the lake of fire.

W. D. Mounce

See also Gehenna; Hell; Death, The Second; Judgment; Eternal Punishment.

Bibliography. R. H. Mounce, *The Book of Revelation;* G. E. Ladd, *The Revelation of John;* G. Vos, *ISBE,* III, 1822.

Lamb of God. Twice in the NT Jesus is called the Lamb of God, and on each occasion by John the Baptist (John 1:29, 35). The word *amnos* (lamb) is found also in Acts 8:32; I Pet. 1:19; and in the LXX version of Isa. 53:7. This last reference suggests Isa. 53 as the immediate context for John's declaration concerning Christ, the Messiah, as the Lamb of God who takes away the sin of the world. The Baptist's quotation from Isa. 40 on the previous day shows that such Isaianic passages were on his mind. Before their polemic against Christians, which drove Jewish commentators to seek another explanation, the lamb of Isa. 53 was identified with the Messiah as the servant of God. This identity of Jesus as Messiah with the Lamb of God was sure for the Baptist (John 1:20, 23, 29).

The use of the genitive of possession—the lamb *of God*—specifically relates Christ to God in the act of sin-bearing. He is at once the sacrificial victim presented to God and the victim provided by God. In this relationship he bears the world's sin, removes it by taking it on himself. As in Isa. 53 he bears "on himself alone the iniquity of us all," by being "led as a lamb to the slaughter, as a sheep before her shearers is dumb."

Some scholars prefer to see the paschal lamb of Exod. 12 as the background for the Baptist's word on the score that it holds no expiatory overtones, while others reject the reference on precisely the same grounds. However, it is not evident that the paschal sacrifice is without an expiatory character in view of the declaration of Exod. 12:13: "The blood shall be to you a token... and when I see the blood I will pass over you." The paschal sacrifice is basic to the whole sacrificial system. There is, therefore, good reason to allow the paschal allusion, since when the Baptist spoke, the Passover was not far off (John 2:12–13), and our Lord was afterward identified therewith (John 19:36, cf. I Cor. 5:7). The two figures, that of Isa. 53:7 and that of Exod. 12, consequently coalesce in the designation. They are not contradictory but complementary. "All the utterances of the NT regarding the Lamb of God are derived from this prophecy (Isa. 53:7), in which the dumb type of the Passover now finds a tongue" (A. F. Delitzsch). All the ideas surrounding the figure of the lamb built up through the progressive revelation of the OT may indeed go into the concept as it occurs in the NT. In Genesis there is the necessity of the lamb—Abel brought the firstlings of his flock (cf. Heb. 9:22); in Exodus, the efficacy of the lamb—the blood-sprinkled door posts (cf. Rev. 7:14; I Pet. 1:12); in Leviticus, the purity of the lamb—without blemish (cf. I Pet. 1:19); in Isaiah, the personality of the lamb—"he," the lamb, as the servant of the Lord (John 1:29; Rev. 5:12–13). Nowhere, therefore, does the figure merely suggest "the meekness and gentleness of Christ" (II Cor. 10:1); it always carries with it a sacrificial sense (cf. Rev. 5:6, 12; 13:8).

In the book of Revelation the unqualified designation lamb (*arnion*) occurs eight times in symbolic reference to Christ and unites the two ideas of redemption and kingship. On one side are such statements as a Lamb which has been slain (5:6, 12); those "who have washed their robes and made them white in the blood of the Lamb" (7:14); "they overcame him by the blood of the Lamb, and by the word of their testimony" (12:11); "they which are written in the Lamb's book of life" (21:27). The stress here falls upon the redeeming work of Christ as the Lamb of God. On the other side, connected with the title is the idea of sovereignty. It is the Lamb that was slain that has power to take the book and loose its seals (5:6–7); there is reference to the wrath of the Lamb (6:16); and the Lamb is seen in the midst of the throne (7:17); the throne in heaven is the throne of God and the Lamb (22:1, 3); the wicked make war against the Lamb but the Lamb is victorious (17:14). In the general term "lamb," then, two ideas unite: victorious power and vicarious suffering. At the heart of God's sovereignty there is sacrificial love.

H. D. McDonald

Bibliography. C. H. Dodd, *The Interpretation of the Fourth Gospel;* L. Morris, *The Apostolic Preaching of the Cross.*

Landmarkism. A term representing a number of convictions maintained by some Baptists, mostly in the southern United States, concerning the nature of the church. With other Baptists, the adherents of Landmarkism are firmly congregational, believing that ecclesiastical authority is limited to the local assembly. More distinctively, they hold that the NT model for the church is only the local and visible congregation and that it violates NT principles to speak of a universal, spiritual church. Landmark Baptists also believe that Communion should be restricted to members of the local assembly and that baptism is valid only when administered in a properly constituted local Baptist congregation. They further believe that a historic "Baptist succession" may be traced from John the Baptist to modern Baptist churches in which believer's baptism and Landmark principles have prevailed. With this belief they also feel that the Roman Catholic Church and the denominations arising from the Reformation are not true churches according to NT standards.

The Landmark emphasis was propounded by James R. Graves (1820–93), influential editor of the *Tennessee Baptist,* and takes its name from a pamphlet by James M. Pendleton, *An Old Landmark Re-Set* (1856), based on Prov. 22:28: "Remove not the old landmark." It is the position of the million-member American Baptist Association, of the much smaller United Baptists, and of some independent Baptist churches.

M. A. Noll

See also Baptist Tradition, The.

Bibliography. J. R. Graves, *Old Landmarkism, What Is It?* A. C. Piepkorn, *Profiles in Belief,* II.

Last Adam, The. *See* Adam, The Last.

Last Day, Days. OT prophets often predict that "in that day" (e.g., Amos 8:9–11; 9:9–12) the Lord will act in a mighty way to judge evil and redeem his people. Usually the order is judgment followed by redemption, which we may designate F^1 (Future[1]) and F^2 (Future[2]) respectively. In prophetic poetry the two themes are repeated and interwoven as highly charged eschatological warnings and promises that often refer to historical events just past or soon to come, as well as to the long-range messianic age. The essential meaning of judgment/redemption is common to both, where the first is analogous to the second, while the significance of the essential meaning is applied in each case to the appropriate age. Several OT examples are Isa. 2:2–21; 3:18–4:6; 10:20–23; Hos. 1–2; Joel 1–3. The latter prophecy is especially instructive because it typically speaks of the dire judgment to come ("For the day of the Lord is great and very terrible; who can endure it?" Joel 2:11*c,* F^1), then prophesies of the blessings to follow ("For behold, in those days and at that time, when I restore the fortunes of Judah and Jerusalem, I will gather all nations," 3:1–2, F^2).

The NT continues the OT theme of judgment/redemption and announces the inauguration of the final eschatological day or time. Jesus proclaims that "the time is fulfilled" and parallels that announcement with the news that "the kingdom of God is at hand," in light of which he calls for repentance and belief in the good news (Mark 1:15). At Nazareth he announces that he is fulfilling the prophecy of Isa. 61:1–2: "Today this Scripture has been fulfilled in your hearing" (Luke 4:18–21). There can be little doubt that Jesus saw the prophesied age of judgment/salvation as having been initiated by his invasion of the demonic realm ("But if it is by the Spirit of God that I cast out demons, then the kingdom of God has come upon you," Matt. 12:28). Yet it is inaugurated, not fully realized, eschatology, for Jesus says that something greater than Jonah and Solomon is here (namely himself), but that there is a coming judgment when the men of Nineveh and the queen of the South will arise and condemn the present generation. Hence in the new age now begun there is a further division of F^1 and F^2, where F^1 is Jesus' inaugurated judgment/salvation and F^2 is the completion of that inaugurated reign.

Paul also identifies the OT prophecies regarding the last day with Jesus, seeing in him the fulfillment of time: "When the time had fully come, God sent forth his Son" (Gal. 4:4). The writer to the Hebrews opens his epistle with a contrast between OT prophets and Christ, demonstrating the superiority of the new over the old and the arrival of the last days (Heb. 1:1–2). It is clear that the NT understands the last days to have begun in the person and work of Jesus Christ, as Peter attests on the day of Pentecost when he quotes Joel 2:28–32 and associates the fulfillment of the prophecy with the ministry of Jesus, calling upon his hearers to repent and be baptized (Acts 2:14–39).

Yet because of the continuation of suffering and demonic opposition to the gospel the NT writers were given to understand that the eschatological day had been initiated but not consummated by Jesus (following his own dominical authority), hence a second coming of Christ will complete the day. Peter expresses this tension when he writes of God's great mercy by which "we have been born anew to a living hope through the resurrection of Jesus Christ from the dead [F[1]], and to an inheritance which is imperishable, undefiled, and unfading, kept in heaven for you, who by God's power are guarded through faith for a salvation ready to be revealed in the last time [F[2]]" (I Pet. 1:3–5). In the interim, suffering accompanies rejoicing and tests the genuineness of faith (I Pet. 1:6–7), making vigilance a virtue, just as Jesus warned: "Take heed to yourselves lest . . . that day come upon you suddenly like a snare" (Luke 21:34). Paul follows the same form of F[1] and F[2], proclaiming the finished work of Christ but anticipating the "day of wrath" (Rom. 2:5), confident of being sealed in the Holy Spirit for "the day of redemption" (Eph. 4:30; cf. John 6:39), but never boastful or complacent. One of the most impressive statements about the tension and paradox of NT F[1] and F[2] is Paul's appeal to the Philippians to have the mind of Christ and to shine as lights in a crooked and perverse generation, "so that in the day of Christ I may be proud that I did not run in vain or labor in vain" (Phil. 2:16). Viewed in this manner, the last day, now inaugurated, is a time of testing for Christians, and is moving inexorably toward its conclusion when each will receive either judgment or fulfillment.

R. G. GRUENLER

See also ESCHATOLOGY; KINGDOM OF CHRIST, GOD, HEAVEN; AGE, AGES; SECOND COMING OF CHRIST; TRIBULATION; DAY OF CHRIST, GOD, THE LORD; LAST JUDGMENT, THE.

Bibliography. C. H. Dodd, *The Parables of the Kingdom;* M. Erickson, *Contemporary Options in Eschatology;* W. Hendriksen, *Lectures on the Last Things;* A. A. Hoekema, *The Bible and the Future;* G. E. Ladd, *The Last Things: An Eschatology for Laymen;* G. Vos, *The Pauline Eschatology.*

Last Judgment, The. Judgment at history's end is the climax of a process by which God holds nations and persons accountable to him as Creator and Lord.

The OT centers ultimate judgment in the day of Yahweh (or the day), when the Lord rids his world of every evil: haughtiness (Isa. 2:12–17), idolatry (Isa. 2:18–20), compromise with paganism (Zeph. 1:8), violence, fraud (Zeph. 1:9), complacency (Zeph. 1:12), and all that brands people as sinners (Isa. 13:9). Both the nations (Amos 1:2; Joel 3:2) and Israel (Amos 9:1–4; Mal. 3:2–5) are targets of judgment, which the OT sees as purification of God's people and world so that his creative and covenantal purposes are fulfilled: "The earth shall be full of the knowledge of the Lord as the waters cover the sea" (Isa. 11:9).

The intertestamental period focuses on the punishment—usually by disaster—of God's enemies, human and supernatural (Eth. Enoch 10:6; 105:3–4). Where such judgment did not take place in history, where the wicked flourished and the righteous suffered (cf. Pss. 37; 73), divine justice was questioned. The problem was solved with the view that judgment was not limited to history but could occur after death (Ps. Sol. 3:1ff.; Eth. Enoch) when God or the Son of man would execute judgment in the last day (II Esd. 7; Eth. Enoch).

The NT builds on OT and intertestamental teaching, expanding it in light of Christ's incarnation. In the Synoptics, Jesus announces himself as the eschatological judge (Mark 15:62) and calls attention to the day of judgment (Matt. 10:15; 11:22, 24; 12:36, 41–42; 23:33), describing it as a final separation of the evildoers from the righteous (Matt. 13:41–43, 47–50). Jesus' parables indicate that his purpose is not to frame an eschatological timetable but so to teach the fact of judgment that his hearers face their present decisions for or against the kingdom with utter seriousness. In the longest judgment parable Jesus' point is that the ultimate outcome will be determined by whether the nations receive or reject his "brethren" who come to them with the gospel message (Matt. 25:31–46).

John's Gospel underscores the tie between present human decisions and future divine judgment: believers do not go through judgment but have already crossed from death to life (5:24); the disobedient will not see life but are already under wrath (3:36). Final judgment, committed by the Father to the Son (5:26–27), will follow the resurrection of both the evil and the good (5:28–29), sealing the decree that human faith or disobedience has already determined.

Paul amplifies these themes: judgment is connected with Christ's coming and the resurrection of the dead (I Cor. 15:22–25); Christ is judge (II Tim. 4:1); Christians share in the judging (I Cor. 6:2–3); judgment is fair (Rom. 2:11), universal (Rom. 2:6), thorough (Rom. 2:16); through justification, judgment is robbed of terror for believers, whose sins have been judged on the cross (Rom. 3:21–26; 8:1, 31–34); believers' judgment consists of rewards for good works (Rom. 14:10; II Cor. 5:10) manifested when the purging fires clear away all dross (I Cor. 3:13–15); final judgment of unbelievers, exclusion from God's presence, is a recurrent theme, much of it stated in OT language (I Thess. 5:3; II Thess. 1:9; Phil. 1:28; 3:19; Rom. 6:21); divine judgment is both present and future reality (Rom. 1:18–32).

Jude and II Peter use some of the Bible's fiercest language to depict the fate of the wicked teachers (incipient Gnostics?) who misled the faithful by mocking their hope of a second coming and encouraging licentious living because they did not fear a final judgment (II Pet. 3:3–7; Jude 3–4). These letters see the final judgment as the ultimate act in a historical pattern (II Pet. 2:4–10; Jude 5–7), an act that should prompt righteous living by its cosmic power to destroy even the very heavens (II Pet. 3:11–13).

Revelation pictures a tribulation poured out on the earth as a judgment just before the final judgment (seven trumpets, 8–11; seven bowls, 16). As the first step in the final judgment the evil leaders whose blasphemous activities sparked the tribulation are captured in battle by the triumphant Christ and consigned to the lake of fire (19:20–21). Next Satan, the ultimate source of evil, is seized and bound for the duration of the millennium (20:1–3). His release results in further deception of the nations, a clear sign that God's final judgment is deserved—even after a thousand years of Christ's perfect rule the nations persist in their sin. The throne and the books symbolize a careful, accurate process based on well-kept records (20:11–15). The scene is cosmic in scope: earth and sky flee to be replaced by a new heaven and earth (20:11; 21:1); the damage to creation done by human sin is reversed, as the OT prophets foresaw (Isa. 11:6–9; 65:17–25) and Paul depicted (Rom. 8:22–23).

The theological implications of the biblical teaching are that final judgment is (1) the ultimate triumph of God's will and the consummate display of his glory in history—the sign that all he intended has been accomplished; (2) the cosmic declaration that God is just—all affronts to his glory are punished and all recognition of it is rewarded; (3) the climax of Christ's ministry, as the Apostles' Creed affirms; (4) the reminder that human and cosmic history move toward a goal, measured by the purposes of God; (5) the absolute seal of human accountability—all believers are held responsible for their works, all unbelievers for their rebellion; (6) the most serious motive for Christian mission—in the face of such judgment the world's only hope is Christ's salvation (Acts 4:12).

Belief in the last judgment was uniformly endorsed in the early creeds and the Reformation confessions. Except where the various ancient and modern forms of universalism have held sway, Christians have accepted the fact of final judgment, though its form and timing have been strongly debated. D. A. Hubbard

See also Eschatology; Last Day, Days; Second Coming of Christ; Tribulation; Day of Christ, God, the Lord; Judgment.

Bibliography. D. G. Bloesch, *Essentials of Evangelical Theology,* II, 211–34; A. A. Hoekema, *The Bible and the Future;* G. E. Ladd, *A Theology of the NT;* J. P. Martin, *The Last Judgment;* W. Schneider, *NIDNTT,* II, 361–67.

Last Supper. *See* Lord's Supper.

Last Times. *See* Last Day, Days.

Latimer, Hugh (*ca.* 1485–1555). English Protestant martyr. Educated at Cambridge, he was ordained about 1510 as a Roman Catholic priest, and in 1524 was still opposing the Lutheran teaching. The following year, however, he was converted to Protestantism through the influence of Thomas Bilney, and in 1531 was inducted to the parish of West Kington in Wiltshire.

Latimer's attitudes were sometimes unpredictable. Preacher rather than scholar, he had a great concern for the poor and he attacked their oppressors, whether clergy or landlords. He supported Henry VIII's efforts to get his first marriage annulled. He drew disciplinary charges for alleged criticism of traditional beliefs such as pilgrimages, the existence of purgatory, and the veneration of saints. Latimer, who protested that his preaching agreed with that of the fathers, said he did not object to certain traditions but he did not regard them as essential. He was excommunicated and jailed for three months until he made complete submission. Nevertheless, he was appointed in 1534 to preach before the king every Wednesday in Lent and, through the influence of his friend Thomas Cromwell, was consecrated Bishop of Worcester in 1535. He told the king that the dissolution of the monasteries could be justified only on acceptance of the view that purgatory was a delusion. A reaction in favor of Rome led to his resignation in 1539, and for the rest of Henry's reign he lived quietly.

Under Edward VI he declined to exercise his bishopric because he felt it might inhibit his preaching, which attracted large crowds. On Mary's accession (1553) he was arrested. He declared he acknowledged the Catholic Church but denied the Church of Rome. When condemned to death, he raised the possibility of an appeal to the next general council of the church. In 1555 he was burnt in Oxford with Nicholas Ridley, whom he encouraged with words that became famous: "We shall this day light such a candle, by God's grace, in England as I trust shall never be put out." J. D. Douglas

Bibliography. H. S. Darby, *Hugh Latimer;* A. G. Chester, *Hugh Latimer, Apostle to the English.*

Latitudinarianism. This critical label became attached to a group of Anglican divines in the late seventeenth century whose thought displayed a high regard for the authority of reason and a tolerant, antidogmatic temper ("gentlemen of a wide swallow"). In many ways products of the Cambridge Platonists (to whom the term was originally applied), they nevertheless lacked their mystical and imaginative depth. Moreover, though mostly Cambridge men, they became prominent churchmen. They included John Tillotson, Archbishop of Canterbury; Edward Stillingfleet, Bishop of Worcester; Simon Patrick, Bishop of Chichester and Ely; Gilbert Burnet, Reformation historian and Bishop of Salisbury; and Thomas Tenison, Archbishop of Canterbury. They reacted against the Calvinism of the Puritans and were broadly Arminian in outlook. They aligned themselves with progressive and liberal movements in the contemporary intellectual world. Hostile to scholasticism and Aristotelianism, they drew inspiration more from Descartes's new "mechanical" philosophy. Respect for "the theatre of nature" led them to support scientific developments such as the Royal Society. Thomas Sprat, Bishop of Rochester, was its historian, and Joseph Glanvill was a fellow of the Society as well as rector of Bath and the author of *The Vanity of Dogmatizing* and *The Agreement of Reason and Religion.* The new mathematics of Isaac Barrow and Isaac Newton they hailed as signs of a new age of light.

Their comprehensiveness allowed only a narrow core of fundamentals in religion. They resisted the Laudian or High Church insistence on conformity in nonessentials such as church order and liturgy. Stillingfleet's *Irenicum* advocated "comprehension" between Anglicans and Presbyterians; Burnet tried to incorporate Nonconformists into the Church of England. They approved "that vertuous mediocrity which our Church observes between the meretricious gaudiness of the Church of Rome, and the squalid sluttery of Fanatick conventicles" (Patrick). Above all they held that "true philosophy can never hurt sound divinity," which in practice normally meant harmonizing Scripture and the fathers with the light of reason. Theologically vague and spiritually insubstantial, their religion was strongly moralistic. Their emphasis on reasonableness looked forward to the skepticism of Hume and the reductionist theology of the next century. They were also the precursors of the Broad Churchmen of the nineteenth century, e.g., the contributors to *Essays and Reviews* (1860), and of the modernists and radicals of more recent Anglican divinity. D. F. Wright

See also Low Church; Cambridge Platonists.

Bibliography. G. R. Cragg, *The Church and the Age of Reason* and *From Puritanism to the Age of Reason;* B. Willey, *The Seventeenth Century Background;* M. H. Nicolson, "Christ's College and the Latitude Men," *MP* 27:35–53.

Latria. In Roman Catholic theology the adoration given to God alone. It differs from any adoration given to either the Virgin Mary or the saints, a point settled by the Second Council of Nicaea. Dulia differs from latria in the sense that it is an honor given to distinguished persons other than God. Thomas Aquinas developed this doctrine. Forms of latria could be bowing and kneeling directed toward either God alone or the Godman in the sacrament of the Eucharist. If latria were given to a creature it would be idolatry.

T. J. German

See also Dulia; Hyperdulia.

Bibliography. Aquinas, *Summa Theologica,* 2a–2ae, 84–100; B. Häring, *The Law of Christ;* W. Palmer, *An Introduction to Early Christian Symbolism.*

Latter Days. *See* Last Day, Days.

Laud, William (1573–1645). Archbishop of Canterbury and adviser to Charles I, Laud served at the same time as a member of the King's Privy Council, on the Court of High Commission, and as chief of the Star Chamber Court. His life was marked by a clear, if limited, vision of a church efficiently ordered, a uniformity of worship, and an obedient populace. He lacked both the craftiness of Richelieu and the human warmth of Archbishop Ussher to succeed by force or by consent.

His policies alienated both Puritans and Parliament in England and the general populace in Scotland. His reforms centered on the attempt to suppress the Puritan lectureships and to institute ceremonial practices thought by many to be "papist."

He was, however, a loyal member of the Church of England, diligently upholding the catholic nature of the Protestant reform in England against Roman Catholic claims, as is recounted in his "Conference with Fisher the Jesuit." His use of the Star Chamber Court to bring about uniformity in England gave the connotation of tyranny to that court in the history of constitutional law. His attempt to impose the Prayer Book upon Scotland precipitated the events which led to his imprisonment and execution and to civil war.

Laud was an able scholar with exceptional liturgical skills. His prayer "For the Church" is still used today in abbreviated form. He was too busy in matters of statecraft to continue his early theological promise, but it is noteworthy that in his description of Anglican differences with Rome there is no mention of justification, that "grand question," according to Richard Hooker, which lies "betwixt us and the Church of Rome." His name has been given to that high church movement at the Restoration that was in reaction to the Puritan rule, and the early Tractarians in the nineteenth century perceived themselves as building upon Laud's view of Anglicanism. His biographers have tended to be uncritical clerical apologists, with the exception of Hugh Trevor-Roper, who approaches Laud from the point of view of a secular humanist. C. F. ALLISON

See also CAROLINE DIVINES; HIGH CHURCH MOVEMENT; ANGLO-CATHOLICISM.

Bibliography. E. C. B. Bourne, *The Anglicanism of William Laud;* H. R. Trevor-Roper, *Archbishop Laud;* P. Heylyn, *Cyprianus Anglicus;* A. S. Duncan-Jones, *William Laud.*

Lauds. *See* OFFICE, DAILY (DIVINE).

Law, Biblical Concept of. The truest window we possess into the mind and life of the OT believer is the book of Psalms. Here we meet the saints of the old covenant in their joys and sorrows; we feel the weight of their problems and covet the richness of their spirituality. At the center lies the law of the Lord. Taking verses at random from Ps. 119 we find God's law is a delight (vs. 92), an object of love (vs. 97), venerated as truth (vs. 142), a means of peace (vs. 165) and liberty (vs. 45), and a treasure above all earthly wealth (vs. 72). To say that we do not customarily think of OT law in these terms is to admit that we have fallen into the error of identifying the Pharisees of the NT with the saints of the OT, forgetful that to the Lord Jesus, Pharisaic Judaism was a plant which his heavenly Father had not planted (Matt. 15:13) and that he himself was the perfect example of life under the law.

God's Law in God's World. From the beginning God's law lay at the center of his dealings with man. The major stress in Gen. 2—the Creator's benevolence and bounty toward his chief creature—does not obscure the fact that man in the garden was man under law and that it was through obedience that he entered into life. The balance of things is seen in the contrast between "every tree" that is there for man's enjoyment and the single tree that is forbidden. Yet in that single tree was enshrined the principle of law. Thus at the outset the Bible joins together that enduring partnership, obedience and life. Obedience safeguarded the enjoyment of the life that was life indeed; disobedience not only forfeited that life but replaced it by a death-bearing opposite. In Gen. 3, with disobedience came the birth of a bad conscience (vs. 8), the replacement of love by resentment (vs. 12), the corruption of marriage (vs. 16), and, most notably from our present point of view, the dislocation of man from his environment (vss. 17–19), which turns to fight against him and only grudgingly and at great cost furnishes a sufficiency for life.

The rest of the OT perpetuates this view of man in his environment: only by obedience to God's law can man live successfully and prosperously in God's world. The very environment itself turns against the disobedient. The earth is defiled by lawbreakers (Lev. 18:24–30) and "vomits out" those who fail to keep the law (Lev. 20:22). Behind this concept of the moral vitality of the environment lies one aspect of the OT theology of the Spirit of the Lord: he was operative in creation (Gen. 1:2; Ps. 33:6) and his activity is seen in both the renewal and decay of plants (Ps. 104:30; Isa. 40:7). The life which vitalizes the environment is God's life, full of his holiness.

Thus the OT has a distinct environmentalism to share with us, and at its center lies the law of God the Creator.

The Two Images of God. *Man in the Image of God.* Man is the crown of the creativity of God. The threefold use of the verb "to create" in Gen. 1:27 marks man as both the creature *par excellence* and the perfect creative act. This human uniqueness is summed up in the description "in our image, after our likeness," words that are used uniformly throughout the OT of outward form or shape, and this must be their leading idea here too. This does not mean that visibility, form, and shape are part of the divine essence, for God is Spirit. Nonetheless, the OT reveals (e.g., Judg. 13:3, 6, 10, 15) that there is an outward shape uniquely suited to (though not essential to) the divine perfection, and in that image (*ṣelem*) and likeness (*dĕmût*) man was created. But every other aspect also of man's nature is related, directly or indirectly in the Genesis narrative, to the image of God: matrimonial (1:26–27; 5:1–2), governmental (1:28), spiritual (subject to personal address by God: 1:28, contrast the bare fiat of 1:22), moral (2:15–17), and rational (2:19–20). The uniqueness of the divine image permeates human nature and constitutes a definition of what man truly is.

Law in the Image of God. Turning now to a very different genre of Scripture, we find in Lev. 19 that God has provided another image of himself on earth. Every aspect of human experience is gathered into this rich review of man's life under God's law: filial duty (vs. 3), religious commitment (vs. 4), ritual exactness (vs. 5), care of the needy (vs. 9), honesty in deed and word (vss. 11–12), and many more, touching on relationships and even on dress, hygiene, and horticulture. Yet all this variety suspends from one central truth: "I am the Lord." Lord is the divine name, the "I am what I am" (Exod. 3:14), so that the significance of the recurring claim is not "You must do what I tell you" (i.e., "lord" as an authority word) but "You must do this or that because I am what I am"; every precept of the law is a reflection of "what I am." Man is the living, personal image of God; the law is the written, preceptual image of God. The intention of Lev. 19 is declared at the outset: "You shall be holy, for I the Lord your God am holy" (vs. 2). The Lord longs for his people to live in his image, and to that end he has given them his law.

A Truly Human Life. When man in the image of God and law in the image of God come together in the fully obedient life, then man is indeed "being himself." His nature is the image of God, and the law is given both to activate and to direct that nature into a truly human life; any other life is subhuman. Of course, it is true that in a world of sinners the law, regrettably, has to give itself to the task of curbing and rebuking antisocial and degrading practices, but OT law has, to a far greater extent, the function of liberating man to live according to his true nature. For it is only when man finds the law of liberty that he becomes free. For this reason the OT asserts that the law has been given for our good, to bring us to a hitherto unrealized fullness of life (Deut. 4:1; 5:33; 8:1).

The Pillars of True Religion. The full flowering of the law of God in the OT came through the ministry of Moses and in the context of that foundational series of events which began with the Exodus and climaxed at Mount Sinai.

Grace and Law. A major truth emerges simply in the way in which the Exodus story is told. Egypt was the scene of a twofold act of God: liberation and redemption. The former was achieved by the tenth plague (Exod. 11:1) and actually brought to Israel all they had sought in crying to the Lord (Exod. 2:23). But the Lord himself had something further in mind: he promised also redemption (Exod. 6:6) as a distinct exercise on his part and, to accomplish it, added the passover. In this way Israel became the people who took shelter beneath the blood of the lamb (Exod. 12:13, 22–23) and who, by sheltering, were saved from the wrath of God (Exod. 12:12) and were initiated into a life of pilgrimage (Exod. 12:11). Pharaoh would have made them outcasts (Exod. 11:1); the blood and the flesh of the lamb made them the Lord's redeemed pilgrims. It was this people—the people liberated and redeemed by grace—who came to Mount Sinai.

Sinai was not a chance stopping place on the journey but an intended, primary destination (Exod. 3:12), and thither they were led by the pillar of cloud and fire (Exod. 13:21–22). The people redeemed by blood were brought by their Redeemer to the place of lawgiving (Exod. 20:2). Grace precedes law; the law of God is not a system of merit whereby the unsaved seek to earn divine favor but a pattern of life given by the Redeemer to the redeemed so that they might know how to live for his good pleasure. Such is the biblical understanding of the place and function of law.

The Way of Holiness by Obedience. The law which God gave through Moses had many aspects—e.g., civil, dealing with the legal system of the people of God considered as a state, with courts and penalties; moral, the law of holy living; and religious, the law of the ceremonies and sacrifices. It is the latter two which concern us here.

The first desire of the redeemer God is that his redeemed should be obedient. To keep the law is not a new bondage but a proof that the old bondage was past (Exod. 20:2). The lawgiving led up to a pledge of obedience (Exod. 24:7) that matched the longing of the Lord (Deut. 5:29).

With the law so central to life, it is understandable that the OT should develop a rich legal vocabulary. In logical order, the first word descriptive of God's law is "testimony" (*'ēdâ*, e.g., Ps. 119:2). In his law the Lord has "testified" regarding himself and his requirements. This self-revelation was given in "teaching" (*tôrâ*, e.g., Ps. 119:1) such as a loving parent would impart (cf., e.g., Prov. 3:1; 6:20). Once given, the teaching is a "word" (*dābār*, e.g., Ps. 119:28) to live by, an intelligible body of truth to be pondered and applied. But the Lord's testimony is also imperative, taking the form of "statute" (*hōq*, a permanent enactment, e.g., Ps. 119:5), "judgment" (*mišpāṭ*, authoritative decision, e.g., Ps. 119:7), "precept" (*piqqûd*, e.g., Ps. 119:4), and "commandment" (*miṣwâ*, e.g., Ps. 119:10), applying the law to the details of life. As a whole, God's law is a "way" (*derek*, e.g., Ps. 119:37) or characteristic life style.

In the OT as in the NT (e.g., Acts 5:32) obedience is a means of grace. The narrative of Gen. 2–3 provides a historical visual aid: obedience gave access to the tree of life; disobedience promised self-enhancement (Gen. 3:5) but brought death. Throughout the OT this remains the mirror of the true. A life based on the law of the Lord is constantly nourished by secret springs and is consistently fruitful (Ps. 1:2–3); it is under the blessing of God (Ps. 1:1), for by his law the Lord has made his people secure from bondage (Exod. 20:2). The psalmist speaks for every true believer when he testifies that the way of obedience is the way of true liberty (Ps. 119:45).

The Way of Fellowship. In the covenant ceremony of Exod. 24:4–8 the ritual of the blood matches the two focal points of the passover: the people sheltering beneath the blood both enjoy peace with God and also are committed to pilgrimage. Thus it is that Moses first sprinkles the blood on the altar—a Godward movement reflecting the central passover theology of propitiation. But next, as soon as the people have committed themselves to the way of obedience, the rest of the blood is sprinkled over them; the blood covers the needs of the redeemed throughout their walk of pilgrim-obedience.

In the covenant ceremony it is also to be noted that the presence of the Lord in the midst of his people is symbolized by an altar, for it is the blood of sacrifice which alone secures and maintains fellowship between Redeemer and redeemed. The permanence of the people in the divine presence is symbolized by stone pillars—stone for durability—but, while thus in his presence, their activity is to offer burnt offerings and peace offerings. Blood had brought them into peace with God, and blood would maintain his fellowship by means of the appointed offerings.

The other side of the same reality is seen in Lev. 9. The Aaronic priesthood has just been introduced into its sacred function (Lev. 8) and now for the first time celebrates the full round of levitical sacrifices: the sin offering (9:8), the burnt offering (vs. 12), and the peace offering (vs. 18). The climax follows: "The glory of the Lord appeared to all the people" (vs. 23), this being the foretold purpose of the sacrifices (vs. 6). The sacrifices are thus designed for the expression, enjoyment, and maintenance of fellowship with God.

Three main sacrifices were enjoined: the burnt offering, the peace offering, and the sin offering. The burnt offering expressed the double idea of acceptance before God and dedication to God. Its savor is sweet to the Lord (Lev. 1:9), indicating his delight to accept it and the one who offers it (cf. Gen. 8:20–21). The truth of acceptance is underlined when the burnt offering reappears in token form in the peace offering; the fat of the offering (Lev. 3:3ff.) is regarded as a burnt offering in miniature and is called "the bread of the offering" (Lev. 3:11; cf. 21:8). This means that the Lord, accepting the offering and the offerer, is delighted to sit at table with him, condescending to participate in the feast of reconciliation. But the burnt offering also expresses dedication. In Gen. 22 the Lord exercised his right to claim all, and in responding with a burnt offering Abraham was holding nothing back (vs. 12). The story of the offering of Isaac, ruling out forever the admissibility of human sacrifice, established at the same time the heart-searching standard of devotion which the burnt offering expressed.

The peace offering looked both Godward and manward. Godward, it expressed thanksgiving and personal love (Lev. 7:12, 16), but it was commanded that this joyous response to God's goodness should be marked also by fellowship with others: the priest has his share (Lev. 7:31–34), and we find the command of Lev. 7:16 fulfilled in the family celebration of Deut. 12:7.

The object of the sin offering was forgiveness. Awareness of a particular fault brought the individual sinner with his offering (Lev. 4:23), and the result was divine forgiveness (Lev. 4:20, 26, 31, 35).

Two acts are common to all three main categories of sacrifice: the laying on of hands (Lev. 1:4; 3:2; 4:4) and the ritual of the blood (Lev. 1:5; 3:2; 4:5–6). In connection with burnt offerings and sin offerings these acts are explicitly linked with making atonement (Lev. 1:4; 4:20, 26), and the sacrifices thus find their focus in the price-paying concepts of a substitution-based theology.

That the OT concept of law is, in fact, the biblical concept of law is nowhere seen more clearly than in the continuance throughout the Bible of the same pillars of true religion: grace and law. For the purpose of God remains the same, the obedience of his people, and it remains true that those who thus walk in the light find that the blood of Jesus Christ keeps cleansing them from all their sin. J. A. MOTYER

See also OFFERINGS AND SACRIFICES IN BIBLE TIMES; CIVIL LAW AND JUSTICE IN BIBLE TIMES; CRIMINAL LAW AND PUNISHMENT IN BIBLE TIMES.

Bibliography. F. D. Kidner, *Sacrifice in the OT;* J. A. Motyer, *Law and Life* and *The Image of God, Law and Liberty in Biblical Ethics;* B. N. Kaye and G. J. Wenham, eds., *Law, Morality and the Bible;* G. J. Wenham, *The Book of Leviticus; IBD.*

Law, William (1686–1761). English theologian and devotional writer. Born at King's Cliffe in Northamptonshire, Law entered Emmanuel College, Cambridge, in 1705 and graduated B.A. in 1708. In 1711 he was elected to a fellowship in his college and ordained as a deacon of the Church of England. In 1714, for refusing to take the oath of allegiance to George I, the newly arrived Hanoverian king, he was deprived of his fellowship and became a nonjuror, though remaining in communion with the Church of England. From 1723 until 1737 he acted as a tutor to Edward Gibbon, father of the historian. In 1740 he retired to King's Cliffe, where he remained until his death, living a disciplined life of prayer and good works, particularly the establishment of much-needed schools and almshouses.

Law participated actively in the religious controversies which agitated the Church of England during the eighteenth century. In 1717 Benjamin Hoadly, Bishop of Bangor, published a sermon entitled "The Nature of the Kingdom of Christ," based on John 18:36. In this sermon he denied that in the NT there is a visible church of Jesus Christ, and he defined Christianity as merely "sincerity." In *Three Letters to the Bishop of Bangor* (1717–19), Law argued that the church is a unique organism, founded by Jesus Christ, having its own special ordinances and its distinctive ministry going back to the NT apostles. In 1730 Matthew Tindal published "the deists' Bible," *Christianity as Old as the Creation,* whose thesis was that Christianity was simply a republication of the religion of nature as apprehended by human reason. In 1731 Law issued *The Case of Reason,* in which he contended that however important reason may be in religion, it alone cannot fathom the mysteries of God's providence, but must be supplemented by special divine revelation.

Law's most enduring contribution was in the realm of Christian devotion. Here his most important work was *A Serious Call to a Devout and Holy Life* (1729). Its argument is that if Christians really desire to follow their Lord Jesus Christ, it must be in every area of activity, in business and leisure as well as in strictly devotional practices. The Christian life, he maintains, must be a continual practice of humility, self-denial, and renunciation of the world; and he illustrates his thesis by a vivid series of imaginary characters who embody various virtues and vices. This treatise became a favorite with Christian leaders as different as John Wesley, George Whitefield, and Samuel Johnson and the great Scottish nineteenth century preacher Alexander Whyte.

N. V. Hope

See also Mysticism.

Bibliography. W. S. Palmer, *Selected Mystical Writings of William Law;* J. H. Overton, *William Law, Non-Juror and Mystic;* A. W. Hopkinson, *About William Law;* S. H. Hobhouse, *William Law and Eighteenth Century Quakerism;* E. P. Rudolph, *William Law* and *William Law on Christian Perfection.*

Law and Grace. *See* Law, Biblical Concept of.

Law and Justice in Ancient Times. *See* Civil Law and Justice in Bible Times.

Lawless One. *See* Antichrist.

Laying on of Hands. An act performed in different ways and with various meanings in the OT, NT, Judaism, and the Christian church. The simple placing (Heb. *śîm* or *šît*) of hands on a person was practiced when pronouncing a blessing (Gen. 48:14–22; cf. Jesus' blessing of the children, Matt. 19:13, 15; Mark 10:13, 16; Luke 18:15). Healing was accompanied by touching in Jesus' ministry and in Acts (e.g., Mark 1:41; 5:23; 6:5; 8:23, 25; Matt. 8:15; Luke 4:40; Acts 28:8). The bestowal of the Spirit was accompanied by an imposition of hands also (Acts 8:14–17; 19:1–7). It is debated whether this was a normative situation. The meaning of Heb. 6:2 is disputed, but this is often linked with the passages just cited as part of the "initiation" into the life of the church, perhaps at baptism. The laying on of hands accompanies Paul's healing (Acts 9:17), at which time he also was filled with the Spirit.

Ultimately the laying on of hands was associated mainly with ordination. Acts 6:6; 13:3; I Tim. 4:14; and II Tim. 1:6 are often cited in this connection. Daube suggests that this action was to be linked with the Hebrew *sāmak* rather than with *śîm,* as above. *Sāmak* was a leaning rather than merely a touching action. This term was also used in the OT with respect to the offering of sacrifices. The appointment of Joshua as Moses' successor was accompanied by this imposition of hands (*sāmak,* Num. 27:18, 23), as was the appointment of the Levites (Num. 8:10). Joshua had the Spirit, as did the seven in Acts 6:1–6, but apparently, according to Deut. 34:9, he received an additional gift of the spirit of wisdom. It is questionable whether this appointment of a successor is a true antecedent of the later ordination of authoritative teachers. The installation of elders (Num. 11:16–17, 24–25) did not include the laying on of hands. The setting apart of the Levites to a special service (Num. 8:14, 19) has some similarity to the setting apart of Paul and Barnabas for a special work (Acts 13:2), and hands were imposed in each case (Num. 8:10;

Acts 13:3). In each case also the laying on of hands was done by a group of peers; in neither was it an ordination to teach (Paul and Barnabas had already been in Christian ministry, and Paul viewed his authority as coming directly from God, not from men or even through the agency of men, Gal. 1:1).

It is difficult to assess the significance of the imposition of hands in the case of Timothy (I Tim. 4:4; II Tim. 1:6). Most commentators assume that the Jewish practice of ordination of rabbis stands as a precedent. However, although it is traditional to think of that Jewish practice as extending continuously back to the time of Moses, evidence is lacking that ordination of teachers existed in the time of Christ. The Jewish examples of the laying on of hands that are usually cited are not necessarily those of ordination. Laying on of hands was also used to admit people to the Sanhedrin (M. Sanh. 4.4), but this was not equivalent to rabbinical ordination. Timothy received a charisma through prophetic utterance with the laying on of hands; Paul does not say that the hands conveyed the spiritual gift. Later ordination, Jewish and Christian, was to an authoritative teaching ministry and was characteristically accompanied not by prophecy but by prayer. Daube sees "the laying on of hands of the presbytery" (I Tim. 4:14) as reflecting the *sĕmîkat zĕqēnîm* (Bab. Sanh. 13b), which he understands to be the laying (or leaning) on of hands not by elders but to make elders. It may be questioned whether this was in mind, whether the practice had yet become common in Judaism, and whether it is in fact the word *sāmak* with its associations, rather than *śîm*, which provides the background. I Tim. 5:22 may refer to the same conferral as Timothy received or, less likely, to the reception of penitents. Apparently the ordination Rabbi Yohanan ben Zakkai conferred was the earliest example known to later writers.

Paul and Barnabas "appointed" (*cheirotoneō*, lit. "stretch out the hand") elders in every city (Acts 14:23), and a brother was "chosen" (same verb) by the churches to accompany Paul in carrying the collection (II Cor. 8:18–19). This verb, *cheirotoneō*, which could mean "elect" or "point out," became, along with its cognate *cheirotonia*, a major term for the laying on of hands at ordination. So did the similar *cheirothesia*, although this word was not so used in the Apostolic Constitutions. The laying on of hands, along with prayer, has continued in Christian ordination until today, whereas the laying on of hands ceased to be used for ordination in Judaism sometime after the second century.

Various Christian churches have also used the laying on of hands in such ceremonies as confirmation, healing, and absolution. In the third century the laying on of hands and the anointing with oil using the sign of the cross (chrism or chrismation) took a strong place alongside of baptism. The following centuries, especially in the Eastern churches, saw even more importance placed on chrismation, which vied with baptism as a means of the bestowal of the Holy Spirit. Confirmation with chrismation continued as a separate rite, and the laying on of hands decreased in significance in connection with baptism, although it continued to be important in other rites, especially ordination.

A basic theological issue is whether the laying on of hands conveys any special power in itself. Daube sees it as an extension of one's personality, even in the case of offering sacrifices. Naturally the widespread concept of conveying power by touching a person is never far from mind. However, Scripture itself does not attribute power to the act except in the case of healing. Even here it is not magical, though people may have had such thoughts when approaching Jesus or the apostles through touching them or their possessions, or even through proximity to them (Acts 5:15–16; 19:11–12). The woman in Matt. 9:20–22; Mark 5:25–34; Luke 8:43–48 drew power from Jesus by touching his clothes. Timothy's gift was received through (*dia*) prophecy, but with (*meta*), not through, the laying on of hands (I Tim. 4:14). Some think that the emphasis on prayer in such circumstances and in later ordination, along with the fact that prayer was commonly associated with the raised hand, should indicate to us an act of benediction rather than of any kind of transfer. Certainly Paul and Barnabas were sent off to a specific work in an atmosphere of worship, prayer, and fasting (Acts 13:1–3), an action by which, according to Acts 14:26, they were "committed to the grace of God." It is inappropriate to read other meanings, especially those which developed later, into this text.

W. L. Liefeld

Bibliography. D. Daube, *The NT and Rabbinic Judaism.*

Lector. *See* Minor Orders.

Leibniz, Gottfried Wilhelm (1646–1716). The brilliant son of a philosophy professor at Leipzig University, Leibniz at first studied law at Leipzig but soon turned his attention to philosophy and mathematics, interests that would consume him for the rest of his life. From 1673 to the end of his life he worked for the Duke of Brunswick assembling and cataloging the vast archives of the House of Brunswick as he wrote a large history of the family. A man with many interests and intellectual contacts, he founded the Prussian Academy in 1700 and tried to promote peace between Protestant and Roman Catholic theologians as well as to unite Protestant churches in general. He was devoted to the cause of international peace.

Although he was a rationalist, Leibniz took to task Spinoza's philosophy, denouncing it as an attack on personal immortality and lacking a place for divine purpose and creativity. He was not content with Descartes's dualism in regard to "spiritual substance" mysteriously interacting with "material substance," and he disliked the mechanistic view of the universe proposed by Newton. Leibniz viewed God as a free and rational being, a being who could have created any type of world that he desired. He believed that God must have created the best of all possible worlds, one in which men are rewarded and punished according to their conduct. God is not responsible for evil. Evil is the result of human freedom. Leibniz had a theistic optimism that was ridiculed by Voltaire but was a precursor to the optimism of the Enlightenment in general. He was the first to use the term "theodicy" (in the title of a work he published in 1710), explaining that the existence of evil is a necessary condition of the existence of the greatest moral good.

In *Monadology* (1720) Leibniz agrees that matter consists of atoms, but contends that beyond and beneath the divisible physical atoms are the indivisible metaphysical atoms. These spiritual force centers he called *monads.* These monads are independent of each other but are brought into a rational organization through a predetermined harmony arranged by the mind and will of God. His system allowed him to defend traditional proofs of God's existence (with modification) and to uphold some scholastic principles that had been attacked by other philosophers. He believed that his doctrine of substance could be brought into harmony with both transubstantiation and consubstantiation. Christianity, he noted, was the summation of all religions.

Leibniz has been viewed as Germany's greatest seventeenth century philosopher and one of the most universal minds of all times. He is indicative of the great diversity within early modern rationalism. D. A. Rausch

See also Rationalism; Enlightenment, The; Theodicy; Spinoza, Benedict de.

Bibliography. C. D. Broad and C. Lewy, *Leibniz: An Introduction;* M. Hooker, ed., *Leibniz: Critical and Interpretive Essays.*

Leipzig Disputation (1519). Debate held at the University of Leipzig between June 27 and July 16, 1519, which involved Johann Eck, Martin Luther, and Andreas von Carlstadt. Eck, a professor of theology at the University of Ingolstadt, was a distinguished scholar and a feared disputant. Although he was originally a friend of Luther's, his criticism of the Ninety-five Theses aroused Luther's anger and provoked a vehement attack by Luther's colleague, Carlstadt. This eventually resulted in Eck challenging Carlstadt to a public disputation. Originally Luther was not expected to participate, but he became involved in the pamphlet war which preceded the debate. Seemingly Eck wanted Luther included because he hoped to expose the radicalness of Luther's position and to discredit the Reformer.

Eck and Carlstadt began the debate by discussing the questions of grace and free will. Although Carlstadt defended his position nobly, Eck proved the more skillful debater. When Luther entered the contest on July 4, the subject was changed to the question of papal authority. Before the debate Luther had written that papal primacy was of recent origin and that it was contrary to the teaching of Scripture, the decrees of the Council of Nicaea, and the evidence of church history. This gave Eck the opportunity to associate Luther's views with those of the Bohemian heretic Jan Hus, who had been condemned by the Council of Constance and burned at the stake in 1415. It was a particularly serious accusation in Leipzig because, following the death of Hus, his followers had fled into Saxony. When Luther stated that "among the articles of John Hus, I find many which are plainly Christian and evangelical, which the universal church cannot condemn," Eck pointed out that the Council of Constance had not been of that opinion. Luther responded by stating that councils could err and had erred in the past and that only the Scriptures were infallible. During the closing days of the debate Luther and Eck dealt with the subjects of purgatory, penance, and indulgences. The disputation concluded with Carlstadt and Eck returning to the questions of grace and free will.

Both sides claimed victory in the debate, but the Universities of Erfurt and Paris, the appointed judges, never rendered a clear verdict. The debate was a tactical success for Eck because he had succeeded in identifying Luther with a condemned heretic. For Luther the Leipzig disputation was a turning point in his career, as it revealed the extent of his estrangement from the official position of the church and helped to clarify his thought on the central issues.

R. W. Heinze

See also LUTHER, MARTIN; ECK, JOHANN.

Bibliography. E. G. Schwiebert, *Luther and His Times;* W. H. T. Dau, *The Leipzig Debate in 1519.*

Lent. A forty-day period of penitence and prayer which begins on Ash Wednesday and prepares for the feast of Easter. It is a form of retreat for Christians preparing to celebrate the paschal mystery. It became a forty-day retreat during the seventh century to coincide with the forty days spent by Christ in the desert; before this Lent usually lasted only a week. Every Friday of Lent is a day of abstinence. Fasting probably originated from the custom of fasting by those who were expecting to be baptized after being catechumens. The third, fourth, and fifth Sundays of Lent refer to the process of preparing for baptism.

Penitential works are very important during Lent. These include not only abstinence and fasting but also prayers and charitable works. Ash Wednesday is one of the greatest days of penitence. Vatican Council II in the *Constitution on the Sacred Liturgy* describes how penitence will lead one closer to God. People should not become overly involved in the penitence itself, however, but realize that the penitence is in preparation for celebrating the death and resurrection of Jesus Christ. Christians seek a change of heart during Lent in their relationship to God.
T. J. GERMAN

See also EASTER; ASH WEDNESDAY; CHRISTIAN YEAR.

Bibliography. N. Hordern and J. Otwell, *Lent;* H. Franke, *Lent and Easter.*

Leo I, the Great. The pontificate of Leo I (440–461) was seminal in the development of the medieval papacy. The pope was probably Italian though not Roman-born. His education was entirely Latin and Christian and his world view completely Roman. He led the Western church at the very end of imperial dominion in the West. It was a period ripe for the advance of papal power in both theory and reality.

Leo I was a great administrator who sought to control all of Christendom. The chaos left by invading barbarians, especially the Vandals and Huns, made local churches turn to Rome for help and advice. Leo made significant inroads into imperial power in the West, even to assuming the old imperial title Pontifex Maximus (chief priest), which the emperors had dropped. In the Eastern empire, where imperial power was intact and the invaders held at bay, this was more difficult. However, the East was beset with Christological heresies, and the Roman church's reputation for impeccable orthodoxy enabled the pope to insinuate himself into the situation.

Scholars disagree as to the exact meaning of Leo's papacy. However, several points seem clear. It was he who put previous claims of papal supremacy based on the Petrine doctrine into a highly structured legal setting. His letters and decretals made clear his vision of a hierarchical church with everything converging on Rome. He provided the indispensable idea of *plenitudo potestatis* (plentitude of power) for the See of Peter where the pope, as heir of Peter, ruled over the whole church. His claims were rejected in the East, where in 451 the Council of Chalcedon gave the Patriarch of Constantinople equal status. This was a blow to Leo, but where imperial power remained strong he could not achieve his aims.

In 455 Leo I, representing the people of Rome, persuaded Attila the Hun and his hordes to stop a brief raid on the city. Attila withdrew beyond the Danube, where he died one year later. Such events as this help explain the enormous power assumed by a pope who was also performing the duties of a defunct imperial authority. When he died in 461, Leo left in the papal archives powerful documentation upon which later popes from Gregory the Great to Innocent III could draw in order to achieve ultimate power in Western Christendom.
C. T. MARSHALL

See also PAPACY.

Bibliography. G. Barraclough, *The Medieval Papacy;* T. G. Jalland, *The Life and Times of Saint Leo the Great; The Letters and Sermons of Leo the Great,* tr. C. Feltoe, in *NPNF.*

Lessing, Gotthold Ephraim (1729–1781). German dramatist, critic, and writer. Son of a pastor in Saxony, he was originally trained in Lutheran orthodoxy, but after studying in Leipzig and Berlin he adopted the popular philosophy of the Enlightenment. He early distinguished himself as a writer and held various positions in which he exercised his literary skills. In 1770 he was placed in charge of the Duke of Brunswick's library at Wolfenbüttel, where he soon stirred up a storm of controversy by publishing fragments from a manuscript by the Hamburg orientalist H. S. Reimarus (1694–1768). The *Wolfenbüttel Fragments* (1774–78) was essentially a deist tract that rejected the validity of biblical revelation and explained the origins of Christianity from a naturalistic standpoint. Lessing responded to his critics in a series of polemical writings but was silenced by the Brunswick censor in 1778. His theological ideas were further developed in his most mature dramatic work, *Nathan the Wise*

(1779), and his essay *The Education of the Human Race* (1780).

Although Lessing is best known for his contributions in literature and the evolution of the German language, he is a landmark figure in the history of theology as well. By publishing the *Fragments* he opened the door to critical study of the Bible, especially the NT. He insisted that the life and personality of Jesus might be different from that portrayed in the Gospels and the subsequent teaching of the church. Applying critical tests to the Gospels, he suggested the existence of an Aramaic original of Matthew which was later condensed in Greek and which Mark and Luke supplemented with new material. But Lessing went further to question whether authentic belief could properly be bound up with particular historical events. No historical truth, he said, could be demonstrated nor could it be used to demonstrate anything. Thus, he rejected the idea of revelation in history, arguing that if religious truth is genuine, it must be so universally and is of a different order from that of historical events. He called upon men to adopt a "natural" or "positive" religion, one that recognizes God, forms noble conceptions of him, and directs individuals to keep these in mind in all of their thoughts and deeds. The "inner truth" of religion cannot be derived from a written tradition but is something capable of being felt and experienced. The miraculous power of all faiths may be assumed to be real, but it cannot be proven at the present time. Truth is something for which we always seek but cannot expect to find, because there is no such thing as a lord of history within history who will provide us with final truth. By portraying the essence of religion as purely humanitarian morality apart from all historical revelation, Lessing laid the foundations for Protestant liberalism. R. V. PIERARD

See also ENLIGHTENMENT, THE; LIBERALISM, THEOLOGICAL.

Bibliography. H. Chadwick, ed., *Lessing's Theological Writings;* H. E. Allison, *Lessing and the Enlightenment;* K. Barth, *Protestant Thought from Rousseau to Ritschl;* O. Mann, *RGG,* III, 327–30; C. Bertheau, *SHERK,* VI, 464–65; C. Brown, *NIDCC,* 593; *NCE,* VIII, 676–78.

Lewis, Clive Staples (1898–1963). Anglican scholar-novelist and Christian apologist, perhaps best known for his literary fantasies that explore theological concepts. Born near Belfast in Northern Ireland, he received his B.A. from University College, Oxford, in 1924, and was fellow and tutor in English literature at Magdalen College, Oxford, from 1925 until 1954. He then accepted the Chair of Medieval and Renaissance English at Cambridge. Among his works in literary criticism the most significant are *The Allegory of Love: A Study in Medieval Tradition* (1936) and *English Literature in the Sixteenth Century, Excluding Drama* (1954) in the Oxford History of English Literature series.

Converted in the late 1920s first to theism and then to Christianity, he saw himself as an "empirical theist" who arrived at the existence of God through induction. In his two autobiographical works, *The Pilgrim's Regress* (1933) and *Surprised by Joy* (1955), he presents the concept of *sehnsucht,* or sense of longing for the infinite, as the motivating factor in his conversion. This becomes a basic element in all his apologetics.

Lewis's theological writings are renowned for their lucidity of style and force of logic. His theology is predominantly romantic. *Miracles: A Preliminary Study* (1947) and *The Problem of Pain* (1940) are his most well known volumes of direct theological exposition. *The Abolition of Man* (1943) is a philosophical statement arguing for the existence of the Tao, or objective moral and natural law. *The Screwtape Letters* (1943)—which quickly sold over one million copies—and *The Great Divorce* (1946) are fictional explorations of the nature of temptation and of redemption.

Impressive as these are, Lewis is at his best in his mythopoeic writings. He uses the term "myth" to designate that which is ultimately true but ineffable, that is, nondescribable in rational terms, able to be glimpsed only by the imagination. His chief mythopoeia are *Till We Have Faces: A Myth Retold* (1956); his trilogy of space travel, *Out of the Silent Planet* (1938), *Perelandra* (1943), and *That Hideous Strength* (1945); and his seven-volume *Chronicles of Narnia* (1950–56). Experts in children's literature rank the latter as among the finest stories of our time.

The death of his wife of four years is poignantly considered in *A Grief Observed* (1961, under the pseudonym N. W. Clerk). His final book was *Letters to Malcom: Chiefly on Prayer* (1965).

Lewis's orthodox theology and inductivist apologetics have large appeal to evangelicals, although he takes a somewhat lower view of the inspiration of the Bible than evangelicals generally do (he holds the Bible to be a literary vehicle containing the Word of God), and he is not against theistic evolution. Lewis's thought is influenced considerably by that of George MacDonald. R. N. HEIN

See also MACDONALD, GEORGE.

Bibliography. C. S. Carnell, *Bright Shadow of Reality: C.S. Lewis and the Feeling Intellect;* R. L.

Green and W. Hooper, *C. S. Lewis;* M. P. Hannay, *C. S. Lewis;* T. Howard, *The Achievement of C. S. Lewis;* C. S. Kilby, *The Christian World of C. S. Lewis;* R. L. Purtill, *C. S. Lewis's Case for the Christian Faith;* R. J. Reilly, *Romantic Religion;* R. H. Smith, *Patches of Godlight;* C. Walsh, *The Literary Legacy of C. S. Lewis;* W. L. White, *The Image of Man in C. S. Lewis.*

Lex Talionis. *See* CIVIL LAW AND JUSTICE IN BIBLE TIMES.

Liberal Evangelicalism. The term refers historically to those (1) who have based their understanding of the Christian faith in the evangelical tradition of the church, but (2) who have understood their responsibility to the modern world as demanding their acceptance of a scientific world view with its specific commitment to historical and psychological methodology. Used particularly in the early decades of the century by some within the Church of England (e.g., T. Guy Rogers, V. F. Storr, E. W. Barnes) to clarify their continuing evangelical orientation, the term has sometimes been adopted to describe other theological moderates who have sought a synthesis of the gospel and modern knowledge.

With evangelicals, these pastors and teachers have emphasized the need for a personal relationship with God, the freedom of the Spirit, the authority of the Bible, the person of Jesus as God incarnate, the centrality of the cross, and the need for conversion. However, with liberals, they have agreed that in a world forever changed by the Enlightenment the message of Christianity must be recast. Bemoaning the decline of evangelicalism in the wider church, liberal evangelicals have seen a major reason as being a lack of sensitivity to the modern age and its thought forms.

While the term "liberal evangelical" is an imprecise one, allowing for a wide range of theological distinctiveness, it has often included the following: (1) The authority of Scripture is understood as residing not in the letter of the text (this would be bibliolatry) but in its dynamic revelation of God in Christ. (2) Older and what is believed cruder penal theories of the atonement have sometimes been replaced by those stressing the redeeming love of God in Christ. (3) Scientific theories such as evolution have been embraced and understood as being compatible with a Christian view of creation. (4) Higher critical conclusions concerning the Bible (e.g., the dating of Daniel, the authorship of II Peter, the redaction of Matthew) have been accepted.

The English liberal evangelicals of the 1920s (the terms "modern evangelicals" and "younger evangelicals" have also been used) sometimes diverged on these and other specific issues, but they found a unity in their desire to be concurrently evangelical and modern. Their precursors were such British moderates as P. T. Forsyth, R. W. Dale, and James Denney; their colleagues outside the Church of England, theologians such as H. R. Mackintosh; and their successors (though the term was seldom applied), such luminaries as T. W. Manson, J. S. Whale, Donald and John Baillie, and perhaps even C. S. Lewis.

In America, owing perhaps to the early acrimony of the fundamentalist-modernist controversy, no comparable turn-of-the-century moderating group of evangelical scholars emerged. Charles Briggs and Henry Preserved Smith began their careers as evangelicals but in the process of speaking to the modern age repudiated much of their earlier beliefs. In the 1960s and 1970s the influence of C. S. Lewis and Dietrich Bonhoeffer, the need for a more responsible biblical criticism, the stress on human fulfillment, and a renewed commitment to social justice have combined to produce a group of younger evangelicals who share with their earlier British counterparts a joint commitment to the evangelical faith and the modern age. R. K. JOHNSTON

See also EVANGELICALISM; LIBERALISM, THEOLOGICAL; FORSYTH, PETER TAYLOR; DENNEY, JAMES; MACKINTOSH, HUGH ROSS; MANSON, THOMAS WALTER; BAILLIE, JOHN; LEWIS, CLIVE STAPLES.

Bibliography. T. G. Rogers, ed., *Liberal Evangelicalism;* P. T. Forsyth, *The Person and Place of Jesus Christ;* D. M. Baillie, *God Was in Christ;* J. S. Whale, *Christian Doctrine;* R. Quebedeaux, *The Young Evangelicals.*

Liberalism, Theological. Also known as modernism, this is the major shift in theological thinking that occurred in the late nineteenth century. It is an extremely elusive concept. A variety of shades of liberal thinking exist, it has changed in character during the passage of time, and the distinctions between liberalism in Europe and North America are considerable.

Main Features. The major distinctive is the desire to adapt religious ideas to modern culture and modes of thinking. Liberals insist that the world has changed since the time Christianity was founded so that biblical terminology and creeds are incomprehensible to people today. Although most would start from the inherited orthodoxy of Jesus Christ as the revelation of a savior God, they try to rethink and communicate the faith in terms which can be understood today. As Harry Emerson Fosdick put it, we must express the essence of Christianity, its "abiding experiences," but we must not identify them with the "changing categories" by which they were expressed in the past. Liberals maintain that Christianity has always adapted its forms and language to particular cultural situations and the "modernists" in any given age have merely been those who were most candid and creative in doing this.

A second element of liberalism is its rejection of religious belief based on authority alone. All beliefs must pass the tests of reason and experience, and one's mind must be open to new facts and truth, regardless of where these may originate. No questions are closed or settled and religion must not protect itself from critical examination. As the Bible is the work of writers who were limited by their times, it is neither supernatural nor an infallible record of divine revelation, and thus does not possess absolute authority. The "essence of Christianity" replaces the authority of Scripture, creeds, and the church. This means there is no inherent contradiction between the kingdoms of faith and natural law, revelation and science, the sacred and the secular, or religion and culture.

A central idea of liberal theology is divine immanence. God is seen as present and dwelling within the world, not apart from or elevated above the world as a transcendent being. He is its soul and life as well as the creator. Thus God is found in the whole of life and not just in the Bible or a few revelatory events. Because he is present and works in all that happens, there can be no distinction between the natural and supernatural. The divine presence is disclosed in such things as rational truth, artistic beauty, and moral goodness. Although most liberals attempt to hold on to a core of Christian doctrine, some did carry immanence to its logical end, which is pantheism.

Immanence contributed to such common liberal beliefs as the existence of a universal religious sentiment that lay behind the institutions and creeds of particular religions and the superiority of good works (both in individual and collective terms) over professions and confessions. God is seen as the one who enables man to integrate his personality and thereby achieve perfection. This of course required the restatement of many traditional Christian doctrines. The incarnation was the entrance into the world through the person of Jesus Christ of a molding and redeeming force in humanity, and it signified and ratified the actual presence of God in humanity. His prophetic personality is the clearest and most challenging demonstration of the divine power in the world, and he is both the revelation of God and the goal of man's longing. Just as Jesus' resurrection was the continuation of his spirit and personality, so it is with all mortals after the death of the physical body. Sin or evil is seen as imperfection, ignorance, maladjustment, and immaturity, not the fundamental flaw in the universe. These hindrances to the unfolding of the inner nature may be overcome by persuasion and education, and salvation or regeneration is their removal. Religion represents the dimension of life in which personal values receive their highest expression, and its power possesses spiritually therapeutic qualities. Prayer, for example, heightens one's spiritual sensitivity and confers the moral benefits of stability, self-control, and peace of mind.

Liberalism also manifests a humanistic optimism. Society is moving toward the realization of the kingdom of God, which will be an ethical state of human perfection. The church is the movement of those who are dedicated to following the principles and ideals set forth by Jesus, the one who provided the ultimate example of an unselfish life of love, and the members of this fellowship work together to build the kingdom. Liberal eschatology views God's work among men as that of redemption and salvation, not punishment for sin, and this end will be reached in the course of a continuous, ascending progress.

Sources and Development. Theological liberalism originated in Germany, where a number of theological and philosophical currents converged in the nineteenth century. German thought had a profound impact on British and American theology, but indigenous movements in both places, the Broad Church tradition in Britain and Unitarianism in America, significantly shaped liberalism's development there.

Kant's ethical idealism and rejection of all transcendental reasoning about religion had the effect of limiting knowledge and opening the way for faith. Schleiermacher introduced the idea of religion as a condition of the heart whose essence is feeling. This made Christian doctrine independent of philosophical systems and faith a matter of individual experience of dependence upon God. Jesus was the perfect realization of the ideal of a new life of spiritual communion with God, and this possibility also existed for those who were drawn into fellowship with him in the church.

Hegel went off in another direction with his absolute idealism, as this emphasized the existence of a rational structure in the world apart from the individual minds of its inhabitants. That which is real is rational, and all reality is the manifestation of the absolute idea or the divine mind. Through a dialectical process of the ebb and flow of historical struggle, reason is gradually overcoming the irrational and good is triumphing over evil. The main contributions of Hegelian idealism were support for the idea of divine immanence and the fostering of historical and biblical criticism.

The ideas of F. C. Baur and the Tübingen School on the origins and early development of Christianity and the NT followed the principles of Hegelian historical evolution, and the same was true with Graf and Wellhausen in OT studies. Higher criticism questioned the authorship and dating of much of the biblical literature and rejected the traditional understanding of the Scriptures as divinely revealed oracles. Christianity was simply seen as the historical fulfillment of natural religion, the culminating self-disclosure of immanent Spirit. Beginning with D. F. Strauss, carried forward by E. Renan and J. R. Seeley, and reaching a high point with Harnack, the "life of Jesus" was studied with the intent of stripping off the dogmatic formulations of the church and getting back to the concrete, historical human personage. They found hidden behind the smokescreen of theology and hellenistic philosophy the teaching of a simple ethical religion summed up in the fatherhood of God and brotherhood of man. Insisting that Christianity must be founded upon the exact type of person he was, they felt it necessary to get behind the "Christ of the creeds" to the "Jesus of history."

The sway of Hegel was broken by Ritschl, who emphasized the importance of faith and religious experience. He upheld Christianity's claim to uniqueness but argued that Christian experience should be based on the objective data of history, not personal feeling. He saw Christianity as a life of action which would free man from the enslaving passions of his own nature and the determinism of his physical environment. Religious statements are value judgments relating to one's spiritual situation and have practical consequences. His theology of moral values relates the gospel to two poles—the redemptive work of Christ and the fellowship of redeemed persons (the kingdom of God). In the kingdom one achieves moral perfection and thus is like Christ. God is immanent, transcendent, and personal all at the same time.

Liberals welcomed the findings of science and readily accommodated to the challenge of Darwinism. Evolution vindicated divine immanence, since this explained how God had slowly built the universe through natural law. He also revealed himself through an evolutionary process, as the Israelites began with backward, bloodthirsty ideas and gradually came to understand that the righteous God could be served only by those who are just, merciful, and humble. At last, Jesus portrayed him as the loving Father of all men. Thus, redemption was the gradual transformation of man from a primitive state to that of obedient sonship to God. The scientific approach was applied to theology and biblical criticism, and they were regarded as open to all truth. Just like the physical realm, culture and religion had evolved, and there was no fundamental antagonism between the kingdoms of faith and natural law.

Liberalism was prevalent in French Protestantism, where Auguste Sabatier taught that religion must be understood as life rather than doctrine. It is to be grasped through religious psychology and the historical study of the documents in which the religious consciousness of the past has left an imprint. According to the Catholic Alfred Loisy, the essence of Christianity is in the ongoing faith of the church rather than exclusively in the teachings of Jesus, and it is constantly reshaped by the present. Catholic modernism had a strong foothold in France as well as in Britain and to a lesser extent in the United States, but it was effectively quashed by papal action in the early twentieth century.

British liberalism was related to the latitudinarian tradition and was found among the Broad Churchmen such as Benjamin Jowett, who stressed a loose definition of dogma. Anglican modernism was distinctly British, individualistic and compromising, tending to combine Jesus' natural manhood with a doctrine of his divinity. Perhaps the most controversial liberal was R. J. Campbell, a Methodist who criticized orthodox doctrine for its "practical dualism" in making people think of God as above and apart from his world instead of expressing himself through his world. He stressed instead the inward unity of God, man, and the universe almost to the point of pantheism. By and large, British liberalism tended to be theoretical and academic and more subdued in its overt humanistic enthusiasm.

In the United States the major source of liberal religious ideas was Unitarianism, and it had already modified the doctrines of divine sovereignty, human sin, and biblical revelation before German thought began to make itself felt. By the 1890s most of the major theologians had studied in Germany, and many of them had come to accept the principles of higher criticism and Darwinism. American liberalism was characterized by a strong sense of activism and a feeling that God is present and active in the great forward movements of human culture.

Liberal theologians concerned themselves

with building the kingdom of God and promoting the applied liberalism known as the social gospel. This emphasized the need to modify the corrupt society that in turn was corrupting man. Social gospelers talked of the kingdom where men would live as brothers in a spirit of cooperation, love, and justice. The church must turn from saving individual sinners to the collective action of saving society. Achieving a better life on earth replaced the concern for the afterlife, and it was expected that Christ and Christian values would conquer the world. Progress could be seen in the advance of political democracy, the movement for world peace, and efforts to end racial discrimination.

Decline and Persistence. By the time of World War I liberalism had made considerable inroads in the Protestant churches in Europe and North America, but it rested on shaky foundations. World War I shattered the heady optimism that was its stock in trade, while conservatives counterattacked. Often referred to as fundamentalists, confessionalists, or pietists, they denounced liberalism for being, as J. G. Machen put it, "Not Christianity at all, but a religion which is so entirely different from Christianity as to belong in a distinct category." Although the fundamentalist challenge was more or less beaten back, a more serious threat came from the sophisticated theologians of neo-orthodoxy who called for the recovery of divine transcendence and a realistic doctrine of sin. Liberalism with its emphasis on the freedom and self-determination of man gave religious sanction to modern man's efforts to control his life by autonomous reason and improve conditions by relying on his own goodness, but it tried to deny the overwhelming power of sin and evil which repeatedly thwart human aspirations. The neo-orthodox suggested that liberals failed to grasp either the actual condition of men or the doctrine of God that could provide a remedy for this. Christianity was transformed into a high-minded ethical humanism that offered little for those caught up in the travail of modern life, and in its efforts not to separate the sacred from the secular it too closely identified the one with the other.

Liberalism had also become too dependent on finding the historical Jesus, and, as Albert Schweitzer showed, the Jesus that researchers were uncovering possessed an apocalyptic world view and assumptions that were quite at variance with their conception of his teaching. The history of religions school carried the idea of historical development to its logical end and portrayed Christianity as the syncretistic religion of the ancient Near East. This meant the denial of its distinctiveness and the authority of the biblical canon. Christianity was merely one among many religions, all of which were relative to their time and circumstance, and thus it had no claim to finality.

In the 1930s some adherents moved much further to the left and broke almost completely with Christianity. Some turned to secular humanism, and in their 1933 manifesto repudiated the existence of God, immortality, and the supernatural in general, and substituted faith in man and his capabilities. Others identified with an empirical philosophy of religion based entirely on the scientific methods and experience.

Nevertheless, liberalism did not die out. A group of "evangelical liberals" in the United States, among them H. E. Fosdick, William A. Brown, Rufus Jones, and Henry Sloane Coffin, preached a God who was both immanent and transcendent, that Jesus, the Bible, and Christianity were unique, and that Jesus should be accepted as Lord of one's life. A new generation of "neoliberals" criticized the old modernism for its excessive preoccupation with intellectualism, sentimentality, a watered-down concept of God, and accommodation to the modern world that prevented it from launching a moral attack. Such people as W. M. Horton, John C. Bennett, and H. P. Van Dusen called for finding who God really is and securing his help in facing the human predicament, which is sin.

In Germany liberal scholarship was dominated by such giants as Bultmann, with his emphasis on form criticism and demythologizing the NT so modern man could understand what the Christian faith is, and Tillich, who was concerned with the ultimate, the ground of being, and suggested that God cannot be described in symbols that last from age to age but can only be encountered by experience. Bonhoeffer put forth the idea of a religionless Christianity where the church must be concerned with Christ and not religious ideas. We live in a world come of age and must reject the way of religion which is a psychological crutch. Christians must step out in faith and follow the one who is "the man for others" in costly discipleship.

By the 1960s most liberals had abandoned humanistic optimism, progressive cultural immanentism, and the dream of an earthly kingdom, but they gave no ground on the nonliteral interpretation of the Bible. Many had a renewed interest in natural theology and stressed the importance of social change. The "radical" and "secular" theologians talked about the traditional concept of God as being "dead" in this secular age, and gloried in the God who comes to us in the events of social change. They were optimistic about the creative possibilities open to secular man, held up love as the sufficient norm of ethical behavior, and reaffirmed the lordship of Christ and his call to discipleship. R. V. PIERARD

See also HIGHER CRITICISM; SOCIAL GOSPEL, THE; TÜBINGEN SCHOOL; CHICAGO SCHOOL OF THEOLOGY; UNITARIANISM; CATHOLICISM, LIBERAL.

Bibliography. J. Dillenberger and C. Welch, *Protestant Christianity Interpreted Through Its Development;* W. Pauck, *The Heritage of the Reformation;* B. Reardon, *Liberal Protestantism;* D. E. Miller, *The Case for Liberal Christianity;* H. Zahrnt, *The Question of God: Protestant Theology in the Twentieth Century;* W. R. Hutchison, *The Modernist Impulse in American Protestantism;* L. J. Averill, *American Theology in the Liberal Tradition;* K. Cauthen, *The Impact of American Religious Liberalism;* R. J. Coleman, *Issues of Theological Conflict: Evangelicals and Liberals.*

Liberation Theology. This is more a movement that attempts to unite theology and sociopolitical concerns than a new school of theological theory. It is more accurate to speak of liberation theology in the plural, for these theologies of liberation find contemporary expression among blacks, feminists, Asians, Hispanic Americans, and Native Americans. The most significant and articulate expression to date has taken place in Latin America. Theological themes have been developed in the Latin American context that have served as models for other theologies of liberation.

There are at least four major factors that have played a significant role in the formulation of Latin American liberation theology. First, it is a post-Enlightenment theological movement. The leading proponents—such as Gustavo Gutiérrez, Juan Segundo, José Miranda—are responsive to the epistemological and social perspectives of Kant, Hegel, and Marx. Second, liberation theology has been greatly influenced by European political theology and the North American radical theology, finding in J. B. Metz and Jürgen Moltmann and Harvey Cox perspectives which have criticized the ahistorical and individualistic nature of existential theology.

Third, it is for the most part a Roman Catholic theological movement. With notable exceptions such as José Miguez-Bonino (Methodist) and Rubem Alves (Presbyterian) liberation theology has been identified with the Roman Catholic Church. After Vatican II (1965) and the conference of the Latin American episcopate (Celam II) in Medellín, Colombia (1968), a significant number of Latin American leaders within the Roman Catholic Church turned to liberation theology as the theological voice for the Latin American church. The dominating role of the Roman Catholic Church in Latin America has made it a significant vehicle for liberation theology throughout the South American continent.

Fourth, it is a theological movement specifically and uniquely situated in the Latin American context. Liberation theologians contend that their continent has been victimized by colonialism, imperialism, and multinational corporations. Economic "developmentalism" has placed so-called underdeveloped Third World nations in a situation of dependence, resulting in the local economies of Latin America being controlled by decisions made in New York, Houston, or London. In order to perpetuate this economic exploitation, liberationists argue, the powerful capitalist countries, especially the United States, give military and economic support to secure certain political regimes supportive of the economic status quo.

These four factors combine to bring about a distinctive theological method and interpretation.

Theological Method. Gustavo Gutiérrez defines theology as "critical reflection on historical praxis." Doing theology requires the theologian to be immersed in his or her own intellectual and sociopolitical history. Theology is not a system of timeless truths, engaging the theologian in the repetitious process of systematization and apologetic argumentation. Theology is a dynamic, ongoing exercise involving contemporary insights into knowledge (epistemology), man (anthropology), and history (social analysis). "Praxis" means more than the application of theological truth to a given situation. It means the discovery and the formation of theological truth out of a given historical situation through personal participation in the Latin American class struggle for a new socialist society.

Liberation theology accepts the two-pronged "challenge of the Enlightenment" (Juan Sobrino). These two critical elements shape liberation theology's biblical hermeneutic. The first challenge comes through the philosophical perspective begun by Immanuel Kant, which argued for the autonomy of human reason. Theology is no longer worked out in response to God's self-disclosure through the divine-human authorship of the Bible. This revelation from "outside" is replaced by the revelation of God found in the matrix of human interaction with history. The second challenge comes through the political perspective founded by Karl Marx, which argues that man's wholeness can be realized only through overcoming the alienating political and economic structures of society. The role of Marxism in liberation theology must be honestly understood. Some critics have implied that liberation theology and Marxism are indistinguishable, but this is not completely accurate.

Liberation theologians agree with Marx's famous statement: "Hitherto philosophers have explained the world; our task is to change it." They argue that theologians are not meant to be theoreticians but practitioners engaged in the struggle to bring about society's transformation. In order to do this liberation theology employs a Marxist-style class analysis, which divides the culture between oppressors and oppressed. This conflictual sociological analysis is meant to identify the injustices and exploitation within the historical situation. Marxism and liberation theology condemn religion for supporting the status quo and legitimating the power of the oppressor. But unlike Marxism, liberation theology turns to the Christian faith as a means for bringing about liberation. Marx failed to see the emotive, symbolic, and sociological force the church could be in the struggle for justice. Liberation theologians claim that they are not departing from the ancient Christian tradition when they use Marxist thought as a tool for social analysis. They do not claim to use Marxism as a philosophical world view or a comprehensive plan for political action. Human liberation may begin with the economic infrastructure, but it does not end there.

The challenge of the Enlightenment is followed by the challenge of the Latin American situation in formulating liberation theology's hermeneutics of praxis. The important hermeneutical key emerging out of the Latin American context is summarized in Hugo Assmann's reference to the "epistemological privilege of the poor." On a continent where the majority is both poor and Roman Catholic, liberation theology claims the struggle is with man's inhumanity to man and not with unbelief. Liberation theologians have carved out a special place for the poor. "The poor man, the other, reveals the totally Other to us" (Gutiérrez). All communion with God is predicated on opting for the poor and exploited classes, identifying with their plight, and sharing their fate. Jesus "secularizes the means of salvation, making the sacrament of the 'other' a determining element for entry into the Kingdom of God" (Leonardo Boff). "The poor are the epiphany of the Kingdom or of the infinite exteriority of God" (Enrique Dussel). Liberation theology holds that in the death of the peasant or the native Indian we are confronted with "the monstrous power of the negative" (Hegel). We are forced to understand God from within history mediated through the lives of oppressed human beings. God is not recognized analogically in creation's beauty and power, but dialectically in the creature's suffering and despair. Sorrow "triggers the process of cognition," enabling us to comprehend God and the meaning of his will (Sobrino). Combining post-Enlightenment critical reflection with an acute awareness of Latin America's conflict-ridden history results in several important theological perspectives.

Theological Interpretation. Liberation theologians believe that the orthodox doctrine of God tends to manipulate God in favor of the capitalistic social structure. They claim that orthodoxy has been dependent upon ancient Greek notions of God that perceived God as a static being who is distant and remote from human history. These distorted notions of God's transcendence and majesty have resulted in a theology which thinks of God as "up there" or "out there." Consequently the majority of Latin Americans have become passive in the face of injustice and superstitious in their religiosity. Liberation theology responds by stressing the incomprehensible mysteriousness of the reality of God. God cannot be summarized in objectifying language or known through a list of doctrines. God is found in the course of human history. God is not a perfect, immutable entity, "squatting outside the world." He stands before us on the frontier of the historical future (Assmann). God is the driving force of history causing the Christian to experience transcendence as a "permanent cultural revolution" (Gutiérrez). Suffering and pain become the motivating force for knowing God. The God of the future is the crucified God who submerges himself in a world of misery. God is found on the crosses of the oppressed rather than in beauty, power, or wisdom.

The biblical notion of salvation is equated with the process of liberation from oppression and injustice. Sin is defined in terms of man's inhumanity to man. Liberation theology for all practical purposes equates loving your neighbor with loving God. The two are not only inseparable but virtually indistinguishable. God is found in our neighbor and salvation is identified with the history of "man becoming." The history of salvation becomes the salvation of history embracing the entire process of humanization. Biblical history is important insofar as it models and illustrates this quest for justice and human dignity. Israel's liberation from Egypt in the Exodus and Jesus' life and death stand out as the prototypes for the contemporary human struggle for liberation. These biblical events signify the spiritual significance of the secular struggle for liberation.

The church and the world can no longer be segregated. The church must allow itself to be inhabited and evangelized by the world. "A theology of the Church in the world should be complemented by a theology of the world in the

Church" (Gutiérrez). Joining in solidarity with the oppressed against the oppressors is an act of "conversion," and "evangelization" is announcing God's participation in the human struggle for justice.

The importance of Jesus for liberation theology lies in his exemplary struggle for the poor and the outcast. His teaching and action on behalf of the kingdom of God demonstrate the love of God in a historical situation that bears striking similarity to the Latin American context. The meaning of the incarnation is reinterpreted. Jesus is not God in an ontological or metaphysical sense. Essentialism is replaced with the notion of Jesus' relational significance. Jesus shows us the way to God; he reveals the way one becomes the son of God. The meaning of Jesus' incarnation is found in his total immersion in a historical situation of conflict and oppression. His life absolutizes the values of the kingdom—unconditional love, universal forgiveness, and continual reference to the mystery of the Father. But it is impossible to do exactly what Jesus did simply because his specific teaching was oriented to a particular historical period. On one level Jesus irreversibly belongs to the past, but on another level Jesus is the zenith of the evolutionary process. In Jesus history reaches its goal. However, following Jesus is not a matter of retracing his path, trying to adhere to his moral and ethical conduct, as much as it is re-creating his path by becoming open to his "dangerous memory" which calls our path into question. The uniqueness of Jesus' cross lies not in the fact that God, at a particular point in space and time, experienced the suffering intrinsic to man's sinfulness in order to provide a way of redemption. Jesus' death is not a vicarious offering on behalf of mankind who deserve God's wrath. Jesus' death is unique because he historicizes in exemplary fashion the suffering experienced by God in all the crosses of the oppressed. Liberation theology holds that through Jesus' life people are brought to the liberating conviction that God does not remain outside of history indifferent to the present course of evil events but that he reveals himself through the authentic medium of the poor and oppressed.

Theological Critique. The strength of liberation theology is in its compassion for the poor and its conviction that the Christian should not remain passive and indifferent to their plight. Man's inhumanity to man is sin and deserves the judgment of God and Christian resistance. Liberation theology is a plea for costly discipleship and a reminder that following Jesus has practical social and political consequences.

Liberation theology's weakness stems from an application of misleading hermeneutical principles and a departure from historic Christian faith. Liberation theology rightly condemns a tradition that attempts to use God for its own ends but wrongly denies God's definitive self-disclosure in biblical revelation. To argue that our conception of God is determined by the historical situation is to agree with radical secularity in absolutizing the temporal process, making it difficult to distinguish between theology and ideology.

Marxism may be a useful tool in identifying the class struggle that is being waged in many Third World countries, but the question arises whether the role of Marxism is limited to a tool of analysis or whether it has become a political solution. Liberation theology rightly exposes the fact of oppression in society and the fact that there are oppressors and oppressed, but it is wrong to give this alignment an almost ontological status. This may be true in Marxism, but the Christian understands sin and alienation from God as a dilemma confronting both the oppressor and the oppressed. Liberation theology's emphasis upon the poor gives the impression that the poor are not only the object of God's concern but the salvific and revelatory subject. Only the cry of the oppressed is the voice of God. Everything else is projected as a vain attempt to comprehend God by some self-serving means. This is a confused and misleading notion. Biblical theology reveals that God is for the poor, but it does not teach that the poor are the actual embodiment of God in today's world. Liberation theology threatens to politicize the gospel to the point that the poor are offered a solution that could be provided with or without Jesus Christ.

Liberation theology stirs Christians to take seriously the social and political impact of Jesus' life and death but fails to ground Jesus' uniqueness in the reality of his deity. It claims he is different from us by degree, not by kind, and that his cross is the climax of his vicarious identification with suffering mankind rather than a substitutionary death offered on our behalf to turn away the wrath of God and triumph over sin, death, and the devil. A theology of the cross which isolates Jesus' death from its particular place in God's design and shuns the disclosure of its revealed meaning is powerless to bring us to God, hence assuring the perpetuity of our theological abandonment. D. D. WEBSTER

See also HOPE, THEOLOGY OF.

Bibliography. C. E. Armerding, ed., *Evangelicals and Liberation;* H. Assmann, *Theology for a Nomad Church;* L. Boff, *Jesus Christ Liberator;* J. Miguez-Bonino, *Doing Theology in a Revolutionary Situation;*

R. M. Brown, *Theology in a New Key: Responding to Liberation Themes;* I. Ellacuria, *Freedom Made Flesh: The Mission of Christ and His Church;* A. Fierro, *The Militant Gospel: A Critical Introduction to Political Theologies;* R. Gibellini, ed., *Frontiers of Theology in Latin America;* G. Gutiérrez, *A Theology of Liberation;* J. A. Kirk, *Liberation Theology: An Evangelical View from the Third World;* J. P. Miranda, *Marx and the Bible.*

Liberty, Christian. To live is to choose; to choose is to live. The exercise of choice, however, does not in itself make us free. Choice is only the shuttle which weaves the fabric of our lives—into a shroud of death or a chrysalis of new life, depending upon which "god" defines the values, goals, and purposes which attract our choices. Freedom, or liberty (the terms are here synonymous), is not *that* we can choose but *what* we choose; freedom is not, then, a status but an achievement. Indeed, the freedom of the Christian is a divine gift. It is a fatal delusion to confuse ability to choose with an illusory right to choose as we please—all choice is an obedience to some "god." Christian freedom resides in obedience to the only God in whose service is liberty.

Christian liberty emerges out of duty. The sense of duty has its origin in God, who lays the demands of his law upon everyone through the witness of conscience. Some seek relief from the divine presence in assorted forms of pseudo-freedom—philosophies, mysticisms, wealth, power, rebellion. Others pursue oblivion via drugs, busyness, dropping out, the abuse of others. But the witness of God is never stilled, and detached from duty choice becomes freedom's counterfeit "license"—slavery to fad, fashion, passion, whim, greed, megalomania. And license is the dance of death.

The human predicament consists in man's uneasy awareness of the divine pressure for obedience to God's law without finding within himself the resources for obeying it. The good news which is the gospel is that God himself opens the way to obedience through faith in Jesus Christ. Christian liberty thus bears two faces: (1) freedom *from* human disability and enslavement to the devil; and (2) freedom *for* striving to know and do the will of God.

Freedom From. "He has delivered us from the dominion of darkness and transferred us to the kingdom of his beloved Son" (Col. 1:13; cf. Eph. 2:2; John 8:32, 36).

God liberates in Christ. The paradigm of that liberation is the rescue of Israel from Egypt. Unhappily, the "Egypt-event" has become a slogan for liberation theologies which confuse "freedom from" (which by itself is license) with Christian liberty.

Jesus illustrates in physical terms the nature of the liberation he effects through his miracles. He calls the dead to life, illumining the fundamental miracle of the believer's rebirth by the Word through water and Spirit (John 3:5). He makes the deaf to hear—as the believer now can hear his Word. He opens the eyes of the blind—as the newborn now sees all in the light of the Word. He makes the lame to walk—as the believer now walks in his Way. He cures the bodily ill—as the Christian is freed for a more abundant life. He loosens the tongue of the dumb—so believers can sing his praise and make their witness. So Christ's miracles vividly illustrate the "freedom from" which the Christian has in him.

Still more, Jesus frees us from sinking under the burden of suffering and hardship by transmuting these (for those who see) into divine pedagogy (Heb. 12:6; Prov. 3:11–12). He liberates the weak and the poor from the agonies of envy by equalizing all (who hear) before his cross; and he draws the sting of physical death and the seeming triumph of the tomb (for all who believe) by the power of his resurrection (I Cor. 15:54–57).

In Christ the believer is liberated *from* servitude to the gods of this age, but we only enter into a full realization of this gracious liberty as we strive daily to live positively for God.

Freedom For. The pivot which hinges "freedom from" to "freedom for" is the divine law, written by God upon tablets of stone and the flesh of the human heart, summarized in the Decalogue, to which much of the Bible is commentary.

First, the law has pressured us into acknowledgment of sin (Rom. 3:20), and thus driven us through repentance to Christ (Gal. 3:24). Then, once liberated in Christ, the believer finds in the law the goal, values, and purposes summed up in the term "love" (John 14:21, 23; Gal. 5:14). And love weaves, by the power of the Spirit, our choices into freedom.

In a word, the God who liberates us from Egypt sets before our feet the way of life as illumined by his law (Exod. 20:2–17; Ps. 119:105), and grants us, through Christ, the gift of the Spirit by whom we can be free—that is, we can seek to do what God commands.

"Freedom from" by grace and through Christ becomes in the life of the believer a blessed "freedom for" by the Spirit and in Christ. Seeking daily to walk in the light of his Word, along the Way which is himself, Christ's redeemed believer comes to realize in his own experience (where freedom alone can be understood) the Lord's gracious promise: "If you continue in my word, you are truly my disciples, and you will know the truth, and the truth will make you free" (John 8:31–32).

L. De Koster

Liberty, Religious. *See* Tolerance.

Liddon, Henry Parry (1829–1890). A leader of the later Oxford Movement and perhaps the most popular Anglican preacher during the last third of the nineteenth century. Born in North Stoneham, Hampshire, he attended King's College School, London, and Christ Church College, Oxford, where he was graduated in 1850. Following his ordination as a priest in 1853 he served as vice-principal at Cuddleston Theological College near Oxford (1854–59) and St. Edmund's Hall at Oxford (1859–62) before returning to Christ Church College to assume permanent residence (1862–90).

As an undergraduate Liddon converted from the evangelicalism of his youth to Anglo-Catholicism under the influence of his mentor, Edward Pusey. Later the two worked closely together as Oxford theologians and, with John Keble, as leaders of the Oxford (or Tractarian) Movement after the defection of John Henry Newman. Liddon's role in the movement was less that of defending Catholic doctrine than of serving as the chief High Church critic of the mounting liberalizing influence in the church and the secularizing influence in higher education. He vigorously fought efforts to diminish the acceptance of the Athanasian and Nicene creeds, and his 1866 Bampton Lectures defending the divinity of Christ attracted wide attention. Crowds flocked to hear his long but clear, engaging, and persuasive sermons at Oxford and at St. Paul's in London, where he became a canon in 1870. His teaching and preaching slowed the departure from creedal Christianity in England, although when he died in many respects the Oxford Movement died with him.

W. C. Ringenberg

See also Oxford Movement; Anglo-Catholicism.

Bibliography. J. O. Johnston, *Life and Letters of Henry Parry Liddon;* G. W. E. Russell, *Dr. Liddon;* H. P. Liddon, *The Divinity of Our Lord and Saviour Jesus Christ* and *Life of Edward Bouverie Pusey,* 4 vols.

Lie, Lying. A lie is an intentional deception or falsehood. A false or erroneous statement should be classified as a lie only if it includes an intention to deceive. Nor is withholding the truth necessarily a lie, for lying is actively, intentionally conveying a falsehood. While the term "lie" might be appropriate to a broad range of behavior ("living a lie," "lying eyes"), it is most specifically a problem for conscious, intentional communication such as speech and writing. Not only personal speech but corporate advertising, political rhetoric, and the claims of religious groups must be scrutinized in an effort to avoid being guilty of lying.

All false witness and lying is prohibited to the people of God (Exod. 20:16; Prov. 12:22; Col. 3:9). The extreme seriousness of the offense is indicated in Scripture by the fate of Ananias and Sapphira (Acts 5:1–11) and the place of unrepentant liars in the final judgment (Rev. 21:8; 22:15). The biblical opposition to all lying originates in the fact that the people of God owe their life and allegiance to "the only true God" (John 17:3). Jesus Christ is "the truth" (John 14:6). The Holy Spirit is "the Spirit of truth" (John 16:13). The Word is always "the truth" (John 17:17). Conversely, Satan is "a liar and the father of lies" (John 8:44). Fundamental to human sin and alienation from God is the choice to "exchange the truth of God for a lie" (Rom. 1:25). There is no middle ground: the people of God must "put off falsehood and speak truthfully" (Eph. 4:25). The choice is between the way of God and the way of Satan.

Lying is wrong first of all, then, because it alienates us from the God who is truth itself. Second, lying destroys community and interpersonal relations (Prov. 25:18; 26:18–19, 28). This is so not only because of the immediate injury to the recipient of the lie but also because the trust which is essential to community is undermined. A third reason lying is wrong is that it destroys the liar himself. The contradiction between the liar's knowledge of the truth and his participation in the lie is a dehumanizing surrender of personal wholeness and integrity. Furthermore, one lie inexorably leads to further lies to cover up the first. This web of falsehood produces a kind of bondage that is the opposite situation to the knowledge and practice of the truth which sets one free.

This general perspective on lying is very clear and consistent throughout the canon of Scripture. The difficulty with this general approach is raised by situations in which lies appear to be justified after all—either by obedience to a special command of God or by the necessity to violate the prohibition against lying in order to obey another biblical principle (e.g., the preservation of life). Among these cases are Abraham's two lies about Sarah being his sister (Gen. 12; 20), Rahab's lie to protect Israel's spies (Josh. 2), and the deception of the midwives in Egypt (Exod. 1). Abraham's situation falls into the category of a lie apparently justified in the interest of saving a life. Rahab and the midwives raise another common difficulty: whether a lie is justified by the national interest (e.g., during wartime).

One approach (Thielicke, Bonhoeffer) to this set of problems has been to stress the strong relational and contextual character of the biblical teaching on truth and falsehood. Fundamental to this kind of approach is the affirmation that truth is ultimately the person of Jesus Christ. A lie is thus an intentional denial or contradiction of the truth and reality of Jesus Christ in a given situation. It is Jesus Christ to whom truth is owed and by whom truth is measured, not independent, abstract facts in themselves. It follows from this presupposition that both truth and falsehood are also related to one's neighbor. "You shall not bear false witness against your neighbor" (Exod. 20:16). You shall "speak the truth in love" (Eph. 4:15). In short, truth and falsehood are not controlled by isolated facts alone but by those facts in relation to God and to one's neighbor.

The other approach to the problem of the "justified lie" is that of casuistry (Murray). Casuistry attempts to make exceedingly careful distinctions in order to vindicate the principle that one ought never to lie under any circumstances. Thus it is argued that Rahab is not commended for her lie (Heb. 11:31; James 2:25) but rather for her faith and works. Her choice of sinful means (the lie) is not endorsed, though her basic faith is. A similar argument is made in the case of Jacob and Rebekah's deception of Isaac and Esau (Gen. 27). Samuel's deception of the elders at Bethlehem is vindicated in that he stated one truth ("I come here to sacrifice") while concealing his primary purpose—to anoint David as the next king (I Sam. 16).

Both the relational and casuistic approaches to the problem of lying are susceptible to exploitation in the interest of self-justification and the rationalization of subterfuge and falsehood. Yet both approaches preserve important principles by which situations must be judged. With the casuist we must strive to remain true to the facts as we know them. With the relational ethicist we must strive to speak the truth (and avoid lying) with the interests of God and our neighbors always in view. D. W. Gill

See also Ethics; Ethics, Biblical; Casuistry.

Bibliography. A. Flavelle, *NBD*, 734–35; J. M. Gustafson and J. T. Laney, eds., *On Being Responsible*, Pt. II; J. Murray, *Principles of Conduct*, ch. 6; H. Thielicke, *Theological Ethics*, ch. 27.

Life. ***God as the Source.*** As the one being who has no cause outside himself, God is frequently disclosed in both the OT and NT as "the living God" (e.g., Deut. 5:26; Josh. 3:10; Ps. 84:2; Matt. 26:63; John 6:69; Rom. 9:26). "But the Lord is true God; he is the living God and the everlasting King" (Jer. 10:10). "As the Lord lives" was a common formula in oath-taking (e.g., I Sam. 14:39, 45; 19:6) that characterized God's nature as dynamic in contrast with idols which are dumb (Hab. 2:18) and cannot move (Isa. 40:20; cf. 44:9–20; I John 5:21). As the living God he "gives to all men life and breath and everything" (Acts 17:25; cf. Gen. 2:7). And he can therefore withdraw life at his will (Deut. 30:19; cf. Judg. 13:3; Job 34:14–15). All life, whatever its expression, has consequently its source in him.

Fuller study of the OT passages shows that the phrase "the living God" was not intended simply to contrast the God of Israel with the dead idols of the heathen. It is specifically a positive description of him as present and active in the world, and in particular among his chosen people as creator and sustainer of their national existence, as well as being himself the never-failing energy of its life both physical and spiritual.

In the NT the very life which is God's is shared by his Son. Peter's declaration (Matt. 16:16) amounts to the confession that the living God is now revealed in him, and that he is thus the giver of eternal life to such as receive him (cf. John 6:68–69). In John 6:57 Jesus declared that "the living Father" had sent him, "and I live because of the Father." In living his life in the flesh, which involved human weakness, struggle, and suffering, Jesus throughout, and in his every moment, depended on the Father for sustenance and support. In thus referring his life to the living Father, Jesus made explicit the fact that all life on the human plane derives from God, is dependent on him, and is responsible to him.

In the OT. The two most important words translated "life" by the English versions are *hay*, usually in its plural form; *ḥayyîm;* and *nepeš*. Of these *ḥayyîm* is by far the most numerous, while *nepeš* occurs 754 times. The LXX distinguishes between them by translating the former as *zōē* and the latter as *psychē*. The term *rûaḥ*, found 378 times, often as a synonym for *nepeš* (cf. Isa. 26:9), means generally "life energy." As the "breath principle" of both man and beast (Eccles. 3:19; cf. Gen. 6:17; 7:15, 22) it has its source in God. Sometimes the presence of *rûaḥ* is contrasted with its absence, which is a state of death (cf. Gen. 45:27; I Sam. 30:12; Ps. 104:29).

Human Life. As existing, man has *ḥayyîm.* Broadly the term connotes active existence with the idea of movement prominent (cf. Gen. 7:21; Lev. 11:10 AV; Ezek. 47:9 AV; Acts 17:28). The opposite of this life movement is inertia. When God's Spirit moved, life came to be (Gen. 1:2).

Ecclesiastes declares that this life is God-given (5:18; cf. 8:15), and the psalmist speaks of "the God of my life" (42:8), who redeems from the Pit (103:4; cf. Lam. 3:58).

As living, man has *nepeš*. The word is usually translated "soul," sometimes as "breath," and as "life" ninety-nine times. Although common to man and beast (Job 12:10), *nepeš* in man expresses his existence as a living being apart from God (cf. Gen. 2:7; 12:13; Exod. 12:15) in contradistinction to *rûaḥ*, which expresses man as drawing his life from God. Yet man exists as a fully integrated being, a living psychosomatic unity.

Life is thus God's supreme gift. It is the "blessing" of which the opposite, death, is the curse (Deut. 30:19). Because it is good, life has "a moral and spiritual connotation" (Orr). To do good in the love and fear of God is truly to live (cf. Pss. 34:12; 36:9; Prov. 10:11).

Afterlife. There is no clear and constant affirmation of an individual future life in the OT. This may be because of the preoccupation of the nation with its own survival. Yet the belief must always have been in Jewish theological thought; the personal translation of Enoch and Elijah was familiar, as was the Mosaic account of man's creation. According to Josephus it was widely accepted in Judaism that "souls have an immortal vigor." At times the hope did shine forth, dimly and briefly. Job believed he would be vindicated after his skin was destroyed and without his flesh he would see God (19:25–26). If the hope of the future life is not certainly present in Pss. 71:20 and 73:23–26, the language of Ps. 16 concerning "the path of life" does readily lend itself to such an interpretation.

In the NT. Three words are translated "life": *bios, zōē,* and *psychē. Bios,* the few times it is used, connotes life as the present state of existence (Luke 8:14; I Tim. 2:2; II Tim. 2:4; I Pet. 4:2; I John 2:16) as well as the resources by which it is maintained ("living"—Mark 12:44; Luke 8:43 RSV marg.; 15:12, 30; 21:4; "goods"—I John 3:17).

Zōē, a frequently used word, corresponds generally with the OT *ḥayyîm* to denote the state of one possessed of vitality, one who is animate. The term embodies all conceptions of what constitutes life (Luke 12:15; Acts 8:33; 17:25; I Pet. 3:10) and so is constant in the phrase "eternal life" (John 3:15–16, 36; 4:14; Rom. 6:23; I Tim. 6:12).

Psychē generally equates with the OT *nepeš* as the animating principle of life (Acts 20:10) and thus stands for a man's "self" (cf. Acts 2:43; 3:23; Rom. 13:1). *Psychē* may specify life as presently lived on earth (cf. Matt. 10:28; 16:25) and life eternal in the kingdom of God (Luke 21:19; Heb. 10:39).

Present Life. Jesus regarded life as a sacred trust from God, and in that realization he himself lived. He did not come to destroy life but to save it (Luke 9:56 AV) and to give it overflowing zest (John 10:10). He decried overanxiety about the means of living (Matt. 6:25) since even the humblest forms of life were his Father's concern (Matt. 10:31; Luke 12:24). True living is not a matter of bread alone but of obedience to the word of God (Matt. 4:4). To seek to secure one's own life in selfish disregard of its spiritual dimension is finally to lose it; while to lose it for Christ's sake is to save it (Matt. 10:39; 16:25).

Eternal Life. The concept of eternal life is present in the teaching of Jesus (Matt. 19:29; 25:46; cf. 18:8–9; 19:17, and parallels), but it figures most prominently in the Johannine writings and means more than mere everlastingness. It is a life of a new quality—the God-type life. It is best understood in contrast to death, to that which is perishing (John 3:16; 5:24; 10:28). Life apart from God is the ethical destruction of the soul, the forfeiture of man's true destiny as a child of God. But the eternal life of which Christ is the embodiment and the giver is one of fellowship with God which by its nature transcends the limits of space and time. John stresses the present possession of this life. It is something the believer *has* (John 3:36; 6:47; I John 5:12–13, 16). This Christ-communicated life is essentially divine (John 5:26; cf. 1:4), while belief is the one absolute subjective condition of its impartation (John 3:36; 5:24; 6:40, 47).

When expressing the significance of salvation in Christ in terms of life, Paul has the same general account as does John. He uses the phrase nine times. Of this life Christ is at once its source and mediator (Rom. 6:23)—indeed the two, Christ and life, are virtually identified (Gal. 2:20; Phil. 1:21; Col. 3:3–4). Sometimes Paul uses the simple term "life" as containing all the implications of eternal life (Rom. 5:17; II Cor. 5:4; Phil. 2:16).

This life is not, however, imposed on anyone; it has to be taken hold of (I Tim. 6:12, 19). It is procured by faith (I Tim. 1:16), while the inward and outward evidences of its possession are outlined in Rom. 6 and II Cor. 4 (cf. vss. 11, 16).

Phrases such as "newness of life" (Rom. 6:4), "new life of the Spirit" (Rom. 7:6; cf. Gal. 5:25), "life in Christ Jesus" (Rom. 6:23; 8:2; II Cor. 4:10–11; cf. II Tim. 3:12) are alternatives for eternal life.

Resurrection Life. Eternal life is not only a present possession, it carries the hope of future realization. The promise of godliness is for both the life that now is and that which is to come

(I Tim. 4:8). Paul gives prominence to the future aspect and coordinates it with immortality (Rom. 2:7; cf. II Cor. 5:4; II Tim. 1:10), while contrasting it with death (Rom. 6:23) and corruption (Gal. 6:8). As himself the "resurrection and the life" (John 11:25), Christ has "abolished death and brought life and immortality to light through the gospel" (II Tim. 1:10). The hope of life forever more is thus assured in him (II Tim. 1:1; Titus 1:2; 3:7). Christ is the believer's life both present and future (Col. 3:3–4; cf. Gal. 2:20; Phil. 1:21), and because Christ lives so shall he live also (John 14:19). Hope in Christ is not for this life only (I Cor. 15:19), for at his coming again the earthly tent in which we now live will be exchanged for a heavenly dwelling (II Cor. 5:1–2; I Cor. 15:42–43) and so "that which is mortal shall be swallowed up by life" (II Cor. 5:4). H. D. McDonald

See also Eternal Life; Resurrection of the Dead.

Bibliography. J. Calvin, *Institutes of the Christian Religion;* J. G. Hoare, *Life in St. John's Gospel;* J. Orr, *ISBE,* III, 1888–90; A. R. Johnson, *The Validity of the Individual in the Thought of Ancient Israel;* H. W. Robinson, *Corporate Personality in Ancient Israel;* O. A. Piper, *IDB,* III, 124–30; R. Bultmann, *TDNT,* II, 832–75; E. E. Ellis, *NBD;* W. B. Wallis, *ZPEB,* III, 927–32; D. M. Johnson, *Human Life and Human Worth;* H. D. McDonald, *The Christian View of Man.*

Life, Book of. *See* Book of Life.

Life, Everlasting. *See* Eternal Life.

Light. To the ancient Hebrew, surrounded by sun worshipers, light was a holy thing, the natural symbol for deity. In the OT God is pictured as creating light (Gen. 1:3) and being clothed with light (Ps. 104:2), and the term is used in conjunction with life to express that ultimate blessedness which God gives to men (Ps. 36:9). In the NT *phōs* is employed as an expression for the eternally real in contrast to the *skotos* of sin and unreality. Some trace this contrast back to the antithesis between the realms of Ahura Mazda and Angra Mainyu in Zoroastrianism, and it certainly colors the doctrine of the two spirits in the Dead Sea Scrolls. Plato associated the sun with the idea of the good, and Philo regarded the Creator as the archetype of light.

In I John 1:5 it is stated absolutely that *ho theos phōs estin.* James calls God, as Creator of heavenly bodies, *patros tōn phōtōn* (1:17), adding the caveat that he does not change position or suffer eclipse as they do. The Pastorals recall the majesty of God on Sinai by stating that he dwells in *phōs aprositon.* Light in the NT is more often spoken of as residing in the Logos and is described (John 1:3–4) as the life of men. It enters the world, shines in the darkness of error, illumines every man; but only those who receive the Logos become children of light and ultimately enter the Holy City whose *lychnos* is the lamb (*arnion,* Rev. 21:23).

By becoming incarnate the Logos becomes *phōs tou kosmou* (John 8:12). In rabbinic tradition this phrase had been applied to Torah and temple and did not amount to a claim to deity; but for John it implies that Christ is the *phōs alēthinon,* the ultimate reality. By contrast there are many lesser lights or copies of reality, who derive their transitory flame from the Logos; such a *lychnos* was the Baptist (John 5:35). The true Light bears witness to himself, because light is self-evidencing, and by light we see light. The lesser lights witness to the Logos.

Paul's conversion is essentially an encounter with the *phōs ek tou ouranou* (Acts 9:3). The scales of sinful darkness fall from his eyes, and he is commissioned as a light of the Gentiles (Acts 13:47). He puts on the armor of light to contend with the rulers of world darkness, who are led by Satan, metamorphosed into a parody angel of light (II Cor. 11:14). He exhorts his converts to walk as children of light (Eph. 5:8).

During the Exodus God's light was displayed to Israel as his *shekinah* glory in cloud and fire. *Phōs* is also found associated with *doxa* in the LXX of Isa. 60:1–3. The transfiguration accounts contain both themes. Christ's garments become white as *phōs* (Matt. 17:2), and both Peter and John insist that they beheld the *doxa* of God on the mount (John 1:14; II Pet. 1:17). In the Fourth Gospel the light of Christ's glory is manifested not simply on the mount, but by all his signs, and issues in a *krisis* or discrimination by light: evildoers hate the light; truth-seekers come to the light; when light appears, all men pass judgment on themselves (John 3:19–21).

D. H. Tongue

See also Darkness.

Bibliography. C. H. Dodd, *The Interpretation of the Fourth Gospel;* A. Dupont-Sommer, *The Jewish Sect of Qumran;* R. Bultmann, *Zur Geschichte der Lichtsymbolik im Altertum;* H.-C. Hahn *et al., NIDNTT,* II, 484ff.; H. Conzelmann, *TDNT,* IX, 310ff.; E. R. Goodenough, *By Light, Light;* D. Tarrant, "Greek Metaphors of Light," *SJT* 14:172ff.

Likeness of God. *See* Image of God.

Limbo. Derived from a Germanic word for a hem or fringe, limbo was devised by medieval theologians as the place or state of those souls after death who did not fit neatly into either heaven or hell. In fact there were two limbos.

The limbo of the fathers (*limbus patrum*) was for the souls of the saints of the OT; Christ's descent into hell in the creed was interpreted as his liberating these souls and taking them to heaven. In Renaissance art the limbo of the fathers was depicted as a large prison cell. More important was the limbo of infants (*limbus infantum*). The majority of children born before the development of modern medicine died without attaining a maturity sufficient to commit serious personal sin. Augustine believed that all children of Adam have original sin, and hence infants who die without baptism are consigned to hell, although their punishment there will be mild. Many medieval theologians such as Peter Lombard and Thomas Aquinas considered the Augustinian view too harsh and postulated limbo as a perpetual state free from the pain of sense but without supernatural salvation and the enjoyment of God. Partly this view paralleled the development of the concept of original sin as privation of grace rather than as positive guilt.

The Councils of Lyons and Florence stated that those who die with only original sin will be punished differently from those with personal sin. Pius VI rejected the claim of the Jansenist Synod of Pistoia that belief in limbo was Pelagian; but belief in limbo has never been defined by the Roman Catholic Church, although it was the dominant teaching of Catholic theologians for many centuries. Theologians in the Calvinist tradition had little need to postulate a limbo: unbaptized infants go to heaven or hell as God has predestined them.

Many twentieth century Catholic theologians have tended to argue for the salvation of unbaptized infants, some postulating an illumination of the infant at the moment of death and a choice for or against God. Others see death itself as a sort of saving martyrdom. Some argue that the parents or the church provide a kind of baptism by desire. Others see limbo as lasting only until the general judgment, at which souls in limbo are either united to Christ or obdurately reject him. J. P. DONNELLY

See also INTERMEDIATE STATE.

Bibliography. J. Dyer, *Limbo: Unsettled Question;* V. Wilkin, *From Limbo to Heaven;* W. A. Van Roo, "Infants Dying Without Baptism: A Survey of Recent Literature and Determination of the State of the Question," *Greg* 35:406–73.

Limited Atonement. *See* ATONEMENT, EXTENT OF THE.

Literalism. A commitment to strict exactness of words or meanings in translation or interpretation. A literal translation seeks to represent as accurately as possible in one language the words which were written in another. By way of contrast, a paraphrase translation seeks only to reproduce the meaning (or the translator's understanding of the meaning) of the original.

Most often literalism is used in connection with biblical interpretation. Generally it seeks to discover the author's intent by focusing upon his words in their plain, most obvious sense. The Jewish rabbis practiced an extreme form of literalism which stressed external and even minor points of OT or traditional requirements. They gave little thought to the intent or purpose that lay behind the texts with which they dealt and so received the condemnation of Jesus (Matt. 23:23–24; Mark 7:3–23). Medieval interpreters sought a fourfold meaning (the *quadriga*)—literal, moral, allegorical, and anagogical—for every text. The plain, literal meaning was considered the lowest and least important level of meaning and received little attention. Disregard for the literal meaning led many of these theologians into sometimes wild speculations and vastly different allegorical or mystical interpretations for the same text.

Luther and the other Reformers, rejecting multiple meanings for biblical passages, sought the single sense. This Luther described as "the very simplest, . . . the literal, ordinary, natural sense." Literalism in this sense remains as the central focus of conservative Protestant interpretation theory.

Since the Reformation at least two main trajectories of thought have come to be associated with literalism. One attitude seems akin to that of the rabbis. It approaches the text in such a strict, unimaginative way that word and letter are permitted to suppress the spirit of the text. Interpretation becomes a mechanical, grammatical, logical process. In extreme forms this type of literalism makes no room for special consideration for figurative literary forms such as poetry or metaphor nor for the possibility of unique situations addressed by the author.

Other contemporary adherents of literalism, no less devoted to finding the true meaning of the text as intended by the author, employ different attitudes and methodologies. They seek to apply interpretative principles and rules with a sense of appropriateness and sensitivity. In addition to grammatical and philosophical investigations they employ information about the author's historical and cultural situation that may aid in interpretation. Differing literary forms and genres are handled with methods suitable to their type. Individual passages are considered within their immediate context in the writing in which they appear as well as within the totality of Scripture. These interpreters focus upon words and externals in order that these may lead them to the meaning and spirit of the text. For them "literalism" means to seek the plain meaning without exaggeration, distortion, or inaccuracy. J. J. Scott, Jr.

See also Interpretation of the Bible.

Literal Sense of Scripture. *See* Interpretation of the Bible.

Liturgical Year. *See* Christian Year; Worship in the Church.

Liturgies. *See* Worship in the Church.

Locke, John (1632–1704). English philosopher often associated with early modern empiricism and a staunch defender of free inquiry. The son of an attorney, he was educated at Oxford for the ministry, studied chemistry and medicine, and served the family of the Earl of Shaftesbury as doctor, secretary, and tutor. His study of Descartes awakened his interest in philosophy, while his study of Hobbes helped form his ideas. A rationalist at heart, Locke ironically freed philosophy from many of its rationalistic presuppositions, and his philosophic system is a combination of Christian rationalism and empiricism.

In *Essay Concerning Human Understanding* (1690), Locke depicted the human mind as a blank slate, a sheet of white paper "void of all characters, without any ideas." The two fountains of knowledge from which ideas flow are sense-experience and self-reflection. By means of reflection one perceives one's own states and activities, while by sensation one ascertains the effects of other things. Locke dismissed Descartes's Platonist conception of "innate ideas," declaring that knowledge through reason was a "natural revelation." Such knowledge through sense-experience or self-reflection was never absolute or final, but probable and reasonable. Thus, Locke spoke of the "reasonableness" of Christianity, argued for the existence of God, and maintained that God's law gives men their rule of morality. Locke appears to be more interested in the self-reflection aspect, and later empiricists would criticize him for forsaking direct mechanistic conceptions for reflective analysis.

Locke's place in the history of theology is clearly demonstrated in his *Reasonableness of Christianity* (1695). In this treatise he clearly states that the essence of Christianity is the acknowledgment of Jesus Christ as the Messiah, while emphasizing that reason is the final criterion in ascertaining the truth of the Bible. Jesus was sent into the world to give true knowledge of God and to provide an example for man, and Locke maintained that even Christ's miracles were not out of harmony with reason. Locke admitted that Christian dogma was incapable of irrefutable proof, but declared that Christ confirmed a moral law already apparent from nature (a law also enforced by rewards or punishments in another world). The broader implications of this thought are found in his social contract theory, which postulated an ethical society of those who voluntarily accepted a set of moral principles advantageous to society and to self.

While the extremely popular Locke insisted that he was not a deist and that he did not want to dispense with Scripture as revelation (the last years of his life he devoted to study of the Bible), others would carry his ideas to these extremes. His philosophical and theological thoughts would provide a bridge to the natural religion of deism.

D. A. Rausch

See also Deism; Rationalism; Empiricism, Empirical Theology; Enlightenment, The.

Bibliography. R. Aaron, *John Locke;* J. Colman, *John Locke's Moral Philosophy;* J. J. Jenkins, *Understanding Locke.*

Logia. *Logia* (plural of *logion*) occurs four times in the NT (Acts 7:38; Rom. 3:2; Heb. 5:12; I Pet. 4:11).

The singular and plural forms are common in classical literature for "divine oracle." In LXX readings the singular occurs twenty-five times and the plural fourteen times, and the translators of the Pentateuch, Psalms, and Isaiah regularly render *'imrâ* ("utterance") by one or the other when God is the subject. Possibly the translator of Psalms equated *'imrâ* with Torah, especially in Ps. 119. *Logia* is used of human speech only in Ps. 19:14, and this was probably understood as a prayer for prophetic, and thus oracular, utterance.

In hellenistic Jewish literature *logia* designates Scripture (Josephus, *Jewish War* vi. 4), or any part of it (*Letter of Aristeas* 158, 177), including narrative. Of Philo's usage, Warfield says: "All that is in Scripture is oracular, every passage is a *logion*, of whatever character or length; and the whole, as constituted by these oracles, is *ta logia*, or even *to logion*."

These facts fix the meaning in the NT. In Acts 7:38 the living oracles are the law, perhaps the written tablets. Rom. 3:2 refers to the OT as such, not to "those utterances in it which stand out as most unmistakably divine" (Sanday and Headlam), nor to the whole revelation of OT and NT (Kittel). Again, Heb. 5:12 refers most naturally to the OT as the daily food of Christians. In I Pet. 4:11 alone is there no express relation to the OT. Here the Christian who ministers is to comfort himself as the bearer of a "Thus saith the Lord" (although Bigg would paraphrase, "as Scripture speaks").

The fathers use *logia* for the Scriptures (I Clement liii). The words of the Lord were also *logia* (Justin, *Trypho* 18); heretics perverted them (Polycarp, *Phld.* 7:1). Papias wrote an *Exposition of the Lord's Logia,* of which a surviving fragment says: "Matthew wrote the *logia* in Hebrew, and everyone interpreted them as he was able" (Eusebius, *History* iii. 39). Some refer this to the Gospel source Q or to a collection of OT messianic oracles; but Eusebius clearly understands Papias to refer to the First Gospel. He would call it *logia,* either because the teaching was his main concern, or because "oracles" was already a collective title for a recognized Gospel, as it was for the OT. The latter is clearly the sense in II Clement xiii, and probably in Polycarp vii.

Oxyrhynchus Papyrus I was entitled "Logia of Jesus" by the first editors, Grenfell and Hunt.

A. F. WALLS

See also SAYINGS OF JESUS; SCRIPTURE.

Bibliography. A. Debrunner *et al., TDNT,* IV, 69–193; B. B. Warfield, "The Oracles of God," in *Inspiration and Authority of the Bible;* J. W. Doeve in *Studia Paulina;* B. W. Bacon, *Studies in Matthew.*

Logical Positivism. *See* POSITIVISM.

Logos. The most usual Greek term for "word" in the NT: occasionally with other meanings (e.g., account, reason, motive); specifically in the prologue to the Fourth Gospel (John 1:1, 14) and perhaps in other Johannine writings (I John 1:1; Rev. 19:13) it is used of the second person of the Trinity. In ordinary Greek parlance it also means reason.

Johannine Usage. According to John 1:1–18 the Logos was already present at the creation ("in the beginning" relates to Gen. 1:1), in the closest relationship with God ("with" = *pros,* not *meta* or *syn*). Indeed, the Logos *was* God (not "divine," as Moffatt—the anarthrous predicate is grammatically required but may also indicate a distinction between the persons). This relationship with God was effective in the moment of creation (1:2). The entire work of creation was carried out through ("by" =*dia,* vs. 3) the Logos. The source of life (1:4, probable punctuation) and light of the world (cf. 9:5) and of every man (1:9, probable punctuation), and still continuing (present tense in 1:5) this work, the Logos became incarnate, revealing the sign of God's presence and his nature (1:14).

The prologue thus sets out three main facets of the Logos and his activity: his divinity and intimate relationship with the Father; his work as agent of creation; and his incarnation.

In I John 1:1 "the Logos of life," seen, heard, and handled, may refer to the personal Christ of the apostolic preaching or impersonally to the message about him. Rev. 19:12 pictures Christ as a conquering general called the Logos of God. As in Heb. 4:12, it is the OT picture of the shattering effects of God's word (cf. the imagery of vs. 15) which is in mind.

Background of the Term. *OT.* Diverse factors give some preparation for John's usage. God creates by the word (Gen. 1:3; Ps. 33:9) and his word is sometimes spoken of semipersonally (Ps. 107:20; 147:15, 18); it is active, dynamic, achieving its intended results (Isa. 50:10–11). The wisdom of God is personified (Prov. 8—note especially vss. 22ff. on wisdom's work in creation). The angel of the Lord is sometimes spoken of as God, sometimes as distinct (cf. Judg. 2:1). God's name is semipersonalized (Exod. 23:21; I Kings 8:29).

Palestinian Judaism. Besides the personification of wisdom (cf. Ecclus. 24), the rabbis used the word *mēʼmrāʼ,* "word," as a periphrasis for "God." This usage occurs in the Targums.

Greek Philosophy. Among the philosophers the precise significance of Logos varies, but it stands usually for "reason" and reflects the Greek conviction that divinity cannot come into direct contact with matter. The Logos is a shock absorber between God and the universe, and the manifestation of the divine principle in the world. In the Stoic tradition the Logos is both divine reason and reason distributed in the world (and thus in the mind).

Hellenistic Judaism. In Alexandrian Judaism there was full personification of the word in creation (Wisd. Sol. 9:1; 16:12). In the writings of Philo, who, though a Jew, drank deeply from Platonism and Stoicism, the term appears more than 1300 times. The Logos is "the image" (Col. 1:15); the first form (*prōtogonos*), the representation (*charaktēr,* cf. Heb. 1:3), of God; and even "Second God" (*deuteros theos;* cf. Eusebius, *Praeparatio Evangelica* vii. 13); the means whereby God creates the world from the great waste; and, moreover, the way whereby God is known (i.e., with the mind. Closer knowledge could be received directly, in ecstasy).

Hermetic Literature. Logos occurs frequently in the Hermetica. Though post-Christian, these are influenced by hellenistic Judaism. They indicate the Logos doctrine, in something like Philonic terms, in pagan mystical circles.

Sources of John's Doctrine. John 1 differs radically from philosophic usage. For the Greeks, Logos was essentially reason; for John, essentially word. Language common to Philo and the NT has led many to see John as Philo's debtor. But one refers naturally to Philo's Logos as "It," to John's as "He." Philo came no nearer than Plato to a Logos who might be incarnate, and he does not identify Logos and Messiah. John's Logos is not only God's agent in creation; He is *God,* and becomes incarnate, revealing, and redeeming.

The rabbinic *mēʾmrāʾ* hardly more than a reverent substitution for the divine name, is not sufficiently substantial a concept; nor is direct contact with Hermetic circles likely.

The source of John's Logos doctrine is in the person and work of the historical Christ. "Jesus is not to be interpreted by Logos: Logos is intelligible only as we think of Jesus" (W. F. Howard, *IB,* VIII, 442). Its expression takes its suitability primarily from the OT connotation of "word" and its personification of wisdom. Christ is God's active Word, his saving revelation to fallen man. It is not accidental that both the gospel and Christ who is its subject are called "the word." But the use of "Logos" in the contemporary hellenistic world made it a useful "bridge" word.

In two NT passages where Christ is described in terms recalling Philo's Logos, the word Logos is absent (Col. 1:15–17; Heb. 1:3). Its introduction to Christian speech has been attributed to Apollos.

Logos in Early Christian Use. The apologists found the Logos a convenient term in expounding Christianity to pagans. They used its sense of "reason," and some were thus enabled to see philosophy as a preparation for the gospel. The Hebraic overtones of "word" were underemphasized, though never quite lost. Some theologians distinguished between the *Logos endiathetos,* or Word latent in the Godhead from all eternity, and the *logos prophorikos,* uttered and becoming effective at the creation. Origen seems to have used Philo's language of the *deuteros theos.* In the major Christological controversies, however, the use of the term did not clarify the main issues, and it does not occur in the great creeds. A. F. Walls

See also Word, Word of God, Word of the Lord; Jesus Christ; John, Theology of.

Bibliography. R. G. Bury, *The Logos Doctrine and the Fourth Gospel;* C. H. Dodd, *The Fourth Gospel;* W. F. Howard, *Christianity According to St. John;* Commentaries on John by B. F. Westcott, J. H. Bernard, C. K. Barrett; R. L. Ottley, *Doctrine of the Incarnation;* A. Debrunner, *TDNT,* IV, 69ff.; H. Haarbeck *et al., NIDNTT,* III, 1078ff.; F. E. Walton, *The Development of the Logos Doctrine in Greek and Hebrew Thought.*

Loisy, Alfred Firmin (1857–1940). French Catholic modernist and biblical scholar. Born at Ambrières in French Lorraine, Loisy studied for the Catholic priesthood at Chalons-sur-Marne Seminary (1874–79) and then at the Institute Catholique in Paris (1879–81). Ordained in 1879, in 1881 he began to teach Hebrew and Assyrian and then biblical exegesis at this institute. But because he employed the canons of historical criticism in his Bible teaching, he was dismissed in 1893. From 1894 to 1899 he served as chaplain to the Dominican teaching nuns at Neuilly. In 1900 he was appointed lecturer on the science of religion at the École Pratique des Hautes Études.

In 1902 Loisy published *L'évangile et l'église* (*The Gospel and the Church*). It was a reply to the liberal German Protestant Adolf Harnack, who in his book *Das Wesen des Christentums* (*What Is Christianity?*) had maintained that essential Christianity consisted in acceptance of Christ's teaching concerning the fatherhood of God and the brotherhood of man—i.e., the religion *of* Jesus, not the religion *about* Jesus. Christianity with its institutional church represented a perversion of the original gospel. But Loisy contended that Jesus preached a future objective kingdom, of which his messiahship was the central feature. When this kingdom did not immediately materialize, the organized church, with its hierarchy, cultus, and creeds, emerged as the necessary instrument through which the Christian gospel could be proclaimed to the world. But this apologetic argument did not sit well with the church establishment. In 1903 Loisy's *L'évangile et l'église,* along with four of his other books, was put on the Index of prohibited books. In 1904 he resigned his position at the École Pratique, and in 1906 he ceased to exercise his priestly functions. In 1907 Pope Pius X in his decree *Lamentabili* and his encyclical *Pascendi gregis,* "Against the Errors of the Modernists," condemned Loisy's positions as "the synthesis of all heresies." Refusing to accept this papal condemnation, Loisy was excommunicated in 1908.

From 1909 to 1930 Loisy was professor of the history of religions in the Collège de France. Though he continued to publish scholarly works, mainly in the field of early Christianity, he drew no nearer to Catholic orthodoxy and died unreconciled to the church. N. V. Hope

See also CATHOLICISM, LIBERAL.

Bibliography. A. Loisy, *My Duel with the Vatican;* M. D. Petre, *Alfred Loisy, His Religious Significance.*

Lombard, Peter. *See* PETER LOMBARD.

Lord. *See* GOD, NAMES OF.

Lord, Jesus as. "Jesus is Lord" is probably the earliest of the Christian confessions and worked its way into the various acts of Christian worship. In what may well reflect a baptismal liturgy Paul writes, "If you confess with your mouth 'Jesus is Lord'... you will be saved" (Rom. 10:9). Similarly, in the confessional or creedal formula in Phil. 2:11 every tongue shall confess that "Jesus Christ is Lord." Furthermore, only by the Holy Spirit can one say "Jesus is Lord" (I Cor. 12:3).

It is important to note that it is Jesus as the risen and exalted one who is Lord—i.e., the lordship of Jesus is confessed by the believing community in virtue of his exaltation to the right hand of God. In his Pentecost sermon Peter declares that Jesus whom they crucified God has raised and exalted to his right hand; and the whole house of Israel must know assuredly that God by this exaltation has made him Lord and Christ (Acts 2:36). According to Paul, Jesus as Lord is declared Son of God with power through his resurrection from the dead. This must not be taken to mean that lordship is not to be ascribed to the earthly ministry of Jesus but to reinforce the point that the significance of the title in the life of the church is linked to his exaltation. To underscore this, Ps. 110:1 was drawn on heavily (cf. Matt. 22:44; 26:64 and pars; Acts 2:34–35; Heb. 1:3).

Scholars have long debated the origin and significance of the title. Did it arise out of a Palestinian or a hellenistic milieu? Is its significance to be found in the OT or among the religions of the ancient world? In the Palestinian community "Lord" was most commonly linked with Yahweh and became a regular circumlocution for the divine name in the public reading of the Scriptures. In the LXX it is a translation of the Hebrew term "Adonai," a designation for Yahweh. Furthermore, the use of *Maranatha* ("Our Lord, come" or "Our Lord is coming") in I Cor. 16:22 suggests an early Palestinian origin. It is suggested, therefore, that when Jesus is called Lord, it is affirming his oneness with God. Others, most notably Wilhelm Bousset and Rudolf Bultmann, have tried to show the title arose out of the worship of the hellenistic Christian communities, which borrowed the title from the Greek background in which "Lord" is a common reference to the deity to be worshiped. They have argued that the title, which makes Jesus equal with God, could not have arisen in the monotheism of Palestine, and that Jesus was first worshiped in these hellenistic Christian communities. Though the debate is exceedingly complex, the former explanation is probably to be preferred. The recognition by even the enemies of Jesus that he acted and spoke with the authority of the OT Lord is not to be dismissed.

As the title for the exalted one, "Lord" has special reference to the present work of Christ as over against his former work on earth or his future work. The life of the community is lived under Jesus' lordship (Rom. 14:8). The baptism, or gift, of the Spirit is the act of the risen Lord which creates and extends the church. Through the Spirit the lordship of Jesus is exercised so that even the work of the Spirit is to be seen as the work of the risen Lord. Having ascended on high he has given the church its charismatic leadership for the equipping of the saints and the perfecting of his body (Eph. 4:11ff.). The diversity of gifts and the variety of services are the singular activity of the Lord (I Cor. 12:4–5). The empowerment of the church is also expressed in the head-body imagery employed by Paul so that the head sustains the body and keeps it on course in the fulfilling of the divine plan (Eph. 1:22–23; Col. 1:18; 2:10). In the church the risen Lord thereby continues his own ministry begun in the incarnation.

Prayer, praise, thanksgiving, and intercession are carried on in the church by virtue of the presence of the Lord at the right hand of the Father (Rom. 8:34). The church rejoices in the Lord (Rom. 5:11; Phil. 3:1; 4:4). All the promises of the present meaning of ministry and witness are rooted in the lordship of Jesus. The promise of conquest and the certain, present reality of the love of God flow from his presence at the right hand of God (Rom. 8:34–39).

The whole of the created order also comes under the lordship of Jesus. He is the sovereign firstborn over all creation, for it was created through him and is sustained by him (Col. 1:15–16; Heb. 1:3). The structure of the text of Col. 1:15–20 shows that Jesus has the same relationship over the created order that he has over his new creation, the church. Only so do we perceive meaning in both the world and creation. So it is the purpose of God to bring all things to their fulfillment in him (Eph. 1:10).

The lordship of Jesus over history is carried out through the church and its proclamation. By virtue of his lordship the church is free to live in the world as servant. Being free from the necessity of power and achievement, for the victory is sealed, the church functions in terms of faithfulness and obedience, knowing that it is God who gives the increase (I Cor. 3:6) and that the conquest of death as the last enemy is a certainty in the light of the victory of Christ (I Cor. 15:25–26). The gift of freedom is that by which the church bears witness to his lordship. The cross is taken up daily. The same is to be said of the weakness of the church. In Revelation the beast is allowed to make war against the saints and to conquer them (Rev. 13:7), but the final chapter reverses the script. The foolishness of the church also bears witness to the lordship of Jesus, since it is by paradox that the church prospers. Paul's testimony regarding himself is true for the church: When it is weak, then it is strong (II Cor. 12:10).

The consequence of the church's reflection on the lordship of Jesus was to establish—in spite of the threat it might have posed to monotheistic commitments—the oneness of Jesus with God. As L. Goppelt has stated, "He was incorporated into the singularity of God." So a title whose basic thrust is to assert Jesus' present power and authority in the church and in the world leads the church to recognize that the authority is the direct, not mediated, authority of God himself. Jesus as Lord speaks not only of his work but of his person also, a fact made clear by the way the various NT writers use the OT. Thus we see the prominence of the "name" of Jesus (e.g., Phil. 2:9–10; Acts 2:38). During his earthly ministry his lordship is obscured for the sake of redemptive servanthood, but after his resurrection he is declared openly to be what he always has been—one with God in power and person. R. W. Lyon

See also Jesus Christ; Trinity; Christology; God, Doctrine of.

Bibliography. W. Pannenberg, *Jesus—God and Man;* A. E. J. Rawlinson, *The NT Doctrine of the Christ;* H. E. W. Turner, *Jesus: Master and Lord;* P. Toon, *Jesus Christ Is Lord;* E. Schweizer, *Lordship and Discipleship;* O. Cullmann, *The Christology of the NT;* R. J. Knowling, *The Testimony of St. Paul to Christ;* W. Foerster and G. Quell, *TDNT,* III, 1039ff.; F. Hahn, *The Titles of Jesus in Christology;* W. Kramer, *Christ, Lord, Son of God;* R. N. Longenecker, *The Christology of Early Jewish Christianity.*

Lord of Hosts. *See* God, Names of.

Lord's Day. Only once does the phrase "the Lord's day" (Gr. *tē kyriakē hēmera*) occur in the NT and that is in the last book (Rev. 1:10). What it means is debated. Some interpret this as a reference to the eschatological day of the Lord. For others it refers to Easter Sunday. Most, however, understand it as a designation of the first day of the week, Sunday.

Later references in early Christian literature in which the adjective alone (Gr. *kyriakē*) was used seem to support this. Ignatius, bishop of Antioch, wrote to the Magnesians *ca* A.D. 115 urging them to "no longer live for the Sabbath but for the Lord's day [Gr. *kyriakēn*], on which day our life arose" (9:1).

In an early manual of church instruction, the Didache (*ca.* A.D. 120), Christians were directed to assemble on the Lord's day to worship (14:1). According to the apocryphal Gospel of Peter (*ca.* A.D. 130) on the night of the Lord's day the stone was rolled away from the tomb (9:35). At dawn on the same day (Gr. *orthrou de tēs kyriakēs*) the empty tomb was visited by the women (12:50).

The attraction of the phrase was at least twofold. It expressed the Christian conviction that Sunday was a day of resurrection when Christ Jesus conquered death and became Lord of all (Eph. 1:20–22; I Pet. 3:21–22) and a day which anticipated the return of that same Lord to consummate his victory (I Cor. 15:23–28, 54–57).

In the NT Sunday was usually designated as "the first day of the week" (Gr. *mia sabbatōn,* e.g., Matt. 28:1; Mark 16:2; Luke 24:1; John 20:1). The term "sabbath" (Gr. *sabbatōn*) referred to both the seventh day of the week, Saturday, and the week of seven days in its entirety. Since only Saturday was specifically named, the remaining days of the week were distinguished by ordinal numbers with Sunday as "the first."

The term "Sunday" (Gr. *heliou hēmera*), never used by NT writers, first appeared in Christian literature in the work of Justin (*ca* A.D. 150, *First Apology* 67.3), who followed the Roman calendar. The name "Sunday" came to the Romans through the Egyptians, who early adopted a week of days named after the sun, moon, and five planets. The first day of the week to the Romans was the day of the sun (Lat. *dies solis*). In the course of time, however, the Christian designation "the Lord's day" (Lat. *dies dominica*) came to displace the term "Sunday" throughout the Roman Empire. Modern Romance languages, which developed from the ordinary Latin, reflect this change, referring to the first day of the week as *domenica* (Italian), *domingo* (Spanish), and *dimanche* (French).

Early Practice. That the early church customarily met on Sunday during the NT era cannot be unequivocally demonstrated. However, two NT references suggest that this was the case. Paul met with the church at Troas (Acts 20:7) on the first day of the week at what seems to be a regular, although prolonged, meeting. He also directed the Corinthian church to make their contribution to the collection for the needy on a Sunday (I Cor. 16:2), a practice which likely, though not necessarily, coincided with the meeting of the church.

Whether these meetings commenced according to the Jewish scheme of reckoning days (sunset to sunset) on a Saturday evening or according to the Roman (midnight to midnight) on a Sunday is a matter also debated, but the latter was more likely. According to Pliny, a Roman governor in Asia Minor (*ca.* 95–110), Christians met at dawn on a regularly scheduled day (Lat. *stato die*) to worship Christ and then reassembled later the same day to eat a meal (*Letter to Trajan* 10.96.7), a practice which recognized the Roman day. Christians in Corinth similarly met for a communal meal which included the observance of the Lord's Supper (I Cor. 11:17–34). Whether they met morning and evening cannot be determined. If Paul's subsequent comments about worship (I Cor. 14:26–40) were intended to conform Corinthian practice to what obtained elsewhere (cf. 14:33), then the Sunday gathering was also marked by considerable congregational participation including singing, prayer, and proclamation. According to Justin (*First Apology* 67.3–6) Sunday services included a reading of Scripture, exhortation, corporate and individual prayers, the Lord's Supper, and a collection.

Theology of the Lord's Day. When the early church began Sunday worship is not known. Nor do the NT writers offer a rationale for the shift from Saturday's sabbath observance to Sunday's meetings, but several factors may be suggested. (1) The seventh day, Saturday, was no longer regarded as a day to be especially observed by worship and rest from labor (Rom. 14:5–6; Gal. 4:8–11; Col. 2:16–17; cf. Acts 15:28–29). (2) The event of the resurrection, at the heart of the Christian gospel (e.g., Acts 2:31; 4:2, 10, 33; 10:40; 13:33–37; 17:18; Rom. 10:9; I Cor. 15:4, 12–19; I Thess. 1:10), occurred on a Sunday. (3) When the NT writers designated the various days on which the resurrected Christ appeared and spoke to his disciples, it was uniformly a Sunday (e.g., Matt. 28:9; Luke 24:13–34; John 20:19, 26). (4) The coming of the Holy Spirit (Acts 2) occurred on Pentecost, a Sunday. (5) After the NT era the first and "eighth" days of the week (both Sundays) were referred to respectively as the day of God's creation (Justin *First Apology* 67.7) and the day which anticipated the new creation or eternity (Barnabas 15:9; cf. II Enoch 33:7). Sunday was thus seen as a "first fruit" of the future eternal state (cf. I Cor. 15:20). Also, perhaps Christians anticipated the Lord's return on his day (cf. Luke 12:35–36).

Underlying each of these reasons, however, may have been the desire on the part of the early church to distinguish itself from Judaism and its distinctive sabbath observances.

Significance. Within Christianity there are many differences of opinion on how the Lord's day should be observed. Three general distinctions may be noted. First, some Christians believe that the church as a whole was mistaken in leaving a Saturday observance for Sunday worship without a specific command to do so. They continue faithfully to observe the fourth commandment, "Remember the sabbath day by keeping it holy" (Exod. 20:8), and they stress the importance of rest and religiously oriented activity. The Seventh-day Adventists are the most visible members of this group.

A second and larger group transfer the principles of sabbath observance to Sunday. The name "sabbatarian" is commonly given to this position. A classic expression of this is in the Westminster Shorter Catechism, in which Sunday is called "the Christian Sabbath" (Q. 59). This position is marked by a strictness with regard to Sunday activity and usually is characterized by a list of practices to be avoided on that day. Question 60, for example, asks, "How is the Sabbath to be sanctified?" The answer is "by a holy resting all that day, even from such worldly employments and recreations as are lawful on other days."

The trend toward sabbatarianism is as old as Tertullian (*ca.* A.D. 200), who advocated that Christians rest from work on Sunday "so that we may give no place to the devil" (*On Prayer* 23). The Roman emperor Constantine subsequently enacted legislation mandating cessation of most types of labor (agriculture was excepted) on Sunday (Codex Justinian 3.12.3). English and Scottish reformers, however, gave sabbatarianism its most stringent formulation by requiring all persons to attend church "on the Lord's day, commonly called Sunday"; prohibiting all "worldly labor or busyness," excepting only "works of necessity or charity" (Act of Parliament 29, ch. 7, of Charles II). The English Puritans and Scottish Presbyterians who came to the United States in turn enacted similar legislation, including the adoption of "blue laws" restricting Sunday commerce. Some of these laws, despite intensive litigation and extensive relaxation, continue in effect.

Most Christians may be included in a third group, who believe that the sabbath commandment was a part of the ceremonial law of Israel and therefore not applicable to the church. This seems to have been the position of the early church. No hint of cessation from work on Sundays is found until Tertullian. While various factors, including Scripture (Ps. 92:2), may have led to an early morning and late evening meeting schedule, one likely explanation was the need to assemble at times that would not conflict with the workday. The subsequent application of sabbath principles to the church by men like Ambrose (cf. *Homily* on Ps. 47) and Chrysostom (cf. *Homily 10* on Genesis) was in part a consequence of Constantine's imperial edict of 321 prescribing Sunday rest.

Most Christians, therefore, do not consider recreational activity or work on Sunday illegitimate, but they do stress the importance of gathering with other believers for worship, edification, and fellowship. Fellowship with other believers is encouraged in recognition of the fact that Christians are not isolated pilgrims but are members of one body united by faith in Christ, who require mutual intercourse for spiritual vitality (Heb. 10:25; Rom. 1:12). The goal of edification is the spiritual transformation of Christians into Christlikeness in character and conduct. A primary means to this end is the reading, explanation, and application of the Word of God (Eph. 4:11–16). Worship recognizes that the Christian's life was initiated by the graciousness of God the Father, was realized in the loving sacrifice of God the Son, and is advanced by the ministry of God the Spirit (Eph. 1:3–14). This worship is expressed in songs, prayers, and deeds such as giving, but preeminently in the Lord's Supper, which reminds of Jesus' death and anticipates his return (I Cor. 11:23–26). In so doing Sunday becomes the *Lord's* day. D. K. Lowery

See also Sabbatarianism; Worship in the Church.

Bibliography. S. Bacchiocchi, *From Sabbath to Sunday* and *Divine Rest for Human Restlessness;* R. Beckwith and W. Stott, *The Christian Sunday;* C. W. Dugmore, "The Lord's Day and Easter," in *Neotestamentica et Patristica;* W. Foerster, *TDNT,* III, 1095–96; P. K. Jewett, *The Lord's Day;* E. Lohse, *TDNT,* VII, 1–35; H. Oster, *Sacramentum Mundi;* H. Riesenfeld, "The Sabbath and the Lord's Day," in *The Gospel Tradition;* W. Rordorf, *Sunday;* W. Stott, "A Note on the Word *Kyriakē* in Rev. 1:10," *NTS* 12:70–75; D. A. Carson, ed., *From Sabbath to Lord's Day.*

Lord's Prayer. The meaning of Jesus' pattern for prayer in Matt. 6:9–13 needs to be sought in the wider context of the units 6:5–13 and 6:1–18. The larger units indicate that Jesus is contrasting surface language with depth language in worship of God. The prayer is not a set form that he himself prayed or asked his disciples to pray, but illustrates the type of prayer appropriate to the person who worships deeply without hypocrisy. The entire Sermon on the Mount (Matt. 5–7) takes its cue from Jesus' declaration in 5:20: "For I tell you, unless your righteousness exceeds that of the Scribes and Pharisees, you will never enter the kingdom of heaven." Three expressions of genuine worship are given in germinal form in 6:1–18: (1) almsgiving (2–4); (2) prayer (5–6, with 7–15 as pattern); and (3) fasting (16–18). The theme of 5:20 is applied to these three areas and is articulated in the warning, "Beware of practicing your piety before men in order to be seen by them; for then you will have no reward from your Father who is in heaven" (6:1). The warning is against play acting before a human audience; those who give, pray, or fast superficially will have their reward (refrain *a,* repeated in 6:2, 5, 16). Those who pray genuinely will receive their reward from God who sees *en tō kryptō,* "in secret" (refrain *b,* repeated in 6:3–4, 6, 17–18). The sentence and paragraph flow of 6:1–18 (with 6:19–21 as summary) brings out the antithetic contrasts of surface/depth motifs and illustrates the dominical pattern of Jesus' teaching that is picked up by Paul in his contrasts of living *kata sarka,* "according to the flesh," and *kata pneuma,* "according to the Spirit" (e.g., Gal. 5:16–24).

The eschatological age has broken in with the coming of Jesus, and now the law is no longer inscribed in stone but in the heart (Jer. 31:33). True prayer is to be a deep and spontaneous response to God, not a superficial game played out in public simply to curry favor with the world. The flow of thought in the larger unit of 6:1–18, with the summary of 6:19–21, makes clear the serious contrast of opposites in which the Lord's Prayer is to be understood.

Luke's location of the corresponding prayer (Luke 11:1–4) in the immediate context of Mary and Martha ("Martha, Martha, you are anxious and troubled about many things; . . . Mary has chosen the good portion, which shall not be taken away from her," 10:41–42) and the importuned friend and related sayings ("Ask, and it will be given you," 11:9; "how much more will the heavenly Father give the Holy Spirit to those who ask him," 11:13) indicates his similar understanding of the underlying meaning of Jesus' ordering of values in the new age.

Viewed in context of Jesus' eschatological contrasts, the Lord's Prayer provides a summary model for properly ordering the priorities of the kingdom. Both Matt. 6:9–13 and Luke 11:2–4 preserve Jesus' order: first God, then human needs. While Jesus makes use of Jewish sources in forming the prayer, he does not design it to be used as a set liturgical piece but as a model for the responsive heart in view of the demands of the new age. The prayer follows a common outline in both Matthew and Luke:

I. Petition to the Father for his glory
   Introduction: "Our Father who art in heaven" acknowledges the intimate relationship of Jesus and believers to the family of God, which is above transitory earthly values.
   1. First petition: "May thy name be hallowed." This prayer recognizes the sovereign claim of God over the world and anticipates human response and the final consummation in the eschatological age (cf. Rom. 10:13; 15:9; Phil. 2:9–11).
   2. Second petition: "May thy kingdom come." This prayer carries on the eschatological urgency of the "already/not yet" of Jesus' inaugurated kingship.
   3. Third petition: "Thy will be done, on earth as it is in heaven." This is an expansion of the unified theme of the first two petitions, indicating the sovereign goal of God's eschatological plan and the importance of the believer's role (implied) in praying for its completion.

II. Address to the Father for human needs
   4. Fourth petition: "Give us this day our bread for the morrow." Not only are daily needs in focus here but also quite likely a foretaste of the messianic banquet.
   5. Fifth petition: "And forgive us our debts, as we also have forgiven our debtors." The point here is one of proper attitude, as in the larger setting of Matt. 6:1–21. Unless one is in a forgiving mood in the sense of Matt. 6:14–15, he or she is not going to ask for or receive divine forgiveness.
   6. Sixth petition: "And lead us not into temptation, but deliver us from evil." Temptation is to be understood as testing (*peirasmos*); cf. Luke 22:28; I Pet. 1:6. In the NT it is often rendered *thlipsis,* tribulation (e.g., John 16:33; Rom. 12:12), which has not only present but future eschatological connotations in regard to the final test in the end time (Matt. 24:21; Mark 13:24; I Pet. 4:12). Matthew's version may be translated, "but deliver us from the evil one," i.e., from the devil or Antichrist. The petition is fraught with eschatological tension, for Jesus knows that the inauguration of the kingship of God in enemy-occupied territory is going to mean testing and suffering both for himself and for his followers, right to the very end.

The doxology commonly used to conclude the prayer is not well attested in the manuscript traditions, though it is consonant with the original theme. R. G. GRUENLER

See also PRAYER; SERMON ON THE MOUNT.

Bibliography. J. Calvin, *Institutes* 3.20.34ff.; F. Chase, *The Lord's Prayer in the Early Church;* R. Guelich, *The Sermon on the Mount;* J. Jeremias, *The Lord's Prayer;* E. Lohmeyer, *The Lord's Prayer;* W. Luthi, *The Lord's Prayer, an Exposition.*

Lord's Supper. In each of the four accounts of the Lord's Supper in the NT (Matt. 26:26–30; Mark 14:22–26; Luke 22:14–20; I Cor. 1:23–26) all the main features are included. The accounts of Matthew and Mark have close formal affinities. So have those of Luke and Paul. The main differences between the two groups are that Mark omits the words "This do in remembrance of me" and includes "shed for many" after the reference to the blood of the covenant. Instead of the Lord's reference to his reunion with the disciples in the fulfilled kingdom of God, common to the Synoptic Gospels, Paul has a reference to proclaiming the Lord's death "till he come."

The meaning of Jesus' action has to be seen against its OT background. Questions are legitimately raised, however, about the actual nature and timing of the meal. The accounts seem to be at variance. The Fourth Gospel says that Jesus died on the afternoon when the passover lamb was slain (John 18:28). The Synoptic accounts, however, suggest that the meal was prepared for, and eaten, as if it were part of the community celebration of the passover feast that year in Jerusalem after the slaying of the lambs in the temple.

The Synoptic accounts raise further problems. It has been thought unlikely that the arrest of Jesus, the meeting of the Sanhedrin, and the carrying of arms by the disciples could have taken place if the meal had coincided with the official passover date. Could Simon of Cyrene have been met coming apparently from work in the country, or could a linen cloth have been purchased for Jesus' body, if the feast was in progress?

To meet all such difficulties several suggestions have been made. Some have held that the meal took the form of a kiddush—a ceremony held by a family or brotherhood in preparation for the Sabbath or for a feast day. It has also been suggested that the meal could have been the solemn climax, before Jesus' death, of other significant messianic meals which he had been accustomed to share with his disciples, in which he and they looked forward to a glorious fulfillment of hope in the coming kingdom of God.

Such theories present as many new difficulties as those they claim to solve. Moreover, many of the features and details of the meal accounted for indicate that it was a passover meal. (They met at night, within the city; they reclined as they ate; the wine was red; wine was a preliminary dish.) Jesus himself was concerned to explain what he was doing in terms of the passover celebration. Scholars who regard the meal as a passover explain the attendant strange circumstances, and various theories have been produced to harmonize all the accounts. One theory is that disagreement between the Sadducees and the Pharisees led to different dates being fixed for the celebration of the feast in this year. Another theory suggests that Jesus held an irregular passover, the illegality of which contributed to his being betrayed by Judas and arrested. (Such a theory could explain why there is no mention of a passover lamb in the account.) Attention has been drawn to the existence of an ancient calendar in which the calculations of the date of the passover were made on premises different from those made in official circles. The following of such a calendar would have fixed the date of the feast a few days earlier than that of its official celebration.

There is no doubt that Jesus' words and actions are best understood if the meal is regarded as taking place within the context of the Jewish passover. In this the people of God not only remembered, but again lived through, the events of their deliverance from Egypt under the sign of the sacrificed paschal lamb as if they themselves participated in them (see Exod. 12). In this context, giving the bread and wine as his body and blood, with the words, "this do in remembrance of me," Jesus points to himself as the true substitute for the paschal lamb and to his death as the saving event which will deliver the new Israel, represented in his disciples, from all bondage. His blood is to be henceforth the sign under which God will remember his people in himself.

In his words at the table Jesus speaks of himself not only as the paschal lamb but also as a sacrifice in accordance with other OT analogies. In the sacrificial ritual the portion of peace offering not consumed by fire and thus not offered to God as his food (cf. Lev. 3:1–11; Num. 28:2) was eaten by priest and people (Lev. 19:5–6; I Sam. 9:13) in an act of fellowship with the altar and the sacrifice (Exod. 24:1–11; Deut. 27:7; cf. Num. 25:1–5; I Cor. 10). Jesus in giving the elements thus gave to his disciples a sign of their own fellowship and participation in the event of his sacrificial death.

Moreover, Jesus included in the Last Supper the ritual not only of the paschal and sacrificial meal but also of a covenant meal. In the OT the making of a covenant was followed by a meal in which the participants had fellowship and were pledged to loyalty one to another (Gen. 26:30; 31:54; II Sam. 3:20). The covenant between God and Israel at Sinai was likewise followed by a meal in which the people "ate and drank and saw God." The new covenant (Jer. 31:1–34) between the Lord and his people was thus ratified by Jesus in a meal.

In celebrating the Supper, Jesus emphasized the messianic and eschatological significance of the passover meal. At this feast the Jews looked forward to a future deliverance which was foreshadowed in type by that from Egypt. A cup was set aside for the Messiah lest he should come that very night to bring about this deliverance and fulfill the promise of the messianic banquet (cf. Isa. 25–26; 65:13, etc.). It may have been this cup which Jesus took in the institution of the new rite, indicating that even now the Messiah was present to feast with his people.

After the resurrection, in their frequent celebration of the Supper (Acts 2:42–46; 20:7), the disciples would see the climax of the table fellowship which Jesus had had with publicans and sinners (Luke 15:2; Matt. 11:18–19) and of their own day-to-day meals with him. They would interpret it not only as a bare prophecy but as a real foretaste of the future messianic banquet, and as a sign of the presence of the mystery of the kingdom of God in their midst in the person of Jesus (Matt. 8:11; cf. Mark 10:35–36; Luke 14:15–24). They would see its meaning in relation to his living presence in the church, brought out fully in the Easter meals they had shared with him (Luke 24:13–35; John 21:1–14; Acts 10:41). It was a supper in the presence of the risen Lord as their host. They would see, in the messianic miracle of his feeding the multitude, his words about himself as the bread of life, a sign of his continual hidden self-giving in the mystery of the Lord's Supper.

But they would not forget the sacrificial and paschal aspect of the Supper. The table fellowship they looked back on was the fellowship of the Messiah with sinners which reached its climax in his self-identification with the sin of the world on Calvary. They had fellowship with the resurrected Jesus through remembrance of his death. As the Lord's Supper related them to the coming kingdom and glory of Christ, so did it also relate them to his once-for-all death.

It is against this background of thought that we should interpret the words of Jesus at the table and the NT statements about the Supper. There is a real life-giving relationship of communion between the events and realities, past, present, and future, symbolized in the Supper and those who participate in it (John 6:51; I Cor. 10:16). This communion is so inseparable from participation in the Supper that we can speak of the bread and the wine as if they were indeed the body and blood of Christ (Mark 14:22, "This is my body"; cf. John 6:53). It is by the Holy Spirit alone (John 6:53) that the bread and wine, as they are partaken by faith, convey the realities they represent, and that the Supper gives us participation in the death and resurrection of Christ and the kingdom of God. It is by faith alone that Christ is received into the heart at the Supper (Eph. 3:17), and as faith is inseparable from the word, the Lord's Supper is nothing without the word. Christ is *Lord* at his table, the risen and unseen host (John 14:19). He is not there at the disposal of the church, to be given and received automatically in the mere performance of a ritual. Yet he is there according to his promise to seeking and adoring faith. He is present also in such a way that though the careless and unbelieving cannot receive him, they nevertheless eat and drink judgment to themselves (I Cor. 11:27).

In participating by the Holy Spirit in the body of Christ which was offered once-for-all on the cross, the members of the church are stimulated and enabled by the same Holy Spirit to offer themselves to the Father in eucharistic sacrifice, to serve one another in love within the body, and to fulfill their sacrificial function as the body of Christ in the service of the need of the whole world which God has reconciled to himself in Christ (I Cor. 10:17; Rom. 12:1).

There is in the Lord's Supper a constant renewal of the covenant between God and the church. The word "remembrance" (*anamnēsis*) refers not simply to man's remembering of the Lord but also to God's remembrance of his Messiah and his covenant, and of his promise to restore the kingdom. At the Supper all this is brought before God in true intercessory prayer.

R. S. Wallace

See also Lord's Supper, Views of.

Bibliography. J. Jeremias, *The Eucharistic Words of Jesus;* A. J. B. Higgins, *The Lord's Supper in the NT;* G. Wainwright, *Eucharist and Eschatology;* I. H. Marshall, *Lord's Supper and Last Supper;* F. J. Leenhardt and O. Cullmann, *Essays in the Lord's Supper;* J. J. von Allmen, *The Lord's Supper;* M. Thurian, *The Eucharistic Memorial;* E. J. F. Arndt, *The Font and the Table;* M. Marty, *The Lord's Supper;* E. Schillebeeckx, ed., *Sacramental Reconciliation.*

Lord's Supper, Views of. The NT teaches that Christians must partake of Christ in the Lord's Supper (I Cor. 11:23–32; cf. Matt. 26:26–29; Luke 22:14–23; Mark 14:22–25). In a remarkable discourse Jesus said that his disciples had to feed on him if they were to have eternal life (John 6:53–57). The setting of that discourse was the feeding of the five thousand. Jesus used the occasion to tell the multitude that it should not be as concerned about perishable food as about the food that lasts forever, which he gives them. That food is himself, his body and his blood. Those who believe in him must eat his flesh and drink his blood—not literally, but symbolically and sacramentally—in the rite he gave the church. Through faith in him and partaking of him they would live forever, for union with him means salvation.

The setting for the institution of the Lord's Supper was the passover meal that Jesus celebrated with his disciples in remembrance of the deliverance of Israel from Egypt (Matt. 26:17; John 13:1; Exod. 13:1–10). In calling the bread and wine his body and blood, and saying, "Do this in remembrance of me," Jesus was naming himself the true lamb of the passover whose death would deliver God's people from the bondage of sin. Thus Paul writes, "Christ, our paschal lamb, has been sacrificed" (I Cor. 5:7; cf. John 1:29).

Transubstantiation. The doctrine of the Lord's Supper first occasioned discord in the church in the ninth century when Radbertus, influenced by the hankering for the mysterious and supernatural which characterized his time, taught that a miracle takes place at the words of institution in the Supper. The elements are changed into the actual body and blood of Christ. Radbertus was opposed by Ratramnus, who held the Augustinian position that Christ's presence in the Supper is spiritual. The teaching and practice of the church moved in Radbertus's direction—a doctrine of transubstantiation; namely, that in the Supper the substance in the elements of bread and wine is changed into the substance of the body and blood of Christ while the accidents—i.e., the appearance, taste, touch, and smell—remain the same. In the eleventh century Berengar objected to the current idea that pieces of Christ's flesh are eaten during Communion and that some of his blood is drunk. With sensitivity he held that the whole Christ (*totus Christus*) is given the believer spiritually as he receives bread and wine. The elements remain unchanged but are invested with new meaning; they represent the body and blood of the Savior. This view was out of step with the times, however, and transubstantiation was declared the faith of the church in 1059, although the term itself was not used officially until the Fourth Lateran Council in 1215.

The medieval church continued and refined the teaching of transubstantiation, adding such subtleties as (1) concomitance, i.e., that both the body and blood of Christ are in each element; hence, when the cup is withheld from the laity the whole Christ, body and blood, is received in the bread alone; (2) consecration, i.e., the teaching that the high moment in the Eucharist is not communion with Christ but the change of the elements by their consecration into the very body and blood of Christ, an act performed by the priest alone; (3) that, inasmuch as there is the real presence of Christ in the Supper—body, blood, soul, and divinity—a sacrifice is offered to God; (4) that the sacrifice offered is propitiatory; (5) that the consecrated elements, or host, may be reserved for later use; (6) that the elements thus reserved should be venerated as the living Christ. The Council of Trent (1545–63) confirmed these teachings in its thirteenth and twenty-second sessions, adding that the veneration given the consecrated elements is adoration (*latria*), the same worship that is given God.

Luther and Consubstantiation. The Reformers agreed in their condemnation of the doctrine of transubstantiation. They held it to be a serious error that is contrary to Scripture; repugnant to reason; contrary to the testimony of our senses of sight, smell, taste, and touch; destructive of the true meaning of a sacrament; and conducive to gross superstition and idolatry. Luther's first salvo against what he considered to be a perversion of the Lord's Supper was *The Babylonian Captivity of the Church.* In it he charges the church with a threefold bondage in its doctrine and practice concerning the Supper—withholding the cup from the people, transubstantiation, and the teaching that the Supper is a sacrifice offered to God. Luther tells about his earlier instruction in the theology of the sacrament and of some of his doubts: "When I learned later what church it was that had decreed this, namely the Thomistic—that is, the Aristotelian church—I grew bolder, and after floating in a sea of doubt, I at last found rest for my conscience in the above view, namely, that it is real bread and real wine, in which Christ's real flesh and real blood are present in no other way and to no less a degree than the others assert them to be under their accidents. I reached this conclusion because I saw that the opinions of the Thomists, whether approved by pope or by council, remain only opinions, and would not become articles of faith even if an angel from heaven were to decree otherwise (Gal. 1:8). For what is asserted without the Scriptures or proven revelation may be held as an opinion, but need not be believed. But this opinion of Thomas hangs so completely in the air without support of Scripture or reason that it seems to me he knows neither his philosophy nor his logic. For Aristotle speaks of subject and accidents so very differently from St. Thomas that it seems to me this great man is to be pitied not only for attempting to draw his opinions in matters of faith from Aristotle, but also for attempting to base them upon a man whom he did not understand, thus building an unfortunate superstructure upon an unfortunate foundation." (*Works*, XXXVI, 29)

Luther was feeling his way into a new understanding of the sacrament at this time, but he believed it legitimate to hold that there are real bread and real wine on the altar. He rejected the Thomistic position of a change in the substance of the elements while the accidents remain, inasmuch as Aristotle, from whom the terms "substance" and "accidents" were borrowed, allowed no such separation. The "third captivity," the doctrine of the sacrifice of the Mass, Luther declared to be "by far the most wicked of all" for in it a priest claims to offer to God the very body and blood of Christ as a repetition of the atoning sacrifice of the cross, only in an unbloody manner, whereas the true sacrament of the altar is a "promise of the forgiveness of sins made to us by God, and such a promise as has been confirmed by the death of the Son of God." Since it is a promise, access to God is not gained by works or merits by which we try to please him but by faith alone. "For where there is the Word of the promising God, there must necessarily be the faith of the accepting man."

"Who in the world is so foolish as to regard a promise received by him, or a testament given to him, as a good work, which he renders to the testator by his acceptance of it? What heir will imagine that he is doing his departed father a kindness by accepting the terms of the will and the inheritance it bequeaths to him? What godless audacity is it, therefore, when we who are to receive the testament of God come as those who would perform a good work for him! This ignorance of the testament, this captivity of so great a sacrament—are they not too sad for tears? When we ought to be grateful for benefits received, we come arrogantly to give that which we ought to take. With unheard-of perversity we mock the mercy of the giver by giving as a work the thing we receive as a gift, so that the testator, instead of being a dispenser of his own goods, becomes the recipient of ours. Woe to such sacrilege!" (*Works*, XXXVI, 47–48)

In his determination to break the bondage of superstition in which the church was held, Luther wrote four more tracts against the medieval perversion of the Lord's Supper. However, he also fought doctrinal developments on the other side. Some who with him rejected Roman Catholic error were denying any real presence of Christ in the Supper; against them, beginning in 1524, Luther directed an attack. In these five writings he showed that, while he rejected transubstantiation and the sacrifice of the Mass, he still believed that Christ is bodily present in the Lord's Supper and that his body is received by all who partake of the elements. "On this we take our stand, and we also believe and teach that in the Supper we eat and take to ourselves Christ's body truly and physically." While he acknowledged the mystery, he was certain of the fact of Christ's real corporeal presence inasmuch as he had said when he instituted the Supper, "This is my body." If Scripture cannot be taken literally here, it cannot be believed anywhere, Luther held, and we are on the way to "the virtual denial of Christ, God, and everything." (*Works*, XXXVII, 29, 53)

Zwingli. Luther's main opponent among the evangelicals was Ulrich Zwingli, whose reforming activity in Switzerland was as old as Luther's in Germany. While equally opposed to Rome, Zwingli had been deeply influenced by humanism with its aversion to the medieval mentality and its adulation of reason. Luther felt an attachment to the whole tradition of the church, was conservative by nature, and had a deep mystical strain and suspicion of the free use of reason. "As the one was by disposition and discipline a schoolman who loved the Saints and the Sacraments of the Church, the other was a humanist who appreciated the thinkers of antiquity and the reason in whose name they spoke. Luther never escaped from the feelings of the monk and associations of the cloister; but Zwingli studied his New Testament with a fine sense of the sanity of its thought, the combined purity and practicability of its ideals, and the majesty of its spirit; and his ambition was to realize a religion after its model, free from the traditions and superstitions of men. It was this that made him so tolerant of Luther, and Luther so intolerant of him. The differences of character were insuperable." (H. M. Fairbairn, *The Cambridge Modern History*, II, 345–46)

The chief differences between Luther and Zwingli theologically were Luther's inability to think of Christ's presence in the Supper in any other than a physical way and a heavy dualism that runs through much of Zwingli's thought. The latter is seen in Zwingli's doctrine of the Word of God as both inward and outward, the church as both visible and invisible, and his conception of the means of grace as having both an external form and an inward grace given by the Holy Spirit. No physical element can affect the soul, but only God in his sovereign grace. Thus there must be no identification of the sign with that which it signifies, but through the use of the sign one rises above the world of sense to the spiritual reality signified. By contrast, Luther held that God comes to us precisely in physical realities discerned by sense.

Zwingli interpreted the words of Jesus, "This is my body," in harmony with John 6, where Jesus spoke of eating and drinking his body and blood, especially vs. 63: "It is the spirit that gives life, the flesh is of no avail." Therefore, he reasoned, not only is transubstantiation wrong but so is Luther's notion of consubstantiation, that somehow Christ is corporeally in, under, and with the elements. The doctrine of physical eating is absurd and repugnant to common sense. Moreover, God does not ask us to believe that which is contrary to sense experience. The word "is" in the words of institution means "signifies," or "represents," and must be interpreted figuratively, as is done in other "I am" passages in the Bible. Christ's ascension means that he took his body from earth to heaven.

Zwingli's shortcoming was his lack of appreciation for the real presence of Christ in the Supper in his Holy Spirit and a real feeding of the faithful on him. What he needed for an adequate doctrine was Luther's belief in the reality of communion with Christ and a reception of him in the Supper. This was to be found in Calvin.

Calvin. Calvin's view of the Lord's Supper appears to be a mediate position between the views of Luther and Zwingli, but it is in fact an independent position. Rejecting both Zwingli's "memorialism" and Luther's "monstrous notion of ubiquity" (*Inst.* 4.17.30), he held that there is a real reception of the body and blood of Christ in the supper, only in a spiritual manner. The sacrament is a real means of grace, a channel by which Christ communicates himself to us. With Zwingli, Calvin held that after the ascension Christ retained a real body which is located in heaven. Nothing should be taken from Christ's "heavenly glory—as happens when he is brought under the corruptible elements of this world, or bound to any earthly creatures. . . . Nothing inappropriate to human nature [should] be ascribed to his body, as happens when it is said either to be infinite or to be put in a number of places at once" (*Inst.* 4.12.19). With Luther, Calvin believed that the elements in the Supper are signs which exhibit the fact that Christ is truly present, and he repudiated Zwingli's belief that the elements are signs which represent what is absent.

Inasmuch as the doctrine of the real presence of Christ in the Supper was the key issue in the eucharistic debate, it is obvious that Luther and Calvin agreed more than did Calvin and Zwingli. The latter's conception of Christ's presence was "by the contemplation of faith" but not "in essence and reality." For Luther and Calvin communion with a present Christ who actually feeds believers with his body and blood is what makes the sacrament. The question between them was the manner in which Christ's body exists and is given to believers.

In his response to this question Calvin rejected the Eutychian doctrine of the absorption of Christ's humanity by his divinity, an idea he found in some of his Lutheran opponents, and any weakening of the idea of a local presence of the flesh of Christ in heaven. While Christ is bodily in heaven, distance is overcome by the Holy Spirit, who vivifies believers with Christ's flesh. Thus the Supper is a true communion with Christ, who feeds us with his body and blood. "We must hold in regard to the mode, that it is not necessary that the essence of the flesh should descend from heaven in order to our being fed upon it, the virtue of the Spirit being sufficient to break through all impediments and surmount any distance of place. Meanwhile, we deny not that this mode is incomprehensible to the human mind; because neither can flesh naturally be the life of the soul, nor exert its power upon us from heaven, nor without reason is the communion which makes us flesh of the flesh of Christ, and bone of his bones, called by Paul, 'A great mystery'(Eph. 5:30). Therefore, in the sacred Supper, we acknowledge a miracle which surpasses both the limits of nature and the measure of our sense, while the life of Christ is common to us, and his flesh is given us for food. But we must have done with all inventions inconsistent with the explanation lately given, such as the ubiquity of the body, the secret inclosing under the symbol of bread, and the substantial presence on earth." (*Tracts,* II, 577)

Calvin held that the essence of Christ's body was its power. In itself it is of little value since it "had its origin from earth, and underwent death" (*Inst.* 4.17.24), but the Holy Spirit, who gave Christ a body, communicates its power to us so that we receive the whole Christ in Communion. The difference from Luther here is not great, for he held that the "right hand of God" to which Christ ascended meant God's power, and that power is everywhere. The real difference between Luther and Calvin lay in the present existence of Christ's body. Calvin held that it is in a place, heaven, while Luther said that it has the same omnipresence as Christ's divine nature. Both agreed that there is deep mystery here which can be accepted though not understood. "If anyone should ask me how this [partaking of the whole Christ] takes place, I shall not be ashamed to confess that it is a secret too lofty for either my mind to comprehend or my words to declare. . . . I rather experience than understand it." (*Inst.* 4.17.32)

Summary. While each of the positions delineated above sought to do justice to the Holy Supper which the Lord has given his church, and while each has in it elements of truth, Calvin's position has received widest acceptance within the universal church. Moreover, it is the position closest to the thinking of contemporary theologians within both the Roman Catholic and Lutheran traditions. It is a position which sees the Lord's Supper as a rite instituted by Jesus Christ in which bread is broken and the fruit of the vine is poured out in thankful remembrance of Christ's atoning sacrifice, having become, through their reception and the sacramental blessing given by the Holy Spirit, the communion (that is, a partaking) of the body and blood of Christ and an anticipation of full future salvation.

M. E. Osterhaven

See also Lord's Supper.

Bibliography. "The Canons and Decrees of the Council of Trent," in *Creeds of Christendom,* II, ed. P. Schaff; J. Pelikan and H. T. Lehmann, eds., *Luther's Works,* 56 vols.; J. Calvin, *Institutes of the Christian Religion,* ed. J. T. McNeill, and *Tracts Relating to the Reformation,* tr. H. Beveridge, 3 vols.; G. W. Bromiley, ed., *Zwingli and Bullinger;* K. McDonnell, *John Calvin, the Church, and the Eucharist;* D. Bridge and D. Phypers, *Communion: The Meal That Unites?*

Love. Asked which is the greatest commandment, Jesus replied, "You shall love the Lord your God with all your heart, and with all your soul, and with all your mind. This is the great and first commandment. And a second is like it, You shall love your neighbor as yourself. On these two commandments depend all the law and the prophets" (Matt. 22:37–40; cf. Mark 12:29–31; Luke 10:26–27). According to Mark 12:31 Jesus stated that there is no other command greater than these two commands. Hence, love is of preeminent importance in the Bible.

Biblical Terms. *OT.* There are many Hebrew words to express the concept of love. By far the most prominent one (used over two hundred times) is the verb *'āhēb,* denoting both divine and human love as well as love toward inanimate objects such as food (Gen. 27:4), wisdom (Prov. 4:6), sleep (Prov. 20:13), agriculture (II Chr. 26:10), and the good (Amos 5:15). The noun *ahăbâ* (used about thirty times) is used primarily of human love, as seen in its frequent use in Song of Solomon, although it is also used of divine love (Isa. 63:9; Jer. 31:3; Hos. 11:4; Zeph. 3:17). Another frequently used word (over forty times), the noun *dôd,* has the sexual sense of a man being addressed as "lover" or "beloved"; it is frequently used in the Song of Solomon (e.g., 1:13, 14, 16; 2:3). Finally, there is the often used noun, *ḥesed*, which is translated most of the time as "mercy" in the AV, "steadfast love" in the RSV, "lovingkindness" in the NASB, and "love" in the NIV, all of which have the idea of loyal covenantal love.

NT. There are several words for love in the Greek language, but only two are used with any frequency in the NT. Although not prominent in prebiblical Greek, the verb *agapaō*/noun *agapē* is the most common NT word for love. This verb/noun combination is the most frequently used in the LXX in translating *'āhēb/ahabāh*. Basically it is a self-giving love that is not merited. The second most frequently used word for love in the NT is the verb *phileō*. It is the most common word for love in prebiblical Greek, but it is not often used in the LXX. Although this word overlaps with *agapaō/agapē*, it is a love with affection in connection with friendship. Its derivatives such as *philos*, friend (used twenty-nine times), and *philia*, friendship (used only in James 4:4), support this connotation. It is a love that is warm and merited. Two common Greek words for love are never used in the NT: *storgē*, having the idea of family love or affection, as borne out by the negative adjective *astorgos* used only in Rom. 1:31 and II Tim. 3:3; and *erōs*, expressing a possessive love and used mainly of physical love. In contrast to *agapē*, "*erōs* has two principal characteristics: it is a love of the worthy and it is a love that desires to possess. *Agapē* is in contrast at both points: it is not a love of the worthy, and it is not a love that desires to possess. On the contrary, it is a love given quite irrespective of merit, and it is a love that seeks to give" (Leon Morris, *Testaments of Love*, p. 128). Although *erōs* does not always have a bad connotation, certainly *agapaō/agapē* is far more lofty in that it seeks the highest good in the one loved, even though that one may be undeserving, and hence its prominence in the Bible can be understood.

Love of God. *The Attribute of Love.* God in his very essence is described as being not only holy (Lev. 11:44–45; 19:2; I Pet. 1:16), spirit (John 4:24), light (I John 1:5), and a consuming fire (Deut. 4:24; Heb. 12:29); God is also love (I John 4:8, 16). God does not need to attain nor attempt to maintain love; it is the very substance and nature of God. Bultmann rightly states: "The sentence cannot be reversed to read, 'Love is God.' In that case, 'love' would be presupposed as a universal human possibility, from which a knowledge of the nature of God could be derived" (*The Johannine Epistles*, p. 66). It is from this very essence of God's being that the activity of love springs.

The Activity of Love. This comes from God's nature of love. "To say, 'God is love' implies that *all* His activity is loving activity. If He creates, He creates in love; if He rules, He rules in love; if He judges, He judges in love" (C. H. Dodd, *The Johannine Epistles*, p. 110).

(1) Love within the Godhead. For man to understand love, he must perceive its activity within the Godhead. Many verses speak of the Father's love for the Son; however, only John 14:31 explicitly states that Jesus loved the Father. Certainly other passages imply Jesus' love for the Father. Love is demonstrated by the keeping of commandments (John 14:31; cf. vss. 15, 21, 23). Christ alone has seen the Father (John 3:11, 32; 6:46) and known him (Matt. 11:27; Luke 10:22; John 7:29; 8:55; 10:15). They are united to one another (John 10:30, 38; 14:10–11, 20; 17:21–23). Although there are no verses that speak explicitly of the Holy Spirit's love for the other two persons of the Trinity, it is implied in John 16:13–15, where Jesus says that the Spirit will not speak from himself, as Jesus did not speak from himself (John 12:49; 14:10), but will speak and disclose what he hears from Christ and the Father. There is, therefore, a demonstration of love within the Godhead.

(2) Love toward man. In the OT the expression of God's love for man is indicated in four ways. First, the simple statement of God's love for man is given in a few places (e.g., Deut. 10:18; 33:3; I Kings 10:9; Isa. 43:4; 63:9; Jer. 31:3; Hos. 14:4; Zeph. 3:17). Second, there is God's electing love for the nation of Israel (e.g., Deut. 4:37; 7:6–8; 10:15; Hos. 3:1; 11:1, 4; Mal. 1:2). Third, there is the covenant love, which is a loyal or steadfast love (*ḥesed;* e.g., Exod. 20:6; Deut. 5:10; 7:9, 12; I Kings 8:23; II Chr. 6:14; Neh. 1:5; 9:32; Ps. 89:28; Dan. 9:4). This love is readily seen in Ps. 106:45: "And he remembered his covenant for their sake, and relented according to the greatness of his loving kindness." God's covenant with Israel gives assurance of his love toward them (Isa. 54:10). Finally, there are a few references that speak specifically of God's love toward individuals (e.g., Solomon in II Sam. 12:24 and Neh. 13:26; Ezra in Ezra 7:28; Cyrus [?] in Isa. 48:14). Although the OT references to God's love toward man are not many, there are a sufficient number from various portions of the OT to adequately confirm it.

The NT is replete with references of God's love for man. A central passage demonstrating this is I John 4:10: "In this is love, not that we loved God, but that he loved us and sent his Son to be the propitiation for our sins." The demonstration of God's love for man is seen in each of the persons of the Trinity. Those who keep Christ's commandments evidence their love for him and they are loved by the Father (John 14:21, 23; 16:27). As the Father loves Christ, so also he loves the believer (John 17:23). The love of the Father for the believer is assured (Eph. 6:23; II Thess. 2:16; I John 3:1). When God is mentioned, it almost invariably refers to the Father. This is emphasized when some gift or blessing given to the believer is also mentioned, because the gift is usually his Son (e.g., John 3:16; Rom. 5:8; I John 4:9–10, 16) or the Holy Spirit (Rom. 5:5). There are many references to Christ's love for man. While on earth Christ loved Lazarus, Mary, and Martha (John 11:3, 5, 36). There is his love for John the apostle (John 13:23; 19:26; 20:2; 21:7, 20) and for the disciples as a group (John 13:34; 14:21; 15:9, 12). Christ's death is the evidence of his love for the believer (II Cor. 5:14; Gal. 2:20; Eph. 5:2; I Tim. 1:14–15; I John 3:16). In his ascension there is an assurance of his love for believers individually (Rom. 8:35, 37; Eph. 6:23) as well as the church as a body (Eph. 5:25). Finally, the Holy Spirit's love for the believer is mentioned in Rom. 15:30.

In conclusion, the love of God toward man is seen throughout the Bible. It is a love that is unselfish and unmerited. The epitome of this is seen in God's love for sinners who were his enemies and deserved nothing except his wrath, but instead he sent Christ to die for them in order that they might become the sons of God (Rom. 5:6–11; II Cor. 5:14–21). It is God's love that serves as a basis for man's love.

Love of Men. With the entrance of sin man has become a hater and enemy of God (Rom. 1:30; 5:10; John 15:18, 24–25). But because God initiated his love by sending his Son, believers are exhorted, on the basis of God's own love, to love one another (I John 4:10–11, 19). The source of this love is God (I John 4:7–9) and not man. This is substantiated in Gal. 5:22, where it is seen as the fruit of the Holy Spirit. The words immediately following love—"joy, peace, patience, kindness, goodness, faithfulness, meekness, self-control"—further describe the character of love rather than other fruit of the Spirit, for the "fruit" and the verb are singular and the context is about love (cf. vss. 5, 13, 14). This is further confirmed when one analyzes the love chapter (I Cor. 13) and notices that the words used to describe love are the same or similar words as used in Gal. 5:22–23 (many times the noun form in Gal. 5 is the verb form in I Cor. 13). In these passages love is described as being unselfish and sacrificial with no condition of expecting the same in return. It is love that is given and not deserved. God's love is so, and man having experienced God's love is to exhibit this in two directions, namely, toward God and toward man. This is what is commanded in the Bible (Matt. 22: 37–40; Mark 12:29–31; Luke 10:26–27).

Love Toward God. In the OT God commands man to love God with his whole being (Deut. 6:5; 10:12; 11:1, 13, 22; 13:3; 30:6, 16; Josh. 22:5; 23:11; Ps. 31:23), and there are a few explicit references indicating man's love for God (I Kings 3:3; Pss. 5:11; 18:1; 91:14; 116:1; Isa. 56:6). In the NT outside of Jesus' quoting the OT command to love God (Matt. 22:37; Mark 12:30, 33; Luke 10:27) there are no explicit commands for man to love God (possibly I Cor. 16:22; II Thess. 3:5). Only a few passages are concerned with man's response of love toward God (John 21:15–17; I Pet. 1:8; I John 5:2; cf. I John 4:20–21). The references to man's love toward God are comparatively few possibly because it would seem normal for man to love God, who has done so much for him, and because man has experienced God's love. However, the command to love God is important because it shows that God is approachable and desires the dynamic relationship involved in love.

Love Toward Man. The two greatest commandments indicate that man is to love his fellow man as well as God. Although there are not many verses that speak of man's love for God, the Scriptures abound with statements of man's love toward his fellows. This is seen in four ways.

(1) Love for neighbor. The command to love one's neighbor is stated often—first in Lev. 19:18, which is then quoted several times in the NT (Matt. 5:43; 19:19; 22:39; Mark 12:31, 33; Rom. 13:9; Gal. 5:14; James 2:8). Paul states that love for the neighbor is the fulfillment of the law (Rom. 13:8, 10). In giving the command to love one's neighbor, Jesus made it clear in the parable of the good Samaritan that one's neighbors are more than those who are acquaintances or of the same nationality (Luke 10:27–37). This is in keeping with the OT for Moses enjoined the Israelites to love the stranger or alien (Deut. 10:19). Man is to be concerned with other men as God is concerned with man. The command is to love the neighbor to the degree that one loves himself. Since man is basically selfish and is concerned about himself, he should have that same degree of concern for his neighbor.

(2) Love for one's fellow believer. In Gal. 6:10 Paul exhorts the believers to do good to all men and especially to those who are of the household of faith. The believer should love his neighbor, whoever that might be, but he must have a real and deep concern and love for those who are fellow believers. In the OT this is seen in Lev.

19:17–18, where the neighbor is the fellow countryman of the covenanted nation Israel or one who was of the same faith. In the NT, there is to be a definite love between believers. Jesus gave a new commandment: that the believers were to love one another as he had loved them (John 13:34–35; 15:12, 17; cf. I John 3:23; 5:2; II John 5). The command to love one another was not new, but to love one another as Christ had loved them was a new command. This is further elaborated in I John. One who loves his brother abides in light (2:10) and God abides in him (4:12). In fact, one who does not love his brother cannot love God (4:20). The source of love is God (4:7), and because of God's love one should love his brother (3:11; 4:11).

Outside the Johannine literature there is the same command to love the brother in the faith (Eph. 5:2; I Thess. 4:9; 5:13; I Tim. 4:12; Heb. 10:24; 13:1; I Pet. 2:17). This was to be done fervently (Rom. 12:10; I Pet. 1:22; 4:8) and with forbearance (Eph. 4:2), serving one another (Gal. 5:13). Paul loved the believers (I Cor. 16:24; II Cor. 2:4; 11:11; 12:15) and was happy when he heard of the saints' love for one another (Eph. 1:15; Col. 1:4; II Thess. 1:3; Philem. 5; cf. Heb. 6:10). Hence one sees that love for the brother was a dominant theme in the early church. It was evidence to the world that they were truly the disciples of Christ (John 13:35).

(3) Love for family. The Scriptures have a few commands and ample illustrations of love within the family. Husbands are commanded to love their wives (Col. 3:19) as Christ loves the church (Eph. 5:25–33; cf. Eccles. 9:9; Hos. 3:1). The love of the husband for the wife is seen in several accounts (Gen. 24:67; 29:18, 20, 30; II Chr. 11:21; Song of S. 4:10; 7:6). Only one time are wives commanded to love their husbands (Titus 2:4) and in only Song of S. is it mentioned (1:7; 3:1–4; 7:12). Certainly the wife's submission to the husband is evidence of her love for him (Eph. 5:22–24; I Pet. 3:1–6). Also, only once is there a command for parents to love their children, specifically for young wives to love their children (Titus 2:4), but there are several illustrations of such love in the OT (Gen. 22:2; 25:28; 37:3; 44:20; Exod. 21:5). Interestingly, there is no command or example of children loving their parents. However, there is the oft-repeated command for children to honor and obey their parents, which would be evidence of their love for their parents (e.g., Exod. 20:12; Deut. 5:16; Prov. 1:8; Matt. 19:19; Mark 10:19; Luke 18:20; Eph. 6:1; Col. 3:20). In conclusion, although not much is spoken about love within the natural family, it can be assumed that this love would be expected; anyone who does not take care of his family is considered a denier of the faith and worse than an unbeliever (I Tim. 5:8).

(4) Love for enemies. Jesus commanded his followers to love their enemies (Matt. 5:43–48; Luke 6:27–35). This love is demonstrated by blessing those who curse them, praying for those who mistreat them, and giving generously to them. This shows that love is more than friendship based on mutual admiration; it is an act of charity toward one who is hostile and has shown no lovableness. Jesus reminded the disciples that it is natural to love those who love them, but to love their enemies is a real act of charity; it is to be a mark of his disciples as opposed to those who are sinners or Gentiles. An example of this love is seen in God's love and kindness toward evil men by sending them sun and rain as he does for those who love him. The NT epistles reiterate that rather than seeking revenge, believers are to love those who hate and persecute them (Rom. 12:14, 17–21; I Thess. 5:15; I Pet. 3:9).

Conclusion. God in his very essence is love, hence love is expressed toward the undeserving. John 3:16 states this unforgettably: though man has repudiated him God loves the world, and the extent of his love was the sacrifice of his own Son, Jesus Christ, who was willing to lay down his life. On the basis of God's love the believer is enjoined to love God, who is deserving, and to love his fellow man and even his enemy, who are undeserving. God's love is not only basic but it continually extends to the undeserving and unloving, as seen in his continuing love for the wayward believer in both the OT and NT. Thus there is a deep loyalty in God's love toward the undeserving, and this is the basis of God's command for man's love. Therefore, God's love is seeking the highest good in the one loved, and man is enjoined to seek the highest good or the will of God in the one loved. H. W. Hoehner

See also God, Attributes of.

Bibliography. C. Brown, W. Günther, and H.-G. Link, *NIDNTT,* II, 538–51; M. C. D'Arcy, *The Mind and Heart of Love;* V. P. Furnish, *The Love Command in the NT;* V. R. Good, *IDB,* III, 164–68; W. Harrelson, "The Idea of Agape in the NT," *JR* 31:169–82; G. Johnston, *IDB,* III, 168–78; W. Klassen, *IDB* Supplement, 557–58; H. Montefiore, "Thou Shalt Love Thy Neighbor as Thyself," *NovT* 5:157–70; L. Morris, *Testaments of Love;* A. Nygren, *Agape and Eros;* G. Outka, *Agape: An Ethical Analysis;* F. H. Palmer, *NBC,* 752–54; J. Piper, *Love Your Enemies;* G. Quell and E. Stauffer, *TDNT,* I, 21–55; O. J. F. Seitz, "Love Your Enemies," *NTS* 16: 39–54; M. H. Shepherd, Jr., *IDB,* I, 53–54; N. H. Snaith, *The Distinctive Ideas of the OT;* C. Spicq, *Agape in the NT,* 3 vols.; G. Stählin, *TDNT,* IX, 113–71; B. B. Warfield, "The Terminology of Love in the NT," *PTR* 16:1–45, 153–203; D. D. Williams, *The Spirit and the Forms of Love.*

Love Feast. ***In the NT.*** The brotherly love between Christians which was enjoined by Jesus (John 13:34; Gr. *agapē*) found its expression in three practical ways. It was commonly exercised in almsgiving; hence on twenty-six occasions *agapē* is translated in the AV "charity." In church gatherings and in Christian greetings it was displayed by the kiss (I Pet. 5:14; see also Rom. 16:16; I Cor. 16:20; II Cor. 13:12; I Thess. 5:26). And gradually the term came to be applied to a common meal shared by believers. Although these meals are called *agapai* only in Jude 12 and possibly II Pet. 2:13, where there is a variant reading of *agapais* for *apatais* ("deceivings"), there is a considerable amount of other evidence for their existence in the early church.

In Acts 2:42–47 there is an account of the early form of "communism" practiced by the believers, which includes breaking bread from house to house and eating their meat (Gr. *trophē*) with gladness and singleness of heart. The first phrase may refer to the administration of the Lord's Supper, but the second obviously indicates a full meal. Similar "communistic" behavior is mentioned in Acts 4:32. By the time of Acts 6:1ff. the increase of disciples in the Jerusalem church led to the appointment of the seven to serve tables, which presumably refers to the responsibility for arranging the common meals. R. L. Cole (*Love-Feasts, A History of the Christian Agape*) suggests that this number was selected in order that each one might be responsible for a different day of the week. This arrangement arose from the complaint of the hellenists that their widows were being neglected, and so would indicate that already these common meals were being held for charitable purposes, as was indeed the custom later.

When Paul was at Troas (Acts 20:6–12) there took place on the first day of the week both a "breaking of bread" and a full meal (which idea is contained in the verb *geusamenos*, used here for eating, cf. Acts 10:10). Both here and in 2:42 it is difficult to determine whether the phrase "breaking of bread" denotes a common meal or is a more restricted reference to the Lord's Supper: whenever these words occur together in the Gospels they describe the action of Jesus (Matt. 26:26; Mark 14:22; Luke 22:19; 24:30, 35). Certainly by the time of Paul's writing to the Corinthians (*ca.* A.D. 55) it is evident that that church observed the practice of meeting together for a common meal before partaking of the Lord's Supper (I Cor. 11:17–34). This custom, however, does not appear to have been observed always in the spirit of *agapē*, for the apostle complains that some make it an excuse for gluttony, while others go without: in vs. 21 *to idion deipnon* may refer to the fact that they refused to pool their food, or that from such a pool each took as much as possible for himself. At all events the situation described here is possible only in the context of a meal more substantial than, and preceding, the bread and wine of the Lord's Supper.

Various theories have been put forward suggesting that the *agapē* was a development from pagan guilds or Jewish common meals, or that it was necessitated by the common desire to avoid meats offered to idols. From the fact that most early Christian paintings found in the catacombs depicting the *agapē* show seven persons partaking, Cole argues that the custom developed from the incident on the shore of Tiberias, where Jesus shared the breakfast meal with seven of his disciples (John 21), and that the conversation with Peter on that occasion supplied the title of *agapē* for this meal. It is equally possible that the meal may have arisen from a desire to perpetuate the table fellowship which the apostles had enjoyed during their Lord's earthly life, and that later, as the church grew and communal living became impossible, the common meal was continued before the Lord's Supper in an effort to place the receiving of that sacrament in its historical context. The fact that the Johannine account points to the giving of the new commandment of mutual *agapē* at that meal (John 13:34) would be sufficient reason for the application of that name to the rite.

In Church History. Ignatius (*Smyr.* 8:2) refers to the *agapē*, as does the Didache (x.1 and xi.9), the latter suggesting that it still preceded the Eucharist. By the time of Tertullian (*Apology* xxxix; *De Jejuniis* xvii; *De Corona Militis* iii) the Eucharist was celebrated early and the *agapē* later at a separate service, and this may be the practice referred to by Pliny in his letter to Trajan (*Epistles* x.96), though his information is not altogether clear. Clement of Alexandria (*Paedagogos* ii.1 and *Stromata* iii.2) gives evidence also of the separation of the two observances. Chrysostom (*Homily* xxvii on I Cor. 11:17) agrees with the order mentioned by Tertullian, but while he calls the *agapē* "a custom most beautiful and beneficial; for it was a supporter of love, a solace of poverty, and a discipline of humility," he does add that by his day it had become corrupt. In times of persecution the custom grew up of celebrating *agapai* in prison with condemned martyrs on the eve of their execution (see the *Passion of Perpetua and Felicitas* xvii.1, and Lucian *De Morte Peregrini* xii), whence developed the practice of holding commemorative *agapai* on the anniversaries of their deaths, and these gave rise to the feasts and vigils which are observed today. *Agapai* also took place on the occasion of weddings (Gregory of Nazianzus *Epistles* i.14) and funerals (Apostolic Constitutions viii.42).

During the fourth century the *agapē* became increasingly the object of disfavor, apparently because of disorders at the celebration and also because problems were raised by the expanding membership of the church, and an increasing emphasis was being placed on the Eucharist. Augustine mentions its disuse (*Ep. ad Aurelium* xxii.4; see also *Confessions* vi.2), and Canons 27 and 28 of the Council of Laodicea (363) restricted the abuses. The Third Council of Carthage (393) and the Second Council of Orleans (541) reiterated this legislation, which prohibited feasting in churches, and the Trullan Council of 692 decreed that honey and milk were not to be offered on the altar (Canon 57), and that those who held love feasts in churches should be excommunicated (Canon 74).

There is evidence that bread and wine (Didache), vegetables and salt (*Acts of Paul and Thecla* xxv), fish (catacomb paintings), meat, poultry, cheese, milk, and honey (Augustine, *contra Faustum* xx.20), and *pultes,* "a pottage" (Augustine), were consumed on different occasions at the *agapē.*

In Modern Times. In the Eastern Church the rite has persisted, and is still observed in sections of the Orthodox Church, where it precedes the Eucharist, and in the Church of St. Thomas in India. From the Eastern Church it was continued through the Church of Bohemia to John Hus and the Unitas Fratrum, whence it was adopted by the Moravians. From them John Wesley introduced the practice within Methodism (see references in his *Journal*), and it is occasionally observed today in Methodist churches. In the Anglican Prayer Book of 1662 the only survival is probably the collection of alms for the poor during the Communion service, but the practice of the sovereign's distribution of Maundy money is a relic of the *agapē,* and in this connection it is interesting that the epistle appointed for Maundy Thursday is I Cor. 11:17–34. A modern attempt to revive the custom can be seen in the increasing practice of holding a "parish breakfast" following the early Communion service, and experiments at using the *agapē* as an opportunity for interdenominational fellowship are described by Frank Baker in *Methodism and the Love-Feast.*

D. H. Wheaton

See also Lord's Supper.

Bibliography. D. Leclerq in *Dictionnaire d'archéologie Chrétienne;* J. F. Keating, *The Agapē and the Eucharist in the Early Church;* P. Battifol, *Études d'histoire et de théologie positive;* J. C. Lambert, *Sacraments in the NT.*

Lovingkindness. The translation of the Hebrew word *ḥesed* in the AV and ASV. The AV also followed the equivalent given in the Latin translation (*misericordia*), which is preceded by the usage of the LXX ("mercy"). Modern versions render *ḥesed* by "steadfast love," "unfailing love," "lovingkindness," and "love" (cf. RSV, NIV). The word *ḥesed* is found approximately 250 times in the Hebrew OT, and of these there are 125 instances in the Psalms.

The nature of the God of Israel is love. Even when Israel has sinned, they are assured that Yahweh is full of lovingkindness (Exod. 34:6; Num. 14:18; Joel 2:13; Ps. 86:5, 15), on which basis he can and does forgive the sin of his repentant people. The assurance of lovingkindness is given in the legal framework of the covenant. God's love is a distinctive love. Yahweh has promised to be loyal to Abraham and his descendants (Deut. 7:12). The relation between lovingkindness as an expression of commitment (loyalty) and truth (*'ĕmet*) expressing faithfulness is so close that the words occur next to each other some sixteen times: *ḥesed we'ĕmet* (Pss. 25:10; 89:14; cf. vs. 25 with *'ĕmûnâ,* "faithfulness"). The God of the covenant shows his covenantal faithfulness by his loving commitment to his people, regardless of their responsiveness or righteousness (Deut. 7:7–8). As such, lovingkindness can be a synonym for covenant (Deut. 7:9, 12). The blessings are generally described as the divine benefits (Deut. 7:13–16). Hence, lovingkindness is not a mere relational term; it is active. The God who loves showers his benefits on his covenant people. He is active (*'āśâ*) in his love (Ps. 18:50; Deut. 5:10). His lovingkindness also finds expression in righteousness. Righteousness as a correlative to lovingkindness guarantees the ultimate triumph and reward of God's people, and also contains a warning that Yahweh does not tolerate sin, even though he may forbear for a long time. The quality of lovingkindness is also assured by its durability. It is from generation to generation (Exod. 34:7). Twenty-six times we are told that "his lovingkindness is forever" (cf. Pss. 106:1; 107:1; 118:1–4; 136). He remembers his love, even when he for a period has withdrawn it in order to discipline (Ps. 98:3).

On the other hand, the God who is love also expects his people to be sanctified by demonstrating lovingkindness to their covenant God and to their fellow men. The call for a commitment of love to God finds expression in Deut. 6:5, and was repeated by our Lord (Matt. 22:37). Man's response to God's lovingkindness is love. On a horizontal plane the believer is called upon to show both lovingkindness (as David did, II Sam. 9:1, 3, 7) and love (Lev. 19:18, cf. Matt.

22:39). In man's response to lovingkindness and all that it entails, he shows that he belongs to the Heavenly Father (Matt. 5:44–48).

W. A. Van Gemeren

See also God, Attributes of.

Bibliography. N. H. Snaith, *The Distinctive Ideas of the OT;* L. J. Kuyper, "Grace and Truth," *RR* 16:1–16; N. Glueck, *Ḥesed in the Bible;* K. D. Sakenfeld, *The Meaning of Ḥesed in the Hebrew Bible.*

Low Church. A term used to describe those who do not place great emphasis on the corporate or historically continuous or doctrinally orthodox nature of the church (or a part or denomination within it), but who usually emphasize the rights and faith of the individual Christian. The technical usage relates to the eighteenth century Church of England, where Low Church was contrasted with High Church as two schools of thought at each end of the Anglican spectrum of theological emphasis. To be Low Church was to be a latitudinarian or a broad churchman (a term which replaced low churchman in the nineteenth century).

After the rise of the evangelical movement in the Church of England, and after its controversy with the Tractarian movement, evangelicals were often called Low Church because in comparison with tractarians they appeared to have a low view of the historical church, its traditions and sacraments. This usage, though common, is technically incorrect, since genuine evangelical Anglicans actually have a high view of the historical church and its liturgy and doctrine.

A good example of a genuine low churchman is Sydney Smith (1771–1845), a canon of St. Paul's Cathedral, London, and a founder of the *Edinburgh Review.* Good examples of later broad (low) churchmen are the Oxford liberals of *ca.* 1850—W. G. Ward, A. H. Clough, Arthur Stanley, A. C. Tait, and Frederick Temple.

Outside Anglicanism the expression Low Church is used imprecisely to refer either to those who do not favor much ritual or ceremonial in worship or to those who oppose high views of clergy or church officials. P. Toon

See also Latitudinarianism.

Bibliography. O. Chadwick, *The Victorian Church,* Pt. 1.

Lucifer. *See* Satan.

Luke, Theology of. ***The Evidence.*** The theology of Luke may be discerned by observing several converging lines of evidence. Since a Gospel lacks the logical sequence of propositional statements characteristic of the epistles, great care is needed to assess this evidence accurately. The following must be considered.

Narrative Structure. The careful statement of purpose inserted before the narrative commences alerts the reader to observe factors that contribute to assurance regarding the truth of the Christian gospel. The inclusion of the birth narratives, in contrast to Mark and John, and with different episodes from those in Matthew, directs the reader to certain themes regarding the messiahship and sonship of Jesus. The use of a chiastic structure in Zechariah's Benedictus (1:68–79) focuses attention on the middle theme—oath/covenant—along with the other repeated themes: God's "coming" (or "visitation"), his "people," "salvation," "prophets," the "hand" of the "enemies," and the "fathers." The introduction of two witnesses Simeon and Anna, according to the accepted pattern of two witnesses, draws attention to and confirms the identity of the baby as the promised Messiah (2:25–38).

Within the narrative of Jesus' ministry certain editorial touches have great effect in featuring theological themes. For example, by omitting most of Mark's narrative of 6:45–8:26, Luke is able to move quickly from the stilling of the storm (Mark 4:35–41; Matt. 8:23–27; Luke 8:22–25), with its significant climactic question, "Who is this?" pausing for only a few incidents, mainly those with messianic significance, to the question of Herod, "Who, then, is this?" (Luke 9:9), and on to the question at Caesarea Philippi, "Who do you say I am?" Another use of structure is the inclusion of the unique central section. This not only contains a collection of Jesus' teachings but features a travel motif. There is a strong sense of movement toward Jerusalem, the city of destiny in God's plan (9:51, 53; 13:22, 33; 17:11; 18:31). Cf. 9:31; 19:11, 28 on Jerusalem, and 9:57; 24:13–17 for examples of Luke's specific references to traveling. The introduction to this section looks ahead specifically to Jesus' ascension ("taken up," Luke 9:51; cf. the same term in Acts 1:2). This is a unique emphasis of Luke, the final event of his Gospel (24:50–53).

Vocabulary. Careful observation of word frequency, especially when it is weighted statistically, provides significant evidence of theological emphasis, especially in comparison with the other Gospels. Observing the relative frequency of such words as "salvation," "sinner," "today," "God," "word," "city," and various words grouped in semantic fields such as those relating to poverty and wealth (to cite just a few) is foundational in assessing the theology of Luke. One example is the unusual frequency of "today" (Luke 2:11; 4:21; 5:26; 12:28; 13:32, 33; 19:5, 9; 22:34, 61; 23:43 and nine times in Acts).

Context. Here we see especially the converging lines of evidence. When several significant words occur together in a passage which clearly has theological importance, especially if it is at a crucial point in the narrative, the reader may be confident that the author is making a major theological statement. Jesus' conversation with Zacchaeus is an example. It occurs shortly before Jesus' triumphal entry, centers on one of the so-called sinners (Luke 19:7), social outcasts, and other unpopular people featured in Luke as the objects of Jesus' concern. The vocabulary includes such key terms as "today" and "salvation." Another significant event occurs at the beginning of Jesus' ministry: his preaching in the Nazareth synagogue. This contains a programmatic statement about Jesus' anointing by the Spirit to preach good news to the poor. The significant use of Isaiah 61 with its jubilee motif (the "year of the Lord's favor") contributes to its theological importance.

Geographical and Historical Background. Other indications of theology are seen in Luke's stress on these features. Luke sets the salvation events within the sweep of human history. His description of Jesus' orientation to Jerusalem from Luke 9:51 on points to the passion, resurrection, and ascension.

In summary, every aspect of the Gospel, from individual words to the larger historical scene, is worth investigating for theological information.

Theological Themes. Some of the specific themes and topics in Luke are:

Christology. As in the other Gospels, Jesus is seen as Messiah (e.g., Luke 9:20). He is also the Son of God, as the angel indicates (Luke 1:35) and as he himself recognizes at age twelve (Luke 2:49). One unique contribution of Luke is the presentation of Jesus as a prophet. He is compared and contrasted with John the Baptist as a prophetic figure. Luke hints at his prophetic role in 4:24–27 and 13:33. Also, the ministry of Elisha comes to mind at the raising of the son of the widow of Nain near where Elisha had raised the son of the "great woman" of Shunem.

Soteriology. Without question, Luke emphasizes the need and provision of salvation. The Gospel focuses on the cross through the passion predictions (9:22, etc.), in common with Matthew and Luke, in the early foreshadowings of 2:35; 5:35; and especially through the sayings at the Last Supper (22:19–22). In Acts the cross is seen as God's will, though accomplished by sinful people (Acts 2:23). If neither the Gospel nor Acts contains the explicit statements familiar from Paul on the theology of atonement, that does not mean Luke's doctrine is deficient. The Gospel presents the need of salvation and the progress of Jesus to the cross vividly; Acts declares the opportunity of forgiveness through Christ (e.g., 2:38; 4:12; 10:43; 13:39).

Glory. Nevertheless, Luke has a very strong theology of glory. He emphasizes the victory of the resurrection, with a declaration of the vindication of Jesus (Acts 2:24; 3:15; 4:10; 10:39–42; 13:26–37; 17:31). The ascension is stressed predictively in the middle of the Gospel (9:51) and in the middle of Luke's two-volume work, Luke 24 and Acts 1.

Doxology. This theology of glory finds practical expression in repeated ascriptions of glory to God. These occur especially at the birth of Christ (2:14) and on the occasions of healing (e.g., Luke 5:25–26; Acts 3:8–10).

The Holy Spirit. The Spirit is prominent from the beginning (Luke 1:15, 41; 2:25–35). Jesus was conceived by the overshadowing of the Spirit (1:35). He was full of the Spirit and led by the Spirit at the time of his temptation (4:1). The Spirit was upon him in his ministry (4:18). The Lord promised the Holy Spirit in answer to prayer (11:13) and in anticipation of Pentecost (24:49; Acts 1:4). The Holy Spirit is, of course, prominent throughout the book of Acts.

Prayer. This is especially significant at times of crisis in the life of Jesus (Luke 3:1; 6:12; 9:18) and in the early perilous days of the church (e.g., Acts 4:23–31; 6:4, 6; 8:15; 9:11; 10:2; 13:3).

The Power of God. Along with the other Gospels, Luke records the miracles of Jesus and uses the word *dynamis.* This emphasis continues throughout Acts.

Sense of Destiny; Prophecy and Fulfillment. This is a unique emphasis of Luke. The verb *dei,* "it is necessary," occurs frequently with reference to the things Jesus "must" accomplish (Luke 2:49; 4:43; 9:22; 13:33; 24:7, 26, 44–47). This is seen both in terms of accomplishment (Luke 1:1, translating *peplērophorēmenōn* as "accomplished" or, with NIV, "fulfilled") and in terms of fulfillment of OT prophecy. "Proof from prophecy" is a significant aspect of Luke's writing.

Eschatology. This aspect of Luke's work has occasioned much discussion. It was the view of H. Conzelmann that Luke wrote against a background of concern because Jesus had not yet returned. Luke supposedly met this alleged "delay of the parousia" by reworking Jesus' teachings to portray an extended period of time in which the church is to continue. Without dealing here with Conzelmann's various ideas on this and other topics, we may note that further study has shown that, while Luke sees a period of faithful service prior to the Lord's return (e.g., the parable of the nobleman, or the ten minas,

Luke 19:11–27), he also retains strong eschatological teachings (e.g., 12:35–40) and a sense of imminency (e.g., 18:8). It is misguided speculation (cf. Luke 17:20–21) which Luke rejected, not the imminency of the Lord's return. It is against this background that Luke's unique emphasis on "today" is to be seen.

Israel and the People of God. The word *laos,* "people," is used with special meaning in Luke. In contrast to the crowds (*ochloi*) and the hostile rulers, the "people" are ready to receive Jesus. Naturally, in the period of Luke-Acts most of these are Jews. Luke seems to be dealing with the nature of the people of God, the position of the church in relation to the unbelieving Jews. He emphasizes that thousands of the Jews believed (Acts 21:20), even though he shows Paul as turning to the Gentiles.

The Word of God. This is a more significant theme in Luke's writings than is generally recognized. *Logos* occurs in the Gospel prologue (1:2), in 4:22, 32, 36, and notably in the parable of the sower, which stresses obedience to the word of God (8:4–15). In Acts the growth of the "word" parallels the growth of the church (Acts 4:31; 6:7; 12:24).

Discipleship. Luke contains teachings not in the other Gospels. In addition to 9:23–26, paralleled in Matthew and Mark, Luke has major sections on discipleship in 9:57–62; 14:25–33.

Poverty and Wealth. The Gospel, addressed to a wealthy person, records Jesus' mission to the poor (4:18). Luke refers to a future reversal of social roles in the Magnificat (1:46–55), the Beatitudes (along with the woes, which only Luke describes; 6:20–26), and the story of the rich man and Lazarus (16:19–31). Luke gives direct teaching on possessions (Luke 12:33), has the only comment on the Pharisees' greed (Luke 16:14), and emphasizes the church's generosity in sharing with those in need (Acts 2:44–45; 4:32–37; 11:27–30).

Recent Study. The study of Luke's theology has been pursued with great vigor during the past several decades. The creative work of Conzelmann spawned a number of treatises on Luke's theology. At issue have been the purpose for which Luke wrote the Gospel and Acts, the extent and significance of his redaction (editing), and the effect the author's theological tendencies may have had on his historical reliability. According to Conzelmann, Luke's purpose was to set forth his scheme of salvation history. Marshall sees Luke's work as a witness to salvation itself. Others have seen an apologetic motive (e.g., defense of Christianity for one or another purpose) or a theological motive (e.g., the identity of the people of God). Evaluation of the extent of Luke's redactional work to serve his purposes depends on one's assessment of several matters. Is "S" given editorial modification due to theology, style, or sources used? If to sources, were there theological reasons for using a given source and for allowing its theological data to stand unmodified? Must it be assumed, as is often done, that Luke's theological purposes affected his historical objectivity adversely? For a defense of Luke's credibility as both a historian and theologian, see Marshall's work below. In conclusion, Fitzmyer's caution against interpreting Luke's theology in terms of one's own thesis about Luke is itself a comment on many contributions to this subject.

W. L. Liefeld

See also New Testament Theology; Matthew, Theology of; Mark, Theology of; John, Theology of.

Bibliography. C. K. Barrett, *Luke the Historian in Recent Study;* H. Conzelmann, *The Theology of St. Luke;* N. A. Dahl, "The Purpose of Luke-Acts," in *Jesus in the Memory of the Early Church;* E. E. Ellis, *Eschatology in Luke;* H. Flender, *St. Luke: Theologian of Redemptive History;* J. A. Fitzmyer, *The Gospel According to Luke I-IX;* E. Franklin, *Christ the Lord: A Study in the Purpose and Theology of Luke-Acts;* J. Jervell, *Luke and the People of God;* L. T. Johnson, *The Literary Function of Possessions in Luke-Acts;* L. E. Keck and J. L. Martyn, eds., *Studies in Luke-Acts;* I. H. Marshall, *Luke: Historian and Theologian;* A. J. Mattill, Jr., *Luke and the Last Things;* J. C. O'Neill, *The Theology of Acts in Its Historical Setting;* N. B. Stonehouse, *The Witness of Luke to Christ;* C. H. Talbert, *Literary Patterns, Theological Themes and the Genre of Luke-Acts,* and (ed.) *Perspectives on Luke-Acts;* D. L. Tiede, *Prophecy and History in Luke-Acts.*

Lust. This word once meant only a strong desire or craving, in a good or bad sense. Now it is used in the sense of craving that which is forbidden, especially sexual passion. The word has been used in the history of English translations, especially in the AV, to render several Hebrew and several Greek words that are basically neutral in ethical overtones and indicate only strong desire. In particular contexts these words may take on the negative aspect found in present usage of "lust."

The Hebrew words with the overtones of lust are: (1) *nepeš,* desire (see Exod. 15:9; Ps. 78:18); (2) *šĕrîrût,* stubbornness (see Ps. 81:12); (3) *ta'ăwâ,* object of desire (see Ps. 78:30); (4) *ḥāmad,* desire for the beauty of the evil woman (see Prov. 6:25); (5) *'āwâ,* to desire (see Ps. 106:14); (6) *'āgab,* have inordinate affection, lust (see Ezek. 23:7, 9, 12; Jer. 4:30).

In short, the OT uses the concept for an inordinate desire for anything—e.g., the desire for specific food in the Exodus experience—and particularly for an intense misdirection of love, whether the individual man to a woman (Prov. 6:25) or the nation of Israel from God her loving husband to her lovers (Ezek. 23). The word of the Lord through Ezekiel says this last tellingly in the memorable statement: "Oholah played the harlot while she was mine; and she lusted after her lovers; . . . with all their idols she defiled herself" (Ezek. 23:5–7).

The Greek terms and their general meanings are: (1) *epithymia,* desire, longing; *epithymeō,* to desire, long for; (2) *hēdonē,* pleasure, enjoyment; (3) *oregō,* to desire; *orexis,* longing, desire; (4) *pathos,* passion.

Epithymia/epithymeō, which is the key concept and virtually incorporates the other concepts in the various passages, indicates basically simply desire. In sinful man the desire becomes inordinate or is set over against God and thus becomes sinful, or is directed to that which is sinful. Thus the term is used for covetousness (Rom. 7:7; 13:9) or for those things that choke out the word of the gospel (Mark 4:19; cf. Luke 8:14, *hēdonē*), and is often indicated to be sinful by the object stated or the adjective supplied or qualification given (e.g., "after evil things," I Cor. 10:6; "of the flesh," Gal. 5:16; Eph. 2:3; II Pet. 2:18; deceitful; hurtful; youthful; worldly; former; fleshly; or ungodly). As the dominant note of one's life the sinful desire to have is marked as a key sin by both James ("You lust, and have not: you kill," 4:2; also *hēdonē,* 4:1, 3) and John in his summary statement of the avarice of sin, "The lust of the flesh and the lust of the eyes and the boastful pride of life ... is not from the Father but is from the world" (I John 2:16), as well as by Paul ("The love of money is a root of all sorts of evil; and some by longing [*oregō*] for it have wandered away from the faith"). More specifically both Paul and the Lord Jesus speak of lust in terms of sexual immorality, i.e., homosexuality (Rom. 1:24; cf. 1:27, *orexis*) and the lustful look which is adultery (Matt. 5:28). Heterosexual immorality Paul speaks of as "lustful passion" (NASB) or "passionate lust" (NIV) by combining two of the terms (*pathei epithymias*) and describing such action as that which the heathen engage in who do not know God (I Thess. 4:5).

Since the particular expression of lust in both OT and NT has been in terms of a compelling sexual immorality, it is understandable that a theology and culture formed by the Bible have virtually reduced the meaning of the word "lust" to that area.

G. W. KNIGHT, III

See also DESIRE.

Bibliography. *TWOT,* I, 18, 294, II, 587–91, 644, 957; F. Büchsel, *TDNT,* III, 167–72; G. Stahlin, *TDNT,* II, 900–926; H. Schönweiss, E. Beyreuther, and J. Guhrt, *NIDNTT,* I, 456–61; W. E. Raffety, *ISBE,* III, 1941–42; R. A. Killan, *WBE,* II, 1057–58; L. Foster, *ZPEB,* III, 1008–9.

Luther, Martin (1483–1546). Major leader of the German Reformation. Luther's father came from peasant background, but achieved success in the mining industry so that he was able to afford an excellent education for his son. Luther began his studies at the Ratschule in Mansfeld and probably attended the Cathedral School at Magdeburg, where he came under the influence of the Brethren of the Common Life. He completed his preparatory education at the Georgenschule in Eisenach before entering the University of Erfurt in 1501. He received his B.A. in 1502 and his M.A. in 1505. In accordance with his father's wishes he had begun study for a law degree when a brush with death in a thunderstorm, July, 1505, caused him to make a vow to become a monk.

While in the monastery Luther began the serious study of theology at Erfurt. In 1508 he was sent to Wittenberg to lecture on moral philosophy at the newly founded University of Wittenberg. In 1509 he returned to Erfurt, where he continued his studies and delivered lectures in theology. His teachers at Erfurt adhered to the nominalist theology of William of Ockham and his disciple, Gabriel Biel, which disparaged the role of reason in arriving at theological truth and placed a greater emphasis on free will and the role of human beings in initiating their salvation than did traditional scholasticism. In 1510–11 Luther made a trip to Rome on a mission for his order. While in Rome he was shocked by the worldliness of the clergy and disillusioned by their religious indifference. In 1511 he was sent back to Wittenberg, where he completed his studies for the degree of Doctor of Theology in October, 1512. In the same year he received a permanent appointment to the chair of Bible at the university.

During the period 1507–12 Luther experienced intense spiritual struggles as he sought to work out his own salvation by careful observance of the monastic rule, constant confession, and self-mortification. Probably as a result of the influence of popular piety and the teachings of nominalism Luther viewed God as a wrathful judge who expected sinners to earn their own righteousness. Partly because of his contact with the vicar general of his order, Johann von Staupitz, and his reading of Augustine, but primarily through his study of the Scriptures as he prepared his university lectures, Luther gradually changed his view of justification. His "tower experience," in which he achieved his major theological breakthrough and came to the full realization of the doctrine of justification by faith alone, has normally been dated before 1517. However, recent scholarship has suggested that Luther was correct when he stated near the end of his life that it did not occur until late 1518. This interpretation maintains that Luther gradually progressed in his understanding of justification from the nominalist view, which gave human beings a role in initiating the process, to the Augustinian view, which attributed the beginning of the process to God's free grace but believed that after conversion human beings could cooperate. The fully developed Lutheran doctrine, which viewed justification as a forensic act in which God declares the sinner righteous because of the vicarious atonement of Jesus Christ without any human merit rather than a lifelong process, was not clearly expressed in Luther's writings until his sermon *Of the Threefold Righteousness,* published toward the end of 1518.

The Reformation began in October, 1517, when Luther protested a major abuse in the sale of indulgences in his Ninety-five Theses. These were translated into German, printed, and circulated throughout Germany, arousing a storm of protest against the sale of indulgences. When the sale of indulgences was seriously impaired, the papacy sought to silence Luther. He was first confronted at a meeting of his order held in Heidelberg on April 26, 1518, but he used the Heidelberg disputation to defend his theology and to make new converts. In August of 1518 Luther was summoned to Rome to answer charges of heresy, even though he had not taught contrary to any clearly defined medieval doctrines. Because Luther was unlikely to receive a fair trial in Rome, his prince, Frederick the Wise, intervened and asked the papacy to send representatives to deal with Luther in Germany. Meetings with Cardinal Cajetan in October, 1518, and Karl von Miltitz in January, 1519, failed to obtain a recantation from Luther, although he continued to treat the pope and his representatives with respect.

In July, 1519, at the Leipzig debate Luther questioned the authority of the papacy as well as the infallibility of church councils and insisted on the primacy of Scripture. This led his opponent, Johann Eck, to identify him with the fifteenth century Bohemian heretic, Jan Hus, in an effort to discredit Luther. After the debate Luther became considerably more outspoken and expressed his beliefs with increasing certainty. In 1520 he wrote three pamphlets of great significance. The first, the *Address to the Christian Nobility of the German Nation,* called upon the Germans to reform the church and society, since the papacy and church councils had failed to do so. The second, *The Babylonian Captivity of the Church,* clearly put Luther in the ranks of the heterodox, because it attacked the entire sacramental system of the medieval church. Luther maintained there were only two sacraments, baptism and the Lord's Supper—or at most three, with penance possibly qualifying as a third—rather than seven sacraments. He also denied the doctrines of transubstantiation and the sacrificial Mass. The third pamphlet, *The Freedom of the Christian Man,* was written for the pope. It was nonpolemical and clearly taught the doctrine of justification by faith alone.

Even before the publication of these pamphlets a papal bull of excommunication was drawn up to go into effect in January, 1521. In December, 1520, Luther showed his defiance of papal authority by publicly burning the bull. Although condemned by the church, Luther still received a hearing before an imperial diet at Worms in April, 1521. At the Diet of Worms he was asked to recant his teachings, but he stood firm, thereby defying also the authority of the emperor, who placed him under the imperial ban and ordered that all his books be burned. On the way home from Worms, Luther was abducted by friends who took him to the Wartburg castle, where he remained in hiding for nearly a year. While at the Wartburg he wrote a series of pamphlets attacking Catholic practices and began his German translation of the Bible. In 1522 Luther returned to Wittenberg to deal with disorders that had broken out in his absence, and he remained there for the rest of his life. In 1525 he married Catherine von Bora, a former nun, who bore him six children. Luther had an extremely happy and rich family life, but his life was marred by frequent ill health and bitter controversies.

Luther often responded to opponents in a polemical fashion, using extremely harsh language. In 1525 when the peasants of south Germany revolted and refused to heed his call to negotiate their grievances peacefully, he attacked them viciously in a pamphlet entitled *Against the Murdering Horde of Peasants.* A controversy with the Swiss reformer Ulrich Zwingli over the Lord's Supper split the Protestant movement when an effort to resolve the differences at a meeting in Marburg failed in 1529. Throughout his life Luther maintained an overwhelming work load, writing, teaching, organizing the new church, and providing overall leadership for the German Reformation. Among his more important theological writings were the Smalcald Articles published in 1538, which clearly defined the differences between his theology and that of the Roman Catholic Church.

Luther never viewed himself as the founder of a new church body, however. He devoted his life to reforming the church and restoring the

Pauline doctrine of justification to the central position in Christian theology. In 1522, when his followers first began to use his name to identify themselves, he pleaded with them not to do this. He wrote: "Let us abolish all party names and call ourselves Christians, after him whose teaching we hold. . . . I hold, together with the universal church, the one universal teaching of Christ, who is our only master." He died at Eisleben on February 18, 1546, while on a trip to arbitrate a dispute between two Lutheran nobles. He was buried in the Castle Church at Wittenberg. R. W. Heinze

See also Luther's Small Catechism; Smalcald Articles, The; Ninety-five Theses, The; Marburg Colloquy; Leipzig Disputation; Lutheran Tradition, The.

Bibliography. J. Pelikan and H. T. Lehmann, eds., *Luther's Works*, 56 vols.; H. T. Kerr, ed., *A Compend of Luther's Theology;* P. Althaus, *The Theology of Martin Luther;* E. G. Rupp, *The Righteousness of God;* U. Saarnivaara, *Luther Discovers the Gospel;* A. G. Dickens, *The German Nation and Martin Luther;* J. Atkinson, *Martin Luther and the Birth of Protestantism;* R. H. Bainton, *Here I Stand: A Life of Martin Luther;* H. Boehmer, *Martin Luther: Road to Reformation;* R. H. Fife, *The Revolt of Martin Luther;* H. Grisar, *Luther,* 6 vols.; H. G. Haile, *Luther: An Experiment in Biography;* E. G. Schwiebert, *Luther and His Times;* J. M. Todd, *Martin Luther: A Biographical Study.*

Lutheran Tradition, The. This term, or "Lutheranism," is employed to refer to the doctrine and practices authoritative in the Lutheran Churches and as a broad term for those churches throughout the world in general. The name "Lutheran" was not self-chosen but was initially applied by the enemies of Martin Luther in the early 1520s. Only when he felt that the identification was understood to mean recognition of the truth of his teaching did Luther suggest, "If you are convinced that Luther's teaching is in accord with the Gospel, . . . then you should not discard Luther so completely, lest with him you discard also his teaching, which you nevertheless recognize as Christ's teaching."

This teaching of Luther—forged from his discovery that the righteousness of God is not a righteousness that judges and demands but the righteousness given by God in grace—found its systematic expression in the formularies incorporated in the *Book of Concord.* All these documents, with the exception of the Formula of Concord, were written between 1529 and 1537 by Luther and Philip Melanchthon. They reflect the emphasis on justification by grace and the correction of abuses in the life of the church while at the same time "conserving" the church's catholic heritage (through explicit commitment to the ancient creeds, traditional forms of worship, church government, etc.). During the years following Luther's death in 1546, theological conflicts increasingly plagued his followers. The Formula of Concord, composed of the Epitome of the Articles in Dispute and the Solid Declaration of Some Articles of the Augsburg Confession, sought to resolve those disputes in terms of the authentic teaching of Luther. Subscription to these "symbolical" writings of the *Book of Concord* as true expositions of the Holy Scriptures has historically marked the doctrinal positions of Lutheranism.

Doctrines. The distinctive doctrines of Lutheran theology have commonly been related to the classical *leitmotifs* of the Reformation: *sola Scriptura, sola gratia, sola fide.*

The theology of Lutheranism is first a theology of the Word. Its principle of *sola Scriptura* affirms the Bible as the only norm of Christian doctrine. The Scripture is the *causa media* by which man learns to know God and his will; the Word is the one and the only source of theology. Lutheranism pledges itself "to the prophetic and apostolic writings of the Old and New Testaments as the pure and clear fountain of Israel, which is the only norm according to which all teachers and teachings are to be judged and evaluated" (Formula of Concord, Epitome). To be sure, the authority of Scripture had been emphasized prior to Luther and the Reformation. However, when Lutheranism referred to the Bible as the divine Word, brought to man through the apostles and prophets, it spoke with a new conviction regarding the primacy of the Word. Luther recognized that the authority of Scripture was valid even where it was opposed by pope, council, or tradition.

The Lutheran understanding of this principle should be distinguished from bibliolatry. Historic Lutheranism viewed Scripture as the organic foundation of faith. It is the source of theology in an instrumental sense. It is not the cause of the being of theology; that would truly be a deification or worship of a book. Rather, God is the first cause of theology; he is the *principium essendi*—its foundation, its beginning, and its end. The Scripture is the *principium cognoscendi,* for from Scripture theology is known and understood. Furthermore, the Lutheran view of the Bible is to be distinguished from a legalistic orientation. Christ is at the center of the Bible. Essential to understanding the Word of God is accepting the promises of the gospel by faith. If this faith is lacking, the Scriptures cannot be correctly understood.

The second doctrinal distinctive of Lutheranism is the doctrine of justification. According to

Luther there are two kinds of righteousness, an external righteousness and an inner righteousness. External righteousness, or civil righteousness, may be acquired through just conduct or good deeds. However, inner righteousness consists of the purity and perfection of the heart. Consequently, it cannot be attained through external deeds. This righteousness is of God and comes as a gift of his fatherly grace. This is the source of justification. The ground for justification is Christ, who by his death made satisfaction for the sins of mankind. The Apology of the Augsburg Confession defines justification as meaning "to absolve a guilty man and pronounce him righteous, and to do so on account of someone else's righteousness, namely, Christ's." Thus God acquits man of all his sins, and he does this not because man is innocent; rather God justifies us and declares man to be righteous for Christ's sake, because of his righteousness, his obedience to God's law, and his suffering and death. When God justifies, he not only forgives sins, but he also reckons to man Christ's perfect righteousness. God declares sinners to be righteous, apart from human merit or work, for the sake of Christ (forensic justification).

Related to this teaching is the third significant hallmark of Lutheranism: *sola fide.* The means whereby justification accrues to the individual is faith. The gospel, as Lutheranism confessed it, made faith the only way by which man could receive God's grace. In the medieval scholastic tradition theologians spoke of faith as something that could be acquired through instruction and preaching (*fides acquisita*). This was distinguished from infused faith (*fides infusa*), which is a gift of grace and implies adherence to all revealed truth. Lutheranism repudiated this distinction. The faith which comes by preaching coincides with that which is justifying; it is wholly a gift of God. Justifying faith is not merely a historical knowledge of the content of the gospel; it is the acceptance of the merits of Christ. Faith, therefore, is trust in the mercy of God for the sake of his Son.

Lutheranism has persistently refused to see faith itself as a "work." Faith is receptivity, receiving Christ and all that he has done. It is not man's accomplishment that effects his justification before God. Faith is instead that which accepts God's verdict of justification: "Faith does not justify because it is so good a work and so God-pleasing a virtue, but because it lays hold on and accepts the merit of Christ in the promise of the holy Gospel" (Formula of Concord, Solid Declaration).

The article of justification by grace through faith challenged the Roman Catholic tradition, which asserted that faith was pleasing to God only if it were accompanied by good works and perfected by love. At the Council of Trent in 1545 the Lutheran view was condemned and the medieval Roman Church reiterated its doctrine that justification is a state of grace in which human good works have merit. For Lutheranism, faith and works certainly cannot be separated; however, they must be distinguished. The righteousness of faith refers to man in his relation to God (*coram Deo*). The righteousness of good works refers to man in relation to his neighbor (*coram hominibus*). These must not be confused so as to intimate that man will seek to become just in the sight of God on the strength of his good deeds, nor in such a way that he will attempt to conceal sin with grace. Thus, with respect to justification strictly speaking, good works must be clearly distinguished. But faith cannot be apart from works. Where there is faith in Christ, love and good works also follow.

In one way or another the three fundamental doctrines of Lutheranism—*sola Scriptura, sola gratia, sola fide*—determine the shape of other distinctive teachings. For example, the position of Lutheranism on man's free will is understood in the light of the doctrine of justification. Man is completely without a free will with respect to the "spiritual sphere" (that which concerns salvation). Salvation depends exclusively on the omnipotent divine will of grace. Man does not have freedom to do the good in the spiritual sense. Similarly, the Lutheran understanding of the Lord's Supper must be viewed in light of the principle of *sola Scriptura.* Lutheranism has consistently battled against every denial of the real and essential presence of Christ's body and blood in the Supper. An important element of Lutheran biblical interpretation is that one takes words of command and promise literally unless there is some compelling reason for not doing so. If the words of institution at the Supper were to be taken figuratively, simply because they appear to conflict with reason or common sense (e.g., the Reformed axiom of the finite being incapable of the infinite), one could do so with any command or promise of God. Thus, Lutheranism has insisted on the doctrine of the "real presence" on the basis of Christ's plain words. Also, the Lutheran view of grace contributed to the retention of infant baptism. Baptism expresses the participation of the Christian in the death and resurrection of Christ. Baptism, like the gospel, is powerful to confer the very faith it calls for with its promises, and in each case the Holy Spirit works faith through the instruments of his choosing, namely baptism and the gospel. In Lutheran understanding it is no more difficult for him to work faith in infants through the gospel promise attached to the water of baptism than in adults alienated from God through the proclamation of the gospel in preaching.

History. These doctrines of Lutheranism were subject to a variegated history in the centuries following the Reformation era. In the seventeenth century they were elaborated in a scholastic mold. Lutheran orthodoxy, whose classical period began about the year 1600, was an extension of the tradition represented by the Lutheran confessional writings. It was, however, profoundly influenced by the neo-Aristotelianism which had secured a foothold in the German universities. This German scholastic philosophy accented the intellectual strain which characterized Lutheran orthodoxy and prompted a more pronounced scientific and metaphysical treatment of theological questions. However, scholastic methodology did not lead to the surrender of Lutheran emphasis on the Bible. The dogmatic works of the orthodox period were based on the principle of *sola Scriptura.* There was an effort to systematize an objective form of theology (theology defined as a "teaching about God and divine things"). Revelation, as codified in the Bible, provided the point of departure for the orthodox theologians. The chief representatives of this period of Lutheranism included Johann Gerhard, Nikolaus Hunnius, Abraham Calov, and David Hollaz.

The period of Lutheran orthodoxy gave way to the pietist movement in the latter part of the seventeenth century. Pietism was a reaction to what was perceived as an arid intellectualism in the orthodox theologians. Philipp Jakob Spener's *Pia desideria* called for a reform movement within Lutheranism. According to Spener, experience is the basis of all certainty. Therefore, the personal experience of the pious is the ground of certainty for theological knowledge. This led to the pietist critique of the metaphysical questions treated by the orthodox fathers as well as their traditional philosophical underpinnings. For the pietist Lutherans inner spiritual phenomena and individual experiences elicited the greatest interest. Since Spener and his followers assumed that theological knowledge could not be acquired apart from the experience of regeneration, their theological expositions dealt mainly with empirical religious events.

In the eighteenth century theological rationalism appeared in Germany. Christian Wolff, utilizing the Leibnizian principle of "sufficient reason," argued that learning must be based on clear and distinct concepts and that nothing should be set forth without proof. Wolff's thought had a great impact on theological activity. Harmony between faith and reason was assumed, and the natural knowledge of God led to the idea of special revelation while the rational proofs for the truth of Scripture demonstrated that the Bible is the source of this revelation. While Wolff intended to defend traditional doctrine, the consequence of his method was the acceptance of reason as a final authority. This conclusion was extended by Johann Semler, who applied a historicocritical method to the Bible and inserted it totally into the framework of human development.

Many Lutherans saw the influence of rationalism behind the Prussian Union of 1817. Frederick William III announced the union of the Lutherans and the Reformed into one congregation at his court in celebration of the three hundredth anniversary of the Reformation and appealed for similar union throughout Prussia. The union was the impetus for a revival of Lutheran confessionalism which reacted to an increasing doctrinal indifference in some quarters of German Lutheranism as well as a growing interest in biblical criticism that threatened to remove the doctrinal foundations of Luther's church. Prominent figures in the effort to restore historical Lutheranism were C. P. Caspari, E. W. Hengstenberg, and C. F. W. Walther. Walther joined an emigration of Saxons to the United States in 1838 to escape the theological legacy of rationalism and the union.

Apart from Germany, where two thirds of the population had accepted Lutheranism by the end of the sixteenth century, the expansion of Lutheranism through Sweden, Denmark, and Norway left national churches that have endured in strength. From these nations Lutherans migrated to the United States and Canada. The earliest Lutherans in America can be traced back to the seventeenth century. In Delaware, Swedish Lutherans had settled as early as 1638. In Georgia, almost a hundred years later, a group of refugee Lutherans from Salzburg established residence. Colonies of Lutherans also settled in upper New York and in Pennsylvania by the time of the Revolution. Henry Melchior Muhlenberg organized the first synod of Lutherans on American soil.

Contemporary Lutheranism seems to have entered on an age of unification. The various waves of immigrants to America led to a proliferation of Lutheran bodies. However, there have been a number of mergers between these groups, which are now mainly included in the Lutheran Church in America (1962), the American Lutheran Church (1960), and the Lutheran Church—Missouri Synod (1847). The Lutheran World Federation, founded in 1947, cultivates world unity and mutual assistance among its fifty or more member churches. Lutheranism throughout the world constitutes the largest of the churches that have come out of the Reformation, numbering some seventy million members, of whom between nine and ten million live in the United States and Canada. J. F. JOHNSON

See also LUTHER, MARTIN; REFORMATION, PROTESTANT; PIETISM; CONCORD, FORMULA OF; CONCORD, BOOK OF; MELANCHTHON, PHILIP; SYNERGISM; MONERGISM; ADIAPHORA, ADIAPHORISTS; MUHLENBERG, HENRY MELCHIOR; WALTHER, CARL FERDINAND WILHELM.

Bibliography. W. Elert, *The Structure of Lutheranism;* E. W. Gritsch and R. W. Jenson, *Lutheranism;* B. Hagglund, *History of Theology;* C. P. Krauth, *The Conservative Reformation and Its Theology;* R. D. Preus, *The Theology of Post-Reformation Lutheranism,* 2 vols.; T. G. Tappert, ed., *The Book of Concord;* R. C. Wolf, ed., *Documents of Lutheran Unity in America;* E. C. Nelson, ed., *The Lutherans in North America.*

Luther's Small Catechism. Martin Luther wrote his Small Catechism, a simple manual of instruction in the Christian faith, in 1529 after one of the great disappointments of his life. In 1527 and 1528 Luther and his associates were asked by their prince to inspect the churches of Saxony. The results were profoundly disappointing. Ignorance reigned among clergy and laity alike, and the schools were in ruins. To meet the need for popular instruction Luther immediately drew up wall charts containing explanations in simple language of the Ten Commandments, the Lord's Prayer, and the Apostles' Creed. When his colleagues delayed in their own efforts at providing educational materials, Luther pulled together his wall charts and published them as a short, simple exposition of the faith.

Luther intended his catechism to be an aid for family worship. In its preface he condemned parents who, by neglecting the Christian education of their children, had become the "worst enemies of God and man." Almost all of the catechism's sections began with remarks directed at the head of the house (e.g., "The Ten Commandments in the plain form in which the head of the family shall teach it to his household").

The catechism contains nine sections, each a series of questions and answers. These sections treat the Ten Commandments, the Apostles' Creed, the Lord's Prayer, baptism, confession and absolution, and the Lord's Supper. They also include instructions for morning and evening prayers, grace at meals, and a "Table of Duties" made up of scriptural passages "selected for various estates and conditions of men, by which they may be admonished to do their respective duties."

Much of the influence of Lutheranism around the world can be traced to the success of this catechism in expressing the profound truths of the faith in a language that all can understand. Unlike some Reformed confessions, Luther's Small Catechism lays out the Ten Commandments before describing the work of Christ. The catechism's exposition of the creed focuses on the free gift of salvation in Christ. And its sections on baptism and the Lord's Supper expound the views—mediating between Catholic sacramentalism and Protestant mere symbolism—which Luther developed fully in lengthy theological works. M. A. NOLL

See also LUTHER, MARTIN; CATECHISMS.

Bibliography. T. G. Tappert, ed., *The Book of Concord.*

Lying. *See* LIE, LYING.

Mm

M'Cheyne, Robert Murray (1813–1843). Widely considered one of the most Christlike men ever to have lived in Scotland. He was born in Edinburgh and educated at the University of Edinburgh, where he won honors in languages and prizes in poetry, music, and drawing. His conversion and call to the ministry followed the death of his saintly young brother, David, who had long prayed for Robert. He studied for the Church of Scotland ministry in Edinburgh under the famous theologian Thomas Chalmers. During this period of the nineteenth century an evangelical reawakening was sweeping the Church of Scotland, ultimately issuing in the "Disruption," which saw nearly one half the membership leave the Established Church to found the more evangelical Free Church of Scotland in 1843, the year of M'Cheyne's death. M'Cheyne's ministry was part of this national ecclesiastical movement. In 1835 he was assistant minister in the parishes of Larbert and Dunipace, near Stirling. In 1836 he was called to St. Peter's Church of Dundee, which had some four thousand members. His ministry there was marked by deep personal holiness, prayer, compassion for the salvation of the lost, powerful evangelical preaching, and tireless counseling. In 1839 he spent six months in Palestine, exploring possible missionary work among the Jews. Revival broke out in his congregation during his absence. Upon his return he threw himself into this work, which soon spread over the country, resulting in the conversion of thousands. He died at age twenty-nine. His biography retains its perennial popularity. D. F. Kelly

Bibliography. M'Cheyne, *The Believer's Joy;* A. A. Bonar, *Memoir and Remains of the Rev. Robert Murray M'Cheyne; Sermons of Robert Murray M'Cheyne.*

MacDonald, George (1824–1905). Scottish theologian and man of letters best known for his fairy tales for young people and his fantasies for adults. He was also a novelist and poet, writing some twenty-six novels in which he scrutinized human behavior and commented on it from a Christian point of view. He also wrote a considerable amount of devotional poetry in the romantic tradition. His poem "The Diary of an Old Soul," composed of a seven-line stanza for each day of the calendar year, is a good work to introduce the reader to his mystical devotional attitudes and convictions.

He was born in Huntly, Scotland, and educated at King's College, Aberdeen, and Highbury Theological Seminary, London. In 1851 he began his ministry in the Trinity Congregational Church at Arundel, West Sussex. Forced to resign when the laity objected to his teachings, he took his family to Manchester, and soon started his writing career. Much of his life was spent in poverty and poor health, but he made a lecture tour of America in 1872–73, and as a mature author he was able to live in the more healthful climate of Italy.

MacDonald published five volumes of theological essays—*The Hope of the Gospel* (1892), *The Miracles of Our Lord* (1870), and three series of *Unspoken Sermons* (1867, 1885, and 1889). Although he was a keen and consistent thinker, he distrusted the ability of any abstract system of thought to contain truth, feeling that the imagination rather than the intellect could approach truth more nearly and embody it more compellingly. Hence an understanding of MacDonald's imaginative writings is necessary for a full appreciation of his thought and influence. In general, his convictions spring from a Scottish Calvinist base, strongly modified by German romantic thought as it came to him mainly through the poetry and fantasies of the German writers Novalis and E. T. A. Hoffmann.

The following ideas are characteristic of MacDonald's writings: Active obedience to the precepts of Christ is the all-important element in Christian experience. It is the essential response to God as our loving heavenly Father who looks impartially upon all people and who expends all his divine energies to bring men "home" to himself. He works first through the agency of Christ, who in his person as Son of God *is* our atonement. The sufferings of God reveal his love. But God speaks as well through the entirety of creation and human experience, as his Spirit is resident in all things, offering to each man that which he needs—although it may be painful or appear terrible—for spiritual growth. Men who are receptive to divine influences are in the process of growing to become full sons of God in will and deed; those who spurn God's loving intentions are diminishing into spiritual grotesques. But MacDonald expresses hope for the eventual repentance of all the inhabitants of hell. He held that, inasmuch as God made man out of his own glory (not *ex nihilo*), the essential self of each man is divine. All unbelievers will one day be afforded opportunity to see both the hideous realities they have made themselves in God's sight and the true beauty of divine love. The inevitable result of this vision will be repentance and turning to God. These souls will then begin the long process of growth into divine sonship. Thus will God's grace be expressed throughout the ages to come, and divine love will in no wise be defeated.

These convictions have imaginative embodiment in the stories for young people—*The Princess and the Goblin* (1872), *The Princess and Curdie* (1883), and *At the Back of the North Wind* (1871)—and in two fantasies for adults, *Phantastes* (1858) and *Lilith* (1895). The fairy tale "The Golden Key" is perhaps his masterpiece.

R. N. HEIN

Bibliography. R. N. Hein, *The Harmony Within: The Spiritual Vision of George MacDonald* and (ed.) *Creation in Christ: The Unspoken Sermons of George MacDonald;* C. S. Lewis, *George MacDonald: An Anthology;* G. MacDonald, *George MacDonald and His Wife;* S. Prickett, *Romanticism and Religion* and *Victorian Fantasy;* R. H. Reis, *George MacDonald;* R. L. Wolff, *The Golden Key.*

McGiffert, Arthur Cushman (1861–1933). The leading church historian of American liberalism at the beginning of the twentieth century. He studied at Union Seminary in New York and with Adolf Harnack at the University of Marburg in Germany, where he received his doctorate in 1888. He then taught church history for five years at Lane Seminary in Cincinnati before succeeding Philip Schaff, founder of the American Society of Church History, as professor of church history at Union in 1893. From 1917 to 1926 he served as president of that institution. McGiffert was an ordained Presbyterian clergyman who left the denomination to become a Congregationalist during a conflict over the nature of his theological views and his approach to history.

McGiffert stood prominently in the rise of theological liberalism in the United States. His three most important principles involved a concentration upon the life of Jesus, a commitment to "scientific history," and a passion for social ethics. For McGiffert, Jesus had possessed "a vivid realization of God as his father and the father of his brethren." Jesus represented a great "ideal," not as a being who communicated the essence of God to humanity, but as a human who lived purely and simply for the betterment of his fellows. The apostle Paul, on the other hand, propounded a faith "totally at variance with Christ's" and established the historic Christian movement which (until the enlightened nineteenth century) deluded people into thinking that Christianity should focus on the divinity of Christ and the reality of an institutional church.

McGiffert's assumptions about history had much to do with the shape of his theology. From study in Germany he returned to the United States with the idea that "scientific" history, which excluded the supernatural, was somehow more "objective" than that which allowed for the possibility of divine involvement in the events of the world. In accounting for this position he expressed the hope that one day people would not be "obliged to ask what Bible or church or creed require, but what the facts teach." Results of historical investigation were thus not to be subject to orthodox traditions. In reality, however, McGiffert's history grew out of a thorough commitment to the truth claims of the late nineteenth century. He believed that "the new scientific spirit, the new historical sense and the new methods of historical criticism, . . . the new emphasis on evolution, the new estimate of nature and the supernatural" had made it possible to reconstitute the past much more factually than had ever been possible before. This method allowed him to jettison as inessential traditional Christian teachings concerning the origin of the race, the fall, the veracity of OT history, and the supernatural aspects of Jesus' teaching.

McGiffert's social ideal extended themes of the social gospel. He believed so thoroughly in the goodness of doing good that virtually every kind of humanitarian service became a form of Christianity. This emphasis also shaped his view of the past, where, for example, Luther became one who exemplified Protestantism because of his "disinterested love to the good of others."

McGiffert's books—including *A History of Christianity in the Apostolic Age* (1897), *Protestant Thought Before Kant* (1911), and *A History of Christian Thought* (1932)—remain forceful examples of church history from a liberal perspective. M. A. NOLL

See also LIBERALISM, THEOLOGICAL; SOCIAL GOSPEL, THE.

Bibliography. W. Bowden, *Church History in the Age of Science.*

Machen, John Gresham (1881–1937). A leading American conservative theologian, NT scholar, and ecclesiastical controversialist. Machen was born in Baltimore of a distinguished southern and Presbyterian family. He graduated with high honors from Johns Hopkins University, where under the guidance of the noted Greek scholar B. L. Gildersleeve he excelled in classical studies. After a year's graduate study at Johns Hopkins, Machen entered Princeton Theological Seminary to study under eminent Calvinist scholars such as Warfield, Patton, Vos, and R. D. Wilson.

During his final year as undergraduate Machen had the distinction of having a series of articles published in the *Princeton Theological Review* entitled "A Critical Discussion of the NT Account of the Virgin Birth of Jesus." Upon graduation from Princeton in 1905 he was still uncertain of a call to the ministry, and so went to Germany for a year's postgraduate work in the universities of Marburg and Göttingen. Although impressed and attracted by the liberal theology of Wilhelm Herrmann, Machen struggled through to a deep commitment to the infallibility of Scripture and to the traditional emphases of historic Reformed theology.

In 1906 Machen returned to Princeton as an instructor in the NT department. He continued in this position until he was installed as professor of NT in 1915. Only in 1913 did he finally decide to seek ministerial ordination. After 1912 he became more widely known as a scholar through the publication of various articles, reviews, and translations.

During World War I he spent several months on the front lines in France serving as a YMCA worker. After the war the theological atmosphere in the Northern Presbyterian Church and in Princeton Seminary was changing from traditional Calvinism to a much more liberal or "modernist" interpretation of Christianity. In the intense struggles between fundamentalists and modernists during the 1920s and 30s Machen emerged as an international champion of biblical authority and evangelical theology.

The faculty of Princeton Seminary split over some of these issues, and ultimately the liberal forces in the Presbyterian Church "reorganized" Princeton Seminary in 1929 in such a way that their viewpoint prevailed administratively. This led to the resignation of Machen, Van Til, Allis, Wilson, and others, who under the guidance of Machen founded Westminster Seminary in Philadelphia in 1929.

Owing to his concern over liberal trends among Presbyterian missionaries, Machen founded the Independent Board for Presbyterian Missions in 1933. This step was to cost him his relationship to the church. He was tried by New Brunswick Presbytery in Trenton, New Jersey, in 1935 for disobeying the order of General Assembly to leave the Independent Board. Machen was not allowed to defend himself from Scripture or to make any reference to the theological implications of his case. He was suspended from the ministry and lost his appeals to synod and to the General Assembly of 1936.

On June 11, 1936, Machen led in the organization of the Presbyterian Church of America (which soon changed its name to the Orthodox Presbyterian Church). This new body did not grow as had been hoped, and within a short time experienced division within its own ranks. Perhaps part of the problem lay with Machen's decision to dissolve the Covenant Union, which was an organization of Bible-believing Christians within the Presbyterian Church. The Rev. Walter Watson of Syracuse, N.Y., requested Machen to maintain relations with this group in the old church even though he was starting a separate body. If this were done, Watson felt that in time many thousands might decide to join with those who had already come out with Machen. The Covenant Union was dissolved, however, and thus evangelicals in the new church and those remaining in the old church failed to benefit from one another's fellowship and common purposes over the years. Nevertheless, evangelical Christianity in the Western world owes a large debt to Machen and to the organizations he founded for their intelligent and courageous explanation of and stand for historical Christian truth.

Machen died on a preaching tour in North Dakota. Among his most influential books are *The Origin of Paul's Religion* (Sprunt Lectures for Union Seminary in Virginia in 1921); *NT Greek for Beginners* (1923); *Christianity and Liberalism* (1923); *What Is Faith?* (1925); *The Virgin Birth of Christ* (Smyth Lectures for Columbia Seminary in 1927); *The Christian Faith in the Modern World* (1936). Two of his booklets were very important: *The Attack upon Princeton Seminary—A Plea for Fair Play* (1927) and *Modernism and the Board of Foreign Missions* (1933). Machen also founded two periodicals, *Christianity Today* and, later, *The Presbyterian Guardian* (both ceased publication many years ago).

D. F. KELLY

See also FUNDAMENTALISM; EVANGELICALISM; PRINCETON THEOLOGY, OLD.

Bibliography. Machen, "Westminster Theological Seminary: Christianity in Conflict," in *Contemporary American Theology,* I, ed. V. Ferm; N. B. Stonehouse, *J. Gresham Machen: A Biographical Memoir;* H. W. Coray, *J. Gresham Machen: A Silhouette;* P. Woolley, *The Significance of J. Gresham Machen Today;* W. D. Livingston, *The Princeton Apologetics Exemplified by the Work of B. B. Warfield and J. Gresham Machen, a Study in American Theology 1880–1930;* F. A. Schaeffer, *The Church Before the Watching World,* ch. 3.

Mackintosh, Hugh Ross (1870–1936). Scottish theologian and author. Born at Paisley, he graduated with honors from the University of Edinburgh and from New College, after which he pursued postgraduate studies at Marburg in philosophy. He was Church of Scotland minister at Tayport from 1897 to 1901, and then at Beechgrove in Aberdeen until he was appointed professor of systematic theology at New College, Edinburgh, in 1904, which post he held until his death. He was elected moderator of the General Assembly of the Church of Scotland in 1932.

Mackintosh had immense knowledge of and considerable sympathy for the liberal theological movement of nineteenth century German Protestantism. His admiration was always mingled, however, with criticism for what he considered its mistakes. Much of his work was an endeavor to make the British public familiar with the results of German scholarship. To accomplish this, he translated (jointly) works of Ritschl and Schleiermacher. He also reformulated the traditional doctrines of Christianity in light of modern scholarship in his lectures and books. In his *Doctrine of the Person of Christ,* he prefers the kenotic theory of the incarnation (Christ being emptied of his deity) to the Chalcedonian formula of Christ having two distinct natures (divine and human) united in one person without confusion. In *The Christian Experience of Forgiveness* he opposes the atonement as a propitiation of the wrath of God, denies its penal character, and in certain respects blends a modified view of the moral influence theory of the atonement with other more traditional theological concepts. His posthumous work, *Types of Modern Theology* (1937), is still a classic survey of German Protestant theology from Schleiermacher to Barth. Some have considered Mackintosh to be a bridge between nineteenth century liberalism and the theology of Karl Barth.

D. F. KELLY

Bibliography. Mackintosh, *Immortality and the Future, The Originality of the Christian Message, The Divine Initiative,* and *Some Aspects of Christian Belief;* J. W. Leitch, *A Theology of Transition;* H. Wyatt, *New College Edinburgh, a Centenary History.*

McPherson, Aimee Semple (1890–1944). Pentecostalist revivalist and radio pioneer, one of America's best-known religious figures in the 1920s and 1930s. She married first the man who had been influential in her conversion, Robert Semple, a Pentecostal minister, with whom she went to China as a missionary in 1908. When Semple died, his wife returned to the United States. She then married Harold McPherson, from whom she was subsequently divorced. A third marriage and another divorce came later. With her mother as companion Aimee Semple McPherson began after World War I a very successful series of revival tours across the United States. "Sister Aimee" was an attractive woman who knew how to exploit her vibrant personality and captivating energy to win the attention of the media. She broke new ground in radio evangelism (1922) and may have participated in a staged kidnaping of herself in 1926, a case which remains clothed in mystery. Her teaching was probably not as important as her personality in her great success, but it did include standard fundamentalistic and Pentecostal emphases: sanctification, baptism of the Holy Spirit and the gift of tongues, Christ as Savior and healer, faith healing, and the imminent return of Christ. In 1922 she settled in Los Angeles, where she preached to thousands each week at her $1.5 million Angelus Temple. The International Church of the Foursquare Gospel arose as a result of her ministry in 1927. It continued under the direction of her son after she died, and now numbers well over 100,000 members worldwide. Part of the sensation surrounding McPherson's career arose from allegations, romantic and otherwise, which she knew how to exploit to her own advantage. She was a force in American popular religion who blazed trails that others, who did not necessarily share her convictions, have followed.

M. A. NOLL

Bibliography. McPherson, *The Story of My Life;* L. Thomas, *Storming Heaven.*

Magnificat. The name given to the first of the three hymns in Luke's infancy narratives (1:46–55), the other two being the Benedictus (1:68–79) and the Nunc Dimittis (2:29–32). The name derives from the opening line of the poem in the Latin Vulgate (*Magnificat anima mea Dominum*).

With the hymn Mary praises the Lord for choosing her to be the mother of the Messiah (although not expressly stated), and for remembering his covenantal promises to Israel. Throughout the hymn runs a note of joy and expectation that now, with the anticipated birth of the Messiah, will begin the reversal of roles associated with the new age which results in the exaltation of the humble and the humiliation of the proud.

The hymn divides into two parts—personal and corporate. In the first part Mary praises God (vss. 46*b*–47), gives her reason for so doing (vss. 48–49), and then states the general principle that lies behind God's action: God is merciful to those who fear him (vs. 50). In the second part Mary applies this general principle to others: just as God exalted Mary, who was of humble state, so also will he exalt all the humble and hungry. Conversely, he will bring down the proud, the rulers, and the rich (vss. 51–53). Specifically, God will remember his covenantal nation Israel and will, it is implied, raise them up from their humble position (vss. 54–55).

The theological consideration behind the hymn is that God deals with men in a consistent pattern—i.e., exaltation of the humble and humiliation of the proud. The historical consideration behind the hymn is that, with the birth of the Messiah, the OT hope of Israel's exaltation is now being realized. Although this is never explicitly stated, it is the basis for the whole hymn (cf. Luke 1:31–33, 35).

It is often said that the Magnificat is similar to Hannah's song (I Sam. 2:1–10) even though the tone of the latter is one of boasting against enemies.

The Magnificat is very Jewish in nature, more Jewish than Christian. In form it is an individual thanksgiving psalm making use of Hebraic parallelism and OT phrases, many from the Psalms. Typical of OT prophetic oracles, the hymn speaks of future deeds as accomplished facts—what God has spoken, he will assuredly bring to pass.

The Semitic form shows that the hymn was in a pre-Lukan tradition. There is no reason that, following the angel's visit, Mary could not have formulated the hymn using traditional materials, perhaps even Hannah's song, and then repeated it in response to Elizabeth's greeting. Luke could even have learned the hymn from Mary herself. Some argue that the speaker was Elizabeth, but the evidence is not sufficient.

Since the time of St. Benedict (sixth century) the hymn has been part of the vespers liturgy of the Western church. It is also read daily in the morning office in the Eastern church.

W. D. MOUNCE

See also LUKE, THEOLOGY OF.

Bibliography. I. H. Marshall, *Commentary on Luke; ODCC*, 858.

Majoristic Controversy. One of various controversies within Lutheranism between Luther's death in 1546 and the definitive formulation of the Lutheran platform in the *Book of Concord* of 1580. The overarching concern of all of them was to maintain purity of doctrine (as Lutheranism saw it) without either relapsing into Catholicism or veering into Calvinism.

One of the concessions made by the Melanchthonians, or Philippists, to the Leipzig Interim after Charles V's defeat of the Smalcald League in 1547 was the assertion of Georg Major, a pupil of Melanchthon, that "good works are necessary to salvation." (Melanchthon had earlier made a like statement but had withdrawn it upon Luther's entreaty.)

The counterattack of the Gnesio-Lutheran ("true Lutheran") party was led by Flacius and Amsdorf, but especially the latter overshot the mark by his counterassertion that "good works are harmful to salvation" (although Luther had on occasion so expressed himself too).

The bitter controversy was settled in Article IV of the Formula of Concord, which pointed out the excesses on both sides. Faith and good works (justification and sanctification) must not be confused in any way, but neither dare the importance of good works as an inevitable consequence of grace be minimized.

H. D. HUMMEL

See also AMSDORF, NICHOLAS VON; CONCORD, BOOK OF; CONCORD, FORMULA OF; FLACIUS, MATTHIAS.

Bibliography. F. H. Bente, *Historical Introduction to the Book of Concord;* A. J. Koelpin, ed., *No Other Gospel: Essays in Commemoration of the 400th Anniversary of the Formula of Concord, 1580–1980;* E. F. Klug and O. F. Stahlke, *Getting into the Formula of Concord;* R. D. Preus and W. H. Rosin, eds., *A Contemporary Look at the Formula of Concord.*

Major Orders. The senior or higher ranks, classes, or grades of the ordained ministry in the church in contradistinction from minor orders (porters, lectors, exorcists, and acolytes). In the Roman Catholic Church there are three major orders—episcopacy, priesthood, and the diaconate. These are seen to be of divine origin: "Christ, whom the Father sanctified and sent into the world, has, through his apostles, made their successors, the bishops, partakers of his consecration and his mission. These in their turn have legitimately handed on to different individuals in the church various degrees of participation in this ministry. Thus the divinely established ecclesiastical ministry is exercised on different levels by those who from antiquity have been called bishops, priests and deacons" (Vatican Council II, Constitution on the Church). Until 1972, when it was abolished, the subdiaconate had been included among the major orders.

All who are in major orders are required to be celibate. To be a priest it is necessary first to be ordained deacon; to be a bishop it is necessary to have been ordained deacon and priest.

In the Eastern, Orthodox, Anglican, and Old Catholic churches there is also agreement that the diaconate, priesthood, and episcopate are essential orders of ministry within the church. The Eastern and Orthodox churches also have various minor orders of ministry. Most Protestant denominations reject the idea of both major and minor orders and recognize only one basic form of ordained ministry. P. Toon

See also Church Officers; Orders, Holy; Minor Orders.

Mammon. The word represents the Aramaic word for riches or wealth. In pre-Christian times the expression "the mammon of unrighteousness" (Luke 16:9) had already become synonymous with the evils of money. In the Aramaic Targums mammon is used for wealth or gain. There is no adequate ground for supposing that this term designated a heathen deity in biblical times.

The NT usage of this word is confined to our Lord's teachings (Matt. 6:24; Luke 16:9, 11, 13). In Luke 16:9–13 "mammon" is used three times in a further exposition of the parable of the unrighteous steward (Luke 16:1–13). The parable itself must not be pressed in every detail; it is primarily an illustration with one point. The central theme is that the disciples of Christ should manifest a prudence and foresight in the use of "the mammon of unrighteousness" that is at least comparable, if not superior, to the unrighteous steward's. If worldly possessions are misused, one cannot expect the real and genuine riches to be committed to him. And, of course, it is morally impossible for one to serve God and mammon (here and in Matt. 6:24 personified) at the same time. W. Broomall

Bibliography. C. Brown, *NIDNTT*, II, 836ff.

Man, Doctrine of. ***In the OT.*** In the Genesis account of creation man's presence in the world is attributed directly to God. By this act alone, as the God of love and power, man was "created" (*bārā'*, 1:27; 5:1; 6:7) and "formed" (*yāṣar*, 2:7–8). By this creative act man was brought into existence in a duality of relationships—at once to nature and to God himself. He was formed of the dust of the earth and was endowed with soul life by the breath of God. God is the source of his life, and dust the material of his being.

Man's Nature. Man, then, did not spring out of nature by some natural evolutionary process. He is the result of the immediate action of God, who used already existing created material for the formation of the earthly part of his being. Man has thus physiological similarities with the rest of the created order (Gen. 18:27; Job 10:8–9; Ps. 103:14, etc.) and consequently shares with the animal world in dependence on God's goodness for his continuance (Isa. 40:6–7; Pss. 103:15; 104, etc.). Throughout the OT the relationship of man to nature is everywhere stressed. As man shares with nature in the constitution of his being, so does nature share with man in the actualities of his living. Thus, while nature was made to serve man, so man on his part is required to tend nature (Gen. 2:15). Nature is therefore not a sort of neutral entity in relation to man's life. For between the two—nature and man—there exists a mysterious bond so that when man sinned the natural order was itself deeply afflicted (Gen. 3:17–18; cf. Rom. 8:19–23). Since, however, nature suffered as a result of man's sin, so does it rejoice with him in his redemption (Ps. 96:10–13; Isa. 35, etc.), for in man's redemption it too will share (Isa. 11:6–9).

But however deeply related man is to the natural order, he is presented nonetheless as something different and distinctive. Having first called the earth into existence with its various requisites for human life, God then declared for the making of man. The impression that the Genesis account gives is that man was the special focus of God's creative purpose. It is not so much that man was the crown of God's creative acts, or the climax of the process, for although last in the ascending scale, he is first in the divine intention. All the previous acts of God are presented more in the nature of a continuous series by the recurring use of the conjunction "and" (Gen. 1:3, 6, 9, 14, 20, 24). "Then God said, 'Let us make man.'" "Then"—when? When the cosmic order was finished, when the earth was ready to sustain man. Thus, while man stands before God in a relationship of created dependence, he has also the status of a unique and special personhood in relation to God.

Man's constituents. The three most significant words in the OT to describe man in relation to God and nature are "soul" (*nepeš*, 754 times), "spirit" (*rûaḥ*, 378 times), and "flesh" (*bāśār*, 266

times). The term "flesh" has sometimes a physical and sometimes a figuratively ethical sense. In its latter use it has its context in contrast with God to emphasize man's nature as contingent and dependent (Isa. 31:3; 40:6; Pss. 61:5; 78:39; Job 10:4). Both *nepeš* and *rûaḥ* denote in general the life principle of the human person, the former stressing more particularly his individuality, or life, and the latter focusing on the idea of a supernatural power above or within the individual.

Of the eighty parts of the body mentioned in the OT the terms for "heart" (*lēb*), "liver" (*kābēd*), "kidney" (*kĕlāyôt*), and "bowels" (*mē'îm*) are the most frequent. To each of these some emotional impulse or feeling is attributed either factually or metaphorically. The term "heart" has the widest reference. It is brought into relation with man's total psychical nature as the seal or instrument of his emotional, volitional, and intellectual manifestations. In the latter context it acquires a force we should call "mind" (Deut. 15:9; Judg. 5:15–16) or "intellect" (Job 8:10; 12:3; 34:10), and is frequently employed by metonymy to denote one's thought or wish with the idea of purpose or resolve. For one's thought or wish is what is "in the heart," or, as would be said today, "in the mind."

These several words do not, however, characterize man as a compound of separate and distinct elements. Hebrew psychology does not divide up man's nature into mutually exclusive parts. Behind these usages of words the thought conveyed by the Genesis account, that man's nature is twofold, remains. Yet even there man is not presented as a loose union of two disparate entities. There is no sense of a metaphysical dichotomy, while even that of an ethical dualism of soul and body is quite foreign to Hebrew thought. By God's inbreathing the man he formed from the dust became a living soul, a unified being in the interrelation of the terrestrial and the transcendental.

Throughout the OT the two concepts of man as a unique and responsible individual and as a social and representative being have emphasis. Adam was both a man and yet mankind. In him individual personhood and social solidarity found expression. At times in Israel's history there is emphasis on individual responsibility (e.g., Ezek. 9:4; 20:38; cf. chs. 18 and 35), while the "Thou shalt" or "Thou shalt not" of the law and the prophets is characteristically singular, being addressed to the individual. Yet generally in Hebrew thought the individual is not viewed atomistically but in intimate connection with, and representative of, the whole community. So does the sin of the single individual involve all in its consequences (Josh. 7:24–26; cf. II Sam. 14:7; 21:1–14; II Kings 9:26). On the other hand, Moses and Phineas stand before God to plead their people's cause because they embody in themselves the whole community. In the intertestamental period, however, this awareness of solidarity passed from being a realized actuality in the social consciousness of the nation to being increasingly an idealistic and theological dogma.

From this perspective of racial solidarity in the first man it follows that Adam's sin involved every individual both in himself and in his social relationships. Because of Adam's transgression everyone is affected in the whole range of his being and in the totality of his societal living.

In the NT. *The Teaching of Jesus.* In formal statements Jesus had little to say about man. But by his attitude and actions among men he showed that he regarded the human person as significant. To Jesus man was not just a part of nature, for he is more precious in God's sight than the birds of the air (Matt. 10:31) and the beasts of the field (Matt. 12:12). His distinctiveness lies in his possession of a soul, or spiritual nature, which to forfeit is his ultimate tragedy and final folly (Matt. 16:26). Man's true life is consequently life under God and for his glory. It does not consist in the plenitude of earthly possessions (Luke 12:15). The sole wealth is therefore the wealth of the soul (Matt. 6:20, 25). Yet while emphasizing the spiritual aspect of man's nature, Jesus did not decry the body, for he showed concern throughout his ministry for total human needs.

This view of man as a creature of value was for Jesus an ideal and a possibility. For he saw all individuals, whether man or woman, as blind and lost and their relationship with God broken off. Although he nowhere specified the nature of sin, he clearly assumed its universality. All men are somehow caught up in sin's plight and enmeshed in its tragic consequences. Thus, all who would live to God's glory and eternal enjoyment must experience newness of life. And it was precisely this purpose that Christ came into the world to accomplish (Matt. 1:21; Luke 19:10). It follows therefore that it is by one's attitude to Christ as the Savior of the world that individual human destiny is finally sealed.

The Pauline Anthropology. Paul's declarations regarding the nature of man are generally stated in relation to salvation so that his anthropology throughout serves the interests of his soteriology. Foremost, therefore, in his teaching is his insistence on man's need of divine grace. Paul is emphatic about the universality of man's sin. Because of Adam's fall sin somehow got a footing in the world to make human life the sphere of its activity. Sin "entered the world through one man" (Rom. 5:12; cf. I Cor. 15:1–2). Consequent on Adam's transgression, "all have sinned and fall short of the glory of God" (Rom. 3:23). To meet man in his plight, Paul sets forth the gospel as a righteousness of God through faith in Jesus Christ for all who believe (cf. Rom. 3:22–25).

In this context Paul contrasts the "old man" of nature (Rom. 6:6; Eph. 4:22; Col. 3:9) who is "after the flesh" (Rom. 8:4, 12; Gal. 4:23, 29, etc.) with the "new man" in grace (Eph. 4:24; cf. II Cor. 5:17; Gal. 6:15) who is "after the Spirit" (Rom. 8:5; Gal. 4:29). He speaks also of the "outer nature" of man which perishes and his "inner nature" which abides and is daily being renewed in Christ (II Cor. 4:16; cf. Eph. 3:16) and of the "natural man" (*psychikos anthrōpos*) and "he who is spiritual" (I Cor. 2:15; cf. 14:37).

In contrast with the second Adam, the first Adam is "from the earth, a man of dust" (I Cor. 15:47), but is yet "a living being" (vs. 45). Though man on his earthly side "bears the image of the man of dust" (vs. 45), he can by grace through faith be made to "bear the image of the man from heaven" (vs. 49). Man in himself is a moral being with an innate sense of right and wrong which Paul speaks of as his "conscience" (21 times). This conscience can, however, lose its sensitiveness for the good and become "defiled" (I Cor. 8:7) and "seared" (I Tim. 4:2).

As the chief exponent of the application of Christ's saving work to personal life Paul can hardly avoid reference to man's essential nature and makeup, and inevitably such allusions reflect the OT usage of terms. At the same time, while he does employ his words with the same general meaning as in the OT, they are more precisely applied in his epistles. The most significant terms in his anthropological vocabulary are "flesh" (*sarx*, 91 times), which he uses in a physical and an ethical sense; "spirit" (*pneuma*, 146 times), to denote generally the higher, Godward aspect of man's nature; "body" (*sōma*, 89 times), most often to designate the human organism as such, but sometimes the carnal aspect of man's nature; "soul" (*psychē*, 11 times), broadly to carry the idea of the vital principle of individual life. Paul has several words translated "mind" in the English versions to specify man's native rational ability which is in the natural man seriously affected by sin (Rom. 1:8; 8:6–7; Eph. 4:17; Col. 2:18; I Tim. 3:8; Titus 1:15). But the mind transformed brings God acceptable worship (Rom. 12:2; Eph. 4:23) and so becomes in the believer the mind of Christ (I Cor. 2:16; cf. Phil. 2:5). The term "heart" (*kardia*, 52 times) specifies for Paul the innermost sanctuary of man's psychical being either as a whole or with one or another of its significant activities—emotional, rational, or volitional.

Sometimes Paul contrasts these aspects—flesh and spirit, body and soul—to give the impression of a dualism of man's nature. At other times he introduces the threefold characterization, body, soul, and spirit (I Thess. 5:23), which raises the question whether man is to be conceived dichotomously or trichotomously. The interchangeable use of the terms "spirit" and "soul" seems to confirm the former view, while the fact that they are sometimes contrasted is held to support the latter. Yet, however used, both terms refer to man's inner nature over against flesh or body, which refers to the outer aspect of man as existing in space and time. In reference, then, to man's psychical nature, "spirit" denotes life as having its origin in God and "soul" denotes that same life as constituted in man. Spirit is the inner depth of man's being, the higher aspect of his personality. Soul expresses man's own special and distinctive individuality. The *pneuma* is man's nonmaterial nature looking Godward; the *psychē* is that same nature of man looking earthward and touching the things of sense.

Other NT Writings. The rest of the NT in its scattered allusions to man's nature and constituents is in general agreement with the teaching of Jesus and of Paul. In the Johannine writings the estimate of man is centered on Jesus Christ as true man and what man may become in relation to him. Although John begins his Gospel by asserting the eternal Godhead of Christ as Son of God, he declares in the starkest manner the humanity of the Word made flesh. Jesus does all that may become a man, all that God intended man should be. What people saw was a "man that is called Jesus" (John 9:11; cf. 19:5). It is against the perfect humanness of Jesus that the dignity of every man is to be measured. By uniting himself with man, God's Son has made it clear for always that being human is no mean condition. For he took upon himself all that is properly human to restore man to his sonship with God (John 1:13; I John 3:1). Such too is the theme of the Epistle to the Hebrews. James declares that man is created in the "likeness" (*homoiōsin*) of God (3:9).

Historical Development. From these biblical statements about man's nature, the history of Christian thought has focused on three main issues.

Content of the Image. The most enduring of these concerns is the content of the image. Irenaeus first introduced the distinction between the "image" (Heb. *ṣelem;* Lat. *imago*) and "likeness" (Heb. *dĕmût;* Lat. *similitudo*). The former he identified as the rationality and free will which inhere in man *qua* man. The likeness he conceived to be a superadded gift of God's righteousness which man, because of his reason and freedom of choice, had the possibility to retain and advance by obedience to the divine commands. But this probationary endowment man was to forfeit by his act of willful disobedience for both himself and descendants. This thesis of Irenaeus was generally upheld by the scholastics and was given dogmatic application by Aquinas. In Aquinas's view, however, Adam had need of divine aid to continue in the path of holiness. But this aid, in its turn, was conditioned on Adam's effort and determination to obey God's law. Thus from the first, in Aquinas's scheme, divine grace was made to depend on human merit.

The Reformers denied this distinction between image and likeness upon which the works-salvation of medievalism was reared in their insistence upon the radical nature of sin and its effect upon the total being of man. Thus did they maintain that salvation is by grace alone and by faith alone as the gift of God.

Some moderns have revived Irenaeus's distinction under new terms. Emil Brunner, for example, speaks of the "formal" image to express the essential structure of man's being, which is not greatly affected by the fall. The "material" image, on the other hand, he regards as quite lost by man's sin. Reinhold Niebuhr has returned to the scholastic distinction more closely as regards both terminology and thesis. Those who do not admit a different connotation for the terms have sought to identify the content of the image as either corporeal form or pure spirit. Schleiermacher speaks of the image as man's dominion over nature, a view expounded in more recent days by Hans Wolff and L. Verdium. Karl Barth conceived of it in terms of male and female, although he stresses at the same time that only in relation to Christ is there a true understanding of man. The Reformed position is that the image of God in man consists in man's rationality and moral competency, but that it is precisely these realities of his being which were lost or marred through sin. Others consider personality as the ingredient of the image, while still others prefer to see it as sonship, contending that man was created for that relationship. But by his sin he repudiated his sonship, which can be restored only in Christ.

The Origin of the Soul. In the light of such passages as Ps. 12:7; Isa. 42:5; Zech. 12:1; and Heb. 12:9, the creationist doctrine that God is the immediate creator of the human soul has been built. First elaborated by Lactantius (*ca.* 240–*ca.* 320), it had the support of Jerome and of Calvin among the Reformers. Aquinas declared any other view to be heretical and so followed Peter Lombard, who in his *Sentences* says, "The Church teaches that souls are created at their infusion into the body."

The alternative view, traducianism (Lat. *tradux,* a branch or shoot), expounded by Tertullian, is that the substances of both soul and body are formed and propagated together. Favored by Luther, it is consequently generally adopted by later Lutheran theologians. In support of the view is the observation that Gen. 1:27 represents God as creating the species in Adam to be propagated "after its kind" (cf. Gen. 1:12, 21, 25). And this increase through secondary causes is implied in the following verse (cf. vs. 22; 5:3; 46:26; John 1:13; Heb. 7:9–10) and in the passages which suggest the solidarity of the race and its sin in the first man (Rom. 5:12–13; I Cor. 15:22; Eph. 2:3).

From its stress on the continuing kinship of God and man, the Eastern church has favored creationism. Here God is regarded as acting immediately to bring individual life into being. The Western church, on the other hand, by emphasizing God's otherness from the created order and the depth of the yawning gulf between the human and divine consequent on man's sin, sees God's contact with man in the world as more distant. Traducianism, therefore, in which God's relation to individual conception and birth is held to be mediated, has had from the third century wide support.

The Extent of Freedom. Consonant with his idea of the *imago Dei* as grounded in man's nature as rational and free, Justin Martyr set in motion the view that every man is responsible for his own wrongdoing, which was to become a characteristic note of the Eastern church. Thus Adam is seen as the primary type of each man's sinning, and his fall is the story of Everyman. Western theology, by contrast, regards Adam's transgression as the fountainhead of all human evil, but against Gnosticism refused to locate its source in individual life in the material of the body. Tertullian traced sin to humanity's connection with Adam, through whom it has become a natural element of every man's nature. Yet he allowed some residue of free will to remain.

In Pelagius and Augustine these two views came into sharp conflict. Pelagius taught that man was unaffected by Adam's transgression, his will retaining the liberty of indifference so that he possesses in himself the ability to choose good or evil. In the light of Rom. 5:12–13 Augustine maintained that Adam's sin has so crippled man that he can act only to express his sinful nature inherited from his first parents. The inevitable compromise appeared in the semi-Pelagian (or semi-Augustinian) synergistic thesis that while all men do inherit a bias to sin, a freedom of decision remains that permits at least some men to take the first step toward righteousness. In the Calvinist-Arminian controversy of the seventeenth century the conflict was reenacted. Calvin contended for the total depravity of man; man "has no good remaining in him." Therefore the will is not free to choose the good; so salvation is an act of God's sovereign grace. Arminius allowed that Adam's sin had dire consequences and that each possesses a "natural propensity" to sin (John Wesley), while maintaining, at the same time, that it belongs to every man of his own free will to ratify this inner direction of his nature. On the other hand, it is possible for any man, by accepting the aid of the Holy Spirit, to opt for God's way, for he still possesses an inner ability so to do.

In the Pelagian-humanist scheme all men are well and need only a tonic to keep them in good health. In the semi-Pelagian (semi-Augustinian)—Arminian doctrine man is sick and requires the right medicine for his recovery. In the Augustinian-Calvinist view man is dead and can be renewed to life only by a divinely initiated resurrection. H. D. McDonald

See also Man, Natural; Man, Old and New; Man, Origin of.

Bibliography. S. B. Babbage, *Man in Nature and Grace;* E. Brunner, *Man in Revolt;* G. Carey, *I Believe in Man;* S. Cave, *The Christian Estimate of Man;* D. Cairns, *The Image of God in Man;* W. Eichrodt, *Man in the OT;* W. G. Kümmel, *Man in the NT;* J. Laidlaw, *The Bible Doctrine of Man;* J. G. Machen, *The Christian View of Man;* H. D. McDonald, *The Christian View of Man;* J. Moltmann, *Man;* J. Orr, *God's Image in Man;* H. W. Robinson, *The Christian Doctrine of Man;* R. F. Shedd, *Man in Community;* C. R. Smith, *The Bible Doctrine of Man;* W. D. Stacey, *The Pauline View of Man;* T. F. Torrance, *Calvin's Doctrine of Man;* C. A. vanPeursen, *Body, Soul, Spirit;* J. S. Wright, *What Is Man?*

Man, Natural. This theme has long been involved in the debate over natural theology, which has sought to define how much knowledge of God (if any) is available to man outside Christ. But as a distinct theological term "natural man" is used by Paul in I Cor. 2:14, where "natural" is a translation of *psychikos* and stands in contrast to "spiritual" (*pneumatikos,* I Cor. 2:13, 15; 3:1) and thus in parallel with "fleshly" (*sarkinos,* I Cor. 3:1). The meaning of "natural man" here is illuminated by I Cor. 15:44–47, where the whole phrase does not appear, but *psychikos* is used a further three times, again in contrast to *pneumatikos,* and with reference to the contrast between Adam and Christ as "living being" (*psychē*) and "life-giving spirit" (*pneuma*) respectively (I Cor. 15:45).

To summarize, the meaning of "natural man" indicates man in the "lower" aspects of his being—i.e., in those aspects which mark him off as creature, as temporally and spatially confined, as limited to this-worldly, "fleshly" modes of perception that cannot penetrate the world of the Spirit. It means much more than "fallen," for it is applied by implication to Adam at the moment of his creation, before the fall (I Cor. 15:45). But the fall is involved, for that had precisely the effect of shackling man irretrievably to those creaturely limitations which for Adam could have been opportunities for discovery and growth but became in fact a sentence of banishment. The contrasting "spiritual man" is not therefore one delivered from all creaturely limitations, but one in whom the indwelling Spirit is beginning to open the doors of perception which Adam slammed shut. S. Motyer

See also Natural Theology; Man, Doctrine of; Man, Old and New.

Bibliography. W. D. Stacey, *The Pauline View of Man;* E. Schweizer, *TDNT,* IX, 662–63; G. E. Ladd, *A Theology of the NT;* A. T. Lincoln, *Paradise Now and Not Yet.*

Man, Old and New. "Old man" and "new man" are terms used by Paul to express the contrast between life without Christ and life in union with him (Rom. 6:6; Eph. 4:22–24; Col. 3:9–10). The use of the word "man" in these contexts is at first sight puzzling, and this explains the RSV translations "self" and "nature," which are attempts to paraphrase the Greek *anthrōpos.* In fact it seems that Paul has something much more far-reaching (and exciting) in mind than merely a contrast between the "before and after" experiences enjoyed by (or expected of) the believer.

The first step to a fuller understanding is to note that in all three contexts the notion of creation appears—explicitly in Eph. 4:24 and Col. 3:10 and implicitly in Rom. 6:6, where the use of *anthrōpos* reminds us of its use with reference to Adam in Rom. 5:12, 19. The next step is to notice that Christ is also called simply *anthrōpos* in Rom. 5:15, in deliberate contrast to Adam. The third step is to recognize that Paul's application of *anthrōpos* to Christ is his adaptation of the great title "Son of man" (*huios tou anthrōpou*), applied to himself by Jesus. This title appears only in the Gospels, and it looks as though missionaries to the Gentiles (like Paul) had to "translate" it into something simpler to understand. We see this translation process at work in I Tim.

2:5–6, which seems to rest upon Mark 10:45 but reduces "Son of man" to just "man."

The final step is to go back to the OT roots of this title (Dan. 7:9–27) and to see that the Son of man is the messianic figure appointed to establish God's kingdom on behalf of his people, who receive the kingdom in and through him. Now put it all together: for Paul, Christ is the "new (Son of) man" of a new creation/kingdom/humanity established in contrast to that of Adam, who is the "old man"; in union with Christ (through baptism into his death and resurrection, Rom. 6:3–5) we are transferred from the old creation to the new. Our "old man"—i.e., our membership in Adam—was crucified with Christ, and now we must seek to reflect in practice the "image" of this new man ("put on"), and to scour out the remaining image of the old ("put off"). I Cor. 15:45–49 sums it all up. S. MOTYER

See also SON OF MAN; MAN, DOCTRINE OF; MAN, NATURAL; NEW CREATION, NEW CREATURE.

Bibliography. A. Richardson, *An Introduction to the Theology of the NT;* C. F. D. Moule, *The Origin of Christology;* J. A. T. Robinson, *The Body;* G. E. Ladd, *A Theology of the NT.*

Man, Origin of. Evolutionists believe that man developed from lower organisms through a series of changes brought about by purely natural processes, that this line of development can be traced from simple, presumably one-cell, living things, through more complex organisms, and finally through organisms which today would be classified as anthropoid apes, to man. Man's closest relatives are believed to be the anthropoid apes because of the great number of similarities between apes and humans. While it is true that there are many similarities and that the similarities between man and the anthropoids are greater than those between man and other animals, it is also true that there are many differences between man and the anthropoids, some quite significant. It is possible to list well over one hundred differences between man and the anthropoids. Probably the most significant biological difference is the fact that man is able to communicate in abstract terms. He has developed language and has a history. Thus, he is able to transmit his culture from one generation to another and to profit from what has been learned by previous generations. These differences suggest a wide gap between man and the anthropoids.

Recent African finds suggest that man was separate from any supposed anthropoid ancestors for a much longer time than was once thought to be the case. Without accepting uncritically the dating of these forms, it is interesting to note that they indicate a separateness of man from any anthropoid forms for a very long period of time; thus they also suggest that the Bible may be correct in emphasizing the separateness of man from anthropoid forms from the beginning.

Fossil evidence of supposed prehuman and early human forms is particularly interesting in a study of man's origin and development. Because of man's understandable interest in the story of his development, this evidence has been carefully studied, with the result that forms which were once classified in a separate genus from man are now usually classified in the genus *Homo* to which modern man is assigned. Thus, most anthropologists classify what was once called *Pithecanthropus erectus* as *Homo erectus, Australopithecus transvaalensis* as *Homo transvaalensis, Sinanthropus pekinensis* as *Homo erectus,* etc. These studies have shown that the differences between prehuman and early human forms are not as great as they were once thought to be.

Particularly interesting has been the careful study on the so-called Piltdown man, *Eoanthropus dawsoni,* once hailed as a link in the evolutionary development of man but now shown to have been a fraud. Its significance is not that it suggests that most of the prehuman and early human forms are similar frauds, but rather that the conclusions of even the most competent anthropologist need to be reexamined, since the Piltdown man was studied and examined by the most competent scientists of the day and pronounced genuine by them.

One of the difficulties in the study of prehuman and early human forms is the paucity of remains. While fossils generally are quite common, the fossils of supposedly early human and prehuman forms are quite rare. A frequent explanation for their rarity is the evidence that man very early practiced earth burial, a procedure that makes fossilization extremely unlikely. This would suggest that man very early had faith in the resurrection of the dead and had a high respect for his dead.

The most common early human form is the Neanderthal man, the "cave man" so frequently pictured in history and biology books and even in comic strips. While supposedly prehuman fossils are rare, a large number of these "cave men" have been discovered and studied. Reconstructions usually represent them as stooped and apelike. It is now known that these forms suffered from osteoarthritis and osteophythosis and that disease accounted for their stooped position. There seems to be evidence too that at least some of them were an erect and lissome people. The arthritis which they contracted and which caused them to develop a pronounced stoop was due to living in damp caves. There is little doubt that these were people who were away from the mainstreams of civilization and took refuge in whatever shelter was available. It is interesting to note that after the fall of Sodom, Lot himself was a "cave man" (Gen. 19:30). When Saul pursued David, David took refuge in the cave of Adullam, where he was joined by a number of other "cave men" (I Sam. 22:1–2).

Today it is generally agreed that the Neanderthal man should properly be classified as *Homo sapiens,* the genus and species to which modern man belongs. If brain size is any measure of intelligence, he was at least as intelligent as modern man; and the form which succeeded him, the Cro-Magnon man, had an average brain size that was significantly higher than that of modern man.

Genesis indicates a "special" creation of man. It tells us that God fashioned him from the dust of the earth and breathed into his nostrils the breath of life so that he became a living soul (2:7). Man was created in the image of God (1:27). The early chapters of Genesis clearly teach that man from the beginning was separate from animal species, that he was morally responsible, and that by his own choice he became alienated from God and a sinner. The Bible from cover to cover describes God's mercy in sending his Son to redeem man from the consequences of the sin for which he was responsible. Scripture teaches that sin is the result of man's choice; evolution suggests that it is the heritage of man's animal ancestry. If indeed man developed by a process of evolution from animal ancestors, and if as a result of this type of development he continues to violate God's law, then God shared some responsibility for man's sinful condition. It is not God's mercy that moves him to send his Son to redeem the world; it is an obligation of simple justice. J. W. Klotz

See also Evolution.

Bibliography. J. W. Klotz, *Genes, Genesis, and Evolution;* W. Lammerts, *Why Not Creation?* H. L. Shapiro, *Peking Man;* J. S. Weiner, *The Piltdown Forgery;* A. E. Wilder-Smith, *Man's Origin, Man's Destiny;* P. A. Zimmerman, *Darwin, Evolution, and Creation.*

Man, Son of. *See* Son of Man.

Mandaeans. Mandaeism is the only form of Gnosticism to survive into modern times as a practiced religion. Its adherents, according to their own tradition, lived in Palestine, possibly in pre-Christian times, whence they emigrated to Haran and subsequently to their present abode in southern Mesopotamia. Modern scholarship, pointing to a Jewish influence, also tends to postulate a Palestinian origin. Jesus is mentioned in Mandaean literature only as the "lying" or "false" Messiah, but John the Baptist figures more positively as a prophet. From this association medieval travelers came to call Mandaeans "Saint John's Christians." Although their sacred writings say little of Christianity, they are vehemently anti-Jewish. Certain scholars have postulated a Mandaean influence upon the Gospel of John. As Mandaean theology is essentially dualistic, it seems doubtful that such an influence was at work on the monotheism of John.

Mandaeism itself, though fundamentally Gnostic, demonstrates elements of Iranian dualism, Platonic thought, astrology, Judaism, and ancient Babylonian and Egyptian lore. The word "Manda" is usually understood to mean "Gnostic," although it is the term applied to the laity. Ordinary priests are known as *tarmidia* or disciples, while those priests who are fully initiated into mystic knowledge and maintain full ritual purity are *nasoraeans.* Members practice frequent baptisms, ritual meals and sacraments, incantations and magic. A high value is placed on ritual observances, ritual purity, marriage, and procreation.

The Mandaean system is peopled with strange celestial powers, intermediary beings, and astrological influences. There is a supreme entity of the universe who produces a cosmic father and mother. The mother, who is essentially evil, is also called the Spirit. One of their numerous offspring creates the physical universe in a sinful action. Thus the Mandaean soul is entrapped in the prison of a physical body but at death ascends through the hostile spirits of the sky to a world of life. Manda-d-Hiia, "Knowledge of Life," is a major savior figure.

The secret writings, some of undoubted antiquity, are fragmentary and sometimes self-contradictory. Written in an Aramaic dialect similar to that of the Babylonian Talmud, some have been published only in the last quarter century. R. C. Kroeger and C. C. Kroeger

See also Gnosticism.

Bibliography. E. S. Drower, *The Mandaeans of Iraq and Iran* and *The Secret Adam;* E. M. Yamauchi, *Gnostic Ethics and Mandaean Origins, Mandaic Incantation Texts, Pre-Christian Gnosticism,* and "The Present Status of Mandaean Studies," *JNES* 25:88–96.

Mani (216–*ca.* 277). Iranian philosopher and painter who synthesized Persian, Christian, and Buddhist ideas to form Manichaeism, a dualistic faith which became one of the major religions of the ancient world. He received his early education in a Gnostic community in southern Babylonia and claimed his first revelation at the age of twelve and his call to apostleship when he was twenty-four. After his efforts to convert his community failed, he traveled to India, where he founded his first religious group. He returned in 242 to preach his faith in Babylonian provinces, and he became a vassal of the new monarch, Shapur I. Although Mani's beliefs were never established as the official state religion, he enjoyed royal protection and sent proselytizers throughout Persia and into foreign lands.

Mani contended that he was the greatest and last prophet or paraclete sent by the Father of Light. His teaching was claimed to be superior to prophets who preceded him because, unlike Zoroaster, Buddha, and Jesus, Mani published an authoritative canon of at least seven major works. His system includes an elaborate mythical cosmogony and eschatology conceived in terms of two absolute principles, Light and Darkness, and an ascetic way of salvation. A unique feature of Manichaeism was paintings which illustrated his system of redemption. Mani claimed continuous revelations and inspiration from an angel, "the Twin," who as his heavenly alter ego prepared and protected him as a teacher and initiated him in the way of salvation. Miraculous healings were also attributed to Mani to authenticate his divine mission.

After the death of Shapur, Mani was charged by Persian priests with perverting the traditional religion. The new king, Vahram I, imprisoned him, and a prolonged trial ensued. Mani was chained (known to his followers as his "crucifixion") and greatly weakened by fasting. He died twenty-six days after giving a final message to his church. His followers memorialized Mani's death in their Bema festival celebrated yearly in March.

W. A. Hoffecker

See also Manichaeism.

Manichaeism. A third century dualistic religion, founded by Mani, who fused Persian, Christian, and Buddhist elements into a major new faith. It was fought in the West as a virulent Christian heresy. Mani's religion was a complex Gnostic system offering salvation by knowledge. The main features of Manichaeism were enunciated in an elaborate cosmogonical myth of two absolute and eternal principles which manifest themselves in three eras or "moments."

The first moment describes a radical dualism in a previous age. Light and darkness (good and evil), personified in the Father of Lights and the Prince of Darkness, were both coeternal and independent. In the middle moment Darkness attacked and became mixed with Light in a precosmic fall of primal man. This resulted in a second creation of the material world and man by the evil powers in which Light is trapped in nature and human bodies. Redemption of Light occurs by a cosmic mechanism in the heavens by which particles of Light (souls) are drawn up and fill the moon for fifteen days. In the last phases of the moon Light is transferred to the sun and finally to Paradise. Ever since the fall prophets have been sent by the Father of Lights, such as Zoroaster in Persia, Buddha in India, and Jesus in the West. But Mani was the greatest prophet who, as the paraclete, proclaimed a salvation by knowledge (*gnōsis*) consisting of strict ascetic practices. In the last days of the second moment a great war is to be concluded with judgment and a global conflagration lasting 1,468 years. Light will be saved and everything material destroyed. In the third moment Light and Darkness will be separated forever as in the primordial division.

In Mani's myth man is lost and fallen in existence, but in essence he is a particle of Light and thus one in substance with God. Individual salvation consists in grasping this truth by illumination from God's Spirit. Christ appears as merely a prophet and is not really incarnate. His teaching about Light and Darkness was falsified by his apostles, who came from Judaism. Mani restored his essential teachings.

Salvation was exemplified in the Manichaean community, a hierarchy of two classes: the Elect, who consisted of Mani's successor, 12 apostles, 72 bishops, and 360 presbyters; and the Hearers. The Elect were "sealed" with a threefold preservative: purity of mouth—abstaining from all ensouled things (meat) and strong drink; purity of life—renouncing earthly property and physical labor which might endanger Light diffused in nature; and purity of heart—forswearing sexual activity. The lower class of Hearers who lived less strenuous lives hoped for later liberation through reincarnation.

Manichaean worship included fasting, daily prayers, and sacramental meals which differed greatly from the Lord's Supper. Hearers served the Elect "alms"—fruit such as melons believed to contain great amounts of Light. Baptism was not celebrated since initiation into the community occurred by accepting Mani's wisdom through preaching. Hymn cycles extolling redeeming knowledge were sung to focus believers' attention on the beauty of Paradise, where rescued souls dwelt.

Manichaeism spread both east and west from Persia. In the West it was vigorously fought by both the Christian church and Roman emperors. Opposition was especially strong in Africa under Augustine, who for nine years had been a Hearer. Augustine challenged Manichaeism by denying Mani's apostleship and condemning his rejection of biblical truth. Other critics accused him of inventing fables which made his ideas not a theology or philosophy but a theosophy. Manichaeism survived into the Middle Ages through such sects as the Paulicians and Cathari, which probably developed from the original tradition.

W. A. Hoffecker

See also Mani.

Bibliography. J. P. Asmussen, *Manichaean Literature;* F. C. Baur, *Das manichaische Religionssystem nach den Quellen neu untersucht und entwikelt;* F. C. Burkitt, *The Religion of the Manichees;* L. J. R. Ort, *Mani: A Religio-Historical Description of His Personality;* G. Widengren, *Mani and Manichaeism.*

Man of Lawlessness. *See* Antichrist.

Man of Sin. *See* Antichrist.

Manson, Thomas Walter (1893–1958). British biblical scholar and author. From 1936 to 1958 Manson was Rylands Professor of Biblical Criticism and Exegesis at the University of Manchester. An ordained Presbyterian minister, he also participated vigorously in Free Church activities in England. Manson criticized liberal biblical scholarship with its dogmas of unbreakable natural law and human moral evolution; liberalism reduced God to an impersonal force and the gospel to general moral platitudes. However, he sought to continue liberalism's "quest for the historical Jesus" in different directions. His earliest and probably most important work, *The Teaching of Jesus* (1931), argued that "the Son of man," as used by Jesus, is not an individual, supernatural savior. Instead, like the OT "remnant," "the servant of the Lord," and the "I" of the Psalms, it stands primarily "for the manifestation of the Kingdom of God on earth in a people wholly devoted to their heavenly King" (p. 227). Jesus first called others to be this "Son of man." But he increasingly had to go the way himself, a way of servanthood and suffering, alone. Thus Jesus alone proved to be the true "Son of man." Yet Manson stressed that Jesus did and still does call people to obedience and servanthood in corporate unity with him—a theme also expressed by the Pauline concept of the church as "the body of Christ."

While Manson wrote occasionally on all parts of the NT, his fundamental approach and interpretations remained fairly consistent throughout his career. His central focus remained the life, and especially the teachings, of Jesus. Jesus was the very presence, the incarnation of the kingdom of God. He proclaimed God's love in contrast to God's judgment. However, Jesus' teachings were neither an afterthought nor an "interim ethic." They described and still describe the way of the kingdom on earth—the way of a people wholly obedient to God's will in union with Christ.

T. N. Finger

Bibliography. Manson, *The Beginning of the Gospel,* "The Failure of Liberalism to Interpret the Word of God," in *The Interpretation of the Bible,* ed. C. W. Dugmore, *Ministry and Priesthood: Christ's and Ours, The Sayings of Jesus, The Servant-Messiah,* and *Studies in the Gospels and Epistles;* C. H. Dodd, "T. W. Manson and His Rylands Lectures," *ExpT* 73:302–3; A. J. B. Higgins, ed., *NT Essays: Studies in Memory of Thomas Walter Manson.*

Many. An adjective used in various English versions to translate several words of the biblical text: Hebrew, *hāmôn* and *rab;* Greek, *hikanos* and *polys* (*pleiōn*). In scriptural contexts "many" may mean a good many, most, a large quantity, or something long.

As to God's creation "many" may help clarify chronological ideas such as many days (Num. 9:19; Acts 9:23); physical things, as many (or surging, niv) waters (Isa. 17:13); many bulls (Ps. 22:12); the spirit world, such as identifying many demons (Mark 1:34) and many angels (Rev. 5:11). Also the Scriptures speak of God's and of Jesus' "many" good and wonderful works/miracles (Ps. 40:5; John 10:32).

The Bible speaks of "many peoples" (Ezek. 3:6) and "many nations" (Neh. 13:26; Jer. 22:8) of the world. On occasion the expression "the many" (Rom. 5:15, "the many died") is to be taken as equivalent to the expression "all men" (Rom. 5:12, "death came to all men"). Such concepts as these are to be distinguished from expressions identifying the great numbers of God's people, such as the redeemed "many nations" of which Abraham is the spiritual father (Gen. 17:16; Rom. 4:17), the "many nations" which Jesus the Messiah will sprinkle with his blood (Isa. 52:15). In speaking of God's external call and ultimate election, Jesus says, "Many are invited, but few are chosen" (Matt. 22:14), and from the great mass of humanity Rev. 7:9–10 speaks of a "great multitude" (*ochlos polys,* a great crowd) "from every nation, tribe, people and language" which will stand in heaven before the throne and the Lamb praising God for his salvation. Of the total population of the Bereans (in Greece) Acts 17:12 says that "many of the Jews believed, as did also a number of prominent Greek women and many Greek men." It is from the mass of humanity that God will "justify many" (Isa. 53:11), on the basis of his Son's bearing "the sin of many" (Isa. 53:12).

W. H. Mare

See also All.

Bibliography. J. Murray, *The Epistle to the Romans;* W. Sanday and A. C. Headlam, *The Epistle to the Romans;* K. H. Rengstorf, *TDNT,* III, 293–96; J. Jeremias, *TDNT,* VI, 536–45.

Marburg Colloquy (1529). The meeting which attempted to resolve the differences between Lutherans and Zwinglians over the Lord's Supper. These differences had been expressed in a bitter pamphlet controversy between 1525 and 1528. While both Luther and Zwingli rejected the Catholic doctrines of transubstantiation and the sacrificial Mass, Luther believed that the words "This is my body, this is my blood" must be interpreted literally as teaching that Christ's body and blood were present in the sacrament "in, with, and under" the elements of bread and wine. Furthermore, he viewed the sacrament as a means of grace by which the participant's faith is strengthened. Zwingli regarded Luther's position as a compromise with the medieval doctrine of transubstantiation and maintained the words of institution must be taken symbolically to mean this represents Christ's body. Although Zwingli believed that Christ was present in and through the faith of the participants, this presence was not tied to the elements and depended upon the faith of the communicants. In contrast to Luther he interpreted the sacrament as a commemoration of the death of Christ, in which the church responded to grace already given, rather than a vehicle of grace.

After three years of bitter polemics Philip of Hesse arranged the meeting at Marburg in order to resolve the doctrinal differences that stood in the way of a united political front. The major participants were Luther, Philip Melanchthon, Zwingli, and John Oecolampadius.

The public colloquy began on October 2 after preliminary private discussions had been held the previous day which paired Luther with Oecolampadius and Melanchthon with Zwingli. Luther based his arguments on the words of institution. His opponents responded that since the body of Christ was "at the right hand of the Father" in heaven, it could not be present simultaneously at altars throughout the Christian world when the Eucharist was celebrated. Although the debate became quite heated at times, it concluded with both sides asking pardon for their harsh words. On October 4, at the request of Philip of Hesse, Luther drew up fifteen articles of faith based on the Schwabach Articles which had been formulated before the colloquy. To his surprise his opponents accepted fourteen of them with only slight modifications. Even the fifteenth article, on the Eucharist, expressed agreement on five points and concluded with the conciliatory statement: "Although we are not at this present time agreed, as to whether the true Body and Blood of Christ are bodily present in the bread and wine, nevertheless the one party should show to the other Christian love as far as conscience can permit."

Despite this hopeful ending unity was not achieved. Shortly afterward both sides were again making critical remarks about the other. Subsequent writings by Zwingli convinced Luther that he had not been sincere in accepting the Marburg Articles. At the Diet of Augsburg in 1530 Zwinglians and Lutherans presented separate confessional statements which reflected the unresolved differences at Marburg.

R. W. Heinze

Bibliography. W. Koehler, *Zwingli und Luther: Ihr Streit über das Abendmahl nach seinen politischen und religiosen Beziehungen,* 2 vols.; H. Sasse, *This Is My Body;* M. E. Lehmann, ed., *Luther's Works,* XXXVIII; G. Beto, "The Marburg Colloquy of 1529: A Textual Study," *CTM* 16:73–94.

Marcion (d. *ca.* 160). Second century heretic, founder of churches that rivaled orthodox Christianity. Marcion came from Sinope, Pontus, to Rome and offered the church a large sum of money. He was disfellowshiped in 144 for his teachings, and his money was returned. He used his wealth and organizing ability to set up a rival church which became widespread and lasted for several centuries.

Marcion rejected the OT and issued his own NT, which consisted of an abbreviated Gospel of Luke and ten Pauline epistles (excluding the Pastorals) edited on a dogmatic basis. His *Antitheses* set forth contradictions between the testaments. His positions are known principally from the five-book refutation by Tertullian, *Against Marcion.*

Marcion distinguished between creator and redeemer Gods; judgment belongs to the Creator and redemption to the Father, the unknown God before the coming of Christ. The OT was the revelation of the Creator, the God of the Jews, who worked evils and was self-contradictory. Jesus Christ was not the Messiah predicted in the OT but a revelation of the God of love. This Christ was not born but simply appeared; he only seemed to suffer and he raised himself from the dead. The original disciples of Jesus had Judaized, so the Father called Paul to restore the true gospel. But his epistles were interpolated by Judaizers, so Marcion had to restore the "true" readings. The flesh is unclean, so only the unmarried were baptized, except at the end of life. Water was substituted for wine in the Lord's Supper. There was no law, and salvation was by grace alone.

Marcion shared many viewpoints with the Gnostics, but he differed from them in his rejection of speculation and allegory, his concern to organize a church, and in taking his stand on a written revelation alone. Reaction to Marcion speeded up the formulation of the orthodox canon, creed, and organization of the church.

E. FERGUSON

See also GNOSTICISM.

Bibliography. A. Harnack, *Marcion: Das Evangelium vom fremden Gott;* M. J. Lagrange, "Saint Paul ou Marcion," *RB* 41:5–30; J. Knox, *Marcion and the NT;* E. C. Blackman, *Marcion and His Influence;* U. Bianchi, "Marcion: Théologien biblique ou docteur gnostique?" *VC* 21:141–49; D. L. Balás, "Marcion Revisited: A 'Post-Harnack' Perspective," in *Texts and Testaments,* ed. W. E. March.

Mariology. The commonly held teachings of Mariology can be derived from her function as Mother of God (*Theotokos*), a term first used around 320 and formally approved by the Council of Ephesus in 431. Mariologists argue that Mary, who enabled God the Savior to be born, has a position more exalted than any other creature. She is the Queen of Heaven. Moreover, since her motherhood was indispensable to God's redemptive activity, Mary is essential to the final, spiritual perfection of every creature. Accordingly, although she was not involved in their original physical creation, Mary is, in this ultimate sense, the Mother of God's Creatures. This includes being Mother of Humans, a title found in Ambrose but popularized around 1100, and Mother of Angels, a term first found in the thirteenth century.

Mary's involvement in salvation makes her co-redemptrix along with Christ. Irenaeus contrasted Eve's disobedience, which brought humanity's downfall, with Mary's obedience, which "became the cause of salvation both for herself and the human race." Beginning in the twelfth century references appear to her redemptive work not only in Christ's birth but also at the cross. Most Mariologists insist on both. While Jesus offered his sinless person to appease God's wrath, Mary, whose will was perfectly harmonious with his, offered her prayers. Both atoned for our sins—although Christ's satisfaction was primary and wholly sufficient. Mary's mediatory role includes her present intercession for sinners. This was seldom mentioned before the twelfth century, when popular piety regarded Mary as more lenient than her Son, the Judge.

Mary's exalted role implies Mariological assertions about her life. If Mary had ever been stained by sin, she would have been God's enemy and unfit to bear him. Consequently, she must have been "immaculate" (wholly free from any sin) from the instant she was conceived. The immaculate conception, hotly debated in the Middle Ages and early modern era, was opposed by Thomas Aquinas and his followers. But in 1854 Pius IX declared it an official dogma.

Mary's immaculate conception implies that she possessed a "fullness of grace" from the first instant. Further, she was immune to the slightest sin throughout her life. Mariologists also stress Mary's perpetual virginity. This includes, first, her virginity *in partu:* that Jesus was born without opening any part of her body; second, that she remained a virgin throughout her life. Though Mary's perpetual virginity, and especially her sinlessness, were challenged by some early fathers, they were generally accepted by Augustine's time. Proponents of perpetual virginity often assumed that anything else would contradict her purity. Finally, Mariologists teach that after her death Mary was assumed bodily into heaven. No clear reference to the assumption of Mary appears before the sixth century. It was not generally accepted until the thirteenth and was promulgated by Pius XII in 1950.

Protestants have criticized Mariology because many assertions apparently lack biblical foundation. Scripture does not mention her immaculate conception or assumption. Her perpetual virginity is challenged by references to Jesus' sisters and brothers (Mark 3:31; 6:3; John 2:12; 7:1–10; Acts 1:14; Gal. 1:19; Mariologists claim they were cousins). Moreover, the Gospels do not present Mary unambiguously as sinless and in continuous accord with Christ's will. Protestants have also argued that Mariology exaggerates the contribution that any human can make to divine redemption. Luther and Calvin saw Mary as a human who in herself was nothing; she was enabled to bear Christ wholly through God's grace. Conservative Protestants argue that most Mariological excesses—her roles as Mother of God's Creatures, co-redemptrix, intercessor; her immaculate conception; and her "fullness of grace"—spring from overestimating the human role in redemption, which was perhaps already implied by Irenaeus. This ancient theological issue may be the most fundamental one surrounding Mariology.

T. N. FINGER

See also MARY, THE BLESSED VIRGIN; MARY, ASSUMPTION OF; MOTHER OF GOD; IMMACULATE CONCEPTION.

Bibliography. S. Benko, *Protestants, Catholics and Mary;* L. Bouyer, *The Seat of Wisdom;* E. A. Carroll, "A

Survey of Recent Mariology," *MarS* 18:103–21, and "Theology on the Virgin Mary: 1966–1975," *TS* 37: 253–89; J. B. Carol, *Fundamentals of Mariology* and *Mariology;* H. Graef, *Mary: A History of Doctrine and Devotion,* 2 vols.; R. Laurentin, *The Question of Mary;* G. Miegge, *The Virgin Mary;* T. A. O'Meara, *Mary in Protestant and Catholic Theology;* O. Semmelroth, *Mary, the Archetype of the Church;* E. Schillebeeckx, *Mary, Mother of the Redemption.*

Maritain, Jacques (1882–1973). Leading exponent of neo-Thomism in twentieth century philosophy, theology, and the humanities. Maritain was born and educated in Paris. He received his university education, chiefly in the sciences, at the Sorbonne, which was at the time dominated almost entirely by positivism. Dissatisfied with this outlook, Maritain first found relief in the philosophy of Henri Bergson. But he did not find full satisfaction until, in 1906, he embraced Catholic Christianity. In his conversion he was accompanied by his wife and fellow student, Raïssa Maritain, who became a respected scholar as well.

Maritain's conversion to Christianity was followed by his initiation into Thomism. He published his first philosophical article in 1910 and began his career of teaching philosophy a year later at the Collège Stanislas. In 1914 came a move to the Institut Catholique of Paris along with his first book, a critique of Bergson. From that time on, book followed upon book, each one of them devoted to shedding light on contemporary issues by means of Thomistic concepts. After World War II Maritain became the French ambassador to the Vatican. In 1948 he moved to Princeton University, from where he stepped into an active retirement in 1956.

As a Thomist, Maritain emphasized the real distinction between the essence of a thing and its prior act of being. This priority of being prompted Maritain to call Thomism the first existentialism. According to his analysis, being is known directly through an intuition.

An intuition also leads Maritain to posit a "sixth way" of demonstrating the existence of God. The realization of our personal finitude directs us to seek the ground of our existence in God's eternal being.

In the face of contemporary totalitarian ideologies Maritain developed a political philosophy based on the distinction between an individual and a person. As an individual (the total preoccupation of the Fascist or Marxist) the human being is merely a part of the greater whole—the state—and so exists for the sake of society. But as a person he has inherent spiritual value and freedom; thus society becomes obligated to support the person. In this way Maritain recognizes democracy as the ideal form of government for this age.

Both Jacques and Raïssa Maritain contributed to the understanding of art. Among other contributions Raïssa has made is a definitive work on Marc Chagall (who shared her roots in Russian Jewry). Jacques Maritain's aesthetic theory focuses on poetic knowledge as emotion-based and nonconceptual, though no inferiority to conceptual knowledge may be inferred.

Maritain was admired by followers and critics alike for his clarity of thought as well as for his consistent personal piety. W. CORDUAN

See also NEO-THOMISM; THOMISM.

Bibliography. Maritain, *Approaches to God, The Degrees of Knowledge, Existence and the Existent, The Person and the Common Good, St. Thomas and the Problem of Evil, Three Reformers: Luther, Descartes, Rousseau, True Humanism,* and *The Peasant of the Garrone;* J. Evans, ed., *Jacques Maritain: The Man and His Achievement;* C. A. Fecher, *The Philosophy of Jacques Maritain.*

Mark, Theology of. A growing consensus has emerged in recent years that the sacred evangelists were both historians and theologians. They produced accurate histories of the life of Christ and at the same time preached its implications for life in the church. Further, each evangelist had a distinctive message, seen in the way he selected and omitted certain scenes and details. It is therefore accurate to speak of a "theology of Mark." His major themes will here be traced and an attempt made to delineate the way in which each is seen throughout his Gospel.

Christology. The book itself declares that it is "the gospel of Jesus Christ, the Son of God." There is a great difference of opinion as to the central emphasis in this regard. Many have thought that Christ/Messiah is predominant and expresses Mark's portrayal of Jesus as the antitype of the suffering servant of Yahweh. This is then linked to a royal stress in King of Israel (15:32)—i.e., in Mark the servant becomes messianic King. While this is no doubt true, it is not the major stress; in fact, Jesus is seen as demanding that this fact be kept secret. Here we find the primary critical problem of the Gospel. Every group with which Jesus is involved is forced to silence: the demons (1:23–25, 34; 3:11–12), those healed (1:40–44; 5:43; 7:36; 8:26), the disciples (8:30; 9:9). In addition, the leaders are kept from the truth (3:22; 4:10–12; 8:11–12), and Jesus withdraws from the crowds (4:10; 7:17; 9:28) and hides from them (7:24; 9:30). Many have thought that Mark created the theme in order to explain why Jesus was never recognized during his life (Wrede) or to oppose the disciples themselves, whom Mark believed were proclaiming a false gospel (Weeden). However, neither explanation is necessary. The crowds were not allowed to hear such teaching because they considered Jesus to be only a "wonder worker," and the disciples could not proclaim it due to their own misunderstanding regarding the meaning of his office—i.e., they interpreted it in light of the Jewish expectation of a conquering king rather than a suffering servant. The demons were silenced as part of the "binding of Satan" theme (cf. 3:27 and further below), and the leaders were kept from understanding as a sign of God's rejection of them. On the whole, Mark stresses that Jesus' messiahship is essentially incognito, hidden from all except those with spiritual insight. In short, while Jesus is indeed a wonder worker, Mark wishes to clarify the implications carefully.

In this regard we must note "Son of God," the title which begins the Gospel (1:1) and occurs at the climax in the centurion's cry (15:39). The stress on sonship occurs at the baptism (1:11) and transfiguration (9:7) and is a key element in Jesus' control over the demonic realm (3:11). Further, Jesus is seen as omniscient (2:8; 5:32, 39; 6:48; 8:17; 9:4, 33; 11:2, 14; 12:9; 13:12) and omnipotent over demons, illness, death, and the natural elements. Yet at the same time Mark stressed his humanity: his compassion (1:41; 6:34; 8:2), indignation (3:5; 9:19; 10:14), and his distress and sorrow (14:33–36). Jesus "sighs" (7:34; 8:12) and shows anger (1:43; 3:5); he becomes weary (4:38) and admits limitations regarding miracles (6:5–6) and knowledge (13:32). The balance between these is important and demonstrates that Mark is probably trying to present a balanced picture in order to correct an overly enthusiastic stress on the supernatural aspects.

Mark's favorite designation is "Son of man," a term which undoubtedly was Jesus' own self-designation but which also went beyond to picture the heavenly figure of Dan. 7:13. In Mark it speaks of his humanity (2:10, 27–28); his betrayal, suffering, and death (the passion predictions of 9:12; 14:21, 41); and his exaltation and future reign (13:26). It is obvious that here we have the correction of misunderstandings regarding his purpose and personhood, especially since it occurs primarily in the second half of the Gospel, where Jesus begins to correct the disciples' views. It seems definite that Mark wishes to combine a *theologia crucis* with a *theologia gloria*. Therefore the so-called messianic secret centers upon the fact that the cross is the path to glory and that Jesus' live exaltation can be understood only by comprehending the significance of his suffering.

The final aspect of Mark's emphases is Jesus as teacher. In the past this designation was usually attributed only to Matthew, but recently it has been more and more recognized that Mark gives Jesus' teaching office prime place in his work. The one who performs such great and mighty deeds is demonstrated as the one who teaches; in fact, the first is subordinate to the second, for it is in his activity as teacher (4:38; 5:35; 9:17, 38; 10:51; 11:21) that both the disciples and the opponents are confronted with the reality of the Christ event. It is in his teaching that the true authority is manifest (1:22), and therefore this may well be the major stress.

Cosmic Conflict. In Mark, Christ is presented as the one who "binds" Satan (3:27). Where Matthew centers upon healing miracles, Mark stresses exorcism. This is nowhere seen better than by comparing Mark and Matthew with respect to the healing of the demon-possessed/epileptic child. Matthew mentions the demon only at the point of the miracle (17:14–18), while Mark relates an amazingly detailed narrative with four separate descriptions of the effects of the possession (9:18, 20, 22, 26). Jesus is pictured as one who violently assaults sin and the cosmic forces of evil. Moreover, he passes on this eschatological ministry to the disciples, who participate with him in his victory (3:15; 6:7, 13; for the problem of 9:18 see below). Implicit in 3:27 also is the idea of "plundering" Satan's realm. This is certainly the thrust of the exorcism miracles (1:23–26; 3:11–12; 5:6–13; 9:14–27). When the demons utter Jesus' name, they are not unwittingly acting as his "PR" agents, but rather are trying to gain control of him. In the ancient world (as in many tribal areas today) one would gain power over a spirit-creature by learning his "hidden name." When Jesus forced silence upon them (1:25, 34; 3:12) or made them reveal their own names (5:9) this signified his mastery over the satanic forces. The authority and other blessings given Jesus' followers are the spoil from that victory.

Eschatology. Many have stated that Mark is primarily a proponent of a futuristic eschatology, perhaps even calling the church to the imminent parousia in Galilee (Marxsen). Yet the Markan emphasis goes beyond this. According to 1:15, the kingdom has already come, and the time of fulfillment is here. Jesus' deeds and words demonstrate the presence of the kingdom within history, and Jesus will continue to mediate this end-time power until the final consummation of the divine plan (8:38; 13:24–27; 14:62). Therefore the disciple exists in present hope, and Mark's eschatology is "inaugurated" rather than final—i.e., it recognizes the "beginning" of the "end" and the fact that the believer lives in a state of tension between the two.

At the same time we must acknowledge the stress on the future parousia in Mark. The three passages mentioned above (8:33; 13:26; 14:62) show that the suffering of Christ could be understood properly only in light of his coming glory at both the resurrection/exaltation and parousia. One event that illustrates the connection between the resurrection and the eschaton is the transfiguration (9:2–8); when one realizes that it is surrounded by passages on suffering, the point made here becomes clear. The same is true of the Olivet discourse (ch. 13), which demonstrates once more that suffering and persecution lead to glory. Yet even here we are not free of the strong realized stress, for it is seen in the great accent on watchfulness (13:5, 9, 23, 33, 35, 37) which permeates the chapter. The true disciple will be characterized by an expectant alertness in light of the imminent inbreaking of the final kingdom.

The Miracles and Soteriology. One cannot ignore the centrality of the miracle stories, for they form one fifth of the Gospel and 47 percent of the first ten chapters. The basic word, as in all the Synoptics, is "power" (*dynamis*), which points to the power of God operative in his Son. Mark, however, is careful to stress that the miracles do not form apologetic proof that Jesus is the Christ. The central theme in Mark is that they can be known only by faith; they cannot produce faith. The disciples misunderstand them (4:40; 6:52; 8:17–18), and their effect is diminished by the apparent humanity of Jesus himself (6:1–3; cf. 3:19–21). With the presence of many miracle workers, many of them false prophets (13:22), the common people could draw only erroneous conclusions. Therefore, they needed his teaching and his person to understand properly (1:37–38; 2:5; 4:40; 5:34). Mark was stressing the hiddenness of God in Jesus and wished to demonstrate that even his miracles were only glimmers of the true reality and as such comprehensible only by faith. Further, they are symbols of God's forgiveness; as the miracle is performed, the spiritual need is met (4:35–41; 6:45–52; 7:31–37; 8:22–26).

The connection of the miracles with faith and forgiveness leads to the further point: when faith is present, the miracles point to the salvific power of God in Christ. By actualizing the power and authority of God in the situation, they make the reader cognizant of the radical demands of God. It has often been said that Mark has no true soteriology. Yet that is to deny the implication of such key passages as 10:45, which presents Christ as the one who gave his life "as a ransom for many." Mark seeks to drive men to decision, which he accomplishes by setting two scenes in contrast, thereby highlighting the issues and demanding encounter with God (e.g., 3:7–12, where the demons acknowledge him, and 3:20–35, where Jesus is called Beelzebub; or 11:12–21, which shows that the cleansing of the temple prefigured the "curse" of God upon Israel). Mark constantly shows men—common people, leaders, and disciples—in the conflict of decision.

Discipleship. The final emphasis in Mark, and in some ways the major emphasis along with Christology, is the discipleship motif. Again there is certainly controversy here, as some have argued that Mark has a negative thrust intended to show the error of the disciples (Weeden). However, this is hardly true of the Gospel as a whole. Mark does wish to stress the radical nature of the call and the difficulties of achieving the goal. However, the reader is expected to identify with the disciples in this dilemma, and it indeed forms the heart of the Gospel.

At the beginning of Mark's Gospel, Jesus fulfills his own message of repentance (1:15) by calling the disciples to be "fishers of men" (cf. Matt. 4:18–22 and Luke 5:1–11, where it comes much later). Then after the conflict narratives (2:1–3:6) Jesus cements his "withdrawal" (3:7) by turning to the disciples and commissioning them (3:13–19), in a scene filled with election terminology and centering upon their authority and responsibility. Finally, the first segment of the Gospel concludes with a missions scene in which Jesus "sends" his disciples, again with authority and in complete dependence upon God (6:7–13). From here, however, the relationship seems to deteriorate, and the central section of Mark (6:7–8:30) has two themes—the withdrawal of Jesus from the crowds combined with his time with the twelve, and the failure of the disciples to comprehend his teaching. They are amazingly obtuse with respect to all aspects of his teaching and are both uncomprehending (6:52; 7:18; 8:17–18) and even "hardened" (6:52; 8:17), a startling term in light of its theological connotations and its presence after the two feeding miracles.

However, once more this failure is not the final point, although it is certainly stressed at the very end, especially if Mark ends at 16:8. Yet in the last section of the Gospel before the passion (8:31–10:52), the solution is seen in the presence of Jesus the teacher, who patiently and lovingly instructs them. Note that in 8:31 Jesus "began to teach" them, an act clearly linked to their failure to understand (8:32–33), which is countered by his instruction (8:34–38). This in itself follows the important healing of the blind man (8:22–26), a two-stage miracle which may have been intended to prefigure a two-stage overcoming of the disciples' blindness (cf. 8:17–21) via first Peter's confession (partial sight, as seen in 8:31–33) and then by the transfiguration, which solidified the revelation of God to the disciples. The passion predictions are followed by very serious failures on their part, and at the healing of the demon-possessed child this comes to a crisis when the disciples are unable to perform that which previously had been a significant sign of their authority (cf. 9:18 with 6:13). The solution is seen in awakened faith (9:24) and its response, prayer (9:29). Steps of this growing awakening are seen in the passion narrative, and there the core of the problem becomes even more evident: discipleship is a call to the cross, and it cannot be understood until the cross. The triumphal entry is an incognito message regarding Jesus' true mission, and it is followed by the judgment on the temple (ch. 11). In three major scenes Jesus begins to lift further the veil, and the disciples are called to understanding—the anointing at Bethany (14:3–9), the eucharistic words at the Last Supper (14:22–25), and Gethsemane (14:32ff.). Finally, at the resurrection failure is still seen (16:8, with most scholars realizing that the women are to be identified with the disciples), but it is obviated by the promise of Jesus' presence (16:7). As the reader identifies first with the problem of discipleship and then with Jesus (the solution), victory becomes an act of faith.

G. R. Osborne

See also Matthew, Theology of; Luke, Theology of; John, Theology of.

Bibliography. P. Achtemeier, *Mark* and "'He Taught Them Many Things': Reflections on Marcan Christology," *CBQ* 42:465–81; G. R. Beasley-Murray, "Eschatology in the Gospel of Mark," *SwJT* 21:37–53, and "The Parousia in Mark," *SwJT* 21:565–81; E. Best, "The Miracles in Mark," *RE* 75:539–54, and *Following Jesus: Discipleship in the Gospel of Mark;* J. L. Blevins, "The Christology of Mark," *RE* 75:505–17; W. D. Carroll, "The Jesus of Mark's Gospel," *BT* 103:2105–12; R. T. France, "Mark and the Teaching of Jesus," in *Gospel Perspectives,* I, ed. R. T. France and D. Wenham; J. J. Kilgallen, "The Messianic Secret and Mark's Purpose," *BTB* 7:62–65; R. Martin, *Mark: Evangelist and Theologian;* W. Marxsen, *Mark the Evangelist;* R. P. Meye, *Jesus and the Twelve;* N. P. Petersen, ed., *Perspectives on Mark's Gospel;* P. S. Pudussery, "The Meaning of Discipleship in the Gospel of Mark," *Jeev* 10:93–110; Q. Quesnell, *The Mind of Mark;* D. Rhoads and D. Michie, *Mark as Story;* J. Rohde, *Rediscovering the Teaching of the Evangelists;* D. Senior, "The Gospel of Mark," *BT* 103:2094–2104; R. C. Tannehill, "The Disciples in Mark: The Function of a Narrative Role," *JR* 57:386–405; T. J. Weeden, *Mark, Traditions in Conflict;* W. Wrede, *The Messianic Secret.*

Mark of the Beast. The importance of this expression is to be seen in its several uses in Revelation (13:16–18; 14:11; 15:2; 16:2; 19:20; 20:4). This mark can be taken to be a brand, stamp, or tag (cf. the philacteries, Deut. 6:8), having economic (Rev. 13:17) and religious significance (Rev. 14:11).

Rev. 13:18 suggests that the mark of the beast is to be identified with the number of the beast, 666. John could be using an ancient system of numerology called gematria, in which the number concepts (e.g., 600, 60, 6, etc.) are identified with their alphabetic letter equivalents, to be translated then into proper names. Thus, 666 has been identified with Titus, or the Latin empire (church), or Nero, or even Nimrod (Gen. 10:8), Napoleon, or Mussolini, etc. In fact, there have been dozens of significant persons throughout history who have been identified as "the beast." Needless to say, all these guesses have been wrong.

The number 666 could well be identified with some future historical antichrist or situation, but history teaches us to be cautious in trying to be too precise.

W. H. Mare

See also Antichrist.

Bibliography. D. G. Barnhouse, *Revelation;* J. M. Ford, *Revelation* (*Anchor Bible*); G. E. Ladd, A *Commentary on the Revelation;* H. B. Swete, *The Apocalypse of St. John;* R. P. Martin, *NIDNTT,* II, 573-74.

Marpeck, Pilgram. *See* Mennonites.

Marriage, Marriage Customs in Bible Times. Marriage began as a custom and symbol recognizing the sexual union of man and wife for the procreation of children as well as the increasing, and thus the strengthening, of the nation. Children assisted in the work of the family and provided sons to be warriors. It was not until early Christian times that marriage came to be regarded as a sacrament.

Eligibility. Marriage within the immediate family group was general, and limits on acceptable consanguinity were imposed. In the early preexilic period a man could marry his half-sister on his father's side (Gen. 20:12); even under David this was so, although probably rare by then, as it was forbidden in Lev. 20:17. The marriage laws of Deut. 25:5 and Lev. 18:16 show some discrepancy, and possibly indicate a mild relaxation of the strict Levitical regulations. Close relatives frequently married, and refusal was difficult (Tob. 6:13; 7:11–12). Isaac and Rebekah were first cousins, as were Jacob and Leah and Rachel. Lev. 18:12–13 and 20:19 would have forbidden the marriage of an aunt and a nephew which produced the infant Moses, or that of Jacob simultaneously to two sisters (Gen. 29:30).

When one was forced to turn outside the tribe or clan, marriage to another Israelite family was easily accepted. However, marriage to a foreigner was fraught with dangers, such as possible dilution of the faith and the Hebrew heritage, as well as the advent of strange gods and religious practices.

Intermarriage with Canaanite women described in I Kings 11:4 was forbidden under Mosaic law (Exod. 34:16; Deut. 7:3–6), although like several other prohibitions this was often ignored. Exceptions were made for women captured in war who were prepared to renounce their country, its customs, and beliefs (Deut. 21:10–14), although it is doubtful whether this was a frequent practice.

Matriarchal marriage occurred when a man went to live with and became part of his wife's family—as Jacob did with Leah and Rachel—either temporarily or permanently. When Samson married a Philistine woman, she continued living with her family, while Samson visited from time to time (Judg. 14:8–20; 15:1–2). Frequent biblical examples show that although marriage to a foreigner was unpopular, it was certainly practiced. Esau married two Hittite women (Gen. 26:34), Joseph an Egyptian (Gen. 41:45), Moses a Midianite (Exod. 2:21), David an Aramean (II Sam. 3:3), Ahab the Tyrian princess Jezebel (I Kings 16:31), and Bathsheba a Hittite (II Sam.11:3).

So great was the concern of the Hebrews that their religion might be diluted by intermarriage with those of other faiths that in postexilic times wholesale divorce was ordered for those married to foreigners (Ezra 9:2; 10:3, 16–17). Purity of the faith was paramount, regardless of the destruction of homes and families. A similar idea was expressed by Paul, who condemned marriage with non-Christians (II Cor. 6:14–15).

Bride and Groom. No precise information exists on the normal age of betrothal or marriage. The bar mitzvah celebrating the coming of age of a young male in later Jewish tradition reflected the earlier idea of a boy being recognized as a man when about thirteen years old. A minimum age of thirteen for boys and twelve for girls was eventually set, although royal families may have held marriages at quite different ages from those considered normal for most people. By early Christian times girls often married between twelve and seventeen, and boys between fourteen and eighteen. Marriages were frequently matters of convenience for the family and rarely a concern of the heart. They were arranged by parents, and in some cases were even considered invalid if parental permission was lacking. Discussions concerning the marriage took place between the parents without the presence, consent, or frequently the awareness of the prospective bride and groom.

It was not necessary for the eldest member of the family to marry first (Gen. 29:26). When Isaac was to be married, a servant was sent by Abraham to his relatives in Mesopotamia to choose a suitable bride and arrange the marriage contract (Gen. 24:33–53), although Rebekah was subsequently asked to give her consent to the proposal (Gen. 24:57–58), a formality which can perhaps be explained by the special interest that a brother might have in his sister's welfare (cf. Gen. 34:5).

Marriages arranged by parents are mentioned frequently in Scripture (Josh. 15:16; Judg. 14:2–3; I Sam. 18:17, 19, 21, 27). In the first century B.C., however, the Bar Manasseh marriage deed formally records the consent of the bride. Where a father did not actually choose the bride for his son, strict guidelines and advice were given (Gen. 28:6–9; Tob. 4:12–13), although not always followed (Gen. 26:34–35). Rare indeed were signs of female initiative, such as Michal, Saul's daughter, expressing her love for David (I Sam. 18:20).

Betrothal. "Betrothed" used in the Pentateuch (Exod. 22:16; Deut. 20:7; 22:23–24) was a legally binding contract between the parents of the bride and groom. It had the legal status of marriage (Deut. 28:30; II Sam. 3:14), and anyone guilty of seducing a betrothed virgin was stoned for violating his neighbor's wife (Deut. 22:23–24). The prospective groom took possession and established control over his bride by the gift of the bride-price to her father (Gen. 34:12; I Sam. 18:25).

The bride-price varied according to the "value" and social status of the bride. In the fifth century B.C. the Elephantine papyri quote sums of 5 and 10 shekels, but the normal bride-price was probably 10 to 30 shekels (Lev. 27:4–5), and by the time of the second temple had become 50 shekels, a sum which was halved for a widow or divorced woman.

The bride-price, often jewelry, was probably returned to the bride at the time of her father's death, or earlier if she became a widow and was in need. Assyrian law required the bride-price to be paid directly to the bride, and the Code of Hammurabi provided a return of double the bride-price to the intended groom where an engagement was broken off. The exchange of gifts was customary among the Hebrews, although few were probably as costly and elaborate as those received by Rebekah (Gen. 24:53). In Babylonian law the husband received gifts from the father of the bride which could be used until the bride became a widow, at which time they became her property.

As the betrothal, which normally lasted one year, was a distinct part of a permanent relationship (Matt. 1:18; Luke 1:27; 2:5), the prospective groom was exempt from military service (cf. Deut. 24:5) and was already termed "son-in-law" by the bride's father from the time of the betrothal (Gen. 19:14). There remained a distinction, however, between betrothal and marriage (Deut. 20:7), and although Mary was considered to be Joseph's wife at the time of their betrothal, he did not have intercourse with her until after the birth of Jesus. If normal Hebrew practices were followed, this would mean after the baby was weaned, usually at about three years of age.

From 1500 B.C. circumcision seems to have been practiced in some areas as an initiatory rite before marriage. It may have been performed at puberty when the Israelites were in Egypt. The legislation given to Moses on Mount Sinai ordered the circumcision of male children on the eighth day (Lev. 12:3), although the practice is mentioned in relation to marriage in Gen. 34.

Marriage Ceremony. The story of Jacob gives the first biblical example of a feast forming part of the marriage celebration (Gen. 29:22; cf. Judg. 14:10), while bridesmaids had a ceremonial place in Samson's marriage festivities (cf. Ps. 45:14). The Elephantine texts record in the marriage ceremony a declaration by the husband, "She is my wife and I am her husband, from this day for ever." In Christian times a simpler format was used, the husband declaring, "Thou shalt be my wife."

There was great family rejoicing at the wedding. Bride and groom acted as royalty for a week of festivity, doing no work. Both were arrayed in special fine clothing (Isa. 61:10; Ezek. 16:9–13), the bridal gown being frequently adorned with jewels. The groom wore a diadem (Song of S. 3:11) and frequently a garland (Isa. 61:10), while the bride wore a veil (Song of S. 4:3). Rebekah was veiled before her fiancé (Gen. 24:65), as the face of the bride always remained covered until she had been escorted by her parents to the bridal chamber. This would also explain the ease with which, on Jacob's wedding night, Laban was able to replace Rachel with Leah (Gen. 29:23–25).

The procession through the streets of the groom and his friends with musical instruments (Jer. 7:34) was the highlight of the wedding ceremony. Closer to the Christian period, both the bride's and the groom's processions would leave their respective houses to meet at a specific location (I Macc. 9:37–39), normally returning to the home of the groom for the actual wedding feast (Matt. 22:2).

The feasting, fine food, and merriment sometimes lasted for seven days (Gen. 29:27; Judg. 14:12), or occasionally even fourteen days (Tob. 8:20). Certain symbolic ceremonies may have been part of the wedding ritual. Ruth requested that Boaz spread his skirt over her as a symbol of taking her as his wife, and the ceremonial removal of the bride's girdle by the groom sometimes took place in the wedding chamber, a room or tent prepared especially for the newly married couple. The marriage was expected to be consummated on the first night (Gen. 29:23; Tob. 8:1), the stained linen being retained as evidence of virginity.

By NT times the wedding of a virgin normally took place on a Wednesday. This provided adequate time for the husband to bring charges against her on Thursday if she were found not to be a virgin. Thursday was the day for weddings of widows and those who were divorced, these newlyweds thus having uninterrupted time before the sabbath. If a husband falsely accused his wife of not being a virgin, or if he had lain with her before their marriage, she could not be divorced (Deut. 22:13–19, 28–29). The Elephantine texts provide evidence of several marriage contracts, although they were also common in Greek times and were first recorded in the book of Tobit (7:12). The marriage was valid only after the couple had lived as man and wife for a week (cf. Gen. 29:27; Judg. 14:12, 18). Before this seven-day period Samson left his bride, whose marriage was then declared void, and she remarried (Judg. 14:20). Although marriage as a sacrament dates only from Christian times, it was considered the sacred fulfillment of God's will and purpose, and as such was holy.

Marital Rights and Responsibilities. Despite the fact that the betrothal seemed to imply the purchase and ownership of the bride by the groom, and although the wife and children are frequently listed with other possessions of the husband (Exod. 20:17; Deut. 5:21), it is unlikely that the position of the wife was as inferior as it sounds. The wife could not be sold, although she could be divorced very easily (Sir. 25:26), whereas she could rarely divorce her husband. The commandment to children to "honor thy father and thy mother" implies an equality of status which was not actually present. Yet the Hebrew wife was treated as a worker and not as a beast of burden, as Arabian women were. The primary role of the wife was to be the mother of sons, and when she had fulfilled this requirement her status rose accordingly. If she was unable to fulfill this role, she would often give her handmaid to her husband for this purpose (Gen. 16:3).

household, fetching water, gathering fuel, reaping straw, providing clothing, preparing food, welcoming guests, and also for the general education and upbringing of children until they were five years old, when the teaching role for the sons was assumed by the father. The wife was not expected to take any part in financial administration, even her own funds being administered by her husband. If she became a widow, however, she might manage funds and property until her sons came of age.

It was the responsibility of the husband to provide for his wife and family. A wife's promise was invalid unless her husband also gave consent to it (Num. 30:4–16). The power and authority came through the male head of the household to the son, who was frequently named after his father, although the right of naming a child, and thereby conveying authority over him, rested almost equally with both parents (cf. Gen. 4:1, 25–26; 5:29; 35:18; I Sam. 1:20; 4:21; Isa. 8:3; Hos. 1:4, 6, 9). Still, the root of the phrase "marry a wife" means to become master (Deut. 21:13), and this was exactly how the husband frequently was treated—and expected to be.

Most marriages in Israel were monogamous, and only in certain periods was polygamy practiced, partly because of the cost that would have been involved in providing several bride-prices. Bigamy was acknowledged in Deut. 21:15–17, although it frequently led to quarrels between wives (I Sam. 1:6) and other problems (Judg. 8:29–9:57; II Sam. 11:13; I Kings 11:1–8). Kings were those most likely to indulge in large numbers of wives. Herod had nine wives (Josephus, *Antiquities* xvii.1.3), David had six wives and concubines (II Sam. 3:2–5; 5:13–16), and Solomon his seven hundred (I Kings 11:1–3), many of which probably represented political alliances.

Levirate Marriage. When a man died without issue, it was considered important to preserve both the family name and the inheritance. Even where there were already children, it became the responsibility of the husband's closest male relative to provide for the widow and orphans. The deceased husband's brother normally entered into a levirate (or "brother-in-law") marriage with the widow (Deut. 25:5–10). If she was childless at the time of this marriage, the firstborn of the levirate marriage was considered to be the child of the deceased. Levirate marriages were also known among other societies in the ancient Near East, including the Canaanites, Assyrians, and Hittites.

The most familiar of levirate marriages in the OT is that of Ruth, who needed to find a male relative to marry her so that the family name could be preserved and the property go to her descendants. In this instance the closest male relative declined the responsibility of both maintaining the widow and purchasing the land, knowing that the firstborn child would not even bear his name. Boaz, the younger brother, agreed to undertake the responsibility for the levirate (Ruth 2:20–4:10). Tamar was also promised under levirate law to be the bride of Onan (Gen. 38:8).

Figurative Use of "Marriage." The terms "bride" and "groom" are used frequently in the OT to refer to the special relationship of the Hebrew people with God (Isa. 62:4–5; Jer. 2:2). In Hosea, God rejects his wife Israel (Hos. 2:2) but is prepared to forgive her and accept her if she again becomes faithful (Hos. 2:19–20). Also in the OT Jeremiah contrasts the desolation and horror about to descend on Judah with the joy of a wedding feast (Jer. 7:34; 16:9; 25:10). In the NT John the Baptist is the first to use such imagery, comparing his feeling of joy with that of a groom at a wedding (John 3:29). The parable of the wise and foolish virgins (Matt. 25:1–12) is probably the best-known parable about the preparations for the wedding procession. The concept of the church as the bride of Christ is continued in Corinthians, Ephesians, and Revelation.

Early in the Christian era, when marriage was still a civil contract rather than a sacrament, virginity became recognized as the highest Christian state. Virginity was pure and acceptable to God. A woman who chose celibacy after the death of her spouse was considered to have chosen the second highest route, with marriage ranking third in a scale of preference to God. Thus for a considerable period of time the early church praised celibacy to the detriment of marriage, despite Christ's own support of the institution of marriage. H. W. PERKIN

Bibliography. W. R. Smith, *Kinship and Marriage in Early Arabia;* E. Westermarck, *History of Human Marriage,* I–III; R. H. Kennett, *Ancient Hebrew Life and Social Custom;* M. Burrows, *The Basis of Israelite Marriage;* L. M. Epstein, *Marriage Laws in the Bible and the Talmud* and *Sex Laws and Customs in Judaism;* E. Neufeld, *Ancient Hebrew Marriage Laws;* A. Van Selms, *Marriage and Family Life in Ugaritic Literature;* L. Köhler, *Hebrew Man;* D. S. Bailey, *The Man-Woman Relation in Christian Thought;* P. H. Goodman, *The Jewish Marriage Anthology;* W. Lacey, *The Family in Classical Greece.*

Marriage, Theology of. Biblical teaching on marriage is epitomized in the statement, "Therefore a man leaves his father and his mother and cleaves to his wife, and they become one flesh" (Gen. 2:24). This sentence is quoted by our Lord (Matt. 19:5) and the apostle Paul (Eph. 5:31) as authority for their teachings on marriage. The key phrase is the expression "one flesh" (*bāśār* *'eḥād*). "Flesh" here implies kinship or fellowship, with the body as a medium, thus setting forth "marriage as the deepest corporeal and spiritual unity of man and woman." On the occasion of Eve's creation God observes, "It is not good that the man should be alone" (Gen. 2:18). In this way he indicates the incompleteness of man or woman apart from one another and sets forth marriage as the means for them to achieve completeness.

An Exclusive Relationship. Marriage is an *exclusive* relationship. The total unity of persons—physically, emotionally, intellectually, and spiritually—comprehended by the concept "one flesh" eliminates polygamy as an option. One cannot relate wholeheartedly in this way to more than one person at a time.

It is also plain from the words of our Lord, "What therefore God has joined together, let no man put asunder" (Matt. 19:6), that marriage is to endure for the lifetime of the two partners. Only under certain special conditions may the principle of indissolubility be set aside.

Promiscuity is likewise ruled out. Such unions are neither exclusive nor enduring. Moreover, they violate the holiness that inheres in biblical marriage. God instituted marriage so that men and women might complete one another and share in his creative work through the procreation of children. (Celibacy is not a higher and holier condition—a viewpoint which finds its roots in Greek dualism rather than in the Bible.) Physical union in marriage has a spiritual significance in that it points beyond itself to the total unity of husband and wife, which is essentially a spiritual union. This is underscored by Paul's use of the conjugal union to symbolize the unity of Christ with his church (Eph. 5:22–33). But to maintain its holiness this union must take place in a relationship committed to enduring exclusiveness. Illicit sexual unions are deemed reprehensible in that they temporarily and superficially establish a one-flesh relationship (I Cor. 6:16) without proper accompanying intentions and commitments. An act with spiritual significance is made to serve improper ends. Another person is selfishly exploited. What should be a constructive relationship serving as the means to deeper interpersonal communion becomes in promiscuous relationships destructive both to one's capacity for personal unity with a member of the opposite sex and to existing marriage relationships, if any. Hence our Lord made adultery the ground for dissolution of a marriage (Matt. 5:32).

A Definition. When is a couple married? Of what does marriage ultimately consist? Some, arguing from I Cor. 6:16, maintain that marriage is effected through sexual intercourse. A person is considered in the eyes of God to be married to that member of the opposite sex with whom he or she first had sex relations. The sex act is viewed as the agent through which God effects marriage in a manner apparently analogous to the way in which adherents of the doctrine of baptismal regeneration see him make the sacrament of baptism the agent in effecting regeneration.

Others consider marriage to be brought about as the result of a declaration of desire to be married accompanied by the expression of mutual intentions of sole and enduring fidelity and responsibility toward the other, preferably undergirded by self-giving love, in the presence of accredited witnesses. This view does not undercut the validity of marriages in which the couple cannot bring about physical consummation. It underscores the fact that marriage never has been regarded as solely the concern of the individual couple. This may be seen, for example, in the prevalence of community laws forbidding incest and regulating the degree of consanguinity permissible for marriage. Since the home is the proper medium for the procreation and nurturing of children, church and community have an important stake in the stability and success of the marriages taking place among their constituents.

Marriage relegates other human ties to a secondary role. Spiritual and emotional satisfactions formerly drawn from the parental relationship the marriage partners are now to find in one another. To sunder one's parental relationships and join oneself in intimate, lifelong union with a person who hitherto has been a stranger demands a considerable degree of maturity—as expressed in a capacity for self-giving love, emotional stability, and the capacity to understand what is involved in committing one's life to another in marriage. Marriage is for those who have grown up. This appears to exclude children, the mentally impaired, and those who are psychotic or psychopathic at the time of entering into marriage.

Marriage and the NT. The chief contributions of the NT to the biblical view of marriage were to underscore the original principles of the indissolubility of marriage and the equal dignity of women (Gal. 3:38; I Cor. 7:4; 11:11–12). By raising women to a position of equal personal dignity with men, marriage was made truly "one flesh," for the unity implied in this expression necessarily presupposes that each person be given opportunity to develop his or her full potentialities. This is not possible in a social system in which either men or women are not accorded full human dignity.

Does not this raise difficulties with the biblical doctrine of subordination of married women (Eph. 5:22–23)? Not at all, for this doctrine refers to a hierarchy of function, not of dignity or value. There is no inferiority of person implicit in the doctrine. God has designated a hierarchy of responsibility, hence authority, within the family, and he has done so according to the order of creation. But woman's dignity is preserved not only in the fact that she has equal standing in Christ, but also in that the command to submit to her husband's headship is addressed to her. She is told to do this willingly as an act of spiritual devotion (Eph. 5:22) and not in response to external coercion. She is to do this because God rests primary responsibility upon her husband for the welfare of the marriage relationship and for the family as a whole. He, in fact, qualifies for leadership in the church in part through the skill he demonstrates in "pastoring" his family (I Tim. 3:4–5). L. I. Granberg

See also Divorce; Marriage, Marriage Customs in Bible Times; Adultery; Separation, Marital.

Bibliography. D. S. Bailey, *The Mystery of Love and Marriage* and *The Man-Woman Relation in Christian Thought;* K. E. Kirk, *Marriage and Divorce;* O. Piper, *The Christian Interpretation of Sex;* E. A. Westermarck, *The History of Human Marriage;* D. Atkinson, *To Have and to Hold;* G. W. Bromiley, *God and Marriage.*

Marriage Feast of the Lamb. The announcement that the wedding supper of the Lamb is at hand is one of the key moments in the drama of the consummation. The picture in Rev. 19:7–9 conforms to the ancient Near Eastern custom of a wedding ceremony in two parts: a procession to the home of the bride and the wedding banquet itself. Here the announcement that the bride has made herself ready and the wedding is at hand forms the prelude to the description of Christ's triumphal procession from heaven to earth.

The imagery of the wedding banquet is a mixture of two distinct biblical figures. The consummation of the kingdom of God and of the Messiah was depicted as a great feast in the OT and in Jewish literature (Isa. 25:6; II Apoc. Bar. 29:1–8; I Enoch 62:13–15). This metaphor is employed by Christ as a description of the consummation of his own messianic reign (Matt. 8:11; 22:1–14; 25:10; Luke 14:15–23; 22:29–30). The other figure is that of the marriage between God and his people. Though already an important OT image, it is enriched in its NT form with Christ the bridegroom and the church his bride (John 3:28–29; II Cor. 11:2; Eph. 5:23–32). As Christ before him (Matt. 22:1–14; 25:1–13), but more explicitly, John joins the images of the messianic banquet and the marriage between Christ and his church so that in Rev. 19:7–9 the church is at once the bride and the guests at the wedding feast.

This complex metaphor is wonderfully suggestive. It expresses the tender love of Christ for his people, the intimacy of their fellowship in the coming age, and the bounty of that future life. It points to the imperfect and provisional aspects of the church's life in the present age—though she is betrothed to Christ, her marriage itself awaits his return. It indicates the necessity and priority of the divine calling in salvation (Rev. 19:9; Matt. 22:9) and the obligation of the called to prepare themselves for the Lord's return with a life of faith and obedience (Rev. 19:7–8; Matt. 22:11–12; 25:7–12; II Cor. 11:2). R. S. Rayburn

Marrow Controversy. Between approximately 1717 and 1722 the Church of Scotland was agitated by a controversy between evangelicals, known as "Marrow Men," and moderates, or "neonomians," over the relationship between law and gospel in salvation. Prominent evangelical ministers such as Thomas Boston and Ralph and Ebenezer Erskine had reprinted *The Marrow of Modern Divinity* (ascribed by some to Edward Fisher of London in 1645), which maintained an immediate, free offer of salvation by looking to Christ in faith. This raised the opposition of the controlling party of the church, who as neonomians held that the gospel is a "new law" (*neonomos*), replacing the OT law with the legal conditions of faith and repentance needing to be met before salvation can be offered. They maintained the necessity of forsaking sin before Christ can be received, whereas the Marrow Men replied that only union to Christ can give us power to be holy. Hence the neonomians considered the call to immediate trust in Christ and to full assurance to be dangerously antinomian. Led by Principal Haddow of St. Andrews, the church condemned *The Marrow of Modern Divinity* in 1720. The evangelicals protested this action without avail. They were formally rebuked by the church's General Assembly in 1722 but not removed from their ministries. Nevertheless, the writings of the Marrow Men (such as Boston's *Fourfold State of Human Nature*) were as influential in the popular piety of Scotland for the next two centuries as was Bunyan's *Pilgrim's Progress* in English and American piety. D. F. Kelly

See also Boston, Thomas.

Bibliography. D. Beaton, *The Marrow of Modern Divinity and the Marrow Controversy;* W. M. Hetherington, *History of the Church of Scotland;* J. MacLeod, *Scottish Theology.*

Martyr, Peter. *See* PETER MARTYR VERMIGLI.

Mary, Assumption of. In principle this doctrine was a part of the Roman Catholic and Byzantine thinking in the Middle Ages. The apostolic constitution *Munificentissimus Deus,* promulgated by Pius XII on November 1, 1950, made it a doctrine necessary for salvation, stating, "The Immaculate Mother of God, the ever-Virgin Mary, having completed the course of her earthly life, was assumed body and soul into heavenly glory."

No basis, biblical, apostolic, or postapostolic, exists in support of the doctrine. Apocryphal documents of the fourth century, Gnostic in character, such as the Passing of Mary hint at it. Gregory of Tours in his *De gloria martyrum* of the sixth century quotes an unfounded legend about Mary's assumption. As the story became popular in both East and West it took two forms. The Coptic version describes Jesus appearing to Mary to foretell her death and bodily elevation into heaven, while the Greek, Latin, and Syriac versions picture Mary calling for the apostles, who are transported to her miraculously from their places of service. Then Jesus, after her death, conveys her remains to heaven. The doctrine was first treated in deductive theology about 800. Benedict XIV (d. 1758) proposed it as a probable doctrine.

Feasts celebrating the death of Mary date from the fifth century. In the East the late seventh century feasts included the assumption. After the eighth century the West followed suit. Nicholas I by edict (863) placed the Feast of the Assumption on the same level as Easter and Christmas. Cranmer omitted it from the *Book of Common Prayer* and it has not since been included.

The 1950 action regarding the assumption of Mary is built upon the declaration of "The Immaculate Conception" (Dec. 8, 1854), which declared Mary free from original sin. Both issue from the concept of Mary as the "Mother of God." Her special state, Pius XII felt, demanded special treatment. If Mary is indeed "full of grace" (cf. Luke 1:28, 44) the assumption is a logical concomitant. Like Jesus, she is sinless, preserved from corruption, resurrected, received into heaven, and a recipient of corporeal glory. Thus Mary is crowned Queen of Heaven and assumes the roles of intercessor and mediator.

The argument in *Munificentissimus Deus* develops along several lines. It emphasizes Mary's unity with her divine Son, for she is "always sharing His lot." Since she shared in the past in his incarnation, death, and resurrection, now, as his mother, she is the mother of his church, his body. Rev. 12:1 is applied to Mary; she is the prototype of the church, for she has experienced anticipatorially corporeal glorification in her assumption. Three times Mary is referred to as the "New Eve," working again the parallel of Christ as the new Adam and presenting the glorified Christ as one with the new Eve.

The assumption of Mary continues to be a fruitful field for Roman Catholic theologians even as biblical renewal, charismatic interest, and liberal theology also make their impact.

W. N. KERR

See also MOTHER OF GOD; IMMACULATE CONCEPTION; MARY, THE BLESSED VIRGIN; MARIOLOGY.

Bibliography. M. R. James, *The Apocryphal NT;* E. L. Mascall and H. S. Box, eds., *The Blessed Virgin Mary; NCE;* L.-J. Suenens, *Mary the Mother of God.*

Mary, The Blessed Virgin. Except for the Gospels, the Scriptures make little explicit reference to Mary. Certain OT prophecies have been thought to refer to her (Gen. 3:15; Jer. 31:22; Mic. 5:2–3; and, most clearly, Isa. 7:14). The symbolic drama of Rev. 12 has often been similarly interpreted. Paul mentions Mary specifically once (Gal. 4:4). For anything more, we must inquire of the Gospel writers. Luke presents the most detailed portrait. While Matthew also tells the nativity story, his references to Mary are brief, even though he strongly stresses her virginity (Matt. 1:18–25). Luke, however, vividly describes her encounter with the angel, her visit to Elizabeth, her beautiful "Magnificat," the birth of Jesus, and her trips to Jerusalem with the infant and the twelve-year-old Jesus (Luke 1:26–2:51). Mary appears humbly obedient in the face of her great task (Luke 1:38), yet deeply thoughtful and somewhat perplexed as to its significance (Luke 1:29; 2:29, 35, 50–51). According to an episode recounted by Matthew, Mark, and Luke, Jesus' mother and his "brothers" stand outside the early circle of disciples (Matt. 12:46–50; Mark 3:19*b*–21, 31–35; Luke 8:19–21; cf. Luke 11:27–28). Elsewhere Jesus complains that he is not without honor save "among his own kin, and in his own house" (Mark 6:4; cf. Matt. 13:53–58; Luke 4: 16–30). John apparently recounts some misunderstanding between Jesus and Mary at the wedding feast in Cana (John 2:1–12). Yet John pictures Mary remaining faithful beside the cross, while Jesus commends her to his "beloved disciple's" care (John 19:25–27). Finally, Luke lists Mary among the earliest post-Easter Christians (Acts 1:14). Traditionally, Catholics have venerated Mary as entirely sinless and as the most glorious of God's creatures. Feeling that this detracts from the centrality of Christ, Protestants have often neglected her unduly. Radical biblical criticism in doubting the infancy narratives' historicity often furthered this neglect. However, the increasing importance of women's issues has spurred new interests in Mary among both Protestants and Catholics alike. T. N. FINGER

See also MARY, ASSUMPTION OF; IMMACULATE CONCEPTION; MARIOLOGY; MOTHER OF GOD.

Bibliography. R. E. Brown *et al.*, eds., *Mary in the NT;* R. E. Brown, "The Meaning of Modern NT Studies for an Ecumenical Understanding of Mary," in *Biblical Reflection on Crises Facing the Church;* W. J. Cole, "Scripture and the Current Understanding of Mary among American Protestants," *Maria in Sacra Scriptura,* VI; A. Greeley, *The Mary Myth;* J. G. Machen, *The Virgin Birth of Christ;* J. McHugh, *The Mother of Jesus in the NT;* H. A. Oberman, *The Virgin Mary in Evangelical Perspective;* R. Ruether, *Mary: The Feminine Face of the Church.*

Mass. The word refers to the Eucharist or Lord's Supper and derives from the Latin *missio,* a term used in churches or law courts to dismiss the people. The expression *Ite, missa est* is the regular ending of the Roman rite. The term has been used in the West as a name for the whole of the service since at least the fourth century, and is presently used by both Roman Catholics and Anglican High Churchmen.

In liturgical terminology there is sometimes a reference to two Masses, referring to a division of the eucharistic service which can be seen as early as Acts 20 and which is clearly developed in third and fourth century texts. The first segment is the service of the word, after which catechumens were dismissed, and therefore termed the Mass of the catechumens; the second is the service of the table (the passing of the peace, the Lord's Prayer, and the Eucharist itself), which was reserved for baptized Christians in good standing and called the Mass of the faithful. In this liturgical use "Mass" indicates which group left the church at the dismissal at the end of that part of the service.

While the use of the term "Mass" does not necessarily indicate any particular theology (as, e.g., in the 1549 *Book of Common Prayer* or Luther's *German Mass*), in common usage it is connected with the Roman Catholic and Anglo-Catholic doctrine of the Mass in which the priest is considered to participate in the sacrifice of the body and blood of Christ, the transubstantiated host and wine. Usually this is not thought of as a resacrifice of Christ, although in some old Catholic theologies that was surely the case, but as a participation in and a making present of the eternal and thus timeless sacrifice of Christ in which the priest represents Christ in terms drawn from Hebrews. Thus the Mass is viewed as eschatological: it is in the here and now the sacrifice offered upon the cross (and indeed all of Christ's work), for in it time is swallowed up in eternity. While this eschatological aspect has never been accepted by Protestants, it allows Catholics to preserve the unity of Christ's work and the sacrificial character of the service. P. H. DAVIDS

See also LORD'S SUPPER, VIEWS OF.

Bibliography. D. B. Stuart, *The Development of Christian Worship;* G. Dix, *The Shape of the Liturgy.*

Mathews, Shailer (1863–1941). Baptist educator, theologian, ecumenist, and evangelist for modernism. Born in Portland, Maine, Mathews was educated at Colby College, Newton Theological Institute, and, briefly, the University of Berlin. After teaching at Colby (1887–94), he joined the faculty of the University of Chicago Divinity School, where in turn he was professor of NT, systematic theology, and historical and comparative theology (1894–1933). In 1908 he became dean.

Mathews was a champion of theological liberalism during the fundamentalist-modernist controversy. His *Faith of Modernism* (1924) was a widely read apology for reconstructing Christianity along liberal lines. Using a sociohistorical approach, he argued that all religion is "functional" (it helps people make sense of their environment) and that all theology is "transcendentalized politics" (it grows out of the church's interaction with the "social mind" of its culture). Thus in order to remain a live option for people in different ages, Christianity must be constantly modernized. In his day, Mathews believed, the faith had to be brought in line with the empirical sciences.

In addition to being a spokesman for the Chicago school of liberal theology, Mathews was an avid churchman. He advocated the social gospel (*The Social Teachings of Jesus,* 1897), served as president of the Federal Council of Churches (1912–16), and promoted the formation of the Northern Baptist Convention, becoming its president in 1915. T. P. WEBER

See also CHICAGO SCHOOL OF THEOLOGY; LIBERALISM, THEOLOGICAL.

Bibliography. Mathews, *The Gospel and Modern Man, The Spiritual Interpretation of History, The Atonement and Social Process, The Growth of the Idea of God,* and *New Faith for Old;* C. H. Arnold, *Near the Edge of Battle;* W. R. Hutchinson, *The Modernist Impulse in American Protestantism.*

Matins. *See* OFFICE, DAILY (DIVINE); MORNING PRAYER.

Matter. In ordinary language, matter means concrete, physical, nonspiritual things, the object of everyday external experience, open to study by physics and chemistry. The Christian faith declares that matter is wholly created by God and subject to his shaping power. Thus, (1) matter is contingent; it does not exist as a coeternal, independent principle; and (2) matter is good and not the principle of evil. It is a permanent element of the world guaranteed by the incarnation and the resurrection of the body.

The idea of a material ingredient common to all things was a central concept in pre-Socratic philosophy beginning with Thales (*ca.* 580 B.C.), who identified fire, earth, air, and water. Aristotle and Plato distinguished sharply between the material substance of which an object was composed and the form imposed on it. Subsequent philosophers have introduced numerous variations into the debate down through the ages. Descartes's fundamental division was between mind and matter as absolutely distinct substances. Today almost all the axioms of earlier philosophy have been qualified because of the findings of Einstein, Planck, Heisenberg, and others.

The term "matter" and its cognates ("material," "materialist," etc.) have been heatedly debated in theological and philosophical circles throughout intellectual history. Matter has often been placed in opposition to life, mind, soul, or spirit. A preoccupation with matter has traditionally meant a preoccupation with worldly pleasures and bodily comforts, as opposed to the "higher" pleasures of the mind.

The doctrine that the divine Logos has become flesh would seem to mean that supreme spirituality has penetrated the material sphere, showing that matter is capable of expressing the concrete reality of God himself.

M. H. MACDONALD

See also EXISTENCE; FORM.

Bibliography. W. Heisenberg, *Philosophical Problems of Nuclear Science;* S. Toulmin and J. Goodfield, *The Architecture of Matter;* G. Gamow, *Biography of Physics;* P. Ricoeur, *Main Trends in Philosophy;* R. Rorty, *Philosophy and the Mirror of Nature.*

Matthew, Theology of. In the literature of the church that remains from the first three centuries the Gospel most often referred to is Matthew's. Its place in the order of the canon as the first Gospel probably reflects the church's estimation of its priority theologically rather than chronologically.

In order to understand the theology of Matthew's Gospel it is helpful to begin at the ending. Its climactic conclusion, the Great Commission (28:16–20), has been called the key to the Gospel's theology. Several important themes are brought together in these verses.

First is the focus on the resurrected Christ. Each of the Gospel writers portrays a facet of Jesus' life and ministry. Prominent in Matthew's Gospel is the picture of Jesus as the Christ, the messianic Son of God who was also the suffering servant.

At this baptism Jesus told John that his ministry was "to fulfill all righteousness" (3:15). Righteousness in Matthew is a term meaning covenant faithfulness, obedience to God. An angel told Joseph that Jesus "will save his people from their sins" (1:21). Later Jesus told his disciples that he had come "to give his life as a ransom for many" (20:28). The prayer of this righteous Son in Gethsemane, "not my will but yours be done" (26:39), was fulfilled on the cross and affirmed by the Roman soldier's confession, "Surely he was the Son of God" (27:54). Christ had fulfilled all righteousness. He had been perfectly obedient to the Father's will. It was this resurrected Christ, possessing the regal authority of God (13:37–42; 26:64), who appeared to the disciples to commission them.

Another aspect of Matthean Christology is the affirmation of Christ's spiritual presence with the disciples. Jesus assured the disciples, "I will be with you" (28:20). The first of a series of OT texts cited by Matthew is Isaiah's prophecy of Immanuel (Isa. 7:14). Its significance is made clear in the phrase "God with us" (1:23; Isa. 8:10). Christ's presence continues. Jesus' promise to the disciples, "Where two or three come together in my name, there am I with them" (18:20), was additional confirmation of his presence. Matthew wanted his readers to know that the regal ascended Christ was also spiritually present with his disciples (cf. Eph. 1:22–23).

This relates also to the Gospel's ecclesiology, the doctrine of the church. Alone among the Gospels Matthew used the word "church" (Gr. *ekklēsia,* 16:18; 18:17). Not without reason has this been called "a pastoral Gospel." Matthew saw that much of what Jesus had taught the disciples was applicable to the church of his own day. Of great importance in this regard was the commission to make disciples of all nations (28:19).

Jesus preached the good news (4:23) to Jews (Galilee and Judea, 4:25) and Gentiles (Decapolis, 4:25). His disciples and the church which they founded (16:18) were to do the same. John's Gospel records Jesus' self-confession, "I am the light of the world" (John 8:12). Matthew, on the other hand, underscored the disciples' missionary responsibility by recording Jesus' statement, "You are the light of the world" (5:14). The disciples, and the church, were to continue the ministry of Christ.

They were to make disciples of all nations.

Israel, indeed, had been temporarily displaced as God's chosen instrument of ministry (21:43). But this displacement was not permanent (19:28; 23:39). However hard of heart most Jews might be to the gospel, the mission to Israel was to continue alongside the mission to the Gentiles until Christ returned at the end of the age (10:23; 28:20; cf. Rom. 11:11–12, 25–26).

Making disciples involved more than preaching the gospel, however. Matthew recorded Jesus' commission to make disciples by "teaching them to obey everything I have commanded you" (28:20). A disciple was to be righteous, to be obedient to God.

The model for the disciple was Jesus, the perfect Son who fulfilled all righteousness by rendering complete obedience to the Father's will (4:4, 10). That same righteousness was to characterize the disciple (5:20). Obedience to God was to be a priority in the disciple's life (6:33). Complete devotion to the Father was the goal (5:48).

The will of the Father was made known in the teaching of Jesus. Matthew devoted a considerable portion of his Gospel to the record of Jesus' teaching. In addition to five distinct units (5–7, 10, 13, 18, 23–25), Jesus' instruction is repeatedly featured in the Gospel elsewhere (e.g., 9:12–17).

But Matthew was under no illusion that knowledge alone would lead to righteousness. Teaching was essential, but it had to be met with faith. Despite their scrupulous observance of the law, Jesus had excoriated the Pharisees for lack of faith (23:23). The righteousness recognized by God was first of all inward and spiritual (6:4, 6, 18; cf. Rom. 2:28–29). Those who believed in Jesus had their lives transformed (8:10; 9:2, 22, 29). Not so much the greatness but the presence of faith was important (17:20).

Where faith existed, however, it might be weak and wavering. Matthew reminded his readers that even in the presence of the resurrected Christ, some of the disciples doubted (28:17). Frequently Jesus addressed the disciples as ones of "little faith" (6:30; 8:26; 16:8). This was exemplified in Peter's experience. He boldly responded to Jesus' call to come to him on the water but then wavered in his faith because of the fearful circumstances (14:30). Without the intervention of Jesus he might have perished.

Matthew likely saw an application in this for his readers. Jesus had warned his disciples of the persecution facing those who proclaimed the gospel (5:11–12; 10:24–25). They would be opposed by Jew and Gentile (10:17–18). The natural response in the face of such opposition was fear (10:26–31). Self-preservation led to denial of Christ (10:32–33). This was what Peter had done at Jesus' trial (26:69–74).

Jesus responded to Peter's failure on the sea by rescuing him. In the same way, failures of faith among the disciples and the sin that resulted should be met not with condemnation but with forgiveness and restoration (18:10–14).

The designation "little ones" in 18:6, 10, 14 may refer to disciples like Peter whose faith was weak in the midst of difficult circumstances. In 10:41–42 Matthew recorded Jesus' description of prophets and righteous men as "little ones." The next verses relate the imprisonment of John the Baptist and his question about Jesus as Messiah (11:2–3). Jesus met John's doubts with assuring words (11:4–6) and went on to commend him (11:7–19). That was the model for ministry to those in need (cf. 10:42; 25:34–40) and the spirit in which the Great Commission could be carried out.

This mission was to continue until the "end of the age" (28:20). When the gospel had been preached to all nations, then the end would come (24:14) and Christ would reign as king (25:31–34). Reference to a kingdom recurs throughout the Gospel. The beginning verses link Jesus to David the king (1:1, 6). Unlike the other Gospels, Matthew uses the phrase "kingdom of heaven" far more frequently (thirty-three times) than the phrase "kingdom of God" (four times). The expressions are probably equivalent with a possible difference in emphasis only. The "kingdom of heaven" may stress the spiritual nature of the kingdom.

The term "kingdom" seems to have a spiritual and a physical aspect to its meaning. The spiritual aspect was present in the ministry of Jesus (12:28) but the physical consummation is anticipated at his return (19:28). The kingdom of heaven about which Jesus preached was entered by repentance (4:17). Forgiveness was based ultimately on Christ's death (26:28).

Opposed to the kingdom of heaven is the kingdom of Satan (4:8–9; 12:26), from whom those with faith in Christ are delivered (12:27–28). While Satan is powerless before the Spirit of God (12:28), nonetheless he will actively hinder and counterfeit the work of God until the consummation (13:38–39).

The ministry of the kingdom carried on by Christ is continued by the church (16:18). The Spirit who enabled Christ to carry out his work (12:28) will enable the disciples to continue it (10:20). The ministry of the church is thus a phase of the kingdom program of God. Ultimately God's program with Israel would also be completed with a positive response to the gospel of the kingdom (19:28; 23:39; cf. Rom. 9:4–6; 11:25–27). Then the "end of the age" (28:20) will come. The king will separate the righteous from the unrighteous (7:21–23), the sheep from the goats (25:31–46), the wheat from the tares (13:37–43). Those who have not done the Father's will (7:21), who have not believed in Christ (18:6), will merit eternal punishment (13:42; 25:46). The righteous will enter into eternal life (13:43; 25:46). Until then, the followers of Christ were to "make disciples of all nations" (28:19). D. K. LOWERY

See also MARK, THEOLOGY OF; LUKE, THEOLOGY OF; JOHN, THEOLOGY OF.

Bibliography. E. P. Blair, *Jesus in the Gospel of Matthew;* P. F. Ellis, *Matthew: His Mind and His Message;* R. H. Gundry, *Matthew: A Commentary on His Literary and Theological Art;* D. Hill, *The Gospel of Matthew;* J. D. Kingsbury, *Matthew: Structure, Christology, Kingdom;* J. P. Meier, *The Vision of Matthew;* E. Schweizer, *The Good News According to Matthew;* R. E. O. White, *The Mind of Matthew.*

Maundy Thursday. The Thursday of Holy Week, said to be named from the command (Lat. *mandatum*) Christ gave his followers at the Last Supper that they love one another (John 13:34). Possibly the name derives from the Latin *mundo,* "to wash," referring to Christ's washing the feet of the apostles, an event still commemorated by Christians, including the Church of the Brethren and Roman Catholics. As the eve of the institution of the Lord's Supper, Maundy Thursday has been kept by Christians from earliest times. By the fourth century it was a feast of the Jerusalem church, and in the sixth century in Gaul it was observed as *Natalis Calicis* ("Birthday of the Chalice"). In medieval England it was known as Chare Thursday (from the scrubbing of the altar) and in Germany as Green Thursday (*Gründonnerstag,* either from the green vestments then worn or from *grunen,* "to mourn"). The day is associated with Tenebrae, a ceremony of the extinguishing of candles in preparation for Good Friday. Observed in the Roman Catholic Church, Maundy Thursday appears on the Lutheran, Anglican, and many Reformed liturgical calendars and is almost universally celebrated with the Lord's Supper. C. G. FRY

See also HOLY WEEK; CHRISTIAN YEAR.

Bibliography. J. G. Davies, *A Select Liturgical Lexicon;* E. T. Horn, III, *The Christian Year;* T. J. Kleinhans, *The Year of the Lord.*

Maurice, John Frederick Denison (1805–1872). Anglican theologian. Son of a Unitarian minister, he was ordained in 1834 only after he had overcome misgivings about the Thirty-nine Articles. In 1840 he became professor of English literature at King's College, London, with which he later combined a post in divinity, but was removed when his *Theological Essays* (1853) disclosed a denial of everlasting punishment. To Maurice, eternal death meant alienation from God because of unrepented sin. At a time when the Tractarians were rising to do battle with evangelicals, his best-remembered book, *The Kingdom of Christ* (1836), denounced theological factions, including the so-called no-party party. He was in some sense a harbinger of the twentieth century ecumenical movement in his emphasis on the visible church as a united body transcending human differences and divisions. He saw baptism, the Eucharist, the historic creeds, Scripture, and the episcopate as the signs of the kingdom. His incarnational theology led him to ally himself with Charles Kingsley, J. M. Ludlow, and others in founding the Christian socialist movement and in organizing workingmen's educational programs. After his ouster from King's College he became the first principal of the Working Men's College (1854); there is reason to suspect that socialist views were as much responsible for his academic deposition as alleged heresy. In 1866 he was elected professor of moral philosophy at Cambridge, and there produced his highly acclaimed *Social Morality* (1869). Amid all the controversies of his time (Tractarianism, the development of Broad Church theology, Darwin and evolutionary theory, Colenso and the issue of biblical criticism), Maurice both made a profound contribution to theological thought and retained a surprisingly simple faith. He maintained habits of regular prayer, and once expressed agreement with Kingsley that "the devil is shamming dead, but was never busier than now." J. D. DOUGLAS

See also SOCIALISM, CHRISTIAN.

Bibliography. A. R. Vidler, *Witness to the Light: F. D. Maurice's Message for Today;* F. McClain, R. Norris, and J. Orens, *F. D. Maurice: A Study.*

Means of Grace. *See* GRACE, MEANS OF.

Meat Offering. *See* OFFERINGS AND SACRIFICES IN BIBLE TIMES.

Mediating Theology (*Vermittlungstheologie*). The name of a program undertaken by widely differing thinkers, mostly in Germany, in the middle third of the nineteenth century. Their conclusions differed greatly, but they shared a commitment to mediation, the attempt to find truth on a middle ground between opposite extremes.

These thinkers tried to mediate between the influences of Hegel and Schleiermacher, between rationalism and supernaturalism, and between innovation and tradition. For them, both feeling and thought were to be taken into account in theology. Christianity was seen as partly natural and partly supernatural in origin. The mediators tended to support the union of Lutherans and Reformed in the state churches of Germany.

The most important members of the mediating school (*vermittelnde Schule*) were I. A. Dorner, Julius Koestlin, Julius Müller, C. I. Nitzsch, Richard Rothe, and Karl Ullmann. Mediating theology was represented at many different universities. It can be dated from 1828 with the founding of the periodical *Theologische Studien und Kritiken.* It was also the theme of *Vierteljahrschrift für Theologie und Kirche* (founded 1845) and *Jahrbücher für deutsche Theologie* (founded 1856).

The most important topic for mediating theology was Christology. The historic doctrine of the person of Christ was being challenged by historical criticism. For philosophical reasons historical criticism began with a picture of Jesus that left no room for his deity and so rejected as unhistorical anything in the Gospels that testified to his deity. The biggest bombshell was the book *Leben Jesu* (*Life of Jesus*) by D. F. Strauss in 1835. This denial of historic Christian doctrine led to a negative reaction from those who wanted to conserve more of the old doctrine.

The mediators attempted to find a middle course that would both retain some elements of historic Christology and accept many of the assumptions and conclusions of historical criticism. They differed radically from one another in doctrine, but in every case the acceptance of historical criticism led them to modify the historic doctrine of the person of Christ fundamentally. In this sense, kenoticism can be seen as a form of mediating theology. But another form was the direct opposite of kenoticism, namely I. A. Dorner's idea of a growing unity between God and Jesus. Dorner saw that kenoticism had lost sight of the immutability of God. He concluded instead that Jesus had originally been a separate person who was only gradually assumed into the unity of the Logos in a process that was completed only at the ascension.

The varieties in mediating theology indicate that its program did not lead to any conclusive results. Indeed, it could lead to new and opposite extremes. It was ambitious but vague, and faded away once Albrecht Ritschl and his disciples became influential in the last part of the nineteenth century. J. M. Drickamer

See also Kenosis, Kenotic Theology; Dorner, Isaac August.

Bibliography. K. Barth, *Protestant Theology in the Nineteenth Century;* J. M. Drickamer, "Higher Criticism and the Incarnation in the Thought of I. A. Dorner," *CTQ* 43:197–206; *God and Incarnation in Mid Nineteenth Century German Theology: G. Thomasius, I. A. Dorner, A. E. Biedermann,* tr. C. Welch, LCC; C. Welch, *Protestant Thought in the Nineteenth Century.*

Mediation, Mediator. The role of a mediator is to bring reconciliation between two parties. The biblical concept of mediation is to bring sinful man to reconciliation with a holy God, a major concern of the Scriptures. The word "mediator" (*mesitēs*) is used only once in the LXX—Job 9:33, where it is translated "daysman," "umpire," or "someone to arbitrate": "He is not man like me that I might answer him, that we might confront each other in court. If only there were someone to arbitrate between us, to lay his hand upon us both, someone to remove God's rod from me, so that his terror would frighten me no more" (9:32–34, NIV).

Mediation in the OT is seen in the function of the offices of prophet and priest. The prophet was a man who spoke for God to man by way of revelation, instruction, and warning (Exod. 4:10–16; Amos 3:8; Jer. 1:7, 17). The priest was a man who spoke for man to God by way of intercession and sacrifices (Deut. 33:10; Heb. 5:1). These offices complemented each other as mediators between God and man.

In the NT "mediator" is used six times. Twice it is used in connection with Moses as being the mediator of the law (Gal. 3:19–20). The word is used three times in Hebrews, where Jesus is shown to be the mediator of a new or better covenant (8:6; 9:15; 12:24). After discussing the superiority of the new covenant over the old covenant, the author of Hebrews states that with the inauguration of the new covenant there needed to be a new mediator, who is identified as Christ (8:6). Christ as the mediator sacrificed his life in order to inaugurate the new covenant and thereby reconciled man to God. A central verse in the mediatorial work of Christ is I Tim. 2:5. Paul states: "This is good and acceptable before God our Savior, who desires all men to be saved and to come to the knowledge of the truth. For there is one God and one mediator between God and men, the man Christ Jesus, who gave himself as a ransom in behalf of all men, the testimony borne in these times" (I Tim. 2:3–6). Again there is death in connection with mediation. Beyond the passages which explicitly use the terminology, the NT is replete with examples of Christ being mediator. He represented God to man as a prophet. That Jesus fulfilled the prophetic office as prophesied by Moses (Deut. 18:15–18) was seen by Philip (John 1:45), Peter (Acts 3:22–23), Stephen (Acts 7:37), the Jewish people who heard Christ (Matt. 21:11; Luke 7:16;

24:19; John 6:14; 7:40), and Christ himself (John 5:45–47). Both God the Father and Jesus stated that those who heard Jesus should heed Jesus' words (Matt. 17:5; John 12:48–50). He came from God and spoke the words of God (John 1:18; 6:60–69; 14:9–10). Not only was he God's greatest prophet, but also he was and is the greatest priest representing man to God. First, in the past he offered himself as the sacrificial lamb, giving himself in behalf of men and their sins (Matt. 1:21; John 1:36; 3:16; Rom. 3:21–26; Heb. 2:17; 9:14–15). He was both the priest and sacrifice (Heb. 2:17; 7:26–27; 9:11–15). Also, in the past he offered prayers in behalf of himself (Matt. 26:39, 42, 44; Mark 14:36, 39; Luke 22:41, 44; John 17:1–5; Heb. 5:7) and in behalf of his disciples (Luke 22:32; John 17:6–26). Second, presently he intercedes in behalf of the saints (Rom. 8:34; Heb. 7:25; 9:24). Thus, he can be a true spokesman for God because he is God (John 1:1–5; II Cor. 5:19; Col. 2:9; Heb. 1:2; 5:5) and yet a true spokesman for man because he is man and can sympathize with man and his problems (Heb. 2:17; 4:15; 5:1–9).

In conclusion, because of sin there is a great gulf between God and man that needs to be bridged. The Bible portrays God and man as brought together by sacrifice and intercession by means of a mediator. However, in today's parlance the word "mediator" may be misleading, for the role of today's mediator is to effect the reconciliation of two conflicting parties by means of compromise. The biblical idea of mediator is really more closely identified as an intermediary; God does not compromise his holiness, but rather, with his holiness intact, he communicates through his intermediaries his righteous demands. God has never been lenient with sin, but in his graciousness he has provided the just payment for sin through the death of the intermediary Jesus Christ, who provided reconciliation for man. Thus the intermediary provides the revelation of God's demands and the means by which man can be reconciled (II Cor. 5:18–21).

H. W. Hoehner

See also Reconciliation.

Bibliography. J. Atkinson, "Mediator, Mediation," *A Dictionary of Christian Theology;* O. Becker, *NIDNTT,* I, 372–75; E. C. Blackman, *IDB,* III, 320–31; E. Brunner, *The Mediator;* D. Guthrie, *NT Theology;* A. H. Leitch, *ZPEB,* IV, 150–58; A. Oepke, *TDNT,* IV, 598–624; V. Taylor, *The Names of Jesus.*

Meister Eckhart (*ca.* 1260–1328). German Dominican mystical theologian. Eckhart studied at Cologne and later at Paris, where he took the master of theology in 1302. In 1304 he became provincial of the Dominican province of Saxony. He taught in Paris from 1311 to 1313 and from 1313 to 1323 served as professor of theology at Strasbourg. At Strasbourg and later at Cologne he developed a reputation as a preacher and spiritual director. Eckhart's significance lies in his elaboration of a mystical theology which stimulated widespread interest and directly influenced such men as J. Tauler and H. Suso. His thought was influenced by Thomas Aquinas, Augustine, Dionysius the Pseudo-Areopagite, and Bernard of Clairvaux. He was cited for heresy in 1326 and died before the proceedings were over. In 1329 John XXII condemned twenty-eight of Eckhart's propositions as heretical.

The essential doctrine which governs Eckhart's whole system is that of divine knowledge. God cannot truly be apprehended by any of the normal means of human knowing, whether by theology, philosophy, or mystical experience, for the unconditioned Godhead transcends all modes of individualized knowledge. Divine knowledge therefore must be an unrestricted knowledge suitable to its transcendent subject. This demands a detached intellection which views all of reality as it were from within the Godhead, from the standpoint of the divine subjectivity.

The possibility for such knowledge lies in a gracious act of the Father whereby he generates his Word in the pure soul. In this man is united with God. The union takes place in the ground of the soul designated the "spark of the soul," *scintilla animae,* although properly it has no name, being free from all modes as God himself is free. The spark is a power for good, and by virtue of it the soul resembles God.

The interpretation of Eckhart is difficult due to his complex and paradoxical style. Many have understood his theology as fundamentally pantheistic, and there are numerous unguarded statements in his works which tend in that direction. In recent years, however, the tendency has been to interpret him in a more orthodox framework.

D. G. Dunbar

See also Mysticism.

Bibliography. J. M. Clark, *Meister Eckhart: An Introduction to the Study of His Works with an Anthology of His Sermons;* C. F. Kelley, *Meister Eckhart on Divine Knowledge.*

Melanchthon, Philip (1497–1560). German Reformer, theologian, and educator. Born in Bretten, Baden, he earned his A.B. from Heidelberg at the age of fourteen and his M.A. from Tübingen when sixteen. He soon demonstrated his skill in the Greek language and established a reputation as a fine grammarian and then as a biblical humanist, eventually being included in the circle of Erasmus. He became a professor at the University of Wittenberg in 1518. His first public lecture established a close tie with Luther which remained throughout their lives. In 1519 he went with Luther to the Leipzig disputation. By 1521 he wrote *Loci Communes,* the first systematic statement of Luther's ideas. It gained widespread circulation due to its clear style and irenic tone—two characteristics of Melanchthon that were typical of his writing and were most helpful in his contacts with other Lutherans, Protestants, and Roman Catholics.

In 1528 his "Visitation Articles" for schools was enacted into law in Saxony and his work as a public educator became an added dimension to his life. At least fifty-six cities sought his help in reforming their schools. He helped to reform eight universities and to found four others. He wrote numerous textbooks for use in schools and later was called "Preceptor of Germany."

At the Marburg Colloquy in 1529 Melanchthon was strongly opposed by Zwingli, particularly over the issue of the real presence in the Lord's Supper. Later Melanchthon would alter his view and would receive the wrath of Lutheran purists. In 1530 he wrote the Augsburg Confession, and its Apology in 1531. These two documents plus the Wittenberg Concord of 1536 soon became the key statements of Lutheran belief. Because of his Christian humanism, which kept him open to new ideas and insights, he changed his position on the Lord's Supper and took a position on the real presence close to that of Calvin. This was revealed in Article X of the 1540 *Variata* of the Augsburg Confession and caused the Gnesio-Lutherans to accuse Melanchthon of being a crypto-Calvinist.

With the defeat of the Protestant forces at Mühlberg in 1547, Melanchthon proposed the Leipzig Interim, an attempt to salvage some Lutheran ideas in a basically non-Lutheran creedal statement. Melanchthon argued here that certain Roman Catholic rites and beliefs were adiaphora, nonessential to the faith, and thus could be accepted. For this effort he was attacked by Matthias Flacius as a traitor to the Lutheran cause. Later Flacius led another attack against Melanchthon because of his synergistic view, in which he argued that man could accept or reject God's grace and the Holy Spirit after grace was given.

Melanchthon's final years were spent in controversy, and many Lutherans looked upon him with suspicion. His brilliant mind, love for Christian humanism, clarity in expression, gentle demeanor, and openness to new ideas made him an ideal co-worker with Luther but also precipitated much of the controversy that filled his last years. Yet his contributions to the Lutheran movement, to Protestantism, and to the German nation are monumental. R. V. SCHNUCKER

See also AUGSBURG CONFESSION; ADIAPHORA, ADIAPHORISTS; SYNERGISM; MARBURG COLLOQUY.

Bibliography. R. Stupperich, *Melanchthon;* C. Manschreck, *Melanchthon, the Quiet Reformer.*

Melchiorites. Term used for the followers of Melchior Hoffman (modernized in German as Hofmann), the Reformer who carried the gospel to Baltic areas such as Estonia and Livonia, to Emden in Friesland, and to Amsterdam. Hoffman was an individualist who did not unite with the Swiss Brethren, and they in turn repudiated him. Nevertheless he did unite with a fringe group of Anabaptists in Strasbourg in 1530. For a time he was a Lutheran, but Luther ultimately repudiated him. In the 1530s he traveled about a great deal. He held to such Swiss Brethren doctrines as believer's baptism, nonresistance, the rejection of oaths, earnest discipleship to Christ, and separation of church and state. He wrote numerous books, mostly on eschatology. He made much of baptism as a covenant (see I Pet. 3:21 in the Luther Bible), and his followers were often called Brethren of the Covenant or "Covenanters."

In addition to the usual Anabaptist doctrines Hoffman was obsessed with eschatology, reveling in the anticipated apocalyptic violence against the wicked after Christ's return, and he was naïvely drawn to "special revelations" through dreams and visions. He also held an eccentric view of the incarnation whereby Mary was understood to be merely a channel through which the "heavenly flesh of Christ made its entrance to the earth." In response to a special revelation through a Melchiorite he hastened back to Strasbourg in 1533, was arrested, and jailed—in the expectation that in six months Christ would return. However, Hoffman lay in prison for ten long years before dying in 1543. His Reformation in the Low Countries slowly matured into two wings: (1) The Peace Wing led by Jan Volkerts Trypmaker (martyred in 1531) and Jacob van Campen (martyred in 1535). Later leaders in this Peace Wing in Friesland were Obbe Philips, his brother Dirk Philips, and from 1536 Menno Simons. (2) The apocalyptic and revolutionary Melchiorites were led by the unstable Jan Matthys, who set up a theocracy in Münster, Germany, and died violently in 1534, and by the unscrupulous "King" Jan van Leyden, who was executed after the 1534–35 Münster "kingdom." Violent Münsterite "ultra-Melchiorism" was kept alive briefly by Jan van Batenburg (executed 1538) and by David Joris, who fled to Basel in 1544 under a false name and successfully posed for the rest of his days as a Zwinglian.

J. C. WENGER

See also RADICAL REFORMATION; ZWICKAU PROPHETS.

Bibliography. *Mennonite Encyclopedia*, II, 778–85, III, 565.

Melitian Schisms. Two schisms are known by this name, each revolving around a different Melitius in a different half of the fourth century. The first involves Melitius, Bishop of Lycopolis, who in 305, during the Diocletian persecution, for some unclear reason took it upon himself to assume some of the responsibilities of Peter, Bishop of Alexandria, while the latter was imprisoned. Most offensive was his unauthorized consecration of presbyters and deacons throughout upper Egypt. Peter soon excommunicated him, refusing to recognize any of his appointments or the baptisms they administered. Melitius took offense at this treatment, especially in light of Peter's generally lenient attitude toward those who apostasized during the persecution.

Returning from a brief imprisonment himself in 311 (during which year Peter was martyred), Melitius set about organizing a schismatic church which by the time of the Council of Nicaea is reported to have had twenty-eight bishoprics. Always opposed to the Bishop of Alexandria, whomever he might be, Melitius found common cause at times with the Arians (Arius himself is reported to have been an early Melitian appointment who was reconciled with Peter); however, the union was political rather than theological.

The Council of Nicaea attempted to heal the division by legitimating the ministry of the Melitian clergy but subordinating it to the authority of the Alexandrian bishop. Melitian bishops were allowed to succeed orthodox bishops only by general election and ordination by the metropolitan. Melitius was allowed the title of bishop but not a see. Unfortunately, the schism was not healed, and the Melitian church continued till the eighth century.

The second Melitian schism concerns Melitius (also Meletius) of Antioch. Prior to his election as Bishop of Antioch he had associated with the semi-Arian party, signing the Creed of Acacius at the synod of Seleucia which ambiguously advocated the *homoion* (likeness) of the Son to the Father while rejecting *homoousion, homoiousion,* and *anomoion.* However, after Melitius came to Antioch (361), he embraced the *homoousion* formulary of the Nicene Creed. His gracious, loving, and holy disposition attracted a loyal following even after his orthodox views brought him exile, during which time the Arian Euzoius was installed as bishop. This split between Arian and orthodox parties was then subdivided by another and more permanent schism on the orthodox side when the older traditional party, retaining the memory of the staunch anti-Arian Eustathius (324), refused to recognize anyone (even if he was orthodox) who had been consecrated by Arians. They elected Paulinus as their bishop. This older conservative party, though small, refused to unite with the Melitians, even after Melitius returned from exile. An arrangement was made, however, that union should be accomplished under the bishop who survived the death of the other. But this arrangement did not hold, for after the death of Melitius, at the Council of Constantinople (381) the council of bishops chose Flavian rather than Paulinus to succeed him. The split remained even after the death of Paulinus until the successor of Flavian, Alexander, achieved the union around 415.

Aside from this schism, Melitius was actually instrumental in reconciling the semi-Arian party to the Nicene. He presided, at the choice of the orthodox emperor Theodosius I, over the initial session of the Council of Constantinople and ordained Gregory of Nazianzus as Bishop of Constantinople. He also ordained a young deacon whom he had taken an interest in by the name of John Chrysostom. C. A. Blaising

See also Nicaea, Council of; Homoousion.

Bibliography. Socrates, *Ecclesiastical History* (*NPNF*); Sozomen, *Ecclesiastical History* (*NPNF*); Theodoret, *Ecclesiastical History* (*NPNF*); P. Schaff, *History of the Christian Church,* II, III.

Melville, Andrew (1545–1622). Scottish educator, biblical scholar, and church reformer. Reared by his brother, who later entered the Reformed ministry, Melville showed intellectual brilliance at St. Andrews University. At nineteen he left Scotland for Paris, where he studied languages and learned the teaching methods of Peter Ramus. After studying civil law and teaching at Poitiers he arrived in 1569 in Geneva to be welcomed by Theodore Beza and installed in the academy's chair of humanity. He returned home in 1574 to lead a striking revival of Scottish higher learning. First at the University of Glasgow and subsequently at St. Andrews, he modernized educational method and curriculum, enlisted superior faculty, and proved to be a talented biblical scholar, exciting teacher, able administrator, and canny disciplinarian. Scottish universities for the first time became generally attractive to European students.

For some time after returning to Scotland, Melville showed little interest in the organization or polity of the kirk. With thirty other ministers, however, in 1576 he became involved in the two-year-long corporate committee process which, under the guidance of the General Assembly, formulated and revised the *Second Book of Discipline* in response to the collapse of the crown's effort to reorganize the church along the lines of the English Elizabethan settlement.

General Assembly approved the work in 1578, but did not receive concurrence from the government. There followed a period in which the General Assembly gradually developed and implemented a presbyterian polity, while the crown repeatedly attempted to restore episcopacy. In this contest Melville rapidly emerged as a major ecclesiastical statesman and champion of the liberties of the kirk against the encroachments of civil authority. A bold, energetic, prophetically articulate, and sometimes tactless leader, for almost thirty years he rallied the ministers to defend the right of assembly and to prevent the reassertion of episcopacy and royal domination of the church. Thus he became viewed as successor to John Knox in leading the Scottish Reformation, was referred to as the "father of the Scottish presbytery," and was credited (erroneously) with almost sole authorship of the *Second Book of Discipline.*

Melville was an internationally recognized Latin poet whose love of writing epigrams led to his final personal defeat. Summoned to London to account for his defense of the ministers' right to assemble freely, he wrote verses satirizing the king's worship, for which treason he was incarcerated in the Tower and eventually exiled to France, where he died. R. M. HEALEY

Bibliography. T. M'Crie, *Life of Andrew Melville,* 2 vols.; W. Morison, *Andrew Melville;* S. Mechie, "Andrew Melville," in *Fathers of the Kirk;* J. Kirk, *Second Book of Discipline* and *"Development of the Melvillian Movement"* (Ph.D. diss., Univ. of Edinburgh).

Mennonites. A large body of Anabaptist groups today, descendants of the Dutch and Swiss Anabaptists (the Swiss Brethren, as they came to be known) of the sixteenth century. The basic doctrines of the original Swiss Anabaptists, as well as the Peace Wing of the Dutch Anabaptists, are reflected in the 1524 *Programmatic Letters* of Conrad Grebel; in the Seven Articles of Schleitheim, 1527; in the voluminous writings of Pilgram Marpeck (d. 1556); in the writings of Menno Simons and of Dirk Philips (*Enchiridion or Handbook of the Christian Doctrine*); in the Swiss Brethren hymn book, the *Ausbund* (1564); and in the huge *Martyrs Mirror* of 1660.

The Swiss Brethren were the Free Church wing of the Zwinglian Reformation. Initially the pioneer leaders such as Conrad Grebel and Felix Mantz had nothing but praise for Zwingli. But by the fall of 1523 they became increasingly uneasy about the tempo of the Reformation in Zurich, and particularly about Zwingli's practice of allowing the Great Council of the 200 to decide what Catholic forms of doctrine, piety, and practice were to be dropped. These young radicals felt that Zwingli was too lukewarm and slow in carrying out his strongly biblical vision for an evangelical Reformed Church in Zurich. But they did nothing until they were ordered to have their infants baptized and forbidden to conduct any more Bible study sessions. It was then that they met, and after earnest prayer ventured to inaugurate believer's baptism and to commission each other to go out as preachers and evangelists. The date of organization of this Swiss Free Church was January 21, 1525.

At this organization meeting the three strongest leaders were Conrad Grebel, who died in 1526; Felix Mantz, who died as a martyr early in 1527; and George Blaurock, who was severely beaten and banished from Zurich in 1527, only to be burned to death in the Tirol in 1529. After the original leaders were off the scene, the mantle of leadership fell upon a former Benedictine monk of South Germany named Michael Sattler. It was Sattler who helped the scattered and sometimes differing Swiss Brethren to settle upon what was a biblical faith and way of life. This was realized at a village in Schaffhausen called Schleitheim in 1527. Seven articles were worked over and finally adopted unanimously by the "brethren and sisters" who were present. These seven articles may be summarized thus:

(1) Baptism is to be given to people who have repented and believed on Christ, who manifest a new way of life, who "walk in the resurrection," and who actually request baptism. (Infants and children are considered saved without ceremony, but infants are often "dedicated.")

(2) Before the breaking of bread (the Lord's Supper), special effort shall be made to reclaim from any form of sin any brothers or sisters who may have strayed from Christ's way of love, holiness, and obedience. Those who are overtaken by sin should be twice warned privately, then publicly admonished before the congregation. The rite of exclusion of impenitent sinners the Swiss Brethren called the ban.

(3) The Lord's Supper is to be celebrated by those who have been united into the body of Christ by baptism. The congregation of believers must keep themselves from the sinful ways of the world in order to be united in the "loaf" of Christ.

(4) Disciples of Christ must carefully avoid the sins of a Christ-rejecting world. They cannot have spiritual fellowship with those who reject the obedience of faith. Accordingly there are two classes of people: those who belong to the devil and live in sin, and those who have been delivered by Christ from this evil way of life. We

must break with every form of sin, and then he will be our God and we will be his sons and daughters.

(5) Every congregation of true Christians needs a shepherd. The shepherd (or pastor) shall meet NT qualifications—"the rule of Paul." He is to read God's Word, exhort, teach, warn, admonish, discipline or ban in the congregation, properly preside in the congregational meetings and in the breaking of bread. If he has financial needs the congregation shall give him support. Should he be led away to martyrdom, another pastor shall be ordained in "the same hour."

(6) The section on being nonresistant sufferers is entitled "The Sword." The sword is ordained of God "outside the perfection of Christ" (the church). The only method the church has to deal with transgressors is the ban (exclusion). Disciples of Christ must be utterly nonresistant. They cannot use the sword to cope with the wicked or to defend the good. Nonresistant Christians cannot serve as magistrates; rather, they must react as Christ did: he refused when they wished to make him king. Under no circumstances can Christians be other than Christlike.

(7) Finally, by the word of Christ, Christians cannot swear any kind of oath. Christian disciples are finite creatures; they cannot make one hair grow white or black. They may solemnly testify to the truth, but they shall not swear.

In the covering letter accompanying the Seven Articles, Sattler acknowledges that some of the brothers had not fully understood God's will aright, but now they do. All past mistakes are truly forgiven when believers offer prayer concerning their shortcomings and guilt; they have perfect standing "through the gracious forgiveness of God and through the blood of Jesus Christ."

In 1693 Jakob Ammann, a Swiss elder in Alsace, founded the most conservative wing of the Mennonites, the Amish.

Down through the centuries the Mennonites have produced numerous confessions of faith, catechisms, printed sermons, and hymn books.

Mennonites hold to the major doctrines of the Christian faith and feel free to confess the Apostles' Creed. They are dissatisfied, however, with the creed's moving directly from the birth of Christ to his atoning death. They feel that it is also important to study Christ's way of life, his beautiful example of love, obedience, and service. They cannot believe that seeking to be faithful to both the letter and the spirit of the NT is legalism, if such obedience is based on love for God and love for man. Indeed, Michael Sattler wrote a moving essay in 1527: *Two Kinds of Obedience.* They are (1) slavish obedience, which is legalism; it involves a low level of performance and produces proud "Pharisees." (2) Filial obedience, which is based on love for God and can never do enough, for the love of Christ is so intense. Mennonites see the will of God revealed in a preparatory but nonfinal way in the OT but fully and definitively in Christ and the NT.

Violent suppression of the Mennonites practically led to their extermination in Germany. In Switzerland they survived chiefly in two areas, the Emme valley of Berne and the mountainous areas of the Jura. William I of the House of Orange brought toleration of a sort to the "Mennists" (the name coined by Countess Anna in Friesland in 1545 to designate the Peace Wing of the Dutch Anabaptists) of the Netherlands about 1575. The severe persecution of the Swiss *Taufgesinnten,* the Dutch *Doopsgezinden,* and the Frisian *Mennists* effectively silenced their evangelistic and mission concerns for several centuries, but these were revived slowly in the nineteenth century, first in Europe and then in North America. Mennonite missions have been most successful in Africa, Indonesia, and in India, and have started in Latin America. J. C. WENGER

See also GREBEL, CONRAD; MENNO SIMONS; RADICAL REFORMATION.

Bibliography. *Mennonite Encyclopedia,* 4 vols.; T. J. van Braght, *Martyrs Mirror;* C. J. Dyck, ed., *Introduction to Mennonite History;* J. Horsch, *Mennonites in Europe;* G. F. Hershberger, *War, Peace, and Nonresistance;* M. Jeschke, *Discipling the Brother;* J. A. Hostetler, *Amish Society;* S. F. Pannabecker, *Open Doors;* J. A. Toews, *Mennonite Brethren Church;* J. C. Wenger, *Introduction to Theology* and *Mennonite Church in America.*

Menno Simons (*ca.* 1496–1561). Best known as the founder of a loosely related group of Reformation believers known today as Mennonites. In the days of Menno family names were not yet established in the Netherlands; the name Simons is simply a patronymic: "son of Simon." We know little more of his life than he himself writes in his book directed to the Reformer Jelle Smit, who wrote under the name Gellius Faber. That brief autobiography was written to demonstrate that Menno had no connection with the Münsterites, the militant wing of the Melchiorites.

Menno was born in the Frisian village of Witmarsum and trained for the Roman priesthood. He was consecrated in 1524 at the age of twenty-eight. His first parish service was from 1524 to 1531 at the neighboring village of Pingjum, and from 1531 to 1536 in his home town of Witmarsum.

In the first year of his priesthood Menno came to doubt the doctrine of transubstantiation, and after much distress he fearfully took up the Scriptures for the first time in his life. As a result of reading the NT, he gave up the doctrine of the miraculous change of the bread and wine into the body and blood of the Lord. In 1531 Menno heard of the execution of Sicke Snijder at Leeuwarden, capital of Friesland, for being rebaptized. This terrified him also, and led to much soul searching. In the end he came to believe that baptism should follow conversion. Finally, Menno's brother joined a nonpeace group of Anabaptists and perished in a struggle with the authorities in 1535. This tragedy broke Menno's heart, and he made a total surrender of himself to Christ. For about nine months he remained in the Catholic Church, preaching his new understanding of the gospel.

On January 31, 1536, Menno renounced his Roman Catholicism and went into hiding. He accepted baptism, probably from the leader of the Peace Wing of the Frisian Anabaptists, Obbe Philips, who also ordained Menno as an elder (bishop) in the province of Groningen in 1537. Menno served in the Netherlands (1536–43), in northwest Germany, mainly in the Rhineland (1543–46), and in Danish Holstein (1546–61). The first major collection of his writings appeared in 1646.

Menno was a good shepherd and leader, and escaped martyrdom only by moving about. He was an evangelical who held to the major doctrines of the Christian faith. He differed from Luther and Calvin by defending the baptism of believers only, by teaching the doctrine of peace and nonresistance, and by rejecting the oath. He assumed the separation of church and state. He held to the Melchiorite doctrine of the incarnation, which taught that Christ brought to earth his own "heavenly flesh," receiving nothing from Mary, not even his humanity. And since no man was the earthly father of Jesus, God must have created a body for him. Our Lord was therefore in Mary prior to his birth, yet he was not of Mary.

J. C. Wenger

See also Mennonites.

Bibliography. J. C. Wenger, ed., *The Complete Writings of Menno Simons;* K. Vos, *Menno Simons;* C. Krahn, *Menno Simons.*

Mental Reservation. These words refer to "veiled speech," statements which, though true, conceal as much as or more than they disclose. In ordinary discourse mental reservation might on occasion be justified if (1) the statement in some way corresponds to the truth as one perceives it, (2) the motivation is genuine love for the truth and for one's neighbor. Mental reservation is exceptional but may be justified. Lying, intentionally conveying a falsehood, is never justified.

Mental reservation is much more problematic in cases where one is asked to confess the Christian faith. Some creeds and confessions uniting a community of faith require affirmation "without mental reservation." It is certain that elements of doubt, uncertainty, and unclarity are part of the human condition. We see now "through a glass darkly" (I Cor. 13:12) owing to human finitude as well as imperfection. Some things in the Bible are "hard to understand" (II Pet. 3:16), and differences in both maturity and conviction must be tolerated (Rom. 14). A degree of mental reservation arising out of partial knowledge and genuine humility may be allowed if it is in the spirit of the epileptic's father, who said to Jesus, "I believe! Help thou my unbelief" (Mark 9:24).

Nevertheless, those who become teachers "shall incur a stricter judgment" (James 3:1) and may properly be required not to be "double-minded" (James 1:8; 4:8) or "double-tongued" (I Tim. 3:8). Our Lord was especially hard on those whose public words and actions were contradicted by inward corruption. The rule of simplicity, sincerity, and honesty in speech is thus especially important for those who are teachers and leaders. While a degree of doubt and difference may be entirely justified within a given confessional community, responsibility to God and to each other means that candor and open communication of such reservations should be the rule, especially for the leadership. Mental reservation per se is not always a problem; dishonesty and a lack of integrity are always problems which must be dealt with in the community of faith.

D. W. Gill

Mercersburg Theology. A romantic Reformed theology which during the midnineteenth century stood opposed to the main developments of American religious thought. It was the work of John Williamson Nevin (1803–86), a theologian, and Philip Schaff (1819–93), a church historian, who taught at the seminary of the German Reformed Church in Mercersburg, Pennsylvania, in the 1840s and 1850s.

Nevin had graduated from Presbyterian Princeton, had lectured there briefly, and then taught for a decade at a Presbyterian seminary in Pittsburgh before joining Mercersburg in 1840. He detailed the theological pilgrimage which undergirded his move away from a Princeton form of Calvinism in *The History and Genius of the Heidelberg Catechism* (1841–42). For Nevin the Heidelberg Catechism, doctrinal standard of the German Reformed, exhibited the Reformation at its best before its modern decline into a rationalistic and mechanical "Puritanism." Nevin criticized the direction of American Protestantism in *The Anxious Bench* (1843), a work which attacked revivalism for being too individualistic, too emotional, and too much concerned with the "new measures" (such as the anxious bench for souls under conviction) which drew attention to human foibles and away from the work of Christ and the church. To remedy these ills Nevin proposed a return to classic Reformed convictions about Christ and his work. *The Mystical Presence* (1846) argued that the views of the Reformers, especially Calvin, provided a means to overcome superficial and subjectivistic Protestantism. It began with the dramatic assertion that "Christianity is grounded in the living union of the believer with the person of Christ; and this great fact is emphatically concentrated in the mystery of the Lord's Supper." Against the view of Communion as a mere memorial, Nevin presented a case for the "real spiritual presence." God, he taught, comes to the church objectively, though not materially, in the Lord's Supper. The Supper in turn should become the focus of worship, and its presentation of the incarnate Christ the center of theology.

When Philip Schaff came to Mercersburg in 1844 from the University of Berlin, he brought along an appreciation for Germany's new idealistic philosophy and for its pietistic church renewal as well. His early work at Mercersburg urged Protestants toward a fuller appreciation of the Christian past. In *The Principle of Protestantism* (1844) he suggested, for example, that the Reformation continued the best of medieval Catholicism. And he looked forward to the day when Reformed, Lutheran, and even eventually Catholic believers could join in Christian union. Such views led to charges of heresy, from which Schaff cleared himself only with difficulty.

The influence of Nevin and Schaff was slight in the 1840s and 1850s. American Protestants were ill at ease with immigrants and with anyone who spoke a good word for any aspect of Roman Catholicism. They were wholeheartedly given to revivalism. They were busy making plans for interdenominational cooperation and did not look kindly on Mercersburg's new reading of history. And America's dominant Protestant philosophy, commonsense realism, had little room for the developmental ideas of Nevin and Schaff.

The two Mercersburg stalwarts were able to work closely together for barely a decade. Nevin, after editing the *Mercersburg Review* from 1849 to 1853, retired because of illness and disillusionment. Schaff left Mercersburg in 1863 for teaching posts at Andover and Union seminaries, where he participated actively in the general evangelical life of America. Nonetheless, the works of the Mercersburg men remain a guidepost for Christians who share their convictions: that the person of Christ is the key to Christianity; that the Lord's Supper, understood in a classic Reformed sense, is the secret to the ongoing life of the church; and that study of the church's past provides the best perspective for bringing its strength to bear on the present. M. A. Noll

See also Schaff, Philip.

Bibliography. J. H. Nichols, *Romanticism in American Theology: Nevin and Schaff at Mercersburg* and (ed.) *The Mercersburg Theology.*

Merciful Acts, Gift of. *See* Spiritual Gifts.

Mercy. The term may designate both character and actions that emerge as a consequence of that character. As a part of character mercy is demonstrated most clearly by such qualities as compassion and forbearance. With respect to action an act of mercy issues from compassion and forbearance; in a legal sense mercy may involve such acts as pardon, forgiveness, or the mitigation of penalties. In each case mercy is experienced and exercised by a person who has another person in his power, or under his authority, or from whom no kindness can be claimed. Thus God may show mercy toward human beings, who are all ultimately within his power, even though they have no direct claim, in terms of their behavior, to attitudes or actions of mercy. And a human being may be merciful to another, to whom neither compassion nor forbearance is due, by free act or thought toward that person.

From a theological perspective the characteristic of mercy is rooted in God and experienced in relation to God, from whom it may be acquired as a Christian virtue and exercised in relation to fellow human beings. In the Bible a variety of Hebrew and Greek words are used which fall within the general semantic range of the English word "mercy." They include such terms as "lovingkindness" (Heb. *ḥesed*), "to be merciful" (Heb. *ḥānan*), "to have compassion" (Heb. *riḥam*), and "grace" (Gr. *charis*).

In the OT mercy (in the sense of lovingkindness) is a central theme; the very existence of the covenant between God and Israel was an example of mercy, being granted to Israel freely and without prior obligation on the part of God (Isa. 63:7; Ps. 79:8–9). Insofar as the covenant was rooted in divine love, mercy was an ever-present quality of the relationship it expressed; the law, which formed a central part of the covenant relationship, came with the promise of forgiveness and mercy, contingent upon repentance, for the breaking of that law. Yet the divine mercy extended beyond the obligations of the covenant, so that even when Israel's sin had exhausted the covenantal category of mercy, still the loving mercy of God reached beyond the broken covenant in its promise and compassion to Israel.

With the new covenant the mercy of God is seen in the death of Jesus Christ; the sacrificial death is in itself a merciful act, demonstrating the divine compassion and making possible the forgiveness of sins. From this fundamental gospel there follows the requirement for all Christians, who are by definition the recipients of mercy, to exercise mercy and compassion toward fellow human beings (Matt. 5:17; James 2:13).

Throughout Christian history the awareness of the continuing human need for divine mercy has remained as a central part of Christian worship. The *kyrie eleison* of the ancient church has continued to be used in many liturgical forms of worship: "Lord, have mercy upon us; Christ, have mercy upon us; Lord have mercy upon us." And from the prayer employed in worship for God's mercy, there must follow the practice of mercy in life.

In the religion of Islam, whose historical origins have been influenced profoundly by both Christianity and Judaism, God is most frequently described as "the Merciful, the Compassionate."

P. C. CRAIGIE

See also GOD, ATTRIBUTES OF.

Bibliography. W. Eichrodt, *Theology of the OT,* I, 232–39; N. Glueck, *Hesed in the Bible;* R. Bultmann, *TDNT,* II, 477–87; H.-H. Esser, *NIDNTT,* II, 593–601.

Mercy Seat. The term used in most English translations of the Bible to translate the Hebrew *kappōret.* This word could have the simpler sense of "cover, lid," but the symbolic significance of the item so designated makes appropriate the more conventional rendition "mercy seat."

The mercy seat was a slab of gold, rectangular in shape, measuring approximately 3½ feet by 2 feet. It was placed over the ark of the covenant, functioning as a cover or lid, in the innermost room of the tabernacle (and of the temple at a later date). On top of the mercy seat were two cherubim, facing each other, their wings extending over the mercy seat and meeting above it. A full account of the mercy seat is provided in Exod. 25:17–22; its construction is described in Exod. 37:6–9.

The symbolic significance of the mercy seat can be seen most dramatically in the events of the day of atonement (Yom Kippur). The high priest entered the inner sanctuary containing the ark and the mercy seat; incense was burned so that the mercy seat was enveloped in smoke. The blood from a bull was sprinkled on the mercy seat (Lev. 16:11–19). The ritual was part of a larger ceremony in which Israel, through solemn repentance, sought God's forgiveness and mercy for sins committed during the preceding year. The mercy seat symbolized God's mercy, overspreading the breaking of the laws that were contained on the tablets in the ark underneath the mercy seat.

In the NT the mercy seat is referred to by the writer of the Epistle to the Hebrews (Heb. 9:5), who demonstrates that the annual sprinkling of blood on the mercy seat in the inner sanctuary is superseded by the more perfect sacrifice of Christ. The shedding of Christ's blood replaced the ancient ritual with bull's blood and served as a final atonement for human sin.

P. C. CRAIGIE

See also ARK OF THE COVENANT.

Bibliography. C. Brown and H.-G. Link, *NIDNTT,* III, 148–66.

Merit. In theology a meritorious human act is one for which a reward from God is appropriate. Occasionally some subapostolic writings (most notably the Didache, the Shepherd of Hermas, and Second Clement) speak as if conversion and baptism bestowed only forgiveness of past sins and a measure of divine strength. Subsequently individuals, with God's assistance, must earn further blessings and eternal life. If they sin, repentance and other virtuous acts may provide atonement. In dealing with penance, Tertullian systematized these notions by employing the Roman legal terms *meritum* (merit) and *satisfactio* (satisfaction). When someone sinned, God was regarded as occupying the position belonging to the injured party under Roman law. Such injury could be set right only by punishment or pardon. But pardon could not occur without a satisfaction, a meritorious act, being paid. For Tertullian, one could not expect forgiveness without paying a price—through confession, self-humiliation, or fasting.

Medieval theologians distinguished merit that strictly deserved a reward (*meritum de condigno*) from that for which a reward was merely appropriate (*meritum de congruo*). The latter could be gained by the nonjustified who heeded God's voice as known through reason and conscience or through the church. Though their actions were tainted with sin and, strictly speaking, could not deserve God's favor, God was pleased to reward them with sanctifying grace. But once aided by sanctifying grace individuals, through the exercise of their free wills, could produce merit *de condigno,* which strictly deserved divine rewards. Medieval theology also elaborated the doctrine of "supererogation." Saintly individuals accumulate merit exceeding that required for their own blessedness. These surplus merits were commonly thought to be stored in a heavenly "treasury" and to be available to others through prayers to saints, indulgences, and other pious acts.

Martin Luther insisted that these teachings encouraged people to assume that they could obey God's law through their own efforts. Instead, he argued, the law's function is to show us our utter inability to do so and drive us to repentance and faith. We are wholly incapable, both before and after we come to faith, of doing anything that could truly merit God's reward. Following Luther, Protestantism as a whole has rejected the notion that humans can earn rewards from God, even when assisted by grace. For orthodox Protestant theology, however, the notions of merit and satisfaction have remained central in explaining Christ's work. God is still regarded as the supreme lawgiver, who can accept sinners only on the basis of the substitutionary merits earned by Christ.

Contemporary Catholic theology still speaks of merit, but usually with a heavy emphasis on divine grace. No one can merit one's original creation, final salvation, nor God's acceptance of one's efforts *de congruo.* Ultimately Christ merited all the grace which God bestows—merit *de condigno.* Hans Küng argues that little real difference exists between Protestants and Catholics on this issue.

However, most contemporary theologians, both Catholic and Protestant, conceptualize God's relationships with humans not in the traditional language of penalties, payments, and rewards, but in relational and developmental terms. Thus Karl Rahner can insist that when the doctrine of merit speaks of individuals being "rewarded" by God (*de condigno*), it means to affirm that those involved in the sanctifying process really do become holy and pleasing to God and experience his increasing favor. But while recent Protestant theologians speak in similar relational language, they tend to avoid discussion of "merit" altogether and to affirm that, despite sanctification, we still remain sinners.

T. N. Finger

See also Grace; Justification; Salvation; Sanctification; Supererogation, Works of.

Bibliography. G. Bertram, *TDNT,* II, 635–65; J. Calvin, *Institutes of the Christian Religion* 3.15; H. Küng, *Justification; Luther's Works,* XXVI, 122–41, 172–85; W. Molinski, "Merit," *Sacramentum Mundi,* IV; J. Morgan, *The Importance of Tertullian in the Development of Christian Dogma;* H. Preisker and E. Würthwein, *TDNT,* IV, 695–728; K. Rahner, "The Comfort of Time," in *Theological Investigations,* III; T. F. Torrance, *The Doctrine of Grace in the Apostolic Fathers;* P. Watson, *The Concept of Grace.*

Messiah. The study of the rise and development of the figure of the Messiah is primarily historical, and then theological. Confusion arises when specifically Christian ideas about the Messiah invade the OT data. Jesus' concept of his messianic mission did not accord with contemporary popular Jewish expectation.

In the OT. "Messiah" is the hellenized transliteration of the Aramaic *mĕšîḥā'.* The underlying Hebrew word *māšîaḥ* is derived from *māšah,* "to anoint, smear with oil." This title was used sometimes of non-Israelite figures—e.g., Cyrus in Isa. 45:1—sometimes of the altar as in Exod. 29:36, sometimes of the prophet as in I Kings 19:16. But most frequently it referred to the king of Israel as in I Sam. 26:11 and Ps. 89:20. It is noteworthy that the word "messiah" does not appear at all in the OT (the AV of Dan. 9:25 is incorrect; it ought to read "an anointed one"), and only rarely in the intertestamental literature. The primary sense of the title is "king," as the anointed man of God, but it also suggests election, i.e., the king was chosen, elect, and therefore honored. It could scarcely be otherwise than that it referred to a political leader, for in its early stages Israel sought only a ruler, visible and powerful, who would reign here and now. But the entire evidence of later Judaism points to a Messiah not only as king but as eschatological king, a ruler who would appear at the end time. David was the ideal king of Israel, and as such he had a "sacral" character, and this sacral characteristic came to be applied to the eschatological king who was to be like David.

How did the national Messiah come to be a future ideal king? After the death of David, Israel began to hope for another like him who would maintain the power and prestige of the country. But Israel came into hard times with the rupture of the kingdom, and with this event there arose a disillusionment concerning the hope for a king like David. Then after the Exile, Zerubbabel, a descendant of David, took the leadership of Judah, but it developed that he was not another David. Gradually the hope was projected into the future, and eventually into the very remote future, so that the Messiah was expected at the end of the age.

This is the mood of the messianic expectations in the latter part of the OT. Such prophecies are common. For example, Jer. 33 promises a continuation of the Davidic line; Isa. 9 and 11 foresee the regal splendor of the coming king; Mic. 5:2 looks forward to the birth of the Davidic king in Bethlehem; and Zech. 9 and 12 describe the character of the messianic kingdom and reign.

The Son of man figure in Daniel is not to be

identified with the Messiah; it is later in the history of Judaism that the two figures were seen to be one. The suffering servant of Isaiah by reason of his role is yet another figure. So the Messiah, or future ideal king of Israel, the Son of man, and the suffering servant were three distinct representations in the OT.

In Intertestamental Writings. The Apocrypha and Pseudepigrapha are the literary remains of the evolution of messianic hopes within Judah between the testaments. As in the OT the formal use of "Messiah" is rare. It is well to remember that in this literature there is a distinction between Messiah and messianic; a book may have a messianic theme but lack a Messiah. The book of Enoch is best known for its doctrine of the Son of man, which has many messianic overtones. Yet he is not the Messiah, but a person much like Daniel's Son of man. It remained to the Psalms of Solomon (*ca.* 48 B.C.) to provide the one confirmed and repeated evidence of the technical use of the term in the intertestamental literature. This literature demonstrates, therefore, a diffuse expectation about the Messiah. It speaks of a Messiah of David, of Levi, of Joseph, and of Ephraim. The Dead Sea Scrolls add to the confusion by referring to a Messiah of Aaron and Israel.

Out of the welter of messianic hopes in this period there emerges a pattern: two kinds of Messiah came to be expected. On one hand, there arose an expectation of a purely national Messiah, one who would appear as a man and assume the kingship over Judah to deliver it from its oppressors. On the other hand, there was a hope for a transcendent Messiah from heaven, part human, part divine, who would establish the kingdom of God on earth. To the popular Jewish mind of the first two centuries before and after Christ these two concepts were not mutually hostile, but tended rather to modify each other. It has been argued by some scholars that the conflation of the concepts of Messiah and suffering servant took place in the intertestamental period, but the sole evidence for this is from the Targums, which are post-Christian.

In the NT. It remained for Jesus to fuse the three great eschatological representations of the OT—Messiah, suffering servant, and Son of man—into one messianic person. Apart from this truth there is no explanation for the confusion of the disciples when he told them he must suffer and die (Matt. 16:21ff.). That Christ knew himself to be the Messiah is seen best in his use of the title Son of man; in Mark 14:61–62 he equates the Christ and the Son of man. "Christ" is simply the Greek equivalent of the Hebrew "messiah." John 1:41 and 4:25 preserve the Semitic idea by transliterating the word "messiah." Jesus willingly accepted the appellation Son of David, a distinct messianic title, on several occasions—the cry of blind Bartimaeus (Mark 10:47ff.), the children in the temple (Matt. 21:15), and the triumphal entry (Matt. 21:9), to name but a few. It has long been wondered why Jesus did not appropriate the title Messiah to himself instead of the less clear title of Son of man. The former was probably avoided out of political considerations, for if Jesus had publicly used "Messiah" of himself it would have ignited political aspirations in his hearers to appoint him as king, principally a nationalistic figure, and to seek to drive out the Roman occupiers. This is precisely the import of the Jews' action at the triumphal entry. Jesus seized on the title Son of man to veil to his hearers his messianic mission but to reveal that mission to his disciples.

The first generation of the church did not hesitate to refer to Jesus as the Christ, and thereby designate him as the greater Son of David, the King. The word was used first as a title of Jesus (Matt. 16:16) and later as part of the personal name (e.g., Eph. 1:1). Peter's sermon at Pentecost acknowledged Jesus not only as the Christ, but also as Lord, and so the fulfillment of the messianic office is integrally linked to the essential deity of Jesus. Acts 2:36 affirms that Jesus was "made" Christ, the sense of the verb being that by the resurrection Jesus was confirmed as the Christ, the Messiah of God. Rom. 1:4 and Phil. 2:9–11 contain the same thought. Other messianic titles attributed to Jesus include Servant, Lord, Son of God, the King, the Holy One, the Righteous One, and the Judge.

D. H. WALLACE

See also CHRISTOLOGY; BRANCH; SON OF MAN.

Bibliography. S. Mowinckel, *He That Cometh;* V. Taylor, *The Names of Jesus;* T. W. Manson, *Jesus the Messiah* and *The Servant-Messiah;* F. Hahn, *The Titles of Jesus in Christology;* R. N. Longenecker, *The Christology of Early Jewish Christianity;* H. Ringgren, *The Messiah in the OT;* H. L. Ellison, *The Centrality of the Messianic Idea for the OT;* H. H. Rowley, *The Servant of the Lord;* B. B. Warfield, "The Divine Messiah in the OT," in *Biblical and Theological Studies;* J. Klausner, *The Messianic Idea in Israel;* E. Schürer, *The History of the Jewish People in the Age of Jesus Christ,* vol. 2 (rev.).

Messianic Banquet. *See* MARRIAGE FEAST OF THE LAMB.

Metaphysics. The branch of philosophy that inquires into the ultimate nature of reality. The term derives from the practice of commentators to call Aristotle's book on such topics the *Metaphysics,* since it came after (*meta*) the book on physics. Since then, it has seemed especially appropriate to use the term to refer to such topics, since they are more fundamental and more abstract than questions about nature.

Metaphysics is widely held to be the central issue in philosophy; central to metaphysics itself is ontology. Ontology is concerned with being as its subject matter. Ontological questions include the following: What is real and what is mere appearance? Is there reality beyond the things that can be seen, tasted, touched, and heard? Are thoughts real? Is the mind real? Is time real? Is there a God? In metaphysics philosophers also inquire into such questions as whether the relation of cause to effect is a feature of events in the world or simply an aspect of our psychological habits of thinking. Also within the scope of metaphysics is the question of human freedom versus universal causal determinism.

Metaphysicians differ as to the goals and methods of metaphysics. Metaphysics has been conceived as a science with nonperceptible reality as the subject matter, as in Leibniz and Wolff, and as an attempt to deduce the complete, all-encompassing system of reality, as in Descartes and Spinoza. This sort of grand-scale metaphysics was dealt a severe blow by Kant, who argued persuasively that human reason was incapable of metaphysical knowledge. More recently logical positivism has denied the meaningfulness of metaphysical language, and analytical philosophy in general has been hostile or indifferent to metaphysics, especially as conceived by the earlier British idealists such as F. H. Bradley. Nonetheless, prominent in contemporary philosophy is P. F. Strawson's "descriptive metaphysics" and the process metaphysics of Alfred North Whitehead and Charles Hartshorne; this latter movement has made itself felt in contemporary theology.

To accept a Christian perspective on reality necessarily involves making metaphysical commitments. A Christian world view that is faithful to Scripture and Christian doctrine will involve, for example, the belief that reality includes far more than is amenable to direct empirical investigation. The Christian will be interested in God and his relation to the world, in the soul and its relation to the body, and in free will in relation to determinism, to name but a few. Insofar as Christians seek not only to give assent but also to exercise judgment and develop understanding they will pursue metaphysical inquiry.

Metaphysical concerns are certainly very close to the core of Christian thinking in theology and philosophy, and it is for good reason that metaphysical investigation has loomed large in philosophy in the Christian tradition. D. B. Fletcher

See also Philosophy, Christian View of.

Bibliography. Aristotle, *Metaphysics;* G. Berkeley, *The Principle of Human Knowledge;* A. F. Holmes, *Faith Seeks Understanding;* G. W. Leibniz, *Monadology;* P. F. Strawson, *Individuals;* R. Taylor, *Metaphysics;* J. Weinberg and K. Yandell, eds., *Metaphysics;* A. N. Whitehead, *Process and Reality.*

Metempsychosis. *See* Reincarnation.

Methodism. A name designating several Protestant groups, Methodism has its roots in the work of John and Charles Wesley, sons of an Anglican rector and his wife, Susannah. A friend and Oxford classmate of the Wesleys, George Whitefield, was also instrumental in forming the Holy Club (*ca.* 1725), which stressed "inward religion, the religion of the heart." These awakenings coupled with the club's insistence on exacting discipline in scholastic as well as spiritual matters earned its members the jeering title of "Methodists" by 1729.

In 1735 the Wesleys sailed to America as missionaries, but not before John, a somewhat troubled young Anglican priest, noted: "My chief motive is the hope of saving my own soul." In the spring of 1738 John Wesley returned to England filled with a troubled sense of failure. He was attracted to the piety and feelings of inward assurance so notably evidenced among the Moravians. Wesley knew this was lacking in his own life despite his outward discipline. He saw himself failing to bear fruits of "inward holiness." Convinced of the necessity for faith and the inner witness, Wesley passed through a torturous spring, fearing that at the advanced age of thirty-five both life and God were passing him by. Unwillingly, he writes later, he was persuaded to attend a Bible study meeting on May 24, 1738, in Aldersgate Street, where an unknown layman was expounding on Luther's commentary on Romans. There, Wesley writes, "I felt my heart strangely warmed. I felt I did trust Christ, Christ alone for salvation; and an assurance was given me that He had taken away my sins." The Aldersgate experience, definitely a turning point in Wesley's life, was not so much an outright conversion experience of the type that came to be associated with the revival movements of England and America as it was a firm receiving of assurance of this priest's own salvation. Aldersgate was what Wesley needed.

By 1739 the distinct and aggressively evangelistic and highly disciplined Methodist movement spread like wildfire through field preaching, lay preaching, bands, and societies. The "Rules of Bands" demanded a highly disciplined life, an exacting schedule of meetings in which the society members were expected to share intimate details of their daily lives, to confess their sins to one another, to pray for each other, and to exhort members of the class toward inner holiness and good works. The enthusiasm of the revivals came under the control of the bands or societies. The weekly prayer meetings; the use of an itinerary system of traveling preachers; the annual conferences; the establishment of chapels; the prolific outpouring of tracts, letters, sermons, and hymns; and the general superintendency of John Wesley became the hallmark of what emerged as a worldwide Methodist movement.

Beginning with Church of England congregations banning John Wesley from their pulpits in 1738—before Aldersgate—tensions with the Established Church were inevitable and eventually disruptive. Wesley's penchant for organization and discipline likely hastened the series of breaks that gave the people called Methodists their several denominations.

As the revivalistic awakening came to include Methodism, work extended from England to Ireland, Scotland, and Wales, where a Calvinistically oriented minority formally established themselves in 1764. Soon lay preachers were active in America, establishing circuits along the mid-Atlantic states under the supervision of Francis Asbury, sent by Wesley in 1771. In 1744 a conference was held in London and standards for doctrine, liturgy, and discipline were adopted. The Wesleys maintained their personal ties (ordination) and devotion to the Church of England with its emphasis on the sacraments and its anti-popery views. Episcopal in its organization, the Methodist Connexion was autocratically controlled by John Wesley. By 1784 Wesley concluded that no one individual would be a suitable successor. He therefore moved to record a "Deed of Declaration" in which he declared a group of one hundred of his most able leaders (the "Legal Hundred") his legal successor. This established that Methodist societies were now duly constituted as legal entities, conceived of as *ecclesicla in ecclesia* but formally separate entities from the Church of England. This also established the Annual Conference as the primary authority in the Methodist system.

In September of that same year Wesley yielded to American pressure to have his preachers administer the sacraments by ordaining two lay helpers as elders and Thomas Coke as general superintendent without consulting with his conference. He was persuaded to this act by Peter King's *Account of the Primitive Church* (1691) that presbyters held the same spiritual authority as bishops to ordain in the early church and by the Bishop of London's refusal in 1780 to ordain any of Methodism's preachers in America. The three newly ordained men were dispatched to build up the full work of Methodism in America. At the Christmas Conference in Baltimore in 1784 Coke ordained Asbury, and the Methodist Episcopal Church was organized. Coke and Asbury were elected general superintendents. A Sunday Service based on the *Book of Common Prayer* and Twenty-five Articles of Religion abridged by Wesley from the Thirty-nine Articles were adopted by the new denomination.

Continuing his work among the various societies, Wesley ordained a number of presbyters in Scotland and England, and for the mission field. Unlike Methodism in America, no formal separation was consummated in England until after Wesley's death in 1791. A conciliar effort by the Church of England in 1793 prompted a formal "Plan of Pacification" in 1795. But final separation occurred in 1797, as the Rubicon had been crossed in 1784, and the formal organization of Methodism was well under way by the beginning of the nineteenth century.

In England a number of Methodist bodies splintered from the main Methodism movement. The Ecumenical Methodist Conferences formalized a renewed conciliar spirit. From 1907 to 1933 various groups united to become part of the Methodist Church. On July 8, 1969, a plan calling for merger of the Methodist and Anglican communions faced defeat at the hands of the Anglican Convocations where the concept of historic episcopacy as an office and not an order proved unacceptable. In Canada the Methodist Church of Canada joined with the Presbyterian Church and selected Union Churches together with the Congregational Churches to form the United Church of Canada.

In the United States numerous Methodist-oriented bodies exist. Some came into being in disputes over doctrinal issues. Others arose out of social concerns. The Wesleyan Methodist Church, organized in the 1840s, drew its inspiration from Orange Scott, a New Englander lacking formal education but committed to the Abolitionist movement. The Methodist Protestant Church, opposing the episcopacy, separated in 1828. By 1860 both doctrinal and social tensions were intense, and the Free Methodist Church was founded, largely under the inspiration of B. T. Roberts. In 1844 the Methodist Episcopal Church, South, was formed over the slavery issue.

Other significant Methodist denominations in the United States are the African Methodist Episcopal (1816), the African Methodist Episcopal Zion (1820), and the Christian Methodist Episcopal (1870), all black, totaling more than

2.5 million members. The year 1939 brought the reunion of the Methodist Episcopal Church, South, the Methodist Protestant Church, and the Methodist Episcopal Church to form The Methodist Church.

A group of German pietists under Jacob Albright were attracted to Methodism and in 1807 organized the Newly-Formed Methodist Conference or the German Methodist Conference. The English-speaking Methodist lay preachers were unable to serve this German-speaking immigrant group, so the Evangelical Association was formed in 1816. During this same period Phillip Otterbein, friend of Asbury, together with Martin Boehm founded the United Brethren in Christ among German-speaking immigrants with its organizing General Conference in 1815. In 1946 these two German immigrant churches merged to form the Evangelical United Brethren (EUB) Church. With its ethnic distinctiveness on the wane, and clearly Methodist in polity and theology, the EUBs merged in 1968 with The Methodist Church to form The United Methodist Church.

Active in social concerns, Methodism has followed in the footsteps of the Wesleys and Richard Watson. The theological mandate espoused in the 1908 Social Creed continues as a challenge to Methodists and other Christian fellowships in the struggle for social justice. In ecumenical circles G. Bromley Oxnam (1891–1963) and Frank Mason North (1850–1935) were instrumental in developing the Federal and National Council of Churches. E. Stanley Jones (1894–1973), evangelist extraordinary, was also instrumental in the worldwide ecumenical and evangelistic efforts of Methodism. Former EUB bishop Reuben H. Mueller (1897–1982) and Glenn R. Phillips (1894–1970) were principals in the formative days of the Consultation on Church Union. John R. Mott (1865–1955) figured prominently in the formation of the World Council of Churches, and Methodist Philip Potter is current general executive secretary of the council. Within Methodism, the World Methodist Council meets at five-year intervals and is composed of some fifty delegates representing some fifty million Methodists.

Long distinguished by an emphasis on practical faith, Methodism and its various offshoots have sought to avoid a strict confessionalism. The addition of a new section to the 1972 *Discipline*—"Our Theological Task," which formalizes a posture of doctrinal pluralism that appeals to Wesley's sermon "Catholic Spirit"—was an acknowledgment of the wide diversity of views within modern Methodism over the proper balance of Wesleyan orthodoxy and a theology of experience.

Concurrent with this development North American Methodism is undergoing the emergence of a neo-Wesleyan theology associated with J. Robert Nelson, Albert Outler, Robert Cushman, and Carl Michalson. African Methodist Episcopal minister James Cone combines the insights of black theology with his Methodist heritage. John B. Cobb, Jr., and Schubert M. Ogden explore their Wesleyan theology from the perspective of process modes of thought. Finally, the Methodist Federation for Social Action urges Methodism to retain its social conscience, and the Good News movement, an evangelically based Methodist renewalist group, seeks to call Methodism to its traditional Wesleyan theological heritage. P. A. Mickey

See also Wesley, John; Wesleyan Tradition, The; Watson, Richard.

Bibliography. F. A. Norwood, ed., *Sourcebook of American Methodism;* E. S. Bucke, ed., *The History of American Methodism,* 3 vols.; H. Bett, *The Spirit of Methodism;* H. Carter, *The Methodist Heritage;* W. J. Townsend, H. B. Workman, G. Eayrs, eds., *A New History of Methodism,* 2 vols.; C. H. Crookshank, *History of the Methodist Church in Ireland,* 3 vols.; G. Smith, *History of Wesleyan Methodism,* 3 vols.; W. F. Swift, *Methodism in Scotland;* W. W. Sweet, *Methodism in American History;* M. Simpson, ed., *Cyclopedia of Methodism;* M. Edwards, *Methodism and England;* G. G. Findlay and W. W. Holdsworth, *The History of the Wesleyan Methodist Missionary Church,* 5 vols.; F. F. MacLeister, *History of the Wesleyan Methodist Church of America;* R. Chiles, *Theological Transition in American Methodism;* T. A. Langford, *Practical Divinity.*

Methodism, Calvinistic. *See* Calvinistic Methodism.

Metropolitan. *See* Church Officers.

Midtribulation Rapture. *See* Rapture of the Church.

Millennium, Views of the. The word "millennium" is derived from the Latin for a thousand (at times the word "chiliasm" taken from the Greek and meaning the same thing is used). It denotes a doctrine taken from a passage in Revelation (20:1–10) in which the writer describes the devil as being bound and thrown into a bottomless pit for a thousand years. The removal of Satanic influence is accompanied by the resurrection of the Christian martyrs, who reign with Christ during the millennium. This period is a time when all of humankind's yearning for an ideal society characterized by peace, freedom, material prosperity, and the rule of righteousness will be realized. The vision of the OT prophets who foretold a period of earthly prosperity for the people of God will find fulfillment during this era.

Millennialism addresses problems that are often overlooked in other eschatological views. Although most Christian theologians discuss death, immortality, the end of the world, the last judgment, the rewards of the just, and the punishment of the damned, they often limit themselves to the prospects for the individual in this world and the next. In contrast, millennialism is concerned with the future of the human community on earth. It is concerned with the chronology of coming events just as history is involved with the study of the record of the past.

Millennialism has appeared within both Christian and non-Christian traditions. Anthropologists and sociologists have found millennialist belief among non-Western people, but they have debated as to whether or not these appearances of the teaching are based upon borrowing from Christian preaching. Most Christian theologians believe that millennialism is based on material written by Judeo-Christian authors, especially the books of Daniel and Revelation. The ideas, events, symbols, and personalities introduced in these writings have reappeared countless times in the teachings of prophets of the end of the world. Each new appearance finds these motifs given fresh significance from association with contemporary events.

Major Varieties of Millennialism. For purposes of analysis and explanation Christian attitudes toward the millennium can be classified as premillennial, postmillennial, and amillennial. These categories involve much more than the arrangement of events surrounding the return of Christ. The thousand years expected by the premillennialist is quite different from that anticipated by the postmillennialist. The premillennialist believes that the kingdom of Christ will be inaugurated in a cataclysmic way and that divine control will be exercised in a more supernatural manner than does the postmillennialist. The premillennialist believes that the return of Christ will be preceded by signs including wars, famines, earthquakes, the preaching of the gospel to all nations, a great apostasy, the appearance of Antichrist, and the great tribulation. These events culminate in the second coming, which will result in a period of peace and righteousness when Christ and his saints control the world. This rule is established suddenly through supernatural methods rather than gradually over a long period of time by means of the conversion of individuals. The Jews will figure prominently in the future age because the premillennialist believes that they will be converted in large numbers and will again have a prominent place in God's work. Nature will have the curse removed from it, and even the desert will produce abundant crops. Christ will restrain evil during the age by the use of authoritarian power. Despite the idyllic conditions of this golden age there is a final rebellion of wicked people against Christ and his saints. This exposure of evil is crushed by God, the non-Christian dead are resurrected, the last judgment conducted, and the eternal states of heaven and hell established. Many premillennialists have taught that during the thousand years dead or martyred believers will be resurrected with glorified bodies to intermingle with the other inhabitants of the earth.

In contrast to premillennialism, the postmillennialists emphasize the present aspects of God's kingdom which will reach fruition in the future. They believe that the millennium will come through Christian preaching and teaching. Such activity will result in a more godly, peaceful, and prosperous world. The new age will not be essentially different from the present, and it will come about as more people are converted to Christ. Evil will not be totally eliminated during the millennium, but it will be reduced to a minimum as the moral and spiritual influence of Christians is increased. During the new age the church will assume greater importance, and many economic, social, and educational problems can be solved. This period is not necessarily limited to a thousand years because the number can be used symbolically. The millennium closes with the second coming of Christ, the resurrection of the dead, and the last judgment.

The third position, amillennialism, states that the Bible does not predict a period of the rule of Christ on earth before the last judgment. According to this outlook there will be a continuous development of good and evil in the world until the second coming of Christ, when the dead shall be raised and the judgment conducted. Amillennialists believe that the kingdom of God is now present in the world as the victorious Christ rules his church through the Word and the Spirit. They feel that the future, glorious, and perfect kingdom refers to the new earth and life in heaven. Thus Rev. 20 is a description of the souls of dead believers reigning with Christ in heaven.

The Rise of Millennialism. Early millennial teaching was characterized by an apocalyptic emphasis. In this view the future kingdom of God would be established through a series of dramatic, unusual events. Such teaching has been kept alive throughout the Christian era by certain types of premillennialism. Apocalyptic interpretation is based upon the prophecies of Daniel and the amplification of some of the same themes in the book of Revelation. These works point to the imminent and supernatural intervention of God in human affairs and the defeat of the seemingly irresistible progress of evil. Numerology, theme figures, and angelology play a major role in these presentations. The apocalyptic world view was very influential among the Jews in the period that elapsed between the OT and the NT. Consequently the audiences to which Jesus preached were influenced by it. The early Christians also embraced this outlook.

The book of Revelation, composed during a period of persecution in the first century, used the Jewish apocalyptic interpretation to explain the Christian era. Daniel's Son of man was presented as Christ, numerological formulas were restated, and the dualistic world of good and evil was provided with a new set of characters. Despite these changes the essential apocalyptic message remained as the book taught the living hope of the immediate direct intervention of God to reverse history and to overcome evil with good. Such an outlook brought great comfort to believers who suffered from persecution by the forces of Imperial Rome. Expressed in a form that has been called historic premillennialism, this hope seems to have been the prevailing eschatology during the first three centuries of the Christian era, and is found in the works of Papias, Irenaeus, Justin Martyr, Tertullian, Hippolytus, Methodius, Commodianus, and Lactantius.

Several forces worked to undermine the millennialism of the early church. One of these was the association of the teaching with a radical group, the Montanists, who placed a great stress on a new third age of the Spirit which they believed was coming among their number in Asia Minor. Another influence which encouraged a change of eschatological views was the emphasis of Origen upon the manifestation of the kingdom within the soul of the believer rather than in the world. This resulted in a shift of attention away from the historical toward the spiritual or metaphysical. A final factor that led to a new millennial interpretation was the conversion of the Emperor Constantine the Great and the adoption of Christianity as the favored Imperial religion.

Medieval and Reformation Millennialism. In the new age brought in by the acceptance of Christianity as the main religion of the Roman Empire it was Augustine, Bishop of Hippo, who articulated the amillennial view which dominated Western Christian thought during the Middle Ages. The millennium, according to his interpretation, referred to the church in which Christ reigned with his saints. The statements in the book of Revelation were interpreted allegorically by Augustine. No victory was imminent in the struggle with evil in the world. On the really important level, the spiritual, the battle had already been won and God had triumphed through the cross. Satan was reduced to lordship over the City of the World, which coexisted with the City of God. Eventually even the small domain left to the devil would be taken from him by a triumphant God.

Augustine's allegorical interpretation became the official doctrine of the church during the medieval period. However, in defiance of the main teaching of the church the earlier apocalyptic premillennialism continued to be held by certain counterculture groups. These millenarians under charismatic leaders were often associated with radicalism and revolts. For example, during the eleventh century in regions most affected by urbanization and social change thousands followed individuals such as Tanchelm of the Netherlands, causing great concern to those in positions of power. In the twelfth century Joachim of Fiore gave fresh expression to the millennial vision with his teaching about the coming third age of the Holy Spirit. During the Hussite Wars in fifteenth century Bohemia the Taborites encouraged the resistance to the Catholic Imperial forces by proclaiming the imminent return of Christ to establish his kingdom. These outbreaks of premillennialism continued during the Reformation era and were expressed most notably in the rebellion of the city of Münster in 1534. Jan Matthys gained control of the community, proclaiming that he was Enoch preparing the way for the second coming of Christ by establishing a new code of laws which featured a community of property and other radical reforms. He declared that Münster was the New Jerusalem and called all faithful Christians to gather in the city. Many Anabaptists answered his summons, and most of the original inhabitants of the town were forced to flee or to live in a veritable reign of terror. The situation was so threatening to other areas of Europe that a combined Protestant and Catholic force laid siege to the place and after a difficult struggle captured the town, suppressing the wave of millennial enthusiasm.

Perhaps the Münster episode led the Protestant Reformers to reaffirm Augustinian amillennialism. Each of the three main Protestant traditions of the sixteenth century—Lutheran, Calvinist, and Anglican—had the support of the state and so continued the same Constantinian approach to theology. Both Luther and Calvin were very suspicious of millennial speculation. Calvin declared that those who engaged in calculations based on the apocalyptic portions of Scripture were "ignorant" and "malicious." The major statements of the various Protestant bodies such as the Augsburg Confession (1, xvii), the Thirty-nine Articles (IV), and the Westminster Confession (chs. 32, 33), although professing faith in the return of Christ, do not support apocalyptic millenarian speculation. In certain respects, however, the Reformers inaugurated changes which would lead to a revival of interest in premillennialism. These include a more literal approach to the interpretation of Scripture, the identification of the papacy with Antichrist, and an emphasis on Bible prophecy.

Modern Millennialism. It was during the seventeenth century that premillennialism of a more scholarly nature was presented. Two Reformed theologians, Johann Heinrich Alsted and Joseph Mede, were responsible for the renewal of this outlook. They did not interpret the book of Revelation in an allegorical manner but rather understood it to contain the promise of a literal kingdom of God to be established on earth before the last judgment. During the Puritan Revolution the writings of these men encouraged others to look for the establishment of the millennial kingdom in England. One of the more radical of these groups, the Fifth Monarchy Men, became infamous for their insistence on the reestablishment of OT law and a reformed government for England. The collapse of the Cromwellian regime and the restoration of the Stuart monarchy discredited premillennialism. Yet the teaching continued into the eighteenth century through the work of Isaac Newton, Johann Albrecht Bengel, and Joseph Priestley.

As the popularity of premillennialism waned, postmillennialism rose to prominence. First expressed in the works of certain Puritan scholars, it received its most influential formulation in the writings of the Anglican commentator Daniel Whitby. It seemed to him that the kingdom of God was coming ever closer and that it would arrive through the same kind of effort that had always triumphed in the past. Among the many theologians and preachers who were convinced by the arguments of Whitby was Jonathan Edwards. Edwardsean postmillennialism also emphasized the place of America in the establishment of millennial conditions upon the earth.

During the nineteenth century premillennialism became popular once again. The violent uprooting of European social and political institutions during the era of the French Revolution encouraged a more apocalyptic climate of opinion. There was also a revival of interest in the fortunes of the Jews. A new element was added to premillennialism during this period with the rise of dispensationalism. Edward Irving, a Church of Scotland minister who pastored a congregation in London, was one of the outstanding leaders in the development of the new interpretation. He published numerous works on prophecy and organized the Albury Park prophecy conferences, thus setting the pattern for other gatherings of premillenarians during the nineteenth and twentieth centuries. Irving's apocalyptic exposition found support among the Plymouth Brethren and led many in the group to become enthusiastic teachers of dispensational premillennialism.

Perhaps the leading early dispensational expositor among the Brethren was John Nelson Darby. He believed that the second coming of Christ consisted of two stages, the first a secret rapture or "catching away" of the saints which would remove the church before a seven-year period of tribulation devastates the earth, and the second when Christ appears visibly with his saints after the tribulation to rule on earth for a thousand years. Darby also taught that the church was a mystery of which only Paul wrote and that the purposes of God can be understood as working through a series of periods, or dispensations, in each of which God dealt with people in unique ways.

Most premillennialists during the early nineteenth century were not dispensationalists, however. More typical of their number was David Nevins Lord, who edited a quarterly journal, *The Theological and Literary Review,* which appeared from 1848 to 1861. This periodical contained articles of interest to premillennialists and helped to elaborate a nondispensational system of prophetic interpretation. Lord believed that a historical explanation of the book of Revelation was preferable to the futurist outlook which characterized the dispensational view. This approach was followed by most premillennialists in the United States until after the Civil War, when dispensationalism spread among their number. Darby's interpretation was accepted because of the work of individuals such as Henry Moorhouse, a Brethren evangelist, who convinced many interdenominational speakers to accept dispensationalism. Typical of those who came to believe in Darby's eschatology were William E. Blackstone, "Harry" A. Ironside, Arno C. Gaebelein, Lewis Sperry Chafer, and C. I. Scofield. It is through Scofield and his works that dispensationalism became the norm for much of American evangelicalism. His *Scofield Reference Bible,* which made the new eschatological interpretation an integral part of an elaborate system of notes printed on the same pages as the text, proved so popular that it sold over three million copies in fifty years. Bible schools and seminaries such as Biola, Moody Bible Institute, Dallas Theological

Seminary, and Grace Theological Seminary, along with the popular preachers and teachers who have utilized the electronic media, have made this interpretation popular among millions of conservative Protestants. The new view replaced the older premillennial outlook to such an extent that when George Ladd restated the historic interpretation in the midtwentieth century it seemed like a novelty to many evangelicals.

While the various forms of premillennialism competed for adherents in nineteenth century America, a form of postmillennialism that equated the United States with the kingdom of God became very popular. Many Protestant ministers fed the fires of nationalism and Manifest Destiny by presenting the coming of the golden age as dependent upon the spread of democracy, technology, and the other "benefits" of Western civilization. Perhaps the most complete statement of this civil millennialism was presented by Hollis Read. Ordained to the Congregational ministry in Park Street Church, Boston, he served as a missionary to India but was forced to return to the United States because of his wife's poor health. In a two-volume work, *The Hand of God in History,* he attempted to prove that God's millennial purposes were finding fulfillment in America. He believed that geography, politics, learning, the arts, and morality all pointed to the coming of the millennium to America in the nineteenth century. From this base the new age could spread to the entire earth. As Ps. 22:27 stated, "All the ends of the earth shall remember and turn to the Lord; and all the families of the nations shall worship before him." In order to accomplish the purpose of global evangelism Read favored imperialism because the extension of Anglo-Saxon control over other nations ensured the spread of the gospel. He cited the prevalence of the English language, which made it easier to preach the Word and to teach the native people the more civilized Western culture, as one example of the benefits of Western control. Technological improvements such as the steam press, the locomotive, and the steamship were also given by God to spread enlightenment and the Christian message to all peoples.

Whenever the United States has faced a time of crisis, there have been those who have revived civil postmillennialism as a means to encourage and comfort their fellow citizens. The biblical content of this belief has become increasingly vague as the society has become more pluralistic. For example, during the period of the Civil War many agreed with Julia Ward Howe's "Battle Hymn of the Republic," which described God as working through the Northern forces to accomplish his ultimate purpose. President Wilson's crusade to "make the world safe for democracy," which led his country into World War I, was based upon a postmillennial vision that gave American ideals the major role in establishing peace and justice on earth. Since World War II several groups have revived civil millennialism to counter communism and to resist domestic changes such as those brought about by the moves for equal rights for women.

In addition to the premillennial, amillennial, and postmillennial interpretations there have been groups such as the Shakers, the Seventh-day Adventists, the Jehovah's Witnesses, and the Latter-day Saints (Mormons) who tend to equate the activities of their own sect with the coming of the millennium. There are also movements including the Nazis and the Marxists who teach a kind of secular millennialism when they speak of the Third Reich or the classless society.

R. G. Clouse

Bibliography. R. G. Clouse, ed., *The Meaning of the Millennium: Four Views;* E. R. Sandeen, *The Roots of Fundamentalism;* G. E. Ladd, *The Blessed Hope;* A. Reese, *The Approaching Advent of Christ;* N. West, *Studies in Eschatology;* R. Anderson, *The Coming Prince;* W. E. Blackstone, *Jesus Is Coming;* R. Pache, *The Return of Jesus Christ;* C. C. Ryrie, *Dispensationalism Today;* J. F. Walvoord, *The Millennial Kingdom;* L. Boettner, *The Millennium;* D. Brown, *Christ's Second Coming;* J. M. Kik, *An Eschatology of Victory;* O. T. Allis, *Prophecy and the Church;* A. A. Hoekema, *The Bible and the Future;* P. Mauro, *The Seventy Weeks and the Great Tribulation;* G. Vos, *The Pauline Eschatology.*

Miller, William (1782–1849). *See* Adventism.

Mind. A concept that is usually defined in contrast with the concept of body. The two terms have received their meanings in the context of lengthy metaphysical disagreements. Thus it is difficult, if not impossible, to define mind in isolation from the theories in which the controversy has been historically embedded. Most modern theories of mind have arisen in response to the views of Descartes.

What Is Mind? Plato was the first to make the distinction between mind and body. The mind was capable of existence before and after its relationship to the body, and was able to rule over the body during its residence. Aristotle proposed a different solution, one that grew out of his understanding of form and matter. What is form in one sense may be matter in another. The physical body is matter in relation to the soul, which is the form of the body. This view was influential during the Middle Ages and was held by Thomas Aquinas and many scholastics.

It was Descartes who first sought to systematically work out the nature and interrelationship of mind and body. The most important views on the nature of mind are given below.

Mental Substance Theory. Body and mind were both substances for Descartes. They were, however, utterly different in nature. Body is extended and unthinking. Mind, on the other hand, is unextended and thinking. Body was the more original and lasting. Mind is mental substance or pure ego. It is an enduring, immaterial, nonextended stuff that changes in the performance of certain acts. Mental acts are all acts of thinking, broadly defined. These acts included doubting, understanding, conceiving, affirming, denying, willing, refusing, imagining, and feeling. Mental substance, since its essence is to think, is always engaged in one of these acts.

The central objection to this view is the inability to give any content to the notion of a substance. Even Locke, who accepted it, admitted that it was an idea of a something-I-know-not-what, which acts in some-way-I-know-not-how. Hume rejected the notion as without meaning. Kant in the paralogisms argued that the notion of substance is based on the confusion of the need for a logical subject for all judgments with a metaphysical determination that some absolute subject exists.

Bundle Theory. This alternative was advocated by Hume. It is called the bundle theory because he views the mind as nothing more than a bundle or collection of perceptions, which follow one another with incredible rapidity and are in constant flux and movement. If all these perceptions were removed, there would not be an enduring substructure. There would be nothing. Hume suggested that these perceptions are related to one another by resemblance, contiguity, and causation, but finally had to admit that he failed to explain the simplicity and identity of the mind. Other conditions for the unity of the perceptions, such as memory, have been advanced, but none have withstood criticism.

Stream-of-Consciousness Theory. William James developed a position somewhere between the mental substance and the bundle theories. Mind is a "stream of consciousness." This view, however, has not resolved the difficulties of definition, because there are states of unconsciousness that are related to the mind. If the stream continues during these states, then there must be some substance. If it does not, then the problem of relating the separate segments becomes the same as in the bundle theory.

The Essence of the Mental. Because of the inability to define what mind is, many philosophers reject talk about minds for mental facts, states, properties, acts, and events. The meaning of such things can be roughly stated by the way in which they are used in reports. From examining these reports it is possible to set out the distinguishing characteristics of the mental.

A popular suggestion for the defining characteristic of the mental is that mental reports are made immediately without inference. This view has been criticized as inadequate in that the same can be said for simple judgments about physical events. For instance, it is possible to judge without inference that one physical event followed another.

This has led to another proposal that the mark of the mental is that reports of mental acts are incorrigible. This means that reports of mental acts are not open to correction in terms of other experience. This is held to be true because the one giving the report has "privileged access" to these events. The objection to this position is that such reports are often corrected by the one reporting or by others.

Franz Brentano argued that the distinctive mark of the mental is intentionality or "intentional inexistence." That is, it is possible for the mind to make some content, existent or nonexistent in reality, the object of mind. The mind can *imagine* a flying horse or a good book. While this view of the mental is widely held in continental philosophy, it is still a matter of dispute.

The Mind-Body Problem. While there are still problems that remain to be worked out concerning what the mind is and what is distinctive about its activities, nevertheless we possess some notion of what the answer to these questions would be. Thus, it is now possible to ask what the relationship between the mind and body is. While there are many theories on this subject, they may be classified under two headings: monistic and dualistic.

Monistic Theories. What follows is a brief description of the major monistic theories of mind-body relation. What characterizes this group of theories is the attempt to reduce either mind or body to the other entity.

Materialism is the oldest mind-body theory. It is the view that matter is fundamental, and that everything that exists is dependent upon it. In its most extreme form materialism is the position that everything that exists is material. When applied to mental events it means that all statements about mind are synonymous or translatable into statements about physical phenomena. The inability to provide this translation has cast doubt on the tenability of this position.

A more sophisticated form of materialism called identity theory is widely held today. At the heart of this view is the distinction between sense/significance and reference, or connotation and denotation. Mentalistic and physicalistic expressions have different senses or connotations, but will be shown as science advances to have the same physical referent or denotation, most likely states of the brain. An example that is similar from another area of knowledge is that the "morning star" and "evening star" both refer to Venus. There is a *de facto* rather than logical identity. There are at least two objections that make this theory unlikely. Physical events have location, but mental events seem to lack this. Moreover, if mental events are in fact reducible to physical events, then this seems to call into question the privileged position that a subject has with respect to his or her mental acts.

There is a monistic theory which attempts to reduce events in the direction of mind. It is called idealism. Bishop Berkeley held that only minds and their perceptions exist. Thus, to exist is either to be perceived or to be a perceiver. So-called physical objects exist only in the mind as constructions of perceptions. Because of its strongly counterintuitive claims, this position has never had many adherents.

Dualistic Theories. What unites dualistic theories is their emphasis on the fact that mentalistic and physicalistic statements differ not only in meaning but in reference.

Interactionism was given its classical formulation by Descartes. He held that there are two kinds of substances in the world, mental and corporeal. Mental events can sometimes cause physical events and vice versa. Man then is so constituted that events in one (e.g., fear) can cause events in the other (e.g., adrenalin in the blood). Two major objections have been repeatedly raised against interactionism. It is thought to violate the principle of the conservation of matter and energy. If interactionism were true, then physical energy would be lost in the production of mental events and gained when mental events caused physical changes. A second objection arises from the fact that mental and physical events are said to be so dissimilar. If this is so, how can there be any causal connection between them? Neither of these objections, however, has been taken to be decisive by a large group of thinkers.

A second dualistic theory of the mind-body relationship is occasionalism. This view grows out of the Cartesian distinction between mind and body and the insistence on their utter dissimilarity. Occasionalists go beyond Descartes in claiming that because of their similarity, there can be no natural causal connection. Therefore, they propose God as the intermediary link between mind and body. For example, one wills to move one's arm, and that is the occasion for God to cause that one's arm to move. There is no real causality, as God's intervention is necessary for one ball to strike another. God becomes the one true cause. Because of this, occasionalism has never had many adherents.

Parallelism is the theory that mental and physical events are correlated in a regular way but without any causal relationship, direct or indirect. To understand how this might be possible Leibniz suggested two clocks with perfect mechanisms and possessing a preestablished harmony as a model. The major objection to this view is that it runs contrary to established empirical procedures. The harmony between the mind and body is merely accidental. However, from observation in science it can be concluded that a high degree of correlation does not occur accidentally. Chance leads to randomness, not harmony.

An old but attractive dualistic theory is epiphenomenalism. Simply put, epiphenomenalism is the view that causality goes in only one direction, from body to mind. Mental events then are effects, never causes, of physical events. How is it that it sometimes appears that a mental event causes a physical change? That, it is argued, is an illusion.

The mind-body problem has implications for a biblical view of man. Traditionally Christian theologians have been dualistic at a minimum. Dichotomy, the view that man has a material and immaterial part, has been widely accepted. The chief alternative to dichotomy until recently has been trichotomy, which sees man as a triparate: body, soul, and spirit.

More recently it has been popular to talk of a unitary view of man. Such discussions are characteristically ambiguous. It is not clear that unitary is synonymous with monistic. If it is, then there is the question as to what survives death and remains of the person between death and resurrection. A number of the advocates of this view accept annihilation. If, on the other hand, those who hold this view mean only that man functions as a unity (i.e., one cannot disassemble mind and body without destroying man), then mind and body may be different parts of a single whole.

P. D. Feinberg

See also Man, Doctrine of; Dichotomy; Trichotomy.

Bibliography. S. L. Jaki, *Brain, Mind, and Computers;* J. C. Eccles., ed., *Brain and Conscious Experience* and *Facing Reality;* G. N. A. Yesey, ed., *Body and Mind;* E. P. Polten, *Critique of the Psycho-Physical Identity Theory;* D. M. MacKay, *Brains, Machines and Persons.*

Minister. It is the consistent NT teaching that the work of ministers is "for the perfecting of the saints, . . . for the edifying of the body of Christ" (Eph. 4:12). The minister is called of God to a position of responsibility rather than privilege, as the words for "minister" show (*diakonos*, "table waiter"; *hypēretēs*, "under-rower" in a large ship; *leitourgos*, "servant," usually of the state or a temple).

There are two passages in the NT which are of especial importance in this connection, I Cor. 12:28 and Eph. 4:11–12. From the former we gather that included in the ministries exercised in the early church were those of apostleship, prophecy, teaching, miracles, gifts of healings, helps, governments, diversities of tongues (possibly also interpretations, vs. 30). The latter adds evangelists and pastors. In every case these appear to be the direct gift of God to the church. Both passages seem to say this, and this is confirmed elsewhere in the case of some of the people mentioned. Thus in Gal. 1:1 Paul insists that his apostolate was in no sense from man. He entirely excludes the possibility of his receiving it by ordination. We are to think, then, of a group of men directly inspired by the Holy Spirit to perform various functions within the church by way of building up the saints in the body of Christ.

But there are others also. Thus from early days the apostles made it a habit to appoint elders. Some hold that the seven of Acts 6 were the first elders. This seems very unlikely, but there were certainly elders at the Council of Jerusalem (Acts 15). It is very striking that even on their first missionary journey Paul and Barnabas appointed elders "in every church" (Acts 14:23). There is every reason for thinking that these men were ordained with the laying on of hands, as in the case of the elders of the Jewish synagogue. Then there were the deacons of whom we read in Phil. 1:1 and I Tim. 3:8ff. We know nothing of their method of appointment, but it is likely that it also included the laying on of hands, as it certainly did somewhat later in the history of the church.

It is sometimes said that the first group of ministers is opposed to the second in that they possessed a direct gift from God. This, however, cannot be sustained. In Acts 20:28 we read, "the Holy Ghost has made you bishops," and in I Tim. 4:14 of "the gift that is in thee, which was given thee by prophecy, with the laying on of the hands of the presbytery." It is clear that the act of ordination was not thought of as in opposition to a gift from God, but as itself the means of the gift from God. Indeed the only reason that a man might minister adequately was that God had given him the gift of ministering. The picture we get then is of a group of ministers who had been ordained, men like bishops and deacons, and side by side with them (at times no doubt the same people) those who had a special gift of God in the way of prophecy, apostleship, or the like. The meaning of some of those gifts has long since perished (e.g., prophecy, apostleship). But they witness to the gifts that God gave his church in the time of its infancy.

There are some who think of the ministry as constitutive of the church. They emphasize that Christ is the head of the body, and that he gives it apostles, prophets, etc., that it may be built up. They infer that the ministry is the channel through which life flows from the head. This does, however, seem to be reading something into the passage. It is better to take realistically the NT picture of the church as the body of Christ, as a body, moreover, with a diversity of functions. The life of Christ is in it, and the divine power puts forth whatever is needed. In the Spirit-filled body there will emerge such ministerial and other organs as are necessary. On this view the ministry is essential, but no more essential than any other function of the body. And it preserves the important truth that the body is that of Christ, who does what he wills within it. His blessing is not confined to any particular channel.

L. MORRIS

See also CHURCH OFFICERS; MINISTRY; ORDAIN, ORDINATION.

Bibliography. H. B. Swete, *Early History of the Church and Ministry;* J. B. Lightfoot, *Commentary on Philippians;* K. E. Kirk, ed., *The Apostolic Ministry;* T. W. Manson, *The Church's Ministry;* S. Neil, ed., *The Ministry of the Church;* L. Morris, *Ministers of God;* D. T. Jenkins, *The Gift of Ministry;* M. Green, *Called to Serve;* J. K. S. Reid, *The Biblical Doctrine of the Ministry;* E. Schweizer, *Church Order in the NT.*

Ministry. The biblical concept of ministry is service rendered to God or to people. Ministry in the church has as its goal the edification of individuals with a view toward corporate maturity in Christ (Eph. 4:7–16).

The concept of ministry as service is seen in the words *diakoneō* ("serve") and *douleuō* ("serve as a slave") and their corresponding nouns. The word *hypēretēs* indicates one who gives willing service to another—e.g., servants of the "word" (Luke 1:2), of Christ (John 18:36; Acts 26:16; I Cor. 4:1), and of Paul and Barnabas (Acts 13:5).

The word *leitourgia* and its corresponding verb, *leitourgeō*, often refer to the priestly service of the OT. They are used figuratively in the NT to indicate financial "ministry" (Rom. 15:27; II Cor. 9:12) and the pouring out of Paul's life sacrificially in his ministry (Phil. 2:17). This terminology describes Christian service in general, but in the postapostolic period it is increasingly applied to the distinctive service of clergy as the Christian counterpart to the OT Levitical ministers. This is seen in I Clement and in the Apostolic Constitutions.

Types of ministry seen in Scripture include the service of priests and Levites in the OT, of apostles, prophets, evangelists, and pastor-teachers in the NT, along with the general ministry of elders and the individual mutual ministries of all believers. The term "ministry" therefore refers to the work both of those commissioned to leadership and of the whole body of believers.

The ideals of ministry are portrayed in the servant-leadership of Christ. Acts 6:3 provides guidelines as to the spiritual qualities sought in leaders, and I Tim. 3:1–13 (cf. Titus 1:6–9) specifies the necessary qualities in greater detail.

There is a considerable difference of opinion regarding the historical development of ministry in the NT and in the early church. Many have seen a development from a simple charismatic ministry, exercised by every Christian in an individual way, to an organized or "official" ministry restricted to a few, ultimately issuing in the monarchial episcopate in the postapostolic period. The Reformation reversed this trend to a degree. From time to time in the history of the church and again in recent times various groups have emphasized the charismatic aspect of ministry. Most recently, concepts of ministry have been modified by such diverse movements as the worker priests, the stress on lay leadership and ministries, the development of multiple church staffs, and the modern charismatic movement.

It is far from certain, however, that the NT church experienced a linear development from charismatic to institutional ministry, and even less plausible that there was an antithesis in the early church between these two forms of ministry such as postulated by E. Käsemann and others. It is true that there is little indication in most of Paul's letters of an institutional ministry, and that elders and deacons are mentioned mainly in the Pastorals (often considered non-Pauline) and Acts (often considered an "early catholic" work). However, the mention in Phil. 1:1 of elders and deacons accords with the picture in Acts of Paul ordaining elders in every church. Also the passages in the Pastorals concerning elders and deacons stress their character and function, not their "office." Further, the specific function exercised by elders, deacons, apostles, prophets, evangelists, and pastor-teachers is never set over against, or intended to eclipse, the mutual ("one another") ministries of the individual Spirit-gifted believers.

There are a number of additional issues surrounding the theology of ministry. These include (1) whether the NT ever described a prerequisite "call" to ministry other than the general commands of Christ and the recognition of the local church; (2) whether women were admitted to ministry in the NT (and consequently should be today); (3) whether life style (e.g., homosexuality) or prior experiences such as divorce should preclude ministry; and (4) what honor and authority should accrue to "full-time" ministers of Christ above those which belong to any faithful follower of the Lord. Some of these questions revolve around the institutional aspect of ministry. A further question is whether there is a sacramental aspect to ministry which is restricted to those ordained as priests by the church.

A dual view of ministry—i.e., that all believers were to exercise a ministry in accordance with their spiritual gift, but that authoritative teaching, leadership, and discipline were limited to a recognized body of elders—paves the way for an answer to the above questions. Paul restricted women from authoritative teaching positions, for example (I Tim. 2:12), but the universal testimony of both the OT and NT is that they exercised a variety of significant ministries. There are some significant instances also of women leaders in the early centuries of the church. Whether Paul's restrictions were intended to apply beyond the time when the NT was completed and when all ministries were more regulated is open to question. Ministry, by whatever persons and in whatever form, is essentially a continuation of the servant ministry of the Lord Jesus Christ. In Protestant evangelicalism it is also largely a ministry of the Word of God. The purpose of ministry extends, of course, even beyond the edification of the church. It is, as in all Christian activity, the glory of God.

W. L. Liefeld

See also Church Officers; Minister; Ordain, Ordination.

Bibliography. P. Achtemeier, "The Ministry of Jesus in the Synoptic Gospels," *Int* 35:157–69; H. W. Beyer, *TDNT,* II, 81–93; F. J. A. Hort, *The Christian Ecclesia;* J. B. Lightfoot, "The Christian Ministry," in *Saint Paul's Epistle to the Philippians;* T. M. Lindsay, *The Church and the Ministry in the Early Centuries;* T. W. Manson, *The Church's Ministry;* J. K. S. Reid, *The Biblical Doctrine of the Ministry;* E. Schillebeeckx, *Ministry;* E. Schweizer, *Church Order in the NT;* E. E. Shelp and A. Sunderland, eds., *A Biblical Basis for Ministry;* H. Strathmann, *TDNT,* IV, 215–31; H. B. Swete, ed., *Essays on the Early History of the Church and the Ministry.*

Minor Orders. Those orders of ministry below the major orders in the Roman and Orthodox churches. In the former, subdeacons were usually reckoned as a minor order until they were officially classed as a major order in 1207. The minor orders since then are acolytes, exorcists, readers or lectors, and doorkeepers or porters.

In the Eastern church acolytes, exorcists, and doorkeepers have been merged with the subdiaconate, but readers and cantors remain. The functions of the acolyte were lighting the candles, carrying them in procession, preparing the water and wine for the Holy Communion, and generally assisting the higher orders. The exorcist originally was concerned with casting out demons. Later he looked after the catechumens. The reader, or lector, as his name denotes, read from the Scriptures. The doorkeeper, or porter, originally had the duty of excluding unauthorized persons.

Nowadays practically nothing of the functions of any of the minor orders survives. They are little more than a steppingstone to the higher orders and are all conferred at the one time. They are conferred usually by the bishop (though others on occasion may do so). There is no laying on of hands, but some symbol of office is delivered—e.g., a candlestick for the acolyte, a key for the doorkeeper. L. Morris

See also Church Officers; Major Orders.

Miracles. It is sometimes claimed that the culture of the late twentieth century is "post-Christian." Those who put forward this claim point out that while the presuppositions and concepts of the historic Christian faith remain intelligible to modern man, they are no longer foundational to our world view. They claim that man has now "come of age," that we now have a scientific and empirical world view that is obviously linked up with reality and which cannot take miracles seriously. In fact, this perspective finds the biblical emphasis on miracles to be somewhat offensive.

It is clear that orthodox Christians cannot accept this world view with its suspicion of miracles. Belief in miracles lies at the heart of authentic Christian faith. Without the miracle of the first Easter, Christianity would no doubt long since have passed from the scene, and would certainly not be around to offend the "modern" man.

It should be equally clear, however, that this world view is a part of the cultural milieu in which modern Christians find themselves. Understanding the role of miracles in the genesis and spread of our faith is therefore an imperative for today's Christian.

Unlike the modern world, the ancient world was not suspicious of miracles. They were regarded as a normal, if somewhat extraordinary, part of life. Ancient people typically believed not only that supernatural powers existed, but also that they intervened in human affairs. Miracles, then, did not present a problem to the early Christians as they attempted to explain and relate their faith to the culture around them.

In understanding miracles it is important to bear in mind that the biblical concept of a miracle is that of an event which runs counter to the observed processes of nature. The word "observed" is particularly important here. This was emphasized as early as Augustine, who stated in his *City of God* that Christians must not teach that miracles are events which run counter to nature, but rather that they are events which run counter to *what is known* of nature. Our knowledge of nature is a limited knowledge. Clearly there may be higher laws which remain unknown to man. In any case, miracles are not correctly conceived of as irrational disruptions of the pattern of nature, but as only the known part of that pattern. This understanding of the biblical conception may well erode some of contemporary man's objections to miracles. It is purely a corrective to the erroneous view that miracles are complete violations of nature.

Biblical miracles have a clear objective: they are intended to bring the glory and love of God into bold relief. They are intended, among other things, to draw man's attention away from the mundane events of everyday life and direct it toward the mighty acts of God.

In the context of the OT, miracles are viewed as the direct intervention of God in human affairs, and they are unquestionably linked to his redemptive activity on behalf of man. They help to demonstrate that biblical religion is not concerned with abstract theories about God's power, but with actual historical manifestations and experiences of that power. The most significant miracle of the OT is God's action on behalf of the Hebrews in opening up the Red Sea as they escaped the Egyptians. This miracle is the centerpiece of Hebrew history and of OT religion. It is a demonstration of God's power and love in action. And this action became the theme of much of the Hebrew religion and literature which came after it. It was the Hebrew view that man does not know the being of God so much as he knows the acts of God. God is therefore known as he acts on man's behalf, and the miracle at the Red Sea is the paradigm of God's acting.

This emphasis on miracles as the redemptive activity of God is continued in the NT, where they are a part of the proclamation of the good news that God has acted ultimately on man's behalf in the coming of Jesus Christ into history. Miracles are a manifestation of the power that God will use to restore all of creation to its proper order, to restore the image of God in man to its full expression, and to destroy death. Again we see the theme of biblical religion as centered not on theory but on action.

The central miracle of the NT, indeed of the Judeo-Christian Scriptures, is the resurrection of Christ. Every book in the NT canon either proclaims or assumes the resurrection of Christ on the third day after his crucifixion. It is discussed thoroughly in each Gospel and is declared by Paul in I Cor. 15 to be the keystone of Christian faith. The reference to it in I Corinthians is much earlier (in date) than those of the Gospels.

When the ancient acceptance of miracles is considered along with the wholly depressing circumstances surrounding the ending of Jesus' mission on the first Good Friday, it can be seen that the best evidence for the resurrection is the existence, energy, and growth of the early church itself. After the crucifixion the apostles were utterly defeated persons, and their movement was sputtering to a humiliating stop. They were completely without hope after watching Jesus die as a criminal. Yet within a few weeks these same men were boldly proclaiming Christ's resurrection to the very people who had brought about the condemnation of Christ. They were preaching that Jesus was the risen Lord to any and to all. And these apostles were normal, rational, sane men. Individually and corporately they had undergone a dramatic change after the crucifixion—from depressed, insecure, and despairing men to confident and bold preachers. Surely it is reasonable, on almost any criterion of reasonableness, to consider that witnessing the risen Christ was what brought about this dramatic change. It should also be noted that one of the earliest acts of Christian worship was the breaking of bread with its attendant symbolism of Christ's broken body. This phenomenon would be unexplainable without the knowledge of the risen Christ—unless, that is, one wishes to dismiss the early apostles as irrational masochists, which they clearly were not.

It should be clear then that the central miracle of NT religion is the resurrection of Christ. Without this miracle the early church would not have come into being, and we who live in the twentieth century would no doubt never have heard of the other NT miracles. Indeed, we would probably never have heard of Jesus of Nazareth, who would have been forgotten along with hundreds of other obscure preachers and miracle workers who wandered about the ancient Middle East.

The Gospels teach that the significance of all the miracles of Christ is that they are the prophesied works of the Messiah. The miracles are signs rather than merely wonderful works. They are, however, signs only to those who have the spiritual discernment to recognize them as such. Without the enlightenment that accompanies Christian commitment they are only "wonders," or wonderful works, and their true theological significance cannot be recognized.

Belief in the biblical miracles has always been a central feature of Christian faith, and this remains the case in the twentieth century. Christian faith is informed by the revelation of God to man in Scripture and in the mighty acts recorded there. Christian faith is not to be conformed to the culture around it but is intended to be a transforming influence in the midst of its cultural milieu. The continuing work of the church in the world may itself be viewed as evidence for the truth of the biblical concept of miracle. Certainly the Christian's experience of God as Redeemer and Sustainer is the experience of miracle. It renders the posture of skepticism untenable.

J. D. Spiceland

Bibliography. C. S. Lewis, *Miracles;* C. F. D. Moule, *Miracles;* H. H. Farmer, *Are Miracles Possible?* H. S. Box, *Miracles and Critics;* A. C. Headlam, *The Miracles of the NT;* E. M. L. Keller, *Miracles in Dispute;* R. M. Burns, *The Great Debate on Miracles;* J. B. Mozley, *Eight Lectures on Miracles.*

Miracles, Gift of. *See* Spiritual Gifts.

Missiology. The term has been variously defined as "the science of the cross-cultural communication of the Christian faith," as "preeminently the scholarly discipline underlying the task of world evangelization," and as "the field of study which researches, records and applies data relating to the biblical origins and history of the expansion of the Christian movement to anthropological principles and techniques for its further advancement."

If missiology is described as a science, it must be recognized as an applied science. The underlying dynamic of the missiological process starts with an actual field situation confronting a church or mission, in which its problems, successes, and failures are clearly known; it ends with the application of missiological perspectives to this same field situation.

The three major disciplines whose input is essential to the missiological process are theology (mainly biblical), anthropology (mainly social, applied, and theoretical but including primitive religion, linguistics, cultural dynamics, and cultural change), and history. Other contributing disciplines include psychology, communication theory, and sociology. All these disciplines interact within the specific structures and problems of the given field situation and with the motivation of the gospel as the driving force of that interaction. Therefore, basic components that later become "missiology" are neither theology nor history, neither anthropology nor psychology, nor the sum total of these fields of study. Hence ethnotheology, ethnohistory, and ethnopsychology emerge. The discipline of missiology then comes into its own, enriched and influenced by such ingredients as ecumenics, non-Christian religion, and even economics.

Major Issues. Missiology is a new discipline with a long history. At no period in its history has the church either totally forgotten its missionary task or failed to engage in a measure of serious reflection on the basic questions which this has raised. In one way or another Christians in every generation have debated these five issues:

Apostolic Practice. How is the apostolicity of the church to be expressed if it is conceived as embracing the evangelistic practice of the apostles as well as their "received" teaching? What is the church's collective responsibility touching the sending forth of laborers to "bring about the obedience of faith . . . among all the nations" (Rom. 1:5)?

Church Structure and Mission. What is the relation between the church's structured congregations, ruled by its ecclesiastical authorities, and those mission structures within its life directed by others, whether voluntary or authorized, whereby the gospel is shared with non-Christians and new congregations are planted?

The Gospel and the Religions. What is the relation between the good news about Jesus Christ and other religious systems which do not acknowledge his lordship? Is there validity to the religious experience of their devotees, or do these religions represent unrelieved Godforsakenness and human rebellion?

Salvation and non-Christians. What is the eternal destiny of those who through no fault of their own have died without ever hearing the gospel? What is the relation between Christ's redemptive work and those who, while ignorant of it, have perceived the divine through nature, conscience, and history and have cried out: "God, be merciful to me a sinner"?

Christianity and Culture. If God is the God of the nations and is at work in all the epochs of human history, what is the validity of each separate culture? Should its elements be "possessed" or "accommodated" or "replaced" when the Christian movement enters and local congregations are being structured?

History. These issues have been discussed for almost two thousand years, because the church has always been aware to some degree of its duty to be missionary. One can hardly have a living congregation that is not to some extent missionary, even if its outreach is only along kinship lines and within racial boundaries. But it was two Roman Catholic writers—the Jesuit José de Acosta in 1588 and the Carmelite Thomas à Jesu in 1613—who were the first to develop comprehensive theories of mission, primarily with reference to Latin America. Their writings greatly stimulated a succession of seventeenth century Dutch Protestants largely concerned with the evangelization of the East Indies: Hadrianus Saravia, Justus Heurnius, Gisbertus Voetius, and Johannes Hoornbeeck. In turn, the writings of these men influenced John Eliot, early missionary to the Indians of New England, and William Carey, the "father of modern missions." Through Jan Amos Comenius, bishop of the Moravians in the Low Countries, their influence reached Count von Zinzendorf, who was prominent in the transformation of the Moravians into a dynamic missionary movement.

However, it was not until the nineteenth century that missiology really came into its own as an academic discipline. Two German Lutherans were responsible: Karl Graul, director of the Leipzig Mission, was (according to Otto Lehmann) "the first German to qualify himself for higher academic teaching in this field"; and Gustav Warneck, who today is regarded as the founder of Protestant missionary science. His *Evangelische Missionslehre* (1892) abundantly confirms this designation. Warneck significantly influenced the great Catholic missiologist Josef Schmidlin (1876–1944) and thereby initiated the sort of stimulating interaction between the two major segments of the church that has continued to the present.

Warneck's death virtually coincided with the World Missionary Conference at Edinburgh in 1910. Since then, the gatherings of this conference's stepchildren—the International Missionary Council (until Ghana, 1958) and the Commission on World Mission and Evangelism of the World Council of Churches (after New Delhi, 1961)—have continued to reflect on a great variety of aspects of the science of mission. In recent years nonconciliar evangelicals have increasingly participated in this scholarly debate because of their concern that a biblical theology of the church must make central its missionary calling, a postulate that has been heavily challenged from 1960 onward with the radicalization of ecumenical theology and the increasing secularization of most World Council of Churches member churches in their service in the world.

In recent decades literature on mission theory has greatly increased, with popular polarizations of competing philosophies of mission dominating the scene. Evangelicals are still chided for a mission theology that ignores the kingdom of God and focuses almost entirely on eternal life. Catholics have been charged with triumphalism, allegedly because all they had to advocate was a theology with a single focus: the expansion of the church. (However, during the 1970s large sections of this church have been a dominant force in the struggle for social justice in the Third World.) Conciliar Protestants are accused of being so captured by the immediate social and human issues that they take unwarranted liberty with the Bible and bend its texts until evangelism is reconceptualized to mean politics, the church's obligation to evangelize "unreached peoples" is dismissed as irrelevant, and religious encounter is confined to the sort of friendly conversation that eschews all thoughts of conversion and church planting.

Evangelicals and the Contemporary Debate. In an effort to reduce this cacophony of discordant diversity and develop a coherent basis for a valid scholarly discipline, evangelicals played a prominent role in the organizing of the American Society of Missiology (ASM) at Scarritt College, Nashville, Tennessee, in June of 1972. They recognized the validity and essentiality of the perspectives of all segments of the Christian movement; the study of missiology would lack balance and be impoverished if any one perspective were denied a fair and full hearing. Hence ASM became a community of scholars drawn from conciliar Protestants, Roman Catholics, the Orthodox, and nonconciliar evangelicals.

Within this forum evangelicals seek to stabilize this emerging discipline with their biblical stress on the Christological center: the gospel has at its heart the affirmation that Jesus Christ alone is Lord and that he offers to enter the lives of all who come to him in repentance and faith. Their overriding concern is the evangelistic task of proclaiming Christ and persuading all peoples everywhere to become his disciples and responsible members of his church. They regard this as a chief and irreplaceable objective in Christian mission. They accent the priority of multiplying structured expressions of the Christian community in which worship can be performed and a supporting *koinonia* deepened and extended. And they encourage the multiplication of voluntary associations (mission structures) to carry out the great variety of tasks God has given to his people.

In addition, evangelicals are increasingly responsive, in the face of the contemporary debate and the anguished cries of the oppressed, to the issues stressed by conciliar Protestants as they call all Christians everywhere to take those priority steps that will demonstrate their authenticity before the world as "salt and light." Their focus is inevitably ecclesiological. They contend that the development of individual and inward faith must be accompanied by a corporate and outward obedience to the cultural mandate broadly detailed in Holy Scripture. The world is to be served, not avoided. Social justice is to be furthered, and the issues of war, racism, poverty, and economic imbalance must become the active, participatory concern of those who profess to follow Jesus Christ. It is not enough that the Christian mission be redemptive; it must be prophetic as well. And it must stress the obligation to express before the world the unity of the people of God. The Christian movement must focus on consolidation while reaching out in expansion.

Roman Catholic and Orthodox missiologists stress the sacramental, liturgical, and mystical ethos that has enriched the church over the centuries. The issues that most concern them are how the church is to fulfill the Vatican II mandate and its essential function as the "Divine Gift," through manifesting and actualizing in this world the eschaton, the ultimate reality of salvation and redemption; how to guarantee that the state, society, culture, and even nature itself are within the real objects of mission; how to achieve truly indigenous congregations; how to enter into the sequence that produces genuine spiritual formation; how to participate in significant and spiritually productive dialogue with the Asian faiths; and how to guard the uniqueness and finality of Jesus Christ while at the same time recognizing that the Christian movement at its best represents what Berdyaev terms "an unfinished revelation about the absolute significance and calling of man."

Missiologists of these three streams of insight into biblical obligation are committed to listen honestly to each other. And this bodes well for missiology as a still-developing "science," "discipline," and "separate field of study." As it becomes more sharply differentiated, and its concepts and tools are better mastered, it will become an increasingly useful instrument to further the understanding and performance of the Christian mission in our day.

Outstanding American evangelical missiologists have been Rufus Anderson, the nineteenth century popularizer of the indigenous church ("Missions are instituted for the spread of a Scriptural, self-propagating Christianity"); Kenneth Scott Latourette and R. Pierce Beaver, two outstanding authorities on the history of missions and younger churches; Donald A. McGavran, the founder of the Church Growth movement;

Eugene A. Nida, the expert on Bible translation and the cross-cultural communication of the Christian faith; J. Herbert Kane, the prolific writer of primary texts on all aspects of the Christian mission; and George W. Peters, the creative biblical theologian in the Mennonite tradition.

A. F. Glasser

See also Warneck, Gustav Adolf.

Bibliography. C. W. Forman, "A History of Foreign Mission Theory in America," in *American Missions in Bicentennial Perspective,* ed. R. P. Beaver; A. F. Glasser, "Missiology—What's It all About?" *MissRev* 6:3–10; J. Glazik, "Missiology," in *Concise Dictionary of the Christian World Mission;* O. G. Myklebust, *The Study of Missions in Theological Education,* 2 vols.; J. Verkuyl, *Contemporary Missiology: An Introduction.*

Modalism. *See* Monarchianism.

Moderator. *See* Church Officers.

Modernism. *See* Liberalism, Theological.

Modernism, Catholic. *See* Catholicism, Liberal.

Moltmann, Jürgen. *See* Hope, Theology of.

Monarchianism. In its most general sense monarchianism (also called patripassianism or Sabellianism) refers to the primarily Western attempts in the third century to defend monotheism against suspected tritheism by denying the personal distinctiveness of a divine Son and Holy Spirit in contrast to God the Father. The term is first used by Tertullian to describe those who desired to protect the monarchy (of the one God) from improper thoughts about the economy (of the three: the Father, Son, and Holy Spirit). There were two forms of monarchianism which were not only distinctly independent but even opposed to each other.

Dynamic, or adoptionistic, monarchianism proposed a monotheism of God the Father in relation to which Jesus was viewed as a mere man who was endowed with the Holy Spirit. This view was first put forward in Rome about 190 by Theodotus of Byzantium and continued by his successor, Artemon (also called Theodotus), who tried to argue that this teaching was the heir of the apostolic tradition. Artemon was refuted by Hippolytus, who condemned the teaching as an innovative attempt to rationalize the Scripture according to the systems of hellenic logic (most likely that taught by the physician and philosopher Galen).

Although there has been some disagreement on exactly how to classify him, it seems most likely that Paul of Samosata held to a more advanced form of this dynamic monarchianism. He depersonalized the Logos as simply the inherent rationality of God, which led him to formulate a doctrine of the *homoousia* of the Logos and the Father which necessarily denied the personal subsistence of the preincarnate Word. It was for this reason that both his teaching as a whole and the use of the word *homoousia* were condemned by the Synod of Antioch in 268. Also in working out the consistency of the dynamic monarchian position, Paul taught that the Holy Spirit was not a distant personal entity but simply a manifestation of the grace of the Father.

Although in basic agreement with dynamic monarchianism on the foundational issue of limiting the term *theos* to the person of the Father alone, modalistic monarchianism, also known simply as modalism, nevertheless attempted to speak of the full deity of the Son. The earlier modalists (operating between the second and third centuries), such as Noetus, Epigonus, and Praxeas, achieved this objective by identifying the Son as the Father himself. This led to the charge of patripassianism, which became another label for modalism. Patripassianism is the teaching that it was the Father who became incarnate, was born of a virgin, and who suffered and died on the cross. Praxeas attempted to soften this charge by making a distinction between the Christ who is the Father and the Son who was simply a man. In this way the Father cosuffers with the human Jesus.

A more sophisticated form of modalism was taught by Sabellius in Rome early in the third century and was given the name Sabellianism. Although much of his teaching has been confused historically with that of Marcellus of Ancyra (fourth century), some elements can be reconstructed. It seems that Sabellius taught the existence of a divine monad (which he named *Huiopator*), which by a process of expansion projected itself successively in revelation as Father, Son, and Holy Spirit. As Father it revealed itself as Creator and Lawgiver. As Son it revealed itself as Redeemer. As Spirit it revealed itself as the giver of grace. These were three different modes revealing the same divine person. Sabellius as well as the modalists preceding him shared the same view of the Logos as that of Paul of Samosata. This along with the fact that modalism was much more popular than dynamic monarchianism (so much so that it alone is sometimes simply called monarchianism) is perhaps why Paul is classified by later patristic writers as a modalist.

C. A. Blaising

See also Homoousion; Antiochene Theology; Paul of Samosata.

Bibliography. Eusebius, *Church History* 5.25; 7.27–30; Hippolytus, *Contra Noetum;* Tertullian, *Against Praxeas;* R. Seeberg, *Text-book of the History of Doctrines;* J. N. D. Kelley, *Early Christian Doctrines.*

Monasticism. The origins of early Christian monasticism are not clearly known and are, therefore, subject to controversy. Some scholars believe that the monastic movement was prompted by late Jewish communal and ascetic ideals, such as those of the Essenes. Still others speculate that Manichaean and similar forms of dualism inspired extremes of asceticism within the Christian family. However, the first Christian commentators on monasticism believed that the movement had truly gospel origins.

Christian monastics drew their spiritual strength from Christ's emphasis on poverty (Mark 10:21) and on the "narrow way" (Matt. 7:14) to salvation. Early monastics believed that Paul preferred celibacy to marriage (I Cor. 7:8). Indeed, the first nuns seem to have been widows of the late Roman period who decided not to remarry. From one point of view, the decision of some Christians to live separate from the community, both physically and spiritually, was regrettable. From another, the commitment and service of the monastics made them the most valued people in early medieval society.

The first monks of whom we have a good record represent an extreme phase in the evolution of monasticism. These are the so-called desert fathers, hermits, living in the eremitical style in the deserts of Egypt, Syria, and Palestine. Enraged by sin and fearful of damnation, they left the towns for a solitary struggle against temptation. Some, like Simeon Stylites, lived very exotic lives and became tourist attractions. More typical, however, was Anthony of Egypt (*ca.* 250–356), whose commitment to salvation led him back to the community to evangelize unbelievers. His extreme asceticism deeply touched the sensibilities of the age.

The word "monk" is derived from a Greek word meaning "alone." The question for the desert fathers was one of the lonely, individual struggle against the devil as opposed to the obvious support that came from living in some sort of community. Pachomius (*ca.* 290–346), an Egyptian monk, preferred the latter. He wrote a rule of life for monks in which he emphasized organization and the rule of elder monks over the newly professed. The rule became popular, and the movement toward communal life was ensured. To the idea of community Basil the Great (*ca.* 330–79) added another element. In his writings, and especially in his commentaries on the Scriptures, this father of Eastern monasticism defined a theory of Christian humanism which he felt was binding on the monasteries. According to Basil, monastics were bound to consider their duty to the whole of Christian society. They should care for orphans, feed the poor, maintain hospitals, educate children, even provide work for the unemployed.

During the fourth through the sixth centuries monasticism spread throughout the Christian world. From Asia Minor to Britain its ideal flourished. However, the Celtic monks tended to espouse the old eremitical tradition, whereas Latin monasticism, under the Great Rule of Benedict of Nursia (*ca.* 480–*ca.* 547), codified itself into a permanent, organized communal form. To the old promises of poverty, chastity, and obedience to Christ the Benedictines added stability. Monks could no longer drift about from monastery to monastery but were bound to one for life. The essence of Benedict's rule is its sensible approach to Christian living. It forbade excess and provided practical advice for every aspect of monastery life. It gave an elaborate description of the role of each person in the community from the abbot, who represented Christ in the community, to the lowliest postulant. For this reason the Benedictine Rule became the standard in western Europe. Because of their devotion to the rule, monks came to be known as the "regular" clergy, from the Latin *regula,* "rule."

The great work of the monasteries of the Middle Ages was the *opus Dei,* the work of God, prayer and praise to the Almighty throughout the day and night. This "work" was organized into the offices of the monastic day. These varied somewhat according to place and season, but generally vigils, lauds, terce, sext, vespers, and compline were chanted throughout Christendom. In addition, monks and nuns performed physical labor, provided charitable services, and kept learning alive. They studied and copied the Scriptures and the writings of the church fathers as well as classical philosophy and literature. They were leaders in the so-called Carolingian Renaissance, during which time (eighth–ninth centuries) writing was reformed and the liberal arts defined. In monastic hands writing became an art. The monasteries had a monopoly on education until the evolution of the cathedral school and the university in the High Middle Ages.

Early medieval monasticism may have reached its height in the foundation of the abbey of Cluny in Burgundy in the tenth century. Cluny set a new standard of liturgical splendor. It also sought to escape corruption by establishing its independence from the feudal system in which all medieval institutions were rooted. Cluny and its "daughters" (houses which it founded and disciplined) exercised enormous spiritual authority in the eleventh century. Though it is no longer acceptable to draw direct connections between the Cluniac reform movement and the reform papacy of Gregory VII (1073–85), both represent institutional responses to the rapid changes in medieval society.

By 1100 monasticism was on the defensive. It was no longer clear that monastic service to God and society was commensurate with the praise and gifts which society had lavished on the monasteries. Great donations of land and other forms of wealth made monks rich at a time when other medieval institutions were assuming societal duties formerly the responsibility of the monasteries. The popularity of the monasteries attracted less than devout postulants, and the aristocracy used the great houses as a repository for spinster daughters and younger sons.

Yet even as monasticism approached its crisis, new reformed orders appeared. The Cistercians, under their most influential leader Bernard of Clairvaux, sought a new life of evangelical purity. They confined membership to adults, simplified services, abandoned all feudal obligations, and tried to restore the contemplative life. The Carthusians tried to recapture the old eremitical spirit of the desert fathers. They retreated from society and became an important feature of the medieval frontier, cutting down forests and opening new ground for agriculture. Their role in the evolution of sheep farming and the wood industry was invaluable.

Perhaps the last great revival of monastic spirit came in the autumn of the Middle Ages with the appearance of the mendicant orders. The Dominicans and Franciscans captured the collective imagination of a society in crisis. Francis of Assisi represented the perfection of both monastic and Christian idealism in his effort to imitate the life of Christ in all its purity and simplicity. By taking the apostolic ideal outside the monastery, Francis gave it one last flowering in the culture which had given it birth.

In modern history monasticism has suffered three great blows; the Reformation, the Enlightenment, and twentieth century secularism. Generally, the leaders of the Reformation believed that the monastics did not in fact conform to a simple gospel rule of life, that their repetitive prayers, fasts, and ceremonies were meaningless and that they had no real value to society. The vast wealth which they had accumulated seemed better spent on general public needs. Those monastics who had kept their vows were seen as cut off from true Christian freedom in lives that were futile and unfulfilled. Wherever the Reformation was triumphant, the monasteries were disestablished. In different terms the eighteenth century Enlightenment would also argue that the monasteries were useless. Liberals saw them as corrupt and unnatural, preserving the superstition of the old regime. The twentieth century has seen the rapid decline of religious orders.

C. T. Marshall

See also Basil the Great; Franciscan Order.

Bibliography. C. Brooke, *The Monastic World;* E. C. Butler, *Benedictine Monachism;* O. Chadwick, *Western Asceticism;* K. Hughes, *The Church in Early Irish Society;* D. Knowles, *Christian Monasticism;* J. Leclercq, *The Love of Learning and the Desire for God;* L. J. Lekai, *The Cistercians: Ideals and Reality;* W. Nigg, *Warriors of God.*

Monergism. The position that "the grace of God is the only efficient cause in beginning and effecting conversion." The opposite of synergism, this position is consistently upheld by the Augustinian tradition within Christianity. Representative is the attitude of Martin Luther. Luther believed that salvation was by grace alone through faith, arriving at this position from his study of Rom. 1:16–17. The believing faith that receives this grace is itself the gift of God. In his explanation of the third article of the Creed, Luther commented: "I believe that by my own reason or strength I cannot believe in Jesus Christ, my Lord, or come to him. But the Holy Spirit has called me through the Gospel, enlightened me with his gifts, and sanctified and preserved me in true faith." The same teaching was embodied in his *Bondage of the Will,* where he affirmed, "Man's will is like a beast standing between two riders. If God rides, it wills and does what God wills. . . . If Satan rides, it wills and goes where Satan wills. Nor may it choose to which rider it will run, or which it will seek; but the riders themselves fight to decide who shall have and hold it." Luther regarded repentance as the work of God in man, citing such texts as Acts 5:31 and II Tim. 2:25. While the human will was free in civil matters, concerning spiritual choices it was bound in sin. This view was reflected in the Formula of Concord, which stated that "man of himself, or from his natural powers, cannot contribute anything or help to his conversion, and that conversion is not only in part, but altogether an operation, gift and present and work of the Holy Ghost alone, who accomplishes and effects it, by his virtue and power, through the Word, in the understanding, heart and will of man."

The implication of this doctrine is that if one is saved, it is entirely the work of God; if one is lost, it is entirely the fault of man, who, while not free to accept the gospel, is by nature able to reject it. Calvin developed his theology in a different direction. Like Luther, upholding the sovereignty of God in conversion, Calvin differed from the German Reformer in affirming the perseverance of the saints (Luther felt it was possible to fall from grace) and in teaching that the lost were condemned because God willed them lost (damnation was a theological, not an anthropological, mystery, as it had been for Luther). Differing from both Calvin and Luther was the predominant position of the Roman Catholic Church, that grace plus faith (itself a good work) brought conversion. Later Protestants such as James Arminius and John Wesley stressed human responsibility as well as divine sovereignty in the matter of conversion. C. G. FRY

See also SYNERGISM.

Bibliography. D. W. H. Arnold and C. G. Fry, *The Way, the Truth, and the Life: An Introduction to Lutheran Christianity;* J. T. Mueller, *Christian Dogmatics;* L. Berkhof, *Systematic Theology.*

Money. *See* WEALTH, CHRISTIAN VIEW OF.

Monism. Although the term was first used by German philosopher Christian Wolff (1679–1754), monism is a philosophical position with a long history dating back to the pre-Socratic philosophers who appealed to a single unifying principle to explain all the diversity of observed experience. Notable among these thinkers is Parmenides, who maintained that reality is an undifferentiated oneness, or unity, and that consequently real change or individuality of things is impossible. Monism is a position taken on the metaphysical question, "How many things are there?"

Substantival monism ("one thing") is the view that there is only one substance and that all diversity is ultimately unreal. This view was maintained by Spinoza, who claimed that there is only one substance, or independently existing thing, and that both God and the universe are aspects of this substance. In addition to having many eminent proponents in the Western philosophical tradition, substantival monism is a tenet of Hinduism and Buddhism. In Hinduism each element of reality is part of *maya* or *prakriti,* and in Buddhism all things ultimately comprise an interrelated network.

Attributive monism ("one category") holds that there is one *kind* of thing but many different individual things in this category. Materialism and idealism are different forms of attributive monism. The materialist holds that the one category of existence in which all real things are found is material, while the idealist says that this category is mental. All monisms oppose the dualistic view of the universe, which holds that both material and immaterial (mental and spiritual) realities exist. Attributive monism disagrees with substantival monism in asserting that reality is ultimately composed of many things rather than one thing. Many leading philosophers have been attributive monists, including Bertrand Russell and Thomas Hobbes on the materialistic side, and G. W. Leibniz and George Berkeley in the idealist camp.

The Christian intellectual tradition has generally held that substantival monism fails to do justice to the distinction between God and creature, and that of attributive monisms only idealism is theologically acceptable. D. B. FLETCHER

Bibliography. F. C. Copleston, "Spinoza," in *A History of Philosophy,* IV; F. H. Bradley, *Appearance and Reality;* R. Hall, "Monism and Pluralism," *Encyclopedia of Philosophy;* J. Passmore, *A Hundred Years of Philosophy;* A. M. Quinton, "Pluralism and Monism," in *EncyBrit;* B. Spinoza, *Ethics.*

Monophysitism. Derived from *monos,* "single," and *physis,* "nature," monophysitism is the doctrine which holds that the incarnate Christ had only a single, divine nature, clad in human flesh. It is sometimes called Eutychianism, after Eutyches (d. 454), one of its leading defenders. Since the Council of Chalcedon, which confirmed as orthodox the doctrine of two natures, divine and human, monophysitism has been considered heretical. Its roots probably go back to Apollinaris (*ca.* 370), who laid tremendous stress on the fusion of the divine and human. Alexandria (as opposed to Antioch) became the citadel of this doctrine, and Cyril, although deemed orthodox, furnished fuel for the fire kindled by his successor, Dioscorus, and Eutyches, who denied that Christ's body was the same in essence as the bodies of men. Their chief opponent was Leo I of Rome, whose formulation of the doctrine of two natures in one person triumphed at Chalcedon.

Monophysites tended to divide into two main groups: Julianists, who held to the immortality and incorruptibility of Christ's incarnate body, and the more orthodox Severians, who rejected the Eutychian view that the human and divine were completely mingled in the incarnation. In the remnant of Syrian Jacobites and in the Coptic and Ethiopian churches (and to a limited extent in the Armenian) it survives to the present day. D. A. HUBBARD

See also MONOTHELITISM.

Bibliography. A. A. Luce, *Monophysitism Past and Present;* R. V. Sellers, *Two Ancient Christologies* and *The Council of Chalcedon;* E. R. Hardy, *Christian Egypt: Church and People;* W. H. C. Frend, *The Rise of the Monophysite Movement;* W. A. Wigram, *The Separation of the Monophysites.*

Monotheism. The belief that there is only one God. Related terms are polytheism (the belief that there are many gods), henotheism (belief in one supreme god, though not necessarily to the exclusion of belief in other lesser gods), monolatry (worship of only one god, though not necessarily denying that other gods exist), and atheism (denying or disbelieving in the existence of any gods at all).

Atheism was not particularly attractive to the Israelite people in ancient times. They were convinced that only fools would be so spiritually ignorant as to deny the existence of a supreme being (Pss. 14:1; 53:1). For the people of God, the fear of the Lord was the beginning of wisdom and knowledge (Ps. 111:10; Prov. 1:7; 9:10). But if the Israelites did not doubt that there was at least one God, the nations on their borders faced them with the tantalizing possibility that there might be more than one. Egypt, Phoenicia, Aram, Ammon, Moab, Edom—these and other nations were polytheistic, henotheistic, or monolatrous throughout their history in ancient times. One of the questions raised by the OT is whether Israel would remain monotheistic or be attracted by the religious options preferred by its pagan neighbors.

Students of comparative religion have suggested that the religions of mankind evolved from lower stages to ever higher stages, the highest of all being monotheism. They have proposed that Israelite religion began as animism, the belief that every natural object is inhabited by a supernatural spirit. After animism, we are told, the idea developed in Israel that some spirits were more powerful than others and deserved to be called "gods." Eventually the most powerful of all became preeminent above the others, and the people believed in his supreme authority and worshiped him alone. Finally, Israel became willing to admit that the lesser gods had no existence whatever. Comparative religion, then, often teaches that Israel's religion underwent a process of evolution from animism to polytheism to henotheism to monotheism.

But it cannot be shown that polytheistic religions always gradually reduce the number of their gods, finally arriving at only one. For example, there are innumerable Hindu deities (estimates range from several hundred thousand to 800 million, depending on how deity is defined), and the number seems actually to be increasing. Since a religion may add more and more deities as its followers become aware of more and more natural phenomena to deify, it is just as plausible to assume that polytheism is the end product of evolution from an original monotheism as it is to assume the reverse.

Monotheism and World Religions. Far from having evolved through the centuries of Israel's history, monotheism is an inspired insight revealed by God to his people. The God of the Bible, the Creator of all that exists, stands outside the universe and is not a part of it. Only three modern religions share this viewpoint, and all of them are based on the revealed religion of ancient Israel. (1) Judaism's synagogue services always begin with Deut. 6:4, a creedal statement known as the *Shema:* "Hear, O Israel: The Lord our God, the Lord is one" (emphatically approved by Jesus in Mark 12:28–29). (2) Christianity's greatest apostle defined monotheism in its most classic form in I Tim. 2:5: "There is one God." (3) Islam (Mohammedanism) claims millions of followers who recite this prayer as they prostrate themselves toward Mecca five times a day: "There is no god but God."

Certain other modern religions, such as Zoroastrianism and Sikhism, teach forms of monotheism that are derived from former dualistic or polytheistic systems. Unlike the three religions based on the Bible, they suggest that God is a part of the universe and not separate from it. Only the OT religion and its derivatives proclaim one God who is transcendent by nature and immanent only by condescension and grace (see Isa. 57:15).

Monotheism and the OT. The book of Genesis begins by assuming that there is only one true God, and that assumption is maintained throughout the OT. Against materialism, which teaches that matter is everything and eternal, Gen. 1 teaches that matter had a beginning and that God created it and is therefore above it. Against pantheism, which teaches that God is (or gods are) in everything, Gen. 1 teaches that God is above everything and separate from it. Against dualism, which posits a continuing struggle between two gods or principles (one evil and the other good), Gen. 1 posits one benevolent God who declares each of his creative works to be "good" and summarizes the week of creation by proclaiming it "very good" (Gen. 1:31).

But other alternatives, commonly held by ancient Near Eastern religion in general, influenced the spiritual struggles of the Hebrew people from the patriarchal period and onward. Polytheism characterized Abraham's ancestors (Josh. 24:2), kinsmen (Gen. 31:19), and descendants (Gen. 35:2). Although all three biblically derived monotheistic religions claim Abraham as their founder, Abraham's monotheism was perhaps more practical than theoretical. God monopolized his allegiance to the extent that Abraham had neither room nor time for competing deities, but nowhere in Genesis does he clearly deny their existence.

By contrast, Moses defined the nature of God in a clearly monotheistic fashion (Deut. 4:35, 39; 32:39). The first of the Ten Commandments, "You shall have no other gods before/besides me" (Exod. 20:3; Deut. 5:7), insists that Israel is to have only one object of faith and worship. Elijah on Mount Carmel likewise demanded that the people choose either the Lord or another god (see also Josh. 24:15), because it was both unseemly and unwise to continue to "waver between two opinions" (I Kings 18:21).

The writing prophets of the eighth century B.C. and afterward strengthened monotheistic doctrine by constantly reminding Israel of the vast gulf that separated the Lord from pagan idols and the so-called gods that they represented (Hos. 4:12; Isa. 2:8, 20; 17:8; 31:7; Jer. 10:5, 10). After Jerusalem was destroyed in 586 B.C. the people of Judah forsook idolatry once and for all. The excessive polytheism of Babylon was revolting to the exiles and helped to make the Jews a truly monotheistic people. Judaism today shares with Christianity a firm belief in the Lord's affirmation as mediated through Isaiah: "There is no God apart from me" (Isa. 45:21).

Monotheism and the Trinity. God did not reveal himself in clearly defined Trinitarian terms in the OT. To do so would have provided needless temptations to polytheism in the light of ancient culture. But the OT prepares for the doctrine of the Trinity in several ways: (1) It uses a plural word for God (*'ĕlōhîm*) with singular verbs (Gen. 1:1 and often). (2) It employs various triadic formulas in reference to God (e.g., the three-man visitation of Gen. 18:2, the triple name of the God of the patriarchs in Exod. 3:15 and often, and the thrice-spoken "Holy" of Isa. 6:3). (3) The "angel of God/the Lord" sometimes refers to God as his sender, sometimes speaks as though he himself were God. (4) Father, Spirit, and Word are all active in creation (Gen. 1:1–3; see also John 1:1–3).

Monotheism and the NT. Although the NT affirms Trinitarianism (see, e.g., Matt. 28:19; II Cor. 13:14), it is outspokenly monotheistic as well (see, e.g., Acts 17:22–31). For the NT writers no conflict existed between the teachings that God is one and that at the same time he is three in one. Paul the monotheist can state with confidence that "there is no God but one" (I Cor. 8:4), and in the very next breath, using a partial Trinitarian formula, he can declare with equal confidence that "there is but one God, the Father, from whom all things came and for whom we live; and there is but one Lord, Jesus Christ, through whom all things came and through whom we live" (8:6).

R. Youngblood

See also God, Doctrine of; Trinity; Theism.

Bibliography. P. Lapide and J. Moltmann, *Jewish Monotheism and Christian Trinitarian Doctrine;* W. F. Albright, *From the Stone Age to Christianity;* R. Youngblood, *The Heart of the OT.*

Monothelitism. A heresy especially prevalent in the Eastern church in the seventh century which said that as Christ had but one nature (monophysitism) so he had but one will (Greek *monos,* "alone"; *thelein,* "to will"). Emperor Heraclius attempted to reconcile the monophysite bishops, who held that the human and divine natures in Christ were fused together to form a third, by offering in his *ecthesis* (statement of faith) in 638 the view that Christ worked through a divine-human energy. This compromise was at first accepted by Constantinople and Rome, but Sophronius, soon to be Bishop of Jerusalem, organized the orthodox opposition to monothelitism. A fine defense of the person of Christ as one in two natures with two wills was given by John of Damascus. The Council of Chalcedon had declared that "Christ has two natures." This was now amended by the Council of Constantinople, which declared that Christ had two wills, his human will being subject to his divine will.

W. N. Kerr

See also Monophysitism.

Bibliography. John of Damascus, *Exposition of the Orthodox Faith,* Bk. III, chs. 3–24; A. Harnack, *History of Dogma,* IV, 252–67; A. A. Luce, *Monophysitism;* H. P. Liddon, *The Divinity of Our Lord.*

Montanism. A prophetic movement that broke out in Phrygia in Roman Asia Minor (Turkey) around 172. It attracted a wide following, chiefly in the East, but won its most distinguished adherent in Tertullian. After a period of uncertainty, especially at Rome, it was condemned by synods of bishops in Asia and elsewhere. A residual sect persisted in Phrygia for some centuries.

The main associates of Montanus, who was a recent convert and held no church office, were the prophetesses Prisca (Priscilla) and Maximilla. What they called "the New Prophecy" was basically a summons to prepare for the return of Christ by heeding the voice of the Paraclete speaking, often in the first person, through his prophetic mouthpieces. They claimed to stand in the line of Christian prophecy well attested in Asia—e.g., by John of Revelation—but their ecstatic manner of utterance was (falsely) alleged to run counter to the tradition of Israelite and Christian prophecy. They also incurred the hostility of church leaders by the women's unusual prominence, a boldness that seemed to court martyrdom, their confident predictions of the imminent consummation (shown in time to be false by their nonfulfillment), the hallowing of obscure Phrygian villages like Pepuza as harbingers of the new Jerusalem, and their stern asceticism which disrupted marriages, protracted fasting, and allowed only a dry diet (xerophagy). Nothing strictly heretical could be charged against Montanism. Any link with monarchianism was accidental. Although none of its catholic opponents doubted the continuance of prophecy in the church, Montanism erupted at a time when consolidation of catholic order and conformity to apostolic tradition preoccupied the bishops. The prophets' extravagant pretensions, while not intended to displace the emergent NT of Christian Scripture, were felt to threaten both episcopal and scriptural authority. Recognition of the Paraclete in the New Prophecy was their touchstone of authenticity.

Tertullian, whose religious rigorism graduated naturally to the New Prophecy, neglected some of the more eccentric features of the Phrygian movement, stressing the development of ethics inculcated by the Spirit in fulfillment of Christ's promises in John 14–16. The "greater things" to come from the Paraclete were the more demanding standards of discipline required of spiritual Christians, such as the denial of remarriage to the widowed and of postbaptismal forgiveness for serious sins. The contemporary African *Passion of Perpetua* similarly exalted recent happenings, especially fearless martyrdoms, as evidence of the superabundant grace of the Spirit decreed for the last days. As Tertullian put it, if the devil's ingenuity escalates daily, why should God's work have ceased advancing to new heights? The New Prophecy seemed almost to claim for itself a special place in salvation history.

D. F. Wright

Bibliography. H. von Campenhausen, *Ecclesiastical Authority and Spiritual Power in the Church of the First Three Centuries,* ch. 8, and *The Formation of the Christian Bible;* D. Powell, "Tertullianists and Cataphrygians," *VC* 29:33–54; D. F. Wright, "Why Were the Montanists Condemned?" *Them* 2:15–22.

Moon, Sun Myung. *See* Unification Church.

Moral Argument for God. *See* God, Arguments for the Existence of.

Moral Inability. *See* Depravity, Total.

Moral Influence Theory of Atonement. *See* Atonement, Theories of the.

Moral Rearmament. In our century the tensions between humanitarian and biblical religion are typified in Frank Buchman (1878–1961) and the Oxford Group movement, later known as Moral Rearmament (MRA). After graduating from the Lutheran Theological Seminary at Philadelphia (1902), Buchman spent a graduate year abroad visiting church institutions in Germany dedicated to social welfare and reform. Filled with a passion to help his fellow men, he founded the first Lutheran hospice for young men in this country and later a settlement house in Philadelphia. In 1908 Buchman had a falling out with the board of trustees who supervised his work; they wanted to balance the budget, whereas his concern was to feed the hungry. As a result he resigned in anger, nursing ill will against the six board members.

In poor health because of overwork, Buchman left for England to attend a Keswick conference on the spiritual life. There in a small church in an English village he heard a simple sermon by a lay woman preacher on the meaning of the cross. For the first time he realized the yawning abyss that separated him from the suffering Christ, and he was convicted of sin—"selfishness, pride, ill-will." He emerged from this life-renewing experience no longer a divided, tormented soul but now devoted exclusively to the service of his Savior and Master. Set free from his resentment against the six members of his board, he proceeded to write to each one individually asking for forgiveness. Though receiving no reply from any of these men, he at once experienced a sense of relief.

Before his conversion Buchman was a humanitarian dedicated to the welfare of his fellow human beings. He believed in God, but he did not yet see that people must be changed inwardly before there can be lasting changes in society. The conviction dawned on him that the disease that was eroding the moral fabric of society was sin in the human heart and that the only cure was Christ. Buchman became known for his "house parties" on university campuses (including Oxford, from which the movement derived its name). On these occasions fun and fellowship were combined with open confession of sin and the public sharing of the joy of emancipation from the burden of guilt.

Buchman was not wrong in his belief that the key to social reformation lies in personal transformation, but his tendency to downplay the continuing effects of sin in the believer tended to make his social policy simplistic and even utopian. Moreover, when the Oxford Group movement became Moral Rearmament in the late 1930s, the experience of personal conversion was even more disassociated from the objective work of Christ's atoning sacrifice on the cross, and a humanistic emphasis began to supplant the evangelical basis that remained central in Buchman's own life. To the end, Buchman insisted that "only God can change human nature"; yet the focus of attention in Moral Rearmament was much more on the realization of the moral ideal than on divine grace.

The first World Assembly of Moral Rearmament was held at Caux, Switzerland, in 1946. Caux remains the center of MRA, but since Buchman's death the movement has lost much of its momentum.

Theological critics of Buchman have been quick to point out the subjectivism and mysticism in his piety without recognizing that in Buchman we have a modern saint, a holy man who was able to read hearts and perform soul surgery even upon a first meeting with people. Moreover, he was a man of prayer who rose early every morning to receive counsel from God. Like Francis of Assisi, with whom he has been compared, he embarked on a vocation of itinerant evangelism, living in celibacy and virtual poverty, depending only on freewill donations for his livelihood. He was often accused of hobnobbing with the wealthy, but it is well to remember that Christ came to seek and save the lost, and this includes the up-and-outs as well as the down-and-outs. Buchman believed that the way to reach those who are crippled by sin is not to demonstrate the superiority of our wisdom but to expose the lie that hides the human condition by speaking the truth in love.

Buchman's life and thought have much to teach evangelical Christianity today, where the emphasis is on correct understanding over practical living. His witness is a timely reminder that life and doctrine belong together. While he tended to neglect the latter, many of his critics have sorely neglected the former. D. G. BLOESCH

Bibliography. Buchman, *Remaking the World;* T. Driberg, *The Mystery of Moral Re-Armament;* P. Howard, *Frank Buchman's Secret;* A. Lunn, *Enigma: A Study of Moral Re-Armament;* J. P. Thornton-Duesbery, *The Open Secret of MRA;* W. H. Clark, *The Oxford Group: Its History and Significance;* A. J. Russell, *For Sinners Only;* H. Begbie, *More Twice-Born Men.*

Moral Theology. The Roman Catholic equivalent to what Protestants commonly call Christian ethics. It is related to dogmatic theology and moral philosophy in Catholic tradition in ways parallel to the Protestant relationship of Christian ethics to systematic theology and philosophical ethics. *General* moral theology deals with the broad questions of what, from the point of view of moral agency and moral action, it means to live as a Christian. Its questions address methods of moral discernment, the definitions of good and evil, right and wrong, sin and virtue, and the goal or end of the Christian life. *Special* moral theology addresses specific issues of life such as justice, sexuality, truth-telling, and the sanctity of life.

While the first five centuries of the church provided important guidance (above all in the works of Augustine) in the development of Catholic moral theology, even more influential was the rise in importance during the sixth century of the sacrament of reconciliation. A series of compendiums known as penitential books was prepared to assist priest-confessors in determining appropriate penance for various individual sins. Despite the great achievement of Bonaventure and Thomas Aquinas in the thirteenth century in developing a systematic, unified philosophy and theology, the tendency to treat morality as a discipline separate from dogmatics was continued and confirmed by the Counter-Reformation, which emphasized the connection between moral teaching and canon law.

During the seventeenth and eighteenth century debates about Jansenism and the precise meaning of the law, Alphonsus Liguori emerged as the most famous and influential moral theologian. Liguori's manuals noted the various alternatives and then urged a prudent, reasonable middle course on various questions. Casuistry in the style of these manuals, aimed primarily toward the preparation of priests for their role as confessors, remained the dominant approach to moral theology in Catholic circles into the twentieth century.

The renewal and reformation of Catholic moral theology that has become so visible since Vatican II is the fruition of the work of such moral theologians as John Michael Sailor (1750–1832), John Baptist Hirscher (1788–1865), Joseph Mausbach (1861–1931), Th. Steinbuchel (1888–1949), and contemporaries Bernard Häring and Josef Fuchs. The new spirit in moral theology since Vatican II is represented by scholars such as Fuchs, Häring, Charles Curran, Timothy O'Connell, Edward Schillebeeckx, and Rudolf Schnackenburg.

Traditionally moral theology was based on the authority of reason, natural law, canon law, and the tradition and authority of the Roman Catholic Church and its *magisterium.* While Scripture has always been acknowledged as divine revelation, it is only in the new Catholic moral theology that the whole shape as well as specific content of moral theology has been aggressively reworked in relationship to authoritative Scripture. Natural law (or general revelation) continues to be important but is now supplemented by attention to the human and social sciences. The parochialism and separatism of the past have given way to ongoing ecumenical dialogue with Protestant ethicists. The traditional preoccupation with specific sins and the role of moral guidance in the confessional have been subsumed in a broader inquiry about the total and positive meaning of the Christian life. The legalism, formalism, rationalism, and traditionalism which used to characterize Catholic ethics are no longer present in anything to the same degree. The prospects have never been better and the need more urgent for Protestants and Catholics to work together on a biblical base, informed by the whole history of the church and responsive to the massive challenges of a secular world.

D. W. GILL

See also ETHICS, BIBLICAL; ETHICAL SYSTEMS, CHRISTIAN.

Bibliography. C. C. Curran, *New Perspectives in Moral Theology;* J. M. Gustafson, *Protestant and Roman Catholic Ethics;* B. Häring, *Free and Faithful in Christ,* 3 vols.; T. E. O'Connell, *Principles for a Catholic Morality.*

Mormonism. The Mormons, as they are usually known, represent one of the most successful of the new religious movements of the nineteenth century. Today they are divided into two main groups, the Church of Jesus Christ of Latter-day Saints, organized from Salt Lake City, Utah, and the Reorganized Church of Jesus Christ of Latter-day Saints, based in Independence, Missouri. In addition to these major groups a number of smaller "fundamentalist" groups exist. Today the Utah church claims over 3 million members, while the Reorganized Church claims about 600,000 adherents.

The Church of Jesus Christ of Latter-day Saints was first organized on April 6, 1830, at Fayette, New York, by Joseph Smith. Soon after its formation its members moved to Kirtland, Ohio, and then Jackson County, Missouri, as a result of the intense opposition they encountered. They finally settled at a place they called Nauvoo on the Mississippi River in Illinois. Here they prospered and built a thriving city.

On July 12, 1843, Smith received a revelation allowing for polygamy, which caused four disillusioned converts to found an anti-Mormon newspaper. Smith was denounced on June 7, 1844, in this paper, the Nauvoo *Expositor,* in its single publication. For that the brothers of Smith burned down the newspaper office. As a result Joseph Smith and his brother Hyrum were placed in Carthage jail, where on June 27, 1844, they were brutally murdered when a mob stormed the jail.

Following the assassination of Joseph Smith the majority of Mormons accepted the leadership of Brigham Young. A minority rallied around Joseph's legal wife and family to form the Reorganized Church. Under the leadership of Young the Mormons left Nauvoo in 1847 and trekked westward to Utah. Here for more than thirty years Brigham Young ruled the Mormon Church and laid the foundation of its present strength.

Mormonism has a dual foundation. The first is the claim of Joseph Smith to have received golden plates upon which ancient scriptures are alleged to have been written. Smith claimed to have translated these plates and subsequently published them in 1830 as *The Book of Mormon.* The second foundation is Smith's claim to have had an encounter with the living Jesus and subsequently to receive continuing revelations from God. The substance of these continuing revelations is to be found in the Mormon publication *The Doctrine and Covenants,* while an account of Joseph Smith's encounter with Jesus and the discovery of *The Book of Mormon* is to be found in *The Pearl of Great Price. The Pearl of Great Price* also contains the text of two Egyptian papyri which Joseph Smith claimed to have translated plus his translation of certain portions of the Bible. Together *The Book of Mormon, Doctrine and Covenants,* and *The Pearl of Great Price* form the basis of the Mormon continuing revelation. Since the death of Smith these revelations have been supplemented by what the church claims to be further revelations given to its leaders.

The Book of Mormon itself is a fairly straightforward adventure yarn written in the style of biblical history. The story concerns two ancient civilizations located on the American continent. The first was founded by refugees from the Tower of Babel. These people crossed Europe and emigrated to the eastern coast of central America. The founders of the second civilization emigrated from Jerusalem around 600 B.C. This group is said to have crossed the Pacific Ocean in arklike boats. After their arrival in America both these groups are said to have founded the great civilizations. The first civilization was known as that of the Jardeites. This was totally destroyed as a result of their corruption. The second group were righteous Jews under the leadership of a man named Nephi. Initially Nephi's group prospered and built great cities. But like their forefathers in Palestine, many apostatized and ceased to worship the true God. As a result their civilization was plagued by civil wars and eventually destroyed itself. The descendants of the apostates remained on the North American continent as native Indians. In

The Book of Mormon the Indians are known as the Lamanites who, as a result of the apostasy, received the curse of a dark skin.

The Book of Mormon claims that Christ visited America after his resurrection and revealed himself to the Nephites, to whom he preached the gospel and for whom he founded a church. The Nephites were eventually destroyed by the Lamanites in a great battle near Palmyra, New York, around A.D. 428. Almost 1,400 years later, according to Mormon claims, Joseph Smith had revealed to him the record of these civilizations in the form of "reformed Egyptian hieroglyphics" written upon golden plates. With the aid of supernatural spectacles, known as the urim and thummim, he translated the unknown language into English and it became *The Book of Mormon*. According to the Articles of Faith of the Mormon Church and to the theology of the *Book of Mormon*, Mormonism is essentially Christian. These present views that are similar to those of many other Christian churches, but this similarity is misleading. Mormon theology is not based upon its declared Articles of Faith or the teachings of *The Book of Mormon*. Rather, the essence of Mormon theology comes from the continuing revelations received by Joseph Smith and later Mormon leaders.

Mormonism teaches that God the Father has a body and that man's destiny is to evolve to Godhood. This teaching is summed up in the popular Mormon saying, "As man is, God once was: as God is, man may become." This belief includes the notion of preexisting souls who gain a body on earth and become human as part of the probationary experience which determines their future heavenly existence. Contrary to the teachings of the Bible man's rebellion against God, known in Christian theology as the fall, is considered necessary. Mormon theology teaches that if Adam had not eaten the forbidden fruit, he would never have had children. Therefore, to propagate the race and fulfill his heavenly destiny Adam had to disobey God. Thus, in a very real sense it is the fall of man which saved man. This doctrine is built into an evolutionary view of eternal progression which reflects popular thinking and scientific speculation at the time of Joseph Smith. In keeping with the idea of a probationary state the doctrine of justification by faith is rejected in Mormon theology in favor of salvation by works as the basis of determining one's future mode of existence. The purpose of Christ's atonement is then said to be the assurance that humans will be raised from the dead. At the resurrection, however, human beings will be assigned a place in one of three heavenly realms according to the life they have lived on earth.

The Mormon Church claims that it is the only true church because its leaders continue to receive revelation from God. In addition it claims to possess the powers of the priesthood of Aaron and Melchizedek into which its male members are expected to be initiated.

As a social organization the Mormon Church exhibits many admirable qualities. It promotes extensive welfare programs for members, operates a large missionary and educational organization, and promotes family life. Mormons are expected to participate in what is known as "temple work." This involves proxy baptism for deceased ancestors and "celestial marriage." Mormons believe that in addition to temporal marriages church members may be sealed to their families "for time and eternity" through a process known as celestial marriage.

During the 1960s the Mormon community was troubled by its denial of the priesthood to blacks. However, in 1978 the president of the church declared that he had received a new revelation which admitted blacks to the priesthood. Today one of the most troublesome issues within the Mormon Church is the place of women, who are also excluded from the priesthood. In addition to these social problems a number of historical challenges have rocked Mormon intellectual life of the past two decades. These include serious questions about the translation of *The Book of Abraham* and *The Pearl of Great Price* and about Joseph Smith, visions, and historical claims.

Much of the criticism has come from ex-Mormons disillusioned by what they see as the refusal of the church hierarchy to face serious questioning. Among the more important ex-Mormon critics are Fawn Brodie, whose biography of Joseph Smith, *No Man Knows My History*, seriously undermines official Mormon histories, and Gerald and Sandra Tanner, whose Modern Microfilm Company has produced numerous documents challenging the official version of early Mormon history and the development of Mormon doctrine. Within the Mormon Church itself a vigorous debate has been conducted in journals such as *Dialog* and *Moonstone*. The rigor with which younger Mormon scholars have addressed the study of their own history in these journals is clear indication of the power of Mormonism to survive sustained criticism.

Although young Mormon missionaries may often present Mormonism as a slightly modified American form of Christianity, this approach does little justice to either Mormon theology or the Christian tradition. As a new religious movement Mormonism represents a dynamic synthesis that combines frontier revivalism, intense religious experience, and popular evolutionary philosophies with a respect for Jesus and Christian ethics. This combination of beliefs holds strong attraction for many people uninterested or unschooled in Christian history and theology.

I. HEXHAM

Bibliography. T. O'Dea, *The Mormons;* G. E. Talmage, *A Study of the Articles of Faith;* G. and S. Tanner, *Mormonism: Shadow or Reality.*

Morning Prayer. "The Order for Daily Morning Prayer" from the *Book of Common Prayer* of the Church of England, long the principal service in Anglican and Episcopal churches. Morning prayer or English matins owes its origin to the work of Thomas Cranmer. Believing daily morning and evening worship to have been the custom of the ancient church, Cranmer developed the offices of morning prayer and evening prayer (evensong). Influenced by Lutheran precedents, the Sarum Breviary, and the monastic offices of matins, lauds, and prime, morning prayer was designed for use on weekdays and on Sundays before Holy Communion. Minor changes were made in 1928; more major ones were authorized in 1965.

C. G. FRY

See also BOOK OF COMMON PRAYER; OFFICE, DAILY (DIVINE); WORSHIP IN THE CHURCH.

Bibliography. S. L. Ollard, ed., *A Dictionary of English Church History;* J. G. Davies, ed., *Westminster Dictionary of Worship.*

Mortality. Man does not need to appeal to an Aristotelian syllogism (all men are mortal, etc.) to demonstrate his mortality. It is self-evident. As certainly as he has been born, just as certainly he will experience death. The fact is incontrovertible; the "why" of mortality needs to be explored. As we probe the NT we find that the cause of mortality is not open to speculation. "The wages of sin is death" (Rom. 6:23); "Sin entered the world and death by sin" (Rom. 5:12). Thus mortality is not a biological problem but a theological one. Man has turned his back upon God, "who gives life to the dead and calls into existence the things that do not exist" (Rom. 4:17), and as a result he has severed himself from the root of his existence and become subject to death. It is only through the substitutionary death and resurrection of Jesus Christ that the power of sin has been broken and the Christian is delivered from the frightful circle of sin and death (Rom. 4:25; 5:6ff.; I Cor. 15:3ff.; II Cor. 5:14ff.; I Thess. 5:10; Heb. 2:9ff.; I Pet. 3:18; Rev. 1:17–18). Those who refuse God's offer of life through Christ choose in its place the "second death," an eternal and irrevocable existence separated from the God whom they have spurned (John 8:21, 24; II Thess. 1:8–9; Heb. 10:26–27, 31; Jude 12–13; Rev. 20:12–15).

Seventh-day Adventist theology sees man as mortal and immortality as bestowed upon the righteous dead at the second coming of Christ. The finally impenitent, including Satan, will be reduced to a state of nonexistence by the fires of the last day.

Christian Science understands man's mortality to be an illusion. Mrs. Eddy stated that the only reality of sin, sickness, and death is the awful fact that unrealities seem real to human, erring belief, until God strips off their disguises.

New Thought, represented by its most prolific exponent, Ernest Holmes, sees man's mortality as real but offers no substantive reason for its existence. Sin is simply a misnomer; there are no sins, only mistakes, and no punishment, only consequences. God does not punish sin. As we correct our mistakes, we are in effect forgiving ourselves.

Karl Rahner, while espousing the view that mortality results from man's sin, moves on to suggest that this does not mean that apart from sin man would have continued endlessly on earth. His life would certainly have ended, but in a manner which would have permitted the perfect consummation of his personal life in bodily form without the violent dissolution of his physical constitution through an external power. His end would have been "a death without dying," the pure, active affirmation of the whole man from *within,* including that openness to the cosmos in its totality which is now possible only to the redeemed.

There are three essential ethical implications to the fact of human mortality. First, although man bears no responsibility for the fact of his existence, there are moral issues implicit in the fact of his mortality. God has reserved for himself the right to determine the hour of man's birth and death. However, when the Decalogue states, "Thou shalt not kill," it implies man's freedom to usurp that authority and precipitate his own death or that of another. For this he *is* responsible.

Second, man's mortality adds ethical dimensions to the experience of human procreation. Married persons who choose to have children must realize that they join in creating not only a new life but also an entity subject to death. The moral responsibility for sustaining the new physical life is certainly implied. Christian families also recognize that they carry the responsibility of Christian witness and nurture for their offspring, who need to be prepared for life's inevitable moment of judgment after death.

Third, implicit in the above are such critical issues as abortion, birth control, euthanasia, organ transplants, the whole spectrum of questions related to war, and many others.

F. R. HARM

See also CONDITIONAL IMMORTALITY; ANNIHILATIONISM.

Bibliography. W. Schmithals, *NIDNTT*, I, 430–41; M. B. Eddy, *Science and Health with Key to the Scriptures;* E. Holmes, *The Science of Mind;* F. R. Harm, *How to Respond to the Science Religions;* F. B. James, *Truth and Health;* K. Rahner, *On the Theology of Death.*

Mortal Sin. *See* SIN, MORTAL.

Moses. Often called the founder of the religion of Israel; one of the most striking and important figures of the OT. The Pentateuch attests to his central role in the exodus of the Israelites from Egypt and in the giving of the law on Mount Sinai.

Although Moses is not mentioned in historical sources outside the Bible, the OT traditions form a rich tapestry of interpretation of his life and mission. His name (derived from the Egyptian *mś*, "to give birth" or "to bear"; cf. Thutmose, "Thoth is born") and the Egyptian provenance of the Exodus account are incontrovertible evidence of the historical basis of Moses' role; and the biblical tradition, while complex, focuses on Moses and no one else for this portion of sacred history.

Traditionally Moses' life has been divided into three forty-year stages (Acts 7:20–34). Moses was threatened at birth by Pharaoh's decree aimed at annihilation of the people of Israel; his mother's daring ploy to save him led to his adoption into the Egyptian royal family (Exod. 2:1–10). The young man Moses, now a man of two national identities, defended a Hebrew slave, killed an Egyptian officer, and fled into exile from Egypt. During the second period of his life Moses was adopted into the Midianite (Kenite) family of Jethro (or Reuel) as a "stranger in a strange land" (Exod. 2:11–22).

God, however, had not forgotten his covenant with the patriarchs and called Moses in the burning bush to be his spokesman before Pharaoh and agent of deliverance for Israel (Exod. 3:1–10). God revealed his sacred name (YHWH) to Moses and equipped him with miraculous powers (Exod. 3:11–7:13). After calling down God's judgment against Egypt in plagues and passover (Exod. 7:14–13:16), Moses led the people out of Egypt, and the Lord saved Israel by the miracle at the Red Sea (Exod. 14–15). Thus the people "believed in the Lord and in his servant Moses." Then at Mount Sinai the Lord revealed himself in a theophany and dictated the Decalogue (Exod. 19:16–20:17); however, the people demanded that Moses conclude God's covenant with them (Exod. 20:18–24). Moses prescribed the law of God (Torah) for Israel: its sanctuary and priesthood (Exod. 25–31; 35–40), its sacrifices and laws of purity (Leviticus), and a census of its tribes (Num. 1:1–10:10). Moses led the people in the wilderness for forty years (Num. 10:11–36) and uttered a final exhortation to obey the Torah as the people gathered on the verge of the promised land (Deuteronomy). Moses himself was not allowed to enter Canaan (cf. Num. 20:2–13; Deut. 1:37; 3:27; 4:21; Ps. 106:32–33) and was buried somewhere in Moab (Deut. 34).

Although Moses is mentioned remarkably infrequently elsewhere in the OT (Josh. 24:5; I Sam. 12:6, 8; Hos. 12:13; Mic. 6:4; Isa. 63:11; Pss. 77, 105–7), his preeminent status and foundational mission are assumed. No other OT figure can compare with Moses (cf. Joshua, Josh. 1:10–11; Elijah, I Kings 19; the prophets, Deut. 34:10). Indeed he is the type par excellence of OT expectation. He is the "servant of the Lord" (Num. 12:7–8; Deut. 34:5; Josh. 1:1). He alone spoke "mouth to mouth" with God; therefore, he is the first and greatest of the prophets (Exod. 33:7–23; Num. 12:6–8; Deut. 18:15–18). As lawgiver he dominates the Pentateuch, which can thus be called "the law of Moses" (I Kings 2:3; Neh. 8:1; Mal. 4:4). His voice is not only authoritative for the wilderness generation, but resounds throughout Israel's history (Deut. 6:20–25; 31:16–22).

Moses is a man zealous for the Lord (Num. 16–17); yet he is also described as "the meekest man on earth" (Num. 12:3). He intercedes on Israel's behalf when it sins, risking his own election for the sake of the people (Exod. 32:32; Num. 11:10–15). He even sets up the bronze serpent as a perpetual sign of God's saving mercy (Num. 21:4–9). Finally, Moses is the founder of the cultic system by which Israel was to seek reconciliation with God, and he and his brother Aaron functioned as priests before the tabernacle (Exod. 40:31–38).

In postbiblical Jewish tradition the role of Moses is extended to that of sage and founder of civilization. Moses is thought to have ascended directly into heaven. For the Jewish *halakah* Moses was giver of the oral law which authoritatively interprets the Pentateuch (cf. Jub; M. Aboth 1:1).

The NT assumes the role of Moses as mediator of the covenant (John 1:17; Gal. 3:19) and author of the Pentateuch (Luke 24:27). Numerous passages compare or allude to Moses and Jesus as type and antitype (e.g., Mark 9:2–10; John

3:14; I Cor. 10). Paul's typology emphasizes the inferiority of the revelation to Moses. At other times Paul likens his own apostleship to the mission of Moses (II Cor. 3:7–18; cf. Rom. 9:3). John likewise sees Jesus as the prophet like Moses (John 6:14); he also sees Moses (and Abraham) as the father of "the Jews" who reject Jesus' revelation (John 9:28). For the Epistle to the Hebrews, the Mosaic covenant is merely a shadow of the true reality, but Moses himself is a model of faith (Heb. 3:1–6; 11:24–28). S. F. Noll

Bibliography. W. F. Albright, *From the Stone Age to Christianity; EJ,* VII, 371–411; R. deVaux, *The Early History of Israel;* D. M. Beegle, *Moses, The Servant of Yahweh;* J. G. Griffiths, "The Egyptian Derivation of the Name Moses," *JNES* 12:225–31.

Most Holy Place. *See* Tabernacle, Temple.

Mother of God. This title was accorded to Mary, the mother of Jesus, at the Council of Ephesus in 431. A bishop named Nestorius—formerly presbyter at Antioch and then made patriarch of Constantinople, but deposed by the council—had found it difficult to accept that the infant born of Mary was "God," and his difficulty came to expression in a refusal to describe Mary as the "Mother of God" as she was now commonly styled to emphasize the deity of Christ. The council decreed that the title could rightly be given to Mary because he who was conceived of her was by the Holy Ghost, and was the Son of God and therefore "God" from the moment of his conception.

Unfortunately, the term soon came to be regarded as expressing an exaltation of Mary, and by the sixth century false notions about Mary, originally framed by Gnostics and a sect known as Collyridians, were taken up by the church itself, and the way was open for the worship of Mary, which has since grown so greatly, especially in the Roman Catholic Church.

In the NT Mary is often referred to as the "mother of Jesus" (e.g., John 2:1; Acts 1:14). She was given special grace by God to perform a service to him that was unique. In this regard she stands alone amongst humankind, and is regarded by all generations as "blessed." But Scripture is silent as regards any special standing of Mary herself. The title "mother of God" (*Theotokos*) is thus to be used with caution as regards its implications for Mary, though evangelical theology recognizes its appropriateness when employed, as at Ephesus, to state the true deity of Jesus Christ even in his incarnate life.

W. C. G. Proctor

See also Mary, The Blessed Virgin; Mariology.

Bibliography. J. McHugh, *The Mother of Jesus in the NT.*

Mott, John Raleigh (1865–1955). The chief architect of twentieth century ecumenism. As a youth he had a Methodist conversion experience and devoted himself to Christian service with boundless enthusiasm and energy. Neither theologically trained nor ordained, he spent his professional career as an official of the American YMCA, first directing the student and foreign work departments and then as general secretary (1915–28). A prodigious speaker, writer, and traveler, he also headed a myriad of committees and boards responsible for missionary and ecumenical ventures.

Deeply influenced by D. L. Moody, from whom he learned the value of total commitment to Christ and the ecumenical ideal, Mott rejected an invitation to direct the evangelist's Chicago Bible institute and concentrated instead on promoting student involvement in foreign missions. In 1888 he founded the Student Volunteer Movement and in 1895 the World's Student Christian Federation, chairing both until 1920. His vision of transforming the world through the advance of Christianity led to the convening of the Edinburgh Missionary Conference in 1910. He was intimately involved in its planning, was a presiding officer, and chaired its Continuation Committee.

A close friend of President Woodrow Wilson, Mott enthusiastically backed American participation in World War I but afterward worked diligently for reconciliation among the foes. He played a key role in the formation of the International Missionary Council in 1921 and chaired it for twenty years. He also took part in the various ecumenical gatherings that culminated in the founding of the World Council of Churches in 1948. He was awarded the Nobel Peace Prize in 1946.

Mott was no systematic theologian, but his beliefs could best be categorized as liberal evangelical with its emphasis upon "now" as the time of crisis, promise, and action. He combined Methodist perfectionism with social Christianity and stressed the primacy of ethics over dogma. Through the missionary outreach of the gospel all nations would be brought into the body of Christ, and every race and people would find expression and be perfected. The task of Christians was to break down every barrier to racial and international understanding and the establishment of world peace. For him the universality of Christian experience and fellowship was more important than doctrinal exclusiveness, and as he said in 1928, he was obliged "to make Jesus Christ known, trusted, loved, and obeyed in the whole range of one's individual life and in all relationships." R. V. Pierard

See also Missiology.

Bibliography. C. H. Hopkins, *John R. Mott 1865–1955: A Biography;* W. R. Hogg, *Ecumenical Foundations.*

Movable Feasts. Those days of the church calendar which depend upon a phase of the moon and thus fall on different dates annually, such as Easter. They are in contrast to fixed feasts, which always occur on the same date, such as Christmas. The contrast is due to the way in which the Christian year developed. Part of it is based on the seven-day week inherited from Judaism. Sunday, the principal day of worship, happens regularly. Other dates, such as Christmas and All Saints, were fixed arbitrarily for annual observance. The dates for the movable feasts are based on cycles of the moon. Chief of these is Easter, the oldest and major festival of the church. Easter is to be "the first Sunday after the first full moon after the vernal equinox" and may fall between March 22 and April 25. The season of preparation for Easter is variable. Lent, which is forty days before Easter (not counting Sundays), starts with Ash Wednesday (which may fall between February 4 and March 10). Major feasts in Lent, including Palm Sunday, Maundy Thursday, Good Friday, and Holy Saturday, are movable. The season of celebration after Easter is variable, including Ascension Day (forty days after) and Pentecost, the climax of "the great fifty days." C. G. Fry

See also Fixed Feasts.

Bibliography. C. Jones, G. Wainwright, E. Yarnold, *The Study of Liturgy;* A. McArthur, *The Evolution of the Christian Year.*

Muhlenberg, Henry Melchior (1711–1787). Patriarch of colonial American Lutheranism. Muhlenberg was born in Eimbeck, Hanover. A lifelong Lutheran, he was baptized the day he was born and confirmed when he was twelve. He was a precocious child, excelling in languages and music, but his poverty seemed to preclude the possibility of advanced study. Receiving "beneficiary aid," however, he enrolled in 1735 at the new and nearby University of Göttingen, where he studied theology and converted to pietism. For fifteen months following his graduation Muhlenberg served at the orphanage in Halle, a city famed for the ministry of Lutheran pietist August Hermann Francke. Though Muhlenberg aspired to be a missionary to India, he accepted a call to pastor a Lutheran congregation in Grosshennersdorf, Saxony, located a few miles from Herrnhut, the center of revived Moravianism under Nikolaus von Zinzendorf. In the autumn of 1739 he was ordained at Leipzig.

On his thirtieth birthday Muhlenberg had dinner with Johann Gotthilf Francke, son of the famed pietist. Francke shared with Muhlenberg a letter from "dispersed Lutherans in Pennsylvania" who needed a pastor. Muhlenberg's missionary fervor returned, and he determined to go to America. On December 9, 1741, "under considerable emotion" he preached his farewell sermon to his congregation, then spent some time with Lutherans in England, sailing for Charleston, South Carolina, on June 13, 1742. A voyage of "unusual peril and exhaustion" followed. Arriving on September 23, Muhlenberg began his American ministry. Historian Henry Eyster Jacobs observed that the history of the Lutheran Church in America from 1742 until Muhlenberg's death was "scarcely more than his biography." After an initial visit with Salzburger Lutherans at Ebenezer, Georgia, Muhlenberg traveled north to Pennsylvania, arriving unannounced in Philadelphia on November 25. He took charge of three Lutheran congregations within a month—one at New Hanover, another at the Trappe, nine miles south of New Hanover, yet another in Philadelphia itself. Installed on December 27, 1742, as the pastor of "the United Congregations," Muhlenberg soon added a fourth charge, Germantown. He began a work of "catechizing, confirming, teaching, reconciling, establishing, building, preaching, and administering the sacraments." His diary, letters, and *Halle Reports* detail his labors. In 1748 Muhlenberg organized the first permanent Lutheran synod in America, later known as the Pennsylvania Ministerium. Founding Christian day schools, Muhlenberg is "the father of Lutheran parochial education." In 1749 he purchased ground for a Lutheran seminary in Philadelphia, though one was not founded in that community until after the Civil War. An orphans' home was established in Philadelphia. The "Savoy Liturgy" of the Lutherans of London was commended to American Lutherans by Muhlenberg in 1748, and in 1782 an American hymnal was prepared under his guidance. A model Lutheran church constitution was adopted by St. Michael's parish, Philadelphia, at his suggestion. Catechists, evangelists, and pastors were trained at his behest.

Soon Muhlenberg had a "ministry of reconciliation" among Lutherans from New York to Georgia, speaking Dutch, German, Swedish, and English. By 1771 some eighty-one congregations were under his oversight. Himself a church planter, frontier preacher, and circuit rider–evangelist, Muhlenberg, according to legend, was called by the Indians "the preacher whose words should go through hard hearts of men like a saw through a gnarled tree." What Francis Asbury was to Methodism and John Carroll to Roman Catholicism, Muhlenberg was to Lutheranism in America. His sound work enabled Lutherans to survive both the American Revolution and the Age of Enlightenment. C. G. Fry

Bibliography. *The Journals of Henry Melchior Muhlenberg,* 3 vols., and *Notebook of a Colonial Clergyman: An Anthology of the Journals of Henry Melchior Muhlenberg,* tr. T. G. Tappert and J. W. Doberstein; W. J. Mann, *Life and Times of Henry Melchior Muhlenberg.*

Münzer, Thomas. *See* Zwickau Prophets.

Murray, Andrew (1828–1917). South African churchman, educator, and author. Son of the Dutch Reformed Church (DRC) minister in the then frontier town of Graaf-Reinet, South Africa, Andrew Murray was educated in Aberdeen, Scotland, and in Utrecht, Holland. He was ordained in the Netherlands and returned to South Africa in 1849, where he became the first regular DRC minister north of the Orange River. His parish covered fifty thousand square miles, and Murray's ministry required frequent long and dangerous journeys to reach the nineteen thousand people in his charge.

After nine years of frontier ministry Murray published his first book, *Jesus the Children's Friend,* in 1858. He opened Grey College, later to become the University of the Orange Free State, in 1859, and became its first rector. In 1860 he returned to the Cape Colony to a parish in Worcester. In 1862 he was elected moderator of the DRC and became involved in a long theological, political, and legal battle with liberal ministers who were attempting to wrest control of the DRC from evangelicals like Murray.

He moved to Cape Town in 1864 and to Wellington in 1871. In 1879 Murray began what was to become the first of seven great evangelistic tours. Adopting the methods of Moody and Sankey, he toured South Africa organizing revival meetings which were an astounding success. These activities, plus his growing stature as a theological writer, led to his being invited to preach at the Northfield, U.S.A., and Keswick, U.K., conventions in 1895.

In South Africa he took great interest in missionary work and education. He helped found the DRC missionary union, a mission institute in Wellington, and several other educational foundations. He encouraged the growth of the Student Christian Association in South Africa and founded an interdenominational prayer union in 1904.

Murray was a systematic thinker who wrote over 250 books and many articles. His best-known works are *Abide in Christ* (1882), *Absolute Surrender* (1895), and *With Christ in the School of Prayer* (1885). Through his mystically inclined theology and *The Second Blessing* (1891) he became associated with the charismatic movement. His book *Divine Healing* (1900) increased his links with Pentecostalism, although following the tragic death of a close friend his views on healing were considerably modified from his earlier ones.

Throughout his life Murray took an active role in South African society. In 1852 he helped organize, and acted as the official interpreter for, the important Sand River Convention, which led to the British recognition of the South African Republic in the Transvaal. He took a keen interest in the welfare and education of Africans and held enlightened views on the race question. One of his last works, *Godsdienst en Politiek* (*Religion and Politics*), was a warning against the practice of Afrikaner Nationalist politicians in promoting their political views, which led to the development of apartheid, as "Christian politics." Later, in the 1930s, followers of Murray were to fight a losing battle against Nationalists in the DRC who ignored Murray's evangelical insights and sought to reform the DRC in terms of Abraham Kuyper's neo-Calvinism. I. Hexham

See also Keswick Convention; Northfield Conferences.

Bibliography. J. du Plessis, *The Life of Andrew Murray;* W. M. Douglas, *Andrew Murray and His Message;* J. Murray, *Young Mrs. Murray Goes to Bloemfontein.*

Mystery. The concept of mystery has played an important role in Christian theology. The best theology has always maintained that the known must be balanced by the unknown, that God is a *mysterium tremendum et fascinans,* compelling the worshiper with awe toward him but remaining ultimately beyond the grasp of human reason and imagination. The mystical tradition, which seeks to use all available means to approach God (reason, prayer, meditation, spiritual imagination, the sacraments), finds its biblical roots in apocalyptic and in such passages as Col. 2:2–3, where Paul longs that his readers may "have all the riches of assured understanding and the knowledge of God's mystery, of Christ, in whom are hid all the treasures of wisdom and knowledge" (RSV).

For Paul "mystery" is an important term. Of the twenty-eight NT occurrences twenty-one are from his pen. It was once widely maintained that he used it because of his contacts in the pagan world with adherents of the mystery religions, ecstatic cults laying much emphasis on personal communion with their deity through knowledge of special secrets, and in fact that his own thinking was considerably shaped by these religions. It is now recognized, however, that there are fundamental differences between Paul's theology and theirs, and that he uses the term "mystery" in a distinctive way. He frequently associates it with words for revelation (e.g., Rom. 16:25; Eph. 3:3–9), and this has led some to assert that, paradoxically, "mystery" is for Paul something no longer mysterious, but clearly revealed. This is certainly true of Eph. 1:9 and Col. 1:26–27 and accounts for the fact that "mystery" is often virtually identical with "gospel" (e.g., I Cor. 2:1; Eph. 6:19; I Tim. 3:9). Other scholars, however, feel that it must indicate a continuing degree of hiddenness, even if it is part of Paul's revelation vocabulary. Paul does seem to use it to convey the ideas of ultimate ungraspability (e.g., I Cor. 2:7; 13:2; Eph. 5:32; Col. 2:2), or of present incomprehensibility (Rom. 11:25; I Cor. 14:2), or of something eschatological which transcends our present experience (I Cor. 15:51; II Thess. 2:7). These two sides of Paul's usage—revealed and hidden—are not of course contradictory. They correspond to the two facets of all our knowledge of God, whose judgments are unsearchable and ways inscrutable (Rom. 11:33), even though "he had made known to us in all wisdom and insight the mystery of his will" (Eph. 1:9, RSV).

S. MOTYER

Bibliography. F. F. Bruce, *Paul and Jesus;* W. D. Davies, *Paul and Rabbinic Judaism;* C. F. D. Moule, *IDB,* III, 479–81; G. Bornkamm, *TDNT,* IV, 802–28; R. E. Brown, *The Semitic Background of the Term "Mystery" in the NT;* G. Finkenrath, *NIDNTT,* III, 501–6.

Mystery of Iniquity. This phrase is the AV translation of the Greek *to mystērion tēs anomias,* which Paul employs in II Thess. 2:7—a passage about which Augustine declared, "I freely confess that I have no idea what he meant." Detailed interpretation is difficult, but the basic outlines of Paul's meaning are clear. He wishes to correct the Thessalonians' mistaken belief that the return of Christ is already past by pointing out that certain events which must precede that day have plainly not taken place. "The rebellion comes first, and the man of lawlessness [*anomias*] will be revealed" (vs. 3). At present this eschatological figure is being "restrained," pending eventual revelation, "for the mystery of lawlessness [iniquity] is already at work." The phrase therefore seems to indicate the presence in the world now, in a veiled but active form, of that which will be the clear characteristic of the "man of lawlessness" when he appears. Because his appearance is eschatological, it seems certain that he is not to be identified with Nero or the pope, as some have maintained. But his precise identity is impossible to determine, as is that of the restrainer, whose activity means that this eschatological "mystery" is prevented from bursting upon the world now. The restrainer has been identified as God, Satan, the Holy Spirit, the Roman Empire, Israel, the principle of order in society, and Paul himself. Certainty is impossible. However, Paul's thought finds a parallel in I John 2:18; 4:3. Antichrist is coming, but "the spirit of antichrist" is already seen in the rejection of Jesus the Christ.

S. MOTYER

See also ANTICHRIST.

Bibliography. G. E. Ladd, *A Theology of the NT;* H. N. Ridderbos, *Paul: An Outline of His Theology.*

Mystery Religions. During the NT and subsequent eras the most popular religious forms in the Greco-Roman world were those of the mystery religions. Some of these had been imported from Egypt and the Orient, while others were indigenous to Greece. The traditional cults of the Olympic gods were no longer perceived as able to fulfill the common person's spiritual needs, and so there was a turning to those religions which promised salvation and a blessed afterlife. Immortality could be obtained through initiation into a secret experience which was intended to save the soul after death. Aristotle said that the initiated did not learn anything so much as they felt certain emotions and were put into a certain frame of mind. Cicero could maintain that Athens had given to the world no greater institution than that of the Eleusinian mysteries. They provided a reason to live with joy and to die with better hopes. Moreover, a civilized way of life had been established through the rites which were properly called "initiation," since they indeed taught the beginnings of life. Women in particular responded to the promise of a brighter future, as well as to the increased recognition and participation which were theirs in the mystery cults.

The essence of the mysteries lay in their secrecy. One could incur the death sentence by revealing the mysteries through speech, pantomime, dance, or depiction. Thus it was that a complete understanding of their secrets perished with the last of their adherents. Their influence permeated ancient society so deeply, however, that the general outlines can be constructed with a considerable degree of certainty. Literally thousands of allusions to the mysteries remain in the form of literary references, vase paintings, reliefs, frescoes, inscriptions, funerary statues, and so forth. We are further aided by the confessions of certain of the church fathers who had been initiated into one or more of the mysteries, although their accounts are far from unbiased. Much religious detective work has been expended upon these ancient mysteries.

Seasonal celebrations marked the birth and death of vegetation gods and of yearly changes in the forces of nature. The mystic rites reenacted a myth concerning a divine figure who suffered some sort of violence, was mourned, and then restored to the grateful worshipers amid general jubilation. Beside the reenactment—which was usually accompanied with music, dancing, and sometimes stunning stage effects—there were acts performed, words spoken, objects revealed, a sacrifice offered, and a sacramental meal shared. Sexual symbols and activities were significantly present. Death, marriage, and adoption by the deity were often simulated, and in some cases the initiate was actually supposed thereby to attain divinity. While noise and wild tumult often accompanied the earlier stages of initiation, silence was attendant upon the ultimate unveiling of the truth. In the Mithras cult the initiate must lay his finger on his lips, address Silence as the symbol of the living, imperishable God, and pray, "Guard me, Silence." The culmination of the Eleusinian rites was said to be the display in complete silence of a newly reaped ear of corn. Such beatific visions guaranteed a blessed afterlife to the initiate.

There were within the mysteries successive grades of initiation in which truth might be perceived in a progressive series. On several occasions Plato likened the discovery of philosophic truth to these levels of initiation. Theon of Smyrna described five stages, the first of which was purification. The second communicated some sort of explanation of the rite and an exhortation. There followed a revelation of a sacred spectacle, after which the initiate was crowned with a garland. Then came the final stage, the happiness of knowing that one was beloved of the gods. The objective was indeed participation in the divine life.

Each of the mysteries had its distinctives, although there were great similarities and much syncretism in late antiquity. The most famous was that of Eleusis, whose cult was officially adopted by Athens. It centered upon Demeter, the Earth Mother, and her daughter Persephone, who was abducted to the underworld by its god, Hades. There she became his bride and queen of the dead. Each year she returned for nine months to her mother, who then caused the corn to grow and returned fertility to the earth. Demeter, bringing her gift of agriculture and civilization, had commanded Eleusis to establish her rites, to which anyone who spoke Greek—even women and slaves—might be admitted. The Isis cult retold the search of the sorrowing Isis for her dead husband, Osiris, who had been slain and dismembered by the wicked Set. The cult, closely associated with Egypt, celebrated the discovery of the god's scattered members and his restoration to life. Apuleius described his own initiation into the mysteries of Isis at Corinth. Wildly popular with women was the cult of Dionysus with its altered state of consciousness and escape from home life. Usually celebrated at night, the rites featured dancing on the mountains, the use of wine and occasionally drugs, ecstatic madness, sex reversal, promiscuity, ritual shouting, the music of flutes and castanets, and in earlier times the rending and eating raw of wild animals. Certain of these rites were accessible only to female adherents, who were called "maenads," or mad women. The cult of Mithras, often embraced by Roman soldiers, admitted only men. The male worshipers of Cybele, great mother of the gods, sometimes castrated themselves in the frenzy of her rites, and the goddess was served by eunuch priests. Both the Cybele and Mithras cults employed the practice of *taurobolium*, the slaughter of a bull whose blood dripped through a grate down onto the worshiper who stood beneath. The singer Orpheus, who managed to descend to the nether world and return to earth, was credited with having instituted various mysteries. Small groups adopted an "Orphic" theology which centered on purification and the means whereby the soul might escape the prison-tomb of the body and ascend to the realm of the blessed.

Christian and pagan authors alike inveighed against some of the gross and barbarous elements associated with the mysteries. Even human sacrifice on a few rare occasions may have played a part. Clement of Alexandria complained that the mysteries gave instruction in "adulterous trickery" and that they consisted of murders and burials. W. M. Ramsay has suggested that the initiate was first exposed to sordid scenes of rape and violence, later to visions of tranquility, civilization, and productivity. Especially after the advent of Christianity, the myths which related the manifold vices of the gods as well as the more offensive practices were spiritualized into allegories of a more sublime nature. Many features of Christianity were adopted into the mysteries of late antiquity. The concept of resurrection, for instance, is not attested in these cults until after the first century A.D.

Scholars have been quick to note the similarities between Christianity and the mystery religions. It should be noted that Christianity is based upon a historical person, while the mysteries were based upon myths of gods whose experiences were repeated yearly. The mysteries were in the main devoid of a written revelation and were constantly subject to change. Nevertheless, Christianity owed a debt to mystery religion. Church fathers such as Eusebius, Justin Martyr, and Ignatius held that the mysteries were a preparatory stage in Christian enlightenment. Just as Philo of Alexandria explained Judaism in terms of Greek mystery religion, so the apostle Paul declared that he imparted the wisdom of God in the form of a mystery (I Cor. 2:7). Examples of mystery concepts applied to Christian truth may be found in Col. 1:26–2:8; Rom. 16:25–26; I Cor. 15:42–49; Phil. 3:12, 15. II Pet. 1:16 contrasts initiation practices with those used in Christian revelation. Here, as elsewhere, technical language is borrowed from the mysteries. While there might be such borrowings of concept and language in the NT, actual vestiges of pagan religion were vigorously denounced. There are numerous indications that many members of the congregation at Corinth were newly converted from mystery cults and still clung to old ways such as ceremonial drunkenness, fornication, participation in an idol's feast, the noisy clamor of worship, and the ritual cries of women. It was a syncretization of Christianity and mystery religion which, according to Hippolytus and others, produced the heresies known as Gnosticism.

R. C. Kroeger and C. C. Kroeger

See also Gnosticism.

Bibliography. U. Bianchi, *The Greek Mysteries;* F. Cumont, *The Oriental Religions in Roman Paganism;* M. Detienne, *Dionysos Slain;* E. R. Dodds, *The Greeks and the Irrational;* L. R. Farnell, *The Cults of the Greek States,* 5 vols.; J. Godwin, *Mystery Religions in the Ancient World;* J. G. Griffiths, *The Isis Book;* W. K. C. Guthrie, *Orpheus and Greek Religion;* S. K. Heyob, *The Cult of Isis among Women in the Greco-Roman World;* C. Kerenyi, *Dionysus: Archetypal Image of Indestructible Life;* I. M. Linforth, *The Arts of Orpheus;* G. Mylonas, *Eleusis and the Eleusinian Mysteries;* M. P. Nilsson, *The Dionysiac Mysteries of the Hellenistic Age;* A. D. Nock, *Conversion* and *Early Gentile Christianity and its Hellenistic Background;* W. F. Otto, *Dionysus: Myth and Cult;* W. M. Ramsay, "The Relation of St. Paul to the Greek Mysteries," in *The Teaching of St. Paul in Terms of the Present Day;* M. I. Rostovtzeff, *Mystic Italy;* M. H. Vermaseren, *Cybele and Attis;* R. E. Witt, *Isis in the Graeco-Roman World;* C. Brown, *NIDNTT,* III, 506–11.

Mystical Sense of Scripture. *See* Interpretation of the Bible.

Mystical Union. *See* Unio Mystica.

Mysticism. As recognized by all writers on this subject, whether they claim direct personal mystical experience or not, both the definition and description of the mystical encounter are difficult. It is clear, however, that mysticism is not the same as magic, clairvoyance, parapsychology, or occultism, nor does it consist in a preoccupation with sensory images, visions, or special revelations. Nearly all Christian mystical writers relegate these phenomena to the periphery. Nearly all Christian mystics avoid the occult arts entirely. Briefly and generally stated, mystical theology or Christian mysticism seeks to describe an experienced, direct, nonabstract, unmediated, loving knowing of God, a knowing or seeing so direct as to be called union with God.

History. A brief historical survey of Christian mysticism is essential to an understanding of the varied ways in which it is explained and defined. Although the terms "mystery" and "mystical" are related etymologically to ancient mystery cults, it is doubtful that NT and patristic writers were dependent theologically upon these sources. A distinct mystical or mystery theology emerged in the Alexandrian school of exegesis and spirituality with Clement of Alexandria and Origen and their search for the hidden meaning of Scripture and their exposition of the mystery of redemption. The Cappadocian fathers, especially Gregory of Nyssa; leading monastics, especially Evagrius of Pontus (346–99) and John Cassian (*ca.* 360–435); Augustine of Hippo; and the obscure personage known as Dionysius the Pseudo-Areopagite created the formative legacy for medieval mysticism. The term generally used until the fourteenth and fifteenth centuries to describe the mystical experience was "contemplation." In its original philosophical meaning this word (Gr. *theōria*) described absorption in the loving viewing of an object or truth.

Only in the twelfth and thirteenth centuries, with the writings of Richard of Saint Victor and Thomas Aquinas, do systematic descriptive analyses of the contemplative life appear. Late medieval concern with practical and methodical prayer contributed to a turning point in the sixteenth century Ignatian and Carmelite schools (Ignatius Loyola, Teresa of Ávila, John of the Cross). Spiritual writers from these traditions were concerned primarily with empirical, psychological, and systematic descriptions of the soul's behavior in order to assist spiritual directors.

Protestants generally rejected mystical theology. Despite his acquaintance with medieval mystical writings, Martin Luther cannot be called a mystic, recent attempts to arrange his theology around a mystical center notwithstanding. Some Protestants in most periods retained an interest in the mystical tradition, although they should not necessarily be considered mystics. But mainstream Protestantism has generally mistrusted or been openly hostile toward a mystical dimension of the spiritual life.

In Catholic circles mystical theology was virtually submerged under a tide of enlightenment rationalism in the eighteenth century. A mystical reaction to rationalism and naturalism, aided by the development of psychological science in the later nineteenth century, is still bearing fruit in the late twentieth century. A controversy over the relation of mystical theology to "ordinary" prayer and the Christian striving for holiness or perfection dominated the early decades of the twentieth century. In general, whereas many Catholic theologians reacted to the challenge of rationalism, naturalism, and modernism with renewed attention to mystical and liturgical spiritual theology, many Protestant evangelicals have responded with a generally rational theology of the letter of Scripture. Others have given renewed attention to spirituality in the 1970s but still prefer a "Reformation faith piety" or "prophetic spirituality" to mystical contemplation, partly because of the rejection of mystery in liturgical and sacramental theology and practice. But contemporary evangelical antipathy toward mysticism is also partly the result of Barthian influence that reduces mysticism (and pietism) to a heretical subjectivity and anthropocentrism that denies the utterly transcendent reality of God.

The Nature of Mysticism. Beyond a general descriptive definition as offered above, explanations of the nature and characteristics of the mystical experience vary widely. Throughout Christian history and especially since the sixteenth century many Roman Catholic authors have distinguished ordinary or "acquired" prayer, even if occurring at a supraconceptual level of love, adoration, and desire for God, from the extraordinary or "infused" contemplation which is entirely the work of God's special grace. Only the latter is mystical in a strict sense, according to this view. Other writers, both Catholic and Protestant, would apply the term "mystical" to all communion with God. In the twentieth century some Catholic theologians (e.g., L. Bouyer, A. Stolz), in conjunction with the movement for liturgical renewal, have sought to locate mystical theology in a scriptural and liturgical context, emphasizing the believer's participation in the mystery of God's reconciliation with his creatures in Christ, especially in the sacraments.

Many attempts have been made to describe the fundamental characteristics of mystical experience. Traditionally it has been asserted that the experiential union of creature and Creator is inexpressible and ineffable, although those who have experienced it seek imagery and metaphors to describe it, however imperfectly. As noted above, it is experienced union or vision, not abstract knowledge. It is beyond the level of concepts, for reasoning, ideas, and sensory images have been transcended (but not rejected) in an intuitive union. Thus it is suprarational and supraintellectual, not antirational or anti-intellectual. In one sense the soul is passive, because it experiences God's grace poured into itself. Yet the union is not quietistic, because the soul consents to and embraces the spiritual marriage. Although some authors also stress the transient and fleeting nature of mystical union, others describe it as lasting for a definite, even prolonged period of time. More recent theological and liturgical understandings of mystical theology, unlike the systematic phenomenological and "empirical" manuals of the early twentieth century, define characteristics less precisely and seek to fit mystical theology more centrally into an ecclesial and soteriological framework.

The various stages of the mystical way have also been described in immensely varying manner. Virtually all writers agree, however, that purification (purgation or cleansing) and discipline are prerequisites. Each of the three classic stages—the path of purification, the phase of illumination, and the mystical union itself (not necessarily occurring in a fixed sequence but rather in interaction with each other)—may be described as consisting of various degrees or gradations. It should not be forgotten that the monastic life, the standard path of ascetic purification throughout much of Christian history, has served as the foundation for much Christian mysticism. Unfortunately, this foundation has been overlooked by some modern scholars who consider mystics to be individualistic seekers after noninstitutional, extrasacramental religious ecstasy.

Teachings about the mystical union have often brought charges of pantheism upon their exponents. Although most mystics seek to transcend the limits of the (false) self, they have been careful to insist on the preservation of the soul's identity in the union with God, choosing such imagery as that of iron glowing in the fire of unitive love, taking on fire in union with the fire, yet without loss of its properties as iron. Indeed, one should rather stress that, far from losing itself, the soul finds its true identity in the mystical union. Many Protestants have found palatable only those mystical writers who are thought to have limited mystical union to a "conformity of human and divine wills," rather than those who teach an ontological union, a union of essence or being. This distinction is problematical, since the meaning of either "ontological union" or "conformity of will" depends on the presuppositions about human nature held by the author in question. Those who stress a "prophetic faith piety" or "Reformation" alternative to supposed pantheistic or panentheistic mysticism (e.g., Heiler, Bloesch, in part under the influence of Brunner and Barth) have circumscribed mysticism so narrowly and connected it so closely to Neoplatonism that few mystics would recognize it. They have also broadened the meaning of "prophetic religion" so much that most mystics would feel at home under its canopy.

Scriptural sources for Christian mysticism are found largely in the Logos-incarnation doctrine of John's Gospel, in imagery such as that of the vine and branches (John 15) or Christ's prayer for union (John 17), as well as in aspects of the Pauline corpus. The latter include the description of Paul's rapture into the third heaven (II Cor. 12:1–4) or statements such as that referring to a life "hid with Christ in God" (Col. 3:3). In all of these the essential theological presuppositions involve belief in a personal God and in the centrality of the incarnation. For medieval mystics Moses' "vision" of God (Exod. 33:12–34:9) and his reflection of God's glory upon leaving Mount Sinai (Exod. 34:29–35; cf. II Cor. 3:7) served as proof texts, and the allegorized spiritual marriage of the Song of Solomon, together with the other OT wisdom literature, provided unlimited scriptural resources until the shift from spiritual to literal-grammatical humanist and Reformation hermeneutics took place.

Anthropologically, Christian mystical theology presupposes a human capacity or fittedness for God, drawing especially upon the doctrine of human beings created in the image of God and on the doctrine of God become human in Christ. Christian mystics have traditionally understood mystical union as a restoration of the image and likeness of God that was distorted or lost at the fall from innocence. The image of God, distorted but not destroyed, remains as the foundation for the journey from the land of unlikeness to restored likeness and union. Especially in the fourteenth century German Dominican school (Eckhart, Tauler) this teaching on the image of God in humans was expressed with terms such as the "basic will" or "ground" (*Grund*) of the soul or the "spark of divinity" in the human soul. In any case, although it stresses union with God who transcends all human limitations, mystical theology is incompatible with either an exclusively transcendent or an exclusively immanent doctrine of God—the God who transcends also became incarnate in Christ and he is immanent in his creatures created in his image. For this reason many representatives of both the social gospel and neo-orthodox theology have been stridently antimystical.

Conclusion. Christian mysticism has often been portrayed as having modified and imported into Christianity the Platonic (Neoplatonic) doctrine of cosmological emanation in creation from the idea of the One and, in mystical union, a corresponding return to the One. While a concern to relate the Creator to creation both immanently and transcendentally has from the earliest centuries led Christian mystics to make use of Neoplatonic philosophy, equally prominent are those (especially in the Franciscan school) whose theology is Christocentric, ecclesial, and liturgical. One of the most cosmologically sophisticated medieval mystics, Nicolas of Cusa (1401–64), drew deeply from Neoplatonic and Eckhartian emanationism but was also profoundly Christocentric. The issue cannot be resolved solely with broad brushstrokes of metahistorical categories such as Neoplatonism.

Of the other issues that have recurred in mystical writings and studies of mystical writings, one of the most enduring is the question of the relation between cognitive, intellectual, or speculative elements, on the one hand, and affective, loving, or supraconceptual and suprarational elements on the other. The negative way that "ascends" by stripping off all cognitions and images until one "sees" God in a "cloud of unknowing" darkness differs from the philosophical systems that claim mystical knowledge to be the human reason (including will, intellect, and feeling) exploring the sphere above that of limited rationalism (Inge), as well as the simple clinging to God in love alone posited by some mystics. Such distinctions, however, are not absolute, and most mystics stress the interrelatedness of love and cognition.

The problem of the objective quality of mystical experience that so preoccupied the psychological-empirical writers of the early twentieth century has become less significant for Christians dealing with mysticism theologically in its scriptural, ecclesial, and liturgical contexts. At the same time, for students of the philosophy of religion the question of objective content has gained renewed attention as nineteenth century naturalism wanes and Western interest in Eastern mysticism and religions grows. D. D. MARTIN

See also ILLUMINATIVE WAY, THE; PURGATIVE WAY, THE; UNITIVE WAY, THE; TERESA OF ÁVILA; JOHN OF THE CROSS; UNIO MYSTICA; HESYCHASM; MEISTER ECKHART; DIONYSIUS THE PSEUDO-AREOPAGITE; UNDERHILL, EVELYN; TAULER, JOHANNES; BOEHME, JAKOB.

Bibliography. M. A. Bowman, comp., *Western Mysticism; A Guide to the Basic Sources;* L. Bouyer, F. Vandenbroucke, and J. Leclercq, *A History of Christian Spirituality,* 3 vols.; *Dictionnaire de spiritualité ascetique et mystique,* II, cols. 1643–2193; A. Louth, *The Origins of Christian Mystical Theology;* T. S. Kepler, comp., *An Anthology of Devotional Literature;* W. James, *The Varieties of Religious Experience;* F. von Hügel, *The Mystical Element of Religion;* E. Underhill, *Mysticism;* R. M. Jones, *Studies in Mystical Religion;* R. Otto, *The Idea of the Holy;* R. C. Zaehner, *Mysticism, Sacred and Profane;* G. Harkness, *Mysticism: Its Meaning and Message;* H. D. Egan, *What Are They Saying about Mysticism?* S. T. Katz, ed., *Mysticism and Philosophical Analysis;* A. Poulain, *The Graces of Interior Prayer;* C. Butler, *Western Mysticism;* P. Murray, *The Mysticism Debate;* T. Merton, *New Seeds of Contemplation;* A. W. Tozer, *The Knowledge of the Holy;* A. Nygren, *Agape and Eros;* F. Heiler, *Prayer;* V. Lossky, *The Mystical Theology of the Eastern Church.*

Myth. The term occurs five times in the NT—four times in the Pastoral Epistles (I Tim. 1:4; 4:7; II Tim. 4:4; Titus 1:14; II Pet. 1:16). In each instance it signifies the fiction of a fable as distinct from the genuineness of the truth (cf. II Tim. 4:4, "turn away their ears from the truth, and turn aside unto myths"). This is in complete harmony with the classical connotation of the term (Gr. *mythos*), which from the time of Pindar onward always bears the sense of what is fictitious, as opposed to the term *logos,* which indicated what was true and historical. This consideration sheds an interesting ray on John's use of the term *Logos* as a title for Christ (John 1:1, 14) and Paul's frequent use of it as a synonym for the gospel which he proclaimed. Thus Socrates describes a particular story as "no fictitious myth but a true logos" (Plato, *Timaeus* 26E). It is also the connotation of the term during the period of the NT. Thus Philo speaks of those "who follow after unfeigned truth instead of fictitious myths" (*Exsecr.* 162), and Pseudo-Aristeas, using an adverbial form, affirms that "nothing has been set down in Scripture to no purpose or in a mythical sense" (*mythōdōs, Letter of Aristeas to Philocrates,* 168). In the English language, too, the "mythical" is ordinarily synonymous with the fabulous, the fantastic, and the historically inauthentic.

In contemporary theological discussion the term "myth" has achieved a special prominence. This is to a considerable degree the result of Rudolf Bultmann's demand for the "demythologization" of the NT—that is, for the excision or expurgation from the biblical presentation of the Christian message of every element of "myth." In Bultmann's judgment this requires the rejection of the biblical view of the world as belonging to "the cosmology of a pre-scientific age" and as therefore quite unacceptable to modern man. In effect, it amounts to the elimination of the miraculous or supernatural constituents of the scriptural record, since these are incompatible with Bultmann's own view of the world as a firmly closed system, governed by fixed natural laws, in which there can be no place for intervention "from outside." John Macquarrie, however, justly criticizes Bultmann for being "still obsessed with the pseudo-scientific view of a closed universe that was popular half a century ago" (*An Existentialist Theology,* 168), and Emil Brunner complains that in claiming "that our faith must eliminate everything that suspends the 'interrelatedness of Nature' and is consequently mythical" Bultmann "is using, as a criterion, a concept which has become wholly untenable" (*The Christian Doctrine of Creation and Redemption,* 190).

It is Bultmann's contention that the central message or *kerygma* of Christianity is incredible to modern man so long as it is presented in the mythical setting of the biblical world view, and that the latter constitutes an offense which is not at all identical with the true and ineradicable offense or *skandalon* of the Christian proclamation. He accordingly finds it necessary to discard such obviously (on his premises) mythical elements as Christ's preexistence and virgin birth, his deity and sinlessness, the substitutionary nature of his death as meeting the demands of a righteous God, his resurrection and ascension, and his future return in glory; also the final judgment of the world, the existence of spirit beings, the personality and power of the Holy Spirit, the doctrines of the Trinity, of original sin, and of death as a consequence of sin, and every explanation of events as miraculous. It is self-evident that this process of demythologization, when carried through with the thoroughness Bultmann displays, mutilates the Christianity of the NT in so radical a manner as to leave it unrecognizable. The stature of Jesus is reduced to that of a mere man, and the Christ event is transformed from an objective divine intervention into "a relative historical phenomenon" (*Kerygma and Myth,* 19). And it is in this, according to Bultmann, that the real offense of Christianity lies: the linking of our redemption with God's choice of an ordinary mortal individual, no different from every other man, and of an event in no way miraculous or supernatural (*Kerygma and Myth,* 43), which in its essential relativity belongs to the normal order of all mundane events.

Bultmann's relativism goes hand in hand with subjectivism. The relevance of the Christ event assumes a merely subjective significance. The incarnation and resurrection of Christ, for example, are not to be understood as datable events of the past, but as "eschatological" events which are to be subjectively experienced through faith in the word of preaching (cf. *Kerygma and Myth*, 41, 209; *Theology of the NT*, 305). It is, in fact, only *my* experience, here and now, that can have any authenticity for me—not anything that has happened in the past or that will happen in the future. In short, the Christian message is compressed within an existentialist mold. History and eschatology are to be understood in terms of pure subjectivism. Pronouncements about the deity of Jesus are not to be interpreted as dogmatic pronouncements concerning his nature but as existential value judgments, not as statements about Christ but as pronouncements about me. Thus, for example, the objective affirmation that Christ helps me because he is God's Son must give place to the subjective value judgment that he is God's Son because he helps me. Truth, in a word, is identified with subjectivity.

While the message of Christianity is, beyond doubt, in the truest sense existential and contemporaneous and demands the subjective response of faith, yet the faith it requires is faith in an objective reality. When robbed of its objectivity, the ground of which is God's free and supernatural intervention through Christ in the affairs of our world, Christianity becomes a drifting idea, an abstraction, a rootless idealism, an ungraspable balloon loosed from its moorings. Bultmann's "confusion of the question of the world-view with that of Myth," criticizes Brunner, "and the effort to adapt the Christian Faith to 'modern' views of life, and to the concepts of existential philosophy, comes out continually in the fact that he 'cleanses' the message of the New Testament from ideas which necessarily belong to it, and do not conflict with the modern view of the world at all, but only with the 'self-understanding,' and in particular with the prejudices, of an Idealistic philosophy"; while in his conception of history Bultmann "is lacking in insight into the significance of the New Testament *eph' hapax*, of the 'once-for-all-ness' (or uniqueness) of the Fact of Christ as an Event on the continuum of history" (*Dogmatics*, I, 267–68).

Yet, while realizing that in Bultmann's program of demythologization "what is at stake is nothing less than the central theological question of revelation, of 'Saving History,' and the knowledge of God as a 'Living God,' who is the Lord of nature and of history" (*Dogmatics*, II, 186), Brunner refuses to "give up the right to criticize this or that recorded miracle, this or that marvel as due rather to the 'myth-forming imagination' than to the historical fact" (*ibid.*, 192). In other words, he is prepared to concur with the judgment that in the NT there are mythical elements which require to be eliminated; but as a demythologizer he is unwilling to proceed to such radical lengths as does Bultmann. When, however, we find him repudiating doctrines like the virgin birth of Christ, his bodily resurrection (whence the unbiblical "liberal" distinction between "the historic Jesus" and "the risen Christ"), his bodily ascension, and the general resurrection at the last day, we perceive that he is definitely moving in the same direction as Bultmann, even though, unlike Bultmann, he seeks to defend his procedure by arguing that these doctrines formed no part of the original kerygma (*ibid.*, 352ff.). But nonetheless, despite his criticisms of Bultmann, "modern science" plays a determinative role in Brunner's thinking. Thus Brunner emphasizes that he "cannot say too strongly that the biblical view of the world is absolutely irreconcilable with modern science" (*ibid.*, 39); and he assures us that "the position of modern knowledge forces us to abandon" the definite picture of space, of time, and of the origins of life given in the biblical story of creation (*ibid.*, 31). And so he rejects as myths the Genesis accounts of creation and Paradise. Likewise he affirms the need for the demythologization of statements concerning the form in which the event of Christ's parousia will take place on the ground that they are "pronouncements of the New Testament which are clearly mythical, in the sense that they are in fact unacceptable to us who have no longer the world-picture of the ancients and the apostles" (*Eternal Hope*). Again, and inversely, new discoveries may reinstate as respectable certain aspects of the biblical world picture which modern science was thought to have exposed as mythical. For example, we are now assured that, thanks to the development of nuclear warheads, the doctrine of the sudden end of human history which "until recently seemed to be only the apocalyptic fantasies of the Christian faith has today entered the sphere of the soberest scientific calculations," with the result, says Brunner, that "this thought has ceased to be absurd, i.e., to be such that a man educated in modern scientific knowledge would have to give it up" (*ibid.*, 127). And so our modern man so educated must now be invited to "dedemythologize" at this point where he had so recently and with such approval demythologized.

Karl Barth, whose approach to the question of the authority of Scripture is governed by premises akin to those accepted by Bultmann and Brunner, wishes to establish a distinction between *myth* on the one hand and *saga* or *legend* on the other. By "legend," however, he means what the other two understand by "myth." Legend, according to Barth, does not necessarily attack the substance of the biblical witness, even though there is uncertainty about what he calls its "general" historicity (i.e., its historical truth as generally conceived), whereas he views myth as belonging to a different category which "necessarily attacks the substance of the biblical witness" inasmuch as it pretends to be history when it is not, and thereby throws doubt on, indeed denies, what he calls the "special" historicity of the biblical narratives (i.e., their special significance as history between God and man), thus relegating them to the realm of a "timeless truth, in other words, a human creation" (*Church Dogmatics* I/1, 375ff.). This however, is principally a matter of definition: where Bultmann and Brunner use the term "myth," Barth prefers to use "legend."

A more recent and no less radical advocacy of theological reductionism or demythologization occurred with the publication of *The Myth of God Incarnate,* a composite volume by seven British academics, in which it is demanded that man be understood as a naturalistic phenomenon, the product of evolutionary development, and the "verbal divine authority" of the Bible is denied. A literal acceptance of the birth of Jesus as the incarnation of the Son of God is, as the title indicates, rejected, and the notion of incarnation is allowed, in existentialist fashion, only as "a mythological or poetic way of expressing his significance for us." Everything again is reduced to merely human dimensions, and we are left with a denial, not an adaptation, of the Christian faith. Everything, by the same token, is reduced to the perspective of subjective relativism as we are offered a "deabsolutized" Scripture and a "deabsolutized" Jesus.

There is one further definition of myth to which attention must be drawn, one which in effect equates it with symbolism and relates it to the inherent inability of human language to express adequately the things of God. Thus Brunner maintains that "the Christian *kerygma* cannot be separated from Myth" since "the Christian statement is necessarily and consciously 'anthropomorphic' in the sense that it does, and must do, what Bultmann conceives to be characteristic of the mythical—'it speaks of God in a human way'" (*Dogmatics,* II, 268). And in the same connection Bultmann explains that "mythology is the use of imagery to express the otherworldly in terms of this world and the divine in terms of human life, the other side in terms of this side" (*Kerygma and Myth,* 10). To eliminate myth in this sense would mean that it would become impossible for man to say anything about God or for God to say anything intelligible to man, for we have no other medium of expression than the terms of this world. But it certainly does not follow that the terms of this side must always be given a symbolical (mythological) meaning, or that they are always inadequate for the purpose intended. While there is indeed much symbolism in the NT, it is evident also that many things there are intended in a literal sense and that events—e.g., Christ's ascension—are described phenomenally (i.e., from the quite legitimate point of view of the observer). Finally, it must be stressed that the concept of myth which we have been discussing in this article is incompatible with the classical doctrine of Holy Scripture. The Christ of the Bible is *the Logos,* not a *mythos;* he needs no demythologization at the hands of human scholars. P. E. Hughes

See also Demythologization; Bultmann, Rudolf; Brunner, Heinrich Emil.

Bibliography. P. E. Hughes, *Scripture and Myth;* I. Henderson, *Myth in the NT;* F. Gogarten, *Demythologizing and History;* N. B. Stonehouse, "Rudolf Bultmann's Jesus," in *Paul Before the Areopagus;* M. Green, ed., *The Truth of God Incarnate.*

Nn

Names in Bible Times, Significance of. The very fact that the word "name" occurs more than a thousand times in the Bible attests to its theological importance. In the ancient world a name was not merely a label but was virtually equivalent to whoever or whatever bore it. I Sam. 25:25 is a key passage: "Nabal . . . is just like his name—his name is Fool, and folly goes with him." The Greek word "names" is correctly translated as "people" in Rev. 3:4 NIV. Name often means (or is translated as) reputation (Mark 6:14; Rev. 3:1), authority/power (Matt. 7:22; Acts 4:7), character (Matt. 6:9). In the OT it is frequently found in parallelism with memory, remembrance, renown (e.g. Exod. 3:15; Job 18:17; Ps. 135:13).

Giving a name to anyone or anything was tantamount to owning or controlling it (Gen. 1:5, 8, 10; 2:19–20; II Sam. 12:28), and changing a name signified promotion to a higher status (Gen. 17:5; 32:28; to this day in orthodox Judaism a dying person's name is sometimes officially changed in the hope that a new name will bring health and a new life) or demotion to a lower status (II Kings 23:34–35; 24:17). Blotting out or cutting off the name of a person or thing meant destroying that person or thing (II Kings 14:27; Isa. 14:22; Zeph. 1:4; see also Ps. 83:4).

The name and being of God are often used in parallelism with each other (Pss. 18:49; 68:4; 74:18; 86:12; 92:1; Isa. 25:1; Mal. 3:16), stressing their essential identity. Belief in Jesus' name is the same as believing in Jesus himself, as John 3:18 demonstrates. Prayer in Jesus' name, therefore, is not mystical reliance on a traditional formula but is praying in accord with Jesus' character, his mind, his purpose. He is just like his name—a name that means Savior (Matt. 1:21), a name "that is above every [other] name" (Phil. 2:9).

R. Youngblood

See also God, Names of.

Bibliography. J. Barr, "The Symbolism of Names in the OT," *BJRL* 52:11–29; H. Bietenhard and F. F. Bruce, *NIDNTT*, II, 648–56; J. Pedersen, *Isr* 1–2:245–59.

Nations, Judgment of. *See* Judgment of the Nations, The.

Naturalism. The view that the "natural" universe, the universe of matter and energy, is all that there really is. This rules out God, so naturalism is atheistic. It rules out other spiritual beings as well as God, so naturalism is materialistic. By ruling out a spiritual part of the human person which might survive death and a God who might resurrect the body, naturalism also rules out survival after death. In addition, naturalism usually but not always denies human freedom on the grounds that every event must be explainable by deterministic natural laws. It usually but not always denies any absolute values because it can find no grounds for such values in a world made up only of matter and energy. And finally, naturalism usually but not always denies that the universe has any meaning or purpose because there is no God to give it a meaning or purpose, and nothing else which can give it a meaning or purpose.

Anyone who accepts the first three denials—of God, spiritual beings, and immortality—might be called a naturalist in the broad sense, and anyone who adds to these the denial of freedom, values, and purpose might be labeled a naturalist in the strict sense, or a strict naturalist. Communists, for instance, are not strict naturalists, for their world view includes a purpose in history—at least in human history—and perhaps in the whole history of the universe. Some religious humanists are not strict naturalists, for they argue for free will and even for values which are independent of known wants and needs. Some opponents of naturalism would argue that naturalists in the broad sense are at least somewhat inconsistent and that naturalism in the broad sense leads logically to strict naturalism. Many strict naturalists would agree with this.

Those who reject naturalism in both the strict and broad sense do so for a variety of reasons. They may have positive arguments for the existence of some of what naturalists deny, or they may have what seem to be decisive refutations of some or all of the arguments for naturalism. But, in addition to particular arguments against naturalist tenets or their grounds of belief, some opponents of naturalism believe that there is a general argument which holds against any form of naturalism. These opponents hold that naturalism has a "fatal flaw" or, to put it more strongly, that naturalism is self-destroying. If naturalism is true, then human reason must be the result of natural forces. These natural forces are not, on the naturalistic view, rational themselves, nor can they be the result of a rational cause. So human reason would be the result of nonrational causes. This, it can be argued, gives us a strong reason to distrust human reason, especially in its less practical and more theoretical exercises. But the theory of naturalism is itself such an exercise of theoretical reason. If naturalism is true, we would have strong reasons to distrust theoretical reasoning. If we distrust theoretical reasoning, we distrust particular applications of it, such as the theory of naturalism. Thus, if naturalism is true, we have strong reasons to distrust naturalism. M. H. MACDONALD

Bibliography. C. S. Lewis, *Miracles;* A. Flew, *God and Philosophy* and *A Rational Animal;* J. N. Jordan, "Determinism's Dilemma," *RevM* Sept. 1969; J. R. Lucas, *The Freedom of the Will;* R. Rorty, *Philosophy and the Mirror of Nature.*

Natural Law. A moral order divinely implanted in mankind and accessible to all persons through human reason. It should not be confused with the "laws of nature," which became so prominent in natural science during the eighteenth and nineteenth centuries—though there was, historically, some overlap and connection between the two. Natural law is chiefly a matter of ethics and is primarily associated with Roman Catholic theology. It has enabled that church to address socioeconomic, legal, moral, and political issues on what is held to be a philosophical foundation common to all mankind.

The roots of this notion lie in antiquity. Aristotle taught that the moral order and human rights should be derived by reason from the objective cosmic order, which he saw best realized in the city-state. The Stoics universalized this idea and heavily influenced Roman ethical and legal thought, which is to say, the intellectual world of the NT and especially the Latin church fathers. In Rom. 2:14–15 Paul describes a law "written in the hearts" of Gentiles by which they will be judged, and elsewhere (Rom. 1:24–27; I Cor. 11:14) refers to certain sexual matters as "against nature." Augustine argued over against pagans and Manichaeans that God's will is the eternal law, both natural and moral, behind the entire cosmos; but he, like Paul, saw this moral order in the light of faith and revelation rather than of reason and philosophy.

It was Thomas Aquinas, the great synthesizer of the gospel and Greek philosophy, who first formulated the notion of natural law in a way still foundational and largely normative for Roman Catholics today. Thomas taught that the "eternal law" by which God established all things became, when impressed upon man and his nature, a "natural law" (*ius naturae*), through which man potentially participated in his divinely ordered true end, but which in his freedom he could also choose to disobey. Because it was of the essence of things, man could perceive and logically deduce it through reason, though it was also taught in Scripture and received simply in faith. For Thomas, the natural law was essentially "to do good and avoid evil," the Golden Rule (Matt. 7:12), and the second Table of the Law, but it included as well such social matters as monogamous marriage and the right to hold property. It was the task of conscience to apply to particular cases the immutable general principles perceived by reason.

Scotus and Ockham located natural law in the will of God rather than in the very essence of things. So also the Protestant Reformers did not reject the term and notion as such, but they equated it with the will of God revealed in Scripture and fundamentally questioned fallen man's ability to reason his way to it. In modern times, beginning perhaps with Hugo Grotius, natural law grew increasingly independent of its religious framework and deeply influenced social and political thought as mankind's universal and inalienable natural rights. Kant and most modern philosophers have denied any demonstrable connection between ethics and a rational law perceivable in the nature of things. Nevertheless, during the past century natural law theory experienced a renaissance in Roman Catholic circles. It underlies much of Pope Leo XIII's social legislation and influenced Pope Paul VI's famous ruling on matters of sexual conduct (*Humanae Vitae*). American Catholic universities still have many institutes and journals which seek to apply natural law theory to contemporary social, moral, and legal issues. Several modern Protestant thinkers (e.g., certain Scottish commonsense realists, Emil Brunner, and, in their own distinctive way, Abraham Kuyper and his disciples) have seen the advantages of natural law theory in treating of social and ethical matters with non-Christians. But most Protestants, especially Karl Barth, continue to hold that ethical matters cannot be known in truth apart from the revelation of God's will in Jesus Christ and Holy Scripture. J. VAN ENGEN

Bibliography. *NCE*, X, 251–71; *LTK*, VII, 821–29; *RGG*, IV, 1359–65.

Natural Man. *See* MAN, NATURAL.

Natural Revelation. *See* REVELATION, GENERAL.

Natural Theology. Truths about God that can be learned from created things (nature, man, world) by reason alone. The importance of natural theology to Christian thought has varied widely from age to age, depending largely upon the general intellectual climate. It first became a significant part of Christian teaching in the High Middle Ages, and was made a fixed part of Roman Catholic dogma in 1870 at Vatican Council I. Its Dogmatic Constitution on the Catholic Faith made it a matter of faith to believe that God has revealed himself in two ways, naturally and supernaturally, and that "God can certainly be known [*certo cognosci*] from created things by the natural light of human reason." The council sought thus to reaffirm, over against nineteenth century secularized skeptics and especially philosophical movements since Kant, that God is indeed knowable by reason and that such philosophical truths are a legitimate and true form of theology. This teaching was one among several factors which stimulated the growth of Neo-Thomism (Gilson, Maritain, etc.) in the early twentieth century. But quite apart from the original intent and later influence of this teaching, the Catholic Church now stands committed to the belief that there are two theologies.

Ancient philosophers spoke of a "natural theology," by which they meant philosophical discourse on the essential, "divine" nature of things as distinguished from the accidental and transient, and also philosophical truths about God as distinguished from state cults and religious myths. Scripture, however, spoke of the world as created in time and sustained by its Creator. Creation points still toward its Creator (what Protestants later called general revelation), but that it does so is chiefly taught by Scripture (that is, special revelation) and confirmed in experience rather than deduced by reason alone. Only when the Judeo-Christian notion of "creation" is made equivalent to the Greek philosophical notion of "nature," something never done directly by the Greek and Latin church fathers, is the stage set for the development of a "natural theology."

The first great proponent of a natural theology distinguishable from revealed theology was Thomas Aquinas, the synthesizer of Greek philosophy and the gospel, who also laid the groundwork for notions of "natural law," the ethical equivalent of natural theology. Aquinas defined theology as a "science" in the Aristotelian sense, that is, a definable body of knowledge with its own sources, principles, methods, and content, and he insisted that beyond the truths derived from the study of Scripture there was another body of (compatible) truths based upon the application of reason to the created world. He supported this, as nearly all Catholics have, with reference to Rom. 1:20–21 and to the actual accomplishments of pagan philosophers, especially Aristotle. Such truths included especially the existence of God, which he laid out in five famous proofs near the beginning of his *Summa* (all of them essentially arguments for an Ultimate Cause) and the attributes (eternity, invisibility, etc.) which described God's nature. These were then complemented and enriched by supernaturally revealed truths such as the trinity of persons in the Godhead and the incarnation of God in Jesus.

Nearly all Catholic scholars of natural theology have built upon, refined, or qualified the position first articulated by Thomas. In doing natural theology, first of all, they do not mean to have reason replace faith or philosophical discourse the grace of God revealed in Christ. Faith and grace remain primary for all believers, but natural theology offers the opportunity to establish certain truths by means common to all persons. Second, those truths are not taken to be "grounds" or "foundations" for additional, revealed truths. Yet if these truths are established, it can be seen as "reasonable" to accept revealed truths as well. And thus Catholics are in fact inclined to see a continuum between natural theology, that which is known of God by the light of natural reason, and revealed theology, that which is known by the light of faith.

The Protestant Reformers objected to the impact of philosophy upon theology and insisted upon a return to Scripture. They assumed that all men had some implicit knowledge of God's existence (Calvin's "sense of divinity"), but they declared it useless apart from the revelation of God's will and grace in Jesus Christ. Several early confessional documents (e.g., the Westminster and the Belgic) do speak of God revealing himself in nature (citing still Rom. 1:20–21), but this is revelation not fully comprehensible apart from Scripture. Orthodox Protestants have generally raised three major objections to natural theology. First, it lacks scriptural basis. Read in context, Rom. 1 and 2 teach that the pagan's natural knowledge of God is distorted and turned only to his judgment, in no way to the reasonable deduction of theological truths. Second, and perhaps most importantly, natural theology effectively exempts human reason from the fall and the effects of original sin. Man's reason is now as perverse as any of his other faculties and therefore is not capable, apart from God's gracious intervention, of finding its way back to God and truly knowing him. This point, which involves quite different anthropological views, will doubtless continue to divide Protestants and Catholics. Third, conceding the knowledge of God arrived at by pagan philosophers (his being, invisibility, omnipotence, etc.), Protestants object that this is wholly abstract and worthless. This Supreme Being has little to do with the God of judgment and mercy, of righteousness and love, revealed all through Scripture and preeminently in Jesus Christ. When Protestants retain descriptions of God's attributes, as they often have at the beginning of formal theologies, they argue and illustrate them from Scripture, not from philosophical discourse.

In modern times the impact of the Enlightenment drove both Catholic and Protestant thinkers to reduce the supernatural, miraculous elements and to construct a "natural theology" open to reason and common to all men. Kant rejected all proofs for the existence of God and sought to place religion "within the bounds of reason." This more liberal form of natural theology became very common in the eighteenth and nineteenth centuries: the famous Gifford Lectures, for instance, are supposed to promote "Natural Theology." Scottish commonsense realism may represent a unique effort to blend philosophy with fairly orthodox Christianity, but in general the miraculous grace of God had disappeared from these forms of theology. In the twentieth century the so-called dialectical theologians vigorously objected against theologies which glossed over the radical intervention of God through Jesus Christ and his Word. Karl Barth in particular saw such natural religion as the great foe of true faith and rejected the Catholic "analogy of being" as an unwarranted jump (rather than deduction) from creation to Creator. Several others in turn, especially Emil Brunner, objected that Barth's exclusive emphasis upon Christ and the Word denied the reality of God's "general revelation" of himself in creation and especially human creatures, his image-bearers, something attested in Scripture.

In recent times natural theology has received comparatively little attention apart from a few Catholic philosophers. One interesting and related development has occurred in the field of the history of religions. Certain such historians (especially G. van der Leeuw and M. Eliade) have discovered patterns of religious belief and practice (a High God, a fall from a past Golden Age, various salvation motifs, etc.) which do not make up a natural theology in the traditional sense, but which they believe could yield an instructive prolegomenon to the study of Christian theology.

J. Van Engen

See also Thomas Aquinas; Neo-Thomism; Revelation, General.

Bibliography. *LTK,* VII, 811–17; *RGG,* IV, 1322–29; *NCE,* XIV, 61–64; M. Holloway, *An Introduction to Natural Theology;* G. Berkouwer, *General Revelation;* R. McInerny and A. Plantinga in the *Proceedings of the American Catholic Philosophical Association,* 1981.

Nazarene. *See* Christians, Names of.

Neander, Johann August Wilhelm (1789–1850). German church historian and theologian. Born David Mendel, he came under the influence of romanticism, especially Schleiermacher, and in 1806 converted from Judaism to Protestantism, taking the name Neander (Greek for "new man"). He then studied theology and from 1813 taught church history at the University of Berlin, where as a member of the "mediating school" he resisted both the extremes of pantheistic metaphysics and rigid orthodoxy and was a determined opponent of the rationalism of F. C. Baur and D. F. Strauss. His pietistic ideal of service was reflected in the part he played in forming the Berlin Missionary Society and his impact on the young J. H. Wichern, founder of the Inner Mission.

Author of the *General History of the Christian Religion and Church* (6 vols., 1825–52) and several monographs on persons and movements in the early and medieval church, Neander is commonly regarded as the founder of modern church historiography. His works were based on extensive use of original sources but tended to concentrate more on personalities than institutions. He saw the main theme of church history as the continuing conflict between the spirit of Christ and the spirit of the world. Functioning in effect as the history of piety, its task was to bring about a higher and purer type of faith by stimulating confidence in the power of the divine Word to overcome the world and spiritually uplift believers. Neander's romantic conception of the role of church history was summed up in his famous phrase: "The heart (*pectus*) is the motivating force of theology." R. V. PIERARD

See also MEDIATING THEOLOGY.

Bibliography. K. Scholder, *RGG,* III, 1388–89; W. W. Gasque, *NIDCC,* 696; E. Simons, *SHERK,* VIII, 95–96.

Necessary Being. *See* BEING.

Necessity. The Greek approach to life was largely shaped by the consciousness of a necessity subject to the laws and norms of fate. The general concept that expresses this feeling of having been consigned to fate (a universal principle which not only embraces human existence but also dominates the lives of the gods themselves) is *anankē. Anankē* was the power which determined all reality, the principle which dominated the universe.

The Greek conception of necessity as fate is foreign to Israel. The OT picture of God conceives him as a divine will powerfully active in history.

In the NT some form of *anankē* occurs thirty-four times. Among its important meanings are (1) to describe a compulsion or a being compelled which does not rest on the use of outward force and (2) to describe a belief in the providence of God governing the processes and events of history. The death of Jesus is a divine necessity and the necessary fulfillment of the Scripture. The way of Christ is not the result of chance or accident. Jesus' suffering is expressly designated as a divine "must." It is the underlying concern of Luke to present the death and resurrection of Jesus as necessary saving acts of God.

Protestantism is not totally unified in its interpretation of the role of necessity. Calvinists stress God's absolute sovereignty—that he is the direct cause of all that is, that no one can stand against his will. Arminians (later Wesleyans) emphasize human freedom—that God through Christ has made provision for the salvation of all human souls who believe. M. H. MACDONALD

See also FREEDOM, FREE WILL, AND DETERMINISM; PREDESTINATION.

Bibliography. Augustine, *City of God,* V, viii, ix; Calvin, *Institutes of the Christian Religion,* 3.3; J. G. Fichte, *The Vocation of Man,* Section I (Doubt); W. Cunningham, "Calvinism and the Doctrine of Philosophical Necessity," in *The Reformers and the Theology of the Reformation;* E. Käsemann, "A Pauline Version of the 'Amor Fati,'" in *New Testament Questions of Today;* R. Morgenthaler, *NIDNTT,* II, 662ff.

Neoevangelicalism. *See* EVANGELICALISM.

Neonomianism. *See* MARROW CONTROVERSY.

Neo-orthodoxy. ***History.*** Neo-orthodoxy is not a single system; it is not a unified movement; it does not have a commonly articulated set of essentials. At best it can be described as an approach or attitude that began in a common environment but soon expressed itself in diverse ways. It began in the crisis associated with the disillusionment following World War I, with a rejection of Protestant scholasticism, and with a denial of the Protestant liberal movement which had stressed accommodation of Christianity to Western science and culture, the immanence of God, and the progressive improvement of mankind.

The first important expression of the movement was Karl Barth's *Römerbrief,* published in 1919. Soon a number of Swiss and German pastors were involved. In the two years 1921–22 Friedrich Gogarten published his *Religious Decision,* Emil Brunner his *Experience, Knowledge and Faith,* Eduard Thurneysen his *Dostoievsky,* and Barth the second edition of his *Commentary on Romans.* In the fall of 1922 they established *Zwischen den Zeiten,* a journal whose title characterized the crisis element in their thinking in that they felt they lived between the time when the Word was made flesh and the imminent appearance of the Word again. Although at this point most of the early members of the movement held to some common points of view, such as the absolute transcendence of God over all human knowledge and work, the sovereignty of the revelation in Jesus Christ, the authority of Scripture, and the sinfulness of mankind, it was not long before their dialectical approach led them to disagreements and a parting of the ways.

However, the disagreements seemed to make the movement all the more vigorous and intriguing. Soon it spread to England, where C. H. Dodd and Edwyn Hoskyns became involved; in Sweden Gustaf Aulén and Anders Nygren became followers; in America the Niebuhr brothers were identified as neo-orthodox; and others in other churches and lands began to read about the movement and watch what was happening. With the rise of the Nazi movement in Germany many of the leaders of the neo-orthodox movement met with other German Christians in Barmen in 1934 and issued a declaration against the evils of Nazism. The resulting crackdown by Hitler forced some into exile, as Paul Tillich; some back to their homeland, as Barth; some underground, as Dietrich Bonhoeffer; and some ultimately into concentration camps, as Martin

Niemoeller. The movement continued throughout the period of World War II and into the postwar period, but with the death of the main leaders it tended to lose its cutting edge in theology.

The movement was called neo-orthodox for a number of reasons. Some used the term in derision, claiming it had abandoned the traditional Protestant creedal formulations and was advocating a new "off" brand of orthodoxy. Others saw the movement as a narrowing of the traditional stance of Protestantism and thus to be avoided in favor of a more liberal stance. Those in sympathy with the movement saw in the word "orthodoxy" the effort to get back to the basic ideas of the Protestant Reformation and even the early church, as a means of proclaiming the truth of the gospel in the twentieth century; and in the prefix "neo" they saw the validity of new philological principles in helping to attain an accurate view of Scripture, which in turn and in combination with orthodoxy would provide a powerful witness to God's action in Christ for those of the new century.

Methodology. The methodological approach of the movement involved dialectical theology, theology of paradox, and crisis theology. The use of dialectical thinking goes back to the Greek world and Socrates' use of questions and answers to derive insight and truth. It was used by Abelard in *Sic et Non,* and is the technique of posing opposites against each other in the search for truth. Barth and the early leaders were probably attracted to the dialectic as the result of their study of Søren Kierkegaard's writings. For Kierkegaard, propositional truths are not sufficient; assent to a series of religious formulations or creeds is not enough. Kierkegaard believed theological assertions of the faith to be paradoxical. This requires the believer to hold opposite "truths" in tension. Their reconciliation comes in an existential act generated after anxiety, tension, and crisis, and which the mind takes to be a leap of faith.

The neo-orthodox took the position that traditional and liberal Protestantism had lost the insight and truth of the faith. The nineteenth century theologians had taken the paradoxes of faith, dissolved their tension, used rational, logical, coherent explanations as a substitute, creating propositions, and thus had destroyed the living dynamic of the faith. For the neo-orthodox, paradoxes of the faith must remain precisely that, and the dialectic method which seeks to find the truth in the opposites of the paradoxes leads to a true dynamic faith. As an example of this consider the statement: "In the No found in God's righteous anger one finds the Yes of his compassion and mercy."

Some of the paradoxes identified by the neo-orthodox movement are the absolute transcendence of God in contrast with the self-disclosure of God; Christ as the God-man; faith as a gift and yet an act; humans as sinful yet free; eternity entering time. How is it possible to have a wholly other God who reveals himself? How is it possible for the man Jesus of history to be the Son of God, the second person of the Trinity? How can one speak of faith as God's gift and yet involve human action? How is it possible for humans to be simultaneously sinful and saved? How is it possible for eternity, which is apart from time, to break in on time? In struggling with these, the temptation is to rationalize answers and avoid the crisis of faith; but the neo-orthodox eschewed such a solution. It is only in crisis/struggling that one can rise above the paradox and be grasped by the truth in such a way as to defy rational explanation. Crisis is that point where yes and no meet. It is that theological point where the human recognizes God's condemnation of all human endeavors in morals, religion, thought processes, scientific discoveries, and so on, and the only release is from God's word. The neo-orthodox, in summarizing their methodology, used dialectics in relation to the paradoxes of the faith which precipitated crises which in turn became the situation for the revelation of truth.

Some Key Beliefs. Perhaps the fundamental theological concept of the movement is that of the totally free, sovereign God, the wholly other in relation to his creation as to how it is controlled, redeemed, and how he chooses to reveal himself to it. Next is God's self-revelation, a dynamic act of grace to which mankind's response is to listen. This revelation is the Word of God in a threefold sense: Jesus as the word made flesh; Scripture which points to the word made flesh; and the sermon which is the vehicle for the proclamation of the Word made flesh. In its first sense, the Word made flesh, it is not a concern for the historical Jesus, as in Protestant liberalism, but a concern for the Christ of faith, the risen Christ testified to and proclaimed by the apostles. In the second sense, Word as Scripture, it is not intended that the two be seen as one. The Scripture contains the Word but is not the Word. In the third sense, the Word is proclaimed and witnessed to, in, and through the body of Christ through the work of the Holy Spirit.

The movement also stressed the sinfulness of mankind. The sovereign, free God who reveals himself does so to a sinful fallen humanity and creation. There is a vast chasm between the sovereign God and mankind, and there is no way that mankind can bridge that chasm. All of mankind's efforts to do so in his religious, moral, and ethical thoughts and actions are as nothing. The only possible way for the chasm to be crossed is by God, and this he has done in Christ. And now the paradox and the crisis: when the paradox of the word's No against mankind's sin is given along with the Yes of the Word of grace and mercy, the crisis mankind faces is to decide either yes or no. The turning point has been reached as the eternal God reveals himself in mankind's time and existence.

Significance. The neo-orthodox movement has made a number of important contributions to twentieth century theology. With its stress on Scripture as the container of the Word it emphasized the unity of Scripture and helped to precipitate a renewed interest in hermeneutics. With its rejection of nineteenth century Protestant liberalism and its return to the principles of the Reformation it helped to rejuvenate interest in the theology of the sixteenth century reformers and in the early church fathers. With its threefold view of the Word the doctrine of Christology has been more carefully examined, and the Word as proclamation has reemphasized the importance of preaching and the church as the fellowship of believers. The use of dialectic, paradox, and crisis introduced an effort to preserve the absolutes of the faith from every dogmatic formulation and, by so doing, aided the cause of ecumenism. Finally, the urgency found in the writings and in the title of its first journal has encouraged a renewed interest in eschatology.

Neo-orthodoxy is tied to its own *Zeitgeist* and thus does not have the popularity it enjoyed earlier in the century. Certain inherent elements have precluded its continuing influence. For example, its dialectic has presented confusing concepts such as "the impossible-possibility" and "the history beyond time"; its view of Scripture, "The Bible is God's Word so far as God lets it be his Word" (Barth, *Church Dogmatics*, I/2, 123), has been seen as a rejection of the infallible *sola Scriptura* of conservative Protestantism. The reliance of some of the neo-orthodox upon existentialism and other nineteenth and twentieth century concepts has meant that when those concepts became unfashionable, neo-orthodoxy became unfashionable. Perhaps the greatest weakness within the movement has been its pessimism concerning the reliability and validity of human reason. If human reason cannot be trusted, then it follows that since neo-orthodoxy relied on human reason, it could not be trusted. Finally, some have criticized neo-orthodoxy for lacking a plan for the reformation of society; most theologies, however, are susceptible to this charge. Neo-orthodoxy's stance toward the conservatives and the liberals has satisfied neither group and the moderates have not embraced it. Thus although one cannot ignore the movement, its ultimate place in the history of theology is not yet clear.

R. V. SCHNUCKER

See also AULÉN, GUSTAF EMANUEL HILDEBRAND; BARTH, KARL; BRUNNER, HEINRICH EMIL; BULTMANN, RUDOLF; KIERKEGAARD, SØREN; GOGARTEN, FRIEDRICH; NIEBUHR, REINHOLD.

Bibliography. J. Pelikan, *Twentieth Century Theology in the Making*, 3 vols.; J. Macquarrie, *Twentieth-Century Religious Thought;* W. Nicholls, *Systematic and Philosophical Theology;* J. M. Robinson, ed., *The Beginnings of Dialectical Theology;* W. Hordern, *The Case for a New Reformation Theology;* H. U. von Balthasar, *The Theology of Karl Barth;* C. Michalson, ed., *Christianity and the Existentialists;* E. Brunner, *The Theology of Crisis;* O. Weber, *Foundations of Dogmatics*, 2 vols.; C. W. Kegley and R. W. Bretall, eds., *Reinhold Niebuhr;* A. J. Klassen, ed., *A Bonhoeffer Legacy;* W. Schmithals, *An Introduction to the Theology of Rudolf Bultmann.*

Neo-Pentecostalism. *See* CHARISMATIC MOVEMENT.

Neoplatonism. The principal form of Greek philosophy from the third to the sixth centuries A.D. It is usually described as founded by Plotinus (205–70), but perhaps a more accurate statement would be that Plotinus was the most creative thinker within later Platonism. Plotinus stands in continuity with second century philosophers such as the middle Platonist Albinus and the Neo-Pythagorean Numenius. Middle Platonism had begun the assimilation of Pythagorean, Aristotelian, and Stoic elements into Platonic thought. Plotinus created a new synthesis by shaping these strands into a coherent religious philosophy.

Plotinus was born in Egypt and studied in Alexandria under Ammonius Saccas. After accompanying the emperor Gordian on a campaign in the East, he settled in Rome about 244 and began his own school there. He wrote essays for his students about their philosophical discussions. His pupil Porphyry collected these and arranged them in a somewhat systematic manner into six *Enneads* (groups of nine), the major source for Plotinus' philosophy. Porphyry published the *Enneads* shortly after A.D. 300 and accompanied them with a *Life of Plotinus.* He reported that Plotinus had the mystical experience of union with the divine on four occasions, and the description of union in the *Enneads* is one of the classics of mysticism.

Plotinus's system begins with the One, the supreme transcendent principle which can be described only by negation. It is immaterial and impersonal. As the number one is different from all other numbers yet makes them possible, so the One is the ground of all being and source of all values. The One transcends all duality, both of thought and reality and of being and nonbeing. Out of the One, but without any change in the One, there proceeded by emanation Mind (*nous*), the intellectual principle. Mind is the principle of divine intelligence, the "eternal consciousness," the highest really knowable entity. This element already partakes of duality, for consciousness contains the knower and the known. The next emanation was the World Soul (*psychē*). This is the moving power behind the whole universe. The World Soul is intermediary between Mind and bodily reality; it is the principle at work in the moving stars, animals, plants, and man, but transcends individual souls. The lowest creative principle is Nature (*physis*). As the descent from the One is characterized by increasing individuation and multiplicity, so Nature finds itself in direct contact with matter. Bare matter is the limiting principle of reality.

Man is a microcosm of reality, containing matter, nature, soul, and mind in himself. Manifoldness longs to be reunited to the One, and man by contemplation has the possibility of return to the One. Contemplation is the most perfect human activity, and by it may be achieved a state of ecstasy, an experience of unification. The importance of mental concentration is the reason for describing Plotinus's view as intellectual mysticism. It is unlike Christian mysticism in that the experience of union is not the result of divine grace. Union is achieved rarely, and then as a result of asceticism and prolonged effort of the will and understanding. One cannot control the experience or determine when it will come. Plotinus thinks, therefore, in a circular movement in which the manifold returns to the One; nothing gets lost in this circular movement of emanation and return.

Evil is not an ontological reality in this system. Nothing is evil in its nature. Rather evil is nonbeing, but Plotinus did not mean by this unreal. Nonbeing is a state of privation, and it is a real possibility for beings to turn away from life toward nonbeing.

After Plotinus and Porphyry, important later Neoplatonists include Iamblichus (*ca.* 250–*ca.* 325), who incorporated theosophy and theurgy into Neoplatonism and wrote works important for the religious thought (influenced by magic) of late antiquity; Sallustius, who *ca.* 362 wrote a manual of Neoplatonic religion in support of Julian's efforts to reestablish paganism; and Proclus (410–485), an encyclopedic thinker who systematized the Greek philosophical inheritance.

Neoplatonism provided the philosophical basis for the pagan opposition to Christianity in the fourth and fifth centuries. Porphyry, in addition to numerous philosophical treatises, wrote a massive work in fifteen volumes, now lost, *Against the Christians.* Julian, emperor from 361 to 363, besides official measures against the Christians wrote *Against the Galilaeans,* which can be reconstructed from Cyril of Alexandria's refutation of it. On the other hand, Neoplatonism provided the intellectual framework for the thought of several Christian theologians: Gregory of Nyssa, Victorinus, Ambrose, Augustine, and especially Dionysius the Pseudo-Areopagite.

The Neoplatonist Damascius was head of the Academy in Athens when Justinian closed it in 529. Neoplatonic influence continued, however, in both the Western and Eastern churches. Neoplatonism inspired the thought of John Scotus Erigena in Gaul in the ninth century, of Michael Psellus in Byzantium in the eleventh century, and of various thinkers in the Renaissance (notably Marsilio Ficino). Elements of the Neoplatonic approach are to be found in as recent a thinker as Paul Tillich. The great minds which have been stimulated by this philosophy are a testimony to its attraction and creative powers. E. Ferguson

See also Augustine of Hippo; Erigena, John Scotus; Dionysius the Pseudo-Areopagite.

Bibliography. E. R. Dodds, *Select Passages Illustrating Neoplatonism* and *Proclus: Elements of Theology;* A. D. Nock, *Sallustius Concerning the Gods and the Universe;* A. H. Armstrong, ed., *The Cambridge History of Later Greek and Early Medieval Philosophy;* J. M. Rist, *Plotinus: the Road to Reality;* J. Geffcken, *The Last Days of Greco-Roman Paganism.*

Neo-Thomism. A twentieth century revival of the thought of Thomas Aquinas. Thomism had been the dominant philosophy undergirding Roman Catholic theology from the fifteenth century. Under the pace-setting interpretations of such thinkers as Cajetan in the early sixteenth century a complex system which spoke to the needs of both theology and contemporary philosophical questions developed. Thomism appeared to have triumphed in 1880 when Pope Leo XIII declared it to be the official (though not exclusive) philosophy of Catholic schools.

However, at the same time it became clear that Thomism's posture was threatened by the increasing popularity of Kantian philosophical principles. In the twentieth century the movement bifurcated. Transcendental Thomism, represented by Joseph Maréchal, Bernard Lonergan, and Karl Rahner, self-consciously adapted itself to Kantian thought. But another wing, under the leadership of Étienne Gilson and Jacques Maritain, sought to recover a pure version of the teachings of Aquinas himself. Eventually this understanding crossed confessional boundaries to include such Protestants as E. L. Mascall. This article will concentrate on this latter movement.

The metaphysical distinctive of neo-Thomism may be found in its insistence on the maxim that "existence precedes essence." For that reason Maritain has claimed that Thomism is the original existentialism. Put simply, this means that one has to know that something exists before one knows what it is, and before one knows that something exists, one has to accept that anything exists. This latter conviction is not the result of a rational deduction; it is an immediate awareness. Thus the act of being, apprehended in a direct intuition, precedes its various modalities.

This apprehension of being leads the Thomist to posit the existence of God via the cosmological argument. For even though the reality of being is an inescapable fact, it is not a logically necessary truth. Being exists, but need not exist. Thus being is inherently contingent, and its contingency makes it finite. If it exists in view of having no inherent necessity to do so, it must be caused to exist. Also, the very forms which being assumes are due to the interplay of various causes; and the fact of change, so characteristic of being, must be the result of causal actions as well. Thus being is bounded by causes wherever it appears. However, since it is a logical absurdity for anything to cause itself, there must be an external cause of being. Now if that cause is also finite, we have not grounded finite being yet, and it still should not exist. A chain of finite causes would carry the same problem with it. Hence the Thomist posits an original uncaused cause of all being, viz. God. It must be noted that this argument is based on the metaphysical necessity for a cause of being, not on a need for explanation, as would be the case with Leibniz's principle of sufficient reason.

The understanding of God as unconditioned necessary existence goes far in providing the basis for Thomistic natural theology. For if God is uncaused, he is unlimited. Then he contains all perfections infinitely; e.g., he is all-good, omnipresent, omniscient, all-loving, perfect person, etc. There can be only one such God, since a God who possesses all perfections cannot differ from any other God who would also possess all the identical possessions. Thus Thomists feel confident that their philosophical arguments concern the same God whom they worship in church.

Thomism understands the relationship between God the Creator and the created order to be analogical. God is the source of all being, and finitude participates in his being, but only with limitations. In the matter of applying language to God, predication proceeds analogically as well. Language is derived from the finite world. But then it is applied to God with the understanding that he is the source of all named properties and that he posseses all those properties without limitation. For example, one may apply the word "love" to God, even though it is a word learned within human finite relationships, because God is pure love and the originator of all human love.

The insistence on being over essence also makes itself felt in Thomism's understanding of the human person. Thomism avoids both a Platonic mind-body dualism and a reductive materialism. With the understanding of the soul as the form of the body, the human is seen as a unit, composed of soul and body in mutual dependence. Thus, for instance, cognition combines both the physical/empirical (sensation) and the spiritual (abstraction). Thomistic writings have consistently defended the dignity and integrity of human personhood, particularly against totalitarian ideologies.

In theology Thomism has usually been linked to conservative expressions of orthodox doctrines, partially due to the close dependence on Aquinas's own formulations. Since the Second Vatican Council it has lost much ground in Catholic circles to philosophies of more recent origin, e.g., phenomenology or process thought, due to a certain impatience with Thomism's supposedly outmoded Aristotelianism. At the same time there has been some movement in evangelical Protestantism to adopt Thomistic philosophical principles for purposes of apologetics and theological enhancement, e.g., by Norman L. Geisler. W. Corduan

See also Thomas Aquinas; Maritain, Jacques; Rahner, Karl.

Bibliography. N. L. Geisler, *Philosophy of Religion;* É. Gilson, *The Christian Philosophy of St. Thomas Aquinas;* J. Maritain, *The Degrees of Knowledge* and *Scholasticism and Politics;* E. L. Mascall, *Existence and Analogy.*

Nestorius, Nestorianism. A native of Germanicia in Syria, Nestorius became Patriarch of Constantinople in 428. Having studied in a monastery in Antioch, probably under Theodore of Mopsuesta, he became a fierce opponent of heterodoxy, his first official act as patriarch being the burning of an Arian chapel.

In 428 Nestorius preached a series of sermons in which he attacked the devotionally popular attribution of the title *Theotokos* ("God-bearing") to the Virgin Mary. As a representative of the Antiochene school of Christology, he demurred at what he understood to be in that title a mixing of the human and divine natures in Christ. This seemed to him Apollinarian. He is reported to have affirmed that "the creature hath not given birth to the uncreatable," "the Word came forth, but was not born of her," and "I do not say God is two or three months old." In place of *Theotokos,* Nestorius offered the term *Christotokos* ("Christ-bearing"). He preferred to attribute human characteristics to the one Christ.

Nestorius's denunciation of *Theotokos* brought him under the suspicion of many orthodox theologians who had long used the term. His most articulate and vehement opponent was Cyril of Alexandria. Apparently a significant portion of the debate between them is traceable to the ecclesiastical rivalry between the two important sees. In any case, the two traded opinions, and when Cyril read of Nestorius's rejection of the term "hypostatic union" as an interpenetration and thus a reduction of both the divine and the human natures of Christ, he understood Nestorius to be affirming that Christ was two persons, one human, one divine. "He rejects the union," stated Cyril.

In August of 430 Pope Celestine condemned Nestorius, and Cyril pronounced twelve anathemas against him in November of the same year. In 431 the General Council at Ephesus deposed Nestorius, sending him back to the monastery in Antioch. Five years later he was banished to Upper Egypt, where he died, probably in 451.

The dispute between Nestorius and Cyril centered in the relationship between the two natures in Christ and represents the divergence between the two major schools of ancient Christology, the Antiochene and the Alexandrian. The former emphasized the reality of Christ's humanity and was wary of any true *communicatio idiomatum,* or communication of the attributes from one nature to the other (hence Nestorius's aversion to the notion of the Logos's being born or suffering; later Reformed theologians have maintained the same kind of concerns). The latter emphasized Christ's essential deity, tended to affirm a real *communicatio,* and was equally wary of what sounded like division in Christ's person (Lutheran theologians have tended to follow the Alexandrian emphases). Cyril rejected Nestorius's notion of the unity of Christ's person consisting in a unity of wills rather than a unity of essence. Both Cyril and Cassian understood this as a kind of adoptionism, wherein the Father adopted the human Jesus, making him his Son (a position similar to the modern so-called Christologies from below). They saw a link between Nestorius's understanding of Christ's person and Pelagius's understanding of Christ as a "mere moral example," and such a connection understandably was anathema to them.

Ironically, modern research has discovered a book written by Nestorius, known as the *Book of Heracleides,* in which he explicitly denies the heresy for which he was condemned. Rather, he affirms of Christ that "the same one is twofold," an expression not unlike the orthodox formulation of the Council of Chalcedon (451). This points to the high degree of misunderstanding which characterized the entire controversy. After 433 a group of Nestorius's followers constituted themselves a separate Nestorian Church in Persia. H. GRIFFITH

See also CYRIL OF ALEXANDRIA; ANTIOCHENE THEOLOGY; ALEXANDRIAN THEOLOGY; COMMUNICATION OF ATTRIBUTES; COMMUNICATIO IDIOMATUM.

Bibliography. K. Baus *et al., The Imperial Church from Constantine to the Early Middle Ages;* J. F. Bethune-Baker, *Nestorius and His Teaching;* A. Grillmeier, *Christ in Christian Tradition,* I; R. V. Sellers, *Two Ancient Christologies.*

New, Newness. The very name "the New Testament" expresses the importance of "newness" for Christianity. This title was plainly intended to summarize the relationship between Christ and what preceded him as that of "new" to "old"; correspondingly, theologians have long grappled with the question, "To what extent, following God's final revelation of himself in Christ, is the same passage from old to new to be a feature of the life of the church?" The question has been revived in this century through the rediscovery of the importance of eschatology, both within the NT and for the church. In addition, renewal movements within the church and Christian groups campaigning for social change have compelled theologians to consider anew the triangular relationship between Christ's establishment of the New Covenant (Testament), the present position and responsibility of the church in the world, and the future hope of the renewal of all things in him.

According to Harrisville, the words for "new" and "newness" in the NT (*kainos, neos, kainotēs, neotēs:* seventy-two times in all) must consistently be interpreted eschatologically, signifying the appearance of the new age in Christ. With qualifications (e.g., *neos* sometimes means simply "young") we must affirm that expressions like "new wine" (Matt. 9:17 etc.), "new commandment" (John 13:34 etc.), "new covenant" (Luke 22:20 etc.), "new creation" (II Cor. 5:17 etc.), "new man" (Eph. 2:15 etc.), "new teaching" (Mark 1:27 etc.), "new heavens and a new earth" (II Pet. 3:13 etc.) all denote this revolution; but they also point ahead to a revolution yet to be. This paradox is typical of NT eschatology and should be carefully maintained in contemporary Christian evaluations of the present and the hoped-for and the passage between them. S. MOTYER

See also ESCHATOLOGY; ISRAEL, THE NEW; MAN, OLD AND NEW; NEW CREATION, NEW CREATURE; NEW HEAVENS AND NEW EARTH.

Bibliography. R. A. Harrisville, "The Concept of Newness in the NT," *JBL* 74:69–79; F. F. Bruce, *IDB,* III, 542–43; J. Moltmann, *A Theology of Hope* and *The Church in the Power of the Spirit.*

New Birth. *See* REGENERATION.

New Commandment. *See* COMMANDMENT, THE NEW.

New Covenant. *See* COVENANT, THE NEW.

New Creation, New Creature. These phrases are translations of *kainē ktisis,* a term used in II Cor. 5:17 and Gal. 6:15. "Creation" (RV, RSV; cf.

NEB "new world") is undoubtedly a better translation than "creature" (AV, Moffatt, NEB mg.), for on only one occasion out of eleven in Paul's writings (Rom. 8:39—RSV misleading) does *ktisis* certainly mean "creature" (i.e., "a created object"). It usually signifies God's act of creation (e.g., Rom. 1:20) or the result of that act, the cosmos (e.g., Rom. 8:19–20). The use of *ktisis* here rather than *ktisma,* which always means "creature" (e.g., I Tim. 4:4), is significant.

Three factors contribute to the meaning of this expression: (1) *The OT background.* In the OT "new" is a word especially associated with the age to come, when God will "do a new thing" (Isa. 43:19), "make a new covenant" (Jer. 31:31), even "create new heavens and a new earth" (Isa. 65:17). Cf. also Isa. 42:9–10; Ezek. 11:19; 18:31; Ps. 96:1. Isa. 43:14–21 especially pictures the redemption of Israel as a new creation/exodus (the two are closely associated). Paul proclaims the fulfillment of these eschatological expectations.

(2) *The balance between future and present in Pauline eschatology.* Paul would not feel that Rev. 21:1ff, where the same OT expectations are used to picture a reality *not yet* fulfilled, contradicted II Cor. 5:17 or Gal. 6:15. He expresses the same future thought himself in Rom. 8:18–23. And it would be wrong to reconcile the two sides of his mind by saying that the man in Christ is "new creation" in that a new life has been conceived in him by the Spirit, a life which must yet grow to fullness. Because Christ is Christ, the promised new creation is *now* a reality: from the eternal perspective the man in Christ is "created" (past tense, Eph. 2:10), just as he is "justified" (Rom. 5:1), "sanctified" (I Cor. 6:11), "glorified" (Rom. 8:30), even though these things are not fully realized in experience.

(3) *The balance between individual and corporate in Pauline anthropology.* Both II Cor. 5:17 and Gal. 6:15 are formally statements about the significance of Christ for the individual, but both are phrased in such a way as to direct the mind beyond the individual. Paul's terse "If any one in Christ, new creation!" (II Cor. 5:17*a,* literally) invites us to see the individual participating in a much greater eschatological reality. In Christ, God has created "one new man" (Eph. 2:15)—a complex expression which moves between the person of Christ himself, who is the new Adam of God's new creation, and the new humanity which is the church "in" Christ; so each must take care to "put on the new man, created after the likeness of God" (Eph. 4:24, cf. Col. 3:10) and to express in practice the "newness of life" (Rom. 6:4) proper to this new creation. S. MOTYER

See also CREATION, DOCTRINE OF; MAN, OLD AND NEW; NEW, NEWNESS.

Bibliography. G. E. Ladd, *A Theology of the NT;* F. F. Bruce, *IDB,* III, 542–43; C. K. Barrett, *The Second Epistle to the Corinthians;* H. Haarbeck, H.-G. Link, C. Brown, *NIDNTT,* II, 669–76.

New England Theology. The name given to a theological tradition arising from the work of Jonathan Edwards (1703–1758) and continuing well into the nineteenth century. The tradition was not unified by a common set of beliefs, for in fact Edwards's nineteenth century heirs reversed his convictions on many important particulars. It was rather united in its fascination for common issues, including the freedom of human will, the morality of divine justice, and the problem of causation behind the appearance of sin.

Jonathan Edwards. Edwards's theological labors grew out of his efforts to explain and defend the colonial Great Awakening as a real work of God. In the process he provided an interpretation of Calvinism that influenced American religious life for over a century.

Edwards's treatment in the *Freedom of the Will* (1754) presented Augustinian and Calvinistic ideas on the nature of humanity and of salvation in a powerful new shape. His basic argument was that the "will" is not an entity, but an expression of the strongest motive in a person's character. He supported the thrust of this work with *Original Sin* (1758), in which he argued that all humankind was present in Adam when he sinned. Consequently, all people share the sinful character and the guilt which Adam brought upon himself.

Earlier, in 1746, Edwards had explored the practical side of theology in *Religious Affections* (or emotions). Here he argued that genuine Christianity is not revealed by the quantity or intensity of religious emotions. Rather, true faith is manifest where a heart has been changed to love God and seek his pleasure. After his death Edwards's friends published *The Nature of True Virtue* (1765), which defined the good life as "love to Being in general." By this he meant that true goodness characterized those actions which honored God as purest Being and other people as derivative beings made in the image of God.

Jonathan Edwards was overwhelmed by the majesty and the splendor of the divine. The major themes of his theology were the greatness and glory of God, the utter dependence of sinful humanity upon God for salvation, and the supernal beauty of the life of holiness. Edwards was not only a fervent Christian person; he was also a theological genius unmatched in American history. Thus, it is little wonder that those who followed him were not successful in maintaining the fullness of his theology. What they did maintain was his revivalistic fervor, his concern for awakening, and his high moral seriousness.

The New Divinity. The next phase of the New England theology was known as the "new divinity." Its leading proponents were Joseph Bellamy (1719–90) and Samuel Hopkins (1721–1803), New England ministers who had studied with Edwards and had been his closest friends. Much as Edwards had, Bellamy argued for the sovereignty of God in redemption and against the idea that humankind could save itself. He also developed Edwards's convictions that churches should allow none into membership who could not testify to a personal experience of God's grace. Hopkins extended Edwards's discussion of virtue into a complete ethical system. He used the phrase "disinterested benevolence" to construct guidelines for practical ethics. Out of this thinking Hopkins developed a vigorous opposition to slavery as an institution which treated people in a way that was not fitting for their character as ones bearing the image of God. Hopkins also maintained a heightened sense of God's sovereignty by insisting that people should be willing even "to be damned for the glory of God."

With Bellamy and Hopkins occurred also the first modifications of Edwards's ideas. Bellamy propounded a "governmental" view of the atonement, the idea that God's sense of right and wrong demanded the sacrifice of Christ. Edwards, by contrast, had maintained the traditional view that the death of Christ was necessary to take away God's anger at sin. Hopkins, again in contrast to Edwards, was more concerned about eternal principles of duty, goodness, and justice than about personal confrontation with the divine. He felt that a Calvinistic theologian should, and could, demonstrate how sin resulted in an overall advantage to the universe. He held that the human sinful nature arose as a product of the sinful acts which all people commit, rather than as a direct result of Adam's guilt. And Hopkins spoke of Christian duties more as legal necessities for the believer than as the natural outflow of a changed heart.

The Nineteenth Century. Modifications made in the New England theology by Hopkins and Bellamy were subtle ones. Their successors moved more obviously beyond the teaching of Edwards. Timothy Dwight (1752–1817), Edwards's grandson and president of Yale College, took a broader view of human abilities in salvation and emphasized more the reasonable nature of the Christian faith. Jonathan Edwards, Jr. (1745–1801), who had studied with Joseph Bellamy, extended Bellamy's idea of a governmental atonement and also placed a stronger emphasis on the law of God for the Christian life. Both he and Dwight continued the general trend to view sin as an accumulation of actions rather than primarily a state of being issuing in evil deeds.

By the time Timothy Dwight's best student, Nathaniel W. Taylor (1786–1858), assumed his position as professor of theology at Yale Divinity School in 1822, the movement from Edwards's specific convictions was very pronounced. Taylor's New Haven theology reversed the elder Edwards on freedom of the will by contending for a natural power of free choice. And he brought to a culmination the teaching that sin lies in the exercise of sinful actions rather than in an underlying condition.

The influence of the New England theology continued to be great throughout the nineteenth century. It set the tone for theological debate in New England and much of the rest of the country. Its questions dominated theological reflection at Yale until midcentury and at Andover Seminary even longer. Andover, founded in 1808 by Trinitarian Congregationalists, had brought together "moderate Calvinists" and the more rigid followers of Samuel Hopkins. Its last great theologian who self-consciously regarded himself as an heir to Edwards was Edwards Amasa Park (1808–1900). Park represented a moderate reaction to the theology of Taylor when he spoke up more strongly for God's sovereignty in salvation. Yet Park also held to a wide variety of nineteenth century assumptions about the capacities of human nature that distanced his thinking from Edwards. Park proved too liberal for the nineteenth century champions of Calvinism at Presbyterian Princeton Seminary, who attacked his ideas as a sell-out of Calvinism to the optimistic spirit of the age. For their part, the Princeton Calvinists, who also attacked Taylor and his like-minded colleagues for their deviations from Calvinism, could respect Edwards but were not able to fathom his sense of God's overmastering beauty.

The New England theology was at its best in careful, rigorous theological exposition. This strength sometimes turned into a weakness when it led to a dry, almost scholastic style of preaching. But with Edwards, Dwight, or Taylor, who did differ markedly among themselves on important questions, there remained a common ability to communicate a need for revival and ardent Christian living.

The changes in the content of the New England theology, and indeed its passing, had much to do with the character of the United States in the nineteenth century. A country convinced of the nearly limitless capabilities of individuals in the New World had increasingly less interest in a theology which had its origin in the all-encompassing power of God. It is significant that when twentieth century theologians like H. Richard Niebuhr and Joseph Haroutunian rediscovered the New England theology, they returned to its fount, Edwards, as the source of its most valuable and enduring insights.

M. A. Noll

See also Edwards, Jonathan; Dwight, Timothy; Taylor, Nathaniel William; New Haven Theology.

Bibliography. J. A. Conforti, *Samuel Hopkins and the New Divinity Movement;* F. H. Foster, *A Genetic History of the New England Theology;* J. Haroutunian, *Piety Versus Moralism: The Passing of the New England Theology;* H. R. Niebuhr, *The Kingdom of God in America;* B. B. Warfield, "Edwards and the New England Theology," in *The Works of Benjamin B. Warfield, Vol. IX: Studies in Theology;* A. C. Cecil, Jr., *The Theological Development of Edwards Amasa Park.*

New Evangelicalism. *See* Evangelicalism.

New Hampshire Confession (1833). Published by a committee of the Baptist Convention in that state, the New Hampshire Confession is one of the most widely used Baptist statements of faith in America. The confession was reissued with minor changes in 1853 by J. Newton Brown of the American Baptist Publication Society, and in this form attracted greater attention among Baptists in America. The confession has influenced many Baptist confessions since, including the influential Statement of Baptist Faith and Message of the Southern Baptist Convention in 1925.

The confession is relatively brief, containing sixteen short articles ranging from "the Scriptures" to "the World to Come." Much of it recapitulates the faith of orthodox Protestants generally. Its article on Scripture, "the supreme standard by which all human conduct, creeds, and opinions should be tried," contains this often repeated statement: "It has God for its author, salvation for its end, and truth, without any mixture of error, for its matter." Similarly evangelical are the articles on God ("the Maker and Supreme Ruler of heaven and earth") and salvation ("wholly by grace; through the Mediatorial Offices of the Son of God").

Other parts of the confession are more baptistic. It defines "a visible Church of Christ" as "a congregation of baptized believers, associated by covenant," and the "only proper officers" for such a church are "Bishops or Pastors, and Deacons." Baptism "is the immersion of a believer in water" as "a solemn and beautiful emblem" of "faith in a crucified, buried, and risen Saviour."

The general tendency of the confession is moderately Calvinistic. It speaks of the "voluntary transgression" of the fall, "in consequence of which all mankind are now sinners." God's election ("according to which he regenerates, sanctifies, and saves sinners") is said to be "perfectly consistent with the free agency of man." The blessings of salvation, furthermore, "are made free to all by the Gospel." True believers "endure to the end."

When it was first published, the New Hampshire Confession provided a common standard for a wide range of Baptists—strict Calvinists and moderate Arminians, revivalistic Separates and orthodox Regulars, Landmarkers and others who did not believe in a universal church along with those who did. Today many modern Baptists, though still unwilling to treat the statement as a binding rule of faith, still find the New Hampshire Confession a sound standard of Christian belief.

M. A. Noll

See also Confessions of Faith; Baptist Tradition, The.

Bibliography. W. L. Lumpkin, ed., *Baptist Confessions of Faith;* R. G. Torbet, *A History of the Baptists.*

New Haven Theology. A late stage of the New England theology that had originated in efforts of Jonathan Edwards to defend the spiritual reality of the first Great Awakening (*ca.* 1740). It was also a theology developed for the needs of the Second Great Awakening (*ca.* 1795–1830). It thus served as a bridge between the Calvinism that dominated American Christianity in the 1700s and the more Arminian theology that came to prevail in the nineteenth century.

Timothy Dwight, grandson of Jonathan Edwards and president of Yale College from 1795 to 1817, laid the groundwork for the New Haven theology. Dwight's concern for revival led him to place more emphasis on the natural abilities of individuals to respond to the gospel than had Edwards. His efforts to provide a rational defense of Christianity led him to stress its reasonable character over the sense of wonder that had been so important for Edwards.

Dwight's best pupil, Nathaniel William Taylor, carried the New Haven theology to its maturity. Taylor was the first professor at the new Yale Divinity School, where he came in 1822 after a successful pastorate in New Haven. Taylor regarded himself as the heir of the tradition of Jonathan Edwards, particularly as he combated the rising tide of Unitarianism in New England. His theology, however, departed from Edwards's, especially in its beliefs about human nature. Most importantly, he argued in a famous phrase that people always had a "power to the contrary" when faced with the choice for God. He also contended—as Edwards's son, Jonathan Edwards, Jr., had suggested—that human sinfulness arose from sinful acts, not from a sinful nature inherited from Adam. Everyone did in fact sin, Taylor believed, but this was not a result of God's action in predetermining human nature. More than other heirs of Edwards, Taylor also accepted the Scottish philosophy of common sense which also made much of innate human freedom and the power of individuals to shape their own destinies.

The New Haven theology was a powerful engine for revival and reform in the first half of the nineteenth century, particularly through the work of Taylor's fellow Yale graduate, Lyman Beecher. Beecher and like-minded colleagues employed the principles of the New Haven theology to promote moral reform, to establish missions and educational institutions, and to win the frontier for Christianity. The New Haven theology arose out of the distinctive Calvinism of New England, but it came to represent—with Methodists, Disciples, and some Baptists—a contribution to the generally Arminian theology which dominated American Christian thought in the nineteenth century. M. A. Noll

See also New England Theology; Dwight, Timothy; Taylor, Nathaniel William; Great Awakenings, The.

Bibliography. S. E. Mead, *Nathaniel William Taylor, 1786–1858;* F. H. Foster, *A Genetic History of the New England Theology;* J. Haroutunian, *Piety Versus Moralism: The Passing of the New England Theology.*

New Heavens and New Earth. The biblical doctrine of the created universe includes the certainty of its final redemption from the dominion of sin. The finally redeemed universe is called "the new heavens and new earth."

In the OT the kingdom of God is usually described in terms of a redeemed earth; this is especially clear in the book of Isaiah, where the final state of the universe is already called a new heaven and a new earth (Isa. 65:17; 66:22). The nature of this renewal was perceived only very dimly by the OT authors, but they did express the belief that man's ultimate destiny is an earthly one. This vision is clarified in the NT. Jesus speaks of the "regeneration" of the world (Matt. 19:28), Peter of the "restoration of all things" (Acts 3:21). Paul states that the universe will be redeemed by God from its current state of bondage (Rom. 8:18–21). This is confirmed by Peter, who describes the new heavens and the new earth as characterized by righteousness and as the Christian's hope (II Pet. 3:13). Finally, the book of Revelation includes a glorious vision of the end of the present universe and of the creation of a new universe, full of righteousness and of the presence of God. The vision is confirmed by God in the awesome declaration: "Behold, I make all things new" (Rev. 21:1–8).

The new heavens and the new earth will be the renewed creation that will fulfill the purpose for which God created the universe. It will be characterized by the complete rule of God and by the full realization of the final goal of redemption: "Behold the dwelling of God is with men" (Rev. 21:3).

The fact that the universe will be created anew shows that God's goal for man is not an ethereal and disembodied existence, but a bodily existence on a perfected earth. The scene of the beatific vision is the new earth. The spiritual does not exclude the created order, and will be fully realized only within a perfected creation.

It has been usual to discuss whether the new heavens and new earth will involve a renewal of the present universe or a complete destruction followed by re-creation *ex nihilo.* Both views have ardent proponents, the Reformed tradition favoring renewal and the Lutheran tradition favoring re-creation. Both views seem to have adequate biblical support (e.g., for renewal, Rom. 8:18–21; Matt. 19:28; Acts 3:21; for re-creation, II Pet. 3:7–13). The best view seems to be that there is both continuity and discontinuity; the universe will be renewed, but this transformation will be so complete as to introduce a radically new order of existence. F. Q. Gouvea

See also Eschatology; Kingdom of Christ, God, Heaven; New, Newness; New Creation, New Creature.

Bibliography. G. C. Berkouwer, *The Return of Christ,* ch. 7; P. E. Hughes, *Interpreting Prophecy;* A. Hoekema, *The Bible and the Future.*

New Hermeneutic, The. A post-World War II development based on Rudolf Bultmann's radical critical methodology in interpreting Scripture. Bultmann had held that the world of the historical is closed to supernatural revelation, since science is normative and does not allow such miraculous intrusions as prophecy, incarnation, resurrection, and eschatology. Working from a radically modern Lutheran interpretation of gospel versus law, he viewed the OT in human terms as the negative background to positive grace in the NT. But NT grace is shrouded in myth, which is unacceptable to the modern mind and accordingly must be demythologized and reinterpreted in existentialist terms. Employing the existentialism of Kierkegaard and Heidegger,

Bultmann emphasized the importance of decision in responding to the kerygma, or proclamation of the NT. In the moment of decision as he hears the Word of God proclaimed, the hearer "stands outside of himself" (*existere,* from Gr. *ek* + *histēmi*) and has the possibility of entering a new understanding of himself. The preaching of the word is therefore central in Bultmann's hermeneutic (Ger. *Hermeneutik*) because it summons one to the possibility of new existence.

The new hermeneutic of Bultmann's disciples accepts the basic truth of his method and affirms the correctness of his interpretation of Luther's "justification by faith alone." Grace lies in the sphere of faith, not in the sphere of historical facts, hence radical biblical criticism can go on relatively unabated without danger to faith, since faith resides largely in a higher realm of history (*Geschichte* or *Urgeschichte;* primal history), while the relative events of the Bible reside in the changing realm of profane history (*Historie*). While Bultmann had extended the older view of hermeneutics far beyond its concern for detailed principles of exegesis and interpretation to a broad inquiry into the meaning of language as existential address, following Heidegger, his disciples felt he had not gone far enough. Ernst Fuchs and Gerhard Ebeling both sought to develop Heidegger's hermeneutical theory of language more comprehensively than had Bultmann and to see that speech itself is profoundly hermeneutical and existential. *Hermeneutik* becomes a deep inquiry into the function of speech and word, and of listening to and being submissive to the call of being itself as being graciously opens itself to *Dasein,* the person who "is there" in the world. For Heidegger, being is not God; but it is an easy step for the followers of Bultmann to adapt this language of "grace" and apply it to Christian proclamation.

The clearest exposition of this new development in post-Bultmannian hermeneutics is to be found in *The New Hermeneutic* (ed. James M. Robinson and John B. Cobb, Jr., 1964), which was written virtually on the scene and contains valuable focal articles by Ebeling and Fuchs, American reactions by Robinson, John Dillenberger, Robert Funk, Amos Wilder, and John Cobb, with a response by Fuchs. In brief, the new hermeneutic took a more positive turn toward the language of Jesus as mediating kerygma, not mere historiography as Bultmann had insisted. Fuchs and Ebeling saw the language of Jesus as "word-happening" or "speech-event" and were ready to argue, in the larger context of Heidegger's hermeneutic, that not just the Easter kerygma but Jesus' word as well mediates an eschatological self-understanding to the listener. Jesus' claim of authority is not limited simply to a point in Palestinian history, as Bultmann required, but speaks today with equal authority in the church's proclamation. Hence the word "kerygma," insofar as it had distinguished the proclamation of the church as over against the historical and no longer relevant proclamation of Jesus, is replaced by the word-event or language-event in the new hermeneutic.

Existentialist interpretation is therefore broadened to bridge the gap which had been created by Bultmann between *Historie* (Jesus) and *Geschichte* (the church's kerygma), to bring together historical and systematic theology in terms of the recurring language-event which moves from Jesus to the contemporary preacher. Ebeling especially, as the historical and systematic theologian deeply immersed in Luther's hermeneutic as well as Heidegger and Bultmann, goes beyond the latter by insisting that all the words of Scripture have to do with the incarnate Son of God, Jesus Christ. Fuchs, his close friend and collaborator on the NT side, speaks of Jesus as standing in the place of God as he speaks of new possibilities for existential self-understanding.

All of the foregoing sounds like a return to orthodox concern for the Jesus of history and his identity with the Christ of faith. But the new hermeneutic is more subtle than to allow for a simple return to classical evangelicalism and too indebted to the basic methodology of Bultmannian radical criticism, which Bultmann himself inherited from his predecessors, notably Dilthey. The critical assumptions of the new hermeneutic remain basically unchanged, only broadened, from those of Bultmann. Fuchs continues to speak of Jesus primarily in terms of his language, but fails to appreciate that language does not have independent status apart from the person who speaks, and therefore cannot be apotheosized or separated from the intentionality of the speaker.

This serious fault in the later Heideggerian hermeneutic—to view language as something which speaks without reference to God or persons—feeds into the abortive attempt of the new quest of the historical Jesus. As long as the school of the new hermeneutic centered upon the event of Jesus' language and did not see that language as revelatory of Jesus' own self-understanding and messianic self-consciousness, it was bound to reflect the same fundamental skepticism regarding the person of Jesus as did Bultmann. James M. Robinson's attempt to undertake a new quest of the historical Jesus was shortly abandoned, mainly because the quest focused upon the understanding of existence which emerges from Jesus' linguistic activity, not on Jesus' self-understanding which is disclosed in that activity. Similarly, Fuchs speaks of Jesus' language and his concept of time, but appears disinterested in what this says of Jesus as person. Amos Wilder has ably criticized Fuchs on this point. One of the foremost new questers, Ernst Käsemann, likewise shows a methodological fault in his desire to allow Jesus a more prominent position than did his mentor Bultmann. Conceding that Jesus makes a good many unusual claims that might suggest a messianic consciousness, he nonetheless holds back and declares that it is his personal opinion that Jesus did not think of himself in those terms.

This has led critics of the school who have been appreciative of the early promise of the new hermeneutic to bemoan the fact that the methodology is too closely allied to Heidegger's notion of language that mysteriously speaks on its own without reference to the intentionality of the speaker. The present writer early expressed his concerns in *Jesus, Persons, and the Kingdom of God* and more recently in *New Approaches to Jesus and the Gospels,* suggesting that a more adequate approach to Jesus' words and activity will need to employ a descriptive phenomenology which views the speaker, and perforce the self-understanding of the person who speaks, as standing within and revealed through what he says and does. Several helpful models may be employed in this more useful enterprise, among them the later Wittgenstein, Marcel, Polanyi, and the British school of person analysts, including G. E. M. Anscombe and P. F. Strawson. This approach is extremely valuable in bringing the new hermeneutic to a satisfactory conclusion in its search for the unity of the Jesus of history and the Christ of faith, and finding that solution in what all along has been the orthodox view of Jesus as the self-conscious Messiah who, in his speaking and acting, is the originator of the church's Christological tradition.

That there have been gains in NT exegesis as a result of the renewed interest in the vitality of Jesus' language, especially the parables, should be gratefully acknowledged by all, in spite of the fact that Jesus' Christological claims implicit in that language have not been widely appreciated. On the theological side of the new hermeneutic, recent developments have reached something of a stalemate over the question of "horizons." The most prominent exponent of the new hermeneutic in the Bultmannian tradition, Hans-Georg Gadamer, and a more recent evangelical interpreter, Anthony Thistleton, argue for a fusion of the church's horizon and ours. This, after all, lay at the center of the new hermeneutic as originally conceived, and it is popularly accepted in theological thought today that the text and the interpreter share in the meaning of the encounter. Evangelicals will want to be wary of speaking too hastily of a fusion of horizons of meaning, however, and will likely be more impressed with E. D. Hirsch's approach to hermeneutics, which allows the original meaning of the speaker or text to remain intact. There can be an appropriation of *significance* for the interpreter which may vary depending on one's setting, but the authoritative *meaning* of the speaker or text is their prerogative to establish. The issue is a serious and fundamental one, for at stake is the very intentionality and authority of Jesus and of the early church. There are signs that, at least from the NT side of the new hermeneutic, the intentionality of Jesus is beginning to receive renewed interest, a fact attested by two recent studies, *New Testament Prophecy,* by David Hill, and *The Aims of Jesus,* by Ben Meyer.

R. G. GRUENLER

See also BULTMANN, RUDOLF; KERYGMA.

Bibliography. H. W. Bartsch, ed., *Kerygma and Myth I* and *Kerygma and Myth II;* S. M. Ogden, ed., *Existence and Faith: Shorter Writings of Rudolf Bultmann;* R. Bultmann, *Jesus Christ and Mythology;* G. Ebeling, *The Nature of Faith* and *Word and Faith;* R. W. Funk, *Language, Hermeneutic, and Word of God;* H.-G. Gadamer, *Truth and Method;* V. A. Harvey, *The Historian and the Believer;* M. Heidegger, *Being and Time;* D. High, *Language, Persons, and Belief;* E. D. Hirsch, Jr., *Validity in Interpretation;* S. M. Ogden, *Christ Without Myth;* M. Polanyi, *Personal Knowledge: Towards a Post-Critical Philosophy;* J. M. Robinson and J. B. Cobb, Jr., *New Frontiers in Theology:* Vol. I: *The Later Heidegger and Theology;* Vol. II: *The New Hermeneutic;* A. Thistleton, *The Two Horizons;* C. Van Til, *The New Hermeneutic.*

New Jerusalem, The. *See* JERUSALEM, THE NEW.

New Light Schism. A division in the Presbyterian and Congregational denominations in the mid-eighteenth century primarily over practical matters of Christian experience. Presbyterian schism occurred in 1741 when the Old Lights, who were predominantly of Scotch-Irish heritage, ejected the New Light faction and formed the Old Side synod of Philadelphia. The New Light party, with their English Puritan background, grew out of the Great Awakening and revived a more experiential interpretation of the Christian life. They organized the New Side presbyteries of New Brunswick and Londonderry.

Both parties professed traditional Calvinist and Puritan doctrine, but they differed substantially on its practical implications. Old Light ministers, interpreting Calvinism in a rationalistic manner, claimed that holding orthodox theology was more important than Christian living. For them God's sovereign decree determined who was elect, and correct theological belief, not manner of life, was the only major practical sign of salvation. Moral laxity often resulted from such deemphasis on religious experience, leading to several Old Light pastors being tried by presbyteries for persistent immoral living and drunkenness.

In contrast, New Lights William and Gilbert Tennent stressed Puritan piety as indispensable to Calvinist theology. They preached conviction of sin, teaching their hearers that true faith in Christ required a vital conversion experience leading to moral obedience and personal holiness. Gilbert Tennent, in "The Danger of an Unconverted Ministry," contended that some Old Light clergy were actually unregenerate, and he encouraged believers to seek spiritual nurture elsewhere. Old Light members countered that New Lights were guilty of "enthusiasm" and defamatory accusations. Their itinerant preaching and their encouragement of laymen to pressure fellow church members into New Light experience violated Presbyterian polity.

During the schism New Siders experienced dramatic growth and founded the College of New Jersey (Princeton) to educate their ministers. Meanwhile the Old Side generally failed in its educational efforts and actually declined in number. In 1758 New Side initiatives produced reunion on conditions favorable to that group.

Congregationalists also experienced schism over the Great Awakening. After George Whitefield's and Gilbert Tennent's evangelistic tours in 1740–41 brought a general revival to New England, James Davenport's incendiary preaching and incitement of emotional excesses brought sharp Old Light reprisals. Charles Chauncey argued that revivals were not the work of God because emotional outbursts were not produced by God's Spirit. Charging New Lights with antinomianism and enthusiasm, he claimed that religion, rather than pertaining to man's emotions, primarily appeals to the understanding and judgment.

Jonathan Edwards defended revivalism. He admitted that instances of doctrinal and ecclesiastical disorder existed. But he argued that believers could distinguish between genuine and counterfeit awakenings by examining whether they brought love for Christ, Scripture, and truth and opposition to evil. Edwards defined the essence of true religion as "holy affections." Religious experience is not limited to the mind. When regenerated by the Holy Spirit, man's whole being—heart, mind, will, and affections—is engaged.

This schism helped Edwards and his followers revive a balanced, vital Calvinism. Chauncey and other Old Lights, on the other hand, broke from Calvinism and began to advocate Arminianism and eventually Unitarianism. W. A. Hoffecker

See also Great Awakenings, The; Edwards, Jonathan; Whitefield, George.

Bibliography. C. Chauncey, *Enthusiasm Described and Cautioned Against* and *Seasonable Thoughts on the State of Religion in New England;* J. Davenport, *The Rev. Mr. Davenport's Confessions and Retractions;* J. Edwards, *The Distinguishing Marks of a Work of the Spirit of God, Some Thoughts Concerning the Present Revival of Religion in New England,* and *A Treatise Concerning the Religious Affections;* E. S. Gaustad, *The Great Awakening in New England;* G. Tennent, *The Danger of an Unconverted Ministry;* L. J. Trinterud, *The Forming of an American Tradition.*

New Man. *See* Man, Old and New.

Newman, John Henry (1801–1890). The most famous English convert to Roman Catholicism in the nineteenth century. First led to personal faith in Christ in his teens in the most Calvinistic section of evangelical Anglicanism, he proceeded to Oxford, where his intellectual ability, subtlety of mind, and singular powers of expression were recognized and developed. Remaining after graduation as a fellow of Oriel College, he was renowned for his piety and preaching. He was also exposed to more liberal currents of thought, which he overtly rejected but which never left him and, once in the secure confines of Catholicism, found a measure of expression.

Repelled by the more extreme forms of liberalism, Newman feared the introduction of such theology to England, and in common with many nurtured in strongly Calvinistic evangelicalism he was critical of the entrepreneurial optimism of much early nineteenth century evangelicalism as well. While many of those of similar background were finding their answer in a return to the Reformation, his romantic temperament sought for an era in which the power of God was even more evident. His brother Francis, who had followed a somewhat similar pilgrimage, sought his orientation in the first century church among the early Plymouth Brethren before shifting to agnosticism. John's friends and patristic studies pointed him to the church of the great fathers of the fourth and fifth centuries. Here he saw an authoritative leadership able to rout the forces of heterodoxy through the effusion of the Spirit vouchsafed to the historic episcopate. In his search for the channel of the

Spirit's presence and power he was in some ways as charismatic as Edward Irving. But he believed that the answer for Christianity lay not in the gifts of the Spirit in general but particularly in the gift of apostleship, which he came to believe had always been present in the apostolic succession of the episcopate.

In 1833 Newman, together with such associates as Keble and Pusey, launched the movement of Catholic Anglicanism known as Tractarianism. Its particular stress lay on the power and authority of the bishop as the way to renewal and strength for the Church of England. Evangelical Anglicans were horrified and Broad Churchmen were appalled. When Newman realized that the Church of England as a whole would not follow the Tractarian program, he joined the Roman Catholic Church in 1845, taking some followers with him but leaving others to create major changes in large sections of Anglicanism.

Settled within the security of the apostolic church, he gave great attention to the development of doctrine. While Newman wished to exalt the pontificate by indicating how the teaching office of the church had taken doctrine from its embryonic NT condition and brought it to rich fullness under the guidance of the Holy Spirit, many traditional Roman Catholics feared that the faith was being undercut by insufficient emphasis on Scripture. As a result, Newman was under something of a cloud during his Roman Catholic experience, although his intellectual brilliance was recognized and he was made a cardinal in his later years. Since his death, and particularly in more recent years, his influence has been of great importance for developments in Roman Catholic theology. I. S. RENNIE

See also OXFORD MOVEMENT; KEBLE, JOHN; PUSEY, EDWARD BOUVERIE; ANGLO-CATHOLICISM; HIGH CHURCH MOVEMENT; VIA MEDIA.

Bibliography. W. Ward, *The Life of John Henry, Cardinal Newman*, 2 vols.; G. Faber, *Oxford Apostles;* C. S. Dessain *et al.*, eds., *The Letters and Diaries of John Henry Newman*, 31 vols.; G. Biemer, *Newman on Tradition;* C. S. Dessain, *John Henry Newman* and *The Spirituality of John Henry Newman;* H. L. Weatherby, *Cardinal Newman in His Age;* N. Lash, *Newman on Development.*

New Morality. *See* SITUATION ETHICS.

New Religious Movements. In the late 1960s and early 1970s a number of religious groups previously unknown in Europe and North America began to gain converts. These groups are often called "cults," but because of problems with the definition of the word and the fact that while a group like the Hare Krishna Movement is a cult to most North Americans but a legitimate branch of an ancient religious tradition to people in India, scholars adopted the term "new religious movements" as a neutral way of referring to the new religions. I. HEXHAM

See also CULTS; SECT, SECTARIANISM.

Bibliography. J. Needleman, *The New Religions;* R. S. Ellwood, *Alternate Altars;* H. Biezais, ed., *New Religions.*

New School Theology. New School Presbyterianism embodied mainstream evangelical Christianity in the middle decades of the nineteenth century. Its modified Calvinist theology, enthusiasm for revivalism, moral reform, and interdenominational cooperation were its most notable characteristics.

New School theology had its remote roots in the Calvinism of Jonathan Edwards, but its immediate predecessor was the New Haven theology of Nathaniel Taylor, who advocated a theology of moral government. He synthesized moralistic elements from Scottish commonsense philosophy with reinterpretations of traditional Calvinism to construct a semi-Pelagian foundation for revivalism. Denying the imputation of Adam's sin and claiming that unregenerate man can respond to moral overtures, especially Christ's death, Taylor argued that men need not wait passively for the Holy Spirit to redeem them. His views reflected a long-standing American faith in human freedom.

While Old School leaders roundly attacked Taylor's theology, revivalists and ministers such as Charles G. Finney, Lyman Beecher, and Albert Barnes popularized it. Finney used Taylor's theology to redefine revivals as works which man can perform using means which God has provided. With such a theological basis he introduced his famous "new measures," such as referring to his hearers as "sinners" and calling them to sit on an "anxious bench" while they contemplated converting to Christ.

Schism divided the two schools of Presbyterians in 1837 when an Old School majority expelled New School members for tolerating theological errors. Differences over a plan of union with Congregationalists and slavery played a secondary role. Those ejected published the Auburn Declaration, which denied sixteen accusations alleged by the Old School. The declaration affirmed a weakened view of imputation—Adam's sinful act was not counted against all men, but all men after Adam were sinners—supported Christ's substitutionary atonement, and asserted that the work of the Holy Spirit, not human choice, was the basis of regeneration.

It was a compromise between New England theology and the Westminster Confession.

This modified Calvinism was used to champion activism in American social life. Voluntary societies consisting of members from various denominations carried out missionary activity and combated social ills. These constructive crusades, in which New School Presbyterians played a leading role, were inspired by postmillennial expectations of progress.

In the decades after 1840 New School theology became more conservative. Its proponents widely criticized Finney's prefectionism. They attacked Darwinism, early biblical criticism, and German philosophy and theology. Henry B. Smith of Union Theological Seminary emerged as the leading spokesman. His defense of systematic theology and biblical infallibility and his perceptions that New Schoolers had become more orthodox were influential in the reunion of the Presbyterian Church in 1869.

W. A. Hoffecker

See also Old School Theology; New Haven Theology; Auburn Declaration; Finney, Charles Grandison; Barnes, Albert.

Bibliography. A. Barnes, *Notes on the Epistle to the Romans;* C. G. Finney, *Lectures on Revivals of Religion;* G. Marsden, *The Evangelical Mind and the New School Presbyterian Experience;* T. L. Smith, *Revivalism and Social Reform;* N. W. Taylor, *Lectures on the Moral Government of God.*

New Testament. *See* Bible.

New Testament Canon. *See* Bible, Canon of.

New Testament Theology. That branch of the Christian disciplines which traces themes through the authors of the NT and then amalgamates those individual motifs into a single comprehensive whole. Thus it studies the progressive revelation of God in terms of the life situation at the time of writing and then delineates the underlying thread which ties it together. This discipline centers upon meaning rather than application, i.e., the message of the text for its own day rather than for modern needs. The term employed most frequently for the current state of biblical theology is "crisis," due to the growing stress on diversity rather than unity and the failure to attain any consensus whatever as to methodology or content. However, this is hyperbolic.

Historical Survey. In the centuries following the apostolic era dogma dominated the church and biblical theology was forced to take a subordinate role. The "rule of faith," or the magisterium of the church, was the guiding principle. The change began with the Reformation, when *sola Scriptura* replaced dogma as the hermeneutic of the church. The true beginning of "biblical theology" came after the Enlightenment within German pietism. The mind replaced faith as the controlling factor, and the historical-critical method developed. J. F. Gabler in 1787 defined the approach in purely descriptive terms, and after him critics treated the Bible like any other book.

In Tübingen, F. C. Baur in 1864 developed "tendency criticism," which reconstructed NT history under Hegel's thesis (Petrine church), antithesis (Pauline church), and synthesis (the later church of the second century). Later in the century the history of religions school with Wilhelm Bousset and William Wrede looked at the sources of Christianity in terms of the surrounding religions. From that time the basis of NT theology was said to be the early church rather than Jesus. The conservative reaction, via Schlatter and Zahn in Germany, the Cambridge trio (Lightfoot, Westcott, and Hort), and the Princetonians (Hodge, Machen, Warfield, and Vos) argued for the interdependence of biblical theology with exegesis and systematics.

Karl Barth and dialectical theology (1919) rescued the old liberalism after its collapse following the First World War. He said that God speaks to man through the Bible. Therefore the testaments were studied along theological rather than historical-critical lines. Oscar Cullmann with his salvation-history approach represented the conservative wing, and Rudolf Bultmann with his demythologization and existential interpretation controlled the liberal faction. Following Bultmann, Ernst Fuchs and Gerhard Ebeling developed the new hermeneutic, an influential school which considered the Bible to be encounter or "word-event." They reacted against the Bible as propositional truth and said that in it man is called to a new relationship with God.

There are several more recent approaches, such as Wolfhart Pannenberg's return to the historical approach as a scientific discipline and Brevard Childs's canon process, which considers the Bible as a unity and states that biblical theology must begin with the final canonical form rather than the developing stages of the biblical books. The major characteristic, however, has been disunity. No voice has gained ascendancy and no single system dominates as did Baur, Bousset, or Bultmann in the past. However, the interest is greater than ever before, and several voices, notably those of the canon-critical camp, are turning interest back to biblical theology.

Relationship to Other Disciples. *To Systematic Theology.* Since biblical theology began as a reaction against dogmatics, there has always been tension between the two. Many like Ernst Käsemann have argued that the fragmentary nature of the NT data makes any attempt to unify the diverse theologies impossible. However, this is doubtful (see below), and the two are interdependent. Biblical theology forces systematics to remain true to the historical revelation, while dogmatics provides the categories to integrate the data into a larger whole. However, the organization itself stems from the text; Scripture must determine the integrating pattern or structure. Biblical theology is descriptive, tracing the individual emphases of the sacred writers and then collating them to ascertain the underlying unity. Systematics takes this material and reshapes it into a confessional statement for the church; it bridges the gap between "what it meant" and "what it means." At the same time, systematics provides the preunderstanding that guides the interpreter, so the two disciplines interact in a type of "hermeneutical circle" as each informs and checks the other.

To Exegesis. There is a constant tension within biblical theology between diversity and unity, and a holistic consideration of the biblical material is a necessary corrective to a fragmented approach to the Bible. Thus biblical theology regulates exegesis (Gaffin). Yet exegesis also precedes biblical theology, for it provides the data with which the latter works. The theologian correlates the results of the exegesis of individual texts in order to discover the unity between them. Therefore the hermeneutical circle is now a three-way enterprise.

To Historical Theology. "Tradition" controls not only Roman Catholic dogma but Protestant thinking as well. All interpreters find their data base in their community of faith. Historical theology makes the theologian aware of the ongoing dialogue and thus functions both as a check against reading later ideas into a passage and as a store of knowledge from which to draw possible interpretations. This discipline also enters the hermeneutical circle, within which the text challenges our preunderstanding and both draws upon and reforms our tradition-derived beliefs.

To Homiletical Theology. Nearly every theologian realizes that theology dare not merely describe the past thinking of the biblical authors. It must demonstrate the relevance of those ideas for contemporary needs. This is the task of homiletical theology. Of course, no one is either a theologian or a homiletician; in a very real sense the two converge. Yet it is still valid to differentiate the levels at which we work, so long as we realize that true interpretation must blend all five aspects—biblical, systematic, exegetical, historical, and homiletical. The task itself has been explained best by missiology's "contextualization." The preacher/missionary takes the results of the first four disciplines and communicates this to the current "context" of the church/mission field.

Specific Problem Areas. *Unity and Diversity.* Many argue that the biblical books are circumstantial and linked to irreversible historical contingency; therefore there was no true unifying theology. Some go so far as to state there was no true "orthodoxy" in the earliest church but only a series of different groups struggling for control. Certainly there is tremendous diversity in the Bible, since most of the books were written to defend God's will for his people against various aberrations. Further, there is a great variety of expressions—e.g., Paul's "adoption" motif or John's "newborn" imagery. However, this does not mean that it is impossible to compile divergent traditions into a larger conceptual whole (cf. Eph. 4:5–6). Through all the diverse expressions a unified perspective and faith shine through. The key is linguistic/semantic; the differences can often be understood as metaphors which point to a larger truth. At this level we can detect unity.

Tradition-History. Many believe that doctrines and traditions developed in stages, and that inspiration should be applied to the originating event, the stages in the subsequent history of the community, and the final stage in which it was "frozen" into the canon. This makes detection of any biblical theology very difficult and usually leads to multiple interpretations. However, there is another way, which depends upon the final form and traces only that which is evident in the text. Moreover, we must not allow a concept of tradition to replace the search for a unifying center. Tradition-critical speculation becomes an end in itself, with very little in the way of fruitful results. Still, when placed within the context of the whole process, the method can highlight individual emphases, e.g., in the four Gospels.

Analogia Fidei and Progressive Revelation. When one places too much stress on unity, "parallelomania" can result, i.e., the tendency to apply any parallel (even if a wrong one) to a text. Actually, as evidenced even in the Reformers, "the faith" or dogma can control our exegesis. A better phrase would be *analogia Scriptura,* "Scripture interpreting Scripture." Here too we must exercise care and stress a proper use of parallels, studying the use of the terms in both passages in order to determine whether the meanings truly overlap. Progressive revelation ties together the seemingly disparate notions of tradition-history and *analogia Scriptura.* One must trace the historical process of revelation and determine the continuities between individual parts.

History and Theology. James Barr says that ambiguity about the connection between revelatory events and historical causation and between revelation and the biblical text itself causes problems for the possibility of biblical theology. Yet history is necessary for theology. While there is theology in narrative sections like the Gospels, this does not obviate the historical core. Lessing's "ugly broad ditch" between "accidental truths of history" and "necessary truths of reason" is based upon the philosophical skepticism of the Enlightenment. In the post-Einsteinian age this position is no longer viable. There is no reason that theology must be divorced from the possibility of revelation in history. Indeed, history and its interpretation are united, and recent approaches to historiography demonstrate not only the possibility of seeing God's revelation in history but the necessity of doing so. In Kings-Chronicles or the Gospels, for instance, history and theology are inseparable. We know Jesus as he has been interpreted for us through the sacred evangelists.

Language, Text, and Meaning. Recent theorists have drawn such a sharp contrast between modern conditions and the ancient world that the interpreter seems forever separated from the intended meaning of the text. They assert that a text once written becomes autonomous from the author, and the interpreter cannot get behind his or her preunderstanding to make an "objective" reading. The world of the interpreter cannot interpenetrate the world of the Bible. Gadamer argues for a fusion of horizons between the interpreter and the text, and Ricoeur speaks of the "world-referential" dimension—i.e., Scripture draws the reader into its own world. More recent approaches such as structuralism go beyond the text to stress the "deeper structure" beneath it—i.e., the universal patterns of the mind which speak to every generation. It is said that we are moving further and further from the original meaning of Scripture. However, this is not necessarily the case. Wittgenstein talked of the "language games" which language plays, and E. D. Hirsch speaks of the "intrinsic genre" of the text—i.e., the rules of the language game which narrow the possibilities and facilitate interpretation. Meaning in the text is open to the interpreter, who must place his preunderstanding "in front of" the text (Ricoeur) and enter its own language game. Within this the original meaning is a possible goal. When we recognize the NT as stating propositional truth, the intended meaning becomes a necessary enterprise.

OT and NT. Any true biblical theology must recognize the centrality of the relationship between the testaments. Again the issue is diversity vs. unity. The various strata of both must be allowed to speak, but the unity of these strata must be recognized. Several aspects demand this unity: the historical continuity between the testaments; the centrality of the OT for the NT; the promise-fulfillment theme of the NT; the messianic hope of the OT and its place as a "pedagogue" (Gal. 3). Many, from Marcion to Bultmann, have posited an absolute dichotomy between the testaments, yet to do so is to separate the NT from its historical moorings and to cause it to founder in a sea of historical irrelevance. Others elevate OT over NT (A. A. van Ruler) or take a purely Christological approach to the OT (Hengstenberg, Vischer). None does full justice to the two testaments. For instance, while a completely Christological approach guards against the tendency to historicize the OT away from promise-fulfillment, it leads to a subjective spiritualizing of the OT which denies its intended meaning. Therefore, I would posit "patterns of unity and continuity" (Hasel) as the OT looks forward to the NT and the NT depends upon the OT for its identity. Both are valid aspects of God's ongoing redemptive activity in history.

Theology and Canon. Brevard Childs has made the final form of the canon the primary hermeneutical tool in determining a biblical theology. He believes that the parts of Scripture must maintain a dialectical relationship with the whole of the canon. Therefore there is no true biblical theology when only the individual voices of the various strata are heard. However, many critics demur, saying that biblical authority and inspiration are dynamic rather than static, centering not only upon the final form of the text but also upon the individual stages within the tradition process, both before the "final" form and after it, even up to the present day. Childs responds that while the tradition process has validity, any true theology must depend upon the canon itself and not upon the speculative results of historical criticism. Childs's concern is valid, but there are certain problems. First, both the original community and the current interpreter have priority over the author and text. Second, Childs admits that with his approach the original meaning of the text cannot be recovered. Many canon critics see the true meaning as encompassing not only the canonical thrust but also the meaning of the original event/saying, subsequent developments, and current interpretations. The text is reduced to a mere voice in a cacophony of sounds. Third, many other critics reduce Scripture to a "canon within the canon" (e.g., Käsemann). One chooses a theme as center and stresses only those passages which fit this so-called core of Scripture. This reductionism must be avoided and the whole of Scripture allowed to speak.

Authority. Since biblical theology is descriptive, dealing with "what it meant," critical scholars deny its authority. True biblical authority, it is said, rests upon its "apostolic effectiveness" in fulfilling its task (Barrett) or upon the community behind it (Knight) or its content (Achtemeier). In actuality the authority of Scripture transcends all these; as the revelation *of God,* it has propositional authority; as the revelation of God *to man,* it has existential authority. The text is primary, and the authority of the interpreter is secondary—i.e., it derives its authority from the text. Theology as interpreted meaning has authority only to the extent that it reflects the true message of the inspired Scriptures. The Barthian separation between the living Word and the written Word, with the latter having only instrumental authority, is an inadequate mode, for it fails to understand properly the claims of Scripture for itself. The Bible is both propositional revelation and the dynamic instrument of the Holy Spirit. The authority of biblical theology stems not just from the fact that it speaks to the contemporary situation (which is the task of systematics and homiletics) but from the fact that it communicates divine truth.

A Proper Methodology. *The Synthetic Method* traces basic theological themes through the strata of Scripture in order to note their development through the biblical period. Its strength is stress on the unity of Scripture. Its weakness is its tendency toward subjectivity: one can force an artificial pattern upon the NT material.

The Analytical Method studies the distinctive theology of individual sections and notes the unique message of each. The strength is the emphasis upon the individual author's meaning. The weakness is the radical diversity, which results in a collage of pictures with no cohesiveness.

The Historical Method studies the development of religious ideas in the life of God's people. Its value is the attempt to understand the community of believers behind the Bible. Its problem is the subjectivity of most reconstructions, in which the scriptural text is at the mercy of the theorist.

The Christological Method makes Christ the hermeneutical key to both testaments. Its strength is its recognition of the true center of the Bible. Its weakness is its tendency to spiritualize passages and force interpretations foreign to them, especially in terms of the OT experience of Israel. One should not read everything in the OT or NT as a "type of Christ."

The Confessional Method looks at the Bible as a series of faith statements which are beyond history. Its value is its recognition of creed and worship in NT faith. Its danger is its radical separation between faith and history.

The Cross-Section Method traces a single unifying theme (e.g., covenant or promise) and studies it historically by means of "cross-sections" or samplings of the canonical record. Its strength is the understanding of major themes that it provides. Its weakness is the danger of arbitrary selection. If one selects the wrong central theme, other themes can be forced into harmony with it.

The Multiplex Method (Hasel) combines the best of these and proceeds hermeneutically from text to theory. It begins with grammatical and historical analysis of the text, attempting to unlock the meaning of the various texts within their life settings. Here a sociological analysis is also helpful, since it studies those life settings in terms of the social matrix of the believing communities. As the data are collected from this exegetical task, they are organized into the basic patterns of the individual books and then further of the individual authors. At this stage the interpreter has delineated the emphases or interlocking forces in the strata. Once these various traditions (e.g., Markan, Johannine, Pauline) have been charted, the student looks for basic principles of cohesion between them, for metaphorical language which discloses larger patterns of unity between the authors. One must seek the unified whole behind statements of election and universal salvific will, on the one hand, or behind realized and final eschatology, on the other. Paul's stress on justification by faith will be united with John's use of new-birth language. These larger unities are charted on two levels, first with respect to overall unity and second concerning the progress of revelation. Finally, these motifs are compiled into major sections and subsections, following a descriptive (biblical) method rather than an artificial reconstruction. In other words, the data rather than the dogmatic presuppositions of the interpreter control the operation. From this will emerge a central unifying theme around which the other subthemes gather themselves. Within this larger unity the individual themes maintain complementary yet distinct roles. The larger cohesive unity must result from rather than become the presupposition of the theological enterprise—i.e., the texts determine the patterns.

Themes in NT Theology. These final two sections will apply the above proposals first to the basical theological messages of individual NT authors and then to the quest for a unifying central theme in the NT. Since there are separate articles in this volume on the theologies of Matthew, Mark, Luke, John, and Paul, we will present here the rest of the NT corpus, namely the themes of the general epistles and of Revelation.

Hebrews was written to a group of Jewish Christians, perhaps in Rome, who were in danger of "apostasizing" due to persecution. As a result, the author stresses the pilgrimage aspect of the Christian life (see Käsemann). The believer is to recognize that he or she lives between two worlds, the present age of trouble and the future age of salvation. The key is a faith which makes hope a concrete reality (11:1) and makes the "powers of the age to come" a present reality (6:4–5). In light of the superiority of Christ over the old Jewish economy, the Christian must cling to the high priest "after the order of Melchizedek" (7:1–2). While many have made the high priestly Christology the major theme of Hebrews, it is more likely that the pilgrimage aspect, rooted in the exhortation passages, is central.

James, probably the first NT book written, is addressed to a Jewish Christian audience, perhaps in Palestine. The church was poor, without influence, and passing through a time of persecution in which wealthy Jews were confiscating their property (2:6, 5:1–6). The book is immensely practical, dealing in a pastoral way with weak believers and their tendencies. It draws upon wisdom themes regarding trials and temptation, social concern, the problem of the tongue, and interpersonal conflicts to underscore the necessity of putting one's faith into practice in the practical Christian life.

I Peter utilizes a great deal of creedal or catechetical material—i.e., formal statements on Christian doctrine composed by the apostles for the early church—to speak to a further situation of persecution on behalf of a mixed church of Jewish and Gentile Christians in northern Galatia. It combines an eschatological perspective (i.e., the end has begun and glory is near) with an ethical emphasis (i.e., exemplary behavior must result from the experience of God's salvation in light of the world's opposition). Christ is the model of the righteous sufferer (3:18), and his exaltation is shared by the one who endures similar hostility. Therefore, in the midst of this evil world the believer is an alien whose true citizenship is in heaven and who rejoices even when suffering (1:6–7) because it is a participation in the humiliation/exaltation of Christ.

II Peter and *Jude* are sister epistles written to combat false teaching of the Gnostic type which rejected the lordship of Christ (II Pet. 2:1) and the parousia (II Pet. 3:3–4) and degenerated into immorality (Jude 4). In light of this, there is a decided emphasis upon the primacy of apostolic teaching (II Pet. 1:16, 20–21; 3:2) and upon the return of Christ in judgment (II Pet. 3:3–4; Jude 5–6). The coming day of the Lord is central in II Peter, and the judgment of those who oppose God, either human or angelic/demonic, comes to the fore in Jude. Both stress the stringent responsibility of the church to oppose the false teachers.

Unifying Themes. Five criteria are necessary to the search for a central motif that binds together the individual emphases and diverse doctrines of the NT: (1) the basic theme must express the nature and character of God; (2) it must account for the people of God as they relate to him; (3) it must express the world of mankind as the object of God's redemptive activity; (4) it must explain the dialectical relationship between the testaments; (5) it must account for the other possible unifying themes and must truly unite the theological emphases of the NT. Many proposed themes will fit one or another of the strata of OT and NT—e.g., the narrative or the poetic or the prophetic or the wisdom or the epistolary portions—but will fail to summarize all. This theme must balance the others without merely lifting one above its fellow motifs.

The Covenant (Eichrodt, Ridderbos) has often been utilized to express the binding relationship between God and his people. It includes both the legal contract and the eschatological hope which results, both the universal dimension of the cosmic God who creates as well as sustains and the specific communion which results. The problem is that this is not universally attested in the testaments as the central core. A better theme might be "election" as expressing the act of God or "promise" as the hope which results (see below).

God and Christ (Hasel) have been stressed a great deal lately, noting the theocentric character of the OT and the Christocentric character of the NT. This is much better than stressing aspects, such as the holiness or lordship or kingship of God, and better than making either God or Christ the center, which would do a disservice to OT or NT respectively. However, while we may view the theme dynamically to allow for the individual expression of subthemes, this too may be narrow since the community of God's people is not a natural part of it.

Existential Reality or Communion has been stressed (Bultmann *et al.*) as the true purpose of the Bible. Proponents argue that this ties together the other themes and expresses the dynamic work of God among his people. Yet as expressed by many it ignores too readily the propositional and creedal content of Scripture. While communion is certainly a primary motif, it is not the unifying theme.

Eschatological Hope (Kaiser) is often stressed, in either the sense of promise or of hope. The strength of this is the way it unites the testaments, since both look to the future consummation of God's activity in history. It also unifies the other three above, which can be said to express aspects of this hope. Its weakness, as often noted by various scholars, is the absence of stress on this in many portions of Scripture, e.g., the wisdom literature or the Johannine writings. Again, this is a major emphasis but not the unifying theme.

Salvation History (von Rad, Cullmann, Ladd) may be the best of the positions, for it recognizes God's/Christ's redemptive activity on behalf of mankind, in terms of both present and future communion. More than the others above, it subsumes each of the categories into itself. Those who oppose this as the unifying theme argue from two directions: (1) its artificial nature, since there is no single instance in OT or NT where it is directly stated; and (2) the lack of emphasis upon it in the entire NT—e.g., it fits Luke-Acts but not John. However, any "unifying theme" is by its very nature artificial, since it is a principle derived from the individual themes of Scripture. Also, while it is not "central" to every book, it is *behind* those diverse motifs and is thereby able to bind them together. Every theme here has a viable claim, so we must see which of the five best summarizes the others. Therefore, salvation-history has the best claim to the title "unifying theme."

G. R. Osborne

See also Old Testament Theology; Mark, Theology of; Matthew, Theology of; Luke, Theology of; John, Theology of; Paul, Theology of.

Bibliography. J. Barr, *The Scope and Authority of the Bible;* C. K. Barrett, "What is NT Theology? Some Reflections," *Horizons in Biblical Theology* 3; H. Boers, *What is NT Theology?* B. Childs, *Biblical Theology in Crisis;* R. Gaffin, "Systematic Theology and Biblical Theology," *The NT Student and Theology III,* ed. J. H. Skilton; D. Guthrie, *NT Theology;* G. Hasel, *NT Theology: Basic Issues in the Current Debate;* U. Mauser, ed., *Horizons in Biblical Theology: An International Dialogue;* E. Käsemann, "The Problem of a NT Theology," *NTS* 19:235–45; G. E. Ladd, *A Theology of the NT;* R. Morgan, *The Nature of NT Theology: The Contributions of William Wrede and Adolf Schlatter;* J. D. Smart, *The Past, Present, and Future of Biblical Theology;* G. Vos, *Biblical Theology.*

Niagara Conferences. A series of summer meetings for Bible study which marked the beginning of the Bible and Prophetic Conference movement in the United States. The idea for holding summer Bible conferences originated in 1868 among a group of American evangelicals associated with the millenarian journal *Waymarks in the Wilderness.* For the next few years conferences were held in different cities, but in 1883 sponsors secured a permanent location at Niagara-on-the-Lake, Ontario.

At first called the Believers' Meeting for Bible Study, the Niagara Conferences met for one week during the summer. The schedule usually commenced with a Wednesday evening prayer meeting. Then for the next week conferees attended two study sessions each morning, two in the afternoon, and one in the evening. On Sunday the slightly abbreviated schedule included a worship service, an observance of the Lord's Supper, and a meeting on missionary themes. Speakers, who were drawn from across the country, emphasized a traditional evangelical understanding of the Bible. Many practiced a new kind of exposition called the "Bible reading." In contrast to more standard preaching and teaching, the Bible reading consisted of a collection of various biblical passages on a given theme which were read together with very few connecting comments. In this way, the audiences were assured, they heard only what the Holy Spirit had to say on the subject.

Because of the nonsectarian spirit of the sessions, the conferences were able to draw a cross-section of North American evangelicals. But the leadership of the meetings remained under the control of millenarian teachers and pastors. Men such as Nathaniel West, H. M. Parsons, A. J. Gordon, W. J. Erdman, A. T. Pierson, George Needham, Robert Cameron, and most importantly James H. Brookes made sure that the still suspect premillennialism was taught alongside more traditional evangelical theological fare. When controversy arose over the doctrinal slant of the 1877 conference, James Brookes issued a fourteen-point "Niagara Creed" in 1878. The statement contained articles on the verbal inerrancy of the Bible, a Calvinist understanding of human depravity, salvation by faith in the blood of Christ, the personality and continuing work of the Holy Spirit in the lives of believers, the need for personal holiness, and the premillennial second coming of Christ.

After the death of James Brookes in 1897 the conference moved from Niagara-on-the-Lake and eventually disbanded in 1901 when its leadership could no longer agree on the timing of the "rapture" in relation to the tribulation of the last days. Nevertheless, the Niagara Conference spawned other Bible and Prophetic Conferences and spread premillennial views, especially the dispensationalism of J. N. Darby. In addition, the conferences forged alliances among conservative evangelicals that played a significant role in the beginnings of the fundamentalist movement after World War I. T. P. WEBER

See also DISPENSATION, DISPENSATIONALISM; FUNDAMENTALISM; MILLENNIUM, VIEWS OF THE.

Bibliography. E. R. Sandeen, *The Roots of Fundamentalism;* G. Marsden, *Fundamentalism and American Culture;* T. P. Weber, *Living in the Shadow of the Second Coming.*

Nicaea, Council of (325). The first ecumenical council in the history of the church was convened by the emperor Constantine at Nicaea in Bithynia (now Isnik, Turkey). The main purpose of the council was to attempt to heal the schism in the church provoked by Arianism. This it proceeded to do theologically and politically by the almost unanimous production of a theological confession (the Nicene Creed) by over three hundred bishops representing almost all the eastern provinces of the empire (where the heresy was chiefly centered) and by a token representation from the West. The creed thus produced was the first that could legally claim universal authority as it was sent throughout the empire to receive the agreement of the churches (with the alternative consequences of excommunication and imperial banishment).

The issue which culminated at Nicaea arose out of an unresolved tension within the theological legacy of Origen concerning the relation of the Son to the Father. On the one hand there was the attribution of deity to the Son in a relationship with the Father described as eternal generation. On the other hand there was clear subordinationism. Almost appropriately, the dispute erupted at Alexandria about 318, with Arius, a popular presbyter of the church district of Baucalis, developing the latter strain of Origenism against Bishop Alexander, who advocated the former line of thinking. Arius was a quite capable logician who attacked Alexander (with motives not entirely scholarly) on the charge of Sabellianism. After a local synod heard his own views and dismissed them and him as unsound, Arius demonstrated his popularizing literary and political talents, gathering support beyond Alexandria. His theological views appealed to left-wing Origenists, including the respected Eusebius, bishop of Caesarea. His closest and most helpful ally was his former fellow student in the school of Lucian, Eusebius, bishop at the imperial residence of Nicomedia. After Constantine's personal envoy, Hosius of Cordova, failed to effect a reconciliation in 322 between the two parties in Alexandria, the emperor decided to convene an ecumenical council.

The teaching of Arianism is well documented. The central controlling idea is the unique, incommunicable, indivisible, transcendent nature of the singular divine being. This is what the Arians referred to as the Father. Logically pressing this definition of the Father and making use of certain biblical language, the Arians argued that if the error of Sabellius was to be avoided (and everyone was anxious to avoid it), then certain conclusions about the Son were inescapable. And it is this view of the Son which is the central significance of Arianism. He cannot be of the Father's being or essence (otherwise that essence would be divisible or communicable or in some way not unique or simple, which is impossible by definition). He therefore exists only by the Father's will, as do all other creatures and things. The biblical description of his being begotten does imply a special relationship between the Father and the Word or Son, but it cannot be an ontological relationship. "Begotten" is to be taken in the sense of "made," so that the Son is a *ktisma* or *poiema*, a creature. Being begotten or made, he must have had a beginning, and this leads to the famous Arian phrase, "there was when he was not." Since he was not generated out of the Father's being and he was, as they accorded him, the first of God's creation, then he must have been created out of nothing. Not being of perfect or immutable substance, he was subject to moral change. And because of the extreme transcendence of God, in the final respect the Son has no real communion or knowledge of the Father at all. The ascription of *theos* to Christ in Scripture was deemed merely functional.

The council of Nicaea opened June 19, 325, with Hosius of Cordova presiding and the emperor in attendance. Despite the absence of official minutes a sketch of the proceedings can be reconstructed. Following an opening address by the emperor in which the need for unity was stressed, Eusebius of Nicomedia, leading the Arian party, presented a formula of faith which candidly marked a radical departure from traditional formularies. The disapproval was so strong that most of the Arian party abandoned their support of the document and it was torn to shreds before the eyes of everyone present. Soon thereafter Eusebius of Caesarea, anxious to clear his name, read a lengthy statement of faith that included what was probably a baptismal creed of the church of Caesarea. Eusebius had been provisionally excommunicated earlier in the year by a synod in Antioch for refusing to sign an anti-Arian creed. The emperor himself pronounced him orthodox with only the suggestion that he adopt the word *homoousios.*

For a long time the confession of Eusebius was believed to have formed the basis of the Nicene Creed, which was then modified by the council. However, it seems clear that such was not the case, the structure and content of the latter being significantly different from the former. Most likely a creed was introduced under the direction of Hosius, discussed (especially the term *homoousia*), and drafted in its final form requiring the signatures of the bishops. All those present (including Eusebius of Nicomedia) signed except two who were subsequently exiled.

It should be noted that this creed is not that which is recited in churches today as the Nicene Creed. Although similar in many respects, the latter is significantly longer than the former and is missing some key Nicene phrases.

The theology expressed in the Nicene Creed is decisively anti-Arian. At the beginning the unity of God is affirmed. But the Son is said to be "true God from true God." Although confessing that the Son is begotten, the creed adds the words, "from the Father" and "not made." It is positively asserted that he is "from the being (*ousia*) of the Father" and "of one substance (*homoousia*) with the Father." A list of Arian phrases, including "there was when he was not" and assertions that the Son is a creature or out of nothing, are expressly anathematized. Thus an ontological rather than merely functional deity of the Son was upheld at Nicaea. The only thing confessed about the Spirit, however, is faith in him.

Among other things achieved at Nicaea were the agreement on a date to celebrate Easter and a ruling on the Melitian Schism in Egypt. Arius and his most resolute followers were banished, but only for a short time. In the majority at Nicaea was Athanasius, then a young deacon, soon to succeed Alexander as bishop and carry on what would become a minority challenge to a resurgent Arianism in the East. However, the orthodoxy of Nicaea would eventually and decisively be reaffirmed at the Council of Constantinople in 381.

C. A. Blaising

See also Arianism; Athanasius; Constantinople, Council of; Melitian Schisms; Monarchianism.

Bibliography. Athanasius, *Defense of the Nicene Council;* Eusebius, *The Life of Constantine* 2.61–3.20; Socrates, *Ecclesiastical History* 1.5–9; Sozomen, *Ecclesiastical History* 1.15–21; Theodoret, *Ecclesiastical History* 1.1–12; A. E. Burn, *The Council of Nicea;* J. Gonzalez, *A History of Christian Thought,* I; H. M. Gwatkin, *Studies of Arianism;* R. C. Gregg and D. E. Groh, *Early Arianism;* A. Grillmeier, *Christ in Christian Tradition;* J. N. D. Kelley, *Early Christian Creeds* and *Early Christian Doctrines;* C. Luibheid, *Eusebius of Caesarea and the Arian Crisis.*

Nicaea, Second Council of (787). The seventh ecumenical council provided the climax (though not yet the end) of the iconoclastic controversy by decisively authorizing the veneration of images of various sorts but especially those of Christ, Mary, the holy angels, and the saints. The controversy had begun when the emperors Leo III (beginning in 725) and his son after him, Constantine V, tried to abruptly end the practice of worshiping images, which had been growing in the church for over three centuries. This seems to have been partly in response to the threat of Islam, which attributed its success to an unidolatrous monotheism. Constantine V convened a council in 754 that rendered an iconoclastic *definitio* based on the second commandment, the earliest fathers, and the concern that images were attempts to circumscribe the divine nature.

These actions were opposed by certain influential figures in the East, including Germanus of Constantinople and John of Damascus, and also by the Roman popes Gregory II, Gregory III, and Hadrian I. After the death of Constantine V his wife, Irene, reversed his policies while acting as regent for their son, Leo IV (whom she later murdered). She convened the council which met at Nicaea in 787, attended by over three hundred bishops. At this council the iconoclasts were anathematized and the worship of images upheld. But a distinction was drawn between worship defined as *proskynesis,* which was to be given to images or rather more properly through the images to their prototypes, and worship defined as *latria,* which was to be given to God alone. The authority for image worship was considered to be the worship of the angel of the Lord in the OT and the incarnate Christ in the NT, the teaching and practice of the latter fathers, and the practice of venerating Mary and the saints that had become so established that not even the iconoclasts opposed it (they only opposed the worship of their images). Despite a brief outbreak of iconoclasm, the position of this council became standard orthodoxy in Greek and Roman churches.

The distinction between *proskynesis* and *latria*—or, as later put in the West, between *dulia* and *latria*—is so fine as to be imperceptible in common practice. As Calvin argued, the biblical usage of the words certainly does not recognize the distinction that Nicaea attempted to establish. Thus the Reformation rejected the decision of this council as encouraging idolatry.

C. A. Blaising

See also Dulia; Latria; Hyperdulia.

Bibliography. H. Bettenson, *Documents of the Christian Church;* J. Calvin, *Institutes of the Christian Religion* 1.11–12; J. Gonzalez, *A History of Christian Thought,* II; E. J. Martin, *A History of the Iconoclastic Controversy;* P. Schaff, *History of the Christian Church,* IV.

Nicene Creed. *See* Nicaea, Council of.

Niebuhr, Helmut Richard (1894–1962). The brothers Reinhold and Richard Niebuhr were the leaders of a new "Christian realism" which represented an American counterpart to European neo-orthodoxy. H. Richard Niebuhr was ordained in the Evangelical and Reformed Church after attending the denomination's schools, Elmhurst College and Eden Theological Seminary. He served three years as a pastor in St. Louis (1916–18), taught theology at Eden Seminary, pursued doctoral studies at Yale University, served as president of Elmhurst, and again as theological professor at Eden. In 1931 he accepted a position at Yale Divinity School, where he remained until his death.

Niebuhr occupied a middle ground between the greatest of nineteenth century liberal theologians, Friedrich Schleiermacher, and the greatest of twentieth century neo-orthodoxy, Karl Barth, even as he embraced aspects of classical orthodoxy. From the older liberalism he took a commitment to the essentially experiential nature of religion and the conviction that humankind, immersed in history, can never grasp truth unbiased and whole. With European neo-orthodox theologians he sharply criticized liberal optimism concerning human potential. And from Augustine, the Protestant Reformers, and Jonathan Edwards he adopted a high view of divine sovereignty and a firm belief in the utter dependency of all existence upon God.

Niebuhr's interests ranged widely. One group of his works treated matters of the church in society. *The Social Sources of Denominationalism* (1929) demonstrated how thoroughly Christian institutions were intertwined with the cultural customs of the West. *The Kingdom of God in America* (1937) provided a brilliant portrait of the way in which the idea of God's kingdom had shifted in American history—from God's sovereignty in the time of Jonathan Edwards, to the kingdom of Christ during the 1800s, and finally to the coming kingdom for twentieth century liberals. The book looks most fondly on the earliest period, when some Americans truly believed in the ultimacy of God. It also contains the best short critical description of theological liberalism ever written: "A God without wrath brought men without sin into a kingdom without judgment through the ministrations of a Christ without a cross." *Christ and Culture* (1951) offered a classic schematization of the different ways in which believers over the centuries have interacted with their surrounding worlds. Its five categories—Christ against culture, the Christ of culture, Christ above culture, Christ and culture in paradox, and Christ the transformer of culture—have become indispensable tools for describing Christian approaches in political, economic, and social affairs.

Niebuhr's more directly theological and ethical works continue to have a broad appeal. *The Meaning of Revelation* (1941) contended that when God reveals himself, all other events and questions become relative. The work has been criticized by evangelicals for slighting Scripture and for making revelation overly subjective, but here and elsewhere Niebuhr pointed to the Christian community as a body providing standards (though they are relative also) for describing and communicating that revelation. *Radical Monotheism and Western Culture* (1960) was Niebuhr's last full statement of his convictions. In it he looked to God as the source of all being, as Being itself, and decried all that would detract from his all-sufficiency. Throughout his work Niebuhr pointed to Jesus Christ as God's supreme revelation. In much the same way as Barth would frame the issue, Niebuhr held that Jesus was the most dramatic manifestation of the Ultimate Being that destroys the estrangement that alienates people from God and from each other.

M. A. Noll

See also Neo-orthodoxy.

Bibliography. J. W. Fowler, *To See the Kingdom: The Theological Vision of H. Richard Niebuhr;* P. Ramsey, ed., *Faith and Ethics: The Theology of H. Richard Niebuhr;* S. E. Ahlstrom, "H. Richard Niebuhr's Place in American Thought," *CCri* 23:213–17; D. B. Meyer, *The Protestant Search for Political Realism, 1919–1941.*

Niebuhr, Reinhold (1892–1971). The best-known spokesman for American "Christian realism" from the early 1930s until his death. Although Niebuhr's position resembled European neo-orthodoxy in its distrust of liberalism, it was more concerned with ethics than with theology proper, it focused more on the doctrine of man than on the doctrine of God, and it showed more concern for life in society than for life in the church.

Niebuhr was the son of a pastor in the Evangelical and Reformed Church. As did his brother H. Richard, who also became an influential theologian and ethicist, Reinhold attended his denomination's college and seminary (Elmhurst and Eden) before doing graduate work at Yale. In 1915 he accepted the pastorate of Bethel Evangelical Church in Detroit, where he served for thirteen years. Niebuhr came of age theologically in this urban church as his liberalism encountered the harsh realities of industrial America. He was particularly troubled by the demoralizing effects of industrialism on the workers. He wondered particularly what hope there was for American civilization when "naïve gentlemen with a genius for mechanics suddenly become the arbiters over the lives and fortunes of hundreds of thousands." While still in Detroit, Niebuhr began to advocate radical solutions to the human crisis as he perceived it—socialism and pacifism for life in society, a new "Christian realism" for theology.

Niebuhr moved to New York's Union Theological Seminary in 1928, where he immediately entered a wider circle of activity. World War II led him to abandon his socialism and pacifism, but he remained a dedicated social activist—serving on scores of committees in the 1930s and 1940s, helping to form Americans for Democratic Action and New York's Liberal Party, editing the journal *Christianity and Crisis,* and writing prolifically for newspapers and magazines.

His theological ethics were developed in a long list of major books, the two most important being *Moral Man and Immoral Society* (1932) and *The Nature and Destiny of Man* (1941, 1943). The first repudiated liberal optimism concerning humanity. It pointed out that social groups are selfish almost by their very definition, and it rebuked the notion that human beings were perfectable as individuals or inherently good in groups. The second provided a more systematic discussion of what Niebuhr called mankind's "most vexing problem: How shall he think of himself?" Here and elsewhere Niebuhr proposed a series of "dialectical" relationships to answer his own question: humanity was both "free and bound, both limited and limitless," sinner and saint, subject to history and social forces but also the shaper of history and society, creature of the Creator but potential lord of the creation, egotistical but capable of living for others. Niebuhr drew on the Bible to expound these paradoxes, especially what he called the biblical "myth" of creation. Scripture shared the human potential, because mankind was made in the image of God, for good and for ill. Humans sinned by failing to believe that God could overcome the bondage to pride and to "the will to power" that is the common human fate. In the person of Christ, Niebuhr found a unique example of power used only for good and not—as with all other people—for evil. The cross of Christ was a particularly important theme for Niebuhr since it revealed the great paradox of powerlessness turned into power, of a love in justice that overcame the sinful world.

Niebuhr showed little concern for traditional theological topics except where they aided his study of humanity. As a result, he has been criticized for showing more interest in the paradoxes of human life than in the salvation offered through Christ. A similar criticism concerns his use of Scripture. The Bible seemed to mean more to him because it was relevant to the modern condition than because it was God's written word. These criticisms notwithstanding, Niebuhr's work remains among the most widely studied of all American theological efforts from the first two thirds of the twentieth century.

M. A. Noll

See also Neo-orthodoxy.

Bibliography. C. W. Kegley and R. W. Bretall, eds., *Reinhold Niebuhr: His Religious, Social, and Political Thought;* J. Bingham, *Courage to Change: An Introduction to the Life and Thought of Reinhold Niebuhr;* E. J. Carnell, *The Theology of Reinhold Niebuhr;* D. B. Meyer, *The Protestant Search for Political Realism, 1919–1941.*

Nihilism. First popularized by the Russian novelist Turgenev, "nihilism" signified total rejection of tradition, morality, authority, and the social order that enshrined them. "What can be smashed should be smashed; what will stand the blow is good, what will shatter is rubbish" (Pisarev) expresses its anarchic, revolutionary application. The czarist order in Russia was oppressive and doomed yet no basis existed for a better.

Later this mood sought justification in total philosophic skepticism, denying objective bases to both truth and morality. Nietzsche declared, "One interpretation of existence [religion] has been overthrown, but since it was held *the* interpretation, it seems no meaning is left in existence." Empiricism engendered agnosticism: all investigation beyond sense-experience being illusory, theological statements are meaningless—expressions of feeling, not truth. Sense-experience being individual, no generalized, objective truth is possible. What cannot be verified by sense-experience cannot be known.

Similarly, moral standards are subjective, arbitrary, emotive, and nonrational. "If God does not exist, everything is permitted" (Dostoevski); alternatively, if God does not exist, "the most meaningful reality is individual freedom, its supreme expression suicide." Morality is the product of social conditioning, mere feeling, or free unmotivated choice.

Some existentialism is nihilistic: man is nothing but what he makes himself; others exist only as related to him, limiting his life; systems, authorities, and obligation are academic fictions. Man's motiveless choices, feeling of responsibility, contradictory paradoxical existence, death, and idea of God are all absurd. We must draw full consequences of God's absence—abandonment. Man, "thrown into the world," lives in anguish, dread, finitude, guilt, and mortality.

Less academic nihilism is expressed in the robotlike, conformist, indifferent attitude of industrial man, relieving toil (or worklessness) with entertainment, stimulants, seeking no meaning, explanation, or future.

Bertrand Russell accepted ultimate nothingness with a dignified stiff upper lip. Camus asserted the dignity and fraternity of men rebelling against absurd predicament; social activists argue for worthwhile personal contributions to society. Christian existentialists seek deeper analysis of Being, personal relationship as clue to existence, and an existential confrontation with God. The value of persons and the presence of purpose in the universe are lines along which nihilism will be answered. "Taking the consequences of atheism seriously serves only to emphasise the importance of the problem of God."

R. E. O. White

See also Atheism.

Bibliography. S. Rosen, *Nihilism, a Philosophical Essay;* H. Thielicke, *Nihilism.*

Ninety-five Theses, The (1517). A series of propositions dealing with indulgences which Martin Luther drew up as the basis for a proposed academic disputation. They were written in reaction to abuses in the sale of a plenary indulgence by Johann Tetzel, who gave the impression that it would not only remit the guilt and penalties of even the most serious sins, but that its benefits could be applied to the dead in purgatory. Luther challenged this teaching because it led people to believe that forgiveness could be bought and to neglect true repentance.

The theses began by arguing that true repentance involves a turning of the entire self to God and not simply the desire to evade punishment. Luther also maintained that only God could remit guilt and that indulgences could only excuse the penalties imposed by the church. In addition, he denied the pope's power over purgatory, stated that the believer always has true forgiveness without indulgences, and condemned the interest shown in money rather than souls. Although written in Latin and not intended for public distribution, the theses were translated into German and soon spread throughout Germany. Even though they do not reveal the full development of Luther's theology, October 31, 1517, the day they were supposedly posted on the Wittenberg Castle Church door, has traditionally been considered the starting point of the Reformation. Recent scholarship has questioned both the dating of the theses and whether they were actually posted. Although the debate has not been resolved, most scholars still accept the traditional interpretation.

R. W. Heinze

See also Luther, Martin.

Bibliography. K. Aland, ed., *Martin Luther's 95 Theses;* H. Grimm, ed., *Luther's Works,* XXXI; E. Iserloh, *The Theses Were Not Posted;* F. Lau, "The Posting of Luther's Theses—Legend or Fact?" *CTM* 38:691–703.

Nominalism. The theory of knowledge that maintains that "universals" (general concepts representing the common elements belonging to individuals of the same genus or species) are empty concepts that have no reality independent of their existence in the thought of an individual. In contrast to Platonic realism, which held that universals had a separate existence apart from the individual object, nominalism insisted that reality was found only in the objects themselves. This debate on universals, found in Porphyry's *Isagogue,* caused great controversy during the Middle Ages. Roscellinus of Compiègne, a teacher and priest in Brittany in the eleventh century, has been called the father of nominalism because he argued that universals are derived from one's observation of individuals and that concepts of genus and species are just abstractions. This affected his theology, because it led him to the belief that "God" was no more than a word, an empty abstraction, and that the divine reality was actually found in the three individuals of the Godhead. He was condemned by the Synod of Soissons (1092) for holding to tritheism.

In the fourteenth century William of Ockham devised a nominalistic system of theology based on his belief that universals were only a convenience of the human mind. According to this view, the fact of a resemblance between two individuals does not necessitate a common attribute; the universals one forms in his mind more likely reflect one's own purposes rather than the character of reality. This led William to question scholastic arguments built upon such abstractions. As he argues in his *Centilogium,* systematization of theology must be rejected, for theology can ultimately be based only on faith and not on fact. Therefore, through grace and not knowledge, he accepted the teachings of the Roman Catholic Church, bowed to the authority of the pope, and declared the authority of Scripture. His follower, Gabriel Biel, would carry his thought to its logical conclusion and declare that reason could neither demonstrate that God was the First Cause of the universe nor make a distinction between the attributes of God, including God's intellect and will. The reality of the Trinity, as well as any theological dogma, can be found only in the realm of faith, not in the realm of reason. This was diametrically opposed to the natural theology of medieval scholasticism.

Nominalism continued to have an effect on theology. Its influence can be discerned in the writings of David Hume and John Stuart Mill.

D. A. Rausch

See also William of Ockham.

Bibliography. D. M. Armstrong, *Universals and Scientific Realism: Nominalism and Realism,* I; F. J. Copleston, *History of Philosophy,* III; R. A. Eberle, *Nominalistic Systems;* R. Seeberg, *Text-book of the History of Doctrines,* II.

Nonconformity. In general terms nonconformity is the refusal to conform to the established or majority religion. Thus Episcopalians are a nonconformist body in Scotland, and Wycliffe and the Lollards are sometimes depicted as England's first nonconformists.

Specifically it denotes those Protestants who could not conscientiously conform to the established religion of the reformed Church of England, especially after 1662, when the Dissenters comprised Independents (Congregationalists), Presbyterians, Baptists, and Quakers. The first three became the main nonconforming denominations, being joined in the eighteenth century by the Methodists and later by other smaller bodies. Since the later nineteenth century they have been known as the English Free Churches. Following a Free Church Congress in 1892, the National Council of the Evangelical Free Churches was formed (1896), followed by the Federal Council of Evangelical Free Churches (1919) on an officially representative basis. The two merged in 1940 in the Free Church Federal Council. A majority of Presbyterians and Congregationalists formed the United Reformed Church in 1972, but other ecumenical schemes have proved abortive.

From *ca.* 1619 "Nonconformists" designated those Puritans who adhered to the doctrine of the established English church but dissented in matters of practice and order, at first chiefly vestments and ceremonies like kneeling at Communion, but soon deeper issues of a set liturgy and episcopal polity. Thomas Fuller's *Church History* (1655) traced Nonconformists back to the reign of Edward VI, when John Hooper, "the father of English Nonconformity," opposed episcopal vestments. Elizabeth's Act of Uniformity (1559), which imposed the 1552 Prayer Book with minor conservative revisions, was not strenuously applied at first. But it provoked Nonconforming "gathered" communities from *ca.* 1567, the first Presbyterian congregational order in 1572, and Separatist Independent churches from *ca.* 1567. Persecution drove many to America and to Holland, from which base the first Baptist congregation in England was organized in London in 1612.

But Nonconformity before 1662 was an inconsiderable minority compared with afterward. During the Commonwealth the established order was Presbyterian (so that Independents remained Nonconformists), but the Restoration of 1660 brought back episcopacy. The Act of Uniformity required of all ministers "unfeigned assent and consent" to the 1662 Prayer book (slightly revised from 1559) and episcopal ordination if not already received. Some two thousand were ejected for refusing to comply. Some, like Richard Baxter, had lost their charges by an act of 1660. In 1661 the Corporation Act effectively excluded Nonconformists from city and town councils, and the Test Act of 1673 extended this to civil or military office under the government. The Conventicle Acts (1664 and later) banned meetings in private houses, and the Five Mile Act (1665) debarred ministers from contact with former congregations.

Nonconformist attitudes and practice varied considerably, as earlier under Elizabeth. Some objected not to episcopal ordination but to renouncing their previous ordination. Episcopacy might be acceptable, but not its English diocesan embodiment. An imposed liturgy was intolerable for others. Baxter's nicely principled Nonconformity was "essentially for the sake of the Church's unity and of others' liberty" (Nuttall) and carefully avoided separatism or sectarianism. Above all, total endorsement of the Prayer Book involved an abandonment of Puritan principles.

Occasional conformity was variously viewed. This was the practice of taking Communion in the established church at least once a year, which from 1661 qualified Dissenters for public office. John Owen opposed it, but Thomas Goodwin allowed it with "godly" Anglican congregations. After 1662 Presbyterians favored it most, as those who most hoped for accommodation within a comprehensive establishment as advocated by some Latitudinarians. Some Dissenters would attend Anglican sermons but not communicate, except perhaps privately with godly fellowships.

Nonconformists campaigned ardently for freedom of conscience and religion. Their fortunes varied with royal and parliamentary policies. Charles II's Declaration of Indulgence (1672) was rejected by Parliament, but the Toleration Act of William and Mary brought relief in 1689 and launched Nonconformity on its independent career. It exempted from the Conventicle Acts ministers and teachers who took the Oaths of Allegiance and Supremacy, but meeting places had to be registered. Ministers had also to subscribe to the Thirty-nine Articles, except on infant baptism. In 1779 subscription was replaced by adherence to the Christian faith and Scriptures. By 1700, 2,500 meeting places had been licensed, Nonconformist denominational lines were hardening (although Independents-Congregationalists and Presbyterians often acted together), a church-chapel distinction was appearing in English life, and Nonconformity's distinguished contribution to education had begun with the first Dissenting academies.

But civil disabilities persisted. Until 1868 Nonconformists had to support the established religion by church rates. The Test and Corporation Acts were repealed only in 1828 (although Dissenters had regularly been excused their penalties), and not until 1871 could Nonconformists graduate from Oxford and Cambridge. After 1836 they no longer had to be married in an Anglican church, although until 1898 a chapel wedding needed a civil registrar.

Behind these advances lay the lobbying of the Protestant Dissenting Deputies, drawn from the three main denominations and first organized in 1732. They aligned naturally with Whigs and later Liberals against Tories. Nonconformist church life was a proving ground for democratic aspirations. By the mid-nineteenth century Nonconformity was a political force, having strongly supported Catholic Emancipation (1829) and the Reform Bill (1832). The Nonconformist conscience found outlet in social reform and philanthropy, just as earlier Nonconformists were pioneers of the modern missionary movement, exporting worldwide England's church divisions. After decline in the later eighteenth century the Free Churches experienced considerable growth in the nineteenth.

Noncomformity's social and political contributions to English life are undoubted. Its significance has been greater for church ("a free church in a free state"), hymnody (Watts and Wesley), and religious experience (what B. L. Manning calls "intensity"—a Puritan legacy) than for theology. Although its ranks have included theologians such as John Owen and P. T. Forsyth, scholars like C. H. Dodd, and churchmen like R. W. Dale and C. H. Spurgeon, it has proved too easy a prey to liberalism, from the Unitarianism of the later eighteenth century to R. J. Campbell's "new theology." Vigorous evangelical groups now operate in all the Free Churches. If Free Churchmen now rarely call for the disestablishment of Anglicanism, an increasing number of Anglicans find the state connection compromising in an era of nuclear militarism. D. F. Wright

See also Puritanism.

Bibliography. W. B. Selbie, *Nonconformity: Its Origin and Progress;* H. Davies, *The English Free Churches;* E. A. Payne, *The Free Church Tradition in the Life of England;* G. F. Nuttall *et al., The Beginnings of Nonconformity;* G. F. Nuttall and O. Chadwick, eds., *From Uniformity to Unity 1662–1962,* esp. Nuttall's essay, "The First Nonconformists"; C. Hill, "Occasional Conformity," *Reformation Conformity and Dissent,* ed. R. B. Knox; B. L. Manning, *The Protestant Dissenting Deputies* and *The Making of Modern English Religion;* I. Sellers, *Nineteenth-Century Nonconformity;* E. K. H. Jordan, *Free Church Unity: History of the Free Church Council Movement 1896–1941.*

Northfield Conferences. A series of summer Bible conferences inaugurated by D. L. Moody in Northfield, Massachusetts. Northfield had been Moody's boyhood home, and after his rise to fame as an evangelist in the 1870s he returned and made Northfield home base. In 1879 he hit upon the idea of using the facilities for summer Bible conferences. Moody planned the conferences for lay people to augment their understanding of the Bible and the Christian faith, to discuss methods of Christian work, and to promote spiritual renewal. He hoped men and women would return to their churches and exert a similar influence there. After a ten-day conference in 1880 and a thirty-day conference in 1881, there was a three-year break while Moody was in the British Isles. The conferences resumed in 1885, and he was their guiding light until his death in 1899.

Although Moody was the dominant personality at these summer conferences, he was not the main speaker. He brought some of the best-known Bible teachers to the Northfield platform, such men as A. T. Pierson, A. J. Gordon, D. W. Whittle, George Needham, W. G. Moorehead, Nathaniel West, William E. Blackstone, James H. Brookes, C. I. Scofield, and R. A. Torrey. But Moody created no small stir by some of the other people he brought to Northfield as speakers: Henry Drummond (synthesizer of evolution and theology), Josiah Strong (proponent of the social gospel), William Rainey Harper (NT critic and later president of the University of Chicago), and George Adam Smith (famous OT critic). Some of Moody's more conservative supporters objected to these men speaking at Northfield, but he would not be dissuaded. Although very conservative in his own theological views, he maintained that these men were true Christians and had much to offer. Moody was also trying to establish a middle ground between extremists on the left and right. During the modernist-fundamentalist debate (in particular 1923–26), the two sides argued in published letters and articles over the significance of Moody's associations with these men.

Themes emphasized at the summer conferences were a reflection of the concerns of Moody and the speakers. There was a strong element of premillennialism and at times dispensationalism. One can even discern in the sermons given at Northfield the beginnings of those stresses that would eventually lead to a break between dispensational and nondispensational premillennialists over the rapture question. Although Moody was not sympathetic to perfectionism or the extremes of the Keswick movement, there was also a Keswick element in the conferences and an emphasis on holiness and the higher life. And there was a strong emphasis on evangelism, both home and foreign.

It is difficult to determine what the precise impact of these conferences was. Did the laity who returned to their churches make a significant impact? Were the conferences effective in the spread of Keswick and dispensational themes? Or were these conferences just an echo of themes and tensions already prevalent in American evangelicalism? Without totally discounting their impact, it must be said that the conferences were a mirror in which these themes and tensions came into focus.

But without question, there was one outgrowth of the Northfield Conferences that had an incalculable impact on not just American but world Christianity. In 1886 the Northfield Conference was expanded to include a month-long conference for college students. From this student conference, the first of many at Northfield, one hundred men dedicated themselves to foreign missionary service when they completed college. By the following June this number had grown to two thousand. Out of this grew the Student Volunteer Movement seeking "the evangelization of the world in this generation." It spread across America to the British Isles and Europe with globe-circling effects. Collegians who visited the Northfield Student Conference and came under Moody's influence included Robert Speer, Robert Wilder, Sherwood Eddy, and John R. Mott. The Northfield student conferences were the birthplace of the SVM and, through that organization, of the early twentieth century ecumenical movement.

The Northfield Conferences continued after Moody's death. But without Moody's vision and magnetic personality they were no longer to have the significance they once had. In fact, the Northfield Conferences gradually became less and less a reflection of their earlier theological themes and emphases. S. N. GUNDRY

See also KESWICK CONVENTION; MILLENNIUM, VIEWS OF THE.

Bibliography. J. F. Findlay, Jr., *Dwight L. Moody: American Evangelist 1837–1899;* S. N. Gundry, *Love Them In: The Life and Theology of D. L. Moody; Northfield Echoes,* 1894–1904 and its successor, *The Record of Christian Work;* T. J. Shanks, ed., *A College of Colleges: Led by D. L. Moody, College Student at Northfield or A College of Colleges No. 2, D. L. Moody at Home,* and *Gems from Northfield.*

Novatian Schism. This began as a debate over the proper treatment which the church should accord to Christians who had denied their faith during times of persecution. In the widespread persecution under Decius, Pope Fabian was martyred in January of 250, but the church was in such dire straits that his successor was not elected until spring of 251. The majority vote was cast for Cornelius, who favored full acceptance of those who had lapsed in the terrible peril. The choice was repudiated by the clergy who had been most staunch during the persecution, and in opposition they consecrated Novatian, a Roman presbyter who was apparently already acclaimed for his important and orthodox theological work, *On the Trinity.* Christendom was thus faced with two rival popes, each seeking support of the wider church.

As each pope defended the legitimacy of his own position, the demarcation became more pronounced. Questions arose as to how the church should deal with those who had purchased from a magistrate false certificates affirming that they had offered a pagan sacrifice as over against those who had actually performed the sacrifice—a practice in which even bishops had engaged. The Novatianists maintained that only God might accord forgiveness for such grievous sin, while the Cornelius party argued for a judicious use of "the power of the keys" in forgiving the lapsed after a proper period of penance. Cyprian of Carthage became the major spokesman for this Catholic position of clemency. He opined that salvation was impossible outside the communion of the church and that true penitents must be received back into the fold as expeditiously as possible, while Novatian and his supporters maintained that the church must be preserved in its purity without the defilement of those who had not proved steadfast. They were later to go so far as to deny forgiveness for any serious offense (such as fornication or idolatry) after baptism, though pardon might be offered to those deemed near death.

When they were excommunicated by a synod of bishops at Rome, the Novatianists, wishing to avoid compromise and complacency with sin, established a separate church with its own discipline and clergy, including bishops. Their emphasis on purity and rigorism as well as a vehement clash of personalities drew significant support throughout the church at large, and especially from a Carthaginian presbyter named Novatus, himself at odds with Cyprian. There was a strong following in Phrygia, especially among Montanist groups. The Novatian Church continued for several centuries and was received by the Council of Nicaea as an orthodox though schismatic group. In particular its affirmation of Christ as being of one substance with the Father was applauded. Later the sect fell under imperial disfavor, was forbidden the right of public worship, and had its books destroyed. The majority of its members were reabsorbed into the mainstream of the Catholic Church, although the Novatian Church was an identifiable entity until the seventh century. R. C. Kroeger and C. C. Kroeger

See also Cyprian.

Bibliography. *ANF,* V, 319–47, 412–20, 611–50, 657–63; Eusebius, *History of the Church,* VI, xliii-xlvi; VII, vii–viii; A. Harnack, *SHERK,* VIII, 197–202.

Numerology, Biblical. Numbers are used in the Bible in much the same way as in other books. They are regularly spelled out, despite the fact that numerical signs were early in use. This would favor accuracy of transmission. The use of the letters of the Greek alphabet to represent numbers is late and belongs to the period of Greek influence.

Numbers are used both exactly, e.g., the three hundred eighteen trained servants of Abram (Gen. 14:14), and inexactly, e.g., the forty years of wandering which include the year and a half before the rejection at Kadesh took place.

Some numbers are used much more frequently than others. Seven is the sacred number because it is the number of the sabbath. Ten is a very natural number, since the fingers and thumbs of the two hands count ten. But we cannot be sure that that is the real explanation of the number which appears most conspicuously in the Decalogue. Twelve is the number of the months, of the sons of Jacob, of the apostles of the Lord. Aside from this, no special significance attaches to the number. The fact that it can be regarded as made up of seven and five has no significance. Many elaborate efforts have been made to attach special meanings to numbers. But none is satisfactory. The number forty, for example, is used in both a good sense (Acts 1:3) and a bad sense (Ps. 95:10). The number seventy is used of the sons of Jacob (Exod. 1:5; 24:1), of the sons of Ahab (II Kings 10:1), and of the years of the Babylonian captivity (Jer. 25:11). Cf. also Ezek. 8:11; Luke 10:1. In prophecy numbers are sometimes used in an enigmatical sense, as in the case of the "seventy weeks" of Dan. 9 or the "two thousand and three hundred" evening-mornings of 8:14. But this does not justify us in taking the numbers themselves in anything other than a literal sense. The only number in Scripture which is declared to be symbolic is 666, which is the number of the beast (Rev. 13:18).

In recent years the name of Ivan Panin has been connected with a most elaborate attempt to find numerical significance in every word and letter in the Bible. But his system is far too complicated to commend itself to the careful student. The Bible does not have an intricate numerical pattern which only a mathematical expert can discover. The strict and obvious meaning of words—and this applies to numbers—should be adhered to unless it is quite plain that some further meaning is involved. We know that the souls that were on the ship which was wrecked at Melita numbered two hundred seventy-six (Acts 27:37, 44). Why this was the number we do not know, and it would be idle to try to find a mysterious or mystical meaning in this simple historical fact.

The desire to find symbolic and significant meanings in numbers can be traced back to ancient times, notably to the Pythagoreans. The Babylonian Creation Tablets record the fifty names of Marduk. Contenau has pointed out that Sargon declared that the number of his name was the same as the circuit of the walls of his palace, 16,283 cubits. A familiar modern example is the attempt of Piazzi Smyth (1867) to find an elaborate and mysterious numerical system in the construction of the Great Pyramid at Gizeh. On the assumption that "the spiritual significance of numbers is seen in their first occurrence," E. W. Bullinger in *How to Enjoy the Bible* worked out an ingenious system of interpretation of the numbers in Scripture. But a little testing makes it quite clear that the first occurrence theory in the case of numbers as of other words, while ingenious, is quite unworkable. To infer from Gen. 14:4 that the number thirteen in Gen. 17:25 is "associated with rebellion, apostasy, and disintegration" (pp. 311–12) will hardly commend itself to the sober-minded student of Scripture.

O. T. Allis

Numinous, The. In his book *The Idea of the Holy* (1917) the German theologian Rudolf Otto investigated, among other things, the basic human experience which on his understanding is the "innermost care" of all religions. This is the experience of "the holy," and it contains a very specific element or "moment" that distinguishes it from man's rational experience and which is in fact inexpressible. This innermost care is clearly there, indeed it is the heart of all religion, yet it cannot be apprehended in terms of concepts, and this of course makes the task of understanding and discussing it very difficult. It is part of the theologian's task, however, to attempt this.

The word "holy" has moral meaning—a holy person is a righteous or good person. It also has a rational aspect. But neither of these isolates the heart of religious experience. The purpose of Otto's investigation is to uncover this "heart" or foundation. When all that can be said about the experience of the holy has been said, there is still something there, something that can only be felt. It is, he says, a "clear overplus of meaning." One is aware that he or she is in the presence of something, or someone, but the awareness is so primitive as to preclude a clear description of what or who. One thing is certain, however: the experiencer stands in awe of that of which he is in the presence.

In his attempt to find a word that will point at this incomprehensible innermost core, and will isolate it from the moral and rational aspects, Otto coined a word adopted from the Latin *numen.* And claiming that since *omen* has given us the word "ominous," there is no reason why *numen* should not form the root of "numinous." There is, then, a numinous state of mind which is perfectly *sui generis* and is irreducible to any other. It is absolutely primary and therefore cannot be strictly defined; it can only be discussed.

One person cannot lead another directly to this experience. But it is possible to lead one through the ways of his or her own mind to the point at which the numinous in the individual begins to stir, begins to *live* in one's consciousness. All of this is to say that numinous cannot be taught; it can only be evoked or awakened.

This experience of the numinous is what lies behind all the world's great religions. It is the experience that generates all the moral and ethical responses of religion, as well as the dogmas and doctrines. It is the experience of the other, the holy, the incomprehensible—of *God.*

J. D. Spiceland

See also Otto, Rudolf.

Oo

Obedience. The whole of biblical theology centers on the notion of divine revelation and the receptive response of man: God speaks his word, man hears and is required to obey. The connection between hearing and obeying is therefore essential. Hearing is always viewed as a process of the mind. When divine revelation is its subject, man must respond with obedience. This connection is borne out in particular by the language of obedience in the Bible. In the OT *šāma'* conveys the meaning of both "to hear" and "to obey." Israel must hear Yahweh's voice and act in obedient response. In the Torah the theme of responsive obedience is underscored (Exod. 19:5, 8; 24:7; Deut. 28:1; 30:11–14). Abraham was blessed because he heard and obeyed the Lord's voice (Gen. 22:18). This theme lies behind the prophetic injunction, "Thus says the Lord." The prophetic word reveals both who God is and what he is calling Israel to do. Disobedience, then, is any hearing which is not attentive, and this too is the story of Israel: "They have ears, but do not hear" (Ps. 115:6; cf. Jer. 3:13; Isa. 6:9–10).

In the LXX *šāma'* is regularly translated by words in the *akouein* word group, and this again expresses the inner relation between hearing and response. Emphatic forms *hypakouein* and *hypakoē* (lit. "to hear beneath") convey the meaning "obey/obedience" (in the NT the verb appears 21 times; the noun 15 times, esp. in Paul). The NT, to be sure, brings out this OT background in full when Jesus demands that he "who has ears to hear, let him hear" (Matt. 11:15; 13:9, 15–16; Mark 4:9, 23; 8:18; Luke 14:35). This kind of constructive response to divine revelation is illustrated well in the parable about the man who built his house on the rock. The story follows the exhortation of Christ: "Why do you call me 'Lord, Lord,' and not do what I tell you?" (Luke 6:46–49). In Matthew this same parable concludes the Sermon on the Mount (Matt. 7:21–27), clearly indicating the seriousness of personal response to Jesus' ethical injunctions.

Jesus stands in the OT prophetic tradition when he calls Israel to a discipleship which essentially involves "doing"—ethics. When a voice in the crowd praises Jesus' mother, the Lord replies by saying, "Blessed rather are those who hear the word of God and keep it"(Luke 11:28; cf. John 10:16, 27; 15:5, 10). Bonhoeffer remarks: "The actual call of Jesus and the response of single-minded obedience have an irrevocable significance. It is only to this obedience that the promise of fellowship with Jesus is given."

Bultmann points out that Jesus' call has radicalized an obedience already well known in Judaism. First century Judaism had emphasized cultic and ceremonial rules to such an extent (365 prohibitions, 278 positive commands) that any notion of virtue was almost unknown. Jesus presses beyond the casuistic rules and expects a true obedience, not blind obedience: "You tithe mint and dill and cummin, and have neglected the weightier matters of the law, justice and mercy and faith" (Matt. 23:23). Man, in effect, must exceed the demands of the law (Matt. 5:20) and perceive for himself what God commands. That is, single-minded obedience grasps the spirit of God's intentions (cf. Mark 10:2–9 on how Jesus applies this to one law) and exceeds God's desires—not with the measured efforts of a servant (Luke 17:7–10), but as people who enjoy a vital and responsive relationship with him. Bultmann sums up: "Radical obedience exists only when a man inwardly assents to what is required of him, . . . when the whole man stands behind what he does; or better, when the whole man is in what he does, when he is not doing something obediently, but is essentially obedient."

Paul regards obedience as being one of the constituent parts of faith. Initially Christ stands as the model of obedience (Phil. 2:5–8), and through his obedience, which is contrasted with Adam's disobedience, "many will be made righteous" (Rom. 5:19; cf. Heb. 5:8–9 for the parallel thought). Paul in fact views his task as bringing about the "obedience of faith" among the nations (Rom. 1:5; 16:26). For him, every thought should be made "captive to obey Christ" so that the Christian's obedience might be complete (II Cor. 10:5–6). This means that Paul too despairs of any faith that is either simply cognitive (a hellenistic weakness) or mechanistically legal (a Jewish fault). Obedience is of the essence of authentic saving faith and should provide evidence of a responsive relation the Christian shares with his God (cf. James 1:22–25; 2:14–20; I Pet. 1:22; I John 3:18).

G. M. Burge

Bibliography. F. W. Young, *IDB*, III, 580–81; W. Mundle, *NIDNTT*, II, 172–80; G. Kittel, *TDNT*, I, 216–25; D. Bonhoeffer, *The Cost of Discipleship;* A. Richardson, *An Introduction to the Theology of the NT;* R. Bultmann, *Jesus and the Word.*

Obedience of Christ. The NT speaks explicitly of the obedience of Christ only three times: "through the obedience of the one man the many will be made righteous" (Rom. 5:19); "he humbled himself and became obedient to death" (Phil. 2:8); and "he learned obedience from what he suffered" (Heb. 5:8). But the concept which these verses contain is clearly alluded to in many other places—e.g., (1) the several contexts in which Christ is called "servant" (Isa. 42:1; 52:13; 53:11; Phil. 2:7; cf. Matt. 20:28; Mark 10:45); (2) the numerous passages where he declares his purpose in coming to earth is to do his Father's will (Ps. 40:7; John 5:30; 8:28–29; 10:18; 12:49; 14:31; Heb. 10:7); (3) the oft-made assertion by himself and both friends and enemies alike of his sinless and righteous life (Matt. 27:4, 19–23; Mark 12:14; Luke 23:4, 14–15; John 8:46; 18:38; 19:4–6; II Cor. 5:21; Heb. 4:15; 7:26); and (4) the passages which affirm his submission to authority (Matt. 3:15; Luke 2:51–52; 4:16).

Evangelical theologians have reasons, other than the mere fact that the Bible teaches that Christ was an obedient servant, to interest themselves with this aspect of Christ's life and ministry. They have rightly discerned that both Christ's own right to minister as God's Messiah-Savior and the salvation of those he came to save directly depend on his personal, perfect, and perpetual obedience to God's holy law. To make this clear, theologians customarily distinguish between the active and passive obedience of Christ. These are not at all satisfactory terms inasmuch as nothing that Christ performed did he do passively, that is, resignedly, without full desire and willingness on his part. Much better are the terms "preceptive" and "penal," which are becoming increasingly preferred respectively to "active" and "passive." By preceptive obedience is meant Christ's full obedience to all the positive prescriptions of the law; by penal obedience is intended his willing, obedient bearing of all the sanctions imposed by the law which had accrued against his people because of their transgressions. By the former—i.e., his preceptive obedience—he made available a righteousness before the law that is imputed or reckoned to those who trust in him. By the latter—i.e., his penal obedience—he took upon himself by legal imputation the penalty due his people for their sin. His preceptive and penal obedience, then, is the ground of God's justification of sinners, by which divine act they are pardoned (because their sins have been charged to Christ, who obediently bears the law's sanctions against sin) and accepted as righteous in God's sight (because Christ's preceptive obedience is imputed to them).

Murray has neatly captured the essence of Christ's obedience in four terms: inwardness, progressiveness, climax, and dynamic. By *inwardness* is meant that Christ's obedience was willingly accomplished from the heart; never was his obedience mechanically, perfunctorily, or just externally carried out. By *progressiveness* is intended what the Scriptures imply when it is said that he "grew . . . in favor with God" (Luke 2:52) and that he "learned obedience" (Heb. 5:8). This does not mean that he learned by moving from disobedience to obedience. Rather, it is to be construed to mean that he moved from obedience at any given stage to an obedience at ever deeper and deeper cost. In other words, his will to obey was being forged throughout his life to face ever stiffer and more severe trials in preparation for his final ordeal of the cross. By *climax* Murray intends to do justice to what he perceives is the unparalleled testing which Christ faced in the Gethsemane experience (Matt. 26:36–46; Mark 14:32–42; Luke 22:39–44) and then in his death on the cross. Finally, by *dynamic* Murray denotes the means by which our Lord was taught obedience—namely, his suffering (Heb. 2:10; 5:8). His trials, temptations, deprivations, etc., became the instrument in his Father's hand by which he was taught obedience and was, as "author of salvation," made thereby perfect, that is, everything he had to be in order to bring many children to glory.

R. L. Reymond

Bibliography. L. Berkhof, *Systematic Theology;* J. O. Buswell, Jr., *A Systematic Theology of the Christian Religion*, II, 110–13; A. Hodge, *The Atonement;* J. Murray, *Redemption—Accomplished and Applied* and "The Obedience of Christ," in *Collected Writings of John Murray*, II.

Oberlin Theology. The fruit of a strong revivalistic, perfectionistic, and reforming tradition in nineteenth century American evangelical life. It was closely associated with the work of Charles Finney, America's most famous antebellum revivalist, and with the faculty at Oberlin College, Ohio (founded 1833), of which Finney was a part. But the theology also contained emphases that were shared widely in American Christianity among New School Presbyterians, Methodists, many Baptists, members of Disciples and Christian churches, and even some Unitarians.

Finney's theology was shaped by his own experience (a dramatic conversion in 1821) and by his early approval of the work of Congregationalist N. W. Taylor. With Taylor, Finney came to conclude that individuals possessed the power within themselves to make the choice for Christ and for holy living. Finney's own evangelism stressed the fact that, with God's help, strenuous personal effort could lead to the spread of the gospel. Early in his ministry he also explored the effects of such conversions on the reform of society. After Finney left the Presbyterians and took a pastorate in New York City, he came to the conclusion, as he put it, "that an altogether higher and more stable form of Christian life was attainable, and was the privilege of all Christians." Shortly after this Finney encountered John Wesley's *Plain Account of Christian Perfection,* which confirmed his belief in "entire sanctification." When Finney became professor of theology at Oberlin College in 1835, he carried with him the outlines of a distinctive theological emphasis. And in 1839, during a revival season at Oberlin, the emphasis received distinct articulation as a perfectionistic theology.

Along with Finney the Oberlin theology was promoted by Asa Mahan, first president of the college and a driving force in its establishment; Oberlin professor Henry Cowles; and many of the students who went out from Oberlin to evangelize and reform America. The theology emphasized a belief in a second, more mature stage of Christian life. This second stage carried different names—"entire sanctification," "holiness," "Christian perfection," or even "the baptism of the Holy Ghost." Finney took it to be more a matter of perfect trust in God and commitment to his way rather than complete sinlessness. And he also came to feel that this state of spirituality would be reached through steady growth rather than through a single, dramatic "second blessing." Other teachers emphasized more a distinct second work of grace and spoke as if the state of the sanctified would be nearly without sin. In these discussions, which also included a consideration of the relative place of human exertion and God's free grace in going on to sanctification, the Oberlin theology showed remarkable parallels with the development of Methodist theology stretching back to the time of John Wesley.

The Oberlin theology represented an immensely important strand of nineteenth century evangelical belief, not only because of its influential convictions but also because of its practical effects. Finney had earlier pioneered new measures in revivalism (including the "anxious bench" and the protracted meeting). And he also had actively encouraged a heightened concern for reforming evils in America like slavery, intemperance, and economic injustice. The perfectionistic emphases of the Oberlin theology greatly aided its revivalistic and reforming concerns. Some of its exponents also believed that the millennial age was at hand, and this conviction also added to the widespread social impact of the theology.

The Oberlin theology retained an important place at Oberlin into the twentieth century. It contributed also to many strands of modern evangelicalism such as the Holiness Movement, more indirectly to Pentecostalism, and to the Higher Life and Keswick movements as well.

M. A. Noll

See also Finney, Charles Grandison; Perfection, Perfectionism; Holiness Movement, American; Pentecostalism.

Bibliography. C. C. Cole, Jr., *The Social Ideas of the Northern Evangelists, 1826–1860;* J. H. Fairchild, *Oberlin: The College and the Colony, 1833–1883;* J. E. Johnson, "Charles G. Finney and Oberlin Perfectionism," *JPH* 46:42–57, 128–38; T. L. Smith, *Revivalism and Social Reform.*

Oblation. *See* Offerings and Sacrifices in Bible Times.

Obscenity. Anything that is filthy, repulsive, impure, lewd, offensive, and indecent. Etymologists debate whether the Latin roots mean "against filth" or "off the scene" (i.e., not worthy of occupying our attention at center stage). The United States Supreme Court, in the 1966 *Fanny Hill* case, gave three tests for obscenity. First, obscene material appeals to prurient interest (i.e., it is intended to arouse lascivious thought and desire). Second, it is patently offensive to prevailing community standards. Third, it is utterly without redeeming social importance. Discussions as well as legal battles have ordinarily restricted the discussion of obscenity to sexual matters, though the essential meaning of the term could well include other forms of obscenity (e.g., violence).

The difficulty of combating obscenity through censorship and prosecution of the merchants of obscenity is due to several reasons. First, there is understandable fear of any encroachments on freedom of speech and assembly. Second, it is sometimes difficult to distinguish between an appeal to artistic or aesthetic interest and an appeal to prurient interest. Third, "redeeming social importance" can be argued on very indirect grounds. Fourth, it is difficult to determine "community standards," especially in an age of great ferment and decline in those standards. As a result, most legal restrictions against obscenity have been eliminated or seriously undermined in recent decades.

A Christian response to obscenity begins with the summary of Paul: "Whatever is true, whatever is noble, whatever is right, whatever is pure, whatever is lovely, whatever is admirable—if anything is excellent or praiseworthy—think about such things" (Phil. 4:8). Much in the Bible, of course, urges us to consider, sometimes in graphic, realistic terms, the problem of evil around us. We are to consider the plight of our neighbor and our city. Obscenity, however, is to leave the situation as it is or, worse yet, to find gratification or pleasure in viewing degradation (sexual or otherwise). The Christian disciple is called to grasp the situation realistically and then to visualize and work toward the redemption of the neighbor. Obscenity is wrong because it dehumanizes both the participant and the observer. Both are left at a level considerably less than what God intends.

A more difficult issue has to do with social policy and the Christian's responsibility outside of the Christian community. Since standards of dress and the meaning of language are historically conditioned (even for the church), and thus the perception of obscenity varies from one generation to the next, it is essential that moral discernment take place in prayerful Christian community. Out of genuine love for one's neighbor, however, it seems clear that Christians ought to struggle for restrictions, including censorship, on obscene material that portrays persons in cruel and dehumanizing fashion and contributes to the rapacious atmosphere of this era. It is also out of genuine neighbor love that Christians would struggle to protect children from the frontal assaults of obscene material on newsstands and television and through the mail.

While sexual sins receive full censure in Scripture, Christians must be careful not to allow their zeal against sexual obscenity to overshadow their zeal to combat violence, dishonesty, greed, and other sins which are also condemned in the Bible. Finally, Christians must remember that their primary calling is not to act negatively as the restrainers of evil but to act positively as the promoters of the gospel and the good. The Christian answer to sexual obscenity is to promote a true appreciation for sexuality in terms established by the Creator and Redeemer. The answer to all forms of obscenity is to promote the interests of the kingdom of God. D. W. Gill

See also Pornography.

Bibliography. P. C. Cotham, *Obscenity, Pornography, and Censorship;* G. D. Everett, *DCE,* 466–68.

Occult, The. The term refers to "hidden" or "secret" wisdom; to that which is beyond the range of ordinary human knowledge; to mysterious or concealed phenomena; to inexplicable events. It is frequently used in reference to certain practices (occult "arts") which include divination, fortune telling, spiritism (necromancy), and magic.

Those phenomena collectively known as "the occult" may be said to have the following distinct characteristics: (1) the disclosure and communication of information unavailable to humans through normal means (beyond the five senses); (2) the placing of persons in contact with supernatural powers, paranormal energies, or demonic forces; (3) the acquisition and mastery of power in order to manipulate or influence other people into certain actions.

In an attempt to achieve legitimation and acceptance from the larger society, advocates of occultism have in recent years portrayed the occult as basically amenable to scientific investigation. Parapsychology and graphology are two fields in which the claim to scientific status is often advanced. There is considerable disagreement in both the academic world and the religious world as to whether parapsychology, for example, is the "scientific" study of occult phenomena. It would appear that the very character of the occult indicates that it deals with contradictory or dissonant knowledge claims that are difficult, if not impossible, to investigate or validate.

However, recent developments not only in science but in the arts, politics, psychology, and religion indicate a broad shift in Western culture to increased acceptance of a common set of presuppositions that parallel the occult/mystical world view, which is in stark contrast to the biblical world view of historic Christianity. The classical systems of occult philosophy and their more recent "new age" variants are fundamentally identical with the "cosmic humanism" that characterizes much of the contemporary world. Likewise, these ideas can be linked with such

Eastern religious practices as yoga and meditation and an accompanying philosophy which asserts a definition of reality that ultimately denies the personal God of the Bible, promotes the essential divinity of man, and rejects any absolute statement of moral values.

The occult/mystical world view and its associated religious expression—especially in the Eastern cults presently active in the West—can be analyzed in terms of the following components:

(1) *The promise of godhood—man is a divine being.* All forms of occult philosophy proclaim that the true or "real" self of man is synonymous with God. Such views are all patterned after the archetypal lie of the serpent in Gen. 3:4, "You will be as gods."

(2) *The notion that "all is one"—God is everything* (pantheism). There is only one reality in existence (monism), and therefore everyone and everything in the material world is part of the Divine. It follows that there is no distinction between supernatural and natural, between good and evil, between God and Satan.

(3) *Life's purpose is to achieve awareness of the Divine within—self-realization.* The path to salvation ("illumination," "enlightenment," "union") is an experiential one. It is the path to *gnosis,* the seeking of experiential "knowledge" through metaphysical insight.

(4) *Humankind is basically good—evil is an illusion or imperfection.* Ignorance, not sin, is at the root of the human dilemma. An "enlightened" person will transcend moral distinctions. There is no need of redemption or forgiveness, only self-realization.

(5) *Self-realization via spiritual technique leads to power—the God-man is in charge.* By employing spiritual technology such as meditation, chanting, and yoga, and through the application of universal laws, the realized being becomes master of his own reality. He attains the status of *guru,* or "light bearer," and can influence the lives of others.

With this broad occult/mystical framework in mind, it can be said that the ultimate objective of psychic/occult power is to validate the lie of Satan—that man is God and that death is an illusion. In the deceptive quest for godhood and power, men and women are brought under the power of Satan himself. They are able to manifest a degree of counterfeit power by engaging in occult experiences. Such paranormal manifestations represent an imitation of authentic spirituality and demonstrate Satan's true nature as the arch deceiver.

Both the OT and the NT proscribe such spiritually impure occultic activities as sorcery, mediumship, divination, and magic. In the OT they are referred to as the "abominable practices" of the pagan cultures which coexisted with the Israelites. Involvement with the occult arts was frequently compared to adultery. Jesus and the NT writers also describe the dynamic of Satan's counterfeit spirituality and call for discernment of spiritist activity.

While Scripture acknowledges both the reality and the power of occultic practices, it proclaims that God through Christ has disarmed the principalities and powers. At the cross of Calvary the works of the devil were destroyed and the powers of darkness were conquered in an ultimate sense. R. M. Enroth

Bibliography. B. Alexander, *Occult Philosophy and Mystical Experience;* K. E. Koch, *Between Christ and Satan* and *Satan's Devices;* J. S. Wright, *Christianity and the Occult; SCPJ,* Winter 1980–81.

Ockham, William of. *See* William of Ockham.

Offerings and Sacrifices in Bible Times. The biblical teaching on offerings and sacrifices lies at the heart of the redemptive history. Any theological attempt to penetrate into the mysteries of reconciliation, ecclesiology, and eschatology presupposes a proper understanding of what God requires from his people before and after Christ.

To begin with, a distinction must be made between offering and sacrifice. The word "offering" denotes several categories of gifts to the Lord: (1) a required offering to be burnt wholly or partially on the altar; (2) a voluntary offering to be burnt partially on the altar and to be consumed by the priests and the Israelites as a communal meal; (3) the tithe of the produce of the land and the offspring of the flocks. The word "sacrifice" denotes the particular way of presenting certain offerings. The word *zebaḥ* ("sacrifice") is related to the word *mizbēaḥ* ("altar"), and both nouns are connected with the Hebrew verb meaning "to slaughter." Only three categories of offerings are to be considered sacrifices: the sin offering, the guilt offering, and the burnt offering. Thus, it can be said that all sacrifices are offerings, but not all offerings are sacrifices. Since the word "offering" also covers sacrifices, reference will be made to the several *offerings.* The word for offering derives from the Hebrew verb meaning "to bring near" (Lev. 7:16), as an expression of the physical act of bringing an object as an offering to the Lord. Offerings are also to be distinguished from the tithe.

The tithe was one of the tributary offerings imposed on Israel. There were strict regulations pertaining to the tithe (*ma'ăśēr,* Lev. 27:30–33; Num. 18:21–32; Deut. 14:22–29; 26:2–15). All crops and the increase in cattle were subject to the tithe. The tithe of grain and fruit could first be exchanged for silver, but the Israelite was required to add 20 percent of the market value before taking the silver to the temple. He was not permitted to redeem the tithe of the herd or flock. In Jerusalem the people were permitted to exchange the silver for grain, wine, oil, and whatever would promote the joy of the people in the presence of their God (Deut. 14:23–27). The Levites and the poor also enjoyed a portion of the tithe. However, every third year the tithe was reserved for the Levites and those in financial need (Deut. 14:28–29). The tithe also functioned as a kind of a tax to support the temple and its personnel. The tithe was retained by the temple personnel, for their own use. Animals were marked to indicate temple ownership, and grain, vegetables, and fruits were stored or sold. An administration was in charge of the storehouse for the continued welfare of the personnel (Neh. 13:13; cf. Mal. 3:10; Neh. 10:38–39; 12:44; 13:5; II Chr. 31:4–14).

The practice of sacrifice has been widely discussed since J. Wellhausen's *Prolegomena to the History of Israel* (1885). According to Wellhausen the sacrificial system was a late development of the custom of enjoying a sacrificial meal (cf. I Sam. 9:13; 16:2–5). In OT circles the assumption prevailed that the OT offering could best be analyzed by reference to the practices of primitive societies such as the bedouin. The study of W. R. Smith (*The Religion of Semites*, 1894) supported Wellhausen's conclusion in that he argued that the sacrificial meal, as an expression of fellowship between God and people, was the rudimentary expression of the sacrificial idea. Wellhausianism held that the idea of sacrifice as atonement for sin developed and was systematized in the postexilic period.

Archaeological excavations have contributed greatly to a better understanding of sacrifice in the ancient Near East. The findings of temples, bones of sacrificial animals, cultic objects, and collections of documents have shown how the nations had elaborate rituals and highly developed ideas on sacrifice. In Mesopotamia the purpose of sacrifices was to provide food for the gods. The Ugaritic materials show a highly developed terminology that has many words in common with Hebrew sacrificial terms. Parallelism in practice and terminology between the OT sacrificial laws and the Near East is instructive, but in this article the sacrificial system will be limited to the OT and its practices in the time of Jesus.

Categories of Offerings. Offerings can be classified as (1) propitiatory (expiatory atonement): sin offering, guilt offering; (2) dedicatory (consecratory): burnt offering, cereal offering, drink offering; (3) communal (fellowship): peace offering, wave offering, thanksgiving offering, vow, freewill offering.

The first mention of an offering in the Bible is in the story of Cain and Abel. Both Cain and Abel offered a type of dedicatory offering (*minḥâ*, Gen. 4:3–4). After the flood Noah presented a dedicatory offering (*'ōlâ*, Gen. 8:20). There is room for discussion as to the nature of the patriarchal offerings. Some scholars argue that it was a communal meal and others argue in favor of the *'ōlâ* (dedicatory) offering. It is significant that the offerings mentioned or alluded to prior to the Mosaic legislation are either dedicatory or communal, not expiatory. The distinction is important because the expiatory offering makes sense only when the law has been introduced.

The OT practice of bringing offerings and sacrifices was carefully regulated. There were certain types of offerings, particular occasions for bringing an offering, qualifications pertaining to the kind of animal and the soundness of that animal, and prescribed rites depending on the offering. The purposes of the prescriptions were to teach Israel that (1) God has ordained ways as to how he is to be approached; (2) because of sin and guilt, one cannot freely approach the Lord; (3) all one possesses has been received from the Lord, and consequently one owes continual recognition to the Lord for his mercies. The presentation of any offering required careful adherence to the prescribed regulations as well as love for the Lord. The prophets often called for obedience rather than sacrifices (I Sam. 15:22–23; Isa. 1:10–20), for praise of the Lord rather than offerings (Hos. 14:2), and for humility (Mic. 6:8). The prophets were not opposed to offerings, as has been posited by some. They were inspired by the vision of a faithful Israel responding freely in faith and obedience to the regulations given in the law.

Several passages in the Pentateuch describe the offerings in great detail (Exod. 20:24–26; 34:25–26; Lev. 1–7; 17; 19:5–8; Num. 15; 28–29; Deut. 12). Lev. 1–7 sets forth the order of the various types of offerings. The order in which the offerings are discussed is neither logical nor chronological. Several offerings are categorized according to their nature. Those offerings which are described as producing "an aroma pleasing to the Lord" (NIV) are detailed in chs. 1–3. They are the burnt offering (1:3–17), the cereal offering (2:1–16), and the peace offering (3:1–17). Lev. 4:1–6:7 describes the two types of expiatory offerings: the sin offering (4:1–5:13) and the guilt offering (5:14–6:7). The remainder of chs. 6 and 7 gives the regulations on the disposal of the priests' portions and the communal meal. The material of the offerings consisted of those possessions with which the Israelites made their living, such as cattle, sheep, goats, grains, wine (grapes). A commonly held misconception is that the Israelites could present to God any food that was ritually clean to them (fish, Lev. 11:9, and wild animals, Deut. 12:22). However, this is not the case, as fish and wild animals were never included in the types of offerings specified by the Lord. Ritually unclean food could not be brought as an offering, and not all "clean" food was to be offered to the Lord.

In addition to the many texts found in the Mosaic legislation, the historical books also provide information regarding the practice of offering to the Lord. The Scriptures suggest that there was a certain order in which offerings were presented to God. The sin or guilt offering had to be presented first as an atonement for sin. The dedicatory offering, either a burnt or cereal offering, could then be presented. In addition to the dedicatory offering, a peace offering was given to symbolize the gratitude of the people and their desire for fellowship with God. This order is exemplified in Exod. 29:10–34, the account of the consecration of the priests. First a bull was sacrificed as a sin offering (vs. 14). A ram was then presented as a burnt offering (vs. 18). Finally, portions of a ram, a loaf of bread, a cake made with oil, and a wafer (vss. 22–23) were presented as a peace offering.

Propitiatory Offerings. An expiatory offering was required when an Israelite had become ritually unclean or had unwittingly sinned against God or his neighbor. The two types of expiatory offering are the sin offering and the guilt offering.

Sin Offering (*ḥaṭṭā't*, Exod. 29:14, 36; Lev. 4). Every Israelite, whether he was a commoner or a high priest, was required to make a sin offering. What was offered depended upon the individual's status within the community. A poor person could satisfy his requirements by sacrificing two pigeons or turtledoves (Lev. 5:7), or he could offer a tenth of an ephah of fine flour (Lev. 5:11; cf. Heb. 9:22). The Israelite of modest income could bring a female goat (Lev. 4:28) or a lamb (4:32) to the altar. The leaders in the community were expected to offer a male goat (4:23) and the high priest as well as the people as a congregation had to sacrifice a young bull (4:3, 14).

A sin offering was presented under three circumstances. First, it was required for ritual cleansing. Women after childbirth (Lev. 12:6–8), victims of leprosy (Lev. 14:13–17, 22, 31), those who suffered from abscesses and hemorrhaging (Lev. 15:15, 30), and Nazirites who had contact with a corpse (Num. 6:11, 14, 16) were among those who needed to make a sin offering in order to be considered ceremonially clean. A second occasion for which a sin offering was required was when an Israelite unintentionally sinned against the law of God (Num. 15:25–29). Finally, sin offerings were made at each of the Hebrew festivals such as passover (Num. 28:22–24), the feast of weeks (Num. 28:30), the feast of booths (Num. 29:16, 19), the new moon festival (Num. 28:15), the festival of trumpets (Num. 29:5), and the day of atonement (Num. 29:11).

Guilt Offering (*'āšām*, Lev. 5:14–6:7; 7:1–7; AV, "trespass offering"). The second kind of expiatory offering was the guilt offering, which consisted of a payment of damages or a fine. The guilt offering was a means of making restitution when social, religious, or ritual expectations had not been observed. It was required of any Israelite who had defrauded God or a fellow Israelite. Whether the offense was against God or another person, the guilty party had to pay full restitution. Furthermore, the offender was required to pay a penalty of a fifth of the value of the goods which he had defrauded. This additional offering was usually a ram (Lev. 5:15).

A guilt offering was necessary whenever a person unknowingly failed to meet his obligation before God in sacrifice, service, or covenantal obedience. Also, if an individual sinned against a fellow Israelite in the same manner, he was expected to make a guilt offering. This entailed sacrificing a ram to God and paying restitution plus a 20 percent penalty to the offended party. The guilty individual was to make his offering while confessing his sin. If his sin was against another Israelite, he had to make full restitution, including the 20 percent penalty, before his offering to God would be accepted (cf. Matt. 5:23–24).

Dedicatory Offerings. Three offerings are characterized as being "pleasant" to the Lord. These are the burnt offering (Lev. 1), the cereal offering (Lev. 2), and the peace offering (Lev. 3). The phrase "an aroma pleasing to the Lord" (NIV) or a "sweet savor" (AV) is a standardized idiom denoting God's acceptance of and pleasure with Israelite offerings. Noah's sacrifice following the flood was such an offering (Gen. 8:21). The dedicatory offerings presuppose the existence and observance of the expiatory offerings in the period of the Mosaic revelation. The dedicatory offerings were not accepted by God unless Israel had first presented any required expiatory offerings.

Burnt Offering (*'ōlâ*, Lev. 1:3–17; 6:8–13). Any Israelite could present a burnt offering. A bull (1:3–5), a sheep or goat (1:10), and a bird (1:14) were all considered to be appropriate sacrifices.

The offering was made by having the offender place his hand upon the animal before it was killed (1:4). After the animal was killed its blood was drained on the altar (1:5) or on the side of the altar (1:15). The priest then carefully washed and cut the offering into pieces and arranged the pieces on the altar (1:6–9, 12–13).

The Scriptures indicate a close association between the burnt offering and the sin offering. These two types of offerings were required together during the new moon festival (Num. 28:11–14), passover (Num. 28:19–24), the feast of weeks (Num. 28:26–29), the festival of trumpets (Num. 29:2–4), day of atonement (Num. 29:8), and the feast of booths (Num. 29:12–38). Also the burnt offering was required in addition to the sin offering following childbirth (Lev. 12:6–8), abscesses (Lev. 15:14–15), hemorrhages (Lev. 15:29–30), and defilement during the Nazirite vow (Num. 6:10–11). The association between the sin and the burnt offering suggests that before the worshiper can fully devote himself to the Lord (symbolized by the burnt offering), he must know that his sins have been atoned for (symbolized by the sin offering).

The relationship that existed between the sin offering, burnt offering, and thank offering can be seen in the scriptural account of II Chr. 29:20–31, in which the offerings were made under the leadership of King Hezekiah. After the cleansing of the temple and the consecration of all the vessels, King Hezekiah and the leaders of Jerusalem brought animals as a sin offering "to atone for all Israel." Burnt offerings were then presented to the Lord. During the sacrifice of the burnt offerings the Levites and priests sang and played their instruments. Following the sacrifices the entire assembly worshiped God. After this time of worship more burnt offerings and thank offerings were made. This combination of sin offering, burnt offering, and thank offering expressed the Israelites' need for atonement, their devotion to God, and their gratitude for his blessing.

Cereal Offering (*minḥâ*, Lev. 2:1–16; AV, "meat offering," NIV, "grain offering"). The Hebrew term *minḥâ* needs further clarification. The root meaning is "offering," and in its most basic sense is found some thirty-five times, meaning tribute or gift (cf. Gen. 43:15; Judg. 3:15–19). In a cultic context it may refer to any sacrifice (Isa. 66:20). As a dedicatory offering the *minḥâ* generally accompanied other consecratory offerings (*'ōlâ* and *nesek*).

The offering was presented by all Israelites, including priests. It consisted mainly of fine flour (Lev. 2:1–3), wafers, unleavened bread, and cakes (2:4–10), or ears of grain (2:14–16). A portion of the cereal offering was burned together with incense (2:1–2). The *'azkārâ* is the technical name of the portion. It is related to the Hebrew verb *zākar*, "to remember" or "token," as it is a reminder to God of the sweet smell of the incense burned together with the cereal offering.

The offering was generally made together with the burnt offering (cf. Num. 28–29) and peace offering (Lev. 7:12–14; Num. 15:4–10). There were additional occasions which called for the cereal offering: the ceremonies associated with the ritual purification of a leper (Lev. 14:10, 20ff.), the completion of a Nazirite vow (Num. 6:15–21), and possibly also with the ritual purification after childbirth, etc. (see the occasions for the burnt offering above). It may be that the offering was not made on the day of atonement (Lev. 16:3ff.). The cereal offering was always made together with the peace offering.

Drink Offering (*nesek*, Num. 28:14; 29:6). As with the cereal offering, anyone could present a drink offering. It accompanied both burnt and peace offerings (Num. 15:1–10). The amount of wine depended on the size of the animal to be sacrificed (half a hin for a bull, a third for a ram, and a fourth for a lamb). The offering was intended to please the Lord (Num. 15:7), and was expected as a daily offering (Num. 28:7) and on the sabbath (28:9), new moon (28:14), and the annual festivals.

Communal Offerings. In addition to the required offerings the worshiper could present voluntary offerings. They did not atone for sins, but were complementary to the expiatory and dedicatory offerings. The communal offerings are at times more difficult to distinguish, since several offerings are aspects of one type of offering.

Peace Offering (*šĕlāmîm*, Lev. 3; 7:11–36; NIV, "fellowship offerings"). Any Israelite could make a peace offering in addition to the sacrifices made for atonement and consecration. Since it was a voluntary offering, some qualifications of the sacrificial animals were more relaxed (both male and female animals were permitted, Lev. 3:1, 6). The animal was killed at the entrance of the outer court (Lev. 3:1–2, 7–8, 12–13) and its blood was thrown against the altar (3:2, 8, 13). The entrails were completely burned. The priest was permitted to take the breast and eat it with his family in a clean place. Before taking it as his own, the priest was required to recognize it as a heave offering (*tĕrûmâ*). He was expected to lift up his portion to signify that it was the Lord's (Lev. 7:34; Exod. 29:27–28). Then he would wave it as a wave offering (*tĕnûpâ*) to symbolize that it was the Lord's and that it became his for food by divine appointment. The offerer also could present unleavened cakes as a part of the thank offering (*zebaḥ tôdâ*, Lev. 7:12; AV, "thanksgiving"; NIV, "expression of thankfulness"). Thank offering is generally viewed as a synonym for peace offering. The priest was also permitted to take one of the unleavened cakes, wave it as a wave offering, and consume it.

The last stage of the peace offering was the communal meal, where the offerer and his family would enjoy those parts of the offering which had not been burned or taken by the priest (Lev. 7:15–17). Strict rules detail that it was to be eaten by ritually clean people, in a place near the sanctuary, a ritually clean place, and detail the time period during which the food could be enjoyed.

The peace offering was regularly made during the feast of weeks (Lev. 23:19–20) as a token of gratitude to God. It was associated with the Nazirite vow (Num. 6:17–20) and the ordination of a priest (Exod. 29:19–34; Lev. 8:22–32). The peace offering was often made during or after periods of national threats, adversity, or spiritual renewal, such as war, famine, pestilence, the dedication of the temple, and reforms.

Voluntary Offerings. These included those gifts presented in fulfillment of a vow (votive offerings, Lev. 7:16–17; 22:21; 27; Num. 6:21; 15:3–16; 30:11). The vow was made either as part of a request of God and then fulfilled when the request was granted, or it could be a voluntary response to the goodness of God. The fulfillment of the latter vow falls together with the thanksgiving offering (*tôdâ*, Lev. 7:12–13, 15; 22:29; II Chr. 33:16; Pss. 50:14, 23; 116:17). Another type of voluntary offering was the freewill offering (*nĕdābâ*, Exod. 35:27–29; 36:3; Lev. 7:16; Num. 15:3; Deut. 12:17; 16:10; 23:23; Ezek. 46:12). Because of the voluntary nature of the freewill offering, an imperfectly developed ox or sheep was acceptable (Lev. 22:23).

The emphasis on sacrifices and offerings in the OT is God's revelation for Israel. It signifies the gravity of sin and the grace of God that by the shedding of blood man's sins can be expiated so that the Israelite could know himself to be reconciled with God. The complex system of sacrifices and offerings made the point that man must know what God requires of man and that man must be sure to please God by the renewal of his heart and motivations as he gives of his possessions to Almighty God. However, the expiatory sacrifices did not atone for all sins. Only unintentional sins, inadvertent acts of default, and particular cases of dishonesty could be atoned for, but any trespass of the Decalogue required the death penalty.

Sacrifices and Offerings in the NT. Jesus upheld the sacrificial system. He went to the temple at passover and participated in the passover meal. He commanded the lepers to go to the priests to undergo ritual cleansing and to bring the required offerings (Matt. 8:4; cf. Luke 17:14). In the Sermon on the Mount our Lord did not reject offerings, but stressed that one must first be reconciled to one's brother before one can be reconciled with God (Matt. 5:23–24). Following the crucifixion and ascension of Jesus, the apostles applied the OT language of sacrifice and expiation to Jesus' sacrifice of himself (Rom. 3:25; 8:3). Especially the Epistle to the Hebrews shows how the OT sacrificial system is fulfilled by Jesus as the high priest of the new covenant, by whose blood all sins can be atoned for and by whom the Christian can be strengthened to do works pleasing to God (Heb. 13:20–21). Paul likewise exhorted the Christians in Rome to offer themselves as a living sacrifice to God as a dedicatory offering (Rom. 12:1–2). W. A. Van Gemeren

Bibliography. G. B. Gray, *Sacrifice in the OT;* H. H. Rowley, "The Meaning of Sacrifices in the OT," *BJRL* 23:74–110; N. H. Snaith, "Sacrifices in the OT," *VT* 7:308–17; B. A. Levine, "The Descriptive Tabernacle Texts of the Pentateuch," *JAOS* 85:307–18, and "Comments on Some Technical Terms of the Biblical Cult," *Lesh* 30:3–11; J. Milgrom, "The Function of the *ḥattat* Sacrifice," *Tar* 40:1–8, "A Prolegomena to Leviticus 17:11," *JBL* 90:149–56, "A Chapter in Cultic History," *Tar* 42:1–11, and "The Alleged Wave-Offering in Israel and in the Ancient Near East," *IEJ* 22:33–38; P. A. H. de Boer, "An Aspect of Sacrifice," *VT* Supplement 23:27–47; M. Haran, "The Passover Sacrifice," *VT* Supplement 23:86–116; D. J. McCarthy, "Further Notes on the Symbolism of Blood and Sacrifice," *JBL* 92:205–10; H. C. Brichto, "On Slaughter and Sacrifice, Blood and Atonement," *HUCA* 47:19–55; D. Davies, "An Interpretation of Sacrifice in Leviticus," *ZAW* 89:387–99; R. Abba, "The Origin and Significance of Hebrew Sacrifice," *BTB* 7:123–38; N. H. Gadegaard, "On the So-called Burnt Offering Altar in the OT," *PEQ* 110:35–45.

Office, Daily (Divine). Prescribed daily services of worship of the Roman Catholic, Anglican, and Lutheran Churches. The word "office" is from the Latin *officium*, meaning performance of duty and implying a religious ceremony. Sometimes called the "hour services," the daily offices have antecedents within Judaism. Jews prayed at the third, sixth, and ninth hours of the day. This custom carried over into the NT. In Acts it is said Peter and John went up into the temple at "the hour of prayer" (Acts 3:1) and that Peter went up on the housetop to pray "about the sixth hour" (Acts 10:9). This Jewish tradition was adopted by Islam, which has five hours of daily prayer (morning, noon, midafternoon, evening, and nighttime). By the fourth century bishops of the Catholic Church were "to charge the people to come regularly to Church in the early morning and evening of each day."

Congregational morning and evening prayers were further developed by the monastic communities. There the daily offices or canonical hours (so-called from the canons or rules of Benedict of Nursia) were regularized. Perhaps the inspiration was a passage in the Psalter: "Seven times a day do I praise thee, because of thy righteous judgments" (Ps. 119:164). Monks prayed together at eight appointed times daily: (1) matins, or nocturns, which began at midnight; (2) lauds, following immediately; (3) prime, at sunrise; (4) terce, at midmorning (9 A.M.); (5) sext, at noon; (6) nones at midafternoon (3 P.M.); (7) vespers, at eventide; and (8) compline, at bedtime. Each office contained readings from Scripture, recitations from the Psalter, prayers, hymns, and perhaps a sermon. Eventually each hour took on a unique character.

While all offices were retained by the Roman Catholics, the Anglican and Lutheran Reformers placed the main emphasis on matins and vespers (or evensong) as acts of congregational worship. Matins (from Lat. "of the morning") had been the opening service of the day. The primary and most popular and varied of the canonical hours, it became normative Sunday worship for Anglicans (morning prayer) and a daily rite for Lutherans (when no communion was celebrated). Vespers (from Lat. "evening") had been a service at twilight. It was retained by Lutherans and Anglicans as evensong or evening prayer. Lauds (from Lat. "praise") was less common, though it has been restored recently as a service of praise among Protestants.

C. G. Fry

See also Morning Prayer; Evening Prayer, Evensong; Worship in the Church.

Bibliography. L. D. Reed, *The Lutheran Liturgy;* J. G. Davies, *A Select Liturgical Lexicon;* L. Duchesne, *Christian Worship, Its Origin and Evolution.*

Officers, Church. *See* Church Officers.

Offices of Christ. As the only Redeemer of his church, Jesus Christ performed his saving work in the threefold role of prophet (Deut. 18:15; Luke 4:18–21; 13:33; Acts 3:22), priest (Ps. 110:4; Heb. 3:1; 4:14–15; 5:5–6; 6:20; 7:26; 8:1), and king (Isa. 9:6–7; Pss. 2:6; 45:6; 110:1–2; Luke 1:33; John 18:36–37; Heb. 1:8; II Pet. 1:11; Rev. 19:16). Theologians refer to these as the three offices of Christ, with all the other Christological designations such as apostle, shepherd, intercessor, and head of the church being subsumed under one of these three general offices.

Fulfilling his office work of prophet, Christ (1) claims to bring the Father's message (John 8:26–28; 12:49–50), (2) proclaims his message to the people (Matt. 4:17) and his disciples (Matt. 5–7), and (3) foretells or predicts future events (Matt. 24–25; Luke 19:41–44). He continues to exercise his work as prophet in "revealing to us, by his word [John 16:12–15] and spirit [I Pet. 1:10–11] the will of God for our salvation" (Westminster Shorter Catechism, Q. 24) and edification (Eph. 4:11–13).

Executing his office work of priest, Christ (1) offered himself up to God as a sacrifice to satisfy divine justice and to reconcile the church to God (Rom. 3:26; Heb. 2:17; 9:14, 28) and (2) makes continual intercession for all those who come unto God by him (John 17:6–24; Heb. 7:25; 9:24).

Performing his office work of king, Christ (1) calls out of the world a people for himself (Isa. 55:5; John 10:16, 27); (2) gives them officers, laws, and censures by which he visibly governs them (I Cor. 5:4–5; 12:28; Eph. 4:11–12; Matt. 28:19–20; 18:17–18; I Tim. 5:20; Titus 3:10); (3) preserves and supports them in all their temptations and sufferings (II Cor. 12:9–10; Rom. 8:35–39); (4) restrains and overcomes all their enemies (Acts 12:17; 18:9–10; I Cor. 15:25); (5) powerfully orders all things for his own glory and their good (Rom. 8:28; 14:11; Col. 1:18; Matt. 28:19–20); and (6) finally takes vengeance on those who know not God and who obey not the gospel (Ps. 2:9; II Thess. 1:8).

This delineation of Christ's execution of his three offices indicates that he exercises his offices in the estates of his humiliation and his exaltation (Isa. 9:6–7; Ps. 2:6; Rev. 19:16). That is to say, one must not think that it was his prophetic and priestly ministries which he exercised before his death and entombment while it is his kingly office which he has exercised since his resurrection from the dead. To the contrary, the Scriptures clearly represent him as exercising all three offices in both estates—both during his earthly ministry prior to his death and now, since his resurrection and ascension.

In filling these offices Christ fulfills all the needs of men. "As prophet he meets the problem of man's ignorance, supplying him with knowledge. As priest he meets the problem of man's guilt, supplying him with righteousness. As king he meets the problem of man's weakness and dependence, supplying him with power and protection" (J. B. Green, *A Harmony of the Westminster Presbyterian Standards*, pp. 65–66).

R. L. Reymond

Oil, Anointing with. *See* Anoint, Anointing.

Old Lights, The. *See* New Light Schism.

Old Man. *See* MAN, OLD AND NEW.

Old Roman Creed. *See* APOSTLES' CREED.

Old School Theology. Old School Presbyterians maintained Calvinist orthodoxy from the 1830s to the 1860s. Princeton theologians Archibald Alexander and Charles Hodge believed that their theology faithfully reflected Reformed beliefs and should be central in American Presbyterianism. They contended that their Calvinism was historically aligned with the Westminster Confession of Faith, John Calvin, Augustine, and the Bible itself. The very term "Old School theology" indicates that its adherents wanted to retain traditional Reformed doctrines. They wanted a "consistent Calvinism" and developed distinct views on confessionalism, revivalism, and church polity. Because of their stand on these issues, the Old School faction expelled the New School from the church in 1837 for having diverged from them.

Believing that doctrinal orthodoxy was of primary importance in Christian faith, Old School men desired a strict confessionalism or subscription to the Westminster Confession. Several New School leaders such as Albert Barnes and Lyman Beecher were accused of holding sub-Calvinist views related to the New Haven theology of Nathaniel W. Taylor. Alexander and Hodge answered Taylor in seven articles in the *Princeton Review* (1830–31) by stressing Reformed doctrines such as the imputation of Adam's sin (Adam acted as a representative for all men and his sin was counted against them), Christ's substitutionary atonement, and the regenerating work of the Holy Spirit.

Many Old School men, including Alexander and Hodge, were greatly influenced by revivals in their younger days and acknowledged a continuing need for revival in the church. But they sharply criticized contemporary revivalists for expressing Taylorite views in their preaching. They condemned emotional excesses and demanded that true revivals be carried out within the church guided by its confessional stance on God's sovereignty and human inability. Charles G. Finney's theology and *Lectures on Revivals of Religion* (1835) were thoroughly criticized. Hodge preferred Horace Bushnell's concept of Christian nurture to revivalism as the primary means of bringing people to faith in Christ.

The Old School party also strongly supported Presbyterian polity as most consistent with a Reformed view of the church. Arguing that church order was a matter of faith, they opposed a plan of union with Congregationalists and claimed that Presbyterian polity provided discipline necessary to prevent errors in doctrine and practice which Congregationalism lacked. They also repudiated the social activism of voluntary societies, preferring that education and mission activities take place within the institutional church, where it also could be guided by the church's confession.

In 1869 New and Old Schools reunited, primarily because during the schism New School theology had become more orthodox.

W. A. HOFFECKER

See also NEW SCHOOL THEOLOGY; NEW HAVEN THEOLOGY; HODGE, CHARLES; ALEXANDER, ARCHIBALD.

Bibliography. A. Alexander, *Evidences of the Authenticity, Inspiration and Authority of the Holy Scriptures;* S. J. Baird, *A History of the New School;* A. A. Hodge, *The Life of Charles Hodge;* C. Hodge, *Systematic Theology,* 3 vols.; *Princeton Review,* 1837–69.

Old Testament. *See* BIBLE.

Old Testament Canon. *See* BIBLE, CANON OF.

Old Testament Theology. A theology of the OT endeavors to set out in something approaching an orderly manner the great statements of divine truth that occur in those writings. Such affirmations can include direct or propositional revelation from God about his nature and purposes, prophetic proclamations relating to his will for Israel and the world, and expositions by prophets and others of specific themes or aspects of the Torah and their meaning for the recipients. Despite its wealth of affirmations about God, the OT does not contain any lists of systematized theological statements about such matters as sin, redemption, and divine grace. Nor does it summarize the affirmations of faith in the form of a creed, which would have furnished an organized statement of theology for acceptance by the believer.

In order to formulate an OT theology with any expectation of success, it is necessary first of all to ascertain the significance that the words or writings had for the original recipients. Hebrew is a language rich in meaning and symbolism, and any attempt at understanding the thought of the OT writers must be firmly based upon as accurate a translation of the original as is possible. The fact that the meaning of some Hebrew words is still unknown has also to be taken into account, as well as certain textual problems that have arisen in process of transmission through the centuries. Such a translation will necessarily proceed from a thorough knowledge of Hebrew grammar and syntax, as well as of ancient Near

Eastern literary traditions and conventions, before it can be trusted as a basis for doctrinal formulations.

A proper balance must also be maintained between an objective historical method of investigation and the concept of an authoritative and final revelation from God in written form. Even then the materials may not respond very well to scholars accustomed to modern attempts at the systematizing of theological concepts. This is especially true if a theology of history is substituted for, or confused with, a theology of being or essence. Finally, the thought of the OT writers must not be restricted to the concerns involving the religion or life of the ancient Hebrews. It must be viewed as part of an ongoing revelation of God that has its culmination in the NT proclamation of his redeeming grace in Christ, the Messiah of Israel and the Savior of mankind. With these considerations in mind it may be possible to outline some of the more important concepts that could be included in an OT theology.

Doctrine of God. The teachings relating to the person and nature of God begin by taking as axiomatic his existence, a fact that only a fool would dispute (Ps. 53:1). God is the ground of all existence, and reveals himself creatively by deeds such as the making of the world and mankind as well as by the verbal communication of his nature and will. Whereas God is necessary Being, having existed from eternity, the earth and its inhabitants are contingent or created entities, depending for their existence upon the sustaining power of the Creator.

While his nature is that of infinite spirit, he permits himself to be described periodically in anthropomorphic terms. He thus has a face—i.e., a presence, from which people can be hidden through the alienation of sin (Gen. 4:14), but which also acts to rescue his people from bondage and lead them to safety (Exod. 33:14). He has hands, with which he creates his marvelous works (Ps. 143:5), and his voice may be heard directly (Exod. 3:4) or through the medium of the prophets (e.g., Isa. 8:1; Jer. 1:4; Ezek. 31:1) as his word is proclaimed. On certain occasions God identifies himself with the physical form and activity of a messenger (Gen. 22:15–18; Isa. 63:9), though with enough difference to enable the messenger to be distinguished from the Creator (cf. Gen. 24:40). In cases such as Gen. 32:24 traditional Christianity has interpreted the "man" or "messenger" as a manifestation of the preincarnate Christ, although this concept is not accepted universally.

The personality of God is also expressed by a variety of names, which in ancient Near Eastern tradition signified a range of character and function. Thus he was worshiped by Melchizedek as the Most High God (Gen. 14:18), while other titles included God Almighty (Exod. 6:3), "a God who sees" (Gen. 16:13), "God is the God of Israel" (Gen. 33:20), and the covenant name YHWH ("I am who I am" or "I will be what I will be"). This name, often transliterated Jehovah or Yahweh, establishes God's existence beyond question and identifies him as the only true and living God (cf. Isa. 45:5), who binds the Israelites to himself in a covenant relationship. It was this act that gave Israel its uniqueness in human society and made it the vehicle of subsequent revelation.

God's names seem to have been revealed in response to specific situations of human need, and at the time when the Israelites were in bondage to the Egyptians the revelation of the covenant name identified God as the deity worshiped by the patriarchs. He was shortly to fulfill earlier covenant promises to liberate Israel from servitude and bring the people into the promised land, where they could serve God as the only true deity and exemplify his character among neighboring peoples. This witness involved manifesting God's essential holiness (Lev. 11:44), righteousness (Amos 5:24), and justice (Mic. 6:8), while warning of the sure judgments of a supremely moral God who was Lord, not merely of Israel, but of the whole earth. God desired all nations to worship in his holy house (cf. Mic. 4:1–3), but also demanded complete separation from idolatry and wickedness. His mercy to sinful humanity would be indicated by the promise of a Messiah, a personage who would be a light to the Gentiles as well as the glory of his people Israel. Though emerging from Hebrew stock (Jer. 23:5–6), he would undertake a work of such spiritual significance that ultimately mankind will be redeemed from bondage to sin.

Throughout the OT God is conceived of as an omnipotent being (cf. Gen. 18:14) who possesses a complete personality and who can be known fully as God at every stage of the historical process. He is omniscient (cf. Prov. 15:3) and has total knowledge of all future events until the end of time (cf. Isa. 46:10). Characteristic of his purposes and deeds is love or mercy (*ḥesed*), which surrounds creation and creature alike (Ps. 145:9) and finds its supreme expression in altruistic activities of blessing and redemption. The idea of God as the Father of his people is connected with the establishing of the covenant nation, who become his adopted children, and is also expressed in relationship to the work of the Messiah, who will ultimately enlarge the family of believers by his work of redemption. As Father,

God requires a response of filial love and obedience from his children (Mal. 1:6), and will punish them if they become apostate.

The OT also describes the activities of God in terms of a vitalizing Spirit (*rûaḥ*) which sustains creation (cf. Job 34:14; Ps. 104:30) and gives distinctive existence to mankind (Gen. 2:7). The notion that the Holy Spirit of God was an active participant in the creation of the world rests upon an evident mistranslation of Gen. 1:2, the Hebrew phrase *rûaḥ 'ĕlōhîm* being more accurately rendered as "an awesome gale." In general, the OT says comparatively little about the nature of God as Spirit, preferring instead to concentrate upon divine activity in the world and in human society.

Doctrine of Man and Sin. OT teachings concerning the nature of mankind are based on the proposition that man is created in the image of God (*imago dei*). Two Hebrew terms, *ṣelem* and *dĕmût*, are used (Gen. 1:26–27; 5:1, 3; 9:6) as synonyms to indicate that man reflects God in a unique manner. Man is thus different from other forms of created organic life, over which he has been given dominion (Gen. 1:28). Although he too is a creature, it is this very fact that clarifies the nature of God's image in man. The Scriptures indicate that mankind does not possess an inherent divinity, but instead was formed originally from the dust (better, "sticky clay") of the ground, and then as a final act of divine creativity became a living being by a process of supernatural inbreathing (Gen. 2:7). By this means man acquired his uniqueness in the universe, which might well be understood by some such term as "selfhood" or "personality." The human spirit derives from God, the progenitor of the spirits of all flesh (Num. 16:22). From Gen. 2:7 it is clear that man is soul—i.e., that the metaphysical principle of his existence interpenetrates and interrelates with the physical in the individual. He is thus not simply a body that "possesses" a soul as some sort of adjunct, but is in fact a living principle of spirituality that has physical extension.

The nature of man as manifesting the clear image of his Maker is consistently connected in the OT with the thought of God as Creator. The concept of an image is meant to show that man is not divine in the sense that God is, but that he manifests a sufficient degree of divinity in his nature to remind the beholder that he reflects the Creator in a way unparalleled by anything else in creation. Against this background the psalmist could extol man as being somewhat lower than God (Ps. 8:5; AV, "the angels"). When man's pristine purity was besmirched by the sin of disobedience to God's will, however, a concomitant was a tarnishing of the image of God in man. Thus it is no longer possible to demonstrate God's nature merely by reference to man's. Godhead can now only be reflected most accurately by Godhead, a fact which the OT narratives make abundantly clear.

It is obvious that the concept of the *imago dei* must be grasped firmly before the significance of other OT observations about sin, grace, human salvation, and the like can be appreciated properly. The *imago dei* is defaced but not destroyed by human rebellion against God in Eden, an episode that defined sin for humanity as a process culminating in rejection of, or disobedience to, the known, revealed will of God. From this point man was recognized as "flesh" (cf. Gen. 6:3), a term implying mortality, frailty, self-centeredness, and transience.

Because of man's sin the penalty of death was imposed upon the race (Gen. 3:19), but the breach between Creator and creature was repaired to some extent by sacrificial procedures which found their fullest definition in the period of Moses. Levitical law prescribed in detail for the restoration of fellowship between the sinner and his God (Lev. 1–7), and one of the most prominent sacrificial observances in Hebrew covenantal religion was the day of atonement (Lev. 16), by which the sins of accident, error, or omission of the nation were forgiven. These offenses were inadvertent transgressions and were distinguished from presumptuous sins (Num. 15:30), which constituted open rebellion against known covenant spirituality and for which there could be no forgiveness.

Doctrine of Redemption. The purpose of blood sacrifice was to make atonement in various ways for human sin, a process which involved a choice animal being presented to God and having the sins of the offender transferred to it symbolically. When the animal was slaughtered, the shed blood was accepted by God as a substitute for the lifeblood of the sinner. The OT shows clearly that animal sacrifice as such has no intrinsic efficacy, but that when the sacrificial offering was presented to God in the manner prescribed, its blood made atonement for the sinner (Lev. 17:11), and fellowship with God was restored. The guilt offering was regarded as "most holy" (Lev. 7:1) because it served to fulfill the holiest of duties. While some prophets appeared to criticize sacrifice (Isa. 1:11; Hos. 6:6; Amos 5:21), they were more concerned with the motivation that prompted the rite than with the institution itself.

The restoration of the sinner is an act of God's grace; the characteristic OT term was *ḥesed.* It is often rendered by "mercy" or "lovingkindness," and represented the motivating force behind the various covenants with the Hebrews (Deut. 7:12). On occasions, however, the term is used independently of covenant association (Jer. 31:3). Where *ḥesed* is used of God, it describes him as initiating the process by which his mercy is bestowed upon man, with emphasis upon fidelity, usually in a covenant context. Another term, *ḥēn*, which carries the sense of "favor," seems often to imply that what is being granted, or is desired, is undeserved (Exod. 33:13). Divine mercy and love are expressed freely in the relationship whereby God bound Israel to himself through a treaty, the form of which has much in common with those used by second millennium B.C. Hittite kings when entering into a relationship with a vassal nation. In his gracious love God offered to care completely for his people if they in turn would obey and revere him as the only true God. As with the Hittite treaties, there were severe penalties threatened for covenant infractions, but the main emphasis was upon a positive relationship between God and his people.

Covenantal theology is of the greatest importance in OT thought because it provides a dimension of formal discipline and spirituality for a people that was expected to exemplify in national life the character of its God. Against this background the ideal of the long-promised Messiah comes gradually to fruition. From the beginning this personage was a fact of history, being conceived of in regal terms, first as an ideal ruler such as David but subsequently as an anointed figure ("messiah") who would appear at the end of the age to usher in the divine kingdom. The splendor of such a person was indicated by Isaiah (9:6–7; 11:1–5), while the historical continuity was especially stressed by Jeremiah (33:14–15). The nature of the messianic kingdom was foretold by Zechariah (9:9–10; 12:7–9), and the precise birthplace of this royal individual was predicted centuries before the event by Micah (5:2). Although the house of David diminished in political importance after the days of Haggai (520 B.C.), the expectation of a coming Messiah had been prominent for some time (cf. the "anointed one" of Dan. 9:25). At the period of Christ's ministry there was a widespread longing for a deliverer from God to come upon the scene and deliver the Jews from bondage to Rome. In a rather different sense the messianic expectation was also prominent in the thought of the Qumran sectaries.

In the OT teachings concerning redemption and restoration there appear some rather enigmatic references to a "servant of the Lord." These are particularly prominent in Isaiah, but in the prophecy they are distributed between an individual and the idea of the nation as the servant, which makes the matter of identification problematical. The nation of Israel as servant (Isa. 41:8; 42:19; 44:1) is replaced elsewhere (Isa. 42:1; 49:1; 52:13; 53:11) by an individual who will restore the nation (Isa. 49:5–6) and glorify God throughout the earth. The righteous character of this personage and his function as the anointed one of God preclude such notable leaders as Isaiah himself or anyone prior to his time because of the future references (Isa. 52:13). Cyrus and Zerubbabel are also excluded because neither died as a divinely ordained sacrifice for Jews and Gentiles alike. The servant was to be a prophet of God, empowered by the Spirit (Isa. 42:1; 61:1) for the work of establishing divine justice in the earth (Isa. 42:4). In his mission he would suffer for others' sins and die dishonorably (Isa. 53:3, 9). His atonement would be that of the priestly *'āšām* or "guilt offering" (Isa. 53:10), which when accepted by God would lead many to be accounted righteous, whatever their race. The servant's work would thus change the old corporate concept of salvation that existed under the Sinai covenant and broaden the scope of God's redemptive activity. It would include the whole human race and place response to God's invitation to forgiveness and fellowship on an individual rather than a corporate basis (Jer. 31:29–30). Just as it was impossible historically for any individual to fulfill the role of an anointed servant, so also the nation was equally unable to achieve that goal, whether in an actual physical or an ideal moral sense.

The suffering servant obviously has much in common with the Messiah, Israel's ideal ruler. Both emerge from the Davidic line (II Sam. 7:15–16; Isa. 11:1) and have a special anointing for their task (Isa. 11:2; 42:1). The ruler, through the Davidic covenant, witnesses about God's nature and saving purposes to those outside the covenant (Isa. 55:3), a function that is also assigned to the servant (Isa. 49:6). Finally, the Messiah, spoken of as the "Branch," is equated with the servant in postexilic prophecy (Zech. 3:8).

Yet another mystic figure relating to the divine plan for Israel's future is that of the son of man. In some occurrences the phrase is the equivalent of a human descendant (Ps. 8:4), or of someone manifesting the appearance of man incarnate (Dan. 10:16, 18). This is in accord with proper Hebrew usage, where the terms *'ĕnôš* and *ben 'ādām* ("son of man") occur occasionally as synonyms (Job 25:6; Pss. 8:4; 90:3; 144:3). Some scholars have regarded the occurrence of "son of man" in Dan. 7:13 as describing either a personification of the ideal nation or as indicating the saints of God. Others think that the term describes a heavenly figure who both represents the nation of Israel and is a sanctified personage at the same time. This in turn suggests a messianic character underlying the reference, and it was doubtless in this sense that Christ interpreted it on occasions.

Eschatology. These topics raise the question of eschatology, an enquiry as to what may occur when the existence of the individual or the nation terminates. The OT recognizes that in both instances the process is of God, and depending upon the relationship with him can portend blessing (Job 19:25–26) or calamity (Ps. 9:17). But in general very little detailed information about individual survival after death is forthcoming, which contrasts markedly with the wealth of conjecture found in Egyptian religion. At death the individual Hebrew was deemed to have gone to Sheol, an underworld region of vague dimensions where the dead existed as shadows of their former selves. Some passages suggest a diminished consciousness of God's presence and activities there (Ps. 88:10–11; Isa. 38:18), but others proclaim God's nearness even in Sheol (Ps. 139:8). The dead were commonly held to be beyond human reach, but on one dramatic occasion the shade of Samuel was raised to give advice to Saul (I Sam. 28:14–19). Teaching about individual resurrection is stated most clearly in Dan. 12:2.

Because Israel's national life was based upon the covenant at Sinai, a corporate concept of survival formed an attractive prospect, especially when associated with the leadership of the Messiah. The possibility of national revival through God's power was seen clearly in Ezekiel's vision (Ezek. 37:1–14), in which a new act of human creation comparable to the first (Gen. 2:7) took place. Despite this encouraging prospect, earlier prophets had pointed sternly to Israel's rebellion against the covenant provisions and had spoken of an apocalyptic day of the Lord, in which impenitent Israel would be punished, not blessed (Amos 5:18–20). Other prophets promised that on that day the whole earth would acknowledge God's righteous overlordship (Isa. 11:9). This emphasis upon the universalism of God's redemptive plan is significant because of the decline of the Davidic monarchy and the ultimate abandonment of the nation because of its apostasy (Zech. 11:10–14). The scene is thus set for God to inaugurate a new age of grace by a sudden revelation of himself in power as he smites the nation's enemies from the Mount of Olives (Zech. 14:3–4). Then he will rule as king over all the earth, and will make his name one among mankind (Zech. 14:9) as he judges in righteousness (Pss. 96:13; 98:9).

R. K. Harrison

See also God, Names of; God, Attributes of; God, Doctrine of; Man, Doctrine of; Image of God; Sin; Son of Man; Offerings and Sacrifices in Bible Times; Messiah.

Bibliography. W. Eichrodt, *Theology of the OT;* Y. Kaufmann, *The Religion of Israel;* J. B. Payne, *The Theology of the Older Testament;* G. F. Hasel, *OT Theology;* G. von Rad, *OT Theology;* H. Schultz, *OT Theology;* T. C. Vriezen, *An Outline of OT Theology;* H. H. Rowley, *The Faith of Israel;* L. Koehler, *OT Theology;* A. B. Davidson, *The Theology of the OT;* O. Baab, *The Theology of the OT.*

Oman, John Wood (1860–1939). A leading British theologian of the early twentieth century. Born at Stenness in the Orkney Islands, he obtained his advanced education at Edinburgh and the United Presbyterian College in his native Scotland, and at Erlangen, Heidelberg, and Neuchâtel on the continent. Oman spent most of his career in the service of the English Presbyterian Church, first in a lengthy pastorate at Alnwick, Northumberland (1889–1907), and then as professor of systematic theology and apologetics at Westminster, the Presbyterian theological college at Cambridge (1907–35).

Oman was strongly influenced by liberal German thought, especially that of Schleiermacher, whose *Speeches on Religion* he translated (1893) and whose emphasis upon the importance of subjective, personal religious experience he reflected. In his major writings, including *Grace and Personality* (1918) and *The Natural and the Supernatural* (1931), he emphasized that each person (1) has the ability to acquire an immediate self-authenticating awareness of the supernatural as he pursues it with sincerity and reverence, (2) is utterly free to interpret the divine meaning of the experiences of his life, and (3) finds liberation from the dominion of his physical environment as he understands and accepts the dominion of the divine.

W. C. Ringenberg

Bibliography. Oman, *Vision and Authority, The Church and the Divine Order,* and *Concerning the Ministry;* F. G. Healey, *Religion and Reality: The Theology of John Oman;* H. H. Farmer, "Memoir of the Author," in Oman, *Honest Religion.*

Omission, Sins of. In both the OT and NT there are a number of Hebrew and Greek words used to convey the concept of sin. This means no single word is able to exhibit the full nature of sin. As these words are used in the various contexts we learn that sin is to miss the mark of God's standard, to fall aside from God's requirements, to pervert that which is right, to trespass against God's law, to rebel against God, to betray a trust, to fail to meet obligations.

However, sin is not only committed when one does that which is wrong; sin is also failing to do what is right. The former would be a sin of commission; the latter a sin of omission. Negligence can also be sin. Ignorance of an offense does not absolve one from guilt (Lev. 4:13, 22, 27; 5:2–4, 17, 19; 6:4; cf. James 4:17).

In Scripture terrible punishments are given because of ignorance and/or negligence. Failure to "help the Lord" resulted in a curse (Judg. 5:23), and an anathema is pronounced upon those who love not the Lord (I Cor. 16:22). Failure to minister to Christ's brethren results in everlasting destruction and damnation (Matt. 25:45–46).

R. P. LIGHTNER

Omnipotence. *See* GOD, ATTRIBUTES OF.

Omnipresence. *See* GOD, ATTRIBUTES OF.

Omniscience. *See* GOD, ATTRIBUTES OF.

Only Begotten. The word *monogenēs* occurs nine times in the NT, referring to Isaac (Heb. 11:17), the widow's son (Luke 7:12), Jairus's daughter (Luke 8:42), the demoniac boy (Luke 9:38), and Jesus Christ (John 1:14, 18; 3:16, 18; I John 4:9). In the LXX it is used to render *yāḥîd,* meaning "only one" (Judg. 11:34, e.g.). Wisdom is *monogenēs* (Wisd. Sol. 7:22), having no peer, unique.

The second half of the word is not derived from *gennaō,* "to beget," but is an adjectival form derived from *genos,* "origin, race, stock," etc. *Monogenēs,* therefore, could be rendered "one of a kind." The translation "only" will suffice for the references in Luke and Hebrews. But what about the passages in the Johannine writings? "The adjective 'only begotten' conveys the idea, not of derivation and subordination, but of uniqueness and consubstantiality: Jesus is all that God is, and He alone is this" (B. B. Warfield, *Biblical Doctrines,* p. 194). Cremer finds a parallel in the Pauline *idios huios* (Rom. 8:32). Since the Synoptists use "beloved" (*agapētos*) of the Son, some have concluded that the two words *agapētos* and *monogenēs* are equivalent in force. But "beloved" does not point to the uniqueness of the Son's relation to the Father as *monogenēs* does.

Though the translation "only" is lexically sound for the Johannine passages, since in all strictness "only begotten" would require *monogennētos,* the old rendering "only begotten" is not entirely without justification when the context in John 1:14 is considered. The verb *genesthai* occurs at the end of 1:13 ("born of God") and *ginesthai* in 1:14. These words ultimately go back to the same root as the second half of *monogenēs.* Especially important is I John 5:18, where the second "born of God" must refer to Christ according to the superior Greek text. As a sample of patristic interpretation, see Justin Martyr, *Dialogue with Trypho* 105. At the very least it is clear that the relationship expressed by *monogenēs* is not confined to the earthly life so as to be adaptable to an adoptionist Christology. The sonship in John is linked to preexistence (17:5, 24, and the many references to the Son as sent of the Father).

In its significance *monogenēs* relates to several areas: (1) being or nature (uniquely God's Son), (2) the revelation of God to man (John 1:18), and (3) salvation through the Son (John 3:16; I John 4:9).

The Apostles' Creed is content with "only Son," which is the usual form of the Old Roman Symbol. In the Old Latin Version of the NT *monogenēs* was rendered by *unicus,* but in the Vulgate it became *unigenitus* due to the influence of the Nicene Christological formulation upon Jerome.

E. F. HARRISON

See also TRINITY.

Bibliography. D. Moody, "God's Only Son: The Translation of John 3:16 in the Revised Standard Version," *JBL* 72:213–19; B. F. Westcott, *Epistles of John;* G. Vos, *The Self-Disclosure of Jesus;* F. Büchsel, *TDNT,* IV, 737ff.; K.-H. Bartels, *NIDNTT,* II, 723ff.; E. Best, *One Body in Christ.*

Ontological Argument for God. *See* GOD, ARGUMENTS FOR THE EXISTENCE OF.

Ontology. *See* METAPHYSICS.

Oppression. The sin of man's inhumanity to man. It is the violation of human rights and dignity, the exploitation of human labor, the repression of moral values, and the robbery of self-identity. Oppressors may arise from an elite who have the power to subjugate others because of their wealth and privileged position, or they may arise from the masses who have the power to oppress a minority because of the strength of their number. Oppression may occur in the family or at the factory or in society at large. Oppressors may be conscious of their efforts to hold down others or they may be oblivious to the consequences of their sinful activities. Their primary motive may be fear, pride, or greed. Oppression is a complex evil bearing psychological, spiritual, economic, and political consequences and frequently renders the oppressed unaware of their true situation and defenseless.

Economic and political oppression is a major concern in contemporary theological thought. Theologies of liberation share the conviction that the essence of the gospel is the liberation of the oppressed from sociopolitical exploitation. It is claimed that material reality provides the proper context for understanding spiritual reality. Salvation is achieved through overcoming unjust social structures and the emergence of exploited and oppressed classes to a place of dignity and equality.

It is claimed that only those who side with the poor and oppressed are able to do authentic theology and identify with the God of the oppressed. According to the broad spectrum of liberation theologies, oppression results from racial, sexual, political, and economic exploitation. Dehumanization is a key concept in understanding the nature of oppression. Whatever prevents people from becoming more fully human is considered oppressive.

Critical awareness of oppressive social structures comes through "conscienticization," a process whereby the oppressed learn to understand their situation and begin their struggle for radical change. Critical awareness of the social situation does not come about before the consciousness of the oppressed has been liberated. Through enculturation the consciousness of the oppressed has been submerged in the mentality of the oppressors. The oppressed have internalized the perspective of their exploiters to the point that sharing the oppressors' way of life becomes an "overpowering aspiration" (Paulo Freire). The poor understand success in the same terms as the rich: to be is to have. Meaning and fulfillment become a matter of possessing material things. The racially oppressed understand their personal identity and worth after the manner of their oppressors: to be is to dominate. Conscienticization is the reversal of this mentality by restoring to the oppressed their human dignity and strengthening their resolve for social justice and equality. Instead of aspiring to be like the oppressors, the oppressed struggle for the full humanity of all people, including the oppressors.

Black theologian James Cone speaks for many theologians of liberation when he writes, "To know Jesus is to know Him as revealed in the struggle of the oppressed for freedom" (*God of the Oppressed*, p. 34). For Cone, oppression is social oppression, and freedom is brought about by political struggle—a struggle in which "the poor recognize that their fight against poverty and injustice is not only consistent with the gospel but is the gospel of Jesus Christ."

The emphasis on social oppression has challenged evangelicals to examine biblical perspectives on oppression and become more aware of the influence of social conditioning in shaping theological perspectives. Words like "tribulation," "suffering," and "affliction," found in many English translations of the Bible, do not convey the social and political impact that the word "oppression" does, even though both the Hebrew and Greek original and the context are clearly concerned with social oppression. The use of the term "oppression" in more recent English translations (e.g., NIV) reveals the importance of the theme throughout the Bible.

Many evangelicals have tended to spiritualize clear biblical references to social and economic oppression. There are a number of reasons for this position, including the biblical stress on patience in suffering, the association of economic struggle with greed and covetousness, the long-standing Christian tradition of obedience to the ruling powers, the dismissal of social action as a worthy pursuit for spiritually minded Christians, the reduction of social concern to works of compassion, and the post–World War II upward social mobility and affluence of the evangelical churches.

While the Bible acknowledges that poverty may result from laziness and divine punishment, it emphasizes in both the OT and NT that its major cause is injustice, exploitation, and class conflict. God is continually portrayed as the defender and refuge of the oppressed. God upholds their human rights and promises judgment on the oppressor. The biblical meaning of oppression exposes the complexity of evil and traces injustice back to a fundamental rejection of God (Rom. 1:18–21). Oppression may be political, racial, sexual, economic, generational, religious, spiritual, or demonic. It is not simply economic, nor is it confined to one social class. Job felt oppressed (Job 10:3), and King David prayed for deliverance and guidance because of his oppressors (Ps. 27:11).

Evangelical theology should not obscure the practical social dimensions of oppression. Poverty results from sin and evil. It is to be neither accepted nor idealized. Concern for man's spiritual condition of lostness and separation from God does not justify indifference toward the justice and well-being of those who are economically poor or racially outcast. The evident complexity of evil in human history does not rationally or spiritually allow for a one-dimensional view of oppression that divorces social realities from personal sin and rebellion against God, and from the dominating and destructive influence of the principalities and powers. To declare that all are oppressed because of man's sinful condition is wrongly motivated if the practice behind the concept reinforces the position of the oppressor. But the concept is true if it is understood that all people stand under God's judgment and are in need of God's forgiveness and deliverance from the suprahuman forces of evil.

Salvation cannot be equated with the emergence of a "new man" who has been set free from a particular social evil through the means of political struggle. Biblically understood, salvation begins with the restoration of man's relationship to God and the reconciliation brought about through the atoning death and resurrection of Jesus Christ. Christ has accomplished victory over the powers of evil and has secured ultimate judgment and justice. Christians are called to work for social justice in the certain hope that the living Lord Jesus will one day rule and reign. Until that day Christians are required to work for the liberation of the oppressed through the power and wisdom of the Spirit.

D. D. WEBSTER

See also LIBERATION THEOLOGY; SOCIAL GOSPEL, THE.

Bibliography. L. Boff, "Christ's Liberation via Oppression: An Attempt at Theological Construction from the Standpoint of Latin America," in *Frontiers of Theology in Latin America*, ed. R. Gibellini; J. H. Cone, *God of the Oppressed;* T. Hanks, *Oppression, Poverty and Liberation;* C. F. H. Henry, *God, Revelation, and Authority*, IV; S. Mott, *Biblical Ethics and Social Change;* W. Scott, *Bring Forth Justice.*

Opus Operatum. The term is used in connection with sacramental theology, particularly that of unreformed Christendom. With the cognate term *ex opere operato*, it sums up the view that the benefit of a sacrament avails "by virtue of the work wrought." As first given by Duns Scotus, it was meant to emphasize the grace of God without the deservings of inward goodness in the communicant, so long as no bar was placed within. Gabriel Biel developed the term to suggest mechanical efficacy of sacraments by virtue of the proper liturgical action by celebrant and receiver. After the Council of Trent incorporated the term into Canon VIII *de Sacramentis* it became authoritative Roman Catholic doctrine. However, Cardinal Bellarmine, for example, accepted the need of faith and repentance instead of a purely passive attitude. Nevertheless, he added that it is "the external act called sacrament, and this is called *opus operatum*," which "actively, proximately, and instrumentally" affects the passive recipient; "it confers grace by virtue of the sacramental act itself, instituted by God for this purpose." The view thus rejects all suggestion of dependence not only on the minister (*ex opere operantis*) but also on the receiver. So much is grace and rite conjoined that the due administration of the latter must necessarily involve the former.

G. J. C. MARCHANT

See also EX OPERE OPERATO; SACRAMENT.

Ordain, Ordination. These words come from the Latin meaning "to set in order," "to arrange." In later Latin they came to mean "to appoint to office." The AV uses the verb "to ordain" to render about thirty different Hebrew and Greek words, which shows that the English word has many different shades of meaning. Some of the more prominent of these meanings are discussed below.

Converted Israel will sing of the peace which Jehovah will "ordain" for it (Isa. 26:12); the idea of "appoint" is in view. God has "ordained" the moon and stars (Ps. 8:3); these heavenly bodies were prepared by God for their work. The idea of arrangement is seen in connection with making one's living by preaching the gospel; the Lord has thus "ordained" (I Cor. 9:14). The king "ordained" or appointed a man (Arioch) to fulfill his dire words of judgment; he specified who was to lose his life. Paul told Titus to "ordain" or set down certain individuals to be elders in the church (Titus 1:5). Jehovah "ordained" Jeremiah to be a prophet to the Gentile nations (Jer. 1:5); this meant he gave Jeremiah to the nations along with his ministry. Certain truths were set aside by the apostles and elders as essential to the faith; these "decrees" were "ordained" of God (Acts 16:4). God "ordained" a specific place for his people to dwell (I Chr. 17:9); that is, he reserved it exclusively for them. Jesus "ordained" twelve men to serve in special ways (Mark 3:14). He set them apart for a specific office and duties; he appointed them.

This sampling illustrates the theological meaning of "ordain" or "ordination." The words have a close relationship with God's word of election and predestination. It is impossible to talk about God's sovereignty without talking about his preparation, his appointment, his choices, and even his predetermined ways. If God's pretemporal selections, appointments, and plans are not seen, he becomes the servant of man and time, both of which he created in the first place. In such a view God is no longer God.

Scripture also speaks of man "ordaining" certain things. The creature "ordains" or appoints in a much different sense than God, the Creator, has done. He has "ordained" as the infinite, all-knowing God; man "ordains" in a very limited way.

There is a nontechnical sense in which local churches and sometimes denominations "ordain" those who minister among them. This is usually accompanied by the laying on of hands. Support is often found for this from the following: (1) Traditionally, group approval has thus been given. (2) The OT speaks of priests, Levites, prophets, and kings being set aside for their work in this way. (3) Christ called, appointed, and commissioned the twelve, though without formal ordination. (4) The apostles gave special recognition to the choice of Matthias to take the place of Judas Iscariot.

The Roman Catholic and Orthodox churches regard ordination as a sacrament instituted by Christ and conferring grace upon the recipient. The ceremony of ordination as practiced by Rome was condemned by Calvin. Lutheran and Reformed confessions stress the need for the individual to be called of God, though these two bodies do practice ordination to the ministry. The Church of England and the Episcopal Church give great prominence to ordination, some of their number believing in apostolic succession. Church bodies associated with what might be called the Free Church movement usually view ordination in a less rigid way and practice it simply as group approval upon the individual after he has been examined doctrinally.

R. P. Lightner

See also Predestination; Orders, Holy.

Bibliography. C. S. Meyer, *WBE*, II, 1252–53; *Unger's Bible Dictionary*, 811–12; D. M. Edwards, *ISBE*, IV, 2199–2200.

Order of Salvation. This phrase (Lat. *ordo salutis*) appears to have been brought into theological usage in 1737 by Jakob Karpov, a Lutheran. But the doctrine is of much greater antiquity. Necessarily, there is a wide divergence between the Roman Catholic and the Reformed view in this connection, for although they both agree that there can be no salvation apart from the work of Jesus Christ, the Roman Catholic Church teaches that it is the divinely appointed dispenser of saving grace through the sacraments, which, of themselves, convey grace to the recipients. The stages of Rome's order of salvation may be taken as marked by its sacraments of (1) baptism, in which the soul is regenerated; (2) confirmation, in which baptized persons receive the gift of the Holy Ghost; (3) the Eucharist, in which they partake of the very body and blood of Christ in the transubstantiated wafer; (4) penance, by which the benefit of Christ's death is applied to those who have fallen after baptism; and (5) extreme unction, which prepares the recipient for death and cleanses him from the remains of sin.

Luther's order of salvation consisted simply in repentance, faith, and good works; but the Lutheran order was elaborated by later theologians into something closely resembling the Reformed order. It rests, however, upon the assumption that Christ's death on the cross was intended to save all men and that grace is resistible.

The Reformed order of salvation may be found in outline in Calvin's *Institutes*, III; but again, this order has been further elaborated by later Reformed theologians. In the Reformed view the application of the redemption wrought by Christ on the cross is an activity of the Holy Spirit, and is to be traced in a series of acts and processes until perfect blessedness is reached. The Reformed order may be taken as (1) effectual calling, issuing in (2) regeneration, (3) faith, leading to (4) justification, and (5) sanctification, ultimately resulting in (6) glorification. Some of these experiences are synchronous, however, and the stages in such cases must be regarded as of logical rather than of chronological sequence.

G. N. M. Collins

Bibliography. H. Kuiper, *By Grace Alone;* J. Murray, *Redemption Accomplished and Applied.*

Orders, Holy. Holy orders usually refers to the major orders of the ministry in an episcopal church. In the Anglican and the Orthodox churches these are the bishops, priests, and deacons. In the Roman Church, where the episcopate and the presbyterate are counted as one order, the three are bishop-priests, deacons, and subdeacons. The minor orders are not usually included in the term "holy orders," for they really refer to laymen set apart for special tasks rather than to clergy in the proper sense of the term. Admission to holy orders is by ordination, the important ceremony being the laying on of hands. It is this which distinguishes ordination to the major orders from that to the minor orders. In the former the minister of ordination is always the bishop (though certain exceptions appear to have occurred occasionally), but the minor orders may sometimes be conveyed by others.

Unlike Roman Catholics and the Orthodox, Anglicans do not officially regard ordination as a sacrament (though some Anglicans do in point of fact hold this view). The official formularies restrict sacraments to ordinances instituted by Christ. Since there is no conclusive evidence that he enjoined ordination, it is not properly a sacrament. It would naturally be expected that a man cannot receive orders outside the church; but, especially in the West, it is usually held that a validly consecrated bishop conveys valid orders, even though he be in heresy or schism. On this principle the Roman Church does not reordain those it receives from Orthodoxy.

L. Morris

See also Major Orders; Ordain, Ordination.

Orders, Major. *See* Major Orders.

Orders, Minor. *See* MINOR ORDERS.

Ordo Salutis. *See* ORDER OF SALVATION.

Origen (*ca.* 185–*ca.* 254). In his fusion of Greek thought with biblical exposition, Origen was the greatest theologian of the early Greek Church. The famed Catechetical School at Alexandria reached its zenith under his tutelage. The son of a martyr, he took Matt. 19:12 literally and castrated himself in order to instruct his female students without fear of scandal. At the request of a church sorely beset by a multiplicity of deviant doctrines, he traveled widely and defended the orthodox faith against pagans, Jews, and heretics. His *Against Celsus,* a response to a pagan treatise attacking Christianity, stands as a monument of Christian apologetic.

His *Fundamental Doctrines* sets forth Christian theology on a scale previously unknown to the church. He argued powerfully for the inspiration and authority of Scripture, though he valued allegorical and typological meanings above the literal sense. In his concern for biblical scholarship he produced the *Hexapla,* an edition of the OT with Hebrew text, Greek transliteration, and available Greek translations in parallel columns—a monumental work. He held that certain cardinal principles were clearly laid out in Scripture, while on other matters Christians were free to speculate. Among his speculations were the beliefs that souls who had erred in a former life were placed upon earth in a human body as part of a purifying process and that all beings, even the devil and his angels, would ultimately be reclaimed and restored by God's grace.

Origen affirmed God as Creator of all things, Christ as eternal Son and Word, and the Holy Spirit—each member distinct from the others yet together forming a unity. This Trinitarianism provided a basis for orthodox thinkers such as Athanasius, Jerome, and the Cappadocians. On the other hand, he sometimes spoke of the Son and Holy Spirit as subject to the Father, a view which led others into subordinationism and ultimately Arianism.

He died as a result of the Decian persecution. Though three centuries later, in 553, he was declared a heretic, Origen must chiefly be remembered for the power and understanding with which he developed, propounded, and defended the major doctrines of the Bible. C. C. KROEGER

See also SUBORDINATIONISM.

Bibliography. C. Bigg, *The Christian Platonists of Alexandria;* H. Chadwick, *Christianity and Classical Tradition;* J. Daniélou, *Origen;* B. Drewery, *Origen on the Doctrine of Grace;* R. M. Grant, *Earliest Lives of Jesus;* R. A. Greer, *Origen;* R. P. C. Hanson, *Allegory and Event* and *Origen's Doctrine of Tradition;* J. M. Rist, *Eros and Psyche: Studies in Plato, Plotinus, and Origen.*

Original Righteousness. *See* RIGHTEOUSNESS, ORIGINAL.

Original Sin. *See* SIN.

Origin of Man. *See* MAN, ORIGIN OF.

Origin of the Soul. *See* SOUL.

Origin of the Universe. Heb. 11:3 tells us that the universe was created by God and implies that our full comprehension of this awesome event, or process, comes by faith.

If there are two laws which are accepted by all scientists, they are the first and second laws of thermodynamics. The first one states that neither energy nor matter can be created or destroyed, but that both are eternally existent in some form. The second may be stated as follows: in a closed system, disorder is always increasing. There are, of course, those who doubt the existence of a God who supernaturally created the universe. If there is no God, the first law of thermodynamics demands that the universe has always existed. But, by the second law, if the universe has always existed, it would have become disordered, or run down, completely by now. Obviously this is not the case. Therefore naturalism leads to a dilemma. Either the laws of thermodynamics are not correct, or the universe is not a closed system. Although this dilemma is not always recognized, it is real. A common method of bypassing this dilemma is to propose that the universe began with a giant explosion. However, the "big bang" theory, whether it is correct or not, does not solve the dilemma. For the Christian there is no dilemma. The universe is not a closed system, but has been acted on by an external God.

Another problem for naturalists is the question of contingency. Why are the laws of nature what they are? There is no rational explanation for them, no reason they could not have been something else, nothing for laws and physical constants to be contingent on. This is no problem for believers, who assume nature's laws and constants to be contingent upon the activity of a supernatural God, who has designed them for the good of his creation.

Belief in a timeless God, who created the universe from nothing, is certainly intellectually defensible as well as taught by Scripture. Some versions of the Bible interpret Gen. 1:1 as referring to the origin of the entire universe, but this interpretation is not certain. It may refer to the creation of the solar system, or the earth in a universe which had been created previously. Gen. 1:14–19 may mean that the universe at large, including the other bodies of the solar system, was created after the earth was. However, this interpretation is not required. It seems more likely that the events of the fourth day are described as if from the earth's surface and that the earth's cloud cover was parted for the first time on the fourth day to reveal heavenly bodies that had already been in existence since the first day, or because of previous creative acts.

Eph. 1:19–20 speaks of the power of God at work in raising Christ from death. Such power is incomprehensible to scientists, economists, and energy experts, because it is power able not just to move something but to reverse time. No governmental agency or university in the world can turn a single fallen brown leaf, however small, into a live green one. But God raised the dead to life. In other words, God's power is somehow able to stop or reverse the effects of the second law of thermodynamics, preventing disorder from occurring or creating order out of disorder. This same divine power was used to create the universe from nothing, again going miraculously above and around this law. An amazing aspect of this concept, according to Eph. 1:19–20, is that this same power, the power that created all things, is working now in Christians.

Since there is ambiguity about whether or not Gen. 1:1, 14–19 refers to the earth or to the entire universe, the role of the Trinity in the origin of the universe is not certain. However, it seems likely that each person of the Trinity played a role in that origin. Gen. 1:2 may refer to the Holy Spirit, and Gen. 1:26 probably refers to all three persons of the Trinity. Certainly the Son was involved as a creative agent (John 1:3–4, 10; Col. 1:15–17). Not only was he involved in the creation, but he continues to sustain it (Col. 1:17).

The Bible teaches that God is separate from, preexistent to, but intimately involved in, the universe he originated. M. La Bar

See also Creation, Doctrine of.

Bibliography. R. E. D. Clark, *The Universe: Plan or Accident?* W. L. Craig, "Philosophical and Scientific Pointers to Creatio ex Nihilo," *JASA* 32:5–12; S. L. Jaki, *The Road of Science and the Ways to God;* C. S. Lewis, *Miracles;* G. Mulfinger, "Examining the Cosmogonies—a Historical Review," in *Why Not Creation?* ed. W. E. Lammerts; F. Schaeffer, *Genesis in Space and Time.*

Orr, James (1844–1913). Noted Scottish theologian. Born in Glasgow, he graduated from Glasgow University as M.A. and then B.D. (1871). For the next twenty years he served as parish minister in the United Presbyterian Church. In 1891 he left his parish in Hawick to become professor of church history in the United Presbyterian Divinity Hall. He became professor of apologetics and dogmatics in the newly formed Trinity College of Glasgow in 1900, retaining this position until his death. An influential writer as well as lecturer, Orr won a prize for *The Sabbath: Scripturally and Practically Considered* (1886). More famous was *The Christian View of God and the World* (1893). In 1897 he gave two series of lectures in the United States (at Western and Auburn theological seminaries), which were later published as *The Progress of Dogma* (his masterpiece) and *Neglected Factors in the Study of the Early Progress of Christianity.*

Orr had profound firsthand knowledge of modern German and British philosophy and theology. Like his colleagues George Adam Smith and James Denney he held a basic evangelical position, but wished to restate the faith in interaction with modern trends in philosophy and theology. He accepted theistic evolution and endeavored to explain the development of Christian doctrine in terms of a divinely implanted law of continual progress. Over against the liberal German Adolf Harnack, who saw the development of dogma as an ultimate "hellenization" and falsification of the original "simple gospel," Orr explained the advance of church doctrine as a natural, wholesome movement, following a divine logic according to which the church discovers more about the inner connections and implications of the living truth recorded in Scripture. Orr believed there was a parallel between the historical course of dogma and the scientific order of the textbooks on systematic theology. Thus textbooks (without knowing it) begin—as did doctrinal history—with apologetics, and develop—as did history—with the doctrine of God; then go to man, to the person of Christ, to salvation, and finally to eschatology. Hence, Orr theorized that by divine inner necessity the logical, systematic statement of theology is a reflection of its temporal development. D. F. Kelly

Bibliography. P. Toon, "James Orr: Defender of the Faith," *GM,* Aug. 1972, and *The Development of Doctrine in the Church.*

Orthodox Tradition, The. The theological tradition, generally associated with the national churches of the eastern Mediterranean and eastern Europe and principally with the Ecumenical

Patriarchate of Constantinople, whose distinguishing characteristic consists in preservation of the integrity of the doctrines taught by the fathers of the seven ecumenical councils of the fourth through eighth centuries. Through medieval times the churches of the Orthodox tradition were mainly Greek-speaking; in modern times they have been predominantly Slavic.

Nature of Orthodox Theology. The first two councils, Nicaea I (325) and Constantinople I (381), laid the foundation of Orthodox theology by adoption of the statement known commonly as the Nicene Creed. This formula established the primary principle of Trinitarianism, declaring the substantial equality of God the Son with God the Father, specifically in refutation of Arianism.

The third council, Ephesus (431), rejected Nestorianism by affirming that in Christ divinity and humanity united in a single person, the Word made flesh. In its primary thrust this affirmation set the premise of Orthodox Christology; it also set the premise for the development of doctrine concerning Mary. In that the Christ was God incarnate, the Virgin was "Mother of God" (*Theotokos,* "god-bearer"); she was not simply mother of an ordinary human. In consequence of this declaration Orthodoxy expressed high regard for Mary, positing her perpetual virginity and sinless life while remaining skeptical of the later Catholic dogmas of the immaculate conception and assumption.

The next three councils, Chalcedon (451), Constantinople II (553), and Constantinople III (680), confronted the heresy of monophysitism in its evolving forms, further defining for Orthodoxy its Christology, which states that in the one person of Christ there are two entire natures, the human and divine, including two wills.

The seventh council, Nicaea II (787), in the midst of the struggle over iconoclasm, defined the doctrine of images representing Christ and the saints, requiring that the faithful venerate, but not worship, them. In the aftermath of this council, whose decrees were not approved by the Roman papacy (although they did not conflict with Catholic teaching), the divergence of Orthodoxy from Western Christian theology became increasingly pronounced. In a special way painted icons became symbols of Orthodoxy, inasmuch as they united correct doctrine and correct worship—the twin meanings of the word—and this perception led to the designation of the final restoration of icons in Byzantine churches on the first Sunday of Lent in 843 as the "triumph of Orthodoxy." For Orthodoxy, the artistic image reiterated the truth that the invisible God had become visible in the incarnate Son of God who was the perfect image of God; the image channeled the presence of the person depicted to the one contemplating it, as the incarnate Word had brought God to man.

Since Nicaea II no genuinely ecumenical council has been possible, owing to the defection (in Orthodoxy's view) of the Roman See, and thus no new absolutely definitive declaration of Orthodox dogma has been possible. From this fact derives Orthodoxy's self-conscious identity as the church of the seven councils and its sense of mission in preserving the faith of the ancient fathers of the church. But Orthodox theology did not stagnate in subsequent centuries, as changing circumstances and developments in others' theologies challenged Orthodox thinkers to refine and restate their conceptions of the faith presupposed by the patristic decrees. Such formulations have acquired considerable authority by approvals enunciated in local councils or by long-term common consent within Orthodoxy, although they do not have the canonical authority of the ecumenical decrees which Orthodoxy views to have been divinely inspired and therefore infallible. When a statement receives widespread acceptance among Orthodox churches, it acquires the status of "symbolic book."

The theological dimension of the schism with Western Catholicism rested primarily in Orthodoxy's rejection of Rome's claim that its bishop was the unique successor of Peter with the consequent prerogative to define dogma. While granting a certain primacy of honor to the papacy, Orthodoxy saw all right-teaching bishops as equally successors of Peter, from which derived the requirement that only genuinely ecumenical, episcopal councils possessed the power of binding the conscience of the faithful. Therefore Orthodoxy has resisted those doctrines which it views as Roman innovations.

The most celebrated point of controversy between Orthodoxy and Western theology arose over the insertion of the *filioque* clause into the Nicene Creed sometime after the eighth century. Besides rejecting this nonconciliar tampering with the decrees of the fathers, Orthodoxy saw in the assertion that the Holy Spirit "proceeds from the Father and the Son" the presupposition of two originating principles within the Godhead, negating the integrity of the Trinity. Most Orthodox thinkers could accept a formulation whereby the Spirit proceeds "from the Father through, or with, the Son," following the chief medieval Orthodox teacher, John of Damascus. But until an ecumenical council acted, this would remain merely "theological teaching" (*theologoumena*).

On the other doctrinal questions where Catholic innovations might be identified, Orthodoxy has been less firm in its denunciations than in the *filioque* issue. Regarding the state of persons after death, Orthodoxy rejects the notion of purgatory as a place distinct from heaven and hell. At the same time it concedes that there is an intermediate period of temporal pain in which penance for sins is carried out by those destined for heaven; moreover, full blessedness, even for saints, is not achieved until after Christ's final judgment. Prayers for the dead, therefore, can have efficacy. Following the Western resolution of the dogma of the real presence in the Eucharist, Orthodox writers adopted the literal translation of "transubstantiation" into Greek (*metousiōsis*). But in a distinction that had both theological and liturgical significance, Orthodoxy insisted that the miracle of transformation did not occur through the celebrant's enunciation of the words, "This is my body," but by the invocation of the Holy Spirit in the *epiclesis:* "Send thy Holy Spirit . . . so as to make the bread to be the body of thy Christ." This difference signifies Orthodoxy's greater sensitivity to the Spirit than has generally been evident in the West.

Orthodoxy agreed with Catholicism in acknowledging seven sacraments while not insisting upon the absolute significance of the number. The two sacraments which were clearly evangelical, baptism and Communion, along with confirmation (called chrismation by Orthodoxy and administered immediately after baptism), occupied a higher place than the rest. Orthodox writers regularly criticized the West's failure to use immersion as the proper mode of baptism, although most acknowledged the validity of aspersion in the Trine name. The Orthodox baptize by triple immersion, baptizing both adults and infants. Orthodoxy's use of leavened bread in the Eucharist, instead of the unleavened wafers of the West, was mostly a liturgical matter, although it was given theological meaning by the explanation that the leaven signified evangelical joy in contrast to the "Mosaic" regime of Catholic practice.

Its doctrine of the church distinguishes Orthodoxy most clearly from all other theologies. According to this doctrine the visible church is the body of Christ, a communion of believers, headed by a bishop and united by the Eucharist, in which God dwells. As such, although individual members are fallible sinners, the church is held to be infallible. This true church by definition is the Orthodox Church, which is "one, holy, catholic, and apostolic," from which other churches are separated. That is, the church consists of those believers who remain in fellowship with, and submission to, the concert of historic patriarchates, Jerusalem, Antioch, Alexandria, Constantinople, and Rome. (When Rome separated from the concert, Moscow assumed membership in the pentarchy, although Rome's place remains reserved for it to resume if it will renounce its obstinacy.)

The infallibility of the church validates the authority of tradition on a par with that of Scripture. Moreover, tradition established both canon and interpretation of that Scripture and thus takes logical precedence over it. How to determine precisely what tradition teaches, however, remains a partially open question for Orthodoxy, since no single office is acknowledged to have definitive authority for the whole church, such as the papacy has for Roman Catholicism. In principle the church speaks authoritatively through episcopal councils; but this claim only moves the issue back one step because it raises the question of what validates which meetings of bishops as genuine rather than "robber" councils (as the Council of Constantinople of 754 is regularly designated). In the end, Orthodoxy trusts that the Holy Spirit abides in the church and in his own mysterious way leads and preserves his people in all truth. This trust produces, in practice, a measure of freedom within what could otherwise be a stifling traditionalism.

History of Orthodox Theology. The history of Orthodoxy may be divided into two periods: Byzantine and modern. During the millennium of the Empire of Byzantium, to 1453, Orthodox theology matured in close association with it. Emperors convoked councils, after the example of Constantine I and the Nicene Council, and pronounced on theological matters, providing some weak basis for speaking of "caesaropapism" in the Byzantine age. In this period three distinctive emphases of Orthodoxy emerged: theology as apophacticism, knowledge as illumination, and salvation as deification.

Relying principally on the sixth century writer Dionysius the Pseudo-Areopagite, Orthodox writers insisted that God in his nature is beyond any understanding. Humans can know nothing about the being of God, and therefore all theological statements must be of a negative, or apophactic, form: God is unchanging, immovable, infinite, etc. Even a seemingly positive affirmation has only negative significance; for example, to say, "God is Spirit," is actually to affirm his noncorporeality. Theology, then, is not a science of God, which is impossible, but of his revelation. That which is known is not necessarily true of God but is what God chooses to disclose, although in that sense it is indeed true knowledge.

Such a theology of negation led to the elevation of spiritual experience to at least an equal role with rationality as an epistemological principle in theology. Maximus Confessor, Orthodoxy's chief twelfth century teacher, affirmed: "A perfect mind is one which, by true faith, in supreme ignorance knows the supremely unknowable one." Knowledge of God comes from illumination, the inner vision of true light, for "God is light." From this perception derived Orthodoxy's characteristic fascination with the transfiguration of Jesus, when the light of his deity was supremely revealed to the apostles. It also fostered heyschasm, in which the mystic's vision of divinity became a theologically significant enterprise. It is for this reason that what is called Orthodox theology is also designated with equal validity "Orthodox spirituality." The chief synthesizer of this aspect of Orthodoxy was Gregory Palamas in the fourteenth century.

The Orthodox concept of salvation as deification undergirded the contemplative methodology implied in the illumination view. Only the "pure in heart" see God, and purity comes only by divine grace in the economy of redemption. Those who are redeemed through the incarnation, whom the NT designates "sons of God" and "partakers of the divine nature," are deified; that is, they become created, in contrast to uncreated, gods. "God became man that we might be made God," said Athanasius of Alexandria; and Maximus Confessor declared: "All that God is, except for an identity in nature, one becomes when one is deified by grace." With this personalistic view of salvation, Orthodoxy diverged from the juridical emphasis which the West inherited through Augustine of Hippo, whom Orthodoxy could not comfortably accept as a Doctor of the Church. Orthodox theology viewed man as called to know God and share his life, to be saved, not by God's external activity or by one's understanding of propositional truths, but by being himself deified.

In sum, the Byzantine period established Orthodoxy's greater mysticism, intuition, and corporatism in contrast to the West's philosophical, scholastic, and forensic orientation.

In the period after 1453 the two events which most influenced the evolution of Orthodoxy were the fall of the Byzantine Empire and the division of Western Christianity. Termination of imperial patronage increased the autonomy of the episcopacy and promoted the Russian contribution to the Orthodox heritage; Reformation theology made it possible for Orthodoxy to select from several alternative expressions of Christian doctrine. To be sure, these developments tended to place Orthodoxy on the defensive and cast it in the role of respondent rather than actor, in which it frequently appeared to be the reactionary wing of Christendom. Nevertheless, that Orthodoxy's vigor remained was evidenced in the writings of several theologians, and the ecumenism of the twentieth century has opened new possibilities for an Orthodox contribution to theology.

Melanchthon made the initial Protestant overture to Orthodoxy when he sent a Greek translation of the Augsburg Confession to Patriarch Joasaph of Constantinople, requesting that the latter find it a faithful rendition of Christian truth. His successor, Jeremiah, responded over twenty years later, condemning numerous Protestant "errors," including justification by faith alone, *sola Scriptura*, rejection of icons and invocation of saints, Augustinian predestination, and *filioque*.

A quite different response to the Reformation came from the patriarch elected in 1620, Cyril Lucaris, who composed a confession which articulated an essentially Calvinist system. Cyril's work proved to be an aberration in the history of Orthodoxy; it was formally condemned after his death in 1638 by a synod of Constantinople and by a patriarchal synod in Jerusalem thirty-four years later. But it elicited two important statements of Orthodox doctrine. In the first, Russian leadership appeared when Metropolitan Peter Mogila of Kiev composed his confession, a thorough refutation of Cyril's, in affirmation of the received body of Orthodoxy. Mogila's work was approved, with amendments, by the Eastern patriarchs in 1643. The second was the confession of Patriarch Dositheos of Jerusalem, approved by the synod of 1672.

These two documents remained the standard definition of Orthodoxy in the modern period. They aligned Orthodoxy with the Catholic side in most of its chief doctrinal disputes with Reformed theology—e.g., the relation of tradition to Scripture, veneration of saints and images, number and meaning of sacraments, faith and works in salvation. On only two questions did they sympathize with Protestants: papal authority and canon of Scripture. Orthodoxy continued to resist both Protestants and Catholics in their mutual agreement on *filioque* and the Augustinian understanding of original sin. Orthodoxy rejects original sin; man is born mortal and therefore sins, instead of the other way around, as the West commonly states the matter.

But the significance of Orthodoxy's agreements with either Catholicism or Protestantism was more apparent than real inasmuch as the respective principles of authority differed fundamentally. For Orthodoxy, dogmatic authority remained rooted in the community of the church, represented by the episcopal succession from the apostles, not in the supremacy of the papacy nor in evangelical exegesis of Scripture, both of which to the Orthodox mind represented the domination of rationalism, legalism, and individualism over the true believing and worshiping fellowship of the faithful. To designate this community principle modern Russian theologians provided the definitive, but untranslatable, word *sobornost'* (approximately, "communion"). "*Sobornost'* is the soul of Orthodoxy," declared the nineteenth century lay theologian Alexis Khomiakov.

After the middle of the nineteenth century the most creative developments within Orthodoxy came from Russian writers, such as Vladimir Solovyev, Nikolai Berdyaev, Sergei Bulgakov, Georges Florvosky, and from professors of the Russian seminaries in Paris and New York, notably Alexander Schmemann and John Meyendorff. Their work is too recent for it to be incorporated into the essence of Orthodoxy, but it testifies to the continuing vitality of the tradition. These men have, each in his own way, worked actively for the reunification of Christendom. The burden of their ecumenical testimony has been that genuine unity can be achieved not on the basis of the least common denominator among Christian churches but in agreement upon the totality of the common tradition contained in the ecumenical councils and authentically preserved only by Orthodoxy. P. D. STEEVES

Bibliography. John of Damascus, *Writings;* G. Maloney, *A History of Orthodox Theology Since 1453;* V. Lossky, *The Mystical Theology of the Eastern Church;* J. Meyendorff, *Byzantine Theology;* J. Pelikan, *The Christian Tradition* III, The Spirit of Eastern Christendom; *The Seven Ecumenical Councils of the Undivided Church, NPNF,* XIV; P. Schaff, ed., *The Creeds of Christendom,* II, 445–542; A. Schmemann, *The Historical Road of Eastern Orthodoxy;* N. Zernov, *Eastern Christendom;* K. Ware, *The Orthodox Way.*

Orthodoxy. The English equivalent of Greek *orthodoxia* (from *orthos,* "right," and *doxa,* "opinion"), meaning right belief, as opposed to heresy or heterodoxy. The term is not biblical; no secular or Christian writer uses it before the second century, though the verb *orthodoxein* is in Aristotle (*Nicomachean Ethics* 1151a19). The word expresses the idea that certain statements accurately embody the revealed truth content of Christianity and are therefore in their own nature normative for the universal church. This idea is rooted in the NT insistence that the gospel has a specific factual and theological content (I Cor. 15:1–11; Gal. 1:6–9; I Tim. 6:3; II Tim. 4:3–4; etc.), and that no fellowship exists between those who accept the apostolic standard of Christological teaching and those who deny it (I John 4:1–3; II John 7–11).

The idea of orthodoxy became important in the church in and after the second century, through conflict first with Gnosticism and then with other Trinitarian and Christological errors. The preservation of Christianity was seen to require the maintenance of orthodoxy in these matters. Strict acceptance of the "rule of faith" (*regula fidei*) was demanded as a condition of communion, and creeds explicating this "rule" were multiplied.

The Eastern church styles itself "orthodox," and condemns the Western church as heterodox for (among other things) including the *filioque* clause in its creed.

Seventeenth century Protestant theologians, especially conservative Lutherans, stressed the importance of orthodoxy in relation to the soteriology of the Reformation creeds. Liberal Protestantism naturally regards any quest for orthodoxy as misguided and deadening. J. I. PACKER

See also HERESY; SCHISM.

Bibliography. H. E. W. Turner, *The Pattern of Christian Faith.*

Osiander, Andreas (1498–1552). German theologian and Reformer, follower of Martin Luther. Osiander was ordained a Roman Catholic priest at Eichstätt in 1520. Within two years he had embraced Lutheranism, attending the Marburg Colloquy of 1529, the Augsburg Diet of 1530, and signing the Smalcald Articles of 1537. His niece, Margaret Osiander, became the wife of English reformer Thomas Cranmer. A biblical scholar, Osiander prepared a revised version of the Vulgate and a harmony of the four Gospels. By the midsixteenth century he was caught up in controversy. In 1548 Emperor Charles V proclaimed as imperial law the Augsburg Interim, a document prepared by theologians of various religious backgrounds and intended to facilitate cooperation between Protestants and Roman Catholics until a national church council could settle "the religious question." Osiander's refusal to consent to the Augsburg Interim caused his removal as preacher and reformer in Nürnberg. Then he became a professor of theology at the newly founded University of Königsberg in Prussia and afterward was appointed vice-president of the bishopric of Samländ.

His work *De Justificatione,* published in 1550, involved Osiander in disputes over the nature of justification. This "Osiandrian controversy" needs to be seen in the broader context of Lutheran church life in this period. Following the death of Martin Luther the Lutherans had divided over several issues. Two parties appeared: the Philippists (followers of Philip Melanchthon) and the Gnesio-Lutherans (followers of Matthias Flacius). One issue caused the adiaphoristic controversy, occasioned by the Augsburg Interim and Melanchthon's willingness to make concessions in what he felt to be adiaphora ("neutral areas"), such as episcopacy and the ceremonies of the Mass. Gnesio-Lutherans denied that there were adiaphora. Then came the Majoristic controversy, when Georg Major maintained that good works were essential to salvation. This led to the antinomian controversy (over the role of the law in the believer's life), the synergistic controversy (over the role of the will in salvation), and the sacramentarian controversy (over the mode of Christ's presence in the Lord's Supper). Into this context came the Osiandrian controversy, over the doctrine of justification. Osiander wrote of the orthodox Lutherans: "They teach [doctrines] colder than ice, that we are accounted righteous only on account of the remission of sins, and not also on account of the righteousness of the Christ dwelling in us by faith. God is not indeed so unjust as to regard him as righteous in whom there is really nothing of true righteousness." For Osiander the justification of the sinner was not simply an imputation of Christ's righteousness through a forensic declaration of innocence; it was an actual impartation of righteousness through the "indwelling" of Christ in the believer. Justification becomes renovation, Christ living within "to recall the dead to life." This position, neither Roman Catholic nor Philippist nor Gnesio-Lutheran, caused Osiander's condemnation. Duke Albert of Prussia executed Osiander in 1552 before a psalm-singing crowd, and in 1556 Osiandrians were banned from Prussia. C. G. FRY

See also ADIAPHORA, ADIAPHORISTS; ANTINOMIANISM; IMPUTATION; MAJORISTIC CONTROVERSY; SYNERGISM.

Bibliography. W. D. Allbeck, *Studies in the Lutheran Confessions;* R. Seeberg, *Text-book of the History of Doctrines.*

Osterwald, Jean Frederic (1663–1747). Swiss pietist preacher who so revived the church at Neuchâtel that his influence spread to Geneva and thence to England, France, and the Netherlands. Osterwald's strength was his ability to teach a vibrant Christianity. He first attracted notice through his effective catechetical instruction of children. His sermons also were primarily a means to teach revival of the church through the cultivation of personal piety and the denunciation of doctrinal disputes. He was such an effective teacher of this view that his sermons were very popular.

Osterwald believed, with the German pietists, that Christianity had become especially vulnerable to atheistical attacks and doctrinal wrangling due to a lack of piety. In 1699 he published a book based on his sermons entitled *A Treatise Concerning the Causes of the Present Corruption of Christians and the Remedies Thereof.* It was so popular that it was republished in England. This book has value for at least three reasons. First, it is a systematic examination of those forces which destroy Christian piety. The book is divided into the study of nine personal and seven external causes for the decline of Christian piety. Each cause is further analyzed into its several parts. Thus it offers a clear analysis that is still useful today. Second, the book is valuable as a compendium of excuses raised by Christians to avoid piety and offers effective answers to those excuses. It is therefore a useful handbook for the pietist who would like to revive his own church. Finally, the book offers a perspective on Christian attitudes of Osterwald's day. He regarded Anabaptists and Quakers as fanatics who were not sufficiently pious. His remedy for notorious sinners in the church, such as drunkards, was to excommunicate them. J. E. MENNELL

Otherworldliness. *See* WORLDLINESS AND OTHERWORLDLINESS.

Otto, Rudolf (1869–1937). German theologian and student of world religions whose work has had considerable influence in the middle and late twentieth century. Otto was born at Peine, near Hanover. He was educated at Erlangen and Göttingen, and in his mature years taught theology at Göttingen, Breslau, and Marburg.

He was a scholar who possessed a broad knowledge of comparative religion, Oriental thought, and the natural sciences. His knowledge of Oriental religion was enhanced by considerable travel in the East. Otto's interests were not merely scholarly, however. He was a committed churchman who believed that there was much room for improvement in the public worship experiences of Lutheran people. Part of the motivation for his scholarly work, therefore, was a concern for the worship experiences of the Lutheran Church. This emphasis on the experience of public worship was only one expression of Otto's wider interest in understanding the basic experience which underlies religious belief and commitment.

This concern and interest led to the research which culminated in *Das Heilige* (1917; ET *The Idea of the Holy*), which was his major work and which was hailed as one of the classics of religious psychology. The book went through fourteen German editions and was translated into several other languages. This work attempts to understand and explain those uncommon but very real moments when the soul is captured by an "ineffable Something." This dramatic religious experience is both nonrational and universal—we all encounter it at some time. Otto's claim is that this experience is the innermost core of all religions.

The claim that this experience is nonrational should not be misunderstood; Otto was aware of the important place of reason in religion. This is seen in the full title of the book: *The Idea of the Holy: An Inquiry into the Nonrational Factor in the Idea of the Divine and its Relation to the Rational.* It is also seen in the fact that he often referred to the rational and the nonrational as the "warp and woof" of religion. It was his conviction, however, that the theologians of his day had so overemphasized the place of reason in religion that a proper understanding of its nonrational aspect had been lost. *The Idea of the Holy* was his attempt to uncover the hidden nonrational experience which lay at the heart of all true religion.

This experience is difficult to define; it is perhaps best expressed as the sense of the Holy, although this too is inadequate. It is inadequate because this experience includes a clear "overplus of meaning," which he associates with the term "numinous," which in turn relates to an awareness of an object, a nonrational apprehension of a presence "out there." It is the awareness of something totally beyond our rational facilities, yet it is certainly "there." Man responds with humility and worship, since he is in the presence of the Holy. This experience, says Otto, is prior to all other religious phenomena. Otto's other works include *The Philosophy of Religion* and *Science and Religion.* J. D. Spiceland

See also Mysticism; Numinous, The.

Bibliography. E. L. Miller, *God and Reason.*

Outward Man. The AV translation of *ho exō anthrōpos,* an expression used by Paul in II Cor. 4:16: "Though our outward man perish, yet the inward man is renewed day by day." At first sight it appears that Paul is adopting the dualistic view of man held, for instance, by the Stoics, who regarded the soul as the "real" part of man and the body as a mere shell shed at death. But the contrast between inner and outer is illuminated by that between "the new man" and "the old man" in Eph. 4:22–24 and Col. 3:9–10. These terms characterize the old and the new life style; similarly, the outward parts of our human makeup are for Paul not merely physical but embody (literally) the power of sin and "the flesh," with which the Christian has to reckon in every part of his nature. Paul's use of the term "man" underlines that he is thinking more of a characteristic, than of part, of the human being. S. Motyer

See also Inner Man; Man, Old and New; Man, Doctrine of.

Bibliography. W. D. Stacey, *The Pauline View of Man.*

Overcome. The Christian idea of overcoming has its basis on the declaration of Jesus that he had overcome the world (John 16:33). The word "world" in this context is to be understood to denote all in the world that is antagonistic to the will of God. A stronger has come and disarmed these antagonistic forces (Luke 11:22), with the result that the Christian need fear them no longer.

This overcoming is described in two ways in I John. Believers are said to overcome (1) the wicked one (2:13–14) and those in whom the spirit of Antichrist breathes (4:4), and (2) the world (5:4–5). In the latter sense the "overcomers" show their genuineness by their attitude toward Jesus as Son of God, thus stressing that moral victory is inseparably linked with soundness of doctrine.

The believer must use good as a means of overcoming evil (Rom. 12:21), and his attitude toward his circumstances should be that of a superconqueror (Rom. 8:37). In the Apocalypse those who endure persecutions and resist false teachers are described as "overcomers" (2:7, 11, 17, 26; 3:5, 12, 21), and the promises of the future are reserved only for these (21:7). The central figure of the book, the slain but royal Lamb, presents the same paradox. As Lion of the tribe of Judah he prevails to open the book (5:5), and as the Lamb he will finally overcome all his enemies (17:14). This power to overcome is in contrast with the temporary power given to the beast (13:7). D. Guthrie

See also Godliness.

Overseer. The Greek word for "overseer," *episkopos,* was used in both religious and secular literature to describe one, divine or human, who watched over others for their good. Jesus is so described in I Pet. 2:25, where the concept of oversight is linked with that of shepherding. The same connection appears in Acts 20:28, addressed to the Ephesian elders. The fact that the *episkopoi* are here called both shepherds and elders (*presbyteroi*) suggests an identity between elder, pastor, and overseer. *Episkopoi* is used in Phil. 1:1 instead of *presbyteroi,* along with *diakonoi* (deacons). In Titus 1:5–9 the same group is called both *presbyteroi* and *episkopoi* (cf. I Tim. 3:1–7). *Episkopos* came to be used of an office of increasingly greater responsibility and dignity, and particularly of the bishop who cared for several congregations and their ministers. W. L. Liefeld

See also Bishop; Elder.

Owen, John (1616–1683). Puritan theologian committed to the congregational way of church government. Educated at Queen's College, Oxford, he became sympathetic to the cause of Puritanism within the Established Church. After his ordination he saw himself first as a presbyterian Puritan, but after careful study he adopted the congregational way and became its chief exponent for the rest of his life. He was a parish minister at Fordham and then Coggeshall in Essex from 1643 to 1651. During this period he accompanied Cromwell with the armies of Parliament first to Scotland and then to Ireland. In 1651 he was appointed dean of Christ Church, Oxford, a position which allowed him to seek to train godly and learned ministers for the Cromwellian state church, of which he was the senior architect. He added to this duty that of the vice-chancellorship of the university from 1652 to 1657. The 1650s saw Owen very influential not only at Oxford but also in matters of state in London. His commitment to congregational church government is seen in the part he played in the writing of the Savoy Declaration of Faith and Order (1658). With the change of political and religious direction in England in 1660, Owen was ejected from Christ Church and became a Nonconformist. He felt unable to minister within the national church, for not only did he reject episcopacy but he also rejected the idea of a written liturgy. For the next twenty years he was a leader of English Nonconformity and a pastor of a congregational church in London.

He is remembered today not primarily because of his important career as an educator and statesman but because of his theological writings, which were numerous and spread over forty years. He wrote on the major themes of high Calvinism (particular redemption, divine election, etc.), of traditional Catholic orthodoxy (Trinitarianism and Christology), of church polity, and of the pursuit of holiness. While he has great depth and insight as a writer, his style is heavy and his thoughts are complex. P. Toon

Bibliography. P. Toon, *God's Statesman, the Life of Dr. John Owen* and (ed.), *The Correspondence of Dr. John Owen.*

Oxford Group Movement. *See* Moral Re-armament.

Oxford Movement. An important religious development within the Church of England in the nineteenth century in response to the critical rationalism, skepticism, lethargy, liberalism, and immorality of the day. Emphasizing a return to the traditions of the church, the leaders of the movement longed for a higher standard of worship, piety, and devotion among clergy and church members.

Guided by and receiving its impetus from Oxford University men, the movement also protested state interference in the affairs of the church. On July 14, 1833, in response to the English government's bill reducing bishoprics in Ireland, John Keble preached the sermon "National Apostacy" from the university pulpit. He accused the government of infringing on "Christ's Church" and of disavowing the principle of apostolic succession of the bishops of the Church of England. Insisting that salvation was possible only through the sacraments, Keble defended the Church of England as a divine institution. During the same year John Henry Newman began to publish *Tracts for the Times,* a series of pamphlets by members of the University of Oxford that supported and propagated the beliefs of the movement. They were widely circulated, and the term "Tractarianism" has often been used for the early stages of the Oxford Movement or, indeed, as a synonym for the movement itself.

It is ironic that these tracts (which were supposed to argue "against Popery and Dissent") would lead some of the writers and readers into embracing the Roman Catholic Church. These men found it increasingly impossible to adhere to church polity and practice on Protestant terms. When Newman argued in Tract 90 (1841) that the Thirty-nine Articles of the Church of England were in harmony with genuine Roman Catholicism, he was attacked with such furor that the series of tracts was brought to an end. Early in 1845, realizing that they would never be allowed to be Anglicans while holding Roman Catholic views, several Oxford reformers joined the Roman Catholic Church. Newman defected later that year, and by 1864 nearly one thousand ministers, theological leaders, and Anglican church members followed his lead. In 1864 Newman's *Apologia pro Vita Sua* was published, explaining his departure from the Church of England and defending his choice of the Roman Church as the one true church. Newman was made a Roman Catholic cardinal in 1879.

After the defections in 1845 the movement was no longer dominated by Oxford men and became more fragmented in its emphases. Edward B. Pusey, professor of Hebrew at Oxford and a contributor to *Tracts,* emerged as the leader of the Anglo-Catholic party, which continued to push for doctrinal modifications and a reunion between the Anglican and Roman churches. Other groups sought to promote High Church ritual within Anglicanism. Many of the sympathizers the Oxford Movement had gained at its inception (before anti-Reformation tendencies were observed) continued to uphold the primary goals and spiritual fervor of the movement. This has had a great significance upon the theological development, polity, and religious life of the Church of England for over a century. Anglican eucharistic worship was transformed, spiritual discipline and monastic orders were revived, social concern was fostered, and an ecumenical spirit has developed in the Church of England.

While the Oxford Movement was opposed in print by traditional churchmen as well as liberal academic thinkers, perhaps no one group matched the evangelicals in their enormous output of literature—printed sermons, tracts, articles, books, and pamphlets against the Tractarians. These dissenting "peculiars," as some Oxford reformers called them, believed that the Oxford "heresy" was both anti-Reformation and antiscriptural. They fought to ensure that the English church would maintain the Protestant character of its theology. And yet even evangelical writers in England at the end of the nineteenth century noted that the Oxford Movement also brought positive contributions to English Christianity—contributions that could not be disregarded. D. A. RAUSCH

See also NEWMAN, JOHN HENRY; PUSEY, EDWARD BOUVERIE; KEBLE, JOHN; ANGLO-CATHOLICISM.

Bibliography. R. W. Church, *The Oxford Movement, 1833–1845;* E. Fairweather, ed., *The Oxford Movement;* P. Toon, *Evangelical Theology, 1833–1856: A Response to Tractarianism;* T. Dearing, *Wesleyan and Tractarian Worship.*

Pp

Pacifism. A term, derived from the Latin word for peacemaking, that has been applied to a spectrum of positions covering nearly all attitudes toward war. On one extreme pacifist designates any person who desires peace, thus describing those who wage war as much as those who refuse participation in war. On the other extreme pacifism also describes renunciation of force and coercion in all forms. A mediating definition sometimes distinguishes nonresistance, which renounces force in all forms, from pacifism, which rejects participation in war but allows the use of nonviolent kinds of force. It makes most sense to reserve the term "pacifism" for that part of the spectrum which includes at least a refusal to participate in war. Those individuals who refuse to do this are called conscientious objectors.

History. Pacifism is one of three historic attitudes of the church toward war. In some form it has existed throughout the entire history of the Christian church. Since the fourth century it has often been overshadowed by the just war theory and the concept of crusade, or aggressive war for a holy cause. The early church was pacifist. Prior to A.D. 170–80 there are no records of soldiers in the Roman army. Following that epoch there are both Christians in the army and also writings which opposed the practice from church fathers such as Tertullian. Some Christian writers sanctioned police functions and military service, provided these did not entail bloodshed and killing. Under Emperor Constantine, who closely identified the interests of the empire with the interests of Christianity, Christian soldiers were common. During the rule of Theodosius II only Christians could serve as soldiers. When confronted by the barbarian invasions that seemed to threaten Roman civilization and thus the Christianity identified with it, Augustine of Hippo developed the idea, rooted in Roman Stoic philosophy and first given a Christian formulation by Ambrose, which has come to be called the just war theory. It intended not to advocate war but to limit the conditions under which Christians could participate in war, accepting it as an unfortunately necessary tool for preserving the civilization to which Christianity belonged. Since Augustine some form of the just war theory has been the majority position of most Christian traditions.

In the Middle Ages the idea of the crusade developed from another attempt by the church to limit warfare. The peace of God and the truce of God limited times for fighting and banned clerical participation in war. To enforce these limitations the church itself came to conduct warring activity. This act associated war with a holy cause, namely the enforcement of peace. This association developed into the crusades, the holy cause of rescuing the Holy Land from the Moslems. Pope Urban II preached the first crusade in 1095. In either religious or secular versions the crusade has been a part of the church's tradition ever since.

During the Middle Ages it was the sectarians who kept alive the pacifist tradition. Groups of Waldensians and Franciscan Tertiaries refused military service. The Cathari were pacifist. The Hussite movement developed two branches, a crusading one under blind general Jan Zizka and a pacifist one under Peter Chelciky.

The period of the Renaissance and Reformation saw assertions of all three attitudes toward war. Renaissance humanism developed a pacifist impulse, of which Erasmus is one of the most important examples. Humanist pacifism appealed to such philosophical and theological principles as the common humanity and brotherhood of all persons as children of God, the follies of war, and the ability of rational individuals to govern themselves and their states on the basis of reason.

All Protestant churches except the Anabaptists accepted the inherited tradition of the just war. Luther identified two kingdoms—of God and of the world. While he rejected the idea of crusade, his respect for the state as ordained by God to preserve order and to punish evil in the worldly realm made him a firm supporter of the just war approach. The Reformed tradition accepted the crusade concept, seeing the state not only as the preserver of order but also as a means of furthering the cause of true religion. Zwingli died in a religious war; Calvin left the door open to rebellion against an unjust ruler; and Beza developed not only the right but the duty of Christians to revolt against tyranny. Cromwell's pronouncement of divine blessing on the massacre of Catholics at Drogheda illustrates the crusade idea in English Puritanism.

Alongside the wars of religion of the sixteenth and seventeenth centuries arose the pacifist traditions which for the most part have preserved their opposition to war until the present time. Pacifism emerged as the dominant position of the Anabaptists, who rejected not only the sword of war but also refused to engage in political life. Although their identification of two kingdoms paralleled Luther's analysis closely, the Anabaptists denied that Christians could in any way exercise the sword of the magistrate in the worldly kingdom. When Alexander Mack organized the Church of the Brethren in 1708, Anabaptism was the major impulse in dialectic with pietism. While Quakers, who emerged in the midseventeenth century, distinguished the kingdom of God from that of the world, they did not utterly despair of the world and involved themselves in its political processes up to the point of war. Appeals to individual conscience played an important role in Quaker nonviolent political activity on behalf of justice and peace. Anabaptists, the immediate predecessors of the Mennonites, were the most withdrawn from participation in government, with the Quakers the least separated. The Brethren occupied a median position.

Wars in North America, from Puritan conflicts with the Indians through the Revolutionary War to the world wars, have all been defended in religious and secular versions of the just war theory or the crusade idea. For example, World War I, fought "to make the world safe for democracy," was a secular crusade. Throughout the North American experience Mennonites, Brethren, and Quakers maintained a continuing if at times uneven witness against war as well as a refusal to participate in it. In the twentieth century they have come to be called the historic peace churches.

The nineteenth century saw the formation of a number of national and international pacifist societies. The Fellowship of Reconciliation was founded as an interdenominational and international religious pacifist organization on the eve of World War I and established in the United States in 1915. It continues today as an interfaith activist force for peace. In reaction to the horror of World War I and buttressed by an optimistic belief in the rationality of humanity, the period between the world wars saw another wave of pacifist sentiment, both inside and outside the churches. These efforts to create peace included political means such as the League of Nations and nonviolent pressure such as the activities of Mohandas Gandhi to influence British withdrawal from India. Spurred by the growing possibility of a nuclear holocaust and the realization that military solutions do not fundamentally resolve conflicts, the era begun in the late 1960s is experiencing another round of increasing attention to pacifist perspectives. In addition to the historic peace churches, denominations which have traditionally accepted the just war theory or the crusade idea have also issued declarations accepting pacifist positions within their traditions. Two significant examples are Vatican II's Pastoral Constitution on the Church in the Modern World, which for the first time endorsed pacifism as compatible with Catholic teaching, and the declaration of the United Presbyterian Church (USA), Peacemaking: The Believer's Calling.

Intellectual Basis for Pacifism. Pacifism encompasses many kinds of oppositions to war, deriving support from a variety of overlapping philosophical, theological, and biblical sources, not all of which are explicitly Christian.

Pacifism may proceed from various pragmatic and utilitarian arguments. Consideration of the destructiveness of modern warfare and the realization that it fails to resolve conflicts can lead to the conclusion that avoidance of war best serves the interests of humanity at all levels, from the individual person to the human race as a whole. The threat of nuclear war has given these arguments particular weight in recent times, resulting in what has been called nuclear pacifism.

Varying individual and collective impulses may support these arguments. Pacifism can appear as the only logical extension of the categorical imperative. Convictions concerning the uniqueness or sanctity of human life, whether based on intuition, logic, or divine revelation, proscribe war. Others may adopt pacifist suffering not only as a means of unilaterally breaking the chain of violence which more violent acts will only prolong but also as an instrument to touch the conscience of the oppressors and turn them into friends.

Pacifism informs or is an outgrowth of a number of social and political strategies. Some argue that political measures such as the negotiation of nuclear weapons bans and promotion of international cooperation are more effective than war in promoting peace. Nonviolent techniques attempt not only to prevent the outbreak of violence but also to move society—even against its will—toward a more just disposition. Notable examples are the efforts of Gandhi and the movement of Martin Luther King, Jr., in the United States to acquire civil rights for black people.

As the dominant view of the early church pacifism stands squarely within the Christian tradition and has theological and biblical bases more specific to Christianity. Pacifists appeal to the authority of the Bible, using specific texts such as the Decalogue and the Sermon on the Mount. The incarnation and the priestly office of Jesus make his specific teachings authoritative and therefore binding on his followers. Pacifism also finds support in broader biblical injunctions such as the call to express God's love to all persons or to witness to the presence of the kingdom of God on earth.

The examples of Jesus and of the early church also support Christian pacifism. The incarnation defines Jesus' actions as reflective of the will of God. The ideas of imitation of Christ and obedience to his command to "follow me" then demand pacifism of those who understand Christians as followers of Jesus. Following includes specifically the idea that with Jesus they will endure suffering for the kingdom of God without violent resistance. Beginning with the generation that experienced Jesus' personal headship, the church of the first century exemplifies obedience to the pacifist example of Jesus.

Theological motifs central to Christianity also support pacifism. For one, since life is sacred and a gift from God, no individual has the right to take it. This divine source of life leads directly to the brotherhood of all persons and their divinely given purpose of living for God as his children. With every human being then either actually or potentially a child of God, no Christian may take the life of a fellow member of the family of God. The presence of the kingdom of God on earth similarly links all persons under God's rule and therefore proscribes violence toward anyone. J. D. Weaver

See also War.

Bibliography. R. H. Bainton, *Christian Attitudes Toward War and Peace;* P. Brock, *Pacifism in the United States;* R. G. Clouse, ed., *War: Four Christian Views;* J. G. Davies, *Christians, Politics and Violent Revolution;* V. Eller, *War and Peace from Genesis to Revelation;* J. Ellul, *Violence: Reflections from a Christian Perspective;* J. Ferguson, *The Politics of Love;* E. Guinan, ed., *Peace and Nonviolence;* G. F. Hershberger, *War, Peace, and Nonresistance;* A. F. Holmes, ed., *War and Christian Ethics;* J.-M. Hornus, *It Is Not Lawful for Me to Fight;* J. Lassere, *War and the Gospel;* M. C. Lind, *Yahweh Is a Warrior;* G. H. C. Macgregor, *The NT Basis of Pacifism;* R. McSorley, *NT Basis of Peace Making;* P. Mayer, ed., *The Pacifist Conscience;* W. R. Miller, *Non-Violence: A Christian Interpretation;* G. Nuttall, *Christian Pacifism in History;* C. G. Rutenber, *The Dagger and the Cross;* G. Sharp, *Exploring Nonviolent Alternatives* and *The Politics of Nonviolent Action;* R. J. Sider, *Christ and Violence;* R. K. Ullman, *Between God and History;* A. Weinberg and L. Weinberg, eds., *Instead of Violence;* J. C. Wenger, *Pacifism and Biblical Nonresistance;* J. H. Yoder, *Nevertheless: Varieties of Religious Pacifism, The Original Revolution,* and *The Politics of Jesus.*

Paedobaptism. *See* Baptism, Infant.

Pain. A series of concepts surround the biblical teaching on pain. The term itself is used most often in Scripture to refer to a physical sensation of ill feeling. It can be used to denote emotional or mental stress as well. A related term which designates such concepts is "anguish." While pain and anguish are portrayed in Scripture as the physical and emotional effects one experiences, affliction, tribulation, and trouble appear as the causes of such pain and anguish. Scripture is rich in its teaching on the subject of pain, and the biblical data concerning pain can be organized around three major topics: (1) the biblical words for pain, anguish, and affliction; (2) the biblical usage of such terms; and (3) the biblical teaching concerning the purposes of such pain and affliction.

Throughout Scripture there are ten basic words for "pain." The OT words are *ḥēbel* (pang, Isa. 66:7), *ḥîl* (writhing, pain, Ps. 48:6), *ḥalḥālâ* (great pain, Isa. 21:3), *kĕʾēb* (pain, Jer. 15:18), *makʾôb* (pain, sorrow, Job 33:19), *mēṣar* (straitness, distress, Ps. 116:3), *ʿāmāl* (labor, Ps. 25:18), and *ṣîr* (pain, pang, I Sam. 4:19). The NT uses two basic words for pain, *ponos* (labor, Rev. 16:10–11) and *ōdin* (pang, Acts 2:24). In verbal forms there is also variety in biblical usage of the terms for pain. For example, the OT uses *ḥûl, ḥîl* (to be pained, to writhe) in such passages as Isa. 13:8 and Mic. 4:10. *Kāʾab* is also used in Job 14:22 to refer to having pain or being in pain. Finally, *ḥālâ* is used in Jer. 12:13 to mean "to become sick, grieved, pained." In the NT *basanizō* is used in Rev. 12:2 to mean "try, torture."

The basic biblical words for "tribulation" are

ṣar (distress, Deut. 4:30) and *ṣārâ* (distress, Judg. 10:14) in the OT and *thlibō* (press, squeeze, afflict, I Thess. 3:4) and *thlipsis* (pressure, affliction, Matt. 13:21; John 16:33) in the NT. There is also a richness of biblical usage for "anguish." The basic words in the OT are *māṣôq* (anguish, Ps. 119:143), *mĕṣûqâ* (anguish, Job 15:24), *ṣar* and *ṣārâ,* which are also used for "tribulation" (in such passages as Job 7:11 and Jer. 4:31 they have the meaning of anguish or distress), *qōṣer* (distress, Exod. 6:9), and *šābāṣ* (anguish and confusion, II Sam. 1:9). In the NT *thlipsis* is sometimes used for pressure and anguish, as in John 16:21. Other NT words are *stenochōria* (Rom. 2:9) and *synochē* (II Cor. 2:4).

Finally, there is a series of words used for "afflict." In the OT such verbs as *yāgâ* (Isa. 51:23), *lāḥaṣ* (Amos 6:14), *'ānâ* (Gen. 15:13; Ps. 88:7), *ṣārar* (Ps. 129:1), and *rā'a'* (Num. 11:11; Jer. 31:28) are used, while in the NT *thlibō* (II Cor. 1:6) is the basic word. The noun "affliction" has various biblical words associated with it. In the OT "affliction" is a rendering of such words as *'āwen* (Jer. 4:15), *laḥaṣ* (I Kings 22:27), *mû'āqâ* (Ps. 66:11), *'ānāh* (Ps. 132:1), *'ŏnî* (Gen. 16:11; I Sam. 1:11; Lam. 1:3, 7, 9), *ṣārâ* (I Sam. 26:24; Jer. 14:8), *šeber* (Jer. 30:15), and *ra'* (Ps. 34:19; Jer. 48:16). In the NT *thlipsis* (Mark 4:17; Phil. 1:16) is the main word, but *kakōsis* (Acts 7:34) and *pathēma* (II Tim. 3:11; I Pet. 5:9) are also used.

Not only is there variety in the words for pain, anguish, and affliction; there is also a multiplicity of usages of such words. In regard to words for pain, one of the most frequent uses is for physical pain (e.g., Job 14:22; 33:19; Jer. 15:18; Rev. 21:4). A second major usage refers to mental and emotional problems or anguish (Ps. 25:18; Isa. 13:8; Jer. 4:19; Joel 2:6). Sometimes mental and emotional pain is referred to as leading to physical pain, as in Isa. 21:3. The most common literary figure in regard to pain—whether physical, emotional, or even national problems—is the pain of childbirth (Isa. 26:17–18; Jer. 22:23; Mic. 4:10). Occasionally pain is used to refer to divine judgment upon a person, city, or nation, or simply to refer to the destruction of that city or nation. Often in such cases pain is used metaphorically to speak of the destruction and judgment (Jer. 51:8; Ezek. 30:16; Nah. 2:10). In one instance (Acts 2:24) there is a reference to the pains of death being loosed, using pain as a general term to refer to the whole death experience. Finally, there is a reference to birth pangs used metaphorically in relation to the nation of Israel "giving birth" to the Messiah (Rev. 12:2).

The biblical words for tribulation seem to be used in four basic ways. (1) Tribulation refers to political and national trouble and problems, and such problems normally refer to a nation's relationships with other nations (Deut. 4:30; Judg. 10:14; I Sam. 10:19). (2) The words for tribulation are used in various passages to refer to the eschatological event, the tribulation (Matt. 24:21, 29; Mark 13:24; Rev. 7:14). (3) In at least one passage (Rom. 2:9) tribulation is used to refer to trouble in the sense of divine judgment. (4) The largest group of references to tribulation deals with personal problems, afflictions, troubles, and persecutions which befall the believer (John 16:33; Acts 14:22; Rom. 5:3; 12:12; II Cor. 1:4; II Thess. 1:4, 6; Rev. 2:9–10, 22).

The biblical words for anguish are also used in various ways. (1) Anguish is used to refer in general to one's problems or troubles (Ps. 119:143; Isa. 30:6). (2) Anguish is used quite often to refer to mental and emotional turmoil (Job 7:11; Gen. 42:21; II Cor. 2:4). Included in such turmoil is despondency or depression and sorrow (Exod. 6:9; II Sam. 1:9). (3) Another type of mental turmoil which is frequently signified by anguish is fear (Deut. 2:25; Job 15:24; Jer. 6:24; 49:24; 50:43). (4) Anguish is used on one occasion to refer to trouble in the sense of divine judgment (Rom. 2:9). (5) On several occasions anguish is used to refer to pain which is seemingly physical in nature (Jer. 4:31; John 16:21).

Finally, the biblical words for affliction seem to be used most often in two broad ways—viz., to refer to national affliction or trouble and to refer to individual problems and suffering. Some such references to national problems concern such events as the Egyptian bondage of Israel (Exod. 1:11; Neh. 9:9). In other cases the reference is to national affliction during the time of the prophets (Lam. 1:5). Some references refer to afflictions and troubles on a national scale during the end times (Hos. 5:15; Mark 13:19). In regard to personal afflictions there is again a wide variety. Affliction is used to refer to the forecast sufferings of Christ (Isa. 53:4, 7). It is also used to refer to the harsh treatment Hagar received at the hands of Sarai because of the contempt she showed Sarai after Ishmael was conceived (Gen. 16:11). In some instances it refers to persecution that the believer undergoes as he takes his stand for Christ and battles Satan (I Pet. 5:9). Clearly, there is richness in usage of the term.

Though there are various words used for pain, affliction, trouble, and anguish, and though they are used in various contexts, there is more to the biblical teaching on pain. Scripture is full of comments about the purposes of suffering. In regard to the unbeliever and the disobedient, Scripture teaches that often God sends pain and affliction as a means of judgment for sin (e.g., Job 4:7–9). Sometimes such pain and affliction may come to turn the individual back to the Lord (e.g., Jonah) or to bring a person or nation to salvation (Israel in the tribulation, Zech. 12). In regard to why the righteous suffer, the Bible is also most helpful. Sometimes the believer will be afflicted as a means of chastisement (Ps. 94:12–13; cf. Heb. 12:6). God uses affliction to keep his servants humble, as in the case of Paul (II Cor. 12:7). On some occasions the purpose of human affliction is to demonstrate to Satan that there are those who serve God because they love him, not because it pays to do so (Job 1–2). According to Peter, suffering promotes sanctification (I Pet. 4:1–2). It does so in various ways such as refining the believer's faith (I Pet. 1:6–7), educating the believer in such Christian virtues as endurance and perseverance (James 1:3–4; Rom. 5:3–4), teaching the believer something more of the sovereignty of God so that he understands his Lord better (Job 42:2–4), and giving the believer an opportunity to imitate Christ (I Pet. 3:17–18). If any of these occurs in the life of the believer, it will be evidence of sanctification, and such sanctification is worked through affliction. Affliction and pain offer an opportunity for the believer to minister to others who are undergoing affliction (II Cor. 1:3–4). On some occasions God's purpose in afflicting the righteous is to prepare them for judgment of their works for the purpose of rewards. Believers someday will give account of their works before the Lord, and affliction helps prepare the believer so that on that day his faith will be found unto honor and glory at the coming of the Lord (I Pet. 1:7). If that happens, the believer will be rewarded, so affliction ultimately is a means to reward in such cases. Finally, God uses affliction as a prelude to exaltation of the believer. The theme of suffering and glory is prevalent throughout Scripture, especially I Peter. The example of Christ is the pattern (Phil. 2:5–11; I Pet. 3:17–22), and God wants to do the same for the believer who will humble himself before God, even if that humbling involves affliction (I Pet. 5:6).

This list of purposes for pain and affliction is not meant to be exhaustive but only indicative of the richness of biblical teaching on the purposes of pain. One does not get the impression from Scripture that pain is purely gratuitous.

J. S. Feinberg

See also Evil, Problem of; Theodicy.

Bibliography. J. Hick, *Evil and the God of Love;* C. S. Lewis, *The Problem of Pain;* E. Madden and P. Hare, *Evil and the Concept of God;* J. Wenham, *The Goodness of God.*

Pain of God Theology. Kazoh Kitamori, a Japanese theologian teaching at the Tokyo Theological Seminary, introduced a new indigenous Japanese theology in his book *Theology of the Pain of God* in 1946, right after World War II when Japan went through a time of devastation and suffering.

To Kitamori the central meaning of the Christian gospel is the pain of God. Kitamori starts with Jer. 31:20: "Ephraim, my dear son, is he a delightful child? Indeed, as often as I have spoken against him, I certainly still remember him; therefore, my heart yearns for him; I will surely have mercy on him, declares the Lord." Here the context of the passage is God suffering for Ephraim, his son. The AV translation reads, "My bowels are troubled for him." The key word in the phrase is the Hebrew verb *hāmâ,* which Kitamori interprets as "pain." He believes that God suffered for Ephraim and God suffers for his people. To him suffering exhausts the meaning of the Christian gospel. The theology of suffering is the entirety of Christian theology.

There are four constituents in the pain of God. First, God's love and forgiveness for sinners who deserve his wrath and judgment engender pain in God. Kitamori writes, "When the love of God bears and overcomes his wrath, nothing but the pain of God takes place. The solution to the wrath of God must be sought in the pain of God before it can be sought in the hidden God." The second constituent is simply human suffering and pain—hunger, thirst, exhaustion, fear, rejection, and the excruciating pain of the historical Jesus at his crucifixion. This pain can be healed, redeemed, and made meaningful only when it unites with the pain of God. The suffering of the historical Jesus as the Son of God is expressed in the *pain* of God. Third, God the Father suffers when he lets his only beloved Son suffer and die on the cross. This suffering of the Father is expressed in the pain of *God.* Fourth, God becomes immanent in the historical reality of human suffering. Jesus' last sermon (Matt. 25:31–46) illustrates his identity with the one who suffers hunger, thirst, sickness, and imprisonment, when he says, "Truly, I say to you, as you did it to one of the least of these my brethren, you did it to me." God does not want us to approach him directly but rather indirectly through love for our neighbors.

After explaining these four constituents in the pain of God, Kitamori goes into the relationships between God's pain and man's pain. Man's pain is the reality of the wrath of God against sin (Rom. 6:23) and is the consequence of his estrangement from God. Man's pain also symbolizes God's pain; therefore, the bridge between God and man is pain. Kitamori explains how the love of God is related to the pain of God by what he calls "three orders of love." The first order is called the immediate "love of God," characterized as smooth, flowing, and intense like parental love. Nevertheless, man's sin has spoiled God's love and has caused the "pain of God." The third order of love is the synthesis of the love and pain of God which is expressed in the phrase "love rooted in the pain of God," which appears more than thirty times throughout his book.

In fact, he makes the astounding claim that due to the influence of Greek philosophy and German theology throughout the centuries the Christian church has failed to discover the centrality of the gospel until this Japanese Christian discovered the truth through the pain of God theology. Kitamori made this discovery because the Japanese concept of *tsurasa* (pain) is deeply rooted in the Japanese mind. The Japanese believe the depth and intelligence of man is measured by his understanding of *tsurasa*.

The significance of the pain of God theology is twofold. First, Kitamori took the tragedies of World War II and sufferings of the Japanese people very seriously. His attempt to contextualize the gospel in the life situation of Japanese at a crucial time was one of the first such attempts in Asia. Furthermore, the concept of suffering and pain is at home in Japan, where the traditional Buddhist teaching of suffering (*dukka*) has been prevalent. Second, Kitamori developed the first significant Asian contextual theology to be widely publicized in the West. His theology pioneered a string of other Asian theologies existing today. B. R. Ro

See also Asian Theology.

Bibliography. D. J. Elwood, ed., *What Asian Christians Are Thinking;* C. Hargraves, *Asian Christian Thinking;* K. Koyama, *Waterbuffalo Theology;* C. Michalson, *Japanese Contributions to Christian Theology.*

Paley, William (1743-1805). Anglican theologian. Graduate of Cambridge, he became a fellow of Christ's College there and lectured in philosophy and divinity. He held that the Thirty-nine Articles of the Church of England contained "about two hundred and forty distinct propositions, many of them inconsistent with each other." He defined virtue as "doing good to mankind, in obedience to the will of God, and for the sake of everlasting happiness." He was a prolific writer, especially after he forsook Cambridge in 1775 and assumed a succession of increasingly lucrative incumbencies in Cumberland, where he was archdeacon of Carlisle from 1782. His most notable work was *A View of the Evidences of Christianity* (1794), which for more than a century was required reading for entrance to Cambridge University. His *Natural Theology* (1802) argued teleologically for God's existence. The exquisite detail in an insect or in a human eye could be explained only in terms of a master craftsman. Only a divine watchmaker could have conceived the mechanical regularity of a watch that kept perfect time.

Often accused of unoriginality, and even of plagiarism, Paley retorted on one occasion that he was writing a textbook, not an original dissertation. Far from laying any claim to creativity, Paley advised his students that they should "make one sermon and steal five." His theology sometimes went beyond liberalism to unitarianism. He was good at whist, conscious of class (he left a sizable fortune), and is immortalized in secular history by a single plaintive question: "Who can refute a sneer?" J. D. Douglas

Bibliography. G. W. Meadley, *Memoirs of William Paley;* D. L. LeMahieu, *The Mind of William Paley;* M. L. Clarke, *Paley: Evidences for the Man.*

Palm Sunday. The Sunday before Easter Sunday, considered to be the second Sunday of the passion of our Lord Jesus Christ. The use of palms was introduced in Rome as late as the twelfth century. The palms help symbolize the last entry of Jesus into Jerusalem before his crucifixion, during which the people strewed palms in his path as a sign of reverence. In today's reenactment of that entrance into Jerusalem people are encouraged to carry palms as part of the liturgical experience.

T. J. German

See also Holy Week; Christian Year.

Bibliography. W. J. O'Shea, *The Meaning of Holy Week.*

Panentheism. A doctrine of God which attempts to combine the strengths of classical theism with those of classical pantheism. The term is particularly associated with the work of Charles Hartshorne. Hartshorne contends, however, that other philosophers and theologians have elaborated panentheistic doctrines of God, especially Alfred North Whitehead but also Nikolai Berdyaev, Martin Buber, Gustaf T. Fechner, Mohammad Iqbal, Charles S. Peirce, Otto Pfleiderer, Sarvepalli Radhakrishnan, Friedrich W. J. von Schelling, Allan Watts, and Paul Weiss.

According to Hartshorne, God, while including an element which may be described as simple, is a complex reality. God knows the world—a world in which change, process, and freedom are real elements. For this freedom and change to be real, and for God's knowledge of this freedom and change to be perfect, Hartshorne reasons that God's knowledge must itself grow and change. That is, as new facts come into being, God comes to know those new facts (some of which are the result of genuinely free will), and thus God's knowledge grows. A perfect knower includes within himself the object which is known. Through perfectly knowing the world, God therefore includes the world (as it comes to be) within himself. As the world grows, God grows. God becomes. Through perfectly knowing and including the world, God is the supreme effect. That is, everything that happens affects God and changes God—e.g., God's knowledge changes. Therefore, the concrete God, the complex God who is actual, is the God who knows, includes, and is changed by the world. This, according to Hartshorne, is the God who loves the world and who shares the joys and sorrows of each creature in the world.

To be the supreme effect, God must not only be affected by each event in the world, he must also retain his own integrity and wholeness during this process. If God's reality were destroyed or his purpose (for goodness) deflected by the events in the world, then God would not be the supreme effect, the perfect receptacle for the world. Therefore, there must be some element in God which remains the same regardless of what happens in the world—i.e., an element that is not affected by any particular event in the world. This element, since it is not changed by any event, is eternal. It is also abstract. (The fact that God's eternal, abstract, essential self-identity is compatible with any state of affairs in the world is the basis for Hartshorne's well-known revival of the ontological argument.) Since God's eternal, abstract self-identity is presupposed by any state of affairs whatsoever, it follows that God is the universal and supreme cause.

It should be noted that while God (as eternal, abstract, essential self-identity) is independent of any particular state of affairs in the world, he (even as abstract self-identity) still requires that a world (of some sort or the other) exist. We may explain as follows. God as supreme cause refers to God's eternal, abstract, essential self-identity which is presupposed by every event in the world. But that which is eternal and abstract is deficient in actuality and can exist only as an element in a larger whole which is temporal and concrete. Thus God's eternal, abstract, essential self-identity exists only as an element in the temporal, concrete, complex reality which is God in his completeness. But God can be temporal, concrete, and complex only if there are contingent states of affairs to which he is related. These states of affairs are the world (which is included in God). These states of affairs are accidental (as opposed to essential) qualifiers of God's character. Thus God even as eternal, abstract, essential self-identity requires some world to exist, without requiring any particular world to exist.

Some of the events in the world are evil. God knows and includes those events within himself. Does it follow that God is evil? Hartshorne answers no. Consider this analogy. A certain event happens in my body. I know and include that event within myself. And yet as a person, while including that event, I remain in an important sense distinct from that event. Not only is my abstract and timeless essence as a man distinct from that event, but even my concrete and changing consciousness (while including that event) is distinct from it. Likewise, God, while including the evil event within himself, is yet distinct from that event. God is distinct from the event not only in his abstract, eternal, essential self-identity but also in his concrete, temporal, and complex consciousness. That is, God's consciousness, while aware of and including the evil event, is more than and distinct from that event.

Is it possible for a panentheistic God to be perfect? The problem is this. If God changes, and if total perfection is not compatible with change, it would follow that the panentheistic God is not perfect. Hartshorne's response runs as follows. The challenge as stated assumes that there is one type of perfection—specifically, changeless perfection. But in fact there are two types of perfection: changeless and changing perfection. God is perfect in both senses. God's abstract, essential, eternal self-identity is perfect. His drive toward goodness in general does not waver. To this extent God's perfection is changeless, but this perfection is abstract. As a concrete reality God changes, as does his perfection. That is, at any time, God infinitely surpasses the perfection of the world, regardless of whether we consider the perfection of the world at that same time, at some previous time, at some future time, or at any combination of these. As time progresses, however, God does surpass his own previous states of perfection—e.g., his knowledge grows, and he has more opportunities to love his creatures. God's perfection changes in that he perfectly surpasses his own previous states of perfection.

While Whitehead's doctrine of God is quite similar to Hartshorne's, Whitehead does have several distinctives worth noting. In Whitehead's metaphysics the basic building blocks of the universe are called actual entities. Actual entities are units of energy/experience. Electrons, rocks, stars, and people are composed of actual entities. For Whitehead, God is a single, everlasting (but continually developing) actual entity. The contemporary theologian John B. Cobb, Jr., argues that on his own principles Whitehead should have conceived God to be a series of actual entities. Cobb's proposal would make God more like a human person which, according to Whitehead, is a series of actual entities. It should be further noted that in Whitehead's system it is the very nature of an actual entity to incorporate other (past) actual entities into its own identity. Therefore, whether on Whitehead's original definition of God as a single everlasting actual entity or on Cobb's revisionary understanding of God as a series of actual entities, it is the very nature of God to include the (past) world within himself as a part of his very identity.

Perhaps the most striking aspect of Whitehead's doctrine of God is his distinction between God and creativity. Creativity is, in Whitehead's metaphysics, the power of being/becoming. Thus the fact that anything exists at all is ascribed not to God but to creativity (which in conjunction with the notions of the "one" and the "many" constitute Whitehead's category of the ultimate). In contrast, God's primary function is to help shape the character of the world. Thus *that* a thing exists must be referred to creativity; *what* a thing is must be referred, in part, to God. As a consequence, in Whitehead's system God's own existence is explained by reference not to God but to creativity. To put it bluntly, we may say that both God and the world are creatures of creativity.

Whitehead's postulation of creativity (in conjunction with the "one" and the "many") as an ultimate that is more fundamental than God is, perhaps, the most problematic aspect of his doctrine of God, not only for evangelical theologians but for other Christian thinkers as well. While a few Christian scholars, such as John Cobb, affirm Whitehead's distinction between God and creativity, others, such as Langdon Gilkey, insist that creativity must be "put back" into God before the panentheistic doctrine of God can really be made available for Christian theology.

S. T. Franklin

See also Process Theology.

Bibliography. J. B. Cobb, Jr., *A Christian Natural Theology;* J. B. Cobb, Jr., and D. R. Griffin, *Process Theology: An Introductory Exposition;* B. Z. Cooper, *The Idea of God: A Whiteheadian Critique of St. Thomas Aquinas' Concept of God;* L. Gilkey, *Naming the Whirlwind: The Renewal of God Language* and *Reaping the Whirlwind: A Christian Interpretation of History;* C. Hartshorne and W. L. Reese, eds., *Philosophers Speak of God;* R. C. Neville, *Creativity and God: A Challenge to Process Theology;* R. E. James, *The Concrete God: A New Beginning for Theology.*

Pantheism. The word, coming from the Greek *pan* and *theos,* means "everything is God." It was coined by John Toland in 1705 to refer to philosophical systems that tend to identify God with the world. Such doctrines have been viewed as a mediating position between atheism and classical theism by some, while others have concluded that pantheism is really a polite form of atheism because God is identified with everything.

Pantheism may be contrasted with biblical theism from a number of perspectives. Pantheism either mutes or rejects the biblical teaching of the transcendence of God in favor of his radical immanence. It is typically monistic about reality, whereas biblical theism distinguishes between God and the world. Because of pantheism's tendency to identify God with nature, there is a minimizing of time, often making it illusory. The biblical understanding of God and the world is that God is eternal and the world finite, although God acts in time and knows what takes place in it. In forms of pantheism where God literally encompasses the world, man is an utterly fated part of the universe which is *necessarily* as it is. In such a world freedom is an illusion. Biblical theism, on the other hand, holds to the freedom of man, insisting that this freedom is compatible with God's omniscience.

It would be erroneous to conclude, however, that pantheism is a monolithic position. The more important forms are as follows:

Hylozoistic pantheism. The divine is immanent in, and characteristically regarded as the basic element of, the world, giving movement and change to the whole. The universe, however, remains a plurality of separate elements. This view was popular among some of the early Greek philosophers.

Immanentistic pantheism. God is a part of the world and immanent in it, although his power is exercised throughout its entirety.

Absolutistic monistic pantheism. God is both absolute and identical with the world. Thus, the world is also changeless though real.

Relativistic monistic pantheism. The world is real and changing. It is, however, *within* God as, for example, his body. God is nevertheless changeless and unaffected by the world.

Acosmic pantheism. God is absolute and makes up the totality of reality. The world is an appearance and ultimately unreal.

Identity of opposites pantheism. Discourse about God must of necessity resort to opposites. That is, God and his relationship to the world must be described in formally contradictory terms. Reality is not capable of rational description. One must go beyond reason to an intuitive grasp of the ultimate.

Neoplatonic or emanationistic pantheism. In this form of pantheism God is absolute in all aspects, removed from and transcendent over the world. It differs from biblical theism in denying that God is the cause of the world, holding rather that the universe is an emanation of God. The world is the result of intermediaries. These intermediaries are for a Neoplatonist like Plotinus ideals or forms. He also sought to maintain the emphasis on immanence by positing a world soul that contains and animates the universe.

From a biblical standpoint pantheism is deficient to a greater or lesser degree on two points. First, pantheism generally denies the transcendence of God, advocating his radical immanence. The Bible presents a balance. God is active in history and in his creation, but he is not identical with it to either a lesser or a greater degree. Second, because of the tendency to identify God with the material world, there is again a lesser or greater denial of the personal character of God. In Scripture, God not only possesses the attributes of personality, in the incarnation he takes on a body and becomes the God-man. God is pictured suprernely as a person.

P. D. Feinberg

See also Neoplatonism; Theism.

Bibliography. C. E. Plumptre, *History of Pantheism*, 2 vols.; W. S. Urquart, *Pantheism and the Value of Life;* J. Royce, *The Conception of God.*

Papacy. As head of the Roman Catholic Church the pope is considered the successor of Peter and the vicar of Christ. He is also, and first of all, the bishop of Rome and, for Eastern Christians, the patriarch of the West. The term *pappa*, from which the word "pope" is derived, originated in ancient colloquial Greek as an endearing term for "father," and was then applied, beginning in the third century, to Eastern patriarchs, bishops, abbots, and eventually parish priests (of whom it is still used today). In the West the term was never very common outside Rome (originally a Greek-speaking church), and from the sixth century became reserved increasingly for the bishop of Rome, until in the later eleventh century Pope Gregory VII made that official. The term "papacy" (*papatus*), meant to distinguish the Roman bishop's office from all other bishoprics (*episcopatus*), also originated in the later eleventh century.

For Catholics the papacy represents an office divinely instituted by Christ in his charge to Peter (Matt. 16:18–19; Luke 22:31–32; John 21:15–17), and therefore something to be revered and obeyed as a part of Christian faith and duty. But the papal role has in fact varied from age to age, and a historical survey is required first to put papal claims into perspective.

History. The first three and a half centuries of papal history have left remarkably little record. That Peter ministered and died in Rome now seems beyond doubt, but a monarchical episcopate emerged there only in the early second century, and a half-century later still came those lists of successive bishops designed to show their preservation of the original apostolic faith. The church at Rome nevertheless enjoyed a certain prominence, owing to its apostolic "founders" and to its political setting, and this eventually inspired its bishops to exercise greater leadership. Victor (*ca.* 190) rebuked the churches of Asia Minor for celebrating Easter on the incorrect date, and Stephan (254–57), for the first known time explicitly claiming to stand on the Petrine deposit of faith, ruled against the churches of North Africa on sacraments administered by heretics.

Between the midfourth and the midfifth centuries, the apogee of the Western imperial church, Roman popes developed and articulated those claims which were to become characteristic. Over against emperors and patriarchs in Constantinople, who claimed that their church in "new Rome" virtually equaled that of "old Rome," the popes asserted vehemently that their primacy derived from Peter and not from their political setting, making theirs the only truly "apostolic see." Siricius (384–98) and Innocent (401–17) issued the first extant decretals, letters modeled on imperial rescripts in which popes ruled definitively on matters put to them by local churches. Leo the Great (440–61), who first appropriated the old pagan title of *pontifex maximus*, intervened with his *Tome* at the Council of Chalcedon to establish orthodox Christology, told a recalcitrant archbishop that he merely "participated in" a "fullness of power" reserved to popes alone (this later to become an important principle in canon law), and provided in his letters and sermons a highly influential description of the Petrine office and its primacy, drawing in part upon principles found in Roman law. Gelasius (492–96), finally, over against emperors inclined to intervene at will in ecclesiastical affairs, asserted an independent and higher pontifical authority in religious matters.

Throughout the early Middle Ages (600–1050) papal claims remained lofty, but papal power diminished considerably. All churches, East and West, recognized in the "vicar of St. Peter" a certain primacy of honor, but the East virtually never consulted him and the West only when it was expedient. In practice, councils of bishops, with kings often presiding over them, ruled in the various Western territorial churches. Reform initiatives came from the outside, even when (as with Boniface and Charlemagne) they sought normative guidance from Rome. Two innovations deserve mention: in the mideighth century the papacy broke with the Eastern ("Roman") emperor and allied itself henceforth with Western royal powers; at the same time popes laid claims to the papal states, lands in central Italy meant to give them autonomy but in fact burdening them with political responsibilities which became very damaging to their spiritual mission during the later Middle Ages and were not finally removed until the forcible unification of Italy in 1870.

The papacy emerged during the High Middle Ages (1050–1500) as the real leader of Western Christendom, beginning with the so-called Gregorian reform movement (its claims neatly epitomized in twenty-seven *dicta* noted down by Pope Gregory VII), culminating initially in the reign of Pope Innocent III (his reforms permanently inscribed in the Fourth Lateran Council), and waning again during the Great Schism and the conciliar movement. In 1059 a new election law (with modifications made in 1179, the same as that in force today) raised the pope above all other bishops, who were in principle still elected by their clergy and people. Henceforth the pope would be elected solely by cardinals, themselves papal appointees given liturgical and administrative responsibilities, and he could be chosen from among all eligible clergymen (preferably cardinals) rather than, as the older law held, only from among Romans. Papal decretals replaced conciliar canons as the routine and normative form of regulation, and this "new law" (little changed prior to the new codes issued in 1917 and 1982) reached down uniformly into every diocese in the West. The papal *curia* or court, reorganized and massively expanded, became the center of ecclesiastical finance and administration. Legates carried papal authority into all parts of Europe. The papal call to crusade brought thousands of laymen to arms, and eventually had important implications in the area of clerical taxation and the issuing of indulgences. Above all, this revitalized papacy constantly asserted the priority of the spiritual over the material world, and adopted for itself a new title as head of the church, that of "vicar [or placeholder] of Christ."

The early modern papacy (1517–1789) began with a staggering defeat. Protestant Reformers, persuaded that the papacy had corrupted the gospel beyond all hope of reform, revolted. The so-called Renaissance papacy had largely lost sight of its spiritual mission, and was forced reluctantly into the reforms articulated by the Council of Trent (1545–63). The papacy then took charge of deep and lasting reforms in, e.g., training clergy, upholding new standards for the episcopal and priestly offices, and providing a new catechism. The number of cardinals was set at seventy (until the last generation), and "Congregations" were established to oversee various aspects of the church's mission.

The critical attack of Enlightenment thinkers (Josephinism in Austria) together with growing national (Gallicanism in France) and episcopal (Febronianism in Germany) resistance to papal authority culminated in the French Revolution and its aftermath, during which time two popes (Pius VI, Pius VII) endured humiliating imprisonments. But the forces of restoration, combined with the official indifference or open hostility of secularized governments, led to a strong resurgence of centralized papal authority known as ultramontanism. Pope Pius IX (1846–78) made this the program of his pontificate, codified it as a part of the Catholic faith in the decrees on papal primacy and infallibility in Vatican Council I (1869–70), and enforced it with an unprecedented degree of Roman centralization that characterized the Catholic Church into the 1960s. Leo XIII (1878–1903), the first pope in centuries to have chiefly spiritual obligations following the loss of the papal states, approved neo-Thomism as an official challenge to modern philosophy and defined a Catholic position on social justice over against radical labor unions. Pius X (1903–14) condemned scattered efforts to bring into the Catholic Church the critical study of Scripture and divergent philosophical views known collectively as "modernism." Pius XII (1939–58) used the papacy's infallible authority for the first time to define the bodily assumption of Mary as Catholic dogma. Throughout the last century mass media, mass transportation, and mass audiences have made the popes far better known and more highly reverenced in their persons (as distinguished from their office) than ever before. Vatican Council II (1962–65) brought deep reforms, in particular a much greater emphasis upon bishops acting collegially with one another and the pope. Protestants are pleased to see a return to Scripture in the papacy's conception of the church's mission and the priest's office, together with a far greater openness toward other Christian churches.

Papal primacy rests upon the power of the keys which Christ conferred upon Peter and his successors, though it has obviously varied in principle and especially in practice throughout the centuries. Leo the Great and the high medieval popes claimed for themselves a "fullness of power" which Vatican Council I defined as "ordinary" and "immediate" jurisdiction over the church and all the faithful in matters of discipline and ecclesiastical authority as well as faith and morals, thus potentially transforming the pope into a supreme bishop and all other bishops into mere vicars, an imbalance which Vatican Council II sought to redress with far greater emphasis upon the episcopal office. The triumph of papal primacy has nevertheless at least three noteworthy results. (1) In the continuing tug of war between papal and conciliar/episcopal authority, the pope has effectively gained the upper hand. He alone has the divinely given power to convoke councils and to authorize their decisions (something reaffirmed at Vatican Council II). (2) Since the fourteenth century, and especially since the nineteenth, episcopal appointments have been removed from local clergy and laymen and reserved to Rome (which tends to preserve loyalty to the pope but also prevents churches from falling prey to local factions and national governments). (3) In general, Rome's approval is needed for all laws which govern the church's institutions, liturgies which shape its worship, courts which enforce its discipline, orders which embody its religious life, and missions sent around the world—though there has been some decentralization in the immediate aftermath of Vatican Council II. Like all monarchical structures, primacy can be and usually is a very conservative force, though it can also initiate sweeping change, as in the reforms of the last two decades.

Until the last century, when papal pronouncements on a host of religious issues first became a regular feature of the Catholic Church, primacy in matters of faith and morals received far less attention than primacy of jurisdiction. Down to the sixteenth century and beyond, popes normally adjudicated matters first argued in schools and local churches, rather than initiating legislation themselves. All bishops originally possessed the *magisterium*, or the authority to preserve and to teach the faith handed down from the apostles, and general councils of bishops were called (usually by emperors) to resolve controverted doctrinal issues. Rome eventually gained a certain preeminence, owing partly to the fame of its apostolic "founders" (Peter and Paul) and partly to its enviable record of orthodoxy, though this was not always above reproach, as in the condemnation of Honorius I (625–38) for his position on monothelitism, something which entered into the debate on infallibility. In the High Middle Ages the unfailing faith Christ promised to pray for (Luke 22:31–32) was understood to apply not to the whole church but to the Roman Church and then more narrowly to the Roman pope. Infallibility was first ascribed to him in the fourteenth century and defined as binding dogma after much debate and some dissent in 1870. This was intended to guarantee and preserve the truths of the apostolic faith. When Protestants disagree about Scripture's teaching on a certain doctrine, they appeal to a famous founder (Calvin, Wesley, etc.), their denominational creeds, or their own understanding; Catholics appeal to the authority they believe Christ conferred upon his vicar. Though popes are careful to distinguish fallible from infallible statements and have in fact made only one of the latter, their Petrine authority and frequent modern pronouncements can tend, as Luther first charged, to generate a new law and obscure the freedom of Christ.

Comparative Views. It is helpful to compare the position of the Eastern Orthodox, contemporary dissenting Catholics, and Protestants with the traditional view of the papacy. The Orthodox considered the church to be organized around five patriarchates, with the see of Peter in the West holding a certain primacy of honor but not final authority. They have consistently refused to recognize any extraordinary magisterial authority (which resides in the teachings of general councils). The catalyst which finally divided the Eastern and Western churches in 1054 was Rome's revitalized claim to primacy, worsened by papal support for the crusades and establishment of a Latin hierarchy in the East. As hostility toward Rome increased, the Orthodox became ever clearer in their exegesis of the keys: the church was built upon Peter's confession of faith (which the Orthodox had preserved intact), not upon Peter himself or his sometime wayward successors. More recently, the Orthodox found the declaration of infallibility almost as offensive as did Protestants.

Catholics have never uniformly reverenced the papacy to the degree that most Protestants believe and that the ultramontane movement of the last century might have suggested. Outright repudiation nevertheless was rare. The so-called Old Catholics split away after the infallibility decree, and a small conservative group has denounced the changes wrought by Vatican Council II. But in the last generation some theologians, led by Hans Küng, have openly questioned infallibility, and many faithful Catholics have rejected the stand on contraception enunciated in Pope Paul VI's *Humanae vitae* (1968). There is increased suspicion of Roman primatial claims and considerable ferment in favor of episcopal and conciliar authority. But whether this is merely a momentary reaction or something of lasting significance is not yet clear.

Until the last generation Protestants have had almost nothing but evil to say of the papacy.

Luther, contrary to popular myth, did not revolt easily against papal authority and for a long time held to the conviction of a Petrine office charged with the care of souls in the church; but when he became convinced that the vicar of Christ had in fact distorted and obstructed the proclamation of the gospel, he labeled him instead the "antichrist," and that label stuck for centuries. Indeed "popery" and its equivalent in other languages came to stand for all that was wrong with the Roman Catholic Church. Liberal Protestants have meanwhile dismissed the papacy as a vestige of superstition, while several extremely conservative groups, often in gross misunderstanding of the papacy and its actual function, continue to link it with all that is evil in the world. Since Vatican Council II evangelical Christians have come better to understand and to appreciate the pope as a spokesman for Christ's church, yet few would go so far as some ecumenically minded Lutherans, who suggested that a less authoritarian papacy could function as the rallying point for a reunited church. Most Protestants still consider the notion of a primatial Petrine office, instituted by Christ and conferred upon the bishops of Rome, to be scripturally and historically unfounded. Therefore the doctrine and office of the papacy will probably continue to divide Catholic from Protestant and Orthodox Christians for the foreseeable future.

J. Van Engen

See also Keys of the Kingdom; Infallibility; Vatican Council I; Vatican Council II.

Bibliography. *NCE,* X, 951–70; XI, 779–81; *LTK,* VIII, 36–48; VI, 884–90; *DTC,* XI, 1877–1944; XIII, 247–391; *RGG,* V, 51–85; T. G. Jalland, *The Church and the Papacy;* K. von Aretin, *The Papacy and the Modern World;* J. D. Holmes, *The Triumph of the Holy See;* S. Hendrix, *Luther and the Papacy;* P. C. Empie, ed., *Papal Primacy and the Universal Church;* C. Mirbt and K. Aland, *Quellen zur Geschichte des Papsttums und des römischen Katholizismus.*

Parables of Jesus. Parables are presented in the OT, in rabbinic literature, and in the Gospels of the NT. The parables taught by Jesus, in comparison to others, are unique. Some scholars count a total of sixty parables and parabolic sayings in the Synoptic Gospels. All told, this number amounts to about one third of all the recorded utterances of Jesus. Therefore, in respect to quantity and variety Jesus is the chief originator of parables.

The parables Jesus taught are marked by brevity and simplicity. Only a few of them are longer than average—e.g., the parable of the talents (Matt. 25:14–30) and the parable of the lost son (Luke 15:11–32). These parables sparkle in their brevity; they come to life; they are the vehicles that convey a profound message in simple terms—the proverbial earthly story with a heavenly message.

A parable is a form of speech, either a story or saying, used to illustrate a point the speaker is trying to make. Conveniently, parables may be divided in three classes: true parables, story parables, and illustrations. The true parable is an illustration taken from daily life, and its teaching is universally acknowledged. Examples of the true parable are children playing in the marketplace (Matt. 11:16–19; Luke 7:31–32), a sheep separated from the flock (Matt. 18:12–14; Luke 15:4–7), a coin lost in a home (Luke 15:8–10). Story parables refer to a particular event that took place in the past and center on one person—the shrewd manager who redeemed himself after wasting his master's possessions (Luke 16:1–9), the judge who eventually administered justice in response to the repeated plea of a widow (Luke 18:2–8). Illustrations are stories that project an example which is to be imitated; the parable of the good Samaritan (Luke 10:30–37) ends with the admonition "Go and do likewise."

Besides these three categories parables also refer to short, pithy sayings which may have circulated as proverbs in Jesus' day: "Physician, heal yourself" (Luke 4:23); "Can a blind man lead a blind man? Will they not both fall into a pit?" (Luke 6:39).

The parables of Jesus are stories that are true to life, even though in some cases either exaggeration is intended (e.g., ten thousand talents by any standard is an astronomical sum of money, Matt. 18:24) or allegorical overtones can be detected (see the parable of the tenants, Matt. 21:33–44; Mark 12:12; Luke 20:9–19). However, the parables Jesus taught are not allegories in which every name, place, and feature is symbolic and demands an interpretation. The parables embody metaphors and similes, but they are never removed from reality and never convey fictitious ideas. They are stories taken from the world in which Jesus lived and are told for the purpose of relating a spiritual truth.

Of the three Synoptics, Matthew and Luke record most of the parables; Mark has only six parables, of which only one is peculiar to his Gospel (the one of the seed growing secretly, 4:26–29). Many of Matthew's parables are introduced as kingdom parables: wheat and weeds (13:24–30), mustard seed (13:31–32), yeast (13:33), hidden treasure (13:44), pearl (13:45–46), fish net (13:47–50), unforgiving servant (18:21–35), workers in the vineyard (20:1–16), wedding banquet (22:1–14), and ten virgins (25:1–13). These ten parables are introduced by the familiar line:

"The kingdom of heaven is like. . . ." The parable of the talents by implication may be considered a kingdom parable (25:14–30). And the context of Matt. 13, in which Jesus teaches the meaning of the coming of the kingdom, may provide a reason to consider the parable of the sower a kingdom parable (13:3–8).

The kingdom parables often reveal an eschatological perspective, especially those of the wheat and weeds, fish net, wedding banquet, ten virgins, and talents. Matthew concludes the eschatological theme in the parable on the last judgment, which portrays the shepherd separating his sheep from the goats (25:31–33). Matthew has grouped parables in certain parts of his Gospel: chapter 13 has a total of seven parables, chapters 24 and 25 feature five of them.

In the parables which Luke has recorded, the theme of repentance and salvation is prominent. Luke portrays Jesus' interest in the outcasts, the poor, the lost, the despised. Luke spells out this theme in the words of Jesus: "For the Son of man came to seek and to save what was lost" (19:10). The emphasis on Jesus' love for the poor is exemplified in the parable of the great supper (14:15–24). The invited guests offer their excuses and refuse to come, but the poor, the crippled, the blind, and the lame are brought in, "so that my house will be full." Luke describes Lazarus in vivid detail: "covered with sores and longing to eat what fell from the rich man's table. Even the dogs came and licked his sores" (16:21). Lazarus was carried by angels to heaven; the rich man died and went to hell. The rich are warned to come to repentance and faith. The rich man who built bigger barns for his bumper crops placed his trust in worldly wealth and not in God. Man is exhorted to live not for himself but for his fellow man and for God in obedience to the summary of the law: Love the Lord your God, and love your neighbor as yourself. This summary comes to expression in the parable of the good Samaritan (10:25–37). The command to love one's neighbor is not invalidated by barriers that race, nationality, language, and culture have erected.

Additional themes stressed by Luke are those of faithfulness, expressed in the parable of the farmer's servant who plowed the field during the day, prepared supper for his master in the evening, and did not even receive a word of thanks (17:7–10); loyalty, as depicted in the parable of the pounds, in which nine servants put their money to work and one buried it in the ground (19:11–27); and prayer, described in the parables of the friend at midnight (11:5–8), the widow and the unjust judge (18:1–8), and the Pharisee and tax collector (18:9–14).

Jesus knew human life in all its forms and manifestations, all its ways and means. He was familiar with the life of the farmer, the vinedresser, the fisherman, the builder, and the merchant. He also was acquainted with the professions of the minister of finance, the judge, the tax collector, and the manager of estates. He knew the Pharisees and the experts in the law. Jesus was at home in all the social levels of society and was able to minister to all people regardless of status, training, or occupation. By means of parables Jesus brought the message of salvation to everyone, called his listeners to repent and to believe, challenged believers to put their faith to work, and urged his followers to exercise watchfulness.

Jesus' parables were not always readily understood by his disciples. He provided an interpretation of some of them. The question whether Jesus hid the meaning of the parables from all except the initiated may be answered by looking at the broader context of the parable of the sower (Mark 4:3–8). In Mark 3 Jesus met the teachers of the law, who charged him with demon possession: "By the prince of demons he is driving out demons" (3:22). Because of their blatant unbelief, those opposed to Jesus were unable and unwilling to understand the meaning of his teaching in parables. Believers accepted the word of Jesus and received his parabolic teaching in faith and understanding, even though full comprehension might not be evident at first. The disciples were perplexed by Jesus' teaching because they had not yet seen the full significance of the person of Jesus the Messiah.

Matthew presents Jesus as the Christ, the Son of God, throughout his Gospel. This is clearly seen in his selection of parables. The application of the parable of the children playing in the marketplace concerns the Son of man who came eating and drinking and was called a glutton, a drunkard, a friend of tax collectors and "sinners." In the parable of the wheat and weeds Jesus explained the details by saying: "The one who sowed the good seed is the Son of man" (13:37). The tenants killed the son of the landowner (21:38–39). The wedding banquet is held to celebrate the wedding of the king's son (22:2). And in the eschatological parable of separating sheep from goats Jesus is described as the Son of man coming in his glory, judging the nations and separating the people from one another (25:31–33). The application of the parable of the burglar refers to the Son of man, who "will come at an hour when you do not expect him" (24:44; Luke 12:40). Numerous parables, including those of the ten virgins and talents, speak of Jesus' imminent return.

Matthew portrays Jesus in many of the parables—something which Luke does not do. Each writer employs his own skills and displays his own interests as he records the parables of Jesus. Nevertheless, these parables originated with Jesus because he created them; they belong to Jesus.
S. J. KISTEMAKER

See also SAYINGS OF JESUS.

Bibliography. K. E. Bailey, *Poet and Peasant* and *Through Peasant Eyes;* C. H. Dodd, *The Parables of the Kingdom;* A. M. Hunter, *Interpreting the Parables;* J. Jeremias, *The Parables of Jesus;* W. S. Kissinger, *The Parables of Jesus;* S. J. Kistemaker, *The Parables of Jesus;* R. H. Stein, *An Introduction to the Parables of Jesus;* D. O. Via, *The Parables: Their Literary and Existential Dimension.*

Paraclete. *See* HOLY SPIRIT.

Paradise. A word probably of Persian origin, appearing as *pardēs* in the OT three times ("orchard," Song of S. 4:13, ASV; "forest," Neh. 2:8, ASV; "parks," Eccles. 2:5). The Greek word *paradeisos* is found from the time of Xenophon, appearing in the papyri, inscriptions, LXX (twenty-seven occurrences, some of which refer to Eden, e.g., Gen. 2:8, 9, 10, 15, 16), Philo, and Josephus. The NT employs *paradeisos* three times, to denote the place of blessedness promised to the thief (Luke 23:43), the third heaven (II Cor. 12:4), and the location of the promised tree of life (Rev. 2:7).

Since the paradise of Eden was the place of bliss man had lost, rabbinical literature used the term to portray the place of blessedness for the righteous dead, in contrast to Gehenna, the place of torment. Elaborate and highly imaginative descriptions were drawn.

Jesus used the term once (Luke 23:43), and some see here only a reference to heaven. However, Jesus may be exhibiting essential agreement with traditional Jewish opinion by employing "Abraham's bosom" as an alternate term for "Paradise" in Luke 16:22. Then Paradise as the abode of the righteous is viewed as a separate section of Hades (a term equivalent to Sheol, Ps. 16:10; cf. Acts 2:27, 31). Because the remaining references to Paradise in the NT are to heaven, some have concluded that since the resurrection and ascension of Christ, Paradise has been removed from Hades to the third heaven, and that the "host of captives" who ascended with Christ were the OT saints (Eph. 4:8, RSV).

If Paradise means heaven as the dwelling place of God in all NT instances, then the choice of the term "Abraham's bosom" may have been deliberate. Then Jesus promised to the thief the bliss of heaven on that very day, which prospect belongs to all Christian believers (Luke 23:43; Phil. 1:23; II Cor. 5:8).
H. A. KENT, JR.

See also ABRAHAM'S BOSOM; HEAVEN.

Bibliography. L. S. Chafer, *Systematic Theology,* VII, 247–48; H. Bietenhard and C. Brown, *NIDNTT,* II, 760ff.; J. Jeremias, *TDNT,* V, 765ff.; H. K. McArthur, *IDB,* III, 655ff.

Paradox. A paradox is (1) an assertion which is self-contradictory, or (2) two or more assertions which are mutually contradictory, or (3) an assertion which contradicts some very commonly held position on the matter in question.

Paradoxes may be either rhetorical or logical. A rhetorical paradox is a figure used to shed light on a topic by challenging the reason of another and thus startling him. The NT contains many effective examples of this use of the paradox (e.g., Matt. 5:39; 10:39; John 11:24; II Cor. 6:9–10).

Logical paradoxes arise from the attempt by the human mind to unify or to coordinate the multiple facets of experience. Because of the diversity and complexity of reality and also because of the limitations of finite and sinful human reason, man's best efforts to know reality bring him only to the production of equally reasonable (or apparently so) yet irreconcilable (or apparently so) truths. In such cases man may be nearer the truth when he espouses both sides of a paradoxical issue than when he gives up one side in favor of the other.

Two differing interpretations of the logical paradox have emerged in the history of the church. One asserts actual paradoxes in which what is really true also really contradicts a right application of the laws of human thought. The other holds that paradoxical assertions are only apparent contradictions. Often this difference resolves itself into a mere difference of psychological attitude. Those who take the first interpretation of the paradox are willing to find rest of mind with incoherent elements lying unresolved in their thinking. Those who take the second believe that all truth must make its peace with the laws of human thought such as the law of contradiction and, therefore, do not find mental rest in incoherencies.

Medieval thought was not uniform on the question of paradox but in its ultimate rejection of double truth seemed to veer away from an acceptance of actual paradoxes in favor of apparent paradoxes. Martin Luther's objection to the denial of double truth by the Sorbonne was in reality a defense of actual paradoxes.

In modern theology the concept of paradox has assumed a prominent role in the writing of

Søren Kierkegaard and his twentieth century followers, Karl Barth, Reinhold Niebuhr, and others. The infinite, timeless, and hidden God can reach into finite time of human history through events which can be discerned only by faith, and even then necessarily appear as logical paradoxes.

For theists of any period, of course, a paradoxical "setting aside" of the laws of logic is understood as provisional; a true synthesis is always to be found in the mind of God. K. S. KANTZER

Bibliography. E. J. Carnell, *A Philosophy of the Christian Religion;* H. De Morgan, *A Budget of Paradoxes;* V. Ferm, ed., *Encyclopedia of Morals; HDB,* 632; H. R. Mackintosh, *Types of Modern Theology;* D. Runes, *Dictionary of Philosophy.*

Paradox, Theology of. *See* NEO-ORTHODOXY.

Pardon. *See* FORGIVENESS.

Parker Society. The London-based Anglican society which printed in fifty-four handsome volumes the works of the leading English Reformers of the sixteenth century. It was formed in 1840 and disbanded in 1855 when its work was completed. Its name is that of Matthew Parker, the first Elizabethan Archbishop of Canterbury, who was known as a great collector of books. The stimulus for the foundation of the society was provided by the Tractarian movement, led by John Henry Newman and Edward B. Pusey. Some members of this movement spoke disparagingly of the English Reformation, and so some members of the Church of England felt the need to make available in an attractive form the works of the leaders of that Reformation. Thus the society represented a cooperation between traditional High Churchmen and evangelical churchmen, both of whom were committed to the Reformation teaching on justification by faith. The society had about seven thousand subscribers who paid one pound each year from 1841 to 1855; thus for fifteen pounds the subscribers received fifty-four volumes. The level of critical scholarship is uneven in the volumes, since twenty-four editors were used and the task of arriving at the best text was far from easy. While some of the volumes have been superseded by more recent critical editions, this collection remains today one of the most valuable sources for the study of the English Reformation.

P. TOON

Bibliography. P. Toon, "The Parker Society," *HMPEC* 46 (Sept., 1977).

Parousia. *See* SECOND COMING OF CHRIST.

Pascal, Blaise (1623–1662). Mathematician, scientist, and religious thinker; one of the greatest figures in Western intellectual history. Pascal was born in Clermont, France, and raised by his widowed father, a brilliant lawyer and civil official who educated his children himself. He spent his formative years in Paris and Rouen, where he moved in intellectual circles and made his earliest scientific and mathematical discoveries. In his work he relied upon the experimental method, and among his contributions were the first mechanical calculator, basic research on vacuums and hydraulics, formulating probability theory, and laying the foundations for differential and integral calculus. His religious training was nominal, but he underwent a "conversion" in 1646 to an austere teaching of world renunciation and submission to God advocated by the disciples of Jean du Vergier. This resulted in a temporary cessation of his intellectual labors, but he soon left the group. In 1654 he experienced a far more significant "second conversion" to the Jansenist doctrine at Port Royal, and he fervently embraced the Christian faith, as seen in his later works, the *Provincial Letters* (1657) and the posthumously published *Pensées (Thoughts on Religion and Some Other Subjects).*

In his religious writings Pascal was an apologist rather than a systematic thinker. In arguing the existence of God he was not a complete fideist, as he felt unbelievers could be shown that religion was not contrary to reason, but he rejected metaphysical proofs like those of Descartes as being inadequate to lead one to the living God. In effect he argued psychologically, believing that the heart was the key. God could be perceived intuitively by the heart, not through reason. This involved combining knowledge, feeling, and will and establishing the personal, mystical relationship with Christ that gives life. As Pascal brings out in his wager argument, probability compels us to take the risk of faith in God. He also saw the human condition as one of "greatness and wretchedness." Rejecting Jesuit Pelagianism, Pascal accepted the Jansenist restatement of the Augustinian view of original sin. He said man possesses a special moral and religious status that elevates him far above animals, but he is controlled by sin and desperately needs God's special grace in order to be saved. Although he felt that "the heart has its reasons, of which reason knows nothing," he nevertheless maintained that the self-validating Scriptures, prophecies, existence of the Jews, miracles, and witness of history all serve to authenticate Christianity.

R. V. PIERARD

See also PASCAL'S WAGER; JANSEN, CORNELIUS OTTO.

Bibliography. Pascal, *Oeuvres complètes*, 14 vols.; M. Bishop, *Pascal: The Life of Genius;* M. Ernest, *Blaise Pascal: The Life and Work of a Realist;* E. Cailliet, *Pascal: The Emergence of Genius;* R. Hazelton, *Blaise Pascal: The Genius of His Thought;* H. M. Davidson, *The Origins of Certainty; Encyclopedia of Philosophy,* VI, 51–55; *NCE,* X, 1046–48; P. M. Bechtel, *NIDCC,* 749.

Pascal's Wager. A famous apologetic advanced by Blaise Pascal in his *Pensées.* Pascal prepares for the ostensibly unreasonable step of faith by pushing reason to its own limits. He argues first that we can know the existence and nature of finite space because we are limited and extended in space, even though we do not know the quality of unboundedness. However, because we do not possess God's attributes of infinity and nonextension and thus cannot know his existence or nature, rational proof of his being is impossible. Moving from rational knowledge to reasonable surmise, Pascal affirms: "Either God exists, or he does not," and proposes that we wager on the matter. To bet that he is means a modest surrender of reason, but to opt for divine nonexistence is to risk the loss of eternal life and happiness. The stake (one's reason) is slight compared to the prize that may be won. If the gambler for God is right, he will win everything, but he loses nothing should this turn out to be wrong. Since the reasonableness of betting has been demonstrated, one can now move from the realm of the probable to the practical action of placing one's faith in God. R. V. PIERARD

See also PASCAL, BLAISE.

Paschal Controversies. Disputes in the Christian church about the dating of Easter (Gr. *pascha*). Differences first arose in the late second century on whether Easter celebrations should be held always on a Sunday or should vary according to the precise day of the Jewish lunar month (the 14th of Nisan) that marked the resurrection of Christ. The Eastern church preferred the latter dating; the Western church rejected this because it clashed with the Jewish Passover and opted for the following Sunday.

Later controversy centered on the different ways in which the paschal moon was calculated, the principal disagreement being initially between Antioch and Alexandria. Antioch followed the Jewish custom; Alexandria always put Easter after the vernal equinox. The Council of Nicaea decided on the latter practice.

Then came differences between Gaul, Rome, and Alexandria. Alexandria used a nineteen-year cycle, Rome an eighty-four-year one. Augustine said in 387 that Easter was observed in Gaul on March 21, in Rome on April 18, and in Alexandria on April 25. The Alexandrian calculation, adopted formally at the instigation of Dionysius Exiguus in 525, remains in use.

Gaul, however, was out of step because in 457 Victorius of Aquitaine had devised a 532-year cycle in Rome which, although never much favored there, caused confusion in Gaul until the time of Charlemagne.

The Celtic churches meanwhile had their own method of computation which led to differences after Roman missionaries came. In the mid-seventh century, for example, those who followed the Roman system were keeping Palm Sunday and fasting while the Celtic adherents were celebrating Easter. The Synod of Whitby (664) decided on the Roman system.

In Eastern Orthodoxy, Easter is often observed on a later Sunday than in the West because the Eastern church follows the Julian calendar. The Second Vatican Council in 1963 said there was no objection to a fixed Sunday (probably early in April) for Easter, but differences still remained two decades later. J. D. DOUGLAS

See also EASTER; CHRISTIAN YEAR.

Passion of Christ. *See* CROSS, CRUCIFIXION.

Passover. The first of three annual festivals at which all men were required to appear at the sanctuary (Exod. 23:14–17). The noun *pesaḥ* is derived from the verb *pāsaḥ,* "to pass over," in the sense of "to spare" (Exod. 12:12–13). Passover is associated with the feast of unleavened bread (*ḥag hammaṣṣôt*), the week during which leaven was rigidly excluded from the diet of the Hebrews (Exod. 23:15).

The historical passover is related to the tenth plague—the death of the firstborn in Egypt. Israel was instructed to prepare a lamb for each household. Blood was to be applied to the lintel and doorpost (Exod. 12:7). The sign of the blood would secure the safety of each house so designated.

On the evening of the 14th of Nisan (Abib) the passover lambs were slain. After being roasted, they were eaten with unleavened bread and bitter herbs (Exod. 12:8), emphasizing the need for a hasty departure and reminiscent of the bitter bondage in Egypt (Deut. 16:3). The passover was a family observance. In the case of small families, neighbors might be invited to share the paschal meal.

The initial instructions concerned the preparation for the historical Exodus (Exod. 12:21–23). Subsequent directions were given for the observance of the seven-day festival of unleavened bread (Exod. 13:3–10). The passover experience was to be repeated each year as a means of instruction to future generations (Exod. 12:24–27).

In subsequent years a passover ritual developed incorporating additional features. Four successive cups of wine mixed with water were used. Psalms 113–18 were sung at appropriate places. Fruit, mixed with vinegar to the consistency of mortar, served as a reminder of the mortar used during the bondage.

The first and seventh days of the week were observed as sabbaths. All work ceased and the people met in holy convocation (Exod. 12:16; Num. 28:18, 25). On the second day of the festival a sheaf of first-ripe barley was waved by the priest to consecrate the opening of harvest (Lev. 23:10–14). In addition to the regular sacrifices, two bullocks, one ram, and seven lambs were offered as a burnt offering and a he-goat as a sin offering each day (Num. 28:19–23; Lev. 23:8).

Passover observances were frequently neglected in OT times. After Sinai (Num. 9:1–14) none took place until after the entrance into Canaan (Josh. 5:10). The reforming kings Hezekiah (II Chr. 30) and Josiah (II Kings 23:21–23; II Chr. 35) gave attention to passover observance. After the dedication of the second temple, a noteworthy passover was celebrated (Ezra 6:19–22).

The death of Christ at the passover season was deemed significant by the early church. Paul calls Christ "our passover" (I Cor. 5:7). The command not to break a bone of the paschal lamb (Exod. 12:46) is applied by John to the death of Christ—"A bone of him shall not be broken" (John 19:36). The Christian must put away the "old leaven" of malice and wickedness, and replace it with "the unleavened bread of sincerity and truth" (I Cor. 5:8).

C. F. Pfeiffer

See also Feasts and Festivals, Old Testament; Lamb of God.

Bibliography. A. Edersheim, *The Temple: Its Ministry and Services;* W. H. Green, *The Hebrew Feasts in Their Relation to Recent Critical Hypotheses;* T. H. Gaster, *Passover: Its History and Traditions;* S. M. Lehrman, *The Jewish Festivals;* J. Lightfoot, *The Temple Service;* The Mishna, ed. H. Danby, tractate *Pesahim;* R. Schaefer, *Das Passah-Mazzoth-Fest;* H. Schauss, *The Jewish Festivals.*

Pastor. *See* Spiritual Gifts.

Patriarch. This term, recalling the OT patriarchs who were heads of their families or of tribes, is an ecclesiastical title used in both Roman Catholic and Eastern Orthodox churches. It describes a bishop who has been exalted over other bishops. The authority and duties of the patriarch differ between Eastern and Western churches. Where the patriarch has significant authority (mainly in the Eastern churches), this would be in legislation, administration, and teaching. The patriarchate is not a universal office; only a few cities have patriarchs. By the fourth/fifth century there were only five such cities: Rome, Alexandria, Antioch, Constantinople, and Jerusalem.

W. L. Liefeld

See also Bishop; Church Officers.

Patripassianism. *See* Monarchianism.

Pattern. *See* Type, Typology.

Paul, Theology of. Paul gives two different accounts of the source of his theology. In Gal. 1:11–12 he insists that he did not receive it from men but "through a revelation of Jesus Christ," referring to his experience on the Damascus Road. But in I Cor. 15:3–8 he pictures himself as simply passing on the tradition he had received about Christ's atoning death, burial, and resurrection. Some scholars (e.g., Drane) maintain that two different Pauls are speaking in these passages: the former an enthusiastic individualist, whose theology was based on the immediate inspiration of the Holy Spirit; the latter an older, more sober Paul, whose individualism has been curbed by the experience of conflict and the need to come to terms with the other apostles' understanding of the faith. Others (e.g., Bruce) argue that Paul's acceptance of the radically new tradition about Jesus, in opposition to "the traditions of my fathers" (Gal. 1:14), was a direct result of the Damascus Road revelation, so that the one complements the other.

Either way, it is a problem to know why Paul presents the gospel in terms so different from those which Jesus himself used. For instance, why is "justification by faith"—scarcely present in Jesus' teaching—so prominent in Paul's, and why does Paul virtually ignore Jesus' great theme of the kingdom of God? Plainly Paul felt himself empowered, as an apostle of Christ, to speak in his name (II Cor. 13:3) under the inspiration of the Holy Spirit (I Cor. 2:12–13, 16) in ways in which the earthly Christ had never spoken. In fact, his thought is a fantastically creative combination of elements drawn together, under the orchestration of the Spirit, from many different sources: from Jesus' earthly teaching (e.g., I Cor. 7:10–11; 9:14), from his own background in Pharisaism (e.g., Rom. 10:6–9; Gal. 4:22–26), from earlier Christian traditions (e.g., I Cor. 15:3–7; Rom. 3:24–25; Phil. 2:6–11), from secular Greek thought (e.g., Rom. 2:15; Col. 3:18–4:1), from his own insight (Eph. 3:4), and above all from the OT (Rom.

15:4; II Tim. 3:15–16). Opinions are of course divided as to whether Paul thus distorted the message of Jesus or not.

The Nature of God. Morris has pointed out that in Romans God is mentioned 153 times, whereas Christ appears 65 times. Statistics can be misleading, but in this case they seem to show where the real foundation of Pauline thought rests. Two key words highlight the center of his thinking about God:

Creation. His belief in the one God who created all that is shaped Paul's theology fundamentally.

He could not accept that God had no purpose for the Gentile nations. "Is God the God of Jews only? Is he not the God of Gentiles also? Yes, of Gentiles also, since God is one" (Rom. 3:29–30). His belief in the equality of Jews and Gentiles before God (Rom. 1:16; 10:12; Gal. 3:28) is based on this oneness of God (cf. Deut. 6:4), who, unlike pagan deities, cannot be bound to a particular geographical area or nation but extends his saving love to all men equally (I Tim. 2:3–5). Paul's whole ministry as apostle to the Gentiles (rejected by many Jewish Christians) grew out of this presupposition.

The foundation for this new Jew-Gentile unity was to be found in the person of Christ, who for Paul was a second Adam (I Cor. 15:47), the head of a newly created humanity balancing and repairing the old. "New creation" thinking often finds expression in Paul (see esp. Rom. 5:12–21; I Cor. 15:42–50): Jews and Gentiles have been united into "one new man," the crucified Christ who breaks down the old barriers (Eph. 1:11–16). This new man has been raised to God's right hand (Eph. 1:20), where he fulfills the role envisaged for man by the OT: he has all things under his feet (Ps. 8:6; Eph. 1:22; I Cor. 15:25–27). As the head of a new humanity, he provides a pattern to be stamped on his descendants, just as Adam's race was marked by his fall (I Cor. 15:49; Rom. 5:18–19; Eph. 4:22–24; Col. 3:10).

God is the one who "calls into existence the things that do not exist" (Rom. 4:17). The light of the gospel, shining in believers' hearts, is comparable to the original light of creation (II Cor. 4:6). Against this background Paul's thought moves on a cosmic scale; God has something more glorious in mind that just a new humanity: the transformation of creation is his ultimate goal (Rom. 8:18–25; Col. 1:15–20; Eph. 1:9–10).

History. For Paul history is purposeful, developing toward a goal and along a route predetermined by its one Lord. Therefore he continued to accept the OT as the word of God and argued strenuously that the "new" in Christ must be integrated into the "old" previously given. He fought tremendous battles over the precise nature of this integration. Jewish Christians who thought that the coming of Christ introduced no alteration into God's purposes with Israel were told that, on the contrary, Christ marks the beginning of the new age in which the gates of salvation are opened to all alike (Rom. 10:13). Gentile Christians who argued that God's purposes with Israel had been annulled or that the new age was fully manifest in their life and worship were told that, on the contrary, God's word to Israel still stands (Rom. 9:6; 11:1, 26), and that a final consummation is yet to be: the Holy Spirit pledges something more glorious to come (II Cor. 1:22; 5:5; Eph. 1:14). Behind all his epistles lies Paul's concern to establish this subtle balance between old and new in different situations of imbalance.

The Son of God. The OT helped Paul to understand how Christ is the last Adam in God's purposes, and led him to see Christ's death as the vital turning point between the two ages. Isa. 53 showed him that Christ's death was substitutionary, for our sins, so that God's people could be made righteous through his righteousness (Rom. 4:25; 5:18; Phil. 2:7–8). Reflection on Deut. 21:23, which seemed at first to speak against Christ, produced the revolutionary view that Christ was "cursed" for us (Gal. 3:13). The ritual of the day of atonement (Lev. 16) helped him to see Christ as God's appointed offering and place of atonement, whereby his people are thoroughly and finally cleansed (Rom. 3:24; 8:3; II Cor. 5:21). The passover ritual of Exod. 12 showed how Christ was "our paschal lamb," sacrificed to redeem the people of God from bondage and set them on the hard road to glory (I Cor. 5:7–8; 11:23–32; Eph. 1:7; Col. 1:11–14). His reflection on Jesus' use of Daniel's "Son of man" vision (Dan. 7) led him to see that, paradoxically, the death that looked like a final defeat was actually a tremendous victory over the powers of this world (Gal. 6:14; Col. 2:15; I Cor. 2:6–8; Rom. 8:31–39). The resurrection he learned to see as God's response to Christ's death (Rom. 1:4; 6:4; I Cor. 15:15; Phil. 2:9–11), and thus as God's response to the whole new humanity, which will likewise be raised to glory (I Thess. 4:14; I Cor. 6:14; 15:20–22; Rom. 6:5; 8:11; Phil. 3:8–11; Eph. 2:4–7; Col. 2:13–14) and must begin to express that new life now (Rom. 6:4, 11; Col. 2:20–3:5).

The People of God. Paul's conversion took him from one "people of God" to another. The tension inevitably produced by these rival claims meant that he had to establish his theology of the church from first principles upward. The most important issue in this struggle was justification, because of the common conviction that

God will one day judge the world (cf. Rom. 3:6). Who will then be acquitted, "justified"? Paul rejected his Jewish contemporaries' view (which he had previously accepted) that God's covenant with Israel assured it of forgiveness and acquittal. If this alone were necessary, why did Christ die (Gal. 2:21)? The bald fact of the death of God's Son showed Paul that justification could not come through "works of the law" (Gal. 2:16; 3:10; Rom. 3:20)—i.e., through mere dependence, however heartfelt and zealous, on the status conferred by God's gift of the law. Even the most impeccable Jewish record, such as Paul himself had (Gal. 1:14; Phil. 3:4–7), was useless. Though prompted to this view by his sudden encounter with Christ, Paul yet came to see that the OT points to its own weakness, by offering nothing more secure than a precarious existence "under a curse" (Gal. 3:10), where human weakness might at any moment trigger the curses listed in Deut. 28:15–68. Christ alone could give assurance of justification, because Christ alone had overcome the sin which has made the law incapable of giving the promised blessing (Rom. 7:7–8; 8:3). But this dethroning of the law as the central salvific principle demolished the barriers of Israel and opened justification to all who would simply embrace Christ and, through reception of his Holy Spirit, begin to evidence the faith and love for God for which the OT longed in vain (Deut. 6:4; 9:13–14; 29:4; Ezek. 18:31; 36:26; Rom. 5:5; 6:17; Gal. 3:14, 23–26). Paul was thus able to claim that he, with his "law-free gospel" offered to all alike, was more faithful to the law (Rom. 3:31) than were those who urged that salvation could be enjoyed only within the borders of Israel. Through Christ, who is its "end" (Rom. 10:4), the law is delivered from its bondage to sin (Rom. 7:10–11) and its nationalist limitations (Gal. 5:3) and restored to its proper role as the guide of the people of God. Hence Paul's confident handling of the OT.

Some scholars (e.g., Knox) argue that Paul's theology contains no essential ethic, because his gospel of justification is about eschatological status before God and does not touch everyday life. This view can be held only when justification is removed from its essential context in Paul's missionary activity—namely, the debate over who are the people of God. For the people of God do not merely exist eschatologically but are also an earthly reality. They will exist supremely at the end, at "the revealing of the sons of God" (Rom. 8:19), but their justification is also present (Rom. 5:1) and constitutes them a distinctive entity. When Paul writes that the Gentiles who did not pursue justification have attained it (Rom. 9:30), he is referring to something obvious here and now, to the incorporation of the Gentiles into the distinctive new life style of the church. Hence the "therefore" of Rom. 12:1 (introducing the practical section of the epistle) is truly logical, and continues the exposition of justification in Rom. 1–11.

The new Christian life style is thus integral to Paul's theology. Its keynotes are the outworking of the love principle (Rom. 12:9–21; I Cor. 13; Col. 3:14; Eph. 5:2) through the formation of a Christian mind (Rom. 8:5; 12:2, 17; I Cor. 2:15–16; Phil. 4:8; Eph. 4:17–24) under the empowering presence of the Holy Spirit (Rom. 8:13; 12:11; I Thess. 1:6; Gal. 5:22–25; Eph. 3:14–18; 5:18–20) in the context of an interdependent community life (Rom. 12; I Cor. 12; Eph. 4:1–16; Col. 3:12–4:1) inspired by a constant awareness of the imminent eschatological goal (I Cor. 7:29–31; Rom. 8:23–25; 13:11–14; II Cor. 5:9–10; Gal. 6:8; Phil. 3:12–14; I Thess. 5:4–11). S. MOTYER

See also PAULINISM.

Bibliography. J. W. Drane, *Paul: Libertine or Legalist?* F. F. Bruce, *Paul and Jesus;* L. L. Morris, "The Theme of Romans," in *Apostolic History and the Gospel,* ed. W. W. Gasque and R. P. Martin; J. Knox, *Chapters in a Life of Paul;* V. P. Furnish, *Theology and Ethics in Paul;* H. N. Ridderbos, *Paul: An Outline of His Theology;* J. A. Ziesler, *The Meaning of Righteousness in Paul;* D. E. H. Whiteley, *The Theology of St. Paul;* G. Bornkamm, *Paul.*

Paulicians. A highly independent Christian sect which arose in the heart of the Eastern church about A.D. 750. They are frequently interpreted as either "early Protestants" or "radical oriental dualists," neither view giving the entire truth. They were the most influential sect of their time, but their formative force on later reform parties is problematical. Though much maligned in contemporary polemical literature, they are seen in the ancient Paulician work, *The Key of Truth,* translated by F. C. Conybeare in 1898, as a true reform party.

They were anti-Romanists, repudiating Mariolatry, intercession of saints, and the use of relics and images. They strongly despised the Roman hierarchy, having themselves only one grade of ministry. In rejecting infant baptism they taught that thirty was the age for immersion, during which ordinance the Holy Spirit was received. Repentance was also a sacrament and the Agape was practiced with the sacrament of "the body and the blood."

In Christology they were adoptionists but not docetics, as often thought. They valued the Pauline writings very highly but made use of other NT and OT books in *The Key of Truth.*

W. N. KERR

Bibliography. W. F. Adeney, *The Greek and Eastern Churches;* R. A. Knox, *Enthusiasm;* C. A. Scott, *HERE;* C. H. Williams, *The Radical Reformers.*

Paulinism. The term is used to describe the type of theology which looks to Paul, rather than to other NT authors, for its chief inspiration. The Reformation was essentially a revival of Paulinism, for the distinctive Pauline doctrine of justification by faith was and has remained for all Protestant churches "the article of faith by which the Church stands or falls" (Luther). In broader terms, however, the whole Western church may be regarded as "Pauline," over against the Orthodox churches of the East, which look rather to John for the NT foundation of their theology. Here Augustine's influence has meant that the Western churches—Catholic and Protestant alike—are partners in a theological tradition which values legal categories of thought and metaphors as the most fruitful way of talking about the relationship between God and the world, and which therefore regards justification as the central soteriological issue, even if Catholic and Protestant interpret Paul's teaching differently.

Lutheran theologians have generally been conscious of the priority they give to Paul, but recently three factors have contributed to a growing feeling that this exaltation is questionable. Ecclesiastically, the ecumenical movement has made Western theologians more aware of the Eastern theological tradition with its very different approach to justification and Pauline theology generally. Theologically, the awareness has grown that religious language can only hint and suggest, never describe—so that perhaps legal language is only one of several possible metaphor groups that may validly be used to talk about God and the world. And in NT scholarship a sharper awareness of the parallel but distinct historical development of the different theological streams within the NT (Pauline, Johannine, Synoptic, etc.) has led to a desire to interpret each within its own terms and not to seek out a "canon within the canon" on the basis of which the rest of the Bible can be interpreted. Ecumenical conversations are therefore found to be mirrored within the NT itself, so that the issue of diversity and unity in the NT has tremendous modern relevance.

Several approaches to this problem are available today. The traditional Lutheran-Protestant solution is still well represented: it distinguishes an original, pure, Pauline gospel from "Early Catholicism," a term used to describe the earliest movements, traceable in the NT itself, toward a Catholic emphasis on the sacraments, ordered ministry, and an ethical Christianity (regarded as a degeneration from the truth). Some scholars even find this degeneration in Paul himself, and so locate pure Paulinism only in the earliest epistles. Another approach identifies a common denominator between Paul and the other NT authors and questions the possibility of finding theological harmony outside this center. For Dunn, the NT authors agree in identifying Jesus of Nazareth with the risen and exalted Christ, but beyond that show very substantial diversity of thought, so that Paulinism is simply one version of Christianity, inevitably existing in tension with other versions. Recently a third approach has appeared, associated particularly with the German scholars Martin Hengel and Peter Stuhlmacher, which asserts a substantial unity between the main NT streams by finding in them the same central theological ideas differently expressed and applied. The heart of Pauline as of Johannine theology is thus the proclamation of Jesus as the messianic Reconciler who dies a sacrificial death for the people of God.

NT scholarship is in a considerable state of flux, matching that in the parallel area of ecumenism. Whatever the outcome, we must affirm that those for whom, like Luther, the Epistle to the Romans contains "the purest gospel" have not misplaced their faith. S. Motyer

See also Paul, Theology of; Justification.

Bibliography. J. D. G. Dunn, *Unity and Diversity in the NT;* E. Käsemann, "The Problem of a NT Theology," *NTS* 19:235–45; J. W. Drane, "Tradition, Law and Ethics in Pauline Theology," *NovT* 16:167–78; M. Hengel, *The Atonement.*

Paul of Samosata. Bishop of Antioch from 260 to 272. Questions about his orthodoxy generated synodal efforts against him early in his tenure. In 268 a large synod was held at Antioch which, under the dominance of Malchion, a local presbyter, excommunicated him. The portions of the synodal letter preserved by Eusebius deal only with Paul's misconduct, but other sources reveal that the real issue was his Christology. Paul refused to be deposed but was finally ejected from the church building by Emperor Aurelian in 272.

Although Paul's beliefs are obscured by the polemical nature of the sources which preserve them, certain features do stand out. His theology was monarchian and his Christology a form of adoptionism. Jesus was a mere man, begotten by the Holy Spirit and born of the Virgin Mary, properly called Christ because of his anointing by the Holy Spirit. The Logos (wisdom) was an impersonal quality of God that came together with and indwelt the man Jesus Christ, but remained in essence distinct. Having enabled Jesus

Christ to become great, the Logos returned to God. For his sinlessness Jesus Christ was granted the titles Redeemer and Savior and secured an eternal union of his will with God. Paul's doctrine of the Holy Spirit is unclear.

Modern attention on the controversy has centered as much on his opponents' theology, which resembled later Apollinarianism, as on Paul's. Eusebius regarded Paul as the theological heir of the heresy of Artemon/Artemas, and there appears to have been some connection between Paul's followers and later Arians.

G. T. Burke

See also Monarchianism.

Bibliography. Eusebius, *Ecclesiastical History* V. 28.1–2, VII.27.1–30.19, 32.5 and 21; H. J. Lawlor, "The Sayings of Paul of Samosata," *JTS* 19:20–45; H. Chadwick, review of *Les actes du procès de Paul de Samosate, JTS* n.s. 4:91–94; R. L. Sample, "The Christology of the Council of Antioch (268 c.e.) Reconsidered," *CH* 48:18–26.

Peace. The primary and basic idea of the biblical word "peace" (OT *šālôm;* NT *eirēnē*) is completeness, soundness, wholeness. It is a favorite biblical greeting (Gen. 29:6; Luke 24:36), and is found at the beginning or end of the NT epistles except James and I John. To this day it is one of the commonest words among the Semites. Dismissal is also expressed by the word (I Sam. 1:17). It means cessation from war (Josh. 9:15). Friendship between companions is expressed by it (Gen. 26:29; Ps. 28:3), as well as friendship with God through a covenant (Num. 25:12; Isa. 54:10). Contentment or anything working toward safety, welfare, and happiness is included in the concept (Isa. 32:17–18).

Peace has reference to health, prosperity, well-being, security, as well as quiet from war (Eccles. 3:8; Isa. 45:7). The prophet Isaiah pointed out repeatedly that there will be no peace for the wicked (Isa. 48:22; 57:21), even though many of the wicked continually seek to encourage themselves with a false peace (Jer. 6:14).

Peace is a condition of freedom from strife whether internal or external. Security from outward enemies (Isa. 26:12), as well as calm of heart for those trusting God (Job 22:21; Isa. 26:3), is included. Peace is so pleasing to the Lord that the godly are enjoined to seek it diligently (Ps. 34:14; Zech. 8:16, 19). It is to be a characteristic of the NT believer also (Mark 9:50; II Cor. 13:11). Peace is a comprehensive and valued gift from God, and the promised and climaxing blessing in messianic times (Isa. 2:4; 9:6–7; 11:6; Mic. 4:1–4; 5:5).

"To hold one's peace" means simply to be silent (Luke 14:4). The words in the OT (e.g., *ḥāraš*) and the NT (e.g., *siōpaō*) have nothing in common with the words now under consideration.

In the NT the word has reference to the peace which is the gift of Christ (John 14:27; 16:33; Rom. 5:1; Phil. 4:7). The word is used many times to express the truths of the mission, character, and gospel of Christ. The purpose of Christ's coming into the world was to bring spiritual peace with God (Luke 1:79; 2:14; 24:36; Mark 5:34; 9:50). There is a sense in which he came not to bring peace, but a sword (Matt. 10:34). This has reference to the struggle with every form of sin. Christ's life depicted in the Gospels is one of majestic calm and serenity (Matt. 11:28; John 14:27). The essence of the gospel may be expressed in the term "peace" (Acts 10:36; Eph. 6:15), including the peace of reconciliation with God (Rom. 5:1) and the peace of fellowship with God (Gal. 5:22; Phil. 4:7).

The innumerable blessings of the Christian revolve around the concept of peace. The gospel is the gospel of peace (Eph. 6:15). Christ is our peace (Eph. 2:14–15); God the Father is the God of peace (I Thess. 5:23). The inalienable privilege of every Christian is the peace of God (Phil. 4:9) because of the legacy of peace left by Christ in his death (John 14:27; 16:33). These blessings are not benefits laid up in eternal glory only, but are a present possession (Rom. 8:6; Col. 3:15). Thus, peace is "a conception distinctly peculiar to Christianity, the tranquil state of a soul assured of its salvation through Christ, and so fearing nothing from God and content with its earthly lot, of whatever sort that is" (Thayer).

C. L. Feinberg

Bibliography. W. Foerster and G. von Rad, *TDNT,* II, 400–401; H. Beck and C. Brown, *NIDNTT,* II, 776ff.; E. Stauffer, *NT Theology.*

Peace Offering. *See* Offerings and Sacrifices in Bible Times.

Pelagius, Pelagianism. Pelagianism is that teaching, originating in the late fourth century, which stresses man's ability to take the initial steps toward salvation by his own efforts, apart from special grace. It is sharply opposed by Augustinianism, which emphasizes the absolute necessity of God's interior grace for man's salvation.

Pelagius was an eminently moral person, who became a fashionable teacher at Rome late in the fourth century. British by birth, he was a zealous ascetic. Whether he was a monk or not we cannot say, but he clearly supported monastic ideals. In his early writings he argued against the Arians but fired his big guns against the

Manichaeans. Their dualistic fatalism infuriated the moralist in him.

While in Rome, Pelagius studied Augustine's anti-Manichaean writings, particularly *On Free Will.* He came to oppose passionately Augustine's quietism, reflected in his prayer in the *Confessions:* "Give what thou commandest—and command what thou wilt" (X,31,45).

When the Visigoths surged upon Rome in 410/411, Pelagius sought refuge in Africa. After avoiding an encounter with Augustine, he moved on to Jerusalem, where he gained a good reputation. No one took offense at his teaching.

Meanwhile in Africa, Pelagius's pupil Coelestius, a less cautious and more superficial man, had pointedly drawn out the consequences of Pelagius's teaching on freedom. Churchmen in the area of Carthage solemnly charged him with heresy. According to Augustine, Coelestius did not accept the "remission of sins" in infant baptism. Such an assertion of "innocence" of newborn babies denied the basic relationship in which all men stand "since Adam." It was claiming that unredeemed man is sound and free to do all good. It was rendering salvation by Christ superfluous.

Augustine sent his own disciple Orosius to the East in an attempt to gain the condemnation of Pelagius. But in the East churchmen were unable to see anything more than an obstinate quarrel about trivialities. They acquitted Pelagius, a decision that infuriated the Africans, who turned toward Rome and compelled Pope Innocent I to expressly condemn the new heresy.

The keystone of Pelagianism is the idea of man's unconditional free will and his moral responsibility. In creating man God did not subject him, like other creatures, to the law of nature but gave him the unique privilege of accomplishing the divine will by his own choice. This possibility of freely choosing the good entails the possibility of choosing evil.

According to Pelagius there are three features in human action: power (*posse*), will (*velle*), and the realization (*esse*). The first comes exclusively from God; the other two belong to man. Thus, as man acts, he merits praise or blame. Whatever his followers may have said, Pelagius himself held the conception of a divine law proclaiming to men what they ought to do and setting before them the prospect of supernatural rewards and punishments. If man enjoys freedom of choice, it is by the express bounty of his Creator; he ought to use it for those ends that God prescribes.

The rest of Pelagianism flows from this central thought of freedom. First, it rejects the idea that man's will has any intrinsic bias in favor of wrongdoing as a result of the fall. Since each soul is created immediately by God, as Pelagius believed, then it cannot come into the world soiled by original sin transmitted from Adam. Before a person begins exercising his will, "there is only in him what God has created." The effect of infant baptism, then, is not eternal life but "spiritual illumination, adoption as children of God, citizenship of the heavenly Jerusalem."

Second, Pelagius considers grace purely an external aid provided by God. He leaves no room for any special interior action of God upon the soul. By "grace" Pelagius really means free will itself or the revelation of God's law through reason, instructing us in what we should do and holding out to us eternal sanctions. Since this revelation has become obscured through evil customs, grace now includes the law of Moses and the teaching and example of Christ.

This grace is offered equally to all. God is no respecter of persons. By merit alone men advance in holiness. God's predestination operates according to the quality of the lives God foresees men will lead.

Theologians often describe Pelagianism as a form of naturalism. But this label scarcely does justice to its religious spirit. Defective though the system is in its recognition of man's weakness, it does reflect an awareness of man's high calling and the claims of the moral law. Yet Pelagianism's one-sidedness remains an inadequate interpretation of Christianity. This was especially so after Coelestius pushed into the foreground the denial of original sin, the teaching that Adam was created mortal, and the idea that children are eligible for eternal life even without baptism. This rosy view of human nature and inadequate understanding of divine grace was finally condemned in 431 at the Council of Ephesus.

B. L. Shelley

See also Augustine of Hippo.

Bibliography. G. Bonner, *Augustine and Modern Research on Pelagianism;* P. Brown, *Religion and Society in the Age of St. Augustine;* R. F. Evans, *Pelagius: Inquiries and Reappraisals;* J. Ferguson, *Pelagius.*

Penal Theory of the Atonement. *See* Atonement, Theories of the.

Penance. Derived from the Latin *poena* ("penalty"), the term refers to disciplinary measures adopted by the church against offenders. In early days it applied to those guilty of such glaring offenses as apostasy, murder, adultery, who were allowed only one chance of restoration after undergoing a course of fastings, etc., on public confession of their sin in renewal of the baptismal profession, and on acceptance of certain lasting prohibitions—e.g., continence in the case of the unmarried. With the barbarian invasions this severe discipline was mitigated, and in the Celtic Penitentials we find that secret confession is allowed and restoration begins to precede the penances, which become much more formal and may be replaced by cash payments according to current notions of satisfaction.

Two notable developments took place in the Middle Ages. First, penance at least once a year was made compulsory from 1215. Second, the whole understanding was developed in a new way which ultimately found codification at the Council of Trent, when penance was officially accepted as a sacrament. It was still agreed that the eternal guilt of mortal sins after baptism could be met only by the atoning work of Christ, true contrition, and the word of absolution. From this angle penance properly speaking remained disciplinary. But it was now argued that the temporal guilt of either mortal or venial sin may be met in part by the actual penances, thus mitigating the final expiation demanded in purgatory. In addition, voluntary alms, Masses, and drawings on the so-called treasury of merit—e.g., by indulgences—could be used for the same purpose and could even take the place of penances. Quite apart from the obviously nonscriptural nature of this whole system, five main evils may be seen in it: (1) it misunderstands the problem of postbaptismal sin; (2) it detracts from the atonement; (3) it promotes related errors such as purgatory, Masses, indulgences, and invocation of saints; (4) it creates legalism and formalism; and (5) it gives rise to the moral evils of the confessional.

The Reformers cut through the whole falsification of theory and practice by insisting that what the NT demands is not penance but penitence or repentance, though they saw a real value in the restoring of true discipline and of course the private counseling of those troubled in conscience as individually required.

G. W. Bromiley

See also Absolution; Penitence; Repentance.

Bibliography. *HERE;* O. D. Watkins, *A History of Penance;* R. C. Mortimer, *The Origins of Private Penance in the Western Church; Canons and Decrees of the Council of Trent; Catechism of Trent.*

Penitence. Among Protestants penitence is considered a synonym for repentance, sorrow for sin and the turning away from it to lead a new life. It should not be confused with penance, a sacrament in the Roman Catholic Church that stresses the performance of ecclesiastically prescribed acts to make satisfaction for postbaptismal sins.

Jesus' message, as well as that of his immediate disciples, was characterized by the call for men to repent (Mark 1:15; 6:12; Luke 10:13). The Greek term *metanoeō* holds two ideas: "to change one's mind" and "to regret or feel remorse." Thus, repentance is one aspect of conversion, the other being faith. Together they form one experience in which a person turns from sin to Christ.

B. L. Shelley

See also Repentance.

Pentecost. A term derived from the Greek *pentēkostos,* meaning fiftieth, which was applied to the fiftieth day after the passover. It was the culmination of the feast of weeks (Exod. 34:22; Deut. 16:10), which began on the third day after the passover with the presentation of the first harvest sheaves to God and which concluded with the offering of two loaves of unleavened bread, representing the first products of the harvest (Lev. 23:17–20; Deut. 16:9–10). After the Exile it became one of the great pilgrimage feasts of Judaism, at which many of those who lived in remote sections of the Roman world returned to Jerusalem for worship (Acts 10:16). For that reason it served as a bond to unite the Jewish world of the first century and to remind them of their history.

In the Christian church Pentecost is the anniversary of the coming of the Holy Spirit. When Jesus ascended, he instructed his disciples to remain in Jerusalem until they should receive power from on high. As a group of 120 were praying in an upper room in Jerusalem fifty days after his death, the Holy Spirit descended upon them with the sound of a great wind and with tongues of fire which settled upon each of them. They began to speak in other languages and to preach boldly in the name of Christ, with the result that three thousand were converted. This tremendous manifestation of divine power marked the beginning of the church, which has ever since regarded Pentecost as its birthday.

In the church year Pentecost covered the period from Easter to Pentecost Sunday. The day itself was observed by feasting, and was a favorite occasion for administering baptism. It was the third great Christian feast after Christmas and Easter. In the liturgy of the Anglican Church it is called Whitsunday, from the custom of wearing white clothing on that day.

M. C. Tenney

See also Christian Year.

Pentecostalism. An evangelical charismatic reformation movement which usually traces its roots to an outbreak of tongue-speaking in

Topeka, Kansas, in 1901 under the leadership of Charles Fox Parham, a former Methodist preacher. It was Parham who formulated the basic Pentecostal doctrine of "initial evidence" after a student in his Bethel Bible School, Agnes Ozman, experienced glossolalia in January, 1901.

Basically Pentecostals believe that the experience of the 120 on the day of Pentecost, known as the "baptism in the Holy Spirit," should be normative for all Christians. Most Pentecostals believe, furthermore, that the first sign of "initial evidence" of this second baptism is speaking in a language unknown to the speaker.

Although speaking in tongues had appeared in the nineteenth century in both England and America, it had never assumed the importance attributed to it by the later Pentecostals. For instance, glossolalia occurred in the 1830s under the ministry of Presbyterian Edward Irving in London, in the services of Mother Ann Lee's Shaker movement, and among Joseph Smith's Mormon followers in New York, Missouri, and Utah. The Pentecostals, however, were the first to give doctrinal primacy to the practice.

Though Pentecostals recognize such sporadic instances of tongue-speaking and other charismatic phenomena throughout the Christian era, they stress the special importance of the Azusa Street revival, which occurred in an abandoned African Methodist Episcopal church in downtown Los Angeles from 1906 to 1909 and which launched Pentecostalism as a worldwide movement. The Azusa Street services were led by William J. Seymour, a black Holiness preacher from Houston, Texas, and a student of Parham.

The Topeka and Los Angeles events took place in a turn-of-the-century religious environment that encouraged the appearance of such a Pentecostal movement. The major milieu out of which Pentecostalism sprang was the worldwide Holiness movement, which had developed out of nineteenth century American Methodism. Leaders in this movement were Phoebe Palmer and John Inskip, who emphasized a "second blessing" crisis of sanctification through the "baptism in the Holy Spirit." English evangelicals also stressed a separate Holy Spirit experience in the Keswick Conventions beginning in 1874.

From America and England "higher life" Holiness movements spread to many nations of the world, usually under the auspices of Methodist missionaries and traveling evangelists. Although these revivalists did not stress charismatic phenomena, they emphasized a conscious experience of baptism in the Holy Spirit and an expectancy of a restoration of the NT church as a sign of the end of the church age.

Other teachings that became prominent in this period were the possibility of miraculous divine healing in answer to prayer and the expectation of the imminent premillennial second coming of Christ. A great interest in the person and work of the Holy Spirit elicited the publication of many books and periodicals devoted to teaching seekers how to receive an "enduement of power" through an experience in the Holy Spirit subsequent to conversion.

In the quest to be filled with the Holy Spirit, many testimonies were given concerning emotional experiences which accompanied the "second blessing," as it was called. In the tradition of the American frontier some received the experience with eruptions of joy or shouting, while others wept or spoke of surpassing peace and quietness.

By 1895 a further movement was begun in Iowa which stressed a third blessing called "the fire," which followed the conversion and sanctification experiences already taught by the Holiness movement. The leader of this movement was Benjamin Hardin Irwin from Lincoln, Nebraska, who named his new group the Fire-Baptized Holiness Church. Other "fire-baptized" groups formed during this period included the Pillar of Fire Church of Denver, Colorado, and the Burning Bush of Minneapolis, Minnesota.

Not only did such Holiness teachers emphasize conscious religious experiences; they tended to encourage persons to seek for them as "crisis" experiences that could be received in an instant of time through prayer and faith. By 1900 the Holiness movement had begun to think of religious experiences more in terms of crises than in gradual categories. Thus the Fire-Baptized Holiness Church taught instant conversion through the new birth, instant sanctification as a second blessing, instant baptism in the Holy Ghost and fire, instant divine healing through prayer, and the instant premillennial second coming of Christ.

Those teachers of the Keswick persuasion tended to speak of the four cardinal doctrines of the movement. This way of thinking was formalized in A. B. Simpson's four basic doctrines of the Christian and Missionary Alliance, which stressed instant salvation, baptism in the Holy Spirit, divine healing, and the second coming of Christ.

Thus, when tongue-speaking occurred in Topeka in 1901, the only significant addition to the foregoing was to insist that tongue-speaking was the biblical evidence of receiving the Holy Spirit baptism. All the other teachings and practices of Pentecostalism were adopted whole cloth from the Holiness milieu in which it was born, including its style of worship, its hymnody, and its basic theology.

After 1906 Pentecostalism spread rapidly in the United States and around the world. Despite its origins in the Holiness movement, the majority of Holiness leaders rejected Pentecostalism, and there were occasional charges of demon possession and mental instability. Leaders of the older Holiness denominations rejected Pentecostal teachings outright. These included the Church of the Nazarene, the Wesleyan Methodist Church, the Church of God (Anderson, Indiana), and the Salvation Army.

Other Holiness groups, however, were Pentecostalized rapidly as leaders went to Azusa Street to investigate the phenomena in evidence there. Among the Azusa Street "pilgrims" were G. B. Cashwell (North Carolina), C. H. Mason (Tennessee), Glen Cook (California), A. G. Argue (Canada), and W. H. Durham (Chicago). Within a year from the opening of the Azusa Street meeting (April, 1906), these and many others spread the Pentecostal message around the nation. Sharp controversies and divisions ensued in several Holiness denominations. The first Pentecostal denominations emerged from these struggles from 1906 to 1908.

This first wave of Holiness-Pentecostal groups included the Pentecostal Holiness Church, the Church of God in Christ, the Church of God (Cleveland, Tennessee), the Apostolic Faith (Portland, Oregon), the United Holy Church, and the Pentecostal Free-Will Baptist Church. Most of these churches were located in the southern states and experienced rapid growth after their Pentecostal renewal began. Two of these, the Church of God in Christ and the United Holy Church, were predominantly black.

Pentecostalism also spread rapidly around the world after 1906. The leading European pioneer was Thomas Ball Barratt, a Norwegian Methodist pastor who founded flourishing Pentecostal movements in Norway, Sweden, and England. The German pioneer was the Holiness leader Jonathan Paul. Lewi Pethrus, a convert of Barratt's, began a significant Pentecostal movement in Sweden which originated among Baptists. A strong Pentecostal movement reached Italy through relatives of American immigrants of Italian extraction.

Pentecostalism was introduced to Russia and other Slavic nations through the efforts of Ivan Voronaev, a Russian-born American immigrant from New York City who established the first Russian-language Pentecostal church in Manhattan in 1919. In 1920 he began a ministry in Odessa, Russia, which was the origin of the movement in the Slavic nations. Voronaev founded over 350 congregations in Russia, Poland, and Bulgaria before being arrested by the Soviet police in 1929. He died in prison.

Pentecostalism reached Chile in 1909 under the leadership of an American Methodist missionary, Willis C. Hoover. When the Methodist Church rejected Pentecostal manifestations, a schism occurred which resulted in the organization of the Methodist Pentecostal Church. Extremely rapid growth after 1909 made Pentecostalism the predominant form of Protestantism in Chile.

The Pentecostal movement in Brazil began in 1910 under the leadership of two American Swedish immigrants, Daniel Berg and Gunnar Vingren, who began Pentecostal services in a Baptist church in Belém, Pará. A schism soon followed, resulting in the first Pentecostal congregation in the nation which took the name Assemblies of God. Phenomenal growth also caused Pentecostalism to be the major Protestant force in Brazil.

Successful Pentecostal missions were also begun by 1910 in China, Africa, and many other nations of the world. The missionary enterprise accelerated rapidly after the formation of major missions-oriented Pentecostal denominations in the United States after 1910.

It was inevitable that such a vigorous movement would suffer controversy and division in its formative stages. Though the movement has been noted for its many submovements, only two divisions have been considered major. These involved teachings concerning sanctification and the Trinity.

The sanctification controversy grew out of the Holiness theology held by most of the first Pentecostals, including Parham and Seymour. Having taught that sanctification was a "second work of grace" prior to their Pentecostal experiences, they simply added the baptism of the Holy Spirit with glossolalia as a "third blessing." In 1910 William H. Durham of Chicago began teaching his "finished work" theory, which emphasized sanctification as a progressive work following conversion with baptism in the Holy Spirit following as the second blessing.

The Assemblies of God, which was formed in 1914, based its theology on Durham's teachings and soon became the largest Pentecostal denomination in the world. Most of the Pentecostal groups that began after 1914 were based on the model of the Assemblies of God. They include the Pentecostal Church of God, the International Church of the Foursquare Gospel (founded in 1927 by Aimee Semple McPherson), and the Open Bible Standard Church.

A more serious schism grew out of the "oneness" or "Jesus only" controversy, which began in 1911 in Los Angeles. Led by Glen Cook and Frank Ewart, this movement rejected the teaching of the Trinity and taught that Jesus Christ was at the same time Father, Son, and Holy Spirit and that the only biblical mode of water baptism was administered in Jesus' name and then was valid only if accompanied with glossolalia. This movement spread rapidly in the infant Assemblies of God after 1914 and resulted in a schism in 1916, which later produced the Pentecostal Assemblies of the World and the United Pentecostal Church.

Through the years other schisms occurred over lesser doctrinal disputes and personality clashes, producing such movements as the Church of God of Prophecy and the Congregational Holiness Church. The large number of Pentecostal sects in America and the world, however, did not result from controversy or schism. In most cases Pentecostal denominations developed out of separate indigenous churches originating in different areas of the world with little or no contact with other organized bodies.

The greatest growth for Pentecostal churches came after World War II. With more mobility and greater prosperity, Pentecostals began to move into the middle class and to lose their image of being disinherited members of the lower classes. The emergence of healing evangelists such as Oral Roberts and Jack Coe in the 1950s brought greater interest and acceptance to the movement. The TV ministry of Roberts also brought Pentecostalism into the homes of the average American. The founding of the Full Gospel Business Men in 1948 brought the Pentecostal message to a whole new class of middle-class professional and business men, helping further to change the image of the movement.

In the post–World War II period the Pentecostals also began to emerge from their isolation, not only from each other but from other Christian groups as well. In 1943 the Assemblies of God, the Church of God (Cleveland, Tennessee), the International Church of the Foursquare Gospel, and the Pentecostal Holiness Church became charter members of the National Association of Evangelicals (NAE), thus clearly disassociating themselves from the organized fundamentalist groups which had disfellowshiped the Pentecostals in 1928. They thus became part of the moderate evangelical camp that grew to prominence by the 1970s.

Intrapentecostal ecumenism began to flourish also during the late 1940s both in the United States and elsewhere. In 1947 the first World Pentecostal Conference (WPC) met in Zurich, Switzerland, and has since met triennially. The next year the Pentecostal Fellowship of North America (PFNA) was formed in Des Moines, Iowa, and has met annually since then.

Pentecostalism entered a new phase in 1960 with the appearance of "neo-Pentecostalism" in the traditional churches in the United States. The first well-known person to openly experience glossolalia and remain within his church was Dennis Bennett, an Episcopal priest in Van Nuys, California. Although forced to leave his parish in Van Nuys because of controversy over his experience, Bennett was invited to pastor an inner-city Episcopal parish in Seattle, Washington. The church in Seattle experienced rapid growth after the introduction of Pentecostal worship, becoming a center of neo-Pentecostalism in the northwestern United States.

This new wave of Pentecostalism soon spread to other denominations in the United States and also to many other nations. Other well-known neo-Pentecostal leaders were Brick Bradford and James Brown (Presbyterian); John Osteen and Howard Irvin (Baptist); Gerald Derstine and Bishop Nelson Litwiler (Mennonite); Larry Christenson (Lutheran); and Ross Whetstone (United Methodist).

In 1966 Pentecostalism entered the Roman Catholic Church as the result of a weekend retreat at Duquesne University led by theology professors Ralph Keiffer and Bill Story. As glossolalia and other charismatic gifts were experienced, other Catholic prayer groups were formed at Notre Dame University and the University of Michigan. By 1973 the movement had spread so rapidly that thirty thousand Catholic Pentecostals gathered at Notre Dame for a national conference. The movement had spread to Catholic churches in over a hundred nations by 1980. Other prominent Catholic Pentecostal leaders were Kevin Ranaghan, Steve Clark, and Ralph Martin. The most prominent leader among Catholics, however, was Joseph Leon Cardinal Suenens, who was named by popes Paul VI and John Paul II as episcopal adviser to the renewal.

In order to distinguish these newer Pentecostals from the older Pentecostal denominations, the word "charismatic" began to be used widely around 1973 to designate the movement in the mainline churches. The older Pentecostals were called "classical Pentecostals." By 1980 the term "neo-Pentecostal" had been universally abandoned in favor of "charismatic renewal."

Unlike the rejection of the earlier Pentecostals, the charismatic renewal was generally allowed to remain within the mainline churches. Favorable study reports by the Episcopalians (1963), Roman Catholics (1969, 1974), and the Presbyterians (1970), while pointing out possible excesses, generally were tolerant and open to the existence of a Pentecostal spirituality as a renewal movement within the traditional churches.

By 1980 the classical Pentecostals had grown to be the largest family of Protestants in the world, according to *The World Christian Encyclopedia.* The 51 million figure attributed to the traditional Pentecostals did not include the 11 million charismatic Pentecostals in the traditional mainline churches. Thus, seventy-five years after the opening of the Azusa Street meeting there were 62 million Pentecostals in over a hundred nations of the world. V. SYNAN

See also AZUSA STREET REVIVAL; SPIRITUAL GIFTS; TONGUES, SPEAKING IN; BAPTISM OF THE SPIRIT; CHARISMATIC MOVEMENT; KESWICK CONVENTION.

Bibliography. M. Poloma, *The Charismatic Movement;* K. McDonnell, ed., *Presence, Power, Praise,* 3 vols.; J. R. Williams, *The Gift of the Holy Spirit Today;* K. and D. Ranaghan, *Catholic Pentecostals;* V. Synan, ed., *Aspects of Pentecostal-Charismatic Origins;* J. T. Nichol, *Pentecostalism;* M. P. Hamilton, ed., *The Charismatic Movement;* S. D. Glazier, *Perspective on Pentecostalism.*

Perfection, Perfectionism. The quest for religious perfection has been an important goal throughout Judeo-Christian history. Both biblical and theological evidence reflects this continuous concern. Although interpretations have varied with reference to methods and chronology of attainment, most Christian traditions recognize the concept.

The Biblical Emphasis. The OT roots for religious perfection signify wholeness and perfect peace. The most frequently used term for "perfect" is *tāmîm,* which occurs eighty-five times and is usually translated *teleios* in the LXX. Of these occurrences fifty refer to sacrificial animals and are usually translated "without blemish" or "without spot." When applied to persons the term describes one who is without moral blemish or defect (Ps. 101:2, 6; Job 1:1, 8; 2:3; 8:20, etc.). This term is also applied to Jehovah's character, and this dual usage may suggest the resemblance between persons and God.

Cognate forms of *tāmîm* are *tōm, tām,* and *tummâ.* These terms have connotations of "integrity," "simple," "uncalculating," "sincere," and "perfect." This spiritual wholeness and uprightness, especially as one is in right relationship to God, reflect a relational/ethical perfection which is patterned after the character of God.

Another Hebrew term for perfect is *šālēm,* an adjectival form of the root *šlm,* which means "peace." This term has a covenant background and indicates the loyalty and purity of motive which are characteristic of a moral and intellectual life of integrity before God (I Kings 8:61; 11:4; 15:3). The root idea connotes fellowship between God and his people and a right relationship with the One who is the model of perfection.

The NT vocabulary reflects the OT interpersonal concepts rather than the Greek ideal of static and dispassionate knowledge. The emphases are on obedience, wholeness, and maturity. The Greek words derived from *telos* reflect the idea of "design," "end," "goal," "purpose." These words describe perfection as the achievement of a desired end. Paul uses *teleios* to describe moral and religious perfection (Col. 1:28; 4:12). He contrasts it to *nēpios,* "childish," which connotes moral immaturity and deficiency. The "perfect man," *teleion,* is the stable person who reflects "the measure of the stature of the fulness of Christ" in contrast to the children who are tossed about by every new wind of doctrine (Eph. 4:13–14). James uses *teleios* to describe the end result of spiritual discipline. The trying of faith develops patience and character that the disciple may be "perfect and entire, wanting in nothing" (James 1:3–4).

Responsible, spiritual, intellectual, and moral development which conforms to the desired pattern is perfection. In the Sermon on the Mount, Jesus uses *teleios* to exhort believers to be perfect as the Heavenly Father is perfect (Matt. 5:48). This use of the future tense indicates a moral obligation, however, and not an absolute perfection identical to that of God. Jesus is emphasizing the need for having right attitudes of love which are acceptable to God, not the accomplishment of perfect conduct.

The concept of corporate perfection seen in a community united in love is expressed by the verb *katartizein.* The moral integrity and spiritual unity of the community are aspects of wholeness and completeness connoted by this term. Interrelatedness in love is a necessary part of the "perfecting of the saints" (I Cor. 1:10; Eph. 4:12; Heb. 13:21). Other usages imply putting into order those things which are imperfect (I Thess. 3:10–13), fitting and adjusting (Heb. 11:3), and mending (II Cor. 13:11; Mark 1:19).

Ethical righteousness is expressed by the words *amemptos* and *amemptōs,* "blameless" or "without fault or defect." The piety of Zacharias and Elisabeth is *amemptoi* (Luke 1:6).

Personal fitness and perfection in the sense of properly using spiritual resources is denoted by *artios* (II Tim. 3:17). The believer who is sound and lacks nothing needed for completeness is *holoklēros* (James 1:4; I Thess. 5:23).

The biblical emphasis on perfection, then,

does not imply absolute perfection but an unblemished character which has moral and spiritual integrity in relationship to God. The goal of spiritual maturity is set forth, and the believer is charged with making sincere and proper use of the spiritual resources available through Christ in order to attain this maturity in fellowship with Christ and the Christian community.

Theological Issues and Historical Heritage. The command of Jesus in the Sermon on the Mount, "Be ye therefore perfect, even as your Father which is in heaven is perfect" (Matt. 5:48), is central to the issue of human perfection. This text has been variously interpreted and even rejected as inauthentic in the attempts to arrive at theological understanding.

Christian Platonism. Clement of Alexandria and the Christian Platonists sought for perfection in the transfiguration of earthly life, a hallowing of the secular. Faith and knowledge lifted some believers to an experience of religious perfection in which the purposes and desires of the soul were harmonized in love. In his *Miscellanies,* the ideal was the attainment of uninterrupted communion with God. Paradoxically, Clement insisted on God's unlikeness to man while insisting on the possibility of the perfected Gnostic's becoming like God. Thus perfection was obedientiary, not absolute, and was attained through obedience to God in prayer and keeping the commandments. The weakness in Clement's view follows from his Platonic tendency to view God as apathetic and without predicates. Although God was active for the salvation of men, Clement emptied both Father and Son of emotions. This hellenization of God is somewhat incongruous with his view of God as the Father persevering in love. His view of perfection, then, emphasizes that the "Christian Gnostic" rises above human emotions by contemplation of God and is "translated absolutely and entirely to another sphere."

Clement's illustrious pupil, Origen, proposed a view of perfection which explicitly reflected the presuppositions of Platonic philosophy. He separated faith and knowledge, with faith being the basis of salvation and knowledge being the means to perfection. A prerequisite to perfection is an ascetic rejection of the external world and all human emotions. His approach was basically humanistic, even though he asserted that human effort must be assisted by grace. Also, his Platonic negative evaluation of the human creature required that perfection be essentially a victory over the body, and more specifically over the sex drive. Furthermore, he anticipated the monastic emphasis of perfection through asceticism and a distinction between the ordinary and the spiritually elite Christian. This tendency toward a double standard of morality reflected the influence of Gnosticism on early Christian thought in that ordinary Christians lived by faith while the enlightened elect lived by *gnōsis.* This dual level of spirituality became more pronounced as the chasm between clergy and laity widened in the medieval period.

Monasticism. One of the most extensive attempts at attaining Christian perfection is found in monasticism. Leaders such as Antony of Egypt and Pachomius went into solitude to practice their disciplines with the aim of achieving spiritual perfection. They were overwhelmed by the sense of their own unworthiness and by the increasing worldliness of the church. The attaining of their goal involved renouncing all encumbrances of the world, taking up their cross, and praying without ceasing. The ideal of perfection became socialized as expressed in the rules of Basil and Benedict. Monastic communities developed which not only sought perfection by resignation from the world and asceticism, but also attempted to transform the world through extensive missionary efforts and the preservation of spiritual, aesthetic, and intellectual life.

Some of the most profound spiritual insights are found in the *Fifty Spiritual Homilies of Macarius the Egyptian.* Greatly admired by William Law and John Wesley, Macarius stressed the worth of the individual human soul in the image of God, the incarnation as the basis of the life of the soul, moral purity, and love as the highest measure of the Christian life. His stress on union with Christ is commendable, but his goal of perfection still is a retreat from reality into ecstasy, lacks a relevant ideal for common humanity, and is excessively individualistic.

Gregory of Nyssa was one of the greatest Eastern leaders in the struggle for perfection. He saw Christ as the prototype of the Christian life in his *On What It Means to Call Oneself a Christian* and *On Perfection.* The responsibility of the Christian is to imitate the virtues of Christ and to reverence those virtues which are impossible to imitate. Gregory saw the truth of the participation in Christ, which results from rebirth "by water and the Spirit." In this interpersonal sharing the Christian perfects the resemblance to Christ which comes through the continual transformation into his image.

Augustine and Pelagius. In the fourth century the reaction against perfectionism was typified by the controversy between Augustine and Pelagius. Although Augustine affirmed an ideal of perfection, the *summum bonum,* it was a perfection attainable only in eternity. He felt that human perfection was an impossible moral ideal in this life because of the sinfulness of mankind resulting from the fall.

Pelagius attributed the moral laxity of the church to the kind of blasphemy which told God that what he had commanded was impossible. He rejected the concept of original sin and asserted that persons are born with the free capacity to perfect themselves or corrupt themselves as they choose. Sin is simply a bad habit which can be overcome by an act of the will. Since sin is avoidable, however, Pelagius tended to judge severely those who fell into the slightest sin.

The response of Augustine was that neither education nor human effort could lead to perfection and the only moral progress persons could make in this life was solely the result of God's grace. He tended to equate sinfulness with humanness in general and with concupiscence in particular, and saw the path to perfection as one of celibacy and virginity. While rejecting the attainment of perfection in this life, Augustine made great contributions to spirituality with his emphasis on contemplation, although he tended to diminish the humanity of Christ because of his aversion to the physical. He was certainly correct in his rejection of Pelagius's exclusive emphasis on moral effort and in his emphasis on grace, but his tendency to identify sinfulness with the physical world is an unnecessary vestige of Greek philosophy.

Aquinas. Often called the "Angelic Doctor," Thomas Aquinas has greatly influenced Roman Catholic theology. He was convinced that although Adam lost the gift of divine grace which enabled mankind to enjoy God fully, the free grace of God can restore humanity to God's favor and enable the Christian to follow God's precepts in perfect love. Final perfection and the beatific vision of God were reserved for the life to come, but through contemplation a perfect vision of God and perfect knowledge of truth can be enjoyed in this life. His concept of perfection, however, involved a disparagement of the world and an understanding of the desires of flesh as evil. Thus the elimination of bodily desires was a prerequisite to perfection, and in this aspect he equated perfection with renunciation. Furthermore, he saw perfection as carrying with it human merit, and thus he contributed to the idea of the treasury of merits from which the imperfect can draw at the discretion of the church. Finally, he formed a hierarchy of the state of perfection which corresponded to the levels of the religious orders. Although he did not deny the possibility of perfection for all persons, religious vows were certainly the shortcut to meritorious perfection. He thus perpetuated the spiritual dichotomy between clergy and laity.

Francis of Sales. The possibility of perfection for all Christians was emphasized by Francis of Assisi and the Friars Minor, and Francis of Sales presented this doctrine with clarity in his treatise *On the Love of God.* He rejected the banishment of the devout life from the experience of common people, and opened up the benefits of spiritual contemplation to all Christians.

François Fénelon. Amid the profligacies of the court of Louis XIV, Fénelon taught his followers to live a life of deep spirituality and introspection. He saw perfection as totally a work of God's grace, not meritorious human effort. The perfect life is carefree and Christlike loving fellowship with others. In *Christian Perfection* he presented single-minded devotion to God as the ideal in attaining perfect love. This perfect life is the imitation of Jesus, and its main obstacle is egocentricity, which must be overcome by an inward act of sanctification by God's Spirit. Thus Fénelon moved the quest for perfection away from its preoccupation with renunciation of the physical and its monopoly by the elite, and focused on God's work of grace which is universally available to the seeker.

The Reformers. Both the Lutheran and Calvinist Reformers reflected the Augustinian position that sin remains in humanity until death, and therefore spiritual perfection is impossible in this life. Calvin explicitly stated that while the goal toward which the pious should strive was to appear before God without spot or blemish, believers will never reach that goal until the sinful physical body is laid aside. Since he saw the body as the residence of the depravity of concupiscence, perfection and physical life are mutually exclusive.

Luther also retained the connection between sin and the flesh. However, he did emphasize a new center of piety—the humanity and work of Jesus Christ. While the previous seekers after perfection focused on the knowledge and love of God which was grasped through contemplation, Luther focused on the knowledge of God through God's revelation in Christ. Faith in Jesus Christ therefore brings an imputed perfection which truly worships God in faith. This true perfection does not consist in celibacy or mendicancy. Luther rejected the distinction between clerical and lay perfection and stressed that proper ethical behavior was not found in renunciation of life, but in faith and love of one's neighbor.

The Pietists. With the pietists arose a Protestant rejection of the pessimism with which the Lutherans and Calvinists viewed the quest for perfection. Marked by the quest for personal holiness and an emphasis on devotion rather than doctrine, seventeenth century leaders such as Jakob Spener and A. H. Francke stressed personal holiness marked by love and obedience. Perfection was reflected in works done solely for the glory of God and in the ability to distinguish good from evil.

While tending toward narrowness and provincialism and often deteriorating into a negative scrupulosity, the pietists developed strong community contexts for nurture and motivated extensive missionary endeavors.

The Quakers. Inspired by a desire to return to the attitude of the NT, George Fox taught both personal responsibility for faith and emancipation from sin in his doctrine of the inner light. He declared a doctrine of real holiness rather than imputed righteousness. This perfection was relative in that it dealt with victory over sin rather than absolute moral development. Fox believed that as a result of the new birth into Christ by the Spirit the believer was free from actual sinning, which he defined as transgressing the law of God, and is thus perfect in obedience. This perfection, however, did not remove the possibility of sinning, for the Christian needed constantly to rely on the inner light and must focus on the cross of Christ as the center of faith. Fox tended toward fanaticism with his teaching that a Christian may be restored to the innocency of Adam before the fall, and could be more steadfast than Adam and need not fall. William Penn and other Quakers qualified the doctrine to guard it from such overstatement.

The strength of Fox's emphasis is that the center of perfection was in the cross of Christ. The cross was no dead relic but an inward experience refashioning the believer into perfect love. This is a celebration of the power of grace. While his refusal to be preoccupied with sin was a needed corrective to the Puritan pessimism over the profound sinfulness of man, Fox did tend to distrust the intellect and to suspect all external expressions of faith such as the sacraments. His refusal to be satisfied with sin and his concentration upon a perfection of life through grace found direct application in commendable attempts at social justice. This message of renewal and hope for the poor and disenfranchised was certainly motivated by the conviction that the quality of life and faith is not predetermined by a radical sinfulness which is resistant to actual moral transformation by grace.

William Law. The author of *A Serious Call to a Devout and Holy Life* and *Christian Perfection,* William Law was an eighteenth century Anglican nonjuring cleric who influenced John Wesley and was admired by Samuel Johnson, Edward Gibbon, John Henry Newman, and many others. Positively, he affirmed the necessity of divine grace for performing the good and the importance of taking up the cross of Christ. He called for absolute dedication of one's life to God and complete renunciation of every aspect of the world. He saw Christian perfection functioning in common ways of life. He rejected the need for retirement to the cloister or the practice of a particular form of life. The whole life is rather an offering of sacrifice to God and praying without ceasing. Christlikeness is the ideal of perfection, and this is accomplished by performing one's human duties as Christ would.

The weaknesses of Law's system are in his somewhat unrealistic ideals for human achievement, his failure to see meaning in actual life itself, and his tendency to see grace as a means of supplanting nature rather than transforming it. Furthermore, he tended to deprecate religious fellowship and all institutional religion.

The Wesleyans. John Wesley was inspired by the perfectionist themes of the early saints and by the devotional literature of Thomas à Kempis, Jeremy Taylor, and William Law. Seeing self-love, or pride, as the root of evil, Wesley taught that "perfect love" or "Christian perfection" could replace pride through a moral crisis of faith. By grace, the Christian could experience love filling the heart and excluding sin. He did not see perfection as sinlessness, nor did he understand it to be attained by merit. He thus combined some aspects of the Catholic emphasis on perfection with the Protestant emphasis on grace.

In contrast to Augustine's Platonic view of sin as being inseparably related to concupiscence and the body, Wesley saw it as a perverted relationship to God. In response to God's offer of transforming grace, the believer in faith was brought into an unbroken fellowship with Christ. This was not only an imputed perfection but an actual or imparted relationship of an evangelical perfection of love and intention. In this life the Christian does not attain absolute Christlikeness but suffers numerous infirmities, human faults, prejudices, and involuntary transgressions. These, however, were not considered sin, for Wesley saw sin as attitudinal and relational. In *A Plain Account of Christian Perfection* he stressed that Christian perfection is not absolute, nor sinless, nor incapable of being lost, is not the perfection of Adam or the angels, and does not preclude growth in grace.

In removing from the idea of perfection any idea of meritorious effort, Wesley resisted any tendency to exclusiveness and elitism. His relational understanding of sin resisted the hellenistic equation of sin with humanity. A reform of personal and social morality resulted to a large degree from the spiritual renewal which accompanied his work. Thus perfection for Wesley was not based on renunciation, merit, asceticism, or individualism. It was instead a celebration of the sovereignty of grace in transforming the sinful person into the image of Christ's love.

Wesleyan perfectionist thought was, however, not without liabilities. Although Wesley defined sin as involving relationships and intentions, he did not adequately guard against allowing it to become understood as a substance or entity which was separate from the person and which must be extricated. Some of his followers did tend to develop this substantialist understanding of sin and a resulting static concept of sanctification. He also tended to narrow sin to include only conscious will and intent. Consequently, some of his interpreters have been led to rationalize serious attitudinal aberrations as expressions of unconscious or unintentional human faults. Finally, Wesley expressed an inward asceticism which tended to derogate the aesthetic, and his emphasis on simplicity was too easily distorted by his followers into a legalistic externalism.

Wesley's emphasis on perfection has been preserved in some circles of Methodism, and continues to be promoted in the denominations associated with the Christian Holiness Association.

Heterodox Sects. In addition to the Gnostic dualism of the early centuries, perfectionism has expressed itself in varying forms on the fringes of Christianity. The second century Montanists taught that men could become gods. In the twelfth through the fourteenth centuries the Albigensian heresy contended that the human spirit was capable of freeing itself from the flesh in order to become one with God. The late medieval period also saw the condemnation of the Brethren of the Free Spirit, who believed that man could advance in perfection beyond God, who then became superfluous. The English Ranters saw it as logically impossible for perfected man to sin. Other communal approaches such as the nineteenth century Oneida community sought for ways of reconciling perfected sinlessness with the impulses of the flesh.

All these heterodox expressions of perfectionism contained forms of antinomianism and egoism. They were condemned by orthodox Christianity with varying degrees of severity. Characterized by utopian views of human ability and by mystical practices, they tended to ignore divine grace and ethical integrity, and deteriorated because of their own inherent weaknesses.

R. L. SHELTON

See also SANCTIFICATION; GODLINESS.

Bibliography. L. Lemme, *SHERK,* VIII, 456–57; L. G. Cox, *John Wesley's Concept of Perfection;* W. S. Deal, *The March of Holiness Through the Centuries;* R. N. Flew, *The Idea of Perfection in Christian Theology;* R. Garrigou-Lagrange, *Christian Perfection and Contemplation;* W. M. Greathouse, *From the Apostles to Wesley;* J. A. Passmore, *The Perfectibility of Man;* W. E. Sangster, *The Path to Perfection;* M. Thornton, *English Spirituality;* G. A. Turner, *The Vision Which Transforms;* B. B. Warfield, *Perfectionism,* 2 vols.; M. B. Wynkoop, *A Theology of Love;* J. K. Grider, *Entire Sanctification.*

Perichoresis. This term and the Latin equivalent, *circumencessio, circuminsessio,* mean mutual indwelling or, better, mutual interpenetration and refer to the understanding of both the Trinity and Christology.

In Trinitarian thought "perichoresis" was used in Greek theology by John of Damascus to describe the inner relation between the persons of the Godhead. Karl Barth says of this, "The divine modes of being mutually condition and permeate one another so completely that one is always in the other two" (*Church Dogmatics* I/1, 370). Trinitarian perichoresis begins with the unity of natures or a strict consubstantiality and affirms a reciprocal interrelation. Each person has "being in each other without any coalescence" (John of Damascus). Perichoresis is a necessary implication of orthodox Trinitarian thought.

For Christology the complementary use of perichoresis was based on the affirmation of the unity of person (hypostasis) and sought to describe the relation of the Lord's two natures as a mutual interpenetration. However, the interpenetration of the incarnate Son is not strictly mutual, since the movement is from the divine to the human. The Cappadocian fathers were apparently the first to use the image of fire (deity) making iron (humanity) glow to explain this concept. In reaction to this form of thinking Antiochene theologians contended that Jesus' humanity was in jeopardy when such interpenetration is allowed.

During the Reformation the interpenetration of the two natures became a burning issue and focused on the nature of Christ's presence in the Lord's Supper. Luther affirmed that the exalted humanity of Christ participated in the omnipresence of his deity in such a way as to communicate his presence at the Lord's Supper. Later Lutheran theology continued to affirm this application of the concept, calling it the *genus maiestaticum,* the communication of divine majesty to Christ's humanity. This was a realistic form of the *communicatio idiomatum.*

Even if the term seems strange, the issue of

the relation of deity and humanity in Christ continues to arouse much interest. Jürgen Moltmann has recently given considerable thought to this issue in relation to the cross. He contends that because of the perichoresis of the divine in the human it can and must be affirmed that God suffered in the death of Christ. New insights into the cross may be forthcoming from this sort of application of the concept of perichoresis.

S. M. Smith

See also Communication of Attributes, Communicatio Idiomatum.

Bibliography. J. Moltmann, *The Crucified God;* W. Pannenberg, *Jesus—God and Man;* K. Adam, *The Christ of Faith;* K. Barth, *Church Dogmatics,* I/1, IV/2.

Perseverance. Although the noun "perseverance" occurs in the AV and RSV only once (Eph. 6:18), the verb is frequent, being translated "continued steadfastly," "devoted," "constant," and the idea of persistence, keeping on, patient endurance occurs very often. Perseverance was an essential virtue in face of persecution. Yet converts were never left to suppose their future depended wholly upon their own endurance. If Jude urges "keep yourselves in the love of God," Peter declares that we "by God's power are guarded through faith for a salvation ready to be revealed in the last time." Final perseverance in a state of grace by no means depended entirely on the virtue of persevering.

Pastoral necessities dictated a dual approach. Converts needed assurance, and it was given: "He who believes has eternal life.... He does not come into judgment but has passed from death to life.... The will of my Father, that every one who sees the Son and believes should have eternal life and I will raise him up at the last day.... I give [my sheep] eternal life and they shall never perish, no one shall snatch them out of my hand, no one is able to snatch them out of the Father's hand. . . . There is no condemnation for those that are in Christ Jesus. . . . Those he foreknew he also predestined to be conformed to the image of his son. . . . Nothing shall separate us from the love of God.... Christ will sustain you to the end.... God is faithful and will not let you be tempted beyond your strength.... Holy Spirit the guarantee of our inheritance. . . . He who began a good work in you will bring it to completion. . . . May you be kept sound and blameless. . . . Whatsoever is born of God overcomes the world.... You may know that you have eternal life."

Upon such assurances could be based not only encouragement but a doctrine of eternal security of every believer—"once a Christian, always a Christian."

But pastoral experience demanded also warning: "Let any one who thinks that he stands take heed lest he fall.... Look to yourself, lest you too be tempted. . . . Watch and pray, lest you enter temptation. . . . Many will fall away, most men's love will grow cold. . . . He who endures to the end will be saved." Judas, Ananias, Demas, some who "by rejecting conscience have made shipwreck of their faith," are remembered. The Colossians are promised presentation before God "provided that you continue in the faith, stable and steadfast, not shifting." The church at Ephesus is warned that Christ may remove its lampstand, and Christ will vomit the lukewarm Laodiceans from his mouth. Most fearful were the warnings to Hebrew Christians: "lest they be judged to have failed," "that no one fail by disobedience." "For if we sin deliberately after receiving the knowledge of the truth, there no longer remains a sacrifice for sins but a fearful prospect of judgement. . . . It is impossible to restore again to repentance those once enlightened, who have tasted the heavenly gift, and have become partakers of the Holy Spirit, and have tasted the goodness of the word of God and the powers of the age to come, if they commit apostasy, since they crucify the Son of God on their own account.... Bearing thorns ... worthless ... near to being cursed ... burned."

History of the Doctrine. In the dual stance of the NT there obviously lay opportunity for divergent views as to whether every Christian can be sure he will continue in a state of grace to the end. There was precedent in Judaism for a positive answer. Many believed that no Israelite could enter Gehenna; all had their portion in the world to come, and all the circumcised were assured of eternal life.

On the other hand, in the postapostolic centuries the baptized were urged, "Let none of you be found a deserter," and the prevailing rigorism denied all comfort to those who fell from the purity conferred in baptism. Hermas and early Tertullian allowed postbaptismal repentance once, Cyprian and others not at all. By the fourth century some delayed baptism until late in life because postbaptismal sin incurred such dire responsibilities. The classification of apostasy with murder and fornication as unpardonable (later, pardonable only after public penance) shows the same deep awareness of the possibility of total defection.

With Augustine a new theme entered the discussion. Convinced of man's utter helplessness through original sin, Augustine traced every thought and motion Godward to the operation of divine grace within those elected to salvation. Nothing was ascribed to man's initiative, or even to man's response. Electing, effectual grace includes not only the call to salvation, the impulse of faith to respond, the inspiring of a good will, but also the *donum perseverantiae,* the gift of enduring to the end. Such being the decree of the unchanging divine will, backed by divine power, it is irresistible; the assurance of persevering in grace is therefore absolute and infallible. The elect, being born of the Spirit, can never finally fall from grace. Eternal security is freely given by God, and is not due to human watchfulness, striving, or endurance.

The obvious fact that not all Christians did persevere led, by hard logic, to the denial of earlier views (Origen) that God willed all men should be saved and to the limitation of election, and so of the gift of perseverance, to some men only. Though Augustine held that "infallible perseverance" did not violate human freedom, others (as Thomasius) contended against the veiled fatalism for human responsibility. In consequence, the later Council of Trent stated Augustine's position more cautiously and obscurely.

Meanwhile, Calvin reaffirmed that Christ died only for the elect and their salvation was guaranteed. God would never allow any to fall away; they are kept in the faith by the almighty power of God. All the regenerate are eternally secure: they have been predestined to eternal glory and are assured of heaven. They do fall into temptation and commit sin, but they do not lose salvation or suffer separation from Christ. The Westminster Confession declared, "They whom God hath accepted in his Beloved, effectually called and sanctified by his Spirit can neither totally nor finally fall away from the state of grace, but shall certainly persevere therein to the end and be eternally saved."

Such dogmatic assurance provoked the Arminian arguments (1) that election itself was conditional, depending upon God's foresight of who would respond in faith of their own free will, and (2) that believers, truly saved, can lose salvation by failing to maintain their faith—the regenerate can by grieving the Spirit fall away and perish.

A twentieth century mediating statement (A. S. Martin) stressed (1) the given religious factors in Christian experience—God's sovereign will, faithfulness, and love; Christ's pattern; the Spirit; the fellowship of saints; and the heavenly inheritance; (2) the moral endeavor, steadfastness, diligence, zeal required: "the great predestinarians were the most Christian men of their generation"; "no perseverance without determined persevering"; (3) all endeavor depends upon the given factors; man cannot be himself except in entire dependence on God for all good initiatives—"the life of perseverance is just the Spirit in the soul." This leaves undefined what happens if the moral endeavor proves insufficient.

A more recent discussion (Steele and Thomas) restates the Calvinist position with vigor, ignoring NT warnings and examples but conceding that perseverance does not apply to all who profess faith, only to those given true faith. Those who fall away were never in grace. This is almost circular: the assurance of perseverance belongs only to those who show their sincerity by persevering.

Value of the Doctrine. Difficult as it is to frame a defensible statement, the Christian values here at stake are precious. Every devout Christian knows that he would not have continued in the faith (as also he would never have begun) but for the unmerited, invasive grace of God, shown to him in innumerable ways. Who has not found wondering comfort, repeatedly, in the words, "He did not begin to love me because of what I was, and he will go on loving me in spite of what I am"? If we fall, we know that is our fault; if we are upheld, we know it is thanks to God's grace. The warnings, exhortations, and tragic examples of the NT do still speak directly to our hearts; had it depended upon us, our waywardness would long ago have snatched us out of God's hands, separated us from God's love. But it has not depended upon anything in us, except our desire to be saved. In this sense God himself, in his freedom, has made perseverance, like salvation, dependent upon human response—so most modern Christians would probably say. But the condition is simply wanting to endure: thereafter, "the perseverance of the saints is nothing else but the patience of God."

R. E. O. White

See also Assurance; Backsliding.

Bibliography. Augustine, *De dono perseverantiae;* Calvin, *Institutes* 3.11–14; G. C. Berkouwer, *Faith and Perseverance;* L. Boettner, *The Reformed Doctrine of Predestination,* ch. 14; A. S. Martin, *HDAC,* II, 186–90; D. L. Moody, *The Word of Truth,* 358–65; D. N. Steele and C. C. Thomas, *The Five Points of Calvinism.*

Person, God as. *See* God, Attributes of.

Person of Christ. *See* Christology.

Peter, Primacy of. Peter's primacy or leadership among the twelve apostles and in the primitive church is now generally accepted by Protestant and Catholic scholars alike. Differences on this matter arise rather between conservative biblical scholars, who accept the texts essentially as they stand, and more liberal ones who argue that a role Peter developed later was projected, somewhat inaccurately, back into the Gospel accounts. Protestants and Catholics do continue to differ, however, on what the implications of Peter's leadership are for later ages and structures of the church.

Simon, son of Jona or John, was among the first of the apostles called (Mark 1:16–18; Matt. 4:18–20), appears first in all biblical lists of apostles (see esp. Matt. 10:2), became part of an inner group especially close to Jesus, and was probably the first apostle to see the resurrected Jesus (I Cor. 15:5; Luke 24:34). Repeatedly he served as an impetuous spokesman for all the apostles, and he also represented their collective desertion. Peter first confessed that Jesus was the Messiah (Mark 8:29; Matt.16:16; Luke 9:20) or Holy One (John 6:69); Jesus surnamed him alone the "rock" upon which he would build his church (Mark 3:16; Matt. 16:18; John 1:42); and the risen Lord charged Peter with the pastoral office (John 21:15–17). In the primitive church, as described in the Acts of the Apostles, Peter clearly emerges as leader, the preacher at Pentecost, the one who receives the vision which opens the way to Cornelius and other Gentiles, and the decisive speaker in this regard at the Council of Jerusalem (Acts 15:7–11). Paul also singled him out (Gal. 1:18). Fragmentary evidence indicates he later did missionary work outside Palestine, beginning in Antioch and ending in Rome. Yet, as Protestants have been quick to point out, James appears actually to have presided in Jerusalem, and after the council there Peter disappears almost completely from the biblical picture.

Christians have interpreted the scriptural image of Peter's "primacy" very differently over the ages. In reaction to the claims of Roman Catholics, Protestants have traditionally lent it no significance whatsoever. Cullmann has argued more carefully that Peter himself was endowed with a special office as the primary eyewitness to our Lord and his resurrection, but that this was unique to him and therefore ceased upon his death. A few more ecumenically minded Protestants have been willing to see in Peter the chief scriptural model for the pastoral office—i.e., the rock upon whose witness the church is built, the one authorized to bind and loose, the spokesman whose own faith is upheld by the Lord's prayer (Luke 22:32), and the shepherd who feeds the sheep.

Roman Catholics believe that Peter's was a permanent office instituted by Christ and conferred upon the apostle's successors in the see of Rome, and that his primacy in the primitive church has fallen now to the bishops (popes) of Rome. Most pointedly, and defined at Vatican Council I in 1870, its First Dogmatic Constitution on the Church of Christ, also known as *Pastor aeternus*, made it a matter of Catholic faith to believe that Christ conferred primacy of jurisdiction over the whole church directly and without mediation (this against conciliarists) upon Peter, that the Petrine office and its primacy persist through the ages in the bishops of Rome, and that they therefore possess universal, ordinary jurisdiction over all of Christ's church. Vatican Council II, in its constitution on the church (*Lumen gentium*), reaffirmed the foregoing, but then went on in fact to place great stress upon all bishops acting together collegially. This Catholic claim to Petrine and Roman primacy rests upon two bases, one historical and the other theological.

The historical claim is that Peter died a martyr as the first bishop of Rome and passed to succeeding bishops there his office and primacy. Protestants once vigorously attacked all stories about Peter's end, but the best evidence, as most scholars now agree, indicates that he in fact died a martyr in the time of Nero and that his cult originated very early in Rome, though Cullmann believes he was probably executed rather than buried at the present St. Peter's on the Vatican Hill. The Roman Church enjoyed a certain preeminence very early (as evidenced, e.g., in I Clement 5; Ignatius, *Rom.* 1; Irenaeus, *Against Heresies* 3.3), but down to the end of the second century Rome was always considered as founded by Peter and Paul, a tradition which never wholly disappeared. Singular emphasis upon Peter as the founder and first bishop of Rome first emerged in the third century and became prominent in the later fourth century, especially as articulated by the popes who reigned between Damasus (366–84) and Leo (440–61). As papal claims expanded to take in the whole church and met stiff resistance from emperors and patriarchs in Constantinople, popes insisted ever more clearly that they were the living embodiment of Peter and therefore enjoyed his primacy over the whole church. Leo's formulation of this in letters and sermons remained fundamental throughout the Middle Ages and beyond. Throughout the early Middle Ages the pope's highest title was vicar (or placeholder) of St. Peter, which gave way in the twelfth century to vicar of Christ. Pope Gregory VII, the first of the powerful high medieval popes, identified almost mystically with Peter, and his excommunication of the emperor took the form of a prayer to St. Peter.

Protestants have always objected that in Scripture especially and in the first century of the church's history there is no concern with Peter's rule in Rome or with provision for his supposed successors. In recent years the most fundamental attacks have come, ironically, from Roman Catholics promoting collegiality. They have produced historical evidence to show that the Roman Church retained a presbyterial structure (making Peter and Clement merely spokesmen, not presiding bishops) into the second century, and that the church as a whole had a decentralized regional structure at least into the fourth, whereby councils of bishops ruled on larger issues and the Roman Church enjoyed at best a primacy of honor.

Theologically the Roman Catholic Church bases its position on Matt. 16:18, claiming that Peter is the "rock" upon which the church is founded, thus giving it the full power of binding and loosing. The first certain application of this text to the Roman Church was by Pope Stephen I (254–57) in argument with Bishop Cyprian of Carthage over the baptism of heretics. This interpretation prevailed in Rome and has been the mainstay of papal documents and claims to this day. But other interpretations persisted elsewhere. The most common Protestant view happens also to be that found in the earliest extant commentary on this text (by Origen), namely, that the "rock" upon which the church stands is Peter's confession of faith. Those concentrating upon the "power of binding and loosing" in that text generally saw it conferred upon the entire episcopate of which Peter was but a symbol or spokesman (this in Cyprian, Augustine, and much of the Eastern Orthodox tradition).

Modern exegesis has produced some surprising twists. Some Protestants say the rock clearly refers to Peter and only by extension to his faith, while liberal Protestants and Catholics claim that this is not an authentic saying of Jesus but rather reflects the coming of "early Catholicism" in the primitive church. Moreover, progressive Catholic theologians concede that this saying, whatever its exact meaning and referent, cannot serve as a direct proof text for the Roman papacy and its primatial claims. Hans Küng has rejected entirely any scriptural basis for a Roman claim to primacy, whereas R. Brown, more cautiously, argues that the scriptural image of Peter's leadership and the Roman Church's early eminence together produce a "trajectory" from which Roman primacy is a defensible conclusion. Conservative Protestants continue to focus upon Peter's confessional recognition of Jesus as the Messiah as the foundational rock of the church and its disciplinary powers. J. Van Engen

See also Papacy; Peter the Apostle.

Bibliography. *NCE,* XI, 201–5; *LTK,* VIII, 334–41; O. Cullmann, *Peter;* R. Brown, K. Donfried, and J. Reumann, eds., *Peter in the NT;* P. Empie and T. Murphy, eds., *Papal Primacy and the Universal Church.*

Peter Lombard (*ca.* 1100–1160). Medieval theologian who taught at the Cathedral School in Paris and later became Bishop of Paris (1159). A student of both Peter Abelard and Bernard of Clairvaux, he combined in his work a skill for using the scholastic logical method with a firm commitment to the Christian faith. Perhaps because he was not as controversial as Abelard or Bernard, he was able to elaborate on the central issues of dogma without arousing great opposition. His fame rests on the *Book of Sentences* (1158), in which he used the logical method to arrive at a definition of orthodoxy. This work consists of numerous citations of the church fathers as well as of medieval writers such as Anselm of Laon, Abelard, Hugh of St. Victor, and Gratian. His lasting achievement was the organization of these materials into a coherent, objective statement of Christian belief. The book is divided into four sections treating God, the creation, the Trinity, and the sacraments. Lombard was one of the first to insist on the view that there are seven sacraments, and he distinguished between sacraments and sacramental signs.

Lombard's work was introduced as the textbook in a theological course by Alexander of Hales (1222), and it gained in popularity to such an extent that for several centuries candidates in theology at European universities were required to comment on it as preparation for the doctoral degree. It continued in use in Roman Catholic institutions until the seventeenth century, when it was replaced by the *Summa* of Thomas Aquinas.

Despite his moderation and popularity Lombard was criticized by a few of his contemporaries. Some accused him of accepting Abelard's teaching that Christ was not man but merely had humanity, while others felt that his Trinitarian statements were inadequate. These critics were silenced at the Fourth Lateran Council (1215), where efforts to have the *Sentences* condemned were defeated and the work was acknowledged as orthodox. R. G. Clouse

See also Scholasticism.

Bibliography. S. J. Curtis, "Peter Lombard, a Pioneer in Educational Methods," in *Miscellanea Lombardiniana;* P. Delhaye, *Pierre Lombard, sa vie, ses oeuvres, sa morale;* E. F. Rogers, *Peter Lombard and the Sacramental System.*

Peter Martyr Vermigli (1499–1562). Major Italian reformer whose flight from Italy in 1542 brought a sophisticated scholastic, rabbinic, and patristic learning to aid a variety of Protestant endeavors in northern Europe. A confidant of cardinals and humanists, he assumed the name of Peter of Verona, martyred in 1252.

In 1518 he entered the University of Padua to study Aristotle. He took his doctorate and was ordained priest in 1525. In 1526 he was promoted to public preacher, and from 1526 to 1533 he taught philosophy and Scripture in the houses of the Lateran Congregation. In 1533 he became abbot of Spoleto for three years. McNair argues plausibly (if only from circumstances) that he next assisted in the remarkable reform proposals which Gasparo Contarini and others presented to Pope Paul III in 1537. From 1537 to 1540 Vermigli served as abbot of S. Pietro ad Aram, Naples. During that time he preached to an audience which overlapped with the reform salon of Juan de Valdés, the Spanish reformer, who became a close friend. His 1540 public lectures on I Corinthians reached only 3:9–17 when he was suspended from preaching for his denial of purgatory. Powerful friends in Rome quashed the local mandate.

Vermigli was elected prior of S. Frediano at Lucca in 1541, a most influential post. He lectured on the Pauline Epistles and the Psalms. The great event was the September, 1541, summit conversations in Lucca between the pope and emperor. Josiah Simler, the contemporary biographer, records that Contarini and Vermigli engaged in daily religious conversations.

The summer of 1542 led to a crisis of conscience when the Inquisition was established in Italy on July 21. Vermigli fled Lucca in August by way of Pisa to Florence. He paused to copy a manuscript of Chrysostom on the Eucharist, to entrust his library to a patrician friend, and to pen a letter to his Lucca canons which concluded with the words, "I am free from hypocrisy through the grace of Christ." Ochino, valued preacher of the Capuchin Order, joined Vermigli in flight across the Alps on August 25.

After some days in Zurich, Vermigli spent a month in Basel. On October 5 he left for Strasbourg at Bucer's invitation. During his five years there he lectured on the OT and later on Romans, publishing comments on the Apostles' Creed in 1544 which clearly deny Roman teaching on the papacy and Eucharist.

Thomas Cranmer invited Vermigli to England in 1547. In spring of 1548 he took up residence in Christ Church, Oxford, as Regius Professor. In the midst of 1549 lectures on I Corinthians, Vermigli held a major Oxford disputation on the Eucharist. He delivered lectures on Romans, served on the Reform Commission for Ecclesiastical Laws, and contributed a prayer to the 1552 Prayer Book.

After Edward VI died, Vermigli returned to Strasbourg late in 1553. There he lectured on Judges to the Marian exiles and was pressed by the Lutheran John Marbach to conform to doctrinal constraints on baptism and Eucharist. He left in 1556 for Zurich.

While in Zurich, Vermigli was twice invited by Calvin to pastor the Genevan Italian congregation and to lecture for him. In 1559 he published the massive *Defense Against Gardiner* at Cranmer's personal request. He dedicated his 1558 *Romans* to Queen Elizabeth. At Zurich he lectured on Samuel, which Beza and Bullinger used in manuscript, and on Kings. He published in 1561 a *Dialogue on the Two Natures in Christ* to answer the Lutheran Brenz.

Vermigli corresponded with Elizabethan bishops such as Jewel, Cox, and Sandys. His Latin writings were excerpted and published in a Latin *Loci Communes* (1576). This was to be expanded and translated into the *Common Places* (1583). *Judges* and *Romans* likewise were translated in 1564 and 1568. Vermigli left a considerable literary deposit for the Elizabethan Puritans. The *Loci* went through thirteen Latin editions by 1656, while the commentaries are extant in thirty-one editions from the *Corinthians* (1551) to *Lamentations* (1629). M. W. Anderson

Bibliography. P. McNair, *Peter Martyr in Italy;* R. M. Kingdon, *The Political Thought of Peter Martyr Vermigli;* J. C. McLelland, ed., *Peter Martyr Vermigli and Italian Reform.*

Peter the Apostle. Simeon (or Simon) bar-Jonah (Matt. 16:17; John 21:15), though his original name continued in use (Acts 15:14; II Pet. 1:1), was known in the apostolic church principally by the name which Jesus conferred on him, "the rock," in either its Aramaic form *Kêpā'* (Gal. 2:9; I Cor. 1:2; 15:5) or Graecized as *Petros* (Gal. 2:7; I Pet. 1:1; II Pet. 2:1). Matthew associates this with the confession of Caesarea Philippi (Matt. 16:18), but we need not assume that this solemn endowment was the first time the name had been given (cf. Mark 3:16; John 1:42).

He was a fisherman from Bethsaida (John 1:43), but had a home in Capernaum (Mark 1:29ff.). His brother Andrew, who introduced him to Jesus, had been a disciple of John the Baptist (John 1:35ff.), and so possibly had he. The seashore call of Jesus (Mark 1:6) was evidently not the first meeting (John 1:41ff.).

One of the original twelve, he is depicted by the Synoptic tradition as their leader and natural spokesman (cf. Matt. 15:15; Mark 1:36; 9:5; 10:28; 11:20; Luke 5:5), particularly in crises. He makes the confession at Caesarea Philippi, expresses their revulsion at the idea of the suffering Messiah, and makes the disastrous representative boast (Mark 14:29–31) and denial (Mark 15:66ff.). Christ chooses him, with James and John, as an inner circle within the twelve (Mark 5:37; 9:2; 14:32).

Peter undoubtedly leads the first Jerusalem church. He is the first witness of the resurrection (I Cor. 15:5; cf. Mark 16:7). He leads in the gathered community before Pentecost (Acts 1:15ff.), and is the first preacher thereafter (Acts 2:14ff.) and the representative preacher of the early chapters of Acts (3:11ff.; 4:8ff.). He presides in judgment (Acts 5:1ff.; 8:20ff.). Paul regards him as a "pillar" of the early church (Gal. 2:9).

In a sense, he is also the first instrument of the Gentile mission (Acts 15:7), and his experience is representative of the intellectual revolution involved for Jewish Christians (Acts 10:1ff.). At the Jerusalem Council he urged the admission of Gentile converts without submission to the Mosaic law (Acts 15:7ff.) and had table fellowship in the mainly Gentile church of Antioch (Gal. 2:12) until, to Paul's disgust, he withdrew in deference to Jewish-Christian opinion. Essentially he was an "apostle of the circumcision" (Gal. 2:7ff.) but remained, despite obvious difficulties, a warm friend of Gentile Christians, whom he addresses in I Peter.

In his lifetime and later, anti-Pauline forces sought to use Peter, without his encouragement. There was a Cephas party at Corinth (I Cor. 1:12), and in the pseudo-Clementine romances Peter confounds Paul, thinly disguised as Simon Magus. Possibly party strife in Rome over the Jewish question (cf. Phil. 1:15) brought him thither.

There is no evidence that he was bishop of Rome or stayed long in the city. I Peter was written there (so probably I Pet. 5:13), doubtless after Paul's death, for Silvanus and Mark were with him. Probably (cf. Eusebius, *Ecclesiastical History*, III.39) Mark's Gospel reflects Peter's preaching. Peter died in Rome in the Neronian persecution (I Clement 5–6), probably by crucifixion (cf. John 21:18). Recent excavations reveal an early cultus of Peter, but the original grave is unlikely ever to be found.

Spurious writings in Peter's name, mainly in heretical interests, caused difficulties in the second century. Canonical works reflecting his teaching (including Mark's Gospel and the Petrine speeches in Acts) unitedly reflect a theology dominated by the concept of Christ as the Suffering Servant and the thought of the ensuing glory. Crises in the life of Christ (e.g., the transfiguration, I Pet. 5:1; II Pet. 1:16ff.) have made a deep impression.

A. F. Walls

See also Peter, Primacy of.

Bibliography. O. Cullmann, *Peter;* J. Lowe, *Saint Peter;* F. H. Chase, *HDB;* H. Chadwick, "St. Peter and St. Paul in Rome," *JTS* n.s. 8:30ff.; T. G. Jalland, *The Church and the Papacy;* J. E. Walsh, *The Bones of St. Peter;* E. Kirschbaum, *The Tombs of St. Peter and St. Paul;* F. F. Bruce, *Peter, Stephen, James and John;* E. J. Goodspeed, *The Twelve.*

Pharisees. An important Jewish group which flourished in Palestine from the late second century B.C. to the late first century A.D.

Sources. Virtually all our knowledge about the Pharisees is derived from three sets of sources: the works of the Jewish historian Flavius Josephus—*The Jewish War* (*ca.* A.D. 75), *The Antiquities of the Jews* (*ca.* A.D. 94), and *Life* (*ca.* A.D. 101); the various compilations of the rabbis (*ca.* A.D. 200 and later); and the NT. Other works—parts of the Apocrypha, the Pseudepigrapha, or the Dead Sea Scrolls—may also contain information concerning the Pharisees. But since the Pharisees are never explicitly mentioned in these works, their use in constructing a picture of the Pharisees is heavily dependent on prior assumptions which are at best speculative.

It should be noted, however, that even the use of the explicit sources is problematical. Most of the NT is written from a point of view that is antagonistic to the tenets of Pharisaism. The rabbinic traditions about the Pharisees are also shaped by polemical forces and are often anachronistic. The value of Josephus's information (traditionally regarded as the most helpful) is diminished by recent studies which suggest that Josephus was not a Pharisee before A.D. 70 and that his eventual conversion was motivated more by political realities than by careful study of the different Jewish sects. It certainly cannot be denied that Josephus's descriptions of the Pharisees are superficial. In short, therefore, our sources provide neither a complete nor a straightforward picture of the Pharisees.

Name. Various etymologies have been proposed for the name "Pharisee." The only one to receive general approval is that which derives the name from the Aramaic passive participle *pĕrîš, pĕrîšayyā',* meaning "separated." The consensus is that the Pharisees regarded themselves, or were regarded, as the "separated ones." From what or whom they were separated is not as clear. The Hasmonean rulers, the Gentiles, the common people, and non-Pharisaic Jews in general have all been suggested as possibilities. Present evidence seems to favor the last two options.

Nature and Influence. The fundamental issue in Pharisaic studies is the twofold question of the nature of the group and its influence within broader Judaism. Two basic positions have been taken on this question. The traditional view holds that the Pharisees were the creators and shapers of late second temple Judaism. They were not so much a sect as a dominant party within Judaism. According to the traditional view, although not all Pharisees were legal experts, Pharisaism was the ideology of the vast majority of the scribes and lawyers. Thus, as a group the Pharisees were the guardians and interpreters of the law. Jewish institutions associated with the law, such as the synagogue and the Sanhedrin, were Pharisaic institutions. While disagreeing over whether the Pharisees were primarily politically or religiously oriented, proponents of the traditional view agree that the Pharisees commanded the loyalty of the masses in both spheres. Indeed, most proponents of the traditional view would accept Elias Bickerman's dictum: "Judaism of the post-Maccabean period is Pharisaic."

The second point of view is a relatively recent development. Proponents of this position argue that when the inherent limitations and tendencies of our sources are taken into account, the Pharisees come across not as the creators and shapers of Judaism but merely as one of its many expressions. In essence, according to this view, the Pharisees were a rather tightly knit sect organized around the observance of purity and tithing laws; on most other issues the Pharisees reflected the range of views present within Judaism. Since Josephus and the Gospels carefully distinguish between the Pharisees and the scribes, scholars of this persuasion argue that it is better not to confuse Pharisaism with the ideology of the scribes. Pharisaism must be seen as a movement which drew from all walks of life. There were Pharisees who were political and religious leaders, but their positions of influence were due to other factors besides sectarian affiliation. Proponents of this second view posit that the Judaism of Christ's day was much more dynamic and variegated than the traditional view allows and that the Pharisees were only one of several sects that influenced the development of Judaism.

Of course, not all scholars subscribe to one of these two views; many hold mediating positions. Nevertheless, these two views constitute the foundations upon which the modern study of Pharisaism is based.

History. The origin of the Pharisaic movement is shrouded in mystery. According to Josephus, the Pharisees first became a significant force in Jewish affairs during the reign of Hyrcanus I (134–104 B.C.). In an earlier work, however, Josephus places the rise of the Pharisees much later, during the reign of Salome Alexandra (76–67 B.C.). Some scholars who view the Pharisees as the shapers of late second temple Judaism have sought to trace the beginnings of the group back to the time of Ezra and beyond. But such reconstructions are speculative at best. It is more likely that the Pharisees were one of several groups to grow out of the revival and resistance movement of the Maccabean period (*ca.* 166–160 B.C.).

Whatever its origins, the Pharisaic movement seems to have undergone a two-stage development. During the reign of Salome Alexandra the Pharisees as a group were heavily involved in politics and national policy making. Sometime after this, possibly when Herod the Great rose to power (37 B.C.), the Pharisees withdrew from politics. Individual Pharisees remained politically involved, but there was no longer any official Pharisaic political agenda. This seems to have been the situation during the time of Christ.

The Pharisees were divided over the issue of Roman rule. Josephus tells us that a Pharisee named Zaddok was instrumental in forming a "fourth philosophy" which was violently opposed to Roman rule. Elsewhere, however, Josephus records that at a later time certain well-placed Pharisees sought to forestall the Jews' rush toward revolt against the empire. It is impossible to tell which tendency reflected the conviction of the majority of the Pharisees.

After the Jewish revolt of A.D. 70 many scholars with Pharisaic leanings gathered at the city of Jamnia to form a school for the preservation and redefinition of Judaism. There is evidence that the Jamnia school was not exclusively Pharisaic. Nevertheless, it can be safely said that the Pharisees were the single most powerful sectarian element at Jamnia. Thus they played an important role at the beginning of the century-long process which transformed second temple Judaism into rabbinic Judaism.

Beliefs. The Pharisees were strongly committed to the daily application and observance of the law. This means they accepted the traditional elaborations of the law which made daily application possible. They believed, moreover, in the existence of spirits and angels, the resurrection, and the coming of a Messiah. They also maintained that the human will enjoyed a limited freedom within the sovereign plan of God.

Yet there is little evidence to suggest that these were distinctively Pharisaic beliefs. To the best of our knowledge these beliefs were the common heritage of most Jews. To some scholars this fact is proof that the Pharisees were the dominant religious force in Judaism; to others it is only another indication that the Pharisees' distinguishing mark was nothing but the scrupulous observance of purity and tithing laws.

The Pharisees and Jesus. The NT does not

present a simple picture of the relationship between the Pharisees and Jesus. Pharisees warn Jesus of a plot against his life (Luke 13:31); in spite of their dietary scruples they invite him for meals (Luke 7:36–50; 14:1); some of them even believe in Jesus (John 3:1; 7:45–53; 9:13–38); later, Pharisees are instrumental in ensuring the survival of Jesus' followers (Acts 5:34; 23:6–9).

Nevertheless, Pharisaic opposition to Jesus is a persistent theme in all four Gospels. This opposition has been explained differently by those who hold differing views on the nature and influence of the Pharisees. Those who see the Pharisees as a class of political leaders posit that Jesus came to be understood as a political liability or threat. Those who understand the Pharisees as a society of legal and religious experts suggest that Jesus became viewed as a dangerous rival, a false teacher with antinomian tendencies. To the extent that there were Pharisaic leaders and scribes, both these factors probably played a part. Yet other scholars point out that according to the Gospels the disputes between Jesus and the Pharisees centered primarily on the validity and application of purity, tithing, and sabbath laws (e.g., Matt. 12:2, 12–14; 15:1–12; Mark 2:16; Luke 11:39–42). In the light of this evidence it would seem that at least part of the Pharisaic opposition to Jesus was occasioned by the obvious disparity between Jesus' claims about himself and his disregard for observances regarded by the Pharisees as necessary marks of piety. In the end, the Pharisees could not reconcile Jesus—his actions and his claims—with their own understanding of piety and godliness.

S. TAYLOR

See also SADDUCEES; ESSENES.

Bibliography. J. Bowker, *Jesus and the Pharisees;* E. Rivkin, "Defining the Pharisees; The Tannaitic Sources," *HUCA* 40–41:205–49, and *A Hidden Revolution;* L. Finkelstein, *The Pharisees: The Sociological Background of Their Faith,* 2 vols.; R. T. Herford, *The Pharisees;* E. Schürer, *The History of the Jewish People in the Age of Jesus Christ;* H. D. Mantel, "The Sadducees and the Pharisees," in *The World History of the Jewish People,* VIII; M. Avi-Yonah and Z. Baras, eds., *Society and Religion in the Second Temple Period;* J. Neusner, *From Politics to Piety: The Emergence of Pharisaic Judaism.*

Philippists. *See* CRYPTO-CALVINISM.

Philosophy, Christian View of. Certain Greek thinkers in the seventh and sixth centuries B.C. were the first to call themselves philosophers, literally "lovers of wisdom." Discounting the traditional myths, doctrines, and common sense of the priests and poets of classical Greece, the first philosophers held that the most important questions all human beings need to answer are those concerning social order and the origin, nature, and development of the material world. Their method of approaching these questions included the critical scrutiny of confessedly human theories about the natural order. Alleged revelation from the gods offered by the religious leaders was explicitly repudiated. Not all philosophers since the first ones in ancient Greece have been antisupernaturalists, but they have all been concerned primarily with the most basic questions common to every human being, and they have adopted a method which tries to be critical of every assertion and the assumptions behind it.

Focusing on the most fundamental and general issues facing mankind, philosophers traditionally have attempted to synthesize all knowledge into a coherent, consistent system. No scientist or group of scientists can accomplish this task, for they are all limited in the scope of their investigations to just parts or certain aspects of the experienced world. The dominance of the scientific method in the modern era has brought with it a skepticism by many, including some scholars in philosophy, about going beyond the methods of science in describing reality. Consequently the synthetic and synoptic function of philosophy is considered less than attainable by some philosophers today.

More in vogue presently is the other characteristic associated with the philosophers from the time of the ancient Greeks onward, namely, their attempt to be analytical. In this role the philosopher gives leadership in the careful evaluation of the assertions, concepts, assumptions, methods, and conclusions of anyone who claims to be describing reality or prescribing for human behavior.

The Four Types of Philosophical Problems. *Logic.* Distinguishing good reasoning from bad cannot be done scientifically, for the ability to make this distinction is presupposed by all thinkers, scientific or otherwise. The philosophical field of logic seeks to ascertain the principles of the thought patterns one ought to follow if reality is to be reflected adequately or if reality is intentionally not being reflected in one's thought or utterances. Thus logic is the normative discipline of correct reasoning as such.

Theory of Knowledge. Although as important as any area in philosophy, the theory of knowledge, also designated epistemology, has seen surprisingly little progress in moving past the issues raised by the first philosophers over two and a half millennia ago. These issues include the definition, criteria, and sources of knowledge.

Equally significant is the question of whether there is a foundational structure of directly known principles of evidence upon which reasoning can be built. Also, there is the problem of deciding on the conditions that must exist for a statement to be true.

Metaphysics and Ontology. The term "metaphysics" was first used to refer to what Aristotle claimed to be "a science which investigates being as being and the attributes which belong to this in virtue of its own nature." He distinguished this "science" from all the "so-called special sciences," for none of them dealt "generally with being as being." Although the etymology and traditional use of the term "ontology" makes it a synonym of "metaphysics," its meaning has become narrowed in contemporary philosophy. This constriction began with Immanuel Kant's theoretical separation of reality from the appearance of reality and the limitation of human knowledge to the latter.

Prior to Kant metaphysics was commonly understood as the theoretical grasp of the overall structure of reality. Following Kant's distinction between reality and appearance metaphysics has been seen by many as the dispelling of illusion about what can be known of reality, assuming the human inability to transcend the realm of appearance.

In the analytically oriented philosophy of today's English-speaking world metaphysics amounts to a rigorous examination of the concepts used when referring to the basic categories of being. The term "ontology" is usually preferred, leaving "metaphysics" for the largely discredited speculative account of reality as a whole. By way of contrast, continental European philosophy considers ontology to be the disclosure of the world of appearance which is reality. Many philosophers, however, reject the Kantian distinction between appearance and reality by striving to grasp reality as a coherent system toward which human thought is advancing. For them metaphysics is understood in its traditional sense.

Value Theory. The fourth major department of philosophy includes ethics and aesthetics. The primary focus of the study of aesthetics is upon the question of whether beauty is relative to the observer. The answer has a direct bearing on the practical problem of whether standards should be imposed upon the creation, appreciation, and criticism of art works.

Ethics is mainly concerned with the grounds warranting human actions to be judged right or wrong, and persons and events good or evil. Ethicists who take moral statements to be cognitively meaningful and who find an objective basis for ethical values are divided into two standpoints in their theory as to what makes human behavior morally right or wrong. The teleological approach looks for the moral quality of an action in its tendency to bring about an intrinsically good state of affairs. Instances of such states that have been proposed include the greatest pleasure for the largest number of people, the full development of one's potential as a rational being, and the attainment of eternal peace. The competing standpoint is that of deontological ethics, which maintains that the rightness or wrongness of some human actions is not based on the results of those actions. Keeping a promise, for example, is thought right in any situation, because it is one's duty or is commanded by God. Traditionally Christian ethics has had both teleological and deontological elements.

The Christian Attitude Toward Philosophy. The apostle Paul's warning to the Colossian believers is clear: "See to it that no one makes a prey of you by philosophy and empty deceit, according to human tradition, according to the elemental spirits of the universe, and not according to Christ" (Col. 2:8). Such a warning was to be expected in light of what passed for philosophy in Paul's time. But he makes a philosophical assertion himself by continuing in the same passage to point out that in Christ "the whole fulness of deity dwells bodily" and that Christ is "the head of all rule and authority" (Col. 8:9–10). Apparently Paul regarded at least some problems of interest to the philosophers of his day worth addressing. For instance, "Christ" and "the elemental spirits of the universe" are taken by Paul to be alternative answers to a philosophical question he considers important.

Secular philosophers began losing the initiative to Christian thinkers within a few centuries after Paul's death. Indeed, during the thousand years prior to the modern era virtually all European philosophers were Christians. They took seriously the need of providing an interpretation of divine revelation in nature, Christ, and Scripture for a culture built on the framework of the ancient Greek philosophers. The basic questions every human must ask had been so clearly articulated by the Greeks that the Christian philosophers sought to formulate equally cogent answers from the standpoint of God's general and special revelation.

Secular philosophy, often anti-Christian, has regained the leadership in the modern period. The foundational issues with which philosophy deals have not changed, but their specific formulations and proposed solutions in the last few centuries have not always been compatible with Christianity. Hence, there is a great need for the insights and truths of divine revelation to be reestablished as being worthy of philosophical consideration.

This goal of contemporary Christian philosophy cannot be attained apart from the assistance of biblical scholarship and theology, however. Since orthodox Christianity is grounded upon, and intended to be consistent with, the events recorded and interpreted in Scripture, the Christian philosopher must come to understand Scripture as it understands itself. Of particular assistance will be theological interpretations of Scripture limited to the problems dealt with by God's inspired prophets and apostles. The Christian in philosophy will build upon this theological framework but will never supplant it.

Since much has been learned from and about both God's and mankind's creative work since the origin of the human race, the Christian thinker must contemplate more than the problems of concern to the biblical writers. Moreover, in order to encompass as much of God's truth as possible from natural revelation within a comprehensive view of the universe created and sustained by the merciful, loving God of Scripture, the Christian must engage in philosophical speculation. This does not entail an outlook inconsistent with Scripture. Specifically, there is no need to repudiate the miraculous, historical events upon which the Christian faith rests. A philosopher's synthetic standpoint is not necessarily secular, much less anti-Christian, even though the first philosophy began this way and has largely reverted to this stance in the modern era. All that a Christian must do to pursue philosophy properly is critically to scrutinize the discoveries, insights, and theories that have increased our knowledge of God's universe, and coherently to weave this knowledge into an adequate whole consistent with Scripture. This will involve a consideration, assessment, and evaluation from the scriptural viewpoint of every area of the human quest for knowledge, for control of the environment, for human governance, and for artistic expression.

The Christian philosopher's overriding purpose is to love God with one's entire being, including the mind. In addition, the Christian philosopher desires to assist the theologian in two important ways. One is to provide leadership in developing techniques of rigorous, critical analysis of both cultural and theological assumptions, concepts, and doctrines and their implications. The other line of assistance is in the formulation of a synthetic and synoptic scheme of thought in order that the systematic theologian, particularly, can show Scripture to be relevant to contemporary life and thought. The simple fact that any systematic theologian must adopt a philosophical system makes it crucial that Christian philosophers make available guidance in the selection and use of one consistent with the teachings of Scripture. S. R. Obitts

See also Philosophy of Religion; Metaphysics; Ethical Systems, Christian; Aesthetics, Christian View of.

Bibliography. R. M. Chisholm *et al., Philosophy;* M. D. Hunnex, *Philosophies and Philosophers;* H. A. Wolfson, *The Philosophy of the Church Fathers;* B. L. Hebblethwaite, *The Problems of Theology;* R. Nash, *The Word of God and the Mind of Man;* W. Corduan, *Handmaid to Theology.*

Philosophy of Religion. The philosophical investigation of the nature and grounds of religious beliefs is one of the oldest and most persistent areas of philosophical endeavor. Religious belief and practice give rise to a variety of philosophical issues, posing epistemological questions about the justification of religious belief, metaphysical questions about the nature of God and the soul, and ethical questions about the relation of God to moral values. So many are the intersecting major philosophical concerns in the religious arena, and so immediate is the interest, that philosophy of religion is one of the most significant fields of philosophical endeavor to both Christian philosophers and those of other persuasions. The classic problems in the philosophy of religion center on the grounds for belief in God, the immortality of the soul, the nature of miracles, and the problem of evil.

Grounds for Belief in God. Religious believers have generally found themselves obliged to defend their belief in such a supersensible reality as God by an appeal to philosophical argument. The classical arguments for God's existence are the five ways of Thomas Aquinas and the ontological argument of Anselm of Canterbury.

Aquinas's arguments are variations of two major forms, the cosmological and teleological arguments. The cosmological argument is based upon the contention that the existence and activity of the universe demand an explanation in an entity beyond itself. On one version propounded by Aquinas and by contemporary philosophers such as Richard Taylor and Frederic Copleston, the universe is seen as a merely contingent or possible being. As a contingent being its existence requires explanation in some being outside itself, a being that is capable of sustaining the universe in existence. According to this argument the universe owes its existence to a being who is "necessary," that is, incapable of nonexistence, which provides an explanation for its own existence. Thus, from the contingent, merely possible existence of the world, it is argued that God can be shown to exist.

The teleological or "design" argument advanced by Aquinas and William Paley, among others, urges us to infer from the well-orderedness of nature the existence of a supreme designer. Paley compares our experience of the intricate order and adaptation of parts to the whole in nature to finding a watch; surely the watch, by virtue of its complexity and apparent purposiveness of design, requires a watchmaker to explain it. No less then does the vastly more remarkable universe require a worldmaker. In Aquinas's more sophisticated version the constant, dynamic adaptation of various aspects of nonintelligent nature to the realization of a stable order in the world demands a granted orchestrator to account for this action.

Cosmological and teleological arguments have come under sustained criticism, notably by Scottish philosopher David Hume, noted empiricist and skeptic. Hume mounted a multipronged attack on the arguments, suggesting among other things that the phenomena in question are capable of alternative explanations, and that the arguments in general prove no single, all-powerful being, but at best a being of limited power or a group of entities far from infinitely wise or powerful, capable merely of bringing about the results in question. Since Hume's day debate has been pursued in philosophical circles with great ingenuity and care, with neither side being able to claim lasting victory. Nonetheless, such arguments on behalf of God continue to exercise a considerable appeal on the popular as well as the academic levels.

Anselm's ontological argument is the only theistic proof to proceed *a priori*, that is, by reflection on the concept of God alone, with no reference to such external evidence as the existence or nature of the world. Anselm observed that if God is defined as "the Being greater than whom nothing can be conceived," then to deny the existence of such a being lands one in a contradiction. One is thus implying that "something greater than God" can be conceived, that is, an *existing* God. This conceivable being would have, in addition to God's properties, a quality lacked by God—i.e., existence—and so would be greater than the being greater than whom nothing could be conceived. In his own day Anselm was criticized by the monk Gaunilo, who reasoned that along similar lines we would be bound to accept the existence of such fantastic entities as a "most perfect island," and later by Immanuel Kant. Briefly, Kant argued that to lack existence is not to be deficient in a property. Thus, the concept of an existing God is not "greater" than a nonexisting God, since the existing God has no properties not shared by a nonexisting God.

In addition to the use of arguments for God's existence, philosophers of religion traditionally have been interested in another avenue of possible knowledge about God—religious experience. Does a mystical experience or other putative encounter with the Divine provide good rational grounds for belief, as believers of all religious traditions have sometimes maintained? As would be expected, skeptics tend to dismiss such experiences as evidence of oversuggestibility in the experiencer, as evidenced by Bertrand Russell's pithy comment that "we can make no distinction between the man who eats little and sees heaven and the man who drinks much and sees snakes."

Status of the Soul. Another classic problem is the status of the soul and its fate after death. Plato's Socrates and others have held that the soul is related to the stable realm of eternal truth and thus is itself eternal, unlike the body, which belongs to the material world of impermanence and decay. Further, since soul is immaterial and has no parts, it, unlike body, is incapable of disintegration. Later philosophers less ambitiously have generally contented themselves with attempting to demonstrate that the soul logically is capable of being conceived as distinct from the mortal human body. Much recent philosophical discussion has been concerned with whether it is intelligible to assert that one could "witness one's own funeral," that is, survive bodily death.

The Miraculous. Much philosophical effort has been expended in subjecting basic theistic, supernaturalistic doctrines to critique or in providing refinements and defense of theism. The concept of miracle has received significant attention in philosophy. Christianity asserts the reality of the miraculous and stresses the importance of biblical miracles to Christian faith and doctrine, especially the conception of Jesus Christ in a virgin's womb and the resurrection of Christ from the dead. In addition, Christ's miraculous deeds are intended to be taken as a sign of his divinity. Hume's monumental work on the miraculous in *An Essay Concerning Human Understanding,* sect. X, depicted miracles as contradictions of our "firm and unalterable" experience in the regularity of natural laws, rendering them improbable in the extreme. It is much more probable that the miracle account is false. Hume's critique of the miraculous has had widespread acceptance in an age dominated by naturalism. Even many Christians have been disinclined to place much importance on miracles, some even explaining them away or preferring to see them as symbolic. Still, many Christian thinkers join C. S. Lewis, who in *Miracles: A Preliminary Study* has argued that an open mind must accept the possibility of divine "interferences" in the ordinary course of nature.

The Problem of Evil. The most potent criticism of theism, both philosophically and personally, arises from the so-called problem of evil. A significant intellectual problem is posed for theism by virtue of the fact that it asserts the existence of a God with unlimited power, wisdom, and goodness in the face of the existence of a world acknowledged to be rife with both moral evil and suffering. In a weak version the problem of evil raises a persistent problem in reconciling the traditional concept of God to the existence of such evils. In a stronger version, such as propounded by J. L. Mackie, it is seen as a positive disproof of God's existence, amounting to what Alvin Plantinga has called "natural atheology." Briefly, the core of the problem of evil is as follows: God is held to be unlimited in power, goodness, and knowledge. However, evil exists, in the form of undeserved suffering, perpetrated by man and nature, unchallenged victimization of weak by strong, pestilence, war, famine, and other horrors. In the face of this, either God is limited in power, goodness, or knowledge, or he does not exist at all; that is, either he is incapable or unwilling to remove evil, or he is unaware of its existence or of solutions to it. The problem of evil presupposes that God would have no reason for permitting evil that is adequate ultimately to outweigh in significance the negative effects of evil. Traditional theistic responses, or theodicies, have focused on this assumption. Augustine's "free will defense" argues that God needed to allow the possibility of evil if he was to create free beings, and a world with free beings is superior to a world of automata. Recently John Hick, taking a cue from Irenaeus, has suggested that God has placed us in a difficult environment that would be suitable for developing moral and spiritual maturity in his creatures rather than creating a maximally comfortable world. While Gottfried Leibniz attempted to argue that every evil in this world is necessary, more modest modern theodicies such as Hick's restrict themselves merely to removing the ground for alleged contradiction, showing that one can consistently affirm both God's existence and the reality of evil.

Contemporary Emphases. Much contemporary philosophy of religion focuses on questions surrounding the use of language in referring to God. Following Hume, contemporary philosophers such as A. J. Ayer and A. G. N. Flew have raised critical questions about religious language. In particular, they have argued that talk about God is as cognitively meaningless as mere gibberish, since it is incapable of empirical verifiability or falsifiability. Also of interest on the contemporary front is the logical coherence of the doctrine of God as he is traditionally understood in Judeo-Christian thought. D. B. FLETCHER

See also GOD, ARGUMENTS FOR THE EXISTENCE OF; EVIL, PROBLEM OF; MIRACLES.

Bibliography. Aquinas, *Summa Theologica*, Pt. 1, Q. 2; A. Flew and A. MacIntyre, eds., *New Essays in Philosophical Theology;* J. Hick, ed., *Classical and Contemporary Readings in the Philosophy of Religion;* W. James, *Varieties of Religious Experience;* J. L. Mackie, "Evil and Omnipotence," *Mind* (April, 1955); B. Mitchell, *The Justification of Religious Belief;* A. Plantinga, *God, Freedom, and Evil;* R. Swinburne, *The Coherence of Theism;* T. W. Tilley, *Talking of God.*

Photian Schism. The name given to a ninth century dispute between Eastern and Western Christianity. It began when Photius, a professor of philosophy, was appointed Patriarch of Constantinople by the emperor Michael III in 858, after the previous incumbent had been deposed. The latter's followers questioned the legality of this and found support from Pope Nicholas I, who took the opportunity to claim dominion also over the Eastern church. The breach was widened by doctrinal differences. These included matters such as celibacy, fasting, and anointing with oil, but concerned more notably the so-called double procession of the Holy Ghost. Rome held that the Holy Ghost proceeds from the Father and the Son (*filioque*). Photius rejected this, and saw in it a reflection of the difference between orthodoxy and heresy.

It seems clear that the schism was exacerbated by a difficulty of communication: neither pope nor patriarch spoke each other's language. The schism extended even to the mission field, where both sides vied for the souls of the Slavs. Bulgaria was a particular bone of contention. A new emperor first deposed, then restored, Photius, and a new pope, John VIII, did not press papal claims that had demonstrably jeopardized the unity of Christendom. But the damage had been done; another emperor in 886 either deposed Photius or compelled him to resign, and the ground was laid for the final split between Eastern and Western Christianity in 1054.

J. D. DOUGLAS

See also FILIOQUE.

Pietism. A recurring tendency within Christian history to emphasize more the practicalities of Christian life and less the formal structures of theology or church order. Its historians discern four general traits in this tendency: (1) its experiential character—pietists are people of the heart for whom Christian living is the fundamental concern; (2) its biblical focus—pietists are, to paraphrase John Wesley, "people of one book" who take standards and goals from the pages of Scripture; (3) its perfectionistic bent—pietists are serious about holy living and expend every effort to follow God's law, spread the gospel, and provide aid for the needy; (4) its reforming interest—pietists usually oppose what they regard as coldness and sterility in established church forms and practices.

Spener and Francke. The German Lutheran Church at the end of the seventeenth century labored under manifold difficulties. Its work was tightly confined by the princes of Germany's many sovereign states. Many of its ministers seemed as interested in philosophical wrangling and rhetorical ostentation as in the encouragement of their congregations. And the devastating Thirty Years War (1618–48), fought ostensibly over religion, had created widespread wariness about church life in general. To be sure, the picture was not entirely bleak. From Holland and Puritan England came stimulation for reform. And in German-speaking lands signs of Christian vitality remained, like the writings of Johann Arndt, whose *True Christianity* (1610) was a strong influence on later leaders of pietism.

But in many places these signs of life were obscured by the formalism and the insincerity of church leaders. This situation was altered by the unstinting work of Philipp Jakob Spener, known often as the father of pietism, who was called in 1666 to be the senior minister in Frankfurt am Main. There he appealed for moral reform in the city. He initiated a far-flung correspondence which eventually won him the title "spiritual counselor of all Germany." Most importantly, he also promoted a major reform in the practical life of the churches. A sermon in 1669 mentioned the possibility of laymen meeting together, setting aside "glasses, cards, or dice," and encouraging each other in the Christian faith. The next year Spener himself instituted such a *collegia pietatis* ("pious assembly") to meet on Wednesdays and Sundays to pray, to discuss the previous week's sermon, and to apply passages from Scripture and devotional writings to individual lives.

Spener took a major step toward reviving the church in 1675 when he was asked to prepare a new preface for sermons by Johann Arndt. The result was the famous *Pia Desideria* (*Pious Wishes*). In simple terms this brief work examined the sources of spiritual decline in Protestant Germany and offered proposals for reform. The tract was an immediate sensation. In it Spener criticized nobles and princes for exercising unauthorized control of the church, ministers for substituting cold doctrine for warm faith, and lay people for disregarding proper Christian behavior. He called positively for a revival of the concerns of Luther and the early Reformation, even as he altered Reformation teaching slightly. For example, Spener regarded salvation more as regeneration (the new birth) than as justification (being put right with God), even though the Reformers had laid greater stress upon the latter.

Spener offered six proposals for reform in *Pia Desideria* which became a short summary of pietism: (1) there should be "a more extensive use of the Word of God among us." The Bible, Spener said, "must be the chief means for reforming something." (2) Spener called also for a renewal of "the spiritual priesthood," the priesthood of all believers. Here he cited Luther's example in urging all Christians to be active in the general work of Christian ministry. (3) He appealed for the reality of Christian practice and argued that Christianity is more than a matter of simple knowledge. (4) Spener then urged restraint and charity in religious controversies. He asked his readers to love and pray for unbelievers and the erring, and to adopt a moderate tone in disputes. (5) Next he called for a reform in the education of ministers. Here he stressed the need for training in piety and devotion as well as in academic subjects. (6) Last he implored ministers to preach edifying sermons, understandable by the people, rather than technical discourses which few were interested in or could understand.

Although these proposals constituted an agenda for reform and renewal, they also posed two difficulties which have ever been troublesome for pietism. First, many clergymen and professional theologians opposed them, some out of a concern to preserve their traditional status, but others out of a genuine fear that they would lead to rampant subjectivity and anti-intellectualism. Second, some lay people took Spener's proposals as authorization for departing from the established churches altogether, even though Spener himself rejected the separatistic conclusions drawn from his ideas.

Spener left Frankfurt for Dresden in 1686, and from there he was called to Berlin in 1691. His time in Dresden was marked by controversy, but it was not a loss, for in Dresden he met his successor, August Hermann Francke. In Berlin, Spener helped to found the University of Halle, to which Francke was called in 1692. Under Francke's guidance the University of Halle showed what pietism could mean when put into practice. In rapid succession Francke opened his own home as a school for poor children, he founded a world-famous orphanage, he established an institute for the training of teachers, and later he helped found a publishing house, a medical clinic, and other institutions.

Francke had experienced a dramatic conversion in 1687, the source of his lifelong concern for evangelism and missions. Under his leadership Halle became the center of Protestantism's most ambitious missionary endeavors to that time. The university established a center for Oriental languages and also encouraged efforts at translating the Bible into new languages. Francke's missionary influence was felt directly through missionaries who went from Halle to foreign fields and indirectly through groups like the Moravians and an active Danish mission which drew inspiration from the leaders of pietism.

The Spread of Pietism. Spener and Francke inspired other varieties of German pietism. Count Nikolas von Zinzendorf, head of the renewed Moravian Church, was Spener's godson and Francke's pupil. Zinzendorf organized refugees from Moravia into a kind of *collegia pietatis* within German Lutheranism, and later shepherded this group in reviving the Bohemian Unity of the Brethren. These Moravians, as they came to be known, carried the pietistic concern for personal spirituality almost literally around the world. This was of momentous significance for the history of English-speaking Christianity when John Wesley was thrown into a company of Moravians during his voyage to Georgia in 1735. What he saw of their behavior then and what he heard of their faith after returning to England led to his own evangelical awakening.

Another group under the general influence of Spener and Francke developed pietistic concern for the Bible within German Lutheranism at Württemberg. Its leading figure, Johann Albrecht Bengel (1687–1752), represented a unique combination of scholarly expertise and devotional commitment to Scripture. Bengel did pioneering study in the text of the NT, exegeted Scripture carefully and piously, and wrote several books on the millennium.

Influences radiating from Halle, Württemberg, and the Moravians moved rapidly into Scandinavia. When soldiers from Sweden and Finland were captured in battle with Russia (1709), pietist commitments migrated to Siberia. Pietism exerted its influence through Wesley in England. The father of American Lutheranism, Henry Melchior Muhlenberg, was sent across the Atlantic by Francke's son in response to requests for spiritual leadership from German immigrants. In addition, pietism also influenced the Mennonites, Moravians, Brethren, and Dutch Reformed in early America. The continuing influence of Spener, Francke, and their circle went on into the nineteenth century. A renewal of interest in Luther and his theology, the active evangelism of the Basel Mission and the Inner Mission Society of Denmark, the revivalistic activity of Norwegian Hans Nielsen Hauge (1771–1824), and the establishment of the Swedish Mission Covenant Church (1878) could all trace roots back to the pietism of an earlier day.

Pietistic Influences. Historians have long studied the relationship between pietism and the Enlightenment, that rationalistic and humanistic movement which flourished during the eighteenth century and which contributed to the eventual secularization of Europe. They have noted that pietism and the Enlightenment both attacked Protestant orthodoxy, that both asserted the rights of individuals, and that both were concerned about practice more than theory. The crucial historical question is whether pietistic antitraditionalism, individualism, and practicality paved the way for a non-Christian expression of these same traits in the Enlightenment. The fact that pietism remained faithful to Scripture and that its subjectivity was controlled by Christian beliefs suggests that, whatever its relationship to the Enlightenment, it was not the primary source of the latter's skepticism or rationalism.

A further historical uncertainty surrounds the tie between pietism and the intellectual movements arising in reaction to the Enlightenment. Striking indeed is the fact that three great post-Enlightenment thinkers—the idealist philosopher Immanuel Kant, the literary genius Johann Wolfgang Goethe, and the romantic theologian Friedrich Schleiermacher—had been exposed to pietism as youths. It is probably best to regard pietism as a movement that paralleled the Enlightenment and later European developments in its quest for personal meaning and its disdain for exhausted traditions. Yet insofar as the heart of pietism was captive to the gospel, it remained a source of distinctly Christian renewal.

Religious movements resembling pietism were active beyond Germany in the seventeenth and eighteenth centuries. In fact, German pietism was but one chord in a symphony of variations on a common theme—the need to move beyond sterile formulas about God to a more intimate experience with him. The English Puritans of the late 1500s and 1600s exhibited this. The New England Puritan Cotton Mather, who corresponded with Francke, strove to encourage pietistic vitality in the New World. Shortly after Mather's death the American Great Awakening of the 1730s and 1740s exhibited pietistic features. In England, William Law's *Serious Call to a Devout and Holy Life* (1728) advocated a kind of pietistic morality. And Wesley's Methodism, with its emphasis on Scripture, its commitment to evangelism and edification, its practical social benevolence, and its evangelical ecumenicity, was pietistic to the core.

Even beyond Protestantism, pietistic elements can be seen in contemporary Roman Catholicism and Judaism. The Jansenist movement in seventeenth century France stressed the concern for heart religion that Spener also championed. The work of Baal Shem Tov (1700–1760) in founding the Hasidic movement in Judaism also sought to move beyond orthodox ritual to a sense of communion with God.

An overall evaluation of pietism must take into consideration the circumstances of its origin in seventeenth century Europe. Whether in its narrow German usage or its more generic sense, pietism represented a complex phenomenon. It partook of the mysticism of the late Middle Ages. It shared the commitment to Scripture and the emphasis on lay Christianity of the early Reformation. It opposed the formalism and cold orthodoxy of the theological establishment. And it was a child of its own times with its concern for authentic personal experience. It was, in one sense, the Christian answer to what has been called "the discovery of the individual" by providing a Christian form to the individualism and practical-mindedness of a Europe in transition to modern times.

In more specifically Christian terms pietism represents a significant effort to reform the Protestant heritage. Some of the fears of its earliest opponents have been partially justified. At its worst the pietistic tendency can lead to inordinate subjectivism and emotionalism; it can discourage careful scholarship; it can fragment the church through enthusiastic separatism; it can establish new codes of almost legalistic morality; and it can underrate the value of Christian traditions. On the other hand, pietism was—and continues to be—a source of powerful renewal in the church. At its best it points to the indispensability of Scripture for the Christian life; it encourages lay people in the work of Christian ministry; it stimulates concern for missions; it advances religious freedom and cooperation among believers; and it urges individuals not to rest until finding intimate fellowship with God himself.

M. A. Noll

See also Spener, Philipp Jakob; Francke, August Hermann.

Bibliography. A. Ritschl, *Geschichte des Pietismus*, 3 vols.; F. E. Stoeffler, *The Rise of Evangelical Pietism*, *German Pietism During the Eighteenth Century*, and (ed.) *Continental Pietism and Early American Christianity;* D. W. Brown, *Understanding Pietism;* R. Lovelace, *The Dynamics of Spiritual Life.*

Pighius, Albert (*ca.* 1490–1542). Roman Catholic apologist. Born in the Netherlands, he graduated from Louvain and lived first in Paris, then from about 1523 in Rome. He defended papal infallibility, denied that the pope could ever become a heretic, and was often cited by the Council of Trent, which valued his concept of tradition but rejected his views on justification and original sin. He wrote a treatise on free will which sought to make predestination dependent on foreknowledge of merits and jeopardized acceptance of original sin. Calvin took Pighius so seriously that his *Upon the Eternal Predestination* (1552) was directed against the latter. Peter Martyr Vermigli, too, wrote rejecting the views of Pighius, who had also engaged in controversy with Luther and Bucer. The Roman scholar, who achieved some fame with his argument that tradition was on a level with Scripture as a source of Christian truth, was also involved in the debate around Henry VIII's divorce project and prepared material for dialogue with the Orthodox Church.

J. D. Douglas

Plato, Platonism. Ancient Greek philosopher, one of the most influential thinkers who ever lived, Plato (*ca.* 427–347 B.C.) came from an aristocratic background which included a number of politically influential members. He was a resident of Athens and was given an excellent education by his family. This was followed by several years spent as a member of the Socratic Circle, a period that was abruptly ended by the death of Socrates in 399.

After Socrates' death, an event which certainly had a profound effect on Plato, he traveled widely in such countries as Greece, Egypt, and Sicily. He did not limit his philosophical studies to Socratic thought, but was also widely exposed to other options such as Pythagoreanism and Heraclitianism. Upon returning to Athens (the date is not exactly known), he set up his famous school of philosophy called the Academy and taught there until his death.

During his career Plato wrote more than two dozen philosophical works which are still extant; almost all of these are written in dialogue form, often with Socrates as the major personality. These dialogues are usually named after one of the debaters or questioners involved in the discussions. Because of this arrangement, there has been some doubt as to the extent to which the expressed views are actually those of the speaker (such as Socrates) or are the teachings of Plato himself.

The chronological order of Plato's works cannot be established with exactitude, but scholars are in general agreement concerning the time frame. The earlier dialogues are chiefly concerned with ethics and revolve around such themes as virtue, right conduct, and obedience to the state, even to the point of death. The later dialogues rely less on dialectical arguments and are more concerned with expositions of his philosophy.

For Plato, sense experience is not a valid means of ascertaining reality, since it is often in error and at best can only perceive facts in this changing world. Rather, he stresses the proper use of reasoning and mathematics, which he holds to be much more reliable than the pursuit of natural science.

Methodologically, the innate knowledge which man is physically born with is rationally reflected upon and extracted from others by means of the so-called Socratic method. This was illustrated by Socrates' well-known dialogue with the slave boy in *Meno* (82–87). Since the boy had no way of learning the principles of geometry, his perception of these truths must have been due to the skillful questioning of Socrates, who drew out the innate knowledge already in the mind of the lad. Through such rational means man may discover the other world of forms.

Three of the most important contributions which Plato made to the philosophy of religion are his theory of forms, his cosmology, and his teaching concerning immortality of the soul.

Forms. For Plato, forms are not physical objects nor are they simply logical or mathematical symbols. Rather, they have objective existence and provide the reality for the physical objects in the sense world, which can only imperfectly imitate these forms. In *Timaeus* the forms appear as the thoughts of God and have often been interpreted this way in both pre-Christian Platonism and in Christian philosophy since Augustine. The sense world is actually patterned after these forms, which provide the ideal copies for living and nonliving things alike, including even manmade objects (*Republic* 595–96).

The forms are ordered according to a hierarchy, of which the highest form is good. Other high forms are truth and beauty, followed by lower but still important ones such as justice, courage, wisdom, and piety (see *Republic* 517; *Philebus* 64–65).

Cosmology. Plato's cosmology includes his concept of the formation of the world, man, and material objects as copies of the eternal forms. Much of this teaching is found in *Timaeus*, which was for a number of centuries Plato's best-known work and exercised great influence.

In *Timaeus* the Demiurge ("craftsman"), who appears to be God, fashions preexisting matter by patterning it after the forms. By the inclusion of mind or soul, the creation shares a little part of divine essence.

In the *Laws* we get an additional glimpse of Plato's natural theology, as he postulates a sort of cosmological argument for God's existence from the presence of motion. In this work Plato rejects the options of atheism and deism (in the later sense of a being who is not interested in his creation). However, in *Statesman* (esp. 273–74) he seems to entertain just such a deistic view, in that God first takes charge of his creation, leaving man to himself.

Immortality of the Soul. Plato's beliefs on this topic are chiefly set forth in *Phaedo*, but they appear in several of his other works as well. For Plato death is marked by the separation of the body and the soul. Until this time the body is a hindrance, as it opposes and even imprisons the soul (*Phaedo* 65–68; 91–94). After death the just will be rewarded with a better destiny than the unjust. While the unjust are judged, penalized, and corrected "under the earth," the just are exalted "in a heavenly place" (*Phaedrus* 248–49). This twofold judgment is illustrated in Plato's famous myth of Er (*Republic* 614–16).

Yet all souls are immortal and acquire much knowledge of both this and the spiritual world. For instance the soul is "born" many times, up to ten thousand years, with philosophers apparently achieving the desired result in a comparatively shorter period of time; after this the soul "speeds away" to heavenly bliss (*Meno* 81; *Phaedrus* 248–49). Therefore, realizing that it leads to the attainment of true wisdom and perfection, the true philosopher should not fear death (*Phaedo* 65–68).

Influence of Platonic Thought. While Plato's concept of forms, his cosmology, and his views of immortality have probably had the greatest influence in the philosophy of religion, his other teachings have also been influential. His political philosophy, outlined in the *Republic*, set forth three classes: philosopher-kings, the military, and workers. His ethical philosophy, stressing the virtue of wisdom, has inspired those who seek intellectual pleasures (*Philebus*). His aesthetic philosophy, which stresses the imitating of ideal beauty rather than temporal, physical realities (*Symposium*), has been a major influence in the history of art.

Plato's academy was closed by Justinian in A.D. 529. Both before and after this time Platonism in various forms has been one of the most influential philosophies. Its influence on Judaism may be seen in Philo in the first century B.C. It inspired the Neoplatonism of Plotinus in the third century A.D., which emphasized the mystical implications of Plato's thought. Christian thought also came under the influence of Platonism, as scholars of the third century such as Clement of Alexandria and Origen mixed this Greek philosophy with their theology. In particular, Augustine's interpretation of Plato dominated Christian thought for the next thousand years after his death in the fifth century.

The Renaissance was partially characterized by a revival of Platonic thought, led by scholars such as Marsilio Ficino and Giovanni Pico of Florence. Later, the seventeenth century Cambridge Platonists promoted these ideas. In modern philosophy Platonism has inspired the works of thinkers such as A. E. Taylor and A. N. Whitehead.

Plato has exercised an enormous influence on Western thought and must therefore be dealt with by those of all philosophical persuasions. Through the centuries scholars have sided both with and against him. Some have questioned the objective existence of forms, others his reliance on the reminiscence of a previous existence. His cosmology has been dismissed by many, especially those of a more empirical persuasion. Christian scholars have rightly objected to the overuse of Plato by some who "Christianized" his thought as the proper vehicle for presenting truth, a practice which led to more problems than it solved in theology. G. R. Habermas

See also Neoplatonism; Augustine of Hippo; Cambridge Platonists.

Bibliography. *The Collected Dialogues of Plato,* ed. E. Hamilton and H. Cairns; I. M. Crombie, *An Examination of Plato's Doctrines,* 2 vols.; D. Gallop, *Plato: Phaedo;* G. M. A. Grube, *Plato's Thought;* W. K. C. Guthrie, *Plato, the Man and His Dialogues: Earlier Period* and *The Later Plato and the Academy;* R. Klibansky, *The Platonic Tradition During the Middle Ages;* T. M. Robinson, *Plato's Psychology;* D. Ross, *Plato's Theory of Ideas;* A. E. Taylor, *Platonism and Its Influence;* W. J. Verdenius, "Plato and Christianity," *Rat* 5:15–32; G. Vlastos, *Platonic Studies, Plato's Universe,* and (ed.) *Plato I: Metaphysics and Epistemology;* N. White, *Plato on Knowledge and Reality.*

Pleasure, God's Good. *See* Will of God.

Plenary Inspiration. This theory of biblical inspiration emerged in the later Reformation period, when serious theological attention was first given to the doctrine of inspiration and concepts of partial and verbal inspiration were also being advocated. The spirit of the Renaissance, developments in philology and textual criticism, and the initial expression of philosophical views which would find their culmination in the Enlightenment all helped to precipitate theological consideration. While verbal inspiration sought to erect bulwarks against the new learning and partial inspiration made a major accommodation, plenary inspiration may be described as a minor accommodation.

Plenary inspiration emerged first among the Jesuits, and was to remain a viable view in certain Roman Catholic circles into the nineteenth century. Among Protestants plenary inspiration was particularly prominent among English-speaking evangelicals.

The main principles of plenary inspiration are (1) God is the author of the Bible, in varied ways. (2) The focus of inspiration is the writers of the Bible. There is author rather than text orientation. (3) The writers have been inspired in all that they have written, though in varied ways. The inspiration of suggestion deals with matters of content which could be known only by divine revelation and in which the writers were inspired in a fashion similar to that of verbal inspiration. The inspiration of elevation relates to humanly accessible knowledge, from which inferences and conclusions had to be drawn. In this mode of inspiration the mental processes are elevated and sharpened. The inspiration of superintendence operates when copying from extant documents, affording accuracy of transmission.

Certain plenarists, refining the theory still further, might advocate several more categories: (4) The data of the Bible are claimed as the source of the theory, both its teaching about itself and its phenomena. (5) The Bible is all of God and all of man, but in varied ways. (6) Human frailty allows for any lapse, infelicity, or inexactitude. (7) Although the word "inerrancy" is not generally used, the Bible is described as without error, without mistake, and infallible. (8) The authority of the Bible extends particularly to the revealed truth of Christianity, but since all was inspired, no part, however apparently incidental, will ever lead astray if properly interpreted.

Plenary inspiration possessed certain concomitants. It could be moderately flexible on matters of biblical criticism and interpretation. For example, it could allow the evangelical social reformers to break through the biblical sanctions which a literalistic hermeneutic appeared to give to slavery. It was also helpful to the evangelists and missionaries of the first and second Evangelical Awakenings (1735–1825), providing them with a fully inspired Bible and yet directing them to concentrate on the central issues of redemptive revelation.

As evangelicalism began to lose some of its

dynamic in the second quarter of the nineteenth century, and as new pressures began to be felt, many plenarists shifted to either partial or verbal inspiration, although among some conservative Wesleyans, for example, the theory appears never to have entirely disappeared. I. S. Rennie

See also Bible, Inspiration of; Bible, Inerrancy and Infallibility of; Verbal Inspiration.

Bibliography. G. T. Ladd, *The Doctrine of Sacred Scripture*, II; J. T. Burtchaell, *Catholic Theories of Biblical Inspiration Since 1810;* B. Vawter, *Biblical Inspiration.*

Pleroma. *See* Fullness.

Plotinus. *See* Neoplatonism.

Polanus, Amandus (1561–1610). Professor of theology and OT exegesis at the University of Basel and one of the leading Reformed theologians of the period of Protestant orthodoxy.

Polanus wrote widely, producing commentaries and "analyses" of OT books—Malachi (1597), Daniel (1593), Hosea (1601), and Ezekiel (1607)—as well as theological works on Christology (1608) and predestination (1600) among others. His systematic theology, *Syntagma Theologiae Christianae* (1609), was published in English as *The Substance of Christian Religion.*

Polanus followed Peter Ramus in dividing theology into two parts: faith and good works. This meant, methodologically, that ethics was a full-fledged part of dogmatics proper. Theology had a practical significance as both faith and observance. This led Polanus to assert that the task of interpreting Scripture is the explication of the "true sense" (*verus sensus*) and the "true use" (*verus usus*) of Scripture. Both interpretation and application are necessary, with the goal being the glory of God and the edification of the church. Polanus stressed the literal sense as the only true and genuine sense of each passage of Scripture. He went on to establish a criterion for interpretation derived from the nature of Scripture. He argued that since the content of the Word of God concerning salvation gives all glory to God and none to humans, this should be the test for interpretation. An interpretation is true or false depending on its making this clear. Polanus quoted John 7:18 as support for this approach and thus set the task of recognizing that in every text the glory given to God should be a foremost concern. Karl Barth called this fundamental rule of Polanus's "unsurpassable."
D. K. McKim

See also Scholasticism, Protestant.

Bibliography. K. Barth, *Church Dogmatics*, I/2; H. Heppe, *Reformed Dogmatics; MSt*, XII; K. L. Sprunger, *The Learned Doctor William Ames;* E. Staehelin, *Amandus Polanus von Polansdorf.*

Polygamy. The practice of having more than one wife at one time. It occurs where women occupy a low station in human society. Islam permits a man four wives, but in recent times in some Mohammedan countries, notably in Turkey, this practice has been abolished by state law. According to the divine institution, lawful marriage consists of one man and one woman (Gen. 2:18, 24). Christ supported monogamy as the only rightful form of marriage (Matt. 19:4–6). While the Bible does not directly condemn the plural marriages that occurred in the OT, it frankly describes the evil effects of polygamy (or polygyny), as in the families of Jacob (Gen. 35:22; 37:18–28), of David (II Sam. 13:1–29; 15:1ff.), and especially of Solomon (I Kings 11:1–12). Abraham's marriage with his wife's maid Hagar, upon Sarah's special request (Gen. 16:1–3), is probably not to be regarded as polygamous, but as motivated by the desire to obtain the promised heir in accord with the custom of the land. His wrong consisted in his lack of enduring trust in the divine promise. Scripture therefore depicts the evils that resulted also from this union (Gen. 16:4–16), while Paul rebukes it even as he censures works-righteousness (Gal. 4:21–31). J. T. Mueller

See also Marriage, Marriage Customs in Bible Times.

Polytheism. The belief in a multitude of distinct and separate deities. It is formally contrasted with pantheism, the belief in an impersonal God identical with the universe, although the two doctrines can sometimes be found in the same religious tradition. Polytheism is distinguished from theism, also called monotheism, on the basis of polytheism's claim that divinity, while personal and distinguished from the universe, is many rather than one. Except for the great monotheisms of Judaism, Christianity, and Islam, the world's religions are overwhelmingly polytheistic. Polytheism characterizes Hinduism, Mahayana Buddhism, Confucianism, Taoism, and Shintoism in the East, and also contemporary African tribal religions. In the ancient world Egyptians, Babylonians, and Assyrians worshiped a plurality of deities, as did the ancient Greeks, Romans, and Norse. Belief in several distinct deities serves to provide a focus for popular religious devotion when the official deity or deities of the religion are remote from the common person.

According to Ninian Smart, deities are formed around a number of aspects of life. These include natural forces and objects such as fertility and atmospheric forces; vegetation such as trees, sacred herbs, and vineyards; animal and human forms such as serpents, cattle, and animal-human hybrids; and assorted functions such as love, agriculture, healing, and war.

The birth of Western philosophy in ancient Greece occurred in a culture with a rich popular polytheism. Socrates was sentenced to death for "impiety" and "atheism" in denying the deities worshiped by Athens and for corrupting the youth. Socrates firmly believed in the divine, and in fact believed himself to have a special mission from the gods. His theology was more philosophically and spiritually sophisticated than that of his contemporaries. It became in fact a matter of indifference in his thought whether gods were one or many, since he denied the distinct personality quirks and moral irregularities that served to differentiate them within the Greek pantheon. His successor Plato carried on this tradition, and held that in a well-run state there would have to be substantial revision in the Homeric mythology before allowing it to be used, because it depicted the gods performing evil and petty acts (*Republic* 376e–383c). Thus the intellectual motive for maintaining a plurality of deities was disappearing from philosophy at an early stage.

Islam erroneously interprets the Christian Trinity as a polytheistic doctrine, and ancient Israel possibly contended with the devotion to other deities in addition to Yahweh. Nonetheless, it is clear that Judaism, Christianity, and Islam represent forms of theism incompatible with polytheism. As the West becomes infiltrated with Eastern religions and their derivative movements, Western Christians will need directly to confront polytheism. D. B. Fletcher

See also Theism; Monotheism.

Bibliography. S. G. F. Brandon, ed., *A Dictionary of Comparative Religion;* L. E. Goodman, *Monotheism: A Philosophical Inquiry;* J. M. Koller, *Oriental Philosophies;* Plato, *Apology* and *Republic;* N. Smart, "Polytheism," *EncyBrit;* G. E. Swanson, *The Birth of the Gods: The Origin of Primitive Beliefs.*

Pope. *See* Papacy.

Pornography. Sex being of almost universal interest, allusions to it are legitimate and necessary if dramatic or literary descriptions of human life are to be truthful or educative; but an enormous market exists for those who exploit sex for gain. The social and moral questions arising from the representation of erotic behavior in books, films, and pictures are manifold.

Psychologically, the overstimulation of imagination by sexual images renders the whole personality oversexed by disproportionately concentrating thought and desire, often to the point of pornographic addiction; it coarsens feelings and attitudes toward the other sex as tools for sexual indulgence, unrefined by affection, tenderness, or respect; it inverts the sex drive into sterile, self-absorbed, physical pleasure alone—"mental masturbation"; and because overstimulation brings diminishing effects, it leads readily to mental indulgence in ever coarser, sadistic perversions—"hard-core" pornography.

Artistically, literary, visual, or dramatic representation of human behavior very powerfully educates, clarifies, "purges" the emotional life of spectators, by secondhand experience. The human body and human love are lovely. The nude statue, the exploration of sexual situations in book or play, have their place in sex education and in appreciation of the human scene. The problem is one of taste, explicitness, intention, and restraint. Deliberate importation of salacious ideas, to appeal to a wider audience or to compensate for want of literary power, is on another level.

Socially, the problems are protection of the immature and unstable; the danger that the emotions stimulated may erupt in antisocial sexual aggressiveness; the tendency to devalue women (mainly) and marriage; and the effect of sensualist displays and opportunities on the whole tone of society.

Legally, suppression of "obscenely offensive" materials has been difficult to enforce because of variable public taste and the unanswerable statement, "The offensiveness is all in the viewer's mind." Suppression of "what tends to deprave and corrupt" (so excluding artistic merit and medical textbooks) faces the difficulty of producing witnesses who admit to being depraved and corrupted. Partial censorship by "certificates of accessibility" make pornography more attractive, as supposedly "adult." Some states have abandoned legal restraint and report diminished interest and crime (e.g., Denmark).

Christians acknowledge the obligation to preserve purity of mind and heart. Jesus condemned the lustful look as equivalent to adultery, and declared the only defilement was that which comes from within (Matt. 5:28; Mark 7:20). The NT abounds in warnings concerning lust of the flesh, lust of the eyes, concupiscence, uncleanness, "following the inclination to sensuality" (II Pet. 2:2), and "the desires of the flesh and of the mind" (Eph. 2:3), on the principle that "as a man thinketh in his heart, so is he," or so he will do (James 1:15).

It is significant that the fullest discussion of "setting the mind on the flesh" (Rom. 8:5–13, almost a definition of pornographic addiction, though Paul includes more), as spiritual death, hostility to God, inability to please him, slavery, contrasts it with the indwelling of the Holy Spirit, whose shrine the Christian's inner life should be.

Not every thought or desire concerning sex is sinful. But Christians "have crucified the flesh with its desires and lusts," will not obey it, or be slaves to it (Rom. 6:12; Titus 3:3), but keep it to its divinely appointed place, subordinate to spiritual ends. Thus the Christian response to pornography is: "Put on the Lord Jesus Christ, and make no provision for the flesh.... Whatever is honorable, pure, lovely, think about these things" (Rom. 13:14; Phil. 4:8). R. E. O. White

See also Obscenity.

Bibliography. A. Burns, *To Deprave and Corrupt;* L. A. Sobel, *Pornography, Obscenity and the Law;* D. Barber, *Pornography and Society.*

Porter. *See* Minor Orders.

Positive Thinking. Over the last decade or so a host of best-selling books have urged people to take a "positive" attitude to life. Some of these have been written from an explicitly Christian perspective, but the majority have been clearly secular. Titles such as Robert Ringer's *Looking Out for No. 1* (1978), David Schwartz's *The Magic of Self-Direction* (1975), and Wayne Dyer's *Pulling Your Own Strings* (1978) are typical of this genre of literature in its secular guise. The most popular religious writer in the new wave of positive thinkers is Robert Schuller with books such as *Move Ahead with Possibility Thinking* (1967) and his numerous seminars for church leaders and members.

Still popular today and a classic of its type is Dale Carnegie's *How to Win Friends and Influence People* (1936). Here the secular brand of positive thinking is seen at its best. Norman Vincent Peale represents the best of the older tradition of religiously motivated positive thinkers. Although he published several books in the 1930s, his first success was *A Guide to Confident Living* (1948), which was followed by his even more successful *The Power of Positive Thinking* (1952). In the writing of these works Peale's mentor was the liberal theologian Harry Emerson Fosdick, whose *On Being a Real Person* (1943) expresses his mature thought on the subject.

The religious roots of positive thinking can be traced back to the revivalism of Charles G. Finney, whose emphasis on the human element in conversion and the ability of men to create revivals broke with the Calvinist heritage of New England. As the inventor of "high pressure revivalism" Finney psychologized conversion and in his *Lectures on Revivals of Religion* (1854) gave his readers techniques for success.

The secular roots of positive thinking are found in New England transcendentalism, especially the works of Henry David Thoreau. His now classic *Walden or Life in the Woods* (1854) develops a vision of faith as a psychological faculty which expresses a profound self-confidence in the ability of men and women to triumph against all odds.

This faith in the will found expression in New Thought and Frank Haddock's best seller, *Power of Will,* published in 1906. Traces of it are also to be found in Christian Science and a host of other nineteenth century new religious movements.

Today the popularity of books like Napoleon Hill's *Think and Grow Rich,* first published in 1937, shows the continuity of this tradition. At the same time a host of television evangelists and other preachers offer the public encouragement through books and cassette tapes that assure them of their self-worth and need to believe in themselves.

Several systems of counseling have developed along these lines, such as the *Psycho-Cybernetics* (1960) of Maxwell Maltz and various techniques of inner healing associated with the charismatic movement.

Psychologically, the need to think in positive ways has been severely criticized by Richard Lazarus in his book *Psychological Stress and the Coping Process* (1966). Sociologically, a telling critique of the trends found in positive thinking is presented in Christopher Lasch's *The Culture of Narcissism* (1979).

Theologically, positive thinking encourages a form of humanism that has often led to the development of heretical movements along the lines of New Thought, Christian Science, and a variety of semi-Christian groups today. It overlooks biblical teachings about sin and the sovereignty of God to emphasize the essential goodness of humanity and the ability of people to solve their own problems through faith in their own abilities. In its Christianized form this self-faith is mediated through reference to Christian symbols, which upon closer examination are devoid of their original meaning. I. Hexham

Bibliography. D. Meyer, *The Positive Thinkers;* P. C. Vitz, *Psychology as Religion.*

Positivism. A distinctive position in contemporary philosophy which stresses the analysis of language as the most important function of philosophy. Positivism, because of its use of recent developments in logic and its emphasis on scientific inquiry as the paradigm of human knowledge, is sometimes called logical positivism or logical empiricism. All three labels can be used interchangeably.

Although its greatest influence was among early twentieth century English-speaking philosophers, positivism can be traced back to the nineteenth century French thinker Auguste Comte, who promoted the claim that the most perfect form of knowledge is simple description of sense experience. This conviction was rooted in his evolutionary view of the growth of human knowledge, which was labeled the "law of three stages." On this account the earliest stage was the theological, in which men explained natural phenomena by appeal to spiritual beings—i.e., gods or God (e.g., "God brought the storm"). The next was the metaphysical, in which these beings become depersonalized forces or essences. In the final, mature stage, called the positive, explanation involves only scientific description (e.g., "The storm was caused by the meeting of two weather fronts"). Although contemporary positivists (of whom there are very few) rely very little on Comte's ideas, they retain his rejection of metaphysics and theology.

Science alone, they claim, generates reliable knowledge of nature, and in promoting this claim they are closely related to naturalism. Positivism differs from naturalism, however, in its explicit and militant rejection of metaphysics. The fact that its analysis of science emphasizes logical principles more than psychological ones also distinguishes positivism from naturalism.

In stressing the analysis of language positivists emphasize the distinction between analytic and synthetic propositions. The truth of analytic propositions depends on their terms—e.g., "All vixens are female foxes." Synthetic propositions, on the other hand, are those which refer to facts and whose truth depends on a relation to them—e.g., "There are books in Oxford." Analytic propositions have no factual content and consist only of tautologies. The determination of their truth and falsehood involves only logical and linguistic analysis. Synthetic propositions as a group contain all propositions having factual meanings and belong entirely to the sciences, there being no factual propositions except scientific ones. A metaphysical statement such as "God exists" is therefore condemned to the positivists' no-man's-land. This statement is not a tautology and it is not scientific, and is therefore not true or false; rather, it is meaningless. Positivists, therefore, are presumably not atheists.

An important, and historically interesting, doctrine developed by positivists is the famous (or infamous) verifiability theory of meaning, which is perhaps the most explicit example of their antimetaphysical bias. Roughly stated, it defines the meaning of an empirical concept by reference to the sensory observations that will confirm or disconfirm it. If a proposition involves such reference, it is obviously meaningful and can be subjected to scientific inquiry. If it does not, and if it cannot be shown to be a logical truth, it is without meaning, is literally nonsense, a pseudostatement—"pseudo" because it may have grammatical form and "look like" a statement, and this is just why we are fooled into thinking that it actually means something. The statement "God exists" would count as such a pseudostatement.

Among other problems positivism has encountered is the issue of the status of the verification principle itself. As a philosophical position its influence on the contemporary scene has waned. Its primary interest to contemporary thinkers is historical.

J. D. SPICELAND

Bibliography. J. Joergensen, *The Development of Logical Empiricism;* A. J. Ayer, *Language, Truth and Logic;* R. von Mises, *Positivism;* E. P. Polten, *Critique of the Psycho-Physical Unity Theory.*

Possession, Demon. *See* DEMON, DEMON POSSESSION.

Postlapsarianism. *See* SUPRALAPSARIANISM.

Postmillennialism. *See* MILLENNIUM, VIEWS OF THE.

Posttribulation Rapture. *See* RAPTURE OF THE CHURCH.

Power, Powers. *See* PRINCIPALITIES AND POWERS.

Pragmatism. The label applied to ideas formulated by three American thinkers, Charles S. Peirce (1839–1914), William James (1842–1910), and John Dewey (1859–1952). Though each developed separate elements in pragmatism, their ideas coalesced, became deeply entrenched in American universities, and affected many fields of inquiry—notably psychology, religion, and education. Early pragmatism was strongest at the University of Chicago, but was popularized in the widely read works of James and Dewey. Also, pragmatism's popularity grew in America because American culture traditionally accepted the pragmatists' dogmas of utility, democracy, and progress.

Charles Peirce created and applied a utilitarian standard in his philosophy as he analyzed ideas for their practical consequences instead of their conformity to an ideal truth. His approach, which he labeled "pragmaticism," stressed logical thinking based on observable facts. The result he envisioned was a clear philosophical method rather than a comprehensive world view, but it was a method closely tied to nineteenth century positivism; thus, his pragmaticism affected more than methodology alone.

William James added to Peirce's ideas by

applying them to conflicts between religion and science. Science, which was positivistic and promoted evolutionary theories, was roundly attacked by many who advocated religious belief based on biblically revealed truths; consequently James proposed a pragmatic solution: opposing philosophies which produced identical results really did not conflict. For example, James believed that if scientific materialism produced belief in deity and traditional religion also produced belief in God, then there was no essential difference between those philosophies.

James advocated his ideas in several widely read books: *The Will to Believe* (1896); *Varieties of Religious Experience* (1902); *Pragmatism* (1907); *A Pluralistic Universe* (1909); and *The Meaning of Truth* (1909). In these works James also developed his thought in additional ways. First, he employed "radical empiricism" to describe the nature of beliefs. That is, in his view beliefs rest on currently observed facts; thus, beliefs are hypothetical and relative rather than dogmatic. Secondly, "humanism" is the route to proper ideas. Ideas are to be based on human experience, not on revelation. Thirdly, truths are relative to experience instead of coming from an absolute source. This latter idea was promoted by Canning Scott Schiller (1864–1937), pragmatism's chief advocate in England. Schiller also wrote several works which employed pragmatic humanism in the discipline of logic.

The third famous philosophical pragmatist, John Dewey, applied the ideas of Peirce and James to educational philosophy in his many books and as a prominent philosopher in the University of Chicago (1894–1904) and Columbia University (1904–29). Dewey's philosophy became known as experimentalism. As the other pragmatists, he emphasized the naturalistic, empirical, and evolutionary aspects of human thought which portrayed humans and their thought patterns as part of nature. That is, in Dewey's view mankind could not escape natural environment; nor could ideals have a transcendent source. For Dewey education was a process of inquiry and human interaction as opposed to a mastery of absolute, fixed truths. Similarly, the traditional use of education to pass on social values was criticized by Dewey; for, with James, Dewey regarded values as hypothetical, not absolute. Given his belief in evolution, Dewey maintained that his educational philosophy promoted true individual growth and would produce true democracy. Also, employing humanism and relativism, Dewey criticized religion as a source of truth. He regarded people as "religious" but rejected values and principles based on any revealed "religion." Some of Dewey's important works are *Psychology* (1871); *The School and Society* (1900); *Ethics* (1908); *Democracy and Education* (1916); *A Common Faith* (1934); *The Theory of Inquiry* (1938); and *Knowing and the Known* (1949).

Pragmatism extensively influenced American life and thought. It fit well with science's popularity and with traditional American notions of democracy and evolutionary progress. Though progressive notions expired in Europe after World War I, America, which escaped the mass destruction and maintained a deep faith in education, provided continued fruitful ground for pragmatist philosophy. Also, though pragmatism denied transcendental sources of truth, it accepted a "religious" aspect in all mankind. Such a philosophy, when not thoroughly critiqued, fit well into America's pluralistic religious environment. R. J. VanderMolen

Bibliography. J. L. Childs, *American Pragmatism and Education;* F. Copleston, *A History of Philosophy,* VIII; S. Hook, *The Metaphysics of Pragmatism;* E. C. Moore, *American Pragmatism;* C. Morris, *The Pragmatic Movement in American Philosophy;* P. P. Wiener, *Evolution and the Founders of Pragmatism;* A. O. Lovejoy, *The Thirteen Pragmatisms.*

Praise. The Bible is full of praise and adoration to God. Praise may be defined as homage rendered to God by his creatures in worship of his person and in thanksgiving for his favors and blessings. Angels that excel in strength render their praise unto the Lord (Ps. 103:20). Their voices were lifted in adoration at the birth of Christ (Luke 2:13–14), and in days of tribulation yet to come they shall join in crying, "Worthy is the Lamb that was slain" (Rev. 5:11–12).

Praise is rendered to God by Israel, especially in the "Hallel Psalms" (Pss. 113–18). Not only Israel, but all who serve God, both heaven and earth, the seas and all that moves therein—in fact, everything that has breath—must rightfully render praise unto the Lord (Pss. 135:1–2; 69:34; 150:6).

God may be praised with musical instruments and with song (Pss. 150:3–5; 104:33). Sacrifice (Lev. 7:13), testimony (Ps. 66:16), and prayer (Col. 1:3) are also activities where praise finds expression. Praise may be public as well as private (Ps. 96:3); it may be an inward emotion (Ps. 4:7) or an outward utterance (Ps. 51:15). It is rendered to God for his salvation (Ps. 40:10) as well as for the greatness of all his marvelous works (Rev. 15:3–4). He should be praised for his inherent qualities, his majesty (Ps. 104:1) and holiness (Isa. 6:3).

Praise occasionally has humanity as its object, in which case the commendation may be worthy (Prov. 31:28, 31) or unworthy (Matt. 6:2). The apostle Paul sought the glory of God rather than the praise of men (I Thess. 2:6), but recognized a legitimate praise as a tribute for distinguished Christian service (II Cor. 8:18). Such praise may become an incentive to holy living (Phil. 4:8).

It is not good to withhold the glory rightfully due God, for he has said, "Whoso offereth praise glorifieth me" (Ps. 50:23). Every believing heart which meditates upon his works (Ps. 77:11–14), which recounts his benefits (Ps. 103:2), and which dwells upon his unspeakable gift (II Cor. 9:15) will find the praise of God not only a duty but a delight. G. B. Stanton

Prayer. Theology that is biblical and evangelical will always be nurtured by prayer. Moreover, it will give special attention to the life of prayer, since theology is inseparable from spirituality. Theology is concerned not only with the Logos but also with the Spirit who reveals and applies the wisdom of Christ to our hearts. John Calvin referred to prayer as "the soul of faith," and indeed faith without prayer soon becomes lifeless. It is by prayer that we make contact with God. It is likewise through prayer that God communicates with us.

Heiler's Typology. Probably the most significant work on the phenomenology of prayer is Friedrich Heiler's *Das Gebet* [*Prayer*], written toward the end of the First World War. Heiler, a convert from Catholicism to Lutheranism and for many years professor of history of religions at the University of Marburg, makes a convincing case that prayer takes quite divergent forms, depending on the kind of religion or spirituality in which it is found. He sees six types of prayer: primitive, ritual, Greek cultural, philosophical, mystical, and prophetic.

In the prayer of primitive man God is envisaged as a higher being (or beings) who hears and answers the requests of humans, though he is not generally understood as all-powerful and all-holy. Primitive prayer is born out of need and fear, and the request is frequently for deliverance from misfortune and danger.

Ritual prayer represents a more advanced stage of civilization, though not necessarily deeper or more meaningful prayer. Here it is the form, not the content, of the prayer which brings about the answer. Prayer is reduced to litanies and repetitions that are often believed to have a magical effect.

In popular Greek religion petition was focused upon moral values rather than simply rudimentary needs. The gods were believed to be benign but not omnipotent. The prayer of the ancient Greeks was a purified form of primitive prayer. It reflected but did not transcend the cultural values of hellenic civilization.

Philosophical prayer signifies the dissolution of realistic or naïve prayer. Prayer now becomes reflection upon the meaning of life or resignation to the divine order of the universe. At its best, philosophical prayer includes a note of thanksgiving for the blessings of life.

According to Heiler, the two highest types of prayer are the mystical and the prophetic. Mysticism in its Christian context represents a synthesis of Neoplatonic and biblical motifs, but it is also a universal religious phenomenon. Here the aim is union with God, who is generally portrayed in suprapersonal terms. The anthropomorphic god of primitive religion is now transformed into a God that transcends personality, one that is best described as the Absolute, the infinite abyss, or the infinite ground and depth of all being. Mysticism sees prayer as the elevation of the mind to God. Revelation is an interior illumination rather than the intervention of God in history (as in biblical faith). Mystics often speak of a ladder of prayer or stages of prayer, and petition is always considered the lowest stage. The highest form of prayer is contemplation, which often culminates in ecstasy.

For Heiler, prophetic prayer signifies both a reappropriation and a transformation of the insights of primitive man. Now prayer is based not only on need but also on love. It is neither an incantation nor a meditation but a spontaneous outburst of emotion. Indeed, heartfelt supplication is the essence of true prayer. Prophetic prayer involves importunity—begging and even complaining. In this category of prophetic religion Heiler places not only the biblical prophets and apostles but also the Reformers, especially Luther, and the Puritans. Judaism and Islam at their best also mirror prophetic religion, though mysticism is present in these movements as well.

The spirituality which Heiler did not consider and which is really a contemporary phenomenon can be called secular spirituality. It signifies a this-worldly mysticism where the emphasis is on not detachment from the world but immersion in the world. This was already anticipated in both Hegel and Nietzsche. J. A. T. Robinson describes secular prayer as the penetration through the world to God. The liberation theologian Juan Luis Segundo defines prayer as reflection on and openness to what God is doing in history. Henry Nelson Wieman, the religious naturalist, sees prayer as an attitude toward life which places us in contact with the creative process in nature. Dorothy Sölle speaks of "political prayer," which is oriented toward praxis rather than either adoration or petition.

Hallmarks of Christian Prayer. In biblical religion prayer is understood as both a gift and a task. God takes the initiative (cf. Ezek. 2:1–2; Ps. 50:3–4), but man must respond. This kind of prayer is personalistic and dialogic. It entails revealing our innermost selves to God but also God's revelation of his desires to us (cf. Prov. 1:23).

Prayer in the biblical perspective is spontaneous, though it may take structured forms. But the forms themselves must always be held to tentatively and placed aside when they become barriers to the conversation of the heart with the living God. True prayer, in the prophetic or biblical sense, bursts through all forms and techniques. This is because it has its basis in the Spirit of God, who cannot be encased in a sacramental box or a ritualistic formula.

In the Bible petition and intercession are primary, though adoration, thanksgiving, and confession also have a role. Yet the petitionary element is present in all these forms of prayer. Biblical prayer is crying to God out of the depths; it is the pouring out of the soul before God (cf. I Sam. 1:15; Pss. 88:1–2; 130:1–2; 142:1–2; Lam. 2:19; Matt. 7:7–8; Phil. 4:6; Heb. 5:7). It often takes the form of importunity, passionate pleading to God, even wrestling with God.

Such an attitude presupposes that God's ultimate will is unchanging, but the way in which he chooses to realize this will is dependent on the prayers of his children. He wants us as covenant partners, not as automatons or slaves. In this restricted sense prayer may be said to change the will of God. But more fundamentally it is sharing with God our needs and desires so that we might be more fully conformed to his ultimate will and purpose.

Meditation and contemplation have a role in biblical religion, though not, however, as higher stages of prayer (as in mysticism) but as supplements to prayer. The focus of our meditation is not on the essence of God or the infinite depth of all being but on God's redemptive deeds in biblical history culminating in Jesus Christ. The aim is not greater detachment from the world of turmoil and confusion but a greater attachment to God and to our fellow human beings.

Biblical spirituality makes a place for silence, yet silence is to be used not to get beyond the Word but to prepare ourselves to hear the Word. Against certain types of mysticism, faith-piety (Heiler) does not seek to transcend reason but to place reason in the service of God. There can be a prayer that consists only in groans or sighs or in shouts and cries of jubilation; yet it is not complete or full prayer until it takes the form of meaningful communication with the living God.

The Paradox of Prayer. Prayer in the Christian sense does not deny the mystical dimension, but neither does it accept the idea of a higher stage in prayer where petition is left behind. The progress that it sees in the spiritual life is from the prayer of rote to the prayer of the heart.

Prayer in biblical or evangelical spirituality is rooted in both the experience of Godforsakenness and in the sense of the presence of God. It is inspired by both the felt need of God and gratitude for his work of reconciliation and redemption in Jesus Christ.

Biblical prayer includes the dimension of importunity and of submission. It is both wrestling with God in the darkness and resting in the stillness. There is a time to argue and complain to God, but there is also a time to submit. Biblical faith sees submission to the will of God coming after the attempt to discover his will through heartfelt supplication. Prayer is both a pleading with God that he will hear and act upon our requests and a trusting surrender to God in the confidence that he will act in his own time and way. But the confidence comes only through the struggle.

Christian prayer is both corporate and individual. We find God in solitariness, but we never remain in this state. Instead, we seek to unite our sacrifices of praise and our petitions and intercessions with those of the company of fellow believers. The man or woman of prayer may find God both in solitude and in fellowship. Even in solitude we believe that the petitioner is not alone but is surrounded by a cloud of witnesses (Heb. 12:1), the saints and angels in the church triumphant.

We are called to present personal and individual needs to God, but at the same time we are urged to intercede for the whole company of the saints (John 17:20–21; Eph. 6:18) and also for the world at large (I Tim. 2:1–2). Biblical spirituality entails not withdrawal from the turmoils of the world but identification with the world in its shame and affliction. Personal petition would become egocentric if it were not held in balance with intercession, adoration, and thanksgiving.

The goal of prayer is not absorption into the being of God but the transformation of the world for the glory of God. We yearn for the blessed vision of God, but even more we seek to bring our wills and the wills of all people into conformity with the purposes of God. We pray not simply for personal happiness or for protection (as in primitive prayer) but for the advancement and extension of the kingdom of God.

D. G. Bloesch

Bibliography. D. G. Bloesch, *The Struggle of Prayer;* J. Ellul, *Prayer and Modern Man;* O. Hallesby, *Prayer;*

P. T. Forsyth, *The Soul of Prayer;* K. Barth, *Prayer;* F. von Hügel, *The Life of Prayer;* T. Merton, *Contemplative Prayer;* H. U. von Balthasar, *Prayer;* P. LeFevre, *Understandings of Prayer.*

Prayer, The Lord's. *See* LORD'S PRAYER.

Prayers for the Dead. No passage in OT or NT enjoins or even implies this practice. Of the single passage in the Apocrypha which appears to allude to it, it may be said that text, translation, and interpretation of II Macc. 12:44 are all uncertain, and that there is considerable evidence that orthodox Jewry of the intertestamental period rejected prayers for the dead. In canonical Scripture the Christian soul is spoken of as at once "with Christ" (II Cor. 5:6, 8; Phil. 1:23); the Lord promised the penitent thief Paradise "today" (Luke 24:43). Scripture everywhere regards death as the end of man's probationary period; after death, even prior to the resurrection of the body and the last judgment, the soul is fixed in a permanent state of bliss or misery (see esp. Luke 16:19–31). Hence prayers for the dead are, at best, irrelevant and unnecessary.

The apostolic fathers do not mention prayers for the dead. The custom seems to have arisen in the church at the end of the second century. In the Roman Catholic Church the practice is an integral part of an erroneous system of salvation and is particularly connected with Roman teaching on purgatory, indulgences, and the Mass. The liturgies and confessions of Protestant churches do not countenance prayers for the dead.

O. R. JOHNSTON

See also PURGATORY.

Preach, Preaching. In the NT a preacher is a person who has the inner call from the Holy Spirit and the external call from the church and has been duly set apart to proclaim the gospel. The preacher's task is to speak as a personal witness to God's revelation, interpreting it, explaining it, and applying it to the needs of the people. The most common definition of preaching is one composed from two quotes from Phillips Brooks: "Preaching is the communication of truth through personality." Bishop Manning gives a more theological definition when he calls preaching "the manifestation of the Incarnate Word from the written word through the spoken word." Henry Sloane Coffin described preaching as "truth through personality to constrain conscience at once." The noted homiletician Andrew W. Blackwood, Sr., gave two worthy definitions: "Preaching is divine truth voiced by a chosen personality to meet human need," and "Preaching means interpreting life today with light from the Scripture so as to meet the needs of the hearer now, and guide the hearer in doing God's will tomorrow."

Preaching in the Bible. In the OT the words used are *qōhelet,* preacher; *bāśar,* to tell good news; *qārā',* to call or proclaim; *qĕrî'â,* preaching. The NT uses *euangelizō,* to announce good news; *kēryx,* herald; *kēryssō,* to proclaim as a herald; *diangellō,* to proclaim or publish abroad; *katangellō,* to proclaim solemnly. In both testaments the words used to denote preaching have the essential element of proclamation or announcing. The preacher is one who tells forth the message which has been received from God. Thus, in one of the Yale lectures on preaching one lecturer said, "Every living preacher must receive his communication direct from God, and the constant purpose of his life must be to receive it uncorrupted and to deliver it without addition or subtraction." Bonhoeffer refers to this when he says, "He has put His Word in our mouth. He wants it to be spoken through us. If we hinder His word, the blood of the sinning brother will be upon us. If we carry out His word, God will save our brother through us."

The earliest beginnings of preaching are found in the OT. There it is said that "Enoch also, the seventh from Adam, prophesied." Then Noah is called a "preacher of righteousness." The blessings of Isaac and of Jacob are examples of formal, religious address in poetical style. The book of Deuteronomy is a series of sermons repeating, expanding, and enforcing much of the legislation of Moses.

From the time of Samuel to that of Jeremiah was the great prophetic period in Israel's history. Within this time appeared Samuel, Nathan, Gad, Azariah, Elijah, Elisha, Joel, Micah, Micaiah, Isaiah, Jeremiah, and others. These "preachers" came to people and kings with their messages from God. Their messages often began with the phrase, "Thus saith the Lord." They pleaded, warned, rebuked, encouraged; they spoke of judgments; they inspired with glowing promises of the glory to come. The glimpses we have of these prophets reveal the greatness of their characters, the strength of their influence, and the lasting value of their messages.

The last period of Hebrew prophecy extended from Ezekiel and Daniel to Malachi, from the Exile to the restoration and later. In this period the character and influence of prophecy did not materially change. It was still the voice of God through chosen persons to his chosen people. It still spoke to the religious life and aspirations of the people, both by preaching to the present and pointing to the future.

During the period between the testaments there was an important development in regard to preaching. This development occurred in connection with the services in the Synagogue. An important part of the service became the explanation of the Scriptures, which were read and then interpreted. Traces of this are found in Nehemiah 8 in reference to the preaching of Ezra. The NT records that both Jesus and the disciples made use of the synagogue service to preach the gospel.

John the Baptist was the connecting link between the OT and the NT. He was the last and greatest of the prophets and the first preacher of the new era. John was marked by strength of character coupled with a powerful personality. He announced the immediate coming of the promised reign of God. The promised Messiah was now about to arrive, and John was only a voice preparing the way. He called for a sincere and demonstrated repentance, to be symbolized by the act of baptism. John did not use the synagogues, but preached in the open air near the rivers where the baptisms took place. He received the highest possible praise from Jesus, who said of him, "Among men born of women there has not arisen a greater than John the Baptist."

The foundation of preaching is found also in the example of Jesus, as George Buttrick showed in his Yale lectures on preaching, *Jesus Came Preaching.* In comparing the preaching of Jesus with that of John one can see both a similarity and a difference. Both spoke of the kingdom of God. But more and more Jesus interpreted the promises as fulfilled in himself. He proclaims himself as the fulfillment of prophecy, as the Son and therefore the revealer of God. He spoke of himself as the Savior and Deliverer of persons: He is the Way to God, the Good Shepherd who gives his life for the sheep, the Redeemer who would give his life a ransom for many. He is his own gospel.

In distinction from John, Jesus calls to faith in the Lord who has now come. He offers himself and his work to the acceptance of his hearers. He is the revelation and embodiment of God's gracious ways with persons, and as such he is to be received and trusted.

Jesus preached in various locations and to various sized audiences. Sometimes he spoke to small groups and at other times to vast crowds. Sometimes he interpreted the Scriptures in a synagogue service, while on other occasions he preached in the field or by the sea. The preaching of Jesus was marked by authority and by quiet confidence in God, in himself, and in his mission and message. Sometimes he thundered judgment, and other times he issued a tender invitation. In his preaching he blended parable, aphorism, argument, and scriptural exposition.

Two occasions are recorded in the Gospels when Jesus sent out groups of disciples on preaching missions. He gave them their message, together with practical instructions as to how they should carry out their ministry. The book of Acts depicts the disciples waiting at Jerusalem for the promise of the Spirit. Acts and the epistles give traces of the apostolic preaching following Pentecost. This preaching was marked by a power seldom seen during the ages since. Possibly this was due to a greater dependence by the apostles on the work of the Holy Spirit. The burden of the early preaching is Christocentric—the life, death, resurrection, and coming again of Jesus Christ. Christ was the central and dominant theme of the gospel. There was a summons to repentance and faith.

In the preaching of the apostles is found the two permanent elements of Christian preaching, evangelism and instruction. There is a free presentation to all people of the claims and demands of the gospel. There is also orderly public instruction of believers in worship based upon the Scriptures. The preaching of John was transitional, the preaching of Jesus was unique, while the preaching of the apostles and the early church becomes our model.

Preaching in Church History. After the death of the apostles and their fellow workers in the early church there is a decline in preaching, until gradually it rises in power to a high level in the fourth and early fifth centuries. Then preaching falls into a long night of obscurity and weakness; with the preaching of the crusades and the rise of scholasticism it begins to revive. It reached its medieval height in the thirteenth century. Then again there is a general falling off in purity and power. The Reformation comes as another high wave gathering forces slowly to its crest in the early part of the sixteenth century. After the Reformation, with the fracturing of the visible church, preaching is marked by diversity as it spreads from country to country and denomination to denomination. Each country, and each denomination, has its peaks of power in preaching.

Contemporary trends in preaching include liturgical preaching, holistic preaching, preaching based on communications theory, liberation preaching (some homileticians include black and feminist preaching in this category), preaching built around language theory, life-situation preaching, inductive preaching, and narrative preaching. There is renewed interest in theological preaching.

John R. W. Stott, in *Between Two Worlds,* begins and ends by saying, "Preaching is indispensable to Christianity." In this he concurs with E. C. Dargan and many others who have studied the history of Christianity. So long as Christianity remains a religion of the word of God, preachers will be needed to interpret that word so that God's people may have God's help for daily life. The Christian church will grow, flourish, and accomplish God's purposes for it only as there are those who respond to God's call to preach that word which brings faith and life. P. T. Forsyth was correct when he said, "With preaching Christianity stands or falls, because it is the declaration of a gospel." J. S. BAIRD

Bibliography. Y. Brilioth, *A Brief History of Preaching;* J. A. Broadus, *Lectures on the History of Preaching* and *On the Preparation and Delivery of Sermons;* E. C. Dargan, *A History of Preaching: From the Apostolic Fathers to the Great Reformers* and *A History of Preaching: From the Close of the Reformation to the End of the Nineteenth Century;* H. Davies, *Varieties of English Preaching 1900–1960;* J. Ker, *Lectures on the History of Preaching;* F. R. Webber, *A History of Preaching in Britain and America,* 3 vols.; J. E. Baird, *Preparing for Platform and Pulpit;* J. D. Baumann, *An Introduction to Contemporary Preaching;* D. W. C. Ford, *The Ministry of the Word;* R. H. Mounce, *The Essential Nature of New Testament Preaching;* H. W. Robinson, *Biblical Preaching;* W. E. Sangster, *The Craft of the Sermon;* R. E. O. White, *A Guide to Preaching.*

Prebendary. *See* CHURCH OFFICERS.

Predestination. The doctrine of predestination as formulated in the history of the Christian church by such theologians as Augustine of Hippo and John Calvin has been a constant cause of discussion and controversy, for many Christians have been unwilling to accept it in any form. Pelagius in the early church and John Wesley in the eighteenth century provide two examples of those who had no use for such teaching. This division concerning the doctrine has continued down to the present.

The doctrine of predestination has both a wider and a narrower aspect. In its wider reference it refers to the fact that the Triune God foreordains whatsoever comes to pass (Eph. 1:11, 22; cf. Ps. 2). From all eternity God has sovereignly determined whatsoever shall happen in history. The narrower aspect or use of the term is that God from all eternity has chosen a body of people for himself, that they should be brought into eternal fellowship with him, while at the same time he has ordained that the rest of humanity should be allowed to go their own way, which is the way of sin, to ultimate eternal punishment. These are known as the doctrines of election and reprobation. While some may accept the idea of God choosing some to eternal life, they reject completely any idea of a decree of reprobation (Rom. 9:16–19).

In the Scriptures there is not one term in either the Hebrew or the Greek which encompasses the term "predestination." In the OT a number of words indicate the divine plan and purpose: *ʿēṣâ* (to counsel, Jer. 49:20; 50:45; Mic. 4:12); *yāʿaṣ* (to purpose, Isa. 14:24, 26–27; 19:12; 23:9); and *bāhar* (to choose, Num. 16:5, 7; Deut. 4:37; 10:15; Isa. 41:8; Ezek. 20:5). In the NT there are even more words which have the meaning of predestine (*proorizō*, Rom. 8:29–30; Eph. 1:5, 11), elect (*eklektos*, Matt. 24:22ff.; Rom. 8:33; Col. 3:12), and to choose (*haireomai*, II Thess. 2:13; *eklegō*, I Cor. 1:27ff.; Eph. 1:4). But the doctrine does not depend upon the use of a few words, for as one studies the Bible as a whole this doctrine is seen to be central to much of the teaching of both testaments.

The foundation of the doctrine of predestination is the biblical doctrine of God. He is the Eternal One, above and beyond time and space, for there never was a time when he did not exist, so he is not subject to changes of time and place (Mal. 3:6; Rom. 1:20–21; Deut. 33:27; Isa. 57:15). Furthermore, God is sovereign over all things as the Creator, Sustainer, and Ruler of the universe. He is Lord over all (Dan. 4:34–35; Isa. 45:1ff.; Rom. 9:17ff.; Eph. 1:11). God is also sovereignly righteous, so that all that he does is according to the perfection of his nature (Jer. 23:6; 33:16; Rom. 1:17; 10:3; II Pet. 1:1). In eternity he sovereignly established his own plan and purpose, which is far above anything that man can think of, conceive, or understand. Man, therefore, may know God's plan only as he reveals it (Jer. 23:18; Deut. 29:29; Ps. 33:11; Isa. 46:10; 55:7ff.; Heb. 6:17).

God has revealed his counsel to men, insofar as it was necessary for them to know it, through the prophets of the OT, through the apostolic writers of the NT, but preeminently through his Son Jesus Christ, to whom both prophets and apostles have borne witness. It was by divine revelation that the prophets could point forward to the coming of the Redeemer (Gen. 3:15; Deut. 18:15; Isa. 53; Mal. 4:2; Heb. 1:1ff.), and it was the apostles who could bear witness to him who had come and explain the meaning of his life, death, resurrection, and ascension (Acts 2:22ff.; John 20:30ff.). Therefore, human beings are limited in their understanding of God's purpose to what he has revealed to them, and the ultimate meanings, purposes, and plans must remain a mystery. Furthermore, because of God's infinitude, eternality, unchanging being, wisdom, power, justice, righteousness, and truth, man simply could not understand him, even should he reveal himself fully and completely to them. This means that God's relationship to time and space cannot be comprehended by spacial-temporal beings, for they do not even know the meaning of eternity (cf. Isa. 26:12ff.; Dan. 4:24ff.; Acts 2:22ff.). This ultimate mystery of the being of God must be kept in mind when studying biblical doctrine.

At this point the question arises of the possibility of individual freedom and responsibility if God is absolutely sovereign. How can these things be? Yet the Scriptures repeatedly assert both. Joseph's remarks to his brothers and Peter's statement concerning Christ's crucifixion highlight this fact (Gen. 45:4ff.; Acts 2:23). Man, in carrying out God's plan, even unintentionally, does so responsibly and freely.

Those who refuse to accept the biblical teaching are faced with the necessity of providing some other explanation. Some Christians attempt to combine God's sovereignty with human independence, but have the difficulty of explaining both the statements in the Bible and also their belief in God's saving work in Jesus Christ. Non-Christians have two choices. They can posit an ultimate chance, which destroys any possibility of human responsibility (for there is no one to whom to be responsible), of logical thought, and thus of scientific knowledge. The other alternative is that of a complete determinism which results in much the same outcome, for it is but solidified chance. Although the biblical point of view cannot be fully rationalized according to our temporal-spacial laws, it is the only one which makes any responsibility or freedom possible.

To understand the biblical teaching concerning predestination, we must commence with the account of man's fall, which was part of God's eternal plan. At the same time, as Paul points out in Rom. 1:18ff., man's refusal to acknowledge God as sovereign and his willful blindness to God's commands brought upon him God's wrath and condemnation. Basically, therefore, all human beings are corrupt because they refuse to acknowledge that God is Lord and that they themselves are only creatures. Yet despite human disobedience and rebellion, God has not let his creatures go. On the one hand he has restrained their sinfulness by his grace, so that even the sinners of this world have accomplished much that is good and true. On the other hand, as soon as man sinned, God promised a redeemer who would crush the tempter and bring restoration (Gen. 3:15). Thus the purpose of redemption was woven inextricably into the fabric of human history from the beginning.

Because of the sinfulness of the creature, however, the creature would not freely seek peace or reconciliation with him who is the Creator. This is shown in the story of Cain, the song of Lamech, and in the sinfulness of antediluvian society (Gen. 2–5). Yet at the same time there was a faithful minority descending from Seth to Noah, who was called to survive the flood and carry on the line of those who were obedient and trusted in God's promise of redemption. One of this line was Abraham, whom God called out of Ur of the Chaldees, and through the descendants of his grandson Jacob established Israel as his people in the pre-Christian world. All this was the result of divine grace which was summed up in Jehovah's covenant with Abraham, Isaac, and Jacob (Gen. 12ff.). Although up to this time little is said in Genesis about God's election and reprobation, when it came to the differentiation between Jacob and Esau it was made quite clear that even before their birth Jacob was chosen and Esau rejected, even though they were twins (Gen. 25:19ff.; Mal. 1:3; Rom. 9:10ff.). Here we find the first clear statement of the doctrine of double predestination.

Throughout the OT the doctrine of election is set forth with increasing clarity. On the one hand it is stated that Israel was chosen, not because of anything it had to offer, but solely because of the grace of God and by his sovereign choice (Deut. 7:7ff.; Isa. 41:8–9; Ezek. 20:5). Furthermore, from both Israel and other nations God freely chose individuals who would do his will in history for the blessing of Israel (I Sam. 16:1ff.; Isa. 45:1ff.; I Chr. 28:1ff.). On the other hand, not all Israel was of the elect, but only a faithful remnant whom God had chosen (Isa. 1:9; 10:21ff.; 11:11ff.; Jer. 23:3; 31:7). These Paul calls "a remnant according to the election of grace" (Rom. 11:5). Those not of the elect remnant were rejected because of their sin to suffer ultimate punishment.

Throughout the OT there is also a constant reference to One who would come to redeem God's people, not only Israel but his elect from every race and tribe. While there are foreshadowings of this universal election and redemption in the histories of such individuals as Ruth and Naaman, the prophets set forth the universality of God's electing grace very clearly (Isa. 11:10; 56; Mic. 5:8; Rom. 9:24, 30; 11:12–13; Acts 15). All those elected and predestined to become God's people, both Jew and Gentile, would indeed enter the covenant relationship. But they would do so only through the One who would be the elect Mediator (Isa. 42:1ff.; 53:1ff.; cf. Matt. 12:18).

In the NT the OT doctrines of election and predestination are expanded and clarified. There was no attempt to reject or alter them, but they are given a more clearly universal scope. Christ claimed that he was the mediator spoken of in the OT, and that to him the Father had given his elect people (Mark 1:15; Luke 4:21; John 5:39; 10:14ff.). Furthermore, he stated very clearly that he had come to lay down his life as redeemer for his people. This is the theme of both his sermon in John 10 and his prayer for his own in John 17. He promised that his people would all come to him and would persevere in their faith unto eternal life (John 6:39, 65; 10:28ff.). True, as the incarnate Son of God his righteousness was such that his life, death, and resurrection were sufficient in their merits for all men, but as he himself pointed out, his mediatorial work was directed to the salvation of his people only (John 17). In this he was fulfilling the teaching of the OT.

Such was also the position of the apostles. The book of Acts gives a number of examples of apostolic teaching on this matter. In his sermon at Pentecost, Peter gives a clear indication of the sovereignty of God and the responsibility of man (Acts 2:14ff.). The speech of Stephen in chapter 7, Peter's call to witness to Cornelius (10:24ff.), and various other passages present the same doctrines. In Peter's and John's letters and in the Apocalypse these themes of God's sovereignty, man's responsibility, and God's election and predestination of people reappear constantly.

The apostolic writer who gives the clearest exposition of the doctrine, however, is Paul. While he refers to the doctrine of predestination in passing in a number of places, he expounds the doctrine in detail in Rom. 8:29–11:36 and throws further light on it in Eph. 1. In these passages he stresses the hopeless condition of man in his sinfulness and the fact that because of man's disobedience and rebellion God not only turns from him but hardens him in his sinfulness (Rom. 9:14ff.). At the same time, however, he reaches out and draws to himself those whom he has chosen from all eternity, redeeming and justifying them in Jesus Christ (Rom. 10:11ff.; Eph. 1:4ff.). Yet in all of this is the mystery of God's sovereign action and man's responsibility (Rom. 9:19; 11:33). And in all things the glory of God's righteousness is made manifest (Rom. 9:16ff.).

These doctrines have continued to raise questions ever since the days of the apostles, but especially since the Protestant Reformation of the sixteenth century, when they were formulated most precisely. Despite their biblical basis both Christians and non-Christians have rejected them on various grounds. If all human beings are sinners and God is sovereign, then he must be the author of sin and is unjust in punishing anyone. Furthermore, what is the basis upon which God makes his choice? Is he not arbitrary; and if not, is he not then a respecter of persons? If these doctrines are true, do they not destroy any desire, even any necessity, for a human being to seek to live a moral life, to do justly, to love mercy, and to walk humbly with God? All these questions are put forward, and many of those who do so feel that they have now answered and condemned the doctrines effectively. They forget, however, that these questions were all raised in the time of Christ and the apostles (John 10:19ff.; Rom. 9:19ff.).

That these doctrines are set forth in both testaments would seem to be clear, along with great stress upon God's sovereign righteousness and holiness. But no further explanation is offered, and beyond what the Scriptures have to say finite man cannot go and, if he accepts the authority of the Bible as God's Word, will not wish to go. All one can say is what Job said when rebuked by God (Job. 42:1–6) or what Paul said when closing his exposition of these doctrines (Rom. 11:33–36). God's wisdom and grace are beyond every creature's comprehension or understanding. One can but bow in worship and praise. Those who do so have within them a sense of comfort and strength which is not their own, but which is a gift of God to enable them to face the world with confidence and peace of mind.

W. S. Reid

See also Elect, Election; Reprobation; Preterition.

Bibliography. L. Boettner, *The Reformed Doctrine of Predestination;* J. Calvin, *Institutes of the Christian Religion* 3:21–24 and *The Eternal Predestination of God;* C. Hodge, *Systematic Theology,* III, ch. 1; J. Murray, *Calvin on Scripture and Divine Sovereignty,* ch. 3, B. B. Warfield, *Biblical Doctrines.*

Preexistence of Christ. The preincarnate existence of Christ may be "only a simple, contemplative inference backwards from the spiritual glory of the present Christ" (Deissmann); certainly its clearest expression is found in later writing reflecting upon the rudimentary messianic, even adoptionist, assessment of Christ in the primitive Christian community (Acts 2:22–23; 10:38). Yet preexistence is at least implied in words of Jesus himself: "The son of man came"; the owner of the vineyard "had still . . . a beloved son: finally he sent him." It is explicit in sayings attributed to Jesus in John's Gospel: "I came down from heaven"; "The glory I had with thee before the world was."

Jewish scholars attributed "ideal" preexistence to things (law, temple) and persons (Adam, Moses) deeply reverenced, echoed perhaps in Paul's calling Christ "last Adam . . . from heaven." Greek thinking, reflected in Philo, was familiar with preexistence of souls. But it is unnecessary to find here more than a source of usable terms. The idea that the Son of God, eternally preexisting in glory with the Father, moved by love became incarnate was too central to Christian faith to depend upon coincidences of language for its basis.

Paul appeals for generosity because Christ,

"though rich, became poor." He pleads that converts live as sons because "God sent forth his son"; argues for self-effacement from the fact that Christ, being in the form of God, "emptied himself"; contends, against the Gnostics' *plērōma* filling the gulf between God and creation, that "all things were created in, through, and for Christ . . . who is before all things." As "Lord from heaven" Christ provides the pattern of our resurrected humanity; as he first descended, so he has ascended—the measure of his triumph and assurance of ours (II Cor. 8:9; Gal. 4:4; Phil. 2:5–6; Col. 1:15–16; Eph. 4:8–9). For such practical, pastoral exhortations one does not argue from fringe speculations, but only from familiar, accepted, foundation truths.

John's Gospel and Epistle, assuming that Christ came from God and went to God (John 13:3), emphasize his being sent by the Father on divine mission, expressing divine love (John 3:16; I John 4:9–10), a revelation of the unseen Father by one belonging "in the bosom of the Father" (John 1:18)—a divine Word, present when God spoke at creation and now again conveying meaning and power to the world (John 1). For John as for Paul, mankind's salvation derives not from any human initiative but from the inbreaking of the eternal Son into time. That is the crucial truth here at issue.

The implications of preexistence are a concern of subsequent Christian thought. Does it impair the manhood of Jesus? (Christological controversies: answer, No—two real natures coexist in one person). Why the delay in Christ's arrival? (medieval: answer, God patiently prepared). Does preexistence imply continuity of memory between the eternal Son and Jesus? (modern: answer, No—a *growing* consciousness of his uniqueness). But the fact of preexistence is not questioned, except where Christ's deity and divine mission are wholly denied. R. E. O. White

See also Christology; Jesus Christ.

Bibliography. D. M. Baillie, *God Was in Christ;* H. R. Mackintosh, *The Doctrine of the Person of Christ;* O. Cullmann, *The Christology of the NT.*

Preexistence of the Soul. *See* Soul.

Prelacy. The term comes from the medieval Latin *praelatus,* a high-ranking civil or religious official. It refers to the type of church government in which control is vested in bishops, archbishops, metropolitans, and patriarchs. In Roman Catholicism such dignitaries as abbots, provosts, nuncios, and apostolic prefects are included among the prelates. In the Church of England bishops and archbishops are considered prelates.

Among nonepiscopal denominations prelacy and related words have often been used invidiously of the episcopal system. This was especially true of the Puritans and Baptists in England and of Scottish Presbyterians in the seventeenth century, when the Stuarts were attempting to impose episcopacy upon them. D. G. Davis

Premillennialism. *See* Millennium, Views of the.

Presbyter. *See* Elder; Church Officers.

Presbyterianism. *See* Church Government.

Presence, Divine. In the Bible the word "face" or "countenance" (Heb. *pānîm;* Gr. *prosōpon* or *enōpion,* "in the face of") is normally used to indicate presence. As applied to God there seem to be three main senses. First, there is the general and inescapable presence of God as described in Ps. 139:7ff. Second, there is the special presence of God among his people or among the nations to save or to judge (cf. Exod. 33:14; Nah. 1:5). This is further expressed by the divine dwelling in the tabernacle and temple (cf. Ps. 48), and especially by the coming of Jesus Christ as Immanuel (Matt. 1:23; John 1:14), his continued presence in and with his disciples by the Holy Spirit (Matt. 28:20; John 14:16–17), and his final coming in glory (I Thess. 2:19). Third, there is the presence of God in heaven, before which the angels stand (Luke 1:19), in face of which there can be no self-righteous boasting (I Cor. 1:29), from which the wicked are to be banished with everlasting destruction (II Thess. 1:9), but before which believers will be presented faultless in virtue of the work of Christ (Jude 24), thus enjoying, as the psalmist dared to hope, the fullness of joy (Ps. 16:11; cf. 73:23–24).

It may be noted that the emphasis of the Bible is not on the divine presence as a general immanence, hence the naturalness with which Jonah can be said to try to flee from God's presence (Jonah 1:3) or worshipers to come before God's presence (Ps. 95:2). For sinful man who cannot see God or abide his presence, the important thing is the special realization of his presence in salvation and the final acceptance of the justified believer in his eternal presence. The presence of God among his people in the new heaven and earth is the goal of the divine work as initiated already by the incarnation and enjoyed in the Holy Spirit but to be consummated only at the last day: "Behold, the tabernacle of God is with men, and he will dwell with them, and they shall be his people, and God himself shall be with them, and be their God" (Rev. 21:3). This ultimate immanence, however, cannot be known and enjoyed by sinners merely in virtue of the divine omnipresence (Rev. 21:8). We are received into God's eternal presence only as we have first received God present to us in Jesus Christ (John 1:12). G. W. Bromiley

See also God, Doctrine of; God, Attributes of.

Preservation. *See* Conservation.

Preterition. A word derived from the Latin *praeter,* meaning beyond or past, and *praeteritus,* meaning that which is passed over. In theology it is used to refer to God's passing over of the nonelect, whom he allows to go their own way and perish for their sins. *Webster's Dictionary* says that it is a doctrine of Calvinism, but this would not seem to be the case, for Calvin spoke in terms of reprobation. It was, however, used by theologians who followed Calvin in the seventeenth century, such as those who composed the Westminster Confession of Faith. In it the stress is laid upon man's decision and action rather than on God's decree. Paul seems to speak of this in Rom. 9:22–23, but as a preliminary to God's hardening and condemnation of the sinner. W. S. Reid

See also Reprobation; Elect, Election; Predestination.

Bibliography. A. A. Hodge, *A Commentary on the Westminster Confession of Faith.*

Pretribulation Rapture. *See* Rapture of the Church.

Prevenient Grace. *See* Grace.

Pride. Usually carrying a negative connotation, the term has been defined as "inordinate and unreasonable self-esteem, attended with insolence and rude treatment of others." It is an attempt to appear in a superior light to what we are, with "anxiety to gain applause, and distress and rage when slighted." "Pride is the high opinion that a poor, little, contracted soul entertains of itself."

Pride is universal among all nations, being variously attributed in the Bible to Israel, Judah, Moab, Edom, Assyria, Jordan, and the Philistines. It is connected with the sin of Sodom (Ezek. 16:49). Indeed, the ambitious pride of Satan was part of the original sin of the universe (Ezek. 28:17; I Tim. 3:6). It may well have been the first sin to enter God's universe, and no doubt will be one of the last to be conquered.

The Bible teaches that pride deceives the heart (Jer. 49:16), hardens the mind (Dan. 5:20), brings contention (Prov. 13:10), compasses about like a chain (Ps. 73:6), and brings men to destruction (Prov. 16:18). A proud heart stirs up strife (Prov. 28:25) and is an abomination unto the Lord (Prov. 16:5). A proud look God hates (Prov. 6:17), and those who engage therein shall stumble and fall (Jer. 50:32).

Pride is the parent of discontent, ingratitude, presumption, passion, extravagance, and bigotry. There is hardly an evil committed without pride being connected in some sense. Augustine and Aquinas held that pride was the very essence of sin. Since God resists the proud (James 4:6), the believer must learn to hate pride and to clothe himself with humility. G. B. Stanton

See also Boasting.

Bibliography. C. Buck, *Theological Dictionary;* L. S. Chafer, *Systematic Theology,* II, 63–64; *MSt;* A. H. Strong, *Systematic Theology,* 569; C. S. Lewis, "The Great Sin," in *Mere Christianity;* E. Güting and C. Brown, *NIDNTT,* III, 27ff.; G. Bertram, *TDNT,* VIII, 295ff.

Priest, Christ as. *See* Offices of Christ.

Priesthood. The term "priest" is identical in origin with the word "presbyter," which literally means "elder"; but in the English language it has become associated for the most part with the religious official whose main function is the offering up of sacrifices, though the English Reformers of the sixteenth century hoped that the retention of the term "priest" in the *Book of Common Prayer* would effect the restoration of its proper meaning of elder. This confusion was occasioned by the strange fact that the English language has not kept in common usage any term corresponding to the Latin *sacerdos,* which precisely designates one who offers up sacrifices (hence "sacerdotal"). In the English of the OT and NT "priest" denotes a *sacerdos* and "priesthood" his sacerdotal ministry. Thus the duty belonging to priesthood is defined in Heb. 5:1 as follows: "Every high priest chosen from among men is appointed to act on behalf of men in relation to God, to offer gifts and sacrifices for sins"; and on the basis of this principle it is argued concerning the priesthood of Christ that "therefore it is necessary for this priest also to have something to offer" (Heb. 8:3). The Christian doctrine of priesthood and of the relationship between the priesthood of the OT and that of the NT is most fully expounded in the Epistle to the Hebrews, which has been called "the Epistle of Priesthood."

The Necessity of Priesthood. It is the universal sinfulness of man which makes a sacrificing priesthood a necessity. The sacrifices offered up effect, or symbolize the means of effecting, reconciliation between sinful man and his holy Creator. The function of priesthood, accordingly, is a mediatorial function. The giving of the law through Moses and the institution of the Aaronic or Levitical priesthood belong together. Law and priesthood are simultaneous in origin and inseparable in operation (Heb. 7:11ff.). The reason for this is that the Israelites, like the rest of mankind, were sinners and therefore when confronted with the law, which is God's standard of righteousness, lawbreakers. Certainly the God-given law is holy and just and good and spiritual (Rom. 7:12, 14) and as such marks out the way of life: by faithfully keeping its precepts a man shall live (Lev. 18:5; Neh. 9:29; Matt. 19:16–17; Rom. 10:5; Gal. 3:12). But man's radical problem is that he is a sinner. The law shows him up for what he is, a lawbreaker, and "the wages of sin is death" (Rom. 6:23; cf. Ezek. 18:4, 20; Gen. 2:17). Consequently Paul writes, "The very commandment which promised life proved to be death to me" (Rom. 7:10)—not that there is anything wrong with the law; the fault is in man who breaks the law (Rom. 7:13). Hence the necessity for the formulation of the law to be accompanied by the institution of a priesthood to mediate redemptively between God and the sinner who has broken his law, and who needs to be restored from death to life.

OT Priesthood. The priesthood of the old covenant could not effect the reality of reconciliation portended by its sacrificial function. Its character was preparatory; it portrayed the principle of propitiatory sacrifice but not the fulfillment of that principle. Its imperfection, which aroused the longing for and the expectation of the provision of the perfect priesthood, was apparent for the following reasons. (1) In the midst of its activity a new priesthood of a different order, that of Melchizedek, was prophetically spoken of (Ps. 110:4). If the existing priesthood had been perfect, there would have been no point in announcing another order of priesthood (Heb. 7:11ff.). (2) During the period when the old or Mosaic covenant was in operation the promise of a new covenant was given, the inauguration of which would mean the placing of God's law in the hearts of his people and the removal of their sins forever (Jer. 31:31ff.). Clearly, "if that first covenant had been faultless, there would have been no occasion for a second" (Heb. 8:7). (3) The very multiplicity of the priests of the old order involved the necessity for a priestly succession because in endless sequence they were carried away by death, and thus "were prevented by death from continuing in office" (Heb. 7:23). This pointed to the need for a priest whose priesthood was perfect and everlasting, one who would be "a priest for ever" (Ps. 110:4). (4) Not only were the priests of the old order mortal, they were also sinful, and thus themselves in need of redemption and reconciliation. Consequently, before offering sacrifices for the people they were obliged to offer sacrifices for their own sins—an action which plainly attested the imperfection of their priesthood (Heb. 5:3; 7:27). (5) The endless repetition of the sacrifices offered by the priesthood of the old order itself demonstrated the inadequacy of those sacrifices to deal fully and finally with sin. Had the perfect sacrifice for all time and all eternity been offered, they would have ceased to be offered: their repetition was a mark of their incompetence (Heb. 10:1–2). (6) The very nature of these sacrifices gave further evidence of their inability to achieve what they foreshadowed. The animals offered up were slain in the sinner's stead, symbolizing the transference of his sin to an innocent victim and his atonement by the substitutionary death of that victim. But an irrational, uncomprehending brute beast can never be a proper substitute for man, who is made in the image of God. That is why "it is impossible that the blood of bulls and goats should take away sins" (Heb. 10:4).

Christ as Priest. The purpose of the old order of priesthood was to teach the people that atonement for sins requires the provision of an innocent victim in the sinner's place and the shedding of blood as that victim dies the death due to the sinner. The Levitical order could not accomplish this atonement, but it kept alive the expectation of the coming of the perfect priest and the offering of the perfect sacrifice in fulfillment of the gospel promises contained in the Scriptures of the OT. The new order of priesthood is that of Melchizedek, and it is comprehended in the single person of our Redeemer Jesus Christ (Heb. 7). The perfection of his priesthood is confirmed by the fact that it is forever (Ps. 110:4), that the sacrifice he offered is once for all (Heb. 7:27), and that, his work of atonement completed, he is now enthroned in celestial glory (Heb. 1:3; 10:12; 12:2). The perfection of his priesthood is established by the sinlessness of his earthly life as the incarnate Son, our fellow human being. This means that in contrast to the first Adam, who suffered defeat and dragged down the human race in his fall, Jesus, "the last Adam" (I Cor. 15:45, 47), took our humanity to himself in order to redeem it and to raise it in himself to the glorious destiny for which it was always intended. It means that in going to the cross he who was without sin took our sins upon himself and suffered the rejection and the death due us sinners, "the righteous for the unrighteous" (I Pet.

2:22–24; 3:18; Heb. 4:15; 7:26–27), as the innocent victim provided by God's grace and mercy (I Pet. 1:18–19). And it means, further, that he is not only our sacrificing priest but also the sacrifice itself, for it was *himself* that he offered up for us, and thus in him we have the provision of the perfect substitute, a genuine equivalent, our fellow man (Heb. 2:14–15), who truly takes our place. Accordingly we are assured that by the will of God "we have been sanctified through the offering of the body of Jesus Christ once for all," who "by a single offering . . . has perfected for all time those who are sanctified" (Heb. 10:10, 14).

The new order of priesthood fulfilled in the single person of Christ has, of course, completely superseded the old order. With Christ as our one great high priest who lives forever there is now no place or need for any succession of sacrificing priests. Now that he has offered up the one perfect sacrifice of himself there is room for no other sacrifice nor for any repetition of sacrifices. In Christ both priesthood and sacrifice have been brought to fulfillment and to finality.

The Priesthood of Believers. There remains, however, a priesthood which belongs to those who through faith have been united to Christ. This has commonly been designated "the priesthood of all believers." Thus Peter describes Christians as "a holy priesthood" whose function is "to offer spiritual sacrifices acceptable to God through Jesus Christ" (I Pet. 2:5; cf. vs. 9). These spiritual sacrifices are not in any sense redemptive sacrifices but sacrifices of gratitude to God for the one all-sufficient redemptive sacrifice of Christ's self-offering at Calvary for us sinners. Thus we are exhorted to "present our bodies," i.e., ourselves, "as a living sacrifice, holy and acceptable to God" (Rom. 12:1); and as we willingly offer ourselves we express our spiritual priesthood in acts of praise and thanksgiving and in the selfless service of our fellow men as we minister to their needs. The exercise of this priesthood is summed up in the words of Heb. 13:15–16: "Through him [Christ] then let us continually offer up a sacrifice of praise to God, that is, the fruit of lips that acknowledge his name. Do not neglect to do good and to share what you have, for such sacrifices are pleasing to God."

In his celebrated essay "The Christian Ministry," J. B. Lightfoot not only insists that "as individuals, all Christians are priests alike," he also draws attention to the fact that in the ministerial offices enumerated in I Cor. 12:28 and Eph. 4:11 "there is an entire silence about priestly functions: for the most exalted office in the Church, the highest gift of the Spirit, conveyed no sacerdotal right which was not enjoyed by the humblest member of the Christian community." His affirmation concerning the kingdom of Christ in the opening paragraph of the essay is no less emphatic: "Above all it has no sacerdotal system. It interposes no sacrificial tribe or class between God and man, by whose intervention alone God is reconciled and man forgiven. Each individual member holds personal communion with the Divine Head. To him immediately he is responsible, and from him directly he obtains pardon and draws strength." These words of a great churchman and NT scholar admirably present the position of the apostolic church on the subject of priesthood. P. E. Hughes

See also Offices of Christ; Offerings and Sacrifices in Bible Times; Priests and Levites.

Priests and Levites. During the OT period the tribe of Levi had particular responsibility for the continuing religious life of Israel. The tribe was divided into two groups, each with distinctive areas of responsibility. (1) The priests, who were the descendants of Aaron, held the principal responsibility for the conduct of worship, initially in the tabernacle and later in the temple. (2) The remainder of the Levites were support staff, being responsible for the maintenance of the temple establishment and certain supplementary religious duties.

The Biblical Period. The priesthood was established by Aaron and his sons in the time of Moses, when Israel's religion was formally instituted in the covenant of Mount Sinai. Aaron, the first high priest, had principal responsibility for the conduct of Israel's worship, for the tabernacle, and for all the sacrifices and festivals that pertained to the continuing religious life of the people. Certain responsibilities were delegated to his sons, who functioned as priests. The office of high priest and the priesthood in general were transmitted throughout OT times on a hereditary basis.

The Levites held less prominent positions but were equally essential in the maintenance of Israel's religious life. They performed a variety of duties, including the service and maintenance of the temple, teaching in the temple, providing music (orchestral and choral) for worship, and various other tasks related to the continuing life of worship in Israel.

The high priest, though initially simply the "greatest priest among his brethren" (the literal sense of Lev. 21:10), came to assume a position of considerable prestige and power in Israel with the passage of time, particularly when the temple was established in Jerusalem and played a central role in the nation's religious life.

In the NT there are frequent references to

priests and Levites; they are referred to as servants of the Jerusalem temple and members of the religious establishment. In most matters their functions were the same as in OT times, but the nature of the high priesthood had changed. Though the office had originally been hereditary and held by the descendants of Aaron (and later of his descendant Zadok), by the midsecond century B.C. the office had become in effect one priest who, among other responsibilities, was president of the Sanhedrin, and a small group of political power struggles. Thus, there was a high priest who was, among other responsibilities, president of the Sanhedrin; and a small group of chief priests. The latter group included former high priests as well as members of influential priestly families.

With the eventual destruction of Jerusalem's temple in A.D. 70, the tradition of priests and Levites came to an end in the Jewish religion. Their principal reason for existence had been the religion of the temple. Without the temple their purpose was gone, and their role as religious leaders within the Jewish community passed into the hands of the rabbis, just as the temple was replaced by the centrality of the synagogue.

Theological Significance. The idea of priesthood is to be interpreted in the context of Israel's religion as a whole. The essence of that religion can be described by the word "relationship," specifically the relationship existing between God and Israel that was given formal expression in the covenant. The priests and Levites were the servants of that covenant relationship and were given the role of mediators. Though their mediatory role functioned in two directions, both in representing God to his people and vice versa, it was the latter role that was most significant. In leading Israel's worship, assisting in the offering of the people's sacrifices, maintaining the temple, and similar duties, they dedicated their entire existence to the spiritual leadership of Israel and the representation of Israel before God. The distinctive responsibility of the high priest—that of entering the holy of holies once each year on the day of atonement—brings out clearly the priestly role as a whole. Standing before the mercy seat, the high priest sought God's forgiveness and mercy for the entire nation (Lev. 16:1–19), for without God's mercy and forgiveness the covenant relationship with Israel could not continue from year to year. P. C. CRAIGIE

See also PRIESTHOOD; OFFERINGS AND SACRIFICES IN BIBLE TIMES.

Bibliography. A. Cody, *A History of OT Priesthood;* J. A. Emerton, "Priests and Levites in Deuteronomy," *VT* 12:129–38; *IBD,* III, 1266–73; G. E. Wright, "The Levites in Deuteronomy," *VT* 4:325–30.

Princeton Theology, Old. The dominant theology of American Presbyterianism, and one of the most influential theologies in all the United States, from the founding of Princeton Seminary in 1812 until the reorganization of that institution in 1929. The first professor at Princeton Seminary, Archibald Alexander, epitomized a great deal of the Princeton tradition in his own life. He was a person of piety and Christian warmth, but his main emphases in theology were the reliability of Scripture and the ability of human reason to understand Christian truth. His intellectual sources were Calvin, the Westminster Confession and Catechisms, the Swiss theologian François Turretin, and the Scottish philosophy of common sense. And he, like his sucessors, was sensitive to trends and fashions in American religious life. His best-known work was a defense of the Bible, *Evidences of the Authenticity, Inspiration, and Canonical Authority of the Holy Scriptures* (1836).

Alexander's pupil, Charles Hodge, extended the Princeton point of view during his fifty-six years at Princeton Seminary. Hodge's particular concerns were taught to thousands of students, expressed regularly in the *Biblical Repertory and Princeton Review,* and were finally written down in his *Systematic Theology* (1872–73). Although he shared many of Alexander's concerns—to proclaim the glory of God, the regenerating power of God's grace in Christ, the helplessness of man apart from God's effectual call, and the all-sufficiency of Scripture—Hodge had a fuller place in his theology for the work of the Holy Spirit. He was also a more effective polemicist in expounding a traditional Calvinism against innovations in American theology.

Although Hodge lived into the period when modernism was beginning to challenge Christian orthodoxy, his theology was most concerned with the errors of Roman Catholicism and the modifications of Calvinism proposed by New England Congregationalists. Hodge's successors, on the other hand, were called upon to deal with the issues posed by liberalism. Hodge's own son, Archibald Alexander Hodge, and Benjamin B. Warfield addressed these critical issues forthrightly, especially where they concerned the Bible. In a famous essay of 1881 A. A. Hodge and Warfield joined to declare that the "original autographs" of Scripture were absolutely without error in everything that they affirmed. Subsequent debate over the nature of Scripture, which continues to the present, has obscured the fact that Warfield in particular made theological contributions on many other fronts. One of the most acute theological minds of his generation, Warfield wrote penetratingly on the person and work of Christ, the contributions of Augustine and Calvin, and the values of the Westminster Confession. He was also a sharp critic of all kinds of Christian perfectionism.

The last of the major Princeton theologians was J. Gresham Machen, student of Warfield and teacher of NT at Princeton Seminary for over twenty years. Machen, like Warfield, was a theologian of wide interests who also became best known as a defender of traditional orthodoxy. His *Christianity and Liberalism* (1923) was one of the strongest twentieth century statements against modernistic trends in American churches. No less a critic than Walter Lippmann called it a "cool and stringent defense of orthodox Protestantism." Yet Machen was not successful in preserving his point of view at Princeton. After the Princeton board was reorganized to the disadvantage of the conservatives in 1929, Machen left to help found Westminster Theological Seminary in Philadelphia. With him went a theological tradition stretching back to Archibald Alexander.

The impact of the Princeton theology lives on at Westminster Seminary, at other seminaries of conservative Presbyterian bodies, and in the confessional Presbyterian denominations. Amongst these groups, however, Reformed influences from Europe, especially Holland, have diluted the insistence upon evidentialist apologetics and an inductive approach to truth which were so characteristic of the Princeton theologians. In the meantime their influence has also been widely extended to other groups who have made extensive use of Princeton arguments to defend the inerrancy of the Bible. This Princeton defense of Scripture—in combination with dispensationalism, an emphasis on "higher Christian living," and a general reaction to modernism—was one of the important elements in the American fundamentalism of an earlier day.

M. A. Noll

See also Alexander, Archibald; Hodge, Archibald Alexander; Hodge, Charles; Machen, John Gresham; Warfield, Benjamin Breckinridge.

Bibliography. *Biblical Repertory and Princeton Review: Index Volume from 1825 to 1868*, 3 vols.; W. A. Hoffecker, *Piety and the Princeton Theologians;* J. C. Vander Stelt, *Philosophy and Scripture: A Study in Old Princeton and Westminster Theology;* M. A. Noll, ed., *The Princeton Theology, 1812–1921.*

Principalities and Powers. The apostle Paul appears to have taken this expression from late Jewish apocalyptic thought, where it was applied to intermediate beings lower than God and higher than man. Apart from passages where the reference is unmistakably to human authorities (Rom. 13:1–3; Titus 3:1), principalities (*archai*) and authorities (*exousiai*) or powers (*dynameis*) refer to cosmic intelligences, occasionally angelic, but usually demonic (Rom. 8:38; I Cor. 15:24; Eph. 1:21; 3:10; 6:12; Col. 1:16; 2:10; 2:15). Other similar spirit powers are dominions (*kyriotētes*, Eph. 1:21; Col. 1:16), thrones (*thronoi*, Col. 1:16), and the rulers (*archontes*) of this age (I Cor. 2:6). It is not possible on the basis of NT evidence to rank these spirit powers or to attribute distinctive meanings to each. On the contrary, Paul was impatient with such questions in his letter to the Colossians, where he refuted the heresy of angelolatry.

Six acts in the drama of the principalities and powers may be delineated:

1. *Creation.* In the creation plan these powers were designed as good spirits. They were created by Christ and subjected to his lordship (Col. 1:16).

2. *Fall.* For reasons undisclosed in the NT some spirit powers separated from Christ (Jude 6) in a rupture of cosmic proportions (II Pet. 2:4), necessitating atonement (Col. 1:20).

3. *Defeat by Christ.* In his ministry Jesus resisted Satanic temptation (Luke 4:1–13) and conquered evil spirits (Luke 4:35), delegating this power to his disciples (Mark 3:15). In his death he disarmed the forces of evil (Col. 2:14–15). In his resurrection and exaltation he subjected them to his lordship (Eph. 1:20–22; 4:8; I Pet. 3:22). Christians are enthroned with Christ and share this victory and ought to live accordingly (Col. 2:20–3:4).

4. *Learning.* The spirit powers, who are not omniscient, learn the manifold wisdom of God by witnessing the historic experience of the church (Eph. 3:10).

5. *Continuing warfare.* Although defeated and under instruction, the spirit powers have not yet surrendered. The vestiges of their power continue to corrupt the disobedient (Eph. 2:2). The Christian's most powerful and deceitful enemies are still demonic (Eph. 6:12), but God's power is stronger (Eph. 6:10–11) and no evil power will separate the Christian from the love of God (Rom. 8:38–39).

6. *Total defeat.* The days of this warfare are numbered and the outcome certain. With the consummation of the kingdom of God the evil powers will be robbed of all malignant efficacy (I Cor. 15:24).

A new understanding of principalities and powers has been supported with increasing confidence by scholars since World War II. Historian Rupp applies the expression to economic, social, and political structures. His justification is that the same helplessness felt by "little people" when events move too quickly for them may be described mythically in terms of demonic powers (as in the NT) or sociologically in terms of dehumanizing structures (as today). Caird applies the term to the powers of the state, legal religion, and nature. Berkhof maintains that while borrowing the expression from Jewish apocalyptic, Paul demythologized it: he viewed principalities and powers not as heavenly spirits but as earthly structures. Influenced by Berkhof, Yoder identifies the powers with abstract religious, intellectual, moral, and political structures which have absolutized themselves and demand unconditional loyalty. On the cross Jesus, who in his life was not the slave of any power, law, custom, community, institution, value, or theory, destroyed the powers' pretensions to sovereignty, thus making authentic living possible.

This new understanding has been questioned by Stott and O'Brien. They insist, first, that the principalities and powers must be supernatural beings, since they are confronted by Christ "in the heavenly places" (Eph. 1:20; 3:10; 6:12). Second, the Christian's warfare is specifically said to be "not with flesh and blood but with principalities and powers" (Eph. 6:12). Third, Jesus believed in angels and exorcism, although it was not inevitable that he should; the Sadducees did not (Acts 23:8).

In spite of Yoder's claim that the new scholarly understanding is the product of a cultural empathy greater than any since the apostolic age, this tendency to identify the principalities and powers with human or abstract, impersonal forces is probably the result of cultural presuppositions determining exegesis. It is more likely that traditional cultures (e.g., the Melanesian), where spirit-worship is common, are better placed to understand Paul's meaning.

It is possible, however, that Paul intended his reference to thrones, dominions, principalities, and authorities in Col. 1:16 to embrace earthly as well as heavenly powers (Lightfoot). The matter invites further research. But for the present, while allowing that all human systems are wide open to corruption from demonic forces, it is safest to avoid identifying principalities and powers with sociopolitical structures.

F. S. Piggin

See also Demon, Demon Possession.

Bibliography. H. Berkhof, *Christ and the Powers;* G. B. Caird, *Principalities and Powers: A Study in Pauline Theology;* J. B. Lightfoot, *Saint Paul's Epistles to the Colossians and to Philemon;* G. H. C. Macgregor, "Principalities and Powers: The Cosmic Background of St. Paul's Thought," *NTS* 1:17–28; J. Michel, in *Encyclopedia of Biblical Theology,* II, 712–16; P. T. O'Brien, "Principalities and Powers and Their Relationship to Structures," *RTR* 40:1–20; E. G. Rupp, *Principalities and Powers;* H. Schlier, *Principalities and Powers in the NT;* J. R. W. Stott, *God's New Society: The Message of Ephesians;* G. Delling, *TDNT,* I, 479–84; J. H. Yoder, *The Politics of Jesus.*

Priscillianism. The movement is named after its originator, Priscillian of Avila, although he probably did not share the views of his successors on the nature of the Trinity. Priscillian himself was a talented layman who began to organize independent Bible study groups in which self-denial and a deeper spiritual life were emphasized along with the need to know the power of the living Word. Women were encouraged to participate in these meetings and to exercise their gifts in ministry. Many attached themselves to this movement. Even bishops and other clergy gave their support. Priscillian's emphasis on celibacy, however, ran afoul of the church, which confused his teaching with Manichaeism and condemned his doctrines at the Council of Sargossa in 380. He was nevertheless ordained as bishop of Avila amid growing controversy. Ultimately, after unsuccessful appeals to Pope Damascus and Ambrose of Milan, Priscillian laid his case before the Emperor Maximus and was beheaded, along with six of his followers, at Triers in 385. This appears to have been the first Christian execution for heresy and caused him to be venerated as a martyr, especially in Galicia.

It is not always easy to separate the beliefs of Priscillian from those of his later followers. Priscillian himself wrote a series of canons which appear in many texts of the Vulgate Bible. He divided the Pauline epistles (in which he included the Epistle to the Hebrews) into a series of texts on theological points and wrote an introduction to each. These canons survived in a form edited by Peregrinus, who considered them an indispensable aid in the study of Scripture. They contain a strong call to a life of personal piety and asceticism, including vegetarianism, teetotalism, and celibacy. Slavery and sexual differences are abolished in Jesus Christ, and the charismatic gifts of all believers affirmed. The elect were called to combat the devil and his evil powers, and to enter into a knowledge of the deep mysteries of God.

Priscillian and his followers placed considerable emphasis upon apocryphal works, which they did not regard as canonical but rather as helpful to the spiritually minded who could discern truth from error. Thus apocryphal writings are quoted significantly in Priscillianist writings. Generally ascribed to the Priscillianist school are the prologues to the four Gospels as they are found in many Old Latin texts. These are strongly monarchian in theology and do not allow for a clear distinction between the persons of the

Godhead. In 1889 G. Schepss published a series of eleven treatises which he had discovered at Wurzburg. Although the text named Priscillian as the author, it seems more probable that these treatises were written by one of his supporters. They too contain a strong emphasis on Bible study, an allegorical interpretation of Scripture, asceticism, and the unity of God rather than the Trinity. Christ is frequently referred to as "Christ-God" and is called "unbegettable."

Closely related to the Wurzburg treatises in both content and thought is a ninth century manuscript of an anonymous treatise, *On the Trinity.* Father and Son are declared to be names for the same person, with Father representing mind and Son word. There is also a fragment of a letter by Priscillian which is quoted by Orosius, a decidedly hostile witness.

The critics of Priscillianism accused the movement of astrology, sorcery, dualism, Manichaeism, Sabellianism, modalism, and outright lying. The strong following of women led to charges of sexual orgies. Priscillianists were also said to teach that preexistent human souls were attached as a punishment to the body, which was the creation of the devil. Thus the bodily humanity of Christ was denied, and fasting instituted on Christmas Day and Sundays. Priscillianism continued at least until 563, when it was officially condemned by the Council of Braga.

R. C. Kroeger and C. C. Kroeger

See also Monarchianism.

Bibliography. H. Chadwick, *Priscillian of Avila;* J. Chapman, *Notes on the Early History of the Vulgate Gospels,* ch. 13.

Probabiliorism. *See* Casuistry.

Probabilism. In moral theology probabilism is the doctrine that where a solid probable opinion favors liberty for a line of action, it may be followed even though a more probable opinion is against it. Originating in the fourteenth century, the view was first developed in the sixteenth under the Dominican Medina. It was adopted by the Jesuits (especially Suárez) and led to considerable laxity where only slight probability was accepted as sufficient. Reaction came in seventeenth century France with Pascal and the Dominicans, the latter favoring probabiliorism, i.e., that only a more probable opinion is to be followed. However, probabilism reestablished itself under Liguori, was adopted with some safeguards by the restored Jesuits after 1814, and is still the predominant teaching in the Roman Catholic Church.

G. W. Bromiley

See also Casuistry.

Probation. The idea that man's life on earth is a period of testing his fitness for fuller life beyond. In this sense, despite its strong appeal to exponents of the reasonableness of Christianity such as Paley and Butler and to Arminian theologians generally, it is only partly biblical. It contains the conviction that this life is incomplete in itself and that man is continually under the eye of the eternal God. Insofar as it expresses the truth that "God will render to every man according to his deeds" as expounded in Rom. 2:6-16, the theory of probation is biblical. But when the Bible speaks specifically of God's probation it is chiefly a testing of his own elect with a view to confirming them in their faith, not a general probation of all men. Thus "God did tempt [ERV prove] Abraham" (Gen. 22:1), his people Israel (Exod. 15:25; 16:4; Deut. 8:16; Judg. 2:22; Ps. 66:10; Zech. 13:9), his servant Job (Job 23:10), and the "righteous one" of the Psalms (Pss. 17:3; 139:23-24).

In the NT it is the Son of God who is tempted, recapitulating in his own person the probation of Israel in the wilderness and exhibiting even to death unswerving faith in his Father. The probation of Christians is viewed consequently as fellowship in the sufferings of Christ to establish their faith (Heb. 12:3-11; I Pet. 4:12-13; cf. I Cor. 10:13; James 1:1-2).

Far from leading us to suppose that man's destiny depends on his ability to earn God's approbation through the trial to which he is put in life, the Bible indicates that the general probation or "trial which is coming on the whole world" is a probation of condemnation from which only those who are Christ's will be delivered (Rev. 3:10, RSV; cf. Matt. 6:13; 26:41; Luke 21:36; II Pet. 2:9).

Probation is also used of testing the suitability of candidates for office within the church (e.g., I Cor. 16:3; I Tim. 3:10).

D. W. B. Robinson

See also Temptation.

Problem of Evil. *See* Evil, Problem of.

Procession of the Spirit. *See* Filioque.

Process Theology. A contemporary movement of theologians who teach that God is dipolar, or has two natures, and that he is integrally involved in the endless process of the world. God has a "primordial" or transcendent nature, his timeless perfection of character, and he has a "consequent" or immanent nature by which he is part of the cosmic process itself. This process is "epochal," i.e., not according to the motion of atoms or changeless substances but by events or units of creative experience which influence one another in temporal sequence.

The method of process theology is more philosophically than biblically or confessionally based, though many of its proponents use process thought as a contemporary way of expressing traditional Christian teachings or seek to relate biblical themes to process concepts. Also the method emphasizes the importance of the sciences in theological formulation. Thus process theology generally stands in the tradition of natural theology, and in particular is associated with the empirical theology tradition in America (Shailer Mathews, D. C. Macintosh, Henry Nelson Wieman) which championed the inductive, scientific approach in liberal theology. Also process theology has some philosophical kinship with the evolutionary thinking of H. Bergson, S. Alexander, C. Lloyd Morgan, and P. Teilhard de Chardin. But its true fountainhead is Whiteheadian philosophy.

The Influence of Whitehead. Alfred North Whitehead (1861–1947), the famed mathematician-philosopher, sought a set of metaphysical concepts that would be able to explain all individual beings, from God to the most insignificant thing. Through philosophical speculation in interaction with science he developed his notable model of the basic unit of reality, which he called the "actual occasion" or "actual entity." All things can be explained as processes of actual occasions, interrelated and varying in degree of complexity. Each actual occasion is a momentary event which is partially self-created and partially influenced by other actual occasions.

Every actual occasion or entity is dipolar, having both physical and mental functions. With its physical pole the actual entity feels or "prehends" the physical reality of other actual entities, and with the mental pole it prehends the "eternal objects" by which actual entities have conceptual definiteness. The eternal objects are the abstract possibilities of the universe, and actual entities are distinct from each other according to the way they realize or actualize these possibilities.

Whitehead uses the term "prehend" to refer to a feeling or grasping of the physical and conceptual data of actual entities. By prehending each other actual entities are internally related (instead of externally related, as in materialistic or mechanistic philosophies). This means that the entities are not isolated or independent beings but are present in other actual entities as interrelated moments of an ongoing process. This characteristic of prehension or feeling is not a conscious or intelligent act except with higher forms of life, but the dipolar structure and the prehensive function are there to some degree in every actual entity, however elementary or complex its level of existence.

Creativity is another of Whitehead's universal concepts; every actual entity has a measure of freedom which is expressed in an individual "subjective aim." The self-creative process by which an actual entity realizes its subjective aim includes unifying its many prehensions of the past and adding to them something new which is the entity's own creative contribution to the cosmic process. When the actual entity has realized its subjective aim, it attains "satisfaction," and thereafter ceases to exist as an experiencing subject, becoming instead the object or datum of the prehensions of subsequent actual entities. Thus the "life" of an actual entity is completed in the moment, and process in the world must be seen as a succession of organically related occasions or momentary experiences.

Hence what traditional philosophy would call an enduring substance, Whitehead calls a succession or "route" of actual occasions with a common characteristic. Change is explained by the creative contribution of each occasion in the series, and endurance is explained by common qualities which are inherited from antecedent occasions. The flux and stability of all things are explained in this way, whether they be electrons, rocks, plants, mammals, or men. Man is an extremely complex route or "nexus" of occasions with memory, imagination, and heightened conceptual feelings.

God is the supreme actual entity, and as such he perfectly exhibits all the functions of the actual entity. Whitehead contends that metaphysical coherence cannot be had by seeing God as an exception to the rules; on the contrary, he is the chief exemplification of the metaphysical principles by which all things are to be explained. Thus God perfectly prehends all entities in the universe and is prehended in part by them. He also has the supreme influence on all actual entities, setting the limits of their creativity and influencing their subjective aims by supplying each one with an ideal "initial aim." God does this by virtue of his mental pole or "primordial nature" in which he envisions all the eternal objects and their graded values relevant to the actual world.

In arguing for the existence of God, Whitehead contends that without the eternal objects there would be no definite rational possibilities or values to be actualized, and yet only that which is actual is able to affect actual entities. Therefore there must be *some* actual entity which grasps and valuates all of the eternal objects and can act as the universal agent and transcendent source of order and value in the world. For Whitehead, then, without God the cosmic process would not be an orderly, creative process, but only a chaos. God, by his primordial nature, acts as the "principle of limitation" or "concretion," enabling the world to become concretely determinate by aiming at certain values within divinely given limits of freedom.

God, as dipolar, also has a physical pole, or "consequent nature," by which he feels the completed actuality of each occasion. (Remember that "physical" does not mean physical substance, as in materialism.) He actually takes the complete entities into his divine life as objects of his perfect prehension and gives them "objective immortality" in his consequent being by his valuation of their achievements. (No actual entity has subjective immortality except God; finite living beings continue subjectively only by virtue of a continuing succession of actual occasions.) Moreover, God "gives back" to the world the data of the objectified entities he has prehended so that the world process will continue and be enriched by the past.

Thus God, by prehending and being prehended, interacts with every being in the world, in every momentary event in the succession of occasions that constitute the "life" of that being. In this way God is radically immanent in the world process itself, leading it on toward greater value and aesthetic intensity, not by coercion but by sympathetic persuasion. And although God in his primordial nature transcends the world, he as actual entity includes the world consequently within himself, and suffers and grows along with it through the creativity which he and the world possess.

The Contributions of Hartshorne. Though Whitehead's philosophy had already reached maturity with the publication of *Process and Reality* in 1929, only a few used Whitehead as a source for theological thought before the 1950s. Most theologians in the intervening years were preoccupied with the rise of neo-orthodoxy, which tended to reject natural theology and compartmentalize theology and science. One notable exception was Charles Hartshorne (1897–), who developed the theological implications of Whitehead's thought and acted as the chief catalyst for the process theology movement of the 60s and 70s.

Like Whitehead, Hartshorne was interested in metaphysics as the study of those general principles by which all particulars of experience are to be explained. But Hartshorne was more rationalistic about this study. For him metaphysics deals with what is externally necessary, or with "*a priori* statements about existence," i.e., statements which are necessarily true of any state of affairs regardless of the circumstances.

Hartshorne took up Whitehead's metaphysical system and, with some modifications, defended it as the most coherent and viable alternative. He agreed with Whitehead on the primacy of becoming (which is inclusive of being, in contrast to classical philosophy), and he emphasized even more than Whitehead the category of feeling as a quality of every entity (panpsychism).

In accordance with the "law of polarity" Hartshorne developed his dipolar view of God, though somewhat differently from Whitehead. Rejecting Whitehead's notion of eternal objects, Hartshorne called the mental pole of God the "abstract nature" of God, which is simply the abstract self-identity of God or his enduring character through all the stretches of time. The consequent nature Hartshorne called God's "concrete nature," which is God in his actual existence in any given concrete state, with all the wealth of accumulated values of the world up to that present state. The attributes of God's abstract nature are those divine qualities that are eternally, necessarily true of God regardless of the circumstances; whereas the qualities of God's concrete nature are those particulars of God's being which he has gained by his interaction with the world in accordance with the circumstances. God in his concrete actuality is a "living person," *in process;* his life consists of an everlasting succession of divine events or occasions. (Here again Hartshorne differs from Whitehead, who viewed God as a single everlasting actual entity.)

The polar opposites in God, therefore, mean that God is necessary according to his abstract nature but contingent according to his concrete nature, and, again, that he is independent in his abstract nature but dependent in his concrete nature. God is independent in the sense that nothing can threaten his existence or cause him to cease acting according to his loving and righteous character, but God is dependent in that what the creatures do affects his response, his feelings, and the content of his divine life.

According to Hartshorne, God's perfection should not be seen exclusively in terms of absoluteness, necessity, independence, infinity, and immutability wholly in contrast to the relativity, contingency, dependence, finitude, and changeability of the creatures. For Hartshorne this is the great mistake of classical theism (of such theologians as Thomas Aquinas), resulting in all sorts of problems like the contradiction of God's necessary knowledge of a contingent world, or God's timeless act of creating and governing a world which is temporal, or God's love for man which supposedly involves God in history yet in no way makes him relative to or dependent on man. Hartshorne contends that if temporal process and creativity are ultimately real, then God himself must be in process in some sense and must be dependent upon the free decisions of the creatures.

In opposition to classical theism, then, Hartshorne develops his "neoclassical" theism in which perfection is understood to mean that God is unsurpassable in social relatedness. If God really is perfect love, then he perfectly feels or has total sympathetic understanding of every creature and responds appropriately to every creature in every event. Thus God is supremely absolute in his abstract nature but supremely relative in his concrete nature. No one can surpass him in the supremacy of his social relatedness to every creature. But God can surpass himself—i.e., he can and does "grow," not to become morally better or more perfect, but to grow in the joy and feeling of the world, in knowledge of actual events, and in the experience of the values created by the world. (Note that for Hartshorne, God cannot foreknow future contingent events, and so his knowledge, which is complete of what *can* be known, nevertheless continues to grow with the process of the world.) Thus God is the "self-surpassing surpasser of all." God is more than just the world in its totality (*contra* pantheism) because he has his own transcendent self-identity; yet God includes the world within himself (*contra* classical theism) by his knowledge and love, which are simply his perfect prehension or taking in of the creative events of the world. Such a view of God is thus termed "panentheism" (all-in-God-ism).

With the panentheistic view of God, Hartshorne has become one of the chief protagonists in the twentieth century reassertion of the ontological argument. He says that the medieval Anselm really discovered something which was fundamental to the theistic proofs, namely the idea of "perfection" and its uniqueness among concepts. But Anselm's argument lacked cogency because it depended on a classical theistic view of perfection. The neoclassical view of perfection, Hartshorne contends, overcomes the objection of modern philosophers that perfection cannot be consistently defined. The thrust of Hartshorne's argument, then, is that perfection or "most perfect being" by definition either exists necessarily or is necessarily nonexistent, and since only the self-contradictory is *necessarily* nonexistent, perfect being, if it is self-consistent to speak of such, is in reality necessarily existent.

Most philosophers still hold that such an argument is defining God into existence by confusing logical necessity with existential necessity. But Hartshorne argues that the relation of logic to existence is unique in the case of perfection; i.e., perfection, if it really is perfection, exists necessarily as the logically required ground of all existence and thought. Here one can see Hartshorne's aprioristic approach to metaphysics very much at work, and the philosophical debate on that issue continues. Nevertheless philosophers (e.g., even a nontheist like J. N. Findlay) admit that Hartshorne has made the concept of perfection rationally conceivable and has reopened the ontological argument which before seemed closed.

Christian Process Thought. After 1960, as the influence of neo-orthodoxy was waning, an increasing number of theologians turned to Whitehead and Hartshorne as new philosophical sources for a contemporary expression of Christian faith. Beginning with the doctrine of God, such theologians as John Cobb, Schubert Ogden, Daniel D. Williams, and Norman Pittenger sought to show that the process view of God is more in accord with the biblical view of God (as dynamically related to human history) than is the more traditional Christian view of classical theism. They argued that the monopolar conception of God as timeless, immutable, impassible, and in every sense independent was more hellenistic than biblical. Williams analyzed the biblical, Christian theme of love and argued that Whitehead's metaphysics helps the theologian to explain God's loving action in ways not possible with classical notions of God as being-itself or absolute predestinator. Ogden argued that the "new theism" of process thought, with its world-affirming emphasis, expresses the relevance of Christian faith to secular man, who needs an ultimate ground for his "ineradicable confidence" in the final worth of human existence. Cobb showed how Whiteheadian philosophy can be the basis of a new Christian natural theology, a theology which by philosophical means demonstrates that the peculiar vision of the Christian community of faith illuminates the general experience of mankind.

Process theologians then began to concentrate on Christology, especially in the 70s, though Pittenger led the way by writing several works on the subject from a process view, the first in 1959. For Pittenger the uniqueness of Christ is seen in the way he actualized the divine aim for his life. Sin is "deviation of aim"; man in his subjective aim distorts or deviates from God's initial aim. In his subjective aims Christ actualized the ideal aim of God (as the cosmic Lover) with such intensity that Christ became the supreme human embodiment of "love-in-action." The deity of Jesus does not mean that he is an eternally preexistent person, but refers to God's act in and through the life of Jesus, who incarnated and transformed the whole of Israel's religion and became the eminent example of God's creative love which is at work universally.

David Griffin has spoken similarly, suggesting that Jesus actualized God's aims in such a way that he became God's decisive revelation; i.e., the "vision of reality" shown in his words and actions was the supreme expression of God's eternal character and purpose.

Cobb emphasizes a Logos Christology. The Logos as the primordial nature of God is present (incarnate) in all things in the form of initial aims for creatures. But Jesus is the fullest incarnation of the Logos because in him there was no tension between the divine initial aim and his own self-purposes of the past. Jesus so prehended God that God's immanence was "coconstitutive" of Jesus' selfhood. Cobb thus suggests (as opposed to other process thinkers) that Jesus was different from others in his "structure of existence" not merely by degree but in kind.

Lewis Ford places emphasis on the resurrection as the basis for a Christology. According to him, what the first disciples experienced was neither a bodily appearance of Christ nor merely a hallucination, but a vision, or an encounter with a "nonperceptual reality" made perceptual by "hallucinatory means." Thus the resurrection is of a spiritual kind; it is a new emergent reality, the "body of Christ," in which mankind is transformed into a new organic unity by the living spirit of Christ. Ford also suggests a process view of the Trinity; the Father is the transcendent unity of God, who by a creative "nontemporal act" generates the Logos (the primordial nature) as the eternal expression of divine wisdom and valuation, and the Spirit is the consequent nature in the sense of the immanent being and providential power of God.

At present, process works continue to abound, dealing with various Christian concepts and concerns: sin and evil, a theodicy, the church, pastoral care, ecology, liberation, and the relation of theology to science, philosophy, and culture. Though process theology has not yet become a major force in the church pew, it is very influential in the intellectual world of the seminaries and graduate schools, and no doubt is the most viable form of neoliberal theology now in the United States.

Some other writers of Christian theology from a process perspective are Bernard Meland, Ian Barbour, Peter Hamilton, Eugene Peters, Delwin Brown, William Beardsley, Walter Stokes, Ewert Cousins, E. Baltazar, and Bernard Lee. Though process theology developed mainly within Protestantism, it now has influence also with Roman Catholic thinkers (as is evident from the last four names just mentioned). Catholic process thinkers have been coming to grips not only with Whitehead but also with Teilhard de Chardin, whose thought is historically separate from, but has some philosophical affinity with, the Whiteheadian tradition.

Evaluation. By philosophical or rational standards process theology has several commendable points. First, it emphasizes metaphysical coherence; i.e., it seeks to express a vision of God and the world by a coherent and clearly defined set of metaphysical concepts. Second, it integrates science and theology. Science provides data and clues for theology, and vice versa; they are together in the same universal sphere of discourse, namely, process metaphysics. Consequently, and in the third place, process theology provides a tenable answer to the charge that theological language is meaningless. The process theologian contends that if metaphysics describes those most general concepts or principles by which all particulars are to be explained, and if God is the chief exemplification of those principles, then talk about God is eminently meaningful and basic to the meaningfulness of everything else. Fourth, process theology eloquently champions natural theology. Fifth, process theology gives clear and plausible form to a dynamic, personal view of God. Personal qualities such as self-consciousness, creativity, knowledge, and social relatedness are attributed to God in the most literal sense.

By rational standards process theology also has its weaknesses or questionable features. First, one may question whether the process model does justice to the self-identity of an individual person in process. Second, process theology has some problems concerning the finitude and temporality of God—e.g., the problem of relating God's infinite, nontemporal, primordial nature to God's finite, temporal, growing, and consequent nature, or the problem of seeing unity of experience in each moment of God's omnipresent existence in view of the teaching of relativity physics that there is no simultaneous *present* throughout the universe. Third, there is the question of the religious adequacy of panentheism. Is the most worthy object of worship a God who needs the world in order to be a complete personal being or a God who is a complete personal being *prior* to the world?

In addition to these philosophical problems, there are some characteristics of process theology which, from the viewpoint of evangelical theology, are contrary to Scripture. These include a nontripersonal view of the Trinity, a Nestorian or Ebionite tendency in Christology, a nonsupernaturalistic view of the Bible and of Christ's works, the denial of divine foreknowledge and predestination, and a weak view of human depravity. D. W. Diehl

See also Panentheism.

Bibliography. J. B. Cobb, Jr., *A Christian Natural Theology;* L. S. Ford, *The Lure of God;* D. Griffin, *A Process Christology;* C. Hartshorne, *The Divine Relativity, The Logic of Perfection,* and *Creative Synthesis and Philosophic Method;* S. Ogden, *The Reality of God;* N. Pittenger, *Christology Reconsidered* and *Process Thought and Christian Faith;* A. N. Whitehead, *Process and Reality;* D. Brown, R. James, and G. Reeves, eds., *Process Philosophy and Christian Thought;* W. Christian, *An Interpretation of Whitehead's Metaphysics;* J. B. Cobb, Jr., and D. Griffin, *Process Theology: An Introductory Exposition;* N. Geisler, "Process Theology," in *Tensions in Contemporary Theology,* ed. S. N. Gundry and A. F. Johnson.

Promise. The English word "promise" derives directly from the Latin *promissa,* meaning exactly what our word means, "a declaration or assurance made to another person with respect to the future stating that one will do or refrain from some specified act, or that one will give or bestow some specified thing, usually in a good sense implying something to the advantage or pleasure of the person concerned" (*Oxford English Dictionary*). Actually, no word in the Hebrew or Greek Scriptures has this exact meaning. The word generally translated "promise" in the OT is *dābar,* rendered "speak" over eight hundred times, or "say" more than one hundred times—to talk, to utter, to pronounce. When these pronouncements embrace the idea of something promised, the word is so used, e.g., in the ordinary promises of men to men, and especially the promises of God to the people of Israel (Deut. 1:11; 6:3; 9:28; 15:6; 19:8, etc.) or to one particular individual, as to Solomon (I Kings 5:12).

In the NT the word is *epangelia,* which in the overwhelming number of instances is simply translated "promise," as a noun and in its verbal form. The root of this word, *angelia,* means something announced; *angelos,* the announcer or the messenger; and *euangelia,* a message of good tidings. On rare occasions the word is used of some incidental promise of man to man, as in Acts 23:21. Its occurrences in the NT may be gathered into three groups. There are, first, the frequent references to God's promises to Abraham concerning an heir (Rom. 4:13–16, 20; 9:8–9; 15:8; Gal. 3:16–22; 4:23; Heb. 6:13–17; 7:6; 11:9, 11, 17). Abraham believed these promises, and they were repeated to his patriarchal descendants Isaac and Jacob, through whom the promised seed should come. The relationship of Christian believers to the promises in Abraham will be considered later.

The second major theme of these promises is David's seed, "a Savior according to promise" (Acts 13:23). Stephen speaks of the time of the advent as that in which "the time of the promise drew nigh" (Acts 7:17). This promise to David of a Savior has been confirmed in Christ (Acts 13:32). It is to this group that we must assign Paul's allusion to "the promise by faith in Jesus Christ" (Gal. 3:22). It is probable that this dual grouping of promises, those to Abraham concerning a seed and those to David concerning a king to reign, are united in Paul's references to this subject as "the promises made unto the fathers" (Rom. 15:8); in the familiar discussion of Israel's future, he refers to the Israelites as "the children of the promise" (Rom. 9:8–9) and reminds them that they are the ones who possess the promises of God (Rom. 9:4). Closely associated with this is the gift of God promised to us in Christ, that is, the promise of life in Christ (II Tim. 1:1), or, as elsewhere expressed, "the promise of eternal inheritance" (Heb. 9:15), or, as John wrote, "the promise which he promised us, even the life eternal" (I John 2:29).

The third group of promises concerns the gift of the Holy Spirit after our Lord's ascension, never referred to as a promise until after the resurrection (Luke 24:49; cf. Acts 1:4; 2:33; Eph. 1:13).

Other subjects related to the promises of God are mentioned only incidentally in the NT: the promise of rest (Heb. 4:1); the fulfillment of the promises of a new heaven and a new earth (II Pet. 3:13, from Isa. 52:11 and Hos. 1:4); the promise of the resurrection (Acts 26:6); "the first commandment with promise," regarding obedience of children to their parents (Eph. 6:2, from Exod. 20:12).

There is some similarity between promise and prophecy. So, e.g., the frequently used phrase "the promises to Abraham, and to Israel" for the most part refers to the prophecies given to Abraham and the patriarchs, beginning with Gen. 12:1–3 (see Rom. 9:4, 8; 15:8; Gal. 3:16–22, 29). But there are some notable differences: (1) All promises relate to the desirable, the good, that which blesses and enriches, while some prophecies refer to judgments, destructions, invasions, the appearance of enemies of Christ, such as the little horn, the man of sin, etc. (2) Promises ordinarily have a more general scope than prophecies, often including the entire human race—though we realize that all mankind is involved in some prophecies also—thus, the fifth commandment is called "the first commandment with promise" (Eph. 6:2), and would seem to refer to all who obey this command. So likewise the "promise of life" (I Tim. 4:8; II Tim. 1:4). (3) Promises have a more continuous fulfillment, generation by generation, than do most prophecies, as in the often repeated phrase, "the promise of the Father" or "the promise of the Holy Spirit" (Luke 24:49; Acts 1:4; 2:33, 39; Gal. 3:14; Eph. 1:13). While there are prophecies relating to Palestine, it is never called "the land of prophecy," but "the land of promise" (Heb. 11:9), and continues to be that down through the ages even though disobedience forfeits for a time the fulfillment of the promise. (4) Many promises are conditional, dependent upon obedience to the word of God, as the Beatitudes, but most prophecies are unconditional, and ultimately will be fulfilled. (5) Generally the concept of promise embraces many utterances of God, as in the phrase "he has granted to us his precious and very great promises" (II Pet. 1:4), whereas prophecies are ordinarily directed to more specific events or individuals. W. M. Smith

See also Prophecy, Prophet; Hope.

Bibliography. E. Hoffmann, *NIDNTT*, III, 68ff.; J. Bright, *Covenant and Promise;* W. G. Kümmel, *Promise and Fulfillment;* J. Schniewind *et al.*, *TDNT*, II, 576ff.; F. F. Bruce, ed., *Promise and Fulfillment;* J. Jeremias, *Jesus' Promise to the Nations.*

Prophecy, Gift of. *See* Spiritual Gifts.

Prophecy, Prophet. The word "prophet" comes from the Greek *prophētēs*, from *pro* ("before" or "for") and *phēmi* ("to speak"). The prophet is thus the one who speaks before in the sense of proclaim, or the one who speaks for, i.e., in the name of (God).

In the OT there are three terms for the prophet: *rō'eh*, *nābî'*, and *ḥōzeh*. The first and last are distinguished by nuances bearing on the habitual or temporary character of the vision. *Nābî'* (he who witnesses or testifies) is best adapted to characterize the prophetic mission.

Prophetic Inspiration. The originality of biblical prophecy derives from the phenomenon of inspiration. As distinct from the sacral figures of pagan antiquity the biblical prophet is not a magician. He does not force God. On the contrary, he is under divine constraint. It is God who invites, summons, and impels him—e.g., Jer. 20:7.

By inspiration God speaks to the *nābî'*, who has to transmit exactly what he receives. The mode of inspiration is verbal. The Bible depicts the mechanism of inspiration as the act by which God puts words (*verba*) in the mouth of the sacred writers. God said to Moses: "I will raise them up a prophet from among their brethren, like unto thee, and will put my words (*verba*) in his mouth" (Deut. 18:18). Similarly to Jeremiah: "I have put my words in thy mouth" (Jer. 1:9). The NT confirms the verbal nature of prophetic inspiration (cf. Gal. 1:11–12; I Cor. 15:1–4; I Thess. 2:13; 4:8).

Yet inspiration does not suppress individuality. It is the miracle of *theopneustia* (II Tim. 3:16). To communicate his thoughts to men, God uses men of different culture, character, and status in order that his word might be accessible to all men. Inspiration safeguards individuality (cf. Moses in Exod. 3–4; Jeremiah in Jer. 20:14–18, etc.).

The Prophets. The writing prophets of the OT are well known. They are usually divided into the four major (Isaiah, Jeremiah, Ezekiel, and Daniel) and the twelve minor (Hosea, Joel, Amos, Obadiah, Jonah, Micah, Nahum, Habakkuk, Zephaniah, Haggai, Zechariah, and Malachi) according to the length of their writings.

In addition there were many other prophets. Moses, who wrote the law of God, was regarded as a *nābî'* without equal (Deut. 34:10–12). Prophetic voices were also raised in the days of the judges (Judg. 2:1–5; 3:9–11; 4:4; 6:8; I Sam. 3:1). Samuel came as a second Moses (Jer. 15:1; Ps. 99:6), and his work was continued by Gad and Nathan (II Sam. 12 and 24; I Kings 1). After the separation of the ten tribes Ahijah (I Kings 2), Elijah, and Elisha (I Kings 18–19; II Kings 5ff.) call for particular mention.

After four centuries of prophetic silence John the Baptist is the last of the prophets of the old covenant and the precursor of Jesus (Matt. 19:1; cf. Matt. 3:7ff.; Luke 3:16ff.; John 1:23, 29). In addition to the Baptist, the NT also refers to a prophetic ministry exercised by both men and women. After Pentecost, mention is made of Agabus (Acts 2:28; 21:10), Jude and Silas (Acts 15:32), and the four daughters of Philip (Acts 21:8–10). We might also cite Anna the daughter of Phanuel (Luke 2:36).

The Prophetic Message. The prophecies of the writing prophets of the OT may be divided into three main groups: (1) Prophecies concerning the internal destiny of Israel. These declare the judgment of God on the unbelief and iniquities of the people, but promise restoration after the testing period of the Exile. (2) Messianic prophecies. These point to the coming Redeemer of Israel and the world. They attain an astonishing clarity and precision in the case of Micah (5:1) and especially Isaiah. The latter gives us a striking summary of the saving life and work of

Christ (52:13–53). (3) Eschatological prophecies. These refer to the last days when the kingdom of God will be set up on earth.

From a different standpoint we might adopt the following classification. (1) Prophecies already fulfilled. Two examples are the Exile, announced by Hosea, Amos, and Micah in the case of northern Israel (deported to Assyria in 722 B.C.) and Isaiah, Jeremiah, Ezekiel, Hosea, Amos, and Micah in the case of Judah (exiled in Babylon in 586 B.C.), and of course the coming of Christ himself. (2) Prophecies in process of fulfillment. A good case in point is the restoration of the modern state of Israel. The prophecy of Jer. 31:31 (cf. Isa. 27:12–13; Ezek. 37:21) found miraculous fulfillment on May 15, 1948, and the physical resurrection of the Israelite nation, as yet incomplete, is a new and up-to-date guarantee that other prophecies will come to realization. (3) Prophecies not yet fulfilled. We may refer to four. The first is the total recovery of Palestine by all the tribes of Israel (Isa. 27:12–13; Ezek. 37:11–14; Jer. 31:1–5, 31; etc.). The second is the destruction of Israel's enemies (Jer. 30:11; Isa. 17:1–3; Ezek. 38–39). The third is the collective conversion of Israel (Ezek. 37:6*b*, 10; Zech. 14:4–5; 12:10). The fourth is the establishment of the kingdom of God on earth. Many prophecies describe the coming of the Messiah, the King of Israel, and the restoration of humanity to righteousness, peace, and happiness under his rule (cf. Isa. 2:4; 11:1–10; 65:19–23), the reconstitution of nature (Ezek. 47:13*a;* 48:1–35; cf. Rom. 8:19–21), and the reestablishment of converted Israel in the prerogatives of its original vocation (cf. Isa. 49:6; Rom. 11:15; Joel 2:28–32; Hab. 2:14; Isa. 55:4–5; Zech. 8:23). Before the kingdom of God is set up, the earth will be the scene of the return and temporary reign of the Messiah (cf. Rev. 20:2*b*-3, 4*b*) and Israel will be God's instrument (Zech. 8:13) for the conversion of the nations.

Prophets and Prophecy of the NT Period. The names of early Christian prophets are few (Acts 11:27–28; 15:30–32; 21:10; Martyrdom of Polycarp 12:3; 16:2), yet these prophets were nonetheless powerful persons within the church who spoke the word of the risen Lord with authority: (1) Their presence and activity were widespread (cf. Acts 20:23 with 21:10–11). (2) They worked within the framework of the church, perhaps becoming active only when Christians were at worship (Hermas, *Mandate* 11:9; Acts 13:1–2). (3) They ranked in importance second only to the apostles (I Cor. 12:28–31; Eph. 4:11), and with them they were considered the foundation upon which the church was built (Eph. 2:20). (4) They belonged to and worked out from bands or brotherhoods which could be considered exclusive groups of charismatics (Acts 11:27; 13:1; Rev. 19:10; 22:9; I Cor. 12:29; cf. Barnabas 16:9). (5) They were people whose minds were saturated with the OT Scriptures. Their prophetic utterances thus were influenced by and couched in the language of the Bible (Acts 7; cf. Rom. 11:27 with Isa. 27:9; I Cor. 15:51, 54–55, with Isa. 25:8; Hos. 13:14). (6) Their ministry was distinguished from that of apostle, miracle worker, etc. (I Cor. 12:28–29), but closely associated with that of teacher (Acts 13:1; Rev. 2:20). Their ministry also included prediction, revelation, identifying specific persons for specific Christian tasks and even equipping them with the spiritual gifts necessary to carry out these tasks (Acts 11:27–28; 13:1–2; I Tim. 4:14). (7) They were people whose words and actions were especially prompted by the Spirit (Acts 11:27–28; 21:11; Hermas, *Mandate* 11:8–9; Didache 11:7).

NT prophecy, therefore, was of more than one kind. It included prophetic words given for the improvement, encouragement, consolation, and general benefit of the Christian community (I Cor. 14:3–4). But it also included another dimension, related directly to a special work of the Spirit upon the prophet by which the Spirit revealed to the prophet a word from the risen and exalted Christ (cf. John 16:12–14; Rev. 1:10 with 4:1–2*a*). When the prophet thus spoke, his word became the command of the Lord (I Cor. 14: 29–30, 37). This part of the prophet's ministry was the result of a direct revelation of an aspect of the divine mind hitherto unknown (Eph. 3:5; Rev. 10:7; 22:6). Like OT prophecy, this new prophetic message was an immediate communication of God's (Christ's) word to his people through human lips (cf. Rev. 16:15; 22:7; see also Rev. 2–3).

Since the prophet was such an authoritative figure and was held in such high regard by the people, abuses were bound to set in. Christ himself predicted that such abuses would arise (Matt. 24:11, 24). Eventually it became necessary for the church to establish regulations that would control not only the prophet's dress and teaching (I Cor. 11:4; 14:29–30), but also how long he could stay in any one place without being judged a false prophet (Hermas, *Mandate* 11:1–21; Didache 11).

A. Lamorte and G. F. Hawthorne

Bibliography. M. Buber, *The Prophetic Faith;* A. B. Davidson, *OT Prophecy;* A. Guillaume, *Prophecy and Divination Among the Hebrews and Other Semites;* J. Lindblom, *Prophecy in Ancient Israel;* J. Skinner, *Prophecy and Religion;* W. R. Smith, *The Prophets of Israel;* A. C. Welch, *Prophet and Priest in Old Israel;* L. J. Wood, *The Prophets of Israel;* E. Boring, "How May We Identify Oracles of Christian Prophets in the Synoptic Tradition?" *JBL* 91:501–21, and "The Influence of Christian Prophecy," *NTS* 25:113–23; W. D. Davies, *Paul and Rabbinic Judaism;* J. D. G. Dunn, *Jesus and the Spirit* and "Prophetic 'I' Sayings and the Jesus of Tradition," *NTS* 24:175–98; E. E. Ellis, "Luke 11:49–51: An Oracle of a Christian Prophet?" *ExpT* 74:157, *Prophecy and Hermeneutic in Early Christianity,* "The Role of the Christian Prophet in Acts," in *Apostolic History of the Gospel,* ed. W. W. Gasque and R. P. Martin, and "'Spiritual' Gifts in the Pauline Community," *NTS* 20:128–44; E. Fascher, *TDNT,* VI, 828–61; G. F. Hawthorne, "Christian Prophecy and the Sayings of Jesus," *SBL Seminar Papers,* II, 105–24; D. Hill, *NT Prophecy* and "On the Evidence for the Creative Role of Christian Prophets," *NTS* 20:262–74; J. M. Meyers and E. D. Freed, "Is Paul Also Among the Prophets?" *Int* 20: 40–53.

Prophet, Christ as. *See* Offices of Christ.

Propitiation. The turning away of wrath by an offering. In the NT this idea is conveyed by the use of *hilaskomai* (Heb. 2:17), *hilastērion* (Rom. 3:25), and *hilasmos* (I John 2:2; 4:10). In the OT the principal verb is *kipper,* usually rendered in the LXX by *exilaskomai.* Outside the Bible the word group to which the Greek words belong unquestionably has the significance of averting wrath. But in recent times it has been suggested that the Bible usage is different. C. H. Dodd argues strongly that, when the word group occurs in the LXX and the NT, it denotes expiation (the cancellation of sin), not propitiation (the turning away of the wrath of God). He denies that "the wrath of God" denotes anything more than a process of cause and effect whereby disaster inevitably follows sin.

For a criticism of his arguments see the works by Nicole and Morris in the bibliography. Here it is sufficient to notice that neither Dodd nor others who argue for "expiation" seem to give sufficient attention to the biblical teaching. The idea of the wrath of God is stubbornly rooted in the OT, where it is referred to 585 times. The words of the *hilaskomai* group do not denote simple forgiveness or cancellation of sin, but that forgiveness or cancellation of sin which includes the turning away of God's wrath (e.g., Lam. 3:42–43). This is not a process of celestial bribery, for the removal of the wrath is in the last resort due to God himself. Of the process of atonement by sacrifice, he says: "I have given it to you" (Lev. 17:11). Note also Ps. 78:38: "Many a time turned he his anger away."

While God's wrath is not mentioned as frequently in the NT as the OT, it is there. Man's sin receives its due reward, not because of some impersonal retribution, but because God's wrath is directed against it (Rom. 1:18, 24, 26, 28). The whole of the argument of the opening part of Romans is that all men, Gentiles and Jews alike, are sinners, and that they come under the wrath and the condemnation of God. When Paul turns to salvation, he thinks of Christ's death as *hilastērion* (Rom. 3:25), a means of removing the divine wrath. The paradox of the OT is repeated in the NT that God himself provides the means of removing his own wrath. The love of the Father is shown in that he "sent his Son to be the propitiation for our sins" (I John 4:10). The purpose of Christ's becoming "a merciful and faithful high priest" was "to make propitiation for the sins of the people" (Heb. 2:17). His propitiation is adequate for all (I John 2:2).

The consistent Bible view is that the sin of man has incurred the wrath of God. That wrath is averted only by Christ's atoning offering. From this standpoint his saving work is properly called propitiation.

L. Morris

See also Atonement; Wrath of God.

Bibliography. C. H. Dodd, *The Bible and the Greeks;* R. Nicole, *WmTJ* 17:117–57; L. Morris, "The Meaning of HILASTĒRION in Rom III.25," *NTS* 2:33–43, and *The Apostolic Preaching of the Cross;* H. G. Link *et al., NIDNTT,* III, 145ff.

Protestantism. In its broadest sense Protestantism denotes the whole movement within Christianity that originated in the sixteenth century Reformation and later focused in the main traditions of Reformed church life—Lutheran, Reformed (Calvinist/Presbyterian), and Anglican-Episcopalian (although Anglicanism par excellence claims to be both Catholic and Protestant)—at Speyer in 1529 in dissenting from a clamptional, Baptist, Methodist, Pentecostal, and many others, down to modern African Independent churches).

The term derives from the "protestation" submitted by a minority of Lutheran and Reformed authorities at the German Imperial Diet at Speyer in 1529 in dissenting from a clampdown on religious renewal. The "protestation" was at once objection, appeal, and affirmation. It asked urgently, "What is the true and holy Church?" and asserted: "There is no sure preaching or doctrine but that which abides by the Word of God. According to God's command no other doctrine should be preached. Each text of the holy and divine Scriptures should be elucidated and explained by other texts. This Holy Book is in all things necessary for the Christian; it shines clearly in its own light, and is found to enlighten the darkness. We are determined by God's grace and aid to abide by God's Word alone, the holy gospel contained in the biblical books of the Old and New Testaments. This Word alone should be preached, and nothing that is contrary to it. It is the only truth. It is the sure rule of all Christian doctrine and conduct. It can never fail or deceive us."

Lutherans and other advocates of reform thus became known as Protestants. The English word originally had the force of "resolute confession, solemn declaration," standing for gospel truth against Roman corruption. "Essentially Protestantism is an appeal to God in Christ, to Holy Scripture and to the primitive Church, against all degeneration and apostasy." The narrowing of "Protestant" to mean anti- or non-Roman has led some to prefer "Evangelical" (though in continental Europe this normally designates Lutherans) and "Reformed" (more commonly used of Calvinist Presbyterians).

Fundamental Principles. The fundamental principles of sixteenth century Protestantism included the following:

Soli Deo Gloria: the justification of God's wisdom and power against papal usurpation and manmade religion, honoring God's sovereign transcendence and providential predestination.

Sola Gratia: redemption as God's free gift accomplished by Christ's saving death and resurrection. This was articulated chiefly in Pauline terms as justification by faith alone, as in the Augsburg Confession: "We cannot obtain forgiveness of sin and righteousness before God by our own merits, works or satisfactions, but receive forgiveness of sin and become righteous before God by grace, for Christ's sake, through faith, when we believe that Christ suffered for us and that for his sake our sin is forgiven and righteousness and eternal life are given to us." Assurance of salvation is therefore a mark of Protestant faith, grounded in the promise of the gospel and released from all pursuit of merit.

Sola Scriptura: the freedom of Scripture to rule as God's word in the church, disentangled from papal and ecclesiastical *magisterium* and tradition. Scripture is the sole source of Christian revelation. Although tradition may aid its interpretation, its true (i.e., spiritual) meaning is its natural (i.e., literal) sense, not an allegorical one.

The Church as the Believing People of God: constituted not by hierarchy, succession, or institution, but by God's election and calling in Christ through the gospel. In the words of the Augsburg Confession, it is "the assembly of all believers among whom the gospel is preached in its purity and the holy sacraments are administered according to the gospel." The sacraments appointed by Christ are two only—baptism and the Lord's Supper—and may be spoken of as "visible words," reflecting the primacy of preaching in Protestant conviction.

The Priesthood of All Believers: the privileged freedom of all the baptized to stand before God in Christ "without patented human intermediaries" and their calling to be bearers of judgment and grace as "little Christs" to their neighbors. Pastor and preacher differ from other Christians by function and appointment, not spiritual status. (Later Protestantism has forgotten this perhaps more than any other foundation principle.)

The Sanctity of All Callings or Vocations: the rejection of medieval distinctions between secular and sacred or "religious" (i.e., monastic) with the depreciation of the former, and the recognition of all ways of life as divine vocations. "The works of monk and priest in God's sight are in no way whatever superior to a farmer laboring in the field, or a woman looking after her home" (Luther). None is intrinsically more Christian than any other—an insight obscured by phrases such as "the holy ministry."

Protestant Developments. Protestantism has developed a distinctive ethos in each of the several traditions derived from the Reformation and also within their historical, cultural, and geographical variations. On some issues, such as the manner (not the reality) of Christ's presence in the Supper, Protestants have disagreed from a very early stage, while agreeing in rejecting transubstantiation and the sacrifice of the Mass and insisting that living faith alone feeds upon Christ's flesh and blood. On others, such as church order, diversity of practice has not always involved disagreement in principle. In this and other areas Protestantism's scriptural principle has itself been articulated in different ways, both to sanction the retention of traditions (e.g., episcopacy) not repugnant to Scripture (a typically Lutheran and Anglican approach) and to debar from the church's life anything not explicitly warranted in Scripture (a tendency of Reformed Protestantism implemented most consistently by Puritanism and some derivative traditions). Nothing has so much promoted the disunity of Protestantism as the inroads of post-Enlightenment rationalism and its offspring in theological liberalism and modernism, which have gravely eroded Protestantism's Reformation and biblical foundations.

Another pattern of Reformation in the sixteenth century, generally called Anabaptist or Radical despite its diversity, sought to restore the precise shape of apostolic Christianity. Pentecostalism has a similar aim, along with other movements, including some Baptists and (Plymouth) Brethren. Some African Independent churches have pursued a restorationist approach even to the OT. Although Anabaptism gave birth to no major Protestant tradition (but note the Mennonites), its rejection of the Constantinian state-church and all its works (endorsed unreservedly by all three primary Protestant traditions) became in time the common property of most of Protestantism, especially outside Europe. (E. Troeltsch has stressed the revolutionary significance of later Protestantism's abandonment of its early ideal of an all-embracing church-civilization, a reformed Christendom.) The Anabaptist "protestation," though persecuted by the authoritarian Protestants—Lutheran, Reformed, and Anglican—is increasingly regarded as a parallel pattern of pristine Protestantism, with perhaps more to contribute to its future than any other pattern.

Despite its divisions the community of Protestantism is still discernible in cross-denominational movements—e.g., missionary expansion, Bible translation, biblical criticism and modern theological study, welfare and relief agencies, and the ecumenical movement itself. Protestants are also held together by common convictions, chief among them the acceptance of the Reformation as an indispensable part of their history. For no Protestants does this exclude a lineage going back to the apostles, but continuity with patristic and medieval Christianity would be variously prized in different Protestant traditions. Protestantism's scriptural principle finds expression in the axiom *Ecclesia reformata sed semper reformanda*—"a church reformed but always open to further reformation." Subjection to the word of God means that no traditions or institutions, secular or religious, not even Reformation or Protestant ones, can be absolutized. Paul Tillich regarded "the Protestant principle" as "the prophetic judgment against religious pride, ecclesiastical arrogance and secular self-sufficiency and their destructive consequences." This was nobly exemplified in the Barmen Declaration of the Confessing Church in Nazi Germany ("Confessing" here being a good modern synonym of sixteenth century "Protestant"). Intellectually, "the co-operation of uninhibited inquiry and religious faith, of theology and science, is possible only on Protestant territory where all human traditions and institutions stand open both to man's scrutiny and to God's" (J. H. Nichols). Finally, Protestantism seeks to draw its life from the gospel of God's grace in Christ. True to its heritage it can tolerate no do-it-yourself Christianity, no ground for human self-confidence before God's face. It will ultimately always value the Christ of faith more than the church of history. D. F. Wright

See also Reformation, Protestant.

Bibliography. H. Wace, *Principles of the Reformation;* E. G. Léonard, *A History of Protestantism,* 2 vols.; W. Pauck, *The Heritage of the Reformation;* J. Dillenberger and C. Welch, *Protestant Christianity Interpreted through Its Development;* P. Schaff, *A History of the Creeds of Christendom,* I, III; R. N. Flew and R. E. Davies, eds., *The Catholicity of Protestantism;* J. H. Nichols, *Primer for Protestants;* W. Niesel, *Reformed Symbolics: A Comparison of Catholicism, Orthodoxy and Protestantism;* L. Bouyer, *The Spirit and Forms of Protestantism;* E. Troeltsch, *Protestantism and Progress;* P. Tillich, *The Protestant Era;* C. S. Carter and G. E. A. Weeks, eds., *The Protestant Dictionary;* J. S. Whale, *The Protestant Tradition.*

Providence of God. "Providence" is one of the words which do not occur in the Bible but which nevertheless represent truly a biblical doctrine. There is no Hebrew equivalent for "providence," and the Greek word translated thus, *pronoia,* is used only of human foresight (Acts 24:2; Rom. 13:14; for the verb *pronoeō,* see Rom. 12:17; II Cor. 8:21; I Tim. 5:8). Rather, the Bible uses *ad hoc* words like "he *giveth food* to all flesh" (Ps. 136:25), or "he *sendeth forth springs* into the valleys" (Ps. 104:10), expressing in concrete situations God's mighty acts toward his children.

We must resist the temptation to think about providence generally and independently of Christ. It would be possible to draw on certain Psalms and the Sermon on the Mount, for example, to make up a doctrine of God's relationship to his creation that had nothing to do with Jesus Christ. But since it is in Christ that this relationship is established, an attempt to understand it apart from him would be a misinterpretation from the start. In Jesus Christ, God has set up the relationship between himself and his creatures, promising to carry through his purpose in creation to its triumphal conclusion. The primal relationship with Adam, renewed with Noah (Gen. 8:21–22), is no less *in Christo* than in the covenant with Abraham or Moses. The Mediator who is the incarnate Word establishes this relationship, and in him God becomes the God of men and they become his people. (The Mediator must also be regarded as setting up the relationship between God and his creatures other than man.) As their God, he will take up the responsibility for their earthly existence.

The doctrine of providence may be viewed from three different aspects.

(1) The creation is the stage on which are enacted God's dealings with mankind. Providence is God's gracious outworking of his purpose in Christ which issues in his dealings with man. We are not at this point slipping over into the doctrine of predestination, but are saying that from the beginning God has ordered the course of

events toward Jesus Christ and his incarnation. From the biblical point of view world history and personal life stories possess significance only in the light of the incarnation. The squalid little story of lust in Judah's dealings with Tamar (Gen. 38) falls into its place in the genealogy of the Messiah (Matt. 1:3). Caesar Augustus was on the throne in Rome for the sake of the unknown baby in its manger.

(2) According to Acts 14:17; 17:22–30; and Rom. 1:18–23, God's providence served also the purpose of bearing witness to God among the heathen. God's fatherly care was a sign, pointing toward himself. Rom. 1:20 makes it clear that the purpose of this witness of providence was simply to render man inexcusable for not knowing God. At this point also, therefore, providence is included in the doctrine of reconciliation.

(3) The God who gives man life also preserves him while he is on the earth. God is not a God of the soul alone, but of the body also. In Matt. 6:25–34 the disciples are reminded (by their Creator himself) of their creaturely relationship to God, and are freed from all anxiety about their earthly future. The other creatures (as exemplified by the birds and the wildflowers) have been set in a definite relationship to God which he faithfully maintains by caring for their needs. Will God bestow less care upon man, to whom he has given a higher place in the creation (cf. Ps. 8:6–8)? Men therefore "glorify their Creator . . . by a daily unquestioning acceptance of His gifts" (D. Bonhoeffer, *The Cost of Discipleship*, 154). Behind this doctrine lies the almighty and loving freedom of God.

In sum, the doctrine of providence tells us that the world and our lives are not ruled by chance or by fate but by God, who lays bare his purposes of providence in the incarnation of his Son.

T. H. L. Parker

Bibliography. "Providence" in *HERE, HDB,* and *Sacramentum Mundi* V, 130–33; J. Calvin, *Institutes* 1.16–18; H. Heppe, *Reformed Dogmatics;* K. Barth, *Church Dogmatics,* III/3, 48; G. C. Berkouwer, *The Providence of God;* W. Eichrodt, *Theology of the OT,* II, ch. 17.

Prudence. *See* Cardinal Virtues, Seven.

Psychology and Christianity. Psychology has always been with us. Throughout history man has reflected on his thoughts and behavior and has attempted to make sense out of these. However, as a distinct discipline psychology has only existed since the last half of the nineteenth century. Since then it has quickly grown to a position of considerable importance and visibility. Some have viewed it as having moved beyond the realm of science to social philosophy. Others go beyond this to describe it as the secular religion of our age. Because of this, Christians have become much more conscious of psychology and the critical question of the relationship of this discipline to Christianity. In order to understand the present tensions and areas of cooperation, the historical development of this relationship should first be examined.

The Pre-1900 Era. Long before psychology developed as a separate discipline from philosophy, Christianity was actively involved in the study, development, and understanding of psychology. Such work is to be found in the theological study of the soul, an important topic in theology since earliest times. Tertullian's third century *De anima* is one good example of this. The works of Gregory of Nyssa in the fourth century continued this early emphasis. Since the word "soul" stems from the Greek *psychē*, from which we also get the word "psychology," this tradition of the study of the soul must be understood as evidence of Christianity's concern with the topics of psychology long before the emergence of psychology as a unique discipline.

This concern continued within Christian theology. The abundant Puritan writings on the soul added much of value to an understanding of psychological topics. The works of John Flavel in the seventeenth century and of Jonathan Edwards in the eighteenth made particularly strong contributions, worthy of the careful study of any modern Christian interested in psychology.

Franz Delitzsch's *A System of Biblical Psychology* might represent the capstone of this tradition. Written in 1855, this work presented a summary and systemization of all the theological works on psychology written to that point. In many ways, however, it represented the last major theological work on psychology. This is reflected even in the treatment given to psychological topics in Bible dictionaries and encyclopedias. Prior to 1920 such works characteristically contained large and sometimes extensive entries on psychology and related topics. James Orr's *International Standard Bible Encyclopedia* (1915) and *The New Schaff-Herzog Encyclopaedia of Religious Knowledge* (1911) are good examples of this. In contrast to this, many modern works such as *The New Bible Dictionary* (1962) and the *Wycliffe Bible Encyclopedia* (1975) do not contain such articles.

1900 to the Present. The end of the first era was not as abrupt as the somewhat artificial designation of these eras suggests. It was, however, clearly tied to the emergence of psychology as a separate discipline and, in particular, its scientific emphasis. Empiricism, determinism, relativism, and reductionism became the major characteristics of modern psychology, and Christians felt immediately alienated from the discipline. Freud's reductionistic views of religion were particularly offensive and threatening. Added to this was the rise of radical behaviorism as led by John B. Watson and later B. F. Skinner. Psychology seemed less and less relevant to theology, and the fruitful interaction of Christians with psychological topics that characterized previous centuries came to a rather abrupt halt.

The reasons that the Christian community gave up its pursuit of a biblically informed psychology are complex. One component was certainly an overreaction to psychology, particularly to Freud. Such a reaction failed to discriminate between Freud's personal religious views (agnostic but not amoral) and his significant clinical discoveries. However, this overreaction was influenced by the reaction of conservative Christians to theological liberalism. Liberal theology tended to accept the findings of modern science, including psychology. In reaction to this, conservative Christians turned away from their previous openness to psychological matters to a defensive posture.

Modern psychology's critique of religion did not end with Freud. In fact it quickly became rather commonplace for psychologists to view religion with at best suspicion and at worst overt hostility. Albert Ellis is a contemporary psychologist who gives prominent voice to such a position. Ellis states clearly and forcefully that orthodox or devout religion is usually a cause and always a symptom of psychological disturbance. His proposed solution to psychological problems is to aid people and society in abandoning such irrational and harmful beliefs.

It has been hard for Christians not to respond to such challenges defensively. To many, psychology has seemed the enemy of the faith. Similarly, religion has looked to many psychologists as enemies of personal well-being. Psychology and Christianity are thus related, to these people, as enemies. One Christian who has prominently identified himself with such a view is Jay Adams.

But other forms of relationship between psychology and Christianity have also emerged in this century. One has been associated with the subfield of psychology of religion. Rather than viewing psychology as the enemy, with irreconcilable differences between the two realms, proponents of this position maintain that there is much common ground between the two. Working from humanistic and often mystical assumptions, they see humans as spiritual-moral beings who cannot be reduced to a collection of naturalistic forces. Psychological insights can aid in spiritual development, and similarly spiritual insights can aid in developing psychological understandings and in promoting psychological growth. Christians whose writings have often reflected this position include Seward Hiltner and John Sanford. Proponents of such a view have been influential in breaking down much of the mistrust of Christians toward psychology. However, because they have tended to come from theologically liberal religious traditions, many conservative Christians have remained unconvinced.

The impact of Christians within this group has been impressive. Hiltner coined the concept of pastoral counseling in 1948, and he and other clergy (including Wayne Oates, Paul Johnson, and Granger Westberg) have continued to give this movement leadership. With the founding of the American Association of Pastoral Counselors and the American Association of Clinical Pastoral Education, clinical training of pastors and chaplains moved ahead aggressively. More and more clergy found themselves serving in hospitals and mental health facilities. One final evidence of this fertile rapprochement of Christians and psychology was the development of a number of scholarly journals devoted to the relationship between the two, including *The Journal of Religion and Health* and *The Journal for the Scientific Study of Religion.*

Closely associated with these developments has been a movement within conservative Protestant Christianity identified by the catch phrase "the integration of psychology and theology." The integrationists have begun with an assumption of the unity of truth. They expect that all knowledge can be interrelated into a single body of truth that will represent a harmonizing of biblical revelation and psychology. In searching for this integrated truth these Christians have held strongly to the ultimate authority of the Scriptures but have not been afraid to face directly the points of tension and apparent conflict. Paul Tournier and Gary Collins are two well-known writers in this tradition. *The Journal of Psychology and Theology* and *The Journal of Psychology and Christianity* contain the writings of many more. Also associated with this position are several organizations. The Christian Association for Psychological Studies is an international group of over a thousand Christian mental health professionals committed to the integration of psychology and theology. Similarly a number of graduate training programs have developed since 1960 with the explicit goal of providing training within the context of the integration of psychology and Christian theology.

Current Status. The last two decades have seen an enormous thawing in the climate of mistrust between Christianity and psychology. Christian pastors, often having received some training in pastoral counseling during seminary, are now much more open to use the services of psychologists (particularly Christian psychologists) and to see that psychological insights can be beneficial to their ministry. Young Christian psychologists now have the option of training in a Christian context that explicitly addresses the integration of psychology and theology and usually includes some formal study of theology. All of this has resulted in an upsurge of publications on the relationship between Christianity and psychology.

This new form of relationship has not been without tension. It is still often easy to forget the differences in meaning attributed to the same words by theologians and psychologists (e.g., guilt) and to see the two positions as contradictory and perhaps mutually incompatible. Nor should all tension be eliminated. Christians should be prepared to speak forcibly against some of the things non-Christian psychologists are advocating. Similarly, psychologists have some critical things that need to be said about aspects of our Christian traditions. Trust will allow this to happen even if tension in the relationship is not eliminated. D. G. Benner

See also Psychology of Religion.

Bibliography. R. K. Bufford, *The Human Reflex: Behavioral Psychology in Biblical Perspective;* J. D. Carter and B. Narramore, *The Integration of Psychology and Theology;* G. R. Collins, *The Rebuilding of Psychology;* C. W. Ellison, "Christianity and Psychology: Contradictory or Complementary?" *JASA* 24: 130–34; M. A. Jeeves, *Psychology and Christianity;* D. G. Jones, *Our Fragile Brains: A Christian Perspective on Brain Research;* J. R. Kantor, *The Scientific Evolution of Psychology,* II; R. L. Koteskey, *Psychology from a Christian Perspective* and *General Psychology for Christian Counselors;* R. E. Larzalere, "The Task Ahead: Six Levels of Integration of Christianity and Psychology," *JPT* 8:3–11; D. G. Myers, *The Human Puzzle: Psychological Research and Christian Belief;* W. E. Oates, *The Psychology of Religion;* R. L. Timpe, "Assumptions and Parameters for Developing Christian Psychological Systems," *JPT* 8:230–39; P. C. Vitz, *Psychology as Religion.*

Psychology of Religion. Religion has provided an important focus for applied psychology in the past century. Currently there is keen interest in the understanding of religious phenomena from the viewpoint of contemporary psychology, i.e., the scientific study of religion from a social science perspective. Such aspects as the origins, the motivations, the expressions, the dynamics, the development, and the effects of religion are popular topics. Broadly defined as the scientific study of faith and/or religion using psychological methods, the psychology of religion is a rich and diverse field that has much to offer individuals concerned with more fully understanding the nature and behavior of man.

The psychology of religion is of particular interest to many Christians in the mental health disciplines. They see it as an opportunity to gather up that part of fact or truth lost in narrow, intradisciplinary pursuits or as a chance to reconcile areas of mutual overlap and concern between psychology and theology. They see this integration as the process of verifying the accuracy of God's truths that are discovered through theology and psychology, relating them, and applying them in one's own life. In other words, integration consists first of the critique and comparison of corresponding psychological and theological facts, and second of commitment to them as truths in one's own faith commitment, a dynamic, evolving, and relational activity.

Researchers and theoreticians in the psychology of religion attempt to read, listen to, and seek to understand the many expressions of both theology and psychology. They attempt to treat both disciplines with mutual respect in order to gain a renewed appreciation of the contributions of each. These individuals ask a number of complex but exciting questions: What does psychology as a science and profession have to do with religious faith commitments and vice versa? What methodologies are appropriate to relate psychological and religious perspectives? How do researchers maintain integrity with their faith and discipline so as to avoid a muddled psychology or a mottled Christianity? In what ways can psychology and religion be related in theory, research, and practice? And finally, how can we best serve persons on their journey toward wholeness and promote their growth and development under the lordship of Jesus Christ?

Definitions. Psychology can be understood as a group of generic efforts to scientifically study human behavior. Religion can be understood in terms of either its functional or substantive definition. The functional definition of religion emphasizes the process wherein humans attempt to answer the enigmas and meaning of life through faith. The substantive definition of religion stresses the product of faith wherein those who gather themselves together around a transpersonal idea are labeled religious. Considerable tension within the field is due to the failure to clarify the manner in which psychology and/or religion is being perceived.

Further, there have been a variety of ways in which psychology and religion have been related, distinguishable by the preposition used to tie the terms together. The psychology "of" religion is defined as either the effort to reduce religion to psychological dynamics or the attempt to more fully understand the significance of these processes for religion. Psychology "through" religion is the reverse of the foregoing, whereby religion or normative analysis of human nature informs the psychological understanding of persons. The psychology "with" religion approach is best understood as an effort to offer psychological and religious interpretation of the same phenomena without engaging in reductionism. Finally, the psychology "for/against" religion perspective is defined as the attempt to use psychology either to authenticate or to invalidate religion. All these approaches are distinguishable in the large literature in the field.

History and Trends. The field can best be understood in terms of three phases: (1) the "psychology of religion" movement, which flourished from 1880 to 1930; (2) the "pastoral psychology" movement, which began in the 1920s and is still strong; and (3) the "psychology and religion" movement, which can be traced back to the 1950s and is still developing.

The first movement was started by psychologists with a strong commitment to the empirical-scientific approach to the study of human behavior and a profound respect for religion as a human and social enterprise. Conversion and religious experience were the most frequently studied topics. Perhaps the most significant work to come out of the movement was William James's *Varieties of Religious Experience.* James epitomizes the attempt to fully understand the significance of psychological processes for religion, and his writings raise issues that ought to be grappled with by Christians committed to the integration of faith and learning. On the other hand, Freud's *The Future of an Illusion,* another highly influential book, represents the other extreme of the movement, or the attempt to reduce religion to psychological dynamics. For a variety of reasons, the movement declined in the late 1920s, and religion became a taboo subject for many psychologists.

The second movement traces its roots to the efforts of Anton Boisen, a minister who suffered from a mental disorder. After a lengthy hospitalization in a psychiatric facility, he regained his mental health and became the first hospital chaplain at a public mental hospital; he eventually established clinical pastoral education, a movement that trains ministers to work with emotionally disturbed individuals. Pastoral psychology has since flourished, with numerous journals and professional societies established, especially since the 1940s. The movement has always had a strong applied thrust (i.e., it is treatment and preventative in its orientation). The insights of mental health professionals have been translated into the language of the laity by pastoral counselors, often to the benefit of the church as well as the individual. Evangelicals have tended to resist the efforts of the clinical pastoral education movement, but parallel developments can be observed.

The final movement can be traced back to the publication of Gordon Allport's *The Individual and His Religion* (1950). Rather than trying to assess the psychological roots of religion or the psychodynamics of religious persons, this approach is more concerned with exploring areas of mutual concern to both theologians and psychologists (e.g., moral development, maturity, dimensions of religiosity, altruism, prejudice). One senses a greater openness to cooperation and cross-disciplinary fertilization in the contemporary movement, as well as greater humility on the part of both psychologists and theologians with reference to their methodologies, orthodoxy, and orthopraxy. Fowler's *Stages of Faith* (1981) and McLemore's *The Scandal of Psychotherapy* (1982) are both examples of excellent attempts by theologically informed and sensitive researchers who are psychologists willing to listen to and seek to understand the expressions of personal faith commitments for both the individual and the community of which he is a part.

Methodology. Psychology has become an enormously sophisticated enterprise methodologically. The scientific study of faith and/or religion, consequently, has shown considerable development from the early efforts of William James. Generally, research efforts have stressed empirical research strategies, although the very nature of religious experience, some argue, necessitates unique, person-oriented methods. Techniques of data collection have been varied, but foremost among these have been the use of questionnaires, interviews, analysis of biographical material, the use of introspection, direct observation, psychological testing, experimental manipulation, participant-observer study, and longitudinal or cross-sectional analysis of attitudes and/or behavior. Examination of any collection of research in mental health and religious behavior will show the many applications of these strategies and methodologies in attempting to more fully understand the nature and behavior of man.

Orientations to Religion. People differ widely in the way they think about religion, the importance they place on it, and the reasons they state for being religious. Consequently, researchers are vitally interested in the effects that religious attitudes have on such nonreligious issues as prejudice. Gordon Allport, for example, was very concerned with the evidence that had accumulated that religious persons were more prejudiced than nonreligious persons. In seeking to understand this issue, he proposed that there are two types of religious persons—those who *use* religion (the extrinsic) and those who *live* religion (the intrinsic). This distinction between types of personal religious orientation undergirds much of the research in the psychology of religion. Numerous scales have been developed to assess religious orientation. Researchers argue that it is not enough to state that someone is religious unless one attempts to clarify the precise manner in which an individual incorporates or introjects those beliefs. Suffice it to say that religion is far more complex than any simple twofold typology, but only by extending our current knowledge about spiritual well-being can we hope to understand better the nature of the abundant life which the Good Shepherd offers to his flock.

Psychodynamics and Religion. How does one's emotionality interact with one's religious faith commitment, and vice versa? What kinds of persons are religious? How do persons differ with respect to personalities, traits, and underlying attitudes in light of their religious commitments? These are the kinds of questions researchers grapple with in respect to psychodynamics and faith, perhaps the most fertile area of investigation in the psychology of religion.

A. E. Bergin, for example, completed an exhaustive study on religiosity and mental health which reviews an extensive empirical (data-based) literature on the topic and concludes that religiosity is a complex phenomenon having numerous correlates and consequences which defy simple interpretation. Of the available studies he reviewed, he found no support for the preconception that religiousness is necessarily correlated with psychopathology, but only slightly positive correlations with measures of mental health. What is necessary in the research, argues Bergin, is better specification of concepts and methods of measuring religiosity, a multidimensional phenomenon having both positive and negative aspects that can be mixed together, thereby leading to generally unimpressive findings.

P. F. Barkman has written about the way in which personality traits influence the unique way in which a person experiences his religion. Some of us conceive of Christianity more readily and easily in words and in verbally mediated concepts such as theologies, which are essentially verbal. For others, Christianity is best conceived of as an experience, as a whole system of feelings and emotionally meaningful behaviors. Still others measure faith and experience in observable behavior, or primarily in a social-relational manner. Finally, some think Christianity can best be understood in its transcendental aspects, specifically in the liturgy of the church and the life of the mystic. Certainly it seems plausible that one's emotional makeup is reflected in one's approach to faith.

Finally, conversion has been extensively studied since the beginnings of the psychology of religion movement. A recent work by two evangelical psychologists (Johnson and Malony, 1982) is an example of the sophisticated work being done today by theologically informed and psychologically sensitive researchers. The model they propose to understand the conversion process merits serious attention.

Religious Experience. How does one decide if what he is experiencing is religious? Is there such a thing as a special religious sense? How does one understand being religious? These are the kinds of questions that researchers ask in reference to religious experience.

Mysticism has always been of a keen interest to researchers in the psychology of religion. These altered states of consciousness have been described by religiously oriented individuals for centuries, but only recently have they been carefully investigated under more controlled situations.

Besides mysticism, religious faith healing, glossolalia, contemplative prayer, fasting, and assorted "charismatic" behaviors have all been carefully researched. Two evangelical journals regularly carry research on these and related topics in the psychology of religion: *The Journal of Psychology and Theology* and *The Journal of Psychology and Christianity.*

Religious Development. A final theme in the psychology of religion has been the function of faith throughout the lifespan. Elkind has written extensively on the origins of religion in the child, Oraker on the religiosity of adolescents, Feldman on changes and stability of religious orientations in college, and Clippinger on adult religious behavior. But perhaps the most significant recent proposal on faith development has been J. Fowler's *Stages of Faith* (1981), a six-stage model of the development of faith throughout the lifespan.

Fowler has a holistic view of humanity which attempts to bring together the significant writings of Erikson, Piaget, and Kolhberg (all major developmental theorists), along with significant theological writings, in order to describe more fully the human quest for meaning.

An emerging theme in the developmental literature is the nature of mature religion, and those factors that facilitate its development or retard its realization. Self-acceptance, acceptance of others, a high level of moral development, a well-defined faith commitment, a strong social conscience, effective interpersonal relationships, commitment to support group, an effective balance emotionally and rationally, the ability to give and to receive feedback, clearly defined goals, a commitment to self-actualization/sanctification, the ability to enjoy recreation, and the desire to live life fully each moment are some of the many qualities that have been discussed in the literature.

Conclusion. Religion is more than mere psychological dynamics. Yet the behavioral sciences provide us with many insights into the multifaceted nature of faith. Although there are tensions between theology and psychology, we must continue to search for ways in which the two might fit together.

In dialoguing with one another, psychologists and theologians must be careful not to collapse either discipline into the other. Each discipline has its unique task and should respect the boundaries of the other's domain. At the same time, there is an interesting and intimate relationship between the task of saving and healing souls and the task of rescuing minds, psyches, and personalities from the grip of despair. This is indeed appropriate, because the church should be concerned with the whole person.

The psychology of religion, then, attempts to bring into the scientific study of religion and/or faith a mutual respect for the insights of both theology and psychology in order to more fully understand the nature and behavior of man.

R. E. Butman

See also Psychology and Christianity.

Bibliography. G. W. Allport and J. M. Ross, "Personal Religious Orientation and Prejudice," *JPSP* 5: 432–43; P. F. Barkman, "The Relationship of Personality Modes to Religious Experience and Behavior," *JASA* 20:27–30; C. D. Batson and W. L. Ventis, *The Religious Experience;* B. Beit-Hallahmi, "Psychology of Religion 1880–1930," *JHBS* 10:84–90; A. T. Boisen, *The Exploration of the Inner World;* J. D. Carter, "Maturity: Psychological and Biblical," *JPT* 2:89–96; J. D. Carter and B. Narramore, *The Interpretation of Psychology and Theology;* W. H. Clark, *The Psychology of Religion;* J. A. Clippinger, "Towards a Human Psychology of Personality," *JRH* 12:241–58; J. Dittes, "Psychology of Religion," in *Handbook of Social Psychology,* ed. G. Lindzey and E. Aronson; W. Donaldson, ed., *Research in Mental Health and Religious Behavior;* D. Elkind, "The Origins of Religion in the Child," *RRR* 12:35–42; K. Farnsworth, *Integrating Psychology and Theology* and "The Conduct of Integration," *JPT* 10: 308–19; K. A. Feldman, "Changes and Stability of Religious Orientations During College," *RRR* 11:40–60; C. B. Johnson and H. N. Malony, *Christian Conversion: Biblical and Psychological Perspectives;* H. N. Malony, ed., *Current Perspectives in the Psychology of Religion;* J. Oraker, *Almost Grown;* O. Strunk, *Mature Religion;* J. R. Tisdale, *Growing Edges in the Psychology of Religion.*

Punishment. Throughout the Bible it is insisted that sin is to be punished. In an ultimate sense God will see that this is done, but temporarily the obligation is laid upon those in authority to see that wrongdoers are punished.The *lex talionis* of Exod. 21:23–25 is not the expression of a vindictive spirit. Rather it assures an even justice (the rich and the poor are to be treated alike) and a penalty proportionate to the crime.

Two important points emerge from OT usage. The verb used in the sense of "punish" is *pāqad,* which means "visit." For God to come into contact with sin is for him to punish it. Of the nouns used, most are simply the words for sin. Sin necessarily and inevitably involves punishment.

In the NT "punishment" is not as common as "condemnation," which may be significant. To be condemned is sufficient. Punishment is implied. The removal of punishment is brought about by the atoning death of our Lord. It is not said in so many words that Jesus bore punishment, unless bearing our sins (Heb. 9:28; I Pet. 2:24) be held to mean this. But that his sufferings were penal seems clearly to be the NT teaching.

L. Morris

See also Eternal Punishment; Criminal Law and Punishment in Bible Times.

Bibliography. C. Brown, *NIDNTT,* III, 98ff., H. Buis, *The Doctrine of Eternal Punishment;* L. Boettner, *Immortality;* H. E. Guilleband, *The Righteous Judge: A Study of the Biblical Doctrine of Everlasting Punishment;* J. Schneider, *TDNT,* III, 814ff.

Punishment, Everlasting. *See* Eternal Punishment.

Purgative Way, The. The purgative way or *via purgativa* refers to the teaching embodied in the classic Christian mystical tradition, especially John of the Cross and Teresa of Ávila, that before one can receive the vision of God one must first purify oneself from all sin and spiritual hindrances. This purification begins with the removal of all outward sin and sensuality (i.e. contrition, sorrow for sin, confession, and amendment of life, according to Luther) and spirals inward through a series of "dark nights" as layer after layer of deeper sins are discovered and confessed. While the classic form of this teaching is found in the monastic and mystical literature, ideas in Protestant literature such as abandonment (*Gelassenheit*), self-emptying, and brokenness either express or presuppose such a process as basic to the fullest experience of redeemed life. P. H. DAVIDS

See also ILLUMINATIVE WAY, THE; UNITIVE WAY, THE.

Bibliography. John of the Cross, *Ascent of Mount Carmel* and *Dark Night of the Soul;* M. Luther, *Theologia Germanica;* W. Nee, *Release of the Spirit;* C. Williams, *Descent of the Dove.*

Purgatory. The teachings of the Roman Catholic and Greek Orthodox churches set forth a place of temporal punishment in the intermediate realm known as purgatory, in which it is held that all those who die at peace with the church but who are not perfect must undergo penal and purifying suffering. Only those believers who have attained a state of Christian perfection are said to go immediately to heaven. All unbaptized adults and those who after baptism have committed mortal sin go immediately to hell. The great mass of partially sanctified Christians dying in fellowship with the church but nevertheless encumbered with some degree of sin go to purgatory where, for a longer or shorter time, they suffer until all sin is purged away, after which they are translated to heaven.

The sufferings vary greatly in intensity and duration, being proportioned in general to the guilt and impurity or impenitence of the sufferer. They are described as being in some cases comparatively mild, lasting perhaps only a few hours, while in other cases little if anything short of the torments of hell itself and lasting for thousands of years. But in any event they are to terminate with the last judgment. Gifts or services rendered to the church, prayers by the priests, and Masses provided by relatives or friends in behalf of the deceased can shorten, alleviate, or eliminate the sojourn of the soul in purgatory.

Protestantism rejects the doctrine since the evidence on which it is based is found not in the Bible but in the Apocrypha (II Macc. 12:39–45). L. BOETTNER

See also INTERMEDIATE STATE; LIMBO.

Bibliography. A. J. Mason, *Purgatory;* E. H. Plumptre, *The Spirits in Prison;* H. W. Luckock, *After Death;* B. Bartmann, *Purgatory;* H. Berkhof, *Well-Founded Hope.*

Purification. Israel, chosen by a holy Jehovah to be his people, was required to be holy (Lev. 11:44–45; 19:2; 21:26). Under the Mosaic legislation the holiness of Israel was from the first recognized as moral separation from sin (Lev. 20:22–26), but it was expressed outwardly by separation from objects designated unclean. Uncleanness contracted through contact with such objects required cleansing. Unclean utensils and clothing were washed in running water; but if a porous earthenware vessel became unclean, it had to be destroyed (Lev. 15:12). Metal was sometimes purified by passing it through fire (Num. 31:32–33).

Israelites who had contracted uncleanness had to separate themselves from the congregation, the length of time depending on the nature of the uncleanness (e.g., Num. 5:2–3; Lev. 12; 15:11–13). They were to wash themselves in water, and for the more serious forms of uncleanness they were required to offer sacrifice (e.g., Lev. 12:6). For persons unclean through leprosy (Lev. 14) or through touching a corpse (Num. 19) more elaborate cleansing by sprinkling with water mingled with blood or ashes was required in addition. The unclean Israelite who would not purify himself was executed (Num. 19:19).

As revelation progressed, the concept of holiness deepened. Ps. 51:7 and Ezek. 36:25 both use terms drawn from the purification ritual to describe the cleansing of the heart from sin. In the NT, though ritual purification is referred to (e.g., Luke 2:22; Acts 21:24), our Lord abolished the uncleanness of certain foods (Mark 7:19; cf. Acts 10:15) and Paul affirmed that this abolition extended to every object formerly designated unclean (Rom. 14:14, 20; Titus 1:15; I Tim. 4:4). The NT writers confine purification to cleansing from sin through the blood of Christ (I John 1:7; Heb. 1:3; 9:14) and interpret OT ritual as foreshadowing this cleansing (Heb. 9:13–14, 23). D. B. KNOX

See also CLEANNESS, UNCLEANNESS.

Puritanism. A loosely organized reform movement originating during the English Reformation of the sixteenth century. The name came from efforts to "purify" the Church of England by those who felt that the Reformation had not yet been completed. Eventually the Puritans went on to attempt purification of the self and of society as well.

History. The theological roots of Puritanism may be found in continental Reformed theology, in a native dissenting tradition stretching back to John Wycliffe and the Lollards, but especially in the theological labors of first-generation English reformers. From William Tyndale (d. 1536) the Puritans took an intense commitment to Scripture and a theology which emphasized the concept of covenant; from John Knox they absorbed a dedication to thorough reform in church and state; and from John Hooper (d. 1555) they received a determined conviction that Scripture should regulate ecclesiastical structure and personal behavior alike.

Puritans achieved a measure of public acceptance in the early years of Queen Elizabeth's reign. They then suffered a series of reverses that lasted through the reigns of her successors James I and Charles I. In the days of James I some Puritans grew discouraged about their reforming efforts and separated entirely from the Church of England. These Separates included the "Pilgrims," who after a sojourn in Holland established in 1620 the Plymouth Colony in what is now southeastern Massachusetts.

When Charles I attempted to rule England without Parliament and its many Puritan members, and when he tried systematically to root Puritans out of the English church, a larger, less separatistic body emigrated to Massachusetts Bay (1630), where for the first time Puritans had the opportunity to construct churches and a society reflecting their grasp of the word of God. In England other Puritans continued the struggle for reform. When war with Scotland forced Charles I to recall Parliament in 1640, civil war was the ultimate result. That conflict ended with the execution of the king (1649), the rise of Oliver Cromwell to the protectorate of England, the production of the Westminster Confession and Catechisms, and the erection of a Puritan Commonwealth. Yet Cromwell, for all his abilities, found it impossible to establish a Puritan state. After his death (1658), the people of England asked the son of Charles I to return, a restoration marking the collapse of organized Puritanism in England. Across the Atlantic a vital Puritanism survived only a little longer. By the time of Cotton Mather (d. 1728) Indian warfare, the loss of the original Massachusetts charter, and a growing secularization had brought an end to Puritanism as a way of life in America.

Convictions. Puritanism generally extended the thought of the English Reformation, with distinctive emphases on four convictions: (1) that personal salvation was entirely from God, (2) that the Bible provided the indispensable guide to life, (3) that the church should reflect the express teaching of Scripture, and (4) that society was one unified whole.

The Puritans believed that humankind was utterly dependent upon God for salvation. With their predecessors in England and with Luther and Calvin they believed that reconciliation with God came as a gift of his grace received by faith. They were Augustinians who regarded humans as sinners, unwilling and unable to meet the demands, or to enjoy the fellowship, of a righteous God apart from God's gracious initiative. But Puritans also made distinctive contributions to the general Reformed idea of salvation. They advocated a "plain style" of preaching, as exemplified in the masterful sermons of John Dod (1555–1645) and William Perkins (1558–1602), which was consciously designed to point out simply the broad way of destruction and the strait gate to heaven. They also placed a new emphasis on the process of conversion. In the journals and diaries of leaders like Thomas Shepard (1605–49) they charted the slow, and often painful, process by which God brought them from rebellion to obedience. They also spoke of salvation in terms of "covenant." In the notes to the Geneva Bible, the translation of proto-Puritans completed during the reign of Mary Tudor, emphasis was on a personal covenant of grace, whereby God both promised life to those who exercised faith in Christ and graciously provided that faith, on the basis of Christ's sacrificial death, to the elect. Later Puritans expanded the idea of covenant to take in the organization of churches, seen most clearly in the rise of Congregationalism (or Independency) and the structuring of all society under God, of which the "Holy Commonwealths" of Massachusetts and Connecticut were the major examples.

With the early English Reformers the Puritans believed, second, in the supreme authority of the Bible. The use of Scripture, however, soon came to be a great cause of offense between Puritans and their Anglican opponents and among Puritans themselves. Puritans, Anglicans, and the many in between all believed in the Bible's final authority. But Puritans came to argue that Christians should do only what the Bible commanded. Anglicans contended rather that Christians should not do what the Bible prohibited. The difference was subtle but profound. Among Puritans considerable differences eventually appeared over what Scripture demanded, especially in questions relating to the church. Some (mostly in England) contended for a presbyterian state-church organization, others (in Massachusetts and Connecticut) supported a congregational organization in league with the state, while still others (English Independents and Baptists as well as Roger Williams in New England) believed that the Bible mandated congregational churches separate from the state. In short, Puritans disagreed with Anglicans about the way to interpret the Bible, but they differed among themselves about which biblical interpretations were best. The former disagreement dominated English religious life so long as the king and his episcopalian allies were in control. The latter came to the fore after the success of the Puritan Revolution, and it led to the disintegration of Puritanism in England.

These disagreements should not hide the Puritans' overriding commitment to the authority of Scripture. They made as serious an attempt as has ever been made in the English-speaking world to establish their lives on the basis of biblical instruction. When Puritan efforts to reform the kingdom of England faltered in the last years of Elizabeth's reign, they turned to the one sphere they could still control, their individual families. It was during this period around 1600 that Puritans began to place new emphasis on the sabbath, to revive family worship, and to encourage personal acts of mercy to the sick and dying. When Puritan prospects brightened in the 1640s, this "spiritualization of the household" emerged into the open.

Puritans believed, third, that the church should be organized from Scripture. Anglicans contended that episcopacy, since it was tried and tested by time and did not violate any command of Scripture, was a godly and appropriate way of organizing the church. Puritans responded that the defenders of episcopacy missed the point, for they neglected to follow the positive teachings of the Bible. Puritans argued that Scripture laid down specific rules for constructing and governing churches. Furthermore, the Bible taught a system of church order that was not based on bishops. Puritans maintained this conviction even when they failed among themselves to agree on what that biblical system was. But even these disagreements were fruitful, for they grounded the modern polity of Presbyterians, Congregationalists, and Baptists as well.

The reason that Puritan beliefs concerning salvation, Scripture, and the church created such upheaval was their fourth basic conviction, that God had sanctioned the solidarity of society. Most Puritans believed that a single, coordinated set of authorities should govern life in society. The result was that Puritans sought nothing less than to make all England Puritan. Only late during the Puritan Commonwealth did ideas of toleration and of what is known today as pluralism arise, but these ideas were combated by most Puritans themselves and firmly set to rest for another generation by the restoration of Charles II.

From a modern vantage point the intolerance entailed by a unified view of society has harmed the Puritans' reputation. From a more disinterested perspective it is possible also to see great advantages. The Puritans succeeded in bursting the bonds of mere religiosity in their efforts to serve God. Puritanism was one of the moving forces in the rise of the English Parliament in the early seventeenth century. For good and for ill, it provided a foundation for the first great political revolution in modern times. It gave immigrants to Massachusetts a social vision whose comprehensively Christian character has never been matched in America. And, for such a putatively uncreative movement, it liberated vast energies in literature as well.

Notable Puritans. The Puritans enjoyed a great number of forceful preachers and teachers. The learned Dr. William Ames explained "the doctrine of living to God" in *The Marrow of Theology*, a book used as a text during the first fifty years of Harvard College. The sermons and tracts of William Perkins outlined with sympathy the steps that a repentant sinner should take to find God. John Preston preached the severity of God's law and the wideness of his mercy fearlessly in the courts of James I and Charles I. John Owen, adviser to Cromwell and vice-chancellor of the University of Oxford, wrote theological treatises on the atonement and on the Holy Spirit which still influence Calvinistic thought in the English-speaking world. His contemporary, Richard Baxter, published nearly two hundred works expounding the virtues of theological moderation and the truths of what C. S. Lewis in the twentieth century would call "mere Christianity." In America, Boston's John Cotton labored to present God's glory in conversion, and Hartford's Thomas Hooker glorified God in the labors of the converted. The Westminster Confession and Catechisms which Puritan divines wrote at the request of Parliament (1643–47) remain a guide to Reformed theology, especially in Presbyterian circles, to this day. Together, the works of the Puritans comprise Protestantism's most extensive library of sacred and practical theology.

Important as the contributions of ministers were, the greatest contribution of Puritans to Christian history probably resided with its laymen. The English-speaking world has never seen such a cluster of thoroughly Christian political leaders as the Lord Protector Oliver Cromwell, the governor of Massachusetts John Winthrop, or the governor of Plymouth William Bradford.

These leaders erred, perhaps often, but they yet devoted their lives to public service, self-consciously and whole-heartedly, out of deepest gratitude to the God of their salvation.

We also glimpse the genius of Puritanism when we look beyond its politicians to its writers. It is all too easy to forget that John Milton, who in *Paradise Lost* dared "assert Eternal Providence/And justify the ways of God to men," had earlier defended the execution of Charles I and served as Cromwell's Latin (or corresponding) secretary. John Bunyan served in Cromwell's army and preached as a layman during the Commonwealth before he was jailed in Bedford for his Puritan beliefs, where he redeemed the time by writing *The Pilgrim's Progress.* In America, Puritanism produced a woman poet of note in Anne Bradstreet (1616–72). It also gave us the poems of Edward Taylor (1645–1729), a retiring country minister. Taylor's meditations, composed to prepare his own heart for quarterly celebrations of the Lord's Supper, are among the finest poems ever written by an American.

Evaluation. The Puritans resemble other groups in Christian history who, in forsaking all for God, have won back not only God but much of the world as well. They stand with the early Franciscans, the Protestant Reformers, the Jesuits, the Anabaptists, the early Methodists, and the Reformed Dutch of the late nineteenth century who, in their own separate ways, were transfixed by the glories of redemption and who went far in redeeming the world around themselves. With these groups the Puritans also verified the truth of the gospel words: they sought first the kingdom of God and his righteousness, and much more was added to them besides.

M. A. Noll

Bibliography. E. H. Emerson, ed., *English Puritanism from John Hooper to John Milton;* D. Neal, *The History of the Puritans;* W. Haller, *The Rise of Puritanism;* P. Collinson, *The Elizabethan Puritan Movement;* C. Hill, *Society and Puritanism in Pre-Revolutionary England;* R. S. Paul, *The Lord Protector: Religion and Politics in the Life of Oliver Cromwell;* R. Baxter, *Reliquiae Baxterianae;* P. Miller and T. Johnson, eds., *The Puritans;* F. J. Bremer, *The Puritan Experiment;* P. Miller, *The New England Mind;* S. Bercovitch, *The Puritan Origins of the American Self;* E. S. Morgan, *The Puritan Family* and *The Puritan Dilemma: The Story of John Winthrop;* W. Bradford, *Of Plymouth Plantation.*

Purpose. The English word "purpose" is the translation for a wide variety of Greek and Hebrew words used in the Scriptures. Frequently only the context gives a clue as to the purposeful element in the word (e.g., *'āmar* in I Kings 5:5 and II Chr. 28:10). The word may refer primarily to a goal set up by choice or conceived of as desirable (Dan. 6:17; Prov. 20:18; Acts 27:43; II Tim. 3:10); or it may refer to the mental act of will by which this goal is chosen or decreed (Dan. 1:8; Jer. 4:28; Lam. 2:8).

The purposes of God are eternal (Eph. 3:11), unchanging (Jer. 4:28), and certain of accomplishment (Isa. 14:24). Salvation is the chief concern (Rom. 8:28–30), characterized by grace and centered in Christ (II Tim. 1:9).

K. S. Kantzer

Pusey, Edward Bouverie (1800–1882). Leader of the Tractarian movement in the Church of England. After the epitome of an English gentleman's education at Eton and Christ Church, Oxford, he became a fellow of Oriel College. He spent two years as one of the first English theological students in Germany after the Napoleonic Wars, and returned home as an accomplished Semitic scholar soon to become Regius Professor of Hebrew. Although he had learned much in Germany, reflection on continental liberal theology led him to commit himself to its opposition.

His initial opposition to liberalism was expressed by his active involvement in the Tractarian movement from its inception in 1833. With Keble and Newman he sought to counter liberalism by a charismatic emphasis which stressed that bishops in apostolic succession—which they claimed Anglican bishops to be—possessed the power and authority of the original apostles. The gift of apostleship was alive and well in the church, and had only to be recognized for the Church of England to become like an army with banners. When Newman and others, sensing the hostility to their program in much of the Church of England, entered the Roman Catholic Church in 1845, Pusey was the acknowledged leader of the remaining Tractarians, who were often called Puseyites.

Pusey's conservatism was further evidenced by his espousal of verbal inspiration, clearly evidenced in his famous commentaries on Daniel and the Minor Prophets. He remained the leader of Tractarianism until his death, and then the most formative influence upon it through his disciple H. P. Liddon, until the more liberal Tractarianism led by Charles Gore came to the center of the stage in *Lux Mundi.* Pusey bequeathed the movement a model of one who embodied personal piety, biblical conservatism, a theology with a strong emphasis on the atonement, the value of ritual, and belief in the indispensability of the historic episcopate.

I. S. Rennie

See also Oxford Movement; Keble, John; Newman, John Henry.

Bibliography. H. P. Liddon, *The Life of E. B. Pusey,* 4 vols.

Qq

Quakers. *See* FRIENDS, SOCIETY OF.

Quenstedt, Johann Andreas (1617–1688). German Lutheran theologian who represents the outlook known as Protestant scholasticism or "high orthodoxy." A nephew of the renowned Johann Gerhard, he was born in Quedlinburg and attended the University of Helmstedt before becoming a professor in the arts faculty at the University of Wittenberg. In addition to teaching he studied theology at Wittenberg, receiving the doctorate in 1650. A quiet, kindly person, he was extremely popular, serving as rector of the university for four terms, as provost of All Saints' Church, and in 1687 as senior professor in the School of Theology.

His outstanding contribution was the massive *Theologia didactica-polemica* (1685), which has been recognized as the major compendium of Lutheran theology in the age of orthodoxy. This work was the result of over thirty years of teaching and study, and displays a broad mastery of seventy-five years of Lutheran theological reflection and writing. A tightly structured volume, it is divided into four major parts. The first section treats theology, the Bible, God, and everlasting life. Section two discusses man made in the image of God, sin, and free will. Section three explains God's goodness, predestination, Christology, redemption, conversion, justification, repentance and confession, union with Christ, and the new life. The last section explains the means of salvation, including the Word of God, the sacraments, faith, good works, suffering, prayer, the ministry, civil government, marriage, and the church. Each chapter contains a didactic section that formulates theses in a positive manner to support the position and a polemic section that refutes objections to the doctrine presented.

In an age of theological polemics and rigid orthodoxy Quenstedt was an individual characterized by warm piety, kindness toward others that extended even to those dismissed as heretics, and great ethical concern. R. G. CLOUSE

See also LUTHERAN TRADITION, THE; SCHOLASTICISM, PROTESTANT.

Bibliography. R. G. Clouse, *The Church in the Age of Orthodoxy and the Enlightenment;* B. Hagglund, *History of Theology;* R. D. Preus, *The Theology of Post-Reformation Lutheranism,* 2 vols.

Quicumque Vult. *See* ATHANASIAN CREED.

Quietism. The term has several connotations and is often used in a broad sense to refer to the emphasis on human inactivity and passivity that has accompanied the mystic experience. In a more specific way it refers to a manifestation of Roman Catholic mysticism in the seventeenth and eighteenth centuries. This movement was inspired by the teachings of Miguel de Molinos, a Spanish priest who lived in Italy and published his views in a book entitled *Spiritual Guide.* According to Molinos the goal of Christian experience is the perfect rest of the soul in God. Such a condition is possible when a person abandons himself completely to God and the will is totally passive. Mental prayer rather than any external activity is the means to the state of absolute rest with God. Molinos was accused of despising Christian virtue and of moral aberration because he believed that in a state of contemplation the soul is unaffected by either good works or sin. The Jesuits led the attack on his doctrine, claiming that it was an exaggerated and unhealthy form of mysticism. Through their efforts he was arrested and imprisoned.

Despite the opposition quietism spread to France, where it found an outstanding proponent in Madame Guyon, a woman from an influential family. Forced to abandon her desire to follow a religious vocation and instead to marry, she was constantly seeking a deeper spiritual life. Following the death of her husband she came under the influence of Molinos's thought and by 1680 felt herself so close to God that she received visions and revelations. Traveling widely through France she won many converts, calling them "spiritual children." Her teaching, elaborated in *A Short and Easy Method of Prayer,* emphasized passive prayer as the major Christian activity. Eventually, she felt, the soul will lose all interest in its own fate, and even the truth of the gospel would be insignificant before "the torrent of the forces of God." On a popular level her teaching led to a disregard for the spiritual activities and the sacraments of the church. The result was a belief in a vague pantheism which is closer to the South Asian religions than to Christianity. Bossuet, bishop of Meaux, warned her to stop propagating these ideas, and others considered her mentally unbalanced, but she continued to win followers. She exchanged a series of letters with Fénelon, who admired and defended her ideas. In 1687 Pope Innocent XI condemned quietism, and Guyon along with many of her followers suffered imprisonment and persecution.

R. G. Clouse

See also Guyon, Madame; Mysticism; Spirituality.

Bibliography. P. Hazard, *The European Mind;* R. A. Knox, *Enthusiasm.*

Quimby, Phineas Parkhurst. *See* Church of Christ, Scientist; Eddy, Mary Baker.

Quinquagesima. The period between Easter Sunday and Pentecost. It celebrates the various appearances of the Lord Jesus Christ to his disciples and friends after he rose from the dead. These appearances are part of the fulfillment of his resurrection. The ascension is celebrated as the Lord is reunited with his Father and the Holy Spirit. This part of the calendar year of the church also anticipates the coming of the Holy Spirit to the early community of Christians on Pentecost.

T. J. German

See also Christian Year.

Bibliography. G. Dix, *The Shape of the Liturgy.*

Qumran. *See* Essenes; Dead Sea Scrolls.

Rr

Racovian Catechism (1605). Published in Polish in Racov, Poland, the catechism was prepared by the followers of Faustus Socinus and was one of the earliest statements of antitrinitarian belief to surface since the Arian heresy of the fourth century. Poland was a center for antitrinitarian sects because of the religious toleration enjoyed there at this time by all religious groups. No strong secular or religious power existed to prevent the discussion and dissemination of unorthodox ideas. A few earlier antitrinitarian catechisms had been published in Poland, the most significant appearing in 1574.

The 1605 catechism was divided into eight sections and was intended more as a collection of beliefs than a confessional creed. In the catechism Christ was represented as more than a great man, but not as one who was divine until after his resurrection. The catechism stated that Jesus was conceived by the Holy Spirit and born of a virgin, although the interpretation of Jesus' conception and birth was not in accord with traditional Catholic or Protestant theology because the Holy Spirit was regarded as a quality or aspect of God and not as a person. Salvation was attained by good works, and followers were called to live a moral life. The catechism stated that all divine knowledge came from the Bible; however, adherents believed that it should be explained and interpreted with "right reason." The use of "right reason" meant that no miracle or quality of God should contradict human understanding.

The Racovian Catechism was a forerunner of deism and Unitarianism. Later antitrinitarian movements broke more completely with traditional Christian beliefs than did the Racovian Catechism. For example, the compilers of the catechism were not willing to completely deny Jesus' divinity or special status, as later Unitarians did. Some scholars believe the critical approach to traditional biblical beliefs evident in the catechism also influenced later higher critical approaches to Scripture in the nineteenth and twentieth centuries. P. KUBRICHT

See also SOCINUS, FAUSTUS.

Bibliography. J. H. S. Kent, "The Socinian Tradition," *Theol* 78:131–40.

Radical Reformation. Also known as the Left Wing of the Reformation and the Third Reformation, it includes all reforming elements not identified with the magisterial reformation. Common to all its participants was disappointment with moral aspects of territorial Protestantism and the rejection of some of its doctrines and institutions. While various interlocking historical connections and doctrinal variations limit the validity of typological and ideological classifications, three main groupings of radicals have been identified: Anabaptists, spiritualists, and evangelical rationalists.

Anabaptists. The Anabaptist movement had a varied cast of characters. From it has evolved the Free Church tradition.

From Luther to twentieth century scholar Karl Holl, the opinion prevailed that Anabaptism began with revolutionaries and spiritualizers such as the Zwickau Prophets and Thomas Münzer and reached its logical conclusion with the violent Münsterites. In the 1940s Harold S. Bender inaugurated a new era in American Anabaptist studies. Using primary sources and following up directions indicated earlier by C. A. Cornelius and other Europeans, Bender distinguished between Anabaptists and revolutionaries. He placed Anabaptist origins in the circle of Conrad Grebel, which left Zwingli's reformation when Zwingli compromised its biblical basis. From Zurich the movement was spread by missionaries from Switzerland to Austria and

Moravia, South Germany, and the Low Countries. Bender described the movement as the logical culmination of the reform begun but left unfinished by Luther and Zwingli. Its principal characteristics were discipleship, biblicism, and pacifism. Beginning in the late 1960s scholars challenged and, to a considerable measure, reoriented Bender's findings. They described a pluralistic rather than a homogenous movement with several points of origin and a multiplicity of reforming impulses.

Swiss Anabaptism. Anabaptism in Switzerland developed from Zwingli's early supporters. These future radicals included the Grebel circle, which gathered in the home of Andreas Castelberger for Bible study, and priests from the outlying towns of Zurich. For different reasons the urban and rural radicals became disillusioned with Zwingli's reform. Seeing the Bible as an alternative authority to Rome, the Grebel circle desired Zwingli to proceed rapidly to purify the city's religious establishment of such corruptions as the Mass. When Zwingli allowed the city council to determine the speed of reformation, it seemed to the radicals the substitution of one oppressive authority for another. The radical movement developed social as well as religious dimensions when its members joined forces with rural priests such as Simon Stumpf at Höngg and Wilhelm Reublin at Wittikon, who sought to establish self-governing *Volkskirchen* in the rural communities, independent of Zurich's central authority, both religious and civil. The rebaptisms which occurred first on January 21, 1525, and from which come the name Anabaptism, originally expressed an anticlerical opposition to civil and religious authority outside of the local parish rather than a Free Church theological concept.

Ultimately the attempts to become a mass movement failed and there emerged the idea of the church of the separated, persecuted, and defenseless minority. The Schleitheim Articles of 1527, edited by Michael Sattler, consolidated this Swiss Anabaptism. Its goal was not the purification of existing Christianity, as it was for the early Zurich radicals, but rather the separation of congregations of believers from the world. Thus at Schleitheim first emerged the idea of a "free church." These Swiss Brethren came to be known for their legalistic approach to the Bible, a salvation manifesting itself in the creation of separated congregations, and baptism which symbolized that salvation and made the baptizand a member of the congregation.

South German Anabaptism. In spite of the mutual practice of adult baptism, Anabaptism in South Germany was a quite different movement from the Swiss Brethren. South German Anabaptism stems from the reformulation of ideas from Thomas Münzer by Hans Hut and Hans Denck (*ca.* 1500–1527). Reflecting a medieval, mystical outlook, Münzer envisioned the inner transformation of persons through the Spirit and an accompanying external transformation of the entire society, with the newly transformed individuals acting in revolutionary fashion to usher in the kingdom of God. This revolution, along with Münzer, died in the May 1525 massacre of peasants at Frankenhausen.

Hans Denck's concept of inner transformation was pacifist in expression, with focus more on the renewal of individuals than of society. This inner, transforming Christ served Denck as an alternative authority both to the Roman hierarchy and to the learned exegesis of the Reformers. Positing the inner Christ as ultimate authority made Denck less than absolute in his approach to adult baptism and the written word, both positions which brought upon him the criticism of the Swiss Brethren.

Hans Hut understood the inner transformation to be accomplished through the experience of both inner and outer struggle and suffering. Hut modified Münzer's revolutionary outlook, commanding the transformed believers to keep the revolutionary sword sheathed until God called for it. Unlike the Swiss Brethren, Hut's practice of rebaptism was not to form separated congregations, but rather to mark the elect for the end-time judgment. Hut's movement gradually died out following his death in a jail fire.

A Hut legacy continued through several metamorphoses. One form developed in Moravia, out of the conflict in the congregation at Nikolsburg between the pacifist *Stäbler* (staff bearers), influenced by Hut and Swiss Brethren refugees, and the *Schwertler* (sword bearers), the majority party under the influence of Balthasar Hubmaier, who had established a state church form of Anabaptism in the city. Forced to leave Nikolsburg in 1529, the *Stäbler* pooled their few possessions as a survival necessity. This community of goods, which became the movement's trademark, soon received a theological justification, making it a social expression of the inner mystical transformation of believers envisioned by Hut. Following the dispute-filled early years Jacob Hutter's strong leadership from 1533 to 1536 consolidated this Anabaptist form. His name still identifies the Hutterites in the twentieth century.

Another form of the Hut legacy developed in South Germany around Pilgram Marpeck. Although he left his native Tyrol after adopting Anabaptism, and while he was forced further to move several times because of his Anabaptist views, Marpeck's skills as a civil engineer enabled him to live in relative security. Marpeck's view was not widely held and therefore is not normative for Anabaptism; but he did develop a mediating position on the Bible, critical both of the legalist Swiss and of spiritualist views. Rather than the radical social separation of the Swiss Brethren, Marpeck held to a separation of church and state which did not withhold all cooperation by believers.

Low Countries Anabaptism. The third major Anabaptist movement was planted in the Low Countries by Melchior Hofmann (*ca.* 1495–1543). An erstwhile Lutheran preacher in Sweden and Schleswig-Holstein, always zealously interested in eschatological speculation, Hofmann found in the Strasbourg Anabaptists influenced by Hans Denck the ideas which precipitated his break with Luther and enabled him to develop his own form of Anabaptism. Hofmann believed in the near inbreaking of God's kingdom into the world, with divine vengeance upon the wicked. The righteous would participate in this judgment, not as agents of vengeance but as witnesses to the coming peace. Hofmann's baptism served to gather the elect into an end-time congregation to build this new Jerusalem. He died after ten years imprisonment in Strasbourg.

Two lines carried on in transformed fashion the Hofmann legacy. One, the revolutionary Melchiorites, founded the short-lived kingdom of Münster, 1534–35. Under Jan Matthys, baptized as a disciple of Hofmann, and then under Jan van Leiden, who seized power at the death of Matthys, the revolutionary Melchiorites in the city of Münster gave a political and social expression to Hofmann's end-time kingdom. They transformed his idea of divine vengeance so that in Münster the members of the kingdom carried out vengeance upon anyone who opposed them. Following the fall of the city revolutionary Melchioritism died out, although it was carried on for a time by personages such as Jan van Batenburg.

The pacifist line from Hofmann runs through Menno Simons, who left the priesthood in 1536 and whose name twentieth century Mennonites carry. After the fall of Münster, Menno rallied the peaceful Melchiorites as well as the surviving Münsterites disillusioned with violence. Menno replaced Hofmann's near end time with the idea of a time of peace which had already begun with Jesus. Using the aberrant "celestial flesh" Christology of Hofmann which he adopted, Menno developed concepts of the transformation of the individual and of the assembly of a spotless church.

Although beginning from different presuppositions, Menno's positions on transformed individuals and a pure, separated church resembled closely the outlook of the Schleitheim Articles. The heirs of the various Anabaptist groups came to recognize their common emphases on the Bible, adult baptism, pacifism, and sense of separation from the state church and worldly society. They had contacts and discussions and divisions. While they never united into one homogeneous body, some sense of unity developed, as represented by the Concept of Cologne signed in 1591 by fifteen preachers, the first confession of faith accepted simultaneously by Dutch and High and Low German Mennonites.

Spiritualists. Radicals characterized as spiritualizers downplayed significantly or rejected altogether external forms of church and ceremonies, opting instead for inner communion through the Holy Spirit. Thus for example Silesian nobleman Kasper Schwenckfeld held that there had been no correct baptism for a thousand years, and in 1526 he recommended suspension of the observance of the Lord's Supper—the *Stillstand* observed by his followers until 1877—until the question of its proper form could be settled. Sebastian Franck (1499–1542) rejected altogether the idea of an external church. He saw external ceremonies as mere props to support an infant church and which in any case had been taken over by the antichrist immediately after the death of the apostles. Franck held the true church to be invisible, its individuals nurtured by the Spirit but to remain scattered until Christ gathered his own at his second coming. Marpeck combated this individualistic, invisible church as the principal threat to South German Anabaptism.

Evangelical Rationalists. Other radicals, given significant weight to reason alongside the Scriptures, came to reject aspects of traditional theology, principally in Christological and Trinitarian matters. Michael Servetus, burned in Calvin's Geneva for his views, is a noteworthy example of antitrinitarianism. Antitrinitarianism attained institutional form in the pacifistic Polish Brethren, later known as Socinians, and in the Unitarian churches in Lithuania and Transylvania. A remnant of the latter survives into the twentieth century. Other modern Unitarians inherit the intellectual if not the historical legacy of antitrinitarianism. J. D. Weaver

See also Ambrosians; Grebel, Conrad; Mennonites; Menno Simons; Melchiorites; Zwickau Prophets; Hubmaier, Balthasar; Socinus, Faustus; Racovian Catechism.

Bibliography. W. R. Estep, ed., *Anabaptist Beginnings;* E. J. Furcha, ed., *Selected Writings of Hans Denck;* L. Harder, ed., *Grebeliana;* W. Klaassen, ed., *Anabaptism in Outline;* W. Klaassen and W. Klassen, eds., *The Writings of Pilgram Marpeck;* J. C. Wenger, ed., *The Complete Writings of Menno Simons;* G. H. Williams and A. Mergal, eds., *Spiritual and Anabaptist Writers;* J. H. Yoder, ed., *The Legacy of Michael Sattler;* R. S. Armour, *Anabaptist Baptism;* R. H. Bainton, "Left Wing of the Reformation," in *Studies in the Reformation,* 2, and *The Travail of Religious Liberty;* H. S. Bender, *The Anabaptist Vision* and *Conrad Grebel;* T. Bergsten, *Balthasar Hubmaier;* C. J. Dyck, *Introduction to Mennonite History* and (ed.), *A Legacy of Faith;* R. Friedmann, *Hutterite Studies;* H. J. Hillerbrand, ed., *A Bibliography of Anabaptism* and *A Fellowship of Discontent;* W. Klassen, *Covenant and Community;* M. Lienhard, ed., *The Origins and Characteristics of Anabaptism; Mennonite Encyclopedia,* I–IV; J. S. Oyer, *Lutheran Reformers Against Anabaptists;* W. O. Packull, *Mysticism and the Early South German–Austrian Anabaptist Movement;* J. M. Stayer, *Anabaptists and the Sword* and "The Swiss Brethren," *CH* 47:174–95; J. M. Stayer and W. O. Packull, eds., *The Anabaptists and Thomas Münzer;* J. M. Stayer, W. O. Packull, and K. Deppermann, "From Monogenesis to Polygenesis," *MQR* 49:83–121; D. C. Steinmetz, *Reformers in the Wings;* G. H. Williams, *The Radical Reformation.*

Radical Theology. *See* DEATH OF GOD THEOLOGY.

Rahner, Karl (1904–). Twentieth century Roman Catholic theologian and one of the leading thinkers behind the Second Vatican Council.

Rahner was born in Freiburg, Germany. He entered the Jesuit order in 1922 and passed through the mandated years of study and practical experience in various locations. He received his ordination in 1932. Two years later he began studying philosophy at Freiburg, where Martin Heidegger was enthralling the intellectual world. Rahner's dissertation on Thomistic epistemology (later published as *Spirit in the World*) was rejected by Martin Honecker in 1936 for its departure from traditional interpretations of Aquinas. That same year Rahner moved to Innsbruck and finished a dissertation in theology (on the origin of the church from the wounds of Christ) which was accepted. From just before until just after the Second World War Rahner carried out a ministry designed both to maintain the church's integrity in the face of official hostility and to maximize the church's contemporaneity. In 1949 he formally became a member of the theological faculty at Innsbruck. He moved to Munich in 1964 and closed out his university career at Münster from 1967 to 1971, only to return to Munich for an active retirement.

Rahner's early work in philosophy gives a clear view of the principles underlying his theology. He is committed to a form of transcendental Thomism, viz., the thought of Thomas Aquinas combined with insights from Kant, Hegel, Heidegger, and Rahner's most immediate intellectual predecessor, Joseph Maréchal. The essence of this philosophy is that being is discovered, not in external objectivity, but in the subjectivity of a human knower.

According to Rahner every act of knowledge is predicated on an implicit knowledge of being, disclosed in the process of questioning, particularly as the questioner asks for the ground of his own existence. This prethematic being is developed further into the thesis that universal being, and thereby the absolute being of God, stands behind all human knowledge (Rahner's notion of the *Vorgriff*). Thus the human person is, by the nature of his intellect, disposed to the knowledge of God.

The possibility of an ever-present potential to relate to God becomes for Rahner the core of his anthropocentric theology. Human beings are not innately divine, but God has implanted in their very nature the potential to receive grace, the "supernatural existential." In fact, Rahner holds that the ability to hear God (*potentia obedientialis*) is the chief characteristic of a human being. To be human means to carry the seeds of union with God.

This doctrine yields several important results. For one thing it means that we get in touch with God internally through our humanity, not through an external confrontation. Consequently one need not be part of the external Christian church in order to be related to God. This expansion of the redemptive perimeter includes adherents of other religions and even atheists, who are all "anonymous Christians."

Secondly Rahner puts a new face on Christology. He sees Jesus Christ as representing the unique fulfillment of the *potentia obedientialis* within human nature. Thus Rahner attempts to avoid the problem of reconciling the apparent paradox of two natures in Christ; the human nature is inherently open to reception of the divine. Further it enables Rahner to place Christ at the pinnacle of human evolution. It may be observed here that Rahner's humanism is in rather sore need of tempering with respect to the fallenness of humanity and the consequences of sin.

Rahner's published works number into the thousands. It is not possible to detail all of his contributions to theology. He stands out as one of the most thorough and influential theologians of this century.

W. CORDUAN

Bibliography. Rahner, *Foundations of Christian Faith; Hearers of the Word;* with K.-H. Weger, *Our Christian Faith: Answers for the Future; Spirit in the*

World; and *Theological Investigations,* 20 vols.; ed., *Mysterium Salutis,* 3 vols.; ed., *Sacramentum Mundi,* 6 vols.; K. Baker, *A Synopsis of the Transcendental Philosophy of Emerich Coreth and Karl Rahner;* W. Corduan, "Hegel in Rahner: A Study in Philosophical Hermeneutics," *HTR* 71:285–98; J. Donceel, *The Philosophy of Karl Rahner;* G. A. McCool, *The Theology of Karl Rahner;* L. Roberts, *The Achievement of Karl Rahner;* H. Vorgrimmler, *Karl Rahner: His Life, Thought and Works;* K.-H. Weger, *Karl Rahner: An Introduction to His Theology.*

Ramus, Peter (1515–1572). A leading French Protestant philosopher of the Reformation period. He was professor of eloquence and philosophy at the Collège de France from 1551 until his death, and held a prestigious position in French Renaissance scholarship. He had close connections with the kings of France. About 1561 he was converted to Protestantism, and thereafter was active in the French Reformed church. Ramus met his death with other Protestants in the St. Bartholomew's Day Massacre in Paris.

Ramus presented himself as an educational reformer dedicated to saving Christianity from the errors of Aristotelianism and scholasticism. His M.A. thesis was a blast against Aristotle: "Everything that was said by Aristotle is fictitious." To replace Aristotle he offered a simplified reorganization of knowledge through logic. Logic is "the art of discoursing well." The logician first invented arguments and then judged or arranged them into intelligent discourse. Protestants gladly accepted Ramism as an alternative to pagan Aristotle or the Roman Catholic scholastic tradition.

Ramus held that all knowledge must be related to God, and having been created by God, the entire spectrum of knowledge (encyclopedia) was divided into the individual liberal arts. Each liberal art had a particular sphere of knowledge, delineated by a Ramist doctrine known as technometry (*technometria* or *technologia* in Latin). Dialectic is the art of discoursing well, grammar the art of speaking well, and so on. Ramus also applied his ideas to religion in a methodical book, *Commentaries on the Christian Religion* (Latin, 1576). Religion became "the art of living well" and took its place alongside the other liberal arts.

An important ingredient of Ramist philosophy was method. Ramus favored dividing each idea into two parts (the dichotomy), and then each was subdivided into two parts again and again, until an idea had been reduced to its most basic components. Not only were the ideas dichotomized in the text, but Ramus favored the use of dichotomized outline charts that would show the skeleton of the arguments in visual form. Proper teaching with proper method, according to Ramus, led to proper action. He stressed the usefulness of knowledge, and his followers made a point of the practical application of education to life. The Ramist system of method and practicality caught the imagination of sixteenth century Protestants as did few other philosophical ideas.

Ramist theology is recognizable by the methodical way that the subject is divided and subdivided into dichotomies and illustrated by diagrammed charts. Ramus had his greatest influence among sixteenth and seventeenth century English Puritans (William Ames, William Perkins) and in New England at Harvard University. Puritans considered him the great and famous Protestant martyr of France. K. L. Sprunger

See also Scholasticism, Protestant.

Bibliography. W. J. Ong, *Ramus, Method, and the Decay of Dialogue;* P. Miller, *The New England Mind;* K. L. Sprunger, *The Learned Doctor William Ames;* C. Walton, "Ramus and Socrates," *PAPS* 114:119–39; L. W. Gibbs, ed., *William Ames, Technometry.*

Ransom. One of the metaphors employed by the early church to speak of the saving work of Christ. It is found on the lips of Jesus in Mark 10:45/Matt. 20:28, "The Son of man came not to be ministered unto, but to minister and to give his life as a ransom for many." Paul also states that Christ gave himself as a "ransom for all" (I Tim. 2:6). As a metaphor ransom commonly points to a price paid, a transaction made, to obtain the freedom of others. These ideas are supported also by such expressions as "buying" and "price" (I Cor. 6:20) and "redeem" (I Pet. 1:18ff.).

The ideas are rooted in the ancient world where slaves and captured soldiers were given their freedom upon the payment of a price. In the OT ransom is linked again with slaves, but also with varied aspects of the cultures as well as the duties of kinsmen (cf. Ruth 4). Most importantly the idea of ransom (redeem) is also linked with the deliverance out of Egypt (e.g., Deut. 7:8) and the return of the exiles (e.g., Isa. 35:10). In both settings the focus is no longer on the price paid but on the deliverance achieved and the freedom obtained. Now the focus is on the activity of God and his power to set his people free. When the ideas of ransom are linked to the saving activity of God, the idea of price is not present.

When the NT, therefore, speaks of ransom with reference to the work of Christ, the idea is not one of transaction, as though a deal is arranged and a price paid. Rather the focus is on the power (I Cor. 1:18) of the cross to save. In the famous ransom saying of Mark 10:45 Jesus speaks of his coming death as the means of release for many. The contrast is between his own solitary death and the deliverance of the many. In the NT the terms of ransom and purchase, which in other contexts suggest an economic or financial exchange, speak of the consequences or results (cf. I Cor. 7:23). The release is from judgment (Rom. 3:25–26), sin (Eph. 1:7), death (Rom. 8:2).

There is no need, then, to ask the question posed so often in the past: To whom was the ransom paid? It is not possible to consider payment to Satan as though God were obligated to meet Satan's demands or "asking price." And since the texts speak always of the activity of God in Christ, we cannot speak of God paying himself. While the sacrifice of Christ is rooted in the holiness and justice of God, it is not to be seen against the background of law only but more especially of covenant. In Christ, God takes upon himself the freedom, the release from bondage, of his people. He meets the demands of his own being. R. W. LYON

See also REDEEMER, REDEMPTION; ATONEMENT, THEORIES OF THE.

Bibliography. D. Hill, *Greek Words and Hebrew Meanings: Studies in the Semantics of Soteriological Terms;* F. Büchsel, *TDNT,* IV, 340–56; L. Morris, *Apostolic Preaching of the Cross.*

Rapture of the Church. A phrase used by premillennialists to refer to the church being united with Christ at his second coming (from the Lat. *rapio,* "caught up"). The main scriptural passage upon which the teaching is based is I Thess. 4:15–17: "For this we declare to you by the word of the Lord, that we who are alive, who are left until the coming of the Lord, shall not precede those who have fallen asleep. For the Lord himself will descend from heaven with a cry of command, with the archangel's call, and with the sound of the trumpet of God. And the dead in Christ will rise first; then we who are alive, who are left, shall be caught up together with them in the clouds to meet the Lord in the air; and so we shall always be with the Lord."

The major divisions of interpretation of Paul's words center on the relationship of the time of the rapture to the tribulation period which marks the end of the age. Pretribulationists teach that the church will be removed before this seven-year period and the revelation of the antichrist. A second group, the midtribulationists, contend that the church will be raptured during the tribulation after the antichrist's rise to power but before the severe judgments that prepare the way for Christ's return to establish his rule on earth. Another approach to the problem is that of the posttribulationists, who believe that the church will continue to exist in the world throughout the entire tribulation and be removed at the end of the period when Christ returns in power.

Pretribulationism and the Origin of the Rapture Debate. Despite the attempt by dispensationalists to identify all premillennialists with peculiar aspects of their thought such as the pretribulation rapture, it is obvious that throughout most of the history of the church those who taught premillennialism did not have such a detailed interpretation of the end times. Until the early nineteenth century those believers who discussed the rapture believed it would occur in conjunction with the return of Christ at the end of the tribulation period. It was the contribution of John Nelson Darby to eschatology that led many Christians to teach that the return of Christ would be in two stages: one for his saints at the rapture and the other with his saints to control the world at the close of the great tribulation. According to this interpretation of Bible prophecy between these two events the seventieth week predicted by Daniel (9:24–27) would be fulfilled and the antichrist would come to power. With the church removed from the scene, God would resume his dealings with Israel at that time.

Darby's ideas had a wide influence in Britain and the United States. Many evangelicals became pretribulationists through the preaching of the interdenominational evangelists of the nineteenth and twentieth centuries. The *Scofield Reference Bible* and the leading Bible institutes and graduate schools of theology such as Dallas Theological Seminary, Talbot Seminary, and Grace Theological Seminary also contributed to the popularity of this view. During the troubled times of the 1960s there was a revival of the pretribulational view on a popular level through the books of Hal Lindsey and the ministries of preachers and Bible teachers who use the electronic media.

If the influence of Darby is obvious in the work of his successors, it is a more difficult task to determine how he arrived at an understanding of the secret pretribulation rapture. Samuel P. Tregelles, like Darby a member of the Plymouth Brethren movement, charged that the view originated during a charismatic service conducted by Edward Irving in 1832. Other scholars maintain that the new understanding of the rapture was the product of a prophetic vision given to a young Scottish girl, Margaret MacDonald, in 1830. She claimed special insight into the second coming and began to share her views with others.

Her ecstatic conduct and apocalyptic teaching led to a charismatic renewal in Scotland. Impressed by the accounts of a new Pentecost, Darby visited the scene of the revival. According to his own testimony in later years he met Margaret MacDonald, but rejected her claims of a new outpouring of the Spirit. Despite his opposition to MacDonald's general approach some writers believe that he accepted her view of the rapture and worked it into his own system.

Other scholars feel that one must accept Darby's own explanation of how he arrived at his eschatological view. He based it upon an understanding that the church and Israel are distinct entities in Scripture. When the church is withdrawn from the world, then the prophetic events involving Israel can be fulfilled. Antichrist will rise to power by promising peace on earth and will make an agreement to protect the restored state of Israel. However, the Jews will be betrayed by their new benefactor, who will suddenly suspend all traditional religious ceremonies and demand that they worship him. Those who do not cooperate will be persecuted. This final holocaust against God's chosen people will lead them to accept Christ as their savior. Plagues will ravage the earth during this time of tribulation, and finally the battle of Armageddon will result in the visible, personal, victorious return to earth of Christ and his saints. The Lord will then bind Satan for a thousand years and rule the world with his followers for a millennium. According to pretribulation premillennialists all the prophecies which were supposed to be fulfilled when Christ came the first time will come to pass at his second coming. The Jewish rejection of Christ in the first century forced the postponement of the kingdom until the second coming. The view that was taken of the church and its place in prophecy is crucial to the acceptance of the pretribulational rapture and the system it supports.

Another argument given in favor of the pretribulation rapture is that the restraining influence of the Holy Spirit must be removed before the antichrist can be revealed (II Thess. 2:6–8). Because the Spirit is particularly associated with the church, it follows that the church must be absent from the scene when the Spirit is gone. Among the other reasons that seem to support pretribulationism is the imminence of the rapture. If it can occur at any time, then no tribulation signs such as the revelation of the antichrist, the battle of Armageddon, or the abomination in the temple precede the "blessed event."

The Midtribulation View. One of the leaders in presenting a different view of the rapture was Harold John Ockenga, a leader in the evangelical movement that developed in the United States after World War II. In a brief personal testimony in *Christian Life* (Feb., 1955) he cited many difficulties associated with pretribulationism. These included the secret aspect of the rapture, the revival to be experienced during the tribulation despite the removal of the Holy Spirit, and the reduction in the importance of the church involved in dispensational eschatology. Other evangelical leaders joined in the criticism of the pretribulation position. The modifications they advocated were slight, involving the limitation of the wrath of God upon the world (Rev. 16–18) to the first three and a half years prior to the battle of Armageddon. Influenced by the repeated mention of three and a half years (forty-two months) in Dan. 7, 9, and 12 and in Rev. 11 and 12, they argued for a shortened tribulation period. To support this argument they cited Dan. 7:25 which indicated that the church will be under the tyrannical rule of the antichrist for three and a half years. Dan. 9:27 also indicates that the world ruler of the end times will make an agreement with Christians and Jews guaranteeing religious freedom, but then he will carry out the second stage of his plan and suppress religious observances. Various NT passages were also believed to support midtribulationism, including Rev. 12:14, which predicts a flight into the wilderness by the church during the first three and a half years of the tribulation period. Also, midtribulationists believed that their view fits into the Olivet discourse (Matt. 24; Mark 13; and Luke 12) better than the pretribulation interpretation.

Midtribulationists claim that the rapture is to take place after the fulfillment of certain predicted signs and the preliminary phase of the tribulation as described in Matt. 24:10–27. The event will not be secret but will be accompanied by an impressive display including a great shout and the blast of the trumpet (I Thess. 4:16; Rev. 11:15; 14:2). This dramatic sign will attract the attention of unsaved people, and when they realize that the Christians have disappeared they will come to Christ in such large numbers that a major revival will take place (Rev. 7:9, 14).

The Posttribulation View. Many other interpreters were uncomfortable with the sharp distinction that the pretribulationists drew between the church and Israel. Christ, they believed, would return to rapture his saints and establish his millennial rule at the same time. They cited numerous passages (Matt. 24:27, 29) which indicate that Christ's second coming must be visible, public, and following the tribulation. This was based upon the fact that much of the advice given to the church in Scripture relative to the last days is meaningless if it does not go through

E022

the tribulation. For example, the church is told to flee to the mountains when certain events occur, such as the setting up of the abomination of desolation in the holy place (Matt. 24:15–20).

Many of the arguments suggested by those who advocate the posttribulation view are stated in opposition to the pretribulation position, which has been the most widely held interpretation among twentieth century American premillennialists. Included in these criticisms are suggestions that the imminent return of Christ does not require a pretribulation rapture. Posttribulationists also point to the difficulty of deciding which passages of Scripture apply to Israel and which are relevant to the church. They also contend that there is a notable lack of explicit teaching about the rapture in the NT.

Advocates of the posttribulation position differ among themselves on the application of the prophetic Scriptures and the details about the return of Christ. John Walvoord has detected four schools of interpretation among their number. The first of these, classic posttribulationism, is represented by the work of J. Barton Payne, who taught that the church has always been in tribulation and therefore the great tribulation has largely been fulfilled. The second main division of posttribulationists is the semiclassic position found in the work of Alexander Reese. Among the variety of views held by these individuals the most common is that the entire course of church history is an era of tribulation, but in addition there is to be a future period of great tribulation. A third category of posttribulational interpretation is called futurist and is ably presented in the books of George E. Ladd. He accepts a future period of three and a half or seven years of tribulation between the present era and the second coming of Christ. He was led to this conclusion by a literal interpretation of Rev. 8–18. A staunch premillennialist, he believes that the pretribulation rapture was an addition to Scripture and as such obscured the truly important event, the actual appearance of Christ to inaugurate his reign. A fourth view is that of Robert H. Gundry, which Walvoord calls the dispensational posttribulational interpretation. Gundry combines in a novel manner the pretribulational arguments and an acceptance of the posttribulation rapture.

The Partial Rapture Interpretation. In addition to the pretribulation, midtribulation, and posttribulation views of the rapture there have been those who contend for a partial rapture theory. This small group of pretribulationists teaches that only those who are faithful in the church will be caught up at the beginning of the tribulation. The rest will be raptured sometime during or at the end of the seven-year period. According to these interpreters those who are most loyal to Christ will be taken first and the more worldly will be raptured later. Although it is condemned by most premillennialists, the respected G. H. Lang advocated this view.

Conclusion. The interpretation of the rapture has introduced a divisive element into evangelicalism. On the surface it would seem that this is a struggle over a very minor point, but on deeper reflection it is a rather basic argument. The pretribulation rapture is one of the major doctrines of dispensationalists, and leads them to adopt a miraculous view of social ethics as well as a negative attitude toward society. Those who hold this view have a narrow outlook toward the church and its mission, culture and education, and current events. Their version of Christ against culture has imparted to twentieth century evangelicals a spirit of withdrawal and of suspicion toward others. R. G. Clouse

See also Second Coming of Christ; Eschatology; Dispensation, Dispensationalism; Millennium, Views of the; Darby, John Nelson.

Bibliography. O. T. Allis, *Prophecy and the Church;* R. Anderson, *The Coming Prince;* E. S. English, *Re-Thinking the Rapture;* R. H. Gundry, *The Church and the Tribulation;* G. E. Ladd, *The Blessed Hope;* D. MacPherson, *The Incredible Cover-Up;* P. Mauro, *The Seventy Weeks and the Great Tribulation;* J. B. Payne, *The Imminent Appearing of Christ;* J. D. Pentecost, *Things to Come;* A. Reese, *The Approaching Advent of Christ;* J. F. Strombeck, *First the Rapture;* J. F. Walvoord, *The Rapture Question;* L. J. Wood, *Is the Rapture Next?*

Rationalism. Philosophical rationalism encompasses several strands of thought, all of which usually share the conviction that reality is actually rational in nature and that making the proper deductions is essential to achieving knowledge. Such deductive logic and the use of mathematical processes provide the chief methodological tools. Thus, rationalism has often been held in contrast to empiricism.

Earlier forms of rationalism are found in Greek philosophy, most notably in Plato, who held that the proper use of reasoning and mathematics was preferable to the methodology of natural science. The latter is not only in error on many occasions, but empiricism can only observe facts in this changing world. By deductive reason, Plato believed that one could extract the innate knowledge which is present at birth, derived from the realm of forms.

However, rationalism is more often associated with Enlightenment philosophers such as Descartes, Spinoza, and Leibniz. It is this form of continental rationalism that is the chief concern of this article.

Innate Ideas. Descartes enumerated different types of ideas, such as those which are derived from experience, those which are drawn from reason itself, and those which are innate and thus created in the mind by God. This latter group was a mainstay of rationalistic thought.

Innate ideas are those that are the very attributes of the human mind, inborn by God. As such these "pure" ideas are known *a priori* by all humans, and are thus believed by all. So crucial were they for rationalists that it was usually held that these ideas were the prerequisite for learning additional facts. Descartes believed that, without innate ideas, no other data could be known.

The empiricists attacked the rationalists at this point, arguing that the content of the so-called innate ideas was actually learned through one's experience, though perhaps largely unreflected upon by the person. Thus we learn vast amounts of knowledge through our family, education, and society which comes very early in life and cannot be counted as innate.

One rationalistic response to this empirical contention was to point out that there were many concepts widely used in science and mathematics that could not be discovered by experience alone. The rationalists, therefore, concluded that empiricism could not stand alone, but required large amounts of truth to be accepted by the proper use of reason.

Epistemology. Rationalists had much to say about knowledge and how one might gain certainty. Although this query was answered somewhat differently, most rationalists eventually got back to the assertion that God was the ultimate guarantee of knowledge.

Perhaps the best example of this conclusion is found in the philosophy of Descartes. Beginning with the reality of doubt he determined to accept nothing of which he could not be certain. However, at least one reality could be deduced from this doubt: *he* was doubting and must therefore exist. In the words of his famous dictum, "I think, therefore I am."

From the realization that he doubted, Descartes concluded that he was a dependent, finite being. He then proceeded to the existence of God via forms of the ontological and cosmological arguments. In Meditations III–IV of his *Meditations on First Philosophy* Descartes argued that his idea of God as infinite and independent is a clear and distinct argument for God's existence.

In fact, Descartes concluded that the human mind was not capable of knowing anything more certainly than God's existence. A finite being was not capable of explaining the presence of the idea of an infinite God apart from his necessary existence.

Next Descartes concluded that since God was perfect, he could not deceive finite beings. Additionally Descartes's own facilities for judging the world around him were given him by God and hence would not be misleading. The result was that whatever he could deduce by clear and distinct thinking (such as that found in mathematics) concerning the world and others must therefore be true. Thus the necessary existence of God both makes knowledge possible and guarantees truth concerning those facts that can be clearly delineated. Beginning with the reality of doubt Descartes proceeded to his own existence, to God, and to the physical world.

Spinoza also taught that the universe operated according to rational principles, that the proper use of reason revealed these truths, and that God was the ultimate guarantee of knowledge. However, he rejected Cartesian dualism in favor of monism (referred to by some as pantheism), in that there was only one substance, termed God or nature. Worship was expressed rationally, in accordance with the nature of reality. Of the many attributes of substance thought and extension were the most crucial.

Spinoza utilized geometrical methodology to deduce epistemological truths which could be held as factual. By limiting much of knowledge to self-evident truths revealed by mathematics, he thereby constructed one of the best examples of rationalistic system-building in the history of philosophy.

Leibniz set forth his concept of reality in his major work *Monadology*. In contrast to the materialistic concept of atoms, monads are unique metaphysical units of force that are not affected by external criteria. Although each monad develops individually, they are interrelated through a logical "preestablished harmony," involving a hierarchy of monads arranged by and culminating in God, the Monad of monads.

For Leibniz a number of arguments revealed the existence of God, who was established as the being responsible for the ordering of the monads into a rational universe which was "the best of all possible worlds." God also was the basis for knowledge, and this accounts for the epistemological relationship between thought and reality. Leibniz thus returned to a concept of a transcendent God much closer to the position held by Descartes and in contrast to Spinoza, although neither he nor Spinoza began with the subjective self, as did Descartes.

Thus rationalistic epistemology was characterized both by a deductive process of argumentation, with special attention being given to mathematical methodology, and by the anchoring of all knowledge in the nature of God. Spinoza's system of Euclidean geometry claimed demonstration of God or nature as the one substance of reality. Some scholars of the Cartesian persuasion moved to the position of occasionalism, whereby mental and physical events correspond to each other (as the perceived noise of a tree falling corresponds with the actual occurrence), as they are both ordained by God. Leibniz utilized a rigorous application of calculus to deductively derive the infinite collection of monads which culminate in God.

This rationalistic methodology, and the stress on mathematics in particular, was an important influence on the rise of modern science during this period. Galileo held some essentially related ideas, especially in his concept of nature as being mathematically organized and perceived as such through reason.

Biblical Criticism. Of the many areas in which the influence of rationalistic thought was felt, higher criticism of the Scriptures is certainly one that is relevant to the study of contemporary theological trends. Spinoza not only rejected the inerrancy and propositional nature of special revelation in the Scriptures, but he was also a forerunner of both David Hume and some of the English deists who rejected miracles. Spinoza held that miracles, if defined as events which break the laws of nature, do not occur.

A number of trends in English deism reflect the influence of, and similarities to, continental rationalism as well as British empiricism. Besides the acceptance of innate knowledge available to all men and the deducing of propositions from such general knowledge, deists such as Matthew Tindal, Anthony Collins, and Thomas Woolston attempted to dismiss miracles and fulfilled prophecy as evidences for special revelation. In fact deism as a whole was largely characterized as an attempt to find a natural religion apart from special revelation. Many of these trends had marked effects on contemporary higher criticism.

Evaluation. Although rationalism was quite influential in many ways, it was also strongly criticized by scholars who noticed a number of weak points.

First, Locke, Hume, and the empiricists never tired of attacking the concept of innate ideas. They asserted that young children gave little, if any, indication of any crucial amount of innate knowledge. Rather the empiricists were quick to point to sense experience as the chief schoolteacher, even in infancy.

Second, empiricists also asserted that reason could not be the only (or even the primary) means of achieving knowledge when so much is gathered by the senses. While it is true that much knowledge may not be reducible to sense experience, this also does not indicate that reason is the chief means of knowing.

Third, it has frequently been pointed out that reason alone leads to too many contradictions, metaphysical and otherwise. For example, Descartes's dualism, Spinoza's monism, and Leibniz's monadology have all been declared as being absolutely knowable, in the name of rationalism. If one or more of these options is incorrect, what about the remainder of the system(s)?

Fourth, rebuttals to rationalistic and deistic higher criticism appeared quickly from the pens of such able scholars as John Locke, Thomas Sherlock, Joseph Butler, and William Paley. Special revelation and miracles were especially defended against attack. Butler's *Analogy of Religion* in particular was so devastating that many have concluded that it is not only one of the strongest apologetics for the Christian faith, but that it was the chief reason for the demise of deism.

G. R. Habermas

See also Enlightenment, The; Deism; Descartes, René; Spinoza, Benedict de; Leibniz, Gottfried Wilhelm.

Bibliography. R. Descartes, *Discourse on Method;* P. Gay, *Deism: An Anthology;* G. Leibniz, *Monadology;* B. Spinoza, *Ethics* and *Tractatus Theologico-Politicus;* C. L. Becker, *The Heavenly City of the Eighteenth-Century Philosophers;* J. Bronowski and B. Mazlish, *The Western Intellectual Tradition: From Leonardo to Hegel;* F. Copleston, *A History of Philosophy,* IV; W. T. Jones, *A History of Western Philosophy,* III; B. Williams, *Encyclopedia of Philosophy,* VII.

Rauschenbusch, Walter (1861–1918). American clergyman and social reformer. "Father of the social gospel," he was born in Rochester, New York, where his father was a professor in the German Department of Rochester's Baptist Theological Seminary. Rauschenbusch lived in Rochester most of the rest of his life, except for one lengthy period which gave him the experiences that altered the course of Protestantism in the United States. In 1886 he became pastor of New York City's largely immigrant Second German Baptist Church, which was located on the lower East Side in an area aptly called Hell's Kitchen. What Rauschenbusch saw there of the immigrants' sordid living conditions, of labor exploitation by industrial giants, and of governmental indifference to the suffering of the poor led him to rethink his religious categories, to begin a fresh study of the Bible, and to explore the views of social critics like socialist Henry George and urban planner Jacob Riis.

When Rauschenbusch returned to Rochester in 1897 as a professor at the seminary, he did not forget his New York experience. His first book, *Christianity and the Social Crisis* (1907), was his response to America's social crisis. It was an immediate sensation. The book recalled the great social concerns of OT prophets and the powerful social effects of the NT church. It called for a faith that applied Christian beliefs to practical social ethics.

In subsequent books Rauschenbusch fleshed out the contours of a social gospel. *Christianizing the Social Order* (1912) contained his most sustained criticism of American capitalism which, according to Rauschenbusch, blinded its practitioners to human needs in a drive for profit, tyrannized over the weak and defenseless, and fostered values through mass marketing that debased the spirit. In the place of capitalism, he called for a social order characterized by justice, collective ownership of most property, democracy in the organization of industry, and a much more equal distribution of goods. Rauschenbusch frequently called himself a Christian socialist, but he also took pains to disavow Marxist formulas for reconstructing American economic life.

Rauschenbusch's last major work appeared shortly before his death, *A Theology for the Social Gospel* (1917). It set out systematically a Christian theology to address the needs of modern society. It was somewhat less optimistic than earlier books about the possibilities for human improvement. Yet Rauschenbusch had never underestimated the reality or permanence of evil. The volume also warned of how dangerous mere social movements could be if they lost the backing of Christian theology. Throughout his work Rauschenbusch stressed the theme of the kingdom of God. He admitted that his conception of the kingdom represented an effort to Christianize Darwinistic evolution, but he also maintained that progress for the kingdom could never take place without the presence of Christ and the work of the Holy Spirit.

Rauschenbusch had no room in his theology for the substitutionary atonement, a literal hell, or a literal second coming. He also encouraged a nearly utopian sense of human potential. And he accepted many of the conclusions of biblical higher criticism. Yet he retained a firm commitment to OT ideals of justice, to the power of Christ as the means for changing society, and to the conviction that evil was not a passing fantasy.

Rauschenbusch lived before the fundamentalist-modernist clashes of the 1920s sharpened lines of combat between evangelical and liberal theology. In his day he was known as an "evangelical liberal" who combined elements of orthodoxy with convictions of the modern age. His reputation as the leader of the *social* gospel has blinded both liberals and evangelicals to how much orthodoxy remained in his social *gospel.* He was undoubtedly the most influential American Christian thinker in the first third of the twentieth century. M. A. NOLL

See also SOCIAL GOSPEL, THE; LIBERALISM, THEOLOGICAL.

Bibliography. R. T. Handy, ed., *The Social Gospel in America, 1870–1920;* B. Y. Landis, ed., *A Rauschenbusch Reader;* D. R. Sharpe, *Walter Rauschenbusch;* C. H. Hopkins, *The Rise of the Social Gospel in American Protestantism, 1865–1915.*

Reader. *See* MINOR ORDERS.

Realism. The theory of knowledge that maintains that "universals" (general concepts representing the common elements belonging to individuals of the same genus or species) have a separate existence apart from individual objects. It stands in contrast to nominalism, which held that universals had no reality apart from their existence in the thought of an individual. Plato's insistence that there is a realm of universals above the material universe as real as individual objects themselves had a great influence on medieval thought.

Anselm's form of realism led him to the belief that by giving proper attention to universal concepts one could prove the truths of theology. He accepted revealed truth, but was convinced that one should exercise reason in apprehending the truth. For example, he was convinced that by "necessary reasons" he could demonstrate the existence of God. Because God is the greatest of beings, Anselm reasoned in his *Proslogion,* he must exist in reality as well as in thought, for if he existed in thought only, a greater being could be conceived of. Thus from consideration of an ideal or universal Anselm believed that he could derive truth about what actually exists.

Augustine had modified Plato's realism by holding that universals existed before the material universe in God's creative mind. This viewpoint was expanded by twelfth century ultrarealists, such as Duns Scotus, Odo of Tournai, and William of Champeaux (in his early years), to posit that the logical and real orders are exactly parallel. By proposing that universals come before individuals, the ultrarealists maintained that the reality of individuals came from the universal. Thus humanity as a universal preceded individual men. In this fashion they explained theological concepts such as transmission of original sin in the human race and the oneness of the Trinity: God comes first; Father, Son and Holy Spirit share together in God.

Thomas Aquinas in his *Summa Theologica* amended this ultrarealist position by developing Aristotle's doctrine that universals have a being only in material objects. According to Aquinas we cannot assert that universals exist wholly apart from individual objects inasmuch as we know of them only through sensory impressions of individual objects. Thus universals are abstracted from the knowledge rooted in individual things. This "moderate realism" stressed that human reason could not totally grasp God's being. One could profitably use reason, then, to determine universals, and one could use reason in theology whenever it was concerned with the connection between universals and individual objects.

Realism had a great effect on the "natural theology" of medieval scholasticism. It affected both the method of demonstration and the shape of the theological dogmas which resulted. One notes its influence to a lesser extent after the Reformation in both Roman Catholic Neo-Thomist circles and among Protestants who emphasize the "unity" of the human race in the passing on of original sin (e.g., W. G. T. Shedd).

D. A. RAUSCH

See also NOMINALISM; DUNS SCOTUS, JOHN; ANSELM OF CANTERBURY; THOMAS AQUINAS.

Bibliography. D. M. Armstrong, *Universals and Scientific Realism: Nominalism and Realism*, II; F. Copleston, *History of Philosophy*, II; R. Seeberg, *Textbook of the History of Doctrines;* M. deWulf, *History of Medieval Philosophy*, I; W. G. T. Shedd, *Dogmatic Theology;* É. Gilson, *History of Christian Philosophy in the Middle Ages.*

Realism, Scottish. *See* SCOTTISH REALISM.

Realized Eschatology. This concept should be contrasted with futurist or thoroughgoing eschatology, in which the teaching of Jesus about the kingdom of God is viewed as significantly influenced by Jewish apocalyptic. While continental scholarship has focused on the latter, the Anglo-American tradition has often urged that the futurist aspects of the kingdom be reduced to a bare minimum. Some have dismissed this apocalyptic note as an early Christian accretion, but many NT scholars have viewed the apocalyptic language as symbolic of a profound theological reality. Instead, they argue, Jesus viewed his ministry as inaugurating the kingdom: that is, this eschatological reality was realized within Christ's own ministry.

C. H. Dodd is often identified with realized eschatology because of his epoch-making challenge to the apocalytic interpreters of Jesus. Dodd's chief contribution was published in 1935 (*The Parables of the Kingdom*), in which he examined various texts that spoke of the kingdom as already present. This does not mean that Jesus merely pointed to the sovereignty of God in human history and labeled this the kingdom, but rather that Jesus viewed the kingdom as arriving in an unparalleled, decisive way. The eschatological power of God had come into effective operation within his present life and was released through his death. Hence in Luke 11:20 we learn that Jesus himself is revealing this new power: "If it is by the finger of God that I cast out demons, then the kingdom of God has come upon you." Luke 17:20ff. is similar in that Jesus seems to deny the observable signs of apocalyptic: "for behold, the kingdom of God is in the midst of you." Dodd particularly stressed the parables of growth (the weeds among wheat, the mustard seed, the sower; see esp. Matt. 13), which find their meaning in a this-worldly event of decisive importance.

To be sure, this alters the entire scheme of futurist eschatology wherein the kingdom ushers in the end. "The eschaton has moved from the future to the present, from the sphere of expectation into that of realized experience" (*Parables of the Kingdom*, p. 50). For Dodd, this must become a fixed point in interpretation because it is these teachings of Jesus that are explicit and unequivocal. "It represents the ministry of Jesus as 'realized eschatology'; as the impact upon this world of the 'powers of the world to come' in a series of events, unprecedented and unrepeatable, now in actual progress" (*ibid.*, p. 51). Thus when Jesus says, "Blessed are the eyes which see what you see" (Luke 10:23), he is referring to his messianic acts which in themselves are ushering in the eschatological kingdom of God. "It is no longer imminent; it is here" (*ibid.*, p. 49).

It must be said at once that realized eschatology has suffered many criticisms. Scholars have quickly pointed out that Dodd was less than fair in his exegesis of many futurist texts (e.g., Mark 9:1; 13:1ff.; 14:25). Still, in a later response to his critics (*The Coming of Christ*, 1951) Dodd accepted the futurist sayings but reinterpreted them as predictions of a transcendent age. Norman Perrin for one has successfully shown how Judaism employed no such transcendent concept of the kingdom and that Dodd again has misrepresented the text by applying a foreign Greek category to Jesus' Hebrew teaching.

Most interpreters have argued for a synthesis of realized and futurist components in eschatology. Dodd convincingly demonstrated that Jesus' appearance brought to bear on history an eschatological crisis in the present; however, we would add that history still awaits its consummation in the future, when the kingdom will come in apocalyptic power. G. M. Burge

See also Dodd, Charles Harold; Eschatology.

Bibliography. G. E. Ladd, *Crucial Questions About the Kingdom of God;* W. G. Kümmel, *Promise and Fulfillment;* G. Lundström, *The Kingdom of God in the Teaching of Jesus;* N. Perrin, *The Kingdom of God in the Teaching of Jesus;* R. Schnackenburg, *God's Rule and Kingdom.*

Real Presence. The reference in this phrase is to the presence of Christ in the sacrament of Holy Communion. In the more general sense it is not objectionable, for all Christians can agree that Christ is really present by the Holy Spirit when they gather in his name. Theologically, however, the word "real" indicates a particular form or understanding of the presence in terms of realist philosophy. On this view, the so-called substance of Christ's body is a reality apart from its "accidents" or specific physical manifestations. It is this substance which is supposed to be present in or under the accidents of bread and wine, and in replacement of (or, as Luther would say, in conjunction with) their own substance. There is, however, no scriptural basis for this interpretation, and in Reformation theology it is rejected and replaced by a more biblical conception of the presence. G. W. Bromiley

See also Transubstantiation; Concomitance; Lord's Supper, Views of.

Reason. The capacity of the human intellect to carry out organized mental activity such as the association of ideas, induction and deduction of inferences, or value judgments. Biblically, the existence of an efficacious human reason is assumed. For example, in Isa. 1:18 God appeals directly to human reason, and this represents a pattern throughout Scripture. The nature of reason, however, is not explicitly described. Consequently there has been a wide diversity within systematic theology on the capabilities of reason, particularly in comparison with the faculty of faith.

History. Over the history of the church few theologians have espoused pure rationalism, viz., the idea that naked reason can without benefit of faith deduce all Christian truth. In the few instances where this approach may have been used (e.g., Socinianism, deism, Hegelianism), technical heresies were almost invariably the direct consequence.

Guarding against potential abuse of reason has led a significant array of Christian thinkers to disparage reason strongly, often specifically by disparaging the systematic expression of reason in a philosophical system. To cite some examples, Tertullian asked the celebrated question, "What has Athens to do with Jerusalem?" and avowed belief in the absurd. Martin Luther called reason a "harlot" and insisted that the gospel was contrary to reason. Blaise Pascal maintained that faith can never be based on purely rational criteria. Finally Søren Kierkegaard opposed the Hegelian system with an appeal to the individual's need to make a decision not based on logical deductions. But in understanding any of these apparent antirationalists it is necessary to realize that they were not themselves irrational; their writings are coherent and analytical. Rather what they have in common is the strict segregation of reason from religious convictions.

Many noted writers utilizing a Platonic expression of Christian theology have held to the clear precedence of faith over reason. "I believe that I may understand," was the slogan attributed to Augustine of Hippo and adopted by Anselm of Canterbury. Under this theory reason is operative only insofar as it has been placed in subjection to prior Christian faith. Paradoxically, however, it appears that once the initial faith commitment has been made, there are few limits to the powers of reason in this tradition. For example, Anselm has given us the ontological argument for God's existence which, though cast in the form of a prayer, is essentially a deduction of God's being purely from concepts of reason. In *Cur Deus Homo* Anselm goes on to deduce the necessity of the incarnation and the atonement. The contemporary successors to Platonic rationalism in this sense may be found in the thought of such presuppositionalist apologetes as Cornelius Van Til and Gordon Clark.

Thomas Aquinas and his disciples have attempted to maintain a delicately balanced view on reason and faith. Reason is seen here as a viable avenue of Christian knowledge, but it is far from omnicompetent. There are a number of truths open to reason—e.g., the existence of God and his goodness. But reason also finds a closed door on many issues; thus it cannot deduce the Trinity, the incarnation, or the necessity of the atonement. These latter issues are known on the authority of faith. Further, reason does not have exclusive reign over its domain. Any of the items open to it can also be known by faith. In fact, for most people it is undoubtedly true that they know God to exist and to be good by faith alone. Moreover Aquinas countered Siger of Brabant, another Aristotelian, who held to a double-truth theory: that reason, if used properly, must not arrive at conclusions opposed to faith.

Conclusion. Thus we see that there have been a great number of opinions on reason in Christian thought. Despite all of this diversity, however, it is possible to draw up some conclusions which should be generally valid within all of conservative Christian theology.

(1) Human reason is adequate to certain tasks and is presently fulfilling them. This truth applies to both Christians and non-Christians. In all spheres of life, whether the reasoning processes are formalized or not, individuals are attaining certain types of knowledge through their reasoning capacities. Minimal examples here might be the balancing of a checkbook or reading a road map. More elaborately, science and technology may be cited as representative of efficacious reason.

(2) Human reason is finite. There are some tasks that human reason cannot fulfill by virtue of its limitations. Our reason stands in contrast to the divine intellect with its omniscience. The limitation applies not only to the mind of any given individual but to human consciousness seen as a totality as well. Consequently reason by itself can never disclose all Christian truth. To illustrate with a drastic example, it is doubtful whether human reason can ever come to know the process of communication among the persons of the Trinity.

(3) Human reason is affected by our sinfulness. Scripture (Rom. 1:20–23) tells us how sin corrupted human minds. As a consequence humans have turned to idolatry and immorality.

(4) The process of becoming saved involves reason but is not completed by it. The recognition that one is lost and needs to place one's faith in Jesus Christ as the sole source of salvation is a reasonable one. But salvation does not occur until a person then actually exercises his will and believes in Christ. Thus, contrary to a Gnostic scheme, redemption can never be due simply to a mental activity.

(5) One of the goals of the Christian life is the renewing of the mind (Rom. 12:2). Hence as a person grows in Christ, his reasoning becomes increasingly captive to the Spirit of God. As a result the effects of sin on reason are removed, and the person's thinking processes are more closely linked to Jesus Christ both in cognition of divine truth and in moral perception.

W. Corduan

Bibliography. Anselm, *Basic Writings;* G. H. Clark, *Religion, Reason and Revelation;* W. Corduan, *Handmaid to Theology: An Essay in Philosophical Prolegomena;* S. Kierkegaard, *Concluding Unscientific Postscript;* M. Luther, *Lectures on Galatians,* 2 vols.; *Great Shorter Works of Pascal;* J. Pelikan, *From Luther to Kierkegaard;* Tertullian, *Apology;* T. Aquinas, *Summa contra Gentiles,* I; C. Van Til, *A Christian Theory of Knowledge.*

Rebaptism. During the second century, the church in Asia Minor, faced with considerable heresy, refused to recognize the validity of heretical baptism. Converts to the orthodox faith from heretical groups were accordingly rebaptized. The church at Rome, however, took the position that the rite was valid when properly performed, i.e., with the correct formula and with the right intention, despite the erroneous views of its administrator. In North Africa, Tertullian, then Cyprian, would not recognize the baptism of heretics. Cyprian carried on a bitter controversy with Stephen, bishop of Rome, on this issue. An anonymous writing, *De rebaptismate,* set forth the position of the church at Rome. It made a distinction between water baptism and Spirit baptism. When a heretic was admitted to the church by the laying on of hands, the Spirit was conveyed, making further application of water unnecessary. The Roman position was endorsed by the Council of Arles (314) and was championed by Augustine in his controversy with the Donatists. Its advocates could point to the fact that Scripture contained no instance of rebaptism, that the analogous rite of circumcision was not repeatable, and that the questioning of the legitimacy of heretical baptism made the efficacy of the rite depend upon man rather than God. The Council of Trent, in its fourth canon on baptism, reaffirmed the Catholic position.

In Reformation times the Anabaptists insisted on baptism for those who had been baptized in infancy, and this has continued to be the position of the Baptist churches. The Roman Catholic Church and the Church of England practice what is known as conditional baptism in cases where there is doubt as to the validity of prior baptism. The formula used in the Church of England begins, "If thou art not already baptized, I baptize thee."

E. F. Harrison

Bibliography. E. W. Benson, *Cyprian; Blunt;* H. G. Wood in *HERE.*

Recapitulation. The doctrine of recapitulation (Lat. *recapitulatio;* Gr. *anakephalaiosis;* a "summing up") was derived from Eph. 1:10. It is especially associated with Irenaeus, although later authors picked up its themes. There are two principal interpretations of the meaning which Irenaeus gave to recapitulation: (1) Christ retraced the steps of Adam and humanity, an interpretation which accords with Irenaeus's presentation of Christ's career; (2) Christ comprehended or brought to a head in himself the whole of humanity, an interpretation which better accords with the meaning of Eph. 1:10. Irenaeus elaborated the parallels between Adam and Christ. Adam was made of virgin soil, was tempted by Satan, and brought sin and death into the world through disobedience at the tree. Christ was born of the Virgin Mary, resisted temptation by Satan, and overcame sin by obedience to death on the cross. Irenaeus further suggested that Christ passed through all ages of life—infant, child, youth, and old man—in order to sanctify all who are born again to God through him. He became what we are in order to make us what he is. As a result of his life, death, and resurrection all that was lost in Adam is regained in Christ. The human race was given a new start, and saved humanity is gathered together as one in Christ. Christ also summed up and completed in himself the revelation of God. The doctrine of recapitulation was important in the context of the Gnostic controversy because it secured the reality of the incarnation, the unity of mankind, and the certainty of redemption. E. FERGUSON

See also IRENAEUS.

Bibliography. J. Lawson, *The Biblical Theology of Saint Irenaeus;* G. Wingren, *Man and the Incarnation;* J. T. Nielsen, *Adam and Christ in the Theology of Irenaeus of Lyons;* J. N. D. Kelly, *Early Christian Doctrines.*

Reconciliation. A doctrine usually ascribed to Paul, although the idea is present wherever estrangement or enmity is overcome and unity restored: Matt. 5:24ff. (brothers, litigants, perhaps man-to-God); bringing lost sheep to fold, prodigal to father, the lost back to God (Luke 19:10; cf. I Pet. 3:18). Indeed reconciliation is exemplified in Jesus' attitude to sinners—the truth in Athanasius's thought that incarnation *is* reconciliation.

The root idea (in Greek) is change of attitude or relationship. Paul applies it to wife and husband (I Cor. 7:11), to Jews and Gentiles reconciled to each other in being reconciled to God (Eph. 2:14ff.), and to the alienated, divisive elements of a fragmented universe "brought under one head" again in Christ (Eph. 1:10; Col. 1:20). His illustrations include those far off made nigh, strangers made fellow citizens of the household, and dividing walls removed. His testimony to reconciliation's results dwells especially upon peace with God (Rom. 5:1; Eph. 2:14; Col. 1:20); upon "access" to God's presence (Rom. 5:2; Eph. 2:18; 3:12; see Col. 1:22) in place of estrangement; "joy in God" replacing dread of "wrath" (Rom. 5:9, 11); and assurance that "God is for us," not against us (Rom. 8:31ff.).

The Central Concept of Christianity. Since a right relationship with God is the heart of all religion, reconciliation which makes access, welcome, and fellowship possible for all may be held the central concept in Christianity. But to describe this experience with doctrinal precision raises questions. Man being made for fellowship with God, what is the difficulty requiring Christ's intervention? Since reconciliation involves "not imputing trespasses," "Christ made sin for us" (II Cor. 5:18ff.), part of the answer must be sin, which separates God and men. This "alienation" from God and from his people (Eph. 2:12; 4:18) deepens into resentment, "enmity" (Rom. 5:10), increased by carnality hostile to God (Rom. 8:7), expressed in rebellious wickedness: "you . . . estranged . . . hostile in mind, doing evil deeds" (Col. 1:21). This total attitude of man needs to be removed.

If this were all, then revelation of truth, the example of Christ, the demonstration of divine love, would remove misunderstanding, effecting reconciliation. But Rom. 11:28 (contrasting "enemies" with "beloved"), repeated references to divine "judicial" wrath (Rom. 1:18; 5:9; 12:19), and the whole case for divine condemnation (Rom. 1–3) suggest that men are "the objects of *divine* hostility" (Denney); that man's sense of estrangement ("a certain fearful looking-for of judgment") witnesses to a barrier on God's side, precluding fellowship—not, certainly, any reluctance in God's mind, which Jesus must change, but a moral, even judicial, barrier that requires the death of Jesus, not merely his message or example, to remove.

Man the Reconciled. Who, then, is reconciled? Certainly man is changed. "We were reconciled . . . being reconciled . . . we received reconciliation . . . he reconciled us . . . be ye reconciled" consistently apply reconciliation to man. Estrangement gives place to prayer and fellowship, hostility becomes faith, and rebellion becomes obedience. Further, man is reconciled to men (Eph. 2:14ff.); and also to life itself, "to the discipline God appoints and the duty he commands" (Oman): reconciliation breeds contentment. The world, too, is reconciled (II Cor. 5:19) or to be reconciled (Eph. 1:10; Col. 1:20).

But this change in man could be affected without Christ by persuasion, example, or education. Yet in the NT the basis of reconciliation is "the death of his Son," "through the cross," "by the blood of his cross," "in his body of flesh by his death" (Rom. 5:10; Eph. 2:16; Col. 1:20, 22); and its means are "through Christ . . . made to be sin" (II Cor. 5:18, 21). Some therefore hold that "God is reconciled, in the sense that his will to bless us is realised as it was not before. . . . God would not be to us what he is if Christ had not died" (Denney). Man's sin affects God, so as to require from him judgment, withdrawal, correction, creating for God too a barrier to fellowship, a problem to be resolved before God and sinful man can be at one again. ("At-one-ment" once meant reconciliation; now atonement means reparation, satisfaction, the basis of reconciliation.) Whether or not God could ignore the separation wrought by sin and embrace men in fellowship without further ado, he did not: "We were reconciled to God by the death of his Son."

Arguments against any reconciliation of God to men stress the absence of that expression from the NT; deny wrath, judgment, atonement; and expound a subjective, moral influence theory of reconciliation.

God the Reconciler. Then who reconciles? In all other religions man propitiates his gods. Christianity declares "God was in Christ reconciling the world to himself" (II Cor. 5:19), an accomplished fact which men are urged to accept. "We have received the reconciliation" (Rom. 5:11). As Christ is our peace; as we are reconciled by his death; as God put forward Christ in expiatory power (Rom. 3:25); and as the sin that separates is ours, not God's—only God *could* reconcile.

The resulting paradox, that God reconciles those he recognizes up to the moment of reconciliation as enemies, is no greater than in the command "Love your enemies." For love always treats its enemies as no enemies at all.

R. E. O. White

See also Paul, Theology of; Man, Old and New; Propitiation; Atonement.

Bibliography. V. Taylor, *Forgiveness and Reconciliation;* J. S. Stewart, *Man in Christ;* J. Denney, *Christian Doctrine of Reconciliation.*

Rector. *See* Church Officers.

Redeemer, Redemption. Though closely allied to salvation, redemption is more specific, for it denotes the means by which salvation is achieved, namely, by the payment of a ransom. As in the case of salvation it may denote temporal, physical deliverance. In the OT the principal words are *pādâ* and *gā'al,* which are usually rendered by *lytrousthai* in the LXX, occasionally by *rhyesthai.* In the NT *lytrousthai* is the usual verb form, and nouns are *lytrōsis* and *apolytrōsis.* Occasionally *agorazein* is used, or *exagorazein,* denoting the act of purchase in the market, especially the slave market. For "ransom" *lytron* and *antilytron* are used.

In the OT. In ancient Israel both property and life could be redeemed by making the appropriate payment. Since the firstborn were spared in the last plague which God visited upon Egypt, he had a special claim on these, so that the firstborn thereafter had to be redeemed by a money payment (Exod. 13:13–15). According to the Pentateuchal legislation, if a man lost his inheritance through debt or sold himself into slavery, he and his property could be redeemed if one near of kin came forward to provide the redemption price (Lev. 25:25–27, 47–54; cf. Ruth 4:1–12). The kinsman-redeemer was also the avenger of blood on occasion.

God's deliverance of his people from Egypt is spoken of as a redemption (Exod. 6:6; 15:13), and he is Israel's Redeemer (Ps. 78:35). The emphasis here may well be upon the great output of strength needed to accomplish this objective—strength which itself serves as a kind of ransom price. Once again God's people are found in captivity (Babylon), and again the language of redemption is used in connection with their release (Jer. 31:11; 50:33–34). The probable meaning of Isa. 43:3 is that the conqueror of Babylon and therefore the liberator of Judah, even Cyrus, is being promised a domain in Africa as a compensation for giving up captive Judah and restoring it to its inheritance in the land of Canaan.

The individual also is sometimes the object of God's redemption, as in Job 19:25, where the sufferer expresses his confidence in a living Redeemer who will vindicate him eventually, despite all present appearances to the contrary. Prov. 23:10–11 presents the same general cast of thought.

It is rather surprising that redemption is verbally so little associated with sin in the OT. Ps. 130:8 contains the promise that Jehovah will redeem Israel from all its iniquities. Isa. 59:20, which Paul quotes in Rom. 11:26, says much the same thing in more general terms (cf. Isa. 44:22). In Ps. 49:7 the impossibility of self-ransom for one's life is emphasized. It is possible that the scarcity of reference to redemption from sin in the OT is due to the ever-present proclamation of redemption through the sacrificial system, making formal statements along this line somewhat superfluous. Furthermore, redemption from the ills of life, such as the Babylonian captivity, would inevitably carry with it the thought that God redeems from sin, for it was sin which brought on the captivity (Isa. 40:2).

The occurrence of numerous passages in the OT where redemption is stated in terms which do not explicitly include the element of ransom has led some scholars to conclude that redemption came to mean deliverance without any insistence upon a ransom as a condition or basis. The manifestation of the power of God in the deliverance of his people seems at times to be the sole emphasis (Deut. 9:26). But on the other hand there is no hint in the direction of the exclusion of a ransom. The ransom idea may well be an assumed factor which is kept in the background by the very prominence given to the element of power needed for the deliverance.

In the NT. This observation affords the necessary bridge to the NT use of redemption. Certain passages in the Gospels reflect this somewhat vague use of the word as implying divine intervention in behalf of God's people without specific reference to any ransom to be paid (Luke 2:38; 24:21).

Mark 10:45, though it does not contain the word "redeem," is a crucial passage for the subject, because it opens to us the mind of Christ concerning his mission. His life of ministry would terminate in an act of self-sacrifice which would serve as a ransom for the many who needed it. The largest development of the doctrine in the NT comes in the writings of Paul. Christ has redeemed from the curse of the law (Gal. 3:13; 4:5; *exagorazein* in both cases). In the apostle's most concentrated section on the work of Christ he couples redemption with justification and propitiation (Rom. 3:24; cf. I Cor. 1:30). One prominent feature of Paul's usage is the double reference to the word—with a present application to the forgiveness of sins based on the ransom price of the shed blood of Christ (Eph. 1:7; cf. I Pet. 1:18–19), and a future application to the deliverance of the body from its present debility and liability to corruption (Rom. 8:23). This latter event is associated with the day of redemption (Eph. 4:30), not in the sense that redemption will then be operative for the first time, but that the redemption secured by Christ and applied to the soul's forgiveness is then extended to include the body as well, so that salvation is brought to its intended consummation.

Redemption, though it includes the concept of deliverance, is a more precise term. Otherwise it would be expected that biblical writers would make more extensive use of words denoting deliverance *per se,* such as *lyein* or *rhyesthai,* to the neglect of words for redeem. Yet such is not the case. It is significant that Paul can content himself with the use of *rhyesthai* when setting forth the relation of Christ's saving work for us with respect to hostile angelic powers (Col. 1:13), yet when he passes to a contemplation of the forgiveness of our sins he must change his terminology to that of redemption (Col. 1:14).

No word in the Christian vocabulary deserves to be held more precious than Redeemer, for even more than Savior it reminds the child of God that his salvation has been purchased at a great and personal cost, for the Lord has given himself for our sins in order to deliver us from them.

E. F. HARRISON

See also MESSIAH; SALVATION.

Bibliography. L. Morris, *The Apostolic Preaching of the Cross;* J. Schneider and C. Brown, *NIDNTT,* III, 177ff.; O. Procksch *et al., TDNT,* IV, 328ff.; R. J. Banks, ed., *Reconciliation and Hope;* V. Taylor, *Forgiveness and Reconciliation;* B. B. Warfield, *The Plan of Salvation;* J. Murray, *Redemption—Accomplished and Applied;* S. Lyonnet and L. Sabourin, *Sin, Redemption, and Sacrifice.*

Redemption, General. *See* ATONEMENT, EXTENT OF THE.

Redemption, Particular. *See* ATONEMENT, EXTENT OF THE.

Reformation, Protestant. A wide-ranging movement of religious renewal in Europe concentrated in the sixteenth century but anticipated by earlier reform initiatives—e.g., by Waldensians in the Alpine regions, Wycliffe and Lollardy in England, and Hussites in Bohemia. Although inseparable from its historical context—political (the emergent nation-states and the tactical interplay of forces and interests in Imperial Germany and in the loose Swiss Confederation), socioeconomic (particularly urban growth, with expanding trade, the transition to a money economy, and new technologies, notably printing, promoting a new assertive middle class, alongside persistent peasant discontents), and intellectual (chiefly the Renaissance, especially in the Christian humanism of northern Europe)—it was fundamentally religious in motivation and objective.

It was not so much a trail blazed by Luther's lonely comet, trailing other lesser luminaries, as the appearance over two or three decades of a whole constellation of varied color and brightness, Luther no doubt the most sparkling among them, but not all shining solely with his borrowed light. The morning star was Erasmus, for most Reformers were trained humanists, skilled in the ancient languages, grounded in biblical and patristic sources, and enlightened by his pioneer Greek NT of 1516. Although Luther in Wittenberg's new university in rural Saxony had a catalytic effect felt throughout Europe, reform was astir in numerous centers. Probably independent in origin was Zwingli's radical reform in Zurich, provoking the thoroughgoing Anabaptist radicalism of the Swiss Brethren. Strasbourg under Bucer's leadership illustrated a mediating pattern of reform, while Geneva, reformed under Berne's tutelage, had by midcentury become an influential missionary center, exporting Calvinism to France, the Netherlands, Scotland, and elsewhere. Much of Germany and Scandinavia followed Luther's or perhaps Melanchthon's Lutheranism, while England welcomed a welter of continental currents, at first more Lutheran, later more Reformed, to energize indigenous Lollard undercurrents.

Protestant Objections. The Reformers' target may be generally described as degenerate late medieval Catholicism, over against which they set the faith of the apostles and the early fathers. Some central target areas may be specified.

Papal Abuses. There was proliferating abuse, theological and practical, connected with penance, satisfactions, and the treasury of merit. These practices were the basis of indulgences, to which were directed Luther's Ninety-five Theses with their pivotal affirmation that "the true treasure of the Church is the most holy gospel of the glory and grace of God." Luther's anguished quest had taught him the bankruptcy of an exuberant piety that never lacked exercises for the unquiet conscience—vows, fasts, pilgrimages, masses, relics, recitations, rosaries, works, etc. The Reformation answer, to which Luther's new understanding of Romans 1 brought him through many struggles, was justification by God's grace in Christ alone received by faith alone. "The righteousness of God is that righteousness whereby, through grace and sheer mercy, he justifies us by faith." Christ's righteousness credited to the believer gave him assurance before God, while he never ceased to be sinful and penitent, for "the whole life of the Christian is one of penitence." Jesus said "Be penitent" (Greek), not "Do penance" (Latin Vulgate). Luther's theology of the cross was a protest against the "cheap grace" of a commercialized, fiscal religion.

The False Foundations of Papal Authority. Lorenzo Valla's exposure of the forged Donation of Constantine combined with fresh biblical and historical study to undermine papal pretensions. The rock on which the church was built was Peter's *faith,* and in the early centuries the Roman bishop enjoyed no more than a primacy of honor. While most Reformers professed a readiness to accept a reformed papacy that served to edify the church, so resistant did it prove to even moderate reform that Antichrist seemed a deserved designation.

The Ecclesiastical Captivity of the Word of God. Whether by papal *magisterium,* church dogma, or the sophistries of schoolmen, canonists, and allegorists, this was a leading target of Luther's "Reformation Treatises" of 1520. In 1519 he had denied the infallibility of general councils. The Reformers liberated the Bible, by vernacular translation (notably Luther's German Bible), expository preaching (recommenced by Zwingli), and straightforward grammaticohistorical exegesis (best exemplified in Calvin's commentaries). Disputations, often critical in the pacing of reform, operated like communal Bible studies. Thus were the Scriptures enthroned as judge of all ecclesiastical traditions and the sole source of authentic doctrine, as well as experienced as the living power of God in judgment and grace.

The Superiority of the "Religious" Life. The Reformers maintained a tireless polemic against monasticism, one of the most prominent features of Latin Christianity. They rejected the distinction between the inferior life of the secular Christian and the higher "religious" world of monk and nun. The Reformation was a strident protest against this distorted set of values. Luther and Calvin both stressed the Christian dignity of ordinary human callings of artisan, housewife, and plowman. Reformers almost insisted on clerical marriage, by their own example elevating the importance of family life. From another angle they objected to clerical intrusion into civil affairs—e.g., the administration of marriage and divorce—and regarded political office as one of the most significant Christian vocations.

Perverted Priesthood and Usurped Mediation. The mediation of Mary (though not necessarily her perpetual virginity) and the intercession of the saints were denied alike by the Reformers. Christ alone was exalted as man's advocate before God and God's appointed priest to bear our sins and minister to our frailty. By rejecting all but two—baptism and Lord's Supper—of the seven medieval sacraments, the Reformation liberated the faithful from the power of the priesthood. The church lost its indispensable role as sacramental dispenser of salvation. Transubstantiation was refuted, along with the sacrificial character of the Mass except as the response of thankful hearts and lives. In accordance with NT usage all believers were declared to be by baptism a royal priesthood, free to fulfill a priestly service to others in need of the Word of life.

The Hierarchical Captivity of the Church. In response to allegations of innovation and disruption of the church's long-lived unity, the Reformers claimed to be renovators, restorers of the primitive face of the church. Such a church was not dependent on communion with the papacy or hierarchical succession but was constituted by its election and calling in Christ and recognized by faithfulness to the word and sacraments of the gospel. Although several Reformers experienced doubts about infant baptism, and both Luther and Bucer hankered after a closer congregation of the truly committed, in the end all stood by the baptism of infants. A major factor was their fear of dividing the civil community which by common baptism could be regarded as coterminous with the visible church. Although the distinction between the church visible (seen by human eyes) and invisible (known only to God) was used by the Reformers, it was not their customary way of acknowledging the mixed character of the church.

The Confusion of Divine and Human. Reformation theology was strongly theocentric, and clearly reasserted the distinction between Creator and creation. Confusion between the two blighted medieval doctrine in various spheres—Eucharist, church, papacy—and made its influence felt in other areas, such as mysticism and anthropology. With a starkly Augustinian understanding of original sin (qualified somewhat by Zwingli), the Reformers asserted mankind's total spiritual inability apart from the renewal of the Spirit. On unconditional election the Reformation spoke almost as one voice. If Calvin related predestination more closely to providence and directed all his theology to the goal of the glory of God, Luther no less saw God's sovereign Word at work everywhere in his world.

The Legacy of the Reformation. Quite apart from the varying hues and shades of their theologies, which owe much to different intellectual and religious formations as well as to temperament, sociopolitical setting, and conviction, the Reformers were not agreed on all issues. Most notoriously they parted company on the Lord's Supper. For Luther the solid objectivity of Christ's presence was created by his word ("This is my body") and could not be vulnerable to the recipient's unbelief. (His position is wrongly called "consubstantiation," because this implies that it belongs to the same conceptual order as "transubstantiation.") Others, even the mature Zwingli, stressed faith's spiritual eating of Christ's body and blood, and Calvin further focused on communion with the heavenly Christ by the Spirit. In reform of worship and church order both Lutherans and Reformed adopted respectively conservative and more radical approaches. A significant difference lay in attitudes toward the Mosaic law. Whereas for Luther its primary function is to abase the sinner and drive him to the gospel, Calvin saw it chiefly as the guide of the Christian life. Again, while for Luther Scripture spoke everywhere of Christ and the gospel, Calvin handled it in a more disciplined and "modern" manner. Overall, "careful Calvin orchestrated Protestant theology most skillfully, but fertile Martin Luther wrote most of the tunes" (J. I. Packer).

Separate attention must be paid to the orthodox Anabaptist Radicals whose Reformation was more sweeping than the "new papalism," as they called it, of the magisterial Reformers. Believers' baptism identified and safeguarded the bounds of the church, the gathered community of the covenanted band. Discipline was essential to maintain its purity (a point not lost on influential Reformed circles). The church's calling was to suffering and pilgrimage, and to total separation from the world. By its accommodation with the empire of Constantine the church had fatally "fallen." The restitution of the apostolic pattern in all particulars entailed the renunciation of the sword and of oaths. By advocating toleration, religious liberty, and separation of church and state, such Anabaptists were ahead of their time, and suffered for it. As Christendom dies out in the West, the attraction of the Radical Reformation option appears in a clearer light.

At times—e.g., *ca.* 1540 in Germany—it seemed as though reform-minded Catholics might prevail. Rome thought otherwise, and in theology the Catholic reforms of Trent were in large measure counter-Protestant reaction. If renewal was more evident elsewhere, in the new Jesuit order, the Spanish mystics, and bishops like Francis of Sales, not until the twentieth century and Vatican Council II did the Roman Church take to heart the theological significance of the Reformation.

D. F. WRIGHT

See also PROTESTANTISM; COUNTER-REFORMATION; LUTHER, MARTIN.

Bibliography. A. C. Cochrane, *Reformed Confessions of the Sixteenth Century;* B. J. Kidd, *Documents Illustrative of the Continental Reformation;* H. J. Hillerbrand, *The Reformation in Its Own Words;* H. A. Oberman, *Forerunners of the Reformation: The Shape of Late Medieval Thought;* W. Cunningham, *The Reformers and the Theology of the Reformation;* B. M. G. Reardon, *Religious Thought in the Reformation;* H. Strohl, *La pensée de la Réforme;* G. W. Bromiley, *Historical Theology: An Introduction;* H. Cunliffe-Jones, ed., *A History of Christian Doctrine;* S. Ozment, *The Age of Reform, 1250–1550;* H. J. Grimm, *The Reformation Era 1500–1650;* A. G. Dickens, *The English Reformation;* I. B. Cowan, *The Scottish Reformation;* G. H. Williams, *The Radical Reformation;* F. H. Littell, *The Anabaptist View of the Church;* G. F. Hershberger, ed., *The Recovery of the Anabaptist Vision;* P. E. Hughes, *The Theology of the English Reformers;* P. D. L. Avis, *The Church in the Theology of the Reformers.*

Reformed Tradition, The. The term "Reformed" is used to distinguish the Calvinistic from the Lutheran and Anabaptist traditions. The Reformed tradition finds its roots in the theology of Ulrich Zwingli, the first reformer in Zurich, and John

Calvin of Geneva, who in his biblical commentaries, his pamphlets, but especially in the *Institutes of the Christian Religion,* developed a Protestant theology. Calvin's teachings have been followed by many different individuals and groups who came out of the Reformation down to the present day, but they have not always followed exactly the same line of thinking or development. Thus in the Reformed tradition Calvinists, while basically agreeing and resembling each other in many ways, have certain differences produced by historical and even geographical circumstances. These differences have resulted in a number of what might be called lines or strains in the tradition.

The Reformation and the Reformed Tradition. The first line of development in the Reformed tradition was that which has been common to northwest Europe, Switzerland, France, Holland, Germany, and has also had an influence to the east in Hungary and to the south in the Waldensian church in Italy. The Reformed churches in the first-named areas were very active in producing the early confessions of faith and catechisms still held as doctrinal standards in many of the churches. Calvin drew up the first Reformed catechism in 1537 and rewrote it in 1541. This work was translated into a number of different languages and was widely influential. Even more important was the Heidelberg Confession of 1563, which is still a standard confessional document in most European Reformed churches. The Helvetic Confessions (1536, 1566), the Gallic Confession (1559), and the Belgic Confession (1561) also set forth a Calvinistic doctrinal position.

Across the channel in the British Isles, Calvinism was a dominant influence in the Reformation. While the Church of England was obliged by Queen Elizabeth to retain a quasi-Romanist liturgy and form of government, Calvinism was the underlying theology as expressed in the Thirty-nine Articles (1563), which were a rewritten version of Archbishop Cranmer's earlier Forty-two Articles (1553). Calvin's *Institutes* also provided English theological students with their basic theological instruction into the seventeenth century. The Puritans, consisting of Independents and Presbyterians and more consistently Calvinistic, sought to have all traces of Roman Catholicism eliminated from the Established Church. At the same time a considerable number of Protestants influenced by Anabaptism, while accepting adult baptism as the only proper method of administering the sacrament, also accepted most Reformed doctrines. Because of their belief in the doctrine of predestination they were known as "Particular" Baptists, as distinguished from the "Freewill" Baptists who rejected the doctrine. These nonconformist groups were responsible for the drawing up of the Westminster Confession of Faith, catechisms, Form of Church Government, and Directory of Worship, which have become the standards of all English-speaking Presbyterian churches. The Presbyterian church in Scotland, the Church of Scotland, which had originally used the Scots Confession (1560) and the Genevan Catechism, adopted the Westminster standards in 1647, after the English Parliament, dominated by the Independents, had refused to agree to their becoming the standards of the Church of England.

The Seventeenth and Eighteenth Centuries. In the European and British colonies throughout the world Reformed and Presbyterian churches from the late seventeenth century on were founded by the colonists who emigrated to Massachusetts, New York, South Africa, Australia, New Zealand, and other places. Although they often received little support from the home churches, at least at first, they nevertheless developed churches of their own, usually following the doctrinal, liturgical, and governmental traditions of the ecclesiastical background from which they had come. Most Presbyterian churches accept the Westminster documents as their subordinate standards, while those in the European Reformed tradition hold to the confessions and catechisms of the bodies from which they came.

The history of the Reformed tradition has been by no means peaceful or noncontroversial. Problems have arisen at times that have required those holding to the Reformed position to reexamine and defend their basic beliefs. One of the best examples and most influential developments was that which began with Dutch theologian James Arminius, who rejected Calvin's doctrines of grace. In 1610 his followers set forth a Remonstrance against those opposing them, bringing the matter to a head. The outcome was a synod held at Dordrecht in the Netherlands in 1618, made up of theologians from a number of countries, who condemned the Arminian teachings, asserting (1) the total depravity of man; (2) unconditional divine election; (3) that Christ's atonement was limited to the elect; (4) that divine grace is irresistible; and (5) the perseverance of the elect until the end. The Arminians were forced out of the Reformed church, but established their own bodies, and have had a wide influence, forming the basis for Wesleyan Methodism and other non- and anti-Reformed Christian groups. The Canons of the Synod of Dort are one of the Three Forms of Unity, the doctrinal standards of most Dutch Reformed churches, the other two being the Belgic Confession and the Heidelberg Catechism.

In England and Scotland a somewhat different conflict took place. In the Puritans' attempts to bring about a complete reform of the Church of England, they found themselves opposed by Elizabeth and her two successors, James I and Charles I. Influential in Parliament, they were able to oppose the monarchy, but eventually this led to war. The actual cause or starting point of the war was in Scotland, where Charles I sought to force episcopacy upon the Presbyterians. They resisted, and when Charles sought to raise an army in England the Puritans in Parliament made such demands upon him that he attempted to overawe them by force. He was defeated, captured, and executed by the Parliament in 1649. For the next nine years Cromwell ruled the country, but shortly after his death Charles II, Charles I's son, ascended the throne and sought to follow his father's policies in both England and Scotland. Although the Puritans in England were forced to submit, the Scots by taking up arms against Charles carried on a type of guerrilla warfare. The Covenanters, so called because they had covenanted together to defend the "Crown Rights of Jesus Christ," continued their opposition when Charles's brother James, a Roman Catholic, became king, and did not lay down their arms until James was forced off the British throne and was succeeded by William, Prince of Orange, in 1688.

While the Reformed tradition has had its conflicts, it also has had a very positive influence in the world. In the eighteenth century it was one of the principal centers of the evangelical revival. In Scotland the movement had begun by 1700 through the influence of Thomas Boston and the Marrow Men, so called because they had been greatly influenced by the Puritan work *The Marrow of Modern Divinity.* The revival associated with the work of this group eventually merged with the Evangelical revival in England through the influence of George Whitefield. At the same time in the American colonies Jonathan Edwards was involved in the Great Awakening, which was again linked to the English movement through Whitefield. In all these cases Calvinistic theology was the underlying influence.

The Reformed Tradition in Recent Times. The revival of evangelical preaching and power did not stop there, for through Scottish influence it was carried to Europe in 1818, when Robert Haldane visited Switzerland on an evangelistic tour. He greatly influenced such men as César Malan and Merle d'Aubigne, and through them the Evangelical revival spread to other parts of Europe. In Holland it had a particularly strong impact, resulting in the labors of Groen van Prinsterer, Herman Bavinck, and Abraham Kuyper. Kuyper was the founder of the Free University of Amsterdam, the leader of the movement that separated from the state church to form the Gereformeerde Kerk, and in 1901, as leader of the Anti-Revolutionary Party, became prime minister. As a result of Kuyper's work a revival of Calvinism took place not only in ecclesiastical circles but in many other aspects of Dutch life, which have had an influence far beyond Holland.

In the British Isles the same Reformed tradition was bearing similar fruit. One of the most important ecclesiastical events was the exodus of a large part of the Church of Scotland to form the Free Church of Scotland. Although the immediate cause was the opposition to the right of patrons to impose ministers on congregations, fundamentally the cause was the fact that the Church of Scotland had largely given up its Reformed position, and those who wished to maintain it insisted that they must be free to choose their own ministers. When this was denied, they withdrew and formed their own denomination. But it was not just in the ecclesiastical sphere that those of Reformed persuasion took action. The Industrial Revolution in Britain had caused great changes, with widespread exploitation of the workers. To counteract this men such as Anthony Ashley Cooper, the Seventh Earl of Shaftesbury in England, the Rev. Thomas Chalmers in Scotland, and others worked to have laws passed to protect factory hands, miners, and those with physical disabilities. Many of these leaders were strong Calvinists, and later in the century many with the same Christian views sat in the British Parliament and were responsible for other laws to ameliorate the condition of the working classes.

This Reformed practice of social and political involvement was carried to America, where those in the Reformed tradition have taken a considerable part in such matters. Many in the Presbyterian and Reformed churches were participants in the movement to abolish slavery, and more recently have been prominent in civil rights and similar movements. Unfortunately in South Africa the Reformed tradition has been involved in support of racial apartheid policies and their application, but this is changing as some of the Reformed elements within the country and Reformed churches outside, through agencies such as the Reformed Ecumenical Synod, are putting pressure on South African churches to change their attitudes toward the government's policies.

The Reformed tradition has always been strongly in favor of the education of church members. Calvin's insistence upon catechetical training of the young, and his establishment of what is now the University of Geneva, was imitated in Scotland by John Knox in the educational provisions in the *First Book of Discipline,* in the Netherlands by the establishment of such institutions as the University of Leiden, and in France by the founding of various seminaries. Similarly in America this educational tradition was responsible for the founding of universities such as Harvard and Yale. In more recent years Calvin College in Grand Rapids, Michigan, Redeemer College in Hamilton, Ontario, and similar institutions indicate that the Reformed tradition in education is still functioning and is fulfilling an important part in developing an educated, Christian citizenry.

During the latter part of the nineteenth and throughout the twentieth centuries, there has been a growing stress upon the importance of Christian scholarship. Although there had always been Reformed scholars, Abraham Kuyper stimulated a strong interest in this field, which was followed in other countries. Outstanding modern scholars include Herman Dooyeweerd, D. H. Th. Vollenhoven, J. H. Bavinck, and others in the Netherlands, particularly in the Free University of Amsterdam; James Orr in Scotland; J. Gresham Machen and Cornelius Van Til in the United States; Pierre Marcel in France; and many others who have devoted themselves to developing a Reformed approach in many learned fields.

From 1850 another noticeable development has been the endeavors of the various Reformed and Presbyterian churches to cooperate in many ways. In 1875 the World Alliance of Reformed Churches holding the Presbyterian system was organized, and still continues. As some of the churches in the alliance, however, have drifted away from a truly Reformed theological position, as evidenced by new confessions and practices which do not seem to be Reformed, a number of Reformed denominations, particularly recently formed bodies, have refused to join the WARC. As a result in the 1960s a new body, the Reformed Ecumenical Synod, was established to ensure that a fully Reformed witness would be maintained. Just prior to this some nonecclesiastical organizations had come into being. In 1953 at Montpellier, France, under the leadership of Pierre Marcel, the International Association for Reformed Faith and Action was founded, and in the United States more recently the National Association of Presbyterian and Reformed Churches was organized. In this way Reformed Christians are increasingly working together to set forth the gospel to the world. The outcome is that the Reformed tradition is exercising an influence not only in the Western world, but even at times more powerfully in such places as South Korea, Indonesia, India, and Africa.

The Reformed tradition has formed an important part of Western culture, influencing many different aspects of thought and life. Gradually, however, much of its contribution has been secularized, the religious roots being discarded and rejected. One cannot help wondering, therefore, if the condition of the Western world today is not the result of this rejection, with self-centeredness taking the place of doing all things "to the glory of God." W. S. Reid

See also Calvin, John; Zwingli, Ulrich; Dort, Synod of; Marrow Controversy; Calvinism; Edwards, Jonathan; Whitefield, George; Kuyper, Abraham.

Bibliography. J. Bratt, ed., *The Heritage of John Calvin;* W. S. Reid, ed., *John Calvin: His Influence in the Western World;* W. F. Graham, *The Constructive Revolutionary;* J. T. McNeill, *The History and Character of Calvinism.*

Regeneration. Regeneration, or new birth, is an inner re-creating of fallen human nature by the gracious sovereign action of the Holy Spirit (John 3:5–8). The Bible conceives salvation as the redemptive renewal of man on the basis of a restored relationship with God in Christ, and presents it as involving "a radical and complete transformation wrought in the soul (Rom. 12:2; Eph. 4:23) by God the Holy Spirit (Titus 3:5; Eph. 4:24), by virtue of which we become 'new men' (Eph. 4:24; Col. 3:10), no longer conformed to this world (Rom. 12:2; Eph. 4:22; Col. 3:9), but in knowledge and holiness of the truth created after the image of God (Eph. 4:24; Col. 3:10; Rom. 12:2)" (B. B. Warfield, *Biblical and Theological Studies,* 351). Regeneration is the "birth" by which this work of new creation is begun, as sanctification is the "growth" whereby it continues (I Pet. 2:2; II Pet. 3:18). Regeneration in Christ changes the disposition from lawless, Godless self-seeking (Rom. 3:9–18; 8:7) which dominates man in Adam into one of trust and love, of repentance for past rebelliousness and unbelief, and loving compliance with God's law henceforth. It enlightens the blinded mind to discern spiritual realities (I Cor. 2:14–15; II Cor. 4:6; Col. 3:10), and liberates and energizes the enslaved will for free obedience to God (Rom. 6:14, 17–22; Phil. 2:13).

The use of the figure of new birth to describe this change emphasizes two facts about it. The first is its *decisiveness.* The regenerate man has forever ceased to be the man he was; his old life is over and a new life has begun; he is a new creature in Christ, buried with him out of reach of condemnation and raised with him into a new life of righteousness (see Rom. 6:3–11; II Cor. 5:17;

Col. 3:9–11). The second fact emphasized is the *monergism* of regeneration. Infants do not induce, or cooperate in, their own procreation and birth; no more can those who are "dead in trespasses and sins" prompt the quickening operation of God's Spirit within them (see Eph. 2:1–10). Spiritual vivification is a free, and to man mysterious, exercise of divine power (John 3:8), not explicable in terms of the combination or cultivation of existing human resources (John 3:6), not caused or induced by any human efforts (John 1:12–13) or merits (Titus 3:3–7), and not, therefore, to be equated with, or attributed to, any of the experiences, decisions, and acts to which it gives rise and by which it may be known to have taken place.

Biblical Presentation. The noun "regeneration" (*palingenesia*) occurs only twice. In Matt. 19:28 it denotes the eschatological "restoration of all things" (Acts 3:21) under the Messiah for which Israel was waiting. This echo of Jewish usage points to the larger scheme of cosmic renewal within which that of individuals finds its place. In Titus 3:5 the word refers to the renewing of the individual. Elsewhere, the thought of regeneration is differently expressed.

In OT prophecies regeneration is depicted as the work of God renovating, circumcising, and softening Israelite hearts, writing his laws upon them, and thereby causing their owners to know, love, and obey him as never before (Deut. 30:6; Jer. 31:31–34; 32:39–40; Ezek. 11:19–20; 36:25–27). It is a sovereign work of purification from sin's defilement (Ezek. 36:25; cf. Ps. 51:10), wrought by the personal energy of God's creative outbreathing ("spirit": Ezek. 36:27; 39:29). Jeremiah declares that such renovation on a national scale will introduce and signal God's new messianic administration of his covenant with his people (Jer. 31:31; 32:40).

In the NT the thought of regeneration is more fully individualized, and in John's Gospel and First Epistle the figure of new birth—"from above" (*anōthen:* John 3:3, 7, Moffatt), "of water and the Spirit" (i.e., through a purificatory operation of God's Spirit: see Ezek. 36:25–27; John 3:5; cf. 3:8), or simply "of God" (John 1:13, nine times in I John)—is integral to the presentation of personal salvation. The verb *gennaō* (which means both "beget" and "bear") is used in these passages in the aorist or perfect tense to denote the once-for-all divine work whereby the sinner, who before was only "flesh," and as such, whether he knew it or not, utterly incompetent in spiritual matters (John 3:3–7), is made "spirit" (John 3:6)—i.e., is enabled and caused to receive and respond to the saving revelation of God in Christ. In the Gospel, Christ assures Nicodemus that there are no spiritual activities—no seeing or entering God's kingdom, because no faith in himself—without regeneration (John 3:1ff.); and John declares in the prologue that only the regenerate receive Christ and enter into the privileges of God's children (John 1:12–13). Conversely, in the Epistle John insists that there is no regeneration that does not issue in spiritual activities. The regenerate do righteousness (I John 2:29) and do not live a life of sin (3:9; 5:18: the present tense indicates habitual law-keeping, not absolute sinlessness, cf. 1:8–10); they love Christians (4:7), believe rightly in Christ, and experience faith's victory over the world (5:4). Any who do otherwise, whatever they claim, are still unregenerate children of the devil (3:6–10).

Paul specifies the Christological dimensions of regeneration by presenting it as (1) a lifegiving coresurrection with Christ (Eph. 2:5; Col. 2:13; cf. I Pet. 1:3); (2) a work of new creation in Christ (II Cor. 5:17; Eph. 2:10; Gal. 6:15). Peter and James make the further point that God "begets anew" (*anagennaō:* I Pet. 1:23) and "brings to birth" (*apokyeō:* James 1:18) by means of the gospel. It is under the impact of the word that God renews the heart, so evoking faith (Acts 16:14–15).

Historical Discussion. The fathers did not formulate the concept of regeneration precisely. They equated it, broadly speaking, with baptismal grace, which to them meant primarily (to Pelagius, exclusively) remission of sins. Augustine realized, and vindicated against Pelagianism, the necessity for prevenient grace to make man trust and love God, but he did not precisely equate this grace with regeneration. The Reformers reaffirmed the substance of Augustine's doctrine of prevenient grace, and Reformed theology still maintains it. Calvin used the term "regeneration" to cover man's whole subjective renewal, including conversion and sanctification. Many seventeenth century Reformed theologians equated regeneration with effectual calling and conversion with regeneration (hence the systematic mistranslation of *epistrephō*, "turn," as a passive, "be converted," in the AV); later Reformed theology has defined regeneration more narrowly, as the implanting of the "seed" from which faith and repentance spring (I John 3:9) in the course of effectual calling. Arminianism constructed the doctrine of regeneration synergistically, making man's renewal dependent on his prior cooperation with grace; liberalism constructed it naturalistically, identifying regeneration with a moral change or a religious experience.

The fathers lost the biblical understanding of the sacraments as signs to sir up faith and seals to confirm believers in possession of the blessings signified, and so came to regard baptism as conveying the regeneration which it signified (Titus 3:5) *ex opere operato* to those who did not obstruct its working. Since infants could not do this, all baptized infants were accordingly held to be regenerated. This view has persisted in all the non-Reformed churches of Christendom, and among sacramentalists within Protestantism.

J. I. PACKER

See also ELECT, ELECTION; CALL, CALLING; SALVATION; ORDER OF SALVATION.

Bibliography. J. Orr, "Regeneration," *HDB;* J. Denney, *HDCG;* B. B. Warfield, *Biblical and Theological Studies;* systematic theologies of C. Hodge, III, 1–40, and L. Berkhof, IV, 465–79; A. Ringwald *et al., NIDNTT,* I, 176ff.; F. Büchsel *et al., TDNT,* I, 665ff.; B. Citron, *The New Birth.*

Regeneration, Baptismal. *See* BAPTISMAL REGENERATION.

Regula Fidei. *See* RULE OF FAITH.

Reid, Thomas. *See* SCOTTISH REALISM.

Reincarnation. The belief that an individual human soul passes through a succession of lives. The idea of reincarnation had its origin in northern India (*ca.* 1000–800 B.C.). Western views of reincarnation popular today are modifications of the ancient theory of transmigration of souls (sometimes called metempsychosis), which holds that the soul may be incarnated not only in human bodies but also in animals and plants. The Western version of transmigration has been redefined to limit cyclic rebirths taking place in human form only.

The concept of reincarnation first appeared in the early Hindu scriptures (Upanishads). It has always been an integral part of classical Buddhism. Reincarnational thinking characterized some Greek philosophers, including Pythagoras and Plato. Because of the influence of the first century Greek mystery religions, the Gnostics, and the Roman Stoics, the theory of transmigration, or reincarnation, became firmly established as a Western as well as Eastern doctrine.

Closely associated with the notion of reincarnation cycles is the Eastern concept of karma. The law of karma asserts that the evil deeds of past lives relate to the present life, and that one's present actions have implications for future lives. Essentially karma is the law of cause and effect, of action followed by reaction. In the Orient the belief in karma has resulted in a basically pessimistic view of life. Human existence is often a dreary, endless cycle of pain, suffering, and rebirth. Karmic reincarnation does not resolve the problem of evil. It requires self-salvation leading to ultimate liberation from the wheel of rebirth. The concepts of divine forgiveness and mercy are absent.

The modern Western expression of reincarnation emerged during the Enlightenment of the eighteenth century and was revived by such nineteenth century occultic movements as Theosophy, founded by the influential Madame H. P. Blavatsky. This westernized version of reincarnation was later popularized by such psychics as Edgar Cayce, Helen Wambach, and Jeanne Dixon. Unlike Eastern proponents of reincarnation, Western reincarnationists stress a more optimistic view of life, holding out the hope of more and better lives.

The ultimate objective of all reincarnation is to fuse with "ultimate reality," to merge with God, to become God. All reincarnation teachings are based on a monistic, mystical-occult world view that promotes the essential divinity of humanity, denies the notion of a sovereign personal God, and offers the promise of esoteric wisdom.

Biblical Christianity, in contrast to reincarnational teaching, emphasizes grace, atonement, and forgiveness for fallen humanity through the once-for-all death and resurrection of Jesus Christ. The Christian's disavowal of reincarnation is anchored in the biblical assertion that "man is destined to die once, and after that to face judgment" (Heb. 9:27).

R. M. ENROTH

Bibliography. M. Albrecht, *Reincarnation: A Christian Appraisal;* R. A. Morey, *Reincarnation and Christianity;* P. J. Swihart, *Reincarnation, Edgar Cayce and the Bible.*

Relativism. Totalistic relativism is (1) an epistemological theory denying any objective, universally valid human knowledge and affirming that meaning and truth vary from person to person, culture to culture, and time to time; (2) a metaphysical theory denying any changeless realities such as energy, space, time, natural laws, persons, or God and affirming that all conceivable meaning rests on activities, happenings, events, processes, or relationships, in which observers are changing participants; and (3) an ethical theory denying any changeless moral principles normative for all people in every situation and so of limited validity. From these three fields relativism pervades every field of meaningful human experience and knowledge.

Limited relativism considers totalistic relativism self-contradictory and wrong in its absolute denials of any absolute truth, and yet accurate in its assertion that much human knowledge is conditioned and slanted by innumerable variables. However, general divine revelation makes clearly known to all people the changeless truths about God's nature and particularly God's changeless plans for changing people in changing cultures in history. Although finite, fallen people may not be able to invent changeless truths, they can discover and receive them through divine revelation and enablement. In this way they can know not only changeless principles, plans, and purposes but also the meaning of unique, once-for-all events with objective validity.

Human cognition does take place in the midst of countless cultural variables: subjectively (Kierkegaard), psychologically (Freud), morally (Fletcher), economically (Marx), politically (Reinhold Niebuhr), historically (H. Richard Niebuhr, W. Dilthey), educationally (Dewey), religiously (Cobb, Starcke, Watts), anthropologically (Kraft), and stylistically (Ricoeur). As a result of the kaleidoscopic impact of these and other influential variables, totalistic relativists have denied any invariable, absolute truth about things in themselves.

Increased consciousness of these cultural variables has generally been of significant value to the fields of interpretation and communication. To grasp the *meaning* of people from other cultures interpreters now realize how crucial it is to seek sympathetic identification with them in terms of their own presuppositions and historical roots. Such cross-cultural understanding is equally indispensable if one seeks to communicate to those of other cultures in terms of their own categories of thought and verbal expressions. Improved ways of grasping and communicating meaning, however, do not settle issues of objective validity.

Agreement has not been reached in regard to the degree of influence the cultural variables bring to bear upon human knowers. According to determinists, given a specific set of conditions present to a person's brain, nothing else could happen. All knowledge is relative to and determined by these situations (Skinner). For others, although all of human knowledge and behavior is predisposed to habitual responses by given sets of stimuli, this conditioning "falls somewhat short of total determination." All propositional assertions are nevertheless held to be time- and culture-bound (Kraft).

Others view persons not only as physical organisms but also as minds, souls, or spirits, with the powers of self-determination and self-transcendence. Hence their knowledge is not all time-bound and they are agents responsible for their own actions (Thomas Reid, J. Oliver Buswell, Jr.). Existentialists affirm that mankind is free from both external determination and internal self-determination by a self with a given, unchangeable nature. To be authentically free a person must, in fact, exercise an arbitrary freedom independent of cultural predispositions and past habitual choices. It seems more likely that some knowledge is predisposed by one's cultural influences and creative knowledge simply occasioned by one's situation.

Totalistic Relativism. Whether the cultural and psychological variables determine, predispose, or occasion certain metaphysical beliefs, totalistic relativists know little about the nature of persons or things as terms or entities in themselves, and much about relationships, functions, and processes. Things and persons are what they do. Distinct, unique persons are reduced to influences, relations, events, or happenings (Arthur F. Bentley). Relational theology also intends to free people from the tyranny of absolutes, but may diminish the value of a person as such.

In Eastern monistic relativism persons are not real, but mere *maya* insofar as they are distinguishable from the One. Differentiations of distinct persons with whom to have relationships are said to be made, not by nature, but by human conceptual assertions distinguishing subjects from predicates. Hence all propositions are illusory and relative to the viewpoints of those who assert them. In "reality" persons, like dew drops, slip into the shining sea, the part never again to be differentiated from the whole. Since all that can be conceived is relative, no permanent objective remains for which to strive and nihilism results. No self-nature can stand by itself, and no lasting distinction can be made between right and wrong. Moral conflicts are a sickness of the mind which should have cultivated a bland indifference. Decisions are to be made without having the faintest understanding of how one decides (Alan Watts).

Totalistic relativism, relationalism, or contextualization ends in amorality, "Asiatic fatalism," meaninglessness, and nihilism. Furthermore radical relativism is self-contradictory. Every human assertion is said to be time-bound and culture-bound, but the assertion that "all is relative" is taken to be universal and necessary. Total relativism absolutely denies any absolutes—and it absolutizes relativity.

Limited Relativism. Less reductive and more open approaches to meaningful human existence acknowledge not only differences among cultures but also similarities. Kraft alludes to over seventy-three constants in human societies in a chapter on human commonality, but concludes the chapter with only one criterion for evaluating cultural systems: their efficiency or adequacy in meeting people's personal, social, and spiritual needs. The forms of a culture, including the Christian missionary's culture, are judged solely in terms of their pragmatic usefulness. Usefulness for what? It sounds good to say, "for properly relating human beings to God." But having held that a hundred percent of human conceptual thought is time-bound, Kraft has no changeless criteria by which to distinguish counterfeit religious experience from authentic conversion to Christ. Apparently dynamically equivalent experiences may be of Satan, who changes himself into an angel of light. The tests of authentic Christian experience, according to Scripture, include conceptually equivalent assertions about the nature of Christ, the eternal Word who became flesh (John 1:1–18; 20:31; I John 4:1–3; II John 9). Relational and functional theologians, succumbing to relativism, undermine the changeless conceptual validity of God's universal revelation in nature and special revelation in the teaching of the incarnate Christ and inspired prophetic and apostolic spokesmen.

What transcultural truths, then, are known through general revelation? (1) People are human. Persons everywhere in all cultures have been, are, and will be human. Dehumanizing and depersonalizing tendencies to the contrary, persons are subjects, not mere objects, and as agents responsibly participate in communities to achieve common, objective goals. (2) People have inalienable human rights and responsibilities. However different physically, economically, educationally, politically, socially, or religiously, people have a right to equal concern and respect. (3) People deserve justice. Whatever the situation, and whenever people are treated unjustly, they cry out against injustice. (4) Unjust people need a just amnesty and forgiving, holy love. (5) People ought to be intellectually honest and faithful to the given data of reality. They ought not bear false witness against others. (6) If human society, mutual trust, and communication is to be meaningful, people ought to be logically noncontradictory in their thought, speech, and writing. Human knowledge and experience are related not only to cultural variables but also to these invariables of morality, fact, and logic.

To argue for but one absolute, love, as did Joseph Fletcher, is to ignore the breadth of the Creator's intelligence and wisdom. To argue for the absoluteness of factual data alone, as with scientism and positivism in their varied forms, overlooks the faithful words of the Logos regarding morality, sin, and salvation, and his own integrity as one who cannot deny himself or contradict himself. But to argue for logical absolutes alone, as rationalists may, blinds one to the given data of experience, the danger of autism, injustice, and irresponsibility in a day of nuclear proliferation.

The Need for Absolutes. Claims to truth, as distinct from mere uninformed opinion, must be justified on the basis of something more than subjective or community feelings of certitude. As Gordon Kaufman has argued, any claim to truth involves the claim to objective validity. Although hesitating to affirm belief in absolutes, Kaufman admits that objectively valid knowledge transcends actual thinking and feeling in three directions—givenness, universality, and logical interconnectedness. These he calls "functioning absolutes." Since they function as absolutes along with justice and love, intellectual honesty, and human worth to make life possible and meaningful, why not call them absolutes?

To acknowledge changeless truths in the midst of changing human experiences, as Augustine realized, is to acknowledge their changeless source and referent, ontologically. Paul Tillich also saw that all such absolutes point beyond themselves to an all-inclusive Absolute. Unfortunately, Tillich's concept of Being itself depersonalized the living and dynamic Logos of Scripture.

The most coherent account of both the variables and the invariables in meaningful human experience, Christians may argue, is the personal, living, moral, just, loving, faithful, and true God revealed not only in the world, history, and human nature, but even more significantly in the Jesus of history and the teachings of Scripture. Although finite, fallen people may not discover objectively valid, normative truths for themselves, as divine image bearers they may be enabled by common or special grace to receive them. Through general revelation from the absolute God, people find out about God's moral principles for justice in society and, through special revelation, about God's loving plans and purposes for unjust people. The living God is not determined by the relative processes of time, space, energy, and humanity. People and nature are relative to, dependent upon, and conditioned by God.

It is commonplace for radical religious relativists to affirm that people can experience God even though no conceptual or propositional truth about God is possible. Even the words of Jesus and the Bible, they hold, are time-bound and culture-bound. They can be taken only noncognitively, as pointers. Such religious relativism, however pious, misses the mark because it fails to take adequate account of mankind's creation in the image of God and renewal in the divine image to know God conceptually (Col. 3:10). Because they are created to know and commune with the Creator and Redeemer who is changeless in essence, attributes, and plans for space and time, humans in a sea of relativism can receive some effable absolutes by divine revelation and illumination.

Denials of propositional revelation may also result from a failure to grasp the relatedness of everything in changing and changeless experience to the Logos of God (John 1:1–3). The divine Logos is eternal and distinct from the universe but not limited to an intellectually other eternity as in Eastern mysticism. The divine Logos is immanent, governing nature and people, but not limited to natural processes as in liberalism. The divine Logos became incarnate as a truly human person but is not limited to noncognitive personal encounters as in neo-orthodoxy. The divine Logos was inscripturated, but is not limited to a mere biblicism as in some extreme fundamentalism. In sum, the Logos of God is transcendent and immanent, incarnate, and inscripturated as in classical orthodox theology.

A verificational apologetic for the absolutes of the divine Logos, general revelation, incarnate revelation, and inscripturated revelation is not itself another absolute. It is not necessary to be divine or an inerrant spokesman for God to verify God's wisdom, power, and morality in the world, divine sinlessness in Christ, or divine revelation in Scripture. The Israelites did not make themselves autonomous by distinguishing between true and false prophets. To check the credentials of one's surgeon is not to presume oneself more wise and capable in practicing surgery than the specialist. Acquainted with the countless variables every human knower faces, we are not surprised that Christian apologists frankly claim no more than an overwhelming probability beyond reasonable doubt.

Similarly, Christians claim only degrees of probability for their interpretations and applications of divinely revealed propositional truths. To affirm the absoluteness of God's understanding in eternity is not to affirm the absoluteness of any believer's understanding of revelation at any given time in his growth in knowledge and grace. Precisely the opposite result follows. To assert the absoluteness of divine revelation in terms of its intended purpose and the standards of accuracy when written for that end is to deny absoluteness to the pronouncements of governments, public schools, the United Nations, and religious institutions. Divine illumination does not result in inerrancy.

Although no interpretation of the Scriptures as given can be regarded as absolute, some interpretations are better informed than others by relevant data, valid hermeneutical principles, and sound criteria of truth. The most reliable checks and balances upon varied interpretive hypotheses are criteria drawn from the invariables found in general revelation: its grammar, literary context, author's purpose, historical and cultural setting, and broader theological context. Furthermore, one must be able to live by that interpretation with integrity while treating people as persons, not things, respecting their rights, treating them justly, and forgiving their injustices.

Untold harm has been done in the name of Christianity by people who have absolutized their relative interpretations of life or of Scripture. Presumptuous prophets who claimed to speak God's word to people, without divine authorization, in the OT administration were subject to the most severe penalties. May God deliver evangelicals today from prophetic ministries not validly drawn from divine revelation. This case for revealed absolutes must not be taken to justify absolutizing merely human ideas, however good.

Similarly, inestimable damage has been done the cause of Christ and Scripture by those who relativize divinely revealed absolutes, which have objective validity for all people of all cultures. Either Christianity is true for all people, or it is true for no one. We can be assured of our view of the major doctrines of Christianity and the realities to which they refer when our interpretations are based on numerous relevant and extensive passages of Scripture, supported by interpreters throughout the history of the church, and attested to us personally by the internal witness of the Holy Spirit to the teaching of the Word. Then we can confidently relate to the realities designated and preach the great doctrines of the faith with joy.

In a day when radical relativism reigns, disciples of the Lord, who is the same yesterday, today, and forever, stand guard against attacks upon the cognitive faith once for all entrusted to the saints (Jude 3) with gentleness, respect, and a clear conscience (I Pet. 3:15–16). G. R. Lewis

See also Apologetics; Contextualization of Theology; Revelation, General; Knowledge; Truth; Bible, Authority of; Christianity and Culture; Situation Ethics.

Bibliography. A. F. Bentley, *Relativity in Man and Society;* G. W. Bromiley, "The Limits of Theological Relativism," *CT,* May 24, 1968, 6–7; J. B. Cobb, Jr., *Christ in a Pluralistic Age;* R. J. Coleman, *Issues in Theological Conflict;* B. A. Demarest, *General Revelation;* J. W. Dixon, Jr., *The Physiology of Faith: A Theory of Theological Relativity;* C. F. H. Henry, *Christian Personal Ethics;* G. Kaufman, *Relativism, Knowledge and Faith;* C. H. Kraft, *Christianity in Culture;* M. Kransz and J. W. Meiland, eds., *Relativism Cognitive and Moral;* G. R. Lewis, "Categories in Collision?" in

Perspectives on Evangelical Theology, and *Testing Christianity's Truth-Claims;* F. Schaeffer, *How Should We Then Live?* B. F. Skinner, *Back to Freedom and Dignity;* J. S. Spong, "Evangelism When Certainty Is an Illusion," *CCen,* Jan. 6–13, 1982, 11–16; W. Starcke, *The Gospel of Relativity;* P. Tillich, *My Search for Absolutes;* D. Turner, *The Autonomous Man.*

Relics. Objects preserved as memorials of the earthly lives of saints, Mary, or Jesus, including their bodies and items which contacted them.

In Catholic and Orthodox traditions relics function as both reminders of those who lived and died for the faith and media for communion with venerable persons, because some of the grace that filled their lives is perceived to remain in surviving objects, evidenced by miracles associated with relics. Biblical intimations of the power of relics may be detected in stories about Elisha's bones (II Kings 13:21) and cloths Paul had touched (Acts 19:12).

Belief in relics spread widely among Christians by the fourth century, receiving approval from such illustrious fathers as Ambrose, Augustine, and Chrysostom. Initially this belief focused on graves of martyrs, which became choice sites for building churches. Later it led to the transporting of objects from graves, including bones and cloths (*brandea*), for enshrinement elsewhere. The seventh ecumenical council decreed that no new church be consecrated without relics in its altar. Relics were also placed in portable reliquaries for use in processions and miracles of healing and protection.

The cult of relics expanded enormously in the Middle Ages, leading to a multitude of pilgrimages and inevitable superstitions and commercial abuses. This was especially so in the Catholic West in contrast to the Orthodox East, where the veneration of images took precedence over relics. Thomas Aquinas summarized Catholic rationale, affirming that as the saints were temples of the Holy Spirit on earth their remains continue as instruments of that Spirit after their glorification. Thus the saint's body merits special honor, and relics are more venerable than images. Nevertheless, such honor must be only that of veneration and never that adoration of which God alone is worthy; nor is the power of the relic anything other than God's power bestowed upon the saint.

The forerunners of Protestantism, Hus and Wycliffe, inveighed against the cult of relics as idolatry, and the Reformers echoed them. Calvin, noting that the preservation of relics inevitably leads to their worship, insisted on the removal of "this heathenish custom." The Council of Trent confirmed the veneration of relics as established by tradition. Catholic canon law now regulates relics through the Congregation of Rites, requiring that relics be authenticated by episcopal certification and forbidding their sale.

P. D. Steeves

Bibliography. J. Calvin, "Inventory of Relics," in *Tracts and Treatises on the Reformation of the Church; Canons and Decrees of the Council of Trent,* Session XXV, in *The Creeds of Christendom,* ed. P. Schaff, II, 201–5; *NCE,* XII, 234–40; W. Smith, *Dictionary of Christian Antiquities,* II, 1768–78; H. Thurston, *HERE,* XI, 51–59.

Religion, Religious. "Religious" is in general the adjective of the noun "religion"; but it is also used, without the noun, in a specialized sense to indicate connection with a monastic order. Thus, a monk may be called a "religious."

The large number, and often contradictory character, of the definitions to be found in modern discussions of religion suggest that scholars find it impossible to formulate a generally acceptable definition. The confusing discussion of this problem in J. H. Leuba's *God or Man?* ch. 2, hardly suggests the amazing variety of the definitions offered. The etymology of the term does not help, both because it is uncertain and because neither *religare* nor *religere* throws much light on the present meaning of religion.

Many of the suggested definitions have been drawn up to serve a particular purpose, e.g., the purpose of psychology, or of sociology, or of some philosophical position such as humanism. Whether they are adequate for such special purposes must be decided by the specialists in that field; but they clearly fail to give a characterization of religion that is useful for more general purposes. This need not cause confusion, provided that their special purpose is noted and that their use is confined to that special purpose. When such a definition is employed as adequate for some other purpose, however, confusion results. Thus F. H. Bradley writes, "I take it to be a fixed feeling of fear, resignation, admiration or approval, no matter what may be the object, provided only that this feeling reaches a certain strength, and is qualified by a certain degree of reflection" (*Appearance and Reality,* p. 438n.). This may or may not be good for the purpose of psychology, but Bradley makes use of it in a discussion that is not confined to psychology. Such confusion is much too common.

The effort to gain a definition by isolating the common characteristics of the recognized religions runs into the following difficulties. (1) There are borderline cases the inclusion or exclusion of which will determine the resulting definition; e.g., including original Buddhism or Marxism in the cases studied will remove from the definition a mention of a supernatural object. But the decision to include or to exclude must in either case seem arbitrary. (2) The characteristics of the various religions differ so widely that it may be impossible, by this method, to find any common features, or, if any are found, they must be so vague as to be of doubtful value. For example, in Bradley's definition, quoted above, note the indefiniteness of the expressions "a certain strength" and "a certain degree of reflection." However, those for example who call Marxism a religion, in spite of its aggressive repudiation of religion, must feel that a satisfactory definition can be attained in this manner.

Perhaps a satisfactory definition can be attained only by confining attention to one or a few of the "higher" religions, the others being treated as defective and so not normative. This would be to apply to religion the method advocated in philosophy by Bernard Bosanquet, namely that reality can be properly understood only from the standpoint of its highest manifestation. One could not, of course, expect anything like unanimous agreement in the selection on the basis of which such a definition would be reached, but a fairly general agreement might be hoped for if the selection were not too rigid, and the actual selection might be capable of defense. Such a method would yield, as definitive characteristics of religion, the acknowledgment of a higher, unseen power; an attitude of reverent dependence on that power in the conduct of life; and special actions, e.g., rites, prayers, and acts of mercy, as peculiar expressions and means of cultivation of the religious attitude. A. K. Rule

Bibliography. P. A. Bertocci, *Religion as Creative Insecurity;* C. J. Ducasse, *A Philosophical Scrutiny of Religion;* H. H. Farmer, *Revelation and Religion;* W. L. King, *Introduction to Religion;* E. C. Moore, *The Nature of Religion;* J. Oman, *The Natural and the Supernatural;* A. Toynbee, *An Historian's Approach to Religion;* A. G. Widgery, *What Is Religion?*

Religionless Christianity. *See* Bonhoeffer, Dietrich.

Religious Liberty. *See* Tolerance.

Remarriage. The question of remarriage is a difficult one, touching, as it does, upon matters of biblical exegesis, moral judgment, and pastoral psychology. Does Scripture allow remarriage? In any particular case would remarriage be morally right? In such a case would remarriage be pastorally wise?

The Exegetical Question. The exegetical question is closely related to the view we take on divorce. Remarriage is presupposed in the Deuteronomic legislation (Deut. 24:1–4), although return to a first husband is forbidden in the one case of a woman also divorced by a second husband. But there are differences of view between Christians about the NT material. In the Synoptic Gospels (Matt. 5:31–32; 19:3–4; Mark 10:2–3; Luke 16:18) is Jesus forbidding all remarriage because it is adultery? Does the "exceptive clause" ("except for the case of *porneia*") in Matt. 5:32 and 19:9 mean that in this one case a husband is free to separate from his wife, but without right of remarriage? Or is Jesus in these passages both affirming God's ideal for marriage as a permanent covenant and also recognizing that sometimes divorce is a tragic reality because of sin? If one takes the latter view, it is arguable that the right of remarriage is also presupposed. Some Christian scholars argue that Jesus is using the word translated "divorce" in the sense of "put away by separation," and that he does not allow remarriage. It would appear, however, that because separation without remarriage was not otherwise known in Jesus' day (though he could be introducing it), and because the context of Jesus' teaching is a discussion of Deut. 24 (in which remarriage is assumed) with the Pharisees (who also assumed the right of remarriage), that Jesus would not have been understood as forbidding remarriage without further explanation.

The apostolic fathers seemingly appeared virtually unanimous in forbidding divorce with right of remarriage, although we need to ask whether that tells us more about their exegesis of Scripture or about the ascetic ideals which prevailed in the patristic age. The Church of Rome has always officially rejected remarriage, in line with its ban on divorce. It has, though, established procedures by which some marriages can be annulled—i.e., declared by the church never to have been proper marriages at all. In those cases the partners after civil divorce are set free to marry again. The Eastern Orthodox churches, the Nonconformist churches, and some parts of the Anglican Church have allowed right of remarriage after divorce in certain circumstances, although until recently the "official" view of the Church of England has been firmly against remarriage of divorced persons in church.

The Moral Question. But suppose we accept that in some circumstances divorce is permitted as a tragic last resort in circumstances of marital breakdown. Does that always justify remarriage? To divorce with someone else in mind (like Herod) may well be the thought behind Luke's strong words in Luke 16:18. There are some whose divorces are the result of blatant refusal to keep their marriage vows; some who early in a youthful marriage sadly come to realize that "we made a mistake"; some who, having tried to keep covenant, find that their partner has not. We cannot have a blanket category "divorcee," as though morally all situations were identical. However, it would seem clear from the NT that—to put it at its highest—remarriage always falls under the cloud of the broken covenant of the first marriage. Further, although a divorced person is no longer married, the "one flesh" has been severed, and in one sense they are free to marry again, we must immediately qualify this sense. The primary moral question is whether or not remarriage cuts into any outstanding covenant obligations of the first marriage which are still capable of fulfillment. If there is any remaining possibility of reconciliation with the first partner, that is decisive. The outstanding obligations of parenthood to any children are also of the highest priority, another moral issue affecting the decision concerning remarriage. Furthermore, the social dimensions to marriage require that we also consider the overall stability of marriage and family patterns in society. We would need to judge that the overall personal good of remarriage in a particular case would justify the threat that a second union would make to the social institution of marriage.

The Pastoral Question. There remains the pastoral question, which may still mean that even if remarriage were judged permissible, it may not be judged wise. Many marriages are broken because of some sort of personal inadequacy in maintaining faithfulness and upholding commitment. A good Christian marriage can provide one of the most fruitful contexts for healing personal immaturities and childhood hurts, but a bad marriage may serve only to deepen wounds and expose hurts undealt with to the consciousness. To add the pain, guilt, and tragedy of divorce to a stock of personal insecurity and need is to make some people very vulnerable indeed, and it is by no means a straightforward question that a second marriage will necessarily be any more successful that the first, unless personal help has been received. A marriage failure should raise for some people the question of personal need and the possibilities of therapy or pastoral ministry on the one hand, and the serious consideration of future celibacy on the other.

That said, however, let it be granted that there are many for whom the experience of a second start has also been an experience of forgiveness from God and a renewed awareness of the need for and resources of his grace. It is part of the church's task to be a healing, supporting, guiding, and enriching environment in which personal needs can be worked through and resources for Christian living made available.

Whether or not remarriage should be blessed in church has been a problem for some churchmen. To do so might seem to be collusion with the serious sin of divorce. To fail to do so might indicate a harder moral line than taken by the Scriptures and a failure to offer a ministry of forgiveness. How best to institutionalize the church's double task in liturgy and church discipline—that of prophet, upholding God's will for the permanence of marriage; that of pastor, proclaiming the gospel of grace and forgiveness—is not an easy task. It might be that any service of blessing for second marriages should include a note, distinct from the normal marriage service, of penitence for past sin—a note in which both couple and congregation should join. This might give liturgical expression to the recognition that a second marriage falls under the shadow of a broken covenant of the first, and also that sin is partly a matter of individual responsibility and partly linked to the social structures which sometimes lay on marriages burdens too great to be borne.

However right remarriage in any particular case may be judged to be, that does not remove from the church one of its primary responsibilities in this area: that of finding ways in which to foster and encourage those personal qualities which make for covenant faithfulness and commitment, even within the pressures of contemporary society, and of finding ways of minimizing in social terms those factors that militate against the permanence of marriage. D. J. Atkinson

See also Divorce; Separation, Marital; Marriage, Theology of.

Bibliography. J. C. Laney, *The Divorce Myth;* S. A. Ellisen, *Divorce and Remarriage in the Church;* D. J. Atkinson, *To Have and to Hold;* A. R. Winnett, *Divorce and Remarriage in Anglicanism* and *Divorce and the Church;* G. W. Bromiley, *God and Marriage.*

Remission of Sins. *See* Forgiveness.

Remnant. The translation of several words in the OT, only two of which are of consequence: *yātar* with its noun *yeter* and *šā'ar* with its derivatives *šĕ'ār* and *šĕ'ērît.* The NT equivalents *loipos* and *leimma* with its compounds are infrequent. In the majority of cases the words concerned are used in a literal and self-explanatory way. They refer merely to things or people left over after famine, conquest, division, passage of time, etc. In the books of the prophets, however, the hope promised for those of the nation left over after the fall of Jerusalem crystallized into a promise not only of preservation for the few people remaining, but also a promise for the kernel of the nation which could be kept in all vicissitudes and at length returned to its land and blessed status in messianic times. For this concept the word *šĕʾērît* is principally used.

The thought perhaps goes back to Deut. 4:27 where the promise is given to the ones left after dispersal, that they will be blessed again if they seek the Lord. Isaiah named one of his sons Shear-jashub, "A remnant shall return" (Isa. 7:3; 8:18). In 10:21 this is interpreted to mean the remnant shall return to God, referring, perhaps, to revival in the days of Hezekiah. Yet in 11:10–16 there is reference to a "second" return from dispersal in which the Gentiles shall join. The quotation in Rom. 15:12 assures us that this refers not to the return from Assyria or Babylon, but a second return at the time of the messianic age.

In Mic. 4:7; 5:7–8; 7:18, the remnant of Jacob is practically a name for Israel in the future days. In Jeremiah the remnant is used in reference to the return from Babylonian captivity in 42:2; 50:20; etc., but it is also used to refer to Israel in the messianic age in 23:3; 31:7. Zechariah also uses the term for the Jews who came back from Babylon (Zech. 8:6, 11–12), as well as for the residue of the people (*yeter hāʿām*) of the messianic age (14:2). The repentant mourning of the Israelite remnant is detailed in Zech. 12:10–13:1 as taking place in the day of Israel's salvation. These verses are quoted in the NT in connection with Christ's second coming (Matt. 24:30; Rev. 1:7).

Much discussed is Amos 9:12, quoted in Acts 15:17. The amillennial view is defended by O. T. Allis (*Prophecy and the Church,* pp. 145–49). In brief, the argument is that the conquest of the "remnant of Edom" in Amos is spiritualized in Acts to refer to the conversion of the Gentiles in this age. An alternative view, presented in Alf and Meyer's Commentary, is that the LXX which Acts 15:17 quotes quite closely had before it a variant Hebrew text. If this be true, the Amos passage prophesied a day when Gentiles and Jews (the remnant of men) would seek the Lord. Heretofore it has often been assumed that when the LXX differed from the Hebrew, the latter was right. Dead Sea Scroll material gives a new perspective on these matters. At least here, where the LXX is supported by the NT, there is good argument that its text is accurate and that it speaks of the promise of salvation for the remnant.

In Rom. 11:5 the remnant of grace appears to be the saved of Israel of Paul's day. It seems equally clear that this age, when Jews are cast off and Gentiles grafted into the stock of the people of God (Rom. 11:15–22), will be followed by an age when the Jews will be reintroduced to the privileges of grace (Rom. 11:25–31). Verse 26 then gives the eventual promise for the Jewish remnant of the last days. R. L. HARRIS

Bibliography. D. Walker in *HDAC;* G. F. Oehler, *Theology of the OT;* W. Günther *et al., NIDNTT,* III, 247ff.; J. C. Campbell, "God's People and the Remnant," *SJT* 3:78ff.; G. F. Hasel, *The Remnant;* J. Jocz, *A Theology of Election;* B. F. Meyer, "Jesus and the Remnant of Israel," *JBL* 84:123ff.; P. Richardson, *Israel and the Apostolic Church.*

Remonstrants. Dutch Protestant group composed of followers of the theological views of Arminius. They presented to the States General in 1610 a "Remonstrance" that reflected their divergence from stricter Calvinism. Rejecting both supralapsarianism and sublapsarianism, the document outlined five articles: (1) Election and reprobation are founded on foreseen faith or unbelief. (2) Christ's death is for all, but only believers enjoy his forgiveness. (3) Fallen man cannot do good or achieve saving faith without the regenerating power of God in Christ through the Holy Spirit. (4) Grace is the beginning, continuation, and end of all good, but is not irresistible. (5) Grace can preserve the faithful through every temptation, but Scripture does not clearly say man may not fall from grace and be lost.

When the matter came before the Synod of Dort it had become a political as well as a theological issue. The Remonstrants, who upheld the principle of free investigation, were ousted from their pulpits. Many of them were expelled from the Netherlands, and their theological position was declared contrary to Scripture. While the rigors of persecution soon died down when the political climate became more favorable, the Remonstrants were not officially tolerated until 1795. The movement has retained its appeal and has had a significant influence on orthodox Dutch Calvinism and on other Christian denominations. The Remonstrance was a modified form of Calvinism which, like the term Arminianism, has been wrongly identified with anti-Calvinist tendencies. J. D. DOUGLAS

See also DORT, SYNOD OF; ARMINIANISM.

Bibliography. A. W. Harrison, *Arminianism;* C. O. Bangs, *Arminius.*

Renan, Joseph Ernest (1823–1892). French Semitic philologist and historian of religion. Of humble origins (a Breton fisherman's family) he received a Catholic education and studied for the priesthood at the seminaries of Issy and St.

Sulplice. As he came under the influence of rationalist philosophy and critical German theology, he grew disillusioned with the church and dropped out in 1845 without receiving ordination. He continued studying philosophy and philology, acquiring a doctorate in 1852, and soon he established a scholarly reputation as an Orientalist. In 1860–61 he went on an archaeological expedition to Lebanon and Palestine, where he wrote the celebrated *Life of Jesus* (1863), the opening volume of *The History of the Origins of Christianity* (7 vols.). Appointed professor of Hebrew at the Collège de France in 1862, he was removed two years later because of the controversy swirling about him but was reinstated in 1870 and became its administrator in 1884. He was a well-known figure on the lecture circuit, author of *History of the People of Israel* (5 vols., 1887–93), and named to the French Academy. His contributions to Semitic philology were significant, but his works on history and exegesis and literary pieces were much more dilettantish.

His fame rested primarily on the *Life of Jesus*, in which D. F. Strauss's myth theory of the origins of Christianity was superseded with a legend theory. Renan presented Jesus in an attractive, vivid style as a romantic figure, a gentle Galilean who preached a simple morality and dreamed of establishing a utopian fellowship of God's people on earth. But under the influence of John the Baptist the vain and ambitious Jesus was transformed into a religious revolutionary who assumed the role of Messiah, battled with evil as he worked to set up the kingdom of God, and died struggling against orthodox Judaism. Both this and his later works were marked by skepticism, rationalism, and rejection of the supernatural dimension of life, divinity of Christ, and the existence of a transcendent God. Although in no way a seminal thinker, he was the major representative of French liberalism in this period.

R. V. Pierard

Bibliography. L. F. Mott, *Ernest Renan;* H. W. Wardman, *Ernest Renan: A Critical Biography;* E. Lachenmann, *SHERK*, IX, 483–85; A. M. Malo, *NCE*, XII, 375; C. T. McIntire, *NIDCC*, 836.

Renewal. This is an integral concept in Christian theology, denoting all those processes of restoration of spiritual strength subsequent to and proceeding from the new birth. It has its roots in the OT (Pss. 5:10; 103:5; Isa. 40:31; 41:1), although it is not predominant in pre-Christian times. The main NT words are *anakainizō* and *ananeoō*. In Rom. 12:2 this renewal (*anakainōsis*) is applied to the mental faculties, and indicates the reinvigorating effect of Christian committal on conduct. This is further illustrated by the apostle's teaching regarding the new man (Col. 3:10), which is represented as in constant need of renewal (II Cor. 4:16). A more specific description is found in Eph. 4:23, where the phrase "renewed in the spirit of your mind" shows the spiritual character of this renewal. "The spiritual principle of the mind must acquire a new youth, susceptible of spiritual impressions" (J. A. Robinson, *St. Paul's Epistle to the Ephesians*).

In the subapostolic age the idea of renewal tended to become linked with that of baptism (cf. Barnabas 6:11, and the apocryphal Acts of Thomas, 132). It was not strange that the initiatory rite should mark in Christian thought the commencement of the process of renewal, but there is nothing in the NT teaching to support any notion of baptismal renewal.

Another word, *palingenesia*, is used of the event of rebirth which leads to renewal. The two ideas are linked together in Titus 3:5, where they appear to describe different aspects of one operation. The linking of *palingenesia* in this passage with "washing" suggests the words may have formed part of a baptismal formula, but gives no basis for the later magical estimate of baptism.

D. Guthrie

See also Regeneration; Baptism.

Bibliography. M. Dibelius, *HZNT* (Titus 3:5); D. Guthrie, *Pastoral Epistles.*

Renewal, Church. A phenomenon which in earlier centuries was described by such words as revival, awakening, and reform. It has been one of the dominant concerns of the American church during the latter half of the twentieth century.

"Renewal" as used here will encompass the larger movement to reform and revitalize the church, a movement that includes such diverse components as mass evangelism; efforts to promote personal witnessing; revivals (in the sense of outpourings of the Holy Spirit); the Faith at Work, charismatic (or neo-Pentecostal), and Church Growth movements; the awakening among youth; efforts for renewal that have emanated from individual congregations; and the larger evangelical renaissance.

There is wide divergence, of course, not only as to what term to use, but as to what constitutes renewal, or whether a given movement should be included. There is wide agreement, on the other hand, on the need for renewal. Some reformers, particularly during the 1960s, have considered the institutional church beyond hope. But the more general agreement is that reform is possible, and, in fact, that the church is the central instrument God uses for the advancement of his kingdom. Indeed, much of the writing on the renewal of the church is marked by a note of optimism, contingent upon the meeting of biblical conditions.

Because efforts for renewal are as old as the story of God's people, reformers today as in earlier centuries have looked to that story for guidelines by which to revitalize the church. For modern evangelicals the primary models have been the early church, the Reformation, and the evangelical awakenings of the post-Reformation era. There are significant antecedents in those models for each of the following emphases.

Present-Day Renewal. The centrality of the Bible in present-day renewal is reflected in almost all facets of the movement, including the greatly increased scholarly activity. The primary emphasis of participants in awakenings is on the truth and authority of the Bible. Rather than being largely an object of study, Scripture is seen as the light for life's pathway, as the Word of God to be understood in order to be obeyed. The Bible serves a special function during awakenings as the objective standard by which to correct the tendency for awakened energies to move in unsound directions.

Prayer and the life of devotion, including such elements as praise and intercession, have formed another prominent theme. Prayer is grounded in the larger resurgence of a supernaturalism that not only accepts the possibility but emphasizes the necessity of divine intervention in human life. The hope of authentic renewal itself rests in the possibility of the appropriation of God's resources through prayer and Bible study.

The experiential dimension of Christian faith, centered in a meaningful personal relationship with God and expressed in such NT pictures as the vine and the branches, the bread of life, and the new birth, continues to be a major current in the stream of vital Christianity. That primary relationship in its turn transforms all other relationships, creating personal wholeness as well as community among believers. That kind of living faith stands in marked contrast to the extremes of dead orthodoxy and shallow experientialism of much of the church.

The Holy Spirit stands at the heart both of the possibility of divine resources and of the experiential dimension of renewal. Both the fruit and the gifts of the Spirit have received strong emphasis as part of the larger empowering or outpouring without which there can be no authentic and powerful renewal of the church.

The Church Growth Movement, arising out of missionary concerns and now focused strongly on the American church as well, has centered attention on the quantitative dimension of church life. And while that emphasis has elicited considerable criticism, the movement has retained strength, partly by clarifying or modifying its position in such qualitative areas as social concern.

In contrast to the common pattern in which the laity are largely spectators and recipients, revitalization of the church results in lay participation in worship, counseling, and evangelistic and social ministries. The clergy serve as enablers or player-coaches, rather than as superstars and authoritarian interpreters of Scripture. Lay witness teams have effectively extended renewal to other congregations.

Small groups, little churches within the church with often forgotten antecedents in earlier evangelical revivals, have played a prominent role in restoring community (*koinōnia*) to the church through such functions as Bible study, prayer, mutual support and accountability, and outreach in evangelism and service.

Evangelism, resurgent in mass form since midcentury, has assumed a significant role in the form of personal witnessing as well, stressing lay participation. Renewal has been marked by spontaneous sharing of the gospel, as well as by highly structured programs of personal evangelism.

Renewal and Social Concern. Social concern and action, practical responsiveness to the entire range of human need, a prominent feature of late twentieth century church renewal, represents a return to the biblical pattern of historic evangelicalism and a reversal of this century's "great reversal" of that tradition.

A growing concern within the large motif of social Christianity has been to attack evil rooted in the systems or structures of society. The renewed church will attend to social as well as individual moral issues, to causes as well as symptoms of social evils.

Partly to counter the centrifugal pressures inherent in the attention devoted separately to devotion, social action, and other emphases, a holistic Christian message has emerged as an additional theme. The Christian person for the modern world must be one whose life reflects a balance of prayer/devotion, evangelism, social concern/action, and rigorous intellectual endeavor.

Indeed, the general renewal has been stimulated by a renaissance of scholarship—biblical, historical, theological—which has enriched the life and theology of the churches and which has been significant in reestablishing evangelicalism as a force in the mainstream of American life. Large-scale awakening seems unlikely to many observers until the gates to the secular mind are opened by a credible and compelling statement of the case for the Christian view of God, humanity, and the world. N. A. Magnuson

See also Church Growth Movement.

Bibliography. D. Bloesch, *Centers of Christian Renewal* and *The Reform of the Church;* L. Christenson, *The Charismatic Renewal Among Lutherans;* R. Coleman, ed., *One Divine Moment;* F. B. Edge, *The Greening of the Church;* W. Fisher, *From Tradition to Mission;* D. R. Hogue, ed., *Understanding Church Growth and Decline: 1960–1978;* W. Howard, *Nine Roads to Renewal;* B. Larson and R. Osborne, *The Emerging Church;* R. F. Lovelace, *Dynamics of Spiritual Life: An Evangelical Theology of Renewal;* J. Kennedy, *Evangelism Explosion;* D. A. McGavran, *Understanding Church Growth;* K. Miller, *The Taste of New Wine;* E. O'Connor, *Call to Commitment;* J. E. Orr, *The Flaming Tongue: The Impact of Twentieth Century Revivals;* B. E. Patterson, ed., *The Stirring Giant: Renewal Forces at Work in the Modern Church;* R. Raines, *New Life in the Church;* L. O. Richards, *Three Churches in Renewal;* S. C. Rose, ed., *Who's Killing the Church?* R. Sider, *Rich Christians in an Age of Hunger;* H. S. Shoemaker, *I Stand by the Door: The Life of Sam Shoemaker;* D. E. Trueblood, *The Company of the Committed, The Incendiary Fellowship,* and *The New Man for Our Time;* G. E. Worrell, ed., *Resources for Renewal;* J. H. Westerhoff, *Inner Growth, Outer Change: An Educational Guide to Church Renewal.*

Repentance. In the OT the verb "repent" (*niham*) occurs about thirty-five times. It is usually used to signify a contemplated change in God's dealings with men for good or ill according to his just judgment (I Sam. 15:11, 35; Jonah 3:9–10) or, negatively, to certify that God will not swerve from his announced purpose (I Sam. 15:29; Ps. 110:4; Jer. 4:28). In five places *niham* refers to human repentance or relenting. The LXX translates *niham* with *metanoeō* and *metamelomai.* Either Greek verb may occur designating either human repentance or divine "relenting" (so the RSV in some places).

However, the background of the NT idea of repentance lies not primarily in *niḥam* (except in Job 42:6; Jer. 8:6; 31:19), but rather in *šûb*, meaning "to turn back, away from, or toward" in the religious sense. The LXX consistently translates *šûb* with *epistrephō* and *apostrephō.* Repentance follows a turning about which is a gift of God (Jer. 31:18–20; Ps. 80:3, 7, 19). Isa. 55:6–7 gives the typical OT call to repentance and conversion. Heartfelt sorrow for sin and conversion are sometimes placed in an eschatological setting, being linked to the remission of judgment, the return from captivity, the coming of the great time of salvation, and the coming of Pentecost (Jer. 31:17–20, 31–34; Joel 12:12–32).

In the NT *metanoia* (noun) occurs twenty-three times and *metanoeō* (verb) thirty-four times. *Metamelomai* occurs seldom and is used almost exclusively in the sense of "regretting, having remorse." *Metanoeō* (*metanoia*) is almost always used in a favorable sense.

Repentance is the theme of the preaching of John the Baptist (Matt. 3:1; Mark 1:4; Matt. 3:8). Baptism in water unto repentance is accompanied by confession of sins (Matt. 3:6; cf. I John 1:8–9). Jesus continues John's theme but adds, significantly, "The time is fulfilled" (Mark 1:15). His coming is the coming of the kingdom in person and is decisive (Matt. 11:20–24; Luke 13:1–5). All life relationships must be radically altered (Matt. 5:17–7:27; Luke 14:25–35; 18:18–30). Sinners, not the righteous, are called to *metanoia* (Matt. 9:13; Mark 2:17; Luke 5:32), and heaven rejoices over their repentance (Luke 15). The preaching of repentance and remission of sins must be joined to the proclamation of the cross and the resurrection (Luke 24:44–49). The apostles are true to this commission (Acts 2:38; 3:19; 17:30; 20:21). Unfaithful churches must repent (Rev. 3:5, 16). Apostates crucify to themselves the Son of God afresh and cannot be renewed to repentance (Heb. 6:5–6).

NT writers often distinguish between repentance and conversion (Acts 3:19; 26:20), and between repentance and faith (Mark 1:15; Acts 20:21). "[*Epistrephō*] has a somewhat wider signification than *metanoeō* . . . [and] always includes the element of faith. *Metanoeō* and *pisteuein* can be alongside of each other; not so *epistrephō* and *pisteuein*" (Louis Berkhof, *Systematic Theology,* p. 482). The distinction between *metanoeō* and *epistrephō* should not be pressed. *Metanoia,* at least, is used to signify the whole process of change. God has granted the Gentiles "repentance unto life" (Acts 11:18) and godly sorrow works "repentance unto salvation" (II Cor. 7:10). Generally, however, *metanoia* can be said to denote that inward change of mind, affections, convictions, and commitment rooted in the fear of God and sorrow for offenses committed against him, which, when accompanied by faith in Jesus Christ, results in an outward turning from sin to God and his service in all of life. It is never regretted (*ametamelēton,* II Cor. 7:10) and it is given by God (Acts 11:18). *Metanoeō* points to the inward conscious change while *epistrephō* directs attention particularly to the changed determinative center for all of life (Acts 15:19; I Thess. 1:9).

Calvin taught that repentance stemmed from serious fear of God and consisted in the mortification of the old man and the quickening of the Spirit. Mortification and renovation are obtained by union with Christ in his death and resurrection (*Institutes* 3.3.5, 9).

Beza (after Lactantius and Erasmus) objected

to the translation of *metanoeō* by "*poenitentiam agite,*" but the attempt to replace this with *resipiscentia* ("a coming to one's self") was infelicitous. Luther occasionally used "*Thut Busse!*" but his thesis was that Jesus, in giving this command, meant that all of life was to be penance before God.

Roman Catholicism teaches that the sacrament of penance consists materially of contrition, confession, and satisfaction. But the judicial pronouncement of absolution by the church is needed to give these elements real validity.

C. G. Kromminga

See also Conversion; Salvation; Order of Salvation; Penitence.

Bibliography. L. Berkhof, *Systematic Theology;* W. D. Chamberlain, *The Meaning of Repentance;* B. H. DeMent, *ISBE,* IV, 2558–59; R. B. Girdlestone, *Synonyms of the OT;* J. Schniewind, *Die Freude der Busse;* G. Spykman, *Attrition and Contrition at the Council of Trent;* G. Vos, *The Teaching of Jesus Concerning the Kingdom of God and the Church;* F. Laubach and J. Goetzmann, *NIDNTT,* I, 353ff.; J. J. von Allmen, ed., *Vocabulary of the Bible;* J. Jeremias, *NT Theology,* I, 152ff.; *TDNT:* J. Behm, IV, 975ff.; O. Michel, IV, 626ff.; G. Bertram, VII, 722ff.

Reprobation. This term is derived from the Latin *reprobatus,* past participle of the verb *reprobare,* to reprove, and refers to the fact that God has eternally condemned the nonelect to eternal punishment for their sins. Calvin set forth this doctrine very clearly and precisely in *The Institutes of the Christian Religion* (III.23.1ff.), and while he regarded it as a dreadful (*horribile*) doctrine, yet he denied that it was to be avoided or rejected, for it is clearly taught in the Scriptures of both the OT and NT. He cites various instances such as the divine choice of Jacob and rejection of Esau, even before the twins were born (Gen. 25:21–23; Mal. 1:2–3; Rom. 9:10ff.), God's hardening of Pharaoh's heart against the Israelites (Exod. 4:21; 10:21, 27; Rom. 9:17), and the apostle Paul's statement in Rom. 9:18ff. concerning God's ability to make one vessel for honor and another for dishonor. He also insists that this is not just a matter of God's "passing over" the nonelect, but an actual hardening so that they are actually strengthened to resist the gospel. Yet while holding this position, he insists that because we cannot comprehend the full counsel of God, we must simply believe and leave the matter in God's hands, knowing that the Judge of all the earth shall do what is right (Gen. 18:25). He also warns that, because of the mystery of God's sovereign will, this doctrine must be dealt with very carefully lest it discourage Christians and give unbelievers an excuse for rejecting the gospel call.

W. S. Reid

See also Preterition; Predestination; Elect, Election.

Responsibility. The relation a free moral agent has to a decision or act for which the agent is answerable, accountable, or responsible. The counterpart to responsibility is imputability, in which the decision or act is chargeable, attributable, or imputable to the agent. Assumed here in both cases are a law imposing an obligation and a sanction enforcing the obligation. A sanction is a promise of reward and the threat of punishment. The lawbreaker deserves the punishment, and the law keeper is entitled to the reward because of merit, or the right of payment. Responsibility and imputability, or culpability, are particularly concerned with the extent to which a decision or act owes its origin to an agent's will guided by reason. Responsibility for a bad act is called guilt. There is no corresponding designation of responsibility for a good act. This is probably accounted for by the fact that responsibility is more often associated with acts of wrongdoing than right doing.

A related concept is justice, the measure of merit. Justice stems from the idea of equality between two persons having some agreement, understanding, or contract between them. If one party fails to keep the agreement, then he or she upsets the equality, thereby owing a compensation to the other party. The person keeping the agreement has something due him or her. Justice is served when the offending party pays the offended party whatever is deserved or merited, that is, whatever is considered to reestablish the state of equality. From the standpoint of the offended party the compensation merited is regarded as a reward. From the standpoint of the offending party the compensation which is owed is seen as a punishment.

Moving beyond the limits of the simple contract situation into the broader context of moral responsibility in general, we find that punishment has several functions, since more than an individual is usually offended by an act of wrongdoing. That act may be a crime against the group or the state. It may also be a sin against God. Retributive punishment serves the offended person by getting back at the offender and restoring the balance which justice demands. Corrective or rehabilitative punishment serves the offender by bringing him or her back to the place of equality with the rest of the group or society. Preventive or deterrent punishment serves the group or society by forestalling future wrongdoing of the type committed. Vindicative punishment serves the law and the lawgiver, both human and divine, by putting down one who has flouted the very ideas of law, equality, and justice. By so doing, that person has offended the holiness and justice of God himself.

Although responsibility is being treated here as a moral phenomenon, we have reflected the biblical approach by looking at it from the standpoint of some of the concerns of legal responsibility. A study of legal responsibility as such would lead into such topics as an offender's intentions (*mens rea*), strict liability, and criminal insanity. Instead we shall focus on a concept which is central to moral responsibility as such, namely, the concept of freedom.

Responsibility and Freedom. No one holds a person responsible for a decision or act when that person's will is not free. Hard determinists believe that the will is never free, hence there is no such thing as moral responsibility. For those who hold the will to be free, a practical criterion is that for any act an agent may be considered to have the freedom required for responsibility if he or she can choose to do otherwise. To be able to choose to do otherwise may be taken to mean that more than one alternative is open to the agent, and the alternative actualized is the one chosen by the agent. The focus here is upon being able to put into effect a decision once it is made. Soft determinists or compatibilists prefer this interpretation. Not wanting to deny the determination of a person's decisions by such factors as the person's heredity, social background, mental history, character, sinful nature, and, some would add, God's foreknowledge or decrees, a soft determinist still maintains that one or more of these determining factors is compatible with the freedom required for responsibility, as long as the agent is not hindered from carrying out his or her decision.

A third position on the freedom of the will is taken by the libertarian. He or she believes that while the determining factors listed by the determinists play a role, the agent of a responsible decision or act must have the kind of freedom in which his or her being able to choose to do otherwise means that no one, not even the agent, can always successfully predict the decision arrived at. It is a new creation arising out of the decision-making process. Some libertarians prefer to think of a free decision to act as having no cause. This is known as indeterminism. Other libertarians refer to the agent's ranking and selecting his or her motives as the cause. This position is called self-determinism.

Another condition necessary for moral responsibility is knowledge of what is expected of one. A person who is ignorant of a rule or law is either not held responsible or is thought to have a reduced degree of responsibility, as long as he or she did not willfully bring about that ignorance.

Responsibility and Scripture. Certainly in Scripture, but also in general usage, responsibility extends to the family, to larger groupings up to a nation, to groups of nations, and to even the entire human race. But the primary focus of responsibility is a person who can be held accountable, i.e., an agent who has the power or ability to make decisions and act on them intentionally. One acts intentionally when one does something for a reason, that is, because of one's beliefs and desires. This is why God is said to judge "the thoughts and intents of the heart."

Specific biblical teachings relative to responsibility include the following: (1) Every human being is held responsible by God for the sin of the first human being (Rom. 5:12). (2) God's giving of the law through Moses created a much greater sense of responsibility in Israel (Rom. 7:7). (3) The rest of the human race is no less responsible, however, for "when they do by nature the things contained in the law . . . [they] show the work of the law written in their hearts" (Rom. 2:14–15). (4) Unless the sinner acknowledges responsibility for sin and repents, he or she cannot be forgiven by God through Jesus Christ (Acts 3:19). S. R. OBITTS

See also ETHICS, BIBLICAL; FREEDOM, FREE WILL, AND DETERMINISM.

Bibliography. J. Feinberg, *Doing and Deserving;* W. K. Frankena, *Ethics;* J. Glover, *Responsibility;* H. L. A. Hart, *Punishment and Responsibility;* H. R. Niebuhr, *The Responsible Self;* H. Morris, ed., *Freedom and Responsibility;* R. Young, *Freedom, Responsibility, and God.*

Restoration of Israel. *See* ISRAEL AND PROPHECY.

Resurrection of Christ. That Jesus Christ died and afterward rose from the dead is both the central doctrine of Christian theology and the major fact in a defense of its teachings. This was true in the earliest church and remains so today.

The Centrality of the Resurrection. It is the witness of the NT that the resurrection of Jesus is the pivotal point of Christian theology and apologetics. Paul reports an early creed in I Cor. 15:3ff. which both includes the resurrection as an integral part of the gospel and reports several eyewitness appearances.

Then Paul relates the importance of this event, for if Jesus did not literally rise from the dead, then the entire Christian faith is fallacious (vs. 14) and ineffective (vs. 17). Additionally, preaching is valueless (vs. 14), Christian testimony is false (vs. 15), no sins have been forgiven (vs. 17), and believers have perished without any Christian hope (vs. 18). The conclusion is that, apart from this event, Christians are the most miserable of all people (vs. 19). Paul even states that without the resurrection we should "eat and drink, for tomorrow we die" (vs. 32). If Jesus was not raised, believers have no hope of resurrection themselves and may as well turn to hedonistic philosophies of life. He thereby strongly implies that it is this event that separates Christianity from other philosophies.

Paul teaches the centrality of the resurrection in other passages as well. In another ancient creed (Rom. 1:3–4) he recites a brief Christology and asserts that Jesus was shown to be the Son of God, Christ, and Lord by his resurrection (cf. Rom. 14:9). This event also provides salvation (Rom. 10:9–10) and ensures the resurrection of believers (I Cor. 15:20; II Cor. 4:14; I Thess. 4:14).

Similarly, Luke's writings relate several instances where the resurrection provided the basis for the Christian proclamation. Jesus taught that his death and resurrection was a central message of the OT (Luke 24:25–27). Peter held that the miracles which Jesus performed, and his resurrection in particular, were the chief indications that God approved of his teachings (Acts 2:22–32). Paul's teaching frequently utilized the resurrection as the basis of the gospel message (cf. Acts 13:29–39; 17:30–31).

Other NT writings share the same hope. Jesus utilized his resurrection as the sign vindicating the authority of his teachings (Matt. 12:38–40). This event both ensures the believer's salvation (I Pet. 1:3) and provides the means by which Jesus serves as the believer's high priest (Heb. 7:23–25).

Even such a brief survey indicates the centrality of the resurrection for the NT writers. Clearly, early believers such as Paul realized that this event provided the central claim of Christianity. With it the Christian message of eternal life is secure, resting on the reality of Jesus' victory over death. Without it the Christian message is reduced to that of one of man's philosophies.

The earliest postapostolic writings held this same message of the centrality of Jesus' resurrection. For example, Clement of Rome asserts that this event both demonstrates the truthfulness of Christ's message (*Cor.* 42) and is an example of the believer's resurrection (24–26). Ignatius insists on the literal facticity of this occurrence as an event in time (*Mag.* 11; *Trall.* 9; *Smyr.* 1), which is the believer's hope (*Trall.*, Introduction) and an example of our resurrection (*Trall.* 9). He also stresses the belief that it was Jesus' flesh that was raised (*Smyr.* 3).

This latter issue of whether it was Jesus' flesh which was resurrected, as supported by Ignatius and later by Tertullian, or whether it was a resurrected body not composed of flesh, as championed by the Alexandrian school and Origen in particular, was a major question in early Christian theology. It was the former position, or forms of it, which gradually became the more widely accepted view in the medieval church and even afterward.

For many scholars today who accept the literal resurrection of Jesus, the emphasis has shifted to stress Paul's concept of the "spiritual body" (I Cor. 15:35–50, e.g.), endeavoring to do justice to both elements. Thus, Jesus was raised in a real body which had new, spiritual qualities.

The Resurrection and Contemporary Theology. There is virtual agreement, even among most critical theologians, that the resurrection of Jesus is the central claim of Christianity. Willi Marxsen asserts that it is still the decisive issue in Christian theology today; to have uncertainty concerning this claim is to jeopardize all of Christianity. Günther Bornkamm agrees that without the message of Jesus' resurrection there would be no church, no NT, and no Christian faith even to this day. Jürgen Moltmann clearly states that Christianity either stands or falls with Jesus' resurrection.

Yet a major issue here concerns the question of whether all that is required is the message of the resurrection, or the literal event itself. This is not only a dispute between evangelicals and higher critical theologians, but also among these critical scholars themselves. The pivotal fact, recognized as historical by virtually all scholars, is the original experiences of the disciples. It is nearly always admitted that the disciples had real experiences and that "something happened." Yet, while contemporary scholars rarely utilize the naturalistic alternative theories, various views exist concerning the exact nature of these experiences. At the risk of oversimplification and partial repetition, at least four major critical positions can be outlined with regard to this question.

First, more radical critics hold that the nature of the original eyewitnesses' experiences cannot be ascertained. For example, Rudolf Bultmann and his followers claim that the actual cause of the disciples' transformation is obscured in the NT text. Regardless, it is not really important to inquire into the object of these experiences. Similarly, Marxsen also believes that the constitution of these encounters cannot be known, including whether the disciples actually saw the risen Jesus. Paul van Buren believes that "something happened" which changed the disciples' outlook from discouragement to faith. Although these experiences were more than subjective and were expressed in terms of actual appearances of Jesus, we still cannot judge their nature.

A second group of scholars is distinguished from the first not only by exhibiting some interest in the nature of the disciples' experiences, but often by the acceptance of the literal resurrection itself. Yet while the naturalistic theories are usually rejected, this group still insists that the event can be known only by faith completely apart from any verification.

The theologians in this second group have usually been influenced by Søren Kierkegaard and more recently by Karl Barth, who held that the resurrection may be accepted by faith as a literal event, but that it cannot be ascertained by any historical investigation. Barth emphatically rejected naturalistic theories and asserted that Jesus appeared empirically to his disciples, yet this event occurred in a different sphere of history and thus cannot be verified by history. Similar views were held by neo-orthodox theologians such as Emil Brunner and Dietrich Bonhoeffer, and are also popular in more contemporary works. For example, Bornkamm notes the invalidity of naturalistic theories but yet, in a manner reminiscent of Barth, states that this event can be accepted only by faith apart from historical examination.

The third position is characterized by a significant interest in more historical aspects of the resurrection. Not only are naturalistic theories usually rejected, but the empty tomb is often held to be a historical fact. Additionally, these scholars proceed a step further by setting forth a more or less abstract reconstruction of the historical nature of the appearances. However, it is still held that the resurrection itself is an eschatological event and is not demonstrable by historical methodology, although some hold that it will be verifiable in the future.

Moltmann holds that the disciples were the recipients of appearances of the risen Jesus, which involved spoken messages and commissioned the hearers to service in the world. These events, which are not strictly verifiable, are placed in eschatological history and are subject to future verification. Ulrich Wilckens likewise concludes that history cannot decide exactly what happened. Thus, while naturalistic theories can be refuted and the facticity of the empty tomb upheld, the appearances themselves were private revelations, indications of a future, eschatological existence.

Reginald Fuller notes that the disciples' transformations necessitate a cause. This cause is Jesus' appearances, which are historically defined as visionary experiences of light and auditions of meaning communicated to the earliest eyewitnesses. The messages both proclaimed that Jesus was risen and imparted a mission to his followers. Such phenomena were not subjective visions but actual experiences. They were the source of the Easter faith and message, but are removed from historical demonstration. Joachim Jeremias similarly taught that the appearances of Jesus were spiritual visions of shining light by which the disciples experienced Jesus as the risen Lord.

The fourth approach to the resurrection is that the available historical evidence demonstrates the probability that Jesus was literally raised from the dead. Perhaps the best-known recent theologian accepting this conclusion is Wolfhart Pannenberg, who both argues against naturalistic theories and concludes that the historical facts demonstrate the empty tomb and the literal appearances of Jesus. Yet Pannenberg argues against a corporeal resurrection body in favor of appearances which are described in terms of a spiritual body which was recognized as Jesus, who appeared from heaven, imparted an audition, and, at least in Paul's case, was accompanied by a phenomenon of light.

A. M. Hunter utilizes historical investigation to conclude that Jesus' resurrection can be demonstrated by the facts. J. A. T. Robinson points out that historical studies cannot ascertain the exact details, but they may be sufficient to formulate a probable case for the probability of this event. Raymond Brown, after an extensive study of the textual data, likewise supports the historical verification of Jesus' resurrection. Additionally, Hunter, Robinson, and Brown all favor the concept of the spiritual body.

It is important to note that of these four critical positions only the first is generally characterized by a rejection of or agnostic attitude toward the literal resurrection of Jesus. Just as significant is the observation that the first position not only appears to be losing ground, but varying positions which support the facticity of the resurrection are presently quite popular.

The Resurrection as History. Historical arguments for the resurrection have traditionally been based on two lines of support. First, naturalistic theories have failed to explain away this event, chiefly because each is disproven by the known historical facts.

Additionally, critics themselves have attacked each theory. For instance, in the nineteenth century David Strauss disarmed the swoon theory while Theodor Keim and others pointed out the weaknesses in the hallucination theory. Form critical studies later revealed the futility of the legend theory popularized by the history of religions school of thought. In the twentieth century such diverse thinkers as Barth, Tillich, Bornkamm, and Pannenberg are examples of higher critical theologians who have rejected these alternative hypotheses.

Second, historical evidences for the resurrection are often cited, such as the eyewitness testimony for Jesus' appearances, the transformed lives of the disciples, the empty tomb, the inability of the Jewish leaders to disprove these claims, and the conversion of skeptics such as Paul and James, the brother of Jesus. When combined with the absence of naturalistic alternative theories these evidences are quite impressive.

However, contemporary apologetics has moved even beyond these important issues to other arguments in favor of the resurrection. One crucial center of attention has been I Cor. 15:3–4, where Paul records material which he had "received" from others and then "delivered" to his listeners. It is agreed by virtually all contemporary theologians that this material contains an ancient creed that is actually much earlier than the book in which it is recorded.

The early date of this tradition is indicated not only by Paul's rather technical terms for receiving and passing on tradition, but also by the somewhat stylized content, the non-Pauline words, the specific names of Peter and James (cf. Gal. 1:18–19), and the possible Semitic idioms used.

These facts have accounted for the critical agreement as to the early origin of this material. In fact, Fuller, Hunter, and Pannenberg date Paul's receiving of this creed from three to eight years after the crucifixion itself. These data are quite significant in that they further indicate that both Paul and the other eyewitnesses proclaimed the death and resurrection of Jesus (I Cor. 15:11) immediately after the events themselves. This anchors their report firmly in early eyewitness testimony and not in legendary reports arising later.

Another extremely strong argument for the resurrection is derived from the known facts that are admitted as historical by virtually all critical scholars who deal with this subject. Events such as Jesus' death by crucifixion, the subsequent despair of the disciples, their experiences which they believed to be appearances of the risen Jesus, their corresponding transformations, and the conversion of Paul due to a similar experience are five facts which are critically established and accepted as historical by most scholars.

Of these facts the nature of the disciples' experiences is the most crucial. As historian Michael Grant asserts, historical investigation demonstrates that the earliest eyewitnesses were convinced that they had seen the risen Jesus. Carl Braaten explains that skeptical historians agree with this conclusion. One major advantage of these critically accepted historical facts is that they deal directly with the issue of these experiences. On a more limited scale these facts are capable both of arguing decisively against each of the naturalistic alternative theories and of providing some strong evidences for the literal appearances of the risen Jesus as reported by the eyewitnesses.

Not only can the historical resurrection be established on this basis, but the additional advantage of these facts is that they are admitted by virtually all scholars as knowable history. Since such a minimum number of facts is adequate to historically establish the literal resurrection as the best explanation for the data, this event therefore should not be rejected even by those critics who disbelieve the reliability of Scripture. Their questions on other issues do not disprove this basic conclusion, which can be established by critical and historical procedures.

Especially when viewed in conjunction with the eyewitness evidence from the early creed, we have a strong twofold apologetic for the historicity of Jesus' resurrection. This contemporary approach also complements the more traditional apologetic summarized earlier, all of which combine to historically demonstrate the fact that Jesus was raised from the dead.

As Paul asserted in I Cor. 15:12–20, the resurrection is the center of the Christian faith and theology. This event signals the approval of Jesus' teachings (Acts 2:22–23) and thus continues to provide a basis for Christian belief today. It guarantees the reality of eternal life for all who trust the gospel (I Cor. 15:1–4, 20).

G. R. Habermas

Bibliography. K. Barth, *Church Dogmatics*, IV/1, 334–52; D. Bonhoeffer, *Christ the Center;* G. Bornkamm, *Jesus of Nazareth;* R. E. Brown, *The Virginal Conception and Bodily Resurrection of Jesus;* E. Brunner, *Dogmatics*, II, 366–72; R. Bultmann, *Theology of the NT;* D. P. Fuller, *Easter Faith and History;* R. H. Fuller, *The Formation of the Resurrection Narratives;* M. Grant, *Jesus: An Historian's Review of the Gospels;* G. R. Habermas, *The Resurrection of Jesus: An Apologetic;* A. M. Hunter, *Bible and Gospel;* J. Jeremias, *NT Theology;* W. Marxsen, *The Resurrection of Jesus of Nazareth;* J. Moltmann, *Revolution and the Future;* J. Orr, *The Resurrection of Jesus;* W. Pannenberg, *Jesus—God and Man;* J. A. T. Robinson, *Can We Trust the NT?* P. M. van Buren, *The Secular Meaning of the Gospel;* U. Wilkens, *Resurrection.*

Resurrection of the Dead. ***In the OT.*** Several considerations moved OT thought away from the early, universal, animistic ideas about postmortem survival which underlay necromancy (I Sam. 28:8–9), funeral provisions, directions for the dead, and Sheol/Hades, the shadowy underworld of ghosts (Ezek. 32:17–32).

Everyday observation, plus the belief that God made man's body in his own image, led to the conviction that man was not "soul" imprisoned within a physical frame but embodied spirit, a unity of body and living self. Sheol's disembodiment in forgetfulness, hopelessness, without knowledge or relationships (II Sam. 12:23; Job 7:9ff.; 10:20–22; Ps. 30:9; Eccles. 9:2, 5, 10) therefore struck horror, as subhuman. Hence Israel's care for the bodies of the dead (Gen. 23; 50:2, 25; Jer. 8:1ff.; 14:16).

At first Yahweh's rule did not extend beyond death (Pss. 6:5; 88:10–12, Isa. 38:18), until prophetic insistence on his universal sovereignty claimed Sheol also within his jurisdiction (Ps. 139:7–8). The emphasis of Jeremiah and Ezekiel on individual relationships with God led to more religious conceptions of the afterlife (Pss. 16:8–11; 73:23–26). No shadow existence could sustain divine fellowship, but only restoration to full personality in resurrection (Matt. 22:31).

Longing for acquittal from the accusation that great suffering implies great sin made Job contemplate waiting in Sheol until God's wrath be past and he, released, would live again (Job 14:7–15). Despite its difficulties, Job 19:25–27 likewise appears to anticipate immortality in some bodily form. Pss. 73:17; 49:14–15; Isa. 53:10ff. similarly relieve the injustice of suffering by the hope of life with God beyond Sheol.

Some think the promises of national vindication and prosperity in the day of the Lord, unless confined to "the final generation," first prompted thoughts of resurrection of intervening generations, although Hos. 6:2; 13:14; Ezek. 37:1–14 use resurrection language as already familiar. Isa. 24–27 (especially 25:6–8; 26:19ff.) and Dan. 12:1–4 anticipate the return of men in bodily integrity to share Israel's glory. Isa. 26:14 denies resurrection to foes; Daniel includes resurrection "to life" (for Jews faithful under persecution), and "to everlasting contempt" (for Jews who joined the persecutors, 11:32ff.). No general resurrection is implied: here, too, justice is the argument.

Zoroastrian, Egyptian, Assyrian, and Babylonian allusions may be either sources or parallels to developing Jewish thought.

Intertestamental Apocalyptic Thought. Intertestamental apocalyptic ranged widely. Some writers applied moral distinctions within Sheol, with reward and punishment implying some degree of judgment. Promises to the faithful, especially martyrs, included earthly glory; justice would likewise resurrect oppressors (with their deformities) to be recognized and punished (II Apoc. Bar.; cf. Mark 9:42ff.).

Hellenized Judaism preferred immortality of the soul, more richly conceived, to resurrection of the body. Palestinian Judaism clung to resurrection. "Garments of glory" (of life) were required for life beyond death (I–II Enoch), "nakedness" (disembodiment) being abhorred. Some speak of a spiritual body, counterpart to the physical and coexistent with it. I Enoch says the body buried will rise "glorious"; II Apoc. Bar. resembles I Cor. 15:35ff. but holds the transformation comes later; most speak of the risen body as "like angels . . . made of the light and glory of God"; others of its needing neither food nor marriage.

Those raised to share Messiah's temporary (earthly) or final (supernatural) kingdom will be righteous (Jews). Other writers assume a general resurrection; II Esdras, a resurrection of Messiah and all men after the messianic age. In I Enoch 22 those already punished remain in Sheol; those not punished move to torturing Gehenna; I Enoch 67 has some wicked raised for judgment. Apocalyptists invent various stages of judgment, kingdom, resurrection. Test. Benj. 10:6ff. makes patriarchs rise first, then sons of Jacob, then all men. II Macc., perhaps following hints of Isa. 24–27 and Daniel, suggests martyrs deserve priority.

By the first century most Jews held to general resurrection; rabbis argued Abraham so believed (Heb. 11:19). Pharisees expected resurrection of the just (Acts 23:8), so probably did Essenes and Qumran covenanters. Sadducees denied resurrection as not "Mosaic," and possibly as a foreign idea (Mark 12:18; Josephus says they believed the soul died with the body). A few, holding matter evil, denied resurrection altogether.

In the NT. New Christian contributions include (1) Jesus' teaching, set against his raising others to resume life, and predictions of his own rising ("third day," not timeless immortality). Jesus utilizes picturesque detail familiar to hearers, especially Pharisees—Sheol/Hades (Luke 16:19ff.; 10:15), morally subdivided, ministry of angels, welcome by patriarchs, torment (Mark 9:43ff.; Matt. 8:12; 10:28), resurrection for fellowship (Matt. 8:11), reward (Luke 14:14). Jesus argues immortality from experience of God and assumes this involves resurrection (Mark 12:18ff.). The risen life is new, angelic, and sexless. His emphasis falls on judgment, which appears to be immediate (Luke 16:23; cf. 12:20), or at the Son of man's coronation (Matt. 25:31ff.). Judgment implies general resurrection (Matt. 25:41; 10:28; Mark 12:26); but Luke 20:35ff.; 14:14 suggest resurrection limited to those qualified. (2) Jesus' own resurrection is the key event in Christian history and the basis of Peter's gospel (Acts 2:32) and Paul's (Acts 17:18; 23:6; 26:6–8). Apostolic testimony (Acts 3:26; 4:2, 33; I Cor. 15:3–11; Rom. 10:9) makes resurrection essential in Christianity. Details of the story (waiting in Sheol, persistent wounds, "flesh and bones" that can be touched, yet "in another form" is unrecognized, passes through doors, vanishes) combine current ideas with a new assertion: an empty tomb. The unquestioned fact creates a new basis for resurrection hope (Rom. 8:11; I Cor. 6:14; 15:20ff.; II Cor. 4:14; I Thess. 4:14; I Pet. 1:3, 21) through Christ "whom God has raised" (sixteen allusions). (3) Pauline reflection likewise begins from current Pharisaic views: the departed share the coming glory (I Thess. 4:15ff.), general resurrection and judgment (Acts 24:15; 17:31; Rom. 2:5–11; II Cor. 5:10), horror of disembodied nakedness (II Cor. 5:4). Paul develops three themes:

Complete Redemption. This includes redemption of the body and argues new ground for resurrection hope. Sexually, Christians must remember that the body is the Lord's, "members of Christ," a temple of the spirit, purchased by Christ (I Cor. 6:12ff.), instrument of righteousness (Rom. 6:12ff.), vehicle of worship (Rom. 12:1). Man being embodied spirit, redemption would remain incomplete without resurrection.

"We Shall All Be Changed." Wishing to be done with the "humiliating" flesh, too long the vehicle of sin (Rom. 7:21–25; Phil. 3:20–21), yet not to be "naked" (II Cor. 5:1–5), Paul argued for deliverance of the body from corruption, but not (as the Greeks) for deliverance of the spirit from the body. Arguing with those who, stressing dissolution, preferred immortality to resurrection, Paul insists first on the bodily resurrection of Jesus (I Cor. 15:1ff.) then faces objectors with the varieties of body in nature (birds, fishes, grain) each adapted to its environment, and asserts God will provide the risen soul with a new body, glorious, incorruptible, immortal (cf. I Thess. 4:16–17). The key words "we shall be changed" imply continuity and difference. As grain disintegrates, that a totally new body may emerge, so human bodies disintegrate that the enduring life may organize new embodiment while retaining identity, as happens (we are told) repeatedly from birth to senility. This effectively meets the objection from dissolution; it has also implications affecting burial and cremation. Paul did not expect such transformation at death, but at the advent (I Thess. 4:14–17; I Cor. 15:23, 51ff.), following an intermediate state which is far better but not final glory (Phil. 1:23; cf. Acts 7:60 "sleep," Luke 23:43 "today").

The Change Has Begun. "Attaining the resurrection" (Phil. 3:11) involves sowing the spiritual, heavenly body in this life by yielding to the Spirit (Rom. 8:11), constantly dying and quickened (II Cor. 4:10ff., 14), reaping life eternal (Gal. 6:8). The counterpart, coexisting spiritual body is being created not "as the angels" but "like unto Christ's glorious body" (Phil. 3:21), as Christians live the risen life now (Rom. 6; Eph. 2:1ff.; Col. 3:1ff.). Nevertheless Paul adheres to physical resurrection as the consummation of the process (I Cor. 15:12–20): the resurrection is not "past already" (II Tim. 2:18).

Johannine reflection moves even nearer than Paul's toward incorporeal immortality. Eternal life is experienced now (John 3:36); the faithful never see death (8:51); believers have already "crossed over" from death to life (5:24), as have those who love (I John 3:14). Faced with Martha's talk about resurrection at the last day, Jesus replies that he himself, and relationship to him, constitute the resurrection and the life (11:25; 17:3) just as belief in him avoids judgment and unbelief *is* judgment (John 3:18–21). As Christ's own life (preexistent, earthly, postmortem) passes through death unquenched, so believers will never die (8:51). Those who disobey the Son do not see life (3:36). As does Paul, John appears to discount physical resurrection, yet 5:25, 28ff. declare a general resurrection, and 6:39–40, 44, 54 a resurrection of believers "at the last day"—hardly an accommodation to earlier views or interpolation, since Lazarus's restoration to this life and Christ's physical resurrection mean so much to John. Faith was still exploratory.

Further Developments. Later thought further illustrates the tension between Hebrew and Greek emphases. Gnostic dualism infiltrated Christian teaching about God, Christ, and morality with the alien Greek principle that matter is inherently evil and must be destroyed, resurrection being impossible. But (except in asceticism) the church rejected dualism. I and II Clement, Barnabas ("a general resurrection"), and Tertullian ("the soul inherently immortal and death unnatural, yet the same body will be raised") express the orthodox view. Ignatius follows John: Christ is eternal life, but "flesh and spirit" will be raised through the Eucharist ("medicine of immortality") and the Spirit. Origen insists that the natural body is dissolved into dust, but will be raised and "advance to a spiritual body"—so striving to reconcile Hebrew and Platonic ideas. Aquinas, too, held our fleshly bodies rise and remain fleshly; like Tertullian, he finds spiritual uses for redundant physical organs.

A typical modern statement runs: "The term

immortality is preferable. The argument that religious experience implies personal survival points to the immortality of the soul and its values rather than to resurrection of the body." This attracts many, who do not always realize the values conserved by the traditional resurrection emphasis: the permanence not only of abstract personality and values but of the individual, with consciousness, relationships, memories, and love, against theories of absorption ("a drop in the eternal ocean of being"), racial survival ("continuing to contribute to ongoing humanity"), or sentimental immortality ("to live in the hearts of those we love is not to die"). Essentially, Christians believe that he who called men into being and into fellowship with himself can sustain all persons under eternal conditions, in complete and enriched humanity, in such bodily garment as eternal life requires. R. E. O. WHITE

See also RESURRECTION OF CHRIST.

Bibliography. D. S. Russell, *Between the Testaments;* J. Baillie, *And the Life Everlasting;* J. H. Leckie, *World to Come and Final Destiny;* Tertullian, *On the Resurrection of the Flesh.*

Retaliation. *See* VENGEANCE.

Revelation, General. That divine disclosure to all persons at all times and places by which one comes to know that God is, and what he is like. While not imparting saving truths such as the Trinity, incarnation, or atonement, general revelation mediates the conviction that God exists and that he is self-sufficient, transcendent, immanent, eternal, powerful, wise, good, and righteous. General, or natural, revelation may be divided into two categories: (1) internal, the innate sense of deity and conscience, and (2) external, nature and providential history.

Summary of Positions. (1) Some scholars flatly deny any reality to general revelation. Postulating an infinite qualitative distinction between God and man and destruction of the *imago Dei* by the fall, Karl Barth refused to acknowledge any revelation outside the Word of God. Revelation for Barth means the incarnation of the Word. (2) Others concede the givenness of general revelation, but deny that it registers as actual knowledge in the sin-darkened mind of the unregenerate. Thus the Dutch Reformed school of Kuyper, Berkouwer, Van Til, and others insists that nature and history point to God only in the experience of those whose hearts and minds have been illumined by the grace of regeneration.

(3) On the other extreme many liberal authorities insist that the light afforded by general revelation is sufficient for salvation. One tradition within this category focuses attention on the illuminatory value of ecstatic religious experience. With but slight modifications Schleiermacher, Otto, Tillich, and Rahner all claim that through a noncognitive, mystical meeting the human soul savingly engages God, the world Soul. A second liberal tradition claims that the human mind, utilizing the scientific method, is capable of ferreting out all the truth man needs to order his life. Here Henry P. Van Dusen, Harold DeWolf, and others argue that since the world order is caused by God and reflects his will, a scientific analysis of man and his environment will lead to God.

(4) Aquinas and the Thomistic tradition claim that the rational mind, aided by the analogy of being between God and man and the law of cause and effect, is capable of proving God's existence and the infinity of his perfectness. By inductive analysis of the space-time world Aquinas constructed a formidable body of natural theology. Although optimistic about natural man's ability to amass knowledge of God, he stressed that salvation is dependent upon higher truths mediated by special revelation.

(5) Authorities such as Augustine, Luther, Calvin, Hodge, Warfield, and Henry argue for the objective reality of general revelation and its limited utility in mediating an elemental knowledge of God's existence and character. Augustine upheld a logos-enabled intuition of God that serves as the basis for the acquisition of further knowledge by rational inspection of the phenomenal world. Luther acknowledged that "all men have the general knowledge that God is, that he has created heaven and earth, that he is just, that he punishes the wicked, etc." Calvin similarly insisted that "even wicked men are forced, by the mere view of the earth and sky, to rise to the Creator." So also the Belgic Confession (II) and the Westminster Confession of Faith (I,1).

Biblical Data. In the OT Elihu's speech to Job (esp. Job. 36:24–37:24) draws attention to the rain that waters the earth, the thunder and lightning that strikes terror in the heart, the fury of a thunderstorm, and the brilliant shining of the sun following the storm's departure. The text suggests that these natural phenomena attest the power, majesty, goodness, and severity of the creator God and that the data are there for all to behold (Job 36:25). Moreover, God's address to Job (esp. Job 38:1–39:30) conveys the idea that natural phenomena (lightning, thunder, rain, snow), the daily rising of the sun, the majestic constellations in the heavens, and the complexity and harmonious interrelationships among the animal kingdom all attest the existence and glory of God.

According to Ps. 19 God reveals himself through the two-volume book of nature (vss. 1–6) and book of the law (vss. 7–13). In the first volume we read, "The heavens declare the glory of God; the skies proclaim the work of his hands" (vs. 1). That which the created order shows forth is the divine "glory" (*kābôd*), namely, the external manifestation of God's inner being and attributes. The revelation of God's glory through the heavens is declared to be perpetual or uninterrupted (vs. 2), wordless or inaudible (vs. 3), and worldwide in scope (vs. 4). That Judaism held to a general revelation in nature is clear from Wisd. Sol. 13:5: "The greatness and beauty of created things give us a corresponding idea of their Creator."

In the prologue to his Gospel, John makes two assertions about the eternal Word. First, "in him was life, and that life was the light of men" (1:4). And second, the Word is "the true light that gives light to every man who comes into the world" (1:9). The Greeks identified the Logos as the divine power that energizes man's intellectual and moral life. Wisdom, the parallel Jewish concept, was viewed as the power of God operative in the world to create, enlighten, and renew (cf. Wisd. Sol. 7:22–9:18). Thus it seems likely that in John 1:4, 9 the apostle has in mind the universal work of the Logos whereby the human mind is divinely illumined so as to perceive God as a first principle, much the same as Calvin's "sense of divinity" or "seed of religion."

Preaching to Gentiles at Lystra, Paul and Barnabas appealed to knowledge they and their hearers held in common as a result of general revelation: namely, that God is the creator of all things (Acts 14:15) and the providential provider of the necessities of life (vs. 17). In his kindly dealings with humankind God "has not left himself without testimony" (*amarturon*, vs. 17). Similarly, in his address to pagan Athenians (Acts 17:24–31) Paul referred, as a point of contact, to truths his audience knew by virtue of God's universal self-disclosure in nature and history. These include (1) God is the creator and sovereign of the universe (Acts 17:24); (2) he is self-sufficient (vs. 25*a*); (3) he is the source of life and all good (vs. 25*b*); (4) he is an intelligent being who formulates plans (vs. 26); (5) he is immanent in the world (vs. 27); and (6) he is the source and ground of human existence (vs. 28).

In Rom. 2:14–15 Paul teaches that a further modality of general revelation is the implanted moral law attested to the heart by the faculty of conscience. All men are guilty of transgressing the law, Paul argues: the Jews because they have violated the law written on stone, and the Gentiles because they have failed to live by the moral law written on their hearts (cf. Rom. 1:32). Communicated to each rational person by the power of conscience is the existence of a supreme Lawgiver and his moral requirements.

The clearest teaching that all people possess a rudimentary knowledge of God as creator occurs in Rom. 1:18–21. Paul argues that through the universal revelation in nature God is "clearly seen" (vs. 20), "understood" (vs. 20), and "known" (vs. 19; cf. vs. 21). That which man gains knowledge of is defined as God's invisible qualities—his eternal power and divine nature (*theiotēs*). The Greek noun *theiotēs*, "divinity," signifies the totality of the perfections that comprise the Godhead. Moreover, the apostle claims that this elemental knowledge of God is acquired by rational reflection on the created order (vs. 20). The word *ginoskō* ("to know") used in vss. 19, 21 connotes to perceive with the senses and to grasp with the mind.

Implications. Scripture teaches that the consistent response of the sinner when confronted with the truth-content of general revelation is to dismiss it from his consciousness (Rom. 1:21–32). Thus instead of worshiping and obeying God, the unregenerate person asserts his own autonomy and fashions lifeless idols which he proceeds to venerate. Whereupon God deliberately gives man over to the sordid impulses of his sinful nature (Rom. 1:24, 26, 28). Instead of proving salvific, general revelation serves only to condemn the sinner and to establish his guiltworthiness before God (Rom. 1:20).

But general revelation serves several salutary ends. (1) The universally implanted moral law provides the only authentic basis by which good and evil can be distinguished. The fact that good is enjoined and evil proscribed provides society with the only viable framework for existence. (2) Since all people possess a rudimentary knowledge of God, the Christian witness is assured that when he speaks to a sinner the notion of God is not a meaningless cipher. And (3) general revelation provides the rational basis for God's saving revelation mediated by Christ and the Bible. In this sense natural theology serves as the vestibule of revealed theology.

B. A. Demarest

See also Revelation, Special.

Bibliography. G. C. Berkouwer, *General Revelation;* E. Brunner, *Revelation and Reason;* B. A. Demarest, *General Revelation.*

Revelation, Special. The midtwentieth century's revival of interest in special divine revelation occurs at a significant time in modern history. Naturalism has become a virile cultural force in both East and West. In previous centuries the chief rivals of revealed religion were speculative idealism and philosophical theism; today the leading antagonists are materialistic communism, logical positivism, atheistic existentialism, and variant forms of Anglo-Saxon humanism. Since communist philosophy refers the whole movement of events to economic determinism, the recovery of the Judeo-Christian emphasis on special historical revelation gains pointed relevance.

The Meaning of Revelation. The term "revelation" means intrinsically the disclosure of what was previously unknown. In Judeo-Christian theology the term is used primarily of God's communication to man of divine truth, that is, his manifestation of himself or of his will. The essentials of the biblical view are that the Logos is the divine agent in all revelation, this revelation being further discriminated as general or universal (i.e., revelation in nature, history, and conscience) and special or particular (i.e., redemptive revelation conveyed by wondrous acts and words). The special revelation in sacred history is crowned by the incarnation of the living Word and the inscripturation of the spoken word. The gospel of redemption is therefore not merely a series of abstract theses unrelated to specific historical events; it is the dramatic news that God has acted in saving history, climaxed by the incarnate person and work of Christ (Heb. 1:2), for the salvation of lost humankind. Yet the redemptive events of biblical history do not stand uninterpreted. Their authentic meaning is given in the sacred writings—sometimes after, sometimes before the events. The series of sacred acts therefore includes the divine provision of an authoritative canon of writings—the sacred Scriptures—providing a trustworthy source of knowledge of God and of his plan.

Despite the distinction of general and special revelation, God's revelation is nonetheless a unity, and it must not be artificially sundered. Even prior to man's fall, Adam in Eden was instructed by specially revealed statutes (e.g., to be fruitful and multiply, to eat and not to eat of certain fruit). In view of man's corruption, after the fall any one-sided reliance simply on general revelation would be all the more arbitrary. Yet we are not on that account to minimize the fact and importance of general revelation, on which the Bible insists (Ps. 19; Rom. 1–2). But taken alone the so-called theistic proofs have led few men to the living God. The assumption of Thomas Aquinas that God can be known by natural reason apart from a revelation of Jesus Christ may be viewed, in fact, as an unwitting preparation for the revolt of early modern philosophy against special revelation and its contrary emphasis solely on general revelation. The many types of speculative theism and idealism arising in the wake of this emphasis were only temporarily able to hold a line against the decline to naturalism.

While the Bible indeed affirms God's general revelation, it invariably correlates general revelation with special redemptive revelation. It declares at one and the same time that the Logos is creator and redeemer (John 1). It does not present general revelation on the thesis that the true knowledge of God is possible to fallen man through the natural light of reason apart from a revelation of Christ, but rather introduces general revelation alongside special revelation in order to emphasize man's guilt. Thus the Scripture adduces God's unitary revelation, general and special, to display man's true predicament; he is a finite creature with an eternal destiny, made for spiritual fellowship with God, but now separated from his maker by sin.

Special revelation is redemptive revelation. It publishes the good tidings that the holy and merciful God promises salvation as a divine gift to man who cannot save himself (OT) and that he has now fulfilled that promise in the gift of his Son in whom all men are called to believe (NT). The gospel is news that the incarnate Logos has borne the sins of doomed men, has died in their stead, and has risen for their justification. This is the fixed center of special redemptive revelation.

False Views of Revelation. Christian theology has had to protect the biblical view of special revelation against many perversions. Platonic preoccupation with "eternal ideas" accessible to men by rational contemplation alone, plus the disregard of history as a meaningful arena of events, tended to militate against essential elements of the biblical view, viz., divine initiative and particularity, and redemptive history as a carrier of absolute revelation. The idealistic notion that God's revelation is given only generally, that it is a universally accessible idea, is destructive of biblical emphases such as the particularity of special revelation and a historical sequence of special saving events (climaxed by the incarnation, atonement, and resurrection of Christ as the unique center of redemptive revelation). Eighteenth century rationalism revived the notion of pre-Christian Greek idealism that historical facts are necessarily relative and never absolute, and that revelation consequently is to be divorced from historical actualities and identified with ideas alone. While still professing to speak of Christian revelation, this form of rationalism dissolved the essential connection of special revelation with historical disclosure. Moreover, it freely abandoned crucial aspects of redemptive history without protest to the destructive critics. And it surrendered the defense of the uniqueness or once-for-allness of special revelation in deference to the notion that revelation is always and only general. Wherever Christianity has been confronted by idealistic speculations of this kind, it has had to contend against a determination to dissolve the central significance of the virgin birth, unique divinity, atoning death, and bodily resurrection of Christ. Since revelation was equated necessarily with a universal manifestation, every historical event was regarded simply as one of many reflections (in lower or higher degree) of this general principle, while an absolute revelation in some particular strand or at some particular point of history was arbitrarily excluded.

Modern evolutionary theory, on the other hand, has attached new importance to the historical process. But this concern for history also has generally been pursued on presuppositions hostile to the biblical view. The tendency to exalt evolution itself into an ultimate principle of explanation works against the recognition of a fixed center or climax of history in the past. While history may be approached with sentimental notions of hidden divinity, and major turning-points in the long sweep of events singled out as providential, the sacred redemptive history of the past is leveled to the plateau of other elements in history, and history as a whole is no longer understood in relation to the unique revelation of God in Christ as its center.

In fact the tendency to view reason itself only as a late emergent in the evolutionary process suppresses the biblical declaration that reality itself has its ultimate explanation in the Logos (John 1:3), and in effect contravenes the doctrine of rational divine revelation. That is why the question of the nature and significance of mind is one of the crucial problems of contemporary philosophy in its bearing upon both Christian and communist philosophy. The modern philosophical revolt against reason, anchored first in skeptical theories about the limitations of human knowledge of the spiritual world and then in evolutionary dogmas, has an obvious bearing upon the Christian contention that God communicates truths about himself and his purposes.

While it is the case that Christianity in contending for special revelation is concerned for spiritual decision between Jesus Christ and false gods, and not merely for an acceptance of certain revealed truths, yet the Christian movement does not on that account demean the importance of divinely revealed doctrines. Christian experience involves both *assensus* (assent to revealed doctrines) and *fiducia* (personal trust in Christ). Moreover, saving trust is impossible without some authentic knowledge of God (Heb. 11:6; I Cor. 15:1–4; Rom. 10:9).

Since Schleiermacher's day Protestant theology has been influenced repeatedly by anti-intellectualistic strands in modern philosophy, especially by such thinkers as Kant, James, and Dewey. Schleiermacher's formulas, that we know God only in relation to us and not as he is in himself, and that God communicates life and not doctrines, have been influential in encouraging an artificial disjunction in many Protestant expositions of special revelation. Although often striving to advance beyond these restrictions, more recent existential and dialectical expositions nonetheless do not consistently rise above the quicksands of a merely relational theology.

Revelation as Rational. Because of its implications for rational revelation the traditional identification of the Bible as the word of God written has been especially repugnant to contemporary neo-orthodox theology. It is contended that Jesus Christ alone should be identified as the Word of God, and that to speak of Scripture in this way demeans Christ. The evangelical Protestant, however, distinguishes carefully between the *logos theou* and the *rhēma theou,* that is, between the ontological Word incarnate and the epistemological word inscripturate. The motives for the neo-orthodox complaint are, in fact, speculative rather than spiritual. For the witness of Scripture, to which neo-orthodox dogmaticians profess to appeal, is specially damaging to their case here. The OT prophets consistently speak of their words as the words of God, using the formula "Thus saith the Lord" with untiring regularity. The NT apostles, moreover, speak of divine revelation in the form of definite ideas and words (cf. I Thess. 2:13, where the Thessalonians are said to have "received the word of God which you heard from us not as the word of men but as . . . the word of God"; cf. also Rom. 3:2, where Paul characterizes the OT as "the oracles of God"). The disciples also spoke of Scripture as divine revelation and, in fact, had the sacred example and authority of Jesus Christ for so doing. Jesus identified his own words with the word of the Father (John 14:34) and spoke of Scripture as the word of God (John 10:35). The Bible nowhere protests against the identification of Scripture with revelation, but rather supports and approves this identification. The neo-orthodox tendency to look upon Scripture as simply witness to revelation, in fact, contravenes the historic Christian view that the Bible itself is a form of revelation specially provided for man in sin as an authentic disclosure of the nature and will of God.

From all this it is clear how significant is the Christian assertion that the laws of logic and morality belong to the *imago Dei* in man. Christian theology has always been under biblical compulsion to affirm the identity of the Logos with the Godhead, and to find a connection between God as rational and moral and the form and content of the divine image in man. That Jesus Christ is himself the truth; that man bears the divine image on the basis of creation and that this image while distorted by sin is not destroyed; that the Holy Bible is a rational revelation of the nature of God and his will for fallen man; that the Holy Spirit uses truth as a means of conviction and conversion—all these facts indicate in some measure the undeniable premium assigned to rationality by the Christian religion. Yet human reason is not viewed as a source of truth; rather, man is to think God's thoughts after him. Revelation is the source of truth, and reason, as illuminated by the Spirit, the instrument for comprehending it.

Contemporary theology is marked by its reaffirmation of the priority of revelation to reason. In this respect it is distinguished from the liberal Protestant dogmatics of the nineteenth century, which tended to view human reason as a self-sufficient and independent criterion. Some neo-Thomistic studies today restate the philosophy even of Thomas Aquinas so as to set the usual summary of his approach, "I understand in order to believe," in a context of faith. The Thomistic hostility to innate ideas, and the Thomistic support for knowledge of God by the way of negation and the way of analogy are, however, firmly reasserted. Protestant theology, heavily influenced by Karl Barth and Emil Brunner, now characteristically reasserts the priority of revelation over reason. Thus the epistemological formulas representative of Augustine ("I believe in order to understand") and of Tertullian ("I believe what is absurd," i.e., to the unregenerate man) are much in the climate of current theological dialogue. But the modern tendency to exaggerate the transcendence of God, by way of revolt against the classic liberal overstatement of divine immanence, subserves the Tertullian more than the Augustinian formula. The historic Christian confidence in a revealed world-and-life view takes its rise from a prior confidence in the reality of rational divine revelation. The modern tendency to veer toward a doctrine of revelation whose locus is to be found in an immediate existential response, rather than in an objectively conveyed Scripture, thwarts the theological interest in biblically revealed doctrines and principles from which an explanatory view of the whole of reality and life may be exposited. Thus it is apparent that a recovery of confidence in the intelligible integration of the whole of life's experiences depends significantly upon a virile sense of the actuality of rational divine revelation.

C. F. H. HENRY

See also REVELATION, GENERAL; BIBLE, INSPIRATION OF; BIBLE, AUTHORITY OF.

Bibliography. J. Baillie, *The Idea of Revelation in Recent Thought;* J. Calvin, *Institutes of the Christian Religion,* 1.6–9; C. F. H. Henry, "Divine Revelation and the Bible," in *Inspiration and Interpretation,* ed. J. F. Walvoord, and (ed.), *Revelation and the Bible;* P. K. Jewett, *Emil Brunner's Concept of Revelation;* H. Kraemer, *Religion and the Christian Faith;* B. B. Warfield, *Revelation and Inspiration;* H. D. McDonald, *Theories of Revelation* and *Ideas of Revelation.*

Revenge. *See* VENGEANCE.

Revivalism. A movement within the Christian tradition which emphasizes the appeal of religion to the emotional and affectional nature of individuals as well as to their intellectual and rational nature. It believes that vital Christianity begins with a response of the whole being to the gospel's call for repentance and spiritual rebirth by faith in Jesus Christ. This experience results in a personal relationship with God.

Some have sought to make revivalism a purely American and even a predominantly frontier phenomenon. Revivalism, however, can be seen as a much broader Christian tradition. Recent studies have discovered a revivalist tradition in the Roman Catholic Church.

The Reformation Roots. Modern revival movements have their historical roots in Puritan-pietistic reactions to the rationalism of the Enlightenment and the formalized creedal expression of Reformation faith that characterized much of seventeenth century Protestantism. Lutherans such as Johann Arndt, Philipp Spener, and August Francke resisted this depersonalization of religion. They discovered a more experiential element in Reformation faith which emphasized personal commitment and obedience to Christ and a life regenerated by the indwelling Holy Spirit. They also emphasized witness and missions as a primary responsibility of the individual Christian and the church. Subjective religious experience and the importance of the individual became a new force in renewing and expanding the church. These concerns gradually permeated much of Protestantism, especially the developing churches in America.

The Eighteenth Century Birth. The appeal for a personal, public response to the gospel that came to characterize revivalism sprang up almost simultaneously in both England and America in the eighteenth century. The initial signs of the First Great Awakening in the American colonies occurred in the congregation of the Dutch Reformed pastor Theodore J. Frelinghuysen in northern New Jersey in 1725, a decade before John Wesley and George Whitefield began their field preaching in England. Frelinghuysen had come under the influence of pietism before coming to America. In 1726 William Tennent, the Presbyterian leader of the Great Awakening, started his "log college" to prepare ministers who would preach a personalized Calvinism which called men and women to repentance.

By the time George Whitefield began recurrent revivalistic tours of the American colonies in 1738, Jonathan Edwards, the theologian of the colonial awakening, had already experienced revival in his Northampton, Massachusetts, Congregational church. Edwards accepted the validity of much of the religious emotion that accompanied the conversions among his parishioners and wrote in defense of the proper role of emotion in true religion. The revival continued to move south until it touched all the colonies. In England the recognized leader of the "Evangelical Revival" was John Wesley, founder of Methodism and close friend of Whitefield. Whitefield had encouraged Wesley to take up the field preaching that brought the gospel directly to the masses of working people.

The success of this appeal to the heart as well as the head could not be doubted. Religious interest was renewed, and people flocked to the churches in significant numbers in both America and England. American historians recognize that the sweep of religious fervor from north to south (prior to the Revolution) was one of the few unifying factors among the otherwise disparate American colonies. In England the revival left an indelible religious and social impact for stability in the midst of the revolutionary unrest which pervaded most of Europe at the time.

The Definitive Stage. The pre-Revolutionary revivals demonstrated the general patterns which characterized all subsequent awakenings; however, it was the Second Great Awakening at the beginning of the nineteenth century that defined the theology and method of the tradition. The revival began at Hampden-Sidney and Washington colleges in Virginia in 1787. It continued at Yale under Timothy Dwight and at Andover and Princeton at the end of the eighteenth century. It was popularized in the great camp meetings on the frontier. The Cane Ridge, Kentucky, camp meeting in August, 1801, became the most famous of all. The strange emotional phenomena which had shown themselves in the earlier colonial revival reappeared in intensified form. "Falling," "jerking," "rolling," and "dancing" exercises engaged many of the twenty thousand worshipers present. These demonstrations moderated as the revival continued, but physical phenomena have always existed in some measure in popular revival movements.

Camp Meetings and Revivalism. The Presbyterians who organized these first camp meetings soon abandoned their use. The Methodists and Baptists, however, continued to use them. The ambience of the natural setting in which the camps were held, the release from the ordinary routines of home and church, the freedom to worship together in a less sectarian context, the family reunion, community-center flavor—all contributed to a mystique that made the camp meeting a continuing factor in future revivalism. The frontier camp meetings declined by the time of the Civil War, but the Holiness revival which began to flourish after the Civil War utilized them extensively in both rural and urban settings. Camp meetings became the religious centers that shaped the theology and ethos of the numerous Holiness churches organized at the end of the century. Although many camp meetings evolved from their original revivalistic commitments into Chautauquas or Christian family resort centers, in Holiness and Pentecostal churches the camp meeting remains an essential expression of their revivalistic worship. Even there, however, the camp meeting has become more of a church family rally or reunion than a time for evangelistic outreach to the unchurched.

Charles Grandison Finney. The outstanding figure in early nineteenth century revivalism was Charles Grandison Finney. Finney took the revival ethos of the frontier camp meeting to the urban centers of the northeast. His success there and his widespread influence as a professor and later president of Oberlin College gave him a platform for propagating a theology and defense of the revival methods he espoused. In his *Revival Lectures* Finney contended that God had clearly revealed the laws of revival in Scripture. Whenever the church obeyed those laws, spiritual renewal resulted. In the minds of many Calvinists this emphasis on human ability greatly modified the traditional concept of the sovereign movement of God in reviving the church. However, the importance which Finney attached to the necessity for prayer and the agency of the Holy Spirit in his revival theory and practice helped to mute such concerns.

Finney's "new methods" raised as much controversy as his attachment to New School Calvinism. Preaching was direct, addressed to the individual, and usually delivered without manuscript or even notes. The public nature of the conversion experience was focused by the introduction of the "anxious bench," by which the serious seeker placed his intentions on record before the congregation. The critics were especially wary of the public platform given to the laity and especially women as they prayed and testified in the revival services. After the dramatic Fulton Street or Layman's Revival of 1858, however, most of the critics were silenced, and revivalized Calvinism joined with the revivalized Arminianism of burgeoning American Methodism to set the predominant pattern of American Protestantism for the remainder of the century.

Perfectionist Revivalism. A significant new development in revivalism between 1835 and 1875 was the rise of perfectionist revivalism. Finney introduced a perfectionist note into his evangelism after his move to Oberlin College in 1835. He and his colleague Asa Mahan, president of Oberlin, joined perfectionist leaders in Methodism, such as lay leaders Walter and Phoebe Palmer, in a new Holiness revivalism in the churches. The movement used revivalistic methods to call Christians to a second crisis of faith and total commitment subsequent to conversion, commonly called among American Calvinists a "second conversion," a "rest of faith," or the "deeper" or "higher life"; to Methodists it was "entire sanctification," "perfection in love," or "the second blessing." Both Calvinist and Methodist wings of the revival ultimately gave prominence to a personal "fullness" or "baptism" of the Holy Spirit in speaking of the experience. The creation of the National Camp Meeting Association for the Promotion of Holiness by John Inskip and other Methodist ministers in 1867 spread the movement beyond Methodism around the world. In England the Holiness revival gave rise to the Salvation Army and the Keswick Movement.

Institutionalization and Decline. Dwight L. Moody dominated the revival movement from 1875 until his death in 1899. Although most of the revivalism of the time was carried on in the local churches and camp meetings of the rapidly growing Baptist and Methodist denominations, Moody's leadership was the stimulus which encouraged the continued use of revivalistic methods in churches not as strongly committed to them. His mass evangelistic campaigns drew vast audiences in Britain and the United States and set the patterns for a more professional revivalism which demanded extensive organization and substantial budgets. Ira Sankey, his musical director, became the best known of the many gospel musicians who formed an essential part of the revivalistic teams which sprang up everywhere in this period. Moody also sponsored educational institutions which furthered his evangelistic aims: the Northfield Institutions in Massachusetts and Moody Bible Institute in Chicago. These institutions were representative of the large number of organizations and movements which sprang out of the many revival movements that looked to Moody for inspiration and leadership at the end of the nineteenth century. Many of these became important components of the growing fundamentalist movement.

Large audiences continued to attend the revival campaigns of William "Billy" Sunday, R. A. Torrey, Gypsy Smith, and others after the turn of the century. However, the change of national mood resulting from the economic upheavals that followed World War I, the persistent attacks of such social critics as H. L. Mencken, and the turn toward a gospel of social concern among the larger denominations led to a decline in the influence of revivalism in the churches and in American life. Nevertheless, the Pentecostal revival which spread swiftly from its center in Los Angeles after 1906 and the effective use of radio by Charles Fuller and other radio evangelists indicated the continuing strength of the revivalist tradition in the churches.

The Modern Period. The rise of Billy Graham in the 1950s and his subsequent recognition as one of the most influential religious leaders of the post–World War II period signaled the latent residual strength of revivalism in the Christian churches. Graham's success in working with a broad spectrum of Protestant churches as well as significant segments of Catholicism reiterated the fact that revivalism is not a sporadic phenomenon in the Christian tradition but rather a steady force which breaks into public prominence whenever churches and society tend to ignore its concerns for experiential religion. Billy Graham emphasized again both the method and theology of the tradition. He played down some of the more strident emotional and psychological aspects of the method; he retained, however, the direct, forceful sermon appeal, the biblically oriented message, the call for personal, public response, the use of gospel music and of large mass meetings.

Graham's ministry represented a general revival of religion, as indicated by the rapid growth of evangelical churches and spread of the charismatic revival in the decades following World War II. The charismatic emphases on the baptism and the gifts of the Spirit—especially glossolalia—have had significant influence upon both Protestant and Catholic churches. The exposure of revivalism with its message and method to the public through television and the dominant role revivalists currently hold in religious broadcasting are additional signs of the contemporary revitalization of the tradition.

The Theology of Revivalism. The intimate historical relationship between the growth of evangelicalism and revivalism indicates many common theological presuppositions. Evangelicalism's commitment to the reliability and authority of Scripture is the basis for revivalism's direct preaching and appeal; the former's belief in the universal need for spiritual rebirth is the basis for the latter's direct call for repentance and faith in Christ. The evangelical's acceptance of Christ's final commission to his disciples as a mandate for personal witness and world mission reinforces the urgency that characterizes revival movements.

Revivals of religion and the theological presuppositions and practices which have accompanied them through their history have consistently raised a common pattern of criticism. The strongly emotional nature of the revivalist's appeal, the critics charge, leads to spiritual instability or even to irrational behavior. They also claim that the revivalist's emphasis upon crisis experience tends to deprecate the place of growth and process in Christian living. Opponents also charge that the importance revivalism attaches to a warm-hearted, spiritual ministry results in a general anti-intellectualism throughout the tradition; they claim as well that the strong appeal to individualized religion leads to a subjectivism that obscures or even denies the social and cultural implications of Christianity. The direct praying and preaching, the tendency to popularize and excite interest by use of promotional psychology, and inclination to judgmentalism and separatism are also common accusations brought against revivalists.

The major response of revival proponents has been to point to the positive results they claim for religious revival and revivalism in church and society since the beginning of the movements in the eighteenth century. The dramatic growth of the churches resulting from special periods of religious revival and the day-to-day revival emphasis in revivalistic churches is part of the historical record. Significant moral, social, and cultural changes have accompanied the major awakenings. The ecumenical spirit of revival efforts has often produced a level of cooperation among churches not achieved in any other way. Expanded Christian benevolence and church extension have always accompanied these periods of spiritual renewal. Religious institutions and organizations to promote Christian causes and social concerns, including most of America's Christian colleges, seminaries, Bible institutes, and many mission bodies, are products of revivalism.

M. E. Dieter

See also Great Awakenings, The; Pietism; Whitefield, George; Edwards, Jonathan; Wesley, John; Finney, Charles Grandison.

Bibliography. R. Carwardine, *Transatlantic Revivalism;* D. W. Dayton, *Discovering an Evangelical Heritage;* M. E. Dieter, *The Holiness Revival of the Nineteenth Century;* J. P. Dolan, *Catholic Revivalism;* J. Edwards, *A Faithful Narrative of the Surprising Work of God;* J. F. Findlay, *Dwight L. Moody: American Evangelist 1837–1899;* C. G. Finney, *Lectures on Revivals of Religion;* E. S. Gaustad, *The Great Awakening in New England;* C. A. Johnson, *The Frontier Camp Meeting;* W. G. McLaughlin, Jr., *Modern Revivalism: Charles Grandison Finney to Billy Graham;* T. L. Smith, *Revivalism and Social Reform in Mid-Nineteenth Century America;* W. W. Sweet, *Revivalism in America;* B. A. Weisberger, *They Gathered at the River.*

Reward. If all of its related forms are included, the word "reward" is found 101 times in our English Bible (AV). Four Greek and several Hebrew words are rendered by this one word.

In present-day usage a reward is a gift given in recognition for some service rendered, either good or evil. Its biblical usage, however, is quite varied, including such ideas as a bribe (Ps. 103:10), punishment (Ps. 91:8), and gift (I Kings 13:7). It includes, therefore, the punishment one experiences in this life for evil deeds (Matt. 6:5) as well as future retribution (Ps. 91:8). Several times the word is used of evil done to a person where good was expected (Gen. 44:4; Ps. 35:12).

Christ often used rewards as an incentive for service. This has been a disturbing thought to some. One need not be troubled by this if one understands the scriptural nature of rewards and dismisses any thought of materialism. Rewards are the result of human effort, to be sure, but as Weiss says: "As the servants of God in the Israelitish theocracy were entitled, by reason of their covenant relationship, to look for the fulfillment of the promise as a reward for their fulfillment of their covenant obligations, so the disciple of Jesus is entitled to look for the completion of salvation as a reward for the fulfillment of the demands which are made upon him in virtue of his being a disciple" (B. Weiss, *Biblical Theology of the New Testament,* I, 144).

For the Christian rewards have an eschatological significance. Paul teaches that every man shall appear before the judgment seat of Christ for the judgment of his works (Rom. 14:12; II Cor. 5:10). This must be kept distinct in our thinking from judgment for sin, for this, as far as the believer is concerned, is forever past (Rom. 5:1). Salvation is a gift (Eph. 2:8–9) whereas rewards are earned (I Cor. 3:14). The two chief passages of Scripture that discuss rewards at length are I Cor. 3:9–15 and I Cor. 9:16–27. Additional information can be found by studying the various passages where rewards for service are depicted as crowns (I Cor. 9:25; Phil. 4:1; I Thess. 2:19; II Tim. 4:8; James 1:12; I Pet. 5:4; Rev. 2:10; 3:11).

Various types of service merit rewards, such as enduring temptation (James 1:12), diligently seeking God (Heb. 11:6), dying for Christ (Rev. 2:10), faithful pastoral work (I Pet. 5:4), faithfully doing God's will and loving his appearing (II Tim. 4:8), soul winning (I Thess. 2:19–20), faithful stewardship (I Cor. 4:1–5), acts of kindness (Gal. 6:10), hospitality (Matt. 10:40–42). Rewards can be lost (Rev. 2:10; II John 8). Then too it is possible to be busy in the Lord's service and receive no rewards at all (I Cor. 3:15; 9:27) or to receive little when one should receive much (II John 8).

H. Z. CLEVELAND

See also CROWN.

Bibliography. D. Walker in *HDAC;* L. S. Chafer, *Systematic Theology,* IV, 396–405; P. C. Böttger *et al., NIDNTT,* III, 134ff.; K. E. Kirk, *The Vision of God.*

Riches. *See* WEALTH, CHRISTIAN VIEW OF.

Righteousness. The Hebrew word regularly translated "righteous" or "just" is *ṣāddîq* and originally meant "straight" or "right." The corresponding Greek term is *dikaios,* and in Greek society referred to that which is in accordance with law or social norm. The noun forms are *ṣedeq* (or *sĕdāqâ*) and *dikaiosynē.* The verbs *ṣādak* and *dikaioō* mean "to do justice," "to be just," "to vindicate," or "to justify" in the forensic sense of "declare righteous" or "treat as just."

OT Usage. The God of Israel is revealed as a God of righteousness, who acts rightly in all his works and judgments (Gen. 18:25; Deut. 32:4; Ps. 11:7; Dan. 9:14). The OT concept of righteousness is closely linked with God's judgeship (Pss. 9:8; 50:6; 143:2). God judges equitably; he does not clear the guilty or forsake the righteous, and the judges of Israel are commanded to act according to his example (Exod. 23:7; Deut. 1:16–17; 10:17–18; Ps. 98:9). Thus, the righteousness of God is revealed in his punishment of the wicked and disobedient (Neh. 9:33; Ps. 7:9–17; Lam. 1:18; Dan. 9:14). But more emphatically God's righteousness is made known in his deliverance of his people from their enemies and oppressors (I Sam. 12:6–11; Pss. 9:7–9; 51:14; Isa. 46:11–13). God as judge comes to the rescue of the poor and the oppressed, delivering them from injustice and restoring their rights (Pss. 34:16–22; 72:1–4; 82; Isa. 11:4). He even treats them as righteous, in the relative sense that they are in the right as over against their wicked oppressors (Pss. 7:6–11; 143:1–3, 11–12). Consequently God's righteous judgment is often expressed in terms of his saving acts. Righteousness many times is closely related to God's salvation, mercy, and lovingkindness, especially in the Psalms and Isaiah (Pss. 40:10; 85:9–10; 98:2–3; Isa. 45:8; 46:13; 51:5; Jer. 9:24).

This emphasis on the righteousness of God in the form of salvation should be understood within the context of God's covenant relationship with Israel. God by his grace made a covenant with Abraham and his descendants, and his righteousness is seen in his faithfulness in keeping that covenant (I Chr. 16:16–17, 35; Isa. 46:9–13; Jer. 33:25–26). The covenant does not make sinful Israel immune from divine judgment, but after chastisement God delivers his people and thus reveals his righteousness (the lesson of the Exile). God justifies his covenant people, declaring them righteous, not because they have perfectly kept the law, but because (or on the condition that) their repentant hearts trust in him and seek to keep his covenant (Gen. 15:6; Pss. 32:10–11; 103:17–18; Isa. 50:8; 53:11). This judgment or forensic act of God is therefore both an act of righteousness and a gift of divine mercy.

Modern Bible scholars often overemphasize the benevolent aspect of God's righteousness in the OT and lose sight of the legal and punitive aspects. But God's righteous judgeship is seen in the punishment of the lawbreaker as well as in the deliverance of the justified. It is noteworthy, however, that the positive aspect of God's righteousness is more common in the OT, while the punitive aspect is more closely associated with God's wrath.

The climax of this positive aspect is found in the theme of Messiah, the one who will be a truly righteous king and will fulfill God's covenant purpose for Israel, bringing it and all nations to God's final righteousness (Ps. 72; Isa. 9:7; 11:3–5; 42:6; Jer. 23:5–6; 33:15–16; Zech. 9:9).

NT Usage. Much of the NT is taken up with the purpose of showing that Jesus of Nazareth is indeed the promised Messiah, and thus God's purposes of righteousness and salvation are spoken of as centered in him. Understandably, then, we find righteousness closely linked to the NT theme of the kingdom of God (Matt. 5:10; 6:33; 13:43; Rom. 14:17), a kingdom and a righteousness for which John the Baptist prepared the way and which Jesus as the righteous Son and Redeemer brings to fulfillment (Matt. 3:15; 5:17–20; 21:32; Acts 3:14, 25–26).

Jesus spoke of a false righteousness which is found in those who trust in themselves as righteous or justified because of their moral accomplishments (Matt. 23:28; Luke 16:15; 18:9), but he taught that the truly justified are those who acknowledge their sin and trust in God for forgiveness and his righteousness (Matt. 5:36; Mark 2:17; Luke 18:14).

Again the forensic understanding of righteousness is the key, and this is brought out most fully by Paul. Following the teaching of Christ, Paul explains that no one seeking to be righteous by the works of the law can be justified in God's sight, since everyone is a sinner and has fallen short of God's righteous standard (Rom. 3:9–10, 20, 23; Gal. 2:16). Therefore the righteousness of God comes as a gift which we do not merit (Rom. 3:24; 5:15–17), a gracious declaration in which God pronounces righteous the one who puts his faith in Jesus Christ (Acts 13:39; Rom. 3:22; 5:1, 18). In this declaration God forgives the sins of the justified on the basis of Christ's atoning death, so that God himself is vindicated as just in his justification of sinners (Rom. 3:25–26; 5:8–9; cf. I John 1:9; 2:2).

However, the NT makes it clear that the one who by faith is declared righteous also by faith seeks to do the deeds of righteousness and to grow in righteousness by God's grace (Rom. 6:12–18; Eph. 4:24; 5:9; Phil. 1:11; Heb. 11; James 2:17–26; I Pet. 2:24; I John 2:29). By this grace God also will bring the justified into a final righteousness (Gal. 5:5; Heb. 12:23; II Pet. 3:13) at the day of Christ when God will judge the whole world (Luke 14:14; Acts 17:31; II Tim. 4:8).

Therefore, as in the OT so also in the NT, God's righteousness, which expresses itself in wrath and judgment against unrepentant sinners (II Thess. 1:5–9; Rom. 2:5–9; Rev. 19:2), triumphs through love in the form of salvation from sin for those who repent and claim God's covenant promise fulfilled in Christ.

Theological Concepts. In systematic theology righteousness or justice is seen, first of all, as an attribute of God's being (one of the moral and communicable attributes), and then derivatively as an attribute of man created in God's image.

God's Righteousness (Justice). Righteousness is that attribute by which God's nature is seen to be the eternally perfect standard of what is right. It is closely related to God's holiness (or moral perfection), on one hand, and to God's moral law or will as an expression of his holiness, on the other hand. Even though there is no distinction between righteousness and justice in the biblical vocabulary, theologians often use the former to refer to the attribute of God in himself and the latter to refer to the actions of God with respect to his creation. Hence, God's justice is seen in the way he subjects the universe to various laws and endows it with various rights according to the hierarchy of beings he created. This is "legislative justice." In addition there is "distributive justice," in which God maintains the laws and rights by giving everything its due, or responding appropriately to created beings according to their value or place in the universe. His distributive justice with respect to moral creatures is expressed in the punishment of sin or disobedience (retributive justice) and the rewarding of good or obedience (remunerative justice; Rom. 2:5–11).

In systematic theology the harmony of God's justice and love is treated primarily under the doctrine of Christ's atonement. In the cross God satisfies the demands of his own justice against our sin, so that by Christ's redemptive act God's "holy love" is seen as both the supreme expression of retributive justice and the supreme expression of forgiving grace.

Man's Righteousness. Doctrinally, human righteousness can be analyzed in the following fourfold way: (1) Original righteousness. God made man upright or morally good (Eccles. 7:29; Gen. 1:31), but man fell from this righteous state into a state of sin. (2) Christ's righteousness. Since Adam's fall Christ is the only human being who has perfectly fulfilled God's moral law and maintained a righteous nature (Matt. 5:17; John 8:29, 46; Heb. 4:15; I Pet. 2:22). Since Christ is the God-man, his righteousness is of infinite value, affording salvation for all who believe. (3) Imputed righteousness (justification). Justification is that step in salvation in which God declares the believer righteous. Protestant theology has emphasized that this includes the imputation of Christ's righteousness (crediting it to the believer's "account"), whereas Roman Catholic theology emphasizes that God justifies in accord with an infused righteousness merited by Christ and maintained by the believer's good works. (4) Renewed righteousness (sanctification). Having been declared righteous, the believer grows in the likeness of Christ (being renewed in the image of God) and becomes righteous in actual moral character, i.e., he becomes sanctified. Most theologians hold that sanctification is progressive and not complete in this earthly life.

D. W. Diehl

See also Righteousness, Original; Sanctification; Justification; God, Attributes of.

Bibliography. J. A. Baird, *The Justice of God in the Teaching of Jesus;* H. Bavinck, *The Doctrine of God;* C. Brown, *NIDNTT,* III, 352–77; E. Brunner, *The Christian Doctrine of God;* P. J. Achtemeier, *IDB,* IV, 80–99; R. Garrigou-Lagrange, *God, His Existence and His Nature;* A. C. Knudson, *The Doctrine of God;* L. Morris, *The Apostolic Preaching of the Cross;* J. I. Packer, *Knowing God;* G. Rupp, *The Righteousness of God;* P. Tillich, *Love, Power, and Justice.*

Righteousness, Civil. *See* CIVIL RIGHTEOUSNESS.

Righteousness, Original. The term refers to the original moral state or condition of man prior to his fall into sin. The Scripture texts which inform the concept are Gen. 1:31; Eccles. 7:29, which speak of man as created "good" and "upright," and Eph. 4:24; Col. 3:10, which speak of the renewal (in Christ) of the image of God in man in "knowledge" and "true righteousness and holiness" (cf. Rom. 8:29; II Cor. 3:18).

Roman Catholicism sees original righteousness as a *donum supernaturale* added to the "natural" image of God. In the fall original righteousness (by which man had supernatural communion with God) was lost, but the natural image (consisting of man's reason, freedom, and spirituality) remained relatively intact. Luther rejected this twofold distinction, and taught that original righteousness was the very essence of man's original nature or image, not a supernatural addition to it. Thus for Luther the image as a whole was lost in the fall. Calvin also rejected the Catholic natural-supernatural distinction, but had a broader view of the image than did Luther. For Calvin the loss of original righteousness in the fall meant the thorough corruption of the image but not its total loss.

Modern liberalism, influenced by evolutionary philosophy, views the Genesis narratives of man's origin as myths and finds the doctrine of original righteousness to be rather lacking in meaning. Neo-orthodoxy, too, rejects a literal, primitive state of righteousness in human history, but finds the concept of original righteousness still valid and important. It refers to man's "essential nature," the God-created law of man's true being (the law of love), standing in contradiction to man's sinful, existential nature (Brunner and Niebuhr). Original righteousness is that of which man is dimly aware through his self-transcendence, and from which he inevitably has fallen through wrong use of freedom. It also is that which man comes to understand most clearly through Christ. D. W. DIEHL

See also FALL OF MAN; IMAGE OF GOD; RIGHTEOUSNESS.

Bibliography. L. Berkhof, *Systematic Theology;* D. G. Bloesch, *Essentials of Evangelical Theology,* I, 88–97, 103–9; E. Brunner, *Man in Revolt;* C. Hodge, *Systematic Theology,* III, 99–102; R. Niebuhr, *The Nature and Destiny of Man,* I, 265–300; P. Schoonenberg, *Man and Sin.*

Righteousness of God. *See* GOD, ATTRIBUTES OF.

Ritschl, Albrecht (1822–1889). German Protestant theologian. Son of a bishop, Ritschl was born in Berlin and studied at various universities. At first an adherent of the Tübingen school, his research in patristics led to his rejection of the theory of the radical conflict between Petrine Judaism and Pauline hellenism. After sixteen years at Bonn he moved to Göttingen in 1864, where as professor of systematic theology he wrote his most important works, *The Christian Doctrine of Justification and Reconciliation* (1870–74), *Instruction in the Christian Religion* (1875), *Theology and Metaphysics* (1881), and *History of Pietism* (3 vols., 1880–86), and founded the important journal, *Zeitschrift für die Kirchengeschichte.*

His theology is often labeled that of "moral value." He explored the ethical implications of Christianity and indicated their relevance for the life and witness of the church. He rejected all forms of natural theology, mysticism, and metaphysics, arguing that theology must concentrate on moral and ethical realities. He said religion cannot be understood on the basis of experience, reason, or doctrines that go beyond verifiable history but rather through apprehension by faith. He distinguished between "value" and "fact" judgments. For example, he said the divinity of Christ is a statement of the revelational value of the church's faith, not something that can be objectively demonstrated.

Central to Ritschl's system is his notion of justification. He defined Christianity as an ellipse with two foci—Jesus, who reveals the love of God for us and reconciles us, and the church, which is the spiritual and ethical community he founded and whose goal is the transformation of human society into the kingdom of God. Justification is the forgiveness of sins, the divine act of lifting the consciousness of guilt (both sin and punishment), but it is achieved in and through the church, the community for which Jesus died. Sin is man's deeds performed in opposition to the action now occurring in the kingdom of God; namely, selfishness, seeking after inferior values, and lack of reverence and trust in God. It restricts man's right to be a child of God and prevents him from achieving life's goal of the kingdom. In justification God assigns a person to his place in the kingdom where he engages in virtuous activity and with God's help overcomes the contradictions running through human existence. Reconciliation is the state of full harmony where God stands before the believer as his father and in turn receives childlike trust. The Christian is given spiritual dominion over the world, engages in the work of the kingdom, and lives a life of faith, humility, patience, prayer, and activity in his vocation and the development of personal virtue.

By rejecting a juridical view of justification Ritschl saw Christ's death not as a propitiation for sins but the result of loyalty to his vocation to bring men into full fellowship with God by sharing in his own consciousness of sonship. He also denied the traditional views of original sin, the incarnation, revelation, resurrection, church, and kingdom of God and created an unbridgeable chasm between the Jesus of history and Christ of faith. R. V. PIERARD

See also LIBERALISM, THEOLOGICAL.

Bibliography. J. Orr, *The Ritschlian Theology and the Evangelical Faith* and *Ritschlianism: Expository and Critical Essays;* A. T. Swing, *The Theology of Albrecht Ritschl;* R. Mackintosh, *Albrecht Ritschl and His School;* P. Hefner, *Faith and the Vitalities of History* and *Three Essays;* K. Barth, *Protestant Thought from Rousseau to Ritschl;* D. L. Mueller, *An Introduction to the Theology of Albrecht Ritschl;* D. W. Lotz, *Ritschl and Luther;* J. Richmond, *Ritschl: A Reappraisal;* C. Brown, *NIDCC,* 850; *ODCC,* 1189; *NCE,* XII, 522–23.

Robinson, Henry Wheeler (1872–1945). English Baptist scholar. After studies in Britain and Germany he was a pastor for six years, became tutor in Rawdon Baptist College in 1906, and principal of his denomination's Regent Park College from 1920 to 1942. The most eminent Baptist scholar of his generation, he had wide-ranging theological interests. His *Christian Doctrine of Man* (1911) upheld religious and moral concepts against the rational and aesthetic emphases found in traditional Greek thinking. *The Christian Experience of the Holy Spirit* (1928) was a salutary corrective of the immanentist approach of Schleiermacher and Ritschl. Significantly, however, Robinson did not oppose this view in favor of an evangelical concept of revelation and inspiration. He put great stress on human response and interpretation.

While he often returned to wider theological fields, as in *Redemption and Revelation* (1942), he is chiefly remembered for contributions to OT scholarship. His first book was a commentary on Deuteronomy and Joshua (1907). *The Religious Ideas of the Old Testament* (1913) was hailed as such a valuable and durable work that it was reissued (with revisions by L. H. Brockington) in 1956. Some hold that his most important work was in the area of Hebrew psychology and OT theology, as found in his *Inspiration and Revelation in the Old Testament* (1946). He was the first non-Anglican chairman of the board of Oxford University theological faculty (1937–39). J. D. DOUGLAS

Bibliography. E. A. Payne, *Henry Wheeler Robinson.*

Roman Catholicism The term has been in general use since the Reformation to identify the faith and practice of Christians in communion with the pope.

Although it has a reputation for conservatism and reaction, Roman Catholicism is a genuinely evolving religious system, valuing the deepening and development of its understanding of the Christian faith. The Ignatian principles of accommodation and J. H. Newman's theory of development have been two expressions of this process. This development sometimes goes beyond biblical data, but Catholic scholars contend that the church's doctrines—e.g., on the sacraments, the blessed Virgin Mary, and the papacy—are suggested by a "trajectory of images" in the NT; postbiblical developments are said to be consistent with the "thrust" of the NT. At other times this evolution has involved the rediscovery of truths that the church once possessed but which it subsequently lost in the course of its long history. The church has even at times recognized as error what it had earlier decreed authoritatively. Vatican Council II's Declaration on Religious Freedom is seen by reputable Catholic scholars to be in conflict with the condemnations of religious freedom in Gregory XVI's encyclical *Mirari vos* of 1832. The conflict was recognized by members of the council, but they supported the declaration on the principle of doctrinal development. Protestants hostile to Catholicism should be wary of attacking allegedly unalterable Catholic positions: the Catholic Church has reversed its position on basic issues.

If, then, Roman Catholicism cannot be fixed within a single monolithic theological system, it is nevertheless helpful to distinguish between two traditions within Catholicism. The mainstream tradition has stressed the transcendence of God and the church as a divinely commissioned institution (the "vertical church"). This authoritarian, centralizing tradition has been variously labeled, mainly by its critics, as "medievalism," "Romanism," "Vaticanism," "papalism," "Ultramontanism," "Jesuitism," "Integralism," and "neoscholasticism." A minority reformist tradition has stressed the immanence of God and the church as community (the "horizontal church"). Reform Catholicism has nourished such movements as Gallicanism, Jansenism, liberal Catholicism, and modernism.

The two traditions coalesced at Vatican II, facilitated by John XXIII's dictum, "The substance of the ancient doctrine is one thing . . . and the way in which it is presented is another." An understanding, then, of modern-day Roman Catholicism requires a description of the characteristics of conservative Catholicism which dominated the church especially from the Council of Trent (1545–63) until Vatican II, plus an outline of the changes in emphasis inaugurated at Vatican II.

The Church. The most distinctive characteristic of Roman Catholicism has always been its theology of the church (its ecclesiology). The church's role in mediating salvation has been emphasized more than in other Christian traditions. Supernatural life is mediated to Christians through the sacraments administered by the hierarchy to whom obedience is due. The church is monarchical as well as hierarchical since Christ conferred the primacy on Peter, whose successors are the popes. Pre–Vatican II theology taught that the Roman Catholic Church is the only true church of Christ, since it alone has a permanent hierarchy (which is apostolic) and primacy (which is Petrine) to ensure the permanence of the church as Christ instituted it. All other churches are false churches insofar as they lack one of the four properties possessed by the Roman Catholic Church: unity, holiness, catholicity, and apostolicity.

The most important document of Vatican II, the Dogmatic Constitution on the Church, transformed rather than revolutionized the church's ecclesiology. The traditional emphasis on the church as means of salvation was supplanted by an understanding of the church as a mystery or sacrament, "a reality imbued with the hidden presence of God" (Paul VI). The conception of the church as a hierarchical institution was replaced by a view of the church as the whole people of God. To the traditional understanding of the church's mission as involving (1) the proclamation of the gospel and (2) the celebration of the sacraments, the council added (3) witnessing to the gospel and (4) service to all in need. The Tridentine emphasis on the church universal was supplemented by an understanding of the fullness of the church in each local congregation.

In the Decree on Ecumenism the council recognized that both sides were at fault in the rupture of the church at the Reformation, and it sought the restoration of Christian unity rather than a return of non-Catholics to "the true Church." For the church is greater than the Roman Catholic Church: other churches are valid Christian communities since they share the same Scriptures, life of grace, faith, hope, charity, gifts of the Spirit, and baptism.

Further, the traditional identification of the kingdom of God with the church, into which everyone must therefore be brought or salvation will elude them, is replaced by an understanding of the church as the sign and instrument by which God calls and moves the world toward his kingdom.

The Pope. The dogmas of papal primacy and infallibility were promulgated as recently as Vatican I (1869–70), but they have a long history which Roman Catholics trace ultimately to the will of Christ (Matt. 16:18–19; Luke 22:32; John 21:15–17) and the roles exercised by the apostle Peter (fisherman, shepherd, elder, rock, etc.) in the NT church. In succeeding centuries the prestige of the church of Rome increased since it was located at the Imperial capital and because of its association with the apostles Peter and Paul. It was increasingly looked to as the arbiter of orthodoxy. Pope Leo I maintained that Peter continues to speak to the whole church through the bishop of Rome, the first known such claim. The rise of the pope's temporal power, which for over a millennium buttressed his claims to supremacy, is commonly traced to the middle of the eighth century, when a vacuum in civil leadership was created by the collapse of the Western Empire.

In 1234 Gregory IX combined and codified all previous papal decisions into the *Five Books of Decretals.* By now the church was understood primarily as a visible hierarchical organization with supreme power vested in the pope. Bishops were required to take an oath of obedience to the pope similar to the feudal oath binding a vassal to his lord. The supreme pontiff was no longer only consecrated; he was also crowned with the triple tiara used originally by the deified rulers of Persia. The coronation rite was continued until 1978, when John Paul I refused the crown, a symbolic action repeated by his successor, John Paul II. The height of papal pretensions was reached in 1302 with Boniface VIII's bull, *Unam Sanctam,* which decreed that the temporal power was subject to the spiritual, and that submission to the Roman pontiff "is absolutely necessary to salvation."

These papal claims were resisted not only by national rulers but by some scholars, notably William of Ockham and Marsilius of Padua, and by conciliarism, a movement in the church to subject the pope to the judgment and legislation of general councils. Its greatest triumph was the Council of Constance (1414–15) with its law *Haec Sancta,* decreeing the supremacy of a general council and the collegiality of bishops. Conciliarism was condemned by succeeding popes until Vatican I declared that the pope's authoritative teachings are not subject to the consent of the entire church. The pope was declared to be infallible (immune from error) when he speaks *ex cathedra* (from the chair) on matters of faith and morals with the intention of binding the whole church.

Vatican II stressed the role of the pope as "perpetual and visible source and foundation of the unity of the bishops and of the multitude of the faithful," a role received sympathetically by some Protestant churches since the council (see, e.g., R. E. Brown *et al*, *Peter in the New Testament*, sponsored by the United States Lutheran-Roman Catholic Dialogue). Vatican II also revived the collegiality of bishops, thus modifying the monarchical governance of the church: "Together with its head, the Roman Pontiff, and never without its head, the episcopal order is the subject of supreme and full power over the universal church."

The Sacraments. The sacramental principle is another characteristic tenet of Roman Catholicism. The sacramental system worked out especially in the Middle Ages by the schoolmen and subsequently at the Council of Trent envisaged sacraments primarily as causes of grace that could be received independent of the merit of the recipient. Recent Catholic sacramental theology emphasizes their function as signs of faith. Sacraments are said to cause grace insofar as they are intelligible signs of it, and that the fruitfulness, as distinct from the validity, of the sacrament is dependent on the faith and devotion of the recipient. Sacramental rites are now administered in the vernacular, rather than in Latin, to increase the intelligibility of the signs.

Conservative Catholicism connected sacramental theology to Christology, stressing Christ's institution of the sacraments and the power of the sacraments to infuse the grace of Christ, earned on Calvary, to the recipient. The newer emphasis connects the sacraments to ecclesiology. We do not encounter Christ directly, but in the church, which is his body. The church mediates the presence and action of Christ.

The number of sacraments was finally fixed at seven during the medieval period (at the councils of Lyons 1274, Florence 1439, and Trent 1547). In addition Roman Catholicism has innumerable sacramentals—e.g., baptismal water, holy oil, blessed ashes, candles, palms, crucifixes, and statues. Sacramentals are said to cause grace not *ex opere operato* like the sacraments, but *ex opere operantis*, through the faith and devotion of those using them.

Three of the sacraments—baptism, confirmation, Eucharist—are concerned with Christian initiation.

Baptism. The sacrament is understood to remit original sin and all personal sin of which the recipient sincerely repents. All must be baptized or they cannot enter the kingdom of heaven. But not all baptism is sacramental baptism by water. There is also "baptism of blood," which is received by dying for Christ (e.g., the "holy innocents," Matt. 2:16–18), and "baptism of desire," which is received by those who, implicitly or explicitly, desire baptism but are prevented from receiving it sacramentally. "Even those who through no fault of their own do not know Christ and his church may be counted as anonymous Christians if their striving to lead a good life is in fact a response to his grace, which is given in sufficient measure to all."

Confirmation. A theology of confirmation was not developed until the Middle Ages. Confirmation was said to be the gift of the Spirit for strengthening (*ad robur*) while baptismal grace is for forgiveness (*ad remissionem*). This distinction has no basis in the Scriptures or the fathers, but has been retained to the present following ratification by the Council of Trent. Today, however, the rite is sometimes administered at the same time as baptism and by the priest, not the bishop, to emphasize that both are really aspects of the one sacrament of initiation.

Eucharist. Distinctively Catholic doctrines on the Eucharist include the sacrificial nature of the Mass and transubstantiation. Both were defined at Trent and neither was modified at Vatican II. The unbloody sacrifice of the Mass is identified with the bloody sacrifice of the cross, in that both are offered for the sins of the living and the dead. Hence Christ is the same victim and priest in the Eucharist as he was on the cross. Transubstantiation, the belief that the substance of bread and wine is changed into the body and blood of Christ, was first spoken of at the Fourth Lateran Council (1215).

Two sacraments—penance and anointing the sick—are concerned with healing.

Penance. By the Middle Ages the sacrament of penance had four components which were confirmed by the Council of Trent: satisfaction (the doing of an act of penance), confession, contrition, and absolution by a priest. All grave sins had to be confessed to a priest who acted as judge. Since Vatican II the role of the priest in penance is understood as healer, and the purpose of the sacrament is reconciliation with the church rather than the restoration of friendship with God. Through contrition the sinner's union with God is restored, but he is still required to seek forgiveness in the sacrament of penance because his sin compromises the mission of the church to be a holy people.

Anointing the Sick. During the Middle Ages the rite of anointing the sick was reserved increasingly for the dying, hence the description of Peter Lombard: *extreme unctio* (last anointing). Vatican II relabeled the sacrament "anointing of the sick," stating explicitly that it "is not a sacrament reserved for those who are at the point of death." The last sacrament is now known as viaticum, received during Mass if possible.

There are two sacraments of vocation and commitment: marriage and orders.

Marriage. The sacramentality of marriage was affirmed by the councils of Florence and Trent. Marriage is understood to be indissoluble, although dispensations, chiefly in the form of annulment (a declaration that a valid marriage never existed), are permitted. The grounds of nullity so carefully delimited in the 1918 Code of Canon Law have now been broadened to embrace many deficiencies of character.

Orders. Vatican II recognized that all the baptized participate in some way in the priesthood of Christ, but confirmed Catholic tradition on the clerical hierarchy by decreeing that there is a distinction between the priesthood conferred by baptism and that conferred by ordination. The ordained priesthood has three orders: bishops, priests, and deacons. The first and third are offices of the NT church. The office of priest emerged when it was no longer practical to continue recognizing the Jewish priesthood (owing to the destruction of the temple and the great influx of Gentiles into the church) and with the development of a sacrificial understanding of the Lord's Supper.

Canon Law. In the eleventh and twelfth centuries a new branch of theological studies, canon law, emerged as an adjunct of papal supremacy. Legal decrees rather than the gospel became the basis for moral judgments. The church was understood primarily as an institution in its juridical aspect. The legal aspects of the sacraments and matrimony were paramount. Until the post–Vatican II period a knowledge of canon law was the chief prerequisite for ecclesiastical advancement.

The Cult of the Blessed Virgin Mary. At the Council of Ephesus (431) Mary was declared to be the Mother of God (*Theotokos*) and not only the mother of Christ (*Christotokos*). This gave an impetus to Marian devotion and by the seventh century four Marian feasts were being observed in Rome: the annunciation, the purification, the assumption, and the nativity of Mary. To these feasts the Eastern churches added the feast of the conception of Mary at the end of the same century. Bernard of Clairvaux influenced Mariology decisively by arguing that while Christ is our mediator he is also our judge, and that therefore we need a mediator with the mediator, so that in popular devotion the merciful Mary was contrasted with the fierce Christ. Marian devotion blossomed between the eleventh and fifteenth centuries. The rosary (three groups of fifty Hail Marys counted on beads) was in popular use by the twelfth century and the angelus also appeared (the recitation of prayers to Mary, morning, noon, and evening, at the sound of a bell). In 1854, following another revival of Marian spirituality, Pius IX promulgated the dogma of the immaculate conception, that Mary was free from original sin from the moment of her conception. In 1950 Pius XII defined the dogma of bodily assumption of the Virgin Mary, that on her death she was preserved from "the corruption of the tomb" and was "raised body and soul to the glory of heaven, to shine refulgent as Queen at the right hand of her Son."

Since Vatican II Catholic scholars have questioned if denial of these two Marian dogmas means exclusion from the Catholic Church, since that denial must be "culpable, obstinate, and externally manifested." Vatican II also tended to disassociate Mariology from Christology, thus removing an emphasis on her involvement in our redemption and attaching her to ecclesiology, so that Mary is seen rather as the type, model, mother, and preeminent member of the church.

Revelation. The Council of Trent declared tradition to be equally authoritative with Scripture and the definitive interpretation of both to be the preserve of the church. In its Dogmatic Constitution on Divine Revelation Vatican II sought to remove the sharp distinction perceived by Protestants between Scripture and tradition by defining tradition as the successive interpretations of the Scriptures given by the church throughout the ages. That the church somehow stood above both sources of revelation was specifically denied: "This teaching office is not above the word of God, but serves it. . . . It is clear, therefore, that sacred tradition, sacred Scripture, and the teaching authority of the Church . . . are so linked and joined together that one cannot stand without the others."

The failure of post–Vatican II Catholicism to give a clear preeminence to the Bible leaves some Protestants dissatisfied, but there is no doubt that the scholarly and popular study of the Bible by Roman Catholics has increased markedly since 1965. Roman Catholicism is no longer simply reacting and polemical, devoted to defending truth through the condemnation of error. It is now an innovative and irenical movement, more devoted to illustrating the Christian faith than defining it. F. S. Piggin

See also TRENT, COUNCIL OF; INFALLIBILITY; PAPACY; COUNTER-REFORMATION; CATHOLICISM, LIBERAL; ULTRAMONTANISM; GALLICANISM; FEBRONIANISM; EXCOMMUNICATION; VATICAN COUNCIL I; VATICAN COUNCIL II.

Bibliography. W. M. Abbott and J. Gallagher, eds., *The Documents of Vatican II;* L. Boettner, *Roman Catholicism; A New Catechism: Catholic Faith for Adults;* G. Daly, *Transcendence and Immanence: A Study in Catholic Modernism and Integralism;* J. Delumeau, *Catholicism Between Luther and Voltaire;* J. P. Dolan, *Catholicism: An Historical Survey;* J. D. Holmes, *The Triumph of the Holy See;* P. Hughes, *A Short History of the Catholic Church;* B. Kloppenberg, *The Ecclesiology of Vatican II;* R. Lawler, D. W. Wuerl, and T. C. Lawler, eds., *The Teaching of Christ: A Catholic Catechism for Adults;* R. P. McBrien, *Catholicism,* 2 vols.

Roman Creed, Old. *See* APOSTLES' CREED.

Romanticism. A movement in art, literature, philosophy, and religion, in the latter eighteenth and early nineteenth centuries, romanticism defies definition. The romantic writers seldom used the term themselves, and controversy has raged among critical and historical scholars of Western culture ever since as to its precise meaning and interpretation. Some, like A. O. Lovejoy, insist there are many "romanticisms" in the sense of artists and writers manifesting its typical features but no clearly definable doctrine or school. Others restrict it to one or more countries, denying that a general movement as such existed. Nevertheless there are identifiable traits that distinguish romanticism from earlier cultural periods, and most contemporary scholars, while disagreeing on details, recognize its descriptive validity. Certainly it characterizes a "temperament" (Crane Brinton) or personality, if not an epoch in cultural history as such.

The term came from the Old French *romanz* (to write), which in the Middle Ages meant writing in the vernacular rather than Latin. It gradually came to be applied to works of fiction and then to the untouched natural landscape. By the eighteenth century it referred to that which was sentimental, full of expression, and melancholy. The movement itself arose in the 1790s as a reaction to the classicism and rationalism of the Enlightenment, but elements of this revolt could be seen in earlier "preromantic" writers like Vico, Rousseau, James Thomson, and the Storm and Stress school in Germany (Klopstock, Herder, and the young Goethe and Schiller). Among the major romantic authors are Coleridge, Wordsworth, Byron, Shelley, Keats, Scott, and Blake in Britain; Madame de Staël, Musset, George Sand, and Victor Hugo in France; and Goethe, August and Friedrich von Schlegel, Novalis, Eichendorff, Kleist, Tieck, the Grimm brothers, and E. T. A. Hoffmann in Germany. There were also romantic composers like Chopin, Schubert, and Schumann, painters like Delacroix and Turner, and the philosophers Fichte, Schelling, Hegel, and Schopenhauer. The main theologian was Schleiermacher. The movement had run its course by the end of the 1830s, but some features continued even past midcentury.

The specific elements of romanticism are difficult to delineate because they exist in differing combinations in the various writers and thinkers, depending on their geographical location, place in time, and personal connections. While acknowledging that there are exceptions, romanticism generally can be said to stress emotionalism, sensualism, fantasy, and imagination over rational order and control. Reality is found not by rational thought but through feeling, immediate experience, spiritual illumination, brooding, and listening to the inner voices. There is a subjectivism that emphasizes self-consciousness, the activity of the ego, introversion, and originality. A sense of mystery arises out of an inner longing for that which is unexperienced and unknown. Each personality should be allowed to unfold itself freely, according to its own genius, individual impulses, and idiosyncrasies. Romantics seek beauty, color, and adventure in out-of-the-way places and events and among the common people. The exotic is preferred over the familiar, rural life over that of the city. Prescribed unities and forms are rejected for that which is different, unconventional, novel, and spontaneous. Romantics have a deep interest in the past, especially the Middle Ages, as well as nonclassical (Nordic) mythology, folklore, and primitivism, and they contributed greatly to recovering and publishing long-forgotten medieval historical records and literature. Finally romantic art seems on the one hand to be sensuous, concrete, and down to earth, yet simultaneously it is much more visionary and even mystical. As Novalis put it, in the romantic view of life "world becomes dream, dream becomes world."

The impact of romanticism on religious and theological developments is significant. To be sure, its emphasis on human self-consciousness, personal creative powers, the natural goodness of man, and the pantheistic interfusion of real and ideal, finite and infinite, spirit and matter leads to a glorification of man's powers of self-expression and to pride. Many romantics refused to believe in any power superior to their own genius, and the objects of their devotion—nature, liberty, beauty, love, brotherhood—essentially circle back to the worshiper and function as ways of asserting human self-sufficiency.

Nevertheless, some did embrace Christianity.

In 1798 Friedrich von Schlegel underwent what approximated a conversion experience, and religion, God, mysticism, and the otherworld began to fill his writings. He was attracted by the shimmering vision of a reality beyond this world whose gates are not opened by critical analysis, and which one does not understand until he has experienced it. Schlegel saw fantasy or the imagination as the point of contact between within and without, the self and God. The poet is the one who illuminates and awakens man to the spark of the divine within him. But in order to find one's way into the higher sphere, he must negate the earthly and finite. This requires self-sacrifice, i.e., death, because only from the perspective of the realm beyond does the purpose of the whole become clear. The flame of eternal life is kindled in death.

Novalis (Friedrich von Hardenberg) argued that the poet must be the priest of this religion, since through fantasy, imagination, and dream he is the one who has been made immortal. In the essay *Christendom or Europe* (1799) Novalis portrayed Christianity as the symbol of a universal world religion, the purest example of religion as a historical phenomenon and the most complete revelation. In the Middle Ages the love of Mary, princely submission to ecclesiastical authority, and sense for the invisible, peace, unity, and inner world reigned supreme. This organic unity disintegrated under the impact of the Reformation, while the Enlightenment squelched imagination and emotion and relegated man merely to first place in the order of created things. But now a new religious surge is sweeping Europe, art is reborn, and imagination and creative will are stirring the universal capability of the inner man. Religion will awaken Europe, install Christendom with new splendor in its old peace-establishing office, and fulfill the comprehensive divine plan.

Both Schlegel and Novalis deeply influenced the young preacher Friedrich Schleiermacher, who moved freely in Berlin's salons. At Schlegel's urging he wrote *On Religion: Addresses to Its Cultured Despisers*, a general analysis and defense of religion commending it to the intellectuals of the day who tended to dismiss it as mere superstition. In this and his main theological work *The Christian Faith* he charts a middle course between traditional orthodoxy and cold rationalism. It reflects his romantic preference for the vital, inward, and spontaneous over the static, outward, and formal. Schleiermacher regarded the essence of religion as experience in the sense of the believer's absolute "dependence" or "God-consciousness." The failure of dependence is sin, but Christ is the man who was utterly dependent on God in every thought, word, and deed. This meant God existed in him and therefore he was divine. Christian doctrines are expressions of one's religious awareness. The Bible shapes and informs the Christian God-consciousness but at the same time is a product of it. The fundamental religious awareness leads necessarily to the development of communities that are marked outwardly by their origins and history and inwardly by the way they provide expression to the essential God-consciousness. In the Christian faith it has received its highest, clearest, and fullest expression because of Jesus' God-consciousness and his redemptive work in bringing believers into a full awareness of God.

Romanticism also influenced Hegel, but he went in a different direction and subsumed theology under philosophy, giving the highest place to reason. His philosophy of idealism sees all reality as incorporated in the all-encompassing mind or spirit which is God. Mind realizes itself in the world through the dialectical pattern of movement which is a clash of opposites, a favorite theme of the romantics. This involves an interplay of diversities, a movement from partial to fuller understanding, and the connection between the outward and inward, the whole and the part, the universal and the individual. The forms of human culture that make up the world advance to ever higher levels of self-realization, and ultimately absolute mind returns to itself.

From a historical perspective romanticism affected trends in the church itself. In Britain the romantics tended to view the church with indifference. In Germany a number of figures turned to Christianity. Some became Roman Catholics, including Friedrich Schlegel, Adam Müller, and Karl Haller, while Clemens Brentano and Joseph Görries returned to Catholicism. The dogmatic church offered a secure resting point for those weary of the restless and vain wanderings into the uncertain, and they viewed it in Novalis's sense as the mystical affirmation of Christianity. The French writer Chateaubriand glorified the Catholic faith in *The Spirit of Christianity* (1802) as a great cultural and moral force. Romanticism thus contributed to the Catholic revival of the early nineteenth century. Interestingly, these converts identified with a conservative view of the state.

This view was reflected in the late romantic tendency toward monarchical legitimacy and political passivity which drew so many of them to the conservative camp after the demise of Napoleon. It flowed out of organic theory which saw the state as rooted in the past, and the state, ruler, people, and church as all parts of one spiritual being or body. Especially in Germany the view was that state and church, throne and altar belong together and that both should be organized in the same manner, the state monarchical and the church episcopal. This, along with conservative Catholicism like that in France, contributed substantially to middle-class alienation from religion.

However, there was another direction in the political realm: the rise of nationalism. In the liberation struggle against Napoleonic rule in Germany concepts like *Volk* (people), fatherland, and freedom were elevated virtually to articles of faith. Such romantics as Arndt and Fichte categorically rejected the cosmopolitanism of the eighteenth century and argued instead for a German national state, one grounded in the organic development of the *Volk*. In the nineteenth century these ideas were linked with a "national Protestantism," but as German society became secularized they were appropriated by the forces of aggressive nationalism, and thus constitute one of the roots of Nazism.

Another point is the manner in which the romantic assumptions of organic development and inner connections within history affected the writing of church history and biblical interpretation. The church itself was seen as a historical phenomenon that should be examined according to the canons of the new scientific history. Growing out of this was both the historical-critical methodology of biblical criticism and the salvation history approach of the Erlangen school.

A final contribution to the emergence of the German *Erweckung* (revival) movement can be mentioned. Whereas the evangelical revival in Britain drew little or no sustenance from romanticism, in Germany this was an important factor. Some of the revival preachers like Kottwitz and Jänicke had contact with the romantic circles in Berlin and picked up their emphases on spirit, mind, feeling, subjectivity, religion of the heart, and uncertainty of the world and their rejection of Enlightenment rationalism and dead orthodoxy. It was not the only or even the decisive element in the *Erweckung* but, as in these other religious developments, the influence of that confusing and contradictory cultural movement labeled romanticism was evident. R. V. Pierard

See also Schleiermacher, Friedrich Daniel Ernst.

Bibliography. I. Babbitt, *Rousseau and Romanticism;* W. T. Jones, *The Romantic Syndrome;* A. O. Lovejoy, *Essays in the History of Ideas;* J. Barzun, *Classic, Romantic, and Modern;* J. G. Robertson, *Studies in the Genesis of Romantic Theory in the Eighteenth Century;* H. M. Jones, *Revolution and Romanticism;* N. Frye, *Romanticism Reconsidered;* J. Engel, *The Creative Imagination: Enlightenment to Romanticism;* R. J. Reilly, *Romantic Religion;* J. Forstman, *A Romantic Triangle: Schleiermacher and Early German Romanticism;* H. H. H. Remak, "West European Romanticism: Definition and Scope," in *Comparative Literature: Method and Perspective,* ed. N. P. Stallknecht and H. Frenz; C. Brinton, "Romanticism," *Encyclopedia of Philosophy,* VII, 206–9; *NCE,* XII, 639–41; C. A. Beckwith, *SHERK,* X, 86–89; N. Geisler, *DCE,* 595.

Rule of Faith (Lat. *regula fidei*). An expression, first used in the theology of the church in the last quarter of the second century, which meant the sure doctrine of the Christian faith. Synonymous expressions were "canon of truth," "rule of truth," "the canon of the church," and "the ecclesiastical canon." In Irenaeus, who writes against the menace of Gnosticism, the appeal is often made to the tradition of the church, but this is not set over against Scripture. Rather the "canon of truth" is the official church teaching that is in agreement with Scripture and is a summary of it. Instead of idle speculation the church, "the pillar and bulwark of the truth" (I Tim. 3:15), teaches living doctrine which is both the "canon of truth" and teaching which is in complete harmony with Scripture from which it is drawn. In Tertullian also church doctrine is seen as stemming from the apostolic tradition that had been given by Christ. It is the "rule of faith" which, agreeing with Scripture, is a clear summary of that which Christians are to believe. It helps in the correct exegesis of Scripture and the discernment of its unity and consistency. Heresy shows a neglect of the rule of faith, and it can be overcome only within the true church where unity and discipline are honored. Whereas many have concluded that Tertullian saw *regula fidei* as church tradition rather than Scripture, J. N. D. Kelly is right in the claim that Tertullian's true position is subtler than that and similar to that of Irenaeus. Aware of the futility of arguing with heretics on the basis of Scripture alone, whose meaning they could twist, he appealed to the *regula* which had been preserved intact in the church since the days of the apostles. This implied no denigration of Scripture, with which the church tradition agreed, but offered a clear, succinct statement about which there could be no debate. This rule of faith was employed in the baptismal formula and otherwise served to indicate what Christians believe.

Whereas a usage similar to that of Irenaeus and Tertullian is found in Hippolytus, Clement of Alexandria, Origen, Novatian, and others in the early church, later usage came to include the whole body of official church teaching. This is the understanding of most Roman Catholic theologians today. The Reformers of the sixteenth century proclaimed Scripture alone to be the "only rule of faith and practice," a position into which they were driven when they repudiated beliefs and practices for which they found no warrant in the Bible. M. E. OSTERHAVEN

Bibliography. J. N. D. Kelly, *Early Christian Doctrines; NCE,* XII, 706ff.; T. Zahn, *SHERK,* IX, 445–46.

Rural Dean. *See* CHURCH OFFICERS.

Ss

Sabaoth. *See* God, Names of.

Sabbatarianism. The view which insists that one day of each week be reserved for religious observance as prescribed by the OT sabbath law. It is most important that we note a distinction between strict or literal sabbatarianism and semisabbatarianism.

Strict or literal sabbatarianism contends that God's directive concerning the OT sabbath law is natural, universal, and moral; consequently the sabbath requires mankind to abstain from all labor except those tasks necessary for the welfare of society. In this view the seventh day, the *literal* sabbath, is the only day on which the requirements of this law can be met. Historically, we see a trend toward sabbatarianism in the Eastern church during the fourth century and the Irish church of the sixth century when, interestingly, a dual recognition of both sabbath and Sunday was stressed. It was not until the Reformation, however, that we meet the quintessence of sabbatarianism. Luther opposed the doctrine, pointing out (in his "Letter against the Sabbatarians") the legalistic pitfalls inherent in the view. Calvin agreed in principle with Luther's stance. The Transylvania unitarians adopted strict sabbath observance during the seventeenth century, later moving to a total acceptance of Judaism. The Seventh-day Baptists originated in 1631, bringing sabbatarianism to England and later to Rhode Island and New York. The most notable proponent of strict sabbatarianism at the present time is the Seventh-day Adventist Church; several smaller adventist groups hold the same or similar views. Adventists believe they have been raised for the express purpose of proclaiming that God requires all men to observe the sabbath. Their arguments for the universally binding character of the sabbath law are these: it (1) is part of the moral law, (2) was given at the creation, and (3) was not abrogated in the NT. Some adventists see in Sunday observance a fulfillment of the prophecy (Rev. 14:9ff.) which states that deluded mankind will be forced to accept the mark of the beast (Sunday observance) in order to survive during the days prior to Christ's second advent.

Semisabbatarianism holds a view essentially the same as strict sabbatarianism but transfers its demands from Saturday, the seventh day, to Sunday, the first day of the week. As early as the fourth and fifth centuries theologians in the Eastern church were teaching the practical identity of the Jewish sabbath and the Christian Sunday. Eusebius's interpretation of Ps. 91 (*ca.* 320) greatly influenced the ultimate transfer of sabbath assertions and prohibitions to the first day of the week. An ancient legend related in the so-called Apocalypse of Peter, and known to Augustine and Prudentius, significantly transfers to Sunday what the original legend said concerning the sabbath: those who suffer the pains of the lost in hell are, for the sake of Christ, permitted to rest from torment on Sunday, the first day of the week!

It was Albertus Magnus who first suggested a structured semisabbatarianism by dividing the sabbath command into (1) the moral *command* to observe a day of rest after six days of labor and (2) the ceremonial *symbol* that applied only to the Jews in a *literal* sense. Thomas Aquinas lifted this formulation to the status of official doctrine, a view later held by a large number of Reformed theologians as well. Semisabbatarianism reached its zenith in English Puritanism, later finding its way to the New World through the early colonists. Sunday restrictions and so-called blue laws in various states are a constant reminder of the influence of this view on the laws of our land. Organizations such as the Lord's Day Observance Society (est. 1831), and the Imperial Alliance for the Defense of Sunday (England) have sought to preserve the principles of semisabbatarianism, but with decreasing success since World War II. F. R. Harm

See also Adventism; Lord's Day.

Bibliography. R. D. Brackenridge, "The Sabbath War of 1865–6," in *RSCHS* 16:1; R. Cox, *Literature of the Sabbath Question;* P. Collinson, "The Origins of English Sabbatarianism," in *Studies in Church History;* C. H. Little, *Disputed Doctrines,* 65–68; M. Luther, *Letter to a Good Friend Against the Sabbatarians;* E. Morgan, *The Puritan Family,* 124–49; E. Plass, *What Luther Says,* III, 1328–31; J. M. Reu, *Christian Ethics,* 117ff., 317ff.; W. Rordorf, *Sunday;* P. Schaff, *The Anglo-American Sabbath;* A. H. Strong, *Systematic Theology,* 408–10; W. Whitaker, *Sunday in Tudor and Stuart Times* and *The Eighteenth Century Sunday.*

Sabbath. The seventh day of the week in which God ceased from his work of creation and declared the day blessed and holy (Gen. 2:1–3). Through the episode of the manna (Exod. 16), the sacred nature of the day was stressed to the Israelites. It was to be "a sabbath of the Lord," a day set apart for God and for rest. The Decalogue forbids work on the sabbath, both for the Israelites and for their servants and guests (Exod. 20:8–11). Deut. 5:12–15 implies that there is a humanitarian motive in the sabbath concept. In God's sight, no man or animal should be required to work seven days a week and to be enslaved as the Israelites were in Egypt. The sabbath is therefore a direct indication of God's consecration of Israel, as well as of his creation.

Violating the sabbath was a serious offense, and the person who worked on the sabbath was to be "cut off from among his people" (Exod. 31:14). During their wandering in the wilderness, the Israelites brought to trial a man found gathering wood on the sabbath. He was stoned to death according to the commandment of the Lord for profaning the sabbath (Num. 15:32–36). A fire was not to be kindled on the sabbath (Exod. 35:3), and admonitions to reverence the day are linked to reverence toward parents (Lev. 19:3) and reverence toward the Lord's sanctuary (19:30; 26:2). The sabbath terminated a week of work and was to be a complete rest unto the Lord, a distinguishing mark of God's choosing the Jewish people.

The sabbath was a joyous holy day, a day of spiritual refreshment and reverent worship. It seems to have been a popular day, an opportunity for man to imitate his Creator, to devote himself to contemplation and to community worship. Those that delighted in the Lord in this fashion were promised that they would "ride on the heights of the earth" (Isa. 58:13–14). Even foreigners who kept from profaning the sabbath and held to God's covenant were promised blessing and deep joy (56:6–8). Jewish tradition held that Isaiah declared the eventual universalization of the sabbath among all nations (note 66:23). Prophets such as Jeremiah and Ezekiel placed such stress on the importance of observing the sabbath that at times the fate of the Jewish people was directly linked in prophecy to attitudes toward the sabbath (note Jer. 17:19–27 and Ezek. 20:12ff.).

Josephus explains that during the first Christian century there were public discourses on the sabbath in the Jewish community. Jesus observed the sabbath, not only worshiping, but also teaching in the synagogue during that time of the week (Mark 6:2). The incidents regarding his disciples' plucking ears of grain or his healing on the sabbath were not a digression from the sabbath law, but were rather an indication that Jesus knew the content of the commandment very well. Not only his disciples, but also the apostle Paul and the early Jewish Christians observed the sabbath.

Jewish tradition has maintained the aspects of Torah observance, community worship, and joyful family participation to the present day. The mother prepares a special meal and kindles the sabbath candles remembering the holy day. As she wafts the aura of the candles toward her and recites the blessing over the candles, she symbolizes the putting of her daily cares from her and acknowledges the historic sacredness of the hour. Two loaves of bread are placed on the dinner table and covered with a cloth to symbolize the double portion of manna given during the wilderness wandering. Guests are often invited to share in this sabbath joy, and special prayers and hymns are recited, led by the father of the household. The family worships at weekly sabbath services at the synagogue. A farewell service is observed in a spirit of sadness that the blessed day has passed. Jewish tradition has proposed that if every Jew kept the sabbath for two consecutive sabbaths, the Messiah would return.

The Bible also made provision for a sabbath year. During the seventh year the land was to lie fallow so that the land might rest, the needy might feed on the aftergrowth, and the animals might eat the surplus. God promised an abundant harvest the sixth year to carry through the sabbatical period. In addition, debts were to be cancelled during that year (note Exod. 23:10–11; Lev. 25:1–7, 18–22; Deut. 15:1–11). At the close of seven sabbatical cycles a year of jubilee was instituted. Land that had been sold was to be returned to its former owner, and there were other sabbatical year provisions. These provisions underscored the fact that ultimately God owned the land. D. A. RAUSCH

See also LORD'S DAY; SABBATARIANISM.

Bibliography. A. E. Millgram, *Sabbath: The Day of Delight;* G. F. Moore, *Judaism in the First Centuries of the Christian Era;* A. J. Heschel, *The Sabbath;* S. Goldman, *Guide to the Sabbath;* D. A. Carson, *From Sabbath to Lord's Day;* R. T. Beckwith and W. Stott, *The Christian Sunday;* N. E. Andreasen, *Rest and Redemption.*

Sabellianism. *See* MONARCHIANISM.

Sacrament. A religious rite or ceremony instituted or recognized by Jesus Christ. Baptism and the Lord's Supper were given a prominent place in the fellowship of the early church (Acts 2:41–42; 10:47; 20:7, 11), along with the proclamation (*kērygma*) and teaching (*didachē*). Both rites were regarded as means appointed by Jesus Christ to bring the members of the church into communion with his death and resurrection, and thus with himself through the Holy Spirit (Matt. 28:19–20; Acts 2:38; Rom. 6:3–5; I Cor. 11:23–27; Col. 2:11–12). They were linked together in our Lord's teaching (Mark 10:38–39) and in the mind of the church (I Cor. 10:1–5ff.) as having such significance. They were the visible enactment of the word proclaimed in the kerygma, and their significance must be understood as such.

The proclamation of the gospel in the NT was no mere recital of the events of the life, death, resurrection, and ascension of Jesus, the Son of God. It was the representation of these events to the hearers in the power of the Spirit so that through such proclamation they could become related to these events in a living way through faith. In the proclamation of the gospel the once-for-all event continued to be effective for salvation (I Cor. 1:21; II Cor. 5:18–19). The word of the kerygma gave men fellowship in the mystery of the kingdom of God brought nigh in Jesus (Matt. 13:1–23; Mark 4:11), and the preacher in fulfilling his task was the steward of this mystery (I Cor. 4:1; Eph. 3:8–9; Col. 1:25). The miracles or signs accompanying the proclamation in the early church were the visible aspect of the living power the word derived from its relation to the mystery of the kingdom of God.

It was inevitable, therefore, that baptism and the Lord's Supper, the other visible counterparts of the kerygma, should also come to be regarded as giving fellowship in the same *mystērion* of the Word made flesh (I Tim. 3:16), and should be interpreted as themselves partaking in the mystery of the relationship between Christ and his church (Eph. 5:32).

The Greek word *mystērion* was later often given the Latin *sacramentum,* and the rites themselves came to be spoken of as *sacramenta.* The word *sacramentum* meant both "a thing set apart as sacred" and "a military oath of obedience as administered by the commander." The use of this word for baptism and the Lord's Supper affected the thought about these rites, and they tended to be regarded as conveying grace in themselves, rather than as relating men through faith to Christ.

A sacrament came later to be defined (following Augustine) as a "visible word" or an "outward and visible sign of an inward and spiritual grace." The similarity between the form of the sacrament and the hidden gift tended to be stressed. Five lesser sacraments became traditional in the church: confirmation, penance, extreme unction, order, matrimony. But the church had always a special place for baptism and the Lord's Supper as the chief mysteries, and at the Reformation these were regarded as the only two that had the authority of our Lord himself, and therefore as the only true sacraments.

Since God in the OT also used visible signs along with the word, these were also regarded as having sacramental significance. Among the OT sacraments the rites of circumcision and the passover were stressed as being the OT counterparts of baptism (Col. 2:11–12) and the Lord's Supper (I Cor. 5:7). R. S. WALLACE

See also BAPTISM; BAPTISM, BELIEVERS'; BAPTISM, INFANT; BAPTISM, MODES OF; BAPTISMAL REGENERATION; EX OPERE OPERATO; LORD'S SUPPER.

Bibliography. Calvin, *Institutes* 4.14; R. Bruce, *Sermons upon the Sacraments;* T. F. Torrance, "Eschatology and the Eucharist," in *Intercommunion;* G. Bornkamm, *TDNT,* IV, 826ff.; O. C. Quick, *The Christian Sacraments;* J. I. Packer, ed., *Eucharistic Sacrifice.*

Sacrifice. *See* ATONEMENT; OFFERINGS AND SACRIFICES IN BIBLE TIMES.

Sadducees. An important Jewish group that flourished in Palestine from the late second century B.C. to the late first Christian century.

Sources. The most reliable information about the Sadducees is found in three bodies of ancient literature: the writings of Flavius Josephus—*The Jewish War* (written *ca.* A.D. 75), *Antiquities of the Jews* (*ca.* A.D. 94), and *Life* (*ca.* A.D. 101); the NT, particularly the Synoptic Gospels and Acts (*ca.* A.D. 65–90; Matt. 3:7; 16:1–12; 22:23–34; Mark 12:18–27; Luke 20:27–38); and the rabbinic compilations (*ca.* A.D. 200 and later; Mishnah, Ber. 9:5; Erub. 6:2; Par. 3:3, 7; Nidd. 4:2; Yad. 4:6–8). Two observations about these sources should be made. First, with the possible exception of Josephus' *War,* all these sources are decidedly hostile towards the Sadducees. Second, many of the rabbinic references, especially those found in the Talmud and later works, are of doubtful historical reliability. Thus, our knowledge of the Sadducees is perforce severely limited and one-sided.

Name and Nature. Historically, the question of the derivation and meaning of the name "Sadducees" has been closely tied to the issue of the nature of the group. Ever since Abraham Geiger argued that the Sadducees were the priestly aristocracy, the majority of scholars have held that their name was derived from "Zadok," the name of the high priest during Solomon's reign (I Kings 2:35; cf. Ezek. 44:15; 48:11). Thus the Sadducees are thought to have been the party of the Zadokite priestly elite. There are problems with this construct, however. The "Zadok" etymology does not explain the doubling of the "d." Moreover, when the Sadducees appeared on the scene, the ruling priests were Hasmoneans, not Zadokites. It is unlikely that the Hasmoneans would have allied themselves with a rival priestly group whose very name called into question the legitimacy of the Hasmonean high priesthood.

More recently, many scholars have argued that the Sadducees were essentially a loose confederation of wealthy and powerful men (this would include members of the priestly aristocracy) who took a secular-pragmatic, rather than a religious-ideological, stance with regard to the nation and its laws. Along with this view, new etymologies for "Sadducees" have been offered. T. W. Manson proposed that behind the name stood the Greek title *syndikoi,* meaning "fiscal officials." R. North suggested that the Sadducees saw themselves as administrators of justice and that their name was derived from an otherwise unattested Piel adjective *ṣaddûq* ("just"). These and other etymologies solve some problems, but raise new ones; at bottom, they all remain speculative. In light of the total absence of Sadducean sources, it would seem wise to admit that both the precise nature of the Sadducees and the derivation of their name remain uncertain.

History. Equally uncertain are the details of Sadducean history. The meager evidence suggests the following outline. The Sadducees solidified as a group soon after the Maccabean revolt (167–160 B.C.). They were heirs to a persistent tendency within the Jewish aristocracy to see Judaism as a temple-centered religion rather than a law-centered way of life. Because they supported the Hasmonean policy of military and economic expansion, they gradually came to exercise tremendous influence in John Hyrcanus's court (134–104 B.C.). Their influence predominated until the end of Alexander Jannaeus's reign (76 B.C.). Under Queen Alexandra (76–67 B.C.) the Sadducees lost their power, and their numbers were greatly reduced. They fared little better under Herod the Great (37–4 B.C.), who deeply mistrusted the native Jewish aristocracy. With the imposition of direct Roman rule (A.D. 6), Sadducean fortunes revived. Between A.D. 6 and 66 the Sadducees not only became a major power within the Sanhedrin, but, for many years, they were able to control the high priesthood as well. The revolt of 66–70 spelled the end for the Sadducees. Although they had sought to forestall the revolt, the Romans had no use for a failed aristocracy. With the destruction of the temple and the dissolution of the nation, the Sadducees faded into oblivion.

Beliefs. The Sadducees are said to have rejected all Jewish observances not explicitly taught in the pentateuchal law. In their legal debates, the Sadducees consistently pushed for a strict and narrow application of the law. They repudiated the notions of resurrection and rewards and punishments after death. According to Josephus, they even denied the immortality of the soul. The Sadducees tended to disassociate God from human affairs. For this reason, they maintained that human choices and actions were totally free—unrestrained by divine interference. Consistent with this emphasis on human autonomy, the Sadducees denied the existence of angels and preterhuman spirits.

Most scholars have held that these beliefs mark off the Sadducees as conservatives who stubbornly resisted the innovations of the Pharisees and others. It should be noted, on the other hand, that these beliefs could just as easily describe hellenized aristocrats who wanted to minimize as much as possible the claims of their ancestral religion on their daily lives.

Sadducees and the NT. Unlike the Pharisees, the Sadducees are consistently painted in a bad light by the NT writers. Their opposition to Jesus and the early church is presented as monolithic and constant. Reasons for the hostility are not hard to imagine. To the Sadducees, Jesus and his early followers would have appeared as destabilizing forces in delicate balance between limited Jewish freedom and totalitarian Roman rule. But just as significantly, the Sadducees could not have had anything but contempt for a movement that proclaimed the present reality of the resurrection and the unconditional necessity of repentance.

S. TAYLOR

See also ESSENES; PHARISEES.

Bibliography. Josephus, *The Jewish War* 2.8.2, 14; *Antiquities of the Jews* 13.5.9, 13.10.6, 18.1.4, 20.9.1; and *Life* 10; A. Geiger, *Sadducäer und Pharisäer;* G. H. Box, "Who Were the Sadducees?" *Exp* 15:19–38; T. W. Manson, "Sadducees and Pharisees—The Origin and

Significance of the Names," *BJRL* 22:144–59; R. North, "The Qumran Sadducees," *CBQ* 17:164–88; J. Le Moyne, *Les Sadducéens;* W. W. Buehler, *Pre-Herodian Civil War and Social Debate;* H. D. Mantel, "The Sadducees and the Pharisees," in *The World History of the Jewish People,* VIII, 99–123; J. M. Baumgarten, "The Pharisaic-Sadducean Controversies about Purity and the Qumran Texts," *JJS* 31:157–70.

Saint, Saintliness. In the OT, the rendering of *ḥāsîd* ("pious, godly") and of *qādôš* ("holy"). The basic idea in *qādôš* is separation unto God, whereas *ḥāsîd* stresses godliness grounded on the reception of God's mercy. The NT word is *hagios* ("holy"). It is regularly used in the LXX to render *qādôš.*

From Ps. 85:8, where the saints seem to be synonymous with the people of God, one concludes that the emphasis does not fall on character to an appreciable degree (for not all were godly) but on divine choice and the bestowal of God's favor. In other passages the godly portion of the nation is often singled out by the term. But if the ethical connotation were paramount, the expectation would be that the word should occur regularly in the absolute form—the saints. Yet, ever and again, we read of "thy saints" or "the saints of the Most High" or, as in the NT, of saints in Christ Jesus.

Saints acquire their status by divine call (Rom. 1:7). Doubtless there is latent in the use of this term the idea that relationship to God involves conformity to his will and character (Eph. 5:3). In this way the term becomes linked with the thought of faithfulness (Eph. 1:1; Col. 1:2).

The next stage of development appears in the book of Revelation, where separation unto the Lord, which characterizes saints, leads to Satan-inspired persecution from the world (Rev. 13:7; 14:12) and even to martyrdom (16:6; 17:6). Here are the seeds for the Roman Catholic concept of saint as a peculiarly holy or self-sacrificing person who is worthy of veneration.

In the NT, however, saint is applied to all believers. It is a synonym for Christian brother (Col. 1:2). Except for Phil. 4:21, it is not used in the singular, and even there it reflects the corporate idea—"every saint." The saints are the church (I Cor. 1:2). In Ephesians, where there is strong emphasis on the unity of the church, "all the saints" becomes almost a refrain (1:15; 3:8, 18; 6:18). The Apostles' Creed enshrines this significance of the word in the statement, "I believe . . . in the communion of saints." E. F. HARRISON

See also CANONIZATION; GODLINESS.

Sainthood. *See* CANONIZATION.

Saints, Invocation of. *See* INVOCATION OF THE SAINTS.

Saints, Veneration of. *See* VENERATION OF THE SAINTS.

Salvation. The saving of man from the power and effects of sin.

The Biblical Idea. The common Hebrew words for salvation, deriving from the root *yāšaʿ* (width, spaciousness, freedom from constraint, hence—deliverance) obviously lend themselves to broad development in application. Literally, they cover salvation from any danger, distress, enemies, from bondage in Egypt (Exod. 14:13; 15:2), exile in Babylon (Isa. 46:13; 52:10–11), adversaries (Ps. 106:10), defeat (Deut. 20:4), or oppression (Judg. 3:31; etc.). Metaphorically, in salvation from social decay (Hos. 1:7) and from want, the meaning approaches moral and personal welfare ("prosperity"; Job 30:15); in Ps. 28:9, religious blessing in general. "The Lord is . . . my salvation" is the heart of OT testimony, always with an overtone of undeserved mercy. Later Judaism anticipated a messianic deliverance, which might include political, national, or religious elements (Pss. Sol. 10:9; T. Benj. 9:10; cf. Luke 1:69, 71, 77).

Sōtēria therefore gathered a rich connotation from LXX to carry into NT. There, too, it means deliverance, preservation, from any danger (Acts 7:25; 27:31; Heb. 11:7). The roots *saos, sōzō,* however, add the notion of wholeness, soundness, health, giving "salvation" a medical connotation—salvation from affliction, disease, demon possession, death (Mark 5:34; James 5:15; etc.). Sometimes this meaning is literal; peace, joy, praise, faith are so interwoven with healing as to give "saved" a religious significance also. Jesus' self-description as "physician" (Mark 2:17) and the illustrative value of the healing miracles in defining his mission show how readily physical and spiritual healing unite in "salvation" (Luke 4: 18–19).

Much of the most frequent use of *sōtēria* and derivatives is for deliverance, preservation from all spiritual dangers, the bestowal of all religious blessings. Its alternative is destruction (Phil. 1:28), death (II Cor. 7:10), divine wrath (I Thess. 5:9); it is available to all (Titus 2:11), shared (Jude 3), eternal (Heb. 5:9). It is ascribed to Christ alone (Acts 4:12; Luke 19:10), "the pioneer of salvation," and especially to his death (Heb. 2:10; Rom. 5:9–10). In that sense salvation was "from the Jews" (John 4:22), though for Gentiles too (Rom. 11:11). It is proclaimed (taught) as a way of thought and life (Acts 13:26; 16:17; Eph. 1:13), to be received from God's favor by faith alone—a confessed confidence and trust (Acts 16:30–31;

Eph. 2:8) focused upon the resurrection and Lordship of Christ (Rom. 10:9), "calling" upon him (Acts 2:21; Rom. 10:13). Once received, salvation must not be "neglected" but "held fast," "grown up to," humbly "worked out" (Heb. 2:3; I Cor. 15:2; I Pet. 2:2; Phil. 2:12), some being only narrowly saved in the end (I Cor. 3:15; I Pet. 4:18).

The Comprehensiveness of Salvation. The comprehensiveness of salvation may be shown

(1) By what we are saved from. This includes sin and death; guilt and estrangement; ignorance of truth; bondage to habit and vice; fear of demons, of death, of life, of God, of hell; despair of self; alienation from others; pressures of the world; a meaningless life. Paul's own testimony is almost wholly positive: salvation has brought him peace with God, access to God's favor and presence, hope of regaining the glory intended for men, endurance in suffering, steadfast character, an optimistic mind, inner motivations of divine love and power of the Spirit, ongoing experience of the risen Christ within his soul, and sustaining joy in God (Rom. 5:1–11). Salvation extends also to society, aiming at realizing the kingdom of God; to nature, ending its bondage to futility (Rom. 8:19–20); and to the universe, attaining final reconciliation of a fragmented cosmos (Eph. 1:10; Col. 1:20).

(2) By noting that salvation is past (Rom. 8:24; Eph. 2:5, 8; Titus 3:5–8); present (I Cor. 1:18; 15:2; II Cor. 2:15; 6:2; I Pet. 1:9; 3:21); and future (Rom. 5:9–10; 13:11; I Cor. 5:5; Phil. 1:5–6; 2:12; I Thess. 5:8; Heb. 1:14; 9:28; I Pet. 2:2). That is, salvation includes that which is given, freely and finally, by God's grace (forgiveness—called in one epistle justification, friendship; or reconciliation, atonement, sonship, and new birth); that which is continually imparted (sanctification—growing emancipation from all evil, growing enrichment in all good—the enjoyment of eternal life, experience of the Spirit's power, liberty, joy, advancing maturity in conformity to Christ); and that still to be attained (redemption of the body, perfect Christlikeness, final glory).

(3) By distinguishing salvation's various aspects: religious (acceptance with God, forgiveness, reconciliation, sonship, reception of the Spirit, immortality); emotional (strong assurance, peace, courage, hopefulness, joy); practical (prayer, guidance, discipline, dedication, service); ethical (new moral dynamic for new moral aims, freedom, victory); personal (new thoughts, convictions, horizons, motives, satisfactions, self-fulfillment); social (new sense of community with Christians, of compassion toward all, overriding impulse to love as Jesus has loved).

Salvation in the NT. Distinctive approaches underline the richness of the concept. Jesus presupposed the universal sin and need of men, originating in rebelliousness (Matt. 7:23; 13:41; 24:12 "lawless"; 21:28–29), and causing "sickness" of soul (Mark 2:17), which lies deep within personality, defiling from within (Matt. 7:15–16; 12:35; cf. 5:21–22, 27–28; 15:19–20; 23:25), and leaving men in debt to God for unpaid duty (6:12; 18:23–24). He therefore called *all* to repentance (Mark 1:15; Luke 5:32; 13:3, 5; 15:10)—to a change of outlook and life style that enthrones God (Luke 8:2; 19:9 [John 8:11]; Matt. 9:9; etc.)—urged daily prayer for forgiveness, himself offered forgiveness (Mark 2:5), and commended humble penitence as the only acceptable basis upon which to approach God (Luke 18:9–10).

In Jesus' openness and friendship toward sinners, the loving welcome of God found perfect expression. Nothing was needed to win back God's favor. It waited eagerly for man's return (Luke 15:11–24). The one indispensable preliminary was the change in man from rebelliousness to childlike trust and willingness to obey. That shown, there followed life under God's rule, described as feasting, marriage, wine, finding treasure, joy, peace, all the freedom and privilege of sonship within the divine family in the Father's world.

Peter also called to repentance (Acts 2:38), promising forgiveness and the Spirit to whoever called upon the Lord. Salvation was especially from past misdeeds and for conformity to a perverse generation (vss. 23–40); and with a purpose, inheritance, and glory still to be revealed (I Pet. 1:3–5; etc.).

In John's thought salvation is from death and judgment. He restates its meaning in terms of life, rich and eternal (thirty-six times in Gospel, thirteen in I John), God's gift in and with Christ, beginning in total renewal ("new birth"); illumined by truth ("knowledge," "light"); and experienced as love (John 3:5–16; 5:24; 12:25; I John 4:7–11; 5:11).

Paul saw his own failure to attain legal righteousness reflected in all men and due to the overmastering power ("rule") of sin, which brought with it death. Salvation is therefore, first, acquittal, despite just condemnation, on the ground of Christ's expiation of sin (Rom. 3:21–22); and second, deliverance by the invasive power of the Spirit of holiness, the Spirit of the risen Christ. The faith which accepts and assents to Christ's death on our behalf also unites us to him so closely that with him we die to sin and rise to new life (Rom. 6:1–2). The results are freedom from sin's power (vss. 7, 18; 8:2); exultation in the power of the indwelling Spirit and assurance of sonship (ch. 8); increasing conformity to Christ.

By the same process death is overcome, and believers are prepared for life everlasting (6:13, 22–23; 8:11).

Further Development. It is evident, even from this brief outline, that need would arise for endless analysis, comparison, systematization, and restatement in contemporary terms of all that salvation means to Christian faith. This is the task of soteriology, the doctrine of *sōtēria*—salvation. How far, for example, did the mystery religions of the first century influence the Christian hope derived from Judaism? They offered salvation, as "all the blessings it is possible to desire," and above all else, immortality. Before becoming absorbed in Christology, patristic reflection probed especially the meaning of the ransom Christ had paid for man's salvation and freedom.

Later, the Eastern Church traced the effect of Adam's fall chiefly in man's mortality, and saw salvation as especially the gift of eternal life through the risen Christ. The Western Church traced the effect of Adam's fall chiefly in the inherited guilt (Ambrose) and corruption (Augustine) of the race, and saw salvation as especially the gift of grace through Christ's death. Divine grace alone could cancel guilt and deliver from corruption.

Anselm and Abelard explored further the relation of man's salvation to the cross of Jesus as satisfaction for sin, or redeeming example of love; Luther, its relation to man's receiving faith; Calvin, its relation to God's sovereign will. Roman Catholic thought has emphasized the objective sphere of salvation within a sacramental church; and Protestantism, the subjective experience of salvation within the individual soul. Modern reflection tends to concentrate on the psychological process and ethical results of salvation, emphasizing the need to "save" society.

R. E. O. White

See also Savior.

Bibliography. L. H. Marshall, *Challenge of NT Ethics;* H. R. Mackintosh, *Christian Experience of Forgiveness;* V. Taylor, *Forgiveness and Reconciliation;* E. Kevan, *Salvation;* U. Simon, *Theology of Salvation.*

Salvation Army. *See* Booth, Catherine; Booth, William.

Sanctification. To make holy. The Hebrew (*qdš*) and Greek (*hagias-*) roots represented in AV by "sanctify, holy, hallow," and varied in RSV by "consecrate, dedicate," are applied to any person, place, occasion, or object "set apart" from common, secular use as devoted to some divine power. Isa. 65:5; 66:17 show heathen, and Gen. 38:21 ("cult prostitute") unmoral, applications of the concept "sacred to deity." With advancing understanding of the intrinsic purity of Yahweh, twofold development followed.

(1) Persons and things devoted to his use must be ritually clean, not merely set apart by taboo, decree, or tribal caste: hence the lustrations, sacrifices, exclusion of the maimed, and laws of "uncleanness," prescribed to ensure sanctity in whatever approaches the shrine. (2) The "fitness" required becomes increasingly moral. Lev. 17–26 demands, "You shall be holy to me, for I the Lord am holy and have separated you from the peoples, that you should be mine." "Be ye holy for I am holy" (20:26; 19:2; I Pet. 1:15–16); the meaning of "holiness" is then worked out in philanthropy, love for God, clean living, compassion, commercial honesty, and love.

Thus God is holy; "separate" from nature, other gods, and sinners; unapproachable except by mediation and sacrifice (Isa. 6:3–5). Men "sanctify" God by obeying his commands (Lev. 22:32; Isa. 8:13; I Pet. 3:15). Israel *is* inherently holy, separated by God from "the peoples" to be his own. Yet Israel must *become* holy, by obedience, fit for the privilege allotted her.

The Nature of Sanctification. *Status Conferred.* These nuances persist. Jesus prays that God's name be "hallowed"; God "sanctifies" the Son, the Son "sanctifies" himself, "setting apart" to special tasks (John 10:36; 17:19). Christians are set apart for God's use: "sanctified . . . saints" (I Cor. 1:2) indicates status, not character; so "chosen . . . destined . . . sanctified" (I Pet. 1:1–2). This is usually the meaning in Hebrews: "We *have been* sanctified . . . *are* sanctified" (timelessly), not by moral transformation, but by the sacrifice of Christ "once for all" (10:10, 29; 2:11; 9:13–14; 10:14; 13:12). The author sees men formerly "standing outside the Temple defiled and banned," now admitted, accepted, their sins expiated, themselves set apart for divine service, all by the sacrifice and intercession of their High Priest—like Israel, *already* sanctified. So I Cor. 6:11, recalling conversion. Christ *is* our sanctification (1:30), and the church *is* sanctified (Eph. 5:25–26).

Process Pursued. Yet even in Hebrews the meaning "moral fitness" emerges. "Strive for sanctity/holiness" (12:14). This is the most common understanding of sanctification, the growth in holiness that should follow conversion (Eph. 1:4; Phil. 3:12). So Paul prays that the Thessalonians be sanctified wholly—spirit, soul, and body being kept sound and blameless—as something still to be accomplished. The first letter says sanctification is the will of God for them in the special matter of sexual chastity (4:3–4).

Similarly, the Romans are exhorted to "present their bodies . . . holy . . ." in their worship; and in I Cor. 6:13–14 the body of the Christian must be kept from immorality because every Christian is a sacred ("sanctified") person, belonging to Christ.

Doubtless the moral tone of first century society necessitated this emphasis. "Let us cleanse ourselves from every defilement of body and spirit, and make holiness perfect" (II Cor. 7:1). One motive urged, beside personal sacredness, is spiritual athletics, with metaphors drawn from the widespread games (I Cor. 9:24–25; Phil. 3:13; etc.), aiming at fitness for service. Another is, to be *worthy* of God, our calling, the Lord, the gospel, the kingdom (I Thess. 2:12; Eph. 4:1; Col. 1:10; Phil. 1:27; II Thess. 1:5). Beside positive motives, Paul stresses positive consecration of the personality so sanctified, in active service and love, with the total dedication of a slave, sacrifice, and man in love.

The addition of "and spirit" in II Cor. 7:1, the transformed "mind" (Rom. 12:1–2) set on things above and filled with all things holy and of good report (Phil. 4:8–9; cf. 2:5; I Cor. 2:16), shows that Paul did not think of holiness only in physical terms.

Everything is to be sanctified (I Tim. 4:4–5). Holiness represents purity before God, as righteousness represents purity before the law, blameless purity before the world (Phil. 2:14–15; Col. 1:22): sanctification includes all three (I Thess. 2:10). Here sanctification broadens into the total personal ethic that some (situationists, e.g.) claim is absent from Christianity, and becomes a technical name for the process of development into which conversion is the entrance, issuing in conformity to Christ (Rom. 8:29–30; II Cor. 3:18; I John 3:1–3).

Theology and Sanctification. *Justification.* An exclusively objective view of the work of Christ tends to regard sanctification as either an addendum to justification, or merely evidence of justifying faith. Yet justification and sanctification are not separate in time (I Cor. 6:11), for God's justifying act sets the sinner apart for service; not separable in experience, but only in thought. Paul's gospel of justification by faith was the moral dynamic of salvation (Rom. 1:16); forgiveness itself has moral force, creating the will to goodness in the forgiven.

To those who wondered whether men counted righteous on the ground of faith might go on sinning with impunity, Paul retorted that the faith expressed in faith-baptism so unites the convert to Christ that he dies with Christ to sin, is buried with Christ to all that belongs to his past life, and rises with Christ to new life in which sin's reign is broken. That new self is yielded to the service of righteousness and of God in a surrender that issues in sanctification (Rom. 6:1–11, 19–22). Sanctification is not merely the completion (correlate or implicate) of justification; it is justifying faith at work. In the faith counted for righteousness, actual righteousness is born. As though to guard against justification without sanctification, John says, "Little children, let no one deceive you. He who does right is righteous" (I John 3:7).

The two experiences must not be identified. In justification, God at the beginning of Christian life declares us acquitted. In sanctification, God accomplishes his will in us as Christian life proceeds. Sanctification never replaces justification. Scholars argue whether Luther taught that "making sinners righteous" was the real ground of justification, as faith led on to good works, penance, saintliness-begun. Not so: Luther's ground remains faith to the end. We are "always being justified, more and more, always by faith." But the faith that justifies, by its very nature as union with Christ in his dying and risen life, sets in motion the sanctifying energies of grace.

The Spirit. Ninety-one times in the NT the Spirit is called "holy," and the implied contrast with the ubiquitous evil spirits that work corruption and death must never be overlooked. "Spirit of Jesus," "Spirit of Christ," designate quality, not source. As, in thought of the Spirit, emphasis moved from spectacular gifts for service to inward equipment for Christian living, so the place of the Spirit in sanctification became central. Constantly, sanctification is said to be of the Spirit: Rom. 15:16; I Cor. 6:11; Eph. 4:30; I Thess. 4:7–8; II Thess. 2:13; I Pet. 1:2.

Sanctification is not primarily negative in the NT, "keeping oneself unspotted," not mainly self-discipline. It is chiefly the outflow of an overflowing life within the soul, the "fruit" of the Spirit in all manner of Christian graces (Gal. 5:22–23), summed up as "sanctification" (Rom. 6:22 lit.). Justification—the privileged status of acceptance—is achieved through the cross; sanctification—the ongoing process of conformity to Christ—is achieved by the Spirit. But not as sudden miraculous gift: the NT knows nothing of any shortcut to that ideal.

Sinless Perfection. How far does sanctification go? References to "perfection" (*teleiotēs*, Col. 3:14); the call to "perfecting holiness" (II Cor. 7:1); misunderstanding of "sanctification" in Hebrews; assurances like "our old self was crucified . . . that the sinful body might be destroyed," "no longer in bondage to sin," "sin will have no dominion over you," "set free from sin . . . slaves of righteousness," "no one who abides in him sins," "anyone born of God does not sin," "he cannot sin"—such thoughts have ever kept alive the dream of sinlessness in this life. Some patristic expressions (Justin, Irenaeus, Origen) have a similar ring, though they scarcely go beyond asserting the obligation not to sin. Augustine and Aquinas sought perfection in the vision of God, and certain evangelical leaders, such as Fénelon, Zinzendorf, or Wesley, stressed perfection as fullness of love, faith, or holiness, respectively.

To dilute the scriptural challenge seems disloyal to the absolute Christian standard, which is certainly not abated in the NT. Yet it must be said that the root *telei-* does not mean "sinless," "incapable of sinning," but "fulfilling its appointed end, complete, mature" (even "all-inclusively complete," Matt. 5:48). Such all-roundness and maturity are clearly part of the Christian's goal. Paul's denial that he is already "perfect," and his exhortations to ongoing sanctification, show that he does not think a final, completed sanctification can be claimed in this life. Though the Christian who has died with Christ is freed from the bondage of sin, and need not, ought not, and at his best does not sin, yet he must continually reaffirm his death with Christ and his yielding to God (Rom. 6:11, 13, 16).

John's warning that "if we say we have no sin, we deceive ourselves, and the truth is not in us," and his insistence on the continual forgiveness and advocacy of Christ available for all Christians (I John 1:7–2:2), shows that he too does not think the Christian sinless. That is also implied in 3:3–10, where John details some fourteen reasons that the Christian ought not to continue to practice sin, as certain Gnostics claimed that the wise man may.

So long as he is "in this body," the Christian continues to be tempted, continues sometimes to fall, growing more sensitive to sin as he lives nearer to God. But he will continue to repent, and to seek forgiveness, never acquiescing, never making excuses, never surrendering, but ever desiring to be further changed into Christ's image, stage by stage, as by the Lord, the Spirit.

Historical Considerations. So rich a theme must have yielded a variety of insights. In the apostolic church, the essence of sanctification was a Christlike purity; in the patristic church, withdrawal from the contaminations of society. This hardened, in the medieval church, into asceticism (a dualistic misapplication of Paul's athleticism). This involved a double standard: "sanctity" and "saintliness" came to be applied only to the "religious" person (priest, monk), whereas a lower attainment, compromising with the world, was tolerated in the "ordinary, secular, or lay" Christian. Luther sought to annul this double standard, making sanctification a matter of inward attitude toward all the affairs of the outside world; he made much, in his expositions, of the transformation in the life of the believer by the work of the Spirit.

Calvin's insistence upon the divine sovereignty, and upon self-discipline, made sanctification a question of ever more complete obedience to the Decalogue as the core of biblical ethics. The Greek Orthodox Church preserved the ascetic view of sanctification as self-denial, nourished by the church and sacraments. The Counter-Reformation, especially in Spain, saw the secret of sanctification as disciplined prayer; while the Puritans sought the divine will, personally revealed as "leadings of the Spirit," and the power to fulfill it, within the recesses of the devout soul. Jonathan Edwards stressed the necessity of grace in sanctification, "infusing" the habits of virtue.

John Wesley, and Methodism after him, laid great emphasis upon complete sanctification, and often on the necessity that Christians seek perfection. Emil Brunner saw faith as essentially active obedience to the divine command, so identifying faith with works in individual sanctification. For most modern Christians, sanctification—if considered at all—is reduced to "the distinctive life-style of the committed soul," a true enough description, but a somewhat thin substitute for the glorious experience of the NT.

R. E. O. White

Bibliography. J. S. Stewart, *A Man in Christ,* ch. 4; V. Taylor, *Forgiveness and Reconciliation,* ch. 5; P. T. Forsyth, *Christian Perfection;* G. C. Berkouwer, *Faith and Sanctification;* J. C. Ryle, *Holiness;* L. Bouyer, *The Spirituality of the NT and the Fathers* and *The Spirituality of the Middle Ages;* L. Bouyer *et al., Orthodox Spirituality and Protestant and Anglican Spirituality.*

Sanday, William (1843–1920). NT scholar. Ordained in 1867, he was principal of Hatfield Hall, Durham, from 1876 until recalled in 1882 to Oxford, where he held theological chairs until his death. He was a pioneer in introducing into English scholarship the work done in biblical criticism on the continent. He was, indeed, often charged with having been too deferential to German scholarship, his regular observations on which R. A. Knox compared with a meteorologist making weather reports. His Bampton Lectures, *Inspiration* (1893), reflect his doubts on biblical authority, yet his attitude to the Gospel miracles evinced in places an unexpected conservatism. While he brought to NT studies wisdom and balance, he was a less reliable guide in dogmatic theology and philosophy, wherein it was said he could be "carried away by too generous enthusiasms" in areas where judgment might have been reserved. He once raised a passing stir by suggesting that "the subliminal consciousness is the proper seat or *locus* of the Deity of the incarnate Christ."

The first of his many published works was *The Authority and Historical Character of the Fourth Gospel* (1872); his later books were progressively more radical, and influenced Anglican clergy in that direction. He wrote extensively on Christology, but he is best remembered for his commentary titled *Romans*, written in collaboration with A. C. Headlam. Sanday's great aim was to write a life of Christ based on the new German critical methods, but he never achieved it. He was a founding fellow of the British Academy.

J. D. Douglas

Sardica, Council of (343–344). The council called by the emperors Constans and Constantius, as well as Pope Julius I, to effect a settlement of the Arian controversy. With various rationalizations and reservations, the Arians and semi-Arians had professed an acceptance of the Nicene Creed and thereby attained to positions of ecclesiastical prominence. The Arian party, led by Eusebius of Nicomedia, succeeded in excommunicating and exiling Athanasius for a second time in 341. Athanasius fled to the West, where he developed a very sizable following. Thus the Eastern prelates inclined toward an Arian view, the Western toward that of Athanasius.

The site of Sardica (modern Sofia in Bulgaria) was chosen as midway geographically between East and West. The Eastern bishops, however, incensed at the arrival of Athanasius and other deposed bishops, withdrew to Philippopolis, where they condemned Athanasius and produced a statement which carefully avoided a declaration of Christ as being of one substance with the Father. The Western bishops, on the other hand, affirmed Athanasius and issued a manifesto strengthening the Nicene position, especially with respect to Christ as truly God, partaker of the same nature as the Father. Although it was an effective anti-Arian statement, it failed to deal with the dangers of Sabellianism. Athanasius himself considered the "Sardican Creed" an unnecessary adjunct to that of Nicaea.

Twenty canons were issued treating of the duties and privileges of the clergy, the most important being the right of a deposed bishop to appeal to the Bishop of Rome. Although Athanasius was restored to his see, the council, with its rival synods, formalized the deepening rift between East and West.

R. C. Kroeger and C. C. Kroeger

See also Arianism; Athanasius; Monarchianism; Nicaea, Council of.

Bibliography. C. J. Hefele, *The History of the Councils*, II, 86ff.; H. Hess, *The Canons of the Council of Sardica, A.D. 343;* H. Chadwick, *The Early Church*; *NPNF:* Athanasius, "Defense against the Arians," IV, 100ff., 119ff.; Theodoret of Cyr, "Ecclesiastical History," II, 76ff.; Socrates Scholasticus, "Ecclesiastical History," II, 46–49; Sozomen, "Ecclesiastical History," II, 288–91; Canons, XIV, 411–36.

Satan (Heb. *śāṭān*, "adversary"). The devil, a high angelic creature who, before the creation of the human race, rebelled against the Creator and became the chief antagonist of God and man. Theologians to a large extent have refused to apply the far-reaching prophecies of Isa. 14:12–14 and Ezek. 28:12–15 to Satan under the contention that they are addressed solely to the king of Babylon in the first instance and to the king of Tyre in the second. Others contend that this interpretation is unwarranted for two reasons. First, it fails to take into account the fact that these prophecies far transcend any earthly ruler and, second, it ignores the close connection Satan has in Scripture with the government of the satanic world system (Dan. 10:13; Eph. 6:12) of which both ancient Babylon and Tyre were an inseparable part. In their full scope these passages paint Satan's past career as "Lucifer" and as "the Anointed Cherub" in his prefall splendor. They portray as well his apostasy in drawing with him a great multitude of lesser celestial creatures (Rev. 12:4), making him "the Evil One" or "the Tempter."

These fallen angels (demons) fit into two classes: those that are free and those that are bound. The former roam the heavenlies with their prince-leader Satan (Matt. 12:24) and as his emissaries are so numerous as to make Satan's power practically ubiquitous. The angels (demons) that are bound are evidently guilty of more heinous wickedness and are incarcerated in Tartarus (II Pet. 2:4; Jude 1:6). Many theologians connect these imprisoned demons with fallen angels who cohabited with mortal women (Gen. 6:1–4).

Satan caused the fall of the human race as "the Serpent" (Gen. 3). His judgment was predicted in Eden (vs. 15), and this was accomplished at the cross (John 12:31–33). As created, his power was second only to God (Ezek. 28:11–16). He is nevertheless only a creature, limited, and permitted to have power by divine omnipotence and omniscience.

The biblical doctrine of Satan is not a copying of Persian dualism as some scholars unsoundly allege. Although Satan, even after his judgment in the cross (Col. 2:15), continues to reign as a usurper (II Cor. 4:4), and works in tempting and accusing men (Rev. 12:10), he is to be ousted from the heavenlies (vss. 7–12) as well as the earth

(5:1–19:16), and is to be confined to the abyss for a thousand years (20:1–3).

When released from the abyss at the end of the thousand years, he will make one last mad attempt to lead his armies against God (Rev. 20:8–9). This will result in his final doom when he is cast into the lake of fire (vs. 10), which has been prepared for him and his wicked angelic accomplices (Matt. 25:41). This will be the one place where evil angels and unsaved men will be kept and quarantined so that the rest of God's sinless universe will not be corrupted in the eternal state.

Satan's present work is widespread and destructive. God permits his evil activity for the time being. Demons must do Satan's bidding. The unsaved are largely under Satan's authority, and he rules them through the evil world system over which he is head and of which the unregenerate are a part (Isa. 14:12–17; II Cor. 4:3–4; Eph. 2:2; Col. 1:13).

As far as the saved are concerned, Satan is in continued conflict with them (Eph. 6:11–18), tempts them, and seeks to corrupt and destroy their testimony, and even their physical life (I Cor. 5:5; I John 5:16). Satanic and demonic fury were unleashed against the incarnate Christ. The power of a sinless humanity called forth special satanic temptation of our Lord (Matt. 4:1–11). The full glow of light manifested in the earthly life of him who was "the light of the world" (John 8:12) exposed the darkness of the powers of evil. This is the explanation of the unprecedented outburst of demonism that is described in the Gospel narratives. It was because God anointed Jesus of Nazareth "with the Holy Spirit and with power" that he "went about doing good and healing all that were oppressed by the devil" (Acts 10:38).

M. F. Unger

See also Abaddon; Baal-zebub; Demon, Demon Possession; Occult, The; Satanism and Witchcraft.

Bibliography. L. S. Chafer, *Systematic Theology,* II, 33–98; W. Robinson, *The Devil and God;* E. Langton, *Satan: A Portrait;* H. Bietenhard *et al., NIDNTT,* III, 468ff.; E. Lewis, *The Creator and the Adversary;* D. W. Pentecost, *Your Adversary, the Devil;* G. von Rad and W. Foerster, *TDNT,* II, 71ff.; R. S. Kluger, *Satan in the OT;* F. A. Tatford, *The Prince of Darkness.*

Satanism and Witchcraft. Worship of Satan and the use of sorcery with evil intent. Probably no subject alarms Christians more than that of satanism and witchcraft. Today many groups claim to be neopagans who belong to such movements. These groups, along with practitioners of ritual magic, are often conceived as belonging to a vast underground movement with its roots in antiquity. In fact, the neopagan movement consists of a large number of small, diverse groups who share the common belief that they are inheritors of ancient religious traditions. Some of these groups are violently anti-Christian, but others claim to be the true inheritors of Gnostic Christianity. The traditions to which they appeal in their attempts to legitimate themselves vary greatly. Some claim to be a revival of Druidism, others of Greek religions, or of ancient Egyptian mysteries. Many simply claim to belong to what they call WICCA, which they assert is the ancient witchcraft religion of Europe. A few groups claim to be satanists who worship the devil of the Christian traditions.

In the new pagans' understanding of the world, Christians have distorted humanity's development by emphasizing the dominance of the intellect over other aspects of the human psyche. Christians, they claim, demand that humans subordinate themselves, their emotions, and will to God. The new pagans argue that humans must live in harmony with nature. Such a harmony represents a cosmic orientation which they claim brings man in contact with the cosmic powers of the universe.

For the new pagans, religion is a practical activity carried out through ritual and ceremonial acts to align the participants with the cosmic order and thus release the mystical power within them. The exact rituals, techniques, and beliefs of the new pagan groups vary greatly. But all are concerned with a quest for power and the desire that humans control their own destiny.

The roots of the new paganism lie in the romantic movement of the nineteenth century and the desire to exalt feelings and imagination over the intellect. Thus the poetry of William Blake is often very important to members of such groups. Contrary to their claims, the history of these pagan movements is relatively short. Rather than representing long historical traditions the majority represent groups only a few decades old.

One of the most important figures in the growth of modern paganism is Alphonse Louis Constant (1810–75), who called himself Eliphas Levi. An ex-Roman Catholic seminarian, he claimed to be an occult initiate and wrote many books that purported to reveal ancient mysteries and occult law. He drew upon theories of magic and the kabbalah, which is an ancient system of Jewish mysticism.

In Britain, the growth of modern paganism was encouraged by the foundation of the Order of the Golden Dawn in 1888. This is the most famous of many esoteric groups that grew out of nineteenth century romanticism. The movement's influence extends to the work of such figures as the poet W. B. Yeats and the notorious black magician Alistair Crowley. Most ritual magic and satanistic groups trace their origins to these sources.

The majority of witchcraft groups have a different and less bizarre history. In England the work of historian Margaret Murray, who claimed to have discovered evidence of a pre-Reformation witchcraft religion, and Gerald Gardiner, the proprietor of a witchcraft museum on the Isle of Man, provides the basis for most WICCA groups. Although these authors give witchcraft an apparently respectable history, their works have not stood the test of time. They are in fact refuted by competent historians. Today witchcraft groups are usually based upon the journalistic writings of self-proclaimed witches who propound a religion based upon the concept of a mother goddess. During the 1970s this movement was greatly reinforced by the writings of some religiously inclined feminists.

Although groups like that of the infamous Manson family are obviously highly dangerous, the majority of witchcraft and ritual magic appear to be relatively innocuous. In attempting to assess such groups it is extremely important to consider carefully their specific claims. Some self-proclaimed "white magic" groups appear to be little more than ill-informed people with vague religious sentiments. Others that practice ritual magic may be more articulate but are still essentially harmless. There remains, however, a small number of social deviants who are psychologically disturbed and potentially socially harmful. It is important to realize, however, that the vast majority of people involved in the neopagan movement repudiate and strongly denounce such deviants. Although a rejection of traditional Christianity, the neopagan movement seems to be essentially no more harmful than many other religious groups which also stand outside the Christian tradition. I. Hexham

See also Demon, Demon Possession; Satan.

Bibliography. J. W. Montgomery, *Principalities and Powers: A New Look at the World of the Occult;* M. F. Unger, *Biblical Demonology;* K. E. Koch, *Christian Counseling and Occultism;* W. Cavendish, *The Black Arts;* W. S. Bainbridge, *Satan's Power: A Deviant Psychotherapy Cult.*

Satisfaction. Compensation, reparation. The word "satisfaction" occurs only twice in the AV (Num. 35:31–32) as the rendering for the Hebrew *kōper,* literally meaning "a price paid as compensation." Theologically the term has played a significant part in the theory of the atonement, especially since the time of Anselm (1033–1109). Prior to his *Cur Deus Homo,* the view of Christ's death which prevailed most widely was that it was a ransom paid to the devil in order to deliver the souls of men over whom he had a legal claim. Anselm by contrast stressed the fact that the death of Christ was a satisfaction rendered to God's justice and honor. Since his time this view has become one of the essential ingredients in the orthodox theory of the atonement for both Roman Catholics and Protestants. In the subsequent Protestant discussion, a distinction has been made between Christ's active and passive obedience. In the former he satisfied the demands of the law by rendering a perfect obedience, and in the latter he satisfied the curse of the law by submitting himself to the ignominious death of the cross.

With the rise of liberalism in Protestant theology, the term "satisfaction" fell under severe criticism and is still suspect in some circles as not being biblical. The fundamental issue, however, is not whether the term as such occurs in Scripture, but whether or not the idea it represents is biblical, and this will be decided ultimately by one's view of God. If the love of God be construed in a way that militates against his justice, then there is no divine wrath that needs propitiation and there is no guilt in the objective sense that must be expiated. Consequently there is no need that a satisfaction be rendered to appease the judicial sentiment in God which man by his guilt and sin has offended.

The Bible, however, plainly teaches that the death of Christ was a sacrifice. This interpretation of Christ's work is imbedded in every important type of NT teaching. To ask, What according to the NT is the nature of Christ's work? is the same as asking, What is the nature of sacrifice? The NT conception of sacrifice, in turn, cannot possibly be understood apart from the OT conception of sacrifice, and there it is very clear that the sacrifice is not simply a gift to God or a mode of communion and fellowship with God. The only explanation which satisfies the OT data is that the sacrifice is propitiatory in character and appeases the wrath of God by removing the guilt of sin through a substitutionary bearing of the penalty. The one who offered the sacrifice placed his hands on the head of the animal victim and thus transferred the guilt to the animal whose blood was shed to satisfy the debt to justice which he owed.

Animal sacrifice was only ceremonial or typical, but it is the ceremonial ritual that is transferred in the NT to the work of Christ and is the basis for the theological teaching that the guilt of our sin is removed by the satisfaction which Christ renders to God against whom the sin is committed. Hence Christ is called the Lamb of God. When God is propitiated by his blood, we are redeemed from the curse of the law and reconciled to him. The concept of satisfaction, then, is a theological term which embraces in its connotation all the major categories used in the Scriptures to describe the meaning of Christ's atoning work, as it relates both to God and to the sinner. The most crucial passage is Rom. 3:21–26.

P. K. JEWETT

See also ATONEMENT, THEORIES OF THE; BLOOD, SACRIFICIAL ASPECTS OF; OFFERINGS AND SACRIFICES IN BIBLE TIMES; PROPITIATION.

Bibliography. Anselm, *Cur Deus Homo?* C. A. Beckwith, *SHERK,* X, 209–10; B. B. Warfield, *Studies in Theology.*

Satisfaction Theory, The. *See* ATONEMENT, THEORIES OF THE.

Sattler, Michael. *See* MENNONITES.

Saumer Academy. *See* AMYRALDIANISM.

Savior. One who saves, delivers.

In the OT. "Savior" represents a participle of *yāša'* ("delivers, sets free"), used frequently of God (Isa. 43:11; 45:21). Cf. Joshua, Jeshua (Gr. *Iēsous*), Hosea, Elisha; all = "God is salvation." It is also used of God's agents (Judg. 3:9). With the participle *gō'ēl* ("redeems, vindicates"—Job 19:25; Isa. 41:14), it emphasizes a quality and initiative in Yahweh as fundamental as creatorhood, sovereignty, and unique in ancient religion. Only later is Messiah called Savior (IV Ezra 12:34; T. Gad. 8).

In the NT (LXX). "Savior" represents *sōtēr* ("deliverer, preserver"), commonly ascribed to pagan deities (Zeus, Aesculapius), to semideities of the mysteries (Serapis, Isis, Heracles), to honored men, and to deified rulers (Ptolemies, Philip, Augustus). Emphasis upon God as Savior continues in Luke 1:47; Jude 25; and the Pastoral Epistles (six times). The title is applied to Christ as constituting, not merely exhibiting, salvation (Luke 2:11; Acts 5:31; 13:23; Phil. 3:20–21; Eph. 5:23; John 4:42; I John 4:14). This predominantly late use and Gentile background suggests contrast with pagan claims as the church moved into Gentile circles.

In the first century, the claim that "there is salvation in no one else . . . no other name under heaven . . . by which we must be saved" (Acts 4:12) gave serious offense, even though made with full acknowledgment that other "faiths," Judaist or not, were in some measure acceptable to God (Acts 10:1–4, 34–35). Christian exclusiveness continues to give offense, yet "the good pagan" needs still the Christian evangelist (vss. 4–5).

R. E. O. WHITE

See also JESUS CHRIST; MESSIAH; SALVATION.

Savonarola, Girolamo (1452–1498). An Italian Dominican religious reformer. Savonarola was born in Ferrara and reacted against his early training in Renaissance humanism. After preaching in several north Italian cities he came to Florence in 1490 to serve as public speaker at San Marco. He rose to prominence by predicting the coming of divine judgment. The French invasion of 1494 seemed to be a fulfillment of his prophecy, and when the Medici abandoned the city he gained great influence through his preaching. He encouraged the establishment of a republican government and assured the people that a golden age was beginning. During the ensuing four years he tried to cleanse the city of vice and sins, often through the use of censorship and violence. Renaissance culture in all its forms, from secular art to frivolous and bawdy drama, had to be repudiated so that a republic of obedience and virtue could be established. Savonarola led the way at the carnival of 1496 when he sponsored the "burning of vanities," including such instruments of sin as false hair, indecent clothing, and lewd books.

For a time Savonarola's position was unchallenged, but soon his sermons lost their effectiveness. His uncompromising nature made many enemies and brought him into conflict with Pope Alexander VI. Unresponsive to papal warnings, he was excommunicated. The Franciscans used the occasion to arrange an ordeal by fire with his followers, and the incident served to discredit him. The Florentine government charged him with treason for which he was convicted and executed. Many early Protestants such as Luther and Beza looked on him as a martyr for the gospel.

R. G. CLOUSE

Bibliography. R. Ridolfi, *The Life of Girolamo Savonarola;* D. Weinstein, *Savonarola and Florence: Prophecy and Patriotism in the Renaissance.*

Savoy Conference (1661). A series of meetings held at the Savoy in the Strand, London, with the aim of reviewing the contents of the *Book of Common Prayer* and hearing criticism of it by leading Presbyterian divines. The participants met from April 15 to July 24, 1661, and included twelve bishops, twelve Presbyterian clergy, and assessors from each party. The conference was called by King Charles II, who had recently regained his crown after being exiled during the protectorate of Cromwell. His return meant the resumption by the established church of episcopalian polity and liturgical worship. This well suited traditional Anglicans who had been pushed into the background during the commonwealth and protectorate periods (1642–60).

Presbyterian Puritans (as contrasted with Congregationalists and Separatists) were ready to participate in an established church governed by bishops as long as certain modifications were made in the contents of the *Book of Common Prayer,* required to be used in every parish. The bishops (supported by the king) were prepared to make only minor concessions, and they further insisted that clergy who had not been episcopally ordained should submit to reordination by this method. As an attempt to keep the Presbyterians in the national church this conference failed, and a large number of them became Nonconformists in 1661–62. However, certain of their requests for change were granted (fifteen in all) and were embodied in the 1662 edition of the *Book of Common Prayer.* This allowed a minority of Presbyterians to stay within the church.

P. Toon

See also Book of Common Prayer.

Bibliography. E. C. Ratcliff, "The Savoy Conference" in *From Uniformity to Unity,* ed. G. F. Nuttall and O. Chadwick.

Saxon Confession (1551). Exposition of the Augsburg Confession written by Philip Melanchthon in 1551 for presentation to the Council of Trent. Originally entitled *Repetition of the Augsburg Confession,* it appeared in print in 1552 under the title, *The Confession of Doctrine of the Saxon Churches.* After the emperor invited the Lutherans to send a delegation to the Council of Trent, which reconvened in May 1551, Elector Maurice of Saxony held a meeting to consider their response. Although Melanchthon placed little hope in the council, he thought it unwise to refuse the emperor's invitation. After agreeing to express their doctrinal stance on the basis of the Augsburg Confession and the catechism, Melanchthon was commissioned to write an explanation of the Augsburg Confession that the envoys could submit in the name of the Lutheran theologians.

Melanchthon wrote the confession at Dessau May 6 to 10, 1551. Despite the fact that it was written after the Lutheran princes had been defeated by the emperor and the Augsburg Interim had been imposed, it does not reveal any retreat from the doctrinal position taken at Augsburg in 1530. In fact, it was considerably less conciliatory than the Augsburg Confession. In addition to stating evangelical doctrine, it specifically detailed the errors of the Roman Catholic Church in twenty-three sections, following the order of the Augsburg Confession. It also emphasized that Reformation theology was in agreement with the position of the ancient church, and it summarized the fundamental principles of that theology under two articles of the Apostle's Creed: "I believe in the forgiveness of sins" and "One Holy Catholic Church." In contrast to the Augsburg Confession, which was signed by the princes, the Saxon Confession was signed only by theologians and the superintendents of the churches in Saxony. Theologians from nine other Lutheran principalities also gave their consent.

Melanchthon never appeared at the Council of Trent, because the threat of war caused him to delay his journey in Nuremburg, and the beginning of hostilities between Maurice and the emperor resulted in the suspension of the council in 1552. The confession was submitted along with Johann Brenz's Würtemberg Confession to a private congregation of the Council in 1552. However, nothing was accomplished. It never received a public hearing, and it did not become a part of the traditional Lutheran Confessions contained in the Book of Concord.

R. W. Heinze

See also Augsburg Confession; Confessions of Faith; Melanchthon, Philip.

Bibliography. P. Schaff, *A History of the Creeds of Christendom,* I, 340ff.; R. Stupperich, *Melanchthon;* E. H. Bindsel, ed., *Corpus Reformatorum,* XXVIII; J. M. Reu, *The Augsburg Confession.*

Saybrook Platform (1708). An effort by Connecticut Congregationalists to strengthen church government at a time when New England's concern for religion seemed to have reached a new low. A similar but unsuccessful effort to shore up ecclesiastical foundations had taken place in Massachusetts in 1705. The founding of Yale College at New Haven, Connecticut, in 1701 was also a response to what many clergymen regarded as spiritual decline. In the spring of 1708 the Connecticut General Court (or legislature) called for an assembly of ministers and lay leaders to correct "defects of the discipline of the churches." The leaders of the colony were troubled by forces that seemed to be fragmenting Connecticut society and that seemed to be undermining traditions in the churches. In September, four laymen and twelve ministers met at Saybrook in response to the General Court's appeal. They prepared fifteen *Articles for the Administration of Church Discipline.* This "platform" committed Connecticut Congregationalists to the doctrine of the Savoy Confession, a modification of the Westminster Confession prepared by English Congregationalists in 1658. But it also incorporated some presbyterian features in the Connecticut churches. County "consociations" of ministers and laymen were empowered to judge disputes arising in local churches. County "associations" and a colony-wide "General Association" of ministers were called into existence, but without carefully defined duties. The acceptance of the Saybrook Platform in Connecticut helped to preserve the influence of the churches in the colony, even as it turned traditional congregationalism in a presbyterian direction. M. A. Noll

See also Creed, Creeds; Confessions of Faith.

Bibliography. W. Walker, *The Creeds and Platforms of Congregationalists.*

Sayers, Dorothy Leigh (1893–1957). Writer of detective fiction, author of religious plays, translator of Dante, arbiter of English usage, and lay theologian, Sayers was an influential exponent of orthodox Christian faith during the middle third of the twentieth century. She was born into the home of an Anglican minister, displayed an early aptitude for languages, and studied medieval literature at Somerville College, Oxford. While teaching secondary school in England and France and working at an advertising agency, she began her career as author and lecturer. Sayers first came to public notice through her detective novels, featuring Lord Peter Wimsey, which were published from 1923 through 1938. The success of these books gave her the financial stability to turn to her first love—religious verse plays and translations of medieval literature, of which her edition of Dante's *Divine Comedy* (published 1949, 1955, 1962) was the major effort. A radio play, *The Man Born to Be King* (performed on the BBC, 1941–42, published 1943), was both a successful drama and a creative, respectful presentation of the life of Christ. Earlier her play for the 1937 Canterbury Festival, *The Zeal of Thy House*, had revealed her imaginative skill at historical drama. Her occasional essays and a book-length treatment of God and the creative process, *The Mind of the Maker* (1942), constituted a forceful body of theology as well.

Sayers, a lifelong member of the Church of England, published her learned, yet eminently readable, theological essays to promote a basic understanding of historic orthodoxy. Her theology reflected her historical studies in medieval Christianity, her particular love for Dante, and the influence of contemporaries like the Catholic writer G. K. Chesterton and the Anglican novelist and critic Charles Williams. The essays defended the intellectual fiber of traditional dogma, proposed canons of literary common sense for reading the Bible, offered Christian reflections on the changing roles of women in the modern world, and during the years of World War II reminded British citizens of Christian values that superseded the virtues of patriotism.

In *The Mind of the Maker* Sayers provided extended exposition of a theme that she had treated in several occasional papers. The creative process, she argued, can be regarded profitably as an analogy to the way in which the Trinitarian God governs the world. If we think of God as an author of a drama, in which humans are the actors, we can learn much about human freedom, divine sovereignty, and the history of salvation. Sayers was not above using her own experience in writing detective stories to explain how God may govern the destiny of his "characters" even as they take on a life of their own in fulfilling the Divine Author's sublime and harmonious plot. M. A. Noll

Bibliography. Sayers, *Christian Letters to a Post-Christian World;* J. Brabazon, *Dorothy L. Sayers;* R. E. Hone, *Dorothy L. Sayers: A Literary Biography;* A. S. Dale, *Maker and Craftsman: The Story of Dorothy L. Sayers.*

Sayings of Jesus. NT scholarship often addresses two major issues with regard to the sayings of Jesus. (1) A serious endeavor has been made to verify the authenticity of the sayings, and frequently this way of phrasing the subject has implied the endeavor's results: finding the genuine sayings of Jesus. (2) Scholars have sought to discover a unifying center to Jesus' sayings. That is, what is the essence of Christ's message? Needless to say, evangelical scholarship has taken a more or less defensive posture regarding the initial question and focused most of its energies on a theological exposition of the meaning of Christ's words.

Since the severely negative and skeptical results of Rudolf Bultmann and the early form critics have been reappraised (esp. E. Käsemann, J. Robinson), scholars have embarked on a "new quest of the historical Jesus" in which the evidence could be sifted once more—but this time, with greater optimism. Typically, while Bultmann could offer barely thirty pages on the teaching of Jesus in his NT theology, Joachim Jeremias could supply an entire volume. Günther Bornkamm, a student of Bultmann, even produced an entire book entitled *Jesus of Nazareth* (1956), thus exhibiting the growing confidence of the field.

Modern study has been especially interested in developing a methodology for uncovering the authentic sayings of Jesus. Here the well-known criteria of authenticity have been employed. Chief among them (and the most used) is the criterion of dissimilarity, wherein only those sayings of Jesus dissimilar to Judaism and the early church are rendered "authentic." But this criterion, like the others, is severely limiting. Can Jesus be divorced from his environment? Did not the early church employ his thoughts? As Morna Hooker, a Cambridge scholar, has accurately claimed, we may discover only what is distinct in Jesus' sayings—not what is characteristic and pivotal.

In this discussion it becomes evident that one's predisposition toward the sayings is important. Indeed, the most important question is, Who owns the burden of proof? Are Jesus' sayings inauthentic till proven otherwise? Or must the critic first demonstrate grounds for his reserve? For the evangelical, the Gospel accounts are clearly innocent until proven guilty.

Fortunately greater agreement is found when we examine the content of Jesus' sayings. Studies will generally tend to begin by studying the form of Jesus' teaching (parable, paradox, poetry, etc.) and find in this a key that unlocks either Semitic background or possible Aramaic antecedents. Here the recent work of scholars such as Jeremias has been indispensable.

A consensus may be at hand concerning the central message of Jesus. The "kingdom of God/heaven" is a frequent theme in the Gospels (when we allow for parallels, it appears about eighty times) and the evangelists imply that this message inaugurates Jesus' ministry (Matt. 4:17; Mark 1:15; Luke 4:43) as well as sums it up (Matt. 9:35; Luke 8:1). Even the Twelve and the Seventy are instructed to proclaim it (Matt. 10:5–7; Luke 10:8–9).

But when we seek a definition for this "kingdom" concise categories seem elusive. Certainly there is no going back to the nineteenth century denial of eschatology in the word. Jesus is announcing a climactic inbreaking of God's sovereign rule in history. But is this image entirely dependent on futurist expectations of Jewish apocalyptic (A. Schweitzer), or should we find here a present working of God within a personal "eschatological" crisis for the believer (C. H. Dodd; existentialism)? No doubt both elements must be held at once. To employ the categories of George Ladd, God's reign has already broken into history in the hearts of men and women who are obedient to Christ. But in addition, God's realm is still future. The church eagerly awaits a genuine eschaton when Christ will bring his thoroughgoing rule into history. While the church enjoys the promise of this kingdom, it awaits the kingdom's future fulfillment (so Kümmel).

But the sayings of Jesus go beyond even this description of God at work in history. Jesus reveals that God is at work in him. Jesus' sayings bear a unique self-revelation. He is the Son who alone knows the Father intimately (Matt. 11:27ff.) and can in turn reveal the Father fully (John 1:18; 14:8–11). In this fashion, the kingdom is entirely dependent on Jesus: He inaugurates the Kingdom and exhibits its presence through his powerful works (Luke 11:20; cf. 17:20–21). Therefore the chief message of the sayings of Jesus may be that God is not only powerfully at work in Israel, but that he is at work through his Son, the Messiah. G. M. BURGE

See also LOGIA; PARABLES OF JESUS.

Bibliography. T. W. Manson, *The Sayings of Jesus* and *The Teaching of Jesus;* W. G. Kümmel, *Promise and Fulfillment;* H. Anderson, *Jesus and Christian Origins;* C. F. H. Henry, ed., *Jesus of Nazareth, Savior and Lord;* C. C. Anderson, *Critical Quests of Jesus;* C. H. Dodd, *The Founder of Christianity;* J. Jeremias, *NT Theology, The Proclamation of Jesus;* M. Hooker, "On Using the Wrong Tool," *Theol* 75:575–81; A. M. Hunter, *The Work and Words of Jesus;* G. E. Ladd, *The Presence of the Future;* P. Henry, *New Directions in NT Study;* I. H. Marshall, "Jesus in the Gospels," in *The Expositor's Bible Commentary,* I, 517–41; R. H. Stein, "The Criteria of Authenticity," in *Gospel Perspectives,* ed. R. T. France and D. Wenham; D. E. Aune, *Jesus and the Synoptic Gospels: A Bibliographic Study Guide.*

Scapegoat. *See* ATONEMENT, DAY OF.

Schaff, Philip (1819–1893). Theologian, church historian, ecumenist. A Swiss carpenter's son, he was converted under Lutheran pietist auspices and studied at Tübingen, Halle, and Berlin. He absorbed the Hegelian approach to church history and biblical studies, and came under the evangelical influence of Tholuck and Neander and the confessionalism of Hengstenberg. A promising young Berlin theologian who identified with the broader union church ideal, he was called in 1844 to a professorship at the obscure theological seminary of the German Reformed Church in Mercersburg, Pennsylvania.

With his colleague John W. Nevin, Schaff quickly became known as the exponent of the intellectually profound and controversial Mercersburg Theology. This stressed Christ and the incarnation as the starting point for theology, the organic growth of the church, liturgical worship, and ecumenism; and in effect it was the first attempt to reconcile German idealism and American Protestantism. In his inaugural address *The Principle of Protestantism* (1844) he set forth the developmental principle, arguing that the Reformation was a flowering of the best in medieval Catholicism and that Protestantism and Catholicism will eventually merge into a renewed, evangelical faith. In *What Is Church History?* (1846) he identified with the new "historical school" that united past and present in the development of the church. Schaff strongly criticized the American propensity to subjectivism, sectarianism, and revivalism, and insisted that the most dangerous enemy was not the Roman pope but the "numberless popes" who would enslave Protestantism to human authority. His vision of the church was ecumenical—one spirit, one body, one shepherd, one flock.

An attempt to convict him of heresy failed, but the Mercersburg movement soon passed from the scene. Schaff moved to Andover Seminary in 1863 and then to Union Theological Seminary in New York in 1870 where he finished out his career. His scholarly contributions were legion. Not only was he a major interpreter of the American religious scene (essays on America, 1854; the Civil War, 1865; and religious liberty, 1888), but also he was the country's leading church historian and a prolific writer of biblical and theological works. Noteworthy are his eight volume *History of the Christian Church*, the indispensable *Creeds of Christendom* (3 vols., 1877), a multivolume edition of the church fathers, the *Schaff-Herzog Encyclopedia of Religious Knowledge* (1884), an American edition of Lange's massive commentary (1864–80), a study of hymnody (1868), and a refutation of the Strauss-Renan view of Christ (1865). Ecumenical involvements included the Sunday school movement, the Evangelical Alliance, and working on the Revised Version of the Bible. In 1888 he helped found the American Society of Church History and was its first president. R. V. PIERARD

See also MERCERSBURG THEOLOGY.

Bibliography. D. S. Schaff, *The Life of Philip Schaff;* J. H. Nichols, *Romanticism in American Theology: Nevin and Schaff at Mercersburg;* C. Yrigoyen and G. Bricker, eds., *Reformed and Catholic: Selected Historical and Theological Writings of Philip Schaff;* R. Schnucker, *NIDCC*, 881–82.

Schism (Gr. *schisma*, meaning "division"). The word is used eight times in the NT. From this usage the theological meaning of the term can be derived. Immediately one popular misconception can be removed. Schism and heresy are two different terms and cannot be used interchangeably, yet they are often so used. Heresy is not schism, for heresy is, at its base, doctrinal, and is opposed to the Christian faith itself. Schism is opposed to charity and is not doctrinal at heart.

Often the departure of Reformers like Martin Luther and John Calvin has been relegated to the area of schism. This is far from the truth. To the Roman Church this was not schism but heresy. To the Reformers it was also heresy, but heresy entertained by Rome which drove them from its fold. Hence John Calvin in his *Institutes of the Christian Religion* argued that the Roman Church was not a true church since it was defective in the true preaching of the gospel and the administration of the sacraments. Therefore he was not leaving the true church. In fact, Calvin argued strongly that whatever the defects of any true church, so long as it continued the marks of a true church, no one should leave its fold.

The Roman Church allowed for the distinction between schism and heresy. A schismatic bishop of that church could continue to ordain priests, and schismatic priests could continue to celebrate the Eucharist. But heretical bishops and priests could not do so legitimately. Rome recognized that schism is a breach of love, a factious spirit, or a factious division, but not doctrinal divergence. Thus it is that the Roman Church has always recognized the Greek Orthodox Church as essentially orthodox, but schismatic. The Greek Church has sinned against love.

Among the various schisms of the Christian church three can be mentioned briefly: the Donatist schism, the Great Schism (the break between East and West in 1054), and the papal schism (some historians also speak of this as the Great Schism). In the case of the Donatists, the problem was one of ecclesiastical discipline in which they opposed internal corruption in the church. This party arose during the Diocletian persecution when some Christians surrendered the Scriptures. Augustine wrote against the Donatists because they persistently separated themselves from the fellowship of the church, insisting on rebaptism of Catholics as a condition of communion with them. Narrow and intolerant, the Donatists were nevertheless recognized as connected with the true church, but were regarded as schismatic or sinning against charity.

The Great Schism relates to the Eastern and Western churches. This occurred by reason of the growing strength of Rome as against that of Constantinople. Several centuries passed before the church was rent. At last in 1054 the separation was completed. Pope Leo IX was angered by an encyclical of the patriarch of Constantinople. When the patriarch refused to submit the papal legates laid down a sentence of anathema.

The third schism (also called the Babylonian Captivity) occurred in the fourteenth and fifteenth centuries and was complicated by strange proceedings. The schism took place shortly after the death of Gregory XI in 1378. There was one pope at Avignon and one at Rome. At the Council of Pisa in 1409 both popes were deposed and a third one elected. Instead of two popes the church now had three. At the Council of Constance the legitimate pope, Gregory XII, resigned with the agreement that his pontificate would be regarded as legal. In 1417 Oddo Colonna was elected pope and reigned as Martin V (1417–31).

Biblically it appears clear that the rending of the body of Christ is sin and that there is no excuse for schism, which is related to love and not to doctrine. But when doctrine is involved, it takes on different dimensions and is not so much schism as heresy. Heretics are to be cut off from the church or excommunicated, and this distinction is not one of schism.

In I Cor. 1:10 schism developed from the party spirit or factiousness in which individuals identified themselves as supporters of Paul or Apollos or Cephas. Outwardly the church was one, but internally it was marked by divisiveness. The schismatic tendency noted in 11:18 was based largely on social distinctions rather than doctrinal differences. In chapter 12 Paul makes the point that the divine wisdom which has established harmony between the members of the human body points to a similar purpose in the body of Christ (see vs. 25). Diversity of gifts should not invite to envy but to cooperation.

By way of summary it may be said that division based upon primary considerations of essential doctrine is not schism and is not per se wrong. Divisions which are not doctrinal, however, but which yield to other considerations, are reprehensible. They rise from a sin against charity and are contrary to the Spirit of Christ.

H. Lindsell

See also Heresy; Schism, The Great.

Bibliography. T. A. Lacey, *Unity and Schism.*

Schism, The Great (1054). The first permanent severing of the Christian community. Its beginnings lay in the division of the Roman Empire at the end of the third century. Thereafter, the Greek (Eastern) and Latin (Western) sections of the Roman world were administered separately. Their cultural and economic differences intensified. When the political institutions of the Latin empire collapsed in the fifth century, the Greek empire, centered in Constantinople, continued to flourish.

The sustaining institution during this period was the Christian church. Its theology dominated all forms of thought in both the united East and the disintegrating West. Important issues, even worldly ones, were transposed into theological questions.

Two fundamental differences between the Latin Catholic and Greek Orthodox traditions developed during the early Middle Ages. The first was the Petrine Doctrine—absolute in the West—resisted in the East. And the second was a Western addition to the Nicene Creed which provoked the *filioque* controversy. Other divisive issues such as the celibacy of the priesthood, use of unleavened bread in the Eucharist, episcopal control over the sacrament of confirmation, and priestly beards and monkish tonsures were the source of conflict but not schism.

Of all the institutions that the medieval Christian empire shared, the political was the first to collapse. In the West during the fifth century imperial authority fell before invading barbarian kings. Increasingly the Roman patriarch, the pope, filled the power vacuum left by retreating politicians. The lines between secular and ecclesiastical authority were hopelessly blurred. On the other hand, in Constantinople, where imperial power was still strong, Christian emperors continued to preside over an integrated Christian society. As heirs of Constantine, Byzantine emperors dominated the administration of church and state in the style still known as caesaropapism.

Theology in the East was speculative, with important decisions submitted to a collegial-conciliar system in which all the patriarchs—the bishops of Constantinople, Antioch, Alexandria, Jerusalem, and Rome—played an important role. It was fully acknowledged that the bishop of Rome had pride of place and certain rights of review over the other four. As early as the pontificate of Leo I (440–61), however, Roman patriarchs demanded more power. Matters were made more difficult by the rise of Islam and new barbarian attacks in the seventh and eighth centuries. The West became even more isolated, and when contacts between Rome and Constantinople were resumed the gulf between East and West had widened.

The *filioque* controversy seems to have originated in sixth century Visigothic Spain where the Arian heresy was endemic. The Arians claimed that the first and second persons of the Trinity were not coeternal and equal. In an effort to enforce traditional theology, Spanish churchmen added a phrase to the Nicene Creed, "*ex Patre Filioque*," which amended the old form to state that the Holy Spirit proceeded from the Son as well as from the Father. However, it had been agreed in the fourth century that no change in the wording of the creed, except by conciliar consent, was possible. To the theologically sophisticated East, the *filioque* phrase seemed to challenge not only the universal creed, but also the official doctrine of the Trinity. When the issue was raised during the reign of Charlemagne (768–814), the papacy seemed to agree. Pope

Leo III, while approving the spirit of the *filioque*, warned against any alteration in the wording of the creed.

It was the fusion of the *filioque* controversy with the rise of papal power that created the great crisis of 1054. The "reform" papacy of the eleventh century established itself on the right of the pope, as apostolic heir of Peter, to absolute power over all Christian people and institutions. Such claims had been rejected by the early church councils. To Eastern patriarchs Christ's charge to Peter in Matt. 16:18–19 was shared by all the apostles and their spiritual heirs, the bishops. In 1054 Pope Leo IX (1048–54) sent a delegation headed by Cardinal Humbert of Silva Candida to discuss the problems between the papacy and Constantinople. Disaster followed. The Patriarch of Constantinople, Michael Cerularius, rejected both papal claims and the *filioque*. The Western legates accused Constantinople of having altered the Nicene Creed. In the end, Cardinal Humbert deposited a Bull of Excommunication against Michael Cerularius on the altar of the Hagia Sophia, and the Great Schism was official.

Thereafter, efforts were made at reunion. As the Muslim Turks advanced on the Byzantine Empire in the high Middle Ages, Eastern Christians were in desperate need of relief from their Western brethren. However, all such hopes ceased when, in 1204, an army of crusading knights from the West sacked Constantinople. Eastern Christians never recovered from this outrage. In recent years efforts to reconcile the Roman Catholic and Greek Orthodox churches have failed. In 1965, Pope Paul VI lifted the ban of excommunication against Michael Cerularius. However, the problem of papal rule has been rendered more difficult by nineteenth century Roman declarations of papal infallibility. The wording of the creed has not been settled.

C. T. MARSHALL

See also FILIOQUE.

Bibliography. F. Dvornik, *Byzantium and the Roman Primacy;* J. Pelikan, *The Spirit of Eastern Christendom (600–1700);* S. Runciman, *The Eastern Schism;* P. Sherrad, *The Greek East and the Latin West;* T. Ware, *The Orthodox Church.*

Schlatter, Adolf von (1852–1938). German NT scholar and theologian. Born in St. Gallen and educated at Basel and Tübingen where he apparently was influenced by the conservative biblicist J. T. Beck, Schlatter entered the pastorate in his native Switzerland and then began teaching at Bern in 1880. Professorships followed at Greifswald (1888), Berlin (1893), and finally Tübingen (1898), where he spent his most productive years.

Schlatter was one of the most respected voices of conservative scholarship in early twentieth century Germany. He felt that a precise knowledge of the religion of late Judaism and history of the intertestamental period was necessary for a proper understanding of the NT, and his research opened new paths for NT exegesis. Besides several large commentaries and numerous *Erläuterungen* designed to assist ordinary Bible readers, he authored major historical studies of Israel (1901) and the early church (1926, *The Church in the NT Period*). He distinguished himself in systematics with substantial works in dogmatics (1911), ethics (1914), and NT theology (1921–22). He prepared the way for the rejection of idealism by modern theologians by emphasizing the facts of faith in the life of Jesus rather than speculative thought. He also copublished an important theological journal, *Beiträge zur Förderung christlicher Theologie.*

Although he identified with no ecclesiastical party and was ecumenical in his outlook—in effect a mediator between the two Protestant confessions, Reformation and modern thought, and liberalism and pietism—Schlatter sided with the conservative view of the priority of Matthew's Gospel and stressed the crucial role of God and his acts in history. He was concerned with the social aspects of Christianity, as evidenced by his lifelong friendship with Friedrich von Bodelschwingh of the Bethel Institution. To be sure, little of his material is available in English, but his commentaries and popular works continue to enjoy a wide audience among pietistic circles in present-day Germany. R. V. PIERARD

Bibliography. R. Morgan, *The Nature of NT Theology: The Contribution of William Wrede and Adolf Schlatter.*

Schleiermacher, Friedrich Daniel Ernst (1768–1834). The most influential theologian of the nineteenth century, often called the father of liberal Protestant theology or theology of religious experience. Born in Breslau in 1768, son of a Reformed military chaplain, he was educated in Moravian schools where he was deeply impressed by mystical pietism. In 1787 he entered the University of Halle and studied the writings of Kant and Spinoza.

Schleiermacher's intellectual development was profoundly influenced after 1796 by his association in Berlin with the flowering romantic movement, which revolted against classical norms in literature and art and the arid rationalism of the Enlightenment. Prodded by Friedrich Schlegel, a leader of the new movement, Schleiermacher wrote *On Religion: Speeches to Its Cultured Despisers* in 1799 to address his fellow romantics. He claimed that they had renounced religion because rationalists had wrongly reduced its essence either to knowledge acquired through reason and expressed in doctrines, or morality perceived through conscience and demonstrated in moral behavior. In doing so they had ignored feeling, not only a primary component of romanticism, but the very essence of religion. Schleiermacher therefore redefined religion as a unique element of human experience, not located in the cognitive or moral faculties, which produce only an indirect knowledge of God by inference, but in feeling which yields immediate experience of God.

Such a redefinition of the essence of religion did not reduce it to mere psychological emotion or mystical absorption, but it did make religion radically subjective. His claim that piety arises from the experience of God (the Infinite) through our experience of the world (the finite), not from rational metaphysics or doctrinal reflection, paralleled a dominant romantic theme. People understand the world in which they live more through imagination and intuitive experiences in nature than by studying it through rational analysis or scientific method. Schleiermacher's emphasis on God's immanence, his presence in the world, and the believer's subjective experience of God rather than God's transcendence and objective reality led traditionalists repeatedly to charge him with pantheism. *On Religion* is significant because it introduced a new conception of religion that inverted traditional methods of theology. Rather than religious experience growing out of doctrinal expressions or ecclesiastical life, religion itself was posited as the unique, primal experience of human existence.

Schleiermacher left Berlin in 1804 to become a professor of theology at the University of Halle, where he demonstrated his breadth of learning by teaching every subject in the curriculum except OT. In 1807 he returned to Berlin, lectured on Greek philosophy, and began preaching in Trinity Church, where he continued until two weeks before he died in 1834. He helped plan the University of Berlin and became professor of theology when the school was founded in 1810.

Just as Kant had subjectivized knowledge by reducing its apprehension to the categories of human understanding, and subsequently reinterpreted Christianity in *Religion Within the Limits of Reason Alone* as a deistic moralism, so Schleiermacher recast Christian theology in *The Christian Faith* (1821) in keeping with his romantic redefinition of religion. In his mature thought he defined religion as "the feeling of absolute dependence" or "God-consciousness." Theological statements do not describe God in any objective manner but rather are ways in which the Christian feeling of absolute dependence is related to God. Theology is a historical discipline whose task is to record the religious experience of each new generation.

Schleiermacher broke from Reformed, Augustianian, and Pauline theology on original sin by denying a historical fall. Rather than an actual event, the fall in Genesis is a story which illustrates how individual acts of sin result from the sinful nature in all people. He denied both that original sin is an inherited corruption and that Adam was created righteous and by sinning plunged the human race into sin. Human nature has always been a mixture of "original righteousness" (potential God-consciousness) and "original sinfulness" (God-forgetfulness). Righteousness and sin coexist within human nature from the beginning; they do not distinguish between man as originally created and man after the fall. Sin in Gen. 3 is not a willful rebellion against a sovereign Creator but merely a shortcoming in which one subordinates his feeling of absolute dependence to such temporal concerns as pleasure and pain.

Despite their potential for God-consciousness humans are unable to save themselves. Christianity's superiority to other religions is found in its provision of redemption through Jesus Christ. Schleiermacher criticized traditional discussions of Christ's person and work because they stressed belief in ideas about Christ, not the experience of redemption itself. As redeemer Christ is both the ideal example and source of God-consciousness which overcomes sin. He contended that believers experience regeneration (Jesus' God-consciousness) by participating in the corporate life of the contemporary church rather than by merely believing in Christ's death and resurrection in history. He pointed out that Jesus' disciples were drawn into Jesus' God-consciousness prior to their belief in the resurrection. He called his view of redemption "mystical" to distinguish it from the Reformed view that focuses on Christ's substitutionary work, a transaction between Christ and the Father external to the believer's religious experience. Such a view is too objective and individualistic, and it neglects the role the community of believers plays in mediating redemption. At the same time he also rejected natural views such as Kant's that reduced redemption to moral obedience.

Schleiermacher's revision of Christian theology had its most radical impact on the issue of authority. No external authority, whether it be Scripture, church, or historic creedal statement, takes precedence over the immediate experience of believers. This contributed to a more critical approach to the Bible by questioning its inspiration and authority, and to a rejection of doctrines he believed unrelated to people's religious experience of redemption such as the virgin birth, the Trinity, and the return of Christ—tenets which implied a cognitive and thus indirect knowledge rather than immediate God-consciousness.

These ideas gained wide acceptance in the nineteenth century. Schleiermacher's influence was evident not only in the demise of Enlightenment deism in Europe, but also in the rise of theological liberalism in America, where disputes between modernists and fundamentalists concerning the deity and resurrection of Christ raged in the 1920s. His ideas were sharply challenged after World War I by the neo-orthodox theologian Karl Barth, who charged that not only were essential doctrines reinterpreted, but Christianity's uniqueness was compromised by making it merely one among many forms of religion. W. A. HOFFECKER

See also LIBERALISM, THEOLOGICAL; ROMANTICISM.

Bibliography. Schleiermacher, *Brief Outline on the Study of Theology;* K. Barth, *Protestant Thought from Rousseau to Ritschl;* R. R. Brandt, *The Philosophy of Schleiermacher;* J. Hick, *Evil and the God of Love;* H. R. Mackintosh, *Types of Modern Theology;* R. R. Niebuhr, *Schleiermacher on Christ and Religion;* M. Redeker, *Schleiermacher: Life and Thought;* C. Welch, *Protestant Thought in the Nineteenth Century,* I.

Schleitheim, Seven Articles of. *See* MENNONITES.

Schmucker, Samuel Simon (1799–1873). Leader of "American" or "New School" Lutheranism in the United States in the fifty years before the Civil War. As opposed to "European" or "Old" Lutheranism, Schmucker sought an accommodation between American Protestantism and traditional Lutheran distinctives. Schmucker, a graduate of Presbyterian Princeton Seminary, gave his life to serving Lutherans with the aim of benefiting American Christianity generally. He was a founder, professor of theology, and president of Gettysburg Lutheran Seminary and a vital force in the General Synod of Lutheran churches that had been formed in 1820. At the same time, he moved beyond traditional Lutheranism by supporting revivalism, aiding the development of interdenominational agencies like the American Sunday School Union, and speaking out on national issues (like many of his fellow Americans he expressed fears about immigrants and Roman Catholics).

What was most upsetting to traditional Lutherans, however, were Schmucker's proposed modifications to the Augsburg Confession. Schmucker did not believe in a real presence of Christ's body in the Lord's Supper; he rejected private confession; he doubted the Lutheran teaching on baptismal regeneration; he desired a much stronger emphasis on keeping the sabbath. Schmucker's Lutheran opponents soon came to regard him as a dangerous advocate of "modern American Puritanism."

Schmucker's views were widely shared by American Lutherans until about the time of the Civil War. Then, however, growing numbers of immigrants from Germany and Scandinavia, who brought to America a renewed interest in the heritage of the Reformation, greatly lessened Schmucker's influence. His own works, like *A Fraternal Appeal to the American Churches* (1838), combined traditional Lutheranism and modern American emphases. The anonymous *Definite Synodical Platform* of 1855, which proposed a revision of the Augsburg Confession along lines favored by Schmucker, precipitated a clash of interests which eventually led to the triumph of European Lutheranism over Schmucker's American variation. M. A. NOLL

Bibliography. Schmucker, *Fraternal Appeal to the American Churches;* V. Ferm, *American Lutheran Theology: A Study of the Issue Between American Lutheranism and Old Lutheranism;* C. E. Nelson, ed., *The Lutherans in North America.*

Scholasticism. A form of Christian philosophy and theology developed by scholars who came to be called schoolmen. It flourished during the medieval period of European history. The heart of scholasticism insisted upon a system that was clear and definitional in tone. The system attempted to synthesize ideas expressed in classical Roman and Greek writings and in Christian Scripture, the writings of the patristic fathers, and other Christian writings preceding the medieval period. Aristotle's views helped give scholasticism a systematic structure, but Platonism also played a large part in the enterprise.

Some persons consider scholasticism to have been a boring, dry system emphasizing sheer memorization. However, in many respects it was dynamic, truly seeking to settle questions concerning reality. The *Disputed Questions* of Thomas Aquinas, rather than his *Summa,* point out the vibrancy of the system. The philosophical aspects of scholasticism were not dictated strictly by a set of theological dogmas but rather worked with both faith and reason in an attempt to understand reality from the viewpoint of a human being.

The method of scholasticism sought to understand the fundamental aspects of theology, philosophy, and law. Apparently contradictory viewpoints were offered in order to show how they possibly could be synthesized through reasonable interpretation. A problem would first be "exposed," and then it would be "disputed" in order to cause a new "discovery" in the mind of the person who was seeking new personal knowledge. Each text investigated had a commentary. The master helped the student to read the text in such a way that he could really understand what it was saying. This experience was to be much more than just memorative. There were yes-and-no positions to various texts, which sought to keep the student from merely memorizing the text. Abelard developed the yes-and-no method with great precision. The two most exciting types of disputations were the *quaestio disputata*, which was a disputed question, and the *quodlibet*, which was a very subtle form of disputed question that could be publicly disputed only by a truly great master, whereas the disputed questions could be talked about by lesser minds still growing in knowledge.

Anselm of Canterbury is the first great developer of scholasticism. His *Monologion* investigates problems surrounding God from a reasonable and yet prayerful viewpoint. He developed the famous principle "faith seeking to know."

Peter Abelard sought to show various ways in which contradictory texts could be synthesized. He became involved in the disputed question concerning whether "universals" were really things or merely names.

Gilbert de la Porree continued to develop various views in a scholastic manner. Hugh of St. Victor sought to give scholasticism more of a mystical flare; he was criticized by many because of his lack of reasonableness. He was deeply indebted to Augustine for his views. Bernard of Clairvaux developed a psychological view in scholasticism which, although wedded to a form of mysticism, sought to be more reasonable than mystical.

Peter Lombard developed a series of "sentences" that were to be taught to seminarians studying for the priesthood in the twelfth century. These scholastic sentences were usually simple and also capable of being memorized by the students. It is this form of scholasticism that has caused many persons to discredit it as an uncreative experience.

Albert the Great (Albertus Magnus) was not much of an improvement over Peter Lombard, but he deeply influenced Thomas Aquinas, who was the apogee of scholastic thought. Thomism has many forms, but they are all trying to interpret the system of thought developed by Thomas Aquinas. His great effort was to combine what could be called non-Christian philosophy with both Christian philosophy and theology. Christian Scripture could be combined with elements of ideas discovered by natural thought unaided by the grace of Scripture. Thomas Aquinas was heavily influenced by not only Aristotelianism but also Platonism. He also attempted to combine the thought of Averroes into his system. Some of his contemporaries considered some of his ideas to be heretical. Cardinal Tempier of Paris was especially disturbed by his view concerning the resurrection of the body as it was presented in his *Disputed Questions*.

Bonaventure was another great schoolman, but his style of presentation is turgid and pales somewhat in relation to the presentations of Aquinas. Bonaventure was quite polemical in his attacks against Aristotelianism, which undermined his attempt to be reasonable.

In the fourteenth century Giles of Rome presented some brilliance within the scholastic tradition, but he was not very consequential in relation to Aquinas. The great scholastic thinker of the fourteenth century was John Duns Scotus. He had an extremely subtle understanding of the use of words. He was chiefly interested in the problem of epistemology. His school of thought, Scotism, influenced many people in later ages, including Martin Heidegger and Ludwig Wittgenstein. William of Ockham rounds out the glorious age of scholasticism. He was called a nominalist because he wondered if exterior reality to the human mind was given a series of words which remained primarily in the mind. For William of Ockham it was unclear that the human mind could actually know exterior reality.

Scholasticism went into desuetude in the fifteenth century, but it was revived in the sixteenth century. The twentieth century has experienced a renewed attempt to make the Thomistic form of scholasticism credible as a system of thought. This movement within Roman Catholic circles has been partially successful.

T. J. German

See also Abelard, Peter; Albertus Magnus; Anselm of Canterbury; Bonaventure; Duns Scotus, John; Peter Lombard; Thomas Aquinas; William of Ockham.

Bibliography. J. Pieper, *Scholasticism;* É. Gilson, *The Christian Philosophy of St. Thomas Aquinas* and *The Unity of Philosophical Experience.*

Scholasticism, Protestant. A method of thinking developed in early Protestantism, which grew stronger in the seventeenth century and became a widely accepted way to create systematic Protestant theologies. Even though the major Protestant Reformers attacked the theology of the medieval schoolmen and demanded total reliance on Scripture, it was impossible either to purge all scholastic methods and attitudes derived from classical authors or to avoid conflicts that required intricate theological reasoning as well as biblical interpretation.

Several factors account for the growth of Protestant scholasticism: formal education, confidence in reason, and religious controversy. Reliance on logical methods derived from Greek and Roman authors was not purged from sixteenth century educational institutions. Aristotle, for example, upon whom the medieval scholastics had relied, continued to be taught by Protestants: Melanchthon at Wittenberg, Peter Martyr Vermigli at Oxford, Jerome Zanchi at Strassburg, Conrad Gesner at Zurich, Theodore Beza at Geneva. Though these teachers did not accept Thomas Aquinas's medieval scholastic theology, which also relied heavily on Aristotle's logic and philosophy, they did teach Aristotle's deductive logic and gave reason an important place in theology.

Though Luther (following William of Ockham) and Calvin (following French humanists) decried scholastic reliance on reason and wanted instead to limit their theology to humanist linguistic analysis of Scripture, the Protestant scholastics, without breaking from the major Reformers, were more amenable to human reason. Reason became a means to develop coherent theology out of the great variety of biblical texts. Further, Renaissance learning, though it stressed textual analysis, also placed confidence in human rationality. The Protestant use of scholastic techniques and attitudes consequently kept them in the mainstream of early modern philosophy, which, though it moved away from deductive logic, maintained confidence in reason. Protestant theologians, especially the Calvinists, could use scholastic methods to inquire beyond biblical texts into the intricacies and implications of Protestant theology, especially when election and the will of God were considered.

Theological controversy also encouraged Protestant scholasticism. When Luther and Zwingli disagreed over the Lord's Supper and when Calvinists entered great controversies over predestination, protagonists often resorted to scholastic logic. The controversies themselves called for thorough, intricate argumentation; for biblical texts on the issues were interpreted in a variety of ways. Also, those who won the controversies embodied victory in tightly reasoned doctrinal statements. Thus, there is strong evidence of Protestant scholasticism in the Canons of Dort, the Westminster Confession, and the Helvetic Confession of 1675.

The influence of Protestant scholasticism was both immediate and long-range. Among Lutherans, the essential doctrine of justification by faith was transformed into a rather complicated theory of conversion by the most famous Lutheran scholastic, Johann Gerhard (1582–1637). Gerhard used Aristotelian and scriptural proof in his *Loci Theologicae* (9 vols.). While this work was important for shaping Lutheran orthodoxy, in the seventeenth century German pietists replaced scholasticism with a greater emphasis on experiential Christianity. Among the Reformed, two scholastic traditions were developed. Peter Ramus modeled his logic on Plato and Cicero in an attempt to avoid too great an emphasis on metaphysics. Though his work was banned in various continental Protestant centers (Wittenberg, Leiden Helmstedt, Geneva), Ramus had a great influence on Puritan thought in England and America. The dominant Reformed scholastics, however, were Beza, Vermigli, Adrianus Heerebout, and, most importantly, Francis Turretin (1623–87). Turretin's *Institutio* became the standard work for modern Protestant scholastics, as it was used as a textbook to shape the modern Princeton Theology. Reformed scholasticism in this tradition led to what is generally labeled Calvinist orthodoxy.

The theology of this branch of Protestant scholasticism was, as in the case of Gerhard, dependent on scriptural evidences and Aristotelian logic. The Reformed scholastics concentrated for the most part on questions evolving from predestination, and thus produced a rather rigid Calvinism. At the same time, the movement was amenable to the use of reason, thus allowing the Reformed to adapt to modern rationalist and Enlightenment philosophy quite easily. Noteworthy in this regard is the rather easy accommodation of philosophy and theology in the Scottish Enlightenment. The impact of Protestant scholasticism's methods and outlook was threefold: it created a systematic, well-defined, and aggressive Protestant theology; it led to a reaction by those who emphasized the emotional character of Christian piety; and it encouraged accommodation to early modern philosophy.

R. J. VanderMolen

See also Beza, Theodore; Gerhard, Johann; Peter Martyr Vermigli; Ramus, Peter; Turretin, Francis.

Bibliography. B. Armstrong, *Calvinism and the Amyraut Heresy;* J. W. Beardslee, III, ed. and tr.,

Reformed Dogmatics; J. P. Donnelly, "Italian Influences on the Development of Calvinist Scholasticism," *SCJ* 7:81–101; J. H. Leith, *An Introduction to the Reformed Tradition; NCE,* III, 162ff.; O. Grundler, "The Influence of Thomas Aquinas upon the Theology of G. Zanchi," in *Studies in Medieval Culture;* B. Hall, "Calvin Against the Calvinists," in *John Calvin,* ed. G. E. Duffield; P. O. Kristeller, *Renaissance Thought: The Classic, Scholastic, and Humanist Strains;* R. Scharlemann, *Aquinas and Gerhard: Theological Controversy and Construction in Medieval and Protestant Scholasticism.*

Schoolmen. *See* SCHOLASTICISM.

Schwabach, Articles of (1529). Lutheran confessional document, prepared by Melanchthon and other Wittenberg theologians. In their final form the seventeen constituent articles provided the basis for the first part of the Augsburg Confession (1530). They were directed against Roman Catholics, Zwinglians, and Anabaptists, and set forth the Lutheran understanding of the Eucharist. The tenth article, for example, declared that "in the bread and wine the body and blood of Christ are truly present, according to the word of Christ." With the exception of the section on the Eucharist, the articles were accepted at the Colloquy of Marburg in 1529, and were regarded as a touchstone of Lutheran orthodoxy. The purpose of the confession, which had been commissioned by the elector of Saxony, John the Steadfast, was to provide a unifying document for the various Reformers and their followers. It was accepted by the rulers of Saxony and Brandenburg, and John presented it to Emperor Charles V in 1530, prior to the Diet of Augsburg, as Saxony's official confession of faith.

J. D. DOUGLAS

See also AUGSBURG CONFESSION; CONFESSIONS OF FAITH; MARBURG COLLOQUY.

Schweitzer, Albert (1875–1965). German theologian, medical missionary, and musicologist. Born into a Lutheran pastor's family in Alsace, he studied organ as a child and took degrees in theology and philosophy at the University of Strasbourg. He then served in a clerical post in the city and taught at the university. His early theological work was devoted to the messiahship and suffering of Jesus (*The Mystery of the Kingdom of God,* 1901), and his most noteworthy book, *The Quest of the Historical Jesus* (1906), established his theological reputation. He also distinguished himself as a student of the baroque organ with the study *J. S. Bach* (1908), an eight-volume critical edition of Bach's organ works, and a book on German and French organ construction (1906).

His experience in charitable work among the homeless and exprisoners in Strasbourg stimulated an interest to devote himself to the service of humanity, and after reading about the Congo mission in the Paris Mission Society magazine, he decided to study medicine. After eight years of study and completion of a dissertation refuting the theory that Jesus was paranoid (*The Psychiatric Study of Jesus*), he received an M.D. at Strasbourg in 1913 and left immediately for the mission at Lambaréné in Gabon. With his wife, a nurse, he founded a jungle hospital which eventually became world famous. Expelled from Africa as an enemy alien in 1917, Schweitzer spent the next seven years discussing his medical endeavors and preparing a two-volume work on the philosophy of religion, *The Philosophy of Civilization* (1923).

In the subsequent years he expanded his hospital complex through funds raised in lecture tours and recitals. He also authored books on the mysticism of Paul (1930), Goethe (1932), and Indian thought (1935); and popularized his famous ethical principle of reverence for life in several autobiographical works and in *The Light Within Us* (1959) and *The Teaching of the Reverence for Life* (1965). He received the Nobel Peace Prize in 1952 and in later life was a strong opponent of atomic weapons. Many criticized him for exercising a paternalistic control over his hospitals and not maintaining modern standards of sanitation.

Schweitzer believed he had found the real historical Jesus, but he differed from that conceived of by liberal Protestants. Schweitzer said Jesus preached the message of the coming kingdom of God as understood in contemporary Jewish apocalyptic thinking and mistakenly tried to provoke the intervention of God and bring about the end of history by challenging the powers of his own day. He was crushed by the wheel of history, and the eschatology by which he had lived was destroyed. But his "spirit" lives on, and we are called to share it. Schweitzer's work in Africa was a monument to his understanding of what following the spirit of Jesus means. Although he was uncertain about traditional Christian dogma, he strongly emphasized the ethical side of life and the necessity for discipleship.

R. V. PIERARD

Bibliography. Schweitzer, *On the Edge of the Primeval Forest, Memoirs of Childhood and Youth, Out of My Life and Thought, African Notebook,* and *More from the Primeval Forest;* C. R. Joy, ed., *Albert Schweitzer: An Anthology* and *The Animal World of Albert Schweitzer: Jungle Insights into Reverence for Life;* G. Seaver, *Albert Schweitzer: The Man and His Mind;* N. Cousins, *Dr. Schweitzer of Lambaréné;* G. McKnight,

Verdict on Schweitzer; J. L. Ice, *Schweitzer: Prophet of Radical Theology;* J. Brabazon, *Albert Schweitzer: A Biography;* H. Willmer, *NIDCC*, 888.

Schwenckfeld, Kasper von Ossig (1489–1561). Mystic, lay theologian, and Silesian nobleman. Schwenckfeld was a university-educated courtier and early supporter of Lutheran reforms in Silesia, *ca.* 1520–26. He broke with Luther and other Reformers initially over the nature and meaning of the Lord's Supper, and advocated a suspension of reforms until the major parties could agree. His own spiritualized concept of the Supper focused on an inward partaking of Christ's heavenly flesh, and was denounced by Luther. Schwenckfeld hoped to develop a "royal" or middle course between Lutheranism and Catholicism, both of which he felt were overly concerned with outward practices.

Political pressure forced Schwenckfeld to resign his post as religious advisor to Duke Frederick II and to go into voluntary exile in 1529. He spent the next few years in Strasbourg, where he at first enjoyed the support of Reformers Capito and Bucer. However, the Marburg Colloquy (1529), which attempted to settle the controversy between Luther and Zwingli and others on the Lord's Supper, dismissed Schwenckfeld's views. While in Strasbourg he also came into contact with various Anabaptist leaders, especially Pilgram Marpeck. Although he chided their emphasis on external baptism, church discipline, and radical eschatology, Schwenckfeld was himself critical of infant baptism, participation in war, and swearing oaths.

At the center of Schwenckfeld's thought was the conviction that all religious life should be an internal spiritual quality. He stressed the necessity of a rebirth and inner experience of faith rather than justification by faith. All outward creeds and forms were unnecessary and should be avoided. The true church is invisible—neither the "mixed multitude" (territorial church) continued by the mainline Reformers, nor the visible, voluntary sect stressed by the Anabaptists.

Schwenckfeld was forced to leave Strasbourg in 1534 and Ulm in 1539. He thereafter wandered from place to place preaching and writing, evading his persecutors and seeking refuge with sympathizers. His doctrines were condemned by a gathering of evangelical Reformers led by Melanchthon in 1540 (Smalcald Convention) and the Formula of Concord (1575). He died at Ulm in December 1561.

Although Schwenckfeld's evangelical spiritualism anticipated later developments in pietism and the Society of Friends, he refused to organize his followers. A Schwenckfelder Church developed after 1540 out of spiritualists who treasured his numerous writings. Small groups of "Confessors of the Glory of Christ" developed in Silesia, Swabia, Prussia, and elsewhere. One center at Goldberg in Silesia flourished till about 1720, when they were denied toleration and forced to seek refuge in Saxony. Some eventually migrated to eastern Pennsylvania in 1735 where a Society of Schwenckfelders was organized in 1782.

D. B. Eller

Bibliography. *Corpus Schwenckfeldianorum*, 19 vols.; H. W. Kriebel, *The Schwenkfelders in Pennsylvania;* F. W. Loetscher, *Schwenckfeld's Participation in the Eucharistic Controversy of the 16th Century;* P. L. Maier, *Casper Schwenckfeld on the Person and Work of Christ;* J. S. Rothenberger, *Casper Schwenckfeld von Ossig and the Ecumenical Idea;* S. G. Schultz, *Casper Schwenckfeld von Ossig;* J. H. Sexpel, *Schwenckfeld, Knight of Faith.*

Scientia Media. Literally "middle knowledge." Many theologians have said that God knows the world by knowing himself. He knows what is possible or impossible in the world by knowing what he can or cannot do: this knowledge is called the knowledge of simple intelligence or necessary knowledge (since it follows from the very nature of God's being). He also knows what actually takes place in the world (whether past, present, or future from our point of view) by knowing his own plan, his decree for the world: this knowledge is called the knowledge of vision or free knowledge (since it follows from God's free decisions concerning the world process). Such a distinction was made by Thomas Aquinas and his Dominican followers. But in the sixteenth century the theologians of the new Jesuit order, seeking to restate the Roman Catholic theology in opposition to the challenges of Protestantism and Jansenism, found this distinction inadequate to do justice to human freedom. They introduced a third form of divine knowledge, a middle knowledge or *scientia media*. This knowledge (a) is a knowledge of what *would* happen under such-and-such conditions, and (b) is based, neither upon God's nature nor upon his decree, but upon the free decisions of created beings. Thus God knows what will happen *if* David remains in Keilah, and what will happen if he does not (I Sam. 23:1–13); and he knows it, not because he controls the course of history, but because he knows what free decisions people will make independently of his controlling decree. This concept found favor with Lutherans (e.g., Quenstedt) and with Arminius and some of his followers. The Reformed agree that God knows what would happen under all conditions, but they reject the notion that this knowledge is ever ultimately based on man's autonomous decisions. Human decisions, they argue, are themselves the effects of God's eternal decrees (see Acts 2:23; Rom. 9:10–18; Eph. 1:11; Phil. 2:12–13). J. M. FRAME

See also FOREKNOWLEDGE.

Bibliography. H. Bavinck, *The Doctrine of God;* H. Heppe, *Reformed Dogmatics;* C. Hodge, *Systematic Theology,* I, 397–401.

Scofield, Cyrus Ingerson (1843–1921). Congregational minister and writer. Scofield was born in Mississippi on August 19, 1843, and was raised in Tennessee. He served with distinction in the Confederate Army and then studied law. President Grant appointed him U.S. Attorney for Kansas. Responding to the witness of Thomas McPheeters, a YMCA worker, he was converted in 1879. In 1882 he accepted a Congregational pastorate in Dallas, Texas. His theological education was directed informally by James H. Brookes, a Presbyterian minister who had read widely in J. N. Darby and other Plymouth Brethren writers. Scofield accepted premillennialism and dispensationalism immediately, and his preaching and teaching were shaped by this commitment. His pastoral ministry, both in Dallas (1882–95) and, at D. L. Moody's urging, in East Northfield, Maine (1895–1902), was marked by strong public response and spiritual blessing. Scofield was an imposing figure, godly in demeanor and personable. In an age of spiritual decline and modernism he was a faithful herald of foundational evangelical theology. He despised theological compromise, saying, "I would rather spend Sunday morning in a saloon than sitting in a church under the preaching of a modern Higher Critic." Before the Sea Cliff Conference of 1906 he wrote, "God help us to meet the seriousness of the days in which we live, with an apostate church, an undernourished body, a lost world, and an impending advent as our environment." From 1902 to 1907 he returned to the Dallas church, which freed him to write and teach.

As impressive as his pulpit ministry was, Scofield's greatest impact came through his writings. In 1885 he issued *Rightly Dividing the Word of Truth.* This set the direction for his teaching and, through numerous editions, the agenda for a major segment of American fundamentalism. Two publications reinforced this basic work. *The Comprehensive Bible Correspondence Course* issued first in 1896 supplied a curricular base for churches and Bible schools. However, *The Scofield Reference Bible* was his most important work. Nine years were devoted to this project prior to publication by Oxford University Press in 1909, and over two million have been sold. The seven consulting editors agreed on a plan for the work. The text was to be the AV, but "passages which . . . miss the meaning will be amended." Believing the Bible to be a "self-interpreting book," he provided a "new system of reference" to assist the scholar. Definitions on "the great pivotal words of scripture," such as atonement, justification, sanctification, kingdom, and church, were to be given. The outline of each book was to appear in the text along with dispensational divisions. Fulfilled and unfulfilled prophecies, types, and important themes were to be indicated and discussed in footnotes. Scofield did a revision in 1917 at which time Ussher's dates were added.

In 1967 a committee of nine produced *The New Scofield Reference Bible.* The doctrinal system remains the same but the book introductions have been revised, the language updated, the definition of "dispensation" restated, and the early dating by Ussher dropped.

Scofield's system was dispensational, premillennial, and pretribulational. The dispensations, seven in number, were periods of time, each governed by a particular principle. These are innocence, conscience, human government, promise, law, grace, and kingdom. For Scofield the dispensations are seen in the light of God's program of redemption. Contrasting the dispensation of law with that of grace, Scofield says, "The point of testimony is no longer legal obedience as the condition of salvation, but acceptance or rejection of Christ, with good works as the fruit of salvation." The dispensations, says Scofield, show "the majestic, progressive order of the divine dealings of God with humanity, 'the increasing purpose' which runs through and links together the ages, from the beginning of the life of man to the end in eternity." *The New Scofield Reference Bible* allows the dispensations to overlap and is more flexible in interpretation.

Scofield's teaching has received wide acceptance and considerable criticism. Liberal attacks like that of J. W. Bowman are vitriolic and often miss the point. The reply by C. E. Mason shows where the lines are drawn. The Reformed response to dispensationalism is summarized in O. T. Allis, *Prophecy and the Church* (1945).

Scofield's zeal for mission must be noted. While studying with Brookes he ran a mission for railroaders and mechanics. He enthusiastically promoted world missions and founded the Central American Mission. In an age when denominational missions suffered from liberal malaise, Bible school people in large numbers went into all the world taking Scofield's works with them. Today his teachings form the theological core in Bible schools around the world.

W. N. KERR

See also DISPENSATION, DISPENSATIONALISM; FUNDAMENTALISM.

Bibliography. L. S. Chafer, "Dr. C. I. Scofield," *BS,* Jan. 1943; A. C. Gaebelein, *The History of the Scofield Reference Bible;* C. C. Ryrie, *Dispensationalism Today;* C. G. Trumbull, *The Life Story of C. I. Scofield;* J. W. Bowman, "Dispensationalism," *Int* 10:170–87; C. E. Mason, "A Review of 'Dispensationalism' by John Wick Bowman," *BS* 144:10–20, 102–22.

Scopes Trial (1925). A legal confrontation over the teaching of evolution in a Tennessee high school and one of the turning points in American religious history. The technical side of the trial was simple in the extreme. The state of Tennessee in March 1925 passed a law forbidding the teaching of evolution in its schools. The next month, John T. Scopes, age twenty-four, a biology teacher at Rhea County High School in Dayton, assigned a text that linked mankind with the evolution of vertebrate mammals. Scopes was indicted, tried in July, convicted by a jury that deliberated a total of nine minutes, and given a one-hundred-dollar fine by Judge John Raulston. The conviction was later overturned by the Tennessee Supreme Court on the technical grounds that the jury, rather than the judge, should have set the amount of the fine. Tennessee's antievolution law continued on the books, though not enforced, until 1967.

The real confrontation at Dayton, however, involved the counsel imported into Tennessee for the event—for the prosecution, three-time presidential candidate William Jennings Bryan, who had emerged as the champion of antievolutionary forces after World War I; for the defense, the famous Clarence Darrow, who had only recently defended the Chicago murderers Leopold and Loeb. Bryan seemed to stand for traditional American values—a simple trust in the Bible, a commitment to "simple facts," and a distrust of new "hypotheses"; Darrow for enlightened science, modern thought, and urbane culture.

The trial itself was intensely theatrical. It lasted twelve days, and most of the time was spent arguing whether expert scientific witnesses should be accepted in court. Its climax came on the afternoon of July 20 when the court, recessed to the out-of-doors, allowed Clarence Darrow to call Bryan as a witness for the defense. The questioning of Bryan by Darrow, as prosecutor Arthur Thomas Stewart objected repeatedly, had nothing to do with the trial proper. It had, however, everything to do with the fate of popular evangelicalism in America.

The interrogation rapidly degenerated into nitpicking, as Darrow subjected Bryan to a thorough grilling about the latter's knowledge of the Bible and science. Bryan concluded that the defense had come to Dayton "to cast ridicule on everybody who believes in the Bible. I am perfectly willing," he went on, "that the world shall know that these gentlemen have no other purpose than ridiculing every Christian who believes in the Bible." Darrow replied, "We have the purpose of preventing bigots and ignoramuses from controlling the education of the United States and you know it, and that is all."

Darrow sounded the depths of Bryan's ignorance about the age of the earth, the creation and flood myths of other world religions, the story of Jonah, and the supposedly assured results of modern science. Bryan stuck solidly to his conviction that a simple faith coúld best understand and interpret Scripture. At the end of the one and a half hour exchange Darrow was swarmed by his supporters. Bryan, ironically, was left mostly to himself, for he had alienated the largely fundamentalistic audience when he admitted that the Bible's six days of creation were probably not meant to be understood literally.

Those who read the transcript of the trial, and not the distorted play and movie based on it, know that neither Bryan nor Darrow carried the day. Bryan did make something of a fool of himself by trying to speak as an expert on science and biblical interpretation. But Darrow was mean-spirited in his attack. Those who read the major newspapers in New York, Atlanta, Los Angeles, Chicago, and Baltimore received an unfair picture of Bryan and his supporters as downright fools, of Darrow and his allies as paragons of enlightenment. H. L. Mencken, in dispatches to the *New York Times* and his own *Baltimore Sun,* was an extreme example of prejudice. He called the Tennessee residents "Babbitts," "peasants," "yokels," "morons," and "hillbillies" before threats of violence induced him to flee Dayton. When Bryan died in his sleep the Sunday after the trial closed, Mencken expressed the glee of many by chortling, "We killed the son-of-a-bitch."

The Scopes Trial had a major impact on American religious life. It gave fundamentalists a reputation for cultural backwardness that lingers to the present. It solidified the issue of evolution as a focus for concern among theological conservatives. And, although the reality may have been different, it fixed in the popular mind a sharp distinction between rural, evangelical, traditional America and an urban, educated, and secular counterpart.

M. A. NOLL

See also EVOLUTION; FUNDAMENTALISM.

Bibliography. P. E. Coletta, *William Jennings Bryan: Political Puritan, 1915–1925,* III; R. Ginger, *Six Days or Forever? Tennessee v. John Thomas Scopes;* G. M. Marsden, *Fundamentalism and American Culture.*

Scots Confession (1560). The first confession of faith of the Reformed Church of Scotland. It was drawn up in four days by six Scottish Reformers—Knox, Spottiswood, Willock, Row, Douglas, and Winram, each of whom bore the Christian name of John. Knox undoubtedly played the predominant role in this preparation. The Scottish Parliament adopted the confession in 1560 with little opposition. Queen Mary, who still resided in France, refused to ratify the decision, with the result that it did not become the official confession until 1567, when Parliament reenacted it after her deposition. The Scots Confession remained the official confession of the Scottish Reformed Church until it adopted the Westminster Confession of Faith in 1647.

The theology of the Scots Confession is Calvinistic and in general agreement with other creeds of the Reformed churches. In formulating the confession, Knox and his colleagues took into account the thinking and statements of a number of Reformers, e.g., Calvin's *Institutes,* John à Lasco's *Compendium,* and Valerian Poullain's *Liturgia Sacra.* It does not, however, merely restate what the Reformers on the continent had said, but has some of its own special characteristics. Though the Scots Confession lacks the systematic thoroughness of the larger Westminster Confession, it is a fresh document that bears witness to the living faith of the Scottish reformation.

The Scots Confession contains twenty-five articles of which twelve treat the basic doctrines of the Christian faith: God and Trinity; the creation and fall of humanity and the promises of redemption; the incarnation; the passion, resurrection, and ascension of Christ, and his return to judge the earth; atonement through the death of Christ; and sanctification through the Holy Ghost. Though traces of Calvinist emphases are noticeable in these articles, Reformed distinctives arise elsewhere. Justification by faith is assumed; the doctrine of election is affirmed; Christ's spiritual presence in the Lord's Supper is emphasized, while transubstantiation and the view that the elements are bare signs are condemned. The "Kirk" is defined as "catholic"; it consists of the elect, and outside of it there is no salvation. The marks of the true kirk on earth are the true preaching of the word and the right administration of the sacraments and of discipline. Civil magistrates are stated to be lieutenants of God, whose duty it is to conserve and purge the church when necessary; but supreme authority is ascribed to the word of God.

R. KYLE

See also CONFESSIONS OF FAITH; KNOX, JOHN; WESTMINSTER CONFESSION OF FAITH.

Bibliography. G. D. Henderson, ed., *The Scots Confession 1560;* P. Schaff, *The Creeds of Christendom,* III, 479–85; J. H. S. Burleigh, *A Church History of Scotland;* K. Barth, *The Knowledge of God and the Service of God According to the Teaching of the Reformation.*

Scottish Realism. A popular movement in eighteenth and nineteenth century Britain, which attempted to overcome the epistemological, metaphysical, and moral skepticism of the Enlightenment philosophy of David Hume (1711–76) with a philosophy of common sense and natural realism. The founder of Scottish Realism was a moderate (as opposed to evangelical) Presbyterian clergyman, Thomas Reid (1710–96), born in Strachan, Kincardineshire, and educated at Marischal College. He became professor at King's College, Aberdeen, in 1751. Reid was disturbed by studying Hume's *Treatise of Human Nature* (1739), which he thought denied the objective reality of external objects, the principle of causation, and the unity of the mind. In answer, Reid wrote *An Inquiry into the Human Mind on the Principles of Common Sense* in 1764, and the same year was appointed professor in Glasgow. In 1785, he wrote *Essays on the Intellectual Powers of Man,* and in 1788, *Essays on the Active Powers of Man.*

Reid traced Hume's skepticism to what he considered a common fallacy in the great philosophers Descartes, Locke, and Berkeley: representational idealism, which postulates that "the mind knows not things immediately, but only by the intervention of the ideas it has of them" (*Essay on Intellectual Powers,* IV,4,3). That is, ideas are an intermediary between the mind and things, which prevents direct knowledge of the actual things, so that we do not immediately know the external reality in itself, but only the idea (or representation or impression) that it causes in us.

On the contrary, the human mind, argued Reid, perceives external objects directly through intuitive knowledge. We know reality, not by a "conjunction" of separated sense experiences, but by immediate "judgments of nature," which we make because our mind is constituted by God to know reality directly. These "original and natural judgements" (by which we know real objects) "make up what is called *the common sense of mankind;* and what is manifestly contrary to any of those first principles is what we call *absurd*" (*Inquiry,* VII,4). These first principles, of course, cannot and need not be proved: they are "self-evident" to the common experience of mankind. Among these principles are the existence of external objects, cause and effect, and the obligations of morality. Any philosophy that denies these commonly accepted principles on which all men must base their lives is of necessity defective.

Dugald Stewart (1753–1828), professor at Edinburgh and a distinguished successor of Reid, laid more stress on observation and inductive reasoning, and subscribed to an empiricist approach to psychology. Stewart's successor, Thomas Brown, moved even further in an empiricist direction, and is considered a bridge between Scottish Realism and the empiricism of J. S. Mill. Sir William Hamilton (1791–1856), Edinburgh professor, attempted the impossible task of uniting the epistemologies of Reid and Kant (who tried to meet the skepticism of Hume in an entirely different way, by asserting that unity and structure are imposed upon the phenomena of sensation by forms in the mind). J. S. Mill's *Examination of Sir William Hamilton's Philosophy* administered an empiricist death blow to Scottish Realism. Empiricism in Britain and idealism in Germany drove realism from the field.

The Scottish philosophy, however, had wide and profound effects. Royer-Collard, Cousin, and Jouffroy gave it wide circulation in early nineteenth century France. Sydney Ahlstrom has shown that it exercised supreme influence over American theological thought in the nineteenth century. While it has long been recognized that the conservative Calvinist theologians of Princeton adopted Scottish Realist epistemology wholesale, Ahlstrom demonstrates a less noted fact: moderate Calvinists of Andover, liberals of Yale, and Unitarians of Harvard were also deeply indebted to the same commonsense realism. Thus it provided the epistemological structure utilized by both "liberals" and "conservatives" in nineteenth century America. D. F. Kelly

See also Hume, David; Princeton Theology, Old.

Bibliography. T. Reid, *Works,* ed. W. Hamilton, 2 vols., *Essays on the Intellectual Powers of Man,* ed. A. D. Woozley, and *Philosophical Orations,* ed. W. R. Humphries; S. E. Ahlstrom, "The Scottish Philosophy and American Theology," *CH* 24:257–72; S. Grave, *The Scottish Philosophy of Common Sense;* R. Metz, *A Hundred Years of British Philosophy,* ch. 1; J. McCosh, *The Scottish Philosophy;* A. Seth, *Scottish Philosophy;* J. S. Mill, *Collected Works,* IX.

Scripture. The rendering of *graphē,* a Greek term occurring in the NT in reference to the canonical OT literature. Its plural form denotes the entire collection of such compositions (Matt. 21:42; I Cor. 15:3–4), but when used in the singular, *graphē* can mean either a specified passage (Mark 12:10) or the constituent body of writings (Gal. 3:22). The (Holy) Scriptures were referred to by the term *hiera grammata* on one occasion (II Tim. 3:15), while in the Pauline literature the word *gramma* ("writing") refers consistently to the Hebrew Torah or law. The content of a particular verse, or group of verses, is sometimes described as *to gegrammenon* (Luke 20:17; II Cor. 4:13). The term "book" can describe a single composition (Jer. 25:13; Nah. 1:1; Luke 4:17), while the plural could indicate a collection of prophetic oracles (Dan. 9:2; II Tim. 4:13), both forms being used as a general designation of Scripture. The divine author of this material is the Holy Spirit (Acts 28:25), and the writings that are the result of divine revelation and communication to the various biblical authors are said to be inspired (*theopneustos,* II Tim. 3:16). Though grammatically passive, this term is dynamic in nature, meaning literally "God-breathed" in an outward rather than an inward direction. God has "breathed out" Scripture as a function of his creative activity, making the revealed word of God authoritative for human salvation and instruction in divine truth. R. K. Harrison

See also Bible.

Bibliography. E. J. Young, *Thy Word Is Truth;* R. Mayer, *NIDNTT,* III, 482–97.

Scripture, Authority of. *See* Bible, Authority of.

Second Advent of Christ. *See* Second Coming of Christ.

Secondary Separation. *See* Separation.

Second Chance. Another chance after death to profess Christ. Some theologians (Marcion and Origen in the ancient church, Schleiermacher, Dorner, Godet, and others in more recent times) have argued that some (or all) who die unsaved will have a second chance. The Jehovah's Witnesses also maintain this view. Chief arguments for it: (1) general considerations about divine love and justice; (2) the position (defended by texts like John 3:18, 36) that conscious, deliberate unbelief in Jesus is the only legitimate ground for condemnation; therefore, those at least who have never heard of Christ or who have not seriously considered him ought to have another chance;

(3) texts like Matt. 12:32; I Pet. 3:19; 4:6 taken to teach a probation after death.

This view is rejected by all orthodox Protestant churches. The mainstream of Protestant theology urges that death is the *end* of man's probation and that the spiritual condition of man after death is fixed, not fluid (Luke 16:19–31; John 8:24; Heb. 9:27). God's judgment is based upon deeds done in the body, i.e., on earth (Matt. 7:22–23; 10:32–33; 25:34ff.; II Cor. 5:9–11; Gal. 6:7–8; II Thess. 1:8). The idea of a second chance is inconsistent with the urgent call in Scripture to repentance and obedience *now* (II Cor. 6:2; Heb. 3:7–19; 12:25–29).

In reply to these arguments in favor of a second probation: (1) God owes man nothing; he has already given to us a fair probation (in Adam); that any of us has opportunity to hear the gospel is an extraordinary divine kindness. (2) John 3:18 and similar passages teach that Jesus is the only way to salvation, but not that disbelief in him is the only ground for condemnation; we are condemned by all of our sin, including our corporate sin in Adam (Rom. 3:23; 5:12–17; 6:23). (3) These texts are far too difficult and isolated to provide an adequate basis for so significant a hypothesis. Further, on any responsible interpretation, they do not teach a second probation. Matt. 12:32 does not say that any sins will be forgiven after death, only that some will *not* be. First Pet. 3:19 has been understood in different ways: (1) Jesus' preaching the gospel to OT saints; (2) Jesus' proclaiming judgment to dead unbelievers (common among Lutheran interpreters); (3) Jesus' proclaiming his triumph to fallen angels (a common interpretation among contemporary scholars, based on parallels with the Book of Enoch); (4) Jesus' preaching through Noah to those living before the flood (cf. 1:11; Eph. 2:17—Augustine, Beza, some Reformed). *None* of these interpretations permits the conclusion that a second chance is given to the dead in general. First Pet. 4:6 probably refers to the preaching of the gospel in this world to people subsequently martyred for the name of Christ.

J. M. Frame

Bibliography. L. Berkhof, *Systematic Theology;* L. Boettner, *Immortality;* W. J. Dalton, *Christ's Proclamation to the Spirits;* B. Reicke, *The Disobedient Spirits and Christian Baptism.*

Second Coming of Christ. The doctrine that Jesus Christ, who left earth and ascended to the father, will one day again return to earth.

The Fact of the Second Coming. This belief is based upon several portions of Scripture. Jesus himself in his great discourse on last things (Matt. 24 and 25) spoke of his return, both in parables and in more direct teaching. He promised the disciples that he was going to prepare a place for his followers and would one day come again to receive them to himself, that they might be together forever (John 14:3). The angels at the time of the ascension told the disciples that the Lord would come again in the same manner in which he had gone away (Acts 1:11). The return of Christ was part of the kerygma (3:21). It is mentioned in Paul's writings, especially the letters to the Thessalonians (I: 2:19; 3:13; 4:15–17; II: 1:7). Other references include I Cor. 15:23; Phil. 3:20; Col. 3:4; II Tim. 4:8; Titus 2:13; Heb. 9:28.

The second coming is a topic of progressive revelation. While there are allusions in the OT to the second coming, they are not clear and explicit, and consequently the Jewish rabbis found the messianic references apparently contradictory. On the one hand, they seemed to depict the coming of the Messiah as triumphant and powerful. On the other hand, this Messiah appeared as the suffering servant (Isa. 53, etc.). What were actually two comings had been collapsed into one through the foreshortening effect of the time perspective. Only in the NT is the revelation clear enough for the two to be distinguished in large part because the first had already occurred. Yet even here, the references to the second coming are often found within genres that are not completely clear, making interpretation difficult.

If the fact of the second coming is clearly revealed in Scripture, the time of it certainly is not. Jesus himself confessed that even he, during the period of his earthly incarnation, did not know the time of his return. This was not even known by the angels, but only by the Father in heaven (Matt. 24:36). At no point do the prophecies give any specific dating for the return of Christ, although there are indications of signs to be watched for. In response to an inquiry from his disciples as to whether he would at that time restore the kingdom to Israel, Jesus seemed to indicate in a more general way that this information about times and seasons was not for his disciples to know (Acts 1:6–7).

The Nature of the Second Coming. The second coming will be personal and bodily. Some maintain that the coming of Christ was fulfilled by the promised coming of the Holy Spirit at Pentecost. On those grounds, when Jesus said, "We will come to him" (John 14:23), he was referring to a presence that would be mediated by the Holy Spirit. Others see Jesus' statement in Matt. 16:28 as being fulfilled at his resurrection. Others generalize the reference somewhat, maintaining that Jesus' statement, "I am with you always, even to the end of the age," gives us the sense in which the coming of Christ is fulfilled. Another reference cited is Rev. 3:20, where Jesus says, "Behold, I stand at the door and knock. If anyone hears my voice and opens the door, I will come in to him and eat with him and he with me." This would make the second coming of Christ virtually equivalent to conversion. Yet a different twist is given by the Jehovah's Witnesses, who teach that Jesus has already returned, in 1914, but not visibly. Rather, he began to reign on his heavenly throne.

There seems little doubt, however, upon examining the biblical data, that Jesus' return will be personal and bodily, and thus perceivable and unmistakable. This is seen in the circumstances attaching to it in the predictions of the second coming. Jesus seemed to suggest that his coming would be spectacularly visible and unmistakable, when he warned against those who would say that he was present "in the wilderness" or "in the inner rooms." They were not to be believed, for "as the lightning comes from the east and shines as far as the west, so will be the coming of the Son of Man" (Matt. 24:26–27). The Son of man would be seen "coming on the clouds of heaven, with power and great glory" (vs. 30). Paul's description of the second coming includes similarly unmistakable circumstances: "For the Lord himself will descend from heaven, with a cry of command, with the archangel's call and with the sound of the trumpet of God. And the dead in Christ will rise first" (I Thess. 4:16). Finally, the two men dressed in white (angels?) at the ascension said, "This same Jesus, who was taken from you into heaven, will come in the same way as you saw him go into heaven" (Acts 1:11). Since this ascension was bodily, personal, and visible, it seems reasonable to assume that the return will be similar.

Terms for the Second Coming. Several NT terms represent the event.

Parousia. The most frequently used term is parousia, literally, "being by." It means "presence, coming, or arrival." It is used in I Thess. 4:15 to designate his coming to raise the righteous dead and catch believers up to be with him. This coming will also result in the destruction of the man of lawlessness, the antichrist (II Thess. 2:8). It will not be a secret event; it will be a glorious outshining. Paul prays for God to strengthen the hearts of the believers, so that they may be "unblamable in holiness before God and Father, at the coming of our Lord Jesus with all his saints" (I Thess. 3:13).

Apocalypse. This word means, literally, "revelation." Paul speaks of waiting for "the revealing of our Lord Jesus Christ" (I Cor. 1:7). It appears from II Thess. 1:6–7 and I Pet. 4:13 that this will be a time of relief from great trial and will produce great rejoicing on the part of believers.

Epiphany. This word means "manifestation." This will be a coming of Christ at the end of the tribulation. It will involve judgment upon the world and slaying of the man of lawlessness. Believers place their hope in this and keep the commandments of Christ, waiting for the rewards to be received at that time (I Tim. 6:14; II Tim. 4:8). It is the completion of their salvation (Titus 2:13–14).

The Purpose of the Second Coming. The purpose of Christ's second coming is the establishment, in the fullest sense, of the kingdom of God. The kingdom does not primarily mean a realm, characterized by a geographically bound domain, so much as it means reign. Wherever Christ reigns in the hearts of people, there is the kingdom. It is both present and future. In one very real sense, it came with the coming of Christ the first time. In another sense, however, it is yet future. Although Christ was a king when he came the first time, relatively very few accepted him as that. The time is coming when "every knee should bow, and every tongue confess that Jesus Christ is Lord, to the glory of God the Father" (Phil. 2:10–11). That will involve joyous celebration by Christians, but also reluctant submission by unbelievers. Even the devil, the beast, and the false prophet will be thrown into the lake of fire (Rev. 20:10). It is significant that in his great message on the last things, in Matt. 24 and 25, Jesus refers to himself as the Son of man until he comes to 25:34. Having said that the Son of man will come in his glory, and his angels with him, and will sit on his throne, he then begins to refer to himself in vs. 34 as the King. He again uses the expression "the King" in vs. 40. He does not again use the term Son of man of himself until he returns to the discussion of the past and immediate future, in 26:2: "After two days the Passover is coming, and the Son of man will be delivered up to be crucified." Thus the setting of the second coming is one in which the kingdom is prominent, for it is the fulfillment of the kingdom.

Preparation for the Second Coming. It is apparent, particularly from Jesus' teaching about the second coming, that it has great practical import. For Jesus did not simply affirm the event as something about to occur. He also emphasized the appropriate behavior in the light of this fact. Many of Jesus' parables were associated with this great fact. Three responses are particularly related to this impending event.

Watchfulness is urged. Because no one knows the time of Jesus' coming, it is essential that one be alert to the possibility at any time (Matt.

24:42). He will come at an hour that one is not expecting (vs. 44). The wicked servant who assumed that it will be a long time until the master's return did not conduct himself appropriately (vss. 45–51).

If watching is to protect one against the error of assuming that the second will be a long time off, waiting is the precaution against the opposite error, believing that it must necessarily be soon. So the five foolish virgins apparently were not prepared for a long wait (Matt. 25:1–13). They then fell asleep. When the bridegroom finally came, their supply of oil was depleted. While they went out and bought oil, the bridegroom came and entered, and they were left out. Peter tells of scoffers who in the last days, because such a long time has elapsed, will say, "Where is the promise of his coming? For ever since the fathers fell asleep, all things have continued as they were from the beginning of creation" (II Pet. 3:3–4). Thus, it is necessary, not only to be watchful, but to sustain that watchfulness in the face of apparently negative indications.

Finally, the follower of the Lord is to be *working* in view of the certain fact of his return. The parable of the talents (Matt. 25:14–30) makes this especially clear. The master gave five talents to one servant, two to another, one to a third. The first two servants put to work what had been entrusted to them, thus doubling these resources, but the third merely hid away what he had received, preserving but not increasing it. When the master returned after a long time, he spoke words of commendation to the first two servants and gave them even greater responsibility. He rebuked and punished the wicked servant, however, terming him lazy. It is clear that watchful waiting is not to be idleness. Paul's words to the Thessalonians (II Thess. 3:6–13) underscore this.

While it is clear that we have not been told, and thus will not know, the time of the Lord's return in an absolute sense, there are some indicators in Scripture that may enable us to ask about the relative time, that is, when it will occur in relation to two other important future events.

Millennial Views. These deal with the question of the relationship of Christ's return to the thousand-year period of which John writes in Rev. 20:4–6.

Amillennialism. This view does not expect any earthly reign of Christ between his return and the final judgment. It maintains that the thousand years is symbolic, either of the completeness of Christ's reign when he returns, or of the condition of believers during the intermediate state between death and resurrection. Amillennialists note that the thousand years is mentioned only in one passage, and that in a highly symbolical book.

Postmillennialism. This is the view that through the successful preaching of the gospel, the reign of God will gradually become complete upon earth, evil will cease, and peace will come. At the end of this period, which is not necessarily exactly a thousand years, Christ will return. The parables such as the mustard seed and the leaven, which depict the kingdom as growing progressively larger, are cited by this view.

Premillennialism. This holds that Christ will return at the beginning of the millennium and will resurrect dead believers; they, together with believers still alive at Christ's coming, will reign with him on earth. At the end of this period of time there will be a brief flareup of evil, followed by the resurrection of unbelievers, and the final judgment. This view rests heavily upon the contention that the two resurrections in Rev. 20, being described in identical fashion, must both be bodily; and upon OT passages such as the lion and the lamb lying down together, which must occur within this period.

Tribulational Views. These relate the time of the second coming to the great tribulation of Matt. 24.

Pretribulationism. This holds that Christ will come for the saints to remove them from the world (the rapture) before the seven years of tribulation, returning with the saints at the end of the tribulation.

Posttribulationism. This teaches that the church will not be removed from the world, but will go through the tribulation, although preserved within it.

Midtribulationism. The church will go through the first three and a half years (the tribulation) but will be removed before the great tribulation (or wrath of God).

Other Issues. *The Second Coming—One Phase or Two?* Some theologians, especially dispensationalists, see two phases or stages to the second coming. The first, basically a secret coming, is to remove the church before the tribulation. The second phase, at the end of the tribulation, is Christ's triumphant return to set up his earthly millennial kingdom. They base this upon a distinction among parousia, epiphany, and apocalypse. Others find this distinction artificial and believe there will be simply one return, at the end of the tribulation.

Imminence of the Second Coming. Some teach that the second coming could occur at any moment. No additional prophecies remain to be fulfilled. They believe that the injunctions, "Watch, you do not know the time," require this.

Others speak of imminence in a more general way. They note that at the time Jesus spoke the words they could not mean that he could come at any time, since certain events, such as the aging and infirmity of Peter (John 21:18), the fall of Jerusalem, and destruction of the temple, had to occur first. They argue that if the words could not denote any-moment imminency when spoken, they do not require that meaning now. Thus, the second coming may be very near, but certain events, such as the tribulation (which may not require a full seven calendar years), would have to occur first.

Conclusion. The doctrine of the second coming sometimes is made a topic of quarreling among Christians. It is instead, as Paul indicated, an encouragement to hope and comfort (I Thess. 4:18).

M. J. Erickson

See also Judgment; Judgment of the Nations, The; Judgment Seat; Marriage Feast of the Lamb; Millennium, Views of the; Rapture of the Church; Resurrection of the Dead; Tribulation.

Bibliography. G. C. Berkouwer, *The Return of Christ;* R. G. Clouse, ed., *The Meaning of the Millennium;* A. A. Hoekema, *The Bible and the Future;* G. E. Ladd, *Crucial Questions About the Kingdom of God* and *The Blessed Hope;* S. Travis, *I Believe in the Second Coming of Jesus;* D. Pentecost, *Things to Come;* R. Pache, *The Return of Jesus Christ;* A. Reese, *The Coming Advent of Christ.*

Second Death, The. *See* Death, The Second.

Second Great Awakening. *See* Great Awakenings, The.

Sect, Sectarianism (Lat. *secta,* "party, school, faction," perhaps deriving from the past participle either of *secare,* "to cut, to separate," or of *sequi,* "to follow"). A group whose identity partially consists of belonging to a larger social body, typically a religious body. The sect's identity is further derived from its principal leader or from a distinctive teaching or practice. The term has regularly been applied to groups that break away from existing religious bodies, such as the early Christians who separated from Judaism or the Protestants who separated from Roman Catholicism. The term has also been applied to such groups as maintain their identity without separating from the larger religious body, for example, the Pharisees among the Jews or the Puritans in the Church of England. In the broadest sense even an unorganized popular religious movement can be called a sect. Occasionally some condemnation or criticism of the group so named may be implied.

"Sectarianism" in a narrow sense denotes zeal for, or attachment to, a sect. Likewise, it connotes an excessively zealous and doctrinaire narrow-mindedness that would quickly judge and condemn those who disagree. In a broader sense, however, "sectarianism" denotes the historical process by which all the divisions in major world religions have come about. In the history of Christianity, for example, sectarianism is a prevalent theme from the Judaizers and Nicolaitans of the NT to the many new denominations emerging in recent times.

Sociologists of religion have appropriated the term "sect" as a label for a specific type of religious movement. In the typology of religious movements that has developed from the pioneering work of Ernst Troeltsch, the sect is a formally organized religious body that arises in protest against and competition with the pervasive religion of a society. The pervasive religion, whether Jewish, Islamic, or Christian, is classified as a "church" or "denomination." The pervasive religion is highly organized and deeply integrated into the society's social and economic structure, but it makes few demands on members for active participation or personal commitment. The sect, however, demands a high degree of participation and a suitable display of individual loyalty and spiritual commitment. While the church has compromised and accommodated its doctrines and practices to the secular society, the sect rejects all such accommodations or compromises and sets itself against both church and secular society to defend a purer doctrine and practice. Comparative study of the many Christian sects has led scholars to suggest several different categories of sect types such as the conversionist, the adventist, and the gnostic. The organization and government of most sects are more democratic than that of a church or denomination; likewise, the leadership is frequently less experienced and nonprofessional.

The life span of a sect is usually short. Many, but not all, sects gradually lose their sectarian character and acquire the status of a church after a generation or two. Thus, modern Protestant denominations began as sects. Yet, not all sects mature into churches. The so-called established sect manages to avoid accommodation and compromise and keeps its spirit of religious protest and opposition to secular society viable indefinitely.

H. K. Gallatin

See also Cults; Denominationalism.

Bibliography. R. K. Mac Master, *NCE,* XIII, 30–31; T. F. O'Dea, *International Encyclopedia of the Social Sciences,* XIV, 130–36; H. R. Niebuhr, *Encyclopedia of Social Sciences,* XIII, 624–31, and *The Social Sources of Denominationalism;* W. J. Warner, *A Dictionary of the Social Sciences,* 624–25; W. J. Whalen, *NCE,* XIII, 31–34; W. T. Whitley, *HERE,* XI, 315–29; E. Troeltsch, *The Social Teachings of the Christian Churches;* B. R. Wilson, *Sects and Society: A Sociological Study of the*

Elim Tabernacle, Christian Science, and Christadelphians; J. Wilson, *Religion in American Society: The Effective Presence;* J. M. Yinger, *Religion in the Struggle for Power.*

Secular Clergy. Clergy in the Roman Catholic Church not bound by the rules of any particular religious community such as the Society of Jesus or the Benedictines. The secular clergy are more directly supervised by a local bishop, or "ordinary," than are members of a religious community who take on occasion monastic vows and are sometimes confined to a particular monastery.

The word "secular" refers to the world as partially distinct from the sacral, which comes from a transcendent God. The secular clergy are viewed as working quite directly *in* the world, while yet not being *of* the world.

The secular clergy are called to lead a holy life in the world. They should make a daily meditation and be deeply devoted to the Mass and the Holy Eucharist. They must not only be obedient to their local ordinary, but also have a certain degree of reverence toward him. They should stay in their particular diocese or area unless there arises a special reason for them to be elsewhere. They are an essential link in the chain of being comprising the church of God.

T. J. German

Bibliography. M. Ramstein, *A Manual of Canon Law;* C. Dawson, *America and the Secularization of Modern Culture.*

Secularism, Secular Humanism. A way of life and thought that is pursued without reference to God or religion. The Latin root *saeculum* referred to a generation or an age. "Secular" came to mean "belonging to this age, worldly." In general terms, secularism involves an affirmation of immanent, this-worldly realities, along with a denial or exclusion of transcendent, otherworldly realities. It is a world view and life style oriented to the profane rather than the sacred, the natural rather than the supernatural. Secularism is a nonreligious approach to individual and social life.

Historically, "secularization" first referred to the process of transferring property from ecclesiastical jurisdiction to that of the state or other nonecclesiastical authority. In this institutional sense, "secularization" still means the reduction of formal religious authority (e.g., in education). Institutional secularization has been fueled by the breakdown of a unified Christendom since the Reformation, on the one hand, and by the increasing rationalization of society and culture from the Enlightenment to modern technological society, on the other. Some analysts prefer the term "laicization" to describe this institutional secularization of society, that is, the replacement of official religious control by nonecclesiastical authority.

A second sense in which secularization is to be understood has to do with a shift in ways of thinking and living, away from God and toward this world. Renaissance humanism, Enlightenment rationalism, the rising power and influence of science, the breakdown of traditional structures (e.g., the family, the church, the neighborhood), the technicization of society, and the competition offered by nationalism, evolutionism, and Marxism have all contributed to what Max Weber termed the "disenchantment" of the modern world.

While institutional secularization and ideological secularization have proceeded simultaneously over the past few centuries, the relationship between the two is not causally exact or necessary. Thus, even in a medieval, Constantinian setting, formally religious in character, men and women were not immune from having their life, thought, and work shaped by secular, this-worldly considerations. Likewise, in an institutionally secular (laicized) society it is possible for individuals and groups to live, think, and work in ways that are motivated and guided by God and religious considerations.

Secularization, then, is itself a fact of history and a mixed blessing. Secularism, however, as a comprehensive philosophy of life expresses an unqualified enthusiasm for the process of secularization in all spheres of life. Secularism is fatally flawed by its reductionist view of reality, denying and excluding God and the supernatural in a myopic fixation on the immanent and the natural. In contemporary discussion, secularism and humanism are often seen in tandem as secular humanism—an approach to life and thought, individual and society, which glorifies the creature and rejects the Creator. As such, secularism constitutes a rival to Christianity.

Christian theologians and philosophers have grappled in various ways with the meaning and impact of secularization. Friedrich Schleiermacher was the first theologian to attempt a radical restatement of Christianity in terms of the Renaissance and Enlightenment humanist and rationalist motifs. While his efforts were brilliant and extremely influential in the development of theology, critics charged that rather than salvaging Christianity, Schleiermacher betrayed crucial aspects of the faith in his redefinition of religion in terms of the human feeling of dependence.

No contemporary discussion of Christianity and secularism can escape dealing with the provocative *Letters and Papers from Prison* penned by Dietrich Bonhoeffer. Primarily because the work is fragmentary and incomplete, Bonhoeffer's concepts such as "Christian worldliness," "man-come-of-age," the world's arrival at "adulthood," and the need for a "non-religious interpretation of Biblical terminology" have been subject to heated debate about their meaning and implication. Friedrich Gogarten (*The Reality of Faith,* 1959), Paul van Buren (*The Secular Meaning of the Gospel,* 1963), Harvey Cox (*The Secular City,* 1965), Ronald Gregor Smith (*Secular Christianity,* 1966), and the "death-of-God" theologians are examples of those who have pursued one possible course by restating Christianity in terms of a secular world. Kenneth Hamilton (*Life in One's Stride,* 1968) denies that this is the best way to interpret Bonhoeffer and argues that the German theologian never wavered in his basic, orthodox stance.

While discussions among theologians during the 1950s and 1960s tended to focus on adapting Christian theology to secularization, the 1970s and 1980s saw a vigorous new resistance to secularism in many quarters. Jacques Ellul (*The New Demons,* 1975) was among several voices arguing that secularism was itself a form of religion and was antagonistic both to Christianity and to a true Christian humanism. Francis A. Schaeffer (*How Should We Then Live?* 1976) and other fundamentalists and conservative evangelicals attacked secular humanism as the great contemporary enemy of Christian faith.

From the perspective of biblical Christian theology, secularism is guilty for having "exchanged the truth of God for a lie, and worshiped and served the creature rather than the Creator" (Rom. 1:25). Having excluded the transcendent God as the absolute and the object of worship, the secularist inexorably makes the world of man and nature absolute and the object of worship. In biblical terms, the supernatural God has created the world and sustains its existence. This world (the *saeculum*) has value because God has created it, continues to preserve it, and has acted to redeem it. While God is Lord of history and the universe, he is not identifiable with either (pantheism). Men and women exist in freedom and responsibility before God and for the world. Stewardship and partnership define man's relationship to God and the world.

The sacral, theocratic character of ancient Israel is modified with the coming of Christ. With the work of Christ, the city and the nation are secularized (desacralized), and the church as the temple of the Holy Spirit is what is now sacralized. The relationship of the church to the society around it is not defined in terms of a mission to resacralize it by imposing ecclesiastical rule upon it. The relationship is one of loving service and witness, proclamation and healing. In this sense, then, secularization of society is a Christian calling. That is, society must not be divinized or absolutized, but viewed as something historical and relative. Only God is finally sacred and absolute. Reestablishing the sacredness of God will, however, imply the proper, relative valuation of this world.

In no sense, of course, is the distinction between the sacred and the secular an unbridgeable gap. In the same way that God speaks and acts in the *saeculum,* Christians must speak and act creatively and redemptively. This means that the secular world must not be abandoned to secularism. In all cases, Christian life in the secular world is to be carried out under the Lordship of Jesus Christ and in obedience to the will of God rather than the will of the world. And in situations, such as the United States, where the general populace is enfranchised and invited to have a voice in public policy, public education, social services, and so on, Christians may work to ensure that the Word of God is heard and is given room among the many other voices which will constitute the heterogenous whole. To insist that the Word of God be imposed on all without exception is to fall once again into an unbiblical authoritarianism. To fail to articulate the Word of God in the *saeculum,* however, is to acquiesce in a secularism which, by excluding the Creator, can lead only to death. D. W. Gill

See also Death of God Theology; Enlightenment, The; Humanism, Christian; Liberalism, Theological; Situation Ethics.

Bibliography. P. L. Berger, *The Sacred Canopy;* K. Hamilton, *DCE,* 609–10.

Security of the Believer. *See* Perseverance.

Self-Esteem, Self-Love. The estimate that one makes of oneself. Self-love is such an estimate as is self-hate. Kenneth Wuest's translation of Rom. 12:3 encapsulates the biblical viewpoint of self-esteem: "For I am saying through the grace which is given to everyone who is among you, not to be thinking more highly of one's self, beyond that which one ought necessarily to be thinking, but to be thinking with a view to a sensible appraisal [of one's self] according as to each one God divided a measure of faith." To make a sensible appraisal of one's worth is to evaluate oneself according to one's strengths as well as one's weaknesses, one's potential for growth as well as one's vulnerabilities.

Self-love involves an acceptance of oneself,

yet is not complacency. It involves a comfortableness with one's being, but is not devoid of impetus for growth. Arrogance is not true self-love, rather it is a reflection of a low self-estimate. A person who is sure of himself need not say, "I am the best." The insecure declare their greatness. Those with a good self-image simply go on and focus on their task. Trying to prove one's greatness to others is often an effort to prove it to oneself.

On the other hand, humility is not synonymous with low self-esteem. True humility is an absence of occupation with oneself. It implies a good self-image, good enough to realize one's finiteness and to be able to be self-forgetful. In contrast, low self-esteem involves groveling, self-denigration, and self-hate. Low self-esteem is really quite contrary to the biblical view of how a Christian should view himself. Psychologist Rollo May states the unattractiveness of a low self-image quite succinctly and strikingly in *Man's Search for Himself.* In circles where self-contempt is preached, it is of course never explained why a person should be so ill-mannered and inconsiderate as to force his company on other people if he finds it so dreary and deadening himself. And furthermore the multitude of contradictions is never explained in a doctrine which advises that we should hate the one self, "I," and love all others, with the obvious expectation that they will love us, hateful creatures that we are; or that the more we hate ourselves, the more we love God who made the mistake, in an off moment, of creating this contemptible creature, "I."

In essence Christianity is not a theology of self-hate, for there is a vast difference between self-hate and the old nature of Rom. 6. For the Christian the old nature, that which is fallen and judicially condemned by God, has been put away by the blood of Christ. Thus without compromise the Scriptures can command us to love our neighbor as we love ourselves, implying a degree of legitimate self-love. For in such self-love we are praising the work of God in us, a work which according to Romans has established a new nature that is of God. This is the principle of self-love as declared by the Bible. But too often, as practicing Christians, we resemble more closely the description of Rollo May and "hate the one self 'I,' and love all others."

Even within Protestant circles, it is important to differentiate at times between church teaching and biblical theology. At times we are very contradictory about such a topic as self-esteem. We tend to emphasize self-denigration, and yet trust explicitly the literal inspiration of a Bible that teaches God made us in his own image for fellowship with him. Then, because the fall of man could have obliterated that original act, God used his plan of redemption to ensure his purpose.

The Scriptures are full of examples of men of God who dared to experience and express self-love. In Genesis the story of Joseph and his brothers is deeply illustrative of a man who knew he was right and acted accordingly, in spite of the accusations of his brothers. God's appraisal of such behavior is indicated by Joseph's vindication, the accuracy of his God-given visions and their interpretations, his place of earthly authority, and ultimately the recognition by his brothers of their own sin and Joseph's righteousness.

Job is a good example of a man deeply tested by God in his multiple afflictions. Yet once again the purpose was just that—testing, not punishment, and certainly not self-denigration. Job was never to believe he was no good because of his afflictions. It is true that God sometimes corrects us when we are wrong, for example, in his denial of Moses' desire to enter into the promised land, but more often than not God afflicts so that he may do some extraordinary work. As in the case of Job, he will pick the person he can trust the most. He could trust Job more than most men; and then, at the end, God gave him back more than he ever took away. Job would have been remiss had he interpreted his afflictions as a sign of low self-worth, even though his do-gooder friends tried to make him believe that.

Always in the Scriptures there is balance. Paul speaks of his great sin against the church in his early persecutions of Christians. That recognition was not neurotic low self-esteem. It was an honest estimate of himself at that time. Later, however, that same man, with strong self-acceptance and a deep trust in God, does not falter in his authoritative posture with the NT church. Paul was honest in his self-estimate as it related to his fellowman and to God. At no time did he lose a sense of dependence upon God as the source of his worth.

For there are times, too, when we must all fall abjectly before the presence of God. That does not indicate neurotic low self-esteem. Actually such a humble posture before God is a realistic view of our position before him; and the greater a man's sense of self-worth, the easier it will be for him to realize his humbleness before God.

Thus throughout the Scriptures there is the consistency of godly teaching that we are to evaluate ourselves honestly before man and God. God's aim is that we be in his image and have a high sense of self-esteem that is not contrived or phony but real.

E. R. Skoglund

See also Humility; Love.

Bibliography. J. Dobson, *Hide or Seek;* V. E. Frankl, *The Doctor and the Soul;* W. Glasser, *Reality Therapy: A New Approach to Psychiatry;* C. S. Lewis, *The Weight of Glory;* R. May, *Man's Search for Himself;* E. R. Skoglund, *Loving Begins with Me;* P. Tournier, *Guilt and Grace;* W. Trobisch, *Love Yourself.*

Self-Examination. The scrutiny of one's inner self to determine his spiritual status, motives, and attitudes is largely a NT teaching. In the OT the searching of innermost thoughts and intents was primarily the responsibility of the Almighty (Exod. 20:20; Deut. 8:2, 16; 13:3; Ps. 26:2; which thought is repeated in I Thess. 2:4). The believer is "to examine himself" (*dokimazō*) to make sure he is in proper relationship to God and to man so that he may partake of the Lord's Supper (I Cor. 11:28). The same verb is translated "to prove" ten times and is rendered "to try" four times, such as: "proving what is acceptable to the Lord" (Eph. 5:10), proving one's work (Gal. 6:4), and proving all things (I Thess. 5:21).

Likewise the Christian is taught "to judge" (*diakrinō*) himself lest he be judged (I Cor. 11:31–32). In thus judging himself and accepting the correction (chastening) of the Almighty he is not under condemnation. Self-judgment leads to confession and forgiveness.

In borderline practices allowed by some Christians and disallowed by others, the believer is not "to judge" (*krinō*) his fellow believer; rather, he is to examine himself lest he be a stumbling block (Rom. 14:13). Because one can "believe in vain" (I Cor. 15:2), and thus not have a faith that is "unfeigned" (I Tim. 1:5; II Tim. 1:5), the Christian is "to examine" (*peirazō*) himself whether he be in the faith (II Cor. 13:5). Thus by careful, prayerful, self-examination he is to prove himself that the Savior dwells within.

The lukewarm Christian is counseled to judge himself so as to realize his backslidden condition and to prove what values are true and everlasting (Rev. 3:18). The purpose of self-examination is always positive—to know oneself, one's weaknesses and frailties, so as to appropriate the grace of God in Christ. Self-examination is a stimulus to faith and holy living (Heb. 12:1–2; I Pet. 2:21–23). It is not morbid introspection for "if our heart condemn us, God is greater than our heart, and knoweth all things" (I John 3:20).

V. R. Edman

Self-Existence of God. *See* God, Attributes of.

Self-Righteousness. The concept of a personally developed ethic as one's standard for salvation. However, once the term "righteousness," in relation to God, is properly understood to imply a faithfulness to his covenantal relationship, "self-righteousness" is revealed to be a dramatic misstatement of biblical principles.

While this concept can be viewed positively as an individual's attempt to establish a moralistic life style, the accompanying attitude usually associated with such an attempt involves one's vain estimate of self-worth before God. This usually leads to a rejection of Christ's saving work as well.

It is only God himself who may lay claim to this term. For, as related to the Hebrew *sedeq,* God is found to be righteous intrinsically. Thus, all other members of the created order can be so designated only in proper relationship to his judgment, and not by their own.

In Judaism, self-righteousness could be understood as a necessary evaluation of one's "balance," with regard to merit accumulated through good works as opposed to one's inherited sinfulness. A Jew's conformity to the Torah, plus his active development of his *yēṣer haṭṭôb* (good impulse) and restraint of his *yēṣer hāra'* (evil impulse), would be the standards by which he could judge his own righteousness.

However, this is precisely the type of righteousness, coveted by the Pharisees, which Jesus rejects in contrast to the righteousness of the kingdom (Matt. 5:20ff.; 6:33ff.; cf. Luke 18:9ff.). The shocking news of the gospel is that God had declared man righteous only in Christ. Thus any attitude of self-righteousness is excluded (Eph. 2:9) and categorically condemned (Matt. 6:1ff.). Righteousness is shown to be impossible as man's own accomplishment but has become a gracious gift to man because of Christ's accomplishment.

S. E. McClelland

Bibliography. F. F. Bruce, *Paul: Apostle of the Heart Set Free;* W. C. Kaiser, *Toward an OT Theology;* G. Schrenk, *TDNT,* II, 192–210; G. E. Ladd, *A Theology of the NT.*

Semi-Arianism. The doctrine of Christ's sonship as held by fourth century theologians who were reluctant to accept either the strict Nicene definition or the extreme Arian position. After the Council of Nicaea (A.D. 325) a single term came to identify each position. Orthodox theologians, led by Athanasius, used the term *homoousios* to express the doctrine that Christ, the Logos, was "of one substance" with the eternal Father. The Arian party held that Christ was a created being, in substance unlike the Father. The term for this view was *anomoios.* Semi-Arians, the third group, avoided either extreme and adopted the term *homoiousios,* which defined Christ as "of like substance" with the Father, but left vague the extent to which Christ differed from other created beings. Semi-Arians called Christ "Divine," but in effect denied that he is truly God, that he is "equal to the Father as touching his Godhead."

Some students of the controversy have argued that the term "Semi-Arianism" is an unfair term, associating the movement too closely with Arianism, and that "Semi-Nicene" might better represent the movement's tendency toward orthodoxy. The term "Anti-Nicene" has been used as often, however, because Semi-Arians did, in fact, deny that Christ was fully one with the Father.

The Semi-Arian position arose at the Council of Nicaea, called by Emperor Constantine to deal with the Arian question, which had raised enough controversy to threaten the unity of the church. All but two of the bishops present at the council signed the orthodox statement, though many did so with reservations. Semi-Arians also came to be called "Eusebians" after Eusebius, bishop of Nicomedia and later patriarch of Constantinople. As a young man Eusebius had studied with Arius. Though he signed the creed at the Council of Nicaea, he later became a key leader in the reaction against it.

The most prominent leader of the Semi-Arians at the Council, however, was Eusebius, bishop of Caesarea, the early church historian. Following the council the Semi-Arian position remained prominent, but a resurgence of the Old Arians, seeking to reinstate the original heresy, led to the disintegration of Semi-Arian support. In August 357, a small but important synod met at Sirmium in Illyricum. The creed that emerged from the synod condemned the term *ousia* in any form and clearly subordinated the Son to the Father. This creed split the opponents of Nicaea so decisively that it turned sentiment in favor of the orthodox view. Many bishops renounced their errors and subscribed to the Nicene Creed. After this point Semi-Arians never existed in significant numbers. Some became Arian and many reaffirmed orthodoxy at the Council of Constantinople in 381.

B. L. Shelley

See also Arianism; Athanasius; Nicaea, Council of.

Bibliography. E. R. Hardy, ed., *Christology of the Later Fathers;* J. N. D. Kelly, *Early Christian Doctrines;* G. L. Prestige, *Fathers and Heretics.*

Semi-Pelagianism. Doctrines, upheld during the period from 427 to 529, that rejected the extreme views both of Pelagius and of Augustine in regards to the priority of divine grace and human will in the initial work of salvation. The label "Semi-Pelagian," however, is a relatively modern expression, which apparently appeared first in the Lutheran *Formula of Concord* (1577), and became associated with the theology of the Jesuit Luis Molina (1535–1600). The term, nevertheless, was not a happy choice, because the so-called Semi-Pelagians wanted to be anything but half-Pelagians. It would be more correct to call them Semi-Augustinians who, while rejecting the doctrines of Pelagius and respecting Augustine, were not willing to follow the ultimate consequences of his theology.

Church councils condemned Pelagianism in 418 and again in 431, but this rejection did not mean the acceptance of everything in the Augustinian system. Augustine's teaching on grace may be summarized as follows: Humanity shared in Adam's sin and therefore has become a *massa damnationis* from which no one can be extricated save by a special gift of divine grace that cannot be merited; yet God in his inscrutable wisdom chooses some to be saved and grants graces that will infallibly but freely lead them to salvation. The number of the elect is set and can be neither increased nor decreased. Nevertheless, Vitalis of Carthage and a community of monks at Hadrumetum, Africa (*ca.* 427), contested these principles, asserting that they destroyed freedom of the will and all moral responsibility. They, in turn, affirmed that the unaided will performed the initial act of faith. In response Augustine produced *Grace and Free Will* and *Rebuke and Grace,* which contain a resume of his arguments against the Semi-Pelagians, and stress the necessary preparation of the will by prevenient grace.

The issue became heated in the fifth century when some monks in southern Gaul, led by John Cassian, Hilary of Arles, Vincent of Lerins, and Faustus of Riez, joined in the controversy. These men objected to a number of points in the Augustinian doctrine of sin and grace, namely, the assertion of the total bondage of the will, of the priority and irresistibility of grace, and of rigid predestination. They agreed with Augustine as to the seriousness of sin, yet they regarded his doctrine of predestination as new, therefore in conflict with tradition and dangerous because it makes all human efforts superfluous. In opposition to Augustinianism, Cassian taught that though a sickness is inherited through Adam's sin, human free will has not been entirely obliterated. Divine grace is indispensable for salvation, but it does not necessarily need to precede a free human choice, because, despite the weakness of human volition, the will takes the initiative toward God. In other words, divine grace and human free will must work together in salvation. In opposition to the stark predestinarianism of Augustine, Cassian held to the doctrine of

God's universal will to save, and that predestination is simply divine foreknowledge.

After Augustine's death, the controversy became more heated; and Prosper of Aquitaine became his champion, replying to the Gallic monks, including Vincent of Lerins. Vincent incorrectly understood Augustine's doctrines of perseverance and predestination to mean that God's elect cannot sin. Nevertheless, he was not entirely wrong in recognizing the practical dangers inherent in Augustine's teaching on grace, and that this teaching deviated from Catholic tradition.

Prosper appealed to Rome on behalf of his master, and though Celestine I praised Augustine, he gave no specific approval to the bishop's teachings on grace and predestination. Hence, Semi-Pelagian beliefs continued to circulate in Gaul with Faustus of Riez as the outstanding spokesman. He condemned the heresy of Pelagianism, teaching instead that natural powers were not sufficient to attain salvation. The free will, while not extinct, was weak and could not be exercised for salvation without the aid of grace. Faustus, however, rejected the predestinarian conception of a divine monergism and taught that human will, by virtue of the freedom left in it, takes the beginning step toward God. Salvation, therefore, is accomplished by the cooperation of human and divine factors, and predestination is merely God's foreknowledge of what a person has freely decided. Grace, to Faustus, meant the divine illumination of human will, and not, as it did to Augustine, the regenerative power of grace in the heart.

The debate about Semi-Pelagianism continued well into the sixth century, when Caesarius of Arles convened the Synod of Orange (529). Here Caesarius succeeded in dogmatizing a number of principles against the Semi-Pelagians. In doing so, however, the synod did not accept Augustine's full doctrine of grace, especially not his concept of divine grace that works irresistibly in the predestinated. In 531, Boniface II approved the acts of this council, thus giving it ecumenical authority. Semi-Pelagianism, as a historical movement, subsequently declined, but the pivotal issue of Semi-Pelagianism—the priority of the human will over the grace of God in the initial work of salvation—did not die out. R. KYLE

Bibliography. P. DeLetter, *Prosper of Aquitaine: Defense of St. Augustine;* N. K. Chadwick, *Poetry and Letters in Early Christian Gaul;* E. Amann, "Semi-Pélagiens," *DTC,* XIV, 1796–1850; L. Duchesne, *l'Église au VI siècle.*

Senses of Scripture. *See* INTERPRETATION OF THE BIBLE.

Sensus Deitatis, Sensus Divinitatis. A term used by Calvin to describe man's innate knowledge of God. Calvin argues that God as creator has revealed himself universally to man both in nature and in the human consciousness. This latter is a constitutional awareness impressed upon the human mind by the creator and takes two forms: conscience and the sense of deity (also called "the seed of religion"). The sense of deity is not merely a capacity for the knowledge of God, nor is it the product of reflection upon natural revelation. It is an immediate intuition of the existence and majesty of the one true God, which, though obscured by human sinfulness, can never be completely eradicated. The effects of this awareness are seen in the universality of religious phenomena and in the slavish fear of God present even in the most infamous of sinners.

The significance of the sense of deity is that man cannot escape God and is therefore held accountable for the revelation given and inexcusable for its rejection. On the other hand, this knowledge will not serve as a foundation for erecting a Christian theology. So universal is the effect of sin that, although God has sown the seed of religion in all men, there are scarcely any who foster its growth and none in whom it comes unaided to fruition. Man's blindness, vanity, and obstinacy combine so that at best he worships not God but a figment and dream of his own heart. D. G. DUNBAR

See also REVELATION, GENERAL.

Bibliography. J. Calvin, *Institutes* 1.3–5; B. A. Demarest, *General Revelation;* E. A. Dowey, Jr., *The Knowledge of God in Calvin's Theology.*

Sentences. An attempt to make the beliefs of the faith partially reasonable within the framework of *Fides quaerens intellectum* (faith seeking to understand). The notion of sentences originated from the writings of the early Christian fathers who wished to explain in a disciplined and authoritative manner the various truths that emanate from the Holy Scriptures as the word of God. The sentences of the medieval period sought to organize more clearly the thoughts of the fathers of the church.

The sentences dealt with both dogma and morals since these two areas of thought were held to be central in both the understanding and execution of faith. There were various forms of sentences dependent upon the choices made by a particular author in relation to the doctrines of Christianity.

Anselm of Laon wrote a very complicated set of sentences in the twelfth century. The famous, or infamous, Abelard wrote a very complex and sophisticated set of sentences. His *Sic et Non* is a classic work concerning affirmative and negative views about dogmatic and moral questions of Christianity. Hugh of St. Victor also wrote an interesting series in the twelfth century, but most experts agree that the sentences of Peter Lombard were the most interesting and unusual of the period.

Most sentences examine the creation of the universe with special emphasis upon man and his free will in relation to original sin. The incarnation of our Lord Jesus Christ is also examined at length with special reference to his influence upon the sacraments as expressions of his grace. God as triune and one is also investigated at length.

Most medieval students studied the sentences assiduously in order to gain their degrees. Students usually considered Peter Lombard to be the master of the sentences. If a student knew the sentences well he was considered to be in possession of the truth concerning theological matters. T. J. GERMAN

See also PETER LOMBARD.

Separation. A reference to the life style of the Christian. Having been redeemed and regenerated by the Lord, the Christian's life is to be different from that of the non-Christian world. Certain actions, attitudes, and thoughts are to be different from what they formerly were and from the conduct of the world. Holiness, not evil, is to be the characteristic feature of the believer's life. As such, separation is the negative aspect of sanctification.

Biblical Teaching. Numerous teachings of Scripture support the idea of separation. The people of Israel were reminded that they were God's chosen people, and that he was a holy God who expected the lives of his people to be similar. They were not to engage in the practices of the ungodly nations around them. Indeed, the most common word for holy is one which means separated, set apart for a particular use, but also set apart from the contaminated things.

In the OT, the people of Israel were to practice separation of life in several ways. They were, for instance, not to engage in the religious practices of the neighboring heathen nations: offering their children as sacrifices, practicing various means of fortune telling, and consulting mediums, witches, and such (Deut. 18:9–14). They were not to intermarry with these nations about them, because of the danger that they would adopt the foreign religious practices. They were also to abstain from eating certain unclean or ceremonially forbidden foods (Lev. 11). Certain objects and persons in certain conditions (e.g., those infected with leprosy) were unclean and were not to be touched (Lev. 12–15).

In the NT, the emphasis is even stronger on the fact that God has called his people to be unique, selected by him as his temple, to be indwelt by him. The emphasis upon this choosing (I Pet. 2:9), upon the Lord (Col. 1:10), upon the calling (Eph. 4:1), is then applied in terms of abstaining from passions of the flesh (I Pet. 2:11), putting off the old nature and the practices of the Gentiles (Eph. 4:17–32) and the evil acts appropriate to the old nature (Col. 3:5). Again and again, the argument is advanced that they are now new creatures, they belong to the Lord, and they have the Holy Spirit dwelling within them. Thus, they should conduct themselves according to this new principle.

There is a conflict between this new nature or life in the spirit and the old nature or flesh still dwelling within the person after regeneration. Paul depicts in vivid terms the struggle, in which he does the evil he does not want to do and does not do the good he wishes to do (Rom. 7:21–25). There are whole lists of activities that are not the fruit of the Spirit, but rather are the works of the flesh (Gal. 5:19–21). These the believer is to shun. Paul even goes so far as to say that those who do such things shall not inherit the kingdom of God.

Some actions cannot be classified right or wrong by so simple a means as consulting a list, however. Here the Spirit-led believer will have to measure them against certain principles: Whether they can be done to the glory of God (I Cor. 10:31); whether they can be done in the name of Christ, on his behalf and invoking his blessing (Col. 3:17); whether this is what Christ would have been likely to do (I John 2:6); whether this will contribute positively to the spiritual welfare of others (I Cor. 10:23–30).

Sometimes separation has been made a matter of external acts, so that lists of forbidden activities were compiled. While separation includes this, it also goes beyond. Jesus extended the law by pointing to the importance of thoughts and attitudes (Matt. 5:17–30). Many of the sins of the flesh that Paul speaks against are not primarily physical or bodily sins but rather are attitudinal or spiritual sins (e.g., strife, jealousy, anger, selfishness, dissension, party spirit, envy). His appeal to believers not to be conformed to the world speaks of the renewing of their *minds* (Rom. 12:1–2). It is the love of money, not the possession of it, that is the root of all evils (I Tim. 6:10). We are not to love the world or the things in the world (I John 2:15). Thus, it is possible to live a life that is very separated in action, but very worldly or unseparated so far as attitudes are concerned. Indeed, this seems to have been precisely the case with the Pharisees (Matt. 23). It is not enough to ask merely what one does or does not do, but why one does it.

Secondary Separation. What one does and thinks oneself with respect to certain wrong and evil matters may be termed primary separation. There is also the question of whether one should separate oneself from others who are not consistently Christian. This is then secondary separation.

There are a number of scriptural injunctions to practice this type of separation. Paul talks about not being mismated with unbelievers (II Cor. 6:14). The believer is to come out from them and be separate and touch nothing unclean (vs. 17). The apostle also speaks of taking note of those who create dissensions and difficulties—who, in other words, are engaged in certain works of the flesh—and having nothing to do with them (Rom. 16:17). He instructed the Corinthian church to drive out the immoral wicked person, who is living in sin, from the church (I Cor. 5:13), delivering him to Satan for the destruction of his flesh (vs. 5). They were to cut themselves off from these people, by practicing church discipline or putting them out of the church. Just how serious a sin calls for such action has been a subject of debate for a long time in the church. Augustine and the Donatists had a major dispute over this matter in the early fifth century. There is always a tension between wanting to preserve the purity of the church and wanting to pursue the restoration of the person to Christ.

It should be noted that in some cases there is what might even be termed tertiary separation: for example, some of those who refuse to cooperate with Billy Graham, not because such a ministry is sinful, or even because they would be thrown into contact with those who do not have sufficiently high standards, but rather because Billy Graham, himself practicing primary separation, is not separated from certain others who do not practice separation in their own lives. Therefore, they must shun Billy Graham, because of those with whom he associates.

Ecclesiastical Separation. What of the situation where the Christian is part of a minority within a church congregation or denomination? Here the believer is unable to have discipline administered, since true and separated Christians are a minority. What then? When should the Christian or a congregation separate from a congregation or church fellowship? Here the issue is one of *ecclesiastical* separation. There are arguments both for and against remaining in the fellowship.

Reasons favoring separation: (1) The Bible clearly states that heresy is not to be tolerated (Gal. 1:8–9; II Tim. 3:5; Titus 3:10–11; I John 4:1ff.; II John 7–11; Rev. 2:14). (2) By remaining in, one shares in the responsibility for it. (3) Remaining in seems to be a tacit endorsement and even recommendation of evil. (4) It is poor stewardship to give one's money to help support Christian ministries that are not unequivocally Christian.

Arguments favoring remaining in the group: (1) By remaining in, one has an opportunity to influence, and perhaps reform, the group and perhaps win it back. Withdrawing writes off the larger group. (2) Separation often leads to additional splitting, fragmenting the body of Christ even further. (3) The church's witness to the world is stronger where it is united, rather than when scandalizing through the inability to function together.

Each believer will have to seek the Holy Spirit's guidance in reaching conclusions for his own convictions. All seem to agree that if one is prohibited from holding beliefs or engaging in practices that the Lord prescribes, or if the gospel is not being preached and cannot be, separation must take place. Those who recommend remaining within the group, however, focus upon the healing ministry, whereas those who advocate separation stress the surgical approach.

While Christians may differ at some points regarding the nature and proper areas of separation, they are agreed that the motivation stems from their belonging to the Lord. In the OT, places, buildings, articles, and days were holy, being set apart for the exclusive use of the Holy God. And in the NT, this God dwells, not in temples made with human hands, but in Christians (I Cor. 3:16; 6:19). And they will desire their lives to be pure and clean, appropriate to his habitation and use.

M. J. Erickson

Separation, Marital. Legal dissolution in whole or in part of a marriage. Some parts of the Christian church have forbidden divorce with right of remarriage (divorce *a vinculo*), although they have recognized legal separation "from bed and board" (*a thoro et mensa*) as permitted in some circumstances of marital breakdown. This was apparently the view of most of the early fathers. The Church of Rome does not recognize divorce, but does allow legal separation without right of remarriage. In the 1603 canon law of the Church of England, regulation is given only for "divorce" in the sense of separation *a thoro et mensa*, and "the parties so separated shall live chastely and continently; neither shall they, during each others' life, contract matrimony with another person." However, had Cranmer's revised canons proposed in 1553 (*Reformatio Legum Ecclesiasticarum*) ever reached the statute book, they would have allowed divorce *a vinculo* for a variety of causes. Different parts of the Church of England have tended to either of these views at different times. The Nonconformist churches, however, and the Eastern Orthodox churches do recognize divorce *a vinculo.*

It is extremely unlikely that legal separation from bed and board without right of remarriage was known to the writers of the OT or the NT. In Deut. 24, the reference is to divorce with (restricted) right of remarriage. The Synoptic divorce material has been variously interpreted. There are those who believe that Jesus is abrogating the Deuteronomic law and is teaching a radically more strict view, namely, all divorce is forbidden, but separation without right of remarriage may be permitted "for the cause of unchastity" (Matt. 19:9). Others believe that Jesus *is* speaking about divorce *a vinculo.* Some also wish to find biblical support for legal separation without remarriage from the teaching of Paul in I Cor. 7:10–11. "To the married I give charge, not I but the Lord, that the wife should not separate from her husband (but if she does, let her remain single or else be reconciled to her husband)—and that the husband should not divorce his wife." The main point of Paul's teaching, here, as in Rom. 7:1–3, is the divine rule for the permanence of marriage, against which all separation and all divorce must be measured as wrong. The concession in I Cor. 7:10 ("but if she does") seems to be more a recognition that the divine ideal is not always kept, and that failure needs to be regulated, rather than a sanction for legal separation without divorce *a vinculo.* D. J. ATKINSON

See also DIVORCE; MARRIAGE, THEOLOGY OF; REMARRIAGE.

Separation of Church and State. *See* CHURCH AND STATE.

Septuagesima (Lat. for "seventieth"). The third Sunday before Lent. Septuagesima, sexagesima, and quinquagesima are the names traditionally assigned in the calendar of the Western Christian church to the three Sundays leading up to Lent. They arise (somewhat inconsistently) from the fact that quinquagesima was literally the fiftieth day before Easter: obviously it has been convenient, though incorrect, to call the preceding Sundays the sixtieth and seventieth respectively; the names are known from the eighth century. The *Book of Common Prayer* in 1662 added the subtitle "or the Third Sunday before Lent."

D. H. WHEATON

See also CHRISTIAN YEAR; LENT.

Bibliography. A. A. McArthur, *The Evolution of the Christian Year.*

Seraph, Seraphim. *See* ANGEL.

Sermon on the Mount. The discourse of Jesus in Matt. 5–7, containing the epitome of his ethical teaching. The shorter but parallel sermon in Luke 6:20–49 is usually known as the Sermon on the Plain, because of a different description of the setting. No other block of Jesus' teaching has enjoyed such wide influence and intense examination. Its uniqueness derives not only from its impact as a whole, but also from the fact that some of its parts have attained classical status on their own.

The sermon has been called anything from essential Christianity to Jesus' manifesto, but it is best seen as the height of Jesus' ethical demands on his disciples occasioned by the nearness of the kingdom. Since Matt. portrays Jesus as seated in rabbinic posture teaching his disciples, the term "sermon" is an unfortunate, though now unavoidable, one.

Contexts of the Sermon. *Matthew.* (1) Structure. The body of Matt. is organized around five discourses of Jesus, each ending with a transitional formula beginning, "When Jesus finished. . . ." The sermon is the first of these discourses, and, coupled with the narrative section which follows in chs. 8–9, forms a characterization of Jesus' early Galilean ministry. Some of the Beatitudes have corresponding woes in ch. 23, whereas in Luke these appear in the sermon itself.

(2) Theology. The sermon meshes well with the theology of Matt. in several respects, especially in parallels with the Pentateuch and emphasis on the kingdom. The initial verse calls to mind early statements in Gen., and as he presents Jesus' preadult life, certain similarities with Moses are quite striking. The sermon is set on a mountain, and Jesus comes to fulfill the law (5:17) and sets himself up as the authoritative interpreter of its true meaning in the antitheses of ch. 5. The kingdom theme combines with that of righteousness in 5:20 and 6:33, but its importance is seen above all in the Beatitudes, which begin and end with a promise of the kingdom, thus indicating that this is their overriding focus.

Synoptic Gospels. Various attempts to place the sermon precisely in Jesus' ministry have proven problematic, but it certainly belongs early. That it bears some relationship to Luke's Sermon on the Plain is evident, especially from the overall agreement in the ordering of parallel material. The greatest difference is the absence in Luke of the Palestinian Jewish or OT background to the sayings and of the whole block of material where Jesus' teaching is set over against some of contemporary Judaism (5:17–6:18). Of the various explanations of the relationship between the two sermons, the most satisfactory one is that they represent two separate teaching occasions reflecting different versions of a discourse Jesus gave on several occasions, but adapted to each situation. This allows for the redactional activity in Matt., but ascribes the basic sermon as it stands to Jesus himself.

NT as a Whole. The position of the sermon on the continuum of NT theology may be seen in light of the commonly perceived extremes—James and Paul. There are more close parallels between the sermon and James than with any other NT writing, and both of them belong in the Wisdom tradition. Because of the widespread belief that Paul and Jesus, in the sermon, taught faith-righteousness versus works-righteousness, the two are often seen as poles apart theologically.

Theological Assessment. *Famous Sections.* Three parts of the sermon have wielded considerable influence in their own right on Christian consciousness and liturgy. The Beatitudes have the kingdom as their primary theme, but they also introduce other of the sermon's emphases. In contrast to their consoling nature in Luke, in Matt. they assume the character of ethical demands, and the focus of the blessings themselves is eschatological. The Matthean version of the Lord's Prayer is poetic with beautiful symmetry and has heavily influenced Christian liturgy. Jesus uses it as an illustration of the need for simplicity in prayer, and some of its words suggest his follow-up principle of reciprocal forgiveness. The Golden Rule (7:12) brings to their apex the sermon's earlier teachings on interpersonal relations. Its interpreters have often stressed Jesus' positive mode of formulating this principle in contrast to the negative way by other great religious teachers. In the context of Jesus' thought as a whole, the Golden Rule is his way of expressing Lev. 19:18*b*, which he elsewhere calls the second great commandment (Matt. 22:39), for he sees both as the epitome of the law and the prophets.

Troublesome Passages. Several of Jesus' precepts are presented in such an absolute form that many interpreters have questioned the sermon's applicability to the average Christian. Tolstoi, on the other hand, while failing to recognize Jesus' use of such techniques as hyperbole, found here maxims the serious person must literally observe. Certainly the person who literally destroys an eye or a hand (5:29–30) has not solved his problem, because he still has another left. Hyperbole here serves to underscore the urgency of radical action to remove the source of a temptation. Jesus' forbidding of judging (7:1) has led some to conclude that a Christian cannot be a judge or serve on a jury; however, he is not giving the word a legal meaning, but is talking about being judgmental in interpersonal relations. The prohibition against swearing (5:34) has led some to refuse to swear, even in court, but Jesus' words are best seen against the background of the elaborate rabbinic system of loopholes that precluded simple honesty in personal dealings. Jesus himself took an oath (Mark 8:12). Finally, Jesus' principle of nonresistance (Matt. 5:39) has been applied even to military and police force, whereas, again, Jesus relates it to interpersonal relationships.

Influence and Interpretation. *Influence.* Since the second century no block of Scripture of comparable size has exerted as great an influence as the sermon. In the pre-Nicene period, passages from this discourse were quoted or alluded to more than from any other part of the Bible. To the present day these words still profoundly challenge Christians and non-Christians alike. They caused Tolstoi to change completely his social theory and influenced the development of Gandhi's use of nonviolence as a political force. Even Nietzsche, who objected to the teachings of the sermon, did not ignore them.

History of Interpretation. The arresting nature of the sermon has produced numerous diverging efforts to explain, or even explain away, Jesus' words. Many have resisted efforts to limit the sermon's applicability. One approach sees Jesus teaching an obedience-righteousness that cannot be reconciled with Paul. Anabaptists did not go so far, but insisted that Jesus' words are so absolute that their obedience precludes Christian participation in certain social and political institutions. Bonhoeffer reacted against those who would analyze and interpret but fail to do the sermon. It must be done, but the power to do it comes only from the cross. Luther attempted to avoid what he regarded as the extremes of both the Roman and Anabaptist interpretations and stressed the obligation to keep the sermon's commandments. Liberal Protestantism has seen the sermon as the heart of the gospel and as Jesus' program for reforming society.

Others have attempted to limit the sermon's applicability. The predominant Lutheran view, though not of Luther himself, is that the sermon presents an impossible ideal which cannot be realized, so its function is to show man his inadequacy so he will be prepared for the gospel. What is sometimes called the existential position sees Jesus as attempting to change attitudes, not actions. The medieval Catholic interpretation called these precepts "evangelical counsels" for the few who would seek perfection, rather than commandments for every Christian. Two approaches limit the full applicability of the sermon to the breaking in of the kingdom, but with different results: Schweitzer saw Jesus primarily as an eschatological figure, so he coined the term "interim ethics" to emphasize that the stringent requirements of the sermon could apply only to the stress-packed times immediately before God introduced his kingdom, an event which never occurred, so the sermon does not apply to our modern situation. Dispensationalists also limit the sermon's focus to the kingdom, so for them Jesus' teachings will fully apply only at its future coming.

Meaning of the Sermon. Jesus concludes the sermon by setting up certain requirements that relate directly to one's being saved or lost. He divides mankind into three classes: those who (1) follow him (7:13–14, 17, 21, 24–25), (2) do not follow him (vss. 13–44, 26–27), and (3) pretend to follow him (vss. 15–20, 21–23). To be saved one must actually follow the teachings of the sermon, but Jesus does not say they must be performed perfectly. The saved are those who accept and actually attempt to direct their lives by the sermon; the lost are those who pretend to follow or who reject these teachings. Is this any different from Paul's man of faith? Was Paul not scandalized by the notion that a person may live the way he wants? The person who rests his faith in Jesus determines to follow him. This is Jesus and Paul. Mere profession of belief, without the following, will secure Jesus' condemnation, "I never knew you. You evildoers, depart from me" (vs. 23). An unfortunate feature of much post-Reformation Christianity has been the interpretation of Jesus in light of Paul rather than the converse. One of the contributions of Bonhoeffer's treatment of this sermon is his insistence on reading Paul in light of Jesus and, hence, his stressing the necessity of *doing* the sermon. Perfection is not demanded and aid is provided, but still the true disciple is "the one who does the will of the Father" (vs. 21). G. T. BURKE

See also GOLDEN RULE; JESUS CHRIST; LOGIA; LORD'S PRAYER; PARABLES OF JESUS.

Bibliography. Augustine, *Our Lord's Sermon on the Mount;* M. Luther, *The Sermon on the Mount;* H. K. McArthur, *Understanding the Sermon on the Mount;* W. S. Kissinger, *The Sermon on the Mount; A Dictionary of the Bible,* extra vol., 1–45; K. Grayston, *IDB,* IV, 279–89; G. Friedlander, *The Jewish Sources of the Sermon on the Mount;* C. G. Montefiore, *Rabbinic Literature and Gospel Teachings;* D. Bonhoeffer, *The Cost of Discipleship;* A. N. Wilder, *IB,* VII, 155–64; J. Jeremias, *The Sermon on the Mount;* W. D. Davies, *The Setting of the Sermon on the Mount* and *The Sermon on the Mount;* R. M. Grant, "The Sermon on the Mount in Early Christianity," *Sem* 12:215–31; R. Guelich, *The Sermon on the Mount;* J. R. W. Stott, *Christian Counter-Culture.*

Serpent. *See* SATAN.

Servant of the Lord. The expression *'ebed yhwh,* "servant of Jehovah," designating devoted worshipers as Abraham (Ps. 105:6), or others who fulfilled God's purposes, as Nebuchadrezzar (Jer. 25:9). But the preeminent "servant of Jehovah" appears as Isaiah comforted Israel, ravaged by Sennacherib, 701 B.C. Twenty times in Isa. 40–53 the *'ebed yhwh* is prophesied, even as vividly present, spoken to, or speaking.

The identity of the servant varies. Sometimes it refers to the whole nation, "Israel, my servant" (41:8), though sinfully deaf and blind (42:19). In Isaiah's "servant songs" (42:1–7; 49:1–9; 50:4–9; 52:13–53; and probably 61:1–3), however, this national meaning disappears, replaced by a *righteous* servant who restores Jacob (49:5). Superficial criticism has accordingly questioned the Isaianic authenticity of the songs. But Isaiah recognized a pious remnant (10:20–22), which included his prophetic circle (44:26; 8:16). In the songs, however (except for 49:3), the servant cannot be the collective remnant but only an individual. By his objective description, moreover (42:1), he cannot be Isaiah himself. The future reference (52:13) demonstrates that he cannot be Moses, the dying-god Tammuz(!), the king performing ritualistic service, or some other past leader. Finally, his sinless character (53:9) and the magnitude of his work (42:4) forbid his equation with any merely human leader in the future, such as Jehoiachin or Zerubbabel. The NT (John 12:38, 41; Acts 8:32–35) specifies Jesus Christ as the only embodiment of ideal Israel, the final accomplishment of the remnant (Isa. 49:6).

The mission of the servant is (1) that of a humanly born prophet (49:1–2; cf. Jer. 1:5), empowered by God's Holy Spirit (Isa. 42:1; 61:1; Luke 4:21), with a nonself-assertive ministry (Isa. 42:2–3; Matt. 12:18–21). (2) He suffers vicariously, bearing the cares of others (Isa. 53:4; cf. Christ's healings, Matt. 8:17). (3) Meeting disbelief (Isa. 53:1), he becomes subject to reproach (49:7; 50:6; Matt. 26:67; 27:26). (4) Condemned as a criminal, he gives up his life, punished for the sins of others (Isa. 53:5–8; I Pet. 2:22–25), God making his soul a priestly *'āšām,* "guilt offering" (Isa. 53:10). He atoningly "sprinkles many nations"

loss meant "Ichabod [no glory]" (I Sam. 4:21), the cloud again filled Solomon's temple (I Kings 8:11; cf. II Chron. 7:1). Ezekiel visualized its departure because of sin (10:18) before this temple's destruction, and Judaism confessed its absence from the second temple. The shekinah reappeared with Christ (Matt. 17:5; Luke 2:9), true God localized (John 1:14: *skēnē*, "tabernacle"; cf. Rev. 21:3, = *šĕkînâ?*), the glory of the latter temple (Hag. 2:9; Zech. 2:5). Christ ascended in the glory cloud (Acts 1:9) and will some day so return (Mark 14:62; Rev. 14:14; cf. Isa. 24:3; 60:1).

J. B. Payne

See also Glory; Tabernacle, Temple.

Bibliography. R. E. Hough, *The Ministry of the Glory Cloud;* G. Kittel and G. von Rad, *TDNT*, II, 237ff.; R. A. Stewart, *Rabbinic Theology.*

Sheol. An intermediate state in which souls are dealt with according to their lives on earth. The noun *šĕ'ôl* occurs sixty-five times in the Hebrew OT. English translations render the word as "grave" (AV, 31 times; NIV), "hell" (AV, 3 times), or as the transliteration "Sheol" (ASV; RSV; NIV, marg.). Most lexicons relate "Sheol" etymologically to *šā'al,* "to ask," thus making Sheol a place of asking—continually asking for more dead from the land of the living, or where the dead are asked for either information (divining) or grace. Some linguists have argued in favor of a relation to *šō'al* ("hollow of the hand"), whereby Sheol is explained as a "hollow or empty place." However, it is impossible to explain "Sheol" by a root meaning or etymology.

"Sheol" is found most often in the Writings (35 times; 7 in the Law and 19 in the Prophets), and it occurs sixteen times in Pss. and seventeen in the Wisdom Literature. Because the vast majority of occurrences are in the poetic genre, our approach to its theological significance must be one of caution. Its precise meaning in any given passage depends upon the context in which it occurs. In the OT there are six ways "Sheol" is used.

(1) It is predicated by various characteristics. Sheol is a place from which no one can save himself (Ps. 89:48). Once there, a person has no hope of returning to the realm of the living (Job 7:9; 17:13–16). In Sheol there is no activity of work, planning, knowledge, or wisdom (Eccl. 9:10); no one praises God from there (Pss. 6:5; 88:10–12; Isa. 38:18). Other passages do not explicitly use the word "Sheol," but clearly describe it as a place of darkness (Job 10:21–22) and a place of silence (Pss. 94:17; 115:17).

(2) The place where all people go upon death. The phrase "I will go down to Sheol in sorrow" occurs four times in Gen. (37:35; 42:38; 44:29, 31).

(3) A place where the wicked go upon death (Job 21:13; 24:19; Pss. 9:17; 31:17; 49:14). David prays that his enemies will go there alive (Ps. 55:15). Proverbs teaches that "the steps" and the house of an adulteress lead to Sheol (5:5; 7:27).

(4) A place from which the righteous are saved (Ps. 49:15; 86:13; Prov. 15:24). Moreover, Sheol has no lasting hold upon the righteous because God will ransom them from its power (Hosea 13:14; cf. I Cor. 15:55). He does not abandon the righteous to Sheol (Ps. 16:10).

(5) A place over which God has absolute sovereignty. Sheol "lies open ["naked"] before" God (Prov. 15:11; Job 26:6) so much so that he is there (Ps. 139:8). No one can escape from God in Sheol (Amos 9:2), because God himself brings people down to it (I Sam. 2:6). Job asks to be hidden from God's anger in Sheol (Job 14:13), yet Moses teaches that God's wrath burns even there (Deut. 32:22).

(6) "Sheol" is used as a metaphor or image for greed (Hab. 2:5; Prov. 27:20; 30:16), murder (Prov. 1:12), jealosy (Song of S. 8:6), troubles of life (Ps. 88:3), near-death situations (II Sam. 22:6; Pss. 18:5; 30:3; 116:3; Jonah 2:2), and great sin (Isa. 28:15, 18; 57:9). In two places, the prophets use "Sheol" in connection with the mythological views of Babylonia (Isa. 14:9, 11, 15) and Egypt (Ezek. 32:21, 27).

The above usages clarify how the word "Sheol" has varied meanings in the OT. Contrary to some opinion, the OT saints had a hope of a life hereafter. Both the righteous and the wicked go to Sheol. When the righteous go to the grave (Sheol) they are delivered from it, whereas the wicked remain there (grave or hell). Because relevant Scriptures seem to teach a marked difference between the ultimate end of the wicked and righteous with respect to Sheol, one might assert that the OT supports neither a general view of an underworld where all souls go nor a soul sleep of the wicked.

The word "Sheol" was translated into Greek by *hadēs* sixty-one times in the LXX; "Hades" occurs ten times in the NT. In the Gospels it represents a place of punishment (Matt. 11:23; Luke 10:15) and a place whose power cannot withstand the church (Matt. 16:18). In Acts 2:27–31, Peter quotes Ps. 16:8–11 in order to prove that the OT predicted Jesus' resurrection from Hades. In the context, Hades means grave or the place of bodily decay. Hades is never found in the Epistles, but in Rev. the word is used three times, in each case followed by *thanatos* ("death"). The writer thus distinguishes death ("grave") from Hades, the latter being a place of punishment for the wicked. Hence, the NT concept of Hades, which primarily involves punishment of the wicked, is much more limited than the OT idea of Sheol.

This shift is apparent even in Jewish apocalyptic writings during the intertestamental period. The apocalyptic writings begin to make a moral distinction with respect to Sheol (II Bar. 54:15). Moreover, many apocalyptic books teach that man's final destiny is determined in his earthly life (I Enoch; II Enoch 62:2; 53:1). In other words, Sheol is a place where men experience rewards or punishments that will come to them in a final judgment (II Esd. 7:75ff.). Some books even state that Sheol is the final state of punishment for the wicked (Jub. 7:29; 22:22; 24:31).

W. A. VAN GEMEREN

See also DEAD, ABODE OF THE; HADES; INTERMEDIATE STATE.

Shepherding Movement. *See* DISCIPLESHIP MOVEMENT.

Shroud of Turin. *See* TURIN, SHROUD OF.

Shrove Tuesday. The name traditionally given to the day before Ash Wednesday and the beginning of Lent. On this day in the Middle Ages the faithful were expected to attend confession with a priest for the purpose of being absolved or shriven in order to begin Lent in the right spiritual state.

Because people were expected to fast during Lent the custom grew up of using up oddments of fat to make and fry pancakes, and from this pancakes on Shrove Tuesday became traditional. A number of other customs, e.g., the annual pancake race at Olney in Buckinghamshire, England, have developed from the same source.

D. H. WHEATON

See also CHRISTIAN YEAR; LENT.

Signs. *See* MIRACLES.

Simons, Menno. *See* MENNO SIMONS.

Simplicity of God. *See* GOD, ATTRIBUTES OF.

Sin. ***The Biblical Understanding of Sin.*** In the biblical perspective, sin is not only an act of wrongdoing but a state of alienation from God. For the great prophets of Israel, sin is much more than the violation of a taboo or the transgression of an external ordinance. It signifies the rupture of a personal relationship with God, a betrayal of the trust he places in us. We become most aware of our sinfulness in the presence of the holy God (cf. Isa. 6:5; Ps. 51:1–9; Luke 5:8). Sinful acts have their origin in a corrupt heart (Gen. 6:5; Isa. 29:13; Jer. 17:9). For Paul, sin (*hamartia*) is not just a conscious transgression of the law but a debilitating ongoing state of enmity with God. In Paul's theology, sin almost becomes personalized. It can be thought of as a malignant, personal power which holds humanity in its grasp.

The biblical witness also affirms that sin is universal. "All have sinned and fall short of the glory of God," Paul declares (Rom. 3:23 RSV). "There is not a righteous man on earth who does what is right and never sins" (Eccles. 7:20 NIV). "Who can say, 'I have kept my heart pure; I am clean and without sin'?" (Prov. 20:9 NIV). "They have all gone astray," the psalmist complains, "They are all alike corrupt; there is none that does good, no, not one" (Ps. 14:3 RSV).

In Reformed theology, the core of sin is unbelief. This has firm biblical support: in Gen. 3 where Adam and Eve trust the word of the serpent over the word of God; in the Gospels where Jesus Christ is rejected by the leaders of the Jews; in Acts 7 where Stephen is martyred at the hands of an unruly crowd; in John 20:24–25 where Thomas arrogantly dismisses the resurrection of Jesus.

Hardness of heart, which is closely related to unbelief (Mark 16:14; Rom. 2:5), likewise belongs to the essence of sin. It means refusing to repent and believe in the promises of God (Ps. 95:8; Heb. 3:8, 15; 4:7). It connotes both stubborn unwillingness to open ourselves to the love of God (II Chr. 36:13; Eph. 4:18) and its corollary—insensitivity to the needs of our neighbor (Deut. 15:7; Eph. 4:19).

Whereas the essence of sin is unbelief or hardness of heart, the chief manifestations of sin are pride, sensuality, and fear. Other significant aspects of sin are self-pity, selfishness, jealousy, and greed.

Sin is both personal and social, individual and collective. Ezekiel declared: "Now this was the sin of your sister Sodom: She and her daughters were arrogant, overfed, and unconcerned; they did not help the poor and needy" (16:49 NIV). According to the prophets, it is not only a few individuals that are infected by sin but the whole nation (Isa. 1:4). Among the collective forms of sin that cast a blight over the world today are racism, nationalism, imperialism, agism, and sexism.

The effects of sin are moral and spiritual bondage, guilt, death, and hell. James explained: "Each person is tempted when he is lured and enticed by his own desire. Then desire when it has conceived gives birth to sin; and sin when it is full-grown brings forth death" (1:14–15 RSV). In Paul's view, "The wages of sin is death" (Rom. 6:23 RSV; cf. I Cor. 15:56).

According to Pauline theology, the law is not simply a check on sin but an actual instigator of sin. So perverse is the human heart that the very prohibitions of the law that were intended to deter sin serve instead to arouse sinful desire (Rom. 7:7–8).

Biblical faith also confesses that sin is inherent in the human condition. We are not simply born into a sinful world, but we are born with a propensity toward sin. As the psalmist says, "The wicked go astray from the womb, they err from their birth, speaking lies" (Ps. 58:3; cf. 51:5). Church tradition speaks of original sin, but this is intended to convey, not a biological taint or physical deformity, but a spiritual infection that in some mysterious way is transmitted through reproduction. Sin does not originate from human nature, but it corrupts this nature.

The origin of sin is indeed a mystery and is tied in with the problem of evil. The story of Adam and Eve does not really give us a rationally satisfactory explanation of either sin or evil (this was not its intention), but it does throw light on the universal human predicament. It tells us that prior to human sin there was demonic sin which provides the occasion for human transgression. Orthodox theology, both Catholic and Protestant, speaks of a fall of the angels prior to the fall of man, and this is attributed to the misuse or abuse of the divine gift of freedom. It is the general consensus among orthodox theologians that moral evil (sin) sets the stage for physical evil (natural disaster), but exactly how the one causes the other will probably always remain a subject of human speculation.

Sin and Hubris. The biblical understanding of sin has certain parallels with the Greek tragic concept of "hubris," and yet there are also profound differences. Hubris, which is sometimes translated as "pride" (not wholly accurate), is not to be equated with the idolatrous pride that proceeds from a corrupted heart. Rather, it is the unwise self-elevation that proceeds from the vitalities of nature. Whereas hubris signifies the attempt to transcend the limitations appointed by fate, sin refers to an unwillingness to break out of our narrow limitations in obedience to the vision of faith. While hubris connotes immoderation, sin consists in misplaced allegiance. Hubris is trying to be superhuman; sin is becoming inhuman. Hubris means rising to the level of the gods; sin means trying to displace God or living as if there were no God.

In Greek tragedy, the hero has a quite different standing from the sinner portrayed in the Bible. The tragic hero is punished for authentic greatness, not for unwarranted exaltation. While the tragic hero is to be admired, the sinner, insofar as he persists in sin, is to be justly condemned. Both are to be pitied, but for different reasons. The tragic hero is a victim of fate, and is not really responsible for his predicament. The sinner, on the other hand, knows the good but does not do it. The tragic hero is tormented by the sorrow of being blind to the forces that brought about his undoing. The sinner is troubled by the guilt of knowing that he has no one to blame but himself. The fault of the tragic hero is inevitable; that of the sinner is inexcusable. The tragic hero is a pawn in the hands of fate. The sinner is a willing accomplice in evil. In Greek tragedy, the essential flaw is ignorance. In the biblical perspective, the tragic flaw is hardness of heart.

Historical Controversy over Sin. In the fifth century, Augustine challenged the views of the British monk Pelagius, who saw sin basically as an outward act transgressing the law and regarded man as free to sin or desist from sin. Appealing to the witness of Scripture, Augustine maintained that sin incapacitates man from doing the good, and because we are born as sinners we lack the power to do the good. Yet because we willfully choose the bad over the good, we must be held accountable for our sin. Augustine gave the illustration of a man who by abstaining from food necessary for health so weakened himself that he could no longer eat. Though still a human being, created to maintain his health by eating, he was no longer able to do so. Similarly, by the historical event of the fall, all humanity has become incapable of that movement toward God—the very life for which it was created.

Pelagius held that one could raise oneself by one's own efforts toward God, and therefore grace is the reward for human virtue. Augustine countered that man is helpless to do the good until grace falls upon him, and when grace is thus given he is irresistibly moved toward God and the good.

At the time of the Reformation, Luther powerfully reaffirmed the Pauline and Augustinian doctrine of the bondage of the will against Erasmus, who maintained that man still has the capacity to do the right, though he needs the aid of grace if he is to come to salvation. Luther saw man as totally bound to the powers of darkness—sin, death, and the devil. What he most needs is to be delivered from spiritual slavery rather than inspired to heroic action.

In our own century, the debate between Karl Barth and Emil Brunner on human freedom is another example of the division in the church through the ages on this question. Though firmly convinced that man is a sinner who can be saved only by the unmerited grace of God as revealed and conveyed in Jesus Christ, Emil Brunner nonetheless referred to an "addressability" in man, a "capacity for revelation," that enables man to apprehend the gospel and to respond to its offer. For Barth, not even a capacity for God remains within our fallen nature; therefore, we must be given not only faith but also the condition to receive faith. In this view, there is no point of contact between the gospel and sinful humanity. Brunner vehemently disagreed, contending that there would then be no use in preaching. Barth argued that the Spirit must create this point of contact before we can believe and obey. In contrast to Brunner he affirmed the total depravity of man; yet he did not believe that human nature is so defaced that it no longer reflects the glory of God. In his later writings, Barth contended that sin is alien to human nature rather than belonging to this nature. Nonetheless, he continued to affirm that every part of our nature is infected by the contagion of sin, and this renders us totally unable to come to God on our own.

Modern Reappraisals of Sin. In the nineteenth century, theologians under the spell of the new world consciousness associated with the Enlightenment and romanticism began to reinterpret sin. For Friedrich Schleiermacher, sin is not so much the revolt of man against God as the dominance of the lower nature within us. It is the resistance of our lower nature to the universal God-consciousness, which needs to be realized and cultivated in every human soul. Sin is basically a minus sign, the inertia of nature that arrests the growth of God-consciousness. Schleiermacher even saw sin in a positive light, maintaining that evil has been ordained in corporate human life as a gateway to the good. Sin has occurred as a preparation for grace rather than grace occurring to repair the damage of sin. Schleiermacher did acknowledge a corporate dimension to sin.

Albrecht Ritschl, in the same century, understood sin as the product of selfishness and ignorance. He did not see the human race in bondage to the power of sin, but instead believed that people could be effectively challenged to live ethical, heroic lives. His focus was on actual or concrete sins, not on man's being *in* sin. He even allowed for the possibility of sinless lives, though he did not deny the necessity of divine grace for attaining the ethical ideal. For Ritschl, religion is fundamentally the experience of moral freedom, a freedom that enables man to be victorious over the world. At the same time, he acknowledged the presence of radical evil, though, as in the case of Kant, this did not significantly alter his vision of a new social order characterized by the mastery of spirit over nature. He also tried to do justice to the collective nature of evil, but this was never quite convincing.

In Twentieth Century America. Reinhold Niebuhr pioneered in reinterpreting sin. Rejecting the Reformation understanding of sin for its biblical literalism and determinism, he also disputed the liberal view, which confused sin with human weakness and finitude. For Niebuhr, sin is inevitable because of the tension between human freedom and human finitude, but it is not a necessary implication of human nature. Our anxiety over our finitude provides the occasion for sin; our ability to transcend ourselves is the source of the possibility of sin. We are tempted either to deny the contingent character of our existence (in pride) or to escape from the responsibilities of our freedom (in sensuality). Niebuhr sought to preserve the paradox of the inevitability of sin and human culpability for sin.

Paul Tillich saw the sin of man as consisting in estrangement from his true self and the ground of his selfhood. Virtually making sin an invariable concomitant of human finitude, he spoke of an ontological fall in addition to an immanent fall. Tillich made generous use of psychological and sociological categories (such as "alienation" and "estrangement") to illumine the mystery of sin. Just as sin is a fall from our ontological ground, so salvation lies in reunion with this ground. For Tillich, the universal experience of estrangement from the creative depth and ground of all being is the tie that links Christians and non-Christians.

In liberation theology, sin is redefined in terms of social oppression, exploitation, and acquiescence to injustice. It is also seen as greed for financial gain at the expense of the poor. Just as sin is that which dehumanizes and oppresses people, so salvation is that which humanizes them, that which liberates them for meaningful and creative lives.

Closely related is feminist theology, which sees the essence of sin in passivity to evil, in timidity and cowardice in the face of intimidation. Sin consists not so much in self-affirmation as in self-contempt. The need for women who have been subjugated by a patriarchal ethos is for self-assertion, and their sin lies in resignation to the social system that relegates them to an inferior status.

The understanding of sin has also undergone

a profound transformation in popular culture religion, where psychology is more significant than theology. Under the influence of "new thought" and other neotranscendentalist movements, media religion reinterprets sin as negative thinking or defeatism. In some other strands of culture religion, also showing the impact of "new thought," sin is equated with sickness or instability. The cure lies in self- or group therapy rather than in a sacrifice for sin. The way to overcome guilt is through catharsis rather than repentance. Atonement is reinterpreted to mean at-one-ment with the self or the world.

Overcoming Sin. Christian faith teaches that sin cannot be overcome through human ingenuity or effort. The solution to the problem lies in what God has done for us in Jesus Christ. The penalty for sin is death, judgment, and hell, but the gospel is that God has chosen to pay this penalty himself in the sacrificial life and death of his Son, Jesus Christ (cf. John 3:16–17; Acts 20:28; Rom. 3:21–26; 5:6–10; II Cor. 5:18, 19; Col. 2:13–15).

Through his atoning sacrifice on Calvary, Christ set humankind free by taking the retribution of sin upon himself. He suffered the agony and shame that we deserve to suffer because of our sin. He thereby satisfied the just requirements of the law of God and at the same time turned away the wrath of God from fallen humankind. His sacrifice was both an *expiation* of our guilt and a *propitiation* of the wrath of God. It also signifies the *justification* of the sinner in the sight of God in that Christ's righteousness is imputed to those who have faith. Likewise, it represents the *sanctification* of the sinner by virtue of his being engrafted into the body of Christ through faith. The cross and resurrection of Christ also accomplish the *redemption* of the sinner, because he has been brought back out of the slavery of sin into the new life of freedom.

Humankind is objectively delivered through the cross and resurrection victory of Christ over the powers of sin, death, and the devil; but this deliverance does not make contact with the sinner until the gift of the Holy Spirit in the awakening to faith. The outpouring of the Spirit completes the salvific activity of Christ. His atoning work is finished, but the fruits of his redemption need to be applied to the people of God by the Spirit if they are to be saved de facto as well as de jure. It is through *regeneration* by the Spirit, the imparting of faith and love, that the sinner is set free from bondage to sin and enabled to achieve victory over sin in everyday life.

Reformation theology insists that Christ saves us, not only from the power of sin, but also from its dire consequences—physical and eternal death. We are given both immortality and the remission of sins. The Christian does not suffer further penalties for sins committed after baptism and conversion, for the punishment for sin has already been borne by Christ. The Christian has been delivered from the guilt of sin, but he still suffers the interior pain of guilt or feelings of guilt insofar as he continues to sin while in the state of grace. The remedy lies, not in acts of penance prescribed by the church, but in the act of repentance by which we claim again the assurance of forgiveness promised in the gospel. The suffering that accompanies the sin of the Christian is to be understood, not as a penalty for sin, but as a sting that reminds him of his deliverance from sin and also as a spur that challenges him to persevere and overcome.

Sin in Evangelical and Legalistic Religion. The meaning of sin is quite different in a religion based on the gospel from one based on law. Sin, in evangelical perspective, is not so much the infringement of a moral code as the breaking of a covenantal relationship. Sin is not an offense so much against law as against love. In legalistic religion, sin is the violation of a moral taboo. In evangelical religion, sin is wounding the very heart of God. The opposite of sin is not virtue, but faith.

Biblical faith acknowledges the legal dimension of sin, recognizing that the just requirements of the law have to be satisfied. Yet it also perceives that sin is basically the sundering of a personal relation between God and man and that the greatest need is not the payment of debt but reconciliation.

The deepest meaning of the cross is that God out of his incomparable love chose to identify himself with our plight and affliction. The suffering of Christ was the suffering of vicarious love, and not simply a penal suffering canceling human debt. Salvation means that the merits of Christ are transferred to the deficient sinner and also that the forgiveness of God is extended to the undeserving sinner. Christ not only pays the penalty for sin, but he does more than the law requires: he accepts the sinner unto himself, adopting that person into his family as a brother or sister. He gives the sinner a writ of pardon and embraces him as a loving shepherd who has found the lost sheep.

Just as sin is deeper than the infringement of law, so love goes beyond the requirements of law. The answer to sin is a forgiveness that was not conditional on the sacrifice of Christ but one that was responsible for this sacrifice. God did not forgive because his law was satisfied; yet because he chose to forgive, he saw to it that the demands of his law were fulfilled.

D. G. Bloesch

See also Augustine of Hippo; Guilt; Idolatry; Justification; Omission, Sins of; Pelagius, Pelagianism; Pride; Sanctification.

Bibliography. D. Bloesch, *Essentials of Evangelical Theology,* I, 88–119; G. P. Hutchinson, *The Problem of Original Sin in American Presbyterian Theology;* E. Brunner, *Man in Revolt;* E. Brunner and K. Barth, *Natural Theology;* K. Barth, *Church Dogmatics* IV/1; G. C. Berkouwer, *Sin;* R. Niebuhr, *The Nature and Destiny of Man* and *Moral Man and Immoral Society;* E. La B. Cherbonnier, *Hardness of Heart;* J. Haroutunian, *The Lust for Power;* Augustine, *On Original Sin;* M. Luther, *The Bondage of the Will;* J. Calvin, *Institutes;* F. R. Tennant, *The Sources of the Doctrines of the Fall and Original Sin;* P. Schoonenberg, *Man and Sin;* W. G. T. Shedd, *Dogmatic Theology,* II.

Sin, Conviction of. The biblical teaching revolving chiefly around *elenchō peri hamartias* and equivalents. The concept of "conviction" does not cover all shades of meaning of *elenchō.* The word sometimes entails the ideas of "exposing" and "correcting" in addition to that of "proving wrong" or "showing the guilt of."

A sinless person cannot be the object of this conviction (John 8:46; I Pet. 2:22). The world can, however, notably for its disbelief in Christ (John 16:8–9). A sinning member of the Christian community can be an object of conviction, too (Matt. 18:15; Eph. 5:11). Similarly a whole congregation may be reproved (I Tim. 5:20; II Tim. 3:16; Titus 1:9, 13; 2:15; James 2:9; Rev. 3:19).

Conviction originates with the persons of the Godhead: the Father (Heb. 12:5), the Son (Jude 15; Rev. 3:19), and the Holy Spirit (John 16:7–11). It is mediated through Christian witnesses, especially preachers, as they spread and implement the word of God (Matt. 18:15; John 16:7, 8; Eph. 5:11, 13; I Tim. 5:20; II Tim. 4:2; Titus 1:9, 13; 2:15), as an outworking of brotherly love (Lev. 19:17–18, LXX). Their witness intensifies the convicting work already present through the Mosaic law (James 2:9) and self-revelation to the conscience resulting from illumination by Christ's first advent (John 3:20).

The outcome of this convicting work varies. In one sense, it is always effective because the object invariably receives divine illumination to see issues clearly (John 16:7–8). In another sense, it is only relatively effective because the object may respond with repentance (Matt. 18:15; I Cor. 14:24) or rejection (Luke 3:19). What conviction does is to make clear the dire results if the guilty party persists in his wrongdoing. Without conviction he remains a victim of satanic blindness (II Cor. 4:4). Once convicted, he must respond with a choice.

Typical sins that occasion conviction include illegitimate marriage, ungodly deeds, and false teaching. The guilty are shown the wrongness of such activity and are pointed away from it toward repentance. Conviction of sin implies an educative discipline. The inflexible standard of divine righteousness is brought to bear on sin, and a turning in obedience to God is shown to be the desirable alternative to remaining in a sinful state.

R. L. Thomas

See also Sin.

Bibliography. C. K. Barrett, *The Gospel According to St. John;* R. E. Brown, *Gospel According to John,* II, 705–6, 711–14; F. Büchsel, *TDNT,* II, 473–76; L. S. Chafer, *Systematic Theology,* VII, 94–96; H.-G. Link, *NIDNTT,* II, 140–42.

Sin, Man of. *See* Antichrist.

Sin, Mortal. Sin causing spiritual death. The biblical teaching is clear: all sin is mortal inasmuch as its intrusion into human experience is the cause of every man's death (Rom. 5:12; 6:23). Roman Catholic moral theology sees sin as twofold: mortal and venial. Mortal sin extinguishes the life of God in the soul; venial sin weakens, but does not destroy that life. In venial sin the agent freely decides to perform a specific act; however, in doing so he does not purpose to become a certain type of person. In venial sin the individual performs an act, but deep within himself he yearns to be the type of individual who opposes that action. Thus, in venial sin there is a tension between the action and the individual performing the act. Mortal sin involves the agent totally. He determines not only to act in a specific manner, but expresses therein the type of individual he wishes to be in and through that action. The result is spiritual death.

Evangelical Christians take seriously the biblical evaluation of the grave nature of certain sins. Our Lord spoke of the "sin that has no forgiveness" (Matt. 12:31–32; Mark 3:28–30; Luke 12:10); Paul teaches that those who participate in certain specified sins are excluded from the kingdom (I Cor. 6:9; Gal. 5:21; I Thess. 4:6); John gives clear instructions concerning prayer for those who have committed the "sin unto death" (I John 5:16; cf. Heb. 6:4–6). These passages cannot be dismissed lightly; they impinge decidedly upon our theme and call for the closest exegetical attention.

F. R. Harm

See also Sin, Unpardonable; Sin unto Death.

Bibliography. J. Greenwood, *Handbook of the Catholic Faith;* R. B. McBrien, *Catholicism,* II; *NCE,* XIII; L. Berkhof, *Systematic Theology;* C. C. Ryrie, *The Holy Spirit;* A. H. Strong, *Systematic Theology;* H. C. Thiessen, *Lectures in Systematic Theology;* J. T. Mueller, *Christian Dogmatics;* F. Pieper, *Christian Dogmatics,* I, 571ff.; C. F. W. Walther, *The Proper Distinction Between Law and Gospel.*

Sin, Unpardonable. Christian teaching about the unpardonable sin stems from a saying of Jesus recorded in all three Synoptic Gospels. In Mark 3:28–29 Jesus remarks, "Truly, I say to you, all sins will be forgiven the sons of men, and whatever blasphemies they utter; but whoever blasphemes against the Holy Spirit never has forgiveness, but is guilty of an eternal sin." An added difficulty comes when we compare the saying to its parallels in Luke 12:10 (which evidences an independent Q tradition) and Matt. 12:31–32 (which no doubt reflects a synthesis of Q and Mark). Matt. and Luke refer to forgiveness of "words against the Son of Man" (namely, Jesus) while Mark mentions "blasphemies of the sons of men." Scholars often resolve this difficulty by suggesting that the earliest saying involved the Aramaic generic idiom for "man" (*bar nāšā'* = "son of man"). When the phrase gained titular importance for Jesus, Mark introduced the plural form to avoid any confusion (plural, "sons of men" is without parallel in any of the Gospels; elsewhere it is only in Eph. 3:5). Nevertheless, in Matt. and Luke the generic form is absent, and the saying claims that an offense to the Son of man will be forgiven.

One must keep in mind that the historical setting of the saying in Mark and Matthew is the Beelzebul controversy (cf. Luke 11:14–23). Jesus' exorcisms stirred up major discussions both during his ministry and within the apologetics of the earliest church. His opponents misrepresented his successful rulership over the demonic and implied that Jesus' exorcisms evidenced some sort of collusion with Satan. Jesus' response is a blunt rebuttal. His power stemmed from the Spirit of God. The saying brings a severe warning about the profound danger of attributing the good things of God to an act of Satan. "Here we see coming to clear expression Jesus' sense of the awesomeness, the numinous quality, the eschatological power which possessed him. In him, in his action, God was present and active in a decisive and final way—to reject his ministry was to reject God and so to reject forgiveness" (J. Dunn). According to Jesus this rejection implied total rejection and spurned the divine presence (cf. a similar severe dishonoring in John 8:48ff.).

But in what fashion could a sin against the Son of man be "forgivable"? In the historical setting of early Christianity, the time of Jesus' earthly ministry was a time of ambiguity *even for the disciples* (Mark 9:30–31). No sin in this period fell outside the realm of forgiveness. If even the Q form of the saying incorporates the generic sense, the evangelists may be saying that unknowing criticisms of Jesus as *bar nāšā'* (a man) were pardonable. But in the post-Easter setting, the presence of the Spirit and the presence of Jesus were rarely distinguished (II Cor. 3:18; cf. Acts 16:7). This was a time of Spirit-inspired understanding (John 12:16; 13:7; 16:12–13; cf. I Cor. 2:1–16); apostasy against the Son would have similarly dire consequences (Heb. 6:4–6; 10:26-31; cf. I John 5:10, 14ff.; Gospel of Thomas, logion 44).

The meaning of this sin in Christian thought is best viewed as a total and persistent denial of the presence of God in Christ. It reflects a complete recalcitrance of the heart. Rather than a particular act, it is a disposition of the will. "This sin is committed when a man recognises the mission of Jesus by the Holy Spirit but defies and resists and curses it. The saying shows the seriousness of the situation. It is the last time... in which the lordship of God breaks in" (W. Grundmann).

Having said this, however, two cautions must be sounded especially when we recall the serious pastoral problems that derive from this teaching. First, this in no way should come in the way of the full implications of the grace of God in Christ. The unpardonable sin refers to complete apostasy (Calvin). If one seeks God's grace he can be assured that he will discover it (I John 2:1ff.). It is interesting that in Luke 12 the saying is immediately followed by another Spirit text bringing reassurance (vss. 11–12). Second, this sin does not refer to a particular act for which one may later feel regret, but instead describes a blatant hostility to God and a serious rejection of Jesus after one has been exposed to the knowledge of the truth. This corrective should help avoid many traumatic problems so frequent among Christians and reassure that God's forgiveness is free and gracious to all who come to him with a contrite heart.

G. M. Burge

See also Sin unto Death.

Bibliography. C. R. Smith, *The Bible Doctrine of Sin;* J. Denney, *The Christian Doctrine of Reconciliation;* O. E. Evans, "The Unforgivable Sin," *ExpT* 68: 240–44; P. E. Davies, *IDB*, IV, 733–34; W. Grundmann, *TDNT*, I, 304; O. Procksch, *TDNT*, I, 104; G. C. Berkouwer, *Sin;* J. D. G. Dunn, *Jesus and the Spirit;* I. H. Marshall, *Kept by the Power of God* and *The Epistles of John.*

Sin, Venial (Lat. *venia*, "pardon, favor, kindness, forgiveness"). Sin that can be forgiven. The term does not occur in Scripture, but the basic idea does. Essentially a Roman Catholic concept, venial sin is invariably used in contrast with mortal sin. Mortal sins are those which exclude from the kingdom; venial are those sins which do not exclude from it (cf. Gal. 5:19–21; Eph. 5:5; with James 3:2; I John 1:8).

Thomas Aquinas expressed the difference between mortal and venial in terms of the diversity of the disorder seen in the essence of the deed. There are two types of such disorder: (1) that which violates the basic principle of order, and (2) that which does not touch the principle but introduces disorder within the soul. When the soul has become so disordered that it turns from its God, mortal sin has occurred. Aquinas likened the turning from God in mortal sin to death, in which the principle of life is gone, and the disorder of venial sin to sickness, which is reparable because the life principle remains.

Venial sin differs from mortal sin in the punishment it entails. Venial merits temporal punishment expiated by confession or by the fires of purgatory, mortal sin merits eternal death.

Lest one become complacent, it is pointed out that venial sin can lead to mortal sin. When one becomes so engrossed in his sin that it is an obsession that leads him ultimately to turn from God, the source of his life, he has entered the domain of mortal sin—and eternal death.

F. R. Harm

See also Sin, Mortal.

Bibliography. T. Aquinas, *Summa Theologica,* I, a2ae, 71–89; J. G. McKenzie, *Guilt: Its Meaning and Significance;* P. V. O'Brien, *Emotions and Morals;* W. E. Orchard, *Modern Theories of Sin;* P. Palazzini, *Sin, Its Reality and Nature;* J. Regnier, *What Is Sin?* H. Rondet, *The Theology of Sin.*

Sinlessness of Christ. The teaching that Jesus Christ was sinless (impeccable). This has been a universal conviction of the Christian church. Even heretics in the early centuries and during the later period of rationalism (1650–1920), who attacked the orthodox Christology of Nicaea and Chalcedon, left this teaching alone. Based on the apostolic witness (II Cor. 5:21; Heb. 4:15; 7:26; I Pet. 2:22; 3:18; James 5:6; I John 3:5), it has both a negative and a positive meaning. Negatively, it means that Christ was kept free from all transgression of the law of God. He whose "meat" it was "to do the will of him who sent [him] and to accomplish his work" (John 4:34) could challenge his enemies to convict him of sin (John 8:46). Positively, this implies the holiness of Christ (Luke 1:35; 4:34; John 6:69; 10:36; Acts 3:14; 4:27, 30; Heb. 7:26), i.e., his wholehearted commitment to his Father (John 5:30; Heb. 10:7) and to that mission for which he had been sent into the world (John 17:19).

The question which arises, given the fact of Christ's sinlessness, is whether his alleged temptations were real. The NT narrates a testing immediately after his baptism and before his public ministry (Matt. 4; Luke 4), and it teaches elsewhere that he is one "who in every respect has been tempted as we are" (Heb. 4:15; cf. Luke 22:28). Thus it has been felt important to maintain the reality of temptation against every effort to undermine it, while maintaining Jesus' sinlessness. The phrases used in the ancient debates between which opinions wavered were whether the Savior was "able not to sin" (*potuit non peccare*) or "not able to sin" (*non potuit peccare*), the first emphasizing his identification with sinful humanity and consequent struggle, and the second his identification with God and God's eternal purpose for the salvation of the world. The position taken by some, that sinlessness and ability to be tempted are mutually exclusive, has been seen as resting on a false assumption. It proceeds "on the assumption that what applies to us applies to Christ; that if there be a close connection for us between our capacity for sin and our struggles, then there must be such a connection for Christ" (Berkouwer). In Christ, however, there is not the inner propensity to sin that there is in every other member of the human race. He had the Holy Spirit without measure to sustain him in his earthly ministry. The temptation narrative in the Gospels is preceded and followed by references to the Holy Spirit: Jesus was "full of the Holy Spirit . . . and was led by the Spirit for forty days in the wilderness, tempted by the devil" (Luke 4:1–2). Thereafter "Jesus returned in the power of the Spirit into Galilee" (vs. 14). Throughout his earthly sojourn, while temptation was real, the God whose life he fully shared (Col. 1:19; 2:9) and who he was (John 1:1; 10:30) kept him from committing any sin and, as important, dedicated to his messianic mission. This latter is the context in which Christ's temptation and sinlessness must be studied. His struggle was primarily to be a faithful high priest that he, through suffering, might bring many unto God (Luke 24:26; John 12:27; Heb. 2:17–18).

M. E. Osterhaven

See also Christology; Jesus Christ.

Bibliography. G. C. Berkouwer, *The Person of Christ;* A. B. Bruce, *The Humiliation of Christ;* W. Pannenberg, *Jesus—God and Man;* W. G. T. Shedd, *Dogmatic Theology,* II.

Sin Offering. *See* Offerings and Sacrifices in Bible Times.

Sins, Seven Deadly. At an early stage in the life of the church, the influence of Greek thought (with its tendency to view sin as a necessary flaw in human nature) made it necessary for the church to determine the relative seriousness of various moral faults. This ultimately gave rise to what is commonly referred to as the seven deadly sins—a concept which occupies an important place in the order and discipline of the Roman Catholic Church.

These sins are pride, covetousness, lust, envy, gluttony, anger, sloth. K. E. Kirk stresses that they are to be understood as "capital" or "root" sins rather than "deadly" or "mortal" (viz., sins which cut one off from his true last end). They are the "sinful propensities which reveal themselves in particular sinful acts." The list represents an attempt to enumerate the primary instincts which are most likely to give rise to sin.

Even though the original classification may have been monastic in origin (cf. Cassian, *Collationes Patrum*, vs. 10), under the influence of Gregory the Great (who has given us the classical exposition on the subject: *Moralia* on Job, esp. XXXI.45) the scope was widened and along with the seven cardinal virtues they came to constitute the moral standards and tests of the early Catholic Church. In medieval scholasticism they were the subject of considerable attention (cf. esp. Aquinas, *Summa Theologica*, II.ii.).

R. H. Mounce

Bibliography. Fr. Connell, *New Baltimore Catechism;* J. Stalker, *The Seven Deadly Sins;* H. Fairlie, *The Seven Deadly Sins Today.*

Sins of Omission. *See* Omission, Sins of.

Sin unto Death. Unpardonable sin. The precise nature of *hamartia pros thanaton* in I John 5:16 was no longer known even in patristic times, but may be surmised in its exegetical context to mean some form of final impenitence, since every sin repented of is forgiven. Two major sins of impenitence are mentioned in the NT, one in connection with the invasion of the demonic realm by Jesus' exercise of the power of the Holy Spirit, whose presence is rejected by the Pharisees and referred to Beelzebul. This constitutes the unforgivable blasphemy against the Holy Spirit (Matt. 12:22–32). The other reference is to those who have once been enlightened by the Holy Spirit and through unbelief crucify Christ and hold him up to contempt (Heb. 6:4–6; 10:26–29). In these texts the Spirit of grace is outraged, and there is no further access to forgiveness. Behind the sin unto death is the spirit of antichrist, the source of false and counterfeit teaching in the opponents of John (I John 2:18–23; 3:10; 4:1–3; II John 7–9), and of Paul (II Cor. 11:12–15; Gal. 1:6–9).

R. G. Gruenler

See also Blasphemy Against the Holy Spirit.

Situation Ethics. The position that every significant moral decision has to be taken "in the light of the circumstances."

Introduction. Consequences, cost, risk, contrary considerations—all have to be weighed to make moral decisions. There never are exact precedents; every situation is unique in some particular. Every system of moral rules, laws, and principles therefore gives rise to casuistry, formal and authoritative, like the Jesuit *Summae de Poenitentia,* or informal and advisory, like the Puritan Baxter's *Christian Directory.* These adjust general principles to particular circumstances, allow exceptions, and discuss "cases of conscience." There can be no absolute, invariable moral rules which govern all situations; even so brief a law as "Thou shalt not kill" did not apply equally to murderers, adulterers, war, sacrifices, or food. "Circumstances alter cases," it is said, and from this it is an easy step to pronounce all moral codes out of date in a world "come of age."

This position is of course attractive to the modern revolt against authority of all kinds, but it accords also with two other contemporary influences. First, the shrinking of the world through communication and travel into one "global village" has emphasized the great variety and inconsistency of existing ethical systems, undermining all. Second, the increasing complexity of modern life, with multiplying moral dilemmas (nuclear war, abortion, contraception, drug addiction, genetic engineering, and the like), has exposed the inadequacy of all existing codes to answer questions posed by contemporary situations.

This lack of adequate, predetermined directions is the essential truth which situation ethics erects into the *only* principle in ethical theory. It builds thereon a so-called new morality, which repudiates all rules, guidelines, laws, principles, or enshrining of past experience or superior authority, and reduces morality to instant, individual, intuitive, and isolated decisions, varying with every situation.

To distinguish "moral" behavior from merely capricious, anarchic, amoral reactions to circumstances, it is necessary to presuppose some standard or "norm" of morality, by reference to which the quality of a given decision may be described. Various single norms have been proposed—self-consistency, compassion, utility, truth, pleasure—or even a scale of norms; but situation ethics has generally selected *love* as the sole and all-sufficient norm of moral action.

Major ethical studies had focused upon "the-will-of-God-for-community" (Brunner), "openness to the demand of love" (Barth), or "letting the love of God flow through us" (Nygren). This emphasis was consonant with the search of a divided world for social cohesiveness, a collectivist reply to excessive individualism, and a deeper understanding of man as "person in relationship." Nygren's summary, "Where love is, no other precepts are requisite," enshrines the theme of situation ethics.

Popular Forms. In its popularized form, situation ethics does not, however, depend upon Christian insights. Its chief exponent, Joseph Fletcher, quotes scriptural phrases and precedents whenever convenient, and cites eight "proof texts" for his "love norm," including words of Jesus about the great commandment and Paul on love's fulfilling the law, but he sees nothing particularly different or unique in a Christian's choices. Lovingness is the motive at work with full force behind the decisions of many non-Christians.

Moreover, Fletcher rejects all revealed norms but the command to love. Nothing outside a situation, such as historical revelation, can enter into a situation to prejudge it. Jesus had no rules or system of values; revered principles, even the Ten Commandments, may be thrown aside if they conflict with love. To break the seventh commandment may be good: it depends whether love is fully served. Sexual intercourse before marriage—if the decision is made "Christianly"—could be right. There is no personal ethic, since morality rests on love-relationship: which makes the Sermon on the Mount largely superfluous. Paradoxically, by resting all upon the agent's instant, intuitive reaction to circumstances, situation ethics precludes any generalized pattern of morality applicable to others, or to society—another distinctly un-Christian flavor.

"Faith working through love" offers a foundation for the love norm, but it is not essential; a sincere, intelligent, and wise man may reject Christ without affecting his situationist morality. The basis of the norm is our decision that it shall be love; for some, this will rest on a previous *decision* (not disclosure) that God is love.

Support is found in a famous saying of Augustine, "Love, and do what you like"—"six blessed monosyllables, part of the stock-in-trade of the emancipated," which make Augustine patron saint of the "new morality." This well illustrates the danger of slogan morality, for in context (*Homilies*, I John 7:8, 10:7) Augustine is contending that it is *loving* to use the forces of the state to compel Donatist heretics to "come in" to the orthodox gospel feast; the argument of an uneasy conscience seeking sadly to prove that a "loving" end justifies any means used, and a principle that laid foundation for all religious persecution thereafter. Plainly everything depends upon what is included in loving conduct.

But in situation ethics only one thing is intrinsically good—love, "a way of relating to persons and using things." The end sought, love, is the only criterion, and alone justifies the means. There are no prescribed rules—only love. The only question to be raised in any situation is, What will produce the most love? One does not recite texts, duties, commandments, virtues, obligations, nor estimate consequences: one reacts in every situation as the free self, exercising responsible love, and does or avoids as love requires. This attitude simplifies, liberates, suffices. No other guidance is necessary or possible in so new an age. And because modern situations can be so very complex, love may well find itself sacrificing others (to preserve war secrets); telling lies; stealing; indulging homosexual, autosexual, promiscuous, or adulterous practices; dropping atomic bombs; approving abortion, prostitution, or polygamy.

Evaluation. On the surface there is much that is attractive to Christians. "The only law is Christ's law of love"; but the master criterion remains essentially vague, because what love aims at is left undefined. It is wholly individualist, impulsive, born-of-the-situation; all obligations are dissolved in loving impulse. It may be true that such "love" is not peculiar to Christians: however, *Christian* love is.

If the norm is claimed to be the love taught by Jesus, then it is inconsistent to desert his concept of love as the fulfilling, not the abrogating, of divine law; to argue that Jesus was right only about love, but wrong on chastity, divorce, self-discipline, the commandments of God; and quite false to claim his authority for whatever "love" excuses—abortion, extramarital sex, lies, and the rest. Where Christ's authority is claimed, Christ's meaning must be retained. Fletcher nowhere reasons out what love requires; the Gospels are full of illustrations of what Jesus meant by it, while it is abundantly clear from the whole NT that Christian love positively forbids fornication, adultery, murder, falsehood, stealing, and much else. What love requires, and excludes, is not left to intuitive, uninstructed impulse.

Thus, though the apparent simplification is also attractive, the love norm, rightly paramount, is not self-sufficient. A greal deal must be assumed about the Christian goal for life, and for individuals, about the Christian scale of values, about what is truly good for our neighbors, and about the will of God in each situation, before love knows what to do. The "situation," too, is itself no accident, but an opportunity into which providence has brought the Christian, with indications of duty and divine guidance. Considerable insight, knowledge, and spiritual maturity is presupposed. Situation ethics is at best a final stage in moral growth, succeeding earlier stages that need guidelines, borrowed experience, and clear instruction. Fletcher tacitly acknowledges this, by supposing love to include intelligence, information, foresight, prudence, and much more.

Finally, the practical immediacy of situation ethics is attractive to Christians. It suggests that the individual is "open to the inspiration of the moment" as to what he ought to do. But the Christian self is not totally open to on-the-spot prompting of capricious love—just because he is Christian. He confronts every situation with mind and heart already shaped by Christian experience, inheriting (to some degree) the long Christian tradition of what is right, and committed to Christian belief and obedience. With the example of Jesus before his eyes, he enters every new situation having "the mind of Christ." His norm of behavior, therefore, though it must certainly be applied to varied and unprecedented situations, is in fact rooted in the past, expressed in the incarnation of the ideal in Christ.

The alert modern Christian does face each novel situation afresh, and looks to the inspiration of the Spirit of Jesus to know how to act in love: but the guidelines are clear. His norm for all circumstances is the imitation of Christ. Shorn of exaggeration, and focused upon Jesus, situation ethics has much to teach those who imagine quotation of ancient texts a sufficient guide to contemporary problems. R. E. O. WHITE

See also ETHICAL SYSTEMS, CHRISTIAN; ETHICS, BIBLICAL; LOVE.

Bibliography. J. Fletcher, *Situation Ethics;* G. Woods, "Situation Ethics," *Christian Ethics and Contemporary Philosophy,* ed. I. T. Ramsey; A. Nygren, *Agape and Eros;* G. H. Clark, *DCE,* 623–24; N. H. G. Robinson, *Groundwork of Christian Ethics.*

Six Articles, The (1539). One of a series of regulations designed to maintain unity in the Church of England under Henry VIII, during that period when the church was independent of the pope but still not officially Protestant. Henry (reigned 1509–47) had broken with the pope in 1533 over his divorce from Catherine of Aragon and over the question of who had ultimate sovereignty in England. He did not, however, have any desire to abandon Catholic theology. His counselors, however, including Thomas Cromwell and the new Archbishop of Canterbury, Thomas Cranmer, wished to see a doctrinal reformation in England as well as an ecclesiastical one. One of their tactics was to encourage Henry to negotiate with the Lutherans of Germany. The Ten Articles of 1536 emerged from such negotiations. They were still generally Roman Catholic, but also reflected Protestant influence—they neglected to mention Catholic teaching on transubstantiation in the Lord's Supper; they gave a nearly Protestant definition of justification by faith; and they mentioned only three of the seven traditional sacraments.

Henry was not pleased with the unrest this and similar reforming measures stimulated. At the same time, moreover, Henry's negotiations with Lutheran princes, which had once seemed promising, were turning sour. As a result he urged his new parliament in 1539 to pass legislation reaffirming Catholic doctrine in England. The result was the Six Articles, revised personally by the king who also argued for them before Parliament. The articles reaffirmed transubstantiation, ordered lay people to refrain from the cup in Communion, and upheld the celibacy of the clergy. They also proclaimed the immutability of monastic vows, defended the saying of private masses, and stressed the importance of auricular confession. Protestants, understandably, called this "the bloody whip with six strings." Hugh Latimer, who would later be burned at the stake under the Catholic Queen Mary, was forced out of his bishopric as a result of these articles. And Archbishop Cranmer felt compelled to send his wife back to her native Germany. The Six Articles were eloquent testimony to Henry's desire to slow the pace of reform in England and to preserve order in his country. M. A. NOLL

See also TEN ARTICLES, THE.

Bibliography. A. G. Dickens, *The English Reformation;* G. R. Elton, *Reform and Reformation: England 1509–1558.*

Slavery. A state of involuntary servitude. Slavery was an accepted fact in the ancient world and a significant factor in economic and societal life. Slaves were frequently the product of defeats in wars. Often entire populations, as well as soldiers, were enslaved. The sale of slaves became a cornerstone of business in the Graeco-Roman world reaching its peak in the pre-Christian second century. Delos, in 100 B.C., was an important slave mart where as many as ten thousand slaves were imported and sold in a day. The Emperor Titus after his Palestinian campaign sold ninety thousand Jews into bondage.

The state of the slave varied. Some were impressed into gangs that worked the fields and mines. Others were highly skilled workers and trusted administrators. Frequently slaves were far better off than free laborers. Roman laws were passed to protect slaves and to allow rights, even of private possessions, which were sometimes used to ransom the slave and his family

(Acts 22:27–28). By the first century the slave population had become so large in the Roman world it created problems. Uprisings were frequent and owners were fearful and suspicious. If a slave attacked his master, every slave in the household was killed. In 136 B.C. some seventy thousand slaves in Sicily withstood Rome for four years. The penalty for rebellion was crucifixion until the time of Christian emperors. Due to the need for free citizens to perform civil duties, including military, between 81 and 49 B.C. five hundred thousand slaves were manumitted. The capital had a population of only eight hundred thousand at that time. Among those freed in Rome, many were Jews who took Roman names, as evidenced in catacomb inscriptions.

In the OT. In the OT slavery was a legally prescribed institution and generally more humanitarian than in the Near East. Since in Israel it was economically preferable to have work done by laborers, slavery was less extensive. Slaves generally performed household duties or labored with the family in the fields. Slaves were acquired by purchase, in payment of debt, by inheritance, by birth, and as prisoners of war. OT instances show a father selling a daughter (Exod. 21:7, Neh. 5:5), a widow selling children (II Kings 4:1), people selling themselves (Lev. 25:39; Deut. 15:12–17). A person might be freed by purchase (Lev. 25:48–55), sabbatical year law (Exod. 21:1–11; Deut. 15:12–18), the jubilee year (Lev. 25:8–55), the death of the master (Gen. 15:2). Slaves were considered part of the owner's family and, if Hebrews, had the right to the sabbath rest and to participate in the religious feasts. They were allowed possessions, even slaves. Often the wife and the slave-concubine had the same privileges and were indistinguishable. The slave was protected from cruel practices, especially life-threatening acts (Exod. 21:20). Man stealing was condemned strongly (Exod. 21:16). Israel as a nation knew bondage in Egypt and thus the exodus experience plays a major role in both the OT and the NT. Likewise, it is a significant theme in the liberation theologies.

In the NT. The early church did not attack slavery as an institution. It did, however, reorder the relationship of slave and masters (Phil.), indicate that in God's sight there was neither "slave nor free" (Gal. 3:28), and state that both were accountable to God (Eph. 6:5–9). The interpersonal relationship was recast in terms of the character of Christ and his kingdom. The full impact of this did not fully appear until after the Reformation when the biblical truth of the personal dignity of man was asserted.

In Church History. In the first Christian centuries slavery was an accepted fact as custom evidences. Slaves could not be baptized without the master's testimony if the master was a Christian. Nor could the slave be ordained unless his master was a Christian and allowed freedom to serve. Similarly the slave could not marry or enter a monastery unless the master permitted. Easter was an occasion when in celebration of the resurrection slaves were frequently freed. Despite Justinian's (527–65) effort to eliminate slavery, the number of slaves again grew, and after the empire's collapse merged into serfdom. The Crusades accentuated slavery on both sides, with Rome serving as a slave trade center and Venice selling even Christian slaves to Muslims. In the fifteenth century the modern slave trade emerged, principally under the Portuguese. The discovery of America called for black labor, causing the trade to flourish.

Some fifteen million slaves were transported to the Americas mostly to the West Indies and South America. Among the minor elements of Christianity opposition to slavery was voiced against great odds. The Quakers (1671), Moravians, Methodists, and evangelicals in England and America raised a standard against the evil of slavery. John Wesley wrote an antislavery tract. Often unfortunately, conservative voices in the churches opposed abolition and all too slowly came to see the light. These forces frequently united with selfish political and economic interest in support of slavery without fully realizing the implications of their actions. Under the efforts of evangelical leaders such as Granville Sharp, William Wilberforce, and Thomas Clarkson slavery was outlawed in Britain in 1807 and 1827 in the empire. The U.S. Congress brought the slave trade to a close in January 1808, but interstate slave trade and the breeding of slaves flourished. In the U.S. the Roman Catholic and Protestant Episcopal churches did not take a stand on slavery, but most other bodies split North and South on the issue. W. N. KERR

See also ABOLITIONISM.

Bibliography. G. W. Barnes, *The Anti-Slavery Impulse;* D. B. Davis, *The Problem of Slavery in Western Culture* and *The Problem of Slavery in the Age of Revolution;* M. I. Finley, ed., *Slavery in Classical Antiquity;* J. Mendlesohn, *Slavery in the Ancient Near East;* W. L. Westermann, *The Slave Systems of Greek and Roman Antiquity;* T. Wiedemann, *Greek and Roman Slavery.*

Smalcald Articles, The (1537). Articles of belief named for the town in Hesse-Nassau, Germany, where they were presented to Protestant leaders; now part of the *Book of Concord,* the normative collection of Lutheran confessions. The Articles were occasioned by the call of Pope Paul III for a council at Mantua. Invited to attend, the German Protestants through Elector John Frederick of Saxony asked Luther to prepare a confession for them to submit. Luther wrote them during Christmas, 1536. Together with his Small and Large catechisms, they comprise his contribution to the *Book of Concord.* Illness prevented Luther's attendance when the princes and theologians met in February, 1537, at Smalcald. Luther's articles were subscribed by most of the theologians in attendance. The princes delayed action, declaring their refusal to recognize the council, which never did convene. The Smalcald Articles are grouped in three parts: (1) those concerning "the chief articles" of "the Divine Majesty," about which there was no controversy with Rome, as the Trinity; (2) those concerning "the articles which refer to the office and work of Jesus Christ or our redemption," about which there was controversy with Rome and no compromise was possible, as justification by grace alone through faith; (3) those concerning miscellaneous matters, about which there was controversy but which were open to negotiation, as monastic vows and the marriage of priests. The articles were valued as "a bold, clear-cut testimony of the Lutheran position" and as a testimony of Luther's personal faith, for he wrote them at a time when he felt his death was near. Published by Luther in 1538, a Latin translation appeared in 1541. By 1553 they were named the Smalcald Articles in an edition issued at Weimar. Within a generation they won wide approval in Lutheran Germany and were included in the *Book of Concord.* Attached to them was the "Treatise on the Power and Primacy of the Pope" (1537) by Philip Melanchthon. It was officially adopted at Smalcald and, while intended to supplement the Augsburg Confession, it became associated with the articles. C. G. FRY

See also AUGSBURG CONFESSION; CONCORD, BOOK OF.

Bibliography. T. G. Tappert *et al.*, trs. and eds., *The Book of Concord;* W. D. Allbeck, *Studies in the Lutheran Confessions;* R. D. Preus, *Getting into the Theology of Concord;* D. P. Scaer, *Getting into the Story of Concord.*

Small Catechism, Luther's. *See* LUTHER'S SMALL CATECHISM.

Smith, Hannah Whitall (1832–1911). Writer, teacher, and social reformer. Hannah Whitall Smith was one of the outstanding women in her time. Her best-known book, *The Christian's Secret of a Happy Life,* after appearing in her husband's magazine *The Christian's Pathway of Power* (Feb. 1874–Jan. 1875) in serial form, was published by the Willard Tract Repository, Boston, and Morgan and Scott, London, in 1875. It has gone through numerous editions and been translated into most of the major languages of the world.

Born in Philadelphia in 1832, Hannah married Robert Pearsall Smith, also a Quaker. They "joined successively the Methodists, the Plymouth Brethren and the Baptists; and then they set out . . . to preach the Higher Life."

The Smiths both preached extensively in Europe and played an important part in founding the Keswick Conferences and leading the Higher Life Movement, but severed their connections with it after some years, and returned to America. After an unfortunate incident between Robert and a young woman, he discontinued preaching and later abandoned his faith entirely.

Hannah, however, continued preaching and writing, and worked eagerly in the Women's Christian Temperance Movement and in the Women's Suffrage Movement.

She and her husband returned to England permanently in 1886, where she continued to write—and occasionally to preach.

In her widely disseminated book, the secret of a happy, Christian life is explained as "a life of inward rest and outward victory." It exists when a Christian is saved not only from sin's "guilt" but "from the power and dominion of sin." She speaks of "the infiniteness of God's power for destroying that which is contrary to Him (which is 'sin')" and extols "God's power," which "comes to help us and to redeem us out of sin." Consistent with failures, and with temptation, it is an obtainment the believer receives through faith, with consecration to God as a prerequisite to faith.

The Holiness Movement, stemming out of John Wesley, has claimed Smith as a popularizer of its doctrine of entire sanctification as a second definite work of grace. J. K. GRIDER

See also HOLINESS MOVEMENT, AMERICAN; KESWICK CONVENTION.

Bibliography. Smith, *Difficulties of Life, Religious Fanaticism,* and *The Unselfishness of God and How I Discovered It: A Spiritual Autobiography;* R. Strachey, *A Quaker Grandmother: Hannah Whitall Smith* and *Group Movements of the Past and Experiments in Guidance;* B. Strachey, *Remarkable Relations;* L. P. Smith, *A Religious Rebel: The Letters of "H. W. S."*

Social Ethics. The study of questions of good and evil, right and wrong, obligation and prohibition as these arise in a social context.

Introduction and Definition. Public policy,

politics, economics, war, poverty, education, racism, ecology, and crime: these are examples of the subject matter of social ethics. The task of social ethics can best be understood in contrast to other related fields. In contrast to social history studies, what *was* the situation in the past, and social science, what *is* the situation, social ethics is concerned with what *ought to be*—with the values and norms against which the past and present are to be judged. While social ethics has a task distinctive from those of social history and social science, it cannot be successful in this endeavor without an ongoing interaction with these related fields.

As in the case of other subfields of ethics, social ethics may be approached *descriptively* (What is the character of this morality? This ethical language?) or *prescriptively* (I propose this set of values, these norms and principles, this way of resolving an ethical dilemma). A further distinction must be made between ethical *discernment* and ethical *implementation.* Social ethics includes reflection both on the problem of analysis and discernment of the social good and on the problem of strategy and implementation of the social good. Just as dogmatic theology exists to serve the church in its proclamation and worship, social ethics exists to serve the world by means of social reforms that will bring it into closer conformity to what is just, good, and right.

It is impossible to maintain a clear and precise distinction between social ethics and personal (individual) ethics. No individual behavior is without social implications. No social situation or problem is without individual repercussions. Nevertheless, for analytical purposes it is helpful to treat social ethics as a field in its own right and to direct primary attention to the ethical aspects of social groups, institutions, and corporate problems (racial, economic, political, etc.). By contrast, then, personal ethics focuses on the individual moral agent.

As in the case of personal ethics, social ethics addresses two general sets of questions (each of which has a discernment and an implementation aspect as noted above). The first has to do with *being* (character) and the second with *doing* (specific decision and action). While the latter (reflection on specific, immediate ethical dilemmas) is an often urgent task for social ethics, the former is at least equally important. That is, behind specific acts and dilemmas exist ongoing attitudes, arrangements, and processes which may be just or unjust, good or evil. This is the problem of corporate and structured evil. For social ethics, good and evil are not located merely in individual moral agents nor in specific decisions and actions: they are also attributes of institutions, traditions, social arrangements, and processes.

Only in the last century has social ethics come into its own as an academic specialization in philosophy, theology, and religious studies departments. For Christian social ethics, however, it is essential to recognize that the subject matter of social ethics has received great attention throughout the Bible, from Genesis to Revelation. So too, most leaders and teachers of the Christian church over the past two millennia have given attention to social ethics, even if the label itself has not been employed. A contemporary Christian social ethics should be rooted in and governed by Holy Scripture as the word of God. It should be informed by the witness and experience of the church throughout history. And it should be in fruitful dialogue with social history and social science as suggested earlier.

Analysis and Discernment. The first task of Christian social ethics is the analysis of structures and situations and the discernment of good and evil in relation to these.

Revelation and Observation. Christian social ethical analysis proceeds in a dialectic between revelation, the word of God "from above," and observation and experience "from below." A sociological realism must probe beneath surface problems to a correct discernment of the fundamental forces and problems of our society. What is the framework and what are the main-currents just under the surface of current events and dilemmas? At the same time, analysis and discernment are informed by biblical revelation, by the word of God. From the Genesis account of God's questioning of Adam, Eve, and Cain, through Jesus Christ's questioning of Peter and the disciples, social ethics is rooted in this word of God. God not only illuminates, corrects, and deepens our observations of social reality, he also raises new issues and problems often undetected by even the most realistic sociological analysis. Thus Christian social ethics has a distinctive role to play in the broader society by giving expression to God's revealed perspectives on human affairs.

Creation. Much of traditional theological social ethics has been shaped by appeals to orders of creation (or "spheres" or "mandates"). The orders of the family and marriage, politics and the state, work and economics, and sometimes others have been understood not only by reference to biblical revelation but also by common sense, reason, and natural law. Each order or sphere has its own distinctive purpose and corresponding ethical framework. All orders are under the final sovereignty of God. Critics of this position have argued that (1) we live in a fallen world in which appeals to a lost creation are misguided, and (2) the Bible itself rarely, if ever, develops an "ethics of creation."

Whether or not social ethics is founded primarily on orders of creation, certain elements of the biblical revelation on creation have ongoing importance for Christian social ethics (cf. Gen. 1–2). The ethical "good" is defined by the will, word, and work of God. Humanity is intended to be cohumanity: a social, joyful partnership of human beings before God ("It is not good that man should dwell alone"). A positive view of politics and the state sees them as rooted in, and implied by, the social nature of created humanity. Marriage is implicitly monogamous and characterized by partnership before God. Work is fundamentally a matter of creativity (in the image of the Creator) and stewardship ("till the earth and subdue it").

Fall. As important as the doctrine of creation for Christian social ethics is the revelation concerning the fall. The fall (Gen. 3) indicates that evil originates in rebellion against God and disobedience to his command. Evil is manifested in accusation, division, and the domination of one human being over another (Adam and Eve, Cain and Abel). Cain's departure from the presence of God in favor of building his own city and society (Gen. 4) and the subsequent revelation concerning the city (Babel/Babylon, Nineveh, etc.) complete this initial description of social evil. Its essential characteristics are pride, disobedience to God, accusation, division, domination, exploitation, violence, and the will to power.

Later perspectives in Hebrew-Christian thought developed this view of the fall in terms of the enmity of cosmic "principalities and powers" against the purposes of God. Social structures and forces can have a demonic, corporate aspect. Evil is not merely an individual phenomenon but a corporate, structural matter. In this light, the state (or work, or money) is ethically ambiguous: it can be the promoter of cohumanity, the restrainer of social evil, or the habitat of the rebellious powers. Both social history and social science, using different terminology and research methods, corroborate the biblical revelation on the ambiguous, transpersonal, and structural potential of the state (and other social institutions).

Law and Justice. Christian social ethics, indeed all social ethics, often centers on the problem of justice and its institutionalization in law. The relationship between divine, revealed moral law and positive, civil law has been the subject of extensive reflection by Thomas Aquinas, John Calvin, and many other classical Christian thinkers. Christian social ethics must be informed, not only by the example of ancient Israel's theocracy (in which the connections between the Ten Commands and the Book of the Covenant and Holiness Code are fairly direct), but also by the example of Israel in exile and captivity (where the people of the word live in an alien situation).

In any case, justice (righteousness, judgment) is one of the most important ethical norms for Christian social ethics. "I am the Lord who practices steadfast love, justice, and vindication in the earth; for in these things I delight" (Jer. 9:24). God "works justice for all who are oppressed" (Ps. 103:6). Biblical justice is more than fairness and equality. It is revealed to be a redress of grievances on the part of the oppressed. It is not so much in tension with love as inclusive of love and mercy. In an era in which justice and law have been reduced, in many respects, to quantitative, technical terms, Christian social ethics must give voice to the biblical concept of justice: qualitative, of divine origin and human concern.

The Kingdom of God. Even the most intransigent orders-of-creation social ethicists acknowledge that a new order of redemption takes its place in society with the coming of Jesus Christ and the founding of the church. This church is (or is supposed to be) the primary exemplar of the kingdom of God which is in tension with the kingdom of this world. In Augustine's terms, the most important constitutive factors in social history are the city of God and the earthly city. The former is powered by *charitas*, love for God, and the latter by *cupiditas*, love for self. For Martin Luther, the two kingdoms are distinctive in that the kingdom of God is a matter of interior faith, while the civil kingdom concerns external affairs. For Augustine, Luther, and others, of course, the picture is considerably more complex than these summaries. Nevertheless, there remains a distinction to be made in Christian social ethics between the corporate reality that takes Jesus Christ as its point of departure, and everything else.

It is in Jesus Christ that the word of God is most clearly and fully revealed—for social ethics as for everything else. The social teaching of Jesus is given in his "platform" statement (Luke 4:18–21), in the temptation (Matt. 4), in his parables and discourses, in the Sermon on the Mount (chs. 5–7), in his farewell discourse (John 13–17), and in the events of the crucifixion and resurrection. The great commands to love God and love one's neighbor, the call to unqualified servanthood and sacrifice, the Golden Rule, the call to simplicity and away from worship of mammon, and so on give the essential dimensions of Jesus' social ethics. Christian social ethics must reflect not only on the traditional, mainline interpretations of the meaning of Jesus Christ, the kingdom of God, and the love command, but also on the interpretation and application of this social teaching by Franciscans, Anabaptists, Quakers, and others who have developed a social ethic based on Jesus Christ.

Eschatology. Christian social ethics is fundamentally eschatological in nature. That is, it leans toward the future and complete arrival of the judgment and grace of God. More than the original creation, it is the new creation which is invoked for ethical guidance in the NT. The kingdom of God, which is truly here (in part), will be (fully) revealed at the end. Jesus Christ is the new Adam. The Holy Spirit is the down payment on the future—not merely the echo of the original creation. History moves toward the new Jerusalem, not back to a golden age in Eden. For these reasons, the Apocalypse has particular social ethical significance in revealing God's final ethical judgment on human society in terms of Babylon (Rev. 18) and the new Jerusalem (ch. 21).

It is in this final judgment that the principalities and powers are finally, completely dethroned, completing the work of Jesus Christ, who, "having disarmed the powers and authorities, . . . made a public spectacle of them, triumphing over them by the cross" (Col. 2:15 NIV). Babylon is the habitation of Satan and the principalities and powers. It is condemned for allowing the merchants of the earth to grow rich from her excessive luxuries, for her pride and power, for her mistreatment of saints, prophets, and apostles, for trafficking in the bodies and souls of human beings, for violence and bloodshed. The new Jerusalem, by contrast, is the place where God dwells, where death, mourning, and pain are eliminated, where the thirsty and hungry are satisfied, where nothing shameful or deceitful occurs, where the city gates are open to all the nations. Given the prominent eschatological thrust of biblical social ethics, Christian ethics takes seriously this final apocalyptic scenario in discerning what is good and evil socially.

Strategy and Implementation. The first task of Christian social ethics, then, is the analysis and discernment of social good and evil, drawing on social history, social science, and, above all, biblical social ethics. The second task is to reflect on the relation between Christ and culture—that is, between the ethical command of God and the social situation. It is the problem of strategy and implementation.

Traditional Perspectives. Contemporary reflection on how Christian (or religious) conviction relates to society has been influenced a great deal by social historians and social scientists. While Karl Marx, Émile Durkheim, and others have also had considerable influence, this reflection is most often indebted to pioneering studies done by Max Weber, Ernst Troeltsch, and H. Richard Niebuhr. Weber's studies of the role of prophetism and charisma, his fourfold typology of the relation of religious groups to the world (innerworldly and otherworldly asceticism, innerworldly and otherworldly mysticism), and his classic study *The Protestant Ethic and the Spirit of Capitalism* continue to be an important point of departure for reflection on problems of strategy and implementation of Christian social ethical concern.

Ernst Troeltsch's *The Social Teaching of the Christian Churches* proposed and gave voluminous historical illustration to a threefold typology of church, sect, and mystical association. H. R. Niebuhr elaborated and modified Troeltsch's typology into five categories which remain influential in many current discussions. "Christ against culture" is represented by the sectarian, Anabaptist approach. "The Christ of culture" is represented by Ritschl and the accommodationist approach. "Christ above culture" is represented by Thomas Aquinas and a synthetic approach. "Christ and culture in paradox" is represented by Luther and the dualist approach. "Christ the transformer of culture" is represented by Augustine and the conversionist approach.

Social scientific and historical typologies such as the above are not able to do full justice to individual traditions. Nor do they take adequate account of the "denominational" and "laicized" character of contemporary society. Sixteenth (or even nineteenth) century categories and divisions are not directly transferable and applicable to the late twentieth century. Nevertheless, reflection of contemporary strategy and implementation is greatly impoverished without taking into account these traditional perspectives.

Prayer and Evangelism. From the point of view of biblical social ethics, the two activities of prayer and evangelism must not be underestimated as strategies for social change. Basic to the Judeo-Christian world view is the conviction that God participates and intervenes in human history, partly, at least, in response to the prayer of the people. Entreaties, prayers, petitions, and thanksgivings are to be made in behalf of all people, including those with political authority (I Tim. 2:1–2). Prayer is thus, among other things, a political and social activity of great importance.

It is also basic to the Christian outlook to proclaim the gospel of Jesus Christ in the hope that men and women will come to know him as Savior, Lord, and God. While social ethics is concerned primarily with corporate and structural good and evil, it is partly by means of individual moral agents that corporate, institutional reality is affected. Evangelism, among other things, brings about social change by means of the transformation of social actors, individual moral agents.

Alternative Community. Far from being an uncaring, irresponsible withdrawal from social responsibility, the formation of alternative Christian community plays an important role in implementing social ethical change. The primary alternative community is the church (in both its local and broader senses). Intentionally Christian businesses, schools, political groups, and other associations are other means by which this strategy may be employed.

Alternative Christian communities have a fivefold significance for the implementation of social concern. First, the community is an essential context for moral deliberation and discernment. The individual gifts and abilities of members of the community combine to discern the best possible responses to the complex issues and dilemmas of contemporary society. Second, the very existence of the community (with its ultimate commitment to Jesus Christ) contributes to the health of society by "opening up" the social order. Totalitarian, monistic tendencies are held in check by the existence of alternative communities in society. Third, the Christian community furnishes society with an example of "another way" of dealing with various social problems (leadership patterns, welfare activities, and so on). Fourth, the community can function as a laboratory in which various reforms can be tested, refined, and demonstrated. Fifth, the community prepares and assists individuals who go out from the community into the various structures and situations in the broader society. It is a resource not only for discernment but for social action.

Institutional Participation. As Moses, Daniel, Paul, and other biblical figures demonstrate, direct participation in the political (and other) structures and institutions of society is another strategy available for the implementation of social ethical concern. Especially in circumstances where Christians (along with others) are invited to exercise political and social responsibility, it is appropriate to regard institutional participation as a valid means of implementing ethical conviction. Electoral politics, legislative reforms, business and professional activities, and public education are examples of institutional spheres where participation might be called for. The boundaries of such participation are established by two criteria. First, no Christian is ever authorized to violate the command of God: we ought always, in cases of conflict, to "obey God rather than men" (Acts 5:29). Second, no Christian individual or group is ever authorized to unilaterally impose (coercively) the moral standards of the kingdom of God on the world. Christians are to be the salt of the earth, the light of the world, and sheep among wolves: they have presence and impact, but not by way of coercion and domination.

Means and Ends. Biblical Christian social ethics, in both discernment and implementation, defies easy categorization as deontological (doing what is right without regard to consequences) or teleological (the end justifies the means) ethics. In particular, however, a teleological approach violates the biblical message. Under no circumstances are evil means justified or permissible (Rom. 6). The Christian is called to "overcome evil with good" (12:21). Since the means chosen affect the character of the end, a good end can be achieved only by the use of good means. Justice will be achieved only with just means; peace with peaceful means; freedom or equality with means that are characterized by freedom and equality. Christian reflection on strategy and implementation of the good that is discerned will always stress this indissoluble relationship between means and ends. D. W. Gill

See also Abortion; Ethical Systems, Christian; Ethics, Biblical; Situation Ethics.

Bibliography. P. C. Cotham, ed., *Christian Social Ethics;* C. F. H. Henry, *Aspects of Christian Social Ethics;* S. C. Mott, *Biblical Ethics and Social Change;* H. R. Niebuhr, *Christ and Culture;* G. Winter, ed., *Social Ethics;* J. H. Yoder, *The Politics of Jesus.*

Social Gospel, The. The term "social gospel," with its present association with theologically liberal, moderately reformist Protestant social thought, came into use about 1900 to describe that Protestant effort to apply biblical principles to the growing problems of the emerging urban-industrial America during the decades between the Civil War and World War I.

Considered to be probably a uniquely American movement in theology, the social gospel also stands as part of a rich Judeo-Christian heritage of response to human need, with roots in the OT and the NT, and with antecedents in every era of church history. Its more immediate debt included the writings and programs with which English and continental churchmen and theologians like Charles Kingsley and John Frederick Denison Maurice had begun responding to similar social distress. In the United States, social gospel roots included such nineteenth century clergymen as Stephen Colwell, whose *New Themes for the Protestant Clergy* was published in 1851, and the revivalists whose story Timothy L. Smith has related in *Revivalism and Social Reform in Mid-Nineteenth Century America.*

The uniqueness of the social gospel resided, then, not in its discontinuity from the past, but in its resourcefulness in applying Christian principles to complex and massive problems during a critical transition in American social history.

A major part of the difficulty encountered in that application was the opposition by advocates of the dominant laissez faire individualism of the nineteenth century. The intense struggle resulted in overreaction on the part of advocates of the new order; the twentieth century came to be as one-sided in its emphasis on social causes and cures as the nineteenth had been in its stress on the individual.

Equally significant in the unfolding identity of Protestant social Christianity in the progressive era were the large-scale defections from historic Christian orthodoxy that resulted from developments in the sciences and in biblical studies. Many of the clergy who led in the accommodation to the new science and to the conclusions of the "higher critics" were also advocates of the social gospel, a fact which increasingly polarized conservative Christians against the movement.

Historians have tended to identify three kinds of responses within the social Christianity of that era, including conservative individualism, socialistic/radical, and progressive/moderately reformist. The latter was, of course, the track taken by the social gospel. That general analysis should be qualified by the fact that there was no direct correlation between social concern and theological stance, and that the lines were not very clearly drawn until well into the era. The Salvation Army, an organization occasionally cited as an example of conservative social Christianity, received strong support from prominent social gospelers and was itself an aggressive champion of social service and reform.

The distinctive ideas of the social gospel clustered around the prevailing social and economic crises, and the responses contained within the Bible and Christian history. Opposing the dominant laissex faire individualism in economic life, with its sanctioning of unrestrained competition, social gospelers pressed for brotherhood that included cooperation between management and labor. They saw in the OT prophets' denunciation of injustice, in the life and teachings of Jesus, and in the immanence of a God of love in human society the sanctions for a contrasting human order. That order would be realized in the kingdom of God, a kingdom in which God's will would be done as human lives expressed his love across the range of their relationships and of society's institutions. And because man was essentially good and perfectible, marked by sin that was a quite curable selfishness, the kingdom would indeed come. To social gospel advocates the early years of the twentieth century appeared to be ushering it in with increasing rapidity.

With immediate antecedents in the mid-nineteenth century, social Christianity began to take its new shape during the 1870s and 1880s in response to the first of a series of industrial crises, and in the preaching, writing, and organizational activities of a growing number of Protestant clergy. One of the first was Washington Gladden, a Congregationalist minister who has been called the father of the social gospel, and whose lectures on the labor question, published in 1876 as *Working People and Their Employers,* was one of the first social gospel writings. During the 1880s, in addition to Gladden's ongoing contributions, Josiah Strong and Richard T. Ely published, respectively, *Our Country* and *Social Aspects of Christianity, and Other Essays.*

Joining the increasingly prominent movement after 1890 was a young German Baptist pastor, Walter Rauschenbusch, who was to become perhaps the most influential prophet of the social gospel. He and other earnest young clergymen formed the Brotherhood of the Kingdom, one of an increasing number of organizations dedicated to the cause of social Christianity. Settlement houses brought Christian workers into tenement areas. The Social Gospel novel, epitomized in Charles M. Sheldon's phenomenally popular *In His Steps,* carried the message of social Christianity to the laity. And the Salvation Army, *Christian Herald,* and other evangelical organizations formalized and expanded their social outreach programs, spearheading a growing evangelical foray into the arena of social service and reform.

The high tide of the social gospel movement occurred during the years after 1900 as individuals like Lyman Abbott, Charles Henderson, Shailer Mathews, Frances Peabody, Charles Stelzle, Graham Taylor, and a host of institutional churches and other organizations began or continued their efforts. Walter Rauschenbusch burst into national prominence with his *Christianity and the Social Crisis* (1907), followed a few years later by *The Social Principles of Jesus* (1916), and *A Theology for the Social Gospel* (1917). The major supporting denominations—Baptists, Congregationalists, Episcopalians, Methodists, and Presbyterians—established commissions, while the churches in concert in 1908 formed the Federal Council of Churches, an agency that gave high priority to the social gospel as expressed in its "social creed." A new and Christian century appeared to be well underway.

The deaths of Washington Gladden and Walter Rauschenbusch in 1918 symbolized the dramatic change that came with World War I and its aftermath of political and economic chaos abroad and isolationism and reaction in the United States. While the social gospel continued into the 1930s, it was increasingly undermined by a changing national temper that included the gradual decline of liberal theology in the mainline churches.

The demise of the social gospel movement did not mean the death of its central emphasis upon applying Christian principles to social problems and to human need. In the civil rights and antiwar movements of recent decades, and in the radical social stance of the National and World councils of churches, some see continuity with the classical social gospel. Evangelicals have returned, meanwhile, to the social concern and action that had marked them until near the eve of World War I. In both cases the ongoing social Christianity appears to be less marked by utopianism and narrowly industrial concerns, and more by social action than was the social gospel itself. N. A. MAGNUSON

See also LIBERALISM, THEOLOGICAL; GLADDEN, WASHINGTON; RAUSCHENBUSCH, WALTER.

Bibliography. A. Abell, *The Urban Impact in American Protestantism* and *American Catholicism and Social Action: A Search for Social Justice 1865–1950;* R. T. Handy, *The Social Gospel in America;* C. H. Hopkins, *The Rise of the Social Gospel in American Protestantism;* N. A. Magnuson, *Salvation in the Slums: Evangelical Social Work, 1865–1920;* H. F. May, *Protestant Churches and Industrial America;* R. M. Miller, *American Protestantism and Social Issues, 1919–1939;* R. Allen, *The Social Passion: Religion and Social Reform in Canada, 1914–1928;* P. A. Carter, *Decline and Revival of the Social Gospel* and *The Spiritual Crisis of the Gilded Age;* G. Harkness, *The Methodist Church in Social Thought and Action;* S. P. Hayes, *The Response to Industrialism, 1885–1914;* R. D. Knudten, *Systematic Thought of Washington Gladden;* R. C. White, *The Social Gospel: Religion and Reform in Changing America.*

Social Implications of the Gospel. *See* GOSPEL, SOCIAL IMPLICATIONS OF.

Socialism, Christian. An application of the social principles of Christianity. The concept had unconventional origins in the French social reformer Henri de Saint-Simon (1760–1825), who predicted a much more greatly industrialized age wherein social problems would be resolved by science and technology. Only later did he introduce a religious note. His *Nouveau Christianisme,* published in the year of his death, held that religion "should guide the community toward the great aim of improving as quickly as possible the conditions of the poorest class." Having seen what France had suffered first under the Revolution in all its ferocity, and then under Napoleon, he urged European rulers to unite for the suppression of war, and to return to that true Christianity that concerns itself with the plight of the poor. Saint-Simon's views were often unordered and imprecise, but they were to influence an improbable combination of thinkers that included Thomas Carlyle, John Stuart Mill, Heinrich Heine, Auguste Comte, Friedrich Engels, and Walter Rauschenbusch, and were to find echoes in the work of the more recent American theologians Paul Tillich and Reinhold Niebuhr.

As well as having an impact on France, Christian socialism was a force in many other European countries, prompting the founding of groups which held that the working man had a right to social and economic justice, and that these were areas in which Christians should be active. In Germany it sadly deviated into anti-Semitism, which resulted in imperial condemnation in 1894. Five years earlier had seen the formation in the United States of the Society of Christian Socialists, but the idea had been there since Henry James, Sr., had expounded similar principles in 1849.

The term "Christian socialism" was popularized in midnineteenth century England when, after the failure of the Chartist movement, a group of Anglicans sought the application of Christian principles in the organization of industry. Its leaders were J. M. F. Ludlow (who had been educated in France), J. F. D. Maurice, and Charles Kingsley. They helped finance cooperative societies, started associations for different trades, and in 1854 founded the Working Men's College in London, with Maurice as principal. Kingsley's novels, notably *Yeast* and *Alton Locke* (both published in 1850), played a not inconsiderable part in a movement which, however, never really caught the imagination of ecclesiastical England, and soon declined. It left a valuable legacy, nonetheless, in principles and practices that benefited a wide area of social concern, including cooperatives, workers' educational institutes, and trade unions. J. D. DOUGLAS

Bibliography. C. E. Raven, *Christian Socialism 1848–54;* M. B. Reckitt: *Maurice to Temple: A Century of Social Movement in the Church of England;* A. J. Booth, *Saint-Simon and Saint Simonism.*

Society of Jesus, The (Jesuits). Monastic order founded by Ignatius of Loyola and approved as a Roman Catholic religious order in 1540. The Jesuits are classified as mendicant clerks regular. Unlike most earlier orders there is no parallel branch for women.

In 1534 Loyola and six companions, all students of theology at the University of Paris, took vows of poverty and chastity and promised to devote their lives to missionary work in Palestine if that were possible. Since war between Venice and the Ottoman Empire kept them from Palestine, they began preaching, teaching catechism, and doing various charitable works in the cities of northern Italy. Gradually they gathered new recruits, and since they wished to give permanent structure to their way of life, they sought approval from Pope Paul III as a religious order. Initially membership was restricted to sixty professed priests, but this was soon lifted, and the popes conferred many privileges on the new order and relied on it for many special tasks, including diplomatic missions to Ireland, Sweden, and Russia. Jesuit-professed fathers take a special vow of obedience to the pope.

Loyola was elected the first superior general in 1540 and spent his remaining years directing the new order and writing its Constitutions. The new order had several distinctive features. The superior general is elected for life and appoints all subordinate superiors, hence the Jesuits are highly centralized. Obedience is especially stressed. There is no distinctive religious habit or uniform, such as earlier orders had, no special fasts or bodily austerities, no common singing of the divine office. Loyola demanded that recruits be carefully selected and trained and that those who did not measure up be dismissed. Later the training normally lasted fifteen years. Two years at the beginning (novitiate) and a year at the end of the training (tertianship) were devoted to the spiritual development of the members in contrast to a one year novitiate in the old orders. Since the Jesuits were to be active in working with outsiders, monastic discipline had to be interiorized by vigorous training. Loyola's *Spiritual Exercises* shaped the Jesuits' interior life, and one hour's private meditation daily has been mandatory for most of the order's history. The Jesuits were in the forefront in spreading systematic meditation, a characteristic of Counter-Reformation piety. For the Jesuit, prayer and activity were to be mutually reinforcing. Popularization of the *Spiritual Exercises* in the retreat movement has been a major contemporary Jesuit apostolate; as many as five million Catholics annually make retreats.

Loyola stressed quality rather than quantity, but the Society of Jesus grew rapidly. There were about a thousand Jesuits by the founder's death in 1556, mainly in Spain, Italy, and Portugal, but also in France, Germany, and Belgium, as well as missionaries in India, Africa, and Latin America. By 1626 there were 15,544 Jesuits. Growth was steady but somewhat slower until 1773 when Clement XIV, under pressure from the Bourbon monarchs of France, Spain, and Naples, suppressed the society. A few Jesuit houses survived in Prussia and Russia where the monarchs refused to promulgate the suppression. In 1814 Pius VII restored the Jesuits worldwide. Despite being exiled from most European Catholic countries at one time or another, the Jesuits grew steadily in numbers during the next hundred years and peaked at 36,038 in 1964. Membership declined after the Second Vatican Council, reaching 27,027 in 1981 with roughly one-third in Europe, one-third in the United States and Canada, and one-third in Asia, Africa, and Latin America.

Education quickly became the largest single Jesuit apostolate. Loyola supervised the founding of a dozen colleges in the order's first decade. By 1626 the Jesuits directed five hundred colleges or seminaries, a number which nearly doubled by the mideighteenth century. Most of the Jesuit colleges approximated modern prep schools, but some were full-fledged universities. During the seventeenth and eighteenth centuries a high percentage of educated Catholic males, particularly the nobility, were graduates of these schools. The basic charter of these schools was the *Ratio Studiorum* (the Plan of Studies) of 1599, which tried to purify and simplify Renaissance humanism. Classical languages and literatures and religion provided the core curriculum with Aristotelian philosophy for advanced students. Attendance was compulsory and a planned curriculum carried students forward step by step in contrast with many contemporary schools. The rod was largely replaced by friendly rivalry as a stimulus to study. The Jesuit schools used drama, often with lush pageantry, to inculcate moral and religious values. Education remains a major Jesuit apostolate today; the Jesuits run some four thousand schools worldwide, mainly in mission countries, as well as eighteen American universities.

The Jesuits adopted Thomas Aquinas as their official theologian but freely modified his system, as in the theology of Francisco Suárez (1548–1617). Generally they stressed human action in the process of salvation in contrast to the Dominicans, who put more emphasis on the primacy of grace. Blaise Pascal attacked their casuistry as laxist. The Jesuits overwhelmingly rejected the principle that the end justifies the means, which was often attributed to them. Prominent among recent Jesuit theologians are Pierre Teilhard de Chardin, Karl Rahner, and Bernard Lonergan. The Jesuits presently edit some one thousand periodicals, including *NT Abstracts*, *Theology Digest*, and *Theological Studies*.

Traditionally the Jesuits have reserved their highest regard for missionary work. Francis Xavier (1506–52), the first and greatest Jesuit missionary, laid the basis for Jesuit activity in India, Indonesia, and Japan. The Japanese mission particularly flourished until it was wiped out by savage persecution in the early seventeenth century. In China Matteo Ricci (1552–1610) founded the Jesuit mission where he and his successors won the protection of the Ming emperors by introducing Western scientific and technical knowledge to court circles at Peking. They pioneered the adaptation of the gospel to Chinese traditions and thought forms, although in this many Catholic critics felt that they had gone too far. Their writings introduced China to the West. The goal of the Peking mission was the conversion of the emperor, but the Jesuits never found their Chinese Constantine. Ricci's idea of adapting Christianity to local culture was applied to India by Robert De Nobili (1577–1658). Jesuits such as Jacques Marquette and Issac Jogues worked among the Indians of North America. Eusebio Kino (1644–1711) established a string of mission stations which introduced the Indians of northern Mexico and the present southwestern United States to advanced agriculture. The Jesuits Christianized and civilized the Indians of Paraguay and Brazil in organized towns (reductions), which flourished for more than a century until the Jesuits were suppressed.

Although the Jesuits were not founded to combat Protestantism, they were quickly drawn into the struggle. Many Jesuits published controversial works, for instance, Peter Canisius and Robert Bellarmine, both of whom also wrote catechisms that enjoyed wide use for three centuries. Other Jesuits influenced policy as court preachers or as confessors to the emperor; the kings of France, Spain, and Poland; and the dukes of Bavaria. Well over a thousand Jesuits died as martyrs both in Europe and in the missions. The Roman Catholic Church has canonized thirty-eight Jesuits, including twenty-two martyrs. J. P. DONNELLY

See also IGNATIUS OF LOYOLA.

Bibliography. J. Brodrick, *The Origins of the Jesuits;* W. Bangert, *A History of the Society of Jesus;* D. Mitchell, *The Jesuits;* J. de Guibert, *The Jesuits: Their Spiritual Doctrine and Practice.*

Socinus, Faustus (1539–1604). Anti-Trinitarian theologian, Socinus was born in Siena, Italy, on December 5, 1539. His early education was limited until two of his uncles began tutoring him. One uncle, Laelius Socinus, was caught up in the Protestant movement and later adopted anti-Trinitarian beliefs. Upon his uncle's death, Faustus took his dead uncle's papers, devoted himself to the study of theology, and also became an advocate of anti-Trinitarian beliefs.

After spending time in several European countries, Socinus settled in Poland in 1578 where a strong anti-Trinitarian community existed. In Poland he was initially refused membership in the Anabaptist-Unitarian sect, because he held that baptism was not a necessary act. As a result, he did not immediately exert influence among Polish Unitarians, although he joined with them in worship. Later he persuaded them to adhere to his theological beliefs and eventually was recognized as their principal leader. His stay in Poland was not altogether peaceful; from time to time he faced persecution for his beliefs from Catholics and Protestants.

Socinus believed that Scripture should be interpreted rationally. This philosophical framework led him to deny the deity of Christ. In his view Christ had a human nature and did not become God until after his resurrection when the Father delegated some of his divine power to the risen Jesus. Socinus accepted the miracles and virgin birth of Christ, seeing them as signs given to mankind to show Jesus' unique role in becoming divine. Socinus did not believe Christ's death on the cross brought forgiveness of sins because God could forgive sins without the necessity of Jesus' atonement. Repentance and good works brought forgiveness from God. Socinus denied original sin, predestination, and the resurrection of the body (except for a select few who were particularly conscientious followers of Jesus). He also regarded the Lord's Supper as purely commemorative.

Socinus's ideas laid the foundation for later unitarian movements, although he did not go as far as future anti-Trinitarians in denying the miraculous or divine role of Jesus. He was also among the first who subjected Scripture to rational criticism. P. KUBRICHT

See also RACOVIAN CATECHISM.

Bibliography. O. Chadwick, *The Reformation;* J. H. S. Kent, "The Socinian Tradition," *Theol* 78: 131–40; E. M. Wilbur, *A History of Unitarianism;* G. H. Williams, *The Radical Reformation.*

Solafidianism (Lat. *sola fide* "faith alone"). The doctrine that salvation is by faith only. The term emerged as a consequence of Luther's translation of Rom. 3:28 in which he added the word "alone" to the phrase "man is justified by faith [alone] apart from works of the Law" (NASB). He was severely castigated for this, but Erasmus defended him. The translation is justifiable in view of the only alternative, namely justification by works, which Paul expressly repudiated. The Council of Trent (1545–63), on the other hand, vigorously opposed Luther's translation and all that it implied by declaring: "If anyone saith that justifying faith is nothing else than confidence in the divine mercy which remits sins for Christ's sake, or that this confidence alone is that whereby we are justified, let him be anathema" (Session 6, Can. 12).

Implicit in solafidianism is the doctrine of divine monergism, which declares that man's salvation is totally dependent upon God's activity and is in no way conditioned by the action of man. Man's choice of sin has rendered him incapable of spiritual action; he is spiritually dead. Unless rescued by a source outside himself, he would eternally perish in this state. God has taken the initiative by restoring mankind to himself through the death of Christ (Christ's passive obedience to the law), which removes man's guilt, and by imputing Christ's righteousness (which he achieved while on earth through his active obedience to the law) to those who believe. Saving faith is not an innate quality of fallen man but a gift of God (Eph. 2:8; Phil. 1:29) communicated through hearing the gospel (Rom. 10:17). The *ordo salutis* ("order of salvation") is God's activity in grace from inception to consummation. Understandably solafidianism is opposed to Pelagianism, semi-Pelagianism, and synergism, all of which attribute justification or the apprehension of it, in one way or another, to the action of man. F. R. Harm

Bibliography. L. Berkhof, *Systematic Theology;* E. L. Lueker, *Lutheran Cyclopedia,* 726; F. E. Mayer, *The Religious Bodies of America;* C. S. Meyer, *NIDCC,* 914; F. Pieper, *Christian Dogmatics,* II, 397–415; A. H. Strong, *Systematic Theology;* H. C. Thiessen, *Lectures in Systematic Theology.*

Solidarity of the Race. A theological teaching that all humans are of the same species and shape, with Adam as a common ancestor. This teaching is not so much positively affirmed as it is assumed in all of Scripture. Most of the scriptural evidence for the solidarity of the race is found in passages dealing with the imputation of Adam's sin to all his posterity. Even prior to NT teaching on the significance of Adam's sin, however, the OT established the unity of the human race. The very use of *'ādām* for man presents strong evidence that the word refers to the class of men (Gen. 6:1). Therefore, *'ādām* can be translated by "Adam" and by "mankind" or the plural "men."

Particular OT passages presuppose the solidarity of the race. Gen. 3:15ff. recounts God's judgment on the serpent and on Adam and Eve. The language of the judgments on Adam and Eve implies that they are to be experienced by all mankind throughout history. Sometimes the referent of *'ādām* is not unambiguous. It may refer to people as a class or to the first man, and as such has a bearing on the issue of the solidarity of the human race. When Job states, "If I have concealed my sin as *men* do," did he intend to say "as Adam did"? When Yahweh charged the people: "Your first father sinned; your spokesmen rebelled against me" (Isa. 43:27, NIV), did he refer to Adam? The concern of the OT is with Abraham and his descendants, rather than all the nations. Therefore, it is not always clear whether the reference is to the patriarchs and their descendants or to Adam and his descendants.

Whereas the OT does not deal explicitly with the solidarity of the human race, but assumes it, the NT, on the other hand, more explicitly teaches the doctrine of solidarity. In Acts 17:26 Paul, standing before the Areopagus, says, "From one man he made every nation of men, that they should inhabit the whole earth." Paul goes on to quote one of the Greek poets, that "We are his offspring." These statements are, of course, in the context of the kerygma, and are addressed to a Gentile audience. Paul affirms that Jews and Gentiles together need Jesus, because all have sinned *in Adam.* This brings us to the classic passage on the imputation of Adam's sin (Rom. 5:12–21). The apostle's use of "all men" clearly demands the doctrine of the unity of the race in order for his argument to be complete (cf. also I Cor. 15:21–22, 45).

The implication of the doctrine of solidarity involves more than just one's view of original sin, whether mediately or immediately imputed. If the human race has a common ancestor in Adam, then all humans have the image of God. For this reason, then, the one gospel of salvation in Christ is truly relevant to all men not only because it proclaims that God's wrath is propitiated by the sacrifice of his Son, and hence that there is hope for our "human" condition. There is also a proclamation of hope in that it calls us to be a part of the new humanity in Jesus Christ.

W. A. Van Gemeren

See also Man, Doctrine of.

Bibliography. R. Shedd, *Man in Community.*

Son of God (*huios tou theou*). A title or a means of expressing a relationship—especially of Jesus—

which can be indicated in other ways. As a title it was relatively rare, especially in hellenistic and Jewish circles, but as a relationship indicating physical descent, numerous examples can be cited in ancient Near Eastern, hellenistic, and Roman sources, especially with reference to kings. Its Christian uses of Jesus as God's Son, however, can be explained only in light of a Jewish background and peculiarly Christian additions.

In the OT. *Israel as God's Son.* Whereas both celestial beings (e.g., Job 1:6; 2:1; Pss. 29:1; 89:6) and Israel (e.g., Deut. 14:1; Hos. 1:10) can collectively be called sons of God, Israel's unique relationship with God enabled it to be referred to in the singular as God's firstborn son (Exod. 4:22) or simply as his son (e.g., Exod. 4:23; Jer. 31:20; Hos. 11:1). The relationship is also indicated by God's referring to himself as Israel's father (e.g., Jer. 31:9; Mal. 1:6) and Israel to God as Father (e.g., Isa. 63:16; 64:8; Jer. 3:4).

The King as God's Son. In Ps. 2:7 God is quoted at the coronation of the king as saying, "You are my son; today I have begotten you." David's descendants in particular are given divine approval in Ps. 89:26–27, where God called the Davidic king "firstborn" and had the king refer to him as "my Father." This special filial relationship for David's dynasty goes back ultimately to II Sam. 7:14, where of Solomon, the beginning of a perpetual line of Davidic kings, God says through Nathan, "I will be his Father, and he will be my son."

In Intertestamental Literature. The title "son of God" occurs, though infrequently, in nonmessianic intertestamental texts. In Wis. Sol. 2:18 the wicked who conspire against the righteous man refer to him as "son of God" and assert that he calls God "father" (2:16). Philo used the phrase of the Logos. In a nonmessianic reference in the Dead Sea Scrolls, a figure is referred to as both "the son of God" and "the son of the Most High." The curious fact, however, in light of the OT justification for it, is that there is no undisputed example of the title in a pre-Christian messianic text. The references in IV Ezra (7:28–29; 13:32, 37, 52; 14:9) and Enoch (105:2) which are often adduced are generally questioned by modern scholars either on linguistic grounds or as suspected Christian corruptions. Reverence for the divine name, opposition to Hasmonean regal claims, and reaction against the non-Jewish practice of regarding the king as physically descendent from a god have all been suggested as possible explanations for the absence of "son of God" as a messianic *title,* when the *relationship* is clearly ascribed to the king in OT passages.

None of this, however, proves that the connection between the Messiah and Son of God was not made in pre-Christian Judaism. In fact, two passages in John suggest that some Jews made the identification. Nathanael, who had had no prior contact with Jesus, had as his initial reaction to him, "Rabbi, you are the Son of God; you are the king of Israel" (1:49). Martha's confession of Jesus as "the Christ, the Son of God, who is coming into the world" (11:27), seems to reflect some type of messianic expectation. The present state of the evidence, nevertheless, renders the point moot.

In the NT. *Jesus' Own Claims.* Although Jesus preferred to refer to himself as the Son of man, there is sufficient evidence that his identity as Son of God goes back ultimately to his own assertions. This is especially true of John, but instances of it are also found in the Synoptics. When the high priest asked Jesus, "Are you the Christ, the Son of the Blessed?" he answered, "I am," and then proceeded to refer to himself as the Son of man (Mark 14:61–62). Earlier he had identified God as the Father of the Son of man (Mark 8:38), and in Matt. he referred to God as "my Father" (7:21; 10:32–33; 20:23; 26:29, 53). In a passage reminiscent of John, Jesus strongly expressed his filial relationship with God (Matt. 11:25–27 = Luke 10:21–22) and implied it in his parable of the wicked tenants (Mark 12:6 and par.). Even as a boy of twelve Jesus recognized that God was his Father (Luke 2:49).

At the heart of Jesus' identity in John is his stated divine sonship. In John 10:36 he admitted saying, "I am the Son of God." Frequently he referred to God as "my Father" (e.g., 5:17; 6:40; 8:54; 10:18; 15:15). Such assertions as "I and the Father are one" (10:30) and "the Father is in me and I am in the Father" (vs. 38) show that Jesus conceived of his divine sonship as unique and unparalleled.

Others' Recognition of Jesus' Divine Sonship. The NT presents a remarkably large and diverse group of individuals who referred to Jesus as the Son of God. At both Jesus' baptism and transfiguration, God himself identified Jesus as his Son in statements reminiscent of Ps. 2:7 (Mark 1:11; 9:35; and par.). Before Jesus' birth Gabriel appeared to Mary and identified the child as the "Son of the Most High" and "Son of God" (Luke 1:32, 35). At his temptation the devil twice challenged Jesus with the words, "If you are the Son of God" (Matt. 4:3, 6 = Luke 4:3, 9). During Jesus' ministry unclean spirits or demons directly asserted his divine sonship (Mark 3:11 = Luke 4:41; Mark 5:7; and par.). At the beginning of Jesus' ministry John the Baptist testified, "This one is the Son of God" (John 1:34), and at the cross, the centurion exclaimed, "Truly, this was [the] son of God" (Mark 15:39 = Matt. 27:54).

Understandably, the assertion and development of Jesus' divine sonship in the NT came principally from his disciples. During his ministry they did this as a group (Matt. 14:33) and as individuals: Peter (16:16), Nathanael (John 1:49), and Martha (11:27). Saul of Tarsus' initial preaching in Damascus emphasized this point (Acts 9:20). Jesus' divine sonship occupies an important position in the Pauline and Johannine epistles and in Hebrews. In Paul, "Lord" and "Christ" are the more frequently used Christological titles, but "his Son" or "Son of God" appears in most of his epistles, especially in contexts dealing with eschatology, Jesus' messianic rule, and salvation. The Johannine epistles represent a special case, where Jesus' divine sonship was constantly asserted as a corrective to the Docetic heresy. The Hebrews writer applied OT messianic texts to Jesus as God's Son, but more importantly, Jesus' sonship is at the heart of his argument that Jesus was superior to angels, Moses, and the Levitical priests.

Associated Themes. The key to understanding what NT writers meant by the title "Son of God" is found in the contexts in which the title occurs. Heading the list are those passages which connect Jesus' divine sonship with his royal office as Messiah. Jesus did this himself in response to the high priest's question (Mark 14:61–62), as God had earlier done at his baptism and transfiguration, using the language of Ps. 2:7. Paul (Acts 13:33) and the Hebrews writer (1:5; 5:5) also applied this verse to Jesus, as he did (II Sam. 7:14). Gabriel told Mary that her son not only would be called God's Son but would reign on David's throne (Luke 1:32–33). Later in Luke the demons' recognition of Jesus as Son of God was associated with their knowledge that he was the Messiah (4:41). The connection of the two occurs three times in the Gospel of John (1:49; 11:27; 20:31), as it does in Paul's letters (Rom. 1:3–4; I Cor. 15:28; Col. 1:13). It surfaced in Peter's confession (Matt. 16:16) and in Luke's summary of Saul's initial Damascus preaching (Acts 9:20, 22).

While Son of God and Messiah are connected in the Gospel of John, the major theological point brought out by Jesus' divine sonship is his own divinity. Other themes underscored in the NT by this relationship include salvation (John and Paul) and Jesus' high priesthood (Hebrews). The question of at what point the Son actually became God's Son is not addressed in the NT so much as the points at which he was designated Son. These are at or in connection with his birth (Luke 1:32, 35), baptism (Mark 1:11; and par.), transfiguration (Mark 9:7; and par.), resurrection (Rom. 1:4; Acts 13:33), and second coming (I Thess. 1:10). Hence, there is no formal adoption Christology implied by his divine sonship; rather, numerous passages present the son as clearly preexistent (e.g., Gal. 4:4; Rom. 8:3; Col. 1:13–17; and John *passim*).

Sons of God. Just as Israelites in the OT were sons of God, so are disciples of Jesus in the NT, although Jesus is Son in a unique sense (John 3:16, 18; I John 4:9). Jesus himself used this phrase of his followers (Matt. 5:9, 45), but it is in Paul that the doctrine became most fully developed. Here it is a part of Paul's doctrine of adoption (Gal. 4:1–7; Rom. 8:14–17), which has a pagan, probably Roman, background, rather than Jewish, because the practice of levirate marriage in ancient Judaism neutralized the social dynamic for adoption. Faith is the vehicle for this adoption (Gal. 3:26), and the outcome is that the adopted sons of God become his heirs along with Christ and thus address him as "Abba, Father," as Jesus did in the garden (Mark 14:36). G. T. BURKE

See also CHRISTOLOGY; JESUS CHRIST; MESSIAH.

Bibliography. E. Huntress, "'Son of God' in Jewish Writings Prior to the Christian Era," *JBL* 54:117–23; S. E. Johnson, *IDB*, IV, 408–13; W. Kramer, *Christ, Lord, Son of God;* W. Bousset, *Kyrios Christos;* P. W. von Martitz *et al.*, *TDNT*, VIII, 334–97.

Son of Man. Title for the Christ, Messiah (Gr., *huios tou anthrōpou;* Aram., *bar nāšā';* Heb. *ben 'ādām*). This Christological title appears sixty-nine times in the Synoptic Gospels and thirteen times in John and meets the most demanding tests of authenticity because of its original use by Jesus. There is no evidence of a well-defined Son of man Christology in Judaism before the time of Jesus. Appearances of the term in Eth. Enoch and II Esd. are inconclusive, though its presence in Dan. 7:13 seems the natural background for Jesus' creative use of the expression as an enigmatic title. Since nothing in Judaism corresponds precisely to the nuances of meaning Jesus gives to the term, and as the early church makes no use of it in its own theology, attempts by radical critics to discount Jesus' originality in applying the title to himself run counter to the fact that it satisfies especially well their own criterion of dissimilarity as the basic test of authentic sayings of Jesus. Rejection of the title in any of its three shades of meaning may thus be seen to rest on presuppositional, not exegetical, grounds, since no other title used by Jesus so clearly attests his messianic self-consciousness; while numerous contemporary schools of interpretation begin with the *a priori* assumption that the church, not Jesus, is responsible for a high Christology.

Son of Man as Pronoun. The first intentional use of Son of man by Jesus functions as a substitute for his personal pronoun "I," and as such conveys extraordinary claims of authority on his part, quite different from its ordinary and simple reference to "man" in the psalms and as a form of address in Ezek. As Jesus uses the title in Mark 2:10, he claims the authority to forgive sins, indicating that he is consciously and creatively investing the title with deep Christological meaning, tantamount to sharing the prerogatives of God. Similarly his use of the title in the grain-field episode of Mark 2:28 indicates his authority over the sacred sabbath, another claim of correlativity with God. The explicitly redemptive character of his ministry is evidenced by his personal claim that "the Son of man also came not to be served but to serve, and to give his life as a ransom for many." Of the passages in so-called Q (Matt. 8:20; 11:19; 12:32), the first indicates his servanthood, the second sounds his familiar theme of open table fellowship with outcasts, and the third concludes a powerful passage on his binding of Satan and a warning about "the unforgivable sin" against the Holy Spirit, by whose power Jesus is invading the demonic kingdom—another personal claim to correlativity with God. Special Matthew (M) sayings are two in number (13:3; 11:13) and imply respectively that Jesus as Son of man is the one who plants the good seed (that is, he is the Lord of the harvest), and that he knows who he is and asks of his disciples the leading question, "Who do men say that the Son of man is?" Special Luke (L) sayings in the first category are also two in number (6:22; 10:10) and again reflect Jesus' awareness of his centrality in the suffering ministry of his disciples, and in the salvation of the lost. It goes without saying that the stakes are high in either accepting or discounting these sayings as authentic, for since the Christology is so high and Jesus so aware of his equality with God, radical redaction criticism must be completely reassessed as to the originality of Jesus and the creativity of the early church if these sayings are accepted as genuine.

Son of Man as Prophecy. This is equally true of the second group of Son of man sayings in which Jesus prophesies of his future suffering. If the first group is accepted as authentic, the second follows coherently. If on *a priori* grounds the first is rejected, then the second group will be rejected as "prophecies" of the church created after the fact. Of the eleven passages in this category, eight are in Mark (8:31; 9:12, 31; 10:33; 14:21, 41) and all disclose Jesus' messianic awareness that he is to suffer as a ransom for many. In considerable detail Jesus foretells his betrayal, condemnation, death, and resurrection. The temptation of the naturalistic critic will be to explain these prophecies as church created, but only if the reality of biblical prophecy and the incarnation are discounted. On the assumption that the evangelist is giving an authentic account of Jesus' prophecies about himself, a coherent picture of Jesus emerges which confirms his personal awareness of his redemptive mission and his authority as the true prophet (Deut. 18:15–22). Three other references complete the suffering Son of man sayings (Matt. 26:2, M; Luke 22:48; 24:7, L).

Son of Man in Third Person. The third group appears to be more enigmatic in the sense that Jesus refers to the Son of man in the third person. A number of more radical interpreters take this to mean that Jesus was referring to another than himself, and since the sayings, interpreted in this fashion, would not suggest his messianic self-consciousness, they are willing to allow the possibility of authenticity. There are nineteen of these sayings, all of which portray the Son of man as a glorified divine being, whereas in the first two groupings Jesus generally speaks of himself in terms of humility and suffering. Again, however, it is likely that nonsupernaturalist assumptions lie behind the refusal to allow that these sayings are Jesus' own prophetic vision of his vindication and glorification in the coming judgment. Certainly there is no suggestion elsewhere in the Gospels that he anticipated any other figure to appear after him. In fact, among the Markan sayings in this category (8:38; 9:9; 13:26; 14:62), 9:9 clearly refers to his own rising as the Son of man from the dead; and 14:62, the scene before the high priest, couples his "I am" confession that he is the Christ, the Son of the Blessed, with the surrogate for "I," the Son of man, "sitting at the right hand of Power, and coming with the clouds of heaven." This further evidences Jesus' messianic self-awareness and is exegetically the proper intent of the passage.

The Q passage Matt. 12:40 also clearly refers to Jesus as Son of man, and there is no good reason for not accepting the other Q sayings as authentic (Matt. 24:27, 37, 39, 44), as well as special M sayings (13:41; 19:28; 24:30; 25:31) and special L (12:8; 17:22; 18:8; 21:36). Matt. 19:28 is especially instructive on the matter of who the glorified Son of man is, for Jesus promises his disciples with the authoritative "Truly, I say to you" that "in the new world, when the Son of man shall sit on his glorious throne, you who have followed me will also sit on twelve thrones judging the twelve tribes of Israel." Surely Jesus, whom they have followed and in terms of whom they shall reign, will not be excluded from reigning with them. Are there then to be two enthroned central figures, the Son of man and Jesus? The sense of the passage exegetically would imply that only one central person is assumed, namely, Jesus the Son of man.

There remain but two sayings in the third group, and since they are difficult and have occasioned considerable controversy, they have been reserved for final comment. Both occur only in Matt. (10:23; 16:28). Since Dan. 7:13 is the likely background to Jesus' creative adaptation of Son of man terminology, it is important to note how the term is used in the larger sense of that passage. In 7:13–14 it is a single person, the Son of man, who is given everlasting dominion and glory and kingdom by the Ancient of Days, while in vss. 18, 21, and 27 it is the saints of the Most High who receive the everlasting kingdom. The difficulty is resolved if the title Son of man is understood as both individual and corporate, like Israel (Jacob) and the people of Israel. We may suppose that Jesus selected the image to fulfill prophecy, to express his messiahship in appropriate hiddenness until the proper time of revealing, and to disclose the individual and corporate nature of his mission. Jesus consciously personifies the Son of man, and as he draws his disciples about him and empowers them to participate in his redemptive reign he allows them to share in the corporate Son of man as saints of the Most High, and in his reign as he as king inaugurates the kingdom of God. Son of man and kingdom of God appear to be nearly interchangeable in both individual and corporate senses. Hence one possible interpretation of Matt. 10:23 is that when the disciples share in the redemptive ministry of Jesus and invade the demonic realm through the power of the coming kingdom, the Son of man has in that corporate sense and to that degree come. Jesus' prophecy is true and is fulfilled (Luke's parallel account regarding the Seventy describes their exultant return as they successfully claim power over demons in Jesus' name, whereupon Jesus sees the fall of Satan "like lightning from heaven," Luke 10:17–18).

The remaining problematic text, Matt. 16:28 ("Truly, I say to you, there are some standing here who will not taste death before they see the Son of man coming in his kingdom"), is also to be exegeted as eschatology in process of realization, for Jesus is the Son of man whose ministry, now incorporating the disciples as the saints of the Most High, invades the kingdom of Satan. That is why the denial that this is indeed occurring through the power of the Spirit of God constitutes the unpardonable sin (12:22–32); and it explains why Mark 9:1 has Jesus making a similar prophecy but using the term kingdom of God in place of the Son of man. The terms are virtually interchangeable. While the vocabulary comes from the OT, Jesus consciously gives it deeper meaning associated with the mysterious disclosure of his own person and the corporate body he is bringing into being. The Son of man and the kingdom of God have come, personified in Jesus; but there is yet more to come as God's redemptive plan is unfolded with power in the cross and resurrection. Hence the irony and mystery of Jesus' favorite title, Son of man, which both reveals and conceals and is penetrated only by the eyes of faith and obedient response.

At the completion of his earthly ministry when Jesus' redemptive work was fulfilled and the Holy Spirit was poured out in power at Pentecost, the disciples were given to see that Christ was now to be preached openly without reference to the enigmatic title Son of man or the veiled connotations of the kingdom of God. Obediently they proclaimed Christ, and true to form Son of man and kingdom of God virtually disappear from the apostolic vocabulary.

R. G. Gruenler

See also Christology; Jesus Christ.

Bibliography. I. H. Marshall, *The Origins of NT Christology;* R. H. Stein, *The Method and Message of Jesus' Teaching;* R. T. France, *Jesus and the OT;* C. F. D. Moule, *The Origin of Christology;* F. H. Borsch, *The Son of Man in Myth and History;* M. Hooker, *The Son of Man in Mark;* R. G. Gruenler, *New Approaches to Jesus and the Gospels;* R. Bultmann, *The History of the Synoptic Tradition;* H. Tödt, *The Son of Man in the Synoptic Tradition;* N. Perrin, *A Modern Pilgrimage in NT Christology;* C. Colpe, *TDNT,* VIII, 402.

Soteriology. *See* Salvation.

Soul. Living being, life principle, person, or individual spiritual nature. It may be ascribed to animals (Gen. 1:30; Rev. 8:9) and to God (Lev. 26:11; Isa. 42:1). It is often used interchangeably with spirit, although distinctions that begin to appear in the OT are carried forward in the NT. Thus while soul in the NT normally means an individual spiritual entity with a material body so that a person is thought of as a body-soul, spirit is the special gift of God which places one in relationship to him. Scripture states that Jesus gave his spirit to his Father (Luke 23:46; John 19:30), but elsewhere it is said that he gave his soul as a ransom for many (Matt. 20:28; John 10:15). In general terms then it can be said that soul in Scripture is conceived to be an immaterial principle created by God, which is usually united to a body and gives it life; however, the soul continues to exist after death in human beings (Matt. 10:28; James 5:20; Rev. 6:9; 20:4), a condition which is ended at the close of this age (I Cor. 15:35–55).

The Early Church. Speculation about the soul in the subapostolic church was heavily influenced by Greek philosophy. This is seen in Origen's acceptance of Plato's doctrine of the preexistence of the soul as pure mind (*nous*) originally, which, by reason of its fall from God, cooled down to soul (*psychē*) when it lost its participation in the divine fire by looking earthward. It is also seen in Tertullian's repudiation of Greek ideas and his insistence on the biblical teaching of the union of the soul, an immaterial creation of God, with the material body which has been made for it.

Augustine's great influence was felt in the church in his teaching about the soul as in other matters. Condemning the heathen notions that the soul was originally a part of God—an idea which he calls blasphemy—that it is corporeal, or that it becomes polluted through the body, he saw the soul as a rational-spiritual substance made "like God," and made by him, sustaining and directing the body (*The Greatness of the Soul,* XIII, 22). Concerning its origin and whether it was created by God or transmitted by parents, Augustine might be unsure (*On the Soul and Its Origin,* I, 27), but of its "proper abode" and "homeland" he was certain, and that is God (*The Greatness of the Soul,* I,2).

Origin of the Soul. Augustine's reluctance to take sides in the debate on the origin of the soul was not shared by his contemporaries. Some Greek church fathers shared Origen's theory that the soul preexisted with God and that it was assigned to a body as a penalty for its sin of looking downward. Most, however, accepted the creationist view that God created each individual soul at the moment that he gave it a body, while some, like Tertullian, held the traducianist theory that each soul is derived, along with the body, from the parents.

Arguments cited in favor of creationism were (1) that Scripture distinguishes the origin of man's soul and body (Eccl. 12:7; Isa. 42:5; Zech. 12:1; Heb. 12:9); (2) that creationism preserves the idea of the soul as a simple, indivisible substance better than traducianism, which requires the idea of the division of the soul and its derivation from the parents; and (3) that it makes more credible Christ's retention of a pure soul than does traducianism.

In behalf of traducianism it was said (1) that certain Scripture supports it (Gen. 2:2; Heb. 7:10; cf. I Cor. 11:8); (2) that it offers the best theory for the whole race having sinned in Adam; (3) that it is supported by the analogy of lower life in which numerical increase is obtained by derivation; (4) that it teaches that parents beget the whole child, body and soul, and not just the body; and (5) that it was necessary for Christ to have received his soul from the soul of Mary in order to redeem the human soul.

Augustine carefully weighed the arguments on each side of the controversy, leaning toward traducianism for a time even while he saw the difficulty of retaining the soul's integrity with this hypothesis; later he admitted that he was perplexed and baffled by the question.

A contemporary theologian who takes essentially the same stance is G. C. Berkouwer, who calls the controversy "unfruitful," inasmuch as it wrongly assumes that the issue is one of horizontal *or* vertical relations. "Such a way of putting it is far too feeble an attempt to render adequately the greatness of the work of God" (*Man: The Image of God,* 292). The God of Israel does not create only in the distant past, but he is constantly active in human history, the Creator in horizontal relationships as well as others. To speak about a separate origin of the soul he sees as impossible biblically, inasmuch as this creationist theory sees the relationship to God as "something added to the 'essentially human,' which later is defined independently as 'soul' and 'body.' Both soul and body can then be viewed in different 'causal' relationships without reference to some intrinsic non-causal relationship to God. If, however, it is impossible to speak of the essence of man except in this latter religious relationship, then it also becomes impossible to introduce duality into the origin of soul and of body within the unitary human individual" (303).

M. E. Osterhaven

See also Body, Biblical View of the; Dichotomy; Man, Doctrine of; Spirit; Trichotomy.

Bibliography. G. C. Berkouwer, *Man: The Image of God;* A. Dihle *et al., TDNT,* IX, 608–66; C. A. Beckwith, *SHERK,* XI, 12–14; C. Hodge, *Systematic Theology,* II; L. Berkhof, *Systematic Theology.*

Soul Sleep. Psychopannychy, the doctrine that the soul sleeps between death and resurrection. It has been held sporadically in the church. It is not a heresy in the narrower sense, due to the paucity of Scripture teaching on the intermediate state, but it may be called a doctrinal aberration. Some Anabaptists endorsed it. In the Forty-two Articles of Edward VI, which preceded the Thirty-nine Articles, the following statement, as the Fortieth Article, was included: "They which say that the souls of those who depart hence do sleep being without all sense, feeling or perceiving till the Day of Judgment, do utterly dissent from the right belief disclosed to us in Holy Scripture."

The case for soul sleep rests principally on these considerations: (1) Human existence demands the unity of soul and body. If the body ceases to function, so must the soul. (2) The use of the term "sleep" in Scripture for death is alleged to point to the cessation of consciousness. (3) A state of consciousness between death and resurrection, characterized by bliss or woe, unwarrantably anticipates the judgment of the last day, when the basis for these experiences is provided.

On the contrary view, while the normal state of man is admittedly a union of soul and body, the possibility of disembodied conscious existence is firmly held, both on the analogy of God's existence as pure spirit (man being made in his image) and on the basis of such passages as Heb. 12:23 and Rev. 6:9–11. As to the word "sleep," it is intended to apply to the body, even though the individual as such may be said to sleep in death. This is clear from Matt. 27:52; John 11:11; Acts 13:36, etc. On the third point it may be replied that the exclusion of the possibility of bliss or woe from the intermediate state, on the ground that the divine judgment which justifies such reactions will not yet have been pronounced, would logically rule out the joyful assurance of salvation in this life as well as the foreboding of judgment to come. But see John 5:24; Phil. 1:28.

Continuing consciousness after death seems to be a necessary (rather than an accidental) element in Jesus' account of the rich man and Lazarus, and also in our Lord's promise to the dying thief. The clearest and strongest passages, however, are in Paul's writings (Phil. 1:23; II Cor. 5:8). If it be contended in the case of the former passage that the sleep of the soul so effectually erases the interval between death and resurrection that the prospect of being with Christ, even though actually long delayed, could produce joyful anticipation, in any event the same thing can hardly be said for the second passage, where not only the resurrection body but the intermediate state is directly contemplated, being a less desirable alternative than the change to the resurrection body without death (vs. 4).

E. F. Harrison

See also Adventism; Conditional Immortality; Intermediate State.

Bibliography. J. Calvin, *Psychopannychia;* O. Cullmann, *Immortality of the Soul or Resurrection of the Dead?* E. Lewis, *Christ, the First Fruits;* R. Whately, *A View of the Scripture Revelations concerning a Future State.*

Sovereignty of God. The biblical teaching that God is king, supreme ruler, and lawgiver of the entire universe.

Biblical Statements. He "has established his throne in heaven, and his kingdom rules over all" (Ps. 103:19 NIV). As the "Most High," God is "sovereign over the kingdoms of men and gives them to anyone he wishes" (Dan. 4:17, 25, 34; 5:21; 7:14). Israel's King David acknowledges "the greatness and the power and the glory and the majesty and the splendor" of God "for everything in heaven and earth" is his (I Chr. 29:11). This prayerful acknowledgment of God's sovereignty is echoed in the traditional conclusion of the Lord's prayer: "for yours is the kingdom, and the power and the glory forever" (Matt. 6:13 NIV). God is indeed the "only Ruler, the King of kings and Lord of lords" (I Tim. 6:15; cf. Rev. 19:16). The sovereignty of God thus expresses the very nature of God as all-powerful and omnipotent, able to accomplish his good pleasure, carry out his decreed will, and keep his promises.

Several divine names express God's sovereignty. He is called "God Most High" (*'elyôn,* Gen. 14:18–20), "God almighty" (*'ēl šadday,* 17:1; cf. Exod. 6:2), "Sovereign Lord" (*'ădōnāy yhwh,* Gen. 15:2; Deut. 3:24 NIV), and "Lord God Almighty" (*kyrios pantokratōr,* Rev. 1:8). See also "Sovereign Lord" for *despota* or "Master" in Luke 2:29; Acts 4:24; II Pet. 2:1; Jude 4; and Rev. 6:10.

God's sovereignty is *expressed* in the comprehensive plan or decree for world history; he "works out everything in conformity with the purpose of his will" (Eph. 1:11). His sovereignty is *exercised* and *displayed* in history in the work of creation, providence, and redemption. The "Sovereign Lord" has "made the heavens and the earth" and "nothing is too hard" for him (Jer. 32:17–23), indeed, "all things are possible with God" (Mark 10:27; 14:35; Luke 1:37). God also sovereignly upholds and governs the created world in his providence. He rules the destiny of men and nations (Acts 14:15–17; 17:24–28). Adam's fall occurred within the context of his arrangement (Gen. 2:16–17) as did Christ's crucifixion (Acts 2:23; 4:27–28) and all other events. His providential rule is all-comprehensive. "I form the light and create darkness, I bring prosperity and create disaster; I, the Lord, do all these things (Isa. 45:7; cf. Eph. 1:11).

The gracious work of redemption also manifests God's sovereignty. He promises, covenants, and works redemptive history. The Messiah is himself "Mighty God" (Isa. 9:6–7), "the Son of the Most High" whose "kingdom will never end" (Luke 1:33). From the beginning of his public ministry to its end Jesus' message concerns "the kingdom of God" (Mark 1:15; Acts 1:3; more than 100 instances in the Synoptics). After the resurrection Christ claims "all authority in heaven and earth" (Matt. 28:18), and the ascended Christ is exalted "far above all rule and authority, power, and dominion" (Eph. 1:19–21; Phil. 2:9–11; I Cor. 15:24–28; Rev. 5:9–14). Hence the earliest Christian confession was simply: "Jesus is Lord" (Rom. 10:9).

The gospel itself displays God's sovereignty; it is "the power of God for the salvation of everyone who believes" (Rom. 1:16), and "to those whom God has called" Christ is "the power of God" (I Cor. 1:24; cf. Eph. 1:18–22). The authority of Scripture is also an expression of the sovereignty of God since all Scripture is "God-breathed" (II Tim. 3:16). That is why "the Scripture cannot be broken" (John 10:35) and why everything in it will be fulfilled and accomplished (Matt. 5:18; Luke 24:44).

Theological Considerations. Theologians generally consider "sovereignty" one of God's communicable attributes; "sovereignty" expresses an inherent characteristic of God, and a distinction is sometimes made between "sovereign will" and "sovereign power." God's sovereign will and power are not arbitrary, despotic, or deterministic; his sovereignty is characterized by his justice and holiness as well as by his other attributes.

Divine sovereignty and human responsibility are paradoxical and beyond human comprehension, but not contradictory. Divine sovereignty and human *sovereignty* are certainly contradictory, but divine sovereignty and human *responsibility* are not. God uses human means in history to accomplish his purposes, yet such means do not involve coercion. God commands us to live according to his sovereign law (Gen. 2:16–17; Exod. 20; Matt. 22:37–38). Yet God effectuates his will even through sinful, disobedient human actions (Gen. 45:5, 7–8; 50:19–20). The crucifixion of Jesus Christ, certainly the most heinous crime in history, occurred within the boundaries of "the determinate counsel and foreknowledge of God," for the crucifiers did what God's "power and will had decided beforehand should happen" (Acts 2:23; 4:27–28; cf. John 19:11).

The doctrine of the sovereignty of God is emphasized especially in the Augustinian-Calvinistic tradition and is denied or compromised in the Pelagian, Arminian, and liberal traditions, which claim varying degrees of human autonomy. The confession of the sovereignty of God has become the hallmark of authentic Calvinism. It is not, however, its central principle; sovereignty is not the basic principle from which Calvin's whole theology was deduced. That is a caricature of Calvin and Calvinism. Actually the term "sovereignty" is found only a few times in the *Institutes;* the same is true of the Reformed confessions. Yet the doctrine is indeed part of authentic Reformed thought. The key to Calvin's theology was to speak where the Scriptures speak and to be silent where they are silent. That is why he wrote of God's sovereignty and defended predestination and other controversial doctrines.

Classic Calvinism does not minimize the role of human responsibility in history. Only in extreme forms of supralapsarian thought and hyper-Calvinism is sovereignty emphasized in ways that compromise human responsibility and curtail the universal proclamation of the gospel. The confession of the sovereignty of God should occasion the praise and glory of God and encourage a life lived in obedient love within the kingdom of the King. As in the case of all God's attributes, so God's sovereignty should be reflected in the Christian's life. The Christian who is being renewed in the image of God and progressing in sanctification should again exercise dominion over creation as God's vicegerent in promoting the kingdom of God in human history to the glory of the Sovereign Lord (cf. Gen. 1:28).

F. H. Klooster

See also Calvinism; Decrees of God; Elect, Election; God, Attributes of; God, Doctrine of; God, Names of; Predestination; Reformed Tradition, The; Reprobation; Supralapsarianism.

Bibliography. L. Berkhof, *Systematic Theology;* J. Calvin, *Institutes;* P. Toon, *Hyper-Calvinism;* J. I. Packer, *Evangelism and the Sovereignty of God;* A. W. Pink, *The Sovereignty of God.*

Special Revelation. *See* Revelation, Special.

Spener, Philipp Jakob (1635–1705). Founder of German pietism. Spener was born in Rappoltsweiler, Upper Alsace, and died in Berlin. He is generally regarded as the founder of German pietism, though his ideas were a combination of viewpoints acquired from his teachers and from sixteenth century Reformers. He received a strict, pious upbringing and took his university training in Strasbourg (1651–59), where he concentrated on biblical languages and historical studies. Professors at Strasbourg stressed spiritual rebirth and ethical concerns, and these emphases became important factors in Spener's preaching as he assumed successive pastoral positions in Strasbourg (1663), Frankfurt-on-Main (1666), Dresden (1686), and Berlin (1697). Spener was also influenced by Genevan Calvinism, for he visited Geneva in 1659 and met Jean de Labadie, the mystical Reformed preacher. Labadie strengthened Spener's beliefs that a conversion experience (*Wiedergeburt*) was essential in the Christian life and that the true Christian must apply religion to all aspects of life.

Though Spener deemphasized the theological dogmatism and controversies of the Protestant scholastics, his view of conversion and its necessary implementation were controversial wherever he preached. His attacks on ignorance and moral laxness among the clergy were not welcomed by that group, and his proposed system of reform was a real threat to established Lutheran churches. These ideas were first published in 1675 in *Pia desideria* (*Heartfelt Desires for a God-Pleasing Reform of the True Evangelical Churches*). The theology in this work stressed the unity between faith and works, a notion that was always important in Reformed theology. By contrast, seventeenth century Lutheran theology (especially in northern Germany) stressed theological dogma, not the purified life. Equally important was the means Spener proposed for implementing change—a church within the church. Spener founded small groups (*collegia pietatis*) to advance the participants' closeness to God through prayers, songs, spiritual reading, and discussion. Though all these activities were regarded as good in themselves, the small groups often challenged contemporary ecclesiastical systems and were usually viewed as hypocritical and divisive. In fact, Spener's successors in German pietism often were quite contentious, even though Spener himself stressed cooperation and tolerance.

Spener also called for the reform of seminary education. In place of systematic theology, with its natural emphasis on dogmatic precision, Spener wanted seminarians to increase their piety by spiritual reading. Further, he emphasized going directly to the scriptural sources instead of relying on the theological formulations of scriptural commentators. The fruit of this phase of Spener's work is seen in the theological faculty established at Halle. With direction from Spener and organization from August Hermann Francke, Halle became the intellectual center of early German pietism; and the movement spread with the founding of *collegia pietatis* groups throughout German Lutheranism. Though Spener's original goals were modest, German pietism influenced Protestantism throughout the Western world; spiritual revival and religious controversy became commonplace in Protestant communities. R. J. VanderMolen

See also Pietism.

Bibliography. D. W. Brown, *Understanding Pietism;* J. O. Duke, "Pietism versus Establishment: The Halle Phase," *CQ,* Nov. 1978, 3–16; P. Grünberg, *Philipp Jakob Spener* and *SHERK,* IX, 53–57; M. Kohl, "*Wiedergeburt* As the Central Theme in Pietism," *CQ,* Nov. 1974, 17–20; J. T. McNeill, *Modern Christian Movements; NCE,* XII, 562; M. E. Richard, *Philip Jacob Spener and His Work;* K. J. Stein, "Philipp Jacob Spener's Hope for Better Times for the Church—Contribution in Controversy," *CQ,* Aug. 1979, 3–20; F. E. Stoeffler, *The Rise of Pietism* and (ed.) *Continental Pietism and Early American Christianity.*

Spinoza, Benedict de (1632–1677). Dutch philosopher. Spinoza was born in Amsterdam, Holland, to Jewish refugees who had fled from religious persecution in Portugal. As a youth he became a serious rabbinical student, but also studied Latin and classical literature privately under Francis van den Ende. Because he questioned Jewish beliefs concerning angels, the nature of God, and the soul's immortality, Spinoza was accused of heresy and expelled by the synagogue in 1656. Subsequently he supported himself as a lens polisher and received some stipends from Dutch friends; but in 1673 he declined substantial financial support by not accepting the chair of philosophy at Heidelberg. During his life Spinoza's reputation as philosopher and ethicist was established by his 1663 work on Descartes, *Principles of Descartes' Philosophy Geometrically Demonstrated,* and his most famous work, *Tractatus Theologico-Politicus* (1670). He became publicly known through a government mission to France and his attachment to the anti-Orangist Dutch political leaders Cornelius and Jan de Witt, who were assassinated in 1672. Spinoza also carried on an extensive correspondence with Henry Oldenburg, secretary of England's Royal Society. Several of Spinoza's writings were published after his death; they helped advance his reputation as a profound thinker and led many writers of the romantic movement to see Spinoza as their intellectual forefather.

As a philosopher Spinoza alienated many religious contemporaries by removing biblical ideas about God and many religious beliefs (such as acceptance of miracles) from the supernatural sphere; further, he alienated empiricists with his emphasis on geometrical order and his denial that physical facts are the basis of true generalizations about reality. Spinoza's method, contrary to that of the empiricist followers of John Locke, was to arrive at truths from axioms by using deductive logic. Also, his approach to philosophy and theology ran counter to traditional religious dependence on divine Scriptures. What resulted was a philosophy that denied supernatural occurrences as well as orthodox beliefs based on biblical revelation. In place of traditional Christian explanations came rationalistic ideas about nature and reason: nature replaced God (or "God" became "nature"); and reason replaced divine revelation.

In applying this philosophy to ethics, Spinoza saw the highest good as understanding and becoming one with nature. This was to produce conformity to natural law, which in turn meant living the ethically good life in all spheres. In this untraditional way Spinoza became something of a pantheist and determinist, two features which put him at odds with most of his contemporaries in philosophy and theology. Romanticist philosophers and writers, however, as well as modern theologians who rely on romantic philosophy, have found Spinoza's ethics and basic ideas very attractive. In spite of many attractive ethical ideas, Spinoza's philosophy is criticized by those who acknowledge a personal, transcendent God.

R. J. VanderMolen

Bibliography. Spinoza, *Correspondence*, tr. A. Wolf, and *Chief Works*, tr. R. H. M. Elwes; F. Copleston, *A History of Philosophy*, IV; L. S. Feuer, *Spinoza and the Rise of Liberalism;* S. Hampshire, *Spinoza;* S. Kashap, ed., *Studies in Spinoza;* J. Ratner, *The Philosophy of Spinoza;* R. L. Saw, *The Vindication of Metaphysics, a Study in the Philosophy of Spinoza.*

Spirit (Heb. *rûaḥ*, "breath of mouth," Pss. 33:6; 135:17; then "breath of air, or wind," Job 4:15; Gen. 3:8). In biblical usage, the breath of mankind that gives life to the body (Gen. 7:22; Job 27:3). It is the seat of rationality (Mal. 2:15; Deut. 34:9), determination (Jer. 51:1; Hag. 1:14), attitude in general (Num. 14:24), courage (Josh. 2:11; 5:1), religious understanding (Job 20:3), emotions (Zech. 12:10; Pss. 77:3; 143:4), pride (Ps. 76:12), jealousy (Num. 5:14, 30), and various other inner dispositions. As the principle of life, spirit is ascribed to beasts also (Gen. 6:17; 7:15).

The spirit of mankind fulfills its true destiny when it lives in conscious relationship to God its creator. Himself the eternal Spirit who out of nothing made the heavens, the earth, and "all the host of them by the breath [spirit] of his mouth," with man made in his image and likeness (Gen. 1:27–28; 2:7), God is called "spirit" and "Father of spirits" in the NT (John 4:24; Heb. 12:9). Mankind has breath, or spirit, because it has been given by God's Spirit (Job 27:3; 33:4; 34:14); when a person dies the spirit is returned to God (Eccles. 12:7). Life and death, therefore, are represented in the Bible as a giving and a withdrawing of God's breath, or spirit, for all created life, including humanity, is utterly dependent on him (Ps. 104).

The NT carries forward the teaching of the OT on spirit with important developments. The human spirit is seen even more sharply as having been made by God and for him so that his children may live in fellowship with him through the Holy Spirit. Thus the Spirit of God witnesses to our spirits that "we are children of God, and if children, then heirs, heirs of God and fellow heirs with Christ" (Rom. 8:16–17). It is the spirit that is given back to God in death, not the soul, which seems to sustain a less intimate relationship to God, even though there are instances in the NT where the two are used synonymously (John 10:15; 19:30). The difference between spirit and soul is seen clearly in Paul's contrast of the spiritual (*pneumatikos*) with the unspiritual (RSV) or natural (*psychikos*, i.e., soulish) person (I Cor. 2:13–15). The first knows God because that person has received the Spirit of God, not the spirit of the world, so that he may understand the things of God (vs. 12). The second knows only human wisdom and is unable to understand the spiritual truth which must be "spiritually discerned"; to him the latter is folly (vs. 14). "The contrast is especially sharp because Paul recognizes no neutral ground between them. Not to have the *pneuma* (spirit) of God is to be controlled by the *pneuma tou kosmou* (spirit of the world)." Spiritual things (knowledge, or other gifts) are held to be from God, effected by his Spirit. Natural (physical, unspiritual) things, while from God as a part of his creation, manifest the reality of a sinful world and do not bring one to God and his grace. Paul exhorts the Corinthians to covet the "spiritual gifts" bestowed on the church by the Holy Spirit as that which is most to be valued and lasting (I Cor. 14:1).

As the aspect of life which lies in one's inmost being, spirit can be overwhelmed (Ps. 143:4), broken (51:17; Prov. 15:13), renewed (Ps. 51:10), and revived (Gen. 45:27). Because of sin one can have a spirit of fear (II Tim. 1:7), error (I John 4:6), counsel (Isa. 11:2), or a dumb or foul spirit (Mark 9:17, 25; Rev. 18:2), an unclean one (Zech. 13:2; Matt. 12:43, *passim*), or one of whoredom (Hos. 4:12). One can be hasty in spirit (Eccles. 7:9) or faithful in spirit (Prov. 11:13), patient or proud (Eccles. 7:8), poor in spirit (Matt. 5:3), or perverse (Isa. 19:14). Thus as the heights and depths of human existence are experienced mankind's spirit is drawn to either God or the devil; it receives blessing or the subtle influences of evil and ultimate condemnation.

M. E. Osterhaven

See also God, Doctrine of; Holy Spirit; Man, Doctrine of.

Bibliography. R. Jewett, *Paul's Anthropological Terms;* W. P. Dickson, *St. Paul's Use of the Terms Flesh and Spirit;* C. Brown *et al., NIDNTT*, III, 689–709; E. Schweizer, *TDNT*, VI, 332–455 (esp. 437).

Spirit, Holy. *See* Holy Spirit.

Spirit, Unclean. *See* DEMON, DEMON POSSESSION.

Spirits, Discernment of. *See* SPIRITUAL GIFTS.

Spirits in Prison. The phrase occurs in I Pet. 3:19 and has provoked considerable discussion. Some have held that the reference is to people of Noah's time who heard preaching by the Spirit through his lips but rejected it and now, at the time Peter is writing, are disembodied spirits imprisoned and awaiting final judgment. Against this is the movement of thought which seems to place the preaching after the death and quickening of Christ and prior to his resurrection. Further, the word "spirit" is rarely used of the dead, especially in the absolute form of statement.

Some see in the passage a preaching by Christ to the dead between his death and resurrection, whether simply to announce his victory to OT saints or to give further opportunity for people who died unrepentant. It is highly improbable that a doctrine so important as "the larger hope" would be set forth in such enigmatical language, especially when it is tacitly contradicted by statements of Scripture (e.g., Heb. 9:27).

There is much to commend the view that the spirits are the angels who sinned in the time of Noah (Gen. 6:1–5). Not only are good angels called spirits (Heb. 1:14), but demons also (Luke 10:20). Whereas the word "prison" is hardly a natural term to apply to the state of the human dead, it is appropriate to evil spirits (II Pet. 2:4; Jude 6). To these Christ proclaimed his triumph. The context appears to support this (I Pet. 3:22).

E. F. HARRISON

Bibliography. E. G. Selwyn, *The First Epistle of Peter;* B. Reicke, *The Disobedient Spirits and Christian Baptism;* E. H. Plumptre, *The Spirits in Prison and Other Studies on the Life after Death.*

Spiritual Body (Gr. *sōma pneumatikon*). The resurrected spiritual body in contrast to the physical body (*sōma psychikon*), which is subject to sin and death (I Cor. 15:44). Paul's teaching, like that of Jesus, (1) stands in contrast to the denial of the afterlife by the Sadducees (cf. Matt. 22:23–33; Acts 23:6–8), and (2) contrasts with the Greek notion of the bare immortality of the soul, separated from the tomb of the body. On analogy of God's revelation in nature, where the sown seed dies and rises to something that bears identity with the seed but is immeasurably different, Paul describes the resurrection of the dead. For Paul, again as with Jesus in his resurrected state, the person is conceived as a gestalt unity of body-spirit, not as a soul separated from the body. The whole person is lifted to a new level of existence, from the fallen and death-prone body-soul of Adam to the imperishable body-spirit of life in Christ (I Cor. 15:35–50). Jesus in his resurrection appearances embodies the new imperishable existence, and though not of flesh and blood of the old order, nor limited by physical parameters of that order (John 20:19–20), nevertheless has identifiable characteristics of flesh and bones, hands, and side, and can partake of food (Luke 24:36–43). This mysterious and "logically odd" language of the apostolic witness is not contradictory but complementary, as Jesus, John, Luke, Paul, and the other NT witnesses convey the divinely revealed fact that the new existence is like, yet different from, the old, on analogy of the identity and difference between the seed and the full grain. *Sōma pneumatikon* is Paul's way of saying that the believer's personal identity as a body-spirit unity will be raised to a new life like that of Christ himself.

R. G. GRUENLER

See also RESURRECTION OF THE DEAD.

Spiritual Gifts. Gifts of God enabling the Christian to perform his (sometimes specialized) service. There are several words in the NT used for spiritual gifts. *Dōrea* and *doma* are so used but are rare (Eph. 4:8; Acts 11:17). *Pneumatikos* and *charisma* are frequently found, with *charisma* being the most common.

The term *charisma* ("spiritual gift"), except for I Pet. 4:10, is used only by Paul. *Charisma* signifies redemption or salvation as the gift of God's grace (Rom. 5:15; 6:23) and a gift enabling the Christian to perform his service in the church (I Cor. 7:7), as well as defining a special gift enabling a Christian to perform a particular ministry in the church (e.g., 12:28ff.).

Paul offers instruction on spiritual gifts in Rom. 12:6–8; I Cor. 12:4–11, 28–30; Eph. 4:7–12. Spiritual gifts were unusual manifestations of God's grace (*charis*) under normal and abnormal forms. Not every spiritual gift affected the moral life of the one who exercised it, but its purpose was always the edification of believers. The exercise of a spiritual gift implied service in the church. This practical approach is never lost sight of in the NT, these spiritual gifts often being divided into miraculous and nonmiraculous; but since some are synonymous with specific duties, they should be classified according to their significance for preaching the word, on the one hand, and exercising practical ministries, on the other.

The Gifts of the Spirit. There are five gifts of the Spirit.

Working of Miracles (I Cor. 12:10, 28–29). "Miracles" is the rendering of *dynameis* (powers). In Acts *dynameis* refers to the casting out of evil spirits and the healing of bodily ailments (8:6–7, 13; 19:11–12). This may explain "working of powers," but this gift is not synonymous with "gifts of healing." Probably the former was much more spectacular than the latter, and may have signified raising the dead (Acts 9:36ff.; 20:9ff.). Paul himself exercised this gift of working of powers, and it was for him proof of his apostleship (II Cor. 12:12), and authenticated both the good news he preached and his right to proclaim it (Rom. 15:18ff.).

Gifts of Healing (I Cor. 12:9, 28, 30). As already suggested, gifts of healing resembled "working of miracles" (powers). Witness the ministry of our Lord (Matt. 4:23–24), of the Twelve (Matt. 10:1), and of the Seventy (Luke 10:8–9). Gifts of healing were also prominent in the church after Pentecost (Acts 5:15–16; cf. also James 5:14–15). "Gifts" (plural) indicates the great variety of both the sicknesses healed and the means used in the healings. The person who exercised the gift, and the patient who was healed, had one essential in common—faith in God. The writings of the church fathers prove that "the gifts of healings" were exercised in the church centuries after the apostolic period. Since then, this gift has appeared intermittently in the church. For long gifts of healing have been in abeyance, but today there are recognized branches of the church which believe that they are beginning to reappear. Unfortunately the manner in which some act who claim to have received the gift has brought it into disrepute. The kind of ailments that were healed in the NT period, the nature and place of faith, the significance of suffering in God's economy, the importance of the subconscious and the nature of its influence upon the body, the relations between gifts of healings and medical science (a doctor was numbered among Paul's traveling companions!)—these have not received the attention they require today. Gifts of healings are a permanent gift of the Spirit to the church but are properly exercised only by men of the Spirit, and of humility and faith.

The Gift of Helpers (I Cor. 12:28). What spiritual gift was signified by "helper" may be gathered from Acts 20:35, where Paul exhorts the Ephesian elders to labor "to help the weak" and constantly to remember the Lord's own words, "It is more blessed to give than to receive." Paul supports this exhortation from his own example. The early church seems to have had a special concern for the needy among her members, and those who helped the indigent were considered to have been endowed by the Spirit for this ministry. It is not impossible that the office of elder originated in the gift of government or rule. By the same token, the office or duty of deacon may have originated in this gift of helpers. The deacon was one who ministered to the needy (Acts 6:1–6).

The Gift of Governments or Administration (I Cor. 12:28; cf. Rom. 12:8). The church's organization was still fluid. Official offices had not been established, nor were duly appointed officials yet ruling the churches. It was necessary, therefore, that certain members should receive and exercise the gift of ruling or governing the local assembly of believers. This gift would take the form of sound advice and wise judgment in directing church affairs. Gradually, of course, this gift of guiding and ruling in church affairs would come to be identified so closely with certain individuals that they would begin to assume responsibilities of a quasipermanent nature. They would become recognized officials in the church, fulfilling well-defined duties in the administration of the Christian community. At the beginning, however, it was acknowledged that some Christians had received the gift of ruling and had liberty to exercise it. In addition to administration, practical matters in the conduct of public worship would require wisdom and foresight, and here again those who had recognizably received the gift of ruling would be expected to legislate.

The Gift of Faith (I Cor. 12:9). The gift of faith should probably be included among the gifts closely related to the practical life and development of the church. These spiritual gifts would naturally strengthen the believers in their faith, and convince the unbelievers of the authenticity of the church's message. The Spirit's gift of faith could effect mighty things (Matt. 17:19–20), and keep believers steadfast in persecution. These five spiritual gifts, then, had special reference to the practical aspects of the church's life, the physical well-being of believers, and orderliness of their worship and conduct.

The remainder of the gifts of the Spirit concern the ministry of the word of God. To that extent, they were more important than the foregoing; but the latter were, nevertheless, spiritual gifts. In origin and nature they were the result of special endowments of the Spirit.

Apostleship. Concerning the gifts especially meaningful for the preaching of the word, Paul gives pride of place to the grace of apostleship: "God hath set some in the church, first apostles" (I Cor. 12:28). The designation "apostle" began to be applied to NT personalities other than the Twelve, especially to Paul. So highly did he value the gift of apostleship which the Holy Spirit had conferred upon him that on occasion he was at pains to prove its validity (cf. I Cor. 9:1ff.; Gal.

1:12). The apostles conceived that they had received this spiritual gift to enable them to fulfill the ministry of the word of God; nothing, therefore, should be allowed to prevent their fulfilling that all-important function (Acts 6:2). We also gather from Paul that the gift of apostleship was to be exercised principally among unbelievers (I Cor.1:17), while other spiritual gifts were more closely related to the needs of believers. Paul's apostleship was to be fulfilled among Gentiles; Peter's ministry of the word was to be exercised among Jews (Gal. 2:7–8). Obviously the Spirit's gift of apostleship was not confined to a strictly limited group of men whose gift of apostleship made them *ipso facto* special units of a divine grace or authority. Their function was doubtless conceived to be the most important so far as the ministry of the word was concerned, but we shall see presently that theirs was only one of a number of such spiritual gifts. The church was built upon prophets as well as apostles (Eph. 2:20), the first ministering in the word to the church, the latter preaching the word to non-Christians. Since, then, the gift of apostleship was spiritual, so also was the authority of the apostles. It remained the prerogative of the Holy Spirit and never became official in the sense that one could communicate it to others of his own volition. The authority exercised by the apostles was exercised democratically, not autocratically (Acts 15:6, 22). They were careful to include the elders and brethren when substantiating the validity of the directives they were issuing to the church. Even when Paul was asked to legislate for the churches he had founded, his authority was not his apostleship but a word from the Lord (I Cor. 7:10).

Prophets. Prophets stand next in importance to apostles in Paul's enumeration of the spiritual gifts (I Cor. 12:2ff.). The gift of prophecy has already been differentiated from the grace of apostleship on the ground of the sphere in which each was exercised. In a sense Moses' desire (Num. 11:29) had been realized in the experience of the church *as a whole* (Acts 2:17–18; 19:6; I Cor. 11:4–5), but some individuals seem to have been specially endowed with this grace (Acts 11:28; 15:32; 21:9–10). These prophets in the NT church seem often to have been itinerant preachers. Moving from church to church, they built up believers in the faith by teaching the word. Their ministry would probably be characterized by spontaneity and power, since it seems to have included speaking by revelation (I Cor. 14:6, 26, 30–31). In these passages, however, the prophet's utterances were clearly understood compared with the utterances in tongues. On occasion God would make his will known through the prophet (Acts 13:1ff.), or a future event would be foretold (Acts 11:28; 21:10–11); but the prophet's special gift was the edification, exhortation, consolation, and instruction of the local churches (I Cor. 14). In the subapostolic period the prophet could still take precedence over the local minister, but the day was not far off when this gift of prophecy passed to the local ministers who preached the word to edify the members of the Christian fellowship.

The nature of this gift of prophecy was such that the danger of false prophets must always have been present. The Spirit, therefore, communicated a gift that enabled some among those who listened to the prophets to recognize the truth or falsity of their utterances. This was not natural insight or shrewd judgment but a supernatural gift. Paul describes this spiritual gift as a "discerning of the spirits." The fact that the prophet spoke by revelation made the appearance of false prophets almost inevitable; while, therefore, Paul urged his converts not to despise prophesyings, they were, nevertheless, to prove all things (I Thess. 5:20–21).

The Gift of Discernment of Spirits. Believers had to be able to discriminate between the false and the true spirits, when an itinerant prophet claimed to be inspired to speak by revelation (I Cor. 14:29).

The Gift of Teaching. Clearly related to, but carefully distinguished from, the gift of prophecy is the gift of teaching (I Cor. 12:28–29; Rom. 12:7). The prophet was a preacher of the word; the teacher explained what the prophet proclaimed, reduced it to statements of doctrine, and applied it to the situation in which the church lived and witnessed. The teacher would offer systematic instruction (II Tim. 2:2) to the local churches. In Eph. 4:11 Paul adds the idea of pastor to that of teacher, because no one is able to communicate effectively (teach) without loving those who are being instructed (pastor). Likewise, to be an effective pastor, one must also be a teacher.

The Gift of Exhortation (Rom. 12:8). The possessor of the gift of exhortation would fulfill a ministry closely allied with that of the Christian prophet and teacher. The difference between them would be found in the more personal approach of the former. If his exhortations were to succeed, they would have to be given in the persuasive power of love, understanding, and sympathy. His aim would be to win Christians to a higher way of life and to a deeper self-dedication to Christ. The Spirit, therefore, who bestowed the gift of exhortation would with the gift communicate spiritual persuasiveness and winsomeness.

The Gift of Speaking the Word of Wisdom (I Cor. 12:8). An important part of the Spirit's endowment so far as the Christian community was concerned was wisdom. This gift would communicate ability to receive and explain "the deep things of God." In God's dealings with men much is mysterious, and the ordinary Christian is often in need of a word that will throw light upon his situation; and the person fitted by the Spirit to fulfill this ministry is through the Spirit given the word of wisdom. Because of the strong sense of revelation or insight implied in the phrase, perhaps this gift was akin to a revelational utterance by the Christian prophet.

The Gift of Speaking the Word of Knowledge (I Cor. 12:8). Speaking the word of knowledge suggests a word spoken only after long and careful consideration. This would be a word that the Christian teacher would ordinarily speak. Of course, this mental activity would not be entirely unaided; a point being reached when the Spirit would give knowledge, understanding, insight, that might be described as intuition. But since Paul points out that both the word of wisdom and the word of knowledge are given through or according to the Spirit, the emphasis is on the reception of the word, not on its interpretation.

The Gift of Tongues. Yet another spiritual gift is mentioned by Paul. The Spirit gives "kinds of tongues" (I Cor. 12:10, 28). The nature of this gift is explained in I Cor. 14. (1) The tongue in which the person spoke was unintelligible, and therefore unedifying to the Christian assembly (vss. 2–4); (2) the tongue (*glōssa*) was not a foreign language (*phōnē,* vss. 10–12); (3) The tongue speaker addressed himself to God to whom he probably offered prayer and praise (vss. 14–17); (4) The tongue edified the speaker (vs. 4); (5) The tongue speaker lost the control of intellectual faculties (vss. 14–15), the tongue being probably a disjointed, highly pitched, ecstatic series of ejaculations, similar to the tongues spoken in times of spiritual awakening experienced intermittently by the church.

The Gift of Interpretation of Tongues (I Cor. 12:10, 30). A necessary corollary to speaking in tongues was the interpretation of tongues. The tongue speaker might also exercise the gift of interpreting, but usually others exercised it (vss. 26–28; 12:10); though Paul's advice in I Cor. 14:13 is interesting. This would imply giving meaning to unmeaningful ecstatic ejaculations as an art critic interprets a play, a symphony, or a canvas to the uninitiated; though the tongue interpreter did not depend on natural knowledge.

The Evangelist. Another gift to the church is the evangelist. Timothy is called an evangelist in II Tim. 4:5, as is Philip, one of the seven, in Acts 21:8. The task of preaching the gospel, although theoretically everyone's responsibility, is entrusted specifically to certain individuals by the Holy Spirit. They are to exercise their ministry in the full realization that the power comes from God, making faddish and manipulative techniques not only unnecessary but wrong. When such are present, it is a clear indication that the Spirit is absent. Converts from the evangelist's ministry are to be funneled into the church where they are to be built up by those exercising the other gifts.

Service (Gr., *diakonia*). Service is called a gift in Rom. 12:7. This term is used in a number of ways in the NT, from a generalized idea of ministry (II Cor. 5:18, where Paul's preaching is called a ministry of reconciliation) to a specific office or task (I Tim. 1:12). It is difficult to know exactly how Paul means it here. It is perhaps a generalized gift of power to anyone exercising a specific function in the church.

Contributing. Paul speaks of contributing as a gift (Rom. 12:8). All are to give to the needs of the church, its ministry, and the poor, but a special gift enables some to make joyous sacrifice in this area. Paul adds that this gift should be exercised "without grudging" or "in liberality."

Acts of Mercy (Rom. 12:8). Merciful acts are to be performed with cheerfulness under the guidance of the Spirit. It might be wondered why such a noble act would require charismatic endowment, but the circumstances of the time explain it. To render aid was dangerous. Such identification with other Christians in need branded one as a Christian as well, opening up the possibility of persecution for oneself.

Giving Aid (Rom. 12:8). Giving aid, also mentioned as a gift, is to be exercised with zeal. It is possible that this gift is another form of administrative gift. If so, this is not new. If not, it more closely parallels acts of mercy.

Conclusion. In instructing Christians on the exercise of these gifts, Paul is concerned to stress their practical nature. The Spirit bestows his *charismata* for the edification of the church, the formation of Christian character, and the service of the community. The reception of a spiritual gift, therefore, brought serious responsibility, since it was essentially an opportunity for self-giving in sacrificial service for others.

The more spectacular gifts (tongues, healings, miracles) necessitated some degree of order that would prevent their indiscriminate use (I Cor. 14:40). The spirits of the prophets must be subjected to the prophets (vs. 32). Paul clearly insists that spectacular gifts were inferior to those that instructed believers in faith and morals and evangelized non-Christians. Tongue speaking was not forbidden (vs. 39), but intelligent exposition of the word, instruction in faith and morals, and preaching the gospel were infinitely superior. The criteria used to judge the relative values of spiritual gifts were doctrinal (I Cor. 12:3), moral (I Cor. 13), and practical (I Cor. 14).

The problem was where to strike the balance. The greatest peril lay in overemphasizing the gifts, which tended to exalt the offices that grew out of them. That led inevitably to institutional ecclesiasticism and the inevitable corresponding loss of the church's awareness of the Spirit's presence and experience of the Spirit's power.

J. G. S. S. Thomson and W. A. Elwell

See also Baptism of the Spirit; Charismatic Movement; Holy Spirit; Tongues, Speaking in.

Bibliography. L. Morris, *Spirit of the Living God;* H. W. Robinson, *The Christian Experience of the Holy Spirit;* J. R. W. Stott, *The Baptism and Fullness of the Holy Spirit;* C. Williams, *The Descent of the Dove;* M. Griffiths, *Grace-Gifts;* K. Stendahl, *Paul Among Jews and Gentiles;* J. R. Williams, *The Gift of the Holy Spirit Today;* A. A. Hoekema, *Tongues and Spirit Baptism;* F. D. Bruner, *A Theology of the Holy Spirit;* E. E. Ellis, *Prophecy and Hermeneutics.*

Spiritual Healing. *See* Heal, Healing.

Spirituality. The state of deep relationship to God. The interest among evangelical Christians in spirituality is new and yet also a deeply based consciousness. It is new because the word "spirituality" is not commonly used, nor does it occur in biblical or theological dictionaries. For some Christians there has been reluctance to speak of spirituality, lest we isolate such expressions as "spiritual formation, spiritual health, spiritual discipline" from other aspects of life and living. In the past, expressions such as "holiness, holy living, godliness, walking with God, discipleship" seemed more acceptable because they emphasized a formal commitment, a deepening relationship with Christ, and a life of personal obedience to the word of God. "Spirituality" is more abstract, even misleading, when used of the asceticism of any religion, including specific traditions of Roman Catholic devotion. But the decline of the sacred even among evangelical Christians and the deep penetration of secularism into every aspect of life are causing alarm and the need to reconsider devotion to Christ much more seriously.

Spirituality in Other Religions. Modern exemplars of spiritual life, such as depicted in the film *Gandhi,* remind us that all mankind has the potential attributes for being spiritual. In primitive religions there is no distinction between the sacred and the secular, as in animism, and when all is viewed in terms of magic, the concept of spirituality probably does not arise. But in the more advanced religions, where the distinction is made between the sacred and the secular, then human choice, personal discipline, and ascetic practice lead to advanced experiences of spirituality. Rudolf Otto in his classic study *The Idea of the Holy* categorizes the experience of religion as the tremendous with its sense of overwhelming awe, the mysterious with its awareness of something numinous, the portentous with its fear that is qualitative, the fascinating with its motive for self-reflection, and with energy as power that elevates the worshiper. These provide the experience of the sacred that encourage the worshiper to incorporate in himself what is different from himself. Yet the gulf between the worshiper and the sacred remains. The deep, earnest, sustained desire to make the leap between the human and the sacred is characteristic of the advanced Eastern religions, although it may also be more loosely used to describe the inspiration of the poet, the vision of the philosopher, or even the ideal of youth.

Indeed, the advanced standards of asceticism in Eastern religions today are often contrasted favorably with the self-interest, materialism, and hedonism of Western life. Asian religions are often marked by a contempt for materialism and by a concept of spirituality as a sustained and consistent way of life that shames Western Christians. The endless vigil, the extreme asceticism, and the simplicity of a mullah, guru, or fakir seem to excel any standards of ascetic spirituality in the West. Indeed, Hindu people are often looked upon as the most prayerful of people, whose whole lives are made up of prayer. A fakir will live all his life entirely dependent on alms and in absolute contempt for all worldly goods. A sannyasi will devote himself to continual journeyings, in a life lived entirely apart. Such have chosen to devote their lives entirely to the sacred. Other great Eastern religions—Buddhism, Zoroastrianism, the religions of China and Japan—have this strong ascetical character of the contemplative life. Some Western Roman Catholic contemplatives have therefore entered into dialogue with such holy men as an aid in deepening their own understanding of the spiritual life.

Spirituality in Christian Heresies. Within Christianity, the early heresies all won popularity more by their ascetic and mystical practices than by any teaching that they professed. Almost all of them were either infiltrations of Eastern thought or the result of Greek mystic thought. Gnosticism, Mithracism, Neoplatonism, and later also Manichaeism all had Eastern origins. They sought the world's regeneration in outdoing Christianity in ascetic and mystical efforts. Likewise, Islam as a heresy of Judaism has produced some of the greatest spiritual poetry, while its Arab philosophers have profoundly influenced Western thought. Its spiritual masters have been among the greatest, the most severe, and the most faithful in the history of asceticism. Thus it is not just in doctrine that such Eastern faiths have challenged the West, but in their practices of spirituality. As the East intermingles with the West today, so we can anticipate the intensification of such challenges to the postmodern consciousness of the West, disillusioned by the aridity of rationalism, technocracy, and the loss of spiritual values.

The Nature of Christian Spirituality. (1) Asceticism as such does not define Christian spirituality. There is much asceticism that is based on contempt for the material world. The biblical doctrine of creation recognizes that God has created all things "good." Thus, living in God's world, there can be no motive for detachment from this good life.

(2) The biblical revelation of God as a personal God leaves no place for the deductions of human wisdom, as in Eastern thought, nor for the human reasoning, as in Greek thought. The will and purpose of God has been given to us in the Holy Scriptures. The Ten Commandments and Israel's worship of Yahweh, the God of covenant, gave its people a very different orientation from those of the surrounding peoples. Conscious intercourse with God, as Moses "spoke with God face to face," the temple, the shekinah, and the prophets all manifested the ways of God and developed an Israelite mysticism very different from anything hitherto known in the ancient world.

(3) Christian spirituality is Christocentric. The apostle Paul frequently describes the life of the believer "in Christ" to emphasize the union Christians enjoy with Jesus Christ. This is a dynamic union which the Synoptic writers describe as following Jesus, the Johannine writings as union in love, and Heb. and I Pet. as a pilgrimage. These and other metaphors imply the growth and dynamism of the life of Christ in the believer. For God's original purpose to create man in the image and likeness of God (Gen. 1:26–28) is reinterpreted by redemption as being "conformed to the image of his Son" (Rom. 8:29).

(4) Christian spirituality is life in the Trinity. The Christian lives in the acceptance of sonship knowing God as Father. He realizes this in the Sonship of Jesus Christ, his saving work of forgiveness, and his gift of eternal life. He actualizes this by the gift of the Holy Spirit who enables the believer to cry "Abba Father" (Rom. 8:15; Gal. 4:6).

(5) Christian spirituality is the outworking, then, of the grace of God in the soul of man, beginning with conversion to conclusion in death or Christ's second advent. It is marked by growth and maturity in a Christlike life. It implies community and fellowship (Eph. 4:15–16), a life of prayer (Matt. 6:5–15; I Thess. 5:17), a sense of the eternal dimension in all one's existence (Gen. 50:19–20; Rom. 8:28), and an intense awareness of life lived in the present before God (Matt. 6:34). The Spirit-filled life is one that manifests practically the Spirit of Jesus, with the fruit of love that is joyful, peaceful, patient, kind, good, faithful, gentle, and self-controlled (Gal. 5:22–23). This is true spirituality. It is a continuous command, "Be filled with the Spirit," that should be neither quenched (I Thess. 5:19) nor grieved (Eph. 4:30).

(6) Christian spirituality engenders fellowship, and the communion of saints deepens its character. As social beings, the reality of our spirituality is tested by the quality of our public worship (Acts 2:42). Godliness and spiritual friendship reinforce each other, as a horizontal and a vertical way respectively, to inspire and to embody the love of God in human hearts. For Christian worship is not primarily a matter of special practices but of life style (Rom. 12:1; 14:6; I Cor. 10:31). Spiritual autobiography, so rich and extensive in the Bible, especially in the Psalter, inspires and integrates our own search for models of the biblical faith. Likewise, devotional writing throughout history, such as Augustine's *Confessions,* Teresa of Ávila's *Life,* John Bunyan's *Grace Abounding to the Chief of Sinners,* or C. S. Lewis's *Surprised by Joy,* help us develop our views of God and of ourselves, so that we keep growing in our faith in God and in our distrust of ourselves.

Orthodox Spirituality. It is often said the Gospel of John has been the prevailing scriptural influence in the Orthodox Church. For its simple faith combined with its deep intellectual character has attracted minds like Origen (185–254) John Chrysostom (347–407), Basil (*ca.* 330–79), Theodore the Studite, and others. One aspect of its importance has been the motif of witness and the importance of martyrdom, which has never been far from the spirit of Eastern life. The creation of a school for catechumens in Alexandria in the third century stimulated an intellectual and speculative type of spirituality. It owed much to Philo, who sought to combine Judaism and Platonism. This led to a dualistic view of matter and spirit, scriptural allegorism, the method of abstraction in apophatic attitudes and in a tendency to think dialectically.

To this was added a Christocentric mysticism by Athanasius (296–373) completing what Irenaeus had emphasized beforehand, of the recapitulation of man's purpose in Christ. There is also a strong asceticism, influenced by the desert fathers such as John Cassian (*ca.* 360–435), Evagrius (*ca.* 346–399), John Climacus (*ca.* 570–649), who considered the monastic model of *apatheia* as the ideal. This is not the apathy of the Stoics, but the fiery love of God, that both burns up the passions and possessiveness of men and flames in living desire for God. Orthodox piety is also deeply liturgical in its dispensing of the sacraments and the celebration of the church calendar, which frames the whole year with its commemoration of all the stages of the Savior's earthly life and ministry. No doubt the ceremony of the Byzantine court also added the richness of Orthodox liturgy and iconic art. There is the strong contemplative element in the tradition of hesychasm (*hesychia,* "quiet"). "Prayer without ceasing" goes back to the contemplative life of the desert fathers, but it was richly developed by Symeon the New Theologian (949–1022). The Jesus Prayer, "Lord Jesus Christ, Son of God, have mercy upon me," became a repetitive spiritual practice with controlled breathing and other exercises. There has been a revived interest in the Jesus Prayer by Russian emigrants in recent decades. Finally, there is in Orthodox spirituality a strong emphasis on man's union with God and "deification." The latter term does not mean pantheism, but a sharing, through the grace of God, of the divine life (II Pet. 1:4). In the Son "we are made sons of God," declares Athanasius. It is a supernatural life which man can never achieve naturally, although as in all human traditions, this has often been lost sight of.

Today there is a growing interest in Orthodox spirituality within the West, as evidenced in the evangelical Orthodox movement. Theologians like T. F. Torrance have redirected us to their Alexandrine fathers. The heroic spirit of Russian Christians today and the recognition of nineteenth century men of prayer like John of Kronstadt, Anthony Bloom, and Timothy Ware are exemplars of a twentieth century renaissance of Orthodoxy.

Western Medieval Spirituality. Until Augustine (354–430), Western spirituality was much influenced by the desert fathers, and the more erudite monasticism of the fourth century Cappadocian fathers—Basil, his brother Gregory of Nyssa, and their friend Gregory of Nazianzus. But their mysticism was tempered in the West by Jerome, who advocated the historical study of the Scriptures, and by Tertullian, who was a Roman jurist. But the key man is Augustine, who rejected the Eastern doctrine of deification of man and emphasized the reality of a personal God to whom he addressed his *Confessions* in humility and trust. His emphasis on the human share in the divine life by grace is also discussed in the *City of God* (bks. 13–14), and in the *Enarrationes,* dialogue between the church as the bride and Christ as the bridegroom, develops the theme of the communal growth of the believers.

However, it is Gregory the Great (540–604) who is the father of medieval spirituality. He systematized Western monasticism, and developed the imagery of the vision of God. To experience this, he emphasized the need of purity of heart, with the associated virtue of humility. Practical service was another Western trait of Gregory's teachings. Isidore (*ca.* 560–636), bishop of Seville, and the Venerable Bede (*ca.* 673–735) developed Gregory's ideas further, with stress on reading (*lectio*), meditative memory (*meditatio*), prayer (*oratio*), and practice (*intento*), as guides for the spiritual life in the dark ages of the barbarians. Maximus the Confessor (*ca.* 580–662) was the first to give expression to the Catholic tradition of the three ways to God of purgation, illumination, and union. The Celtic church emphasized the need of a penitential life. John Scotus Erigena (*ca.* 810–77) introduced Greek mystical thought into the West, translating Dionysius, Gregory of Nyssa, and others.

The high Middle Ages (1000–1300) are primarily concerned with monastic reform, the clash between scholasticism and the contemplative life, and the laicization of the church. An intensely affective expression of spirituality was promoted by Bernard of Clairvaux (1090–1153) and his followers. The Victorines, Hugh of St. Victor (1097–1141) and especially Richard of St. Victor (d. 1173), attempted a synthesis of love and knowledge which has deeply influenced subsequent mystical thought. Popularity was aroused by the examples of the friars, notably Francis of Assisi (1181–1226) and his followers, Bonaventure (1221–74) and Raymond Lull (1235–1315). More speculative in their theology were the Dominicans. Dominic (*ca.* 1173–1221) saw the great need of spiritual direction for the laity, an emphasis perhaps eclipsed by the great Dominican theologian Thomas Aquinas (1224–74), who had reservations as to how far mystical theology could take one.

The late Middle Ages (1300–1500) are marked by a dramatic change of mood to one of pessimism in Western life with famines, plagues, intellectual sterility, and skepticism, and the breakup of feudal society. Individual mysticism deepens, although regional associations of mystics are discernible.

In the Rhineland, the Dominicans Meister Eckhart (1260–1328), Johannes Tauler (*ca.* 1300–1361), and Henry Suso (*ca.* 1295–1366), with the Augustinian John Ruysbroeck (1293–1381), all exerted a profound influence. Tauler was related to Nicholas of Basel, a leader of the movement called Friends of God and later a significant influence on Martin Luther. In England, the Lollards and other disaffected mystics gave great impetus to lay piety. Richard Rolle (*ca.* 1290–1349), Julian of Norwich (late fourteenth century), Margery Kempe (*ca.* 1373–1433), Walter of Hilton (d. *ca.* 1396), and the unknown writer of *The Cloud of Unknowing* and other works all express the anti-intellectualism and affective needs of the period. In the Netherlands, Gerard Groote (1340–84) and his disciple Thomas à Kempis (1379–1471) gave birth to the *Devotio Moderna,* whose classic, *The Imitation of Christ,* had an immense influence on subsequent generations. In northern Italy, there were Catherine of Genoa (1447–1510) and Lorenzo Scupoli (*The Spiritual Combat*), who have had profound influence.

Modern Catholic Spirituality. More than anywhere else, the founders of the tradition of modern Catholic spirituality are the Spanish mystics. Ignatius of Loyola (1491–1556) was the founder of the Jesuits. Teresa of Ávila (1515–82) and John of the Cross (1542–91) were reformers of the Carmelites. A precursor was Cardinal Cisneros (1475–1516), whose *Spiritual Exercises* shows the influence of the *Devotio Moderna.* Ignatius in turn wrote his *Spiritual Exercises* to introduce to others what he had experienced in 1582 when he awaited God's direction for his life. Teresa's *Life* and *The Interior Castle* describe her autobiographical experiences in prayer, two of the most balanced descriptions of prayer that are still deeply mystical. John of the Cross, perhaps Spain's most famous lyricist, expanded his poems into four treatises on the contemplative life. He is profoundly biblical and yet speculative in his mysticism of "darkness."

While the Renaissance, much less the Reformation, never touched Spain, Italy was in the heart of the first movement and was also affected by the second. Those persecuted for their reforming zeal were Girolamo Savonarola (1452–98); a Dominican, Aonio Palaerio, who was in touch with Calvin; and Lorenzo Scupoli (1530–1610), whose book *The Spiritual Combat* ran into over two hundred editions in Slavic and Balkan languages. Robert Bellarmine (1542–1621), a Jesuit, was influenced by it in western Europe.

In France there was sharp conflict between the more rationalistic views of men like Bossuet and the quietist views of Francis Fénelon (1651–1715). Before him the great influence on French spirituality was Francis of Sales (1567–1622), who followed the combined influences of Ignatius and Teresa. Sales focused on the spiritual needs of the laity in a gentle, fragrant manner. A more theological emphasis on spiritual renewal of the clergy was made by Pierre de Brulle (1575–1629), who founded the Oratory for that purpose in 1611. Blaise Pascal (1623–62) with his specific attack on the intellectualism of René Descartes is best known for his *Pensées.*

Caroline Spirituality. In England, the spirituality of the Anglican Church is associated with the *Book of Common Prayer,* first issued by Archbishop Cranmer in 1549 and revised in 1552. The petitionary emphasis of Bishop Jewel, the communal liturgy of Richard Hooker (*ca.* 1554–1600), the confessional bias of John Donne (*ca.* 1572–1631), the catechetical aim of Lancelot Andrewes (1555–1626), the lyrics of George Herbert and of other metaphysical poets, and the astringent emphasis of Jeremy Taylor and William Law (1686–1761) have all contributed to a rich cultural life around the communal piety of Anglican devotion. Although "Caroline" indicates the reign of Charles I and II, it is still characteristic of much Anglicanism today. Its balance between the contemplative life of prayer and the vocal liturgy of communal prayer is the genius of its spiritual continuity in the life of the church.

Puritan Spirituality. While the Reformation of Martin Luther (1483–1546) and John Calvin (1509–64) developed into classical Protestantism, the subsequent reforms of Puritanism, pietism, and Methodism were distinct, and sometimes divergent. At first influenced by the mystics, notably Tauler and the unknown writer of the *Theologia Germanica,* Luther later became more antimystical, so that his prayer life is practical and simple. To him the essence of spiritual life could be sustained on the actualization of the Ten Commandments, the Lord's Prayer, and the Apostles' Creed. Calvin is a much more sophisticated spiritual guide, and in the third book of his *Institutes* he has left rich teaching on the spiritual life. He was possibly originally inspired by Jean Gerson's teachings on personal piety and by the *Devotio Moderna,* though very soon Calvin gave his own distinctive alternative to the Catholic model of purgation-illumination-union with the biblical themes of justification-sanctification-glorification.

It was out of Calvinist teaching that Puritan spirituality developed in England and later in New England. It focused on the centrality of the word of God and its preaching, the preparation of heart to receive the word, the need for a godly walk and accountability to God, and the strength and watchfulness required in pilgrimage and conflict. The heavenly hope of the believer enabled him to anticipate heaven while still on earth. The strong theological understanding of scriptural authority by John Rogers (1500–1555), the prayerful life of John Bradford (1510–55), and the synthesis of Tudor Puritan theology by William Greenham established a framework for Puritan life. Later the affectivity of Richard Sibbs and Thomas Goodwin (1600–1680), the theological clarity of John Owen, and the pastoral insights of Richard Baxter (1615–91) established the heyday of Puritan spirituality in the middle of the seventeenth century. Why Puritanism collapsed as a cultural force is a complex issue, but one suggestion is that prayer was vocalized like the preaching that was central to its witness. Meditation did have a significant emphasis, as the works of Hall and Baxter attest, but the contemplative life was suspect by its association with popery. It might have been a richer, more sustained spirituality if the contemplative life had also been considered. The movement lasted longer in New England.

German Pietism. In reaction to the sterile theology of Lutheranism in the seventeenth and eighteenth centuries, pietism was somewhat anti-intellectual and reactionary. Philipp J. Spener (1635–1705) was its classical exponent, although it is agreed Johann Arndt (1555–1621) was its founder. Arndt's *True Christianity* was widely read as an inspiration for "a new life." His favorite phrase was "It is faith that fashions the love of Christ in the faithful heart"—faith that was an act of thinking as well as feeling. The name "pietism" was unfortunate, for the movement would be better described as "devotionalism." But the group that met in Spener's house was called the college of piety, and so the name stuck. August H. Francke (1663–1727), the organizing genius of the lay movement, became professor of Greek and Oriental languages at Halle University. Both Spener and Francke practiced their devotion in the establishment of poor schools, orphanages, farms, printing shops, and other enterprises. Count Nikolaus L. von Zinzendorf (1700–1760) later constituted remnants of a pre-Reformation group into the Moravian Brethren in his state in 1727. Gerard Tersteegen (1697–1769) was perhaps the last of the great Protestant spiritual theologians; his hymns have had a lasting impact on the church, though the Clapham Sect and William Wilberforce's *Practical View of . . . Real Christianity* were to continue the echoes of the pietist movement into nineteenth century England.

Methodism and Modern Holiness Movements. John Wesley (1703–91), who lived and died an Anglican pastor, nevertheless was founder of the Methodist movement. Eclectic in his spiritual life, he was read in William Law, Teresa of Ávila, Francis of Sales, Thomas à Kempis, Fénelon, and others. While preaching was the main emphasis of his ministry, he developed hymnody with his brother Charles as an instrument of spirituality, and developed class organization as a means of instruction. But his doctrine of Christian perfection was developed carefully, leaving the possibility of Feuerbach's later teaching on religion as feeling to overwhelm liberal Methodism in a later period. While George Whitefield (1714–70) is commonly associated with the Wesleys, his teachings are closer to the Puritans and Jonathan Edwards, with whom he was also associated during his visits to New England.

The Keswick Convention was established in England in the late 1800s to promote the message of victorious Christian living. Watchman Nee's influential book *The Normal Christian Life,* based on Rom. 8, taught Christians what to expect when the power of the Holy Spirit was operative in their lives. Both have been influential movements among contemporary evangelicals.

Pentecostalism, beginning in the early part of this century out of holiness teaching, and the more interdenominational charismatic movement since World War II have been significant renewal movements. The focus on direct illumination of the Holy Spirit has been claimed by other movements in the history of the church, but none has grown so fast. The pentecostal movement today is the fastest church growth movement in modern times. The release of self-consciousness, the exercise of touch, the emphasis on spiritual gifts, the strong awareness of the satanic and the need of exorcisms, the ministry of all believers—these have marked the character of its spirituality. There is a felt vibrancy in the reality of the living and present God, like children rediscovering the reality of the fatherhood of God.

Conclusion. In spite of the renewal movements, there is a dearth today of spiritual leadership and direction in the evangelical world. Catholics can look to Mother Teresa in Calcutta, and the Orthodox to the unnamed martyrs of modern Russia, but evangelical Protestants are largely secularized by their politics, their obsession with growth, and their interests in administration and parachurch activities. The loss of the practice of prayer, the ignorance of the rich traditions of spirituality, and the need to develop a cultural framework for the practice of devotion are challenges worthy of the most serious consideration at the end of the twentieth century.

J. M. Houston

See also Beatific Vision; Boehme, Jakob; Brethren of the Common Life; Devotio Moderna; Francis of Assisi; Godliness; Hesychasm; Holiness Movement, American; Illuminative Way, The; Keswick Convention; Mysticism; Perfection, Perfectionism; Pietism; Purgative Way, The; Quietism; Sanctification; Unitive Way, The.

Bibliography. L. Bouyer, *History of Christian Spirituality;* U. T. Holmes, *A History of Christian Spirituality;* R. Lovelace, *Dynamics of Spiritual Life;* R. Payne, *The Holy Fire: The Story of the Fathers of the Eastern Church;* E. Kodloubousky and G. E. H. Palmer, eds. and trs., *Early Fathers from the Philokalia* and *Writings from the Philokalia;* P. Pourrat, *Christian Spirituality;* E. Stoeffler, *The Rise of Evangelical Pietism;* J. Tiller, *Puritan, Pietist and Pentecostalist;* G. S. Wakefield, *Puritan Devotion: Its Place in the Development of Christian Piety.*

Sprinkle, Sprinkling. *See* Baptism, Modes of.

Spurgeon, Charles Haddon (1834–1892). Influential Baptist minister in England. Spurgeon was born at Kelvedon, Essex, on June 19, 1834, and became apart of the Nonconformist tradition from his early childhood. His grandfather, James, and his father, John, were both ministers of Independent congregations. He spent his early years at his grandfather's home, but attended schools at Colchester and Newmarket.

Although he had been reared as an Independent and converted in a primitive Methodist chapel, he was baptized and joined a Baptist church in 1849. In 1850 he enrolled in a school near Cambridge and became an active member of a Baptist church. At the age of sixteen he preached his first sermon in a cottage at Teversham, near Cambridge. By 1851 he was preaching regularly to a Baptist congregation at Waterbeach, a village near Cambridge.

In April 1854, he accepted a call to the Baptist chapel at New Park Street in London and began a ministry which lasted thirty-eight years. He received some unfavorable publicity at first because of his lack of a formal education and his rural origins. The congregation began to grow, however, and soon he was preaching at Exeter Hall while the church building was being enlarged. Then some members of the church rented the Surrey Gardens Music Hall, and at age twenty-two Spurgeon was perhaps the most popular preacher of his day.

In 1861 the Metropolitan Tabernacle at Elephant and Castle streets was built, a church that would seat six thousand people. The building was completely paid for when the congregation occupied the site, and Spurgeon ministered there continually until his death. The tabernacle became a center for the religious life of the area, housing a pastor's college and a colportage society which emphasized the distribution of religious literature. The congregation grew yearly, and it has been estimated that fourteen thousand members were added during Spurgeon's ministry.

Spurgeon was married to Susannah Thompson in 1856, and they had two sons, Charles and Thomas. A liberal in politics, he supported the liberal-unionist party and their opposition to home rule in Ireland. He refused the title of "reverend" as a matter of principle, and he refused to be ordained. He lived well, but was generous to those in need, and was responsible for founding an orphanage in 1867. He died at Mentone in France after a lengthy illness.

Spurgeon was a product of his Calvinist upbringing, and the Metropolitan Tabernacle was the center of Nonconformist activity during the 1870s and 1880s. He took pride in the fact that his Calvinist theology did not change during his years of ministry, and he claimed roots from Paul, Augustine, Calvin, and John Knox. One of his many biographers described him as an heir of the Puritans.

He was involved in doctrinal controversies on at least two occasions. In 1864 he preached a sermon against infant baptism and offended a large group of evangelicals who had been his supporters. A pamphlet war ensued and subsequently Spurgeon withdrew from the Evangelical Alliance, a group supported by the low church party of the Anglican Church. On October 26, 1887, he withdrew from the Baptist Union, pointing to what he considered to be doctrinal aberrations. He was particularly concerned about the development in modern biblical criticism and the lack of stress on the deity of Christ. This so-called downgrade controversy came near the close of his ministry and led to a great deal of pamphlet writing, a host of news articles, and the writing of a great many letters.

A prolific writer, he published some 2,241 of his weekly sermons during his lifetime, and some 3,800 in all were published. From 1865 on he edited a monthly magazine entitled *The Sword and the Trowel.* His primary emphasis was always focused on evangelism. Often criticized for not having received formal college training, his sermons revealed that he did a great deal of reading, and his personal library contained more than ten thousand volumes. J. E. Johnson

Bibliography. A. R. Meredith, "The Social and Political Views of Charles Haddon Spurgeon" (Diss., Michigan State University); *C. H. Spurgeon's Autobiography,* 4 vols.; G. H. Pike, *The Life and Work of Charles Haddon Spurgeon,* 6 vols.; W. Smith, *The Best of C. H. Spurgeon,* 9–19.

State. *See* GOVERNMENT.

States of Jesus Christ. The different relationships Jesus Christ had to God's law for mankind, to the possession of authority, and to receiving honor for himself. Generally two states (humiliation and exaltation) are distinguished. Thus, the doctrine of the twofold state of Christ is the teaching that Christ experienced first the state of humiliation, then the state of exaltation. Within each of these states four aspects may be distinguished.

The Humiliation of Christ. The four aspects of Christ's humiliation are (1) incarnation, (2) suffering, (3) death, and (4) burial. Sometimes a fifth aspect (descent into hell) is included.

Incarnation. The incarnation, or Christ's taking to himself a human nature, was itself a step of humiliation. He gave up the honor and glory that belonged to him in heaven (John 17:5). He also gave up his right to exercise divine authority for his own benefit and the right to enjoy his Lordship over all things in heaven and on earth (II Cor. 8:9; Phil. 2:6–7; Heb. 2:9). Thus he gave up the status of ruler and took on the status of a servant. Furthermore, he subjected himself to the demands of living under the law (Gal. 4:4), thus making it necessary for him to obey perfectly the OT laws which God had commanded of his people (John 8:46; Matt. 3:15). He took on himself the obligation to obey God perfectly *as a man,* as our representative, in order to earn salvation for us through a record of perfect lifelong obedience (Rom. 5:18–19). This he had to do in the strength of his human nature, without miraculous assistance from his divine powers (cf. Matt. 4:3–4).

It was a true human nature which the Son of God took to himself. It was not merely a human body, but also a human mind (which learned as we learn, Luke 2:52), and a human soul (which could be troubled as we are troubled, John 12:27; 13:21). Thus, Jesus was *fully* man, made like us "in every respect" (Heb. 2:17). He had to be fully man in order to become the sacrifice who was offered for man's sins: if he was not fully man, we could not have been saved. Nevertheless, the human nature of Christ was not subject to sin (Rom. 8:3; Heb. 4:15; I John 3:5). Thus, his human nature was like Adam's human nature before the fall.

Yet Jesus did not give up any of his divine attributes or become less fully God when he took on a human nature. He remained fully God (John 1:1, 14; Col. 1:19; 2:9), omnipotent (Matt. 8:26–27; Isa. 9:6), omniscient (John 2:25; 6:64; 16:30; 21:17), eternal (8:58), and incapable of dying (2:19; 10:17–18). However, these attributes were veiled, not generally manifested during Jesus' earthly ministry (Matt. 13:55–56), and never used for his own benefit or to make the path of obedience easier for him (4:1–11).

Thus, Jesus remained fully God and became fully man as well. It is sometimes said, "while remaining what he was, he became what he was not." (It should be remembered that it is God's Son, the second person of the Trinity, who became man. God the Father did not become man, nor did the Holy Spirit: Matt. 3:16–17; John 1:1; 3:16; Gal. 4:4). It is the most amazing fact in all history that one who was eternal and infinite God should take to himself the lowly nature of a man and should then continue to exist for all eternity as fully God and fully man as well, united in one person.

It is important to insist that even while existing in these two natures, Jesus Christ remained one person. His human nature was not an independent person by itself (capable, e.g., of talking to the divine nature or acting in opposition to it). In a manner that surpasses our understanding, the human and divine natures of Christ were integrated into one person, and he remains as both God and man, and yet one person, forever.

Suffering. Jesus' sufferings lasted throughout his whole life, though they culminated in his trial and death on the cross. He experienced the ordinary sufferings of living in a fallen world. He was weary (John 4:6), thirsty (19:28), hungry (Matt. 4:2), sorrowful (John 11:35), and lonely (Matt. 26:56). He felt great grief at human sin and its terrible effects (Matt. 23:37; Mark 3:5; 8:12; John 11:33–35, 38). He endured human opposition and intense hatred against himself (Luke 11:53–54; John 15:18, 24–25). He was "a man of sorrows and acquainted with grief" (Isa. 53:3).

Moreover, he "learned obedience through what he suffered" (Heb. 5:8); that is, his moral strength and ability to resist temptation increased with the successful meeting of each more difficult temptation, especially those connected with hardship and suffering. He experienced the sufferings of enduring great temptations without yielding (Matt. 4:1–11; Luke 11: 53–54; 22:28; Heb. 2:18; 4:15; I Pet. 2:21–23), especially in the Garden of Gethsemane just prior to his death (Matt. 26:37–38; Heb. 5:7; 12:3–4). Here it must be remembered that one who does not yield to temptation most fully feels its force, just as someone who successfully holds a heavy weight overhead feels its force much more than someone who drops it at once.

Jesus' humiliation increased in intensity at the time of his trial and death. Physical sufferings connected with crucifixion were terrible, as were the mocking and shame connected with such a death. But even worse were the sufferings in spirit which Jesus experienced when God the Father put on him the guilt of our sins (II Cor. 5:21; Gal. 3:13; I Pet. 2:22; Isa. 53:6). The Father turned away his face, so that Jesus was left alone with the blackness of sin and guilt upon him (Matt. 27:46; Hab. 1:13). Then, as Jesus fulfilled the role of propitiatory sacrifice (Rom. 3:25; I John 2:2; 4:10), he bore the fury of the intense wrath of God against sin, and bore it to the end.

Death. Since the penalty for sin was death (Gen. 2:17; Rom. 6:23), it was necessary that Jesus himself die to bear our penalty. His death was similar to ours, and is the pattern for us. Jesus' physical body died (Matt. 27:50), and his human spirit (or soul) was separated from his body and passed into the presence of the Father in heaven (Luke 23:43, 46). Thus, he experienced a death that is like the one we as believers will experience if we die in this present age. The knowledge that Jesus has gone through death before us should remove from us the fear of death (I Cor. 15:55–57; Heb. 2:14–15).

It is not correct to say that Jesus' divine nature died, or could die, if "die" implies a cessation of activity, a cessation of consciousness, or a diminution of power (John 2:19; 10:17–18). Yet by virtue of union with Jesus' human nature, his divine nature experienced what it was like to go through death. Whether the divine nature was ever itself the object of divine wrath against sin is not explicitly stated in Scripture. (For the idea that Jesus "descended into hell" after his death on the cross, see below.)

Burial. Jesus' body was laid in a tomb (Matt. 27:59–60), and he continued under the state of death for a time. Thus, Jesus' humiliation was complete in that he suffered all the punishment and shame due to fallen mankind as a result of sin.

"Descent into Hell." It does not seem correct to say that Jesus descended into hell, at least not according to any sense in which that phrase can be understood today, apart from specialized meanings which may be assigned to the word "hell." He did not experience further conscious suffering after he died on the cross, for he cried, "It is finished" (John 19:30). The statement from Ps. 16:10, "Thou dost not give me up to Sheol," quoted of Christ in the NT (Acts 2:27; cf. 13:35) is best understood to mean that God did not abandon him in the grave or in the state of death, for the Hebrew word *šĕʾôl* can certainly have those meanings.

Nor did Christ proclaim a second chance for salvation for those who were dead. I Pet. 4:6, "this is why the gospel was preached even to the dead," is best understood to mean that the gospel was preached to believers who had died before the time Peter was writing, and that the reason it was preached to them during their lifetime was not to save them from physical death, but to save them from final judgment.

It is also unlikely that any NT text can be understood to teach that Jesus after his death and before his resurrection went to proclaim his triumph to rebellious spirits in prison (a common Lutheran view) or to bring OT believers into the presence of God in heaven (a Roman Catholic view). In Eph. 4:9, where Paul says that Christ descended into "the lower parts of the earth," it is best understood as a genitive of apposition, meaning "the lower parts, namely, the earth" (compare NIV: "the lower, earthly regions"). Thus, the text refers to the incarnation. I Pet. 3:18–20, admittedly a difficult text, says that Christ "went and preached to the spirits in prison, who formerly did not obey, when God's patience waited in the days of Noah, during the building of the ark." When it is realized that Peter saw the spirit of Christ as active in the OT prophets (I Pet. 1:10–11), and saw Noah as a "'preacher" of righteousness (II Pet. 2:5), this text is probably best understood to mean that Christ in spirit was preaching through Noah while the ark was being built. Thus, no "descent into hell" is contemplated here either.

In the Apostles' Creed, the phrase "descended into hell" is a late addition, appearing only around A.D. 390, and probably originally having the meaning, "descended into the grave."

The Exaltation of Christ. The four aspects of Christ's exaltation are (1) resurrection, (2), ascension, (3) session, and (4) return in glory.

Resurrection. The resurrection was the transition point into Jesus' state of exaltation. It was the person of Christ that was exalted, not just his human nature, but the focus of this activity of exaltation was the change in his human nature to a new, much more glorious state.

The resurrection was not just a restoration to life, but the beginning of a new, better kind of life, a "resurrection life" (Rom. 6:9–10). After the resurrection, Jesus still had a physical body that could be touched and held (Matt. 28:9; John 20:17, 27), could break bread (Luke 24:30), prepare breakfast (John 21:12–13), and eat (Luke 24:42–43). It was a body of "flesh and bones," for Jesus said, "A spirit has not flesh and bones as you see that I have" (vs. 39).

Yet this physical body of Jesus was no longer subject to weakness, sickness, aging, or death. It was imperishable and glorious and powerful

(I Cor. 15:42–44; the term "spiritual" here means not "nonmaterial" but "conformed to the character of the Holy Spirit"). It is possible that John 20:19 implies that Jesus had the ability to enter a locked room miraculously. It is clear, however, that since Jesus was the "firstfruits" of the resurrection, we will be like him when we are raised from the dead (I Cor. 15:20, 23, 49; Phil. 3:21; I John 3:2).

The resurrection demonstrated the approval of God the Father and his satisfaction with Christ's work of redemption (Isa. 53:11; Phil. 2:8–9). Now Christ was exalted to a new status with respect to the law as well: he was no longer under the law in the sense of being obligated to obey the OT as our representative, for his work of obedience in our place was complete (Rom. 5:18–19).

The resurrection also was the initiation of a new relationship with God the Father, for Jesus was exalted to the role of messianic "Son" with new power and authority which were not his before as God-man (Matt. 28:18; Acts 13:33; Rom. 1:4; Heb. 1:5).

Ascension. Forty days after his resurrection (Acts 1:3), Jesus ascended up to heaven and entered more fully into the privileges of his state of exaltation. The NT clearly presents Jesus' ascension as a bodily ascension and therefore as ascension to a place (Luke 24:51; John 14:1–3; 16:28; 17:11; Acts 1:9–11), though it is a place ordinarily hidden from our physical eyes (Acts 7:55–56; cf. II Kings 6:17). Thus, Jesus retained his human nature when he returned to heaven and will retain it forever (cf. Heb. 13:8). However, Jesus' human nature is now worthy of worship by all creation, unlike our human nature.

When Jesus ascended into heaven he received glory, honor, and authority which were not his before as God-man (Acts 2:33, 36; Phil. 2:9–11; I Tim. 3:16; Heb. 1:3–4; 2:9), especially the authority to pour out the Holy Spirit on the church in greater fullness and power than before (Acts 1:8; 2:33).

After Jesus ascended into heaven he also began his high priestly work of representing us before God the Father (Heb. 9:24) and of interceding for us before God (7:25; Rom. 8:34). (Lutherans have taught that Jesus' human nature also became omnipresent upon his ascension to heaven, but this teaching does not receive clear support from Scripture, and appears largely to be affirmed in order to support a particular view of the presence of Christ's body in the Lord's Supper.)

Sitting (Session) at the Father's Right Hand. A further stage in the exaltation of Christ was his sitting down at the right hand of the Father in heaven (Acts 2:33; Eph. 1:20–22; Heb. 1:3). This action shows both the completion of Christ's work of redemption and his reception of new authority as God-man to reign over the universe. Christians presently share in this session of Jesus at God's right hand (Eph. 2:6) largely in terms of sharing in spiritual authority over demonic forces (6:10–18; II Cor. 10:3–4) and power to gain increasing victory over sin (Rom. 6:11–14).

In this exalted state of reigning at God's right hand, Christ will reign until the end of the age, when all his enemies will be conquered (I Cor. 15:24–25).

Return in Glory. When Jesus Christ returns to the earth in glory, his exaltation will be complete, and he will receive all the glory that is due to him as the God-man who has purchased our redemption and is worthy of eternal and infinite honor. Whether this future culmination of Christ's exaltation occurs in only one stage (as amillennialists hold) or two stages separated by a millennium (as post- and premillennialists hold), all agree that Jesus Christ will some day return to the earth to reign in triumph (Acts 1:11; Rev. 1:7), publicly and finally to defeat all his enemies (II Thess. 1:7–8; Rev. 19:11–21), and to sit as judge of all the earth (Matt. 25:31–46; Rev. 22:12). Then his kingdom will be established forever, and, exalted with the Father and the Holy Spirit, "he shall reign for ever and ever" (Rev. 11:15; 22:3–5). W. A. GRUDEM

See also JESUS CHRIST; OFFICES OF CHRIST.

Bibliography. L. Berkhof, *Systematic Theology;* E. A. Litton, *Introduction to Dogmatic Theology;* C. Hodge, *Systematic Theology,* II, 610–38.

Stealing. *See* CRIMINAL LAW AND PUNISHMENT IN BIBLE TIMES.

Steiner, Rudolf (1861–1925). *See* ANTHROPOSOPHY.

Stewardship (Gr. *oikonomia,* meaning "management of a household"). Administration of duties or goods in one's care. The person who administers the household is called a steward (*oikonomos,* "law of the house") or an overseer (*epitropos*). The idea has its roots in the institution of slavery. The master appointed a slave to administer his household, which might include the teaching and disciplining of the members of the house, especially other slaves and the children. A classic example is the position of Joseph in Potiphar's house (Gen. 39:4–6). The ordinary idea of stewardship is found in several passages in the NT, notably the story of the unjust steward (Luke 16:1–8; cf. Matt. 20:8; Luke 12:42). The guardian of a minor child could also be called a steward (Gal. 4:3). This is a most common use in the papyri. A public official could be called a steward (*oikonomos*, Rom. 16:23) or an overseer (*epitropos*, Luke 8:3).

The idea that man is a steward of God in his relation to the world and his own life is inherent in the creation story (Gen. 1–3) in which he is appointed lord of all things except himself. In the NT, the word, when not used in its ordinary sense, refers to the administration of the gifts of God, especially preaching the gospel. By metonymy, stewardship may refer to God's provision for the Christian age (Eph. 1:10; 3:9), the context implying that this plan includes the entrustment of the gospel message to man. This idea is explicit in I Cor. 9:17; Eph. 3:2; Col. 1:25; I Cor. 4:1–2; Titus 1:7. Stewardship is broadened to include all Christians and all the gracious gifts of God in I Pet. 4:10. An unusual use of the word is found in I Tim. 1:4, where it seems to refer to the discipline and training of the Christian in the realm of faith. The requirement of stewards of God, as well as of stewards of men, is faithfulness, i.e., administration of trust according to directions.

The modern emphasis on the stewardship of possessions, while true, may tend to obscure the fact that the Christian's primary stewardship is that of the gospel and includes the use of his whole life as well as his money. F. L. Fisher

Bibliography. J. Goetzmann, *NIDNTT*, II, 247ff.; J. Reumann, "Oikonomia—Terms in Paul in Comparison with Lucan Heilsgeschichte," *NTS* 13:147ff.

Stoddard, Solomon (1643–1729). One of the most influential leaders in American Protestantism from the settlement of Massachusetts (1630) to the colonial Great Awakening (*ca.* 1740). From his pulpit in Northampton, Massachusetts, where he served from 1672 to 1729, Stoddard's ideas exerted a powerful influence, not only in the Connecticut River valley, but in Boston and in New England as a whole.

"Pope" Stoddard, as his opponents called him, was best known for his innovations in church discipline. By his day many New England Congregational churches had adopted the Halfway Covenant. This allowed baptized members who had not made a personal profession of faith to bring their infants for baptism even as it kept all except those who could personally confess their faith from participating in the Lord's Supper. Stoddard proposed that all who lived outwardly decent lives should be allowed to take Communion. At the same time he also urged the churches of Massachusetts to develop a "connectional" or "presbyterian" plan of oversight in order to ensure the orthodoxy of local churches and ministers. These different aspects of Stoddard's thought have led some historians to praise him for his democratic principles (in opening up the Lord's Supper) and others to condemn him as autocratic (for proposing tighter outside control of local churches).

In fact, Stoddard was most interested in revivals and the conversion of the lost. He regarded the Lord's Supper distributed at an open Communion as a converting ordinance. He claimed that participation in Communion was an excellent way for people to "learn the necessity and sufficiency of the Death of Christ in order to [find] Pardon." Likewise, Stoddard intended tighter control over the churches to preserve the purity of the gospel. For his labors, Stoddard experienced five "harvests" of souls in Northampton. In general, however, those who followed his teachings on church discipline were not as eager as he was to promote evangelism. Stoddard's concern for revival was shared by his grandson, Jonathan Edwards, who became his associate minister in 1724 and his successor in 1729. Edwards did eventually repudiate his grandfather's ideas on church membership, for which he lost the pulpit in Northampton. But his efforts in the 1730s and 1740s to promote the revival that came to be known as the Great Awakening would have earned Stoddard's warm commendation. M. A. Noll

Bibliography. P. Miller, "Solomon Stoddard, 1643–1729," *HTR* 34:277–320; T. Schafer, "Solomon Stoddard and the Theology of Revival," in *A Miscellany of American Christianity*, ed. S. C. Henry; P. R. Lucas, *Valley of Discord: Church and Society Along the Connecticut River, 1636–1725*.

Stoics, Stoicism. Stoicism was a major school of hellenistic thought. The Stoics derived their name from the Painted Porch (*stoa*) in Athens where their founder taught. Though the school, begun by Zeno of Citium (335–263 B.C.), continued to maintain its headquarters in Athens, throughout the more than half a millennium of its existence, its major thinkers and practitioners were not drawn from the Greek mainland. After Zeno's death, Cleanthes of Assos (331–232) assumed leadership of the school, but he seems to have done little more than pass on the teachings of his master. The real systematizer of the Early Stoa was the school's next head, Chrysippus of Soli (*ca.* 280–207), who also expanded Zeno's thought.

The Middle Stoa, which continued the Stoic mainstream during the last two centuries before Christ, introduced some Platonic elements, but its most far-reaching contribution was made by Panaetius of Rhodes (*ca.* 185–110 B.C.), who extended the teachings so they could be appropriated by those in public life, not just philosophers.

Hence the Late Stoa of the two centuries after Christ could become predominantly Roman and could concentrate almost entirely on ethics. From this period Seneca (*ca.* 4 B.C.–A.D. 65), Epictetus (*ca.* 55–*ca.* 135) and Marcus Aurelius (A.D. 121–180) stand out. After Marcus Aurelius, Stoicism as a distinct school gradually declined into extinction, but some of its features continued to be assimilated into the predominantly Platonic philosophies of both pagans and Christians.

The tripartite division of Stoic thought into logic, physics, and ethics is said to derive from Zeno himself. Logic was the framework that supported the other two branches, and its principles of deduction have only recently regained appreciation, having long been overshadowed by those of Aristotle. Stoic physics, which included theology, has been variously described as either monism or pantheism. God is totally immanent in the world, and this leads to a strong belief in providence (*pronoia*). Fate (*heimarmenē*) also plays a key role and underlies the belief in the cyclical character of the natural order, in which each cycle is identical to all the others. Stoic ethics gained its chief prominence during the Late Stoa, both in theoretical developments and in practice. Man becomes virtuous through knowledge, which enables him to live in harmony with nature and thereby achieve a profound sense of happiness (*eudaimonia*) and freedom from emotion (*apatheia*) which insulates him from the vicissitudes of life.

Stoic influence on Jewish writers is seen principally in Philo, who, as other middle-Platonists, borrowed both Stoic terminology and concepts. Of principal interest in the NT is Paul's sensitivity to his Stoic auditors' belief in divine immanence, as he in his Areopagus speech quoted from Zeno's friend Aratus to support the doctrine (Acts 17:28).

While some Stoic influence on later Christian theologians is detectable, it is Christian middle-Platonists of the second century like Justin and Clement of Alexandria and Western theologians like Minucius Felix and Tertullian who exhibit the greatest debt to the Stoa. In some of their writings the doctrines of providence and natural law are to be found in Stoic-like formulations. Christians also probably derived some of the terminology in their Logos theology from the Stoics but appear to have used it in their own middle-Platonic manner. Christians also found the Stoic view of a unified world compatible with their own, but it is in the area of ethics that the strongest affinities are found. Galen, the second century physician-philosopher, provided ample testimony to this when he classed Christians with philosophers on the basis of their ethics, in spite of the fact that they could not follow a demonstrative argument. Christians, however, differed with Stoics on suicide and found certain other Stoic teachings objectionable, including their materialism, fatalism, doctrine of endless world cycles, and belief in total divine immanence.

G. T. BURKE

Bibliography. K. von Fritz, *The Oxford Classical Dictionary,* 1015–16; P. P. Hallie, *Encyclopedia of Philosophy,* VIII, 19–22; H. E. W. Turner, *The Pattern of Christian Truth;* H. Chadwick, *Early Christian Thought and the Classical Tradition;* F. H. Sandbach, *The Stoics.*

Storch, Nicholas. *See* ZWICKAU PROPHETS.

Strauss, David Friedrich (1808–1874). German theologian. Born in Ludwigsburg near Stuttgart, he studied under F. C. Bauer at Tübingen and spent a brief time in Berlin where he became an enthusiast for Hegelian speculative philosophy. In 1832–35 he served as a tutor at the Tübingen *Stift,* but the controversy over his *Life of Jesus* resulted in his dismissal. He obtained an appointment at the University of Zurich in 1839, which was blocked by clerical opposition, and he spent the remainder of his life as a free-lance writer.

Strauss's most influential work was the *Life of Jesus, Critically Examined* (2 vols. 1835–36). Refusing to accept either the historical accuracy of miracle accounts in the Gospels or that the narratives were pure fabrications, he introduced the idea of "myth," a concept from Hegel's philosophy of religion, and applied it to the supernatural elements. The Gospel accounts of the life of Jesus had been embellished by pious reflections by his followers so as to make it repeat and fulfill the legends and predictions of the OT. These "myths," although historically inaccurate, were in harmony with their religious feelings and ideas. They were not falsehoods, as such, but truths about Jesus indirectly stated. In a Hegelian sense they expressed the awareness of the writers that Jesus as the founder of Christianity had discovered that God and man are one. Thus the true God-man is not an individual but humanity as a whole. Jesus must be understood symbolically as the realization of the Absolute Idea or Spirit in the human race. Man is the union of the finite and infinite, of spirit and nature, and mankind is destined for perfection in its onward and upward march, symbolized in the NT in terms of death, resurrection, and ascension.

A heated debate over the book followed, and Strauss essentially repudiated any commitment to theism in its sequel *Die christliche Glaubenslehre* (1840–41), which maintained that biblical teaching could not be harmonized with modern knowledge. For the next twenty years he turned from theology, dabbled briefly in politics, and published a number of biographies, the best-known being *Ulrich von Hutten* (1861). He issued a new version of the *Life of Jesus* in 1864 in which he backed away from some of the more extreme Hegelianism of the 1835 work and called for the restoration of the picture of the historical Jesus in his simple, human features as much as possible. However, neither it nor his attack on Schleiermacher (1865) bridged the chasm between the Jesus of history and the Christ of faith. In his last work, *The Old and the New Faith* (1872), Strauss set forth a Darwinian theory of faith in natural science which rejected religious belief in a personal God and immortality, insisting all that remains is the feeling of absolute dependence on the universe.

R. V. PIERARD

See also HEGEL, GEORG WILHELM FRIEDRICH; TÜBINGEN SCHOOL.

Bibliography. A. Schweitzer, *The Quest of the Historical Jesus;* K. Barth, *Protestant Thought from Rousseau to Ritschl;* L. E. Keck, ed., *The Christ of Faith and the Jesus of History;* H. Harris, *David Friedrich Strauss and His Theology;* C. Brown, *NIDCC,* 934.

Strong, Augustus Hopkins (1836–1921). Theologian, educator, and author. Strong was born at Rochester, New York. His father, a devout layman, was the publisher of the *Rochester Democrat.* Early in life, the son learned from his father the value of consistent church attendance but was not converted until after he had entered college. Graduating from Yale in 1857 and Rochester Theological Seminary in 1859, he spent a year at the University of Berlin.

On his twenty-fifth birthday he was ordained to the gospel ministry, having been called to the pastorate of the First Baptist Church of Haverhill, Massachusetts, which he served from 1861 to 1865. From 1865 to 1872 he was pastor of the First Baptist Church of Cleveland, Ohio, which numbered John D. Rockefeller among its members. In 1872, Strong was elected president of the Rochester Theological Seminary and professor of theology. In these dual roles he served for forty years, retiring in 1912 as president emeritus. He embarked on a world tour in 1916–17, which resulted in a book, *A Tour of Missions, Observations, and Conclusions.*

Strong's great influence was due to his personal contact with students and prominent laymen and to his writings. Apparently, he was the catalyst that moved Rockefeller to found the University of Chicago. Through the various editions of his books, *Systematic Theology* (1886, 1907–46), *Philosophy and Religion* (1888), *Christ in Creation and Ethical Monism* (1899), and *What Shall I Believe?* (1922), one can trace the development of Strong's theology. By 1894, according to C. F. H. Henry, Strong abandoned federal theology for what he termed ethical monism. It is also referred to as qualitative monism, metaphysical monism, and personalistic idealism. In his theology, which was a synthesis of historic Christian faith with personal idealism, Strong was attempting to undergird a biblical theology with a modified form of Platonism. The center of his system was Christ. "The person of Christ was the clue I had followed; his deity and atonement were the two foci of the great ellipse." He considered his most original contribution to theology his explanation of the imputation of the sins of the race to Christ. "The atonement then is not only possible but necessary, because Christ is from the beginning the life of humanity." Strong also rejected all forms of determinism. "The author has come progressively to the conviction that a monism which makes room for the transcendence of God and the separate personality of man—a monism which recognizes the great ethical facts of freedom, responsibility, sin, and guilt—affords the only key to the great problems of philosophy and theology." Strong was apparently indebted to Ezekiel Robinson, Herman Lotze, and Borden P. Bowne, among others, for some aspects of his theology. In turn, two Southern Baptist theologians, E. Y. Mullins and W. T. Conner, reflect a reliance upon Strong. Therefore, it is not without reason that Strong has been ranked among the foremost Baptist theologians of his day.

W. R. ESTEP, JR.

Bibliography. W. H. Allison, in *Dictionary of American Biography;* C. F. H. Henry, *Personal Idealism and Strong's Theology;* C. Douglas, ed., *Autobiography of A. H. Strong.*

Stübner, Markus. *See* ZWICKAU PROPHETS.

Subdiaconate. An order of ministry found in the church from the third century. In the hierarchy of ordained clergy the subdeacon followed the bishop, priest, and deacon. His duty was primarily liturgical, especially at High Mass, when he chanted the Epistle reading, presented the bread (paten) and wine (chalice) to the presiding priest, and cleaned the holy vessels afterward.

The churches of the Reformation in the sixteenth century abolished this order, but it was retained by the Roman Church until 1972, when it went as part of the reforms following the Second Vatican Council. It is still found, however, in the Orthodox and Eastern churches, where it functions within the liturgy. Sometimes

the word is used today to describe the role of laity who assist in the Eucharist, but this usage is nontechnical.
P. TOON

See also CHURCH OFFICERS; MAJOR ORDERS.

Sublapsarianism. *See* INFRALAPSARIANISM.

Subordinationism. A doctrine that assigns an inferiority of being, status, or role to the Son or Holy Spirit within the Trinity. Condemned by numerous church councils, this doctrine has continued in one form or another throughout the history of the church. In the early centuries, the struggle to understand the human and divine natures of Christ often led to placing the Son in a secondary position to the Father. Justin Martyr, Origen, and Tertullian all evidence a certain amount of subordinationism in their writings. This incipient subordinationism, especially that of Origen, eventually led to Arianism and other systems such as Sabellianism, Monarchianism, and Macedonianism. Arius, who would allow no intermediary being between the supremacy of the One God and his creatures, denied the full deity of Christ. From this it followed that Christ the Word was less than God incarnate and was instead a subordinate image of the Father. In subordinationism lay the roots from which modern unitarianism and related theologies were to spring.

The Nicene fathers ascribed to the Son and Spirit an equality of being or essence, but a subordination of order, with both deriving their existence from the Father as primal source. Athanasius insisted upon the coequality of the status of the three Persons of the Trinity, and Augustine that these Persons are coequal and coeternal. Ancient and modern theologians have argued for a subordination in the role of Son and Spirit to the Father and cite in support such passages as Matt. 11:27; John 5:26–27; 6:38; 8:28; 14:28. Some apply a doctrine of subordination of woman to man on the basis of a similar relationship within the Trinity (I Cor. 11:3). Others argue that passages that seem to teach a subordination of Son to the Father speak of Christ's voluntary humiliation when he assumed human form (Phil. 2:5–8). In his exaltation, however, he returned to the equality of the eternal relationship expressed in such passages as John 1:1; 5:17–23; 10:15, 30; Titus 2:13; Rom. 9:5; I John 5:7. The Athanasian Creed declared that in the Trinity "none is before or after another: none is greater or less than another," and the Second Helvetic Confession, the second most influential confession in Reformed tradition, condemns as heretics any who teach a subordination of Son or Holy Spirit (III, v).
R. C. KROEGER and C. C. KROEGER

See also ARIANISM; MONARCHIANISM; NICAEA, COUNCIL OF.

Bibliography. E. H. Bickersteth, *The Trinity;* H. M. Gwatkin, *Studies in Arianism;* T. C. Hammond, *In Understanding Be Men;* B. and A. Mickelsen, "What Does 'Head' Mean in the NT?" *CT,* Feb. 1981; P. Schaff, *History of the Christian Church;* W. W. Stevens, *Doctrines of the Christian Religion.*

Substance (Lat. *substantia,* Gr. *hypostasis,* "standing under"). Essential nature, essence. The key Greek word for substance from Aristotle on, which was also rendered in Latin as *substantia,* is *ousia.* Although *ousia* was brought into philosophy by Plato, it has been the Aristotelian criteria for substance that have shaped the Christian development of the concept. In much of modern philosophy, substance is no longer seen as a meaningful category.

The matter of substance played an important role in Christian theology in both the patristic and medieval periods. During the former it was a central issue in the interrelated Trinitarian and Christological controversies.

In defining the nature of the Godhead, the East generally emphasized its threefold nature, while in the West the stress was on its unified substance. This and translation problems between Greek and Latin made it difficult to realize that an actual consensus was being reached. In Greek, *hypostasis* and *ousia* were synonyms, as can be seen in the Creed at Nicaea (325). The Cappadocian fathers found them too ambiguous. Hence, they arrived at a Trinitarian formula which distinguished them, as Origen had already done and as John of Damascus would later do: three *hypostaseis* (individuals), one *ousia* (substance). In the West, where in the fourth century the formula was expressed as one *substantia* (substance), three *personae* (persons), this caused difficulties. Augustine regarded *essentia* (essence) and *substantia* (substance), which usually translated *ousia* and *hypostasis* respectively, as synonyms, so when the Eastern fathers talked of three *hypostaseis,* it sounded as if they meant three substances. The difference, however, was merely semantic. The meaning was the same: three persons of the Godhead share a common substance.

Of Aristotle's several definitions of substance, the one rather uniformly followed during the patristic period was substratum. Augustine, however, differed from his predecessors on the precise application to the Godhead. For Tertullian, Basil, and the Creed at Nicaea, for example, the Father was the common substratum of the Son and Holy Spirit. This avoided the problem of having this substance exist separately from the

Trinity as a fourth divine entity. Augustine solved this problem by having the substance of the Godhead derived from neither the Father nor an external source, but from the eternal constitution of the Trinity itself.

It was a compound form of *ousia* around which much of the Christological controversy of the fourth century East revolved. The Creed at Nicaea, in opposition to Arian Christology, asserted that Jesus Christ was "of the same substance [*homoousios*] with the Father." In the ensuing decades, this formula came under increasing attack, because its ambiguity made it susceptible to heretical interpretation and the key word, *homoousios*, was nonbiblical. Other formulas were suggested, such as that Jesus Christ was "of *like* substance with the Father," but by the time of the Council of Constantinople (381), *homoousios* was firmly fixed in the East, and Arianism was effectively defeated. With Christ's consubstantiality with the Father now established, the Creed at Chalcedon (451) added the final chapter by affirming his complete humanness: He is "of the same substance (*homoousios*) with us."

Since the patristic period, substance has been an important component in theological discussions of the doctrine of Christ's incarnation, but it has appeared most extensively in connection with the eucharistic doctrine of transubstantiation. Thomas Aquinas has given the doctrine its most extensive theoretical development, beginning from, but not limited to, Aristotle's distinction between substance and accident. According to the doctrine, which received formulation before Aquinas at the Fourth Lateran Council (1215) and after him at the Council of Trent, in the Eucharist the substance of the bread and wine are changed into the substance of the body and blood of Christ. At the level of accidents or species, however, no change takes place, because such accidents as color, shape, taste, and the like remain. Hence, it is only at the level of faith that one can know that this actual change in substance has taken place. G. T. BURKE

Bibliography. M. Wiles, "*Homoousios Hēmin*," *JTS* n.s. 16:454–61; *Encyclopedia of Philosophy*, VIII, 36–40; *NCE*, XIII, 766–70; J. L. González, *A History of Christian Thought*, I; H. A. Wolfson, *The Philosophy of the Church Fathers*.

Suffering. *See* EVIL, PROBLEM OF; PAIN.

Suffering Servant. *See* SERVANT OF THE LORD.

Sufficient Grace. *See* GRACE.

Suffragan Bishop. *See* CHURCH OFFICERS; BISHOP.

Sunday. *See* LORD'S DAY.

Supererogation, Works of. Voluntary works over and above what God commands. *Supererogare* means "to pay out more than is necessary." In Roman Catholic ecclesiastical matters *supererogatio* means doing more than God requires. The term goes back to the Vulgate of Luke 10:35 (*quodcumque supererogaveris*), but was not used in its present technical sense until the Middle Ages. The conception is based upon a distinction between works which are necessary and those which are voluntary. In doing the latter (such as accepting vows of poverty, celibacy, and obedience), we can do more than God requires. Such works of supererogation are meritorious and can avail for the benefit of others, hence the so-called treasury of merit and the possibility of indulgences. R. J. COATES

Superintendent. *See* CHURCH OFFICERS.

Supper, Lord's. *See* LORD'S SUPPER.

Supplication. *See* PRAYER.

Supralapsarianism. The doctrine that God decreed both election and reprobation before the fall. Supralapsarianism differs from infralapsarianism on the relation of God's decree to human sin. The differences go back to the conflict between Augustine and Pelagius. Before the Reformation, the main difference was whether Adam's fall was included in God's eternal decree; supralapsarians held that it was, but infralapsarians acknowledged only God's foreknowledge of sin. Luther, Zwingli, and Calvin were agreed that Adam's fall was somehow included in God's decree; it came to be referred to as a "permissive decree," and all insisted that God was in no way the author of sin. As a result of the Reformers' agreement, after the Reformation the distinction between infra- and supralapsarianism shifted to differences on the logical order of God's decrees.

Theodore Beza, Calvin's successor at Geneva, was the first to develop supralapsarianism in this new sense. By the time of the Synod of Dort in 1618–19, a heated intraconfessional controversy developed between infra- and supralapsarians; both positions were represented at the synod. Francis Gomarus, the chief opponent of James Arminius, was a supralapsarian.

The question of the logical, not the temporal, order of the eternal decrees reflected differences on God's ultimate goal in predestination and on the specific objects of predestination. Supralapsarians considered God's ultimate goal to be his own glory in election and reprobation, while infralapsarians considered predestination subordinate to other goals. The object of predestination, according to supralapsarians, was uncreated and unfallen humanity, while infralapsarians viewed the object as created and fallen humanity.

The term "supralapsarianism" comes from the Latin words *supra* and *lapsus;* the decree of predestination was considered to be "above" (*supra*) or logically "before" the decree concerning the fall (*lapsus*), while the infralapsarians viewed it as "below" (*infra*) or logically "after" the decree concerning the fall. The contrast of the two views is evident from the following summaries. The logical order of the decrees in the supralapsarian scheme is: (1) God's decree to glorify himself through the election of some and the reprobation of others; (2) as a means to that goal, the decree to create those elected and reprobated; (3) the decree to permit the fall; and (4) the decree to provide salvation for the elect through Jesus Christ.

The logical order of the decrees according to infralapsarians is: (1) God's decree to glorify himself through the creation of the human race; (2) the decree to permit the fall; (3) the decree to elect some of the fallen race to salvation and to pass by the others and condemn them for their sin; and (4) the decree to provide salvation for the elect through Jesus Christ. Infralapsarians were in the majority at the Synod of Dort. The Arminians tried to depict all the Calvinists as representatives of the "repulsive" supralapsarian doctrine. Four attempts were made at Dort to condemn the supralapsarian view, but the efforts were unsuccessful. Although the Canons of Dort do not deal with the order of the divine decrees, they are infralapsarian in the sense that the elect are "chosen from the whole human race, which had fallen through their own fault from their primitive state of rectitude into sin and destruction" (I,7; cf. I,1). The reprobate "are passed by in the eternal decree" and God "decreed to leave [them] in the common misery into which they have willfully plunged themselves" and "to condemn and punish them forever . . . for all their sins" (I,15).

Defenders of supralapsarianism continued after Dort. The chairman of the Westminster Assembly, William Twisse, was a supralapsarian but the Westminster standards do not favor either position. Although supralapsarianism never received confessional endorsement within the Reformed churches, it has been tolerated within the confessional boundaries. In 1905 the Reformed churches of the Netherlands and the Christian Reformed Church in 1908 adopted the Conclusions of Utrecht, which stated that "our Confessional Standards admittedly follow the infralapsarian presentation in respect to the doctrine of election, but that it is evident . . . that this in no wise intended to exclude or condemn the supralapsarian presentation." Recent defenders of the supralapsarian position have been Gerhardus Vos, Herman Hoeksema, and G. H. Kersten.

F. H. KLOOSTER

See also CALVINISM; DECREES OF GOD; ELECT, ELECTION; INFRALAPSARIANISM; PREDESTINATION; REPROBATION; SOVEREIGNTY OF GOD.

Bibliography. L. Berkhof, *Systematic Theology;* H. Heppe, *Reformed Dogmatics;* H. Hoeksema, *Reformed Dogmatics;* G. H. Kersten, *Reformed Dogmatics;* B. B. Warfield, "Predestination in the Reformed Confessions," in *Studies in Theology.*

Swedenborg, Emanuel (1688–1772). Swedish scientist and religious teacher. Swedenborg was the son of a devout bishop of the Lutheran Church in Sweden. He studied first at Uppsala and then in England, France, and Holland in pursuit of a scientific career. For much of his adult life he was an assessor of the Royal Board of Mines in his homeland and wrote works on science and philosophy. In his fifties his interest shifted to religion and theology as he claimed to have special communication with angels and spirits. Holding that he had been granted by God a special knowledge in the interpretation of the Bible, he wrote several works unfolding a system of thought which rejects or alters many traditional Christian beliefs.

Swedenborg's theological views include the following:

(1) Neoplatonic view of the God-world relationship. Creation out of nothing is rejected; God is the one and only true substance, the ultimate love and wisdom from which all things proceed. Yet the world is not God (pantheism being disavowed); the world derives its being from God by "contiguity," not continuity.

(2) Theory of correspondence. The physical world images the spiritual world; animals and physical things reflect or correspond to moral and spiritual qualities or ideas.

(3) Literal and spiritual interpretation of the Bible. Based on the theory of correspondence every Scripture has a literal meaning and a spiritual meaning. Swedenborg claimed that his special mission was to reveal the true spiritual meaning of Scripture.

(4) Monopersonal Trinity. The Godhead consists, not of three persons, but of three essential principles. The Father is the inmost principle, the "ineffable Love" of God; the Son is the divine

Wisdom; and the Holy Spirit is the divine Power. All three principles are the same divine person, Jesus Christ himself.

(5) Example theory of atonement. Christ's saving work is not a sacrifice to make satisfaction for divine justice, but a triumph over temptation and spiritual evil as the example, and reconciling power, of God by which all men can overcome evil.

(6) Freedom of the will in spiritual matters.

(7) Salvation by faith plus works. Though God is the ultimate source of all merit and good works, man must choose to cooperate with God's power of love and seek self-reformation and spiritual health through a life of doing good.

(8) Choice of all between heaven and hell in the intermediate state.

(9) The continuance of true marital love in heaven.

(10) The spiritual realization of the Second Advent and Last Judgment in 1757 (from which doctrine the Church of the New Jerusalem was formed). D. W. DIEHL

Bibliography. J. H. Spalding, *Introduction to Swedenborg's Religious Thought;* S. Toksvig, *Emanuel Swedenborg Scientist and Mystic;* G. Trobridge, *Swedenborg, Life and Teaching;* S. M. Warren, ed., *A Compendium of the Theological Writings of Emanuel Swedenborg.*

Swete, Henry Barclay (1835–1917). Anglican scholar. Theological professor in London (1882–90) and Cambridge (1890–1915), he published works on the OT and NT, and on Christian doctrine. Though he espoused modern critical methods in biblical studies, he respected those who reached different conclusions from his own. He himself was oddly conservative on occasion: on some of the Johannine discourses, for example, and on miracles. He edited various Greek texts, including the LXX, stimulated his students to undertake serious research, and founded the prestigious *Journal of Theological Studies* (1899). His work in *The Holy Spirit in the Ancient Church* (1912) was long used as a standard textbook. He was the chief architect of the work known popularly as *Cambridge Theological Questions* (1905), a symposium written by leading scholars of the day. In it Swete commented on what he saw as the most important work of the twentieth century church: to assimilate new truth without sacrificing the primitive message, and "to state in terms adapted to the needs of a new century the truths which the ancient Church expressed in those which were appropriate for its own times." A sequel, *Cambridge Biblical Questions,* followed in 1909. In it Swete rejected the suggestion that the spread of knowledge would shake the credit of the Bible in the public estimation. J. D. DOUGLAS

Synagogue. The Jewish house of assembly, study, and prayer. Its origins are shrouded in mystery. While some have suggested that it dates back to Moses and others have identified the "meeting places" in Ps. 74:8 as synagogues, it has been traditionally traced to the period of the Babylonian exile when the Jewish people were deprived of the temple and assembled together for worship in a strange land. Jewish tradition has maintained that the reference to "little sanctuary" in Ezek. 11:16 is a direct reference to the synagogues of these exiles and that Ezekiel's repeated allusion to the assembly of the elders (8:1; 14:1; 20:1) also indicates synagogue worship. Ezekiel appears to be answering those who taunted the exiles because they were far away from the Jerusalem temple, and he explains to them that God had provided sanctuaries of worship among the nations. When the exiles returned and rebuilt the temple, it is believed that the synagogue continued as an institution of Palestinian Judaism. The Talmud ascribes to Ezra and his successors, the men of the Great Synagogue, the formulation of the earliest liturgical prayers such as the *Amidah.*

By the first Christian century the synagogue was a well-established institution, giving every indication of centuries of growth as a center of religious and social life of the Jewish community. Before the destruction of the temple by the Romans in A.D. 70, the synagogue maintained an important functioning relationship with the temple. After the destruction, the synagogue emerged as the central institution. The NT documents both Jesus' use of the synagogue and that of the disciples and early Christians. Missionaries, such as the apostle Paul, made great use of the first century synagogues as well. The synagogue service, in turn, had a great impact on Christian worship and church government (cf. the office of "elder").

The reading of both the law and the prophets was a central element in the synagogue service. The scrolls of Scripture were kept in a receptacle called an ark which was generally raised above the floor level and located on the wall facing the Temple Mount. In the center of the synagogue was an elevated platform (*bîmâ*) upon which stood a reading desk. Worshipers sat on wooden seats which surrounded the *bîmâ.* The Scripture was read from a standing position, but was explained from a sitting position. Luke 4:16–27 indicates that Jesus properly followed this pattern.

In addition to the reading and explanation of

Scripture during the synagogue service, the basic structure included the recitation of the *Shema* ("Hear O Israel, the Lord Our God, the Lord is One") and the *Amidah*. The *Shema* included the reading of Deut. 6:4–9, which the rabbis maintained was the acceptance of the yoke of God's rulership; 11:13–21, which the rabbis maintained was the acceptance of the yoke of commandments; and Num. 15:37–41, which the rabbis called the exodus from Egypt (because of the last verse). The *Amidah* was a central silent prayer contemplating God and thanking him for the sabbath and human blessings (such as the opportunity to worship). The synagogue liturgy developed from two talmudic principles that worked side by side, i.e., *qeba'* (fixed times and fixed liturgy) and *kawwānâ* (inwardness and spontaneity). Through a synthesis of *qeba'* and *kawwānâ*, one generation's expression of *kawwānâ* became the next generation's heritage of *qeba'*.

The earliest remains of a synagogue have been discovered at Shedia near Alexandria, Egypt. A marble slab states that the Jewish community dedicated this synagogue to Ptolemy III Euergetes (246–221 B.C.) and his queen Berenice. One of the popular synagogues found in Israel is that discovered at the ancient site of Capernaum which dates back to the third Christian century. The oldest remains of a synagogue in Israel are those discovered on the royal citadel of Masada, built by Herod the Great and used by the Zealots against Rome during the Jewish War.

D. A. RAUSCH

Bibliography. J. Gutmann, *The Synagogue: Studies in Origins, Archeology and Architecture;* A. Eisenberg, *The Synagogue Through the Ages;* M. Friedländer, *Synagoge und Kirche;* L. A. Hoffmann, *The Canonization of the Synagogue Service;* W. O. E. Oesterley and G. H. Box, *The Religion and Worship of the Synagogue;* L. I. Levine, ed., *Ancient Synagogues Revealed;* M. Kadushin, *Worship and Ethics: A Study in Rabbinic Judaism;* C. W. Dugmore, *The Influence of the Synagogue upon the Divine Office.*

Syncretism. The process by which elements of one religion are assimilated into another religion resulting in a change in the fundamental tenets or nature of those religions. It is the union of two or more opposite beliefs, so that the synthesized form is a new thing. It is not always a total fusion, but may be a combination of separate segments that remain identifiable compartments. Originally a political term, "syncretism" was used to describe the joining together of rival Greek forces on the Isle of Crete in opposition to a common enemy.

Syncretism is usually associated with the process of communication. It can originate with either the sender or the receptor of the message. The sender may introduce syncretistic elements in a conscious attempt for relevance or by the presentation of a limited and distorted part of the message. It may happen unconsciously as the result of an inadequate or faulty grasp of the message. The receptor will interpret the message within the framework of his world view. This may distort the data but fit his values.

Specifically we are faced with a problem of meaning. What is actually understood by words, symbols, or actions as expressed in creeds, or application to certain needs, is the test of the presence of syncretism. The receptor is the one who assigns meaning. It is therefore essential that the sender communicate with words or symbols that are not merely approximate equivalents, but dynamic equivalents, of meaning.

Syncretism of the Christian gospel occurs when critical or basic elements of the gospel are replaced by religious elements from the host culture. It often results from a tendency or attempt to undermine the uniqueness of the gospel as found in the Scriptures or the incarnate Son of God. The communication of the gospel involves the transmission of a message with supracultural elements between a variety of cultures. This includes the disembodiment of the message from one cultural context and the reembodiment of it in a different cultural context.

Cross-cultural communication of the gospel always involves at least three cultural contexts. The gospel message was originally given in a specific context. The receiver/sender assigns meaning to that message in terms of his own context. The receptor seeks to understand the message within a third context. The problem of syncretism will be encountered with each new outreach of the church and also as the culture changes around an established church.

The Bible reveals syncretism as a long-standing tool of Satan to separate God from his people. It strikes at the heart of the first commandment. Beyerhaus notes a threefold answer in the OT to the challenge of external syncretism: segregation, eradication, and adaptation. Pressures from early Canaanite practices with Baal and Asherah were followed by the demands of the national gods of Assur and Babylon. Internally the prophets of Israel sought to enforce the obligatory nature of Israel's holy traditions, to apply the revealed will of God to actual situations, and to forcefully present the eschatological vision of God's continuing control, justice, and promises.

The NT was born in a melee as rulers sought to blend cultures through syncretistic monotheism—all forms of the same God. All the gods of Egypt, Persia, and Babylon became Greek. The influence of Mani spread from Africa to China. Esoteric knowledge vied with unique, historical revelation. Rome harbored all cults and mystery religions. Antioch, Ephesus, and Corinth each boasted syncretistic gods seeking to absorb the church. NT confrontations include Simon Magus, the Jerusalem Council, the Epistle to the Colossians, combating Jewish thought mixed with early Gnosticism, and the rebuke of the church at Pergamum. Against these forces the church developed its creeds, canon, and celebrations. The Christmas celebration date was set over against the festival of the birth of the sun god, Sol Invictus, in protest against a major attempt to create a syncretistic imperial religion.

Visser 't Hooft discusses the many syncretistic pressures of the NT times exerted by Judaism, Gnosticism, emperor worship, and the mystery cults. It is helpful to study the books of Hebrews, I John, and the Revelation from the perspective of defending against syncretism. The NT canon and the recognized creed became the church's two greatest weapons against the growth and transmission of syncretism. Church history is filled with the struggle against syncretism from political, social, religious, and economic sources. Syncretistic pressure can be seen today. In our global-village context secular humanism seems to be the common ground for solving shared problems. The values of this world view strive for a place in the church's response to both the demands for conformity and the cries for liberation confronting it.

In the striving by missionaries for an indigenous national church with a contextualized gospel, the danger of syncretism is ever present in attempts at accommodation, adjustment, and adaptation. Tippett reminds us that while striving for relevance we must remember that in communication only *message* is transmitted, not *meaning*. Beyerhaus points out three steps in biblical adaptation:

(1) Discriminating selection of words, symbols, and rites, e.g., "Logos."

(2) Rejection of that which is clearly incompatible with biblical truth.

(3) Reinterpretation by a complete refilling of the selected rite or symbol with a truly Christian meaning.

The supracultural teachings of Scripture must be judge of both culture and meaning as God works through men using various forms to bring all creation under his lordship.

In the history of theology the term "syncretism" is used specifically to define two movements aimed at unification. In the Lutheran tradition, George Calixtus (1586–1656) attempted to reconcile Lutheran thought with Roman Catholicism on the basis of the Apostles' Creed. This precipitated a syncretistic controversy that was to last for many years. In Roman Catholicism "syncretism" refers to the attempt to reconcile Molinist and Thomist theology. S. R. Imbach

Bibliography. W. A. Visser 't Hooft, *No Other Name;* H. Kraemer, *Religion and the Christian Faith;* T. Yamamori and C. R. Taber, eds., *Christopaganism or Indigenous Christianity;* H. Lietzmann, *The Beginnings of the Church Universal.*

Synergism (Gr. *synergos*, "working together"). Reference to the doctrine of divine and human cooperation in conversion. Synergism seeks to reconcile two paradoxical truths: the sovereignty of God and man's moral responsibility. Nowhere do these two truths so intersect as in the theology of conversion. One tradition within Christianity, the Augustinian, emphasizes the sovereignty of God in conversion (monergism or divine monergism). Calvin and Luther stood within this heritage. In the Small Catechism Martin Luther wrote: "I believe that by my own reason or strength I cannot believe in Jesus Christ, my Lord, or come to him. But the Holy Spirit has called me through the Gospel, enlightened me with his gifts, and sanctified and preserved me in true faith." The other tradition, the Pelagian, emphasizes man's moral responsibility. Modified by such Roman Catholics as Erasmus of Rotterdam and such Protestants as James Arminius and John Wesley, this position stresses the freedom of the will. Erasmus said, "Free will is the power of applying oneself to grace." During the Lutheran Reformation the synergistic controversy occurred. Scholars debate whether or not Philip Melanchthon was a synergist. Certainly he wrote that "man is wholly incapable of doing good" and that in "external things" (secular matters) there is free will, but not in "internal things" (spiritual matters). In the second edition of his *Loci,* however (published in 1535), Melanchthon wrote that in conversion "Three causes are conjoined: The Word, the Holy Spirit and the Will not wholly inactive, but resisting its own weakness.... God draws, but draws him who is willing ... and the will is not a statue, and that spiritual emotion is not impressed upon it as though it were a statue." His followers were called Philippists. His opponents were called Gnesio- or Genuine Lutherans. Melanchthon's position was embodied in the Leipzig Interim (1548). John Pfeffinger (1493–1573), the first Lutheran superintendent of Leipzig, sought to expound the Philippist position in *De libertate voluntaris humanae* and *De libero arbitrio* in 1555, ascribing conversion's active concurrent causes to "the Holy Spirit moving through the Word of God, the mind in the act of thinking, and the will not resisting, but complying whenever moved by the

Holy Spirit." Nicholas von Amsdorf, friend of Luther, called the "Secret Bishop of the Lutheran Church," attacked Pfeffinger in 1558 for teaching synergism. Victorinus Strigel (1524–69), professor at Jena, and John Stoltz (*ca.* 1514–56), court preacher at Weimar, became involved. Matthias Flacius, professor at Jena, became the major adversary of the Philippists. He taught that the "natural man" is comparable to a block of wood or a piece of stone and is hostile toward the work of God. Due to his influence John Frederick II drafted the Weimar *Book of Confutations* (1558–59), causing Strigel to be imprisoned for opposing it. Enforced strictly by the clergy, John Frederick in 1561 deprived ministers the right to uphold it, vesting that power in the consistory at Weimar. Flacius opposed this change and was expelled from Jena in 1561, while Strigel was reinstated in his professorship, signing an ambiguous document. John Stössel (1524–78), striving to justify Strigel's position, merely fueled the controversy. John William succeeded John Frederick in 1567. Desiring to resolve the controversy, he issued an edict on January 16, 1568, causing the Philippists to leave Jena, and the Flacianists (but not Flacius) to return. An Altenburg Colloquy (1568–69) failed to solve the controversy. By 1571, however, the *Final Report and Declaration of the Theologians of Both Universities*—Leipzig and Wittenberg—affirmed "consideration and reception of God's Word and voluntary beginning of obedience in the heart arises out of that which God has begun graciously to work in us." The Formula of Concord (1577) rejected synergism, endorsed Augustinianism, avoided the rhetoric of Flacianism and the tendencies of Philippianism, teaching "through . . . the preaching and the hearing of his Word, God is active, breaks our hearts, and draws man, so that through the preaching of the law man learns to know his sins . . . and experiences genuine terror, contrition and sorrow . . . and through the preaching of . . . the holy Gospel . . . there is kindled in him a spark of faith which accepts the forgiveness of sins for Christ's sake." C. G. Fry

See also Concord, Formula of; Flacius, Matthias; Melanchthon, Philip; Monergism.

Bibliography. T. G. Tappert, ed., *The Book of Concord;* C. Manschreck, *Melanchthon: The Quiet Reformer;* H. L. J. Heppe, *Geschichte der lutherischen Concordienformel und Concordie* and *Geschichte des deutschen Protestantismus in den Jahren 1555–1581;* G. F. Schott, *The Encyclopedia of the Lutheran Church,* III, 2313–14.

Synod (Gr. *synodos,* "a group of people traveling together"). The coming together of Christians for the purpose of discussing the church's business (the coming together for worship was known as the *synaxis*). The word is technically used of a local church meeting for this purpose: general meetings attended by representatives of the church throughout the world were in the early days known as ecumenical (from the Gr. for "inhabited") councils. It is believed that the first official synod (calling together the clergy of a diocese) was held by Bishop Siricius in Rome in 387. Subsequently Pope Benedict XIV ruled that a synod was a convocation of the diocese, while the gathering of all the bishops of the catholic world was to be called a council.

Different denominations use the word in different ways today. Episcopalians have varying systems of synodical government in their various provinces, while since Vatican II the Church of Rome has had biennial synods (starting in 1969) of representative bishops. Presbyterians use the synod, composed of ministers and elders from the presbyteries, as the next stage up in their chain of church government. Lutheran churches also organized themselves originally in regional synods. D. H. Wheaton

Systematic Theology. An attempt to reduce religious truth to an organized system.

Definition and Relations. The word "theology" does not occur in Scripture, although the idea is very much present. In secular Greek use *theologia* signified the discussions of the philosophers about divine matters. Plato referred to the poets' stories about the gods as "theologies," and Aristotle taught a threefold division of the sciences: physics, the study of nature; mathematics, the study of number and quantity; and theology, the study of God. Aristotle regarded theology as the greatest of the sciences since its subject, God, is the highest reality.

Etymologically theology derives from the Greek words *theos* (God) and *logos* (reason or speech), and thus means rational discussion about God. B. B. Warfield advanced the classic short definition: "Theology is the science of God and his relationship to man and the world." In greater detail theology might be defined as the discipline that (1) presents a unified formulation of truth concerning God and his relationship to humanity and the universe as this is set forth in divine revelation and that (2) applies such truths to the entire range of human life and thought. Systematic theology thus begins with divine revelation in its entirety, applies the Spirit-illumined mind to comprehend the revelation, draws out the teachings of Scripture via sound grammatical-historical exegesis, provisionally respects the development of the doctrine in the church, orders the results in a coherent whole, and applies the results to the full scope of human endeavor.

The discipline sometimes is designated "dogmatic theology" (Shedd, Pieper, Bavinck, Barth), the leading idea being truth established by competent authority. The governing authority is variously viewed as inspired Scripture, creedal standards, or the church's *magisterium*. Other common designations are Christian theology (Clark, Headlam, Wiley) and Christian faith (Rahner, H. Berkhof, and many Dutch theologians).

Some mistakenly view systematic theology as a deposit of divine truths that is timeless and unalterable. Although the Scriptures are inviolable, fresh theological understanding and reformulation are required in every generation. First, because as language and cultural forms change the body of Christian truth must be clad in contemporary dress to remain intelligible; and second, because new issues and problems continually arise to challenge the church. Hence the biblical text periodically needs to be reinterpreted and reapplied to the modern context.

The relation of systematic theology to other disciplines deserves mention. Since philosophy and theology both engage in critical analysis of the meaning of terms, follow a strict process of observation and reasoning to reach conclusions, and traditionally have sought to formulate a consistent world view, philosophy and theology may be regarded as overlapping disciplines. Religion, on the other hand, is defined as a set of beliefs, attitudes, and practices that are given a particular institutionalized expression. Every religion, whether simple or sophisticated, *has* a theology. Hence religion is larger in scope than theology. Ethics, defined as the science of religious conduct, works within the descriptive framework of systematic theology and assumes its results. Apologetics develops a reasoned defense of a Christian's basic presuppositions concerning God, Christ, and the Bible against basic assumptions of conflicting world views (metaphysics) and ways of knowing (epistemologies).

The Possibility and Necessity of Systematic Theology. Contrary to those who assert that human knowledge of metaphysical realities is not possible, the Christian asserts that knowledge of God is eminently feasible for several reasons: (1) The God who exists has revealed himself in a meaningful disclosure to his creatures (I Cor. 2:10); (2) Man created in the image of God is a rational being endowed with the ability to think God's thoughts after him (James 3:9); (3) The believer enjoys the restoration of his epistemic powers by the grace of regeneration (Col. 3:10); and (4) The Christian is enabled to perceive spiritual truths through the gift of Holy Spirit illumination (Ps. 119:18; I Cor. 2:14–15). It follows that only the Spirit-guided Christian can do theology in a way pleasing to God.

It has been mentioned that systematic theology works with the full range of divine revelation. Thus it focuses on God's saving history with his chosen people, the utterances of divinely ordained prophets and teachers, and supremely the life, teachings, death, and resurrection of Jesus Christ—all of which are inerrantly recorded in the Scriptures. Systematic theology also takes into account data mediated by secondary modes of revelation as, for example, the created order (Ps. 19:1–6; Rom. 1:18–21), the flow of providential history (Acts 17:26), and the moral imperatives mediated by conscience (Rom. 2:14–15).

Although the person and especially the believer is able to acquire knowledge of God and thus to construct a systematic theology, it does not follow that such knowledge is fully identical to God's knowledge of himself and the universe (complete univocal knowledge). Rather the partial knowledge that finite man receives of the infinite God is a knowledge mediated by both images and symbols (analogical knowledge) and propositional assertions (cognitive, univocal truth). Even "picture language" about God, for example, God as "heavenly Father," is true and valid knowledge since the analogy includes a core of univocal truth. In sum, systematic theology claims that God can be known and truths about God communicated in meaningful everyday language.

The church undertakes the task of constructing a systematic theology for three principal reasons. (1) That the church might be edified. The people of God are spiritually enriched by those teachings that systematic theology upholds as verily to be believed (II Tim. 3:16). (2) That the gospel in its fullness might be proclaimed. Without the foundation of a solid theology there can be no effective gospel preaching, evangelism, missionary outreach, or Bible translation. And (3) that the truth content of the faith might be preserved. It is the express task of systematic theology to expound the whole counsel of God as given by divine revelation. Where systematic theology is devalued numerous cults and false sects abound.

The Method of Systematic Theology. One way of doing systematic theology is the so-called confessional method, by which the teachings of Scripture are expounded and proclaimed. Thus Lutheran confessional theologies, Reformed confessional theologies, and neo-orthodox confessional theologies have been produced from the perspectives of the host system. The difficulty of the confessional method is that few reasons are given *why* one confessional position should be accepted as the norm vis-à-vis all the others. Preferable is the method that respects all the confessional views as hypotheses to be tested by the criteria of logical consistency, coherence with the facts of revelation, and existential viability. The task of the theologian is to show that the body of truth as he formulates it from revelation fits the facts with fewest problems and satisfies human needs to a greater degree than the alternatives. The virtues of this method are (1) a higher degree of openness and communication are maintained with others inside and outside the church; and (2) a rationale is provided why one should accept the Christian doctrine as stated in the face of competing truth claims. In sum, by this method both the content of revelation is expounded in orderly fashion for the church and a convincing case for the validity of the gospel is offered to the world.

The church traditionally has viewed systematic theology not only as a scientific endeavor, but also, for centuries, as the queen of the sciences. Kant, however, argued that the science of God is impossible since objective knowledge of noumenal realities is not attainable. Modern logical positivism and theological liberalism for various reasons deny that systematic theology is properly a science. But the fact is that systematic theology, like all scientific endeavors, follows a reliable *method*, namely the method of research that observes, records data, formulates hypotheses, tests the hypotheses, and finally relates the resultant body of knowledge to life. Systematic theology also deals with a *product*, namely an integrated body of reliable information in a particular field. In this respect theology is no less a science than any of the social sciences. The point is that systematic theology is not a bogus discipline that deals with private opinions and fables, but a discipline that operates with accurate information secured by reliable means.

In pursuing its task systematic theology utilizes the results of other branches of theological science. Exegetical theology unfolds the meaning of specific biblical texts and so provides systematic theology with its basic building blocks. Biblical theology sets forth the doctrinal message of the books of the Bible in their historical setting. Historical theology traces the science of God through the various eras of the church's history. Here the principle of organization is not logical or topical, but chronological. Systematic theology, then, incorporates the data of exegetical, biblical, and historical theology to construct a coherent explication of the Christian faith. As Origen put it, "God gives the truth in single threads which we must weave into a finished texture." Finally, practical theology applies the results of systematic theology to preaching, teaching, and counseling.

Theologians have organized the data of revelation in various ways. Some (Schleiermacher, Tillich, Marquarrie) have begun with man and his existential situation and so have constructed a "theology from below." Others (most orthodox and some neo-orthodox) posit God as the primary datum and thus construct a "theology from above." The latter approach is preferred, if only for the reason that "man only knows who he is in the light of God" (Bonhoeffer). More particularly, theologians such as Aquinas and Calvin have organized the material of theology according to the Trinitarian pattern. Others, such as Barth, follow a Christological model and seek to relate the data to God's self-disclosure in the Word. It is more difficult in these two schemes to do justice to all the subject matter of theology, although the first is preferred to the second. Preferable is the logical ordering espoused by Berkhof, Hodge, Strong, and others that organizes the data beginning with God and his revelation, followed by man and his predicament in sin, then by God's saving work through Christ, the society of redeemed people, and finally the consummation and the eternal state. B. A. Demarest

See also Dogma; Dogmatics.

Bibliography. L. Berkhof, *Introduction to Systematic Theology;* J. J. Davis, *Theology Primer* and (ed.) *The Necessity of Systematic Theology;* G. R. Lewis, *Decide for Yourself: A Theological Workbook;* J. W. Montgomery, "The Theologian's Craft," *CTM* 39:67–98; J. G. Skilton, ed., *The NT Student and Theology;* B. B. Warfield, "The Idea of Systematic Theology," in *Studies in Theology.*

Tt

Tabernacle, Temple. Structures built for the worship of gods. The use of temples is both ancient and widespread in human culture. In Mesopotamia the "house" or "palace" of the gods was placed on a massive artificial platform (ziggurat) where the gods were thought to reside on their journeys from the heaven to the lower world (cf. Gen. 11:4). The Canaanites also constructed local shrines on loose stone platforms, as is clear from the striking excavations at Hazor. Altars (but not necessarily temples) crowned these "high places" (*bāmôt*). The high places existed concurrently and competitively with Israelite sanctuaries in the preexilic period and were only systematically suppressed by King Josiah (II Kings 23).

Tabernacle and Temple in History. The patriarchs worshiped at various cultic places in Canaan, such as Shechem, Bethel, Hebron, and Beersheba. These unenclosed sites would usually contain a sacred tree or stone (*maṣṣēbâ*) and an altar. Each site commemorated an appearance of God to the patriarchs (see Gen. 18:1; 28:10ff.; 33:18).

The essential elements of biblical temple worship derive from the Sinai covenant. The Bible attributes to this period the central features of the later Jerusalem temple—the tent of meeting (*'ōhel mô'ēd*), or tabernacle (*miškān*), and the ark of the covenant—although scholars debate the exact provenance of and relationship between these institutions.

As described in Exod. 25–31, the wilderness tabernacle was the prototype of the later temple in Jerusalem with certain unique features. It was half the size of the temple and was portable. Its walls consisted of a framework of boards; from these, linen curtains were suspended, and skins covered the whole structure. The courtyard was likewise enclosed with a linen screen upheld by wooden pillars.

During the period of the judges Israelite temples were established throughout the land at Gilgal, Shiloh, Bethel, Dan, Mizpah of Benjamin, Ophrah, Hebron, Bethlehem, Nob, and several lesser sites. The ark is primarily associated with Shiloh, although it also resided for a time at Gilgal and Bethel. The Philistines destroyed Shiloh and captured the ark; however, they soon returned it, and it probably remained at Kiriath-jearim (Baalah) until David determined to install it in a new temple in Jerusalem (I Sam. 4–7; II Sam. 6; cf. I Chron. 16:39). Solomon's temple (or the first temple) became preeminent as a symbol of national and religious unity. However, the rival temples died hard: King Jeroboam I reestablished Dan and Bethel as shrines for the northern tribes. Surprisingly, a small temple complex has been found in Solomon's own border fortress at Arad. During and after the Exile, Jewish temples were built in Egypt at Elephantine (sixth to fifth centuries B.C.) and Leontopolis (second century B.C.), and the Samaritans also built a temple on Mount Gerizim (fourth to second century B.C.).

The first temple in Jerusalem was destroyed by the Babylonians in 587 B.C. and the second temple completed on the same site in 515 B.C. The second temple was understandably modest in comparison with Solomon's temple—until King Herod's total remodeling along grand hellenistic lines in 20 B.C. Control of the temple continued to have strong political overtones; both Antiochus IV of Syria and the Roman general Pompey set up pagan insignia within it as signs of their authority over the Jews. The second temple itself was destroyed in A.D. 70 by the Romans, who erected their own temple on the spot. Today the site is occupied by the Muslim shrine, Dome of the Rock.

The basic shape of the temple was that of a "long house" subdivided into two rooms, the holy place and the holy of holies, separated by doors in Solomon's day and later by a curtain. Inside the holy place stood the incense altar, the table(s) for showbread, and the golden lampstand(s). In Solomon's temple the inner sanctum contained the ark, the cherubim, and perhaps the mercy seat (*kappōret*); in the postexilic second temple the holy of holies was presumably bare. Once a year on the day of atonement the high priest entered and cleansed the holy of holies. The temple was flanked by various outbuildings for priests and by one or two courtyards. To the east of the temple porch with its twin pillars stood the sacrifice altar and bronze laver. Here worshipers and priests performed the prescribed sacrifices according to the Torah.

Theological Significance. The institution of the tabernacle is set within the context of the giving of the covenant on Mount Sinai. The tabernacle signifies to Israel crucial aspects of this covenant. First of all, it is a sign of *election*—God has graciously chosen Israel; she has not chosen him. Likewise God personally prescribes the form, furnishings, clergy, and ceremonial of the tabernacle; he also promises to choose the future site of his dwelling (Deut. 12:5). Any deviation from these exact prescriptions is a breach of the covenant and leads to death (Exod. 32).

The tabernacle is a sign of *unity:* as God is one, so God's people, gathered in diverse tribes and ranks, are united around the tabernacle (Num. 1–10). Conversely, those temples erected outside Jerusalem indicate both the disunity of the nation and its idolatry; and the prophets look toward the day when worship will be unified in Jerusalem and purified (Ezek. 28:25–26). Indeed the temple on Mount Zion even points to the eventual reconciliation of the human race (Isa. 2:1–5).

God is holy and calls Israel to be a holy nation. The temple and its priesthood remind her of this vocation to *holiness.* The sacrificial system provides atonement for the sins of the people and for the sanctuary (Lev. 16). The holy God reveals his name, his glory, and his presence to Israel at Mount Sinai. However, the tabernacle is to be the ongoing locus of God's presence throughout her history. God is seen as permanently dwelling (*šākan*) in the tabernacle or temple (Exod. 29:43–46; I Kings 6:13); but he also manifests his glory, in blessing or wrath, at critical moments in Israel's life (Exod. 40:34–38; Num. 14:10ff.; 16:19ff.; Ezek. 1–10; 43:1–7; Mal. 3:1). The rebuilding of the temple is an indispensable token of God's continuing will to bless Israel (Hag. 2:18–19; Zech. 4:9–10).

God is cosmic king, and the temple is the sign of his *kingship.* The enthronement psalms and the Zion psalms acclaim God as reigning from his abode in Zion over the whole earth (Pss. 29; 46–48; 76; cf. Isa. 6:1–3). The messianic king is God's delegate in his kingdom (Ps. 2); sometimes a messianic figure is pictured as serving before God in his sanctuary (II Sam. 6; Ps. 110; Dan. 9:24–26; Zech. 4).

The temple is also seen as the earthly pattern of the *heavenly kingdom* (Exod. 25:8–9; I Chr. 28:19; Isa. 6:1–3). During the Exile, Ezekiel is given a visionary tour of the New Jerusalem and its temple (Ezek. 40–48). Ezekiel's temple does not conform to the reality of the first and second temples. Many scholars likewise see the priestly prescriptions in the Pentateuch as idealizations of the temple and its appurtenances. Along with such spiritualization of the temple idea goes the expectation of an eschatological temple (Isa. 2:1–5; Ezek. 37:27; Hag. 2:9). Both these tendencies to look for a final, glorious temple are extended in the apocalyptic literature (I Enoch 14; 90:28–29; T. Levi 2–3). The Qumran sectarians, for instance, collected visions of the New Jerusalem, including the lengthy Temple Scroll. They also described their own community in exile as "the house of holiness for Israel . . . a most holy dwelling for Aaron" (1QS 8:5–9).

The true Israelite continually longed to be in the "courts of the Lord" (see Pss. 27; 122); at the same time the people of Israel were continually tempted to respond to God's institution of the temple with a false confidence in the unconditional character of his grace. The prophets repeatedly warned the people that trust in the temple could derive only from trust in God and obedience to the terms of his covenant. Otherwise God would destroy the temple (cf. Jer. 7:1–15; Ezek. 9; Amos 9:1). But when the temple was devastated in 587 B.C. and A.D. 70, it then became the object of hope for future restoration (Ps. 137; Seventeenth Benediction of the synagogue liturgy).

Tabernacle and Temple in the NT. The NT reflects the same devotion toward the temple—not to mention the same ambivalence and apocalyptic expectation—expressed by Jews of the time; however, the NT writers, convinced that the kingdom of God has come and that Jesus has fulfilled the messianic prophecies of the OT, heighten and deepen the meaning of the temple idea.

Jesus himself assumed the divine institution of the temple and called it "my Father's house" (John 2:16). At the same time he saw God's judgment impending upon it, and he predicted its imminent destruction (Mark 13:1–2). In a manner reminiscent of the prophets, Jesus "cleansed" the temple, recalling its holiness and its universal destiny ("a house of prayer for all nations"—Matt. 21:13). He also claimed that were the temple to be destroyed, he would raise up a new one (John 2:19). While Jesus intended this claim parabolically, it was used against him at his trial (Matt. 26:61; cf. 27:40). Ironically, the trial and crucifixion of Jesus seal the fate of the temple and open the way to a new Gentile community confessing Jesus as the Son of God (Mark 15:37–39).

The Gospel of John employs the OT imagery of the tabernacle to emphasize that God himself, the Word, is present in human form (John 1:14). The new temple, Christ's exalted body, will become the focus of true worship for those who receive the Spirit (John 2:18–22; 4:19–24; 7:37–38). The book of Acts illustrates the movement of the church from the first Jerusalem community—still worshiping at the temple—outward to Samaria, and at last to Rome, the capital of the Gentile world.

While it is possible that the book of Acts refers to the church as a new temple (15:13–18), it is Paul who develops this image fully. Paul calls his converts to a holiness of life intended for the true Israel, because "you are the temple of the living God" (II Cor. 6:16–7:1; cf. I Cor. 6:19–20). Sometimes he likens the church to a building founded on Christ within which the Holy Spirit dwells and gives unity (I Cor. 3:10–17; Eph. 2:20–22). Similarly Peter calls believers to appropriate the OT promises to Israel by coming to Christ the cornerstone and being built into a spiritual edifice (I Pet. 2:4–10).

The Epistle to the Hebrews is a thoroughgoing representation of OT types with strong emphasis on the heavenly realities underlying them. Thus the regulations for worship in the OT were earthly and transient; Christ as the true high priest entered into the heavenly sanctuary and offered once for all the perfect sacrifice of his blood. For this reason Christians can draw near to God with confidence (Heb. 9–10). While we remain, in one sense, on pilgrimage in the world, through our forerunner, we have come already by faith to the eschatological feast in heaven (Heb. 11–12).

The author of the Revelation elaborates on this eschatological fulfillment in vivid imagery. John assures the beleaguered churches that Christ the Lamb has already entered the heavenly tabernacle and received authority over the future (Rev. 4–5). They are already a royal and priestly temple, and by martyrdom they will enter proleptically into heaven (Rev. 7:1–12; 11:1–13).

The ultimate fulfillment of all God's promises in space and time is to come in the New Jerusalem (Rev. 21–22). It is a new world order, a new creation for all eternity. God Almighty and the Lamb are its temple, and all the elect will see him face to face. S. F. Noll

See also Altar; Offerings and Sacrifices in Bible Times; Priests and Levites.

Bibliography. R. deVaux, *Ancient Israel,* II; M. Haran, *Temples and Temple-Service in Ancient Israel;* J. Comay, *The Temple of Jerusalem;* R. J. McKelvey, *The New Temple.*

Tauler, Johannes (*ca.* 1300–1361). Medieval preacher and mystic. Born in a well-to-do family in Strasbourg, Tauler entered the Dominican Order in that city *ca.* 1315. His pastoral education was taken at Strasbourg; contrary to frequent assertion, he did not study scholastic theology in Cologne. Unlike Meister Eckhart, he never taught theology but spent his life as a Dominican preacher and spiritual counselor, primarily in Strasbourg, but also in Basel and Cologne. Tauler left no Latin writings and none of the German treatises once ascribed to him are genuine; his literary legacy consists of German sermons. Tauler's nineteenth century reputation as a "Reformer before the Reformation" was based in large part on the spurious treatises.

Tauler can scarcely be considered a disciple of Eckhart. He learned much from Eckhart's writings but probably did not know this fellow Dominican personally. Although they share the common goal of union with God that is made possible by the existence of a divine *Grund* ("ground, center, fundament") or "spark" of divineness in the human soul, Tauler's approach may with caution be described as that of a pastoral *Lebemeister* ("master of living") rather than that of a pastoral *Lese-* or *Lehrmeister* ("lector or scholastic-mystical master of teaching"). Tauler's mystical theology is based less explicitly on a metaphysical system than on the existence of the image of God in humans. Whereas Eckhart speaks of the eternal birth of the Word in the soul, Tauler focuses on a transforming or "hyperforming" (*Überformung*) of the human being in the divine image. Thus Tauler's mystical theology is more personalistic and anthropological, stressing the affective resources of the soul (the *Gemüt* or "basic will") to a greater degree than the intellectual faculties of the soul. Tauler also pays greater attention to the preparation for union, to the purgative path of growth in love and in freedom from selfness and creatureliness: one cannot run before walking.

Untainted by the stigma of heresy that Eckhart's writings carried, Tauler's sermons were widely transmitted and frequently printed. Thus they were read and recommended by subsequent spiritual writers, including Martin Luther and various pietists. The assumption that Tauler limited the mystical union to a conformity of divine and human wills by grace alone has made

Protestant authors sympathetic to Tauler, but this interpretation, even when based on genuine Taulerian sermons, must be understood in the context of his assumption that an innate likeness to God within the human soul makes possible a union of essence or being, and also in view of his emphasis on human cooperation with divine grace in the path toward union. D. D. MARTIN

See also MEISTER ECKHART; MYSTICISM.

Bibliography. G. Hofmann, tr., *Johannes Tauler, Predigten;* E. Filthaut, ed., *Johannes Tauler, ein deutscher Mystiker: Gedenkschrift zum 600. Todestag;* J. M. Clark, *Great German Mystics,* 36–54; R. M. Jones, *The Flowering of Mysticism,* 86–103; I. Weilner, *Johannes Taulers Bekehrungsweg;* D. Mieth, *Die Einheit von vita activa und vita contemplativa in . . . Meister Eckhart und bei Johannes Tauler;* G. Wrede, *Unio Mystica: Probleme der Erfahrung bei Johannes Tauler.*

Taylor, Nathaniel William (1786–1858). Founder of the New Haven Theology, he contributed to the rise of evangelical theology by modifying Calvinism, rendering it compatible with revivalism in the opening decades of the nineteenth century. He was born in 1786 in New Milford, Connecticut, into a family rich in both material things and religious heritage. Taylor entered Yale in 1800, but an eye ailment deferred his graduation until 1807.

Taylor was profoundly influenced while a student by revivalist Timothy Dwight, the president of Yale. Taylor lived with the Dwight family for two years after his graduation, serving as the president's secretary and studying theology. In 1812 Taylor was ordained and installed at First Church in New Haven, the most prestigious pulpit in the state, where he commanded admiration for ten years as a preacher and defender of revivalism. He worked closely with Lyman Beecher, who preached throughout New England to promulgate the Second Great Awakening, not only to win souls, but to launch a moral crusade against such social ills as sabbath breaking and drunkenness. Taylor contributed by publishing his sermons as doctrinal tracts against Old Calvinists, Episcopalians, and the growing Unitarian movement, all opposed to the revival.

In 1822 Taylor was appointed Dwight Professor of Didactic Theology at Yale, where he taught until his death in 1858. Taylor was prompted to revise Calvinism by the increasing charges from Unitarians that Calvinistic determinism actually promoted immorality by denying human freedom. In response to these attacks he altered the Reformed doctrines of revelation, human depravity, God's sovereignty, Christ's atonement, and regeneration in order to harmonize Calvinist theology with actual revival practices. He accepted the humanistic teaching of commonsense realism that reason provides not only proof of God's existence but also the first principles of morality that make man a free, moral agent. He insisted that men are lost but denied that Adam's sin was imputed to all men and that everyone inherits a sinful nature which causes one to sin. Even though a person sins, he has power to do otherwise, thus remaining morally responsible. God made man with a proper self-love, a natural desire for happiness, which motivates all choices.

Taylor also reinterpreted Calvin's teaching on God's sovereignty by calling God a moral governor who rules, not by determining the destiny of all men through election, but rather by establishing a moral universe and judging its inhabitants. God promotes moral action by a system of means and ends in which man can respond to ethical appeals for repentance. He opposed the legal view of the atonement that stressed Christ's substitutionary death on the cross in the place of sinners to satisfy God's justice. Instead, God as benevolent moral governor sent Christ to die so that his death could be preached as a means to urge sinners to turn freely from their sin out of self-love and be converted. Taylor blurred the distinction between the Holy Spirit's sovereign work of regeneration and human repentance that Jonathan Edwards maintained in his defense of the First Great Awakening in the 1740s.

Taylorism was popularized by revivalists such as Charles G. Finney, who demonstrated wide appeal to New School Presbyterians and Congregationalists anxious for revivals in their parishes. However, Old School opponents such as Charles Hodge at Princeton Theological Seminary accused Taylor of Pelagianism and Arminianism and defended traditional Calvinism.

W. A. HOFFECKER

See also NEW HAVEN THEOLOGY.

Bibliography. S. E. Ahlstrom, "The Scottish Philosophy and American Theology," *CH* 24:257–72; J. Haroutunian, *Piety versus Moralism: The Passing of the New England Theology;* G. M. Marsden, *The Evangelical Mind and the New School Presbyterian Experience;* S. E. Mead, *Nathaniel William Taylor;* Taylor, *Concio ad Clerum: On Human Nature, Sin, and Freedom* and *Lectures on the Moral Government of God.*

Teaching, Gift of. *See* SPIRITUAL GIFTS.

Teilhard de Chardin, Pierre (1881–1955). Controversial Jesuit paleogeologist who absorbed theology into a scheme of cosmic evolution. Teilhard was born in Sarant, France. At the Jesuit boarding school he attended from the age of ten, he developed an early interest in geology, leading eventually to his taking the doctorate in that field at the Sorbonne in 1922. In the meantime he had taken the Jesuit vow and served as stretcher bearer in World War I. In 1926 he was relieved of his teaching duties at the Catholic Institute in Paris for his unorthodox views. The next twenty years saw his major activities in Asia, where his work included participation in the discoveries of Sinanthropus (Peking Man) and Pithecanthropus. During the last decade of his life he lectured widely in Europe and America to acclaim from outside of the church; but ecclesiastical authorities continued to forbid publication of his ideas. Thus most of Teilhard's published views from his lifetime are scientific; his major theological works saw print only posthumously.

Teilhard's central work is *The Phenomenon of Man,* written in 1938. The focus of the book is on seeing the human person as a unique scientific phenomenon. Humanity in all its aspects needs to be brought into the total picture of the universe, and that picture is described by evolution.

The Phenomenon of Man is divided into three parts corresponding to Teilhard's tripartite conception of evolution: prelife, life, and thought. For him, the evolutionary process is orthogenetic: evolution, rather than being merely the result of chance adaptation, proceeds along a "correct" line that the universe is compelled to follow. Thus the material realm already tends toward consciousness. Physical matter, however, is enveloped by the "biosphere," the manifestation of all the various forms of life beginning with the simplest and concluding with the most complex: the human being.

In the area of human development the most remarkable features of evolution are accented. All along, evolution has defied the second law of thermodynamics by increasing complexity in the system and by raising similarity in forms. But now in the human person complexity is highly intensified, and all of human evolution converges into the development of culture and thought. Thereby is created the third layer beyond matter and the biosphere: the "noosphere." The noosphere is the ever-increasing collectivity of human knowledge as well as of humanistic attitudes, especially love. It too develops, and it also has a goal: the unification of all humankind under the commitment of love. Teilhard refers to this certain destiny as "omega point." It becomes identical with Jesus Christ.

Teilhard has few true disciples, but his thought has been a great stimulant for dialogue. Many of his ideas are reflected in the Vatican II documents. Scientists have found inspiration in his transmaterial view of the world.

Nonetheless, in many specifics, he stands scathed by strong critiques. Contemporary biology is leery of orthogenetics and the teleology it implies. On the other side, conservative theologians would find fault with his doctrines of creation, sin, and Christ, among others. In sum, Teilhard de Chardin epitomizes the twentieth century myth: a combination of science and theology that does justice to neither. W. CORDUAN

See also EVOLUTION.

Bibliography. Teilhard de Chardin, *The Divine Milieu, The Future of Man, Hymn of the Universe,* and *The Phenomenon of Man;* H. de Lubac, *The Religion of Teilhard de Chardin;* R. G. North, *Teilhard and the Creation of the Soul.*

Teleological Argument for God. *See* GOD, ARGUMENTS FOR THE EXISTENCE OF.

Temperance. *See* CARDINAL VIRTUES, SEVEN.

Temple. *See* TABERNACLE, TEMPLE.

Temple, William (1881–1944). Commonly adjudged one of the greatest church leaders of the twentieth century and possibly the most gifted teacher ever to fill the See of Canterbury. Son of Frederick Temple, Archbishop of Canterbury, William was educated at Rugby School (1894–1900) and Balliol College, Oxford (1900–1904), graduating B.A. with first class honors in *literae humaniores.* He was ordained priest in 1909. His appointments included: Fellow of Queen's College, Oxford (1904–10); Headmaster of Repton (1910–14); Rector of St. James's, Piccadilly (1914–17), where his preaching through the Gospel of John laid the foundation for his most popular devotional work, *Readings in St. John's Gospel* (1939); Canon of Westminster (1919–20); Bishop of Manchester (1921–29); Archbishop of York (1929–42); and Archbishop of Canterbury (1942–44).

Of massive intellectual and spiritual power, Temple's most important writings are on philosophical theology (*Mens Creatrix,* 1917; *Christus Veritas,* 1924; *Nature, Man and God,* 1934) and social theology (*Christianity and Social Order,* 1942). Influenced by the neo-Hegelian idealism of T. H. Green and Edward Caird, Temple sought a unifying spiritual principle by which apparently contradictory or independent intellectual and social movements might be reconciled or related. This principle, he believed, was the Christian doctrine of the Logos. Indeed, the starting point of his philosophical theology was faith in God, which, he maintained, cannot be demonstrated by philosophical argument but makes the best sense of human experience. He agreed with Augustine that the motto of theology is "I believe in order to understand." A corollary was Temple's optimism about the meaningfulness of human life, including the experience of evil and suffering. The fall, he suggested, was a "fall upwards," since through it man acquired self-will, and only through the conquest of self-will could man make progress from innocence to self-sacrifice, which is virtue. In the incarnation of the Logos, God offers man not explanation, but salvation, which is the divine summons to loving, self-sacrificial action to eradicate evil in the lives of individuals and in the structures of society. So, particularly in his later thinking, the unifying principle of the Logos was understood, not as a static concept, but as a dynamic process in which men and institutions cooperate with God in the renovation of the world. Temple's Christocentric metaphysic and his stress on the theology of incarnation have placed him outside the mainstream of twentieth century theological thought with its emphasis on a dogmatic theology of redemption.

Consistent with his position, Temple was committed to a large number of social, political, and economic, as well as ecclesiastical, movements: (1) Educational reform: Temple was president of the Workers' Educational Association from 1908 to 1924, and he was instrumental in the passage of the influential Education Act of 1943. (2) Student work: Temple had a long association with the Student Christian Movement, which he promoted in Australia in 1910 on the invitation of John R. Mott. In his many university missions, he demonstrated the intellectual respectability of Christianity and helped stem the drift away from the churches fashionable after World War I. (3) Christian renewal: Temple traveled for the Life and Liberty Movement in 1918–19 advocating a reformed establishment. The consequent Enabling Act of 1919 created a new Church Assembly made up of bishops, clergy, and laity. (4) Social justice and reform: Temple was attracted to socialism, was a lifelong friend of R. H. Tawney and a short-term member of the Labor Party. He was an ardent champion of the church's right to intervene in social and economic matters and was chairman of the interdenominational Conference on Politics, Economics, and Citizenship (COPEC) in Birmingham in 1924. (5) The ecumenical movement: Temple's involvement dated from the 1910 Edinburgh Conference until his death. He was first president of both the World Council of Churches "in process of formation" (1938) and of the British Council of Churches (1943).

In spite of his brilliance, Temple's was a serene and simple faith, grounded in a life of prayer. His profound humanity may be attributed partly to a lifelong affliction with gout. He was a popular evangelist with the capacity to express deep truths in simple words and was known as the people's archbishop.

F. S. Piggin

Bibliography. F. A. Iremonger, *William Temple, Archbishop of Canterbury; Theol* 84; O. C. Thomas, *William Temple's Philosophy of Religion.*

Temptation. The act of tempting or the state of being tempted. In the OT the specific verb indicating the act of tempting is the Piel form *nissâ.* In I Sam. 17:39 the word is used of proving or testing armor. In Gen. 22:1 *nissâ* characterizes God's command to Abraham to offer Isaac as a burnt offering in the land of Moriah. A similar use of the term in application to God's testing of men is found in Exod. 16:4; 20:20; Deut. 8:2, 16; 13:3; II Chr. 32:31; Ps. 26:2; etc. Related to this sense of the term is that which is given to it when it is applied to the terrible and wonderful acts of God against Egypt (Deut. 4:34).

The same technical term is applied to those acts of men which challenge God to demonstrate his veracity and justice.

The term *nissâ* is rarely, if ever, applied in the OT to Satan's act of enticing men to sin. Nevertheless, the essence of temptation in this sense is clearly revealed in the account of the fall and in the record of Satan's role in the affliction of Job (Gen. 3:1–13; Job 1:1—2:10). Eve tells God, "The serpent beguiled me (*hiššî'anî*), and I did eat" (Gen. 3:13; cf. *exapataō* in II Cor. 11:3; I Tim. 2:14). Deception plays an important part in satanic temptation. Satan avoids making a frontal attack immediately on God's probationary command and its threatened penalties. Instead, he sows the seeds of doubt, unbelief, and rebellion. The temptation of Eve is typical. She is made to feel that God has unwisely and unfairly withheld a legitimate objective good from man. In Job's trials the strategy is different, but the end sought is the same—the rejection of God's will and way as just and good.

The NT reflects the translation of *nissâ* with *ekpeirazō*, etc., in the LXX (Matt. 4:7; I Cor. 10:9; Heb. 3:8–9). In these passages the sinful tempting of God is referred to by way of the OT. However, the same sense is employed by Peter in connection with the sin of Ananias and Sapphira (Acts 5:9) and the prescriptions to be given to Gentile Christians (Acts 15:10).

The additional use of *peirazō* and related forms is complex. The words may refer to exterior circumstances which try the believer's faith and are designed to strengthen that faith (James 1:2; I Pet. 1:6). Although these circumstances are held to be under the absolute control of God, the explicit causal ascription of them to God is not prominent. Perhaps some reasoning by analogy is permissible here. Paul, e.g., recognizes that his "thorn in the flesh" is under God's sovereign control (II Cor. 12:8–9). But the "thorn" is "a messenger of Satan" (vs. 7). The same phenomenon may be viewed from two aspects. The *peirasmon* is a trial of one's faith controlled and, even in some sense, sent by God. But God is not the author of the prompting to sin that such trial seems to bring with it. The believer may rejoice in trial because he detects God's good purpose in it (James 1:2–4, 12). But the subjective use of trying situations, the internal incitement to sin in connection with trials and testings, is not and cannot be the work of God. Enticement to sin and to impatient rebellion is the work of Satan (I Pet. 5:8–9; Rev. 2:9; cf. I Thess. 3:5). In this he is immensely aided by the deceptive power of *epithymia,* lust, in the old nature (James 1:14–15). While Satan's role in temptation is usually assumed rather than stated, in I Cor. 7:5 Paul explicitly warns Christians to observe his charge with respect to marital relationships, "that Satan tempt you not because of your incontinency" (cf. Matt. 4:1; Mark 1:13; Luke 4:2).

Jesus teaches the disciples to pray, "And bring us not into temptation, but deliver us from the evil *one*" (Matt. 6:13), and the Bible is replete with warnings to be watchful because of the ever-present danger of falling into temptation (Luke 22:40; Gal. 6:1; I Pet. 5:8–9). But the Bible assures the believer that God will make a way of escape from temptation (I Cor. 10:13), and that "the Lord knoweth how to deliver the godly out of temptation . . ." (II Pet. 2:9*a*).

Jesus was repeatedly "tempted" by the Jewish leaders (Mark 8:11; etc.). But these temptations were designed either to force Jesus to prove his messiahship in terms of the preconceptions of his enemies or to compel him to show himself incapable of being a true rabbi (Luke 10:25) or to cause him to make self-incriminating statements (Mark 12:15; cf. Luke 23:2).

Very likely Jesus was subject to temptation throughout his ministry (cf. Luke 4:13; 22:28). But the great temptation is the crucial temptation in redemptive history (Matt. 4:1, and parallels). This temptation confronts one with the question, How could the sinless Son of God be really tempted? Granted that appeal could be made to legitimate desires in his human nature, what force could temptation have on a divine person who cannot be tempted? Efforts to solve the problem run the risk either of impairing the "without sin" of Heb. 4:15 or of making the temptation unreal. Our understanding of the matter is beclouded by the fact that our awareness of being tempted immediately involves us in at least a momentary inclination to yield to the temptation. This was not true of Jesus, and yet the temptation was real, so that he is able to "succor them that are tempted" (Heb. 2:18).

The necessity of the temptation in view of Adam's fall is evident. Jesus *triumphed* over Satan with his immediate and obedient use of the word of God. He thereby proved that he was qualified to be the "last Adam." "To this end was the Son of God manifested, that he might destroy the works of the devil" (I John 3:8*b*).

C. G. Kromminga

Bibliography. L. Berkhof, *Systematic Theology,* 219–26; H. Seesemann, *TDNT,* VI, 23ff.; W. Schneider, *et al., NIDNTT,* III, 798ff.; R. C. Trench, *Synonyms of the NT;* P. Dobble, "Temptations," *ExpT* 72:91ff.; E. Best, *The Temptation and the Passion;* W. J. Foxell, *The Temptation of Jesus;* C. Ullmann, *The Sinlessness of Jesus.*

Tempter. *See* Satan.

Ten Articles, The (1536). A doctrinal statement resulting from the religious revolution of King Henry VIII of England. After declaring himself supreme head of the English Church in 1534, Henry strove for a middle way between Roman Catholicism and Lutheranism: the English Church would still be catholic, but without the pope. This was acceptable to most Englishmen because Henry did not interfere with their traditional Catholic beliefs. There was, however, a small but growing group of insistent Protestant reformers who were determined to bring Lutheranism into the English Church. Henry did not want to suppress these reformers because they were militant defenders of his break with the pope. However, unless Henry pronounced *ex cathedra* on their Protestant notions, he risked growing theological ferment in England. Thus the Ten Articles were issued in 1536.

In deference to his Protestant supporters, Henry's Ten Articles reduced the number of sacraments from seven to three; denied the efficacy of prayers for souls in purgatory; and condemned religious images, prayers to the saints, and the use of holy water and ashes.

Protestants increasingly demanded more reforms; so in 1539 Henry was forced to issue the Six Articles to restrain them. These essentially prohibited any Protestant reforms beyond the Ten Articles. As a result, Henry was able to maintain a precarious balance between the two theologies for the rest of his reign.

J. E. Mennell

See also Six Articles, The.

Bibliography. A. G. Dickens, *The English Reformation;* P. Hughes, *The Reformation in England.*

Ten Commandments, The. The basic law of the covenant formed between God and Israel at Mount Sinai; though the date of the event is uncertain, the commandments may be dated provisionally in the early part of the thirteenth century B.C. In Hebrew, the commandments are called the "Ten Words," which (via Greek) is the origin of the alternative English title of the commandments, namely the Decalogue. The commandments are recorded twice in the OT; they appear first in the description of the formation of the Sinai Covenant (Exod. 20:2–17) and are repeated in the description of the renewal of the covenant on the plains of Moab (Deut. 5:6–21).

The commandments are described as having been written on two tablets. Each tablet contained the full text; one tablet belonged to Israel and the other to God, so that both parties to the covenant had a copy of the legislation. The first five commandments pertain basically to the relationship between Israel and God; the last five are concerned primarily with the forms of relationships between human beings.

The commandments must be interpreted initially within the context of the Sinai Covenant, which was in effect the constitution of the state in process of formation during the time of Moses and his successor Joshua. Because God was the one who enabled Israel to move toward statehood, as a consequence of his liberating the chosen people from slavery in Egypt, he was also to be Israel's true king. As such, he had the authority to establish Israel's law, as is made clear in the preface to the commandments. Thus, the commandments were initially part of a constitution and served as state law of the emerging nation of Israel.

The fundamental principle upon which the constitution was established was *love.* God had chosen his people and freed them from slavery only because he loved them. In turn, he had one fundamental requirement of Israel, that they love God with the totality of their being (Deut. 6:5). This commandment to love is provided with a commentary and explanation. As to how the commandment to love might be fulfilled, the first five commandments indicated the nature of the relationship with God which would be an expression of love for God. The second five commandments go further and indicate that love for God also has implications for one's relationships with fellow human beings.

The interpretation of the commandments in their initial context is the source of debate; the following comments indicate in broad outline their primary thrust.

(1) The Prohibition of Gods Other Than the Lord (Exod. 20:3; Deut. 5:7). The first commandment is in negative form and expressly prohibits the Israelites' engaging in the worship of foreign deities. The significance of the commandment lies in the nature of the covenant. The essence of the covenant was a relationship, and the essence of relationship was to be faithfulness. God's faithfulness to his people had already been demonstrated in the Exodus, as is indicated in the preface to the commandments. In turn, God required more than anything else, a faithfulness in the relationship of his people with him. Thus, though the commandment is stated negatively, it is full of positive implications. And its position as first of the ten is significant, for this commandment establishes a principle which is particularly prominent in the social commandments. The contemporary significance of the commandment can thus be seen in the context of faithfulness in relationship. At the heart of human life, there must be a relationship with God. Anything in life that disrupts the primary relationship breaks the commandment. Foreign "gods" are thus persons, or even things, that would disrupt the primacy of the relationship with God.

(2) The Prohibition of Images (Exod. 20:4–6; Deut. 5:8–10). The possibility of worshiping gods other than the Lord has been eliminated in the first commandment. The second commandment prohibits the Israelites from making images of the Lord. To make an image of God, in the shape or form of anything in this world, is to reduce the Creator to something less than his creation, and to worship such an image would be false. The temptation for Israel to worship God in the form of an image must have been enormous, for images and idols occurred in all the religions of the ancient Near East. But the God of Israel was a transcendent and infinite being, and could not be reduced to the limitations of an image or form within creation. Any such reduction of God would be so radical a misunderstanding, that the "God" so worshiped would no longer be the God of the universe. In the modern world, the shape of the temptation has changed. Few are tempted to take tools and shape from wood an image of God, but the commandment is still applicable. One can construct an image of God with words. If we use words about God and say, "This is exactly what God is like, no less" (and, we imply, no more), and if we work out the minute details of our understanding of God, then we are in danger of creating an image of God no less fixed or rigid than the image of wood or stone. Of course, we are not prohibited from using words about God, or religion would become impossible. But if the words become set firmly, like cement, and our understanding of God sets with those words, an image has been constructed. To worship God in the form of a word image is to break the commandment. God is transcendent and infinite, and always greater than any words a creature can use of him. The second commandment thus guards the ultimate greatness and mystery of God.

(3) The Prohibition Against the Improper Use of God's Name (Exod. 20:7; Deut. 5:11). There is a popular understanding that the third commandment prohibits bad language or blasphemy; however, it is concerned with a more grave matter—the use of God's name. God had granted to Israel an extraordinary privilege; he had revealed to them his personal name. The name is represented in Hebrew by four letters, *yhwh,* variously rendered in English Bibles as: Lord, Yahweh, or Jehovah. The knowledge of the divine name was a privilege, for it meant that Israel did not worship an anonymous and distant deity, but a being whose personal name was known. Yet the privilege was accompanied by a danger, namely, that the knowledge of God's personal name could be abused. In the ancient Near Eastern religions, magic was a common practice, involving the use of a god's name, which was believed to control the god's power, in certain kinds of activity designed to harness divine power for human purposes. Thus the kind of activity prohibited by the third commandment is magic, attempting to control God's power through his name for a personal and worthless purpose. God may give, but must not be manipulated or controlled. Within Christianity, the name of God is equally important. It is in the name of God, e.g., that the privilege of access to God in prayer is granted. The abuse of the privilege of prayer, involving calling upon the name of God for some selfish or worthless purpose, is tantamount to the magic of the ancient world. In both, God's name is abused and the third commandment broken. The third commandment is a positive reminder of the enormous privilege given to us in the knowledge of God's name; it is a privilege not to be taken lightly or abused.

(4) The Observation of the Sabbath (Exod. 20:8–11; Deut. 5:12–15). This commandment also has no parallels in ancient Near Eastern religions; it is also the first of the commandments to be expressed in a positive form. While most of life in Israel was characterized by work, the seventh day was to be set aside. Work was to cease and the day was to be kept holy. The holiness of the day is related to the reason for its establishment; two reasons are given, and though at first they appear different, there is a common theme linking them. In the first version (Exod. 20:11), the sabbath is to be kept in commemoration of creation; God created the world in six days and rested on the seventh day. In the second version (Deut. 5:15), the sabbath is to be observed in commemoration of the Exodus from Egypt. The theme linking the two versions is *creation;* God created not only the world, he also "created" his people, Israel, in redeeming them from Egyptian slavery. Thus, on every seventh day throughout the passage of time, the Hebrew people were to reflect upon creation; in so doing, they were reflecting upon the meaning of their existence. For most of Christianity, the concept of "sabbath" has been moved from the seventh to the first day of the week, Sunday. The move is related to a change in Christian thought, identified in the resurrection of Jesus Christ on Sunday. The change is appropriate, for Christians now reflect each Sunday, or sabbath, on a third act of divine creation, the "new creation" established in the resurrection of Jesus Christ from the dead.

(5) The Honor Due to Parents (Exod. 20:12; Deut. 5:16). The fifth commandment forms a bridge between the first four, concerned primarily with God, and the last five, concerned primarily with interhuman relationships. On first reading, it appears to be concerned with family relationships only; children were to honor their parents. Although the commandment establishes a principle of honor, or respect, in family relationships, it is probably also related to a specific concern. It was the responsibility of parents to instruct their children in the faith of the covenant (Deut. 6:7), so that the religion could be passed on from one generation to another. But instruction in the faith required an attitude of honor and respect from those who were being instructed. Thus, the fifth commandment is not concerned only with family harmony, but also with transmission of faith in God throughout subsequent generations. With the fifth commandment, there is little need to convert its meaning into contemporary relevance. In a century, however, in which so much education is undertaken beyond the confines of the family unit, the commandment serves a solemn reminder, not only of the need for harmonious family life, but also of the responsibilities with respect to religious education that rest upon both parents and children.

(6) The Prohibition of Murder (Exod. 20:13; Deut. 5:17). The wording of this commandment simply prohibits "killing"; the meaning of the word, however, implies the prohibition of murder. The word used in the commandment is not related primarily to killing in warfare or to capital punishment; both those matters are dealt with in other portions of the Mosaic Law. The word could be used to designate both murder and manslaughter. Since manslaughter involves accidental killing, it cannot be sensibly prohibited; it, too, is dealt with in another kind of legislation (Deut. 19:1–13). Thus, the sixth commandment prohibits murder, the taking of another person's life for personal and selfish gain. Stated positively, this preserves for each member of the covenant community the right to live. In the modern world, a similar statute, prohibiting murder, exists in almost all legal codes; it has become a part of state law, rather than purely religious or moral law. Jesus, however, pointed to the deeper meaning implicit in the commandment; it is not only the act but also the sentiment underlying the act that is evil (Matt. 5:21–22).

(7) The Prohibition of Adultery (Exod. 20:14; Deut. 5:18). The act of adultery is fundamentally an act of unfaithfulness. One or both persons in an adulterous act are being unfaithful to other persons. It is for this reason that adultery is included in the Ten Commandments, while other sins or crimes pertaining to sexuality are not included. Of all such crimes, the worst signifies unfaithfulness. Thus the seventh commandment is the social parallel to the first. Just as the first commandment requires absolute faithfulness in the relationship with the one God, so the seventh requires a similar relationship of faithfulness within the covenant of marriage. The relevance is apparent, but again, Jesus points to the implications of the commandment for the mental life (Matt. 5:27–28).

(8) The Prohibition of Theft (Exod. 20:15; Deut. 5:19). This commandment establishes a principle within the covenant community concerning possessions and property; a person had a right to certain things, which could not be violated by a fellow citizen for his or her personal advantage. But while the commandment is concerned with property, its most fundamental concern is human liberty. The worst form of theft is "manstealing" (somewhat equivalent to modern kidnapping); i.e., taking a person (presumably by force) and selling him or her into slavery. The crime and the related law are stated more fully in Deut. 24:7. The commandment is thus not only concerned with the preservation of private property, but is more fundamentally concerned with the preservation of human liberty and freedom from such things as slavery and exile. It prohibits a person from manipulating or exploiting the lives of others for personal gain. Just as the sixth commandment prohibits murder, so the eighth prohibits what might be called social murder, the cutting off of a man or a woman from a life of freedom within the community of God's people.

(9) The Prohibition of False Witnessing (Exod. 20:16; Deut. 5:20). The commandment is not a general prohibition against lies or mistruths. The wording of the original commandment sets it firmly in the context of Israel's legal system. It prohibits perjury, the giving of false testimony within the proceedings of the law court. Thus, it establishes a principle of truthfulness and carries implications with respect to false statements in any context.

Within any nation, it is essential that the courts of law operate on the basis of true information; if law is not based on truth and righteousness, then the very foundations of life and liberty are undermined. If legal testimony is true, there can be no miscarriage of justice; if it is false, the most fundamental of human liberties are lost. Thus, the commandment sought to preserve the integrity of Israel's legal system and it was, at the same time, a guard against encroachments on a person's liberties. The principle is maintained in most modern legal systems; it is evident, e.g., in the taking of an oath before giving evidence in court. But, in the last resort, the commandment points to the essential nature of truthfulness in all interhuman relationships.

(10) The Prohibition of Coveting (Exod. 20:17; Deut. 5:21). The tenth commandment is curious, in its initial context. It prohibits coveting, or desiring, persons or things belonging to a neighbor (i.e., a fellow Israelite). It is curious to find such a commandment in a code of criminal law. The first nine commandments prohibited *acts,* and a criminal act can be followed by prosecution and legal process (if the act is detected). But the tenth commandment, in contrast, prohibits *desires,* or covetous feelings. Under human law, it is not possible to prosecute upon the basis of desire (proof would be impossible!). And yet Hebrew law was more than a human system. There were indeed courts, police officers, judges, and attorneys. But there was also a chief judge, God. The crime involved in the tenth commandment could not be prosecuted within the limitations of the Hebrew system; it was known, nevertheless, by God. The genius of the commandment lies in its therapeutic nature. It is not enough merely to deal with crime once it has been committed; the law must also attempt to attack the roots of crime. The root of almost all evil and crime lies within the self; it lies in the desires of the individual. Thus evil desires are prohibited; if the tenth commandment is fully and profoundly understood, then the significance of the first nine is much better understood. If covetous desires are gradually eliminated, then that natural desire which is rooted within each person may be directed more and more toward God.

The Ten Commandments functioned first as a part of the constitutional law of a nation; in the teaching of Jesus, they became the ethic of the kingdom of God, adding substance and direction to the "first and great commandment," that we love God with the totality of our beings (Matt. 22:37–38). The commandments as such are not the basis of salvation; rather, to those who have found salvation in the gospel of Jesus Christ, they are a guide toward that fullness of life in which love for God is given rich expression.

P. C. Craigie

See also Civil Law and Justice in Bible Times; Law, Biblical Concept of.

Bibliography. W. Harrelson, *The Ten Commandments and Human Rights;* E. Nielsen, *The Ten Commandments in New Perspective;* A. Phillips, *Ancient Israel's Criminal Law: A New Approach to the Decalogue;* J. J. Stamm and M. E. Andrew, *The Ten Commandments in Recent Research.*

Tennant, Frederick Robert (1866–1957). One of the major figures in British theology during the first half of the twentieth century. He began his career as a scientist but was drawn into the issue of the verification of Christianity through the attacks on the faith by Thomas Henry Huxley (1825–95) and others. Tennant was educated at Cambridge and spent his academic career as a Fellow of Trinity College and University Lecturer in the philosophy of religion from 1913 until his retirement in 1938.

Tennant contributed works in theology in the areas of sin and miracles. During the first third of the twentieth century when the prevailing liberal theology did not treat the doctrine of sin in a major way, Tennant produced three works on the subject: *The Origin and Propagation of Sin* (1902), *The Sources of the Doctrine of the Fall and Original Sin* (1903), and *The Concept of Sin* (1912). In 1925 his *Miracle and Its Philosophical Presuppositions* was published. Tennant's *Philosophy of the Sciences* (1932) arose from his Tarner Lectures at Cambridge, a lectureship usually reserved for experts in the philosophy of science. His greatest work was his two-volume *Philosophical Theology* (1928/1930) in which he argued that there is a theistic world view that can be shown to be more reasonable than other interpretations of reality and more congruent with the knowledge by which life and science is guided. His *Nature of Belief* was published in 1943.

Tennant's philosophical and apologetic works were based solidly in the British empirical tradition. He rejected the efforts of rationalism, religious *a priorism,* and revelation to provide the groundwork for belief in God and religious faith. Instead, belief should be constructed in the same general way as are the laws of science. Tennant began with religious experience at its most basic level and then examined psychologically how this experience develops and the new elements added to it. The two most basic notions on which all religion rests are the soul and God. Tennant's argument for God's existence, dependent heavily on natural theology, stemmed from what he called the wider or cosmic teleology. He advanced upon views of the "argument from design" as formulated by William Paley by maintaining that the complexity of life is so great that the appearance of life *in itself* points one beyond the thought that mere chance or blind force alone is at work in the universe. For Tennant, theology is the final link in a chain of belief that begins with interpretations of empirical data. Theistic belief is a continuation of the curve of knowledge constructed by natural science and is built upon the hypotheses of these sciences. Metaphysics and science should not be separated according to Tennant for "science and theism spring from a common root."

Tennant's writings on the doctrine of sin exhibit an attack on the traditional Christian view of original sin as the source of sin and the cause of its universality. He stressed the concept of responsibility. His argument was that any inherited bias toward sin as being prior to one's own volitional choices cannot be sin since one cannot rightly be held responsible for it and thus is not guilty. Sin should be seen only as disobedience to the moral law that the sinner understands at the moment of sinning. For this one can properly be held morally accountable. Tennant rejected as too harsh and unbalanced the description of sin as enmity toward God as well as the Augustinian view of humanity's corrupt moral condition. Rather, sin for Tennant was imperfect compliance with the moral ideal. It occurs when one has made a choice for something of lower ethical worth when one could have chosen for something of higher ethical worth. D. K. McKim

Bibliography. P. A. Bertocci, *The Empirical Argument for God in Late British Theology;* C. D. Broad, "Frederick Robert Tennant, 1866–1957," *PBA* 44; J. O. Buswell, *The Philosophies of F. R. Tennant and John Dewey; Encyclopedia of Philosophy,* VIII, 93–94; B. Ramm, *Varieties of Christian Apologetics;* D. L. Scudder, *Tennant's Philosophical Theology;* N. Smart, "F. R. Tennant and the Problem of Evil," in *Philosophers and Religious Truth.*

Teresa of Ávila (1515–1582). Spanish mystic, born Teresa de Cepeda y Ahumada at Ávila on March 28, 1515. Her stepmother died when Teresa was thirteen years of age. Three years later, upon the marriage of her oldest sister, she was sent to the Augustinian convent in Ávila, but illness forced her to leave. After a prolonged spiritual struggle, accompanied by poor health, she entered the Carmelite Convent of the Incarnation at Ávila on November 2, 1535. Here she was treated with deference because of her personality and family status. However, in 1555, her spiritual pilgrimage took a more serious turn. This second conversion, as it is sometimes called, was marked by "mental prayer" and ecstatic visions. Some of her spiritual advisors thought her visions were diabolical, but others reassured her that they were, indeed, from the Lord. She found support from the Jesuits, particularly her father confessor, Baltasar Álvarez. In 1559, Teresa reported a remarkable vision known as the "transverberation of her heart," in which an angel with a fire-tipped lance pierced her heart. Growing increasingly disillusioned with her own Carmelite order, Teresa felt compelled to launch a reform movement with Carmelite nuns who would follow an austere rule. Her plans met with stiff resistance from a number of sources, including the city of Ávila. However, wealthy friends offered their support. In spite of stout opposition, Teresa sought and found approval from Pope Paul IV. Her convent was to be small, numbering no more than thirteen, following the rule prepared by Fray Hugo in 1248. Thus on August 24, 1562, the resolute nun founded the convent of Discalced ("barefoot") Carmelite Nuns of the Primitive Rule of St. Joseph. After a visit by the General of the Carmelites, she was encouraged in her work and given permission to form other houses of the Discalced Carmelites, not only for nuns, but for monks also. With the backing of Philip II, she managed to escape the Inquisition, and spent the remainder of her life establishing new convents all over Spain.

Teresa was a remarkable person, combining mystic contemplation and a fervent activism with a literary career. She wrote two autobiographical works, the *Life* and the *Book of Foundations.* Two were written for her nuns: *The Way of Perfection* and *The Interior Castle.* It was her conviction that contemplation should lead to action, not lethargy. In spite of a frail body, beset by continuing bouts of illness, she became the personification of this conviction. Teresa was canonized by Gregory XV in 1622.

W. R. Estep, Jr.

See also Mysticism.

Bibliography. E. A. Peers, *Handbook to the Life and Times of St. Teresa and St. John of the Cross;* "Teresa of Jesus, Saint," *Catholic Encyclopedia,* XIV.

Terminism. The doctrine that God has eternally determined a time limit (*terminus*) in the life of the individual after which he no longer wills the conversion and salvation of that person. After that time the individual may no longer repent and come to faith. Terminism was a doctrine of some pietists and therefore went along with the idea of human free will in spiritual matters.

The difference between strict terminism and other doctrines is that the time limit is set by God, not by the individual's hardening his own heart. Terminism is also not a matter of the sin against the Holy Ghost. Different theologians may have combined these elements with terminism in varying ways. Pietism in general was not characterized by a high degree of doctrinal unanimity.

As expressed by the pietist J. C. Boese (d. 1700), terminism led to a controversy between the pietists and the orthodox Lutherans in the late seventeenth and early eighteenth centuries. Terminism is best considered a peculiar point of historic pietism, though a similar idea has been held by some Quakers.

In the history of philosophy, terminism is sometimes used to refer to nominalism.

J. M. Drickamer

See also Pietism.

Territorialism. The claim that the ruler of a country has a natural right to fix the type of state church and to control the ecclesiastical affairs of his people. It is based on the theories of Hugo Grotius (1583–1645) and Christian Thomasius (1655–1725), and rests on the idea that the state has its origins in the natural right of the people to form a society and then to form a church in that society. Thus the state being primary in idea and time has power over the church, a power usually exercised through its ruler.

In practice territorialism means much the same as the earlier principle of *cuius regio, eius religio* ("in the prince's country, the prince's religion"), which was adopted as the formula of the Peace of Augsburg in 1555. However, it is best to compare and contrast it with collegialism, with which it shares common ideas. The differences lie in the degree of power of the state over the church; territorialism draws the lines wider than does collegialism. This kind of thinking was important in Europe from the seventeenth to the nineteenth centuries.

P. Toon

See also Collegialism.

Tertullian (*ca.* 155–220). An early Latin father of the church. He was born Quintus Septimus Florens Tertullianus at Carthage in modern Tunisia. The son of pagan parents, he was sent to

Rome to study law. There he was converted to Christianity and rejected his licentious mode of life. Returning to Carthage, he gave himself passionately to the propagation and defense of the gospel. Ultimately disenchanted with the laxity of the Roman Church, he broke away and espoused the rigorous asceticism and enthusiasm of Montanism.

A man of vast erudition, he employed the classical rhetorical arts and freely cited Greek and Latin authors, although he disclaimed a reliance on Greek philosophy. Increasingly he wrote in the Latin vernacular and became the first great Latin church father. He set the concepts of Scripture in new language, and much of his terminology became normative in the theological discussions of the Western church. He was peculiarly apt at pithy sayings, the most famous of which is, "The blood of Christians is the seed of the church." It was Tertullian who coined the term "Trinity." His postulation that the Godhead was "one substance consisting in three persons" helped spare the West much of the bitter Christological controversy that raged in the Eastern church.

His view of original sin was also to influence Western theology profoundly. Probably because of his early Stoic training, Tertullian held that the soul was actually material and that both body and soul were procreated simultaneously by an individual's parents. The inclination to sin was thus transmitted from Adam to successive generations of progeny.

There are thirty-odd extant treatises by Tertullian. His *Apology*, addressed to Roman magistrates, defends Christians against slanderous charges and demands for them the same due process of law afforded to other citizens of the empire. Other works deal with practical aspects of Christian living, vindications of Montanism, the failings of early Catholicism, and polemic arguments against the heathen and heretics. These latter writings contained powerful and innovative expressions of Christian dogma that came to be regarded as definitive for orthodoxy. His *Against Praxeas* was famed in particular for its affirmation that Jesus Christ had two natures joined in one person.

R. C. Kroeger and C. C. Kroeger

See also Montanism.

Bibliography. T. D. Barnes, *Tertullian: A Historical and Literary Study;* G. L. Bray, *Holiness and the Will of God: Perspectives on the Theology of Tertullian;* J. Morgan, *The Importance of Tertullian in the Development of Christian Dogma;* R. A. Norris, Jr., *God and World in Early Christian Thought;* R. E. Roberts, *The Theology of Tertullian;* C. de L. Shoritt, *The Influence of Philosophy on the Mind of Tertullian;* J. Quasten, *Patrology*, II, 246–319; B. B. Warfield, *Studies in Tertullian and Augustine; ANF*, III, IV.

Testament. The biblical term derived from the Latin *testamentum.* It was used in Jerome's Vulgate to render the Hebrew *bĕrît*, "covenant," in a few instances, as in Num. 14:44, and the Greek *diathēkē*, as in II Cor. 3:14. Since Tertullian's time it has been used to designate the two main divisions of Holy Scripture—the Old Testament and the New. This represents the literary use of the word.

As used in biblical theology, the term may denote the era from the arrangement given through Moses (Exod. 19:5–8; Jer. 31:32; Heb. 8:9) to the death of Christ. This is the old testament, or covenant, in contrast to the new, which began legally with the death of Christ, as may be inferred from Luke 22:20 and I Cor. 11:25.

The AV uses the term "testament" as well as "covenant" for the Hebrew and Greek originals *bĕrît* and *diathēkē*, but the ASV uses the word "covenant" regularly, apart from the exceptional use of "testament" in Heb. 9:16–17. The Roman testament, in order to go into effect, required "the death of the testator" (see above), but this was not necessarily so in Semitic practice, as is illustrated in the parable of the prodigal son and elsewhere.

The old testament or covenant had its tabernacle or temple and its ceremonial and civil laws, but when the death of Jesus introduced the new testament or covenant, these provisions of the old order became antiquated and were "nigh unto vanishing away." In fact, in A.D. 70 the temple did vanish away with the destruction of Jerusalem. Meanwhile, the moral law of the Ten Commandments, written in the old testament "in tables of stone" (see below), but in the new testament "in fleshly tables of the heart" (II Cor. 3:3; cf. vs. 6), still stands and abides.

M. J. Wyngaarden

See also Covenant.

Bibliography. L. Berkhof, *Systematic Theology;* L. S. Chafer, *Systematic Theology;* G. Vos, *Biblical Theology;* M. J. Wyngaarden, *The Future of the Kingdom.*

Testimonium Spiritus Sancti Internum. *See* Internal Testimony of the Holy Spirit.

Testimony. *See* Witness, Witnessing.

Tetragrammaton. The designation for the four (*tetra*) letters (*grammata*) in the Hebrew Bible for the name of the God of Israel, *yhwh.* The name was God's particular revelation to Moses and the Israelites (Exod. 6:2–3). It signifies that the God of Israel, unlike pagan deities, is present with his people to deliver them, to fulfill his promises to them, and to grant them his blessings. The pronunciation of the tetragrammaton *yhwh* was lost when the Jews avoided its usage for fear of desecrating the holy name (cf. Exod. 20:7). In OT times the name was pronounced and was at times used in theophoric names, which can be recognized in our Bibles by the prefixes Jo- or Jeho- (cf. *Jo*nathan and *Jeho*iada) and the suffix -jah (Adoni*jah*). The pronunciation fell into disuse after the Exile when the Jews began to pay careful attention to the practice of the law. The translators of the Septuagint consistently avoided the name and substituted the title *Kyrios* ("Lord"). This reflects the Jewish practice of reading *Adonai* (Heb. *'ădōnāy*) "Lord" for *yhwh* or reading *Elohim* (Heb. *'ĕlōhîm*) in place of the Hebrew compound *yhwh 'ădōnāy* to avoid the duplication of *'ădōnāy*. The vowels of *'ădōnāy* (*ă-ō-ā*) were placed under the tetragrammaton to remind the reader that he was not to pronounce *yhwh* but instead was to read the word as *'ădōnāy*. Christians who were unaware of this substitution read the vowels as if they actually belonged to *yhwh*, which resulted in the English form "YeHoWaH" or "JeHoVaH" (the *ă* of *'ădōnāy* having been reduced to *ĕ* under the *y* of *yhwh*). The ASV of 1901 adopted the practice of using the name "Jehovah," whereas most English versions continued the established practice of translating the tetragrammaton by LORD (capital letters) to distinguish it from "Lord" (*Adonai*). Many scholars accept the widely held opinion that the tetragrammaton is a form of the root *hyh* ("be") and should be pronounced as "Yahweh" ("He who brings into being"; cf. Exod. 3:12, "I will be with you" and "I will be who I will be," vs. 14). Regardless of the editorial decision of substituting LORD for *yhwh* or of using the divine name "Yahweh," the reader must keep in mind that LORD, Yahweh, or *yhwh* is the *name* of God that he revealed to his ancient people. In reading the text of the OT, one should develop a feeling for the usage of the name itself over against such usages as "God" or "Lord" (Exod. 3:15; 6:3; Pss. 102:16, 22; 113:1–3; 135:1–6; 148:5, 13). The Messiah has a name, Jesus, so the God of the OT has revealed himself by a name *yhwh* and a blessing is lost when no attention is paid to the difference in usage of a title and the actual name of the God of Israel.

> Let them praise the name of the LORD,
> for his name alone is exalted;
> his splendor is above the earth and the heavens.

W. A. VAN GEMEREN

See also GOD, NAMES OF.

Tetrapolitan Confession (1530). A conciliatory gesture, the confession was composed during the Diet of Augsburg by Martin Bucer and Wolfgang Capito. Both men sought to effect a conclusion to the bitter animosities between Lutheranism and Zwinglianism. Bucer, originally drawn powerfully to Luther's teachings, later moved toward Zwingli's position emphasizing the crucial work of the Holy Spirit to guide the believer into truth; also, he came to embrace a more symbolic interpretation of the Lord's Supper: the humanity of Christ is in heaven, but the sacrament remains nonetheless a means of grace. At the Diet of Augsburg (1530), Capito, who shared a tolerance toward the left-wing reformers, joined Bucer in penning the confession on behalf of the four southern German cities Strasbourg, Constance, Memmingen, and Lindau (i.e., four cities = tetrapolitan), not represented at the Diet of Augsburg.

The confession's structure parallels the twenty-three chapters of the Augsburg Confession, but it attempts to provide a compromise treatment of the Lord's Supper (ch. 18) that might hold the Lutheran and Reformed sacramental theories in working tension. As a theological formula it failed in its attempts to gain a Protestant and evangelical union. P. A. MICKEY

See also BUCER, MARTIN; CAPITO, WOLFGANG FABRICIUS; CONFESSIONS OF FAITH.

Bibliography. D. Steinmetz, *Reformers in the Wings;* P. Schaff, *The Creeds of Christendom,* I, 526–29.

Thank Offering. *See* OFFERINGS AND SACRIFICES IN BIBLE TIMES.

Theism. Literally, belief in the existence of God. Though the concept seems to be as old as philosophy, the term itself appears to be of relatively recent origin. Some have suggested that it appeared in the seventeenth century in England to take the place of such words as "deism" and "deistic" when referring to belief in God. "Theism" is often used as the opposite of "atheism," the term for denial of the existence of God, and distinguishes a theist from an atheist or agnostic without attempting any technical philosophical or theological connection. The term is also used as a label for religious believers, though again, there is no attempt to imply a particular theological or philosophical position. Finally, the term is used to denote certain philosophical or theological positions, regardless of whether this involves a religious relationship to the God of whom individuals speak.

God as Ultimate Reference Point. In its broadest sense theism denotes a belief in some ultimate reference point that gives meaning and unity to everything. However, the God postulated in this sense is totally depersonalized and thoroughly transcendent, almost an abstract concept. There are philosophical and theological positions that seem to use "God" and "theism" in this way.

(1) Paul Tillich's concept of theism is that God is whatever becomes a matter of ultimate concern, something that determines our being or nonbeing. Consequently, God is identified by Tillich as the ground of all being, or being-itself. While being-itself is certainly objective and not a mere creation of the mind, Tillich's God is totally depersonalized and abstract. This is demonstrated by Tillich's claim that the only nonsymbolic statement one can make about God is that he is being-itself or the ground of being. All words traditionally used to denote the attributes of God are entirely symbolic.

(2) This broad sense of theism is also found in Hegel, who actually has several concepts of God, but at least one that fits this category. In Hegel's thought, one concept is that God is equivalent to the infinite. Philosophy, he says, rises to divinity or a divine viewpoint. Here "God" seems to be equivalent to transcendent, all-encompassing thought, but is not a personal God.

God as Immanent. A narrower concept of theism sees God also as depersonalized and as the ultimate reference point, but gives God some kind of concrete manifestation. Nevertheless, the God of such theistic views is entirely immanent.

One example is *pantheism,* the view that everything is God. The most famous philosophical form is that of Spinoza, who held there is only one substance in the universe—God. Consequently, everything is merely a mode of that one substance. Such a God is not abstract but immanent.

By contrast, the biblical concept speaks of God as infinite, meaning, among other things, that God has being to an infinite *degree,* but not to an infinite *amount,* a view that is qualitative but not quantitative being. Scripture further teaches that God is everywhere simultaneously (immensity) and is present at every spatial location in the totality of his being (omnipresence), i.e., God is present *at* but not *as* every point in space.

The broad difference between the pantheistic and biblical concepts on these matters is that the pantheist thinks God is present, not only *at* every point in space, but *as* every point. Furthermore, pantheism denies omnipresence, since the totality of God's being is present in no one place.

Another example of this concept is *process theism,* based on the process metaphysics of Alfred North Whitehead (*Process and Reality*), sometimes known as bipolar or dipolar theism. Some of the better-known process theologians are Charles Hartshorne, Schubert Ogden, John Cobb, and David Griffin. According to this school, there are in God two poles: a primordial, eternal, potential pole, and a temporal, consequent, actual pole. In addition, there are certain eternal objects that may ingress into the world to become actual entities. Such eternal objects are pure potentials, and, as such, cannot order and relate themselves as actual entities can. To order these eternal entities some nontemporal actual entity is needed, and this is God in his primordial nature. Here God is like a backstage director who lines up the forms, getting them ready to ingress onto the stage of the temporal world. However, God's primordial nature should not be seen as distinct from the order of eternal objects; which means the order is his primordial nature. Consequently, God is not a creator before creation, but with it in its concrescence at its very beginning. In his primordial pole, God is the principle of concretion; and this entirely depersonalizes God and makes him finite.

The same is true for God in his actual pole. According to bipolar theism, every actual entity (and God is perceived as such) needs a physical pole to complete the "vision" of its potential pole. The consequent nature of God, then, refers to all the entities in being in the temporal order. Given such a view, God can change and develop as his temporal pole does, and he is clearly finite. Moreover, God in his actual pole can perish, since all actual things can perish. In such a concept God is not the creator of the world, but rather the director of a world process. He is interdependent in the sense of being mutually dependent. Moreover, he does not have all perfections eternally and concurrently, but attains them successively and endlessly.

A final example of this form of theism is found in Hegel's conception of God as Spirit. This notion of Spirit does not allow God to be a person in the Judeo-Christian sense, but sees him as a force, or general consciousness, uniting all finite consciousnesses. In other words, he is not just all finite consciousnesses taken together, but rather the force that underlies and unites all intersubjectivity. Such a God is clearly immanent and not personal.

God as Personal. A third sense of theism is that God is not an abstract concept nor even a concrete manifestation of some depersonalized idea. In this sense, the concept of God does take on personhood, though this is not to suggest that in all forms of this view God has interactions with persons. Despite the fact that such a God is an individual object (rather than a compilation of objects), he is not the equivalent of the Judeo-Christian concept. Normally, such a concept of God sees him in some way as finite. Two examples will illustrate this sense of theism.

(1) Polytheism, of which the best known is perhaps the Greco-Roman pantheon of gods. Here there is a multiplicity of gods, each representing and personifying some aspect of life or of the created universe. In spite of the fact that each god may represent only one quality of life (love, war, etc.), each is perceived as a person. As such, the gods are perceived as separate from, but participating in, the world and interacting with men and with one another. In fact, the gods were perceived as having many of the foibles and failings of human beings. Such polytheistic perceptions of God view him as personal, but definitely finite. Such concepts are not equivalent to the Judeo-Christian notion of God.

(2) There is also deism. According to this view, God is an individual being (personal in that sense), but one who does not interact with the world. He initially created the world, but since then has withdrawn himself from it (impersonal in that sense). He does not act in the world or sustain it, but remains thoroughly transcendent from it. There is a sense in which such a view renders God's existence inconsequential and certainly not equivalent to the Judeo-Christian conception.

God as Personal Creator and Sustainer. A final perception is of God as creator and sustainer of the universe. He is infinite in attributes, and he is the only God. This monotheistic concept of God is held within the Judeo-Christian tradition, and there are three ways in particular that have appeared.

(1) *Theonomy.* According to this view, God is the law in the universe, and in particular, his will is law. Whatever rules of ethics, epistemology, etc., there are result from what God wills and could be otherwise if he so chose. No action in the universe is intrinsically good or evil or better or worse, but has its value in regard to the value God places upon it. The necessary rules are known through divine revelation rather than reason.

(2) *Rationalism.* This school of thought is represented by the work of Leibniz. According to his system, all the laws of logic, ethics, and the like are necessary laws in the universe and are so in virtue of the principle of sufficient reason in accord with which everything must happen. In such a system God must create a world, and he must create the best of all possible worlds (for Leibniz, the best world is intelligible). The circumstances in such a universe are discernible by the light of pure reason unaided by revelation. If in theonomy the concept of God is prior to logic, in rationalism logic is prior to theology.

(3) *Modified Rationalism.* There is a mediating position which, like theonomy, does not claim that everything is discernible by reason alone, nor that what is discernible is an expression of some necessary law. Modified rationalism does not demand that God create a world, but asserts that creating a world is something fitting for God to do. For a modified rationalist, there is no best possible world, only good and evil worlds. Modified rationalism differs from theonomy in that it claims that certain things are intrinsically good and intrinsically evil, apart from what God says about them. In such a universe, things are as they are according to reason, and in many cases one can discern why something is the case and what the case is by means of reason, though some things can be known only by revelation, a view historically typical of Judeo-Christian theologies.

Conclusion. More needs to be said about theism as a philosophy, especially about certain questions traditionally attached to the philosophy of theism. For example, in speculating on theism, one of the questions that arises is about the relation of human language to God, i.e., How is human language (with its reference to finite beings) predicable of an infinite being? Another question deals with whether it is possible to demonstrate rationally, or at least to justify rationally, belief in God's existence. Philosophers of religion also ask whether a particular mode of experience is specifically religious. Likewise, they ask about the relation of the providence and sovereignty of God to the freedom and responsibility of man. Finally, there is the question about the internal consistency of theological systems that hold to the existence of an all-powerful, all-loving God along with the presence of evil in the world. Though many philosophers and theologians in our century (Barthians, existentialists, logical empiricists, e.g.), and at other times, have argued that it is impossible to give a rational justification of theism, nonetheless, many are ready to answer to the contrary.

J. S. Feinberg

See also Deism; God, Arguments for the Existence of; God, Attributes of; God, Doctrine of; Panentheism; Pantheism; Polytheism.

Bibliography. A. M. Farrar, *Finite and Infinite;* É. Gilson, *God and Philosophy;* J. Maritain, *The Range of Reason;* E. L. Mascall, *Existence and Analogy;* S. Ogden, *The Reality of God and Other Essays;* W. Reese and E. Freeman, *Process and Divinity;* B. Spinoza, *Ethics;* P. Tillich, *Systematic Theology.*

Theistic Evolution. *See* Evolution.

Theocracy. Derived from the Greek *theos,* "God," and from *kratein,* "to rule," the word denotes the rule of God. Josephus apparently coined the word, according to Thackeray, and gave it a political connotation (*Against Apion* II, 165). But the idea goes back to the OT (Exod. 19:4–9; Deut. 33:4–5). The law of the king (Deut. 17:14–20) recognizes the ultimate control of the Lord God. Saul's trend was antitheocratic, but David's was theocratic, and to him was given the promise of the great Son of David (II Sam. 7:13–16).

Although the political sense is essential to the word "theocracy," as coined by Josephus, a broader meaning is usually implied, to include every sphere and relationship of life as governed in OT times by the contemporaneous and continuing special revelation of God. The human agencies provided to enable Israel to carry out Jehovah's will included, not only kings, but also a succession of prophets, culminating in the great prophet like Moses (Deut. 18:14–15). Priests and Levites were also included, to whom God gave the duties of presenting the typically redemptive sacrificial blood to the Lord, pointing forward to the blood of Christ, and the duty of teaching the people the moral law, the statutes, the judgments, the sacred history, prophecy, and poetry of the OT (Lev. 10:8–11; Deut. 31:9–11).

M. J. Wyngaarden

Bibliography. M. G. Kyle, *The Problem of the Pentateuch;* M. J. Wyngaarden, *The Future of the Kingdom.*

Theodicy. From *theos,* "God," and *dikē,* "justice"; a term used to refer to attempts to justify the ways of God to man. A successful theodicy resolves the problem of evil for a theological system and demonstrates that God is all-powerful, all-loving, and just, despite evil's existence.

Nature of Theodicies. Six basic points are relevant to the nature of a theodicy.

(1) A theodicy is a response to a problem of the logical consistency of a theological position. Most attacks on theistic systems charge that their key theological claims, e.g., God is omnipotent, God is all-loving, and evil exists in a world created by God, taken together are self-contradictory. The theodicist's task is to structure an answer which demonstrates that these propositions taken together are logically consistent. It should be noted that the theodicist is required to demonstrate only that there is no contradiction in his own theological position given his own views of God and evil. It is irrelevant if the critic objects on the grounds that the theodicy incorporates intellectual commitments about God and evil that he does not accept, for the theodicist needs only to demonstrate that his theology squares with itself. This means also that the theodocist must not structure a defense of God incorporating propositions that produce internal inconsistency.

(2) A successful theodicy must be relevant to the problem of evil it addresses, and there are many variations: moral evil, physical evil, the problem of an individual's relation to God in view of experiencing specific evil, as well as problems of the degree and intensity of evil. The theodicist must construct a system relevant to the problem of evil confronting him. One cannot, e.g., answer the problem of natural evil by an appeal to the free will of human beings. Free human action is irrelevant to the occurrence of earthquakes and droughts. On the other hand, free human action is relevant to the problem of moral evil, a problem about evil produced at the hands of moral agents.

(3) A theodicy must be relevant to the specific theology it addresses, and not all theologies, even within the sphere of orthodox Christian theism, hold identical positions concerning God and evil. Each theological position incorporates a particular concept of divine benevolence, divine power, the nature of evil, and the nature of free human action. The theodicist must construct a defense of God's ways as they are portrayed in his theological system. The free will defense, e.g., is an inappropriate answer to the problem of moral evil that faces a Calvinistic theology, since the notion of freedom involved in the free will defense (incompatibilism) contradicts the notion of freedom involved in a Calvinistic system (compatibilism).

(4) The problem of evil in its various forms is always a problem of logical consistency, and as such is intellectually interesting only for theologies that incorporate a notion of God's omnipotence according to which he may do any logically consistent thing. If one holds, e.g., that God can do anything whatsoever, even actualize contradictions, then there is no sense in talking about the logical consistency. Most, if not all, theodicies are structured for theological positions that interpret God's omnipotence as the ability to do the logically consistent.

(5) Most theodicies (and systems of ethics in general) adopt a particular axiom with regard to moral agency and moral blameworthiness; viz., that a person is not morally responsible for that which he cannot do or which he does under constraint or compulsion.

(6) The pattern of most theodicies is indicated by the preceding principles. They attempt to resolve the apparent contradiction by arguing that God, in spite of his omnipotence, cannot remove

evil. Since he cannot remove evil, he is not morally responsible for its presence in the world. Such an argument rests on the concept of God's omnipotence according to which God can do only the logically consistent. The strategy is to specify something that God does accomplish—a value of the first order—which he could not do if he were to remove evil. The free will defender argues, e.g., that God cannot accomplish two ends simultaneously—give man free will *and* remove evil—without contradicting his intentions to do one or the other. Since God cannot do both simultaneously, he is not guilty of the evil present in the world, for no moral agent is guilty for failing to do that which he could not do.

Views of Theodicy. Several interesting theodicies have been offered by well-known thinkers for the moral problem of evil.

Gottfried Leibniz's theodicy was structured for his extreme rationalistic theological system. Accordingly, there are not only reasons that God does whatever he does, but such reasons are necessary laws. These reasons are discernible by the light of pure reason unaided by revelation. Moreover, for Leibniz, God is the only metaphysically necessary being. There are an infinite number of contingent finite possible worlds God could actualize, but there is only one that is the best possible world. God is obligated to create the best. In addition to this metaphysic, Leibniz's system has its own concept of ethics: "good" and "evil" are *pros hen* equivocal terms whose primary sense is a metaphysical one. All other senses of "good" and "evil" relate to this primary one. Metaphysical evil is finitude or lack of being, and metaphysical good is plenitude of being. Moral goodness in God consists therefore in willing the best, metaphysically speaking. For such a theological system the problem of evil arises as follows: If it can be shown that God has willed less than the best world, metaphysically speaking, then God is shown not to be a good God. However, if it can be shown that God has willed the best metaphysically, then he is morally praiseworthy, despite the presence of moral and physical evil in the world. In response, Leibniz argues that God always operates on the basis of sufficient reason, i.e., God will not do something without a sufficient reason (discernible by pure reason). In the case of actualizing a world, the reason for choosing one over another is that it is best. Leibniz's system demands that there be a best possible world. Moreover, God, the supremely rational being, knows what that world is, and being all-powerful, he can actualize it. Since he is all-good, he is inclined to do so, and in fact has actualized the best of all possible worlds. Of course, the metaphysically richest world must contain the greatest number and variety of beings, but that means that a world with moral and physical good and evil is richer metaphysically than a world with only moral and physical good. Thus, since God is obligated to create the best, and since Leibniz explains that he has, we can see that the best of all possible worlds, metaphysically speaking, must contain moral and physical evil. If God had refused to create such a world, however, he would be morally reprehensible, for his supreme moral obligation is to create the best world. The existence of moral and physical evil in the world God actualized is justified, then, and God is shown to be just, omnipotent, and omnibenevolent.

Given the basic tenets of this system, Leibniz does not contradict himself with his theodicy. Consequently, he has solved his problem of evil, a problem of internal consistency. One may reject his theodicy and his theology, but not on grounds that it fails to remove the alleged contradiction.

Other well-known theodicies rest upon a modified rationalistic theology. Such a metaphysic lies behind the free will defense, the basic theodicy in the Augustinian tradition of theodicy; and also behind the soul-building theodicy, the basic theodicy in the Irenaean tradition. There are four basic points here. (1) In a modified rationalist's universe, God is not obligated to create any world, for his own existence is the supreme good. (2) Creating a world is a fitting thing for God to do, but not the only fitting thing for him to do. Whatever he chooses to do is done on the basis of reason, but such reasons are not necessary laws in this universe. (3) There is an infinite number of finite contingent possible worlds. Some by their very nature are inherently evil, so God could not create them. However, there is more than one good possible world which God could have created. There is no such thing as a best possible world. (4) God was free with respect to whether or not he should create and with respect to which of the good possible worlds he would create, if he chose to create. For such a theological position, the problem of evil arises as follows: Is the contingent possible world that God created one of the good possible worlds (despite the evil in it)? The modified rationalist theologian must specify a reason that this world is one of those good possible worlds.

There is a basic ethic behind modified rationalistic theologies. The notion of evil and good presupposed by a free will defense is some form of nonconsequentialism, i.e., good and evil are not determined on the basis of the consequences of the act. In regard to the problem of evil, this means that the world as created from the hand of God must not contain any evil and that evil in the world has been introduced by the actions of agents whom God created. Soul-building theodicies follow a consequentialist account of ethics in which the good or evil of an act is determined by its results. The world as created from the hand of God did contain evil, but that causes no stain on God, since he will ultimately use evil to bring good.

The theodicist using the free will defense begins by pointing out that God is not the cause of evil in the world; the abuse of human free will is. Then, the question is whether God is not guilty for giving man free will when he knew that man could abuse it to commit evil. The answer is no. Free will is a value of the highest order, which God should have given. However, God is not the one who uses such free will to commit evil; man does, so man is responsible for evil. Moreover, God is still good for giving man something which he could, and in fact did, abuse because a world in which there are significantly free beings (even though they produce evil) is a far better world than one that contains no evil but is populated by automatons. In other words, God cannot both create significantly free beings *and* make it the case that they always freely do good. On the free will defender's account of free human action, if God makes it the case that man does anything, man cannot do it *freely*. Genuine free will, then, involves evil, but God is justified in what he did, for free will is a good that far overbalances any evil produced by the use of such a will.

Note that (1) if the free will defender is granted his concepts of God, evil, and free human action (and he must be, given the nature of a problem of evil), he can answer his problem of evil. His system is internally consistent. He has proved that this world is one of those good possible worlds God could have created. (2) The theodicy follows the basic strategy outlined previously. The free will defender holds to divine omnipotence, but argues that it means God can do whatever is logically consistent. The free will defender then argues that God was faced with two choices, neither of which could be actualized simultaneously with the other. God had the choice of either making man free or removing evil. He chose the former, and the good produced by such a choice far overbalances the evil man can and does produce with free will. However, God is not guilty for evil that remains in the world, for, having given man free will, God cannot remove that evil, and no one is guilty for failing to do what he could not do.

Soul-building theodicy also rests on a modified rationalist theology, but it incorporates a consequentialist ethic. The most noteworthy form of this view in recent years is that of John Hick, who begins by suggesting that God's intent in creating man was not to create a perfect creature, but rather to create a being in need of moral development. God intended for man's time on earth to be spent in building his moral and spiritual character in preparation for his participation in the kingdom of God. Hick asks, What sort of environment would be most conducive to soul-building? Would a world in which no evil ever confronts man be better for developing character, or would man be more likely to develop spiritually if he lived in a world where he would be confronted by problems and evil? Hick argues that the answer is obviously the latter. If God wants to use the world to build souls, he cannot place man in an Edenic paradise where nothing ever goes wrong. Consequently, there is evil in the world, but God is not to be blamed for it, since he intends to use it to build souls and ultimately develop men to a point where they are ready for the kingdom of God. Hick recognizes that if God's purpose with the world is to build souls, many will argue he has severely failed. Evil in the world often turns people away from God rather than encouraging them to grow spiritually. Therefore, it does not seem that the evil in the world accomplishes its purpose, and God must be guilty for creating such a world. Hick answers that though it seems that souls are not being built, God will nonetheless see to it that everyone ultimately makes it to the kingdom of God. No soul will finally go unbuilt; no evil will prove to be unjustified or unjustifiable.

Note first that if we allow—as we must—Hick's concepts of God and evil he can answer the problem of evil that confronts his theology. Some may not accept his theology as a whole, but he has shown a way to render it internally consistent. He has proved that this is one of the good possible worlds God could have created. Second, as in the preceding examples, Hick's theodicy follows the basic strategy outlined. God was faced with two choices, neither of which could be actualized simultaneously with the other. God could remove evil from the world, but then he would not be able to build the souls of his creatures; or he could build the souls of his creatures, but then he would have to include evil in the world, for that is the way to build souls. Building souls and preparing them for the kingdom of God is a value of the first order which makes it worth the evil present in the world. However, God cannot be guilty for not removing evil, for he could not both build souls and remove evil, and no one is guilty for failing to do that which he could not.

Value of Theodicy. *Apologetics.* An initial value of theodicies is that many answer the problems of evil that face the theologies for which they are constructed. Most rejections of theodicies tend to be on grounds external to the theological system, i.e., the critic refuses to adopt the intellectual commitments of the system. Such a rejection is not made on the grounds of a problem of evil, for that is always a problem of the internal consistency of a system. The theodicies presented above render their theologies internally consistent and thereby solve their problem of evil. As a result, atheists are mistaken who claim that all theistic positions are hopelessly irrational because self-contradictory on this matter. Moreover, their claims that no theist can solve his problem of evil are contradicted by the fact that many theists can do so. The ways of God are defensible, and they are defensible in such a way that no theist should have to give in to the charge of irrationality due to a problem of evil.

Intellectual Clarity. The one who structures a theodicy must be clear about the intellectual commitments his theology entails. Each theology incorporates particular views on God, evil, and free human action. It is valuable for the theologian to understand that he works within the broad stream of Christian theism, even though his views are not necessarily identical to every other Christian theist's.

Human Creativity. The former benefit leads to another. Obviously, there is only one God, but there are many theologies and theodicies about that God. One of the values of theodicy making is that it helps the theologian recognize that his system is just one way of perceiving the nature of God and the world. Insofar as his views square with reality, his theology is correct; nonetheless, it is still a human construct. Consequently, when someone rejects a theology or theodicy, he is not actually rejecting God (unless the theology and theodicy accurately portray God), but rather a human construction about the nature of God and the world.

Internal Consistency. Since the intent in writing a theodicy is to avoid self-contradiction, the theist strives to remove any potential or actual contradictions in his system. Many theologians, nonetheless, seem to do only fragments of theology, and they wind up holding views in one area that contradict views in another. Theodicy making reminds the theologian that he must think holistically and synthetically as well as analytically; and he must seek to avoid creating a theological position that contains contradictions.

J. S. Feinberg

See also Evil, Problem of; Pain.

Bibliography. M. B. Ahern, *The Problem of Evil;* J. S. Feinberg, *Theologies and Evil;* P. T. Geach, *Providence and Evil;* J. Hick, *Evil and the God of Love;* G. W. Leibniz, *Theodicy,* tr. E. M. Huggard; J. L. Mackie, "Evil and Omnipotence," in *Philosophy of Religion,* ed. B. Mitchell; E. Madden and P. Hare, *Evil and the Concept of God;* M. Peterson, *Evil and the Christian God;* A. Plantinga, *God, Freedom, and Evil.*

Theologia Crucis ("Theology of the Cross"). Martin Luther's most profound contribution to theological thought. Five months after he nailed the ninety-five theses to the door of the Castle Church at Wittenberg, Luther formulated the *theologia crucis.* Standing in opposition to the theology of glory, the theology of the cross is best understood in concert with the *Deus Absconditus* ("the hidden God") and the *Deus Revelatus* ("the revealed God").

Before the fall (*lapsus*) man was capable of knowing God directly or immediately. He was the *Deus Revelatus* who communed with man in the cool of Eden's garden. The consequence of man's fall into sin included much more than personal death and moral deterioration; it also changed man's ability to know and commune with the Creator. The revealed God became the hidden God (*Deus Absconditus*). The only way the shattered fellowship could be restored was by means of redemption. Throughout the OT period, in spite of miraculous interventions, military conquests, magnificent temples, and elaborate palaces, the only place God met with his people was at the mercy seat (*"There* will I meet with you," Exod. 25:22), the place of sacrifice and redemption. God's consummate meeting place was unveiled at the cross of Christ. God is known and understood, not in strength, but in weakness, not in an awesome display of majesty and power, but in the exhibition of a love willing to suffer in order to win man back to itself.

Unfortunately modern man is determined to know God as the Revealed One. The heathen sees God's power in the created cosmos, but is led from one degree of idolatry to another. The civilized religionist thinks he finds God in displays of pageantry and expressions of personal moral accomplishment. All are tragically in error. God is ever and only known to man at the cross. With great insight Luther expostulated: *Solus praedica Sapientium crucis.* "This one thing preach, the wisdom of the Cross."

F. R. Harm

See also Luther, Martin; Theologia Gloriae.

Bibliography. P. Althaus, *The Theology of Martin Luther;* W. von Loewenich, *Luther's Theology of the Cross; The Encyclopedia of the Lutheran Church,* I, 641; G. Wuensch, *Luther und der Gegenwart.*

Theologia Gloriae ("Theology of Glory"). One of Martin Luther's many theological insights, the theology of glory is the antithesis of the theology of the cross. So strongly did Luther feel about the distinction between these theologies that he stated unequivocally that only those who hold to and teach the theology of the cross deserve to be called theologians.

The theology of glory comes to know God by means of his works. Natural theology and speculative metaphysics fit into this category, as does the triumphalistic view expressed by some modern-day charismatics who see God revealing himself in dramatic interventions (visions, miracles, healings, etc.), and the Christian life as one that is lived on a constant spiritual "high." With this view, proponents of the theology of the cross resoundingly disagree. God wishes to be known and revered on the basis of another principle. The theology of glory feels that it knows God immediately through his expressions of divine power, wisdom, and glory; whereas the theology of the cross recognizes him in the very place at which he has hidden himself—the cross and its suffering, all of which is esteemed to be weakness and foolishness by the theology of glory.

The potential danger that the theology of the cross sees in its antithesis is that the theology of glory will lead to a form of moralistic works righteousness, a propensity to strike a bargain with God on the basis of personal achievement. The theology of the cross repudiates man's own accomplishments and permits God to do everything to effect and preserve his salvation. Such theology redirects from moralistic activism to genuine receptivity. F. R. HARM

See also LUTHER, MARTIN; THEOLOGIA CRUCIS.

Bibliography. P. Althaus, *The Theology of Martin Luther;* R. Prenter, *Luther's Theology of the Cross;* W. von Loewenich, *Luther's Theology of the Cross;* M. Luther Works, Amer. ed., XXXI and LII, theses 19 and 20 of the Heidelberg Disputation; L. Pinomaa, *Faith Victorious;* H. Preus, *A Theology to Live By,* ch. 1.

Theophany. A theological term used to refer to either a visible or auditory manifestation of God. Visible manifestations include an angel appearing in human form (Judg. 13); a flame in the burning bush (Exod. 3:2–6); or fire, smoke, and thunder on Mount Sinai (Exod. 19:18–20). Auditory manifestations include the voice of God in the garden (Gen. 3:8), the still small voice to Elijah (I Kings 19:12ff.), or the voice from heaven at the baptism of Jesus (Matt. 3:17). Normally the physical aspects are not described with any detail because it is the message of God that is emphasized. However, the physical aspects are there to impress the recipients and authenticate the revelation. This is not to imply that everything is immediately obvious to the recipients. Samson's father, Judg. 13:15–22, does not know he is speaking to the angel of the Lord until after the angel disappears in the flames of the sacrifice. In many cases the one seen seems to the recipient as a normal human being and only what is said and done indicates otherwise.

God takes the initiative in theophany, never revealing himself completely, and usually only in a temporary rather than permanent way. A permanent manifestation like the incarnation of Christ made theophanies less necessary and accounts for their diminished importance in the NT. In the OT theophanies are concentrated in Genesis, in the exodus and conquest events, in Judges, and in the prophets, often in relation to their initial call.

The literary description of theophany varies somewhat from one occasion to another. However, Kuntz has been able to show that there is often a definite literary form. Gen. 26:23–25 would be a typical example. It includes an introductory description (Yahweh appeared), divine self-asseveration ("I am the God of Abraham your father"), quelling of human fear ("fear not"), assertion of gracious divine presence ("I am with you"), *hieros logos* ("holy word"; "I will bless you"), and concluding description (he built an altar there).

Some label the expressions "angel of the Lord" or "angel of God" as a theophanic angel. These expressions occur over fifty times in the OT; some of the most important passages include Exod. 23:20–23; 32:34; and Isa. 63:9. Various interpretations have been suggested including an appearance of God himself, an appearance of a messenger or one of God's many angels, or an appearance of the preincarnate Christ. Each interpretation has difficulties, and there is no consensus. J. C. MOYER

See also ANGEL OF THE LORD.

Bibliography. J. A. Borland, *Christ in the OT;* J. K. Kuntz, *The Self-Revelation of God;* W. G. MacDonald, "Christology and 'The Angel of the Lord,'" in *Current Issues in Biblical and Patristic Interpretation,* ed. G. F. Hawthorne.

Theotokos. *See* MOTHER OF GOD.

Thirteen Articles, The (1538). A doctrinal statement by a committee of German Lutheran and English theologians, written in Latin at London in the summer of 1538. The product of negotiations that had been carried on since 1535, they were based on the Augsburg Confession (1530)

and on a set of articles drawn up in Wittenberg in 1536 at an earlier stage in the discussions. The Thirteen Articles were never accepted by the civil or ecclesiastical authorities in England, but Thomas Cranmer preserved them, and they became in part the basis for the Forty-two Articles approved in the reign of Edward VI.

The influence of the Augsburg Confession is clear throughout the Thirteen Articles. Some statements were taken almost verbatim from the earlier document. The material was organized in a similar way, and most of the topics of the Augsburg Confession's twenty-one doctrinal articles found their way into the Thirteen Articles. The latter document did not deal with the abuses rejected in the confession's other articles because Henry VIII was about to express himself on some of them.

There is a large measure of doctrinal agreement between the Augsburg Confession and the Thirteen Articles. This agreement even includes the real presence of the body and blood of Jesus in the Lord's Supper. But there are important differences, too. For instance, the Thirteen Articles say that good works are necessary for salvation (article IV, on justification).

J. M. Drickamer

See also Augsburg Confession.

Bibliography. P. Schaff, *The Creeds of Christendom,* I, 611–27; N. Tjernagel, *Henry VIII and the Lutherans.*

Thirty-nine Articles, The (1563). The historical doctrinal standard of the Church of England and the worldwide network of Episcopal churches in communion with the Archbishop of Canterbury. The articles arose as one of the manifestations of the sixteenth century English Reformation, and more specifically from the liturgical genius of Thomas Cranmer, who served as Archbishop of Canterbury from 1533 to 1556. Cranmer and like-minded colleagues prepared several statements of more or less evangelical faith during the reign of Henry VIII, whose divorce from Catherine of Aragon provided the political impetus for the English Reformation. But it was not until the reign of Edward VI that England's reformers were able to proceed with more thorough efforts. Shortly before Edward's death, Cranmer presented a doctrinal statement consisting of forty-two topics, or articles, as the last of his major contributions to the development of Anglicanism. These Forty-two Articles were suppressed during the Catholic reign of Edward's successor, Mary Tudor, but became the source of the Thirty-nine Articles which Elizabeth the Great and her Parliament established as the doctrinal position of the Church of England. The 1563 Latin and 1571 English editions of the articles, which benefited from the consultation of the queen herself, are the definitive statements. Elizabeth promoted the articles as an instrument of national policy (to solidify her kingdom religiously) and as a theological *via media* (to encompass as wide a spectrum of English Christians as possible). Since her day much controversy has swirled over their theological significance. In more recent years they have been of greatest interest to the evangelical and Catholic wings of the Anglican-Episcopalian community who, though they differ between themselves over the meaning of the articles, still consider them valid, in contrast to the more liberal (or "broad") groupings within Anglicanism for whom the articles are little more than a venerated historical document.

The Thirty-nine Articles have been justly praised as a moderate, winsome, biblical, and inclusive statement of Reformation theology. The articles repudiate teachings and practices that Protestants in general condemned in the Catholic church—they deny, e.g., supererogation of merit (XIV), transubstantiation (XXVIII), the sacrifice of the Mass (XXXI), and implicitly the sinlessness of Mary (XV). On the other hand, they affirm with the continental reformers that Scripture is the final authority on salvation (VI), that Adam's fall compromised human free will (X), that justification is by faith in Christ's merit (XI), that both bread and wine should be served to all in the Lord's Supper (XXX), and that ministers may marry (XXXII). The articles borrow some wording from Lutheran confessions, especially on the Trinity (I), the church (XIX), and the sacraments (XXV). But on baptism (XXVII, "a sign of Regeneration") and on the Lord's Supper (XXVIII, "The Body of Christ is given, taken, and eaten, in the Supper, only after an heavenly and spiritual manner"), the articles resemble Reformed and Calvinistic beliefs more than Lutheran. Article XVII on predestination and election is much debated, for it pictures election unto life in terms very similar to those used by Reformed confessions, and yet—like the Lutherans—is silent on the question of reprobation to damnation. The Thirty-nine Articles mute considerably the attack on extreme views from the radical reformation which is present in the Forty-two Articles of 1553. Thus, the Thirty-nine Articles do not contain the repudiations of antinomianism, soul sleep, chiliasm, and universalism that the early statement did. But they do retain affirmations concerning the propriety of creeds (VIII), the necessity of clerical ordination (XXIII), the right of the sovereign to influence religion (XXXVII), the right of private property (XXXVIII), and the legitimacy of official oaths (XXXIX), which had been challenged by some radical reformers.

The articles take on a more expressly English cast when they address matters of special relevance to the sixteenth century. Articles VI and XX allow the monarch considerable space for regulating the external church life of England. Article XX also sides more with Luther than with Zwingli in treating the authority of Scripture as the *final* and *last* word on religious matters rather than as the *only* word. Article XXXIV upholds the value of traditions that "be not repugnant to the Word of God." And Article XXXVII maintains the sovereign's right to "chief government" over the whole realm, including the church, even as it restricts the monarch from exercising strictly clerical functions of preaching or administering the sacraments (in 1801 the American Episcopal Church exchanged this article for one more in keeping with New World views on the separation of church and state).

The Thirty-nine Articles remain a forthright statement of sixteenth century reform. They are Protestant in affirming the final authority of Scripture. They are at one with common Reformation convictions on justification by grace through faith in Christ. They lean toward Lutheranism in permitting beliefs and practices that do not contradict Scripture. They contain statements which, like Zwingli in Zurich, give the state authority to regulate the church. They are "catholic" in their respect for tradition and in their belief that religious ceremonies should be everywhere the same within a realm. They are ambiguous enough to have provided controversy for a thousand theologians, but compelling enough to have grounded the faith of millions.

M. A. Noll

See also Confessions of Faith; Anglican Communion.

Bibliography. E. J. Bicknell, *A Theological Introduction to the Thirty-nine Articles of the Church of England;* P. Schaff, *The Creeds of Christendom,* I, III; J. H. Newman, *Tract 90;* W. H. Griffith Thomas, *The Principles of Theology: An Introduction to the Thirty-nine Articles.*

This Age, The Age to Come. Terms characterizing the biblical concept of time. Biblical thought views time as linear (or horizontal) and contrasts the present age with a future age to come. Greek thought, on the other hand, finds a vertical dualism in the order of the world: this world is contrasted with another superior world coexisting with the present one. The use of the terms *kosmos* ("world") and *aiōn* ("aeon, age") bears this out. Hellenistic and Gnostic thought found the *kosmos* divided into two spheres: this present world order and that of God and eternity. *Aiōn* described the mediating powers bridging this absolute distinction. Biblical thought looks for the transformation of the present age in a future time. This age and the age to come will both appear in the same historical plane; their distinction for the most part is chronological.

Among the evangelists Matthew brings out clearly this horizontal dualism (12:32). In the climax to the parable of the wheat and tares (13:36ff.), "the close of the age" is viewed in terms of apocalyptic. There will be a climactic conclusion to the present historical order: the Son of man/Jesus Christ will return, initiate judgment, and establish his kingdom (cf. Matt. 24:3; Luke 20:34–35). Paul similarly emphasizes this two-age structure (Eph. 1:21) and affirms that the two ages are interlocked; Jesus Christ is the turning point in eschatology.

And yet an aspect of the future age is already present. Especially in the Fourth Gospel, a vertical eschatology is evident that claims a present reality for elements of the age to come (e.g., eternal life, judgment; 3:19; 5:24). Even spatial language (e.g., above/below) is common (3:3, 31; 8:23). According to Paul, because the new creation has begun (II Cor. 5:17), Christ can deliver us already from the present evil age (Gal. 1:4; II Cor. 6:2). Therefore the ages also overlap (cf. Luke 17:21). Christ's reign (to use Ladd's expression) is here in the present world, but his rule is incomplete; his realm is still coming in the future. In the interim, the "powers of the age to come" are with us (Heb. 6:5). In the present age, Christ has given the believer the Spirit to sustain him until the promises of the future age are fully realized (Eph. 1:13; 4:30; cf. II Cor. 1:22).

In brief, the present age is characterized by the rulership of Satan (Eph. 6:12; II Cor. 4:4), the sin of men, and death (Eph. 2:1–2). Followers of Christ are called to not be conformed to this age (Rom. 12:2), but to be renewed by the Spirit in anticipation of the age to come. Once this age is consummated, the coming age will be hallmarked by the rulership of Christ and eternal life.

G. M. Burge

See also Age, Ages.

Bibliography. G. E. Ladd, *The Presence of the Future;* H. Ridderbos, *The Coming of the Kingdom;* W. G. Kümmel, *Promise and Fulfillment;* J. W. Bowman, *IDB,* II, 135–40; O. Cullmann, *Christ and Time;* H. Sasse, *TDNT,* I, 197–209; J. Guhrt, *NIDNTT,* I, 521–26; III, 826–33.

Tholuck, Friedrich August Gottreu (1799–1877). German Protestant theologian. Of humble origins, he showed great proficiency in languages and took oriental studies at Breslau and Berlin.

At the age of twenty Tholuck was converted from skepticism and pantheism after coming under the influence of such pietists as Neander and Baron von Kottwitz, and he switched to theology. In 1820 he began lecturing at Berlin while at the same time holding positions in Jänicke's missionary training school, a mission to Jews, and the Prussian Bible Society. His first theological work, *The Doctrine of Sin and the Propitiator* (1823), helped check the spread of rationalism in Germany. In 1826 he was appointed professor of theology at Halle over the strenuous objections of the rationalists who predominated there, and in a few years he succeeded in turning the faculty around. Except for a stint as chaplain of the Prussian embassy in Rome (1827–29), he spent the remainder of his academic career at Halle.

Among Tholuck's most influential writings were commentaries on Romans (1824), John (1827), the Sermon on the Mount (1833), Hebrews (1836), and the Psalms (1843); the republication of Calvin's *Institutes* and commentaries on the Gospels and epistles, together with an essay on his hermeneutics (*The Merits of Calvin as an Interpreter of the Holy Scriptures*); and numerous collections of sermons, the best-known in English being *Hours of Christian Devotion, Light from the Cross,* and *Festal Chimes and Sabbath Musings.* His later works dealt with German church history since the Reformation.

A champion of conservative biblical scholarship, Tholuck sharply attacked D. F. Strauss in 1837. As both a teacher and preacher, he concentrated more on spiritual edification than on the scientific side of theology. His close ties with the German revival movement (*Erweckung*), the vital pastoral ministry among his students (the most famous being Martin Kähler), and his propagation of *Vermittlungstheologie* (a system which stressed personal piety and downplayed confessionalist dogma) made him without doubt the leading pietist theologian of the nineteenth century. His works were well received in the Anglo-Saxon world and are still read today in pietist circles in Germany. R. V. Pierard

See also Mediating Theology.

Bibliography. P. Scharpff, *History of Evangelism; RGG,* V, 854–55; D. S. Schaff, *SHERK,* XI, 420–21; *NIDCC,* 970; *ODCC,* 1369.

Thomas à Kempis (*ca.* 1379–1471). A German monk and spiritual writer. Thomas Hemerken (Hämmerlein or "little hammer") left Kempen near Krefeld on the Lower Rhine *ca.* 1392 to attend school in Deventer in the Netherlands. There he came into contact with Florent Radewijns (*ca.* 1350–1400), one of the founders of the Brethren of the Common Life. In 1399 Thomas entered the monastery at Agnietenberg (Mount Saint Agnes near Zwolle), which was affiliated with the Windesheim Congregation of Augustinian regular (monastic) canons. He spent most of his life at Mount Saint Agnes, where he was ordained priest (1413–14) and served as subprior and director of novices. He was a prolific copyist.

Thomas wrote or compiled more than thirty works, which may be arranged in the following categories: (1) several volumes of monastic sermons; (2) biographies of the founders of the *Devotio Moderna* (Gerard Groote, Florent Radewijns, and others) intended for the edification of novices; (3) a chronicle of his monastery that includes much historical and biographical information on the *Devotio Moderna;* and (4) numerous works on the spiritual life (e.g., *On the Exaltation of the Spirit* [*De elevatione mentis*]; *The Soul's Soliloquy;* various *Prayers and Meditations on the Life and Passion of the Lord; On True, Heartfelt Remorse; Valley of Lillies; Garden of Roses; On the Training of Monks* [*De disciplina claustralium*]). Like other leaders in the Windesheim monastic reform, Thomas's concern was for practical methods to achieve genuine devotion and a true observance of the monastic rule.

Thomas à Kempis is best known, however, for the compilation of the four books of the *Imitation of Christ.* Although long disputed, general scholarly consensus since the late 1950s ascribes it to Thomas. Widely transmitted, translated, and read by Catholics and Protestants alike, the *Imitation* expresses a contemplative and monastic emphasis on the interior life and its disciplines. Thus, unlike the semimonastic spirituality of the Brethren of the Common Life, who sought to live devout lives in the middle of bustling cities, the spiritual teaching of the *Imitation* emphasizes withdrawal from the distractions and dangers of the world. It warns against placing confidence in one's own prudence and calls for knowledge of oneself, continual self-judgment, and other traditional monastic virtues. It is also critical of speculative theologizing, preferring study that inflames the heart with love for God. The first book is a collection (*rapiarium*) of spiritual meditations; the second and third books, the heart of the *Imitation,* offer counsel on growth in virtues such as humility, patience, and obedience and on the fluctuations of the interior life. The fourth book is devoted to eucharistic piety. D. D. Martin

See also Brethren of the Common Life; Devotio Moderna; Spirituality.

Bibliography. J. P. Arthur, *et al., Works of Thomas à Kempis;* R. R. Post, *The Modern Devotion: Confron-*

tation with Reformation and Humanism; DTC, XV; F. Vandebroucke, *The Spirituality of the Middle Ages;* A. Hyma, *The Christian Renaissance;* J. E. G. de Montmorency, *Thomas à Kempis: His Age and Book;* J. van Ginneken, *The Following of Christ or the Spiritual Diary of Gerard Groote.*

Thomas Aquinas (1225–1274). Italian theologian and Doctor of the Church, born at Roccasecca near Aquino, Italy. He was inducted into a Benedictine monastery at age five but later was forcibly removed by his family and enrolled at the new secular University at Naples (1239) where he joined the Dominicans. Sometime after 1245 he began studies under Albert the Great at the Convent of St. James, Paris. In 1248 Aquinas and Albert started a school in Cologne. Aquinas returned to Paris in 1252 to teach at the university. From 1259 to 1268 he taught at the papal *Curiae* in Italy, where he met the translator, William Moerbeke. The Latin Averroeist controversy called him back to Paris (1268–72). His final years were spent in Naples, teaching in a Dominican house. He died at Fossanova on the way to the Council of Lyons, March 7, 1274.

Aquinas was canonized in 1326, made a Doctor of the Church in 1567, commended for study by Pope Leo XIII (*Aeterni Patris*) in 1879, and declared patron of Catholic schools in 1880.

Major Writings. Thomas is credited with some ninety-eight works, though nine are of doubtful authenticity. His writings were produced steadily from 1252 until the year of his death. The greatest and most influential of his works was *Summa Theologica,* a systematic presentation of Christian doctrine in philosophical terms. His system was declared the official teaching of the Catholic Church by Leo XIII.

Thought. The views of Aquinas cover most philosophical and theological categories.

Faith and Reason. Like Augustine, Aquinas believed faith was based in God's revelation in Scripture. Support for faith was found in miracles and probable arguments. Although God's existence is provable by reason, sin obscures man's ability to know, and so belief (not proof) that God exists is necessary for most. Reason, however, is never the basis for faith in God. Demanding reasons for belief in God actually lessens the merit of one's faith. Believers, nonetheless, should reason *about* and *for* their faith. There are five ways to demonstrate God's existence by reason. (1) From motion to an Unmoved Mover, (2) from effects to a First Cause, (3) from contingent being to a Necessary Being, (4) from degrees of perfection to a Most Perfect Being, and (5) from design in nature to a Designer. There are, however, mysteries (e.g., Trinity, Incarnation) that cannot be known by human reason but only by faith.

Epistemology. Aquinas held that all knowledge begins in experience. We are, however, born with an *a priori,* innate capacity to know. Certainty about reality is possible by means of first principles: (1) identity—being is being, (2) noncontradiction—being is not nonbeing, (3) the excluded middle—either being or nonbeing, (4) causality—nonbeing cannot cause being, and (5) finality—every being acts toward an end. So nothing is in the mind that was not first in the senses—*except the mind itself* with its capacity to know by means of first principles. These first principles are self-evident, once they are understood.

Metaphysics. Like Aristotle, Aquinas believed it was the function of the wise man to know order. The order reason produces in its own acts is *logic.* That which it produces through acts of will is *ethics.* The order produced by reason in external things is *art.* But the order reason contemplates (but does not produce) is *nature.* When nature is contemplated insofar as it is sensible, one is studying the *physical sciences.* Nature studied insofar as it is quantifiable is *mathematics.* But nature studied insofar as it is being is *metaphysics.*

The heart of Aquinas's metaphysics is the real distinction between essence and existence in all finite beings. Aristotle had distinguished between actuality and potentiality, but he applied this only to form and matter, not to the order of being. Aquinas argued that only God is pure being, pure actuality, with no potentiality whatsoever. Hence, the central premise of Thomistic thought is "act in the order in which it is act is unlimited and unique, unless it is cojoined with passive potency." God alone is pure act(uality) without form. Angels are completely actualized potentialities (pure forms), and man is a composition of form (soul) and matter (body) with progressive actualization.

God. God alone *is* being (I Am-ness). Everything else *has* being. God's essence is identical to his existence, it is of his essence to exist. God is a necessary being. He cannot *not* exist. Neither can God change, since he is without potentiality to be anything other than he is. Likewise, God is eternal, since time implies a change from a before to an after. But as the I-*Am* (Exod. 3:14), God has no befores and afters. God also is simple (indivisible) since he has no potential for division. And he is infinite, since pure act as such is unlimited, having no potentiality to limit it. Besides these metaphysical attributes, God is also morally perfect and infinitely wise.

Analogy. God is known by analogy. Univocal

(totally the same) knowledge of God is impossible, since our knowledge is limited and God is unlimited. Equivocal (totally different) knowledge of God is impossible, since creation resembles the Creator (Ps. 19:1; Rom. 1:19–20); the effect resembles its efficient cause. Because there are great differences between God and creatures, the way of negation (*via negativa*), is necessary. We must take only the perfection signified (goodness, truth, etc.), without the finite mode of signification, when we apply it to God. So the attribute will have the same definition for creatures and Creator, but it will have a different application or extension, since creatures are finitely good, while God is infinitely good. So before we can appropriately apply the term "good" to God we must negate the finite *mode* (how) in which we find good among creatures and apply the *meaning* (what) to God in an unlimited way.

Creation. God created the world out of nothing (*ex nihilo*). Although Aquinas believed that an eternal creation was logically possible, since there is no logical reason an eternal cause cannot be causing eternally; nevertheless, he believed that Scripture teaches a beginning of the universe. Time did not exist before God created—only eternity. God did not create *in* time; rather, with the world there was the creation *of* time. So there was no time before time began.

Man. Man is a hylomorphic unity of soul and body. Adam was directly created by God at the beginning, and God directly creates each new soul in the womb of its mother. Despite this unity of soul and body, there is no identity between them. The soul survives death and awaits the reunion with the body at the resurrection.

Ethics. Just as there are first principles of thought, so there are first principles of action called laws. Aquinas distinguishes four kinds. *Eternal* law is the plan by which God governs creation. *Natural* law is the participation of rational creatures in this eternal law. *Human* law is a particular application of natural law to a local community. And *divine* law is the revelation of God's law through Scripture and the church.

Virtues are in two classes: natural and supernatural. The former include prudence, justice, courage, and temperance. These are part of the natural law. Supernatural virtues are faith, hope, and love.

N. L. Geisler

See also Neo-Thomism; Thomism.

Bibliography. V. J. Bourke, *Aquinas' Search for Wisdom* and *Thomistic Bibliography: 1920–1940;* M. D. Chenu, *Toward Understanding St. Thomas;* G. K. Chesterton, *St. Thomas Aquinas;* K. Foster, *The Life of St. Thomas Aquinas;* É. Gilson, *The Christian Philosophy of St. Thomas Aquinas;* M. Grabmann, *The Interior Life of St. Thomas Aquinas;* J. Maritain, *St. Thomas Aquinas, Angel of the Schools;* A. Walz, *Saint Thomas Aquinas, A Biographical Study;* R. J. Deferrari, *A Complete Index of the Summa Theologica of St. Thomas Aquinas, Latin-English Dictionary of Thomas Aquinas, etc.,* and *A Lexicon of St. Thomas Aquinas Based on Summa Theologica and Select Passages of His Other Work;* P. Mandonnet and J. Destrez, *Bibliographie thomiste; Repertoire bibliographique.*

Thomism. The school of philosophy and theology following the thought of Thomas Aquinas. It developed in various phases and has experienced periods of support and neglect.

When Aquinas died he left no direct successor, but his system was adopted by various individuals, most notably by many of his confreres in the Dominican order and by his own original teacher, the eclectic Albertus Magnus. Nonetheless, there was still much opposition to his Aristotelianism on the part of church authorities, and in 1277 in Paris and Oxford several propositions derived from Thomas's teachings were condemned. It was primarily due to Dominican efforts that the system of Aquinas was not only eventually rehabilitated, but that he himself was canonized in 1323.

From this time period on, Thomism became one of the several competing schools of medieval philosophy. In particular, it set itself off against classical Augustinianism with its reliance on Aristotle, most eminently by insisting on a unified anthropology whereby the soul is the form of the body. What St. Thomas was to the Dominicans, Duns Scotus became to the Franciscans, and Scotism debated with Thomism on such issues as freedom of the will and the analogy of being. Finally, Thomism, along with the other two schools mentioned, maintained a moderate realism in contrast to nominalism. At the same time, the followers of St. Thomas did not remain uniform, but took on individual traits with particular commentators and in terms of national movements. This tendency is illustrated most interestingly by the Dominican Meister Eckhart (*ca.* 1260–1328), who developed a mysticism that was to become characteristic of German theological life for more than a century.

A central figure of developing Thomism was Thomas de Vio Cardinal Cajetan (1469–1534). His high ecclesiastical standing contributed to the authoritativeness of his expositions of Aquinas. Cajetan's brand of Thomism bears several distinctives. Among these is his analysis of analogy; he argues that this concept is best understood as the proportionality of an attribute to two essences rather than as the predication of an attribute primary in one essence and derived in a second. Further, Cajetan thought more in terms of abstract essences than his predecessors, who majored on existing substances. Third, he raised doubt concerning the provability of both God's existence and the immortality of the soul.

Thomism became the leading school of Catholic thought in the sixteenth century. Several factors contributed to its ascendancy. The Jesuit order (approved in 1540), known for its aggressive teaching, aligned itself with Aquinas; also, the Council of Trent (first convened in 1545), which self-consciously styled many of its pronouncements in Thomistic phraseology.

Thomism entered the seventeenth century triumphantly, but exited void of power and originality. John of St. Thomas (1589–1644) is a good representative of the early century. He was a creative teacher and interpreter of Aquinas's thought; he was a careful and compassionate official of the Spanish Inquisition; and he was an intimate advisor to King Philip IV. Thus in him the intellectual, theological, and political machinations of Thomism are brought to a focus. But Thomism's primacy bore the seeds of its own demise. Due to lack of competition Thomism became too self-contained to cope with the rise of rationalism and empirical science on their own ground. Thomism would not adapt itself; and so the alternatives left were obscurantism or non-Thomistic philosophy. Consequently, though Thomism was still alive, primarily in Dominican circles, in the eighteenth century, it was essentially a spent force.

But the early nineteenth century saw another abrupt change in the fortunes of Thomism. Catholic thinkers increasingly began to see that in Thomas's works there were viable responses to topical questions not answered elsewhere. Particularly the questions of human dignity in the face of rising industrialism revived Thomism. Dramatically the schools returned to the authority of Aquinas. By the time of Vatican I (1869/70), Thomistic principles were again in vogue. And Thomism triumphed in 1879 when Pope Leo XIII in *Aeterni Patris* recalled the church to St. Thomas. The result was the movement known as neo-Thomism which has persisted well past the middle of the twentieth century. W. CORDUAN

See also CAJETAN, THOMAS DE VIO; NEO-THOMISM; SCHOLASTICISM; THOMAS AQUINAS.

Bibliography. V. J. Bourke, *Thomistic Bibliography: 1920–1940;* É. Gilson, *The Christian Philosophy of St. Thomas Aquinas;* H. John, *Thomist Spectrum;* T. L. Miethe and V. J. Bourke, *Thomistic Bibliography: 1940–1978.*

Thornwell, James Henley (1812–1862). Distinguished Southern Presbyterian theologian and educator, born in Marlborough District, South Carolina. He was educated at South Carolina College (now University of South Carolina), then attended Andover Seminary, Harvard University, and Columbia (S.C.) Seminary. Converted to Calvinism through reading the Westminster Confession of Faith, he was later described by Charles Hodge of Princeton, during the heat of ecclesiastical debate, as "hyper-hyper-hyper Calvinist." He served as pastor of the influential First Presbyterian Church in Columbia, and eventually became president of South Carolina College, which he purged of strong deist and unitarian influences. Afterward, Thornwell became professor in Columbia Theological Seminary.

His theology, which was traditional, evangelical Calvinism, displays a vast erudition in classical and modern philosophy, as well as in the history of thought. Thornwell, according to Thornton Whaling, endeavored to bring reason and faith, theology and philosophy, dogma and ethics, into a systematic unity. Like Calvin, he held that the major theme of religious thought is the relationship between God and man. Whaling shows that Thornwell summarized theological science in terms of "The Moral Government of God in its Essential Principles; as Modified by the Covenant of Works; and as Modified by the Covenant of Grace." Although Thornwell died too early to compose a systematic theology, he was a prolific theological writer, and also edited the *Southern Quarterly Review.*

Thornwell's ecclesiology has perhaps attracted more interest than his theology. He held to a pure spirituality of the church, entailing an absolute separation of church and state, and thus opposed church sanction of movements of social reform. In opposition to Charles Hodge, he did not favor the introduction of boards into church government. He was a vigorous defender of slavery as scriptural and of state's rights, and was a founder of the Southern Presbyterian Church (P.C.U.S.), which separated from the national body in 1861 over the Civil War. D. F. KELLY

Bibliography. B. M. Palmer, *Thornwell's Life and Letters; Collected Writings of James Henley Thornwell,* 4 vols.; M. H. Smith, *Studies in Southern Presbyterian Theology;* T. W. Rogers, "James Henley Thornwell," *JCR* 7:175–205; T. Whaling, "Dr. Thornwell as a Theologian," in *Centennial Address Commemorating the Birth of the Rev. James Henley Thornwell;* E. B. Holifield, *The Gentlemen Theologians: American Theology in Southern Culture, 1795–1860.*

Tillich, Paul (1886–1965). One of the most widely read and influential Protestant theologians of the twentieth century. Tillich was born in the village of Starzeddel near Guben in Prussia. According to his own account his early years had a great influence on both his theological interest and development. His father was a Lutheran minister who was of a conservative temperament and nurtured in his son a respect for traditional beliefs and values. His mother, on the other hand, encouraged openness of mind and a spirit of intellectual adventure. As he put it, therefore, he was brought up "on the boundary" between these two temperaments. He formed a deep attachment to the country life of his childhood, with its stable rural pace and closeness to nature. When, however, the family moved to Berlin when Tillich was fourteen, he was equally fascinated by the excitement and vitality of the big city. These early experiences of conservatism and openness, of the quiet life of a rural area and the pressing human environment of a large and busy world capital, placed a permanent stamp on his life and thought. Throughout his long career he retained a deep respect for nature while being actively involved in the human affairs of his time. And while he appreciated traditional beliefs and values, he constantly strained to move beyond them. He studied philosophy and theology and took his Ph.D. degree at Breslau, writing a dissertation on Schelling. He was ordained to the Lutheran ministry in 1912.

The First World War, in which he served as a chaplain in the German forces, also had an important influence on his development. The war provided the newly ordained Tillich with a vivid experience of the destructive underside of human nature, as well as the conviction that Christians must be involved in the affairs of the life around them. His war experience also drove him to seek relief from its cruelty, and he found this in art. His openness to art and the larger cultural context in which it had its genesis was an important aspect of his mature thought. If it is fair to attach any label at all to Tillich's thought, it is a theology of culture.

He spent his professional life teaching theology and philosophy. In the troubled late 1920s he became interested in the religious-socialist movement, and his open opposition to Hitler and the political-cultural views he represented led to Tillich's dismissal from the philosophy faculty at the University of Frankfurt in 1933. Not long after leaving Frankfurt he came to the United States. His academic career in America spanned thirty-three years, during which he authored several books and taught at Union Theological Seminary (New York), Columbia University, Harvard University, and the University of Chicago. He became an American citizen in 1940.

His interests and research were wide ranging, and the influences on his thought were correspondingly diverse. They include Platonism, medieval mysticism, German idealism, and existentialism. The latter philosophical perspective, which he encountered in-depth while teaching at Marburg, was perhaps the greatest single influence on his work. Tillich's theological methodology has been called the "method of correlation," and proposes that philosophy and theology should play a complementary role to each other. Philosophy's task is to pose problems and ask questions, while the challenge of theology is to enter into dialogue with philosophy, understand its questions, and struggle to come up with answers.

Perhaps the most important work of his career was the three-volume *Systematic Theology* (1963). Here it is argued that God should be viewed as the ground of being, known to man as ultimate concern. It is by participation in this ground of being that man receives his own being. Man must face nonbeing. When he does so, and courageously affirms himself in the face of nonbeing, he is expressing ultimate concern. The "New Being" for man is Jesus Christ. When Jesus gave himself on the cross, he became "transparent" to the ground of being, i.e., the Christ, the New Being. Jesus the Christ is therefore the answer to man's existential need.

The structure and meaning of reality can be grasped only by myths or symbols, which are signs that actually participate in the reality to which they point. *How* they participate in this reality is not as clear as it should be. This leaves one with the impression that Tillich's philosophy of religious language is not only difficult to understand—it may indeed be impossible to understand. It is in any case not as clear as one would hope for from a theologian of his stature.

Tillich was a prolific writer in both German and English. His published works include *Interpretation of History* (1936); *The Protestant Era* (1936); *The Courage to Be* (1952); *The New Being* (1955); *Theology of Culture* (1959); and *Morality and Beyond* (1963). *On the Boundary* (1966) is a revision of part 1 of *The Interpretation of History.* It is a brief and very readable autobiographical sketch offered by Tillich to the public.

J. D. Spiceland

Bibliography. C. W. Kegley and R. W. Bretall, eds., *The Theology of Paul Tillich;* J. R. Lyons, ed., *The Intellectual Legacy of Paul Tillich;* W. and M. Pauck, *Paul Tillich: His Life and Thought.*

Time (Gr. *chronos*). One of the most vexing problems of philosophy. The Bible presents a distinctive conception of time, reflected especially by its peculiar use of the terms *kairos* and *aiōn.* Instead of viewing time abstractly as a problem, it regards time as a created sphere in which God's redemptive plan is actualized.

In the usual secular sense, *kairos* refers to a

definite point of time especially appropriate for a given undertaking (Acts 24:25), *aiōn* to an extent of time (stipulated or unstipulated). The NT builds on this usage with a special eye to redemptive history (John 7:6), in which divine determination (Acts 1:7), not human deliberation, constitutes a given moment or age the appropriate time of God's working. "Because . . . the divine plan of salvation is bound to such time points or *kairoi* chosen by God, . . . it is . . . redemptive *history*. Not all fragments of ongoing time constitute redemptive history in the narrower sense, but rather . . . these *kairoi* singled out from time as a whole" (Cullmann, 40–41).

While the NT gives prominent scope to the future *kairoi* associated with the eschatological drama, its central *kairos* is the life and death and resurrection of the incarnate Christ, which is decisively significant for the kingdom of God. The terms "day [of the Lord]" and "hour," "now," and "today" likewise gain dramatic significance in the NT context whenever the eternal order and redemptive history impinges upon the sweep of ordinary events. The interconnected redemptive *kairoi* supply the threadline of salvation history. Yet the divine *kairoi* at the same time secretly enfold the entire secular movement of time (Acts 17:26) for the fulfillment, often unwittingly, of God's ultimate purposes.

As the *kairos* is a decisive momentary unveiling of the eternal, so the *aiōn* discloses the Lord of ages who divides the long sweep of time according to his own purposes. The *kairoi* are decisive turning points within the larger *aiōna*. The Bible brackets history with an eye on the age of promise, the age of fulfillment, and the age to come.

Man's transition to the eternal order will not involve him in the supersession of temporal experience since, although redeemed, he remains a creature (Rev. 10:6, "there will be no more time," teaches not the cessation of time, but the expiration of opportunity. The word here means "delay").

Modern philosophy characteristically affirms that it takes time more seriously than did ancient or medieval philosophy. Classic Greek thought dissolved the significance of the temporal world, depicting it as illusory shadow alongside the eternal ideas and forms. The influence of Platonic and Aristotelian thought upon medieval scholars served to divert attention from the unique biblical view of history to the revealed truths of Judeo-Christian religion, although the importance of historical revelation and redemption remained central in the great creeds. Modern idealistic philosophy shunned the historical and temporal as bearing eternal meaning and significance at any point, and therefore was hostile, even if often in a concealed manner, to the doctrines of Christ's unique incarnation and atonement. Led by Hegel, however, modern idealism placed time and history in the very nature of the Absolute. Thus it simultaneously minimized the uniqueness of biblical history and exaggerated the spirituality of history in general by viewing all as divine process. In two ways this profoundly unbiblical speculation retained nonetheless a debt to the biblical view. Against the depreciation of the temporal by classic ancient philosophy, it stressed God's aggressive interest in history; and against cyclical views of history as a process of recurring ages, it emphasized that the time process moves toward a perfect goal.

Equally significant, evolutionary naturalism, returning to the Greek cosmocentric outlook at the expense of theistic interpretations of reality, appealed to modern evolutionary views as lifting time to decisive importance. Its notion that time itself actualizes new forms of life was more popularly held in the first half century after Darwin than today, when speculative interest in emergent evolution is enlarging. Both approaches usually retain the expectation of a higher goal to which the temporal process moves, thus reflecting a secret indebtedness of modern theories of progress to the biblical doctrine of the kingdom of God, which speculative expositions strip of its supernatural features.

Outside the stream of biblical theology, virtually the whole movement of ancient religion and philosophy depreciated the significance of the temporal order. Not all religions of the Orient indeed shared the notion of nirvana, peculiar to Buddhism, with its emphasis on history and personal existence as evil and its expectation of bliss through annihilation or by absorption into the divine rather than through historical redemption; but none of them rose to the biblical emphasis that history displays a purposive movement to an intelligent, moral goal. The nonbiblical religions and speculations of antiquity did not escape the cycle theory of history as a series of recurring ages; in fact, this conception was sometimes spiritualized by designating the process "God" along pantheistic lines. While Zoroastrianism made more room for ethical teleology through its insistence on two eternal principles, good and evil, its unrelieved dualism excluded an abiding significance for history. In fact, while shunning the notion of eternal recurrence, Zoroastrianism nonetheless divided the world movement into four ages.

Nowhere does the importance of time come into view as in biblical teaching. While time is not ultimate, it is the divinely created sphere of God's preserving and redemptive work, and the arena of man's decision on his way to an eternal destiny. History moves toward a divine goal involving the redemption of the elect by the Creator and Lord of the universe. Within this historical matrix, every thought, word, and deed has repercussions in the eternal moral order. Richard Kroner aptly summarizes the biblical philosophy: "History has a beginning in God, it has its center in Christ and its end in the final consummation and the Last Judgment" (*ER*, 582). Oscar Cullmann emphasizes that, as against the Jewish conception of a linear history still awaiting its climax (the Christ event coinciding with the parousia), in the Christian view the center of history lies in a past event rather than in the eschatological future (the death and resurrection of Jesus of Nazareth decisively controls the timeline thereafter).

Cullmann properly warns against excessive disjunctions of time and eternity by Kierkegaard, Barth, Brunner, and Bultmann. But his own alternative impairs the unique eternity of God. Moreover, Cullmann's biblical realism is threatened by concessions to the notion of "temporal, non-historical myth" to which he reduces much in the biblical narratives of the beginning and the end. If such myth actually preserves the continuity of the temporal line, why may not all biblical events be reduced to this status, and the second Adam be dismissed on the same pattern as the first Adam? C. F. H. HENRY

See also AGE, AGES; ETERNITY; THIS AGE, THE AGE TO COME.

Bibliography. O. Cullmann, *Christ and Time;* J. Barr, *Biblical Words for Time;* J. Guhrt *et al., NIDNTT,* III, 826ff., H. Sasse, *TDNT,* I, 197ff.

Tindal, Matthew (*ca.* 1655–1733). English deist, a native of Devonshire. He was educated in Oxford University, and in 1678 became a law fellow in All Souls College. Tindal advocated high-church Anglicanism, but was associated with the small group of deists in that movement. He developed a reputation as an expert in international law, and published a controversial work, *The Rights of the Christian Church Asserted* (1706). To this work he added several political tracts, which gradually came to support the whig faction in politics.

Tindal's greatest fame, however, came as a deist leader; and he labeled himself a Christian deist. His reputation on this score was secured by his 1730 publication, *Christianity as Old as the Creation, or the Gospel a Republication of the Religion of Nature.* This work especially criticized alliances between church and state, alliances that, according to Tindal, corrupted Christianity. He argued that earliest Christianity was pure but that politics subverted its original natural principles, which were understandable to any rational man. Such ideas were common among deists, and Tindal had supported them often, though unpopularly, at Oxford; but he went farther by adding skeptical critiques of the Bible. He attacked traditional ideas of biblical inspiration and asserted that the rational person need not reply on special revelation.

Tindal's writings were very important in summarizing English deism's development from the late seventeenth century to the 1730s. The movement was very attractive to critics of all contemporary forms of Christianity and spurred many responses (Tindal's major work is said to have drawn one hundred fifty published replies). Also, Tindal's combination of deist and whiggish views influenced Voltaire's religious outlook and his descriptions of English life as well. Tindal's work, however, also marked the exhaustion of the English deist movement, for virtually all elements of historic Christianity had been subjected to negative critique. Few positive religious ideas remained in deism in spite of deists' claims that the basics of Christianity were as valid as "natural religion" and that any "right-thinking" person could believe those basic notions. Critics of deism continued to insist on a supernatural God, on belief in divine revelation, and on many doctrines derived from biblical writings.

R. J. VANDERMOLEN

See also DEISM; ENLIGHTENMENT, THE.

Bibliography. G. R. Cragg, *Reason and Authority in the Eighteenth Century* and *The Church in the Age of Reason, 1648–1789; NB,* XIX; P. Gay, *The Enlightenment: An Interpretation;* J. Orr, *English Deism: Its Roots and Fruits;* L. Stephen, *History of English Thought in the Eighteenth Century;* R. Stromberg, *Religious Liberalism in Eighteenth-Century England;* N. L. Torrey, *Voltaire and the English Deists.*

Tithe. *See* OFFERINGS AND SACRIFICES IN BIBLE TIMES.

Tithing. The practice of giving a tenth of one's property or produce to support religious institutions or the priesthood. It is an ancient practice, widespread in antiquity and found in Judaism as well as in surrounding cultures of the ancient Near East.

Commandments to tithe in the OT emphasize the quantity (one-tenth) of the gift. In this is the belief that God is entitled to share directly in the grain, wine, and oil that humans are permitted to produce. At different times in Israel's history, varying regulations governed the tithe. Before the time of the Deuteronomic code, tithes were used to celebrate a cultic festival at the local holy place, as when Amos mentions the tithes brought to Bethel (4:4), probably because of the vow made by Jacob (Gen. 28:22). The firstborn of flocks and a tithe of the fruits of the field provided for the festive meal. The priest of the holy place, strangers, widows, and orphans shared in the meal with those who brought the provisions. The remainders from the meal were given to the priests and their assistants as well as to the needy (Deut. 14:22ff.).

In the book of Deuteronomy, the firstborn of the flocks and the tithes are to be brought to the central holy place in Jerusalem ("the place which he will choose, to make his name dwell there," 14:23). Families and the Levites of the towns were to travel to Jerusalem for the festive meal. If the journey was too long and carrying the tithe too difficult, one could sell the tithe and buy what was needed in Jerusalem (vss. 24ff.). Yet this system did not adequately provide for the needs of the poor, so the code stipulated that every third year the tithe should be kept in the local town (vss. 28–29; 26:12–15). It would be distributed to Levites, sojourners, the fatherless, and widows who could not produce food for themselves.

The trip and tithe in Jerusalem changed the nature of the tithe from a harvest sacrifice to more of a cultic tax. The concentration of worship in Jerusalem also meant that temple priests required a somewhat regular income. During the exilic period the tithe became a type of tax paid to the priests. In postexilic texts, the cultic meal is no longer mentioned. At this time tithes were stored in warehouses (Neh. 10:38; Mal. 3:10). Then too, tithes no longer were required to be brought to Jerusalem, but rather were collected by local Levites (Neh. 10:37–38). This in effect made the tithe a tax.

References to the tithe are few in the NT. Jesus attacked the Pharisees for paying the tithe (Gr. *apodekatoō*) exactly while neglecting the more important parts of the law: justice, mercy, and faith (Matt. 23:23; cf. Luke 11:42). The Pharisee is shown praying in the temple, "I give tithes of all that I get" (Luke 18:12). There are three references to Genesis 14:17–20 in Heb. 7:6, 8–9.

The early church prescribed a tithe for its members. Yet this differed from OT regulations in that the tithe was seen as an absolute minimum, and it was to be given from one's total income. The Didache prescribed that firstfruits be given of "money, clothes, and of all your possessions" (13:7).

In the later history of the church, the obligation to tithe was always held in tension with Christ's command to sell all and renounce possessions (Matt. 19:21) along with Paul's teaching that Christ brings freedom from legal prescriptions (Gal. 5:1). By the fifth and sixth centuries, the practice of tithing was well established in old areas of Christianity in the West. In the eighth century, Carolingian rulers made the ecclesiastical tithe part of secular law.

By the twelfth century, monks who previously had been forbidden to receive tithes and required to pay them obtained a measure of freedom in being able to receive tithes while being freed from the obligation of payment. Controversies over tithes often arose when people sought to evade payment while others sought to appropriate tithe revenues for themselves.

Medieval tithes were divided into *predial*, due from the fruits of the earth; *personal*, due from labor; and *mixed*, due from the produce of livestock. These were further divided into *great*, derived from corn, hay, and wood to go to the rector or incumbent priest of the parish; and *small*, from all other predial tithes, plus mixed and personal tithes to go to the vicar.

In England, particularly by the sixteenth and seventeenth centuries, the issue of tithes was a source of intense conflict since a state church depended on tithes for its livelihood. Social, political, and economic implications were considerable in Archbishop Laud's attempts to increase tithe payments prior to 1640. English Puritans and others wanted the abolition of tithes in favor of voluntary contributions to support clergy. But the question of the tithe aroused some of the fiercest passions and bitterness of all issues associated with the English Civil War. After the war, the legislative tithe survived in England until the twentieth century. D. K. McKim

Bibliography. G. Constable, *Monastic Tithes from Their Origins to the Twelfth Century;* C. Hill, *Economic Problems of the Church from Archbishop Whitgift to the Long Parliament;* L. Vischer, *Tithing in the Early Church.*

Toland, John (1670–1722). English deist, born near Londonderry, Ireland; educated in a dissenter school at Redcastle and in the Enlightenment centers at Glasgow, Edinburgh (M.A. 1690), and Leiden. He concluded his formal education at Oxford University. Toland's reputation as a controversial thinker commenced in 1696, when he published *Christianity Not Mysterious.* This work was attacked by English clerics and by members of the House of Commons as well. Toland returned to Ireland and was publicly defended by William Molyneaux and John Locke.

Toland supported himself by editing the works of others (Milton, Harrington), by publishing political tracts supporting whig policies, and by gaining the support of wealthy patrons.

Because of the controversy stirred by his work, Toland had a precarious existence. He visited Hanover, Holland, Prussia, and Austria in search of patrons, but had little success. Of greater value to him were his political tracts against English Jacobites and high churchmen, for he was given financial support by Harley, Earl of Oxford. Toland's fortunes improved with the Whig ascendancy under King George I, to the extent that he speculated in the South Sea Company. He died at Putney after a brief illness.

Toland became one of the best-known English deists and was quite popular among continental writers. His writings gave English deism a new, controversial direction in that he rejected Christian mysteries and miracles that lacked rational proofs. Such a rejection meant criticism of orthodox ideas about the Trinity and the incarnation, and also opened the Scriptures to rationalistic criticisms. In Toland's view it was necessary to purge from Christianity what had been introduced by converted Jews and "superstitious" Gentiles. The resultant religion would be the original, simple, pure Christianity which conformed to modern rationalism. Toland did not deny the existence of revelation, but did reduce its role to a supplementary one. This was not what John Locke and English churchmen advocated, but it did become characteristic of deist thought. Toland popularized deist ideas, but he also created widespread opposition in the English church. Ultimately John Locke's rejection of skepticism and his reliance on revelation prevailed, while Toland's deism remained the possession of a few intellectuals.

R. J. VanderMolen

See also Deism; Enlightenment, The.

Bibliography. J. C. Biddle, "Locke's Critique of Innate Principles and Toland's Deism," *JHI* 37:411–23; G. R. Cragg, *Reason and Authority in the Eighteenth Century; DNB,* XIX; P. Gay, *The Enlightenment: An Interpretation;* J. Orr, *English Deism: Its Roots and Fruits;* L. Stephen, *History of English Thought in the Eighteenth Century;* R. Stromberg, *Religious Liberalism in Eighteenth-Century England.*

Tolerance. Indulgence of belief or conduct other than one's own. The term is variously defined from being an attitude of forbearance in judging the beliefs and behavior of others to one of respect for the opinions and practices of others when they are in conflict with one's own. The problem of tolerance is deeply rooted in the history of religions, in which coercion, intolerance, and persecution have played a prominent role. Religious intolerance, generally born out of the denial of the right of dissent in faith or practice, is as old as religious diversity.

Throughout human history, religion and tolerance have not been natural allies. Intolerance, not tolerance; conformity, not nonconformity; and assent, not dissent; have been hallmarks in the history of religions. More wars have been fought, more persecutions have been carried out, and more lives have been lost in the name of religion than probably for any other single cause. Religious intolerance has, in turn, been made the basis of racial prejudice and acts of political and social discrimination against nonadherents or nonconformists to established religious faith. Among the causes of religious intolerance are the following: (1) a religion that is viewed as false and/or dangerous to the prevailing religious community; (2) a religion perceived to be in conflict with the mores and moral values of a particular society; (3) a religion judged to be subversive because its teachings threaten the pattern of political authority or the political policy being advanced; and (4) a religion believed to be alien to the culture in which it is being promulgated or one identified with a foreign power.

Tolerance in History. The ultimate concerns of religious traditions have in a sense precluded the tolerance of opposing views of faith and practice. Because of the will to demand conformity to unify the empire or nation, religious differences or expressions of dissent were treated with intolerance which became the basis of persecution. Generally speaking, diversity was abhorred because it represented a threat to the unity and solidarity of the tribe, the state, the empire, or the nation. The denial of tolerance is usually characterized by the following: (1) the absolutizing of the formulations of a particular faith and the necessity of defending it; (2) fear of the consequences of tolerating moral and religious error; (3) abhorrence of unorthodox views and practices; and (4) intense hostility toward those who are nonconformists with respect to the legally and socially accepted norms of religious faith and practice.

These characteristics, deeply embedded in interfaith and international relations throughout the history of religions, have been manifestly present in the waves of intense persecution carried on throughout the centuries in Christianity's relations with Jews and Judaism, in the confrontations between Islam and Christianity, and in the encounters between Catholicism and Protestantism.

For several thousand years the history of religion has been marked by intolerance, which has clearly not been restricted to any one era or to any one religion. Examples include: persecution of the adherents of Amon by Ikhnaton (Ahmenhotep IV), of the Canaanites by the Israelites, of Jesus and the early Christians by the Romans, of Buddhists by Shintoists, of Sufis by Islamic orthodoxy, of heretics and Jews by Christians, of Protestants by Catholics and of Catholics by Protestants, of Anabaptists by Martin Luther, of religious sectarians by Protestant established churches (in the Old World and New), of "witches" and Quakers by the Puritans in early Massachusetts, and, when fused with political power, of religious dissenters by religious fundamentalists, as in present-day Iran.

As long as religions were tribal or national in character, tolerance of another religion within the tribe or nation could not be countenanced, since another religion threatened the unity of the group, which had to be preserved in order to maintain the state's solidarity. While an outward tolerance, i.e., acknowledgment of other gods and religions identified with other people, constituted no problem in the ancient world, veneration of foreign gods or criticism or dissent with respect to the religion of one's own tribe or nation was not tolerated. Even in ancient Greece, a relatively liberal and syncretistic culture, Socrates had to drink the cup of poison for having undermined belief in the Greek gods and the state religion, thereby endangering the unity of the Greek state. For this reason, Plato wrote, "If a person be proven guilty of impiety, not merely from childish levity, but such as grown-up men may be guilty of, . . . let him be punished with death."

The Romans persecuted Christians, not because the Christian faith lacked religious truths or good ethical and moral teachings, but because Christians refused to worship the emperor of Rome. Christianity was thereby a threat to Roman unity, to the sacred institution of *Imperium Romanum.* Thus, later in the alliance of Christianity with Rome, following the espousal of Christianity by Constantine in the Edict of Milan of A.D. 313, Christianity became the persecutor of rival faiths within the Roman Empire, since once again rival faiths threatened the unity of the empire. Non-Christian temples were destroyed, and a death penalty was imposed upon those who continued to offer sacrifices to pagan gods.

The concept of the Christian state prevailed throughout the Middle Ages. With the establishment of the Holy Roman Empire by Charlemagne in 800, the concept attained ultimate application. To be a citizen of the empire was to be a member of the church, and to be a member of the church was the foundation of one's citizenship in the empire. Enemies of the church, such as heretics and sectarians, were regarded as enemies of the empire. Non-Christians, such as Jews, were therefore aliens without any real citizenship and hence were treated as outcasts without human status or civil rights.

Augustine, Bishop of Hippo, had provided a theological rationale for intolerance. Indeed, for more than a millennium, Augustine's text, "Compel them to come in" (Luke 14:23), was used to authorize the use of force by the church against heretics and infidels, since liberty of error is the ultimate destroyer of the soul. Augustine furnished theological justification for the right of the state to suppress heresy and schism. Where persuasion failed, persecution could be used, as in the case of the Donatists, "to accomplish by the help of the terror of judges and laws," Augustine wrote, "whereby they may be preserved from falling under the penalty of eternal judgment." While Augustine was opposed to the death penalty, he saw persecution as a duty of the church in its defense of truth against error. "I persecute openly," he declared, "because I am a son of the Church."

Because of its acceptance of the Christian state, the Protestant Reformation brought neither religious toleration nor church-state separation. In Protestant countries, those who did not accept the authority of the established church were excluded also from the political community with which the church was identified. Protestantism was not tolerated in Catholic countries, and Catholicism was not tolerated in Protestant countries. The right of religious dissent was politically prohibited. Nonconformists were persecuted as heretics of the church and traitors of the state. The notion of the Christian state, including the European pattern of an established church, was transplanted to the New World, where in New England the Puritans and in Virginia the Anglicans denied the right of religious dissent.

Tolerance in Modern Times. The concept of tolerance, rooted in the concept of "liberty of conscience," a phrase of modern origin, emerged slowly. The major advances toward tolerance came not from church confessions of faith, councils, or synods, but from constitutions, legislatures, and courts of law. While the Protestant Reformation did not espouse tolerance as such, it did represent a revolt against authority in the final dismemberment of a united Christendom or *mundus Christianus*, and it fostered the emergence of new nation-states and a new national spirit throughout Europe and Great Britain. Ecclesiastical or religious authority was weakened to a degree beyond which it could never recover. Religious liberty came to be proclaimed as both a natural and a divine right. The spirit of tolerance was greatly accelerated in principle and in practice by international relations that resulted in the ratification of treaties between states, and by the emergence of pluralistic societies resulting from constitutional governments and the shifting of many large and ethnic communities.

Since the adoption in 1948 of the Universal Declaration of Human Rights, religious tolerance has been recognized as a part of international law.

J. E. Wood, Jr.

Bibliography. J. E. E. D. Acton, *The History of Freedom and Other Essays;* R. Bainton, *The Travail of Religious Liberty;* M. S. Bates, *Religious Liberty: An Inquiry;* S. W. Cobb, *The Rise of Religious Liberty in America;* W. K. Jordan, *The Development of Religious Toleration in England;* H. Kamen, *The Rise of Toleration;* J. Lecler, *Toleration and the Reformation;* J. Locke, *Epistola de Tolerantia: A Letter on Toleration;* G. Mensching, *Tolerance and Truth in Religion;* F. Ruffini, *Religious Liberty.*

Tongues, Gift of. *See* Spiritual Gifts.

Tongues, Speaking in ("Glossolalia"). One of the nine *charisma*, or "grace-gifts," of the Spirit in I Cor. 12:4–11. It has two functions: in the Acts of the Apostles, it is an initiation or authentication gift meant as a divine affirmation of a new group entering the church; and in I Cor. 12–14 or Rom. 12 it is a "spiritual gift" bestowed upon sovereignly chosen individuals within the church. It is vigorously debated whether the NT favors unknown or known languages, with a slight majority favoring the former. Many others opt for a both/and rather than an either/or.

The Biblical Data. *OT Evidence.* Two specific OT passages are utilized as proof texts in the NT, Joel 2:28–30 (Acts 2:15–21) and Isa. 28:11 (I Cor. 14:21). Scholars debate the extent to which the two passages prophesy a future outpouring of the Spirit as the sign of the new age, with the consensus favorable in terms of the Joel passage and doubtful in terms of the Isaiah passage, which originally prophesied foreign rule during the Exile. Further, the Joel passage was only partially fulfilled at Pentecost, and many believe that it refers to the eschaton as its final denouement. The latter part (vss. 30–31) contains the cosmic signs associated in the NT with the return of Christ. This relates to the NT belief that in salvation history the events of the first advent inaugurated the last days and that believers now live in a state of tension between the ages.

Other OT precursors are Num. 11:24–29; I Sam. 19:18–24; and I Kings 18:28–29. In Num. 11 the seventy elders upon whom the Spirit rested "prophesied," which many take to be an ecstatic experience since the action is an external manifestation of the Spirit's descent upon them. However, it is difficult to draw too much out of the passage because the text does not clearly indicate the outward results. In light of extrabiblical parallels some sociologically oriented commentators believe that ecstatic utterances were one of the chief characteristics of the prophetic office. Again, however, this reads too much into the biblical data. In I Sam. 19 such behavior may be read into the actions of the group of prophets and of Saul and his men (vss. 20–24). Clearly this is the major OT passage that may relate to ecstatic experiences as a prophetic attribute (note that Saul "lay all day and night" prophesying, vs. 24). However, Samuel does not exhibit this conduct, and neither do the other oral prophets (e.g., Elijah and Elisha). In I Kings 18 the prophets of Baal cut themselves with knives and "frantically prophesy." While there is no explicit statement of glossolalia, most recognize it in their behavior. Yet again, this is clearly not associated with the prophetic office. Therefore, we would conclude that this phenomenon, although perhaps present at times, was in no way a primary characteristic of the true prophet.

Extrabiblical Evidence. In the ancient world, pagan prophets were commonly associated with ecstatic utterances, trances, and frenzied behavior. There are records of ecstatic speech and the like in Egypt in the eleventh century B.C. In the hellenistic world the prophetess of Delphi and the Sibylline priestess spoke in unknown or unintelligible speech. Moreover, the Dionysian rites contained a trancelike state as well as glossolalia. Many of the magicians and sorcerers of the first century world exhibit similar phenomena, as in the case of the "spirit of divination" (or possibly ventriloquism) at Philippi in Acts 16:16–18.

NT Evidence. In Matt. 3:11 John the Baptist prophesies that the Messiah "will baptize you with the Holy Spirit and with fire." Pentecostals often see in this a precursor of their doctrine of "baptism by the Spirit," but the passage more likely looks forward to Pentecost. James Dunn argues that this is a metaphorical expression for that "baptism" into the kingdom that was an extension of John's own ministry of baptism. It is true that neither Jesus nor his disciples speak in tongues in the Gospels, and there is no hint there of a connection between tongues and the activity of the Holy Spirit. The only passage that may do so is Mark 16:17, which makes "new tongues" one of the "signs" that will accompany the Christian. However, most scholars agree that this "longer ending" of Mark was added in the second century and so refers back to the apostolic gifts. Nevertheless as such it is evidence that the second century church still accepted the validity of these supernatural gifts.

The Acts of the Apostles is naturally a key portion of Scripture on this issue. Pentecost (Acts 2) has been the focus of much debate. First, there is the "Johannine Pentecost" (John 20:22), which some say contradicts the Acts account and others say is proleptic, promising the later event. Neither fits the evidence. Most likely, when Jesus breathed on them and said, "Receive the Holy Spirit," he was providing a private infusing of the Spirit, while Acts 2 was the public empowering, which inaugurated the new age of the Spirit. Second, others argue that the miracle was one of hearing rather than speaking and that this ecstatic utterance was meant as the obverse to the Babel incident regarding the confusion of tongues (Gen. 11:1–9). This too is unlikely, for the tenor of the passage favors a miracle of speaking. While the Babel theme may be present, the major theological emphasis deals with the universal mission. The catalogue of nations in Acts 2:9–11 sweeps from east to west, stressing the future redemptive mission of the church (cf. 1:8).

The rest of Acts builds upon this, as we have the Samaritan Pentecost (8:14–19), the Gentile Pentecost (10:44–46), and the Ephesian Pentecost (19:6). Two misconceptions need to be explained. First, some say that Acts presents the Pentecost-type of encounter as the necessary initial experience for one who is filled or baptized with the Spirit. The problem is twofold: (1) the historical passages cannot be used to establish dogma unless they are corroborated by teaching material, since historical narratives tell what happened rather than what always must be. (2) There are too many episodes in Acts where tongues are not the necessary initiatory experience (e.g., 4:31; 8:17; 9:17–18). While the Samaritan Pentecost probably included tongues (Simon's reaction shows that something spectacular had occurred), it is not the main stress of the passage and does not support the weight placed upon it by proponents of the thesis above.

Second, others argue that tongues were sign gifts intended to authenticate the apostolic message and so this gift ceased at the end of the apostolic age. This too goes beyond the evidence of Acts. In actuality, they authenticated the addition of new groups to the church, not for the sake of non-Christians but rather for the sake of the Jewish Christians in Jerusalem. There is no hint that the supernatural gifts had so narrow a purpose. Therefore both of these theories must await further data from the NT.

The next major source is I Cor. 12–14. The purpose of the gift has obviously changed drastically. It is no longer apologetic proof, but has now become part of the cultic worship of the church. The problem at Corinth was the tendency of the enthusiasts there to elevate glossolalia to the greatest of the gifts. Paul in these chapters corrects this error and puts the gift in its proper place. The gifts are given, not to everyone , but only to those sovereignly chosen by the Spirit (12:11). Moreover, in any hierarchical order, tongues is the least of the gifts; the use of "first, second, third" in vs. 28 reflects just such a pattern. In vss. 29–30 it is clear that Paul denies the contention of the enthusiasts that everyone truly spiritual should speak in tongues: "All are not apostles, are they? . . . All do not speak in tongues, do they?"

Chapter 13 explores the basic problem of this group, the lack of love, and chapter 14 stresses the problematic value of this gift for the church. Without "interpretation" it is incomprehensible and will not "edify" like the gift of prophecy. Moreover, as a "sign" it seems to the outsider to typify madness (vss. 21–23). Paul at the same time recognizes the validity of glossolalia as a spiritual gift (vs. 12) and rejoices that he has been chosen to excel in it (vs. 18). Nevertheless, tongues are often best relegated to private devotions (vs. 28) and must be utilized in corporate worship with dignity and order (vss. 26–33). Finally, Paul commands that in spite of the problems enumerated above, the church dare not "forbid" glossolalia, so long as it is expressed in a "fitting and orderly manner" (vss. 39–40).

In other NT epistles, there are perhaps references to tongues. Eph. 5:19 and Col. 3:16 speak of "songs and hymns and spiritual songs," which some take to be charismatic singing. While most remain dubious regarding this, it is a possibility. Also, many interpret Rom. 8:26, which describes the Spirit praying "with groanings too deep for words," in terms of "Spirit-filled prayer." While this is growing in popularity, it must remain more conjecture than likelihood, since the context speaks of the Spirit's intercession rather than the believer's charismatic prayer. Finally, Heb. 2:4 asserts that "God bears witness with [the apostles] . . . by gifts of the Holy Spirit on the basis of his will." This is a crucial verse for those who wish to see the supernatural charisms as sign gifts meant only for the apostolic age. However, it does not state that *the* purpose of the gifts was authentication, only that *a* purpose is to affirm the apostles' message. Building a doctrine on a single statement from Scripture without recognizing other passages is a misuse of biblical data.

Church History. The supernatural gifts like glossolalia gradually declined during the patristic period. Several fathers, e.g., Irenaeus or Tertullian, speak favorably of it, and groups like the Montanists make it central to their worship experience. This group followed Montanus of Phrygia, who said he was the chosen instrument of the Spirit to prepare the church for the second coming. He taught a strict asceticism, which soon developed into a legalism. The antiestablishment attitude of the Montanists led to denunciation and then rejection and the movement disappeared. By the middle of the fourth century the practice seems to be a thing of the past. Chrysostom was quite negative, and Augustine declared that it had been given only for the NT times. It appears that in the pressures of the dogmatic controversies and the debates with pagan hellenism, interest in such suprarational gifts as tongues or prophecy gradually diminished.

The Eastern church, with a more mystical and enthusiastic religious experience, continued to be open to tongues, and many believe that it was practiced unabated in Greek Orthodox monasteries throughout the Middle Ages. It was quite a different case in the Western church. Such experiences were viewed with suspicion, perhaps even taken as evidence of the demonic. Several possible examples of tongues may be adduced: the abbess Hildegard, whose use of unknown tongues is recorded in the *Lingua Ignota,* or missionaries like Vincent Ferrer or Francis Xavier, who described their miraculous ability to communicate with various groups as glossolalia.

Luther and Calvin both spoke positively of the gift, and some believe Luther actually had such experiences. However, the passages which discuss the gift primarily think of it in terms of missionary preaching, and it is difficult to connect the Reformers to any actual experience. The best one can say is that they accepted the continuing validity of tongues. The next widespread outbreak occurred among a group of persecuted Huguenots in southern France at the end of the seventeenth century. This lasted a little over a decade, and in the 1730s a similar occurrence took place among the Jansenists, a group of Catholic pietists.

Two eighteenth century movements, the early Quakers and the Methodists, are often placed among those who have exhibited glossolalic traits. Both claims, however, are disputed, and the evidence is not conclusive. Wesley does appear positive toward tongues and certainly believed that such gifts were valid, but we cannot be certain whether he himself participated. The Irvingites from the 1830s to the end of the century made such expressions the hallmark of their church life. The example of the Huguenots and the Irvingites led to similar occurrences among the Shakers and the Mormons in America, and in Russia a pentecostal-type movement began in the 1850s and apparently continued throughout the century.

Modern Pentecostalism developed out of the revivalist movement, within which several such experiences were recorded in the nineteenth century. In 1901, in a small Bible school in Topeka, Kansas, a group made up of several Baptist ministers and students in a Bible study came to the conclusion that tongues always accompanied Spirit baptism in Acts. After much prayer they apparently received the gift. For the first few years, in spite of much publicity, only sporadic outbreaks occurred. The "breakthrough" came in Los Angeles in 1906, and the resulting Azusa Street Mission became the center for Pentecostalism. Meanwhile, glossolalia arose in the 1904 Welsh revival and in Pentecostal meetings throughout both Europe and America in ensuing years.

In the first half of this century Pentecostals were rejected by the other denominations. The normal result of such an occurrence was a church split. However, in the 1960s the phenomenon simultaneously developed within both mainline Protestant and Roman Catholic groups, and what has become known as the charismatic movement began. Today there are movements within both Pentecostalism and the charismatic groups toward a mediating position on tongues.

The Current Issue. We may delineate three basic positions today with respect to the tongues controversy, and there are two issues within the positions. (1) Are tongues for every age? (2) Are tongues the necessary sign of baptism by the Holy Spirit?

The Positive School. Pentecostals and most charismatics answer yes to both questions. They make clear distinction between baptism (in Acts) and the gift of tongues (I Cor.). The former is for everyone, while the latter is given to those whom the Spirit chooses. Even in the latter instance, however, the common belief is that all the gifts are open to everyone, and it is only a matter of the faith to claim it. Since glossolalia is the *only* initial evidence of Spirit baptism, everyone must seek the gift in that sense. It is the key to greater spiritual power in one's life and so must be sought. For this reason "tarrying" meetings developed within Pentecostalism, as groups of people would "tarry" and be taught how to expand their consciousness in order to bypass the intellect and to open themselves to the baptism of the Spirit.

The Negative School. This group answers no to both questions above. Some believe that the supernatural gifts ceased at the end of the apostolic age, others that they gradually diminished and ended in the fourth century. There are two basic approaches. (1) The Reformed scholar Benjamin B. Warfield at the turn of the century argued that glossolalia was among the sign gifts intended to authenticate the message of the apostles. Therefore, when the NT message was complete, they no longer were necessary. (2) The dispensational scholar Merrill F. Unger asserted that the "perfect" in I Cor. 13:10 meant the canon, and therefore at the close of the canon tongues "ceased in and of themselves" (the middle voice). There are quite a few differences among proponents of this position. Some state that God allows tongues as an emotional release, and so we should not be too negative toward adherents. Others say that God never allows them, and some go so far as to declare them demonic.

The Middle Position. A growing number take a position similar to that of A. B. Simpson, founder of the Christian and Missionary Alliance: "This gift is one of many gifts and is given to some for the benefit of all. The attitude toward the gift of tongues held by pastor and people should be, 'Seek not, forbid not.'" Those of this persuasion would answer yes to the first question, no to the second. They would be leery of developing a system that would involve the violation of I Cor. 14:39*b,* "Do not forbid to speak in tongues." They would also be afraid to disregard 12:30*b,* "All do not speak in tongues, do they?" Therefore, while speaking in tongues is not the initial sign of Spirit baptism, it can be experienced as a gift, if the Spirit so determines. Moreover, scholars of this school are leery of utilizing 13:9–10 against glossolalia, since the verb itself simply means "cease" in the middle voice and since "perfect" as "canon" is doubtful in this context. Rather, "perfect" refers to the "perfect age" when we will see Christ "face to face" (vs. 12).

Conclusion. The key, of course, is Scripture itself more than experience, even from church history. Many Pentecostals go so far as to accept the demise of the gift down through the ages but believe that the outbreak of glossolalia in this century is the "latter rain" (Joel 2:23) prophesied for the last days in Acts 2:16–21. Therefore one must consider all the passages that deal with tongues and see which position best interprets the data.

G. R. Osborne

See also Charismatic Movement; Holy Spirit; Pentecostalism; Spiritual Gifts.

Bibliography. 1. *Pentecostal Works.* L. Christensen, *Speaking in Tongues;* H. M. Ervin, *These Are Not Drunken, As Ye Suppose;* W. H. Horton, ed., *The Glossolalia Phenomenon;* J. L. Sherrill, *They Speak with Other Tongues.* 2. *Anti-Pentecostal Works.* A. A. Hoekema, *What About Tongue-Speaking?* C. R. Smith, *Tongues in Biblical Perspective;* M. F. Unger, *NT Teaching on Tongues;* B. B. Warfield, *Miracles: Yesterday and Today.* 3. *Works from the Middle Position.* G. W. Bromiley, "The Holy Spirit," in *The Fundamentals of the Faith,* ed. C. F. H. Henry; J. D. G. Dunn, *Baptism in the Holy Spirit;* M. T. Kelsey, *Tongue Speaking: An Experiment in Spiritual Experience;* C. Pinnock and G. R. Osborne, "A Truce Proposal for the Tongues Controversy," *CT,* Oct. 8, 1971.

Torgau Articles, The. Three documents composed by Lutheran theologians in the sixteenth century. They are named for a town on the Elbe River in Germany.

(1) The Torgau Articles of 1530 were prepared by Martin Luther, Philip Melanchthon, and Justus Jonas and presented to Elector John the Constant in anticipation of the Diet at Augsburg. They contained an introduction and ten articles, dealing primarily with abuses in Roman Catholic practice (e.g., the invocation of saints, prohibition of clerical marriage, communion in one kind) and defending worship in the vernacular. Melanchthon incorporated these (along with the Schwabach Articles) into the Augsburg Confession.

(2) The Torgau Articles or Confession of 1574 were prepared by various Lutheran theologians and subscribed by the Wittenberg faculty. They dealt with the Lord's Supper and contained both positive and negative articles. A high Lutheran view of the Eucharist is affirmed, for "by the sacramental union the bread is the body of Christ, and the wine is the blood of Christ." Alternative interpretations, especially those of the Swiss, are said to be "dangerous errors" that "ought to be refuted and condemned in our churches."

(3) The Torgau Articles or Book of Torgau of 1576 were occasioned by controversies within the Lutheran churches and composed by a convention held at Torgau between May 28 and June 7, 1576, which included Jacob Andreae, Andreas Musculus, Martin Chemnitz, David Chytraeus, and Nicholas Selnecker. It drew heavily on previous documents, especially the Maulbronn Formula and the Swabian-Saxon Concord, and was submitted to Elector Augustus, who circulated the document widely among the Lutheran states. After receiving many suggestions from the territorial churches, the Book of Torgau was thoroughly revised in 1577 at Bergen, Germany, and

called the Bergen Book. It was incorporated into the Formula of Concord, the statement of 1577, which provided a consensus of doctrinal views and ecclesiastical unity for the Lutherans.

C. G. Fry

See also Concord, Formula of.

Bibliography. W. D. Allbeck, *Studies in the Lutheran Confessions.*

Total Abstinence. *See* Abstinence.

Total Depravity. *See* Depravity, Total.

Tractarianism. *See* Oxford Movement.

Tradition. The entire process by which normative religious truths are passed on from one generation to another. As such, tradition is found in all religious communities, whether its form be oral or written, its contents embodied in a closed canon or a living organism. Even evangelical Protestants, inclined though they may still be to overlook it, must recognize that oral tradition preceded and shaped the canon of written Scripture and that their own understanding of Scripture and consequently their own community life have been molded, consciously or unconsciously, by particular traditions. This article will treat the meaning of tradition in Scripture, and then examine the way in which tradition has been understood and employed in the early Christian, Orthodox, Roman Catholic, and Protestant communities.

Most scholars see recorded in the OT numerous traditions regarding persons, places, events, and cults crucial to the full story of God's dealings with his chosen people. The act of handing these on is specifically enjoined or mentioned only rarely (Deut. 6:20–25; 26:5–9; Josh. 24:2–13), but the very text entirely presupposes it. How these traditions were passed on, how and when written texts came into being, and how the canon was finally formed remains in part a matter of speculation, though conservative Christians and Jews continue to look first of all for God's word faithfully delivered to his people over generations. The Qumran texts have proven the existence of differing Hebrew text traditions, including one closer to that used for the Greek LXX. The Jewish canon was not closed until very late (A.D. 90), resulting as well in two different versions, one originating in Palestine and the other in the Diaspora, the first accepted eventually by Protestants and the second (with the deuterocanonical or apocryphal books) by Catholics. The standard Hebrew Bible comes from the early tenth century when Jews in Babylon set the readings and pointed the vowels in a text known as the Masoretic, which means literally "traditional."

By the third century B.C., at least, Jewish rabbis had produced a "traditional" interpretation of the scriptural text known as the Mishnah, of which scribes and Pharisees became the keepers and teachers. This continued to grow until it was codified in the fourth and sixth centuries as the Talmud, which provided until modern times the traditional (and therefore binding) Jewish interpretation of the OT.

In the NT the word for tradition (*paradosis*) is used, in the main, negatively by Christ and positively by the apostles. Christ repudiated "human traditions" (Matt. 15:3; Mark 7:9, 13), doubtless parts of the Mishnah, as distortions or even contradictions of God's law. But the apostles, sometimes in the style of rabbis, passed on and explicated the gospel tradition they had received from the Lord. Often in formulaic utterances taken up into his text (Rom. 1:1–4; 6:7; Phil. 2:5–11; I Thess. 4:14–17; I Tim. 3:16), Paul repeats this tradition and enjoins his flock to receive and keep it (I Cor. 11:2; II Thess. 2:15; Col. 2:6ff.). Sometimes this tradition is the very heart of the gospel (esp. I Cor. 15:1–9), while elsewhere it concerns cultic matters such as the Lord's Supper (11:23) or ethical matters such as divorce (7:10). In writings that some critics consider later this tradition comes to be called the received "deposit of faith" (I Tim. 1:10; 6:20; II Tim. 1:12, 14; Titus 1:9). The power of the apostolic witness, as Cullmann and Bruce have argued, is that what they were called to "pass on" was not of men but of God (Gal. 1:1).

The question of how the apostolic witness came to be written down and the canon of inspired texts formed is very complicated and controversial. Form critics have tended to dissolve the text into several contradictory or even unreliable sources, while redaction critics sometimes make the texts reflect more of the late first century church (which they call "early Catholicism") than of the earlier and original events. But more conservative scholars have scored considerable advances recently by pointing up the relatively short time lapse involved and the NT's concern with maintaining the true tradition (Luke 1:1–4). This is not to deny that traditions concerning Jesus, especially his sayings, soon varied in Christian communities and that a text like the Gospel of Thomas, though essentially Gnostic, might not contain the echo of some authentic sayings. Well into the second century, the OT remained the early Christians' only authorized text, but the needs of churches and the assaults of heretics led to a relatively rapid formation of the canon of the NT by the late second century and its fixation by the mid-fourth. The essential criterion was that these writings contain authentic *apostolic tradition.*

Even before the NT canon was fixed, early church fathers appealed to its individual books and to sayings of Christ (a lost exegesis of them by Papias). But they likewise saw the original apostolic tradition preserved in other ways. They often appealed to an orthodox "rule of faith," a kind of summary of the gospel possibly related to early baptismal creeds and later issuing in full-fledged creedal documents; this rule was not originally fixed in writing or anything contrary to or wholly outside of Scripture. They also appealed to "apostolic succession," the public teaching (as distinguished from the Gnostics' secret wisdom) in those churches where bishops stood in a direct line with their apostolic founders, especially the see of Rome "founded" by Peter and Paul. And they prepared, between the first and fourth centuries, a whole series of anonymous manuals (Didache) that claimed to contain the apostles' teachings, especially on cultic and ethical matters. These were not set over against Scripture, but they rather constituted the means by which the living church carried forward its witness.

Once the NT canon was fixed and the whole Bible complete, the great church fathers of the fourth and fifth centuries distinguished tradition and Scripture more clearly, but not antithetically. Tradition was understood as the church's enriching and interpretative reflection on the original deposit of faith contained in Scripture. This pertained preeminently to Christological interpretation of the OT. But it included as well the writings of earlier "fathers," considered a product of the Spirit's guidance and used to buttress the true faith; the decisions of bishops met in council under the Spirit's aegis; and various rites which had become central to the practice of the faith. A few fathers (notably Basil) recognized that certain matters were not clearly, or even remotely, prescribed in Scripture and ascribed these separately to apostolic tradition: e.g., to pray facing East, to baptize infants, to immerse three times, to fast on certain days, and the like. To count as authentic apostolic tradition, the fathers (Augustine and Vincent of Lerins in the West, e.g.) required that these be recognized and practiced throughout the whole church. What constituted authoritative tradition nevertheless became something on which the East and West eventually parted ways.

The Eastern Orthodox came to define tradition as the whole of the church's witness, based on Scripture, but expressed chiefly in the seven ecumenical councils, the writings of the fathers, and liturgical worship. In principle, Scripture remained fundamental and the church alive with its witness; in practice, the weight of tradition became preponderant and the church tended to stagnate in its fixation on what had been wrought between the fourth and seventh centuries. Outside Scripture, ecumenical councils represented the highest authority in defining tradition.

During most of the Middle Ages, the Western view differed only slightly, placing somewhat greater emphasis upon written Scripture as fundamental and an ever-increasing emphasis upon the papacy (rather than councils) as the normative spokesman for apostolic tradition. But in the fourteenth century the realization that certain doctrines (Christ's absolute poverty, e.g., or Mary's immaculate conception) could not be proved even remotely from Scripture, together with theologians' increased sophistication about their sources, inspired several of them to posit tradition as a separate, unwritten *source* handed down by apostolic succession, especially through an infallible papacy. The Protestant revolt against all tradition transformed this view, despite protest, into the church's official position at the Council of Trent: The truths and discipline of the gospel are contained in written Scripture *and* in unwritten traditions given to the church by Christ or the Spirit through the apostles, and both deserve *equal* respect. Vatican Council I completed this line of thought when it declared the church's teaching office to be centered in an infallible papacy.

Ever since the sixteenth century there has been dissent among Catholics, and that has received much attention in the last century and a half. A romantic school, associated with Möhler in Germany and Newman in England, preferred to speak of "living tradition" in which understanding and fullness grew over centuries, rather than of a distinctly separate source. Geiselmann, noting that Trent rejected a preliminary "partly . . . partly" formulation, argued for the "material sufficiency" of Scripture, meaning it contained the entire deposit of faith in whole or in germ; and in various forms this has been very influential among contemporary Catholics. Still others (Congar) refer to a single apostolic tradition being handed down in the church through written Scripture as well as teaching, discipline, and rites. Vatican Council II, while not rejecting earlier pronouncements on tradition as a source, gave much more emphasis to Scripture, and described Scripture and tradition as forming a unity through which the faithful are brought to a full knowledge of God's truth.

Protestants have nearly always rejected tradition in principle, while necessarily allowing it to reappear in practice in some other form. Luther rejected ecclesiastical traditions as distortions of the true gospel found in Scripture alone, and he thus, and for nearly all Protestants ever since, radically sundered apostolic authority from ecclesiastical tradition, now rendered merely human. Calvin confronted the question of interpretation squarely and insisted that the Spirit interacts with the word to illuminate believers—this was recognized by Catholics too, but placed under the strict supervision of the church. The word, all Reformers asserted, brought forth the church, not the other way around, and that word was "perspicuous," requiring no apostolic traditions to interpret it correctly. While Anglicans and Lutherans retained many rites and customs "not contrary to Scripture" (the Swedish Lutherans even claiming to stand still in the apostolic succession), Calvinists and later free churches attempted to ground all ecclesiastical and devotional practices in biblical teaching.

In practice, most Protestant groups formed traditions nearly as binding as the Catholics and established similar sets of authorities: ecumenical councils, confessional creeds, synodical legislation, church orders, and theologians (esp. founders) of a particular church. Those free churches, particularly in America, that claim to stand on Scripture alone and to recognize no traditional authorities are in some sense the least free because they are not even conscious of what traditions have molded their understanding of Scripture. Yet there is a decided difference between Protestants and Catholics. All Protestants insist that these traditions must ever be tested against Scripture and can never possess an independent apostolic authority over or alongside of Scripture. In recent years, scholarly research into the formation of Scripture and the course of church history has inspired greater thoughtfulness and honesty among Protestants on the subject of tradition. The word of God does not and cannot operate in a vacuum, as an isolated text; it comes alive through the Spirit in the context of gathered believers who make up Christ's church. Preaching is in fact the chief Protestant form of perpetuating tradition, i.e., authoritative interpretations and applications of the word. Protestants should therefore, at the very least, come to some understanding of how particular traditions of preaching were formed, and then proceed to consider devotional practices, church polities, and forms of worship. Protestants will never grant these apostolic authority, which resides alone in the written and inspired apostolic witness, but they can greatly enrich their own understanding and continuation of that witness by examining how the church has done it down through the ages.

J. Van Engen

Bibliography. H. Berkhof, *Christian Faith;* F. F. Bruce, *Tradition Old and New;* R. P. C. Hanson, *Tradition in the Early Church;* O. Cullmann, *La tradition;* Y. Congar, *Tradition and Traditions; LTK,* X, 290–99; *DTC,* XV, 1252–1350; *RGG,* VI, 966–84; *NCE,* XIV, 223–28; H. E. W. Turner, *The Pattern of Christian Truth.*

Traducianism. One of four theories of the origin of the individual soul, i.e., that the soul, as well as the body, comes from the parents. Alternatives are: (1) preexistence of all souls, held by, e.g., Origen and Mormons; (2) reincarnation; (3) creationism, whereby God creates a fresh soul for each body.

Direct biblical evidence is nonexistent, and conclusions must be based on deductions. In favor of traducianism: (1) God's breathing into man the breath of life is not said to be repeated after Adam (Gen. 2:7); (2) Adam begat a son in his own likeness (Gen. 5:3); (3) God's resting (Gen. 2:2–3) suggests no fresh acts of creation *ex nihilo;* and (4) original sin affects the whole man, including the soul; this is simply accounted for by traducianism.

Traducianism was held by Tertullian and many Westerns; since the Reformation by Lutherans; also by the Eastern church. Roman Catholics and most Reformed theologians are creationists, though Shedd and Strong favor traducianism. Modern studies in heredity and psychosomatic unity are indecisive, but can easily be interpreted on the traducianist side.

J. S. Wright

See also Soul.

Bibliography. A. H. Strong, *Systematic Theology,* V. I. iv.

Transcendence of God. *See* God, Attributes of; God, Doctrine of.

Transcendentalism. An idealistic philosophy that in general emphasizes the spiritual over the material. By its very nature, the movement is hard to describe and its body of beliefs hard to define. Its most important practitioner and spokesman in the New England manifestation, Ralph Waldo Emerson, called it "the Saturnalia or excess of Faith." That which is "popularly called Transcendentalism among us," he wrote, "is Idealism; Idealism as it appears in 1842." That description mentions two of the very elements—an emphasis upon heightened spiritual awareness and an interest in various types of philosophical idealism—that make transcendentalism so difficult to describe.

In actuality, we cannot speak of a well-organized and clearly delineated transcendentalist movement as such. Instead, we find a loosely knit group of authors, preachers, and lecturers bound together by a mutual loathing of Unitarian orthodoxy, a mutual desire to see American cultural and spiritual life freed from bondage to the past, and a mutual faith in the unbounded potential of American democratic life. Located in the Concord, Massachusetts, area in the years between 1835 and 1860, the transcendentalists formed not a tight group but, rather, a loose federation.

Though a movement such as transcendentalism cannot be said to have had one distinct leader, Emerson (1803–82) was clearly its central figure. The publication of his *Nature* in 1836 is generally considered to mark the beginning of an identifiable movement. The next two decades were to see numerous new works from Emerson and poems, essays, and books from other transcendentalist figures, such as Henry David Thoreau (1817–62), Orestes Brownson (1803–76), Amos Bronson Alcott (1799–1888), Margaret Fuller (1810–50), George Ripley (1802–80), and Theodore Parker (1810–60). Never forming an official affiliation, these figures and others associated with them banded together for the formation of an informal discussion group called the Transcendental Club; the publication of the transcendentalist literary and philosophical journal, *The Dial;* and the establishment of an experiment in utopian communal living, Brook Farm.

One thing almost all those associated with the movement did share, however, was a common heritage of Unitarianism. Perhaps more than anything else, this fact helps to explain the development of transcendentalism and its later and larger significance for American culture. The transcendentalists broke with Unitarianism for two reasons. First, they objected to the Unitarian desire to cling to certain particulars of Christian history and dogma. Emerson called this clinging a "noxious" exaggeration of "the personal, the positive, the ritual," and he asked instead for a direct access to God, unmediated by any elements of Scripture and tradition. And second, the transcendentalists lamented the sterility of belief and practice they found in the Unitarian faith. According to Thoreau, it is not man's sin but his boredom and weariness that are "as old as Adam." The American Adam needs to exchange his bondage to tradition for a freedom to experiment: "old deeds for old people, and new deeds for new."

In some ways transcendentalism attempted to recapture for the American spirit the fervor of the original Puritan enterprise. That zeal, with its attendant bliss and agony, had been suppressed or exiled to the wilderness of the American religious experience by the end of the eighteenth century. Transcendentalism was one of the first and most dramatic protests against civil religion in America. Though it did not live up to the expectations of its adherents—many of them expected nothing less than a total regeneration of social and spiritual life through the application of the principles of idealism in America—transcendentalism has had a lasting impact. In the years immediately preceding the Civil War, several of the transcendentalists were important participants in the abolitionist movement, and in the decades to follow, widely divergent individuals and movements would find inspiration in the transcendental protest against society. For example, Henry Ford, who once said "history is bunk" and declared Emerson's essays to be his favorite reading, dwelt upon the transcendentalists' disdain for convention and their exaltation of self-reliant power, while both Mahatma Gandhi and Martin Luther King drew deeply upon the resources of Thoreau's famous essay, "Civil Disobedience."

Perhaps even more significantly, transcendentalism marked the first substantial attempt in American history to retain the spiritual experience and potential of the Christian faith without any of the substance of its belief. By claiming an essential innocence for man, by substituting a direct intuition of God or truth for any form of revelation, and by foreseeing a future of ill-defined but certain glory for humankind, transcendentalism paved the way for the many romantic notions about human nature and destiny that have become such a central part of the American experience in the last hundred years.

R. LUNDIN

See also EMERSON, RALPH WALDO.

Bibliography. P. Miller, "From Edwards to Emerson," *NEQ* 13:587–617, and (ed.) *The Transcendentalists: An Anthology;* O. B. Frothingham, *Transcendentalism in New England: A History;* F. O. Matthiessen, *American Renaissance: Art and Expression in the Age of Emerson and Whitman;* L. Buell, *Literary Transcendentalism: Style and Vision in the American Renaissance;* J. Myerson, *The New England Transcendentalists and The Dial.*

Transcendental Meditation (TM). An Eastern meditative practice popularized in the West by Maharishi Mahesh Yogi. Born in India in 1918, Maharishi (which means "great sage") was a disciple of Swami Brahmananda Saraswati (or "Guru Dev") before he began teaching in the West as a Hindu holy man. As part of a series of world tours, Maharishi first came to the United

States in 1959. The TM movement has become the largest and fastest growing of the various Eastern spiritual disciplines that have taken root in the West.

The simplified and Westernized set of yoga techniques that Maharishi has introduced and marketed in the West is presented to the public as a nonreligious practice designed to enable a person to make use of his/her full mental potential while at the same time achieving deep rest and relaxation. TM claims to offer people absolute happiness, perfect bliss, and "restful alertness" through a technique that requires a minimum of meditation—twenty minutes twice a day.

The claim that TM is not religious, that it is merely a scientific technique, has been questioned by Christian and secular observers alike. Maharishi and his carefully trained instructors assert that the benefits of TM can be enjoyed without compromising one's religion. Critics of the TM movement argue that transcendental meditation is essentially Hindu religious practice in disguise.

An initiation ceremony is required of all novice meditators. TM instructors contend that this is merely a secular ceremony of gratitude. The religious nature of this ceremony (called the *puja*), however, is quite clear. The participant is asked to bring flowers, fruit, and a white cloth and to bow before the image of Maharishi's late teacher, Guru Dev. The *puja* is a Sanskrit hymn of adoration and worship, although its meaning is not revealed to the novice. The initiation ceremony, therefore, is by Christian definition the worship of false gods. From the perspective of TM, the *puja* is intended to alter the consciousness of both instructor and novice so that the mind is opened to the influence of the "great masters."

At the time of initiation, the candidate is given a supposedly secret mantra, a Sanskrit word or syllable, which is claimed to have special vibrational qualities and which is regularly used by the meditator thereafter. TM instructors state that the mantras are merely "meaningless sounds." However, an examination of the source of the mantras, the Hindu religion, reveals that these sounds are the code names of deities. Therefore, the repetition of a mantra constitutes an act of worship.

The use of a mantra is one of the standard means of inducing the classical mystical experience of God-consciousness or unity. The twice-daily routine of TM is said to enable the person to achieve an altered or "transcendental" state of consciousness with the goal of ultimately reaching "enlightenment." Its objective is the elimination of all consciously directed thought, an emptying of the mind. Like all Eastern mysticism, TM involves the negation of the mind and an increased reliance on subjective feelings.

Transcendental Meditation is in reality a form of pantheism. It does not teach the existence of one eternal, personal God, the Creator of the universe. It is part of the monist tradition in that it teaches belief in the essential oneness of all reality and therefore the possibility of man's unity with the divine. The practice of TM itself leads the meditator toward the idolatry of self-worship because of the identification of the self with the higher "Self" of the creation. In short, TM promotes an experience involving the loss of one's distinctive identity under the false pretense of a scientific technique. R. M. ENROTH

Bibliography. D. Haddon and V. Hamilton, *TM Wants You! A Christian Response to Transcendental Meditation;* D. Haddon, "Transcendental Meditation," in *A Guide to Cults and New Religions,* ed. R. M. Enroth.

Transgression. *See* SIN.

Transmigration of Souls. *See* REINCARNATION.

Transubstantiation. The theory accepted by Rome as a dogma in 1215, in an attempt to explain the statements of Christ: "This is my body" and "This is my blood" (Mark 14:22, 24) as applied to the bread and wine of the Lord's Supper. It is insisted that the "is" must be taken with the strictest literalism. But to our senses the bread and wine seem to remain exactly as they were even when consecrated. There is no perceptible miracle of transformation. The explanation is found in terms of a distinction between the so-called substance (or true reality) and the accidents (the specific, perceptible characteristics). The latter remain, but the former, i.e., the substance of bread and wine, is changed into that of the body and blood of Christ. This carries with it many serious consequences. If Christ is substantially present, it is natural that the elements should be adored. It can also be claimed that he is received by all who communicate, whether rightly to salvation or wrongly to perdition. There also arises the idea of a propitiatory immolation of Christ for the temporal penalties of sin, with all the associated scandals of private masses. The weaknesses of the theory are obvious. It is not scriptural. On sharper analysis it does not even explain the dominical statements. It contradicts the true biblical account of Christ's presence. It has no secure patristic backing. It stands or falls with a particular philosophical understanding. It destroys the true nature of a sacrament. And it certainly perverts its proper use and gives rise to dangerous superstitions inimical to evangelical faith. G. W. BROMILEY

See also Concomitance; Lord's Supper, Views of; Real Presence.

Bibliography. J. Calvin *Institutes* 4.18; T. Cranmer, *The True and Catholic Doctrine of the Lord's Supper;* N. Dimock, *Doctrine of the Lord's Supper;* W. H. Griffith Thomas, *The Principles of Theology,* 388–410.

Trent, Council of (1545–1563). Official Roman Catholic response to the Lutheran Reformation. The Council of Trent did not begin until twenty-five years after Martin Luther's symbolic rejection of papal authority when he publicly burned *Exsurge Domine* (1520), the papal bull condemning his teachings. This fateful delay in the history of Christianity permitted the consolidation of Protestantism and ensured that, when the council did eventually meet to define doctrines, it would do so in conscious reaction to Protestant doctrines. Though some Protestants attended the council, the majority of those attending were motivated by a desire to counter, rather than conciliate, the Protestants. Hence, even Catholic historians who emphasize the continuity of Trent's doctrinal definitions with traditional Catholic theology concede that Trent did not restore the medieval equilibrium so much as evolve a new system synthesizing Catholic tradition and the altered historical situation. The new system was rigid and exclusive, but also rich and energetic, drawing on the spiritual and theological revival that characterized the Counter-Reformation.

Reasons for the repeated delays in convening the council were chiefly, but not solely, political. Even Pope Paul III (1534–49), who was elected on the understanding that he would call a council and who acknowledged that it was desperately needed, was forced into repeated postponements by a growing appreciation of the complexity of the issues at stake. So complex and voluminous was its agenda that the council took eighteen years, spanning the reigns of five popes, to complete. Its sittings alone took over four years, and it produced a greater volume of legislation than the combined output of all the previous eighteen general councils recognized by the Roman Catholic Church.

The Council's history has three periods:

1. Sessions 1–10 (Dec. 13, 1545, to June 2, 1547), during the pontificate of Paul III.
2. Sessions 11–16 (May 1, 1551, to April 28, 1552), under Julius III.
3. Sessions 17–25 (Jan. 17, 1562, to Dec. 4, 1563), under Pius IV.

It was decided at the outset to deal with both disciplinary reforms (which Holy Roman Emperor, Charles V, saw as the first priority) and the definition of dogma (the primary concern of Paul III). A repentant episcopate acknowledged that the Lutheran revolt was occasioned by the "ambition, avarice and cupidity" of bishops. The council accordingly condemned pluralism and absenteeism by bishops and priests. Clergy were to "avoid even the smallest faults, which in them would be considerable." Bishops were to establish seminaries for the training of clergy in every diocese. In nothing was the Roman Catholic Church more indelibly scarred by its fear of Protestantism than in the council's decision to make the curriculum in the new seminaries scholastic rather than biblical. On indulgences, the issue which ignited the Lutheran explosion, the council abolished indulgence sellers and decreed that the giving of alms was never to be the necessary condition for gaining an indulgence.

The article on justification was perceived as the most difficult of the doctrinal issues, partly because it had not been dealt with in previous councils. Thirty-three canons condemned Protestant errors concerning justification. Most were errors held by Protestant extremists, but the bishops certainly understood that they had condemned Luther's doctrine that Christ's righteousness is extrinsic to the justified person and only imputed to him. The Tridentine doctrine on justification was expressed in sixteen chapters. Chapters 1–9 stress man's incapacity to save himself but confirm the necessity for the cooperation of his free will, including his resolve to receive baptism and begin a new life. Justification results not only in the remission of sin but also in "sanctification and renewal of the whole man." Chapters 10–13 affirm the increase of justifying grace through obedience to the commandments and deny that predestination to salvation can be known with certainty. Chapters 14–16 declare that grace is forfeited by any grievous sin (not just faithlessness) and must be recovered through the sacrament of penance. Salvation is given to the justified as a reward as well as a gift, since, on the basis of his union with Christ, he has meritoriously fulfilled God's law by good works performed in a state of grace.

In the belief that Lutheran heresy was based on a misunderstanding of the sacraments, the council devoted more time to them than any other doctrinal issue. The council confirmed that there are seven sacraments instituted by Christ (baptism, confirmation, communion, penance, unction, orders, marriage) and condemned those who said that sacraments are not necessary for salvation or that through faith alone, and without any sacrament, man can be justified. Sacraments contain the grace they signify and confer it *ex opere operato,* irrespective of the qualities or merits of the persons administering or receiving them. The council confirmed transubstantiation, that the substance of bread and wine is changed into the body and blood of Christ while the appearance of bread and wine remains. Luther's real presence doctrine; the symbolist doctrine of Zwingli, Karlstardt, and Oecolampadius; and Calvin's medial position (presence is real but spiritual) were all condemned; as were those who denied that the whole of Christ is received when the bread alone is taken at communion. The council also affirmed that in the Mass, which must be said in Latin, the Son is offered anew to the Father, a sacrifice by which God is appeased and which is efficacious for the living and the dead.

In its article on Scripture the council again rejected Lutheran teaching. Tradition was said to be equally authoritative with Scripture; the correct interpretation of the Bible was the preserve of the Catholic Church; the Vulgate was to be used exclusively in public readings and doctrinal commentaries.

The Tridentine decrees enjoyed great prestige and determined Catholic belief and practice for four centuries. F. S. PIGGIN

See also COUNTER-REFORMATION; PAPACY.

Bibliography. G. Alberigo, "The Council of Trent: New Views on the Occasion of Its Fourth Centenary," *Con* 7.1:28–48; J. Delumeau, *Catholicism between Luther and Voltaire: A New View of the Counter Reformation;* P. Hughes, *The Church in Crisis: A History of the General Councils;* H. Jedin, *A History of the Council of Trent;* H. J. Schroeder, *Canons and Decrees of the Council of Trent.*

Trespass. *See* SIN.

Trespass Offering. *See* OFFERINGS AND SACRIFICES IN BIBLE TIMES.

Tribulation. ***General Biblical Meaning.*** "Tribulation" is the general term in the Bible to denote the suffering of God's people. In the OT the words *ṣārâ* and *ṣar* ("straits" or "distress") pertain variously to intense inner turmoil (Pss. 25:17; 120:1; Job 7:11), the pain of childbirth (Jer. 4:31; 49:24), anguish (Job 15:24; Jer. 6:24), and punishment (I Sam. 2:32; Jer. 30:7). The Greek *thlipsis* from *thlibō* ("to press" or "to hem in") often serves to translate *ṣārâ* in the LXX, and refers generally to the oppression and affliction of the people of Israel or the righteous (Deut. 4:30; Ps. 37:39), while in the NT *thlipsis* is usually translated "tribulation" or "affliction."

Varieties of Tribulation. In the NT tribulation is the experience of all believers and includes persecution (I Thess. 1:6), imprisonment (Acts 20:23), derision (Heb. 10:33), poverty (II Cor. 8:13), sickness (Rev. 2:22), and inner distress and sorrow (Phil. 1:17; II Cor. 2:4). Frequently tribulation is connected with deliverance, which implies that it is a necessary experience through which God glorifies himself in bringing his people to rest and salvation.

Tribulation in the Purpose of God. Tribulation may be a means by which God disciplines his people for their unfaithfulness (Deut. 4:30). More often, especially in the NT, tribulation occurs in the form of persecution of believers because of their faithfulness (John 16:33; Acts 14:22; Rev. 1:9).

The sufferings of Christ provide the model for the believer's experience (I Pet. 2:21–25), and in some sense they participate thus in the sufferings of Christ (Col. 1:24). Tribulations are viewed by Scripture as entirely within the will of God, serving to promote moral purity and godly character (Rom. 5:3–4). As such, they must be endured with faith in the goodness and justice of God (see James 1:2–4, where "trials" or "temptations" labels what appears to be the same experience), thus serving as a test of the believer's faith and leading to greater stability and maturity.

Jesus promised tribulation as the inevitable consequence of his followers' presence in the evil *kosmos* (John 16:33), something they could expect as a way of life. The Apostle Paul echoes this viewpoint when he warns that godly believers will certainly suffer persecution (II Tim. 3:12–13). Jesus nevertheless encouraged his followers through his overcoming of the world to seek their victory through the application of his victory.

The Great Tribulation. *The Teaching of Jesus.* The precise expression, "great tribulation" (Matt. 24:21; Rev. 2:22; 7:14—Gr. *thlipsis megalē*), serves to identify the eschatological form of tribulation. These words are Jesus' caption for a worldwide, unprecedented time of trouble that will usher in the parousia, Jesus' return to earth in great glory (see parallels Mark 13:19, "tribulation," and Luke 21:23, "great distress"; also Rev. 3:10, "hour of trial").

This period of time will be initiated by the "abomination of desolation" (Matt. 24:15) predicted in Dan. 9:27, a desecration of the "holy place" by one whom many scholars believe is the same as the "man of lawlessness" of II Thess. 2:3, 4. Jesus gives specific instructions to inhabitants of Judea for their escape and warns that the intensity of its calamities would almost decimate all life (Matt. 24:15–22).

Views of the Great Tribulation. Though some modern interpreters, along with many ancient commentators and early fathers, are inclined to regard Jesus' predictions as totally fulfilled during the destruction of Jerusalem in A.D. 70, the words of Matt. 24:29, "But immediately after the tribulation of those days," seem to connect them with the parousia. Jesus' words in verse 21 are probably an allusion to Dan. 12:1 because of the reference there to unparalleled trouble (LXX, *thlipsis*). The Daniel passage strengthens the case for the eschatological view of the great tribulation, because it places this period prior to the resurrection of Daniel's people.

Since Jesus made this prophecy, major wars, catastrophes, and cosmic phenomena have stimulated belief in the presence of the great tribulation. Such a tendency is typified by Hesychius of Jerusalem in some correspondence with Augustine. Augustine disagreed, preferring to interpret such things instead as characteristics of history as a whole with no particular eschatological significance. In modern times some premillennialists have speculated on the trend of current events as possible precursors of the great tribulation, some even attempting to identify the antichrist with such candidates as Kaiser Wilhelm II and Mussolini.

Adherents of the major millennial views place the great tribulation at different points in relation to the millennium. Both postmillennialists and amillennialists regard it as a brief, indefinite period of time at the end of the millennium, usually identifying it with the revolt of Gog and Magog of Rev. 20:8–9. Postmillennialists view history as moving toward the Christianization of the world by the church and a future millennium of undetermined length on earth culminating in the great tribulation and final return of Christ. In contrast, amillennialists consider the millennium to be a purely spiritual reality from the first advent to the second, a period lasting already two thousand years and to culminate in the great tribulation, a somewhat less optimistic view of history and the progress of the gospel witness.

To premillennialists the millennium is a future, literal thousand years on earth, and the great tribulation a chaotic period toward which history is even now moving, a decline, i.e., to be terminated by the return of Christ before the millennium. One group, which describes itself as "historic" premillennialists, understands the great tribulation to be a brief but undetermined period of trouble. Another group, dispensational premillennialists, connects it with the seventieth week of Dan. 9:27, a period of seven years whose latter half pertains strictly to the great tribulation.

Within the premillennial movement another issue, the time of the rapture of the church, has given rise to three views. Pretribulationists (rapture prior to the seventieth week) and midtribulationists (rapture at the middle of the seventieth week) perceive the great tribulation as characterized by the wrath of God upon an unbelieving world from which the church is necessarily exempt (I Thess. 5:9).

Posttribulationists believe that the great tribulation is merely an intensification of the kind of tribulation the church has suffered throughout history, through which the church logically must pass. A more recent, novel view in the posttribulation camp seeks to maintain the imminence of the rapture despite the fact that notable tribulational events would necessarily intervene. In order to do so, the events of the great tribulation would be "potential" but uncertain in their fulfillment. Jesus could come at any moment, and one could look back into recent history to see events that fulfilled the great tribulation.

W. H. Baker

See also Last Judgment, The; Millennium, Views of the; Rapture of the Church; Second Coming of Christ.

Bibliography. R. Anderson, *The Coming Prince;* L. Boettner, *The Millennium;* M. J. Erickson, *Contemporary Options in Eschatology;* R. N. Gundry, *The Church and the Tribulation;* S. N. Gundry, "Hermeneutics or *Zeitgeist* as the Determining Factor in the History of Eschatology," *JETS* 20:45–55; A. A. Hoekema, *The Bible and the Future;* J. E. Hartley, *TWOT,* II, 778–79; R. Schippers, *NIDNTT,* II, 807–9; H. Schlier, *TDNT,* III, 140–48; T. Weber, *Living in the Shadow of the Second Coming;* D. Wilson, *Armageddon Now! The Premillenarian Response to Russia and Israel Since 1917;* J. Walvoord, *The Rapture Question.*

Trichotomy. The term, signifying a division into three parts (Gr. *tricha,* "in three parts"; *temnein,* "cut"), is applied in theology to the tripartite division of human nature into body, soul, and spirit. This view developed from Plato's twofold division, body and soul, through Aristotle's further division of the soul into an (1) animal soul, the breathing, organic aspect of man's being, and a (2) rational soul, the intellectual aspect.

Early Christian writers, influenced by this Greek philosophy, found confirmation of their view in I Thess. 5:23, "And the very God of peace sanctify you wholly; and . . . your whole spirit and soul and body be preserved blameless unto the coming of our Lord Jesus Christ." Origen even took the words *sōma* ("body"), *psychē* ("soul"), and *pneuma* ("spirit") as clues to the proper method of interpreting all Scripture, suggesting that each Scripture should be interpreted (1) in its natural or somatic meaning, (2) its symbolic or psychical meaning, and finally (3) in its spiritual or pneumatic meaning. Such piecemeal interpretation of Scripture or of human nature is likely to miss the tremendous biblical emphasis upon wholeness and unity, where even in the Thessalonian proof text Paul prays that they may be sanctified *wholly* and that their *whole* spirit, soul, and body may be preserved blameless.

Both Tertullian and Augustine held to the dichotomy of body and soul but leaned almost to the threefold analysis of man by making the Aristotelian distinction between the animal and rational soul. Present theological and psychological emphasis is almost altogether upon the fundamental wholeness or unity of man's being as against all philosophical attempts to divide it.

W. E. Ward

See also Body, Biblical View of the; Dichotomy; Man, Doctrine of; Soul; Spirit.

Bibliography. J. B. Heard, *The Tripartite Nature of Man;* R. E. Brennan, *History of Psychology, from the Standpoint of a Thomist;* D. E. Roberts, *Psychotherapy and a Christian View of Man;* W. M. Horton, *A Psychological Approach to Theology.*

Trinity. The term designating one God in three persons. Although not itself a biblical term, "the Trinity" has been found a convenient designation for the one God self-revealed in Scripture as Father, Son, and Holy Spirit. It signifies that within the one essence of the Godhead we have to distinguish three "persons" who are neither three gods on the one side, nor three parts or modes of God on the other, but coequally and coeternally God.

The main contribution of the OT to the doctrine is to emphasize the unity of God. God is not himself a plurality, nor is he one among many others. He is single and unique: "The Lord our God is one Lord" (Deut. 6:4), and he demands the exclusion of all pretended rivals (Deut. 5:7–11). Hence there can be no question of tritheism.

Yet even in the OT we have clear intimations of the Trinity. The frequent mention of the Spirit of God (Gen. 1:2 and *passim*) may be noted, as also, perhaps, the angel of the Lord in Exod. 23:23. Again, the plural in Gen. 1:26 and 11:7 is to be noted, as also the plural form of the divine name and the nature of the divine appearance to Abraham in Gen. 18. The importance of the word (Ps. 33:6), and especially the wisdom, of God (Prov. 8:12ff.) is a further pointer, and in a mysterious verse like Isa. 48:16, in a strongly monotheistic context, we have a very close approach to Trinitarian formulation.

In the NT there is no explicit statement of the doctrine (apart from the rejected I John 5:7), but the Trinitarian evidence is overwhelming. God is still preached as the one God (Gal. 3:20). Yet Jesus proclaims his own deity (John 8:58) and evokes and accepts the faith and worship of his disciples (Matt. 16:16; John 20:28). As the Son or Word, he can thus be equated with God (John 1:1) and associated with the Father, e.g., in the Pauline salutations (I Cor. 1:3, etc.). But the Spirit or Comforter is also brought into the same interrelationship (cf. John 14–16).

It is not surprising, therefore, that while we have no dogmatic statement, there are clear references to the three persons of the Godhead in the NT. All three are mentioned at the baptism of Jesus (Matt. 3:16–17). The disciples are to baptize in the name of Father, Son, and Holy Ghost (Matt. 28:19). The developed Pauline blessing includes the grace of the Son, the love of God, and the communion of the Holy Ghost (II Cor. 13:14). Reference is made to the election of the Father, the sanctification of the Spirit, and the sprinkling of the blood of Jesus Christ (I Pet. 1:2) in relation to the salvation of believers.

The fact that Christian faith involves acceptance of Jesus as Savior and Lord meant that the Trinity quickly found its way into the creeds of the church as the confession of faith in God the Father, Jesus Christ his only Son, and the Holy Ghost. The implications of this confession, especially in the context of monotheism, naturally became one of the first concerns of patristic theology, the main aim being to secure the doctrine against tritheism on the one side and monarchianism on the other.

In the fully developed doctrine the unity of God is safeguarded by insisting that there is only one essence or substance of God. Yet the deity of Jesus Christ is fully asserted against those who would think of him as merely adopted to divine sonship, or preexistent, but in the last resort created. The individuality of Father, Son, and Holy Spirit is also preserved against the notion that these are only modes of God for the various purposes of dealing with man in creation or salvation. God is one, yet in himself and from all eternity he is Father, Son, and Holy Ghost, the triune God.

Trinitarian analogies have been found by many apologists both in nature generally and in the constitution of man. These are interesting, but are not to be thought of as providing a rationale of the divine being. More pregnant is the suggestion of Augustine that without the Trinity there could be no fellowship or love in God, the divine Triunity involving an interrelationship in which the divine perfections find eternal exercise and expression independent of the creation of the world and man.

Rationalist objections to the Trinity break down on the fact that they insist on interpreting the Creator in terms of the creature, i.e., the unity of God in terms of mathematical unity. More scientifically, the Christian learns to know God from God himself as he has acted for us and attested his action in Holy Scripture. He is not surprised if an element of mystery remains which defies ultimate analysis or understanding, for he is only man and God is God. But in the divine work as recorded in the Bible the one God is self-revealed as Father, Son, and Holy Ghost, and therefore in true faith he must "acknowledge the glory of the eternal Trinity."

G. W. BROMILEY

See also GOD, ATTRIBUTES OF; GOD, DOCTRINE OF.

Bibliography. K. Barth, *Church Dogmatics,* I/1, 8–11; J. F. Bethune-Baker, *An Introduction to the Early History of Christian Doctrine,* 139ff.; W. H. Griffith Thomas, *The Principles of Theology,* 20–31; J. Moltmann, *The Trinity and the Kingdom;* R. W. Jensen, *The Triune Identity;* P. Toon and J. Spiceland, *One God in Trinity;* E. J. Fortman, *The Triune God;* D. M. Baillie, *God Was in Christ;* C. W. Lowry, *The Trinity and Christian Devotion;* E. Jungel, *The Doctrine of the Trinity;* K. Rahner, *What Is the Trinity?* C. F. D. Moule, "The NT and the Doctrine of the Trinity," *ExpT* 78:16ff.; T. F. Torrance, "Toward an Ecumenical Consensus on the Trinity," *TZ* 31:337ff.

Troeltsch, Ernst (1865–1923). German theologian, philosopher of history, and social theorist. Son of an Augsburg physician, he studied theology at Erlangen, Berlin, and Göttingen (under Ritschl), served as a curate in Munich briefly, and took an appointment at Göttingen in 1890. He then went to Bonn and in 1894 to Heidelberg, where he was named a full professor at age twenty-nine. In 1915 he became professor of philosophy at Berlin. A liberal, he was active in politics as a state legislator and held a post in the Prussian ministry of cultural affairs.

Closely linked with the history of religions school (a movement that questioned the distinctiveness of Christianity and stressed gaining insights from the comparative study of other religions) and profoundly influenced by the historicism of Dilthey, Troeltsch grappled with problems raised by the scientific historical method. He saw the modern awareness of history as the key to understanding our culture, but yet a conflict existed between the ceaseless flux and manifold contradictions within history and the demand of the religious consciousness for certainty, unity, and peace. He concluded that all the world religions were unique and relative to a given historical situation, and conscience is valid for each individual who subscribes to a faith. Although no religion can be shown historically to be absolute or final, Troeltsch functioned as a Christian theologian because he held to a Hegelian perspective of history as movement of the spirit which is on the way back to its home in God. He saw all religion as a reflection and intimation of the ultimate reality of God, and from a rational standpoint Christianity is valid since its ethical values are shaped by living decisions made by its adherents in the historical setting of Western culture.

His concern with social and political questions led to a sociological treatment of the history of Christianity in his best-known work, *The Social Teaching of the Christian Churches* (1912). It examined the areas of family, economics, politics, and learning and revealed Christianity as exhibiting two contradictory but complementary tendencies—compromise and rejection of compromise. This rhythm of accommodation and protest was expressed in three forms of religious institution—the *church* which compromises with society and culture, the *sect* which rejects all compromise with the world, and individual religious spontaneity which expresses itself in *mysticism.* Each type in turn was conditioned by social and cultural variables.

R. V. PIERARD

Bibliography. Troeltsch, *The Absoluteness of Christianity and the History of Religions, Protestantism and Progress: A Historical Study of the Relation of Protestantism to the Modern World;* and *The Social Teaching of the Christian Churches;* R. Morgan and M. Pye, eds., *Ernst Troeltsch: Writings on Theology and Religion;* T. Ogletree, *Christian Faith and History: A Critical Comparison of Ernst Troeltsch and Karl Barth;* B. A. Rust, *Toward a Theology of Involvement: The Thought of Ernst Troeltsch;* W. Pauck, *Harnack and Troeltsch: Two Historical Theologians;* T. F. O'Dea, "Ernst Troeltsch," *International Encyclopedia of the Social Sciences,* XVI, 151–55.

Trust. *See* FAITH.

Truth. Fundamental or spiritual reality. The first Christian theologian to attempt any systematic exposition of the concept of truth was Augustine. His immediate aim was to refute skepticism. If man's mind is incapable of grasping truth, particularly if man is incapable of grasping the truth about God, then morality and theology are impossible. Augustine distinguished four senses of the term "truth." First, truth is the affirmation of what is, e.g., three times three is nine, and David was king of Israel. Second, every reality (particularly the immutable, supersensible ideas) can be considered as an affirmation of itself: it is true when it merits the name it claims. In this sense beauty and wisdom are truth. Third, the Word of God, Jesus Christ, is the Truth because he expresses the Father. And fourth, in the realm of sensible objects, such as plants and animals, there is a resemblance, but only a resemblance, to the primary realities of point two above. Strictly speaking, a visible tree is not a true tree. But as the resemblance is real, even sensible objects have a degree of truth.

Many contemporary students of the Bible,

fearing that Augustine or others are too deeply influenced by Greek philosophy, attempt to specify the several senses in which truth is used in the Scripture. Hoskyns and Davey, *The Riddle of the NT,* after quoting Eph. 4:20–24, seek for a conception of truth that will have "not an intellectual but a moral and spiritual effect upon them." The common conception of truth as "a fact" or "what is real," so they assert, "has no moral or spiritual significance." The Hebrew notion of truth, with its close relation to God, is considered un-Greek. So also Gerhard Kittel distinguishes, more cautiously perhaps, between Hebrew and Greek usage, citing several passages in the Platonic dialogues.

One should, however, bear in mind that the technical concepts of the philosophers are hardly ever used by the majority of the population, whether in ancient Greece or modern America. The Bible, too, is written in colloquial language, and the senses in which it uses the term truth are not so different from colloquial usage anywhere.

One should also bear in mind that moral and spiritual truth is as much truth as mathematical, scientific, and historical truth. It is all equally "intellectual." Nonintellectual truth is unthinkable. It is not true that the common conception of truth as a fact or what is real "has no moral or spiritual significance." We need only to recall that God gave the Ten Commandments.

Furthermore, the Greek philosophers did not divorce truth from moral and spiritual values. Plato went so far as to teach, to the consternation of many readers, that a knowledge of the truth automatically guarantees a moral life. Both Pythagoreanism and Neoplatonism were systems of salvation; and even the Stoics and Epicureans made ethics the culmination of philosophy.

The differences between the Hebrew Scriptures and the Greek philosophies are rather to be sought in the nature and the method of the salvation proclaimed, in the concepts of sin, of redemption, and the specific norms of morality; and not in the usage of the word "truth." The relation between God and truth in the Scriptures is indisputably quite different from anything found in Greek philosophy, mainly because the concept of God is so different. It is in such theological content, not in philological usage, that the important distinctions are to be found.

The usage of the words in the Scripture supports this conclusion. Plain, ordinary, factual truth is the point of Gen. 42:16, "Ye shall be kept in prison, that your words may be proved, whether there be any truth in you" (Cf. Deut. 13:14; 17:4; 22:20; Prov. 12:19; Jer. 9:3). Esth. 9:30 concerns legally certified information, and Josh. 2:12 points to a private oath.

It is not a different meaning but precisely the same meaning when the veracity of divine revelation is asserted. God tells the truth; he tells what is so; his assertions are correct. Cf. Pss. 19:9; 119:160; Dan. 8:26; 10:1, 21.

For the NT Kittel lists six different meanings of the word "truth," but adds that "in many individual cases the distinction is not certain." One of the six meanings is "that which has existence or duration." It is true that truth exists or endures, but it is not in this sense that Gal. 2:5, 14 and Eph. 4:21 define truth.

Similarly one can rely on the truth without defining truth as "that on which man can rely." Rom. 15:8 is not thus to be pressed; nor with the connotation of "sincerity" can II Cor. 7:14; 11:10; and Phil. 1:18 be used for this purpose.

Rather, all these usages are derivative from the basic meaning of "the actual fact" or "the truth of an assertion." Cf. Mark 12:14, 32; Luke 4:25; Acts 26:25; Rom. 1:18, 25. It is not another and different meaning of the term, but exactly the same meaning, in the NT as in the OT, when it is applied to correct doctrine or right belief. Cf. II Cor. 4:2; 6:7; 13:8; I Tim. 2:4; II Tim. 3:7.

Like other words, truth too can be used figuratively, by metonymy, in which the effect is substituted for the cause. Thus when Christ says, "I am the Way, the Truth, and the Life," the word "truth" is just as figurative as the word "life." As Christ is the cause of life, so is he the cause of truth. That water freezes and that a sinner may be justified by faith are true because Christ creatively said, Let it be so. G. H. Clark

Bibliography. Augustine, *Contra Academicos;* N. de Malebranche, *Recherche de la Vérité;* J. Locke, *Essay Concerning Human Understanding;* I. Kant, *Kritik der reinen Vernunft;* B. Blanshard, *The Nature of Thought.*

Tübingen School. In the late eighteenth and early nineteenth centuries a conservative school of theology existed at Tübingen fostered by G. C. Storr (1746–1805) that stressed the supernatural character of revelation and biblical authority. Also, a Catholic "Tübingen school" attempted in the late nineteenth century to reconcile the church's teaching with modern philosophy and biblical studies. By far the best known, however, is the one headed by Ferdinand Christian Baur (1792–1860), which opened up new avenues in NT study and was the most controversial movement in biblical criticism in the midnineteenth century. Its major contribution was calling attention to the distinct strands and theologies within the NT itself and establishing the principle of a purely historical understanding of the Bible. The contrasts between the Synoptic Gospels and John, the various letters attributed to Paul, and

Paul and the other early church leaders were carefully examined. Baur, much influenced by idealist philosophy, rejected supernaturalism and applied Hegelian dialectic to the NT. He found that it reflected, not a homogeneous development, but a fundamental tension between the Jewish church of Peter and the hellenistic Gentile church of Paul. The NT documents attempted to reconcile the conflict between an earlier Petrine and a later Pauline theology by formulating a new synthesis. Baur believed that the authenticity of the various books could be determined by the degree to which they revealed "tendencies" of this conflict. He also traced out a similar kind of dialectical movement in the history of the church.

Although Baur began teaching at Tübingen in 1826, the school's founding is properly dated from the appearance of his pupil D. F. Strauss's *Life of Jesus* in 1835. This marked the formal break between the old conservative school and the new radical antisupernaturalism. Bauer himself viewed Jesus in Hegelian terms as the exemplary embodiment of an idea that had greater universal significance than the concrete person of Jesus himself. Soon a circle of young lecturers formed under the leadership of Eduard Zeller and in 1842 founded the principal mouthpiece of the school, the *Tübinger theologische Jahrbücher.* (It went under in 1857 but was revived as the *Zeitschrift für wissenschaftliche Theologie* [1858–1914] under the auspices of Adolf Hilgenfeld, one of Baur's most extreme followers.)

By the late 1840s the Tübingen School came under severe attack and the various members gradually drifted away. Baur himself became isolated within the Tübingen faculty as well as the German academic community, and spent his last years defending his views and producing a multivolume history of the church from a naturalistic standpoint, which explained all events by a combination of political, social, cultural, and intellectual causes but without any consideration of divine influence. Although relatively short-lived, the school with its emphasis on dialectical conflict within the early church, rejection of Pauline authorship of most of his epistles, and completely antisupernaturalistic outlook contributed significantly to the development of a historical-critical approach to the Bible that completely ignored the divine element in it. R. V. PIERARD

See also BAUR, FERDINAND CHRISTIAN; LIBERALISM, THEOLOGICAL; STRAUSS, DAVID FRIEDRICH.

Bibliography. N. Harris, *The Tübingen School;* P. C. Hodgson, *The Formation of Historical Theology: A Study of F. C. Baur;* K. Barth, *Protestant Theology in the Nineteenth Century;* A. Heron, *A Century of Protestant Theology;* C. Brown, *NIDCC,* 987–88.

Turin, Shroud of. A linen cloth, which measures 14′3″ by 3′7″, housed at Turin, Italy. On the material is a double, head-to-head image of a man, revealing the obverse and reverse of the body.

Known to exist since at least 1354, there are indications that the shroud is much older. Pollen studies point to its presence in Palestine at a much earlier date, while the weave and type of linen is compatible with first century cloth. It is also quite possible that a coin over the right eye is a lepton of Pontius Pilate, minted *ca.* A.D. 29–32.

While some have raised biblical questions concerning various aspects of the shroud, such a burial is well supported. Evidence reveals that the head napkin was rolled up and wrapped around the head as indicated in the Gospel of John (11:44; 20:5–7), the Mishnah (*Shabbath* 23:5), and the *Code of Jewish Law,* "Laws of Mourning" (chs. 351–52). The lengthwise wrapping and positioning of the body is supported by Qumran burial procedures and the "Laws of Mourning" (ch. 364).

The lack of bodily washing is explained by the "Laws of Mourning" in that those who are executed by the government or who die violent deaths are not to be washed. The use of several strips of linen described in John is also confirmed by the shroud, where pieces were also used. Additionally, the hasty burial recorded in the Gospels (Mark 15:42; 16:1–3; Luke 23:54–56; 24:1–4) explains a number of these issues.

In October, 1978, the Shroud of Turin was the subject of an intense scientific investigation revolving around such questions as the nature of the bloodstains and the composition and cause of the image. It was found that the shroud is very probably not a fake of any kind. There is no sign of paint, dye, powder, or any other foreign substance on the cloth that can account for the image. Additionally, the image was found to be three-dimensional, superficial, and nondirectional, each quite an enigma to the explanation of the image.

The man buried in the shroud apparently died from crucifixion, and his body is in a state of rigor mortis. The Gospels, which have been shown to be trustworthy on historical grounds, present reliable accounts of Jesus' crucifixion. A comparison of the man of the shroud with Jesus reveals that they suffered the same wounds, even in several points that were not normal crucifixion procedure.

Both men received a series of punctures throughout the scalp from a series of sharp objects, a badly bruised face, a severe whipping (over 120 wounds are visible on the shroud), shoulder abrasions from a heavy object, and knee contusions. There are punctures in both wrists and both feet, the absence of broken ankles, and a postmortem chest wound with a clear flow of blood and watery fluid. Both were buried hastily, individually, and in fine linens. There certainly are strong indications that the two men might be one and the same since they agree in such features and disagree in none.

Most significantly, there is no decomposition on the cloth, meaning that the body exited comparatively quickly. Many of the bloodstains are intact, including the blood clots, meaning that the body probably was not unwrapped, since this would have disturbed the stains. Additionally, it is very possible that a light or heat scorch caused the image. The convergence of the data certainly indicates that the dead body appears to have left the cloth in some mysterious manner.

It is still possible that the shroud is a fake, or that it is a genuine ancient shroud but simply not the burial garment of Jesus. Yet, the evidence thus far indicates the probable conclusions that the shroud is ancient (perhaps from the first century), that it does not contradict the NT accounts, and that the image is not a fake. It may well be the actual burial garment of Jesus, as indicated especially by the similarities in areas of abnormal crucifixion practice. Lastly, the image on the shroud may have resulted from Jesus' resurrection, which is complemented by the demonstrable historical evidence and reliable Gospel testimony for this event, as well. However, no absolute conclusions are possible at present concerning the shroud with regard to some of these matters. G. R. Habermas

Bibliography. P. Barbet, *A Doctor at Calvary;* G. M. Cocoris, "The Shroud of Turin: Fact or Fake?" *BRM,* June, 1980, 22–24; B. J. Culliton, "The Mystery of the Shroud of Turin Challenges 20th-Century Science," *Sci,* July, 1978, 235–39; V. J. Donovan, "The Shroud and the Laws of Probability," *CathDi,* April, 1980, 49–52; F. L. Filas, "The Dating of the Shroud of Turin from Coins of Pontius Pilate," private monograph, 1980; G. R. Habermas and K. E. Stevenson, *Verdict on the Shroud;* G. R. Habermas, "The Shroud of Turin and Its Significance for Biblical Studies," *JETS* 24:47–54; T. Humber, *The Sacred Shroud;* C. Murphy, "Shreds of Evidence," *Harper's,* November, 1981, 42–65; D. Sox, *Is the Turin Shroud a Forgery?* H. Thurston, "The Holy Shroud," *Catholic Encyclopedia,* XIII, 762–63; P. Vignon, *The Shroud of Christ* and "The Problem of the Holy Shroud," *SciAm,* March, 1937, 162–64; K. F. Weaver, "The Mystery of the Shroud," *NatGeo,* June, 1980, 730–52; R. Wilcox, *Shroud;* I. Wilson, *The Shroud of Turin.*

Turretin, Francis (1623–1687). Calvinist theologian. Turretin was the grandson of an Italian Protestant who emigrated to Geneva and the son of a leading Swiss theologian in the early seventeenth century. Benedict Turretin was a proponent of the orthodox Calvinism formulated at the Synod of Dordt (1618–19), and he promoted the Canons of Dordt in Switzerland and France. Francis advocated the same sort of Calvinism as his father, and is most widely known for presenting orthodox Calvinism in a scholastic manner.

Francis was born and died in Geneva, but was educated in a variety of theological centers: Geneva, Leiden, Utrecht, Paris, Saumer, Montauban, Nimes. In 1647 he became pastor to the Italian congregation in Geneva, and in 1653 he was named a professor of theology as well. He was known for his mild and friendly personality as well as for his unbending interpretation of Calvinism. In 1675 he published the *Formula Consensus Helvetica,* and in 1688 his famous four-volume work, the *Institutio,* one of the fullest expressions of Calvinist scholasticism. Francis died in Geneva and was succeeded in his pastoral and teaching positions by his son, Jean Alphonse (1671–1737). Jean Alphonse, contrary to his father, worked to remove the scholastic Calvinist standards.

Francis Turretin's theology is generally what became known as Calvinist orthodoxy in the tradition of Theodore Beza and the Dutch theologians who opposed Arminius. In addition, it reflected the idea of verbal biblical inspiration as written into the Helvetic Consensus Formula of 1675. Turretin's contribution to this theology was to create precise and complete doctrinal positions. Calvin's theology provided the framework, and Turretin developed carefully worded dogmas based on scripturally derived principles. Though Calvin, using a more humanist scholarship, allowed contradictions and problems to stand, Turretin sought to present the most complete set of logical deductions possible in order to reject unorthodox interpretations and to present a biblical and complete theology. Doctrines deduced from the "decrees of God" provided Turretin with his basic approach to all theology; thus, Calvinist orthodoxy concentrated for the most part on ideas about predestination, reprobation, and salvation by unmediated grace.

This orthodoxy was not maintained in the eighteenth century. Questions about biblical texts were raised by theologians who continued to use humanist exegesis and by others who questioned orthodox ideas of verbal inspiration (Helvetic Consensus) and infallibility (Belgic Confession). Also, theologians such as Turretin's son played down the use of precise doctrines that tended to divide Protestants; instead, they identified basic beliefs (as the Apostles' Creed) in order to promote unity. Francis's theology was revived, however, in the nineteenth century by the American Presbyterians of the Princeton school of theology, most notably Charles Hodge. Turretin's *Institutio* was reprinted in 1847, and became a standard textbook for orthodox training in American Presbyterianism. R. J. VanderMolen

See also Princeton Theology, Old; Scholasticism, Protestant.

Bibliography. J. W. Beardslee, III, ed. and tr., *Reformed Dogmatics* and "Theological Development at Geneva Under Francis and Jean-Alphonse Turretin, 1648–1737," Ph.D. diss., Yale University; J. Good, *History of the Swiss Reformed Churches since the Reformation;* J. H. Leith, *An Introduction to the Reformed Tradition;* G. Marsden, *Fundamentalism and American Culture; NCE,* XIV, 348; H. Heppe, *Reformed Dogmatics.*

Twelve Articles of the Peasants (1525). Produced in South Germany, the articles are a demand for religious, social, and economic rights in the face of continuation of the manorial system under which the peasant was virtually a slave. Europe had seen peasant uprisings from 1381 on. John Ball, an English priest, rejected the medieval theological justification of serfdom and made a social application of Wycliffe's *Dominion.* Similarly in Germany the uprisings of 1524–25 drew from Luther, but gave also a secular interpretation of *The Liberty of the Christian Man.*

In a period of unrest among the towns and the upper level of peasants, the *Twelve Articles* were published by Sabastian Lotzer of Memminge on March 1, 1525. They may have been revised by Balthasar Hubmaier, who approved the peasants' goals. Among his papers was found an annotated copy with NT support for each article.

The articles open with a petition for the right of "the entire community" to choose and dismiss pastors. The purpose was to guarantee the teaching of "the Holy Gospel pure and simple" to the end that "His grace may increase within us and be confirmed in us." The second article agrees to a tithe but insists it be gathered and controlled by the elders and used to support the minister and his family. The third article asks for personal freedom. It begins, "It has been the custom, hitherto for men to hold us as their own property." But because Christ died for all, all are free though under authority in an ordered state. The fourth and fifth ask the right to fish, hunt, and gather wood. Numbers six, seven, and eight ask deliverance from excessive service, personal oppression, and rents. Nine asks for cessation of "the great evil in the constant making of new laws." Ten requests the return of "common lands" which have been confiscated. Eleven wants the abolishing of the law of heriot, the nobles' right to choose any item from an estate, thus robbing widows and orphans.

The articles emerged as the Christian Union of peasants attempted to establish an evangelical state in which special privileges were to be abolished and all men equal. The peasants took the NT quite literally, applying the teaching to the Christian community to society at large. Unfortunately, radical elements under Thomas Müntzer became violent, causing a crusade by the princes who crushed the peasant forces. In the end, towns and peasants suffered and the Reformation lost face. Only the princes profited.

The witness of the peasants to the civil rights implicit in the gospel was at least a hundred years ahead of its time. The *Twelve Articles* stand with Hubmaier's *Heretics and Their Burners* as a call for religious liberty and social justice.

W. N. Kerr

See also Hubmaier, Balthasar; Radical Reformation; Zwickau Prophets.

Bibliography. H. J. Hillerbrand, *The Reformation in Its Own Words;* B. J. Kidd, *Documents Illustrative of the Continental Reformation,* #83; R. W. Scribner, "The German Peasants War," in S. Ozment, *Reformation Europe: A Guide to Research.*

Twofold State of Jesus. *See* States of Jesus Christ.

Two Swords Theory. *See* Church and State.

Type, Typology. From the Greek word for form or pattern, which in biblical times denoted both the original model or prototype and the copy that resulted. In the NT the latter was labeled the antitype, and this was especially used in two directions: (1) the correspondence between two historical situations like the flood and baptism (I Pet. 3:21) or two figures like Adam and Christ (Rom. 5:14); (2) the correspondence between the heavenly pattern and its earthly counterpart, e.g., the divine original behind the earthly tent/tabernacle (Acts 7:44; Heb. 8:5; 9:24). There are several categories—persons (Adam, Melchizedek), events (flood, brazen serpent), institutions (feast), places (Jerusalem, Zion), objects (altar of burnt offering, incense), offices (prophet, priest, king).

In addition we might note the parallel use of image along with type to denote a moral example to be followed. This latter is an important part of the NT stress on imitation of the divinely ordained pattern exemplified first in Christ (John 13:15; I Pet. 2:21), then in the apostolic band (Phil. 3:17; II Thess. 3:9), the leaders (I Tim. 4:12; Titus 2:7; I Pet. 5:3), and the community itself (I Thess. 1:7). As such all believers are to consider themselves models or patterns of the Christlike life.

It is important to distinguish types from symbol and allegory. A symbol has a meaning apart from its normal semantic field and goes beyond it to stand for an abstract concept, e.g., cross = life, fire = judgment. Allegory is a series of metaphors in which each one adds an element to form a composite picture of the message, e.g., in the good shepherd allegory (John 10) each part carries meaning. Typology, however, deals with the principle of analogous fulfillment. A symbol is an abstract correspondence, while a type is an actual historical event or person. An allegory compares two distinct entities and involves a story or extended development of figurative expressions while a type is a specific parallel between two historical entities; the former is indirect and implicit, the latter direct and explicit. Therefore, biblical typology involves an analogical correspondence in which earlier events, persons, and places in salvation history become patterns by which later events and the like are interpreted.

Hermeneutical Significance. It has increasingly been recognized that typology expresses the basic hermeneutic, indeed the attitude or perspective, by which both OT and NT writers understood themselves and their predecessors. Each new community in the ongoing development of salvation history viewed itself analogously in terms of the past. This is true within the OT as well as in the NT use of the OT. The two major sources, of course, were creation and the Exodus. Creation typology is especially seen in Rom. 5 and the Adam-Christ parallel, while Exodus or covenant typology predominates in both testaments. Positively, the Exodus was behind the redemptive imagery in Isa. 51–52 as well as NT salvific concepts (e.g., I Cor. 10:1–6). Negatively, the wilderness wanderings became the model for future admonition (e.g., Ps. 95:7–8; Heb. 4:3–11).

The church fathers combined typology and allegory, linking the former with general religious truths expressed in terms of Greek philosophical concepts. This continued until the Reformation (with periodic opposition such as the Antiochene School of the fourth century or the Victorenes of the twelfth); the Reformers espoused a system which viewed the OT literally with a Christological hermeneutic, i.e., as pointing forward messianically to Christ. During the critical period after the seventeenth century, the whole concept of promise-fulfillment was played down and the OT became religious experience rather than history. In recent decades, however, typology properly conceived has become again a valid tool, based upon the biblical perspective regarding the recurring pattern in God's acts within history, thereby establishing continuity between the stages of redemptive history.

Current Debate. The debate today concerns the possible distinction between innate and inferred types. An innate type is explicitly stated as such in the NT; an inferred type is not explicit but is established by the general tone of NT teaching, e.g., the Epistle to the Hebrews, which uses typology as its basic hermeneutic. Many deny the latter because of the danger of fanciful eisegesis which subjectively twists the text.

Both type and antitype should be based upon genuine historical parallels rather than timeless mythological parallels. Typology should not redefine the meaning of the text or suggest superficial rather than genuine correspondence. Both OT and NT passages should be exegeted before parallels are drawn.

Further, one should study the specific correspondences as well as the differences between type and antitype. Here typology is similar to parable research, necessitating a consideration of exegetical details in both OT and NT passages. In what way, e.g., was the brazen serpent a type of Jesus' death in John 3:14–15? Were the peripheral details of Num. 21:4–9 part of the typology? There will always be a single central point, and secondary details must be noted with care before they are applied to the analogy. Noting the dissimilarities provides a control against an overly imaginative, allegorical rendering of the type.

It is well to avoid dogmatizing types. It is difficult and extremely subjective to establish doctrine on the basis of typology. Even in Heb., typology is utilized for illustrative effect rather than for dogmatic considerations. Therefore, only when typology has a direct doctrinal purpose may we affirm such.

Finally, one must not seek types where the context does not warrant them. As in all exegetical study, we want to arrive at the author's intended meaning rather than a generalized subjective interpretation. As stated above, while the NT writers undoubtedly used typology that is not recorded in canon, we do not have the revelatory stance necessary to extend that approach beyond the text itself. The allegorical, subjective results seen in many modern sermons testify eloquently to the dangers. G. R. Osborne

See also Interpretation of the Bible.

Bibliography. E. Achtemeier, *IDB* Supplement, 926–27; D. L. Baker, "Typology and the Christian Use of the OT," *SJT* 29:137–57; E. C. Blackman, "Return to Typology," *CongQ* 32:53–59; J. W. Drane, "Typology," *EvQ* 50:195–210; E. E. Ellis, "How the NT Uses the Old," in *NT Interpretation*, ed. I. H. Marshall; A. M. Fairbairn, *The Typology of Scripture;* F. Foulkes, *The Acts of God: A Study of the Basis of Typology in the OT;* L. Goppelt, *Typos: The Typological Interpretation of the NT* and *TDNT*, VIII, 246–59; S. Gundry, "Typology as a Means of Interpretation," *JETS* 12:233–40; H. Hammel, "The OT Basis of Typological Interpretation," *BR* 9:38–50; G. H. Lampe and K. J. Woolcombe, *Essays on Typology;* R. B. Laurin, "Typological Interpretation of the OT," in *Baker's Dictionary of Practical Theology,* ed. R. Turnbull; H. Müller, *NIDNTT,* III, 903–7; N. H. Ridderbos, "Typology," *VoxT* 31:149–50; J. Stek, "Biblical Typology: Yesterday and Today." *CTJ* 5:133–62.

Tyrrell, George (1861–1909). A Roman Catholic modernist, Tyrrell was born in Dublin. He forsook his early Anglicanism and entered the Jesuit Order in 1880. Ordained priest in 1891, he taught philosophy at Stonyhurst College, where his superiors disapproved of his emphasis on Aquinas, and where he began to question whether his order was speaking to the condition and needs of the modern church. He was transferred to Jesuit headquarters in London, and in 1899 provoked censure with a published article that challenged traditional doctrine on everlasting punishment. Removed to Yorkshire (1900–1905), he attacked his church's view of authority and suggested that Roman Catholicism, like Judaism, might "have to die in order that it may live again in a greater and grander form." Rather than recant and submit, Tyrrell chose dismissal from the Jesuits, and complained that "mendacity seems to have eaten into the whole heart of the system."

In 1907 he was deprived of the sacraments. He rejected papal infallibility and defended modernism in his *Medievalism* (1908). To him, modernism meant "the acknowledgment on the part of religion of the rights of modern thought: of the need of effecting a synthesis . . . between what . . . is found to be valid in the old and in the new." Tyrrell held that the most subtle and dangerous form of atheism was his church's rejection of the world as God-forsaken. To him, this was a denial of God's working and self-revelation in human history. He developed his thought in *Christianity at the Cross-Roads* (1909), but refused to join Roman Catholic priests who were received into the Church of England. He died at forty-eight, was refused a Roman Catholic burial, and lies in an Anglican churchyard in Sussex.

J. D. Douglas

See also Von Hügel, Friedrich.

Bibliography. D. G. Schultenover, *George Tyrrell in Search of Catholicism;* M. D. Petre, *Autobiography and Life of George Tyrrell;* J. L. May, *Father Tyrrell and the Modernist Movement.*

Uu

Ubiquity of God. *See* God, Attributes of.

Ultradispensationalism. Dispensationalists distinguish Israel from the church and so look for a point in history at which God's redemptive program changed from the one form of administration to the other. The most common dispensationalism finds the beginning of the church in Acts 2 with the Spirit's coming at Pentecost. From the standpoint of Acts 2 dispensationalism two other views seem extreme, or "ultra." According to Acts 13 dispensationalism the church began when Paul started his mission to Jews and Gentiles (Acts 13:2). According to Acts 28 dispensationalism the church began toward the end of Paul's ministry with his reference to Israel's rejection of the kingdom of God and the sending of God's salvation to the Gentiles (Acts 28:26–28).

Acts 28 dispensationalism is sometimes called Bullingerism after its leading proponent, Ethelbert William Bullinger (1837–1913). Other writers holding this position include Charles H. Welch, A. E. Knoch, Vladimir M. Gelesnoff, and Otis R. Sellers. Bullinger's analysis of the NT led to three dispensations where Acts 2 dispensationalism has two (Israel before Pentecost and the church after Pentecost). Bullinger's first administration encompassed the time of the Gospels when Christ offered the kingdom to Jews only and entrance was signified by water baptism. Second was the transitional period in Acts and the earlier NT epistles when the apostles offered the Jews participation in the "bride church" and practiced two baptisms, in water and in the Spirit. Third was the oneness of Jew and Gentile in the body of Christ addressed in Paul's prison epistles (Ephesians, Colossians, Philippians, I Timothy, Titus, and II Timothy) and entered by Spirit baptism alone.

Bullinger based some of his arguments upon dichotomies of words that did not refer to incompatible realities. For example, the ordinances of baptism and the Lord's Supper had to do with the flesh only and so had no place in the body of Christ alleged to be of the Spirit only. Bullinger failed to understand that just as the inner and outer man can be one man, so the inner Spirit baptism and outer water baptism can constitute one baptism. The church, as many recent studies have indicated, is made up of tangible people in bodies meeting together in visible gatherings for the purposes of ministering to the whole person, both spirit and body. Christ's reference to baptism in the Great Commission need not exclude it from application to today's church.

Spokesmen for the Acts 13 dispensationalism are J. C. O'Hair, C. R. Stam, and Charles F. Baker, author of a major textbook, *A Dispensational Theology.* Baker's name is associated with the Grand Rapids Grace Bible College, which prepares people for ministry in Grace Gospel Fellowship and the Worldwide Grace Testimony.

Answering the Acts 28 dispensationalism, Baker notes that Paul's statement (Acts 28:28) does not mark the beginning of the body of Christ but should be understood in the past tense, the gospel *had been* sent to the Gentiles (RSV, NIV, and others). Baker also argues effectively for the unity of all the Pauline epistles in their teaching about the church. In Paul's letters he finds support for the practice of the Lord's Supper (I Cor. 11) but not water baptism. Paul's transitional use of water baptism for Jews (he assumes) is not regarded as normative for Gentiles (I Cor. 1:13–17). Baker interprets baptism in Rom. 6:3–4 as mere Spirit baptism, but as has been noted, it may best be understood as both inner Spirit baptism and outer water baptism.

In defense of Acts 2 dispensationalism Charles C. Ryrie argues that the question is when God initially formed the church, not when it was first understood. Baker replies that God plainly stated what he was doing earlier—bringing in the consummation of all prophecy and offering the kingdom to Israel (Acts 2:16; 3:24). As late as Acts 11:16, he writes, the apostles preached only to Jews. However, Baker failed to quote Acts 3:25, which explains that through the Jews all people on earth will be blessed. Is the message in the early chapters of Acts to the Jews exclusively, or to the Jews first, in order that Samaritans and Gentiles also may be added to the church? Baker's attempt to divorce the Pentecostal reception of power from the Spirit's baptism cannot stand in the light of the total development in Acts. The church began when believers in the crucified and risen Christ were baptized by the Spirit into one body (Acts 2:38, 41, 44, 47; cf. I Cor. 12:13) to which the Spirit added Samaritans (Acts 8:17) and Gentiles (Acts 10:28, 34–35, 45–48; 11:18).

Baker's chief reason for objecting to Acts 2 dispensationalism is that what happened prior to Paul had been prophesied by the prophets, but nothing about the body of Christ was revealed before Paul. Such all or nothing reasoning is imposed upon Scripture, not drawn from it. The fact that Paul most fully understood, explained, and received the mystery of uniting Jew and Gentile in one body need not imply that Peter, Cornelius, and the Jerusalem church had grasped nothing of this truth (Acts 10:30–38; 11:1–18). Did not Jesus Christ lay the one foundation for the church and prepare the disciples to establish it? Robert L. Saucy shows that the church is built upon the entire work of Christ's first coming and is sustained through his present leadership. But he also finds that the actual historical formation of the church occurred in Jerusalem on the day of Pentecost. G. R. Lewis

See also Dispensation, Dispensationalism.

Bibliography. E. W. Bullinger, *How to Enjoy the Bible;* A. H. Freundt, Jr., *Encyclopedia of Christianity,* II, 214–15; L. S. Chafer, "Bullingerism," *BS* 104:257–58; C. F. Baker, *A Dispensational Theology;* C. C. Ryrie, *Dispensationalism Today;* J. B. Graber, *Ultradispensationalism* (Diss., Dallas Theological Seminary); R. L. Saucy, *The Church in God's Program.*

Ultramontanism. Literally "beyond the mountains" (Alps), the term usually refers to a movement within the Roman Catholic Church in the nineteenth century that opposed conciliar and nationalist decentralization and advocated centralization of power in the papacy in order to restore the spiritual vigor of the church. The concept itself actually dates from the Middle Ages, when the papacy sought increased power in order to free itself from secular control, as in the investiture controversy of the eleventh century—a movement which some call "old ultramontanism." Coined as a term of derision in the seventeenth century, "ultramontanism" was resurrected in the post-Napoleonic era to refer to an attempt spearheaded by French Catholic romantics to terminate the influence of Enlightenment rationalism and secular governments in church affairs and to restore papal power—a movement which some call "new ultramontanism."

However, it was in Germany that the movement became political and eventually touched off the *Kulturkampf*—literally the "struggle for civilization"—between the papacy and the German government led by Chancellor Otto von Bismarck. The conflict was brief but bitter, beginning in the 1860s and ending by 1890. Diplomatic relations between Germany and the Vatican were restored in 1880, and most of the laws passed against Catholics during the period were repealed by 1886.

The movement aided and abetted the growing administrative authority of the popes and the tightening of the hierarchical structure of the church under their direction. Ultramontanists everywhere applauded such unilateral papal acts as the declaration of the immaculate conception in 1854 and the promulgation of the Syllabus of Errors in 1864. The movement culminated with Vatican I in 1869–70 and its decree of papal infallibility.

Even though Vatican II (1962–65) reaffirmed papal infallibility, it also weakened ultramontanism with its approval of an increased role in ecclesiastical affairs for the college of bishops and a greater voice for the laity in congregational life. On the other hand, the tone of the papacy since John Paul II took office in 1978 has been one of reassertion of the ultramontane principles of centralization of power and strong papal leadership. It remains to be seen if a revitalized ultramontanism will emerge in Catholicism at large.

R. D. Linder

See also Papacy; Vatican Council I; Vatican Council II.

Bibliography. E. E. Y. Hales, *Pio Nono: A Study in European Politics and Religion in the Nineteenth Century* and *Papacy and Revolution, 1769–1846;* A. R. Vidler, *The Church in an Age of Revolution;* A. M. J. Kloosterman, *Contemporary Catholicism;* D. J. Holmes, *The Triumph of the Holy See;* P. Hebblethwaite, *The New Inquisition?*

Unbelief. Within the context of Christianity and of Western culture, "unbelief" refers to the turning away of individuals and groups from the traditional Christian faith and world view. Unbelief can be understood from a broad cultural perspective as the secularization of Western society and a defection from belief in the theistic, personal God of the Judeo-Christian heritage. We may also speak of a relative unbelief within the church that is in evidence when certain cardinal doctrines of the faith are denied and attacked from within Christendom. In this sense theological liberalism in at least its extreme forms represents a sort of unbelief.

By the time of the close of the Roman period in Western history, Europe had become Christianized to the extent that the theistic world view had become dominant. This consensus continued without significant challenge throughout the medieval period, and even the Reformation with its powerful affront to the domination of the Roman Church did little directly to shake the basic consensus. Differences between the Reformers and Rome were primarily ecclesiological, soteriological, and regarding authority.

Unbelief in Western culture began to constitute a serious challenge during the Renaissance with the rise of science and in the Enlightenment. In the seventeenth and eighteenth centuries, thinkers began to express militant religious skepticism, anticlericalism, and scientism, and rejected the influence of the medieval synthesis of Christian doctrine and Aristotelian science. It can properly be said that Christianity had been tied so tightly to this antiquated cosmology that as it began to lose its grip over the intellectual life of the West, Christianity declined in spiritual and cultural influence. Leading secularists such as Denis Diderot, Voltaire, and Baron d'Holbach persuasively challenged the Christian world view.

Still, Christians were inclined to support the faith with a broad appeal to reason, especially to natural theology, and to Christianity's positive moral impact. William Paley was typical of many, believing that there was ample evidence for a designer in the marvelous order of the universe. Then skeptic David Hume began to mount the first concentrated opposition to natural theology, undercutting the traditional program of grounding religious beliefs in reason. Hume subjected to rigorous criticism Paley's design argument and also the cosmological, or first-cause, argument for God's existence in its popular form, derived ultimately from Thomas Aquinas in the medieval period. In Germany, Immanuel Kant attacked arguments that attempted to rest faith on reason as part of his general attack on metaphysical reasoning. In particular, he opposed the ontological argument, the attempt to prove God's existence *a priori* based upon the concept of God, as used by Anselm of Canterbury, René Descartes, and Gottfried Leibniz. While today philosophers consider the validity of the arguments as still open to question, the historical effect of such critiques was to convince Western thinkers to reject the rational attempt to base belief on reason.

While eighteenth century unbelief challenged the intellectual grounds for faith, nineteenth century unbelief moved beyond this and assumed the falsehood of theism. While John Stuart Mill could still argue against the reasons for Christianity, Ludwig Feuerbach, Sigmund Freud, and Friedrich Nietzsche took for granted Christianity's falsehood and rational groundlessness and so turned to speculation as to the nonrational causes for the belief. Freud argued that man, in need of a "father figure" to enable him to feel at home in the world, projected the concept of God to meet this need, while Nietzsche criticized Christianity at its point of pride, its moral impact on society. For Nietzsche the ethical doctrines of Christianity were a "slave morality" responsible for inhibiting the development of human excellence.

The spread of unbelief in the twentieth century has continued apace. Atheists, among others, turned to existentialism in Europe, as advocated by atheist Jean-Paul Sartre, while Anglo-American thinkers entertained logical positivism as represented by A. J. Ayer. Sartre argued that God's existence was to be denied because it was incompatible with human freedom, while Ayer and Anthony Flew urged that it was linguistically meaningless even to refer to God in language. Varieties of Marxism have risen to power in major areas of the world, invariably antagonistic to religious belief. In Western society the powerful established churches of the nineteenth century have seen in the twentieth a drastic decline in attendance and influence, as Søren Kierkegaard had predicted. A secularized outlook dominates the major intellectual centers and communications media of Western societies, and naturalistic humanism has asserted itself in *The Humanist Manifestoes I and II* and the *Secular Humanist Declaration.* Within Christianity itself relative unbelief has made significant inroads into theology as some have attempted to reinterpret traditional theology to accord with the modern secularistic outlook—none perhaps so clearly as John A. T. Robinson in *Honest to God.*

Even as unbelief has made significant advances in the past several centuries, there is also a vital resurgence of Christianity around the world. Large numbers are being added to the church in many areas, and evangelical activism and scholarship have borne fruit in a new, greater influence in the American cultural and religious scene.

D. B. Fletcher

See also Agnosticism; Atheism; Death of God Theology.

Bibliography. P. Angles, *Critiques of God;* C. Brown, *Philosophy and Christian Faith;* O. Guiness, *The Dust of Death;* P. Kurtz, ed., *The Humanist Manifestoes I and II; The Secular Humanist Declaration;* J. Sire, *The Universe Next Door;* J. Thrower, *A Short History of Western Atheism;* J. Hick, ed., *The Myth of God Incarnate;* P. van Buren, *The Secular Meaning of the Gospel;* M. Marty, *Varieties of Unbelief.*

Unchangeability of God. *See* God, Attributes of.

Unclean. *See* Cleanness, Uncleanness.

Underhill, Evelyn (1875–1941). British spiritual writer. The product of a middle-class and nominally Anglican upbringing, she experienced a gradual conversion from self-styled "agnosticism" (through a fascination with Neoplatonic philosophy and "occult" and mystical theism) to religious devotion that led her, shortly before her marriage in 1907, seriously to consider becoming a Roman Catholic. By 1909 she had written a number of short stories and three highly symbolic novels.

The appearance of *Mysticism* (1911) marked the beginning of her life's work of explaining the mystical traditions. Initially she intentionally avoided an explicitly Christian viewpoint in order to reach a broader readership. *The Mystic Way* (1913) attempted what *Mysticism* had not: to establish the mystical character of NT Christianity. Her romantic, empirical, and psychological approach both contrasted with and built upon previous historical, theoretical, and philosophical introductions to mysticism and, coupled with her contemporaries' fascination with psychology and the vitalistic philosophies of Henri Bergson and Rudolf Eucken, helped stimulate a wave of interest in mysticism before and during the First World War. Underhill's *Practical Mysticism* (1920) appeared at the same time as several translations and studies of medieval mystical writings. Underhill translated or edited a few of these; for most of them she provided encouragement for other translators and introductions to their translations. She also published two volumes of mystical verse (*Immanence,* 1912; *Theophanies,* 1916).

After World War I Underhill became active in the Church of England, while placing herself (1922–25) under the spiritual direction of the Roman Catholic Friedrich von Hügel. Called upon to give numerous retreats, she shifted her focus increasingly toward the liturgical life of the church; this culminated in her second main work, *Worship* (1936).

Underhill's spiritual insight and learning were remarkable, but these gained their impact from her literary gifts. She had limited academic training, especially in regard to the German mystics, and relied on the help of others more skilled than she in the early vernacular literatures. Although she understood her purpose as a practical one and was content to leave theologizing and philosophizing to others, her work is far from superficial. D. D. Martin

See also Mysticism; Spirituality.

Bibliography. C. J. R. Armstrong, *Evelyn Underhill;* T. S. Kepler, ed., *The Evelyn Underhill Reader;* C. Williams, ed., *Letters of Evelyn Underhill;* L. Menzies, ed., *Collected Papers of Evelyn Underhill;* M. Cropper, *Life of Evelyn Underhill;* O. Wyon, *Desire for God;* M. Vernon in *DNB;* L. Barkway and L. Menzies, eds., *An Anthology of the Love of God from the Writings of Evelyn Underhill.*

Understanding. A cognitive activity that surpasses in depth and richness any mere acquaintance with facts or events. Whereas "to know" generally signifies perception and observation in an impersonal, objective mode, "to understand" means to grasp the meaning of phenomena that are meaningful to persons either because they are expressions of persons or because they form an important part of persons' lives. To understand means to see the cause-and-effect relations and the purposes of the phenomenon in question, and to be able to place this phenomenon into the broader context of human choices and actions. "To understand" cannot be reduced to the familiar concept "to know," since understanding is richer and more oriented toward persons and their interests than is knowledge. Despite the distinctness of the concept of understanding, it generally has been ignored in epistemological discussions of the nature and grounds of human cognitive activity. More recently it has received significant attention in hermeneutical theory.

Wilhelm Dilthey (1833–1911) distinguished between the natural sciences and those disciplines that deal with the inner reality of persons—i.e., the social sciences and humanities, which he termed the *Geisteswissenschaften,* or human sciences. Dilthey distinguished the two types of inquiry by their epistemological methods; we *know* in the natural sciences, which deal with impersonal facts and phenomena, but in the human sciences the goal is to *understand* others as individuals in their inner experiences. Thus the impersonal epistemological objectivity sought in the natural sciences can never gain a true understanding of persons or their doings.

Developing such ideas, Karl Jaspers (1883–1969) argues that the social sciences can only describe man in his "mundane" relationships, in which he is seen as an organism in the environment, as a conscious user of concepts, or as a cultural being. These modes of knowledge cannot penetrate one's true inner self, which Jaspers calls *Existenz*. Understanding of *Existenz* comes only through "elucidation" via such means as communication and "loving struggle" with others in community.

For Martin Heidegger (1889–1976) understanding is a literal "standing under" everything; it is our way of coming to grips with our life situations, of using language to apprehend meanings, and of "feeling at home" in the world. Understanding is, for Heidegger, presupposition-laden.

Biblical understanding is a very lively field of intellectual interest, as philosophers and theologians have come to realize that there is more to understanding the biblical texts than merely to exegete them. To understand is to engage in a hermeneutical task involving an attempt to enter into the "horizon" of interpretations and presuppositions of the biblical writer while of course retaining our own "horizon." Any naïve view of understanding Scripture is to be rejected, such as those that see the text as having a single, transparent meaning for all persons in all times, merely awaiting proper exegesis to be manifest. The questions in biblical understanding have now become, To what extent is there a definite and objective meaning in Scripture, and To what extent do our own personal "horizons" of contemporary concepts shade our understanding? Can there be a biblical message to be understood, or does our act of understanding either create or radically shape the message?

D. B. Fletcher

See also Interpretation of the Bible.

Bibliography. W. Cerf, "To Know and to Understand," *PPR* 12:83–94; R. E. Palmer, *Hermeneutics;* M. Polanyi, *Personal Knowledge;* A. C. Thiselton, *The Two Horizons;* P. Ziff, *Understanding Understanding.*

Unforgiveable Sin. *See* Sin, Unpardonable.

Unification Church. The original and official name of this new religious movement founded by the Rev. Sun Myung Moon is the Holy Spirit Association for the Unification of World Christianity. Despite its relatively small size (less than 500,000 members worldwide), it has received considerable publicity and media attention because of its controversial beliefs and practices.

Moon was born to Presbyterian parents in Korea in 1920. He claims that on Easter Sunday, 1936, while in prayer on a Korean hillside, Jesus appeared to him and revealed that he had been chosen to complete the work which Jesus had begun. This experience was the first in a series of revelatory encounters with God in which Moon states that he received new truth for a new age. The new revelations and teachings of Rev. Moon were subsequently set forth in the *Divine Principle,* first published in 1957. Moon officially established his new church in 1954 with the avowed purpose of bringing salvation to the world and initiating a truly international family.

The doctrine of the Unification Church is highly eclectic and spiritistic in nature. It reflects the peculiarities of Korea's religiously fertile soil and Moon's lifelong interest in spiritualistic phenomena. The presence of much biblical and Christian terminology in Unification theology has led casual observers to conclude that Moon's church is just another variant of Christianity. However, Moon himself has admitted that his teachings are heretical from the standpoint of traditional, orthodox Christianity. He maintains that because of sectarian divisions and the inability of conventional churches to meet the needs of today's complex world, God desires to communicate a new revelation of truth which, assisted by the spirit world and the movement's loyal followers (popularly known as "Moonies"), will bring about a spiritual revolution. Such a movement will result in the true, lasting unification of the family of man and the world.

At the core of Unification theology is Moon's teaching on the fall of Adam and Eve. According to the *Divine Principle,* the primary theological document of the Unification Church, no one has truly understood the fall until Moon's revelation, which brought illumination and clarification to the existing biblical account. Moonies believe that Lucifer seduced Eve and that this sexual union caused the spiritual fall of mankind as well as the fall of Lucifer. Eve then entered into a sexual relationship with Adam, which resulted in the physical fall of man.

This dual aspect of the fall—spiritual and physical—requires a restoration to God (salvation) which is likewise both spiritual and physical in nature. Unificationists teach that God's original intention for humankind at the time of creation was for men and women to mature to perfection in God, to be united by God in a marriage centered on God's love, and to produce perfect children, thereby establishing a sinless family and ultimately a sinless world. God's plans were thwarted by the fall, however, and it then became

God's desire to restore all things in order to bring about the earthly and heavenly kingdom of God.

In order to accomplish this, Unificationists teach that a Messiah, a Christ, is required. According to the *Divine Principle,* God finally found an obedient man—Jesus—who came in Adam's place to restore mankind. Moonies teach that Jesus was not God, but a perfect man without original sin. God's intention was for Jesus to take a perfected bride in Eve's place, marry, and produce sinless children. Ultimately, other perfect families would be formed and God's plan for the restoration of the whole of society would be accomplished. This is the essence of the *Divine Principle*—God's plan for the restoration of humanity—which once was hidden but, Unificationists believe, now has been made plain.

A central teaching of the Unification Church is that God's will was thwarted by the crucifixion of Jesus. Moonies teach that it was not God's original intention that Jesus die. In this sense Jesus failed to complete his mission; he did not marry; he did not achieve physical redemption. Because Jesus saved mankind spiritually but not physically, it is necessary, according to Unification thought, for another Messiah, the Lord of the Second Advent, to bring about physical redemption. This will occur during the messianic age (also referred to as the completed testament age or the new age), which is now upon the earth.

The *Divine Principle* implies that the Lord of the Second Advent will be born in Korea and that all religions will unite under him. Unification Church members feel that the Messiah is already on earth, although many are reticent about publicly declaring that Sun Myung Moon is that Messiah. Moon himself is evasive on the topic, claiming that his mission is to proclaim the coming of the messianic age and that God will reveal the identity of the Messiah, the "central figure," to the hearts of sincere seekers.

R. M. Enroth

Bibliography. J. Bjornstad, *The Moon Is Not the Son;* R. M. Enroth, *Youth, Brainwashing and the Extremist Cults* and *The Lure of the Cults;* F. Sontag, *Sun Myung Moon and the Unification Church;* J. I. Yamamoto, *The Puppet Master* and "Unification Church," in *A Guide to Cults and New Religions,* ed. R. M. Enroth.

Uniformity, Acts of. Four parliamentary enactments designed to ensure uniformity of theology and worship in the Church of England on the basis of required use of the *Book of Common Prayer.*

The Act of 1549 (Edward VI) established the first *Book of Common Prayer,* prepared by Thomas Cranmer and others, for exclusive use in the Mass and all public services. Enacted on January 21, 1549, to take effect the following Whitsunday (June 9), it provided penalties for noncompliance and for speaking against the Prayer Book that ranged up to life imprisonment for a third offense. Public services were to be held in English, with the exception that at the universities services other than the Mass could employ Latin, Greek, or Hebrew.

The Act of 1552 (Edward VI) reflected a shift in Cranmer's position, as the Prayer Book was revised in a Zwinglian direction. Passed on March 9 to take effect the following All Saints Day, this act extended regulations and penalties to the laity, requiring attendance at all public services and prohibiting attendance at unauthorized gatherings. It eliminated the requirement for ministers to wear ecclesiastical vestments in services of worship.

The Act of 1559 (Elizabeth I) reestablished the Prayer Book of 1552 as of June 24, 1559, repealing the legislation of Mary's reign which had restored Roman practice in worship. Modifications of the Act of 1552 included intensified penalties as well as reinstatement of the use of clergy vestments as they had been during the second year of the reign of Edward VI. This act regulated the worship and discipline of the English church for more than a century.

The Act of 1662 (Charles II) reestablished Anglicanism as part of the Restoration settlement after the collapse of the Puritan revolution. It required universal adoption of a somewhat revised version of the Elizabethan Prayer Book of 1559, including a public declaration of support as well as episcopal ordination for those not already so ordained, before the ensuing St. Bartholomew's Day (August 24). It thereby effected the "Great Ejection" of approximately two thousand noncomplying Presbyterian, Independent, and Baptist clergymen, marking the beginning of English Nonconformity. The first of several acts of repression known as the Clarendon Code, the Act of 1662 was rendered largely inoperative for Dissenters by the Toleration Act of William and Mary, passed in 1689. It remained in force for Anglican ministers, although it was modified by later legislation.

N. A. Magnuson

Bibliography. H. Davies, *Worship and Theology in England From Cranmer to Hooker, 1534–1603* and *Worship and Theology in England From Andrewes to Fox, 1603–1690;* A. G. Dickens, *The English Reformation;* H. Gee, comp., *Documents Illustrative of English Church History;* J. R. H. Moorman, *A History of the Church in England;* C. E. Whiting, *Studies in English Puritanism from the Restoration to the Revolution, 1660–1688.*

Unio Mystica. Although a doctrine of union with God or Christ is not limited to mystical theologies, the term "mystical union" refers to a direct union or communion with God that is quite different from the general union in Christ that is the privilege of all believers. Students of Christian mysticism have assembled various categories for the mystical unions described by mystics. One set of categories distinguishes between a habitual or frequently recurring union and an ecstatic, transient union. Some authors also speak of a unitive life, a more or less permanent state of living in bliss in God's presence that is granted in the present life on earth to a very few as a sort of extension of habitual union.

Another distinction is that between abstractive union that removes the human spirit from consciousness of the ordinary world of sense phenomena and a nonabstractive union that is fully compatible with ordinary consciousness. Some writers have also distinguished between an ontological union or union of essence, on the one hand, and a conformity of wills, on the other hand. Most Christian mystics, however, take care to deny a monistic annihilation of the human soul or personality, even in the ontological or essentialist union. One might also distinguish between a union that results in a clear, affirmative vision of God and a union of negativity wherein God is seen through a cloud of darkness or enigmatically, as in a clouded mirror. Virtually all Christian mystics reserve the clear vision of God, a vision of God as he is, to the beatified saints in heaven. Emphasis on the priority of the speculative or cognitive aspect of the human spirit in comparison to the affective or loving aspect, or vice versa, varies from mystic to mystic and is not necessarily related to a particular view of union, although the affective aspect is often stressed by those describing a voluntaristic rather than an essentialist union or by those experiencing a nonabstractive, transient union. Many mystics offer combinations of the above categories—the distinctions serve the scholar-taxonomist far better than the practitioner.

D. D. Martin

See also Mysticism.

Bibliography. R. Kieckhefer, "Meister Eckhart's Conception of Union with God," *HTR* 71:203–25; S. E. Ozment, *Homo Spiritualis: A Comparative Study of the Anthropology of Johannes Tauler, Jean Gerson, and Martin Luther (1508–16) in the Context of Their Theological Thought;* G. Wrede, *Unio Mystica: Probleme der Erfahrung bei Johannes Tauler;* W. A. Mueller, "Basic Christian Doctrines, 31: The Mystical Union," *CT* 6:22–23.

Union, Hypostatic. *See* Hypostatic Union.

Union with Christ. *See* Identification with Christ.

Union with God. *See* Unio Mystica.

Unitarianism. The origin of this ancient heresy, sometimes called antitrinitarianism, is to be found in the Arian controversy of the early fourth century when Arius, presbyter in the church at Alexandria, set forth the system of thought which bears his name. He denied the orthodox doctrine of the Trinity and asserted that there was a time when God was not the Father and Jesus Christ was not the Son. Because God foresaw the merit of Jesus the man, Christ was accorded a kind of divinity, but he was never of the same substance as the Father although he is worthy of worship. This early and rather high form of Unitarianism was condemned by the Council of Nicaea in 325 and by the Council of Constantinople in 381. Throughout the Middle Ages, Unitarianism in any form was regarded as heretical. It reappeared in a somewhat different guise in the writings of Michael Servetus and was accepted by some of the more radical of the Anabaptist groups.

It received a new impetus and theological foundation in the Socinianism of Laelius and Faustus Socinus and in the Racovian Catechism of 1605. Although they rejected the deity of Christ and the orthodox doctrine of the Trinity, the Socinians held to a kind of supernaturalism and even insisted on the worship of Jesus Christ as a divine person, believing in his resurrection from the dead and his ascension. But his divine nature was the result of his perfect obedience. They denied the orthodox position on the fall of man and held that man still possesses a full freedom of the will. Thus the redeeming work of Christ is to be found in his life and teachings rather than in his vicarious death upon the cross.

With the coming of the Enlightenment and the appearance of deism, Unitarianism in the hands of Joseph Priestly and others became more rationalistic and less supernaturalistic in its outlook. Nature and right reason replaced the NT as the primary sources of religious authority, and what authority the Scriptures retained was the result of their agreement with the findings of reason.

Unitarianism came to New England as early as 1710, and by 1750 most of the Congregational ministers in and around Boston had ceased to regard the doctrine of the Trinity as an essential Christian belief. In 1788 King's Chapel, the first Anglican church in New England, became definitely Unitarian when its rector, with the consent of the congregation, deleted from the liturgy all mention of the Trinity. The triumph of Unitarianism in New England Congregationalism seemed complete with the election of Henry Ware, an avowed opponent of the Trinitarian position, to the Hollis chair of divinity at Harvard.

In the nineteenth century, under the impact of transcendentalism, Unitarianism became steadily more radical. Its later leaders such as Ralph Waldo Emerson and Theodore Parker rejected those remaining supernatural elements which William Ellery Channing had seen fit to retain. Modern Unitarianism has become increasingly humanistic. Many members of the American Unitarian Association, founded in 1825, have come to the conclusion that their movement is not a part of the Christian church. In 1961 they merged with the Universalists. C. G. SINGER

See also ARIANISM; SOCINUS, FAUSTUS; RACOVIAN CATECHISM; CHANNING, WILLIAM ELLERY; TRANSCENDENTALISM.

Bibliography. S. H. Fritchman, *Together We Advance;* J. Orr, *English Deism: Its Roots and Fruits;* E. M. Wilbur, *History of Unitarianism,* 2 vols.; C. Wright, *Beginnings of Unitarianism in America.*

Unitive Way, The. The last and highest stage of the three ways of the spiritual life in classical mystical theology, following on the purgative and illuminative ways. While the basis of these categories is found in the NT (e.g., I Cor. 3:1–3; Heb. 5:12–14; I John 2:12–14), they developed in the later fathers, especially Evagrius Pontieus and Augustine. The classic expression of the unitive way is in John of the Cross's *Dark Night of the Soul.*

The unitive way, or *via unitiva,* is pictured as being pursued either along with or subsequent to the other two ways. While the purgative way deals with the outer life (the removal of sins) and the illuminative way with the inner life (in terms of prayer and love), the unitive way goes beyond them to the direct contemplation of God, usually thought of in terms of love (although in Eastern thought ceaseless prayer or the prayer of the heart are the normal terms). On this journey one passes through the dark night of the soul in which all spiritual rewards or blessings are withdrawn. As one continues in contemplation all that is left is pure love of God, for one does not "get anything" experiential. God rewards this disinterested, wordless, contemplative love at his will and in his time with a deep spiritual communion with him, sometimes spoken of as the beatific vision. But since this cannot be produced, it is not a motive. The only goal is to present oneself in love before the only worthy object of love and in that union of love to rest content in peace. Out of this union one can then act in the world, but again the union in love with God, not the resulting action, is the goal.

P. H. DAVIDS

See also ILLUMINATIVE WAY, THE; PURGATIVE WAY, THE; MYSTICISM; ASCETICAL THEOLOGY.

Bibliography. Bonaventure, "The Triple Way, or Love Enkindled," *Works,* I, ed. J. de Vinck; R. Garrigon-Lagrange, *The Three Ages of the Interior Life;* W. H. Capps and W. M. Wright, *Silent Fire.*

Unity. This word is very rare in the Bible, but the thought behind the term, that of the one people of God, is extremely prominent. Already in the OT Israel is descended from the one father, and although the tribes are later divided the psalmist commends unity (Ps. 133:1) and Ezekiel looks to the time when there shall be "one stick" (Ezek. 37:17). Nor is this merely a political or natural unity, for Abraham is divinely elected, and Isaac is the child of special promise and miracle.

In the NT this unity is expanded in accordance with the original promise. The wall of partition between Jew and Gentile, and indeed between Greek and barbarian, bond and slave, male and female, is broken down. There is now the one people of God embracing men of all nations (Eph. 2:12–13; Gal. 3:28).

But this new unity is not one of mere good will, or common interests, or ecclesiastical organization. It is a unity of expansion because of contraction. It is a unity in the one seed (Gal. 3:16) who has come as the true Israelite and indeed the second Adam (Rom. 5:12–13). The old and estranged men are made one in Jesus Christ (Eph. 2:15). The one Jesus Christ is the basis of the unity of his people.

But they are one in Jesus Christ as the one who reconciled them by dying and rising again in their stead. As divided men they first meet in his crucified body, in which their old life is put to death and destroyed. They are reconciled in one body by the cross (Eph. 2:16). "We thus judge, that if one died for all, then were all dead" (II Cor. 5:14). But Jesus Christ rose as well as died, and as the Resurrected he is the one true life of his people (Col. 3:3–4). They thus meet in his risen body, in which they are the one new man.

Yet if this unity is centered in Jesus Christ, it is necessarily a unity of the Holy Spirit. Believers have their new life in Christ as they are all born of the one Spirit (John 3:5; Eph. 4:4). But this means that they are brothers of Jesus Christ and of one another in the one family of God. They have the one God and Father of all (Eph. 4:4). They have not only a common birth, but a common mind which is the mind of Christ (Phil. 2:5). They are led by the one Spirit, being built up as a habitation of God through the Spirit (Eph. 2:22).

How full and real this unity is emerges in the fact that the church is called the bride of Christ, and is therefore one body and one spirit with him (cf. I Cor. 6:17; Eph. 5:30). It can thus be described quite simply as his body, of which Christians are the different members (Rom. 12:4). Since it is by faith that Christians belong to Christ, their unity is a unity of faith (Eph. 4:13). It is expressed in the two sacraments, for as there is only one baptism (Eph. 4:5), so there is only one loaf and cup (I Cor. 10:17).

Since unity belongs so essentially to the people of God, it is right that it should find expression in the creed (one church), and that in all ages there should be a concern for Christian unity according to the prayer of Christ himself (John 17:21). For the attainment of genuine unity, however, it is necessary that the following point should be observed.

Christian unity is a given fact of the new life to be believed and accepted in faith in Christ. It is not first the unity created, safeguarded, or enforced by a human institution or association. Nor can it be simply equated with a particular structure of the church or form of ministry, practice, or dogma. Like the righteousness of the Christian, it is found first and primarily and exclusively in Christ.

Again, Christian unity is not identical with uniformity. It does not allow division. But it does not exclude variety. The one Spirit gives different gifts (I Cor. 12:4–5). In the one body of Christ there are many members. The unity grounded in Christ leaves scope for diversity of action and function, the only conformity being to the mind of Christ and direction of the Spirit.

Finally, the unity received in faith must find expression in historical life and action. There must be no antinomian acquiescence in divided or competitive Christian bodies. To this extent, it is right and necessary that there should be an active pursuit of practical unity, but only on the basis of the unity already given, and therefore with a fuller looking to Christ and readier subjection to his Spirit. G. W. Bromiley

See also Church, The; Ecumenism.

Universalism. A belief which affirms that in the fullness of time all souls will be released from the penalties of sin and restored to God. Historically known as *apokatastasis,* final salvation denies the biblical doctrine of eternal punishment and is based on a faulty reading of Acts 3:21; Rom. 5:18–19; Eph. 1:9–10; I Cor. 15:22; and other passages. Belief in universal salvation is at least as old as Christianity itself and may be associated with early Gnostic teachers. The first clearly universalist writings, however, date from the Greek church fathers, most notably Clement of Alexandria, his student Origen, and Gregory of Nyssa. Of these, the teachings of Origen, who believed that even the devil might eventually be saved, were the most influential. Numerous supporters of final salvation were to be found in the postapostolic church, although it was strongly opposed by Augustine of Hippo. Origen's theology was at length declared heretical at the fifth ecumenical council in 553.

In Western Europe universalism almost completely disappeared during the Middle Ages, save for the Irish scholar John Scotus Erigena and some of the lesser-known mystics. Following Augustine, the Protestant Reformers Luther and Calvin also rejected final salvation. Some spiritualist and Anabaptist writers of the Radical Reformation, however, revived the doctrine. In the sixteenth century it was embraced by the south German scholar Hans Denck and spread through his convent Hans Hut. The impact of Denck's universalism for the wider Anabaptist movement has probably been overemphasized. Mennonites and Hutterites, for example, have largely rejected a belief in the restoration of all things.

In America universalism developed out of roots from both radical German pietism and the English evangelical revival. The pietist influence was strongly shaped by the mystic Jakob Boehme. Several noted radical pietists such as Johann Wilhelm Peterson (1649–1727) and Ernst Christoph Hochmann (1670–1721) were Boehmist in their development of final restoration, which became one of the most distinguishing characteristics of radical pietist theology. This type of universalism was brought to the colonies by the physician George DeBenneville (1703–1793) and, to a lesser extent, by the German Baptist Brethren. DeBenneville, who had close contacts with Hochmann, is widely regarded as the father of American universalism. As a separatist he preached frequently, but neither belonged to nor founded any church. As with most radical pietists, universalism was an implicit but not central focus of his faith.

Universalism which was explicit and the center of doctrine emerged out of Calvinism in England. Several sects which embraced final salvation developed out of seventeenth century Puritanism, among them the Philadelphians, founded by Jane Lead. It was not, however, until a century later, when James Relly broke with the Wesley-

Whitefield revival, that an organized universalist movement appeared. His *Union* (1759) rejected Calvinism and argued that all souls are in union with Christ. Christ's sacrificial punishment and death therefore brought salvation to all, not merely an elect few. One of Relly's converts was John Murray, another Methodist preacher, who was excommunicated for his universalist views. While Murray believed that all souls were corrupted with original sin, his view of universalism was based on Christ as the head of the human family. Just as all men had participated in Adam's sin, so through Christ's sacrifice all would receive salvation. Murray arrived in New England in 1770 and organized the first Universalist congregation at Gloucester, Massachusetts, in 1779. A General Convention was formed a few years later. Organized Universalism thus became primarily an American phenomenon.

Meanwhile similar ideas were emerging elsewhere. Certain liberal Congregationalist clergy such as Jonathan Mayhew and Charles Chauncy helped to prepare the foundation for the spread of universalism. The latter's *Salvation of All Men* (1784) completely rejected a "limited" atonement view. The former Baptist Elhanan Winchester founded a Universalist congregation in Philadelphia in 1781 and developed a compelling restorationist position in his *Dialogues on the Universal Restoration* (1788). Winchester, an Arminian, argued that future punishment is measured for each sin and results ultimately in the eternal happiness of all souls.

Although DeBenneville, Murray, and Winchester approached universalism from different theological positions, all were restorationists in that they denied eternal punishment in hell. Otherwise eighteenth century universalism was a diverse and noncoherent movement. A loosely agreed-upon statement of faith, the Winchester Profession (adopted at Winchester, New Hampshire), was drawn up in 1803. Doctrinal statements were also formulated in 1899 and 1935.

Hosea Ballou, another former Baptist, proved to be the dominant theological spokesman for the movement in the early nineteenth century. His *Treatise on the Atonement* (1805) posited a "moral" view of Christ's sacrifice rather than the "legal" or substitutionary position of Relly and Murray. Christ suffered on behalf of mankind but not in their place. Christ's death demonstrated God's unchangeable loving concern for the restoration of the soul from sin. Ballou also taught what opponents called a "death and glory" view that death brings the unregenerate soul to repentance. Because of his stress on reason and his rejection of miracles, the Trinity, and the deity of Christ, Ballou moved the Universalists closer to Unitarianism. His "no hell" theology struck most orthodox Christians, however, as one that would lead to immorality.

Nineteenth century universalism took on the familiar characteristics of an American denomination. It grew steadily in several midwestern and New England states, and in frontier and rural areas it assumed a more evangelical posture than has commonly been recognized. Several periodicals were started and state or regional associations formed. Tufts College (1852) and a theological school (1869) at Medford, Massachusetts, became the leading educational institutions. Controversy over the future punishment question led to the formation of a minority restorationist faction in 1831. This was dissolved in 1841, however, as most universalists placed less and less emphasis on the earlier doctrine of *apokatastasis*.

Twentieth century universalism, now clearly a liberal faith, was largely shaped by the theologian Clarence Skinner. A wider conception of universalism was articulated which rejected the deity of Jesus and which sought to explore the "universal" bases of all religions. Accordingly, closer ties were sought with the major world non-Christian and native American religions. Universalists continue to stress such beliefs as the dignity and brotherhood of mankind, tolerance of diversity, and the reasonableness of moral actions. Because of the close kinship which many universalists felt toward Unitarians, there had always been a close cooperation between the two groups. This cooperation led to a formal merger and the organization of the Unitarian Universalist Association in 1961, having a combined membership of 70,500 in nearly four hundred congregations.

Clearly, however, many who have professed a belief in final salvation have remained outside the Unitarian Universalist tradition. In the twentieth century universalism (*apokatastasis*) has been associated with the neo-orthodox theology as shaped by the Swiss theologian Karl Barth. Although he did not teach final salvation directly, certain passages of his massive *Church Dogmatics* stress the irresistible universal triumph of God's grace. Barth was led in this direction by the doctrine of double predestination. In Christ, the representative of all men, adoption and reprobation merge. There are not two groups—one saved and the other damned. Mortal man may still be a sinner, but the election of Christ demands a final judgment of salvation. Other neo-orthodox writers have suggested that divine punishment is a purifying or disguised form of God's love, which results ultimately in restoration.

Some from a more conservative Protestant

tradition have also defended a universalist view. One position is that a "Hades Gospel" gives a second chance for those who did not have an opportunity to confess Christ in the world. Another approach has been articulated by Neal Punt in *Unconditional Good News* (1980). Punt reverses the traditional Calvinist view that all are lost except those whom the Bible indicates are among the elect. His "biblical universalism" counters that all are saved in Christ except those whom the Bible directly declares are lost. Clearly universalism, in a variety of forms, continues to have appeal for contemporary faith, in both liberal and conservative circles. D. B. ELLER

See also APOKATASTASIS; UNITARIANISM.

Bibliography. J. H. Allen and R. Eddy, *History of the Unitarians and the Universalists in the United States;* H. Ballou, *Ancient History of Universalism;* A. D. Bell, *The Life and Times of Dr. George DeBenneville, 1703–1793;* R. Eddy, *Universalism in America, a History,* 2 vols.; T. Engelder, "The Hades Gospel" and "The Argument in Support of the Hades Gospel," *CTM* 16:293–300, 374–96; R. E. Miller, *The Larger Hope;* W. O. Pachull, *Mysticism and Early South German-Austrian Anabaptist Movement, 1525–1531;* C. R. Skinner and A. S. Cole, *Hell's Ramparts Fell: The Life of John Murray;* C. R. Skinner, *A Religion for Greatness* and *The Social Implications of Universalism;* T. Whittmore, *The Modern History of Universalism;* G. H. Williams, *American Universalism.*

Universalism, Hypothetical. *See* ATONEMENT, EXTENT OF THE.

Universe, Origin of. *See* ORIGIN OF THE UNIVERSE.

Unpardonable Sin. *See* SIN, UNPARDONABLE.

Ursinus, Zacharias (1534–1583). One of the authors of the Heidelberg Catechism. Ursinus was born in Breslau and studied in Wittenberg under Melanchthon and then with Calvin in Geneva. In 1558 he returned to his hometown to teach, but after a year was dismissed from his post since he espoused Calvinist views on the Lord's Supper.

In 1561 as Frederick III the Pious embarked upon church reform in Heidelberg and the Palatinate, he sought Reformed faculty for the Collegium Sapientiae, the main theological school in Heidelberg. Upon the recommendation of Peter Martyr Vermigli, Ursinus was employed. Ursinus became head of Collegium Sapientiae, holding the main theology chair there. He also preached, and was charged by Frederick to develop a new Reformed church liturgy. Ursinus wrote a *Summa Theologica* and a *Catechismus Minor* in preparation for this task.

In the meantime Frederick came under attack for his Reformed position. He called upon his new faculty at the Collegium Sapientiae plus the preachers in Heidelberg to help in his defense. As head of the school Ursinus worked closely with one of the leading preachers of the city, Caspar Olevianus, and others, including Frederick, in writing what came to be called the Heidelberg Catechism. From this point on, Ursinus was drawn into controversies with the Lutherans, something he did not enjoy. With the death of Frederick in 1578, he was dismissed from the school, and Lutheran theology again held sway in Heidelberg. Frederick's younger son, Casimir, hired Ursinus to teach at Neustadt-on-Hardt, and here Ursinus wrote a Calvinist critique of the Formula of Concord and the *Book of Concord.* By this time his health had weakened, and shortly after completing the critique, he died.

R. V. SCHNUCKER

See also HEIDELBERG CATECHISM.

Ussher, James (1581–1656). Irish Protestant churchman and scholar. Born in Dublin, he was one of the earliest graduates of the newly founded Trinity College, and gained appointment there as professor of theological controversies in 1607. Strongly in favor of a national church, he drafted the articles approved by the first convocation of the Irish Episcopal Church in 1615—an adaptation and amplification of the Anglican Thirty-nine Articles with an emphasis upon the Calvinist and Puritan elements of the English tradition. In 1621 he was appointed bishop of Meath and in 1626 Archbishop of Armagh (primate of Ireland). His authority declined after 1633, however, when Thomas Wentworth became deputy and pursued Archbishop Laud's policy of enforcing conformity with England. He nonetheless remained on good terms with both men, even while opposing their efforts.

Rebellion broke out in Ireland shortly after Ussher had left for England in 1640. Most of his personal property was lost and, given the tense situation there, he never returned. In England he declined an offer to participate in the work of the Westminster Assembly but contributed a scheme for a modified episcopacy combining bishops and advisory clerical symbols. Although a strong proponent of divine-right monarchy, he counseled Charles I not to approve the execution of Wentworth (now Lord Strafford) in 1641. And yet when Ussher died in 1656, Oliver Cromwell (a republican) honored his memory with a state funeral in Westminster Abbey.

Wentworth echoes most of his contemporaries in speaking of "so learned a prelate and so good a man." Ussher was a vehement opponent of Roman Catholicism and denounced toleration as a "grievous sin," yet he was respected by all parties for his sweet temper and the astonishing range of his scholarship. In patristic studies he distinguished the genuine parts of the epistles of Ignatius from the spurious and also argued the case for the continuity of British Protestantism with the church of the fathers. Undoubtedly he is best known for his scriptural chronology (with the creation of the world dated in 4004 B.C.) since it was eventually inserted in the marginal notes of the Authorized Version.

Ussher was regarded as an outstanding preacher in the "plain" style. He also collected a magnificent library of books and manuscripts (including the famous Book of Kells) now housed at Trinity College, Dublin. He was much sought after by contemporaries for his knowledge and beauty of character, and his personal impact was probably even greater than his scholarly legacy.

R. K. BISHOP

See also IRISH ARTICLES.

Bibliography. C. R. Elrington and J. H. Todd, eds., *The Whole Works*, 17 vols.; R. B. Knox, *James Ussher, Archbishop of Armagh;* T. W. Moody, F. X. Martin, and F. J. Byrne, *A New History of Ireland*, III.

Utilitarianism. The ethical theory according to which the rightness of actions is determined by the net balance of benefits produced. The principle of utility is seen by utilitarians as the sole moral criterion by which to judge actions, this principle being that we should always produce the greatest possible balance of good over evil.

Utilitarianism is a teleological or consequentialist moral theory, holding that rightness of actions is a function of the consequences, "the greatest good for the greatest number." Consequences are to be distributed as widely as possible; the moral agent is not to look only to his own welfare nor to that of those he especially cares for, but to all persons. In some versions the class of beneficiaries is extended to include nonhuman sentient beings as well.

As a consequentialist theory, utilitarianism proper is not necessarily tied to any specific view about "the good" that is to be produced. One prominent type of utilitarianism is hedonistic, advocating the maximization of pleasure and avoidance of pain. Other types include G. E. Moore's agathistic utilitarianism, promoting but refusing to analyze "the good," and eudaimonistic utilitarianism, maximizing happiness.

Utilitarianism is traced historically to Jeremy Bentham (1748–1832), although David Hume was a significant precursor of the theory. Bentham advanced utilitarianism as an ethic primarily for social reform. Christian utilitarians such as John Austin (1790–1859) attempted to see God's law as pointing the way to utility. In John Stuart Mill (1806–73) utilitarianism emerged as a specifically personal ethic. Mill believed, incidentally, that the theory accorded well with Christian morality, directing our efforts toward the welfare of all. Utilitarianism's most careful and articulate spokesman was Henry Sidgwick (1873–1958), who saw utilitarianism as capable of reconciling the various "methods of ethics" (intuitionism or deontology, egoism, and utilitarianism itself) and thus of philosophically justifying "common sense morality."

Utilitarianism has recently dominated ethics in the English-speaking world, claiming under its banner many prominent ethicists as well as making a deep impression in public policy decision-making. The theory has, however, been heartily criticized. Early versions of the theory held that the specific case, the selection of alternatives in the situation, was properly the realm for application of the principle of utility. Strictly speaking, then, we are incapable of morally evaluating a type of action, such as lying or keeping promises, until we understand the situation in which the action is to be performed so that we could calculate outcomes. W. D. Ross objected that this would lead to highly counterintuitive moral judgments. If two alternatives produced the same net balance of good over evil, but one involved lying and the other truthtelling, the utilitarian would be unable to prefer one to another, since their consequences were equivalent. In response to such objections, rule utilitarianism proposed that certain moral rules should be followed because those rules promote utility. This sort of utilitarianism is widely supported, although R. M. Hare argues that the distinction is unclear and J. J. C. Smart contends that rule utilitarianism is a form of "rule worship."

Utilitarianism is very much in the midst of philosophical debate at the present time. Detractors argue that it fails to provide an adequate protection for the claims of justice, since it would seem that on utilitarian principles the rights of the few could be violated to realize a gain in utility for the greater number. Its defenders argue that utilitarianism fares far better than any deontological system in commanding one's allegiance and in providing a reason to do as morality requires. Contemporary Christian ethicists are generally disinclined to see utilitarianism as an adequate Christian moral theory.

D. B. FLETCHER

See also ETHICAL SYSTEMS, CHRISTIAN; ETHICS, BIBLICAL; SOCIAL ETHICS.

Bibliography. M. D. Bayles, ed., *Contemporary Utilitarianism,* J. Bentham, *Introduction to the Principles of Morals and Legislation;* W. K. Frankena, *Ethics;* J. S. Mill, *Utilitarianism;* G. E. Moore, *Ethics;* H. Sidgwick, *The Methods of Ethics;* J. J. C. Smart and B. Williams, *Utilitarianism: For and Against.*

Utopianism. The ideal of a perfect, present, earthly society—organic, harmonious, virtuous, satisfying—has a lengthy history. As far as Christianity is concerned, where it has been conceived of as realizable at all, it has been only in the microcosm. Where these tiny minorities have been sanctioned, it has stemmed from the conviction that the Holy Spirit can so bring the life of the heavenly community into this age that, with the response of a few heroic souls, something more approaching the society of the eternal state can be realized than the church has hitherto exhibited. These are eschatological communities, with special realization of their hope. Morally the Spirit gives particular grace to forget self and share both possessions and one's inmost spirit. The Spirit present in such measure also bestows his gifts, so that a charismatic community emerges. In the dynamic phase of these communities there is frequently also an apocalyptic element. Such pouring out of the Spirit is the brief latter-rain manifestation indicating the imminence of the return of Jesus Christ and the ushering in of the supramundane community, either celestial or millennial. Abilities and skills are also given. In its totality the Christian utopian community is filled with worship, and with joy that it is uniquely the dwelling place of God by the Spirit.

In the Early and Medieval Church. Monasticism has been the supreme form of Christian utopianism. In the cloister the graces of poverty, confession, obedience, and peace are implemented. Charismatic activity has varied greatly over the centuries, but even at its most minimal the abbot or abbess occupied a quasi-prophetic role. And there have always been those like Joachim of Fiore, in his twelfth century Sicilian cloister, who have regarded monasticism as a sign of that soon-coming age when the whole world would be a monastery. So monasteries have been a window into and a preparation for heaven. As Roman Catholic monasteries have been in relationship with ecclesiastical authority, a balance has been given that has allowed this form of utopianism to survive and thrive through the centuries. In the Middle Ages there were many utopian groups influenced by monasticism, but their apocalypticism frequently drove them to dissent, which tended to mark the end of the road in a closed society.

In the Reformation. At the time of the Reformation the magisterial Protestants, in their reaction, often possessed only a moderate expectation of what the Spirit could accomplish in believers individually or corporately. The keynote of "O wretched man that I am," even if it should continually impel to Christ, did not radiate great anticipation, while the whole matter of the charismatic was virtually banished. As a result it was quite consistent that monasticism should be dissolved, along with any other form of utopianism.

Anabaptists, on the other hand, gave more indication of continuing emphases of piety which comported well with monasticism. This was particularly true of the Hutterites, whose communitarian structures in Moravia exhibited a family-oriented Protestant monasticism, and have continued to do so to this day on the American plains and the Canadian prairies.

As the Reformation proceeded, Calvinism embodied some of the Anabaptist concern for a disciplined life, and this came to particular expression in the English Puritans. Their intense concern with sanctification began to create a desire in some quarters for a life akin to perfection. Not finding these aspirations met in mainstream Protestantism, the left wing of Puritanism, during the Cromwellian interregnum, displayed a lush spiritual vegetation of utopianism. Perhaps the Quakers were the most moderate, believing only that means of grace and official ecclesiastical ministries were no longer necessary for those who possessed the Spirit in such immediacy and fullness. There were also primitivists who believed that in their age of the Spirit the restrictions of private property could no longer apply, and in addition to apocalyptic Fifth Monarchy men there were antinomian Ranters, who interpreted their lack of conscience over sexual irregularities as a certain sign that they had been lifted far beyond mundane restriction into a new realm of liberty in the Spirit. How desperately a Protestant pope was needed in such a situation. But failing such a provision, the antics in these purported vestibules of heaven did little to convince Englishmen, unspiritual or simply less spiritual, that utopianism was a desirable option. Yet in spite of this reaction the longing for heaven on earth could not be entirely quenched.

In Modern Times. The search for utopias in the late eighteenth and nineteenth centuries had many stimuli. The eighteenth century was an age of optimism; among the figures of the Enlightenment there were advocates of human perfection, and John Wesley reached back behind the Reformation and sought to rehabilitate moral perfection in his teaching on perfect love.

And of course he had Holiness descendants who believed in the ontological eradication of evil in those redeemed and sanctified. In such a setting Shakers and the Oneida community were only the tip of the utopian iceberg.

The Shakers, remembered best for their artifacts and tranquility, were so filled with the Spirit that there was neither marrying nor giving in marriage and there was open confession of sin, community of possessions, pacifism, equality of the sexes, and consecrated work. Their utopianism was also charismatic, with their dancing in the Spirit and the founder, Ann Lee, being such a unique prophet of God that she was actually the incarnation of the feminine side of deity. In upstate New York was the Oneida community, directed by the Andover Seminary graduate John Humphrey Noyes. Led by the apparent success of revivalism and Christian social reform, Noyes founded a community in which the Spirit's gift of love was so all-encompassing that it had to be expressed among all, even sexually. Though this expression was restricted and regimented, it did not require many such instances to bring utopianism into disrepute. And there it languished for many years.

During the first two thirds of the twentieth century one of the few new and viable Christian utopian communities was the Bruderhof, which patterned much of its life after the Hutterites. Then came the social upheaval of the late 1960s and early 70s and the emergence of the Jesus Movement. Communitarian experiments multiplied. Some simply existed as centers of nurture, but others shared something of the dreams of Christian utopianism. A few, picking up the ideology of Latter Rain Pentecostalism, believed that this was the age of the manifestation of the sons of God, and that they were uniquely in the forefront of the new and glorious end-time humanity. Most of these communities lacked a counterbalance and quickly vanished from the scene.

But the utopian Christian continues to express his challenge: there is more, much more, of the life of God that is to be unleashed on earth.

I. S. Rennie

See also Perfection, Perfectionism; Friends, Society of.

Bibliography. L. Bouyer *et al., A History of Christian Spirituality,* 3 vols.; N. Cohn, *The Pursuit of the Millennium;* E. L. Tuveson, *Millennium and Utopia;* W. Cross, *The Burned-Over District;* D. Hayden, *Seven American Utopias;* B. Zablocki, *The Joyful Community;* C. Wiesbrod, *The Boundaries of Utopia.*

Utrecht, Declaration of (1889). A policy statement made by the five Old Catholic bishops, which in 1897 was adopted as the doctrinal basis of the Old Catholic Churches. It affirmed loyalty to Catholicism rightly understood—that is, as found in the beliefs of the primitive church and the decrees of the ecumenical councils up to the Great Schism between Rome and Constantinople in 1054. Made at a time soon after Vatican Council I controversies had augmented the ranks of dissidents, the declaration condemned what it regarded as Roman deviations from orthodoxy. Prominent among these were the decrees on immaculate conception (1854) and papal infallibility (1870), and the Syllabus of Errors (1864), which had condemned liberal doctrines. The Declaration of Utrecht was in large part the work of those who had earlier unsuccessfully tried to persuade Roman Catholicism to subject its history and traditions to modern criticism.

J. D. Douglas

Vv

Van Prinsterer, Guillaume Groen (1801–1876). Educated at the University of Leyden, Groen van Prinsterer was referendary to the cabinet of William I of the United Netherlands from 1827 to 1829 and cabinet secretary from 1829 to 1833. Following a breakdown in his health he experienced an evangelical conversion. After recovering from the breakdown he was appointed the official archivist to the House of Orange. He published his major work, *Unbelief and Revolution,* in 1847 and played an active role in Dutch political life until his death. A strong advocate of Christian education, van Prinsterer helped create a political grouping which led to the formation of the Anti-Revolutionary Party. He had a profound influence on Abraham Kuyper, and is one of the shapers of modern Calvinism. I. HEXHAM

See also KUYPER, ABRAHAM.

Bibliography. B. Zylstra, *Who Was Groen.*

Vatican Council I (1869–1870). The First Vatican Council, convened by Pope Pius IX in Rome, is reckoned by Roman Catholics to be the twentieth ecumenical church council. It was the first to meet since the Council of Trent (1545–63), which had responded to the sixteenth century Protestant movement. Vatican I sought to define authoritatively the church's doctrine concerning the faith and the church, especially in response to new challenges from secular philosophical and political movements and theological liberalism. However, its work was cut short by the Franco-Prussian War and the invasion and capture of Rome by the army of the Italian government in September, 1870. The council completed only two major doctrinal statements, leaving another fifty-one unfinished. Vatican I is remembered almost exclusively for its doctrinal definition of papal infallibility.

Context and Structure The council befitted Pius IX's devout spirituality and expressed the aspirations of the papal-oriented revival of Catholic faith and practice in progress since the 1840s. It also reflected the wide-felt need of the hour to counteract the religious, philosophical, and political beliefs identified by the *Syllabus of Errors* (1864). Closest to home, the council sought to undergird the authority of the papacy that could appear to be damaged by the loss of the pope's temporal power, except for Rome and its surrounding region, to the kingdom of Italy (1859–61). The need was to regather the church and reaffirm its faith, its authority, and in particular its head, the papacy.

Pius first mentioned the possibility of a council in 1864, and he set some cardinals to work on it in 1865. He formally announced it in 1867 and issued a bill convening it in 1868. When it met in 1869, the council included 737 archbishops, bishops, and other clerical members. The council considered drafts of documents prepared in advance, debated them, and changed them. The results were undoubtedly the work of the council assembled, although what degree of freedom the council members enjoyed was questioned then as it continues to be today.

Constitution "De Fide Catholica." The first doctrinal definition, "On the Catholic faith" (approved Apr. 1870; also called "Dei Filius"), expressed a consensus of the Catholic revival concerning God, faith, and reason. In its four chapters it defined as a doctrine of divine revelation the existence of a free, personal, creator God who was absolutely independent of the universe he created. The religious truth concerning the existence of this God, it affirmed, could be known by human reason alone, so that all people had no excuse for unbelieving. Nevertheless, other truths about God and this creation could only be known by faith through divine revelation via

Scripture and the tradition of the church. Properly understood, faith and reason were not in conflict. The errors that were specifically mentioned in an appendix—notably atheism, pantheism, rationalism, fideism, biblicism, traditionalism—were either utterly wrong (atheism) or wrong in emphasizing merely one element of the whole truth (rationalism). This definition provided the basis for Catholic theology and philosophy for the next several generations.

Constitution "On Papal Primacy and Infallibility." The proposal of this second definition (also called *Pastor aeternus*) divided the council into a majority and a minority (140 at its fullest) and began a controversy that has troubled the Roman Catholic Church to this day. Originally the council was to discuss a well-rounded statement of fifteen chapters "On the Church of Christ"—as body of Christ, as a true, perfect, supernatural society, as united under the primacy of the pope, as related to civil society, etc. But when a new section on papal infallibility was introduced later, the majority considered it urgent to treat immediately the sections on papal primacy and papal infallibility as a separate unit. The result was a statement of four chapters which defined both papal primacy and papal infallibility as doctrines of divine revelation.

The passage on papal infallibility, after crucial amendments, carefully circumscribed in what sense the *magisterium* (doctrinal authority) of the pope was infallible: "The Roman Pontiff when he speaks *ex cathedra*, i.e. when, exercising the office of pastor and teacher of all Christians, according to his supreme Apostolic authority, through the divine assistance promised to him in St. Peter, he defines doctrine concerning faith and morals to be held by the universal Church, then under those circumstances he is empowered with that infallibility with which the divine Redeemer willed his Church to be equipped in defining doctrine concerning faith and morals." The statement concluded, against Gallicanism and conciliarism, that "such definitions by the Roman Pontiff were in themselves, and not by virtue of the consensus of the Church, not subject to being changed."

Eighty-eight bishops voted against the definition in the first round, and fifty-five bishops formally absented themselves at the final vote (July 18, 1870). Eventually, after the council, every bishop submitted to the definition, and the debate transmuted into differences over its interpretation. The definition encouraged Catholic revival, gave Protestants new evidence of papal superstition, and convinced secularists that the papacy was indeed utterly incompatible with modern civilization. To this day the doctrine of papal infallibility continues to trouble many Catholics and to complicate Roman Catholic consultations with Anglicans, Lutherans, and others. C. T. McIntire

See also Papacy; Vatican Council II; Infallibility.

Bibliography. *Pii IX P.M. Acta*, Pt. I, Vol. 5, 177–94, 208–20 (the council documents); R. Aubert, *Vatican I;* C. Butler, *The Vatican Council*, 2 vols.; F. J. Cwiekowski, *The English Bishops and the First Vatican Council;* H. Küng, *Infallible? an Enquiry;* A. B. Hasler, *How the Pope Became Infallible: Pius IX and the Politics of Persuasion;* J. Hennessey, *The First Vatican Council: The American Experience.*

Vatican Council II (1962–1965). Regarded by Roman Catholics as the twenty-first ecumenical church council, Vatican II was a deliberate attempt to renew and bring up to date (*aggiornamento*) all facets of church faith and life. It was convened in October of 1962 by Pope John XXIII, and reconvened in September 1963 by his successor, Pope Paul VI. Altogether the council held four annual fall sessions, finally adjourning after approving sixteen major texts that were promulgated by the pope. At the opening session 2,540 bishops and other clerical members of council attended, and an average of 2,300 members were present for most major votes. The council took on a profound and electrifying life of its own. Before the eyes of the world it succeeded in initiating an extraordinary transformation of the Roman Catholic Church.

Occasion and Characteristics. In January, 1959, Pope John XXIII announced his intention to convene an ecumenical council. After one full year of gathering suggestions throughout the church he established ten commissions to prepare draft documents for the council to consider. He formally called the council in December, 1961, and opened it in St. Peter's Basilica, Rome, on October 11, 1962.

In various communications, including his opening speech, Pope John indicated the needs of the hour. The Western world had experienced during the 1950s stupefying technical, scientific, and economic expansion that had given countless people occasion to put their trust in material goods even while other millions of people lived in devastating poverty and suffering. Militant atheism abounded, and the world was undergoing grave spiritual crisis. But, proclaimed Pope John—and herewith he set the character of the entire council—the world needs not the condemnation of its errors but the full supply of "the medicine of mercy." The church, via the council, aimed to help the world by rejuvenating its own faith and life in Christ, by updating itself, by promoting the unity of all Christians, and by directing Christian presence in the world to the works of peace, justice, and well-being.

Chief among the council's characteristics was a pastoral spirit which dominated throughout. There was also a biblical spirit. From the very beginning the bishops indicated that they would not accept the rather abstract and theologically exact drafts prepared for them. Instead, they desired to express themselves in direct biblical language. Moreover, there was an evident awareness of history—the history of salvation, the pilgrim church, the ongoing tradition, the development of doctrine, the openness to the future. The council was ecumenical in its outreach to non-Catholic Christians (represented by observers from twenty-eight denominations) and humble in relation to non-Christian religions. It was remarkably open to the whole world, especially through massive global press coverage and by directly addressing the world in an opening "Message to Humanity," and in a series of closing messages to political rulers, intellectuals and scientists, artists, women, the poor, workers, and youth. Yet the council kept the church thoroughly consistent with its Roman Catholic identity and tradition.

On the Church. Undoubtedly the central theme of the promulgated documents was the church. The "Dogmatic Constitution on the Church" (Nov. 1964) was the pivotal doctrinal statement of the entire council. A second dogmatic constitution was "On Divine Revelation." A third, called simply a constitution, was "On Liturgy," and a fourth, called a pastoral constitution, was "On the Church in the Modern World." In addition, nine practical decrees and three declarations of principle were promulgated. Of these, five concerned the vocations of the church as fulfilled by bishops, priests (two), members of religious orders, and the laity. Three treated education, missions, and the media. Four covered the church's relations with Eastern Catholics, ecumenism, non-Christian religions, and civil governments (religious liberty).

The constitution "On the Church," in eight chapters (also called *Lumen gentium*), was the first ever issued on the subject by a council. In a direct way it explicitly continued and completed the work of Vatican I. In particular it incorporated (ch. 3) almost verbatim the controversial statement on papal infallibility, with the addition that infallibility also resided in the body of bishops when exercising the *magisterium* (doctrinal authority) in conjunction with the pope. The primacy of the Roman pontiff was again affirmed, but, significantly, the centrality of the bishops was also affirmed. This was the principle of collegiality—that the bishops as a whole were the continuation of the body of the apostles of which Peter was head. By placing episcopal collegiality in union with papal primacy and by shared infallibility the council resolved the ancient tension of pope versus councils.

The same document (ch. 4) introduced the biblical teaching that the church as a whole was the people of God, including both clergy and laity. This reversed centuries of virtually explicit assertion that the clergy alone were the church. Both laity and clergy, the document affirmed, shared in the priestly, prophetic, and kingly functions of Christ. The decree "On the Laity" and the constitution "On the Church in the Modern World" (also called *Gaudium et spes*) charged lay people to undertake their work in the world in all walks of life as Christian vocations, as a lay apostolate which shared directly in the continuation of the work of the apostles of Christ. This too undid centuries of emphasis on the clergy, monks, and nuns as virtually the sole possessors of Christian calling.

On Divine Revelation. This second dogmatic constitution continued the work of Vatican I, but profoundly modified it. As continuation, it stressed the necessity of the *magisterium* of the church functioning within the ongoing sacred tradition "which comes from the apostles [and] develops in the Church with the help of the Holy Spirit." The profound modification was the new *de facto* primacy given to sacred Scripture. Four of the six chapters define the Scriptures of the OT and the NT as the sacred communication by God, under the inspiration of the Holy Spirit, of "those things which he wanted." While use of critical methods is appropriate, "serious attention must be given to the content and unity of the whole of Scripture." Sacred Scripture is properly interpreted within the context of the sacred tradition and of the *magisterium* of the church; all three together and each differently are due to the action of the same Holy Spirit. The biblical emphasis is made explicit here and in other decrees by the centrality given to Scripture in the revised liturgy, in the education of clergy, in the exposition of the council's teachings, and in the insistence that all persons be given full and easy access to Scripture. The results were immediately experienced most dramatically in the transformation of parish worship into the vernacular languages throughout the world.

On Ecumenism. The decree "On Ecumenism" likewise continued traditional teaching, but adapted it dramatically. The council reaffirmed that "it is through Christ's Catholic Church alone, which is the all-embracing means of salvation, that the fullness of the means of salvation can be obtained." Yet for the first time Protestants and Anglicans are explicitly regarded as Christians ("separated brethren"), and Eastern Orthodox are treated as directly descendant from the apostles. Most significantly, the Catholic Church, for the first time, did not claim that the solution to these divisions lies in a "return" of these churches to Rome, but in an open future in which all may be "tending toward that fullness with which our Lord wants His body to be endowed in the course of time." Pope Paul made the point concrete by creating a permanent Secretariat for Promoting Christian Unity, and by issuing (Dec. 1965) with Patriarch Athenagoras, head of Eastern Orthodoxy, a declaration committing the mutual excommunications of A.D. 1054 to oblivion and hoping for restoration of full communion of faith and sacramental life.

C. T. McIntire

See also Vatican Council I; Papacy; Infallibility.

Bibliography. Walter M. Abbott, ed., *The Documents of Vatican II;* J. H. Miller, ed., *Vatican II: An Interfaith Appraisal;* B. Pawley, ed., *The Second Vatican Council;* G. C. Berkouwer, *Reflections on the Vatican Council;* A. C. Outler, *Methodist Observer at Vatican II;* E. Schillebeeckx, *The Real Achievement of Vatican II.*

Veneration of Relics. *See* Relics.

Veneration of the Saints. Celebration of the virtuous life or heroic death of persons whose souls reside in heaven with Christ. Such honor includes the respectful memory and imitation of the virtues of departed believers as well as verbal communion with them. It includes both private and public devotion.

Veneration of saints began as recognition of early martyrs, at whose graves Christians conducted memorial services of worship of God. By the fourth century Christians inaugurated similar honor of other deceased, called "confessors," whose piety they esteemed as a sacrifice equivalent to that of martyrs. Subsequently use of images and relics as conveyers of personal presence multiplied the places where this form of the communion of saints was practiced by Orthodox and Catholic faithful.

Evangelical critics of veneration, from as early as the twelfth century Waldensians, have argued that it is unbiblical, pagan, and potentially blasphemous. Defenders generally concede the lack of direct scriptural warrant, although they claim it follows logically from the doctrines of immortality and the unity of the body of Christ (Eph. 2:19). They deny similarity to pagan practice because veneration does not imply divinity in saints. Saints are humans who, by grace, enjoy God's special love and friendship. In veneration the pious glorify God's grace displayed in both the earthly and the heavenly works of saints.

To differentiate between worship of God and veneration of saints Augustine proposed the distinction, elaborated by later writers, between *latria* and *dulia. Latria* ("worship") belongs to deity alone (Matt. 4:10); *dulia* ("honor") may be merited by human beings by virtue of their office or deeds (Rom. 13:7).

Three historical stages in defining who are the venerable may be identified. Initially ordinary believers honored the dead on general repute. After the third century bishops supervised the public cult of saints. From the later Middle Ages centralized authority (papacy in catholicism; synod in Orthodoxy) assumed sole power to designate saints. Currently an elaborate judicial procedure is required to determine sainthood, entailing two degrees: "beatification" confirms that the deceased reigns with Christ and merits local devotion; subsequent "canonization" prescribes veneration by all faithful. In such determination, miracles in response to prayers to the individual constitute primary evidence.

P. D. Steeves

See also Latria; Dulia; Beatification; Canonization; Invocation of the Saints.

Bibliography. Augustine, *City of God,* X,1; P. Brown, *The Cult of the Saints;* J. Calvin, *Institutes of the Christian Religion,* 3.20.21–27; P. Molinari, *NCE,* III, 55–59; J. Pelikan, *The Growth of Medieval Theology,* III, 174–84; Thomas Aquinas, *Summa Theologica,* II.II.84.1; II.II.103.1–3.

Vengeance. In the earliest biblical story Cain assumed that vengeance would pursue him (Gen. 4:14); the pagan citizens of Malta thought the same concerning Paul (Acts 28:4 AV), as would most of the Greek world, for whom Nemesis or the fates ensured that wrongdoing met its due reward.

In Jewish-Christian thought this impersonal vengeance is seen as the deliberate act of God: "God of vengeance, . . . God of vengeance, . . . Rise up, O judge of the earth. . . . How long shall the wicked exult?" (Ps. 94:1–3). So even the sensitive Jeremiah: "O Lord . . . who judgest righteously, who triest the heart and the mind, let me see thy vengenace; . . . to thee have I committed my cause" (Jer. 11:20). In Deut. 32:35, 43 God is praised precisely because vengeance is his, and recompense, "for the Lord will vindicate his people. . . . He avenges the blood of his servants." Thus Jesus, too: "Will not God vindicate his elect. . . ? I tell you, he will vindicate them speedily" (Luke 18:7–8; literally "make vengeance for them"). Throughout Scripture a final "day of vengeance" is foreseen, associated with avenging God's people, with requital, recompense, anger, wrath (Mic. 5:15), "not clearing the guilty" (Nah. 1:3), repayment of wrong (Rom. 12:19), and punishment (II Thess. 1:8–9).

These explicative words and phrases illumine a complex idea. (1) Vengeance may include anger, fury (Prov. 6:34), vindictiveness, hatred, and reacting passionately to injury suffered. This is *revenge,* demanding "satisfying" reprisal, exhausting emotion in violence or cunning. (2) But "taking vengeance" is nearer to avenging, fulfilling a duty owed to the injured in assertion of loyalty or affection; it seeks to vindicate a friend, brother, or colleague for injury inflicted or dishonor done. To this extent vengeance may be selfless, even self-sacrificing, the recognition of a moral bond. For such divine vindication, or recompense, the godly wait and pray, when their cause will be shown to be right and victorious; hence the day of vengeance is for some a day of comfort (Isa. 61:2).

(3) This will, however, involve punishment of the evildoer, requital, "doing to [Babylon] as she has done" (Jer. 50:15), and repayment. Such is retribution, or *retaliation,* returning evil upon the head of the evildoer. (4) In God's vengeance, this is no mere expression of personal antipathy or spitefulness, no vestige of revenge; rather it is the reaction of positive holiness, of active righteousness, asserting the moral order of the world, vindicating truth, right, and goodness against all that is corrupt, false, and evil. For this divine justice, because in time words change their nuances, "vengeance" is probably no longer the appropriate term.

Among men, instinctive personal revenge aims at relief of anger, self-defense, and deterrence. Usually unrestrained in primitive societies, it was limited by the ancient *lex talionis* (as in the legal codes of Hammurabi and Moses) to equal, or proportionate, reprisal—*only* "an eye for an eye," where once any insult might bring death.

But Christian teaching outlawed revenge entirely; the Christian reaction to injury is forgiveness, love, turning the other cheek, and overcoming evil with good. Incentives to this total repudiation of private vengeance are four: (1) feelings of anger, hatred, and malice being forbidden (Sermon on the Mount), no action for emotional release is contemplated; (2) retaliation changes nothing in the situation, producing only a vicious circle, injury breeding further injury; (3) Christ's superb example (Luke 9:51–56; 19:41; 23:34); (4) our own dependence as sinners on God's forgiving love—only the merciful obtain mercy, only the forgiving are forgiven (Matt. 5:7; 6:14–15).

Nevertheless, protection and vindication of others oppressed, out of love toward them and indignation against wrong, remain a Christian duty. This is implemented wherever possible through the community's judicial system, as God's agency of vengeance (Rom. 13:1–4; I Pet. 2:13–14), helping to insure impartiality, equity, punishment without malice, examination of circumstances, motive, and background of the offender. Ultimate vindication of the moral order of the world is best left in more competent hands (Rom. 12:19; I Thess. 4:6).

By such careful distinctions Christianity effectively eschews all personal vengeance, without sentimentally destroying the moral basis of social order.

R. E. O. White

Venial Sin. *See* Sin, Venial.

Verbal Inspiration. From the early church until the Reformation, Christians expressed themselves on the inspiration of the Bible in what might be called pretheological fashion. What they stated was not necessarily in conflict with the later and well-developed theory of verbal inspiration—in fact, their statements contained some essential constituents of the theory—but in the matter of inspiration their reflection had not evidenced the intensity which made possible the construction of self-consistent theories.

Even in the early Reformation period detailed theories of inspiration were not broached, but by 1580 the situation was changing. Orthodox Christianity, both Protestant and Roman Catholic, sensed that it was being forced to face certain new questions and that these related especially to the Bible and its inspiration. The spirit of the Renaissance, developments in philology and textual criticism, the emergence of ideas of the partial inspiration of the Bible in some quarters, and the initial expression of philosophical views that would find their culmination in the Enlightenment—all helped to precipitate theological consideration. And the theories of plenary and then verbal inspiration were among the consequences.

The Nature of Verbal Inspiration. The exponents of verbal inspiration usually shared in the Aristotelian philosophical orientation that was once again sweeping Europe, while in most cases they also shared Augustinian theological propensities. Both continental Protestants and Roman Catholics were involved, although, as has frequently happened, the English Channel provided a barrier, and the British at the time did not get immersed in the new developments.

There are a number of entities which comprised the theory of verbal inspiration. (1) God is the author of the Bible in the sense of being the formal cause. (2) The focus of inspiration is the words of the Bible; it is text rather than author oriented. (3) All the words and all the verbal relationships are inspired by God. This includes all seemingly peripheral statements as well as those more obviously germane to the matter under consideration. All are of significance in the totality of inspired Scripture. Even accounts known beforehand by the writers from other sources are inspired in the same verbal way for inclusion in the Bible. Thus the totality of Scripture partakes of uniform verbal inspiration. (4) The data of the Bible are claimed as the source of the theory—not the data in the sense of the phenomena, but the teaching of the Bible about its own nature. In this way it is affirmed as inductive, although deduction is then operative to spell out the assumption of what should be the consequences of a God-breathed and Spirit-borne inspiration. (5) Dictation is not involved; there is no violation of the personality of the writer. God had sovereignly and concursively been preparing the writers for the instrumental task so that they willingly and naturally recorded God's revelation in the way he required. Thus the Bible may be described as all of God and all of man. (6) Conscious accommodation on God's part accounts for any lapse, infelicity, or inexactitude. (7) The autographs of the biblical books are solely thus inspired. (8) Inerrancy is the quality of such a Bible; it speaks with exactitude on all matters, save where accommodation has obviously taken place. (9) Authority flows from such a Bible on all matters which it touches, thus guaranteeing that divine teaching is communicated on all matters concerning what a Christian is to believe and how he is to live.

Verbal inspiration has usually been accompanied by certain corollaries. It has tended to encourage a relatively literalistic hermeneutic and to be very cautious on the subject of biblical criticism. Its literalism has encouraged the view that societal hierarchicalism was divinely established, and thus it has frequently been a buttress to social conservatism. It has often been staunch in its defense of Christian orthodoxy in difficult days, and its supporters have usually been convinced that it was the only view of the Bible which could properly maintain the faith.

Verbal Inspiration in History. The forces which drove Christians to produce theories of inspiration by reaction continued in such strength that during the eighteenth century they virtually engulfed verbal inspiration except in certain restricted quarters. Partial inspiration became a common view during this century among those who made significant accommodation to the Enlightenment, whereas the Christians of the dynamic first and second evangelical awakenings, from 1735 to 1825, almost invariably held to plenary inspiration. During their two finest generations the evangelicals, although they adhered to the full inspiration of the Bible, did not propagate the verbal theory.

Verbal inspiration received a new lease on life after the close of the Napoleonic Wars in 1815, particularly in the movement known as Protestant confessionalism. Its supporters were increasingly unhappy with the way in which much of evangelicalism appeared to be disregarding the divine initiative. And at the same time liberal theology appeared to be advancing with new vigor. A return to the Reformation confessions and their theology appeared to be the necessary strategy, and in this endeavor verbal inspiration was rediscovered.

In the English-speaking world, where verbal inspiration was for the first time to find a significant welcome, the first prominent nineteenth century Protestant advocate was Robert Haldane, the wealthy Scottish lay evangelist, who after his exposure to the rationalism of Genevan Protestantism in 1817 determined that a new line of biblical defense was necessary. His views were particularly expressed in his frequently reprinted *The Books of the Old and New Testaments Proved to be Canonical and Their Verbal Inspiration Maintained and Established.* His outlook on inspiration was embraced by his friend Andrew Thomson, the leading evangelical in the Church of Scotland, and was regularly expressed in the *Christian Instructor,* becoming the accepted view in the Free Church of Scotland among the generation following the disruption of 1843. Henry Cooke, another close friend of Haldane's and the powerful champion of orthodoxy in Irish Presbyterianism, espoused and promulgated similar views. In the United States, Charles Hodge introduced the verbal theory—silently jettisoning the plenary view of his venerated predecessor at Princeton Seminary, Archibald Alexander—making it the accepted view among Old School Presbyterians in the middle Atlantic and southeastern states and a position of long continuance among northern and southern Presbyterians of Old School lineage.

Robert Haldane's influence ran in other directions as well. His nephew, Alexander, became a power among the English evangelical Anglicans and helped to stamp verbal inspiration on an important section of the party. From these evangelical Anglicans came the founders of the

Plymouth Brethren, who though they transmuted Protestant Anglican confessionalism into what was assumed to be first century restorationism, nonetheless remained strong advocates of the verbal theory. When Robert Haldane's peripatetic evangelism proved unacceptable to the preevangelical leadership of the Church of Scotland, he became a Baptist, as did his Irish ghost writer Alexander Carson, and both promulgated verbal inspiration through their Baptist links. Perhaps the most important individual in the popular spread of verbal inspiration was Haldane's Genevan convert, Louis Gaussen, whose *Theopneustia* is still reprinted. And while this was happening in the English-speaking world, Lutheran confessionalism was resuscitating verbal inspiration in the Germanic lands.

On the other hand, the majority of mid-nineteenth century evangelicals clung to plenary inspiration. Among denominations such as Methodists and Congregationalists there was little concern with verbal inspiration.

The second wave of reaction to liberalism was fundamentalism, which emerged in the late nineteenth and carried on into the twentieth century. Although it differed from confessionalism in certain important aspects, they were at one in championing verbal inspiration and worked together for the dissemination of this concept. One of the ablest upholders of verbal inspiration appeared at this time in the person of B. B. Warfield of Princeton Seminary. Although he added nothing particularly new to the theory, his numerous articles and book reviews shed the light of his brilliant mind upon his specially chosen theme. As the modernist-fundamentalist controversy developed in intensity and polarization, particularly in North America, many conservatives found themselves shifting from plenary and accepting verbal inspiration. In many quarters the phrase "plenary verbal inspiration" began to be used, but this was only a change in wording, implying no change in the content of verbal inspiration. However, an interesting contrast occurred in the United Kingdom, where it was almost impossible to find a recognized conservative evangelical spokesman who in the first half of the twentieth century taught verbal inspiration.

In Roman Catholicism the late nineteenth century saw a new form of verbal inspiration advocated by the famous French exegete M. J. Lagrange, but it was too open to the recognition of literary forms in the Bible to escape the extremely conservative reaction precipitated by Catholic modernism in the pontificate of Pius X. Henceforth, for more than a generation, official Catholic teaching on the subject of inspiration assumed an almost pretheological posture.

Since World War II evangelical Protestants and Roman Catholics, until very recently, have been almost the only Christians interested in the subject of biblical inspiration. While Roman Catholics have been shifting from any view akin to verbal inspiration, among evangelicals the concept received new strength in the United Kingdom following J. I. Packer's *"Fundamentalism" and the Word of God* in the mid-1950s. But in recent years, as evangelicalism has grown and lost something of its siege mentality, there are many voices within the movement advocating a rethinking of inspiration. And even among scholars who profess to wish to maintain verbal inspiration and inerrancy, many appear to be adopting a sophisticated posture in relation to the language and literary forms of Scripture reminscent of Lagrange, which may point to a new evangelical synthesis. I. S. RENNIE

See also PLENARY INSPIRATION; ENLIGHTENMENT, THE; LIBERALISM, THEOLOGICAL; FUNDAMENTALISM; BIBLE, INSPIRATION OF; BIBLE, AUTHORITY OF; BIBLE, INERRANCY AND INFALLIBILITY OF.

Bibliography. G. T. Ladd, *The Doctrine of Sacred Scripture,* II; B. B. Warfield, *The Inspiration and Authority of the Bible;* R. Preus, *The Inspiration of Scripture;* J. F. Walvoord, ed., *Inspiration and Interpretation;* J. T. Burtchaell, *Catholic Theories of Biblical Inspiration Since 1810;* E. R. Sandeen, *The Roots of Fundamentalism;* B. Vawter, *Biblical Inspiration;* J. W. Montgomery, ed., *God's Inerrant Word;* J. B. Rogers and D. K. McKim, *The Authority and Interpretation of the Bible;* N. Geisler, *Inerrancy;* D. F. Wright, "Soundings in the Doctrine of Scripture in British Evangelicalism in the First Half of the Twentieth Century," *TB* 31:87–106; J. Woodbridge, "Biblical Authority," *TJ* 2:165–236.

Vermigli, Peter Martyr. *See* PETER MARTYR VERMIGLI.

Vermittlungstheologie. *See* MEDIATING THEOLOGY.

Vespers. *See* OFFICE, DAILY (DIVINE); EVENING PRAYER, EVENSONG.

Via Analogia. An approach to the human conceptualization about God that uses analogy. It seeks to escape the limitations imposed by the *via negativa,* which denies all positive attribution of God. The direct opposite of the *via negativa* is the *via eminentia,* according to which all positive qualities in the world have their origin in God, who thus possesses them preeminently, thereby allowing us to predicate properties directly of

God, knowing that they are first of all his as creator.

However, the *via eminentia* by itself does not take into account the limitations of finitude in contrast to divine infinity. Hence it must be said that God possesses properties in compliance with his essence, viz., infinitely in both quality and quantity, whereas creatures possess them finitely and only as derived from God. Thus analogy seeks to steer a middle course between univocity (where the properties are all alike) and equivocation (where the properties are entirely dissimilar).

Refinement of the doctrine of analogy has led to many divergent points of view. Some thinkers hold that there is a fundamental analogy of being, whereas others say that analogy extends only to concepts while being remains univocal. Still others maintain that concepts are univocal; only the predication of a concept is analogical. Finally, the literature abounds with attempts by advocates of all the above versions of analogy to make analogy logically plausible in the face of philosophical and theological critique.

Analogy has been widely criticized among Protestants for its apparent reliance on natural theology, particularly since analogy is devised by Aristotle and adapted by Thomas Aquinas. Karl Barth in particular claims that analogy denies God's free self-expression in his revelation. Barth sought to replace the *via analogia* with a Christological analogy in which Christ is the midpoint between God and creation. In defense of analogy it can be pointed out that all attempts to avoid univocation and equivocation are in fact analogies, regardless of whether they are based on natural or revealed theology. W. CORDUAN

See also VIA NEGATIVA.

Bibliography. A. Farrer, *Finite and Infinite;* N. L. Geisler, *Philosophy of Religion;* E. L. Mascall, *Existence and Analogy;* B. Mondin, *The Principle of Analogy in Protestant and Catholic Theology;* N. C. Nielsen, Jr., "Analogy and the Knowledge of God: An Ecumenical Appraisal," *RUS* 60:21–102; E. Przywara, *Analogia Entis.*

Via Eminentia. *See* VIA ANALOGIA.

Via Illuminativa. *See* ILLUMINATIVE WAY, THE.

Via Media. Doctrinal justification for the Anglican Church as representing a middle way between the Roman Catholic Church and dissenting Protestantism. Though the term first appears in the seventeenth century, it was made most popular by John Henry Newman during his career as tractarian with the Oxford Movement, 1833 to 1841. The tractates were written by Newman and others as a series of polemics against incipient modernization of the Church of England. Thus the Oxford Movement attempted to reestablish a high church view of Anglicanism in the face of possible disestablishment of the church as a whole. The concept of the *via media* served to provide the theological underpinning for this ecclesiology.

As Newman himself tells it in *Apologia Pro Vita Sua,* the *via media* was based on three ideas: dogma, sacrament, and anti-Romanism. The first is directed against liberalism, the second against evangelicalism, and here Newman often sided with Roman ideas. But throughout this phase he also maintained the third notion, opposition to the Roman Church.

Newman describes the *via media*'s attitude toward Rome with two concepts: apostolicity and antiquity. He had no doubt that the Roman Church was apostolic, though he did not deny Anglican apostolicity either. However, he felt that the Church of England had the advantage when it came to antiquity, i.e., faithfulness to biblical and patristic doctrine. In particular, Newman objected to the Roman practice of worshiping Mary and the saints.

However, the *via media,* which was after all only a theoretical notion, was to die at Newman's own hands. He became increasingly convinced that his own arguments were working against him. Any arguments for the apostolicity of the Anglican Church could be made *a fortiori* for Romanism. And doctrinal rectitude has historically been found on the side of Rome as well. Newman discovered to his great chagrin that an attempt at a *via media* in the fifth century would have left him as a monophysitist heretic. With his *Essay on Doctrinal Development,* Newman overcame his last objections to Roman dogma, and he converted to Rome. The *via media* had died.

The leading issue concerning the *via media* was always ecclesiological: Which church is the right one? Evangelical theologians may rightly ask if a greater commitment to doctrinal truth wherever it may be found might not have left Newman a Protestant and allowed him to serve Christendom better in the long run.

W. CORDUAN

See also NEWMAN, JOHN HENRY; OXFORD MOVEMENT.

Bibliography. C. F. Harrold, ed., *A Newman Treasury;* P. Misnar, *Papacy and Development: Newman and the Primacy of the Pope;* J. H. Newman, *Apologia pro Vita Sua, An Essay on the Development of Christian Doctrine,* and *The Via Media of the Anglican Church,* 2 vols.; L. H. Yearly, *The Ideas of Newman.*

Via Negativa. The "way of remotion"—an approach to the knowledge of God that denies the strict applicability of any human concepts to God. Originating in the Neoplatonic tradition, it became an important consideration in the Christian theology of the Middle Ages.

Although Plato never drew up an explicit system on this point, it is clear from his writings that he considered the forms to be ordered hierarchically with such mundane ones as tallness and heat toward the bottom and the good at the apex. All the forms specify modes or characteristics of reality. One of the innovations of Neoplatonism, that of Plotinus, consisted in the addition of the source for all the forms, the "One." Since it is from the One that all the forms originate (frequently envisioned in a sequence of emanations, e.g., by Proclus), the One itself is not subject to any of the restrictions or specifications imposed by the forms. Hence no attributes can be applied to the One.

In medieval theology the role of the One was taken over by God, who was thus thought to be beyond conceptualization. A leading advocate of the *via negativa* was Dionysius the Pseudo-Areopagite. He summarized his views in his short work *The Mystical Theology.* Dionysius recognized a way of affirmation in which it is realized that God possesses all attributes as First Cause; he explicated this notion in *On Divine Names.* This way of affirmation begins with God and sees all creaturely attributes as derived from him. But if we attempt to reverse this process and try to reapply those attributes to God, we find that he is beyond such predication, and all we have left is the darkness of skepticism concerning his attributes.

Aquinas and other later medieval scholars retained the idea of the *via negativa,* but only insofar as it reveals to us the uniqueness of God. Rather than leading to skepticism, they saw the remoteness of God as necessitating analogical predication. A revival of the *via negativa* can be seen in the skepticism engendered by the extreme nominalists of the fifteenth century.

W. Corduan

See also Via Analogia; Neoplatonism; Dionysius the Pseudo-Areopagite.

Bibliography. Dionysius Areopagus, Collected Writings, *Patrologia Graeca,* III; A. Farrer, *Finite and Infinite: A Philosophical Essay;* F. C. Harrold, *Mysticism;* E. O'Brien, ed., *The Essential Plotinus;* T. Whittaker, *Neo-Platonists.*

Via Purgativa. *See* Purgative Way, The.

Via Unitiva. *See* Unitive Way, The.

Vicar. *See* Church Officers.

Vicarious Atonement. *See* Atonement.

Violence. That "the earth was corrupt in God's sight, and . . . filled with violence" is the reason given in Gen. 6:11 for the punitive flood. Repeatedly the charge recurs in the OT that the city is full of violence (Ezek. 7:23), princes do violence (Ezek. 45:9), and men of violence have their way in society. The rich seize by violence houses and fields of the impoverished "because it is in their power," thereby becoming "full of violence" (see Mic. 2:2; 6:12), while great houses are stored with treasures taken by violence (Amos 3:10). Eccles. 5:8 expresses the realistic view of the candid observer of society: "If you see in a province the poor oppressed and justice and right violently taken away, do not be amazed. . . . The high official is watched by a higher." Violence is often coupled with plunder, often with deceit, as two ways of stealing. Hab. 2:8 extends the thought significantly, warning those guilty of the blood of men, doing "violence to the earth, to cities, and all who dwell therein." It is declared that the Lord's soul hates him that loves violence (Ps. 11:5); that the servant of the Lord will do no violence (Isa. 53:9; cf. 42:2); eventually, in God's time, the land shall be purged of violence (Isa. 60:18). At the opening of the NT, with its announcement of the divine reign, armed soldiers of the occupying power are warned to "rob no one by violence" (Luke 3:14).

Scripture thus consistently identifies violence with ruthless exercise of power, by actions involving physical force or unlawful intimidation, resulting in loss, injury, or constraint to the unprotected. Its condemnation as evil and retrograde is assumed to follow, alike from its irrationality and its injustice.

But violence may also be both rational and just—e.g., in duly authorized, impartial, and controlled law enforcement, in restraint of unlawful violence such as rioting, and in benevolent constraint of the insane. Society cannot always wait upon assent to secure order: "The passions of men must be restrained by fear until they can be disciplined by love." It is false, therefore, to equate the violence socially authorized to agents of justice and control with that of the antisocial individual and the anarchic terrorist cell.

A refinement of violence is expressed in moral blackmail, in the coercion of threats, in play upon imaginary fears, or social ostracism; and still more subtly in intellectual dogmatism, brainwashing, withholding information, dictatorial pronouncements coupled with threats (the so-called "violence of principle"), and all denial of freedom of thought, speech, expression, and persuasion.

Violence may be defended (1) psychologically, as the only form of protest available to the inarticulate, untrained in more intellectual forms of self-expression and persuasion; (2) sociologically, as the only weapon within reach of the unprivileged, the only avenue of protest open to political groups suppressed by dictatorship or smothered by insensitive democratic majorities. It can be defended (3) morally, as necessary to any progressive movement in order to assert its independence of conventional standards, to define its distinctive position, and to eliminate lukewarm supporters. Thus, early Christianity welcomed deliberate confrontation with paganism, rejecting all compromise; it embraced persecution in preference to toleration on the state's terms. In time the church itself adopted inquisition, physical torture, and persecution "to save the souls of unbelievers"; and later still, it imposed severer intellectual demands on the faithful (the bodily assumption of Mary, papal infallibility) in "violent" opposition to the rational teaching of science and the "reasonable compromises" of modernism.

Violence has always been present in society, in law enforcement and in war, and may always be so until all mankind share identical intellectual convictions. Christian moralists will therefore distinguish the springs, grounds, and aims of violence before condemning all violent actions for reasons of academic superiority, cultural taste, or fear. Christians will sympathize with (but not approve) the violence that expresses personal frustration of the physically or mentally handicapped, but will still insist that for a rational and moral creature like man, violence will always be subnormal. For society, violence will ever breed insecurity, never arriving at truth, justice, or equilibrium, but always reproducing endless counterviolence.

Christian wisdom will condemn the exploitation of violence for entertainment, rejecting the claim that theater and literature may "reflect society" without incurring responsibility for portraying the intolerable as "normal," and so lowering social standards. Most of all, the Christian must condemn the manipulation, by the social and intellectual activist, of the frustrated and envious passion of the mob for his own selfish or political ends.

R. E. O. White

Bibliography. G. Sorel, *Reflections on Violence;* J. Ellul, *Violence: Reflections from a Christian Perspective;* M. Hengel, *Victory over Violence;* T. Merton, *Faith and Violence.*

Virgin Birth of Jesus. Matt. 1:18, 22–25 and Luke 1:26–38 teach that the birth of Jesus resulted from a miraculous conception. He was conceived in the womb of the Virgin Mary by the power of the Holy Spirit without male seed. This is the doctrine of the virgin birth, which must be distinguished from other doctrines concerning Mary such as perpetual virginity, her immaculate conception, her assumption, which are rejected by most Protestants, and from views in which the phrase "virgin birth" is taken to indicate some sort of divine involvement in the incarnation without affirming the biological virginity of Jesus' mother. Views of the latter sort are common enough in modern liberal theology, but it is an abuse of language to call them affirmations of the virgin birth; they are denials of the virgin birth, though they may indeed be affirmations of something else.

Possibility and Probability. If one rejects the possibility of miracle in general, as does, e.g., Bultmann, then one must reject the virgin birth as well. But such a generalized rejection of miracle is arbitrary and indefensible on any ground, and it is contrary to the most fundamental presuppositions of Christian thought. The virgin birth is no more miraculous than the atonement or the resurrection or the regeneration of sinners. If miracle is rejected, then nothing important to Christianity can be retained.

If one accepts the general possibility of miracle, one must still ask about the possibility and probability of the virgin birth in particular. For an evangelical Christian the fact that this doctrine is taught in God's inerrant Word settles such questions. Yet this fact does not make historical investigation superfluous. If indeed Scripture is inerrant, it is consistent with all historical discovery. To illustrate this consistency can only be helpful—not only to convince those who doubt the authority of Scripture, but also to confirm the faith of those who accept it. But such investigation must be carried out on principles compatible with the Christian revelation, not (as with Bultmann) on principles antagonistic to it from the outset.

The NT Accounts. On that basis, then, let us examine the credibility of the NT witnesses, Matthew and Luke. Both Gospels are often dated from A.D. 70–100, but if we grant the assumption that Jesus was able to predict the fall of Jerusalem (A.D. 70; and why would a Christian deny this?), there is ample evidence for dating these Gospels in the 60s or earlier. In any case, the two accounts are generally thought to be independent of each other and thus to be based on a tradition antedating both.

Confirming the antiquity of this tradition is the remarkably "Hebraic" character of both birth accounts: the theology and language of these chapters seem more characteristic of the

OT than the NT, as many scholars have noted. This fact renders very unlikely the hypothesis that the virgin birth is a *theologoumenon*—a story invented by the early church to buttress its Christological dogma. There is here no mention of Jesus' preexistence. His title "Son of God" is seen to be future, as is his inheritance of the Davidic throne (Luke 1:32, 35). In the birth narratives Jesus is the OT Messiah—the son of David, the fulfillment of prophecy, the one who will rescue God's people through mighty deeds, exalting the humble and crushing the proud (Luke 1:46–55). The writers draw no inference from the virgin birth concerning Jesus' deity or ontological sonship to God; rather, they simply record the event as a historical fact and (for Matthew) as a fulfillment of Isa. 7:14.

Not much is known about the author of Matthew, but there is much reason to ascribe the third Gospel to Luke the physician (Col. 4:14), a companion of Paul (II Tim. 4:11; cf. the "we" passages in Acts, such as 27:1ff.) who also wrote the Acts of the Apostles (cf. Luke 1:1–4; Acts 1:1–5). Luke claims to have made a careful study of the historical data (1:1–4), and that claim has been repeatedly vindicated in many details even by modern skeptical scholars such as Harnack. Both his vocations—historian and physician—would have prevented him from responding gullibly to reports of a virgin birth. The two birth narratives have been attacked as inconsistent and/or erroneous at several points: the genealogies, the massacre of the children (Matt. 2:16), the census during the time of Quirinius (Luke 2:1–2); but plausible explanations of these difficulties have also been advanced. Jesus' Davidic ancestry (emphasized in both accounts) has been under suspicion also; but as Raymond Brown argues, the presence of Mary and Jesus' brothers, especially James (Acts 1:14; 15:13–21; Gal. 1:19; 2:9), in the early church would probably have prevented the development of legendary material concerning Jesus' origin. All in all, we have good reason, even apart from belief in their inspiration, to trust Luke and Matthew, even where they differ from the verdicts of secular historians ancient and modern.

The Rest of Scripture. Much has been said concerning the "silence" of Scripture about the virgin birth outside of the passages mentioned. This silence is real, but it need not be explained by any ignorance or denial of the virgin birth by other NT writers. It is significant that even the Gospels of Matthew and Luke are "silent" about the virgin birth through fifty of their combined fifty-two chapters. The silence of the rest of the NT can be explained in essentially the same ways as one would explain the partial silence of Matthew and Luke. The NT deals chiefly with (1) Jesus' preaching, life, death, resurrection (the Gospels and to some extent the epistles); (2) the preaching and missionary work in the early church (Acts especially); (3) teaching concerning the theological and practical problems of the church (Acts, epistles); (4) assurances of the triumph of God's purposes and visions of the end times (Revelation, other NT books). The virgin birth was not part of Jesus' preaching or that of the early church. It was not a controversial matter such as might have been addressed in the epistles (Christology in general was not a particularly controversial matter among the Christians, and even if it had been, the virgin birth most likely was not seen as a means of supporting Christological dogma). The main function of the virgin birth in the NT, to show the fulfillment of prophecy and to describe the events surrounding Jesus' birth, is appropriate only to birth narratives, and only two birth narratives have been preserved in the canon. We must also assume that the early church maintained a certain reserve about public discussion of these matters out of respect for the privacy of Jesus' family, especially Mary.

Is there anything in the NT that *contradicts* the virgin birth accounts? There are passages where Jesus is described as the son of Joseph: John 1:45; 6:42; Luke 2:27, 33, 41, 43, 48; Matt. 13:55. Clearly, though, Luke and Matthew had no intention of denying the virgin birth of Christ, unless the birth narratives are later additions to the books, and there is no evidence of that. These references clearly refer to Joseph as the legal father of Jesus without reference to the question of biological fatherhood. The same is true in the Johannine references, with the additional fact that the words in question were spoken by those who were not well acquainted with Jesus and/or his family. (The text of Matt. 1:16, saying that Joseph begat Jesus, is certainly not original.)

It is interesting that the Markan variant of Matt. 13:55 (Mark 6:3) eliminates reference to Joseph and speaks of Jesus as "Mary's son," an unusual way of describing parentage in Jewish culture. Some have thought that this indicates some knowledge of the virgin birth by Mark, or even some public knowledge of an irregularity in Jesus' origin, even though Mark has no birth narrative as such. Cf. John 8:41, where Jesus' opponents hint his illegitimacy, a charge which apparently continued to be made into the second century. Brown remarks that such a charge would not have been fabricated by Christians, nor would it have been fabricated by non-Christians probably, unless Jesus' origin were known to be somehow unusual. Thus it is possible that these incidental references to Jesus' birth actually confirm the virgin birth, though this evidence is not of great weight.

Is Isa. 7:14 a prediction of the virgin birth? Matt. 1:22 asserts that the virgin birth "fulfills" that passage, but much controversy has surrounded that assertion, turning on the meaning of the Isaiah passage in context, its LXX translation, and Matthew's use of both. The arguments are too complicated for full treatment here. E. J. Young has mounted one of the few recent scholarly defenses of the traditional position. I would only suggest that for Matthew the concept of "fulfilment" sometimes takes on aesthetic dimensions that go beyond the normal relation between "prediction" and "predicted event" (cf. his use of Zech. 9:9 in 21:1–4). For Matthew, the "fulfillment" may draw the attention of people to the prophecy in startling, even bizarre ways which the prophet himself might never have anticipated. It "corresponds" to the prophecy in unpredictable but exciting ways, as a variation in music corresponds to a theme. It may be that some element of this takes place in Matt. 1:23, though Young's argument may prevail in the long run.

Postbiblical Attestation. Belief in the virgin birth is widely attested in literature from the second century. Ignatius defended the doctrine strongly against the docetists, who held that Jesus only "appeared" to have become man. Some have thought that Ignatius shows acquaintance with a tradition independent of the Gospels affirming the virgin birth. The virgin birth was denied only by Gnostic docetists and by Ebionites, who held Jesus to be a mere human prophet. The silence of some church fathers, like the silence of Scripture, has been cited as evidence of a tradition contrary to this doctrine, but there is no clear evidence of any such things, and the argument from silence can easily be countered as above.

Pagan or Jewish Background? Occasionally someone will suggest that the virgin birth narratives are based not on fact but on pagan or Jewish stories of supernatural births. Such a hypothesis is most unlikely. There is no clear parallel to the notion of a *virgin* birth in pagan literature, only of births resulting from intercourse between a God and a woman (of which there is no suggestion in Matthew and Luke), resulting in a being half-divine, half-human (which is far different from the biblical Christology). Further, none of the pagan stories locates the event in datable history as the biblical account does. Nor is there any precise parallel in Jewish literature. The closest parallels would be the supernatural births of Isaac, Samson, and Samuel in the OT, but these were not *virgin* births. Isa. 7:14 was not considered a messianic passage in the Jewish literature of the time. It is more likely that the event of the virgin birth influenced Matthew's understanding of Isa. 7:14 than the reverse.

Doctrinal Importance. The consistency of this doctrine with other Christian truth is important to its usefulness and, indeed, to its credibility. For Matthew and Luke the chief importance of the event seems to be that it calls to mind (as a "sign," Isa. 7:14) the great OT promises of salvation through supernaturally born deliverers, while going far beyond them, showing that God's *final* deliverance has come. But one can also go beyond the specific concerns of Matthew and Luke and see that the virgin birth is fully consistent with the whole range of biblical doctrine. The virgin birth is important because of: (1) The doctrine of Scripture. If Scripture errs here, then why should we trust its claims about other supernatural events, such as the resurrection? (2) The deity of Christ. While we cannot say dogmatically that God could enter the world only through a virgin birth, surely the incarnation is a supernatural event if it is anything. To eliminate the supernatural from this event is inevitably to compromise the divine dimension of it. (3) The humanity of Christ. This was the important thing to Ignatius and the second century fathers. Jesus was *really* born; he *really* became one of us. (4) The sinlessness of Christ. If he were born of two human parents, it is very difficult to conceive how he could have been exempted from the guilt of Adam's sin and become a new head to the human race. And it would seem only an arbitrary act of God that Jesus could be born without a sinful nature. Yet Jesus' sinlessness as the new head of the human race and as the atoning lamb of God is absolutely vital to our salvation (II Cor. 5:21; I Pet. 2:22–24; Heb. 4:15; 7:26; Rom. 5:18–19). (5) The nature of grace. The birth of Christ, in which the initiative and power are all of God, is an apt picture of God's saving grace in general of which it is a part. It teaches us that salvation is by God's act, not our human effort. The birth of Jesus is like our new birth, which is also by the Holy Spirit; it is a new creation (II Cor. 5:17).

Is belief in the virgin birth "necessary"? It is possible to be saved without believing it; saved people aren't perfect people. But to reject the virgin birth is to reject God's Word, and disobedience is always serious. Further, disbelief in the virgin birth may lead to compromise in those other areas of doctrine with which it is vitally connected.

J. M. Frame

See also Jesus Christ; Christology.

Bibliography. T. Boslooper, *The Virgin Birth;* R. E. Brown, *The Birth of the Messiah* and *The Virginal Conception and Bodily Resurrection of Jesus;* F. F. Bruce, *Are the NT Documents Reliable?* H. von Campenhausen, *The Virgin Birth in the Theology of the Ancient Church;* R. G. Gromacki, *The Virgin Birth: Doctrine of Deity;* J. G. Machen, *The Virgin Birth of Christ;* J. Murray, *Collected Writings,* II, 134–35; O. Piper, "The Virgin Birth: The Meaning of the Gospel Accounts," *Int* 18:131ff.; B. B. Warfield, "The Supernatural Birth of Jesus," in *Biblical and Theological Studies;* E. J. Young, *Commentary on Isaiah.*

Virgin, Assumption of the. *See* Mary, Assumption of.

Virtue, Virtues. The concept of moral excellence fills Scripture as it does the universe, for it is rooted in the being of the Eternal God. Man as the creation of God was initially good, and this goodness was purposefully stamped on him by the Creator (Gen. 1:27). The drama of history is marked indelibly by this factor and the fall of man by which moral perfection was lost. Yet perfection remains a demand of God's law (Lev. 20:26; Matt. 5:28). The human predicament then is that the *imago* seeks, longs for, and calls for perfection, yet man in his fallenness is denied fulfillment (Rom. 7). The saving act of God in Christ alone rectifies this dilemma. Only by the complete work of Jesus, the God-man, can God's righteousness become man's. The burdened Augustine lifted the Word to read, "Clothe yourselves with the Lord Jesus Christ" (Rom. 13:14). Sanctifying grace renews the believer in God's image, and he experiences the moral excellence of the Lord who called him out of darkness into light (I Pet. 2:9; Col. 3:10; Eph. 4:17). God has "given us everything we need for life and godliness through our knowledge of him who called us by his own glory and goodness" (moral perfection; II Pet. 1:3).

The classical pagan concept of virtue (*aretē*) and its achievement differs radically from the biblical view. For Plato there were four inherent virtues: wisdom, courage, temperance, and justice. Aristotle extended the number and taught that these were learned. Stoicism, common in NT times, concurred with the Platonic. All omitted "benevolence," which is foundational in Christian morality. As classical learning entered the church, leaders like Ambrose of Milan adapted the Platonic view of virtue to the Christian system. During the Middle Ages the four "natural" virtues were combined with the "theological" virtues (faith, hope, and love) and were called the seven cardinal virtues. Christian theology universally insists that virtue came from above and is not the product of human effort. In common practice, however, a diluted doctrine of grace allowed a works-system to pollute both the doctrines of justification and sanctification, and virtue came to be seen as the result of human effort. Contrary to such deviation, the NT declares that moral perfection is not inherent, does not have happiness as its primary goal, and is not self-justifying. Rather, Christian character is the work of the Holy Spirit in the believer's life as the Word of God is applied and the means of grace employed. The danger of anthropocentrizing Christian experience and so placing enjoyment and personal satisfaction above a moral excellence offered to God for his glory is present in every age.

The biblical use of *aretē* gives the scope of the concept. It is variously translated virtue (Phil. 4:8; II Pet. 1:5, KJV), excellence (Phil. 4:8, RSV, NIV), wonderful deeds (I Pet. 2:9, RSV), goodness (II Pet. 1:3, 5, NIV). Translators have been assisted by the LXX use of *aretē* for *hôd* ("splendor, majesty, vigor") in Hab. 3:3; Zech. 6:13; and *tĕhillâ* ("praise, adoration, thanksgiving") in Isa. 42:12; 43:21; and 63:7. The combination of ideas that are commonly held apart in Western society is enlightening. God's perfection unites excellence, splendor, and power, and produces praise, adoration, and thanksgiving. The "divine power" gives "life and godliness" through "knowledge of him that called us to glory and virtue" (II Pet. 1:3).

The NT gives several lists of qualities that can be called virtues (I Cor. 13; Gal. 5:22–23; Phil. 4:8; Col. 3:12–16). These are more personal than a "household table" (Eph. 5:21–6:9) or a "community table" (I Tim. 2:1–15; 5:1–21; 6:1–12). Jonathan Edwards in *Charity and Its Fruits* writes that "all virtue that is saving, and that distinguishes true Christians from others, is summed up in Christian love." Such virtue is practical and marked by inward sanctity and outward charity (Eph. 2:8–10). The Bible does not speak about virtue as moral improvement or as an adornment for unregenerate man but only as a concomitant of regeneration and for God's glory and service.

W. N. Kerr

See also Cardinal Virtues, Seven.

Bibliography. E. Brunner, *The Divine Imperative;* A. B. Bruce, *The Moral Order of the Word;* K. E. Kirk, *The Vision of God;* C. S. Lewis, *The Abolition of Man;* J. Stalker, *The Seven Cardinal Virtues;* J. G. Machen, *The Christian View of Man.*

Visible Church. *See* Church, The.

Vision of God, Visio Dei. *See* BEATIFIC VISION.

Vitringa, Campegius (1659–1722). Dutch Reformed biblical scholar. Born at Leeuwarden, Frisia (modern Netherlands), he was the son of the recorder of the Supreme Council of Friesland. He learned Greek and Hebrew at an early age, and studied philosophy and theology at the universities of Franeker (1675–78) and Leiden (1678–79). Shortly thereafter he became professor of Oriental languages at Franeker. He turned down more prominent and financially attractive positions at Leiden and Utrecht to remain at Franeker, teaching theology and sacred history, until his death.

Theologically, Vitringa's views were consistent with post-Reformation orthodoxy; he held high views of the Bible and its inspiration, and upheld the doctrine of absolute predestination. His greatest significance was as an exegete. His most prominent work was his commentary on Isaiah. He also began a work on Zechariah, but died having written only the introduction and the commentary as far as Zech. 4:6. He did complete a commentary on Revelation, *Anakrisis Apocalypseos Ioannis Apostoli* (1705), in which he combined the recapitulation and millenarian interpretations and used prophecy in polemics against the Roman Catholic Church. This work had a wide influence in making millenarianism (labeled heresy by the Augsburg and Helvetic Confessions) a popular idea among German pietist groups. Vitringa's Latin lectures on the parables of Christ, in which he compared the parabolic characters to historical figures, were published in Dutch under the title *Verkaeringe van de evangelische parabolen* (1715).

Next to the commentary on Isaiah, Vitringa's chief work was *De synagoga vetere libri tres* (1696), published in English as *The Synagogue and the Church.* This work was a thorough volume covering the deficiencies of an earlier controversial work, *Archisynagogus observationibus novis illustratus* (1685), which sought to trace the functions of early church officers to the Jewish synagogue.

Two of Vitringa's sons also authored theological works. Horatius, who died at the age of nineteen, wrote *Animadversiones ad Johnannem Vorstium de Hebraismis Novi Testamenti.* Campegiusfils, who in 1715 became professor of theology at Franeker, wrote *Epitome theologiae naturalis* and *Dissertationes sacrae.*

B. L. SHELLEY

Vocation. Derived from the Latin *voco,* "I call," the word is used to describe God's calling to his people both individually and corporately.

In the OT God is seen as calling individuals to special tasks of obedience and leadership; Abraham, Moses, Samuel, David, and Jeremiah are differing examples of this activity. He also called Israel as a nation to enter into covenant with him at Sinai, and when in wickedness they turned from his ways he constantly kept calling them to return to him. This was the regular refrain of the message of the prophets.

Jesus called people to follow him as disciples. For some this meant leaving all they had in order to join his band, while others were left to continue witnessing for him in their natural locality (e.g., Luke 8:39; John 9:13ff.; cf. Mark 1:17, 20; 2:14).

The teaching of the NT epistles is consistent in maintaining that the Christian's call to follow Christ has a moral dimension. The Christian is to be like Jesus, to grow into his likeness (I Pet. 1:16; II Cor. 3:18; I John 3:2–3). So Paul stresses that the Christian is called to be a saint (Rom. 1:7; I Cor. 1:2) and also partakes of a holy calling (II Tim. 1:9). Much of the epistles is taken up with the ethical implications and outworkings of this demand. Because the Christian is seen to be on a pilgrimage to heaven, the NT writers also refer to it as a "high" (Gk. lit. "upward"; Phil. 3:14) calling and a "heavenly" calling (Heb. 3:1; it is unclear whether this adjective refers to the calling as having heaven as its source or destination; the original could be deliberately ambiguous).

Christians are also encouraged to see their daily occupations, however menial, as God's vocation for them in this world. Thus one's career should always be a matter for prayerful consideration of "where does God want *me* to be, and what does he want *me* to do?" An ancient prayer of the Western church prays for "all your faithful people; that each in his vocation and ministry may serve you in holiness and truth to the glory of your Name."

Finally, in the most restricted and technical sense, the word has been used to refer to God's call to the work of Christian ministry in its various aspects, including the "religious" life of the monk or nun. All these usages challenge every Christian to a constant review of his life in the light of God's Word and under the promptings of his Spirit to ensure that he or she is in the place and doing the work of God's choosing.

D. H. WHEATON

See also CALL, CALLING.

Voluntarism. Stemming from the Latin word *voluntas,* meaning will, voluntarism is a general name for a variety of philoscphical positions united in their emphasis on will. In contrast to the dominant rationalistic, intellectualist stream of Western thought reaching back to Plato and beyond, voluntarism boldly asserts the superiority or importance of the exercise of will to the deliberations of reason. Voluntarism is expressed in the work of David Hume, who argued that the conflict traditional since Plato between reason and will was strictly impossible; reason is capable of selecting only means toward ends, not the ends themselves. Will alone by affirming them can choose ends, and reason is to be the "slave" of the will in helping to achieve those willed ends. Nietzsche and Schopenhauer placed will at the center of their philosophies. For Nietzsche, human reality is a scene of conflicting forces, of the will-to-power of each individual as the sole driving force which leads each of us to assert ourselves over others, either overtly or subtly. Schopenhauer saw will as a blind force permeating all living things, impelling them to struggle to survive and reproduce. The extent to which he emphasized will is evidenced by the title of his major work, *The World as Will and Idea.*

In theology and religious philosophy voluntarism is significant in several contexts. Some have claimed that logic and the laws of reason hold only because God wills them so; God could assert his will and change them were he so to choose. This position, held by the medieval Peter Damien and others, was discussed by Descartes, and has been soundly opposed by contemporary evangelical Gordon Clark in his *Reason, Religion, and Revelation.* Other voluntarists hold that we need not have rational grounds for religious belief, but may justifiably assert our wills to make a religious commitment, a view titled fideism. Such a doctrine in various forms has a long history in Christian thought, and finds expression in Pascal, Kierkegaard, William James, and many contemporary evangelicals of a pietistic leaning.

Theological voluntarism with respect to ethics is generally called the "divine will" or "divine command" theory. This view is held by William of Ockham, Carl F. H. Henry, Emil Brunner, and many others, and was criticized as early as Plato's *Euthyphro.* Theological voluntarists argue that God's mere assertion of a command to do or refrain from doing an action or type of action renders these either right or wrong. Theological voluntarists in ethics explicitly deny that God commands actions because they are good, believing that this would compromise God's sovereignty by binding him to an independent moral standard. Critics of this view within and without the Christian community argue that it makes ethics arbitrary. They suggest that if it were true, then God could by his mere act of willing render an evil action good or obligatory. Most Christian ethicists have been ill at ease with ethical voluntarism and have sought rational grounds for ethics. D. B. Fletcher

Bibliography. V. J. Bourke, *Will in Western Thought;* É. Gilson, *Reason and Religion in the Middle Ages;* D. Hume, *Treatise on Human Nature;* C. F. H. Henry, *Christian Personal Ethics;* W. James, *The Will to Believe;* S. Kierkegaard, *Purity of Heart;* G. R. Lewis, *Testing Christianity's Truth Claims;* A. Schopenhauer, *The Will to Live;* R. Taylor, "Voluntarism," *Encyclopedia of Philosophy;* P. Helm, ed., *Divine Commands and Morality.*

Von Hügel, Friedrich (1852–1925). Roman Catholic philosopher and writer. The child of an Austrian-Scottish marriage, he lived in England from 1867 and inherited the title of Baron of the Holy Roman Empire. Multilinguist and biblical and patristics scholar, he lamented his church's modern retreat from intellectual culture and rich mental training and its reluctance to wrestle with contemporary problems (a view shared by his friend George Tyrrell, and later by Teilhard de Chardin). He greatly admired Augustine, wrote a definitive study of Catherine of Genoa (1908), and often referred to the saintliness of the Middle Ages. He followed Aquinas in seeking to interpret traditional faith according to "what appears the best and the most abiding elements in the philosophy and the scholarship and science of the later and latest times," a policy developed in his *Essays and Addresses* (1921) and *The Reality of God* (1931).

This gifted layman was a leader of the modernist movement within his church, and to it gave generously of his money, learning, and advice. Ecclesiastical authorities who disliked his tendencies recognized that his preoccupation with contemporary science and philosophy deepened his devotional life. He ministered through correspondence with the highly placed, as his *Selected Letters* (1928) shows, and he is chiefly remembered as a wise counselor of souls. The man for whom God was both "other" and near acknowledged his childlike dependence by words inscribed on his tombstone: "Whom have I in heaven but Thee?" J. D. Douglas

See also Catholicism, Liberal; Tyrrell, George.

Bibliography. L. V. Lester-Garland, *The Religious Philosophy of Baron F. von Hügel;* B. Holland, ed., *Selected Letters of B. von Hügel, 1896–1924;* L. F. Barmann, ed., *The Letters of Baron F. von Hügel and N. K. Smith;* M. D. Petre, *Von Hugel and Tyrrell;* M. de la Bedoyère, *The Life of Baron von Hügel.*

Vow. By a vow is meant a voluntary obligation or promise made to God. It is generally taken on condition of receiving special favors from God. Often during sickness or other kinds of affliction the vow is made to God. It is then to be carried out when the calamity is over or the desire is granted (Gen. 28:20–22; Num. 21:2; I Sam. 1:11; II Sam. 15:8). The conditions of the vow are the following: (1) a consciousness of entire dependence upon the will of God and of obligation of gratitude; (2) that it is something which in itself is lawful; (3) that it is something which is acceptable to God; (4) that it is something which tends to the spiritual edification of the one who makes the vow.

Who may take such a vow? (1) The person assuming the vow must be competent, that is, having sufficient intelligence. A child or a person with an unbalanced mind may not take it. (2) The vow may be assumed only after due deliberation. Being an act of worship, it may not be taken rashly. (3) It must be voluntary and be taken cheerfully.

Is the vow lawful? On this subject there is little or no diversity of opinion. That the vow is lawful appears from the following considerations. First, from the nature of a vow, being a promise made to God. It may be an expression of gratitude for some favor already granted or a pledge to manifest gratitude for some blessings desired, should God see fit to grant them. Jacob vowed that if God would bring him back to his father's house, he would consecrate one tenth of all he possessed to Jehovah. Various parts of the Bible, the Psalms especially, abound with such vows to God (Ps. 65:1; 76:11). These are expressions of thanks to God. Second, the vow is lawful because the Bible contains many examples and many injunctions to their faithful observance. This is sufficient proof that on proper occasions vows are acceptable in the sight of God (Deut. 12:6; Eccl. 5:4; Gen. 28:20). Third, the lawfulness of the vow is also evident from the fact that the baptismal covenant is in the nature of a vow. An element of vow is also clearly implied in the celebration of the Lord's Supper. In both sacraments there is a consecration to Christ and a vow to be faithful to him. The same is true of the marriage covenant, because the promises therein made are not merely promises made between two parties, but an oath and a vow taken before God.

Vows may never be taken rashly. This principle was enforced by the example of Jephthah and clearly stated in Prov. 20:25. W. Masselink

Bibliography. C. Hodge, *Systematic Theology,* III (on the Third Commandment); R. de Vaux, *Ancient Israel;* J. Pederson, *Israel: Its Life and Culture,* IV, 265ff., 324ff.

Ww

Waldenses. A movement that began in the city of Lyons in the decade 1170–80. During these years a wealthy merchant of the city, Peter Waldo, underwent a deeply felt personal religious experience. Following this, he gave away his property and adopted a life of strict gospel simplicity and poverty. Touched by his example, many men and women became his followers. Thus, the most perfect example of reformist dissent in the twelfth century was composed of simple lay people, many of whom were illiterate.

These "Poor Men of Lyons" did not intend to challenge the authority of the church, but the hostility of first the local clergy and finally the papacy drove them into opposition. Their condemnation by the Archbishop of Lyons in 1181 was formalized in 1184 when Pope Lucius III declared the movement heretical and called for its destruction. Thereafter, although they were subject to periodic persecutions of great violence, the Waldenses developed quickly in Languedoc and the Piedmont. From here they spread throughout central and eastern Europe.

In common with most popular religious movements of the period the Waldensian ethic was personal and anticlerical. In search of an authentic gospel ethic, they had the NT, the prophets, and selections from the fathers translated into the vernacular. They believed that the Bible should be the supreme authority in their lives, and insofar as the established clergy did not conform to the teachings of the Gospels, it was condemned. Ultimately the Waldenses declared themselves a counterchurch, the "true church," in opposition to the Roman Church, whose clergy and sacraments were renounced as invalid.

Waldensian thought changed and altered throughout the Middle Ages. In 1207 a significant number of the membership were brought back into the Roman Church following a debate with Catholic clergy. Those who returned were given special dispensations to practice their rigorous life style as the "Catholic poor." In addition, there were disagreements within the brotherhood over articles of faith. However, the general requirements of Waldensian belief emerge clearly from the source materials of the period.

Waldo believed that he and his followers must abandon all other activities in order to spend their time as evangelists in the apostolic mold. Therefore, he required the leaders of the movement, the "perfect," to give up traditional jobs and to live by begging. Waldo also recommended celibacy, following, he believed, the injunctions of Paul, but also because he believed it would facilitate the evangelistic endeavor.

The Waldenses believed in the divinity of Jesus Christ and salvation by Christ. They accepted, at least in theory, that all true believers were entitled to preach, evangelize, and give the sacraments. They celebrated the Eucharist, though at one point it was reduced to an annual (Holy Thursday) occasion. An initiation ceremony or baptism, which seems to have resembled the Cathar sacrament, was also common. Their reading of the NT convinced the Waldenses that purgatory was a myth. From this they concluded that prayers for the dead and indulgences were worthless. They banned the taking of oaths, despised lies, and condemned the death penalty.

In many areas the Waldenses resembled the Cathari. Both dissenting groups rejected the Roman Church, believed in evangelism and poverty, and abstained from killing and oaths. However, the Waldenses were not dualists; they did not reject creation and engaged in many debates with the Cathari concerning this issue. Still the two groups were often confused. The division of Waldensian society into the "perfect" and the "believers," in the Cathar tradition, may reflect this.

In spite of persecution by the revived and militant medieval papacy, whose incarnation was Innocent III (1198–1216), Waldensianism survived to stimulate and challenge the atmosphere in which the Protestant Reformation began. Many of its beliefs entered the mainstream of the Protestant tradition. C. T. MARSHALL

See also CATHARI.

Bibliography. Bernard of Gui, *Manuel de l'Inquisiteur;* E. Comba, *History of the Waldenses of Italy,* 2 vols.; E. Montet, *Histoire littéraire des Vaudois du Piémont;* W. L. Wakefield, *Heresy, Crusade and Inquisition in Southern France;* G. Tourn, *The Waldensians.*

Waldenstrom, Peter Paul (1838–1917). Swedish theologian, preacher, and writer who was a key leader in the organization of the pietist revivals into the permanent Swedish Mission Covenant. He was also a major figure in the establishment and early life of two American denominations with Swedish roots—the Evangelical Covenant Church and the Evangelical Free Church. The Covenant has retained significant continuity with Waldenstrom's pietism and modified Lutheranism.

Born in Lulea, Waldenstrom studied theology and classical languages at Uppsala University. His ordination as a priest in the Lutheran state church took place in 1863. Later he resigned his clerical standing as theological and practical differences with the Lutheran hierarchy increased.

From the beginning Waldenstrom opposed the liturgism of the state church, which too often replaced rather than enhanced a genuine, personal faith in Jesus Christ. In the pietist tradition of Spener, Francke, Zinzendorf, and Wesley, he approved the gathering of devout Christians and serious seekers into small conventicles for mutual prayer, Bible study, and conversation. From this starting point Waldenstrom's journey illustrates the worst fears of the orthodox critics of pietism. While retaining a fully Lutheran understanding of the sacraments, he approved—and occasionally presided at—celebrations of the Lord's Supper in these small gatherings of the devout. This meant celebrating the Eucharist outside the regular parish structure of the state church. This in turn led to the demand for a regenerate church in which only believers would be admitted, where one's status as a believer was determined by one's conversion to Jesus Christ and not by the affirmation of a creed or by participation in certain sacraments. In short, the mark of the true church, in Waldenstrom's opinion, was neither a proper creed nor the preaching of a doctrinally correct gospel nor the celebration of the sacraments; rather, living faith was the central mark of the church. Waldenstrom emphasized, in consistency with this position, the primacy of the local congregation, and he rejected the authority of the great Lutheran and ecumenical creeds on which the Swedish state church was based. In place of the creeds he substituted a simple biblicism. The status of any doctrine could be determined, according to him, by asking, "Where in the Bible is it written?" Any form of higher criticism would threaten such a biblicism, and Waldenstrom, even after his study in Germany, rejected it furiously.

While Waldenstrom's theology annoyed the Swedish Lutheran hierarchy, it won approval in other places. In 1889 Yale University—responding apparently to his emphasis on congregational polity—awarded him a doctorate of divinity during the first of his three trips to the United States. True to the pietist impulses in his heritage, Waldenstrom strongly encouraged evangelism and missions and supported various social projects, serving from 1884 to 1905 in the Swedish House of Representatives. In 1913 his own university, Uppsala, bestowed upon him the Jubilee doctorate of philosophy.

Waldenstrom is best remembered for his doctrine of the atonement, which foreshadowed many of the emphases of twentieth century Scandinavian work on this doctrine, especially Gustaf Aulén's *Christus Victor.* The specific form of Waldenstrom's restatement of the atonement, however, illustrates both the strengths and weaknesses of his biblicism. The state church had been teaching that the atonement on the cross, among other effects, reconciled God to man. Waldenstrom at first continued to teach the doctrine of the state church; but when challenged, "Where is it written?" he discovered that it was nowhere stated in Scripture. This caused him to rethink the issue.

The least controversial thesis in Waldenstrom's restatement of the atonement was that the incarnation, the cross, the resurrection, and Christ's atoning work proceeded fundamentally from God's love and not his wrath. Even theologians such as Luther (in most of his emphases) and Calvin (clearly and repeatedly) agreed that the foundation of Christ's atonement is the love of God. But Waldenstrom added the claim that in no sense did the cross reconcile God to man; rather, the atonement only reconciled man to God. This conflicted with the Lutheran confessions; but Waldenstrom rejected them, and he challenged anyone to find a biblical text that asserted that the cross reconciled God to man. (As a part of his argument, he denied that the term "propitiation" is anywhere found in the Greek text in reference to Christ's relation to the Father.) When asked what took place on the cross, Waldenstrom answered that Christ had won the victory over death, evil, and Satan.

Waldenstrom's biblicism, however, prevented him from giving a clear picture of this victory. He was asked where in Scripture it is written that the world is already reconciled to God, and he could not find a text. He could not appeal to the creeds of the church, for he had rejected their authority. And appeals to philosophical, speculative, or conceptual considerations were inconsistent with his biblicism. In the end Waldenstrom concluded that the atonement (and not just the application of the atonement) is a continuing process and that as each person is newly converted, through faith, to Christ, the new convert is reconciled to God. It is quite unclear, however, what sort of victory Christ won on the cross if the atonement is a process which is not completed until the last convert is won for Christ. Throughout his life Waldenstrom wanted to say that Christ did win a decisive and completed victory on the cross; but he was never able to explicate that victory in the sense of showing its integral relation to the ongoing process of the atonement and reconciliation of man to God.

In fact, Waldenstrom was not so isolated from the creeds and the history of theology as his biblicistic methodology might lead one to expect. Apart from the pietist emphases mentioned previously and his restatement of the atonement, he lived quite faithfully within the theological structure of classical Lutheranism. And his memory and contributions have been most cherished by those standing in a basically Lutheran tradition who appreciate his emphasis on renewal and new life within that context.

S. T. Franklin

Bibliography. K. A. Olsson, *By One Spirit.*

Waldo, Peter. *See* Waldenses.

Walloon Confession. *See* Belgic Confession.

Walther, Carl Ferdinand Wilhelm (1811–1887). Lutheran clergyman and theologian. Born at Langenschursdorf in Saxony, where his father served as the local pastor, Walther as a young man decided that he was "born for nothing but music." But his father had other plans for him, and in 1829 he entered the University of Leipzig to study theology. During his student days Walther experienced serious doubts about his salvation and received help from Martin Stephan, the popular though erratic preacher of St. Johannes Church, near Dresden. Following his graduation in 1833 Walther spent four years as a private tutor. In 1837 he was ordained as pastor at Braünsdorf, but he was frustrated by the indifferent and rationalistic atmosphere of the Saxon state church. Consequently, in 1838 he joined a group of approximately seven hundred Lutherans emigrating to the United States under the leadership of Martin Stephan.

Most of this group eventually settled in Perry County, Missouri. Shortly after their arrival Stephan's fanaticism led to his expulsion from the community and Walther succeeded him as their spiritual leader. Under his direction several churches were built, including two at Dresden and Johannesburg, which he served as pastor. With others Walther also founded in December of 1839 a log college which was moved to St. Louis in 1850 and named Concordia Theological Seminary. Before his death Concordia had become the largest Protestant theological seminary in the United States.

In 1841 Walther moved to St. Louis, where he served as pastor of the Trinity congregation and as professor of theology at Concordia Seminary. In connection with the seminary Walther also established the Concordia Publishing House. In 1844 he founded a biweekly publication, *Der Lutheraner,* as the voice of a strict confessional Lutheranism. The publication became the rallying point for Lutherans of similar convictions and soon led to the organization of the German Evangelical Lutheran Synod of Missouri, Ohio, and Other States, familiarly known as the Missouri Synod. Walther served as its president from 1847 to 1850 and from 1864 to 1878. When the Missouri Synod joined with several other midwestern synods in 1872, he became the first president of the expanded Evangelical Lutheran Synodical Conference of North America, the largest body of Lutherans in the United States. As a prolific author, a powerful preacher and debater, and a masterful organizer and leader, Walther emerged as the most influential Lutheran clergyman of the nineteenth century.

R. L. Troutman

See also Lutheran Tradition, The.

Bibliography. A. R. Suelflow, ed., *Selected Writings of C. F. W. Walther,* 6 vols.; L. W. Spitz, *The Life of Dr. C. F. W. Walther;* C. S. Meyer, ed., *Letters of C. F. W. Walther.*

War. A term referring to a struggle between rival groups, carried on by arms, which can be recognized as a legal conflict. According to this definition riots or individual acts of violence are not considered wars, but armed rebellion within particular sovereignties and violent struggles between nations would be included.

Scriptural Background. The OT contains many statements which support armed conflict, including Deut. 7 and 20 and the war narratives of Joshua, Judges, and Samuel. These passages have been cited by some Christians to justify war, but others have cautioned believers that many laws given to ancient Israel are not meant to be applied to later times. In the teaching of Jesus the kingdom is no longer confined to a single state but exists in an international body, the Christian church. The change in the form of God's kingdom means that many passages that applied to Israel cannot be used in the new situation. It is also evident that the OT contains many passages such as Isa. 2:4 that emphasize peace.

The NT has very few specific statements about war, but from its pages one can draw some general statements about armed conflict. In the Sermon on the Mount, Jesus encouraged his followers to live in a nonviolent manner: "But if any one strikes you on the right cheek, turn to him the other also" (Matt. 5:39); "Love your enemies and pray for those who persecute you" (Matt. 5:44). Yet Jesus seemed to accept war as part of the world system (Matt. 24:6), and his followers who were soldiers were not condemned (Acts 10). The first disciples included Zealots, although Jesus tried to channel their energies into nonpolitical tasks. Soldiers were recognized as some of the heroes of the faith (Heb. 11:32), but Jesus clearly explained that the cause of God was not to be advanced through the use of physical force (John 18:36) and he criticized Peter for violently defending him at his arrest (Matt. 26:52–54). The epistles use military terms and metaphors to describe the Christian life, and the believer is called a soldier who must struggle against evil with spiritual weapons that are analogous to those used by the Roman army (II Tim. 2:3; I Pet. 2:11; Eph. 6:10–20). Victory will come for the Christian cause at the return of Christ, when evil will be defeated in a series of battles described in the book of Revelation.

Early Church Pacifism. Because of the difficulty in applying the biblical statements about war the example of the early church has been extremely important in subsequent discussions on the matter among Christians. Those who favor nonresistance find strong support from the fact that there is no evidence of a single Christian soldier in the Roman army from NT times until *ca.* A.D. 170. It would be helpful if statements about war had been preserved from this early period, but because the Romans did not have universal conscription there was no pressure on Christians to serve; thus they did not seem to comment on the subject. The closing years of the second century brought changes in the situation, and there is evidence of Christians in the imperial service despite the protests of church leaders. Many members of the military forces were converted, and others joined the army because they felt that a person should support the empire.

Others opposed the blurring of distinctions between the church and the world. They called attention to the idolatrous oath of allegiance to the emperor, which was required of those who joined the army, and they pointed out the incompatibility between the quality of love taught by Jesus and the need for a soldier to kill the enemy. Yet the Canons of Hippolytus, a guide for church discipline written in the third century, indicate that military life is acceptable if one does not kill. The apparent contradiction between serving as a soldier and not killing is resolved when it is understood that during the *Pax Romana* the army performed services provided by the police and fire departments in modern times. During that era it was possible to be in the Roman legions and never take life. But because most of them refused to serve in the military and the government, Christians were charged with disloyalty. In response to these accusations Origen wrote in *Against Celsus* that believers performed alternative service for the state by improving the moral fiber of society and by praying for the government. Prayer would combat the spiritual forces of evil that were responsible for violence and conflict.

The Just War. Roman society was Christianized during the fourth and fifth centuries through the work begun by the Emperor Constantine. This made the pacifist position difficult to maintain. In earlier times believers had benefited from Rome but had largely ignored imperial claims upon them. As long as the church was a minority in the state, its attitudes could be overlooked; but when believers became more numerous, there was increasing pressure for them to serve in the army. Augustine gave expression to a new attitude toward conflict on the part of Christians by formulating the just war theory. He adapted the rules of warfare developed by classical thinkers such as Plato and Cicero to the Christian position. War, he taught, should be fought to secure justice and to reestablish peace. It must be conducted under the direction of the ruler and be characterized by an attitude of love for the enemy. Promises to the opposition should be honored, noncombatants respected, and there was to be no massacre, looting, and burning. Those engaged in God's service, including monks and priests, were not to take part in warfare. In spite of Augustine's argument for war he continued to be influenced by the nonviolent approach of the early church. There is a mood of gloom and resignation about much of his teaching regarding the state and its coercive powers.

The Crusade and Medieval Christianity. It was not until the eleventh century that the pacifism of the early church died out and the glorification of the fighting man, the knight, took its place. The explanation for this change can be found in the influx of Germanic people with their martial spirit. The clearest example of the outlook which resulted from the fusion of the barbarian religion of war and the Christian belief in peace was the crusade. In 1095 Pope Urban II urged his listeners to undertake a holy war under the auspices of the church to free the Holy Land from pagan control. The appeal succeeded, and the First Crusade was launched. This campaign resulted in the conquest of Jerusalem (1099) and the establishment of European states in the Middle East. There were more crusades to bolster these outposts, but by 1291 the last of them had fallen to the Muslims.

The crusades were the most obvious example of the merger between violence and holiness which took place in the medieval church. The liturgy was expanded to include the blessing of battle standards and weapons. Knights were consecrated in a sacral fashion through ceremonies based on old pagan customs. There were new religious orders such as the Templars founded for the purpose of fighting the enemies of God. Western peoples came to look upon groups that professed another faith as enemies of the kingdom of God who should be destroyed or converted. It was considered wrong to show mercy to these people, and the code of the just war could be suspended when fighting them. A favorite text of the crusaders summed up this attitude: "Cursed is he who keeps back his sword from bloodshed" (Jer. 48:10).

The acceptance of violence by medieval Christians is demonstrated by the theologians of the time, who tended to believe that war was a necessary condition of society. Aside from minor sects there was little consideration of nonresistance. Scholars such as Gratian and Thomas Aquinas expressed the just war teaching in a manner that made it useful for aggressive action. Perhaps their greatest weakness was not what they wrote but what they did not write. They composed reams of material on the doctrine of angels but few lines on the problem of violence. Consequently the discussion of war was left to those who looked on it favorably as an aspect of chivalry. The "heroic" knight of the time became the basis of later glorification of war. Geoffrey Chaucer illustrates this point of view in the *Canterbury Tales,* where the knight is the natural leader of the pilgrims and is endowed with all that is graceful and noble in an individual.

Renaissance and Reformation Developments. The technological and political changes of fifteenth and sixteenth century Europe created the conditions in which many Christians were forced to reconsider their attitudes toward war. The major technological change was the development of cannons. These were able to destroy medieval fortresses and, when adapted for field use, made the knight obsolete. The Middle Ages saw not only new methods of warfare but also the rise of larger dynastic monarchies. The territorial ambition of these states led to large-scale warfare.

Christian humanists such as Thomas More and Erasmus condemned the new violence. They pointed out that Christ did not advance his kingdom by force but through love and kindness. Erasmus reminded his readers that once wars are accepted as just, they tend to become glorious. The humanists accused the church of missing the true meaning of Scripture and instead becoming the obedient servant of ambitious, bloodthirsty princes. The early Protestant Reformers (Luther, Zwingli, and Calvin) did not add their voices to this protest, however. In fact, when religious fanaticism was added to the new munitions, the religious wars that followed the Reformation were some of the most violent in all of European history. Only one group of Reformers, the Anabaptists, practiced nonresistance. They advocated a literal return to the Sermon on the Mount and an imitation of the peacefulness of Christ.

Total War and the Modern World. The Peace of Westphalia (1648) settled the last major European religious war and ushered in a period when dynastic monarchs on the pattern of Louis XIV gained great power. The states led by these kings suppressed local war bands and organized standing armies. These actions threatened the nobles because their traditional position was based upon military service and now they were losing this function. In an effort to preserve their status they became the officers of the new forces and thus became an interest group who encouraged a larger military establishment. The most famous of these nobles were the Junkers in Prussia. Such individuals continued the medieval notions of chivalry, honor, and martial virtues.

During the eighteenth century there was much criticism of war, but with the coming of the French Revolution a new wave of violence swept over Europe. Napoleon diverted the revolution into a campaign to build a vast empire. He formed an alliance between nationalism and democratic idealism. His idea of organizing the entire nation for the purpose of warfare was ominous for later times. Although defeated, he wielded great influence through his example and the humiliation he created among those he defeated. Challenged by the Napoleonic victories, a Prussian military instructor, Karl von Clausewitz, articulated the theory of "total war." He believed that it is necessary to push conflict to its "utmost bounds" in order to win. At the time he expressed these ideas the industrial revolution began increasing the power of armaments so that an enemy could be totally defeated in a manner never before possible.

Christians in the nineteenth century responded to the danger caused by new armaments by encouraging international cooperation and humanitarian endeavors. Despite a strong current of nationalism these attempts led to international gatherings including the Hague Conferences of 1899 and 1907. These meetings produced a series of recommendations protecting the rights of prisoners of war, insisting on care for the sick and wounded, ensuring the rights of neutrals, and attempting in other ways to limit the cruelty of war.

The forces that worked toward harmony and peace failed, however, and with World War I Clausewitz's view moved closer to reality. The two sides used mines, machine guns, poison gas, submarines, and aerial bombardment, thus taking the conflict to land, sea, and air. The churches supported the war. The rhetoric of leaders such as Woodrow Wilson made them feel that they were involved in a crusade to help humankind. But reality came home to these church people when, after the Peace of Versailles which ended the conflict, nothing seemed to go as planned. Totalitarian regimes came to power in many countries, and the Great Depression spread among the liberal democracies of the West. The years between the global conflicts were characterized by a spirit of weariness and pacifism in the United States and western Europe. The League of Nations, organized for the purpose of keeping peace, was unable to prevent another crisis, and the world was plunged into the maelstrom of another war.

The attitude of Christians toward World War II was closer to the just war theory. The struggle differed from the First World War because it was a clash between antagonistic social and political systems. Fascism with its bizarre biological racism led many former Christian pacifists, including Reinhold Niebuhr, to urge believers to participate in the conflict. New technology produced weapons that made war more destructive than ever before. The atomic bomb seemed to represent the ultimate in destructive capability. When the war ended, the rivalry between the United States and the Soviet Union continued to threaten world peace. The United Nations has tried to keep peace, but the arms race has become a fact of life and the production of weapons has been woven into the texture of modern technological society. The situation is made even more difficult because of a decline in Christian influence in a more secular society.

Christian Responses to War. As history demonstrates, it is difficult to formulate the Christian position on war. The early church, certain Christian humanists, and the majority of Anabaptists have taken a nonresistant or pacifist stance. The majority, however, have followed Augustine and claimed that certain wars are just. Denominations including the Church of the Brethren, Quakers, and Mennonites maintain a nonresistant position, but the larger groups such as Lutherans, Presbyterians, Baptists, Roman Catholics, Methodists, and Reformed adhere to the just war interpretation. In certain rare instances Christians have even supported crusades. The medieval popes urged such action against the Turks, and in the twentieth century some fundamentalist Protestants in the United States have supported such an attitude toward the Soviet Union.

One of the more interesting developments in recent times is the effect that the threat of global conflagration is having on Christian attitudes toward war. Leaders in many denominations have come to realize that the use of nuclear bombs makes a mockery of the just war position because they automatically result in the slaughter of noncombatants. In the minds of these "nuclear pacifists" such weapons invalidate war as a rational policy. R. G. Clouse

See also Pacifism.

Bibliography. R. H. Bainton, *Christian Attitudes Toward War and Peace;* L. Boettner, *The Christian Attitude Toward War;* P. Brock, *Pacifism in Europe to 1914, Pacifism in the United States from the Colonial Period to the First World War,* and *Twentieth Century Pacifism;* D. W. Brown, *Brethren and Pacifism;* C. J. Cadoux, *The Early Christian Attitude Toward War;* R. G. Clouse, ed., *War: Four Christian Views;* P. C. Craigie, *The Problem of War in the OT;* G. F. Hershberger, *War, Peace and Nonresistance;* A. F. Holmes, ed., *War and Christian Ethics;* R. Niebuhr, *Christianity and Power Politics* and *Moral Man and Immoral Society;* G. Nuttall, *Christian Pacifism in History;* R. B. Potter, *War and Moral Discourse;* P. Ramsey, *The Just War* and *War and the Christian Conscience;* R. J. Sider and R. K. Taylor, *Nuclear Holocaust and Christian Hope;* M. Walzer, *Just and Unjust Wars;* R. Wells, ed., *The Wars of America: A Christian View;* Q. Wright, *A Study of War;* J. Yoder, *Nevertheless: The Varieties of Religious Pacifism* and *The Original Revolution: Essays on Christian Pacifism;* G. C. Zahn, *An Alternative to War* and *War, Conscience and Dissent.*

Warfield, Benjamin Breckinridge (1851–1921). The last of the great conservative theologians who defended Calvinistic orthodoxy from the chair of theology at Princeton Seminary. After his education at Princeton College and Princeton Seminary, Warfield traveled in Europe and taught NT at Western Seminary in Allegheny, Pennsylvania. He succeeded Archibald Alexander Hodge as professor of didactic and polemic theology at Princeton in 1887. Warfield wrote a vast number of articles, reviews, and monographs for the popular press and learned journals. His scholarship was precise, wide-ranging, and well grounded in scientific literature. He was one of the great academic theologians at the turn of the century, and his work remains alive today among theologically conservative Protestants who share particularly his attitudes toward Scripture.

Like his Princeton predecessors, Archibald Alexander and the Hodges, Warfield was a strict Calvinist. He wrote numerous studies on Calvin, Augustinian theology, and the Westminster Confession, both to illuminate the theological history and to advocate the positions thus illuminated. He set his Calvinism against the tides of liberalism, which he faulted for subverting God's activity in salvation and divine authority in revelation. He was heartened by the spiritual zeal of the fundamentalists, but felt that they were forfeiting rich theological resources by drifting toward anti-intellectualism. He was especially antagonistic toward the defenders of revelational religious experience, whether the rationalistic piety of Albrecht Ritschl and A. C. McGiffert, the perfectionism of the "Higher Life" and Keswick movements, or the insistence on special spiritual gifts in modern Pentecostalism. To him these substituted subjective religiosity for the completeness of Scripture. Warfield found himself increasingly isolated in his later years. He shared with the modernists a commitment to learned theological inquiry but rejected their conclusions. He shared with the fundamentalists a commitment to supernatural faith yet questioned their methods.

Warfield is best known today for his painstakingly careful efforts to defend the inerrancy of the Bible. In 1881 with A. A. Hodge he wrote a famous essay, "Inspiration," which set out a carefully stated reassertion of traditional Protestant belief in the full infallibility and truthfulness of Scripture. In countless essays and reviews thereafter Warfield labored to clarify the Bible's own testimony to its inspiration and to oppose those who detracted from Scripture's infallible authority. This work on the Bible has made Warfield an important guide for conservative evangelicals in the twentieth century, even for those who do not share his Calvinism (he never wavered in rejecting the pretensions of "free will"), his eschatology (he regarded premillennialism and dispensationalism as aberrations), or his views on science (he believed evolution could be reconciled with the inerrancy of early Genesis). M. A. Noll

See also Princeton Theology, Old; Hodge, Archibald Alexander; Hodge, Charles.

Bibliography. *The Works of Benjamin B. Warfield,* 10 vols.; J. E. Meeter, ed., *Selected Shorter Writings of Benjamin B. Warfield,* 2 vols.; J. E. Meeter and R. Nicole, *A Bibliography of Benjamin Breckinridge Warfield 1851–1921;* M. A. Noll, ed., *The Princeton Theology 1812–1921;* J. H. Gerstner, "Warfield's Case for Biblical Inerrancy," in *God's Inerrant Word,* ed. J. W. Montgomery.

Warneck, Gustav Adolf (1834–1910). German Protestant missiologist. Trained at the Francke School and the University of Halle, Warneck entered the pastorate in 1862. As he spent his free time studying missionary theory and practice, he was soon attracted to an administrative post in the Rhenish Missionary Society in Barmen. Health problems necessitated a return to parish work in 1875, and he accepted a charge in the Saxon village of Rothenschirmbach which allowed him to continue his scholarly endeavors. In 1874 he founded the *Allgemeine Missionszeitschrift,* the main missiological journal in Germany, and in 1879 he started sponsoring annual missions conferences that brought pastors and laymen together. In 1885 he helped form the German Protestant Missions Committee to promote cooperation among the various societies and served as its secretary from 1885 to 1901. Upon retiring from the ministry he was given an honorary lectureship in missions at Halle. His major works include *Modern Missions and Culture: Their Mutual Relations* (1879), *Outline of a History of Protestant Missions from the Reformation to the Present Times* (1882), and the untranslated *Evangelical Mission Doctrine* (1892–1903). He made contributions in popularizing missions among church leaders and laity alike and fostering cooperation in overseas efforts.

Theologically Warneck was a conservative and strongly influenced by pietist thought. He saw Christianity as the "life" which penetrates into all the "orders of life." Through the new birth in Christ a principle of life flows into all aspects of human existence. He divided reality into two spheres, the realms of nature and spirit. To the latter belong problems of Christ, salvation, the church, and the kingdom of God; to the former are the questions of nature, history, man, and the world. In nature occurs the organic growth of a people (*Volk*) which has its uniqueness and character. Effective missionary work involves the penetration of a people with the gospel and the establishment of a church that reflects its organic character and development. Forming such *Volkskirchen* (people's churches) should lead to the Christianization of whole nations and the ultimate victory of Christianity over paganism. The church stands on the word of God and must therefore be incorporated into the lives of the peoples if the world is to be won. Unlike Anglo-Saxon missiology, which emphasized individual conversion, Warneck saw church planting as crucial because the object of missions is "all the nations" as nations. They are to be Christianized in their organic structures through a gradual process with the reborn taking the leading role. When self-supporting and self-governing native churches are established, the leaven of Christianity will spread through the nation until all are won to Christ and the second coming takes place. R. V. Pierard

See also Missiology.

Bibliography. H. Kasdorf, "Gustav Warnecks Missiologisches Erbe" (Diss., Fuller Theological Seminary); J. C. Hoekendijk, *Kirche und Volk in der deutschen Missionswissenschaft;* M. Schlunk, "Gustav Warneck," *IRM* 23:395–404; *SHERK,* XII, 273–74; R. V. Pierard, *NIDCC,* 1030.

Washing of Feet. *See* Foot Washing.

Watson, Richard (1781–1833). Early Wesleyan theologian and missions secretary. Born at Barton-upon-Hunter, in Lincolnshire, Watson was converted under the preaching of William Dodwell, and preached his first sermon one day after his fifteenth birthday. His extemporaneous preaching style endeared him to congregations, and in 1796 he became a Methodist traveling preacher. He enjoyed taking the role of devil's advocate in doctrinal matters to sharpen his debater's skills and to deepen his understanding of Wesleyan orthodoxy. However, this action was misunderstood, and Watson was charged with heterodoxy and accused of being an Arian. He resigned as itinerant preacher in spring of 1801 and was admitted into the Methodist New Connexion in 1803. Appointed secretary of the New Connexion conference, he held the position until a chronic respiratory ailment forced his resignation in 1809.

In 1810 he again took appointment and in 1811 became conference secretary. He collaborated with Jabez Bunting to defeat a bill before Parliament that would radically curtail the freedom of ministers except those who were "substantial" (financially and politically). As English Wesleyan missions secretary he gave staunch support to the abolition of slavery.

Watson's theological commitment to Wesleyan orthodoxy and the Arminian position pitted him against a doctrine of predestination and special election: "Our Lord Jesus Christ did so die for all men, as to make salvation attainable by all men." A major argument in his *Theological Institutes* (1823) was that Christ died for all men, that his death was for those who obtain salvation as well as for those who reject Christ by "their own opposing wills" and thereby fail to obtain salvation.

Of such importance was Watson's *Institutes* as the first systematic treatment of the theological motifs of Wesley's thought that it was required as a core text in the Course of Study School in both the Methodist Episcopal Church and the Methodist Episcopal Church, South, from the 1870s until the turn of the century. Watson's theological orthodoxy and social activism stand as a significant influence in British and American Wesleyan thought. P. A. Mickey

See also Wesleyan Tradition, The; Methodism; Arminianism.

Bibliography. Watson, *Anecdotes of the Life of Richard Watson; The Works of the Reverend Richard Watson in Thirteen Volumes; The History of American Methodism,* II.

Watson, Thomas (d. *ca.* 1686). Puritan minister and writer. Educated at Emmanuel College, Cambridge (called by C. H. Spurgeon "the nursing mother of gigantic evangelical divines"), he was known there as a most diligent student. In 1646 he became rector of St. Stephen's, Walbrook, London, where he combined considerable learning with popular preaching. An Anglican bishop who heard him there once asked for a copy of a prayer Watson had offered, and was incredulous when told it was extempore. His incumbency of St. Stephen's came to an end by ejection for nonconformity under the 1662 Act of Uniformity. It was an ironic development, for Watson had continued to be a Royalist under Cromwell and his son, was briefly imprisoned for this, and had been active in supporting the restoration of the monarchy in 1660.

For several years he ministered secretly until

the easing of repressive legislation permitted Nonconformists to conduct public worship in their own meeting places, in one of which Watson was for a time copastor with Stephen Charnock. Details of Watson's life are generally sparse; it seems that he retired to Essex about 1680. A prolific writer, he is remembered chiefly for his *Body of Practical Divinity*, published posthumously in 1692. Comprising 176 sermons, this work was still highly regarded, especially among ordinary people, in the nineteenth century, probably because of its lucid and succinct presentation of material. Spurgeon, though taking issue with Watson on infant baptism, describes his work as "a happy union of sound doctrine, heart-searching experience and practical wisdom."

J. D. Douglas

Watts, Isaac (1674–1748). English hymnwriter. Born in Southampton and educated at the famous Nonconformist academy in Stoke Newington, he ministered in a London church (1699–1712), during which time he wrote *Horae Lyricae* (1706), a book of religious poetry that ensured his inclusion in *Johnson's Lives of the Poets.* His hymns first appeared in *Hymns and Spiritual Songs* (1707) and ran through numerous editions in his lifetime. He was a pioneer in writing for the young. His *Divine Songs Attempted in Easy Language for the Use of Children* (1715) aimed to be "a constant furniture for the minds of children, that ... may sometimes give their thoughts a divine turn, and raise a young meditation."

In *The Psalms of David Imitated in the NT* (1719) he aimed to make David a Christian. This work included "O God, Our Help in Ages Past" (from Ps. 90), still used on great national occasions, and "Jesus Shall Reign" (Ps. 72). Among his other hymns are "When I Survey the Wondrous Cross," called by Matthew Arnold the finest hymn in the English language.

Though Edinburgh University gave him an honorary D.D. (1728), Watts was an uneasy Calvinist, unhappy with the doctrines of total depravity and reprobation. Some saw Arian tendencies in his published works. At a conference in 1719 he voted with the minority who refused to impose acceptance of the doctrine of the Trinity on independent ministers. He did not believe this necessary to salvation. He sought to heal the breach between Arianism and orthodoxy in a number of theological works. In views expounded also by others including Henry More, he argued that the human soul of Christ had been created before the creation of the world and united with the divine principle in the Godhead known as the Sophia or Logos, and that the personality of the Holy Spirit was metaphorical rather than literal.

It was reported that Watts became Unitarian in his last years, but this has never been substantiated. What is certain is that many of his compositions have an austere OT quality, notably in their contemplation of God's glory in nature as well as in his revelation in Christ.

Watts, who broke the stern embargo on the use of hymns in Nonconformist churches, also published works on philosophy, astronomy, and social concerns. His educational handbooks, notably *Catechisms* (1730) and *Scripture History* (1732), were still used long after his death. His *Collected Works* was published in 1810.

J. D. Douglas

Bibliography. A. P. Davis, *Isaac Watts;* S. L. Bishop, *Isaac Watts's Hymns and Spiritual Songs (1707): A Publishing History and a Bibliography.*

Wave Offering. *See* Offerings and Sacrifices in Bible Times.

Way, Follower of the. *See* Christians, Names of.

Way International, The. A cultic organization founded in the mid-1950s by a former Evangelical and Reformed minister, Victor Paul Wierwille. The Way claims it is not a church or a denomination but merely a "biblical research and teaching organization."

Like most cultic groups, The Way's history and theology revolve around its founder and long-time president. A graduate of Princeton Theological Seminary, Wierwille holds a doctorate from a reputed degree mill, Pike's Peak Seminary. He first taught his "Power for Abundant Living" class in 1953 and began to attract attention and followers during the Jesus Movement of the late 1960s and 1970s. The class (PFAL) continues to be the primary means by which potential converts are introduced to the unorthodox teachings of the movement, and has become the cornerstone of The Way's doctrinal position.

In 1958 Wierwille resigned from the ministry, disillusioned with the institutional church, and continued his spiritual search as an ecclesiastical loner. He claims to have had a life-changing experience during which God spoke to him audibly and promised that he would teach Wierwille the Word as it had not been known since the first century.

After this "revelation" encounter with God, Wierwille pursued a career of writing, preaching, and teaching that included the denial of the Trinity, the deity of Jesus Christ, and other major doctrines of orthodox Christianity. He is revered as a prophet by his followers and views himself as an apostle, "one who brings new light to his generation."

Wierwille's theology is a strange admixture of Unitarianism, dispensationalism, Pentecostalism, and Calvinism. While he claims to teach the "rightly divided" Word in a manner that was lost to Christianity until he rediscovered it, Wierwille's preconceived theology is essentially an accumulation of ancient heresies in modern dress combined with some biblical truth. The Way, in reality, is an organization that is built around one man's interpretation of the Bible.

Critics claim that Wierwille misdefines Greek words, employs inferior study tools, promotes false principles of textual criticism, and routinely distorts biblical teaching. A presupposition underlying much of Wierwille's questionable exegesis is the primacy of the Aramaic. Way researchers assert that the NT was originally written in Aramaic, not Greek. They make extensive reference to Syriac versions and to the Peshitta version translated by George Lamsa, an inferior biblical text. Wierwille also manipulates Orientalisms to reinforce his own preferred doctrine.

Members of The Way do not accept the deity of Christ. Wierwille regularly asserts, "Jesus Christ is not God—never was and never will be." The Way teaches that Jesus is the son of God, but he is not God the Son. Consistent with Wierwille's unitarian monotheism is his rejection of the Holy Spirit as the third person of the Godhead. In his view, the Holy Spirit is the Father (God) and just another name for God. When the words "holy spirit" are not capitalized, Wierwille is referring to a spiritual ability of power. Therefore, according to Way theology, the Holy Spirit is not a person but an impersonal power or enablement.

Speaking in tongues is central to The Way's theology. Wierwille teaches that speaking in tongues constitutes the true worship of God and that the practice is a necessary indicator of the new birth. As part of the Power for Abundant Living course Way members are taught how to speak in tongues, following Wierwille's rather mechanical instruction.

Other errant doctrines of The Way include the belief that there is no glory in death and that the dead remain dead until the final resurrection ("soul sleep"); the teaching that water baptism is not for Christians; and the view that faith is a spiritual thing given to man only after Pentecost and therefore it is the faith *of* Jesus Christ that saves, not our faith *in* Jesus.

The Way International has headquarters in New Knoxville, Ohio. Its outreach program includes Word Over the World (WOW) Ambassadors, a leadership training program called The Way Corps, and publication of *The Way Magazine.* The organization espouses a very conservative political ideology and has been accused by some parents of mind manipulation and aggressive recruitment tactics. R. M. Enroth

See also Cults.

Bibliography. R. M. Enroth, *Youth, Brainwashing and the Extremist Cults;* J. MacCollam, "The Way," in *A Guide to Cults and New Religions,* ed. R. M. Enroth; D. V. Morton and J. C. Juedes, *The Integrity and Accuracy of The Way's Word;* J. L. Williams, *Victor Paul Wierwille and The Way International.*

Wealth, Christian View of. The term "wealth" originates in a less commonly recognized form, *weal,* an Anglo-Saxon word now meaning a general state of well-being. For an individual the word "wealth" signifies well-being resulting from outward rather than inward causes such as health or contentment. So a man who has $100 is wealthier than a pauper with only 50 cents, even if the rich man is Dives and the pauper Lazarus. Adam Smith used the word to signify the material well-being produced and consumed in the community. Both uses of the term, whether pertaining to an individual or a community, are concerned with the evaluation of things according to priorities.

The value of an item of wealth is measured by the market price. If there is no market, the value can only be appraised. Because a railway and a share of stock in the same railway are not separate items of wealth, counting paper wealth such as equities and securities together with the underlying physical nonhuman goods involves double counting. When debits and credits for all forms of wealth are summed for a community, paper wealth cancels out and double counting is eliminated.

Individual Wealth. For the Christian, wealth is not an innate evil but an opportunity for godly service. While not the greatest value on earth, wealth can be a good thing. We should not put our trust in it because it can be lost or stolen. Among the many things more important than wealth the Bible mentions the fear of the Lord, wisdom, knowledge, understanding, integrity, a lowly spirit, righteousness, and peace. As in the case of Solomon, if we receive these things, wealth often accompanies them.

Abraham was a very wealthy man who owned gold, silver, and cattle. Lot was also very wealthy. Job was a wealthy man before his ordeal and twice as wealthy afterward because God prospered him with cattle and livestock and blessed the work of his hands. God in no way questioned the legitimacy of their wealth. Although wealth is sometimes associated with violence and oppression, it is sometimes a gift from God representing a blessing on his people. Sometimes wealth can help us when there is trouble, although it cannot shield us from God's judgment. Wealth can tempt us to forget God and prevent us from enjoying things.

God entrusts his wealth to individuals and institutions in order to increase its value. As compassionate stewards of God's property we are fully responsible to him for the proper administration of his wealth. At the same time we are the legitimate owners during the period of our stewardship. Complete economic self-sufficiency for an individual or even a small community is difficult, if not impossible, because of the curse of the ground. This forces us to cooperate with other men of all types to increase our own per capita wealth. This is a way in which our interdependence as human beings is demonstrated. How we manage our cooperation with other people will determine to a large extent the value of our wealth.

Studies for the United States and other countries generally show that a relatively small percentage of the population (1–2 percent) owns a high percentage of wealth (20–70 percent). Although there are many motives for accumulating wealth, most of the population has no significant accumulation. Most people tend to live above or at their income and run down what little liquid wealth they own. They may do this in reaction to those who love money and wealth for its own sake rather than for what it can do or in reaction to examples of the tyrannical use of wealth. Nevertheless, wealth can be enjoyed for the prospect of family continuity it offers, the status it provides, and the opportunity for the exercise of power.

In recent times the importance of providing for one's children as a motive for accumulating wealth has diminished. Public and private security and pension plans; taxes; and geographical, occupational, and marital mobility have all contributed to this general tendency. When a family has managed to maintain a certain position in a community for a long time, however, there may be an element of pleasure in perpetuating the position for another generation. In these cases there may be exceptions to the general tendency of not providing much for one's children, especially if a stock of wealth is necessary to maintain estates and other inherited possessions associated with family continuity.

Some men enjoy the process of accumulating wealth because it demonstrates that they have the ability to grapple with the vicissitudes of life and win. A man who puts together a successful deal may even feel the same kind of inner satisfaction as a poet or a mathematician who has just completed a creative endeavor. For him it is not so much the enjoyment of using wealth that motivates as the fun of accumulating it.

The owner of a successful business may enjoy identifying himself with the success or wealth of his business, especially if it dominates a market. The accumulation of wealth in this case accompanies successful activity and enlarges the individual's influence. Directing great affairs, putting one's ideas into practice, or only doing good for mankind may be important motivating factors which impel a Christian man to devote his energy, capital, and time to subduing the portion of the earth under his sphere of responsibility.

One's world and life view affects one's attitude toward wealth and its accumulation. Aristotle and Thomas Aquinas perpetuated a dualism causing men to think that being spiritual was something distinct from the practical issues of life. Those following them emphasized a difference between wealth and the spiritual world. When the highest purpose of man is seen as the attainment of spiritual union with God, wealth may be regarded with a certain amount of disdain. The accumulation of wealth beyond the minimum to keep an ascetic alive may then harm the individual and subvert his spiritual union with God. Because the desire for wealth and the things wealth allows can defile the spirit, the struggle of life is to mortify any desire for wealth and to escape any attachments to wealth. This antagonism between spirit and wealth is unnecessary, however, and may ultimately be understood as anti-Christian.

For others who accept this same dichotomy, spirit is something obscure and unreal if it exists at all, while the practical issues of business are real. Under this view wealth is seen as real but also dead and inert because it is totally unrelated to the spiritual issues of life. For this reason such people fail to relate to wealth except to use, manipulate, or destroy it. This attitude directed toward the physical world leads to the depletion and destruction of the earth's wealth. Only by having one's mind renewed can we come to a true and joyous repentance of our anti-Christian attitude toward wealth, our rape of the environment, and our disdain of God's creation.

Still others believe we are caught up in an inevitable process of evolutionary advancement to which all means of wealth should be directed. Only the best in civilization as confirmed by repeated human judgments should be encouraged. Some holding this view, however, suspect that a greater flow of wealth retards human creation, knowledge, and experience and causes decay in civilization. For the evolutionists this is evidenced by a coarsening of cultural tastes, an atrophy of conscience, and a frenzied search for sensual pleasures which satisfy only for a moment. For the Christian these phenomena, while real, are the results of turning from God rather than the accumulation of wealth.

When the Christian begins with God creating the heavens and the earth and pronouncing it good, all the earth is full of the beauty, goodness, and love of a holy God. The Christian sees a world of spirit and wealth flowing together in oneness without antagonism. Through Jesus Christ all wealth is clean, and both spirit and wealth are to be respected. The Christian way of unity is for people to be fulfilled and expressed through material wealth in an abundant and prosperous life. In the biblical view the Spirit of God naturally flows through everything the Christian is and does, and the Christian is a blessing purely because he is. The Lord then blesses everything his child touches. Guided with purity, honesty, and integrity, and with the burden of his fellow laborers on his heart, he works as unto the Lord, realizing that nothing is secular.

The view that God is active in wealth and present in the whole of creation removes the sense of guilt associated with the accumulation and use of wealth. For the Christian human passion is not opposite to the life of the spirit but the very medium through which we grow to be fully human. It is in the use of wealth that we learn to choose between the wrong passions of the flesh and the pure passions of the spirit. John Wesley's injunction to Christians was, Make as much as you can; save as much as you can; give as much as you can. The Christian view frees us in our pursuit of wealth and permits us to bring a greater sense of well-being to the hungry as part of the task of bringing the kingdom of God to reality on earth.

The wealthy person derives benefits from his wealth that he divides among different forms in accordance with his priorities. Five different forms in which wealth can be held are (1) money, (2) securities, (3) equities, (4) physical nonhuman goods, and (5) human capital. The primary benefit from holding money is derived from its liquidity, which gives the holder command over goods and services and the power to provide for exigencies. Securities (bonds, notes, and bills) yield a fixed interest and capital gains, or losses if sold before maturity. Investors in equities receive dividends and capital gains. Physical nonhuman goods such as art objects, furniture, vehicles, and property yield benefits in their use, while investment in human wealth through education or health-related services increases the potential income from labor.

Money. Money is a form of wealth which serves as a temporary medium of purchasing power. It is accepted in payment of debts and in exchange for goods and services because people know others will accept it in like circumstances. It thus overcomes the difficulties of barter. Many objects such as cattle, salt, shells, cigarettes, cognac, and even women have been used as money, but precious metals, especially gold, have been the most popular historically. The Bible records the long history of silver and gold as forms of wealth. In *Strong's Concordance* there are three columns of references to silver and three and a half to gold. God calls attention to the gold of Havilah. He expects men to recognize the special nature of this gift, which is almost universally recognized as valuable. Gold was one of the three gifts brought by the magi to honor the child Jesus. Gold is the highest earthly standard by which we can compare God's judgments. Even the New Jerusalem is to be constructed of gold. So from Eden to the New Jerusalem gold is a valuable form of wealth.

Despite its special characteristics among forms of wealth, money is still a marketable good and is not equally useful or valuable in every possible situation. Neither gold nor any other form of wealth has absolute value but is subject to the laws of God. For instance, if faith in market institutions fails, and men give up their hope in their earthly futures, the value of money will be affected. What has formerly been valuable will fall to zero value, demonstrating that there is no ultimate, infallible, all-purpose "store of value" in economics. In a world of uncertainty no single commodity, not even gold, can successfully preserve value under all contingencies. This is what Christ pointed to when he cautioned men to lay up treasure in heaven, since there alone is a man's treasure safe from the flux of human events.

Community Wealth. Economic development began when God drove Adam from the Garden of Eden and said that he would earn his living under conditions of scarcity by the sweat of his brow. Adam and his sons set out to lighten the burden of this curse by using stone, copper, bronze, iron, and steel to make tools to farm, hunt, and build shelters. Progress was slow, but they learned to replace their muscles with natural sources of power and to organize people and processes to increase production. Civilizations rose only to fall by war, catastrophe, plague, or exhaustion of natural resources.

In the fifteenth century the Italians adopted Arabic symbols and double-entry bookkeeping for business records. In the same century the joint stock company, the stock exchange, and deposit-credit banks emerged to separate ownership from control of business. This facilitated transfers of ownership and provided a payments and lending mechanism. These institutions, while facilitating larger economic enterprises, tended to obfuscate most people's understanding of the fundamentals of economic life.

In the 1850s the legal invention of the limited liability corporation expanded the concept of the joint stock company by limiting the investor's risk and liability to the extent of his ownership. Since ownership could be divided into small portions, many people participated. In the 1890s investment banking houses underwrote security issues by guaranteeing to furnish funds at a given time whether or not the securities were sold. They raised capital for financing large-scale enterprises by selling bonds and stocks to many people. These institutions facilitated an unprecedented economic expansion.

Today financiers who trade paper wealth every day live in a world of symbols where a very important factor is the reaction of other financiers. Because of this their actions can lead to more volatility in prices of paper wealth than would take place if only the underlying real wealth were exchanged. This overreaction is also more apparent because there is usually a liquid market for paper wealth where the rights to use, derive income from, or control are evaluated and discounted continuously.

In the last two hundred years men have learned to organize production in factories, to apply steam and water power to production and transportation, and to facilitate development with new financial institutions. But the new element enabling men to use their ingenuity and determination was an unprecedented license for free enterprise. This produced a degree of economic freedom never before attained. From 1775 to 1850 the United States in particular threw off society's long-standing restrictions on individuals and witnessed an unprecedented surge in material wealth. Freedom of choice produced the opportunity and incentive for productive activity and economic development.

Under the free enterprise system the variety of products and services available to the public increases constantly as a result of scientific discovery, experimentation, and risk taking. The possibility of accumulating wealth stimulates individuals to develop new products and more efficient production methods. Everyone has the opportunity and motivation to exploit new ideas, while competition exerts pressure on management to improve productive processes. Workers are free to select their occupations and offer their services to whomever they wish, while businesses are free to choose their products, workers, manufacturing techniques, and locations. Consumers who are free to buy or not determine what will be produced and how much. Businessmen must respond to this competition or fail. While no nation has ever had wholly unrestricted free enterprise, the most rapid economic progress has occurred in those nations which have given it the most latitude.

Why did this freedom appear so fully on the American scene? Francis Schaeffer traces how the biblical teaching in the Reformation not only opened the approach to God through Jesus Christ but brought forth political and economic freedom in society without chaos.

Although many of the U.S. founding fathers were not Christians, they functioned within the Christian consensus. The U.S. Constitution permits the ordinary citizen on the basis of biblical teaching to call the majority wrong. A majority is prevented from becoming a final authority to the extent that biblical teaching is practiced in the community. And yet amid this freedom there was no chaos because the freedom took place within a consensus based upon the Bible.

Unfortunately, the wealth accumulated in England and the United States from the Industrial Revolution under this freedom was not used compassionately. The greater flow of goods was accompanied by the increasing exploitation of women and children, the rise of slums, and a growing inequality of wealth. Our ability to produce enough to meet the basic needs of all did not lead to economic wealth for everyone. It was not that the majority of people were worse off but that the dignity of many suffered. New economic problems such as unemployment and depressions arose. Individual efforts of charity, while frequent, did not suffice. Unfortunately, the churches were silent about the Bible's emphasis on a compassionate use of wealth.

Because of the negative side effects occurring in communities as a result of the lack of compassion accompanying rapid economic development in a free economy, some claimed that we were making no real economic progress and that our present attainments were in jeopardy. Jeremy Bentham's utilitarianism and Thomas Malthus's and David Ricardo's views of the inevitability of poverty stifled the teaching of Christ and the Bible on the compassionate use of accumulated wealth. Around 1850 John Stuart Mill and Karl Marx agreed that there was little hope for improving the welfare of the masses under existing institutions. Mill had no solution, while Marx called for revolution. Around 1870 Henry George attracted attention by claiming that wealth increases poverty. By the 1930s some believed that we were heading for economic depression because our economy was "mature" and the opportunities for invention and production were exhausted.

If the church had been faithful at this time, it might not have lost so many workers and intellectuals. If it had spoken clearly against the uninhibited use of wealth, the "survival of the fittest" concept might not have taken over so fully. Pessimism in the face of abuses real and threatened and mistrust of businessmen have led to the growth of government corporations and regulation. In the past fifty years this government regulation has increased vastly, leading to a whole new set of problems, limiting the precious freedom spawned by the Reformation, and retarding economic growth.

Conclusion. Because God made the world and everything in it, wealth as a part of God's creation is not inherently evil and therefore to be refused. In the Bible it is often depicted as a blessing from God and a sign of his favor. However, because this is a fallen world, wealth also partakes of our fallenness. If it is used to exploit, dominate, or persecute, it becomes a great evil. Covetousness is equivalent to idolatry (Col. 3:5), and the love of money is the root of all evil (I Tim. 6:10). Thus the Bible admonishes us not to become anxious over our possessions, exhausting ourselves to pile up treasures on earth where moth and rust corrupt. Our heavenly Father knows we have needs, and whether we abound or suffer want, we should be content with what his kind hand has provided (Phil. 4:11–13).

D. K. Adie

Bibliography. E. von Böhm-Bawerk, *Capital and Interest,* 3 vols.; C. Carter, *Wealth, an Essay on the Purposes of Economics;* J. B. Clark, *The Philosophy of Wealth;* R. R. Doane, *The Anatomy of American Wealth;* R. T. Ely, *Property and Contracts in their Relations to the Distribution of Wealth;* I. Fisher, *The Nature of Capital and Income;* M. Friedman, *The Optimum Quantity of Money and Other Essays;* R. W. Goldsmith and R. E. Lipsey, *Studies in the National Balance Sheet of the United States,* 2 vols.; R. J. Lampman, *The Share of Top Wealth-Holders in National Wealth 1922–56;* G. North, *The Dominion Covenant: An Economic Commentary of the Bible;* F. A. Schaeffer, *How Should We Then Live?* J. A. Schumpeter, *History of Economic Analysis;* E. L. H. Taylor, *Economics, Money and Banking.*

Wesley, John (1703–1791). The primary figure in the eighteenth century Evangelical Revival and founder of Methodism. Wesley was born in Epworth, England, to Samuel and Susanna Wesley, one of nineteen children. Although both his grandfathers distinguished themselves as Puritan Nonconformists, his parents returned to the Church of England, where his father for most of his ministry held the livings of Epworth (1697–1735) and Wroot (1725–35). Wesley spent his early years under the careful direction of his remarkable mother, who sought to instill in him a sense of vital piety leading to a wholehearted devotion to God.

Life. Wesley was educated at Charterhouse, a school for boys in London, and then Christ Church, Oxford, where he received the B.A. degree in 1724 and the M.A. degree in 1727. Although a serious student in both logic and religion, Wesley was not to experience his "religious" conversion until 1725. He was then confronted with what to do with the rest of his life. He decided (through the influence of his mother, a religious friend, and the reading of Jeremy Taylor and Thomas à Kempis) to make religion the "business of his life." He was ordained deacon (1725), elected to a fellowship at Lincoln College, Oxford (1726), and served as his father's curate at Wroot (1727–29). He then returned to Oxford and became the leader of a small band of students organized earlier by his younger brother, Charles. This band, dubbed the "Holy Club," would later be called "Methodist" for their prescribed method of studying the Bible and for their rigid self-denial which included many works of charity. During this period (1729–35) both John and Charles fell under the influence of the nonjuror and mystic William Law. Although Wesley confessed that he did not at that time understand justification by faith (seeking instead justification by his own works-righteousness), it was during this period that he formulated his views on Christian perfection—the hallmark of Methodism.

In 1735 (Wesley's *Journal* begins at this point and continues until shortly before his death) Wesley went to Georgia as a missionary to the Indians. Although the Indians eluded him, he did serve as priest to the Georgia settlers under General James Oglethorpe. During a storm in crossing Wesley was deeply impressed with a group of Moravians on board ship. Their faith in the face of death (the fear of dying was constantly with Wesley since his youth) predisposed Wesley to the Moravian evangelical faith. After a disastrous experience in Georgia, he returned to England (1738) and met the Moravian Peter Böhler, who exhorted him to trust Christ alone for salvation. What had earlier been merely a religious conversion now became an "evangelical" conversion. At a Moravian band meeting on Aldersgate Street (May 24, 1738), as he listened to a reading from Luther's preface to his commentary on Romans, Wesley felt his "heart strangely warmed." Although scholars disagree as to the exact nature of this experience, nothing in Wesley was left untouched by his newfound faith. After a short journey to Germany to visit the Moravian settlement of Herrnhut, he returned to England and with George Whitefield, a former member of the Holy Club, began preaching salvation by faith. This "new doctrine" was considered redundant by the sacramentalists in the Established Church, who thought people sufficiently saved by virtue of their infant baptism. The established churches soon closed their doors to their preaching. The Methodists (a name which carried over from their Oxford days) began preaching in the open air.

In 1739 Wesley followed Whitefield to Bristol, where a revival broke out among the miners of Kingswood. At that point Wesley's true genius surfaced through his ability to organize new converts into Methodist "societies" and "bands" which sustained both them and the revival. The revival continued under Wesley's direct leadership for over fifty years. He traveled some 250,000 miles throughout England, Scotland, Wales, and Ireland, preaching some 40,000 sermons. His influence also extended to America as he (after considerable reluctance) ordained several of his preachers for the work there, which was officially organized in 1784. Wesley literally established "the world as his parish" in order to spread "scripture holiness throughout the land." He remained fearlessly loyal to the Established Church all his life. Methodism in England did not become a separate denomination until after his death.

Theology. Although Wesley was not a systematic theologian, his theology can be described with reasonable clarity from the study of his published sermons, tracts, treatises, and correspondence. In essence, Wesley's theology, so akin to the Reformation, affirms God's sovereign will to reverse our "sinful, devilish nature," by the work of his Holy Spirit, a process he called *prevenient, justifying,* and *sanctifying* grace (grace being nearly synonymous with the work of the Holy Spirit).

Prevenient or preventing grace for Wesley describes the universal work of the Holy Spirit in the hearts and lives of people between conception and conversion. Original sin, according to Wesley, makes it necessary for the Holy Spirit to initiate the relationship between God and people. Bound by sin and death, people experience the gentle wooing of the Holy Spirit, which prevents them from moving so far from "the way" that when they finally understand the claims of the gospel upon their lives, he guarantees their freedom to say yes. This doctrine constitutes the heart of Wesley's Arminianism.

Justifying grace describes the work of the Holy Spirit at the moment of conversion in the lives of those who say yes to the call of prevenient grace by placing their faith and trust in Jesus Christ. Wesley understood such conversion as two phases of one experience. The first phase—justification—includes the Spirit attributing or imputing to the believer the righteousness of Jesus Christ. The second phase—the new birth—includes the Spirit launching the process of sanctification or imparted righteousness. These two phases identify, in part, the Wesleyan distinctive. Here he combines the "faith alone" so prevalent in the Protestant Reformation (Wesley insisted that he and Calvin were but a hair's breadth apart on justification) with the passion for holiness so prevalent in the Catholic Counter-Reformation.

Sanctifying grace described the work of the Holy Spirit in the lives of believers between conversion and death. Faith in Christ saves us *from* hell and sin *for* heaven and good works. Imputed righteousness, according to Wesley, entitles one to heaven; imparted righteousness qualifies one for heaven. It is here that Wesley goes to great lengths to describe his views on Christian perfection.

The process of sanctification or perfection culminates in an experience of "pure love" as one progresses to the place where love becomes devoid of self-interest. This second work of grace is described as the one purpose of all religion. If one is not perfected in love, one is not "ripe for glory." It is important, however, to note that this perfection was not static but dynamic, always improvable. Neither was it angelic or Adamic. Adam's perfection was objective and absolute, while Wesley's perfection was subjective and relative, involving, for the most part, intention and motive.

Although Wesley talks about an instantaneous experience called "entire sanctification" subsequent to justification, his major emphasis was the continuous process of going on to perfection. Perhaps first learned from the early church fathers like Macarius and Ephraem Syrus, this emphasis upon continuous process was enforced by Wesley to prevent the horrible expectation of backsliding. Wesley soon learned that the only way to keep Methodists alive was to keep them moving. This same concept of continuous process was later polished by the influence of mystics like François Fénelon, whose phrase *moi progressus ad infinitum* (my progress is without end) greatly impressed Wesley and became a major tool for the perpetuation of the Evangelical Revival. The watchword for the revival became: "Go on to perfection: otherwise you cannot keep what you have."

Prevenient grace, therefore, is a process. Justifying grace is instantaneous. Sanctifying grace is both a process and instantaneous. Although

Wesley's theology went through some subtle shifts later in life (for example, he placed more and more emphasis on good works as the inevitable fruit of saving faith), this is fairly representative of Wesley's theology throughout. Generally speaking, Wesley was a practical theologian. In a very practical way his theology was geared primarily to his own needs and to the needs of those given into his care. R. G. TUTTLE, JR.

See also METHODISM; WESLEYAN TRADITION, THE; ARMINIANISM; WHITEFIELD, GEORGE; REVIVALISM.

Bibliography. Wesley, *Journal*, ed. N. Curnock, 8 vols.; *Letters*, ed. J. Telford, 8 vols.; *Standard Sermons*, ed. E. H. Sugden, 2 vols.; *Works*, ed. T. Jackson, 14 vols; W. R. Cannon, *The Theology of John Wesley;* M. L. Edwards, *John Wesley and the Eighteenth Century;* V. H. H. Green, *The Young Mr. Wesley;* H. Lindström, *Wesley and Sanctification;* A. C. Outler, ed., *John Wesley;* M. Piette, *John Wesley in the Evolution of Protestant Discipline;* R. G. Tuttle, *John Wesley, His Life and Theology;* L. Tyerman, *The Life and Times of The Reverend John Wesley*, 3 vols.; C. W. Williams, *John Wesley's Theology Today.*

Wesleyan Tradition, The. In the broad sense of the term, the Wesleyan tradition identifies the theological impetus for those movements and denominations (and their name is Legion) who trace their roots to a theological tradition finding its initial focus in John Wesley. Although its primary legacy remains within the various Methodist denominations (the Wesleyan Methodist, the Free Methodist, the African Methodist Episcopal, the African Methodist Episcopal Zion, the Christian Methodist Episcopal, and the United Methodist), the Wesleyan tradition has been refined and reinterpreted as catalyst for other movements and denominations as well—e.g., Charles Finney and the Holiness movement; Charles Parham and the Pentecostal movement; Phineas Bresee and the Church of the Nazarene.

In the more narrow sense of the term, the Wesleyan tradition has been associated with Arminianism, usually in contrast to Reformed Calvinism. This could be misleading. Historically, Calvinists have feared that Wesleyans have strayed too close to Pelagianism. On the other hand, Wesleyans have feared that Calvinists have strayed too close to antinomianism. In fact, neither is necessarily true. Calvin was no antinomian and neither Arminius nor Wesley a Pelagian. Justification by faith is pivotal for both traditions. Although free will is an issue, in many respects the two traditions are not that far apart. For example, Wesley stated that he and Calvin were but a hair's breadth apart on justification. Sanctification, not free will, draws the clearest line of distinction. Good theology, for Wesley, was balance without compromise. This balance is most evident in Wesley's understanding of faith *and* works, justification *and* sanctification. Those who espouse such a tradition like to think of this as their peculiar genius.

Wesleyan Distinctives. In a phrase, the Wesleyan tradition seeks to establish justification by faith as the gateway to sanctification or "scriptural holiness." Taken separately, justification by faith builds the foundation. Wesley himself in a sermon entitled "Justification by Faith" makes an attempt to define the term accurately. First, he states what justification is not. It is not being made actually just and righteous (that is sanctification). It is not being cleared of the accusations of Satan, nor of the law, nor even of God. We have sinned, so the accusation stands. Justification implies pardon, the forgiveness of sins. God justifies not the godly but the ungodly. They that are righteous need no repentance so they need no forgiveness. This pardon or forgiveness comes by faith. Then Wesley states what faith is and what it is not. It is not that faith of a heathen, nor of a devil, nor even that of the apostles while Christ remained in the flesh. It is "a divine supernatural, *evidence* or *conviction*, 'of things not seen,' not discoverable by our bodily senses." Furthermore, "justifying faith implies a sure trust and confidence that Christ died for *my* sins, that He loved *me* and gave Himself for *me*" (*Works*, V, 60–61). This faith is received by repentance and our willingness to trust Christ as the one able to deliver us from all our sins.

With justification by faith as the foundation the Wesleyan tradition then builds a doctrine of sanctification upon it. The doctrine develops like this. Man and woman were created in the image of God's own eternity. They were upright and perfect. They dwelt in God and God dwelt in them. God required full and perfect obedience, and they were (in their unfallen state) equal to the task. They then disobeyed God. Their righteousness was lost. They were separated from God. We, as their seed, inherited a corruptible and mortal nature. We became dead, dead in spirit, dead in sin, dead to God, so that in our natural state we hastened on to death everlasting. God, however, was not to be undone. While we were yet sinners Christ died for the ungodly. He bore our sins that by his stripes we might be healed. The ungodly, therefore, are justified by faith in the full, perfect, and sufficient sacrifice. This is not the end, however. This is only the beginning. Ultimately for the true Wesleyan salvation is completed by our return to original righteousness. This is done by the work of the Holy Spirit. Although we are justified by faith alone, we are sanctified by the Holy Spirit—the Spirit that makes us holy.

The Wesleyan tradition insists that grace is not contrasted with law but with the works of the law. Wesleyans remind us that Jesus came to fulfill, not destroy, the law. God made us in his perfect image, and he wants that image restored. He wants to return us to a full and perfect obedience through the process of sanctification. As we continually yield to the Spirit's impulse, he roots out those things that would separate us from God, from ourselves, and from those around us. Although we are not justified *by* good works, we are justified *for* good works. To be sure, no good works precede justification, as they do not spring from faith in Christ. Good works follow after justification as its inevitable fruit. Wesley insisted that Methodists who did not fulfill all righteousness deserved the hottest place in the lake of fire. Fulfilling "all righteousness" or being restored to our original righteousness became the hallmark of the Wesleyan tradition.

To fulfill all righteousness describes the process of sanctification. Wesley insisted that imputed righteousness must become imparted righteousness. God grants his Spirit to those who repent and believe that through faith they might overcome sin. Wesleyans want deliverance from sin, not just from hell. Wesley speaks clearly of a process that culminates in a second definite work of grace identified as entire sanctification. Entire sanctification is defined in terms of "pure or disinterested love." Wesley believed that one could progress in love until love became devoid of self-interest at the moment of entire sanctification. Thus, the principles of scriptural holiness or sanctification are as follows: sanctification is received by faith as a work of the Holy Spirit. It begins at the moment of new birth. It progresses gradually until the instant of entire sanctification. Its characteristics are to love God and one's neighbor as oneself; to be meek and lowly in heart, having the mind which was in Christ Jesus; to abstain from all appearance of evil, walking in all the commandments of God; to be content in every state, doing all to the glory of God.

Wesleyanism. The Wesleyan tradition's defense has normally exercised four basic proofs: Scripture, reason, tradition, and experience. Although these "proofs" represent only a construct of Wesley's theology, the principles can be clearly identified.

Scripture. Wesley insisted that Scripture is the first authority and contains the only measure whereby all other truth is tested. It was delivered by men divinely inspired. It is a rule sufficient of itself. It neither needs, nor is capable of, any further addition. The Scripture references to justification by faith as the gateway to scriptural holiness are well known to true Wesleyans: Deut. 30:6; Ps. 130:8; Ezek. 36:25, 29; Matt. 5:48; 22:37; Luke 1:69; John 17:20–23; Rom. 8:3–4; II Cor. 7:1; Eph. 3:14; 5:25–27; I Thess. 5:23; Titus 2:11–14; I John 3:8; 4:17.

Reason. Although Scripture is sufficient unto itself and is the foundation of true religion, Wesley writes: "Now, of what excellent use is reason, if we would either understand ourselves, or explain to others, those living oracles" (*Works,* VI, 354). He states quite clearly that without reason we cannot understand the essential truths of Scripture. Reason, however, is not a mere human invention. It must be assisted by the Holy Spirit if we are to understand the mysteries of God. With regard to justification by faith and sanctification Wesley said that although reason cannot produce faith, when impartial reason speaks we can understand the new birth, inward holiness, and outward holiness. Although reason cannot produce faith, it shortens the leap.

Tradition. Wesley writes that it is generally supposed that traditional evidence is weakened by length of time, as it must necessarily pass through so many hands in a continued succession of ages. Although other evidence is perhaps stronger, he insists: "Do not undervalue traditional evidence. Let it have its place and its due honour. It is highly serviceable in its kind, and in its degree" (*Works,* X, 75). Wesley states that men of strong and clear understanding should be aware of its full force. For him it supplies a link through 1,700 years of history with Jesus and the apostles. The witness to justification and sanctification is an unbroken chain drawing us into fellowship with those who have finished the race, fought the fight, and who now reign with God in his glory and might.

Experience. Apart from Scripture, experience is the strongest proof of Christianity. "What the Scriptures promise, I enjoy" (*Works,* X, 79). Again, Wesley insists that we cannot have reasonable assurance of something unless we have experienced it personally. John Wesley was assured of both justification and sanctification because he had experienced them in his own life. What Christianity promised (considered as a doctrine) was accomplished in his soul. Furthermore, Christianity (considered as an inward principle) is the completion of all those promises. Although traditional proof is complex, experience is simple: "One thing I know; I was blind, but now I see." Although tradition establishes the evidence a long way off, experience makes it present to all persons. As for the proof of justification and sanctification Wesley states that Christianity is an experience of holiness and happiness, the image of God impressed on a created spirit, a fountain of peace and love springing up into everlasting life.

Development of Wesleyan Thought. The emphasis on justification by faith as the foundation and sanctification as the building upon it kept the people called Methodist moving perpetually toward God. Even entire sanctification as an instantaneous experience was never cause to sleep. Not to improve it was to lose it. One was to grow in love. Perfect love continually plumbed some new depth of the human experience. These distinctives of the Wesleyan tradition were powerful tools for the perpetuation of the Evangelical Revival. Unfortunately, many of these doctrines have been either lost or misdirected. Many within the Wesleyan tradition have slipped into legalism, for example. Their understanding of sanctification has become too closely identified only with the form of godliness. Wesley intended that sanctification should be a disposition of the mind or a condition of the heart from which spring all good works. Wesley would be grieved to see good works become an end in themselves.

Ironically, in spite of an emphasis on "doing," many within the Wesleyan tradition have lost their social vision as well. Originally Wesley championed the fight against injustices like slavery and the lack of prison reform. Many followed in his footsteps. The cry of the early Holiness movement (which carried the banner of the Wesleyan tradition throughout the nineteenth century) was "Repent, believe, and become an abolitionist." Unfortunately, many within the Wesleyan tradition lost their social consciences when the Holiness movement became defensive and ingrown during the late 1800s. When such movements lose their theological head (Finney died in 1875), they tend to become more and more rigid. The social gospel became associated with liberalism, and many within the Wesleyan tradition overreacted. There was also a period of infighting. At the turn of the century the Wesleyan tradition, then deeply embedded within the Holiness movement, splintered. Now the Wesleyan tradition can be traced through many different movements and denominations which still hold, in one form or another, a view to justification by faith as the gateway to sanctification. Admittedly, there might have been some improvements on Wesley's legacy, but much has been lost as well. Wesley's own question—"How to reunite the two so long divided, knowledge and vital piety?"—strikes a relevant chord. The principles of scriptural holiness still have meaning and contain much that is yet precious and important for our contemporary world.

R. G. TUTTLE, JR.

See also WESLEY, JOHN; SANCTIFICATION; METHODISM; HOLINESS MOVEMENT, AMERICAN; ARMINIANISM.

Bibliography. J. Wesley, *Works*, ed. T. Jackson, 14 vols.; H. Lindström, *Wesley and Sanctification;* P. A. Mickey, *Essentials of Wesleyan Theology;* J. B. Behney and P. H. Eller, *The History of the Evangelical United Brethren Church;* F. A. Norwood, *The Story of American Methodism.*

Westcott, Brooke Foss (1825–1901). One of the foremost NT scholars of the nineteenth century. A fellow of Trinity College, Cambridge, for several years as a young man, he spent almost two decades as a master at the famous Harrow School. In 1870, primarily at the instigation of his close and learned friend, the renowned NT scholar J. B. Lightfoot, he was invited to return as Regius Professor of Divinity. Here his greatest NT work was done. With F. J. A. Hort he worked in textual criticism, publishing the Westcott-Hort edition of the Greek testament, and he produced famous commentaries on the Gospel of John, the Epistles of John, and the Epistle to the Hebrews. His work reflects the best of the English exegetical tradition which he and his colleagues did so much to develop. Based on massive historical and theological learning, the approach was conservative and spiritual, as expressed in the introduction to the Epistles of John: "the sense of rest and confidence which grows firmer with increasing knowledge."

He was also deeply involved in social issues, and was the first president of the Christian Social Union. Abhorring the raw brutalities of unfettered capitalism, he found his answer in an organic view of society based on an incarnational model similar to that of F. D. Maurice. Since Jesus Christ in his incarnation assumed humanity and then glorified it in his resurrection, so all humanity is already bound together in Jesus Christ. The need is for this corporate reality to be recognized. The sacraments play an important part in this scheme, for the incarnation of Christ is expressed through the sacraments, which sanctify all of human life in community. Through this emphasis Westcott became one of the progenitors of the famous school of Anglican Christian Socialists, which would include Stewart Headlam, Scott Holland, Charles Gore, and William Temple.

After two decades at Cambridge, Westcott succeeded Lightfoot as Bishop of Durham in 1890. In the industrial northeast of England his social consciousness, as well as his intelligence, scholarship, and spirituality, helped to make him a great bishop.

I. S. RENNIE

See also SOCIALISM, CHRISTIAN.

Bibliography. A. Westcott, *Life and Letters of Brooke Foss Westcott,* 2 vols.; P. d'A. Jones, *The Christian Socialist Revival 1877–1914;* F. Olofsson, *Christus Redemptor et Consummator: A Study in the Theology of B. F. Westcott.*

Westminster Catechisms. After the Westminster Assembly completed its work on the confession, it focused its attention on preparation of a catechism. Its early attempts were frustrated, and a consensus developed that two catechisms would be needed, "one more exact and comprehensive, another more easie and short for new beginners." The Larger was intended for pulpit exposition, while the Shorter was intended for the instruction of children. These were completed, the Shorter in 1647 and the Larger in 1648. Both function as official standards of doctrine in many denominations today within the Reformed tradition. The Larger has, to a considerable extent, fallen into disuse, while the Shorter has been greatly used and loved, though many have found it too difficult to be an effective teaching aid for children.

The theology of the catechisms is the same as that of the confession. The catechisms (especially the Shorter) also share the confession's conciseness, precision, balance, and thoroughness. Neither breathes the warm, personal spirit of the Heidelberg Catechism, but it may be argued that some of the answers are equally memorable and edifying. Both are structured in two parts: (1) what we are to believe concerning God, and (2) what duty God requires of us. The first part recapitulates the basic teaching of the confession on God's nature, his creative and redemptive work. The second part contains (a) exposition of the Decalogue, (b) the doctrine of faith and repentance, and (c) the means of grace (word, sacrament, prayer, concluding with an exposition of the Lord's Prayer).

The Larger is sometimes thought to be overdetailed, even legalistic, in its exposition of the law. One emerges with an enormous list of duties that are difficult to relate to the simple commands of the Decalogue. There is truth in such criticisms, but those who urge them often fail to realize the importance of applying scriptural principles authoritatively to current ethical questions. Whatever we may think of their conclusions, the Westminster divines provide us with a good example of zealousness at that task.

J. M. Frame

See also Westminster Confession of Faith; Catechisms.

Bibliography. G. I. Williamson, *The Shorter Catechism.*

Westminster Confession of Faith (1647). The Westminster Assembly (so called because of its meeting place) was summoned by the English Parliament in 1643. Its mission was to advise Parliament in restructuring the Church of England along Puritan lines. To the assembly were invited 121 ministers (the "divines"), 10 members of the House of Lords, 20 of the Commons, plus 8 nonvoting (but influential) representatives of Scotland, which was allied to the English Parliament by a treaty, the "Solemn League and Covenant." Different views of church government were represented, presbyterianism being the dominant position. On theological matters, however, there was virtual unanimity in favor of a strong Calvinistic position, unequivocally rejecting what the assembly saw as the errors of Arminianism, Roman Catholicism, and sectarianism.

The assembly's Confession of Faith, completed in December, 1646, is the last of the classic Reformed confessions and by far the most influential in the English-speaking world. Though it governed the Church of England only briefly, it has been widely adopted (sometimes with amendments) by British and American Presbyterian bodies as well as by many Congregational and Baptist churches. It is well known for its thoroughness, precision, conciseness, and balance. Notable elements are: (1) The opening chapter on Scripture, called by Warfield the best single chapter in any Protestant confession. (2) The mature formulation of the Reformed doctrine of predestination (chs. III, V, IX, XVII). It is noncommittal on the debate between supra- and infralapsarianism, but teaches clearly that God's will is the ultimate cause of all things, including human salvation. It teaches the doctrine of reprobation in very guarded terms (III. vii. viii.). It is careful to balance this teaching with a chapter on human freedom (IX). (3) The emphasis on covenants as the way in which God relates to his people through history (VII, esp.). (4) Its doctrine of redemption structured according to God's acts (X–XIII) and human response (XIV–XVII), thus underscoring its "covenantal" balance between divine sovereignty and human responsibility. (5) Its Puritan doctrine of assurance (XVIII)—a strong affirmation, yet more sensitive than other Reformed confessions to the subjective difficulties believers have in maintaining a conscious assurance. (6) Its strong affirmation of the law of God as perpetually binding the conscience of the believer, even though certain ceremonial and civil statutes are no longer in effect (XIX), balanced by a careful formulation of the nature of Christian liberty of conscience (XX). (7) Its Puritan view of the sabbath, regarding the day as a perpetual obligation, contrary to

Calvin's *Institutes* and other Reformed writings. (8) The first clear confessional distinction between the visible and invisible church (XXV).

J. M. Frame

See also Westminster Catechisms; Confessions of Faith.

Bibliography. D. Laing, ed., *The Letters and Journals of Robert Baillie;* S. W. Carruthers, *The Westminster Confession of Faith;* G. Hendry, *The Westminster Confession for Today;* W. Hetherington, *History of the Westminster Assembly of Divines;* A. Mitchell and J. Struthers, *Minutes of the Sessions of the Westminster Assembly;* J. Murray, "The Theology of the Westminster Confession of Faith," in *Scripture and Confession,* ed. J. Skilton; B. B. Warfield, *The Westminster Assembly and Its Work;* G. I. Williamson, *The Westminster Confession of Faith for Study Classes.*

Whitby, Daniel (1638–1726). Anglican minister and scholar. Born in Northamptonshire and educated at Trinity College, Oxford, Whitby held a series of church appointments leading to the position of rector of St. Edmund's, Salisbury, in 1669. Although he was a popular preacher, his reputation mainly rests upon his voluminous writings—thirty-nine volumes filled with controversial material. At first his work, such as a collection of materials that attacked Roman Catholicism, was quite popular, but when he published a plea for concession to Nonconformists in order to win them to the Church of England (*The Protestant Reconciler,* 1683), this changed. The violent opposition aroused by his suggestion led to the burning of his book at Oxford. Among his other writings were attacks on Calvinism and a defense of Bishop Hoadly in the Bangorian controversy.

Whitby's most notable work was the two-volume *Paraphrase and Commentary on the NT* (1703), which continued to be popular throughout the eighteenth and nineteenth centuries. In the latter part of this commentary he placed an elaborate twenty-six page "hypothesis" on the millennial reign of Christ. According to Whitby, the world would be converted by the gospel, the Jews restored to the Holy Land, and the papacy and the Muslims defeated. This would lead to the thousand-year period of peace, righteousness, and happiness on earth. At the close of the millennium Christ would return and the last judgment be conducted. Whitby's postmillennialism became the leading interpretation for most of eighteenth century English and American commentators.

R. G. Clouse

See also Millennium, Views of the.

Bibliography. *DNB,* LXI, 28–29; A. A. Sykes, *Short Account,* preface to Whitby, *Last Thoughts.*

Whitby, Synod of (664). English church assembly that brought together the Roman and Celtic streams in English Christianity to discuss differences, notably the question of the date of Easter. This matter had become acute since Scottish monks of the Celtic tradition had settled in parts of northern England. King Oswy of Northumbria, who presided at Whitby, adhered to the Celtic practice; his wife, however, had been brought up in Kent and observed the Roman Easter. The Celts claimed their usage was derived from the apostle John and from Columba of Iona. The Romans referred to Rome and Peter, and argued that "a corner of a remote island had no business to stand out against the custom of the rest of the Catholic Church." The prestige of Rome won the day; the king decided that uniformity was crucial and that those who served one God should observe one rule of life. A majority assented. The dissenters withdrew to Scotland. There was, however, no schism. Rome had won a victory over the old Irish Church, but it was well into the Middle Ages before the Celtic Church was completely Latinized.

J. D. Douglas

See also Paschal Controversies.

White, Ellen Gould (1827–1915). Seventh-day Adventist leader. Born Ellen Gould Harmon in Maine and brought up in a Methodist family, she with them was influenced by addresses given in Portland by the Adventist William Miller. In 1843 the family was expelled from Methodist membership for accepting premillennial views. Soon after joining the Adventists Ellen, who had little formal education, claimed to have seen in the first of many "revelations" the triumph and vindication of the Adventists over earthly persecution. Before her death seventy years later she was said to have experienced "two thousand visions and prophetic dreams." Her early followers regarded these visions as partially fulfilling Joel 2:28–32. The Adventist movement suffered a severe setback when two dates in 1844 set by Miller for Christ's return proved to be mistaken.

Ellen became a "sabbathkeeper" in 1846, soon after her marriage to James White. The Seventh-day Adventist Church as an official denomination was established at Battle Creek, Michigan, in 1863, with Ellen as leader and her writings and counsels accepted as the "spirit of prophecy" (Rev. 19:10). This, according to *Fundamental Beliefs of Seventh-day Adventists,* is "one of the identifying marks of the remnant church." Modern Seventh-day Adventism denies that Mrs. White's writings are to be equated with the biblical canon which closed nearly two thousand years ago, though a leading Adventist says that "just as God enlightened Moses . . . he enlightened Ellen G. White."

Mrs. White herself declared that all teaching is to be judged by the Bible and that "the Spirit was not given . . . to supersede the Bible." Acceptance of her writings is not to be made a matter of church discipline, but Adventists hold that in her life and ministry the "gift of prophecy" was restored in these last days of the Christian church. Through more than sixty works (100,000 handwritten pages) Ellen G. White still dominates the movement seventy years after her death, even though the leadership carefully refers to her as "a lesser light to lead men and women to the greater light." Nonetheless, at the denomination's World Congress in Vienna in 1975 her writings were commended as timeless and realistic, for they "lift up Christ and His Word, foster Biblical doctrines and standards, encourage personal piety, devotion and sacrifice, spiritual and physical health, church unity and effectual methods of work, provide a clearer understanding of our times and coming events, and offer needed warnings, admonitions, and reproof."

Among her publications are the nine-volume *Testimonies for the Church* (1855–1909) and *Steps to Christ,* which has sold more than twenty million copies in more than a hundred languages. W. R. Martin, a careful modern researcher, concludes that despite all her misinterpretations and deficiencies, Ellen G. White was "true to the cardinal doctrines of the Christian faith regarding the salvation of the soul and the believer's life in Christ." Not all evangelical scholars accept Martin's assessment.

Having lectured throughout America, Mrs. White took Seventh-day Adventism to Europe (1885–87) and Australia (1891–1900).

J. D. Douglas

See also Adventism.

Bibliography. D. M. Canright, *Life of Mrs. E. G. White;* L. E. Froom, *The Prophetic Faith of Our Fathers;* F. D. Nichol, *Ellen G. White and Her Critics;* W. R. Martin, *The True Story of Seventh-day Adventism* and *The Kingdom of the Cults;* W. T. Rea, *The White Lie;* A. A. Hoekema, *The Four Major Cults.*

Whitefield, George (1714–1770). The best-known evangelist of the eighteenth century and one of the greatest itinerant preachers in the history of Protestantism. Whitefield, an ordained minister of the Church of England, cooperated with John and Charles Wesley in establishing at Oxford during the 1720s the "Holy Club," a group of young men dedicated to seriousness in religion and a methodical approach to Christian duties. Whitefield showed the way to the Wesleys in preaching out of doors and in traveling wherever he could to air the message of salvation. He visited Georgia briefly in 1738 to aid in the founding of an orphanage. When he returned to the colonies in 1739, his reputation as a dramatic preacher went before him. His visit became a sensation, especially when it culminated in a preaching tour of New England during the fall of 1740 when Whitefield addressed crowds of up to eight thousand people nearly every day for over a month. This tour, one of the most remarkable episodes in the whole history of American Christianity, was the key event in New England's Great Awakening. Whitefield returned often to the American colonies, where in 1770 he died as he had wished, in the midst of yet another preaching tour.

Whitefield was a decided, if unscholarly, Calvinist. In his one visit to Northampton, Massachusetts, in 1740 he moved Jonathan Edwards to tears by the emotional and evangelistic power of his Calvinistic message. Whitefield also moved Charles Wesley to tears, but to tears of frustration at a Calvinism that was too harsh for Wesley's more Arminian views. Whitefield and John Wesley broke with each other over Calvinistic-Arminian issues in 1741, but they soon mended their differences enough to establish a peaceful truce, and at a memorial service in England after Whitefield's death, John Wesley praised his colleague as a great man of God. Whitefield was not a skilled theologian. Although he preached on the bound will, the electing power of God, and the definite atonement—all themes of traditional Calvinism—he confessed in a letter to John Wesley early in his career that "I never read anything Calvin wrote; my doctrines I had from Christ and His apostles: I was taught them of God." Whitefield did acknowledge, however, that his views had been shaped by the Reformed theology of the English Puritans.

Whitefield's greatest significance may have resided in his innovative approach to pulpit speech. Unlike the Wesleys, he was not a good organizer, so those quickened through his preaching found their own ways to Anglican or Methodist congregations in England or to Congregational, Presbyterian, and Baptist churches in America. Whitefield did, however, know how to address plain people in plain language. And he did so in a much freer context than was customary. His appeal to the heart and to the emotional nature, though within a Calvinistic framework, and his casual approach to denominational traditions aided the move toward a more democratic and popular style of religion that would shape American Christianity after his death. Whitefield remained in his own estimation only a herald of the gospel. To the work of public preaching he devoted his entire adult life. The fifteen thousand times that he preached in a ministry of thirty-three years remain his most enduring monument. M. A. NOLL

See also AWAKENINGS, THE GREAT; REVIVALISM.

Bibliography. A. Dallimore, *George Whitefield;* S. C. Henry, *George Whitefield: Wayfaring Witness;* E. S. Gaustad, *The Great Awakening in New England;* A. S. Wood, *The Inextinguishable Blaze: Spiritual Renewal and Advance in the Eighteenth Century.*

Whitehead, Alfred North. *See* PROCESS THEOLOGY.

Whitsunday. *See* PENTECOST.

Wicked, Wickedness. Since the first and all-important demand that God makes upon man is perfect obedience to his revealed will (Gen. 2:16–17), it follows that any want of conformity to or transgression of the law of God is sin. In the OT as in the NT a number of different words are used to describe the sinful condition of fallen man. They are rendered by such English words as evil, sin, iniquity, transgression, and wickedness. "Wicked" (wickedness) is the rendering of more than a dozen Hebrew words and of five Greek words. Of the former, it most frequently renders *rāšā'* (252 times). Wicked apparently always involves a moral state, unlike *ra'* (usually rendered by "evil"), which may describe misfortunes and distresses resulting from sin as well as sin itself. Wicked is contrasted with "righteous" (*ṣaddîq*), especially in Proverbs (e.g., 12:5; 13:5; 29:2) and in Ps. 37. Wickedness is an active, destructive principle (Prov. 21:10; 29:16). This active opposition to God and his people causes suffering and distress (Ps. 10). But it is vain; the wicked shall perish in his wickedness (Ps. 9:16). It is the confident prayer and expectation of the righteous that this may be true (Pss. 11; 68:13). The prosperity of the wicked tries and tests the faith of the righteous (Ps. 73). "Wicked" is used less frequently in the NT, where it usually renders the strong word *ponēros* (e.g., Matt. 13:19, 38, 49). But the word "sinner" (*hamartōlos*), which frequently renders *rāšā'* in the LXX, is also frequently used in the NT. O. T. ALLIS

See also SIN; EVIL.

Will. The Scriptures manifest greater interest in the will of God than in the will of man. The latter is not treated in analytic fashion any more than heart or other psychological terms. Yet the material warrants consideration. The notion of inclination is expressed in the OT by *'ābâ,* nearly always in negative form, whereas the other leading words for will, *rāṣôn* and *ḥāpēṣ,* emphasize the element of good pleasure. In the NT the chief verbs are *thelō* and *boulomai,* which mean to wish or to will according to the demands of the context. The noun *thelēma* is used mainly of God. Decision or plan is the force of the rarely used *boulē* (Luke 24:51; Acts 5:38). To will in the sense of coming to a decision is sometimes expressed by *krinō* (I Cor. 5:3). Among the more striking passages in which *thelēma* is used of man are Eph. 2:3, where the word has the force of desire, and II Pet. 1:21, where it denotes an act of the will.

Of supreme import is Luke 22:42, the Gethsemane declaration of Jesus' submission to the will of the Father. Here is the pattern for the capitulation of the will of the believer to God. But this does not mean the adoption of an attitude of passivity such as may be suggested by the motto: "Let go . . . let God." It means rather the determination that the individual shall actively cooperate with the revealed purpose of God for him. The power of the flesh is so great that even in the Christian the will to do the will of God may be largely immobilized (Rom. 7:15ff.). The aid of the Holy Spirit is needed (Rom. 8:4). Continued dependence on the Spirit results in the strengthening of the will so that the meeting of the divine requirement becomes more constant.

The present trend in psychology is away from the notion of will as a faculty and toward the viewpoint that it is an expression of the total self or personality. Normal life includes the capacity for making decisions, and one is responsible for his choices. That choice which makes all others the more meaningful is commitment to Christ.

E. F. HARRISON

See also FREEDOM, FREE WILL, AND DETERMINISM; WILL OF GOD; MAN, DOCTRINE OF.

Bibliography. D. Müller, *NIDNTT,* III, 1015ff.; G. Schrenk, *TDNT,* I, 629ff.; III, 44ff.

William of Ockham (*ca.* 1280–1349). Medieval English theologian. He was born in Ockham, Surrey, sometime between 1280 and 1285. His ambition was to enter the order of Friars Minor, and in 1306 he received lesser orders and began a rigorous course of study at Oxford. Ockham was deeply influenced by John Duns Scotus, also at Oxford, whose ideas were very popular during the early fourteenth century. Scotus's theology centered on the thesis that God is omnipotent and infinite, and therefore cannot be bound by the limitations of human reason, which is finite.

Ockham's first major work was his commentary on the *Sentences* of Peter Abelard. It created a sensation at Oxford. The chancellor of the university, John Lutterell, remanded selections from the commentary to the papacy at Avignon. There Ockham's ideas were censured, and he was summoned to explain his views in person. While at Avignon, he continued to write. Of special importance were his *Summa Logicae* and *De Sacramento Altaris.*

Ockham believed himself to be a devout Christian. However, Pope John XXII found it difficult to accept the wholesale attack on Thomism which Ockhamism represented. Ockham insisted that faith and reason could never be reconciled, that reason could construct universals with regard to nature alone. Nothing about God, faith, or doctrine could be known in this way. Knowledge of God came by way of revelation and intimate personal experience.

Nevertheless, Ockham was relatively secure in spite of argument and censure until he sided with the head of his order against the pope in a debate over apostolic poverty. Michael of Cesena, the head of the Franciscan Order, attempted to return his friars to the ideals of strict poverty advocated by Francis of Assisi. He and his followers, including Ockham, were excommunicated. In 1328 they fled to the protection of the German emperor, Ludwig of Bavaria.

Ultimately it was not Ockham's attack on Thomism and the scholastic intellectual order that forced his separation from the established church. Rather it was his insistence on supporting a life style which he believed to be of true Gospel origin and which stood in harsh contrast to the extravagance and corruption of the late medieval church. Ockham's situation was rendered untenable when John XXII declared belief in apostolic poverty heretical.

Thereafter, Ockham questioned both papal and conciliar authority and seems to have concluded that individual conscience was the final test of faith. His ideas stimulated the growth of mysticism and fed the spiritual environment in which the Reformation occurred. Ockham was reconciled to the Roman Church before his death. C. T. Marshall

See also Nominalism.

Bibliography. Ockham, *Predestination, God's Foreknowledge and Future Contingents,* tr. M. Adams and N. Kretzmann; P. Boehner, *Collected Articles on Ockham;* G. Leff, *William of Ockham: The Metamorphosis of Scholastic Discourse;* D. Webering, *Theory of Demonstration According to William Ockham.*

Will of God. Scripture frequently mentions the "will" of God. Various words are used to set forth that idea. In the OT they are mainly *ḥāpēṣ, rāṣôn,* and *'ābâ;* in the NT *thelō/thelēma, boulomai/boulē,* and *eudokia,* with the meanings to will, desire, favor, enjoy, have pleasure, counsel. Eph. 1:5, 9, 11 is an instance where the three major Greek words are used. In the introduction to his letters Paul often attributes his calling as an apostle to the will of God (I and II Cor. 1:1; Eph. 1:1; Col. 1:1; II Tim. 1:1), and the expression is used in numerous other places to indicate God's will as the final ground of all things. Since Scripture is primarily the history of God's redemptive purpose, most allusions to the divine will refer to that purpose, but there are instances where God's will is seen as the ultimate cause of the entire created world (e.g., Rev. 4:11).

It is necessary to make distinctions within the will of God. Thus God's will may be said to be both necessary and free. It is necessary with respect to himself; it is free over against creation. God's necessary will means that he cannot deny himself but that he must act consistently with his own nature. There are some things which he wills necessarily, some things which he cannot do (II Tim. 2:13; Heb. 6:18; James 1:13; I Sam. 15:29; Num. 23:19). God's will is not arbitrary, as the medieval theologian Duns Scotus said it is. Scotus held that God can save by an act of will alone without satisfaction for sin through atonement. Since the sovereign God has absolute freedom and power, he can do whatsoever he desires. Even the moral order, Duns Scotus said, is based on a decree which could have been altered. This view threatened the biblical picture of God, the foundation of Christian morality, and other doctrine; hence it had to be withstood in the church. Herman Bavinck gives the biblical position: "God's will is identical with his being, his wisdom, his goodness, and with all his attributes. And it is for this reason that man's heart and mind can rest in that will, for it is the will not of blind fate, incalculable fortune, or dark energy of nature, but of an omnipotent God and merciful Father" (*The Doctrine of God,* 235).

God's will is free with respect to creation. He did not have to make the world; to deny this is to slip into pantheism. Creation, preservation, and salvation are free acts of God. It can be said that whereas God had to react against sin—because of his holy nature—he did not have to save. Redemption, which culminated in the coming into the world of Jesus Christ, his suffering, and death, are acts of God which are grounded in free grace.

The will of God is also distinguished as decretive and preceptive, or hidden and revealed. God's decretive, or hidden, will, sometimes called his secret will, is that attribute of God by which he has determined what he will do; it is known to him alone. His preceptive, or revealed, will is that attribute by which he tells us what to do. This latter is revealed in Scripture; thus the law of God is correctly said to be an expression of God's holy will. Deut. 29:29 refers to this distinction within the will of God; Ps. 115:3; Dan. 4:17, 25, 32, 35; Rom. 9:18–19; 11:33–34; Eph. 1:5, 9, 11 refer to his secret will; and Matt. 7:21; 12:50; John 4:34; 7:17; Rom. 12:2; 10:8; Deut. 30:14 refer to his revealed will.

Another more dubious distinction within the one will of God has been called his antecedent and subsequent, or consequent, will. Some, following the same pattern of reasoning, have distinguished between God's intentional, circumstantial, and ultimate will. From Tertullian until today there are those who favor this distinction because they believe that God offers sufficient saving grace to all mankind; then, after the personal decision of the creature, God adjusts his will to that decision and determines that he will save those who believe, condemn those who do not believe, and determine what else he will do under the new circumstances. In the case of misfortune it is reasoned that God's antecedent, or intentional, will did not encompass this, but because of the entrance of sin into the world it is included within his circumstantial will. Because God is God he will reach his final goal; thus his ultimate will, or consequential will, is accomplished.

This distinction has seemed inadequate to many because it compromises the biblical picture of God Almighty in complete control of the world and of mankind as having a will which is only contingently free. While it recognizes the awesome reality of evil as running counter to God's intended purpose and that God permits certain things without desiring them, it fails to see that God's will is more than a mere "willingness" and that its most usual meaning in Scripture is his good pleasure (*eudokia*) which is sovereignly efficacious, immutable, and identical with God's very being.

The above may seem to suggest that God's will is the reason for the fact of sin in the world and that therefore God can be said to be its author, whereas Scripture holds that sin is the very antithesis of his holy nature. In the face of this difficulty some have claimed that God has only foreknowledge of future evil and that in no sense can it be said to be related to his will. Others with such Scripture as Acts 2:23; 4:28 in mind have felt constrained to confess that somehow even wickedness must be comprehended within the permissive will of God. He is the Lord, even of a world in rebellion against him, and he will accomplish his purpose.

> Remember this and consider,
> recall it to mind, you transgressors,
> remember the former things of old;
> For I am God, and there is no other;
> I am God, and there is none like me,
> declaring the end from the beginning
> and from ancient times things not yet done,
> saying, "My counsel shall stand,
> and I will accomplish all my purpose,"
> calling a bird of prey from the east,
> the man of my counsel from a far country.
> I have spoken, and I will bring it to pass;
> I have purposed, and I will do it.
> (Isa. 46:8–11 RSV)

Whereas there is much that is obscure in the subject under consideration, with Scripture affirming that no one can plumb the depths of the counsel of God (Job 9:10; 38; Rom. 11:33), the teaching about the importance of doing God's will and the detailed exposition of his preceptive will are crystal clear. God's children are called to obedience. Faith, by which one is accepted of God (Heb. 11:6; Rom. 3:24–28; Gal. 2:16), means trusting in God's promise of salvation in Christ and obedience; the rule for discipleship is "trust and obey." That which is to be obeyed is the will of God expressed in his law. The law of God is set forth in a variety of forms in Scripture: the Ten Commandments; the Beatitudes and other teachings of Jesus; summaries given by Christ (e.g., Mark 12:30–31), Paul (e.g., Rom. 13:8–10), and John (I John 4:7–21); other hortatory passages (e.g., Rom. 12; James 1:22–2:26; I Pet.); and the new commandment which Jesus gave his disciples before his death (John 15:12, 14).

Although Christian duty is set forth clearly, human ability is impaired by sin so that obedience at best is imperfect and one is cast on the mercy of God. Through the Holy Spirit, however, as believers mature in faith, they have an increasing desire to give obedience and are enabled to make some small beginning in this life. Thus, however feebly, they come to be conformed to the image of Christ, whose delight it was to do the will of his Father.

In the transition from doctrine to Christian living in the Epistle to the Romans, the apostle asks Christians by God's mercy to give themselves as a "living sacrifice, dedicated and fit for his acceptance, the worship offered by mind and heart. Adapt yourselves no longer to the pattern of this present world, but let your minds be remade and your whole nature thus transformed. Then you will be able to discern the will of God, and to know what is good, acceptable, and perfect" (Rom. 12:1–2 NEB).

M. E. Osterhaven

Bibliography. L. Berkhof, *Systematic Theology;* O. Jager, *What Does God Want, Anyway?*

Wisdom. In the OT the English word "wisdom" represents the translation of many Hebrew words, but by far the most common is *hokmâ* (150 times). More than half of these references are found in the so-called Wisdom literature (Job, Proverbs, and Ecclesiastes).

Outside this Wisdom literature the word seldom refers to God or even purely "spiritual" wisdom but to human skills or abilities which may or may not be God-given. Such skills were involved in the tabernacle preparation (Exod. 28:3; 31:3, 6), in warfare (Isa. 10:13), in sailing (Ps. 107:27), and in ruling (Deut. 34:9; Ezek. 28:4; I Kings 2:6; and very frequently with reference to Solomon). Wisdom (skill) may be bad and condemned by God (Ezek. 28:17; Isa. 29:14; Jer. 8:9; II Sam. 20:22; Isa. 47:10).

In the Wisdom literature the word often refers to a mere humanly derived knowledge (Eccles. 1:13; Job 4:21), which brings only grief and frustration (Eccles. 1:12; 2:9–11). In contrast with this human wisdom, however, there is a divine wisdom, given by God, which enables man to lead a good and true and satisfying life. Such divine wisdom keeps the commandments of God (Prov. 4:11), is characterized by prudence (Prov. 8:12), discernment (Prov. 14:8), humility (Prov. 10:8), is based on the fear of the Lord (Job 28:28; Prov. 9:10), and is of inestimable value (Job 28:13ff.). Only God, of course, possesses this wisdom in the absolute sense (Job 12:13). It cannot be derived by human intelligence (Job 28:12; Eccles. 7:23; Job 2:21). The scoffer will never find it (Prov. 14:6); but God, whose attribute it is (I Kings 3:28; Dan. 2:20), freely gives it to those who seek it (Prov. 2:6; Eccles. 2:26).

The controversial passage in Proverbs (8:22–31) has often been interpreted as a proof of the Trinity in the OT. In its context, however, it is better taken as a personification of the divine attribute which God exercised in the creation of all things and which also he wishes to impart to men in order to lead them into a righteous life.

In the OT the concept of divine wisdom must not be abstracted from its practical implications for men. The truly wise man is the good man, and the truly good man is he who at the very beginning wisely chooses to give God his proper place in his life.

In the OT Apocrypha three books, the Wisdom of Solomon, Ecclesiasticus, and Baruch, are also to be included in the Wisdom literature. In postbiblical times the Jews developed this type of literature still further. Its culmination is to be found in the works of the Jewish philosopher Philo (d. A.D. 50).

In the NT the Greek word *sophia* occurs frequently and repeats most of the OT usages supplemented by the relation which Christ bears to the divine wisdom. Wisdom is an attribute of God (Luke 11:49), the revelation of the divine will to man (I Cor. 2:4–7), a religious and spiritual understanding of the will of God on man's part (Matt. 13:54; James 1:5; and often ascribed to Christ in an absolute sense as perfect humanity), and the human intellectual capacity (Matt. 12:42; 11:25). There is also a proud human wisdom which spurns the divine wisdom and which leads only to destruction (I Cor. 1:19–20).

The distinctive element in NT wisdom is its identification of Jesus Christ as the wisdom of God (I Cor. 1:24), who becomes the ultimate source of all the Christian's wisdom (I Cor. 1:30).

K. S. Kantzer

Bibliography. W. R. Harvey-Jellie, *The Wisdom of God and the Word of God;* J. L. Crenshaw, ed., *Studies in Ancient Israelite Wisdom;* H. Conzelmann, *IDB* Supplement; R. L. Wilken, ed., *Aspects of Wisdom in Judaism and Early Christianity;* J. Goetzmann *et al.*, *NIDNTT,* III, 1023ff.; M. Noth and D. W. Thomas, eds., *Wisdom in Israel and in the Ancient Near East.*

Wisdom, Gift of. *See* Spiritual Gifts.

Witness, Witnessing. Properly, a "witness" (*martys*) is "one who testifies" (*martyreō*) by act or word his "testimony" (*martyrion*) to the truth. This act of testifying is called his "testimony" (*martyria*). In ancient days, as at the present, this was a legal term designating the testimony given for or against one on trial before a court of law. In Christian usage the term came to mean the testimony given by Christian witnesses to Christ and his saving power. Because such testimony often means arrest and scourging (cf. Matt. 10:18; Mark 13:9), exile (Rev. 1:9), or death (cf. Acts 22:20; Rev. 2:13; 17:6) the Greek was transliterated to form the English word "martyr," meaning one who suffers or dies rather than give up his faith. However, in the NT suffering was an incidental factor in the word.

A thorough study of witnessing would necessitate a study of the whole Bible. Such words as preaching, teaching, and confessing would have to be included. Greek words (fifteen in number) stemming from "witness" (*martys*) are used over two hundred times in the NT. The most common usage is found in the Johannine writings, in which seventy-six instances are found. Acts has thirty-nine instances and the Pauline writings thirty-five.

Leaving aside those uses of the word that refer to man's witness to men (cf. III John 12), God's witness to men (cf. Acts 13:22), man's witness against men (cf. Matt. 18:16), and miscellaneous uses (cf. John 2:25), we will consider the distinctively Christian use of the words.

First, there are those testimonies which are meant to establish the incarnation and the truth of Christianity. In John's Gospel, where this is primary, we find instances of all the main witnesses. John the Baptist "bears testimony" (*martyreō*) to Jesus as the coming Savior of the world (John 1:7–8, 15, 32, 34; 3:26; 5:32). The works that Jesus did were a testimony that he came from the Father (John 5:36); this explains why John called the miracles "signs" (*sēmeion*). The OT Scriptures are a testimony to Jesus (John 5:39); this thought is behind most of the NT quotations from the OT. After the resurrection the main evidences of the truth of Christianity are the ministry of the Holy Spirit (John 15:26), the witness of the disciples to the resurrection (Acts 1:22), and the signs and wonders by which God attested the ministry of the apostles and the churches (Heb. 2:4).

The pattern of Christian missionary and evangelistic activity is set in the NT. Several principles emerge. (1) Witnessing is the universal obligation of all Christians (Luke 24:48; Acts 1:8). That the act of witnessing was not restricted to the apostles or ministers is shown by those references in Acts which speak of all the disciples giving testimony (cf. Acts 2:4). This is one of the most needed emphases for modern Christianity. (2) The testimony to be given centered in the facts and the meaning of the earthly ministry of Jesus (Acts 10:39–41) and his saving power (Acts 10:43). The primary witnesses were the apostles, who had personal knowledge of this ministry from its beginning (Acts 1:22). This knowledge they delivered to others who gave testimony to it also (Heb. 2:3–4). They, in turn, were to entrust this message to others who would continue to give witness to it (II Tim. 2:2). The primary message was this Christian "tradition" (*paradosis;* I Cor. 15:1–3). (3) Christian witnesses were to be faithful without regard to their personal safety or comfort (Matt. 10:48). (4) Christian testimony was attended by the ministry of the Holy Spirit and the manifestation of God's presence and power (Heb. 2:3–4).

F. L. Fisher

Witness of the Holy Spirit. *See* Internal Testimony of the Holy Spirit.

Wittenberg, Concord of (1536). An agreement on the Lord's Supper between Saxon Lutherans and southern German Protestants. Discussions had been initiated by Martin Bucer in 1529, aimed at establishing a united evangelical position, and as a result he and Luther had been drawing closer together. Briefly, the concord (or articles) declared: (1) That the Eucharist has both an earthly and a heavenly reality; thus Christ's body and blood are "truly and substantially present and presented and received" with the bread and wine. (2) That while no transubstantiation takes place, "by the sacramental union the bread is the body of Christ . . . present and truly presented." (3) The sacrament is "efficacious in the Church" and independent of the worthiness of minister or recipient.

This achieved a substantial measure of agreement; indeed, the only point unsettled was that of ubiquity. It was this which prevented the Swiss Protestants from accepting the concord. While the Zwinglians continued to insist on the symbolic interpretation of the Lord's Supper, they sought to live on cordial terms with their Lutheran brethren.

While Bucer had set himself up as honest broker between Lutherans and Swiss Zwinglians, some suggest that this success was bought at the cost of his integrity, or at least by the exercise of "evasive weakness," as he sought to explain and commend one side's views to the other. The Concord of Wittenberg is perhaps most vulnerable on two fronts: the ambiguity surrounding the word "substantial" and the somewhat disingenuous attempt by Bucer to distinguish between the unworthiness of the godless unbeliever and that of the unspiritual unbeliever.

J. D. Douglas

See also Bucer, Martin.

Woman, Biblical Concept of. The place of women in the family, in society, and in the church has been the object of much attention in the latter part of the twentieth century. It is important to have clear biblical moorings in an area where positions vary to an extreme degree. The Scripture provides a wholesome contrast with the oppressive attitude and practice which prevailed in biblical times in the nations surrounding the Jews and which (alas) often prevail to this day around the world.

The Creation of Woman. In the first chapter of Genesis we have an account of the creation of humanity as the climax of God's creative activity. The supreme dignity of human beings is expressed in the concept that they are created "in the image of God." This is immediately related to both male and female (Gen. 1:27). If anyone were to doubt whether the image of God terminology applies to women (perhaps by some misunderstanding of I Cor. 11:7), it is quite apparent from Gen. 9:6 and James 3:9 that the term applies to females as well as to males, since the sinfulness of murder or of cursing is not different if women are the object than if men are in view.

Gen. 2:4–25 provides fuller detail concerning

the precise order of events and circumstances of the creation of humanity, somewhat as in an automobile map one might have an insert with fuller details concerning the roads in and around the city. Here it is apparent that Adam was created first (cf. I Cor. 11:8; I Tim. 2:13) and received the task of classifying and naming animals. Many of these may have been presented to him in pairs, and Adam's loneliness must have been painfully apparent to him: there was no "helper" suitable for him. It is in response to the yearning that Adam must have felt that God supernaturally created Eve as his counterpart; and when Adam saw her, he was naturally enthralled and saluted the wonderful gift of God with the well-known words: "This is now bone of my bones and flesh of my flesh" (Gen. 2:23). This account, therefore, emphasizes the fundamental unity of male and female. The very nature of Adam from the start called for a counterpart that God graciously provided. While chronologically Eve followed Adam, in the purpose of God there appears to be an equal ultimacy for both sexes.

The creation of Eve is also the origin of the institution of monogamous marriage. The unity between husband and wife into "one flesh" is asserted in Gen. 2:24 and referred to in the NT on several occasions (Matt. 19:5; Mark 10:8; I Cor. 6:16; Eph. 5:31; cf. Luke 16:18). It is this unity which is the fundamental bond at the root of society. Its closeness, perennial character, and importance in humanity can scarcely be exaggerated.

When Adam and Eve fell in disobedience and unbelief (Gen. 3), the first rift appears between them, for in answer to God's questions Adam in a cowardly manner accuses his wife and by implication God himself: "The woman *you* put here with me" (Gen. 3:12). The rift which opened up at the point of the fall has tended to increase in the passing of the years and centuries and has poisoned even the beneficial institution of marriage. In the punishment meted out to Eve is the statement, "Your desire will be for your husband and he will rule over you" (Gen. 3:16). This was a divine description of what would occur, not a mandate which obedient servants of God should attempt to carry out. Subordination is not enjoined here any more than it is mandated that women should suffer a maximum of pain in childbearing, or men a maximum of discomfort and toil in earning their living. God has graciously provided means whereby even the curse of evil may be alleviated, and those who wish to carry out his will can and should as much as possible counteract the painful effects of evil. It is to be noted also that the promise of the redeemer through a descendant of Eve precedes the statement of the curse incurred by women at the fall (Gen. 3:15).

After the narrative of the fall the movement is steadily downward. Gen. 4 records the first instance of polygamy on the part of Lamech, descendant of Cain, and the context shows him to have been otherwise fearfully unprincipled. A consideration of human societies, primitive and civilized, leads us to the painful observation that women have very frequently been abused and oppressed, degraded to playthings, sexual objects, and beasts of burden. Whenever a human being is debased, civilization is damaged.

Human corruption called for the flood, that fearful judgment of God in which humanity was wiped out except for Noah and his immediate family. We note here a reaffirmation of the principles of monogamous marriage in that four men and four women were preserved in the ark by the gracious appointment of God.

The Mosaic Economy and Onward. To understand properly the significance of the provisions of the Mosaic economy it is important to view them in contrast to the surrounding civilizations. When this is done, we note a special concern to recognize the dignity of women, the significance of motherhood, and the importance of appropriate safeguards for the welfare and security of women.

Mothers are frequently recognized along with fathers. This is the case in the fifth commandment (Exod. 20:12) and also at many points in the book of Proverbs (1:8; 6:20; 10:1) and elsewhere. Mothers have a right and an obligation to share in the trial of a rebellious child (Deut. 21:18–19). Frequently daughters are listed with sons both in the narrative and in legal prescriptions (e.g., Exod. 20:10). Merciful laws protect women in slavery (Deut. 21:10–14) and widows (e.g., Exod. 22:22; Deut. 14:29; 24:17, 19; 27:19). Sins against women are very seriously dealt with—notably, the death penalty is imposed on both parties who are found guilty of adultery (Lev. 20:10; Deut. 22:20–24, etc.). The case of David's sin with Bathsheba may also be viewed as an expression of God's sharp condemnation of adultery, this in contrast to nations surrounding Israel. When a male heir was not present in the family, daughters could be counted as heirs (Num. 27:1–11, etc.).

In the OT women could occupy exalted positions such as that of prophetess (Miriam in Exod. 15:20 and Num. 12:2, Deborah in Judg. 4:4, Huldah in II Chr. 34:22); of judge (Deborah shared with Barak in this office, Judg. 4–5); of queen (Athaliah in II Kings 11, Esther).

In spite of these notable advantages in the

OT, there were some circumstances and regulations that seemed to be detrimental to women. In the first place, women did not, as men did, receive in their body the sign of the covenant (circumcision). They were surely encompassed in God's covenant, but their participation in it was not physically signified in the same intensive way. No women were admitted to the priesthood, perhaps because in surrounding nations the presence of priestesses was almost invariably tied up with immorality, but undoubtedly women felt somewhat disenfranchised by this exclusion. Lev. 12 provides regulations for purification after childbirth. Perhaps the suggestion that there is impurity connected with birth may be due to the bleeding during and after the delivery. A period of thirty-three days was assigned in connection with the birth of a boy and sixty-six days in connection with the birth of a girl. This also might appear discriminatory. Unquestionably, the OT society was a patriarchal society, and the word "father" is used in OT Scripture about five times as often as the word "mother." God is also represented as a male. To do otherwise would have undoubtedly severely curtailed the understanding of his majesty, and the licentious developments in religions where female deities are found would manifest the appropriateness of avoiding this representation in OT times.

Jewish Attitude Toward Women. Outside the canon it would appear that frequently the Jewish attitude toward women was severely discriminatory. Quotations are often cited from Jewish writings that manifest a contemptuous attitude. While this may be at times exaggerated, there is nevertheless an attitude which frequently demeans women. For instance, rabbis were encouraged not to teach them and not even to speak to them. This may be epitomized in the passage "From garments cometh a moth and from a woman the iniquities of a man. For better is the iniquity of a man than a woman doing a good turn" (Ecclus. 42:13–14). While there are passages in Ecclesiasticus that are more appreciative of women, this may stand as a sample of the things that were sometimes said among the Jews.

Jesus and Women. The birth and infancy narratives in Matthew and Luke feature a remarkable number of women in addition to Mary, the virgin mother of our Lord. Thus, from the very start the record stresses a place for women that goes well beyond what was ordinary in Jewish life. This is made even more manifest in the three years of the public ministry of our Lord. He was willing to speak to women (as in the conversation with the Samaritan woman in John 4), to teach women (as in the ministry at the home of Martha and Mary in Luke 10:38–42), to admit women as his followers (Luke 8:2–3) in spite of the objections and suspicions that might arise.

In his teaching our Lord featured women in a number of ways. They are the central figures in some parables—e.g., the leaven (Matt. 13:33), the importunate widow (Luke 18:1–5), the ten virgins (Matt. 25:1–13), the lost drachma (Luke 15:8–10). He pointed to the place of women in the descriptions of the times of the end (Matt. 24:19, 41); he observed the significance of the widow's mite (Luke 21:1–4).

Christ manifested a special compassion to women in distress. His ministry of healing extended to females as well as to males. In Luke 13:10–17 he was willing to affront the anger of the Jewish leaders in refusing to wait one more day to heal a woman who had been crippled for eighteen years. He called her a "daughter of Abraham." Similarly, he manifested special graciousness to the woman who touched his garment, risking thereby to make him ceremonially unclean (Matt. 9:20–22). Yet our Lord had words of commendation for her faith. He responded to the plea of a Gentile mother who desperately craved the healing of her daughter (Matt. 15:21–28). He raised the daughter of Jairus (Matt. 9:18–26), and the other two resurrections on record are related to the women who were bereaved: the widow of Nain (Luke 7:11–17) and Martha and Mary (John 11). Jesus furthermore showed compassion to women of dubious reputation whom others would have shunned (Luke 7:36–50, and possibly the incident of the adulterous woman, if indeed John 8:1–11 belongs to the text or at least represents an authentic incident).

Jesus safeguarded the rights of women in a remarkable way in his instructions on marriage and divorce (Matt. 5:27–32; 19:3–9).

After the resurrection our Lord first appeared to women and made them the bearers of the good news even to the apostles (Matt. 28:8–10; cf. John 20:14–16).

It is true that our Lord appointed only males as his apostles, but this does not necessarily represent a discrimination, since the ministry of the apostles needed to be readily received and for that purpose the attitude of some of those to whom it would be addressed needed to be considered. Jesus used extensively the "Father language" in his teaching, but once again this does not imply any contempt for motherhood. In its totality the attitude of our Lord was revolutionary even though the primary point of his ministry does not appear to have been to precipitate a revolution in this area. Women who aspire to a greater fulfillment of their own humanity and those who sympathize with them in this yearning can hardly look for a better ally than Jesus.

Women in the Early Church. The broadening brought about by the attitude of Jesus is reflected at many levels in the early church. Mary the mother of Jesus is listed among those who worshiped in the upper room (Acts 1:14). Baptism—the sign and seal of the covenant of grace—is now administered to women as well as to men (Acts 8:12; 16:15). Women may perform the ministry of prophecy (Acts 2:18; 21:9; I Cor. 11:5). Widows who were often eking out a miserable existence in society are now recognized in the church, almost to the point of having a special office (I Tim. 5:3–16). The apostle Paul was surrounded by women co-workers. In Rom. 16 it would appear that ten of the twenty-nine persons mentioned are women. There is some question whether Junia (16:7) should be rendered Junias. This particular understanding has arisen very late (end of the thirteenth century) and appears a desperate effort to avoid saying that a woman was "among the apostles." Junia was a very common name; Junias does not seem to have any established precedent. The way in which Paul characterizes the women that he lists here is also interesting, for a number of them are presented in the same terms as his male collaborators—Timothy, Apollos, Epaphras, Titus. The verb "work very hard" (16:6, 12) is used of ministerial service. Phoebe is called a deacon and one who presides. Priscilla is associated with her husband, Aquila, here as well as in the book of Acts (Acts 18:18–19, 26). This whole approach is climaxed by Paul's great declaration that "in Christ there is . . . no male or female" (Gal. 3:28). In I Pet. 2, Christians of both sexes are represented as "living stones . . . built into a spiritual house to be a holy priesthood," and in the book of Revelation Christians in general are presented as "a kingdom and priests" (Rev. 1:6; 5:10). Thus with respect to our position in Christ the NT obliterates any distinction of rank between male and female.

Passages Articulating Distinction. In the light of these practices and specific texts certain passages that appear to enjoin some distinctions must be considered.

I Cor. 7. In this passage the apostle deals with the Christian attitude toward marriage, and he seems to refer to this issue as if the decisions were always the prerogative of the males, whether husbands or fathers of the women to be married. This indeed may be in conformity with the prevailing usage of the time, but it does not constitute a mandate. What needs to be carefully observed is the complete mutuality in the marital relationship emphasized here, which is stunning when considered against the Greek background of the Corinthians (I Cor. 7:2–5, 10–11, 15–16).

I Cor. 11:3–16. The necessity of decent attire for women and the importance of retaining a sense of submission related to her position in the home is here emphasized. Again we notice a special emphasis of Paul to balance his statements (11:11–12) lest women's rights might be considered abridged by what he has said. It is also noteworthy that this passage emphasizes that women may pray and prophesy in public (11:5, 13).

I Cor. 14:33–36. This passage has often been construed as forbidding a woman to speak in the public gatherings of the church. This understanding would put the passage in direct contradiction with 11:5, 13. Taken strictly it would also prevent women from sharing in the congregational singing. This makes a different interpretation imperative. One could perceive that what Paul is forbidding is a kind of disruptive babbling and questioning that would interfere with a worshipful attitude in the church. Questions must be asked at home, not during the service. The reason that women rather than men are mentioned here may be due to the fact that in Corinth women were the primary disturbers. Obviously the injunction would apply to males as well as to females if a worshipful atmosphere is to be maintained.

Eph. 5:22–33. This has often been considered to be disparaging to women because submission is enjoined by the apostle upon the wives. However, it is preceded by a commandment for general submission (5:21). That which applies to the wives is only a particular case of the basic principle. The context is the home and carries no implication of roles in society, in the church, or in other relationships that do not affect the home. This is obvious in connection with the other two types of relationships which Paul considers: children and parents, slaves and masters. The submission enjoined at the home level in these relationships manifestly does not bear an implication for church offices or society. It is not a violation of God's order when a son has a higher army rank than his father, or a higher place in a corporation, or a pastoral office in a church in which his parents are members. Similarly, the submission required of wives in Eph. 5 could not be interpreted to include anything that lies outside of the home realm. Within the home when ordinary circumstances prevail God has given to the husbands a special responsibility for leadership. To use a modern phrase, he has put the husband in the driver's seat. This in no wise precludes the exercise of leadership by women in society and in the church.

Meanwhile, by comparing the role and the love of husbands to those of Christ, this passage places a much greater demand upon husbands than upon wives. Specifically, it is not difficult to imagine circumstances where a wife might say, "I have obeyed the injunction of Eph. 5; I have shown submission beyond question." Few if any husbands will be in a position to say, "I have perfectly obeyed this command. I have loved my wife as Christ loved the church." In fact, the very nature of the love of Christ is manifested in that he gave himself (John 15:13; I John 3:16) and took the form of a servant (Phil. 2:7; John 13:1–20). The husband's love is not one which revels in lording it over his wife, but rather one which is prepared to be subservient. This ought to make the duty of submission on the part of wives much easier to bear.

The passage does elevate marriage to unprecedented heights, for it compares the union between husband and wife to the union between Jesus Christ and the church; there is no loftier comparison that could well be presented, since here the purpose and climax of the whole redemptive plan is in view.

I Pet. 3:1–7. This passage is written in very much the same spirit as Eph. 5. It enjoins submission for wives, but it ennobles their function in the home and commends as supreme not physical beauty, which only some may possess, but spiritual beauty that any Christian woman may exhibit by virtue of the work of God's grace in her heart. As men may rejoice in being "sons of Abraham," women may take comfort in calling themselves "daughters of Sarah," and they are described as "heirs . . . of the gracious gift of life."

I Tim. 2:9–15. This is generally recognized as the passage which constitutes the clearest restriction on the activity of women. The context favors an interpretation of the directions given as applying to church life, although the mention of childbearing might also suggest that the reference is to life in the home and in society. Certainly the instructions concerning a woman's attire have a wider relevancy than the church context.

Here the apostle enjoins quietness and full submission and forbids teaching and usurpation of authority. The quietness in view is not spelled out, but a ready explanation of the term may well be silence, as indeed it is translated in the NIV in verse 12.

Some have suggested that the passage was not written by Paul but represents a stiffening that occurred after the death of the apostle (e.g., Swidler). This explanation is unacceptable for those who hold strongly to the canonicity of Timothy together with its assertion of Pauline authorship. Some have been so bold as to say that the author of this passage, whether Paul or any other, was simply wrong at this point (e.g., Jewett); but this is obviously in conflict with the doctrine of the truthfulness and normative character of Scripture. Still others have thought that the passage does not represent a permanent mandate but relates to a cultural situation in Ephesus, tied perhaps to the kind of disorders brought about by some women mentioned in II Tim. 3:6–7 (e.g., Howe). The great difficulty with this position lies in the fact that Paul builds his argument on the order of creation and (as we perceive it) on the order of the fall. It would appear that Paul's reasoning is, generally speaking, as follows: Eve was created second and she fell first; therefore, women are under some restriction. If this is the correct understanding of the passage, the question arises: What is it that Paul (and the Holy Spirit through Paul) forbids?

Perhaps one way to respond to this question may be to recognize at once some areas where the prohibition cannot be lodged: (1) Paul could not forbid mothers to teach their children since this is enjoined in Prov. 1:8; 6:20; 31:26 and implicitly in Deut. 6:7. This would also be in conflict with the commendation given to Lois and Eunice (II Tim. 1:5), who guided Timothy toward the faith. (2) It would appear that Paul does not refer here to the teaching profession *per se,* since probably a majority of all teachers have been women and have often been blessed in this function. In Paul's day quite often teachers were slaves, so the act of teaching did not involve taking undue authority. (3) It is difficult to think that Paul would disallow the religious teaching of women in situations such as the Sunday school. God has been pleased to bless this ministry immensely, which could hardly be the case if he had expressly forbid it. The suggestion that the Sunday school pupils should not be adult males might be given consideration, but it is not clearly borne by the context. (4) A similar remark might be made with respect to the religious teaching done by women in the mission field, for here again the blessing of God has been evident beyond question.

If these considerations are deemed valid, it remains to assess precisely what Paul does forbid, and if no assured results can be reached on that score, it will be important not to curtail the ministry of women which God has clearly blessed on the basis of a passage which we simply do not understand too well. It is certainly unwise to "doubt in the dark what one has seen in the light."

This should be particularly emphasized here because of a number of problems that remain in the interpretation of this pericope. It is not clear, for instance, why only men are enjoined to pray (2:8) when this activity surely should be open to women both at home and in the church (I Cor. 11:5). It is not clear why the fact that Eve was deceived when Adam was not is construed to warrant a restriction on women. The person who sins with eyes open would appear to be even less reliable than one who succumbs to deception. For this reason we may interpret the passage to refer to the order of the fall rather than a special type of failure in the fall, but this is not absolutely evident. Verse 15 furthermore has a strange shift in the number of the verb. The first verb, "she shall be saved," agrees with the previous statement, "the woman . . . was deceived." But afterward a plural verb comes in somewhat unaccountably. Under no condition can we assume that here Paul speaks of salvation by childbearing instead of salvation by faith, but precisely what he has in view may be difficult to ascertain with assurance. Since he deals with the early chapters of Genesis, it appears plausible that his reference to childbearing points to the protevangel and the entrance of our Lord into humanity through a woman, the Virgin Mary. If this be the correct view, Paul would then complete his discussion with a reminder of the dignity of women and their place in the saving economy of grace that would counterbalance a restriction previously imposed.

But what is the restriction? The present writer is unable to make an assertion here. Some inordinate assumption of authority in teaching appears to be in view, but it is not clear under what circumstances this would actually arise. When we read in II Tim. 3:16–17 that all Scripture is God-breathed and is useful for "teaching, rebuking, correcting and training in righteousness," we might have expected that after these descriptions of ministry Paul would use a term for "the man of God" that emphasizes distinctive maleness, but, in fact, the language he uses is that of generic humanity and applies to women as well as to men. One can hardly forget this when attempting to understand the meaning of I Tim. 2:9–15.

Conclusion. In view of all the above it is clear that the Scripture provides for women a place of unusual dignity and significance. It never demeans the activities in which primarily women are engaged, such as functioning as wife, homebuilder, mother, educator of children. To engage in these notable activities according to Scripture is not to choose some second-best option, manifestly inferior to the pursuit of an independent career. In this respect some of the emphases of certain forms of modern feminism are doing a great disservice to a very large number of women by failing to recognize the worth and dignity of their tasks. Meanwhile, there is no scriptural reason to consider women as inferior, as too often has been done in human culture.

Created in the image of God to be man's helpmate, "not made out of his head to rule over him, nor out of his feet to be trampled upon by him, under his arm to be protected and near his heart to be beloved" (Matthew Henry), woman has a glorious place and destiny in God's purpose.

Although encompassed in the ruin of the fall, she is the object of God's compassion and grace. It is through a woman, the Virgin Mary, that the Lord Jesus Christ made his entrance into our race. Women were among the first to respond to his ministry and the first to witness his resurrection. Women, in even greater number than men, have responded to the invitation of the gospel and to the mandate of the Great Commission. In Revelation, the concluding book and climax of Scripture, the church as the body of all God's redeemed people is represented as a woman, the bride of Jesus Christ. R. NICOLE

See also WOMEN, ORDINATION OF; WOMEN IN THE CHURCH; EVE.

Bibliography. S. B. Clark, *Man and Woman in Christ;* E. Elliot, *Let Me Be a Woman;* S. Foh, *Women and the Word of God: A Response to Biblical Feminism;* G. W. Knight, *The NT Teaching on the Role Relationship of Men and Women;* J. B. Hurley, *Man and Woman in Biblical Perspective;* E. Deen, *The Bible's Legacy for Womanhood;* P. Gundry, *Woman, Be Free* and *Heirs Together;* E. M. Howe, *Women and Church Leadership;* P. K. Jewett, *Man as Male and Female;* L. Scanzoni and N. Hardesty, *All We're Meant to Be: A Biblical Approach to Women's Liberation;* L. Swidler, *Biblical Affirmations of Women.*

Women, Ordination of. The ordination of women to Christian ministry has become a topic of great importance in the second half of the twentieth century. The issue is complicated by the fact that biblical guidelines are sparse and ancient traditions have often been molded by fear and prejudice. Ordination itself is a rite by which a community appoints an individual to a leadership role. In the NT period this was often associated with the laying on of hands (Acts 6:6; 13:3), although such an act did not always imply public office (Acts 28:8). In this way the community demonstrated visibly its acceptance of the leader. The act also signified God's gracious bestowal of spiritual power (Acts 8:17; 19:6).

NT Evidence. Leadership structures were not clearly defined in the early church. The NT speaks of bishops, deacons, and elders (I Tim. 3:1–13; 5:17–22). The term "elder" may have been a general term having reference to a bishop or a deacon rather than being an indication of a separate office. Leadership title and function varied from one geographical region to another during the NT period and in the early Christian centuries. There is in the NT no blueprint of leadership that might be considered applicable to all times and places. Each church in every era must structure its own leadership in order to best suit the needs of its members. The NT does, however, provide principles which may be used as guidelines in this endeavor.

Women feature in the NT as leaders of community worship, as specially appointed church officials, and as co-workers with the apostles. In I Cor. 11:2–16 Paul gives careful directives concerning how men and women leading congregational worship were to be dressed. He assumes that women will be leading mixed congregations in prayer and prophecy. Prophecy, as Paul explains here (I Cor. 14:3, 24–25), involves preaching and teaching. Today we associate these functions with those of the ordained minister. Paul refers to Phoebe as a deacon of the church in Cenchrea (Rom. 16:1). Elsewhere the word here translated "deacon" is understood to mean "minister," and in those places it is so translated in the RSV (I Tim. 4:6; Col. 1:7; Eph. 6:21). Probably Phoebe was entrusted with the letter to the church in Rome. The matters which she had in mind as the purpose of her visit merited the cooperation of the whole church. Paul speaks of women as his coworkers (Phil. 4:3), and it is possible that the Junias (or Junia) mentioned in Rom. 16:7 was herself an apostle.

The Problem of Women's Leadership. Why then has the church not affirmed the leadership role of women more consistently through the centuries? The answer to this question lies partly in the complex forces which molded early Christian leadership structures. Christianity was born and spread in a world in which women were sadly oppressed. While it is true that the Christians believed in freedom and equality (Gal. 3:28), sometimes historical circumstances and social pressures hampered the development of these commendable virtues.

One factor which adversely affected the ordination of women was the gradual trend toward regarding the leadership role as a priestly office. The minister who had once been simply "first among equals" now became a person set apart from the congregation. As a priest, his prime duty was to offer the sacrifice of the bread and wine in the Eucharist. In OT times women were not members of the priesthood. Indeed, they were forbidden to enter the inner sanctuary. Thus when church leadership came to be conceived in terms of priesthood, women found themselves once more outsiders as far as sacred office was concerned.

Another factor was the low regard in which sexuality was held in the early centuries. Lax moral standards in the pagan world frequently resulted in unwanted pregnancies, abortions, and the exposing of infants. Lewdness and lust were certainly not commendable virtues as far as the Christians were concerned. In their reaction against all of this, some Christians began to advocate the ascetic life. Rather than affirming sexuality as an enriching part of human experience, early church fathers began to speak of it in derogatory terms. Even sexual expression within marriage was regarded with distaste, and celibacy began to be exalted as a significant Christian virtue. The church has had difficulty overcoming this sadly negative attitude toward sexuality, and in some areas it has persisted up to the present day. As a result, women came to be viewed as objects of temptation. Men who had devoted themselves to a life of "purity" were advised to avoid their company.

The rise of monasticism encouraged this trend. Although it was not originally intended that the monastic communities should be the training schools for priests, it did in fact work out that way. In the Dark Ages, when education was hard to acquire, it was natural that the church should turn to educated monks for leadership. And so there came about a tradition of celibacy for clergy. The principle was not uncontested—indeed some Christian communities were much opposed to this idea—but it won out among large segments of the church, and is still a requirement for Roman Catholic priests today. And so women were removed one stage further away from the priestly office, and the Christian priesthood became an all-male institution. As the centuries passed, church leadership was perpetuated by appointments which came not from the congregations but from the leaders themselves. As these leaders were all men, the result was that women did not even have a voice in the making of these appointments. The all-male priesthood had become self-perpetuating. There was no possibility of challenge from within the organized structure, unless that challenge came from the men themselves.

Conclusion. Old attitudes are hard to efface, even when they are seen to be unhealthy. However, the church of today is boldly reassessing these old traditions and is seeking to come to grips more realistically with the biblical narratives. It is widely recognized that when Paul said, "The women should keep silence in the churches. For they are not permitted to speak. . . . It is shameful for a woman to speak in church" (I Cor. 14:34–35), he could not have been addressing the issue of church leadership. In the same letter he had assumed that women would be speaking openly in mixed church gatherings (I Cor. 11:5). He must therefore have been addressing some local problem involving women who were interrupting congregational worship with distracting questions. The pastoral injunction, "I permit no woman to teach or to have authority over men" (I Tim. 2:12), may have had local or even temporary significance. When weighed against the rest of the NT it is not found to be regular Pauline practice. The church leadership model presented in the NT is that of the leader as a servant. The exercise of authority is not the significant issue. In any case, the NT affirms the equality of men and women and gives ample precedent for placing women in leadership positions. There seems to be no biblical basis for the common church practice of placing both men and women in leadership positions but reserving ordination and pay only for the men. Consequently many Christian denominations are reinstating women in ordained ministries. In these denominations women participate in the same areas of ministry as their male counterparts and they are paid equally.

There are ordained women today in many Protestant denominations, including Assemblies of God, American Baptist Convention, Southern Baptist Convention, Christian Church (Disciples of Christ), the recently merged American Lutheran Church and Lutheran Church in America, United Methodist Church, and Presbyterian Church, USA. The Eastern Orthodox and Roman Catholic churches have entered into serious discussion on these issues. In both groups there are men and women who strongly affirm the leadership roles of women and who would like to see women ordained to ministry in their churches. As yet, however, there is no legislation in these churches to support such action.

E. M. Howe

See also Woman, Biblical Concept of; Women in the Church.

Bibliography. E. M. Howe, *Women and Church Leadership;* P. K. Jewett, *The Ordination of Women;* D. Kuhns, *Women in the Church;* D. Williams, *The Apostle Paul and Women in the Church.*

Women in the Church. ***In the Bible.*** The roots of the church lie in early Israel, where women occupied a high position and had a strong influence both in the home and in the believing community. The leadership of Miriam (Exod. 15:20–21) is viewed as a special gift to Israel (Mic. 6:4). Deborah served as judge, general, and prophetess (Judg. 4–5), while Hulda the prophetess declared an old scroll to be indeed the Word of God and called the nation to a repentance which resulted in a great revival (II Kings 22:8–20; II Chr. 34:14–28). "Wise women" played a considerable role in the moral and political life of Israel (II Sam. 14:1–20; 20:14–22; Prov. 14:1), and female cult officials served in both the tabernacle and the temple (Exod. 38:8; I Chr. 25:5–6; Ezra 2:65; Neh. 7:67, 73; 10:39; Ps. 68:24–25; Luke 2:36–37). Female prophets functioned throughout the history of Israel (Exod. 15:20; Neh. 6:7, 14; Isa. 8:3; Ezek. 13:17–23; Luke 2:36–37), and the courage and fidelity of Esther caused many to convert to the Jewish faith in the postexilic period (Esth. 8:17).

Attitudes toward women, and concomitantly their position, sank in later Judaism as it came into contact with hellenistic misogyny. Although one may point to the heroism of Judith and the highly able leadership of Queen Salome in the intertestamental period, women were frequently denigrated and forbidden the study of Scripture. By contrast, Jesus accepted women as both students and disciples and demonstrated a rare sympathy for their interests and concerns.

The first women in the church were the group of female followers who were attached to Jesus and traveled about with him (Luke 8:1–3; Matt. 27:55–56; Mark 15:40–41). We are not told that they were sent out on separate missions but rather that theirs was a significant ministry in the presence of Jesus. Some of the women are named and appear to form a cohesive and purposeful unit (Luke 8:2; Acts 1:13–14). Luke notes that these women, along with others, followed Jesus to Jerusalem, the cross, and the tomb (23:27, 49, 55–56). After the body was interred, they maintained watch over it and noted the exact location (Matt. 27:59–61; Mark 15:47). On Easter morning the women were instructed by an angel to proclaim the resurrection, a task for which Christ had prepared them (Luke 24:6–8). After the departure of Peter and John, Jesus showed himself first to Mary Magdalene, then to the other women, with the specific direction that they convey the news to the male disciples, especially Peter. Thus women are attested as the primary witnesses of the birth, crucifixion, burial, and resurrection of Jesus Christ. This witness, together with their confession of him as Messiah and Son of God (John 4:27–42; 11:27), is biblical testimony essential to the formulation of the church's basic beliefs.

Women were significantly present in the upper room at the choice of Matthias (Acts 1:13–14). On the day of Pentecost the Holy Spirit fell equally upon men and women (Acts 2:17–18), and women had a pronounced role in the ministry of the early church (Acts 9:36–43; 21:8–9; Rom. 16). Churches are identified as meeting in the homes of women, who apparently gave them leadership (Acts 12:12; 16:40; Rom. 16:3–5; I Cor. 1:11; 16:19; Col. 4:15; II John). Euodia and Syntyche are mentioned as colleagues of the apostle Paul (Phil. 4:2–3), as is Priscilla. She enjoyed an outstanding ministry along with her husband, Aquila, whose name usually stands second (Acts 18:1–4, 18–28; Rom. 16:3–4; I Cor. 16:19; II Tim. 4:19). The early fathers understood Junia (Rom. 16:7) to be a female apostle, although modern translators frequently give the masculine "Junias," a name unattested in the ancient world. There was a strong tradition of Thecla as apostle and associate of Paul, and there is indeed evidence for her life and ministry.

In Church History. Tertullian wrote that there were four orders of female church officers, all of whom were mentioned in the Bible. These appear to be female deacons, virgins, widows, and eldresses. Some of these women were considered clerics, given ecclesial authority, and seated with the other clergy (*Testament of the Lord* I.23). The NT speaks twice of women deacons (Rom. 16:1–2; I Tim. 3:11), and Pliny reports two *ministrae*, or deaconesses, as leaders of a Christian community (*Epistles* 10.96,8). The ordination service of deaconesses is still preserved in the Apostolic Constitutions (VIII.19–20). Women elders are mentioned in I Tim. 5:2 or Titus 2:3, where they must be *hieroprepeis*, "worthy of holy office." The title "eldress" was applied by the early church to those in the order of widows, whose qualifications are given in I Tim. 5:5–10. Early catacomb paintings show women in the authoritative stance of a bishop, conferring blessing on Christians of both sexes. Two frescoes appear to show women serving Communion. Beginning about 350 the following prohibitions were issued against women's activities: Council of Laodicea—serving as priests or presiding over churches, establishing presbyteresses or presidents in the churches, approaching the altar; Fourth Synod of Carthage—teaching men or baptizing; First Council of Orange and the councils of Nimes, Epaons, and Orleans—the ordination of deaconesses. These prohibitions provide indication of the previous existence of such offices for women.

Although deprived of official status, women continued to serve the church in many ways. The responsible behavior of Christian wives and mothers won from the pagan Libanius the exclamation, "What women these Christians have!" Jerome once referred a hermeneutical dispute to the great Bible scholar Marcella; and the Empress Pulcheria, a prime mover in the Council of Chalcedon, was declared by Pope Leo I to be the major defender of orthodoxy against both Nestorianism and Eutychianism. Women exerted tremendous influence in the Reformation, Counter-Reformation, and Great Awakenings. In the American church they were in the forefront of evangelism and of the Sunday school, missionary, Holiness, and Pentecostal movements. The first woman to be ordained by a recognized denomination was Antoinette Brown (1853), a convert of Charles Finney. The ordination of women still remains a controversial issue in evangelical churches.

In Evangelical Thought. Within Protestant evangelicalism there are significantly differing views as to the proper activities, role, and status of women in the church. Perhaps three major stances may be discerned. The first embraces the traditional thinking of the last millennium and a half in assigning women a subordinate status. Proponents argue that the priority of man's creation gives him a superiority over woman (I Cor. 11:8–9; I Tim. 2:13). As she led him into sin, God has ordained that he should rule rather than she (Gen. 3:16; I Tim. 2:14). Because of Eve's misdemeanor the earlier church fathers, most notably Tertullian, had concluded that women were weak, degraded, depraved, and an obstacle to the spiritual development of men. Although considerably modified, the doctrine of woman's inferiority has been eloquently expressed by modern theologians as well. Women are viewed as less capable of good judgment, while decision-making and leadership in ministry become male prerogatives. There is a strong emphasis on the prohibition against women teaching or exercising authority over men (I Tim. 2:11–14), and there is the command for them to be silent in the congregation (I Cor. 14:34–35; I Tim. 2:12).

Some stress the subordination of women as following implicitly from the subordination of Christ to the Father and draw on the headship concepts of I Cor. 11:3–15. Others accord women a full equality of being but an inferiority of status both in the family and in the church. The subjection of wife to husband in Christian marriage (Eph. 5:22; Col. 3:18; I Pet. 3:1) is transposed to general male-female relationships in the church. Women who have no husbands are encouraged to seek out a male figure, such as a father or pastor, who may serve as intermediary in her access to God. Certain evangelicals hold that the submission of wife to husband must extend even to obedience if he commands her to perform a sinful act and that the moral choice and guilt are his rather than hers.

In contradistinction, there has grown up a so-called biblical feminism. Although the roots of this stance are older than the last century, D. L. Moody, A. J. Gordon, C. G. Finney, and J. Blanchard all found the equality of women to be a biblical concept and urged full utilization of women in the church. Phoebe Palmer, an associate evangelist with D. L. Moody and herself credited with the conversion of 25,000 souls, declared the church to be a sort of potter's field in which the talents of women are buried. Although largely ignored, much scholarship was expended and an extensive literature developed. One contemporary group lays great stress on Gen. 1:27; I Cor. 11:11–12; and above all on Gal. 3:28 in its affirmation of women as the equals of men in Jesus Christ. These universal statements, it is maintained, supersede the narrower dictates of Paul, who is sometimes viewed as a victim of rabbinic prejudice and somewhat misguided. The contradictory nature of Paul's statements is explored and a distinction made between those which are universally normative and those which are culturally relative. Just as certain statements regarding slavery are no longer applicable today, so certain statements regarding women better served another age. God is affirmed as no respecter of persons (Acts 10:34) and as having maternal aspects (Ps. 131:2–3; Deut. 32:18; Isa. 42:14; 49:15; 66:9–13; Matt. 23:37). This maternal and feminine image allows women as well as men to serve in the gospel ministry. For some, theological justification for ordination rests upon the leadership roles of women in both the OT and the NT. Egalitarian marriage is set forth as a biblical and humanitarian principle involving mutual submission (Eph. 5:21). Allied in some respects with liberation theology, this group has produced a radically new theology that is highly controversial in the evangelical world.

A more irenic school of thought, seeking to uphold both the authority of Scripture and the equality of women within the church, holds that the "difficult" passages are no less inspired by God than I Cor. 11:11–12 and Gal. 3:28. Adherents demand that texts be studied in their linguistic, religious, historical, social, and geographical setting. The Greek word for "head," for instance, unlike its English and Hebrew counterparts, did not convey the meaning of "chief" or "boss." Thus the concept of "head" in Eph. 5:23 and I Cor. 11:3 must be studied in the light of its accepted Greek meanings as integrating source (Eph. 4:15–16; Col. 2:19), topmost bodily member (Eph. 1:22–23), interdependent with the body (I Cor. 12:21; Eph. 5:23–30), and the part which is usually born first (Col. 1:15–18). Gen. 3:16 is viewed as a divine prediction of sinful dominance (Matt. 20:25–28; Mark 10:42–45; Luke 22:24–27) rather than a divine decree and is countered with Jer. 31:22, 31–34 in the new covenant.

Research into the cult patterns of ancient women has a high priority in an understanding of Paul as missionary to the Gentiles. The ceremonial shouts of women, obligatory in certain pagan practices, contained no meaning but aroused considerable religious awe in the hearers. These sacred cries are attested in Corinth; thus it is understandable that the apostle, in seeking to curtail meaningless noise and confusion during worship (I Cor. 14), would ask women to refrain from such utterances while allowing them to pray and prophesy meaningfully (I Cor. 11:5). The possibility of alternative translations of I Tim. 2:12 is raised, especially since *authentein,* generally rendered "to bear rule," had several more common meanings in the NT era. Proponents suggest that it may be a directive against women involved in false teaching (I Tim. 4:7; 5:15; II Tim. 3:5–7; Rev. 2:20). The entire passage (I Tim. 2:5–15) must be studied in the wider context of the Pastoral Epistles with their concern over heretical opposition to the truth and need for suppression of false teachers (I Tim. 1:3–4; Titus 1:10–11). In particular there is evidence that there may have been a distortion of the Adam and Eve story (I Tim. 1:4; II Tim. 4:4; Titus 1:14; II Cor. 11:2–4, 13–15) similar to Gnostic theologies which portrayed Eve as a celestial power and as the one who brought life and light to Adam through the serpent's gift of knowledge. I Tim. 2:11–15 may then be a refutation of such doctrines rather than a rationale for the restriction of women.

In any event, the proper utilization of the talents of gifted Christian women remains a pressing contemporary issue and one that requires much thought, study, and reflection.

R. C. Kroeger and C. C. Kroeger

See also Woman, Biblical Concept of; Women, Ordination of.

Bibliography. R. H. Bainton, *Women of the Reformation,* 3 vols.; J. and R. Boldrey, *Chauvinist or Feminist? Paul's View of Women;* K. Bushnell, *God's Word to Women;* E. Clark, *Jerome, Chrysostom and Friends;* J. Daniélou, *The Ministry of Women in the Early Church;* J. J. Davis, "Ordination of Women Reconsidered: Discussion of I Tim. 2:8–15," *PC,* Nov.–Dec. 1979; D. W. and L. S. Dayton, "Women as Preachers: Evangelical Precedents," *CT,* May 23, 1975; E. Deen, *Great Women of the Christian Faith;* V. B. Demarest, *Sex and Spirit: God, Woman, and Ministry;* A. J. Gordon,

"The Ministry of Women," *Eter,* July-Aug. 1980; R. Gryson, *The Ministry of Women in the Early Church;* N. A. Hardesty, *Great Women of Faith;* A. R. Hay, *The Woman's Ministry in Church and Home;* G. E. Harkness, *Women in Church and Society: A Historical and Theological Inquiry;* V. Hearn, ed., *Our Struggle to Serve;* R. Hestenes and L. Curley, eds., *Women and the Ministries of Christ;* K. T. Malcolm, *Women at the Crossroads;* L. Mercadante, *From Hierarchy to Equality: I Corinthians 11:2–16;* M. McKenna, *Women in the Church: Role and Renewal;* B. and A. Mickelsen, "Does Male Dominance Tarnish our Translations?" *CT,* Oct. 5, 1979, and "The 'Head' in the Epistles," *CT,* Feb. 20, 1981; J. Morris, *The Lady Was a Bishop;* V. Mollenkott, *Women, Men, and the Bible;* A. Oepke, *TDNT,* I, 776–89; D. R. Pape, *In Search of God's Ideal Woman;* J. Penn-Lewis, *The Magna Charta of Woman;* R. C. Prohl, *Woman in the Church;* C. C. Ryrie, *The Place of Women in the Church;* D. Sayers, *Are Women Human?* L. A. Starr, *The Bible Status of Woman;* K. Stendahl, *The Bible and the Role of Women;* L. Swidler, "Jesus Was a Feminist," *CW* 212:177–83, and *Women in Judaism;* G. H. Tavard, *Woman in Christian Tradition;* B. Trude, *A Woman More Precious Than Jewels;* E. Verdesi, *In But Still Out;* C. J. Vos, *Woman in OT Worship;* P. Wilson-Kastner *et al., A Lost Tradition: Women Writers of the Early Church;* F. Zerbst, *The Office of Woman in the Church.*

Wonders. *See* MIRACLES.

Woolman, John (1720–1772). Quaker social reformer and mystic; one of the most effective advocates for peace and the abolition of slavery in colonial America. Woolman's family helped settle Quaker West Jersey. Here John Woolman earned his living as a tailor, and from this same location he embarked after 1746 on a series of tours to argue against slaveholding and war. His diplomacy was mild but firm. He retained compassion for the slaver as well as for the slave. But he would brook no compromise with the evils of the slave system, insisting, for example, on paying slaves when they performed personal services for him or eventually rejecting food which they grew or cloth which they dyed. His antislavery efforts had an impact in Rhode Island, where wealthy Quaker shipowners had long taken part in the slave traffic, but especially in Pennsylvania, where Woolman's resolutions against slaves (first introduced in 1758) led to the final disavowal of slavery by the Philadelphia Yearly Meeting in 1776. Woolman's *Considerations on the Keeping of Negroes,* written in two sections in 1754 and 1762, contended that slavery affronted common humanity and the "inner light of Christ" that had been placed in all people.

Woolman also was influential in Quaker withdrawal from Pennsylvania politics during the French and Indian War (1756–63). Under pressure from Woolman and other fervent Quakers in England and America, most Quaker members of the Pennsylvania legislature resigned their seats rather than compromise their "peace testimony" through the promotion of war with the French and their Indian allies. Woolman published also a *Plea for the Poor,* which urged those who had enough of the world's goods to care for those who did not.

Woolman's mystical piety represented an important development in Quaker thought as well as in Quaker social action. His *Journal* reveals one who saw physical life as an intimate reflection of the spiritual world, and who devoutly reverenced the work of God in both nature and other humans. He was a man of rare spiritual sensitivity who, without fanfare or posturing, exerted more of an influence on public moral values, at least among the Quakers, than many of the would-be reformers that so filled America during the Revolutionary period. M. A. NOLL

See also FRIENDS, SOCIETY OF.

Bibliography. P. P. Moulton, ed., *The Journal and Major Essays of John Woolman;* R. Jones, *The Quakers in the American Colonies.*

Word, Word of God, Word of the Lord. Of the three Hebrew terms used in the OT to express God's communications, that of *peh* ("mouth"), generally translated "word" in these contexts, is the most vivid. It specifies the source of the declarations as coming directly from God himself. Both Moses (Num. 3:16, 51; cf. 4:5; Josh. 22:9) and Joshua (Josh. 19:50) received instructions from the mouth of the Lord for their people. They consequently declared their word to be his.

Every instance of the term *'imrâ,* including the occurrence of its one plural form (Ps. 12:6), has God's word in view, while the term itself focuses on the act of speech as such. Only four of its twenty-seven references are outside the Psalms (Deut. 33:4; II Sam. 22:31; Prov. 30:5; Isa. 5:24, which in the NEB appears between vss. 4 and 5 of ch. 10). As the speech of God his word is "tried" (Ps. 18:30, AV), or "proves true" (RSV, cf. Pss. 105:19; 119:140; II Sam. 22:31), having "stood the test" (Prov. 30:5, NEB). Such a word laid up in the heart is a sure safeguard against sinning (Ps. 119:11).

There are 394 occurrences of the word *dābār* to characterize a communication as the *word* "of God" or "of the Lord." Here the emphasis falls upon the matter of the utterance, on the what is said. As *dābār,* God's word is the virtual concrete expression of his personality. God is what he says. Therefore did the Lord reveal himself to Samuel by "the word of the Lord" (I Sam. 3:21). As the expression of his being and character the word of the Lord is the supreme means by which God makes himself known to his creatures. By such a word the world was brought into existence and history set in motion. This *dābār* of the Lord can be trusted (Ps. 119:42) as the source of life (Ps. 119:25), light (Ps. 119:105), and understanding (Ps. 119:169).

In the LXX the words *rhēma* and *logos* are used to translate the Hebrew *dābār*. In the familiar phrase "the word of the Lord came" it is rendered *logos* in II Sam. 24:11; I Kings 6:11; etc., and *rhēma* in I Sam. 15:10; II Sam. 7:4; I Kings 17:8, etc. In the prophetic books the LXX translators favor *logos* to denote God's message to the prophets to be proclaimed to the people.

The NT uses both *rhēma* and *logos* with apparent indifference to any significant nuance of meaning. In addition to the word "of God" and "of the Lord" there is that "of Jesus" (Matt. 26:75; cf. John 2:22; 4:50; etc.) and "of Christ" (Col. 3:16; cf. John 5:24; 17:17; etc.). One and the same, then, with "the word of God" and "the word of the Lord" is the "word"—the *logos*—of Jesus Christ; so are his words (*rhēmata*) spirit and life (John 6:63).

In three contexts in the NT the designation "the word of God" appears. The preached word of the gospel is spoken of in such terms. There was a time when the NT as we now have it was not in existence. But "the word of God" was there—the saving message of Christ. The first disciples spoke "the word of God" with boldness (Acts 4:31) and so "the word of God" increased (Acts 6:7; cf. 19:20). At Salamis, Paul and Barnabas "proclaimed the word of God in the synagogues" (Acts 13:5), which "word of God" Sergius Paulus desired to hear (vs. 7). This "good word of God" (Heb. 6:5, KJV) is "the word of the truth" (Col. 1:5) and is consequently God's gospel (Rom. 1:1; 15:16; I Thess. 2:2, 8, 9; I Pet. 4:17; cf. I Tim. 1:11; Acts 20:24) and Christ's (Mark 1:1; Rom. 1:16; 15:19, 29; I Cor. 9:18; II Cor. 2:12; etc.). It is the *logos* of promise (Rom. 9:9) and of wisdom and knowledge (I Cor. 12:8), therefore the *rhēma* of faith (Rom. 10:8). By this "living and abiding" *logos* of God man is born anew (I Pet. 1:23) and by this *rhēma* of God man lives (Phil. 2:16; cf. Matt. 4:4; John 6:63). Such a "word of God" is the "word of the good news" of the apostolic gospel (I Pet. 1:25), being preeminently the word of reconciliation (II Cor. 5:19) and the word of salvation (Acts 13:26), which find their summary and dynamic in "the word of the cross" (I Cor. 1:18).

The word of God proclaimed orally by its first witnesses is one with the word finally embodied in written form in the NT.

In Rev. 19:13 the exalted Christ is specifically designated "The Word of God." The title naturally associates itself with the same author's *logos* doctrine either by way of an approach to it or as an application of it. In John 1:1–2 the term *logos*—Word—is used in an absolute sense of Christ as the incarnate Son of God. In the person of Christ, John thus affirms, God's essential being became actual, comprehensive, and historical. As the Word—*logos*—Christ was among men as the incarnate speech of God; and as such communicates to those who receive him eternal life. John declares that this Word had an existence beyond the limits of time. He stresses both his separate personality—"the Word was with [*pros*, "toward"] God" in the intimacy of an eternal relationship—and his true deity—"the Word was God" in the actuality of his essential nature. Precisely because the Word was personally distinct from God and yet truly God, he made God known.

Throughout John's prologue, then, the *logos* is set forth as the personal self-disclosure of God in his total being. Thus is the Word more than divine reason. In Jesus Christ, the Word made flesh, there is a real incarnation of God; an actual forth-coming in human actuality of the innermost nature of eternal deity. Thus is Jesus Christ the perfect medium of God's self-revelation. To speak of him as "the Word" is consequently to affirm more about him than that he is *ho legōn*, "the he who speaks." He was not just a teacher sent from God. As *Logos* Jesus Christ is the Son of God in his everlasting relationship with his divine Father and in his continued function of divine revealer.

The source of John's Word-*logos* doctrine has been much discussed. Seeing that John was a Palestinian Jew, some regard the OT as its source, since the idea of God's self-manifestation by means of an intermediary agent, more or less personal and blending with the divine personality, was clearly present in Jewish thought. The "wisdom" of Prov. 8, for example, is given personal attributes and at the same time wears the aspect of divinity. Others see John's *logos* doctrine heavily indebted to Philo, the Jewish Alexandrian philosopher, who in his turn was much influenced by Plato. From the time of Heraclitus a *logos* doctrine was developed in Greek thought with a view to explaining how the deity could relate to the world, but the Greek *logos* was generally understood as impersonal reason.

It was with this understanding that it was introduced into early Christian thinking by the Greek apologists of the second century. Thus did Theophilus and Athenagoras speak of the *logos* as immanent in God, but uttered, or "belched forth," prior to creation to become the agent of the creative process. Justin Martyr likewise refers to Jesus the Christ "being of old the *Logos*, ... now by the will of God having become man for the human race." Among the Alexandrians the *logos* doctrine reached its ascendancy. According to Origen the *logos*-Word had its being eternally in God but was brought forth by the Father's will to an existence as Son of God, thereby to accomplish God's purpose of redemption for the world. Seen in retrospect, however, the use made of logology by the apologists and Alexandrians was a desperate expedient which in the course of Christological development was to result in the unacceptable notion that the *logos*-Son was somehow *caused* by God. In this way the filial subordinationism of the NT was substituted for that of the Son's essential inferiority to God the Father, being at best for Origen "a second God," and at worst "a thing made." Such a Word-*logos* Christology failed to secure what the dictates of biblical revelation require—the hypostatic preexistence of Christ and the reality of his eternal and essential divine personhood.

In several NT passages "the word of God" is used to designate in principle the written Scriptures themselves. Our Lord authenticated this use by declaring that Scripture as the word of God cannot be broken (John 10:35). It is "the sure word of prophecy" of which Peter speaks (II Pet. 1:19, AV) because it results from God's "outbreathing" (II Tim. 3:16; cf. II Pet. 1:21).

By characterizing the Scriptures of the OT as the word of God, Jesus incidentally yet specifically affirmed the identity: what is Scripture is the word of God, and vice versa. Into this category the canonical writings of the NT eventually came. Its writers frequently allude to the divine revelation preserved in the OT as the word of God, and they regarded the message of the gospel as the true meaning and fulfillment of that former testament. They had learned from their Lord himself that Moses and all the prophets wrote of him (Luke 24:27). The fathers of the early church and the Reformers of the later church were at one in affirming faith in the biblical writings as the word of God. Augustine of Hippo states the general conviction of the former. "What is the Bible else but a letter of God Almighty addressed to his creatures, in which letter we hear the voice of God, and behold the heart of our Heavenly Father?" The Reformation brought to a focus once again this valuation of the Bible as the word of God. Luther's identity of Holy Scripture with the word of God is generally assumed and sometimes explicitly stated. In fact, in the opening words of his *Table Talks* he declares that "the Bible is God's Word and book I prove this." Elsewhere he asks rhetorically, "Where do we find God's word except in the Scriptures?" to require the reply "Nowhere." For Calvin, too, the Bible is specifically God's word, at once sure and true. The Thirty-nine Articles of the Church of England state that the Bible is "God's word written" (XX), while the Westminster Confession later affirms that since God is the author of Scripture, "it ought to be received because it is the Word of God." The Longer Catechism poses the question, "What is the word of God?" The answer is explicit, "The Holy Scriptures of the Old and New Testament are the Word of God, the only rule of faith and obedience." For the Puritans the same sure faith in Scripture was constant. And from their evangelical successors there have been renewed affirmations of confidence in the Bible as truly and fully the word of God. To speak of the Scriptures is indeed to use a term which etymologically specifies the word of God in written form. Without the writing there would be no Scriptures, and therefore no word of God. The Bible is God's word written.

It is, however, this identification of Scripture as a written form with the word of God that has been called in question in recent times. Some contend that the Bible merely contains the word of God, and then only insofar as it speaks inspiringly to the individual human soul. To regard the Bible in its full extent as the word of God would be to posit for its composition the sovereign action of the Holy Spirit. But it is precisely this action of the Spirit on the writers of the Scriptures that they themselves claim and which requires for their production the designation "the word of God."

Others consider the biblical writings to be at most a witness to God's revelation disclosed in the moment of the divine encounter. Those passages in the Bible which "find me" may be regarded as the word of God *for me;* but objectively, and in themselves, they cannot carry the designation. No such word-of-God type of language, it is presently affirmed, is appropriate. At best the OT can be referred to as the word of Israel and the NT as the word of some leading Christians of the first century. But the prophets of the OT were sure that they were recording God's word for Israel, and leading NT Christians, like Paul, believed themselves to be stating God's word for the churches.

The designation "the word of God, word of the Lord," appears then in three distinct contexts. It refers in particular to Jesus Christ, in general to the divinely disclosed message through God's chosen spokesmen, and in principle to the biblical writings. These three meanings are not, however, unrelated. Rather, they lie one within another on three concentric circles. Christ himself is the ultimate, the total, Word. As the normative expression of God he is consequently the Word in an absolute and personal sense. For the apostolic church the OT read from the perspective of the Word made flesh validated his presence as "he who should come," and so is properly designated the word of God. Against this background and in obedience to their Lord's command the apostolic preachers went forth with the gospel of God's salvation sure in the conviction that they proclaimed the word of God. In summary, then, "the word of God, word of the Lord" belongs in turn to God's own revelation of himself made known personally in Christ, to the proclamation of Christ in the apostolic ministry, and to the truth of Christ embodied in written form in the Scriptures. H. D. McDonald

See also Logos.

Bibliography. A. Debrunner *et al., TDNT,* IV, 69ff.; H. Haarbeck *et al., NIDNTT,* III, 1078ff.; G. Bornkamm, "God's Word and Man's Word in the NT," in *Early Christian Experience;* R. E. Brown, *The Gospel According to John,* I, 519ff.; G. Vos, "The Range of the Logos Title in the Prologue to the Fourth Gospel," *PTR* 11:365ff., 557ff.; S. Wagner, *TDOT,* I, 238ff.

Work. Throughout the Bible there are many references to work, the words used to designate it being divided into two classes. There is the term which has no moral or physical implications as, for instance, when God works in creation, or when reference is made generally to man's works in this life. *Mĕlā'kâ* (Gen. 2:2; Exod. 20:9; I Chr. 4:23; Hag. 1:14) and *ma'ăśeh* (Gen. 5:29; Exod. 5:13; Prov. 16:3; Eccles. 1:14) in the Hebrew, and *ergon* in the Greek are the usual words employed for this purpose. There are, however, other words—*yĕgîa'* (Gen. 31:42; Deut. 28:33; Ps. 128:2; Isa. 55:2; Ezek. 23:29) and *'āmāl* (Ps. 90:10; Eccles. 1:3; 2:10; Jer. 20:18) in the OT, and *kopos* in the NT (Matt. 11:28; John 4:38; I Cor. 4:12; 15:58; I Thess. 1:3; II Thess. 3:8) which imply weariness, trouble, and sorrow.

Work and labor of themselves are never held to be evil, but rather are thought of as man's natural occupation in the world. Even in the state of innocency man as the apex of creation, the representative of all creation before God (Gen. 2:15ff.), was given work to perform as part of his normal existence. This is contrary to much modern thinking which adopts the attitude that man should regard work as something evil and to be avoided if at all possible.

That man's sin has corrupted and degraded work is at the same time continually repeated in the Bible. Gen. 3:17–18 specifically states that work will, because of sin, change its character to become the cause of man's ultimate physical disintegration. This would seem to be the reason for work in subsequent portions of the Bible frequently embodying the idea of weariness. Indeed, this is the theme of the book of Ecclesiastes, in which the preacher states that all man's labor that he does under the sun is vanity. Man as a sinner works solely with worldly ends in view, the outcome being a sense of frustration and hopelessness, for ultimately he will disappear from this earth and his works with him (Eccles. 2). Only as he interprets his work in the light of eternity will his understanding of it change.

Yet even sinful man possesses great gifts and abilities with which to subdue and use the physical world. In Exod. 31:1ff.; Judg. 3:10 (cf. also Isa. 45); and many other places it is stated that it is the Holy Spirit who gives man these endowments. Certain OT characters are also said to have received special gifts from God that would enable them to do their work: the judges, Saul, and even the heathen king Cyrus (Judg. 3:10; I Sam. 10:6–7; Isa. 45). The NT writers assume the point of view of the OT, but stress it particularly in connection with gifts and abilities possessed by members of the church (I Cor. 12; Eph. 4:11ff.). Moreover, they continually emphasize that God calls all men to work and positions in life in which they are to serve him. While this appears in the OT, as in the case of Esther (Esth. 4:13–14), the apostle Paul repeats it with great frequency in his writings (Eph. 6:5ff.; I Tim. 6:1–2; Philem.).

Work, however, even though a man may be richly endowed with gifts, cannot be anything but ultimately empty unless man realizes that its true purpose is to glorify God. Paul makes this very plain in speaking to both servants and masters (Eph. 6:5ff.; I Tim. 6:1–2), summing it all up in his instruction to Christians to be not "slothful in business, but fervent in spirit serving the Lord" (Rom. 12:11), and in his exhortation to do all things to the glory of God (I Cor. 10:31).

In practice, such a view of work means that the Christian must always regard his work as a divinely appointed task in which, as he fulfills his calling, he is serving God. This requires him to be honest and diligent in all that he does, whether as employee or employer. Such, for instance, is the central point in the parable of the talents (Matt. 25:15). If he is a servant, he is to be faithful and obedient, doing all things as in God's sight

(Eph. 6:5ff.), while if he is an employer God lays upon him the responsibility of fair dealing and consideration toward his employees. He is to pay them adequately and not to defraud them of their wages, "for the laborer is worthy of his hire" (Lev. 19:13; Deut. 24:14; Amos 5:8ff.; Luke 10:7; Col. 4:1; James 5:4–5). Thus all honest work is honorable and to be performed as a divinely given commission to God's eternal glory (Rev. 14:13). W. S. Reid

See also Vocation.

Bibliography. J. Calvin, *Institutes of the Christian Religion,* 3.7; A. Kuyper, *The Work of the Holy Spirit;* J. Murray, *Principles of Conduct;* P. Marshall *et al., Labor of Love: Essays on Work;* G. Baum, *The Priority of Labor;* G. Wingren, *Luther on Vocation;* K. Barth, *Church Dogmatics,* III/4, 595ff.; J. Ellul, "Work and Calling," *Kat,* Fall/Winter, 1972; H. C. Hahn and F. Thiele, *NIDNTT,* III, 1147ff.; A. Richardson, *The Biblical Doctrine of Work.*

Works. The works of both God and mankind receive prominent attention in the Bible. God's works, mentioned early in Genesis and throughout the giving of special revelation, consist of creation, providence (including the preservation and government of the world), and redemption. Jesus' comment that his Father was still working (John 5:17) is reinforced by Paul (Phil. 1:6; Rom. 14:20), who considers his activity as an aspect of the work of God (I Cor. 16:10; Phil. 2:30; cf. Acts 13:2).

Although human labor was originally given as a divine commission and privilege (Gen. 2:15), the intervention of sin gave it a negative connotation in biblical usage. Man now eats and lives by the sweat of his brow (Gen. 3:17–19; cf. 5:29), and his works are seen increasingly in the OT as being marked by vanity and sin. This negative attitude toward mere human action was accentuated by an emphasis in the opposite direction in late Judaism: the righteousness of works and their deserving a reward. The NT teaching on works must be seen against this background. Here human works are characterized in general as of the devil (I John 3:8; John 8:41), of darkness (Rom. 13:12), of the flesh (Gal. 5:19), as evil (Jude 15; Matt. 23:3), lawless (II Pet. 2:8), and dead (Heb. 6:1; 9:14). The only works that will stand the scrutiny of God are those which are effected by his Spirit and are grounded in faith (John 3:21; 6:29; I Thess. 1:3; Rom. 2:6–7; Acts 26:20). Such are not only approved by Jesus (Matt. 5:16; 7:21; 21:28ff.) and Paul (Rom. 2:6–7) but expected of God's people (Matt. 25:37–40). What is condemned is the expectation of payment from God for doing what he has commanded men to do. After they have done all that he has commanded them to do—as though that were possible—they must still say, "We are unworthy servants; we have only done what was our duty" (Luke 17:10). The chief work that God desires is the obedience of humble belief (John 6:29), which then begets a life full of good deeds (Titus 3:14).

Good Works. Soon after the apostolic age, a drifting from the biblical view of good works is noticeable. Whereas the NT had taught that the kingdom is built on God's grace, not human merit, and that God rewards according to his grace, not merit (Matt. 20:1–16), leaders in the church held that baptized persons must obey the commandments, and when they do God rewards them. Thus Tertullian, a former lawyer, saw God related to mankind as lawgiver; he commands, and we obey and obtain merit. God is the rewarder of merit. "If God is the acceptor of good works, he is also the rewarder.... A good deed has God as its debtor, just as has also the evil deed, since the judge is the rewarder of every matter." Although all service to God is meritorious, he has decreed that certain good works give one merit when freely done. Penances, fasting, virginity, martyrdom, and other good deeds please him and receive his reward.

Soon merit was said to be transferable; salvation was seen as grace and as something merited; by free will we obtain merit, and by merit, operating within the context of grace, salvation. Peter Lombard, whose *Sentences* was the standard theological textbook in the late Middle Ages, saw grace and free will cooperating in salvation to produce good works and thus obtain salvation. Good works produce merit; "without merits to hope for, anything cannot be called hope but presumption." This theology was refined, and merit was said to be "that property of a good work which entitled the doer to receive a reward from him in whose service the work is done.... In the theological sense a supernatural merit can only be a salutary act to which God in consequence of his infallible promise owes a supernatural reward, consisting ultimately in eternal life" (*The Catholic Encyclopedia*). The merit of human good works in the scheme of salvation ordained by God was associated with and dependent on the merit of the passion of Christ so that there was seen to be a congruence of the two. Thus the Catechism of the Council of Trent in the sixteenth century reads: "It is his passion also that imparts to our good actions the twofold most excellent quality of meriting the rewards of eternal glory, so as that even a cup of cold water given in his name shall not be without its reward, and of satisfying for our sins" (Ch. IV, Q.67).

This unbiblical teaching, combined with a

semi-Pelagian doctrine of free will and human ability, was the fundamental reason for the necessity of doctrinal reformation in the late medieval period, as Luther declared in his debate with Erasmus. The problems of the papacy, purgatory, and indulgences he calls mere trifles compared with the real issue: the condition of mankind in the state of sin. Before his rediscovery of the gospel he had struggled to acquire merit by good works. "I was a good monk and kept my order so strictly that I could say that if ever a monk could get to heaven through monastic discipline, I should have entered in. All my companions in the monastery who knew me would bear me out in this. For if it had gone on much longer I would have martyred myself to death with vigils, prayers, readings, and other works." Luther became a doctor of theology and "did not yet know that we cannot expiate our sins." So he, and others, tried the impossible, to expiate them by themselves through good works. This was changed for Luther and a large part of the church with the development of the doctrine of justification by faith in the merits of Christ alone and not those of the believer obtained through good works. The Reformers declared that the only righteousness which can stand before the judgment of a holy God is one which is "absolutely perfect and wholly in conformity with the divine law. But even our best works in this life are all imperfect and defiled with sin" (Heidelberg Catechism Q.62). If God marks iniquities, who can stand? But he forgives and reckons sinners righteous. This is the teaching of Rom. 4. The reckoning, or imputation, of the righteousness of Christ does not mean that God observes how well the sinner has done and then declares him a fit citizen of his kingdom. Rather, the Bible, and the Reformation with it, declares that God justifies the ungodly (Rom. 5:6, 9–10, 16–21). Christ came not to call the righteous but sinners to repentance (Matt. 9:13). It was the publican who smote his breast, asking God to be merciful to him, a sinner, who went home justified, rather than the self-righteous Pharisee (Luke 18:14). Sinners are justified freely, as a gift, through the redemption—i.e., the good work—of Jesus, says the apostle, after which he asks, "Then what becomes of our boasting?" He answers, "It is excluded. On what principle? On the principle of works? No, but on the principle of faith. For we hold that a man is justified by faith apart from works of law. . . . The wages of sin is death, but the free gift of God is eternal life in Christ Jesus our Lord" (Rom. 3:24–28; 6:23). Salvation freely given does not mean that good works are unimportant. They are commanded and are the fruit of faith (Titus 2:14; Eph. 2:10; Matt. 5:16). They are known of God and will be taken into account in the final judgment (Rom. 2:6; I Cor. 3:14; II Cor. 5:10; Rev. 22:12).

M. E. Osterhaven

Bibliography. G. Bertram, *TDNT,* II, 654ff.; K. Thieme, *SHERK,* V, 19–22; G. Rupp, *The Righteousness of God.*

World. In the OT *'ereṣ,* which is properly earth in contrast to heaven (Gen. 1:1), is occasionally rendered "world," but the more usual term is *tēbēl,* which signifies the planet as having topographical features, as habitable and fruitful (Pss. 19:4; 90:2). The NT words are *oikoumenē,* denoting the populated world (Luke 4:5); *aiōn,* which is usually rendered age, but which occasionally combines with the concept of time that of space (Heb. 1:2; 11:3); and *kosmos,* which contains the thought of order or system. The latter word may denote the material world (Rom. 1:20) or even the totality of heaven and earth (Acts 17:24); the sphere of intelligent life (I Cor. 4:9); the place of human habitation (I Cor. 5:10); mankind as a whole (John 3:16); society as alienated from God and under the sway of Satan (I John 5:19); and the complex of ideas and ideals which govern men who belong to the world in this ethical sense (I John 2:15–17; James 4:4).

Since *kosmos* is the leading term involved, it calls for further consideration. Among the Greeks, *kosmos* became used for the universe, since it suitably expressed the order noted there. The Hebrews, on the other hand, were not hospitable to the concept of universe, but thought in terms of the heavens (the abode of God) and the earth (the realm of human existence). God was the author of both, and the regularity of the movements of the heavenly bodies and the rhythm of the seasons bore witness to his creative wisdom and the power of his sustaining control. NT writers follow this pattern of OT thought, avoiding, with rare exceptions, the use of the word *kosmos* for the heavens and the earth combined (Acts 17:24 is explicable as an adaptation of the message in terms congenial to the hearers, who were Greeks). The word *kosmos* then, in the NT, prevailingly denotes the earth, and by an extension of thought is used for mankind which dwells on the earth. Perhaps this process was assisted by the fact that, owing to human intelligence and the drive for social integration, life presents considerable order.

But the most striking fact about the NT use of *kosmos* is the readiness with which the term is employed in an evil sense. Again and again, especially in the Johannine writings, the world is presented as something hostile to God. This seems to spell disorder. How, then, can *kosmos* be used to describe such a state of affairs? The answer is likely to be found in the fact that the powers of spiritual evil, which have Satan as their head and appear to be organized on a vast scale and with great efficiency (Eph. 6:12), dominate the life of unredeemed humanity. Satan rules a kingdom which is opposed to the kingdom of God (Luke 11:18).

We are not dropped into the depths of a hopeless dualism by reason of this opposition, for the word teaches that the sphere of divine control embraces "all things." Therefore, even over the world which is marred by the love of evil and by the sinister hold of the devil, God is still sovereign. Satan's kingdom exists by permission, not by reason of divine helplessness. Reconciliation has been provided for the world (II Cor. 5:19), whereby men may leave the realm of darkness and be transferred into the kingdom of the Son of God's love. Those who will not do so must share the fate of Satan.

Worldliness, though not a scriptural term, is certainly a scriptural concept. It is an affection for that which is unlike God and contrary to his will (James 4:4; I John 2:15–16). The refusal to live an ascetic life is not a proof of worldliness, nor is the love of the beautiful. The determination of what is worldly should not rest solely upon the nature of an activity or habit viewed as a thing-in-itself, but also upon the spirit of the one who indulges himself. If one is actuated by selfishness or neglect of God, he may be more worldly in God's sight than another whose outward acts are more questionable, but whose heart does not condemn him, because he is not consciously disobeying his Lord. E. F. Harrison

See also Worldliness and Otherworldliness; Age, Ages; This Age, The Age to Come.

Bibliography. G. Bornkamm, *Early Christian Experience;* J. M. Robinson, "World in Modern Theology and in NT Theology," in *Soli Deo Gratia;* R. Morgenthaler *et al., NIDNTT,* I, 517ff.; H. Sasse, *TDNT,* III, 867ff.; O. Michel, *TDNT,* V, 157ff.; G. Johnston, "*Oikoumenē* and *Kosmos* in the NT," *NTS* 10:352ff.

Worldliness and Otherworldliness. Israel's world-affirming outlook—God is creator and ruler of *this* world—was reinforced by incarnation of the ideal in flesh, in Jesus Christ. He rejected the austerities of the Baptist and proclaimed the rule of God in this world. Nevertheless, he sharply criticized his "evil and adulterous generation": disciples must be different ("it shall not be so among you") yet must love their neighbor. So Peter and Paul exhorted converts to protective "separation" from the world, while stressing involvement in human needs and the mission to save the world. John was uncompromisingly world-renouncing: society organized against God "lies in the evil one"; love of the world contradicts love for the Father; yet Christ, the Savior of the world God loves, dies for the world (I John 2:2).

Tension grew between world-affirming ministry and world-renouncing concentration upon the world above (mysticism) or upon the world to come (adventism), as Christians resisted the theaters, games, and debauchery rampant in the Roman world yet cared for the world's unwanted. Separation strengthened into rejection of the world and ultimately into escape, as anchorites and monastics despised marriage, cleanliness, and all human comforts, in an otherworldly search for deeper truth and the vision of God. Simultaneously, the conversion of Rome fostered a new kind of worldliness, ambition for all the rewards of power. Two types of Christians emerged—the religious, withdrawn from the world, and the lay, active in the world.

Augustine held Christians should use but not enjoy the world; Aquinas would impose natural law upon it. Luther's "kingdom of grace" (the church) was paralleled by "the kingdom of God's left hand," the secular world, ruled by law: Christians live within *both.* Calvin would restore the world to God's rule by discipline, making the world one vast monastery. For Puritans, the world is Vanity Fair, to be traveled through toward the Celestial City, not dwelt in. Yet not the world but worldliness is sinful, the desire for the world's ways and prizes when the heart's true loyalties lie elsewhere.

Nineteenth century social gospel reformers, firmly rooted in the kingdom (Maurice), in compassion (Gladden), or in a liturgical vision of God's glory (Holland, Temple), strove to embody their spiritual vision within the everyday world of wages, houses, work, and peace. But Bonhoeffer insisted that the world is already spiritual, reconciled, needing "religionless," unseparated Christians to plunge into its life to prove it is not godless.

In the tensions of such unworldly worldliness the Christian ever lives, not of the world, redeemed from it, independent of it, but sent back to minister to it, living within it in the power of the world to come, knowing that the world is God's. R. E. O. White

Worldwide Church of God. *See* Armstrongism.

Worms, Diet of (1521). One of the most dramatic events of the Reformation. Martin Luther, the miner's son, confessed his faith before Charles V, scion of the house of Hapsburg. Elected Holy Roman Emperor in 1519, Charles scheduled his first meeting with the German princes for a diet (parliament) at Worms in 1521. A major concern was Martin Luther. Upon the urging of Luther's prince, Frederick the Wise, Luther was invited on March 6 to appear at the diet. Charles gave a safe conduct pass. Luther was determined to go to Worms even if there were "as many devils in it as there were tiles on the roofs of the houses." Accompanied by Nicholas von Amsdorf, a fellow professor; Peter Suaven, Pomeranian nobleman and student; John Petzensteiner, another Augustinian friar; and Caspar Sturm, the imperial herald, Luther left for Worms on April 2. Justus Jonas, canon at Erfurt, joined them. For two weeks Luther made a triumphal tour across Germany, arriving at Worms toward noon on April 16. Greeted by a trumpet blast from the cathedral, Luther entered town in his two-wheeled cart, greeted by more than two thousand people, who accompanied him to his lodging at the Hospital of the Knights of St. John.

April 17 at 4 P.M. Luther entered the diet to be questioned by the Archbishop of Trier, who pointed to a table of writings and asked if the Reformer had written them and if he recanted any of them. "The books are all mine, and I have written more," Luther responded. "Do you defend them all, or do you care to reject a part?" he was asked. "This touches God and his Word. This affects the salvation of souls. . . . To say too little or too much would be dangerous. I beg you, give me time to think it over," Luther answered. Allowed a day for reflection, Luther reappeared at 6 P.M. on April 18. The same questions were posed once more. Luther explained that his books were of several types—pastoral, polemical, theological. Denied the opportunity to further explain, Luther was asked for a simple reply. He stated: "Since then your Majesty and your lordships desire a simple reply, I will answer without horns and without teeth. Unless I am convicted by Scripture and plain reason—I do not accept the authority of popes and councils, for they have contradicted each other—my conscience is captive to the Word of God. I cannot and I will not recant anything, for to go against conscience is neither right nor safe. God help me. Amen." Some accounts add: "Here I stand, I cannot do otherwise." Confusion followed. Compromise was impossible. On April 23 Luther was permitted to leave Worms. His supporters left. Charles then issued the Edict of Worms on May 26 accusing Luther of heresy and treason, placing him under the imperial ban.

Worms marks Luther's complete break with the past—excommunicated by pope and banned by emperor—and the birth of Lutheran Protestantism outside the Church of Rome.

C. G. Fry

See also Luther, Martin.

Bibliography. R. H. Bainton, *Here I Stand: A Life of Martin Luther;* H. J. Grimm, *The Reformation Era, 1500–1650;* H. Boehmer, *Martin Luther: Road to Reformation.*

Worry. *See* Anxiety.

Worship. Our English word means "worthship," denoting the worthiness of an individual to receive special honor in accordance with that worth. The principal biblical terms, the Hebrew *šāḥâ* and the Greek *proskyneō*, emphasize the act of prostration, the doing of obeisance. This may be done out of regard for the dignity of personality and influenced somewhat by custom (Gen. 18:2), or may be based on family relationship (Gen. 49:8) or on station in life (I Kings 1:31).

On a higher plane the same terms are used of divine honors rendered to a deity, whether to the gods of the nation (e.g., Exod. 20:5) or to the one true and living God who reveals himself in Scripture and in his son (Exod. 24:1). The tutelage of Israel in the wilderness laid great stress on the sinfulness of idolatrous worship and its dire consequences (e.g., Deut. 8:19). No injury to God compares with the denial of his uniqueness and the transfer to another of the recognition due to him. In this light must be understood his references to himself as a jealous God (Exod. 20:5).

Perversion of worship is seen in Satan's avid effort to secure for himself what belongs properly to God alone (Matt. 4:9), as well as in the blasphemous figure of the beast (Rev. 13:4). Undue deference paid to men verges at times on worship and is resisted by the godly (Acts 10:25–26). Barnabas and Paul protested the attempt to worship them at Lystra based on the impression that they were gods who had come down to men (Acts 14:11–14). Loyal angels refuse veneration (Rev. 22:9).

It is useful to distinguish between a broad and a restricted meaning of worship as applied to God. In general he may be honored with prayer and praise and the bringing of sacrificial gifts (I Sam. 1:3). This cultic worship is especially appropriate in the house of God (Ps. 138:2) and when it is carried on with a desire to be clothed in his holiness (Ps. 29:2). In a still broader sense the service which issues from worship and derived therefrom its inspiration may be included (Matt. 4:10).

In the narrower sense worship is pure adoration, the lifting up of the redeemed spirit toward God in contemplation of his holy perfection. Matthew distinguishes between the presentation of gifts by the magi to the Christ child and their worship of him (Matt. 2:11).

Jesus made an epochal statement on this subject (John 4:24). To worship God in spirit involves a contrast with worship in the letter, in the legalistic encumbrance so characteristic of the Jew; to worship him in truth contrasts with the Samaritan and all other worship which is false to a greater or lesser extent.

Our Lord made possible a more intelligent worship of God by revealing the Father in his own person. As the incarnate Son, he himself is deserving of the same veneration (John 9:38; 20:28; Heb. 1:6; Rev. 5:6–14). E. F. HARRISON

See also WORSHIP IN THE CHURCH.

Bibliography. R. Abba, *Principles of Christian Worship;* A. B. Macdonald, *Christian Worship in the Primitive Church;* R. P. Martin, *Worship in the Early Church;* W. D. Maxwell, *A History of Christian Worship;* G. Wainwright, *Doxology;* J. F. White, *Introduction to Christian Worship;* W. Hahn, *Worship and Congregation;* E. Underhill, *Worship.*

Worship in the Church. To worship God is to ascribe to him the worth of which he is worthy. The church of Jesus Christ is by definition a worshiping community called into being by God to be "a spiritual house, to be an holy priesthood, offering spiritual sacrifices acceptable to God through Jesus Christ" (I Pet. 2:5). The Christian church has from the very beginning gathered regularly for corporate worship. The most basic acts of worship in the early church—the reading and exposition of Scripture; the prayers; the singing of psalms, hymns, and spiritual songs; and the observance of the sacraments—are all derived from the example and command of Jesus himself. However, with the exception of the celebration of the Lord's Supper, Jesus did not originate these practices. They were derived from the synagogue worship of the Jews.

The Early Church. The first Christian community in Jerusalem was essentially Jewish in orientation and as such accepted the OT as the Word of God. What distinguished these early Christians from the Jews was their conviction that Jesus was the promised Messiah and that salvation was found only in him. They continued to worship in a basically Jewish fashion, but added the Lord's Supper (Acts 2:42, 46) and prayers in the name of Jesus (Acts 4:24–30).

Although the Christians gathered daily for prayer, fellowship, preaching, and teaching (Acts 2:46; 5:42), the chief day for services of worship in the church was changed from the Jewish sabbath to the first day of the week almost from the beginning, because it was the day of resurrection.

It is not clear what the order of worship in the church as established by the apostles was, but the service was basically a simple one. All the early evidence (NT and noncanonical writings) indicates that while the elements of the service had no fixed sequence, the climactic event of the weekly service on the Lord's Day was the sacrament of the Lord's Supper. One early source, the Didache (*ca.* 95–150), gives us a detailed description of how the Lord's Supper was celebrated, including the prayers to be used, as well as other liturgical directions and usages. Fixed forms of prayer were included, but provision was made for free prayers in some places in the liturgy. Confession of sin was required before partaking of the Lord's Supper (Didache 14:1).

Justin Martyr's *First Apology,* written somewhere near the middle of the second century, describes the Lord's Supper as the Eucharist (meaning thanksgiving), as does the Didache (14:1). In describing a service of worship Justin says, "The memoirs of the Apostles [the Gospels] and the writings of the prophets were read aloud as long as time allowed" (*First Apology* 67). The writings of the prophets were undoubtedly the books of the OT. From Justin's writing it is clear that the churches had a definite order of service established by tradition but the service was still very simple.

In the primitive church there were gatherings in which the believers who had been baptized celebrated the Lord's Supper along with a full-scale meal. At a very early date, however, the meal was separated from the sacrament (Clement of Alexandria, *Paedagogos* 2:1; *Stromata* 3:2; Tertullian, *Apology* 39; *Chaplet* 3) and was called the agape, i.e., love feast. By the fourth century the observance of the agape had largely died out because of disorders in its conduct (Augustine, *Letter to Aurelium* 22:4).

The observance of festivals throughout the year by the Jews gave rise among the Christians to the idea of a "church year," now referred to as the "liturgical year," but this effort to sanctify the entire year by a succession of sacred festivals developed slowly. The festivals of Christmas and Epiphany were not added until the fourth century, and the liturgical year as it is now observed was not completed until the end of the sixth century.

The apostle Paul mentions revelations, speaking in tongues, and the interpretation of tongues as present within the worshiping congregation. The exercise of these special spiritual gifts (charismata) was strictly regulated so that the service could be carried on in good order and the believers edified (I Cor. 14:40). Thus the free expression of the Spirit went hand in hand with liturgical restrictiveness in the same service. This free expression of the Spirit in tongues and prophecy seems to have died out very early, in all probability concurrent with the recognition of the final authority of the writings of the apostles as canonical. As early as the time of Justin Martyr prophesying, speaking in tongues, and the interpretation of tongues had disappeared. What remained was a service of two divisions, the first part being an adaptation and expansion of the synagogue service of praise, prayer, and instruction, and the second the observance of the Lord's Supper.

A process of steady departure from the evangelical faith and free worship which the NT describes had its beginning in the second century. This departure was sufficient gradually and progressively to change the character of Christianity itself. It is clear from the Church Order of Hippolytus, compiled before the year 236, that considerable development had taken place by the middle of the third century. Some liturgical forms had been established this early, but the worship was still quite simple and relatively brief and some of the prayers were free.

The Middle Ages and Reformation. When the Emperor Constantine made Christianity the official religion of the Roman Empire in 313, the new public image of the Christians encouraged the building of splendid churches and the creation of longer and more colorful services. The results were not uniformly beneficial. As pagans professed to embrace Christianity in great numbers, they began to have influence, especially in the introduction of an emphasis upon the "mystery" of the Lord's Supper. Rather than perpetuation of the simplicity of early Christian worship, form and ceremony became the important thing. The way was prepared for the radical change of the Lord's Supper into the Roman Mass with all the abuses which developed from this in the medieval Roman Church.

Originally the Roman Mass was a simple rite with two main divisions, the Liturgy of the Word and the Liturgy of the Upper Room. Gradually, however, the communion table gave way to the altar, which was placed against the wall, and the officiating clergyman became a priest who went to the altar to offer a sacrifice for the people which they were not allowed to offer themselves. By the end of the fourth century, as the reality of Christ's presence in the Communion service yielded to an extremely localized view of his presence in the bread and wine, barriers began progressively to be raised between the altar and the people. The Lord's Supper was no longer a joyful service of evangelical thanksgiving; it had become an awesome objective sacrifice of the body and blood of Christ. The importance of this radical departure from NT teaching and practice cannot be overestimated. It represents a watershed in the history of the worship of the Christian church. It resulted in the elimination of most of what is characteristic of evangelical worship. The worshipers became mere spectators observing the activity of the priest at the altar. Doctrinal errors such as transubstantiation, penance, and meritorious works contributed to the decline of worship and the growing dissatisfaction of the worshipers which became major factors in the Reformation.

The Reformers were more concerned with doctrine than with worship materials, and most of them gave comparatively little attention to the development of liturgy. A wide variety of worship services came into being. Luther at first used only a shortened version of the Roman Mass, later making some significant changes to recover the NT idea of fellowship in the observance of Communion. Zwingli denounced the Mass and eradicated everything suggesting the Roman practice. He even eliminated congregational singing and use of the organ. Calvin's aim was to return to the worship practices of the primitive church. While he too eliminated everything indicating that the Mass was a sacrifice and all prayers to the saints or to the Virgin Mary, he endorsed congregational singing, especially the use of metrical versions of the Psalms. He gave the sermon an important place in the service. His liturgy became the norm of worship in the Calvinistic churches of Europe.

In the Protestant Reformation on the continent the break with the Roman Church was more complete than in England. Henry VIII did not embrace the doctrines of the continental Reformers. He simply wanted to be free from the authority of the pope. Services in the English Church continued to be conducted according to the practices of the Roman Church before the break. The continental Reformation had its effect, however, for Thomas Cranmer, Archbishop of Canterbury, headed a commission which changed the Latin Mass into an English Communion service, a revision approved by Parliament. A revised edition of Cranmer's work, known as the Second Prayer Book of Edward VI, was published in 1552. It included a number of changes brought about by strong Puritan pressures. It was sufficiently purged of Romish elements that it was endorsed by John Knox for use in Scotland. The final edition of the *Book of Common Prayer* was published in 1662, and has remained authoritative in the Church of England to the present.

In 1643 Parliament called together the Westminster Assembly of divines which produced not only a confession of faith and catechisms but also the Directory for the Public Worship of God. Although accepted by Parliament, the liturgical directions of the directory never enjoyed widespread acceptance in England, but were followed as a standard in Scotland until late in the nineteenth century. As far as worship practices are concerned, the Protestant Reformation came to an end in England in 1662.

The American Churches. Throughout the seventeenth century Protestants moving from Europe to America carried with them their Reformation principles, but with some exceptions their worship practices were modified by the circumstances associated with their colonial life and the struggles they endured as they fought for independence and then developed and expanded a new nation. Three principal types of worship were transferred to the American colonies. First there were those churches which retained a fixed liturgy such as had been known in the Anglican Church. This allowed maximum opportunity for formal corporate participation and, while deemphasizing the preaching function of the minister, encouraged frequent individual participation in Communion. A second type was characteristic of those churches that stemmed from what might be termed radical Puritanism. They rejected all forms in worship as quenching the Spirit and felt that men should be as free as possible in praising God and communicating his message to others. A third type of worship, distinct from the other two, might be characterized as an attempt to worship according to the Word. This was the emphasis of the Calvinistic churches which followed the dictum of Calvin that nothing was to be allowed in worship except that which the Scripture commanded. The preaching of the Word of God became predominant in their services, but because of the example of Calvin and Knox they did not hesitate to produce liturgies for their congregations.

A number of different aspects of colonial life influenced the early settlers. Nearly all settlements had their beginnings without church buildings, so worship took on the informality of the schoolhouse or the home or the grove where it was conducted. It was characterized by a very simple pattern of unskilled singing, extempore prayer, Scripture reading, and a sermon when a minister was present. United worship with Christians of other churches played a significant part in lessening the emphasis upon the distinctive worship practices of the various sects.

As the frontier was pushed westward, most of the American denominations holding solid historical connections with Old World churches were strongly influenced by revivalism as it spread through the new land. Many of America's free churches have their roots in the American revival tradition. The revival meeting began with a song service of three or more songs chosen to raise the emotional pitch of the congregation. Prayers were offered, but they were intensely personal. An offering was received in conformity with the tempo of the service, and after a highly subjective musical number, usually a solo, the congregation was prepared for the climax of the service, the evangelistic sermon, which was always followed by some form of the "altar call."

While not many churches follow this pattern today, it did have a strong impact on most evangelical churches of the eighteenth and nineteenth centuries, and its effects remain to this day. Strong revivalistic and judgmental preaching tended to completely overshadow the experience of corporate worship. The balance between Word and sacrament was largely lost. The Lord's Supper was limited to semiannual or quarterly or sometimes monthly observance. There was very little experience of common prayer. The pastor's sermon was the all-important part of the service.

Another movement which had a strong effect upon evangelical Christian worship in America was the Chautauqua, which rose in the nineteenth century for the distinct purpose of raising the cultural level of the country by informing and entertaining the public. Chautauqua spread widely over the country, but when it began to dwindle the only organization able adequately to provide for community cultural growth was the church. The minister, who was often the best educated member of the community, was expected to carry on these educational and entertainment functions. Thus the personality and ability of the preacher became vitally important. Churches began to be built like theaters with banked seats, so that what was taking place in the pulpit area and choir loft could be more readily observed. People became more and more adjusted to being mere spectators in their worship services.

The combination of the effect of the highly subjective emphasis of the revival movement with the entertainment aspect of the Chautauqua has been felt strongly in the evangelical churches of America in the twentieth century. The choir and soloists often seem to be providing Christian entertainment for the congregation, while individual participation in the service is limited to the singing of hymns. While the central and all-important part of the service is the sermon, in line with an appropriate emphasis on the Word of God, the potential richness of common worship for the individual worshiper is often unrealized.

Among the growing number of independent,

nondenominational churches as well as many evangelical churches in denominations with Old World roots there is not presently any evident widespread concern for developing richer corporate worship. The structure of their worship services is without any particular scriptural or historical significance. However, in some of the evangelical denominations there is widespread interest in worship renewal. Even some of the denominations that have been traditionally antiliturgical are now seeking ways to enrich their worship experiences, not by simply introducing one or more ancient elements into their liturgy, but by a careful effort to develop services in harmony both with NT standards and with historic, prophetic, evangelical Christianity.

R. G. RAYBURN

See also CHRISTIAN YEAR; WORSHIP.

Bibliography. T. Klausner, *A Short History of the Western Liturgy;* R. P. Martin, *Worship in the Early Church;* W. D. Maxwell, *A History of Christian Worship;* R. G. Rayburn, *O Come, Let Us Worship;* J. J. von Allmen, *Worship: Its Liturgy and Practice;* B. Thompson, ed., *Liturgies of the Western Church.*

Wrath of God. Wrath, anger, and indignation are integral to the biblical proclamation of the living God in his opposition to sin. While God's love is spontaneous to his own being, his wrath is called forth by the wickedness of his creatures. Thus it is the wounding of his gracious love, the rejection of his proffered mercy, which evokes his holy wrath. God's act of wrath is his strange work (Isa. 28:21). C. H. Dodd has well observed, "Wrath is the effect of human sin: mercy is not the effect of human goodness, but is inherent in the character of God."

On the other hand, the exhaustive studies of Fichtner in the OT and of Staehlin in the NT do not sustain the thesis that wrath is an impersonal retribution, an automatic, causal working out of an abstract law. In the OT wrath is the expression of the personal, subjective free will of Yahweh who actively punishes sin, as in the NT it is the personal reaction of God, not an independent hypostasis. In the face of evil the Holy One of Israel does not dodge the responsibility of executing judgment. He demonstrates his anger at times in the most personal way possible. "I the Lord do smite" (Ezek. 7:8–9). In such NT passages as John 3:36; Rom. 1:18; Eph. 5:6; Col. 3:6; Rev. 19:15; 11:18; 14:10; 16:19; 6:16; cf. Rom. 9:22, wrath is specifically described as God's wrath, his wrath, thy wrath, or the wrath of the Lamb. The wrath of God is being continually revealed from heaven, actively giving the wicked up to uncleanness, to vile passions, to reprobate minds, and punishing them in the day of wrath and revelation of the just judgment of God (Rom. 1:18–2:6). In II Thess. 1:7–9 Paul writes as personal a description of the Lord Jesus' action in directly punishing the disobedient as can be penned.

In the total biblical portrayal the wrath of God is not so much an emotion or an angry frame of mind as it is the settled opposition of his holiness to evil. Accordingly, the wrath of God is seen in its effects, in God's punishment of sin in this life and in the next. These inflictions include pestilence, death, exile, destruction of wicked cities and nations, hardening of hearts, and the cutting off of the people of God for idolatry or unbelief. They reach into the life to come in Jesus' descriptions of everlasting punishment, of a hell of fire, where the worm dieth not and the flame is not quenched. The day of wrath is God's final judgment against sin, his irrevocable condemnation of impenitent sinners.

The OT description of God as "slow to anger and plenteous in mercy" is best understood as a blessed revelation full of wonder and awe. For only he who apprehends the reality of God's wrath is overpowered by the magnitude of his mercy, as it is declared in Isa. 54:7–10 or in the ASV reading of Ps. 30:5: "His anger is but for a moment, his favor is for a lifetime." As mercy gets the upper hand in these OT passages, so the ultimate NT word is the grace of our Lord Jesus Christ, the love of God the Father made ours in the fellowship of the Holy Spirit.

Accordingly, the way of escape from the wrath of the Almighty is abundantly presented in both testaments. While man's puny efforts are insufficient, God's own heart of love provides a way of salvation. He calls men to repent, to return unto himself, to receive his forgiveness and renewal. He receives the intercession of his servants—Abraham, Moses, Eleazar, and Jeremiah—for his people, and himself provides the OT sacrificial system by which his wrath may be averted.

In the NT the call is to faith, to repentance, to baptism in the name of the Lord Jesus who saves us from the wrath to come (I Thess. 1:9–10). For when we are justified by his blood and reconciled by his death we shall be saved from the wrath by his life (Rom. 5:9–10). The most poignant word about God's punishment is that it is the wrath of the Lamb who took upon himself and bore the sins of the world.

W. C. ROBINSON

See also JUDGMENT; ETERNAL PUNISHMENT.

Bibliography. H. Schönweiss and H.-C. Hahn, *NIDNTT,* I, 105ff.; G. Bornkamm, *Early Christian Experience;* A. T. Hanson, *The Wrath of the Lamb;* H. Kleinknecht *et al., TDNT,* V, 382ff.; R. V. G. Tasker, *The*

The Biblical Doctrine of the Wrath of God; L. Morris, *The Apostolic Preaching of the Cross;* G. H. C. Macgregor, "The Concept of the Wrath of God in the NT," *NTS* 7:101ff.

Würtemberg Confession (1552). A Lutheran statement of faith used alongside the Augsburg Confession and the Formula of Concord in Swabia. It was mainly the work of theologian John Brenz (1499–1570), "Luther's most reliable friend in South Germany." A Swabian, Brenz was educated at Heidelberg, where he came to know Philip Melanchthon, Martin Bucer, and Eberhardt Schnepf. He met Luther at the Heidelberg Disputation in 1518 and embraced the Reformation. Attending the Marburg Colloquy (1529), supporting the Augsburg Confession (1530), he introduced Lutheran Church orders into several German territories. Although the Reformation had spread early to the imperial free cities of the south—Reutlingen, Esslingen, Ulm, Hall, and Biberbach—it was only upon Brenz's return in 1534 that the thorough reform of Würtemberg began. Influences were felt from both the Swiss and Saxon Reformations. Brenz reformed the University of Tübingen (1537), attended the meeting at Smalcald (1537), emerging as "the chief Reformer of Würtemberg," and becoming provost of the cathedral in Stuttgart in 1554. The convening of the Council of Trent (1545–63) impelled the Swabians to restate their faith. Brenz was the chief author of the Würtemberg Confession, which he took to the council in March, 1552, though he was not permitted to read it. Viewed by many Lutherans as "a restatement of the Augsburg Confession," the Würtemberg Confession was described as "an excellent statement of positive Lutheranism, presented in mild, popular, and moderate language" and directed chiefly toward the Roman Catholics. By 1559 the confession was incorporated into the Great Church Order which was used by the Lutherans in Würtemberg for centuries. C. G. Fry

See also Confessions of Faith; Lutheran Tradition, The.

Bibliography. P. Schaff, *The Creeds of Christendom,* I, 343ff., 627ff.; H.-M. Maurer, *Johannes Brenz und die Reformation in Württemberg.*

Wycliffe, John (*ca.* 1330–1384). English scholar and theologian who is often called "the Morning Star of the Reformation." A native of Yorkshire, he attended Oxford University, receiving the doctorate in theology in 1372. Supported by church positions, he spent most of his life teaching at Oxford. A brilliant scholar who mastered the late medieval scholastic tradition, he came to the attention of the government. The Duke of Lancaster, John of Gaunt, son of Edward III, enlisted his services on several occasions. Gaunt was the effective ruler of England from the death of his father (1377) until Richard II was old enough to reign (1381). Wycliffe performed diplomatic duties for the crown and wrote in support of civil government. His work denied the validity of clerical ownership of land and property as well as papal jurisdiction in temporal affairs. The doctrine of dominion, which he set forth in *On Divine Dominion* (1375) and *On Civil Dominion* (1376), declared that all people are the tenants of God and only the righteous as God's true stewards ought to have political authority because they alone have the moral right to rule and hold possession. The wicked on the other hand, even if they are nobles, kings, or popes, have no such right despite the fact that at times God may allow them to temporarily hold power or property. Wycliffe believed that churchmen who lived in mortal sin relinquished their right as God's stewards and should be deprived of their wealth and authority.

These views led to his condemnation by a series of papal bulls issued in 1377 which indicated that Oxford University should stop such teaching. Opposition drove Wycliffe to more extreme positions, and he moved from an attack on the wealth and temporal power of the church to criticism of the central dogmas of medieval Catholicism. He rejected all ceremony and organization not specifically mentioned in the Bible, condemned transubstantiation, renounced the sacramental power of the priesthood, and denied the efficacy of the Mass. He also dismissed the whole structure of rituals, ceremonies, and rites that pervaded the church on the grounds that they were not only false but they interfered with the true worship of God. He came to agree with Augustine that the church is the predestined body of true believers and that salvation comes through divine grace rather than through people's efforts to save themselves.

In 1381 the Peasants' Revolt in England forced the church and the aristocracy to cooperate in restoring law and order. Although Wycliffe was not involved in the rebellion, those who opposed him claimed that it was the result of his teaching. Taking advantage of the situation, the leaders of the English church forced his followers from Oxford. Wycliffe went to live at his parish in Lutterworth (1382), where he died of a stroke in 1384.

Wycliffe's writings, in addition to his work on the problems of church and state, include logical and metaphysical treatises and numerous theological books and sermons. He is best known, however, for instigating a translation of the Vulgate into English. According to his doctrine of dominion, Christians are directly responsible to God. Therefore, in order to know and obey God's law it is necessary for them to read the Bible. For Wycliffe, the Holy Scriptures were the only standard of faith and source of authority. That is why he felt that it was so important to make them available in the vernacular. He spent the last few months of his life on that task, leaving the completion of the Wycliffe Bible to his followers.

The followers of Wycliffe, known as Lollards, were made up of scholars from Oxford, the lesser gentry, and many poor people from both rural and urban areas. They based their preaching on the Bible and counseled disobedience to unjust churchmen, attacked the priesthood, affirmed the idea of the invisible church, and condemned monasticism and ritualism. This message led to their persecution, which some scholars feel was effective in destroying the movement by the end of the fifteenth century. Others argue that Lollard sentiments were preserved in certain places and led to an enthusiasm for the Reformation of the next century.

If Wycliffe's influence on Protestantism is difficult to trace in England, it is somewhat clearer in continental thought. His ideas spread to Bohemia through Czech students who attended Oxford University. In Prague, John Hus adopted his teachings, and the Hussites kept them alive for many years. One of the early proposals of Luther was that justice should be done to the Hussites, who he believed were wrongly condemned. Through the Bohemian connection Wycliffe was indeed a forerunner of the Protestant Reformation. R. G. CLOUSE

Bibliography. E. A. Block, *John Wyclif: Radical Dissenter;* K. B. McFarlane, *John Wycliffe and the Beginnings of English Nonconformity;* J. Stacey, *Wyclif and Reform;* H. B. Workman, *John Wyclif;* G. Lechler, *John Wycliffe and His English Reformers.*

Yahweh. *See* GOD, NAMES OF.

Zz

Zeller, Eduard (1814–1908). German Protestant theologian and philosopher. Born in Württemberg, he studied with F. C. Baur at Tübingen and later became his son-in-law. Zeller also became close friends with D. F. Strauss there and fully accepted his explanation of the Bible as a collection of myths which obscured the person of the historical Jesus. After completing his doctorate, he began lecturing at his alma mater in 1840 and within two years emerged as the leader and guiding force of the "Tübingen School" by editing its literary organ, the *Tübinger Theologische Jahrbücher* (1842–57). He spent two stormy years at Bern (1847–49) and then went to Marburg, where after some controversy he was appointed to the philosophical faculty. Next he taught in Heidelberg (1862–72) and finally Berlin (1872–95). He devoted his later years largely to writing and revising his landmark work on Greek thought, *A History of Greek Philosophy* (5 vols., 1844–52), and the shorter *Outlines of the History of Greek Philosophy* (1883), but he continued to hold Strauss in high regard, publishing a study of Strauss and Renan in 1864 and a biography in 1874.

In a lengthy commentary, *The Contents and Origin of the Acts of the Apostles, Critically Investigated* (1854), Zeller utilized the critical views advanced by Baur and Strauss to call into question the historicity of the book of Acts. As a theologian he rejected the orthodox view of God as the personal, transcendent Creator of the world, and in a pantheistic fashion regarded him as the creative basis of all life and existence. The supernatural person of Christ was the mythical embellishment of the early church, life after death was only a matter of speculation, and the fundamental beliefs of the church were little more than hair-splitting scholasticism. Although philosophically a Hegelian in early life, he became a neo-Kantian in his middle years.

R. V. PIERARD

See also TÜBINGEN SCHOOL.

Bibliography. H. Harris, *The Tübingen School; RGG,* V; W. W. Gasque, *NIDCC,* 1070.

Zinzendorf, Nikolaus Ludwig von (1700–1760). German religious reformer and founder of the Moravian Church. Born in Saxony to a noble family, he was educated at the Francke school in Halle and studied law at Wittenberg, where he attempted unsuccessfully to reconcile Lutheran orthodoxy and pietism. Foreign travels helped to broaden his understanding of Christendom, although he always regarded himself basically as a Lutheran. He accepted a civil service position, but a turning point in his life came in 1722 when he invited a group of Bohemian Brethren (*Unitas Fratrum*) refugees to settle on his estate in Saxony. He organized them into a community named Herrnhut (The Lord's Watch) and devoted full attention to its development. In 1727 he left government service to become a lay preacher and evangelist as well as spiritual leader of Herrnhut. Following a period of theological study he was formally ordained a bishop in 1737, after opposition from orthodox Lutherans had forced his group to assume a separate existence. In numerous trips to other lands, including two visits to America, he founded and nurtured churches and kindled a missionary vision hitherto unknown in Protestantism. He also wrote hymns and prayers, created liturgical forms, and prepared daily "watch words" (*Losungen*) to foster spiritual growth.

Zinzendorf held to the essentials of Lutheran theology, accepting without question God's revelation in Jesus Christ, the distinction between law and gospel, justification by faith, sanctification of life, and Christ's real presence in the Lord's Supper. His distinctive emphasis, however, was on "heart religion." One must live in communion with God, and in turn this meant a living communion with Christ since God was revealed only in him. When one's existence was oriented to the person and work of Christ, that would lead not only to the blessedness mediated through Christ but also to participation in the common work to advance the kingdom of God. The more unions like the one at Herrnhut that could be introduced into the church, the more the Christian life could be realized historically. Zinzendorf envisioned the revitalization of the existing Lutheran Church through the cultivation of an intense community religious life. This included frequent worship services, organizing the community into groups with spiritual supervisors, setting up schools, the use of choral and instrumental music, and an active program of evangelism and missions to the heathen world.

The Moravian piety differed from that of Halle in that it contained much more of the element of joy and less emphasis upon the struggle with sin and a conscious conversion experience. Although Zinzendorf advocated an experiential religion, he rejected perfectionism. The conception of the church as a fellowship bound together by a common salvation, obedience, and joy kept his movement within the mainstream of Protestantism, while the stress on proclamation of the gospel, the realization of brotherhood, fostering Christian living on a voluntary basis, the missionary imperative, and an ecumenical outlook transcended the boundaries of countries and churches and made him one of the most influential eighteenth century preachers. R. V. Pierard

See also Pietism.

Bibliography. Zinzendorf, *Hauptschriften*, 7 vols., ed. E. Beyreuther and G. Meyer, *Sixteen Discourses on Jesus Christ our Lord* (1740), and *Nine Public Lectures on Important Subjects in Religion*, ed. G. W. Forell; H. Renkewitz, *Im Gespräch mit Zinzendorfs Theologie;* J. R. Weinlick, *Count Zinzendorf;* A. J. Lewis, *Zinzendorf, the Ecumenical Pioneer.*

Zionism. This term refers to the philosophy of the Jewish people's restoration to "Zion," which early in Jewish history was identified with Jerusalem. After the Roman expulsion of the Jews from Jerusalem in A.D. 135 this "Zion" idea was never divorced from Jewish thinking, and Jewish prayers (both individual and corporate) emphasized the desire to return to their homeland. The religious Jew dreamed of an end period of ultimate release from his dispersion among the nations and a return to the land of promise. A handful of Jews had always remained in Palestine, and their numbers were augmented by refugees of the Spanish Inquisition in 1492. Nevertheless, to many Jews the notion of a physical return to Palestine seemed an illusive, if not impossible, dream.

During the nineteenth century the rise of Hebrew literature, Jewish nationalism, and most importantly a fresh outbreak of anti-Semitism stimulated groups such as *Hoveve Zion* ("Lovers of Zion") to raise money to send Jewish settlers to Palestine. Pogroms in czarist Russia after 1881 resulted in thousands of panic-stricken refugees who realized that Palestine was their safest place of refuge. Agricultural settlements were also sponsored by benefactors such as Baron Edmond de Rothschild.

Premodern Zionism emphasized a religious motive and quiet territorial settlement. With the publication of *Der Judenstaat* ("The Jewish State") by Theodor Herzl in 1896, however, political Zionism was born and with it the modern conception of Zionism. A new era in Jewish history unfolded when Herzl, an Austrian journalist, changed from an advocate of Jewish assimilation to a belief that anti-Semitism was inevitable as long as the majority of Jewish people lived outside their homeland. He expounded political, economic, and technical efforts that he believed were necessary to create a functioning Jewish state. The first Zionist Congress met in 1897, and over two hundred delegates from all over the world adopted the Basel Program. This stressed that Zionism sought to create a legal home in Palestine for the Jewish people and would promote settlement, create worldwide organizations to bind Jews together, strengthen Jewish national consciousness, and obtain consent of the governments of the world.

Herzl's thinking was purely secular; in fact, he was an agnostic. The majority of his followers, however, were Orthodox southeastern Europeans, and while Herzl opposed turning Zionism into a cultural, religious, or piecemeal settlement society, he did make concessions to these advocates. This fragile alliance indicates the many facets of Zionism during the twentieth century. To Herzl, the main goal of Zionism was to obtain a political charter granting Jews sovereign rights in their homeland. Shortly after his death in 1904 approximately seventy thousand Jews had settled in Palestine. A majority (at least 60 percent) lived in the cities. Zionism was metamorphized into a mass movement and political power during World War I. In 1917 the British issued the Balfour Declaration, which bestowed favor upon the establishment in Palestine of a Jewish national home.

Zionism was a minority movement and encountered opposition even within the Jewish community. American Reform Judaism, for example, believed that Jews were not suited for the rigors of Palestine, where disease and famine were rampant. Furthermore, they claimed that Palestine was no longer a Jewish land and that the United States was "Zion." To these non-Zionist Jews, Zionism was damaging to the fabric of Judaism and only served to stir up the Russians. It was only the horror of the mass murder of a hundred thousand Jews by Russian army units from 1919 to 1921 and, ultimately, the horror of the Nazi Holocaust during World War II in which six million Jews were exterminated that drew Zionists and non-Zionists together in support of Palestine as a Jewish commonwealth—a haven for the persecuted and homeless. In November, 1947, a partition plan creating a Jewish state, endorsed by both the United States and the Soviet Union, was adopted by the General Assembly of the United Nations. The State of Israel was formally recognized on May 14, 1948, when British rule ended. As the young state strengthened, the definition of Zionism and what its current goals and purpose should be have been heatedly debated within the World Zionist Organization itself. Since 1968 the emphasis of aliyah (personal migration to Israel) has been seen by many as an ultimate, yet controversial, goal.

Zionism has been aided in the nineteenth and twentieth centuries by "Christian Zionists." Because of their premillennial eschatology fundamentalist evangelicals have been particularly supportive of the restoration of the Jewish people to Israel and of Israel itself in the twentieth century.

D. A. Rausch

See also Zionism, Christian.

Bibliography. W. Laqueur, *A History of Zionism;* A. Hertzberg, *The Zionist Idea: A Historical Analysis and Reader;* N. W. Cohen, *American Jews and the Zionist Idea;* I. Cohen, *Theodor Herzl: Founder of Political Zionism; EJ,* XVI, 1031–1162.

Zionism, Christian. Christians have had an important part in supporting the Jewish people's restoration to "Zion." Within the millenarian tradition the conviction that the Jews would return to Palestine became an important dogma. As premillennialism gained ground during the nineteenth century, forming the core of the early fundamentalist movement, adherents not only believed that the Jewish people would return, but also vocally supported the right of the Jews to be restored to their former homeland. Even before Theodor Herzl's *Der Judenstaat* fundamentalist-evangelical William E. Blackstone advocated the reestablishment of a Jewish state and circulated a petition urging the United States to return the land of Palestine to the Jewish people. The Blackstone Petition of 1891 was signed by 413 outstanding Christian and Jewish leaders and through the State Department was distributed to the principal nations of the world. During World War I, Blackstone urged a new petition on Woodrow Wilson, and in 1918 he was invited to address a Zionist mass meeting in Los Angeles.

Other Christians, such as Herzl's close friend William H. Hechler, worked diligently to promote political Zionism as the ultimate solution to the Jewish question. Hechler tried to encourage heads of state (including the Turkish sultan who controlled Palestine) to support Herzl's proposals, and he accompanied Herzl to Palestine in 1898 to meet with the kaiser. The active support of such Christian Zionists in many countries influenced political action, and even the Balfour Declaration of 1917 was the product of religious as well as political activity. Individual Christian Zionists came from a broad spectrum of theological traditions. Even liberal Protestantism, which has historically opposed Zionism, contributed clergymen through organizations such as the Christian Council of Palestine during World War II.

Nevertheless, because of their premillennial eschatology fundamentalist evangelicals have been particularly supportive of the restoration of the Jewish people to Israel and of Israel itself in the twentieth century. In his periodical *Our Hope,* Arno C. Gaebelein advocated from 1894 to 1945 that the Jewish people would not only return to Palestine, but that they had an inherent right to that land as well. When Israel became a state in 1948, prophetically minded Christians viewed it as a miracle of God. In the 1960s liberal Protestantism called for the "internationalization" of the city of Jerusalem, but the fundamentalist evangelical declared that the Bible gave it to the Jewish people. After the 1967 Six-Day War the National Council of Churches denounced Israel's annexation of the old city of Jerusalem. In contrast, fundamentalist evangelicals rejoiced and insisted that God had seen to it that the Jewish people had come out on top in spite of world oppression and obstacle.

On October 30, 1977, Billy Graham enhanced decades of support for Israel by addressing the National Executive Council meeting of the American Jewish committee and calling for the rededication of the United States to the existence and safety of Israel. At the Bicentennial Congress of Prophecy in Philadelphia the year before, a proclamation in support of Israel had been signed by eleven prominent fundamentalist evangelicals. It then quickly received seven thousand additional signatures and was presented to the ambassador of the State of Israel. Statements of support have also appeared in full-page newspaper advertisements—several in the *New York Times.*

Such unequivocable Christian Zionism has not gone without attack. It has been criticized even within evangelicalism as an erroneous political philosophy based on a spurious interpretation of the Bible which dictates that modern Palestine is the Jew's own special piece of real estate. These critics argue that Christian Zionism totally ignores the rights of the Palestinian Arab people and that the Jews forfeited their title to the Promised Land through unfaithfulness long ago. D. A. RAUSCH

See also ZIONISM.

Bibliography. H. Fishman, *American Protestantism and a Jewish State;* D. A. Rausch, *Zionism Within Early American Fundamentalism.*

Zoroastrianism. A religion that developed in Iran from about the sixth century B.C., generally ascribed to Zoroaster (Zarathustra), who was born in Iran "258 years before Alexander." The date of Zoroaster's birth has been given variously as 6000 B.C., 1400 B.C., and 1000 B.C., but Herzfeld accepts the traditional date, approximately, as now confirmed (Herzfeld, 570–500 B.C.; Jackson, 660–583 B.C.). Accordingly, Zoroaster was contemporary with other great religious personages, including Buddha, Confucius, Lao Tze, and several Hebrew prophets. That Zoroaster used Vedic materials found in early Hinduism can hardly be denied; that he was a polytheist like Darius, Xerxes, and others who were probably Zoroastrians (at least, their inscriptions pay homage to Ahura Mazda) seems most likely. But Zoroaster was protesting against the false and cruel in religion, and followed the principle, "If the gods do aught shameful, they are not gods." Accordingly, he exalted Ahura Mazda ("wise Lord," often improperly translated "Lord of light") as supreme among the gods or spirits, and viewed the world as an agelong struggle between Ahura Mazda and Angra Mainyu (or Ahramanyuš, Ahriman, "Spirit of evil"), both of whom came into existence independently in the distant past. Zoroastrianism is therefore called a dualism—but it is a limited dualism. Zoroaster calls upon human beings to join in this conflict on the side of Ahura Mazda, the key words of such religion being "good thoughts, good works, good deeds." The ultimate victory of Ahura Mazda, however, was not to be accomplished by human assistance but by the advent of a messiahlike figure, the Saoshyant. The duration of the struggle was to be six thousand years (three thousand had already passed when Zoroaster was born), following which was to be the resurrection and judgment. Many of the details of Zoroastrianism are later developments, some post-Christian and even post-Mohammedan, and scholars are divided on what elements are to be traced to Zoroaster's own teaching.

Because of the fact that the revelation of the doctrines of resurrection, angels, Satan, and the Messiah comes late in the OT or even in the intertestamental period in early Judaism, scholars have frequently traced these ideas to Zoroastrian influence exerted upon the Jewish people after the Babylonian exile. Moulton examined these points in detail and concluded that they were "not proven." The discovery of the Dead Sea Scrolls has reopened the discussion, due to the presence of marked "Zoroastrian" influences in the Qumran literature. Some of the most striking parallels to Jewish-Christian eschatology can be shown to be very late developments in Zoroastrianism. On the other hand, it would not do violence to a high view of inspiration to admit that God could have used Zoroastrianism as a means of stimulating the Jewish mind to think on these subjects even as he used hellenism to prepare the Jewish mind for the Christian revelation (witness Saul of Tarsus). The magi ("wise men") of the birth narrative may have been Zoroastrian priests. W. S. LASOR

Bibliography. J. H. Moulton, *HDB;* A. V. W. Jackson, *Jewish Encyclopedia;* E. Herzfeld, *Zoroaster and His World,* 2 vols.; R. P. Masani, *The Religion of the Good Life, Zoroastrianism;* J. J. Modi, *The Religious Ceremonies and Customs of the Parsees;* M. Boyce, "Zoroastrianism," in *Historia Religionum,* ed. C. J. Bleeker and G. Widengren.

Zurich Agreement (1549). The statement on the Lord's Supper that prevented a split between Calvinists and Zwinglians in Switzerland; also called *Consensus Tigurinus,* after the Latin name of the city. Calvin expressed himself differently on the Lord's Supper than Zwingli had done. Calvin spoke of a true, though only spiritual, communication of Christ in the Lord's Supper. Heinrich Bullinger, Zwingli's successor at Zurich, spoke of the Lord's Supper in merely symbolic terms. After Luther renewed his attack on Zwinglianism in 1544, Calvin and Bullinger negotiated more seriously. Calvin and William Farel met with Bullinger in Zurich in 1549, and the Zurich Agreement was the result. Calvin was the main author, but Bullinger's influence was evident throughout. In twenty-six articles the agreement presented a unified doctrine that became the basis for unity among all the Reformed in Switzerland.

The document was more Zwinglian than Calvinist in its expressions, but it affirmed the spiritual presence of Christ in the Lord's Supper. The sacraments, it said, were not "empty symbols" but seals and attestations of grace. The Spirit was said to work independently of the eating and drinking in the Lord's Supper, and believers were said to have communion with Christ outside of and before the use of the sacraments. The document clearly limited any divine operation to the elect.

The Zurich Agreement rejected both Lutheran and Roman Catholic views on the Lord's Supper as well as consubstantiation. It said that Jesus' body was confined to heaven and that a literal interpretation of "This is my body" was preposterous. J. M. Drickamer

Bibliography. "Confessions," *HERE; P. Christ, SHERK*, XII, 536–37; J. T. McNeill, *The History and Character of Calvinism;* T. H. L. Parker, *John Calvin;* P. Schaff, *The Creeds of Christendom.*

Zwickau Prophets. The "Zwickau prophets" were Nicholas Storch, Markus Stübner, and Thomas Drechsel, three refugees from the conventicle movement of Zwickau, who visited Wittenberg shortly after Christmas, 1521. For a brief time their extravagant claims perplexed and excited the Wittenbergers. These disturbances contributed to Luther's decision to return from the Wartburg and also fixed the prophets' long-term notoriety. Storch, a weaver with impressive but informal knowledge of the Bible, acted as leader of the conventicle movement of Zwickau, along with Thomas Müntzer. Stübner had studied theology in Wittenberg. Drechsel was an unlettered weaver.

The conventicle movement had divided Zwickau into two sharply conflicting camps, with the situation degenerating on occasion into rock-throwing incidents. Lay persons from the lower-class laborers made up the conventicles. Their main idea was the conviction that God spoke directly to people and revealed his will through visions and dreams rather than through the church or the Scriptures. Storch's party claimed to hold familiar conversations with God. As a result, they predicted that within five to seven years the Turks would invade Germany and destroy priests and all the godless. Storch saw himself at the head of a new church, designated by God to complete the reformation left unfinished by Martin Luther. Reliance on the direct voice of God led to the rejection of Scripture as authority in itself and the rejection of the sacraments as means of grace. Storch rejected infant baptism, believing that *fides aliena* as taught by Luther could not substitute for the absent faith of an infant, and that Mark 16:16 required baptism only after faith is engendered. However, Storch did not advocate rebaptism as did the Anabaptists.

The long-term significance of the Zwickau prophets falls into two related areas. (1) They formed part of the backdrop for some early positions of Martin Luther. Against their spiritualism Luther asserted that spirits must be tested by Scripture and that they would say nothing which contradicted the Bible. To defend infant baptism Luther not only asserted the tradition of the church, but also affirmed the presence of latent faith in infants through which they responded to the grace of baptism. (2) The Zwickau prophets have been part of the discussion of Anabaptist origins. They formed the image of Anabaptists for Luther and Melanchthon, who believed that the prophets, along with Thomas Müntzer and Andreas Carlstadt, were the fathers of Anabaptism. This view of origins prevailed until the twentieth century, when Harold S. Bender made prominent the view which totally divorced Anabaptist origins from these radicals. Early modern scholarship credited Storch with causing Müntzer's break from Lutheran ideas during Müntzer's pastoral activity in Zwickau, May 1520 to April 1521. More recent work discounts Storch's influence and attributes the break to Müntzer's mysticism, his spiritualism discovering a like-minded individual in Storch. While recent scholarship on Anabaptist origins does consider some Müntzerian ideas a source of South German Anabaptism, it is true that the Zwickau prophets contributed little if anything to Anabaptism. J. D. Weaver

Bibliography. H. S. Bender, "The Zwickau Prophets, Thomas Muentzer, and the Anabaptists," *MQR* 27:3–16; M. U. Edwards, Jr., *Luther and the False Brethren;* E. Gritsch, *Reformer Without a Church: The Life and Thought of Thomas Muentzer;* J. S. Oyer, *Lutheran Reformers Against Anabaptists;* G. H. Williams, *The Radical Reformation.*

Zwingli, Ulrich (1484–1531). After Luther and Calvin, the most important early Protestant reformer. Zwingli was born in Wildhaus, St. Gall, Switzerland, and showed early promise in education. He studied at Berne and Vienna before matriculating at the University of Basel, where he was captivated by humanistic studies. At Basel he also came under the influence of reformer Thomas Wyttenbach, who encouraged him in the directions that would eventually lead to his belief in the sole authority of Scripture and in justification by grace through faith alone. Zwingli was ordained a Catholic priest and served parishes in Glarus (1506–16) and Einsiedeln (1516–18) until called to be the people's (or preaching) priest at the Great Minster in Zurich.

Sometime around 1516, after diligent study in Erasmus's Greek NT and after long wrestling with the moral problem of sensuality, he experienced an evangelical breakthrough, much like Luther was experiencing at about the same time. This turned him even more wholeheartedly to the Scriptures, and it also made him hostile to the medieval system of penance and relics, which he attacked in 1518. One of the great moments of the Reformation occurred early in 1519 when Zwingli began his service in Zurich by announcing his intention to preach exegetical sermons beginning with the Gospel of Matthew. In the final decade of his life he shepherded Zurich to its declaration for reform (1523). He wrote numerous tracts and aided in the composition of confessions to promote the course of the Reformation (e.g., the Ten Theses of Berne, 1528); he established solid relationships with other Swiss reformers, including Oecolampadius in Basel; he inspired and then broke with the rising Anabaptist movement; and he had a momentous disagreement with Luther over the Lord's Supper (expressed most sharply at the Colloquy of Marburg in 1529). Zwingli lost his life while serving as a chaplain to Zurich troops engaged in warfare with other Swiss cantons.

Zwingli's Protestantism was a more rationalistic and biblicistic variation of Luther's theology. His discussions with German Protestants about the Lord's Supper led him to doubt Luther's belief in a sacramental real presence of Christ in Communion, and even Martin Bucer's belief in a real spiritual presence, in favor of a nearly memorialistic view. To Zwingli the Lord's Supper was primarily an occasion to remember the benefits purchased by Christ's death. In his approach to theology and practice Zwingli looked for strict and specific scriptural warrant, even though this led him into embarrassment when early Anabaptists demanded proof texts for the practice of infant baptism. Zwingli's strict adherence to the Bible led him in 1527 to remove the organ from the Great Minster, since Scripture nowhere mandated its use in worship (and this in spite of the fact that Zwingli was an accomplished musician who otherwise encouraged musical expression). He was strongly predestinarian in his theology, but did not display the consummate sense of Scripture's thematic relationships which Calvin employed in the discussion of election. Zwingli had no qualms in seeking reform through the authority of the Zurich council. Even after his death the Zurich city government under his successor, Heinrich Bullinger, exercised a dominant role in church affairs. This model of church-state relations eventually appealed to England's Queen Elizabeth, even as reformers Calvin and John Knox fought for the autonomy of the church over its own affairs.

Zwingli's noble character, his firm commitment to scriptural authority, and his diligent propagation of evangelical reform, even more than his writings, marked him as one of the Reformation's most appealing leaders. M. A. Noll

See also Marburg Colloquy.

Bibliography. G. W. Bromiley, ed., *Zwingli and Bullinger;* G. R. Potter, *Zwingli;* G. R. Potter, ed., *Huldrych Zwingli;* O. Farner, *Huldrych Zwingli,* 2 vols.; C. Carside, *Zwingli and the Fine Arts.*